UNITED STATES

POLYCONIC PROJECTION

SCALE OF MILES

0   50   100   200   300   400

SCALE OF KILOMETERS

0   100   200   300   400

Capitals of Countries .... ✪
State Capitals .... ⊙
International Boundaries .... ——

ATLANTIC

OCEAN

GULF OF MEXICO

BAHAMAS

CUBA

Tropic of Cancer

Havana

HAMMOND INCORPORATED, Maplewood, N.J.

WORLDMARK ENCYCLOPEDIA OF THE STATES

A practical guide to the geographic, demographic, historical, political, economic, and social development of the United States.

WORLDMARK
ENCYCLOPEDIA
OF THE STATES

WORLDMARK PRESS, LTD.

HARPER & ROW, PUBLISHERS

Goode projection of the world Copyright by the University of Chicago.

Typography by U.S. Lithograph Inc., New York, N.Y.

Production by the Maple-Vail Book Manufacturing Group, New York, N.Y.

Map endsheets prepared by Hammond Incorporated, Maplewood, N.J.

Preparation of lithographic negatives for black-and-white maps by John Dreyer & Co., Inc., New York, N.Y.

Printed in the United States of America.

DISTRIBUTED IN THE UNITED STATES OF AMERICA BY HARPER & ROW, PUBLISHERS, INC., NEW YORK, N.Y. DISTRIBUTED IN CANADA BY FITZHENRY & WHITESIDE LIMITED, TORONTO.

LIBRARY OF CONGRESS CATALOGING IN PUBLICATION DATA

WORLDMARK ENCYCLOPEDIA OF THE STATES

1. United States—Dictionaries and encyclopedias.
E156.W67   973   80–8218
ISBN 0–06–014733–4   AACR1

Staff

Editor and Publisher	MOSHE Y. SACHS
Executive Editor	GEOFFREY M. HORN
Senior Editor	LOUIS BARRON
Managing Editor	DEBORAH GALE
Chief Copy Editor and Consulting Editor	MARY JANE ALEXANDER
Staff Editors	DONNA AMOS LANGDON HAMMER
Contributing Editors	ANTONINA W. BOUIS WALTER R. FOX EDMUND GREKULINSKI THOMAS L. HARRISON WILLIAM A. McGEVERAN, JR. KATHRYN PAULSEN CHARLES PIERRE DEBBIE WEISMAN
Cartographer	ATTILA SIORETI
Associate Cartographers	HARRIS GRABER LUBA PROKOP ELEONORA SIORETI
Cartographic Editor	MIKLOS PINTHER
Proofreaders	DONNE FLORENCE MARCIA D. HORN MARTIN MITCHELL
Artists	HIDEO IETAKA KATSUMI SUZUKI
Typist	ROSEMARIE T. KRIST

Contributors

ALLEN, HAROLD B. Emeritus Professor of English and Linguistics, University of Minnesota (Minneapolis–St. Paul). LANGUAGES.***

BASSETT, T. D. SEYMOUR. Former University Archivist, University of Vermont (Burlington). VERMONT**

BENSON, MAXINE. Curator of Document Resources, Colorado Historical Society. COLORADO.**

BROWN, RICHARD D. Professor of History, University of Connecticut (Storrs). MASSACHUSETTS.**

CASHIN, EDWARD J. Professor of History, Augusta College. GEORGIA.*

CHANNING, STEVEN A. Professor of History, University of Kentucky (Lexington). KENTUCKY.**

CLARK, CHARLES E. Professor of History, University of New Hampshire (Durham). MAINE.*

COGSWELL, PHILIP, JR. Forum Editor, *The Oregonian.* OREGON.*

CONLEY, PATRICK T. Professor of History and Law, Providence College. RHODE ISLAND.**

CORLEW, ROBERT E. Dean, School of Liberal Arts, Middle Tennessee State University (Murfreesboro). TENNESSEE.*

CREIGH, DOROTHY WEYER. Author and historian; member, Nebraska State Board of Education. NEBRASKA.**

CUNNINGHAM, JOHN T. Author and historian. NEW JERSEY.**

FISHER, PERRY. Director, Columbia Historical Society. DISTRICT OF COLUMBIA.**

FRANTZ, JOE B. Professor of History, University of Texas (Austin). TEXAS.**

GOODELL, LELE. Member, Editorial Board, *Hawaiian Journal of History.* HAWAII (in part).**

GOODRICH, JAMES W. Associate Director, State Historical Society of Missouri. MISSOURI.**

HAMILTON, VIRGINIA. Professor of History, University of Alabama (Birmingham). ALABAMA.**

HAVIGHURST, WALTER. Research Professor of English Emeritus, Miami University (Oxford). OHIO.**

HINTON, HARWOOD P. Editor, *Arizona and the West,* University of Arizona (Tucson). ARIZONA.**

HOOGENBOOM, ARI. Professor of History, Brooklyn College of the City University of New York. PENNSYLVANIA.**

HOOVER, HERBERT T. Professor of History, University of South Dakota (Vermillion). SOUTH DAKOTA.**

HUNT, WILLIAM R. Historian; former Professor of History, University of Alaska. ALASKA.*

JENSEN, DWIGHT. Author and historian. IDAHO.*

JENSEN, RICHARD J. Professor of History, University of Illinois (Chicago). ILLINOIS.*

LARSON, ROBERT W. Professor of History, University of Northern Colorado (Greeley). NEW MEXICO.**

MAPP, ALF J., JR. Author and historian; Associate Professor of English, Creative Writing, and Journalism, Old Dominion University (Norfolk). VIRGINIA.**

MAY, GEORGE S. Professor of History, Eastern Michigan University (Ypsilanti). MICHIGAN.*

MEYER, GLADYS. Professor emeritus, Columbia University. ETHNIC GROUPS.***

MOODY, ERIC N. Historian, Nevada Historical Society. NEVADA.**

MUNROE, JOHN A. H. Rodney Sharp Professor of History, University of Delaware. DELAWARE.**

MURPHY, MIRIAM. Associate Editor, *Utah Historical Quarterly.* UTAH.**

O'BRIEN, KATHLEEN ANN. Project Director, Upper Midwest Women's History Center for Teachers. MINNESOTA.**

PADOVER, SAUL K. Distinguished Service Professor Emeritus, Graduate Faculty, New School (New York City). UNITED STATES OF AMERICA.**

PECKHAM, HOWARD H. Professor emeritus, University of Michigan. INDIANA.**

PRYOR, NANCY. Research consultant and librarian, Washington State Library. WASHINGTON.**

RAWLS, JAMES J. Instructor of History, Diablo Valley College (Pleasant Hill). CALIFORNIA.**

RICE, OTIS K. Professor of History, West Virginia Institute of Technology (Montgomery). WEST VIRGINIA.*

RICHMOND, ROBERT W. Assistant Executive Director, Kansas State Historical Society. KANSAS.**

RIGHTER, ROBERT W. Assistant Professor of History, University of Wyoming (Laramie). WYOMING.**

ROTH, DAVID M. Director, Center for Connecticut Studies, Eastern Connecticut State College (Willimantic). CONNECTICUT.*

SCHEFFER, BARBARA MOORE. Feature Writer. OKLAHOMA (in part).*

SCHEFFER, WALTER F. Regents' Professor of Political Science and Director, Graduate Program in Public Administration, University of Oklahoma (Norman). OKLAHOMA (in part).*

SCHMITT, ROBERT C. Hawaii State Statistician. HAWAII (in part).**

SCUDIERE, PAUL J. Senior Historian, New York State Education Department. NEW YORK.**

SKATES, JOHN RAY. Professor of History, University of Southern Mississippi (Hattiesburg). MISSISSIPPI.**

SMITH, DOUG. Writer, *Arkansas Gazette* (Little Rock). ARKANSAS.**

STOUDEMIRE, ROBERT H. Professor of State and Local Government and Senior Research Associate, Bureau of Governmental Research, University of South Carolina (Columbia). SOUTH CAROLINA.*

SULLIVAN, LARRY E. Librarian, New-York Historical Society. MARYLAND.**

TAYLOR, JOE GRAY. Professor of History, McNeese State University (Lake Charles). LOUISIANA.**

TEBEAU, CHARLTON W. Emeritus Professor of History, University of Miami. FLORIDA.**

THOMPSON, WILLIAM FLETCHER. Director of Research, State Historical Society of Wisconsin. WISCONSIN.**

VIVÓ, PAQUITA. Author and consultant. PUERTO RICO.**

WALL, JOSEPH FRAZIER. Professor of History, Grinnell College. IOWA.**

WALLACE, R. STUART. Assistant Director/Editor, New Hampshire Historical Society. NEW HAMPSHIRE.**

WATSON, HARRY L. Assistant Professor of History, University of North Carolina (Chapel Hill). NORTH CAROLINA.*

WEAVER, KENNETH L. Associate Professor of Political Science, Montana State University (Bozeman). MONTANA.**

WILKINS, ROBERT P. Professor of History, University of North Dakota (Grand Forks). NORTH DAKOTA.**

WOODS, BOB. Editor, *Sierra Club Wildlife Involvement News.* FLORA AND FAUNA.***

*Full contributor.

**Consultant contributor.

***Special contributor.

Contents

Preface

More than two decades ago, the editors of Worldmark Press set out to create a new kind of reference work—one that would view every nation of the world as if through a "world mirror" and not from the perspective of any one country or group of countries. To that work, the *Worldmark Encyclopedia of the Nations*, we now offer a companion volume, the *Worldmark Encyclopedia of the States*.

The fitness of the United States of America as a subject for encyclopedic study is plain. No discussion of world politics, economics, culture, technology, or military affairs would be complete without an intensive examination of the American achievement. What is not so obvious is why we chose to present this work as an encyclopedia of the *states* rather than of the United States. In so doing, we emphasize the fact that the United States is a federal union of separate states with divergent histories, traditions, resources, laws, and economic interests. The flourishing activities of state and local historical societies, partly stimulated by the bicentennial celebrations of 1976, serve to remind us of that truth. More personal reminders, for those of us who worked on this project, were the many hundreds of telephone calls to every part of the Union, confirming in a very direct way the extraordinary variety of accents and attitudes this nation embraces.

Every state, large or small, is treated in an individual chapter, within a framework of 50 standard subject headings; generally, the more populous the state, the longer the article. The District of Columbia and the Commonwealth of Puerto Rico each has its own chapter, and two additional articles describe in summary form the other Caribbean and Pacific dependencies. The concluding chapter is a 50-page overview of the nation as a whole. Supplementing this textual material are tables of conversions and abbreviations, a glossary, and 58 black-and-white maps prepared especially for this edition.

The editors invited more than 50 distinguished historians, political scientists, scholars, and journalists—all of them intimately familiar with their own states—to examine the text for general accuracy, fairness, and completeness. We recognized three categories of contributors. Consultant contributors (the majority) reviewed the chapters on their respective states and in most cases each also wrote part of the article; full contributors wrote entire articles on their respective states and then reviewed and corrected the edited manuscript; and three special contributors prepared sections for every state on the complex and rapidly changing fields of *flora and fauna*, *ethnic groups*, and *languages*. We encouraged our contributors to amend and amplify the text, but responsibility for the completed articles remained that of the editors.

Publication of this encyclopedia brings to a close a collective effort that enlisted the talents of scholars, editor-writers, artists, cartographers, typesetters, proofreaders, and many others. Perhaps only those involved in the production of reference books fully appreciate how complex that endeavor can be. We ourselves relied on many reference books in the course of this project, assuming their accuracy in every case though painfully aware of the possibilities of error. (Some of these are discussed in the notes that follow.) Readers customarily expect that a reference book will be correct in every particular; and yet, by the time the first edition has been on the shelves for a few months, a conscientious editor may already have a long list of improvements and corrections to be made in a second edition. Although the editors of Worldmark Press cannot acknowledge all comments and questions personally, we do invite you, the reader, to add your suggestions to our list.

THE EDITORS

Notes

GENERAL NOTE: Although the following comments refer repeatedly to "the states" and "state sources" in describing the process by which official information was gathered for the *Worldmark Encyclopedia of the States*, the editors also wish to acknowledge the kind assistance provided by the governments of the District of Columbia, the Commonwealth of Puerto Rico, the other US Caribbean and Pacific dependencies, and the United States as a whole. Space does not permit a complete listing of all federal, national, and state sources used in preparation of this encyclopedia. We have therefore confined ourselves to source notes that clarify a statistical problem or give due credit to a nongovernmental organization.

MAPS: Each state map shows principal topographic features, including drainage and elevations (the latter as adapted by Richard Edes Harrison from the *National Atlas of the United States*); county names, county lines, and county seats; the state capital; major cities and metropolitan areas; and, wherever possible, other topographical features, points of interest, place-names, and regional designations mentioned in the text. The key to city populations is based on 1970 census data and on estimates available in early 1980.

FLAGS AND SEALS: Depictions of the flag and official seal at the head of each state article are based on reproductions solicited from that state and current as of 1980.

LEGAL HOLIDAYS: Lists of legal holidays in each state were compiled from official state sources. A legal holiday is defined as a day (other than a Saturday or Sunday) on which the transaction of government business is limited by law.

WEIGHTS AND MEASURES: Recognizing the trend toward use of the metric system throughout the United States, the text provides metric equivalents for customary measures of length and area, and both Fahrenheit and Centigrade expressions for temperature. Production figures are expressed exclusively in the prevailing customary units.

LOCATION, SIZE, AND EXTENT: The lengths of interstate boundary segments and the total lengths of state boundaries appear in roman type when derived from official government sources or supplied by an individual serving as an agent or designee of a state or federal body; italic type indicates data derived from other sources. Discrepancies in the boundary lengths of neighboring states as specified by official sources (and hence in roman type) arise from divergent methodologies of measurement.

FLORA AND FAUNA: Discussions of endangered species are based on the *List of Endangered and Threatened Wildlife and Plants* maintained by the Fish and Wildlife Service of the US Department of the Interior, and on data supplied by the states.

POPULATION: Data from the 1980 census are in many cases preliminary and subject both to revision and to transmission error. Tables of counties, county seats, county areas, and county populations accompany the articles on states of 5 million population or more; the editors regret that space limitations prevented the publication of such a table for each state.

LANGUAGES: Examples of lexical and pronunciation patterns cited in the text are meant to suggest the historic development of principal linguistic features, and should not be taken as a comprehensive statement of current usage.

RELIGIONS: For data on the members and adherents of Christian denominations, the editors are indebted to *Churches and Church Membership in the United States, 1971*, published in 1974 by the Glenmary Research Center, and to the *Official Catholic Directory* (1979 edition), an annual publication of P. J. Kenedy & Sons; for Jewish population estimates, the editors relied on the *American Jewish Year Book* (vol. 80), issued annually by the Jewish Publication Society of America and the American Jewish Committee.

POLITICAL PARTIES: Data on elections prior to 1979 were compiled from reports supplied by state sources and from *Congressional Quarterly's Guide to U.S. Elections*, published in 1975 (with a supplement for 1976). Election results for 1980 are based on a telephone survey of state election officials; vote totals are subject to revision and transmission error.

JUDICIAL SYSTEM: *Uniform Crime Reports for the United States*, published annually by the Federal Bureau of Investigation and embodying the FBI Crime Index (tabulations of offenses known to the police), was the principal source for the crime statistics cited in the text.

ARMED FORCES: Estimates published by the Veterans Administration of the number of veterans of US military service living in each state as of 30 September 1979 represent extrapolations from 1970 census data.

ENERGY AND POWER: Data for proved reserves and production of fossil fuels were derived from publications of the American Gas Association, American Petroleum Institute, National Coal Association, and US Department of Energy.

HEALTH: The principal statistical sources for hospitals and medical personnel were annual publications of the American Dental Association, American Hospital Association, and American Medical Association.

LIBRARIES AND MUSEUMS: In most cases, library and museum names are as listed in the *American Library Directory* (32d ed.), published in 1979 by R. R. Bowker, and the *Official Museum Directory, 1980*, compiled by the National Register Publishing Co. in cooperation with the American Association of Museums.

PRESS: Circulation data follow the *1979 Editor & Publisher International Yearbook*.

FAMOUS PERSONS: Entries are current through December 1980. Where a person described in one state is known to have been born in another, the state of birth follows the personal name, in parentheses.

BIBLIOGRAPHY: Bibliographies are intended as a guide to further reading and not as a listing of sources used in preparing the articles. Such listings would have far exceeded space limitations, inasmuch as each article draws upon at least 75 documents.

Acknowledgments

The editors wish to express their deepest thanks to the many hundreds of federal, state, and local officials without whose cooperation this project would not have been possible. The editors are especially grateful to the staff of the US Bureau of the Census, who gave generously of their time in supplying us in person and by telephone with preliminary 1980 census results, and to the Eastern Mapping Center of the US Geological Survey for assistance in determining the lengths of certain interstate boundaries. We are also indebted to cartographer Richard Edes Harrison for permitting us to adapt for our purposes the map elevations that appeared in the *National Atlas of the United States*, and for preparing relief drawings of Puerto Rico and the other US Caribbean dependencies.

Grateful acknowledgment is offered to Fredric M. Kaplan, Executive Editor of the Fifth Edition of the *Worldmark Encyclopedia of the Nations* and now President and Publisher of Eurasia Press, and to Richard Zeldin, General Manager of the Encyclopedia Division, John Wiley & Sons, for impressing upon us the need for this encyclopedia. The editors are profoundly indebted to M. S. Wyeth, Jr., Vice President and Executive Editor, and to Patrick Barrett, Senior Editor, both of Harper & Row, who offered many helpful suggestions at every stage. The advice and assistance of Robert Famighetti, Managing Editor at Macmillan Educational Co., were also of enormous benefit. Lastly, the editors note with sorrow the passing of Edmund Grekulinski, who died shortly after completing his assignments as Contributing Editor.

Key to Subject Headings

All information contained within a state article is uniformly keyed by means of small superior numerals to the left of the subject headings. A heading such as "Population," for example, carries the same key numeral (6) in every article. Thus, to find information about the population of Oklahoma, consult the table of contents for the page number where the Oklahoma article begins and look for section 6 thereunder.

Introductory matter for each state includes: Origin of state name
Nickname
Capital
Date and order of statehood
Song
Motto
Flag
Official seal
Symbols (animal, tree, flower, etc.)
Legal holidays
Time

FLAG COLOR SYMBOLS

 gold/ yellow   red   green   blue   orange   brown   white   black

SUBJECT HEADINGS IN NUMERICAL ORDER

1 Location, size, and extent	26 Forestry
2 Topography	27 Mining
3 Climate	28 Energy and power
4 Flora and fauna	29 Industry
5 Environmental protection	30 Commerce
6 Population	31 Consumer protection
7 Ethnic groups	32 Banking
8 Languages	33 Insurance
9 Religions	34 Securities
10 Transportation	35 Public finance
11 History	36 Taxation
12 State government	37 Economic policy
13 Political parties	38 Health
14 Local government	39 Social welfare
15 State services	40 Housing
16 Judicial system	41 Education
17 Armed forces	42 Arts
18 Migration	43 Libraries and museums
19 Intergovernmental cooperation	44 Communications
20 Economy	45 Press
21 Income	46 Organizations
22 Labor	47 Tourism, travel, and recreation
23 Agriculture	48 Sports
24 Animal husbandry	49 Famous persons
25 Fishing	50 Bibliography

SUBJECT HEADINGS IN ALPHABETICAL ORDER

Agriculture	23	Insurance	33
Animal husbandry	24	Intergovernmental cooperation	19
Armed forces	17	Judicial system	16
Arts	42	Labor	22
Banking	32	Languages	8
Bibliography	50	Libraries and museums	43
Climate	3	Local government	14
Commerce	30	Location, size, and extent	1
Communications	44	Migration	18
Consumer protection	31	Mining	27
Economic policy	37	Organizations	46
Economy	20	Political parties	13
Education	41	Population	6
Energy and power	28	Press	45
Environmental protection	5	Public finance	35
Ethnic groups	7	Religions	9
Famous persons	49	Securities	34
Fishing	25	Social welfare	39
Flora and fauna	4	Sports	48
Forestry	26	State government	12
Health	38	State services	15
History	11	Taxation	36
Housing	40	Topography	2
Income	21	Tourism, travel, and recreation	47
Industry	29	Transportation	10

EXPLANATION OF SYMBOLS

Data not available: NA
Nil (or negligible)—
Subtotals on tables are usually given in parentheses ( ).
A fiscal or split year is indicated by a stroke (e.g., 1981/82).
The use of a small dash (e.g., 1981–82) normally signifies the full period of calendar years covered (including the end year indicated).

Conversion Tables*

LENGTH

1 inch	2.540005 centimeters
1 foot (12 inches)	30.4801 centimeters
1 US yard (3 feet)	0.914402 meter
1 statute mile (5,280 feet; 1,760 yards)	1.609347 kilometers
1 British mile	1.609344 kilometers
1 nautical mile (1.1508 statute miles or 6,076.10333 feet)	1.852 kilometers
1 British nautical mile (6,080 feet)	1.85319 kilometers
1 centimeter	0.3937 inch
1 centimeter	0.03280833 foot
1 meter (100 centimeters)	3.280833 feet
1 meter	1.093611 US yards
1 kilometer (1,000 meters)	0.62137 statute mile
1 kilometer	0.539957 nautical mile

AREA

1 sq inch	6.451626 sq centimeters
1 sq foot (144 sq inches)	0.092903 sq meter
1 sq yard (9 sq feet)	0.836131 sq meter
1 acre (4,840 sq yards)	0.404687 hectare
1 sq mile (640 acres)	2.589998 sq kilometers
1 sq centimeter	0.154999 sq inch
1 sq meter (10,000 sq centimeters)	10.76387 sq feet
1 sq meter	1.1959585 sq yards
1 hectare (10,000 sq meters)	2.47104 acres
1 sq kilometer (100 hectares)	0.386101 sq mile

VOLUME

1 cubic inch	16.387162 cubic centimeters
1 cubic foot (1,728 cubic inches)	0.028317 cubic meter
1 cubic yard (27 cubic feet)	0.764559 cubic meter
1 cord (128 cubic feet)	3.62458 cubic meters
1 cubic centimeter	0.061023 cubic inch
1 cubic meter (1,000,000 cubic centimeters)	35.31445 cubic feet
1 cubic meter	1.307943 cubic yards

LIQUID MEASURE

1 US quart	0.946333 liter
1 imperial quart	1.136491 liters
1 US gallon	0.037853 hectoliter
1 imperial gallon	0.04546 hectoliter
1 liter	1.05671 US quarts
1 liter	0.8799 imperial quart
1 hectoliter	26.4178 US gallons
1 hectoliter	21.9975 imperial gallons

TEMPERATURE

Fahrenheit (F)	9/5 Centigrade + 32
Centigrade (C)	Fahrenheit-32 x 5/9

WEIGHT

1 avoirdupois ounce	0.0283495 kilogram
1 troy ounce	0.0311035 kilogram
1 avoirdupois pound	0.453592 kilogram
1 avoirdupois pound	0.00453592 quintal
1 hundredweight (cwt, 112 lb)	0.50802 quintal
1 ton (short ton, 2,000 lb)	0.907185 metric ton
1 long ton (2,240 lb)	1.016047 metric tons
1 kilogram (1,000 grams)	35.27396 avoirdupois ounces
1 kilogram	32.15074 troy ounces
1 kilogram	2.204622 avoirdupois pounds
1 quintal (100 kg)	220.4622 avoirdupois pounds
1 quintal	1.9684125 hundredweights
1 metric ton (1,000 kg)	1.102311 (short) tons
1 metric ton	0.984206 long ton

BUSHELS

	LB	% OF SHORT TON	BUSHELS PER SHORT TON
Barley (US)	48	2.4	41.667
(UK)	50	2.5	40.0
Corn (UK, US)	56	2.8	35.714
Linseed (UK)	52	2.6	38.462
(Australia, US)	56	2.8	35.714
Oats (US)	32	1.6	62.5
(Canada)	34	1.7	58.824
Potatoes (UK, US)	60	3.0	33.333
Rice (Australia)	42	2.1	47.619
(US)	45	2.25	44.444
Rye (UK, US)	56	2.8	35.714
(Australia)	60	3.0	33.333
Soybeans (US)	60	3.0	33.333
Wheat (UK, US)	60	3.0	33.333

BALES OF COTTON

	LB	% OF SHORT TON	BALES PER SHORT TON
India	392	19.6	5.102
US (net)	480	24.0	4.167

ELECTRIC ENERGY

1 horsepower (hp)	0.7457 kilowatt
1 kilowatt (kw)	1.34102 horsepower

PETROLEUM

One barrel = 42 US gallons = 34.97 imperial gallons = 158.99 liters = 0.15899 cubic meter (or 1 cubic meter = 6.2898 barrels).

*Includes units of measure cited in the text, as well as certain other units employed in parts of the English-speaking world.

ALABAMA

State of Alabama

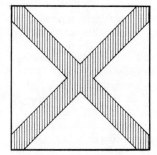

ORIGIN OF STATE NAME: Probably after the Alabama Indian tribe. **NICKNAME**: The Heart of Dixie. **CAPITAL**: Montgomery. **ENTERED UNION**: 14 December 1819 (22d). **SONG**: "Alabama." **MOTTO**: *Audemus jura nostra defendere* (We dare defend our rights). **COAT OF ARMS**: Two eagles, symbolizing courage, support a shield bearing the emblems of the five governments (France, England, Spain, Confederacy, US) that have held sovereignty over Alabama. Above the shield is a sailing vessel modeled upon the ships of the first French settlers of Alabama; beneath the shield is the state motto. **FLAG**: Crimson cross of St. Andrew on a square white field. **OFFICIAL SEAL**: Map of Alabama, including names of major rivers and neighboring states, surrounded by the words "Alabama Great Seal." **BIRD**: Yellowhammer. **FISH**: Tarpon. **FLOWER**: Camellia. **TREE**: Southern (longleaf) pine. **STONE**: Marble. **MINERAL**: Hematite. **LEGAL HOLIDAYS**: New Year's Day, 1 January; Robert E. Lee's Birthday, 3d Monday in January; Washington's Birthday, 3d Monday in February; Mardi Gras, February or March; Thomas Jefferson's Birthday, 14 April; Confederate Memorial Day, last Monday in April; Jefferson Davis's Birthday, 1st Monday in June; Independence Day, 4 July; Labor Day, 1st Monday in September; Columbus Day, 2d Monday in October; Veterans Day, 11 November; Thanksgiving Day, 4th Thursday in November; Christmas Day, 25 December. **TIME**: 6 A.M. CST = noon GMT.

¹LOCATION, SIZE, AND EXTENT

Located in the eastern south-central US, Alabama ranks 29th in size among the 50 states.

The total area of Alabama is 51,609 sq mi (133,667 sq km), of which land constitutes 50,708 sq mi (131,334 sq km) and inland water 901 sq mi (2,333 sq km). Alabama extends roughly 200 mi (320 km) E–W; the maximum N–S extension is 300 mi (48 km).

Alabama is bordered on the N by Tennessee; on the E by Georgia (with part of the line formed by the Chattahoochee River); on the S by Florida (with part of the line defined by the Perdido River) and the Gulf of Mexico; and on the W by Mississippi (with the northernmost part of the line passing through the Tennessee River).

Dauphin Island, in the Gulf of Mexico, is the largest offshore island. The total boundary length of Alabama is 1,044 mi (1,680 km). The state's geographic center is in Chilton County, 12 mi (19 km) SW of Clanton.

²TOPOGRAPHY

Alabama is divided into four major physiographic regions: the Gulf Coastal Plain, Piedmont Plateau, Ridge and Valley section, and Appalachian Plateau. The physical characteristics of each province have significantly affected settlement and industrial development patterns within the state.

The coastal plain of southern Alabama consists primarily of lowlands and low ridges. Included within the coastal plain is the Black Belt—historically, the center of cotton production and plantation slavery in Alabama—an area of rich, chalky soil that stretches across the entire width of the state. The piedmont of east-central Alabama contains rolling hills and valleys. Alabama's highest elevation, Cheaha Mountain, 2,407 feet (734 meters) above sea level, is located at the northern edge of this region. North and west of the piedmont is a series of parallel ridges and valleys running in a northeast-southwest direction. Mountain ranges in this area include the Red, Shades, Oak, Lookout, and other noteworthy southern extensions of the Appalachian chain; elevations of 1,200 feet (366 meters) are found as far south as Birmingham. The Appalachian Plateau covers much of northern Alabama, with some portion of the Highland Rim in the extreme northwest near the Tennessee border. The flood-plain of the Tennessee River cuts a wide swath across both these northern regions.

The largest lake wholly within Alabama is Guntersville Lake, covering about 108 sq mi (280 sq km) and formed during the development of the Tennessee River region by the Tennessee Valley Authority. The TVA lakes—also including Wheeler, Pickwick, and Wilson—are all long and narrow, fanning outward along a line that runs from the northeast corner of the state westward to Florence. The longest rivers are the Alabama, extending from the mid-central region to the Mobile River for a distance of about 160 mi (260 km); the Tennessee, which flows across northern Alabama for about the same distance; and the Tombigbee, which flows from north-central Alabama to Mobile for some 150 mi (240 km). The Alabama and Tombigbee rivers, which come together to form the Mobile River, and the Tensaw River all flow into Mobile Bay, an arm of the Gulf of Mexico.

About 450 million years ago, Alabama was covered by a warm, shallow sea. Over millions of years, heavy rains washed gravel, sand, and clay from higher elevations onto the rock floor of the sea to help form the foundation of modern Alabama. The skeletons and shells of sea animals, composed of limy material from rocks that had been worn away by water, settled into great thicknesses of limestone and dolomite. Numerous caves and sinkholes formed as water slowly eroded the limestone subsurface of northern Alabama. Archaeologists believe that Russell Cave, in northeastern Alabama, was the earliest site of human habitation in the southeastern US. Other major caves in northern Alabama are Manitou and Sequoyah; near Childersburg is DeSoto Caverns, a huge onyx cave once considered a sacred place by Creek Indians.

Wheeler Dam on the Tennessee River is now a national historic monument. Other major dams include Guntersville, Martin, Millers Ferry, Jordan, Mitchell, and Holt.

³CLIMATE

Alabama's three climatic divisions are the lower coastal plain, largely subtropical and strongly influenced by the Gulf of Mexico; the northern plateau, marked by occasional snowfall in winter; and the Black Belt and upper coastal plain, lying between the two extremes. Among the major population centers,

Birmingham has an annual mean temperature of 62°F (17°C), with a normal maximum of 90°F (32°C) and a normal minimum of 34°F (1°C). Montgomery has an annual mean of 65°F (18°C), with a normal maximum of 91°F (33°C) and a normal minimum of 37°F (3°C). The mean in Mobile is 67°F (19°C), the normal maximum 91°F (33°C) and the normal minimum 41°F (5°C). The record low temperature for the state is –27°F (–33°C), registered at New Market, in the northeastern corner, on 30 January 1966; the all-time high is 112°F (44°C), registered at Centreville, in the state's midsection, on 5 September 1925. Mobile is one of the rainiest of US cities, recording an average precipitation of 67 in (170 cm) a year.

Two of the most destructive hurricanes to hit Alabama were Camille in August 1969 and Frederic in September 1979, the latter causing extensive property damage in the Mobile Bay area.

⁴FLORA AND FAUNA

Alabama was once covered by vast forests of pine, which still forms the largest proportion of the state's forest growth. Alabama also has an abundance of poplar, cypress, hickory, and various gum trees. Red cedar grows throughout the state; southern white cedar is found in the southwest, hemlock in the north. Other native trees include hackberry, ash, and holly, with species of palmetto and palm in the Gulf Coast region. There are more than 150 shrubs, mountain laurel and rhododendron among them. Cultivated plants include wisteria and camellia, the state flower.

In a state where large herds of bison, elk, bear, and deer once roamed, only the white-tailed deer remains abundant. Other mammals still found are the Florida panther, bobcat, beaver, muskrat, and most species of weasel. The fairly common raccoon, opossum, rabbit, squirrel, and red and gray foxes are also native, while nutria and armadillo have been introduced to the state. Alabama's birds include golden and bald eagles, osprey and various other hawks, yellowhammer or flicker (the state bird), and black and white warblers; game birds include quail, duck, and goose. Freshwater fish such as bream, shad, bass, and sucker are common. Along the Gulf Coast there are seasonal runs of tarpon (the state fish), pompano, redfish, and bonito.

Animals listed by the state as rare and threatened include the Atlantic sturgeon, dusky gopher frog, Atlantic leatherback turtle, and American alligator, among others. On the endangered list are four species of sea turtle, the ivory-billed woodpecker, the northern and Florida black bears, and the Florida panther.

⁵ENVIRONMENTAL PROTECTION

State agencies concerned with environmental protection include the Alabama Surface Mining Reclamation Commission, the Department of Conservation and Natural Resources, and the Alabama Coastal Area Board, whose Coastal Area Management Program became in 1979 the first of the Gulf states' programs to gain federal approval. The most active environmental groups in the state are the Alabama Conservancy, Safe Energy Alliance, Sierra Club, and League of Women Voters.

The leading environmental controversy as the 1980s began was over the proposed Tennessee-Tombigbee Waterway Project, which faced court challenges because of its alleged threat to river species. Nuclear power was also a source of conflict in Alabama, the site of a fire that forced the shutdown of one Browns Ferry reactor in 1975; in 1980, the controversy focused on the proposed construction of a nuclear processing plant near Prattville. A major concern of environmentalists in the state was the improvement of land-use planning, including the protection of the state's rapidly diminishing farmlands from loss to erosion and development.

⁶POPULATION

Alabama ranked 21st in population among the 50 states in 1970, with a census total of 3,444,165. By 1978, Alabama's population had grown to an estimated 3,742,000.

Alabama experienced its greatest population growth between 1810 and 1820, following the defeat of the Creek Nation by General Andrew Jackson and his troops. Population in what is now Alabama boomed from 9,046 in 1810 to 127,901 in 1820, as migrants from older states on the eastern seaboard poured into the territory formerly occupied by the Creek Indians and taken over by the US. Thousands of farmers, hoping to find fertile land or to become wealthy cotton planters, brought their families and often their slaves into the young state, more than doubling Alabama's population between 1820 and 1830. By 1860, Alabama had almost 1,000,000 residents, about one-half of whom were black slaves. The Civil War brought Alabama's population growth almost to a standstill, largely because of heavy losses on the battlefield; the total population gain between 1860 and 1870 was only about 30,000. Between 1870 and 1970, Alabama's population rose 150,000–300,000 every decade.

In 1978, Alabama had an estimated population density of 74 persons per sq mi (29 per sq km). More than 3 out of every 5 Alabamians lived in metropolitan areas. First in size among Alabama's metropolitan areas comes Birmingham (47th in the US), which had 805,000 residents in 1977. According to federal figures, other major metropolitan areas were Mobile, 425,000; Montgomery, 254,000; and Huntsville, 201,000. Birmingham proper had a population of 282,000 (51st in the US) in 1977; Mobile and Montgomery followed with 205,000 and 156,000, respectively.

⁷ETHNIC GROUPS

Alabama's population is largely divided between whites of English and Scotch-Irish descent and blacks descended from African slaves. The 1970 census counted only 2,443 Indians, mostly of Creek or Cherokee descent. Creek Indians are centered around the small community of Poarch in southern Alabama; most of the Cherokee live in the northeastern part of the state.

The black population of Alabama in 1976 was estimated at 959,000, about one-fourth of the total population. As of 1970, Birmingham was 42% black, Mobile 36%, and Montgomery 34%. As before the Civil War, rural blacks are most heavily represented in the Black Belt of central Alabama.

In 1970, Alabama had 1,079 Japanese, 626 Chinese, and 540 Filipinos; the Hispanic population was 13,313. All told, the foreign-born and their native-born children numbered 64,000 (1.9% of the state's population) in 1970, Germany, the United Kingdom, and Italy being the leading countries of origin.

Alabama's Cajuns, of uncertain racial origin (Anglo-Saxon, French, Spanish, Choctaw, Apache, and African elements may all be represented), are ethnically unrelated to the Cajuns of Louisiana. Numbering perhaps 3,000, they live primarily in the pine woods area of upper Mobile and lower Washington counties. Many Alabama Cajuns suffer from poverty, poor health, and malnutrition.

⁸LANGUAGES

Four Indian tribes—the Creek, Chickasaw, Choctaw, and Cherokee—occupied the four quarters of Alabama as white settlement began, but by treaty agreement they were moved westward between 1814 and 1835, leaving behind such placenames as Alabama, Talladega, Mobile, and Tuscaloosa. In 1970, only 248 Alabama residents claimed an Indian language as their mother tongue.

Alabama English is predominantly Southern, with a transition zone between it and a smaller area into which South Midland speech was taken across the border from Tennessee. Some features common to both dialects occur throughout the state, such as *crocus sack* (burlap bag), *batter cakes* (made of corn meal),

LOCATION: 30°10′59″ to 35°N; 84°51′ to 88°28′24″ w. **BOUNDARIES**: Tennessee line, 148 mi (238 km); Georgia line, 298 mi (480 km); Florida line, 219 mi (352 km); Gulf of Mexico coastline, 53 mi (85 km); Mississippi line, 326 mi (525 km).

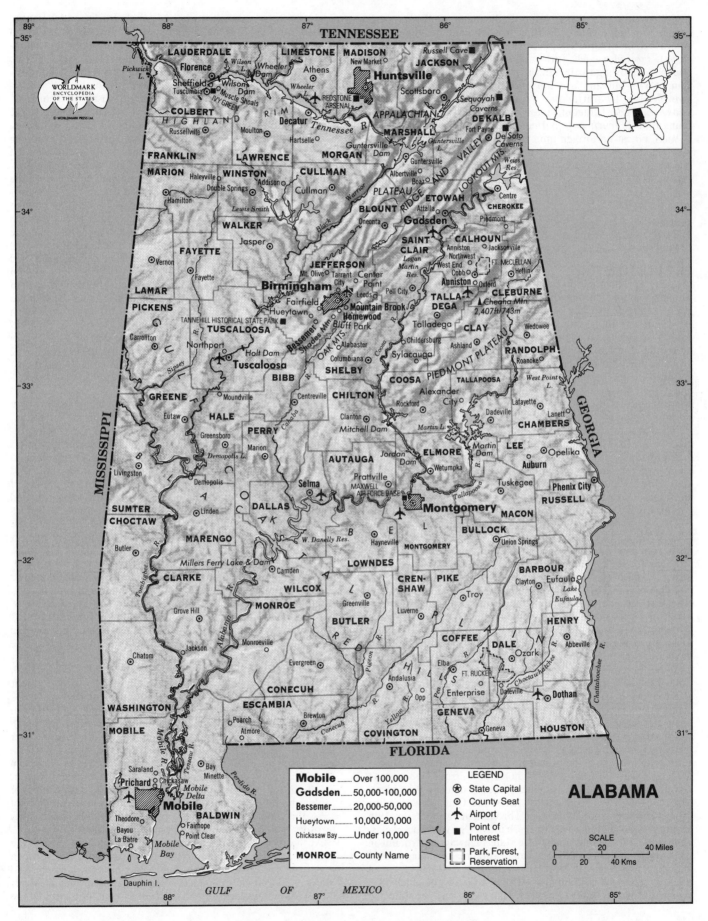

LEGEND

⊛ State Capital
⊙ County Seat
✈ Airport
■ Point of Interest
⬚ Park, Forest, Reservation

Mobile_____Over 100,000
Gadsden_____50,000-100,000
Bessemer_____20,000-50,000
Hueytown_____10,000-20,000
Chickasaw Bay_____Under 10,000

MONROE_____County Name

ALABAMA

SCALE
0   20   40 Miles
0   20   40 Kms

See US political: front cover J4; physical: back cover J4.

harp (harmonica), and *snap beans*. In the major Southern speech region are found the decreasing loss of final /r/, the /boyd/ pronunciation of *bird, soft peach* (freestone), *press peach* (clingstone), *mosquito hawk* (dragonfly), *fire dogs* (andirons), and *gopher* (burrowing turtle). In the northern third of the state are found South Midland *arm* and *barb* rhyming with *form* and *orb*, *redworm* (earthworm), *peckerwood* (woodpecker), *snake doctor* and *snake feeder* (dragonfly), *tow sack* (burlap bag), *plum peach* (clingstone), *French harp* (harmonica), and *dog irons* (andirons).

With almost no foreign immigration, 97% of the native-born residents and 94% of all residents reported in 1970 that English was their mother tongue. Principal groups reported their mother tongue as follows:

	NATIVE-BORN	FOREIGN-BORN
English	3,232,193	3,948
German	12,167	3,911
French	6,341	832
Spanish	6,059	1,311

⁹RELIGIONS

Although predominantly Baptist today, Alabama was officially Roman Catholic throughout most of the 18th century, under French and Spanish rule. A century passed between the building of the first Catholic church in 1702 and the earliest sustained efforts by Protestant evangelists. The first Baptist church in the state, the Flint River Church in Madison County, was organized in 1808; the following year, the Old Zion Methodist Church was founded in the Tombigbee area. During the second decade of the 19th century, settlers from the southeastern states brought the influence of the Great Revival to Alabama, along with the various Methodist, Presbyterian, and Baptist sects that had developed in its wake. The first black church in Alabama probably dates from 1820. As in other southern states, black slaves who had previously attended the churches of their masters formed their own churches after the Civil War. One of the earliest of these, the Little Zion Methodist Church, was established in 1867 in Mobile; most freed blacks became Baptists, however.

As of 1971, the major Protestant denominations were the Southern Baptist Convention, with 1,054,917 adherents, and the United Methodist Church, with 274,531. Other Protestant groups had a combined total of 230,355 known adherents. In 1979, Roman Catholics in Alabama numbered 99,597, and there were an estimated 8,805 Jews.

¹⁰TRANSPORTATION

The first rail line in the state—the Tuscumbia Railroad, chartered in 1830—made its first run, 44 mi (71 km) around the Muscle Shoals from Tuscumbia to Decatur, on 15 December 1834. By 1852, however, Alabama had only 165 mi (266 km) of track, less than most other southern states. Further development awaited the end of the Civil War. Birmingham, as planned by John T. Milner, chief engineer of the South and North Railroad, was founded in 1871 as a railroad intersection in the midst of Alabama's booming mining country; it subsequently became the state's main rail center, followed by Mobile. As of 1974, Alabama had 4,541 mi (7,308 km) of track. Amtrak passenger trains connect Birmingham and Tuscaloosa with Atlanta and New Orleans.

In settlement days the principal roads into Alabama were the Federal Road, formerly a Creek horse path, from Georgia and South Carolina; and the Natchez Trace, bought by the federal government (1801) from the Choctaw and Chickasaw, leading from Kentucky and Tennessee. Throughout most of the 19th century, road building was in the hands of private companies. Only after the establishment of a state highway department in 1911 and the securing of federal aid for rural road building in 1916 did Alabama begin to develop modern road systems. As of 1978 there were 87,015 mi (140,037 km) of roads, of which 78% were rural and 96% were surfaced. That same year, the state had

2,054,436 registered automobiles, 713,628 trucks, and 2,159,612 licensed drivers. The major interstate highways in Alabama all intersect at Birmingham: I-65, running from the north to Montgomery and Mobile, and I-59 from the northeast and I-20 from the east, which, after merging at Birmingham, run southwestward to Tuscaloosa and into Mississippi.

By the 1970s, Alabama had the 4th-longest system of navigable waterways of any state in the US. The coming of the steamboat to Alabama waters, beginning in 1818, stimulated settlement in the Black Belt; however, the high price of shipping cotton by water contributed to the eventual displacement of the steamboat by the railroad. Thanks to the Tennessee Valley Authority, the Tennessee River has been transformed since the 1930s into a year-round navigable waterway. The Tennessee-Tombigbee project, scheduled to be about 50% finished by the end of 1980, would provide a new barge route, partly through Alabama, from the Midwest to the Gulf of Mexico, for which the US Army Corps of Engineers would have to cut a 39-mi (63-km) canal and build 10 locks and dams; Tenn-Tom, as it is called, had an estimated cost as of mid-1980 of at least $1.8 billion. When and if completed, this would be not only the largest civilian engineering project in the US during the 1980s but also by far the largest earth-moving project in US history, displacing more earth than was moved to build the Panama Canal. Mobile, on the Gulf of Mexico, is Alabama's only international port.

At the end of 1978, Alabama had 147 airfields (95 public, 52 private): 134 airports and 13 heliports. The largest and busiest facility is Birmingham Municipal Airport.

¹¹HISTORY

The region now known as Alabama has been inhabited for some 90–100 centuries. The earliest evidence of human habitation, charcoal from an ancient campfire at Russell Cave in northeastern Alabama, is about 9,000 years old. These early peoples, probably descended from humans who crossed from Asia to North America via the Bering Strait, moved from caves and open campsites to permanent villages about AD 1000. Some of their descendants, popularly called Mound Builders, erected huge earthen temple mounds and simple huts along Alabama's rivers, beginning around 1100. Moundville (near Tuscaloosa), one of the most important Mound Builder sites in the southeastern US, includes 20 "platform mounds" for Indian buildings, dating from 1200 to 1500. When the first Europeans arrived, Alabama was inhabited by Indians, half of them either Creek or members of smaller groups living within the Creek confederacy. Cherokee Indians inhabited northeastern Alabama; Chickasaw lived in the northwest, and Choctaw settled in the southwest.

During the 16th century, five Spanish expeditions entered Mobile Bay or explored the region now called Alabama. The most extensive was that of Hernando de Soto, whose army marched from the Tennessee Valley to the Mobile Delta in 1540. In 1702, two French naval officers—Pierre Le Moyne, Sieur d'Iberville, and Jean Baptiste Le Moyne, Sieur de Bienville—established Ft. Louis de la Mobile, the first permanent European settlement in present-day Alabama. Mobile remained in French hands until 1763, when it was turned over to the British under the terms of the Treaty of Paris. Because the majority of Mobile's residents remained loyal to England during the American Revolution, that city was captured in 1780 by the forces of Spain, an ally of the rebellious American colonists. Spanish control of Mobile lasted until the city was again seized during the War of 1812, this time by American troops in 1813. Mobile was the only territory added to the US as a result of that war.

At the start of the 19th century, Indians still held most of the present State of Alabama. War broke out in 1813 between American settlers and a large Creek faction known as the Red Sticks, who were determined to resist white encroachment. After General Andrew Jackson and his Tennessee militia crushed the

Red Sticks in 1814 at the Battle of Horseshoe Bend, in central Alabama, he forced the Creek to sign a treaty ceding some 40,000 sq mi (103,600 sq km) of land to the US, thereby opening about three-fourths of the present state to white settlement. By 1839, nearly all Alabama Indians had been removed to Indian Territory.

From 1814 onward, pioneers, caught up by what was called "Alabama fever," poured out of the Carolinas, Virginia, Georgia, Tennessee, and Kentucky into what Andrew Jackson called "the best unsettled country in America." Wealthy migrants came in covered wagons, bringing their slaves, cattle, and hogs. But the great majority of pioneers were ambitious farmers hoping to acquire fertile land in the newly opened area. In 1817, Alabama became a territory; on 2 August 1819, a state constitution was adopted; and the following 14 December, Alabama was admitted to statehood.

During the antebellum era, 95% of white Alabamians lived and worked in rural areas, primarily as farmers, planting and harvesting cotton, corn, sorghum, oats, and vegetables and raising razorback hogs and cattle; by 1860, 80% of Alabama farmers owned the land they tilled. Only about one-third of all white Alabamians were slaveowners. Large planters (owners of 50 slaves or more) made up less than 1% of Alabama's white population in 1860. However, they owned 28% of the state's total wealth and occupied one-fourth of the seats in the legislature. Dominant in Alabama's economic, political, and social life, these planters led in the secession movement. Most white farm folk, fearing the consequences of an end to slavery, eventually embraced the Confederate cause, although 2,500 white Alabamians did serve in the Union Army and an estimated 8,000–10,000 others acted as Union scouts, deserted Confederate units, or hid from conscription agents.

Alabama seceded from the Union in January 1861 and shortly thereafter joined the Confederate States of America. The Confederacy was organized in Alabama's senate chamber in Montgomery, and Jefferson Davis was inaugurated president on the steps of the capitol. Montgomery served as capital of the Confederacy until May, when the seat of government was moved to Richmond, Va.

Remote from major theaters of war, Alabama experienced only occasional Union raids during the first three years of the conflict. In the summer of 1864, however, Confederate and Union ships fought a major naval engagement in Mobile Bay which ended in surrender by the outnumbered southern forces. During the Confederacy's dying days in the spring of 1865, federal troops swept through Tuscaloosa, Selma, and Montgomery. Their major goal, Selma, one of the Confederacy's main industrial centers, was left almost as heavily devastated as Richmond or Atlanta. Estimates of the number of Alabamians killed in the Civil War range from 25,000 upward.

During Reconstruction, Alabama was under military rule until readmitted to the Union in 1868. For the next six years, Republicans held most top political positions in the state. With the help of the Ku Klux Klan, Democrats regained political control of the state in November 1874.

Like many other southerners, Alabamians sought to create a "New South" in which agriculture would be balanced by industry. In the 1880s and 1890s, at least 20 Alabama towns were touted as ironworking centers. Birmingham, founded in 1871, became the New South's leading industrial center. Its promoters invested in pig iron furnaces, coal mines, steel plants, and real estate. Small companies merged with bigger ones, which were taken over, in turn, by giant corporations. In 1907, Birmingham's Tennessee Coal, Iron, and Railroad Co. was purchased by the nation's largest steelmaker, US Steel.

Another major Alabama enterprise was cotton milling. By 1900, 9,000 men, women, and children were employed in Alabama mills; most of these white workers were farm folk who had lost their land after the Civil War because of mounting debts and low cotton prices. Wages in mills were so low that entire families had to work hours as long as those they had endured as farmers.

As thousands of other Alabama farmers lost their land and became sharecroppers and tenants, farm unrest mounted. Discontented farmers and factory workers allied during the 1890s in the Populist Party, in an attempt to overthrow the Bourbon Democrats who had dominated Alabama politics for two decades. Although a number of Populists were elected to the Alabama legislature, no Populist candidate succeeded in winning the governorship, primarily because Democrats manipulated the black vote to their own advantage. In 1901, Alabama adopted a new state constitution containing numerous restrictions on voting—supposedly to end vote manipulation and restore honest elections. The tangible result of these new rules was to disfranchise almost all Alabama black voters and thousands of poor whites. As recently as 1941, fewer than one-fourth of Alabama adults were registered voters. In 1960, no blacks voted in Lowndes or Wilcox counties, 80% and 78% black, respectively.

During the 1950s and 1960s, national attention focused on civil rights demonstrations in Alabama, including the Montgomery bus boycott of 1955, the Birmingham and University of Alabama demonstrations of 1963, and the voting rights march from Selma to Montgomery in 1965. The primary antagonists were Dr. Martin Luther King, Jr., head of the Southern Christian Leadership Conference, and Governor George C. Wallace, an opponent of integration. These black protests and the sometimes violent reactions to them—such as the 1963 bombing of a church in Birmingham in which four young black girls were killed—helped influence the US Congress to pass the Civil Rights Act of 1964 and the Voting Rights Act of 1965.

Once the most tightly segregated city in the nation, Birmingham has become thoroughly integrated in public facilities and in 1979 elected its first black mayor, Richard Arrington. The civil rights era brought other momentous changes to Alabama. Hundreds of thousands of black voters are now an important force in state politics. Blacks attend schools, colleges, and universities of their choice and enjoy equal access to all public facilities. New racial attitudes among most whites have contributed to a vast improvement in the climate of race relations since 1960.

¹²STATE GOVERNMENT

Alabama has had six constitutions, the most recent one dating from 1901. That document was 123,900 words long by the end of 1977—longer than that of any other state except Georgia—and had been amended 371 times.

Alabama's bicameral legislature consists of a 35-seat senate and a 105-seat house of representatives, all of whose members are elected at the same time for four-year terms. Senators must be at least 25 years of age, representatives 21.

Elected executive officials are the governor and lieutenant-governor (separately elected), secretary of state, attorney general, treasurer, auditor, commissioner of agriculture and industries, eight members of the Board of Education, and three members of the Public Service Commission. The governor, who serves for four years, must be at least 30 years of age and must have been a US citizen for 10 years and a citizen of the state for 7.

A bill becomes a law when it is passed by at least a majority of a quorum of both houses and is signed by the governor, left unsigned for 6 days while the legislature is in session, or passed over the governor's veto by a majority of the elected members of each house. The governor may pocket veto a measure submitted fewer than 5 days before adjournment by not signing it within 10 days after adjournment. The submission of a constitutional amendment to the electorate requires the approval of three-fifths of the membership of each house.

Voters in Alabama must be US citizens, at least 18 years of age, and must have resided in the state at least 30 days prior to the election.

13 POLITICAL PARTIES
The major political parties in Alabama are the Democratic and Republican parties, each affiliated with the national party organization.

Pre–Civil War political divisions in the state reflected those elsewhere in the South. Small and subsistence farmers, especially in the northern hill country and pine forest areas, tended to be Jacksonian Democrats, while the planters of the Black Belt and the river valleys often voted Whig. After a period of Radical Republican rule during Reconstruction, the Bourbon Democrats, whose party then served largely the interests of wealthy property owners, businessmen, and white supremacists, ran the state for the rest of the century, despite a challenge in the 1890s by the Populist Party.

During the 20th century, the Democratic Party has continued to command virtually every statewide office, major and minor. The continued strength of the party during the 1960s and 1970s depended, in part, on the allegiance of black voters; the number of registered black voters increased from 111,000 in 1960 to about 321,000 in 1976. In the 1980 elections, Republican Ronald Reagan won a slim majority of Alabama's popular vote, while Jeremiah Denton, a former prisoner of war in Viet-Nam, became the first Alabama Republican since Reconstruction to win election to the US Senate.

On two occasions, 1948 and 1964, the Alabama Democratic Party bolted the national Democratic ticket, each time because of disagreement over civil rights. Barry Goldwater in 1964 was the first Republican presidential candidate in the 20th century to carry Alabama. In 1968, George Wallace carried Alabama overwhelmingly on the American Independent Party slate.

14 LOCAL GOVERNMENT
Alabama has 67 counties, more than 400 municipalities, and at least 300 special districts. Counties are governed by county commissions, usually consisting of three to seven commissioners, elected by district. Other county officials include a clerk, assessor, tax collector, sheriff, and superintendent of education.

Until the late 1970s, the predominant form of municipal government, especially in the larger cities, was the commission, whose members may be elected either at-large or by district. Partly in response to court orders requiring district elections in order to permit the election of more black officials, there has since been a trend toward the mayor-council form—though a US Supreme Court ruling in May 1980 that Mobile may elect its public officials at-large places in doubt the movement toward greater representation of blacks at the local level.

An alteration in local government had a significant effect on the racial climate in Birmingham during the 1960s, when the Young Men's Business Club led a movement to change to the mayor-council system, in order to oust a commission (including Eugene "Bull" Connor as public safety commissioner) that for nearly a decade had reacted negatively to every black demand. After a narrow vote in favor of the change, a moderate was elected mayor in April 1963, but the former commissioners then contested the initial vote that had changed the system. At the height of Birmingham's racial troubles, both the former commissioners and the newly elected council claimed to govern Birmingham, but neither did so effectively. When peace came, it was as the result of an unofficial meeting held between local black leaders and 77 of the city's most influential whites, with federal officials serving as mediators. Although the council, like the commissioners, publicly opposed these negotiations, once they were over and the council's election confirmed, the new moderate leadership permitted peaceful racial accommodation to go forward.

15 STATE SERVICES
Alabama's Ethics Commission administers the state's ethics laws, makes financial disclosure records available to the public, and receives monthly reports from lobbyists. Educational services are administered primarily by the Department of Education and the Alabama Commission on Higher Education, which manages the state's student financial aid programs. The Department of Aeronautics, Highway Department, and Public Service Commission administer transportation services; driver's licenses are issued by the Department of Public Safety.

Health and welfare services are offered primarily through the Medical Services Administration, Department of Public Health, Department of Mental Health, Department of Veterans Affairs, the Commission on Aging, Alabama Women's Commission, Department of Youth Services, and Department of Adult Blind

Alabama Presidential Vote by Political Parties, 1948–80

YEAR	ELECTORAL VOTE	ALABAMA WINNER	DEMOCRAT	REPUBLICAN	STATES' RIGHTS DEMOCRAT	PROHIBITION	PROGRESSIVE
1948	11	Thurmond (SRD)	—	40,930	171,443	1,026	1,522
1952	11	Stevenson (D)	275,075	149,231	—	1,814	
					UNPLEDGED		
1956	11	Stevenson (D)	279,542	195,694	20,323	—	—
					NAT'L. STATES' RIGHTS		
1960	11	*Kennedy (D)	318,303	236,110	4,367	—	—
					UNPLEDGED DEMOCRAT		
1964	10	Goldwater (R)	—	479,085	210,782	—	—
					AMERICAN IND.		AM. IND. DEMOCRAT
1968	10	Wallace (AI)	195,918	146,591	687,664	3,814	10,518
					AMERICAN		
1972	9	*Nixon (R)	256,923	728,701	11,928	8,559	—
					AMERICAN IND.		COMMUNIST
1976	9	*Carter (D)	659,170	504,070	9,198	6,669	1,954
1980	9	*Reagan (R)	636,730	654,192	—	—	—

*Won US presidential election.

and Deaf. Planning for the state's future health-care needs is carried out by the Health Planning and Development Agency.

Public protection services are administered by the Military Department, Board of Corrections, Alabama Law Enforcement Planning Agency, and Department of Public Safety, among other agencies. Numerous government bodies offer resource protection services: the Department of Conservation and Natural Resources, Alabama Coastal Area Board, Alabama Forestry Commission, Oil and Gas Board, Surface Mining Reclamation Commission, and Alabama State Soil and Water Conservation Committee.

[16] JUDICIAL SYSTEM

The high court of Alabama is the supreme court, consisting of a chief justice and eight associate justices, all elected for staggered six-year terms. It issues opinions on constitutional issues, has appellate jurisdiction over major civil cases, and may review decisions of the two lower courts of appeal. The court of civil appeals hears suits involving sums up to $10,000; its three judges are elected for six-year terms, and the one who has served the longest is the presiding judge. The five judges of the court of criminal appeals are also elected for six-year terms.

Circuit courts, of which there were 39 systems with 110 judgeships in 1979, have exclusive original jurisdiction over civil actions involving sums of more than $5,000, exclusive original jurisdiction in criminal cases (concurrent with district courts in noncapital cases in which the defendant pleads guilty), and appellate jurisdiction over cases from lower courts.

A new system of district courts replaced county and juvenile courts as of January 1977. There are 66 district court systems in 73 locations. At least one judge is elected per county (except that Clay and Coosa counties share a single judge), and nine counties elect two or more judges, who, like circuit court judges, serve six-year terms.

During 1978, 5,524 prisoners were held in state and federal prisons in Alabama, including 1,342 inmates held in local jails because of overcrowding. In 1976, US Districct Court Judge Frank M. Johnson, Jr., ruled that conditions in Alabama prisons inflicted "cruel and unusual punishment" upon inmates, spurring the process of prison reform.

Alabama had an FBI Crime Index rate in 1978 of 3,939 crimes per 100,000 population, including 419 violent crimes and 3,520 property crimes; all these rates were below the national averages. However, Alabama had the 5th-highest murder rate in the nation—13.3 per 100,000 population—and Mobile's murder rate, 18.6, was among the highest for US metropolitan areas.

An Alabama case that became internationally notorious was that of the nine "Scottsboro boys," eight of whom were sentenced to death and one to life imprisonment in 1931 for the alleged rape of two white girls, one of whom later recanted her charges. After multiple appeals and reversals, five indictments were subsequently dropped; of the four remaining defendants, all sentenced to lengthy jail terms, three were paroled and one escaped to Michigan, which refused extradition.

[17] ARMED FORCES

The US Department of Defense had 59,918 authorized personnel in Alabama during 1977/78. The major installation was the US Army's Redstone Arsenal at Huntsville, with 21,586 personnel. Redstone is the center of the Army's missile and rocket programs and contains the George C. Marshall Space Flight Center of the National Aeronautics and Space Administration, which directs all private contractors for the space program. Among the spacecraft developed there were the Redstone rocket, which launched the first US astronaut, and Explorer I, the first US earth-orbiting satellite. Other installations include Ft. Rucker (near Enterprise), Ft. McClellan (Anniston), and Maxwell Air Force Base (Montgomery), site of the US Air University and national headquarters for the Civil Air Patrol. During 1977/78, Alabama firms received defense contract awards totaling $480 million.

There were 422,000 veterans of US military service in Alabama as of 30 September 1979, 8,000 of whom served in World War I, 171,000 in World War II, 91,000 in the Korean conflict, and 125,000 during the Viet-Nam era. During 1977/78, benefits paid to Alabama veterans amounted to $395.9 million.

Alabama maintained 191 Army and 26 Air National Guard Units as of 1980 at a strength of approximately 21,000. State and local police forces numbered 8,185 during 1977.

[18] MIGRATION

After 1814, Alabama was the mecca of a great migratory wave, mainly of whites of English and Scotch-Irish descent (some with their black slaves) from Virginia, Georgia, and the Carolinas. Since the Civil War, migration to Alabama has been slight. Many blacks left Alabama from World War I through the 1960s to seek employment in the East and Midwest, but following the civil rights revolution, the trend began to reverse; more blacks chose to remain in the state, and some who had gone elsewhere returned. Overall, Alabama lost 944,000 residents through migration between 1940 and 1970, but enjoyed a net gain from migration of 51,000 between 1970 and 1977.

[19] INTERGOVERNMENTAL COOPERATION

Among the interstate compacts and commissions in which Alabama participates are the Appalachian Regional Commission, Gulf States Marine Fisheries Compact, Interstate Mining Compact, Interstate Oil and Gas Compact, Southeastern Forest Fire Protection Compact, Southern Growth Policies Compact, Southern Interstate Energy Compact, Southern Regional Education Compact, and Tennessee-Tombigbee Waterway Development Compact. The Office of State Planning and Federal Programs coordinates planning efforts by all levels of government.

During 1978/79, Alabama received federal aid amounting to nearly $1.4 billion, of which $108.8 million was general revenue sharing.

[20] ECONOMY

Cotton dominated Alabama's economy from the mid-19th century to the 1870s, when large-scale industrialization began. The coal, iron, and steel industries were the first to develop, followed by other resource industries such as textiles, clothing, paper, and wood products. Although Alabama's prosperity has increased, particularly in recent decades, the state still lags in wage rates and per capita income. One factor that hindered the growth of the state's own economy was the ownership of resource industries by large corporations outside the state.

By the mid-1960s, the state had begun to take steps toward overcoming another important obstacle to its economic progress—the problem of race. One dramatic and influential gesture made early in 1965 was the placing of an advertisement in several national journals and 22 Alabama dailies by the state government, 10 local chambers of commerce, and leading Alabama business groups affirming the right of blacks to vote and advocating communication between the races.

Economic projections from the mid-1970s indicated that between 1974 and 1985, employment in fisheries, metal mining, and agriculture would decline, while employment in the mining sector as a whole would grow more than 65%, largely because of expansion in the coal, oil, and natural gas industries. Major gains were also expected in finance, services (with the largest increases in business, automobile repair, and medical and health services), manufacturing (especially in electrical machinery, professional and scientific instruments, and petroleum and coal products), and state and local government. The total growth in employment was expected to be 18% for the period.

[21] INCOME

Alabama's per capita personal income in 1978 was $6,247, for a rank of 47th among the 50 states—the same position it held in 1960, when the per capita figure was $1,510. Measured in constant 1972 dollars, Alabamians' total income more than doubled during the same period, and current per capita income rose from 69% of the US average to 80%. Median family income was $11,785 in 1975 (45th in the US), when some 587,000 Alabamians (more than 16% of the population) were living below the federal poverty level. There is an apparent correlation between poverty and race, especially in rural Alabama: the 8 counties with the highest percentage of nonwhites in 1970—Bullock, Greene, Hale, Lowndes, Macon, Perry, Sumter, and Wilcox— all were among the 10 poorest counties, their highest per capita average being $1,817, as against the state average of $2,578.

²²LABOR

Alabama's civilian labor force in 1978 numbered 1,592,000, of whom 962,000 were males and 630,000 females. Alabama's total employment was 1,492,000, yielding an unemployment rate of 6.3%, 4.7% for whites and 12.4% for blacks.

A federal census of workers covered by unemployment insurance in March 1977 revealed the following nonfarm employment pattern in Alabama:

	ESTABLISH- MENTS	EMPLOYEES	ANNUAL PAYROLL ('000)
Agricultural services, forestry, fishing	698	4,285	$ 34,186
Mining, of which:	330	14,552	237,952
Bituminous coal, lignite	(174)	(11,213)	(190,809)
Contract construction	6,645	71,908	831,413
Manufacturing, of which:	5,257	345,071	3,872,407
Primary metals	(156)	(41,424)	(709,557)
Transportation, public utilities	2,649	53,905	713,494
Wholesale trade	5,607	64,218	730,776
Retail trade	20,772	184,136	1,199,802
Finance, insurance, real estate	5,274	54,521	561,596
Services	16,744	158,259	1,270,688
Other	1,127	1,625	16,982
TOTALS	65,103	952,480	$9,469,296

Government employees, not included in this survey, numbered about 247,000 in 1978.

In 1871, James Thomas Rapier, a black Alabamian who would later serve a term as a US representative from the state, organized the first black labor union in the South, the short-lived Labor Union of Alabama. The Knights of Labor began organizing in the state in 1882. A serious obstacle to unionization and collective bargaining was the convict leasing system, which was not ended officially until 1923 and in practice not until five years later. In 1888, the Tennessee Coal, Iron, and Railroad Co. (later taken over by US Steel) was granted an exclusive 10-year contract to use the labor of all state convicts, paying the state $9–18 a man per month. Until the beginning of World War II, US Steel paid its workers in metal scrip called "clackers," which could be redeemed only at company stores. Child labor was also exploited. Alabama had limited a child's working day to 8 hours in 1887, but a Massachusetts company that was building a large mill in the state secured the repeal of that law in 1895. A weaker measure passed 12 years later limited the child's workweek to 60 hours and set the minimum working age at 12.

As of 1976, 290,000 Alabamians belonged to unions or employee associations; unions were especially strong in the northern industrial cities and in Mobile. About 19% of all nonagricultural workers were unionized—the highest rate among states with right-to-work laws. In 1980, the state legislature repealed a law that had required companies bidding for government contracts to pay the highest prevailing wage for the kind of labor employed.

²³AGRICULTURE

Alabama ranked 26th among the 50 states in agricultural income in 1978, with $1.9 billion.

There was considerable diversity in Alabama's earliest agriculture. By the mid-19th century, however, cotton had taken over, and production of other crops dropped so much that corn and other staples, even work animals, were often imported. In 1860, cotton was grown in every county, and one-crop agriculture had already worn out much of Alabama's farmland.

Diversification began early in the 20th century, a trend accelerated by the destructive effects of the boll weevil on cotton growing. As of 1979 there were some 56,000 farms in Alabama, occupying approximately 13 million acres (5 million hectares), or roughly two-fifths of the state's land area. Soybeans and livestock are raised in the Black Belt; peanuts in the southeast; vegetables, livestock, and timber in the southwest; and cotton and soybeans in the Tennessee River Valley. In 1979, Alabama ranked 2d in the US in production of peanuts for nuts, with 595,335,000 lb, worth $122,044,000. Other crops included soybeans, 56,250,000 bushels, $343,125,000; corn for grain, 30,622,000 bushels, $88,804,000; tomatoes for fresh market, 516,000 hundredweight, $18,277,000; and watermelons, 1,122,000 hundredweight, $6,225,000. The 1978 cotton crop, 320,000 bales, was valued at about $85,000,000.

²⁴ANIMAL HUSBANDRY

The principal livestock-raising regions of Alabama are the far north, the southwest, and the Black Belt, where the lime soil provides excellent pasturage. During 1979, Alabama produced 626.9 million lb of cattle and calves, valued at $409.4 million, and 297.2 million lb of hog and pigs, valued at $129.3 million. At the close of 1979 there were 1,730,000 cattle and 880,000 hogs on Alabama farms and ranches. In addition, 78,000 milk cows yielded 603 million lb of milk during the same year.

Alabama is a leading producer of chickens, broilers, and eggs. In broiler production, the state was surpassed only by Arkansas and Georgia in 1979, with 1.9 billion lb, valued at $459 million. That year, Alabama ranked 3d in chicken production, with 1.9 billion lb, worth $468.2 million; and 4th in egg production, with 3.3 billion, worth $180.7 million.

²⁵FISHING

Alabama's commercial fish catch was estimated at 31,553,000 lb, worth $35,922,000, in 1978. The principal fishing port is Bayou La Batre, which brought in about 22,200,000 ib, worth $25,100,000. Catfish farming is of growing importance.

²⁶FORESTRY

Forestland in Alabama, predominantly pine, covering 21,361,000 acres (8,645,000 hectares), was nearly 3% of the nation's total in 1977. Nearly all of that was classified as commercial timberland, 95% of it privately owned. Shipments of lumber and wood products were valued at $1.2 billion in 1977; of paper and paper products, $1.9 billion.

²⁷MINING

Alabama ranked 19th among the 50 states in mineral output during 1978, with nearly $1.3 billion worth. The most valuable minerals include coal, petroleum, natural gas, and lime. The mining of iron, the foundation of the state's large steel industry, had virtually ceased by the late 1970s, as steelmakers substituted cheaper foreign iron.

Output in 1978 (excluding fossil fuels) was as follows: stone, 26,114,000 tons; sand and gravel, 14,500,000 tons; cement, 3,281,000 tons; clays, 2,755,000 tons; and lime, 1,167,000 tons.

²⁸ENERGY AND POWER

Electrical generating plants in Alabama had an installed capacity of 18.6 million kw in 1978, when production totaled 71.6 billion kwh. About half of the capacity and production came from private sources, with most of the remainder attributable to the Tennessee Valley Authority, which also owned three of the state's four nuclear reactors.

Significant petroleum finds in Alabama date from the early 1950s. The 1978 output was 11,188,000 barrels; proved reserves as of 31 December 1978 totaled 33,107,000 barrels. During the same year, 55.9 billion cu feet of natural gas were extracted, leaving reserves of 751.2 billion cu feet. Coal production, which began in the 19th century, reached 20,553,000 tons in 1978, of which 70% was surface mined. Coal reserves in 1976 totaled 3.1 billion tons, two-thirds bituminous and one-third lignite.

[29]INDUSTRY

Alabama's industrial boom, which began in the 1870s with the exploitation of the coal and iron fields in the north, quickly transformed Birmingham into the number-one industrial city in the South, producing pig iron more cheaply than its American and English competitors. Although Birmingham remains highly dependent on steel, the state's industry has diversified considerably since World War II. An important stimulus to manufacturing in the north was the development of ports and power plants along the Tennessee River.

As of 1977, the principal employers among industry groups were apparel and textiles, primary metal industries, and fabricated metal products, together accounting for 47% of the state's manufacturing jobs. The total value added by manufacture exceeded $8.3 billion, of which apparel and textiles contributed 16%; primary metals, 12%; paper and allied products, 11%; chemicals and chemical products, 10%; and rubber and miscellaneous plastic products, 9%. The following table shows value added in 1972 and 1977 by selected industries:

	1972	1977
Tires and inner tubes	$251,800,000	$589,900,000
Blast furnaces and basic steel products	412,200,000	369,200,000
Men's and boys' apparel	159,800,000	304,600,000
Paperboard mill products	NA	278,600,000
Agricultural chemicals	55,700,000	167,100,000
Meat products	94,600,000	150,600,000
Motor vehicles and equipment	NA	144,900,000

[30]COMMERCE

With sales of $7.5 billion, Alabama ranked 27th among the 50 states in wholesale trade in 1972. As of 1977, Alabama ranked 22d in retail trade, with sales of $10.7 billion. The leading types of businesses were automotive dealers, 24%; grocery stores, 22%; department stores, 8%; gasoline service stations, 8%; and eating and drinking places, 6%. Among counties, Jefferson had the largest share of retail sales, 23%; Birmingham, within it, led all the cities with 12%. Alcoholic beverages, except for beer and wine, are sold in ABC (Alcoholic Beverage Control) stores, run by the state. Prohibition is by local option.

Alabama exported $832 million worth of manufactured goods in 1976 (25th in the US). Foreign exports of agricultural products totaled $332 million in 1976/77 (22d).

[31]CONSUMER PROTECTION

The Office of Consumer Protection, established in 1972, was transferred to the Office of the Attorney General in 1979. Because Alabama did not as of mid-1980 have a consumer protection law—it was the only state without one—the office served mainly as a mediator, although in 1979/80 it did bring suit successfully in a limited number of cases.

[32]BANKING

Alabama's 312 insured commercial banks had assets exceeding $14.7 billion in 1978; outstanding loans totaled $5.1 billion and savings deposits were nearly $12.7 billion. There were 61 insured savings and loan associations, with combined assets of $4.3 billion, savings capital of $3.7 billion, and outstanding mortgage loans of $3.6 billion. During the same year, Alabama also had 114 state-chartered credit unions, with assets exceeding $436.5 million. There were 535 finance companies licensed in the state under the Consumer Credit Act during 1979, some 200 finance companies licensed under the Small Loan Act, and about 7,000 merchants extending consumer credit.

[33]INSURANCE

During 1978, life insurance in force per family in Alabama averaged $34,100, slightly below the national average. A total of 12,375,000 policies were in force, amounting to $46 billion. Benefits paid by life insurance companies to Alabamians totaled $359.4 million, of which $185.3 million consisted of death benefits paid to 106,800 beneficiaries.

Property and liability insurers wrote premiums amounting to more than $1 billion in 1978. Of that total, $226.9 million was automobile liability insurance.

[34]SECURITIES

Alabama has no securities exchanges. New York Stock Exchange member firms had 29 sales offices and 247 registered representatives in the state during 1978. Alabamians reported $256.6 million in dividend income on their 1977 federal tax returns.

[35]PUBLIC FINANCE

The Division of the Budget within the Department of Finance prepares and administers the state budget, which the governor submits to the legislature for amendment and approval. The fiscal year runs from 1 October through 30 September.

The following table summarizes consolidated revenues and expenditures for 1979/80 (estimated) and 1980/81 (recommended), in millions:

REVENUES	1979/80	1980/81
General fund	$ 296.7	$ 298.4
Federal and local funds	1,417.5	1,628.0
Special educational trust fund:		
Income tax	508.2	582.0
Sales tax	479.4	514.5
Utility tax	107.6	120.5
Other receipts	148.7	157.1
Special mental health fund	52.0	57.1
TOTALS	$3,010.1	$3,357.6
EXPENDITURES		
Highway Department	$ 334.2	$ 473.7
Medical Services Administration	314.8	305.8
Department of Industrial Relations	268.0	291.0
Department of Pensions and Security	221.1	236.3
Department of Mental Health	98.3	103.7
Other general, federal, and local fund outlays	477.8	515.9
Special educational trust fund	1,243.9	1,350.6
Special mental health fund	82.5	83.2
TOTALS	$3,040.6	$3,360.2

As of mid-1977, the total debt of Alabama state and local governments was $3.1 billion, or $849 per capita.

[36]TAXATION

Alabama ranked 23d in the US in total tax receipts in 1978, with $1.6 billion. Per capita tax revenues of all state and local governments, $507 in 1977, were less than those of every other state except Arkansas, and receipts from property taxes ($60 per capita) were the lowest in the nation.

As of 1980, the personal income tax, which is designated for education, ranged from 1.5% on the first $1,000 to 5% on amounts over $5,000. The tax on corporate net income was 5% for most enterprises, but 6% for financial institutions. Corporate income taxes in 1978 supplied 5.2% of Alabama's total tax revenues, much less than the nationwide rate of 9.5%. The state also imposes a sales tax of 4%; most cities in the state charge an additional 2%. Other state levies include a value-added tax, severance taxes on coal and timber, and taxes on oil production, gasoline sales, cigarettes, and railroads.

Alabama paid $4 billion in federal taxes in 1975/76 and received federal expenditures totaling $5.4 billion, for a spending/tax ratio of 1.35, one of the highest in the US. State residents filed 1.3 million federal income tax returns in 1977, paying $1.9 billion in tax.

[37] ECONOMIC POLICY

Alabama seeks to attract out-of-state business by means of tax incentives and plant-building assistance. The Alabama Industrial Development Training Institute, within the Department of Education, provides job training especially designed to suit the needs of new or expanding industries in the state. The state Foreign Trade Relations Commission seeks to promote international markets for Alabama products.

[38] HEALTH

Alabama ranked 45th among the 50 states in average life expectancy during 1969–71 at 69.05 years, 73.41 for females and 64.90 for males. The infant death rate in 1977, 16.9 per 1,000 live births, was the 5th highest in the US; the rate for whites was 13.4, for blacks 23.6. Rates for births, marriages, and divorces all exceeded the national averages for 1977, but the abortion rate in Alabama was only about half the national norm.

The state's overall death rate in 1977, 9.4 deaths per 1,000 population, included the nation's 2d-highest death rate from cerebrovascular disease, 109 per 100,000 population; the 7th-highest from accidents, 67 per 100,000; and, with two other states, the 7th-highest from early infancy diseases, 13 per 100,000. Alabama also ranked above the national average in death rates from pneumonia, influenza, and diabetes mellitus, but below it for heart disease, cancer, and arteriosclerosis; the state had the 6th-lowest rate of death by suicide (10.7 per 100,000 population), and, with Tennessee, the 9th-lowest death rate from cirrhosis of the liver (9.6). In 1970, Alabama was estimated to have the 2d-lowest rate of alcoholism in the US, 1,830 per 100,000 population. The East Alabama Sickle Cell Association, a private nonprofit diagnostic service that receives state and federal funds, attempts to screen residents of a 10-county area of east-central Alabama. No other agency or clinic provides sickle-cell screening in the area, in which 200,970 out of a population of 521,400 were at risk in 1980.

Alabama had 148 hospitals in 1978; there were 25,242 beds and 752,371 admissions, for a 76% average occupancy rate. Hospital personnel included 8,395 registered nurses and 5,844 licensed practical nurses. The average cost of hospital care was $154 per day and $1,094 per stay, both figures being more than 20% below the US average. Approximately one-third of Alabama women receive maternity care in local health department clinics, and in 1978, about 70,000 persons received family planning services in these clinics. Alabama had 4,330 licensed physicians in 1977 and 1,314 professionally active dentists in 1979.

Beginning in 1932, a number of black men in Macon county were unknowingly the subjects of experimentation on syphilis by the US Public Health Service. A suit brought on their behalf in 1973 was resolved two years later: $37,500 was to be paid to living survivors of the study who had had syphilis, $16,000 to living controls, $15,000 to heirs of deceased syphilitics, and $5,000 to heirs of deceased controls. As of 1980, a search was still under way for eligible beneficiaries.

[39] SOCIAL WELFARE

Until the federal government became involved in social welfare programs during the 1930s, welfare in Alabama had been primarily private, through such organizations as the Community Chest. Public welfare expenditures in Alabama are still low by national standards: spending on the five largest programs totaled $501 million in 1976, with the federal government providing nearly 84% of the funds.

Payments of approximately $78 million were made in 1978 to 174,400 recipients of aid to families with dependent children; the average monthly payment, $112 per family, was 5th lowest in the US. During 1977, $193 million was paid under Medicaid, the state's fastest-growing welfare program. In 1978/79, food stamps were issued to a monthly average of 130,685 families (420,888 persons), at a total cost of $159 million. In addition,

283,101 victims of Hurricane Frederic were issued $14.3 million in emergency food stamps. During 1977/78, Alabama's rate of participation in the national school lunch program was the 5th highest in the US; 638,000 students, or 83% of the enrollment at participating schools, were served at a federal cost of $49.5 million.

During 1977, Social Security benefits exceeding $1.3 billion were paid to 615,200 Alabamians: $735.6 million to 347,600 retired workers, $225 million to 105,100 disabled workers, and $357.6 million in survivors' benefits to 162,400 recipients. The average monthly payment to retired workers (excluding persons with special benefits) was $215.20, 4th lowest among the 50 states. Supplemental Security Income payments in 1978 totaled $164.4 million, including $85.4 million to the aged, with an average monthly payment of $86, and $76.1 million to the disabled, for an average of $128 a month. Under additional programs that were entirely state-financed in 1980, the aged received average monthly stipends of $56, and the permanently and totally disabled received $72. In 1978, payments of $43 million under the Black Lung Benefit program were paid by the Social Security Administration to 19,000 Alabama beneficiaries.

More than 600 visually and aurally handicapped persons were expected to receive rehabilitation services from the Department of Adult Blind and Deaf during 1980/81. In 1977, workers' compensation payments totaled $72 million. Vocational rehabilitation expenditures amounted to $24.8 million in 1978, when unemployment insurance benefits reached $111 million, with an average of 32,000 beneficiaries per week.

[40] HOUSING

At the time of the 1970 census there were 1,120,220 housing units in Alabama, of which 1,034,113 were occupied. Two-thirds of these were owner-occupied, and only 84% had full plumbing.

A total of 61,800 new units valued at more than $1.3 billion were authorized between 1976 and 1978. During 1977/78, Alabama received $51 million in aid from the US Department of Housing and Urban Development for low-income housing and $52.3 million in HUD community development block grants.

The Fairhope Single Tax Corp., near Point Clear, was founded in 1893 by Iowans seeking to put into practice the economic theories of Henry George. Incorporated under Alabama law in 1904, this oldest and largest of US single-tax experiments continues to lease land in return for the payment of a rent (the "single tax") based on the land's valuation; the combined rents are used to pay all government taxes and to provide and improve community services.

[41] EDUCATION

Public education in Alabama was slow to gain state support. During the first half of the 19th century, the state failed in its attempts to fund education by land sales. The success of the public school system in Mobile, founded in 1852, influenced the legislature to appropriate $100,000 for a state system two years later. Today, state funding for education is provided through a special trust fund that accounted for about 40% of consolidated state government expenditures in 1980/81.

In 1970, Alabama had the 6th-highest illiteracy rate in the US—2.1% of the population aged 14 and older. By 1976, 55.5% of Alabamians 18 and older were high school graduates, the 5th-lowest rate in the nation. Nearly 7% of adult Alabamians had no more than 4 years of grade school, and the median number of school years completed was 12.2, well below the national average.

The total enrollment in Alabama's public schools during 1978/79 was 773,051: 382,037 in kindergarten and elementary grades, 211,711 in junior high school, and 179,303 in high school. In fall 1977, estimated enrollment in nonpublic schools was 20,000 in elementary grades and 4,000 in secondary grades, well below the estimates of 37,000 and 12,000, respectively, for 1975. As of 1976, more than 41% of all minority public-school students were in schools with less than 50% minority-group enrollment; 24% were in schools with 99–100% minority enrollment. Despite George Wallace's opposition, court-ordered integration began early in Wallace's first term as governor (1963–67) at all state universities and large public-school systems.

As of 1979 there were 58 institutions of higher education in Alabama, 36 public and 22 private; 28 of them were two-year institutions, many of them community colleges founded under Governor George Wallace. The major state universities are Auburn (founded in 1856), with a 1977/78 enrollment of 17,977, and the three campuses of the University of Alabama: the main campus near Tuscaloosa (1831), 16,821; Birmingham (1966), 12,540; and Huntsville (1950), 4,011. Tuskegee Institute, founded as a normal and industrial school in 1881 under the leadership of Booker T. Washington, soon became one of the nation's most famous black colleges; its 1977/78 enrollment was 3,296. Another well-known black college in the state is Talladega, founded in 1867, with an enrollment of 586. The Alabama Commission on Higher Education manages the State Student Assistance Program and the Alabama Student Grant Program.

42 ARTS

The Alabama State Council on the Arts and Humanities, established by the legislature in 1967, provides aid to local arts organizations; there were 70 local arts councils in 1980. The Alabama Shakespeare Festival in Anniston, the only nonprofit professional theater in the state, has a summer season and a fall tour. The Birmingham Festival of Arts was founded in 1951, and the city's Alabama School of Fine Arts has been state-supported since 1971. Birmingham also has a professional symphony orchestra and an active chamber music society.

Sacred Harp a cappella "sings" of old hymn tunes are held regularly, and there is a Sacred Harp gathering each fall at Addison in Winston County. The Tennessee Valley Old Time Fiddlers Convention takes place on the first Saturday in October at Athens State College. Every June, the annual Memorial and Country Music Celebration is held near the birthplace of Hank Williams at the Mt. Olive West community in Butler County.

43 LIBRARIES AND MUSEUMS

As of 1980, Alabama had 182 local public libraries and 25 county and multicounty regional libraries. Alabama public libraries had a combined total of 4,706,979 volumes in 1977/78, when the total circulation was 13,309,363. The Amelia Gayle Gorgas Library of the University of Alabama had 965,153 volumes; the Birmingham Public and Jefferson County Free Library had 19 branches and 975,448 volumes. The Alabama Department of History and Archives Library, at Montgomery, has about 250,000 volumes, with special collections on Alabama history and the Civil War. Collections on aviation and space exploration in Alabama's libraries, particularly its military libraries, may be the most extensive in the US outside of Washington, D.C. Memorabilia of Wernher von Braun are deposited in the library at the Alabama Space and Rocket Center at Huntsville, and the Redstone Arsenal's Scientific Information Center holds some 200,000 volumes and 1,200,000 technical reports.

Alabama has nearly 50 museums and historic sites. The most important art museum is the Birmingham Museum of Art. Other museums include the George Washington Carver Museum at Tuskegee Institute, the Women's Army Corps Museum at Ft. McClellan, the Army Aviation Museum at Ft. Rucker, the Pike Pioneer Museum at Troy, and the Museum of the City of Mobile. Russell Cave National Monument has an archaeological museum. In Florence is the W. C. Handy Restored Birthplace and Museum; at Tuscumbia, Helen Keller's birthplace, Ivy Green.

There is a zoo in Birmingham and planetariums in Montgomery and Birmingham. The spectacular gardens of the Bellingrath mansion at Theodore (near Mobile) feature thousands of rose bushes, azalea, and boxwood.

44 COMMUNICATIONS

At the end of 1978 there were 2,419,979 telephones, 1,849,732 residential and 570,247 business. Only in Mississippi and Louisiana did a smaller percentage of households have telephone service than in Alabama, with 89%.

During the same year, Alabama had 207 commercial radio stations (138 AM, 69 FM) and 17 television stations. The state Educational Television Commission operated, as of 1980, 9 television transmitters, 47 microwave relay stations, a public radio broadcasting station at Huntsville, and two 24-hour-a-day radio transmitters for weather broadcasts. In 1978, 86 cable television systems served 241,299 subscribers in 138 communities.

45 PRESS

The earliest newspaper in Alabama, the short-lived *Mobile Centinel* (sic), made its first appearance on 23 May 1811. The oldest newspaper still in existence in the state is the *Mobile Register*, founded in 1813.

As of 1978, Alabama had 7 morning dailies, with a combined circulation of 204,753; 18 evening dailies, with 534,069; and 17 Sunday papers, with 684,941. The following table shows the leading dailies with their 1978 circulations:

AREA	NAME	DAILY	SUNDAY
Birmingham	News (e,S)	174,392	218,647
	Post-Herald (m)	67,374	
Huntsville	Times (e,S)	51,400	55,613
Mobile	Register (m,S)	47,488 }	96,547
	Press (e,S)	54,259 }	
Montgomery	Advertiser (m,S)	48,038	74,987
	Alabama Journal (e)	25,723	

46 ORGANIZATIONS

National organizations with headquarters in Alabama include Civitan International (a service club), the National Federation of State Poetry Societies, and the Life Insurance Society of America, in Birmingham; the National Speleological Society, Huntsville; and the Montgomery Cotton Exchange and Southern Poverty Law Center, Montgomery. The last-named was one of the major civil rights organizations active in Alabama in 1980, along with the Southern Christian Leadership Conference (SCLC), the National Association for the Advancement of Colored People (NAACP), and the Committee Against the Death Penalty. Two branches of the Ku Klux Klan were also active in Alabama: the United Klans of America, with headquarters in Tuscaloosa, and the Invisible Empire, Knights of the Ku Klux Klan, which organized extensively in northern Alabama in late 1978 and 1979.

47 TOURISM, TRAVEL, AND RECREATION

During 1977, some 7,705,000 persons took trips to and through Alabama, 41% of them to destinations within the state. The number-one tourist attraction, with more than 750,000 visitors yearly, is the Alabama Space and Rocket Center at Huntsville, the official museum for the US space program. Among the many antebellum houses and plantations to be seen in the state are Magnolia Grove (a state shrine) at Greensboro, Gaineswood and Bluff Hall at Demopolis, Arlington in Birmingham, Oakleigh at Mobile, Sturdivant Hall at Selma, and Shorter Mansion at Eufaula. The celebration of Mardi Gras in Mobile, which began in 1704, predates that in New Orleans and now occupies 10 days before Ash Wednesday; since 1939, blacks in Mobile have held a special carnival and parade. Point Clear, across the bay from Mobile, has been a fashionable resort, especially for southerners, since the 1830s. The state fair is held at Birmingham every October.

During 1980/81, 7,200,000 visitors were expected at 21 state parks covering a total of 45,014 acres (18,217 hectares). Tannehill Historical State Park features ante- and postbellum dwellings, a working iron furnace that dates to 1830, and a museum of the iron and steel industry.

As of 1 June 1979, world fishing records had been set for

spotted bass at Lewis Smith Lake in the southeast. The Alabama Deep Sea Fishing Rodeo, founded in the summer of 1928 at Dauphin Island, attracts about 2,500 visitors a year. In 1977/78, licenses were issued to 342,831 hunters and 583,516 fishermen.

48 SPORTS
Although Alabama has no major league professional teams, there is a Class AA baseball club at Birmingham. Two major professional stock car races, the Winston 500 and Talladega 500, in May and August respectively, are held at Alabama International Motor Speedway in Talladega. Dog racing was legalized in Mobile in 1971. Three of the major hunting-dog competitions in the US are held annually in the state.

Football reigns supreme among collegiate sports, especially at the University of Alabama, a perennial top-10 entry. Competing in the Southeastern Conference, Alabama's Crimson Tide won the Sugar Bowl in 1962, 1964, 1967, 1978, 1979, and 1980, and the Orange Bowl in 1943, 1953, 1963, and 1966. Alabama coach Paul "Bear" Bryant was named College Football Coach of the Year for 1961, 1971, and 1973. Auburn also has a major football program. The Blue-Gray game, an all-star contest, is held at Montgomery on the last Saturday in December, and the North-South game is played in Mobile.

The Heritage Classic National Championship Boat Races for outboards are held during the Lake Eufaula Festival in August. The Guntersville Boat Race, in its 42d season during 1980, claims to the oldest continuously held regatta in the US. The Alabama Sports Hall of Fame is located at Birmingham.

49 FAMOUS ALABAMIANS
William Rufus De Vane King (b.North Carolina, 1786–1853) served as a US senator from Alabama and as minister to France before being elected US vice president in 1852 on the Democratic ticket with Franklin Pierce; he died six weeks after taking the oath of office. Three Alabamians who served as associate justices of the US Supreme Court were John McKinley (b.Virginia, 1780–1852), John A. Campbell (b.Georgia, 1811–89), and Hugo L. Black (1886–1971). Campbell resigned from the court in 1861, later becoming assistant secretary of war for the Confederacy; Black, a US senator from 1927 to 1937, served one of the longest terms (1937–71) in the history of the court and is regarded as one of its most eminent justices.

Among the most colorful figures in antebellum Alabama was William Lowndes Yancey (b.Georgia, 1814–63), a fiery orator who was a militant proponent of slavery, states' rights, and eventually secession. During the early 20th century, a number of Alabamians became influential in national politics. Among them were US senators John Hollis Bankhead (1842–1920) and John Hollis Bankhead, Jr. (1872–1946); the latter's brother, William B. Bankhead (1874–1940), who became speaker of the US House of Representatives in 1936, and US Senator Oscar W. Underwood (b.Kentucky, 1862–1929), a leading contender for the Democratic presidential nomination in 1912 and 1924. Other prominent US senators from Alabama have included (Joseph) Lister Hill (b.1894) and John Sparkman (b.1899), who was the Democratic vice-presidential nominee in 1952. Alabama's most widely known political figure during the 1960s and 1970s was George Corley Wallace (b.1919), who served 12 years as governor. An outspoken opponent of racial desegregation, Wallace was a candidate for the Democratic presidential nomination in 1964; four years later, as the presidential nominee of the American Independent Party, he carried five states. While campaigning in Maryland's Democratic presidential primary on 15 May 1972, Wallace was shot by a would-be assassin.

Civil rights leader Martin Luther King, Jr. (b.Georgia, 1929–68), winner of the Nobel Peace Prize in 1964, first came to national prominence as leader of the Montgomery bus boycott of 1955; he

also led demonstrations at Birmingham in 1963 and at Selma in 1965. His widow, Coretta Scott King (b.1927), a former concert singer, is a native Alabamian. Federal judge Frank M. Johnson, Jr. (b.1918), has made several landmark rulings in civil rights cases.

Helen Keller (1880–1968), deaf and blind as the result of a childhood illness, was the first such multihandicapped person to earn a college degree; she later became a world famous author and lecturer. Another world figure, Negro educator Booker T. Washington (b.Virginia, 1856–1915), built Alabama's Tuskegee Institute from a school where young blacks were taught building, farming, cooking, brickmaking, dressmaking, and other trades into an internationally known agricultural research center. Tuskegee's most famous faculty member was George Washington Carver (b.Missouri, 1864–1943), who discovered some 300 different peanut products, 118 new ways to use sweet potatoes, and numerous other crop varieties and applications. Among Alabama's leaders in medicine was Dr. William Crawford Gorgas (1854–1920), head of sanitation in Panama during the construction of the Panama Canal; he later served as US surgeon general. Brought to the US after World War II, the internationally known scientist Wernher von Braun (b.Germany, 1912–77) came to Alabama in 1950 to direct the US missile program.

Two Alabama writers, (Nelle) Harper Lee (b.1926) and Edward Osborne Wilson (b.1929), have won Pulitzer Prizes. Famous musicians from Alabama include blues composer and performer W(illiam) C(hristopher) Handy (1873–1958), singer Nat "King" Cole (1917–65), and singer-songwriter Hank Williams (1923–53). Alabama's most widely known actress was Tallulah Bankhead (1903–68), the daughter of William B. Bankhead.

Among Alabama's sports figures are track and field star Jesse Owens (James Cleveland Owens, 1913–80), winner of four gold medals at the 1936 Olympic Games in Berlin; boxer Joe Louis (Joseph Louis Barrow, b.1914), world heavyweight champion from 1937 to 1949; and baseball stars Willie Mays (b.1931) and (Louis) Henry Aaron (b.1934), all-time US home-run leader.

50 BIBLIOGRAPHY
Agee, James, and Walker Evans. *Let Us Now Praise Famous Men*. New York: Ballantine, 1966.
Alabama, State of. Office of the Governor. *Executive Budget, Fiscal Year, 1980–81*. Montgomery, 1980.
Barnard, William D. *Dixiecrats and Democrats: Alabama Politics, 1942–1950*. University, Ala.: University of Alabama Press, 1974.
Carter, Dan T. *Scottsboro: A Tragedy of the American South*. Baton Rouge: Louisiana State University Press, 1969.
Federal Writers' Project. *Alabama: A Guide to the Deep South*. New York: Hastings House, 1975 (orig. 1941).
Griffith, Lucille, ed. *Alabama: A Documentary History to 1900*. Rev. ed. University, Ala.: University of Alabama Press, 1972.
Hackney, F. Sheldon. *Populism to Progressivism in Alabama*. Princeton: Princeton University Press, 1969.
Hamilton, Virginia V. *Alabama: A Bicentennial History*. New York: Norton, 1977.
Hamilton, Virginia V. *Hugo Black: The Alabama Years*. Baton Rouge: Louisiana State University Press, 1972.
Harlan, Louis R. *Booker T. Washington: The Making of a Black Leader, 1856–1901*. New York: Harper and Row, 1971.
McMillan, Malcolm C. *Constitutional Development in Alabama, 1798–1901: A Study in Politics, the Negro and Sectionalism*. Chapel Hill: University of North Carolina Press, 1955.
Rogers, William Warren, and Robert David Ward. *August Reckoning: Jack Turner and Racism in Post–Civil War Alabama*. Baton Rouge: Louisiana State University Press, 1973.
Rosengarten, Theodore. *All God's Dangers: The Life of Nate Shaw*. New York: Knopf, 1974.

ALASKA

State of Alaska

ORIGIN OF STATE NAME: From the Aleut word *alakshak*, meaning "peninsula" or "mainland." **CAPITAL**: Juneau. **ENTERED UNION**: 3 January 1959 (49th). **SONG**: "Alaska's Flag." **MOTTO**: North to the Future. **FLAG**: On a blue field, eight gold stars form the Big Dipper and the North Star. **OFFICIAL SEAL**: In the inner circle, symbols of mining, agriculture, and commerce are depicted against a background of mountains and the northern lights. In the outer circle are a fur seal, a salmon, and the words "The Seal of the State of Alaska." **BIRD**: Willow ptarmigan. **FISH**: King salmon. **FLOWER**: Wild forget-me-not. **TREE**: Sitka pine. **GEM**: Jade. **MINERAL**: Gold. **SPORT**: Dogteam racing (mushing). **LEGAL HOLIDAYS**: New Year's Day, 1 January; Lincoln's Birthday, 12 February; Washington's Birthday, 3d Monday in February; Seward's Day, last Monday in March; Memorial Day, last Monday in May; Independence Day, 4 July; Labor Day, lst Monday in September; Alaska Day, 18 October; Veterans Day, 11 November; Thanksgiving Day, 4th Thursday in November; Christmas Day, 25 December. **TIME**: noon GMT = 4 A.M. PST, 3 A.M. Yukon Standard Time, 2 A.M. Alaska-Hawaii Standard Time, 1 A.M. Bering Standard Time.

¹LOCATION, SIZE, AND EXTENT

Situated at the northwest corner of the North American continent, Alaska is separated by Canadian territory from the contiguous 48 states. Alaska is the largest of the 50 states, with a total area of 589,757 sq mi (1,527,470 sq km). Land takes up 569,600 sq mi (1,475,263 sq km) and inland water 20,157 sq mi (52,207 sq km). Alaska is more than twice the size of Texas, the next-largest state, and occupies 16% of the total US land area; the N-S extension is 2,261 mi (3,639 km); the maximum E-W extension is 1,358 mi (2,185 km).

Alaska is bounded on the N by the Arctic Ocean and Beaufort Sea; on the E by Canada's Yukon Territory and province of British Columbia; on the S by the Gulf of Alaska, Pacific Ocean, and Bering Sea; and on the W by the Bering Sea, Bering Strait, Chukchi Sea, and Arctic Ocean.

Alaska's many offshore islands include St. Lawrence, St. Matthew, Nunivak, and the Pribilof group in the Bering Sea; Kodiak Island in the Gulf of Alaska; the Aleutian Islands in the Pacific; and some 1,100 islands comprising the Alexander Archipelago, extending SE along the Alaska panhandle.

The total boundary length of Alaska is 6,230 mi (10,026 km), including a general coastline of 5,580 mi (8,890 km); the tidal shoreline extends 31,383 mi (50,506 km). Alaska's geographic center is about 60 mi (97 km) NW of Mt. McKinley. The northernmost point in the US—Point Barrow, at 71°23′30″N, 156°28′30″W—lies within the state of Alaska, as does the westernmost point—Cape Wrangell on Attu Island in the Aleutians, at 52°55′30″N, 172°28′E. Little Diomede Island, belonging to Alaska, is less than 2 mi (3 km) from Big Diomede Island, belonging to the Soviet Union.

²TOPOGRAPHY

Topography varies sharply among the six distinct regions of Alaska. In the southeast is a narrow coastal panhandle cut off from the main Alaskan landmass by the St. Elias Range. This region, featuring numerous mountain peaks of 10,000 feet (3,000 meters) in elevation, is paralleled by the Alexander Archipelago. South-central Alaska, which covers a 700-mi (1,100-km) arc along the Gulf of Alaska, includes the Kenai Peninsula and Cook Inlet, a great arm of the Pacific penetrating some 200 mi (320 km) to Anchorage. The southwestern region includes the Alaska Peninsula, filled with lightly wooded, rugged peaks, and the 1,700-mi (2,700-km) sweep of the Aleutian Islands, barren masses of volcanic origin. Western Alaska extends from Bristol Bay to the Seward Peninsula, an immense, treeless tundra dotted with lakes and containing the great deltas of the Yukon and Kuskokwim rivers, the longest in the state at 1,875 mi (3,018 km) and 800 mi (1,287) respectively. Interior Alaska extends north of the Alaska Range and south of the Brooks Range, including most of the drainage of the Yukon and its major tributaries, the Tanana and Porcupine rivers. The Arctic region extends from Kotzebue, north of the Seward Peninsula, east to the Canadian border. From the northern slopes of the Brooks Range, the elevation falls to the Arctic Ocean.

Eleven of the 20 highest mountains in the US—including the highest, Mt. McKinley (20,320 feet, or 6,194 meters), located in the Alaska Range—are in the state, which also contains half the world's glaciers; the largest, Malaspina, covers more area than the entire state of Rhode Island. More than one-fourth of all the inland water wholly within the US lies inside Alaska's borders; the largest lakes are Iliamna, occupying about 1,000 sq mi (2,600 sq km), and Becharof, 458 sq mi (1,186 sq km).

The most powerful earthquake in US recorded history, measuring 8.5 on the Richter scale, struck the Anchorage region on 27 March 1964, resulting in 114 deaths and $500 million in property damage in Alaska and along the US west coast.

³CLIMATE

Americans who called Alaska "Seward's icebox" when it was first purchased from the Russians were unaware of the variety of climatic conditions within its six topographic regions. Although winter temperatures in the Arctic region and in the Brooks Range average –20°F (–29°C) and the ground at Point Barrow is frozen permanently to 1,330 feet (405 meters), summer temperatures in the Alaskan lowlands average above 60°F (16°C) and have been known to exceed 90°F (32°C). The southeastern region is moderate, ranging from a daily average of 35°F (2°C) in January to 56°F (13°C) in July; the south-central zone has a similar range, but winters are harsher in the interior. The Aleutian Islands have chilly, damp winters and rainy, foggy weather for most of the year; western Alaska is also rainy and cool. The all-time high for the state was 100°F (38°C), recorded at Ft. Yukon on 27 June 1915; the reading of –79.8°F (–62°C) registered at Prospect Creek Camp, in the northwestern part of the state, on 23 January 1971 is the lowest temperature ever officially recorded in the US.

Juneau receives an average of 55 in (140 cm) of precipitation each year. The average annual snowfall is 108 in (274 cm).

⁴FLORA AND FAUNA

Life zones in Alaska range from grasslands, mountains, and tundra to thick forests, in which Sitka spruce, western hemlock, tamarack, white birch, and western red cedar predominate. Various hardy plants and wild flowers spring up during the short growing season on the semiarid tundra plains. Species of poppy and gentian are endangered.

Mammals abound amid the wilderness. Great herds of caribou, reindeer, elk, and moose migrate across the state. Kodiak, polar, black, and grizzly bears, Dall sheep, and an abundance of small mammals are also found. The sea otter and musk ox have been successfully reintroduced. North America's largest population of bald eagles nests in Alaska, and whales migrate annually to the icy bays. Pristine lakes and streams are famous for trout and salmon fishing. Endangered species listed by the state include the Eskimo curlew, Arctic peregrine falcon, Aleutian Canada goose, and short-tailed albatross; numerous species considered endangered in the conterminous US remain common in Alaska.

⁵ENVIRONMENTAL PROTECTION

Land-use planning is the liveliest controversy in Alaska today, pitting developers against those who consider the state the last unspoiled US region. When Alaska became a state, the federal government owned 99.8% of the land. Under the terms of the Statehood Act of 1959, the state was authorized to select 103 million acres (42 million hectares), or 28% of the total, for its own use. By 1968, the state had chosen 26 million acres (11 million hectares), including the oil-rich Prudhoe Bay area, when all claims were frozen pending action on land claims of Alaskan natives. The resulting federal Native Claims Settlement Act of 1971 not only gave Alaska's Native Americans the right to choose 44 million acres but also required the US secretary of the interior to withdraw up to 80 million acres of "National Interest Lands" from public use and gave Congress until 1978 to decide how much of this land would be protected from development. When Congress could not reach a decision, Interior Secretary Cecil Andrus, citing a different law, withdrew 114 million acres (46 million hectares) from public use. A federal law imposing development restrictions on 104 million acres (42 million hectares) and superseding Andrus's decision was enacted in 1980.

Both the state and federal governments have opened the shorelines of the Gulf of Alaska and the Bering and Beaufort seas to oil leasing and development, under strict environmental standards.

⁶POPULATION

Alaska, with a land area one-fifth the size of the contiguous US, ranked 50th in population in 1970, with a census figure of 302,173, only 0.15% of the US total. The preliminary 1980 census total was 400,331, less than 1 person per sq mi. Regions of settlement and development constitute less than 0.001% of Alaska's total land area.

Historically, population shifts in Alaska have directly reflected economic and political changes. The Alaska gold rush of the 1890s resulted in a population boom from 32,052 in 1890 to 63,592 a decade later; by the 1920s, however, when mining had declined, Alaska's population had decreased to 55,036. The region's importance to US national defense during the 1940s led to a rise in population from 72,524 to 128,643 during that decade. Oil development, especially the construction of the Alaska pipeline, brought an 87% population increase between 1960 and 1978. Almost all of this gain was from migration; as of 1976, 41% of all state residents had moved there within the last five years, and only 21% had lived in Alaska their whole lives. The state's population is much younger than that of the nation as a whole, and only 2.5% of all Alaskans were 65 years of age or older, the lowest such percentage of any state. Alaska is also one of the few states where men outnumber women, 52.7% to 47.3% in 1976.

About half of all state residents live in and around Anchorage, whose population, according to preliminary 1980 census data, was 173,992. Other leading cities in 1980 were Fairbanks, 22,538, and Juneau, 19,483.

⁷ETHNIC GROUPS

Indians, primarily Athapaskan, Tlingit, Haida, and Tsimshian living along the southern coast, constitute Alaska's largest minority group. Eskimos and Aleuts, the other native peoples, live mostly in scattered villages to the north and northwest. Taken together, Alaskan natives numbered 50,554 in 1970, less than 17% of the population. The Native Claims Settlement Act of 1971 gave 13 native corporations nearly $1 billion in compensation for exploration, mining, and drilling rights, and awarded them royalties on oil and the rights to 12% of Alaska's land area. The black, Asian, and Hispanic populations are small. As of 1970, the foreign-born and their native-born children made up 11% of the state population; Canada, Germany, and the United Kingdom were the leading countries of origin.

⁸LANGUAGES

From the Tlingit, Haida, and Tsimshian groups of lower Alaska almost no language influence has been felt, save for *hooch* (from Tlingit *hoochino*); but of the native words known to the sourdough, some have escaped into general usage, notably Eskimo *mukluk* and Aleut *parka*. Native place-names abound: Skagway and Ketchikan (Tlingit), Kodiak and Katmai (Eskimo), and Alaska and Akutan (Aleut).

The extraordinary population influx brought about by the petroleum industry makes an adequate description of the dialectal mixture of Alaska English impossible at present.

In 1970, 77% of the native-born had English as their mother tongue, as did 76% of foreign-born residents. Mother tongues of major resident groups were as follows:

	NATIVE-BORN	FOREIGN-BORN
English	224,855	2,055
Native American languages	6,649	75
German	5,192	1,256
Spanish	3,117	445
French	2,074	396

⁹RELIGIONS

The largest religious organization in the state is the Roman Catholic Church, which had 39,730 members in 1978. Southern Baptists constitute the largest Protestant denomination, with 15,995 adherents in 1971. Other major groups are the Latter-day Saints, 6,630; United Methodists, 5,996; United Presbyterians, 5,802; and Episcopalians, 5,084. The very small Jewish population numbered 920 in 1979.

Many Aleuts were converted to the Russian Orthodox religion during the 18th century, and small Russian Orthodox congregations are still active on the Aleutian Islands, in Kodiak and southeastern Alaska, and along the Yukon River.

¹⁰TRANSPORTATION

Alaska had no rail service until 1923, when the 495-mi (797-km) Alaska Railroad linked Seward, Anchorage, and Fairbanks. This federally operated railroad, subsequently extended to 538 mi (866 km), is still the only one in the state and is not connected to any other North American rail line.

The Alaska Highway, 1,422 mi (2,288 km) from Dawson Creek, British Columbia, to Delta Junction, is the only road link with the rest of the US. In-state roads are few and far between; only 12,115 mi (19,497 km) of roads were in use as of 1978, including 4,205 mi (6,767 km) of military roads. During the same year, the state had 274,159 registered vehicles and 220,696 licensed drivers. A state-operated ferry, used by 187,000 passengers in 1977, connects the southeastern ports to Seattle. The state's major port, the Port of Anchorage, handled 2,100,000 tons of cargo in 1978.

Air travel is the primary means of trans-state transportation, with several bush carriers serving the remote communities. Anchorage International Airport, the state's largest, emplaned

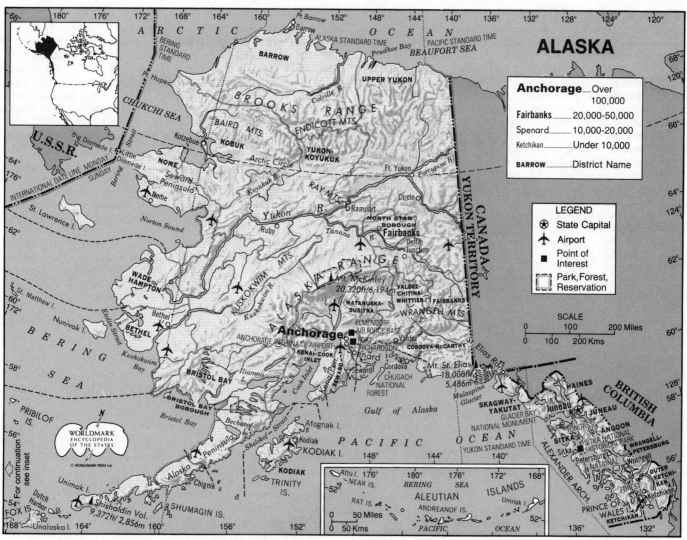

ALASKA

Anchorage	Over 100,000
Fairbanks	20,000-50,000
Spenard	10,000-20,000
Ketchikan	Under 10,000
BARROW	District Name

LEGEND
- ⊛ State Capital
- ✈ Airport
- ■ Point of Interest
- ▢ Park, Forest, Reservation

See US political: front cover C5; physical: back cover C5.
LOCATION: 51°13′05″ to 71°23′30″N; 129°59′W to 172°28′E. **BOUNDARIES:** Arctic Ocean and Pacific Ocean (Gulf of Alaska/Bering Sea) coastlines, 5,580 mi (8,980 km); Canadian line, 650 mi (1,046 km).

860,380 passengers and 115,077 tons of cargo in 1978, when Alaska had a total of 537 public airfields (1st in the US) and 219 private facilities.

¹¹HISTORY

At some time between 10,000 and 40,000 years ago, the ancestors of all of America's aboriginal peoples trekked over a land bridge that connected northeastern Siberia with northwestern America. These early hunter-gatherers dispersed, eventually becoming three distinct groups: Aleut, Eskimo, and Indian.

Ages passed before overseas voyagers rediscovered Alaska. Separate Russian parties led by Aleksei Chirikov and Vitus Bering (who had sailed in 1728 through the strait that now bears his name) landed in Alaska in 1741. Within a few years, the discoverers were followed by the exploiters, who hunted the region's furbearing animals. In 1784, the first permanent Russian settlement was established on Kodiak Island; 15 years later, the Russian American Company was granted a monopoly over the region. Its manager, Aleksandr Baranov, established Sitka as the company's headquarters. In 1802, the Tlingit Indians captured Sitka, but two years later lost the town and the war with the Russian colonizers.

Fluctuations in the fur trade, depletion of the sea otter, and the Russians' inability to make their settlements self-sustaining limited their development of the region. Increasingly, the czarist government viewed the colonies as a drain on the treasury. In 1867, as a result of the persistence of Secretary of State William H. Seward, a devoted American expansionist, Russia agreed to sell its American territories to the US for $7,200,000. From 1867 until the first Organic Act of 1884, which provided for a federally appointed governor, Alaska was administered first by the US Army, then by the US Customs Service. Federal officials were occupied chiefly in enforcing prohibition of liquor traffic and supervising the fur seal industry of the Pribilof Islands.

The pace of economic development quickened after the discovery of gold in 1880 at Juneau. Prospectors began moving into the eastern interior after this success, leading to gold strikes on Forty Mile River in 1886 and at Circle in 1893. But it was the major strike in Canada's Klondike region in 1896 that sparked a mass stampede to the Yukon Valley and other regions of Alaska, including the Arctic. The gold rush led to the establishment of permanent towns in the interior for the first time. Nome and Fairbanks became major population centers, while towns like Circle, Rampart, Valdez, and Ruby rose and declined in pace with the local mineral production.

Subsequent development of the fishing and timber industries increased Alaska's prosperity and prospects, though the region suffered from a lack of transportation facilities. A significant achievement came in 1914 when construction started on the Alaska Railroad connecting Seward, a new town with an ice-free port, with Anchorage and Fairbanks. Politically there were advances as well. In 1906, Alaskans were allowed to elect a nonvoting delegate to Congress for the first time. Congress granted territorial status to the region in 1912, and the first statehood bill was introduced in Congress two years later.

Mineral production declined sharply after 1914. Population declined too, and conditions remained depressed through the 1920s, although gold mining was helped by a rise in gold prices in 1934. World War II provided the next great economic impetus for Alaska: the Aleutian campaign following the Japanese invasion of the islands, though not as pivotal as the combat in other areas of the Pacific, did show American policymakers that Alaska's geography was in itself an important resource. Thus the spurt of federal construction and movement of military personnel continued even after the war ended, this time directed at the Soviet Union—only 40 mi (64 km) across the Bering Strait—rather than Japan. The US government built the Alaska Highway and many other facilities, including docks, airfields, and an extension of the Alaska Railroad. Population soared as thousands of civilian workers and military personnel moved to the territory. The newcomers added impetus to a new movement for statehood, and the Alaska Statehood Act was adopted by Congress in June 1958 and ratified by Alaska voters that August. On 3 January 1959, President Dwight Eisenhower signed the proclamation that made Alaska the 49th state.

Since statehood, Alaska has often been the center of national attention. In 1971, the Native Claims Settlement Act provided an extensive grant to the state's natives, but also precipitated a long federal-state controversy over land allocations. A major oil field was discovered in 1968, and in 1974, over the opposition of many environmentalists, construction began on the 789-mi (1,270-km) trans-Alaska pipeline from Prudhoe Bay to Valdez. The oil that began flowing through the pipeline in 1977 made Alaska almost immediately one of the nation's leading energy producers.

12 STATE GOVERNMENT

Under Alaska's first and only constitution, adopted in 1956 and effective since the time of statehood, the house of representatives consists of 40 members elected for two-year terms; the senate has 20 members elected for four-year terms. The minimum age is 21 for a representative, 25 for a senator; legislators must have resided in the state for at least 3 years prior to election.

Alaska's executive branch, modeled after New Jersey's, features a strong governor who appoints all cabinet positions and judges subject to legislative confirmation. The lieutenant governor is the only other elected executive. The governor must be a US citizen, at least 30 years of age, and must have been an Alaska resident for seven years.

After a bill has been passed by the legislature, it becomes law if signed by the governor; if left unsigned for 15 days while the legislature is in session or for 20 days after it has adjourned; or if passed by a three-fourths vote of each house over a gubernatorial veto. Constitutional amendments require a two-thirds vote of the legislature and ratification by the electorate.

Any US citizen at least 18 years of age who has been a resident of a voting district for 30 days may register to vote in that district.

13 POLITICAL PARTIES

When Congress debated the statehood question in the 1950s, it was assumed that Alaska would be solidly Democratic, but this expectation has not been borne out. As of 1979, of 240,121 registered voters, 28% were Democrats, 15% Republicans, 3% belonged to other parties, and 54% were nonpartisan. Republicans controlled the governorship, one US Senate seat, and Alaska's lone House seat. Democrats held the state house of representatives, Republicans the state senate.

In the 1980 presidential election, Alaskans voted Republican for the fourth consecutive time, choosing Ronald Reagan by a two-to-one popular majority over the incumbent, Jimmy Carter. Republican Frank H. Murkowski was elected to the US Senate, polling about 55% of the vote, and the state's Republican House member was reelected. Among minor party presidential candidates, Ed Clark, running on the Libertarian line, garnered 18,479 votes; independent candidate John Anderson won a total of 11,156 votes.

Alaska Presidential Vote by Major Political Parties, 1960–80

YEAR	ELECTORAL VOTE	ALASKA WINNER	DEMOCRAT	REPUBLICAN
1960	3	Nixon (R)	29,809	30,953
1964	3	*Johnson (D)	44,329	22,930
1968	3	*Nixon (R)	35,411	37,600
1972	3	*Nixon (R)	32,967	55,349
1976	3	Ford (R)	44,058	71,555
1980	3	*Reagan (R)	41,842	86,112

*Won US presidential election.

14 LOCAL GOVERNMENT

Unlike most other states, Alaska has no counties. Instead, the needs of its small, scattered population are met by eight boroughs, governed by elected assemblies. As of 1979 there were 139 cities, most of them governed by elected mayors and councils. Juneau, Sitka, and Achorage, known as Alaska's three unified municipalities, consolidated city and borough functions. Much of the state remains unorganized.

15 STATE SERVICES

By law, Alaska's government may contain no more than 20 administrative departments. As of 1980 there were 14: Administration, Commerce and Economic Development, Community and Regional Affairs, Education, Environmental Conservation, Fish and Game, Health and Social Services, Labor, Law, Military Affairs, Natural Resources, Public Safety, Revenue, and Transportation and Public Facilities. In addition, the state has an ombudsman with limited powers to investigate citizen complaints against state agencies.

16 JUDICIAL SYSTEM

The supreme court, consisting of a chief justice and 4 associate justices, hears appeals from the superior court, whose 20 judges are organized among the four state judicial districts. The lowest court is the district court, composed of 17 judges. All judges are appointed by the governor, but are thereafter subject to voter approval; supreme court justices serve terms of 10 years, superior court judges 6, and district judges 4.

In 1978, according to the FBI Crime Index, Alaska had the nation's highest rate of forcible rape and the 5th-highest rate for murder. Overall, the rate was 6,046 crimes per 100,000 population: murder and nonnegligent manslaughter, 12.9; forcible rape, 55.6. Crime rates in a few remote mining areas are even higher. Alaska has no capital punishment statute.

17 ARMED FORCES

A huge buildup of military personnel occurred after World War II, as the cold war with the Soviet Union led the US to establish a Distant Early Warning (DEW) System, Ballistic Missile Early Warning System, and Joint Surveillance system in the area. The 1970s saw a cutback in personnel, however, from a high of 40,214 in 1962 to 25,001 in 1978. Anchorage is the home of both the largest Army base, Ft. Richardson, and the largest Air Force base, Elmendorf. Along the Pacific coast are several Navy and

Coast Guard facilities. Alaska firms received defense contracts worth $195 million in 1977/78.

About 40,000 veterans were living in Alaska as of 30 September 1979, of whom fewer than 1,000 served in World War I, 13,000 in World War II, 8,000 during the Korean conflict, and 15,000 during the Viet-Nam era. Expenditures on veterans amounted to $25.8 million in 1977/78.

The Alaska State Troopers provide police protection throughout the state, except in the larger cities, where municipal police forces have jurisdiction. National Guard personnel numbered about 2,800 in 1978.

[18]MIGRATION

The earliest immigrants to North America, more than 10,000 years ago, likely came to Alaska via a land bridge across what is now the Bering Strait. The Russian fur traders who arrived during the 1700s found Aleuts, Eskimos, and Indians already established there. Despite more than a century of Russian sovereignty over the area, however, few Russians came, and those that did returned to the mother country with the purchase of Alaska by the US in 1867.

Virtually all other migration to Alaska has been from the continental US—first during the gold rush of the late 19th century, most recently during the oil boom of the 1970s. Between 1950 and 1977, Alaska's net gain from migration was 125,000, about half of that during the 1970–77 period.

[19]INTERGOVERNMENTAL COOPERATION

Alaska participates with Washington and Oregon in the North Pacific Fishery Management Council. The WAMI Medical Education Program (including Washington, Montana, and Idaho) enables Alaskan students to pursue medical studies in the State of Washington. Alaska also belongs to other western regional agreements covering energy, corrections, and education. The most important federal-state effort, the Joint Federal-State Land Use Planning Commission, was involved with the Alaska lands controversy throughout the 1970s.

Federal aid to Alaska was an estimated $388.6 million in 1978/79, of which $22 million was general revenue sharing.

[20]ECONOMY

When Alaska gained statehood in 1959, its economy was almost totally dependent on the US government. Fisheries, limited mining (mostly gold and gravel), and some lumber production made up the balance. That all changed with development of the petroleum industry during the 1970s. Construction of the trans-Alaska pipeline brought a massive infusion of money and people into the state. Construction, trade, and services boomed—only to decline when the pipeline was completed. As of 1977, the federal government still employed nearly one-third of all Alaska workers. Nevertheless, the state was beginning to use its oil revenues to develop new industry and create a viable private sector.

[21]INCOME

Alaska boasts the highest per capita income in the US: $10,851 in 1978. Measured in constant dollars, Alaska's total personal income tripled between 1960 and 1978. On the other hand, living costs are high: in 1977, Anchorage's family living costs were 40% above the US average, and costs in some other cities were even higher. Not quite 7% of all Alaskans were living below the federal proverty level in 1975.

[22]LABOR

Following completion of the trans-Alaska pipeline in 1977, the state entered a period of high unemployment which lasted through the end of the decade. Of the 180,000 in the civilian labor force in 1978, 20,000 were unemployed. The rate of 11.1% was the highest in the US, and the rate for Alaskan natives was much higher.

A federal census of workers covered by unemployment insurance in March 1977 revealed the following nonfarm employment pattern in Alaska:

	ESTABLISH-MENTS	EMPLOYEES	ANNUAL PAYROLL ('000)
Agricultural services, forestry, fishing	61	636	$ 9,265
Mining, of which:	127	4,430	140,622
Oil and gas extraction	(81)	(3,516)	(101,290)
Contract construction	1,248	16,582	580,315
Manufacturing, of which:	359	8,672	176,625
Food products	(101)	(3,433)	(62,192)
Lumber and wood products	(67)	(2,055)	(42,350)
Transportation, public utilities	616	14,000	308,242
Wholesale trade	605	6,054	119,290
Retail trade	2,240	24,409	293,430
Finance, insurance, real estate	741	7,511	116,164
Services	2,380	23,506	342,335
Other	287	445	9,730
TOTALS	8,664	106,245	$2,096,018

Government employees, not included in this survey, numbered nearly 49,000 in 1977, with US military personnel additional.

About 36% of all nonagricultural employees belonged to labor unions or employee associations in 1977, the 7th-highest percentage in the US. About one-third of them belonged to the International Brotherhood of Teamsters, which is especially strong in Alaska, covering a range of workers from truck drivers to school administrators. Wage rates—averaging $9.12 per hour for production workers in 1977—are the highest in the US, as they must be to compensate for Alaska's isolation and high living costs.

[23]AGRICULTURE

Hampered by a short growing season and frequent frosts, Alaska has very limited commercial agriculture. Farm income in 1978 was only $12 million, the lowest of any state's. Hay, greenhouse and nursery items, and potatoes are the main commodities produced. The 1,115 workers employed on the state's 310 farms in 1978 received the highest agricultural wages in the US. Nevertheless, Alaska produces only about 5% of the food it consumes.

[24]ANIMAL HUSBANDRY

Dairy and livestock products account for about one-third of Alaska's agricultural income. In 1979, 13 million lb of milk, valued at more than $2 million, were produced by 1,200 milk cows. Meat and poultry production is negligible by national standards. Production of reindeer meat of 312,000 lb dry weight had a value of $275,000 in 1977.

[25]FISHING

Although Alaska has long been the number-one fishing state, the industry has an uncertain future because of overfishing in the past. The state acted to limit commercial fishing permits in 1973 in order to prevent further depletion—a successful conservation measure, if the increased salmon and crab landings of the late 1970s are any evidence. The salmon catch, the staple of the industry, amounted to 80.2 million fish (341.4 million lb) in 1978, the largest catch in 35 years. King crab, a major export item, followed with more than 119 million lb. Landings of snow crab reached a record-high 130.5 million lb. On the other hand, the shrimp catch declined to 73.3 million lb, with a drastic drop in shrimp stocks (for reasons that were unclear) in the Kodiak area. In all, Alaska's commercial catch in 1978 totaled 745.6 million lb, valued at $438.6 million. By value of catch, Dutch Harbor and Kodiak were the top US fishing ports, together accounting for 10% of the national total.

[26]FORESTRY

Alaska's timber resources are vast, but full-scale development of the industry awaits fundamental land-use decisions at the federal and state levels. In 1977, Alaska had 119,145,000 acres (48,216,000 hectares) of forestland, 16% of the US total. Only 11,150,000 acres (4,512,000 hectares), or 2% of the US total, were classified as commercial timberland, and three-fourths of that was federally controlled. Alaska contains the nation's two largest national forests, Tongass in the southeast and Chugach along the gulf coast.

Lumbering and related industries employed about 3,500 workers in 1977 (most of them not covered by unemployment insurance). In 1973, the fledgling industry reached a peak production of 678.8 million board feet, but the closing of some areas to production and the vagaries of the foreign market led to a decline in the timber harvest to 602.4 million board feet in 1977. Shipments of lumber and wood products that year were valued at $142.5 million.

[27] MINING
Within a year after oil began flowing via pipeline from Prudhoe Bay to Valdez, Alaska became the nation's 9th-leading mineral producer, with an output worth over $2.9 billion in 1978.

As of 1978, more than 90% of the oil produced in Alaska came from Prudhoe Bay, where a huge field was discovered in 1968. By 1980, vast new finds had been made, including one estimated to hold from 1 billion to 4 billion barrels of oil. How soon any of that oil—or any from the 117 Beaufort Sea tracts for which leases were sold in December 1979—would be extracted depended on the outcome of court cases that remained unresolved in 1980. The main gas fields are in the Prudhoe Bay and Cook Inlet regions. Especially in the Prudhoe Bay field, most of the gas produced is reinjected for storage until transportation facilities—specifically, a gas pipeline from Prudhoe Bay to Valdez—become a reality.

Except for gold, the metal mining industry is very limited; the gold output of 18,962 troy oz had a value of $2.8 million in 1977. Some mining of copper and base metals occurs in the Brooks Range, and of radioactive minerals in the Seward Peninsula, Yukon-Tanana, and southeast regions. Production of sand and gravel reached 66,426,000 tons in 1977, valued at $134.3 million.

[28] ENERGY AND POWER
Despite its vast oil wealth, Alaska is not self-sufficient in energy. The planned construction by private companies and consortiums of two oil refineries at Valdez and a gas liquefaction plant on the Kenai Peninsula would sharply reduce Alaska's need to import petroleum refinery products.

Electric power production totaled 3.2 billion kwh in 1978; installed capacity was 1.1 million kw, and almost all generating facilities were government owned. Alaska's enormous fossil-fuel resources were estimated in 1978 at 9.2 billion barrels of oil (33% of the US total) and 31.6 trillion cu feet of natural gas (16%). New oil finds since 1978 make that year's estimate very conservative. Alaska also had proved coal reserves totaling 6.2 billion tons in 1976: 11% bituminous, 89% subbituminous. Production of fossil fuels in 1978 included 447.5 million barrels of oil, 214 billion cu feet of natural gas, and 731,000 tons of coal.

[29] INDUSTRY
Alaska's small but growing manufacturing sector is centered on the processing of lumber and food products; petroleum refining, natural gas liquefaction, and fertilizer production offered the greatest potential for industrial development during the 1980s. As of 1977, Anchorage led all regions with 18% of industrial employment, followed by Kodiak, 15%; Ketchikan, 14%; and Kenai–Cook Inlet, 10%. Employment in manufacturing increased by 52% between 1972 and 1977, and value added by manufacture rose from $170.4 million to $479.3 million. The following table shows value added for selected industries in 1972 and 1977:

	1972	1977
Fresh or frozen packaged fish	$19,100,000	$103,000,000
Canned and cured seafood	29,800,000	78,600,000
Lumber and wood products	30,200,000	69,500,000

[30] COMMERCE
Wholesale trade in 1976 amounted to $717 million. Retail sales in 1977 exceeded $1.8 billion, 138% higher than in 1972, with the increase attributable to the pipeline boom. More than half of all retail sales were in the Anchorage metropolitan area. Grocery stores accounted for 22% of all sales, followed by eating and drinking places, 14%; automotive dealers, 13%; department stores, 8%; and gasoline service stations, 6%.

During the first 10 months of 1978, about $632 million worth of goods passed through the Anchorage customs district, a 40% increase over the same period in 1977. Exports for January–October 1978 jumped to $521 million, four times the 1970 total; imports declined to $111 million for the same 10-month period as the need for construction material dropped. Overall, fishery products represented 35% of all direct exports, followed by 27% for forest products, with natural gas, urea, and anhydrous ammonia among the other important export items; many of Alaska's resource products, especially salmon and king crab, pass through the Seattle customs district. Japan alone received 74% of all direct exports in 1977, with other Asia-Pacific countries accounting for 11%, the Americas for 9%, and the rest of the world for 6%. Singapore was the major supplier, followed by Canada.

[31] CONSUMER PROTECTION
The Consumer Protection Section of the Department of Law maintains offices in Anchorage, Fairbanks, Juneau, and Ketchikan and is charged with enforcement of the state's Unfair Trade Practices and Consumer Protection Act.

[32] BANKING
As of 1978, Alaska had 12 insured commercial banks with assets totaling $1.9 billion, outstanding loans of $823 million, and deposits of more than $1.5 billion. There were 4 savings and loan associations (all of them federally chartered) with combined assets of $289.9 million and mortgage loans amounting to $242 million. Also under the regulatory authority of the Department of Commerce and Economic Development's Division of Banking, Securities, and Corporations were 12 small-loan companies with 11,225 outstanding loans totaling $14.7 million as of 31 December 1977.

[33] INSURANCE
Premiums written in 1977 totaled $452.5 million, including $353.4 million for property, casualty, and disability coverage, $59.5 million for life insurance, and $7.8 million for title insurance. Some 642,000 life insurance policies worth $5.6 billion were in force in 1978. The average coverage per family was $39,800, 13% above the US average.

[34] SECURITIES
There are no securities exchanges in Alaska. As of 30 June 1978, 577 broker-dealers, investment advisers, and agents were registered with the Division of Banking, Securities, and Corporations of the Department of Commerce and Economic Development. Alaskans reported $15.5 million in dividend income on their 1977 federal tax returns.

[35] PUBLIC FINANCE
Alaska's annual budget is prepared by the Division of Budget and Management, within the Office of the Governor, and submitted by the governor to the legislature for amendment and approval. The fiscal year runs from 1 July through 30 June. The following table summarizes estimated revenues and expenditures for 1979/80 (revised) and 1980/81, in millions:

REVENUES	1979/80	1980/81
Petroleum revenues	$1,801.3	$2,488.3
Taxes	215.2	280.0
State resources	114.1	189.8
Licenses and permits	19.8	20.9
Other receipts	8.6	8.7
TOTALS	$2,159.0	$2,987.7

EXPENDITURES	1979/80	1980/81
Public education	$ 385.4	$ 395.7
University of Alaska	174.1	185.3
Transportation	143.2	171.5
Social services	142.0	163.2
Natural resources management	94.2	119.3
Health	89.9	116.8
Other outlays	283.4	332.9
TOTALS	$1,312.2	$1,484.7

As of 30 June 1977, the outstanding debt of Alaska state and local governments was $2.3 billion, or $5,651 per capita, by far the highest of any state and more than double that of New York State, which ranked 2d.

36 TAXATION
The huge sums generated by the sale of oil leases and oil and gas royalties make Alaska's tax structure highly atypical. In April 1980, the state legislature abolished the personal income tax; the business tax was ended in 1979.

Alaska's share of the federal tax burden in 1975/76 was $718 million, while its share of federal tax benefits exceeded $1.3 billion. Alaskans filed 182,141 federal income tax returns in 1977, paying $580.9 million in tax.

37 ECONOMIC POLICY
The Department of Commerce and Economic Development co-ordinates a loan program for small businesses, especially those in the tourism and fishing industries. The Commercial Fisheries and Agricultural Bank, a state-owned facility, offers business loans for enterprises in those two sectors; industrial revenue bonds are made available through the Alaska Industrial Development Corp.

38 HEALTH
Alaska ranked 43d among the 50 states in average life expectancy during 1969–71 at 69.31 years: 66.05 for men and 74.03 for women. The infant mortality rates were 14.7 per 1,000 live births for whites and 16.3 for nonwhites. Alaska's overall death rate was less than half the US average, but the death rate from accidents (97.8 per 100,000 population) was the highest in the US, and the suicide rate ranked 3d behind Nevada's and Arizona's. The major public health problem is alcoholism.

Alaska's 26 hospitals (9 federal) in 1978 had 1,697 beds and an average daily occupancy rate of 62%; hospital personnel included 867 registered nurses and 306 licensed practical nurses. The average cost of medical care in 1977 was $359 per day (highest in the US) and $1,831 per stay. There were 442 licensed nonfederal physicians in Alaska in 1977 and 232 active dentists in 1979.

39 SOCIAL WELFARE
Because Alaska is the smallest state in population, expenditures on social services are the lowest for any state. About 13,000 Alaskans received $18 million in aid to families with dependent children in 1978, when the school lunch program fed 35,000 students at a federal cost of $1.6 million and 11,000 Alaskans used food stamps with a federal subsidy of $6 million. Approximately $3.6 million was spent on vocational rehabilitation in 1978, and $51.6 million on workers' compensation in 1977. Unemployment benefits for 84,000 claimants totaled $93 million in 1978.

Social Security benefits for 18,800 Alaskans totaled $45 million in 1977. Two years later, Alaska became the first state to withdraw its government workers from the Social Security system.

40 HOUSING
Despite the severe winters, housing designs in Alaska do not differ notably from those in other states. Builders do usually provide thicker insulation in walls and ceilings, but the high costs of construction have not encouraged more energy-efficient adaptation to the environment. In 1980, the state legislature passed several measures to encourage energy conservation in housing and in public buildings.

In native villages, traditional dwellings like the half-buried huts of the Aleuts and others have long since given way to conventional, low-standard housing. In point of fact, Alaska's Eskimos never built snow houses as did those of Canada; in the Eskimo language, the word *igloo* refers to any dwelling.

The 1970 census counted 79,000 occupied housing units, 86% of them with full plumbing. From 1970 to 1978, 43,009 building permits were issued, as construction boomed during the years of pipeline building. After completion of the pipeline, however, the construction industry went into a decline, with average employment dropping from 30,233 in 1976 to 11,925 in 1978, and housing starts down 36% in 1978 from the previous year.

The Alaska State Housing Authority supervises construction of publicly funded residences in rural areas.

41 EDUCATION
In 1970, 1.5% of Alaska's population was illiterate, half the 1960 figure. The median number of school years completed as of 1976 was 12.7; in 1970, the median was slightly over 10 years, and in the Arctic and northwestern regions the figure was much lower. Much of the overall improvement derives from the migration to Alaska of better-educated, skilled workers, but in recent years the Department of Education has been working with the state's 51 school districts to improve the public schools, particularly in the more remote regions, through the use of broadcast instruction and increased financial support.

Enrollment in public elementary schools was 48,573 in 1979/80; in secondary schools, 36,854. The University of Alaska is the state's leading higher educational institution. The main campus at Fairbanks, established in 1917, had 2,949 students in fall 1977, while the Anchorage campus had 4,343. Ten community colleges, supported by the state, enrolled 16,732 students. The Alaska Postsecondary Commission oversees the state's student loan program.

42 ARTS
The Council on the Arts sponsors tours by performing artists, supports artists' residences in the schools, aids local arts projects, and purchases the works of living Alaskans for display in state buildings. Fairbanks and Anchorage have community orchestras and theater groups.

43 LIBRARIES AND MUSEUMS
Alaska public libraries had a combined book stock of about 500,000 and a circulation of 1,000,000 in 1976/77; facilities are located in seven boroughs and in most larger towns. Anchorage has the largest public library system, with eight branches and 228,254 volumes in 1976/77. Also notable are the State Library in Juneau and the library of the University of Alaska at Fairbanks.

Alaska has about two dozen museums and 68 national historic sites. The Alaska State Museum in Juneau offers an impressive collection of native crafts and Alaskan artifacts. Sitka National Historical Park features Indian and Russian items, and the nearby Museum of Sheldon Jackson College holds important native collections. Noteworthy historical and archaeological sites include the Heritage Center in Ketchikan.

44 COMMUNICATIONS
Considering the vast distances traveled and the number of small, scattered communities, the US mail is a bargain for Alaskans; 1,239 postal service workers moved the state's mail in 1978. All of Alaska's 240,000 telephones (144,000 residential, 96,000 business) were operated by RCA Alaska Communications Inc. or the small General Telephone Co. of Alaska. On average, 92% of Alaska households had service in 1978; 51% of all phones were in Anchorage. The telephone system employed 153,269 mi (246,663 km) of radio relays, nearly half the US total.

In 1978 there were 41 radio stations (26 AM, 15 FM), 11 of them public, along with 11 television stations (4 public). At the end of 1978, 14 cable television systems served 20 communities with 15,541 subscribers.

[45] PRESS

Two of Alaska's seven daily newspapers and its only Sunday newspaper are in Anchorage. Total newspaper circulation as of mid-1978 was 88,267 daily and 51,658 Sunday; the most widely read paper was the *Anchorage Times*, published daily (circulation 46,081) and Sunday (51,658). The *Tundra Times*, also published in Anchorage, is a statewide weekly devoted to native concerns.

[46] ORGANIZATIONS

There are no major national organizations based in Alaska. The largest statewide organization, the Alaska Federation of Natives, with headquarters in Anchorage, represents and gives assistance to the state's Eskimos, Aleuts, and Indians.

[47] TOURISM, TRAVEL, AND RECREATION

With thousands of miles of unspoiled scenery and hundreds of mountains and lakes, Alaska has vast tourist potential. An estimated 525,000 travelers visited the state in 1978, of whom 430,000 came for pleasure. Travel-related industries employed about 6,000 full-time workers, had a payroll of $49 million, and earned revenues of $762 million. Some 68% of all visitors came by air.

Cruise travel along the Gulf of Alaska is one of the fastest-growing sectors in the tourist trade. One of the most popular tourist destinations is Glacier Bay National Monument. In all, 422,000 persons visited the state's five national parks and monuments in 1978. Public recreation sites during that year included 21 alpine ski areas, 1,876 mi (3,019 km) of hiking trails, and 3,450 camp units. Licenses were issued to 179,306 fishermen and 69,124 hunters in 1977/78.

[48] SPORTS

The only professional sports team in Alaska is a basketball franchise in Anchorage. Fans follow wintertime college basketball in Fairbanks and Anchorage and summertime semipro baseball.

Skiing and fishing are favorite participant sports, and dogteam racing, or mushing, is the official state sport.

[49] FAMOUS ALASKANS

Alaska's best-known federal officeholder was Ernest Gruening (b.New York, 1887–1974), a territorial governor from 1939 to 1953 and US senator from 1959 to 1969. Alaska's other original US senator was E. L. "Bob" Bartlett (1904–68). Walter Hickel (b.Kansas, 1919), the first Alaskan to serve in the US cabinet, left the governorship in 1969 to become secretary of the interior.

Among historical figures, Vitus Bering (b.Denmark, 1680–1741), a seaman in Russian service who commanded the discovery expedition in 1741, and Aleksandr Baranov (b.Russia, 1746–1819), the first governor of Russian America, are outstanding. Secretary of State William H. Seward (b.New York, 1801–72), who was instrumental in the 1867 purchase of Alaska, ranks as the state's "founding father," although he never visited the region.

Sheldon Jackson (b.New York, 1834–1909), a Presbyterian missionary, introduced the reindeer to the region and founded Alaska's first college in Sitka. Carl Ben Eielson (1897–1929), a famed bush pilot, has become a folk hero. Benny Benson (1913–72), born at Chignik, designed the state flag at the age of 13.

[50] BIBLIOGRAPHY

Alaska, State of. Department of Commerce and Economic Development. Division of Economic Enterprise. *The Alaska Economy*. Vol. 7. Juneau, 1979.

Alaska, State of. Department of Education. Division of State Libraries and Museum. *Alaska Blue Book, 1979*. Juneau, 1979.

Alaska, State of. Office of the Governor. Division of Budget and Management. *Executive Budget, Fiscal Year 1980–81*. Juneau, 1980.

Brooks, Alfred Hulse. *Blazing Alaska's Trails*. Fairbanks: University of Alaska Press, 1972.

Drucker, Philip. *Indians of the Northwest Coast*. New York: American Museum of Natural History, 1963.

Golder, Frank A. *Russian Expansion to the Pacific*. Gloucester, Mass.: Peter Smith, 1960.

Gruening, Ernest. *State of Alaska*. New York: Random House, 1968.

Hunt, William R. *Alaska: A Bicentennial History*. New York: Norton, 1976.

Hunt, William R. *North of 53°: The Wild Days of the Alaska-Yukon Mining Frontier*. New York: Macmillan, 1974.

McPhee, John. *Coming into the Country*. New York: Farrar, Straus, and Giroux, 1977.

Naske, Claus-M., and Herman E. Slotnick. *Alaska: A History of the 49th State*. Grand Rapids, Mich.: Eerdmans, 1979.

Oswalt, Wendell H. *Alaskan Eskimos*. San Francisco: Chandler, 1967.

Vanstone, James. *Athapaskan Adaptations*. Chicago: Aldine, 1974.

ARIZONA

State of Arizona

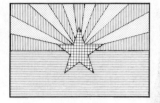

ORIGIN OF STATE NAME: Probably from the Pima Indian word *arizonac*, meaning "small springs," or "few springs." **NICKNAME**: The Grand Canyon State. **CAPITAL**: Phoenix. **ENTERED UNION**: 14 February 1912 (48th). **SONG**: "Arizona." **MOTTO**: *Ditat Deus* (God enriches). **FLAG**: A copper-colored, five-pointed star symbolic of the state's copper resources rises from a blue field; six yellow and seven red segments radiating from the star cover the upper half. **OFFICIAL SEAL**: Depicted on a shield are symbols of the state's economy and natural resources, including mountains, a rising sun, and a dam and reservoir in the background, irrigated farms and orchards in the middle distance, a quartz mill, a miner, and cattle in the foreground, as well as the state motto. The words "Great Seal of the State of Arizona 1912" surround the shield. **BIRD**: Cactus wren. **FLOWER**: Blossom of the saguaro cactus. **TREE**: Paloverde. **OFFICIAL NECKWEAR**: Bola tie. **LEGAL HOLIDAYS**: New Year's Day, 1 January; Lincoln's Birthday, 1st Monday in February; Washington's Birthday, 3d Monday in February; Memorial Day, last Monday in May; Independence Day, 4 July; Labor Day, 1st Monday in September; Columbus Day, 2d Monday in October; Veterans Day, 11 November; Thanksgiving Day, 4th Thursday in November; Christmas Day, 25 December. **TIME**: 5 A.M. MST = noon GMT.

¹LOCATION, SIZE, AND EXTENT

Located in the Rocky Mountains region of the southwestern US, Arizona ranks 6th in size among the 50 states.

The total area of Arizona is 113,909 sq mi (295,024 sq km), of which land takes up 113,417 sq mi (293,750 sq km) and inland water 492 sq mi (1,274 sq km). Arizona extends about 340 mi (547 km) E–W; the state's maximum N–S extension is 395 mi (636 km).

Arizona is bordered on the N by Utah and on the E by New Mexico (with the two borders joined at Four Corners, the only point in the US common to four states); on the S by the Mexican state of Sonora; and on the W by the Mexican state of Baja California Norte, California, and Nevada (with most of the line formed by the Colorado River). The total boundary length of Arizona is *1,478 mi (2,379 km)*. The state's geographic center is in Yavapai County, 55 mi (89 km) ESE of Prescott.

²TOPOGRAPHY

Arizona is a state of extraordinary topographic diversity and beauty. The Colorado Plateau, which covers two-fifths of the state in the north, is an arid, upland region characterized by deep canyons, notably the Grand Canyon, a vast gorge more than 200 mi (320 km) long, up to 18 mi (29 km) wide, and more than 1 mi (1.6 km) deep. This region also embraces the San Francisco Mountains, whose foremost summit, Humphreys Peak, an extinct volcano, is the highest point in the state, at 12,633 feet (3,851 meters). The Plateau of Arizona, Kaibab, Shivwit, and Kaibito plateaus, Painted Desert, Petrified Forest, and Black Mesa also lie within the Colorado Plateau area.

The Mogollon Rim separates the northern plateau from a central region of alternating basins and ranges with a general northwest-southeast direction. Ranges in the Mexican Highland in the southeast include the Chiricahua, Gila, and Mazatzal mountains. The Sonoran Desert, in the southwest, contains the lowest point in the state, 70 feet (21 meters) above sea level, on the Colorado River near Yuma.

The Colorado is the state's major river, flowing southwest from Glen Canyon Dam on the Utah border through the Grand Canyon and westward to Hoover Dam, then turning south to form the border with Nevada and California. Tributaries of the Colorado include the Little Colorado and Gila rivers. Arizona has few natural lakes, but there are several large artificial lakes formed by dams for flood control, irrigation, and power development. These include Lake Mead (shared with Nevada), formed by Hoover Dam; Roosevelt Lake, formed by the Theodore Roosevelt Dam; and the San Carlos Reservoir, created by the Coolidge Dam.

³CLIMATE

Arizona has a dry climate, with little rainfall. Temperatures vary greatly from place to place, season to season, and day to night. Temperatures at Yuma, in the southwestern desert, range from 43° to 67°F (6–19°C) in January and from 81° to 106°F (27–41°C) in July. At Flagstaff, in the interior uplands, January temperatures range from 14° to 41°F (–10–5°C), and July temperatures range from 50° to 81°F (10–27°C). The maximum recorded temperature was 127°F (53°C), registered at Parker on 7 July 1905; the minimum, –40°F (–40C), was set at Hawley Lake on 7 January 1971.

The northern and western parts of the state receive less than 10 in (25 cm) of precipitation a year, and the rest, for the most part, less than 20 in (50 cm). The driest area is the extreme southwest, which receives less than 3 in (8 cm) a year. Snow, sometimes as much as 100 in (254 cm) of it, falls on the highest peaks but is rare in the southern and western lowlands.

The greatest amount of sunshine is registered in the southwest, with the proportion decreasing progressively toward the northeast; overall, the state receives more than 80% of possible sunshine, among the highest in the US. The normal growing season on some of the highest plateaus is fewer than 120 days a year. Lower areas in the southwest have a growing season of more than 200 days.

⁴FLORA AND FAUNA

Generally categorized as desert, Arizona's terrain also includes mesa and mountains, and consequently the state has a wide diversity of vegetation. The desert is known for many varieties of cacti, from the saguaro, whose blossom is the state flower, to the cholla and widely utilized yucca. Desert flowers include the night-blooming cereus; among medicinal desert flora is the jojoba, also harvested for its oil-bearing seeds. Northern temperate zones are well timbered with varieties of fir, juniper, oak, birch, and piñon. Rare plants, some of them endangered or threatened, include various cacti of commercial or souvenir value.

Arizona's fauna range from desert species of lizards and snakes to the deer, elk, and antelope of the northern highlands. Mountain lion, jaguar, coyote, and black and brown bears are found in the state, along with the badger, black-tailed jackrabbit, and gray fox. Small mammals include various cottontails, mice, and squirrels; prairie dog towns dot the northern regions. Rattlesnakes are abundant, and the desert is ripe with reptiles such as the collared lizard and chuckwalla. Native birds include the thick-billed parrot, white pelican, and cactus wren (the state bird). Arizona counts the osprey, desert bighorn, desert tortoise, spotted bat, and Gila monster among its threatened wildlife. Officially listed as endangered are the southern bald eagle, peregrine falcon, gray hawk, tiger salamander, Sonoran pronghorn, Mexican wolf, and black-footed ferret.

5ENVIRONMENTAL PROTECTION

Arizona has always been noted for its clean air, open lands, and beautiful forests. The main environmental concern of the state is to protect these resources in the face of growing population, tourism, and industry.

State agencies with responsibility for the environment include the Land Department, which oversees land management and natural resource conservation; the Game and Fish Commission, which administers state wildlife laws; the Department of Health Services, which supervises sanitation engineering projects and air pollution prevention programs; the Department of Water Resources, formed in 1980, concerned with the development, management, and conservation of water; and the Water Quality Control Council, which supervises and controls water standards for the state.

Legislation enacted in 1980 attempts to apportion water use among cities, mining, and agriculture, the last of which, through irrigation, accounts for about 90% of Arizona's annual water consumption. The new conservation program calls for registration of all wells and is aimed at such high-use areas as Phoenix, Tucson, Prescott, and Pinal County. Tucson has reduced water consumption through voluntary programs, with average daily use dropping by 60 gallons per household from 1977 to 1980.

6POPULATION

Arizona ranked 33d in the US with a 1970 census population of 1,775,399, 36% more than in 1960. The state estimate for 1979 was 2,631,000, 48% more than in 1970; the preliminary 1980 census total was 2,714,013. Arizona's population growth rate is one of the highest in the nation.

In 1978, nearly 73% of the population was white, 18% Hispanic, 6% Indian, and 3% black. In that year, 49.4% of the population was male and 50.6% female. Arizonans 65 years of age or older increased from 9.1% of the population in 1970 to 10.8% in 1978, reflecting to some extent the state's increasing popularity among retirees. During the same period, according to state data, there were 323,900 births, and 137,700 deaths, and a net increase from migration of 585,600. Despite its rapid population growth, Arizona still had a population density of only 22 persons per sq mi (8 per sq km) in 1978.

Three out of four Arizonans live in metropolitan areas. The largest cities are Phoenix, with an estimated 1978 population of 716,100; Tucson, 311,400; Mesa, 130,000; Tempe, 106,765; Scottsdale, 85,070; and Glendale, 80,000. More than half the state's population resides in Maricopa County, which includes every leading city except Tucson.

7ETHNIC GROUPS

Arizona claims both the nation's largest Indian population and the greatest expanse of Indian lands.

The largest single American Indian nation, the Navaho, with an estimated 1978 population of 87,300, is located in northeastern Arizona. The Navaho reservation, covering about 14,000 sq mi (36,000 sq km) within Arizona, extends into Utah and New Mexico and comprises desert, mesa, and mountain terrain.

Herdsmen by tradition, the people are also famous for their crafts. Especially since 1965, the Navaho have been active in economic development; reservation resources in uranium and coal have been leased to outside corporations, and loans from the US Department of Commerce have made possible roads, telephones, and other improvements. There are 14 other tribes and 17 other reservations. After the Navaho, the leading tribes are the Pima-Papago in the south, Apache in the east, and Hopi in the northeast. All together, the Indian population was 142,636 in 1978, when Indian lands exceeded 28,000 sq mi (73,000 sq km).

The southern part of Arizona has most of the state's largest ethnic minority, a Hispanic population totaling 468,300 by 1978. There are some old, long-settled Spanish villages, but the bulk of Hispanics are first- and second-generation Mexicans. These make up most of the unskilled and semi-skilled urban and rural labor force.

There were an estimated 72,900 black Americans in Arizona in 1978. Filipinos, Chinese, Japanese, and other Pacific peoples together made up much less than 1% of the population.

8LANGUAGES

Although Arizona has the largest Indian population of the 50 states, the linguistic influence of its Papago, Pima, Apache, Navaho, and Hopi tribes is almost totally limited, except possibly for Navaho *hogan*, to some place-names: Arizona itself, Yuma, Havasu, Tucson, Oraibi. Indian loanwords spreading from Arizona derive from the Nahuatl speech of the Mexican Aztecs—for example, *coyote, chili, mesquite,* and *tamale.* Spanish, dominant in some sections, has given English *mustang, ranch, stampede, rodeo, marijuana, bonanza, canyon, mesa, patio,* and *fiesta.*

English in the state represents a blend of North Midland and South Midland dialects without clear regional differences, although new meanings developed in the north and east for *meadow* and in the southern strip for *swale* as terms for flat mountain valleys. The recent surge from eastern states has produced an urban blend with a strong Northern flavor. In 1970, 72% of the native-born residents had English as the mother tongue, as did 70% of all residents. Mother tongues claimed by major groups were as follows:

	NATIVE-BORN	FOREIGN-BORN
English	1,218,803	12,450
Spanish	224,709	34,361
Indian languages	71,601	68
German	32,582	7,511
Italian	9,598	2,653

9RELIGIONS

The first religions of Arizona were the sacred beliefs and practices of the Indians. Catholic missionaries began converting Arizona Indians (Franciscan among the Hopi and Jesuits among the Pima) to the Christian faith in the late 17th century. By the late 18th century, the Franciscans were the main missionary force, and the Roman Catholic Church was firmly established. In 1979, the state had about 449,000 Catholics.

The Church of Jesus Christ of Latter-day Saints (Mormons) constitutes the 2d-largest Christian denomination. Mormons were among the state's earliest Anglo settlers; in 1971 there were 106,323 known Mormon adherents. Other major denominations include the Southern Baptist Convention, 85,173; and the United Methodist Church, 53,148. The total number of Protestant adherents was 324,348 in 1971.

In 1979, Arizona's estimated Jewish population was nearly 40,000, virtually all of whom lived in Phoenix or Tucson.

10TRANSPORTATION

More people and goods pass through Arizona than actually go to the state. The automobile is the main mode of transportation but air transport is of increasing importance.

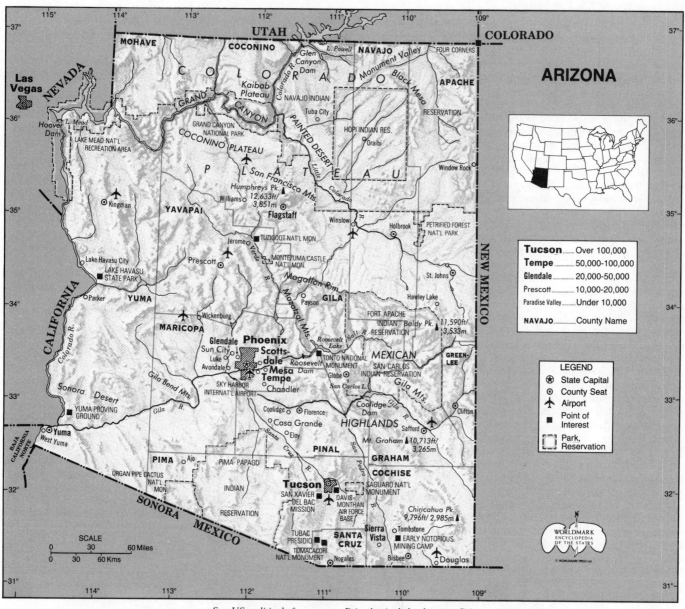

ARIZONA

MOHAVE · COCONINO · NAVAJO · APACHE · YAVAPAI · YUMA · MARICOPA · GILA · GREENLEE · PINAL · GRAHAM · PIMA · COCHISE · SANTA CRUZ

Tucson	Over 100,000
Tempe	50,000-100,000
Glendale	20,000-50,000
Prescott	10,000-20,000
Paradise Valley	Under 10,000
NAVAJO	County Name

LEGEND
State Capital
County Seat
Airport
Point of Interest
Park, Reservation

See US political: front cover D4; physical: back cover D4.

LOCATION: 31° to 36°59′56″N; 109°2′40″ to 114°50′W. **BOUNDARIES**: Utah line, *277 mi (446 km)*; New Mexico line, *389 mi (626 km)*; Mexico line, *373 mi (600 km)*; California line, *234 mi (377 km)*; Nevada line, *205 mi (330 km)*.

Until the last decade of the 19th century, the principal reason for the development of transportation in Arizona was to open routes to California. The most famous early road was El Camino del Diablo (Devil's Highway), opened by the Spanish missionary Eusebio Kino in 1699. The first wagon road across Arizona was the Gila Trail (Cooke's Wagon Road), opened in 1846 as a southern route to California; Beale's Road was inaugurated in 1857. Also in 1857, the first stagecoach began operations. Until the coming of the railroads in the 1880s, however, the bulk of territorial commerce was by water transport on the Colorado River. Railroad construction reached its peak in the 1920s and declined rapidly thereafter. Railroad trackage totaled 2,034 mi (3,273 km) in 1974. Amtrak provides limited passenger service through Flagstaff, Kingman, and other cities in the north, and through Tucson, Phoenix, and Yuma on the southern route.

In 1978, the state had 57,513 mi (92,558 km) of roads and streets, of which 46,733 mi (75,210 km) were classified as rural

and 10,780 mi (17,349 km) as municipal. Of the 2,227,865 motor vehicles registered, 1,192,021 were passenger vehicles, 584,850 trucks, 377,531 trailers, 68,359 motorcycles, and 5,104 buses and taxis. There were 1,612,555 licensed drivers, of whom 892,597 were male and 719,958 female. Total highway expenditures in 1977/78 were $460.9 million.

Arizona had 97 public and 112 private airfields in 1978. The leading air terminal was Phoenix Sky Harbor International Airport, which handled 5,931,900 arriving and departing passengers; Tucson International Airport ranked second with 1,694,500. Both totals were more than double the 1968 passenger volume.

¹¹HISTORY

Evidence of a human presence in Arizona dates back more than 12,000 years. The offshoot of migrations across the Bering Strait, the first Arizonans were large-game hunters; their remains have been found in the San Pedro Valley in the southeastern part of the state. By AD 500, their descendants had acquired a rudimentary agriculture from what is now Mexico and divided into several cultures. The Basket Makers (Anasazi) flourished in the northeastern part of the state; the Mogollon hunted and foraged in the eastern mountains; the Hohokam, highly sophisticated irrigators, built canals and villages in the central and southern valleys; and the Hakataya, a river people, lived south and west of the Grand Canyon. For reasons unknown—a devastating drought is the most likely explanation—these cultures were in decay and the population much reduced by the 14th century. Two centuries later, when the first Europeans arrived, most of the natives were living in simple shelters in fertile river valleys, dependent on hunting, gathering, and small-scale farming for subsistence. These Arizona Indians belonged to three linguistic families: Uto-Aztecan (Hopi, Paiute, Chemehuevi, Pima-Papago), Yuman (Yuma, Mohave, Cocopa, Maricopa, Yavapai, Walapai, Havasupai), and Athapaskan (Navaho-Apache). The Hopi were the oldest group, their roots reaching back to the Anasazi; the youngest were the Navaho-Apache, migrants from the Plains, who were not considered separate tribes until the early 18th century.

The Spanish presence in Arizona involved exploration, missionary work, and settlement. Between 1539 and 1605, four expeditions crossed the land, penetrating both the upland plateau and the lower desert in ill-fated attempts to find great riches. In their footsteps came Franciscans from the Rio Grande to work among the Hopi, and Jesuits from the south, led by Eusebio Kino in 1692, to missionize among the Pima. Eight years later, Kino established a major mission station at San Xavier, near present-day Tucson. In 1736, a rich silver discovery near the Pima village of Arizonac, about 20 mi (32 km) southwest of present-day Nogales, drew Spanish prospectors and settlers northward. To control the restless Pima, Spain in 1752 placed a military outpost, or presidio, at Tubac on the Santa Cruz River north of Nogales. This was the first major European settlement in Arizona. The garrison was moved north to the new fort at Tucson, also on the Santa Cruz, in 1775. During these years, the Spaniards gave little attention to the Santa Cruz settlements, administered as part of the Mexican province of Sonora, regarding them merely as way stations for colonizing expeditions traveling overland to the highly desirable lands of California. The end of the 18th century and the beginning of the 19th were periods of relative peace on the frontier; mines were developed, and ranches begun. Spaniards removed hostile Apache bands onto reservations and made an effort to open a road to Santa Fe.

When Mexico revolted against Spain in 1810, the Arizona settlements were little affected. Mexican authorities did not take control at Arizpe, the Sonoran capital, until 1823. Troubled times followed, characterized by economic stagnation, political chaos, and renewed war with the Apache. Sonora was divided into *partidos* (counties), and the towns on the Santa Cruz were designated as a separate *partido*, with the county seat at Tubac. The uninhabited area north of the Gila River was vaguely claimed by New Mexico. With the outbreak of the Mexican War in 1846, two US armies marched across the region: General Stephen W. Kearny followed the Gila across Arizona from New Mexico to California, and Colonel Philip Cooke led a Mormon battalion westward through Tucson. The California gold rush of 1849 saw thousands of Americans pass along the Gila toward the new El Dorado. In 1850, northern Arizona became part of the new US Territory of New Mexico; the southern strip was added by the Gadsden Purchase in 1853.

Anglo settlement in Arizona began in 1854. Two years later, the Sonora Exploring and Mining Co. organized a large party, led by Charles D. Poston, to open silver mines around Tubac. A boom followed, with Tubac becoming the largest settlement in the valley; the first newspaper, the *Weekly Arizonian*, was launched there in 1859. The great desire of California for transportation links with the rest of the Union prompted the federal government to chart roads and railroad routes across Arizona, erect forts there to protect Anglo travelers from the Indians, and open overland mail service. Dissatisfied with their representation at Santa Fe, the territorial capital, Arizona settlers joined those in southern New Mexico in 1860 in an abortive effort to create a new territorial entity. The outbreak of the Civil War in 1861 saw the declaration of Arizona as Confederate territory and abandonment of the region by Union troops. A small Confederate force entered Arizona in 1862 but was driven out by a volunteer Union army from California. On 24 February 1863, President Abraham Lincoln signed into law a measure creating the new Territory of Arizona. Prescott became the capital in 1864, Tucson in 1867, and finally Phoenix in 1889.

During the early years of territorial status, the development of rich gold mines along the lower Colorado River and in the interior mountains attracted both people and capital to Arizona, as did the discovery of silver bonanzas in the Tombstone and other districts in the late 1870s. Additional military posts were constructed to protect mines, towns, and travel. This activity, in turn, provided the basis for a fledgling cattle industry and irrigated farming. Phoenix, established in 1868, grew steadily as an agricultural center. The Southern Pacific Railroad, building east from California, reached Tucson in 1880, and the Atlantic and Pacific (later known as the Santa Fe), stretching west from Albuquerque through Flagstaff, opened service to California in 1882. By 1890, copper had replaced silver as the principal mineral extracted in Arizona. In the Phoenix area, large canal companies began wrestling with the problem of supplying water for commercial agriculture. This problem was resolved in 1917, with the opening of the Salt River Valley Project, a federal reclamation program that provided enormous agricultural potential.

As a creature of Congress, Arizona Territory was presided over by a succession of governors, principally Republicans, appointed in Washington. In reaction, the populace was predominantly Democratic. Within the territory, a merchant-capitalist class, with strong ties to California, dominated local and territorial politics until it was replaced with a mining-railroad group whose influence continued well into the 20th century. A move for separate statehood began in the 1880s but did not receive serious attention in Congress for another two decades. After a federal act was passed in 1910, a convention met at Phoenix and drafted a state constitution. On 14 February 1912, Arizona entered the Union as the 48th state.

During the first half of the 20th century, Arizona shook off its frontier past. World War I spurred the expansion of the copper industry, intensive agriculture, and livestock production. Goodyear Tire and Rubber established large farms in the Salt River Valley to raise pima cotton. The war boom also generated high prices, land speculation, and labor unrest; at Bisbee and Jerome local authorities forcibly deported more than 1,000 striking miners to Mexico during the summer of 1917. The 1920s brought depression: banks closed, mines shut down, and agricultural production declined. To revive the economy, local boosters pushed highway construction, tourism, and the resort business. Arizona also shared in the general distress caused by the Great Depression of the 1930s and received large amounts of federal aid for relief and recovery. A copper tariff encouraged the mining industry, additional irrigation projects were started, and public works were begun on Indian reservations, in parks and forests, and at educational institutions. Prosperity returned during World War II, as camps for military training, prisoners of war, and displaced Japanese-Americans were built throughout the state. Meat, cotton, and copper markets flourished, and the construction of processing and assembly plants suggested a new direction for the state's economy.

Arizona emerged from World War II a modern state. War industries spawned an expanding peacetime manufacturing boom that soon provided the principal source of income, followed by tourism, agriculture, and mining. During the 1950s, the political scene changed. Arizona Republicans captured the governorship, gained votes in the legislature, won congressional seats, and brought a viable two-party system to the state. The rise of Barry Goldwater of Phoenix to national prominence further encouraged Republican influence. Meanwhile, air conditioning changed lifestyles: no longer fearful of the fierce summer heat, 924,000 migrants from other states flocked to Arizona between 1950 and 1977. In that period, the population more than tripled.

¹²STATE GOVERNMENT

The constitution of Arizona, drafted in 1910 at the height of the Progressive era, contained reform provisions that were very advanced for the time: initiative, referendum, workers' compensation, short terms for elected officials, suffrage for women, and the barring of trusts and monopolies from the state. This constitution, as amended, still governs Arizona today.

Legislative authority is vested in a 30-member senate and a 60-member house of representatives. All senators and representatives serve 2-year terms and are chosen at the general election in November of each even-numbered year. A legislator must be a US citizen, at least 25 years of age, and must have been an Arizona resident for at least 3 years.

Chief executive officials elected statewide include the governor, secretary of state, state treasurer, attorney general, and superintendent of public instruction, all of whom serve 4-year terms. The three members of the Corporation Commission, which regulates public services and utilities, are elected for staggered 6-year terms, and the state mine inspector is elected for 2 years. Candidates for executive office must be US citizens, at least 25 years of age, and have been residents of Arizona for at least 5 years.

Bills may originate in either house of the legislature and must be passed by both houses and approved by the governor in order to become law. A two-thirds vote in each house is necessary to override the governor's veto. Under the initiative procedure, legislation and proposed constitutional amendments can be placed on the ballot by petition. Voters may also petition to make any act of the legislature subject to referendum.

In order to vote in Arizona, a person must be 18 years of age, a US citizen, and have been a resident of the state for 50 days.

¹³POLITICAL PARTIES

Of Arizona's 17 territorial governors, all federally appointed, 14 were Republicans and 3 Democrats. Statehood meant a prolonged period of Democratic dominance. From 1912 through 1950, the state had 9 Democratic and 3 Republican governors, and during that 49-year period Republicans held the statehouse for only 6 years.

Republican Party fortunes improved dramatically after 1950, largely because of the rise to state and national prominence of a conservative Republican, Barry Goldwater, first elected to the US Senate in 1952. From 1951 to 1980, 3 Republican governors occupied the state house for 18 years, and 5 Democratic governors for 12. Arizonans gave the nod to Republican presidential candidates in every election from 1952 through 1976. Several Arizona Republicans were appointed to high office during the Nixon years, and in 1973, another Republican, John J. Rhodes, became minority leader of the US House of Representatives.

Arizonans, who had favored Republican presidential nominees in the seven previous races, made it eight in a row in 1980 by giving more than 60% of the popular vote to Ronald Reagan. Goldwater barely won reelection to the Senate, defeating his Democratic opponent by only 1% of the total votes cast, despite the generally Republican tide. The election left the Republicans with one of the state's two Senate seats, two of Arizona's four US House seats, a narrow majority in the state senate, and a sizable majority of the state house of representatives. Independent presidential candidate John Anderson captured 76,952 votes, or not quite 9% of the total votes cast. A state-operated lottery was approved.

¹⁴LOCAL GOVERNMENT

Each of Arizona's 14 counties has a sheriff, county attorney, county recorder, treasurer, assessor, superintendent of schools, and three or five supervisors. Each official is elected to a four-year term.

Local governmental units include towns, cities, and charter cities. Towns generally follow the council-mayor form of government. They elect five-member councils if under 1,500 in population, and seven-member councils if over 1,500. Each council chooses one member as mayor, and appoints a clerk (treasurer), marshal (tax collector), and engineer. A town attaining a population of 3,000 or more may become a city in title and organization, if the voters and town council approve. In a city,

Arizona Presidential Vote by Political Parties, 1948–80

YEAR	ELECTORAL VOTE	ARIZONA WINNER	DEMOCRAT	REPUBLICAN	PROGRESSIVE
1948	4	*Truman (D)	95,251	77,597	3,310
1952	4	*Eisenhower (R)	108,528	152,042	—
1956	4	*Eisenhower (R)	112,880	176,990	—
1960	4	Nixon (R)	176,781	221,241	—
1964	5	Goldwater (R)	237,753	242,535	—
					AMERICAN IND.
1968	5	*Nixon (R)	170,514	266,721	46,573
					AMERICAN
1972	6	*Nixon (R)	198,540	402,812	21,208
					LIBERTARIAN
1976	6	Ford (R)	295,602	418,642	7,647
1980	6	*Reagan (R)	246,843	529,688	18,784

*Won US presidential election.

the mayor may be elected either by the council or at large; state law requires that cities appoint a city clerk (treasurer), attorney, police chief or marshal, physician, and engineer. With the approval of the voters and the governor, cities may adopt charters. These charter cities may adopt their own government structure and assessment system, and levy revenue and sales taxes. All of Arizona's largest cities are charter cities.

Each of the 18 Indian reservations in Arizona has a tribal council or board with members elected by the people.

¹⁵STATE SERVICES
Arizona's eight-member Ethics Board receives and may initiate complaints and charges against public officials other than members of the judiciary and legislature. There are also ethics committees in both the senate and the house of representatives.

The Arizona Department of Education regulates the public school system. The Arizona Board of Regents governs the state's three public universities. The Department of Transportation administers the highway and air-transport systems.

The Department of Health Services operates programs for environmental health, behavioral health (including alcohol abuse, drug abuse, and mental illness treatment facilties), and family health services. The National Guard falls under the jurisdiction of the Department of Emergency and Military Affairs, while prisons and rehabilitation programs are administered by the State Department of Corrections. The Department of Public Safety oversees the state highway patrol.

Natural resources are the responsibility of several agencies, including the Game and Fish Commission, Department of Mineral Resources, Oil and Gas Conservation Commission, Arizona State Parks Board, and Arizona Water Commission. The Department of Economic Security handles employment services, manpower planning, and public-assistance programs.

¹⁶JUDICIAL SYSTEM
The supreme court is the highest court in Arizona and has administrative responsibility over all other courts in the state. The five supreme court justices, elected for staggered six-year terms, choose a chief justice and vice chief justice to preside over the court. When a vacancy occurs, the governor appoints a new justice who serves until the next regular election.

The court of appeals, established in 1964, is organized in two geographical divisions which together comprise four departments of three judges each. All appeals court judges are elected for terms of six years.

The superior court is the general trial court of the state, and there must be at least one superior court judge in every Arizona county. Superior court judges (76 in 1979) are elected to four-year terms.

Counties are divided into precincts, each of which has a justice court. Every incorporated city and town has a police court. The jurisdiction of justice courts and police courts is limited to minor civil and criminal cases. Local judges are elected for terms of four years.

According to the FBI Crime Index of 1978, Arizona's crime rate of 7,603.8 per 100,000 population ranked 2d only to Nevada's among the 50 states. Rates for murder and nonnegligent manslaughter, forcible rape, aggravated assault, breaking and entering, larceny, and motor vehicle theft were all above the national average. Both Phoenix (8,716.3) and Tucson (8,342.9) ranked among the most crime-ridden metropolitan areas.

¹⁷ARMED FORCES
In 1978, Arizona had a total of 34,276 federal military personnel. Major military installations include Fort Huachuca at Sierra Vista; Luke, Williams, and Davis Monthan Air Force bases; and Yuma Proving Ground. Defense Department expenditures in Arizona exceeded $1.4 billion in 1977/78.

As of 1979, about 329,000 veterans lived in the state; 7,000 saw service in World War I; 137,000 in World War II; 66,000 in the Korean conflict; and 102,000 during the Viet-Nam era. Veterans' benefits totaled $293.2 million in 1977/78.

In 1978, about 5,500 National Guard personnel were authorized. There were 7,023 state and local police and 2,866 state and local corrections personnel in 1977.

¹⁸MIGRATION
Arizona's first migrants were the ancient peoples who came from Asia via the Bering Strait more than 12,000 years ago. Hispanic settlers began arriving in the late 17th century. The Anglo migration, especially from the South, became significant as the US developed westward to California, and increased at an even faster rate with the building of the railroads during the 1880s. Migration has accelerated since World War II, and according to state data, Arizona showed a net gain of 585,600 immigrants (23% of the 1978 population) from 1970 to 1978. Increasingly, the new arrivals are northerners seeking the favorable weather and good business climate of a Sunbelt state. Mexico is the main source of foreign immigrants.

¹⁹INTERGOVERNMENTAL COOPERATION
Arizona is a signatory to a boundary agreement with California (1963) and to such interstate accords as the Colorado River Compact, Interstate Oil and Gas Compact, Upper Colorado River Basin Compact, Western Interstate Energy Compact, and Western Regional Education Compact.

The most important federal project in the state is the Central Arizona Project, approved by Congress in 1968, and designed to divert water from the Colorado River to the Phoenix and Tucson areas for agriculture, energy, and other purposes. Federal aid to Arizona totaled $809.5 million in 1978/79, of which $78.4 million was general revenue sharing.

²⁰ECONOMY
Mining and cattle raising were the principal economic activities in Arizona during the territorial period. With the introduction of irrigation in the early 1900s, farming assumed a greater importance. Improvements in transportation during the 20th century led to the development of manufacturing and tourism. State sources estimated the value of manufacturing in 1979 at $4.8 billion; tourism and travel, $3.9 billion; mining, $2.2 billion; and agricultural marketings, $1.6 billion. Leading products include electronic components and nonelectrical machinery from the manufacturing sector, copper from the mining sector, and cattle and cotton from the farming sector.

Arizona's economy compiled a remarkable growth record during the 1970s. Between 1968 and 1978, the state population increased by 51% (1st in the US); nonfarm wage and salary employment grew by nearly 87%, and total personal income by 246% (both 3d). During the same period, retail sales increased 250%, value added by manufacturing 245%, and bank deposits 211%. Most forecasts called for a slowdown in the early 1980s. Despite the Central Arizona Project, it was questionable whether the state had sufficient water resources to sustain anything approaching its 1970s growth rates for very much longer.

²¹INCOME
In 1978, Arizona ranked 30th among the 50 states with a per capita income of $7,374. Total personal income was $17.4 billion in 1978, of which $10.3 billion was concentrated in Maricopa County and $3.4 billion in Pima County (Tucson). The other 12 counties, all rural and including most of the state's Indian lands, accounted for the rest. Per capita income in these 12 counties was far below that in Maricopa and Pima. In 1975, 314,000 persons (about 14% of the population) were below the federal poverty level.

²²LABOR
In 1979, the civilian labor force totaled 1,047,200, 61% of it in Maricopa County and 18% in Pima. A federal census of workers covered by unemployment insurance in March 1977 revealed the following nonfarm employment pattern for Arizona:

	ESTABLISH-MENTS	EMPLOYEES	ANNUAL PAYROLL ('000)
Agricultural services forestry, fishing	729	4,375	$ 36,596
Mining, of which:	185	23,480	352,552
Metals	(69)	(20,906)	(302,470)
Contract construction	4,883	44,793	646,718
Manufacturing	2,554	111,948	1,488,008
Transportation, public utilities	1,259	34,494	495,782
Wholesale trade	3,461	39,796	495,928
Retail trade	13,889	158,577	1,027,124
Finance, insurance, real estate	4,537	45,131	494,017
Services	14,234	142,398	1,219,591
Other	816	1,176	13,810
TOTALS	46,547	606,168	$6,270,126

This survey excluded government workers, of whom there were nearly 330,000 in 1979.

Employees in the high-paying electronics and military-related industries are predominantly Anglo, while much of the Indian, Hispanic, and black populations hold seasonal jobs in agriculture and services. Unemployment in 1979 was 5.9%, but the figure was much higher among the minorities.

Organized labor has a long history in Arizona. A local of the Western Federation of Miners was founded in 1896, and labor was a powerful force at the constitutional convention in 1910. Nevertheless, the state's work force is much less organized than that of the nation as a whole. In 1976, 117,000 Arizonans belonged to labor unions, and 39,000 to employee associations. The state has a right-to-work law.

[23] AGRICULTURE

Arizona's agricultural output was valued at nearly $1.5 billion in 1978 (29th in the US). Cash receipts from farming alone amounted to $753.3 million.

In 1979 there were about 6,000 farms covering 41 million acres (17 million hectares), or about 56% of the state's total area. The average size of nearly 7,000 acres (2,800 hectares) per farm was by far the highest in the US. In general, Arizona's farms are intensely cultivated and highly productive. About 95% of all farmland is dependent on irrigation provided by the state's many dams and water projects.

Cotton is the leading cash crop in Arizona. In 1978, the state produced 1,074,000 bales on 572,200 acres (231,600 hectares), with a total value of $320,021,000. Alfalfa hay is the 2d-leading item; total hay production was 1,397,000 tons in 1979. Other important crops include wheat, sorghum, barley, vegetables, and citrus fruits.

[24] ANIMAL HUSBANDRY

Livestock production in 1978 was valued at $717.9 million. The total inventory of cattle and calves was 1.2 million in 1979, with an estimated value of $462 million. At the close of 1979, the state had 400,000 sheep and lambs and 149,000 hogs and pigs.

In 1978, 785,800 head of cattle were shipped out of Arizona, and 279,500 head were slaughtered within the state; the livestock slaughter also included 182,500 hogs and pigs. The wool clip totaled 2,595,000 lb in 1978.

[25] FISHING

Arizona has no commercial fishing. The state's lakes and mountain streams lure sport fishermen and are an increasingly important tourist attraction.

[26] FORESTRY

The lumber industry in Arizona began during the 19th century, when the building of the transcontinental railroad created a demand for railroad ties. During the 20th century, Arizona's forests have been more valuable for conservation and recreation than for lumber.

The main forest regions stretch from the northwest to the southeast, through the center of the state. All together, in 1977 there were 18,494,000 acres (7,484,000 hectares) of forestland in Arizona, 25% of the state's area and 2.5% of the US total. Commercial timberland accounted for only 3,896,000 acres (1,577,000 hectares), however, and less than 5% of that was privately owned.

National forests covered nearly 12 million acres (5 million hectares) as of 30 September 1979.

[27] MINING

Arizona ranked 11th in the US in mineral production in 1978, with output valued at nearly $2 billion.

Arizona produces nearly two-thirds of the nation's copper. The major copper mines are in Pima, Pinal, and Greenlee counties, in the south and southeast. In 1978, the state produced 982,606 tons of copper, with a value of $1.3 billion.

Molybdenum is the next most valuable mineral, followed by sand and gravel, silver, gold, and stone. In 1978, mineral output included 23,000,000 tons of sand and gravel, 5,250,000 tons of stone, 6,638,000 troy oz of silver, and 92,989 troy oz of gold.

[28] ENERGY AND POWER

In 1978, Arizona produced 30.5 billion kwh of electric power; installed capacity was 9.3 million kw. The state had 28 power plants, of which 11 were hydroelectric, accounting for 24% of power output. Electric energy sales in the state were 26.6 million kwh; the surplus production was exported to other states, primarily California.

Arizona's fossil-fuel potential remains largely undeveloped, though oil and natural gas exploration was under way as the 1980s began. Coal production in 1978 was 9,054,000 tons, all of that by surface mining.

Energy resource development in the state is encouraged by the Department of Mineral Resources, Power Authority Commission, and the Solar Energy Research Commission.

[29] INDUSTRY

Manufacturing has grown rapidly since World War II, and in the 1970s became the state's leading economic activity. Factors contributing to this growth included favorable tax structure, available labor, plentiful electric power, and low land costs. The major manufacturing centers are the Phoenix and Tucson areas. Principal industries include nonelectrical machinery, electrical and electronic equipment, aircraft equipment, food products, and printing and publishing. Military equipment accounts for much of the output.

The total value added by manufacture was $3.4 billion in 1977, and the value of industry shipments was $7.1 billion. Value added by manufacturing for selected industries in 1977 was as follows:

Office and computing machines	$591,100,000
Semiconductors, related devices	329,900,000
Communication equipment	150,200,000
Instruments and related products	147,000,000
Primary nonferrous metals	139,600,000

The total value added was estimated at $3.9 billion in 1978; the 1980 forecast was $5.4 billion.

[30] COMMERCE

In 1972, wholesale establishments in Arizona had sales of $4.3 billion. Most wholesale establishments were concentrated in Maricopa and Pima counties. Retail sales in 1978 exceeded $10.7 billion, of which 62% took place in Maricopa County and 17% in Pima. Of the 1977 retail sales total, $8.2 billion, food stores accounted for 23%; automotive dealers, 21%; general merchandise stores, 13%; eating and drinking places, 9%; gasoline service stations, 8%; and other establishments, 26%. Retail sales of $12.6 billion were estimated for 1979; the 1980 projection was $13.9 billion.

Manufactured goods worth $639 million were exported in 1976, and agricultural products valued at $285 million were sent abroad in 1976/77.

[31] CONSUMER PROTECTION

The Department of Law, headed by the attorney general, has primary responsibility for consumer protection.

[32] BANKING

In 1978 there were 20 insured commercial banks in Arizona with total assets of nearly $10.2 billion, and 16 savings and loan associations with total assets of $4.5 billion. Deposits in all Arizona banks totaled $8.9 billion at the close of 1978, and outstanding loans exceeded $6.5 billion.

The banking industry in Arizona is regulated by the Department of Banking, which annually examines each financial organization in the state.

[33] INSURANCE

More than $30 billion of life insurance was in force in Arizona in 1978. The average amount of life insurance per family increased from $19,600 in 1970 to $34,900 in 1978. Purchases of ordinary life insurance in Arizona totaled $3.3 billion in 1977, when life insurance companies owned nearly $1.3 billion in mortgages in the state. Receipts from premiums totaled $345 million for life insurance and $317 million for health insurance. About $215.5 million in benefits were paid in 1978. In 1976, approximately 1,320,000 Arizonans were protected by some form of hospital insurance; 1,216,000 had surgical coverage, 1,148,000 had regular medical coverage, and 907,000 had major medical insurance. Automobile liability and physical damage premiums totaling $367 million were written in 1978; homeowners' premiums were $88 million.

The Department of Insurance regulates the state's insurance industry and examines and licenses domestic insurance companies.

[34] SECURITIES

In 1978, the New York Stock Exchange had 48 offices and 478 full-time registered representatives in Arizona. State residents declared $306.4 million in dividend income on their 1977 tax returns. Sales of securities are regulated by the Corporation Commission. The state has no securities exchanges.

[35] PUBLIC FINANCE

The state budget is prepared annually and submitted by the governor to the legislature for amendment and approval. The fiscal year runs from 1 July to 30 June.

The following table summarizes consolidated revenues and expenditures for 1978/79 (actual) and 1979/80 (estimated):

REVENUES	1978/79	1979/80
Taxes	$1,069,694,000	$1,145,390,000
Interest	28,736,000	42,000,000
Licenses and fees	12,267,000	12,945,000
Sales and services	5,862,000	5,900,000
Other receipts	781,473,136	877,426,700
TOTALS	$1,898,032,136	$2,083,661,700
EXPENDITURES		
Education	$1,061,214,300	$1,152,635,400
Health and welfare	329,264,500	364,314,600
Transportation	215,441,200	260,160,000
Protection and safety	93,618,500	107,684,600
General government	63,594,700	79,021,700
Other expenses	193,430,200	275,192,500
TOTALS	$1,956,563,400	$2,239,008,800

The total debt of state and local government as of mid-1977 was nearly $2.9 billion, or $1,242 per capita.

[36] TAXATION

State tax receipts for the general fund in 1978/79 exceeded $1 billion, of which income taxes accounted for $322.4 million. The personal income tax ranged from 2% on the first $1,000 to 14.5% on income over $200,000. For corporations the maximum rate was 10.5% on net income over $6,000. The state sales and use tax of 4% raised nearly $136 million in 1978/79. An estate tax, luxury tax, pari-mutuel tax, and transport fuel tax are also levied.

In 1976, Arizona's share of the federal tax burden was $3.1 billion; of federal tax benefits, $3.8 billion. In 1976/77, Arizonans filed 908,342 federal income tax returns, paying more than $1.4 billion in taxes.

[37] ECONOMIC POLICY

The Office of Economic Planning and Development has primary responsibility for encouraging business expansion and relocation in Arizona. Its programs emphasize manpower planning, energy conservation, and development of the motion-picture industry. Specific incentives include tax exemptions on goods in transit and on raw materials used in manufacturing.

[38] HEALTH

Arizona ranked 31st among the 50 states in average life expectancy during 1969–71, at 70.55 years—66.57 for males, 75.04 for females. In 1978 there were 43,058 live births and 19,097 deaths. Infant mortality in 1977 was 12.4 per 1,000 live births among whites, and 19.3 among nonwhites. There were 9,700 legal abortions in 1977/78; the rate of 226 per 1,000 live births was far below the national average. Arizona's overall death rate was below the US norm in 1977, and especially low for heart disease and cardiovascular diseases. Deaths from suicide and cirrhosis of the liver were above average, however. Serious health problems include glaucoma and coccidioidomycosis—a disease marked by a high fever—especially among the Indian population.

In 1978 there were 78 hospitals, with 11,339 beds. Hospital personnel included 6,738 registered nurses and 2,177 licensed practical nurses. The state had 4,615 licensed physicians in 1977, and 1,173 dentists in 1979; 90% of the physicians and 82% of the dentists were in Pima and Maricopa counties. The average cost of a hospital stay in 1977 was $228 per day, 15% above the US average.

[39] SOCIAL WELFARE

In 1978, aid to families with dependent children totaled $30 million. About 97,000 persons participated in the federal food stamp program, at a federal cost of $38.4 million. Some 269,000 pupils (56% of the eligible enrollment) took part in the school lunch program, at a cost to the federal government of $18.6 million.

In 1977, $929 million in Social Security benefits was paid to 371,700 beneficiaries; the average monthly benefit for retirees was $249. About 29,000 Arizonans received $41.7 million in federal Supplemental Security Income benefits during 1978. A total of $221 million in hospital and medical insurance was paid under the Medicaid program in 1977; $10.9 million was spent on vocational rehabilitation in 1978, when unemployment insurance benefits totaled $32 million. Workers' compensation payments amounted to $79.6 million in 1979.

[40] HOUSING

The 1970 census counted 578,000 units of year-round housing in Arizona, of which 539,000 were occupied. Of the latter, 65% were owner-occupied, and 95% had complete plumbing facilities. Overcrowding was a serious problem. More than 10% of occupied units averaged more than a person per room; only five states had a higher percentage.

The 1970s saw a boom in housing construction, with 204,032 units authorized from 1974 through 1978. In 1978 alone, 69,351 units were authorized, of which 78% were in the Phoenix and Tucson metropolitan areas. Building permits valued at $2.4 billion were issued.

[41] EDUCATION

Arizona's illiteracy rate was 1.8% in 1970, well above the national norm. Nearly 73% of adult Arizonans were high school graduates in 1976.

The first public school in the state opened in 1871 at Tucson, with 1 teacher and 138 students. By 1977/78, average daily attendance at public schools was 496,418, including 181,556 students in elementary districts, 84,235 in high school districts, and 230,627 in unified school districts. There were 24,400 public-school teachers in 1979, 70% of them in the elementary grades. Private schools enrolled some 29,000 students in 1977.

The leading public higher educational institutions, the University of Arizona at Tucson and Arizona State University (originally named the Arizona Territorial Normal School) at Tempe, were both established in 1885. As of 1978, the state had 6 colleges and universities (3 private) and 16 community colleges, with a total enrollment of more than 191,000. The Graduate School of International Management, a private institution, is located in Glendale.

[42]ARTS

Arizona has traditionally been a center for Indian folk arts and crafts. The Arizona State Museum (Tucson), Colorado River Indian Tribal Museum (Parker), Heard Museum of Anthropology and Primitive Art (Phoenix), Mohave Museum of History and Arts (Kingman), Navaho Tribal Museum (Window Rock), and Pueblo Grande Museum (Phoenix) all display Indian creations, both historic and contemporary. Modern Arizona artists are featured at the Tucson Museum of Art and the Yuma Art Center.

Musical and dramatic performances are presented in Phoenix, Tucson, Scottsdale, and other major cities. Phoenix and Tucson have symphony orchestras.

[43]LIBRARIES AND MUSEUMS

In 1978, Arizona's public libraries had a combined book stock of 3.5 million volumes and total circulation of 10.8 million. Principal public libraries include the Phoenix Public Library and the State Library and Department of Archives in Phoenix, and the Arizona Historical Society Library in Tucson. The largest university libraries are located at the University of Arizona and Arizona State University.

Arizona has at least 75 museums and historic sites. Attractions in Tucson include the Arizona State Museum, University of Arizona Museum of Art, Arizona Historical Society Museums, Arizona–Sonora Desert Museum, and Flandreau Planetarium. Phoenix has the Heard Museum of Anthropology and Primitive Art, Arizona Mineral Museum, Phoenix Art Museum, Pueblo Grande Museum, and Desert Botanical Garden. The Museum of Northern Arizona and Lowell Observatory are in Flagstaff.

Archaeological and historical sites include the cliff dwellings at Montezuma Castle, Tonto, and Tuzigoot; the town of Tombstone, the site of the famous O. K. Corral gunfight in the early 1880s; the restored mission at Tumacacori; and San Xavier del Bac Church near Tucson.

[44]COMMUNICATIONS

In the late 1970s there were some 120 post offices and 6,000 postal employees in Arizona. Postal receipts in Phoenix in 1977/78 were $62.1 million; in Tucson, $18.4 million. Of the 1,795,955 telephones in service in 1978, 1,316,749 were residential and 479,206 business. On average, 99% of residences had telephone service.

There were 92 radio stations broadcasting in Arizona in 1978, 60 AM and 32 FM. The state also had 11 commercial television stations, 5 in Phoenix, 4 in Tucson, and 1 each in Flagstaff and Yuma, as well as 2 educational television stations, one at Arizona State University and the other at the University of Arizona. In 1978, 46 cable television systems were serving 82,112 subscribers in 77 communities.

[45]PRESS

The *Weekly Arizonian*, started in Tubac in 1859, was the first newspaper in the state. The *Daily Arizona Miner*, the state's first daily, was founded at Prescott in 1866. As of 1978 there were 2 morning dailies with a combined circulation of 292,667 and 15 evening dailies with 282,655 circulation. The following table shows 1978 circulations for leading dailies:

AREA	NAME	DAILY	SUNDAY
Phoenix	Arizona Republic		
	(m,S)	228,085	347,801
	Gazette (e)	97,750	
Tucson	Citizen (e)	58,747	
	Arizona Daily Star		
	(m,S)	64,582	119,368

At least 35 magazines and periodicals are published in Arizona. Among the most notable are *Arizona and the West*, published quarterly by the University of Arizona Library in Tucson, and *Arizona Highways*, a beautifully illustrated monthly published by the Department of Transportation in Phoenix.

In a case that attracted nationwide attention, Don Bolles, a reporter for the *Arizona Republic*, was murdered on 2 June 1976 after writing articles exposing the influence of organized crime in the state. Shortly thereafter, a team of 36 reporters from newspapers and broadcast news services throughout the US came to Arizona to investigate the murder case and to pursue the leads that Bolles had been unable to explore. Two men were convicted in the murder case, but their convictions were overturned on appeal, and another man was convicted in August 1980.

[46]ORGANIZATIONS

Service organizations with headquarters in Arizona include the Boys Club Professional Association (Tucson) and the National Employment and Training Association (Phoenix). Among the educational, scientific, and health organizations are the American Society for Ethnohistory (Tucson), Council of Community Blood Centers (Scottsdale), National Foundation for Asthma (Tucson), and the National Foundation for the Prevention of Oral Disease (Glendale). Commercial, trade, and professional groups include the American Institute of Landscape Architects (Phoenix), National Association of State Park Directors (Phoenix), and Pianists Foundation of America (Tucson). The US Gymnastics Federation has its headquarters in Tucson.

[47]TOURISM, TRAVEL, AND RECREATION

Tourism is the 2d-leading industry in Arizona. In 1978, tourism accounted for $3.4 billion in income, of which about $1.4 billion came from highway travelers to the state, $1.5 billion from air travelers to the state, and $500 million from intrastate travelers. Most tourists were Americans, but travelers from Mexico spent nearly $348 million in the state. Total direct employment in tourism in 1978 was 71,614, and the industry indirectly employed another 119,595 Arizonans.

There are 19 national parks and monuments located entirely within Arizona. By far the most popular is Grand Canyon National Park, which had 2,986,174 visitors in 1978. Petrified Forest National Park had 957,771 visitors, and Saguaro National Monument, 549,112. There are also 16 state parks; Lake Havasu, the overwhelming favorite, had 979,047 visitors in 1978.

Arizona offers excellent camping on both public and private land, and there are many farm vacation sites and dude ranches, particularly in the Tucson and Wickenburg areas. Popular for sightseeing and shopping are the state's Indian reservations, particularly those of the Navaho and Hopi.

Licenses were issued to 188,936 hunters and 447,498 fishermen in 1977/78. Boat registrations in 1978 totaled 86,018.

[48]SPORTS

The Phoenix Suns, the state's lone major league professional team, play in the National Basketball Association. Several major league baseball teams hold spring training in Arizona, and Phoenix and Tucson have entries in the Pacific Coast League. There is horse racing at Turf Paradise in Phoenix, and dog racing at Phoenix Greyhound Park. Auto racing is held at Bee Line

Dragway, Manzanita Park, and Phoenix Fastrack Raceway. Both Phoenix and Tucson have hosted tournaments on the Professional Golfers Association's nationwide tour.

Rodeos are held throughout the state. Phoenix hosts the Rodeo of Rodeos, while Tucson has La Fiesta de los Vaqueros (Festival of the Cowboys).

The Sun Devils of Arizona State won Western Athletic Conference football titles five times between 1969 and 1977, and shared the title twice (once with the University of Arizona Wildcats). Both Arizona State and the University of Arizona joined the Pacific 10 Conference in 1978. The Wildcats captured NCAA Division I baseball championships in 1975 and 1980.

[49] FAMOUS ARIZONANS

Although Arizona entered the Union relatively late, many of its citizens have achieved national prominence, especially since World War II. William H. Rehnquist (b.Wisconsin, 1924) was appointed associate justice of the US Supreme Court in 1971. Arizona natives who became federal officeholders include Lewis Douglas (1894–1974), a representative who served as director of the budget in 1933–34 and ambassador to the Court of St. James's from 1947 to 1950; Stewart L. Udall (b.1920), secretary of the interior, 1961–69; and Richard G. Kleindienst (b.1923), attorney general, 1972–73, who resigned during the Watergate scandal. Another native son was Carl T. Hayden (1877–1972), who served in the US Senate from 1927 to 1969. Barry Goldwater (b.1909), son of a pioneer family, was elected to the US Senate in 1952, won the Republican presidential nomination in 1964, and returned to the Senate in 1968. His Republican colleague, John J. Rhodes (b.Kansas, 1916), has been minority leader of the US House of Representatives since 1973. Raul H. Castro (b.Mexico, 1916), a native of Sonora, came to the US in 1926, was naturalized, served as Arizona governor from 1975 to 1977, and has held several ambassadorships to Latin America. Morris K. Udall (b.1922), first elected to the US House of Representatives in 1960, contended for the Democratic presidential nomination in 1976.

Prominent state officeholders included General John C. Frémont (b.Georgia, 1813–90), who was territorial governor of Arizona from 1878 to 1883, and George W. P. Hunt (1859–1934), who presided over the state constitutional convention in 1910 and was elected governor seven times during the early decades of statehood. Eusebio Kino (b.Italy, 1645?–1711) was a pioneer Jesuit who introduced missions and European civilization to Arizona. Also important to the state's history and development were Charles D. Poston (1825–1902), who in the late 1850s promoted settlement and separate territorial status for Arizona; Chiricahua Apache leaders Cochise (1812?–74) and Geronimo (1829–1909), who, resisting the forced resettlement of their people by the US government, launched a series of raids that occupied the Army in the Southwest for over two decades; John C. Greenway (1872–1926), copper magnate and town builder who was a nominee on the Democratic ticket in 1924 for US vice president; and Frank Luke, Jr. (1897–1918), a World War I flying ace who was the first American airman to receive the Medal of Honor.

Distinguished professional people associated with Arizona have included James Douglas (b.Canada, 1837–1918), metallurgist and developer of the Bisbee copper district; Percival Lowell (b.Massachusetts, 1855–1916), who built the Lowell Observatory in Flagstaff; and Andrew Ellicott Douglass (b.Vermont, 1867–1962), astronomer, university president, and inventor of dendrochronology, the science of dating events and environmental variations through the study of tree rings and aged wood. Cesar Chavez (b.1927) is president of the United Farm Workers of America.

Writers whose names have been associated with Arizona include novelist Harold Bell Wright (b.New York, 1872–1944), who lived for an extended period in Tucson; Zane Grey (b.Ohio, 1875–1939), who wrote many of his western adventure stories in his summer home near Payson; and Joseph Wood Krutch (b.Tennessee, 1893–1970), an essayist and naturalist who spent his last two decades in Arizona. Well-known performing artists from Arizona include singers Marty Robbins (b.1925) and Linda Ronstadt (b.1946). Joan Ganz Cooney (b.1929), director of the Children's Television Workshop, was one of the creators of the award-winning children's program *Sesame Street*.

[50] BIBLIOGRAPHY

Arizona: Its People and Resources. 2d ed., rev. Tucson: University of Arizona Press, 1972.

Arizona Yearbook, 1979–80: A Guide to Government in Arizona. Yuma: Arizona Information Press, 1979.

Barnes, Will C. *Arizona Place Names.* Revised by Byrd H. Granger. Tucson: University of Arizona Press, 1960.

Faulk, Odie B. *Arizona: A Short History.* Norman: University of Oklahoma Press, 1970.

Federal Writers' Project. *Arizona: The Grand Canyon State.* Rev. ed. New York: Hastings House, 1968 (orig. 1940).

Krutch, Joseph Wood. *The Desert Year.* New York: Viking, 1963 (orig. 1951).

Lamar, Howard R. *The Far Southwest, 1846–1912: A Territorial History.* New Haven: Yale University Press, 1966.

Powell, Lawrence C. *Arizona: A Bicentennial History.* New York: Norton, 1976.

Valley National Bank of Arizona. *Arizona Statistical Review.* 35th ed. Phoenix, 1979.

Wagoner, Jay J. *Arizona's Heritage.* Layton, Utah: Peregrine Smith, 1977.

Wagoner, Jay J. *Arizona Territory 1863–1912.* Tucson: University of Arizona Press, 1970.

Wagoner, Jay J. *Early Arizona: Prehistory to Civil War.* Tucson: University of Arizona Press, 1975.

Walker, Henry P., and Don Bufkin. *Historical Atlas of Arizona.* Norman: University of Oklahoma Press, 1980.

Wallace, Andrew, ed. *Sources and Readings in Arizona History.* Tucson: Arizona Pioneers' Historical Society, 1965.

Wyllys, Rufus K. *Arizona: The History of a Frontier State.* Phoenix: Hobson and Herr, 1950.

ARKANSAS

State of Arkansas

ORIGIN OF STATE NAME: French derivative of *Akansa* or *Arkansas*, name given to the Quapaw Indians by other tribes. **NICKNAME:** The Land of Opportunity. **CAPITAL:** Little Rock. **ENTERED UNION:** 15 June 1836 (25th). **SONG:** "Arkansas." **MOTTO:** *Regnat populus* (The people rule). **COAT OF ARMS:** In front of an American eagle is a shield displaying a steamboat, plow, beehive, and sheaf of wheat, symbols of Arkansas's industrial and agricultural wealth. The angel of mercy, the goddess of liberty encircled by 13 stars, and the sword of justice surround the eagle, which holds in its talons an olive branch and three arrows, and in its beak a banner bearing the state motto. **FLAG:** On a red field, 25 stars on a blue band border a white diamond containing the word "Arkansas" and four blue stars. **OFFICIAL SEAL:** Coat of arms surrounded by the words "Great Seal of the State of Arkansas." **BIRD:** Mockingbird. **FLOWER:** Apple blossom. **TREE:** Pine. **GEM:** Diamond. **INSECT:** Honeybee. **LEGAL HOLIDAYS:** New Year's Day, 1 January; Robert E. Lee's Birthday, 19 January; George Washington's Birthday, 3d Monday in February; Memorial Day, last Monday in May; Independence Day, 4 July; Labor Day, 1st Monday in September; Veterans Day, 11 November; Thanksgiving Day, 4th Thursday in November; Christmas Eve, 24 December; Christmas Day, 25 December. **TIME:** 6 A.M. CST = noon GMT.

¹LOCATION, SIZE, AND EXTENT

Located in the western south-central US, Arkansas ranks 27th in size among the 50 states.

The total area of Arkansas is 53,104 sq mi (137,539 sq km), of which land takes up 51,945 sq mi (134,537 sq km) and inland water 1,159 sq mi (3,002 sq km). Arkansas extends about 275 mi (443 km) E–W and 240 mi (386 km) N–S.

Arkansas is bordered on the N by Missouri; on the E by Missouri, Tennessee, and Mississippi (with part of the line passing through the St. Francis and Mississippi rivers); on the S by Louisiana; on the SW by Texas (with part of the line formed by the Red River); and on the W by Oklahoma. The total boundary length of Arkansas is *1,168 mi (1,880 km)*. The state's geographic center is in Pulaski County, 12 mi (19 km) NW of Little Rock.

²TOPOGRAPHY

The Boston Mountains (an extension of the Ozark Plateau, sometimes called the Ozark Mountains) in the northwest and the Ouachita Mountains in the west-central region not only constitute Arkansas's major uplands but also are the only mountain chains between the Appalachians and the Rockies. Aside from the wide valley of the Arkansas River, which separates the two chains, the Arkansas lowlands belong to two physiographic regions: the Mississippi Alluvial Plain and the Gulf Coastal Plain. The highest elevation in Arkansas, at 2,753 feet (839 meters), is Magazine Mountain, standing north of the Ouachitas in the Arkansas Valley. The state's lowest point, at 55 feet (17 meters), is on the Ouachita River in south-central Arkansas.

Arkansas's largest lake is the artificial Lake Ouachita, covering 63 sq mi (163 sq km); Bull Shoals Lake, occupying 71 sq mi (184 sq km), is shared with Missouri. Principal rivers include the Mississippi, forming most of the eastern boundary; the Arkansas, beginning in Colorado and flowing 1,450 mi (2,334 km) through Kansas and Oklahoma and across central Arkansas to the Mississippi; and the Red, White, Ouachita, and St. Francis rivers, all of which likewise drain south and southeast into the Mississippi. Numerous springs are found in Arkansas, of which the best known are Mammoth Spring, near the Missouri border, one of the largest in the world, with a flow rate of 36 million gallons an hour, and Hot Springs, in the Ouachitas.

Crowley's Ridge, a narrow strip of hills running west of and parallel to the St. Francis River for about 180 mi (290 km), is rich in fossils.

³CLIMATE

Arkansas has a temperate climate, warmer and more humid in the southern lowlands than in the mountainous regions. At Little Rock, the normal daily temperature ranges from 40°F (4°C) in January to 81°F (27°C) in July. A record low of –29°F (–34°C) was set on 13 February 1905 at the Pond weather station, and a record high of 120°F (49°C) on 10 August 1930 at the Ozark station. A state of emergency was declared during the summer heat wave of 1980, with 115 deaths attributed to the heat by mid-July.

Average yearly precipitation is approximately 45 in (114 cm) in the mountainous areas and greater in the lowlands; Little Rock receives an annual average of 49 in (124 cm) and has an average relative humidity ranging from 84% at 7 A.M. to 57% at 1 P.M. Snowfall in the capital totals some 5 in (13 cm) a year.

⁴FLORA AND FAUNA

Arkansas lists at least 2,600 native plants, and there are many naturalized exotic species. Cypresses, water oak, hickory, and ash grow in the Mississippi Valley, while the St. Francis Valley is home to the rare cork tree. Crowley's Ridge is thick with tulip trees and beeches. A forest belt of oak, hickory, and pine stretches across south-central and southwestern Arkansas, including the Ozark and Ouachita mountains. The Mexican juniper is common along the White River's banks. The state has at least 26 native varieties of orchid; the passion flower is so abundant that it was once considered for designation as the state flower, but the apple blossom was finally named.

Arkansas's native animals include 15 varieties of bat, and 3 each of rabbit and squirrel. Also common throughout the state are mink, armadillo, white-tailed deer, and eastern chipmunk. Some black bear still roam the forest, swamp, and mountain regions. Among 300 native birds are such game birds as the eastern wild turkey, mourning dove, and bobwhite quail. Among local fish are catfish, perch, and gar, a nemesis to fishermen. Arkansas counts 20 frog and toad species, 23 varieties of salamander, and 36 kinds of snake.

The Arkansas Game and Fish Commission lists the leopard

darter and fat pocketbook pearly mussel as threatened species. The peregrine falcon and American alligator are listed as endangered, along with the Indiana and gray bats and eastern puma.

⁵ENVIRONMENTAL PROTECTION

The Department of Pollution Control and Ecology, the state's principal environmental protection agency, was established in 1971. A survey by the department in 1980 indicated that the two environmental issues Arkansans were most concerned about were water pollution control and solid waste disposal; as of the late 1970s, the state's water quality standards were among the strictest in the US. Citizens' groups actively involved with environmental issues include the Arkansas Ecology Center, Arkansas Community Organizations for Reform Now (ACORN), the League of Women Voters, the Ozark Society, Ducks Unlimited, and some local chapters of the US Wildlife Federation. The Federation of Water and Air Users presents industries' viewpoints on environmental issues.

The Buffalo, designated as a national wild river, flows through northern Arkansas. One of the wildest areas in the state is the 113,000-acre (46,000-hectare) White River Wildlife Refuge, which contains more than 100 small lakes. The Department of Arkansas Natural and Cultural Heritage was established in 1975 for, among other purposes, the preservation of rivers and other natural features in an unspoiled condition.

⁶POPULATION

At the time of the 1970 census, Arkansas had a population of 1,923,322 (32d in the US). Provisional figures for 1979 showed Arkansas ranking 33d, with 2,180,000 residents; the average population density was 42 per sq mi (16 per sq km). The preliminary 1980 census total for Arkansas was 2,280,687.

As of 1978, Arkansas was 2d only to Florida in percentage of population aged 65 or over—13.4%—partially reflecting the large numbers of retirees who settled in the state during the 1970s. At the same time, an above average percentage of Arkansans were 17 or under. Arkansans are somewhat more mobile than residents of other states: as of 1976, 15% had lived in Arkansas for five years or less.

About 38% of all state residents lived in metropolitan areas in 1977. The largest city in Arkansas is Little Rock, which had an estimated 1979 population of 194,824. Other major cities include Ft. Smith, 68,006; North Little Rock, 62,004; Pine Bluff, 57,389; and Hot Springs, 35,631. The Little Rock–North Little Rock metropolitan area had some 369,000 residents in 1977.

⁷ETHNIC GROUPS

Arkansas's population is predominantly white, composed mainly of descendants of Scotch-Irish immigrants. The only significant minority group consists of black Americans, numbering 366,000 in 1976. The 1970 census listed 2,014 American Indians, 743 Chinese, 587 Japanese, and 289 Filipinos. The Hispanic population is also small. The foreign-born and the native-born children of foreign or mixed parentage accounted for less than 2% of Arkansas's 1970 population; Germany, the United Kingdom, and Canada were the leading countries of origin.

As of 31 December 1975, 2,042 Vietnamese refugees had been resettled in Arkansas. Ft. Chaffee, with barracks capable of accommodating 24,000 people, was opened as a receiving and processing center for Indochinese refugees in May 1975, and again for Cuban refugees in the spring of 1980. Local protests were mounted against each group, especially the latter.

⁸LANGUAGES

A few place-names, such as Arkansas itself, Choctaw, and Ouachita, attest the onetime presence of American Indians, mostly members of the Caddoan tribes, in the Territory of Arkansas. In 1970, only 572 persons claimed an Indian language as their mother tongue.

Arkansas English is essentially a blend of Southern and South Midland speech, with South Midland dominating the mountainous northwest and Southern the southeastern agricultural areas. Common in the east and south are *redworm* (earthworm), *mosquito hawk* (dragonfly), and *cold drink* (soft drink). In the northwest appear South Midland *whirlygig* (merry-go-round) and *sallet* (garden greens).

In 1970, 93% of native-born Arkansans and of all state residents claimed English as their mother tongue. Major resident groups claimed the following first languages:

	NATIVE-BORN	FOREIGN-BORN
English	1,789,331	1,747
German	11,784	2,151
Spanish	4,792	470
French	3,022	413

⁹RELIGIONS

Although French Roman Catholic priests had worked as missionaries among the Indians since the early 18th century, the state's first mission was founded among the Cherokee by a Congregationalist, Cephas Washburn, in 1820. When the Cherokee were removed to Indian Territory (present-day Oklahoma), the mission moved there as well, remaining active through the Civil War. William Patterson may have been the first Methodist to preach in Arkansas, around 1800, in the area of Little Prairie; the first Methodist circuit, that of Spring River, was organized in 1815. The first Baptist church was likely that of the Salem congregation, begun in 1818 near what is now Pocahontas.

The largest denomination in Arkansas is the Southern Baptist Convention, which had 435,183 known adherents in 1971. Other leading Protestant groups are the United Methodist Church, with 184,724 adherents in 1971, and the Baptist Missionary Association of America, with 59,024. As of 1979, the Roman Catholic population of Arkansas was 54,312; the estimated Jewish population, 3,395.

¹⁰TRANSPORTATION

Although railroad construction began in the 1850s, not until after the Civil War were any lines completed. The most important railroad, the St. Louis, Iron Mountain, and Southern line, reached Little Rock in 1872 and was subsequently acquired by financier Jay Gould, who added the Little Rock and Ft. Smith line to it in 1882. By 1890, the state had about 2,200 mi (3,500 km) of track; in 1974, trackage totaled 3,559 mi (5,728 km). As of 1980, Arkansas was served by four major railroads, and Amtrak passenger trains serviced Little Rock.

Intensive road building began in the 1920s, following the establishment of the State Highway Commission and the inauguration of a gasoline tax. By 1978, Arkansas had 74,208 mi (119,426 km) of highways, of which 87% were surfaced. During the same year, 974,123 automobiles and 478,102 trucks were registered in Arkansas, and there were 1,366,869 licensed drivers.

Beginning in the 1820s, steamboats replaced keelboats and flatboats on Arkansas rivers. Steamboat transportation reached its peak during 1870–90, until supplanted by the railroads that were opened during the same two decades. Development of the Arkansas River, completed during the early 1970s at a cost of $1.2 billion, made the waterway commercially navigable all the way to Tulsa.

In 1978, Arkansas had 160 airports, 1 heliport, and 2 seaplane bases. The principal airport in the state, Adams Field at Little Rock, emplaned 555,942 passengers and handled 13,494 scheduled departures.

¹¹HISTORY

The bluff dwellers of the Ozark Plateau were among the first human beings to live in what is now Arkansas, making their homes in caves and beneath overhanging rock cliffs along the banks of the upper White River. Farther south are the remains of another primitive people, the Mound Builders. The most significant of the Stone Age monuments they left are those of the

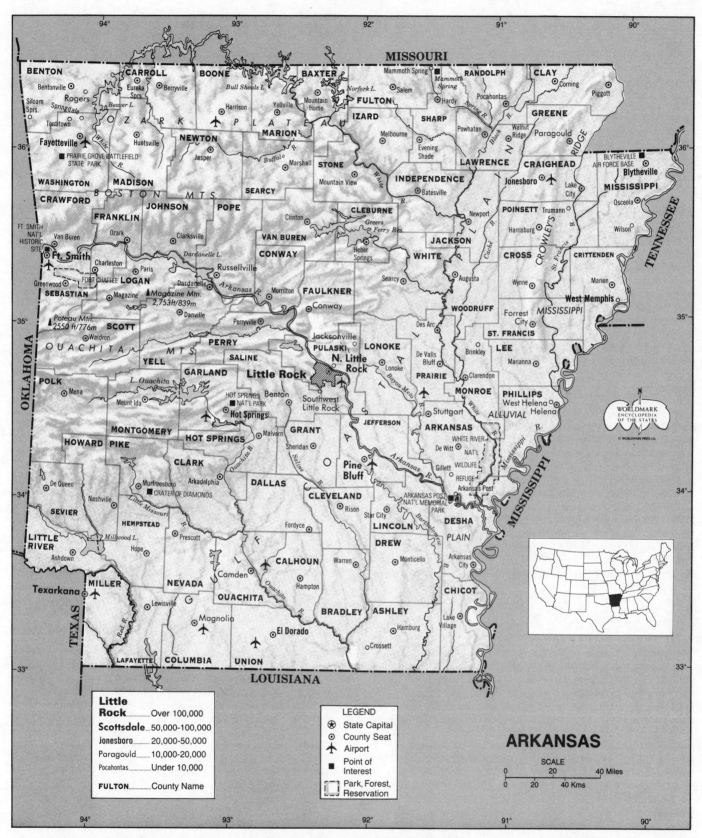

LEGEND

- ⊗ State Capital
- ⊙ County Seat
- ✈ Airport
- ■ Point of Interest
- Park, Forest, Reservation

Little Rock _____ Over 100,000
Scottsdale _____ 50,000-100,000
Jonesboro _____ 20,000-50,000
Paragould _____ 10,000-20,000
Pocahontas _____ Under 10,000

FULTON _____ County Name

ARKANSAS

SCALE

0 — 20 — 40 Miles
0 — 20 — 40 Kms

See US political: front cover H3; US physical: back cover H3.

LOCATION: 33° to 36°31′N; 89°41′ to 94°42′W. **BOUNDARIES**: Missouri line, *331 mi (533 km)*; Tennessee line, *163 mi (262 km)*; Mississippi line, *208 mi (335 km)*; Louisiana line, *166 mi (267 km)*; Texas line, *102 mi (164 km)*; Oklahoma line, *198 mi (319 km)*.

Toltec group in Lonoke County, some 25 mi (40 km) southeast of Little Rock. Eventually, both ancient peoples vanished, for reasons that remain unclear.

Foremost among the Indian tribes in Arkansas were the Quapaw (meaning "downstream people"), agriculturists who had migrated to southern Arkansas in the early 16th century; the Caddo, fighters from Texas, who claimed the western region between the Red and Arkansas rivers; the warlike Osage, who hunted north of the Arkansas River and in present-day Missouri; and the Choctaw and Chickasaw of the northeast. Another prominent tribe, the Cherokee, arrived in the early 19th century, after federal and state authorities had taken their land east of the Mississippi and driven them westward. Nearly all these Indians had been expelled to what is now Oklahoma by the time Arkansas became a state.

The first Europeans to set foot in Arkansas were Spaniards, led by Hernando de Soto. They crossed the Mississippi, probably near present-day Helena, in the spring of 1541, roamed the land for a year or so, and then returned to the mighty river, where De Soto was buried in 1542. More than 100 years later, in 1673, a small band of Frenchmen led by Jacques Marquette, a Jesuit missionary, and Louis Jolliet, a fur trader and explorer, ended their voyage down the Mississippi at the mouth of the Arkansas River and returned north after being advised by friendly Indians that hostile tribes lay to the south. Nine years later, Robert Cavelier, Sieur de la Salle, led an expedition from Canada down the Mississippi to the Gulf of Mexico, stopping at Indian villages in Arkansas along the way and, on 9 April 1682, claiming all the Mississippi Valley for his king, Louis XIV.

Henri de Tonti, who had been second in command to La Salle, came back to Arkansas in 1686 to claim a land grant at the confluence of the Arkansas and White rivers, a few miles inland from the Mississippi. He left six men there; the log house they built was the beginning of Arkansas Post, the first permanent white settlement in the lower Mississippi Valley. Though tiny and isolated, Arkansas Post upheld the French claim to the Mississippi Valley until 1762, when France ceded the territory to Spain. Restored to France in 1800, the territory was sold to the US in the Louisiana Purchase of 1803. White settlers soon began arriving in Arkansas, and in 1806, the Louisiana territorial legislature created the District of Arkansas as a separate entity. When the Louisiana Purchase was further subdivided, Arkansas became part of the Missouri Territory. In 1819, Arkansas gained territorial status in its own right, and its boundaries were fixed by Congress. The territorial capital was moved from Arkansas Post to Little Rock in 1821. By 1835, Arkansas Territory had a population of 52,240, including 9,838 slaves. It was admitted to the Union in 1836 as a slave state, paired with the free state of Michigan in accordance with the Missouri Compromise.

Increasing numbers of slaves were brought into the largely agricultural state as the cultivation of cotton spread. Arkansas, like the rest of the South, was headed for secession, although it waited until the Civil War had begun to commit itself. There was considerable Union sentiment in the state, especially in the hilly northern and western counties, which lacked the large plantations—and the slaves—of southern and eastern Arkansas. But the pro-Union sympathies crumbled after Confederate guns fired on Ft. Sumter, S.C., and a secession convention was held at Little Rock on 6 May 1861. The final vote to leave the Union was 69–1; the lone holdout was Isaac Murphy of Madison County, who became the first Republican governor at the end of the war.

The largest Civil War battle fought in Arkansas, and one of the most significant battles of the war west of the Mississippi, was at Pea Ridge, in the northwest corner of the state. After three days of fighting and 2,500 casualties, the engagement ended with the Confederate forces relinquishing the field. By September 1863, the Union Army had taken Little Rock, and the capital

was moved to Washington, in Hempstead County, until the conclusion of hostilities in 1865.

Like virtually all white southerners, Arkansas's white majority hated the postwar Reconstruction government and repudiated it thoroughly at the first opportunity. Reconstruction officially ended in 1874, when the reenfranchised white Democratic majority adopted a new state constitution, throwing out the carpetbagger constitution of 1868. The most colorful figure in postwar Arkansas was federal judge Isaac C. Parker, known as the Hanging Judge. From his court at Ft. Smith, he had sole jurisdiction over Indian Territory, which had become a gathering place for the nation's worst cutthroats. Parker and his deputy marshals fought them relentlessly. From 1875 through 1896, the judge hanged 79 men, as many as 6 at a time, on his Ft. Smith gallows. The struggle was not one-sided: 65 of Parker's deputy marshals were killed in the line of duty.

Industrialization, urbanization, and modernization did not come to Arkansas until after the depression of the 1930s. Following World War II, the state became the first in the South to integrate its public colleges and universities. Little Rock's school board decided in 1954 to comply with the US Supreme Court's desegregation decision. Nevertheless, in September 1957, Governor Orval E. Faubus called out the National Guard to block the integration of Central High School at Little Rock. US President Dwight D. Eisenhower enforced a federal court order to integrate the school by sending in federal troops. The 1957 crisis brought years of international notoriety to Arkansas, as Faubus, then in his second term, was elected to a third term, and then to three more.

By the end of the Faubus administration, the public mood had changed, and the contrast between Faubus and his successor could not have been greater. Winthrop Rockefeller, millionaire scion of a famous family, moved to Arkansas from New York in the early 1950s, established himself as a gentleman rancher, and devoted himself to luring industry into his adopted state and building a Republican Party organization in one of the most staunchly Democratic states in the Union. Elected governor in 1966, Rockefeller thus became the first Republican to capture the Arkansas statehouse since Reconstruction. The specific accomplishments of his two terms were relatively few—he and the Democratic-controlled legislature warred incessantly—but he helped immeasurably in bringing a new image and a new spirit to the state. Rockefeller's successors, all Democrats (his efforts to build a grassroots Republican Party never succeeded), have continued the progressive approach he took. New industry has moved into the state, along with new people; during the 1960s and 1970s, Arkansas gained in population, reversing a long-term trend.

12 STATE GOVERNMENT

Arkansas's fifth constitution, enacted in 1874, and amended 58 times through 1979, has survived several efforts to replace it with a more modern charter. In November 1980, voters turned down yet another proposed new constitution.

Arkansas's bicameral legislature, the general assembly, consists of a 35-member senate and a 100-member house of representatives. Senators serve four-year terms and must be at least 25 years of age; representatives serve for two years and must be at least 21. Each legislator must be a US citizen and have resided for at least two years in the state and one year in the county or district prior to election.

Under the 1874 constitution, the executive officers elected statewide are the governor, lieutenant governor, secretary of state, treasurer, auditor, and state land commissioner, all of whom serve two-year terms. The governor and lieutenant governor, who run separately, must be US citizens, at least 30 years old, and must have resided in Arkansas for seven years before election.

A bill passed by both houses of the legislature becomes law if signed by the governor, if passed over his veto by a majority of all elected members of each house, or if neither signed nor returned by the governor within five days when the legislature is in session. Under an initiative procedure, 8% of those who voted for governor in the last election may propose a law, and 10% may initiate a constitutional amendment; initiative petitions must be filed at least four months before the general election in order to be voted upon at that time. A referendum on any measure passed by the general assembly or any item of an appropriations bill or other measure may be petitioned by 6% of the voters; referendum petitions must be filed within 90 days of the session in which the act in question was passed. A successful referendum measure may be repealed by a two-thirds vote of all elected members of the general assembly. Constitutional amendments may also be proposed by the general assembly or by constitutional convention, subject to ratification by the electorate.

To vote in Arkansas, one must be a US citizen at least 18 years of age; registration closes 20 days before an election.

[13]POLITICAL PARTIES

The principal political groups in Arkansas are the Democratic Party and the Republican Party, each affiliated with the national party organizations.

Prior to the Civil War, politics in Arkansas were fraught with violence, and differences between politicians and judges commonly were resolved by dueling. As late as 1858, one Arkansas newspaper, the *True Democrat*, asserted that "Arkansas has never to this day had a Senator or Representative in the councils of the nation who has not once, if no more, periled his life on the so-called 'field of honor.'"

Republicans ruled during Reconstruction, which ended in Arkansas after the election of 1872. During that campaign, the Liberal Republicans, nicknamed Brindletails, opposed the Radical Republicans, or Minstrels. After the Minstrel candidate, Elisha Baxter, was elected, he proved so independent a governor that some of the party leaders who had supported him attempted to oust him through a court order in April 1874, declaring his defeated opponent, Joseph Brooks, the winner. Supported by a militia of about 300 blacks under white command, Brooks took over the statehouse; Baxter, bolstered by his own 300-man black army, set up his headquarters three blocks away. The so-called Brooks–Baxter War finally ended with President Ulysses S. Grant's proclamation of Baxter as the lawful governor, followed by Baxter's abdication in favor of Augustus H. Garland, the first of a long series of Bourbon Democrats who were to rule the state well into the 20th century.

After Reconstruction, blacks in Arkansas continued to vote and to be elected to public office; under what became known as the fusion principle, black Republicans and white Democratic leaders in the plantation belt often agreed not to oppose each other's candidates. Segregation in public places was still outlawed, and Little Rock was perhaps the most integrated city in the South. During the 1890s, however, as in the rest of the South, Democrats succeeded in passing laws imposing segregation and disfranchising blacks as well as poor whites. In 1898, the Democrats instituted a nominating primary for whites only.

Not until 1948 and the election of Sidney McMath as governor did Arkansans enjoy relatively progressive government. Although elected to the governorship as a progressive in 1954, McMath's protégé Orval Faubus took a segregationist stand in 1957. In subsequent years, poor whites tended to support Faubus, and blacks and more affluent whites to oppose him. Faubus's successor, progressive Republican Winthrop Rockefeller, was strongly supported by blacks. Rockefeller was followed by three more progressives, all Democrats: Dale Bumpers, David Pryor, and—after Bumpers and Pryor had graduated to the US Senate—Bill Clinton. In a major upset, Clinton was defeated in the November 1980 elections by a Republican, Frank White. In other races, Ronald Reagan captured Arkansas's 6 electoral votes, Democratic Senator Dale Bumpers easily won reelection to a second term, and the Democrats retained large majorities in both houses of the state legislature.

[14]LOCAL GOVERNMENT

There are 75 counties in Arkansas, some of them with two county seats, a legacy of settlement days when transportation and communications were difficult. Each county is governed by a quorum court, consisting of 9–15 justices of the peace, elected for two-year terms; the county judge, who presides, does not vote but has veto power, which may be overridden by a three-fifths vote of the total membership. Elected county executives, who serve two-year terms, include the sheriff, assessor, coroner,

Arkansas Presidential Vote by Political Parties, 1948–80

YEAR	ELECTORAL VOTE	ARKANSAS WINNER	DEMOCRAT	REPUBLICAN	STATES' RIGHTS DEMOCRAT
1948	9	*Truman (D)	149,659	50,959	40,068
1952	8	Stevenson (D)	226,300	177,155	—
					CONSTITUTION
1956	8	Stevenson (D)	213,277	186,287	7,008
					NAT'L STATES' RIGHTS
1960	8	*Kennedy (D)	215,049	184,508	28,952
1964	6	*Johnson (D)	314,197	243,264	2,965
					AMERICAN IND.
1968	6	Wallace (AI)	188,228	190,759	240,982
					AMERICAN
1972	6	*Nixon (R)	199,892	448,541	2,887
1976	6	*Carter (D)	498,604	267,903	—
					LIBERTARIAN
1980	6	*Reagan (R)	398,041	403,164	8,970

*Won US presidential election.

treasurer, and county supervisor. Each township elects a constable for a two-year term.

¹⁵STATE SERVICES
Educational services in Arkansas are administered primarily by the Department of Education (which also operates the state schools for the deaf and blind at Little Rock) and the Department of Higher Education. The State Highway and Transportation Department has primary responsibility for roads, rails, and public transit; the offices of motor vehicle registration and driver services are in the Department of Finance and Administration.

Health and welfare services are under the jurisdiction of the Department of Health and the Department of Human Services. Public protection is provided primarily through the Department of Public Safety, which includes the Office of Emergency Services, State Police, National Guard, and Civil Air Patrol; and the Department of Correction, which operates three prisons and three work-release centers. The Public Service Commission, within the Department of Commerce, regulates utilities in the state. Housing services are provided through the Housing Development Agency and the Department of Local Services, whose Division of Manpower offers employment and training programs.

¹⁶JUDICIAL SYSTEM
Arkansas's highest court is the supreme court, consisting of a chief justice and six associate justices, elected for staggered eight-year terms. An appeals court of six judges, also elected for eight-year terms, was established in 1978.

Arkansas's courts of original jurisdiction are the circuit courts (law) and the chancery courts (equity), of which there are 86 each; their judges are elected for four-year terms. Courts of limited jurisdiction include justice of the peace, county, municipal, and police courts, and courts of common pleas.

Arkansas had an FBI Crime Index rate of 3,462 per 100,000 population in 1978, placing well below the national averages for both violent and nonviolent crimes. In 1977, per capita expenditures on criminal justice were only $43, the lowest in the US. The state's once notorious prisons, which had been under federal jurisdiction for more than a decade, were returned in 1978 to state authority, subject to monitoring by an independent ombudsman. By then, the decaying system of the 1960s had been almost entirely replaced by modern facilities, although allegations of overcrowding and inhumane treatment persisted.

¹⁷ARMED FORCES
As of mid-1978, the principal military installations in Arkansas were Little Rock Air Force Base, with 8,914 personnel; Blytheville Air Force Base, with 3,009; and the Army's Pine Bluff Arsenal, with 1,105. Firms in the state received $85 million in defense contract awards in 1978.

As of 30 September 1979, some 270,000 Arkansans were veterans of US military service; 7,000 saw service in World War I, 122,000 in World War II, 48,000 during the Korean conflict, and 79,000 during the Viet-Nam era. Arkansas veterans received $293.7 million in benefits in 1977/78, including $161.2 million in compensation and pensions.

Army and Air National Guard units had 10,500 personnel in 1978. Arkansas had a total in 1977 of 4,048 police employees, 79% of them local.

¹⁸MIGRATION
Near the end of the 18th century, Indians from east of the Mississippi, displaced by white settlement, entered the area now known as Arkansas. However, as the availability of cheap land drew more and more white settlers—in particular, veterans of the War of 1812, who had been promised 160-acre (65-hectare) tracts—to Louisiana Territory, the Indians were pressured to cross the border from Arkansas to present-day Oklahoma.

After the end of the Mexican War, thousands of Arkansans emigrated to Texas, and others were attracted to California in 1849 by the gold rush. Because of a law passed in 1859 requiring free blacks to leave the state by the end of the year or risk being enslaved, Arkansas's population of freedmen dropped from 682 in 1858 to 144 in 1860. During Reconstruction, the state government encouraged immigration by both blacks and whites. Literature sent out by the Office of State Lands and Migration, under the tenure of William H. Grey, a black leader, described the state as a new Africa. Railroads were especially active in encouraging immigration after Reconstruction, in order to find buyers for the lands they had acquired through government grants. Later immigrants included Italians who settled in Tontitown and started making wine there near the turn of the century and midwestern farmers of German extraction who came to Arkansas to grow rice in the early 1900s.

During the depression years and thereafter, Arkansas lost a substantial proportion of its farm population, while blacks left the state for the industrial cities of the Midwest and the east and west coasts; the net loss from migration totaled 919,000 between 1940 and 1970. Between 1970 and 1977, however, the state gained 135,000 residents through migration, as the Ozarks became by mid-decade the fastest-growing rural area in the US.

¹⁹INTERGOVERNMENTAL COOPERATION
Among the many interstate agreements in which Arkansas participates are the Arkansas River Basin Compact of 1970 (with Oklahoma), Interstate Oil and Gas Compact, Red River Compact, South Central Forest Fire Protection Compact, Southern Growth Policies Compact, Southern Interstate Energy Compact, and Southern Regional Education Compact. There are boundary agreements with Mississippi, Missouri, and Tennessee.

Preliminary figures for 1978/79 indicate that Arkansas received $846.9 million in federal aid, of which $66.8 million was general revenue sharing.

²⁰ECONOMY
During the 19th century, Arkansas's economic growth was hindered by credit problems. When the state's two central banks, the Arkansas State Bank and the Real Estate Bank, failed during the 1840s, the government defaulted on bonds issued by the latter and amended the constitution to prohibit all banking in Arkansas. Although banking was restored after the Civil War, the state defaulted on its obligations once more in 1877, this time following a decision by the Arkansas supreme court that $10 million worth of railroad bonds issued during Reconstruction were unconstitutional. Not until 1917 did New York banks again accept Arkansas securities.

Cotton dominated Arkansas's agricultural economy until well into the 20th century, when rice, soybean, poultry, and fish farming diversified the output. Coal mining began in the 1870s, bauxite mining near the turn of the century, and oil extraction in the 1920s; lumbering developed in the last quarter of the century, reached its peak about 1909, and then declined until the 1920s, when reforestation started. Industrialization was limited however, and resources were generally shipped out of state for processing. Not until the 1950s did Arkansas enjoy significant success in attracting industry, thanks in large part to the efforts of Winthrop Rockefeller. Although the Little Rock integration crisis of 1957 was a severe setback to the state's industrial growth, development resumed during the next two decades. As the 1980s began, Arkansas, though still one of the poorest of the 50 states, was clearly narrowing the gap between its own standard of living and that of the nation as a whole.

²¹INCOME
In 1978, Arkansas ranked 49th among the 50 states in per capita personal income, with $6,183; since 1960, only Mississippi has ranked lower. On the other hand, the 1978 figure represented 79% of the US average per capita income for that year, a large improvement over the 62% recorded in 1960 and the 43% registered in 1929. Total personal income was $13.5 billion in 1978; measured in constant 1972 dollars, total income increased more

than 70% during 1960–70 and 54% for 1970–78, both far above the respective national percentages. An estimated 392,000 Arkansans, or nearly 19% of the population, were living below the federal poverty level in 1975, when median family income was $10,106 (49th in the US).

22 LABOR

Arkansas's civilian labor force totaled 926,000 in 1978, based on a participation rate of 58.5%, one of the lowest such rates in the US. About 868,000 Arkansans were employed and 58,000 unemployed, for an overall unemployment rate of 6.3%. The rate for black women, 17.4%, was 2d only to that of Mississippi.

A federal census of workers covered by unemployment insurance in March 1977 revealed the following nonfarm employment pattern in Arkansas.

	ESTABLISH-MENTS	EMPLOYEES	ANNUAL PAYROLL ('000)
Agricultural services, forestry, fishing	483	4,140	$ 32,535
Mining, of which:	307	4,635	64,643
Oil, gas extraction	(212)	(2,162)	(30,370)
Contract construction	4,593	29,542	305,857
Manufacturing	3,190	196,559	1,948,799
Transportation, public utilities	1,908	29,269	374,304
Wholesale trade	3,562	35,193	378,439
Retail trade	13,759	105,967	689,529
Finance, insurance, real estate	2,939	26,187	264,600
Services	10,462	93,201	666,945
Other	628	757	7,041
TOTALS	41,831	525,450	$4,732,692

Government employees, not covered by this survey, numbered about 116,000 in 1978.

Chartered in 1865, the Little Rock Typographical Union, consisting of *Arkansas Gazette* employees, was the first labor union in the state. The United Mine Workers was established in the Ft. Smith area by 1898; six years later, the UMW led in the founding of the Arkansas Federation of Labor. Between 1904 and World War I, a series of progressive labor laws was enacted, including a minimum wage, restrictions on child labor, and prohibitions against blacklisting and payment of wages in scrip. Union strength waned after the war, however, and the labor movement is not a powerful force in the state today. There were 122,000 members of labor unions and employee associations in Arkansas in 1976; of these, 102,000 were union members, 87,000 belonging to AFL-CIO affiliates. Hourly wages of field workers, livestock workers, and production workers in manufacturing are all below the US average. Arkansas has a right-to-work law.

23 AGRICULTURE

Agricultural income in Arkansas exceeded $2.7 billion in 1978 (15th in the US), of which crops accounted for about 48%. The state is the leading producer of rice and is among the leaders in cotton, soybeans, and grain sorghum.

Cotton was first grown in the state about 1800, along the river valleys, which often had to be drained for cultivation. Confined mainly to slaveholding plantations before the Civil War, cotton farming became more widespread in the postwar period, expanding into the hill country of the northwest and eventually into the deforested areas of the northeast, which proved to be some of the most fertile farmland in the nation. As elsewhere in the postbellum South, sharecropping by tenant farmers predominated well into the 20th century, until mechanization and diversification gradually brought an end to the system. Rice was first grown commercially in the early 1900s; by 1920, Arkansas had emerged as a poultry and soybean producer.

During 1979, Arkansas produced 144,200,000 bushels of soybeans, valued at $915,670,000; 1,552,000 tons of hay, worth $66,736,000; 14,700,000 bushels of wheat, worth $54,390,000; and 10,912,000 bushels of sorghum for grain, valued at $24,116,000. The rice harvest in 1978 was 48,505,000 hundredweight, worth $410,837,000; the estimated cotton crop, 660,000 bales, $192,000,000.

As of mid-August 1980, state agriculturists estimated the farm losses attributable to the drought that year at roughly $750 million, about three-quarters of it in crops.

24 ANIMAL HUSBANDRY

Poultry farms are found throughout Arkansas, but especially in the northern and western regions. Arkansas is the top-ranked broiler-producing state in the US: in 1979, 678,208,000 broilers brought a gross income of $639,889,000. During the same year, the state ranked 3d in the value of egg production, with $218,175,000 for 4.1 billion eggs; 4th in turkeys, with $91,566,000; and 4th in chickens, with $14,399,000. A rough estimate of the drought loss to Arkansas's poultry industry as of mid-August 1980 was $25,000,000.

In 1979, Arkansas ranchers produced 612,030,000 lb of cattle and calves valued at $430,968,000, and 205,305,000 lb of hogs and pigs worth $85,612,000. At the close of the year, the livestock inventory included 2,000,000 cattle and calves and 600,000 hogs and pigs. The dairy yield was 720,000,000 lb of milk.

25 FISHING

Commercial fish landings in 1978 were estimated at 6,495,000 lb, worth $2,055,000. Of far greater economic importance to Arkansas is fish farming. As of 1980, the state ranked 1st in the US in minnow farming, 1st in total acreage devoted to fish farming, and 2d only to Mississippi in catfish farming. A telephone survey by the Arkansas Game and Fish Commission indicated that during 1978, fish farms occupied a total of 41,612 acres (16,480 hectares) and produced 38,230,783 lb of fish, valued at $35,711,396. Some producers rotate fish crops with row crops, periodically draining their fish ponds and planting grains in the rich and well-fertilized soil.

26 FORESTRY

Forestland comprised 18,282,000 acres (7,398,000 hectares), or 55% of the state's total land area in 1977. Of that total, 18,207,000 acres (7,368,000 hectares) were commercial timberland, 84% of it in private hands. The southwest and central plains, the state's timber belt, constitute one of the most concentrated sources of yellow pine in the US. Shipments of lumber and wood products were valued at more than $1 billion in 1977. Three national forests in Arkansas covered a total of 2,469,214 acres (999,259 hectares) of National Forest System lands in 1979.

27 MINING

Arkansas ranked 27th among the 50 states in mineral production in 1978, with an output valued at $574 million. The state produced 84% of all bauxite mined in the US in 1979, and is also a leading producer of bromine, vanadium, and abrasive stone. The only diamond fields in the US are located in Pike County in southwestern Arkansas.

Leading minerals in 1978 (excluding fossil fuels) were stone, 19,114,000 tons; sand and gravel, 16,500,000 tons; clays, 1,242,000 tons; and lime, 171,000 tons. An estimated 1,574,000 tons of bauxite were mined in 1979.

28 ENERGY AND POWER

Although Arkansas possesses substantial and varied energy resources—petroleum, natural gas, coal, and water—the state was slow to develop them. As late as 1935, only 1% of Arkansas farms had electric power. The struggle that began during the 1930s over whether Arkansas's rivers would be publicly developed for the production of electricity (in the manner of the Tennessee Valley Authority) was won by the advocates of private power development. As of 1978, Arkansas power plants had a combined capacity of 5.7 million kw, of which about three-fourths was privately owned; production totaled 19.7 billion kwh.

During that same year, 19,419,000 barrels of crude petroleum were produced, leaving proved reserves of 94,038,000 barrels. Production of natural gas exceeded 105.7 billion cu ft, with 1.6 trillion cu ft of reserves remaining. As of 1 January 1976, Arkansas's known coal reserves were 392,000,000 tons: 270,000,000 bituminous, 96,000,000 anthracite, and 26,000,000 lignite. About 519,000 tons of bituminous coal were mined in 1978.

29 INDUSTRY

Manufacturing in Arkansas is diverse, ranging from blue jeans to bicycles, though resource industries such as rice processing and woodworking still play a major role. The total value added by manufacturing in 1977 was nearly $4.9 billion, of which food and food products contributed 13%; electric and electronic equipment, 12%; lumber and wood products, 9%; paper and allied products, 8%; fabricated metals products, 8%; and chemicals and chemical products, 7%. The following table shows value added for selected industries in 1972 and 1977:

	1972	1977
Sawed lumber	$129,400,000	$185,600,000
Preserved fruits and vegetables	101,700,000	156,400,000
Household furniture	99,100,000	133,500,000
Poultry dressing plants	NA	120,800,000
Tires and inner tubes	NA	110,700,000
Grain-mill products	54,000,000	109,000,000
Refrigeration, heating equipment	35,500,000	93,200,000
Valves and pipe fittings	25,200,000	82,500,000

30 COMMERCE

Arkansas ranked 34th in the US in wholesale trade during 1972, with sales of $3.2 billion. Retail establishments recorded $6.4 billion in sales in 1977 (32d in the US). The leading retail categories were automotive dealers, 24%; grocery stores, 22%; department stores, 9%; gasoline service stations, 8%; and eating and drinking places, 6%. Of the counties, Pulaski (including Little Rock and North Little Rock) had the highest percentage of sales, 21%; Little Rock had 12%, highest among the cities.

During 1976/77, Arkansas ranked 11th in the US in agricultural exports, valued at $907 million, or more than one-third of all farm sales. Arkansas is the principal US exporter of rice. In 1976, Arkansas's manufactured exports, worth $651 million, ranked 28th among the 50 states.

31 CONSUMER PROTECTION

Under the mandate of the Consumer Protection Act of 1971, the Consumer Protection Division of the Office of the Attorney General has principal responsibility for consumer affairs.

32 BANKING

In 1836, the first year of statehood, the legislature created the Arkansas State Bank and the Real Estate Bank, which was intended to promote the plantation system. Fraud, mismanagement, and the consequences of the financial panic of 1837 ruined both banks and led to the passage in 1846 of a constitutional amendment prohibiting the incorporation of any lending institution in Arkansas. Money grew scarce, with credit being rendered largely by suppliers and brokers to farmers and planters until after the Civil War, when the prohibition was removed.

Arkansas had 259 insured commercial banks with $9.3 billion in assets and $8 billion in deposits at the end of 1978. The combined assets of 75 insured savings and loan associations amounted to $3.7 billion; they held $3.3 billion in savings accounts and more than $3 billion in outstanding mortgage loans and contracts. As of the late 1970s, Arkansas's usury law, imposing a 10% ceiling on interest rates, was among the most rigid in the US. The rise of the federal discount rate well above that limit caused a considerable outflow of capital from Arkansas during 1979 and 1980.

33 INSURANCE

Arkansans held 2.8 million life insurance policies worth $19.6 billion at the close of 1978. The average of $23,900 in life insurance per family was the lowest of any state. Benefits paid in 1978 amounted to $169.7 million, including $74.6 million in death payments. During the same year, premiums were written for $149.4 million in automobile liability insurance, $122.4 million for automobile physical damage coverage, and $80.8 million for homeowners insurance. Flood insurance in force as of mid-1979 exceeded $131 million.

34 SECURITIES

There are no securities exchanges in Arkansas.

35 PUBLIC FINANCE

Under the 1874 constitution, state expenditures may not exceed revenues. The mechanism adopted each biennium to prevent deficit spending is a Revenue Stabilization Act, allocating a proportion of actual state revenues for each program and agency up to the amount appropriated, and categorizing programs according to priority as A, B, or C. All A programs must be funded first; then, revenue permitting, B and C programs are funded in that order. In the event of a shortfall, agencies share according to their established proportions.

The Arkansas state budget covers two years, each fiscal year running from 1 July through 30 June. The following table summarizes estimated general fund revenues and appropriations for 1979/80 and 1980/81 (in millions):

	1979/80	1980/81
REVENUES		
Sales and use taxes	$402.3	$461.4
Individual income tax	322.6	374.4
Corporate income tax	98.4	113.6
Other net receipts	58.4	54.4
TOTALS	$881.7	$1,003.8
EXPENDITURES		
Department of Education	$414.6	$475.9
Institutions of higher education	165.9	185.0
Department of Human Services	161.8	171.4
Other outlays	139.4	171.5
TOTALS	$881.7	$1,003.8

The total outstanding debt of Arkansas state and local governments was $1.2 billion, or about $547 per capita, in mid-1977.

36 TAXATION

As of 1977, Arkansas's state tax revenues per capita was $494, the lowest in the US. The state income tax ranges from 1% on amounts under $3,000 to 7% on amounts over $25,000; the corporate income tax ranges from 1% on the first $3,000 to 6% on amounts over $25,000. The state sales tax, 3%, was lifted from prescription drugs in 1979 but is still applied to food. The state also imposes severance taxes on oil, gas, and other natural resources, along with levies on liquor, gasoline, and cigarettes. City and county property taxes in Arkansas are among the lowest in the nation.

During 1975/76, Arkansans paid federal taxes totaling nearly $2.3 billion and received federal expenditures of more than $2.8 billion. State residents filed 742,572 federal income tax returns in 1977, paying $976,388,000 in tax.

37 ECONOMIC POLICY

First as chairman of the Arkansas Industrial Development Commission and later as governor of the state, Winthrop Rockefeller succeeded in attracting substantial and diverse new industries to Arkansas. In 1979, Governor Bill Clinton established the Department of Economic Development for the purpose of finding new export markets and stimulating the growth of small business.

38 HEALTH

As of 1970, Arkansas ranked 27th in the US in average life expectancy, relatively high among the southern states. For both sexes, average life expectancy was 70.66 years: 74.97 for females, 66.68 for males. The infant death rate in 1977 was 12.3 per 1,000 live births for whites and 24.4 for nonwhites. About

3,600 legal abortions were performed during 1977/78, when the state's abortion rates were among the lowest in the US. During the same year, however, Arkansas's death rate, 10 per 1,000 population, was the nation's 6th highest, and the incidence of cerebrovascular disease—123 per 100,000 population—led the US. Death rates from heart disease, cancer, accidents, pneumonia and influenza, and early infancy diseases also exceeded the national norm.

Arkansas's 96 hospitals had 12,650 beds and recorded 437,193 admissions in 1978, for an occupancy rate of 71%; personnel included 4,135 registered nurses and 3,759 licensed practical nurses. Hospital costs in 1977—$141 per day and $902 per stay—were among the lowest in the US. At the end of 1977, the state had 2,506 licensed physicians; there were 714 professionally active dentists in 1979.

39 SOCIAL WELFARE
Social welfare payments in Arkansas generally fall well below national norms. During 1978, payments in aid to families with dependent children totaled $51 million; the average payment per family was $143 monthly, 8th lowest among the 50 states. The food stamp program had 188,000 participants at a federal cost of $63.9 million, and the school lunch program served 349,000 students with a federal outlay of $24.1 million.

Some 427,900 Arkansans received Social Security benefits totaling $886.5 million in 1977; the average monthly benefit for retired workers of $208.20 ranked 49th, exceeding only that of Mississippi. Supplemental Security Income payments of $93.9 million were made to 82,500 Arkansans in 1978, when expenditures on vocational rehabilitation reached $15.6 million, and $59 million in unemployment insurance benefits were paid. Workers' compensation payments totaled $48.4 million in 1977.

40 HOUSING
The 1970 census counted some 673,000 year-round housing units in Arkansas, 615,000 of them occupied. Only 83% of the occupied units had full plumbing. From 1976 through 1978, 30,000 new units worth $802 million were authorized.

41 EDUCATION
At the time of the 1970 census, 1.9% of Arkansans were illiterate—the 8th highest rate in the US. By 1976, 56% of all Arkansans 18 years of age and older were high school graduates (7th lowest in the US) and 6% had less than four years of schooling; the median for school years completed was 12.2.

Public school enrollment during 1978/79 totaled 475,261: special education, 5,056; kindergarten, 29,073; elementary, 219,338; grades 7–9, 117,717; and grades 10–12, 104,077. Nonpublic school enrollment was 20,922.

In some ways, Little Rock was an unlikely site for the major confrontation over school integration that occurred in 1957. The school board had already announced its voluntary compliance with the Supreme Court's desegregation decision, and during Governor Faubus's first term (1955–56), several public schools in the state had been peaceably integrated. Nevertheless, on 5 September 1957, Faubus, claiming that violence was likely, ordered the National Guard to seize Central High School to prevent the entry of nine black students. When a mob did appear following the withdrawal of the National Guardsmen in response to a federal court order later that month, President Dwight Eisenhower dispatched federal troops to Little Rock, and they patrolled the school grounds until the end of the 1958 spring semester. Although Faubus's stand encouraged politicians in other southern states to resist desegregation, in Arkansas integration proceeded at a moderate pace. By 1980, Central High School had a nearly equal balance of black and white students, and the state's school system was one of the most integrated in the South.

In 1979, Arkansas had 34 higher educational institutions, 19 public and 15 private, of which the largest, the University of Arkansas at Fayetteville (established in 1871) had a fall 1977 enrollment of 14,789. Student aid is provided by the State Scholarship Program within the Department of Higher Education, by the Arkansas Student Loan Guarantee Foundation, and by the Arkansas Rural Endowment Fund, Inc.

42 ARTS
Little Rock is the home of the Arkansas Symphony and the Arkansas Arts Center, which holds art exhibits and classes and community theater performances. The best-known center for traditional arts and crafts is the Ozark Folk Center at Mountain View; every evening from late spring through October, folk music of the Ozarks may be heard. The Ozark Folk Festival is held there during three weeks in April, and the Family Harvest Festival for three weeks in October. Arkansas College at Batesville sponsors two-week summer workshops in Ozark crafts, music, and folklore in association with the center. The Grand Prairie Festival of Arts is held at Stuttgart in September.

43 LIBRARIES AND MUSEUMS
During 1978/79, Arkansas had 33 county or multiregional libraries and 9 municipal libraries. That year, public libraries held a total of 2,642,803 volumes and circulation amounted to 6,680,484. Important collections include those of the University of Arkansas at Fayetteville (860,000 volumes), Arkansas State University at Jonesboro (273,028), the Central Arkansas Library System of Little Rock (446,729), and the News Library of the *Arkansas Gazette*, also in Little Rock.

There are some 50 museums and historic sites. Principal museums include the Arkansas Arts Center and the Museum of Science and History, both at Little Rock; the Arkansas State University Museum at Jonesboro; and the University of Arkansas Museum at Fayetteville, specializing in archaeology, anthropology, and the sciences. Also of interest are the Arkansas County Agricultural Museum at Stuttgart; the Arkansas Post County Museum at Gillette, whose artifacts are housed in recreated plantation buildings; Hampson Museum State Park, near Wilson, which has one of the largest collections of Mound Builder artifacts in the US; and the Saunders Memorial Museum at Berryville, with an extensive collection of firearms. Civil War battle sites include the Pea Ridge National Military Park (Helena), the Prairie Grove Battlefield State Park, and the Arkansas Post National Memorial. The Ft. Smith National Historic Site includes buildings and museums from the days when the town was a military outpost on the border of Indian Territory.

44 COMMUNICATIONS
In 1978, the state had 1,389,618 telephones, 1,049,157 residential and 340,461 business. Only in Mississippi did a lower percentage of households have telephones than in Arkansas (88%).

Arkansas's first telegraph line was laid in 1861. The first radio station, WOR at Pine Bluff, began broadcasting in 1921, and the first television station, KRTV in Little Rock, in 1953. By 1978 there were 139 commercial radio stations (86 AM, 53 FM) and 8 television stations. Cable television systems served 160,392 subscribers in 141 communities during that year.

45 PRESS
The first newspaper in Arkansas, the *Arkansas Gazette*, established at Arkansas Post in 1819 by William E. Woodruff, is the state's most widely read and influential journal. In 1978 there were 5 morning dailies with a combined circulation of 181,694, and 30 evening papers with 297,565 paid subscribers (these totals include 2 all-day newspapers); 15 Sunday papers had a circulation of 462,381. The following table shows the 1978 circulations of the leading dailies:

AREA	NAME	DAILY	SUNDAY
Ft. Smith	Southwest Times		
	Record (all day, S)	38,792	43,452
Little Rock	Arkansas Democrat		
	(m,S)	54,281	98,759
	Arkansas Gazette		
	(m,S)	127,997	154,601

⁴⁶ORGANIZATIONS

Among the national organizations with headquarters in Arkansas are the National Association for Gifted Children, in Hot Springs; American Crossbow Association, at Huntsville; the Ozark Society, American Association of Anatomists, American Parquet Association, Catfish Farmers of America, and Federation of American Hospitals, all at Little Rock; the American Fish Farmers Federation, at Lonoke; and the Aluminum Extruders Council, at Rogers. ACORN, founded in Little Rock in 1970 as the Arkansas Community Organizations for Reform Now, has since spread to some 20 other states and become one of the most influential citizens' lobbies in the US.

⁴⁷TOURISM, TRAVEL, AND RECREATION

During 1977, 7,255,000 persons took trips to and through Arkansas. National parks in Arkansas attracted 2,040,900 visitors in 1979.

Leading attractions are the mineral waters and recreational facilities at Hot Springs, Eureka Springs, Mammoth Spring, and Heber Springs. The Crater of Diamonds, near Murfreesboro, is the only known public source of natural diamonds in North America. For a fee, visitors may hunt for diamonds and keep any they find; more than 100,000 diamonds have been found in the area since 1906, of which the two largest are the 40.42-carat Uncle Sam and the 34.25-carat Star of Murfreesboro.

During 1977/78, licenses were issued to 331,649 hunters and 627,320 fishermen. The World's Championship Duck Calling Contest is held at the beginning of the winter duck season in Stuttgart.

⁴⁸SPORTS

Arkansas has no major league professional sports teams, but does claim a class AA minor league baseball entry in the Texas League. Hot Springs has a 50-day Thoroughbred racing season at the Oaklawn Jockey Club, and dog races are held in West Memphis during the summer. The Rodeo of the Ozarks is held each 1–4 July at Springdale.

The Razorback football team of the University of Arkansas won the Cotton Bowl in 1947, 1965, and 1976, the Orange Bowl in 1978, and the Sugar Bowl in 1969. The university's basketball team won the Southwest Conference championship in 1979.

⁴⁹FAMOUS ARKANSANS

Arkansas has yet to produce a US president, vice president, or Supreme Court justice, but one Arkansan came close to the latter two offices. US Senator Joseph T. Robinson (1872–1937) was the Democratic nominee for vice president in 1928, on the ticket with Al Smith; later, he was Senate majority leader under President Franklin D. Roosevelt. At the time of his death, Robinson was leading the fight for Roosevelt's bill to expand the Supreme Court's membership and had reportedly been promised a seat on the court if the bill passed. Robinson's colleague, Hattie W. Caraway (b.Tennessee, 1878–1950), was the first woman elected to the US Senate, serving from 1931 to 1945. After World War II, Arkansas's congressional delegation included three men of considerable power and fame: Senator John L. McClellan (1896–1977), investigator of organized labor and organized crime and champion of the Arkansas River navigation project; Senator J. William Fulbright (b.Missouri, 1905), chairman of the Senate Foreign Relations Committee; and Representative Wilbur D. Mills (b.1909), chairman of the House Ways and Means Committee until scandal ended his political career in the mid-1970s. Other federal officeholders include Brooks Hays (b.1898), former congressman and special assistant to Presidents John F. Kennedy and Lyndon B. Johnson, as well as president of the Southern Baptist Convention, the nation's largest Protestant denomination; and Frank Pace, Jr. (b.1912), secretary of the Army during the Truman administration. General Douglas MacArthur (1880–1964), supreme commander of Allied forces in the Pacific during World War II, supervised the occupation of Japan and was supreme commander of UN troops in Korea until relieved of his command in April 1951 by President Truman.

Orval B. Faubus (b.1910) served six terms as governor, a record, drew international attention during the 1957 integration crisis at Little Rock Central High School, and headed the most powerful political machine in Arkansas history. Winthrop Rockefeller (b.New York, 1912–73) was Faubus's most prominent successor. At the time of his election in 1978, Bill Cinton (b.1946) was the nation's youngest governor.

Prominent business leaders include the Stephens brothers, W. R. "Witt" (b.1907) and Jackson T. (b.1923), whose Stephens, Inc., investment firm in Little Rock is one of the 10 largest in the US and largest off Wall Street; and Kemmons Wilson (b.1913), founder of Holiday Inns. Other distinguished Arkansans include Edward Durrell Stone (1902–78), renowned architect; C. Vann Woodward (b.1908), Sterling Professor of History at Yale University; and the Right Reverend John M. Allin (b.1921), presiding bishop of the Episcopal Church of the United States. John H. Johnson (b.1918), publisher of the nation's leading black-oriented magazines—*Ebony, Jet,* and others—is an Arkansan, as is Helen Gurley Brown (b.1922), editor of *Cosmopolitan.* Harry S. Ashmore (b.South Carolina, 1916) won a Pulitzer Prize for his *Arkansas Gazette* editorials calling for peaceful integration of the schools during the 1957 crisis; the *Gazette* itself won a Pulitzer for meritorious public service that same year. Paul Greenberg (b.Louisiana, 1937), of the *Pine Bluff Commercial,* is another Pulitzer Prize–winning journalist.

John Gould Fletcher (1886–1950) was a Pulitzer Prize–winning poet. Other Arkansas writers include Dee Brown (b.Louisiana, 1908), Maya Angelou (b.Missouri, 1928), Charles Portis (b.1933), and Eldridge Cleaver (b.1935).

Arkansas planter Colonel Sanford C. Faulkner (1803–74) is credited with having written the well-known fiddle tune "The Arkansas Traveler" and its accompanying dialogue. Perhaps the best-known country music performers are Johnny Cash (b.1932) and Glen Campbell (b.1938). Film stars Dick Powell (1904–63) and Alan Ladd (1913–64) were also Arkansans.

Notable Arkansas sports personalities include Jerome Herman "Dizzy" Dean (1911–74) and Bill Dickey (b.1907), both members of the Baseball Hall of Fame; Brooks Robinson (b.1937), considered by some the best-fielding third baseman in baseball history; and star pass-catcher Lance Alworth (b.Mississippi, 1940), a University of Arkansas All-American and member of the Professional Football Hall of Fame.

⁵⁰BIBLIOGRAPHY

Angelou, Maya. *I Know Why the Caged Bird Sings.* New York: Bantam, 1971.

Arkansas, University of. Industrial Research and Extension Center. *State and County Economic Data for Arkansas.* Little Rock, 1980.

Ashmore, Harry S. *Arkansas: A Bicentennial History.* New York: Norton, 1978.

Du Vall, Leland. *Arkansas: Colony and State.* Little Rock: Rose, 1973.

Federal Writers' Project. *Arkansas: A Guide to the State.* New York: Hastings House, 1941.

Fletcher, John Gould. *Arkansas.* Chapel Hill: University of North Carolina Press, 1947.

Holley, Donald. *Uncle Sam's Farmers.* Urbana: University of Illinois Press, 1975.

Moore, Waddy William, ed. *Arkansas in the Gilded Age.* Little Rock: Rose, 1976.

Ross, Margaret. *Arkansas Gazette: The Early Years, 1819–66.* Little Rock: Arkansas Gazette Foundation, 1969.

Taylor, Orville W. *Negro Slavery in Arkansas.* Durham, N.C.: Duke University Press, 1958.

CALIFORNIA

State of California

ORIGIN OF STATE NAME: Probably from the mythical island California in a 16th-century romance by Garcí Ordóñez de Montalvo. **NICKNAME:** The Golden State. **CAPITAL:** Sacramento. **ENTERED UNION:** 9 September 1850 (31st). **SONG:** "I Love You, California." **MOTTO:** Eureka (I have found it). **FLAG:** The flag consists of a white field with a red star at upper left and a red stripe and the words "California Republic" across the bottom; in the center a brown grizzly bear stands on a patch of green grass. **OFFICIAL SEAL:** In the foreground is the goddess Minerva; a grizzly bear stands in front of her shield. The scene also shows the Sierra Nevada, San Francisco Bay, a miner, a sheaf of wheat, and a cluster of grapes, all representing California's resources. The state motto and 31 stars are displayed at the top. The words "The Great Seal of the State of California" surround the whole. **COLORS:** Yale blue and golden yellow. **ANIMAL:** California grizzly bear. **BIRD:** California valley quail. **FISH:** Golden trout. **FLOWER:** Golden poppy. **TREE:** California redwood. **ROCK:** Serpentine. **MINERAL:** Native gold. **REPTILE:** Desert tortoise. **INSECT:** California dog-face butterfly (flying pansy). **MARINE MAMMAL:** California gray whale. **FOSSIL:** California saber-toothed cat. **LEGAL HOLIDAYS:** New Year's Day, 1 January; Lincoln's Birthday, 12 February; Washington's Birthday, 3d Monday in February; Memorial Day, last Monday in May; Independence Day, 4 July; Labor Day, 1st Monday in September; Admission Day, 9 September; Columbus Day, 2d Monday in October; Veterans Day, 11 November; Thanksgiving Day, 4th Thursday in November; Christmas Day, 25 December. **TIME:** 4 A.M. PST = noon GMT.

¹LOCATION, SIZE, AND EXTENT

Situated on the Pacific coast of the southwestern US, California is the nation's 3d-largest state (after Alaska and Texas).

The total area of California is 158,693 sq mi (411,015 sq km), of which land takes up 156,361 sq mi (404,975 sq km) and inland water 2,332 sq mi (6,040 sq km). California extends about 350 mi (560 km) E–W; its maximum N–S extension is about 780 mi (1,255 km).

California is bordered on the N by Oregon; on the E by Nevada; on the SE by Arizona (separated by the Colorado River); on the S by the Mexican state of Baja California Norte; and on the W by the Pacific Ocean.

The eight Santa Barbara islands lie from 20 to 60 mi (32–96 km) off California's southwestern coast; the small islands and islets of the Farallon group are about 30 mi (48 km) W of San Francisco Bay. The total boundary length of the state is 2,050 mi (3,299 km), including a general coastline of 840 mi (1,352 km); the tidal shoreline totals 3,427 mi (5,515 km). California's geographic center is in Madera County, 38 mi (61 km) E of the city of Madera.

²TOPOGRAPHY

California is the only state in the US with an extensive seacoast, high mountains, and deserts. The extreme diversity of the state's landforms is best illustrated by the fact that Mt. Whitney (14,494 feet, or 4,418 meters), the highest point in the contiguous US, is situated no more than 80 mi (129 km) from the lowest point in the entire country, Death Valley (282 feet, or 86 meters, below sea level). The mean elevation of the state is about 2,900 feet (900 meters).

California's principal geographic regions are the Sierra Nevada in the east, the Coast Ranges in the west, the Central Valley between them, and the Mojave and Colorado deserts in the southeast. The mountain-walled Central Valley, more than 400 mi (640 km) long and about 50 mi (80 km) wide, is probably the state's most unusual topographic feature. It is drained in the north by the Sacramento River, about 320 mi (515 km) long, and in the south by the San Joaquin River, about 350 mi (560 km). The main channels of the two rivers meet at and empty into the northern arm of San Francisco Bay, flowing through the only significant break in the Coast Ranges, a mountain system that extends more than 1,200 mi (1,900 km) alongside the Pacific. Lesser ranges, including the Siskiyou Mountains in the north and the Tehachapi Mountains in the south, link the two major ranges and constitute the Central Valley's upper and lower limits.

California has 41 mountains exceeding 10,000 feet (3,048 meters). After Mt. Whitney, the highest peaks in the state are Mt. Williamson, in the Sierra Nevada, at 14,375 feet (4,382 meters), and Mt. Shasta (14,162 feet, or 4,317 meters), an extinct volcano in the Cascades, the northern extension of the Sierra Nevada. Lassen Peak (10,457 feet, or 3,187 meters), also in the Cascades, is a dormant volcano. Beautiful Yosemite Valley, a narrow gorge in the middle of the High Sierra, is the activities center of Yosemite National Park. The Coast Ranges, with numerous forested spurs and ridges enclosing dozens of longitudinal valleys, vary in height from about 2,000 to 7,000 feet (600–2,100 meters).

Melted snow from the Sierra Nevada feeds the state's principal rivers, the Sacramento and San Joaquin. The Coast Ranges are drained by the Klamath, Eel, Russian, Salinas, and other rivers. In the south, most rivers are dry creek beds except during the spring flood season; they either dry up from evaporation in the hot summer sun or disappear beneath the surface, like Death Valley's Amargosa River. The Salton Sea, in the Imperial Valley of the southeast, is the state's largest lake, occupying 374 sq mi (969 sq km) as of December 1976. This saline sink was created accidentally in the early 1900s when Colorado River water, via an irrigation canal, flooded a natural depression 235 feet (72 meters) below sea level in the Imperial Valley. Lake Tahoe, located in the Sierra Nevada at the angle of the California-Nevada border, covers 192 sq mi (497 sq km).

The California coast is indented by two magnificent natural harbors, San Francisco Bay and San Diego Bay, and two smaller bays, Monterey and Humboldt. Two groups of islands lie off the California shore: the Santa Barbara Islands, situated west of Los Angeles and San Diego; and the rocky Farallon Islands, off San Francisco.

The Sierra Nevada and Coast Ranges were formed more than 100 million years ago by the uplifting of the earth's crust. The Central Valley and the Great Basin, including the Mojave Desert and Death Valley, were created by sinkage of the earth's crust; inland seas once filled these depressions but evaporated over eons of time. Subsequent volcanic activity, erosion of land, and movement of glaciers until the last Ice Age subsided some 10,000 years ago gradually shaped the present topography of California. The San Andreas Fault, extending from north of San Francisco Bay for more than 600 mi (970 km) southeast to the Mojave Desert, is a major active earthquake zone and was responsible for the great San Francisco earthquake of 1906.

Because water is scarce in the southern part of the state and because an adequate water supply is essential both for agriculture and for industry, more than 1,000 dams and reservoirs have been built in California. In 1979, the state's reservoirs had an aggregate capacity of 44,158,982 acre-feet of water. In that year, the major dams and their reservoir capacities were (in acre-feet) Shasta, on the Sacramento River, 4,500,000 (completed in 1949); Oroville, Feather River, 3,558,000 (1968); Trinity, Trinity River, 2,448,000 (1960); and New Melones, Stanislaus River, 2,400,000 (1979).

³CLIMATE

Like its topography, California's climate is varied and tends toward extremes. Generally there are two seasons—a long, dry summer, with low humidity and cool evenings, and a mild, rainy winter—except in the high mountains, where four seasons prevail and snow lasts from November to April. The one climatic constant for the state is summer drought.

California has four main climatic regions. Mild summers and winters prevail in central coastal areas, where temperatures are more equable than virtually anywhere else in the US; in the area between San Francisco and Monterey, for example, the difference between average summer and winter temperatures is seldom more than 10 Fahrenheit (6 Centigrade) degrees. During the summer there are heavy fogs in San Francisco and all along the coast. Mountainous regions are characterized by milder summers and colder winters, with markedly low temperatures at high elevations. The Central Valley has hot summers and cool winters, while the Imperial Valley is marked by very hot, dry summers, with temperatures frequently exceeding 100°F (38°C).

Average annual temperatures for the state range from 47°F (8°C) in the Sierra Nevada to 73°F (23°C) in the Imperial Valley. The highest temperature ever recorded in the US was 134°F (57°C), registered in Death Valley on 10 July 1913. The state's lowest temperature was –45°F (–43°C), recorded on 20 January 1937 at Boca, near the Nevada border.

Among the major population centers, Los Angeles has an average annual temperature of 65°F (18.3°C), with an average January minimum of 47°F (8.3°C) and an average July maximum of 83°F (28.3°C). San Francisco has an annual average of 57°F (13.9°C), with a January average minimum of 46°F (7.8°C) and a July average maximum of 64°F (17.8°C). The annual average in San Diego is 63°F (17.2°C), the January average minimum 46°F (7.8°C), and the July average maximum 75°F (23.9°C). Sacramento's annual average temperature is 60°F (15.6°C), with January minimums averaging 37°F (2.8°C) and July maximums of 93°F (33.9°C).

Annual precipitation varies from only 2 in (5 cm) in the Imperial Valley to 68 in (173 cm) at Blue Canyon, near Lake Tahoe. San Francisco has normal annual precipitation of 21 in (53 cm); Sacramento, 17 in (43 cm); Los Angeles, 14 in (36 cm); and San Diego, 9 in (23 cm). The largest one-month snowfall ever recorded in the US—390 in (991 cm)—fell in Alpine County in January 1911. Snow averages between 300 and 400 in (760–1,000 cm) annually in the high elevations of the Sierra Nevada, but is rare in the coastal lowlands.

In 1978, Los Angeles, San Francisco, and San Diego were free of frost throughout the year, and Sacramento had a frost-free period of 307 days; the Alturas Ranger station, in the northeast, had only 54 frost-free days. Sacramento has the greatest percentage (79%) of possible annual sunshine among the state's largest cities; Los Angeles has 73%, and San Francisco 67%. San Francisco is the windiest, with an average annual windspeed of 11 mph (18 km/hr).

Severe tropical rainstorms occur often in California during the winter. In late February 1980, six storms struck the southern coast within nine days, killing 24 persons and causing an estimated $425 million in property damage, chiefly in the residential suburbs of Los Angeles, where the downpours produced extensive mudslides.

⁴FLORA AND FAUNA

Of the 48 contiguous states, California embraces the greatest diversity of climate and terrain. The state's six life zones are the lower Sonoran (desert); upper Sonoran (foothill regions and some coastal lands); transition (coastal areas and moist northeastern counties); and the Canadian, Hudsonian, and Arctic zones, comprising California's highest elevations.

Plant life in the arid climate of the lower Sonoran zone features a diversity of native cactus, mesquite, and paloverde. The Joshua tree (*Yucca brevifolia*) is found in the Mojave desert. Flowering plants include the dwarf desert poppy and a variety of asters. Fremont cottonwood and valley oak grow in the Central Valley. The upper Sonoran zone includes the unique chapparal belt, characterized by forests of small shrubs, stunted trees, and herbaceous plants. Nemophila, mint, phacelia, viola, and the golden poppy (*Eschscholtzia californica*)—the state flower—also flourish in this zone, along with the lupine, more species of which occur here than anywhere else in the world.

The transition zone includes most of the state's forests, with such magnificent specimens as the redwood (*Sequoia sempervirens*) and "big tree" or giant sequoia (*Sequoia gigantea*), among the oldest living things on Earth (some are said to have lived at least 4,000 years). Tanbark oak, California laurel, sugar pine, madroña, broad-leaved maple, and Douglas fir are also common. Forest floors are carpeted with swordfern, alumroot, barrenwort, and trillium, and there are thickets of huckleberry, azalea, elder, and wild currant. Characteristic wild flowers include varieties of mariposa, tulip, and tiger and leopard lilies.

The high elevations of the Canadian zone are abundant with Jeffrey pine, red fir, and lodgepole pine. Brushy areas are covered with dwarf manzanita and ceanothus; the unique Sierra puffball is also found here. Just below timberline, in the Hudsonian zone, grow the whitebark, foxtail, and silver pines. At approximately 10,500 feet (3,200 meters) begins the Arctic zone, a treeless region whose flora includes a number of wild flowers, including Sierra primrose, yellow columbine, alpine buttercup, and alpine shootingstar.

Common plants introduced into California include the eucalyptus, acacia, pepper tree, geranium, and Scotch broom. Among the numerous species classified by California as rare and endangered are the Contra Costa wallflower, Antioch Dunes evening primrose, Milo Baker lupine, July gold, Pismo clarkia, Mono milkvetch, McDonald's rock-cress, and Monterey clover.

Mammals found in the deserts of the lower Sonoran zone include the jackrabbit, kangaroo rat, squirrel, and opossum. The Texas nightowl, roadrunner, cactus wren, and various species of hawk are common birds, and the sidewinder, desert tortoise, and horned toad represent the area's reptilian life. The upper Sono-

LOCATION: 32°32' to 42°N; 114°08' to 124°25'W. **BOUNDARIES:** Oregon line, 220 mi (354 km); Nevada line, 612 mi (985 km); Arizona line, 234 mi (376 km); Mexico line, 144 mi (232 km); Pacific Ocean coastline, 840 mi (1,352 km).

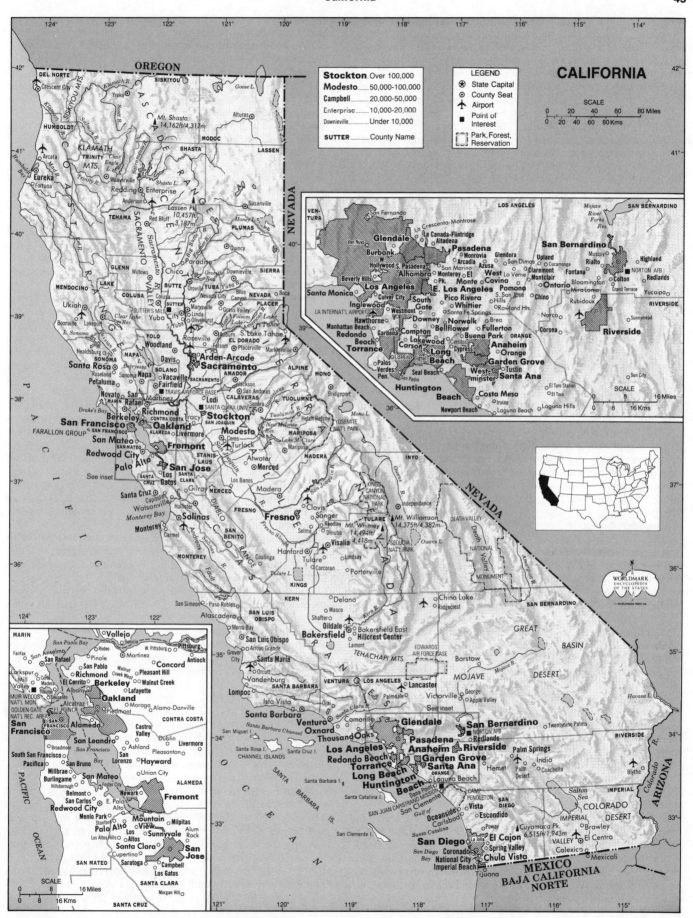

See US political: front cover B3; physical: back cover B3.

ran zone is home to such mammals as the antelope, brown-footed woodrat, antelope, and ring-tailed cat. Birds distinctive to this zone are the California thrasher, bush tit, and California condor.

Animal life is abundant amid the forests of the transition zone. Colombian black-tailed deer, black bear, gray fox, cougar, bobcat, and Roosevelt elk are found. Garter snakes and rattlesnakes are common, as are such amphibians as the water-puppy and redwood salamander. The kingfisher, chickadee, towhee, and hummingbird represent the bird life of this region.

Mammals of the Canadian zone include the mountain weasel, snowshoe hare, Sierra chickaree, and several species of chipmunk. Conspicuous birds include the blue-fronted jay, Sierra hermit thrush, water ouzel, and Townsend solitaire. Birds become scarcer as one ascends to the Hudsonian zone, and the wolverine is now regarded as rare. Only one bird is native to the high Arctic region—the Sierra rosy finch—but others often visit, including the hummingbird and Clark nutcracker. Principal mammals of this region are also visitors from other zones, though the Sierra coney and white-tailed jackrabbit make their homes here. The bighorn sheep also lives in this mountainous terrain. Among fauna found throughout several zones are the mule deer, coyote, mountain lion, red-shafted flicker, and several species of hawk and sparrow.

Aquatic life in California is abundant, from the state's mountain lakes and streams to the rocky Pacific coastline. Many trout species are found, among them rainbow, golden, and Tahoe; migratory species of salmon are also common. Deepsea life forms include sea bass, yellowfin tuna, barracuda, and several types of whale. Native to the cliffs of northern California are seals, sea lions, and many types of shorebirds, including several migratory species.

The Resources Agency of California's Department of Fish and Game is especially active in listing and providing protection for rare, threatened, and endangered fauna. Joint efforts by state and federal wildlife agencies have established an ambitious—if somewhat controversial—recovery program to revitalize the dwindling population of the majestic condor, the largest bird native to the US.

Considered as rare are the San Joaquin kit fox, Southern rubber boa, black toad, and Cottonball marsh pupfish. Among threatened animals are the San Clemente sage sparrow, Paiute cutthroat trout, and Southern sea otter. Seven species of whale—including the gray whale, the official state marine mammal—are on the state's endangered list, as are two subspecies of bighorn sheep. Other endangered animals include the Morro Bay kangaroo rat, southern bald eagle, California least tern, San Francisco garter snake, desert slender salamander, Mohave chub, Lost River sucker, and Tecopa pupfish.

5 ENVIRONMENTAL PROTECTION

Efforts to preserve natural wilderness areas in California go back at least to 1890, when the US Congress created three national parks in the Sierra Nevada: Sequoia, Grant (now part of Kings Canyon), and Yosemite; three years later, some 4 million acres (1.6 million hectares) of the Sierra Nevada were set aside in national forests. In 1892, naturalist John Muir and other wilderness lovers founded the Sierra Club, which with other private groups of conservationists has been influential in saving the Muir Woods and other stands of redwoods from the lumberman's ax. By 1978 there were 20,359,000 acres (8,239,000 hectares) of California land in the federal forest system.

California's primary resource problem is water: the southern two-thirds of the state accounts for about 75% of annual water consumption but only 30% of the supply. Water has been diverted from the Sierra Nevada snow runoff and from the Colorado River to the cities and dry areas largely by means of aqueducts, some 700 mi (1,100 km) of which have been constructed in federal and state undertakings. In 1960, California embarked on

one of the largest public works programs ever undertaken in the US, when voters approved a bond issue to construct the California Water Project, designed to deliver annually 1.4 trillion gallons of water to central and southern California for residential, industrial, and agricultural use. Other purposes of the project were to provide flood control, generate electric power, and create recreation areas.

Air pollution has been a serious problem since July 1943, when heavy smog enveloped Los Angeles for the first time; smog conditions in October 1954 forced the closing of the city's airport and harbor. Smog is caused by an atmospheric inversion of cold air that traps unburned hydrocarbons at ground level; perhaps two-thirds of the smog particles are created by automobile exhaust emissions. In 1960, the state legislature passed the first automobile antismog law in the nation, requiring that all cars be equipped with antismog exhaust devices within three years. (Federal laws controlling exhaust emissions on new cars came into effect in the 1970s.) The city's smog problem has since been reduced to manageable proportions, but pollution problems from atmospheric inversions still persist there and in other southern California cities.

State land-reclamation programs have been important in providing new agricultural land and controlling flood damage. One of the earliest such programs, begun shortly before 1900, reclaimed 500,000 acres (200,000 hectares) by means of a network of dams, dikes, and canals in the swampy delta lying within the fork of the Sacramento and San Joaquin rivers. In 1887, a state law created irrigation districts in the southeastern region; the Imperial Valley was thus transformed from a waterless, sandy basin into some of the most productive agricultural land in the US. Flood control was one of the main purposes of the $2.6-billion Feather River Project in the Central Valley, completed during the 1970s.

In 1972, the state legislature enacted stringent controls on toxic waste disposal. California has also been a leader in recycling waste products—for example, using acid waste from metal-processing plants as a soil additive in citrus orchards. According to a federal survey in 1979, there were 177 potentially hazardous abandoned dump sites in the state.

The California Department of Water Resources is responsible for maintaining adequate groundwater levels, enforcing water quality standards, and controlling floodwaters. The state Department of Conservation has overall responsibility for conservation and protection of the state's soil, mineral, petroleum, geothermal, and marine resources. In the 1980 fiscal year, the state budget included $324 million for the preservation and development of natural resources, including $144 million for state parks and forests, $35 million for air pollution control, $20 million for water projects, $19 million for solid waste disposal, $16 million for the California Conservation Corps, and $90 million for other projects.

6 POPULATION

At least 1 out of every 10 Americans lives in California, which ranks 1st in population among the 50 states. California replaced New York as the decennial census leader in 1970, with a total of 19,971,069 residents, and has lengthened its lead ever since. Los Angeles is the 3d most populous city in the US, and Los Angeles County ranks 1st in population amoung all US counties.

When Europeans first arrived in California, at least 300,000 Indians lived in the area. By 1849, the Indian population had been reduced to about 7,000. Although Spanish missions and settlements were well established in California by the late 18th century, the white population numbered only about 7,000 until the late 1840s. The gold rush brought at least 85,000 adventurers to the San Francisco Bay area by 1850, however, and the state's population increased rapidly thereafter. California's census population grew to 379,994 by 1860, and had passed the 1 million mark within 30 years. Since 1890, the number of state residents just about doubled every two decades until the 1970s, when the population continued to increase, though at a slower pace. Although the state's annual growth rate fell from 4% during the 1950s to 2.3% during the 1960s, and then to 1.4% between 1970 and 1978, when the estimated population was 22,297,000, census projections indicate a steady increase to 26,292,000 by 1990 and to 29,287,000 by the year 2000.

In 1977, California led the 50 states in the proportion of residents living in metropolitan areas, nearly 93%. At the 1970 census, the population was 49.2% male and 50.8% female. The population density in 1970 was 128 persons per sq mi (49 per sq km), or more than double the US average; by 1978, the density was 143 per sq mi (55 per sq km), 15th in the US but the highest of any western state. Densities in urban areas were much higher —1,751 per sq mi (676 per sq km) in Los Angeles County in 1978, and 14,638 per sq mi (5,652 per sq km) in San Francisco.

Census estimates for 1978 indicated that Californians were not conspicuously younger than the US as a whole; the population curve showed a slight bulge toward those between 18 and 64, while the proportions of very young and very old were slightly below the US norms. Californians are highly mobile, however. According to the 1970 census, 57% of state residents 5 years of age or older had moved within the previous 5 years. Only one-third of all Californians in 1970 had lived in the state their whole lives. California gained 2,113,000 people through migration during the 1960s, and about 2,123,000 through net natural increase. The birthrate per 1,000 residents dropped from 23.7 in 1960 to 15.8 in 1977, while the death rate declined from 8.6 to 7.8.

Three out of four Californians live in urban areas located within 20 mi (32 km) of the ocean; three out of five reside in metropolitan San Francisco and Los Angeles. In 1979, the state had 23 cities with more than 100,000 population. Los Angeles had an estimated population of 2,801,900; San Diego, 825,700; San Francisco, 657,200; San Jose, 598,000; Long Beach, 349,000; Oakland, 329,000; Sacramento, 264,400; and Anaheim, 207,500.The first 4 all placed among the 20 most populous cities in 1978, and San Jose, ranked 20th, showed the fastest population growth of any leading US city between 1970 and 1978 (24%). First results from the 1980 census showed Los Angeles with a population of 2,950,010; San Francisco, 674,063.

Los Angeles, which expanded irregularly and lacks a central business district, nearly quadrupled its population from 319,000 in 1910 to 1,240,000 in 1930, and then doubled to 2,479,000 by 1960. A major component of the city's population growth has been an upsurge in the number of blacks, especially since World War II. Between 1960 and 1970, the number of blacks increased from 335,000 to 504,000, many of them crowded into the deteriorating Watts section. During the same period, San Francisco's black population increased from 74,000 to 96,000, while the white population declined from 666,000 to 620,000.

In 1977, the Los Angeles–Long Beach urban complex, with a total population of 7,031,000, was the 2d most populous metropolitan area in the country (after New York City). In that year, the San Francisco–Oakland area ranked 7th with 3,182,000; Anaheim–Santa Ana–Garden Grove had a combined population of 1,801,000 (19th); metropolitan San Diego, 1,683,000 (20th).

[7]ETHNIC GROUPS

California has the nation's largest Mexican-American, Chinese, and Filipino populations, and more Japanese than any state except Hawaii.

The westward movement of American settlers in the third quarter of the 19th century, followed by Germans, Irish, North Italians, and Italian Swiss immigrants, overshadowed but did not obliterate California's Spanish heritage. In 1976, Hispanics were the largest ethnic minority; California had 3,343,000 Spanish-speaking Americans, more than any other state. The majority

California Counties, County Seats, and County Populations

COUNTY	COUNTY SEAT	LAND AREA[1] (SQ MI)	POPULATION (1 JULY 1978)
Alameda	Oakland	733	1,101,900
Alpine	Markleeville	723	1,000
Amador	Jackson	593	17,900
Butte	Oroville	1,663	131,800
Calaveras	San Andreas	1,027	18,200
Colusa	Colusa	1,153	13,000
Contra Costa	Martinez	734	613,400
Del Norte	Crescent City	1,003	17,100
El Dorado	Placerville	1,714	75,000
Fresno	Fresno	5,964	477,700
Glenn	Willows	1,317	20,700
Humboldt	Eureka	3,573	107,400
Imperial	El Centro	4,284	89,500
Inyo	Independence	10,091	17,900
Kern	Bakersfield	8,152	368,700
Kings	Hanford	1,395	71,000
Lake	Lakeport	1,256	31,700
Lassen	Susanville	4,547	19,900
Los Angeles	Los Angeles	4,060	7,108,300
Madera	Madera	2,144	52,900
Marin	San Rafael	520	222,900
Mariposa	Mariposa	1,455	10,300
Mendocino	Ukiah	3,507	63,900
Merced	Merced	1,982	125,400
Modoc	Alturas	4,092	8,600
Mono	Bridgeport	3,028	8,200
Monterey	Salinas	3,324	275,000
Napa	Napa	758	94,000
Nevada	Nevada City	978	44,500
Orange	Santa Ana	782	1,832,500
Placer	Auburn	1,424	106,500
Plumas	Quincy	2,570	15,700
Riverside	Riverside	7,177	606,200
Sacramento	Sacramento	983	738,500
San Benito	Hollister	1,396	21,400
San Bernardino	San Bernardino	20,131	772,600
San Diego	San Diego	4,255	1,738,000
San Francisco	[2]	45	658,700
San Joaquin	Stockton	1,409	313,700
San Luis Obispo	San Luis Obispo	3,316	140,000
San Mateo	Redwood City	454	585,100
Santa Barbara	Santa Barbara	2,738	292,500
Santa Clara	San Jose	1,302	1,227,500
Santa Cruz	Santa Cruz	439	173,900
Shasta	Redding	3,798	108,600
Sierra	Downieville	958	3,400
Siskiyou	Yreka	6,312	38,000
Solano	Fairfield	827	208,300
Sonoma	Santa Rosa	1,579	271,600
Stanislaus	Modesto	1,500	247,400
Sutter	Yuba City	607	49,200
Tehama	Red Bluff	2,976	36,200
Trinity	Weaverville	3,191	11,700
Tulare	Visalia	4,838	224,700
Tuolumne	Sonora	2,274	31,500
Ventura	Ventura	1,851	482,100
Yolo	Woodland	1,034	106,200
Yuba	Marysville	637	47,500
TOTALS		156,573	22,297,000

[1]Total area, based on a 1965 state study, differs slightly from the 1970 census estimate.

[2]The city and county of San Francisco are coterminous.

were first- and second-generation Mexican-Americans; in 1970 there were also 46,078 Puerto Ricans, double the number in 1960, and 138,859 Filipinos. After World War II, the Hispanic communities of Los Angeles, San Diego, and other southern California cities developed strong political organizations. Increasing numbers of Mexican-Americans have won local, state, and federal elective office, though their potential remains unrealized.

Nearly 50% of all Mexican-Americans in the US are farm laborers. In California, with its large corporate growers, fewer than 10% of the growers employ three-fourths of the laborers; it was this concentration of labor that made possible the successful unionization of field workers. California in 1970 had the highest state minimum wage for pickers and was the only one of five western states with substantial Hispanic labor to provide unemployment insurance and workers' compensation for field workers.

Chinese workers were imported into the state betwen 1849 and 1882, when the Chinese Exclusion Act was passed by Congress. In 1970, the state's Chinese population was 170,131, double that of New York State and by far the highest in the US. The nation's oldest and largest Chinatown is in San Francisco. Although Chinese-Americans, as they prospered, moved to suburban areas, the seats of the powerful nationwide and worldwide merchant and clan associations are in that city. Los Angeles also has a Chinese district.

The Japanese, spread throughout the western seaboard states, were engaged mainly in agriculture, along with fishing and small business, until their removal and internment during World War II. After the war, some continued in market gardening and other family agriculture, but most, deprived of their landholdings, entered urban occupations, including the professions, and many dispersed to other regions of the country. In 1970 there were 213,280 Japanese in California.

California had 178,671 other Asians in 1970; 27,199 Vietnamese resettled there in 1975. The total Asian population of the state in 1975 (exclusive of Filipinos) was very nearly 600,000.

American Indians numbered 91,000 in 1970. This figure includes Indians native to California and many others coaxed to resettle there under a policy that sought to terminate tribal status. Along with the remaining indigenous tribes in California; there is also a large urban Indian population, especially in Los Angeles, which has more Indians than any other US city. Many of the urban Indians were unprepared for the new kind of life and unable to earn an adequate living; militant Indians have made dramatic, but on the whole unsuccessful, protests aimed at bettering their condition.

Black Americans constitute a smaller proportion of California's population than of the nation's as a whole: less than 8% in 1976. Considerable migration of blacks took place during World War II, when defense industries on the West Coast offered new opportunities. Many California blacks are middle-class business people and professionals. The Watts district of Los Angeles is a ghetto of low-income blacks; many low-income blacks also live in Oakland.

8 LANGUAGES

The speakers of Russian, Spanish, and English who first came to what is now California found an amazing diversity of Indian tribes ranging from the Wiyot in the north to the Yokuts in the central valley and the Diegueño in the south, and of Indian languages, representing four great language families—Athapaskan, Penutian, Hokan-Siouan, and Aztec. Yet, except for place-names such as Shasta, Napa, and Yuba, they have not lent any of their words to California speech. In 1970, 18,033 Californians claimed an Indian language as their mother tongue.

As in much of the West, California English is a composite of the eastern dialects and subdialects brought by the continuing westward migration from the eastern states, first for gold and timber, then for farming, for diversified manufacture, for Holly-

wood, and for retirement. The interior valley is Midland-oriented with such retained terms as *piece* (a between-meals lunch), *quarter till, barn lot* (barnyard), *dog irons* (andirons), and *snake feeder* and *snake doctor* (dragonfly), but generally, in both northern and southern California, Northern dominates the mixture of North Midland and South Midland speech in the same communities. Northern *sick to the stomach,* for example, dominates Midland *sick at* and *sick in,* with a 46% frequency; Northern *angleworm* has 53% frequency, as compared with 21% for Midland *fishworm;* and Northern *string beans* has 80% frequency, as compared with 17% North Midland *green beans* and South Midland and Southern *snap beans.* Northern *comforter* was used by 94% of the informants interviewed in a state survey; Midland *comfort* by only 21%. Dominant is Northern /krik/ as the pronunciation of *creek,* but Midland *bucket* has a greater frequency than Northern *pail,* and Midland /greezy/ for *greasy* is scattered throughout the state. Similarly, the distinction between the /hw/ in *wheel* and the /w/ of *weal* is lost in the use of simple /w/ in both words, and *cot* and *caught* sound alike, as do *caller* and *collar.*

There are some regional differences. San Francisco, for instance, has *sody* or *soda water* for a soft drink; there the large sandwich is a *grinder,* while in Sacramento it is either a *poor Joe* or a *submarine.* Notable is the appearance of *chesterfield* (meaning sofa or davenport), found in the Bay region and from San Jose to Sacramento; this sense is common in Canada but now found nowhere else in the US. Boonville, a village about 100 mi (160 km) north of San Francisco, is notorious for "Boontling," a local dialect contrived in the mid-19th century by Scotch-Irish settlers who wanted privacy and freedom from obscenities in their conversation. Now declining in use, Boontling has about 1,000 vocabulary replacements of usual English words, together with some unusual pronunciations and euphemisms.

Three major foreign-language populations—Spanish, Chinese, and Japanese—along with a large number of recent South Asian refugees—have posed major educational problems. In 1974, a landmark San Francisco case, *Lau* v. *Nichols,* brought a decision from the US Supreme Court that children who do not know English should not thereby be handicapped in school, but should receive instruction in their native tongue while learning English.

As the nation's major motion picture, radio, and television entertainment center, Los Angeles has influenced English throughout the nation, even the world, by making English speakers of many dialects audible and visible and by making known new terms and new meanings. It has thus been instrumental in reducing dialectal extremes and in developing increased language awareness.

Major language groups reported their first language as follows:

	NATIVE-BORN	FOREIGN-BORN
English	13,979,915	285,946
Spanish	1,575,530	575,070
German	400,178	163,068
Italian	261,894	84,447
French	145,280	55,504
Japanese	116,113	43,358
Yiddish	104,926	40,082
Chinese	71,929	73,102

9 RELIGIONS

The first Roman Catholics in California were Spanish friars who established 21 Franciscan missions from San Diego to Sonoma between 1769 and 1823. After an independent Mexican government began to secularize the missions in 1833, the Indian population at the missions declined from about 25,000 to only about 7,000 in 1840. With the American acquisition of California in 1848, the Catholic Church was reorganized to include the archdiocese of San Francisco. Protestant ministers accompanied migrant miners during the gold rush, founding 32 churches in San

Francisco by 1855. These early Protestants included Baptists, Congregationalists, Methodists, Presbyterians, Episcopalians, and Unitarians; a group of Mormons had arrived by ship via Cape Horn in 1846. Small Jewish communities were established throughout California by 1861, and in 1880, the Jewish population was estimated at 18,580. The midwesterners who began arriving in large numbers in the 1880s were mostly Protestants who settled in southern California. By 1900, the number of known Christians in the state totaled 674,000, out of a population of nearly 1,500,000.

The mainstream religions did not satisfy everybody's needs, however, and in the early 20th century many dissident sects sprang up, including such organizations as Firebrands for Jesus, the Psychosomatic Institute, the Mystical Order of Melchizedek, the Infinite Science Church, and Nothing Impossible, among many others. Perhaps the best-known founder of a new religion was Canadian-born Aimee Semple McPherson, who preached her Foursquare Gospel during the 1920s at the Angelus Temple in Los Angeles, won a large radio audience and thousands of converts, and established 240 branches of her church throughout the state before her death in 1944. She was typical of the many charismatic preachers of new doctrines who gave—and still give—California its exotic religious flavor. In the postwar era, religions such as Zen Buddhism and Scientology have won enthusiastic followings, along with various cults devoted to self-discovery and self-actualization.

Nevertheless, the large majority of religious adherents in California continue to follow traditional faiths. In 1979 there were 4,778,302 Roman Catholics (2d only to New York); the archdiocese of Los Angeles had 1,964,000, the San Francisco archdiocese had 620,250, and the remainder were divided among 9 dioceses. In 1971, the latest year for which detailed information is available, the state had 2,753,033 known Protestant adherents. The largest non-Catholic Christian denominations were the Church of Jesus Christ of Latter-day Saints, with 367,521 adherents; United Methodist, with 361,116; United Presbyterian, 318,858; Southern Baptist, 314,217; Episcopal, 199,685; American Baptist, 184,052; Lutheran Church–Missouri Synod, 172,030; American Lutheran Church, 143,150; and Seventh-Day Adventist, 128,080. In 1979, the Jewish population was estimated at 698,995 (2d in the US), nearly two-thirds of whom lived in the Los Angeles metropolitan area.

[10] TRANSPORTATION

California has—and for decades has had—more motor vehicles than any other state, and ranks 2d only to Texas in interstate highway mileage. An intricate 5,400-mi (8,700-km) network of urban freeways is one of the engineering wonders of the modern world—but the traffic congestion in the state's major cities during rush hours may well be the worst in the country.

In pioneer days, the chief modes of transportation were sailing ships and horse-drawn wagons; passage by sea from New York took three months, and the overland route from Missouri was a six-week journey. The gold rush spurred development of more rapid transport. The state's first railroad, completed in 1856, was a 25-mi (40-km) line from Sacramento northeast to Folsom, in the mining country. The Central Pacific–Union Pacific transcontinental railroad, finished 13 years later, was financed in part by several Sacramento business leaders, including Leland Stanford, who became governor of the state in 1861, the same year he assumed the presidency of the Central Pacific. Railroad construction crews, mostly imported Chinese laborers, started from Sacramento and dug and blasted the route through the solid granite of the Sierra Nevada and then across the Nevada desert, linking up with the Union Pacific at Promontory, Utah, on 10 May 1869; Stanford himself helped drive the golden spike that marked the historic occasion. The Southern Pacific completed a line from Sacramento to Los Angeles in 1876, and another to Texas the following year. Other railroads took much longer to build; the

coastal railroad from San Francisco to Los Angeles was not completed until 1901, and another line to Eureka was not finished until 1914. The railroads dominated transportation in the state until motor vehicles came into widespread use in the 1920s.

As of 1977, California had 36 railroad companies operating about 7,300 mi (11,700 km) of track. Railways with the largest track mileage are the Southern Pacific, Santa Fe, Western Pacific, and Union Pacific. Amtrak passenger trains connect the state's major population centers. In 1979, Amtrak's Los Angeles–San Diego commuter line carried 1,177,000 passengers, 43% more than in 1978; the increase was attributed to a decline in automobile traffic because of a gasoline shortage.

Urban transit began in San Francisco in 1861 with horse-drawn streetcars. Cable-car service was introduced in 1873; a few cable cars are still in use, mainly for the tourist trade. The 71-mi (14-km) Bay Area Rapid Transit System, or BART, connects San Francisco with Oakland by high-speed, computerized subway trains via a 3.6-mi (5.8-km) tunnel under San Francisco Bay and runs north-south along the San Francisco peninsula. Completed in the 1970s despite many mechanical problems and costly delays, BART carried an average of 131,000 passengers daily during the mid-1970s.

Public transit in the Los Angeles metropolitan area was provided by electric trolleys beginning in 1887. By the early 1930s, the Los Angeles Railway carried 70% of the city's transit passengers, and in 1945, its trolleys transported 109 million passengers. Competition from buses—which provided greater mobility, but aggravated the city's smog and congestion problems—forced the trolleys to end service in 1961. Today, Los Angeles lacks an adequate urban transit system, although interurban railroads do connect the city with surrounding suburbs.

California's extensive highway system had its beginnings in the mid-19th century, when stagecoaches began hauling freight to the mining camps from San Francisco, Sacramento, and San Jose. In the early 1850s, two stagecoach lines, Adams and Wells Fargo, expanded their routes and began to carry passengers; by 1860, some 250 stagecoach companies were operating in the state. The decline of stagecoach service corresponded with the rise of the railroads. In 1910, at a time when only 36,000 motor vehicles were registered in the state, the California Highway Commission was established. Among its first acts was the issuance of $18 million in bonds for road construction, and the state's first paved highway was constructed in 1912. The number of automobiles surged to 604,000 by 1920; by 1929, about 1 of every 11 cars in the US belonged to a Californian. Ironically, in view of the state's subsequent traffic problems, the initial effect of the automobile was to disperse the population to outlying areas, thus reducing traffic congestion in the cities.

The Pasadena Freeway, the first modern expressway in California, opened in 1941. During the 1960s and 1970s, the state built a complex toll-free highway network linking most cities of more than 5,000 population, tying in with the federal highway system, and costing more than $10 billion. In the 1977/78 fiscal year, total expenditures on roads by state, county, and city governments amounted to nearly $1.4 billion, and federal aid for highway construction in California totaled about $360 million.

The new freeways, by providing easy access to beach and mountain recreation areas, and in combination with the favorable climate and low price of gasoline, further encouraged the use of the automobile—and led to massive traffic tie-ups, contributed to the decline of public transit, and worsened the coastal cities' air-pollution problems. Los Angeles County claims more automobiles, more miles of streets, and more intersections than any other city in the US. The greatest inducement to automobile travel in and out of San Francisco was the completion in 1936 of the 8-mi (13-km) San Francisco–Oakland Bay Bridge. The following year saw the opening of the magnificent Golden Gate

Bridge, which at 4,200 feet (1,280 meters) was the world's longest suspension bridge until New York's Verrazano-Narrows Bridge opened to traffic in 1964.

In 1978, California had 176,309 mi (283,742 km) of roads. Included in this total were 38,634 mi (62,176 km) of federal highways, 15,235 mi (24,518 km) of state highways, 71,371 mi (114,861 km) of county roads, 48,605 mi (78,222 km) of city streets, and 2,464 mi (3,965 km) of other state roads. In that year, the state registered 18,165,594 motor vehicles—about 81 for every 100 state residents—including 12,319,392 passenger vehicles, 3,088,028 commercial vehicles, 2,102,224 trailers and semitrailers, and 655,950 motorcycles. There were 15,020,183 California driver's licenses in force in 1978. In 1978, California led the nation in number of traffic injuries, 317,916, and fatalities, 5,296.

The large natural harbors of San Francisco and San Diego monopolized the state's maritime trade until 1912, when Los Angeles began developing port facilities at San Pedro by building a breakwater that eventually totaled 8 mi (13 km) in length. In 1924, Los Angeles surpassed San Francisco in shipping tonnage handled, and became the busiest port on the Pacific coast. In 1978, the value of foreign trade handled by California's ports exceeded $35 billion, of which the Los Angeles Customs District accounted for 63%, San Francisco 33%, and San Diego 4%.

In 1978, California had 822 airfields, 297 public and 525 private; 51 airports were served by 27 regularly scheduled air carriers. More than 23,000 general aviation aircraft, greater than the number in any other state and nearly 13% of the US total, were registered in California in 1977. Six of the nation's 10 busiest airports are located in the state. California's most active air terminal—and the nation's 3d most active in 1978—is Los Angeles International Airport, which handled 152,122 departing passenger aircraft and emplaned 12,913,589 passengers in 1978. Also among the nation's 25 busiest airports, with more than 450,000 landings and takeoffs of all types of aircraft, were those at Santa Ana, Long Beach, Van Nuys, Oakland, San Jose, Torrance, Hayward, San Francisco, Concord, and San Diego. Value of airborne export and import shipments handled by the Los Angeles, San Francisco, and San Diego customs districts exceeded $10.5 billion.

¹¹ HISTORY

The region now known as California has been populated for at least 10,000 years, and possibly far longer. Estimates of the prehistoric Indian population have varied widely, but it is clear that California was one of the most densely populated areas north of Mexico. On the eve of European discovery, at least 300,000 Indians lived there. This large population was divided into no fewer than 105 separate tribes or nations speaking at least 100 different languages and dialects, about 70% of which were as mutually unintelligible as English and Chinese. No area of comparable size in North America, and perhaps the world, contained a greater variety of native languages and cultures than did aboriginal California.

In general, the California tribes depended for their subsistence on hunting, fishing, and gathering the abundant natural food resources. Only in a few instances, notably along the Colorado River, did the Indians engage in agriculture. Reflecting the mild climate of the area, their housing and dress were often minimal. The basic unit of political organization was the village community, consisting of several small villages. For the most part, these Indians were sedentary peoples; they occupied village sites for generations, and only rarely warred with their neighbors.

European contact with California began early in the Age of Discovery, and was a product of the two great overseas enterprises of 16th-century Europe: the search for a western passage to the East and the drive to control the riches of the New World. In 1533, Hernán Cortés, Spanish conqueror of the Aztecs, sent a naval expedition northward along the western coast of Mexico in search of new wealth. The expedition led to the discovery of Baja California (now part of Mexico), mistakenly described by the pilot of the voyage, Fortún Jiménez, as an island. Two years later, Cortés established a settlement on the peninsula at La Paz but, because Baja California seemed barren of any wealth, the project was soon abandoned. The only remaining interest in California was the search for the western mouth of the transcontinental canal—a mythical waterway the Spanish called the Strait of Anian. In 1542, Juan Rodríguez Cabrillo led a voyage of exploration up the western coast in a futile search for the strait. On 28 September, Cabrillo landed at the bay now known as San Diego, thus becoming the first European discoverer of Alta (or Upper) California.

European interest in the Californias waned in the succeeding decades. There was a brief revival of interest following the landing of Francis Drake in 1579; the British navigator put in for repairs probably at what is now Drake's Bay, north of San Francisco, and called the region New Albion, claiming it for England. At about this time, the Spanish made preliminary plans to settle the California coast as a way station for the Manila galleons plying the trade route between Mexico and the Philippines. This project too was abandoned, however, and California remained for generations beyond the periphery of European activity in the New World. Subsequent contact was limited to occasional landfalls by Manila galleons, such as those of Pedro de Unamuno (1587) and Sebastián Cermeño (1595), and the tentative explorations of Sebastián Vizcaíno in 1602–3.

Spanish interest in California revived during the late 18th century, largely because Spain's imperial rivals were becoming increasingly aggressive. For strategic and defensive reasons, Spain decided to establish permanent settlements in the north. In 1769, José de Gálvez, visitor-general in New Spain, selected the president of the Franciscan missions in Baja California, Father Junípero Serra, to lead a group of missionaries on an expedition to Alta California. Accompanying Serra was a Spanish military force under Gaspar de Portolá. This Portolá-Serra expedition marks the beginning of permanent European settlement in California. Over the next half-century, the 21 missions established by the Franciscans along the Pacific coast from San Diego to San Francisco formed the core of Hispanic California. Among the prominent missions were San Diego de Alcalá (founded in 1769), San Francisco de Asís (1776), Santa Barbara (1786), and San José (1797). During most of the Spanish period, Mission San Carlos Borromeo (1770), at Carmel, was the ecclesiastical headquarters of the province, serving as the residence of the president-general of the Alta California missions.

These missions were more than just religious institutions. The principal concern of the missionaries was to convert the Indians to Christianity—a successful enterprise, if the nearly 88,000 baptisms performed during the mission period are any measure. The Franciscans also sought to bring about a rapid and thorough cultural transformation. The Indians were taught to perform a wide variety of new tasks: making bricks, tiles, pottery, shoes, saddles, wine, candles, and soap; herding horses, cattle, sheep, goats, and other livestock; and planting, irrigating, and harvesting.

In addition to transforming the way of life of the California Indians, the missions also reduced their number by at least 35,000. About 60% of this decline was due to the introduction of new diseases, especially those of the nonepidemic and venereal type. Alfred Kroeber, founder of the American Anthropological Society, remarked that it "must have caused many of the Fathers a severe pang to realize, as they could not but do daily, that they were saving souls only at the inevitable cost of lives. And yet such was the overwhelming fact. The brute upshot of missionization, in spite of its kindly flavor and humanitarian root, was only one thing, death."

Spain also established several military and civilian settlements in California. The four military outposts, or presidios, at San Diego (1769), Monterey (1770), San Francisco (1776), and Santa Barbara (1782) served to discourage foreign influence in the region and to contain Indian resistance. The presidio at Monterey also served as the political capital, headquarters for the provincial governors appointed in Mexico City. The first civilian settlement, or pueblo, was established at San José de Guadalupe in 1777, with 14 families from the Monterey and San Francisco presidios. The pueblo settlers, granted supplies and land by the government, were expected to provide the nearby presidios with their surplus agricultural products. The second pueblo was founded at Los Angeles (1781), and a third, Branciforte, was established near present-day Santa Cruz in 1797.

During the 40 years following the establishment of the Los Angeles pueblo, Spain did little to strengthen its outposts in Alta California. The province remained sparsely populated and isolated from other centers of Hispanic civilization. During these years, the Spanish-speaking population of 600 grew nearly fivefold, but this expansion was almost entirely due to natural increase rather than immigration.

Spanish control of California ended with the successful conclusion of the Mexican revolution in 1821. For the next quarter-century, California was a province of the independent nation of Mexico. Although California gained a measure of self-rule with the establishment of a provincial legislature, the real authority still remained with the governor appointed in Mexico City. The most important issue in Mexican California was the secularization of the missions, the replacement of the Franciscans with parish or "secular" clergy, and the redistribution of the vast lands and herds the missions controlled. Following the secularization proclamation of Governor José Figueroa in 1834, the Mexican government authorized more than 600 rancho grants in California to Mexican citizens. The legal limit of an individual grant was 11 square leagues (about 76 sq mi, or 197 sq km), but many large landholding families managed to obtain multiple grants.

The rancho economy, like that of the missions, was based on the cultivation of grain and the raising of huge herds of cattle. The rancheros traded hides and tallow for manufactured goods from foreign traders along the coast. As at the missions, herding, slaughtering, hide tanning, tallow rendering, and all other manual tasks were performed by Indian laborers. By 1845, on the eve of American acquisition, the non-Indian population of the region stood at about 7,000.

During the Mexican period, California attracted a considerable minority of immigrants from the US. Americans first came to California in the late 18th century in pursuit of the sea otter, a marine mammal whose luxurious pelts were gathered in California waters and shipped to China for sale. Later, the hide and tallow trade attracted Yankee entrepreneurs, many of whom became resident agents for American commercial firms. Beginning in 1826, with the arrival overland of Jedediah Strong Smith's party of beaver trappers, the interior of California also began to attract a growing number of Americans. The first organized group to cross the continent for the purpose of settlement in California was the Bidwell-Bartleson party of 1841. Subsequent groups of overland pioneers included the ill-fated Donner party of 1846, whose members, stranded by a snowstorm near the Sierra Nevada summit, resorted to cannibalism so that 47 of the 87 travelers could survive.

Official American efforts to acquire California began during the presidency of Andrew Jackson in the 1830s, but it was not until the administration of James K. Polk that such efforts were successful. Following the American declaration of war against Mexico on 13 May 1846, US naval forces, under command of Commodores John D. Sloat and Robert F. Stockton, launched an assault along the Pacific coast, while a troop of soldiers under

Stephen W. Kearny crossed overland. On 13 January 1847, the Mexican forces in California surrendered. More than a year later, after protracted fighting in central Mexico, a treaty of peace was signed at Guadalupe-Hidalgo on 2 February 1848. Under the terms of the treaty, Mexico ceded California and other territories to the US in exchange for $15 million and the assumption by the US of some $3 million in claims by Mexican citizens.

Just nine days before the treaty was signed, James Wilson Marshall discovered gold along the American River in California. The news of the gold discovery, on 24 January 1848, soon spread around the globe, and a massive rush of people poured into the region. By the end of 1848, about 6,000 miners had obtained $10 million worth of gold. During 1849, production was two or three times as large, but the proceeds were spread among more than 40,000 miners. In 1852, the peak year of production, about $80 million in gold was mined in the state, and during the century following its discovery, the total output of California gold amounted to nearly $2 billion. California's census population quadrupled during the 1850s, reaching nearly 380,000 by 1860, and continued to grow at a rate twice that of the nation as a whole in the 1860s and 1870s.

The new population of California was remarkably diverse. The 1850 census found that nearly a quarter of all Californians were foreign-born, while only a tenth of the national population had been born abroad. In succeeding decades, the percentage of foreign-born Californians increased, rising to just under 40% during the 1860s.

One of the most serious problems facing California in the early years of the gold rush was the absence of adequate government. Miners organized more than 500 "mining districts" to regulate their affairs; in San Francisco and other cities "vigilance committees" were formed to combat widespread robbery and arson. The US Congress, deadlocked over the slavery controversy, failed to provide any form of legal government for California from the end of the Mexican War until its admission as a state in the fall of 1850. Taking matters into their own hands, 48 delegates gathered at a constitutional convention in Monterey in September 1849 to draft a fundamental law for the state. The completed constitution contained several unique features, but most of its provisions were based on the constitutions of Iowa and New York. To the surprise of many, the convention decided by unanimous vote to exclude slavery from the state. After considerable debate, the delegates also established the present boundaries of California. Adopted on 10 October, the constitution was ratified by the voters on 13 November 1849; at the same time, Californians elected their first state officials. California soon petitioned Congress for admission as a state, having bypassed the preliminary territorial stage, and was admitted after southern objections to creation of another free state were overcome by adoption of the stringent new Fugitive Slave Law. On 9 September 1850, President Millard Fillmore signed the admission bill, and California became the 31st state to enter the Union.

The early years of statehood were marked by racial discrimination and considerable ethnic conflict. Indian and white hostilities were intense; the Indian population declined from an estimated 150,000 in 1845 to less than 30,000 by 1870. In 1850, the state legislature enacted a foreign miners' license tax, aimed at eliminating competition from Mexican and other Latin American miners. The Chinese, who replaced the Mexicans as the state's largest foreign minority, soon became the target of a new round of discrimination. By 1852, 25,000 Chinese were in California, representing about a tenth of the state's population. The legislature enacted new taxes aimed at Chinese miners, and passed an immigration tax (soon declared unconstitutional) on Chinese immigrants.

Controversy also centered on the status of the Mexican ranchos, those vast estates created by the Mexican government which totaled more than 13 million acres (5 million hectares) by 1850. The Treaty of Guadalupe-Hidalgo had promised that property belonging to Mexicans in the ceded territories would be "inviolably protected." Nevertheless, in the early years of statehood, thousands of squatters took up residence on the rancho lands. Ultimately, about three-fourths of the original Mexican grants were confirmed by federal commissions and courts; however, the average length of time required for confirmation was 17 years. During the lengthy legal process, many of the grantees either sold parts of their grants to speculators or assigned portions to their attorneys for legal fees. By the time title was confirmed, the original grantees were often bankrupt and benefited little from the decision.

Despite the population boom during the gold rush, California remained isolated from the rest of the country until completion of the transcontinental railroad in 1869. Under terms of the Pacific Railroad Act of 1862, the Central Pacific was authorized by Congress to receive long-term federal loans and grants of land, about 12,500 acres per mi (3,100 hectares per km) of track, to build the western link of the road. The directors of the California corporation, Leland Stanford, Collis P. Huntington, Charles Crocker, and Mark Hopkins, who became known as the Big Four, exercised enormous power in the affairs of the state. Following completion of the Central Pacific, the Big Four constructed additional lines within California, as well as a second transcontinental line, the Southern Pacific, providing service from southern California to New Orleans.

To a degree unmatched anywhere in the nation, the Big Four established a monopoly of transportation in California and the Far West. Eventually the Southern Pacific, as the entire system came to be known after 1884, received from the federal government a total of 11,588,000 acres (4,690,000 hectares), making it the largest private landowner in the state. Opponents of the railroad charged that it had established not only a transportation monopoly but also a corrupt political machine and a "land monopoly" in California. Farmers in the San Joaquin Valley became involved in a protracted land dispute with the Southern Pacific, a controversy that culminated in a bloody episode in 1880, known as the Battle of Mussel Slough, in which seven men were killed. This incident, later dramatized by novelist Frank Norris in *The Octopus* (1901), threw into sharp relief the hostility between many Californians and the state's largest corporation.

In the late 19th century, California's economy became more diversified. The early dependence on gold and silver mining was overcome through the development of large-scale irrigation projects and the expansion of commercial agriculture. Southern California soon was producing more than two-thirds of the nation's orange crop, and more than 90% of its lemons. The population of southern California boomed in the 1880s, fueled by the success of the new citrus industry, an influx of invalids seeking a warmer climate, and a railroad rate war between the Southern Pacific and the newly completed Santa Fe. For a time, the tariff from Kansas City to Los Angeles fell to a dollar a ticket. Real estate sales in Los Angeles County alone exceeded $200 million in 1887.

During the early 20th century, California's population growth became increasingly urban. Between 1900 and 1920, the population of the San Francisco Bay area doubled, while residents of metropolitan Los Angeles increased fivefold. On 18 April 1906, San Francisco's progress was interrupted by the most devastating earthquake ever to strike California. The quake and fires which raged for three days killed at least 452 people, razed the city's business section, and destroyed some 28,000 buildings. The survivors immediately set to work to rebuild the city, and completed about 20,000 new buildings within three years.

By 1920, the populations of the two urban areas were roughly equal, about 1 million each. As their populations grew, the need for additional water supplies became critical, and both cities became involved in bitter "water fights" with other state interests. Around the turn of the century, San Francisco proposed the damming of the Tuolumne River at the Hetch Hetchy Valley to form a reservoir for the city's water system. Conservationist John Muir and the Sierra Club objected strongly to the proposal, arguing that the Hetch Hetchy was as important a natural landmark as neighboring Yosemite Valley. The conservationists lost the battle, and the valley was flooded. (The dam there is named for Michael O'Shaughnessy, San Francisco's city engineer from 1912 to 1932 and the builder of many of California's water systems.) When Los Angeles began its search for new water supplies, it soon became embroiled in a long controversy over access to the waters of the Owens River. The city constructed a 250-mi (400-km) aqueduct which eventually siphoned off nearly the entire flow of the river, thus jeopardizing the agricultural development of Owens Valley. Residents of the valley dramatized their objection to the project by dynamiting sections of the completed aqueduct.

Important movements for political reform began simultaneously in San Francisco and Los Angeles in the early 20th century. Corruption in the administration of San Francisco Mayor Eugene Schmitz led to a wide-ranging public investigation and to a series of trials of political and business leaders. Meanwhile, in Los Angeles, a coalition of reformers persuaded the city to adopt a new charter with such progressive features as initiative, referendum, and recall. In 1907, reformers throughout the state combined forces and organized the Lincoln-Roosevelt League, dedicated to the election of Progressive candidates to public office. Hiram Johnson, the Progressive Republican candidate for governor in 1910, toured the state with his promise to "kick the Southern Pacific Railroad out of politics." Johnson won the election, and reformers gained control of both houses of the state legislature in 1911. Subsequent reform legislation established effective regulation of the railroads and other public utilities, greater governmental efficiency, female suffrage, closer regulation of public morality, and workers' compensation.

During the first half of the 20th century, California's population growth far outpaced that of the nation as a whole. The state's climate, natural beauty, and romantic reputation continued to attract many, but new economic opportunities were probably most important. In the early 1920s, major discoveries of oil were made in the Los Angeles Basin, and for several years during the decade California ranked 1st among the 50 states in production of crude oil. The population of Los Angeles County more than doubled during the decade, rising to 2,208,492 by 1930. Spurred by the availability and low price of petroleum products and by an ever expanding system of public roadways, Los Angeles also became the most thoroughly motorized and automobile-conscious city in the world. By 1925, Los Angeles had one automobile for every three persons—more than twice the national average.

Even during the 1930s, when California shared in the nationwide economic depression, hundreds of thousands of refugees streamed into the state from the dust bowl of the southern Great Plains. The film industry, which offered at least the illusion of prosperity to millions of Americans, continued to prosper during the depression. By 1940 there were more movie theaters in the US than banks, and the films they showed were almost all California products. Politics in the Golden State in the 1930s spawned splinter movements like the Townsend Plan, and the "Ham 'n' Eggs" Plan, both of which advocated cash payments for the elderly. In 1934, Socialist author Upton Sinclair won the Democratic gubernatorial nomination with a plan called End Poverty In California (EPIC), but he lost the general election to the Republican incumbent, Frank Merriam.

During World War II, the enormous expansion of military installations, shipyards, and aircraft plants attracted millions of new residents to California. The war years also saw an increase in the size and importance of ethnic minorities. By 1942, only Mexico City had a larger urban Mexican population than Los Angeles. During the war, more than 93,000 Japanese-Americans in California —most of whom were US citizens and American-born—were interned in "relocation centers" throughout the Far West.

California continued to grow rapidly during the postwar period, as agricultural, aerospace, and service industries provided new economic opportunities. Politics in the state were influenced by international tensions, and the California legislature expanded the activities of its Fact-Finding Committee on Un-American Activities. The University of California became embroiled in a loyalty-oath controversy, culminating in the dismissal in 1950 of 32 professors who refused to sign an anti-Communist pledge. The early 1950s saw the rise to the US vice-presidency of Richard Nixon, whose early campaigns capitalized on fears of Communist subversion.

At the beginning of 1963, California (according to census estimates) became the nation's most populous state; its population continued to increase at a rate of 1,000 net migrants a day through the middle of the decade. By 1970, however, California's growth rate had slowed considerably. During the 1960s, the state was beset by a number of serious problems which apparently discouraged would-be immigrants. Economic opportunity gave way to recessions and high unemployment. Such rapid-growth industries as aerospace experienced a rapid decline in the late 1960s and early 1970s. Pollution of air and water called into question the quality of the California environment. The traditional romantic image of California was overshadowed by reports of mass murders, bizarre religious cults, extremist social and political movements, and racial and campus unrest.

By the mid-1970s, migration to California had resumed at a more modest annual rate. The political importance of California's preeminence in population can be measured in the size of its congressional delegation and electoral votes. Defeated in his quest for the presidency in 1960, former Vice President Nixon in 1968 became the first native Californian to win election to the nation's highest office. Both Ronald Reagan, governor of the state from 1967 to 1975, and Edmund G. Brown, Jr., elected governor in 1974 and reelected in 1978, were active candidates for the US presidency in 1980, with Reagan the Republican presidential winner.

12 STATE GOVERNMENT

The first state constitution, adopted in 1849, outlawed slavery and was unique in granting property rights to married women in their own name. A new constitution, drafted in 1878 and ratified the following year, sought to curb legislative abuses—even going so far as to make lobbying a felony—and provided for a more equitable system of taxation, stricter regulation of the railroads, and an eight-hour workday. Of the 152 delegates to the 1878 constitutional convention, only 2 were natives of California, and 35 were foreign-born; no Spanish-speaking persons or Indians were included. This second constitution, as amended, is the basic document of state government today.

The California legislature consists of a 40-member senate and an 80-member assembly. Senators are elected to four-year terms, half of them every two years, and assembly members are elected to two-year terms. As a result of a 1972 constitutional amendment, the legislature meets in a continuous two-year session, thus eliminating the need to reintroduce or reprint bills proposed in the first year of the biennium. Each session begins on the 1st Monday in December of even-numbered years. Special sessions may be called by the governor to consider certain specific matters.

Members of the senate and assembly must be US citizens, over 18 years of age, and have been residents of the state for at least three years and of the districts they represent for at least one year prior to election. Legislative salaries in 1980 were $23,232 annually, plus a $30 per diem and a transportation allowance during the legislative session.

Bills, which may be introduced by either house, are referred to committees, and must be read before each house three times. Legislation must be approved by an absolute majority vote of each house, except that appropriations bills, certain urgent measures, and proposed constitutional amendments require a two-thirds vote for passage. Gubernatorial vetoes may be overridden by two-thirds majority votes in both houses. The legislature considers approximately 6,000 bills during each two-year session. Constitutional amendments and proposed legislation may also be placed on the ballot through the iniative procedure. For a constitutional amendment, petitions must be signed by at least 8% of the number of voters who took part in the last gubernatorial election; for statutory measures, 5%. In each case, a simple majority vote at the next general election is required for passage.

Officials elected statewide include the governor and lieutenant governor (who run separately), secretary of state, attorney general, controller, treasurer, and superintendent of public instruction. Each serves a four-year term, without limitation. As chief executive officer of the state, the governor is responsible for the state's policies and programs, appoints department heads and members of state boards and commissions, serves as commander-in-chief of the California National Guard, may declare states of emergency, and may grant executive clemency to convicted criminals. The governor's annual salary in 1980 was $49,100.

The lieutenant governor acts as president of the senate and may assume the duties of the governor in case of the latter's death, resignation, impeachment, inability to discharge the duties of the office, or absence from the state. The annual salary of the lieutenant governor was $35,000 in 1980. Salaries of other elected officials also were $35,000, except for the attorney general, who received $42,500.

In order to vote in California, one must be a US citizen, at least 18 years old, and have been a resident of the state for at least 29 days prior to the election.

13 POLITICAL PARTIES

As the state with the largest number of US representatives, 43, and electoral votes, 45, Calfornia plays a key role in national and presidential politics.

In 1851, the year after California entered the Union, the state Democratic Party was organized. But the party soon split into a pro-South faction, led by US Senator William Gwin, and a pro-North wing, headed by David Broderick. A political leader in San Francisco, Broderick became a US senator in 1857 but was killed in a duel by a Gwin stalwart two years later. This violent factionalism helped switch Democratic votes to the new Republican Party in the election of 1860, giving California's four electoral votes to Abraham Lincoln. This defeat, followed by the Civil War, demolished Senator Gwin's Democratic faction, and he fled to exile in Mexico.

The Republican Party itself split into liberal and conservative wings in the early 1900s. Progressive Republicans formed the Lincoln-Roosevelt League to espouse political reforms, and succeeded in nominating and electing Hiram Johnson as governor on the Republican ticket in 1910. The following year, the legislature approved 23 constitutional amendments, including the initiative, referendum, recall, and other reform measures. Johnson won reelection on a Progressive Party line in 1915. After Johnson's election to the US Senate in 1916, Republicans (both liberal and conservative) controlled the state house uninterruptedly for 22 years, from 1917 to 1939. Democratic fortunes sank so low that in 1924 the party's presidential candidate, John W. Davis, got only 8% of the state's votes, leading humorist Will Rogers to quip, "I don't belong to any organized political party—I am a California Democrat." An important factor in the Progressive Republicans' success was the cross-filing system, in effect from 1913 to 1959, which blurred party lines by permitting candidates to appear on the primary ballots of several parties. This favored such Republican moderates as Earl Warren, who won an unprecedented three terms as governor—in 1946, he won both Republican and Democratic party primaries—before being elevated to US chief justice in 1953.

Political third parties have had remarkable success in California since the secretive antiforeign, anti-Catholic Native American Party—called the Know-Nothings because party members were instructed to say they "knew nothing" when asked what they stood for—elected one of their leaders, J. Neely Johnson, as governor in 1855. The Workingmen's Party of California, as much anti-Chinese as it was antimonopolist and prolabor, managed to elect about one-third of the delegates to the 1878 constitutional convention. The most impressive third-party triumph came in 1912, when the Progressive Party's presidential candidate, Theodore Roosevelt, and vice-presidential nominee, Governor Hiram Johnson, defeated both the Republican and Democratic candidates among state voters. The Socialist Party also attracted support in the early 20th century. In 1910, more than 12% of the vote went to the Socialist candidate for governor, J. Stitt Wilson. Two years later, Socialist congressional nominees in the state won 18% of the vote, and a Socialist assemblyman was elected from Los Angeles. In the election of 1914, two Socialist assemblymen and one state senator were elected. During the depression year of 1934, the Socialist Party leader and author Upton Sinclair won the Democratic nomination for governor on his End Poverty In California program and received nearly a million votes while losing to Republican Frank Merriam. Splinter groups and nonparty political movements have also won followings: several southern California congressmen were members of the ultraconservative John Birch Society during the 1960s, and in 1980 the Grand Dragon of the Ku Klux Klan won the Democratic Party nomination for a US House seat. Even when they lost decisively, third parties have won enough votes to affect the outcome of elections. In 1968, for example, George Wallace's American Independent Party received 487,270 votes, while Republican presidential candidate Richard Nixon topped Democrat Hubert Humphrey by only 223,346.

In 1978, California had 10,129,986 registered voters, including 5,729,959 Democrats, 3,465,384 Republicans, 84,895 American Independent Party members, 31,408 Peace and Freedom Party members, 27,600 supporters of other parties, and 790,740 independents. Even with a 3–2 advantage in voter registration, however, the Democrats managed to carry California in presidential elections only twice between 1948 and 1978, and to elect only two governors, Edmund G. "Pat" Brown (in 1958 and 1962) and his son, Edmund G. "Jerry" Brown, Jr. (in 1974 and 1978), during the same period. Three times Californians gave their electoral votes to a California Republican, Richard Nixon, though they turned down his bid for governor in 1962. They elected one former film actor, Republican George Murphy, as US senator in 1964, and another, Republican Ronald Reagan, as governor in 1966 and 1970.

As of early 1980, Democrats held majorities in both houses of the state legislature, and held a 25–18 advantage in the state's delegation to the US House. California's representation in the US Senate was evenly divided. In November 1980, Reagan carried California's 45 electoral votes. The Republicans also won a 22–21 edge in the state's House delegation, but Democratic Senator Alan Cranston was reelected, and the Democrats kept control over both houses of the state legislature. Independent presidential candidate John Anderson won 727,655 votes.

The state's direct primary law had a salutary effect on local politics by helping to end the power of political machines in the large cities. In 1910, Los Angeles voters adopted the nonpartisan primary and overthrew the corrupt rule of Mayor A. C. Harper in favor of reformer George Alexander. At the same time, voters were revolting against bossism and corruption in San Francisco, Sacramento, Oakland, and other cities.

Minority groups of all types are represented in California politics. In 1979 there were 227 black elected officials, the most prominent of whom was Los Angeles Mayor Thomas Bradley, first elected in 1973 at a time when the city's population was only 18% black. In 1974, Californians elected a black state senator, Mervyn Dymally, as lieutenant governor, and a woman of Asian ancestry, March Fong Eu, as secretary of state. In 1976, a former college president of Japanese extraction, S. I. Hayakawa, was elected US senator. During the 1970s, organized groups of avowed homosexuals began to play an important political role in

California Presidential Vote by Political Parties, 1948–80

YEAR	ELECTORAL VOTE	CALIFORNIA WINNER	DEMOCRAT	REPUBLICAN	STATES' RIGHTS	PROGRESSIVE	SOCIALIST	PROHIBITION
1948	25	*Truman (D)	1,913,134	1,895,269	1,228	190,381	3,459	16,926
					CONSTITUTION		SOC. LABOR	
1952	32	*Eisenhower (R)	2,197,548	2,897,310	3,504	24,692	273	16,117
1956	32	*Eisenhower (R)	2,420,135	3,027,668	6,087	—	300	11,119
1960	32	Nixon (R)	3,224,099	3,259,722	—	—	1,051	21,706
1964	40	*Johnson (D)	4,171,877	2,879,108	—	—	489	—
					AMERICAN IND.		PEACE & FREEDOM	
1968	40	*Nixon (R)	3,244,318	3,467,664	487,270	—	27,707	—
						AMERICAN	PEOPLE'S	LIBERTARIAN
1972	45	*Nixon (R)	3,475,847	4,602,096	—	232,554	55,167	980
						COMMUNIST		
1976	45	Ford (R)	3,742,284	3,882,244	51,096	12,766	41,731	56,388
						CITIZENS	PEACE & FREEDOM	
1980	45	*Reagan (R)	3,039,532	4,444,044	—	9,687	60,059	17,797

*Won US presidential election.

San Francisco. Women were mayors of two of the state's four largest cities, San Francisco and San Jose, as of 1980.

14 LOCAL GOVERNMENT

As of 1977, California had 58 counties, 413 municipalities, 1,109 school districts, and 2,227 special districts.

County government is administered by an elected board of supervisors, which also exercises jurisdiction over unincorporated towns within the county. Government operations are administered by several elected officials, the number varying according to the population of the county. Most counties have a district attorney, assessor, treasurer–tax collector, superintendent of schools, sheriff, and coroner. Larger counties may also have an elected planning director, public defender, public works director, purchasing agent, and social welfare services director.

Municipalities are governed under the mayor-council, council-manager, or commission system. Most large cities are run by councils of from 5 to 15 members, elected to four-year terms, which are responsible for taxes, public improvements, and the budget. An elected mayor supervises city departments and appoints most city officials. Other elected officials usually include the city attorney, treasurer, and assessor. Los Angeles and San Francisco have the mayor-council form of government, but in San Francisco the city and county governments are consolidated under an elected board of supervisors, and the mayor appoints a manager who has substantial authority. San Diego and San Jose have both an elected mayor and city manager chosen by an elected city council.

15 STATE SERVICES

In accordance with the Political Reform Act of 1974, the Fair Political Practices Commission investigates political campaign irregularities, regulates lobbyists, and enforces full disclosure of political contributions and public officials' assets and income.

Educational services are provided by the Department of Education, which administers the public school system. The department, which is headed by the superintendent of public instruction, also regulates special schools for blind, deaf, and handicapped children. The University of California system is governed by a board of regents headed by the governor.

Transportation services are under the direction of the Department of Transportation (CALTRANS), which oversees mass transit lines, highways, and airports. Intrastate rate regulation of pipelines, railroads, buses, trucks, airlines, and waterborne transportation is the responsibility of the Public Utilities Commission, which also regulates gas, electric, telephone, water, sewer, and steam-heat utilities. The Department of Motor Vehicles licenses drivers, road vehicles, automotive dealers, and boats.

Health and welfare services are provided by many state agencies. The Department of Health Services provides health care for about 3 million persons through the state's Medi-Cal program. The department's public health services include controlling infectious disease, conducting cancer research, safeguarding water quality, and protecting the public from unsafe food and drugs. The department also has licensing responsibility for hospitals, clinics, and nursing homes. Care for the mentally ill is provided through the Department of Mental Health by means of state hospitals and community outpatient clinics. Handicapped people receive counseling, vocational training, and other aid through the Department of Rehabilitation. Needy families receive income maintenance aid and food stamps from the Department of Social Services (formerly the Department of Benefit Payments). Senior citizens can get help from the Department of Aging, which allocates federal funds for the elderly and, as of 1979, ran 80 nutrition projects serving more than 55,000 hot meals daily at 662 meal sites. The Commission on the Status of Women reports to the legislature on women's educational and employment needs, and on statutes or practices that infringe their rights. The Youth Authority, charged with the rehabilitation of juvenile offenders,

operates training schools and conservation camps. The Department of Alcohol and Drug Abuse coordinates prevention and treatment programs.

Public protection services are provided by the Military Department, which includes the Army and Air National Guard and the California Cadet Corps, and by the Department of Corrections, which maintains institutions and programs to control and treat convicted felons and narcotics addicts. The California Highway Patrol has its own separate department. The State and Consumer Services Agency has jurisdiction over the Department of Consumer Affairs, the Department of Veterans Affairs, the California Public Broadcasting Commission, and several other state departments. A state innovation was the establishment in 1974 of the Seismic Safety Commission to plan public safety programs in connection with California's continuing earthquake problem.

Housing services are the responsibility of the Department of Housing and Community Development, which regulates housing standards and helps communities to provide residential facilities for low-income families, the elderly, and handicapped persons.

Programs for the preservation and development of natural resources are centralized in the Department of Conservation. State parks and recreation areas are administered by the Department of Parks and Recreation. California's vital water needs are the responsibility of the Department of Water Resources. In 1975, as a result of the national oil shortage, the state established the Energy Resources Conservation and Development Commission to develop contingency plans for dealing with fuel shortages, to forecast the state's energy needs, and to coordinate programs for energy conservation. The California Conservation Corps provides employment opportunities for young people in conservation work.

The Department of Industrial Relations has divisions dealing with fair employment practices, occupational safety and health standards, workers' compensation, apprenticeship, and arbitration of labor disputes. The Employment Development Department provides unemployment and disability benefits and operates job-training and work-incentive programs.

16 JUDICIAL SYSTEM

California has a complex judicial system and a very large correctional system, which in 1978 ranked 3d in the US in number of prisoners but 1st—by a wide margin—in number of personnel. Crime rates in the state are among the nation's highest; and among the largest US cities in 1978, San Francisco ranked 4th in violent crimes, Los Angeles 7th, and San Diego 13th.

The state's highest court is the supreme court, which may review appellate court decisions and superior court cases involving the death penalty. The high court has a chief justice and six associate justices, all of whom serve 12-year terms; justices are appointed by the governor, confirmed or disapproved by the Commission on Judicial Appointments (headed by the chief justice), and then submitted to the voters for ratification. The chief justice also chairs the Judicial Council, which seeks to expedite judicial business and to equalize judges' caseloads.

Courts of appeal, organized in five appellate districts, review decisions of superior courts and, in certain cases, of municipal and justice courts. As of 1979 there were 56 district court judgeships, 4 of which were temporarily vacant. All district court judges are appointed by the governor, reviewed by the Commission on Judicial Appointments, and subject to popular election for 12-year terms.

Superior courts in each of the 58 county seats have original jurisdiction in felony, juvenile, probate, and domestic relations cases, as well as in civil cases involving more than $15,000. They also handle some tax and misdemeanor cases and appeals from lower courts. Municipal courts, located in judicial districts with populations of more than 40,000, hear misdemeanors (except those involving juveniles) and civil cases involving $15,000 or less. In districts with less than 40,000 population, justice courts have jurisdiction similar to that of municipal courts. All trial court judges are elected to six-year terms.

As of 31 December 1977 there were 17,338 prisoners in state and federal prisons in California. The State Department of Corrections maintains 12 correctional institutions, 1 community correctional center, 19 conservation camps, and more than 60 parole offices. At the end of 1978 there were 19,116 men and 878 women in state prisons; 9,102 former prisoners (8,685 men, 417 women) were on parole. As of the same date, 4,741 juvenile offenders were in youth correction facilities, and 6,700 former inmates were on parole. California had 33,749 state and local corrections personnel in 1977, 33% more than New York State, which ranked 2d; Texas, with 5,179 more prisoners than California, had less than one-third the personnel.

According to the FBI, California's crime rate in 1978 was 7,116 crimes per 100,000 population, 41% above the US average. In that year, 1,586,483 crimes were reported to the police, including 165,626 violent crimes and 1,420,857 crimes against property. The 1978 rate per 100,000 population included murder and manslaughter, 12; forcible rape, 51; robbery, 306; assault, 374; burglary, 2,193; larceny-theft, 3,489; and motor vehicle theft, 691. In 1978, Los Angeles reported 233,344 crimes (including 651 murders); San Francisco, 70,385 (118 murders); and San Diego, 66,838 (68 murders).

California's death penalty statute received its most serious challenge after the 1948 conviction of Caryl Chessman on a charge of forcible rape. Chessman served 12 years on death row at San Quentin, got eight stays of execution, and wrote a best-seller about his ordeal. Despite highly publicized attempts to overturn capital punishment and save Chessman's life, the legislature refused to act, and he was executed in 1960. The death penalty was carried out 30 times in California from 1960 to 1967—more than in any other state—but, as of early 1980, it had not been used since that time.

17 ARMED FORCES

California leads the 50 states in defense contracts received, numbers of National Guardsmen and military veterans, veterans' benefit payments, and funding for police forces.

In 1976, the US Department of Defense had 330,544 personnel in California, including 197,438 servicemen and 133,106 civilians. Army military personnel totaled 23,778, the Navy (including Marines) 118,748, and the Air Force 54,912. The Army's principal base, Fort Ord at Monterey, had 18,807 personnel in 1978; other bases are located at Oakland and San Francisco. Naval facilities in the San Diego area had more than 88,000 personnel in 1978; there are weapons stations at Concord and Seal Beach, and supply depots at Oakland and San Pedro. The Marine Corps training base, Camp Pendleton at Oceanside, had 32,706 personnel. The Air Force operates three main bases—McClellan AFB at Sacramento, Travis AFB at Fairfield, and Norton AFB at San Bernardino—and numerous smaller installations. In 1978, California companies were awarded $10.5 billion in defense contracts, twice the total for Texas (which ranked 2d), and about 17% of the US total.

As of 30 September 1979, 3,343,000 veterans of US military service, 11% of the national total, were living in California. Of those, 56,000 served in World War I, 1,430,000 in World War II, 734,000 in the Korean conflict, and 995,000 during the Viet-Nam era. Veterans' benefits paid to Californians in 1977/78 exceeded $1.9 billion, or 10% of the US total. About 40% went for compensation and pensions, 29% for medical services and administrative costs, 23% for education and training, and 8% for insurance and other payments.

California's military forces consist of the Army and Air National Guard, the naval and state military reserve (militia), and

the California Cadet Corps. National Guard strength was about 22,000 in 1978. The governor summons National Guardsmen to active duty in order to fight forest fires, to help people evacuate their homes during floods or earthquakes, or to deal with other emergencies: about 14,000 Guardsmen helped restore order in the Watts section of Los Angeles during riots by black residents in August 1965.

In 1977, state and local police forces totaled 62,745, a figure that was ranked 2d only to New York's and represented 11% of the US total. Of these employees, 82% worked for county sheriff's offices and city police departments, and 18% for the state. Expenditures for police protection by state and local governments in 1976/77 were nearly $1.4 billion, or almost 14% of national expenditures.

18 MIGRATION

A majority of Californians today are migrants from other states.

The first great wave of migration, beginning in 1848, brought at least 85,000 prospectors by 1850. Perhaps 20,000 of them were foreign-born, mostly from Europe, Canada, Mexico, and South America, plus a few from the Hawaiian Islands and China. Many thousands of Chinese were brought in during the latter half of the 19th century to work on farms and railroads. When Chinese immigration was banned by the US Congress in 1882, Japanese migration provided farm labor. These ambitious workers soon opened shops in the cities and bought land for small farms. By 1940, about 94,000 Japanese lived in California. During the depression of the 1930s, approximately 350,000 migrants came to California, most of them looking for work. Many thousands of people came there during World War II to take jobs in the burgeoning war industries; after the war, some 300,000 discharged servicemen settled in the state. All told, between 1940 and 1977, California registered a net gain from migration of 8,722,000, representing about 60% of its population growth during that period.

Although the 1970s brought an influx of refugees from Indochina, the bulk of postwar foreign immigration has come from neighboring Mexico. At first, Mexicans—as many as 750,000 a year—were imported legally to supply seasonal labor for California growers. Later, hundreds of thousands—perhaps even millions—of illegal Mexican immigrants crossed the border in search of jobs and then, unless they were caught and forcibly repatriated, stayed on. Counting these state residents for census purposes is extremely difficult, since many of them are unwilling to declare themselves for fear of being identified and deported.

Intrastate migration has followed two general patterns: rural to urban until the mid-20th century, and urban to suburban thereafter. In particular, the percentage of blacks increased in Los Angeles, San Francisco, and San Diego between 1960 and 1970, as black people settled or remained in the cities while whites moved into the surrounding suburbs. In the 1970s, intrastate migration spilled over from the suburbs into outlying rural areas. From 1970 to 1977, metropolitan Los Angeles–Long Beach actually lost 389,000 people, and metropolitan San Francisco–Oakland suffered a net loss of 27,000. But metropolitan San Diego, where living space was more plentiful, gained 237,000 through migration during the same period.

19 INTERGOVERNMENTAL COOPERATION

The Commission on Interstate Cooperation, established in the late 1970s, develops plans for improved cooperation between California and other states, and with the federal government, and represents California in the Council of State Governments and its allied organizations. The Colorado River Board of California represents the state's interests in negotiations with the federal government and other states over utilization of Colorado River water and power resources. California also is a member of the Western States Water Council, the Klamath River Compact Commission (with Oregon), and the Tahoe Regional Planning

Agency (with Nevada). Regional agreements signed by the state include the Pacific Marine Fisheries Compact, Western Corrections Compact, Western Interstate Energy Compact, and Western Regional Education Compact. The Arizona-California boundary accord dates from 1963. California also is a member of the Commission of the Californias, along with the State of Baja California Norte and the territory of Baja California Sur, both in Mexico.

In 1978, federal aid to California exceeded $8.2 billion, including more than $774 million in general revenue sharing.

20ECONOMY

California leads the 50 states in economic output and total personal income. In the 1960s, when it became the nation's most populous state, California also surpassed Iowa in agricultural production and New York in value added by manufacturing. In 1978, the state ranked 1st in the US in such important industries as food products, machinery, electric and electronic equipment, aerospace, dairy production, and beef cattle. California also leads the nation in retail sales, foreign trade, and corporate profits. If California were an independent country, it would be one of the world's leading economic powers, outranking Canada, Italy, and Brazil.

The gold rush of the mid-19th century made mining (which employed more people than any other industry until 1870) the principal economic activity and gave impetus to agriculture and manufacturing. Many unsuccessful miners took up farming or went to work for the big cattle ranches and wheat growers. In the 1870s, California became the most important cattle-raising state and the 2d-leading wheat producer. Agriculture soon expanded into truck farming and citrus production, while new manufacturing industries began to produce ships, metal products, lumber, leather, cloth, refined sugar, flour, and other processed foods. Manufacturing outstripped both mining and agriculture to produce goods valued at $258 million by 1900, and 10 times that by 1925. Thanks to a rapidly growing work force, industrial output continued to expand during and after both world wars, while massive irrigation projects enabled farmers to make full use of the state's rich soil and favorable climate.

By the late 1970s, a highly diversified economy appeared to make California less vulnerable to national recession than most other states. In 1978, the booming economy produced an increase of nearly 14% in total personal income, created about 500,000 new jobs, reduced the unemployment rate from 8.2% to 7.1%, and produced a record $22.6 billion in pretax corporate profits. The 1977 gross state product exceeded $220 billion, or 12% of the gross national product. In the late 1970s, one of every four California workers was employed in high technology industry. On the other hand, inflation has hit Californians harder than residents of most other states. In 1979, the consumer price index in Los Angeles rose 15.7%, compared with the US rate of 13.3%; the city was especially vulnerable to rising gasoline prices and housing costs.

A report published in March 1978 by the Wells Fargo Bank predicted that high economic growth rates would continue into the 1980s. Assuming an increase in population to 26 million by 1990, the survey forecasted rises in personal income to $253 billion in constant dollars (for an annual rate of 3.6%), in per capita income to $9,900, in median family income to almost $23,000, and in jobholders to 12.5 million. The analysts concluded that the state would keep its lead in advanced technologies for military and space applications, and that demand for the state's farm products would continue to grow. The report warned, however, that increasing labor costs and higher taxes might dampen economic growth by reducing productivity.

21INCOME

With a per capita income of $8,850 in 1978, California ranked 5th among the 50 states and 13% above the national average.

Total personal income exceeded $197 billion—nearly 12% of the US total, one-third more than in New York State, and nearly double the total for Texas. Measured in constant 1972 dollars, total personal income increased 60% during the 1960s and 37% between 1970 and 1978. Median family income was $15,069 in 1975 (11th in the US).

Despite California's relatively high average personal income, 2,192,000 state residents in 472,000 families were below the federal poverty level in 1975. On a percentage basis, however, these totals were slightly below the national averages. California is justly noted for its large number of wealthy residents, particularly in the Los Angeles, Sacramento, and San Francisco metropolitan areas. In 1972, 1,237,600 individuals were among the nation's top wealthholders; only New York had more. According to federal income tax returns for 1977, 39,376 Californians had adjusted gross incomes of more than $100,000, including 324 with incomes exceeding $1,000,000.

In 1978, total disposable income, after state and federal income taxes, amounted to $172.5 billion, or $7,738 per capita. The major sources of personal income were wages and salaries, 64%; property, 14%; transfer payments, 13%; proprietor's income, 7%; and other sources (net), 2%.

The following table shows the sources of Californians' earned income (without property income and transfer payments) for 1975 and 1978 (in millions):

	1975	1978
Manufacturing	$ 22,523	$ 32,758
Services	19,584	30,470
Government	22,081	27,357
Wholesale and retail trade	18,278	26,159
Transportation, communications, and public utilities	7,650	10,915
Finance, insurance, and real estate	5,416	9,400
Contract construction	5,435	8,933
Agriculture	3,551	4,005
Mining	633	960
Other	670	1,758
TOTALS	$105,821	$152,715

22LABOR

California has the largest work force in the nation and the greatest number of employed workers. During the 1970s, its work force also grew at a higher annual rate than of any other state in the US.

In 1978, the state's labor force totaled 10,632,000, of whom 9,877,000 (92.9%) were employed and 755,000 (7.1%) unemployed. The labor force increased by more than 4% in 1978, compared with the US rate of 3%, and the number of employed workers rose by 6%.

Of the total 1978 labor force, 58% was male and 42% female. A large majority of the 1978 work force was employed in metropolitan areas, including 3,216,100 (33% of all employees) in the Los Angeles–Long Beach area, 1,475,200 (15%) in the San Francisco–Oakland area, 644,100 (7%) in the San Diego area, and 621,600 (6%) in metropolitan San Jose.

All together, 6,696,345 workers covered by unemployment insurance were employed in nonagricultural industries in 1977. The following table shows insured employment data for principal industry groups in 1977:

	ESTABLISH-MENTS	EMPLOYEES	ANNUAL PAYROLL ('000)
Agricultural services, forestry, fishing	6,054	43,294	$ 426,176
Mining, of which:	1,192	38,749	711,436
Oil, gas extraction	(746)	(22,980)	(409,126)
Contract construction	39,837	374,270	6,420,365

	ESTABLISH-MENTS	EMPLOYEES	ANNUAL PAYROLL ('000)
Manufacturing, of which:	40,232	1,751,309	25,084,336
Food products	(2,370)	(148,200)	(2,139,197)
Apparel and textiles	(3,588)	(104,141)	(801,736)
Printing and publishing	(5,154)	(101,950)	(1,310,262)
Fabricated metals	(3,946)	(134,226)	(1,350,044)
Nonelectrical machinery	(6,006)	(172,952)	(2,606,468)
Electric, electronic equipment	(2,683)	(224,379)	(3,199,925)
Transportation equipment	(1,682)	(267,443)	(4,689,543)
Transportation, public utilities, of which:	15,760	442,887	7,400,965
Trucking and warehousing	(7,628)	(102,504)	(1,573,411)
Wholesale trade	35,697	467,281	6,848,014
Retail trade	126,517	1,431,332	11,236,304
Finance, insurance, real estate, of which:	47,158	532,481	6,305,511
Banking	(4,193)	(142,683)	(1,478,991)
Real estate	(22,784)	(111,778)	(1,125,494)
Services, of which:	145,546	1,601,967	16,732,856
Health services	(37,364)	(445,302)	(5,202,880)
Other	7,951	12,775	163,632
TOTALS	465,944	6,696,345	$81,329,595

Among the workers not covered by this federal census were government employees, of whom California had 1,762,600 in 1978; 314,900 were federal employees, and 1,447,700 were employed by state and local governments. Full-time workers in the state civil service, 115,052 as of 31 March 1979, were studied in detail by the California State Personnel Board. Of these state workers, 38% were women and 62% men. Women most often were employed in clerical, nonsupervisory, and subprofessional categories; their average salary represented 80% of the average for all full-time employees. In the same year, 76% of the work force was white and 24% of other races: 14% were Hispanic, 6% black, 2% Asian, and the remaining 2% Filipino, American Indian, or other. Whites were most often employed as craftsmen, tradesmen, technicians, labor supervisors, administrators, and professional persons. Minority workers, on the other hand, were most heavily represented in the unskilled and semiskilled, nonsupervisory, clerical, and subprofessional categories.

The unemployment rate during most of the 1970s ranged from the 1978 low of 7.1% to a high of 9.9% in 1975, but the average rate was considerably higher than the 5–6% rate registered in the 1960s. From 1967 to 1976, an average of 226,000 Californians entered the labor market each year, but the economy generated only about 175,000 jobs annually, so unemployment rose steadily. Although the unemployment rate was 9.2% in 1976, the number of Californians working that year increased by a record 358,000.

The labor movement in California was discredited by acts of violence during its early years. On 1 October 1910, a bomb explosion at a *Los Angeles Times* plant killed 21 workers, resulting in the conviction and imprisonment of two labor organizers a year later. Another bomb explosion, this one killing 10 persons in San Francisco on 22 July 1916, led to the conviction of two radical union leaders, Thomas Mooney and Warren Billings; the death penalty for Mooney was later commuted to life imprisonment (the same sentence Billings had received), and after evidence had been developed attesting to his innocence, he was pardoned in 1939. These violent incidents led to the state's Criminal Syndicalism Law of 1919, which forbade "labor violence" and curtailed militant labor activity for more than a decade.

Unionism revived during the depression of the 1930s. In 1934, the killing of two union picketers by San Francisco police during a strike by the International Longshoremen's Association led to a three-day general strike that paralyzed the city, and the union eventually won the demand for its own hiring halls. In Los Angeles, unions in such industries as automobiles, aircraft, rubber, and oil refining obtained bargaining rights, higher wages, and fringe benefits during and after World War II. In 1958, the California Labor Federation was organized, and labor unions have since increased both their membership and their benefits. As of July 1977 there were 3,412 union locals with 2,173,100 members, of whom 26% worked in manufacturing, 15% in construction, 14% in government, 14% in commerce, 9% in transportation and warehousing, 7% in food processing, and 15% in other sectors. Of the total union membership, 38% worked in Los Angeles County and 23% in the San Francisco–Oakland metropolitan area. Women, who comprised 27% of union members, were most heavily represented in services, government, and food processing. About 476,000 Californians belonged to employee associations in 1976, when organized workers made up 32% of all nonfarm labor.

Of all working groups, migrant farm workers have been the most difficult to organize because their work is seasonal and because they are largely members of minority groups, mostly Mexicans, with few skills and limited job opportunities. During the 1960s, a Mexican-American "stoop" laborer named Cesar Chavez established the National Farm Workers Association (later the United Farm Workers Organizing Committee, now the United Farm Workers of America), which after a long struggle, won bargaining rights from grape, lettuce, and berry growers in the San Joaquin Valley. Chavez's group was helped by a secondary boycott against these California farm products at some grocery stores throughout the US. When his union was threatened by the rival Teamsters Union in the early 1970s, Chavez got help from the AFL-CIO and from Governor Brown, who in 1975 pushed through the state legislature a law mandating free elections for agricultural workers to determine which union they wanted to represent them. The United Farm Workers and Teamsters formally settled their jurisdictional dispute in 1977 with a five-year agreement.

In 1978, production workers in manufacturing industries worked an average of 40.1 hours per week and earned average weekly wages of $257.84, ranging from a low of $147.90 in the clothing industry to a high of $382.82 in the oil industry. Average weekly earning in industries other than manufacturing ranged from $196.42 in retail trade to $493.85 for electrical work in contract construction. In 1977, California had 409 strikes and other work stoppages, involving 144,000 workers and 2,911,200 workdays lost; the aerospace industry was the hardest hit.

23 AGRICULTURE

California leads the 50 states in agricultural production. With only 3% of the nation's farms and farm acreage, the state accounts for 10% of US cash farm receipts. Unique in having no single crop that dominates the agricultural economy, California ranked 1st among the 50 states in production of no fewer than 48 farm commodities in 1978. Famous for its specialty crops, California produces virtually all the almonds, apricots, avocados, broccoli, dates, figs, nectarines, olives, pomegranates, safflower, and walnuts grown commercially in the US. California's total agricultural production was valued at $10.4 billion in 1978, up 11% from the previous year.

Agriculture has always thrived in California. The Spanish missions and Mexican ranchos were farming centers until the mid-19th century, when large ranches and farms began to produce cattle, grain, and cotton for the national market. Wheat was a major commodity by the 1870s, when the citrus industry was established and single-family farms in the fertile Central Valley and smaller valleys started to grow large quantities of fruits and vegetables. European settlers planted vineyards on the slopes of the Sonoma and Napa valleys, thus beginning the important California wine industry, which now provides some 70% of US domestic wines. Around 1900, intensive irrigation transformed the dry, sandy Imperial Valley in southeastern California into a garden of abundance for specialty crops. Since World War II, large corporate farms, or agribusinesses, have largely replaced the small one-family farm. Today, the state grows about 40% of all fruits marketed in the US, as well as much of its grains and vegetables, and farm commodities account for one-fifth of the state's foreign exports.

Less than one-third of California's total land area was devoted to farming in 1979, when some 60,000 farms comprised about 32 million acres (13 million hectares). According to US Department of Agriculture estimates, the average size of a farm was 538 acres (218 hectares), well above the US average of 450 acres (182 hectares). Approximately one-fourth of all farmland is used to grow crops, and some 95% of all cropland is under irrigation.

The leading cash crops in 1978 were grapes (used for the table, for raisins, and especially for wine), cotton, and lettuce. The following table shows harvested acreage, production, value, and US rank of the 15 leading cash crops in 1978:

	ACRES (1,000)	PRODUCTION (1,000 TONS)	VALUE (1,000)	US RANK
Grapes	621.4	3,879.0	$863,936	1
Cotton	1,445.1	1,270.6	690,501	2
Lettuce	159.4	2,217.5	456,320	1
Hay	1,610.0	6,955.0	413,823	6
Tomatoes	262.7	5,672.1	481,138	1
Nursery products	—	—	357,573	1
Flowers and plants	—	—	290,996	1
Almonds	300.0	90.0	252,000	1
Oranges	187.4	1,575.0	247,920	2
Walnuts	179.8	160.0	217,600	1
Rice	499.0	1,312.4	201,847	2
Wheat	715.0	1,374.8	149,066	13
Strawberries	13.7	256.9	147,814	1
Peaches	63.3	815.5	136,310	1
Sugar beets	195.0	4,778.0	126,139	2

In recent years, increased capitalization and the use of advanced technology have enabled agribusiness to control the entire agricultural process from planting through marketing. The number of corporate farms increased by 35% from 1969 to 1974. Agribusiness now employs about 750,000 workers, of whom only 40% are involved in field work. Some 80% of all farm labor is hired.

Irrigation is essential for farming in California, and agriculture consumes 85% of the state's water supply. The major irrigation systems include the Colorado River Project, which had irrigated 500,000 acres (200,000 hectares) in the Imperial Valley by 1913; the Central Valley Project, completed by 1960, which harnessed the runoff of the Sacramento River; the Feather River Project, also in the Central Valley and finished during the 1970s; and the largest of all, the California Water Project, begun in 1960 and completed in its essentials by 1973. On 16 June 1980, the US Supreme Court ended 13 years of litigation by ruling that federally subsidized irrigation water in the Imperial Valley could not be limited to family farms of fewer than 160 acres (65 hectares) but must be made available to all farms regardless of size; the ruling represents a major victory for agribusiness interests.

[24] ANIMAL HUSBANDRY

California is a leading producer of livestock and dairy products, which together accounted for 31% of the state's farm income in 1978. In that year, cash receipts for meat animals totaled $1.4 billion; dairy products, $1.2 billion; and poultry and eggs, $631 million.

Beef cattle, raised principally in the Central Valley, were California's chief farm product in 1978, when sales of cattle and

calves totaled more than $1.3 billion (7th in the US); 1979 sales were $1.8 billion (6th). At the end of 1979 there were 4,550,000 cattle and calves, 1,175,000 sheep and lambs, and 180,000 hogs and pigs on California farms and ranches. In 1979, cash sales of sheep and lambs for slaughter totaled $55.4 million (3d in the US); hogs and pigs, $36 million.

California is the 2d-leading milk producer (behind Wisconsin) among the 50 states. In 1978, milk and cream products ranked 2d among the state's farm commodities by value, with sales of more than $1.2 billion. Milk cows, raised mainly in the southern interior, totaled 860,000 head in 1979.

California ranked 1st among the 50 states in egg production in 1979, with total sales of $368.6 million, based on an output of 8.7 billion eggs. The state was 3d in production of turkeys; the 18.9 million birds sold weighed 377.1 million lb and were valued at $154.6 million. In 1978, 122 million chickens (both broilers and fryers) were produced for market, bringing cash receipts of $168.1 million (9th in the US). Laying hens and turkey breeder hens, raised chiefly in the central part of the state, numbered 37.1 million in 1979.

California is the nation's leading producer of honey and beeswax, and ranks 3d in production of wool. In 1978, output of honey totaled 31,248,000 lb (valued at $13,999,000); beeswax, 554,000 lb ($981,000); and wool, 10,117,000 lb ($7,385,000).

[25] FISHING

The Pacific whaling industry, with its chief port at San Francisco, was important to the California economy in the 19th century, and commercial fishing is still central to the food-processing industry. In 1978, California ranked 3d in the US in commercial fishing, with a catch of 722.3 million lb; the value of the catch, $228.2 million, ranked 2d only to Alaska's.

As of March 1978, the California fishing fleet numbered 8,261 vessels; there were 16,911 commercial fishermen. In 1977, principal species caught and total landings included tuna, 326,785,000 lb; anchovy, 222,953,000 lb; mackerel, 112,283,000 lb; shellfish, 51,809,000 lb (mostly crab and shrimp); sole, 31,603,000 lb; squid, 28,244,000 lb; rockfish, 24,135,000 lb; bonito, 22,548,000 lb; and salmon, 5,921,000 lb.

The fish-processing industry in 1977 produced 13,284,552 cases of canned fish, 42,216 tons of fish meal, and 1,358,450 gallons of fish oil. Fish canneries are located at San Francisco, San Diego, San Pedro, and Monterey.

Deep-sea fishing is a popular sport. Anglers fishing from licensed party boats landed 5,149,493 saltwater fish in 1976; rockfish accounted for 70% of the catch.

[26] FORESTRY

California has more forests than any other state except Alaska. Forested lands in 1977 covered 40,152,000 acres (16,249,000 hectares), representing 40% of the state's land area and 5.4% of the US total. Nearly 41% of the state's forested area is used to produce commercial timber, and California ranks 2d among the 50 states in lumber production and 3d in volume of standing timber.

Forests are concentrated in the northwest part of the state and in the eastern Sierra Nevada. Commercial forestland in private hands was estimated at 7,628,000 acres (3,087,000 hectares) in 1977; an additional 8,569,000 acres (3,468,000 hectares) of nationally owned or managed forests and 106,000 acres (43,000 hectares) of state forests were available for commercial cutting. In that year, the growing stock of commercial timber was estimated at 49.7 billion board feet. Production of timber totaled 4.4 billion board feet in 1978. The volume of sawtimber totaled 263.7 million board feet, mostly such softwoods as fir, pine, cedar, and redwood.

According to the US census of manufactures, the lumber and wood products industry in 1977 employed 58,500 production workers, paid them a total of $677.4 million, and shipped finished wood products valued at more than $4.5 billion. Principal wood products in that year included finished lumber, $1.7 billion; wood mobile homes, $570 million; wooden household furniture, $375 million; and kitchen cabinets, $203 million. Production of wood pulp for paper products is also important; shipments of paper and paper products had a value of $3.3 billion in 1977.

About half of the state's forests are protected as national forests and state parks or recreational areas. Although stands of giant redwood trees have been preserved in national and state parks since the late 19th century, only about 15% of the original 2,000,000 acres (800,000 hectares) of redwoods between Monterey Bay and southern Oregon remain.

Reforestation of public lands is supervised by the National Forest Service and the California Department of Forestry. In 1924–25, more than 1.5 million redwood and Douglas fir seedlings were planted in the northwestern corner of the state. During the 1930s, the Civilian Conservation Corps replanted trees along many mountain trails, and the California Conservation Corps performed reforestation work in the 1970s.

In California's dry climate, forests are particularly vulnerable to devastating fires. In 1978, 326 forest fires caused by lightning and 8,170 human-caused fires burned 88,586 acres (35,850 hectares) of forested land.

[27] MINING

California ranks 3d among the 50 states in value of mineral production and is the nation's leading producer of sand and gravel, asbestos, and boron ores. In 1978, California's mineral output was estimated at $4.4 billion, of which fossil fuels accounted for $3 billion and all other minerals $1.4 billion.

Some 40 minerals are mined in commercial quantities in California, chiefly in the Sierra Nevada range in the eastern part of the state. Gold and silver are still extracted, though not in the quantities of the gold rush days; in 1978, 4,560 troy oz of gold (valued at $879,000) and 55,000 troy oz of silver ($297,000) were produced. Other metals include copper (260 tons in 1978, valued at $345,000), mercury, tungsten, iron, lead, and zinc. Industrial boron ores have been mined in Death Valley and other desert areas since 1885.

Most mining and quarrying centers around such basic construction minerals as cement, gypsum, lime, clays, stone, and sand and gravel. In 1977 there were 1,192 mining establishments, of which 61 mined minerals, 311 produced nonmetallic minerals (except fuels), and 746 extracted oil and gas. In that year, 38,749 employees covered by unemployment insurance were engaged in mining, including 6,916 workers in nonmetallic minerals and 22,980 in oil and gas extraction.

The following table shows preliminary 1978 production and value figures for the state's principal nonmetallic minerals:

	VOLUME (TONS)	VALUE
Cement	8,989,000	$445,045,000
Boron ores	1,520,000	260,000,000
Sand and gravel	110,000,000	258,000,000
Stone	34,025,000	81,120,000
Diatomite	389,000	44,648,000
Lime	523,000	19,219,000
Asbestos	69,000	17,402,000
Clays	2,461,000	13,428,000
Gypsum	1,590,000	9,323,000
Talc	109,816	5,630,000
Pumice	640,000	4,040,000

[28] ENERGY AND POWER

In 1980, petroleum supplied an estimated 60% of the state's energy needs, natural gas 25%, nuclear power 6%, hydroelectric power 5%, coal 3%, and geothermal sources 1%. California ranks 2d among the 50 states in production of electric power, 3d in crude oil, and 6th in natural gas. Despite its ample energy re-

sources, California is a net importer of electric power because of its extensive industrial, residential, and commercial requirements.

Installed electric power capacity in 1978 was 37.1 million kw, of which 68% was privately owned. In that year, according to the California Energy Commission, electrical output totaled 150.6 billion kwh. About 40% was generated from oil, 25% from hydroelectric plants, 20% from natural gas, 7% from coal, 5% from nuclear power plants, 2% from geothermal sources, and the remaining 1% from other sources. When licensed for commercial operation, two Diablo Canyon nuclear reactors, completed in San Luis Obispo County during the late 1970s, would increase the number of nuclear power plants in the state to five and boost the combined nuclear electric-generating capacity to 3.6 million kw.

In 1977, sales of electric power in the state totaled 158.8 billion kwh, of which 34% went to commercial businesses, 32% to industries, 29% to home consumers, and 5% to other users. The state's private electric utilities in 1978 sold 116.7 billion kwh of electricity to 7 million customers. Largely because of the mild California climate, utility bills are lower than in many other states. According to the California Public Utilities Commission, of the 25 largest US cities in June 1978, San Francisco had the lowest average monthly bill for home electric, gas, and telephone service ($28.85), Los Angeles ranked 3d lowest ($34.54), and San Diego was the 5th least expensive ($36.39).

The petroleum and natural gas industries are of paramount importance in supplying California's energy requirements. Although crude oil was discovered in Humboldt and Ventura counties as early as the 1860s, it was not until the 1920s that large oil strikes were made at Huntington Beach, near Los Angeles, and at Santa Fe Springs and Signal Hill, near Long Beach. These fields added vast pools of crude oil to the state's reserves, which were further augmented in the 1930s by the discovery of large offshore oil deposits in the Long Beach area. The state's attempts to retain rights to tideland oil reserves as far as 30 mi (48 km) offshore were denied by the US Supreme Court in 1965; state claims were thus restricted to Monterey Bay and other submerged deposits within a 3-mi (5-km) offshore limit. In late 1979, oil from the US Navy's petroleum reserves at Elk Hills, in Kern County, was sold by the US Department of Energy to private oil companies at a cost of $41 a barrel—a move that helped to alleviate the domestic oil shortage but also to drive up crude oil prices throughout the US. The state's largest oil company in 1979 was Standard Oil of California, with headquarters in San Francisco; its sales totaled $29.9 billion (4th among US oil companies, and 6th among all US industrial corporations) and assets $18.1 billion.

California's proved oil reserves as of 31 December 1978 were estimated at nearly 3.5 billion barrels, more than 12% of the US total and 3d behind Alaska and Texas. Petroleum production totaled 347 million barrels, representing more than 11% of the domestic output. Production of natural gas totaled 305 billion cu feet, 1.6% of the US total, and proved reserves exceeded 5 trillion cu feet (2.5%). In 1977 there were 42,292 producing oil wells and 1,123 active natural gas wells in the state. Virtually all the coal consumed for electric power generation is shipped in from other states.

California has been a leader in developing solar and geothermal power as alternatives to fossil fuels. State tax credits encourage the installation of solar energy devices in commercial and residential property.

[29] INDUSTRY

California is the nation's leading industrial state, ranking 1st in almost every general manufacturing category—number of establishments, number of employees, total payroll, value added by manufacture, and value of shipments—and 2d only to Texas in new capital spending. Specifically, California ranks among the leaders in machinery, fabricated metals, food processing, computers, aerospace technology, and many other industries.

With its shipyards, foundries, flour mills, and workshops, San Francisco was the state's first manufacturing center. The number of manufacturing establishments in California nearly doubled between 1870 and 1900, and the value of manufactures increased almost tenfold from 1900 to 1925. New factories for transportation equipment, primary metal products, chemicals, and food products sprang up in the state during and after World War II. Second to New York State in industrial output for many years, California finally surpassed that state in most major manufacturing categories in the 1972 census of manufactures.

According to the 1977 census, value added by manufacture totaled $55.5 billion, the value of manufactures' shipments was $121.4 billion, and new capital spending amounted to nearly $3.5 billion. Of the total value added, transportation equipment accounted for 17%; electric and electronic equipment, 12%; food and food products, 12%; nonelectrical machinery, 10%; fabricated metal products, 7%; chemicals and chemical products, 6%; printing and publishing, 5%; clothing and textiles, 4%; and other sectors, 27%. The following table shows value added by manufacturing for selected industries in 1972 and 1977:

	1972	1977
Guided missiles, space vehicles	NA	$2,690,100,000
Radio and television equipment	NA	2,572,500,000
Aircraft	NA	2,543,600,000
Petroleum refinery products	$594,600,000	2,345,200,000
Electronic computing equipment	888,200,000	2,154,200,000
Semiconductors, related devices	NA	1,120,600,000
Newspapers	654,700,000	1,050,200,000
Aircraft equipment	835,700,000	1,014,800,000
Commercial printing	533,000,000	874,200,000
Canned fruits and vegetables	521,800,000	847,300,000
Bakery products	454,600,000	727,600,000
Drugs	245,900,000	660,800,000
Household furniture	395,500,000	657,000,000
Blast furnace products	345,300,000	527,600,000
Paperboard containers and boxes	310,800,000	521,700,000
Metal cans	NA	513,000,000
Meat products	286,100,000	499,400,000
Toys and sporting goods	229,400,000	464,100,000
Wines and brandies	297,600,000	406,600,000

Nearly half of all industrial employees were engaged in manufacturing transportation equipment, electrical and electronic equipment, nonelectrical machinery, and food products; more than two-thirds worked in the Los Angeles–Long Beach, Oakland–San Francisco, and San Jose metropolitan areas. Los Angeles is among the nation's leading cities in aircraft and automobile production. Among the many new industries established in San Diego, Oakland, Fresno, and Stockton, as well as Los Angeles, after World War II were the western plants of such corporate giants as Aluminum Co. of America, Carnation, Goodyear Tire and Rubber, Heinz, International Harvester, Johns-Manville, Kraft, Lever Brothers, Procter and Gamble, Swift (now Esmark), and US Steel.

The important aerospace and electronics industries in southern California produce highly sophisticated missiles and space vehicles. Major commercial aircraft plants located in the region include those of McDonnell Douglas and Lockheed, which has corporate headquarters in Burbank; other principal aerospace contractors include Rockwell International, Hughes, General Dynamics, and TRW. These six companies received 40% of all contracts awarded by the National Aeronautics and Space Administration in 1978. Another center of the state's electronics industry is in Santa Clara County, known as "Silicon Valley." Memorex, National Semiconductor, and Intel are among the firms based in the region. Of the $10 billion in defense contracts received by all California firms in 1976/77, 27% went for missile

and space systems, 20% for military aircraft, and 18% for electronic and communications equipment.

The Wells Fargo study issued in 1978 forecast that the aerospace, electronic, chemical, and food-processing industries would continue to grow steadily during the 1980s, while the primary metals and forest industries would not show significant expansion.

³⁰COMMERCE

Reflecting its rank in population, California led the nation in retail trade in 1977, but was 2d to New York State in wholesale trade in 1972 (the latest year for which data were available).

California's wholesale trade in 1972 totaled $62.3 billion, about 9% of the US total. Durable goods accounted for 53% of total wholesale sales, and nondurable goods for the remaining 47%. Of the total sales of durable goods in that year, motor vehicles and automotive parts made up 27%; metals and minerals (excluding petroleum), 11%; sporting goods and recreational supplies, 4%; furniture and home furnishings, 3%; and other categories, 55%. Of the nondurable goods, groceries and related products accounted for nearly 40%; petroleum products, 14%; clothing and fabrics, 6%; agricultural raw materials, 5%; and other items, 35%.

The state's 1977 retail sales amounted to $81.1 billion, for 11% of the US total. Of total 1977 sales, food stores accounted for 21%; automobile dealers, 20%; general merchandise stores, 13%; eating and drinking places, 10%; gasoline service stations, 7%; and other establishments, 29%. Taxable 1978 sales at all outlets totaled $113.5 billion, of which Los Angeles accounted for 11%; San Francisco, 4%; San Diego, 3%; and San Jose, 2%. The principal retail commodities in 1978, in order of sales volume, were automobiles, department store merchandise, gasoline, food and liquor, building materials, household furnishings, and drugs.

Foreign trade is important to the California economy. About 400,000 workers are employed directly and indirectly in foreign trade. In 1976, California's foreign exports were estimated at $11.5 billion and imports at $15.3 billion. The state's leading trade partner was Japan, which took 17% of its exports and supplied 32% of its imports. Australia, Oceania, and other Asian countries together took 56% of California's exports, West European countries received 15%, and the rest of the world purchased 12%. Of 1976 exports by value, aerospace and electronics equipment accounted for 36%, food products for 20%, machinery 18%, and other commodities 26%. California's principal import in 1976 was petroleum, which comprised 21% of the state's imports by value; the major source of petroleum was Indonesia, which accounted for 10% of all the state's 1976 imports. Electrical machinery and equipment made up 17% of the import value, and transportation equipment (mostly automobiles) added 14%.

California's customs districts are the ports of Los Angeles, San Francisco, and San Diego. San Francisco and San Jose have been designated as federal foreign-trade zones, where imported goods may be stored duty-free for reshipment abroad, or customs duties avoided until the goods are actually marketed in the US.

³¹CONSUMER PROTECTION

The State and Consumer Services Agency, headed by the secretary for state and consumer affairs, embraces the Department of Consumer Affairs, Department of Veterans Affairs, State Personnel Board, public employees and teachers' retirement systems, and certain other state agencies. The Department of Consumer Affairs administers the California Consumer Affairs Act and oversees the administrative and financial affairs of the various state agencies that regulate automotive, radio, and television repair shops, collection agencies, employment services, tax preparers, funeral establishments, cemeteries, and boxing, wrestling, and karate matches. The department also supervises the licensing boards for physicians, nurses, dentists, pharmacists, optometrists, veterinarians, civil engineers, construction contractors, social workers, accountants, barbers, cosmetologists, and other professionals who serve the public. The Consumer Advisory Council recommends to the director of the department those laws it considers necessary to protect and promote the interests of consumers.

The assistant attorney general for consumer law, within the Department of Justice, pursues criminal cases affecting consumers, while the assistant attorney general for environment and consumer protection has responsibility in civil matters.

³²BANKING

In 1848, California's first financial institution—the Miners' Bank—was founded in San Francisco. Especially since 1904, when A. P. Giannini founded the Bank of Italy, now known as the Bank of America, California banks have pioneered in branch banking for families and small businesses. Today, California is among the leading states in branch banking, savings and loan associations, and credit union operations.

In 1978, California's 230 commercial banks, with 3,911 branches, employed about 240,000 persons. Of the total number of institutions, 77% were state banks and 23% were national banks. These banks had total assets of $143 billion, 2d only to New York State, and held more than 11% of all US commercial bank assets; state banks had 26% of the total, and national banks 74%. Loans in 1978 totaled $82.9 billion, 35% of which were mortgage loans and 30% commercial and industrial loans. In the same year, commercial bank deposits exceeded $113.4 billion, 64% time deposits and 36% demand deposits.

The largest bank in California—and the world's largest in 1978—was the Bank of America, with deposits of $79 billion. BankAmerica Corp., the bank's holding company, held $102.9 billion in assets as of 31 March 1980, 2d behind Citicorp (the parent company of Citibank) in New York City. Security Pacific National Bank and United California Bank, both of Los Angeles, and Wells Fargo Bank and Crocker National Bank, both of San Francisco, were also among the nation's top 20 commercial banks in 1978.

California's savings and loans associations, whose assets consist largely of home mortgage loans, benefited during the 1970s from the booming real estate market. In 1977, these institutions accounted for nearly 19% of outstanding mortgage loans and 17% of total savings deposits of all US savings and loan associations; these percentages far exceeded those of any other state. As of 31 December 1978 there were 170 such institutions in California, with total assets of $95.5 billion. Their outstanding mortgage loans totaled $80.8 billion, and their savings deposits amounted to $74.9 billion.

California credit unions accounted for more than 13% of the national totals for both loans outstanding and deposits at the end of 1975. As of 31 December 1977, the state's 1,720 credit unions had 4,597,507 members, had issued loans totaling $4.5 billion, and held assets of $8.2 billion. From 1969 to 1976, they registered annual growth rates of nearly 14% for deposits and 12% for loans.

A forecast by Wells Fargo projected that by 1990, deposits of commercial banks would grow to $310 billion; of savings and loans, $260 billion; and of credit unions, $25 billion. Wells Fargo's analysts predicted a similar growth in total loans outstanding to $211 billion by 1990 for both commercial banks and savings and loan associations, and to more than $20 billion for credit unions.

The State Banking Department administers laws and regulations governing state-chartered banks, foreign banking corporations, and trust companies.

³³INSURANCE

Insurance companies provide a major source of California's investment capital by means of premium payments collected from policyholders. Life insurance companies also invest heavily in real estate; in 1975, life insurance firms held an estimated $12 billion in mortgage debt on California properties. Insurance carriers employed more than 112,000 Californians in 1977.

In 1978, California's 54 life insurance companies paid benefits of $2.8 billion (2d in the US). Nearly 30.7 million policies were in force, with a total value of $280.1 billion. The average California family held $31,300 worth of life insurance, 11% below the US norm.

Multiline companies offer fire, casualty, and health insurance. In 1978, premiums paid for health insurance totaled $4.3 billion; automobile casualty insurance, $1.2 billion; and fire insurance, $317 million.

The Department of Insurance licenses insurance companies and brokers, reviews policy forms, regulates rates for workers' compensation, and collects taxes on insurance premiums.

³⁴SECURITIES

California's Pacific Stock Exchange (PSE), the largest securities market in the US outside New York City, is an association of some 300 member brokers who provide an auction market for the stocks, options, and bonds of national and local corporations. The exchange, which operates trading floors in Los Angeles and San Francisco, was established in 1957 to combine the separate exchanges in those cities. Between 1957 and 1979, the volume of shares traded increased tenfold, to more than 357 million.

As of April 1980, the PSE listed 1,060 stocks, warrants, and bonds for trading. The total included 87 issues traded exclusively on the PSE; virtually all of the remainder were also traded on New York stock exchanges. Because of the time difference between the east and west coasts, the PSE begins trading at 7 A.M. PST and stays open until 2:30 P.M. PST, one and a half hours after the New York exchanges have closed. As of 21 April 1980, a seat on the Pacific Stock Exchange cost $16,000.

In 1978, New York Stock Exchange member firms had 406 sales offices and 5,677 full-time registered representatives in California. State residents reported $3.1 billion in dividend income on their federal income tax returns in 1977.

The Department of Corporations enforces laws and regulations governing the sale of securities and the activities of agents, brokers, and investment advisers.

³⁵PUBLIC FINANCE

California's general budget is the largest of all the states' in both expenditures and revenues. The state's public finances became the focus of national attention when, on 6 June 1978, California voters approved Proposition 13, a constitutional amendment that reduced local property taxes by more than 50%. This new measure—which slashed the average tax rate per $100 of assessed value from $10.68 in 1977/78 to $4.78 in 1978/79—threatened to impair the public services of county and municipal governments, whose funds came largely from property taxes, by cutting their total revenues by $6.8 billion. The state legislature acted promptly to save essential public services by funding $4.2 billion from the state government's budget surplus to the counties, cities, towns, and school districts, and by increasing user fees and other public charges. Two byproducts of Proposition 13 were the reduction of government employment by 30,000 as of November 1978, and drastic cuts in the state's budget surplus for 1979/80 and future years. Proposition 9, a constitutional amendment that would have cut the state's personal income tax by half, was defeated by the voters in June 1980.

The state budget is prepared by the Department of Finance and presented by the governor to the state legislature for approval. The fiscal year lasts from 1 July through 30 June. The governor's budget request more than doubled from $11.3 billion in 1975 to about $24 billion in 1980, largely because of inflation and because of the state's increased aid to local governments as a result of Proposition 13. Consolidated state revenues for the

1977/78 fiscal year totaled $15.7 billion, state expenditures $13.8 billion.

The following table summarizes consolidated revenues and expenditures for 1978/79 (estimated) and 1979/80 (recommended), in millions:

	1978/79	1979/80
REVENUES		
Sales and use taxes	$ 5,700.0	$ 6,375.0
Personal income tax	4,747.0	4,840.0
Bank and corporation tax	2,287.0	2,460.0
Motor vehicle license and registration fees	955.7	1,057.6
Motor vehicle fuel tax	885.5	913.0
Insurance tax	432.0	480.0
Inheritance and gift taxes	405.3	452.4
Cigarette tax	274.2	281.4
Alcoholic beverage tax	141.5	150.2
Horse racing fees	119.0	126.0
Other receipts	1,193.1	1,155.6
TOTALS	$17,140.3	$18,291.2
EXPENDITURES		
General government[1]	$ 6,665.9	$ 2,360.2
Local fiscal relief	—	4,378.0
Education	5,628.5	5,799.9
Health and welfare	4,739.4	5,139.5
Business and transportation	1,122.5	1,129.7
Resources	512.7	396.2
State and consumer services	234.3	203.4
Other expenditures	326.8	259.0
TOTALS	$19,230.1	$19,665.9

[1]Includes $4.3 billion in emergency relief to localities in 1978/79.

A comparison of city budgets for 1976/77 shows that Los Angeles ranked 2d (behind New York City) among large US cities in expenditures with $1.7 billion, San Francisco 7th with $910 million, and San Diego 31st with $257 million. The following table shows consolidated revenues and expenditures for Los Angeles in 1977/78 (estimated) and 1978/79 (proposed), in millions:

	1977/78	1978/79
REVENUES		
Property taxes	$ 302.8	$ 337.1
Sales tax	117.5	144.1
Utilities tax	70.0	90.3
Business tax	75.9	84.7
Licenses, permits, fees, fines	65.4	71.0
Other receipts and transfers	408.8	448.5
TOTALS	$1,040.4	$1,175.7
EXPENDITURES		
Police	$ 224.0	$ 223.3
Public works	159.2	166.3
Fire and police pensions	116.1	146.1
Fire protection	97.6	98.7
City employees' retirement	60.2	68.7
Personnel	51.7	49.1
Recreation and parks	29.7	29.9
Other expenditures	250.6	393.6
TOTALS	$989.1	$1,175.7

California's total public debt exceeded $21.1 billion as of 30 June 1977, 2d only to New York State's. The per capita debt of $965 ranked only 26th among the 50 states, however. At the end of 1978, bonds outstanding from the California state government totaled $5.8 billion.

[36] TAXATION

In the mid-1970s, Californians were paying more in taxes than residents of any other state. On a per capita basis, California ranked 3d among the 50 states in state and local taxation in 1977, but this heavy tax burden of $1,089 per person was reduced by the passage in 1978 of Proposition 13. The state ranked 12th in federal income tax per capita in 1977.

In 1979/80, California's revenues from state taxes and fees totaled nearly $18.3 billion. Of this total, the state sales tax provided 35%, personal income tax 26%, bank and corporation tax 13%, and other taxes 26%.

The state's progressive income tax rates in 1979 ranged from 1% on the 1st $2,000 to 11% on net taxable income over $15,000. Low-income tax credits exempted single people with earnings of less than $5,000 and married couples earning less than $10,000 from paying state income taxes. An income tax credit of 55% or $3,000, whichever was less, applied to the cost of purchasing and installing solar energy systems in the home. The state corporate franchise and income tax was 9% of net income from California sources; a minimum franchise tax of $200 applied to all firms except banks, whose net income was taxed at rates ranging up to 13%.

The state sales tax in 1979 was 6% on retail sales (excepting food for home consumption and prescription medicines); of that 6%, 4.75% represented the basic state rate, 1% was designated for localities, and 0.25% was a county tax for the support of local transit systems. A surtax of 0.5% was levied in the San Francisco, Santa Clara, and Santa Cruz transit districts, of which half was used for metropolitan transit systems. Other state taxation includes inheritance and gift taxes, insurance tax, motor vehicle fees, cigarette tax, alcohol beverage tax, and pari-mutuel betting fees.

Localities derive most of their revenue from property taxes, which were limited in 1978 by Proposition 13 to 1% of market value, with annual increases in the tax not to exceed 2%. The drastic revision reduced property tax collections by about 57% to an estimated $4.9 billion in the 1978/79 fiscal year. The tax rate per $100 of assessed property value for Los Angeles County fell from $12.40 in 1977/78 to $4.78 in 1978/79; for San Francisco County, from $11.82 to $5.06; and for Alameda County, from $12.59 to $5.19. In 1978/79, the state provided $4.2 billion in fiscal relief for local governments to make up for local revenues lost by property tax reductions that were mandated by the adoption of Proposition 13.

In 1977, California bore a heavier share of the federal tax burden than any other state, contributing $38.3 billion in federal taxation, or 11% of the US total. But California also received more federal expenditures than any other state—$47.2 billion, for a net benefit of $8.9 billion. In that year, California ranked 1st among the states in federal income tax payments, which exceeded $17.6 billion, based on 9.3 million returns.

[37] ECONOMIC POLICY

In 1978, California established the Department of Economic and Business Development. The department seeks to stimulate the economy and to serve as an ombudsman between business and government. Responsible both for encouraging new businesses to locate in the state and for assisting established industries to expand, the department supplies information to interested companies concerning site locations, labor conditions, wage rates, and other relevant factors. It provides loan guarantees for small businesses and long-term loans to industries that create permanent jobs. The department also prepares studies on the potential economic impact of a new business, and assists manufacturers and agribusinesses to expand their foreign trade.

Several other state agencies administer business aid programs. The California Pollution Control Financing Authority helps businesses to install mandated antipollution devices by providing long-term low-cost loans from the sale of state revenue bonds. The Office of Permit Assistance expedites the review of permit applications for community development projects submitted to public agencies for approval. Local nonprofit corporations in many communities help to finance industrial development in cooperation with the federal government.

Perhaps the most important tax incentive offered to business during the 1970s was the large reduction in local property taxes as a result of Proposition 13; nearly 60% of the total tax reduction affected industrial and commercial properties. In addition, a tax credit applies to the cost of installing solar energy equipment in commercial and industrial buildings.

38 HEALTH

California ranked 17th among the 50 states in average life expectancy in 1969–71. The average for both sexes was 71.71 years, nearly a year above the national average. Women lived an average of 75.37 years, men 68.19 years.

Vital statistics bear out, to some extent, California's reputation for unconventional life-styles. In 1977, California had the lowest marriage rate—6.8 per 1,000 population—of any state. All told, 140,000 licensed marriages were registered (3d behind Texas and New York); another 32,008 nonlicensed marriages were also recorded. California's divorce rate, 6 per 1,000 population, was 20% above the national average, and the state had far more divorces (132,200) than any other. California also led the US in number of legal abortions, with 209,900 during 1977/78, although its abortion rates of 612 per 1,000 live births and 42 per 1,000 women 15–44 years of age both ranked 2d to New York State's. Because of its large population, California led the nation in live births in 1977 with 348,000; the birthrate of 15.9 was slightly above the US average. The infant death rate in 1977 was 15 per 1,000 live births for nonwhites and 11.4 for whites; both rates were well below the US norm.

California registered 176,578 deaths in 1978, including 4,188 infant deaths, 2,726 neonatal deaths, and 36 maternal deaths. California ranked below the national average in death rates for 8 of the 10 leading causes of deaths (the exceptions were cirrhosis of the liver and suicide), according to data compiled for 1977 by the US National Center for Health Statistics. In that year, the leading causes of death were heart diseases, which accounted for 35% of all deaths, and cancer, which caused 22%. Principal causes of death and their rates per 100,000 population during 1977, as compiled for the US National Center for Health Statistics, included diseases of the heart, 60,263 (275); malignant neoplasms, 37,256 (168); cerebrovascular diseases, 16,688 (76); accidents, 10,078 (48); cirrhosis of the liver, 4,399 (20); pneumonia and influenza, 4,196 (19); and suicide, 3,918 (18). California led the US in number of homicide victims, with 2,559.

In 1978, the California Department of Health recorded 146,195 cases of venereal disease: 135,064 cases of gonorrhea and 11,083 of syphilis, with 31 deaths. Other reported diseases included 19,723 cases of streptococcal infections, with 23 deaths; 9,459 viral hepatitis, 81 deaths; 4,084 shigellosis; 3,353 tuberculosis, 235 deaths; 2,719 salmonellosis, 16 deaths; 1,100 German measles or rubella; and 1,096 coccidioidomycosis, 47 deaths. More than 5,000 persons were treated for narcotic addiction at California rehabilitation centers. According to 1970 estimates the state had 833,400 alcoholics; only Nevada had a higher estimated rate per 100,000 population. The state declared as rehabilitated 1,036 alcoholics and 455 drug addicts in 1977/78.

As of 30 June 1979, six state hospitals for the mentally disordered had 5,208 patients. During the 1978/79 fiscal year, these hospitals admitted 20,238 patients and discharged an estimated 19,070. In recent years, an increasing number of patients have been treated through community mental health programs rather than in state hospitals; 3,437,586 outpatient visits were reported by local facilities in 1976/77.

In 1978, California had 562 general care hospitals, with 107,889 beds; 50 psychiatric hospitals, 11,468 beds; 1,160 skilled nursing facilities, 106,470 beds; and 36 intermediate care institutions, 2,040 beds. Outpatient care was offered by 560 institutions. The state's hospitals admitted more than 3,300,000 patients and had an average of nearly 80,000 patients daily, with a bed occupancy

rate of 69%. Hospital personnel included more than 59,000 registered nurses and 24,000 licensed practical nurses. Total operating costs were $8 billion. Health insurance payments to community hospitals in 1977 exceeded $4.4 billion. The average cost per patient was $291 a day, highest in the US and far above the national average cost of $198. The average cost per stay, $1,918, was less than that in the District of Columbia, Massachusetts, and New York, but higher than that of 47 states.

Medical personnel licensed to practice in California included 50,088 physicians (1977) and 14,052 dentists (1979). California had some 3,500 nursing homes with 124,500 resident patients in 1976.

Under Medi-Cal, a statewide program that pays for the medical care of individuals who otherwise could not afford it, 2,776,779 Californians received more than $2.8 billion in medical benefits. Enrolled in the program were 403,999 elderly persons, 379,876 disabled persons, and 13,278 blind persons. Also through Medi-Cal, the state funded renal dialysis for a monthly average of 77 patients, at an annual cost of $592,387. California has also been a leader in developing new forms of health care. One increasingly popular system, called the health maintenance organization (HMO), provides preventive care, diagnosis, and treatment for which the patient pays a fixed annual premium.

39 SOCIAL WELFARE

A greater number of Californians receive public assistance than do residents of any other state. Federal, state, and local outlays for the five largest welfare programs in California exceeded $4.8 billion in 1976, 2d only to New York State and 13.5% of the US total.

In June 1978, payments in aid to families with dependent children (AFDC) went to 429,162 families with 965,650 children. Total AFDC payments in 1977/78 were nearly $1.8 billion, for an average monthly cost of $314.15 per family and $154.38 per child. During the same year, California county welfare departments granted basic subsistence payments for food, shelter, and clothing (general home relief) to 44,668 persons for a monthly average of $142.65 per person and an annual total of $76,462,065. A monthly average of 26,687 dependent children lived in boardinghouses and institutions; aid to their families totaled $131,194,186 during 1977/78 for an average monthly grant of $409.96 per child.

As of June 1978, food stamps were issued to 428,600 households comprising 1,230,014 persons, of whom 70% were receiving other forms of public assistance. In 1977/78, the value of food stamps issued totaled $631,014,566, of which 49% was paid by the recipients and 51% was provided by federal funds. The federal government also paid $161,700,000 in 1977/78 for the state's school lunch program, in which 1,850,000 pupils participated. This was double the number of pupils involved in the program in 1969/70, and the federal cost was nearly 15 times as great. Even so, the participation rate, 45% of eligible enrollment, was one of the lowest in the US. During 1977/78, 2,607 schools took part in a school breakfast program serving more than 330,000 breakfasts daily.

Federal Social Security benefits were paid in 1977 to 3,056,900 persons (9% of the US total), of whom 65% were retired workers, 20% received survivors' benefits, and 15% were disabled persons. In that year, payments totaled $7.9 billion—nearly equal with New York State—for an average monthly benefit to retired workers of $246.90.

As of February 1979, 700,047 Californians were enrolled in federal Supplemental Security Income (SSI) and state supplemental income programs. Of that number, 46% were aged, 52% disabled, and 2% blind. SSI monthly payments averaged $50.21 for the aged, $97.50 for the blind, and $109.20 for the disabled; the state supplements were $95.59, $138.37, and $109.20, respectively.

During 1977/78, 40,864 disabled persons received vocational training, of whom 14,028 were rehabilitated; the total cost of vocational training was nearly $90 million. California led the 50 states in workers' compensation payments in 1977 with a total of $1.1 billion, 13% of the national total and more than twice as much as the 2d-ranking state, New York. In that year, an average of 310,000 workers received weekly unemployment insurance benefits. Payments totaled $963 million, and the average monthly benefit was $75.84, 9% below the national average.

⁴⁰HOUSING

California leads the US both in the number of housing units built annually and in the value of their construction. The state also ranks 1st in the average cost of a new house: new homes in the Los Angeles area averaged more than $100,000 in 1980, nearly 50% above the national norm. Housing construction boomed at record rates during the 1970s but slowed down at the beginning of the 1980s because rising building costs and high mortgage interest rates made it difficult for people of moderate means to enter the housing market.

The earliest homes in southern California were Spanish colonial structures renowned for their simplicity and harmony with the landscape. These houses were one story high and rectangular in plan, with outside verandas supported by wooden posts; their thick adobe walls were covered with whitewashed mud plaster. In the north, the early homes were usually two stories high, with thick adobe walls on the ground floor, balconies at the front and back, and tile roofing. Some adobe houses dating from the 1830s still stand in coastal cities and towns, particularly Monterey.

During the 1850s, jerry-built houses of wood, brick, and stone sprang up in the mining towns, and it was not until the 1870s that more substantial homes, in the Spanish-mission style, were built in large numbers in the cities. About 1900, the California bungalow, with overhanging eaves and low windows, began to sweep the state and then the nation. The fusion of Spanish adobe structures and traditional American wooden construction appeared in the 1930s, and "California style" houses gained great popularity throughout the West. Adapted from the functional international style of Frank Lloyd Wright and other innovative architects, modern domestic designs, emphasizing split-level surfaces and open interiors, won enthusiastic acceptance in California. Wright's finest California homes include the Freeman house in Los Angeles and the Millard house in Pasadena. One of Wright's disciples, Viennese-born Richard Neutra, was especially influential in adapting modern design principles to California's economy and climate.

California continues to be a trend setter in housing construction. Since 1960, more than 4 million houses and apartments have been built in the state, comprising nearly half of California housing stock. The annual number of new dwelling units authorized during that period ranged from 322,018 in 1963 to a low of 99,375 in 1968, averaging about 215,000 a year throughout the 1970s. In 1978, 243,684 new units were authorized, of which 58% were single-family dwellings and 42% were multifamily units. The value of housing construction totaled $10.6 billion, of which single-unit structures accounted for $6.8 billion, multiunit structures $2.9 billion, and additions and alterations of existing homes more than $900 million.

Of the state's 6,574,000 occupied housing units in 1970, nearly 55% were occupied by the owner; 98.3% had full plumbing facilities. New houses have excellent electric and water supplies, and even old dwellings are usually well equipped with air conditioning, washing machines, television sets, and other amenities. By 1976, the state's housing stock had risen to an estimated 8,053,000 units, of which 64% were single-family dwellings, 33% were multifamily dwellings, and 3% were mobile homes.

According to US Bureau of Labor Statistics, the cost of a new home for urban workers in Los Angeles increased during 1979 by 30%, well above the national average. As of December 1979, it was estimated that 24,000 homes and condominiums in the Los Angeles metropolitan area remained unsold. The rapid rise in housing costs that began in 1975 was attributed not only to inflation but also to increased demand, restrictive housing codes that reduced the availability of home sites, and heavy speculative investment in the housing market by foreign buyers.

Analysts for the Wells Fargo Bank forecast that more than 200,000 new dwelling units would be required annually to meet housing needs during the 1980s. Of the total units, 55% would be single-family dwellings, assuming that state residents would continue to prefer—and could still afford—real property as a hedge against inflation. The forecasters maintained that the cost of new housing would continue to increase more rapidly than the overall cost of living, but not at the rapid rates of the late 1970s, unless there were severe construction restrictions. Expectations were that numerous townhouse condominiums would be built during the 1980s because of their relatively low-cost construction and maintenance, and that about 10% of all new housing units would be mobile homes.

California housing policies have claimed national attention on several occasions. In 1964, state voters approved Proposition 14, a measure repealing the Fair Housing Act and forbidding any future restrictions on the individual's right to sell, lease, or rent to anyone of his own choosing. The measure was later declared unconstitutional by state and federal courts. In March 1980, a Los Angeles city ordinance banned rental discrimination on the basis of age. A municipal court judge had previously ruled it was illegal for a landlord to refuse to rent an apartment to a couple simply because they had children. Ordinances banning age discrimination had previously been enacted in the cities of San Francisco, Berkeley, and Davis, and in Santa Monica and Santa Clara counties.

⁴¹EDUCATION

California ranks 1st among the states in number of public and private schools, public school pupils, college students, high school and college graduates, and total funding for educational purposes. According to the US National Center for Education Statistics, California's current expenditure on public schools in 1977/78 was $1,674 per pupil (20th in the US), based on average daily attendance.

The history of public education in California goes back at least to the 1790s, when the governor of the Spanish colony assigned retired soldiers to open one-room schools at the Franciscan mission settlements of San Jose, Santa Barbara, San Francisco, San Diego, and Monterey. Most of these schools, and others opened during the next three decades, were short-lived, however. During the 1830s, a few more schools were established for Spanish children, including girls, who were taught needlework.

Easterners and midwesterners who came to California in the 1840s laid the foundation for the state's present school system. The first American school was opened in an old stable at the Santa Clara mission in 1846, and the following year a schoolroom was established in the Monterey customhouse. San Francisco's first school was founded in April 1848 by a Yale graduate, Thomas Douglass, but six weeks later, caught up in the gold rush fever, he dropped his books and headed for the mines. Two years after this unauspicious episode the San Francisco city council passed an ordinance providing for the first free public school system in California. Although the first public high school was opened in San Francisco in 1856, the California legislature did not provide for state financial support of secondary schools until 1903.

The state's first colleges, Santa Clara College (now the University of Santa Clara), founded by Jesuits, and California Wesleyan (now the University of the Pacific), located in Stockton, both opened in 1851. A year later, the Young Ladies' Seminary was founded at Benicia. The nucleus of what later became the University of California was established at Oakland in 1853 and moved to nearby Berkeley in 1873. Subsequent landmarks in education were the founding of the University of Southern California (USC) at Los Angeles in 1880 and of Stanford University in 1885, the opening of the first state junior colleges in 1917, and the establishment in 1927 of the Department of Education, which supervised the vast expansion of the California school system in the years following.

Perhaps the outstanding characteristics of public education in the state have been the emphasis placed on practical knowledge, through extensive vocational training programs, and the establishment of coordinating councils representing various community groups to work with educators in shaping school policies. More recent innovations include a state program to ensure educational continuity for some 70,000 children of migrant Mexican farm workers by enabling them to carry their school records back and forth between Mexico and California.

As of 1970, the illiteracy rate among Californians was 1.1%, slightly better than the national average. About 74% of the state's adult population were high school graduates in 1976; of the population aged 18–24, more than 80% were high school graduates. In addition, about 2,474,000 Californians were college graduates, representing nearly 17% of the adult population. The percentage of adults with no more than 4 years of grade school was small—only 3.3% in 1976—but the numerical total, 482,000, was 2d only to that in Texas. Adult Californians had completed a median of 12.7 school years in 1976.

During the 1977/78 school year, California's 7,471 public schools enrolled 4,157,000 pupils. Elementary schools had 2,815,552 pupils, and high schools 1,341,448. In that year, the number of high school graduates totaled 278,553. There were 183,470 teachers and 29,665 other professionals in the public school system. Also in 1977/78, 2,967 private schools enrolled 450,611 pupils, and had 22,879 full-time teachers. During the 1978/79 school year there were 587 Roman Catholic elementary schools with 181,405 pupils, and 72 parochial and diocesan high schools with 43,356 pupils.

As of 1 March 1979, the University of California, a state university, enrolled 127,881 students; the California state college and university system (which should not be confused with the University of California), 306,175; private colleges and universities, 177,851; community colleges, 1,170,773; and private two-year colleges, 6,058. Academic degrees conferred by state and private four-year colleges in 1977/78 totaled 117,359, including 82,364 baccalaureate degrees, 30,689 masters degrees, and 4,306 doctorates.

The University of California has its main campus at Berkeley and branches at Davis, Irvine, Los Angeles (UCLA), Riverside, San Diego, San Francisco, Santa Barbara, and Santa Cruz. California's 16 state universities include those at Los Angeles, Sacramento, San Diego, San Francisco, and San Jose; state colleges are located at Bakersfield, San Bernardino, and Stanislaus.

Privately endowed institutions with the largest student enrollments are USC (with 15,319 undergraduates in 1978) and Stanford University (6,559). Other independent institutions include Occidental College in Los Angeles, Mills College at Oakland, Whittier College, Claremont University Center (including Harvey Mudd College, Pomona College, and Claremont Men's College), and the California Institute of Technology at Pasadena. Thirteen Roman Catholic colleges and universities, including Loyola Marymount University of Los Angeles, enrolled 29,879 students in 1979.

California's public school system is directed by the Department of Education, which is headed by the state superintendent of public instruction, elected on a nonpartisan ballot every four years. The University of California is governed separately by a board of regents which includes, ex officio, the state governor, lieutenant governor, speaker of the assembly, and superintendent of public instruction, along with the university president and the president and vice president of the alumni association.

The four state officials also serve on the board of trustees which administers the state colleges and universities. The California Student Aid Commission supervises three financial assistance programs: Cal Grant A, for needy and academically able undergraduates; Cal Grant B, specifically for disadvantaged students; and Cal Grant C, for students in occupational programs. Funding for these programs in 1980/81 was budgeted at more than $88 million, of which the federal government contributed more than $12 million. There were nearly 69,000 grants, more than three-fifths of them Grant A scholarships; the average scholarship was $1,368 per student per year. The commission also administers the California Guaranteed Student Loan Program and the State Graduate Fellowship Program. All recipients must have been California residents for at least 12 months.

Revenues for the public schools in 1977/78 totaled $9 billion, of which local property taxes furnished about 52%, state aid 40%, federal assistance 6%, and miscellaneous sources 2%; local contributions fell and state aid increased as a result of Proposition 13. State general fund expenditures totaled $1.7 billion for public schools in 1977/78. About 71% of that went for teachers' and other employees' salaries, 12% for employee benefits, 8% for school operating expenses, 6% for books and supplies, and 3% for other outlays. Elementary school teachers were paid an average annual salary of $16,328, and high school teachers averaged $17,909.

[42] ARTS

The arts have always thrived in California—at first in the Franciscan chapels with their religious paintings and church music, later in the art galleries, gas-lit theaters, and opera houses of San Francisco and Los Angeles, and today in seaside artists' colonies, regional theaters, numerous concert halls, and, not least, in the motion-picture studios of Hollywood.

In the mid-19th century, many artists came from the East to paint western landscapes, and some stayed on in California. The San Francisco Institute of Arts was founded in 1874; the E. B. Crocker Art Gallery was established in Sacramento in 1884; and the Monterey-Carmel artists' colony sprang up in the early years of the 20th century. Other art colonies developed later in Los Angeles, Santa Barbara, Laguna Beach, San Diego, and La Jolla. Notable art museums and galleries include the Los Angeles County Museum of Art (founded in 1910), Huntington Library, Art Gallery and Botanical Gardens at San Marino (1919), San Francisco Museum of Modern Art (1921), the Norton Simon Museum of Art at Pasadena (1924), and the San Diego Museum of Art (1925).

The theater arrived in California as early as 1846 in the form of stage shows at a Monterey amusement hall. The first theater building was opened in 1849 in Sacramento by the Eagle Theater Co. Driven out of Sacramento by floods, the company soon found refuge in San Francisco; by 1853, that city had seven theaters. During the late 19th century many famous performers, including dancer Isadora Duncan and actress Maude Adams, began their stage careers in California. Today, California theater groups with national reputations include the American Conservatory Theater of San Francisco, Berkeley Repertory Theater, Mark Taper Forum in Los Angeles, and Old Globe Theater of San Diego.

The motion-picture industry did not begin in Hollywood—the first commercial films were made in New York City and New Jersey in the 1890s—but within a few decades this Los Angeles suburb had become synonymous with the new art form. California became a haven for independent producers escaping an East-Coast monopoly on patents related to filmmaking. (If patent infringements were discovered, the producer could avoid a lawsuit by crossing the border into Mexico.) In 1908, an independent producer, William Selig, completed in Los Angeles a film he had begun in Chicago, *The Count of Monte Cristo*, which is now recognized as the first commercial film produced in California. He and other moviemakers opened studios in Los Angeles, Santa Monica, Glendale, and—finally—Hollywood, where the sunshine was abundant, land was cheap, and the work force plentiful. These independent producers developed the full-length motion picture and the star system, utilizing the talents of popular actors like Mary Pickford, Douglas Fairbanks, and Charlie Chaplin again and again. In 1915, D. W. Griffith produced the classic "silent," *The Birth of a Nation*, which was both a popular and an artistic success. Motion-picture theaters sprang up all over the country, and an avalanche of motion pictures was produced in Hollywood by such increasingly powerful studios as Warner Brothers, Fox, and Metro-Goldwyn-Mayer. Hollywood became the motion-picture capital of the world. By 1923, film production accounted for one-fifth of the state's annual manufacturing value; and in 1930, the film industry was one of the 10 largest in the US.

Hollywood flourished by using the latest technical innovations and by adapting itself to the times. Sound motion pictures achieved a breakthrough in 1927 with *The Jazz Singer*, starring Al Jolson; color films appeared within a few years; and Walt Disney originated the feature-length, animated cartoon with *Snow White and the Seven Dwarfs* (1937). Whereas most industries suffered drastically from the depression of the 1930s, Hollywood prospered by providing, for the most part, escapist entertainment on a lavish scale. The 1930s saw the baroque spectacles of Busby Berkeley, the inspired lunacy of the Marx Brothers, and the romantic historical drama *Gone With the Wind* (1939). During World War II, Hollywood offered its vast audience patriotic themes and pro-Allied propaganda.

In the postwar period, the motion-picture industry fell on hard times because of competition from television, but it recovered fairly quickly by selling its old films to television and producing new ones specifically for home viewing. In the 1960s, Hollywood replaced New York City as the main center for the production of television programs. Fewer motion pictures were made, and those that were produced were longer and more expensive, including such top box-office attractions as *The Sound of Music* (1965), *The Godfather* (1972), *Jaws* (1975), *Star Wars* (1977), and *The Empire Strikes Back* (1980). No longer are stars held under exclusive contracts, and the power of the major studios has waned as the role of independent filmmakers like Francis Ford Coppola and George Lucas has assumed increased importance.

Among the many composers who came to Hollywood to write film music were Irving Berlin, George Gershwin, Kurt Weill, George Antheil, Ferde Grofe, and Erich Korngold; such musical luminaries as Igor Stravinsky and Arnold Schoenberg were long-time residents of the state. Symphonic music is well established. In addition to the renowned Los Angeles Philharmonic, whose permanent conductors have included Zubin Mehta and Carlo Maria Giulini, there are the San Francisco Symphony and other professional symphonic orchestras in Oakland and San Jose. Some 160 semiprofessional or amateur orchestras have been organized in other communities. Resident opera companies perform regularly in San Francisco and San Diego. Annual musical events include the Monterey Jazz Festival and summer concerts at the Hollywood Bowl.

California has also played a major role in the evolution of popular music since the 1960s. The "surf sound" of the Beach Boys dominated California pop music in the mid-1960s, and was supplanted by the "acid rock" of bands like the Grateful Dead, the Jefferson Airplane (now the Jefferson Starship), and the Doors, which had started to gain national recognition by 1967—heralded as the "summer of love" in San Francisco. It was at the Monterey International Pop Festival, also in 1967, that Jimi Hendrix began his rise to stardom. During the 1970s, California was strongly identified with a group of resident singer-songwriters, including Neil Young, Joni Mitchell, Randy Newman, Jackson Browne, and Warren Zevon, who brought a new sophistication to rock lyrics. Los Angeles is a main center of the popular-music industry, with numerous recording studios and branch offices of the leading record companies.

California has nurtured generations of writers, many of whom moved there from other states. In 1864, Mark Twain, a Missourian, came to California as a newspaperman. Four years later, New York–born Bret Harte published his earliest short stories, many set in mining camps, in San Francisco's *Overland Monthly*. The writer perhaps most strongly associated with California is Nobel Prize–winner John Steinbeck, a Salinas native. Hollywood's film industry has long been a magnet for writers, and San Francisco in the 1950s was the gathering place for a group, later known as the Beats (or "Beat Generation"), that included Jack Kerouac and Allen Ginsberg. The City Lights Bookshop, owned by poet Lawrence Ferlinghetti, was the site of readings by Beat poets during this period.

[43] LIBRARIES AND MUSEUMS

In 1978, California had 156 main public libraries with 543 branches, 448 smaller library stations, and 98 bookmobiles; the book stock exceeded 45 million volumes. The state's 182 academic libraries contained 38.3 million volumes; in addition, 483 special libraries had nearly 5.7 million volumes. Circulation of all library materials in 1977/78 totaled 152.7 million.

California has three of the largest public library systems in the nation, along with some of the country's finest private collections. The Los Angeles Public Library System had 5,364,882 volumes in 1977/78; the San Francisco Public Library, 1,642,683; and the San Diego Public Library, 1,560,443. Outstanding among academic libraries is the University of California's library at Berkeley with its Bancroft collection of western Americana. Stanford's Hoover Institution has a notable collection of research materials on the Russian Revolution, World War I, and worldwide relief efforts thereafter. Numerous rare books and manuscripts, as well as many valuable documents on American history, are held in the Huntington Library in San Marino.

California has more than 300 museums and historical sites. Outstanding museums include the California Museum of Science and Industry, Los Angeles County Museum of Art, and Natural History Museum, all in Los Angeles; the San Francisco Museum of Modern Art, Fine Arts Museums of San Francisco, and Asian Art Museum of San Francisco; the San Diego Museum of Man; the California State Indian Museum in Sacramento; and the Norton Simon Museum in Pasadena. Among historic sites are Sutter's Mill, northeast of Sacramento, where gold was discovered in 1848; and a restoration of the Mission of San Diego de Alcala, where in 1769 the first of California's Franciscan missions was established. San Diego has an excellent zoo, and San Francisco's Strybing Arboretum and Botanical Gardens has beautiful displays of Asian, Mediterranean, and California flora.

[44] COMMUNICATIONS

Mail service in California, begun in 1851 by means of mule-drawn wagons, was soon taken over by stagecoach companies. The need for speedier delivery led to the founding in April 1860 of the Pony Express, which operated between San Francisco and Missouri. On the western end, relays of couriers picked up mail in San Francisco, carried it by boat to Sacramento, and then conveyed it on horseback to St. Joseph, Mo., a hazardous journey of nearly 2,000 mi (3,200 km) within ten days. The Pony Express functioned for only 16 months, however, before competition from the first transcontinental telegraph line (between San Francisco and New York) put it out of business; telegraph service between San Francisco and Los Angeles had begun a year earlier. Today, mail is conveyed by the US Postal Service, which had 72,500 employees in the state in 1977. Postal receipts in Los Angeles were nearly $252 million in 1977/78.

California has more telephones than any other state. In 1978 there were 19,123,465 telephones, 13,608,641 residential and 5,514,824 business. About 78% of the state's telephones were owned and operated by Bell System affiliates. On average, 99% of all households had telephone service. In 1978, the telephone system had 106,485,329 mi (171,371,839 km) of wire in cable—farther than the distance from the earth to the sun—121,574 mi (195,655 km) of aerial wire, 23,879 mi (38,430 km) of coaxial cable, and 14,986 mi (24,118 km) of radio relay system. Californians made 24.7 billion local calls and 3.8 billion toll calls during the same year.

The state's first radio broadcasting station, KQW in San Jose, began broadcasting speech and music on an experimental basis in 1912. California stations pioneered in program development with the earliest audience-participation show (1922) and the first "soap opera," *One Man's Family* (1932). When motion-picture stars began doubling as radio performers in the 1930s, Hollywood emerged as a center of radio network broadcasting. Similarly, Hollywood's abundant acting talent, experienced film crews, and superior production facilities enabled it to become the principal production center for television programs from the 1950s onward.

California ranks 1st in the US in the number of commercial television stations, and 2d only to Texas in radio stations. In 1978 there were 231 AM and 194 FM radio stations, and 56 television stations; Los Angeles alone had 35 radio and 8 television stations. Los Angeles is also the home of the Pacifica Foundation, which operated 6 listener-sponsored radio stations (2 in Berkeley, one in Los Angeles, and 3 outside the state). Affiliates of the Public Broadcasting System serve Los Angeles, San Francisco, and Sacramento. In 1978, 284 systems provided cable television service to 1,814,516 subscribers in 811 communities.

⁴⁵PRESS

California's newspapers rank 1st in number and 2d in circulation among the 50 states. Los Angeles publishes one of the nation's most influential dailies, the *Los Angeles Times*, and San Francisco has long been the heart of the influential Hearst newspaper chain.

In August 1846, the state's first newspaper, the *Californian,* first published in Monterey, printed (on cigarette paper—the only paper available) the news of the US declaration of war on Mexico. The *Californian* moved to San Francisco in 1847 to compete with a new weekly, the *California Star*. When gold was discovered both papers failed to mention the fact, and both soon went out of business as their readers headed for the hills. On the whole, however, the influx of goldseekers was good for the newspaper business. In 1848, the *Californian* and the *Star* were resurrected and merged into the *Alta Californian*, which two years later became the state's first daily newspaper; among subsequent contributors were Mark Twain and Bret Harte. Four years later there were 57 newspapers and periodicals in the state.

The oldest continuously published newspapers in California are the *Sacramento Bee* (founded in 1857), San Francisco's *Examiner* (1865) and *Chronicle* (1868), and the *Los Angeles Times* (1881). *Times* owner and editor Harrison Gray Otis quickly made his newspaper preeminent in Los Angeles—a tradition continued by his son-in-law, Henry Chandler, and by the Otis-Chandler family today. Of all California's dailies, the *Times* is the only one with a depth of international and national coverage to rival the major east coast papers. In 1887, young William Randolph Hearst took over his father's *San Francisco Daily Examiner* and introduced human interest items and sensational news stories to attract readers. The *Examiner* became the nucleus of the Hearst national newspaper chain, which later included the *News–Call Bulletin* and *Herald Examiner* in Los Angeles. The *Bulletin*, like many other newspapers in the state, ceased publication in the decades following World War II because of rising costs and increased competition for readers and advertisers.

In 1978 there were 29 morning dailies with an average circula-

tion of 3,499,428 and 97 evening dailies with 2,702,310 circulation (these figures include all-day newspapers), plus 47 Sunday newspapers with 5,484,375 average circulation. The *Los Angeles Times* is the only California paper whose daily circulation exceeds 1 million. The following table shows California's leading newspapers, with their average circulations for 1978:

AREA	NAME	DAILY	SUNDAY
Fresno	Bee (m,S)	120,909	143,259
Long Beach–	Independent (m,S)	64,263⎱	135,200
Huntington Beach	Press Telegram (e,S)	77,120⎰	
Los Angeles	Herald Examiner (e,S)	316,206	320,721
	Times (m,S)	1,018,490	1,302,395
Oakland	Tribune (all day, S)	164,481	189,850
Orange County–	Register(m,e,S)	100,778(m)⎱	238,962
Santa Ana		109,566(e)⎰	
Sacramento	Bee (m,S)	176,604	210,360
	Union (m,S)	103,252	103,621
San Diego	Evening Tribune (e)	130,148	
	Union (m,S)	198,334	320,754
San Francisco	Chronicle (m,S)	493,948⎱	663,303
	Examiner (e,S)	157,192⎰	
San Jose	Mercury (m,S)	145,379⎱	254,497
	News (e,S)	67,332⎰	

⁴⁶ORGANIZATIONS

Californians belong to thousands of nonprofit societies and organizations, many of which have their national headquarters in the state.

National service organizations operating out of California include the National Assistance League, in Hollywood; Braille Institute of America, Los Angeles; and Knights of the Round Table International, Pasadena. Cultural and educational groups headquartered in the state are the Association for the Arts and Psychology, Sacramento; American Aviation Historical Society, Garden Grove; American Battleships Association, San Diego; American Society of Zoologists, Thousand Oaks; Childbirth Without Pain League, Dana Point; International Association for Childbirth at Home, Cerritos; and the Comparative and International Education Society, Los Angeles.

Environmental and scientific organizations include the Sierra Club, Friends of the Earth, and Save-the-Redwoods League, all with headquarters in San Francisco; American Ecologist Society and Animal Protection Institute of America, both in Sacramento; Geothermal Resources Council, Davis; and the Seismological Society of America, Berkeley.

Among entertainment-oriented organizations centered in the state are the Academy of Motion Picture Arts and Sciences and the Academy of Television Arts and Sciences, both in Beverly Hills; Directors Guild of America, Writers Guild of America (West), and National Association of Composers, all in Los Angeles; Screen Actors Guild and American Society of Cinematographers, both in Hollywood; and the National Academy of Recording Arts and Sciences, Burbank. Other commercial and professional groups include the Institute of Mathematical Statistics, San Carlos; Manufacturers' Agents National Association, Irvine; National Association of Civil Service Employees, San Diego; Pacific Area Travel Association, San Francisco; and Women's Army Corps Veterans Association, Oceanside.

The many national sports groups with California headquarters include the Association of Professional Baseball Players of America, Long Beach; Amateur Fencers League of America, Albany; US Hang Gliding Association, Los Angeles; National Hot Rod Association, Hollywood; International Jugglers Association, Anaheim; International Skateboard Association, Costa Mesa; Soaring Society of America, Santa Monica; American Surfing Association, Huntington Beach; and US Swimming Association, Fresno.

California also has Gamblers Anonymous, Los Angeles; Overeaters Anonymous, Torrance; and the National Investigations Committee on UFOs, Van Nuys.

⁴⁷TOURISM, TRAVEL, AND RECREATION

California's cornucopia of scenic and man-made wonders attracts millions of state residents, out-of-state visitors, and foreign tourists each year. In 1977, the state's travel industry received 11 cents of every travel dollar spent by Americans, earned about $13.5 billion in total receipts, and employed some 400,000 persons. Nearly 22 million people took trips to and through California, the highest total for any state. About 33% of all trips to the state were to visit relatives or friends, 25% for recreation, sightseeing, and entertainment, 20% for conventions or business reasons, and 22% for other purposes. California is the main destination of foreign visitors from Canada, Mexico, and Japan.

While the state's mild, sunny climate and varied scenery of seacoast, mountains, and desert lure many visitors, the San Francisco and Los Angeles metropolitan areas offer the most popular tourist attractions. San Francisco's Fisherman's Wharf, Chinatown, and Ghirardelli Square are popular for shopping and dining; tourists also frequent the city's unique cable cars, splendid museums, Opera House, and Golden Gate Bridge. The Golden Gate National Recreation Area, comprising 68 sq mi (176 sq km) on both sides of the entrance to San Francisco Bay, includes Fort Point in the Presidio park, Alcatraz Island (formerly a federal prison) in the bay, the National Maritime Museum with seven historic ships, and Muir Woods, located 17 mi (27 km) north of the city. This popular region had about 9 million visitors in 1978. South of the city, the rugged coastal scenery of the Monterey peninsula attracts many visitors; to the northeast, the wineries of the Sonoma and Napa valleys offer their wares for sampling and sale.

The Los Angeles area has the state's principal tourist attractions: the Disneyland amusement center at Anaheim, and Hollywood, which features visits to motion-picture and television studios and sight-seeing tours of film stars' homes in Beverly Hills. One of Hollywood's most popular spots is Mann's (formerly Grauman's) Chinese Theater, where the impressions of famous movie stars' hands and feet (and sometimes paws or hooves) are embedded in concrete. The New Year's Day Tournament of Roses at Pasadena is an annual tradition. Southwest of Hollywood, the Santa Monica Mountain National Recreation Area was created by Congress in 1978 as the country's largest urban park, covering 150,000 acres (61,000 hectares). The *Queen Mary* ocean liner, docked at Long Beach, is now a marine-oceanographic exposition center and hotel-convention complex.

The rest of the state offers numerous tourist attractions, including some of the largest and most beautiful national parks in the US. In the north are Redwood National Park and Lassen Volcanic National Park. In east-central California, situated in the Sierra Nevada, are Yosemite National Park, which drew 2.7 million visitors in 1978; towering Mt. Whitney in Sequoia National Park, which had 1 million visitors; and Lake Tahoe, on the Nevada border. About 80 mi (129 km) east of Mt. Whitney is Death Valley. Among the popular tourist destinations in southern California are the zoo and Museum of Man in San Diego's Balboa Park and the Mission San Juan Capistrano, to which, according to tradition, the swallows return each spring. The San Simeon mansion and estate of the late William Randolph Hearst is now a state historical monument.

As of 1 January 1979 there were more than 230 state parks, historic parks, reserves, and recreation areas of all types, covering more than 888,000 acres (359,000 hectares). In 1978/79, the state issued 2,763,684 angling licenses and 501,722 hunting licenses. Special permits to hunt wild fowl on public lands numbered 87,596, and deer and bear tags 303,534.

⁴⁸SPORTS

California is more heavily represented in professional sports than any other state, with five major league teams in baseball, four in football, two in basketball, and one in ice hockey. Los Angeles is represented by clubs in all these sports, and leads US cities in total sports attendance.

Los Angeles' baseball Dodgers (which moved from Brooklyn, N.Y., at the end of the 1957 season) play in Dodger Stadium, the football Rams in Anaheim Stadium, and the basketball Lakers and ice hockey Kings at the Forum arena. The neighboring California Angels baseball team uses Anaheim Stadium. San Francisco's baseball Giants (formerly of New York City) and football 49ers play in Candlestick Park. Oakland's baseball A's (Athletics) and football Raiders occupy the Oakland–Alameda County Coliseum; the Golden State Warriors' basketball team uses the Oakland Coliseum Arena. The baseball Padres and football Chargers both play at San Diego Stadium.

From 1972 to 1974, the Oakland A's, led by Jim "Catfish" Hunter, Vida Blue, and Reggie Jackson, won three World Series; between 1959 and 1978, the Los Angeles Dodgers captured seven National League pennants and three world championships with teams whose stars included Sandy Koufax, Don Drysdale, and Steve Garvey. The Giants, led by Hall of Famer Willie Mays, won a National League title in 1962. The Lakers have won two National Basketball Association championships, in 1972 (with Wilt Chamberlain) and 1980 (behind Kareem Abdul-Jabbar), and the Warriors one, in 1975. The Oakland Raiders defeated the Minnesota Vikings in the Super Bowl (played in Pasadena) in 1977. The Los Angeles Rams dominated their division throughout the 1970s, reaching the Super Bowl in 1980 but losing to the Pittsburgh Steelers.

Another popular professional sport is horse racing at such well-known tracks as Santa Anita and Hollywood Park. Because of the equable climate, there is racing in California virtually the whole year round. A pari-mutuel license fee of 5.5–7.45% returned $113 million to the state treasury in 1979/80, out of the total betting estimated at $1.7 billion.

California's teams have fielded powerhouses in collegiate sports. USC's baseball team won six national championships between 1970 and 1979, and the UCLA basketball team, coached by John Wooden, won seven consecutive NCAA Division I titles from 1967 through 1973; in all, UCLA captured an unprecedented ten NCAA titles in 12 years (1964–75). During the 1970s, three California collegiate football teams played in 9 of the 10 Rose Bowl games, winning 8: USC took 5 and suffered the only loss, Stanford won 2, and UCLA 1. In track and field, California colleges have also done exceptionally well.

Californians also excel at individual sports, especially golf, tennis, and swimming. Other popular sports are surfing, sports-car racing, archery, badminton, and hang gliding. Los Angeles hosted the summer Olympic Games in 1932 and was scheduled to repeat that role in 1984. The winter games took place in Squaw Valley in 1960.

⁴⁹FAMOUS CALIFORNIANS

Richard Milhous Nixon (b.1913) is the only native-born Californian ever elected to the presidency. Following naval service in World War II, he was elected to the US House of Representatives in 1946, then to the US Senate in 1950. He served as vice president during the Eisenhower administration (1953–61) but failed, by a narrow margin, to be elected president as the Republican candidate in 1960. Returning to his home state, Nixon ran for the California governorship in 1962 but was defeated. The next year he moved his home and political base to New York, from which he launched his successful campaign for the presidency in 1968. As the nation's 37th president, Nixon withdrew US forces from Viet-Nam while intensifying the US bombing of Indochina, established diplomatic relations with China, and followed a policy of détente with the Soviet Union. In 1972, he scored a resounding reelection victory, but within a year his administration was beset by the Watergate scandal. On 9 August

1974, after the House Judiciary Committee had voted articles of impeachment, Nixon became the first president ever to resign the office.

The nation's 31st president, Herbert Hoover (b.Iowa, 1874–1964), moved to California as a young man. There he studied engineering at Stanford University and graduated with its first class (1895) before beginning the public career that culminated in his election to the presidency on the Republican ticket in 1928. Former film actor Ronald Reagan (b.Illinois, 1911) served two terms as state governor (1967–75) before becoming the Republican president-elect in 1980.

In 1953, Earl Warren (1891–1974) became the first Californian to serve as US chief justice (1953–69). Warren, a native of Los Angeles, was elected three times to the California governorship and served in that office (1943–53) longer than any other individual. Following his appointment to the US Supreme Court by President Eisenhower, Warren was instrumental in securing the unanimous decision in *Brown* v. *Board of Education of Topeka* (1954) that racial segregation was unconstitutional under the 14th Amendment. Other cases decided by the Warren court dealt with defendants' rights, legislative reapportionment, and First Amendment freedoms.

Prior to the appointment of Earl Warren, California had been represented on the Supreme Court continuously from 1863 to 1926. Stephen J. Field (b.Connecticut, 1816–99) came to California during the gold rush, practiced law, and served as chief justice of the state supreme court from 1859 to 1863. Following his appointment to the highest court by President Lincoln, Field served what was at that time the longest term in the court's history (1863–97). Joseph McKenna (b.Pennsylvania, 1843–1926), was appointed to the Supreme Court to replace Field upon his retirement. McKenna, who moved with his family to California in 1855, became US attorney general in 1897 and was then elevated by President McKinley to associate justice (1898–1925).

Californians have also held important positions in the executive branch of the federal government. Longtime California resident Victor H. Metcalf (b.New York, 1853–1936) served as Theodore Roosevelt's secretary of commerce and labor. Franklin K. Lane (b.Canada, 1864–1921) was Woodrow Wilson's secretary of the interior, and Ray Lyman Wilbur (b.Iowa, 1875–1949) occupied the same post in the Hoover administration. Californians were especially numerous in the cabinet of Richard Nixon. Los Angeles executive James D. Hodgson (b.Minnesota, 1915) was secretary of labor; former state lieutenant governor Robert H. Finch (b.Arizona, 1925) and San Francisco native Caspar W. Weinberger (b.1917) both served terms as secretary of health, education, and welfare; and Claude S. Brinegar (b.1926) was secretary of transportation. Weinberger and Brinegar stayed on at their respective posts in the Ford administration. An important figure in several national administrations, San Francisco-born John A. McCone (b.1902) was chairman of the Atomic Energy Commission (1958–60) and director of the Central Intelligence Agency (1961–65).

John Charles Frémont (b.Georgia, 1813–90) led several expeditions to the West, briefly served as civil governor of California prior to statehood, became one of California's first two US senators (serving only until 1851), and ran unsuccessfully as the Republican Party's first presidential candidate in 1856. Other prominent US senators from the state have included Hiram Johnson (1866–1945), who also served as governor from 1911 to 1917; William F. Knowland (1908–74); and more recently, former state controller Alan Cranston (b.1914) and former college president and semanticist Samuel Ichiye Hayakawa (b.Canada, 1906). Governors of the state since World War II include Reagan, Edmund G. "Pat" Brown (b.1905), and 4th-generation Californian Edmund G. "Jerry" Brown, Jr. (b.1938). Other prominent state officeholders are Rose Elizabeth Bird (b.Arizona, 1936),

the first woman to be appointed chief justice of the state supreme court; and Wilson Riles (b.Louisiana, 1917), superintendent of public instruction, the first black Californian elected to a state constitutional office. Prominent among mayors are Thomas Bradley (b.Texas, 1917) of Los Angeles, Pete Wilson (b.Illinois, 1933) of San Diego, Dianne Feinstein (b.1933) of San Francisco, and Janet Gray Hayes (b.Indiana, 1926) of San Jose.

Californians have won Nobel Prizes in four separate categories. Linus Pauling (b.Oregon, 1901), professor at the California Institute of Technology (1927–64) and Stanford (1969–74), won the prize for chemistry in 1954, and the Nobel Peace Prize in 1962. Other winners of the Nobel Prize in chemistry are University of California (Berkeley) professors William Francis Giauque (b.Canada, 1895), in 1949, and Edwin M. McMillan (b.1907) and Glenn T. Seaborg (b.Michigan, 1912), who shared the prize in 1951. Members of the Berkeley faculty who have won the Nobel Prize for physics include Ernest Orlando Lawrence (b.South Dakota, 1901–58), in 1939; Emilio Segrè (b.Italy, 1905) and Owen Chamberlain (b.1920), who shared the prize in 1959; and Luis W. Alvarez (b.1911), in 1968. Stanford professor William Shockley (b.England, 1910) shared the physics prize with two others in 1956. The only native-born Californian to win the Nobel Prize for literature was novelist John Steinbeck (1902–68) in 1962.

Other prominent California scientists include world-famed horticulturist Luther Burbank (b.Massachusetts, 1849–1926) and nuclear physicist Edward Teller (b.Hungary, 1908). Naturalist John Muir (b.Scotland, 1838–1914) fought for the establishment of Yosemite National Park. Influential California educators include college presidents David Starr Jordan (b.New York, 1851–1931) of Stanford; and Robert Gordon Sproul (b.1891–1975) and Clark Kerr (b.Pennsylvania, 1911) of the University of California.

Major figures in the California labor movement were anti-Chinese agitator Denis Kearney (b.Ireland, 1847–1907); radical organizer Thomas Mooney (b.Illinois, 1882–1942); and Harry Bridges (b.Australia, 1901), leader of the San Francisco general strike of 1934. The best-known contemporary labor leader in California is Cesar Chavez (b.Arizona, 1927).

The variety of California's economic opportunities are reflected in the diversity of its business leadership. Prominent in the development of California railroads were the men known as the Big Four: Charles Crocker (b.New York, 1822–88), Mark Hopkins (b.New York, 1813–78), Collis P. Huntington (b.Connecticut, 1821–1900), and Leland Stanford (b.New York, 1824–93). California's long-standing dominance in the aerospace industry is a product of the efforts of such native Californians as John Northrop (b.1895) and self-taught aviator Allen Lockheed (1889–1969), along with Glenn L. Martin (b.Iowa, 1886–1955); the San Diego firm headed by Claude T. Ryan (b.Kansas, 1898) built the monoplane, *Spirit of St. Louis*, flown by Charles Lindbergh across the Atlantic in 1927. Among the state's banking and financial leaders was San Jose native Amadeo Peter Giannini (1870–1949), founder of the Bank of America. Important figures in the development of California agriculture include Edwin T. Earl (1856–1919), developer of the first ventilator-refrigerator railroad car, and Mark J. Fontana (b.Italy, 1849–1922), whose California Packing Corp., under the brand name of Del Monte, became the largest seller of canned fruit in the US. Leaders of the state's world-famous wine and grape-growing industry include immigrants Ágostan Haraszthy de Mokcsa (b.Hungary, 1812?–69), Charles Krug (b.Prussia, 1830–94), and Paul Masson (b.France, 1859–1940), as well as two Modesto natives, Ernest (b.1910) and Julio (b.1911) Gallo. It was at the mill of John Sutter (b.Baden, 1803–80) that gold was discovered in 1848.

Leading figures among the state's newspaper editors and publishers were William Randolph Hearst (1863–1951), whose publishing empire began with the *San Francisco Examiner*, and Harrison Gray Otis (b.Ohio, 1837–1917), longtime owner and publisher of the *Los Angeles Times*. Pioneers of the state's electronics industry include David Packard (b.Colorado, 1912) and William R. Hewlett (b.Michigan, 1913). Other prominent business leaders include clothier Levi Strauss (b.Germany, 1830–1902), paper producer Anthony Zellerbach (b.Germany, 1832–1911), cosmetics manufacturer Max Factor (b.Poland, 1877–1938), and construction and manufacturing magnate Henry J. Kaiser (b.New York, 1882–1967).

California has been home to a great many creative artists. Native California writers include John Steinbeck, adventure writer Jack London (1876–1916), novelist and dramatist William Saroyan (b.1908), and novelist-essayist Joan Didion (b.1934). One California-born writer, whose life and works were divorced from his place of birth, was Robert Frost (1874–1963), a native of San Francisco. Many other writers who were residents but not natives of the state have made important contributions to literature. Included in this category are Mark Twain (Samuel Langhorne Clemens, b.Missouri, 1835–1910); local colorist Bret Harte (b.New York, 1836–1902); Ambrose Bierce (b.Ohio, 1842–1914?); novelists Frank Norris (b.Illinois, 1870–1902), Mary Austin (b.Illinois, 1868–1934), and Aldous Huxley (b.England, 1894–1963); novelist-playwright Christopher Isherwood (b.England, 1904); and poets Robinson Jeffers (b.Pennsylvania, 1887–1962) and Lawrence Ferlinghetti (b.New York, 1920). California has been the home of several masters of detective fiction, including Raymond Chandler (b.Illinois, 1888–1959), Dashiell Hammett (b.Connecticut, 1894–1961), Erle Stanley Gardner (b. Massachusetts, 1889–1970), creator of Perry Mason, and Ross Macdonald (b.1915). Producer-playwright David Belasco (1853–1931) was born in San Francisco.

Important composers who have lived and worked in California include natives Henry Cowell (1897–1965) and John Cage (b.1912), and immigrants Arnold Schoenberg (b.Austria, 1874–1951), Ernest Bloch (b.Switzerland, 1880–1959), and Igor Stravinsky (b.Russia, 1882–1971). Immigrant painters include landscape artists Albert Bierstadt (b.Germany, 1830–1902) and William Keith (b.Scotland, 1839–1911), as well as abstract painter Hans Hofmann (b.Germany, 1880–1966). Contemporary artists working in California include Berkeley-born Elmer Bischoff (b.1916), Wayne Thiebaud (b.Arizona, 1920), and Richard Diebenkorn (b.Oregon, 1922). San Francisco native Ansel Adams (b.1902) is the best known of a long line of California photographers that includes Edward Curtis (b.Wisconsin, 1868–1952), famed for his portraits of American Indians; and Dorothea Lange (b.New Jersey, 1895–1965), chronicler of the 1930s migration to California.

Many of the world's finest performing artists have also been Californians. Violinist Ruggiero Ricci (b.1920) was born in San Francisco, while fellow virtuosos Isaac Stern (b.Russia, 1920) and Yehudi Menuhin (b.New York, 1916) were both reared in the state. Another master violinist, Jascha Heifetz (b.Russia, 1901), makes his home in Beverly Hills. California jazz musicians include Dave Brubeck (b.1920) and Los Angeles–reared Stan Kenton (b.Kansas, 1912). Among the many popular musicians who live and record in the state are California natives David Crosby (b.1941), Randy Newman (b.1943), and Beach Boys Brian (b.1942) and Carl (b.1946) Wilson.

The list of talented and beloved film actors associated with Hollywood is enormous. Native Californians on the screen include child actress Shirley Temple (Mrs. Charles A. Black, b.1928) and such greats as Gregory Peck (b.1916) and Marilyn Monroe (Norma Jean Baker, 1926–62). Other longtime residents of the state include Douglas Fairbanks (b.Colorado, 1883–1939), Mary Pickford (Gladys Marie Smith, b.Canada, 1894–1979), Harry Lillis "Bing" Crosby (b.Washington, 1904–77), Cary Grant (Archibald Leach, b.England, 1904), John Wayne (Marion Michael

Morrison, b.Iowa, 1907–79), Bette Davis (b.Massachusetts, 1908), and Clark Gable (b.Ohio, 1901–60). Hollywood has also been the center for such pioneer film producers and directors as D. W. Griffith (David Lewelyn Wark Griffith, b.Kentucky, 1875–1948), Cecil B. DeMille (b.Massachusetts, 1881–1959), Samuel Goldwyn (b.Poland, 1882–1974), and master animator Walt Disney (b.Illinois, 1901–66).

California-born athletes have excelled in every professional sport. A representative sampling includes Baseball Hall of Famers Joe Cronin (b.1906), Vernon "Lefty" Gomez (b.1908), and Joe DiMaggio (b.1914), along with Richard A. "Pancho" Gonzales (b.1928) and Billie Jean (Moffitt) King (b.1943) in tennis, Gene Littler (b.1930) in golf, Frank Gifford (b.1930) and Orenthal James "O. J." Simpson (b.1947) in football, Mark Spitz (b.1950) in swimming, and Bill Walton (b.1952) in basketball.

[50]BIBLIOGRAPHY

Bean, Walton. *California: An Interpretive History*. Rev. ed. New York: McGraw-Hill, 1978.

Bowman, Lynn. *Los Angeles: Epic of a City*. Berkeley: Howell-North, 1974.

Bronson, William. *How to Kill a Golden State*. Garden City, N.Y.: Doubleday, 1968.

California, State of. *California Roster, 1979–80*. Sacramento, 1979.

California, State of. *California Statistical Abstract 1979*. Sacramento, 1979.

California, State of. *Governor's Budget Summary for 1979–80*. Sacramento, 1979.

Caughey, John W. *California: A Remarkable State's Life History*. Rev. ed. Englewood Cliffs, N.J.: Prentice-Hall, 1970.

Cleland, Robert Glass. *From Wilderness to Empire: A History of California*. Edited by Glenn S. Dumke. New York: Knopf, 1959.

Conot, Robert. *Rivers of Blood, Years of Darkness*. New York: Morrow, 1967.

Cook, Sherburne Friend. *The Indian Versus the Spanish Mission: The Conflict Between the California Indian and White Civilization*. Berkeley: University of California Press, 1943.

Cook, Sherburne Friend. *The Population of the California Indians, 1769–1970*. Berkeley: University of California Press, 1976.

Dana, Richard Henry. *Two Years Before the Mast*. Edited by John H. Kemble. Los Angeles: Ward Ritchie Press, 1964.

Dasmann, Raymond F. *The Destruction of California*. New York: Macmillan, 1969.

Davie, Michael. *California: The Vanishing Dream*. New York: Dodd Mead, 1972.

DeVoto, Bernard. *Year of Decision: 1846*. Boston: Houghton Mifflin, 1943.

Federal Writers' Project. *California: A Guide to the Golden State*. Rev. ed. New York: Hastings House, 1967 (orig. 1939).

Griswold, Wesley S. *A Work of Giants: Building the First Transcontinental Railroad*. New York: McGraw-Hill, 1962.

Hart, James D. *A Companion to California*. New York: Oxford University Press, 1978.

Harte, Bret. *The Letters of Bret Harte*. New York: AMS Press, 1975 (orig. 1926).

Jackson, Donald Dale. *Gold Dust*. New York: Knopf, 1980.

Lavender, David. *California: A Bicentennial History*. New York: Norton, 1976.

Lavender, David. *California: Land of New Beginnings*. New York: Harper and Row, 1972.

Lee, William Storss. *The Great California Deserts*. Illustrations by Edward Sanborn. New York: Putnam, 1963.

Lillard, Richard. *Eden in Jeopardy, Man's Prodigal Meddling with His Environment: The Southern California Experience*. New York, Knopf, 1966.

Lotchin, Roger A. *San Francisco, 1846–56.* New York: Oxford University Press, 1974.

MacCann, Richard Dyer. *Hollywood in Transition.* New York: Houghton Mifflin, 1962.

McWilliams, Carey. *California: The Great Exception.* New York: Wynn, 1949.

McWilliams, Carey. *Southern California Country.* New York: Duell, Sloan and Pearce, 1946.

Mowry, George. *The California Progressives.* Berkeley and Los Angeles: University of California Press, 1951.

Nadeau, Remi. *California: The New Society.* Santa Barbara and Salt Lake City: Peregrine Smith, 1974 (orig. 1963).

Nash, Gerald D. *The American West in the Twentieth Century.* Englewood Cliffs, N.J.: Prentice-Hall, 1973.

Nash, Gerald D. *State Government and Economic Development: A History of Administrative Policies in California, 1849–1933.* Berkeley and Los Angeles: University of California Press, 1964.

Paul, Rodman W. *California Gold.* Cambridge: Harvard University Press, 1947.

Pitt, Leonard. *The Decline of the Californios: A Social History of the Spanish-Speaking Californians, 1846–1900.* Berkeley and Los Angeles: University of California Press, 1966.

Robinson, W. W. *Land in California.* Berkeley and Los Angeles: University of California Press, 1948.

Robinson, W. W. *Los Angeles: From the Days of the Pueblo.* San Francisco: California Historical Society, 1959.

Rolle, Andrew. *California: A History.* Arlington Heights, Ill.: AHM, 1978.

Roske, Ralph J. *Everyman's Eden: California.* New York: Macmillan, 1968.

Saxton, Alexander. *The Indispensable Enemy: Labor and the Anti-Chinese Movement in California.* Berkeley and Los Angeles: University of California Press, 1971.

Seidenbaum, Art. *This Is California: Please Keep Out!* New York: Wyden, 1975.

Starr, Kevin. *Americans and the California Dream.* New York: Oxford University Press, 1973.

Stewart, George R. *The California Trail.* New York: McGraw-Hill, 1962.

Thompson, Warren S. *Growth and Changes in California's Population.* New York: Haynes Foundation, 1955.

Turner, Henry A., and John A. Vieg. *The Government and Policies of California.* New York: McGraw-Hill, 1964.

Watkins, T. H. *California: An Illustrated History.* Palo Alto: American West, 1973.

Wells Fargo Bank, N.A. *California to 1990: State Economic Forecast.* Wells Fargo and Co., 1978.

Weston, Charis Wilson and Edward. *California and the West.* New York: Duell, Sloan and Pearce, 1940.

COLORADO

State of Colorado

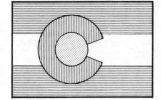

ORIGIN OF STATE NAME: From the Spanish word *colorado*, meaning red or reddish brown. **NICKNAME**: The Centennial State. **CAPITAL**: Denver. **ENTERED UNION**: 1 August 1876 (38th). **SONG**: "Where the Columbines Grow." **MOTTO**: *Nil sine numine* (Nothing without providence). **COAT OF ARMS**: The upper portion of a heraldic shield shows three snow-capped mountains surrounded by clouds; the lower portion has a miner's pick and shovel, crossed. Above the shield are an eye of God and a Roman fasces, symbolizing the republican form of government; the state motto is below. **FLAG**: Superimposed on three equal horizontal bands of blue, white, and blue is a large red "C" encircling a golden disk. **OFFICIAL SEAL**: The coat of arms surrounded by the words "State of Colorado 1876." **ANIMAL**: Rocky Mountain bighorn sheep. **BIRD**: Lark bunting. **FLOWER**: Rocky Mountain columbine. **TREE**: Colorado blue spruce. **GEM**: Aquamarine. **LEGAL HOLIDAYS**: New Year's Day, 1 January; Lincoln's Birthday, 12 February; Washington's Birthday, 3d Monday in February; Memorial Day, last Monday in May; Independence Day, 4 July; Colorado Day, 1st Monday in August; Labor Day, 1st Monday in September; Columbus Day, 2d Monday in October; Election Day, 1st Tuesday after 1st Monday in November in even-numbered years; Thanksgiving Day, 4th Thursday in November; Christmas Day, 25 December. **TIME**: 5 A.M. MST = noon GMT.

¹LOCATION, SIZE, AND EXTENT

Located in the Rocky Mountain region of the US, Colorado ranks 8th in size among the 50 states.

The state's total area is 104,247 sq mi (270,000 sq km), of which 103,766 sq mi (268,754 sq km) consist of land and 481 sq mi (1,246 sq km) comprise inland water. Shaped in an almost perfect rectangle, Colorado extends 387 mi (623 km) E–W and 276 mi (444 km) N–S.

Colorado is bordered on the N by Wyoming and Nebraska; on the E by Nebraska and Kansas; on the S by Oklahoma and New Mexico; and on the W by Utah (with the New Mexico and Utah borders meeting at Four Corners). The total length of Colorado's boundaries is *1,307 mi (2,103 km)*. The state's geographic center lies in Park County, 30 mi (48 km) NW of Pikes Peak.

²TOPOGRAPHY

With a mean average elevation of 6,800 feet (2,100 meters), Colorado is the nation's highest state. Dominating the state are the Rocky Mountains. Colorado has 53 peaks higher than 14,000 feet (4,300 meters), including Elbert, the highest in the Rockies at 14,433 feet (4,399 meters), and Pikes Peak, at 14,110 feet (4,301 meters), one of the state's leading tourist attractions.

The entire eastern third of the state is part of the western Great Plains, a high plateau that rises gradually to the foothills of the Rockies. Colorado's lowest point, 3,350 feet (1,021 meters), on the Arkansas River, is located in this plateau region. Running in a ragged north–south line, slightly west of the state's geographic center, is the Continental Divide, which separates the Rockies into the Eastern and Western slopes. The Eastern Slope Front (Rampart) Range runs south from the Wyoming border and just west of Colorado Springs. Also on the Eastern Slope are the Park, Mosquito, Medicine Bow, and Laramie mountains. Western Slope ranges include the Sawatch, Gore, Elk, Elkhead, and William Fork mountains. South of the Front Range, crossing into New Mexico, is the Sangre de Cristo Range, separated from the San Juan Mountains to its west by the broad San Luis Valley. Several glaciers, including Arapahoe, St. Mary's, Andrews, and Taylor, are located on peaks at or near the Continental Divide.

Colorado's western region is mostly mesa country—broad, flat plateaus accented by deep ravines and gorges, with many subterranean caves. Running northwest from the San Juans are the Uncompahgre Plateau, Grand Mesa, Roan Plateau, the Flat Tops, and Danforth Hills. The Yampa and Green gorges are located in the northwestern corner of the state.

The man-made John Martin Reservoir on the Arkansas River is Colorado's largest lake. Six major river systems originate in Colorado: the Colorado River, which runs southwest from the Rockies to Utah; the South Platte, northeast to Nebraska; the North Platte, north to Wyoming; the Rio Grande, south to New Mexico; and the Arkansas and Republican, east to Kansas. Dams on these rivers provide irrigation for the state's farmland and water supplies for cities and towns. Eighteen hot springs are still active in Colorado; the largest is at Pagosa Springs.

³CLIMATE

Abundant sunshine and low humidity typify Colorado's highland continental climate. Winters are generally cold and snowy, especially in the higher elevations of the Rocky Mountains. Summers are characterized by warm, dry days and cool nights.

The average annual temperature statewide is 45°F (7°C), ranging from 54°F (12°C) at Lamar in the Arkansas Valley to about 32°F (0°C) at the top of the Continental Divide; differences in elevation account for significant local variations on any given day. Denver's annual average is 50°F (10°C); normal temperatures range from 16° to 44°F (−9 to 7°C) in January and from 59° to 87°F (15–31°C) in July. Bennett recorded the highest temperature in Colorado, 118°F (48°C), on 11 July 1888; the record low was −60°F (−51°C), on 1 February 1951 at Taylor Park.

Annual precipitation ranges from a low of 7 in (18 cm) in the San Luis Valley to a high of 27 in (69 cm) in Silverton, with Denver receiving about 16 in (41 cm). Denver's snowfall averages 59 in (150 cm) yearly; up to 200 in (508 cm) of snow falls in the Rockies.

⁴FLORA AND FAUNA

Colorado's great range in elevation and temperature contributes to a variety of vegetation, distributed among five zones: plains, foothills, montane, subalpine, and alpine. The plains teem with grasses and as many as 500 types of wild flowers. Arid regions contain two dozen varieties of cacti. Foothills are matted with berry shrubs, lichens, lilies, and orchids, while fragile wild flowers, shrubs, and conifers thrive in the montane zone. Aspen and Engelmann spruce are found up to the timberline.

In the late 1970s, Colorado counted 347 common and 147 uncommon wildlife species. Principal game species are the elk, Rocky Mountain bighorn sheep (the state animal), antelope, black bear, and white-tailed and mule deers; the mountain goat, introduced in 1948, is the only nonnative big-game quarry. The lark bunting is the state bird; blue grouse and mourning doves are numerous, and 28 duck species have been sighted. Scores of lakes and rivers contain bullhead, salmon, and a diversity of trout. Rare Colorado fauna include the Arctic grayling, black-bellied plover, and mountain lion. The lesser prairie chicken and Arkansas darter are listed among threatened species. The greater prairie chicken, Canada lynx, wolverine, and river otter are among endangered species.

[5]ENVIRONMENTAL PROTECTION

The Department of Natural Resources, with an estimated budget of $38.3 million in 1978/79, has primary responsibility for state environmental programs. The first efforts to protect Colorado's natural resources were the result of federal initiatives. On 16 October 1891, US President Benjamin Harrison set aside the White River Plateau as the first forest reserve in the state. Eleven years later, President Theodore Roosevelt incorporated six areas in the Rockies as national forests. By 1906, 11 national forests covering about one-fourth of the state had been created. Mesa Verde National Park, founded in 1906, and Rocky Mountain National Park (1915) were placed under the direct control of the National Park Service. In 1978, Colorado became the first state in the US to encourage taxpayers to allocate part of their state income tax refunds to wildlife conservation; about $500,000 was collected for this purpose in 1979.

Air pollution and water supply problems head the list of current environmental concerns. Carbon monoxide, ozone, particulates, and nitrogen dioxide pollution are serious problems for metropolitan Denver, Colorado Springs, Pueblo, and other Front Range areas. Legislation designed to reduce levels of vehicular emissions, a major cause of air pollution, was enacted in 1980 shortly after the Environmental Protection Agency temporarily cut off federal funds because of the state's failure to meet clean air standards. Formal efforts to ensure the state's water supply date from the Newlands Reclamation Act of 1902, a federal program designed to promote irrigation projects in the semiarid plains areas; its first effort, the Uncompahgre Valley Project, reclaimed 146,000 acres (59,000 hectares) in Montrose and Delta counties. One of the largest undertakings, the Colorado–Big Thompson Project, begun in the 1930s, diverts a huge amount of water from the Western to the Eastern Slope.

Colorado's rapid population growth during the 1970s taxed an already low water table. The questions of whether and how to augment metropolitan Denver's water supply was an environmental controversy vexing state residents as the decade of the 1980s began.

[6]POPULATION

The 6th-fastest-growing state in the US, Colorado rose from 33d in population in 1960 to 30th in 1970, and to 28th in 1978. The 1970 census population was 2,207,259; the 1978 estimate, 2,670,000. According to the 1970 census, Colorado's population was 50.7% female and 49.3% male. In 1977, 81% lived in metropolitan areas. The population density in 1977 ranged from 5,130 per sq mi (1,981 per sq km) in Denver to less than 1 per sq mi (.39 per sq km) in Hinsdale County in southwest Colorado. The statewide average was 25 per sq mi (10 per sq km). The estimated median age in 1977 was 29 years; nearly 30% of the population was under 18 years of age, and less than 9% was over 65. Preliminary data from the 1980 census put the state's population at 2,877,726, 30% more than in 1970.

Denver is the state's largest city and was, in 1977, the 26th-largest US city. Its preliminary 1980 population was 488,765, but its metropolitan area (including Boulder) encompassed nearly

1,500,000, or more than half the state's population. Other major cities with their 1980 preliminary census populations are Colorado Springs, 206,939, and Pueblo, 101,504.

[7]ETHNIC GROUPS

Once the sole inhabitants of the state, Indians numbered only 8,836 as of 1970. About 4,100 lived in Denver, fewer than 3,000 on the 782,000 acres (316,000 hectares) under the jurisdiction of the Bureau of Indian Affairs, and the rest in other cities. The black population is also a relatively small proportion of the state total, less than 4% in 1977. Of far greater importance to the state's history, culture, and economy are its Hispanic residents, of whom there were 354,540, comprising more than 13% of the population, in 1977. As of 1970, about 19% lived in the southern part of the state, along the New Mexico border. Of the 81% who lived in urban areas, most were in central Denver.

The 1970 census counted 19,660 Asian-Pacific peoples, of whom 7,831 were Japanese. In 1975, some 1,790 Indochinese refugees were resettled in the state. By 1977, the total estimated Asian population was 32,680.

Second-generation Coloradans of European descent made up nearly 13% of the state population in 1970. The largest groups were of German, Russian, and British descent.

[8]LANGUAGES

The first whites to visit Colorado found Arapaho, Kiowa, Comanche, and Cheyenne Indians roaming the plains and often fighting the Ute in the mountains. Despite this diverse heritage, Indian place-names are not numerous: Pagosa Springs, Uncompahgre, Kiowa, and Arapahoe. In 1970, 3,574 Coloradans claimed an Indian language as their mother tongue.

Colorado English is a mixture of the Northern and Midland dialects, in proportions varying according to settlement patterns. Homesteading New Englanders in the northeast spread *sick to the stomach, pail,* and *comforter* (tied and filled bedcover), which in the northwest and the southern half are Midland *sick at the stomach, bucket,* and *comfort.* South Midland *butter beans* and *snap beans* appear in the eastern agricultural strip. Denver has *slat fence, Heinz dog* (mongrel), and *submarine* (large sandwich). A mountain meadow is a *park.* In the southern half of the state, the large Spanish population has bred many loanwords such as *arroyo* and *penco* (pet lamb).

Among native-born residents in 1970, English was the first language for 80%, as it was for 78% of all residents. Mother tongues reported by major resident groups were as follows:

	NATIVE-BORN	FOREIGN-BORN
English	1,716,567	10,979
Spanish	186,847	7,838
German	77,286	16,139
Italian	18,103	3,390
French	9,389	2,449

[9]RELIGIONS

The Spanish explorers who laid claim to (but did not settle in) Colorado were Roman Catholic; but the first American settlers were mostly Methodists, Lutherans, and Episcopalians. Some evangelical groups sought to proselytize the early mining camps during the mid-19th century.

Roman Catholics comprise the single largest religious group in the state today, with 398,419 in 1979. Protestant denominations had 539,529 adherents in 1971, of which the largest was the United Methodist Church, with 103,926. Other major denominations included United Presbyterian, 61,092; Southern Baptist, 50,385; Lutheran Church—Missouri Synod, 47,808; Protestant Episcopal, 44,658; and Church of Jesus Christ of Latter-day Saints, 38,256. The World Evangelical Fellowship has its headquarters in Colorado Springs.

According to 1979 estimates there were 41,765 Jews in Colorado, nearly all of them in the Denver area.

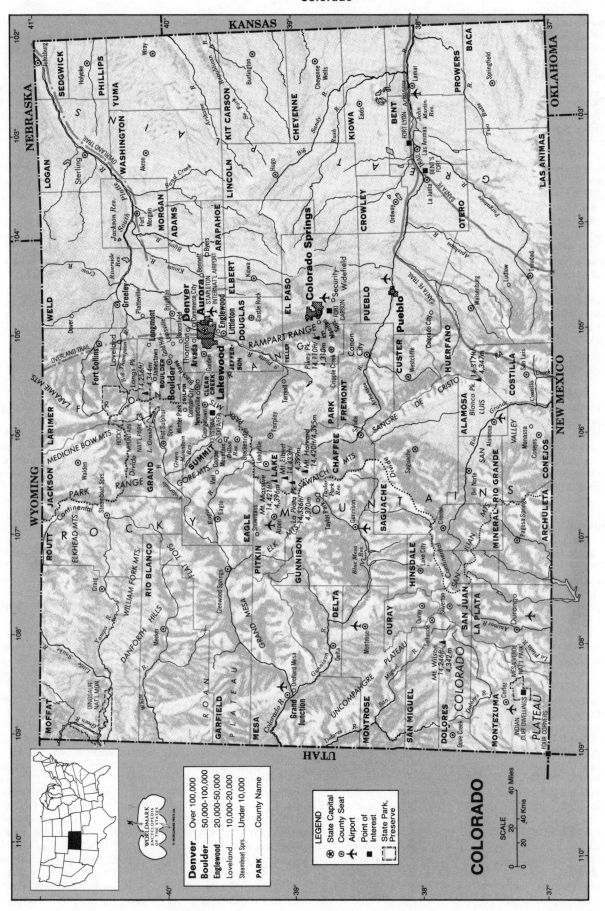

See US political: front cover: E3; physical: back cover E3.

LOCATION: 36°59'35" to 41° N; 102°02'31" to 109°02'58" W. **BOUNDARIES:** Wyoming line, 260 mi (419 km); Nebraska line, 173 mi (278 km); Kansas line, 207 mi (333 km); Oklahoma line, 58 mi (93 km); New Mexico line, 333 mi (536 km); Utah line, 276 mi (444 km).

KANSAS

NEBRASKA

WYOMING

UTAH

OKLAHOMA

NEW MEXICO

COLORADO

SEDGWICK
PHILLIPS
YUMA
WASHINGTON
LOGAN
MORGAN
ADAMS
WELD
LARIMER
JACKSON
ROUTT
MOFFAT
RIO BLANCO
GARFIELD
MESA
DELTA
MONTROSE
OURAY
SAN MIGUEL
DOLORES
MONTEZUMA
LA PLATA
SAN JUAN
HINSDALE
MINERAL
ARCHULETA
CONEJOS
RIO GRANDE
ALAMOSA
SAGUACHE
GUNNISON
PITKIN
EAGLE
GRAND
SUMMIT
LAKE
CHAFFEE
FREMONT
PARK
TELLER
JEFFERSON
CLEAR CREEK
GILPIN
BOULDER
GRAND
DOUGLAS
ELBERT
ARAPAHOE
EL PASO
PUEBLO
CROWLEY
KIOWA
LINCOLN
CHEYENNE
KIT CARSON
CUSTER
HUERFANO
COSTILLA
LAS ANIMAS
PROWERS
BACA
BENT
OTERO
KIOWA

LINES

Denver .... Over 100,000
Boulder 50,000-100,000
Englewood 20,000-50,000
Loveland 10,000-20,000
Steamboat Sprs. .. Under 10,000
PARK .... County Name

LEGEND
⊗ State Capital
✦ County Seat
✈ Airport
■ Point of Interest
State Park, Preserve

SCALE
0   20   40 Miles
0   20   40 Kms

WORLDMARK ENCYCLOPEDIA OF THE STATES
© WORLDMARK PRESS Inc.

¹⁰TRANSPORTATION

As the hub of the Rocky Mountain states, Colorado maintains extensive road and rail systems, including some of the highest roadways in the country.

Because of its difficult mountain terrain, Colorado was by-passed by the first transcontinental railroads. In 1870, however, the Denver Pacific built a line from Denver to the Union Pacific's cross-country route at Cheyenne, Wyo. Several intrastate lines were built during the 1870s, connecting Denver with the mining towns. In particular, the Denver and Rio Grande built many narrow-gauge lines through the mountains, including a track across Marshall Pass; this track went out of service in the 1950s. Denver finally became part of a main transcontinental line in 1934. As of 1974 there were 3,499 mi (5,631 km) of track in the state, a number that includes many miles of unused trackage. Amtrak provides service connecting Denver with Greeley and Cheyenne, Wyo., to the north.

Colorado has an extensive network of roads, including 29 mountain passes. As of 1978 there were 9,087 mi (14,624 km) of municipal roads and 78,201 mi (125,853 km) of rural roads. The major state roads are I-70, US 40, and US 50, all crossing the state from east to west, and I-25, running north-south through the Front Range cities; I-70 and I-25 intersect at Denver. I-76 connects Denver with Nebraska's I-80 to Omaha. Of the 2,652,862 motor vehicles registered in 1978, 1,905,613 were automobiles, 623,161 trucks, 118,753 motorcycles, and 5,335 buses. There were 1,996,420 licensed drivers in 1978.

A total of 87 public and private airfields served the state in 1980. Stapleton International Airport in Denver is the state's busiest. In the year ending 30 June 1978, it handled 8,024,123 passengers and 91,471 tons of cargo.

¹¹HISTORY

A hunting people lived in eastern Colorado at least 20,000 years ago, but little is known about them. The Basket Makers, who came to southwestern Colorado after 100 BC, grew corn and squash and lived in pit houses. By AD 800 there were Pueblo tribes who practiced advanced forms of agriculture and pottery making. From the 11th through the 13th centuries (when they migrated southward), the Pueblo Indians constructed elaborate apartmentlike dwellings in the cliffs of the Colorado canyons and planted their crops both on the mesa tops and in the valleys.

In the 1500s, when Spanish conquistadores arrived in the Southwest, northeastern Colorado was dominated by the Cheyenne and Arapaho, allied against the Comanche and Kiowa to the south. These plains dwellers also warred with the mountain-dwelling Ute Indians, who were divided into Capote, Moache, and Wiminuche in the southwest; Yampa, Grand River, and Uintah in the northwest; and Tabeguache and Uncompahgre along the Gunnison River.

The exact date of the first Spanish entry into the region now called Colorado is undetermined; Juan de Oñate is believed to have traveled into the southeastern area in 1601. More than a century later, in 1706, Juan de Uribarri claimed southeastern Colorado for Spain, joining it with New Mexico. Meanwhile, French traders did little to stake out their claim to the Colorado region, which included most of the area east of the Rocky Mountains. In 1763, France formally ceded the Louisiana Territory to Spain, which returned it to the French in 1801. Two years later, as part of the Louisiana Purchase, Colorado east of the Rockies became US land; the rest of Colorado still belonged to Spain.

Formal boundaries had never been demarcated between the lands of French Louisiana and Spanish New Mexico. In 1806, the US government sent out a group led by Lieutenant Zebulon M. Pike to explore this southwestern border. Pike's group reached Pueblo on 23 November 1806 and then attempted—without success—to scale the peak that now bears his name. Not until 1819 did the US and Spain agree to establish the boundary along the Arkansas River and then northward along the Continental Divide. The following year, Major Stephen Long explored this new border, and Dr. Edwin James made the first known ascent of Pikes Peak.

Eastern Colorado remained a wilderness for the next few decades, although traders and scouts like Charles and William Bent, Kit Carson, and Jim Bridger did venture into the largely uncharted and inhospitable land, establishing friendly relations with the Indians. It was at Bent's Fort, the area's major trading center, in 1840, that the four major eastern tribes ended their warfare and struck an alliance, a bond that lasted through their later struggle against the white settlers and US government. Between 1842 and 1853, John C. Frémont led five expeditions into the region, the first three for the US government. In 1842, he traveled along the South Platte River; on the next two trips, he crossed the Rockies. In his fourth expedition, he and a few of his party barely survived severe winter conditions. Finally, in 1853, Frémont led an expedition over a route traveled by Captain John Gunnison earlier that year—through the San Luis Valley over Cochetopa Pass and along the Gunnison River. The 1853 trips were made five years after western and southern Colorado had come into US possession through the Mexican War.

The magnet that drew Americans to Colorado was the greatly exaggerated report of a gold strike in Cherry Creek (present-day Denver) in July 1858. Within a year, thousands of prospectors had crossed the plains to seek their fortune. Many were disappointed and headed back east, but those who stayed benefited from a second strike at North Clear Creek, some 40 mi (64 km) to the west. The subsequent boom led to the founding of such mining towns as Central City, Tarryall, Golden, Blackhawk, Boulder, Nevadaville, Colorado City, and Gold Hill. By 1860, the population exceeded 30,000. A bill to organize a territory called Colorado, along the lines of the state's present-day boundaries, was passed by the US Congress on 28 February 1861. Colorado City, Golden, and Denver served at various times as the territorial capital until 1867, when Denver was selected as the permanent site. Colorado sided with the Union during the Civil War, though some settlers fought for the Confederacy. Union troops from Colorado helped defeat a contingent led by Confederate General Henry H. Sibley at La Glorieta Pass in New Mexico in 1862.

The 1860s also saw the most serious conflict between Indians and white settlers in Colorado history. Cheyenne and Arapaho chiefs had ceded most of their tribal holdings to the US government in 1861. Sent to a reservation in the Arkansas Valley, these tribes were expected to farm the land. Unsuccessful at farming, the Indians rebelled against the poor rations supplied them by the US government, and sought to resume a nomadic life-style, hunting buffalo, raiding towns, and attacking travelers along the Overland and Sante Fe trails. Colonel John Chivington was placed in charge of controlling the Indian unrest in the summer of 1864 as Territorial Governor John Evans departed for Washington, D.C., leaving the situation in the hands of the military. On 29 November of that year, Chivington led his forces to Sand Creek, on the reservation's northeastern border, where they brutally massacred perhaps 200 Indian men, women, and children who thought they were under the protection of US military forces at nearby Ft. Lyon. Five more years of warfare followed, with the Indians finally defeated at Beecher Island (1868) and Summit Spring (1869). By 1874, most Plains Indians were removed to reservations in what is now Oklahoma. After gold and silver were discovered in areas belonging to the Ute in 1873, they too were forced off the land. By 1880, a series of treaties limited the Ute to a small reservation in the barren mesa country.

The first bill to admit Colorado to statehood was vetoed in 1866 by President Andrew Johnson, who at that time was in the midst of an impeachment fight and feared the entry of two more Republicans into the US Senate. Colorado finally entered the Union as the 38th state on 1 August 1876—less than a month after the nation's 100th birthday—during the presidency of Ulysses S. Grant.

In the early years of statehood, silver strikes at Leadville and Aspen brought settlers and money into the state. Rail lines, smelters, and refineries were built, and large coalfields were opened up. The High Plains attracted new farmers, and another new industry—tourism—emerged. As early as the 1860s, resorts had opened near some of the state's mineral springs. By the mid-1870s, scenic canyons and towns became accessible by train. One of the first major spas, Colorado Springs, recorded 25,000 tourists in 1878, and by the mid-1880s, Denver was accommodating up to 200,000 visitors a year.

Colorado's boom years ended with a depression during the early 1890s. Overproduction of silver—coupled with the US government's decision to adopt a gold standard in 1893—wiped out the silver market, causing the closing of mines, banks, and some businesses. Coinciding with this economic disaster was a drought that led to the abandonment of many farms. A more positive development was a gold find at Cripple Creek in 1891.

By the dawn of the 20th century, farmers were returning to the land and making better use of it. Immigrants from Germany and Russia began to grow sugar beets in the Colorado, Arkansas, and South Platte river valleys. Huge reclamation projects brought water to semiarid cropland, and dry-land farming techniques also helped increase yields. The development of the automobile and good roads opened up more of the mountain areas, bringing a big boom in tourism by the 1920s.

Following World War I, the agricultural and mining sectors fell into depression. From 1920 to 1940, statewide employment declined, and the population growth rate lagged behind that of the US as a whole. World War II brought military training camps, airfields, and jobs to the state. After the war, the expansion of federal facilities in Colorado led to new employment opportunities. The siting of both the North American Air Defense Command and the US Air Force Academy in Colorado Springs helped stimulate the growth of defense, federal research, and aerospace-related industries in the state.

¹²STATE GOVERNMENT

Colorado's state constitution, ratified on 1 July 1876, is a complex and extremely detailed document specifying the duties and structure of state and local government. Despite numerous amendments and revisions, such anachronisms as the prohibition of dueling still remain on the books.

The general assembly, which meets annually, consists of a 35-member senate and 65-member house of representatives. In even-numbered years, the legislators may consider only revenue bills or measures submitted by the governor (the "governor's call"); in odd-numbered years, they may consider any measure. There is no limit on the length of a session, and the governor may call special sessions. Members of the legislature must be US citizens, at least 25 years old, and have been Colorado residents for at least one year.

The executive branch is headed by the governor, who submits the budget and legislative programs to the general assembly, and appoints judges, department heads, boards, and commissions. The governor must be a US citizen, at least 30 years old, and have been a resident of the state for two years or more. Elected with the governor is the lieutenant governor, who assumes the governor's duties when the governor is out of state, and also serves as the president of the senate. Other elective officers include the secretary of state, attorney general, and state treasurer, all of whom serve four-year terms. Members of the state Board of Education and of the Board of Regents of the University of Colorado are elected from each of the state's congressional districts and serve six-year terms.

Bills may originate in either house of the general assembly and become law when passed by majority vote of each house and signed by the governor; a bill may also become law if the governor fails to act on it within 10 days after the legislature adjourns. A two-thirds vote in each house is needed to override a gubernatorial veto.

The state constitution may be amended in several ways. An amendment may be introduced in the legislature, passed by a two-thirds majority in both houses, and submitted to the voters for approval. Alternatively, an initiative amendment, signed by a number of eligible voters equaling at least 8% of the number of votes cast for secretary of state in the previous election and then

Colorado Presidential Vote by Political Parties, 1948–80

YEAR	ELECTORAL VOTE	COLORADO WINNER	DEMOCRAT	REPUBLICAN	PROGRESSIVE	SOCIALIST	SOC. LABOR
1948	6	*Truman (D)	267,288	239,714	6,115	1,678	—
						CONSTITUTION	
1952	6	*Eisenhower (R)	245,504	379,782	1,919	2,181	—
1956	6	*Eisenhower (R)	263,997	394,479	—	759	3,308
						SOC. WORKERS	
1960	6	Nixon (R)	330,629	402,242	—	563	2,803
1964	6	*Johnson (D)	476,024	296,767	—	2,537	—
					AMERICAN IND.		
1968	6	*Nixon (R)	335,174	409,345	60,813	235	3,016
					AMERICAN		
1972	7	*Nixon (R)	329,980	597,189	17,269	666	4,361
							LIBERTARIAN
1976	7	Ford (R)	460,801	584,278	397	1,122	5,338
					STATESMAN	CITIZENS	
1980	7	*Reagan (R)	368,009	652,264	1,180	5,614	25,744

*Won US presidential election.

published in every county, may be filed no later than four months before the general election. If approved by the voters, it then becomes law.

Any US citizen 18 or older who is a resident of a Colorado county 32 days prior to an election may register to vote.

13 POLITICAL PARTIES

The Democratic and Republican parties are the major political organizations in Colorado. Although both parties were in existence when Colorado achieved statehood, the Republicans controlled most statewide offices prior to 1900. Since then, the parties have been more evenly balanced. Of the 1,345,006 registered voters in 1978, 470,858 were Democrats, 373,270 were Republicans, and 500,878 were unaffiliated. As of early 1980, the state had one Democratic and one Republican US senator, and three Democratic and two Republican US representatives; the Democrats controlled the statehouse, the Republicans the state legislature. In November, more than 55% of all Coloradans voting in the presidential election cast their ballots for Ronald Reagan, the seventh time the state had gone Republican since 1952; Democrat Jimmy Carter won only 31% of the vote, while independent candidate John Anderson won 11%, one of his best performances outside the Northeast. Bucking the national Republican trend, Gary Hart was reelected to a second term, thus becoming one of the few liberal Democratic senators in the West to survive fierce conservative opposition.

14 LOCAL GOVERNMENT

As of 1980 there were 63 counties, 261 cities and towns, 181 school districts, and 950 special districts in Colorado.

The administrative and policymaking body in each county is the board of county commissioners, whose three members are elected to staggered four-year terms. Other county officials include the county clerk, treasurer, assessor, sheriff, coroner, superintendent of schools, surveyor, and attorney.

Statutory cities are those whose structure is defined by the state constitution. Power is delegated by the general assembly to either a council-manager or mayor-council form of government. Increasingly, Colorado municipalities have opted for home rule, taking control of local functions from the state government. Of the 40 cities operating under their own charters as of 1976, 8 had mayor-council systems of government; the rest had council-manager systems. Towns, which generally have fewer than 2,000 residents, are governed by a mayor and a six-member board of trustees. The major source of revenue for both cities and towns is the property tax.

Denver, the only city in Colorado that is also a county, exercises the powers of both levels of government. It is run by a mayor and city council; a city auditor, independently elected, serves as a check on the mayor.

15 STATE SERVICES

The Board of Education supervises and makes policy decisions for all public elementary and secondary schools. The Board of Regents of the University of Colorado governs the operations of that institution as well as its affiliates, the Colorado General Hospital, Children's Diagnostic Center, Psychiatric Hospital, and schools of medicine, nursing, and dentistry. All other state-run colleges, as well as the Colorado Historical Society and Council on the Arts and Humanities, are under the jurisdiction of the Department of Higher Education.

The Department of Highways builds, operates, and maintains state roads. The Department of Social Services administers welfare, medical assistance. rehabilitation, and senior-citizens programs. Manpower planning and development are under the Department of Labor and Employment, and health conditions are monitored by the Department of Health. The Department of Institutions oversees mental health, youth services, and developmental disabilities programs. The state's 10 correctional facilities are administered by the Department of Corrections.

All programs concerned with the protection and control of Colorado's natural resources are the responsibility of the Department of Natural Resources. The Department of Local Affairs coordinates such local government services as housing, planning, and development. Other state agencies include the Department of Agriculture, Department of Military Affairs, Department of Regulatory Agencies, Office of State Planning and Budgeting, and Office of Energy Conservation.

16 JUDICIAL SYSTEM

The supreme court, the highest court in Colorado, consists of seven justices elected on a nonpartisan ballot. They select a chief justice, who also serves as the supervisor of all Colorado courts. The next highest court, the court of appeals, consists of six judges, and is confined to civil matters. District courts have original jurisdiction in civil, criminal, and probate cases.

All judges in state courts are appointed to 2-year terms by the governor from a list of names recommended by a judicial nominating commission. The appointees must then be elected by the voters: supreme court justices for 10-year terms, appeals court judges for 8 years, and district court judges for 6. The mandatory retirement age is 72.

County courts hear minor civil disputes and misdemeanors. In Denver, probate and mental health matters fall under the jurisdiction of the Denver probate court, and juvenile cases come before the juvenile court; appeals from the Denver county courts are heard in Denver's superior court. Municipal courts throughout the state handle violations of municipal ordinances, such as traffic tickets.

Colorado's FBI Crime Index crime rate in 1978 was 6,832 per 100,000 people; the violent crime rate was 498 (slightly above the US average), the property crime rate 6,334 (well above the US average). Denver's metropolitan area crime rate (including Boulder) was 7,954 per 100,000: the violent crime rate was 594, the property crime rate 7,360.

17 ARMED FORCES

As of December 1978, 54,537 personnel, of whom 11,303 were civilians, were stationed at the six military facilities in the state. The largest Army base is Ft. Carson in Colorado Springs, headquarters of the 4th Infantry Division, with 23,495 personnel. There were 404 personnel at the Army's Rocky Mountain Arsenal near Denver, where chemical weapons (including 888 Weteye nerve-gas bombs) have been produced and stored. Colorado Springs is the site of the US Air Force Academy; of the 4,156 cadets in 1980, 437 were women. Peterson Air Force Base is also located in Colorado Springs, as is the North American Air Defense Command (NORAD). Lowry Air Force Base, an important training center, is in the Denver area. Defense contracts awarded in 1977/78 totaled $435 million.

About 375,000 veterans lived in Colorado as of 30 September 1979. Of those who served in wartime, 6,000 were veterans of World War I, 141,000 of World War II, 73,000 of the Korean conflict, and 128,000 of the Viet-Nam era. They received more than $264 million in benefits, of which $110 million was for compensation and pensions.

About 3,800 Coloradans served in the state's National Guard. State police numbered 1,022 in 1977; there were 6,268 local police.

18 MIGRATION

The discovery of gold in 1858 brought an avalanche of prospectors, first from Kansas, Iowa, and Missouri, later from such eastern states as Pennsylvania, Kentucky, and Ohio. Some of these migrants returned to the east, but others moved westward into the Rockies and Colorado River canyons. In 1873, another gold strike brought settlers into the Ute territory, eventually driving the Indians into a small reservation in the southwestern corner of the state. During the late 19th and early 20th centuries the sparsely populated eastern plains were settled by farmers from Kansas and Nebraska and by immigrants from Scandinavia, Germany, and Russia. Five years of drought, from 1933 to 1938, helped drive many rural Coloradans off the land into the cities or westward to California.

Since World War II, migration into the state has been substantial, totaling 634,000 between 1950 and 1977. Growth has been evident in both urban and rural areas, but the largest increase has been in the Denver metropolitan area. A number of migrant workers, mostly Chicanos, work seasonally in the western orchards and fields.

[19]INTERGOVERNMENTAL COOPERATION

Among the most important interstate agreements for Coloradans are those governing water resources. Colorado participates with New Mexico in the Animas–La Plata, Costilla Creek, and La Plata River compacts; with Kansas in the Arkansas River Compact of 1949; and with Nebraska in the South Platte River Compact. Multistate compacts allocate water from the Colorado and Republican rivers and the Rio Grande. Colorado also is a signatory to such regional agreements as the Interstate Oil and Gas Compact, Western Corrections Compact, and Western Regional Education Compact. The Western Interstate Commission for Higher Education has its headquarters in Boulder, as does the National Conference of State Legislatures.

Federal aid to Colorado totaled $942.9 million in 1978/79, including $75.6 million in general revenue sharing.

[20]ECONOMY

During the late 1880s, Colorado was the nation's leading silver producer, and an important source of gold. With its abundant reserves of coal, natural gas, and other minerals—and the economic potential of its vast oil-shale deposits—Colorado remains a major mining state, although the mineral industry's share of the state economy has declined throughout this century. Agriculture, primarily livestock, retains its historic importance.

Trade, services, government, and manufacturing were responsible for close to 75% of new jobs created in the 1970s. Trade is the leading source of employment, while manufacturing (2d in employment) is the principal contributor to the gross state product. Electronics, instruments, and food processing have been the foremost industrial growth sectors.

A major driving force behind Colorado's economy is the US government, whch employs more workers in Colorado than anywhere other than the District of Columbia. As the regional headquarters of many federal agencies, Denver is sometimes referred to as "little Washington." Tourism has expanded rapidly in all areas of the state, and the banking industry nearly doubled in size during the 1970s.

[21]INCOME

In 1978, Colorado ranked 15th among the 50 states (tied with Kansas) in per capita income, with $8,001. Personal income that year reached $21.4 billion, or 1.3% of the US total. State sources estimated personal income for 1980 at more than $27 billion.

Only 9% of all Coloradans (and 6% of Colorado families) were below the federal poverty level in 1975. Median family income was $14,992, 13th in the US. As of 1972, 1.4% of the top US wealthholders lived in the state.

[22]LABOR

In 1978, an average of 1,221,000 Coloradans were employed in the civilian labor force. Of that number, 18% were clerical workers, 15% professional and technical personnel, 14% service workers, 13% craftsmen, 13% nonfarm managers and administrators, 11% equipment operators, 7% salespeople, 5% nonfarm laborers, and 4% farm workers. The state's unemployment rate has been consistently below the US average, and about 154,000 new jobs were created during 1978–79.

A federal census of workers covered by unemployment insurance in March 1977 revealed the following nonfarm employment pattern in Colorado:

	ESTABLISH-MENTS	EMPLOYEES	ANNUAL PAYROLL ('000)
Agricultural services, forestry, fishing	639	2,571	$ 24,997
Mining, of which:	902	25,431	460,056
Metals	(140)	(7,045)	(117,777)
Oil, gas extraction	(548)	(10,854)	(190,970)
Contract construction	7,698	60,555	931,107
Manufacturing	3,526	156,013	2,197,360
Transportation, public utilities	1,966	55,235	881,021
Wholesale trade	5,282	60,780	821,672
Retail trade	17,664	194,816	1,311,305
Finance, insurance, real estate	6,691	61,214	696,405
Services	18,657	187,358	1,591,872
Other	1,061	1,269	15,135
TOTALS	64,086	805,242	$8,930,930

The census did not include government employees, of whom Colorado had 224,600 in October 1979. Federal employees accounted for 22% of the total; state, 27%; and local, 51%.

Colorado's labor history has been marked by major disturbances in the mining industry. From 1881 to 1886, the Knights of Labor led at least 35 strikes in the mines; during the 1890s, the Western Federation of Miners struck hard-rock mines in Telluride and Cripple Creek. The United Mine Workers, who came into the state in 1899, shut down operations at numerous mines in 1900 and 1903. Violence was common in these disputes. In one well-known episode, after striking miners and their families set up a tent colony at Ludlow, near Trinidad, the governor called out the militia; in the ensuing conflict, on 20 April 1914, the miners' tents were burned, killing 2 women and 11 children, an event that touched off a rebellion in the whole area. Federal troops restored order in June, and the strike ended with promises of improved labor conditions. In 1917, the state legislature created the Colorado Industrial Commission to investigate all labor disputes.

As of 1976 there were 218,000 members of unions and employee associations in Colorado, nearly 22% of nonagricultural employment.

[23]AGRICULTURE

Colorado ranked 14th among the 50 states in agricultural income in 1978, with $2.7 billion, of which more than $560 million came from crops.

As of 1979 there were 26,500 farms and ranches covering about 38 million acres (15 million hectares); Colorado's average of 1,434 acres (580 hectares) per farm ranked 7th in the US. Of the 51,000 farm workers, 33,000 were family workers and 18,000 were hired hands. The major crop-growing areas are the east and east-central plains for sugar beets, beans, potatoes, and grains; the Arkansas Valley for grains and peaches; and the Western Slope for grains and fruits.

Colorado ranked 5th in the US in production of dry edible beans in 1978, with 1,530,000 hundredweight; 7th in sugar beets, with 1,538,000 bushels; 8th in barley, with 15,360,000 bushels; 10th in potatoes, with 11,400,000 hundredweight; and 10th in wheat, with 57,268,000 bushels. Other field crops include corn, hay and sorghum. Also in 1978, Colorado produced 252,000 tons of fresh market vegetables, 35,950 tons of vegetables for processing, 45,000,000 lb of commercial apples, 5,500,000 lb of peaches, and 1,300,000 lb of tart cherries. Colorado is also a major grower of carnations and poinsettias.

[24]ANIMAL HUSBANDRY

The leading sheep-producing state, Colorado is also a major area for cattle and other livestock. Nearly four-fifths of all farm income in 1978 came from livestock products.

From 1858 to about 1890, cattle drives were a common sight in

Colorado, as a few cattle barons had their Texas longhorns graze on public-domain lands along the eastern plains and Western Slope. This era came to an end when farmers in these regions fenced in their lands, and the better-quality shorthorns and Herefords took over the market. Today, huge tracts of pastureland are leased from the federal government by both cattle and sheep ranchers, with cattle mostly confined to the eastern plains and sheep to the western part of the state.

The following table shows livestock output for 1979 (except where indicated):

	VOLUME (LB)	CASH RECEIPTS	US RANK
Cattle and calves	1,641,340,000	$2,154,502,000	5
Sheep and lambs	65,811,000	67,566,000	2
Hogs and pigs	147,585,000	52,801,000	22
Turkeys	98,679,000	40,458,000	11
Wool (1978)	7,689,000	5,613,000	3

Other livestock products in 1979 included chickens, 4,572,000 lb; eggs, 481,000,000; milk, 857,000,000 lb; butter, 4,851,000 lb; and ice cream, 9,066,000 lb. Production of honey in 1978 was 2,613,000 lb; of beeswax, 55,000 lb.

25 FISHING
There is virtually no commercial fishing in Colorado. The state's many mountain streams lure sport fishermen with perch, silver and blue bass, and trout.

26 FORESTRY
About 22,271,000 acres (9,013,000 hectares) of forestland, 3% of the US total, are located in Colorado, most of it in the Rocky Mountains. Of this amount, 11,315,000 acres (4,579,000 hectares) were commercial timberland, 70% of that owned or managed by the federal government. Despite the vast supply of wood, commercial forestry is not a major element in the state's economy. Shipments by the lumber and wood products industry totaled $226.9 million in 1977, only 2% of all manufactured goods.

27 MINING
Colorado's mineral output in 1978 was valued at $1.5 billion, 17th in the US. Estimates for 1980 placed the total at $1.9 billion.

Colorado is one of the nation's leading sources of molybdenum, vanadium, and uranium. Although silver output is far below the boom years of the late 1800s, Colorado still ranked 3d in the US in 1978, producing 4,217,000 troy oz of silver; gold output was 32,094 troy oz, 5th in the US. Other minerals (excluding fossil fuels) were zinc, 20,146 tons; lead, 13,744 tons; and copper, 1,313 tons.

28 ENERGY AND POWER
An abundant supply of coal, oil, and natural gas makes Colorado a major energy-producing state.

During 1978, 21.2 billion kwh of electricity were generated in Colorado, about 78% of that in coal-fired plants; installed capacity was 4.8 million kw. There is one nuclear power plant, at Platteville.

Petroleum production in 1978 was 36,280,000 barrels from 3,260 wells; proved reserves were 198,012,000 barrels. Natural gas production in 1978 reached 185.6 billion cu feet from 2,169 wells; reserves were nearly 2 trillion cu feet.

Colorado ranked 14th in coal production in 1978, with 13.8 million net tons of bituminous coal, two-thirds of it from surface mines. The 16.3 billion tons of demonstrated coal reserves ranked 7th in the US in 1978.

Colorado holds nearly 75% of the nation's proved oil-shale reserves. Production has been delayed, however, as companies await federal assistance to underwrite the huge cost of plant construction and until improved technology makes refining oil from shale more economical. Because of its ample sunshine, Colorado is also well suited to solar energy development. Among the many energy-related facilities in the state is the Solar Energy Research Institute in Denver.

29 INDUSTRY
Accounting for about 15% of all nonagricultural employment in 1979, manufacturing is a major segment of the economy. Colorado is the main manufacturing center of the Rocky Mountain states; value added by manufacturing in 1977 exceeded $4.5 billion, up 82% from 1972. The major sectors were food and food products, 16%; instruments and related products, 16%; nonelectrical machinery, 11%; printing and publishing, 7%; fabricated metal products, 7%; primary metal products, 6%; transportation equipment, 6%; rubber and plastics, 6%; electric and electronic equipment, 5%; and other sectors, 20%.

The following table shows value added by manufacturing for selected industries in 1972 and 1977:

	1972	1977
Beverages	$154,300,000	$227,100,000
Office and computing machines	NA	175,300,000
Meat products	143,600,000	175,200,000
Communications equipment	NA	140,300,000
Construction and related machinery	70,400,000	100,600,000

Leading corporations headquartered in the state in 1979 included the Adolph Coors brewery in Golden; Storage Technology in Louisville, computers; and Monfort of Colorado in Greeley, food products. Of equal or greater importance to the local economy, however, are the branches of such national corporations as Martin Marietta, Dow Chemical, IBM, Hewlett Packard, Western Electric, Honeywell, and Beech Aircraft.

30 COMMERCE
Colorado is the leading wholesale and retail distribution center for the Rocky Mountain states. Wholesale trade totaled $7.9 billion in 1972; retail sales reached $9.8 billion in 1977. Major retail sectors included automotive dealers, 21%; food stores, 20%; department stores, 11%; eating and drinking places, 10%; gasoline service stations, 7%; and other establishments, 31%. Metropolitan Denver (including Boulder) accounted for three-fifths of all retail sales.

Colorado's foreign exports included $238 million in agricultural products in 1976/77, and $616 million in manufactured goods in 1976.

31 CONSUMER PROTECTION
The Consumer Section of the Department of Law, under the jurisdiction of the attorney general, administers the state's Uniform Consumer Credit Code and Consumers Protection Act.

32 BANKING
In 1978, Colorado had 299 insured commercial banks with nearly $13 billion in assets, and 48 savings and loan associations with $7.9 billion in assets. Most of these institutions were concentrated in metropolitan Denver, the leading banking center between Kansas City and the Pacific.

33 INSURANCE
As of April 1980, 86 insurance carriers were licensed by the Colorado commissioner of insurance. Coloradans purchased $4.6 billion in ordinary life insurance during 1978, when 4,798,000 policies worth $40 billion were in force. The average Colorado family had $39,400 in life coverage.

34 SECURITIES
There are no stock or commodity exchanges in Colorado.

35 PUBLIC FINANCE
The governor's annual budget is presented to the general assembly in early January. The fiscal year runs from 1 July to 30 June. Since 1977/78 there has been a 7% limitation on state budget increases; excess revenues must be placed in a special reserve fund for tax relief.

The following table summarizes consolidated revenues and expenditures for 1979/80 (estimated) and 1980/81 (recommended):

REVENUES	1979/80	1980/81
Excise taxes	$ 598,000,000	$ 588,000,000
Income taxes	650,000,000	680,000,000
Other revenues	151,000,000	141,000,000
Revenue sharing	26,000,000	7,000,000
Rebates[1]	(169,000,000)	(156,000,000)
Balance from previous year	293,000,000	335,000,000
TOTALS	$1,549,000,000	$1,595,000,000
EXPENDITURES		
Education	$ 540,100,000	$ 582,300,000
Higher education	244,600,000	261,800,000
Social services	156,200,000	177,400,000
Tax relief	69,800,000	111,200,000
Capital construction	22,400,000	34,800,000
Other expenses	158,900,000	145,500,000
TOTALS	$1,192,000,000	$1,313,000,000

[1]For budgeting purposes, rebates are treated as negative revenues and should be subtracted from the total.

During 1976/77, Denver's revenues were $404 million and expenditures $411 million. Total public debt for all levels of Colorado government as of 30 June 1977 was $2.2 billion, or $838 per capita.

[36] TAXATION

As of 1980, Colorado's state income tax ranged from 3% of the first $1,000 to 8% on income over $10,000. The corporate income tax was 5% of net income, based on a formula taking into consideration both total profits and those derived solely from state sources. The state also imposed a 3% sales and use tax, along with taxes on cigarettes, alcoholic beverages, pari-mutuel racing, fossil fuel production, motor fuel sales, insurance premiums, and inheritances and gifts.

In 1977, Colorado ranked 26th in federal taxes paid, with $4 billion, and 26th in federal outlays, with $5.2 billion. Coloradans filed 1,147,110 federal income tax returns in 1977, paying a total of more than $2 billion.

[37] ECONOMIC POLICY

Colorado provides funds for development-related public works and recreational projects, training programs, and programs to encourage new industry. Tax incentives include a reduction of the inventory tax on goods in transit, and a reduction of taxes on raw materials used in manufacturing.

[38] HEALTH

As of 1969–71, Colorado ranked 12th among the 50 states in average life expectancy, at 72.06 years—68.40 for males and 75.43 for females. Colorado's birthrate was slightly above the US average in 1977, and the infant mortality rate (11.9 for whites and 14.3 for nonwhites) was well below it. There were 18,700 legal abortions in 1977/78. Colorado's death rate from all causes was 23% below the national average; specific death rates for heart disease and cancer were far below the US norm, while those for accidents and suicide were considerably above it.

In 1978, Colorado had 101 hospitals, with 14,666 beds and an occupancy rate of 71%; hospital personnel included 7,752 registered nurses and 2,790 licensed practical nurses. The average cost per day in Colorado hospitals, $199, nearly equaled the US average. The state had 5,299 licensed physicians in 1977, and 1,701 practicing dentists in 1979. The state's only medical school is the University of Colorado Medical Center in Denver.

[39] SOCIAL WELFARE

During 1978, more than $300 million was spent on public assistance programs in Colorado, including $73 million to 77,900 recipients of aid to families with dependent children. Some 112,000 Coloradans received food stamps, at a cost to the federal government of $44.8 million. The school lunch program served 295,000 pupils (57% of the eligible enrollment), at a federal cost of $16.4 million.

Social Security benefits totaling $770.4 million were paid to 313,800 Coloradans in 1977; retirement benefits amounted to $486.8 million, survivors' benefits $185.4 million, and disability payments $98.2 million. In 1978, $9.1 million was spent on vocational rehabilitation programs, and $50 million on unemployment insurance payments. Workers' compensation benefits totaled $60.8 million in 1977.

[40] HOUSING

Colorado's housing is an eclectic mixture of styles transplanted from the East and those adapted from native dwellings. In the southern regions, adobe structures were first built by Indians, modified by the Spanish, and later adapted by the white settlers. The mining towns built log homes of native timber; miners who prospered added false fronts to give their homes a grander appearance.

The 1970 census counted about 742,000 year-round housing units, of which 691,000 were occupied; more than 96% of the occupied units had full plumbing. Housing accounted for nearly 60% of the dollar value of all new construction during the 1970s, and employed a large percentage of the state's construction work force. From 1976 through 1978, 108,600 new housing units worth more than $3.3 billion were authorized.

[41] EDUCATION

Colorado residents are better educated than the average American. The 1970 illiteracy rate, 0.7%, was well below the US average. In 1976, Colorado tied with Utah for 1st place in median school years completed, with 12.8; more than 78% of all adult Coloradans were high school graduates (3d in the US).

In fall 1979, Colorado public schools had 307,105 pupils in elementary grades and 243,422 in secondary grades; there were 14,200 elementary and 15,100 secondary school teachers. Nonpublic school enrollment was about 38,000 for all grades.

More than 106,000 students were enrolled in state-supported colleges and universities in the fall of 1978. The oldest state school is the Colorado School of Mines, founded in Golden in 1869; it had a 1977 enrollment of 2,584. Although chartered in 1861, the University of Colorado did not open until 1876; its Boulder campus is now the largest in the state, with a fall 1978 enrollment of 20,221. Colorado State University, founded at Ft. Collins in 1870, had 17,661 students in 1978. The University of Denver, chartered in 1864 as the Colorado Seminary of the Methodist Episcopal Church, had 7,753 students. The Aspen Institute for Humanistic Studies holds seminars in the mountain resort town.

[42] ARTS

From its earliest days of statehood, Colorado has been receptive to the arts. Such showplaces as the Tabor Opera House in Leadville and the Tabor Grand Opera House in Denver were among the most elaborate buildings in the Old West. Among the newest US performing arts centers are Denver's Boettcher Concert Hall, which opened in 1978 as the home of the Denver Symphony, and the adjacent Helen G. Bonfils Theater Complex, which opened in 1980 and houses a repertory theater company.

Other artistic organizations include the Colorado Springs Symphony and Colorado Opera Festival of Colorado Springs, and the Central City Opera House Association, which sponsors a summer opera season in this old mining town. Aspen is an important summer music center. The amphitheater in Red Rocks Park near Denver, formed by red sandstone rocks, provides a natural and acoustically excellent concert area.

[43] LIBRARIES AND MUSEUMS

In 1977, public libraries in the state held 5 million volumes and circulated nearly 13 million. The largest system was the Denver Public Library, with 1.7 million volumes in 30 branches. The leading academic library is at the University of Colorado at Boulder, with nearly 1.8 million volumes.

Colorado has more than 120 museums and historic sites. One of the most prominent museums in the West is the Denver Art Museum, with its large collection of American Indian, South Seas, and Oriental art. Another major art museum is the Colorado Springs Fine Arts Center, specializing in southwestern and western American art. Other notable museums include the Denver Museum of Natural History, University of Colorado Museum in Boulder, Western Museum of Mining and Industry in Colorado Springs, and the Colorado Ski Museum–Ski Hall of Fame in Vail. Museums specializing in state history include the Colorado Heritage Center of the Colorado Historical Society in Denver, Ute Indian Museum in Montrose, Ft. Carson Museum of the Army in the West, Bent's Old Fort National Historic Site in La Junta, Georgetown–Silver Plume Historic District, Healy House–Dexter Cabin and Tabor Opera House Museum in Leadville, and Ft. Vasquez in Platteville.

44 COMMUNICATIONS

Colorado's first mail and freight service was provided in 1859 by the Leavenworth and Pikes Peak Express. As of 1977 there were 8,800 postal workers in the state.

Virtually all the state's households have telephone service, more than 98% of it provided by Mountain States Telephone and Telegraph and the Continental Telephone Co. of the West. In 1978, Colorado had 2,180,695 telephones, 1,546,552 residential and 634,143 business.

Of the 113 radio stations in operation in 1978, 70 were AM and 43 FM. There were 11 commercial television stations. Forty-three cable television systems served 99,108 subscribers.

45 PRESS

As of 1978 there were 4 morning dailies with a circulation of 338,649, 24 afternoon dailies with a circulation of 503,462, and 9 Sunday papers with a circulation of 873,792. The leading newspapers were the *Denver Post*, 269,261 evenings, and 354,342 Sundays; and the *Rocky Mountain News*, 258,825 mornings, and 279,892 Sundays.

46 ORGANIZATIONS

The Education Commission of the States and its affiliate, the National Assessment of Educational Progress, have their headquarters in Denver.

Environmental associations include the National Environmental Health Association in Denver, and the American Humane Association in Englewood. The American College of Allergists and US Metric Association are located in Boulder, as is the International Association of Meteorology and Atmospheric Physics.

Among the many professional and trade groups in the state are the Geological Society of America in Boulder, the American School Food Service Association, American Sheep Producers Council, College Press Service, National Cattlemen's Association, and National Live Stock Producers Association, all in Denver.

Colorado Springs is the home of several important sports organizations, including the US Olympic Committee, the Amateur Basketball Association of the USA, Amateur Hockey Association of the US, and Professional Rodeo Cowboys Association. Skiing groups include the International Ski Racers Association in Aspen and the US Ski Association in Denver. Also in Denver is the Sports Car Club of America.

47 TOURISM, TRAVEL, AND RECREATION

Scenery, history, and skiing combine to make Colorado a top-flight tourist mecca. In 1979, the industry accounted for an estimated 8.3 million tourists and $890 million in revenues.

Skiing brings about 20% of all visitors into the state. Vail is the most popular ski resort center, followed by Winter Park, Snowmass (Aspen), Breckenridge, Steamboat, Keystone, and Copper Mountain. Skiing aside, the state's most popular attraction is the US Air Force Academy near Colorado Springs. Nearby are Pikes Peak, the Garden of the Gods (featuring unusual red sandstone formations), and Manitou Springs, a resort center. Besides its many museums, parks, and rebuilt Larimer Square district, Denver's main attraction is the US Mint.

All nine national forests in Colorado are open for camping, as are the state's two national parks: Rocky Mountain, encompassing 263,809 acres (106,760 hectares) in the Front Range; and Mesa Verde, 52,085 acres (21,078 hectares) of mesas and canyons in the southwest. In the western part of the state are the fossil beds at Dinosaur National Monument, Indian cliff dwellings at Mesa Verde, the Durango-Silverton steam train, and white-water rafting on the Colorado, Green, and Yampa rivers. In 1977/78, licenses were issued to 315,411 hunters and 611,656 fishermen.

48 SPORTS

There are three major league professional sports teams in Colorado, all in Denver: the Broncos of the National Football League, the Nuggets of the National Basketball Association, and the Colorado Rockies of the National Hockey League. Denver's minor league baseball team competes in the American Association.

49 FAMOUS COLORADANS

Fort Collins was the birthplace of Byron R. White (b.1917), who, as an associate justice of the US Supreme Court since 1962, has been the state's most prominent federal officeholder. Colorado's first US senator, Henry M. Teller (b.New York, 1830–1914), also served as secretary of the interior.

Charles Bent (b.Virginia, 1799–1847), a fur trapper and an early settler in Colorado, built a famous fort and trading post near present-day La Junta. Early explorers of the Colorado region include Zebulon Pike (b.New Jersey, 1779–1813) and Stephen Long (b.New Hampshire, 1784–1864). John Evans (1814–97) was Colorado's second territorial governor and founder of the present-day University of Denver. Ouray (1820–83) was a Ute chief who ruled at the time when mining districts were being opened. Silver magnate Horace Austin Warner Tabor (b.Vermont, 1830–99) served as mayor of Leadville and lieutenant governor of the state, spent money on lavish buildings in Leadville and Denver, but lost most of his fortune before his death; the story of Tabor and his second wife, Elizabeth McCourt Doe Tabor (1862–1935), is portrayed in Douglas Moore's opera *The Ballad of Baby Doe* (1956).

Among the performers born in the state were actors Lon Chaney (1883–1930) and Douglas Fairbanks (1883–1939), and band leader Paul Whiteman (1891–1967). Singer John Denver (Henry John Deutschendorf, Jr., b.New Mexico, 1943) is closely associated with Colorado and lives in Aspen.

Colorado's most famous sports personality is Jack Dempsey (b.1895), born in Manassa and nicknamed the "Manassa Mauler," who held the world heavyweight boxing crown from 1919 to 1926.

50 BIBLIOGRAPHY

Abbott, Carl. *Colorado: A History of the Centennial State.* Boulder: Colorado Associated University Press, 1976.
Casewit, Curtis W. *Colorado.* New York: Viking, 1973.
Federal Writers' Project. *Colorado: A Guide to the Highest State.* Rev. ed. New York: Hastings House, 1970 (orig. 1941).
Hafen, Leroy R. *The Indians of Colorado.* Denver: State Historical Society of Colorado, 1952.
Lavender, David. *Bent's Fort.* Garden City, N.Y.: Doubleday, 1954.
Michener, James. *Centennial.* New York: Random House, 1974.
Sprague, Marshall. *Colorado: A Bicentennial History.* New York: Norton, 1976.
State of Colorado. *1980/81 Executive Budget Summary.* Denver, 1980.
Ubbelohde, Carl, Maxine Benson, and Duane A. Smith. *A Colorado History.* Rev. ed. Boulder: Pruett, 1972.
Walton, Roger A. *Colorado: A Practical Guide to Its Government and People.* Ft. Collins: Publishers Consultants, 1976.

CONNECTICUT

State of Connecticut

ORIGIN OF STATE NAME: From the Mahican word *quinnehtukqut*, meaning "beside the long tidal river." **NICKNAME**: The Constitution State. (Also: the Nutmeg State.) **CAPITAL**: Hartford. **ENTERED UNION**: 9 January 1788 (5th). **SONG**: "Yankee Doodle." **MOTTO**: *Qui transtulit sustinet* (He who transplanted still sustains). **COAT OF ARMS**: On a rococo shield, three grape vines, supported and bearing fruit, stand against a white field. Beneath the shield is a streamer bearing the state motto. **FLAG**: The coat of arms appears on a blue field. **OFFICIAL SEAL**: The three grape vines and motto of the arms surrounded by the words *Sigillum reipublicæ Connecticutensis* (Seal of the State of Connecticut.) **ANIMAL**: Sperm whale. **BIRD**: American robin. **FLOWER**: Mountain laurel. **TREE**: White oak. **GEM**: Garnet. **INSECT**: European praying mantis. **LEGAL HOLIDAYS**: New Year's Day, 1 January; Martin Luther King Day, 15 January; Lincoln Day, 12 February; Washington's Birthday, 3d Monday in February; Good Friday, March or April; Memorial Day, last Monday in May; Independence Day, 4 July; Labor Day, 1st Monday in September; Columbus Day, 2d Monday in October; Veterans Day, 11 November; Thanksgiving Day, 4th Thursday in November; Christmas Day, 25 December. **TIME**: 7 A.M. EST = noon GMT.

¹LOCATION, SIZE, AND EXTENT

Located in New England in the northeastern US, Connecticut ranks 48th in size among the 50 states.

The state's area, 5,009 sq mi (12,973 sq km), consists of 4,862 sq mi (12,592 sq km) of land and 147 sq mi (381 sq km) of inland water. Connecticut has an average length of 90 mi (145 km) E–W, and an average width of 55 mi (89 km) N–S.

Connecticut is bordered on the N by Massachusetts; on the E by Massachusetts and Rhode Island (with part of the line formed by the Pawcatuck River); on the S by New York (with the line passing through Long Island Sound); and on the W by New York. On the SW border a short panhandle of Connecticut territory juts toward New York City. The state's geographic center is East Berlin in Hartford County. The total boundary length of Connecticut is 328 mi (528 km).

²TOPOGRAPHY

Connecticut is divided into four main geographic regions. The Connecticut and Quinnipiac river valleys form the Central Lowlands, which bisect the state in a north–south direction. The Eastern Highlands range from 500 feet (150 meters) to 1,100 feet (335 meters) near the Massachusetts border and from 200 feet (60 meters) to 500 feet (150 meters) in the southeast. Elevations in the Western Highlands, an extension of the Green Mountains, range from 200 feet (60 meters) in the south to more than 2,000 feet (600 meters) in the northwest; within this region, near the Massachusetts border, stands Mt. Frissell, the highest point in the state at 2,380 feet (725 meters). The Coastal Lowlands, about 100 mi (160 km) long and generally 2–3 mi (3–5 km) wide, consist of rocky peninsulas, shallow bays, sand and gravel beaches, salt meadows, and good harbors at Bridgeport, New Haven, New London, Mystic, and Stonington.

Connecticut has more than 6,000 lakes and ponds. The two largest bodies of water—both artificial— are Lake Candlewood, covering about 5,000 acres (2,000 hectares), and Barkhamsted Reservoir, a major source of water for the Hartford area. The main river is the Connecticut, New England's longest river at 407 mi (655 km), of which 69 mi (111 km) lie within Connecticut; this waterway, which is navigable as far north as Hartford by means of a 15-foot (5-meter) channel, divides the state roughly in half before emptying into Long Island Sound. Other principal rivers include the Thames, Housatonic, and Naugatuck.

Connecticut's bedrock geology and topography are the product of a number of forces: uplift and depression, erosion and deposit, faulting and buckling, lava flows, and glaciation. About 180 million years ago, the lowlands along the eastern border sank more than 10,000 feet (3,000 meters); the resultant trough or fault extends from northern Massachusetts to New Haven Harbor and varies in width from about 20 mi (32 km) to some 4 mi (6 km). During the Ice Ages, the melting Wisconsin glacier created lakes, waterfalls, and sand plains, leaving thin glaciated topsoil and land strewn with rocks and boulders.

³CLIMATE

Connecticut has a generally temperate climate, with mild winters and warm summers. The January mean temperature is 27°F (–3°C) and the July mean is 70°F (21°C). Coastal areas have warmer winters and cooler summers than the interior. Norfolk, in the northwest, has a January mean temperature of 22°F (–6°C) and a July mean of 66°F (19°C), while Bridgeport, on the shore, has a mean of 30°F (–1°C) in January and of 71°F (22°C) in July. The highest recorded temperature in Connecticut was 105°F (41°C) in Waterbury on 22 July 1926; the lowest, –32°F (–36°C) in Falls Village on 16 February 1943. The annual rainfall is about 44–48 in (112–122 cm) and is evenly distributed throughout the year. The state receives some 36–60 in (90–150 cm) of snow each year, with heaviest snowfall in the northwest.

Weather annals reveal a remarkable range and variety of climatic phenomena. Downtown Hartford was inundated by a flood in March 1936. On 21 September 1938, a particularly violent hurricane struck about 10 mi (16 km) west of New Haven and followed the Connecticut Valley northward, causing 85 deaths and property losses of more than $125 million. Particularly severe droughts were experienced in 1749 and 1762, and during the 20th century the state was hard hit in 1929–33, the early 1940s, 1948–50, and 1956–57. The worst drought in recent Connecticut history took place from 1963 to 1966, when the forest-fire hazard was high, crops seriously damaged, and water had to be rationed.

⁴FLORA AND FAUNA

Connecticut has an impressive diversity of vegetation zones. Along the shore of Long Island Sound are tidal marshes with saltgrasses, glasswort, purple gerardia, and sea lavender. On slopes fringing the marshes are black grass, switch grass, marsh elder, and sea myrtle.

The swamp areas contain various ferns, abundant cattails, cranberry, tussock sedge, skunk cabbage, sweet pepperbush, spicebush, and white hellebore. The state's hillsides and uplands support a variety of flowers and plants, including mountain laurel (the state flower), pink azalea, trailing arbutus, Solomon's seal, and Queen Anne's lace. Beaton's quillwort is threatened, while the climbing fern, North American wall rue, and Fries' pondweed are on the endangered list.

The first Englishmen arriving in Connecticut in the 1630s found a land teeming with wildlife. Roaming the forests and meadows were black bear, white-tailed deer, red and gray foxes, timber wolf, cougar, panther, raccoon, and enough rattlesnakes to pose a serious danger. The impact of human settlement on Connecticut wildlife has been profound, however. Only the smaller mammals—the woodchuck, gray squirrel, cottontail, eastern chipmunk, porcupine, raccoon, and striped skunk—remain common. Deer can still be seen, but not often, and hunting is restricted. Snakes remain plentiful but mostly harmless, except for the northern copperhead and timber rattlesnake. Freshwater fish are abundant and aquatic life in Long Island Sound even more so. Common birds include the robin (the state bird), bluebird, blue jay, song sparrow, wood thrush, and many waterfowl; visible in winter are the junco, pine grosbeak, snowy owl, and winter wren.

Threatened and endangered wildlife listed by the US Department of the Interior include shortnose sturgeon, five species of turtle, American peregrine falcon, Indiana bat, humpback and right whales, and eastern cougar.

5ENVIRONMENTAL PROTECTION

Although Connecticut was one of the first states to attempt a comprehensive state water pollution control program, establishing a State Water Commission in 1925, Connecticut still had severe water and air pollution in the early 1970s. Its air quality was poor, with high levels of carbon monoxide, sulfur dioxide, and ozone. Many streams were below the federal government's "swimmable-fishable" standards, and the state was releasing 461 million gallons of partly treated sewage and 13 million gallons of raw sewage each day into Long Island Sound.

More recently, progress in environmental protection has been substantial. In 1971, Connecticut reorganized its state antipollution programs under the State Department of Environmental Protection. Between 1972 and 1977, Connecticut committed $321 million in federal and $249 million in state funds for sewage and waste treatment. About half of the state's 600 mi (970 km) of inland waterways now meet federal standards, but problem areas as of 1980 included two-thirds of the state's segment of the Connecticut River, all 17 mi (27 km) of the Thames River, and about two-thirds of the 86 mi (138 km) of coastal basin waterways.

Connecticut was able to reduce sulfur dioxide levels between 1971 and 1975 by aggressive regulation of the sulfur levels in fuels burned in the state. Less progress was made in controlling other pollutants, however. In 1977, levels of carbon monoxide exceeded federal standards at eight of nine sampling sites, and ozone levels ranged from 2.5 to 3.5 times the amount specified by federal health standards; during the summer months, about one-third of the days were registered as "unhealthful." According to federal estimates, the airborne transport of pollutants from New York and New Jersey accounts for 30% of Connecticut's pollution problems, but engineers with the state's Department of Environmental Protection claim that the proportion is much higher, from 50% to 70%.

Legislation encouraging the recycling of beverage containers and banning the use of "fliptop" cans with disposable tabs took effect in 1980.

6POPULATION

Connecticut ranked 24th among the 50 states in population in 1970, with 3,032,217 residents.

The preliminary 1980 census total for Connecticut was 3,096,951, representing a gain of only 2% for the entire decade of the 1970s. One sign of the population lag is that Connecticut tied with Massachusetts for the lowest birth rate in the US, 11.8 live births per 1,000 population in 1977.

The population density in 1970 was 624 persons per sq mi (241 per sq km); about 77% of all Connecticut residents lived in urban areas and 23% in rural areas. As of 1978, some 73% of Connecticut's population resided on only 26% of the state's land area.

Major cities with preliminary 1980 populations are Bridgeport, 142,459; Hartford, 136,319; New Haven, 125,187; Waterbury, 102,230; and Stamford, 101,636. Despite urban renewal projects, the three largest cities have lost population since 1960 largely because of the exodus of middle-class whites to the suburbs, which have increased rapidly in population. For example, Bloomfield, to the north of Hartford, gained in population from 5,700 in 1950 to more than 18,000 in 1970, and Trumbull, near Bridgeport, increased from 8,641 in 1950 to 31,394 in 1970; in 1980, Bridgeport, Hartford, and New Haven all had growing percentages of minority populations (with relatively low per capita incomes) and shrinking tax bases.

7ETHNIC GROUPS

Connecticut has large ethnic populations of 2d-generation European descent, comprising 32% of the state's residents in 1970. The biggest groups came from Italy, Ireland, and Poland, and Quebec, Canada; most of these immigrants clustered in the cities of New Haven, Hartford, Bridgeport, and New London. The number of Roman Catholic newcomers drew the hostility of many native-born Connecticuters, particularly during the decade 1910–20, when state officials deported 59 "dangerous aliens" on scant evidence of radicalism, and Ku Klux Klan chapters enrolled some 20,000 members.

Especially since 1950, ethnic groups of non-Yankee ancestry have exercised leadership roles in all facets of Connecticut life, especially politics. Connecticut elected a Jewish governor in 1954, and its three subsequent governors were of Irish or Italian ancestry. A wave of newcomers to the state during and after World War II consisted chiefly of blacks and Hispanics seeking employment opportunities. In 1976, the black population numbered 213,000, about 7% of the state total. According to federal data, there were also some 81,000 Hispanic residents in 1976, of whom perhaps three-fourths were Puerto Ricans; state estimates placed the total much higher. Smaller groups include American Indians (about 4,000 in 1979), Japanese, Chinese, Filipinos, Greeks, Portuguese, and Vietnamese refugees.

8LANGUAGES

According to the 1970 census, 418 Connecticuters claimed an Indian language as their mother tongue. Only place-names such as Naugatuck and Willimantic remain to evidence the Native American speech of the Pequots and the Mahican.

Connecticut English is basically that of the Northern dialect, but features of the eastern New England subdialect occur east of the Connecticut River. In the east, *half* and *calf* have the vowel of *father*, *box* is /bawks/ and *cart* is /kaht/, *yolk* is /yelk/, *care* and *chair* have the vowel of *cat*, and many speakers have the intrusive /r/, as in *swaller it* (swallow it). In the western half, *creek* is /krik/, *cherry* may be /chirry/, *on* has the vowel of *father*, and /r/ is heard after a vowel, as in *cart*. Along the Connecticut River, *butcher* is /boocher/, and *tomorrow* is pronounced /tomawro/. Along the coast, the wind may be *breezing on*, and a *creek* is a saltwater inlet. The sycamore is *buttonball*, one is *sick to his stomach*, gutters are *eavestroughs*, a lunch between meals is a *bite*, and in the northwest an earthworm is an *angledog*.

In 1970, 72% of the native-born residents had English as their mother tongue, as did 67% of all residents. Major resident groups claimed the following as their mother tongues:

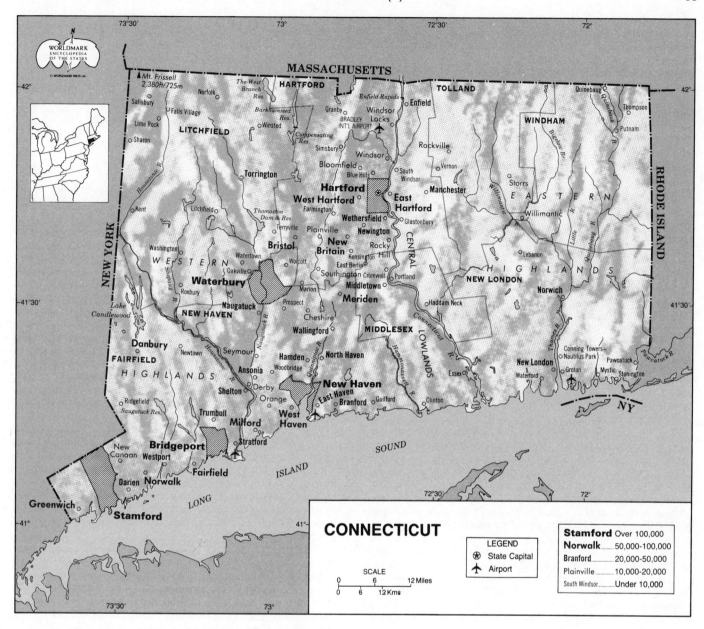

CONNECTICUT

LEGEND
⊛ State Capital
✈ Airport

SCALE
0   6   12 Miles
0   6   12 Kms

Stamford Over 100,000
Norwalk 50,000-100,000
Branford 20,000-50,000
Plainville 10,000-20,000
South Windsor Under 10,000

See US political: front cover M2; US physical: back cover M2.

LOCATION: 40°57′ to 42°03′N; 71°47′05″ to 73°43′05″W. **BOUNDARIES**: Massachusetts line, 94 mi (151 km); Rhode Island line, 54 mi (87 km); New York line, 180 mi (290 km).

	NATIVE-BORN	FOREIGN-BORN
English	1,995,398	45,892
Italian	165,099	57,325
French	116,001	26,117
Polish	91,187	22,993
German	47,021	22,220
Spanish	46,355	12,017

⁹RELIGIONS

Connecticut's religious development began in the 1630s with the designation of the Congregational Church as the colony's "established church." The Puritan fathers enacted laws decreeing church attendance on Sundays and other appointed days, and requiring all residents to contribute to the financial maintenance of local Congregational ministers. Educational patterns, business practices, social conduct, and sexual activities were all comprehensively controlled in accordance with Puritan principles. "Blue laws" provided penalties for offenses against God's word, such as profanation of the Sabbath and swearing, and capital punishment was mandated for adultery, sodomy, bestiality, lesbianism, harlotry, rape, and incest.

Connecticut authorities harassed and often persecuted such non-Congregationalists as Quakers, Baptists, and Anglicans. However, the church was weakened during the 18th century by increasing numbers of dissenters from the Congregational order. A coalition of dissenters disestablished the church by the Connecticut constitution of 1818. The final blow to Congregational domination came in the late 19th and early 20th centuries, with the arrival of many Roman Catholic immigrants.

Since World War I, Roman Catholics have been the most numerous religious group in the state. As of 1979 there were 1,323,673 Roman Catholics, representing 42% of the total population. In 1971 there were 466,253 known adherents of Protestant denominations. Leading groups included Congregationalists (United Church of Christ), 147,870; Episcopalians, 126,303; and United Methodists, 54,426. In 1979, the state's estimated Jewish population was 101,375.

¹⁰TRANSPORTATION

Because of both the state's traditional conservatism and the opposition of turnpike and steamboat companies, rail service did not fully develop until the 1840s. Hartford and New Haven were connected in 1839 and the New Haven line was completed to Northampton, Mass., in 1850. In the late 1840s and the 1850s, a network of lines connected Hartford with eastern Connecticut communities. Railroad expansion peaked during the 1890s when total trackage reached 1,636 mi (2,633 km). The giant in Connecticut railroading from the 1870s until its collapse in 1969 was the New York, New Haven, and Hartford Railroad. As of 1980, the state's rail passenger service was provided by Conrail and Amtrak, which together encompassed 506 route mi (814 km) of track and supplied direct service to 33 of the state's 169 towns.

Local bus systems provide intracity transportation. These services, which carried 36 million passengers in 1979, are generally subsidized by the state and, in some instances, by the federal Urban Mass Transportation Administration. Intercity bus service (not subsidized by the state or the federal government) is provided in 32 municipalities by 39 companies.

Connecticut has an extensive system of expressways, state highways, and local roads encompassing 19,104 mi (30,745 km) of roads in 1978; 99% of the roads are either paved or hard-surfaced. Major highways include I-95, which crosses the entire length of the state near the shore; I-91, linking New Haven and Springfield, Mass.; I-84 from Hartford southwestward through Waterbury and Danbury to New York State; and I-86, connecting I-84 and the Massachusetts Turnpike. As of 1978 there were 2,006,252 automobiles, 166,080 trucks, 73,109 motorcycles, and 8,439 buses registered in the state. Connecticut had 2,060,965 licensed drivers during the same year.

Most of Connecticut's waterborne traffic is handled through the three major ports of New Haven, New London, and Bridgeport, and at the shallow-draft terminals in Norwalk and Stamford. Petroleum products account for 90% of the volume of the commodities shipped through the state's ports.

There were 107 licensed air landing places in Connecticut in 1979, including 26 commercial and 35 private airports, 8 commercial and 28 private heliports, and 3 commercial and 7 private seaplane bases. Connecticut's principal air terminal is Bradley International Airport at Windsor Locks, located 14 mi (23 km) north of Hartford. Served by eight major airlines, Bradley handled 3.1 million passengers during 1978–79.

¹¹HISTORY

The first people known to have lived in the area now called Connecticut were Indians, whose forebears may have come to New England as many as 10,000 years ago. By the early 17th century, Connecticut had between 6,000 and 7,000 Indians organized into 16 tribes, all members of the loose Algonkian Confederation. The most warlike of these tribes were the Pequot, who apparently had migrated not long before from the Hudson River region to escape the Mohawk and had settled along the Connecticut coast. There was also a heavy concentration of Indian groups in the Connecticut River Valley, but fear of Mohawk hunting parties kept them from occupying most of western and northwestern Connecticut.

Because of their fear of the Pequot along the shore and of the Mohawk to the west, most of Connecticut's Indians sought the friendship of English newcomers in the 1630s. The Indians sold land to the English and provided instruction in New World agricultural, hunting, and fishing techniques. The impact of English settlers on Connecticut's friendly Indians was devastating, however. The Indians lost their land, were made dependents in

their own territory, and were decimated by such European imports as smallpox and venereal disease. The Pequot, who sought to expel the English from Connecticut by a series of attacks in 1636–37, were destroyed during the Pequot War by a Connecticut-Massachusetts force, aided by a renegade Pequot named Uncas. By the 1770s, Connecticut's Indian population was less than 1,500.

The first recorded European penetration of Connecticut was in 1614 by the Dutch mariner Adriaen Block, who sailed from Long Island Sound up the Connecticut River, probably as far as the Enfield Rapids. The Dutch established two forts on the Connecticut River, but they were completely dislodged by the English in 1654.

The early English settlers were part of a great migration of some 20,000 English Puritans who crossed the treacherous Atlantic to New England between 1630 and 1642. The Puritans declared that salvation could be achieved only by returning to the simplicity of the early Christian Church and the truth of God as revealed in the Bible. They sailed to America in order to establish a new society that could serve as a model for the rest of Christendom. Attracted by the lushness of the Connecticut River Valley, the Puritans established settlements at Windsor (1633), Wethersfield (1634), and Hartford (1636). In 1639, these three communities joined together to form the Connecticut Colony, choosing to be governed by the Fundamental Orders, a relatively democratic framework for which the Reverend Thomas Hooker was largely responsible. (According to some historians, the Fundamental Orders comprised the world's first written constitution—hence the state nickname, adopted in 1959.) A separate Puritan colony was planted at New Haven in 1638 under the leadership of John Davenport, a Puritan minister, and Theophilus Eaton, a successful merchant.

In 1662, the Colony of Connecticut secured legal recognition by England. Governor John Winthrop, Jr., persuaded King Charles II to grant a charter that recognized Connecticut's existing framework of government and established its north and south boundaries as Massachusetts and Long Island Sound, and its east and west borders as Narragansett Bay and the Pacific Ocean. In 1665, New Haven reluctantly became part of the colony because of economic difficulties and fear of incorporation into Anglican New York.

Connecticut had acrimonious boundary disputes with Massachusetts, Rhode Island, New York, and Pennsylvania. The most serious disagreement was with New York, which claimed the entire area from Delaware Bay to the Connecticut River. The issue was resolved in 1683 when the boundary was set 20 mi (32 km) east of and parallel to the Hudson River, although it was not until 1881 that Connecticut, New York, and Congress established the exact line.

Connecticut functioned throughout the colonial period much like an independent republic. It was the only American colony that generally did not follow English practice in its legislative proceedings, nor did it adopt a substantial amount of English common and statute law for its legal code. Connecticut's autonomy was threatened in 1687 when Sir Edmund Andros, appointed by King James II as the governor of the Dominion of New England, arrived in Hartford to demand surrender of the 1662 charter. Connecticut leaders protected the colony's autonomy by hiding the charter in an oak tree that subsequently became a landmark known as the Charter Oak.

With its Puritan roots and historic autonomy, Connecticut was a Patriot stronghold during the American Revolution. Tories numbered no more than 7% of the adult male population—2,000 to 2,500 out of a total of 38,000 males. Connecticut sent some 3,600 men to Massachusetts at the outbreak of fighting at Lexington and Concord in April 1775. Jonathan Trumbull, who served as governor from 1769 to 1784, was the only colonial governor in office in 1775 who supported the Patriots. He served throughout the Revolutionary War, during which Connecticut troops participated in most of the significant battles. Connecticut's privateers captured more than 500 British merchant vessels, and its small but potent fleet captured at least 40 enemy ships. Connecticut also produced arms and gunpowder for state and Continental forces, thus beginning an arms-making tradition that would lead to the state's unofficial designation as the "arsenal of the nation." It was also called the Provisions State, in large part because of the crucial supplies of foodstuffs it sent to General George Washington throughout the war. The state's most famous Revolutionary War figure was Nathan Hale, executed as a spy by the British in New York City in 1776.

On 9 January 1788, Connecticut became the 5th state to ratify the Constitution. Strongly Federalist during the 1790s, Connecticut ardently disagreed with the foreign policy of Presidents Thomas Jefferson and James Madison, opposed the War of 1812, and even refused to allow its militia to leave the state. Connecticut's ire over the war was exacerbated by the failure of the government to offer significant help when the British attacked Essex and Stonington in the spring and summer of 1814. The politically vulnerable Federalists were defeated in 1817 by the Toleration Party. This coalition of Republicans and non-Congregationalists headed the drive for the new state constitution (1818) that disestablished the Congregational Church, a Federalist stronghold.

Long before the Civil War, Connecticut was stoutly antislavery. In the early years of independence, the general assembly enacted legislation providing that every black born after 1 March 1784 would be free at age 25. Connecticut had a number of antislavery and abolition societies whose members routed escaped slaves to Canada via the Underground Railroad. The state's pro-Union sentiment was reflected in the enormous support given to the Union war effort; some 55,000 Connecticut men served in the Civil War, suffering more than 20,000 casualties. Arms manufacturers such as Colt and Winchester produced desperately needed rifles and revolvers, and the state's textile, brass, and rubber firms turned out uniforms, buttons, ponchos, blankets, and boots for Union troops. The contribution by Connecticut industries to the war effort signaled the state's emergence as a manufacturing giant. Its industrial development was facilitated by abundant waterpower, the growth of capital held by banks and insurance companies, a sophisticated transportation network, and, most important, the technological and marketing expertise of the people. The first American hat factory was established in Danbury in 1780, and the nation's brass industry had its roots in the Naugatuck Valley between 1806 and 1809. Connecticut clocks became known throughout the world. Micah Rugg organized the first nut and bolt factory in Marion in 1840; Elias Howe invented the first practical sewing machine in Hartford in 1843; and the International Silver Co. of Meriden developed from the efforts of the Rogers family, which had devised a method of silver plating in 1847. Perhaps the most important figure in the development of Connecticut manufacturing was Eli Whitney, best known for inventing the cotton gin (1793). Whitney also developed a system of interchangeable parts while operating a firearms factory near New Haven from the late 1790s until he died in 1825.

Seventy-five years after Whitney's death, Connecticut was a leader in the production of hats, typewriters, electrical fixtures, machine tools, and hardware. The state's textile industry ranked 6th in the nation in 1900, with an annual output of $50 million. By 1904, Connecticut's firearms industry was producing four-fifths of the ammunition and more than one-fourth of the total value of all firearms manufactured by nongovernment factories in the US. These great strides in manufacturing transformed Connecticut from a rural, agrarian society in the early 1800s to an increasingly urban state.

The state's contribution to the Allied forces in World War I more than equaled its Civil War effort. Four Liberty Loan drives raised $437 million, more than from any other state. About 66,000 Connecticuters served in the armed forces, and the state's manufacturers produced 450,000 Enfield rifles, 45,000 Browning automatic rifles, 2 million bayonets, and much other war matériel. By 1917–18, four-fifths of Connecticut's industry was involved in defense production.

The prosperity sparked by World War I continued, for the most part, until 1929. During the 1920s, Connecticuters enjoyed a rising standard of living, as the state became a national leader in the production of specialty parts for the aviation, automotive, and electric power industries. The only soft spot was the textile industry; from 1919 to 1929, Connecticut lost 14 of its 47 cotton mills to southern states.

The stock market crash of 1929 and the subsequent depression of the 1930s hit highly industrialized Connecticut hard. By the spring of 1932, the state's unemployed totaled 150,000, and cities such as Bridgeport fell deeply in debt. The economic reversal led to significant political change: the ousting of a business-oriented Republican administration, which had long dominated the state, by a revitalized Democratic Party under the leadership of Governor Wilbur L. Cross (1931–39). During his tenure, Connecticut reorganized its state government, improved facilities in state hospitals and penal institutions, and tightened state regulation of business.

Connecticut was pulled out of the unemployment doldrums in 1939, when the state's factories were once again stimulated by defense contracts. The value of war contracts placed in Connecticut was $8 billion by May 1945, and industrial employment increased from 350,000 in 1939 to 550,000 by late 1944. Connecticut's factories turned out submarines, Navy Corsair fighter aircraft, helicopters, 80% of all ball bearings manufactured in the US, and many thousands of small arms. Approximately 220,000 Connecticut men and women served in the US armed forces.

The principal developments in Connecticut since 1945 have been substantial population growth, economic diversification, an increasingly liberal trend in politics, the expansion of middle-class white suburbs, and an influx of black and Hispanic migrants to the major cities. Urban renewal projects in Hartford and New Haven have resulted in expanded office and recreational facilities, but not much desperately needed new housing. The major challenge facing Connecticut in the 1980s is, once again, how to effect the social and economic integration of this latest wave of newcomers.

¹²STATE GOVERNMENT

Connecticut has been governed by four basic documents: the Fundamental Orders of 1639, the charter of 1662, the constitution of 1818 (which remained in effect until 1964, when a federal district court, acting on the basis of the US Supreme Court's "one man, one vote" ruling, ordered Connecticut to reapportion and redistrict its legislature), and the constitution of 1965. This last document adjusted representation to conform with population, and provided for mandatory reapportionment every ten years.

The state legislature is the general assembly, consisting of a 36-member senate and 151-member house of representatives. Legislators, who must be 21 years old and qualified voters in Connecticut, are elected to both houses for two-year terms from single-member districts of substantially equal populations.

Elected members of the executive branch are the governor and lieutenant governor (who run jointly and must each be at least 30 years of age); secretary of state, treasurer, comptroller, and attorney general. All are elected for four-year terms and may be reelected. The governor, generally with the advice and consent of the general assembly, selects the heads of state departments, commissions, and offices.

A bill becomes law when approved by both houses of the general assembly and signed by the governor. If the governor fails to sign it within 5 days when the legislature is in session, or within 15 days when it has adjourned, the measure also becomes law. A bill vetoed by the governor may be overridden by a two-thirds vote of the members of each house.

A constitutional amendment may be passed in a single legislative session if approved by three-fourths of the total membership of each house. If approved in one session by a majority but by less than three-fourths, the proposed amendment requires approval by majority vote in the next legislative session following a general election. After passage by the legislature, the amendment must be ratified by the voters in the next even-year general election in order to become part of the state constitution.

To vote in state elections, residents must be US citizens, at least 18 years of age, and must satisfy a 21-day registration requirement.

¹³POLITICAL PARTIES

Connecticut's major political groups during the first half of the 19th century were successively the Federalist Party, the Democratic-Republican coalition, the Democrats, and the Whigs. The political scene also included a number of minor political parties—the Anti-Masonic, Free Soil, Temperance, and Native American (Know-Nothing) parties—of which the Know-Nothings were the most successful, holding the governorship from 1855 to 1857. The Whig Party collapsed during the controversy over slavery in the 1850s, when the Republican Party emerged as the principal opposition to the Democrats.

From the 1850s to the present, the Democratic and Republican parties have dominated Connecticut politics. The Republicans held power in most of the years between the Civil War and the 1920s. Republican hegemony ended in 1930 when the Democrats elected Wilbur L. Cross as governor. Cross greatly strengthened the Connecticut Democratic Party by supporting organized labor and providing social legislation for the aged and the needy. The success of the increasingly liberal Democrats in the 1930s prodded Connecticut Republicans to become more forward-looking, and the two parties were fairly evenly matched between 1938 and 1954. Connecticut's Democrats have generally held power since the mid-1950s under the leadership of Hartford's John Moran Bailey, chairman of the state's Democratic Party

from 1946 to 1975. As of October 1978, Democratic Party registration in Connecticut was 613,225, Republican, 410,675.

In the November 1980 elections, Republican Ronald Reagan carried the state with 48% of the popular vote; Jimmy Carter won more than 38%, and John Anderson 12%. Christopher Dodd, son of former US senator Thomas Dodd, won the Connecticut Senate seat vacated by Abraham Ribicoff, who retired.

¹⁴LOCAL GOVERNMENT

As of 1979, Connecticut had 8 counties, 150 towns, 18 consolidated towns and cities, 11 boroughs, and 206 other municipal and special districts. Counties in Connecticut have been geographical subdivisions without governmental functions since county government was abolished in 1960.

Connecticut's cities generally use the council-manager or mayor-council forms of government. The council-manager system provides for an elected council which determines policy, enacts local legislation, and appoints the city manager. The mayor-council system employs an elected chief executive with extensive appointment power and control over administrative agencies.

In most towns, an elected, three-member board of selectmen heads the administrative branch; the town meeting, in which all registered voters may participate, is the legislative body. Boroughs are generally governed by an elected warden, and borough meetings exercise major legislative functions.

¹⁵STATE SERVICES

The Department of Education administers special programs for the educationally disadvantaged, the emotionally and physically handicapped, and non-English-speaking students. The Department of Transportation operates state-owned airports, oversees bus system operations, and provides for snow removal from state highways and roads. The Department of Human Resources has a variety of social programs for state residents, including special services for the physically handicapped. The Department of Children and Youth Services administers programs dealing with child protection, adoption, juvenile corrections and rehabilitation, and prevention of delinquency. The Department of Aging has state and regional ombudsmen to handle problems involving nursing homes. Among programs sponsored by the Health Services Department are ones that help people to stop smoking, increase their nutritional awareness, improve their dental health,

Connecticut Presidential Vote by Political Parties, 1948–80

YEAR	ELECTORAL VOTE	CONNECTICUT WINNER	DEMOCRAT	REPUBLICAN	PROGRESSIVE	SOCIALIST
1948	8	Dewey (R)	423,297	437,754	13,713	6,964
1952	8	*Eisenhower (R)	481,649	611,012	1,466	2,244
1956	8	*Eisenhower (R)	405,079	711,837	—	—
1960	8	*Kennedy (D)	657,055	565,813	—	—
1964	8	*Johnson (D)	826,269	390,996	—	—
					AMERICAN IND.	
1968	8	Humphrey (D)	621,561	556,721	76,660	—
						AMERICAN
1972	8	*Nixon (R)	555,498	810,763	—	17,239
						US LABOR
1976	8	Ford (R)	647,895	719,261	7,101	1,789
					LIBERTARIAN	CITIZENS
1980	8	*Reagan (R)	541,732	677,210	8,570	6,130

*Won US presidential election.

prevent the spread of influenza, and control hypertension. The Labor Department provides a full range of services to the unemployed, jobseekers, and disadvantaged workers.

[16] JUDICIAL SYSTEM

Connecticut's judicial system has undergone significant streamlining in recent years, with the abolition of municipal courts (1961), the circuit court (1974), the court of common pleas (1978), and the juvenile court (1978). Currently, the Connecticut judicial system consists of the supreme court, superior court, and probate courts.

The supreme court comprises the chief justice and five associate justices, all of whom are also judges of the superior court. The high court reviews, upon appeal, decisions of the superior court to determine whether any material error has been committed, as well as decisions of the appellate session of the superior court at the request of that body. Justices of the supreme court, as well as all superior court judges, are nominated by the governor, and appointed by the general assembly for eight-year terms.

The superior court, the sole general trial court, has the authority to hear all legal controversies except those over which the probate courts have exclusive jurisdiction. The superior court sits in 11 state judicial districts and is divided into trial divisions for civil, criminal, and family cases. As of 1979, there were 119 superior court judges (including the 6 supreme court justices).

Connecticut has 130 probate courts. These operate on a fee basis, with judges receiving their compensation from fees paid for services rendered by the court. Each probate district has one probate judge, elected for a four-year term.

Connecticut had 10 correctional institutions with an inmate population of 3,257 as of January 1979. State law provides for the death penalty (by electrocution), but as of 1980, there had been no executions in the state for 20 years. Crime rates in 1978 were below the national averages in every category of violent crime, and for most nonviolent crimes except motor vehicle theft.

[17] ARMED FORCES

The principal military installation in Connecticut is the US Navy Submarine Base at Groton, with 15,934 personnel in 1978. Across the Thames River in New London is one of the nation's four service academies—the US Coast Guard Academy. Founded in 1876 and located at its present site since 1932, this institution offers a four-year curriculum leading to a B.S. degree and a commission as ensign in the Coast Guard. Women were first admitted to the academy in 1976 as members of the class of 1980.

Connecticut ranks first among the 50 states in value of defense contracts per capita. In 1977/78, the total value of defense contracts was $3.5 billion (4th in the US). Nearly 12% of the state's manufacturing employment was dependent on prime defense contracts.

As of 30 September 1979, some 463,000 veterans were living in Connecticut, of whom 8,000 were veterans of World War I, 196,000 of World War II, 98,000 of the Korean conflict, and 131,000 of the Viet-Nam era. Veterans' benefits in 1977/78 exceeded $204.7 million.

In 1978, the Connecticut National Guard consisted of 58 Army and Air units, with total personnel of 7,291. The Connecticut State Police consisted of 857 troopers in 1979.

[18] MIGRATION

Connecticut has experienced four principal migrations: the arrival of European immigrants in the 17th century, the outmigration of many settlers to other states beginning in the 18th century, renewed European immigration in the late 19th century, and the intrastate migration of city dwellers to the suburbs since 1945.

Although the first English settlers found an abundance of fertile farmland in the Connecticut Valley, later newcomers were not so fortunate. It is estimated that in 1800, when Connecticut's population was 250,000, nearly three times that many people had moved away from the state, principally to Vermont, western New York, Ohio, and other midwestern states.

The influx of European immigrants increased the number of foreign-born in the state from 38,518 in 1850 to about 800,000 by World War I. After World War II, the rush of middle-class whites (many from neighboring states) to Connecticut suburbs, propelled in part by the "baby boom" that followed the war, was accompanied by the flow of minority groups to the cities. All told, Connecticut had a net increase from migration of 561,000 between 1940 and 1970, followed by an estimated net loss of 23,000 from 1970 to 1977.

[19] INTERGOVERNMENTAL COOPERATION

Among the regional interstate agreements to which Connecticut belongs are the Atlantic States Marine Fisheries Compact and the New England Higher Education Compact. Boundary agreements are in effect with Massachusetts, New York, and Rhode Island. Connecticut participates with New York in the Railroad Passenger Transportation Compact.

In 1978/79, federal aid to Connecticut totaled $1.1 billion, of which $86 million was general revenue sharing.

[20] ECONOMY

Connecticut has had a strong economy since the early 19th century, when the state, unable to support its population by farming, turned to a variety of nonagricultural pursuits. Shipbuilding and whaling were major industries: in the 1840s and 1850s, New London ranked behind only New Bedford and Nantucket, Mass., among US whaling ports. Connecticut has been a leader of the insurance industry since the 1790s. As of 1979, Connecticut insurance companies had worldwide assets of nearly $70 billion and accounted for 55,000 jobs in the state.

Connecticut's most important economic pursuit is manufacturing. In 1980, Connecticut was a leader in the manufacture of aircraft engines and parts, bearings, hardware, submarines, helicopters, typewriters, electrical equipment, guns and ammunition, optical instruments, and watches and clocks.

Because defense production is so important to the state, the economy has fluctuated with the rise and fall of international tensions. Connecticut's unemployment rate stood at 8.7% in 1949, dropped to 3.5% in 1951 during the Korean conflict, and rose sharply after the war to 8.3% in 1958. During the height of the Viet-Nam era, from 1966 to 1968, unemployment averaged between 3.1% and 3.7%, but the rate subsequently rose to 8.6% in 1972 and peaked at 9.5% in 1976. Connecticut has lessened its dependence on the defense sector somewhat by attracting nonmilitary domestic and international firms to the state. As of 1979, more than 120 international companies employed 15,000 Connecticut workers.

[21] INCOME

Connecticut is one of the wealthiest states, ranking 4th in per capita personal income during 1978 with $8,914.

For the 1978/79 fiscal year, the state's personal income increased by nearly 11% to $29.1 billion. On a per capita basis, the average Connecticuter received $9,314 during that period, 12% above the US average. Real income per capita in 1978/79 was $4,539 (in 1967 dollars), compared with the US figure of $4,050.

Only 6.7% of all state residents and 5.6% of Connecticut families were below the federal poverty level in 1975, percentages bettered by no state except Alaska. In 1972, about 266,600 (2%) of the nation's top wealthholders were Connecticuters.

[22] LABOR

The state's civilian labor force in 1978 totaled 1,512,000, of whom 94.8% were employed and 5.2% unemployed. The unemployment rate for all males in 1978 was 4.1%; for females, 6.7%; and for minority workers, 11.2%.

A federal census of workers covered by unemployment insurance in March 1977 revealed the following nonfarm employment pattern in Connecticut:

	ESTABLISH-MENTS	EMPLOYEES	ANNUAL PAYROLL ('000)
Agricultural services, forestry, fishing	802	2,660	$ 28,064
Mining	93	963	18,977
Contract construction	6,911	37,330	696,540
Manufacturing, of which:	6,047	417,430	5,901,192
Fabricated metal products	(943)	(50,672)	(646,787)
Nonelectrical machinery	(1,268)	(54,418)	(798,102)
Transport equipment	(149)	(77,444)	(1,293,501)
Transportation, public utilities	2,052	49,611	716,706
Wholesale trade	4,620	60,642	887,041
Retail trade	18,290	192,077	1,329,498
Finance, insurance, real estate, of which:	5,870	97,912	1,180,681
Insurance	(1,389)	(55,055)	(722,528)
Services	19,535	228,278	2,089,047
Other	614	599[1]	16,466
TOTALS	64,834	1,087,502	$12,864,212

[1]Employment as of March 1977.

Among categories of workers excluded by this survey is government workers, of whom Connecticut had 182,320 (21,460 federal, 160,860 state and local) in February 1980.

During the early 20th century, Connecticut was consistently antilabor and was one of the leading open-shop states in the northeastern US. But great strides were made by organized labor in the 1930s with the support of New Deal legislation recognizing union bargaining rights. Labor union membership totaled 309,000 in 1976; another 68,000 Connecticuters belonged to employee associations.

23AGRICULTURE
Agriculture is no longer of much economic importance in Connecticut. The number of farms declined from 22,241 in 1945 to only 3,600 in 1978, when the average farm covered 125 acres (51 hectares). Total agricultural income was $233 million in 1978 (45th in the US).

Cash farm income from crop sales in 1978 was $98 million. Connecticut ranked 10th in tobacco production, valued at $23 million. Other principal crops are hay, silage, greenhouse and nursery products, potatoes, sweet corn, tomatoes, apples, pears, and peaches.

24ANIMAL HUSBANDRY
Cash farm income from the sale of livestock and livestock products totaled $135 million in 1978, or 58% of the state's total farm production. In 1979 there were 104,000 cattle on Connecticut farms; marketings totaled $24 million. Also during 1979, poultry farmers received $51.3 million from the sale of eggs, $1.7 million for chickens, and $604,000 for turkeys. About 605 million lb of milk were produced.

25FISHING
Commercial fishing does not play a major role in the economy. In 1978, the value of commercial landings was $12 million. Included in the catch were 3,200,000 lb of edible finfish and 971,000 lb of lobster.

During 1978/79, the Conservation and Preservation Division of the Department of Environmental Protection released 876,510 catchable trout, 395,000 Kokanee fry, and 184,198 Atlantic salmon smelts into Connecticut waters. The state also operates a broodstock improvement program at the Quinebaug Valley Hatchery.

26FORESTRY
By the early 20th century, the forests that covered 95% of Connecticut in the 1630s were generally destroyed. Woodland recovery has been stimulated since the 1930s by an energetic reforestation program. More than half of the state's 1,861,000 acres (753,000 hectares) of forestland in 1977 was wooded with new growth. Shipments of lumber and wood products were valued at $75.3 million in 1977, and the paper and wood furniture industries are also substantial.

State woodlands include 88 state parks and 30 state forests covering some 175,000 acres (71,000 hectares).

27MINING
In 1978, Connecticut ranked only 46th among the 50 states in value of mineral production, which totaled $46 million.

Formerly, there were working iron mines at Salisbury, Sharon, and Kent (iron from these mines was used for cannon and shot during the Revolutionary and Civil wars); copper mines at Granby, Bristol, and Cheshire; nickel mines at Litchfield; and granite quarries and garnet mines at Roxbury. Between the Civil War and World War I, a superior grade of red sandstone was quarried at Portland and barged via the Connecticut River and Long Island Sound to become the "brownstone fronts" of New York City.

At present, the state's commercial mining is limited to lime and silica for low-grade glass and traprock, which is crushed for use in building and highway construction.

28ENERGY AND POWER
In 1978, Connecticut's fuel bill was $2.8 billion, of which 60% was for petroleum products, 9% for natural gas, and the remainder for electricity. Energy prices were 79% higher than the national average for natural gas, 48% higher for coal, and 23% higher for electricity.

Production of electricity increased from 20 billion kwh in 1970 to 26 billion kwh in 1978; installed capacity increased from 4.6 million kw to 6.4 million kw during the same years. The use of coal to generate electric power declined from 85% of the total fuel used in 1965 to zero in 1978 because of the increased utilization of nuclear energy and oil, each of which accounted for about half of all electrical production in 1978. As of 1979, Connecticut had three nuclear reactors, one at Haddam Neck (575,000 kw) and two at Waterford (1,490,000 kw). Electricity consumption increased from 36.2 trillion Btu in 1965 to 71.3 trillion Btu in 1978.

Having no petroleum or gas resources of its own, Connecticut must rely primarily on imported oil from Saudi Arabia, Venezuela, Nigeria, and other countries. About 90% of the natural gas used in Connecticut is piped in from Texas and Louisiana.

29INDUSTRY
One of the most highly industrialized states, Connecticut ranks 6th in percentage of nonfarm workers engaged in manufacturing and 4th in value added by manufacture per capita.

Connecticut is a leading producer of aircraft engines and parts of submarines, with the largest employers being United Technologies (its Pratt and Whitney Aircraft Division has headquarters in East Hartford) and the General Dynamics Corp. Electric Boat Division in Groton. The state is also a leading producer of military and civilian helicopters.

The state's value added by manufacture totaled $11 billion in 1977, an increase of nearly 9% from 1976. The following table shows the value added by manufacture for Connecticut's major industries in 1976 and 1977:

	1976	1977
Transport equipment	$2,125,900,000	$2,342,000,000
Nonelectrical machinery	1,414,100,000	1,602,200,000
Fabricated metal products	1,305,800,000	1,332,900,000
Electric and electronic equipment	990,500,000	857,100,000
Chemicals and allied products	723,600,000	857,100,000
Instruments and related products	588,300,000	663,400,000
Primary metals	532,900,000	606,100,000
Printing and publishing	474,800,000	510,600,000
Food and food products	370,600,000	406,500,000
Rubber and plastic products	264,100,000	300,300,000
Paper and allied products	241,100,000	242,400,000
Textile mill products	200,200,000	182,400,000

Leading corporations with headquarters in Connecticut include, in order of assets in 1979, General Electric, Conoco, United Technologies, Xerox, American Can, Continental Group, Champion International, AMAX, Combustion Engineering, Singer, Uniroyal, Kennecott Copper, and Olin. Connecticut has been particularly successful in attracting big corporations, especially from New York City; 58 corporations moved to Connecticut between 1969 and 1973.

³⁰COMMERCE
Considering its small size, Connecticut is a busy commercial state. Its wholesale trade in 1972 totaled $8.8 billion, and retail trade in 1977 amounted to $10.4 billion. Of total retail sales in that year, food stores accounted for 23%, automotive dealers 17%, department stores 11%, restaurants and taverns 9%, gasoline service stations 8%, and other establishments 32%.

The estimated value of Connecticut's manufactures exported abroad was $4.6 billion in 1979, representing an increase of 56% over 1976. Shipments of transport equipment, nonelectrical machinery, and instruments accounted for more than 70% of the state's 1979 foreign sales.

³¹CONSUMER PROTECTION
In 1959, Connecticut established a Department of Consumer Protection charged with protecting consumers from injury by product use or merchandising deceit. The department conducts regular inspections of wholesale and retail food establishments, drug-related establishments, bedding and upholstery dealers and manufacturers, and commercial establishments that use weighing and measuring devices. The department also issues and reviews licenses, conducts investigations into alleged fraudulent activities, provides information and referral services to consumers, and responds to their complaints. Regional offices were established in 1978 in Stamford and Norwich.

³²BANKING
The first banks in Connecticut were established in Hartford, New Haven, Middletown, Bridgeport, Norwich, and New London between 1792 and 1805. By 1850, the state had 45 commercial and 15 savings banks. As of 1979, Connecticut's banking institutions included 19 national banks, 46 state banks and trust companies, and 65 savings banks. Assets of the state's insured commercial banks amounted to $11.5 billion at the end of 1978; their outstanding loans totaled $4.5 billion. The leading commercial bank was Hartford National Bank and Trust, with total resources worth $2.6 billion as of 31 December 1979.

In 1978 there were 37 state and federal savings and loan associations. Their combined assets totaled $3.4 billion; savings capital, $3 billion; and mortgage loans, $2.8 billion. Connecticut also had 17 state credit unions and 282 federal credit unions in 1979.

Banking operations are regulated by the Division of Banking of the State Department of Business Regulation.

³³INSURANCE
Connecticut's preeminence in the insurance field and Hartford's title as "insurance capital" of the nation date from the late 18th century, when state businessmen agreed to bear a portion of a shipowner's financial risks in return for a share of the profits. Marine insurance companies were established in Hartford and major port cities between 1797 and 1805. The state's first insurance company had been formed in Norwich in 1795 to provide fire insurance. The nation's oldest fire insurance firm is the Hartford Fire Insurance Co., active since 1810. Subsequently, Connecticut companies have been leaders in life, accident, casualty, automobile, and multiple-line insurance.

In 1979 there were 47 insurance companies with headquarters in Connecticut. Life insurance in force in 1978 totaled 5,836,000 policies valued at $49.7 billion, divided about evenly between individual and group policies. Connecticut families averaged $44,000 in life insurance coverage in 1978 (4th in the US). Property and liability insurers wrote premiums totaling $1.3 billion, of which automobile insurance accounted for $524.5 million and homeowners' insurance $152.1 million. No-fault automobile insurance has been in effect since 1 January 1973.

The insurance industry is regulated by the Division of Insurance of the State Department of Business Regulation.

³⁴SECURITIES
There are no securities or commodities exchanges in Connecticut. New York Stock Exchange member firms had 72 sales offices and 783 registered representatives in the state in 1978. Connecticuters reported $889 million in dividend income on their 1977 federal tax returns.

³⁵PUBLIC FINANCE
Although Connecticut ranks high in per capita income, its unwillingness to impose a personal income tax has kept state expenditures—especially on education—at a relatively low level.

The state budget is prepared annually by the Budget and Financial Management Division of the Office of Policy and Management and submitted by the governor to the general assembly for consideration. The fiscal year runs from 1 July to 30 June. The following is a summary of general revenues and expenditures for 1977/78 and 1978/79:

REVENUES	1977/78	1978/79
Taxes	$1,438,652,000	$1,593,592,000
Other revenues	327,917,000	334,718,000
Grants-in-aid	243,885,000	293,842,000
Restricted revenues	243,799,000	248,063,000
TOTALS	$2,254,253,000	$2,470,215,000

EXPENDITURES		
Education, libraries, and museums	$ 527,415,000	$ 583,642,000
Public welfare	475,581,000	537,024,000
Health and hospitals	148,286,000	167,989,000
Department of transportation	131,587,000	141,569,000
General government	115,976,000	115,866,000
Corrections	51,618,000	83,237,000
Regulation and protection of persons and property	58,293,000	62,866,000
Judicial	35,196,000	45,362,000
Natural resources and recreation	16,882,000	28,186,000
Legislative	6,969,000	8,927,000
Debt service, grants, miscellaneous	582,489,000	628,196,000
TOTALS	$2,150,292,000	$2,402,864,000

The state's public debt totaled $2.3 billion as of 30 June 1979. The consolidated debt of Connecticut state and local governments surpassed $5 billion in mid-1977; per capita debt averaged $1,639 (9th in the US).

³⁶TAXATION
Connecticut is one of the few states without a personal income tax. It ranked 20th in state and local taxation in 1977, with receipts of $2.8 billion, or $885 per capita.

Principal taxes are a sales and use tax levied at a rate of 7.5% in 1980, a corporation business tax levied at the basic rate of 10%, and a motor fuels tax of 11 cents per gallon. Other state taxes are levied on capital gains and dividends, inheritances, cigarettes, alcoholic beverages, and theater admissions. Property taxes are the main source of local revenue.

In 1977, Connecticuters filed 1,252,643 federal income tax returns and paid more than $3 billion in tax.

³⁷ECONOMIC POLICY
Connecticut's principal economic goal is to strengthen employment in the manufacturing sector and urban areas. Toward that end, the Department of Economic Development in 1978/79 approved $200 million in low-cost industrial loans to enable companies to construct or expand facilities in the state. Business recruitment missions were sent to industrialized Europe and Japan to stimulate the state's export program. Officials of the

department cooperate with the state's Office of Employment and Training and with the labor and education departments to develop job-training programs in order to meet the needs of new and expanding employers. Such measures succeeded in motivating 352 firms to expand their Connecticut facilities or to relocate operations from other states or countries in 1978/79.

³⁸HEALTH

Connecticut is one of the healthiest states in the US, according to federal data. Average life expectancy in 1969–71 was 72.48 years, 9th highest among the 50 states; life expectancy for men was 69.04 years, for women 75.94 years. The infant mortality rates in 1977 were 12.2 per 1,000 live births for whites and 22.2 for blacks; both were close to the national average. There were 16,800 legal abortions in 1977/78, a rate of nearly one abortion for every two live births. The two leading causes of death in 1977 were heart disease and cancer. Death rates for heart disease, stroke, accidents, pneumonia and influenza, diabetes, suicide, and early childhood disease were below the respective national norms, while rates for cancer, cirrhosis of the liver, and arteriosclerosis were above them.

Connecticut's four public mental hospitals, in Newington, Middletown, Newtown, and Norwich, admitted 16,157 patients in 1978/79. In 1977/78, the most frequent diagnoses upon admission were alcoholism, 44%; schizophrenia and paranoid states, 23%; affective disorders, 10%; and drug abuse, 8%. Other state medical facilities in 1979 included 2 state training schools and 12 regional centers for the mentally retarded, and 4 other institutions. In 1979, Connecticut had 219 nursing homes, 72 rest homes with nursing supervision, and 148 homes for the aged.

In 1978, Connecticut had 64 hospitals, with 18,791 beds; among the 46,993 personnel were 8,986 registered nurses and 2,817 licensed practical nurses. Hospital costs in 1977 averaged $242 per day and $1,818 per stay, among the highest in the nation. According to state sources, Connecticut had 5,942 physicians and 2,151 dentists in 1979. Outstanding medical schools are those of Yale University and the University of Connecticut.

³⁹SOCIAL WELFARE

In 1976, public assistance by the state, local, and federal governments in Connecticut exceeded $431 million. Aid to families with dependent children was paid to 136,400 state residents, including 95,700 children, and totaled $174 million in 1978. The national school lunch program provided nutritional assistance during 1978/79 to 275,874 pupils. In that year, 155,000 persons participated in the food stamp program, at a federal cost of $40.4 million. In 1977, 455,800 state residents received federal Social Security benefits totaling $1.3 billion. Medicare programs provided health care and helped subsidize nutritional programs, senior-citizen centers, and home-care services.

The Department of Human Resources provided a wide range of social services to individuals of all ages in the course of administering $12 million in state funds and $38 million in federal funds during 1978/79. The department's Hispanic Services Division administered a grant program of $300,000, in cooperation with 14 Hispanic agencies in major towns, to design pilot programs for youth training and education.

As of 1980, unemployment insurance in Connecticut provided $122 to $183 per week to recipients for a maximum duration of 26 weeks. Payments totaled $138 million in 1978.

⁴⁰HOUSING

On 1 January 1978, the Department of Community Affairs Management Information reported that there were 1,114,729 housing units in Connecticut, an increase of 133,126 units, or nearly 14%, over the 1970 census total. Virtually every town increased its housing stock during that period; the smallest increases were in the big cities, however, and in Hartford the number of units declined from 58,495 to 57,703.

As of 1970, year-round housing units in Connecticut had a median number of 5.2 rooms and 3.2 people per unit; the median value of owner-occupied dwellings was $25,500. The proportion of all housing units having full plumbing facilities was 97%, compared with 85% at the 1960 census.

⁴¹EDUCATION

Believing that the Bible was the only true source of God's truths, Connecticut's Puritan founders viewed literacy as a theological necessity. A law code in 1650 required a town of 50 families to hire a schoolmaster to teach reading and writing, and a town of 100 families to operate a school to prepare students for college. Despite such legislation, many communities in colonial Connecticut did not provide sufficient funding to operate first-rate schools. Public education was greatly strengthened in the 19th century by the work of Henry Barnard, who advocated free public schools, state supervision of common schools, and the establishment of schools for teacher training. By the late 1860s and early 1870s, all of Connecticut's public elementary and high schools were tuition free. In 1865, the Board of Education was established.

The 1970 census determined that 1.1% of adult Connecticuters were illiterate, slightly lower than the national average. As of 1976, 70.3% of adult state residents were high school graduates, and 18.3% had completed four or more years of college. As of 1978, Connecticut had 1,087 public schools, with 34,703 teachers and 581,246 students. During that same year, nonpublic schools had 4,955 teachers and 84,060 students. In 1979, Connecticut had 178 Roman Catholic parochial schools with 55,236 pupils. The state's private preparatory schools include Choate (Wallingford), Taft (Watertown), Westminster (Simsbury), Loomis (Windsor), and Miss Porter's (Farmington).

Public institutions of higher education include the University of Connecticut at Storrs, with 21,349 students in 1978/79; four state colleges at New Britain, New Haven, Danbury, and Willimantic, with a combined total of 31,659 students; 12 regional community colleges with 33,342 students; and 5 state technical colleges with 6,854.

Connecticut's 18 private colleges and universities had 57,491 students in 1978/79. Among the oldest are Yale, founded in 1701 and settled in New Haven between 1717 and 1719; Trinity College (1823), Hartford; and Wesleyan University (1831), Middletown. Other private institutions include the University of Hartford, University of Bridgeport, Fairfield University, and Connecticut College in New London.

A characteristic of public school financing in Connecticut has been high reliance on local support for education. Differences among towns in their wealth bases and taxation were compounded by the mechanism used to distribute a majority of state funds for public education—the flat-grant-per-pupil formula. After the Connecticut supreme court in *Horton* v. *Meskill* (1978) declared this funding mechanism to be unconstitutional, the general assembly in 1979 replaced it with an equity-based model in order to reduce the disparity among towns in educational expenses per pupil.

⁴²ARTS

Art museums in Connecticut include the Wadsworth Atheneum in Hartford, the oldest (1842) free public museum in the US; the Yale University Art Gallery in New Haven; the New Britain Museum of American Art; and the Lyman Allyn Museum of Connecticut College in New London. The visual arts are easily accessible through these and 26 other art museums, 60 galleries, and more than 150 annual arts shows and festivals.

The theater is vibrant in contemporary Connecticut. In 1979, 37 new theater pieces were presented in the state, which has numerous dinner theaters, at least 100 community theater groups, and many college and university theater groups, among them the Yale Repertory Theater. Nationally recognized professional theaters include the American Shakespeare Festival Theater in Stratford, the Long Wharf Theater in New Haven, the Hartford

Stage Company, and Eugene O'Neill Memorial Theater Center in Waterford.

The state's foremost metropolitan orchestras are the Hartford and New Haven symphonies. Professional opera is presented by the State Opera in Stamford, the Connecticut Grand Opera in Darien, and the Connecticut Opera, Hartford. Prominent dance groups include the Connecticut Dance Company in New Haven, the Hartford Ballet Company, and the Pilobolus Dance Theater in the town of Washington.

[43]LIBRARIES AND MUSEUMS

As of 1980, Connecticut had more than 200 public libraries. The leading public library is the Connecticut State Library (Hartford), which houses about 650,000 bound volumes, 2 million manuscripts, and 1 million other items, as well as the official state historical museum. Connecticut's most distinguished academic collection is the Yale University library system (6.8 million volumes), headed by the Sterling Memorial Library and the Beinecke Rare Book and Manuscript Library. Special depositories include the Hartford Seminary Foundation's impressive material on Christian-Muslim relations, the Connecticut Historical Society's especially strong collection of materials pertaining to state history and New England genealogy, the Trinity College Library's collection of church documents, the Indian Museum in Old Mystic, the maritime history collections in the Submarine Library at the US Naval Submarine base in Groton, and the G. W. Blunt White Library at Mystic Seaport. In all, Connecticut libraries held 9.2 million volumes and had a combined circulation of 16.6 million in 1977/78.

Connecticut has more than 100 museums and historic sites. The Peabody Museum of Natural History at Yale includes an impressive dinosaur hall. Botanical gardens include Harkness Memorial State Park in Waterford, Elizabeth Park in West Hartford, and Hamilton Park Rose Garden in Waterbury. Connecticut's historical sites include the Henry Whitfield House in Guilford (1639), said to be the oldest stone house in the US; the Webb House in Wethersfield, where George Washington met with the Comte de Rochambeau in 1781 to plan military strategy against the British; Noah Webster's birthplace in West Hartford; and the Jonathan Trumbull House in Lebanon.

[44]COMMUNICATIONS

Connecticut's communications needs are served by the US Postal Service, four telephone companies, and two telegraph companies.

Virtually every household has telephone service. In 1978 there were 2,583,453 telephones, of which 99% were owned and operated by Bell System affiliates. Of the total number, 1,925,792 were residential and 657,661 business.

In 1979, Connecticut had 39 AM and 34 FM radio stations, and 9 television stations. There were educational television stations in Bridgeport, Hartford, New Haven, and Norwich. In addition, in 1978, 17 cable television companies served 189,091 subscribers in 68 communities.

[45]PRESS

The *Hartford Courant*, founded in 1764, is generally considered to be the oldest US newspaper in continuous publication. The leading Connecticut dailies in 1978 were the *Courant*, with an average morning circulation of 214,766 (Sundays, 284,968); and the *New Haven Register*, with an average evening circulation of 101,268 (Sundays, 142,616). Statewide, there were 6 morning newspapers with 374,072 circulation, 19 evening newspapers (543,631), and 7 Sunday newspapers (680,446). In 1979, Connecticut also had 57 weekly papers with a total circulation of 562,434.

Leading periodicals are *American Scientist, Connecticut Magazine, Teacher Magazine*, and the *Yale Review*.

[46]ORGANIZATIONS

The best-known national organization with headquarters in Connecticut is the Knights of Columbus (New Haven), with 1,316,543 members (29,918 of them state residents) as of 31 January 1980. Most national organizations have chapters in Connecticut, and there are hundreds of local, civic, humane, professional, business, and cultural organizations in the state. The Connecticut Citizens Action Group has been instrumental in the passage of environmental and civil liberties legislation. Among the leading statewide historical groups are the Acorn Club, the Association for the Study of Connecticut History, the Antiquarian and Landmarks Society of Connecticut, and the Connecticut League of Historical Societies. There are also scores of local ethnic societies.

[47]TOURISM, TRAVEL, AND RECREATION

Tourism has become an increasingly important part of the state economy in recent decades, with tourist expenditures climbing from $77 million in 1956 to more than $800 million in 1979/80, when Connecticut entertained an estimated 25 million visitors from other states and nations. Popular tourist attractions include the Mystic Seaport restoration and its aquarium, the Mark Twain House and state capitol in Hartford, the American Clock and Watch Museum in Bristol, the Lock Museum of America in Terryville, and the Yale campus in New Haven. Outstanding events are the Harvard-Yale regatta held each June on the Thames River in New London, and the 50 fairs held in Danbury, Guilford, and other towns between June and October.

Connecticut abounds in outdoor recreational facilities. As of 1979 there were 70 golf courses open to the public, 118 state parks and forests, and more than 100 freshwater and saltwater boat-launching sites, along with ski resorts and snowmobile trails for winter recreation. The state issued licenses to 81,453 hunters and 183,826 fishermen in 1977/78.

[48]SPORTS

Connecticut's only major league professional team is the Hartford Whalers of the National Hockey League. New Haven has a minor league hockey franchise. Bristol, Waterbury, and West Haven compete in baseball's Class AA Eastern League. Auto racing takes place at Lime Rock Race Track, Salisbury, and at East Thompson Raceway, Thompson.

The state runs daily and weekly lotteries, and licenses off-track betting facilities for horse racing and pari-mutuel operations for greyhound racing and jai-alai. In 1978/79, the state treasury received $76 million from these activities.

Connecticut schools, colleges, and universities provide amateur athletic competitions, highlighted by Ivy League football games on autumn Saturdays at the Yale Bowl in New Haven.

[49]FAMOUS CONNECTICUTERS

Although Connecticut cannot claim any US president or vice president as a native son, John Moran Bailey (1904–75), chairman of the state Democratic Party (1946–75) and of the national party (1961–68), played a key role in presidential politics as a supporter of John F. Kennedy's successful 1960 campaign.

Two Connecticut natives have served as chief justice of the US, Oliver Ellsworth (1745–1807) and Morrison R. Waite (1816–88). Associate justices include Henry Baldwin (1780–1844), Stephen J. Field (1816–99), and William Strong (1808–95). Other prominent federal officeholders were Oliver Wolcott (1760–1837), secretary of the treasury; Gideon Welles (1802–78), secretary of the Navy; Dean Acheson (1893–1971), secretary of state; and Abraham A. Ribicoff (b. 1910), secretary of health, education, and welfare. An influential US senator was Orville H. Platt (1827–1905), known for his authorship of the Platt Amendment (1901) making Cuba a virtual protectorate of the United States. Also well known are Connecticut senators Ribicoff (served 1963–81) and Lowell P. Weicker, Jr. (b.France, 1931), brought to national attention by his work during the Watergate hearings in 1973.

Notable colonial and state governors include John Winthrop, Jr. (b.England, 1606–76), Jonathan Trumbull (1710–85), William A. Buckingham (1804–75), Simeon Eben Baldwin (1840–1927), Marcus Holcomb (1844–1932), Wilbur L. Cross (1862–

1948), Chester Bowles (b.1901), and Ribicoff. Ella Tambussi Grasso (b.1919), elected in 1975 and reelected in 1979, but forced to resign for health reasons at the end of 1980, was the first woman governor in the US who did not succeed her husband in the post.

In addition to Winthrop, the founding fathers of Connecticut were Thomas Hooker (b. England, 1586–1647), who was deeply involved in establishing and developing Connecticut Colony; and John Davenport (b.England, 1597–1670) and Theophilus Eaton (b.England, 1590–1658), cofounders and leaders of the strict Puritan colony of New Haven. Other famous historical figures are diplomat Silas Deane (1737–89); Israel Putnam (b.Massachusetts, 1718–90), Continental Army major general at the Battle of Bunker Hill, who supposedly admonished his troops not to fire "until you see the whites of their eyes"; and Benedict Arnold (1741–1801), known for his treasonous activity in the Revolutionary War but also remembered for his courage and skill at Ft. Ticonderoga and Saratoga. Roger Sherman (b.Massachusetts, 1721–93), a signatory to the Articles of Association, Declaration of Independence (1776), Articles of Confederation (1777), Peace of Paris (1783), and the US Constitution (1787), was the only person to sign all these documents; at the Constitutional Convention, he proposed the "Connecticut Compromise," calling for a dual system of congressional representation. Connecticut's most revered Revolutionary War figure was Nathan Hale (1755–76), the Yale graduate who was executed for spying behind British lines. Radical abolitionist John Brown (1800–1859) was born in Torrington.

Connecticuters prominent in US cultural development include painter John Trumbull (1756–1843), son of Governor Trumbull, known for his canvases commemorating the American Revolution. Joel Barlow (1754–1812) was a poet and diplomat in the early national period. Lexicographer Noah Webster (1758–1843) compiled the *American Dictionary of the English Language* (1828). Frederick Law Olmsted (1822–1903), the first American landscape architect, planned New York City's Central Park. Harriet Beecher Stowe (1811–96) wrote one of the most widely read books in history, *Uncle Tom's Cabin* (1852). Mark Twain (Samuel L. Clemens, b.Missouri, 1835–1910) was living in Hartford when he wrote *The Adventures of Tom Sawyer* (1876), *The Adventures of Huckleberry Finn* (1885), and *A Connecticut Yankee in King Arthur's Court* (1889). Charles Ives (1874–1954), one of the nation's most distinguished composers, used his successful insurance business to finance his own career and to help other musicians. Eugene O'Neill (b.New York, 1888–1953), the playwright who won the Nobel Prize for literature in 1936, spent summers in New London during his early years. A seminal voice in modern poetry, Wallace Stevens (b.Pennsylvania, 1879–1955), wrote the great body of his work while employed as a Hartford insurance executive. James Merrill (b.New York, 1926), a poet whose works have won the National Book Award (1967), Bollingen Prize (1973), and numerous other honors, makes his home in Stonington.

Native Connecticuters important in the field of education include Eleazar Wheelock (1711–79), William Samuel Johnson (1727–1819), Emma Willard (1787–1870), and Henry Barnard (1811–1900). Shapers of US history include Jonathan Edwards (1703–58), a Congregationalist minister who sparked the 18th-century religious revival known as the Great Awakening; Samuel Seabury (1729–96), the first Episcopal bishop in the US; Horace Bushnell (1802–76), said to be the father of the Sunday school; Lyman Beecher (1775–1863), a controversial figure in 19th-century American Protestantism who condemned slavery, intemperance, Roman Catholicism, and religious tolerance with equal fervor; and his son Henry Ward Beecher (1813–87), also a religious leader and abolitionist.

Among the premier inventors born in Connecticut were Abel Buel (1742–1822), who cast the first American foundry type in 1769; David Bushnell (1742–1824), who designed the first American submarine; Eli Whitney (1765–1825), inventor of the cotton gin and a pioneer in manufacturing; Charles Goodyear (1800–60), who devised a process for the vulcanization of rubber; Samuel Colt (1814–62), inventor of the six-shooter; and Frank Sprague (1857–1934), who designed the first major electric trolley system in the US.

Other prominent Americans born in Connecticut include clock manufacturer Seth Thomas (1785–1859), circus impresario Phineas Taylor "P. T." Barnum (1810–91), jeweler Charles Lewis Tiffany (1812–1902), financier John Pierpont Morgan (1837–1913), pediatrician and social activist Benjamin Spock (b.1903), cartoonist Al Capp (1909–79), soprano Eileen Farrell (b.1920), and consumer advocate Ralph Nader (b.1934). Leading actors and actresses are Ed Begley (1901–70), Katharine Hepburn (b.1909), Rosalind Russell (1911–76), Robert Mitchum (b.1917), and Ernest Borgnine (b.1917).

Walter Camp (1859–1925), athletic director of Yale University who contributed to the formulation of the rules of US football, was a native of Connecticut.

⁵⁰BIBLIOGRAPHY

Anderson, Ruth O. M. *From Yankee to American: Connecticut, 1865–1914.* Chester, Conn.: Pequot Press, 1975.

Bingham, Harold J. *History of Connecticut.* 4 vols. New York: Lewis, 1962.

Bixby, William. *Connecticut: A New Guide.* New York: Scribner, 1974.

Bushman, Richard L. *From Puritan to Yankee: Character and the Social Order in Connecticut, 1690–1765.* Cambridge: Harvard University Press, 1967.

Connecticut, State of. Secretary of State. *Register and Manual 1979.* Hartford, 1979.

Janick, Herbert F. *A Diverse People: Connecticut, 1914 to the Present.* Chester, Conn.: Pequot Press, 1975.

Lee, W. Storrs. *The Yankees of Connecticut.* New York: Holt, 1957.

Morse, Jarvis Means. *A Neglected Period of Connecticut's History: 1818–1850.* New Haven: Yale University Press, 1933.

Niven, John. *Connecticut for the Union: The Role of the State in the Civil War.* New Haven: Yale University Press, 1965.

Peirce, Neal R. *The New England States: People, Politics, and Power in the Six New England States.* New York: Norton, 1976.

Roth, David M. *Connecticut: A Bicentennial History.* New York: Norton, 1979.

Roth, David M., and Freeman Meyer. *From Revolution to Constitution: Connecticut, 1763–1818.* Chester, Conn.: Pequot Press, 1975.

Stuart, Patricia. *Units of Local Government in Connecticut.* Storrs: Institute of Public Service, University of Connecticut, 1979.

Taylor, Robert J. *Colonial Connecticut.* Millwood, N.Y.: KTO Press, 1979.

Trecker, Janice Law. *Preachers, Rebels, and Traders: Connecticut, 1818–1865.* Chester, Conn.: Pequot Press, 1975.

Van Dusen, Albert E. *Connecticut.* New York: Random House, 1961.

Van Dusen, Albert E. *Puritans Against the Wilderness: Connecticut to 1763.* Chester, Conn.: Pequot Press, 1975.

Warren, William L. *Connecticut Art and Architecture: Looking Backwards Two Hundred Years.* Hartford: American Revolution Bicentennial Commission of Connecticut, 1976.

Whipple, Chandler. *The Indian in Connecticut.* Stockbridge, Mass.: Berkshire Traveller Press, 1972.

Zeichner, Oscar. *Connecticut's Years of Controversy, 1750–1776.* Chapel Hill: University of North Carolina Press, 1949.

DELAWARE

State of Delaware

DECEMBER 7, 1787

ORIGIN OF STATE NAME: Named for Thomas West, Baron De La Warr, colonial governor of Virginia; the name was first applied to the bay. **NICKNAME:** The First State. **CAPITAL:** Dover. **ENTERED UNION:** 7 December 1787 (1st). **SONG:** "Our Delaware." **COLORS:** Colonial blue and buff. **MOTTO:** Liberty and Independence. **COAT OF ARMS:** A farmer and a rifleman flank a shield that bears symbols of the state's agricultural resources—a sheaf of wheat, an ear of corn, and a cow. Above is a ship in full sail; below, a banner with the state motto. **FLAG:** Colonial blue with the coat of arms on a buff-colored diamond; below the diamond is the date of statehood. **OFFICIAL SEAL:** The coat of arms surrounded by the words "Great Seal of the State of Delaware 1793, 1847, 1907." The three dates represent the years in which the seal was revised. **BIRD:** Blue hen's chicken. **FLOWER:** Peach blossom. **TREE:** American holly. **ROCK:** Sillimanite. **INSECT:** Ladybug. **LEGAL HOLIDAYS:** New Year's Day, 1 January; Lincoln's Birthday, lst Monday in February; Washington's Birthday, 3d Monday in February; Good Friday, March or April; Memorial Day, last Monday in May; Independence Day, 4 July; Labor Day, 1st Monday in September; Columbus Day, 2d Monday in October; Veterans Day, 11 November; General Election Day, 1st Tuesday after the 1st Monday in November in even-numbered years; Thanksgiving Day, 4th Thursday in November; Christmas Day, 25 December. **TIME:** 7 A.M. EST = noon GMT.

¹LOCATION, SIZE, AND EXTENT

Located on the eastern seaboard of the US, Delaware is the smallest of the 8 South Atlantic states and ranks 49th in size among the 50 states.

The total area of Delaware is 2,057 sq mi (5,328 sq km), of which land takes up 1,982 sq mi (5,134 sq km) and inland water 75 sq mi (194 sq km). Delaware extends 35 mi (56 km) E–W at its widest; its maximum N–S extension is 96 mi (154 km).

Delaware is bordered on the N by Pennsylvania; on the E by New Jersey (with the line passing through the Delaware River into Delaware Bay) and the Atlantic Ocean; and on the S and W by Maryland.

The boundary length of Delaware, including a general coast-line of 28 mi (45 km), totals 200 mi (322 km). The tidal shoreline is 381 mi (613 km). The state's geographic center is in Kent County, 11 mi (18 km) S of Dover.

²TOPOGRAPHY

Delaware lies entirely within the Atlantic Coastal Plain except for its northern tip, above the Christina River, which is part of the Piedmont Plateau. The state's highest elevation is 442 feet (135 meters) on Ebright Road, near Centerville, New Castle County. The rolling hills and pastures of the north give way to marshy regions in the south (notably Cypress Swamp), with sandy beaches along the coast. Delaware's mean elevation, 60 feet (18 meters), is the lowest in the US.

Of all Delaware's rivers, only the Nanticoke, Choptank, and Pocomoke flow westward into Chesapeake Bay. The remainder—including the Christina, Appoquinimink, Leipsic, St. Jones, Murderkill, Mispillion, Broadkill, and Indian—flow into Delaware Bay. There are dozens of inland freshwater lakes and ponds, but none larger than 220 acres (90 hectares).

³CLIMATE

Delaware's climate is temperate and humid. The normal daily mean temperature in Wilmington is 54°F (12°C), ranging from 32°F (0°C) in January to 76°F (24°C) in July. Both the record low and the record high temperatures for the state were established at Millsboro: –17°F (–27°C) on 17 January 1893 and 110°F (43°C) on 21 July 1930. The average annual precipitation is 40 in (102 cm), and about 20 in (50 cm) of snow falls each year. Wilming-

ton's average share of sunshine—53%—is one of the lowest among leading US cities.

⁴FLORA AND FAUNA

Delaware's mixture of northern and southern flora reflects its geographical position. Common trees include black walnut, hickory, sweetgum, and tulip poplar. Shadbush and sassafras are found chiefly in southern Delaware. Two subspecies of orchid are threatened, and one member of the sedge family is considered endangered.

Mammals native to the state include the white-tailed deer, red and gray foxes, eastern gray squirrel, muskrat, and common cottontail. The robin, wood thrush, cardinal, and eastern meadowlark are representative birds, while various waterfowl are common. The southern bald eagle is an endangered species.

⁵ENVIRONMENTAL PROTECTION

Protection of wetlands and marine resources is Delaware's most pressing environmental problem. The Coastal Zone Act, proposed by then Governor Russell W. Peterson (who later headed the US Council on Environmental Quality) and passed in 1971 by the state legislature after much public debate, outlaws all new heavy industry "incompatible with the protection of the natural environment" of shore areas. In 1979, however, the act was amended to permit offshore oil drilling and the construction of a pipeline and oil production support bases along the Delaware coast. The heavy traffic of oil tankers into Delaware Bay represents another environmental hazard.

State environmental protection agencies include the Department of Natural Resources and Environmental Control, Coastal Zone Industrial Control Board, and Council on Soil and Water Conservation.

⁶POPULATION

Delaware ranked 46th among the 50 states with a 1970 census population of 548,104. The preliminary census figure for 1980 was 594,711, an increase of 8.5% for the decade.

About 70% of all Delawareans live in metropolitan areas. The largest city is Wilmington, with 76,152 residents in 1975, a 21% drop since 1960. Other leading cities are Newark, with 26,645, 134% more than in 1960; and Dover, the capital, with 22,480. Wilmington's population declined to 70,363 in 1980.

⁷ETHNIC GROUPS

Black Americans constitute Delaware's largest racial minority, numbering 77,000 in 1976. There is a sizable Hispanic American element, and small numbers of American Indians and Asians.

The foreign-born and their native-born children made up 12% of the state's population in 1970. Italy, the United Kingdom, and Poland were the leading countries of origin.

⁸LANGUAGES

English in Delaware is basically North Midland, with Philadelphia features in Wilmington and the northern portion. In the north, one *wants off* a bus, lowers *curtains* rather than blinds, pronounces *wharf* without /h/, and says /noo/ and /doo/ for *new* and *due* and /krik/ for *creek*. In 1970, 87% of native-born residents claimed English as a first language, as did 85% of all residents. The major first-language groups were as follows:

	NATIVE-BORN	FOREIGN-BORN
English	463,650	4,035
Italian	9,514	2,146
Polish	8,590	1,221
German	6,992	1,926

⁹RELIGIONS

The earliest permanent European settlers in Delaware were Swedish and Finnish Lutherans and Dutch Calvinists. English Quakers, Scotch-Irish Presbyterians, and Welsh Baptists arrived in the 18th century, though Anglicanization was the predominant trend. The Great Awakening began at Lewes with the arrival of George Whitefield, an Anglican preacher, on 30 October 1739, and the colony soon became a center of early Methodist activity. The Methodist Church was the largest denomination in Delaware by the early 19th century. Subsequent immigration brought Lutherans from Germany, Roman Catholics from Ireland, Germany, Italy, and Poland, and Jews from Germany, Poland, and Russia; most of the Catholic and Jewish immigrants settled in cities, Wilmington in particular.

As of 1979 there were 121,070 Catholics and an estimated 10,000 Jews living in Delaware. The number of known adherents of Protestant groups reached 134,102 in 1971. The leading groups were the United Methodist Church, 61,849; United Presbyterian Church, 21,296; and Episcopal Church, about 20,000.

¹⁰TRANSPORTATION

The New Castle and Frenchtown Railroad, a portage route, was built in 1832; the state's first passenger line, the Philadelphia, Wilmington, and Baltimore Railroad, opened six years later. As of 1974 there were 291 mi (468 km) of track. Amtrak provides passenger service to Wilmington on the Philadelphia-Baltimore route, and Conrail and the Chesapeake and Ohio Railroad are the main freight carriers. The Delaware Authority for Regional Transit (DART) provides state-subsidized bus service.

In 1978, the state had more than 5,240 mi (8,430 km) of roads and streets, 394,354 registered vehicles, and 402,907 licensed drivers. Delaware's first modern highway, running about 100 mi (160 km) from Wilmington to the southern border, was financed by industrialist T. Coleman du Pont between 1911 and 1924. The twin spans of the Delaware Memorial Bridge connect Delaware highways to those in New Jersey; the Delaware Turnpike section of the John F. Kennedy Memorial Highway links the bridge system with Maryland.

The Port of Wilmington, Delaware's chief port, received special state appropriations in 1979 and 1980 to enable it to handle containerized cargo. The Delaware River is the conduit for much of the oil brought by tanker to the US east coast.

Delaware had 32 airfields (3 public, 29 private) in 1978, of which Greater Wilmington Airport was the largest and busiest.

¹¹HISTORY

Archaeological evidence shows that Delaware was inhabited nearly 10,000 years ago, and that a succession of various cultures occupied the area until the first European contact. At that time, the Leni-Lenape (Delaware) Indians occupied northern Delaware, as well as nearby New Jersey and Pennsylvania, while several tribes, including the Nanticoke and Assateague, inhabited southern Delaware. The Dutch in 1631 were the first Europeans to settle in what is now Delaware, but their little colony (at Lewes) was destroyed by Indians. Permanent settlements were made by the Swedes in 1638 (at Wilmington, under the leadership of a Dutchman, Peter Minuit) and by the Dutch in 1651 (at New Castle). The Dutch conquered the Swedes in 1655, and the English conquered the Dutch in 1664. Eighteen years later, the area was ceded by the duke of York (later King James II), its first English proprietor, to William Penn. Penn allowed Delaware an elected assembly in 1704, but the colony was still subject to him and to his deputy governor in Philadelphia; ties to the Penn family and Pennsylvania were not severed until 1776. Boundary quarrels disturbed relations with Maryland until Charles Mason and Jeremiah Dixon surveyed the western boundary of Delaware (and the Maryland-Pennsylvania boundary) during the period 1763–68. By this time, virtually all the Indians had been driven out of the territory.

In September 1777, during the War for Independence, British soldiers marched through northern Delaware, skirmishing with some of Washington's troops at Cooch's Bridge, near Newark, and seizing Wilmington, which they occupied for a month. In later campaigns, Delaware troops with the Continental Army fought so well that they gained the nickname "Blue Hen's Chickens," after a famous breed of fighting gamecocks.

On 7 December 1787, Delaware, seeking the security of a strong union in which its equality with other states would be protected, became the first state to ratify the federal Constitution. Although Delaware had never abolished slavery, it remained loyal to the Union during the Civil War. By that time, it was the one slave state in which a clear majority of blacks (about 92%) were already free. However, white Delawareans generally resented the Reconstruction policies adopted by Congress after the Civil War, and by manipulation of registration laws denied blacks the franchise until 1890.

The key event in the state's economic history was the completion of a railroad between Philadelphia and Baltimore through Wilmington in 1838, encouraging the industrialization of northern Delaware. Wilmington grew so rapidly that by 1900 it encompassed 41% of the state's population. Considerable foreign immigration contributed to this growth, largely from the British Isles (especially Ireland) and Germany in the mid-19th century and, in great numbers, from Italy, Poland, and Russia in the early 20th century.

Although flour and textile mills, shipyards, carriage factories, iron foundries, and morocco leather plants were Wilmington's leading enterprises for much of the 19th century, the city eventually became famous as an administrative and research center for the chemical industry, which developed from gunpowder manufacturing. E. I. du Pont de Nemours and Co., founded near Wilmington in 1802, controlled such a large share of the explosives business by 1912 that it was split by court order into three companies, all based in that city. All three firms—Du Pont, Hercules, and Atlas (later largely absorbed into ICI America)—soon became primarily manufacturers of chemicals.

During this same period, Delaware's agricultural income rose, although the number of farmers declined. Peaches and truck crops flourished in the 19th century, along with corn and wheat; poultry and soybeans became major sources of agricultural income in the 20th century. Another economic stimulus was improved transportation.

During the 1950s, Delaware's population grew by an unprecedented 40%. The growth was greatest around Dover, site of a large air base, and on the outskirts of Wilmington. Wilmington itself lost population after 1945 because of the proliferation of suburban housing developments, as well as of suburban shopping centers, offices, and factories, including two automobile assembly plants and an oil refinery. Although many neighborhood schools became racially integrated during the 1950s, massive busing was instituted by court order in 1978 to achieve a racial balance in schools throughout northern Delaware.

12 STATE GOVERNMENT

Delaware has had four state constitutions, adopted in 1776, 1792, 1831, and 1897. Under the 1897 document, as amended, the legislative branch is the general assembly, consisting of a 21-member senate and a 41-member house of representatives. Senators are elected for four years, representatives for two.

Delaware's major elected executives include the governor and lieutenant governor (separately elected), treasurer, attorney general, auditor of accounts, and insurance commissioner. All serve four-year terms, except the treasurer and auditor, who are elected for two years. The governor, who may be reelected only once, must be at least 30 years of age, and must have been a US citizen for 12 years and a state resident for 6 years prior to taking office. The legislature may override a gubernatorial veto by a three-fifths vote of the elected members of each house. An amendment to the state constitution must be approved by a two-thirds vote in each house of the general assembly in two successive sessions with an election intervening; Delaware is the only state where amendments need not be ratified by the voters.

Voters must be US citizens at least 18 years of age. There is no minimum residency requirement.

13 POLITICAL PARTIES

The Democrats were firmly entrenched in Delaware for three decades after the Civil War; a subsequent period of Republican dominance lasted until the depression of the 1930s. Since then, the two parties have been relatively evenly matched.

As of 1978, the Democrats held an edge of 123,361 to 90,936 in voter registration; there were 63,959 other voters registered as independents or with minor parties. In November 1980, Delaware, generally regarded as a "swing state," gave Ronald Reagan a narrow victory, while Republican Governor Pierre du Pont IV easily won reelection. The Republicans gained control of the state house of representatives, while Democrats retained their majority in the state senate.

Delaware Presidential Vote by Major Political Parties, 1948–80

YEAR	ELECTORAL VOTE	DELAWARE WINNER	DEMOCRAT	REPUBLICAN
1948	3	Dewey (R)	67,813	69,588
1952	3	*Eisenhower(R)	83,315	90,059
1956	3	*Eisenhower(R)	79,421	98,057
1960	3	*Kennedy (D)	99,590	96,373
1964	3	*Johnson (D)	122,704	78,078
1968	3	*Nixon (R)	89,194	96,714
1972	3	*Nixon (R)	92,283	140,357
1976	3	*Carter (D)	122,596	109,831
1980	3	*Reagan (R)	105,700	111,185

*Won US presidential election.

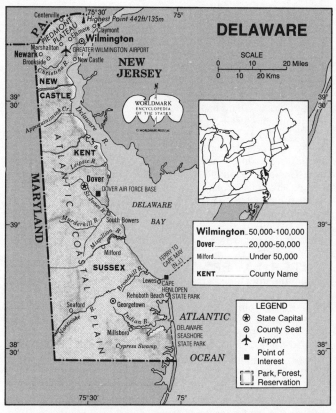

See US political: front cover L3; US physical: back cover L3.
LOCATION: 38°27′ to 39°50′N; 75°02′ to 75°47′W. **BOUNDARIES:** Pennsylvania line, 23 mi (37 km); New Jersey line, 27 mi (44 km); Atlantic coastline, 28 mi (45 km); Maryland line, 122 mi (196 km).

14 LOCAL GOVERNMENT

Delaware is divided into three counties. In New Castle, voters elect a county executive and a county council; in Sussex, the members of the elective county council choose a county administrator, who supervises the executive departments of the county government. Kent operates under an elected levy court, which sets tax rates and runs the county according to regulations spelled out by the assembly. Most municipalities elect a mayor and council.

15 STATE SERVICES

Public education is supervised by state boards of education and vocational education. Highways are the responsibility of the Department of Transportation, while medical care, mental health facilities, and help for the aging fall within the jurisdiction of the Department of Health and Social Services. Public protection services are provided primarily through the Department of Public Safety and Department of Correction. The Department of Labor has divisions covering employment services, vocational rehabilitation, unemployment insurance, and equal employment opportunity.

16 JUDICIAL SYSTEM

The state's highest court is the supreme court, composed of a chief justice and 4 associate justices, all appointed by the governor and confirmed by the senate for 12-year terms, as are all state judges. Other state courts are the court of chancery, comprising a chancellor and two vice-chancellors, and the superior court, which has a president judge and 10 associate judges.

Delaware was the last state to abolish the whipping post. During the 1900–1942 period, 1,604 prisoners (22% of the state's prison population and two-thirds of them black) were beaten with a cat-o'-nine-tails. The whipping post, nicknamed "Red Hannah," was used for the last time in 1952 but was not formally abolished until 1972.

[17] ARMED FORCES

Delaware's main defense facility is the military airlift wing at Dover Air Force Base, with 8,944 personnel in 1977/78. There were some 79,000 veterans living in Delaware as of 30 September 1979; about 1,000 were veterans of World War I, 33,000 of World War II, 12,000 of the Korean conflict, and 25,000 of the Viet-Nam era. Veterans' benefits totaled $52.4 million in 1977/78.

The National Guard had 2,900 members in 1977. There were 649 state police and 850 local police personnel during the same year.

[18] MIGRATION

Delaware has attracted immigrants from a variety of foreign countries: Sweden, Finland, and the Netherlands in the early days; England, Scotland, and Ireland during the later colonial period; and Italy, Poland, and Russia, among other countries, during the first 130 years of statehood. The 1960s and 1970s saw the migration of Puerto Ricans to Wilmington, some from the island and others from New York and Philadelphia. Delaware enjoyed a net gain from migration of 127,000 persons between 1940 and 1977.

[19] INTERGOVERNMENTAL COOPERATION

Among the interstate agreements to which Delaware subscribes are the Delaware River and Bay Authority Compact, Delaware River Basin Compact, Atlantic States Marine Fisheries Compact, Middle Atlantic Forest Fire Protection Compact, and Southern Interstate Energy Compact.

Federal aid to Delaware was estimated at $232.6 million in 1978/79, including $21.2 million in general revenue sharing.

[20] ECONOMY

Since the 1930s, Delaware has been one of the nation's most prosperous states. Manufacturing—preeminently the chemical industry—is the major contributor to the state's economy.

[21] INCOME

Average personal income per capita in Delaware was $8,604 in 1978, 8th highest among the 50 states; in 1960, Delaware had ranked 4th with an average of $2,735.

Median family income increased from $10,209 in 1969 (14th in the US) to $15,732 in 1975 (7th). Also in 1975, some 47,000 Delawareans, or 8% of the state's residents, were living below the federal poverty level.

[22] LABOR

Of the 273,000 members of the civilian labor force in 1978, 160,000 were male and 112,000 female. Some 21,000 Delawareans were unemployed for an unemployment rate of 7.7%, 3d highest in the US for that year. A federal census of workers covered by unemployment insurance in March 1977 revealed the following nonfarm employment pattern for Delaware:

	ESTABLISH-MENTS	EMPLOYEES	ANNUAL PAYROLL ('000)
Agricultural services, forestry, fishing	138	859	$ 6,309
Mining	15	96	2,006
Contract construction	1,378	15,055	240,237
Manufacturing	575	66,314	1,190,337
Transportation, public utilities	461	9,684	147,563
Wholesale trade	769	11,190	159,368
Retail trade	3,608	39,274	264,889
Finance, insurance, real estate	1,214	11,472	130,114
Services	3,333	38,971	335,189
Other	169	333	3,917
TOTALS	11,660	193,248	$2,479,929

Government workers, not covered by this survey, numbered about 37,000 in 1978.

Only 49,000 Delawareans—about 21% of all nonagricultural employees—belonged to labor unions in 1976. Employee associations enrolled another 8,000 persons.

[23] AGRICULTURE

Though small by national standards, Delaware's agriculture is efficient and productive. In 1978, according to state sources, only Arizona and California had higher net incomes per farm. Total farm receipts were $323.2 million in 1978 (42d in the US).

Tobacco was a leading crop in the early colonial era, but was soon succeeded by corn and wheat. Peaches were a mainstay during the mid-19th century, until the orchards were devastated by "the yellows," a tree disease. Today, the major field crops are corn, soybeans, wheat, and melons. Production in 1979 included corn for grain, 17,034,000 bushels, valued at $47,695,000; soybeans, 7,950,000 bushels, $48,781,000; wheat, 1,020,000 bushels, $4,233,000; and watermelons, 265,000 hundredweight, $1,381,000.

[24] ANIMAL HUSBANDRY

Livestock and livestock products account for about two-thirds of Delaware's farm income, with poultry farming by far the leading sector. Sales of chickens and broilers in 1979 totaled 759,963,000 lb, valued at $197,140,000; egg production was 130,000,000, valued at $7,931,000. There were 11,700 milk cows in 1979, when 129,000,000 lb of milk were produced.

[25] FISHING

Fishing, once an important industry in Delaware, has declined in recent decades. In 1956, 1,257 commercial fishermen landed 360,014,000 lb of fish, worth $6,206,000; in 1975, there were only 487 fishermen, and their landings of 7,055,300 lb were worth $1,716,894. The 1978 catch totaled 1,056,000 lb, worth $500,000.

The catch consists mainly of weakfish, bluefish, and blue crabs. Clams, which were plentiful until the mid-1970s, are in short supply because of overharvesting.

[26] FORESTRY

Delaware had 392,000 acres (159,000 hectares) of forestland in 1977, of which 384,000 acres (155,000 hectares) were classified as commerical forest. Sussex County has large stands of southern yellow pine, nearly all of it privately owned.

[27] MINING

In colonial times, iron was taken from bogs in Sussex County and also mined in the Newark area. Today, however, mining is of scant importance to Delaware's economy.

In 1978, the state's mineral output was only $2 million, last among the 50 states. Production in that year included 1,400,000 tons of sand and gravel and 9,000 tons of clays.

[28] ENERGY AND POWER

Installed electric capacity totaled 1.7 million kw in 1978, when production of electric power reached 7.3 billion kwh. Most of the power is supplied by oil-fired plants. Delaware has no nuclear reactors, nor does it have any fossil fuel resources.

[29] INDUSTRY

From its agricultural beginnings, Delaware has developed into an important industrial state. Today, Wilmington is called the "Chemical Capital of the World," largely because of E. I. du Pont de Nemours and Co., a chemical industry giant originally founded as a powder mill in 1802. As of 1979, the company was the 16th-largest US industrial corporation.

The Chrysler Corp., another leading employer, was offered a $5-million loan by the state under the recommended 1980/81 budget, to help keep that financially troubled company afloat. Notable Delaware manufactures during the 1970s, in addition to chemicals and transportation equipment, included cash registers, luggage, Jell-O, and seafood products.

The total value added by manufacture in 1977 was $1.6 billion. Major sectors and their value added in 1972 and 1977 were:

	1972	1977
Chemicals, chemical products	NA	$473,600,000
Food, food products	$209,900,000	286,800,000
Paper, allied products	NA	92,800,000
Rubber, miscellaneous plastics products	118,400,000	83,400,000

Data on several leading sectors was withheld by the US Bureau of the Census to avoid disclosing individual company operations.

³⁰COMMERCE

Wholesale trade in Delaware totaled $2.5 billion in 1972. Retail establishments had sales exceeding $2.1 billion in 1977, with Wilmington accounting for about one-seventh of the total. The leading retail sectors were food stores, 22%; automotive dealers, 17%; and department stores, 13%.

In 1976, Delaware exported $188 million worth of transportation equipment, chemicals, and other manufactured products to foreign markets.

³¹CONSUMER PROTECTION

The Division of Consumer Affairs within the Department of Community Affairs and Economic Development is responsible for enforcing state and federal consumer protection laws, representing consumer interests before local, state, and federal agencies, and maintaining consumer information and education programs. Other executive agencies with consumer protection responsibilities are the Consumer Affairs Board and the Council on Consumer Affairs.

³²BANKING

Delaware had 20 banks in 1979: 12 state-chartered commercial banks had assets of $3.4 billion, 2 mutual savings banks had $933.1 million, and 6 national banks had $83.8 million. There were 18 savings and loan associations: 16 state-chartered, with assets of $77.5 million, and 2 federally chartered, with assets of $202.7 million. As of 30 June 1979, Delaware had 71 small-loan companies holding 75,343 loans worth nearly $127 million.

The state government holds controlling interest in the Farmers Bank, the legal depository for all state funds.

³³INSURANCE

As of 31 December 1978, a total of 2,412,000 life insurance policies valued at $10.8 billion were in force. The average of $50,800 in life insurance per family ranked 2d only to Hawaii among the 50 states and was 45% above the US average. Life insurance benefits totaling $94.1 million were paid in 1978; death payments constituted 44% of the total.

³⁴SECURITIES

Delaware has no securities exchanges.

³⁵PUBLIC FINANCE

Delaware's annual state budget is prepared by the Office of the Budget and submitted by the governor to the general assembly for amendment and approval. The fiscal year runs from 1 July through 30 June. The following table summarizes state general revenues and expenditures for 1979/80 (budgeted) and 1980/81 (recommended), in millions:

REVENUES	1979/80	1980/81
Individual income taxes	$261.0	$291.0
Franchise taxes	61.5	62.4
Business and occupational licenses	47.0	53.4
Corporation income taxes	52.0	49.0
Other receipts	174.2	185.1
TOTALS	$595.7	$640.9
EXPENDITURES		
Public education	$193.5	$212.6
Higher education	62.5	71.3
Health, social services	109.3	115.3
Transportation	51.0	46.1
Other outlays	178.8	183.6
TOTALS	$595.1	$628.9*

*Excluding grants-in-aid.

As of mid-1977, the outstanding debt of Delaware state and local governments was more than $1.1 billion, or $1,979 per capita (5th among the 50 states).

³⁶TAXATION

Delaware's state tax revenues come primarily from levies on personal and corporate income, inheritances and estates, motor fuels, cigarettes, pari-mutuel betting, and alcoholic beverages. In 1979, personal income taxes were cut by more than $20 million, providing a reduction of 2% for most workers and lowering the top rate from 19.8% to 13.5%, a move welcomed by those who had complained that Delaware's top-bracket tax rate was the highest in the US (it ranked 3d as of early 1980). The corporate tax rate remained 7.2%. There is no state sales tax.

Delaware paid $1.1 billion in federal taxes in 1975/76 and received $698 million in federal expenditures, for a spending/tax ratio of 0.63, the lowest in the US for that year. State residents filed 239,419 federal income tax returns in 1977, paying $501,145,000 in tax.

³⁷ECONOMIC POLICY

Legislation passed in 1899 permits companies to be incorporated and chartered in Delaware even if they do no business in the state and hold their stockholders' meetings elsewhere. Another incentive to chartering in Delaware is the state's court of chancery, which has extensive experience in dealing with stockholders' suits and other corporate problems.

The Economic Development Division of the Department of Community Affairs and Economic Development seeks to create jobs by encouraging businesses to relocate to Delaware.

³⁸HEALTH

Average life expectancy in Delaware during 1969–71 was 70.06 years—66.29 for men, 74.07 for women—ranking the state 41st in the US. The infant mortality rate in 1977 was 11.4 per 1,000 live births for whites and 20.8 for nonwhites, in both cases below the US averages. With an overall death rate of 9.4 per 1,000 residents, Delaware had lower death rates than the nation as a whole for stroke, accidents, and pneumonia and influenza, but higher death rates for diabetes and cirrhosis of the liver.

Delaware's 15 hospitals had 83,440 admissions and 4,099 beds in 1978, for an occupancy rate of 83.8%. Hospital personnel included 1,823 registered nurses and 728 licensed practical nurses. The average cost of hospital care was $205 per day and $1,725 per stay in 1977, both above the US average. Delaware had 936 physicians in 1977 and 265 dentists in 1979.

³⁹SOCIAL WELFARE

Delaware does not have a history of expansive social programs. A survey made in 1938 found that the state, which then ranked 4th nationally in per capita income, spent little more than the poorest southern states on public assistance. Outlays for the five largest welfare programs in 1976 totaled $62 million, of which the federal government contributed 63%.

Expenditures on aid to families with dependent children reached $28 million in 1978, and $27 million was expended under Medicaid in 1977. Some 29,000 Delawareans participated in the food stamp program at a federal cost of $9 million; the school lunch program served 74,000 pupils, at a cost of $4.3 million.

Social Security benefits totaling $212.3 million went to 81,000 state residents in 1977; the average monthly payment for retired workers was $254.50. Federal Supplementary Security Income payments totaled $9.1 million in 1978, when unemployment payments amounted to $33 million. Delaware, the only state in 1938 not to have a vocational rehabilitation program, spent $2.7 million for that purpose in 1978. Workers' compensation payments amounted to $13.4 million in 1977.

⁴⁰HOUSING

The 1970 census counted 180,212 housing units in 1970, of which 164,804 were occupied. Owner-occupied units accounted for two-thirds of the latter total; blacks lived in only 9.5% of the owner-occupied units, but in 19.7% of the rented units. Only 4.5% of the housing units lacked full plumbing. From 1976 through 1978, 9,000 new units were authorized.

⁴¹EDUCATION

Delaware's school system was slow to develop. The first state school law, passed in 1829, divided the state into many independent school districts; black children were excluded. Compulsory school attendance legislation was not passed until 1907, and it required a mere three months a year. The development of public support and financing for an adequate public educational system was the handiwork of industrialist-Progressive Pierre S. du Pont, who undertook the project in 1919. Today's schools compare favorably with those of neighboring states. The adult illiteracy rate was only 0.9% in 1970; nearly 70% of adult Delawareans were high school graduates in 1976, and the median for school years completed was 12.5.

As of 30 September 1978 there were 111,034 students enrolled in public elementary and secondary schools, 53,041 in grades K–6 and 57,993 in grades 7–12. Another 22,150 children were enrolled in private and parochial schools. Delaware has two public four-year institutions: the University of Delaware (Newark), with a total enrollment of 19,029 in 1977/78; and Delaware State College (Dover), with 2,135. The Delaware Technical and Community College has four campuses. There are two four-year private colleges, Wesley (Dover) and Wilmington.

42 ARTS
Wilmington has a local symphony orchestra, opera society, and drama league. The restored Grand Opera House in Wilmington, which is Delaware's Center for the Performing Arts, presents a season of symphonic and chamber music concerts, as well as popular music and ballet. Many Delawareans also enjoy the cultural resources of nearby Philadelphia, Pa.

43 LIBRARIES AND MUSEUMS
Delaware had 29 public libraries and branches in 1977/78, with a combined book stock of 1,001,672 and circulation of 1,875,551. The University of Delaware's Hugh M. Morris Library is the largest academic library in the state, with 1,113,688 volumes. Other distinguished libraries include the Eleutherian Mills Historical Library; the Winterthur Library, and Historical Society of Delaware Library (Wilmington).

Notable among the state's museums and historical sites are the Hagley Museum and Delaware Art Museum, both in Wilmington, where the Historical Society of Delaware maintains a museum in the Old Town Hall. The Henry Francis du Pont Winterthur Museum features a collection of American antiques and decorative arts. The Delaware State Museum is in Dover.

44 COMMUNICATIONS
Delaware had 501,332 telephones—367,578 residential, 133,754 business—as of 31 December 1978. All telephone service in the state was supplied by Bell system affiliates, and virtually every household had a telephone. Also during 1978, the state had 10 AM and 8 FM radio stations. While Delaware has no commercial television stations of its own, Philadelphia and Baltimore stations are within range, and the state also had 9 cable systems serving 33 communities with 75,506 subscribers in 1978.

45 PRESS
Delaware's three leading newspapers, all published in Wilmington by the News-Journal Co. (an affiliate of the Gannett chain), are the *Morning News*, with an average daily circulation of 48,648 in 1978; the *Evening Journal*, 83,623; and the *News-Journal*, 117,485 on Saturdays, 96,032 on Sundays.

46 ORGANIZATIONS
Among national organizations headquartered in Delaware are the International Reading Association, Jean Piaget Society, American Philosophical Association, and American Astronomical Society, all in Newark.

47 TOURISM, TRAVEL, AND RECREATION
Delaware's travel and recreation industry is second only to manufacturing in economic importance.

Rehoboth Beach on the Atlantic Coast bills itself as the "Nation's Summer Capital" because of the many federal officials and foreign diplomats who summer there; annual festivities include an Easter sunrise service. Among other events are the Delaware Kite Festival at Cape Henlopen State Park (east of Lewes) every Good Friday, Old Dover Days during the first weekend in May, and Delaware Day ceremonies (7 December) throughout the state.

Fishing, clamming, crabbing, boating, and swimming are the main recreational attractions. Licenses were issued to 13,350 hunters and 27,854 fishermen in 1977/78.

48 SPORTS
Horse racing at Delaware Park (Wilmington) and other racetracks brought $3 million in pari-mutuel sales and admissions revenues to the state in 1979.

49 FAMOUS DELAWAREANS
Three Delawareans have served as US secretary of state: Louis McLane (1786–1857), John M. Clayton (1796–1856), and Thomas F. Bayard (1828–98). Two Delawareans have been judges on the Permanent Court of International Justice at The Hague: George Gray (1840–1925) and John Bassett Moore (1860–1947). James A. Bayard (b.Pennsylvania, 1767–1815), a US senator from Delaware from 1805 to 1813, was chosen to negotiate peace terms for ending the War of 1812 with the British.

John Dickinson (b.Maryland, 1732–1808), the "penman of the Revolution," and Caesar Rodney (1728–84), wartime chief executive of Delaware—and uncle of Caesar A. Rodney (1772–1824), later a US attorney general—were notable figures of the Revolutionary era. George Read (b.Maryland, 1733–98) and Thomas McKean (b.Pennsylvania, 1734–1817) were, with Rodney, signers for Delaware of the Declaration of Independence. Naval officers of note include Thomas Macdonough (1783–1825) in the War of 1812 and Samuel F. Du Pont (b.New Jersey, 1803–65) in the Civil War.

Morgan Edwards (b.England, 1722–95), Baptist minister and historian, was a founder of Brown University. Richard Allen (b.Pennsylvania, 1760–1831) and Peter Spencer (1779–1843) established separate denominations of African Methodists. Welfare worker Emily P. Bissell (1861–1948) popularized the Christmas seal in the US, and Florence Bayard Hilles (1865–1954) was president of the National Woman's Party.

Among scientists and engineers were Oliver Evans (1755–1819), inventor of a high-pressure steam engine; Edward Robinson Squibb (1819–1900), physician and pharmaceuticals manufacturer; Wallace H. Carothers (b.Iowa, 1896–1937), developer of nylon at Du Pont; and Daniel Nathans (b.1928), who shared the Nobel Prize in medicine in 1978 for his research on molecular genetics. Eleuthère I. du Pont (b.France, 1771–1834) founded the company that bears his name; Pierre S. du Pont (1870–1954) was architect of its modern growth.

In addition to Wilson, Delaware authors include Robert Montgomery Bird (1806–54), playwright; Hezekiah Niles (b.Pennsylvania, 1777–1839), journalist; Christopher Ward (1868–1944), historian; Henry Seidel Canby (1878–1961), critic; and novelists Anne Parrish (b.Colorado, 1888–1957) and J(ohn) P(hillips) Marquand (1893–1960). Howard Pyle (1853–1911) was known as a writer, teacher, and artist-illustrator.

50 BIBLIOGRAPHY
Dolan, Paul, and James R. Soles. *The Government of Delaware.* Newark: University of Delaware, 1976.

Federal Writers' Project. *Delaware: A Guide to the First State.* New York: Hastings House, 1955 (orig. 1938).

Hoffecker, Carol E. *Delaware: A Bicentennial History.* New York: Norton, 1977.

Mosley, Leonard. *Blood Relations: The Rise and Fall of the Du Ponts of Delaware.* New York, Atheneum, 1980.

Munroe, John A. *Colonial Delaware: A History.* Millwood, N.Y.: KTO Press, 1978.

Munroe, John A. *History of Delaware.* Newark: University of Delaware Press, 1979.

Weslager, C. A. *The Delaware Indians: A History.* New Brunswick, N.J.: Rutgers University Press, 1972.

FLORIDA

State of Florida

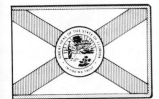

ORIGIN OF STATE NAME: Named in 1513 by Juan Ponce de León, who landed during *Pascua Florida*, the Easter festival of flowers. **NICKNAME**: The Sunshine State. **CAPITAL**: Tallahassee. **ENTERED UNION**: 3 March 1845 (27th). **SONG**: "Old Folks at Home" (also known as "Swanee River"). **MOTTO**: In God We Trust. **FLAG**: The state seal appears in the center of a white field, with four red bars extending from the seal to each corner; the flag is fringed on three sides. **OFFICIAL SEAL**: In the background, the sun's rays shine over a distant highland; in the foreground are a Sabal palmetto, a steamboat, and an Indian woman scattering flowers on the ground. The words "Great Seal of the State of Florida" and the state motto surround the whole. **BIRD**: Mockingbird. **FISH**: Largemouth bass (freshwater), Atlantic sailfish (saltwater). **FLOWER**: Orange blossom. **TREE**: Sabal palmetto. **GEM**: Moonstone. **MARINE MAMMALS**: Manatee, dolphin. **SHELL**: Horse conch. **BEVERAGE**: Orange juice. **LEGAL HOLIDAYS**: New Year's Day, 1 January; Martin Luther King's Birthday, 15 January; Robert E. Lee's Birthday, 19 January; Lincoln's Birthday, 12 February; Susan B. Anthony's Birthday, 15 February; Washington's Birthday, 3d Monday in February; Shrove Tuesday, February; Good Friday, March or April; Pascua Florida Day, 2 April; Confederate Memorial Day, 26 April; Memorial Day, last Monday in May; Jefferson Davis's Birthday, 3 June; Independence Day, 4 July; Labor Day, 1st Monday in September; Columbus Day and Farmers' Day, 2d Monday in October; General Election Day, 1st Tuesday after the 1st Monday in November in even-numbered years; Veterans Day, 11 November; Thanksgiving Day, 4th Thursday in November; Christmas Day, 25 December. **TIME**: 7 A.M. EST=noon GMT; 6 A.M. CST=noon GMT.

¹LOCATION, SIZE, AND EXTENT

Located in the extreme southeastern US, Florida is the 2d-largest state (after Georgia) east of the Mississippi River, and ranks 22d in size among the 50 states.

The total area of Florida is 58,560 sq mi (151,670 sq km), of which land takes up 54,090 sq mi (140,093 sq km) and inland water 4,470 sq mi (11,577 sq km). Florida extends 361 mi (581 km) E–W; its maximum N–S extension is 447 mi (719 km). The state comprises a peninsula surrounded by ocean on three sides, with a panhandle of land in the NW.

Florida is bordered on the N by Alabama and Georgia (with the line in the NE formed by the St. Marys River); on the E by the Atlantic Ocean; on the S by the Straits of Florida; and on the W by the Gulf of Mexico and Alabama (separated by the Perdido River).

Offshore islands include the Florida Keys, extending from the state's southern tip into the Gulf of Mexico. The total boundary length of Florida is 1,799 mi (2,895 km). The state's geographic center is in Hernando County, 12 mi (19 km) NNW of Brooksville.

²TOPOGRAPHY

Florida is a huge plateau, much of it barely above sea level. The highest point in the state is believed to be a hilltop in the panhandle, 345 feet (105 meters) above sea level, near the city of Lakeland, in Walton County.

Most of the panhandle region is gently rolling country, much like that of southern Georgia and Alabama, except that large swampy areas cut in from the Gulf coast. Peninsular Florida, which contains extensive swampland, has a relatively elevated central spine of rolling country, dotted with lakes and springs. Its east coast is shielded from the Atlantic by a string of sandbars. The west coast is cut by numerous bays and inlets, and near its southern tip are the Ten Thousand Islands, a mass of mostly tiny mangrove-covered islets. At the southwestern end of the peninsula lies Key West, which, at 24°33′N, is the southernmost point of the US mainland.

Almost all the southeastern peninsula and the entire southern end are covered by the Everglades, the world's largest sawgrass swamp, with an area of approximately 5,000 sq mi (13,000 sq km). The Everglades is, in a sense, a huge river, in which water flows south-southwest from Lake Okeechobee to Florida Bay. No point in the Everglades is more than 7 feet (2 meters) above sea level. Its surface is largely submerged during the rainy season—April to November—and becomes a muddy expanse in the dry months. Slight elevations, known as hammocks, support clumps of cypress and the only remaining stand of mahogany in the continental US. To the west and north of the Everglades is Big Cypress Swamp, covering about 2,400 sq mi (6,200 sq km), which contains far less surface water.

Lake Okeechobee, in south-central Florida, is the largest of the state's approximately 30,000 lakes, ponds, and sinks. With a surface area of about 700 sq mi (1,800 sq km), it is the 4th-largest natural lake located entirely within the United States. Like all of Florida's lakes, it is extremely shallow, having a maximum depth of 15 feet (5 meters), and was formed through the action of groundwater and rainfall in dissolving portions of the thick limestone layer that underlies Florida's sandy soil. The state's numerous underground streams and caverns were created in a similar manner. Because of the high water table, most of the caverns are filled, but some spectacular examples thick with stalactites can be seen in Florida Caverns State Park, near Marianna. More than 200 natural springs send up some 7 billion gallons of groundwater a day through cracks in the limestone. Silver Springs, near Ocala in north-central Florida, has the largest average flow of any inland spring, 823 cu feet (23 cu meters) per second.

Florida has more than 1,700 rivers, streams, and creeks. The longest river is the St. Johns, which empties into the Atlantic 19 mi (42 km) east of Jacksonville; estimates of its length range from 273 to 318 mi (439–512 km), a clear-cut figure being elusive because of the swampy nature of the headwaters. Other major rivers are the Suwannee, which flows south from Georgia for 177 mi (285 km) through Florida and empties into the Gulf of Mexico; and the Apalachicola, formed by the Flint and Chattahoochee rivers at the Florida-Georgia border, and flowing south-ward across the panhandle for 94 mi (151 km) to the Gulf. Jim Woodruff Lock and Dam is located on the Apalachicola about 1,000 feet (300 meters) below the confluence of the two feeder rivers. Completed in 1957, the dam created Lake Seminole, most of which is in Georgia.

More than 4,500 islands ring the mainland. Best known are the Florida Keys, of which Key Largo—about 29 mi (47 km) long and less than 2 mi (3 km) wide—is the largest. Key West—less than 4 mi (6 km) long and 2 mi (3 km) wide—a popular resort, is the westernmost.

For much of the geological history of the US, Florida was under water. During this time, the shells of countless millions of sea animals decayed to form the thick layers of limestone that now blanket the state. The peninsula rose above sea level perhaps 20 million years ago. Even then, the southern portion remained largely submerged, until the buildup of coral and sand around its rim blocked out the sea, leaving dense marine vegetation to decay and form the peaty soil of the present-day Everglades.

³CLIMATE

A mild, sunny climate is one of Florida's most important natural resources, making it a major tourist center and a retirement home for millions of transplanted northerners. Average annual temperatures range from 65° to 70°F (18–21°C) in the north, and from 74° to 77°F (23–25°C) in the southern peninsula and on the Keys. At Jacksonville, the average annual temperature is 68°F (20°C); the average low is 59°F (15°C), the average high is 78°F (26°C). At Miami, the annual average is 76°F (24°C), with a low of 68°F (20°C) and a high of 83°F (28°C). The record high temperature, 109°F (43°C), was registered at Monticello on 29 June 1931; the record low, –2°F (–19°C), at Tallahassee on 13 February 1899.

Florida's proximity to the Atlantic and the Gulf of Mexico, and the state's many inland lakes and ponds, together account for the high humidity and generally abundant rainfall, although precipitation can vary greatly from year to year and serious droughts have occurred. At Jacksonville, the average annual precipitation is 54 in (137 cm) and the average annual relative humidity (at 1 P.M.) is 55%. At Miami, precipitation averages 60 in (152 cm), humidity 62%. Rainfall is unevenly distributed throughout the year, more than half generally occurring from June through September; periods of extremely heavy rainfall are common. The highest 24-hour total ever recorded in the US, 38.7 in (98.3 cm), fell at Yankeetown, west of Ocala on the Gulf coast, on 5–6 September 1950. Thus, despite the high annual precipitation rate, the state also receives abundant sunshine—61% of the maximum possible at Jacksonville, and 75% at Miami and Key West. Snow is virtually unheard of in southern Florida but does fall on rare occasions in the panhandle and the northern peninsula. Frost may occur throughout the state.

Winds are generally from the east and southeast in the southern peninsula; in northern Florida, winds blow from the north in winter, bringing cold snaps, and from the south in summer. Average wind velocities are 8.5 mph (13.7 km/hr) at Jacksonville and 9.1 mph (14.6 km/hr) at Miami. Florida's long coastline makes it highly vulnerable to hurricanes and tropical storms, which may approach from either the Atlantic or the Gulf coast, bringing winds of up to 150 mph (240 km/hr). Hurricane Donna, which struck the state 9–10 September 1960, considered the most destructive in Florida's history, caused an estimated $300 million in damage. Tornadoes and waterspouts are not uncommon.

⁴FLORA AND FAUNA

Generally, Florida has seven floral zones: flatwoods, scrublands, grassy swamps, savannas, salt marshes, hardwood forests (hammocks), and pinelands. Flatwoods consist of open forests and an abundance of flowers, including more than 60 varieties of orchid.

Small sand pines are common in the scrublands; other trees here include the saw palmetto, blackjack, and water oak. The savannas of central Florida support water lettuce, American lotus, and water hyacinth. North Florida's flora includes longleaf and other pines, oaks, and cypresses; one giant Seminole cypress is thought to be 3,500 years old. The state is known for its wide variety of palms, but only 15 are native and more than 100 have been introduced; common types include royal and coconut. Although pine has the most commercial importance, dense mangrove thickets grow along the lower coastal regions, and northern hardwood forests include varieties of rattan, magnolia, and oak. Numerous rare plants have been introduced, among them bougainvillea and oleander. All species of cacti and orchids are regarded as threatened, as are most types of ferns and palms. Thirty plant species are listed as endangered, including the prickly apple cactus and the cowhorn orchid.

Florida once claimed more than 80 land mammals. Today the white-tailed deer, wild hog, and gray fox can still be found in the wild; such small mammals as the raccoon, eastern gray and fox squirrels, and cottontail and swamp rabbits remain common. Florida's bird population includes many resident and migratory species. The mockingbird was named the state bird in 1927; among game birds are the bobwhite quail, wild turkeys, and at least 30 duck species. Several varieties of heron are found, as well as coastal birds such as gulls, pelicans, and frigates. The Arctic tern stops in Florida during its remarkable annual migration between the North and South poles.

Common Florida reptiles are the diamondback rattler and various water snakes. Turtle species include mud, green, and loggerhead, and various lizards abound. More than 300 native butterflies have been identified. The peninsula is famous for its marine life: scores of freshwater and saltwater fish, rays, shrimps, live coral reefs, and marine worms.

The American alligator and the brown pelican, though common in Florida, are classified as threatened by the state and endangered by the US government. All of Florida's lands have been declared sanctuaries for the bald eagle, of which Florida has about 300 pair (2d only to Alaska among the 50 states). The state's unusually long endangered list includes the crocodile, shortnose sturgeon, Atlantic ridley turtle, Pine Barrens tree frog, dusky seaside sparrow, red-cockaded woodpecker, Florida panther, Key deer, and manatee.

⁵ENVIRONMENTAL PROTECTION

Throughout the 20th century, a rapidly growing population, the expansion of agriculture, and the exploitation of such resources as timber and minerals have put severe pressure on Florida's natural environment.

The state agency principally responsible for safeguarding the environment is the Department of Environmental Regulation, created by the Environmental Reorganization Act of 1975. Its duties include implementing state pollution control laws and improving water-resource management. The department's Division of Environmental Programs oversees and coordinates the activities of the state's five water-management districts, which have planning and regulatory responsibilities. The Department of Natural Resources protects the state's coastal and marine resources. Its Division of Recreation and Parks is authorized by the Conservation Act of 1972 to acquire environmentally endangered tracts of land; the division also administers state parks and wilderness lands. The Department of Agriculture and Consumer Services' Division of Forestry manages four state forests plus the Talquin State Lands. The Game and Fresh Water Fish Commission manages nature preserves and regulates hunting and fishing.

LOCATION: 24°33′ to 31°N; 80°02′ to 87°28′W. **BOUNDARIES:** Alabama line, 219 mi (353 km); Georgia line, 230 mi (370 km); Atlantic Ocean coastline, 580 mi (933 km); Gulf of Mexico coastline, 770 mi (1,239 km).

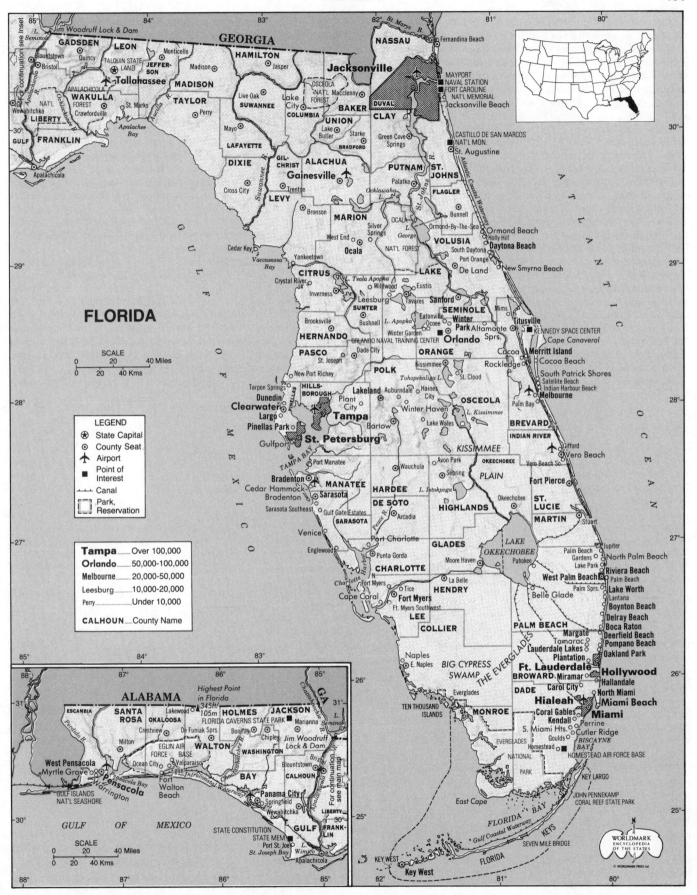

State spending for environmental protection in 1976/77 was $14.8 million, about half of that for water quality control. Local government spending was far greater. The city of Jacksonville spent nearly $50 million for environmental quality control in 1976/77, and Dade County and the city of Miami together spent more than $120 million. As of 30 June 1978, the face value of state capital bonds outstanding for environmental conservation and pollution control projects was $620.5 million. Federal aid in 1977/78 included $147.4 million from the Environmental Protection Agency (EPA) and $6.4 million for land and water conservation from the Department of the Interior.

Water quality is the state's most serious environmental problem. In 1971, an estimated 120 million gallons of raw or partially treated sewage were dumped into the Atlantic along the 60-mi (97-km) stretch of coast from Palm Beach to Miami. Local government spending on sewage treatment and disposal in 1976/77 was $435.6 million; of the 1977/78 federal aid from the EPA, $139.6 million was for construction of sewage treatment plants.

Sewage is not the state's only water problem. The steadily increasing demand for water for both residential and farm use has reduced the subterranean runoff of fresh water into the Atlantic and the Gulf of Mexico. As a result, salt water from these bodies has begun seeping into the layers of porous limestone that hold Florida's reserves of fresh water. This problem has been aggravated in some areas by the cutting of numerous inlets by developers of coastal property.

The conversion of large areas of the northern Everglades into farmland has reduced the flow of water to the southern part of the swamp, threatening its delicate ecological balance. To protect crops and create new agricultural land, networks of dikes, levees, spillways, and canals were constructed in the mid-20th century to prevent the seasonal flooding by Lake Okeechobee of the region to its south. In an effort to protect a portion of the Everglades from encroachment, Everglades National Park, covering 1,400,533 acres (566,777 hectares), was created in 1947 at the swamp's southern tip.

In 1960, the only undersea park in the US, the John Pennekamp Coral Reef State Park, was established in a 75-sq-mi (194-sq-km) sector off the Atlantic coast of Key Largo, in an effort to protect a portion of the beautiful reefs, rich in tropical fish and other marine life, that adjoin the Keys. Untreated sewage from the Miami area, runoff water polluted by pesticides and other chemicals, dredging associated with coastal development, and the removal of countless pieces of live coral by growing numbers of tourists and souvenir dealers have severely damaged large areas of the reefs.

⁶POPULATION

Florida, the most populous state in the southeastern US, is also one of the fastest growing of the 50 states. In 1970, it ranked 9th in the nation, with a census population of 6,789,443.

The first US census to include Florida, in 1830, recorded a total population of only 34,730. By 1860, on the eve of the Civil War, the population had more than quadrupled, to 140,424 people; about 80% of them lived in the state's northern rim, where cotton and sugarcane plantations flourished. The population migrated southward in the late 19th and early 20th centu-

Florida Counties, County Seats, and County Populations

COUNTY	COUNTY SEAT	LAND AREA (SQ MI¹)	POPULATION (1978)	COUNTY	COUNTY SEAT	LAND AREA (SQ MI¹)	POPULATION (1978)
Alachua	Gainesville	916	135,962	Leon	Tallahassee	670	133,817
Baker	Macclenny	585	13,045	Levy	Bronson	1,083	16,609
Bay	Panama City	747	96,525	Liberty	Bristol	839	4,267
Bradford	Starke	294	17,293	Madison	Madison	703	14,566
Brevard	Titusville	1,011	264,327	Manatee	Bradenton	739	135,415
Broward	Ft. Lauderdale	1,219	929,584	Marion	Ocala	1,600	102,722
Calhoun	Blountstown	561	8,863	Martin	Stuart	556	53,895
Charlotte	Punta Gorda	703	50,219	Monroe	Key West	1,034	55,793
Citrus	Inverness	560	40,148	Nassau	Fernandina Beach	650	31,686
Clay	Green Cove Springs	593	54,339	Okaloosa	Crestview	944	110,106
Collier	East Naples	2,006	74,572	Okeechobee	Okeechobee	777	18,759
Columbia	Lake City	784	30,232	Orange	Orlando	910	430,680
Dade	Miami	2,042	1,494,276	Osceola	Kissimmee	1,313	38,084
DeSoto	Arcadia	648	18,396	Palm Beach	West Palm Beach	2,023	534,551
Dixie	Cross City	692	7,382	Pasco	Dade City	742	150,153
Duval	Jacksonville	796	574,004	Pinellas	Clearwater	265	708,068
Escambia	Pensacola	665	231,133	Polk	Bartow	1,858	284,388
Flagler	Bunnell	487	8,405	Putnam	Palatka	779	45,045
Franklin	Apalachicola	536	8,388	St. Johns	St. Augustine	605	44,550
Gadsden	Quincy	512	37,275	St. Lucie	Ft. Pierce	584	77,477
Gilchrist	Trenton	346	5,837	Santa Rosa	Milton	1,032	50,284
Glades	Moore Haven	753	5,788	Sarasota	Sarasota	587	183,426
Gulf	Port St. Joe	565	11,081	Seminole	Sanford	305	149,802
Hamilton	Jasper	514	8,685	Sumter	Bushnell	555	21,781
Hardee	Wauchula	629	17,827	Suwannee	Live Oak	686	20,645
Hendry	La Belle	1,187	16,783	Taylor	Perry	1,051	15,090
Hernando	Brooksville	484	35,031	Union	Lake Butler	241	10,758
Highlands	Sebring	997	45,120	Volusia	DeLand	1,062	229,291
Hillsborough	Tampa	1,038	615,844	Wakulla	Crawfordville	601	9,307
Holmes	Bonifay	482	13,978	Walton	De Funiak Springs	1,053	19,059
Indian River	Vero Beach	506	52,333	Washington	Chipley	585	15,362
Jackson	Marianna	935	38,413				
Jefferson	Monticello	605	10,011				
Lafayette	Mayo	549	4,337	TOTALS		54,125	8,966,395
Lake	Tavares	961	94,315				
Lee	Ft. Myers	785	181,208				

¹Total, derived from a 1960 census of land areas considered more accurate than the 1970 census estimates, differs from the total cited elsewhere in the article and most often used by federal sources.

ries, following the railroads. A land boom in the early 1920s sharply increased the state's population; the 1930 census was the first in which the state passed the million mark. Migration from other states, especially of retirees, caused a population explosion in the post–World War II period, with much of the increase occurring along the south Atlantic coast. From 1950 to 1960, Florida's population increased 79%—the fastest rate of any US state. From 1960 to 1970, the growth rate was 37%; from 1970 to 1978, 32%, 4th highest in the US.

Of the 1970 census population, nearly 81% lived in urban areas; the average population density was 126 per sq mi (49 per sq km). Females constituted 51.8% of the population, males 48.2%. Nearly 15% of the 1970 population was 65 years of age or over.

By 1 July 1978, Florida's population had increased to 8,966,395 (8th in the US), according to state estimates. The proportion of females had increased to 52.3%, and the proportion of people 65 or over was 17.5%—by far the highest such percentage of any state (no other state had more than 14%). The population density had increased to 166 per sq mi (64 per sq km). By 1980, according to preliminary census data, Florida's population was 9,579,495, an increase of 41% since 1970.

The most populous city in Florida is Jacksonville, the 23d-largest city in the US in 1976. Its population, as measured by the 1970 census, was 504,265; the 1 July 1978 estimate was 544,215, an increase of nearly 8%. Miami is Florida's 2d-largest city, with a 1978 population of 344,393. However, Miami is the center of the state's largest metropolitan region, with an estimated 1,441,000 residents (22d in the US) in mid-1977; Jacksonville's metropolitan population was 694,000, for a rank of 4th in the state and 56th in the US. Florida's 2d-largest metropolitan area was Tampa–St. Petersburg, with 1,380,000 residents (25th in the US); the city of Tampa had 274,604 people in 1978, and St. Petersburg had 238,450. Ft. Lauderdale, with a city population of 154,365 in 1978, was the center of the state's 3d-largest metropolitan area, Ft. Lauderdale–Hollywood (864,000 in mid-1977, 42d in the US). Tallahassee, the state capital, had an estimated 1978 population of 83,773.

7 ETHNIC GROUPS
Florida's population consists mainly of whites of northern European stock, blacks, and Hispanics. European immigrants came primarily from Germany and the United Kingdom. Germans were particularly important in the development of the citrus fruit industry. Since World War II, the development of southern Florida as a haven for retired northerners has added new population elements to the state, a trend augmented by the presence of numerous military bases.

The largest group of first- and second-generation residents are Cubans, who represented nearly 4% of Florida's population in 1970. Puerto Ricans, Central Americans, and Filipinos have also settled in Florida. The total Hispanic population was 668,000 in 1976 and much higher than that by 1980, when more than 100,000 Cubans claiming refugee status arrived on Florida shores.

The black population, as reported in 1976, was 1,319,000, or more than 15%. Black-white relations in the 20th century have been tense. There were race riots following World War I, and the Ku Klux Klan was openly active until World War II. One of the worst race riots in US history devastated black areas of Miami in the spring of 1980.

Florida Indians resisted white encroachment longer and more militantly than Indians in other seaboard states. The leaders in resistance were the Seminole, most of whom by the 1850s had been killed or removed to other states, had fled to the Florida swamplands, or had been assimilated as small farmers. No peace treaty was signed with the Seminole until 1934, following the Indian Reorganization Act that attempted to establish tribal integrity and self-government for Indian nations. In 1939, the Indian population was reported as only 600, but the 1970 census reported a figure of 6,677. The difference is too large to be explained by natural increase, and there is no evidence of marked in-migration; presumably, then, it reflects a growing consciousness of Indian identity. There are four Indian reservations, three for the Seminole (Hollywood, Big Cypress, and Brighton) and one for the Mikasuki (Tamiami Trail).

A modest number of Chinese and Japanese have settled in Florida. In 1970 there were 4,090 Japanese, 3,133 Chinese, and 9,457 other Asians (not including 5,092 Filipinos). To these, 5,323 Vietnamese refugees were added in 1975.

8 LANGUAGES
Spanish and English settlers found what is now Florida inhabited by Indians recently separated from the Muskogean Creeks, who, with the addition of escaped black slaves and remnants of the Apalachee Indians of the panhandle, later became known as the Seminole Indians. Although the bulk of the Seminole were removed to Indian Territory in the 1840s, enough remained to provide the basis of the present population. In 1970, 1,566 residents claimed an Indian language as their mother tongue. Florida has such Indian place-names as Okeechobee, Apalachicola, Kissimmee, Sarasota, Pensacola, and Hialeah.

Such rapid population change has occurred in Florida since World War II that accurate statements about the language must await completion of research projects under way in 1980. Massive migration from the North Central and North Atlantic areas, including a large number of speakers of Yiddish, has materially affected the previously rather uniform Southern speech of much of the state. Borrowing from the Spanish of the expanding number of Cubans and Puerto Ricans in the Miami area has had a further effect.

Representative words in the Southern speech of most native-born Floridians are *light bread* (white bread), *pallet* (temporary bed on the floor), *fairing off* (clearing up), *serenade* (shivaree), *tote* (carry), *snap beans* (green beans), *mosquito hawk* (dragonfly), *crocus sack* (burlap bag), *pullybone* (wishbone), and *comforter* (tied and filled bedcover), especially in south Florida. Largely limited to the northern half of the state are *pinder* (peanut), *croker sack* instead of crocus sack, *fire dogs* (andirons); also in the Tampa Bay area, *comfort* (tied and filled bedcover), and, in the panhandle, *whirlygig* (merry-go-round). Some north Florida terms are clearly imported from Georgia: *mutton corn* (green corn), *lightwood* (kindling), and *co-wench!* (a call to cows).

English was the mother tongue claimed by 86% of the native-born residents in 1970, and by 80% of all residents. Major groups reported their mother tongues as follows:

	NATIVE-BORN	FOREIGN-BORN
English	5,347,491	93,121
Spanish	137,894	243,261
German	110,766	48,963
Italian	60,571	20,782
Yiddish	46,766	28,329
French	45,100	19,278

9 RELIGIONS
Protestant denominations claim the majority of church members in Florida. The state also has sizable Roman Catholic and Jewish populations.

Dominican and Franciscan friars, intent on converting the Indians, arrived with the Spanish conquistadores and settlers in the 1500s, and for some 200 years Florida's white population was overwhelmingly Catholic. Protestant colonists from Britain arrived in the late 1700s, and a significant influx of Protestant settlers from the southern US followed in the early 1800s. Sephardic Jews from the Carolinas also moved into Florida around this time, although the largest influx of Jews has occurred during the 20th century.

In 1971, the latest year for which detailed statistics are available there were 1,881,665 known adherents of Protestant groups in Florida. The largest denominations were Southern Baptist Convention, with 806,088 members; United Methodist Church, 385,051; Episcopal Church in the USA, 150,542; Presbyterian Church in the US, 116,705; United Presbyterian Church in the USA, 53,696; Lutheran Church–Missouri Synod, 49,950; and Lutheran Church in America, 43,510. The Roman Catholic population of Florida in 1979 was 1,306,782. The state has one archdiocese (Miami) and four dioceses (Orlando, Pensacola-Tallahassee, St. Augustine, and St. Petersburg).

The estimated number of Jews in Florida in 1979 was 435,580, about 5% of the state's total population and more than 7% of all Jews in the US. About nine-tenths of Florida's Jewish population was concentrated along the south Atlantic coast, from Palm Beach to Miami, including 225,000 in the Miami area. Florida's Jewish population increased by 45% between 1973 and 1979.

¹⁰TRANSPORTATION

Railroad building in the 19th century opened southern Florida to tourism and commerce. During the 20th century, long-distance passenger trains and, more recently, planes and automobiles have brought millions of visitors to the state each year.

The first operating railway in Florida was the St. Joseph Railroad, which inaugurated service on an 8-mi (13-km) track between St. Joseph Bay and Lake Wimico on 14 April 1836—using mules to pull the train. The railroad soon put into operation the state's first steam locomotive, on 5 September 1836. By the time the Civil War broke out, railroads connected most of northern Florida's major towns, but the rapid expansion of the state's railroad system—and with it the development of southern Florida—awaited two late-19th-century entrepreneurs, Henry B. Plant and Henry M. Flagler. Plant's South Florida Railroad extended service to Tampa in 1884. Flagler consolidated a number of small lines in the 1880s into the Florida East Coast Railway, with service as far south as Daytona. He then extended service down the Atlantic coast, reaching Palm Beach in 1894, Miami in 1896, and after construction of an extensive series of bridges, Key West in 1912. The "overseas" railway down the Keys was abandoned in 1935 after a hurricane severely damaged the line.

Florida's most extensive railroad is the Seaboard Coast Line, with 4,766 mi (7,670 km) as of 1 January 1978; the total trackage in use on that date was 6,556 mi (10,551 km). As of early 1980, Amtrak provided passenger service to 16 Florida cities.

On 7 June 1979, construction began on a surface rail system for Miami and surrounding areas of Dade County. The first stage of this mass transit system (known as Metrorail), a 20.5-mi (33-km) line serving Hialeah, Miami International Airport, downtown Miami, and areas to the south, was scheduled for completion in 1984.

As of 1 January 1979, Florida had about 95,500 mi (154,000 km) of public roads. Of this total, more than 12,000 mi (19,000 km) constituted the state highway system, including 1,460 mi (2,350 km) of interstate highways and the 315-mi (507-km) Florida Turnpike, a toll road. The turnpike's 265-mi (426-km) main section extends from Wildwood in north-central Florida to Ft. Pierce on the Atlantic coast and then south to Miami; there is also a 50-mi (80-km) extension to Homestead. The Overseas Highway down the Keys, using the bridges of the abandoned overseas railroad and including the famous Seven Mile Bridge (which is actually 35,716 feet, or 10,886 meters—6.8 mi—in length), is part of the state highway system. Florida also had more than 58,000 mi (93,000 km) of county roads as of 1 January 1979, of which nearly 28,000 mi (45,000 km) were paved. There were some 25,500 mi (41,000 km) of city streets and local roads, nearly 21,000 mi (34,000 km) of which were paved.

Florida had 7,068,875 registered motor vehicles in 1978:

5,738,031 automobiles (15% more than in 1977), 26,065 buses, 1,151,844 trucks, and 152,935 motorcycles. As of 9 July 1979, 7,148,085 people held active Florida driver's licenses, 3,861,979 men and 3,286,106 women.

Inland waterways in Florida include the southernmost section of the Atlantic Intracoastal Waterway and the easternmost section of the Gulf Intracoastal Waterway; both are navigable, federally maintained coastal channels for commercial vessels and pleasure craft. Construction began on 27 February 1964 on a barge canal across northern Florida to connect the two intracoastal systems; however, work was ordered stopped by President Richard Nixon on 19 January 1971 because of the threat the canal posed to flora and fauna in the surrounding area.

Florida has several commercially important ports. By far the largest port is Tampa, which handled 48,375,316 tons of cargo in 1978. Other major ports and their 1977/78 tonnage handled include Port Manatee, south of Tampa, 4,270,099; Pensacola, 2,582,417; Jacksonville, 1,965,871; and Miami, 1,922,864.

Florida's air lanes are among the busiest in the US. The state has 444 airports, including 14 used by scheduled airlines; in 1977, these 14 airports handled some 17,250,000 passengers. Florida's busiest airport is Miami International, which handled 245,472 scheduled airline flights in 1977/78. That same year, Tampa International had 127,988 such flights; Fort Lauderdale–Hollywood International, 84,370; and Orlando Jetport, 83,690. The Carter administration's policy in the late 1970s of encouraging airline competition and reducing government regulation of the industry sparked an increase in the number of flights and airlines on lucrative routes to and from Florida.

¹¹HISTORY

Indians entered Florida from the north 10,000–12,000 years ago, and had reached the end of the peninsula by 1400 BC. They subsisted mainly on large prehistoric animals until around 5000 BC, when they began to hunt smaller animals, as the huge ones became extinct, and to live in villages and, in the north, to practice some agriculture. As they grew in number, the Indians developed more complex economic and social organization. In northeastern Florida and nearby Georgia they apparently invented pottery independently about 2000 BC, some 800 years earlier than any other Indian group in North America.

In north Florida, an agricultural and hunting economy organized around village life was typical by this time. South of Tampa Bay and Cape Canaveral, Indians lived mostly along the coast and relied heavily on wild plants and on a large variety of aquatic and land animals for meat. The southern groups did not practice agriculture until about 450 BC, when they began to plant corn in villages around Lake Okeechobee. Huge mounds of shells along the southwest coast attest to the importance of clams, conch, and oysters in their diet.

As they spread over Florida and adjusted to widely different local conditions, the Indians fell into six main divisions, with numerous subgroups and distinctive culture traits. When Europeans arrived in the early 16th century, they found nearly 100,000 Indians: 25,000 Apalachee around Tallahassee; 40,000 Timucua in the northeast; on Tampa Bay, 7,000 Tocobaga; on the southwest coast and around Lake Okeechobee, 20,000 Calusa; on the lower southeast coast, 5,000 Tequesta; and in the Jupiter area, 2,000 Ais and Jeaga.

The Spanish who began arriving in the 16th century found the Indians in upper Florida to be relatively tractable, but those in the lower peninsula remained uniformly hostile and resisted to the last. The Spaniards sought to Christianize the Indians and settle them around missions—to grow food, to supply labor, and to help defend the province. By 1674, 70 Franciscan friars were working in dozens of missions and stations in a line running west from St. Augustine and north along the sea island coast to Carolina.

The impact of the Europeans on the Indian population was, on the whole, disastrous. Indians died of European-introduced diseases, were killed in wars with whites or with other Indians, or moved away. Raids from South Carolina by the Creeks, abetted by the British, between 1702 and 1708 completely destroyed the missions. When the Spanish departed Florida in 1763, the remaining 300 of the original 100,000 Indians left with them.

As early as 1750, however, small groups of Creek tribes from Georgia and Alabama had begun to move into the north Florida area vacated by the first Indian groups. They came in small bands, from widely separated places, at wide intervals, to settle in scattered parts of Florida. Called Seminole—the Creek word for runaway or refugee—these Indians did not then constitute a tribe and had no common government or leadership until resistance to white plans to resettle them brought them together. They numbered only 5,000 when Florida became part of the US.

Pressures on the US president and Congress to remove the Seminole intensified after runaway black slaves began seeking refuge with the Indians. In 1823, the Seminole accepted a reservation north of Lake Okeechobee. Nine years later, an Indian delegation signed a document pledging the Seminole to move within three years to lands in present-day Oklahoma. The Indians' subsequent resistance to removal resulted in the longest and most costly of Indian wars, the Seminole War of 1835–42. The warfare and the Indians' subsequent forced migration left fewer than 300 Seminole in Florida.

The history of the twice-repeated annihilation of Florida Indians is, at the same time, the history of white settlers' rise to power. After Christopher Columbus reached the New World at Hispaniola in 1492, the Caribbean islands became the base for wider searches, one of which brought Juan Ponce de León to Florida. Sailing from Puerto Rico in search of the fabled island of Bimini, he sighted Florida on 27 March 1513 and reached the coast a week later. Ponce de León claimed the land for Spain and named it La Florida, for *Pascua Florida*, the Easter festival of flowers; sailing southward around Florida, he may have traveled as far as Apalachicola, on the shore of the panhandle. In 1521, he returned to found a colony at Charlotte Harbor, on the lower Gulf coast, but the Indians fought the settlers. After Ponce was seriously wounded, the expedition sailed for Cuba, where he died that same year.

Other Spaniards seeking treasure and lands to govern came after Ponce. Pánfilo de Narváez arrived in 1528. Landing near Tampa Bay, he marched inland and northward to Tallahassee, finding only difficult terrain and hostile Indians with little surplus food. Missing a rendezvous with ships at St. Marks, on Apalachee Bay south of Tallahassee, he built five crude boats and took to the Gulf, but the party ran into a storm on the Texas coast that left no boats and only 80 survivors, 4 of whom, marching overland, reached Mexico City in 1536.

Hernando de Soto, a rich and famous associate of Francisco Pizarro in the conquest of Peru, found many men eager to try the same with him in Florida. Appointed governor of Cuba and *adelantado* (loosely, conqueror) of Florida, he followed the route of Narváez to Tallahassee in 1539, finding some food but no promise of wealth.

In 1559, Spain sought to establish a settlement on Pensacola Bay, as well as one at Santa Elena on Port Royal Sound, in South Carolina, to protect the trade route along Florida's east coast. Tristan de Luna led a large expedition to Pensacola Bay, landing on 14 August, but he lost most of his ships and supplies in a storm shortly after he arrived. A smaller expedition thence to Santa Elena was wrecked en route. Unable to find or produce food, Tristan de Luna abandoned the Pensacola settlement at the end of two years.

In 1562, Jean Ribault, with a small expedition of French Huguenots, arrived at the St. Johns River, east of present-day Jacksonville, and claimed Florida for France. Another group of French Huguenot settlers built Ft. Caroline, 5 mi (8 km) upriver, two years later. In the summer of 1565, Ribault brought in naval reinforcements, prepared to defend the French claim against the Spaniards, who had sent the redoubtable Pedro Menéndez de Avilés to find and oust the intruders. Menéndez selected St. Augustine as a base, landing on 28 August, and with the aid of a storm withstood the French effort to destroy him. He then marched overland to take Ft. Caroline by surprise, killing most of the occupants, and later captured Ribault and his shipwrecked men, most of whom he slaughtered. St. Augustine—the first permanent European settlement in the US—served primarily, under Spanish rule, as a military outpost, maintained to protect the wealth of New Spain. Attesting to its importance was the construction of Castillo de San Marcos, the stone fort that still stands guard there. The Spanish established a settlement at Pensacola in 1698, but it too remained only a small frontier garrison town. In 1763, when Spain ceded Florida to England in exchange for Cuba, about 3,000 Spaniards departed from St. Augustine and 800 from Pensacola, leaving Florida to the Seminole.

British Florida reached from the Atlantic to the Mississippi River and became two colonies, East and West Florida. Settlers established farms and plantations, traded with the Indians, and moved steadily toward economic and political self-sufficiency. These settlers did not join the American Revolution, but Florida was affected by the war nonetheless, as thousands of Loyalists poured into East Florida. In 1781, Spain attacked and captured Pensacola. Two years later, Britain ceded both Floridas back to Spain, whereupon most of the Loyalists left for the West Indies.

The second Spanish era was only nominally Spanish. English influence remained strong, and US penetration increased. Florida west of the Perdido River was taken over by the US in 1810, as part of the Louisiana Purchase (1803). Meanwhile, renegade whites, runaway slaves, pirates, and political adventurers operated almost at will.

Present-day Florida was ceded to the US in 1821, in settlement of $5 million in claims by US citizens against the Spanish government. At this time, General Andrew Jackson—who three years earlier had led a punitive expedition against the Seminole and their British allies—came back to Florida as military governor. His main tasks were to receive the territory for the US and to set up a civilian administration, which took office in 1822. William P. DuVal of Kentucky was named territorial governor, and a legislative council was subsequently elected. The new council met first in Pensacola and in St. Augustine, and then, in 1824, in the newly selected capital of Tallahassee, located in the wilderness of north-central Florida, from which the Indians had just been removed. Middle Florida, as it was called, rapidly became an area of slave-owning cotton plantations, and was for several decades the fastest-growing part of the territory. Of the 70,000 people in the state by 1845, Middle Florida had 47% of the total, and four Middle Florida counties with Negro majorities—Jackson, Gadsden, Jefferson, and Leon—were producing 80% of the cotton. The war to remove the Seminole halted the advance of frontier settlement, however, and the Panic of 1837 bankrupted the territorial government and the three banks whose notes it had guaranteed. Floridians drew up a state constitution at St. Joseph in 1838–39, but, being proslavery, had to wait until 1845 to enter the Union, paired with the free state of Iowa.

In 1861, Florida—which had only 140,000 people, about 40% of them blacks (mostly slaves), only 400 mi (644 km) of railroad, and no manufacturing—seceded from the Union and joined the Confederacy. Some 15,000 whites (one-third of whom died) served in the Confederate army, and 1,200 whites and almost as many blacks joined the Union army. Bitterness and some violence accompanied Republican Reconstruction government in

1868–76. The conservative Bourbon Democrats then governed for the rest of the century. They encouraged railroad building and other forms of business, and they kept taxes low by limiting government services. Cotton production never recovered prewar levels, but cattle raising, citrus and vegetable cultivation, forestry, phosphate mining, and, by late in the century, a growing tourist industry took up the slack.

The Spanish-American War in 1898, during which Tampa became the port of embarkation for an expedition to Cuba, stimulated the economy and advertised the state nationwide, not always favorably. Naval activity at Key West and Pensacola became feverish. Lakeland, Miami, Jacksonville, and Fernandina were briefly the sites of training camps.

In 1904, Napoleon Bonaparte Broward was elected governor on a moderately populist platform, which included a program to drain the Everglades lands which the state had received under the Swamp and Overflowed Lands Act of 1850. Drainage did lower water levels, and settlements grew around Lake Okeechobee—developments whose full environmental impact was recognized only much later. By the time Broward took office, Jacksonville had become the state's largest city, with Pensacola and Tampa not far behind, and Key West had dropped from 1st to 4th. During World War I, more than 42,030 Floridians were in uniform.

Boom, bust, blow, and depression characterized the 1920s. Feverish land speculation brought hundreds of thousands of people to Florida in the first half of the decade. Cresting in 1925, the boom was already over in 1926, when a devastating hurricane struck Miami, burying all hope of recovery. Yet population jumped by more than 50% during the decade, and Miami rose from 4th to 2d place among Florida cities. Florida's choice of Republican Herbert Hoover over Al Smith in the 1928 presidential election reflected the Protestant and prohibitionist attitudes of most of the state voters at that time.

The 1930s were marked first by economic depression, then by recovery, new enterprise, and rapidly growing government activity. The Florida depression that began in 1926 was compounded by the national depression that hit late in 1929. Bank and business failures, as well as defaults on city and county bond issues and on mortgage payments, produced growing economic distress. The state joined the federal government in assuming responsibility for relief and recovery. The legalization of parimutuel betting in 1931 created a new industry and a new tax source. The state's first paper mill opened in the same year, revolutionizing the forest industry. Private universities in Miami, Tampa, and Jacksonville were started during the depression years.

The 1940s opened with recovery and optimism, arising from the stimulus of production for World War II, production that began well before the actual entry of the US into the war. New Army and Navy installations and training programs brought business growth. After 1941, Florida seemed to become a vast military training school. The number of Army and Navy airfield flying schools increased from 5 to 45. Tourist facilities in all major cities became barracks, mess halls, and classrooms, with 70,000 rooms in Miami Beach alone being used to house troops in 1942. Families of thousands of trainees visited the state. Florida was on the eve of another boom.

First discovered but near last to be developed, the 27th state reached a rank of 27th in population only in 1940. But it was 7th by 1980, with well over 9 million people. Most of the increase was the result of migration, with enough of the migrants being 65 years of age or over to make the proportion of senior citizens in Florida nearly twice the national average by the late 1970s.

¹²STATE GOVERNMENT
Florida's first constitutional convention, which met from December 1838 to January 1839, drew up the document under

which the state entered the Union in 1845. A second constitutional convention, meeting in 1861, adopted the ordinance of secession that joined Florida to the Confederacy. After the war, a new constitution was promulgated in 1865, but not until still another document was drawn up and ratified by the state—the fourteenth amendment to the US Constitution—was Florida readmitted to statehood in 1868. A fifth constitution was framed in 1885; extensively revised in 1968, this is the document under which the state is now governed.

The 1968 constitutional revision instituted annual (rather than biennial) regular sessions of the legislature, which consists of a 40-member senate and a 120-member house of representatives. Senators serve four-year terms, with half the senate being elected every two years; representatives serve two-year terms. All legislators must be US citizens, at least 21 years of age, must have been residents of Florida for at least two years, and must be registered voters and residents of the district. A legislator's salary in 1979 was $12,000 a year. The maximum length of a regular session is 60 calendar days, unless it is extended by a three-fifths vote of each house. Special sessions may be called by the governor or by joint action of the presiding officers of the two houses (the president of the senate and speaker of the house of representatives). In addition, a special session may be convened by a three-fifths vote of all legislators, the poll being conducted by mail by the secretary of state upon a written request from at least 20% of the members.

The governor is elected for a four-year term; a two-term limit is in effect. The lieutenant governor is elected on the same ticket as the governor. A six-member cabinet, consisting of the secretary of state, attorney general, comptroller, insurance commissioner and treasurer, commissioner of agriculture, and commissioner of education, is independently elected. Each of these officials must be at least 30 years old, a US citizen, a registered voter, and have been a resident of Florida for at least seven years; in addition, the attorney general must have been a member of the Florida bar for at least five years. Each cabinet member heads an executive department. The governor appoints the heads of 11 departments and shares supervision of five additional departments with the cabinet. The governor and cabinet also share management of or membership in several other state agencies. These provisions make Florida's elected cabinet one of the strongest such bodies in any of the 50 states.

The Public Service Commission, an arm of the legislative branch with quasi-judicial powers, sets rates for and otherwise regulates (consistent with Interstate Commerce Commission rulings) railroads, motor carriers, canal companies, telephone and telegraph companies, and privately owned electric, gas, water, and sewer utilities. The PSC's five members are appointed by the governor from lists prepared by the Florida Public Service Nominating Council, a nine-member body selected, for the most part, by the legislative leadership.

Passage of legislation requires a majority vote of those present and voting in both houses. A bill passed by the legislature becomes law if it is signed by the governor; should the governor take no action on it, it becomes law 7 days after receipt if the legislature is still in session, or 15 days after receipt if the legislature has adjourned. The governor may veto legislation and, in general appropriations bills, may veto individual items. Gubernatorial vetoes may be overridden by a two-thirds vote of the legislators present in each house.

Amendments to the constitution may originate in three ways: by a joint resolution of the legislature passed by a three-fifths majority of the membership of each house; by action of a constitutional revision commission which, under the constitution, must be convened every 20 years; or by initiative petition. A proposed amendment becomes part of the constitution if it receives a majority vote in a statewide election.

To be eligible to vote in state elections, a person must be at least 18 years of age, a US citizen, and a resident in the county of registration; the registration books close 30 days prior to a general election.

¹³POLITICAL PARTIES

The Democratic and Republican parties are Florida's two principal political organizations. The former is the descendant of one of the state's first two political parties, the Jeffersonian Republican Democrats; this party, along with the Florida Whig Party, was organized shortly before statehood.

Florida's Republican Party was organized after the Civil War and dominated state politics until 1876, when the Democrats won control of the statehouse. Aided from 1889 to 1937 by a poll tax, which effectively disenfranchised most of the state's then predominantly Republican black voters, the Democrats won every gubernatorial election but one from 1876 through 1962; the Prohibition Party candidate was victorious in 1916.

By the time Republican Claude R. Kirk, Jr., won the governorship in 1966, Florida had already become, for national elections, a two-party state, although Democrats retained a sizable advantage in party registration. Beginning in the 1950s, many registered Democrats became "presidential Republicans," crossing party lines to give the state's electoral votes to Dwight D. Eisenhower in 1952 and 1956 and to Richard M. Nixon in 1960 (the only presidential candidate between 1928 and 1976 to carry Florida but lose the presidency).

A presidential preference primary, in which crossover voting is not permitted, is held on the 2d Tuesday in March of presidential election years. Because it occurs so early in the campaign season, this primary is closely watched as an indicator of candidates' strength. Primaries to select state and local candidates are held in September, with crossover voting again prohibited; runoff elections are held in October for races in which no candidate receives a majority in the first round.

As of 7 October 1978, the state had 2,812,217 registered Democrats (of whom 405,102 were black) and 1,178,671 registered Republicans (including only 12,725 blacks). Other organized groups include the American, Constitution, Conservative, Libertarian, and Socialist Workers parties. Minor parties can qualify by obtaining petition signatures from 3% of the state's voters.

Democratic candidate Reubin Askew was elected governor in 1970, and four years later became the first Florida governor to succeed himself for a second full term (as permitted by the 1968 constitutional revision). In the 1978 general election, Democrat Bob Graham won the governorship. Democrat Wayne Mixson was elected lieutenant governor on the same ticket, and Democrats captured all six cabinet posts. In late 1979, both US Senators were Democrats, and Florida's US House delegation had 12 Democrats and 3 Republicans. The state senate contained 29 Democrats and 11 Republicans, and the state house of representatives had 89 Democrats and 31 Republicans.

In the 1980 elections, Floridians favored Ronald Reagan for president and elected another Republican, Paula Hawkins, to the US Senate. Democrats retained control of Florida's US House delegation and of the state legislature. Voters in Dade County approved a resolution banning the use of county funds for bilingual (that is, English-Spanish) road signs and public notices, an action generally viewed as a majority backlash against the recent influx of Cuban immigrants.

¹⁴LOCAL GOVERNMENT

Florida has 67 counties. As of 1977, the state also had 393 municipalities, 119 school districts, and 468 special districts.

Generally, legislative authority within each county is vested in a five-member elected board of county commissioners, which also has administrative authority over county departments, except those departments headed by independently elected officials. In counties without charters, these elected officials usually include a sheriff, tax collector, property appraiser, supervisor of elections, and clerk of the circuit court. County charters may provide for a greater or lesser number of elected officials, and for a professional county administrator (analogous to a city manager). Much state legislation restricting county government operations has been repealed since 1968. Counties may generally enact any law not inconsistent with state law. However, the taxing power of county and other local governments is severely limited.

Municipalities are normally incorporated and chartered by an act of the state legislature. Except where a county charter specifies otherwise, municipal ordinances override county laws. Municipal governments may provide a full range of local services, but as populations rapidly expand beyond municipal boundaries, many of these governments have found that they lack the jurisdiction to deal adequately with area problems. Annexations of surrounding territory are permissible but difficult under state law. Some municipal governments have reached agreement with

Florida Presidential Vote by Political Parties, 1948–80

YEAR	ELECTORAL VOTE	FLORIDA WINNER	DEMOCRAT	REPUBLICAN	STATES' RIGHTS DEMOCRAT	PROGRESSIVE
1948	8	*Truman (D)	281,988	194,280	89,755	11,620
1952	10	*Eisenhower (R)	444,950	544,036	—	—
1956	10	*Eisenhower (R)	480,371	643,849	—	—
1960	10	Nixon (R)	748,700	795,476	—	—
1964	14	*Johnson (D)	948,540	905,941	—	—
					AMERICAN IND.	
1968	14	*Nixon (R)	676,794	886,804	624,207	—
1972	17	*Nixon (R)	718,117	1,857,759	—	—
					AMERICAN	
1976	17	*Carter (D)	1,636,000	1,469,531	21,325	—
						LIBERTARIAN
1980	17	*Reagan (R)	1,417,637	2,043,006	—	30,457

*Won US presidential election.

county or other local governments for consolidation of overlapping or redundant services or for provision of service by one local government to another on a contract basis. Complete consolidation of a municipal and a county government is authorized by the state constitution, requiring state legislation and voter approval in the area affected. As of 1979, one such consolidation effort had been successful, involving Jacksonville and Duval County.

The problem of overlapping and uncoordinated service is most serious in the case of special districts. These districts, established by state law and by approval of the voters affected, provide a specified service in a specified geographic area. An urban area may have dozens of special districts. State legislation in the 1970s attempted to deal with this problem by permitting counties to set up their own special-purpose districts, whose operations could be coordinated by the county government.

[15] STATE SERVICES

A "sunshine" amendment to the constitution and a statutory code of ethics require financial disclosure by elected officials and top-level public employees; the code prohibits actions by officials and employees that would constitute a conflict of interest. The Commission on Ethics, established in 1974, is empowered to investigate complaints of breach of public trust or violation of the code of ethics. In addition, an auditor general appointed by the legislature conducts financial and performance audits of state agencies.

Educational services are provided by the State Department of Education, which sets overall policy and minimum performance standards, operates the state university and community college systems, and issues bonds (as authorized by the state constitution) to finance capital projects. The Department of Transportation is responsible for developing long-range transportation plans and for construction and maintenance of the state highway system. The Department of Highway Safety and Motor Vehicles licenses drivers and regulates the registration and sale of motor vehicles.

Health and welfare services are the responsibility primarily of the Department of Health and Rehabilitative Services. In 1978, this department operated 18 major institutions and 65 other facilities, including mental hospitals, institutions for the mentally retarded, alcoholic treatment centers, and training schools for juvenile delinquents. In addition, the department administers such social welfare programs as Medicaid, aid to families with dependent children, food stamps, and foster care and adoption. It is also responsible for disease prevention and for assisting localities in performing health services.

The Department of Corrections maintained 24 major correctional institutions and 55 smaller facilities in 1979. The Department of Law Enforcement is responsible for maintaining public order and enforcing the state criminal code; enforcement activities emphasize combating organized crime, vice, and racketeering. The state's Army and Air National Guard are under the jurisdiction of the Department of Military Affairs. The Florida Highway Patrol, within the Department of Highway Safety and Motor Vehicles, is the only statewide uniformed police force.

No statewide agency has the provision of housing services as its primary responsibility. The Northwest Florida Regional Housing Authority provides housing for low-income and other residents of that area. The Department of Community Affairs' Division of Technical Assistance helps localities formulate housing policies and regulations.

The Department of Labor and Employment Security enforces legislation protecting the state's workers (including child labor and industrial safety laws) and administers the federally funded workers' compensation and unemployment insurance programs and the State Employment Service, whose nearly 100 offices provide employment counseling and assist in job placement. The

Department of Community Affairs' Office of Manpower Planning administers the federal Comprehensive Employment and Training Act program. The state civil service (called the Career Service), which has some 70,000 employees, is administered by the Department of Administration's Division of Personnel.

The Department of State manages state historic sites, archives, libraries, and fine arts centers.

[16] JUDICIAL SYSTEM

The state's highest court is the supreme court, a panel of seven justices which sits in Tallahassee; every two years the presiding justices elect one of their number as chief justice. All justices are appointed to six-year terms by the governor upon the recommendation of a judicial nominating commission. They may seek further six-year terms in a yes-no vote in a general election; however, there is a mandatory retirement age of 70. Supreme court justices, who prior to nomination must have been members of the Florida bar for at least 10 years, received an annual salary in 1979 of $45,350.

The supreme court has appellate jurisdiction only. The state constitution, as amended, prescribes certain types of cases in which an appeal must be heard, including those in which the death penalty has been ordered and those in which a lower appellate court has invalidated a state law or a provision of the state constitution. The court also hears appeals of state agency decisions on utility rates and may, at its discretion, hear appeals in many other types of cases.

Below the supreme court are four district courts of appeal, which sit in Tallahassee, Lakeland, West Palm Beach, and Miami. Each court has seven judges, who hear cases in three-judge panels. The method of their selection and retention in office is the same as for supreme court justices. District courts hear appeals of lower court decisions and may review the actions of executive agencies. District court decisions are usually final, since most requests for supreme court review are denied.

The state's principal trial courts are its 20 circuit courts, which have original jurisdiction in many types of cases, including civil suits involving more than $1,500, felony cases, and all cases involving juveniles. Circuit courts may also hear appeals from county courts if no constitutional question is involved. Circuit court judges are elected for six-year terms and must have been members of the Florida bar for at least five years prior to election. In 1979 there were 292 such judges, the number in each district varying from 50 (Greater Miami) to 3 (the Keys), depending on district population and caseload.

Each of Florida's 67 counties has a county court with original jurisdiction in misdemeanor cases, civil disputes involving $1,500 or less, and traffic-violation cases. County court judges are elected for four-year terms and must be members of the bar only in counties with populations of 40,000 or more. In 1979 there were 191 county court judges, the number in each county again varying according to population and caseload.

Florida has one of the highest crime rates in the US. In 1978, the number of FBI Index crimes reported in the state was 607,552. Of this total, 65,792 were violent crimes (murder, rape, robbery, and aggravated assault), and 541,760 were nonviolent (breaking and entering, larceny, and auto theft). According to the FBI, Florida's crime rate per 100,000 population was 7,069.5 in 1978, when only four states had higher crime rates—Arizona, California, Hawaii, and Nevada. Among US metropolitan areas, Daytona Beach had the 2d-highest crime rate in 1977. Miami was 6th overall, and 2d in violent crime; Orlando ranked 15th overall and Gainesville 18th. As of 30 June 1978, a total of 19,794 persons were serving prison sentences in institutions run by the Florida Department of Corrections. The state has a capital punishment statute, which was upheld by the US Supreme Court in 1976. The first execution under the statute took place in the state on 25 May 1979.

¹⁷ARMED FORCES

In 1977/78 there were 15 US Navy and 11 US Air Force installations in Florida. Naval personnel stationed in the state (military and civilian) exceeded 93,000, including some 30,000 based at facilities in Jacksonville, 21,470 at the Orlando Naval Training Center, nearly 18,000 at facilities in Pensacola, and over 14,000 at the Mayport Naval Station. In October 1979, the Key West Naval Air Station was made the headquarters of a new Caribbean Joint Task Force, established to coordinate US military activities in the Caribbean. The state had more than 51,000 Air Force personnel in 1977/78; the largest installations were Eglin Air Force Base in Valparaiso and Homestead Air Force Base in Homestead. The US Air Force Missile Test Center at Cape Canaveral (called Cape Kennedy from 1963 to 1973) has been the launching site for most US space flights, including all manned flights. US Department of Defense military spending in Florida in 1977/78 was nearly $3.9 billion (3.7% of the US total).

Some 1,318,000 US military veterans lived in Florida as of 30 September 1979; of those who saw wartime service, 41,000 served during World War I, 626,000 during World War II, 269,000 during the Korean conflict, and 352,000 during the Viet-Nam era. US Veterans Administration spending in Florida in 1977/78 totaled about $901.8 million, including $506 million for income security (primarily pensions); $169.8 million for education, training, and rehabilitation; and $211.5 million for hospital and medical care.

The state's Army and Air National Guard contained approximately 9,800 officers and enlisted personnel in 1978. Federal spending for Florida's National Guard that year totaled $30.8 million.

Florida's police forces had 24,649 full-time-equivalent employees in October 1977: state, 3,125; county, 7,862; and municipal, 13,662. The two largest municipal police forces were those of Miami and Jacksonville, with 1,148 and 1,132 employees, respectively. Spending for police protection in 1976/77 totaled $411.1 million. In 1977/78, law enforcement assistance grants totaling $19.9 million were received from the US Department of Justice.

¹⁸MIGRATION

Florida is populated mostly by migrants. In 1976, only 22% of all residents 14 years old or over were Florida-born—less than half the averages for the South and for the US as a whole. Among the Sunbelt states, only Arizona had a lower proportion of native residents in 1976. Migration from other states accounted for more than 90% of Florida's population increase in the 1970s.

The early European immigrants to Florida—first the Spanish, then the English—never populated the state in significant numbers. Immigration from southern states began even before the US acquisition of Florida, and accelerated thereafter. In the 20th century, US immigrants to Florida have come, for the most part, from the Northeast and Midwest. Their motivation has often been to escape harsh northern winters, and a large proportion of the migrants have been retirees and other senior citizens. Between 1970 and 1978, the number of Floridians 65 or over increased by almost 60%, nearly twice the rate of increase for the population as a whole.

In the 1960s and 1970s, Florida also experienced large-scale migration from the Caribbean and other parts of Latin America. Although the state has had a significant Cuban population since the 2d half of the 19th century, the number of immigrants surged after the Cuban revolution of 1959. From December 1965 to April 1973, an airlift agreed to by the Cuban and US governments landed a quarter of a million Cubans in Miami. By 1980, more than 500,000 Cubans were living in southern Florida, mostly in and around Miami, where the Cuban section had become known as "Little Havana." Another period of large-scale immigration from Cuba, beginning in April 1980, brought more than

100,000 Cubans into Florida harbors. At the same time, Haitian "boat people" were arriving in Florida in significant numbers—often reaching the southern peninsula in packed, barely seaworthy small craft. The number of Haitians in south Florida was estimated at 12,000 in early 1980. The US government classified most of them as illegal aliens, fleeing extreme poverty in their native country, but the immigrants claimed to be political refugees and sued to halt deportation proceedings against them.

The US Immigration and Naturalization Service reported 2,098 apprehensions of illegal aliens in Florida in 1978/79. The number of legal aliens living in the state in 1978 was 370,000, more than 7% of the US total; 17,478 Florida aliens were naturalized in 1977, 11% of the US total and 3d behind New York and California.

¹⁹INTERGOVERNMENTAL COOPERATION

In 1953, Florida became a signatory to the Alabama-Florida Boundary Compact. Among the interstate regional organizations in which Florida participates are the Southeastern Interstate Forest Fire Protection Compact Commission, Coastal Plains Regional Commission, Gulf of Mexico and South Atlantic regional fisheries management councils, and Gulf States marine fisheries commissions. The Central and South American and Caribbean Trade and Development Commission, within Florida's Department of Commerce, was created in 1978 to foster cooperation between Florida and Latin America.

Federal aid to Florida's state and local governments in 1978/79 totaled $2.4 billion, including general revenue-sharing funds of $202.4 million. Florida ranked 45th among the US states in per capita federal aid in 1977/78.

²⁰ECONOMY

Farming and the lumbering and naval stores industries, all concentrated in northern Florida, were early mainstays of the economy. In the late 19th century, the extension of the railroads down the peninsula opened up an area previously populated only by Indians; given the favorable climate, central and southern Florida soon became major agricultural areas. Tourism, aggressively promoted by the early railroad builders, became a major industry after World War I and remains so today.

Tourists and winter residents with second homes in Florida contribute billions of dollars annually to the state economy and make retailing and construction particularly important economic sectors. However, this dependence on discretionary spending by visitors and part-time dwellers also makes the economy—and especially the housing industry—highly vulnerable to recession. The economic downturn of the mid-1970s hit Florida harder than the US generally. New housing starts, for example, which fell by about 50% in the US from 1973 to 1975, dropped by more than 80% in Florida during the same period.

An extremely low level of unionization among Florida workers encouraged growth in manufacturing in the 1970s—but may also help explain Floridians' below-average income levels. At the end of the decade, the aerospace and electronics industries were expanding rapidly. Also at that time, the state's economy—particularly that of the Miami area—was benefiting from an influx of Latin American investment funds. Miami was said to have one of the largest "underground economies" in the US, a reference both to the sizable inflow of cash from illicit drug trafficking and to the large numbers of Latin American immigrants working for low, unreported cash wages.

The gross state product in 1977, according to preliminary estimates, was $59.7 billion, or about 3% of the gross national product. Contributions to the 1977 gross state product comprised wholesale and retail trade, 20%; finance, insurance, and real estate, 18%; services, 16%; government, 15%; manufacturing and mining, 12%; transportation, communications, and public utilities, 11%; contract construction, 5%; and farms, 3%.

²¹INCOME

In 1978, according to preliminary estimates, Florida's per capita income was $7,505, 27th among the 50 states but 2d in the Southeast, behind Virginia's. Total personal income was $64.5 billion. Personal income in 1977 was $58.3 billion, of which wages and salaries accounted for 54%; other labor income (principally fringe benefits), 5%; dividends, interest, and rent, 19%; transfer payments, 17%; and proprietors' income, 5%. The largest component of transfer payments was Social Security. Total retirement and disability benefits in 1977 (including those paid by private firms and by the military) exceeded $7 billion. Florida's median family income in 1975 was $12,205, 38th in the US.

In 1975, some 1,225,000 Floridians (more than 14%) lived below the federal poverty level. In the black population, 38% were below the poverty level; in the Hispanic, 18%. For all persons 65 or over the proportion was 11%, but for the elderly living alone it was 24%, and for those living with nonrelatives (i.e., in institutions), 31%.

The state's most affluent county in 1977 was Sarasota, on the Gulf coast, with a per capita income of $8,249. Next came the three counties encompassing the so-called Gold Coast of southeastern Florida: Palm Beach, $7,878; Broward, $7,834; and Dade, $7,755. Franklin, in the panhandle, was the poorest county, with a per capita income of $3,332. Union County, in northern Florida, was the 2d poorest ($3,529), despite the fact that it had registered nearly a 130% increase in per capita income since 1970.

²²LABOR

Florida's civilian labor force totaled 3,712,800 as of August 1978. Of that total, 3,468,200 were employed and 244,600 unemployed, for an unemployment rate of 6.6%. As in the US generally, unemployment was higher among nonwhites and among teenagers than among white adults—and highest among black teenagers.

Florida's labor force participation rate is well below the US average. In 1977, about 55% of the state's civilian noninstitutionalized population 16 years of age or older was in the labor force, compared with 62% for the US as a whole. The major reason for the difference is the extremely low participation rate for Floridians 65 or older, reflecting the fact that many people migrate to the state for their retirement years.

Reflecting the importance of tourism to Florida's economy, a higher proportion of the state's workers are employed in the trade and service industries than for the US as a whole; the proportion of workers in manufacturing is about half the US average. A federal census of workers covered by unemployment insurance in March 1977 revealed the following nonfarm employment pattern for Florida:

	ESTABLISH-MENTS	EMPLOYEES	ANNUAL PAYROLL ('000)
Agricultural services, forestry, fishing	2,732	23,773	$ 153,543
Mining	276	9,411	126,476
Contract construction	19,964	167,446	1,912,148
Manufacturing, of which:	10,912	369,400	4,196,558
Food products	(689)	(48,674)	(487,040)
Electric, electronic equipment	(439)	(37,908)	(474,413)
Transportation equipment	(567)	(36,766)	(530,416)
Transportation, public utilities	6,155	165,687	2,433,596
Wholesale trade	14,929	159,585	1,906,823
Retail trade	55,305	609,600	4,034,824
Finance, insurance, real estate	20,166	210,085	2,156,263
Services, of which:	57,518	617,308	5,166,748
Health	(13,271)	(161,674)	(1,779,400)
Hotels, lodgings	(3,465)	(88,790)	(414,560)
Other	3,632	5,892	60,891
TOTALS	191,589	2,338,187	$22,147,870

The federal survey excluded the self-employed, government workers, and several other employment categories. In 1978, 586,700 workers were employed in government: 384,900 by localities, 116,800 by the state, and the remaining 85,000 by the federal government.

In 1977, the average wage and salary income of Florida nonagricultural workers was $10,032. Average income was highest in the transportation, communication, and utilities sector ($14,576), and lowest in wholesale and retail trade ($8,163). Some 365,000 Florida workers belonged to labor unions in 1976, about 13% of the total nonagricultural work force and far below the national average. The state has a right-to-work law. Another 48,000 Floridians belonged to employee associations. Overall, less than 15% of the work force was organized, giving the state a rank of 46th in the US.

²³AGRICULTURE

Florida's most important agricultural products, and the ones for which it is most famous, are its citrus fruits. That fame is well deserved: nearly four-fifths of all the oranges produced in the US and three-fourths of all the grapefruits are grown in Florida. But the state is also an important producer of other fruits, vegetables, and sugarcane.

The total value of Florida's crops in 1977 was nearly $1.9 billion, 7th highest among the 50 states. Total agricultural income, including livestock marketings and government payments, exceeded $3.2 billion in 1978 (12th in the US). There were about 35,000 farms covering some 14 million acres (6 million hectares) in 1979; the total represented more than 40% of the state's entire land area.

The orange was introduced to Florida by Spanish settlers around 1570. Oranges had become an important commercial crop by the early 1800s, when the grapefruit was introduced. In 1886, orange production for the first time exceeded 1 million boxes (one box equals 90 lb). Much of this production came from groves along the northern Atlantic coast and the St. Johns River, which offered easy access to maritime shipping routes north. The expansion of the railroads and severe freezes in the 1890s encouraged the citrus industry to move farther south. In the late 1970s, Polk, Lake, St. Lucie, Orange, and Indian River counties in central Florida were the largest producers of citrus fruits. As of January 1976 there were about 70.5 million citrus trees in Florida, covering a total of more than 850,000 acres (344,000 hectares).

The value of Florida's citrus crop was about $1 billion in 1977. The orange crop totaled 164 million 90-lb boxes in the 1978/79 season. The grapefruit crop was 50 million 85-lb boxes; tangerines, 3.5 million 95-lb boxes; and tangelos and temple oranges, 8.9 million 90-lb boxes. About four-fifths of Florida's citrus production is processed into canned or chilled juice, frozen or pasteurized concentrate, or canned fruit sections. Production of frozen concentrate totaled 166,290,000 gallons in the 1976/77 season, when chilled juice production was 124,577,000 gallons. Stock feed made from peel, pulp, and seeds is an important by-product of the citrus-processing industry; feed production exceeds 1 million tons a year.

Florida is the 2d-leading producer, after California, of vegetables and melons. Vegetable farming is concentrated in central and southern Florida, especially in the area south of Lake Okeechobee, where drainage of the Everglades had left exceptionally rich soil. In 1977, the combined value of the state's vegetable, melon, tomato, and strawberry crops was $560.9 million, with tomatoes accounting for nearly 28% of that total. In 1977/78, Florida farmers harvested 8,565,000 hundredweight of tomatoes, 8,000,000 hundredweight of watermelons, and 5,658,000 hundredweight of potatoes. Florida's tomato and vegetable growers, who had at one time enjoyed a near monopoly of the US winter vegetable market, began in the late 1970s to face increasing competition from Mexican growers, whose lower-priced produce had captured about half the market by 1980.

Florida's major field crop is sugarcane (mostly grown near Lake Okeechobee), which enjoyed a sizable production increase in the 1960s and 1970s, following the cutoff of imports from Cuba. In 1979, Florida's sugarcane production, estimated at 10,240,000 tons, nearly equaled that of Hawaii, the leading US producer. Florida's 2d-largest field crop is soybeans (13,137,000 bushels in 1979), followed by peanuts, tobacco, and hay.

24 ANIMAL HUSBANDRY

Florida is an important cattle-raising state. The Kissimmee Plain, north of Lake Okeechobee, is the largest grazing area. Florida ranked 10th in the US in number of beef cattle in 1978, and 15th in number of dairy cows. Most of the beef cattle are sold to out-of-state feedlots; cash receipts from marketings totaled $422,199,000 in 1979 for 534,460,000 lb of marketed product. Other types of livestock raised commercially include hogs and pigs ($51,676,000), sheep, and rabbits.

Production of honey and eggs and the raising of Thoroughbred horses are also major industries. Honey production in 1978 totaled 23,852,000 lb, valued at $11,783,000. Florida ranked 8th in egg production in 1978, with an output of nearly 3 billion, or more than 4% of the US total.

25 FISHING

Florida's extensive shoreline and numerous inland waterways make sport fishing a major recreational activity. Commercial fishing is also economically important.

In 1978, Florida's commercial fish catch was 171,462,000 lb, nearly 3% of the US total. The value of Florida's catch was $97,519,000, more than 5% of the US total. The most important commercial species are shrimp, black mullet, Spanish mackerel, and blue crabs. In 1977/78, 24,805 commercial fishing vessels were registered in Florida.

Both freshwater and saltwater fishing are important sports. Tarpon, sailfish, and bonefish are major saltwater sport species; largemouth bass and panfish (including bream, speckled perch, and red-finned pike) are the leading freshwater sport fish.

26 FORESTRY

Nearly half of Florida's land area—17,040,000 acres (6,896,000 hectares)—was forested in 1977, when the state had 2.3% of all forested land in the US. A total of 15,330,000 acres (6,204,000 hectares) was commercial timberland, of which 86% was privately owned. The most common tree is the pine, which occurs throughout the state but is most abundant in the north.

Florida's forestry industry, concentrated in the northern part of the state, produced $13,165,000 worth of products in 1977. The most important forestry product is pulpwood for paper manufacturing; production in 1977 was 3.2 million cords. Lumber production was 467 million board feet; veneer log production, 60 million board feet. As of 1 January 1978, 6,413,753 acres (2,595,562 hectares) of Florida's forested land consisted of tree farms. In 1978, employment in the forestry and major wood-using industries, including paper and furniture manufacturing, exceeded 37,000.

Three national forests—Apalachicola, Ocala, and Osceola—covering 1,094,275 acres (442,839 hectares) are located in Florida. Four state forests plus the forested Talquin State Lands encompass 319,000 acres (129,000 hectares). Some timbering is permitted in the state forests, which are also used for recreational activities and wildlife protection.

Virtually all of Florida's natural forest had been cleared by the mid-20th century; the forests existing today are thus almost entirely the result of reforestation. Since 1928, some 3 billion seedlings have been planted in the state.

27 MINING

Although Florida is not generally considered a major mining state, it ranked 13th among the 50 states in mineral output value

in 1978, according to preliminary US Bureau of Mines data. Production totaled nearly $1.8 billion, about 2% of the US output.

Florida's principal minerals (exluding fossil fuels) are phosphate rock, limestone, dolomite, clays, and sand and gravel. The state is the leading US producer of phosphate rock (used largely for fertilizer), accounting for about five-sixths of US output and about one-third of world production. Production is concentrated in northern Hamilton and Gilchrist counties and central Polk, Marion, and Citrus counties. In 1977/78, 187,430,000 tons of phosphate rock were produced, of which 54,400,000 tons were marketable. Florida is also the dominant US producer of staurolite (used in portland cement manufacturing) and the leading producer of titanium minerals (rutile and ilmenite), accounting for 100% and 44%, respectively, of 1977 US production. During the same year, Florida also ranked 2d in production of fuller's earth (a type of clay), with 31% of US output, and 6th in stone production (5%). Total estimated production of clays in 1978 was 725,000 tons. Portland cement production was 3,062,000 tons; sand and gravel, 21,000,000 tons; and stone, more than 54,200,000 tons. Limestone, found throughout the state, is used largely in road building and cement manufacture. A variety of limestone known as coquina, consisting partly of mollusk shells (which are easily visible in the stone), was used as a building material by the first Spanish settlers at St. Augustine; a number of structures made from coquina still survive in the city.

28 ENERGY AND POWER

In 1978, a total of 2,266.5 trillion Btu of energy was consumed in Florida. About 37% of that total was used in transportation, 23% in residences, 17% by commercial establishments, 16% by industry, and 7% for other purposes. The primary source of 73% of the energy consumed in 1976 was petroleum. Other sources included natural gas, 15%; coal, 7%; and nuclear power, 5%. Although Florida produces some oil and natural gas, it is a net importer of energy resoures. Its mild climate and abundant sunshine offer great potential for solar energy development, but this potential had not been extensively exploited by the end of the 1970s.

More than 40% of all the primary energy sources consumed are used to produce electricity. In 1978, Florida had an installed generating capacity of 28.4 million kw; production in 1977 was 94.6 billion kwh. About 84% of output and 82% of capacity were in privately owned utilities. About 48% of electricity produced in 1977 came from fuel oil, 20% from nuclear power, 17% from coal, and 14% from natural gas; hydropower accounted for much less than 1%. Electricity generation from nuclear plants more than doubled in 1977, largely because the state's 4th such plant, the 825,000-kw Crystal River facility, operated by the Florida Power Corp. on the northern Gulf coast, went on line in March 1977. The state's three other nuclear plants, all owned by the Florida Power and Light Co., are Turkey Point Units 1 and 2, each with a capacity of 666,000 kw, located in Dade County; and St. Lucie Unit 1, with a 777,000 kw capacity, located south of Ft. Pierce. Residential customers used 49% of all electricity sold by utilities in 1977, commercial customers 28%, and industrial customers 20% (the remainder went for other purposes).

Petroleum production is centered in the northwest and to a lesser extent in the south. Production in 1978 was 47,262,000 barrels; proved reserves as of 31 December 1978 were 169,361,000 barrels. Petroleum production in Florida accounts for less than one-fifth of the amount of petroleum products used. Natural gas production in 1976 was 43.2 billion cu feet, or slightly more than 16% of consumption for that year. In 1978, production totaled 60 billion cu feet, and proved reserves were 160.3 billion cu feet.

29 INDUSTRY

Florida ranked 21st among the 50 states in value added by manufacturing in 1976, and 19th in number of manufacturing employees. The state is not a center of heavy industry, and many of its manufacturing activities are related to agriculture and exploitation of natural resources. Leading industries include food processing, production of lumber, furniture, and paper, and manufacture of stone, clay, and glass products. Value added by manufacturing in 1977 totaled $9.3 billion, up from $3.7 billion a decade earlier. The state's major industrial categories, in terms of value added, were food and food products, 17%; electric and electronic equipment, 12%; transportation equipment, 11%; chemicals and chemical products, 10%; printing and publishing, 8%; fabricated metal products, 7%; nonelectrical machinery, 6%; paper and paper products, 5%; stone, clay, and glass products, 5%; apparel and other textile products, 4%; and other industries, 15%.

Value added by manufacture for selected industries in 1972 and 1977 was as follows:

	1972	1977
Radio and television equipment	NA	$663,700,000
Preserved fruits and vegetables	$267,700,000	543,200,000
Newspapers	267,100,000	473,700,000
Phosphate fertilizers	130,800,000	304,500,000
Guided missiles, space vehicles	319,700,000	278,800,000
Ship and boat building and repairs	144,200,000	276,600,000
Office and computing machines	100,200,000	168,400,000

The cigar-making industry, traditionally important in Florida, has declined considerably with changes in taste and the cutoff of tobacco imports from Cuba. In the late 1930s, the Tampa area alone had well over 100 cigar factories, employing some 10,000 people. The 1977 Census of Manufactures found just 46 plants statewide, with total employment of about 2,600. Value added by the cigar industry declined from $49.6 million in 1972 to only $31.3 million in 1977.

Manufacturing is currently concentrated in and around Florida's three largest cities. Dade and Broward counties (Greater Miami), Hillsborough County (Tampa), and Duval County (Jacksonville) accounted for nearly half of all manufacturing employment in 1977.

³⁰COMMERCE

Wholesale and retail trade together account for about one-fifth of the gross state product and more than one-fourth of all non-agricultural employment. According to the 1977 US Census of Retail Trade, the state ranked 8th in the US in retail sales volume and 7th in number of retail establishments. The fashionable shops lining Palm Beach's Worth Avenue make it one of the nation's most famous shopping streets.

Sales by Florida's wholesale establishments in 1972, as measured by that year's US Census of Wholesale Trade, totaled nearly $20 billion, or close to 3% of the US total. Reflecting the importance of agriculture in the state, sales of groceries and produce accounted for 22%, compared with 15% for the US as a whole.

Retail sales in 1977 were $31.4 billion, more than 4% of the US total. At least 29% of retail trade employees worked in the more than 13,600 restaurants, cafeterias, bars, and similar establishments—a reflection, in part, of the importance of the travel business in Florida's economy. Sales at eating and drinking places represented 9% of total retail sales. Food stores accounted for 22%; automotive dealers, 21%; department, variety, and other general merchandise stores, 13%; gasoline service stations, 8%; furniture, home furnishing, and equipment stores, 5%; building material, hardware, garden supply, and mobile home dealers, 5%; apparel and accessories stores, 5%; drug and proprietary stores, 4%; and other establishments, 8%. The Miami metropolitan area had retail sales of $5.6 billion in 1977, or 18% of the state total. Retail sales in the Tampa–St. Petersburg area were about $4.9 billion (16%); in the Ft. Lauderdale–Hollywood area, $3.8 billion (12%); in the Jacksonville area, $2.4 billion

(8%); and in the Orlando area, $2.3 billion (7%).

Florida manufactures worth nearly $1.4 billion were exported to foreign customers in 1976. Exports of Florida agricultural products totaled $390 million in 1976/77. The value of all imports entering the US through Florida was $4.7 billion in 1978, 2.7% of the US total. The value of American exports leaving the US through Florida that year was $6.2 billion (4.3%). Duty-free goods for reshipment abroad pass through Port Everglades—a free-trade zone, established to bring international commerce to the state. In the late 1970s, Florida was believed to be the principal entry point for marijuana, cocaine, and other illicit drugs being smuggled into the US from Latin America.

³¹CONSUMER PROTECTION

In 1969, the Department of Agriculture was renamed the Department of Agriculture and Consumer Services. Its Division of Consumer Services disseminates consumer information, conducts educational programs for consumers, and acts as a clearinghouse for consumer complaints, referring them to the appropriate agency. The Florida Consumers' Council advises the commissioner of agriculture on consumer legislation.

The public counsel to the Public Service Commission (PSC), appointed by a joint committee of the legislature, represents the public interest in commission hearings on transportation and utility rates and other regulations. The public counsel can also seek judicial review of PSC rulings, and may appear before other state and federal bodies on the public's behalf in utility and transportation matters.

The Department of Business Regulation oversees pari-mutuel betting; land sales; the operations of condominiums, hotels, restaurants, mobile homes, parks, collection agencies, and repair services for electronic goods; and alcoholic beverage and tobacco sales.

³²BANKING

As of March 1978, Florida had a total of 2,640 banking and credit institutions, employing nearly 80,000 persons. The state's banking center is Miami, where the industry benefited in the late 1970s from an influx of funds from Latin America, some of which may represent "laundered" money derived from drug smuggling. The state's largest commercial bank, and the 79th-largest US commercial bank in 1979, is Miami's Southeast First National Bank, with total deposits of more than $1.5 billion as of 30 June.

At the end of 1977 there were 686 commercial banks (including nondeposit trust companies) in the state; 423 were state chartered, and 263 federally chartered. All but 4 were federally insured, and 293 were members of the Federal Reserve System. The largest bank holding companies were Southeast Banking Corp., with 45 banks, and Flagship Banks, with 38.

Assets of Florida's commercial banks as of 31 December 1978 exceeded $37 billion. Deposits totaled $32.2 billion, up more than 200% from a decade earlier, and loans outstanding totaled $11.2 billion. Banks in Dade County accounted for more than twice the shares of deposits and loans of any other county.

The state had 120 federally insured savings and loan associations in 1978. Their total assets on 31 December exceeded $41 billion; savings deposits were $35.2 billion, and mortgages exceeded $33.2 billion. Institutions in Greater Miami accounted for about 30% of each of those figures. Florida savings and loan associations made $5.3 billion worth of mortgage loans in 1977, about 5% of the US total; Miami area institutions accounted for nearly a quarter of Florida's total.

International banking grew in Florida during the late 1970s with the establishment of Edge Act banks in Miami. These banks have headquarters outside Florida and must engage exclusively in international banking.

The state had 584 credit unions in 1978, with 1,267,800 members (10% more than in 1977). The value of shares outstanding was nearly $1.8 billion (up 19% from 1977); assets exceeded $2 billion (up 19%); and loans outstanding, $1.6 billion (up nearly 22%).

The Department of Banking and Finance charters state banks and also oversees state savings and loan associations, credit unions, finance companies, trust companies, and mortgage brokerage firms.

³³INSURANCE

Florida's insurance industry employed nearly 56,000 people as of March 1978, including some 17,000 agents and brokers. More than 30% of insurance-carrier employment was concentrated in Duval County (which includes Jacksonville), and another 15% in Dade County. More than a quarter of the state's insurance agents and brokers were based in Dade County. Insurance premiums written in 1977 totaled nearly $5.7 billion. Florida companies accounted for $572 million, or about 10% of that total.

More than 16 million life insurance policies were in force in 1978, carrying a total face value, as of 31 December, of $100.3 billion. Benefits paid during the year were about $1.3 billion, consisting of the following: death payments, $467.1 million; annuity payments, $284.3 million; matured endowments, $38.6 million; disability payments, $25.3 million; surrender values, $226.8 million; and policy dividends, $234.5 million. Average life insurance in force in 1978 was $28,700 per Florida family.

Fire, casualty, and other types of insurance premiums written in 1977 totaled $4.2 billion; direct losses paid during the year came to nearly $2.3 billion. Of the total premiums written, automotive policies accounted for $1.4 billion; accident and health policies, $1.2 billion; homeowner multiple-peril policies, $290.7 million; commercial multiple-peril policies, $231.7 million; and other policies, nearly $1.1 billion.

Within the accident and health category, group policies accounted for $808.8 million worth of premiums, or two-thirds of the total. Hospital medical insurance premiums written in 1977 by Blue Cross and Blue Shield of Florida came to $352.8 million, and net losses paid totaled $319.7 million. As of 31 December 1976, 4,570,000 Floridians under age 65 were insured for hospital expenses, 4,263,000 for surgical expenses, 4,219,000 for regular medical expenses, and 3,058,000 for major medical coverage.

Not surprisingly for a state with so many inland waterways and such a lengthy coastline, marine insurance accounted for more than $89.4 million in premiums written during 1977. Direct losses paid during the year were $37.3 million.

The insurance industry is regulated by the state's Department of Insurance.

³⁴SECURITIES

No securities exchanges are located in Florida, but there were 126 security brokerage firms doing business in the state as of 30 September 1977. Employment in securities and commodities brokerage houses and related businesses exceeded 6,000 persons in March 1978; the vast majority of these people, more than 5,800, were employed by securities brokers and dealers. Nearly half of the industry's total employment was concentrated in the three Gold Coast counties—Dade, Broward, and Palm Beach. New York Stock Exchange member firms had 249 sales offices and 2,604 registered representatives in Florida as of 31 December 1978.

The Department of Banking and Finance, headed by the comptroller, oversees the securities industry.

³⁵PUBLIC FINANCE

Florida's general budget, the 9th-largest in the US, exceeded $6 billion in 1977/78. The Division of Planning and Budget of the Governor's Office prepares and submits to the legislature the budget for each fiscal year, which runs from 1 July to 30 June. The largest expenditure items are aid to localities, education, public welfare, and highways. By prohibiting borrowing to finance operating expenses, Florida's constitution requires a balanced budget.

The following table shows general revenues and expenditures for the 1977 and 1978 fiscal years:

REVENUES	1976/77	1977/78
Sales and use tax	$1,398,589,657	$1,644,746,777
Other state taxes and fees	2,189,054,090	2,513,153,680
Federal aid	1,253,129,833	1,335,494,575
Other receipts	487,407,032	606,682,798
TOTALS	$5,328,180,612	$6,100,077,830
EXPENDITURES		
State operations	$3,354,598,704	$3,980,659,596
Aid to cities	200,806,234	201,833,780
Aid to counties	1,772,775,674	1,917,584,454
TOTALS	$5,328,180,612	$6,100,077,830

Consolidated state revenues and disbursements exceeded $11 billion in 1977/78.

For county governments, total revenues in the year ending 30 September 1978 were $2,284,256,000; total expenditures came to $2,326,678,000. The county with by far the largest budget was Dade: revenues, $741,113,000; expenditures, $742,424,000. For the consolidated Jacksonville–Duval County government, revenues were $504,266,000 and expenditures $484,965,000. Other major city budgets included those of Miami, with revenues of $167,350,000, and expenditures of $177,867,000; Tampa, with revenues of $161,825,000 and expenditures of $282,707,000; and Tallahassee, with revenues of $132,717,000 and expenditures of $137,260,000.

The issuance of state bonds is overseen by the State Board of Administration, which consists of the governor, the state treasurer, and the comptroller. Three principal types of bonds are issued. The first consists of bonds backed by the "full faith and credit" of the state and payable from general revenue. Issuance of such bonds generally requires voter approval. The second type consists of revenue bonds, payable from income derived from the capital project financed—for example, from bridge or highway tolls. The third type consists of bonds payable from a constitutionally specified source—for example, higher education bonds backed by the state gross receipts tax, or elementary and secondary education bonds backed by the motor vehicle license tax. The face value of all state bonds outstanding as of 30 June 1978 was $2.4 billion, of which $1.3 billion comprised education bonds of all types.

The total public debt of all Florida state and local governments in 1978 exceeded $6 billion. The face value of state bonds outstanding was more than $2.4 billion. County governments' long-term debt came to nearly $1.4 billion, and city governments' long-term debt exceeded $2.2 billion.

³⁶TAXATION

Florida ranked 39th among the 50 states in per capita taxation in 1977/78, with a tax burden of $438.01 per person. The 4% sales and use tax is the largest single source of state revenue; property taxes make up the bulk of local receipts. The state constitution prohibits a personal income tax. The 1977 session of the legislature, after narrowly defeating a state sales tax hike, increased taxes on mining, and on cigarettes, beer, and wine. However, by the end of the decade, legislature emphasis had shifted to property tax relief. The 1979 legislature reduced the ceiling on school district taxes from $8 to $6.75 per $1,000 of assessed valuation, and limited increases in city and county property tax revenues to 5% a year. In addition, a constitutional amendment approved by voters in March 1980 raised the homestead exemption from school taxes from the first $5,000 of assessed valuation ($10,000 for senior citizens) to the first $25,000. For city and county taxes, the exemption remained $5,000.

The state sales tax applies to most retail items (but excludes groceries, medicines, and certain other items), as well as to car and hotel room rentals and theater admissions. The use tax is levied on wholesale items brought into Florida for sale. A 5% tax is levied on corporations' net incomes over $5,000. Other taxes include those on gasoline and other motor fuels, cigarettes, alcoholic beverages, driver's licenses and motor vehicles, and pari-mutuel betting. An estate tax is also levied. All told, taxes accounted for more than two-thirds of state revenues in 1977/78.

In 1977, Floridians filed more than 3.4 million federal income tax returns and paid nearly $6 billion in federal taxes.

37 ECONOMIC POLICY

In the late 1970s, the state government intensified its efforts to attract manufacturing industries to Florida, aiming to decrease the economy's vulnerability to fluctuations in tourism and other discretionary spending. The Division of Economic Development within the Department of Commerce opened offices in New York City, Europe, and Japan to promote Florida as a business relocation site and attract foreign investment funds. This department, in conjunction with the Department of Education, provides occupational training for new employees of firms relocating in Florida and requiring workers with particular skills. At the same time, the state continues to promote tourism, primarily through the Department of Commerce's Division of Tourism. The division conducts national advertising campaigns, publishes promotional materials, and otherwise seeks to publicize the state's attractions.

A special state Department of Citrus assists the important citrus industry with both research and product promotion. Its promotional activities have increasingly emphasized frozen and chilled juice, as growing citrus production threatens to outstrip demand for whole fruit.

38 HEALTH

For the period 1969–71, Florida (along with Arkansas) ranked 27th among the 50 states in life expectancy, with an average of 70.66 years. For men the average was 66.61; for women, 74.96.

Reflecting the age distribution of the state's population, Florida has a relatively low birthrate and a high death rate. Florida's birthrate was 13.1 per 1,000 population in 1977, 45th among the 50 states and well below the overall US figure of 15.4. The state's 1977 infant mortality rate among whites was 12.2 per 1,000 live births; among nonwhites, 24 (well above the US average). Some 57,500 legal abortions were performed in Florida in 1977; there were 520 abortions per 1,000 live births, well above the US average.

Florida's 1977 death rate, 10.9 per 1,000 population, was the highest of any state and 24% above the national norm. In that year, Florida exceeded the national averages in deaths from all major causes except early childhood diseases, and the death rate from cerebrovascular diseases was 28% higher than in the nation as a whole. The leading causes of death in 1978 were cardiovascular disease and cancer. The former accounted for about half of all deaths in the state, 47,519 out of 95,424. Cancer claimed 21,605 lives, nearly 23% of the total.

The most common types of infectious diseases in 1977 were gonorrhea, with 58,839 reported cases; influenza, 17,458; streptococcal infections, 11,951; chicken pox, 4,953; and syphilis, 4,543. In 1970, an estimated 160,000 Floridians were alcoholics, 132,500 men and 27,600 women.

Four state mental hospitals admitted 6,832 patients in 1977/78, of whom 4,230 were males and 2,602 females; nonwhite males accounted for more than 18% of the admissions, three times their proportion of the population as a whole. The number of resident patients as of 30 June 1978 was 5,673.

In 1978 there were 245 hospitals in Florida, including 219 general hospitals. The total number of beds available was 54,211, and the average daily census was 39,922, for an occupancy rate of nearly 74%. Florida's hospitals had 127,416 full-time-equivalent employees in 1978, including 24,085 registered nurses and 9,977 practical nurses. In 1976 there were 335 nursing homes, with 33,100 beds and 29,600 resident patients.

As of 31 December 1977, the total number of licensed physicians in the state (excluding armed forces, Veterans Administration, US Public Health Service, and other federally employed doctors) was 17,740. There were 212 physicians per 100,000 population, 8th in the US. More than one-fourth of all physicians were practicing in Dade County. Three Florida counties—Dixie, Glades, and Lafayette—had no practicing physicians in 1977. There were 4,323 dentists in 1979.

Private health insurance benefits paid to hospitals in 1977 exceeded $1.1 billion. The average cost of a hospital stay was $1,442; per day, $195. Florida ranked 19th among the 50 states in number of Medicaid recipients in 1978, with 135,000; Medicaid payments came to $16.8 million. In 1977, the state ranked 4th in number of residents enrolled in the Medicare program. As of 1 July 1977, 1,463,000 Floridians were eligible for Medicare hospital benefits, and 1,455,000 for medical benefits. For 1977, Medicare hospital benefits paid were $900 million; medical benefits, $462 million.

39 SOCIAL WELFARE

More than one-fifth of all Floridians receive Social Security payments. In 1977, the state ranked 4th in the US in both number of beneficiaries and total benefits received.

Public assistance payments to Floridians in 1977/78 totaled $359,751,320, including $138,359,800 in aid to families with dependent children (AFDC). As of December 1978 there were some 231,500 AFDC recipients. Gadsden, Madison, Jefferson, and Hamilton counties—all in the panhandle—had the highest percentages of the population receiving AFDC benefits.

In June 1978, 227,172 households, containing 645,675 persons, were participating in the federal food stamp program. Stamps worth $344,440,359 were purchased for $90,903,406 in 1977/78; the federal subsidy was $253,536,953. In 1978, some 1,039,000 students (about two-thirds of the total enrollment) were taking part in the national school lunch program; federal spending for this program came to $79,700,000.

Recipients of old age, survivors, and disability insurance (OASDI) payments from the Social Security Administration as of December 1977 numbered about 1,845,500, consisting of some 1,302,800 retired workers and their dependents, 323,500 survivors of covered workers, and 219,200 disabled workers and their dependents. OASDI payments in 1977 totaled more than $4.6 billion, including $3.2 billion to retirees and their dependents, $866.3 million to survivors, and $546.8 million to the disabled and their dependents. Retirees' average monthly benefits in December 1977 were $244.60. At the end of 1978, about 167,900 Floridians were receiving Supplemental Security Income. Payments in 1978 totaled $229.9 million: $105.1 million to the aged, $120.7 million to the disabled, and $4.1 million to the blind.

Federally supported vocational training programs enrolled some 997,000 persons in 1977/78, the 4th-highest total among US states. Federal spending for these programs was $16.1 million; state and local spending, $332.8 million. Nearly 41,000 Floridians took part in vocational rehabilitation programs, at a cost to the federal and the state governments of $35.1 million. In 1977, workers' compensation benefits totaled $301.4 million. Unemployment insurance benefits paid in 1978 came to $112 million; the average number of weekly beneficiaries was about 59,000.

40 HOUSING

Florida's housing market fluctuated widely in the 1970s. During the mid-decade recession, home buying dropped off markedly, and much newly completed housing could not be sold. By late in the decade, however, the unused housing stock had been depleted, and a new building boom was under way. Dade County, in particular, was experiencing a housing shortage.

The 1970 census counted 2,488,968 housing units in Florida as of 1 April 1970. Of that total, 69% were owner-occupied, and 95% had full plumbing facilities. As of 1 January 1979 there were 29,622 apartment buildings with 572,340 units, and 3,011 rooming houses with 24,224 units. Multifamily housing ranges from beachfront luxury high rises along the Gold Coast to dilapidated residential hotels in the South Beach section of Miami Beach, which has become a ghetto for the aged poor.

The assessed value of condominiums (almost certainly well below the market value) as of 1 January 1978 exceeded $10.7 billion. Dade, Broward, and Palm Beach counties, which had one-third of the state's 1978 population, accounted for nearly two-thirds of the total assessed valuation. Large retirement communities, often containing thousands of condominium units, are commonplace in the three counties. For cooperatives, the statewide assessed valuation was $635 million; more than 60% of that was in Broward County.

The Division of Florida Land Sales and Condominiums, within the Department of Business Regulation, registers all sellers of subdivided land and oversees the advertising and selling of land, condominiums, and cooperatives. A major controversy involving condominiums in the early 1970s centered on so-called "rec leases." Until the practice was outlawed in mid-decade, condominium developers often retained ownership of such recreational facilites as the swimming pool, clubhouse, and tennis courts, requiring apartment purchasers to pay rent for their use. The rents were generally set quite low at the time of sale, but raised sharply soon after.

In 1977 there were 35,069 tenant-occupied low-income housing units, 46% of them occupied by the elderly; 64% of the occupants were black, 28% white, and 8% Hispanic. The number of mobile homes licensed in 1977/78 was 366,981. The Mobile Home Tenant-Landlord Commission, within the Department of Business Regulation, hears complaints by mobile home park tenants concerning rate increases and service cutbacks.

An estimated 163,900 new housing units were authorized in 1978, more than double the 1976 total. Residential construction contracts in 1978 were valued at nearly $5 billion, 2d only to California and more than 8% of the US total.

41 EDUCATION

In the 1970s, Florida was an innovator in several areas of education, including competency testing, expansion of community colleges, and school finance reform. On the other hand, the state ranked below national norms in educational expenditures and attainments, although it compared well with most southern states.

As of 1970, 1.3% of Florida's adult population was illiterate—slightly above the US percentage, but the lowest in the Deep South. The median number of school years completed by Floridians 18 or older was 12.4 in 1976, when nearly 65% of state residents were high school graduates.

Student achievement in reading, writing, and mathematics is measured by the State Student Assessment Test (SSAT), given annually to all 3d, 5th, 8th, and 11th graders. Schools must make test results available to parents and the general public. Under state law, 11th graders must pass the SSAT Part II, which tests ability to apply reading and math skills in practical situations, in order to obtain a regular high school diploma. However, in 1979, a federal court prohibited withholding diplomas until 1982/83, on the grounds that poor test scores by nonwhites before that time could be the result of prior discrimination. In 1977/78, 64% of all 11th graders passed the SSAT Part II in math, and 92% in communications skills; 91,412 high school diplomas were awarded that year.

There were 2,179 public schools, 74,908 classroom teachers, and 10,702 other instructional personnel in 1977/78. The full-time-equivalent enrollment was 1,621,531, including 1,380,971 students in basic education, 157,038 in vocational education,

28,802 in adult education, and 54,720 in exceptional education. The basic-education total consisted of 435,502 students in grades K–3, 673,237 in grades 4–9, and 272,232 in grades 10–12. In fall 1978, nearly 70% of public school students were white, 23% black, and almost 7% Hispanic; there were small percentages of Asian and American Indian students. In Dade County, nearly one-third of the student body was Hispanic.

There were 207,616 students enrolled in nonpublic prepri-mary, elementary, and secondary schools in 1977/78. The full-time instructional staff of these schools totaled 12,789, including 9,946 teachers. Nonpublic school enrollment, especially in northern Florida, increased markedly in the early 1970s, apparently in response to public school desegregation.

Florida has nine state universities, with a total fall 1978 enrollment of 120,552. The largest, the University of Florida (Gainesville), had a fall 1978 enrollment of 31,027, of whom 26,372 were full-time students. Also part of the state university system are 15 university centers, which provide advanced and graduate courses away from the main university campuses. In 1972, Florida completed a community college system that put a public two-year college within commuting distance of virtually every resident. The state's 28 community colleges had a 1976/77 enrollment of more than 535,000. About one-third of these students were in academic programs, intended to lead ultimately to the baccalaureate degree; slightly more than one-third were in occupational training programs; and the remainder were in adult education and other noncredit programs.

Florida's 37 accredited private colleges and universities enrolled more than 65,000 students in fall 1978. By far the largest nonpublic institution is the University of Miami (Coral Gables), which had a fall 1978 enrollment of 14,572.

The Board of Education, consisting of the governor and the cabinet, is responsible for the state's educational system. The commissioner of education (a cabinet member) is also the administrative head of the Department of Education. The policy-making body for the state university system is the Board of Regents; the chancellor is the system's chief adminstrative officer. The Florida Student Financial Assistance Commission provides student assistance grants and guaranteed loans for Florida residents enrolled in higher educational institutions within the state. Special scholarships for Indians, descendants of Confederate soldiers or sailors, and children of deceased or disabled veterans are also offered.

In 1977/78, the state government provided about 51% of the funding for public education; local governments, 38%; and the federal government, 11%. Estimated operating expenditures in 1977/78 were $2.2 billion. Spending per pupil in average daily attendance was $1,594 (22d in the US); spending per capita was $316 (36th, tied with Louisiana). Florida's school finance law, enacted in 1978, establishes a funding formula aimed at equalizing both per-pupil spending statewide and the property tax burdens of residents of different school districts.

42 ARTS

Key West has long been a gathering place of creative artists, ranging from John James Audubon and Winslow Homer to Ernest Hemingway and Tennessee Williams. On 24 January 1980, the Tennessee Williams Fine Arts Center at Florida Keys Community College, located in Key West, opened with the world premiere of a Williams play, *Will Mr. Merriwether Return from Memphis?* In addition to the playhouse, the center contains gallery space and a cinema.

The Asolo Theater, which is located in Sarasota and is the site of an annual theater festival, was designated the state theater of Florida by the 1965 legislature.

Regional and metropolitan symphony orchestras include the Florida Philharmonic (Miami), Florida Symphony (Orlando), Jacksonville Symphony, Florida Gulf Coast Symphony (St. Petersburg), Florida West Coast Symphony (Sarasota), Ft. Lauderdale Symphony, Miami Beach Symphony, and Greater Palm Beach Symphony. Opera companies include the Asolo Opera Company, Civic Opera of the Palm Beaches, and Greater Miami Opera Association.

43 LIBRARIES AND MUSEUMS
There were 9 county public library systems and 23 multicounty systems serving a total of 52 Florida counties in 1977/78; the book stock was 9.3 million, and circulation totaled 30.6 million. The largest public library systems are those of Miami–Dade County (1.4 million volumes and 19 branches in 1978) and Jacksonville (1 million volumes and 10 branches). The State Library in Tallahassee housed more than 166,000 books and 134,000 state and federal documents in 1976/77; the State Library also distributes federal aid to local libraries and provides other assistance. In 1977/78, federal aid to Florida public libraries totaled $4.8 million. The largest university library is that of the University of Florida, with 2.1 million volumes in 1978. Other major university libraries include those of the University of Miami (1.2 million volumes in 1976/77) and Florida State University (1.1 million).

Florida has more than 100 museums, galleries, and historical sites. One of the best-known museums is the John and Mabel Ringling Museum of Art (Sarasota), a state-owned facility which houses the collection of the late circus entrepreneur, featuring Italian and North European Renaissance paintings. Also in Sarasota are the Ringling Museum of the Circus and the Circus Hall of Fame. The estates and homes of a number of prominent former Florida residents are now open as museums. The Villa Vizcaya Museum and Gardens in Miami, originally the estate of International Harvester founder James R. Deering, displays his collection of 15th–18th century antiques. Railroad developer Henry Morrison Flagler's home in Palm Beach is now a museum in his name. The Society of the Four Arts is also in Palm Beach. On Key West, Ernest Hemingway's home is also a museum. The Miami Seaquarium and Jacksonville zoo are among the state's leading zoos and aquariums.

The largest historic restoration in Florida is in St. Augustine, where several blocks of the downtown area have been restored to their 18th-century likeness under the auspices of the Historic St. Augustine Preservation Board, a state agency. Castillo de San Marcos, the 17th-century Spanish fort at St. Augustine, is now a national monument under the jurisdiction of the National Park Service and is open to the public. Other Florida cities having historic preservation boards include Pensacola, Tallahassee, and Tampa.

44 COMMUNICATIONS
In 1977/78, Florida had 175 first-class post offices. Postal receipts totaled $451.3 million, with Miami accounting for nearly one-fifth of that amount. The US Postal Service employed nearly 22,000 people in Florida as of mid-March 1978.

There were 7,272,155 telephones in the state in 1978, an increase of more than 75% since 1970. Of the 1978 total, 1,874,699 were business phones and 5,397,456 residential. On average, 100% of Florida households had telephone service. About 65% of all phones were part of the Bell System.

Florida's first radio station was WFAW (later WQAM) in Miami, which went on the air in 1920. In 1978, the state had 200 commercial AM stations and 111 FM. Miami was also the site of the state's first television station, WTVJ, which began broadcasting on 27 January 1949. There were 31 commercial TV stations by 1978; Miami, with 6 stations, had more than any other Florida city. Nine educational television stations were operating in 1980, serving virtually the entire state.

In 1979, Florida had 127 cable television systems, serving 571,430 residents in 366 communities.

45 PRESS
The *East Florida Gazette*, published in St. Augustine in 1783–84,

was Florida's earliest newspaper. The oldest paper still publishing is the *Jacksonville Times-Union*, which first appeared in February 1883.

In 1978, the state had 50 daily newspapers. There were 17 morning papers, with a combined circulation of 1,641,492; 32 evening papers, with a circulation of 808,599; 1 all-day paper (whose circulation is included in the morning and evening totals); and 33 Sunday papers with circulation of 2,483,444. The leading English-language dailies and their circulations in 1978 were:

AREA	NAME	DAILY	SUNDAY
Jacksonville	Times-Union (m,S)	150,758	188,483
	Journal (e,S)	52,026	
Miami	Herald (m,S)	419,960	529,291
	News (e,S)	66,714	
Orlando	Sentinel Star (all day, S)	186,920	213,813
St. Petersburg	Times (m,S)	197,499	245,555
	Independent (e,S)	38,083	
Tampa	Tribune (m,S)	179,477	210,043
	Times (e,S)	23,992	

There were 144 weekly newpapers in 1980. Of these, the most widely read was the sensationalist *National Enquirer*, published in Lantana, with a national circulation of more than 5 million. Another 177 periodicals of various types were also published in Florida as of 1980. Eleven Spanish-language newspapers and other periodicals were being published in Miami.

46 ORGANIZATIONS
Commercial, trade, and professional organizations based in Florida include the American Accounting Association (Sarasota), American Welding Society (Miami), American Electroplaters' Society (Winter Park), National Police Reserve Officers Association (Venice), American Law Enforcement Officers Citizen's Band Radio Patrol (North Miami), Florida Citrus Mutual (Lakeland), and Florida Fruit and Vegetable Association (Orlando).

Sports groups include the National Association for Stock Car Auto Racing, better known as NASCAR (Daytona Beach), the American Water Ski Association (Winter Haven), and the International Game Fish Association (Ft. Lauderdale).

Among other organizations with headquarters in Florida are the American Euthanasia Foundation (Ft. Lauderdale) and the American Sunbathing Association, formerly the International Nudist Conference (Orlando).

47 TOURISM, TRAVEL, AND RECREATION
Tourism is a mainstay of the state's economy. In 1977, Florida had more than 29 million visitors—who collectively spent nearly $11.3 billion there. At least 20 million visitors entered the state by car, more than three-quarters of them for vacations. Most of Florida's tourists are from elsewhere in the US, although, by the end of the 1970s, Miami was attracting large numbers of affluent Latin American travelers, lured at least in part by the Latin flavor the large Cuban community has given the city.

More than 355,000 Floridians worked in tourist- and recreation-related businesses as of March 1978. In January 1979, the state had 887 licensed hotels, with a total of 84,204 units. More than half of these facilities were located in Dade County, where hotels and other tourist accommodations stretch for miles along Collins Avenue in Miami Beach and communities to the north, in the heart of the state's tourist industry. In addition, there were 4,990 licensed motels, with 182,501 units.

Florida's biggest tourist attractions are its sun, sand, and surf. According to the state's Department of Commerce, leisure-time activity is the principal reason why more than four-fifths of auto travelers enter the state. Aside from the beaches and resorts, major tourist attractions include Walt Disney World, a huge amusement park near Orlando; the Kennedy Space Center at Cape Canaveral; and the St. Augustine historic district.

Nine parks and other facilities in Florida operated by the National Park Service drew some 7,564,700 visitors in 1978. The most popular destination was the Gulf Islands National Seashore, located near Pensacola (3,971,600 visitors), followed by Everglades National Park (1,136,100). In 1977/78, 11,350,332 people visited 89 facilities operated by the Division of Recreation and Parks of the state's Department of Natural Resources. These facilities included 27 state parks, 28 state recreation areas, and 17 state historical sites.

Fishing and boating are major recreational activities. In 1977/78, 434,818 pleasure craft were registered in the state. In 1977/78, licenses were sold to 750,052 fishermen and 263,136 hunters.

In the 1970s, the Miami Beach tourist hotels faced increasing competition from Caribbean and other Latin American resorts. The city's business community, seeking to boost tourism, strongly backed a 1978 statewide referendum to authorize casino gambling along part of Collins Avenue in Miami Beach and Hollywood; however, the proposal was defeated by a wide margin. In a local advisory referendum in March 1980, Miami Beach voters approved development in South Beach of an $850-million, 250-acre (100-hectare) complex that would include hotels and a convention center.

⁴⁸SPORTS

Florida has two National Football League teams, the Miami Dolphins and the Tampa Bay Buccaneers, and two North American Soccer League teams, the Fort Lauderdale Strikers and Tampa Bay Rowdies. Of these, the Dolphins have been the most successful, winning Super Bowls in 1973 (climaxing an undefeated season) and 1974. Although no major-league baseball teams play their home games in Florida during the regular season, many have their training camps in the state and play exhibition games (the "grapefruit league") there in the spring.

Thoroughbred, harness, quarter-horse, and greyhound racing are popular spectator and gambling sports, as is jai alai; the pari-mutuel tax yielded more than $88 million in state revenue in 1977/78. Paid attendance at greyhound tracks in 1977/78 was 8,938,093; jai alai frontons, 4,714,851; horse-racing tracks, 2,452,618; harness-racing tracks, 594,822; and quarter-horse-racing tracks, 89,549. The Hialeah Park Race Track, site of the annual Flamingo Stakes, is considered one of the most beautiful in the US.

Several tournaments on both the men's and the women's professional golf tours are played on Florida courses. In stock-car racing, the Daytona 500 is a top race on the NASCAR circuit. Three major collegiate football bowl games are played in the state: the Orange Bowl (Miami), Gator Bowl (Jacksonville), and Tangerine Bowl (Orlando).

⁴⁹FAMOUS FLORIDIANS

The first Floridian to serve in a presidential cabinet was Alan S. Boyd (b.1922), named the first secretary of transportation (1967–69) by President Lyndon Johnson. Florida also produced one of the major US military figures of World War II, General Joseph Warren Stilwell (1883–1946), dubbed "Vinegar Joe" for his strongly stated opinions. Graduated from West Point in 1904, he served in France during World War I. First posted to China in the 1920s, he became chief of staff to General Chiang Kai-shek and commander of US forces in the China-Burma-India theater during World War II. He was promoted to full general in 1944 but forced to leave China because of his criticism of the Chiang Kai-shek regime.

David Levy Yulee (b.St. Thomas, 1810–86) came to Florida in 1824 and, after serving in the US House of Representatives, was appointed one of the state's first two US senators in 1845, thereby becoming the first Jew to sit in the Senate. He resigned in 1861 to serve in the Confederate Congress. Yulee built the first cross-state railroad, from Fernandina to Cedar Key, in the late 1860s. Ruth Bryan Owen Rohde (b.Illinois, 1885–1954), a longtime Miami resident and member of the US House of Representatives (1929–33), became, in 1933, the first woman to head

a US diplomatic office abroad, when she was named minister to Denmark.

Prominent governors of Florida include Richard Keith Call (b. Virginia, 1792–1862), who came to Florida with General Andrew Jackson in 1821 and remained to become governor of the territory in 1826–39 and 1841–44. In the summer of 1836, Call commanded the US campaign against the Seminole. Although a southerner and a slaveholder, he steadfastly opposed secession. Napoleon Bonaparte Broward (1857–1910) was, before becoming governor, a ship's pilot, and owner of St. Johns River boats. He used one of these, *The Three Friends*, a powerful seagoing tug, to run guns and ammunition to Cuban rebels in 1896. As governor (1905–9), he was noted for a populist program that included railroad regulation, direct elections, state college reorganization and coordination, and drainage of the Everglades under state auspices. As governor in 1955–61, Thomas LeRoy Collins (b.1909), met the desegregation issue by advocating moderation and respect for the law, helping the state avoid violent confrontations. He served as chairman of both the southern and national governors' conferences, and he was named by President Johnson as the first director of the Community Relations Service under the 1964 Civil Rights Act.

Military figures who have played a major role in Florida's history include the Spanish conquistadores Juan Ponce de León (c. 1460–1521), the European discoverer of Florida, and Pedro Menéndez de Avilés (1519–74), founder of the first permanent settlement, St. Augustine. Andrew Jackson (b.South Carolina, 1767–1845), a consistent advocate of US seizure of Florida, led military expeditions into the territory in 1814 and 1818 and, after US acquisition, served briefly in 1821 as Florida's military governor before leaving for Tennessee. During the Seminole War of 1835–42, one of the leading military tacticians was Osceola (c. 1800–1838), who although neither born a chief nor elected to that position, rose to the leadership of the badly divided Seminole by force of character and personality. He rallied them to fierce resistance to removal, making skillful use of guerrilla tactics. Captured under a flag of truce in 1837, he was imprisoned; already broken in health, he died in Fort Moultrie in Charleston harbor. During the Civil War, General Edmund Kirby Smith (1824–93), a native of St. Augustine who was graduated from West Point in 1845, served as commander (1863–65) of Confederate forces west of the Mississippi River. He surrendered the last of the southern forces at Galveston, Texas, on 26 May 1865.

Among the late-19th century entrepreneurs who played significant roles in Florida's development, perhaps the most important was Henry Morrison Flagler (b.New York, 1830–1913). Flagler made a fortune in Ohio as an associate of John D. Rockefeller in the Standard Oil Co. and did not even visit Florida until he was in his 50s. However, in the 1880s, he began to acquire and build railroads down the length of Florida's east coast and to develop tourist hotels at various points, including St. Augustine, Palm Beach, and Miami, helping to create one of the state's major present-day industries. Henry Bradley Plant (b.Connecticut, 1819–99) did for Florida's west coast what Flagler did for the east. Plant extended railroad service to Tampa in 1884, built a huge tourist hotel there, developed the port facilities, and established steamship lines.

Among Floridians prominent in science was Dr. John F. Gorrie (b.South Carolina, 1802–55), who migrated to Apalachicola in 1833 and became a socially and politically prominent physician, specializing in the treatment of fevers. He blew air over ice brought in by ship from the north to cool the air in sickrooms, and he independently developed a machine to manufacture ice, only to have two others beat him to the patent office by days.

The noted labor and civil rights leader A. Philip Randolph (1889–1979) was a native of Crescent City. Mary McLeod Bethune (b.South Carolina, 1875–1955) was an adviser to President Franklin D. Roosevelt on minority affairs, became the first president (1935) of the National Council of Negro Women, and was a consultant at the 1945 San Francisco Conference that founded the UN. A prominent black educator, she opened a school for girls at Daytona Beach in 1904. The school merged with Cookman Institute in 1923 to become Bethune-Cookman College, which she headed until 1942 and again in 1946–47.

Prominent Florida authors include James Weldon Johnson (1871–1938), perhaps best known for his 1912 novel *Autobiography of an Ex-Colored Man*. He was also the first black to be admitted to the Florida bar (1897) and was a founder and secretary of the NAACP. Marjory Stoneman Douglas (b.Minnesota, 1890), who came to Miami in 1915, is the author of several works reflecting her concern for the environment, including *The Everglades: River of Grass* (first published in 1947), *Hurricane* (1958), and *Florida: The Long Frontier* (1967). Marjorie Kinnan Rawlings (b.Washington, D.C., 1895–1953) came to Florida in 1928 to do creative writing. After her first novel, *South Moon Under* (1933), came the Pulitzer Prize–winning *The Yearling* (1938), the poignant story of a 12-year-old boy on the Florida frontier in the 1870s. Zora Neale Hurston (1901–60), born in poverty in the all-Negro town of Eatonville and a graduate of Barnard College, spent four years collecting folklore, which she published in *Mules and Men* (1935) and *Tell My Horse* (1938).

Florida's most famous sports figure is Chris Evert Lloyd (Christine Marie Evert, b.1953), who became a dominant force in women's tennis in the mid-1970s. After turning pro in 1973, she won the Wimbledon singles title in 1974 and 1976 and the US Open from 1975 to 1978.

⁵⁰BIBLIOGRAPHY

Douglas, Marjory Stoneman. *The Everglades: River of Grass*. Rev. ed. Miami: Banyan, 1978.

Douglas, Marjory Stoneman. *Florida: The Long Frontier*. New York: Harper and Row, 1967.

Federal Writers' Project. *Florida: A Guide to the Southernmost State*. New York: Oxford University Press, 1939.

Florida, State of. Division of Economic Development. *An Analysis of the Florida Economy As It Pertains to Economic Development, 1979*. Tallahassee, 1979.

Gannon, Michael V. *The Cross in the Sand*. Gainesville: University of Florida Press, 1965.

Hanna, Alfred Jackson, and James Branch Cabell. *The St. Johns: A Parade of Diversities*. New York: Farrar and Rinehart, 1943.

Hanna, Kathryn T. Abbey. *Florida: Land of Change*. Chapel Hill: University of North Carolina Press, 1948.

Harris, Michael H. *Florida History: A Bibliography*. Metuchen, N.J.: Scarecrow Press, 1972.

Jahoda, Gloria. *Florida: A Bicentennial History*. New York: Norton, 1976.

Johns, John E. *Florida During the Civil War*. Gainesville: University of Florida Press, 1963.

Lyon, Eugene. *The Enterprise of Florida: Pedro Menéndez de Avilés and the Spanish Conquest of 1565–68*. Gainesville: University Presses of Florida, 1976.

MacDonald, John D. *Condominium*. Philadelphia: Lippincott, 1977.

Mahon, John K. *The Second Seminole War*. Gainesville: University of Florida Press, 1967.

Morris, Allen, comp. *The Florida Handbook 1979–80*. Tallahassee: Peninsular Publishing, 1979.

Patrick, Rembert W. *Florida Under Five Flags*. Gainesville: University of Florida Press, 1960.

Rawlings, Marjorie Kinnan. *The Yearling*. New York: Scribner, 1938.

Shofner, Jerrell M. *Nor Is It Over Yet: Florida in the Era of Reconstruction, 1863–77*. Gainesville: University Presses of Florida, 1974.

Smiley, Nixon. *Knights of the Fourth Estate: The Story of the Miami Herald*. Miami: Seemann, 1974.

Smiley, Nixon. *Yesterday's Florida*. Miami: Seemann, 1974.

Tebeau, Charlton. *A History of Florida*. Coral Gables: University of Miami Press, 1980 (orig. 1971).

Thompson, Ralph B., ed. *Florida Statistical Abstract 79*. 14th ed. Gainesville: University Presses of Florida, 1979.

Wood, Roland, and Edward A. Fernald. *The New Florida Atlas: Patterns of the Sunshine State*. Tampa: Trend House, 1974.

Wright, J. Leitch, Jr. *Florida in the American Revolution*. Gainesville: University Presses of Florida, 1975.

GEORGIA

State of Georgia

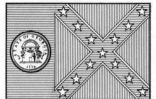

ORIGIN OF STATE NAME: Named for King George II of England in 1732. **NICKNAME**: The Empire State of the South. (Also: Peach State.) **CAPITAL**: Atlanta. **ENTERED UNION**: 2 January 1788 (4th). **SONG**: "Georgia." **MOTTO**: Wisdom, Justice, Moderation. **COAT OF ARMS**: Three columns support an arch inscribed with the word "Constitution"; intertwined among the columns is a banner bearing the state motto. Right of center stands a soldier with a drawn sword, representing the aid of the military in defending the Constitution. Surrounding the whole are the words "State of Georgia 1776." **FLAG**: At the hoist, on a blue bar, is the coat of arms. The remainder comprises the battle flag of the Confederacy. **OFFICIAL SEAL**: Obverse: same as the coat of arms. Reverse: a sailing vessel and a smaller boat are offshore; on land, a man and horse plow a field, and sheep graze in the background. The scene is surrounded by the words "Agriculture and Commerce 1776." **BIRD**: Brown thrasher. **FISH**: Largemouth bass. **FLOWER**: Cherokee rose. **WILDFLOWER**: Azalea. **TREE**: Live oak. **GEM**: Quartz. **INSECT**: Honeybee. **FOSSIL**: Shark tooth. **LEGAL HOLIDAYS**: New Year's Day, 1 January; Robert E. Lee's Birthday, 19 January; Washington's Birthday, 3d Monday in February; Confederate Memorial Day, 26 April; National Memorial Day, last Monday in May; Jefferson Davis's Birthday, 3 June; Independence Day, 4 July; Labor Day, 1st Monday in September; Columbus Day, 2d Monday in October; Veterans Day, 11 November; Thanksgiving Day, 4th Thursday in November; Christmas Day, 25 December. **TIME**: 7 A.M. EST = noon GMT.

¹LOCATION, SIZE, AND EXTENT

Located in the southeastern US, Georgia is the largest state east of the Mississippi River, and ranks 21st in size among the 50 states.

The total area of Georgia is 58,876 sq mi (152,489 sq km), of which land comprises 58,073 sq mi (150,409 sq km) and inland water 803 sq mi (2,080 sq km). Georgia extends 254 mi (409 km) E–W; the maximum N–S extension is 320 mi (515 km).

Georgia is bordered on the N by Tennessee and North Carolina; on the E by South Carolina (with the line formed by the Chattooga, Tugaloo, and Savannah rivers) and by the Atlantic Ocean; on the S by Florida (with the line in the SE defined by the St. Marys River); and on the W by Alabama (separated in the SW by the Chattahoochee River). The state's geographic center is located in Twiggs County, 18 mi (29 km) sw of Macon.

The Sea Islands extend the length of the Georgia coast. The state's total boundary length is 1,039 mi (1,672 km).

²TOPOGRAPHY

Northern Georgia is mountainous, the central region is characterized by the rolling hills of the Piedmont Plateau, and southern Georgia is a nearly flat coastal plain.

The Blue Ridge Mountains tumble to an end in northern Georgia, where Brasstown Bald, at 4,784 feet (1,458 meters), is the highest point in the state. The piedmont slopes slowly to the fall line, descending from about 2,000 feet (600 meters) to 300 feet (90 meters) above sea level. Stone Mountain, where a Confederate memorial has been carved into a mass of solid granite 1,686 feet (514 meters) high, is the region's most famous landmark.

The piedmont region ends in a ridge of sand hills running across the state from Augusta to Columbus. The residue of an ancient ocean was caught in the vast shallow basin on the Florida border, known as the Okefenokee Swamp, which filled with fresh water over the centuries. The coastal plain, thinly populated except for towns at the mouths of inland rivers, ends in marshlands along the Atlantic Ocean. Lying offshore are the Sea Islands, called the Golden Isles of Georgia, the most important of which are, from north to south, Tybee, Ossabaw, St. Catherines, Sapelo, St. Simons, Sea Island, Jekyll, and Cumberland.

Two great rivers rise in the northeast: the Savannah, which forms part of the border with South Carolina, and the Chattahoochee, which flows across the state to become the western boundary. The Flint joins the Chattahoochee at the southwestern corner of Georgia to form the Apalachicola, which flows through Florida into the Gulf of Mexico. The two largest rivers of central Georgia, the Ocmulgee and Oconee, flow together to form the Altamaha, which then flows eastward to the Atlantic. Perhaps the best-known Georgia river, though smaller than any of the above, is the Suwanee, flowing southwest through the Okefenokee Swamp, across Florida, and into the Gulf of Mexico and famous for its evocation by Stephen Foster in the song "Old Folks at Home." Huge lakes created by dams on the Savannah River are Clark Hill Reservoir and Hartwell Lake; man-made lakes on the Chattahoochee River include Lake Seminole, Walter F. George Reservoir, Lake Harding, West Point Reservoir, and Lake Sidney Lanier.

³CLIMATE

The Chattahoochee River divides Georgia into separate climatic regions. The mountain region to the northwest is colder than the rest of Georgia, averaging 39°F (4°C) in January and 78°F (26°C) in July. The remainder of the state experiences mild winters, ranging from a January average of 44°F (7°C) in the piedmont to 54°F (12°C) on the coast. Summers are hot in the piedmont and on the coast, with July temperatures averaging 80°F (27°C). The record high is 113°F (45°C), set at Greenville on 27 May 1978; the record low is −17°F (−27°C), registered in Floyd County on 27 January 1940.

Humidity is high, ranging from 83% in the morning to 57% in the afternoon in Atlanta. Rainfall averages 50 in (127 cm) annually in the lowlands, increasing to 75 in (191 cm) in the mountains; snow falls occasionally in the interior. Tornadoes are an annual threat in mountain areas, and Georgia beaches are exposed to hurricane tides.

The growing season is approximately 185 days in the mountains and a generous 300 days in southern Georgia.

⁴FLORA AND FAUNA

Georgia has some 250 species of trees, 90% of which are of commercial importance. White and scrub pines, chestnut, northern red oak, and buckeye cover the mountain zone, while lob-lolly and shortleaf (yellow) pines and whiteback maple are found throughout the piedmont. Pecan trees grow densely in southern Georgia, and white oak and cypress are plentiful in the eastern part of the state. Trees found throughout the state include red cedar, scaly-bark and white hickories, red maple, sycamore, yellow poplar, sassafras, sweet and black gums, and various dogwoods and magnolias. Common flowering shrubs include yellow jasmine, flowering quince, and mountain laurel. Spanish moss grows abundantly on the coast and around the streams and swamps of the entire coastal plain. The state lists 58 protected plants, of which 24—including buckthorn, golden seal, spider-lily, fringed campion, and star-flower—are endangered.

Prominent among Georgia fauna is the white-tailed (Virginia) deer, found in some 50 counties. Other common mammals are the black bear, muskrat, raccoon, opossum, mink, common cottontail, and three species of squirrel—fox, gray, and flying. No fewer than 160 bird species breed in Georgia, among them the mockingbird, brown thrasher (the state bird), and numerous sparrows; the Okefenokee Swamp is home to the sandhill piper, snowy egret, and white ibis. The bobwhite quail is the most popular game bird. There are 79 species of reptile, including such poisonous snakes as the rattler, copperhead, and cotton-mouth moccasin. The state's 63 amphibian species consist mainly of various salamanders, frogs, and toads. The most popular freshwater game fish are trout, bream, bass, and catfish, all but the last of which are produced in state hatcheries for restocking. Dolphins, porpoises, shrimp, oysters, and blue crabs dwell off the Georgia coast.

Rare or threatened animals include the indigo snake and Georgia's blind cave salamander. The state classifies at least 21 animals as endangered, among them the Colonial and Sherman's pocket gophers, right and humpback whales, brown pelican, American alligator, three species of sea turtle, shortnose sturgeon, and southern cave fish.

⁵ENVIRONMENTAL PROTECTION

Erosion of Georgia's farmlands left red clay exposed all across the once-fertile piedmont by the 1930s. The Soil Conservation Acts of 1936 and 1956 paid farmers to grow restorative crops and even to put their lands into tree production. The result was that Georgia's countryside had become green again by 1980.

In the early 1970s, environmentalists pointed to the fact that the Savannah River had been polluted by industrial waste and that an estimated 58% of Georgia's citizens lived in districts lacking adequate sewage treatment facilities. In 1972, at the prodding of Governor Jimmy Carter, the general assembly created the Environmental Protection Division (EPD) within the Department of Natural Resources. This division is responsible for enforcing the Water Quality Control Act of 1964, which forbids any person or agency to discharge polluted waste into the state's waters without a permit. A permit is also required before any person or agency may attempt to withdraw or divert more than 100,000 gallons a day of surface water. Persons who refuse to obey an order issued by the EPD director are subject to a fine of $10,000 a day and imprisonment for up to one year.

A spate of laws has added other areas to EPD's jurisdiction. The Safe Drinking Water Act of 1977 gives EPD control over the quality of drinking water in the state, and the Georgia Safe Dams Act of 1978 empowers EPD to inspect and regulate the safety of all dams in the state. Moreover, the Air Quality Act of 1978 requires EPD to establish and maintain air quality standards. It is unlawful to render inoperable a motor vehicle emission control device, just as it is illegal to operate a motor vehicle producing excessive exhaust emissions.

The Oil and Gas and Deep Drilling Act of 1975 regulates drilling in environmentally sensitive areas, and prohibits the waste of oil and gas. The Erosion and Sedimentation Act of 1975 prohibits "land-disturbing" activities that may result in soil erosion or the movement of sediment into state waters. The Shore Assistance Act of 1979 is designed to protect coastal sand dunes, beaches, sandbars, and shoals by forbidding any commercial activity that might endanger the fragile coastal environment. Other measures regulate surface mining; set standards for waste disposal and mandate stiff penalties for noncompliance; regulate the labeling, distribution, storage, transportation, use, and disposal of pesticides; forbid the storage of radioactive waste without a permit; and set forth standards for the treatment and transportation of radioactive materials.

⁶POPULATION

Georgia ranked 15th among the 50 states in 1970 with a population of 4,589,575. The estimated population in 1978 was 5,084,000, yielding an average density of 88 per sq mi (34 per sq km), 42% above the US average.

During the first half of the 18th century, restrictive government policies discouraged settlement. In 1752, when Georgia became a royal colony, the population numbered only 3,500, of whom 500 were blacks. Growth was rapid thereafter, and by 1773 there were 33,000 people, almost half of them black. The American Revolution brought free land and an influx of settlers, so that by 1800 the population had swelled to 162,686. Georgia passed the million mark by 1860, the 2 million mark by 1900, and by 1960, the population had doubled again. Georgia's population increased 29% between 1960 and 1978, well above the US average. Census figures for 1980 (preliminary) put Georgia's population at 5,396,425, an increase of nearly 18% since 1970.

According to the 1970 census, the population was 51.4% female and 48.6% male. Georgia residents were somewhat younger than the national average but rather less mobile: as of 1976, nearly 63% of all Georgians 14 years of age or older had been there all their lives, a higher percentage than in Florida, Virginia, and Arkansas among southern states.

About 60% of all Georgians lived in urban areas in 1970, and 40% in rural areas. There has always been a strained relationship between rural and urban Georgians, and the state's political system long favored the rural population. Since before the American Revolution, the city people have called the country folk "crackers," a term that implies a lack of good manners and which may derive from the fact that these pioneers drove their cattle before them with whips.

Preliminary census counts for the state's four largest cities in 1980 were Atlanta, 405,437; Columbus, 168,598; Savannah, 133,672; and Macon, 116,044. The Atlanta metropolitan area had an estimated population of 1,851,000 in 1978.

⁷ETHNIC GROUPS

Georgia has been fundamentally a white/black state, with minimal ethnic diversity. Most Georgians are of English or Scotch-Irish descent. Only 33,000 Georgians were foreign-born in 1970, and no more than 79,000 (1.7%) were 2d-generation Americans, chiefly from Germany, Britain, and Canada. There were also 8,838 Asian/Pacific peoples. In 1975, 1,351 Vietnamese refugees were resettled in Georgia.

Georgia's black population declined from a high of 47% of the total population in 1880 to about 26% in 1970, when there were 1,187,149 blacks. Black citizens comprised 27% of the total population and numbered 1,336,000 in 1976. Atlanta, which had 255,000 black residents (51%) in 1970, has been a significant center for the development of black leadership, especially at Atlanta University. With its long-established black elite, Atlanta

LOCATION: 30°21′ to 35°N; 80°51′ to 85°36′W. **BOUNDARIES**: Tennessee line, 73 mi (118 km); North Carolina line, 70 mi (113 km); South Carolina line, 266 mi (428 km); Atlantic Ocean coastline, 100 mi (161 km); Florida line, 242 mi (389 km); Alabama line, 288 mi (463 km).

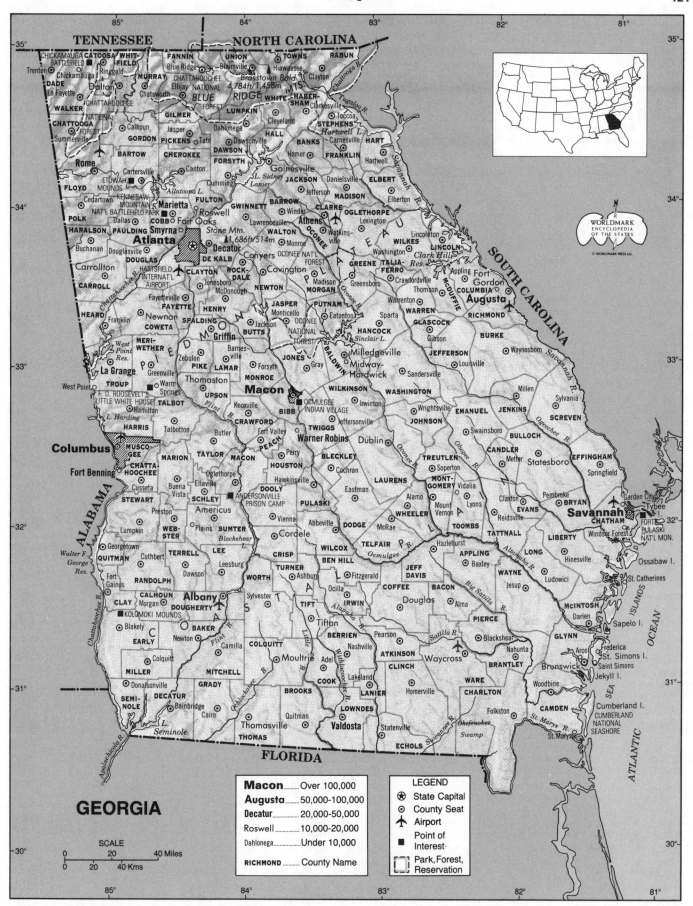

GEORGIA

Macon	Over 100,000
Augusta	50,000-100,000
Decatur	20,000-50,000
Roswell	10,000-20,000
Dahlonega	Under 10,000
RICHMOND	County Name

LEGEND
- ⊛ State Capital
- ⊙ County Seat
- ✈ Airport
- ■ Point of Interest
- ⌐ Park, Forest, Reservation

WORLDMARK
ENCYCLOPEDIA
OF THE STATES
© WORLDMARK PRESS Ltd.

SCALE
0   20   40 Miles
0   20   40 Kms

See US political: front cover K4; physical: back cover K4.

has also been the locus of some large black-owned business enterprises. There are elected and appointed blacks in the state government, and in 1973, Atlanta elected its first black mayor, Maynard Jackson.

There were only 2,347 Indians in Georgia in 1970. The great Cherokee nation and its collateral linguistic relatives had been effectively removed from the state 140 years earlier.

⁸LANGUAGES

The first Europeans entering what is now Georgia found it occupied almost entirely by Creek Indians of the Muskogean branch of Hokan-Siouan stock. Removed by treaty to Indian Territory after their uprising in 1813, the Creek left behind only such place-names as Chattahoochee, Chattooga, and Okefenokee. In 1970, only 479 Georgians claimed an Indian tongue as their first language.

Except for the South Midland speech of the extreme northern up-country, Georgia English is typically Southern. Loss of /r/ after a vowel in the same syllable is common. The diphthong /ai/ as in *right* is so simplified that Northern speakers hear the word as *rat*. *Can't* rhymes with *paint*, and *borrow*, *forest*, *foreign*, and

Georgia Counties, County Seats, and County Populations[1]

COUNTY	COUNTY SEAT	LAND AREA (SQ MI)	POPULATION (EST. 1976)	COUNTY	COUNTY SEAT	LAND AREA (SQ MI)	POPULATION (EST. 1976)
Appling	Baxley	513	14,600	Fayette	Fayetteville	199	18,700
Atkinson	Pearson	318	5,900	Floyd	Rome	514	78,500
Bacon	Alma	293	9,200	Forsyth	Cumming	219	22,500
Baker	Newton	355	3,600	Franklin	Carnesville	263	13,900
Baldwin	Milledgeville	255	32,800	Fulton	Atlanta	530	[3]
Banks	Homer	231	6,800	Gilmer	Ellijay	439	10,500
Barrow	Winder	171	19,400	Glascock	Gibson	143	2,400
Bartow	Cartersville	461	36,800	Glynn	Brunswick	412	47,900
Ben Hill	Fitzgerald	255	14,000	Gordon	Calhoun	358	27,200
Berrien	Nashville	468	12,400	Grady	Cairo	466	19,200
Bibb	Macon	254	143,400	Greene	Greensboro	403	10,500
Bleckley	Cochran	219	10,600	Gwinnett	Lawrenceville	437	119,700
Brantley	Nahunta	447	7,600	Habersham	Clarkesville	282	23,700
Brooks	Quitman	491	14,200	Hall	Gainesville	378	68,100
Bryan	Pembroke	443	8,300	Hancock	Sparta	478	9,300
Bulloch	Statesboro	685	32,700	Haralson	Buchanan	285	17,500
Burke	Waynesboro	831	18,400	Harris	Hamilton	465	12,100
Butts	Jackson	185	12,300	Hart	Hartwell	231	16,500
Calhoun	Morgan	289	6,700	Heard	Franklin	297	5,900
Camden	Woodbine	653	12,200	Henry	McDonough	331	28,900
Candler	Metter	250	6,900	Houston	Perry	380	72,800
Carroll	Carrollton	495	54,000	Irwin	Ocilla	372	8,400
Catoosa	Ringgold	167	32,500	Jackson	Jefferson	346	23,700
Charlton	Folkston	796	6,600	Jasper	Monticello	373	6,700
Chatham	Savannah	445	186,400	Jeff Davis	Hazlehurst	331	11,000
Chattahoochee	Cusseta	253	20,300	Jefferson	Louisville	530	16,500
Chattooga	Summerville	317	22,500	Jenkins	Millen	351	8,000
Cherokee	Canton	415	40,300	Johnson	Wrightsville	313	7,800
Clarke	Athens	116	69,800	Jones	Gray	402	15,500
Clay	Ft. Gaines	200	3,500	Lamar	Barnesville	181	11,600
Clayton	Jonesboro	149	133,700	Lanier	Lakeland	177	5,200
Clinch	Homerville	797	6,700	Laurens	Dublin	810	34,100
Cobb	Marietta	343	243,800	Lee	Leesburg	355	9,700
Coffee	Douglas	612	24,800	Liberty	Hinesville	514	23,400
Colquitt	Moultrie	563	33,600	Lincoln	Lincolnton	193	6,100
Columbia	Appling	290	31,100	Long	Ludowici	402	3,400
Cook	Adel	233	12,400	Lowndes	Valdosta	508	62,700
Corveta	Newnan	442	36,400	Lumpkin	Dahlonega	292	9,500
Crawford	Knoxville	315	6,600	Macon	Oglethorpe	403	12,800
Crisp	Cordele	292	18,900	Madison	Danielsville	281	15,600
Dade	Trenton	168	11,500	Marion	Buena Vista	365	6,200
Dawson	Dawsonville	211	4,600	McDuffie	Thomson	253	17,700
Decatur	Bainbridge	575	24,800	McIntosh	Darien	426	8,200
DeKalb	Decatur	269	1,024,800[2]	Meriwether	Greenville	499	20,600
Dodge	Eastman	498	16,600	Miller	Colquitt	287	6,100
Dooly	Vienna	395	10,900	Mitchell	Camilla	510	19,300
Dougherty	Albany	324	92,000	Monroe	Forsyth	398	11,800
Douglas	Douglasville	202	45,700	Montgomery	Mt. Vernon	237	6,200
Early	Blakely	524	13,200	Morgan	Madison	356	10,600
Echols	Statenville	425	2,100	Murray	Chatsworth	342	16,500
Effingham	Springfield	480	15,800	Muscogee	Columbus	220	162,500[4]
Elbert	Elberton	358	18,000	Newton	Covington	271	32,300
Emanuel	Swainsboro	686	20,400	Oconee	Watkinsville	186	9,400
Evans	Claxton	186	8,400	Oglethorpe	Lexington	435	8,100
Fannin	Blue Ridge	394	14,500	Paulding	Dallas	318	22,000

orange all have the /ah/ vowel as in *father*. However, a highly unusual variety of regional differences, most of them in long vowels and diphthongs, makes a strong contrast between northern up-country and southern low-country speech. In such words as *care* and *stairs*, for example, many up-country speakers have a vowel like that in *cat*, while many low-country speakers have a vowel like that in *pane*.

In general, northern Georgia *snake doctor* contrasts with southern Georgia *mosquito hawk* (dragonfly), *goobers* with *pinders* (peanuts), *French harp* with *harmonica, plum peach* with *press*

COUNTY	COUNTY SEAT	LAND AREA (SQ MI)	POPULATION (EST. 1976)
Peach	Ft. Valley	151	19,000
Pickens	Jasper	225	10,800
Pierce	Blackshear	342	10,800
Pike	Zebulon	230	8,300
Polk	Cedartown	312	31,300
Pulaski	Hawkinsville	253	8,000
Putnam	Eatonton	339	8,800
Quitman	Georgetown	156	2,000
Rabun	Clayton	368	9,600
Randolph	Cuthbert	436	8,800
Richmond	Augusta	323	156,800
Rockdale	Conyers	128	29,000
Schley	Ellaville	162	3,000
Screven	Sylvania	651	13,000
Seminole	Donalsonville	246	8,200
Spalding	Griffin	201	44,500
Stephens	Toccoa	173	22,300
Stewart	Lumpkin	452	5,600
Sumter	Americus	488	27,800
Talbot	Talbotton	390	6,400
Taliaferro	Crawfordville	195	2,200
Tattnall	Reidsville	490	17,100
Taylor	Butler	403	8,100
Telfair	MacRae	440	11,300
Terrell	Dawson	329	11,200
Thomas	Thomasville	541	37,400
Tift	Tifton	266	31,500
Toombs	Lyons	368	21,400
Towns	Hiawassee	166	4,800
Trentlen	Soperton	194	6,100
Troup	La Grange	415	45,200
Turner	Ashburn	293	8,900
Twiggs	Jeffersonville	364	7,900
Union	Blairsville	309	8,400
Upson	Thomaston	334	24,100
Walker	La Fayette	445	54,700
Walton	Monroe	330	29,200
Ware	Waycross	912	35,100
Warren	Warrenton	284	6,200
Washington	Sandersville	674	17,000
Wayne	Jesup	645	19,000
Webster	Preston	195	2,300
Wheeler	Alamo	306	4,900
White	Cleveland	243	8,700
Whitefield	Dalton	281	59,400
Wilcox	Abbeville	383	6,800
Wilkes	Washington	468	10,100
Wilkinson	Irwinton	458	9,800
Worth	Sylvester	579	16,600
	TOTALS	58,073	4,970,200

[1]Totals may not add because of rounding.
[2]Includes Fulton.
[3]Included in DeKalb.
[4]Metropolitan Columbus population.

peach (both clingstone peaches), *nicker* with *whicker* for a horse's neigh, and *sallet* with *salad*. Atlanta calls the big sandwich a *poorboy*; in Savannah, a peach pit is a *kernel*.

A distinctive variety of black English, called Gullah, is spoken in the islands off the Georgia and South Carolina coast, to which Creole-speaking slaves escaped from the mainland during the 17th and 18th centuries. Characteristic grammatical features include lack of inflection in the personal pronoun, the invariant form of the *be* verb, and the absence of *–s* in the third person singular of the present tense. Many of the private personal names stem directly from West African languages.

In 1970, 93% of native-born Georgians as well as of all state residents gave English as their mother tongue. Speakers of principal first languages were as follows:

	NATIVE-BORN	FOREIGN-BORN
English	4,254,323	7,413
German	19,230	7,980
Spanish	13,665	4,920
French	8,862	1,846

[9]RELIGIONS

The Church of England was the established church in colonial Georgia. During this period, European Protestants were encouraged to immigrate, and German Lutherans and Moravians took advantage of the opportunity. Roman Catholics were barred and Jews were not welcomed, but persons of both denominations came anyway. In the mid-18th century, George Whitefield, called the Great Itinerant, helped touch off the Great Awakening, the religious revival out of which came the Methodist and Baptist denominations. Daniel Marshall, the first "separate" Baptist in Georgia, established a church near Kiokee Creek in 1772. Some 16 years later, James Asbury formed the first Methodist Conference in Georgia.

The American Revolution resulted in the lessening of the authority of Anglicanism and a great increase in the numbers of Baptists, Methodists, and Presbyterians. During the 19th century, fundamentalist sects were especially strong among blacks. Roman Catholics from Maryland, Ireland, and Hispaniola formed a numerically small but important element in the cities, and Jewish citizens were active in the leadership of Savannah and Augusta. Catholics and Jews enjoyed general acceptance from the early 1800s until the first two decades of the 20th century, when they became the targets of political demagogues, notably Thomas E. Watson.

In 1971 there were 2,014,482 known Protestant adherents. Leading denominations were Southern Baptist Convention, 1,276,081; United Methodist, 390,240; Presbyterian, 94,946; and Episcopal, 54,187. In 1979, Georgia had 138,860 Roman Catholics and an estimated 33,610 Jews.

[10]TRANSPORTATION

Georgia's location between the Appalachian Mountains and the Atlantic Ocean makes it the link between the eastern seaboard and the Gulf states. In the 18th century, Carolina fur traders crossed the Savannah River at the site of Augusta and followed trails to the Mississippi River. Pioneer farmers soon followed the same trails and used the many river tributaries to send their produce down to Savannah, Georgia's first great depot. Beginning in 1816, steamboats plied the inland rivers, but they never replaced the older shallow-drafted Petersburg boats, propelled by poles.

From the 1830s onward, businessmen in the eastern cities of Savannah, Augusta, and Brunswick built railroads west to maintain their commerce. The two principal lines, the Georgia and the Central of Georgia, were required by law to make connection with a state-owned line, the Western and Atlantic, at the new town of Atlanta, which thus became in 1847 the link between Georgia and the Ohio Valley. By the Civil War, Georgia, with more miles of rail than any other Deep South state, was a vital link between the eastern and western sectors of the Confederacy. After the war, the railroads contributed to urban growth as towns sprang up along their routes. Trackage increased from 4,532 mi (7,294 km) in 1890 to 7,591 mi (12,217 km) in 1920. But with competition from motor carriers, the total declined to 5,408 mi (8,703 km) in 1974. In 1979, Atlanta inaugurated the first mass transit system in the state, including the South's first subway.

Georgia's old intracoastal waterway carries about 1 million tons of shipping annually and is also used by pleasure craft and fishing vessels. Savannah's modern port facilities handle about $700 million worth of imports and exports a year; the coastal cities of Brunswick and St. Marys also have deepwater docks. Locks and dams permit barge traffic to Augusta on the Savannah River, to Bainbridge on the Flint River, and to Columbus on the Chattahoochee.

In the 1920s, Georgia became the gateway to Florida for motorists. Today, I-75 is the main route from Atlanta to Florida, and I-20 is the major east–west highway; both cross at Atlanta with I-85, which proceeds southeast from South Carolina to Alabama. I-95 stretches along the coast from South Carolina through Savannah to Jacksonville, Fla. In 1978, Georgia had 103,038 mi (165,824 km) of roads, 3,757,779 registered vehicles, and 3,213,660 licensed drivers. Atlanta's Hartsfield International Airport is the hub of air traffic in the Southeast; it emplaned 18,226,652 passengers and handled 146,269 tons of freight in 1978. In that year, Georgia had 121 public airports and 157 private airfields.

11 HISTORY

The history of what is now Georgia was influenced by two great prehistoric events: first, the upheaval that produced the mountains of the north, and second, the overflow of an ancient ocean that covered and flattened much of the rest of the state. Human beings have inhabited Georgia for at least 12,000 years. The first nomadic hunters were replaced by shellfish eaters who lived along the rivers. Farming communities later grew up at these sites, reaching their height in the Master Farmer culture around AD 800. These Native Americans left impressive mounds at Ocmulgee, near Macon, and at Etowah, north of Atlanta.

During the colonial period, the most important Indian tribes were the Creek, who lived along the central and western rivers, and the Cherokee, who lived in the mountains. By clever diplomacy, the Creek were able to maintain their position as the balance of power between the English on the one hand and the French and Spanish on the other; with the ascendancy of the English and the achievement of statehood, however, the Creek lost their leverage and were expelled from Georgia in 1826. The Cherokee sought to adopt the white man's ways in their effort to avoid expulsion or annihilation. Thanks to their remarkable linguist Sequoyah, they learned to write their own language, later running their own newspaper, the *Cherokee Phoenix,* and their own schools. Some even owned slaves. Unfortunately for the Cherokee, gold was discovered on their lands; the Georgia state legislature confiscated their territory and outlawed the system of self-government the Cherokee had developed during the 1820s. Despite a ruling by the US Supreme Court, handed down by Chief Justice John Marshall, that Georgia had acted illegally, federal and state authorities expelled the Cherokee between 1832 and 1838. Thousands died on the march to Indian Territory (Oklahoma), known ever since as the Trail of Tears.

Georgia's first European explorer was Hernando de Soto of Spain, who in 1540 crossed the region looking for the fabled Seven Cities of Gold. French Huguenots under Jean Ribault claimed the Georgia coast in 1562 but were driven out by the Spanish captain Pedro Menéndez de Avilés in 1565. By 1700, Jesuit and Franciscan missionaries had established a chain of missions along the Sea Islands and on the lower Chattahoochee.

From Charles Town, in Carolina colony, the English chal-

lenged Spain for control of the region, and by 1702 they had forced the Spaniards back to St. Augustine, Fla. In 1732, after the English had become convinced of the desirability of locating a buffer between the valuable rice-growing colony of Carolina and Indian-held lands to the south and west, King George II granted a charter to a group called the Trustees for Establishing the Colony of Georgia in America. The best known of the trustees was the soldier-politician and philanthropist James Edward Oglethorpe. It was his original intention to send debtors from English prisons to Georgia, but Parliament refused to support this idea. Instead, Georgia was to be a place where the industrious poor would produce those things England needed, such as silk and wine, and would guard the frontier. Rum and slavery were expressly prohibited.

Oglethorpe and the first settlers landed at Yamacraw Bluff on 12 February 1733 and were given a friendly reception by a small band of Yamacraw Indians and their chief, Tomochichi. Oglethorpe is best remembered for laying out the town of Savannah in a unique design, featuring numerous plazas, that still delights tourists today; however, as a military man, his main interest was defending the colony against the Spanish. Ater war was declared in 1739, Oglethorpe conducted an unsuccessful siege of St. Augustine. The Spaniards counterattacked at Oglethorpe's fortified town of Frederica on St. Simons Island in July 1742 but were repulsed in a confused encounter known as the Battle of Bloody Marsh, which ended Spanish threats to the British colonies. Soon afterward, Oglethorpe returned permanently to England.

The trustees' restrictions on rum and slavery were gradually removed, and in 1752, control over Georgia reverted to Parliament. Georgia thus became a royal colony, its society, like that of Carolina, shaped by the planting of rice, indigo, and cotton. After the French and Indian War, settlers began to pour into the Georgia backcountry above Augusta. Because these backcountry pioneers depended on the royal government for protection against the Indians, they were reluctant to join the protests by Savannah merchants against new British mercantile regulations. When war came, however, the backcountry seized the opportunity to wrest political control of the new state away from Savannah.

Georgians spent the first three years of the Revolutionary War in annual attempts to invade Florida, each of them unsuccessful. The British turned their attention to Georgia late in 1778, reestablishing control of the state as far as Briar Creek, midway between Savannah and Augusta. After a combined French and American force failed to retake Savannah in October 1779, the city was used by the British as a base from which to recapture Charleston, in present-day South Carolina, and to extend their control further inland. For a year, most of Georgia was under British rule, and there was talk of making the restoration permanent in the peace settlement. However, Augusta was retaken in June 1781, and independent government was restored. A year later, the British were forced out of Savannah.

With Augusta as the new capital of Georgia, a period of rapid expansion began. Georgia ratified the US Constitution on 2 January 1788, the 4th state to do so. The invention of the cotton gin by Eli Whitney in 1793 made cotton cultivation profitable in the lands east of the Oconee River, relinquished by the Creek Indians under the Treaty of New York three years earlier. A mania for land speculation was climaxed by the mid-1790s Yazoo Fraud, in which the state legislature sold 50 million acres (20 million hectares), later the states of Alabama and Mississippi, to four land companies of which many of the same legislators were members. Although a subsequent reform-minded legislature moved to nullify the deal, the US Supreme Court ruled in 1810, in the case of *Fletcher* v. *Peck,* that the original sale was valid.

Georgia surrendered its lands west of the Chattahoochee River to the federal government in 1802. As the Indians were removed to the west, the lands they had occupied were disposed of by successive lotteries. The settlement of the cotton lands brought prosperity to Georgia, a fact that influenced Georgians to prefer the Union rather than secession during the constitutional crises of 1833 and 1850, when South Carolina was prepared to secede.

After South Carolina actually did secede in 1860, Georgia also withdrew from the Union and joined the Confederate States of America. Union troops occupied the Sea Islands during 1862. Confederate forces defeated the Union Army's advance into northern Georgia at Chickamauga in 1863, but in 1864, troops under General William Tecumseh Sherman moved relentlessly upon Atlanta, capturing it in September. In November, Sherman began his famous "march to the sea," in which his 60,000 troops cut a swath of destruction 60 mi (97 km) wide, devastating factories, mills, railroads—anything of value to the Confederacy. Sherman presented Savannah as a Christmas present to US President Abraham Lincoln.

Georgia did not fit the Reconstruction stereotype of a crushed state languishing under blacks and carpetbaggers. The leaders of the weak and short-lived Republican regime (1868–71), which moved the capital to Atlanta, were either Georgia-born or state residents before the war. There were only 29 Negroes among the 172-member house, and but 3 among the 44-member senate. After ratifying the 14th and 15th amendments, Georgia was readmitted to the Union on 15 July 1870.

Commercial interests were strong in antebellum Georgia, but their political power was balanced by that of the great planters. After the Democrats recovered control of the state in 1871, business interests dominated politics. Discontented farmers supported an Independent Party in the 1870s and 1880s, and then the Populist Party in the 1890s. Democratic Representative Thomas E. Watson, who declared himself a Populist during the early 1890s, was defeated three times in congressional races by the party he had deserted. Watson subsequently fomented anti-Negro, anti-Jewish, and anti-Catholic sentiment in order to control a bloc of rural votes with which he dominated state politics for ten years. In 1920, Watson finally was elected to the US Senate, but he died in 1922. Rebecca L. Felton was appointed to succeed him, thus becoming the first woman to serve in the US Senate, although her career lasted only one day before Walter F. George took her place.

Franklin D. Roosevelt learned the problems of Georgia farmers firsthand when he made Warm Springs his second home in 1924. However, his efforts to introduce the New Deal to Georgia after he became president in 1933 were blocked by Governor Eugene Talmadge, who advertised himself as a "real dirt farmer." It was not until the administration of Eurith D. Rivers (1937–41) that progressive social legislation was enacted. Governor Ellis Arnall gained national attention for his forward-looking administration (1943–47), which revised the outdated 1877 state constitution and gave the vote to 18-year-olds. Georgia treated the nation to the spectacle of three governors at once when Eugene Talmadge was elected for a fourth time in 1946 but died before assuming office. His son Herman was then elected by the legislature, but the new lieutenant governor, M. E. Thompson, also claimed the office, and Arnall refused to step aside until the issue was resolved. The courts finally decided in favor of Thompson.

The Supreme Court order to desegregate public schools in 1954 provided Georgia politicians with an emotional issue they exploited to the hilt. Govenors Herman Talmadge, Marvin Griffin, and Ernest Vandiver were all elected on pledges to resist integration. A blow was dealt to old-style politics in 1962, however, when the US Supreme Court declared the county-unit system unconstitutional. Under this sytem, state officers and members of Congress had been elected by county units instead of by popular vote since 1911; the new ruling made city voters as important as those in rural areas. During the 1960s, Atlanta was the home base for the civil-rights efforts of Martin Luther King,

Jr., though his campaign to end racial discrimination in Georgia focused most notably on the town of Albany. Federal civil rights legislation in 1964 and 1965 changed the state's political climate by guaranteeing the vote to black citizens. A black man, Julian Bond, was elected to the state legislature in 1965; in 1973, Maynard Jackson was elected mayor of Atlanta, thus becoming the first black mayor of a large southern city. For decades the belief that defense of segregation was a prerequisite for state elective office cost white southerners any chance they might have had for national leadership. Governor Jimmy Carter's unequivocal renunciation of racism in his inaugural speech in 1971 thus marked a turning point in Georgia politics, and was a key factor in his election to the presidency in 1976.

[12] STATE GOVERNMENT

Georgia's first constitution, adopted in 1777, was considered one of the most democratic in the new nation. Power was concentrated in a unicameral legislature; a senate was added in 1789. The Civil War period brought a flurry of constitution making in 1861, 1865, and 1868. When the Democrats displaced the Republicans after Reconstruction, they felt obliged to replace the constitution of 1868 with a rigidly restrictive one. This document, adopted in 1877, modified by numerous amendments, and revised in 1945 and 1976, continues to govern the state today.

The legislature, called the general assembly, consists of a 56-seat senate and a 180-seat house of representatives; all the legislators serve two-year terms. The legislature convenes on the 2d Monday in January and stays in session for 45 days in odd-numbered years and 40 days in even-numbered years. These limits are not absolute: if the legislators find themselves pressed for time, they simply stop the legislative clock and prolong the session for as long as necessary. Since 1962, the legislature has been engaged in a series of attempts to redistrict itself to provide equal representation based on population.

Elected executives include the governor, lieutenant governor, secretary of state, attorney general, state school superintendent, comptroller general, commissioner of agriculture, and commissioner of labor. Each serves a four-year term. To be eligible for office, the governor and lieutenant governor must have been US citizens for 15 years, Georgia citizens for six years preceding the election, and at least 30 years of age. The governor appoints six of the state's eight constitutional boards and commissions. The exceptions are the Public Service Commission, elected by the people, and the State Transportation Board, chosen by the general assembly.

To become law, a bill must be passed by both houses of the legislature and approved by the governor or passed over the executive veto by a two-thirds vote in both houses. All revenue measures originate in the house, but the senate can propose, or concur in, amendments to these bills. Amendments to the constitution may be proposed by two-thirds votes of the elected members of each chamber and must then be ratified by popular vote.

To vote, a person must be a citizen of the US, at least 18 years old, and must have resided in the state for at least 30 days immediately preceding the election.

[13] POLITICAL PARTIES

The first political group to emerge in the state was the Federalist Party, but it was tainted by association with the Yazoo Fraud of the 1790s. The reform party at this time was the Democratic-Republican Party, headed in Georgia by James Jackson (whose followers included many former Federalists), William Crawford, and George Troup. During the presidency of Andrew Jackson (1829–37), one wing, headed by John Clark, supported the president and called itself the Union Party. The other faction, led by Troup, defended South Carolina's right to nullify laws and called itself the States Rights Party. Subsequently the Union Party affiliated with the Democrats, and the States Rights Party merged with the Whigs. When the national Whig Party collapsed, many

Georgia Whigs joined the Native American (Know-Nothing) Party. During Reconstruction, the Republican Party captured the governor's office, but Republican hopes died when federal troops were withdrawn from the state in 1870.

Georgia voted solidly Democratic between 1870 and 1960, despite challenges from the Independent Party in the 1880s and the Populists in the 1890s. Georgia cast its electoral votes for the Democratic presidential candidate in every election until 1964, when Republican Barry Goldwater won the state. Four years later, George C. Wallace of the American Independent Party received Georgia's 12 electoral votes. Republican Richard Nixon carried the state in 1972, as the Republicans also became a viable party at the local level. In 1976, Georgia's native son, Jimmy Carter, returned the state to the Democratic camp in presidential balloting. Another native Georgian and former Georgia governor, Lester Maddox, was the American Independent candidate in 1976.

Georgians for the most part remained loyal to President Carter in the 1980 general election, but they turned out US Senator Herman Talmadge, the Democratic incumbent (who had been involved in a financial scandal), in favor of Republican Mack Mattingly. The state's congressional delegation and legislature remained overwhelmingly Democratic, however.

¹⁴LOCAL GOVERNMENT

In 1758, colonial Georgia was divided into eight parishes, the earliest political districts represented in the royal assembly. By the constitution of 1777, the parishes were transformed into counties, and as settlement gradually expanded, the number of counties grew to 159. The Georgia constitution of 1877 granted counties from one to three seats in the house of representatives, depending on population. This county-unit system was used in counting votes for elected state and congressional offices until ruled unconstitutional by the US Supreme Court in 1962. Originally administered by judges of county courts, all Georgia counties but one, Towns County, have since adopted a commission system. Commissioners are elected for terms ranging from one to six years.

Georgia has some 575 incorporated cities, towns, and villages. In 1965, the legislature passed a home-rule law permitting these local governments to amend their own charters. The traditional and most common form of municipal government is the mayor-council form. But city managers are employed by some communities, and a few make use of the commission system.

During the 1970s there were efforts to merge some of the larger cities with their counties. However, most county voters showed an unwillingness to be burdened with city problems, and only Columbus and Muscogee County had achieved consolidated government by 1980.

The Intergovernmental Relations Council was established in 1975 to advise the governor and general assembly of local government needs. The governor is chairman of the council, on which the president of the Georgia Municipal Association and the president of the Association of County Commissioners also serve. The Department of Community Affairs, which replaced the Bureau of Community Affairs in 1977, serves as the governor's representative to local governments.

¹⁵STATE SERVICES

In 1977, the State Ethics Commission was renamed the Campaign and Financial Disclosure Commission. As the title indicates, this commission is charged with providing procedures for public disclosure of all state and local campaign contributions and expenditures.

Educational services are provided by the Board of Education, which exercises jurisdiction over all public schools, including teacher certification and curriculum approval. The superintendent of schools is the board's executive officer. The public colleges are operated by the Board of Regents of the University System of Georgia, whose chief administrator is the chancellor. Air, water, road, and rail services are administered by the Department of Transportation, established in 1916 as the State Highway Board.

The Reorganization Act of 1972 made the Department of Human Resources a catch-all agency for health, rehabilitation, and social welfare programs. The department, which employs some 28,000 people in 2,000 locations, offers special services to the mentally ill, drug abusers and alcoholics, neglected and abused children and adults, juvenile offenders, the handicapped, the aged, and the poor.

Public protection services are rendered through the Department of Defense, created in 1955. Responsibility for natural resource protection is lodged with the Department of Natural Resources, into which 33 separate agencies were consolidated in

Georgia Presidential Vote by Political Parties, 1948–80

YEAR	ELECTORAL VOTE	GEORGIA WINNER	DEMOCRAT	REPUBLICAN	STATES' RIGHTS DEMOCRAT	PROGRESSIVE
1948	12	*Truman (D)	254,646	76,691	85,135	1,636
1952	12	Stevenson (D)	456,823	198,961	—	—
1956	12	Stevenson (D)	444,688	222,778	—	—
1960	12	*Kennedy (D)	458,638	274,472	—	—
1964	12	Goldwater (R)	522,163	616,584	—	—
					AMERICAN IND.	
1968	12	Wallace (AI)	334,440	380,111	535,550	—
1972	12	*Nixon (R)	289,529	881,490	—	—
						AMERICAN
1976	12	*Carter (D)	979,409	483,743	1,071¹	1,168¹
					LIBERTARIAN	
1980	12	Carter (D)	890,955	654,168	15,627	—

*Won US presidential election.

¹Write-in votes.

1972. The Environmental Protection Division is charged with maintaining air, land, and water quality standards; the Game and Fish Division manages wildlife resources; and the Parks and Historic Sites Division administers state parks, recreational areas, and historic sites. Labor services are provided by the Department of Labor, which oversees workers' compensation and unemployment compensation programs.

¹⁶ JUDICIAL SYSTEM

Georgia's highest court is the supreme court, created in 1845 and consisting of a chief justice, presiding justice (who exercises the duties of chief justice in his absence), and five associate justices. Each is elected by the people to a six-year term.

As of 1980 there were 159 superior courts, grouped into 42 circuits. Each circuit has from 1 to 9 judges, depending on its population; there are 68 superior court judges, all of them elected for four-year terms. Superior courts have exclusive jurisdiction in cases in divorce and land title, and in major criminal cases. Cases from local courts can be carried to the superior court of appeals, consisting of 9 judges elected for six-year terms.

Georgia has 63 county courts, 53 small claims courts, a juvenile court in each county, and 11 miscellaneous courts. Most judges of the county and city courts are appointed by the governor with the consent of the senate.

Georgia's penal system is contained within the Georgia Department of Offender Rehabilitation, which operates all state correctional institutions, offers rehabilitation services to prisoners, and directs probation operations. In 1978, Georgia's prison population numbered 11,948. Of this total, 11,442 were males (4,443 white, 6,999 nonwhite) and 506 were females (179 white, 327 nonwhite).

According to the FBI Crime Index, the crime rate per 100,000 inhabitants for 1978 was 4,771, up 14% from 1977. Rates for murder, nonnegligent manslaughter, and forcible rape were well above the US average, but property crime rates were generally below it. Metropolitan Atlanta had a crime rate of 6,917 per 100,000 inhabitants.

¹⁷ ARMED FORCES

There were 11 military installations in the state in 1979. Major facilities included Dobbins Air Force Base, Ft. Gillem, Ft. McPherson, and a Naval Air Station, all located in the Atlanta area; Ft. Stewart and Hunter Army Air Field in Savannah; Ft. Gordon at Augusta; Moody Air Force Base at Macon; and a Navy Supply School in Athens. Three-fourths of the $1.2 billion spent for military purposes in Georgia in 1978 went to support these bases. During the same year, Georgia firms received defense contracts worth $793 million.

There were 637,000 veterans of the US armed forces living in Georgia as of 30 September 1979. Of these, 9,000 served in World War I, 231,000 in World War II, 134,000 in the Korean conflict, and 215,000 during the Viet-Nam era. In all, 77,000 Georgians fought and 1,503 died in World War I, and 320,000 served and 6,754 were killed in World War II. In 1977/78, Georgia veterans received benefits amounting to $520.2 million, of which $261.7 million was spent for compensation and pensions.

The National Guard consisted of 12,400 active members in 1978, with an annual budget of $44.2 million. In that year, state and local police numbered 12,867 persons; expenditures totaled $167 million. The Department of Public Safety patrols all public roads, administers the Motor Vehicle Inspection Law, and establishes regulations governing the issuance of driver's licenses. The department includes the Georgia Bureau of Investigation, which provides special criminal investigative support services for local law enforcement agencies. The bureau operates the Georgia Crime Laboratory, one of the oldest and largest in the US.

¹⁸ MIGRATION

During the colonial period, the chief source of immigrants to Georgia was England; other important national groups were Germans, Scots, and Scotch-Irish. The number of African slaves increased from 1,000 in 1752 to nearly 20,000 in 1776. After the American Revolution, a large number of Virginians came to Georgia, as well as lesser numbers of French refugees from Hispaniola and immigrants from Ireland and Germany. Following the Civil War, there was some immigration from Italy, Russia, and Greece.

The greatest population shifts during the 20th century have been from country to town and, after World War I, of black Georgians to northern cities. Georgia suffered a net loss through migration of 502,000 from 1940 to 1960, but enjoyed a net gain of 187,000 new residents during the next 18 years.

¹⁹ INTERGOVERNMENTAL COOPERATION

Georgia's Interstate Cooperation Commission, established in 1937, consists of five members from the senate, five from the house, and five appointed by the governor. Specialized commissions established since then have lessened the importance of this group.

Multistate agreements in which Georgia participates include the Southern Regional Educational Compact, Southeastern Interstate Forest Fire Protection Compact, and the Southern Interstate Energy Compact. Georgia also participates in the Southern Regional Environmental Conservation Council.

In 1978/79, federal aid to Georgia totaled $2.2 billion, of which $150.5 million was general revenue sharing.

²⁰ ECONOMY

According to the original plans of Georgia's founders, its people were to be sober spinners of silk. The reality was far different, however: during the period of royally appointed governors, Georgia became a replica of Carolina, a plantation province producing rice, indigo, and cotton. After the Revolution, the invention of the cotton gin established the plantation system even more firmly by making cotton planting profitable in the piedmont. Meanwhile, the backcountry produced deerskins and other furs and lumber; rice remained an important staple along the coast; turnpikes, canals, and railroads were built; and textile manufacturing became increasingly important, especially in Athens and Augusta.

At the end of the Civil War, the state's economy was in ruins, and tenancy and sharecropping were common. Manufacturing, especially of textiles, was promoted by "New South" spokesmen like Henry Grady of Atlanta and Patrick Walsh of Augusta. Atlanta, whose nascent industries included production of a thick sweet syrup called Coca-Cola, symbolized the New South idea—then as now. Farmers did not experience the benefits of progress, however. Many of them flocked to the mills, while others joined the Populist Party in an effort to air their grievances. To the planters' relief, cotton prices rose from the turn of the century through World War I. Meanwhile, Georgians lost control of their railroads and industries to northern corporations. During the 1920s, the boll weevil wrecked the cotton crops, and farmers resumed their flight to the cities. Not until the late 1930s did Georgia accept Social Security, unemployment compensation, and other relief measures.

Georgia's economy underwent drastic changes as a result of World War II. The raising of poultry and livestock became more important than crop cultivation, and manufacturing replaced agriculture as the chief source of income. By 1978, only about 2% of the labor force was employed in agriculture; among the leading sectors, manufacturing employed 22%, wholesale and retail trade 20%, government 17%, and services 13%. Georgia is a leader in the making of paper products, tufted textiles products, processed chickens, naval stores, lumber, and transportation equipment.

Georgia's oldest industry, textile manufacturing, remains its most important, though ownership of the mills has passed from local to national corporations. After World War II, many northern industries moved to Georgia to take advantage of low wages and low taxes, conditions that meant low benefits for Georgians. A chronic problem for workers in the textile industry has been how to organize labor unions for the purpose of collective bargaining. As of 1980, national unions had not been very successful in their attempts to organize mill workers. A recent barrier to the employment of economically disadvantaged Georgians has been the gradual movement of manufacturing plants from the inner cities to the suburbs.

21 INCOME

The per capita income of Georgians has been low historically, at least since the Civil War. In 1940, the average income was below $350 a year; the average doubled during World War II and stood at $1,034 in 1950. In relative terms, Georgians in 1940 received only 57% as much as other Americans but by 1950, they were earning nearly 70% of the national average. The growth rate continued during the next two decades until, by 1970, per capita income averaged $3,318, or 84% of the national level.

Georgia's per capita income rose from $1,645 in 1960 to $6,700 in 1978, boosting the state's national rank from 42d to 37th. The median income for four-person families increased from $9,650 in 1969 to $16,835 in 1977, a rise of nearly 75%. Moreover, the number of persons below the federal poverty level declined from 924,000 in 1969 to 883,000 in 1975, although their share of the total population, 18% in 1975, was well above the US average and among the highest in the South.

Income appears to be directly related to educational attainment. Whereas nearly 60,000 persons with no more than an elementary education made under $4,000 in 1976, only about 2,000 with college educations were in that bracket. More than 90,000 college-educated Georgians earned $25,000 or more during 1976, while only about 5,000 Georgians with elementary educations earned that much. Racial and sexual disparities are also evident: in 1970, adult black men earned only about half as much as white men, white women earned 16% less than black men, and black women earned 44% less than white females. In 1977, median income in metropolitan Atlanta was $7,352, the highest in the state.

22 LABOR

Georgia's civilian labor force was estimated at 2,452,000 in 1980. Of this total, 156,000 workers, or 6.4%, were unemployed. White males constituted 43.5% of the labor force, white females 30%, nonwhite males 13.5%, and nonwhite females 13%. The most remarkable change in the labor force since World War II has been the rising proportion of women, whose share increased from less than 28% in 1940 to an estimated 43% in 1980.

The trend during the 1970s was toward increased employment in service industries and toward multiple-job holding. Employment in agricultural production, the leading industry prior to World War II, continued its long-term decline, decreasing between 1970 and 1978 by 20,400 workers, or nearly 27%. The mining, construction, and manufacturing industries registered employment increases but declined in importance relative to such sectors as trade and government.

A federal census of workers covered by unemployment insurance in March 1977 revealed the following nonfarm employment pattern for Georgia:

	ESTABLISH-MENTS	EMPLOYEES	ANNUAL PAYROLL ('000)
Agricultural services, forestry, fishing	986	5,336	$ 43,628
Mining	197	6,979	91,775
Contract construction'	9,873	86,309	961,436
Manufacturing, of which:	7,771	487,005	5,162,793
Textile mill products	(646)	(115,320)	(1,071,975)
Apparel, other textiles	(573)	(74,216)	(488,109)
Transportation, public utilities	3,406	107,648	1,640,978
Wholesale trade	9,968	125,884	1,650,155
Retail trade	30,490	300,979	2,056,020
Finance, insurance, real estate	8,958	95,845	1,085,859
Services	26,349	262,714	2,166,660
Other	1,375	2,370	24,369
TOTALS	99,373	1,481,069	$14,883,673

Among the workers not covered by this survey were government employees, of whom Georgia had 426,200 (80,500 federal, 345,700 state and local) in February 1980.

Georgia has not been hospitable to union organizers, partly because of a mistrust of "outside agitators," a suspicion reinforced by conservative politicians like Eugene Talmadge who convinced many people that union organizers were promoters of racial equality. Among state laws strictly regulating union activity is a right-to-work law enacted in 1947. Union membership in Georgia did grow from 166,000 in 1964 to 261,000 in 1976. As a proportion of the total labor force, however, the number of union members remained only 14%. In addition, 51,000 Georgians were members of employee associations in 1976. In 1962, the legislature denied state employees the right to strike.

The average earnings for Georgia workers in manufacturing industries climbed from $2.01 an hour in 1965 to $4.88 an hour in 1978. The latter figure was about 21% below the national average. Strikes in Georgia tend to be fewer than in most heavily industrialized states. In 1977, 23,000 workers were involved in 58 work stoppages.

One of the earliest state labor laws was an 1889 act requiring employers to provide seats for females to use when resting. A child-labor law adopted in 1906 prohibited the employment of children under 10 years of age in manufacturing. A general workers' compensation law was enacted in 1920.

23 AGRICULTURE

In 1978, Georgia's farm income reached $2.6 billion (16th in the US). Georgia ranked 1st in the production of peanuts and pecans, harvesting 51% of all the pecans grown in the US and 44% of the peanuts.

Cotton was the mainstay of Georgia's economy through the early 20th century, and the state's plantations also grew corn, rice, tobacco, wheat, and sweet potatoes. World War I stimulated the cultivation of peanuts along with other crops. By the 1930s, tobacco and peanuts were challenging cotton for agricultural supremacy, and Georgia had also become an important producer of peaches, a product for which the "peach state" is still widely known.

After 1940, farm mechanization and consolidation were rapid. The number of tractors increased from 10,000 in 1940 to 85,000 by 1955. In 1940, 6 out of 10 farms were tenant-operated; by the mid-1960s, less than 1 in 6 was. The number of farms declined from 226,000 in 1945 to 54,000 in 1979, when the average farm size was 291 acres (118 hectares). Georgia's farmland area of 15.7 million acres (6.4 million hectares) represents 42% of its land area. Total farm operating expenses, including feed, seed, and labor, were $1.7 billion in 1978. The cost for fertilizer and lime was $209.6 million.

The following table shows acreage and value for leading crops in 1978:

	ACREAGE	VALUE
Peanuts	526,000	$364,518,000
Soybeans	1,680,000	188,160,000
Corn for grain	1,500,000	183,750,000
Tobacco (flue-cured)	61,000	179,191,000
Cotton	115,000	32,501,000

Other crops and their values in 1978 included hay, $53,675,000; cottonseed, $4,644,000; oats, $4,479,000; rye, $4,048,000; and sorghum, $2,270,000.

There are 94 cooperatives headquartered in the state; and a total of 107 cooperatives do business in Georgia. These include agricultural cooperatives and those that provide services to farmers, such as land bank associations and rural electric cooperatives. In 1978, membership totaled 154,488 and the co-ops did a net business totaling $843,525,000.

24 ANIMAL HUSBANDRY
Georgia's cash receipts from livestock and livestock products totaled $1.5 billion in 1978, or nearly three-fifths of the total farm income. Georgia ranks 1st in the US in total cash receipts from chickens, eggs, and broilers; and 2d only to California in eggs, and to Arkansas in broilers produced.

At the close of 1979, Georgia farms had 1,600,000 cattle and calves, and 2,280,000 hogs and pigs. Some 462,660,000 lb of cattle valued at $309,898,000 were produced in 1979; the totals for hogs were 610,126,000 lb and $238,559,000.

Cows kept for milk production numbered 127,000 in 1979, when Georgia dairies produced 1.3 billion lb of milk. Poultry farmers sold $525,506,000 worth of broilers and $283,221,000 of eggs; the total egg production was nearly 5.7 billion. The 2,516,000 turkeys raised in 1979 brought $24,758,000.

The value of honey and beeswax for 1978 was $2.1 million, and the estimated value of queen bees and package bees was $2.9 million.

25 FISHING
Georgia's total commercial catch of fish and shellfish in 1978 was 17,493,000 lb, valued at $14,567,000. Although Georgia ranked 19th among the 50 states in value of commercial fishing, the volume represented less than 1% of the national catch. Commercial fishing in Georgia involves more shellfish—mainly shrimp and crabs—than finfish, the most important of which are caught in the nets of shrimp trawlers. Leading finfish are flounder, king whiting, grouper, porgy, red snapper, and shad.

Georgia ranks 1st in the South in sport fishing. In brisk mountain streams and sluggish swamps, fishermen catch bass, catfish, jackfish, bluegill, crappie, perch, and trout. Fishery habitats include 29 major reservoirs covering 282,179 acres (114,194 hectares), 60,000 farm ponds and small lakes, 21,252 mi (34,202 km) of warm-water streams, and 882 mi (1,419 km) of prime trout streams wider than 10 feet (3 meters). Georgia ranked 2d only to Texas in hatchery production of striped bass and the striped-white bass hybrid in 1979.

26 FORESTRY
In 1977, Georgia, which occupied 1.6% of the total US land area, had nearly 3.4% of the nation's forestland and 5.1% of the nation's commercial forests. Georgia's total forest area, 25,256,000 acres (10,221,000 hectares), ranked 4th in the US, and its 24,812,000 acres (10,041,000 hectares) of commercial forests ranked 1st.

Forests cover more than two-thirds of the state's land area. The most densely wooded counties are in the piedmont hills and northern mountains. Ware and Charlton counties in southeastern Georgia, containing the Okefenokee Swamp, are almost entirely forested. Six percent of all Georgia's forestland is government-owned, 17% is owned by industry, and 77% belongs to other private interests.

Georgia's timber industry in 1979 consisted of 241 sawmills, 24 plywood plants, 39 treatment plants, and 15 pulp and paper mills. The chief products were pine lumber and pine plywood for the building industry, hardwood lumber for the furniture industry, and pulp for the paper and box industry. Georgia produced approximately 2.5 billion board feet of lumber, of which 84% was softwood (pine), and 6 million cords of pulpwood, of which 87% was softwood. The combined value of all forestry products was $4 billion in 1979.

The two chief recreational forest areas are Chattahoochee National Forest, in the northern part of the state, and Oconee National Forest, in the central region. The Georgia Forest Commission employs about 800 persons, including more than 100 professional foresters. Georgia was one of the first states to provide free fire protection. There are nine nurseries, three state-owned and six owned privately. Nurseries operated by the state produced 60 million trees in 1979, and the forest industry planted another 90 million.

27 MINING
The estimated value of minerals produced in Georgia in 1978 was $587 million, 25th in the US. Georgia ranks 1st in the production of marble, kaolin, and crushed granite.

About three-fourths of the nation's supply of kaolin, or "white clay," is produced in Georgia; used mostly for filler and coating in white paper, kaolin is also employed in pottery making. The most important minerals commercially are the clays found along the sand hills at the southern edge of the piedmont. Marble is found chiefly in northeastern Georgia; the marble quarried at Tate is noted for its texture and durability. Small quantities of iron ore are mined in the coastal plain, and coal is found in northwestern Georgia. Other minerals include mica, barite, bauxite, and talc. Estimated output of principal minerals (excluding fossil fuels) in 1978 included stone, 42,065,000 tons; clays, 8,158,000 tons, and sand and gravel, 5,500,000 tons.

Gold was discovered in 1827 in the hills around Dahlonega, and a US mint was established there in 1838. The dome of the state capitol at Atlanta is painted with Dahlonega gold leaf. Gold is no longer mined commercially but tourists still come to Dahlonega to try their luck.

28 ENERGY AND POWER
Georgia is an energy-dependent state which in 1979 produced only 3% of its energy needs, most of it through hydroelectric power. There are no commercially recoverable petroleum or natural gas reserves, and the state's coal deposits are of no more than marginal importance. Georgia does have large amounts of timberland, however, and it has been estimated that 20–40% of the state's energy demands could be met by using wood that is currently wasted. In 1980, Georgia led the nation in the number of houses heated primarily by wood, with 66,000 units. The state's southern location and favorable weather conditions also make solar power an increasingly attractive energy alternative; nearly 400 solar power units of varying sizes were in operation in 1980. Georgia's extensive river system also offers the potential for further hydroelectric development.

Transportation is the state's largest energy user, accounting for 44% of total energy consumed; industry uses 27%, residences 15%, commercial enterprises 12%, and other sectors 2%. Transportation and industry are the most rapidly increasing users of energy, reflecting Georgia's poorly developed public transportation system and energy-wasteful industrial plant. Automobiles consume 32% of the state's energy, trucks 11%, and railroads only 1%.

In 1978, Georgia produced 55.2 billion kwh of electricity and had an installed capacity of 15.6 million kw, of which 92% was privately owned. The state's major electric utilities include the Georgia Power Co., Savannah Electric and Power Co., Municipal Electric Authority of Georgia, and Oglethorpe Electric Membership Cooperative. Georgia Power had two atomic reactors near Baxley with a combined capacity of 1,581,000 kw in 1978. All utilities are regulated by the Georgia Public Service Commission, which must approve their rates.

Petroleum accounted for 55% of all fuel used in Georgia in 1973. Exploration for oil off the coast goes on, but the state's offshore oil resources are expected to be slight. Georgia's demonstrated coal reserves were less than 500,000 tons in 1977, and production was 113,000 tons in 1978.

In 1978, the state created the Office of Energy Resources to develop a plan for energy conservation and energy resource development. State universities have cooperated with this agency to determine and meet Georgia's future energy needs.

29 INDUSTRY

Georgia's manufactured goods in 1979 had a total value of nearly $35 billion. Important products include textiles, clothing, aircraft, soft drinks, paper, paints and varnishes, bricks and tiles, glassware, and ceramics.

Georgia was primarily an agrarian state before the Civil War, but afterward the cities developed a strong industrial base by taking advantage of abundant water power to operate factories. Textiles have long been dominant, but new industries have also developed. Charles H. Herty, a chemist at the University of Georgia, discovered a new method of extracting turpentine which worked so well that Georgia led the nation in producing turpentine, tar, rosin, and pitch by 1928. Herty also perfected an economical way of making newsprint from southern pines that was adopted by Georgia's paper mills. With the onset of World War II, meat-processing plants were built at rail centers, and fertilizer plants and cottonseed mills were expanded.

The state's—and Atlanta's—most famous product was created in 1886, when druggist John S. Pemberton developed a formula which he sold to Asa Griggs Candler, who in 1892 formed the Coca-Cola Co. In 1919, the Candlers sold the company to a syndicate headed by Ernest Woodruff, whose son Robert made "Coke" into the world's most widely known commercial product. The transport equipment, chemical, food-processing, apparel, and forest-products industries today rival textiles in economic importance.

The total value added by manufacturing increased from $9.8 billion in 1975 to $12.5 billion in 1977. The following table shows value added by manufacture for major industries:

	1975	1977
Textile mill products	$1,688,900,000	$2,435,000,000
Transportation equipment	962,100,000	1,577,100,000
Food and food products	1,157,000,000	1,295,500,000
Chemicals and products	759,100,000	1,126,500,000
Apparel	721,600,000	975,200,000
Paper and paper products	808,100,000	958,700,000
Lumber and wood products	342,100,000	542,400,000
Electric and electronic equipment	346,300,000	530,500,000
Fabricated metal products	321,600,000	483,800,000
Stone, clay, glass products	810,200,000	462,400,000

Georgia's heavily forested northern region is dominated by carpet mills, especially around Dalton. In the piedmont plateau, manufacturing is highly diversified, with textiles and transportation equipment being the most significant.

In 1980, five of the nation's 500 largest industrial corporations listed by *Fortune* magazine had headquarters in Georgia: Coca-Cola, Gold Kist, National Service Industries, and Royal Crown Companies, all in Atlanta; and the West Point–Pepperell Co. in West Point.

30 COMMERCE

Georgia ranked 11th among the 50 states in 1972, with total sales of $19.5 billion in 1972. The state ranked 14th in retail trade in 1977, with sales totaling $15.9 billion. The most important categories (and their sales shares) were food stores, 22%; automotive dealers, 22%; department stores, 10%; gasoline service stations, 8%; and eating and drinking places, 8%. Nearly 43% of all retail sales were concentrated in the Atlanta metropolitan area.

Georgia exported manufactured goods worth $1.4 billion in 1976, and farm products worth $476 million in 1976/77, ranking among the top 20 states in both categories. Savannah is Georgia's most important export-import center; it handled 9,875,678 tons of commercial goods in 1977.

31 CONSUMER PROTECTION

The Consumer Advisory Board, established in 1975, protects consumers and legitimate business enterprises from unfair and deceptive practices. The Fair Business Practices Act of 1975 forbids representing products as having official approval when they do not, outlaws advertising without the intention of supplying a reasonable number of the items advertised, and gives the Consumer Advisory Board the power to investigate complaints and to penalize unfair practices up to $25,000 per violation. Georgia's basic consumer protection law dates from 1953.

32 BANKING

The state's first bank was the branch of the Bank of the US established at Savannah in 1802. Eight years later, the Georgia legislature chartered the Bank of Augusta and the Planters' Bank of Savannah, with the state holding one-sixth of the stock of each bank. The state also subscribed two-thirds of the stock of the Bank of the State of Georgia, which opened branches throughout the region. To furnish small, long-term agricultural loans, the state in 1828 established the Central Bank of Georgia, but this institution collapsed in 1856 because the state kept dipping into its reserves. After the Civil War, the lack of capital and the high cost of credit forced farmers to borrow from merchants under the lien system. By 1900 there were 200 banks in Georgia; with an improvement in cotton prices, their number increased to nearly 800 by World War I. During the agricultural depression of the 1920s, about half these banks failed, and the number has remained relatively stable since 1940. Georgia banking practices came under national scrutiny in 1979, when Bert Lance, President Carter's former budget director and the former president of the National Bank of Georgia, was indicted on 33 counts of bank fraud. The federal government dropped its case after Lance was acquitted on 9 of the charges and most of the rest were dismissed.

In 1978 there were 376 state-chartered banks with total assets of $10.5 billion. In 1979, the state's 98 savings and loan associations had total assets of almost $10 billion. The duty of supervising all financial institutions is entrusted to the Department of Banking and Finance.

33 INSURANCE

In 1978 there were 27 life insurance companies doing business in Georgia. Insurance in force at the end of the year totaled more than $48.2 billion, and premiums paid amounted to $657.4 million. Death benefit payments were $266.6 million in 1978, and total benefit payments, including death, disability, and annuity as well as policy dividends and matured endowments, amounted to $553.4 million. The average family had $38,400 in life insurance coverage, 9% above the national norm.

Premiums written by other types of insurance firms in 1978 included $450.8 million for automobile liability coverage, $284.8 million for automobile physical damage coverage, $176.7 million for homeowners insurance, and $125.5 million for commercial multiple-peril insurance. Georgians held $386.2 million in flood insurance as of 30 June 1979.

34 SECURITIES

There are no stock or commodity exchanges in Georgia. In 1978, New York Stock Exchange member firms had 60 sales offices and 837 registered representatives in the state. Georgians reported $460.1 million in dividend income on their 1977 federal tax returns.

35 PUBLIC FINANCE

Since the Georgia constitution forbids the state to spend more than it takes in from all sources, the governor attempts to reconcile the budget requests of the state department heads with the revenue predicted by economists for the coming fiscal year. The governor's Office of Planning and Budget prepares the budget, which is then presented to the general assembly at the beginning of each year's session. The assembly may decide to change the revenue estimate, but it usually goes along with the governor's forecast. The fiscal year begins on 1 July, and the first question for the assembly when it convenes the following January is whether to raise or lower the current year's budget estimate. If the revenues are better than expected, the legislators enact a supplemental budget; if the income is below expectations, cuts can be made.

The Georgia budget more than doubled between 1969/70 and 1975/76, when state revenues totaled nearly $3.4 billion and expenditures amounted to $3.3 billion. The following table summarizes general revenues and expenditures for 1974/75 and 1975/76:

REVENUES	1974/75	1975/76
Taxes	$1,547,774,000	$1,676,007,000
Federal grants	888,555,000	965,097,000
Local governments	10,122,000	11,437,000
Other receipts	485,937,000	704,972,000
TOTALS	$2,932,388,000	$3,357,513,000
EXPENDITURES		
Education	$1,146,408,000	$1,229,076,000
Public welfare	492,151,000	480,784,000
Highways	423,769,000	384,188,000
Health and hospitals	245,669,000	247,169,000
Natural resources	98,553,000	99,139,000
Public safety	83,039,000	89,904,000
General administration	54,559,000	59,744,000
Debt interest	48,638,000	56,522,000
Employment security	22,379,000	27,996,000
Other expenditures	420,837,000	649,879,000
TOTALS[1]	$3,036,002,000	$3,324,401,000

[1]Expenditure totals include supplementary federal funds.

With the refusal by Governor George Busbee to raise taxes during the late 1970s, revenues declined to $2.9 billion by 1979/80, when recommended expenditures were $2.8 billion.

The Atlanta municipal budget for 1976/77 estimated general revenues at $214 million, of which property and other taxes provided 42%; and expenditures at $211 million, of which police and fire protection accounted for 20%.

Georgia's state and local debt totaled nearly $4.2 billion in mid-1977, or $826 per capita. Under state law, Georgia cannot issue a bond without amending the constitution. Such an amendment, enacted in 1968, permits the state to issue bonds for the purpose of making loans available to college students. The only other obligations the state may incur are debts of up to $500,000 to cover temporary shortages and debts up to $3,000,000 for the payment of teachers.

[36] TAXATION

Georgia was the last of the 13 original colonies to tax its citizens, but today its state tax structure is among the broadest in the US. The first comprehensive state tax was provided by the Property Tax Act of 1852, which allocated 50% of the tax to the counties; as of 1980, only 1% of property taxes went to the state. Motor vehicle license fees began in 1910; motor fuel has been taxed since 1921, tobacco since 1923. In 1929, Georgia began taxing incomes; a withholding tax on incomes has been required since 1960. In 1951, Georgia enacted what at that time was the most all-inclusive sales tax in the US; by 1980, this 3% tax was the state's largest source of revenue. State law gives counties the option of charging an additional 1% state tax and of using the money to roll back property taxes. Since the law does not specify what share should accrue to cities within those counties that use the tax, this provision has led to frequent litigation between county and city governments.

In 1978, state tax revenues were nearly $2.2 billion, 18th highest among the 50 states. In that year, sales taxes amounted to $1.3 billion; individual income taxes, to $643.4 million; and corporation income taxes, $203.8 million. As of 1980, the personal income tax ranged from 1% on the first $1,000 to 6% on taxable income over $10,000; the basic corporate tax rate was 6%.

The US Office of Management and Budget estimated that in 1978/79 Georgians paid only 66 cents for every dollar of federal money received, and 87 cents for every dollar from federal revenue sharing. Georgians filed 1.9 million federal income tax returns in 1977, paying $2.9 billion in tax.

[37] ECONOMIC POLICY

Since the time of Henry Grady, spokesman for the New South, Georgia has courted industry. Corporation taxes have been traditionally low, wages also low, and unions weak. Georgia's main attractions for new businesses, as summarized in a 1974 study, are a favorable location for air, highway, and rail transport, a mild climate, a rapidly expanding economy, tax incentives and competitive wage scales, and an abundance of recreational facilities. During the 1970s, Georgia governors aggressively sought out domestic and foreign investors, and German, Japanese, and South American corporations were lured to the state.

The Department of Industry and Trade promotes international trade, cultivates new industry, and is responsible for developing tourism. The state funds city and county development plans, aids recreational projects, promotes research and development, and supports industrial training programs.

[38] HEALTH

Georgia's public health facilities developed only after the turn of the century. The Ellis Health Law of 1914 placed the responsibility for public health with the counties, but by 1936, only 36 of the state's 159 counties had full-time health departments. Not until after federal funds became available during the 1940s was malaria, one of the oldest afflictions in Georgia, brought under control through the eradication of mosquito-breeding places. Federal funds also enabled every county to receive public health nursing services and X-ray clinics.

Despite these advances, federal data for 1969–71 put the average lifespan in Georgia at 68.54 years (48th in the US). State statistics put average longevity even lower—in 1977, just under 62 years for white males, just below 70 for white females, 55.6 years for black males, and 60.6 for black females. Georgia's birthrate declined to a record low of 15.9 per 1,000 population in 1976, but the 1977 birthrate rose to 16.8. Fetal deaths have increased dramatically since 1973, when abortion laws were liberalized in Georgia. Of the 30,264 fetal deaths in 1977, induced abortions accounted for 26,290. Georgia's infant mortality rates in 1977—12.5 per 1,000 live births for whites, 20.4 for nonwhites—were close to the national averages. Heart disease, cancer, cerebrovascular disease, accidents, and respiratory diseases were the leading causes of death in 1977. The number of cases of gonorrhea reported from 1 January through 19 May 1980 was 16,721, a figure surpassed by only five other states.

In 1978 there were 189 hospitals, 17 of them psychiatric, employing 74,156 persons, of whom 11,652 were registered nurses and 6,680 licensed nurses. The number of hospital beds increased from 9,673 in 1950 to 31,146 in 1978. The average cost of hospital care in 1977 was $174 per day and $1,113 per stay, in each case well below the US average. There were 312 nursing care facilities in Georgia, with 28,959 beds in 1977; these homes provided care for 27,704 residents and employed 14,431 persons. Georgia had 6,928 physicians in 1977 and 2,167 active dentists in 1979.

The Medical College of Georgia, established at Augusta in 1828, is one of the oldest medical schools in the US and the center of medical research in the state. The federal Center for Disease Control was established in Atlanta in 1973.

[39] SOCIAL WELFARE

As a responsibility of state government, social welfare came late to Georgia. The state waited two years before agreeing to participate in the federal Social Security system in 1937. Eighteen years later, the state was distributing only $62 million to the aged, blind, and disabled, and to families with dependent children; by 1970, the amount had risen to $150 million, but Georgia still lagged far behind the national average. The state's general assistance payments at the local level were $37.03 monthly in 1976, well under the US average of $115.25.

In 1978, 208,500 Georgians received $103 million in aid to families with dependent children. In that year, 390,000 Georgians participated in the federal food stamp program, at a total cost of $137.6 million. Some 912,000 pupils, or 85% of the eligible enrollment, took part in the federal school lunch program, which cost about $65.4 million.

Social Security benefits paid to 730,500 Georgians totaled nearly $1.6 billion in 1977. Of that amount, 55% went to retired workers, 25% to survivors of deceased workers, and 20% to the disabled. The average monthly Social Security benefit for retired workers was $214.40, nearly 12% below the national average. Supplemental Security Income benefits, distributed to 158,700 Georgians, totaled $196.5 million in 1978.

In 1977, workers' compensation payments totaled $109.4 million. Unemployment insurance benefits averaged $90 weekly for a maximum duration of 26 weeks; $118 million in benefits were paid during 1978.

[40] HOUSING

The advent of television and air conditioning, which coincided with the massive move by Georgians to the suburbs after World War II, influenced both housing design and social patterns, as the den replaced the front porch as a place for the family to gather in the evening. More generally, postwar housing developments provided ordinary Georgia families with modern, comfortable, and affordable dwellings. The home-loan guarantee programs of the Federal Housing Administration and the Veterans Administration made modest down payments, low interest rates, and long-term financing the norm in Georgia. The result was a vast increase in both the number of houses constructed and the percentage of families owning their own homes.

Between 1940 and 1970, the number of housing units in the state doubled to 1,470,557. In 1940, only 3 in 10 Georgia homes were owner-occupied; by 1970, 6 in 10 were. However, in 1970, 13% of all Georgians were still living in units that lacked full plumbing.

In 1970 there were 896,432 housing units in urban areas and 574,125 in rural areas. The state required 695,000 additional housing units by 1980, but that goal was made inaccessible by rising costs. Many families chose mobile homes as an alternative; in 1976, three-fourths of housing units priced under $30,000 were mobile homes. Between 1976 and 1978, 95,500 new housing units worth nearly $2.6 billion were authorized by the state.

[41] EDUCATION

During the colonial period, education was in the hands of private schoolmasters. Georgia's first constitution called for the establishment of a school in each county; the oldest school in the state is Richmond Academy (Augusta), founded in 1788. The nation's oldest chartered public university, the University of Georgia, dates from 1784. Public education was inadequately funded, however, until the inauguration of the 3% sales tax in 1951. By 1960, rural one-teacher schools had disappeared, and children were riding buses to consolidated schools. In the 1953/54 school year, Georgia spent $190 per white student and $132 per black student; by 1978, 24 years after the US Supreme Court outlawed public school segregation, the overall cost per pupil had increased to $1,341. Reported receipts for the operation of Georgia's public schools in 1977/78 totaled $1.3 billion, funding for which was 11.6% federal, 50.7% state, and 37.7% local.

Despite increased expenditures, Georgia continues to lag behind the nation in academic achievement. The illiteracy rate, 2% in 1970, is one of the highest in the US. In 1976, 8% of adult Georgians had less than five years of grade school. Georgia also has one of the highest dropout rates in the nation: only 58% of those entering first grade in 1958 graduated from high school. Among Georgians 35 years of age or older in 1976, 22% had completed four years of high school, and only 6% had completed four years of college.

In fall 1977, Georgia public schools enrolled an estimated 1,766,000 students, of whom 1,284,000 were in elementary schools, 438,000 in secondary schools, and 44,000 in special schools. Private schools had 254,000 students in all grades.

Georgia had 67 institutions of higher learning, 34 public and 33 private, with a total of 169,618 students in 1978/79. Thirty-two public colleges are components of the University System of Georgia; the largest of these is the University of Georgia (Athens), with a 1977 enrollment of 22,974. The largest private university is Emory (Atlanta), with 7,572 students in 1977. Financial aid to college students in 1977/78 amounted to $56,834,736, distributed among 78,073 awards. A scholarship program was established in 1978 for minority students seeking graduate and professional degrees.

[42] ARTS

During the 20th century, Atlanta has replaced Savannah as the major art center of Georgia, while Athens, the seat of the University of Georgia, has continued to share in the cultural life of the university. The state has eight major art museums, as well as numerous private galleries; especially notable is the High Museum of Art in Atlanta. The Atlanta Art Association exhibits the work of contemporary Georgia artists; the Atlanta Memorial Arts Center was dedicated in 1968 to the 100 members of the association who lost their lives in a plane crash.

The theater has enjoyed popular support since the first professional resident theater troupe began performing in Augusta in 1790. Atlanta has a resident theater, and there are community theaters in some 30 cities and counties. Georgia has actively cultivated the filmmaking industry, and an increasing number of films for cinema and television are being produced in the state.

Georgia has more than 20 symphony orchestras, ranging from the Atlanta Symphony, under the direction of Robert Shaw, to community and college ensembles throughout the state. Atlanta and Augusta have professional ballet touring companies, and choral groups and opera societies perform in all major cities.

Macon has become a major recording center, especially for popular music. The north Georgia mountain communities retain their traditional folk music: one may still hear the "fa-so-la" singsong, and ancient sacred harp songs have been collected and preserved.

[43] LIBRARIES AND MUSEUMS

In 1976, the Georgia public library system included 36 regional and 11 county systems, each operating under its own board.

The holdings of all public libraries totaled 8,459,366 volumes in 1977/78, when the combined circulation was 19,201,745 volumes. The University of Georgia had by far the largest academic collection, including 1,811,235 books in addition to government documents, microforms, and periodicals. Emory University in Atlanta has the largest private academic library, with about 1,531,620 bound volumes.

Georgia has more than 80 museums and historic sites, including the Telfair Academy of Arts and Sciences in Savannah, the Georgia State Museum of Science and Industry in Atlanta, the Columbus Museum of Arts and Sciences, and the Augusta–Richmond County Museum in Augusta. Atlanta's Cyclorama depicts the 1864 Battle of Atlanta. The Crawford W. Long Medical Museum in Jefferson is a memorial to Dr. Long, a pioneer in the use of anesthetics. A museum devoted to gold mining is located at Dahlonega.

Georgia abounds in historic sites, 100 of which were selected for acquisition in 1972 by the Georgia Heritage Trust Commission. Sites administered by the National Park Service include the Chickamauga battlefield, Kennesaw Mountain battlefield, Ft. Pulaski National Monument, and Andersonville prison camp near Americus, all associated with the Civil War, as well as the Ft. Frederica National Monument, an 18th-century English barracks on St. Simons Island. Also of historic interest are Factors

Wharf in Savannah, the Hay House in Macon, and Franklin D. Roosevelt's "Little White House" at Warm Springs. The state's most important archaeological sites are the Etowah Mounds at Carterville, the Kolomoki Mounds at Blakely, and the Ocmulgee Indian village near Macon.

⁴⁴COMMUNICATIONS

Airmail service was introduced to Georgia around 1930, and since then the quantity of mail has increased enormously. In 1977/78, postal receipts for the metropolitan Atlanta area amounted to $168,176,256. The US Postal Service had 13,100 employees in Georgia during 1977.

Atlanta is the communications center of Georgia and has the largest toll-free dialing system in the entire Bell network. As of 31 December 1978 there were 3,904,785 telephones, 2,906,935 residential and 997,850 business, 86% of them owned by Southern Bell Telephone and Telegraph. On average, 93% of Georgia households had telephone service.

In 1980, Georgia had 288 radio stations and 30 television stations, of which 15 were part of the State Education Department's system. More than 200 radio and television stations have combined to form the Georgia Association of Broadcasters.

Cable television systems served 321,234 subscribers in 178 communities in 1978. On 1 June 1980, Atlanta businessman Ted Turner inaugurated the independent Cable News Network, which made round-the-clock news coverage available to 4,100 cable television systems throughout the US.

⁴⁵PRESS

Georgia's first newspaper was the *Georgia Gazette*, published by James Johnston from 1763 until 1776. When royal rule was temporarily restored in Savannah, Johnston published the *Royal Georgia Gazette*; when peace came, he changed the name again, this time to the *Gazette of the State of Georgia*. After the state capital was moved to Augusta in 1785, Greensburg Hughes, a Charleston printer, began publishing the *Augusta Gazette*. Today's *Augusta Chronicle* traces its origin to this paper and claims the honor of being the oldest newspaper in the state. In 1817, the *Savannah Gazette* became the state's first daily. After the Indian linguist Sequoyah gave the Cherokee a written language, Elias Boudinot gave them a newspaper, the *Cherokee Phoenix*, in 1828. Georgia authorities suppressed the paper in 1835, and Boudinot joined his tribe's tragic migration westward.

After the Civil War, Henry Grady made the *Atlanta Constitution* the most famous newspaper in the state, with his "New South" campaign. Joel Chandler Harris's stories of Uncle Remus appeared in the *Constitution*, as did the weekly letters of humorist Charles Henry Smith, writing under the pseudonym Bill Arp. In 1958, Ralph E. McGill, editor and later publisher of the *Constitution*, won a Pulitzer Prize for his editorial opposition to racial intolerance.

As of 1978, Georgia had 8 morning dailies with 452,145 combined circulation, 29 evening dailies with 608,708, and 15 Sunday newspapers with 1,038,802. The following table shows leading daily newspapers with their 1978 circulations:

AREA	NAME	DAILY	SUNDAY
Atlanta	Constitution (m,S)	216,002	529,220
	Journal (e,S)	217,450	
Augusta	Chronicle (m,S)	55,365	79,849
	Herald (e,S)	19,022	
Columbus	Enquirer (m,S)	33,689	69,164
	Ledger (e,S)	31,309	
Macon	News (e,S)	23,847	87,538
	Telegraph (m,S)	52,118	
Savannah	News (m,S)	55,934	71,820
	Press (e,S)	21,608	

There were 122 periodicals published in Georgia in 1979. They included the *Southern Automotive Journal, Atlanta Magazine, Farmers and Consumers Market Bulletin, Rural Georgia,* and *Southern Accents.*

⁴⁶ORGANIZATIONS

There were at least 138 organizations headquartered in Georgia in 1979. General and service organizations include the Law Students Civil Rights Research Council, Industrial Development Research Council, and the Association of Information and Dissemination Centers. Among the cultural and educational organizations are the National Association of College Deans, Registrars, and Admissions Officers, Southern Association of Colleges and Schools, Southern Education Foundation, Southern Regional Council, and Association of Art Museum Directors. The Southern Christian Leadership Conference, led by Martin Luther King, Jr., had a key role in the civil rights movement of the 1960s, and the Voter Education Project helped to increase black voter registration and participation during the 1970s. Medical, health, and charitable organizations include the American Rheumatism Association, Arthritis Foundation, Calorie Control Council, International Association of Pacemaker Patients, and American Dermatological Association. Among the many commercial, trade, and professional organizations are the American Risk and Insurance Association, American Academy of Psychotherapists, American Business Law Association, American Real Estate and Urban Economics Association, Federation of Southern Cooperatives, International Association of Financial Planners, National Association of Market Developers, National Economic Association, Southern Wholesalers Association, and the Textile Quality Control Association.

⁴⁷TOURISM, TRAVEL, AND RECREATION

Georgia's travel industry earned $5.6 billion in 1979, when 182,370 people were employed in tourist-related industries and services. Some 23.1 million people made recreational trips to or within Georgia during the same year.

Major tourist attractions include 2 national forests, 6 national parks, and about 60 state parks. Other places of interest include the impressive hotels and convention facilities of downtown Atlanta, the Okefenokee Swamp in southern Georgia, Stone Mountain near Atlanta, President Jimmy Carter's home in Plains, and the historic squares and riverfront of Savannah. The varied attractions of the Golden Isles include fashionable Sea Island; primitive Cumberland Island, now a national seashore; and Jekyll Island, owned by the state and leased to motel operators and to private citizens for beach homes. Since 1978, the state, under its Heritage Trust Program, has acquired Ossabaw and Sapelo islands, and strictly regulates public access to these wildlife sanctuaries.

Georgia has long been a hunters' paradise. Waynesboro calls itself the "birddog capital of the world," and Thomasville in South Georgia is a mecca for quail hunters. In 1977/78, Georgia issued licenses to 617,367 fishermen and 373,965 hunters.

⁴⁸SPORTS

Most major professional sports are represented in Georgia. Atlanta–Fulton County Stadium, completed in 1965 at a cost of over $18 million, serves as the home field for three professional teams: baseball's Atlanta Braves, for whom Henry Aaron hit many of his record 755 home runs; the Atlanta Falcons of the National Football League; and the Atlanta Chiefs of the North American Soccer League. The Omni International Sports Complex houses the Atlanta Hawks of the National Basketball Association.

The Atlanta 500 is one of the Winston Cup Grand National auto races. The Masters Golf Tournament, brainchild of golfing great Bobby Jones, has been played at the Augusta National Golf Club since 1934. The Atlanta Open is also listed on the professional golfers' tour.

Football is king of the college sports. The University of Georgia Bulldogs play in the Southeastern Conference, and Georgia Tech's "Rambling Wrecks" compete in the Atlantic Coast Conference. The Peach Bowl has been an annual postseason football game in Atlanta since 1968.

Professional fishing, sponsored by the Bass Anglers Sportsman's Society, is one of the fastest-growing sports in the state. A popular summer fad is rafting. Massive raft races on the Chattahoochee at Atlanta and Columbus, and on the Savannah River at Augusta, draw many spectators and participants.

⁴⁹FAMOUS GEORGIANS

James Earl "Jimmy" Carter (b.1924), born in Plains, was the first Georgian to serve as president of the US. He was governor of the state (1971–75) before being elected to the White House in 1976. Georgia has not contributed any US vice presidents; Alexander H. Stephens (1812–83) was vice president of the Confederacy during the Civil War.

Georgians who served on the US Supreme Court include James M. Wayne (1790–1867) and Joseph R. Lamar (1857–1916). Several Georgians have served with distinction at the cabinet level: William H. Crawford (b.Virginia, 1772–1834), Howell Cobb (1815–68), and William G. McAdoo (1863–1941) as secretaries of the treasury; John M. Berrien (b.New Jersey, 1781–1856) as attorney general; John Forsyth (1781–1841) and Dean Rusk (b.1909) as secretaries of state; George Crawford (1798–1872) as secretary of war; and Hoke Smith (b.North Carolina, 1855–1931) as secretary of the interior.

A leader in the US Senate before the Civil War was Robert Toombs (1810–85). Notable US senators in recent years were Walter F. George (1878–1957), Richard B. Russell (1897–1971), Herman Talmadge (b.1913), and Sam Nunn (b.1938). Carl Vinson (b.1883) was chairman of the House Armed Services Committee.

Many Georgians found fame in the rank of the military. Confederate General Joseph Wheeler (1836–1906) became a major general in the US Army during the Spanish-American War. Other Civil War generals included W.H.T. Walker (1816–64), Thomas R.R. Cobb (1823–62), who also codified Georgia's laws, and John B. Gordon (1832–1904), later a US senator and governor of the state. Gordon, Alfred Colquitt (1824–94), and wartime governor Joseph E. Brown (b.South Carolina, 1821–94) were known as the "Bourbon triumvirate" for their domination of the state's Democratic Party from 1870 to 1890. Generals Courtney Hicks Hodge (1887–1966) and Lucius DuBignon Clay (b.1897) played important roles in Europe during and after World War II.

Sir James Wright (b.South Carolina, 1714–85) was Georgia's most important colonial governor. Signers of the Declaration of Independence for Georgia were George Walton (b.Virginia, 1741–1804), Button Gwinnett (b.England, 1735–77), and Lyman Hall (b.Connecticut, 1724–90). Signers of the US Constitution were William Few (b.Maryland, 1748–1828) and Abraham Baldwin (b.Connecticut, 1754–1807). Revolutionary War hero James Jackson (b.England, 1757–1806) organized the Democratic-Republican Party (today's Democratic Party) in Georgia.

The first Georgians, the Indians, produced many heroes. Tomochichi (c.1664–1739) was the Yamacraw chief who welcomed Oglethorpe and the first Georgians. Alexander McGillivray (c.1759–93), a Creek chief who was the son of a Scottish fur trader, signed a treaty with George Washington in a further attempt to protect the Creek lands. Osceola (1800–1838) led his Seminole into the Florida swamps rather than move west. Sequoyah (b.Tennessee, 1773–1843) framed an alphabet for the Cherokee, and John Ross (Coowescoowe, b.Tennessee, 1790–1866) was the first president of the Cherokee republic.

Among influential Georgian educators were Josiah Meigs (b.Connecticut, 1757–1822), the first president of the University of Georgia, and Milton Antony (1784–1839), who established the Medical College of Georgia in Augusta in 1828. Crawford W. Long (1815–78) was one of the first doctors to use ether successfully in surgical operations. Paul F. Eve (1806–77) was a leading teacher of surgery in the South, and Joseph Jones (1833–96) pioneered in the study of the causes of malaria.

Distinguished black Georgians include churchmen Henry M.

Turner (b.South Carolina, 1834–1915) and Charles T. Walker (1858–1921), educators Lucy Laney (1854–1933) and John Hope (1868–1936), and civil rights activists William Edward Burghardt DuBois (b.Massachusetts, 1868–1963) and Walter F. White (1893–1955). One of the best-known Georgians was Martin Luther King, Jr. (1929–68), born in Atlanta, leader of the March on Washington in 1963, and winner of the Nobel Peace Prize in 1964 for his leadership in the campaign for civil rights; he was assassinated in Memphis, Tenn., while organizing support for striking sanitation workers. Black Muslim leader Elijah Muhammad (Elijah Poole, 1897–1975) was also a Georgian. Other prominent black leaders include former UN Ambassador Andrew Young (b.Louisiana, 1932), Atlanta Mayor Maynard Jackson (b.Texas, 1938), and Georgia Senator Julian Bond (b.Tennessee, 1940).

Famous Georgia authors include Sidney Lanier (1842–81), Joel Chandler Harris (1848–1908), Lillian Smith (1857–1966), Conrad Aiken (1889–1973), Erskine Caldwell (b.1902), Caroline Miller (b.1903), Frank Yerby (b.1916), Carson McCullers (1917–67), and Flannery O'Connor (1925–1964). Also notable is Margaret Mitchell (1900–1949), whose Pulitzer Prize–winning *Gone With the Wind* (1936) typifies Georgia to many readers.

Entertainment celebrities include songwriter Johnny Mercer (1909–76); actors Charles Coburn (1877–1961) and Oliver Hardy (1877–1961); singers and musicians Harry James (b.1916), Ray Charles (Ray Charles Robinson, b.1930), Little Richard (Richard Penniman, b.1935), Jerry Reed (b.1937), Gladys Knight (b.1944), and Brenda Lee (b.1944); and actors Melvyn Douglas (b.1901), Sterling Holloway (b.1905), Ossie Davis (b.1917), Barbara Cook (b.1927), Jane Withers (b.1927), Joanne Woodward (b.1930), and Burt Reynolds (b.1936).

Major sports figures include baseball's "Georgia peach," Tyrus Raymond "Ty" Cobb (1886–1961), and Robert Tyre "Bobby" Jones (1902–71), winner of the "grand slam" of four major golf tournaments in 1930. Robert E. "Ted" Turner (b.Ohio, 1939), an Atlanta businessman-broadcaster, owns the Atlanta Hawks and the Atlanta Braves franchises and skippered the *Courageous* to victory in the America's Cup yacht races in 1977.

⁵⁰BIBLIOGRAPHY

Bartley, Nunan V. *From Thurmond to Wallace: Political Tendencies in Georgia, 1948–68.* Baltimore: Johns Hopkins Press, 1970.

Coleman, Kenneth. *Georgia History in Outline.* Athens: University of Georgia Press, 1960.

Coleman, Kenneth, et al. *A History of Georgia.* Athens: University of Georgia Press, 1977.

Georgia, State of. Department of Archives and History. *Georgia Official and Statistical Register, 1977/78.* Atlanta: Perry Communications, 1978.

Georgia, University of. College of Business Administration. Division of Research. *1978 Georgia Statistical Abstract.* Edited by Lorena M. Akioka. Athens, 1978.

Grady, Henry W. *The New South.* Savannah: Beehive Press, 1971.

King, Coretta Scott. *My Life with Martin Luther King.* New York: Holt, Rinehart & Winston, 1970.

Lane, Mills. *The People's Georgia: An Illustrated Social History.* Savannah: Beehive Press, 1975.

Maguire, Jane. *On Shares: Ed Brown's Story.* New York: Norton, 1976.

Malone, Henry. *Cherokees of the Old South.* Athens: University of Georgia Press, 1956.

Martin, Harold H. *Georgia: A Bicentennial History.* New York: Norton, 1977.

Saye, Albert B. *Georgia History and Government.* Austin: Steck Vaughn, 1973.

Woodward, C. Vann. *Tom Watson: Agrarian Rebel.* New York: Oxford University Press, 1970 (orig. 1938).

HAWAII

State of Hawaii

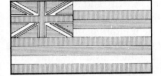

¹LOCATION, SIZE, AND EXTENT

The State of Hawaii is an island group situated in the northern Pacific Ocean, about 2,400 mi (3,900 km) wsw of San Francisco. The smallest of the 5 Pacific states, Hawaii ranks 47th in size among the 50 states.

The 132 Hawaiian Islands have a total area of 6,450 sq mi (16,706 sq km), including 6,425 sq mi (16,641 sq km) of land and only 25 sq mi (65 sq km) of inland water. The island chain extends over 1,576 mi (2,536 km) N–S and 1,425 mi (2,293 km) E–W . The largest island, Hawaii (known locally as the "Big Island"), extends 76 mi (122 km) E–W and 93 mi (150 km) N–S; Oahu, the most populous island, extends 44 mi (71 km) E–W and 30 mi (48 km) N–S.

The eight largest islands of the Hawaiian group are Hawaii (4,038 sq mi—10,458 sq km), Maui (729 sq mi—1,888 sq km), Oahu (608 sq mi—1,575 sq km), Kauai (553 sq mi—1,432 sq km), Molokai (261 sq mi—676 sq km), Lanai (140 sq mi—363 sq km), Niihau (73 sq mi—189 sq km), and Kahoolawe (45 sq mi—117 sq km). The general coastline of the island chain is 750 mi (1,207 km); the tidal shoreline totals 1,052 mi (1,693 km). The state's geographic center is off Maui, at 20°15′ N, 156°20′ w.

²TOPOGRAPHY

The 8 major and 124 minor islands that make up the State of Hawaii were formed by volcanic eruptions. Mauna Loa, on the island of Hawaii, is the world's largest active volcano, at a height of 13,675 feet (4,168 meters). Kilauea, on the eastern slope of Mauna Loa, is the world's largest active volcanic crater: beginning on 24 May 1969, it spewed forth 242 million cu yards (185 million cu meters) of lava spreading over an area of 19.3 sq mi (50 sq km). Further indications of Hawaii's continuing geological activity are the 14 earthquakes, each with a magnitude of 5 or more on the Richter Scale, that shook the islands from 1969 to 1979; one quake, at Puna, on Hawaii, at 4:47 A.M. on 29 November 1975, reached a magnitude of 7.2.

Hawaii, Maui, Kauai, and Molokai are the most mountainous islands. The highest peak in the state is Mauna Kea (13,796 feet—4,205 meters), on Hawaii; the largest natural lake, Halulu (182 acres—74 hectares), Niihau; the largest artificial lake, Waiia Reservoir (422 acres—171 hectares), Kauai; and the longest rivers, Kaukonahua Stream (33 mi—53 km) in the north on Oahu and Wailuku River (32 mi—51 km) on Hawaii. While much of the Pacific Ocean surrounding the state is up to 20,000 feet (6,100 meters) deep, Oahu, Molokai, Lanai, and Maui stand on a submarine bank at a depth of less than 2,400 feet (730 meters).

³CLIMATE

Hawaii has a tropical climate cooled by trade winds. Normal daily temperatures in Honolulu average 72°F (22°C) in January and 80°F (27°C) in July; the average wind speed is a breezy 11.8 mph (19 km/hr). The record high for the state is 100°F (38°C), set at Pahala on 27 April 1931, and the record low is 14°F (–10°C), set at Haleakala, Maui.

Rainfall is extremely variable, with far more precipitation on the windward (northeastern) than on the leeward side of the islands. Waialeale, Kauai, is reputedly the rainiest place on earth, with a mean annual total of 460 in (1,168 cm); only a few miles away, on the same island, the annual rainfall is only 20 in (51 cm), and Puako, Hawaii, receives only 9.5 in (24 cm). Snow falls at the summits of Mauna Loa and Mauna Kea.

⁴FLORA AND FAUNA

Formed over many centuries by volcanic activity, Hawaii's topography—and therefore its flora and fauna—have been subject to constant and rapid change. Relatively few indigenous trees remain; most of the exotic trees and fruit plants have been introduced since the early 19th century. Of 2,200 species and subspecies of flora in 1977, more than half were considered endangered, threatened, or extinct; the koa is an indigenous tree under state protection.

The only land mammal native to the islands is the Hawaiian bat, now endangered; there are no indigenous snakes. The endangered humpback whale migrates to Hawaiian waters in winter;

135

other marine animals abound. Listed as threatened are Newell's shearwater and the green sea turtle. Animals considered endangered by the state but not on the federal list include the Hawaiian storm petrel, Hawaiian owl, Maui 'amakihi (*Loxops virens wilsoni*), and 'i'iwi (*Vestiaria coccinea*).

5 ENVIRONMENTAL PROTECTION

Environmental protection responsibilities are vested in the Department of Land and Natural Resources and in the Environmental and Health Services Division of the Department of Health. In 1974, the legislature enacted the Hawaii Environmental Policy Act of 1974, establishing environmental guidelines for state agencies, and mandated environmental impact statements for all government and some private projects. Noise-pollution standards in Honolulu are among the strictest in the US, and air and water purity levels are well within federal standards. The state's Solid Waste Energy and Resources Task Force has explored methods of recovering energy from garbage and agricultural wastes.

6 POPULATION

According to the 1970 census, Hawaii had a resident population of 769,913, 22% more than in 1960 and 40th among the 50 states. Estimates for mid-1978 give a population of 896,600, including members of the armed forces and their dependents; counting an average of 96,000 visitors and 7,900 Hawaii residents abroad, the estimated de facto population was 984,700. More than four-fifths of the population lives on Oahu, giving the island a density (de facto) of 1,315 persons per sq mi (508 per sq km) in 1978; the figure for the entire state was 153 per sq mi (59 per sq km). Preliminary 1980 census data credited the state with 964,680 residents.

In 1900, 74.5% of Hawaii's inhabitants were rural; by 1970, only 16.5% lived outside urban areas. By far the largest city is Honolulu, with a 1980 population of 365,114, according to preliminary census data. Federal data placed metropolitan Honolulu 55th among US metropolitan areas in 1978, with an estimated population of 719,600.

7 ETHNIC GROUPS

According to federal census data, Hawaii had the nation's largest Japanese population in 1970, ranked 2d only to California in numbers of Filipino residents, and placed 3d behind California and New York in Chinese inhabitants. Under the state's own system of ethnic classification, 72% of all residents were of unmixed ethnic stock in 1979: 26% Caucasians, 25% Japanese, 11% Filipinos, 4% Chinese, about 1% each for Hawaiians, Koreans, Samoans, and blacks, and 2% all others. Of the 28% who were of mixed ethnic stock, 19% were part Hawaiian and 9% were not.

The earliest Asian immigrants, the Chinese, were superseded in number in 1900 by the Japanese, who have since become a significant factor in state politics. The influx of Filipinos and other Pacific island peoples is largely a 20th-century phenomenon. In recent decades, ethnic Hawaiians have been increasingly intent on preserving their cultural identity.

8 LANGUAGES

Although massive immigration from Asia and the US mainland since the mid-19th century has effectively diluted the native population, the Hawaiian lexical legacy in English is conspicuous. Newcomers soon add to their vocabulary *aloha* (love, good-bye), *haole* (white foreigner), *malihini* (newcomer), *lanai* (porch), *tapa* (bark cloth), *mahimahi* (a kind of fish), *ukulele, muumuu,* and the common directional terms *mauka* (toward the mountains) and *makai* (toward the sea), customarily used instead of "north," "east," "west," and "south." Native place-names are numerous: Waikiki, Hawaii, Honolulu, Mauna Kea, Molokai.

According to a state survey, 93% of all residents understand English easily. Most native-born residents of Hawaiian ancestry speak one of several varieties of Hawaiian pidgin, a lingua franca incorporating elements of Hawaiian, English, and other Asian

and Pacific languages. In 1970, major first languages were reported as follows:

	NATIVE-BORN	FOREIGN-BORN
English	439,100	5,407
Japanese	105,498	20,079
Spanish	9,691	1,160
German	4,434	1,658

9 RELIGIONS

Congregationalist missionaries arrived in 1820, and Roman Catholics in 1827; the constitution of 1840 guaranteed freedom of worship for all religions. Subsequent migration brought Mormons and Methodists, and Anglican representatives were invited by King Kamehameha IV in 1862. Confucianism, Taoism, and Buddhism arrived with the Chinese during the 1850s; by the turn of the century, Shinto and five forms of Mahayana Buddhism were being practiced by Japanese immigrants.

A survey conducted in 1979 by the Oahu Public Communications Council of the Church of Jesus Christ of Latter-day Saints showed that 31% of Hawaiians considered themselves Roman Catholics, 34% Protestants, 12% Buddhists, and 3% Mormons; the remaining 20% included Jews, nonbelievers, and followers of Hawaiian traditional religions and other faiths.

10 TRANSPORTATION

Hawaii's only operating railroad is the Lahaina, Kaanapali & Pacific on Maui, with 6 mi (10 km) of track, which carried 103,206 passengers in 1979. Oahu and Hawaii islands have public bus systems. By the end of 1979, Hawaii's 542,905 licensed drivers traversed 3,874 mi (6,235 km) of roads and streets, 92% paved and 73% of that on the two most populous islands. There were 510,353 passenger cars registered that year, along with 84,578 trucks, 3,267 buses, and 77,979 bicycles.

All scheduled interisland passenger traffic and most transpacific travel is by air. In 1980, the state had 10 commercial airports, 15 other nonprivate airfields, and 13 civilian heliports. The busiest air terminal, Honolulu International Airport, accounted for about half of all aircraft operations. In 1977, Hawaii's seven deepwater ports and other harbors handled 12,647,133 tons of overseas cargo and 4,542,847 tons of interisland cargo.

11 HISTORY

Hawaii's earliest inhabitants were Polynesians who came to the islands in double-hulled canoes between 1,000 and 1,400 years ago, either from Southeast Asia or from the Marquesas in the South Pacific. The Western world learned of the islands in 1778, when an English navigator, Captain James Cook, sighted Oahu; he named the entire archipelago the Sandwich Islands after his patron, John Montagu, 4th earl of Sandwich. At that time, each island was ruled by a hereditary chief under a caste system called *kapu*. Subsequent contact with European sailors and traders exposed the Polynesians to smallpox, venereal disease, liquor, firearms, and Western technology—and fatally weakened the *kapu* system. Within 40 years of Cook's arrival, one of the island chiefs, Kamehameha (whose birthdate, designated as 11 June, is still celebrated as a state holiday), had consolidated his power on Hawaii, conquered Maui and Oahu, and established a royal dynasty in what now became known as the Kingdom of Hawaii.

The death of Kamehameha I in 1819 preceded by a year the arrival of Protestant missionaries. One of the first to come was the Reverend Hiram Bingham, who, as pastor in Honolulu, was instrumental in the christianizing of Hawaii. Even before he came, however, Liholiho, successor to the throne under the title of Kamehameha II, had begun to do away with the *kapu* system. After the king's death of measles while on a state trip to England in 1824, another son of Kamehameha I, Kauikeaouli, was proclaimed King Kamehameha III. His reign saw the establishment of public schools, the first newspapers, the first sugar plantation, a bicameral legislature, and Honolulu as the kingdom's capital

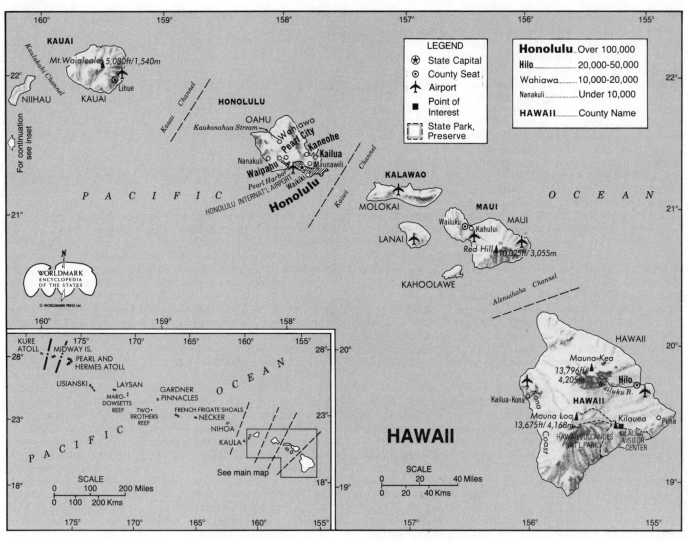

See US political: front cover F5; physical: back cover F5.

LOCATION: 18°54′ to 28°15′N; 154°40′ to 178°75′ W. **BOUNDARIES**: Pacific coastline, 750 mi (1,207 km).

city. Hawaii's first written constitution was promulgated in 1840, and in 1848 a land reform called the Great Mahele abolished the feudal land system and legitimized private landholdings, in the process fostering the expansion of sugar plantations. The power behind the throne during this period was Dr. Gerrit P. Judd, a medical missionary who served as finance minister and interpreter for Kamehameha III.

Diplomatic maneuverings during the 1840s and 1850s secured recognition of the kingdom from the US, Britain, and France. As the American presence on the islands increased, however, so did pressure for US annexation—a movement opposed by Alexander Liholiho, who ruled as Kamehameha IV after his father's death in 1854. His brief reign and that of his brother Lot (Kamehameha V) witnessed the arrival of Chinese contract laborers and of the first Japanese immigrants, along with the continued growth of Hawaii as an international port of call (especially for whalers) and of the increasing influence of American sugar planters. Lot's death in 1872 left no direct descendant of Kamehameha, and the legislature elected a new king, whose death only a year later required yet another election. The consequent crowning of Kalakaua, known as the Merry Monarch, inaugurated a stormy decade during whch his imperial schemes clashed with the power of the legislature and the interests of the planters. The

most significant event of Kalakaua's unstable reign was the signing of a treaty with the US in 1876, guaranteeing Hawaii an American sugar market. The treaty was renewed in 1887 with a clause leasing Pearl Harbor to the US.

Kalakaua died during a visit to San Francisco in 1891 and was succeeded by his sister, Liliuokalani, the last Hawaiian monarch. Two years later, after further political wrangling, she was deposed in an American-led revolution that produced a provisional government under the leadership of Sanford B. Dole. The new regime immediately requested annexation by the US, but the treaty providing for it bogged down in the Senate, and died after the inauguration of President Grover Cleveland, an opponent of expansionism. The provisional government then drafted a new constitution and on 4 July 1894 proclaimed the Republic of Hawaii, with Dole as president. The Spanish-American War, which fanned expansionist feelings in the US and pointed up the nation's strategic interests in the Pacific, gave proponents of annexation the opportunity they had been seeking. The formal transfer of sovereignty took place on 12 August 1898, Dole becoming Hawaii's first territorial governor when the act authorizing the annexation became effective in June 1900.

Notable in the territorial period were a steady US military buildup, the creation of a pineapple canning industry by James D.

Dole (the governor's cousin), the growth of tourism (spurred in 1936 by the inauguration of commercial air service), and a rising desire for statehood, especially after passage of the Sugar Act of 1934, which lowered the quota on sugar imports from Hawaii. The Japanese attack on Pearl Harbor on 7 December 1941, crippling the US Pacific fleet and causing some 4,000 casualties, quickly turned Hawaii into an armed camp, under martial law. The record of bravery compiled by Nisei of the 442d Regiment on the European front did much, on the other hand, to allay the mistrust that some mainlanders felt about the loyalties of Hawaiians of Japanese ancestry. Hawaii also bore a disproportionate burden during the Korean confict, suffering more casualties per capita than any of the 48 states.

Hawaiians pressed for statehood after World War II, but Congress was reluctant, partly because of racial antipathy and partly because of fears that Hawaii's powerful International Longshoremen's and Warehousemen's Union was Communist-controlled. The House of Representatives passed a statehood bill in 1947, but the Senate refused. Not until 1959, after Alaska became the 49th state, did Congress vote to let Hawaii enter the Union. President Eisenhower signed the bill on 18 March, and the question was then put to the Hawaiian electorate, who voted for statehood on 27 June 1959 by a margin of about 17 to 1. Hawaii became the 50th state on 21 August 1959. Since then, defense and tourism have been the mainstays of Hawaii's economy, with the state playing an increasingly important role as an economic, educational, and cultural bridge between the US and the nations of Asia and the Pacific.

12 STATE GOVERNMENT

The constitution of the state of Hawaii was written by the constitutional convention of 1950 and ratified by the people of the Territory of Hawaii that year and then amended by the 1959 plebiscite on the statehood question.

There is a bicameral legislature of 25 senators, elected from eight senatorial districts for four-year terms, and 51 representatives, elected from 25 representative districts for two-year terms. The legislature meets annually on the 3d Wednesday in January. To be eligible to serve as a legislator, a person must have attained the age of majority, be an American citizen, have been a resident of the state for at least three years, and be a qualified voter of his district.

The governor and lieutenant governor are elected for concurrent four-year terms and must be of the same political party. They are the only elected officers of the executive branch, except for members of the Board of Education. There are 17 executive departments, each under the supervision of the governor and headed by a single appointed executive.

Voters in Hawaii must be US citizens at least 18 years of age; there is no minimum residency requirement.

13 POLITICAL PARTIES

Both Republicans and Democrats established party organizations early in the 20th century, when Hawaii was still a territory. Prior to statehood, the Republican Party dominated the political scene; since the 1960s, however, Hawaii has been solidly Democratic. As of 1980, most local officials were Democrats, as were the governor and majorities of both houses of the state legislature. Of the state's 395,262 registered voters, 241,456 were Democrats, 37,663 Republicans, and 116,143 members of minor parties or unaffiliated. Hawaii was one of only six states to cast its electoral votes for Jimmy Carter in 1980.

14 LOCAL GOVERNMENT

The state is divided into four principal counties: Hawaii, including the island of Hawaii; Maui, embracing the islands of Maui, Kahoolawe, Lanai, and Molokai; Honolulu, covering all of Oahu, including the city of Honolulu, plus the northwestern Hawaiian Islands, from Nihoa to Kure Atoll; and Kauai, including the islands of Kauai and Niihau. Since there are no further subdivi-

Hawaii Presidential Vote by Major Political Parties, 1960–80

YEAR	ELECTORAL VOTE	HAWAII WINNER	DEMOCRAT	REPUBLICAN
1960	3	*Kennedy (D)	92,410	92,295
1964	4	*Johnson (D)	163,249	44,022
1968	4	Humphrey (D)	141,324	91,425
1972	4	*Nixon (R)	101,433	168,933
1976	4	*Carter (D)	147,375	140,003
1980	4	Carter (D)	135,879	130,112

*Won US presidential election.

sions, the counties provide some services traditionally performed in other states by cities, towns, and villages, notably fire and police protection, refuse collection, and street maintenance and lighting. On the other hand, the state government provides many functions normally performed by counties on the mainland. Each principal county has an elected council and a mayor.

A fifth county of Kalawao forms that part of Molokai more commonly known as the Kalaupapa Settlement, primarily for the care and treatment of persons suffering from leprosy. Kalawao is entirely under the jurisdiction of the Department of Health; the only county officer is an appointed sheriff.

15 STATE SERVICES

Hawaii's first ombudsman, empowered to investigate complaints by the public about any officer or employee of state or county government, took office in 1969. The State Ethics Commission, a legislative agency, implements requirements for financial disclosure by state officials and investigates alleged conflicts of interest and other breaches of ethics.

The Department of Education (headed by an elected Board of Education) operates the public schools, administers the statewide library system, regulates private schools, and certifies teachers. The Board of Regents of the University of Hawaii oversees the state's higher educational institutions. Highways, airports, harbors, and other facilities are the concern of the Department of Transportation.

The Department of Health operates 10 public hospitals, the Kalaupapa leper colony, and various programs for the mentally ill, the mentally retarded, and alcoholics. Civil defense and the Air and Army national guards are under the jurisdiction of the Department of Defense.

The Corrections Division of the Department of Social Services and Housing operates the state prison system, along with programs for juvenile offenders. Also within this department are divisions of public welfare and vocational rehabilitation, as well as the Hawaii Housing Authority. The Executive Office on Aging works with state and county departments to coordinate programs for senior citizens. Unemployment insurance, occupational safety and health laws, and workers' compensation programs are run by the Department of Labor and Industrial Relations.

16 JUDICIAL SYSTEM

The supreme court, the highest in the state, consists of a chief justice and four associate justices, all of them appointed by the governor with the advice and consent of the senate. All serve 10-year terms, up to the mandatory retirement age of 70.

The state is divided into four judicial circuits with 20 circuit court judges, also appointed by the governor to 10-year terms. Circuit courts are the main trial courts, having jurisdiction in most civil and criminal cases. District courts, whose judges are appointed by the chief justice to 6-year terms, function as inferior courts within each judicial circuit; district court judges may also preside over family court proceedings. Hawaii also has a land court and a tax appeal court.

According to the FBI Crime Index, Hawaii's crime rates in 1978 were 270.1 per 100,000 population for violent crimes, well below the US average, and 6,866 for property crimes, far above it. Only Arizona had a higher incidence of larceny-theft in 1978 than did Hawaii.

17 ARMED FORCES

Hawaii is the nerve center of US defense activities in the Pacific. CINCPAC (Commander-in-Chief Pacific), headquartered at Camp H. M. Smith in Honolulu, directs the US Pacific Command, largest of the six US unified commands and responsible for all US military forces in the Pacific and Indian oceans and southern Asia. Total US Defense Department expenditures in Hawaii in 1979 were $1.3 billion, and military prime contract awards totaled $307 million.

As of 1 April 1980, Hawaii was home base for about 61,000 members of the armed forces and 64,000 dependents. The US Navy accounted for 23,500 personnel, of whom 11,500 worked in shore installations and 12,000 on the 60 ships whose home port is Pearl Harbor. The major Army bases, all on Oahu, are Schofield Barracks, Ft. Shafter, and Ft. DeRussy; Air Force bases include Hickam and Wheeler. Military reservations occupy nearly one-fourth of Oahu's land area.

There were 94,000 veterans living in Hawaii as of 30 September 1979. About 1,000 were veterans of World War I, 30,000 of World War II, 20,000 of the Korean conflict, and 33,000 of the Viet-Nam era. Veterans' benefits totaled $63.7 million in 1977/78. Hawaii's National Guard had 5,394 personnel in 1979, and state and local police forces had 2,539 in 1978.

18 MIGRATION

The US mainland and Asia have been the main sources of immigrants to Hawaii since the early 19th century. Immigration remains a major source of population growth: between 1950 and 1980, Hawaii's net gain from migration was 91,000, most of it in the last 10 years.

Since the early 1970s, about 40,000 mainland Americans have come each year to live in Hawaii. More than half are military personnel and their dependents, on temporary residence during their term of military service. During 1977/78, 9,053 foreign immigrants were admitted, of whom 4,398 were from the Philippines and 1,965 from Korea. Nearly 28,000 persons were naturalized between 1970 and 1978, according to records compiled by the US Immigration and Naturalization Service.

19 INTERGOVERNMENTAL COOPERATION

Among the interstate accords in which Hawaii participates are the Western Corrections Compact and the Western Regional Education Compact. Total federal expenditures in Hawaii exceeded $2.6 billion in 1978/79, with $1.3 billion allocated for purposes other than defense. Federal aid was estimated at $407.9 million in fiscal year 1979, of which $33.8 million was general revenue sharing.

20 ECONOMY

Hawaii's gross state product was $8 billion in 1977, when direct income from the state's three leading export industries—tourism, national defense (treated as an export industry because funds to pay for it come entirely from overseas), and agriculture—totaled $3.3 billion. By 1979, direct income from export industries was about $4.4 billion, to which visitors' expenditures (excluding transpacific transportation costs) contributed $2.6 billion; defense programs (mostly for wages, salaries, and supplies), $1.2 billion; raw sugar and molasses, $346 million; and fresh and processed pineapple, $190 million. Manufacturing is a relatively insignificant sector of the Hawaiian economy, though the garment industry grew rapidly during the 1970s. Agricultural diversification—including the cultivation of flowers and nursery products, papaya, and macadamia nuts—aquaculture, manganese nodule mining, and film and television production also promised to broaden the state's economic base. Nevertheless,

tourism will almost certainly remain Hawaii's leading employer, revenue producer, and growth sector for the foreseeable future.

21 INCOME

Average per capita income in Hawaii in 1978 was $8,380 (11th in the US); total personal income was $7.4 billion, representing a real increase of 145% since statehood but of only 29% since 1970. Although Hawaii's per capita income was 7% above the US average in 1978, the cost of living on the islands was 20–30% higher. Of all leading US cities only Anchorage, Alaska, is more expensive to live in than Honolulu. In 1979, an average family budget was 26–31% higher in Honolulu than in a typical mainland city, and costs for a retired couple were at least 13% above the US urban average.

As of 1976, 7.9% of all Hawaii residents were below the federal poverty level. About 53,700 state residents were counted among the nation's leading wealthholders in 1972, nearly five times the 1962 total.

22 LABOR

The civilian labor force in 1979 averaged 399,000, of whom 374,000 were employed and 25,000 were unemployed, for an unemployment rate of 6.3%. The large number of Hawaii's women in the labor force—57.4% of adult women, 2d only to Alaska among the 50 states—is mostly attributable to wives' working outside the home because of the high cost of living throughout the islands.

A federal census of workers covered by unemployment insurance in March 1977 revealed the following nonfarm employment pattern in Hawaii:

	ESTABLISH-MENTS	EMPLOYEES	ANNUAL PAYROLL ('000)
Agricultural services, forestry, fishing	186	1,542	$ 13,448
Mining	9	247	3,949
Contract construction	1,548	20,016	308,249
Manufacturing, of which:	837	23,711	273,291
Food products	(204)	(9,362)	(108,040)
Transportation, public utilities	806	26,278	405,423
Wholesale trade	1,522	15,388	193,387
Retail trade	5,230	75,159	507,116
Finance, insurance, real estate	2,510	23,275	244,793
Services, of which:	5,533	78,581	698,221
Hotels, lodgings	(210)	(18,785)	(141,129)
Health services	(1,146)	(13,160)	(161,498)
Other	479	560	8,902
TOTALS	18,660	264,757	$2,656,779

Full- and part-time civilian employees of federal, state, and county governments, not included in this survey, numbered 87,050 in 1978.

Unionization was slow to develop in Hawaii. After World War II, however, the International Longshoremen's and Warehousemen's Union (ILWU) organized workers in the sugar and pineapple industries and then on the docks. The Teamsters Union is also well established. All together, 129,000 Hawaii workers belonged to labor unions in 1976, and another 12,000 were members of employee associations, yielding a combined labor organization rate of 40% (3d in the US). The garment industry was, by the late 1970s, one of the few economic sectors in which the labor movement continued to show weakness.

23 AGRICULTURE

Export crops—especially sugarcane and pineapple—dominate Hawaiian agriculture, which, with farm receipts of $381.2 million, ranked 40th in the US in 1978. Hawaii produced only 41% of its locally consumed fresh-market vegetables, 28% of the fresh fruits, 36% of the beef, and 24% of the chickens. The following table shows data for major crops in 1978:

	ACREAGE ('000)	VOLUME (TONS)	SALES
Sugarcane	220.7	9,263,000	$182,700,000
Pineapples	44.0	675,000	63,000,000
Flowers and nursery products	—	—	17,458,000
Vegetables and melons	4.0	35,995	16,463,000
Macadamia nuts	10.2	11,000	10,714,000
Fruits (excluding pineapples)	5.2	39,110	10,321,000

The Kona district of the island of Hawaii is the only place in the US where coffee is grown commercially; another tropical product, papaya, has also become a substantial export crop, with an output totaling 48.8 million lb in 1980.

[24] ANIMAL HUSBANDRY
Livestock products account for less than one-fifth of Hawaii's farm income. Sales of cattle and calves totaled $28 million in 1979; of hogs and pigs, $7 million; and of chickens and broilers, $3.7 million. Poultry farms produced 229 million eggs in 1979, or 91% of domestic consumption—one of the very few farm commodities in which the state is close to self-sufficient. Most of the cattle farms are in Hawaii and Maui counties.

[25] FISHING
Though expanding, Hawaii's commercial catch remains surprisingly small: 13.3 million lb, worth $12.2 million, in 1978. The most important fish caught are aku (skipjack), accounting for 36% of the total value in 1978, followed by ahi (yellowfin and bigeye). There were 2,409 licensed fishermen, operating 1,377 fishing vessels and serving 35 fishery establishments. Aquacultural industries produced 110,000 lb of prawns and 100,000 lb of catfish in 1978, and the prawn harvest reached 205,000 lb in 1979. Sport fishing is extremely popular, with bass, bluegill, tuna, and marlin among the most sought-after varieties.

[26] FORESTRY
As of 1977, Hawaii had 1,986,000 acres (804,000 hectares) of forestland, but less than half of that was classified as commercial forest, most of it on the island of Hawaii. Production of lumber and plywood falls far short of local demand. Specialty woods include *Eucalyptus robusta*, used for making pallets for shipping, and blue gum eucalyptus, converted to chips for use by papermakers in Japan.

[27] MINING
Mineral production in Hawaii had a value of $51 million in 1978 (44th in the US). Only cement and stone are of commercial significance: in 1979, an estimated 5,085,000 tons of stone worth $19.9 million were quarried, and 479,000 tons of cement ($32.3 million) were produced. Local jewelry makers use olivines (green gems formed by lava explosions) and black, pink, red, and golden coral. Among the state's underexploited resources are mineral nodules (usually about 25–35% manganese) on the ocean floor off the coast. Commercial harvesting of nodules began in 1978.

[28] ENERGY AND POWER
Devoid of indigenous fossil fuels and nuclear installations, Hawaii depends on imported petroleum for more than 92% of its energy needs; sugarcane wastes contribute 7%, and hydroelectric power 1%. Transportation accounts for over half the petroleum used in Hawaii; jet fuel alone represents 36% of fuel consumption, compared with 6% on the mainland.

Generation of electricity accounts for 25% of the state's fuel consumption (9% on the mainland). Installed capacity reached 1.5 million kw in 1979, when production totaled 6.2 billion kwh. All of Hawaii's electric power plants are privately owned.

[29] INDUSTRIES
Of the total value added by manufacturing—$790.9 million in 1977—food and food products account for nearly 50%. Other major industries are clothing and shipbuilding. The following table shows value added for selected industries in 1972 and 1977:

	1972	1977
Sugar, confectionery products	$76,700,000	$159,000,000
Canned fruits and vegetables	69,000,000	87,100,000
Ladies' dresses	15,800,000	22,200,000
Shipbuilding and repairing	NA	16,400,000

Hawaii's publicly held corporations include Amfac, involved in food processing, merchandising, and land development, with revenues exceeding $1.7 billion in 1979; Castle & Cook, which owns the Dole and Bumble Bee food product lines, $1.6 billion; Dillingham, maritime industries and land development, $1.2 billion; and Brewer (owned by IU International), which produces 20% of the state's sugar and more than half the world's macadamia nuts, $274 million.

[30] COMMERCE
In 1977, Hawaii's wholesale trade amounted to $2.6 billion, of which groceries and related products contributed 27% and petroleum and petroleum products 20%. Honolulu County absorbed 84% of the sales and 85% of the wholesaling jobs. Retail establishments had sales of $3.3 billion in 1977, 79% of that in Honolulu County. The leading shopping centers, all on Oahu, are the Ala Moana Center, Pearlridge Center, and Kahala Mall. Oahu's 19 department stores had sales totaling $403.7 million in 1979.

Hawaii's central position in the Pacific ensures a sizable flow of goods through the Honolulu Customs District. Foreign imports to Hawaii totaled $1.3 billion in 1979, while exports exceeded $176 million. Merchandise imported from the US mainland amounted to nearly $2.2 billion in 1978; exports, $495 million. Hawaii's major trading partners in 1979 were Japan for imports and Australia for exports.

[31] CONSUMER PROTECTION
Hawaii's Office of Consumer Protection, under the Office of the Governor, coordinates the state's consumer protection activities and deals with landlord-tenant disputes.

[32] BANKING
As of 30 June 1980, Hawaii had 9 commercial banks with 173 branches, 8 savings and loan associations with 139 branches, 4 trust companies, 249 industrial loan or small loan licensees, and 159 credit unions. In 1978, the combined assets of all commercial banks exceeded $4 billion; the largest commercial institution, the Bank of Hawaii, had 76 branches and $1.6 billion in assets, while the First Hawaiian Bank had 43 branches and $1.3 billion. Honolulu Federal, the largest of the savings and loan associations, had 19 branches and $944.6 million in assets, with $840.5 million in mortgage loans outstanding; assets of all savings and loan associations totaled $2.9 billion. Loan companies held assets of $776.7 million; trust companies, $60 million; and credit unions, more than $600 million.

[33] INSURANCE
The 556 insurance companies authorized to do business in Hawaii received premiums in 1978 of $555.4 million and paid losses, claims, and benefits of $240.3 million. As of 31 December 1978, insurance firms held Hawaiian investments totaling nearly $2.1 billion; 93% of that total was controlled by out-of-state US firms, 5% by Hawaiian companies, and 2% by foreign insurers.

Hawaii residents held about 1,709,000 life policies with a face value of $15.9 billion in 1978; the average coverage of $51,500 was the highest in the US. Insurance payouts totaled $157.7 million, of which $50.5 million was in death payments. Property and casualty companies wrote premiums in 1978 for $96.6 million in automotive liability insurance, $44.9 million in automotive physical damage insurance, and $20.3 million for homeowners' coverage. A total of $309.1 million in flood insurance was in effect as of mid-1979. By the end of 1979, 528,362 Hawaii residents had prepaid health coverage through the Hawaii Medical Service Association, and 115,225 were covered by the Kaiser Foundation Health Plan.

³⁴SECURITIES
Of Hawaii's "Big 13"—major companies listed on mainland stock exchanges or on the national over-the-counter market—only 5 companies have more than 50% of their total shares held by Hawaiians. The Honolulu Stock Exchange, established in 1898, discontinued trading on 30 December 1977.

³⁵PUBLIC FINANCE
Development and implementation of Hawaii's biennial budget is the responsibility of the Department of Budget and Finance. The fiscal year runs from 1 July through 30 June. The following table summarizes operating revenues and expenditures for 1976/77 and 1977/78 (in thousands):

	1976/77	1977/78
REVENUES		
Excise taxes	$ 446,225	$ 487,771
Income taxes	225,762	251,052
Federal grants	327,607	376,233
Other receipts	312,726	306,204
TOTALS	$1,312,320	$1,421,260
EXPENDITURES		
Public schools	$ 256,114	$ 254,979
Higher education	155,758	164,851
Public welfare	203,520	241,795
Debt service	108,698	118,264
Other outlays	667,067	679,712
TOTALS	$1,391,157	$1,459,601

The combined debt of the Hawaii state and county governments as of 30 June 1977 was $1.8 billion, or $2,023 per capita, 5th in the US.

³⁶TAXATION
Hawaii's per capita tax burden is one of the highest in the US. The personal income tax ranges from 2.25% on the first $500 to 11% on taxable income over $30,000; there is a capital gains tax of 4%. The business income tax is 5.85% on net income up to $25,000 and 6.435% above that amount. There is a broad-based general excise tax of 0.5% on wholesaling and manufacturing activities and 4% on retail sales of goods and services. Taxes on estates, fuel, liquor, and tobacco are also levied, and the property tax is a major source of county income.

Hawaii's total federal tax burden in 1977/78 was $1.2 billion. For 1977, Hawaiians filed 377,112 federal income tax returns, paying $690,786,000 in tax.

³⁷ECONOMIC POLICY
Business activity in Hawaii is limited by physical factors: land for development is scarce, living costs are relatively high, heavy industry is environmentally inappropriate, and there are few land-based mineral operations. On the other hand, Hawaii is well-placed as a trading and communications center, and Hawaii's roles as a defense outpost and tourist mecca seem secure for the foreseeable future. The state has actively encouraged tourism and aquaculture. A free trade zone, authorized by the US government in 1966, is managed and promoted by the Foreign Trade Zone, a division of the Department of Planning and Economic Development.

³⁸HEALTH
State residents enjoyed, as of 1969–71, the highest average life expectancy in the US: 76.79 years for women, 71.02 for men, and 73.60 overall. The infant mortality rate in 1979 was 10.2 per 1,000 live births. In 1979, the birthrate (19.2 per 1,000 population) was more than triple the death rate (5.6); death rates from heart disease, stroke, and arteriosclerosis are less than half the national average. Thirty-three new cases of leprosy were reported in 1979; the state leprosarium is on Molokai.

A total of 11,642 people were served by state mental health facilities in 1978, when Hawaii also had 22 civilian hospitals, with 2,241 beds, and 32 skilled nursing and intermediate care facilities, with 2,133 beds. During the same year, the state had 2,254 physicians and surgeons, 788 dentists, 6,818 registered nurses, and 513 pharmacists. The average cost of hospital care in 1977 was $213 per day and $1,513 per stay, slightly above the national norm.

³⁹SOCIAL WELFARE
Approximately 8% of the resident population of Hawaii was served by major public welfare programs in 1979. Direct public assistance costs reached $245 million in 1978/79, of which federal funds paid about two-fifths. Some 59,400 state residents received $85 million in aid to families with dependent children in 1978; Medicaid payments totaled $76 million in 1977. In 1979, 90,000 people participated in the food stamp program at a federal cost of $37.2 million; the school lunch program served 164,000 students, with a federal subsidy of $8.3 million. Other programs included Social Security (1978), $273.6 million; Supplemental Security Income (1978), $16.4 million; vocational rehabilitation (1978), $3.1 million; unemployment insurance (1979), $40 million; and workers' compensation (1979), $42.6 million.

⁴⁰HOUSING
Although statehood set off a building surge in Hawaii, housing remained in short supply throughout the 1970s. In 1980 there were an estimated 334,000 housing units, of which almost 70,000 were condominiums, a type of housing first authorized in 1961; military and public housing accounted for another 26,000 units. The mean selling price for a single-family house on Oahu in 1979 was $152,000, and two-bedroom, two-bath apartments in Honolulu generally sold for $70,000 to $200,000 in 1978. As of 1975, virtually every housing unit in Hawaii had full plumbing.

⁴¹EDUCATION
Education has developed rapidly in Hawaii. Although the adult illiteracy rate remained high at 1.9% in 1970, 73% of all state residents 18 years of age or older had completed high school by 1976, 17% had at least 4 years of college, and the median number of school years completed had reached 12.7.

Hawaii is the only state with a single, unified public school system, founded in 1840. In 1979/80 there were 229 public schools with 8,291 teachers and 168,393 students; in addition, 140 private schools had 3,059 teachers and 37,187 pupils. The University of Hawaii maintains three campuses—Manoa (by far the largest), Hilo, and West Oahu—with an enrollment of 24,190 in fall 1979, when six community colleges enrolled 19,185. Four private colleges—Brigham Young University–Hawaii Campus, Chaminade University of Honolulu, Hawaii Loa College, and Hawaii Pacific College—had a combined enrollment of 6,133 during the same year. Scholarships for needy students are offered by the Hawaiian Trust Co.; graduate students generally receive low-interest loans rather than grants.

⁴²ARTS
The Neal Blaisdell Center in Honolulu has a 2,100-seat theater and concert hall, an 8,400-seat arena, and display rooms. Other performance facilities in Honolulu include the John F. Kennedy Theater at the University of Hawaii, the Waikiki Shell for outdoor concerts, and the Hawaii Opera Theater, which presents three operas each season. The Honolulu Symphony Orchestra performs both on Oahu and on the neighboring islands. Other Oahu cultural institutions include the Honolulu Community Theater, Honolulu Theater for Youth, Windward Theater Guild, and Polynesian Cultural Center.

⁴³LIBRARIES AND MUSEUMS
The Hawaii state library system had 46 facilities in 1978/79 (22 on Oahu), with a combined book stock of 1,924,572 and total circulation of 5,008,477. During the same year, the University of Hawaii library system had 2,004,995 volumes, five-sixths of them on the Manoa campus.

Total attendance at Hawaii's 32 major museums and cultural attractions was 10,609,600 (77% on Oahu) in 1979. Among the most popular sites are the *USS Arizona* Memorial at Pearl Harbor, Polynesian Cultural Center, Sea Life Park, Bernice P. Bishop Museum (specializing in Polynesian ethnology and natural history), Kahuku Sugar Mill, and Honolulu Academy of Arts. Outside Oahu, the Kilauea Visitor Center (Hawaiian Volcanoes National Park) and Kokee Natural History Museum (Kauai) attract the most visitors.

⁴⁴COMMUNICATIONS

Hawaii's 76 post offices handled 276 million pieces of mail and had gross receipts of $55.3 million in 1978/79. Commercial interisland wireless service began in 1901, and radiotelephone service to the mainland was established in 1931. By 1979 there were 684,812 telephones in service (nearly double the number in 1969), 79% of them on Oahu. Hawaii residents made 1.8 billion local calls, 10 million interisland calls, and 15.2 million transpacific calls during the same year.

Hawaii had 25 AM radio stations and 10 FM stations as of 1 January 1980, as well as 12 television stations (10 commercial and 2 educational). The state's 10 cable television companies served 114,790 subscribers in 1979.

⁴⁵PRESS

In 1980, Hawaii had six daily newspapers. Three were published in English: the *Honolulu Advertiser* and *Honolulu Star-Bulletin*, the latter owned by the Gannett chain, and the *Hawaii Tribune-Herald*. *Hawaii Hochi* and the *Hawaii Times* are bilingual in Japanese and English, and the *United Chinese Press* is published in Chinese. The combined circulation of all English-language dailies in 1980 was 216,497 weekdays, 218,169 Sundays. Another 6 newspapers are published semiweekly or weekly, and 63 magazines and other periodicals are also in circulation. In 1979, the University Press of Hawaii issued 34 new books and 5 scholarly journals.

⁴⁶ORGANIZATIONS

Leading organizations headquartered in Honolulu are the East-West Center, a vehicle of scientific and cultural exchange; the International League of Women Composers; and the American Surfing Association.

⁴⁷TOURISM, TRAVEL, AND RECREATION

Jet air service has fueled the Hawaii travel boom in recent decades. In 1959, 243,000 travelers visited Hawaii, and more than 1,527,000 in 1969; as of 1979, 3,960,531 visitors stayed at least one night in Hawaii, spending nearly $2.6 billion exclusive of transpacific air fare. Of these visitors, about 2,600,000 came from other states, 300,000 from Canada, and 580,000 from Japan. Resort complexes and hotels employed 23,700 people in 1979.

Visitors come for scuba diving, snorkeling, swimming, fishing, and sailing; for the hula, luau, lei, and other distinctive island pleasures; for the tropical climate and magnificent scenic beauty; and for a remarkable variety of recreational facilities, including, as of 1979, 5 national parks and historic sites, 65 state parks, 595 county parks, 39 golf courses, and 1,600 recognized surfing sites.

⁴⁸SPORTS

Hawaii's professional baseball team, the Hawaii Islanders, competes in the Pacific Coast League. The Hula Bowl takes place in Hawaii, and the Pro Bowl (the National Football League's all-star game) has also been played there. Hawaii is also the site of an annual Professional Golfers' Association tournament, and the yearly Duke Kahanamoku and Makaha surfing meets attract surfers from all over the world. The Transpacific Yacht Race is held biennially from California to Honolulu. Kona is the site of the International Billfish Tournament, and the Hawaii Big Game Fishing Club holds two statewide tournaments each year. Football, baseball, and basketball are the leading collegiate and school sports.

⁴⁹FAMOUS HAWAIIANS

Hawaii's best-known federal officeholder is Daniel K. Inouye (b.1924), a US senator since 1962 and the first person of Japanese ancestry ever elected to Congress. Inouye, who lost an arm in World War II, came to national prominence through the Senate Watergate investigation of 1973. George R. Ariyoshi (b.1926), elected governor in 1974, was the first Japanese-American to serve as chief executive of a state.

Commanding figures in Hawaiian history are King Kamehameha I (1758?–1819), who unified the islands through conquest, and Kamehameha III (Kauikeaouli, 1813–54), who transformed Hawaii into a constitutional monarchy. Two missionaries who shaped Hawaiian life and politics were Hiram Bingham (b.Vermont, 1789–1869) and Gerrit Parmele Judd (b.New York, 1803–73). Sanford B. Dole (1844–1926) and Lorrin Andrews Thurston (1858–1931) were leaders of the revolutionary movement that overthrew Queen Liliuokalani (1838–1917), established a republic, and secured annexation by the US. Dole was the republic's first president and the territory's first governor. Another prominent historical figure is Bernice Pauahi Bishop (1831–88), of the Kamehameha line, who married an American banker and left her fortune to endow the Kamehameha Schools in Honolulu; the Bishop Museum was founded by her husband in her memory.

Don Ho (b.1930) is the most prominent Hawaiian-born entertainer; singer-actress Bette Midler (b.1945) was also born on the islands. Duke Kahanamoku (1889–1968), a swimmer and surfer, held the Olympic 100-meter free-style swimming record for almost 20 years.

⁵⁰BIBLIOGRAPHY

Daws, Gavan. *Shoal of Time: A History of the Hawaiian Islands.* Honolulu: University Press of Hawaii, 1974.

Hawaii, State of. Department of Planning and Economic Development. *The Economy of Hawaii 1979: Annual Economic Report and Outlook.* Honolulu, 1979.

Hawaii, State of. Department of Planning and Economic Development. *The State of Hawaii Data Book 1980—A Statistical Abstract.* Honolulu, 1980.

Joesting, Edward. *Hawaii: An Uncommon History.* New York: Norton, 1972.

Kuykendall, Ralph S., and A. Grove Day. *Hawaii: A History—From Polynesian Kingdom to American State.* Rev. ed. Englewood Cliffs, N.J.: Prentice-Hall, 1961.

Wenkam, Robert. *Hawaii.* Chicago: Rand McNally, 1972.

IDAHO

State of Idaho

ORIGIN OF STATE NAME: Apparently coined by a lobbyist-politician, George M. Willing, who claimed the word came from an Indian term meaning "gem of the mountains." **NICKNAME**: The Gem State. **CAPITAL**: Boise. **ENTERED UNION**: 3 July 1890 (43d). **SONG**: "Here We Have Idaho." **MOTTO**: *Esto perpetua* (May it endure forever). **FLAG**: On a blue field with gilt fringe, the state seal appears in the center and the words "State of Idaho" on a red band below. **OFFICIAL SEAL**: With cornucopias at their feet, a female figure (holding the scales of justice in one hand and a pike supporting a liberty cap in the other) and a miner (with pick and shovel) stand on either side of a shield depicting mountains, rivers, forests, and a farm; the shield rests on a sheaf of grain and is surmounted by the head of a stag above whose antlers is a scroll with the state motto. The words "Great Seal of the State of Idaho" surround the whole. **BIRD**: Mountain bluebird. **FLOWER**: Syringa. **TREE**: Western white pine. **GEM**: Star garnet. **HORSE**: Appaloosa. **LEGAL HOLIDAYS**: New Year's Day, 1 January; Washington's Birthday, 3d Monday in February; Memorial Day, last Monday in May; Independence Day, 4 July; Labor Day, 1st Monday in September; Columbus Day, 2d Monday in October; Veterans Day, 11 November; Thanksgiving Day, 4th Thursday in November; Christmas Day, 25 December. **TIME**: 5 A.M. MST = noon GMT; 4 A.M. PST = noon GMT.

¹LOCATION, SIZE, AND EXTENT

Situated in the northwestern US, Idaho is the smallest of the 8 Rocky Mountain states and ranks 13th in size among the 50 states.

The total area of Idaho is 83,557 sq mi (216,412 sq km), of which land comprises 82,677 sq mi (214,133 sq km) and inland water 880 sq mi (2,279 sq km). With a shape described variously as a hatchet, a snub-nosed pistol, and a pork chop, Idaho extends a maximum of 305 mi (491 km) E–W and 479 mi (771 km) N–S.

Idaho is bordered on the N by the Canadian province of British Columbia; on the NE by Montana; on the E by Wyoming; on the S by Utah and Nevada; and on the W by Oregon and Washington (with part of the line formed by the Snake River). The total boundary length of Idaho is 1,787 mi (2,876 km). The state's geographic center is in Custer County, SW of Challis.

²TOPOGRAPHY

Idaho is extremely mountainous. Its northern two-thirds consists of a mountain massif broken only by valleys carved by rivers and streams, and by two prairies: the Big Camas Prairie around Grangeville and the Palouse Country around Moscow. The Snake River Plain extends east–west across Idaho from Yellowstone National Park to the Boise area, curving around the southern end of the mountain mass. A verdant high-mountain area encroaches into the southeastern corner; the rest of Idaho's southern edge consists mostly of low, dry mountains. Among the most important ranges are the Bitterroot (forming the border with Montana), Clearwater (the largest range), Salmon River, Sawtooth, Lost River, and Lemhi mountains. More than 40 peaks rise above 10,000 feet (3,000 meters), of which the highest is Mt. Borah, at 12,662 feet (3,859 meters), in the Lost River Range. Idaho's lowest point is 710 feet (216 meters) near Lewiston, where the Snake River leaves the Idaho border and enters Washington.

The largest lakes are Pend Oreille (180 sq mi—466 sq km), Coeur d'Alene, Payette, and Bear (on the Utah border). The Snake River—one of the longest in the US, extending 1,038 mi (1,671 km) across Wyoming, Idaho, and Washington—dominates the southern part of the state. The Salmon River—the "River of No Return," a salmon-spawning stream that flows through wilderness of extraordinary beauty—separates northern from southern Idaho. The Clearwater, Kootenai, Bear, Boise, and Payette are other major rivers.

There are ice caves near Shoshone and American Falls, and a large scenic cave near Montpelier. Near Arco is an expanse of lava, craters, and caves called the Craters of the Moon, another scenic attraction.

³CLIMATE

The four seasons are distinct in all parts of Idaho, but not simultaneous. Spring comes earlier and winter later to Boise and Lewiston, which are protected from severe weather by nearby mountains and call themselves "banana belts." Eastern Idaho has a more continental climate, with more extreme temperatures; climatic conditions there and elsewhere vary with the elevation. Mean temperatures in Boise range from 29°F (–2°C) in January to 75°F (24°C) in July. The record low, –60°F (–51°C), was set at Island Park Dam on 16 January 1943; the record high, 118°F (48°C), at Orofino on 28 July 1934. The corresponding extremes for Boise are –23°F (–31°C) and 111°F (44°C).

Humidity is low throughout the state. Precipitation in southern Idaho averages 13 in (33 cm) per year; in the north, about 40 in (100 cm). Boise gets more than 21 in (53 cm) of snow per year, with much greater accumulations in the mountains.

⁴FLORA AND FAUNA

With 10 life zones extending from prairie to mountaintop, Idaho has some 3,000 native plants. Characteristic evergreens are Douglas fir and western white pine (the state tree); oak/mountain mahogany, juniper/piñon, ponderosa, and spruce/fir constitute the other main forest types. Syringa is the state flower.

Classified as game mammals are the elk, moose, mule and white-tailed deer, pronghorn antelope, bighorn sheep, mountain goat, black bear, mountain lion, cottontail and pigmy rabbit. Several varieties of pheasant, partridge, quail, and grouse are the main game birds, and there are numerous trout, salmon, bass, and whitefish species in Idaho's lakes and streams. Rare animal species include the wolverine, kit fox, and pika. The caribou is listed as threatened, while the grizzly bear, gray (timber) wolf, and whooping crane are endangered.

⁵ENVIRONMENTAL PROTECTION

The environmental protection movement in Idaho dates from 1897, when President Grover Cleveland established the Bitterroot Forest Preserve, encompassing much of the northern region. In the early 1930s, the US Forest Service set aside some 3 million acres (1.2 million hectares) of Idaho's roadless forestland as primitive areas. The Taylor Grazing Act of 1934 regulated grazing on public lands, for the first time providing some relief from the overgrazing that had transformed much Idaho grassland into sagebrush desert. Thirty years later, Idaho Senator Frank Church was floor sponsor for the bill creating the National Wilderness System, which now contains most of the primitive areas earlier set aside. Many miles of Idaho streams are now in the Wild and Scenic Rivers System, another congressional accomplishment in which Senator Church played a leading role. In 1970, Governor Cecil Andrus (later US secretary of the interior) was elected partly on a platform of environmental protection.

Despite these signs of progress, pollution from automobile emissions still plagues Boise, and airborne lead pollution is a problem at Kellogg. The Department of Health and Welfare, responsible for enforcing environmental standards, is kept underfunded by an industry-oriented legislature. Idaho has no genuine land-use planning program; urban sprawl is the rule, and scenic areas are being subdivided. Since 1953, nuclear waste has been buried at the Idaho National Engineering Laboratory west of Idaho Falls or discharged in liquid form into the underground aquifer; some isotopes are migrating toward the boundaries of the site.

⁶POPULATION

Idaho's population at the 1970 census was 712,567, 42d among the 50 states. The preliminary census total for 1980 was 943,134, yielding a density of more than 11 per sq mi (4 per sq km). The population is 98% white, slightly younger than the national average, and more than 54% "urban"—although no part of Idaho except Boise is genuinely urban, and even Boise does not have much of a central city. Boise's preliminary 1980 census population was 102,125; Pocatello was next with 46,359, Idaho Falls had 39,601, and Lewiston 27,972.

⁷ETHNIC GROUPS

The 1970 census counted 6,687 American Indians; there are five reservations, the most extensive being that of the Nez Percé in northern Idaho, on which nearly 2,600 Indians live; about 3,000 Shoshoni survive on the Ft. Hall Reservation north of Pocatello.

There is a very small population of black Americans (only about 2,000 in 1970) and a somewhat larger number of Asian-Pacific peoples, about half of them (2,255) Japanese. There are 23,000 Hispanic Americans, and a very visible Basque community in the Boise area, with an organization devoted to preserving their language and culture.

The foreign-born and their native-born American children comprised about 10% of Idaho's population in 1970. Canada, the United Kingdom, and Germany were the principal countries of origin.

⁸LANGUAGES

Only a few place-names, such as Nampa, Pocatello, and Benewah, reflect in the general word stock the presence on Idaho reservations of Indians of the Nez Percé, Shoshoni, and Coeur d'Alene tribes, 82% of whom claimed an Indian language as their first in 1970. In all, 2,471 Idaho residents reported an Indian language as their mother tongue.

In Idaho, English is a merger of Northern and North Midland features, with certain Northern pronunciations marking the panhandle. Major resident groups reported their mother tongues as follows:

	NATIVE-BORN	FOREIGN-BORN
English	626,104	3,352
German	15,155	2,151
Spanish	11,165	2,042
Indian languages	2,458	13

⁹RELIGIONS

Roman Catholic and Presbyterian missionaries first came to Idaho between 1820 and 1840. The Church of Jesus Christ of Latter-day Saints (Mormon) has been the leading religion in Idaho since 1860, although Catholicism predominates north of Boise. According to 1976 estimates, Idaho has about 213,000 Mormons, 65,500 Catholics, 25,000 members of various Lutheran denominations, 19,000 Methodists, 10,500 Presbyterians, 10,500 Episcopalians, and 25,000 persons of other faiths, including about 500 Jews.

¹⁰TRANSPORTATION

In 1978, Idaho had 63,991 mi (102,984 km) of roads and streets, 94% of them rural, including about 15,000 mi (24,000 km) managed by the US Forest Service. The major east–west highways are I-90, I-84 (formerly I-80N), and US 12; US 95, Idaho 55, US 93, and I-15 are among the most traveled north–south routes. Idaho had 809,750 registered vehicles—including 471,065 automobiles, 289,174 trucks, and 2,796 buses—in 1978, when there were 587,583 licensed drivers. Only Boise has a mass transit system—a bus line.

There were 2,544 mi (4,094 km) of operating rail lines in 1979. Among freight carriers, the Union Pacific Railroad serves southern Idaho, and the Burlington Northern crosses the panhandle; Amtrak provides limited passenger service to Pocatello, Boise, and Sandpoint, among other cities, along each line. United, Republic Airlines, Frontier, and several smaller airlines serve Boise's modern airport, the busiest of the state's 128 public and 62 private air terminals in 1978. Other transport facilities are 6,100 mi (9,800 km) of pipeline, carrying virtually all the natural gas and 80% of the gasoline consumed in Idaho, and a port at Lewiston that links Idaho, Montana, and the Dakotas with the Pacific via 464 mi (747 km) of navigable waterways in Washington State.

¹¹HISTORY

Human beings came to the land now known as Idaho about 15,000 years ago. Until 1805, only Indians and their ancestors had ever lived in the area, scratching a bare living from seeds and roots, insects, small animals, and what fishing and big-game hunting they could manage. At the time of white penetration, Shoshoni and Northern Paiute lived in the south, and two linked tribal families, the Salishan and Shapwailutan (including the Nez Percé), lived in the north. It was the Nez Percé who greeted the Lewis and Clark expedition when it entered Idaho in 1805, and it was their food and canoes that helped these explorers reach the Columbia River and the Pacific.

Fur trappers—notably David Thompson, Andrew Henry, and Donald Mackenzie—followed within a few years, and then missionaries; Henry Harmon Spalding founded a mission among the Nez Percé in 1836. The Oregon Trail opened in 1842, but for two decades people merely crossed Idaho on it; virtually no one settled. In 1860, 14 years after Idaho had officially become US land through the Oregon Treaty with the United Kingdom, Mormons from Utah established Franklin, Idaho's first permanent settlement, and began farming. Gold was discovered that summer in northern Idaho; a gold rush, lasting several years, led directly to the organizing of Idaho Territory on 10 July 1863.

Boise became the capital of Idaho in 1864, and the following decade saw the inauguration of telegraph service, the linking of Franklin with the transcontinental railway, and the birth of the territory's first daily newspaper. Idaho's population nearly doubled between 1870 and 1880, and the pressure of white settlement impinging on Indian hunting and fishing grounds touched off a series of wars in the late 1870s. The most famous of those was the Nez Percé War, culminating in Chief Joseph's surrender in Montana on 5 October 1877 and in the subsequent confinement of Idaho Indians to reservations.

Lead and silver were discovered in south-central Idaho in 1880 and in the panhandle in 1884, touching off yet another stampede of would-be miners. With a population of 88,548 in 1890, Idaho was eligible to enter the Union, becoming the 43d state on 3 July. Statehood came to Idaho at a time of turmoil, when Mor-

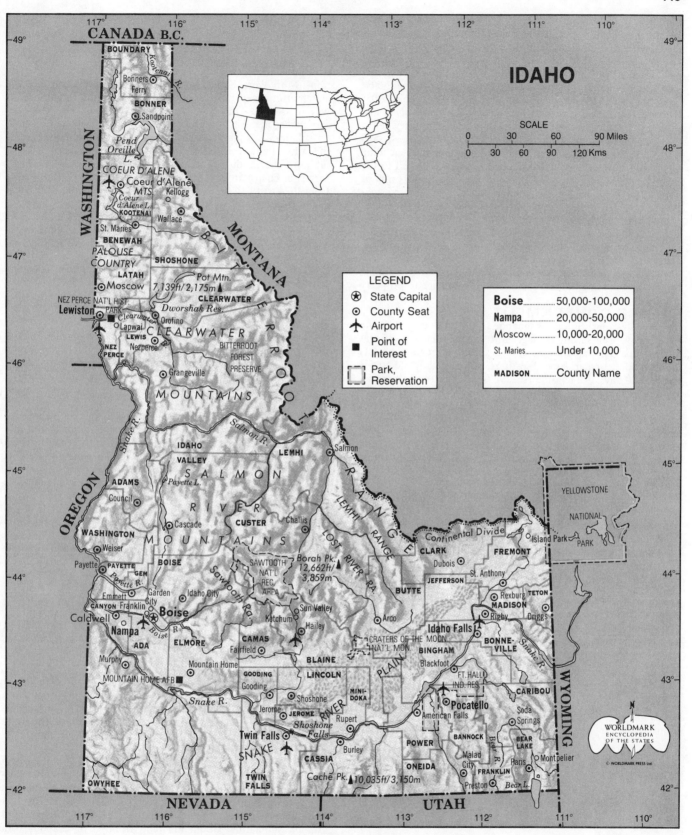

IDAHO

SCALE

0   30   60   90 Miles

0   30   60   90   120 Kms

LEGEND

⊛ State Capital
⊙ County Seat
✈ Airport
■ Point of Interest
Park, Reservation

Boise............50,000-100,000
Nampa............20,000-50,000
Moscow............10,000-20,000
St. Maries............Under 10,000
MADISON............County Name

CANADA B.C.

WASHINGTON

MONTANA

OREGON

NEVADA

UTAH

WYOMING

YELLOWSTONE NATIONAL PARK

WORLDMARK ENCYCLOPEDIA OF THE STATES

© WORLDMARK PRESS Ltd.

See US political: front cover D2; physical: back cover D2.

LOCATION: 42° to 49°N; 111° to 117°w. **BOUNDARIES**: Canadian line, 45 mi (72 km); Montana line, 738 mi (1,188 km); Wyoming line, 170 mi (274 km); Utah line, 153 mi (246 km); Nevada line, 152 mi (245 km); Oregon line, 319 mi (513 km); Washington line, 210 mi (338 km).

mons and non-Mormons were contending for political influence, the Populist Party was challenging the established political organizations, and violent labor disputes were sweeping the mining districts. In 1907, in a case that grew out of the labor conflict, William "Big Bill" Haywood (defended by Clarence Darrow) was acquitted on charges that he conspired to assassinate former Idaho Governor Frank Steunenberg, murdered on 30 December 1905.

From 1895 onward, federal land and irrigation projects fostered rapid economic growth. The modern timber industry began in 1906 with the completion of one of the nation's largest sawmills at Potlatch. By World War I, agriculture was a leading enterprise; however, a farm depression of the 1920s led to the Great Depression of the 1930s and ended only with the onset of World War II. After the war, an agroindustrial base was established, with fertilizers and potato processing leading the way. Population expansion and the push for economic growth collided with a new interest in the environment, creating controversies over land-use planning, mineral development, and dam construction. On 5 June 1976, the new, earth-filled Teton Dam in eastern Idaho collapsed, flooding the region and in the process claiming 10 lives and causing at least $400 million in damage to property and livestock.

¹²STATE GOVERNMENT

Idaho's 1889 constitution, as amended, continues to govern the state today. The bicameral legislature, consisting of a 35-seat senate and a 70-member house of representatives, regularly meets for 60–90 days a year; special sessions, summoned by the governor, last 20 days. All legislators serve two-year terms. The executive branch is headed by seven elected officials: the governor and lieutenant governor (who run separately), secretary of state, attorney general, auditor, treasurer, and superintendent of public instruction. All serve four-year terms. The governor, who must be at least 30 years of age and must have been a state resident for at least two years prior to election, can sign or veto a bill or let it become law without his signature. Vetoes may be overridden by a two-thirds vote of each house.

The state constitution may be amended with the consent of two-thirds of each house and a majority of the voters at the next general election. Provisions for initiative, referendum, and recall were added by amendment to the state constitution in 1912 but not implemented by the legislature until 1933. The initiative procedure was employed in 1974 to pass the Sunshine Act, mandating registration by lobbyists and campaign financing disclosures by candidates for public office.

Idaho Presidential Vote by Major Political Parties, 1948–80

YEAR	ELECTORAL VOTE	IDAHO WINNER	DEMOCRAT	REPUBLICAN
1948	4	*Truman (D)	107,370	101,514
1952	4	*Eisenhower (R)	95,081	180,707
1956	4	*Eisenhower (R)	105,868	166,979
1960	4	Nixon (R)	138,853	161,597
1964	4	*Johnson (D)	148,920	143,557
1968	4	*Nixon (R)	89,273	165,369
1972	4	*Nixon (R)	80,826	199,384
1976	4	Ford (R)	126,549	204,151
1980	4	*Reagan (R)	110,192	290,699

*Won US presidential election.

An Idaho voter must be at least 18 years of age, a US citizen, and a bona fide resident of the state.

¹³POLITICAL PARTIES

The Republican and Democratic parties dominate Idaho's political life. Idahoans usually vote Republican in presidential elections. Moreover, the Republicans have generally controlled the statehouse, except for the mid-1890s—when the Populist Party was at its peak—the New Deal, and the 1970s. The dominant Republican in the 20th century was US Senator William E. Borah, an isolationist-progressive who opposed US entry into the League of Nations but advocated world disarmament and supported prohibition, the graduated income tax, and some New Deal reforms; as chairman of the Senate Foreign Relations Committee from 1924 to 1940, he was one of the most influential legislators in the nation.

One measure of the conservatism of Idaho voters in the 1960s and 1970s is the showings by the American Independent Party in 1968 (12.6% of the total vote) and the American Party in 1972 (9.3% in 1972, the highest of any state). In November 1980, Idahoans voted overwhelmingly for conservative Republican Ronald Reagan for president and denied a bid by Frank Church, a leading Democrat, for a fifth term in the US Senate. The Republicans also increased their majorities in both houses of the state legislature.

¹⁴LOCAL GOVERNMENT

As of 1977, Idaho had 44 counties, 199 incorporated cities (only 11 of which had more than 10,000 residents), 117 school districts, and 612 special districts. Each county elects three commissioners and other officers, usually including an assessor, treasurer, coroner, and sheriff. Nearly all cities have an elected mayor and council.

¹⁵STATE SERVICES

Executive agencies concerned with human resources include the State Board of Education and the departments of health and welfare, employment, correction, and law enforcement, which includes the Idaho State Police. Under the general rubric of physical and natural resources come the departments of energy, transportation, lands, water resources, fish and game, and parks and recreation. The departments of agriculture, finance, insurance, and labor and industrial services oversee economic development and regulation. Within the Executive Office of the Governor are the state's Commission on Human Rights, Office on Aging, and Commission on Women's Programs. The quasi-public Idaho Housing Agency helps support low-income housing.

¹⁶JUDICIAL SYSTEM

Idaho's highest court, the supreme court, consists of five justices, each elected at large, on a nonpartisan ballot, to a six-year term; the justice with the shortest remaining term automatically becomes chief justice. The district court is the main trial court in civil and criminal matters, while magistrates courts handle traffic, misdemeanor, and minor civil cases and preliminary hearings in felony cases.

Idaho's crime rates are among the lowest in the US in almost every category; the rate for robbery, 40 per 100,000 population in 1978, was less than one-fourth the US average. A few murderers have been hanged, but none since the 1950s. The state permits, but has never used, execution by lethal injection.

¹⁷ARMED FORCES

About 2,000 Navy personnel are on short-term duty at the Idaho National Engineering Laboratory, where more than 50 experimental nuclear reactors have been built, among them the first practical nuclear-powered electrical generator, a nuclear-fuel breeder reactor and a prototype engine for the nuclear-powered *Nautilus* submarine. Mountain Home Air Force Base, about 50 mi (80 km) southeast of Boise, has some 4,000 officers and enlisted personnel. Defense contract awards to Idaho firms in 1977/78 totaled $19 million, the least of any state.

Idaho casualties in recent US wars include 1,419 in World War II, 132 in Korea, and 187 in Viet-Nam. As of 30 September 1979,

105,000 veterans of military service were living in Idaho, including, from World War I, 2,000; World War II, 43,000; Korean conflict, 18,000; and Viet-Nam era, 33,000. Benefits paid to Idaho veterans totaled $70.2 million in 1977/78.

As of 1980, the Army National Guard had 2,450 personnel; the Air National Guard, 886; and the Idaho State Police, 185. There were some 1,850 full-time local police and sheriff's officers.

[18] MIGRATION

Idaho's first white immigrants came from Utah, California, and Oregon in the early 1860s. By the end of the Civil War, the chief sources of immigrants were the southern and border states. Homesteaders from the Midwest, Utah, and Scandinavia arrived at the end of the 19th century. Since 1960, immigrants have come largely from California. Idaho suffered a net loss from migration of 109,000 persons between 1940 and 1970, but gained 77,000 during the next seven years.

[19] INTERGOVERNMENTAL COOPERATION

Idaho participates with Utah and Wyoming in the Bear River Compact, with Oregon, Washington, and Montana in the Pacific Northwest Commission, with Wyoming in the Snake River Compact, and with Washington, Alaska, and Montana in the WAMI medical education program. Federal aid in 1978/79 was estimated at $337.2 million, of which $25.2 million was general revenue sharing.

[20] ECONOMY

Fur trapping was Idaho's earliest industry. Agriculture and mining began around 1860, with agriculture dominating since the 1870s. Timber became important after 1900, tourism and manufacturing—especially food processing and forest products—after 1945.

The gross state product in 1977 exceeded $6.4 billion, the major sectors being wholesale and retail trade, 18%; manufacturing, 18%; government, 16%; finance and real estate, 12%; services, 11%; transportation, communications, and public utilities, 9%; agriculture, 7%; contract construction, 7%; and mining, 2%. Idaho has a stable labor supply, expanding by about 8,000 workers a year as of 1980.

[21] INCOME

Per capita income in Idaho in 1978 was $6,813, 36th in the US and up 32% from 1975. Total personal income reached $6 billion, representing an increase in constant dollars of 58% since 1970—one of the fastest growing rates in the US for the period.

Median family income ranked 33d at $12,844 in 1975, when 10% of all state residents were below the federal poverty level. About 67,000 Idahoans were among the nation's leading wealthholders in 1972; largely because of inflated land values, Idaho is said to have more millionaires per capita than any other state.

[22] LABOR

Of Idaho's civilian labor force of 443,000 in early 1980, about 35% were women and nearly 99% were white. By occupation, 14.3% were operatives, 13.5% professional and technical workers, 13.3% clerical workers, 12.7% craftsmen, 12% service personnel, 11.4% farm workers, 9.8% managers and administrators, 6.5% salespeople, 5.4% laborers, and 1.1% household workers. Unemployment in early 1980 was 5.4%.

A federal census of workers covered by unemployment insurance in March 1977 revealed the following nonfarm employment pattern in Idaho:

	ESTABLISH-MENTS	EMPLOYEES	ANNUAL PAYROLL ('000)
Agricultural services, forestry, fishing	263	2,248	$ 14,240
Mining, of which:	98	3,440	54,156
Metals	(42)	(2,122)	(33,824)
Contract construction	2,550	19,340	421,249
Manufacturing, of which:	1,339	51,894	632,900
Food products	(165)	(16,073)	(154,669)
Lumber, wood products	(519)	(15,171)	(220,360)
Transportation, public utilities	914	12,721	163,597
Wholesale trade	1,929	20,233	258,166
Retail trade	5,856	53,284	343,558
Finance, insurance, real estate	1,768	12,759	126,671
Services	4,995	42,986	372,350
Other	326	370	4,136
TOTALS	20,038	219,275	$2,391,023

Government workers, not included in this survey, numbered about 55,000 in 1978.

Idaho was a pioneer in establishing the eight-hour day and in outlawing yellow-dog contracts. By 1980 there were some 45,000 union members in Idaho, accounting for less than 12% of the nonagricultural work force—one of the lowest such percentages in the US. In 1958, Idaho voters rejected right-to-work legislation.

[23] AGRICULTURE

Receipts from farm marketings totaled $1.5 billion in 1978 (28th in the US); net farm income in 1977 was about $200 million, based on gross income of nearly $1.4 billion and production expenses of $1.2 billion. As of 1977, Idaho led the US in potato production, ranked 2d in bluegrass seed, dry edible peas, and alfalfa seed, 3d in dry edible beans, hops, and mint, 4th in sugar beets, and 5th in barley.

Development of the russet potato in the 1920s gave Idaho its most famous crop. In 1977, the state produced 85,050,000 hundredweight of potatoes (25% of the US total), worth $251 million; about three-fourths of the crop is processed into frozen french fries, instant mashed potatoes, and other products. Other leading crops were wheat, 74,140,000 bushels, $261,138,000; hay, 4,126,000 tons, $239,308,000; barley, 49,300,000 bushels, $120,785,000; and dry beans and peas, 3,164,000 hundredweight, $68,189,000.

As of 1979, Idaho had 15.4 million acres (6.2 million hectares) under cultivation, 29% of the state's land area; an estimated 23,000 farms averaged about 670 acres (271 hectares) each and employed about 36,000 persons.

[24] ANIMAL HUSBANDRY

Livestock and livestock products account for 40–45% of Idaho farm marketings. By the close of 1979 there were about 1,860,000 beef cattle and calves, 141,000 dairy cows, 468,000 sheep and lambs, and 110,000 hogs and pigs on the state's farms and ranches. Production of meat animals in 1979 included 778.8 million lb of cattle and calves worth $528.3 million; sheep and lambs, 39 million lb, $22.6 million; and hogs and pigs, 25.6 million lb, $9.7 million. The wool clip comprised 5 million lb in 1978.

Leading dairy and poultry products were 1.7 billion lb of milk, 98 million lb of cheese, and 192 million eggs. Some 100,000 bee colonies in the state produce more than 4.5 million lb of honey each year.

[25] FISHING

Sport fishermen catch about 2 million lb of trout each year, along with salmon, steelhead, bass, and other varieties. Idaho hatcheries produce some 23 million fish a year. The commercial catch amounted to only 400,000 lb, worth $35,000, in 1978.

[26] FORESTRY

As of 30 September 1977, Idaho forests covered 21,727,000 acres (8,793,000 hectares); of the 13,541,000 acres (5,480,000 hectares) classified as commercial forestland, the federal government controlled 71%, including 3,500,000 acres (1,400,000 hectares) of Wilderness System lands. Idaho forests are used increasingly for ski areas, hunting, and other recreation as well as for timber and pulp. The total lumber production in 1978 was nearly 2 billion board feet; shipments of lumber and wood products in 1977 were valued at more than $1 billion.

²⁷MINING

Idaho leads the US in the production of silver, antimony, and garnets, ranks 2d in phosphates and lead, 3d in vanadium and zinc, and 6th in gold. In 1978, the state's mineral output, valued at $280 million (31st in the US), included lead, 47,285 tons; zinc, 34,990 tons; copper, 4,286 tons; gold, 19,500 troy oz; and silver, 18,051 troy oz. There are hard-rock lead-silver mines in the Coeur d'Alene Mountains and phosphate strip mines in the southeast. Cement, clays, gypsum, lime, perlite, sand and gravel, and tungsten are also produced. Rising silver prices produced a silver boom in early 1980.

²⁸ENERGY AND POWER

Idaho's only significant domestic energy sources are hydroelectric power, some natural hot water (used to heat buildings in Boise), and firewood. Installed electrical capacity was 1.8 million kw in 1978, when production (99.9% hydroelectric) totaled 10 billion kwh. About half of Idaho's irrigation depends on electric pumping, and electrical energy consumption regularly exceeds the state's supply.

Idaho's large size, widespread and relatively rural population, and lack of public transportation fosters reliance on motor vehicles and imported petroleum products. Idahoans purchased 551 million gallons of gasoline in 1979—5% less than in 1978, indicating a possible trend toward conservation.

²⁹INDUSTRY

Resource industries—food processing and lumber production—form the backbone of manufacturing in Idaho. Value added by manufacture, which increased from $820.8 million in 1972 to $1.4 billion in 1977, is shown for major sectors in the following table:

	1972	1977
Lumber, wood products	$269,000,000	$467,100,000
Food and food products	257,300,000	336,100,000
Chemicals and allied products	106,200,000	202,100,000
Nonelectrical machinery	11,000,000	50,600,000

Ore-Ida Foods is a leading potato processor, and J. R. Simplot engages in food processing and fertilizer production. Boise Cascade (with headquarters at Boise), Potlatch, Diamond International, and Louisiana-Pacific dominate the wood-products industry; a Bucyrus-Erie plant at Pocatello manufactures mining, construction, and industrial machinery.

³⁰COMMERCE

In 1977, Idaho's wholesale establishments registered $3.2 billion in trade. Retail sales exceeded $3 billion, of which automotive dealers accounted for 23%, food stores 22%, eating and drinking places 9%, gasoline service stations 7%, and department stores 6%. Boise is the headquarters of the Albertson grocery chain.

About two-thirds of Idaho's wheat crop and a substantial amount of its fertilizer, peas, lentils, beans, potatoes, and barley are exported abroad; natural gas and sulfate are imported from Canada in significant quantities. Foreign exports of agricultural products were valued at $262 million in 1976/77 (28th in the US); manufactured exports totaled $169 million (44th).

³¹CONSUMER PROTECTION

The Attorney General's Office is responsible for investigating consumer complaints and enforcing the state Consumer Credit Code and other consumer laws.

³²BANKING

The Idaho First National Bank, first in fact as well as name, was chartered in 1867. As of 31 December 1978, 24 insured commercial banks had $4.3 billion in assets, $3.6 billion in deposits, and $1.5 billion in outstanding loans. The state's 12 insured savings and loan associations (4 state-chartered, 8 federally chartered) had $934.4 million in assets and $816.4 million in outstanding mortgage loans. Idaho also has some 150 credit unions with about $300 million in assets.

³³INSURANCE

Idaho families held, on average, $31,800 in life insurance coverage in 1978, 9% below the US average. A total of 1,318,000 policies in effect that year had a combined value of $10.1 billion; payouts reached $85.9 million, including $34.5 million in death payments. Property and liability companies wrote premiums worth $318.8 million in 1978, of which $62.1 million was for automobile physical damage insurance, $68.4 million for automotive liability insurance, and $25.1 million for homeowners' coverage.

³⁴SECURITIES

Although Idaho has no stock exchanges, New York Stock Exchange member firms had 19 sales offices and 65 registered representatives in the state in 1978. Idahoans reported $68.3 million in dividends on their 1977 federal income tax returns.

³⁵PUBLIC FINANCE

Idaho's annual budget, prepared by the Division of Budget, Policy Planning, and Coordination, is submitted by the governor to the legislature for amendment and approval. The fiscal year runs from 1 October to 30 September.

The following table summarizes estimated revenues and expenditures for 1979/80 and 1980/81 (in millions):

	1979/80	1980/81
REVENUES		
Individual income tax	$180.5	$ 208.0
Corporate income tax	42.2	43.0
Sales tax	100.1	110.5
Other general revenues	45.1	46.1
Federal aid	319.9	331.7
Other funds	295.1	345.1
TOTALS	$982.9	$1,084.4
EXPENDITURES		
Board of Education	$433.1	$467.9
Department of Health and Welfare	168.4	177.1
Department of Transportation	130.7	173.8
Department of Employment	86.6	94.3
Other outlays	156.9	169.9
TOTALS	$975.7	$1,083.0

The outstanding debt of the Idaho state and local governments was $295 million, or $345 per capita, as of mid-1977—the lowest in the US by both measures.

³⁶TAXATION

Idaho's original revenue base of property taxes and a variety of local business license fees has been substantially abandoned. The state instituted an income tax during the 1930s and a sales tax in 1965; as of 1980, the personal income tax ranged from 2% of the first $1,000 to 7.5% on income over $5,000, the corporate income tax was 6.5%, and the general sales tax was 3%. The state also levies taxes on alcoholic beverages, cigarettes, motor fuels, and electric utilities. Property taxes, the only major source of local revenue, brought in $206.4 million in 1978/79.

In 1976/77, Idaho paid federal taxes totaling $1.16 billion and received federal outlays of $1.7 billion. Idahoans filed 333,368 federal income tax returns for 1977, paying $460,255,000 in tax.

³⁷ECONOMIC POLICY

The Division of Tourism and Economic Development, within the Office of the Governor, seeks to widen export markets for Idaho products, encourage film production in the state, and help the state and its localities develop industries and resources consistent with long-range economic goals. Attractions for industry include conservative state fiscal policies and a probusiness regulatory climate.

³⁸HEALTH

As of 1969–71, Idahoans enjoyed an average life span of 71.87 years (14th in the US): 76.10 for women, 68.20 for men. Data for infant mortality are not statistically significant. The live birthrate in 1977 was a very high 22 per 1,000 population, 43% above the national average, while the death rate, 8.4, was slightly below the US norm. There were 2,446 legal abortions in Idaho in 1979. Death rates for all the leading causes of death except accidents, suicide, and arteriosclerosis were below the respective national averages in 1977.

Idaho in 1979 had two mental hospitals with 675 patients; 6,207 patients were treated in community mental health centers, and the state school for the mentally retarded had an enrollment of 390. In all, 51 hospitals had 3,737 beds in 1978, with an occupancy rate of 66%; hospital personnel included 1,717 registered nurses and 1,083 licensed practical nurses. The average cost of hospital care in 1977 was $167 per day and $1,036 per stay, among the lowest in the US. There were 978 licensed physicians in 1977 and 459 active dentists in 1979, when the average Idahoan spent $630 on health care.

³⁹SOCIAL WELFARE

Less than 3% of Idaho's population receives public assistance. Participants and costs of major social welfare programs in 1978 were as follows: aid to families with dependent children, 19,500, $21 million; food stamps, 30,000, federal subsidy of $10 million; school lunch program, 111,000, federal cost $5.3 million; unemployment insurance, 7,000 average weekly beneficiaries, $30 million; and vocational rehabilitation, 5,100, $4.7 million. Idaho public employees received pensions in 1979 totaling $26.7 million; in addition, 123,100 Idahoans were beneficiaries of $297.5 million in Social Security payments during 1977, with an average monthly benefit for retired workers of $236.10.

⁴⁰HOUSING

Single-family housing predominates in Idaho, although the number of apartments increased during the 1960s and 1970s. The state added some 8,100 residential units in 1979, bringing the total to 283,900.

⁴¹EDUCATION

Although Idaho's per-pupil expenditure on education, $1,415 in 1978/79, is one of the lowest in the US, Idaho students generally rank above grade level on standardized tests. The adult illiteracy rate in 1970 was only 0.6%, about half the national average; as of 1976, over 71% of adult Idahoans were high school graduates, and the median number of school years completed was 12.6.

As of fall 1978, public educational institutions enrolled 108,744 elementary school students, 94,278 secondary, and 31,212 postsecondary; the enrollment totals for nonpublic schools were 3,480, 1,778, and 8,472, respectively. The leading public higher educational institutions are the University of Idaho at Moscow, with 8,334 students in 1978/79; Idaho State University (Pocatello), with an enrollment of 6,841; and Boise State University, 10,389. There are three other public colleges and community colleges and four private institutions. The State Board of Education offers scholarships to graduates of accredited Idaho high schools.

⁴²ARTS

The Boise Philharmonic is Idaho's leading professional orchestra. Moscow has a professional ballet company. Notable theaters include the Little Theater of Boise, which has been operating continuously since 1948. The Idaho Commission on the Arts and Humanities, founded in 1966, offers grants to support both creative and performing artists.

⁴³LIBRARIES AND MUSEUMS

Idaho's 123 public libraries had a combined book stock of nearly 1.8 million volumes in 1977/78 and a total circulation of more than 4.1 million. The largest public library system is the Boise Public Library and Information Center, with about 200,000 volumes; the leading academic library, at the University of Idaho (Moscow), has more than 300,000.

The state also has about 40 museums, notably the Boise Gallery of Art, Idaho State Historical Museum (Boise), and the

Idaho Museum of Natural History (Pocatello). The University of Idaho Arboretum is at Moscow, and there is a zoo at Boise. Major historic sites include Cataldo Mission near Kellogg, Spalding Mission near Lapwai, and Nez Percé National Historical Park in north-central Idaho.

⁴⁴COMMUNICATIONS

As of 31 December 1978, Idaho had 662,359 telephones, 486,866 residential and 175,493 business; on average, 97% of all households had telephone service, the leading suppliers being Mountain Bell and the General Telephone Co. of the Northwest. Idaho's first radio station, built by a Boise high school teacher and his students, began transmitting in 1921, was licensed in 1922, and six years later was sold and given the initials KIDO—the same call letters as Idaho's first permanent television station, which began broadcasting in 1953 and subsequently became KTVB. As of 1978, the state had 58 commercial radio stations (42 AM, 16 FM) and 8 commercial television stations. Another 3 television stations—in Boise, Moscow, and Pocatello—were public. Cable systems served 65,573 Idahoans in 83 communities during the same year.

⁴⁵PRESS

Idaho, site of the first printing press in the Northwest, had 15 daily newspapers in 1978, with a combined circulation of 197,967; and 6 Sunday papers, with 162,264 circulation. The most widely read newspaper is the *Idaho Statesman*, published in Boise, with a circulation of 54,520 daily and 67,445 Sundays.

Caxton Printers, founded at Caldwell in 1902, is the state's leading publishing house.

⁴⁶ORGANIZATIONS

Among the few national organizations with headquarters in Idaho are the Food Industries Suppliers Association (Caldwell) and the Appaloosa Horse Club (Moscow).

⁴⁷TOURISM, TRAVEL, AND RECREATION

In 1977, tourism generated $596 million in business revenues and employed 25,000 persons on a payroll of $162 million. Tourists come to Idaho primarily for outdoor recreation—river trips, skiing, camping, hunting, fishing, and hiking. There are more than two dozen ski resorts, of which by far the most famous is Sun Valley, which opened in 1936. Licenses were issued to 217,415 hunters and 377,068 fishermen in 1977/78.

⁴⁸SPORTS

Idaho has no major league professional teams, but Idaho Falls has a minor league baseball franchise, and Boise supports a semiprofessional hockey team. Most county seats hold parimutuel quarterhorse racing a few days a year, and Boise's racing season (including Thoroughbreds) runs three days a week for five months. World chariot racing championships have been held at Pocatello, and polo was one of Boise's leading sports from 1910 through the 1940s. Idaho cowboys have won numerous riding, roping, and steer-wrestling championships. Skiing and golf are among the most popular participant sports.

⁴⁹FAMOUS IDAHOANS

Leading federal officeholders born in Idaho include Ezra Taft Benson (b.1899), secretary of agriculture from 1953 to 1961, and Cecil D. Andrus (b.Oregon, 1931), governor of Idaho from 1971 to 1977 and secretary of the interior from 1977 to 1981. Maverick Republican William E. Borah (b.Illinois, 1865–1940) served in the US Senate from 1907 until his death. Frank Church (b.1924) entered the US Senate in 1957 and became chairman of the Senate Foreign Relations Committee in 1979; he was defeated in his bid for a fifth term in 1980. Important state officeholders were the nation's first Jewish governor, Moses Alexander (b.Germany, 1853–1932), and New Deal governor C. Ben Ross (1876–1946).

Author Vardis Fisher (1895–1968) was born and spent most of his life in Idaho, which was also the birthplace of poet Ezra Pound (1885–1972). Nobel Prize–winning novelist Ernest Hemingway (b.Illinois, 1899–1961) is buried at Ketchum. Gutzon

Borglum (1871–1941), the sculptor who carved the Mt. Rushmore National Memorial in South Dakota, was an Idaho native. Idaho is the only state in the US with an official seal designed by a woman, Emma Edwards Green (b.California, 1856–1942).

Baseball slugger Harmon Killebrew (b.1936) and football star Jerry Kramer (b.1936) are Idaho's leading sports personalities.

⁵⁰BIBLIOGRAPHY

Beal, Merrill D., and Merle W. Wells. *History of Idaho*. 3 vols. New York: Lewis, 1959.

Etulain, Richard W., and Merwin Swanson. *Idaho History: A Bibliography*. Pocatello: Idaho State University Press, 1975.

Federal Writers' Project. *Idaho: A Guide in Word and Picture*. 2d rev. ed. New York: Oxford University Press, 1950.

Idaho, State of. Executive Office of the Governor and Division of Tourism and Industrial Development. *Idaho Almanac*. Boise, 1977.

Idaho, State of. Secretary of State. *Idaho Blue Book, 1979–80*. Boise, 1979.

Peterson, F. Ross. *Idaho: A Bicentennial History*. New York: Norton, 1976.

Walker, Deward E., Jr. *American Indians of Idaho*. Moscow: University of Idaho Press, 1971.

ILLINOIS

State of Illinois

ORIGIN OF STATE NAME: French derivative of *Iliniwek*, meaning "tribe of superior men," an Indian group formerly in the region. **NICKNAME:** The Prairie State. **SLOGAN:** Land of Lincoln. **CAPITAL:** Springfield. **ENTERED UNION:** 3 December 1818 (21st). **SONG:** "Illinois." **MOTTO:** State Sovereignty–National Union. **FLAG:** The inner portion of the state seal and the word "Illinois" on a white field. **OFFICIAL SEAL:** An American eagle perched on a boulder holds in its beak a banner bearing the state motto; below the eagle is a shield resting on an olive branch. Also depicted are the prairie, the sun rising over a distant eastern horizon, and, on the boulder, the dates 1818 and 1868, the years of the seal's introduction and revision, respectively. The words "Seal of the State of Illinois Aug. 26th 1818" surround the whole. **BIRD:** Cardinal. **FLOWER:** Violet. **TREE:** White oak. **MINERAL:** Fluorite. **INSECT:** Monarch butterfly. **LEGAL HOLIDAYS:** New Year's Day, 1 January; Martin Luther King's Birthday, 15 January; Lincoln's Birthday, 12 February; George Washington's Birthday, 3d Monday in February; Memorial Day, last Monday in May; Independence Day, 4 July; Labor Day, 1st Monday in September; Columbus Day, 2d Monday in October; Election Day, 1st Tuesday after the 1st Monday in November in even-numbered years; Veterans Day, 11 November; Thanksgiving Day, 4th Thursday in November; Christmas Day, 25 December. **TIME:** 6 A.M. CST = noon GMT.

¹LOCATION, SIZE, AND EXTENT

Situated in the eastern north-central US, Illinois ranks 24th in size among the 50 states. Its area totals 56,400 sq mi (146,076 sq km), of which land comprises 55,748 sq mi (144,387 sq km) and inland water 652 sq mi (1,689 sq km). Illinois extends 211 mi (340 km) E–W; its maximum N–S extension is 381 mi (613 km).

Illinois is bounded on the N by Wisconsin; on the E by Lake Michigan and Indiana (with the line in the SE defined by the Wabash River); on the extreme SE and S by Kentucky (with the line passing through the Ohio River); and on the W by Missouri and Iowa (with the entire boundary formed by the Mississippi River).

The state's boundaries total 1,297 mi (2,088 km). The geographic center of Illinois is in Logan County, 28 mi (45 km) NE of Springfield.

²TOPOGRAPHY

Illinois is flat. Lying wholly within the Central Plains, the state exhibits a natural topographic monotony relieved mainly by hills in the northwest (an extension of Wisconsin's Driftless Area) and throughout the southern third of the state, on the fringes of the Ozark Plateau. The highest natural point, Charles Mound, tucked into the far northwest corner, is only 1,235 feet (376 meters) above sea level—far lower than Chicago's towering skyscrapers. The low point, at the extreme southern tip along the Mississippi River, is 279 feet (85 meters) above sea level. The average elevation is about 600 feet (180 meters).

Although some 2,700 rivers and streams totaling 9,000 mi (14,500 km) crisscross the land, pioneers in central Illinois confronted very poor drainage. The installation of elaborate and expensive networks of ditches and tiled drains was necessary before commercial agriculture became feasible. Most of the 2,000 lakes of 6 acres (2.4 hectares) or more were created by dams. The most important rivers are the Wabash and the Ohio, forming the southeastern and southern border; the Mississippi, forming the western border; and the Illinois, flowing northeast-southwest across the central region and meeting the Mississippi at Grafton, just northwest of the junction between the Mississippi and the Missouri rivers. The man-made Lake Carlyle (41 sq mi—106 sq km) is the largest body of inland water. Illinois also has jurisdiction over 1,526 sq mi (3,952 sq km) of Lake Michigan.

³CLIMATE

Illinois has a temperate climate, with cold, snowy winters and hot, wet summers—ideal weather for corn and hogs. The seasons are sharply differentiated: mean winter temperatures are 22°F (−6°C) in the north and 37°F (3°C) in the south; summer temperatures are 70°F (21°C) in the north and 77°F (25°C) in the south. The record high, 117°F (47°C), was set at East St. Louis on 14 July 1954; the record low, −35°F (−37°C), was registered at Mt. Carroll on 22 January 1930.

The average farm sees rain one day in three, for a total of 36 in (91 cm) of precipitation a year. An annual snowfall of 37 in (94 cm) is normal for northern Illinois, decreasing to 24 in (61 cm) or less in the central and southern regions. Chicago's record 90 in (229 cm) of snow in the winter of 1978/79 created monumental transportation problems, enormous personal hardship, and even a small political upheaval when incumbent Mayor Michael Bilandic lost a primary election to Jane Byrne in February 1979 partly because of his administration's slowness in snow removal.

Although Chicago is nicknamed the "Windy City," the average inland wind speed, 10.3 mph (16.6 km/hr), is actually lower than that of Buffalo, Honolulu, Oklahoma City, and several other US metropolitan areas. "Tornado alley" cuts diagonally across Illinois from St. Louis to Chicago.

⁴FLORA AND FAUNA

Urbanization and commercial development have taken their toll on the plant and animal resources of Illinois. Northern and central Illinois once supported typical prairie flora, but nearly all the land has been given over to crops, roads, and suburban lawns. About 90% of the oak and hickory forests that once were common in the north have been cut down for fuel and lumber. In the forests that do remain, mostly in the south, typical trees are black oak, sugar maple, box elder, slippery elm, beech, shagbark hickory, white ash, sycamore, black walnut, sweet gum, cottonwood, black willow, and jack pine. Characteristic wild flowers are the Chase aster, French's shooting star, lupine, primrose violet, purple trillium, small fringed gentian, and yellow fringed orchid. Tamarack and ginseng are considered threatened, and white basswood, shortleaf pine, prairie fringed orchid, and white lady's-slipper have been proposed as endangered.

Before 1800, wildlife was abundant on the prairies, but the

bison, elk, bears, and wolves that once roamed freely have long since vanished. The white-tailed deer disappeared in 1910 but was successfully reintroduced in 1933 by the Department of Conservation. Among the state's fur-bearing mammals are opossum, raccoon, mink, red and gray foxes, and muskrat. More than 350 birds have been identified, with such game birds as ruffed grouse, wild turkey, and bobwhite quail especially prized. Other indigenous birds are the cardinal (the state bird), horned lark, blue jay, purple martin, black-capped chickadee, tufted titmouse, bluebird, cedar waxwing, great crested flycatcher, and yellow-shafted flicker. Mallard and black ducks are common, and several subspecies of Canada goose are also found. The state claims 17 types of native turtle, 46 kinds of snake, 19 varieties of salamander, and 21 types of frog and toad. Heavy industrial and sewage pollution have eliminated most native fish, except for the versatile carp and catfish. Coho salmon were introduced into Lake Michigan in the 1960s, thus reviving sport fishing.

In 1973, the Department of Conservation established an endangered and threatened species protection program. Included among threatened animals are the river otter, bobcat, Swainson's warbler, western hog-nosed snake, and lake sturgeon. Endangered species include the gray and Indiana bats, eastern woodrat, white-tailed jackrabbit, little blue heron, red-shouldered hawk, greater prairie chicken, barn owl, bigeye chub, bluebreast darter, dusky salamander, and Higgin's eye pearly mussel.

5 ENVIRONMENTAL PROTECTION

The history of conservation efforts in Illinois falls into three stages. From 1850 to the 1930s, city and state parks were established and the beauty of Chicago's lakefront was successfully preserved. During the next stage, in the 1930s, federal intervention through the Civilian Conservation Corps and other agencies focused on upgrading park facilities and, most important, on reversing the severe erosion of soils, particularly in the hilly southern areas. Soil conservation laws took effect in 1937, and within a year the first soil conservation district was formed; by 1970, 98 districts, covering 44% of the state's farmland, promoted conservation cropping systems, contour plowing, and drainage.

The third stage of environmentalism began in the late 1960s, when Attorney General William J. Scott assumed the leadership of an antipollution campaign, won suits against steel mills, sanitary districts, and utility companies, and secured passage of clean air and water legislation. The Illinois Environmental Protection Act of 1970 created the Pollution Control Board to set standards and conduct enforcement proceedings; the Environmental Protection Agency to issue permits and provide advice; and the Institute for Environmental Research to undertake interdisciplinary studies. The federal Environmental Protection Agency has also helped upgrade water and air quality in Illinois.

The 1970s saw a noticeable improvement in environmental quality. Dirty air became less prevalent—though one by-product was the crippling of the state's high-sulfur coal industry. Vast expenditures for sewage treatment plants and for a $3-billion "deep tunnel" system to carry off rainfall in Chicago contributed to improved water quality, especially in Lake Michigan. Land reclamation and flood control programs remain important, since small cities and suburban tracts lie in flood basins. A controversial issue still unresolved in 1980 was nuclear waste disposal.

The Illinois Audubon Society, founded in 1897, has expanded its interests from bird watching to broad concern with the environment. The Illinois Wildlife Federation has also been active in conservation efforts.

6 POPULATION

Illinois ranked 5th among the 50 states at the 1970 census, with a population of 11,112,772, having ceded 3d place to California by 1950 and 4th place to Texas during the 1960s. The preliminary 1980 census population was 11,321,350, or 203 persons per sq mi (78 per sq km).

The population of Illinois was only 12,282 in 1810. Ten years later, the new state had 55,211 residents. The most rapid period of growth came in the mid-19th century, when heavy immigration made Illinois one of the fastest-growing areas in the world. Between 1820 and 1860, the state's population doubled every 10 years. The rate of population increase slowed somewhat after 1900, especially during the 1930s, although the population more than doubled between 1900 and 1960. Population growth was very slow in the 1970s, less than 0.2% a year; only five states had slower growth during the decade.

The age distribution of the state's population in 1978 closely mirrored the national pattern, with 29% under age 18 and nearly 11% aged 65 or older. The number of households grew to 3,929,000 in 1978, from 3,085,000 in 1960; nearly all the increase was in families headed by women and in households composed of unmarried persons. The number of husband-wife households increased from 2,254,000 in 1960 to 2,405,000 in 1970 but remained constant throughout the 1970s. Illinois's population was 48% male and 52% female in 1976.

The rapid rise of Chicago meant that a large proportion of the state's population was concentrated in cities from a relatively early date. Thus, by 1895, 50% of Illinoisans lived in urban areas, whereas the entire country reached that point only in 1920. By 1970, 81% of the population lived in metropolitan areas of 50,000 or more, compared with 74% nationally; the new lure of rural areas kept these proportions constant during the 1970s. With an estimated population of 7,029,600 in 1978, Greater Chicago was the 3d-largest metropolitan area in the nation and alone accounted for more than three-fifths of the total state population. The state's other major metropolitan areas, with their 1978 populations, were Peoria, 360,600, and Rockford, 269,300. The St. Louis metropolitan area included 577,000 in Illinois as of 1977, while Rock Island and Moline, which are part of the Quad Cities metropolitan area of Illinois and Iowa, had 220,000 residents. Smaller metropolitan areas in 1977 included Springfield with 185,000 residents; Champaign-Urbana, 168,000; and Decatur, 127,000. According to preliminary 1980 census data, Chicago had a population of 2,969,570 within the city limits (2d only to New York City), representing a decline of more than 650,000 since 1950. Rockford had 139,206 residents in 1980, and Peoria had 123,571.

7 ETHNIC GROUPS

The Indian population of Illinois had disappeared by 1832 as a result of warfare and emigration. By 1970, however, Indian migration from Wisconsin, Minnesota, and elsewhere had brought the Native American population to 11,413, concentrated in Chicago.

French settlers brought in black slaves from the Caribbean in the mid-18th century; in 1752, one-third of the small non-Indian population was black. Slavery was slowly abolished in the early 19th century. For decades, however, few blacks entered the state, except to flee slavery in neighboring Kentucky and Missouri. Freed slaves did come to Illinois during the Civil War, concentrating in the southern tip and in Chicago. By 1900, 109,000 blacks lived in Illinois. Most held menial jobs in the cities or eked out a precarious existence on small farms in the far south. Large-scale black migration, mainly to Chicago, began during World War I. By 1940, Illinois had a black population of 387,000; extensive wartime and postwar migration brought the total in 1977 to 1,700,000, 78% of whom lived within the city of Chicago, which was nearly 40% black. Smaller numbers of black Illinoisans lived in Peoria, Rockford, and certain Chicago suburbs.

Illinois's Hispanic population did not become significant until

LOCATION: 36°58′ to 42°30′N; 87°30′ to 91°32′W. **BOUNDARIES:** Wisconsin line, 185 mi (298 km); Indiana line, 397 mi (639 km); Kentucky line, 134 mi (216 km); Missouri line, 367 mi (591 km); Iowa line, 214 mi (344 km).

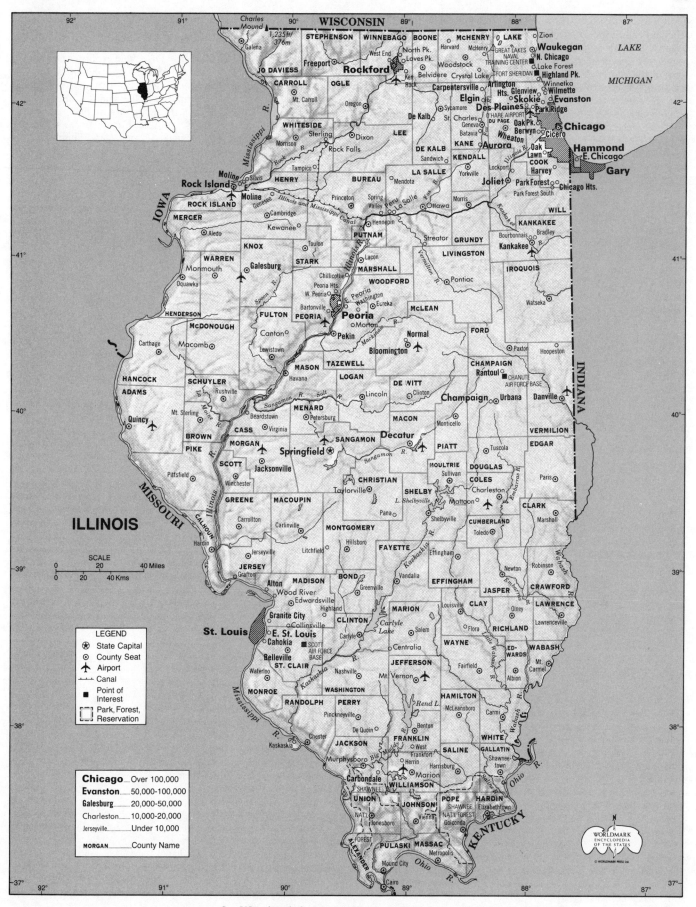

ILLINOIS

LEGEND
- ⊛ State Capital
- ⊙ County Seat
- ✈ Airport
- ⊹ Canal
- ■ Point of Interest
- ⬚ Park, Forest, Reservation

Chicago — Over 100,000
Evanston — 50,000-100,000
Galesburg — 20,000-50,000
Charleston — 10,000-20,000
Jerseyville — Under 10,000
MORGAN — County Name

SCALE
0   20   40 Miles
0   20   40 Kms

WORLDMARK
ENCYCLOPEDIA
OF THE STATES
© WORLDMARK PRESS Ltd.

See US political: front cover J3; physical: back cover J3.

the 1960s. In 1976, the number of Hispanic Americans was officially estimated at 412,000, chiefly in Chicago. There were about 150,000 Puerto Ricans, and 150,000 of Mexican origin (not counting thousands of Mexicans without official papers), with most of the remainder coming from Cuba and other Caribbean and Latin American countries.

In 1970 there were 14,474 Chinese in Illinois, most of whom came to Chicago in the late 19th century; 17,299 Japanese, for the most part brought from the West Coast to Chicago and other cities late in World War II; 12,654 Filipinos, who have come to Illinois throughout the 20th century; and 20,000 Koreans, Polyne-

sians, and other Asian peoples who have come to the state since World War II. In 1975, 3,696 Vietnamese refugees were resettled in the Prairie State.

Members of non-British European ethnic groups are prevalent in all the state's major cities and in many farming areas. In 1970, 19.8% of the population was foreign-born or of foreign-born parentage. The largest groups were Germans (2.8%), Poles (2.7%), and Italians (2.1%), with significant numbers of Scandinavians, Irish, Lithuanians, Serbs, East European Jews, Ukrainians, Slovaks, Hungarians, Czechs, Greeks, and Dutch. Except for the widely dispersed Germans, most of these ethnic groups

Illinois Counties, County Seats, and County Populations[1]

COUNTY	COUNTY SEAT	LAND AREA (SQ MI)	POPULATION (EST. 1977)	COUNTY	COUNTY SEAT	LAND AREA (SQ MI)	POPULATION (EST. 1977)
Adams	Quincy	866	69,300	Lee	Dixon	729	35,800
Alexander	Cairo	224	11,900	Livingston	Pontiac	1,043	41,100
Bond	Greenville	383	14,700	Logan	Lincoln	622	30,200
Boone	Belvidere	283	26,500	Macon	Decatur	576	127,800
Brown	Mt. Sterling	307	5,500	Macoupin	Carlinville	872	46,400
Bureau	Princeton	868	37,000	Madison	Edwardsville	731	246,600
Calhoun	Hardin	259	5,700	Marion	Salem	580	41,200
Carroll	Mt. Carroll	468	18,700	Marshall	Lacon	395	13,500
Cass	Virginia	370	14,100	Mason	Havana	541	19,300
Champaign	Urbana	1,000	168,500	Massac	Metropolis	246	14,600
Christian	Taylorville	709	36,800	McDonough	Macomb	582	39,600
Clark	Marshall	505	16,400	McHenry	Woodstock	611	133,200
Clay	Louisville	464	15,000	McLean	Bloomington	1,173	119,000
Clinton	Carlyle	498	30,800	Menard	Petersburg	312	11,100
Coles	Charleston	507	49,800	Mercer	Aledo	556	18,100
Cook	Chicago	954	5,313,600	Monroe	Waterloo	380	18,800
Crawford	Robinson	442	20,100	Montgomery	Hillsboro	706	30,800
Cumberland	Toledo	346	10,400	Morgan	Jacksonville	565	35,000
DeKalb	Sycamore	636	72,200	Moultrie	Sullivan	345	14,000
DeWitt	Clinton	399	16,700	Ogle	Oregon	757	42,600
Douglas	Tuscola	420	19,300	Peoria	Peoria	624	202,200
DuPage	Wheaton	331	574,900	Perry	Pinckneyville	443	20,800
Edgar	Paris	628	21,800	Piatt	Monticello	437	16,200
Edwards	Albion	225	7,700	Pike	Pittsfield	829	19,000
Effingham	Effingham	482	29,100	Pope	Golconda	381	4,500
Fayette	Vandalia	718	20,800	Pulaski	Mound City	204	8,900
Ford	Paxton	488	14,900	Putnam	Hennepin	166	5,700
Franklin	Benton	434	41,900	Randolph	Chester	594	34,000
Fulton	Lewistown	874	42,900	Richland	Olney	364	17,400
Gallatin	Shawneetown	328	7,500	Rock Island	Rock Island	420	164,600
Greene	Carrollton	543	16,600	Saline	Harrisburg	384	27,000
Grundy	Morris	432	28,600	Sangamon	Springfield	880	175,200
Hamilton	McLeansboro	435	8,800	Schuyler	Rushville	434	8,000
Hancock	Carthage	797	23,200	Scott	Winchester	251	6,000
Hardin	Elizabethtown	183	5,000	Shelby	Shelbyville	772	23,100
Henderson	Oquawka	381	8,500	Stark	Toulon	291	7,400
Henry	Cambridge	826	56,500	St. Clair	Belleville	670	282,300
Iroquois	Watseka	1,122	33,400	Stephenson	Freeport	568	46,700
Jackson	Murphysboro	603	55,500	Tazewell	Pekin	653	128,700
Jasper	Newton	495	11,100	Union	Jonesboro	414	16,500
Jefferson	Mt. Vernon	574	35,600	Vermilion	Danville	898	98,200
Jersey	Jerseyville	374	19,600	Wabash	Mt. Carmel	221	13,800
Jo Daviess	Galena	614	22,600	Warren	Monmouth	542	21,000
Johnson	Vienna	345	9,300	Washington	Nashville	565	15,200
Kane	Geneva	516	271,800	Wayne	Fairfield	715	17,600
Kankakee	Kankakee	680	96,000	White	Carmi	501	16,900
Kendall	Yorkville	320	32,700	Whiteside	Morrison	690	63,800
Knox	Galesburg	728	60,700	Will	Joliet	845	305,900
Lake	Waukegan	457	417,900	Williamson	Marion	427	52,600
La Salle	Ottawa	1,153	108,800	Winnebago	Rockford	520	241,200
Lawrence	Lawrenceville	374	17,700	Woodford	Eureka	537	31,000
				TOTALS		55,748	11,145,000

1. Totals do not add because of rounding.

lived in and around Chicago. A 1968 survey of national origins of Illinois's white population showed that 21% were of German ancestry, 17% British, 12% Irish, 11% Polish, 6% Italian, 6% Scandinavian, 7% other eastern European, 7% other western European, and 13% of uncertain origin or "just American."

Again, except for the Germans, all the ethnic groups maintain a lively identity, with their own newspapers, clubs, festivals, and houses of worship. For the European ethnics, however, these reminders of their cultural heritage are now largely symbolic; they have become highly assimilated into a "melting pot" society. Such was not always the case, however. In 1889, the legislature attempted to curtail foreign-language schools, causing a sharp political reaction among German Lutherans, German Catholics, and some Scandinavians. The upshot was the election of a German-born Democrat, John Peter Altgeld, as governor in 1892. During World War I, anti-German sentiment was intense in the state, despite the manifest American loyalty of the large German element, then about 25% of the state's population. The Germans responded by rapidly abandoning the use of their language and dissolving most of their newspapers and clubs. At about the same time, the US government, educators, social workers, and business firms sponsored extensive "Americanization" programs directed at the large numbers of recent arrivals from Poland, Italy, and elsewhere. The public schools especially played a major role in the assimilation process, as did the Catholic parochial schools, which sought to protect the immigrants' religious but not ethnic identities.

[8]LANGUAGES

A number of place-names—Illinois itself, Chicago, Peoria, Kankakee, and Ottawa—attest the early presence of various Algonkian-speaking tribes, such as the Kickapoo, Sauk, and Fox, and particularly those of the Illinois Federation, the remnants of which moved west of the Mississippi River after the Black Hawk War of 1832.

Nineteenth-century western migration patterns determined the rather complex distribution of regional language features. Excepting the Chicago metropolitan area and the extreme northwestern corner of Illinois, the northern quarter of the state is dominated by Northern speech. An even greater frequency of Northern features appears in the northeastern quadrant; in this region, speakers get *sick to the stomach, catch cold* (take cold), use *dove* as the past tense of *dive*, pronounce *hog, fog, frog, crop,* and *college* with the vowel /ah/, and sound a clear /h/ in *whine, wheel,* and *wheat.*

Settlement from Pennsylvania and Ohio led to a mix of Northern and North Midland speech in central Illinois, with such dominating Northern features as *white bread, pail, greasy* with an /s/ sound, and *creek* rhyming with *stick.* Here appear Midland *fishworm* (earthworm), *firebug* (firefly), *wait on* (wait for), *dived* as the past tense of *dive, quarter till four* (3:45), and *sick at one's stomach* (but *sick on the stomach* in German communities near East St. Louis).

Migration from South Midland areas in Indiana and Kentucky affected basic speech in the southern third of Illinois, known as Egypt. Here especially occur South Midland and Southern *pullybone* (wishbone), *dog irons* (andirons), *light bread* (white bread), and, in extreme southern counties, *loaf bread, snake doctor* (dragonfly), *redworm* (earthworm), *ground squirrel* (chipmunk), *plum peach* (clingstone peach), *to have a crow to pick* (to have a bone to pick) with someone, and the pronunciations of *coop* with the vowel of *put* and of *greasy* with a /z/ sound. Such speech is found also in the northwestern corner around Galena, where Kentucky miners who came to work in the lead mines brought such pronunciations as *bulge* with the vowel of *put, soot* with the vowel of *but,* and /yelk/ for *yolk.*

Metropolitan Chicago has experienced such complex in-migration that, although it still has a basic Northern/Midland mix,

elements of almost all varieties of English appear somewhere. The influx since World War II of speakers of black English, a Southern dialect, and of nonstandard Appalachian English has aggravated language problems in the schools. Foreign-language schools were common in the 1880s and 1890s, but by 1920 all instruction was in English. The policy of monolingual education came into question in the 1970s, when the state legislature mandated bilingual classes for immigrant children, especially Spanish speakers.

In Chicago, rough-and-tumble politics has created a new meaning for *clout; prairie* means a vacant lot, *porch* includes the meaning of *stoop,* and *cornbread* has been generalized to include the meanings of *corn pone* and *hush puppies.* A fuel and food stop on the Illinois tollway system is an *oasis.*

In 1970, English was the mother tongue of 80% of the native-born population and 76% of all state residents. Speakers of major first languages were as follows:

	NATIVE-BORN	FOREIGN-BORN
English	8,412,730	69,422
German	395,406	102,925
Polish	278,630	67,518
Spanish	210,372	84,709
Italian	161,653	61,168
Yiddish	62,079	22,183
French	40,331	11,611

[9]RELIGIONS

Before 1830, little religion of any sort was practiced on the Illinois frontier. Energetic Protestant missionaries set out to evangelize this un-Christian population, and they largely succeeded. By 1890, 36% of the adults in Illinois were affiliated with evangelical denominations—chiefly Methodist, Disciples of Christ, Baptist, Congregationalist, and Presbyterian—while 35%, mostly immigrants, belonged to liturgical denominations (chiefly Roman Catholic, Lutheran, and Episcopal). The remaining adults acknowledged no particular denomination.

Illinois has had episodes of religious bigotry: it was at Carthage in 1844 that Mormon founder Joseph Smith was killed by a mob, and there were strong but brief waves of anti-Catholicism in the 1850s (the "Know-Nothing" movement) and 1920s (the Ku Klux Klan). Nevertheless, tolerance of religious diversity has been the norm for most of the state's history.

Today, the largest Christian denomination is the Roman Catholic Church, with 3,567,541 members in 1979, 2,415,354 of whom were in the archdiocese of Chicago (42% of the regional population). The largest Protestant denomination in 1971 was the United Methodist Church, with 589,975 adherents, followed by the Lutheran Church–Missouri Synod, 351,990; United Presbyterian Church, 234,465; Southern Baptist Convention, 233,863; United Church of Christ, 211,149; and Lutheran Church in America, 204,421. Protestants are most numerous in the Chicago suburbs and in smaller cities and towns downstate. The Jewish population, estimated at 267,525 in 1979, is heavily concentrated in Chicago and its northern suburbs. Chicago is one of the main theological centers of the country, with 15 seminaries and numerous religious publications.

[10]TRANSPORTATION

The fact that Illinois is intersected by several long-distance transportation routes has been of central importance in the state's economic development for a century and a half. Easy access by way of the major rivers and the Great Lakes system facilitated extensive migration to Illinois even before the coming of the railroads in the 1850s. Most of the nation's rail lines converge on Illinois, and Chicago and St. Louis (especially East St. Louis) have been the two main US railroad centers since the late 19th century. Interstate highways, notably the main east–west routes, also cross the state, and Chicago's central location has made it a major transfer point for airline connections.

After several false starts in the 1830s and 1840s, the state's railroad system was begun in the 1850s. The Illinois Central (now the Illinois Central Gulf), aided by the first federal land grants, opened up the prairie lands in the years before the Civil War. By 1890, about 10,000 mi (16,000 km) of track crisscrossed the state, placing 90% of all Illinois farms no more than 5 mi (8 km) from a rail line. The railroads stimulated not only farming but also coal mining, and in the process created tens of thousands of jobs in track and bridge construction, maintenance, traffic operations, and the manufacture of cars, rails, and other railroad equipment.

The rise of automobile and truck traffic in the 1920s and 1930s dealt the railroads a serious blow, but their utter ruin was staved off by complex mergers that incorporated bankrupt or threatened lines into ever larger systems. By 1974, the state had 10,607 mi (17,070 km) of track, 2d only to Texas. Shedding their unprofitable passenger business in the 1970s (except for important commuter lines around Chicago), the railroads concentrated on long-distance freight traffic. The bankruptcy of the Penn Central, Rock Island, and Milwaukee Road systems during the 1970s impelled some companies, notably the Illinois Central Gulf and the Chicago Northwestern, to shift their attention to real estate and manufacturing. Chicago is the hub of Amtrak's passenger service.

Mass transit is of special importance to Chicago, where subways, buses, and commuter railroads are essential to daily movement. The transit systems were built privately but eventually were acquired by the city and regional transportation authorities. Ridership declines every year, as fewer people work in the central city and as more people choose the privacy and convenience of travel by automobile. Federal aid to mass transit, beginning in 1964, and state aid, initiated in 1971, have only partly stemmed the decline. Outside Chicago, bus service is still available in some of the older, larger cities.

The road system of Illinois was inadequate until the 1920s, when an elaborate program to build local and trunk highways first received heavy state aid. In 1978, 133,240 mi (214,429 km) of roadway served 7,340,448 registered vehicles—including 5,883,525 automobiles and 1,184,958 trucks—operated by 6,853,843 licensed drivers. I-80, I-70, and I-64 are the main east–west routes. I-94 links Chicago with Milwaukee, to the north, while I-57 and I-55 connect Chicago with the south and southwest (St. Louis), respectively.

Barge traffic along the Mississippi, Ohio, and Illinois rivers remains important, especially for the shipment of grain. The Port of Chicago no longer sees the sailing ships that brought lumber, merchandise, and people to a fast-growing city. However, the port is still the largest on the Great Lakes, handling about 36 million tons of cargo annually, mostly grain and iron ore.

Midway Airport in Chicago became the world's busiest after World War II, but was superseded by O'Hare Airport, which opened in the late 1950s. With more than 130,000 travelers a day arriving or departing on 2,000 flights by the late 1970s, O'Hare is not only the largest but also the most hectic airport in the country, processing about twice as many passengers as it was built to handle. Efforts to expand its cramped facilities have been blocked by the Defense Department's reluctance to abandon its extensive training facilities there. With 97 municipal airfields and the remarkably large number of 804 private airfields, Illinois is also an important center for general aviation.

¹¹HISTORY

Different tribes of paleo-Indians lived in Illinois as long ago as 8000 BC. By 2000 BC, the cultivation of plants and use of ceramics were known to village dwellers; the first pottery appeared during the Woodland phase, a millennium later. Between 500 BC and AD 500, skilled Hopewellian craftsmen practiced a limited agriculture, developed an elaborate social structure, and con-

structed burial mounds. Huge mounds, which still exist, were built along the major rivers by the Middle Mississippian culture, around AD 900.

It is not known why the early native civilizations died out, but by the time white explorers arrived in the 17th century, the state was inhabited by seminomadic Algonkian-speaking tribes. The Kickapoo, Sauk, and Fox lived in the north, while the shores of Lake Michigan were populated by the Potawatomi, Ottawa, and Ojibwa. The Kaskaskia, Illinois (Iliniwek), and Peoria tribes roamed across the central prairies, and the Cahokia and Tamoroa lived in the south. Constant warfare with tribes from neighboring areas, plus disease and alcohol introduced by white fur traders and settlers, combined to decimate the Native American population. Warfare with the whites led to a series of treaties, the last in 1832, that removed all of the Indians to lands across the Mississippi.

French missionaries and fur traders from Quebec explored the rivers of Illinois in the late 17th century. Father Jacques Marquette and trader Louis Jolliet were the first to reach the area now known as the State of Illinois in 1673, when they descended the Mississippi as far as the Arkansas River and then returned by way of the Illinois River. The first permanent settlement was a mission built by French priests at Cahokia, near present-day St. Louis, in 1699. It was followed by more southerly settlements at Kaskaskia in 1703 and Ft. Chartres in 1719. In 1765, pursuant to the Treaty of Paris (1763) that ended the French and Indian War, the British took control of the Illinois country, but established no settlements of their own. Most of the French settlers were Loyalists during the Revolution. However, they put up no resistance when Virginia troops, led by George Rogers Clark, captured the small British forts at Cahokia and Kaskaskia in 1778. Virginia governed its new territory in desultory fashion, and most of the French villagers fled to Missouri. In 1784, Virginia relinquished its claim to Illinois, which three years later became part of the newly organized Northwest Territory. In 1800, Illinois was included in the Indian Territory. Nine years later, Illinois Territory, including the present state of Wisconsin, was created; Kaskaskia became the territorial capital, and Ninian Edwards was appointed territorial governor by President James Madison. A territorial legislature was formed in 1812. During the War of 1812, British and Indian forces combined in a last attempt to push back American expansion into the Illinois country, and much fighting took place in the area. On 3 December 1818, Illinois was formally admitted to the Union as the 21st state. The capital was moved to Vandalia in 1820 and to Springfield in 1839.

Apart from a few thousand nomadic Indians and the remaining French settlers and their slaves, Illinois was largely uninhabited before 1815; two years after statehood, the population barely exceeded 55,000. The withdrawal of British influence after the War of 1812 and the final defeat of the Indian tribes in the Black Hawk War of 1832 opened the fertile prairies to settlers from the south, especially Kentucky. The federal government owned most of the land, and its land offices did a fast business on easy terms. Before the 1830s, most of the pioneers were concerned with acquiring land titles and pursuing subsistence agriculture, supplemented by hunting and fishing. An effort in 1824 to call a constitutional convention to legalize slavery failed because of a widespread fear that rich slaveholders would seize the best land, squeezing out the poor yeoman farmers. Ambitious efforts in the 1830s to promote rapid economic development led to fiscal disaster. Three state banks failed; a lavish program of building roads, canals, and railroads totally collapsed, leaving a heavy state debt that was not paid off until 1880. Despite these setbacks, the steady influx of land-hungry poor people and the arrival after 1840 of energetic Yankee entrepreneurs, all attracted by the rich soil and excellent water routes, guaranteed rapid growth.

Although Illinois gradually eliminated French slavery and even served as a conduit to Canada for slaves escaping from the South, the state was deeply divided over the slavery issue and remained unfriendly territory for blacks and their defenders. The abolitionist leader Elijah P. Lovejoy was killed in Alton in 1837, and as late as 1853 the state passed legislation providing that free blacks entering Illinois could be sold into slavery. In 1856, however, the new Republican Party nominated and Illinois voters elected a governor, William H. Bissell, on a reform program that included support for school construction, commercial and industrial expansion, and abolition of slavery. During the Civil War, Illinois sent half its young men to the battlefield and supplied the Union armies with huge amounts of food, feed, and horses. The strong-handed wartime administration of Republican Governor Richard Yates guaranteed full support for the policies of Abraham Lincoln, who had been prominent in Illinois political life since the 1840s and had been nominated for the presidency in 1860 at a Republican convention held in Chicago. Democratic dissenters were suppressed, sometimes by force, leaving a legacy of bitter feuds that troubled the "Egypt" section (the southern third of the state) for decades thereafter.

Economic and population growth quickened after 1865, as exemplified by the phenomenal rise of Chicago to become the principal city of the Midwest. Responding to opportunities presented by the coming of the railroads, boosters in hundreds of small towns and cities built banks, grain elevators, retail shops, small factories, ornate courthouses, and plain schools, in an abundance of civic pride. The Democrats sought the support of the working class and small farmers, assuming an attitude of hostility toward banks, high railroad freight rates, protective tariffs, and antiunion employers; but they failed to impose any significant restraints on business expansion. They were more successful, however, in opposing prohibition and other "paternalistic" methods of social control demanded by reformers such as Frances Willard, a leader in the Women's Christian Temperance Union, and the Prohibition Party. In Chicago and other cities the Democrats were less concerned with social reform than with building lucrative political machines on the backs of the poor Irish, Polish, and Czech Catholic immigrants, who kept arriving in large numbers. Statewide, Illinois retained a highly competitive two-party system, even as the excitement and high voter turnouts characteristic of 19th-century elections faded rapidly in the early 20th century.

During the second half of the 19th century, Illinois was a center of the American labor movement. Workers joined the Knights of Labor in the 1870s and 1880s and fought for child labor laws and the eight-hour day. Union organizing led to several spectacular incidents, including the Haymarket riot in 1886 and the violent Pullman strike in 1894, suppressed by federal troops at the behest of President Grover Cleveland. A coalition of Germans, labor, and small farmers elected John Peter Altgeld to the governorship in 1892. After the turn of the century, Illinois became a center of the Progressive movement, led by Jane Addams and Republican Governor Frank Lowden. Lowden reorganized the state government in 1917 by placing experts in powerful positions in state and municipal administrations.

After the great fire of 1871 destroyed Chicago's downtown section (but not its main residential or industrial areas), the city's wealthy elite dedicated itself to rebuilding Chicago and making it one of the great metropolises of the world. Immense steel mills, meat-packing plants, and factories sprang up, and growth was spectacular in the merchandising, banking, and transportation fields. Their fortunes made, Chicago's business leaders began building cultural institutions in the 1890s that were designed to rival the best in the world: the Chicago Symphony, the Art Institute, and the Field Museum of Natural History. The World's Columbian Exposition of 1893 was a significant international exhibition of the nation's technological achievements, and it

focused worldwide attention on what was by then the 2d-largest American city. A literary renaissance, stimulated by the new realism that characterized Chicago's newspapers, flourished for a decade or two before World War I, but the city was recognized chiefly for its contributions in science, architecture, and (in the 1920s) jazz.

The first three decades of the 20th century witnessed almost unbroken prosperity in all sections save Egypt, the downstate region where poor soil and the decline of the coal industry produced widespread poverty. The slums of Chicago were poor, too, because most of the hundreds of thousands of new immigrants arrived virtually penniless. After 1920, however, large-scale immigration ended, and the immigrants' steady upward mobility, based on savings and education, became apparent. During the prohibition era, a vast organized crime empire rose to prominence, giving Chicago and Joliet a reputation for gangsterism, violence, and corruption; the most notorious gangster was Al Capone. Money, whether legally or illegally acquired, mesmerized Illinois in the 1920s as never before—and never since.

The depression of the 1930s affected the state unevenly, with agriculture hit first and recovering first. Industries began shutting down in 1930 and did not fully recover until massive military contracts during World War II restored full prosperity. The very fact of massive depression brought discredit to the probusiness Republican regime that had run the state with few exceptions since 1856. Blacks, ethnics, factory workers, and the undereducated, all of whom suffered heavily during the early years of the depression, responded enthusiastically to Franklin Roosevelt's New Deal. They elected Henry Horner, a Democrat, to the governorship in 1932, reelected him in 1936, and flocked to the new industrial unions of the Congress of Industrial Organizations, founded in 1938.

World War II and its aftermath brought prosperity, a sense of national unity and purpose, and new anxiety about national security in a nuclear age. Most Illinoisans adopted hard-line anti-Communist attitudes in foreign policy, and many (outside the city of Chicago) transferred their allegiance back to the Republican Party. The goals of personal security and prosperity, encapsulated in the dream of owning a house (preferably in the burgeoning suburbs) and a car, holding a steady job, and providing a good education for one's children, dominated Illinois life in the two postwar decades. The chilling events of the 1960s and 1970s—assassinations, the Viet-Nam war, race riots, and the violence that accompanied the 1968 Democratic National Convention in Chicago—coupled with a new awareness of poverty, alienation, and environmental pollution, helped reshape many people's attitudes in Illinois, as the problems attendant on heavy industrialization, particularly air and water pollution and urban decay, began to be addressed for the first time.

[12] STATE GOVERNMENT

Illinois has had four constitutions. The first, written in 1818, was a short document modeled on those of New York, Kentucky, and Ohio. An attempt to rewrite the charter to allow slavery failed in a bitterly contested referendum in 1824. A new constitution in 1848 democratized government by providing for the popular election of judges. A third constitution, enacted in 1870, lasted a century; its unique feature was a voting system for the lower house of the state legislature that virtually guaranteed minority party representation in each electoral district. Important amendments in 1884 and 1904, respectively, gave the governor an item veto over appropriation bills and provided a measure of home rule for Chicago. In 1970, Illinois voters ratified a new constitution by a margin of 57%. It streamlined state offices somewhat, improved accounting procedures, reformed the state tax system, and gave the state, rather than local governments, the major responsibility for financing education. The state bill of rights was expanded to include provisions banning discrimination in housing and employment and recognizing women's rights. An elected judiciary and the state's unique representational system were retained.

Under the 1970 constitution, as amended, the upper house of the general assembly consists of a senate of 59 members, who are elected on a two-year cycle to four-year terms. Up until 1980, the lower house, the house of representatives, consisted of 177 members, with 3 representatives elected for two-year terms from each district. Each voter was empowered to cast three ballots for representatives, giving one vote to each of three candidates, one and a half votes to each of two, or all three to one candidate; each party never nominated more than two candidates in any single district. In November 1980, however, Illinois voters chose to reduce the size of house membership to 118 (2 representatives from each district) and to eliminate the proportional system.

The executive officers elected statewide are the governor and lieutenant governor (who run jointly), secretary of state, treasurer, comptroller, and attorney general. Each serves a four-year term and is eligible for reelection. An important revision of appointive offices in 1917 made most agency heads responsible to the governor. In the 1970s, the governor's office expanded its control over the budget and the higher education complex, further augmenting an already strong executive position. The governor must be a US citizen, at least 25 years of age, and must have been a state resident for three years prior to election.

Bills passed by both houses of the legislature become law if signed by the governor, if left unsigned for 60 days while the legislature is in session or 90 days after it adjourns, or if vetoed by the governor but passed again by three-fifths of the elected members of each house. Constitutional amendments require a three-fifths vote by the legislature for placement on the ballot; either a simple majority of those voting in the election or three-fifths of those voting on the amendment is sufficient for ratification.

Qualified voters must be US citizens at least 18 years of age. There is a 30-day district residency requirement.

¹³POLITICAL PARTIES

The Republican and Democratic parties have been the only major political groups in Illinois since the 1850s. Illinois is a closely balanced state, with a slight Republican predominance from 1860 to 1930 giving way in seesaw fashion to a highly competitive situation statewide. In Chicago and Cook County, an equally balanced division before 1930 gave way to heavy Democratic predominance forged during the New Deal.

The Democrats, organized by patronage-hungry followers of President Andrew Jackson in the 1830s, dominated state politics down to the mid-1850s. They appealed to subsistence farmers, former southerners, and poor Catholic immigrants. Though they advocated minimal government intervention, Democratic officials were eager for the patronage and inside deals available in a fast-growing state. Their outstanding leader, Stephen Douglas, became a major national figure in the 1850s, but never lost touch with his base of support. After Douglas died in 1861, many Illinois Democrats began to oppose the conduct of the Civil War and became stigmatized as "Copperheads." The success of the Republican war policies left the Democrats in confusion in the late 1860s and early 1870s. Negative attitudes toward blacks, banks, railroads, and prohibition kept a large minority of Illinoisans in the Democratic fold, while the influx of Catholic immigrants replenished the party's voter base. However the administration of Governor Altgeld (1893–97), coinciding with a deep depression and labor unrest, split the party, and only one other Democrat held the governorship between 1852 and 1932. The intraparty balance between Chicago and downstate changed with the rise of the powerful Cook County Democratic organization in the 1930s. Built by Mayor Anton Cermak and continued into the 1970s by Mayor Richard J. Daley, the Chicago Democratic machine totally controlled the city, dominated the state party, and exerted enormous power at the national level.

The Republican Party, born amid the political chaos of the 1850s, brought together most former Whigs and some Democrats who favored industrialization and opposed slavery. Abraham Lincoln, aided by many talented lieutenants, forged a coalition of commercial farmers, businessmen, evangelical Protestants, skilled craftsmen, professionals, and later, patronage holders and army veterans. Ridiculing the Democrats' alleged parochialism, the GOP called for vigorous prosecution of the Civil War and Reconstruction and for an active policy of promoting economic growth by encouraging railroads and raising tariffs. However, such moralistic crusades as the fight for prohibition frequently alienated large voting blocs (especially the Germans) from the Republicans.

In the early 20th century, Republican politicians built their own ward machines in Chicago and succumbed to corruption. William "Big Bill" Thompson, Chicago's Republican mayor in the 1910s and 1920s, openly allied himself with the gangster Al Capone. Moralistic Republicans, who were strongest in the smaller

Illinois Presidential Vote by Political Parties, 1948–80

YEAR	ELECTORAL VOTE	ILLINOIS WINNER	DEMOCRAT	REPUBLICAN	SOCIALIST LABOR	PROHIBITION	COMMUNIST	SOCIALIST
1948	28	*Truman (D)	1,994,715	1,961,103	3,118	11,959	—	11,522
1952	27	*Eisenhower (R)	2,013,920	2,457,327	9,363	—	—	—
1956	27	*Eisenhower (R)	1,775,682	2,623,327	8,342	—	—	—
1960	27	*Kennedy (D)	2,377,846	2,368,988	10,560	—	—	—
1964	26	*Johnson (D)	2,796,833	1,905,946				
						AMERICAN IND.		
1968	26	*Nixon (R)	2,039,814	2,174,774	13,878	390,958	—	—
						AMERICAN		
1972	26	*Nixon (R)	1,913,472	2,788,179	12,344	2,471	4,541	—
						LIBERTARIAN		SOC.WORKERS
1976	26	Ford (R)	2,271,295	2,364,269	2,422	8,057	9,250	3,615
					CITIZENS			
1980	26	*Reagan (R)	1,981,413	2,358,094	10,692	38,939	9,711	1,302

*Won US presidential election.

towns, struggled to regain control of their party. They succeeded in the 1930s, when the Republican political machines in Chicago collapsed or switched their allegiance to the Democrats. Since then, the Republicans have become uniformly a party of the middle and upper-middle classes, hostile to machine politics, welfare, and high taxes, but favorable to business, education, and environmental protection. Although the GOP has a stronger formal organization in Illinois than in most other states, its leading candidates have exuded an aura of independence.

The Whigs usually ran a close second to the Democrats from 1832 to 1852. Taken over in the 1840s by a group of professional organizers under Lincoln's leadership, the Whigs simply vanished after their crushing defeat in 1852. Notable among the smaller parties was the Native American Party ("Know-Nothings"), which controlled Chicago briefly in the 1850s. The Prohibitionists, Greenbackers, Union Labor, and Populist parties were weak forces in late-19th-century Illinois. The Socialist Party, strongest among coal miners and central European immigrants, grew to a minor force in the early 20th century and elected the mayor of Rockford for years. In 1912, Theodore Roosevelt's Progressive Party briefly split the GOP, allowing Democrat Edward Dunne's election as governor and Woodrow Wilson's victory in presidential voting.

Illinois provided two important leaders of the national GOP in the 1860s—Abraham Lincoln and Ulysses S. Grant. The only major-party presidential nominee from the state between 1872 and 1976, however, was Governor Adlai Stevenson, the Democratic candidate in 1952 and 1956. In 1980, three native-born Illinoisans actively pursued the Republican Party nomination. The first, US Representative Philip Crane, was the earliest to declare his candidacy but failed in the primaries. The second, US Representative John Anderson, dropped out of the GOP primaries to pursue an independent candidacy, ultimately winning more than 6% of the popular vote nationally and in Illinois, but no electoral votes. The third, Ronald Reagan, a native of Tampico, won both the Republican nomination and the November election, becoming the 40th president of the US.

There is no party registration. At the close of 1980, Republicans held the governorship, 1 of 2 US Senate seats, and 14 of 24 US House seats.

14 LOCAL GOVERNMENT

As of 1977, Illinois had 6,620 units of local government (84% with property-taxing power), far more than any other state. There were 102 counties, 1,274 municipalities, 1,436 townships, 1,063 school districts, and 2,745 special districts.

County government in Illinois dates back to 1778, when Virginia, claiming authority over the territory, established the earliest counties. The major county offices are elective: the county judge (now a judicial officer, but formerly with administrative duties), the county clerk (chief administrative officer), clerk of the circuit court, sheriff, state's attorney, treasurer, coroner, and superintendent of schools. Cook County controls hospital and welfare programs in Chicago, thus spreading the cost over both the city's own tax base and that of the more affluent suburbs. The New England township system was made optional by the 1848 constitution, and eventually 85 counties, including Cook County, adopted the idea. Townships, which elect local judges and administrators, also handle tax collection.

Chicago is governed by an elected mayor, clerk, treasurer, and city council composed of 50 aldermen. The mayor's power depends more on control of the city's Democratic Party organization than on formal authority. Independent candidates get elected to the city council from time to time, but the Democratic machine generally staffs the city with its own members. Other cities may choose either the commission or aldermanic system; most are administered by nonpartisan city managers. In villages, trustees are the principal elected officials.

15 STATE SERVICES

Officials responsible to the governor of Illinois, the mayor of Chicago, and the members of Congress actively provide ombudsman service, although there is no state office by that name. The state has a Board of Ethics, but the US attorney's office in Chicago has far more potent weapons at its disposal: many top political leaders were indicted and convicted in the 1970s, including federal judge and former governor Otto Kerner and, in 1980, Attorney General William Scott.

Educational services provided by the Illinois Office of Education include teacher certification and placement, curriculum development, educational assessment and evaluation, and programs for the disadvantaged, gifted, handicapped, and ethnic and racial minorities. The Board of Higher Education and the Illinois Community College Board oversee postsecondary education. The Department of Transportation handles highways, traffic safety, and airports.

Among state agencies offering health and welfare services are the Department of Children and Family Services, which focuses on foster care, the deaf, the blind, and the handicapped, and the Department of Public Aid, which supervises Medicaid, food stamps, and general welfare programs. The Mental Health and Developmental Disabilities Department operates homes and outpatient centers for the retarded and the mentally ill; it also offers an alcoholism program. Established in 1973, the Department on Aging provides nutritional and field services. The Board of Vocational Rehabilitation operates programs to retrain the disabled, while the Department of Veterans' Affairs administers bonus and scholarship programs and maintains a veterans' home.

State responsibility for public protection is divided among several agencies: the Office of the Attorney General, Department of Corrections (prisons and parole), Department of Law Enforcement (including the State Police and Bureau of Investigation), Dangerous Drugs Commission, and Military and Naval Department. Resource protection is supervised by the Department of Conservation, which oversees fish hatcheries, state parks, nature reserves, game preserves, and forest fire protection. The Department of Mines and Minerals handles mine safety and land reclamation programs.

The Department of Labor mediates disputes and handles unemployment compensation. The Department of Human Rights, created in 1979, seeks to ensure equal employment, housing, and credit opportunities.

16 JUDICIAL SYSTEM

The state's highest court is the supreme court, consisting of seven justices elected by district for 10-year terms; the justices elect one of their number as chief justice for 3 years. The supreme court has appellate jurisdiction generally, but has original jurisdiction in cases relating to revenue, mandamus, and habeas corpus. The chief justice, assisted by an administrative director, has administrative and supervisory authority over all other courts. The appellate court is divided into five districts; appellate judges, also elected for 10-year terms, hear appeals from the 21 circuit courts, which handle civil and criminal cases. Circuit judges are elected for 6-year terms. Repeated efforts to remove the state's judgeships from partisan politics have failed in the face of strong party opposition.

The penal system, under the general supervision of the Department of Corrections (established in 1970), includes large prisons at Joliet (1860), Pontiac (1871), Menard (1878), and Stateville (1919), near Joliet, plus juvenile facilities and an active parole division. The Cook County House of Corrections is highly active, as are federal facilities in Chicago and Marion. Nevertheless, Illinois has surprisingly few prisoners at any one time—10,668 in 1977, fewer than eight other states. Prisoner unrest, demands for legal rights, gang activity, and low guard morale continue to be serious problems in the state's penal institutions.

Illinois has a reputation for lawlessness, born of the gang warfare in Chicago during the prohibition era. In the 19th century, southern Illinois was ravaged by numerous bands of outlaws, and one county still carries the nickname "Bloody Williamson" because of its history of murders, massacres, and assassinations. However, as of 1978, the crime rate in the state was close to the national average, and Chicago's crime rate was actually lower than the rates of most large cities. The number of violent crimes in Chicago fell 2.5% a year during the 1970s, to a total of 897 per 100,000 in 1978. Crime rates per 100,000 population statewide were murder, 9.9; forcible rape, 23.8; robbery, 205; aggravated assault, 227; burglary, 1,339; larceny, 2,902; and motor vehicle theft, 511.

[17]ARMED FORCES

The most important military installations in Illinois are Ft. Sheridan, north of Chicago, the headquarters of the Fifth Army; the nearby Great Lakes Naval Training Center; Scott Air Force Base near Belleville; and Chanute Air Force Base in Rantoul. Total authorized personnel numbered nearly 60,000 in 1977/78, when Illinois firms received defense contract awards amounting to $712 million, only 1.2% of the US total.

About 1,000,000 Illinoisans served in World War II, of whom 30,000 were killed. As of 30 September 1979, 1,545,000 veterans were living in Illinois, of whom 30,000 saw service in World War I, 654,000 during World War II, 308,000 during the Korean conflict, and 428,000 during the Viet-Nam era. Veterans' benefits reached $739.5 million in 1977/78, with cumulative payments totaling $10 billion since 1940.

Illinois's relatively small National Guard comprised 9,700 men and women in 1978. On the other hand, police forces are relatively large, totaling 34,472 men and women in 1977 and costing $638 million; the ratio of 3.1 police employees per 1,000 population was one of the highest in the US.

[18]MIGRATION

Apart from the small French settlements along the Mississippi that were formed in the 18th century, most early white migration into Illinois came from the South, as poor young farm families trekked overland to southern Illinois from Kentucky, Tennessee, and the Carolinas between 1800 and 1840. After 1830, migration from Indiana, Ohio, and Pennsylvania filled the central portion of the state, while New Englanders and New Yorkers came to the northern portion.

Immigration from Europe became significant in the 1840s and continued in a heavy stream for about 80 years. Before 1890, most of the new arrivals came from Germany, Ireland, Britain, and Scandinavia. These groups continued to arrive after 1890, but they were soon outnumbered by heavy immigration from southern and eastern Europe. The opening of prairie farms, the burgeoning of towns and small cities, and the explosive growth of Chicago created a continuous demand for unskilled and semiskilled labor. Concern for the welfare of these newcomers led to the establishment by Jane Addams in Chicago of Hull House (1889), which served as a social center, shelter, and advocate for immigrants. Hull House launched the settlement movement in America, and its activity helped popularize the concept of cultural pluralism. The University of Chicago was one of the first major universities to concern itself with urban ecology and with the tendency to "ghettoize" culturally and economically disadvantaged populations.

The outbreak of World War I interrupted the flow of European immigrants but also increased the economy's demand for unskilled labor. The migration of blacks from states south of Illinois—especially from Arkansas, Tennessee, Louisiana, Mississippi, and Alabama—played an important role in meeting the demand for labor during both world wars. After World War II, the further collapse of the cotton labor market drove hundreds of thousands more blacks to Chicago and other northern cities.

In contrast to the pattern of foreign and black migration to Illinois was the continued westward search by native-born whites for new farmland, a phenomenon that produced a net outflow by this group from 1870 to 1920. After World War II, native whites again left the state in large numbers, with Southern California a favorite mecca. After 1970, for the first time, more blacks began leaving than entering Illinois.

The major intrastate migration pattern has been from farms to towns. Apart from blacks, who migrated considerable distances from farms in the South, most ex-farmers moved only 10-30 mi (16-48 km) to the nearest town or city.

Chicago, with its large Hispanic community, has been a haven for illegal immigrants from Mexico. Estimates vary widely, but 200,000 Mexicans were thought to reside in the city in 1980.

[19]INTERGOVERNMENTAL COOPERATION

Illinois participates in 25 interstate compacts, including such regional accords as the Great Lakes Basin Compact, Midwest Nuclear Compact, and Ohio River Valley Water Sanitation Compact.

General revenue sharing totaled nearly $350 million in 1978/79, when all federal aid to Illinois amounted to $3.8 billion.

[20]ECONOMY

The economic development of Illinois falls into four periods: the frontier economy, up to 1860; the industrial transition 1860-1900; industrial maturity, 1900-50; and the transition to a service economy, 1950 to the present.

In the first phase, subsistence agriculture was dominant; the cost of transportation was high, cities were small and few, and cash markets for farm products hardly existed. The main activity was settling and clearing the land. A rudimentary market economy developed at the end of the period, with real estate and land speculation the most lucrative activities.

The industrial transition began about 1860, stimulated by the construction of the railroad network, which opened up distant markets for farm products and rural markets for manufactured items. The Civil War stimulated the rapid growth of cash farming, commercial and financial institutions, and the first important factories. The last quarter of the 19th century saw the closing of the agricultural frontier in Illinois and the rapid growth of commercial towns and industrial cities, especially Chicago.

Industrial maturity was reached in the early 20th century. Large factories grew, and small ones proliferated. Chicago's steel industry, actually centered in Gary, Ind., became second in size only to Pittsburgh's, while the state took a commanding lead in food production, agricultural implement manufacture, and agricultural finance. The depression of the 1930s stifled growth in the state and severely damaged the coal industry, but with the heavy industrial and food demands created by World War II, the state recovered its economic health. Since 1950, the importance of manufacturing has declined, but a very strong shift into services—government, medicine, education, law, finance, and business—has underpinned the state's economic vigor.

The gross state product reached $113.9 billion in 1978, more than double the 1967 total. The following table shows contributions of the same sectors to the GSP for those two years (in billions):

	1967	1978[1]
Manufacturing	$17.1	$33.1
Trade	8.6	19.5
Finance, insurance, real estate	6.6	17.1
Services	5.8	14.3
Transportation, communications	4.5	10.1
Government	4.1	10.6
Contract construction	2.4	4.6
Agriculture	1.5	3.5
Mining	0.4	1.2
TOTALS	$51.0	$114.0

[1]Preliminary figures.

Trends in the 1970s showed declines in the relative importance of manufacturing and construction, little relative change in transportation and agriculture, and significant proportional increases in the other sectors. Severe competition from Japan wreaked havoc in the state's steel, television, and automotive industries, while Illinois's high-wage, high-cost business climate encouraged the migration of factories to the South. Meat-packing, once the most famous industry in Illinois, dwindled after the closing of the Chicago stockyards in 1972. On the brighter side, Chicago remained the nation's chief merchandising center, and an influx of huge international banks boosted the city's financial strength. The service industries—especially medicine and research—flourished, and though the railroads grew weaker every year, aviation and trucking remained potent.

21 INCOME

Illinois is a rich state and has been for the last century. In per capita income, it ranked 7th in 1978, trailing only California and New Jersey among the most populous states. Per capita income was 19% above the national average in 1960 and, at $8,745, was 12% above the national average in 1978.

Proportionally fewer Illinois residents live in poverty than do Americans as a whole, but the proportions are somewhat higher than in many other midwestern states. In 1975, 10.5% of the entire population and 15.1% of all children were below the poverty line. Blacks and households headed by women or old people were the most likely victims of poverty. On the other hand, 834,200 of the nation's leading wealthholders—7% of the US total—lived in the state in 1972.

Income levels vary by race and geography. In 1969, the average income for white families was 4% higher than the mean income for all families in Illinois. For Hispanic families, it was 17% lower; for blacks, 30%. Suburban families averaged 22% above the mean; families in large cities, 6% below it; in small cities, 15% below it; and in rural areas, 16% below. Residents of southern Illinois had lower incomes than those living in central and northern Illinois, and families headed by a woman had incomes averaging 42% below the state norm.

22 LABOR

In 1978, 5,005,000 Illinoisans (or 44.5% of the state's population) were employed, and 323,000 were unemployed, for an unemployment rate of 6.1%. Women comprised 40.9% of those employed and 48.3% of those unemployed, while nonwhites comprised 11.5% of the employed and 31% of the unemployed.

A federal census of workers covered by unemployment insurance in March 1977 revealed the following nonfarm employment pattern in Illinois:

	ESTABLISH-MENTS	EMPLOYEES	ANNUAL PAYROLL ('000)
Agricultural services, forestry, fishing	1,811	7,756	$ 86,654
Mining, of which:	829	28,169	481,986
Bituminous coal, lignite	(74)	(15,923)	(292,229)
Contract construction	19,416	169,699	3,332,044
Manufacturing, of which:	18,260	1,286,289	18,903,053
Food and food products	(1,180)	(103,300)	(1,465,568)
Printing and publishing	(2,972)	(100,056)	(1,436,319)
Primary metals	(548)	(87,412)	(1,545,168)
Fabricated metals	(2,507)	(142,604)	(2,057,768)
Nonelectrical machinery	(3,262)	(208,709)	(3,320,349)
Electric, electronic equipment	(996)	(153,920)	(1,932,286)
Transportation, public utilities	7,951	224,583	3,751,024
Wholesale trade	20,876	290,996	4,565,333
Retail trade	58,915	768,536	5,514,802
Finance, insurance, real estate, of which:	23,061	297,933	3,752,197
Insurance	(5,813)	(114,850)	(1,538,421)
Services, of which:	59,233	827,729	8,118,716
Health services	(13,359)	(254,501)	(2,774,971)
Business services	(8,229)	(148,430)	(1,619,834)
Other	2,812	4,182	62,018
TOTALS	213,164	3,905,872	$48,567,827

Some 735,000 Illinoisans, not included in this survey, were government employees in 1978; about 42% of these were teachers and other educational personnel.

The first labor organizations sprang up among German tailors, teamsters, and carpenters in Chicago in the 1850s, and among British and German coal miners after the Civil War. The period of industrialization after the Civil War saw many strikes, especially in coal mining and construction, many of them spontaneous rather than union-related. The Knights of Labor organized extensively in Chicago, Peoria, and Springfield in the 1870s and 1880s, reaching a membership of 52,000 by 1886. However, in the aftermath of the Haymarket Riot—at which a dynamite blast at a labor rally killed eight policemen and an unknown number of civilians—the Knights faded rapidly. More durable was the Chicago Federation of Labor, formed in 1877 and eventually absorbed by the American Federation of Labor (AFL). Strongest in the highly skilled construction, transportation, mining, and printing industries, the federation stood aside from the 1894 Pullman strike, led by industrial union organizer Eugene V. Debs, a bitter struggle broken by federal troops over the protest of Governor Altgeld.

Today, labor unions are powerful in Chicago but relatively weak downstate. In 1976, about 34% of nonfarm workers belonged to unions and employee associations (versus 29% nationally); this represented a sharp decline from 1964, when 38% were members. The state's major unions are the International Brotherhood of Teamsters, the United Steelworkers of America, the International Association of Machinists, the United Automobile Workers, the United Brotherhood of Carpenters, and the American Federation of State, County, and Municipal Employees. The Illinois Education Association, though not strictly speaking a labor union, has become one of the state's most militant employee organizations, calling strikes in dozens of school districts each fall and constituting the most active lobby in the state. During the 1970s, firefighters, police officers, hospital workers, and nurses began to organize their own associations. A three-week strike by firefighters in Chicago in February 1980 resulted in the defeat of their union, however.

As of 1978, average weekly wages in manufacturing were $271, 9th in the US and 9% above the national average. Weekly earnings in retail trade, services, education, and government also exceeded the national norms.

23 AGRICULTURE

Total agricultural income in 1978 reached $6.2 billion in Illinois, 4th behind California, Iowa, and Texas. Crops account for nearly two-thirds of the value of farm marketings, with soybeans and corn the leading cash commodities.

Prior to 1860, agriculture was the dominant occupation, and food for home consumption was the leading product. Enormous effort was devoted to breaking the thick prairie soil in the northern two-thirds of the state. Fences and barns were erected, and in the 1870s and 1880s, the drainage of low-lying areas in central Illinois was a major concern. Commercial agriculture was made possible by the extension of the railroad network in the 1860s and 1870s. Corn, wheat, hogs, cattle, and horses were the state's main products in the 19th century. Since then, wheat and poultry have declined greatly in significance, while soybeans and, to a lesser extent, dairy products and vegetables have played an increasingly important role. The mechanization and electrification of agriculture, beginning around 1910, proceeded faster in Illinois than anywhere else in the world. Strong interest in scientific farming, including the use of hybrid corn, sophisticated animal-breeding techniques, and chemical fertilizers, has also fostered a steady, remarkable growth in agricultural productivity.

The number of farms reached a peak at 264,000 in 1900 and began declining rapidly a 'ter World War II, down to 107,000 in 1979. Total acreage in far. ing, 32.8 million acres (13.3 million hectares) in 1900, or 92% of the state's land area, declined slowly to 28.7 million acres (11.6 million hectares), or 80%, in 1979. The average farm size has more than doubled from 124 acres (50 hectares) in 1900 to 268 acres (108 hectares) in 1979. The farm population, which averaged 1.2 million persons from 1880 to 1900, declined to 390,000 in 1979; by then, moreover, about half the people who lived on farms commuted to work in stores, shops, and offices.

The major agricultural region is the corn belt, covering all of central Illinois and about half of northern Illinois; its chief products are corn, soybeans, hogs, and cattle. The following table shows volume, value, and rank of leading field crops in 1979:

	VOLUME (MILLION BUSHELS)	VALUE (MILLIONS)	US RANK
Corn for grain	1,358.1	$3,395.2	2
Soybeans	374.2	2,395.0	1
Wheat	55.9	223.6	14
Hay (million tons)	3.8	205.2	16
Oats	16.2	22.7	12
Sorghum for grain	5.1	10.6	13

Cash sales usually represent less than 10% of the value of hay, and 40% of corn, oats, and sorghum; nearly all wheat and soybeans are sold for cash.

Agriculture is big business in the state, though very few farms are owned by corporations (except "family corporations," a tax device). The financial investment in agriculture is enormous, largely because of the accelerating cost of land. The value of land quadrupled during the 1970s to an average of about $1,800 per acre ($4450 per hectare) statewide, and much more in the prime corn belt counties.

²⁴ANIMAL HUSBANDRY
Livestock is raised almost everywhere in Illinois, but production is concentrated especially in the west-central region. In 1978, livestock marketings and products exceeded $2.1 billion. At the close of 1979, Illinois farms had 6.95 million hogs and pigs (10% of the nation's total) and 2.7 million head of cattle (2.4%). Production of meat animals included 964.7 million lb of cattle worth $625 million and 2.6 billion lb of hogs worth $1.1 billion.

The dairy belt covers part of northern Illinois, providing Chicago's milk supply. Milk production in 1979 totaled 2.4 billion lb. Other dairy products included 3.5 million lb of butter, 97 million lb of cheese, and 38.3 million gallons of ice cream. During the same year, Illinois poultry farmers produced 16.3 million lb of chickens and broilers, worth $1.8 million; 1.3 billion eggs sold for $63.7 million.

²⁵FISHING
Commercial fishing is insignificant in Illinois: only 3.6 million lb of fish, with a value of merely $826,000, made up the commercial catch in 1978. Sport fishing is of modest importance in southern Illinois and in Lake Michigan. Some 450 lakes and ponds and 200 streams and rivers are open to the public, though the lure of Wisconsin is stronger for more serious fishermen.

²⁶FORESTRY
Except for shade trees and occasional orchards, the northern two-thirds of the state is barren of trees. Forests remain in the south, however: as of 1977, 3,810,000 acres (1,542,000 hectares) of forestland covered not quite 11% of the state's land area. Of that, 3,692,000 acres (1,494,000 hectares) were classified as commercial forest, 92% of it privately owned. Lumbering is a minor industry in Illinois, with shipments of lumber and wood products amounting in 1977 to $710.8 million.

²⁷MINING
Illinois ranked 16th among the 50 states in mineral production in 1978, with output valued at $1.6 billion. Fossil fuels, especially coal, were the leading mineral commodities, but stone, sand, and gravel are also important. Excluding fossil fuels, mineral output in 1977 comprised 61,862,000 tons of stone, worth $141,543,000; 38,784,000 tons of sand and gravel, $87,152,000; 1,632,000 tons of Portland cement, $53,524,000; and 142,666 tons of fluorspar, $14,563,000. Lead, zinc, silver, and lime are also mined in small commercial quantities.

²⁸ENERGY AND POWER
Illinois is one of the nation's leading energy producers and consumers. Electric power production reached 108.5 billion kwh (6th in the US) in 1978, up 42% over 1970; installed capacity was 29.7 million kw (5th), nearly all of it privately owned. Total sales of electric energy in 1977 were 92.9 billion kwh (6th), of which industry consumed 36%, residences 30%, commercial establishments 26%, and other users 8%. Commonwealth Edison and Northern Illinois Light and Power are the largest suppliers. Coal-fired plants account for about 60% of the state's power production; nuclear power is also important, particularly for the generation of electricity in the Chicago area. The two largest installations, both owned by Commonwealth Edison, are the Zion Nuclear Generating Station north of Chicago and the Dresden Nuclear Power Station near Joliet.

In 1978, Illinois ranked 3d in natural gas usage, with sales of 1.2 quadrillion Btu to 3.2 million customers, for a total revenue of $2.7 billion. People's Gas, a diversified energy conglomerate based in Chicago, is the largest firm. Illinois's own natural gas reserves were 420.4 billion cu feet as of 31 December 1978; production that year was only 789 million cu feet. Petroleum extraction is more substantial, though steadily declining: in 1978, production totaled 22.6 million barrels and reserves were 137.9 million barrels.

Illinois ranked 5th in the US in bituminous coal production in 1978, with 48.6 million tons, an 18% decline since 1975. Reserves in 1976 were estimated at 68 billion tons. Coal is abundant throughout the state, with the largest mines in the south and central regions. Coal mining reached its peak in the 1920s, but suffered thereafter from high pricing policies, the depression of the 1930s, and the environmental restrictions against burning high-sulfur coal in the 1970s. Most coal is now produced by surface (strip) mining.

²⁹INDUSTRY
Manufacturing in Illinois, concentrated in but not limited to Chicago, has always been diverse. Before 1860, small gristmills, bakeries, and blacksmith shops handled what little manufacturing was done. Industry tripled in size in the 1860s, doubled in the 1870s, and doubled again in the 1880s, until manufacturing employment leveled off at 10–12% of the population. Value added by manufacture grew at a compound annual rate of 8.1% between 1860 and 1900, and at a rate of 6.3% until 1929. The chief industries in 1929 were iron and steel, printing, food, electrical equipment, and machinery.

Nearly five decades later, in 1976, Illinois ranked 5th in the nation in the size of its manufacturing payrolls and 4th in value added by manufacture. As of 1977, the total value added was $40.3 billion, and new capital expenditures amounted to $2.7 billion. Of the major sectors, nonelectrical machinery contributed 18%; food and food products, 12%; electric and electronic equipment, 11%; fabricated metal products, 11%; chemicals and allied products, 9%; printing and publishing, 8%; and primary metal industries, 7%. The following table shows value added by manufacture for selected industries in 1972 and 1977:

	1972	1977
Construction machinery	$1,257,100,000	$2,032,000,000
Blast furnace, basic steel products	1,097,000,000	1,396,000,000
Communications equipment	922,800,000	1,379,800,000
Petroleum refining	277,600,000	1,246,300,000
Commercial printing	811,200,000	1,155,600,000
Soaps, cleaners, toilet goods	816,200,000	1,146,200,000
Metal forgings and stampings	619,600,000	1,046,500,000
Farm machinery and equipment	458,100,000	1,012,300,000
Grain mill products	520,000,000	928,900,000
Miscellaneous plastics products	455,900,000	921,700,000
Metalworking machinery	542,100,000	870,500,000
Motor vehicles and equipment	648,900,000	810,500,000

By far the leading industrial center is Chicago, followed by Rockford, the East St. Louis area, Rock Island and Moline in the Quad Cities region, and Peoria. The leading industrial corporations headquartered in Illinois in 1979 were Standard Oil of Indiana, International Harvester, Beatrice Foods, and Esmark (formerly Swift), all in Chicago; Kraft, in Glenview; and Caterpillar Tractor, in Peoria.

30 COMMERCE
Chicago is the leading wholesaling center of the Midwest. In 1972, the state's 20,085 wholesale establishments employed 251,700 people (3d in the US) and enjoyed sales of $52.1 billion (7.6% of the US total). Chicago is an especially important trade center for furniture, housewares, and apparel.

Retail trade exceeded $39.2 billion (5.4% of the US total) in 1977. The principal retail store groups and their respective shares were automotive dealers, 21%; food stores, 19%; department stores, 11%; eating and drinking places, 9%; and gasoline service stations, 8%. The Chicago metropolitan area accounted for retail sales of $25.2 billion, or 64% of the state total. Leading Chicago retailers as of 1975 were Sears, Roebuck, with 30,000 employees; Jewel (food), 22,000; Montgomery Ward, 15,000; Marshall Field, 14,500; Walgreen (drugs), 9,700; National Tea (groceries), 8,500; Carson Pirie Scott, 6,000; J. C. Penney, 6,000; and Spiegel, 5,500. Except for J. C. Penney, all had their national headquarters in the city.

Exports, especially of soybeans, farm implements, and construction equipment, are of great importance to Illinois. In 1978, 15.1% of the nation's exports and 13.5% of its imports passed through the Chicago customs district, covering most of the Midwest; total trade volume through the district was $45 billion, 2d only to New York. Foreign exports of Illinois's own manufactures reached $6.7 billion (3d in the US) in 1976, while agricultural exports mounted to $2.5 billion (1st) in 1976/77.

31 CONSUMER PROTECTION
Consumer protection became a popular political cause in Illinois during the 1970s. Chicago's consumer commissioner, Jane Byrne, fired for overaggressiveness, used the incident in her successful campaign for the city's mayoralty in 1979.

Statewide, the Office of the Attorney General is the most active protector of consumers. Its Consumer Fraud Section operates 16 offices across the state, and its Consumer Protection Division has 8 offices. The governor controls the Consumer Advocate's Office, and the Department of Insurance also has a Consumer Division. Cook, Madison, and Rock Island counties also have consumer offices, as does the city of Lake Forest.

32 BANKING
Banking was highly controversial in 19th century Illinois. Modernizers stressed the need for adequate venture capital and money supplies, but traditionalist farmers feared they would be impoverished by an artificial "money monster." Efforts to create a state bank floundered in confusion, while the dubious character of most private banknotes inspired the state to ban private banks altogether. The major breakthrough came during the Civil War, when federal laws encouraged the establishment of strong na-

tional banks in all the larger cities, and Chicago quickly became the financial center of the Midwest. Apart from the 1920s and early 1930s, when numerous neighborhood and small-town banks folded, the banking system has flourished ever since.

There were 1,241 commercial banks in Illinois in 1978 (2d only to Texas), an unusually large number attributable to regulations restricting branch banking. Until the 1970s, even the largest banks were allowed only one office. By 1978, commercial banks held $96.8 billion in assets (7.7% of the US total), as well as time deposits of $48.6 billion and demand deposits of $25.6 billion. The largest banks are Continental Illinois, the 7th largest in the US and growing rapidly in mid-1980, with deposits of nearly $26 billion; First National Bank of Chicago (9th), $20.8 billion; Harris Trust and Savings (26th), $4.5 billion; and Northern Trust (32d), $3.9 billion. Many leading world banks have offices in Chicago, and the Federal Reserve district headquarters is of major importance.

In 1978, Illinois had 386 savings and loan associations (234 state-chartered, 152 federally chartered), with total assets of $38.9 billion (3d in the US) and outstanding mortgage loans of $32.2 billion. The largest associations are First Federal, Talman, and Home Federal, all of Chicago, and each with assets of more than $2 billion.

Illinois had 1,102 state-chartered credit unions in 1977. Their assets, exceeding $1.4 billion, belonged to nearly 1.3 million Illinoisans in that year.

33 INSURANCE
Illinois is a major center of the insurance industry, ranking 2d to the New York–Hartford–Newark complex. In 1978, life insurance companies collected $1.9 billion in premiums and paid out $1.8 billion in benefits, including $689.5 million in death benefits and $289.3 million in annuities, to Illinois residents. Illinoisans held 23 million policies, valued at $171 billion, in 1978; the average family had $40,600 in life coverage.

In 1978, 4 of the 89 life insurance companies headquartered in the state had assets of more than $1 billion, though none ranked in the top 20 nationwide. Illinois fire and casualty companies, however, are among the US leaders. State Farm, based in Bloomington, wrote $4.7 billion in premiums in 1978, ranking 1st in its field. Allstate, a Chicago subsidiary of Sears, Roebuck, was 2d nationally with $4 billion in premiums. Inside the state, fire and casualty underwriters wrote premiums totaling $4.8 billion in 1978, including $1.1 billion in automotive liability insurance, $720.7 million in automobile physical damage insurance, and $403.8 million in homeowners' coverage.

Blue Cross–Blue Shield, the nation's largest hospital and medical insurance program, is headquartered in Chicago.

34 SECURITIES
Chicago ranks 2d only to New York as a center for securities trading. The Midwest Stock Exchange, the largest securities exchange outside New York City, has an average monthly volume of 32 million shares. New York Stock Exchange member firms had 181 sales offices and 2,305 registered representatives in Illinois in 1978; state residents reported $1.7 billion in dividend income on their 1977 federal tax returns. Several dozen banks, trust companies, and specialized firms manage tens of billions of dollars of trust, investment, and pension funds.

The most intensive trading in Chicago takes place on the three major commodity exchanges. The Chicago Board of Trade has set agricultural prices for the world since 1848, especially in soybeans, corn, and wheat. The Chicago Mercantile Exchange specializes in pork bellies (bacon), live cattle, potatoes, and eggs; since 1972, it has also provided a market for world currency futures. The Mid-America Commodity Exchange, the smallest of the three, has a colorful ancestry dating back to 1868. It features small-lot futures contracts on soybeans, silver, corn, wheat, and live hogs.

³⁵PUBLIC FINANCE

Among the larger states, Illinois is known for its low taxes and conservative fiscal policy. The Bureau of the Budget, under the governor's control, has major responsibility for the state's overall fiscal program, negotiating annually with key legislators, cabinet officers, and outside pressure groups. The governor then submits the budget to the legislature for amendment and approval; the fiscal year runs from 1 July to 30 June. As in other states, the Illinois budget soared in the 1960s and 1970s, primarily because of planned educational expansion and unexpected increases in welfare payments. The following table summarizes estimated consolidated revenues and expenditures for the 1979 and 1980 fiscal years (in millions):

	1978/79	1979/80
REVENUES		
Sales tax	$ 2,135	$ 2,469
Personal income tax	1,857	2,072
Corporate income tax	535	540
Public utility tax	429	465
Motor fuel tax	438	420
Cigarette tax	180	181
Inheritance tax	140	112
Other taxes	287	287
Federal aid	2,236	2,563
Other receipts and designated funds	3,347	4,499
TOTALS	$11,584	$13,608
EXPENDITURES		
Highways and transportation	$ 2,302	$ 2,855
Primary and secondary education	2,346	2,574
Public welfare	2,282	2,441
Higher education	964	1,057
Capital development	568	608
Mental health	433	475
Environmental protection	315	277
Other outlays	2,374	3,321
TOTALS	$11,584	$13,608

The city of Chicago collected general revenues exceeding $1.23 billion in 1977, of which property taxes supplied 26%, sales taxes 20%, the federal government 20%, and the state government 15%. In the same year, Chicago's expenditures totaled $1.17 billion, of which 27% was spent on police protection. Chicago's budget appears relatively low—less than one-eleventh the size of New York City's in 1977—because it does not include expenditures by the Chicago school board and the welfare agencies of Cook County.

The total debt outstanding for all state and local governments in mid-1977 was $11.7 billion, or $1,043 per capita, slightly below the national average. The state debt was $4.1 billion; the city of Chicago owed $1.4 billion.

³⁶TAXATION

Illinoisans have fiercely resisted the imposition of new and higher taxes. The levying of the first 1% sales tax in 1933 to finance relief programs was bitterly resented, and the inauguration of a state personal income tax in 1970 led to the defeat of Governor Richard Ogilvie in his 1972 reelection campaign. Total state and local revenue in 1977 was $14.4 billion, or $1,277 per capita, 3% below the national average. The tax burden of $174 per $1,000 of personal income ranked 47th among the 50 states; only in Connecticut, Missouri, and Ohio was the relative tax burden lighter.

As of 1980, the state personal income tax was a flat 2.5%. The corporate income tax was 4% and the sales tax 6%, with few exemptions. Excise taxes included charges of 12 cents a pack on cigarettes and 7.5 cents a gallon on gasoline.

Local levies, chiefly property taxes, were relatively light. Indeed, in Chicago the tax burden shrank during the 1970s. Among the nation's 30 largest cities, Chicago ranked 10th in property tax

rates in 1975 ($2.73 per $100) but fell to 23d place in 1977 ($1.71 per $100). The total burden of state and local taxes on a middle-income family in Chicago in 1975 was reckoned at 11.1% of income (6th highest among 30 cities); by 1977, however, the tax burden was only 7.3% (9th lowest), and the effective tax burden on poorer and wealthier families also declined. Three years later, in January 1980, as Chicago's school board faced serious financial problems, Standard & Poor's downgraded the city's bonds from AA to A-plus, citing the use of nonrecurrent revenues to finance operating expenditures.

Low state and local taxes were counterbalanced by high federal payments and a very low return of federal dollars to Illinois. In 1978, $236 of every $1,000 of personal income was sent off to Washington, more than in all but two states (New York and Delaware). The federal government collected $20.4 billion in Illinois in 1975/76, but sent back only $14.4 billion. The net deficit of $6 billion was the highest for any state. Illinoisans filed 4,644,542 federal income tax returns for 1977, paying $10.5 billion in tax.

³⁷ECONOMIC POLICY

The state's policy toward economic development has engendered political controversy since the 1830s. Before the Civil War, the Democrats in power usually tried to slow, though not reverse, the tide of rapid industrial and commercial growth. The Republican ascendancy between the 1850s and the 1930s (with a few brief interruptions) produced a generally favorable business climate, which in turn fostered rapid economic growth. The manufacturing sector eroded slowly in the 1960s and 1970s, as incentives and tax credits for new industry were kept at a modest level.

The Department of Business and Economic Development, describing itself as the "sales department for Illinois," maintains out-of-state offices in Washington, D.C., Brussels, Hong Kong, and São Paulo. The promotion of jobs, tourism, minority-owned enterprises, and foreign markets for Illinois products are the department's major responsibilities.

³⁸HEALTH

In pioneer days, Illinois had a rather insalubrious reputation. The state's many swampy areas harbored malaria, then known as the "Illinois shakes"—a menace that declined late in the 19th century as the swamps and low-lying areas were drained. The cities grew faster than did their sanitation and water purification systems, and bad living conditions exacerbated the medical effects of improper hygiene. Tuberculosis, widespread in the late 19th and early 20th centuries, was the major cause of death and disability during this period. Public health services, strongly promoted by the medical profession, alleviated the threat of most communicable diseases by the 1940s, when penicillin and sulfa drugs finished the job.

Even now, however, health conditions in Illinois do not meet the national norm. Average life expectancy was 70.14 years in 1969–71 (37th in the US); for men the average was 66.48 years, for women 73.96. In 1977, infant mortality was 13 per 1,000 live births for whites and 26 for nonwhites. Although the infant mortality rates declined 40% between 1960 and 1977, they did not decline as rapidly as elsewhere, and since the late 1960s, Illinois has had a slightly higher infant mortality rate than the rest of the country; the 1977 rate among nonwhites was one of the highest in the US. The number of legal abortions climbed rapidly in the 1970s to 72,000 in 1977.

Illinois's marriage and divorce rates were both below the US norms, but the birthrate, 15.8 per 1,000 population in 1977, was marginally higher, as was the death rate, 9.2 per 1,000 residents. The major causes of death in 1977 (with rates per 100,000 population) were heart disease, 382; cancer, 185; stroke, 82; and accidents, 43. Major public health problems in 1980 included rapidly increasing rates of venereal disease and drug abuse. Alcoholism has always been a major problem in Illinois: in 1970, an estimated 5% of the state's adults were alcoholics, the 6th-highest rate in the US. Illinois also had a high proportion of residents receiving psychiatric care; 148,000 persons were treated in 1975, 30% more than the national average.

Hospitals abound in Illinois, with Chicago serving as a diagnostic and treatment center for patients throughout the Midwest. With 285 facilities (many quite large) and 75,484 beds, Illinois hospitals recorded 2,044,783 admissions in 1978. Hospital personnel in 1978 included 35,309 registered nurses and 10,346 licensed practical nurses; the average cost of hospital care in 1977 was $212 per day and $1,694 per stay, well above the US average. The state had 19,592 licensed physicians in 1977 and 5,999 professionally active dentists in 1979.

³⁹SOCIAL WELFARE

Prior to the 1930s, social welfare programs were the province of county government and private agencies. Asylums, particularly poor farms, were built in most counties following the Civil War; they provided custodial care for orphans, the very old, the helpless sick, and itinerant "tramps." Most people who needed help, however, turned to relatives, neighbors, or church agencies. The local and private agencies were overwhelmed by the crisis of the 1930s, forcing first the state and then the federal government to intervene. Social welfare programs are implemented by county agencies, but funded by local and state taxes and federal aid. In 1976, the total outlay for the five largest welfare programs was $2.2 billion, of which the federal government paid 57%, a lower share than for most states, even though the benefits actually received by state residents exceeded national norms.

In 1975, 578,000 children and 225,000 adults received aid to families with dependent children; by 1978, the totals had fallen to 485,000 children and 199,000 adults. Payments, however, increased from $275 million to $698 million during the same period. The food stamp program aided 827,000 persons in 1978, at a federal cost of $284.6 million, while the school lunch program reached 1,124,000 students, with federal outlays totaling $74.1 million. Social Security monthly payments averaged $257.50 for the state's 1,051,000 retired workers; the total paid to all beneficiaries was $4.3 billion. In 1978, disability benefits were paid to 85,300 persons at an average of $136 per month; total Supplemental Security Income payments of $201 million covered 160,000 disabled, aged, and blind persons. Vocational rehabilitation cost $35 million in 1978, and outlays for workers' compensation totaled $395 million in 1977. Unemployment insurance is slightly more generous in Illinois than in most other states: the total payout in 1978 was $690 million, for an average weekly benefit of $97.68 to eligible Illinoisans.

⁴⁰HOUSING

Flimsy cabins and shacks provided rude shelter for many Illinoisans in pioneer days. Later, the balloon-frame house, much cheaper to build than traditional structures, became a trademark of the Prairie State. After a third of Chicago's wooden houses burned in 1871, the city moved to enforce more stringent building codes. The city's predominant dwelling then became the three- or five-story brick apartment house. Great mansions were built in elite areas of Chicago (first Prairie Avenue, later the Gold Coast), and high-rise lakefront luxury apartments first became popular in the 1920s. In the 1970s, Chicago pioneered the conversion of luxury apartment buildings to condominiums, which brought handsome profits to developers and residents alike.

The 1970 census counted 3,693,000 housing units in Illinois, of which 3,502,000 were occupied; of these, more than 59% were owner-occupied (below the ratio for both the Midwest and the US as a whole) and all but 4% had full plumbing. New housing starts fluctuated with economic conditions and mortgage rates during the 1970s. Between 1976 and 1978, more than 207,000 new units worth nearly $7 billion were authorized. Public hous-

ing, serving primarily poor blacks and elderly whites in Chicago, was enmeshed in controversy and court cases throughout the decade, and few new units were built.

⁴¹EDUCATION

The pioneers did not see much use in book learning, and arithmetic was not needed for a subsistence economy. Thus, until the Yankee reformers in the Republican Party secured power in the mid-1850s, there was little public effort to support education. Once in office, the reformers helped create an outstanding public school system in Chicago, although until foreign immigration subsided in the 1920s, the city was hard-pressed to construct enough school buildings to serve the growing numbers of students. Rural Illinois clung to its system of one-room schoolhouses until state-mandated consolidation in the 1940s created large modern schools to which students were bused. By the 1960s, the Chicago public schools had begun to deteriorate, and the system verged on bankruptcy in 1979/80. The suburban school districts outside the city, however, remained among the finest in the US as the 1980s began.

Illinois's adult illiteracy rate was only 0.9% at the 1970 census. Literacy was virtually universal in 1980, though careful studies showed a fourth of the state's adults were "functionally illiterate"—that is, unable to comprehend simple written forms. In 1976, two-thirds of the adult population held high school diplomas, fewer than 3% had less than four years of grade school, and nearly 14% had at least four years of college; school years completed by Illinois adults reached a median of 12.5.

In 1977, Illinois had 3,155 public elementary schools, 1,276 high schools, and 113 schools for the handicapped. Enrollment at the elementary level slipped from 1,539,000 in 1975 to 1,419,000 in 1978; enrollment at the secondary level declined less dramatically from 731,000 in 1975 to 720,000 in 1978. Out of all public school students, 599,300 belonged to minority groups. Of these, 59% were in schools with 90–100% minority enrollment. Chicago schools remained heavily segregated, despite persistent pressure by state and federal officials. Nonpublic schools, dominated by Chicago's extensive Roman Catholic school system, declined sharply in the 1970s. Total enrollment fell from 398,000 to 261,000 between 1975 and 1977. Rising tuition fees, caused in part by higher salaries for lay teachers and a drop in the number of teaching sisters, threatened the parochial schools in the late 1970s. High-tuition private schools continued to flourish in Chicago, however.

Illinois has always been well endowed with colleges. In 1977 there were 56 public and 87 private colleges with some 616,000 students. The Board of Higher Education, created in 1961, attempts to coordinate the crazy-quilt pattern of public university systems. The largest system, the University of Illinois, operates three major campuses—Champaign-Urbana, Chicago Circle, and the Chicago Medical Center—plus branch medical schools in Peoria and Rockford. Known for its leadership in science and engineering, the system operated with an $880 million budget in 1978/79, of which $84 million came from federal grants and contracts. In addition, the state supports Southern Illinois University (with campuses in Carbondale and Edwardsville), Chicago State University, Eastern Illinois University (Charleston), Governors State University (Park Forest South), Northeastern Illinois University (Chicago), Western Illinois University (Macomb), Illinois State University (Normal), Northern Illinois University (De Kalb), and Sangamon State University (Springfield). A flourishing community college network, within easy commuting range of nearly every student, was built up primarily in the 1960s. Major private universities, all in the Chicago area, include the University of Chicago, Northwestern University (Evanston), Illinois Institute of Technology, and Loyola University. Each maintains undergraduate and research programs, as well as nationally recognized professional schools. The Illinois State Scholarship Commission administers general grant and guaranteed loan programs, as well as special awards for the children of firemen and policemen killed in the line of duty, of deceased correctional workers, and of prisoners of war and those missing in action.

Illinois spends heavily for its public elementary and secondary schools. In 1978, per capita school expenditures reached $437, far above the national average of $375 (though not disproportionate to the state's high per capita income). The 1970 constitution gives the state government primary responsibility for the public school system, a mandate that was put to the test in efforts to save the Chicago public schools from financial collapse. Chicago spent $2,594 per student in 1978/79; the remainder of the state spent only $1,870.

⁴²ARTS

Chicago emerged in the late 19th century as the leading arts center of the Midwest, and it continues to hold this premier position. The major downstate facilities include the Krannert Center at the University of Illinois (Champaign-Urbana) and the Lakeview Center in Peoria.

Architecture is the outstanding art form in Illinois, and Chicago—where the first skyscrapers were built in the 1880s—has been a mecca for modern commercial and residential architects ever since the fire of 1871. The Art Institute of Chicago, incorporated in 1879, is the leading art museum in the state. Although its holdings, largely donated by wealthy Chicagoans, cover all the major periods, its French Impressionist collection is especially noteworthy.

Theater groups abound, notably in Chicago, where the Second City comedy troupe has spawned many well-known entertainers; the city's best playwrights and performers, however, usually gravitate to Broadway or Hollywood. The state has some 6,000 cinemas, some housed in ornate palaces. Film production was an important industry in Illinois before 1920, when operations shifted to the sunnier climate and more opulent production facilities of Southern California.

The Chicago Symphony Orchestra, organized by Theodore Thomas in 1891, quickly acquired world stature; its permanent conductors have included Frederick Stock, Fritz Reiner, and Sir Georg Solti. German immigrants founded many musical societies in Chicago in the late 19th century, when the city also became a major center of musical education. Opera flourished in Chicago in the early 20th century, collapsed during the early 1930s, but was reborn through the founding of the Lyric Opera in 1954. Chicago's most original musical contribution was jazz, imported from the South by black musicians in the 1920s. Such jazz greats as King Oliver, Louis Armstrong, Jelly Roll Morton, Benny Goodman, and Gene Krupa all worked or learned their craft in the speakeasies and jazz houses of the city's South Side. More recently, Chicago became the center of an urban blues movement, using electric rather than acoustic guitars and influenced by jazz.

The seamy side of Chicago has fascinated writers throughout the 20th century. Among well-known American novels set in Chicago are two muckraking works, Frank Norris's *The Pit* (1903) and Upton Sinclair's *The Jungle* (1906), as well as James T. Farrell's *Studs Lonigan* (1935) and Saul Bellow's *The Adventures of Augie March* (1953). Famous American plays also associated with Chicago are *The Front Page* (1928), by Ben Hecht and Charles MacArthur, and *A Raisin in the Sun* (1959), by Lorraine Hansberry.

⁴³LIBRARIES AND MUSEUMS

Libraries and library science are particularly strong in Illinois. In 1978 there were some 500 public libraries, nearly all of them members of 18 regional systems; by 1977/78, the state's public libraries had a combined book stock of 22,887,286. The facilities in Peoria, Oak Park, Evanston, Rockford, and Quincy are noteworthy, but the Chicago Public Library (which operates 77 neigh-

borhood branches) is hampered by an inadequate central library crowded into an old warehouse. The outstanding libraries of the University of Illinois (Champaign-Urbana) and the University of Chicago (with 5,622,938 and 4,019,470 volumes, respectively) constitute the state's leading research facilities; both universities have famous library schools. Principal historical collections are at the Newberry Library in Chicago, the Illinois State Historical Society in Springfield, and the Chicago Historical Society.

Illinois has at least 140 museums and historic sites. Chicago's Field Museum of Natural History, founded in 1893, has sponsored numerous worldwide expeditions in the course of acquiring some 13 million anthropological, zoological, botanical, and geological specimens. The Museum of Science and Industry, near the University of Chicago, attracts 5 million visitors a year, mostly children, to see its exhibits of industrial technology. Also noteworthy are the Adler Planetarium, Shedd Aquarium, and the Oriental Institute Museum of the University of Chicago. The Brookfield Zoo, near Chicago, opened in 1934; smaller zoos can be found in Chicago's Lincoln Park and in Peoria, Elgin, and other cities.

Just about every town has one or more historic sites authenticated by the state. The most popular is New Salem, near Springfield, where Abraham Lincoln lived from 1831· to 1837. Its reconstruction was begun by press magnate William Randolph Hearst in 1906 and includes one original cabin and numerous replicas. The most important archaeological sites are the Dixon Mounds, 40 mi (64 km) south of Peoria, and the Koster Excavation in Calhoun County, north of St. Louis.

⁴⁴COMMUNICATIONS

Illinois has an extensive communications system. The US Postal Service has some 46,000 employees in Illinois, and its largest single facility is located in Chicago, which ranked 2d only to New York City·in postal receipts in 1977/78, with $451.7 million. The state's ratio of 87 telephones per 100 people is one of the highest in the nation; in all, there were 9,792,452 telephones (2,477,513 business, 7,314,939 residential) in 1978, when Illinoisans made 12.6 billion local calls and more than 1.1 billion toll calls. The Bell System, which owned 83% of the phones in 1978, has its major manufacturing operation near Chicago.

There were 125 AM and 129 FM commercial radio stations in Illinois in 1978; 22 television stations served the metropolitan areas. The rapid growth of cable systems—in 1978, 98 systems served 402,461 subscribers in 236 communities—has brought good television reception to the small towns. In 1979, WGN-TV in Chicago became a "superstation," with sports programs, movies, and advertising beamed to cable systems across the country. Although the three major networks own stations in Chicago, they originate very little programming from the city. However, as a major advertising center, Chicago produces many commercials and industrial films. Educational broadcasting is badly underdeveloped in Illinois; most local programming comes from state universities and the Chicago public and Catholic school systems.

⁴⁵PRESS

The state's first newspaper, the *Illinois Herald*, was begun in Kaskaskia in 1814. From the 1830s through the end of the 19th century, small-town weeklies exerted powerful political influence. After 1900, however, publishers discovered that they needed large circulations to appeal to advertisers, and so toned down their partisanship and began adding a broad range of features to attract a wider audience.

As of 1978, Illinois had 22 morning newspapers (including all-day papers), with a combined paid circulation of 1,868,960; 70 evening dailies, with 1,493,358, and 22 Sunday papers, with 2,761,788. The Illinois editions of St. Louis papers are also widely read. The following table shows the leading dailies with their 1978 circulation:

AREA	NAME	DAILY	SUNDAY
Chicago	Sun-Times (m,S)	683,573	719,577
	Tribune (all day, S)	793,672	1,139,074
Peoria	Journal Star (all day, S)	103,096	119,863
Rockford	Register Star (all day, S)	54,523	76,346
Springfield	State Journal-Register (m,e,S)	57,820 } 14,043 }	72,786

The most popular magazine published in Chicago is *Playboy*, with a circulation of 5,538,559 as of 1979. *Ebony* magazine, with a circulation of about 1,300,000, also is based in that city. Many specialized trade and membership magazines, such as the *Lion* and the *Rotarian*, are published in Chicago, which is the printing and circulation center for many magazines edited in New York.

⁴⁶ORGANIZATIONS
Before the Civil War, Yankee-dominated towns and cities in northern Illinois sponsored lyceums, debating circles, women's clubs, temperance groups, and antislavery societies. During the 20th century, Chicago's size and central location attracted the headquarters of numerous national organizations, though far fewer than New York or, more recently, Washington, D.C. Major national service and fraternal bodies headquartered in Chicago or nearby suburbs include the Benevolent and Protective Order of Elks of the USA, International Association of Lions Clubs, Loyal Order of Moose, Rotary International, Ancient Arabic Order of the Nobles of the Mystic Shrine (the Shriners), and Kiwanis International.

Chicago has long been a center for professional organizations, among them the most powerful single US medical group, the American Medical Association, founded in 1847, and the American Hospital Association, begun in 1898. Other major groups include associations of surgeons, dentists, veterinarians, osteopaths, and dietitians, as well as the Blue Cross Association and the Easter Seals Society. The American Bar Association has its headquarters in Chicago, as do several smaller legal groups, including the American Judicature Society and Commercial Law League of America. Librarians also have a base in Chicago: the American Library Association, the Society of American Archivists, and the associations of law and medical librarians. The National Parent-Teacher Association is the only major educational group.

A variety of trade organizations, such as the National Restaurant Association, are based in Chicago, though many have moved to Washington, D.C., in recent decades. The American Farm Bureau Federation operates out of Park Ridge. The National Women's Christian Temperance Union, one of the most important of all US pressure groups in the 19th century, has its headquarters in Evanston.

⁴⁷TOURISM, TRAVEL, AND RECREATION
The tourist industry is of special importance to Chicago, the nation's leading convention center. The city's chief tourist attractions are its museums, restaurants, and shops; Chicago also boasts the world's tallest building, the Sears Tower, 110 stories and 1,454 feet (443 meters) high.

For the state as a whole, tourism is a multibillion-dollar enterprise; in 1976, the state had 2,246 public and 277 private parks, together with 16,000 camp sites, 174 beaches, 410 public swimming pools, and 9,400 mooring slips for boats in hundreds of marinas. Swimming, bicycling, hiking, camping, horseback riding, fishing, and motorboating are the most popular recreational activities. Licenses were issued to 718,841 fishermen and 422,579 hunters in 1977/78. More popular than hunting was wildlife observation, an activity that engaged some 2,700,000 Illinoisans in 1977.

⁴⁸SPORTS
Illinois is moderately sport-conscious, but its teams seldom win championships. As of 1980, the Chicago Bears had not won a National Footbal League championship since 1963. The Chicago White Sox last won the American League pennant in 1959 and a World Series in 1917; the Cubs, also representing Chicago, last won the National League pennant in 1945 and the World Series in 1908. The Chicago Bulls won a National Basketball Association divisional championship in 1975, but lost the playoffs; the city's other major teams, the Black Hawks of the National Hockey League and the Sting of the North American Soccer League, also frustrated their fans during the 1970s. The major stadiums in Illinois tend to be old, smallish structures; Wrigley Field, home of the Cubs, still lacks lights for night games.

Horse racing has been profitable (for the owners and a few politicians) since Chicago's first meet was held in 1845. Gambling, both legal and illegal, flourishes, with the pari-mutuel handle approaching $1 billion.

Colleges and high schools offer full sports programs, with the emphasis on football and basketball. The Fighting Illini of the University of Illinois and the Wildcats of Northwestern compete in Big Ten football, neither with much success during the 1970s. In basketball, the Salukis of Southern Illinois won the National Invitation Tournament in 1967, and the DePaul Blue Demons were highly ranked in 1979/80 and 1980/81.

⁴⁹FAMOUS ILLINOISANS
Abraham Lincoln (b.Kentucky, 1809–65), 16th president of the US, is the outstanding figure in Illinois history, having lived and built his political career in the state between 1830 and 1861. The only Illinois native to be elected president is Ronald Reagan (b.1911), who left the state after graduating from Eureka College to pursue his film and political careers in California. Ulysses S. Grant (b.Ohio, 1822–85), the nation's 18th president, lived in Galena on the eve of the Civil War. Adlai E. Stevenson (b.Kentucky, 1835–1914), founder of a political dynasty, served as US vice president from 1893 to 1897, but was defeated for the same office in 1900; his grandson, also named Adlai E. Stevenson (b.California, 1900–65), served as governor of Illinois from 1949 to 1953, was the Democratic presidential nominee in 1952 and 1956, and ended his career as US ambassador to the United Nations. Charles Gates Dawes (b.Ohio, 1865–1951), a Chicago financier, served as vice president from 1925 to 1929 and shared the 1925 Nobel Peace Prize for the Dawes Plan to reorganize German finances. William Jennings Bryan (1860–1925), a leader of the free-silver and Populist movements, was the Democratic presidential nominee in 1896, 1900, and 1908.

US Supreme Court justices associated with Illinois have included David Davis (b.Maryland, 1815–86); Chicago-born Arthur Goldberg (b.1908), who also served as secretary of labor and succeeded Stevenson as UN ambassador; and John Paul Stevens (b.1920). Melville Fuller (b.Maine, 1833–1910) served as chief justice from 1888 to 1910.

Many other politicians who played important roles on the national scene drew their support from the people of Illinois. They included Stephen Douglas (b.Vermont, 1813–61), senator from 1847 to 1861, Democratic Party leader, 1860 presidential candidate, but equally famous as Lincoln's opponent in a series of debates over slavery in 1858; Lyman Trumbull (b.Connecticut, 1813–96), senator from 1855 to 1873, who helped secure passage of the 13th and 14th amendments to the US Constitution; Joseph "Uncle Joe" Cannon (b.North Carolina, 1836–1926), Republican congressman from Danville for half a century and autocratic speaker of the House from 1903 to 1911; Henry Rainey (1860–1934), Democratic speaker of the House during 1933–34; Everett McKinley Dirksen (1896–1969), senator and colorful Republican leader during the 1950s and 1960s; Charles Percy (b.Florida, 1919), Republican senator since 1967; John B. Anderson (b.1922), Republican congressman for 20 years and an independent presidential candidate in 1980; and Robert Michel (b.1923) who became House Republican leader in 1981.

Noteworthy governors of the state, in addition to Stevenson, have included Richard Yates (b.Kentucky, 1815–73), who maintained Illinois's loyalty to the Union during the Civil War; John Peter Altgeld (b.Germany, 1847–1902), governor from 1893 to 1897; and Republican-Progressive leader Frank Lowden (b.Minnesota, 1861–1943). Richard J. Daley (1902–76) was Democratic boss and mayor of Chicago from 1955 to 1976. Jane Byrne (b.1934), a Daley protégée, became mayor in 1979. Phyllis Schlafly (b.Missouri, 1924) of Alton became nationally known as an antifeminist conservative crusader during the 1970s.

An outstanding Illinoisan was Jane Addams (1860–1935), founder of Hull House (1889), author, reformer, prohibitionist, feminist, and tireless worker for world peace; in 1931, she shared the Nobel Peace Prize. Winners of the Nobel Prize in physics included Albert Michelson (b.Germany, 1852–1931), Robert Millikan (1868–1953), Arthur Holly Compton (b.Ohio, 1892–1962), Enrico Fermi (b.Italy, 1901–54), John Bardeen (b.Wisconsin, 1908), and James W. Cronin (b.1931). Chemistry prizes went to Robert Mulliken (b.Massachusetts, 1896), Wendell Stanley (b.Indiana, 1904), and Willard Libby (b.Colorado, 1908). Nobel Prizes in physiology or medicine were won by Charles Huggins (b.Canada, 1901) and George Beadle (b.Nebraska, 1903). A Nobel award in literature went to Saul Bellow (b.Canada, 1915), and the economics prize was given to Milton Friedman (b.New York, 1912), leader of the so-called Chicago school of economists, and to Theodore Schultz (b.South Dakota, 1902) in 1979. Except for Addams, Dawes, and Bardeen, all the Nobel laureates associated with Illinois were on the University of Chicago faculty at one time or another.

Some of the most influential Illinoisans have been religious leaders; many of them also exercised social and political influence. Notable are Methodist circuit rider Peter Cartwright (b.Virginia, 1785–1872); Dwight Moody (b.Massachusetts, 1837–99), the foremost evangelist of his day; Frances Willard (b.New York, 1839–98), leading force in the National Women's Christian Temperance Union and the feminist cause; Mother Frances Xavier Cabrini (b.Italy, 1850–1917), the first American to be canonized; Elijah Muhammad (Elijah Poole, b.Georgia, 1897–1975), leader of the Black Muslim movement; and Jesse Jackson (b.North Carolina, 1941), civil rights leader and one of the most prominent black spokesmen as the 1980s began.

Outstanding business and professional leaders who lived in Illinois include John Deere (b.Vermont, 1804–86), industrialist and inventor of the steel plow; Cyrus Hall McCormick (b.Virginia, 1809–84), inventor of the reaping machine; Nathan Davis (1817–1904), the "father of the American Medical Association"; railroad car inventor George Pullman (b.New York, 1831–97); meat-packer Philip Armour (b.New York, 1832–1901); merchant Marshall Field (b.Massachusetts, 1834–1906); merchant Aaron Montgomery Ward (b.New Jersey, 1843–1913); William Rainey Harper (b.Ohio, 1856–1906), first president of the University of Chicago; lawyer Clarence Darrow (b.Ohio, 1857–1938); public utilities magnate Samuel Insull (b.England, 1859–1938); Julius Rosenwald (1862–1932), philanthropist and executive of Sears, Roebuck; advertising executive Albert Lasker (b.Texas, 1880–1952); and *Chicago Tribune* publisher Robert R. McCormick (1880–1955).

Artists who worked for significant periods in Illinois (usually in Chicago), include architects William Le Baron Jenney (b.Massachusetts, 1832–1907), Dankmar Adler (b.Germany, 1844–1900), Daniel H. Burnham (b.New York, 1846–1912), John Wellborn Root (b.Georgia, 1850–91), Louis Sullivan (b.Massachusetts, 1856–1924), Frank Lloyd Wright (b.Wisconsin, 1869–1959), and Ludwig Miës van der Rohe (b.Germany, 1886–1969). Important writers include humorist Finley Peter Dunne (1867–1936), creator of the fictional saloonkeeper-philosopher Mr. Dooley; and novelists Hamlin Garland (b.Wis-

consin, 1860–1940), John Dos Passos (1896–1970), and Ernest Hemingway (1899–1961). Poets include Harriet Monroe (1860–1936); Edgar Lee Masters (b.Kansas, 1869–1950); biographer-poet Carl Sandburg (1878–1967); Nicholas Vachel Lindsay (1879–1931); Archibald MacLeish (b.1892), also Librarian of Congress and assistant secretary of state; and Gwendolyn Brooks (b.Kansas, 1917), the first black woman to win a Pulitzer Prize. Performing artists connected with the state include opera stars Mary Garden (b.Scotland, 1877–1967) and Sherrill Milnes (b.1935); clarinetist Benny Goodman (b.1909); pop singers Mel Torme (b.1925) and Grace Slick (b.1939); showmen Gower Champion (1921–80) and Robert Louis "Bob" Fosse (b.1927); comedians Harvey Korman (b.1927), Bob Newhart (b.1929), and Richard Pryor (b.1940); and a long list of stage and screen stars, including Gloria Swanson (b.1899), Ralph Bellamy (b.1904), Robert Young (b.1907), Karl Malden (Malden Sekulovich, b.1913), William Holden (b.1918), Jason Robards, Jr. (b.1922), Charlton Heston (b.1924), Rock Hudson (Roy Fitzgerald, b.1925), Donald O'Connor (b.1925), and Bruce Dern (b.1936).

Dominant figures in the Illinois sports world in recent decades have included Ernest "Ernie" Banks (b.Texas, 1931) of the Chicago Cubs; Robert "Bobby" Hull (b.Canada, 1939) of the Chicago Black Hawks; owner George Halas (b.1895) and running backs Harold Edward "Red" Grange (b.Pennsylvania, 1903), Gale Sayers (b.Kansas, 1943) and Walter Payton (b.Mississippi, 1954) of the Chicago Bears; and collegiate football coach Amos Alonzo Stagg (b.New Jersey, 1862–1965).

[50] BIBLIOGRAPHY

Allen, John W. *Legends and Lore of Southern Illinois*. Carbondale: Southern Illinois University Press, 1963.

Bluhm, Elaine (ed.). *Illinois Archaeology*. Urbana: University of Illinois Press, 1964.

Bluhm, Elaine (ed.). *Illinois Prehistory*. Urbana: University of Illinois Press, 1963.

Clayton, John. *The Illinois Fact Book and Historical Almanac, 1673–1968*. Carbondale: Southern Illinois University Press, 1970.

Crane, Edgar G. *Illinois: Political Processes and Governmental Performance*. Dubuque: Kendall-Hunt, 1980.

Cutler, Irving. *Chicago: Metropolis of the Mid-Continent*. Dubuque: Kendall-Hunt, 1976.

Drake, St. Clair, and Horace Cayton. *Black Metropolis*. New York: Harcourt Brace, 1970.

Federal Writers' Project. *Illinois: A Descriptive and Historical Guide*. Rev. ed. New York: Hastings House, 1974 (orig. 1939).

Howard, Robert P. *Illinois: A History of the Prairie State*. Grand Rapids, Mich.: Eerdmans, 1972.

Illinois, State of. Department of Business and Economic Development. *Illinois Data Book, 1978*. Springfield, 1979.

Illinois, State of. Secretary of State. *Illinois Blue Book, 1979–80*. Springfield, 1980.

Jensen, Richard J. *Illinois: A Bicentennial History*. New York: Norton, 1978.

Kenney, David. *Basic Illinois Government*. Carbondale: Southern Illinois University Press, 1974.

Kilian, Michael, Connie Fisher, and F. Richard Ciccone. *Who Runs Chicago?* New York: St. Martin, 1979.

Koeper, Frederick. *Illinois Architecture from Territorial Times to the Present*. Chicago: University of Chicago Press, 1978.

Nelson, Ronald E. *Illinois: Land and Life in the Prairie State*. Dubuque: Kendall-Hunt, 1978.

Sutton, Robert P., (ed.). *The Prairie State*. 2 vols. Grand Rapids, Mich.: Eerdmans, 1976.

Walton, Clyde (ed.). *An Illinois Reader*. De Kalb, Ill.: Northern Illinois University Press, 1970.

Wheeler, Adade, and Marlene Wortman. *The Roads They Made: Women in Illinois History*. Chicago: Kerr, 1977.

INDIANA

State of Indiana

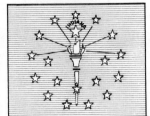

ORIGIN OF STATE NAME: Named "land of Indians" for the many Indian tribes that formerly lived in the state. **NICKNAME**: The Hoosier State. **CAPITAL**: Indianapolis. **ENTERED UNION**: 11 December 1816 (19th). **SONG**: "On the Banks of the Wabash, Far Away." **MOTTO**: The Crossroads of America. **FLAG**: A flaming torch representing liberty is surrounded by 19 gold stars against a blue backgound. The word "Indiana" is above the flame. **OFFICIAL SEAL**: In a pioneer setting, a farmer fells a tree while a buffalo flees from the forest and across the prairie; in the background, the sun sets over distant hills. The words "Seal of the State of Indiana 1816" surround the scene. **BIRD**: Cardinal. **FLOWER**: Peony. **TREE**: Tulip tree (yellow poplar). **STONE**: Indiana limestone. **POEM**: "Indiana." **LEGAL HOLIDAYS**: New Year's Day, 1 January; Lincoln's Birthday, 12 February; Washington's Birthday, 3d Monday in February; Good Friday, March or April; Primary Election Day, Tuesday after 1st Monday in May in even-numbered years; Memorial Day, last Monday in May; Independence Day, 4 July; Labor Day, 1st Monday in September; Columbus Day, 2d Monday in October; Election Day, 1st Tuesday after 1st Monday in November in even-numbered years; Veterans Day, 11 November; Thanksgiving Day, 4th Thursday in November; Christmas Day, 25 December. **TIME**: 7 A.M. EST = noon GMT; 6 A.M. CST = noon GMT.

¹LOCATION, SIZE, AND EXTENT

Situated in the eastern north-central US, Indiana is the smallest of the 12 midwestern states and ranks 38th in size among the 50 states.

Indiana's total area is 36,291 sq mi (93,994 sq km), of which land takes up 36,097 (93,491 sq km) and water the remaining 194 sq mi (502 sq km). Shaped somewhat like a vertical quadrangle, with irregular borders on the s and w, the state extends about 160 mi (257 km) E–W and about 280 mi (451 km) N–S.

Indiana is bordered on the N by Michigan (with part of the line passing through Lake Michigan); on the E by Ohio; on the SE and s by Kentucky (the entire line formed by the north bank of the Ohio River); and on the w by Illinois (with the line in the sw demarcated by the Wabash River). The total boundary length of Indiana is 1,696 mi (2,729 km).

Indiana's geographical center is located in Boone County, 14 mi (23 km) NNW of Indianapolis.

²TOPOGRAPHY

Indiana has two principal types of terrain: slightly rolling land in the northern half of the state and rugged hills in the southern, extending to the Ohio River. The highest point in the state, a hill near Lynn (Randolph County) on the eastern boundary, is 1,257 feet (383 meters) above sea level; the lowest point, on the Ohio River, is 320 feet (98 meters). The richest soil is in the north-central region, where the retreating glacier during the last Ice Age enriched the soil, scooped out lakes, and cut passageways for rivers.

Four-fifths of the state's land is drained by the Wabash River, which flows westward across the north-central region and turns southward to empty into the Ohio, and by its tributaries, the White, Eel, Mississinewa, and Tippecanoe rivers. The northern region is drained by the Maumee River, which flows into Lake Erie at Toledo, Ohio, and by the Kankakee River, which joins the Illinois River in Illinois. In the southwest, the two White River forks empty into the Wabash, and in the southeast, the Whitewater River flows into the Ohio.

In addition to Lake Michigan on the northwestern border, there are more than 400 lakes in the northern part of the state. The largest lakes include Wawasee, Maxinkuchee, Freeman, and Shafer. There are mineral springs at French Lick and West Baden in Orange County, and two large caves, at Wyandotte and Marengo, are located in adjoining Crawford County.

The underlying rock strata found in Indiana are sedimentary, atop which are rocks formed during the Paleozoic era, when the land was submerged. About 400 million years ago, the first uplift of land, the Cincinnati arch, divided the Indiana region into two basins, a small one in the north and a large one in the southwest. The land was steadily elevated and at one time formed a lush swamp, which dried up some 200 million years ago when the climate cooled. During the Ice Ages, about five-sixths of the land lay under ice some 2,000 feet (600 meters) thick. The retreat of the glacier more than 10,000 years ago left excellent topsoil and drainage conditions in Indiana.

³CLIMATE

Indiana has a humid continental climate, marked by distinct seasons.

Temperatures vary widely from the extreme north to the extreme south of the state; the annual mean temperature is 53°F (12°C)—49°F (9°C) in the north and 57°F (14°C) in the south. Although Indiana sometimes has temperatures below 0°F (–18°C) during the winter, the average temperatures in January range between 22°F(–6°C) and 39°F (4°C). Average temperatures during July vary from 63°F (17°C) to 88°F (31°C). The highest recorded temperature was 116°F (47°C) at Collegeville on 14 July 1936; the lowest was –35°F (–37°C) at Greensburg on 2 February 1951.

The growing season averages 155 days in the north and 185 days in the south. Rainfall is distributed fairly evenly throughout the year, although drought sometimes occurs in the southern region. The average annual precipitation in the state is 40 in (102 cm), ranging from about 35 in (89 cm) near Lake Michigan to 45 in (114 cm) along the Ohio River. The annual snowfall averages less than 22 in (56 cm). Average wind speed in the state is 8 mph (13 km/hr), but gales occur occasionally along the shores of Lake Michigan, and there are infrequent tornadoes in the interior.

⁴FLORA AND FAUNA

Because the state has a relatively uniform climate, plant species are distributed fairly generally throughout Indiana. There are 124 native tree species, including 17 varieties of oak, as well as black walnut, sycamore, and tulip tree (yellow poplar), the state tree. Fruit trees—apple, cherry, peach, and pear—are common.

Local indigenous species—now reduced because of industrialization and urbanization—are the persimmon, black gum, and southern cypress along the Ohio River; tamarack and bog willow in the northern marsh; and white pine, sassafras, and pawpaw near Lake Michigan. American elderberry and bittersweet are common shrubs, while various jack-in-the-pulpits and spring beauties are among the indigenous wild flowers. The peony is the state flower. Mountain laurel is considered threatened, the prairie white-fringed orchid endangered.

Although the presence of wolves and coyotes has been reported occasionally, the red fox is Indiana's only common carnivorous mammal. Other native mammals include the common cottontail, muskrat, raccoon, opposum, and several types of squirrel. Many waterfowl and marsh birds, including the black duck and great blue heron, inhabit northern Indiana, while the field sparrow, yellow warbler, and red-headed woodpecker nest in central Indiana. Various catfish, pike, bass, and sunfish are native to state waters.

The state provides protection for the following animals, considered to be rare and endangered: bobcat, badger, otter, Indiana bat, gray myotis, southeastern myotis, and big-eared bat. In keeping with federal statutes, Indiana lists as endangered the eastern timber wolf, Arctic peregrine falcon, Kirtland's warbler, bald eagle, longjaw cisco, and eight types of mussel.

[5] ENVIRONMENTAL PROTECTION
During the 19th century, early settlers cut down much of Indiana's forests for farms, leaving the land vulnerable to soil erosion and flood damage, particularly in the southern part of the state. In 1919, the legislature created the State Department of Conservation (which in 1965 became the Department of Natural Resources) to reclaim worn-out soil, prevent further erosion, and control pollution of rivers and streams. In 1934, the state's newly created Natural Resources Planning Board (now the Natural Resources Commission) made a survey of soil, water, forest, and mineral conditions and outlined conservation practices for their proper future use.

The Department of Natural Resources regulates the use of Indiana's lands, water, forests, and minerals. Specifically, the department manages land subject to flooding, preserves natural rivers and streams, grants mining permits and regulates strip-mining, plugs and repairs faulty oil or gas wells, administers existing state parks and preserves and buys land for new ones, and registers motorboats and snowmobiles. Also, the department is responsible for preventing soil erosion and flood damage, and for conserving and disposing of water in the state's watersheds. In 1978/79, the Department of Natural Resources expended for the above and other purposes an estimated total of $28.7 million, including $3.2 million in federal funds.

Other state agencies assist the department in protecting the environment. In 1972, an 11-member Environmental Management Board was created to coordinate air and water pollution control programs and to serve as the final authority for other environmental activities, including purification of drinking water and disposal of solid wastes. A Pesticide Review Board classifies pesticides according to their use and regulates their handling.

[6] POPULATION
In mid-1978, Indiana had an estimated population of 5,374,000 and ranked 12th in population among the 50 states.

Although the French founded the first European settlement in Indiana in 1717, the census population was no more than 5,641 in 1800, when the Indiana Territory was established. Settlers flocked to the state during the territorial period, and the population rose to 24,520 by 1810 and to 147,178 by 1820. After Indiana became a state, its population grew even more rapidly, quadrupling during the 1820s and 1830s to reach 988,416 by 1850. At the outbreak of the Civil War, Indiana had 1,350,428 inhabitants and ranked 6th in population among the states.

Indiana was relatively untouched by the great waves of European immigration that swept the US from 1860 to 1880. In 1880, when the state's population was 1,978,301, Indiana had fewer foreign-born residents (about 7% of its population) than any other northern state. Indiana doubled its 1900 population to 5,193,669 at the 1970 census; preliminary census results for 1980 showed a population of 5,454,154, a 10-year growth of 5%.

Of the 1970 census population, 65% lived in urban areas and 35% resided in rural areas; 51% was female and 49% male. In 1970, the state's population density was 144 persons per sq mi (56 per sq km), and the median age was 27.2 years. From 1970 to 1977, Indiana had 628,000 live births and 349,000 deaths; the state also lost some 144,000 people through migration. By 1978, about 30% of the population was below the age of 18, 60% was between the ages of 19 and 64, and 10% was 65 years and older.

Indianapolis, the capital and largest city, expanded its boundaries in 1970 to coincide with those of Marion County. It thereby increased its area to 388 sq mi (1,005 sq km) and its population by some 50%. Preliminary data from the 1980 census gave a population count of 695,040 (the city and county limits also include four self-governing communities). Other cities with 1976 populations of more than 100,000 were Fort Wayne, 183,039; Gary, 163,675; Evansville, 133,609; South Bend, 114,103; and Hammond, 107,983. Thirteen other cities in 1976 had populations in excess of 35,000, and 96 cities and 4 towns had populations of more than 10,000.

[7] ETHNIC GROUPS
Originally an agricultural state, Indiana was settled by native Americans moving west, by a small group of French Creoles, and by European immigrant farmers. Although railroad building and industrialization attracted other immigrant groups—notably the Irish, Hungarians, Italians, Poles, Croats, Slovaks, and Syrians—foreign immigration to Indiana declined sharply in the 20th century. As of 1970, foreign-born Hoosiers and those of foreign or mixed parentage numbered 351,000, or less than 7% of the state total. Most of the foreign-stock population was of German, Polish, or British (including Irish) descent.

Restrictions on foreign immigration and the availability of jobs spurred the migration of black Americans to Indiana after World War I; by 1976, the state had 355,000 blacks, also representing about 7% of the total population. Approximately one-fourth of all Indiana blacks live in Gary, which was 53% black in 1970.

The total Hispanic population in 1976 was 84,000. Indiana's Asian residents are few in number: only 2,279 Japanese, 2,115 Chinese, 1,365 Filipinos, and 6,235 other Asian-Pacific peoples. In 1975, 1,785 Vietnamese were resettled in the state.

The Indians of early 19th-century Indiana came from a variety of Algonkian-speaking tribes, including Delaware, Shawnee, and Potawatomi. By 1846, however, all Indian lands in the state had been seized or ceded, and most Indians had been removed. In 1970, only 3,887 Indiana residents identified themselves as Indian.

[8] LANGUAGES
Several Algonkian Indian tribes, including some from the east, met the white settlers who arrived in Indiana in the early 1800s. However, of the Delaware, Potawatomi, Miami, and other groups, only 338 descendants in 1970 claimed an Indian language as their mother tongue. Yet their heritage exists in many place-names, from Kokomo to Nappanee, Muncie, and Shipshewana.

Except for the dialect mixture in the industrial northwest corner and for the Northern-dialect fringe of counties along the Michigan border, Indiana speech is essentially that of the South

LOCATION: 37°47' to 41°46'N; 84°49' to 88°02'W. BOUNDARIES: Lake Michigan shoreline, 45 mi (72 km); State of Michigan line, 99 mi (159 km); Ohio line, 179 mi (288 km); Kentucky line (Ohio River), 848 mi (1,365 km); Illinois line: land, 168 mi (270 km); Wabash River, 357 mi (575 km).

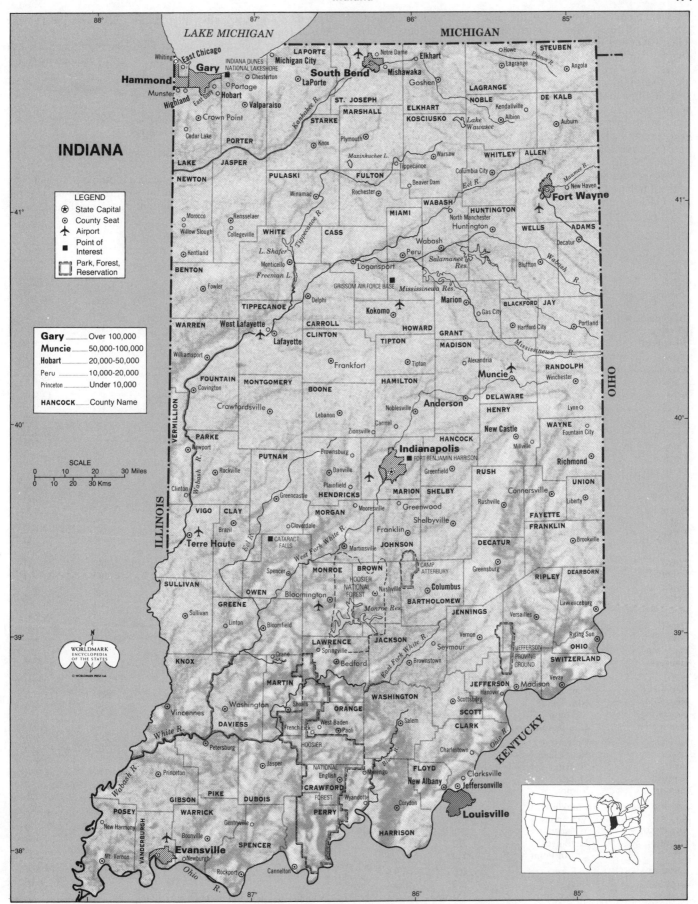

INDIANA

LEGEND
⊛ State Capital
⊙ County Seat
✈ Airport
■ Point of Interest
▢ Park, Forest, Reservation

Gary _____ Over 100,000
Muncie _____ 50,000-100,000
Hobart _____ 20,000-50,000
Peru _____ 10,000-20,000
Princeton _____ Under 10,000

HANCOCK _____ County Name

SCALE
0   10   20   30 Miles
0   10   20   30 Kms

ILLINOIS

OHIO

KENTUCKY

WORLDMARK
ENCYCLOPEDIA
OF THE STATES
© WORLDMARK PRESS Ltd.

See US political: front cover J3; physical: back cover: J3.

Midland pioneers from south of the Ohio River, with a transition zone toward North Midland north of Indianapolis. Between the Ohio River and Indianapolis, South Midland speakers use *evening* for late afternoon, eat *clabber cheese* instead of cottage cheese, are wary of *frogstools* rather than toadstools, once held that *toadfrogs* and not plain toads caused warts, eat *goobers* instead of peanuts at a ball game, and may therefore be *sick at the stomach*. In the same region, some Hoosiers use a few Midland words that also occur north of Indianapolis, such as *rock fence* (stone wall), *French harp* (harmonica), *mud dauber* (wasp), *shucks* (leaves on an ear of corn), and perhaps even some expanding North Midland words, such as *run* (a small stream), *teetertotter* (seesaw), and *fishworm*. North of Indianapolis, speakers with a Midland Pennsylvania background wish on the *pullybone* of a chicken, may use a *trestle* (sawhorse), and are likely to get

their hands /greezy/ rather than greasy. Such was the Hoosier talk of James Whitcomb Riley.

In 1970, a high percentage of Hoosiers (89%) had English as their native language. Major first languages claimed by Hoosiers were as follows:

	NATIVE-BORN	FOREIGN-BORN
English	4,597,993	13,674
German	140,450	13,673
Polish	41,597	6,198
Spanish	40,798	8,590

Italian, French, Yiddish, and Russian were also reported.

[9] RELIGIONS

The first branch of Christianity to gain a foothold in Indiana was Roman Catholicism, introduced by the French settlers in the early 18th century. The first Protestant church was founded near

Indiana Counties, County Seats, and County Populations[1]

COUNTY	COUNTY SEAT	LAND AREA (SQ MI)	POPULATION (1977)[2]	COUNTY	COUNTY SEAT	LAND AREA (SQ MI)	POPULATION (1977)[2]
Adams	Decatur	345	27,700	Marion	Indianapolis	392	769,400
Allen	Fort Wayne	671	286,700	Marshall	Plymouth	443	37,800
Bartholomew	Columbus	402	60,100				
Benton	Fowler	409	10,900	Martin	Shoals	345	11,000
Blackford	Hartford City	167	15,800	Miami	Peru	377	39,000
				Monroe	Bloomington	386	91,900
Boone	Lebanon	427	33,500	Montgomery	Crawfordsville	507	34,200
Brown	Nashville	319	10,100	Morgan	Martinsville	406	49,200
Carroll	Delphi	374	17,600				
Cass	Logansport	415	39,100	Newton	Kentland	413	13,900
Clark	Jeffersonville	384	85,800	Noble	Albion	412	32,900
				Ohio	Rising Sun	87	4,800
Clay	Brazil	364	24,400	Orange	Paoli	405	17,200
Clinton	Frankfort	407	30,600	Owen	Spencer	390	14,200
Crawford	English	312	8,700				
Daviess	Washington	430	25,800	Parke	Rockville	445	15,600
Dearborn	Lawrenceburg	306	32,400	Perry	Cannelton	384	18,100
				Pike	Petersburg	335	12,400
Decatur	Greensburg	370	24,000	Porter	Valparaiso	425	103,700
De Kalb	Auburn	366	31,500	Posey	Mt. Vernon	412	23,600
Delaware	Muncie	396	128,300				
Dubois	Jasper	433	32,000	Pulaski	Winamac	433	12,400
Elkhart	Goshen	468	133,300	Putnam	Greencastle	490	28,100
				Randolph	Winchester	457	29,500
Fayette	Connersville	215	27,500	Ripley	Versailles	442	22,500
Floyd	New Albany	149	57,900	Rush	Rushville	409	20,400
Fountain	Covington	397	18,200				
Franklin	Brookville	394	18,600	St. Joseph	South Bend	466	238,800
Fulton	Rochester	368	17,300	Scott	Scottsburg	193	19,300
				Shelby	Shelbyville	409	38,700
Gibson	Princeton	498	31,700	Spencer	Rockport	396	17,800
Grant	Marion	421	83,100	Starke	Knox	310	20,800
Greene	Bloomfield	549	28,100				
Hamilton	Noblesville	401	73,600	Steuben	Angola	309	23,000
Hancock	Greenfield	305	41,500	Sullivan	Sullivan	457	19,900
				Switzerland	Vevay	221	6,700
Harrison	Corydon	479	25,500	Tippecanoe	Lafayette	500	115,000
Hendricks	Danville	417	64,600	Tipton	Tipton	261	16,000
Henry	New Castle	400	53,700				
Howard	Kokomo	293	87,600	Union	Liberty	168	6,700
Huntington	Huntington	369	35,200	Vanderburgh	Evansville	241	161,300
				Vermillion	Newport	263	17,300
Jackson	Brownstown	520	34,000	Vigo	Terre Haute	415	111,400
Jasper	Rensselaer	562	24,600	Wabash	Wabash	398	35,900
Jay	Portland	386	23,500				
Jefferson	Madison	366	27,300	Warren	Williamsport	368	8,200
Jennings	Vernon	377	20,800	Warrick	Boonville	391	36,600
				Washington	Salem	516	20,200
Johnson	Franklin	315	73,200	Wayne	Richmond	405	76,800
Knox	Vincennes	516	39,200	Wells	Bluffton	368	24,400
Kosciusko	Warsaw	540	53,200				
Lagrange	Lagrange	381	23,300	White	Monticello	497	22,200
Lake	Crown Point	513	540,600	Whitley	Columbia City	337	24,400
LaPorte	LaPorte	607	106,000				
Lawrence	Bedford	459	40,600		TOTALS	36,097	5,330,000
Madison	Anderson	453	137,200				

[1]Columns may not add because of rounding. [2]Provisional.

Charlestown by Baptists from Kentucky in 1798. Three years later, a Methodist church was organized at Springville; in 1806, Presbyterians established a church near Vincennes; and the following year, Quakers built their first meetinghouse at Richmond. The Disciples of Christ, Lutherans, the United Brethren, Mennonites, and Jews were among the later 19th-century arrivals.

A dissident religious sect, the Shakers, established a short-lived community in Sullivan County in 1808. In 1815, some German separatists, led by George Rapp, founded a community called the Harmonie Society, which flourished briefly. Rapp moved his followers to Pennsylvania and sold the town to a Scottish social reformer, Robert Owen, in 1825. Owen renamed the town New Harmony and tried to establish there a nonreligious utopia, but the experiment failed after three years. A group of religious dissidents founded the pentecostal Church of God at Beaver Dam in 1881; the world headquarters of the church, which had 37,902 adherents in 1971, is now at Anderson. The Youth for Christ movement started in Indianapolis in 1943.

In 1971, 44.6% of Indiana's population held church membership, as compared with the US average of 49.6%; there were 6,092 churches in the state. According to the latest church census of 1971, the largest Protestant denominations were the United Methodists, with 415,540 adherents; Christian Churches and Churches of Christ, 157,753; American Baptist Convention, 151,029; United Presbyterian Church, 127,053; and Lutheran Church–Missouri Synod, 116,658. There were 720,081 Roman Catholics in 1979; the estimated Jewish population in that year was 23,690.

¹⁰TRANSPORTATION

Indiana's central location in the US and its position between Lake Michigan to the north and the Ohio River to the south gave the state its motto, "The Crossroads of America." Historically, the state took advantage of its strategic location by digging canals to connect Indiana rivers and by building roads and railroads to provide farmers access to national markets.

The success of the state's first railroad, completed in 1847 between Madison and Indianapolis, led to a tenfold increase in track mileage during the 1850s, and more railroad expansion took place after the Civil War. In 1979, 19 railroad companies operated 8,398 mi (13,515 km) of track in Indiana. Regularly scheduled Amtrak passenger trains connect Fort Wayne, Gary, Lafayette, and Indianapolis with the rest of the country. These and other major cities have public transit systems subsidized heavily by the state and federal governments. The South Shore commuter railroad connects South Bend, Gary, and East Chicago with Chicago, Ill.

The east-to-west National Road (US 40) reached Indiana in 1827, and the north-to-south Michigan road (US 421) was built in the late 1830s. In August 1979, Indiana had 1,134 mi (1,825 km) of interstate highways—more than any other state of comparable size. In that year, there were 10,987 mi (17,682 km) of state highways and 80,518 mi (129,581 km) of county and municipal roads. In 1978, motor vehicle registrations totaled 4,238,839, including 2,810,308 passenger cars, 790,760 trucks, 228,681 trailers, and 154,012 motorcycles. Five of the nation's 10-largest moving companies have their headquarters in Indiana.

Water transportation has been important from the earliest years of European settlement. The Wabash and Erie Canal, constructed in the 1830s from Fort Wayne east to Toledo, Ohio, and southwest to Lafayette, was vital to the state's market economy. In 1836, the state legislature earmarked $10 million for an ambitious network of canals, but excessive construction costs and the financial panic of 1837 caused the state to go virtually bankrupt and default on its bonds. Nevertheless, the Wabash canal was extended to Terre Haute and Evansville by the early 1850s.

The transport of freight via Lake Michigan and the Ohio River helped to spark Indiana's industrial development. A deepwater port on Lake Michigan, which became operational in 1970, provided access to world markets via the St. Lawrence Seaway. Public port facilities on the Ohio River near Mt. Vernon were opened in June 1979, and a second port project was under way near Jeffersonville in 1980.

In 1979, nine national air carriers and five commuter carriers provided scheduled airline service to Indianapolis and 12 other cities in Indiana. In 1978 there were 69 public and 249 private airfields in the state. The number of aircraft registered in Indiana was 4,183 in 1977.

¹¹HISTORY

How early Indiana was occupied by man is not known. Hundreds of sites used by primitive hunters, fishermen, and food gatherers prior to 1000 BC have been found in Indiana. Burial mounds of the Woodland culture (1000 BC to AD 900), when the bow and arrow appeared, have been located across the state. The next culture, called Mississippian and dating about AD 900 to 1500, is marked by gardens, ceramics, tools, weapons, trade, and social organization. It is well illustrated by remains of an extensive village on the north side of the Ohio River near Newburgh. The unidentified inhabitants are believed to have come up from the south about 1300, for reasons not known, and to have migrated back before 1500, again for unknown reasons.

The next Indian invaders, and the first to be seen by white men, were the Miami and Potawatomi tribes who drifted down the west side of Lake Michigan and turned across the northern sector of what is now Indiana after the middle of the 17th century. The Kickapoo and Wea tribes pushed into upper Indiana from northern Illinois. The southern two-thirds of the present state was a vast hunting ground, without villages.

The first European penetration was made in the 1670s by French explorers: Father Jacques Marquette and Robert Cavelier, Sieur de la Salle, followed by nameless French traders. After the founding of Detroit in 1701, the Maumee-Wabash river route to the lower Ohio was discovered. At the portage between the two rivers, Jean Baptiste Bissot, Sieur de Vincennes, lived at Kekionga, the principal village of the Miami and the present site of Fort Wayne. The first French fort was built farther down the Wabash among the Wea, near modern Lafayette, in 1717. Three years later, Fort Miami was erected. Vincennes's son constructed another fort on the Wabash in 1732, at the site of the town later named for him.

English traders venturing down the Ohio River disputed the French trade monopoly, and as a result of the French and Indian War, the whole of Canada to the Mississippi River was given up to the British in 1760. Indians under Chief Pontiac captured the two forts in northern Indiana, and the area was not securely in English hands until 1765. The prerevolutionary turbulence in the Atlantic seaboard colonies was hardly felt in Indiana, although the region did not escape the Revolutionary War itself. Colonel George Rogers Clark, acting for Virginia, captured Vincennes from a British garrison early in 1779 after a heroic march. Two years later, a detachment of troops from Pennsylvania, passing down the Ohio to reinforce Clark, was surprised and taken in camp by a force of French Canadians and Indians under Mohawk Captain Joseph Brant.

Following the Revolutionary War, the area northwest of the Ohio River was granted to the new nation. The first US settlement in Indiana was made in 1784 on land opposite Louisville, Ky., granted to Clark's veterans by Virginia. (The new town, called Clarksville, still exists.) Americans also moved into Vincennes. Government was established by the Continental Congress under the Northwest Ordinance of 1787. Again, Indian unrest endangered all settlements north of the Ohio, and the small US army, with headquarters at Cincinnati, met defeat at what is now Fort Wayne in 1790 and disaster in neighboring Ohio in 1791. General Anthony Wayne was put in command of an enlarged army and defeated the Indians in 1794 at Fallen Timbers (near Toledo, Ohio). British meddling was ended by Jay's treaty later the same year. Wayne then built a new fort— named for him— among the Miami.

In 1800, as Ohio prepared to enter the Union, the rest of the Northwest Territory was set off and called Indiana Territory, with its capital at Vincennes. There Elihu Stout established a newspaper, the *Indiana Gazette*, in 1804. After Michigan Territory was detached in 1805, and Illinois Territory in 1809, Indiana assumed its present boundaries. The federal census counted 24,520 people in Indiana in 1810, including a new Swiss colony on the Ohio, where settlers planted vineyards and made wine.

William Henry Harrison was appointed first governor and, with a secretary and three appointed judges, constituted the government of Indiana Territory. Under the Northwest Ordinance, when the population reached 5,000 adult males, it was allowed to elect an assembly and nominate candidates for an upper house. When the population totaled 60,000—as it did in 1815—the voters were allowed to write a state constitution and to apply for admission to the Union. A short constitution excluding slavery and recommending public schools was adopted, and Indiana became the 19th state on 11 December 1816.

Meanwhile, Indiana had seen Governor Harrison lead US troops up the Wabash in 1811 and beat off an Indian attack at Tippecanoe. The War of 1812 took Harrison away from Indiana, and battles were fought in other theaters. Hoosiers suffered Indian raids, and two forts were besieged for a few days. After the war, new settlers began pouring into the state from the upper South and in fewer numbers from Ohio, Pennsylvania, New York, and New England. A group of German Pietists under George Rapp settled Harmonie on the lower Wabash in 1815 and stayed ten years before selling out to Robert Owen, a visionary with utopian dreams that failed at the village he renamed New Harmony. In 1816, Tom Lincoln brought his family from Kentucky, and his son Abe grew up in southern Indiana from age 7 to 21, his formative years.

Unlike most other states, Indiana was settled from south to north. The inhabitants were called Hoosiers; the origin of the word is obscure, but the term may have come from an Anglo-Saxon word for hill dwellers. Central and northern Indiana was opened up as land was purchased from the Indians. The Potawatomi were forced to go west in 1838, and the Miami left in 1846. Commerce flowed south to the Ohio River in the form of corn, hogs, whiskey, and timber. Indianapolis was laid out as a planned city and centrally located capital in 1820, but 30 years passed before its population caught up to the size of Madison and New Albany on the Ohio.

An overly ambitious program of internal improvements (canals and roads) in the 1830s plunged the state into debts it could not pay. Railroads, privately financed, began to tie Indiana commercially with the East. The Irish came to dig canals and lay the rails, and Germans, many of them Catholics, came to do woodworking and farming. Levi Coffin, a Quaker who moved to Fountain City in 1826, opened a different kind of road, the Underground Railroad, to help escaping slaves from the South.

A new constitution in 1851 showed Jacksonian preferences for more elective offices, shorter terms, a one-term governorship, limited biennial legislative sessions, county government, obligatory common schools, and severe limits on state debt. But this constitution also prohibited Negroes from entering the state.

Hoosiers showed considerable sympathy with the South in the 1850s, and treasonable "copperhead" activity showed itself in the early 1860s. Nevertheless, Indiana remained staunchly in the Union under Governor Oliver P. Morton, sending more than 200,000 soldiers to the Civil War. The state suffered no battles, but General John Hunt Morgan's Confederate cavalry raided the southeastern sector of Indiana in July 1863.

After the Civil War, small local industries expanded rapidly. The first nonfarm enterprises were gristmills, sawmills, meatpacking plants, distilleries and breweries, leatherworking shops, furniture factories, and steamboat and carriage makers. Wagons made by Studebaker in South Bend won fame during the war, as did Van Camp's canned pork and beans from Indianapolis. Discovery of natural gas in several northeastern counties in 1886, and the resultant low fuel prices, spurred the growth of glass factories. Elwood Haynes of Kokomo designed a one-cylinder horseless carriage in 1894 and drove it. As America became infatuated with the new autos, 375 Indiana factories started turning them out. A racetrack for testing cars was built outside Indianapolis in 1908, and the famous 500 mi (805 km) race on Memorial Day weekend began in 1911. Five years earlier, US Steel had constructed a steel plant at the south end of Lake Michigan. The town built by the company to house the workers was called Gary, and it grew rapidly with the help of the company and the onset of World War I. Oil refineries were developed in this same area, known as the Calumet region.

Of the millions of immigrants who flocked to the US from 1870 to 1914, very few settled in Indiana. The percentage of foreign-born residents declined from 9% in 1860 to 7% in 1880, all of them from Northern Europe and over half from Germany. By 1920, the percentage was down to 5%, although some workers from Southern and Eastern Europe had gravitated to the industries of the Calumet. By 1970, the foreign-born comprised only 1.6% of the population. Indiana's black population rose slowly from 2% in 1880 to 2.8% in 1920, and increased to 7% by 1970.

Although many Hoosiers of German and Irish descent favored neutrality when World War I began, Indiana industries boomed with war orders, and public sympathy swung heavily toward the Allies. Indiana furnished 118,000 men and women to the armed forces and suffered the loss of 3,370—a much smaller participation than in the Civil War, from a population more than twice the size.

After 1920, only about a dozen makes of cars were still being manufactured in Indiana, and those factories steadily lost out to the big three carmakers in Detroit. The exception was Studebaker in South Bend, which grew to have more than 23,000 employees in World War II. The company finally closed its doors in 1965. Auto parts continued to be a big business, however, along with steelmaking and oil refining in the Calumet. Elsewhere there was manufacturing of machinery, farm implements, railway cars, furniture, and pharmaceuticals. Meat packing, coal mining, and limestone quarrying continued to be important. In 1860, about 21,000 workers were employed in manufacturing; by 1970, more than 30 times that number were in industrial occupations. With increasing industrialization, cities grew, particularly in the northern half of the state, and the number of farms diminished. The balance of rural and urban population, about even in 1920, tilted in favor of urban dwellers.

World War II had greater impact on Indiana than did the first war. Most factories converted to production of war materials; 300 held defense orders in 1942. Du Pont built a huge powder plant near Charlestown. The slack in employment was taken up, women went into factories, and more rural families moved to cities. Training facilities were created; Camp Atterbury covered 100 sq mi (259 sq km) in Bartholomew County, and two air stations trained aviators. Two large ammunition depots loaded and stored shells; and the enormous Jefferson Proving Ground, north of Madison, tested ammunition and parachutes.

After the war, many locally owned small industries were taken over by national corporations, and their plants were expanded. By 1976, the largest employer in Indiana was General Motors, with 50,000 employees in six cities. Second was US Steel, with 23,000 workers, followed by Radio Corporation of America, International Harvester, General Electric, and Eli Lilly. Although the state's population in 1975 was about two-thirds urban and one-third rural, agriculture retained much of its importance. Nostalgia for an older, simpler, rural way of life pervades much Hoosier thinking. The state stands high in conservation, owing to the vision of Richard Lieber, a state official who from 1933 to 1944 promoted the preservation of land for state parks and recreational areas as well as for state and federal forests.

Hoosiers enjoy politics and participate intensively in conventions and elections. The percentage of registered voters who vote has always exceeded the national average by a wide margin, reaching a peak of 95% in 1876, when the national average was 82%. The evenness of strength between the two major political parties has made Indiana a swing state, eagerly courted by Democrats and Republicans alike.

The state legislature was dominated by rural interests until reapportionment in 1966 gave urban counties more representation. Biennial sessions were then changed to annual, although they are still limited in duration. Indianapolis has extended its boundaries to cover the county, and much of city and county government is unified. The direct primary for nomination of governor, lieutenant governor, and US senator was mandated in 1975. In 1976, for the first time, the governor was allowed to succeed himself, and Republican Otis Bowen was reelected.

¹²STATE GOVERNMENT

The first state constitution took effect when Indiana became a state in 1816. Reportedly written by convention delegates beneath a huge elm tree in Corydon, the first state capital, the brief document prohibited slavery and recommended a free public school system, including a state university.

This constitution did not allow for amendment, however, and a new constitution that did so was adopted in 1851. The second constitution authorized more elective state officials, gave greater responsibility to county governments, and prohibited the state from going into debt (except under rare circumstances). It also established biennial rather than annual sessions of the state legislature, a provision not repealed until 1971. With amendments, the second constitution is still in effect today.

The Indiana general assembly consists of a 50-member senate elected to four-year terms, with half the senators elected every two years; and a 100-member house of representatives elected to two-year terms. A member of the general assembly must be a US citizen and have been a resident of Indiana for at least one year. A senator must be at least 25 years of age, a representative at least 21 years old. Senators and representatives are paid the same salary ($9,600 as of 4 November 1980) and allowances ($44 per day in 1980 during the legislative session, and $12.50 per day, except Sundays, when not in session).

The state's chief executive is the governor, elected to a 4-year term and eligible for reelection, although ineligible to serve more than 8 years in a 12-year period. A governor must be at least 30 years old, a US citizen, and a state resident for 5 years prior to election. The governor may call special sessions of the legislature and may veto bills passed by the legislature. The governor receives an annual salary of $48,000 as of 12 January 1981, and business expenses ($12,000 in 1980).

Indiana's other top elected officials are the lieutenant governor, secretary of state, treasurer, auditor, attorney general, and superintendent of public instruction. Each is elected to a four-year term and receives an annual salary of $34,000 as of 12 January 1981, plus business expenses.

Legislation may be introduced in either house of the general assembly, except that bills for raising revenue must originate in the house of representatives. A bill approved by both houses goes to the governor for signing into law; if the governor declines to sign it within seven days, the bill becomes law, but if the governor vetoes it, majorities of at least 26 votes in the senate and 51 votes in the house are required to override the veto. Should the governor veto a bill after the end of a legislative session, it must be returned to the legislature when that body reconvenes.

An amendment to the state constitution must be approved by two successive legislatures and be submitted to the voters for approval or rejection at the next general election.

In order to vote in Indiana, a person must be a US citizen, at least 18 years old, and have been a resident of the voting precinct for 30 days and of the township for 60 days.

¹³POLITICAL PARTIES

The Democratic Party has been one of the two major political parties since Indiana became a state in 1816, as has the Republican Party since its inception in 1854. In that year, Hoosiers voted for Democrat James Buchanan for president, but in 1860, the voters supported Republican Abraham Lincoln. After voting Republican in four successive presidential elections, Indiana voted Democratic in 1876 and became a swing state. More recently, a

Indiana Presidential Vote by Political Parties, 1948–80

YEAR	ELECTORAL VOTES	INDIANA WINNER	DEMOCRAT	REPUBLICAN	PROGRESSIVE	PROHIBITION
1948	13	Dewey (R)	807,833	821,079	9,649	14,711
1952	13	*Eisenhower (R)	801,530	1,136,259	1,222	15,335
1956	13	*Eisenhower (R)	783,908	1,182,811	—	6,554
1960	13	Nixon (R)	952,358	1,175,120	—	6,746
1964	13	*Johnson (D)	1,170,848	911,118	—	8,266
					AMERICAN IND.	
1968	13	*Nixon (R)	806,659	1,067,885	243,108	4,616
					PEOPLE'S	SOC. WORKERS
1972	13	*Nixon (R)	708,568	1,405,154	4,544	5,575
					AMERICAN	
1976	13	Ford (R)	1,014,714	1,185,958	14,048	5,695
					CITIZENS	LIBERTARIAN
1980	13	*Reagan (R)	844,197	1,255,656	4,852	19,627

*Won US presidential election.

Republican trend has been evident: the state voted Republican in 9 out of 10 presidential elections between 1940 and 1976.

Hoosiers have always taken an active interest in politics; in 1976, 75% of the state's electorate voted in the presidential election—well above the US average of 53%. In that year, Indiana voted for Republican presidential candidate Gerald Ford and reelected Republican Governor Otis Bowen, but Democrats won the state legislature.

Third-party movements have rarely succeeded in Indiana. Native son Eugene Debs, the Socialist Party leader who was personally popular in Indiana, received only 36,931 votes in the state in 1912, while garnering more than 900,000 votes nationally. Even in 1932, during the Great Depression, Socialist candidate Norman Thomas won only 21,388 votes in Indiana. The most successful third-party movement in recent decades was George Wallace's American Independent Party, which took 243,108 votes (11.5% of the Indiana total) in 1968. In the 1976 presidential election, minority party candidates together received less than 1% of the votes cast.

The November 1980 elections proved a disaster for Democratic candidates, as Hoosiers chose Republican Ronald Reagan, elected Republicans to the governorship and the US Senate, and increased Republican majorities in the state legislature.

¹⁴LOCAL GOVERNMENT

In 1816, when Indians controlled central and northern Indiana, the state had only 15 counties. By 1824, the number of counties had grown to 49. All but one of Indiana's 92 counties were established by 1851. The last remaining county—Newton, in the state's northwest corner—was created in 1859.

Counties in Indiana provide law enforcement in rural areas, operate county courts and institutions, maintain county roads, administer public welfare programs, and collect taxes. The county's business is conducted by a Board of County Commissioners, the three members elected to four-year terms. Nine officials also elected to four-year terms exercise executive functions: the county auditor, treasurer, recorder, clerk, surveyor, sheriff, prosecuting attorney, coroner, and assessor. The county's appointed officials include the county superintendent of schools, highway supervisor, highway engineer, extension agent, attorney, and physician. An elected seven-member County Council exercises taxing power and acts as a check on the Board of County Commissioners. The major exception to this general pattern is Marion County, which in 1970 was consolidated with the city of Indianapolis and is governed by an elected mayor and council of 29 members.

Townships (1,008 in 1979) provide assistance for the poor and assess taxable property. Each township is administered by a trustee elected to a four-year term. In a few townships, the trustee oversees township schools, but most public schools are now run by community school corporations.

Indiana had 115 cities in 1979. They are governed by elected city councils varying in membership from five to nine persons. City officials elected for four-year terms are the mayor and the city clerk or clerk-treasurer. In 1979 there were also 450 incorporated towns. Each town is governed by an elected board of trustees (one for each ward) and an elected clerk-treasurer. The board may appoint a town manager and a marshal.

¹⁵STATE SERVICES

In 1974, Indiana's state legislature created the State Ethics and Conflicts of Interest Commission to formulate and regulate a code of ethics for state officials. The commissioner receives and investigates reported cases of misconduct or violations of the code of ethics by any state official or employee. After holding hearings, the commission reports violations to the governor and makes its findings public. Top-level state officials and heads of state departments must provide statements of their financial interests to the commission.

In 1977, the state established an Interdepartmental Board for the Coordination of Human Service Programs. Members include the chief administrative officers of the state's agencies for employment, senior citizens, community services, education, health, corrections, and public welfare. The board provides assistance to persons and families requiring help from one of these agencies and monitors federal service programs in the state. The Indiana Office of Social Services administers programs for the board. An executive assistant to the governor serves as chairman of the board, which also includes the director of the State Budget Agency.

Educational services are provided by the Commission for Higher Education, the Indiana Educational Services Foundation, and the Commission for Postsecondary Proprietary Education, which accredits private vocational, technical, and trade schools in the state. A public counselor, appointed by the governor, represents the public at hearings of the Public Service Commission, which regulates public transportation agencies and public utilities. Health services are supplied by the State Board of Health, Department of Mental Health, and Emergency Medical Services Commission. The Civil Rights Commission enforces state antidiscrimination laws.

¹⁶JUDICIAL SYSTEM

The Indiana supreme court consists of five justices who are appointed by the governor from names submitted by a nonpartisan judicial nominating committee. To qualify for selection, a nominee must have practiced law in the state for at least 10 years or have served as judge of a lower court for at least 5 years. A justice serves for 2 years and then is subject to approval by referendum in the general election; if approved by the voters, the justice serves a 10-year term before being again subject to referendum. The chief justice of the Indiana supreme court is chosen by the nominating commission. Formerly, justices had been chosen through partisan elections, a system abolished by constitutional amendment as of 1 January 1972.

The state court of appeals consists of 12 justices, 3 for each of the four judicial districts in the state. The court exercises appellate jurisdiction under rules set by the state supreme court. Both the clerk and the reporter for the state's high courts are chosen in statewide elections for four-year terms.

There were also 88 circuit courts, 35 superior courts, and 58 county courts in 1979. When the justice of the peace system in the counties was abolished by the state legislature in 1976, small-claims dockets (civil cases involving up to $1,500) were added to circuit and county courts. Circuit and superior court judges are elected for six-year terms; county judges are elected to four-year terms.

The Department of Correction operated 10 penal institutions with about 5,700 inmates in 1979. Indiana State Prison is located at Michigan City, and the Women's Prison is in Indianapolis. For 1978, the FBI Crime Index reported 17,383 instances of violent crime, including murder and manslaughter, 334 (6.2 per 100,000 inhabitants); forcible rape, 1,451; and aggravated assault, 9,072. In nearly every category, Indiana's crime rate was well below the US average for that year.

¹⁷ARMED FORCES

US defense installations in Indiana had 19,368 personnel in 1978. Army installations include Fort Benjamin Harrison and Jefferson Proving Ground; Grissom Air Force Base is the lone Air Force installation. The Navy operates a Weapons Support Center at Crane and an Avionics Center at Indianapolis. The state was awarded $909 million in defense contracts during the 1977/78 fiscal year.

Indiana supported the Union during the Civil War; more than 200,000 Hoosiers served in northern armies, and some 24,400 died while in service. During World War I, a Hoosier reportedly was the first American soldier to fire a shot, and the first American soldier killed was from Indiana; in all, about 118,000 Indiana citizens served and 3,370 lost their lives. In World War II, about 338,000 Hoosiers served in the armed forces and some 10,000 died in line of duty. In 1979, 729,000 veterans were living in Indiana, of whom 14,000 served during World War I, 287,000 in World War II, 132,000 during the Korean conflict, and 230,000 during the Viet-Nam era. After World War II, the state paid a bonus to veterans for the first time; in 1978, veterans' benefits in Indiana totaled $327 million.

Indiana's National Guard units served in World War II, the Korean conflict, and the Viet-Nam war. In 1978 there were 12,600 National Guard personnel in 72 communities in the state.

In 1978, Indiana's police forces consisted of 1,651 state police employees (of whom 548 were civilians), 5,278 city and town police personnel, and 2,091 employees in county sheriffs' departments.

[18] MIGRATION

Indiana's early settlers were predominantly North Europeans who migrated from eastern and southern states. The influx of immigrants to the US in the late 19th and early 20th centuries had little impact on Indiana. In 1860, only 9% of the state's population was foreign-born, mostly Germans and Irish. The percentage was only 5.6% in 1900 and had further declined to 5.2% by 1920. The principal migratory pattern since then has been within the state, from the farms to the cities.

Whereas in 1860 more than 91% of the population lived in rural areas, by 1900 the percentage had fallen to 67%, and in 1920 to 50%. In 1960, about 60% of the population lived in urban areas; by 1975, some 67% of the population was urban and only 33% was rural.

Since World War II, Indiana has lost population through a growing migratory movement to other states, mostly to Florida and the Southwest. From 1960 to 1970, Indiana suffered a net loss of nearly 16,000 persons through migration, and from 1970 to 1977, a net total of 126,000 left the state. Demographic studies indicate that this outmigration will probably continue in the 1980s.

[19] INTERGOVERNMENTAL COOPERATION

Indiana's Commission on Interstate Cooperation promotes cooperation with other states and with the federal government. It acts largely through the Council of State Governments. Indiana is a member of such interstate regulatory bodies as the Great Lakes Commission, the Ohio River Basin Commission, and the Ohio River Valley Water Sanitation Commission. The Indiana-Kentucky Boundary Compact was signed by Indiana in 1943 and received congressional approval the same year.

Federal aid to Indiana totaled $1.3 billion in 1977/78 and $1.4 billion in 1978/79.

[20] ECONOMY

Indiana is both a leading agricultural and industrial state. In 1976, it ranked 8th in the US in farm output and 9th in value added by manufacturing production among the 50 states.

The economy was almost entirely agricultural until after the Civil War, when rapid industrial development tripled the number of factories in the state to 18,000 plants, employing 156,000 workers, by 1900. During that period, the accompanying mechanization of agriculture resulted in the doubling of the number of farms to a peak of 220,000 in 1900. Metals and other manufacturing industries surged during and after World War I, lagged during the Great Depression of the 1930s, then surged again during and after World War II. Between 1940 and 1950, the number of wage earners in the state nearly doubled. Job opportunities brought in many workers from other states and encouraged the growth of labor unions.

The state's industrial development in Indianapolis, Gary, and other cities was based on its plentiful natural resources—coal, natural gas, timber, stone, and clay—and on good transportation

facilities. By 1972, Indiana ranked 1st in mobile homes and recreational vehicles, 2d in steel production, and 3d in motor vehicle parts manufacturing among the 50 states. Other leading manufactures include food and livestock products, pharmaceuticals, phonograph records and tapes, musical instruments, caskets, and books.

Indiana's gross state product in 1978 dollars totaled $51.8 billion, or 2.4% of the US gross national product, and the real economic growth rate was 4%. Of the total, the principal industrial sectors and their values were durable goods, $15.6 billion; trade, $8 billion; finance, insurance, and real estate, $5.5 billion; service industries, $4.8 billion; government, $4.5 billion; nondurable goods, $4.3 billion; transportation, communications, and public utilities, $4.2 billion; contract construction, $2.4 billion; farm products, $1.9 billion; and mining, $571 million.

The chief economic concerns of Hoosiers in the late 1970s were rising unemployment in such major industries as steel and auto and recreational vehicle manufacturing, and the high rate of inflation.

[21] INCOME

In 1978, Indiana ranked 23d among the 50 states in individual income, with an average of $7,696 per capita. In that year, personal income totaled $41.4 billion—11th in the US—representing an increase of 39% since 1975.

The major sources of personal income in 1976 were manufacturing, 32%; trade, 12%; government, 10%; services, 9%; construction, 4%; finance, insurance, and real estate, 3%; agriculture, 3%; transportation, 3%; communications and public utilities, 2%; and other sectors, 22%.

In 1977, the state's median household income was $15,858. The distribution of income by households was as follows: under $10,000, 28%; $10,000–14,999, 18%; $15,000–24,999, 35%; over $25,000, 19%. About 424,000 persons (8% of the population) had incomes below the federal poverty level in 1975.

[22] LABOR

In 1978, the state's civilian labor force totaled 2,571,000 persons, 58.5% male and 41.5% female.

A federal census of workers covered by unemployment insurance in March 1977 revealed the following nonfarm employment pattern in Indiana:

	ESTABLISH-MENTS	EMPLOYEES	ANNUAL PAYROLL ('000)
Agricultural services, forestry, fishing	791	3,171	$ 27,631
Mining, of which:	484	8,626	151,530
Bituminous coal, lignite	(80)	(3,912)	(81,910)
Contract construction	10,308	79,606	1,289,667
Manufacturing, of which:	7,522	700,537	10,471,079
Primary metals	(274)	(101,238)	(1,906,542)
Electric, electronic equipment	(306)	(108,102)	(1,563,699)
Transport equipment	(388)	(101,997)	(1,718,680)
Transportation, public utilities	3,584	86,473	1,310,628
Wholesale trade	8,747	99,376	1,296,140
Retail trade	30,750	340,252	2,251,947
Finance, insurance, real estate	8,775	92,306	950,250
Services	26,682	275,243	2,182,594
Other	1,111	1,656	17,132
TOTALS	98,754	1,687,246	$19,948,598

Principal occupational categories in 1974 (and projections for 1985) were professional people, 253,671 (289,148); managers and proprietors, 206,566 (232,406); sales workers, 135,129 (154,633); clerical workers, 359,072 (435,869); crafts workers, 345,147 (391,809); industrial operatives, 388,888 (423,310); service workers, 285,021 (343,862); laborers, 122,580 (129,982); transport workers, 92,763 (97,907); farmers and farm workers, 66,163 (61,394). Discrepancies between these state totals and the federal data cited in the table above arise from the fact that such occupational categories as government and farm workers and the self-employed were excluded from the federal survey.

In 1978 there were 2,425,000 employed workers (1,437,000 men and 988,000 women) and 146,000 unemployed workers, giving Indiana an unemployment rate of 5.7%, slightly below the US average. In that year, the average weekly wages of workers in manufacturing industries were $295.40; average weekly hours worked, 41.2; and average hourly earnings, $7.17.

Most industrial workers live in Indianapolis and the Calumet area of northwestern Indiana. The AFL first attempted to organize workers at the US Steel Company's plant in Gary in 1919, but a strike to get union recognition failed. Other strikes by Indiana coal miners and railway workers in 1922 had limited success. By 1936, however, the CIO had won bargaining rights and the 40-hour workweek from US Steel, and union organization spread to other industries throughout the state.

In 1976, labor unions had 621,000 members in Indiana, or nearly 31% of the total number of workers, as compared with the US average of 25%. Of that total, 434,000 workers belonged to unions affiliated with the AFL-CIO. Another 55,000 employees belonged to professional and state employee associations. Overall, Indiana's labor force ranked 11th in the US in extent of organization. In 1977 there were 234 strikes and work stoppages, involving 95,000 workers, that resulted in 1,612,000 working days lost.

By 1975, the state had recognized the right of collective bargaining by public employees such as schoolteachers, although police and firemen were excluded and strikes by any public employees were banned.

[23] AGRICULTURE

In 1977, Indiana ranked 8th among the 50 states in cash farm receipts. The state's total farm marketings that year were valued at $3.2 billion. The leading crops were corn, which accounted for 31 cents of every dollar the farmer earned, and soybeans, which provided 22 cents of that dollar.

The golden age of Indiana agriculture was the decade of the 1850s, when Indiana ranked among the four leading states in production of corn, wheat, and hogs. At that time, about 95% of the population lived on farms. The number of farms increased from 132,000 in 1860 to 222,000 in 1900, when about 21.6 million acres (8.7 million hectares) of land were under cultivation. But after 1900, with the rapid mechanization of agriculture and the rise of industry, the number of farms declined. Nevertheless, agriculture remains vital to the state's economy, and nearly three-fourths of its total area is farmland. There were 89,000 farms being worked in 1979, when farmland totaled 17 million acres (7 million hectares), making the size of the average farm 191 acres (77 hectares), more than half again as large as the average 120 acre (49 hectare) farm of 1950. The most productive land is in the broad central region of the state.

In 1977, Indiana ranked 3d among the producing states in output of corn and hogs, and 4th in soybeans; the state also produced one-fourth of the country's popcorn. In 1979, Indiana's principal field crops were as follows:

CROPS	PRODUCTION	VALUE
Corn for grain	664,160,000 bushels	$1,660,400,000
Soybeans	159,120,000 bushels	1,002,456,000
Winter wheat	44,415,000 bushels	177,660,000
Hay	2,150,000 tons	115,025,000
Tobacco (1977)	16,560,000 lb	19,789,000
Oats	8,845,000 bushels	13,710,000
Popcorn (1977)	118,250,000 lb	12,298,000

Federal crop subsidies to Hoosier farmers were estimated at $53.4 million in 1978.

[24] ANIMAL HUSBANDRY

In 1977, Indiana ranked 5th among the 50 states in sales of livestock and livestock products. In that year, about one-third of the state's farm income came from the sale of hogs, cattle, and dairy products.

Production of livestock was valued at $847,156,000; dairy products, $22,751,000; and poultry and eggs, $189,962,000. The number of livestock on Indiana farms at the start of 1979 was hogs and pigs, 4,400,000; cattle and calves, 1,750,000; milk cows, 202,000; and sheep and lambs, 171,000. Indiana poultry farmers raised 15,700,000 chickens and 4,700,000 turkeys in 1978. Other animal products include honey (valued at $2,237,000 in 1977), beeswax, and wool.

[25] FISHING

Fishing is not of commercial importance in Indiana; in 1978, only 162,000 lb of fish valued at $106,000 were landed. Fishing for bass, pike, perch, catfish, and trout is a popular sport.

[26] FORESTRY

About 17% of Indiana land is forested (0.5% of the US total). In 1977, the state had 3,943,000 acres (1,596,000 hectares) of forestland, of which 3,815,000 acres (1,544,000 hectares) were commercial timberland; of the latter total, 239,000 acres (96,800 hectares) were federal land and 169,700 acres (68,700 hectares) were state land. Most forestland is situated in the southern region, where oak, beech, sycamore, poplar, and hickory trees are plentiful. About 89% of the state's commercial timberland is privately owned.

In 1977 there were an estimated 92.3 million cu feet of softwoods and 4.1 billion cu feet of hardwoods on commercial timberlands. The annual growth that year was 106.5 million cu feet, and the annual harvest was 65.7 million cu feet. The lumber and furniture industries employed 35,400 persons and paid wages totaling $315.4 million; the value added by manufacturing was $849.5 million, and factory shipments amounted to nearly 1.9 billion. In that year, the principal wood products and their total shipment values were plywood and millwork, $457 million; mobile homes, $334 million; household furniture, $500 million; office furniture, $106 million.

Indiana ranked 3d in the US in furniture manufacturing during 1979. In that year there were 200 sawmills and 14 veneer mills in the state.

There is one national forest in Indiana, Hoosier National Forest (near Bloomington), with 183,000 acres (74,000 hectares). The largest of the 12 state forests are Harrison-Crawford, Morgan-Monroe, Clark, and Yellowwood.

[27] MINING

In 1978, Indiana ranked 23d among the 50 states in mineral production value, which totaled $702 million, or slightly less than 1% of the US total. Coal accounted for more than half of Indiana's mineral output. Indiana produced about two-thirds of all building limestone quarried in the US, plus significant quantities of other construction materials, including cement, gypsum, sand and gravel, clay, and shale. For the most part, mines are situated in the southern part of the state.

In 1978, the state's principal mineral products (excluding fossil fuels) were stone, 28,840,000 tons; sand and gravel, 26,500,000 tons; and clay, 1,427,000 tons.

[28] ENERGY AND POWER

Indiana is largely dependent upon fossil fuels for its energy supplies. The use of wood, an important source of energy in the 19th century, declined with the increased burning of coal. In recent years, petroleum has become an important power source for automobiles, home heating, and electricity. Nevertheless, coal has continued to be the state's major source of power, meeting about half of Indiana's energy needs.

In 1977, Indiana's gross energy consumption totaled 2,502 trillion Btu, of which 46% was provided by coal, 31% by petroleum products, 16% by natural gas, and 7% by other sources. The state has no nuclear power plants.

Electric power produced in Indiana in 1978 totaled 68 billion kwh; total installed capacity was 16.9 million kw. Privately owned power plants accounted for 97% of Indiana's production and installed capacity. Of total electricity sales in 1977, roughly 54% was sold to industries, 30% to homes, and 16% to commercial users. The major electric utilities in 1978 were Northern Indiana Public Service Co. (serving 357,791 customers), Indiana & Michigan Electric Co. (with 362,682 customers), Public Service Co. of Indiana (515,871), Indianapolis Power & Light Co. (314,587), and Southern Indiana Gas & Electric Co. (98,337).

At the end of 1978, Indiana's estimated proved reserves of petroleum totaled 26.5 million barrels, and its estimated recoverable reserves of natural gas totaled 56.7 billion cu feet. In 1978, 10 petroleum refineries had a daily producing capacity of 655,500 barrels of oil and 300,900 barrels of gasoline. Production of crude petroleum totaled 4.8 million barrels in 1978; of natural gas, 173 million cu feet.

In 1976 there were 2 underground coal mines and 62 strip mines active in the state. Indiana's coal production in 1978 was estimated at 23.9 million tons of coal, 9th in the US and 3.6% of the US total. Land reclaimed from strip-mining by coal operators totaled 13,000 acres (5,300 hectares) in 1978.

29 INDUSTRY

The industrialization of Indiana that began in the Civil War era was spurred by technological advances in processing agricultural products, manufacturing farm equipment, and improving transportation facilities. Meat-packing plants, textile mills, furniture factories, and wagon works—including Studebaker wagons—were soon followed by metal foundries, machine shops, farm implement plants, and a myriad of other durable goods.

New industries included a pharmaceutical house started in Indianapolis in 1876 by a druggist named Eli Lilly, and several automobile manufacturing shops established in South Bend and other cities by 1900. In 1906, the US Steel Co. laid out the new town of Gary for steelworkers and their families.

In 1977, Indiana was the 9th-largest manufacturing state, with a total value added by manufacture of $22.6 billion. The state's leading industry groups in 1972 and 1977, and their value added by manufacture, were as follows:

	1972	1977
Electrical and electronic equipment	$2,324,500,000	$3,583,400,000
Transportation equipment	1,947,900,000	3,383,600,000
Primary metal products	2,192,000,000	3,341,800,000
Nonelectrical machinery	1,305,000,000	2,406,200,000
Fabricated metal products	1,119,800,000	1,850,800,000
Chemicals and chemical products	1,244,800,000	1,771,900,000
Food and food products	972,000,000	1,640,000,000
Drugs	682,200,000	866,400,000
Rubber and plastics	500,600,000	859,300,000
Printing and publishing	447,500,000	679,600,000
Furniture and fixtures	274,900,000	390,400,000
Paper and paper products	224,700,000	384,000,000
Apparel and textile products	119,200,000	174,300,000

According to the 1977 census of manufactures, Indiana led the US in production of storage batteries, small motors, mobile homes, wood furniture, phonograph records and tapes, caskets, and musical instruments. Most manufacturing plants are located in and around Indianapolis and in the Calumet region.

30 COMMERCE

In 1972, Indiana had 8,903 wholesale establishments with 92,676 employees and registered sales totaling $13.4 billion. Of the total sales, merchant wholesalers accounted for 54%, manufacturers for 36%, and merchandise agents and brokers for 10%. Principal goods traded were grains and livestock, food products, motor vehicles and parts, radio and television sets, farm machinery,

and petroleum products. The federal business census of March 1977 listed 8,747 establishments with 99,376 employees and an annual payroll of $1.3 billion.

Retail stores in Indiana had total sales of $18.3 billion in 1977. Of that total, automotive dealers and service stations accounted for 32%; food stores, 20%; general merchandise establishments, 13%; eating and drinking places, 8%; furniture and home appliance outlets, 4%; drugstores, 4%; and other establishments, 19%.

Indiana ranked 7th among the 50 states in agricultural exports in 1978, when farm products shipped abroad were valued at $1.4 billion, or half of the state's total export value. Major farm exports (in order of value) were corn and other feed grains, soybeans, wheat, meat products, lard and tallow, poultry products, and tobacco. Principal nonfarm exports (in order of value) were electronic equipment, construction machinery, electrical apparatus, motor vehicles and parts, transportation equipment, instruments, drugs, medical equipment, and chemicals.

31 CONSUMER PROTECTION

The Division of Consumer Protection of the Office of the Attorney General is empowered to investigate consumer complaints, initiate and prosecute civil actions, and warn consumers about deceptive sales practices. Indiana also has a public counselor, who appears on behalf of the public at hearings of the Public Service Commission in regard to rates charged by public utilities and transportation agencies. The public counselor is appointed by the governor to a four-year term.

In early 1980, the first criminal prosecution of an American corporation because of alleged product defects was brought against the Ford Motor Co. at Winamac. A jury found the company not guilty of reckless homicide in a rear-end collision involving a Pinto automobile in which three young women were killed.

32 BANKING

The large-scale mechanization of agriculture in Indiana after 1850 encouraged the growth of banks to lend money to farmers to buy farm machinery, using their land as collateral. The financial panic of 1893 caused most banks in the state to suspend operations, and the depression of the 1930s caused banks to foreclose many farm mortgages and dozens of banks to fail. The nation's subsequent economic recovery, together with the federal reorganization of the banking system, helped Indiana banks to share in the state's prosperity during and after World War II.

In 1977 there were 407 banks in the state, of which 162 were members of the Federal Reserve System (121 had national charters and 41 were state chartered). Their total assets amounted to $25.6 billion; their liabilities included time deposits of $14.3 billion and demand deposits of $7.5 billion. The state's 166 savings and loan associations held $7.1 billion in mortgage loans and $7.3 billion in savings accounts in 1977; their total assets amounted to $8.4 billion. In the same year, Indiana had 587 credit unions with 876,047 members; these credit unions had outstanding loans totaling $884 million and held savings amounting to $1.1 billion.

The Department of Financial Institutions regulates the operations of Indiana-chartered banks, savings and loans associations, and credit unions. The department is headed by a seven-member board; each board member serves a four-year term, and no more than four members may be of the same political party. A full-time director, also appointed by the governor to a four-year term, is the department's chief executive and administrative officer.

33 INSURANCE

As of 30 June 1977 there were 175 state-licensed insurance companies and 1,089 out-of-state companies with branches in Indiana. Of these 1,264 insurance companies, 562 issued life insurance policies, 437 were multiple-line companies, 75 offered casualty policies, and 190 wrote policies of other types.

In 1978, life insurance companies in the state had in force a total of 10.3 million policies and paid benefits of $669.1 million. In that year, life insurance policies were valued at $72.3 billion, of which $36.5 billion was in ordinary life policies and $30.2 billion in group policies. The average amount of life insurance held by a Hoosier family was $36,900 in 1978.

Health insurance companies in the state collected $622 million in premiums and paid $452 million in benefits in 1975. In addition, Blue Cross–Blue Shield and other hospital and medical plans collected $378 million in premiums and paid benefits totaling $371 million.

Property and liability companies wrote premiums totaling $1.8 billion in 1978, including $768 million in automobile coverage and $218.7 million in homeowners insurance.

The Department of Insurance licenses insurance carriers and agents in Indiana, and it enforces regulations governing the issuance of policies. A 1975 law limited medical malpractice insurance claims.

³⁴SECURITIES

There are no securities exchanges in Indiana. New York Stock Exchange member firms had 65 sales offices and 384 registered representatives in Indiana in 1978. Hoosiers reported $597.7 million in dividend income on their 1977 federal income tax returns. Laws governing the trading and sale of corporate securities are administered by the secretary of state, who also regulates franchise sales and corporate takeover attempts.

³⁵PUBLIC FINANCE

The State Budget Agency acts as watchdog over state financial affairs. The agency prepares the budget for the governor and presents it to the general assembly. The budget director, appointed by the governor, serves with four legislators (two from each house) on the State Budget Committee, which helps to prepare the budget. The State Budget Agency receives appropriations requests from the heads of state offices, estimates anticipated revenues for the biennium, and administers the budget.

The fiscal year runs from 1 July to 30 June of the following year; budgets are prepared for the biennium beginning and ending in an odd-numbered year. The state budget has more than doubled in the decade from 1970 to 1980, mainly because of inflation and the rising cost of government. Federal funds for Indiana were estimated at $2.7 billion for the 1979–81 biennium.

The following is a summary of estimated revenues and requested expenditures for 1979/80 and 1980/81 (in millions):

REVENUES	1979/80	1980/81
Sales and use taxes	$1,025.8	$1,164.0
Individual income taxes	705.1	805.9
Corporate income taxes	519.9	553.0
Other taxes	530.4	552.1
Intergovernmental receipts	1,200.0	1.257.1
Other revenues	238.9	242.2
TOTALS	$4,220.1	$4,574.3

EXPENDITURES		
Local school aid	$1,193.1	$1,308.6
Other aid to education	696.3	768.5
Highways and roads	512.9	488.4
Public welfare	511.2	566.8
Health	441.3	458.9
General government	250.3	266.6
Public safety and regulation	116.8	117.6
Corrections	113.6	115.8
Natural resources	90.8	91.0
Other appropriations	786.1	824.2
TOTALS	$4,712.4	$5,006.4

In the fiscal year 1976/77, local governments spent a total of $3.2 billion. Counties spent $694.4 million; municipalities, $804.7 million; and school districts $1,521.7 million. In that fiscal year,

local governments collected total revenues of $3.4 billion, of which 54% was raised by property taxes and other local taxes, 39% was provided by the state government, and 7% came from the federal government.

The total indebtedness of county and local governments was nearly $2.2 billion in 1977. About 97% of this total represented long-term obligation; 42% of the obligations were backed by the full faith and credit of the issuing body, while 58% were not fully guaranteed.

³⁶TAXATION

The first state property tax in Indiana was levied in 1852 to support public schools. In 1923, a state gasoline tax of 2 cents per gallon (8 cents in 1979) was introduced. In 1933, Indiana instituted the personal income tax, which was the major source of state revenue until 1963, when a 2% retail sales tax was enacted. Also in 1933, with the end of Prohibition, taxes were imposed on the manufacture and sale of alcoholic beverages. In 1973, the state sales tax was doubled to 4% and optional local income taxes of up to 1% were initiated, while local property taxes were reduced by at least 20% to ease the tax burden on property owners. The state's personal income tax in 1980 was 1.9% of adjusted gross income after the first $1,000 for single persons and the first $2,000 for married couples, with exemptions of $500 for each dependent.

In the 1976/77 fiscal year, Indiana's state taxes totaled nearly $3.5 billion; the tax per capita was $653, 20% below the US average. Of total state taxes collected that year, the major sources were retail sales tax, 50%; income tax, 26%; state property tax, 1%; and miscellaneous taxes, 23%.

Taxes levied by local governments in fiscal 1976/77 totaled more than $1.3 billion, of which the local property tax provided 97% of the total. In fiscal year 1974/75, the total tax burden in Indiana amounted to $9.9 billion, of which the federal government received 69%, the state government 21%, and local governments 10%.

Hoosiers filed 2,117,735 federal income tax returns for 1977, paying a total tax of $4.1 billion.

³⁷ECONOMIC POLICY

The state's early economic policy was to provide farmers with access to markets by improving transportation facilities. During the Civil War era, however, the state began to encourage industrial growth. In modern times, the state has financed extensive highway construction, developed deepwater ports on Lake Michigan and the Ohio River, and worked to foster industrial growth and the state tourist industry. Tax incentives to businessmen include a 15-year phaseout, beginning in 1979, of the "intangibles" tax on stocks, bonds, and notes.

The Department of Commerce solicits new businesses to locate in Indiana, promotes sales of exports abroad, plans the development of energy resources, continues to promote the expansion of agriculture, and helps minority-group owners of small businesses. The department's Industrial Development Fund makes loans to municipalities for the purchasing or leasing of property for industrial development.

³⁸HEALTH

Average life expectancy, mortality rates, and infant death rates are all close to the national average in Indiana. In 1977, the live-birth rate for the state was 16 per 1,000 population; the infant mortality rates were 13.3 per 1,000 live births for whites, and 21.6 for other races; and the legal abortion rate was 126 per 1,000 live births (far below the US average of 400).

In 1977, the most common childhood diseases were chicken pox, measles, rubella, scarlet fever, and mumps; the most prevalent adult communicable diseases were influenza, gonorrhea, streptococcal sore throat, pneumonia, impetigo, salmonellosis, syphilis, hepatitis, and meningitis. The principal causes of death in Indiana during 1977 were as follows: heart disease, 17,938;

cancer, 9,251; cerebrovascular diseases, 5,298; arterial disease, 1,782; motor vehicle accidents, 1,323; other accidents, 1,258; pneumonia, 1,098; and diabetes, 1,013.

In the 1970s, the state started new health programs for the care and treatment of chronic kidney disease, sickle-cell anemia, and hemophilia. In 1970, Indiana ranked 20th among the 50 states in alcoholism, with an estimated 124,500 alcoholics (3,940 per 100,000 population).

Indiana had a total of 135 hospitals in 1978, with 33,816 beds; 129 were community hospitals, with 27,521 beds, of which an average of 74% were occupied. Mental hospitals in the state had 8,763 patients in 1978. Hospital personnel totaled 74,829, of whom 12,791 were registered nurses and 4,702 were licensed practical nurses. The state had 6,763 physicians in 1977, of whom 1,622 were general practitioners. There were 2,234 dentists in 1979; the rate of 2,390 people per professionally active dentist was 29% above the US average.

The State Board of Health is responsible for protecting the health and lives of Hoosiers. In the 1977/78 fiscal year, the state spent $286.5 million for health care, more than half of that for mental health.

[39] SOCIAL WELFARE

In 1976, expenditures for public assistance in Indiana exceeded $435 million; the federal government provided more than 68% of the total. Public assistance payments to families with dependent children totaled $148 million in 1978. Food stamps were issued to more than 169,000 persons; the federal cost was $56.2 million. School lunches were provided to 712,000 pupils, at a cost to the federal government of $31.7 million.

In 1977, Social Security benefits were paid to 798,100 persons, of whom 510,700 were retired workers, 181,500 were surviving dependents, and 105,900 were disabled workers. Benefit payments totaled more than $2 billion. The average monthly payment was $254.40 per retired worker, above the US average. Supplemental Security Income was provided to a monthly average of 40,573 recipients in 1978, and totaled $41.1 million, of which about 57% went to the disabled, 41% to the aged, and 2% to the blind. In addition, compensation and pension payments to Indiana veterans amounted to $169.3 million in 1977/78.

In 1978, vocational rehabilitation programs enrolled 13,200 persons, of whom 3,200 were declared rehabilitated; the programs cost $18 million. Workers' compensation payments totaled $76 million in 1977.

In 1978, state unemployment insurance covered 2,055,000 workers in Indiana; weekly payments to 32,000 unemployed workers averaged $75.75 per worker.

[40] HOUSING

The great majority of Indiana families enjoy adequate housing, particularly in newly built suburbs, but inadequate housing exists in the deteriorating central cores of large cities.

In 1977, the state had 1,990,612 housing units, of which 80% were single-family units and 15% were multifamily units; the remainder included 104,303 mobile homes. In 1970, about 65% of all houses were located in urban areas, and 35% in rural areas. Of all rented housing units in 1970, about 82% were occupied by single families, 13% were multifamily dwellings, and 5% were mobile homes.

In 1978, the median sales price of a new house in the north-central states (including Indiana) was $59,200, compared with the US average of $55,700; the median sales price of an existing home was $42,200, compared with $48,700 for the US. The mean sales price of all houses sold in Marion and Hamilton counties (both in the Indianapolis metropolitan area) in 1979 was $48,850.

In 1978, the number of housing units authorized for construction was 35,100, of which 70% were single-family units; the value of new housing units was estimated at nearly $1.3 billion. A total of 251,817 housing starts was authorized between 1970 and 1977;

about 36% were multifamily dwellings. Overall, the state's housing stock increased by about 15% during this period.

[41] EDUCATION

Although the 1816 constitution recommended establishment of public schools, the state legislature did not provide funds for education. The constitution of 1851 more specifically outlined the state's responsibility to support a system of free public schools. Development was rapid following passage of this document; more than 2,700 schoolhouses were built in the state from 1852 to 1857, and an adult literacy rate of nearly 90% was achieved by 1860. The illiteracy rate was reduced to 5.2% for the adult population in 1900, 1.7% in 1950, and to only 0.7% in 1970, when Indiana ranked 14th among the 50 states. In 1976, the median educational level was 12.4 years, and 67% of those aged 18 years and over were high school graduates. Indiana ranked 15th among the states in college enrollment in 1975.

In the fall of 1977, Indiana had 2,057 public schools with 1,143,722 pupils, including 1,547 elementary schools with 766,821 pupils and 510 secondary schools with 376,901 pupils. In that year there were also 336 private schools with 91,756 pupils. Public-school teachers in 1978 numbered about 48,000; their average salary was $13,421.

In the 1977/78 school year there were 32 private colleges with 52,544 students and 6 publicly supported colleges with 165,389 students. Indiana University, the state's largest institution of higher education, was founded in 1820. It was the 10th-largest state university in the US in 1978/79, with a total enrollment on 8 campuses of 75,150; the Bloomington campus alone had 31,526 students. Other major state universities and their 1978/79 enrollments were Purdue University (Lafayette), 31,070; Ball State University (Muncie), 18,875; and Indiana State University (Terre Haute), 11,692. Well-known private universities in the state are Notre Dame (at Notre Dame) and Butler (Indianapolis). Small private colleges and universities include DePauw (Greencastle), Earlham (Richmond), Hanover (at Hanover), and Wabash (Crawfordsville).

In 1965, the general assembly established a program of state college scholarships, at least two for each county. Recipients must be US citizens under 25 years of age, Indiana residents for at least 6 months prior to enrollment, and enrolled full-time in a college or community college.

The state superintendent of public instruction is elected for a four-year term. He serves on the 19-member Board of Education, which is appointed by the governor. The board, which sets basic policy for the public school system, is divided into three commissions dealing, respectively, with general education, textbook adoption, and teacher training and licensing.

In 1977/78, Indiana spent more than $1.8 billion on public schools, for an average expenditure of $1,449 per student based on average daily attendance (33d in the US).

[42] ARTS

The earliest center for artists in Indiana was the Art Association of Indianapolis, founded in 1883. It managed the John Herron Art Institute, consisting of a museum and art school (1906–08). Around 1900, art colonies sprang up in Richmond, Muncie, South Bend, and Nashville. Indianapolis remains the state's cultural center, especially after the opening in the late 1960s of the Lilly Pavilion of the Decorative Arts, the Krannert Pavilion, which houses the paintings originally in the Herron Museum, the Clowes Art Pavilion, and the Grace Showalter Pavilion of the Performing Arts (all collectively known as the Indianapolis Museum of Art). Since 1969, the Indiana Arts Commission has taken art—and artists—into many Indiana communities. Some 40 arts councils in Indianapolis and other cities encourage painters and sponsor art exhibitions.

The state's first resident theater company established itself in Indianapolis in 1840, and the first theater building, the Metropolitan, was opened there in 1858. Ten years later, the Academy of Music was founded as the center for dramatic activities in Indianapolis. In 1875, the Grand Opera House opened there, and the following year it was joined by the English Opera House, where touring performers such as Sarah Bernhardt, Edwin Booth, and Ethel Barrymore held the stage. Amateur theater has been popular since the founding in 1915 of the nation's oldest amateur drama group, the Little Theater Society, which later became the Civic Theater of Indianapolis.

Music has flourished in Indiana. Connersville reportedly was the first American city to establish a high school band, while Richmond claims the first high school symphony orchestra. The Indianapolis Symphony Orchestra was founded in 1930. The Arthur Jordan College of Music is part of Butler University in Indianapolis.

43 LIBRARIES AND MUSEUMS

The state constitution of 1816 provided for the establishment of public libraries. A majority of Indiana counties opened such libraries but neglected to provide adequate financing. Semiprivate libraries did better: workingmen's libraries were set up by a bequest at New Harmony and 14 other towns. After the state legislature provided for township school libraries in 1852, more than two-thirds of the townships established them, and the public library system has thrived ever since. In 1978 there were 49 county libraries, and every county received some form of library service. Federal grants-in-aid totaled $1,690,509; state grants, $832,000. The largest book collections are at public libraries in Indianapolis, Fort Wayne, Gary, Evansville, South Bend, and Hammond; the total book stock of all Indiana public libraries was 13,392,299 volumes in 1978.

The Indiana State Library maintains the state's archives, a complete collection of documents about Indiana's history, and a large genealogical collection. The Indiana University Library has special collections on American literature and history; the University of Notre Dame has a noteworthy collection on medieval history; and Purdue University Libraries contain outstanding industrial and agricultural collections, as well as voluminous materials on Indiana history.

Private libraries and museums include those maintained by historical societies in Indianapolis, Fort Wayne, and South Bend. Also of note are the General Lew Wallace Study museum in Crawfordsville and the Elwood Haynes Museum of early technology in Kokomo. In all, Indiana had more than 120 museums in 1980.

Indiana's historic sites of most interest to visitors are the Lincoln Boyhood National Memorial near Gentryville, the Benjamin Harrison Memorial Home and the James Whitcomb Riley Home in Indianapolis, and the Grouseland Home of William Henry Harrison in Vincennes. Among several archaeological sites are two large mound groups: one at Mounds State Park near Anderson, which dates from about AD 800–900; and a reconstructed village site at Angel Mounds, Newburgh, which dates from AD 1300–1500.

44 COMMUNICATIONS

In 1977, some 24,200 Hoosiers worked in the field of communications, the largest group being about 13,800 postal employees. In 1978 there were 55 telephone companies operating in the state, maintaining 4,042,963 telephones, of which 3,099,101 were residential and 943,862 business phones. About 95% of all households had telephone service, below the US average.

The state's first radio station was licensed in 1922 at Purdue University, Lafayette. Indiana had 86 AM and 95 FM radio stations and 22 television stations in 1978. Powerful radio and television transmissions from Chicago and Cincinnati also blanket the state. As of 31 December 1979, 85 cable television systems served 142 communities and 261,831 subscribers throughout much of the state.

45 PRESS

The first newspaper in Indiana was published at Vincennes in 1804, and a second pioneer weekly appeared at Madison nine years later. By 1830, newspapers were also being published in Terre Haute, Indianapolis, and 11 other towns; the following year the state's oldest surviving newspaper, the Richmond *Palladium,* began publication. Most pioneer newspapers were highly political and engaged in acrimonious feuds; in 1836, for example, the Indianapolis *Journal* referred to the editors of the rival *Democrat* as "the Lying, Hireling Scoundrels." By the time of the Civil War, Indiana had 154 weeklies and 13 dailies.

The last third of the 19th century brought a sharp increase in both the number and quality of newspapers. Two newspapers, which later became the state's largest in circulation, the Indianapolis *News* and the *Star,* began publishing in 1869 and 1904, respectively. In 1941 there were 294 weekly and 98 daily newspapers in Indiana; the number declined after World War II because of fierce competition for readers and advertising dollars, rising operating costs, and other financial difficulties.

In 1978, the state had 7 morning dailies with a paid circulation of about 441,479, and 71 evening dailies with 1,204,344 paid circulation; Sunday papers numbered 18, with paid circulation totaling 1,183,149. In 1979, the Indianapolis morning *Star* had a daily circulation of 217,619 (Sunday circulation, 357,706); the Indianapolis evening *News* had a daily circulation of 152,367; and the Gary evening *Post-Tribune*'s circulation averaged 81,122 daily and 83,675 on Sundays.

Indiana is noted for its literary productivity. A survey of authors claimed by Indiana up to 1966 showed a total of 3,600. Examination of the 10 best-selling novels each year from 1900 to 1940 (allowing 10 points to the top best-seller, down to 1 point for the 10th best-selling book) showed Indiana with a score of 213 points, exceeded only by New York's 218.

Many Hoosier authors were first published by Indiana's major book publisher, Bobbs-Merrill. Indiana University Press is an important publisher of scholarly books.

46 ORGANIZATIONS

National organizations with headquarters in Indiana include the Amateur Athletic Union of the US and the American Legion, both in Indianapolis; and the American Camping Association, at Martinsville. Founded in 1919, the American Legion enrolled 123,487 Hoosiers in 1979, when its total US membership was 2,629,105.

Philanthropic foundations headquartered in the state are the Indianapolis Foundation, the Krannert Charitable Trust, and the Lilly Endowment, all located in Indianapolis; the Ball family foundation at Muncie; the Eugene V. Debs Foundation at Terre Haute; and the Irwin-Sweeney-Miller Foundation in Columbus.

47 TOURISM, TRAVEL, AND RECREATION

Tourism is of moderate economic importance to Indiana. In 1977, 64,947 Hoosiers worked in travel-related industries, and travelers spent $1.8 billion in the state.

Summer resorts are located in the north, along Lake Michigan and in Steuben and Kosciusko counties, where there are nearly 200 lakes. Popular tourist sites include the reconstructed village of New Harmony and Zionsville, the Indianapolis Motor Speedway and Museum, the George Rogers Clark National Historic Park at Vincennes, and 15 state memorials, including the Wilbur Wright State Memorial at his birthplace near Millville. Among the natural attractions are the Indiana Dunes National Lakeshore on Lake Michigan; the state's largest waterfall, Cataract Falls, near Cloverdale; and the largest underground cavern at Wyandotte.

Indiana has 19 state parks and many recreational areas, together comprising more than 320,000 acres (130,000 hectares). The largest state park is Brown County (15,543 acres, or 6,290 hectares), near Nashville. There are 15 state fish and wildlife preserves, totaling about 75,200 acres (30,400 hectares). The largest are Pigeon River, near Howe, and Willow Slough, at Morocco. Game animals during the hunting season include deer, squirrel, and rabbit; ruffed grouse, quail, ducks, geese, and partridge are the main game birds. In 1977/78, the state issued licenses to 650,608 fishermen and 419,761 hunters.

⁴⁸SPORTS

Indiana is represented in professional sports by the Indiana Pacers of the National Basketball Association, and by Indianapolis in baseball's Class AAA league.

The state's biggest annual sports event is the Indianapolis 500, which has been held at the Indianapolis Motor Speedway on Memorial Day every year since 1911 (except for the war years 1917 and 1942–45). The race is now part of a three-day Indiana festival and attracts crowds of over 300,000 spectators; prize money in 1980 amounted to $1,502,425, with $318,019 going to the winning car.

The state's most popular amateur sport is basketball. The high school boys' basketball tournament culminates on the last Saturday in March, when the four finalists play afternoon and evening games to determine the winner before sold-out crowds at Indianapolis's Market Street Arena. A tournament for girls' basketball teams began in 1976. Basketball is also popular at the college level: Indiana University won the NCAA Division I basketball championship in 1940, 1953, and 1976, and the National Invitational Tournament (NIT) in 1979; Purdue University won the NIT title in 1974; and Evansville College won the NCAA Division II championships in 1959–60, 1964–65, and 1971.

Collegiate football in Indiana has a colorful tradition stretching back at least to 1913, when Knute Rockne of Notre Dame unleashed the forward pass as a potent football weapon. Notre Dame, which competes as an independent, was recognized as the top US college football team in 1946–47, 1949, 1966, 1973 (with Alabama), and 1977. Indiana and Purdue compete in the Big Ten, while Indiana State is part of the Missouri Valley Conference.

The Little 500, a 50-mi (80-km) bicycle race, is held each spring at Indiana University's Bloomington campus.

⁴⁹FAMOUS HOOSIERS

Indiana has contributed one US president and four vice presidents to the nation. Benjamin Harrison (b. Ohio, 1833–1901), the 23d president, was a Republican who served one term (1889–93) and then returned to Indianapolis, where his home is now a national historic landmark. Three vice presidents were Indiana residents: Thomas Hendricks (b.Ohio, 1819–85), who served only eight months under President Cleveland and died in office; Schuyler Colfax (b.New York, 1823–85), who served under President Grant; and Charles Fairbanks (b.Ohio, 1852–1918), who served under Theodore Roosevelt. One vice president was a native son: Thomas Marshall (1854–1925), who served two four-year terms with President Wilson. Marshall, remembered for his wit, originated the remark, "What this country needs is a good five-cent cigar."

Other Indiana-born political figures include Eugene V. Debs (1855–1926), Socialist Party candidate for president five times, and Wendell L. Willkie (1892–1944), the Republican candidate in 1940.

A dozen native and adoptive Hoosiers have held cabinet posts. Hugh McCulloch (b.Maine, 1808–95) was twice secretary of the treasury, in 1865–69 and 1884–85. Walter Q. Gresham (b. England, 1832–95) was successively postmaster general, secretary of the treasury, and secretary of state. John W. Foster (1836–1917) was an editor and diplomat before serving as secretary of state under President Benjamin Harrison. Two other postmasters general came from Indiana: Harry S. New (1858–1937), and Will H. Hays (1879–1954). Hays resigned to become president of the Motion Picture Producers and Distributors (1922–45), and enforced its moral code in Hollywood films through what became widely known as the Hays Office. Two Hoosiers served as secretary of the interior: Caleb B. Smith (b.Massachusetts, 1808–64) and John P. Usher (b.New York, 1816–89). Richard W. Thompson (b.Virginia, 1809–1900) was secretary of the Navy. William H. H. Miller (b. New York, 1840–1917) was attorney general. Two native sons and Purdue University alumni have been secretaries of agriculture: Claude R. Wickard (1873–1967) and Earl Butz (b.1909). Paul V. McNutt (1891–1955) was a governor of Indiana, high commissioner to the Philippines, and director of the Federal Security Administration.

Only one Hoosier, Sherman Minton (1890–1965), has served on the US Supreme Court. Ambrose Burnside (1824–81) and Lew Wallace (1827–1905) were Union generals during the Civil War; Wallace later wrote popular historical novels. Oliver P. Morton (1823–77) was a strong and meddlesome governor during the war, and a leader of the radical Republicans during the postwar Reconstruction. Colonel Richard Owen (b.England, 1810–90) commanded Camp Morton (Indianapolis) for Confederate prisoners; after the war, some of his grateful prisoners contributed to place a bust of Owen in the Indiana statehouse. Rear Admiral Norman Scott (1889–1942) distinguished himself at Guadalcanal during World War II. Nearly 70 Hoosiers have won the Medal of Honor.

Dr. Hermann J. Muller (b.New York, 1890–1967), of Indiana University, won the Nobel Prize in physiology and medicine in 1946 for proving that radiation can cause mutation in genes. The Pulitzer Prize in biography was awarded in 1920 to Albert J. Beveridge (b.Ohio, 1862–1927) for his *Life of John Marshall*. Beveridge also served in the US Senate. Booth Tarkington (1869–1946) won the Pulitzer Prize for fiction in 1918 and 1921. A. B. Guthrie (b.1901) won it for fiction in 1950. The Pulitzer Prize in history went to R. C. Buley (1893–1968) in 1951 for *The Old Northwest*.

Aviation pioneer Wilbur Wright (1867–1912) was born in Millville. Other figures in the public eye were chemist Harvey W. Wiley (1844–1930), who was responsible for the Food and Drug Act of 1906; Emil Schram (b.1893), president of the New York Stock Exchange from 1931 to 1951; and Alfred C. Kinsey (b. New Jersey, 1894–1956), who investigated human sexual behavior and issued the famous "Kinsey reports" in 1948 and 1953.

Indiana claims such humorists as George Ade (1866–1944), Frank McKinney "Kin" Hubbard, (b.Ohio, 1868–1930), and Don Herold (1889–1966). Historians Charles (1874–1948) and Mary (1876–1958) Beard, Claude Bowers (1878–1958), and Glenn Tucker (1892–1976) were Hoosiers. Maurice Thompson (1844–1901) and George Barr McCutcheon (1866–1928) excelled in historical romances. The best-known poets were James Whitcomb Riley (1849–1916) and William Vaughn Moody (1869–1910). Juvenile writer Annie Fellows Johnston (1863–1931) produced the "Little Colonel" series.

Other Indiana novelists include Edward Eggleston (1837–1902), Meredith Nicholson (1866–1947), David Graham Phillips (1868–1911), Gene Stratton Porter (1868–1924), Theodore Dreiser (1871–1945), Lloyd C. Douglas (1877–1951), Rex Stout (1886–1975), William E. Wilson (b.1906), Jessamyn West (b.1907), and Kurt Vonnegut (b.1922). Well-known journalists were news analyst Elmer Davis (1890–1958), war correspondent Ernie Pyle (1900–45), and columnist Janet Flanner (1892–1978), "Genêt" of the *New Yorker*.

Among the few noted painters Indiana has produced are Theodore C. Steele (1847–1928), William M. Chase (1851–1927), J. Ottis Adams (1851–1927), Otto Stark (1859–1926), Wayman Adams (1883–1959), Clifton Wheeler (1883–1953), Marie Goth (1887–1975), C. Curry Bohm (1894–1971), and Floyd Hopper (b.1909).

Composers of Indiana origin have worked mainly in popular music: Paul Dresser (1857–1906), Cole Porter (1893–1964), and

Howard Hoagland "Hoagy" Carmichael, (b.1899). Howard Hawks (1896-1977) was a renowned film director. Entertainers from Indiana include actor and dancer Clifton Webb (Webb Hollenbeck, 1896–1966); orchestra leader Phil Harris (b.1906), comedians Ole Olsen (1892–1963), Richard "Red" Skelton (b.1913), and Herb Shriner (b.Ohio, 1918–70); and actresses Marjorie Main (1890–1975) and Carole Lombard (Jane Peters, 1908–42).

Hoosier sports heroes include Knute Rockne (b.Norway, 1888–1931), famed as a football player and coach at Notre Dame. Star professionals who played high school basketball in Indiana include Oscar Robertson (b.Tennessee, 1938) and Larry Bird (b.1956), who at Indiana State University in 1978/79 was honored as college basketball's player of the year.

⁵⁰BIBLIOGRAPHY

Banta, R. E. *Indiana Authors and Their Books, 1816–1916.* Crawfordsville: Wabash College, 1949.

Banta, R. E. *The Wabash.* New York: Farrar & Rinehart, 1950.

Barnhart, John D., and Donald F. Carmony. *Indiana From Frontier to Industrial Commonwealth.* 4 vols. New York: Lewis Historical Publishing, 1954.

Barnhart, John D., and Dorothy L. Riker. *Indiana to 1816: The Colonial Period.* Indianapolis: Indiana Historical Society, 1971.

Bloemker, Al. *500 Miles to Go: The Story of the Indianapolis Speedway.* New York: Coward-McCann, 1961.

Buley, R. C. *The Old Northwest: Pioneer Period, 1815–1840.* Indianapolis: Indiana Historical Society, 1950.

Federal Writers' Project. *Indiana: A Guide to the Hoosier State.* New York: Oxford University Press, 1941.

Indiana State Chamber of Commerce. *Here Is Your Indiana Government.* Indianapolis, 1979.

Latta, William C. *Outline History of Indiana Agriculture.* Lafayette: Purdue University and Indiana County Agricultural Agents Assn., 1938.

Leibowitz, Irving. *My Indiana.* Englewood Cliffs, N.J.: Prentice-Hall, 1964.

Lilly, Eli. *Prehistoric Antiquities of Indiana.* Indianapolis: Indiana Historical Society, 1937.

Lindley, Harlow, ed. *Indiana as Seen by Early Travelers.* Indianapolis: Indiana Historical Commission, 1916.

McCord, Shirley S., ed. *Travel Accounts of Indiana, 1679–1961.* Indianapolis: Indiana Historical Bureau, 1970.

Martin, John Bartlow. *Indiana: An Interpretation.* New York: Knopf, 1947.

Nicholson, Meredith. *The Hoosiers.* New York: Macmillan, 1900.

Nolan, Jeannette C. *Hoosier City: The Story of Indianapolis.* New York: Messner, 1943.

Peat, Wilbur D. *Pioneer Painters of Indiana.* Indianapolis: Art Association of Indianapolis, 1954.

Peckham, Howard H. *Indiana: A Bicentennial History.* New York: Norton, 1978.

Phillips, Clifton J. *Indiana in Transition: The Emergence of an Industrial Commonwealth, 1880–1920.* Indianapolis: Indiana Historical Society, 1968.

Shumaker, Arthur W. *A History of Indiana Literature.* Indianapolis: Indiana Historical Society, 1962.

Starr, George W. *Industrial Development of Indiana.* Bloomington: Indiana University, 1937.

State of Indiana. *Indiana Fact Book 1979.* State Planning Services, 1979.

Thompson, Donald E. *Indiana Authors and Their Books, 1916–66.* Crawfordsville: Wabash College, 1974.

Thornbrough, Emma Lou. *Indiana in the Civil War Era, 1850–80.* Indianapolis: Indiana Historical Society, 1965.

Wilson, William E. *The Angel and the Serpent: The Story of New Harmony.* Bloomington: Indiana University Press, 1964.

Wilson, William E. *Indiana: A History.* Bloomington: Indiana University Press, 1966.

IOWA

State of Iowa

IOWA

ORIGIN OF STATE NAME: Named for Iowa Indians of the Siouan family. **NICKNAME**: The Hawkeye State. **CAPITAL**: Des Moines. **ENTERED UNION**: 28 December 1846 (29th). **SONG**: "The Song of Iowa." **MOTTO**: Our Liberties We Prize and Our Rights We Will Maintain. **FLAG**: There are three vertical stripes of blue, white, and red; in the center a spreading eagle holds in its beak a blue ribbon with the state motto. **OFFICIAL SEAL**: A sheaf and field of standing wheat and farm utensils represent agriculture; a lead furnace and a pile of pig lead are to the right. In the center stands a citizen-soldier holding a US flag with a liberty cap atop the staff in one hand and a rifle in the other. Behind him is the Mississippi River with the steamer *Iowa* and mountains; above him an eagle holds the state motto. Surrounding this scene are the words "The Great Seal of the State of Iowa" against a gold background. **BIRD**: Eastern goldfinch. **FLOWER**: Wild rose. **TREE**: Oak. **STONE**: Geode. **LEGAL HOLIDAYS**: New Year's Day, 1 January; Lincoln's Birthday, 12 February; Washington's Birthday, 3d Monday in February; Memorial Day, last Monday in May; Independence Day, 4 July; Labor Day, 1st Monday in September; Veterans Day, 11 November; Thanksgiving Day, 4th Thursday in November; Christmas Day, 25 December. **TIME**: 6 A.M. CST = noon GMT.

¹LOCATION, SIZE, AND EXTENT

Located in the western north-central US, Iowa is the smallest of the midwestern states situated W of the Mississippi River, and ranks 25th in size among the 50 states.

The total area of Iowa is 56,290 sq mi (145,791 sq km), of which land takes up 55,941 sq mi (144,887 sq km) and inland water 349 sq mi (904 sq km). The state extends 324 mi (521 km) E–W; its maximum extension N–S is 210 mi (338 km).

Iowa is bordered on the N by Minnesota; on the E by Wisconsin and Illinois (with the line formed by the Mississippi River); on the S by Missouri (with the extreme southeastern line defined by the Des Moines River); and on the W by Nebraska and South Dakota (with the line demarcated by the Missouri River and a tributary, the Big Sioux).

The total boundary length of Iowa is 1,151 mi (1,853 km). The state's geographic center is in Story County, near Ames.

²TOPOGRAPHY

The topography of Iowa consists of a gently rolling plain that slopes from the highest point of 1,670 feet (509 meters) in the northwest to the lowest point of 480 feet (146 meters) in the southeast at the mouth of the Des Moines River. About two-thirds of the state lies between 800 feet (244 meters) and 1,400 feet (427 meters) above sea level; the mean elevation of land is 1,100 feet (335 meters).

Supremely well suited for agriculture, Iowa has the richest and deepest topsoil in the US and an excellent watershed. Approximately two-thirds of the state's area is drained by the Mississippi River, which forms the entire eastern boundary, and its tributaries. The western part of the state is drained by the Missouri River and its tributaries. Iowa has 13 natural lakes. The largest are Spirit Lake (9 mi, or 14 km, long) and West Okoboji Lake (6 mi, or 10 km, long), both near the state's northwest border.

The Iowa glacial plain was formed by five different glaciers. The last glacier, which covered about one-fifth of the state's area, retreated from the north-central region some 10,000 years ago, leaving the topsoil as its legacy. Glacial drift formed the small lakes in the north. The oldest rock outcropping, in the state's northwest corner, is about 1 billion years old.

³CLIMATE

Iowa lies in the humid continental zone and generally has hot summers, cold winters, and wet springs.

Temperatures vary widely during the year, with an annual average of 49°F (9°C). The state averages 166 days of full sunshine and 199 cloudy or partly cloudy days. Des Moines, in the central part of the state, has a normal maximum temperature of 75°F (24°C) and a normal minimum of 24°F (–4°C). The record low temperature for the state is –47°F (–44°C), established at Washta on 12 January 1912; the record high is 118°F (48°C), registered at Keokuk on 20 July 1934. Rainfall averages 32 in (81 cm) annually; snowfall, 30 in (76 cm); and relative humidity, 72%.

⁴FLORA AND FAUNA

Although most of Iowa is under cultivation, such unusual wild specimens as bunchberry and bearberry can be found in the northeast, whose loess soil supports tumblegrass, western beard-tongue, and prickly pear cactus. Other notable plants are pink lady's-slipper and twin-leaf in the eastern woodlands, arrowgrass in the northwest, and erect dryflower and royal and cinnamon ferns in sandy regions. More than 80 native plants can no longer be found, and at least 35 others are confined to a single location. Three state plants thought to be endangered are Mead's milkweed, prairie bushclover, and monkshood, which the federal government classified as threatened as of 1978.

Common Iowa mammals include red and gray foxes, raccoon, opossum, woodchuck, muskrat, common cottontail, and gray, fox, and flying squirrels. The bobolink and purple martin have flyways over the state; the cardinal, rose-breasted grosbeak, and eastern goldfinch (the state bird) nest there. Game fish include rainbow trout, smallmouth bass, and walleye; in all, Iowa has 140 native fish species.

Rare animals include the pygmy shrew, ermine, black-billed cuckoo, and crystal darter. The state lists as endangered the red-backed vole, black bear, bobcat, red-shouldered hawk, piping plover, burrowing owl, northern copperhead, and lake sturgeon. The Indiana bat and peregrine falcon, both indigenous to Iowa, are on the federal endangered species list.

⁵ENVIRONMENTAL PROTECTION

Because this traditionally agricultural state's most valuable resource has been its topsoil, Iowa's conservation measures beginning in the 1930s were directed toward preventing soil erosion and preserving watershed runoff. In the 1970s, Iowans began to pay equal attention to improving air quality and preventing chemical pollution.

The Iowa Department of Environmental Quality develops and implements programs to preserve the quality of the state's air, land, and water. Another executive agency, the Iowa State Conservation Commission, administers state parks, preserves, forests, and other conservation areas. The commission coordinates the plans of other state government agencies that receive federal funds for environmental protection.

During the 1977 fiscal year, Iowa's share of federal outlays for pollution control totaled $47,658,000, and for conservation and land management, $14,923,000. Of the state's own expenditures for environmental protection, the Department of Environmental Quality spent an estimated $2,126,386 in 1978/79, and the State Conservation Commission expended an estimated $7,880,200.

⁶POPULATION

Iowa, the 25th in size of the 50 states, also ranked 25th in state population at the 1970 census, with 2,825,041 residents. Iowa's preliminary 1980 census population was 2,908,797.

Iowa's population growth was rapid during the early years of settlement. When the first pioneers arrived in the early 19th century, an estimated 8,000 Indians were living within the state's present boundaries. From 1832 to 1840, the number of white settlers increased from fewer than 50 to 43,112. The population had almost doubled to more than 80,000 by the time Iowa became a state in 1846. The great influx of European immigrants who came via other states during the 1840s and 1850s caused the new state's population to soar to 674,913 at the 1860 census. By the end of the next decade the population had reached nearly 1,200,000; by 1900 it had surpassed 2,200,000.

The state's population growth leveled off in the 20th century. In 1970, Iowa's population was 51.4% female and 48.6% male; 57% of all Iowans lived in urban areas. Of the total 1970 population, over 98% was native-born; only 9% had one or two foreign-born parents.

The population density was 50.5 persons per sq mi (19.5 per sq km) at the 1970 census. The most densely populated area was Polk County (including Des Moines), with 495 persons per sq mi (191 per sq km); the least was Ringgold County, in the south, with 11.8 persons per sq mi (4.6 per sq km).

In 1970, Iowa had 111 cities and towns of more than 2,500 population. Of these, seven cities had populations of over 50,000: Des Moines, 200,587; Cedar Rapids, 110,642; Davenport, 98,469; Sioux City, 85,925; Waterloo, 75,533; Dubuque, 62,309; and Council Bluffs, 60,348. In 1980, according to early census data, Des Moines had 190,410 residents; Cedar Rapids, 110,124.

⁷ETHNIC GROUPS

In 1970, 9% of Iowa's population consisted of second-generation Americans of European descent, chiefly from Germany, Sweden, and Norway. There were 35,000 black Americans in the state in 1976, and no more than 10,000 persons of Asian-Pacific origin. Among these, as of 1975, were 2,593 Indochinese refugees. American Indians numbered only 2,992 in 1970.

⁸LANGUAGES

A few Indian place-names are the legacy of early Siouan Iowa Indians and the westward-moving Algonkian Sauk and Fox tribes who pushed them out: Iowa, Ottumwa, Keokuk, Sioux City, Oskaloosa, Decorah. In all, only 617 Iowans claimed an Indian language as their first in 1970.

Iowa English reflects the three major migration streams: Northern in that half of the state above Des Moines and North Midland in the southern half, with a slight South Midland trace in the extreme southeastern corner. Although some Midland features extend into upper Iowa, rather sharp contrasts exist between the two halves. In pronunciation, Northern features contrast directly with Midland: /hyumor/ with /yumor/, /ah/ in *on* and *fog* with /aw/, the vowel of *but* in *bulge* with the vowel of *put*, and /too/ with /tyoo/ for *two*. Northern words also contrast with Midland words: *crab* with *crawdad*, *corn on the cob* with *roasting*

ears, *quarter to* with *quarter till*, *barnyard* with *barn lot*, and *gopher* with *ground squirrel*.

In 1970, 86% of native-born Iowans reported English as their mother tongue, and 85% of all state residents. Major resident groups reported their mother tongue as follows:

	NATIVE-BORN	FOREIGN-BORN
English	2,405,288	7,055
German	157,727	10,397
Spanish	7,958	2,224
Italian	6,005	1,545
French	4,283	931

⁹RELIGIONS

The first church building in Iowa was constructed by Methodists in Dubuque in 1834; a Roman Catholic church was built in Dubuque the following year. By 1860, the largest religious sects were the Methodists, Presbyterians, Catholics, Baptists, and Congregationalists. Other religious groups who came to Iowa during the 19th century included Lutherans, Dutch Reformers, Quakers, Mennonites, Jews, and the Community of True Inspiration, or Amana Society, which founded seven communal villages.

In 1971, an estimated 62% of Iowans were church adherents. There were 1,233,846 Protestants, including 418,715 Lutherans, 370,513 Methodists, and 120,634 Presbyterians. Roman Catholic church membership totaled 535,291 in 1979. On 4 October 1979, about 350,000 people—the largest such gathering in the state's history—met in a pasture near Des Moines to see and hear Pope John Paul II. Iowa's Jewish population was 8,735 in 1979.

¹⁰TRANSPORTATION

The early settlers came to Iowa by way of the Ohio and Mississippi rivers and the Great Lakes, then traveled overland on trails via wagon and stagecoach. The need of Iowa farmers to haul their product to market over long distances prompted the development of the railroads, particularly during the 1880s. But river traffic continues to play a vital role in the state's transport.

Iowa ranks 4th among the 50 states in miles of first-class railroads. Although total trackage in the state declined slightly from 8,301 mi (13,359 km) in 1960 to 7,532 mi (12,122 km) in 1976, freight carried by first-class railroads increased from 89.7 million to 118 million tons in the same period. Amtrak provides regular passenger service across the state from Burlington to Omaha, Neb. and from Dubuque to Chicago, Ill. All together, 17 railroads operated passenger and/or freight service in Iowa in 1979.

In 1978, Iowa ranked 10th among the states in road mileage, with 112,148 mi (180,485 km) of rural and municipal roads. In 1978, there were 1,716,928 registered automobiles and 601,390 trucks in the state, with 2,021,520 licensed drivers. In 1976, buses carried 1,511,585 passengers, and truck carriers hauled 274,966 tons of freight.

Iowa is bordered by two great navigable rivers, the Mississippi and the Missouri. These provided excellent transport facilities for the early settlers via keelboats and paddle-wheel steamers. Today, freight is still transported by water as far east as Pennsylvania and west to Oklahoma. In 1976, Mississippi riverboats carried 25.6 million tons of Iowa's cargo, including 14.2 million tons of grain. Important terminal ports on the Mississippi are Dubuque and Davenport; on the Missouri, Sioux City and Council Bluffs.

In 1978, Iowa had 257 airports of all types; 115 were public and 142 were privately owned. Air passenger service is supplied by three international airlines (American, United, Braniff) and by 12 domestic carriers (including Ozark and North Central). The busiest airfield is Des Moines Municipal Airport, which handled 16,849 scheduled departures in 1978.

¹¹HISTORY

The fertile land now known as the State of Iowa was first visited

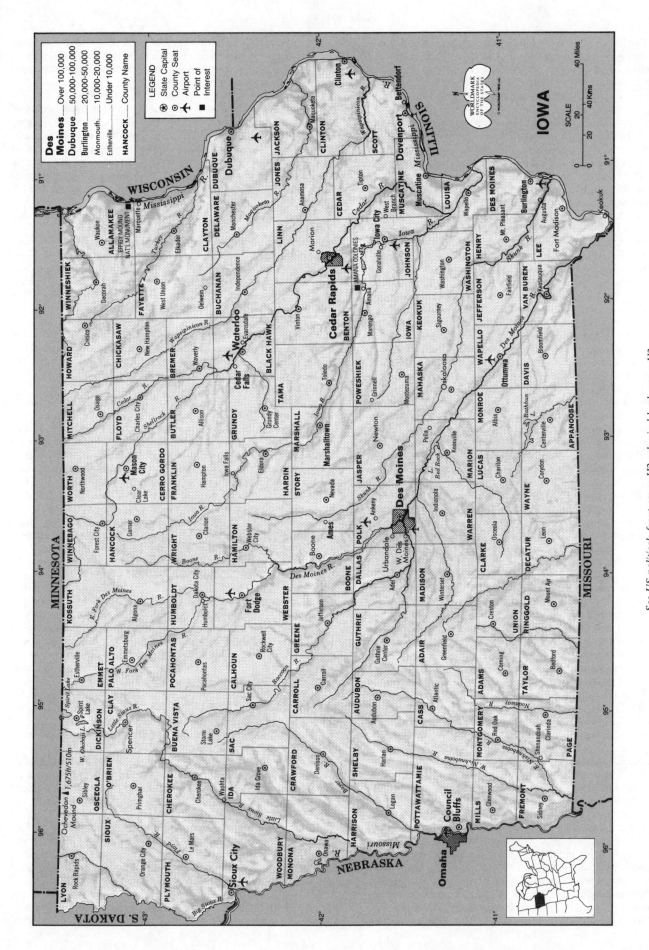

IOWA

See US political: front cover H2; physical:back cover H2.

LOCATION: 40°22′32″ to 43°30′3″ N; 90°8′24″ to 96°38′21″ W. **BOUNDARIES:** Minnesota line, 264 mi (425 km); Wisconsin line, 93 mi (150 km); Illinois line, 219 mi (352 km); Missouri line, 244 mi (393 km); Nebraska line, 200 mi (322 km); South Dakota line, 131 mi (211 km).

by primitive hunting bands of the Paleo-Indian period some 12,000 years ago. The first permanent settlers of the land were the Woodland Indians, who built villages in the forested areas along the Mississippi River, introduced agriculture, and left behind only their animal-shaped burial mounds as evidence of their prehistoric existence.

Not until June 1673 did the first known white men come to the territory. When Louis Jolliet, accompanied by five French voyageurs and a Jesuit priest, Jacques Marquette, stopped briefly in Iowa on his voyage down the Mississippi, the region was uninhabited except for the Sioux in the west and a few outposts of Illinois and Iowa Indians in the east. Iowa was part of the vast, vaguely defined Louisiana Territory ruled by the French until the title was transferred to Spain in 1762. Napoleon took the territory back in 1800, and then promptly sold all of Louisiana to the amazed American envoys who had come to Paris seeking only the purchase of New Orleans and the mouth of the Mississippi. After Iowa had thus come under US control in 1803, the Lewis and Clark expedition worked its way up the Missouri River to explore the land that President Thomas Jefferson had purchased so cheaply. Iowa looked as empty as it had to Jolliet 130 years earlier. The only white man who had come to explore its riches prior to the American annexation was an enterprising former French trapper, Julien Dubuque. Soon after the American Revolution, he had obtained from the Fox Indians the sole right to work the lead mines west of the Mississippi, and for 20 years Dubuque was the only white settler in Iowa.

The first wave of migrants into Iowa were the Winnebago, Sauk, and Fox, driven there by the US Army, which was clearing Wisconsin and Illinois of their Indian populations to make way for white farmers. Although President Andrew Jackson had intended that Louisiana Territory lying north of Missouri should forever be Indian land, the occupation of Iowa by the Indians was to be brief. Following the abortive attempt by an aging Sauk chieftain, Black Hawk, to win his lands in Illinois, the Sauk and Fox were driven westward in 1832 and forced to cede their lands in eastern Iowa to the incoming white settlers.

Placed under the territorial jurisdiction of Michigan in 1834, and then two years later under the newly created Territory of Wisconsin, Iowa became a separate territory in 1838. The first territorial governor, Robert Lucas, extended county boundaries and local government westward, planned for a new capital city to be located on the Iowa River, resolutely resisted Missouri's attempt to encroach on Iowa territory, and began planning for eventual statehood by drawing boundary lines that included not only the present State of Iowa but also southern Minnesota up to present-day Minneapolis.

Because a new state seeking admission to the Union at that time could expect favorable action from Congress only if accompanied by a slave state, Iowa was designated to come into the Union with Florida as its slaveholding counterpart. A serious dispute over how large the state would be delayed Iowa's admission into the Union until 28 December 1846, but by the delay the people of Iowa got what they wanted—all the land between the Mississippi and Missouri rivers—even though they had to abandon Lucas's northern claim.

The settlement of Iowa was rapidly accomplished. With one-fourth of the nation's fertile topsoil located within its borders, Iowa was a powerful magnet that drew farmers by the thousands from Indiana, Ohio, and Tennessee, and even from faraway Virginia, the Carolinas, New York, and New England. Except for German and Irish immigrants along the eastern border and later Scandinavian immigrants during the 1870s and 1880s, Iowa was settled primarily by Anglo-American stock. The settlers were overwhelmingly Protestant in religion and remarkably homogeneous in ethnic and cultural backgrounds. Although New Englanders made up only 5% of Iowa's early population, they

had a cultural influence that far exceeded their numbers. Many small Iowa towns, with their large frame houses, elm-lined streets, and Congregational churches, looked like New England villages faithfully replicated on the prairie.

Fiercely proud of its claim to be the first free state created out of the Louisiana Purchase, Iowa was an important center of abolitionist sentiment throughout the 1850s. The Underground Railroad for fugitive slaves from the South ran across the southern portion of Iowa to the Mississippi River. Radical abolitionist John Brown, a welcome visitor on his frequent trips across Iowa to Kansas, spent the winters of 1857 and 1859 in the small Quaker village of Springdale, preparing for his attack on the US arsenal at Harpers Ferry, in western Virginia.

Although the Democrats had a slight edge over their Whig opposition in the early years of statehood, a majority of Iowa voters in 1856 supported the new Republican Party and, for the most part, have done so ever since. A Republican legislative majority in 1857 scrapped the state's first constitution, which had been written by Jacksonian Democrats 12 years earlier. The new document moved the state capital from Iowa City westward to Des Moines, but it provided that the state university would remain forever in Iowa City.

When the Civil War came, Iowa overwhelmingly supported the Union cause. Iowans fought not only for their ideals, the abolition of slavery, and the preservation of the Union, but also for the very practical objective of keeping open the Mississippi River, the main artery for agricultural transport.

In the decades following the Civil War, Iowans on the national scene, most notably US Senators James Harlan and William B. Allison, his successor, belonged to the conservative Republican camp, but they frequently faced liberal Republican and Populist opposition inside the state. Iowan James B. Weaver broke from the Republican Party to become the Greenback-Labor candidate for president in 1880 and the Populist presidential nominee in 1892. Senator Allison and the conservatives had powerful allies in the railroad entrepreneurs, especially Grenville Dodge of the Union Pacific and Charles Eliot Perkins of the Burlington Railroad, throughout the late 19th century. The railroad had been lavishly welcomed by Iowans in the 1850s; by the 1870s, Iowa farmers were desperately trying to free themselves from the stranglehold of the rail lines. The National Grange was powerful enough in Iowa to put through the legislature the so-called Granger laws to regulate the railroads. In 1886, Allison pushed his protégé, William Larrabee, into the governorship, only to discover that Larrabee was a reformer in disguise. During his four years in office, Larrabee carried on a constant battle with the railroad interests for effective regulatory legislation. At the turn of the century, as the aging Allison's hold on the state weakened, Iowa became a center for Republican progressivism.

Following World War I, the conservatives regained control of the Republican Party. They remained in control until, during the 1960s, new liberal leadership was forced on the party because of the debacle of Barry Goldwater's presidential campaign, controversy over US involvement in Viet-Nam, and effective opposition from a revitalized Democratic Party led by Harold Hughes. After Hughes gave up the governorship in 1969 to become a US senator, he was succeeded in office by Robert Ray, a liberal Republican who dominated the state throughout the 1970s.

[12] STATE GOVERNMENT

Iowa has had two state constitutions. The constitution of 1857 replaced the original constitution of 1846, and is still in effect.

The state legislature, or general assembly, consists of a 50-member senate and a 100-member house of representatives. Senators serve four-year terms, with half the members elected every two years. Representatives are elected to two-year terms. The legislature convenes each year on the 2d Monday in January. Special sessions may be called by the governor or initiated by petition of two-thirds of the members of each house. Each house may introduce or amend legislation, with a simple majority vote required for passage. The governor's veto of a bill may be overridden by a two-thirds majority in both houses. Legislators must be US citizens and must have resided in the state for a year; a representative must be at least 21 years of age, and a senator 25.

The state's only elected executives are the governor, lieutenant governor, secretary of state, auditor, treasurer, attorney general, and secretary of agriculture; since 1974, they have been elected to four-year terms. The governor and lieutenant governor are jointly elected; there is no limit to their number of terms. The governor must be a US citizen, at least 30 years old, and a resident of the state for two years.

To vote in Iowa, one must be a US citizen, at least 18 years old, and a state resident. A voter must register at least 10 days prior to an election, and remains permanently registered if there is no change of residency.

[13]POLITICAL PARTIES
For 70 years following the Civil War, a majority of Iowa voters supported the Republicans over the Democrats in nearly all state and national elections. During the Great Depression of the 1930s, Iowa briefly turned to the Democrats, supporting Franklin D. Roosevelt in two presidential elections. But from 1940 through 1980, the majority of Iowans voted Republican in 9 of 11 presidential elections. Republicans won 31 of the 39 gubernatorial elections from 1900 through 1978, and controlled both houses of the state legislature for 110 of the 126 years between 1855 and 1980.

In the 1960s, however, Iowa showed signs of becoming a two-party state. Harold Hughes, a liberal Democrat, revitalized the party in Iowa and was elected governor for three two-year terms before moving on to the US Senate. During the post-Watergate period of the mid-1970s, Democrats captured both US Senate seats, five of the six congressional seats, and both houses of the Iowa legislature. The tide had reversed by November 1980, when Iowans elected a conservative Republican, Charles Grassley, to the US Senate seat held by a liberal Democratic incumbent, John Culver.

[14]LOCAL GOVERNMENT
The state's 99 counties are governed by boards of supervisors consisting of three or five members. In general, county officials are elected to four-year terms. These officials enforce state laws, collect taxes, supervise welfare activities, and help to manage roads and bridges.

Local government was exercised by 951 municipal units in 1979. The mayor-council system functioned in 920 towns and cities; city managers governed 26 towns and cities. In the 5 cities that had a commission form of government, elected commissioners (including a mayor and council) appointed a city manager. Iowa's towns and cities derive their local powers from the state constitution, but the power to tax is authorized by the general assembly.

[15]STATE SERVICES
The Department of Public Instruction is responsible for educational services in Iowa. It assists local school boards in supplying special educational programs and administers 15 area education agencies (reduced in 1974 from 79 county school systems).

Transportation services are directed by the Department of Transportation, which is responsible for the safe and efficient operation of highways, motor vehicles, airports, railroads, public transit, and river transportation. The department's motor vehicle division licenses drivers, road vehicles, and car dealers.

Health and welfare services are provided by the Department of Health, the Iowa Mental Health Authority, and the Department of Social Services. Public protection is the responsibility of the Departments of Public Defense and of Public Safety. Housing programs are supported by the Iowa Housing Finance Authority.

[16]JUDICIAL SYSTEM
The Iowa supreme court consists of nine justices who are appointed by the governor and confirmed to eight-year terms by judicial elections held after they have served on the bench for at least one year. Judges may stand for reelection before their terms expire. The justices select one of their number as chief justice. The court exercises appellate jurisdiction in civil and criminal cases, supervises the trial courts, and prescribes rules of civil and appellate procedure. The supreme court transfers certain cases to the court of appeals, a five-member appellate court which began reviewing civil and criminal cases in 1977, and may review its decisions. Judges on the court of appeals are appointed and confirmed to six-year terms in the same manner as supreme

Iowa Presidential Vote by Political Parties, 1948–80

YEAR	ELECTORAL VOTE	IOWA WINNER	DEMOCRAT	REPUBLICAN	PROGRESSIVE	PROHIBITION	SOCIALIST LABOR
1948	10	*Truman (D)	522,380	494,018	12,125	3,382	4,274
1952	10	*Eisenhower (R)	451,513	808,906	5,085	2,882	—
							CONSTITUTION
1956	10	*Eisenhower (R)	501,858	729,187	—	—	3,202
1960	10	Nixon (R)	550,565	722,381	—	—	—
1964	9	*Johnson (D)	733,030	449,148	—	1,902	—
					SOC. WORKERS	AMERICAN IND.	
1968	9	*Nixon (R)	476,699	619,106	3,377	66,422	—
						AMERICAN	PEACE AND FREEDOM
1972	8	*Nixon (R)	496,206	706,207	—	22,056	1,332
							LIBERTARIAN
1976	8	Ford (R)	619,931	632,863	—	3,040	1,452
					CITIZENS		
1980[1]	8	*Reagan (R)	508,735	676,556	2,191	NA	12,324

*Won US presidential election.   1. Preliminary returns.

court justices; they elect one of their members as chief judge.

The state is divided into eight judicial districts, each with a chief judge appointed to a two-year term by the chief justice of the supreme court. District court judges are appointed to six-year terms by the governor from nominations submitted by district nominating commissions. Appointees must stand for election after they have served as judges for at least one year, and they may be reelected.

As of 31 December 1978 there were 2,068 prisoners in federal and state institutions. Iowa's crime rates are among the lowest in the US.

[17] ARMED FORCES

Iowa residents in 1979 included 375,000 veterans, of whom 113,000 saw service during the Viet-Nam era and 154,000 served during World War II. The Veterans Administration expended $230 million in Iowa during the 1977/78 fiscal year.

The Iowa National Guard provides reserve units for the US Army and Air Force in case of a national emergency or war. The governor is the commander-in-chief of the state's armed forces, and the adjutant general of Iowa, appointed by the governor, is his chief of staff. In 1978 there were 91 National Guard units stationed in Iowa, with a total enlistment of 9,568.

[18] MIGRATION

Iowa was opened, organized, and settled by a generation of native migrants from other states. According to the first federal census of Iowa in 1850, 31% of the total population of 192,214 came from nearby midwestern states (Illinois, Wisconsin, Indiana, Michigan, and Ohio), 14% from the five southern border states, and 13% from the Middle Atlantic states. In all, 9 of 10 newcomers in 1850 had left their homes in other states to resettle in Iowa.

The remaining 10% of the state's 1850 population consisted of immigrants from northern Europe. The largest group were Germans who had fled military conscription; the next largest group had sought to escape the hardships of potato famine in Ireland or of agricultural and technological displacement in Scotland, England, and Wales. They were joined in the 1850s by Dutch immigrants seeking religious liberty, and in the 1860s and 1870s by Norwegians and Swedes. During and immediately after the Civil War, some former slaves fled the South for Iowa, and more blacks settled in Iowa cities after 1900.

But many of the migrants who came to Iowa did not stay long. Some Iowans left to join the gold rush, and others settled lands in the West. Migration out of the state has continued to this day, as retired Iowans seeking warmer climates have moved to California and other southwestern states; from 1940 through 1977, Iowa's net loss through migration totaled 649,000.

An important migratory trend within the state has been from the farm to the city. Although Iowa is the state with the largest number of farm residents, the urban population surpassed the rural population by 1960 and increased to over 57% of the total population by 1970.

[19] INTERGOVERNMENTAL COOPERATION

Iowa is a signatory to the Midwest Nuclear Compact, the Iowa-Missouri and Iowa-Nebraska boundary compacts, and 11 other interstate compacts and agreements. Federal aid to Iowa amounted to $877.8 million in 1978/79, of which more than $80 million was general revenue sharing.

[20] ECONOMY

Iowa's economy is based on agriculture. Although the value of the state's manufactures exceeds the value of its farm production, manufacturing is basically farm centered. The major industries are food processing and the manufacture of agriculture-related products, such as farm machinery. Iowa's gross state product (GSP) in 1977 totaled $25.3 billion, or 1.34% of the US gross national product in current dollars. Of the 1977 GSP, manufacturing accounted for $7.1 billion; trade, $4.4 billion;

banking, insurance, and real estate, $3.2 billion; agriculture, $3.1 billion; service industries, $2.4 billion; and construction, $1.2 billion.

Periodic recessions—and especially the Great Depression of the 1930s—have afflicted Iowa farmers and adversely affected the state's entire economy. But technological progress in agriculture and the proliferation of manufacturing industries have enabled Iowans to enjoy general prosperity since World War II. Because the state's population is scattered, the growth of light manufacturing has extended to hundreds of towns and cities.

In the late 1970s, the state's major economic problem was inflation, which boosted the cost of farm equipment and fertilizers, and contributed to the continued decline of the farm population. As the farm population decreased by more than one-third between 1960 and 1977, the number of nonfarm workers in the state has increased by more than 58%.

[21] INCOME

With a current income per capita of $7,873 in 1978, slightly above the national average, Iowa ranked 17th in the US.

The following table shows total earned income and components for Iowa in 1972 and 1977 (in millions):

	1972	1977
Total earnings, of which:	$9,500	$14,777
Farm	1,733	1,265
Manufacturing	2,302	3,919
Mining	28	26
Construction	505	1,032
Wholesale and retail trade	1,509	2,663
Finance, insurance, and real estate	421	778
Transportation, communications, utilities	591	1,001
Services	1,077	1,989
Government	1,299	2,057

The state's total personal income is $22.8 billion in 1978 dollars and $15.2 billion in constant dollars. The percentage of families under the federal poverty level is well below the national average.

[22] LABOR

Since 1950, Iowa has consistently ranked above the national average in employment of its work force. Iowa's unemployment rate of 4% for 1978 was well below the overall US rate of 7%. Almost 64% of all Iowans were employed that year, as compared with 59% of the nation as a whole.

The civilian labor force in 1977 totaled 1,385,000, of whom 1,329,000 were employed and 56,000 unemployed. Of the total work force, 58.9% was male and 41.1% female. A federal census of workers covered by unemployment insurance in March 1977 revealed the following nonfarm employment pattern in Iowa:

	ESTABLISH-MENTS	EMPLOYEES	ANNUAL PAYROLL ('000)
Agricultural services, forestry, fishing	775	3,348	$ 31,651
Mining	237	2,630	37,758
Contract construction	7,793	43,127	663,805
Manufacturing, of which:	3,533	245,046	3,402,027
Food and food products	(551)	(45,440)	(677,771)
Nonelectrical machinery	(529)	(61,674)	(1,013,693)
Transportation, public utilities	3,290	44,176	596,701
Wholesale trade	7,507	70,291	861,066
Retail trade	20,463	189,223	1,147,615
Finance, insurance, real estate	5,943	53,550	573,235
Services	17,043	168,511	1,202,353
Other	759	786	7,948
TOTALS	67,343	820,688	$8,524,159

The labor movement generally has not been strong in Iowa, and labor unions have had little success in organizing farm laborers. The Knights of Labor, consisting mostly of miners and railroad workers, was organized in Iowa in 1876 and enrolled 25,000 members by 1885. But the Knights practically disappeared after 1893, when the American Federation of Labor (AFL) established itself in the state among miners and other workers. The Congress of Industrial Organizations (CIO) succeeded in organizing workers in public utilities, meat packing, and light industries in 1937. After 1955, when the AFL and CIO merged, the power and influence of labor unions increased in the state. In 1976, the number of labor union members in Iowa totaled 192,000; another 39,000 workers belonged to employee associations. In 1977 there were 98 work stoppages involving 30,100 workers and 651,700 working days lost.

Iowa did not forbid the employment of women in dangerous occupations or prohibit the employment of children under 14 years of age in factories, shops, or mines until the early 1900s. The state's right-to-work law, enacted in 1947, has been bitterly opposed by labor unions.

23 AGRICULTURE

Iowa ranks 2d among the 50 states (after California) in gross farm income, which totaled $7.7 billion in 1977. More than half that total came from the sale of livestock and meat products; about one-sixth derived from the sale of feed grains. In that year, Iowa ranked 2d in output of corn for silage, corn for grain, and soybeans.

The early settlers planted wheat. Iowa ranked 2d in wheat production by 1870, but as the wheat belt moved farther west, the state's farmers turned to raising corn to feed their cattle and hogs. Two important 20th-century developments were the introduction in the 1920s of hybrid corn and the utilization on a massive scale during World War II of soybeans as a feed grain. Significant postwar trends include the rapid mechanization of farming and the decline of the farm population from 667,823 in 1960 to 424,863 in 1973.

In 1979, Iowa had 121,000 farms, with an average size of 281 acres (114 hectares) per farm. This total represents a marked decrease of 62,000 farms since 1960, although land devoted to farming decreased by only 1.4% during the same period, from about 34,700,000 acres (14,043,000 hectares) to 34,200,000 acres (13,840,000 hectares). Of the total number of farms in 1974 for which data are available, 52% were operated by farm owners and 48% were rented to operators. Farm employment in 1979 totaled 213,000 workers, of whom 46,000 were hired hands.

Nearly all of Iowa's land is tillable, and more than nine-tenths of it is given to farmland. Corn is grown practically everywhere; wheat is raised in the southern half of the state and in counties bordering the Mississippi and Missouri rivers.

In 1979, production of corn for grain totaled 1.6 billion bushels, valued at $3.7 billion; soybeans, 310.5 million bushels, $1.9 billion; oats, 63 million bushels, $88.2 million; and hay, 8.3 million tons, $380.5 million.

24 ANIMAL HUSBANDRY

Iowa produced about 25% of the nation's pork and 7% of its grain-fed beef in 1979. In that year, it ranked 1st among the 50 states in hog production, 3d in beef cattle output, and 3d in production of cheese and butter.

Pigs, calves, lambs, and chickens are raised throughout the state, particularly in the Mississippi and Missouri river valleys, where good pasture and water are plentiful. Iowa farmers were leaders in applying modern livestock breeding methods to produce lean hogs, tender corn-fed cattle, and larger-breasted chickens and turkeys.

Livestock produced for market in 1979 included 23,060,300 hogs and 3,171,400 grain-fed cattle. Cash receipts to farmers for farm animals and livestock products in 1979 included $2.2 billion

for hogs and pigs, $2.8 billion for cattle and calves, and $14,373,000 for sheep and lambs. Receipts for milk products were $440,115,000; gross income for poultry and eggs was $131,295,000. In 1979 there were 7,300,000 beef cattle and 372,000 milk cows.

Iowa dairy farmers produced 3.9 billion lb of whole milk in 1979. In that year, the state's poultry producers raised 7.5 million chickens and 6.2 million turkeys.

25 FISHING

Fishing has little commercial importance in Iowa; the catch in 1978, 3,730,000 lb, was worth only $820,000. Game fishing in the rivers and lakes is a popular sport.

26 FORESTRY

Lumber and woodworking were important to the early settlers, but the industry has since declined in commercial importance. In 1977, Iowa had 1,460,000 acres (591,000 hectares) of commercial timberland, of which over 92% was privately owned. Shipments of paper and paper products totaled $395 million in 1977.

27 MINING

In 1977, the value of Iowa's mineral output was estimated at $264 million, 32d in the US. The principal minerals (in order of value) were cement, stone, sand and gravel, and gypsum.

In 1788, the French explorer Julien Dubuque founded the first white settlement in Iowa at the site of Indian lead mines on the banks of the Mississippi River (later the site of the city named for him), but the supply of lead gave out in the late 19th century. Rich gypsum deposits near Fort Dodge continued to be mined in the 1970s. Limestone is still mined in east-central Iowa, and sand and gravel are found throughout the state's northern half. In 1977, shipments of stone, clay, and glass products were valued at $538.9 million; shipments of cement totaled $105.8 million.

28 ENERGY AND POWER

Although Iowa's fossil fuel resources are extremely limited, the state's energy supply has been adequate for consumer needs. According to 1978 estimates, oil supplied 40% of the state's energy requirements; natural gas, 30%; coal, 22%; electric power, 7%; and solar energy, less than 1%.

The state's production of electricity totaled 17.6 billion kwh in 1978; installed capacity was 6.6 million kw, of which 83% was provided by private utilities. Coal-fired plants supplied 14.4 billion kwh of electricity; nuclear power plants supplied 1.2 billion kwh; and hydroelectric plants less than 1 billion kwh.

Extensive coalfields in southeastern Iowa were first mined in 1840. The boom town of Buxton, in Monroe County, mined sufficient coal in 1901 to support a population of 6,000 people, of whom 5,500 were transplanted southern blacks, but the mines closed in 1918 and Buxton became a ghost town. The state's annual bituminous coal production reached nearly 9 million tons in 1917–18; output in 1978 was only 470,000 tons.

29 INDUSTRY

Because Iowa was primarily a farm state, the first industries were food processing and the manufacture of farm implements. In recent years, Iowa has added a wide variety of manufactures—pens, washing machines, even mobile homes.

The total value added by manufactures was $8.7 billion in 1977. The following table shows value added by manufacturing for selected industries in 1972 and 1977:

	1972	1977
Farm, garden machinery	$643,400,000	$1,223,600,000
Construction machinery	314,200,000	777,100,000
Meat products	487,300,000	677,100,000
Grain mill products	324,900,000	645,700,000
Printing, publishing	227,600,000	413,700,000
Tires, inner tubes	NA	188,100,000
Valves, pipe fittings	77,600,000	167,200,000
Dairy products	115,700,000	137,200,000
Lumber, wood products	72,100,000	134,500,000
Agricultural chemicals	59,700,000	102,800,000

Many of America's corporate giants have plants in Iowa, including Caterpillar Tractor, John Deere, General Electric, General Foods, Procter & Gamble, and US Steel.

³⁰ COMMERCE

In 1972, Iowa's wholesale trade totaled nearly $10 billion. The most valuable categories of goods traded were agricultural raw materials, 34%; groceries and related products, 15%; motor vehicles and automotive parts, 7%; petroleum products, 6%; metals and minerals, 3%; and other items, 35%.

Retail sales in 1977 were $9.8 billion. Of that total, automotive dealers and gas stations accounted for 32%; food stores, 20%; general merchandise stores, 12%; eating and drinking places, 8%; and other establishments, 28%.

Iowa ranked 2d among the 50 states (after Illinois) in 1977 agricultural exports, accounting for $2 billion, or 8.5% of the US total. The leading exported commodities were corn and other feed grains, soybeans and soybean oil, protein meal, and meat products. Iowa's exports of manufactured goods in 1976 had an estimated value of $1.45 billion; the principal categories were machinery, food products, and electrical equipment.

³¹ CONSUMER PROTECTION

Iowa does not have a specific state agency to protect consumers. The Office of the Citizens' Aide, established in 1970 and headed by an ombudsman, may investigate citizens' complaints about violations of consumers' rights that involve state agencies.

³² BANKING

In 1978, Iowa had 650 insured commercial banks with total assets of $17.9 billion and total deposits of $15.6 billion; 70 savings and loan associations had assets totaling $6.3 billion and mortgage loans valued at $5.4 billion. In 1977, there were 297 small loan company offices with 55,754 accounts that made loans totaling $33.5 million, and 423 state-chartered credit unions with total assets of $493 million and outstanding loans of $410 million.

The Department of Banking supervises and controls the state's chartered banks, credit unions, and loan companies.

³³ INSURANCE

In 1977, Iowa had 33 life insurance companies with combined assets of $8.7 billion. Life insurance in force as of 31 December 1977 totaled $34.4 billion. The 46 fire, casualty, and multiple-line insurance companies operating in the state had assets totaling $1.4 billion, liabilities amounting to $887 million, and premiums of $993 million. In 1978, $418.2 million of automobile insurance premiums were written in the state.

The commissioner of insurance, appointed by the governor, supervises all insurance business transacted in the state.

³⁴ SECURITIES

There are no securities exchanges in Iowa. New York Stock Exchange member firms had 67 sales offices and 276 registered representatives in Iowa in 1978. Iowans reported $324.3 million in dividend income on the 1977 federal tax returns.

³⁵ PUBLIC FINANCE

The public budget is prepared by the state comptroller with the governor's approval and is adopted or revised by the general assembly. Each budget is prepared for the biennium of the upcoming fiscal year and the one following; the fiscal year runs from 1 July to 30 June.

Iowa's estimated 1979/80 budget and projected budget for 1980/81 were as follows (in millions):

REVENUES	1979/80	1980/81
Personal income taxes	$ 714.0	$ 793.0
Sales taxes	373.0	402.0
Corporate income taxes	147.8	150.0
Inheritance, use, insurance taxes	147.8	158.0
Federal revenue sharing	28.0	28.0
Other receipts	197.7	202.6
TOTALS	$1,608.3	$1,733.6

EXPENDITURES	1979/80	1980/81
Education	$ 846.8	$ 903.6
Tax credits and refunds	330.9	351.4
Human resources	301.6	321.6
Government	90.4	89.3
Capital investment	34.9	4.7
Other expenditures	53.8	39.6
TOTALS	$1,658.4	$1,710.2

The principal sources of revenue are personal income taxes, the state sales tax, and corporate income taxes; about half of state expenditures are allocated to education. The combined state and local government debt in 1977 was $1.4 billion, or $502 per capita. Only two states—Idaho and North Carolina—had lower per capita debt burdens.

³⁶ TAXATION

In 1980, Iowa's personal income tax ranged from 0.5% on the first $1,000 of income to 13% on amounts over $75,000. The corporate tax rate ranged from 6% on the first $25,000 of net income to 10% on amounts over $100,000. Iowa's retail sales tax was 3% in 1980. The state also taxed gasoline, cigarettes, alcoholic beverages, insurance premiums, inheritances, chain stores, and business franchises.

Iowans filed 1,150,906 federal income tax returns in 1977, paying almost $2 billion in tax.

³⁷ ECONOMIC POLICY

Since World War II, the state government has attracted new manufacturing industries to Iowa by granting tax incentives and by encouraging a favorable business climate. The Iowa Development Commission helps local communities diversify their economies, assists companies already in the state, and helps exporters to sell their products abroad. State law permits city councils to begin industrial development by buying land and building plants.

³⁸ HEALTH

Iowa ranked 7th among the 50 states in life expectancy in 1969–71, with an average expectancy of 72.56 years—68.83 for men and 76.5 for women. The 1977 infant mortality rate was 12.2 per 1,000 live births for whites and 18 for nonwhites; the latter figure was well below the national average. In 1977, 5,097 legal abortions were performed, a rate of 113 per 1,000 live births.

In 1978, Iowa's 141 hospitals admitted 576,577 patients; the average number of hospital patients daily was 15,125, for a bed occupancy rate of 70%. Hospital personnel totaled 43,554, of whom 8,614 were registered nurses and 3,398 were licensed practical nurses. The average hospital stay in 1976 cost $1,151, or $154 per day; both averages were more than 20% below the US norm. Mental hospitals and general hospitals with psychiatric facilities treated 18,763 patients in 1976. As of 30 June 1978 there were 2,010 mentally retarded persons in public institutions. The state's 552 nursing homes had 31,700 patients in 1976.

There were 3,490 physicians in Iowa in 1977 and 1,396 active dentists in 1979.

³⁹ SOCIAL WELFARE

Iowa's per capita expenditures on social welfare are well below the national average. State welfare programs in 1976 totaled $284 million, of which the federal government provided 64%.

In 1978, aid to families with dependent children in Iowa totaled $111 million, or $284 monthly per family. In that year, Supplemental Security Income payments amounted to $10.2 million for the elderly ($69 per person per month) and $16.8 million for disabled persons ($114 per person per month). About 470,000 pupils participated in the federal school lunch program, which cost $19.5 million.

Social Security benefits totaling $824.1 million were paid to 337,300 retired Iowans in 1977. The average monthly payment to retirees was $242.30.

In 1978, state expenditures on vocational training for 313,000 persons totaled $59 million. Workers' compensation payments amounted to $56.5 million in 1977. Unemployment insurance benefits in 1978 went to an average of 22,000 beneficiaries monthly and totaled $114 million.

⁴⁰HOUSING

Iowa ranks high in the number of housing units that are family owned and occupied. According to the 1970 census, there were 964,060 housing units, of which 82% were one-unit structures and 72% were occupied by the owners. Of the total, 57% were located in urban areas and 43% in rural areas. In 1978, the state authorized the construction of 17,200 new housing units, valued at $554 million; 63% of these units were single-unit structures.

⁴¹EDUCATION

In 1979, Iowa ranked 1st among the 50 states in literacy: 99.5% of its population 15 years and older was able to read and write. The median educational level was 12.5 years. Iowa's progressive public school system has been an innovator in school curriculum development, teaching methods, educational administration, and school financing.

In the 1978/79 school year, Iowa had a total of 621,735 pupils enrolled in the public school system. 307,146 students were in grades K–6, 147,475 in grades 7–9, 156,196 in grades 10–12, and 10,918 in special schools. In addition, 232 parochial schools enrolled 53,067 pupils in 1979/80.

In 1978/79, 127,393 students were enrolled in institutions of higher learning. Iowa had 3 state universities, with 56,497 students; 38 private colleges, with 34,423 students; and 15 state community colleges, with 30,849 students. Professional and technical schools enrolled 2,326, and private junior colleges 3,298. Since the public community college system began offering vocational and technical training in 1960, total enrollment has increased tenfold.

The state's small liberal arts colleges and universities include Briar Cliff College, Sioux City; Coe College, Cedar Rapids; Cornell College, Mt. Vernon; Drake University, Des Moines; Grinnell College, Grinnell; Iowa Wesleyan College, Mt. Pleasant; Loras College, Dubuque; and Luther College, Decorah.

Public schools are administered by the state superintendent of public instruction, who is appointed by a nine-member state board to a four-year term. Expenditures for public schools in Iowa totaled $1.3 billion in the 1977/78 school year.

The State of Iowa Scholarship program awarded $3.8 million in scholarship aid to 5,500 Iowa college students from 1966 to 1979. Needy Iowa students are also eligible for tuition grants provided by the Iowa College Aid Commission.

⁴²ARTS

Beginning with the public lecture movement in the late 19th century and the Chautauqua shows in the early 20th century, cultural activities have gradually spread throughout the state. Today there are art galleries, little theater groups, symphony orchestras, and ballet companies in the major cities and college towns.

The Des Moines Arts Center is a leading exhibition gallery for native painters and sculptors. There are regional theater groups in Des Moines, Davenport, and Sioux City. The Writers' Workshop at the University of Iowa has an international reputation. One problem for the arts in Iowa is the continued migration of native artists to cultural centers in New York, California, and elsewhere.

⁴³LIBRARIES AND MUSEUMS

Beginning with the founding in 1873 of the state's first tax-supported library at Independence, Iowa's public library system has grown to include total book holdings of 7,955,188 volumes. Among the principal libraries in Iowa are the State Library in Des Moines, the State Historical Society Library in Iowa City, the libraries of the University of Iowa (also in Iowa City), and the Iowa State University Library in Ames.

Iowa had at least 62 museums in 1979. The Herbert Hoover Presidential Library and Museum, in West Branch, contains the public and private papers of the 31st US president. Other historic sites include the grave of French explorer Julien Dubuque near the city named for him, the girlhood home at Charles City of suffragist Carrie Chapman Catt, and the seven communal villages of the Amana colonies.

⁴⁴COMMUNICATIONS

The first post office in Iowa was established at Augusta in 1836. Mail service developed slowly with the spread of population, and rural free delivery of mail did not begin until 1897. The first telegraph line was built between Burlington and Bloomington (now Muscatine) in 1848. Telegraph service throughout the state is provided by Western Union.

In 1977, Iowa had 74.7 telephones per 100 population, and 98% of all households had telephone service. Of the total of 2,144,352 telephones, 521,531 were business and 1,622,821 residential.

Among the first educational radio broadcasting stations in the US were one established in 1919 at the State University in Iowa City and another in 1921 at Iowa State University in Ames. The first commercial radio station west of the Mississippi, WOC at Davenport, began broadcast in 1921. In 1977 there were 147 commercial radio stations, including 76 AM stations and 71 FM stations. There were also 16 noncommercial stations, of which 13 were FM.

In 1977, Iowa had a total of 15 television stations, including one public broadcasting station. In that year, 64 cable television systems had 107,704 subscribers.

⁴⁵PRESS

Iowa's first newspaper, the *Dubuque Visitor*, was founded in 1836 but lasted only a year. The following year, the *Fort Madison Patriot* and the *Burlington Territorial Gazette* were established; the latter paper, now the *Hawk Eye*, is the oldest newspaper in the state. In 1860, the *Iowa State Register* was founded; as the *Des Moines Register and Tribune*, it grew to be the state's largest newspaper in circulation and influence. In 1978, the *Register* had a morning circulation of 217,584 and a Sunday circulation of 408,826; the *Tribune*'s evening circulation was 87,697.

Overall, Iowa had 41 dailies with a combined circulation of 898,176 in 1978. In addition, there were 9 Sunday papers with a total circulation of 752,397.

⁴⁶ORGANIZATIONS

The National Corn Growers Association has its headquarters in Des Moines, and the National Farmers Organization is located in Corning. Members of the Antique Airplane Association, based in Ottumwa, hold "fly-ins" throughout the state.

⁴⁷TOURISM, TRAVEL, AND RECREATION

In 1977, out-of-state travelers paid 20.3 million visits to Iowa and spent an estimated $697 million. In that year, the state's 18,800 travel-related businesses employed 111,300 workers. Total receipts by the travel industry in 1977 were $2.8 billion.

The Mississippi and Missouri rivers offer popular water sports facilities for both out-of-state visitors and resident vacationers. Iowa's "Little Switzerland" region in the northeast, with its high bluffs of woodland overlooking the Mississippi, is popular for hiking and camping. Notable tourist attractions in the area include the Effigy Mounds National Monument (near Marquette), which has hundreds of prehistoric Indian mounds and village sites, and the Buffalo Ranch (at Fayette), with its herd of live buffalo. Tourist sites in the central part of the state include the state capitol and the Herbert Hoover National Historic Site, with its Presidential Library and Museum.

Iowa has about 85,000 acres (34,400 hectares) of lakes and reservoirs, and 19,000 mi (30,600 km) of fishing streams. There were 96 state parks in 1977, of which 51 had camping facilities. In 1977, the parks recorded 14,209,601 visitors, including 425,731 campers. The state issued 344,938 hunting licenses and 463,518 fishing licenses in 1978. Pheasant, rabbit, squirrel, and quail were the most popular game for hunters.

⁴⁸SPORTS

Iowa has no major-league professional teams. High school and college basketball and football teams draw thousands of spectators, particularly to the state high school basketball tournament at Des Moines in March. Large crowds also fill stadiums and fieldhouses for the University of Iowa games in Iowa City and the State University games in Ames. In intercollegiate competition, the University of Iowa belongs to the Big Ten Conference; and Iowa State University is in the Big Eight. A popular track and field meet for college athletes is the Drake Relays, held every April in Des Moines. Horse racing is popular at state and county fairgrounds, as is stock car racing at small-town tracks. Wagering on sports events is illegal in Iowa.

⁴⁹FAMOUS IOWANS

Iowa was the birthplace of Herbert Clark Hoover (1874–1964), the first US president born west of the Mississippi. Although he was orphaned and left the state for Oregon at the age of 10, he always claimed Iowa as his home. His long and distinguished career included various relief missions in Europe, service as US secretary of commerce (1921–29), and one term in the White House (1929–33). Hoover was buried in West Branch, the town of his birth. Iowa has also produced one US vice president, Henry A. Wallace (1888–1965), who served in that office during Franklin D. Roosevelt's third term (1941–45). Wallace also was secretary of agriculture (1933–41) and of commerce (1945–47); he ran unsuccessfully as the Progressive Party's presidential candidate in 1948.

Two Kentucky-born members of the US Supreme Court were residents of Iowa prior to their appointments: Samuel F. Miller (1816–90) and Wiley B. Rutledge (1894–1949). Iowans who served in presidential cabinets as secretary of the interior were James Harlan (b.Illinois, 1820–99), Samuel J. Kirkwood (b.Maryland, 1813–94), Richard Ballinger (1858–1922), and Ray Lyman Wilbur (1875–1949). Ray Wilbur's brother Curtis (1867–1954) was secretary of the Navy, and James W. Good (1866–1929) was secretary of war. Appropriately enough, Iowans have dominated the post of secretary of agriculture in this century: they included, in addition to Wallace, James "Tama Jim" Wilson (b.Scotland, 1835–1920), who served in that post for 16 years and set a record for longevity in a single cabinet office; Henry C. Wallace (b.Illinois, 1866–1924), the father of the vice president; and Edwin T. Meredith (1876–1928). Harry L. Hopkins (1890–1946) was Franklin D. Roosevelt's closest adviser in all policy matters, foreign and domestic, and served in a variety of key New Deal posts. Prominent US senators from Iowa have included James W. Grimes (b.New Hampshire, 1816–72), whose vote, given from a hospital stretcher, saved President Andrew Johnson from being convicted of impeachment charges in 1868; earlier, Grimes had been governor of the state when its 1857 constitution was adopted. William Boyd Allison (b.Ohio, 1829–1908) was the powerful chairman of the Senate Appropriations Committee for nearly 30 years.

Among Iowa's most influential governors were the first territorial governor, Robert Lucas (b.Virginia, 1781–1853); Cyrus C. Carpenter (b.Pennsylvania, 1829–98); William Larrabee (b.Connecticut, 1832–1912); Horace Boies (b.New York, 1827–1923); and, in recent times, Harold Hughes (b.1922) and Robert D. Ray (b.1928).

Iowa has produced a large number of radical dissenters and social reformers. Abolitionists, strong in Iowa prior to the Civil War, included Grimes, Josiah B. Grinnell (b.Vermont, 1821–91),

and Asa Turner (b.Massachusetts, 1799–1885). George D. Herron (b.Indiana, 1862–1925) made Iowa a center of the Social Gospel movement before helping to found the Socialist Party. William "Billy" Sunday (1862–1935) was an evangelist with a large following among rural Americans. James B. Weaver (b.Ohio, 1833–1912) ran for the presidency on the Greenback-Labor ticket in 1880 and as a Populist in 1892. John L. Lewis (1880–1969), head of the United Mine Workers, founded the Congress of Industrial Organizations (CIO).

Iowa can claim two winners of the Nobel Peace Prize: religious leader John R. Mott (b.New York, 1865–1955) and agronomist and plant geneticist Norman E. Borlaug (b.1914). Two other distinguished scientists who lived in Iowa were George Washington Carver (b.Missouri, 1864–1943) and James Van Allen (b.1914).

Iowa writers of note include Hamlin Garland (b.Wisconsin, 1860–1940), Octave Thanet (Alice French, b.Massachusetts, 1850–1934), Bess Streeter Aldrich (1881–1954), Carl Van Vechten (1880–1964), James Norman Hall (1887–1951), Thomas Beer (1889–1940), Ruth Suckow (1892–1960), Philip D. Strong (1899–1957), MacKinlay Kantor (1904–77), Wallace Stegner (b.1909), and Richard P. Bissell (b.1913). Iowa's poets include Paul H. Engle (b. 1908), who directed the University of Iowa's famed Writers' Workshop, and James S. Hearst (b.1900). Two Iowa playwrights, Susan Glaspell (1882–1948) and her husband, George Cram Cook (1873–1924), were instrumental in founding influential theater groups.

Iowans who have contributed to America's musical heritage include jazz musician Leon "Bix" Beiderbecke (1903–31) and popular composer Meredith Willson (b.1902). Iowa's artists of note include Grant Wood (1892–1942), whose *American Gothic* is one of America's best-known paintings, and printmaker Mauricio Lasansky (b.Argentina, 1914).

Iowa's contributions to the field of popular entertainment include William F. "Buffalo Bill" Cody (1846–1917); circus impresario Charles Ringling (1863–1926) and his four brothers; the reigning American beauty of the late 19th century, Lillian Russell (Helen Louise Leonard, 1860–1922); and one of America's best-loved movie actors, John Wayne (Marion Michael Morrison, 1907–79). Iowa sports figures of note are baseball Hall of Famers Adrian C. "Cap" Anson (1851–1922) and Robert "Bob" Feller (b.1918), and football All-American Nile Kinnick (1918–44).

⁵⁰BIBLIOGRAPHY

Bogue, Allan G. *From Prairie to Cornbelt*. Chicago: University of Chicago Press, 1963.

Federal Writers' Project. *Iowa: A Guide to the Hawkeye State*. New York: Viking, 1938.

Gue, Benjamin F. *History of Iowa*. 4 vols. New York: Century History Co., 1903.

Hamilton, Carl. *In No Time at All*. Ames, Iowa State University Press, 1974.

Iowa Development Commission. *1979 Statistical Profile of Iowa*. Des Moines, 1979.

Iowa, State of. *Iowa Official Register 1979-80*. Vol. 58. Des Moines, 1979.

Ross, Earle D. *Iowa Agriculture*. Iowa City: State Historical Society, 1951.

Sage, Leland. *A History of Iowa*. Ames: Iowa State University Press, 1974.

Schwieder, Dorothy, ed. *Patterns and Perspectives in Iowa History*. Ames: Iowa State University Press, 1973.

Swierenga, Robert P. *Pioneers and Profits*. Ames: Iowa State University Press, 1968.

Wall, Joseph Frazier. *Iowa: A Bicentennial History*. New York: Norton, 1978.

KANSAS

State of Kansas

ORIGIN OF STATE NAME: Named for the Kansa (or Kaw) Indians, the "people of the south wind." **NICKNAME**: The Sunflower State. (Also: the Wheat State; the Jayhawk State.) **CAPITAL**: Topeka. **ENTERED UNION**: 29 January 1861 (34th). **SONG**: "Home on the Range." **MARCH**: "The Kansas March." **MOTTO**: *Ad astra per aspera* (To the stars through difficulties). **FLAG**: The flag consists of a dark blue field with the state seal in the center; a sunflower on a bar of twisted gold and blue is above the seal, the word "Kansas" is below it. **OFFICIAL SEAL**: A sun rising over mountains in the background symbolizes the east; commerce is represented by a river and a steamboat. In the foreground, agriculture, the basis of the state's prosperity, is represented by a settler's cabin and a man plowing a field; beyond this is a wagon train heading west and a herd of buffalo fleeing from two Indians. Around the top is the state motto above a cluster of 34 stars; the circle is surrounded by the words "Great Seal of the State of Kansas, January 29, 1861." **ANIMAL**: American buffalo. **BIRD**: Western meadowlark. **FLOWER**: Wild native sunflower. **TREE**: Cottonwood. **INSECT**: Honeybee. **LEGAL HOLIDAYS**: New Year's Day, 1 January; Lincoln's Birthday, 12 February; Washington's Birthday, 3d Monday in February; Memorial Day, last Monday in May; Independence Day, 4 July; Labor Day, 1st Monday in September; Columbus Day, 2d Monday in October; Veterans Day, 11 November; Thanksgiving Day, 4th Thursday in November; Christmas Day, 25 December. **TIME**: 6 A.M. CST = noon GMT; 5 A.M. MST = noon GMT.

¹LOCATION, SIZE, AND EXTENT

Located in the western north-central US, Kansas is the 2d-largest midwestern state (following Minnesota), and ranks 14th among the 50 states.

The total area of Kansas is 82,264 sq mi (213,064 sq km), of which 81,787 sq mi (211,828 sq km) are land, and the remaining 477 sq mi (1,235 sq km) inland water. Shaped like a rectangle except for an irregular corner in the NE, the state has a maximum extension E–W of about 411 mi (661 km) and an extreme N–S distance of about 208 mi (335 km).

Kansas is bounded on the N by Nebraska, on the E by Missouri (with the line in the NE following the Missouri River), on the S by Oklahoma, and on the W by Colorado, with a total boundary length of 1,219 mi (1,962 km). The geographic center of Kansas is in Barton County, 15 mi (24 km) NE of Great Bend.

²TOPOGRAPHY

Although the popular image of the state is one of unending flatlands, Kansas has a diverse topography. Three main land regions define the state. The eastern third of the state consists of the Osage Plains, Flint Hills, Dissected Till Plains, and Arkansas River Lowlands. The central third of the state comprises the Smoky Hills (which include the Dakota sandstone formations, Greenhorn limestone formations, and chalk deposits) to the north and several lowland regions to the south. To the west are the Great Plains proper, divided into the Dissected High Plains and the High Plains. Kansas generally slopes eastward from a maximum elevation of 4,039 feet (1,231 meters) at Mt. Sunflower (a mountain in name only) on the Colorado border to 680 feet (207 meters) by the Verdigris River at the Oklahoma border. More than 50,000 streams run through the state, and there are hundreds of artificial lakes. Major rivers include the Missouri, which defines the state's northeastern boundary; the Arkansas, which runs through Wichita; and the Kansas (Kaw), which runs through Topeka and joins the Missouri at Kansas City.

The geographic center of the 48 contiguous states is located in Smith County, in north-central Kansas, at 39°50′N and 98°35′W.

Forty miles (64 km) south of this point, in Osborne County at 39°13′27″ N and 98°32′31″ W, is the North American geodetic datum, the controlling point for all land surveys in the US, Canada, and Mexico. Extensive beds of prehistoric ocean fossils lie in the chalk beds of two western counties, Logan and Gove.

³CLIMATE

Kansas's continental climate is highly changeable. The average mean temperature is 55°F (13°C). The record high is 121°F (49°C), recorded near Alton on 24 July 1936; the record low, –40°F (–40°C), was registered at Lebanon on 13 February 1905. The normal annual precipitation ranges from slightly more than 40 inches (1,016 mm) in the southeast to less than 20 inches (508 mm) in the barren west. The overall annual average is 27 inches (686 mm), although years of drought have not been uncommon. Seventy percent of the precipitation falls between 1 April and 30 September. The annual mean snowfall ranges from about 40 inches (1,016 mm) in the extreme southeast to less than 16 inches (406 mm) in the far southwest. Tornadoes are a regular fact of Kansas life, with an annual average of 29 recorded during 1966–77.

⁴FLORA AND FAUNA

Native grasses, consisting of 60 different groups subdivided into 194 species, cover at least one-third of Kansas. Bluestem—both big and little—which grows in most parts of the state, has the greatest forage value. Other grasses include buffalo grass, blue and hairy gramas, and alkali sacaton. One native conifer, eastern red cedar, is found generally throughout the state. Hackberry, black walnut, and sycamore grow in the east, while box elder and cottonwood predominate in western Kansas. There are no native pines. The wild native sunflower, the state flower, is found throughout the state. Other characteristic wild flowers include wild daisy, ivy-leaved morning glory, and smallflower verbena. The prairie white-fringed orchid and Mead's milkweed are protected under federal statutes.

Kansas's indigenous mammals include the common cottontail, black-tailed jackrabbit, black-tailed prairie dog, muskrat, opossum, and raccoon; the white-tailed deer is the state's only big-game animal. There are 12 native species of bat, 2 varieties of shrew and mole, and 3 types of pocket gopher. The western meadowlark is the state bird. Threatened animals include the prairie falcon and Topeka shiner. The black-footed ferret, gray bat, bald eagle, small amphibious snail, and three species of salamander are on the endangered list.

⁵ENVIRONMENTAL PROTECTION

No environmental problem is more crucial to Kansas than water quality. The Water Resources Board was established in 1955 to develop and maintain all water resources in the state. A law passed in 1979 mandates each county with a population of more than 30,000 to establish wastewater treatment plants by July 1983. The State Conservation Commission promotes conservation measures in the state's 105 conservation districts.

⁶POPULATION

Kansas ranked 28th in 1970, with 2,249,071 residents, or 1.1% of the US total.

When it was admitted to the Union in 1861, Kansas's population was 107,206. During the decade that followed, the population grew by 240%, more than 10 times the US growth rate. Steady growth continued through the 1930s, but in the 1940s the population declined by 4%. Since then, the population has risen, though at a slower pace than in the rest of the country.

Of the 1970 population, 49% was male and 51% female. About 66% lived in urban areas and 34% in rural areas, nearly reversing the percentages recorded 50 years earlier. In 1975, the average Kansan was 27.8 years old, close to the national average. The 1980 preliminary census population was 2,355,536, almost 5% more than in 1970.

In 1978, Kansas had 34 incorporated areas of 10,000 population or more. Census returns for 1980 show 279,352 residents of Wichita, 159,972 of Kansas City, and 115,996 of Topeka.

⁷ETHNIC GROUPS

White settlers began to pour into Kansas in 1854, dispersing the 36 Indian tribes that had lived there and precipitating a struggle over the legal status of slavery. Remnants of 6 of the original tribes still make their homes in the state. Some live on reservations covering 27,000 acres (11,000 hectares); others live and work elsewhere, returning to the reservations several times a year for celebrations and observances. There were 8,672 Indians in Kansas as of 1970.

Black Americans in Kansas numbered 125,000—more than 5% of the population—in 1976, when the state also had 43,000 residents of Hispanic origin. The 1970 census recorded 8,661 Asian-Pacific peoples, the largest group being 1,584 Japanese. A total of 1,897 Indochinese refugees were resettled in Kansas in 1975.

The foreign-born and their American-born offspring numbered 175,000 (almost 8% of the population) in 1970. About one-fourth were of German descent.

⁸LANGUAGES

Plains Indians of the Macro-Siouan group originally populated what is now Kansas; their speech echoes in such place-names as Kansas, Wichita, Topeka, Chetopa, and Ogallah. In 1970, 2,029 Kansans claimed Indian languages as their first.

Regional features of Kansas speech are almost entirely those of the Northern and North Midland dialects, reflecting the migration into Kansas in the 1850s of settlers from the East. Kansans typically use *fish(ing) worms* as bait, play as children on a *teetertotter,* see a *snakefeeder* (dragonfly) over a /krik/ (creek), make *white bread* sandwiches, carry water in a *pail,* and may designate the time 2:45 as a quarter *to,* or *of,* or *till* three.

The migration by southerners in the mid-19th century is evidenced in southeastern Kansas by such South Midland terms as *pullybone* (wishbone) and *light bread* (white bread); the expression *wait on* (wait for) extends farther westward.

In 1970, 87% of Kansas residents considered English their native tongue. Speakers of the principal first languages were as follows:

	NATIVE-BORN	FOREIGN-BORN
English	1,962,263	4,576
German	98,866	7,174
Spanish	26,838	4,739

Still other language groups include French, Italian, Polish, and Yiddish.

⁹RELIGIONS

Protestant missions played an important role in early Kansas history. Isaac McCoy, a Baptist minister, was instrumental in founding the Shawnee Baptist Mission in Johnson County in 1831. Later Baptist, Methodist, Quaker, Presbyterian, and Jesuit missions became popular stopover points for pioneers traveling along the Oregon and Santa Fe trails. Mennonites were drawn to the state by a law passed in 1874 allowing exemptions from military service on religious grounds. As of 1971, Mennonites comprised 0.7% of the population.

Religious freedom is specifically granted in the Kansas constitution, and a wide variety of religious groups is represented in the state. In 1971 there were 2,992 Protestant churches with 871,850 adherents. The leading Protestant denominations were United Methodists, 290,792; American Baptist Convention, 81,277; Southern Baptist Convention, 61,098; and Lutheran Church–Missouri Synod, 60,835. Roman Catholics constitute the largest single religious group in the state, with 336,948 church members in 1979. Kansas's estimated Jewish population was 10,755.

¹⁰TRANSPORTATION

In the heartland of the nation, Kansas is at the crossroads of the US road and railway systems. The state ranks 5th in total railroad miles and 3d in total highway miles.

Kansas was literally built on the success of the railroads in the late 1800s. The two major railroads, the Kansas Pacific (now the Union Pacific) and the Santa Fe, acquired more than 10 million acres (4 million hectares) of land in the state and then advertised for immigrants to come and buy it. By 1872, the railroads stretched across the state, creating in their path the towns of Ellsworth, Newton, Caldwell, Wichita, and Dodge City. One of the first "cow towns" was Abilene, the terminal point for all cattle shipped to the East. In 1980, the state had about 7,500 mi (12,000 km) of railroads. Amtrak passenger trains cross Kansas en route from Kansas City to Denver.

As of 1978, the state had 134,855 mi (217,028 km) of roads, some 77% of them paved, of which 123,015 mi (197,974 km) were rural and 11,840 mi (19,055 km) municipal. There were 1,344,319 autos, 586,671 trucks, 84,832 motorcycles, and 3,712 buses registered in Kansas in 1978.

During that same year, the state had 372 airports, 125 private and 247 public. The busiest airport, in Wichita, had 17,364 departing flights involving 572,032 passengers.

¹¹HISTORY

Present-day Kansas was first inhabited by Paleo-Indians approximately 10,000 years ago. They were followed by several prehistoric cultures, forerunners of the Plains tribes—the Wichita, Pawnee, Kansa, Osage, and Plains Apache—that were living in Kansas when the earliest Europeans arrived. These tribes were buffalo hunters who also farmed and lived in small permanent communities. Around 1800, they were joined on the Central Plains by the nomadic Cheyenne, Arapaho, Comanche, and Kiowa.

The first European, explorer Francisco Coronado, entered Kansas in 1541, searching for riches in the fabled land of Quivira. He found no gold but was impressed by the land's fertility. A second Spanish expedition to the Plains was led by Juan de Oñate in 1601. Between 1682 and 1739, French explorers established trading contacts with the Indians. During the mid-1700s, the Spanish relinquished all claims on the land to the French.

Most of Kansas was sold to the US by France as part of the Louisiana Purchase of 1803. (The extreme southwestern corner

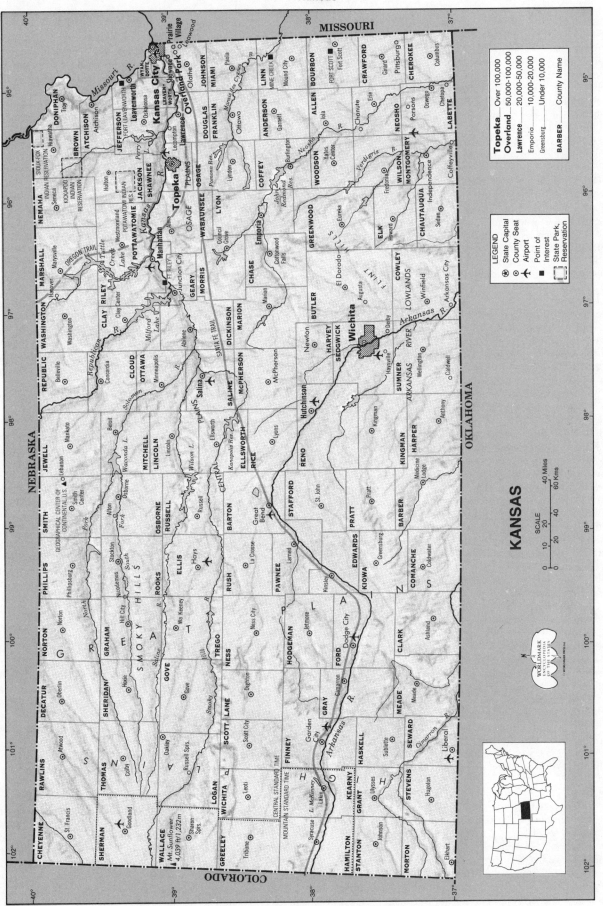

KANSAS

SCALE

| 0 | 10 | 20 | 40 Miles |

| 0 | 20 | 40 | 60 Kms |

See US political: front cover G3; physical: back cover G3.

LOCATION: 36°59'55" to 40° N; 94°37'03" to 102°03'02" W. **BOUNDARIES:** Nebraska line, 357 mi (575 km); Missouri line, 244 mi (393 km); Oklahoma line, 411 mi (661 km); Colorado line, 207 mi (333 km).

LEGEND

⊛ State Capital
⊙ County Seat
✈ Airport
■ Point of Interest
State Park, Reservation

Topeka	Over 100,000
Overland	50,000-100,000
Lawrence	20,000-50,000
Emporia	10,000-20,000
Greensburg	Under 10,000
BARBER	County Name

was gained after the Mexican War.) Lewis and Clark examined the country along the Missouri River in 1804, and expeditions under the command of Zebulon Pike (1806) and Stephen Long (1819) traversed the land from east to west. Pike and Long were not impressed with the territory's dry soil, the latter calling it "unfit for civilization, and of course uninhabitable by a people depending on agriculture for their subsistence."

Largely because of these negative reports, early settlement of Kansas was sparse, limited to a few thousand eastern Indians who were removed from their lands and relocated in what is now eastern Kansas. Included were such once powerful tribes as the Shawnee, Delaware, Chippewa, Wyandot, Ottawa, and Potawatomi. They were joined by a number of Christian missionaries seeking to convert the Indians into Christian farmers.

William Becknell opened the Santa Fe Trail to wagon traffic in 1822, and for 50 years that route, two-thirds of which lay in Kansas, was of commercial importance to the West. During the 1840s and 1850s, thousands of migrants crossed northeastern Kansas on the California-Oregon Trail. In 1827, Fort Leavenworth was established, followed by Fort Scott (1842) and Fort Riley (1853). Forts Leavenworth and Riley remain active and important installations.

Kansas Territory was created by the Kansas-Nebraska Act (30 May 1854), with its western boundary set at the Rocky Mountains. Almost immediately, disputes arose as to whether Kansas would enter the Union as a free or slave state. Both free-staters and proslavery settlers were brought in, and a succession of governors tried to bring order out of the chaos arising from the two groups' differences. Free-staters established an extralegal government at Topeka following the establishment of a territorial capital at Lecompton.

Because of several violent incidents the territory became known as Bleeding Kansas. One of the most memorable attacks came in May 1856, when the town of Lawrence was sacked by proslavery forces. John Brown, an abolitionist who had recently arrived from upstate New York, retaliated by murdering five proslavery settlers. Guerrilla skirmishes continued for the next few years along the Kansas-Missouri border. The final act of violence was the Marais des Cygnes massacre in 1858, which resulted in the death of several free-staters. In all, about 50 people were killed in the territorial period—not an extraordinary number for a frontier community.

After several attempts to write a constitution acceptable to both anti- and pro-slavery groups, the final document was drafted in 1859. Kansas entered the Union on 29 January 1861 as a free state. Topeka was named the capital, and the western boundary was reduced to its present location.

Although Kansas lay west of the major Civil War action, two-thirds of its adult males served in the Union Army and gave it the highest military death rate among the northern states. Kansas units saw action in the South and West, most notably at Wilson's Creek, Cane Hill, Prairie Grove, and Chickamauga. The only full-scale battle fought in Kansas was at Mine Creek in 1864, at the end of General Sterling Price's unsuccessful Confederate campaign in the West. The most tragic incident on Kansas soil came on 21 August 1863, when Confederate guerrilla William C. Quantrill raided Lawrence, killing at least 150 persons and burning the town.

Following the Civil War, settlement expanded in Kansas, particularly in the central part of the state. White settlers encroached on the hunting grounds of the Plains tribes, and the Indians attacked white settlements in retaliation. Treaty councils were held, the largest at Medicine Lodge in 1867, but not until 1878 did conflict cease between Indians and whites. Most of the Indians were eventually removed to the Indian territory in what is now Oklahoma. Also during this period, buffalo, slaughtered for food and hides, all but disappeared from the state.

By 1872, both the Union Pacific and the Santa Fe railroads had crossed Kansas, and other lines were under construction. Rail expansion brought more settlers, who established new communities. It also led to the great Texas cattle drives that meant prosperity to a number of Kansas towns, including Abilene, Ellsworth, Wichita, Caldwell, and Dodge City, from 1867 to 1885. This was when Bat Masterson, Wyatt Earp, Doc Holliday, and Wild Bill Hickok reigned in Dodge City and Abilene—the now romantic era of the Old West. A strain of hard winter wheat that proved particularly well suited to the state's soil was brought to Kansas in the 1870s by Russian Mennonites fleeing czarist rule, and Plains agriculture was thereby transformed. There were also political changes: the state adopted limited female suffrage in 1887. Prohibition, made part of the state constitution in 1880, was a source of controversy until its repeal in 1948.

Significant changes in agriculture, industry, transportation, and communications came after 1900. Mechanization became commonplace in farming, and vast areas were opened to wheat production, particularly during World War I. Some automobile manufacturing took place, and the movement for "good roads" began. The so-called agrarian revolt of the late 19th century, characterized politically by populism, evolved into the Progressive movement of the early 1900s, which focused attention on control of monopolies, public health, labor legislation, and more representative politics. Much of the Progressive leadership came from Kansas; Kansan newspaper editor and national Progressive leader William Allen White devoted considerable energy to Theodore Roosevelt's Bull Moose campaign.

Kansas suffered through the Great Depression of the 1930s. The state's western region, part of the Dust Bowl, was hardest hit. Improved weather conditions and the demands of World War II revived Kansas agriculture in the 1940s. The World War II era also saw the development of industry, especially in transportation. Wichita had been a major center of the aircraft industry in the 1920s and 1930s, and its plants became vital to the US war effort. Other heavy industry grew, and mineral production—oil, natural gas, salt, coal, and gypsum—expanded greatly.

Since World War II, Kansas has become increasingly urban. Agriculture has become highly commercialized, and there are dozens of large industries that process and market farm products and supply materials to crop producers. Livestock production, especially in closely controlled feedlots, is a major enterprise. Recent governors have worked to expand international exports of Kansas products.

[12] STATE GOVERNMENT

The form of Kansas's constitution was a matter of great national concern, for the question of whether Kansas would be a free or slave state was in doubt throughout the 1850s. After three draft constitutions failed to win popular support or congressional approval, a fourth version, banning slavery, was drafted in July 1859 and ratified by Kansas voters that October. Signed by President James Buchanan on 29 January 1861, this constitution (with 77 subsequent amendments) has governed Kansas to the present day.

The Kansas legislature consists of a 40-member senate and a 125-member house of representatives. Senators serve four-year terms and house members serve for two years; elections are held in even-numbered years. Legislative sessions are limited to 90 days in even-numbered years but are unlimited in odd-numbered years.

Officials elected statewide are the governor, lieutenant governor, secretary of state, attorney general, treasurer, and commissioner of insurance. Members of the state Board of Education are elected by districts. All serve four-year terms. Every office in the executive branch is controlled by either the governor or another elected official. The governor appoints the heads (secretaries) of all state departments.

A bill becomes law when it has been approved by 21 senators and 63 representatives and signed by the governor. A veto can be overridden by one more than two-thirds of the members of both houses.

To vote in the state, a person must be a US citizen, 18 years old at the time of the election, and a resident of Kansas. Registration closes 20 days prior to all elections.

13 POLITICAL PARTIES

Kansas was dominated by the Republican Party for the first three decades of statehood. Although the Republicans remain the dominant force in state politics, the Democrats controlled several state offices in the late 1970s.

The Republican Party of early Kansas espoused the abolitionist ideals of the New England settlers who sought to ban slavery from the state. After the Civil War the railroads played a major role in Republican politics and won favorable tax advantages from the elected officials. The party's ranks swelled with the arrival of immigrants from Scandinavia and Germany, who tended to side with the party's by then strongly conservative beliefs.

The Republicans' hold over state life was shaken by the Populist revolt toward the end of the 19th century. The high point of Populist Party power came in 1892, when the insurgents won all the statewide elective offices and also took control of the senate. When electoral irregularities denied them control of the house, they temporarily seized the house chambers. The two parties then set up separate houses of representatives, the Populists meeting one day, the Republicans the next. This continued for six weeks, until the Kansas supreme court ruled that the Republicans constituted the rightful legal body. After a Republican sweep in 1894, the Populists returned to office in 1896, but the party declined rapidly thereafter.

The Democrats rose to power in the state as a result of the split between the conservative and progressive wings of the Republican Party in 1912. Nevertheless, the Democrats were very much a minority party until after World War II. Democrats held the governorship for 14 of the 24 years between 1957 and 1980; Republicans have regularly controlled the legislature, however. In 1979, the state had 361,736 registered Republicans (31% of eligible voters) and 283,952 registered Democrats (24%). The remaining 45% included independents and members of minor parties.

In November 1980, Kansans gave a large majority of their presidential votes to Republican Ronald Reagan. Another Republican, Robert Dole, was reelected to the US Senate, and the Republicans remained firmly in control of the state's US congressional delegation and legislature.

14 LOCAL GOVERNMENT

As of 1980, Kansas had 105 counties, 625 incorporated cities, 1,449 townships, and 307 unified school districts. By law, no county can be less than 432 sq mi (1,119 sq km).

Each county government is headed by three elected county commissioners. Other county officials include the county clerk, treasurer, register of deeds, attorney, sheriff, clerk of district court, and appraiser. Most cities are run by mayor-council systems.

15 STATE SERVICES

The Kansas Governmental Ethics Commission administers all laws mandating ethical practices by state officials.

All education services except higher education are handled by the Board of Education; higher education lies within the jurisdiction of the Board of Regents. Transportation services are supervised by the Department of Transportation. The Department of Human Resources administers employment and worker benefit programs; the Department of Economic Development operates housing and business planning programs. Social, vocational, and children's programs are run by the Department of Social and Rehabilitation Services; the Department of Health and Environment supervises health, environment, and laboratory services. Correctional institutions are administered by the Department of Corrections; a state ombudsman for corrections handles complaints from prisoners.

16 JUDICIAL SYSTEM

The supreme court, the highest court in the state, is composed of a chief justice and six other justices. All justices are elected for six-year terms; there is no limit to the number of terms a justice may serve. An intermediate-level court of appeals consists of a chief judge and six other judges elected to four-year terms.

In January 1977, probate, juvenile, and county courts, as well as magistrate courts of countywide jurisdiction, were replaced by district courts. There are 29 judicial districts served by 70 district judges, 66 associate district judges, and 75 district magistrate judges. All run for four-year terms in elections that are either partisan or nonpartisan depending on the district.

The Department of Corrections administers the state correctional system. Those convicted of major crimes are sent to the

Kansas Presidential Vote by Political Parties, 1948–80

YEAR	ELECTORAL VOTE	KANSAS WINNER	DEMOCRAT	REPUBLICAN	PROGRESSIVE	SOCIALIST	PROHIBITION
1948	8	Dewey (R)	351,902	423,039	4,603	2,807	6,468
1952	8	*Eisenhower (R)	273,296	616,302	6,038	530	6,038
1956	8	*Eisenhower (R)	296,317	566,878	—	—	3,048
1960	8	Nixon (R)	363,213	561,474	—	—	4,138
						SOC. LABOR	
1964	7	*Johnson (D)	464,028	386,579	—	1,901	5,393
					AMERICAN IND.		
1968	7	*Nixon (R)	302,996	478,674	88,921	—	2,192
					AMERICAN		
1972	7	*Nixon (R)	270,287	619,812	21,808	—	4,188
					LIBERTARIAN		
1976	7	Ford (R)	430,421	502,752	4,724	3,242	1,403
1980	7	*Reagan (R)	326,150	566,812	7,555	14,470	—

*Won US presidential election.

Kansas State Penitentiary, which in 1979 housed 959 inmates. The Kansas Adult Authority makes the final decision on parole. Kansas's crime rate is much lower than the national average. The Crime Victims Reparation Board was established in 1978 to compensate victims of violent crime. It paid out $36,127 in 1978/79, its first full year of operation.

17 ARMED FORCES

The US Army's 1st Infantry Division, known as the Big Red One, is located at Fort Riley in Junction City and had 20,834 personnel in 1978. The Army's General Staff College is housed at Fort Leavenworth, which had 7,195 personnel in 1978; McConnell Air Force Base, located in Wichita, had 5,869. That year about $431 million in defense contracts were awarded to state firms.

Kansas had 312,000 veterans in 1979. Of these, 8,000 were veterans of World War I, 136,000 of World War II, 53,000 of the Korean conflict, and 93,000 of the Viet-Nam era. During fiscal year 1977/78, $90,190,284 was paid to veterans for compensation and pensions.

In 1980, Kansas had 1,662 members of the Air National Guard and 7,229 members of the Army National Guard. Of the 5,258 people employed by state and local police in 1977, 4,471 were local police force members.

18 MIGRATION

By the 1770s, Kansas was inhabited by a few thousand Indians, mainly from five tribes: the Kansa (Kaw) and the Osage, both of whom had migrated from the east, and the Pawnee, Wichita, and Comanche, who had come from the southwest. In 1825, the US government signed a treaty with the Kansa and Osage that allowed eastern Indians to settle in the state.

The first wave of white migration came during the 1850s with the arrival of New England abolitionists who settled in Lawrence, Topeka, and Manhattan. They were followed by a much larger wave of emigrants from the eastern Missouri and the upper Mississippi Valley, drawn by the lure of wide-open spaces and abundant economic opportunity.

The population swelled as a result of the Homestead Act of 1862, which offered land to anyone who would improve it and live on it for five years. The railroads promoted the virtues of Kansas overseas and helped sponsor immigrant settlers. By 1870, 11% of the population was European. More than 30,000 blacks, mostly from the South, arrived during 1878–80. Crop failures caused by drought in the late 1890s led to extensive outmigration from the western half of the state. Another period of outmigration occurred in the early 1930s, when massive dust storms drove people off the land.

Steady migration from farms to cities has been a feature of Kansas life throughout this century. Urban population surpassed farm population after World War II, and the trend toward urbanization has continued.

19 INTERGOVERNMENTAL COOPERATION

Kansas is a member of the Ozarks Regional Commission and many other interstate bodies. The Kansas Commission on Interstate Cooperation assists state officials and employees in maintaining contact with governmental units in other states.

In 1977/78, Kansas received $616 million in federal assistance. Of that amount, $138 million was for public assistance, $83 million for medicaid, $77 million for transportation, and $59 million for revenue sharing.

20 ECONOMY

Although wheat has long been the mainstay of the Kansas economy, efforts to bring other industries into the state began as early as the 1870s, when the railroads linked Kansas to eastern markets. Today, agricultural products and meat-packing industries are rivaled by the large aircraft industry centered in Wichita. The Kansas City metropolitan area is a center of automobile production and printing. Metal fabrication, printing, and mineral products industries predominate in the nine southeastern counties.

21 INCOME

In 1978, Kansas tied with Colorado in income per capita with $8,001 (15th in the US).

The following table shows personal income in 1976 and 1977 (in thousands):

	1976	% CHANGE	1977
Total earnings, of which:	$10,606,565	10.8	$11,749,077
Farm	618,078	−5.1	586,721
Agricultural services, forestry, fisheries	33,048	12.6	37,209
Mining	264,434	20.7	319,080
Construction	697,743	17.5	819,982
Manufacturing	2,251,170	11.3	2,506,371
Transportation and public utilities	910,087	12.3	1,021,692
Wholesale and retail trade	1,943,364	8.5	2,107,975
Finance, insurance, and real estate	529,494	15.7	612,624
Services	1,481,172	14.2	1,691,079
Government	1,877,975	9.0	2,046,344

Total personal income was $18.8 billion in 1978, 1.1% of the US total.

22 LABOR

Kansas has traditionally had a fairly low unemployment rate. In 1979, the civilian labor force was 1,204,200, of whom 1,169,400 were employed, yielding an unemployment rate of 2.9%. The unemployment rate for all males was 2.5%; for females, 3.7%; and for nonwhites, 10.4%.

A federal census of workers covered by unemployment insurance in March 1977 revealed the following nonfarm employment pattern in Kansas:

	ESTABLISH- MENTS	EMPLOYEES	ANNUAL PAYROLL ('000)
Agricultural services, forestry, fishing	533	2,028	$ 15,386
Mining, of which:	1,015	12,778	183,382
Oil, gas extraction	(855)	(9,871)	(138,858)
Contract construction	5,701	46,871	614,152
Manufacturing, of which:	3,028	172,414	2,163,742
Food, food products	(346)	(22,193)	(279,311)
Nonelectrical machinery	(518)	(26,815)	(323,856)
Transport equipment	(153)	(37,955)	(537,920)
Transportation, public utilities	2,797	40,785	529,679
Wholesale trade	5,219	54,892	675,742
Retail trade	16,190	150,882	923,780
Finance, insurance, real estate	4,799	42,536	433,420
Services	14,030	132,222	1,002,391
Other	569	929	8,632
TOTALS	53,881	656,337	$6,550,306

In 1976, 125,000 workers, or 15% of the nonfarm work force, belonged to labor unions. In 1977 there were 28 work stoppages involving 8,000 workers. Kansas has a right-to-work law.

23 AGRICULTURE

Known as the Wheat State and the breadbasket of the nation, Kansas produces more wheat and milo (a grain sorghum) than any other state. It also ranks 1st in per capita exports of all farm products, and 7th in total farm income.

Because of fluctuating prices, Kansas farmers have always risked economic disaster. During the 1920s, depressed farm prices forced many new farmers out of business. By World War II, however, Kansas farmers were prospering again, as record prices coincided with record yields. Since then, improved technology has favored large corporate farms at the expense of small landholders. Between 1940 and 1978, the number of farms declined from 159,000 to 76,000, while the average size of farms more than doubled.

In 1977, about 29,984,000 acres (12,134,000 hectares) were in crops, or 62% of all farmland. Current farm operating expenses totaled $2.6 billion, while cash receipts from farm marketings were $3.8 billion. The following table shows several leading crops in 1977:

	VALUE	PRODUCTION (BU)	US RANK
Wheat	$741,428,000	344,850,000	1
Sorghum (grain)	393,660,000	234,000,000	1
Corn (grain)	314,496,000	161,280,000	10
Soybeans	148,302,000	27,720,000	15

Other leading crops include alfalfa, oats, popcorn, edible beans, corn and sorghums for silage, wild hay, red clover, and lespedeza seed for forage. In 1977, Kansas ranked 2d in the US in milled flour production and 2d in dehydrated alfalfa. The state was also a leading producer of soybean oil and meal.

24 ANIMAL HUSBANDRY
Livestock and animal products had a total farm value of $1,307,702,000 in 1977. An estimated 3,071,000 cattle and 1,098,600 hogs were slaughtered for commercial purposes. The following is a summary of livestock production for 1977:

	VALUE	OUTPUT (LB)	US RANK
Cattle	$975,315,000	2,790,210,000	3
Hogs	303,042,000	757,605,000	7
Sheep	5,570,000	11,821,000	17
Chickens	1,165,000	10,995,000	27

The value of meat products was $1,370,600,000, 4th in the US. Kansas's 28 meat-packing plants processed 1,989,670,000 lb of beef, 234,000 lb of veal, 183,938,000 lb of pork, and 237,000 lb of lamb and mutton. The total value of all dairy products was $101,149,000. Thirty plants manufactured 16,154,000 lb of butter, 26,448,000 lb of American cheese, and 7,325,000 lb of ice cream. Milk production brought $140,402,000 in 1977.

25 FISHING
There is little commercial fishing in Kansas. Sport fishermen can find bass, crappie, catfish, perch, and pike in the state's reservoirs and man-made lakes.

26 FORESTRY
Kansas was at one time so barren of trees that early settlers were offered 160 acres (65 hectares) free if they would plant trees on their land. The law was rarely enforced, however, and today much of Kansas is still treeless.

Kansas had about 1,344,000 acres (544,000 hectares) of forest land, 0.18% of the US total, in 1977. There were 1,187,000 acres (480,000 hectares) of commercial timberland, of which 96.9% was privately owned. About $2 million worth of forest products were sold during that same year.

27 MINING
In 1978, the estimated value of all mineral production in Kansas was $1.5 billion, 18th in the US. The state produced 16,600,000 tons of crushed stone, 14,000,000 tons of sand and gravel, 2,113,000 tons of cement, 1,652,000 tons of salt, and 1,429,000 tons of clay.

About two-thirds of all helium produced in the US is extracted from Kansas natural gas. In 1977, 565,000,000 cu feet (16,000,000 cu meters) of helium was refined, with a value of $12,712,000.

28 ENERGY AND POWER
In 1978, Kansas had an installed electric generating capacity of 6,800,000 kw. Electric output was 24.7 billion kwh, a 55% increase over 1970. About 84% of the power was privately produced. Sales in 1977 totaled 18.9 billion kwh, of which 32% was for residences, 30% for commercial establishments, 37% for industrial plants, and 1% for other purposes.

In 1977, Kansas was the nation's 7th-leading oil producer. Output totaled 57,496,000 barrels of crude petroleum, valued at $715,825,000. There were 42,900 producing wells in 1978, when proved reserves totaled 350,000,000 barrels. Ten refineries had a daily capacity of 453,918 barrels.

Natural gas production was 787.9 trillion cu feet (22.3 trillion cu meters), 13% below the 1970 record. However, the 1977 wellhead value of $382,928,000 was an all-time high. Six gas companies served more than 702,000 customers in 1978. Sales totaled $544,462,000, of which 58% went for industrial purposes, 28% for residential use, 12% for commercial applications, and 2% to other purposes.

Kansas was one of the first states to market gasohol in 1979, and many farmers were planning to grow grain for future gasohol production.

29 INDUSTRY
Transportation equipment, nonelectrical machinery, food and food products, and printing and publishing accounted for 59% of all state manufacturing employment in 1977 and 55% of value added by manufacturing, which totaled $5.4 billion in that year. Industries are concentrated in Sedgwick, Wyandotte, Johnson, and Shawnee counties.

The following table shows the value added by manufacturing for major industries in 1976 and 1977:

	1976	1977
Transportation equipment	$1,084,300,000	$1,119,700,000
Nonelectrical machinery	602,200,000	679,600,000
Food and food products	676,400,000	686,800,000
Chemicals and allied products	478,200,000	462,800,000
Printing and publishing	405,400,000	467,000,000
Petroleum and coal products	313,800,000	365,200,000
Stone, clay, glass	242,000,000	302,800,000
Rubber and plastics	221,900,000	320,100,000
Fabricated metal products	181,100,000	235,500,000
Electrical and electronics equipment	160,200,000	204,200,000
Apparel and textile products	121,000,000	127,600,000

Kansas is a world leader in aviation, claiming a large share of both US and world production and sales. Wichita, the home of Beech, Cessna, Gates Learjet, and Great Lakes Aviation, is the center of aircraft construction; Boeing Wichita employs some 12,000 workers.

30 COMMERCE
Domestically, Kansas is not a major commercial state. In 1972, wholesale trade totaled $7.9 billion. Retail sales were $7.7 billion in 1977, divided as follows: automotive dealers, 24%; food stores, 20%; general merchandise stores, 13%; gasoline service stations, 9%; eating and drinking places, 8%; and others, 26%.

Kansas does play an important role in US foreign trade. In 1976/77, the state ranked 1st nationally in the export of wheat and flour, and agricultural exports totaled $998.5 million.

31 CONSUMER PROTECTION
The consumer credit commissioner is responsible for administering the state's investment and consumer credit codes.

32 BANKING
Kansas's 615 commercial banks had assets of $11.4 billion and assigned loans worth $6.1 billion in 1977. In that same year, 84 savings and loan associations reported $5.5 billion in assets and $4.9 billion in first mortgage loans. Credit unions showed a substantial rise in the value of loans granted, from $383 million in 1976 to $533 million in 1977. There were 248 credit unions with 387,872 members.

Records of all banks and trust companies in the state are examined once a year by the bank commissioner (who is appointed by the governor, with the consent of the senate, to a four-year term), by the Federal Deposit Insurance Corporation, or by a federal reserve bank.

33 INSURANCE
Some 20 companies are licensed to sell life insurance in Kansas. In 1978, 4,172,000 policies were in force, worth $30,896,000,000;

benefit payments totaled $288,600,000. The average amount of life insurance per family was $34,300. Of the $867.3 million in premiums written by property and liability insurers in 1978, $184 million was in automobile liability insurance, $150.9 million in automotive physical damage insurance, and $114.2 million in homeowners' coverage.

34 SECURITIES

Grain commodity exchanges are located in Hutchinson, Salina, and Wichita. There are no stock exchanges.

35 PUBLIC FINANCE

The state budget is prepared by the Division of the Budget and is submitted by the governor to the legislature for approval. The fiscal year runs from 1 July to 30 June.

The following is a summary of state revenues and expenditures for fiscal years 1978/79 (actual) and 1979/80 (estimated):

RECEIPTS	1978/79	1979/80
Taxes	$1,004,555,431	$1,111,301,099
Transfers	1,006,782,372	1,095,927,243
Federal grants	481,668,750	619,853,248
TOTALS	$2,493,006,553	$2,827,081,590

EXPENDITURES		
Public welfare	$ 449,661,056	$ 516,042,049
Education, research	923,026,843	1,059,352,025
General government	136,289,561	177,879,280
Public safety	45,070,839	55,718,080
Conservation of agriculture and natural resources	17,724,910	21,522,940
Health and hospitals	94,588,490	112,312,522
Recreational, historical	15,268,646	18,407,933
Transportation (including highways)	354,584,237	392,411,697
TOTALS	$2,036,214,582	$2,353,646,526

According to state law, no Kansas governmental unit may issue revenue bonds to finance current activities; all these must operate on a cash basis. Bonds may be issued for such capital improvements as roads and buildings. The total indebtedness of county and local governments exceeded $2.4 billion as of 30 June 1978.

36 TAXATION

Kansas ranked 29th in total state and local tax revenue in 1977, with receipts of $1.7 billion, or $728 per capita.

The state income tax rate in 1979 ranged from 2% on the first $2,000 to 9.5% on income over $25,000. Receipts from individual income taxes in 1978 were $241 million. Corporate income tax receipts were $129 million.

A statewide 3% sales tax was adopted in 1965; by law, cities and counties may together add up to another 1%. As of 1980, 17 cities and four counties had a 0.5% tax; one county levied a 1% tax. The state also collects liquor and bingo enforcement taxes, cigarette and tobacco products taxes, inheritance taxes, motor vehicle and motor carrier taxes, motor fuel taxes, and royalty taxes on oil, natural gas, and other minerals. Property and school taxes are the largest sources of income for local governments.

In 1977, Kansas filed 952,830 federal tax returns on more than $12.1 billion in gross income and paid nearly $1.7 billion in taxes, or about $715 per capita, slightly below the US average.

37 ECONOMIC POLICY

The first state commission to promote industrial development was formed in 1939. In 1963, this commission was reorganized into the Department of Economic Development, whose agencies conduct economic planning, assist local communities, and encourage minority business enterprise. In 1979/80, a new program to encourage film production in the state was launched.

Kansas has a duty-free foreign trade zone and provides tax-exempt bonds to help finance business and industry. Specific tax incentives include job expansion and investment tax credits; tax exemptions or moratoriums on land, capital improvements, and specific machinery; and certain corporate income tax exemptions.

38 HEALTH

Kansas is one of the healthiest places in the US to live. Life expectancy of 72.58 years during 1969–71 ranked it 6th nationwide. Life expectancy for men was 68.83; for women, 76.54.

As in the rest of the country, the birthrate in Kansas has been decreasing since the mid-1950s; in 1977, it was 15.9 per 1,000 population. The infant mortality rate for that year was 12.8 per 1,000 white live births and 19.4 per 1,000 nonwhite live births; neither figure was far from the US average. There were about 7,400 legal abortions, a rate of 1 for each 5 live births; 82% of these abortions involved white mothers, 75% of whom were unmarried. Heart disease is the leading cause of death in the state, accounting for 39% of all deaths in 1977.

Topeka, a major US center for psychiatric treatment, is home to the world-famous Menninger Clinic as well as numerous state-run psychiatric hospitals and outpatient clinics. As of December 1976, 1,456 inpatients were receiving full-time care in state and county mental hospitals. In 1975, 15,105 Kansans received outpatient psychiatric services; another 14,685 were treated in general hospitals with inpatient psychiatric units. The state sponsors four hospitals and treatment centers for the mentally retarded.

In 1978, Kansas had 164 hospitals with 18,161 beds, 462,395 admissions, and 39,413 personnel, including 6,424 registered nurses and 3,155 licensed practical nurses. Nine counties had no hospitals in 1977. State figures for nursing homes in 1976 showed 393 facilities with about 23,200 beds and 21,900 patients.

Kansas suffers from an overall shortage of doctors; in 1978, for example, six counties reported that no doctors were practicing within their borders. Overall, Kansas had 3,445 physicians in 1977, of whom 676 were general practitioners. Kansas had 1,080 dentists in 1979, most of them in the Kansas City area.

The University of Kansas has the state's only medical and pharmacology schools. The university's Mid-America Cancer Center and Radiation Treatment Center are the major cancer research and treatment facilities in the state. The Menninger Foundation has an extensive research and treatment center for mental health.

39 SOCIAL WELFARE

Public assistance in Kansas is coordinated through the Department of Human Resources and its seven agencies. The Department of Social Rehabilitation Services coordinates social programs through its four divisions.

In 1979/80, public assistance was estimated at $274,798,927, of which $179,655,694 went for medical aid and $72,582,851 to aid for dependent children. The state also granted $1,265,374 to aid Indochinese refugees.

An estimated 48,000 Kansans participated in the federal food stamp program in 1978, at a cost of $14,800,000. About 318,000 children, or 70% of the total eligible school enrollment, took part in the school lunch program at a total cost of $15,600,000.

In 1977, about 370,000 Kansans received Social Security benefits totaling $927,800,000. Of that amount, $635,000,000 went to 258,400 retirees; 78,400 Kansans received $212,100,000 in survivors' benefits; and 33,200 disabled workers received $80,700,000. A total of $21,600,000 in supplemental security income benefits was paid in 1978: $9,300,000 went to the aged, $12,000,000 to the disabled, and $300,000 to the blind.

A total of $9,780,108 in federal funds and $1,216,029 in state funds was spent on vocational rehabilitation in 1978. The Kansas Vocational Rehabilitation Unit offers services to developmentally disabled people. About $47,100,000 was paid in workers' compensation in 1977.

In order to qualify for unemployment compensation, a worker must have worked at least 20 weeks during the previous year. Payments in 1979 were $52,270,175.

[40] HOUSING

Kansas has relatively old housing stock. According to the 1970 census, 54% of all dwellings were built before 1939, and only 21% were built in the 1960s. The overwhelming majority (82%) were one-unit structures, and 64% were owner occupied. There were 224,779 rented houses or apartment units. The median value of a house was $12,100; the median rent was $75. Only 4% of all structures lacked plumbing facilities in 1970.

As the population in the metropolitan areas around Wichita, Topeka, and Kansas City grows, the number of apartment units appears to be increasing. In 1978, 34% of all building permits issued were for multiunit structures. The total value of housing starts in 1978 was $605,119,947, of which permits in Wichita County accounted for $136,924,298.

[41] EDUCATION

Kansans are, by and large, better educated than most Americans. The illiteracy rate as of 1970 was 0.6% of the population, well below the US average of 1.2%. In 1976, adult Kansans had completed a median of 12.6 years of school; 15% were college graduates and 73% were high school graduates, while only 1% had finished less than five years of school.

Enrollment in the state's 1,583 public schools in 1977/78 was 446,189: 131,026 students were in high school, 63,120 in junior high school, and 252,043 in elementary school. There were about 13,800 elementary-school teachers and 11,800 secondary-school teachers. The dropout rate was 2% of total enrollment.

Students' average daily attendance at nonpublic schools in 1977/78 was 28,377, of whom 7,224 were in high schools, 1,309 in junior high schools, 18,972 in elementary schools, 709 in kindergarten, and 163 in special classes.

There are 6 state universities, 19 community colleges, 4 private two-year colleges, 16 church-affiliated colleges, and 14 vocational-technical schools. In addition, Kansas has a state technical school, a municipal university (Washburn University, Topeka), and a federally run junior college for Indians. Kansas State University was the nation's first land-grant institution. Washburn University and the University of Kansas, Lawrence, have the state's two law schools. In fall 1977, 127,447 students were enrolled in institutions of higher education. Of these, 63% were full-time students and 76% were undergraduates. Public institutions enrolled 89%; private, 11%.

During 1977/78, Kansas spent $1,682 per pupil (19th in the US), at a cost of $355 per capita. Total expenditures on education were $824,000,000. The Kansas Board of Regents offers scholarships and tuition grants to needy Kansas students.

In 1954, Kansas was the focal point of a US Supreme Court decision that had enormous implications for US public education. The court ruled, in *Brown* v. *Board of Education of Topeka*, that Topeka's "separate but equal" elementary schools for black and white students were inherently unequal, and it ordered the school system to integrate.

[42] ARTS

The Kansas Arts Commission is a 12-member panel appointed by the governor. In 1978/79, it sponsored 113 touring arts programs. Wichita has a resident symphony orchestra.

[43] LIBRARIES AND MUSEUMS

The Dwight D. Eisenhower Library in Abilene houses the collection of papers and memorabilia from the former president. The Kansas State Historical Society Library (Topeka) contains the state's archives. Volumes of books and documents on the Old West are found in the Cultural Heritage and Arts Center Library in Dodge City. Kansas had 311 public libraries in 1978, with 5,810,370 volumes and a circulation of 11,143,852. Additionally there were 34 county and regional libraries, 10 bookmobiles, 27 college libraries, and 24 junior college libraries. Seven regional library systems serve those state residents who have no local library service.

More than 120 museums, historical societies, and art galleries were scattered across the state in 1978. The Dyche Museum of Natural History at the University of Kansas, Lawrence, was the most visited place in Kansas during that year. The Kansas State Historical Society maintains an extensive collection of ethnological and archeological materials. Among the art museums are the Mulvane Art Center, Helen Foresman Spencer Museum of Art at the University of Kansas, and the Wichita Art Museum. The Dalton Museum in Coffeyville displays memorabilia from the famed Dalton family of desperadoes. LaCrosse is the home of the Barbed Wire Museum, displaying more than 500 specimens of barbed wire. The US Cavalry Museum is on the grounds of Fort Riley.

The entire town of Nicodemus, where many blacks settled after the Civil War, was made a national historic landmark in 1975. The chalk formations of Monument Rocks in western Kansas constitute the state's only national natural landmark.

[44] COMMUNICATIONS

During 1977, Kansas was served by 7,200 postal workers. There were 859,025 telephones in 1978, of which 75% were residential. About 95% of all households had telephone service, slightly below the US average. Telephone service is provided by Southwestern Bell.

The state had 62 AM and 58 FM radio stations, 14 commercial television stations, and 3 public television stations in 1978. With the aid of the Kansas Public Television Board, founded by the state in 1977, new public stations were being built in Hays and Garden City. As of early 1979 there were 134 cable television systems serving 161 communities with 209,778 subscribers.

[45] PRESS

Starting with the *Shawnee Sun*, a Shawnee-language newspaper founded by missionary Jotham Meeker in 1833, the press has been at the heart of Kansas society. The most famous Kansas newspaperman was William Allen White, whose *Emporia Gazette* was a leading voice of progressive Republicanism around the turn of the century. Earlier, John J. Ingalls launched his political career by editing the *Atchison Freedom's Champion*. Captain Henry King came from Illinois to found the *State Record* and *Daily Capital* in Topeka. In 1872, he founded the literary periodical *Kansas Magazine*, now known as the *Kansas Quarterly*.

In 1978, Kansas had 51 daily newspapers with a total circulation of 643,635, and 15 Sunday papers with a circulation of 452,500. Leading newspapers and their circulations in 1979 were as follows:

AREA	NAME	DAILY	SUNDAY
Topeka	Capital (m,S)	59,395 }	73,414
	State Journal (e,S)	26,967 }	
Wichita	Eagle (m,S)	121,849 }	175,002
	Beacon (e,S)	41,540 }	

[46] ORGANIZATIONS

Kansas is the headquarters of several prominent sports associations, including the National Collegiate Athletic Association at Shawnee Mission, the National Junior College Athletic Association at Hutchinson, and the US Collegiate Sports Council in Kansas City. Lefthanders International has its headquarters in Topeka.

[47] TOURISM, TRAVEL, AND RECREATION

During 1977, about 6,297,000 people traveled to and within Kansas. About 45% of the trips were within the state, of which about 50% were for vacation purposes. In 1979, Kansas had 19 state parks, 21 federal reservoirs, more than 100 privately owned campsites, and some 304,000 acres (123,000 hectares) of public hunting and game management lands. During 1978, 4,854,220 visitors used the state park system.

Topeka holds a number of tourist attractions, including the state capitol and the Menninger Foundation. Dodge City offers a reproduction of Old Front Street as it was when the town was the "cowboy capital of the world." Historic Wichita Cowtown is another frontier-town reproduction. In Hanover stands an original Pony Express station. A recreated "Little House on the Prairie," near the childhood home of Laura Ingalls Wilder, is 13 mi (21 km) southwest of Independence.

In 1978, the state issued 317,301 fishing licenses and 225,680 hunting licenses.

⁴⁸SPORTS

There are no major professional sports teams in Kansas. During spring, summer, and early fall, horses race at Eureka Downs.

The University of Kansas and Kansas State are both members of the Big Eight Conference. The National Junior College Basketball Tournament is held in Hutchinson each March. The Kansas Relays take place at Lawrence in April.

A US sporting event unique to Kansas is the International Pancake Race held in Liberal each Shrove Tuesday. Women wearing housedresses, aprons, and scarves run along an S-shaped course carrying skillets and flipping pancakes as they go. The race is also run in Olney, England.

⁴⁹FAMOUS KANSANS

Kansas claims only one US president and one US vice president. Dwight D. Eisenhower (b.Texas, 1890–1969) was elected the 34th president in 1952 and reelected in 1956; he had served as the supreme commander of Allied Forces in World War II. He is buried in Abilene, his boyhood home. Charles Curtis (1860–1936) was vice president during the Hoover administration.

Two Kansans have been associate justices of the US Supreme Court: David J. Brewer (1837–1910) and Charles E. Whittaker (1901–73). Other federal officeholders from Kansas include William Jardine (1879–1955), secretary of agriculture; Harry Woodring (1890–1967), secretary of war; and Georgia Neese Clark Gray (b.1900), treasurer of the US. Prominent US senators include Edmund G. Ross (1826–1907), who cast the crucial acquittal vote at the impeachment trial of Andrew Johnson; John J. Ingalls (1833–1900), who was also a noted literary figure; Joseph L. Bristow (1861–1944), a leader in the Progressive movement; Arthur Capper (1865–1951), a former publisher and governor; Robert Dole (b.1923), who was the Republican candidate for vice president in 1976; and Nancy Landon Kassebaum (b. 1932), elected to the US Senate in 1978. Among the state's important US representatives are Jeremiah Simpson (1842–1905), a leading Populist, and Clifford R. Hope (1893–1970), important in the farm bloc.

Notable Kansas governors include George W. Glick (1827–1911); Walter R. Stubbs (1858–1929); Alfred M. Landon (b. 1887), who ran for US president on the Republican ticket in 1936; and Frank Carlson (b.1893). Other prominent political figures were David L. Payne (1836–84), who helped open Oklahoma to settlement; Carry Nation (1846–1911), the colorful prohibitionist; and Frederick Funston (1865–1917), hero of the Philippine campaign of 1898 and a leader of San Francisco's recovery after the 1906 earthquake and fire.

Earl Sutherland (1915–74) won the Nobel Prize in 1971 for physiology and medicine. Other leaders in medicine and science include Samuel J. Crumbine (1862–1954), a public health pioneer; the doctors Menninger—C. F. (1862–1953), William (1899–1966), and Karl (b.1893)—who established the Menninger

Foundation, a leading center for mental health; Arthur Hertzler (1870–1946), a surgeon and author; and Clyde Tombaugh (b.1906), who discovered the planet Pluto.

Kansas also had several pioneers in aviation, including Clyde Cessna (1880–1954), Glenn Martin (1886–1955), Walter Beech (1891–1950), Amelia Earhart (1898–1937), and Lloyd Stearman (1898–1975). Cyrus K. Holliday (1826–1900) founded the Santa Fe railroad; William Coleman (1870–1957) was an innovator in lighting; and Walter Chrysler (1875–1940) was a prominent automotive developer.

Most famous of Kansas writers was William Allen White (1868–1944), whose son William L. White (1900–73) also had a distinguished literary career; Damon Runyon (1884–1946) was a popular journalist and storyteller. Novelists include Edgar Watson Howe (1853–1937), Margaret Hill McCarter (1860–1938), Dorothy Canfield Fisher (1879–1958), Paul Wellman (1898–1966), and Frederic Wakeman (b.1909). Gordon Parks (b.1912) has made his mark in literature, photography, and music. William Inge (1913–73) was a prizewinning playwright who contributed to the Broadway stage. Notable painters are Sven Birger Sandzen (1871–1954), John Noble (1874–1934), and John Steuart Curry (1897–1946). Sculptors include Robert M. Gage (b.1892), Bruce Moore (b.1905), and Bernard Frazier (1906–76). Among composers and conductors are Thurlow Lieurance (b.Iowa, 1878–1963), Joseph Maddy (1891–1966) and Kirke L. Mechem (b.1926). Jazz great Charlie "Bird" Parker (Charles Christopher Parker, Jr., 1920–55) was born in Kansas City.

Stage and screen notables include Fred Stone (1873–1959), Milburn Stone (b.1904), Charles "Buddy" Rogers (b.1904), Vivian Vance (1912–79), Edward Asner (b.1929), and Shirley Knight (b.1937). The clown Emmett Kelly (1898–1979) was a Kansan. Operatic performers include Marion Talley (b.1906) and Kathleen Kersting (1909–65).

Glenn Cunningham (b.1910) and Jim Ryun (b.1947) both set running records for the mile. Also prominent in sports history were James Naismith (1861–1939), the inventor of basketball; baseball pitcher Walter Johnson (1887–1946); and Gale Sayers (b.1943), a football running back.

⁵⁰BIBLIOGRAPHY

Boyer, Richard O. *The Legend of John Brown*. New York: Knopf, 1973.

Clanton, O. Gene. *Kansas Populism*. Lawrence: Regents Press of Kansas, 1969.

Connelley, William E. *Kansas and Kansans*. 5 vols. Chicago: Lewis, 1918.

Davis, Kenneth S. *Kansas: A Bicentennial History*. New York: Norton, 1976.

Davis, Kenneth S. *Soldier of Democracy: A Biography of Dwight Eisenhower*. New York: Doubleday, 1945, 1952.

Kansas, State of. Office of the Secretary of State. *Kansas Directory 1979*. Topeka, 1979.

Kansas, University of. Center for Public Affairs. *Kansas Statistical Abstract 1978*. 14th ed. Lawrence, 1979.

Richmond, Robert W. *Kansas: A Land of Contrasts*. St. Charles, Mo.: Forum Press, 1974.

Socolofsky, Homer, and Huber Self. *Historical Atlas of Kansas*. Norman: University of Oklahoma Press, 1972.

KENTUCKY

Commonwealth of Kentucky

ORIGIN OF STATE NAME: Derived from the Wyandot Indian word *Kah-ten-tah-teh* (land of tomorrow). **NICKNAME**: The Bluegrass State. **CAPITAL**: Frankfort. **ENTERED UNION**: 1 June 1792 (15th). **SONG**: "My Old Kentucky Home." **MOTTO**: United We Stand, Divided We Fall. **FLAG**: A simplified version of the state seal on a blue field. **OFFICIAL SEAL**: In the center, two men exchange greetings; above and below them is the state motto. On the periphery are two sprigs of goldenrod and the words "Commonwealth of Kentucky." **COLORS**: Blue and gold. **BIRD**: Cardinal. **WILD ANIMAL**: Gray squirrel. **FISH**: Bass. **FLOWER**: Goldenrod. **TREE**: Kentucky coffee tree. **LEGAL HOLIDAYS**: New Year's Day, 1 January, plus one extra day; Washington's Birthday, 3d Monday in February; Good Friday, March or April, half-day holiday; Memorial Day, last Monday in May; Independence Day, 4 July; Labor Day, 1st Monday in September; Thanksgiving Day, 4th Thursday in November, plus one extra day; Christmas Day, 25 December, plus one extra day. **TIME**: 7 A.M. EST = noon GMT; 6 A.M. CST = noon GMT.

¹LOCATION, SIZE, AND EXTENT

Located in the eastern south-central US, the Commonwealth of Kentucky is the smallest of the 8 south-central states and ranks 37th in size among the 50 states.

The total area of Kentucky is 40,395 sq mi (104,623 sq km), of which land comprises 39,650 sq mi (102,693 sq km) and inland water 745 sq mi (1,930 sq km). Kentucky extends about 350 mi (563 km) E–W; its maximum N–S extension is about 175 mi (282 km).

Kentucky is bordered on the N by Illinois, Indiana, and Ohio (with the line following the north bank of the Ohio River); on the NE by West Virginia (with the line formed by the Big Sandy and Tug Fork rivers); on the SE by Virginia; on the S by Tennessee; and on the W by Missouri (separated by the Mississippi River). Because of a double bend in the Mississippi River, about 10 sq mi (26 sq km) of SW Kentucky is separated from the rest of the state by a narrow strip of Missouri. The total boundary length of Kentucky is 1,290 mi (2,076 km). The state's geographic center is in Marion County, 3 mi (5 km) NNW of Lebanon.

²TOPOGRAPHY

The eastern quarter of the state is dominated by the Cumberland Plateau, on the western border of the Appalachians. At its western edge, the plateau meets the uplands of the Lexington Plain (known as the Bluegrass region) to the north and the hilly Pennyroyal to the south. These two regions, which together comprise nearly half the state's area, are separated by a narrow curving plain known as the Knobs because of the shapes of its eroded hills. The most level area of the state is the western coalfields, bounded by the Pennyroyal to the east and the Ohio River to the north. In the far west are the coastal plains of the Mississippi River; this region is commonly known as the Purchase, having been purchased from the Chickasaw Indians.

The highest point in Kentucky is Black Mountain on the southeastern boundary in Harlan County, at 4,145 feet (1,263 meters). The lowest point is 257 feet (78 meters), along the Mississippi River in Fulton County. The state's mean altitude is 750 feet (229 meters).

The only large lakes in Kentucky are artificial. The biggest is Cumberland Lake (79 sq mi, or 205 sq km); Kentucky Lake, Lake Barkley, and Dale Hollow Lake straddle the border with Tennessee.

Including the Ohio and Mississippi rivers on its borders and the tributaries of the Ohio, Kentucky claims at least 3,000 mi (4,800 km) of navigable rivers—more than any other state. Among the most important of Kentucky's rivers are the Kentucky, 259 mi (417 km); the Cumberland, partly in Tennessee; the Tennessee, also in Tennessee and Alabama; and the Big Sandy, Green, Licking, and Tradewater rivers. All, except for a portion of the Cumberland, flow northwest into the Ohio and thence to the Mississippi.

Drainage through porous limestone rock has honeycombed much of the Pennyroyal with underground passages, the best known of which is Mammoth Cave. The Cumberland Falls, 92 feet (28 meters) high and 100 feet (30 meters) wide, are located in Whitley County.

³CLIMATE

Kentucky has a moderate, relatively humid climate, with abundant rainfall.

The southern and lowland regions are slightly warmer than the uplands. In Louisville, the normal daily mean temperature ranges from 33°F (1°C) in January to 77°F (25°C) in July. The record high for the state was 114°F (46°C), registered in Greensburg on 28 July 1930; the record low, –34°F (–37°C), in Cynthiana on 28 January 1963.

Average daily relative humidity in Louisville ranges from 60% to 80%. The normal annual precipitation is 43 in (109 cm); snowfall totals about 18 in (46 cm) a year. Much of Kentucky's rain falls between March and June; thunderstorms are frequent during this period.

⁴FLORA AND FAUNA

Kentucky's forests are mostly of the oak/hickory variety, with some beech/maple stands. Four species of magnolia are found, and the tulip poplar, eastern hemlock, and eastern white pine are also common; the distinctive "knees" of the cypress may be seen along riverbanks. Kentucky's famed bluegrass is actually blue only in May at which time dwarf iris and wild columbine are in bloom. Rare plants include the swamp loosestrife and showy gentian. Goldenseal, used for medicinal purposes, is on the state's endangered list.

Game mammals include the raccoon, muskrat, opossum, mink, gray and red foxes, and beaver; the eastern chipmunk and flying squirrel are common small mammals. At least 300 bird species have been recorded, of which 200 are common. Blackbirds are a serious pest, with some roosts numbering 5–6 million; more desirable avian natives include the cardinal (the state bird), robin, and brown thrasher, while eagles are winter visitors. More than 100 types of fish have been identified.

Rare animal species include the swamp rabbit, black bear, raven (*Corvus corax*), and mud darter. Among Kentucky's threatened species are the river otter, common shrew, and osprey. The Indiana bat, cougar, Kirtland's warbler, bald eagle, and northern coal skink are listed as endangered.

[5]ENVIRONMENTAL PROTECTION

The Department for Natural Resources and Environmental Protection, with broad responsibility, includes the Bureau for Surface Mining Reclamation and Enforcement and the Kentucky Nature Preserves Commission. The Environmental Quality Commission, created in 1972 to serve as a watchdog over the department, is a citizen's group of seven members appointed by the governor. Funding for environmental programs in 1977/78 totaled $23,615,000, or 0.7% of the state budget. Proposed funding for 1979/80 was $37,787,500, or 1% of the budget.

The most serious environmental concern in Kentucky is repairing and minimizing damage to land and water from stripmining. Efforts to deal with such damage are relatively recent. The state has had a strip-mining law since 1966, but the first comprehensive attempts at control did not begin until the passage in 1977 of the Federal Surface Mining Control and Reclamation Act. A program submitted in 1980 by the Bureau for Surface Mining and Reclamation called for the recovery each year of 5,000 acres (2,000 hectares) of surface-mined land.

There are 15 major dams in Kentucky, and more than 900 other dams. Flooding is a chronic problem in southeastern Kentucky, where strip-mining has exacerbated soil erosion.

[6]POPULATION

Kentucky ranked 23d in population among the states in 1970, with a census population of 3,219,311.

During the early decades of settlement, population grew rapidly, from a few hundred in 1780 to 564,317 in 1820, by which time Kentucky was the 6th most populous state. By 1900, however, when the population was 2,147,174, growth had slowed considerably. For most of the 20th century, Kentucky's growth rate has been significantly slower than the national average.

At the time of the 1970 census, Kentucky's population was 52% urban, far below the national norm, but the state's population density, 81 persons per sq mi (31 per sq km), was 41% above the US average. Mobility is low: in 1976, 72% of Kentuckians 14 years of age and older had lived in the state all their lives, a percentage exceeded only in Pennsylvania.

The provisional estimate of Kentucky's population in 1978 was 3,498,000—an 8.7% increase over the 1970 figure, higher than the national average of 6.4% for the same period.The 1978 estimate assumed a net gain through migration of 87,000, reversing a tide of outmigration that had caused a population loss of 153,000 during 1960–70. Preliminary census data for 1980 showed Kentucky with a population of 3,642,143, an increase of more than 13% since 1970.

Louisville is the state's largest city and most densely populated area, with a total of 317,503 residents according to the preliminary 1980 census count. Lexington was next with 190,686, followed by Owensboro, 53,839. The Louisville (Ky.-Ind.) metropolitan area had an estimated population of 887,300 in 1978.

[7]ETHNIC GROUPS

Though a slave state, Kentucky never depended on a plantation economy. This may account for its relatively low black population—296,000 (9%) in 1976. Kentucky was a center of the American (or Know-Nothing) Party, a pre–Civil War movement opposed to slavery and immigration alike. With relatively little opportunity for industrial employment, Kentucky attracted small numbers of foreign immigrants in the 19th and 20th centuries. The state had only 56,000 residents of second-generation foreign

stock in 1970, primarily the children of German, British, and Canadian immigrants.

There were 1,531 American Indians, according to the 1970 census. The census also found 1,095 Japanese, 558 Chinese, and 2,963 other Asian-Pacific peoples. Kentucky accepted 967 Vietnamese refugees in 1975.

[8]LANGUAGES

Kentucky was a fought-over hunting ground for Ohio Shawnee, Carolina Cherokee, and Mississippi Chickasaw Indians. Placenames from this heritage are Kentucky (Iroquois), Etowah (Cherokee), and Paducah (Chickasaw). In 1970, 208 Kentuckians claimed an Indian language as their mother tongue.

Kentucky has received little foreign immigration. Speech patterns in the state generally reflect the first settlers' Virginia and Kentucky backgrounds. South Midland features are best preserved in the mountains, but some common to Midland and Southern are widespread.

Other regional features are typically both South Midland and Southern. After a vowel /r/ may be weak or missing. *Coop* has the vowel of *put*, but *root* rhymes with *boot*. In southern Kentucky, earthworms are *redworms*, a burlap bag a *tow sack* or the Southern *grass sack*, and green beans *snap beans*. A young man may *carry*, not escort, his girl friend to a party. Subregional terms appear in abundance. In the east, kindling is *pine*, a seesaw is a *ridyhorse*, and the freestone peach is an *openstone peach*. In central Kentucky, a moth is a *candlefly*.

In 1970, 93% of all residents as well as of the native-born claimed English as a mother tongue. Other chief groups indicated these mother tongues:

	NATIVE-BORN	FOREIGN-BORN
English	2,983,554	3,638
German	27,993	4,795
Spanish	5,393	1,409

[9]RELIGIONS

Throughout its history, Kentucky has been predominantly Protestant. A group of New Light Baptists who, in conflict with established churches in Virginia, immigrated to Kentucky under the leadership of Lewis Craig, built the first church in the state in 1781, near Lancaster. The first Methodist Church was established near Danville in 1783; within a year, Roman Catholics had also built a church, and a presbytery of 12 churches had been organized. There were 42 churches in Kentucky by the time of statehood, with a total membership of 3,095.

Beginning in the last few years of the 18th century, the Great Revival sparked a new religious fervor among Kentuckians, a development that brought the Baptists and Methodists many new members. The revival, which had begun among the Presbyterians, led to a schism in that sect. Presbyterian minister Barton W. Stone organized what turned out to be the era's largest frontier revival meeting, at Cane Ridge (near Paris), in August 1801. Differences over doctrine led Stone and his followers to withdraw from the Synod of Kentucky in 1803, and they formed their own church, called simply "Christian." The group later formed an alliance with the sect now known as the Christian Church (Disciples of Christ).

As of 1971 there were 1,424,999 known Protestant adherents in Kentucky, of whom 820,739 belonged to the Southern Baptist Convention, 214,322 to the United Methodist Church, 72,276 to the Christian Church (Disciples of Christ), and 69,711 to the Christian Churches and Churches of Christ. The Roman Catholic Church, with 359,312 members at the beginning of 1979, is the 2d-largest denomination in the state. There were an estimated 11,585 Jews in Kentucky in 1979.

[10]TRANSPORTATION

Statewide transportation developed slowly in Kentucky. Although freight and passengers were carried by river and later by rail during the 19th century, mountains and lack of good roads made

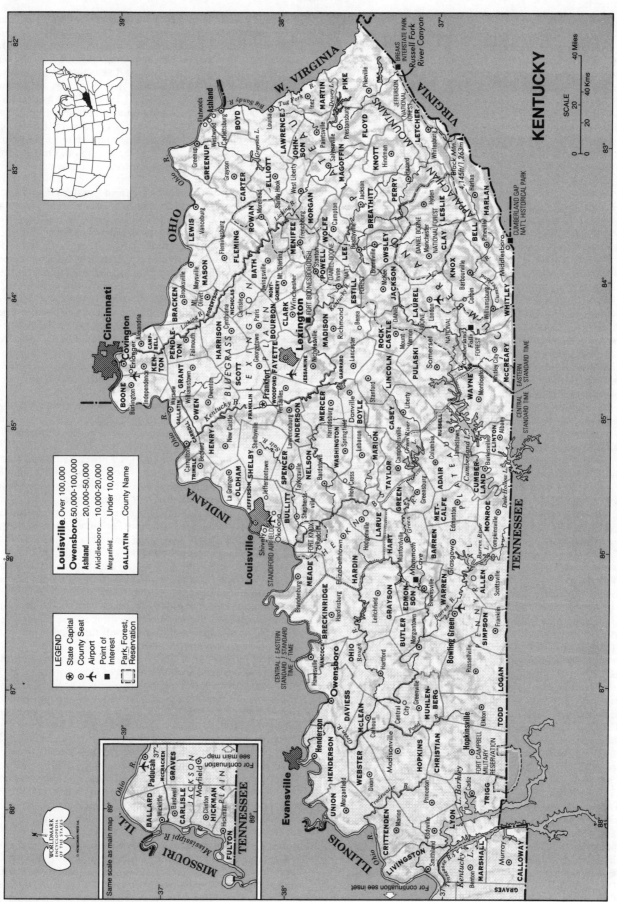

KENTUCKY

Louisville Over 100,000
Owensboro 50,000-100,000
Ashland   20,000-50,000
Middlesboro   10,000-20,000
Morganfield   Under 10,000
GALLATIN   County Name

SCALE
40 Miles
40 Kms

See US political: front cover J3; physical: back cover J3.

LOCATION: 36°30' to 39°08'45"N; 81°58' to 89°34'W. **BOUNDARIES:** Illinois line, 131 mi (211 km); Indiana line, 345 mi (555 km); Ohio line, 167 mi (269 km); West Virginia line, 107 mi (172 km); Virginia line, 127 mi (204 km); Tennessee line, 336 mi (541 km); Missouri line, 77 mi (124 km).

land travel in eastern Kentucky so arduous that the region was for a long time effectively isolated from the rest of the state.

The first railroad in Kentucky, the Lexington and Ohio, opened on 15 August 1832 with a 6-mi (10-km) route from Lexington to Frankfort. Not until 1851 did the railroad reach the Ohio River. In November 1859, Louisville was connected with Nashville, Tenn., by the Louisville and Nashville Railroad; heavily used by the Union, it was well maintained during the Civil War. Railroad construction increased greatly after the conflict ended. By 1900, Kentucky had three times the track mileage it had had in 1870. As of April 1980, Kentucky had 3,126 mi (5,031 km) of track. Rail service to the state, 99% of which was freight, was provided by 15 railroads.

The trails of Indians and buffalo became, the first roads in Kentucky. Throughout the 19th century, roads were maintained—if at all—by private enterprise, as toll roads. This system came to an end as a result of the "tollgate war" of the late 19th and early 20th centuries, a rebellion in which masked Kentuckians, demanding free roads, raided tollgates and assaulted their keepers. Not until 1909, however, was a constitutional prohibition against the spending of state funds on highways abolished. In 1912, a state highway commission was created, and by 1920, roads had improved considerably. In 1978, Kentucky had 68,781 mi (110,692 km) of roads, of which 94% were surfaced. Local governments controlled 63% of Kentucky's roads; the state government, 36%; and the federal government, less than 1%. In the 1977/78 budget, $150 million was allocated to build resource recovery roads for coal transportation. They were intended to supplement rural highways in eastern Kentucky which had been severely damaged by trucks conveying heavy loads of coal the roads were not designed to carry. In 1978, 1,804,146 automobiles, 731,848 trucks, and 60,989 motorcycles were registered in the state.

The Ohio River and its tributaries, along with the Mississippi, were Kentucky's primary commercial routes for trade with the South and the West until gradually displaced by the railroads. The Kentucky Port and River Development Commission was created by the legislature in 1966 to promote river transportation.

In 1978 there were 101 airports and heliports in Kentucky, 55 public and 46 private. The largest of these is Standiford Field in Louisville, which emplaned 1,051,933 passengers in 1978. Seven commuter airlines in Kentucky serve approximately 40,000 passengers a year.

[11] HISTORY

Six distinctive Indian cultures inhabited the region now known as Kentucky. The earliest nomadic hunters occupied the land for several thousand years, and were followed by the seminomadic Woodland and Adena cultures (1000 BC–AD 1000). Remains of the Mississippian and Fort Ancient peoples (AD 1000–1650) indicate that they were farmers and hunters who often dwelled in stockaded villages, subsisting on plentiful game and fish supplemented by crops of beans, corn, and squash.

No Indian nations resided in central and eastern Kentucky when these areas were first explored by British-American surveyors Thomas Walker and Christopher Gist in 1750 and 1751. The dominant Shawnee and Cherokee tribes utilized the region as a hunting ground, returning to homes in the neighboring territories of Ohio and Tennessee. Early descriptions of Kentucky generated considerable excitement about the fertile land and abundant wildlife. The elimination of French influence after the French and Indian War intensified pressures to open the region to American settlement—pressures that were initially thwarted by Britain's Proclamation of 1763, barring such western migration until Native American interests could be protected. This artificial barrier proved impossible to maintain, however, and the first permanent white settlement in Kentucky was finally established at Harrodstown (now Harrodsburg) in 1774 by a group of Virginians.

The most ambitious settlement scheme involved the Transylvania Land Company, a creation of North Carolina speculator Richard Henderson, assisted by the famed woodsman Daniel Boone. Henderson purchased a huge tract of land in central Kentucky from the Cherokee, and established Fort Boonesborough. The first political meeting by whites in Kentucky, held at Fort Boonesborough on 23 May 1775, provided for rule by the Transylvania proprietors and a representative assembly. Henderson then sought approval for creation of a 14th colony, but the plan was blocked by Virginians determined to claim Kentucky as a possession of the Old Dominion. On 1 December 1776, the new state of Virginia incorporated its new County of Kentucky.

Kentucky's image soon changed from "western Eden" to "dark and bloody ground," as it became the scene of frequent clashes between Ohio-based Indians and the growing number of white settlements dotting the central Bluegrass region. Nevertheless, immigrants continued to come westward, down the Ohio River and through the Cumberland Gap. Kentucky became the principal conduit for migration into the Mississippi Valley. By the late 1780s, settlements were gaining in population, wealth, and maturity, and it was obvious that Kentucky could not long remain under the proprietorship of distant Virginia. Its entire orientation was westward, and the majority of its citizens were no longer Virginia-born, but former residents of Pennsylvania, Maryland, and North Carolina. Virginia yielded permission for the drafting of a Kentucky state constitution, and in June 1792, Kentucky entered the Union as the 15th—and first western—state.

Over the next several decades, Kentucky prospered because of its diverse agricultural and processing industries. Although there were 225,483 slaves in the state in 1860, Kentucky was spared the evils of one-crop plantation agriculture. Nevertheless, its economy was tightly linked to the lower South's, a tie facilitated by the completion in 1829 of a canal around the Ohio River falls at Louisville. Hemp was one such connection; the plant was the principal source of rope and bagging used to bind cotton bales. Kentucky was a major supplier of hogs, mules and workhorses, prepared meats, salt, flour, and corn for the plantation markets of the South. The state became a center for breeding and racing fine Thoroughbred horses, an industry that thrives today on Bluegrass horse farms as virtually the state symbol. More important was the growing and processing of tobacco, an enterprise accounting for half the agricultural income of Kentucky farmers by 1860. Finally, whiskey began to be produced in vast quantities by the 1820s, culminating in the standardization of a fine, aged amber-red brew known throughout the world as bourbon, after Bourbon County.

Despite this economic development, several social and cultural problems disturbed the state. Much of the agricultural productivity came from farms employing slave labor, while the less affluent majority of white families often dwelled on less fertile upland farms. Efforts were repeatedly made to consider the slavery question. Leaders such as Henry Clay, Reverend Robert J. Breckinridge, and the fiery antislavery advocate Cassius Marcellus Clay urged an end to the "peculiar institution." Because of racial phobias and hostility to "Yankee meddling," the appeal was rejected. Henry Clay, who had contributed more than any man to the preservation of national unity, died in 1852. Nine years later, Kentuckians were forced to choose sides in a dreaded Civil War between the Union, led in the North by Kentucky native Abraham Lincoln, and the Confederacy, led in the South by Kentucky native Jefferson Davis.

Although the state legislature finally opted for the Union side, approximately 30,000 men went south to Confederate service, while 70,000—including nearly 24,000 black soldiers—served in the Union army. For four years the state was torn with conflict over the collapse of slavery and wracked with guerrilla warfare and partisan feuds. Vigilantism and abuse of black people continued into the turbulent Reconstruction period, until legislative changes in the early 1870s began to restrain Ku Klux Klan violence and bring increased civil rights to black people.

The decades to 1900 saw other progress. Aided by liberal tax exemptions, railroad construction increased threefold, and exploitation of timber and coal reserves began in eastern Kentucky. Industrial employment and productivity increased by more than 200%, drawing rural folk into the growing cities of Louisville and Lexington. In 1900, Kentucky ranked 1st among southern states in per capita income.

An economic and political crisis was developing, however, that would send shock waves across the state. Wealth remained very unevenly distributed. Farmers, expecially western Kentucky "dark leaf" tobacco farmers, were feeling the brunt of a prolonged price depression. The major national farm protest movements—the Grange, the Farmers' Alliance, and the Populist Party—all found support here, for by 1900, a third of all Kentucky farmers were landless tenants, and the size of the average family farm had fallen below 100 acres (40 hectares). Calls for currency inflation, reform of corporate monopolies, and improved rights for industrial workers reached a climax in the gubernatorial election of 1899. Republican William S. Taylor narrowly defeated the more reform-minded Democrat William Goebel, and was sworn into office. Democrats, claiming electoral fraud, instituted a recount. On 30 January 1900, Goebel, a state senator, was shot while approaching the capitol; as he lingered near death, the legislature, controlled by Democrats, declared him governor. Goebel died immediately thereafter, and his lieutenant governor, John Beckham, was given the oath of office. Surprisingly, further bloodshed was averted, the courts upheld the Goebel-Beckman election, and "Governor" Taylor fled the state forever.

Goebel's assassination weighed heavily, however. The state was polarized, outside investment plummeted, and Kentucky fell into a prolonged economic and moral depression. By 1940, the state ranked last among the 48 states in per capita income and was burdened by an image of clan feuding and homicide, poverty, and provincial courthouse politics. The Great Depression hit the state hard, though an end to Prohibition revived the dormant whiskey industry.

Kentucky has changed greatly since World War II. The number of farmers has fallen by half, cropland has declined by more than 1.5 million acres (607,000 hectares), and tobacco has come under attack as a menace to public health. Meanwhile, the number of manufacturing plants has more than doubled, industrial jobs have increased at least fourfold, and since 1960, a majority of Kentuckians have resided in urban areas. Although Kentucky remains one of the poorest states in the nation, positive change is evident even in relatively isolated rural communities, a result of better roads, education, television, and government programs.

12 STATE GOVERNMENT

Kentucky's constitution, first drafted in 1792, was revised in 1799, 1849, and 1891. Between 1891 and 1979, it was amended 24 times.

The state legislature, called the general assembly, consists of the house of representatives, which has 100 members elected for two-year terms, and the senate, with 38 members elected for staggered four-year terms. A constitutional amendment approved by the voters in November 1979 provided for the election of legislators in even-numbered years, a change scheduled for completion by November 1988. The assembly meets in regular sessions of no more than 60 legislative days, beginning in January of each even-numbered year. The governor may also call special sessions; these are of unlimited duration, but may consider only the subjects specified by the governor in his call. Except for revenue-raising measures, which must be introduced in the house of representatives, either chamber may introduce or amend a bill. Most bills may be passed by voting majorities equal to at least two-fifths of the membership of each house. Measures requiring an absolute majority in each house include those that appropriate money or create a debt, summon a constitutional convention, or enact emergency measures to take effect immediately. A majority of the members of each house is required to override the governor's veto.

A member of the senate must have been a citizen and resident of Kentucky for six years preceding election, a representative for two. A senator must be at least 30 and a representative at least 24. The constitutional limit of $12,000 for salaries of public officials, which is thought to apply to legislators, has been interpreted by the courts in terms of 1949 dollars, and thus may be increased considerably—and has been. However, as of 1977, most legislators in Kentucky probably received less than $12,000 per year, including travel and expense allowances.

The elected executive officers of Kentucky are the governor, lieutenant governor, secretary of state, attorney general, treasurer, superintendent of public instruction, auditor of public accounts, the commissioner of agriculture, labor, and statistics, and three members of the Railroad Commission. All serve four-year terms and may not succeed themselves. The governor and lieutenant governor, who are independently elected, must each be 30 years old, US citizens, and residents of Kentucky for six years. As of 1979, the governor's salary was $35,000, and the lieutenant governor's $29,294.

A second constitutional amendment approved in 1979 made the process of amending the constitution somewhat easier by eliminating the prohibition on resubmitting any amendment to the voters within five years of its rejection at the polls. A three-fifths majority of each house plus a voting majority of the electorate must still approve any proposed amendment. Before a constitutional convention may be called, two regular sessions of the general assembly must approve it, and the call must be ratified at the polls by at least one-fourth the number of voters who cast ballots in the previous election.

To vote in Kentucky one must be a US citizen, at least 18 years of age, and have been a resident in the state for one year, in the county for six months, and in the precinct for 60 days before the election.

13 POLITICAL PARTIES

A rift was created in Kentucky politics by the presidential election of 1824, which had to be determined in the US House of Representatives because neither John Quincy Adams nor Andrew Jackson won a majority of the Electoral College. Representative Henry Clay voted for Adams, despite orders by the Kentucky general assembly to support Jackson, thereby splitting the state into two factions: supporters of Clay, who became Whigs, and supporters of Jackson, who became Democrats. The Whigs dominated Kentucky politics until Clay's death in 1852, after which, as the Whigs divided over slavery, most Kentuckians turned first to the Native American (or Know-Nothing) Party and then to the Democrats. Regional divisions in party affiliation during the Civil War era, according to sympathy with the South and slavery (Democrats) or with the Union and abolition (Republicans), have persisted in the state's voting patterns. In general, the poorer mountain areas tend to vote Republican, while the more affluent lowlanders in the Bluegrass and Pennyroyal tend to vote Democratic.

In 1978, Kentucky had 1,637,616 registered voters—1,121,450 Democrats, 463,946 Republicans, and 52,220 independents or members of minor parties. In 1978, fewer than 29% of those registered actually voted (lowest in the US); they represented about 19% of the voting age population. Ronald Reagan carried the state by a slim margin in the November 1980 presidential voting, but Governor Wendell Ford, a Democrat, easily won reelection. At the close of the year, both houses of the state legislature were in Democratic hands.

14 LOCAL GOVERNMENT

The form of Kentucky's county government is of English origin. The state's 120 counties were run in 1978 by about 1,500 county officials. The chief governing body is the fiscal court, consisting of the county judge and from three to eight magistrates. Other elected officials include the sheriff, jailer, treasurer, attorney, and court clerk. All are elected for four-year terms; the sheriff may not succeed himself in office. Many county officials earn their living by collecting a share of the fees for the services they render. As of 1977, the maximum income for a county official was set at $29,000.

Cities are assigned by the general assembly to one of six classes. First-class cities have populations of 100,000 or more; second, 20,000 to 99,999; third, 8,000 to 19,999; fourth, 3,000 to 7,999; fifth, 1,000 to 2,999; and sixth, 999 or fewer. In 1977, Kentucky had only one first-class city, Louisville. There were 8 second-class cities, 18 third, 32 fourth, 111 fifth, and 181 sixth. The mayor or other chief executive officer in the top three classes must be elected; in the bottom classes, the executive may be either elected by the people or appointed by a city council or commission. Mayors serve four-year terms; members of city legislative boards, also provided for in the state constitution, are elected for terms of two years. City officials must be residents of the cities and of the districts in which they are elected.

Other units of local government in Kentucky include urban counties and special-purpose districts, including districts for sewer and flood control and the 15 area-development districts for regional planning. The general assembly may create new local government units, although its power to create new counties is restricted. (Since 1912, it has created only one new county, McCreary.) The constitution provides for local option elections concerning the sale of alcoholic beverages. As of April 1980, alcoholic beverage sales were completely banned in 84 counties.

15 STATE SERVICES

An ombudsman in the Department for Human Resources receives citizens' complaints concerning services offered by that department. The Financial Disclosure Review Board was established in 1975 to review the financial status of government management personnel in order to prevent conflicts of interest.

Educational services are provided through the Education and the Arts Cabinet, which includes the Department of Education, the Advisory Council for Vocational Education, and the Bureau for the Blind. Under the jurisdiction of the Department of Education are the School for the Blind (Louisville) and the School for the Deaf (Danville). The Council for Higher Education oversees the state-supported colleges and universities. Financial aid is offered by the Higher Education Assistance Authority.

Transportation services are administered by the Department of Transportation, which is responsible for highways, public transportation, water transport, railroads, and aviation. Health, welfare, and other human services are provided primarily by the Department for Human Resources, which includes bureaus for social insurance and for health and social services, and by such executive agencies as the Human Rights Commission and the Commission on Women. Rehabilitation services, including the Eastern Kentucky Comprehensive Rehabilitation Center, are under the jurisdiction of the Department of Education.

Among the agencies that provide public protection services are the Department of Military Affairs, including the Kentucky National Guard and Disaster and Emergency Services; the Crime Victims' Compensation Board; and the Consumer Protection Division of the Department of Law. Both corrections and the state police are administered within the Department of Justice.

Housing services for members of minority groups are provided by the Commission on Human Rights. The Community and Regional Development Program (including the Appalachian Regional Commission) within the Development Cabinet aids in long-range economic planning. Also assisting in community development are programs within the Department for Local Government.

Natural resources protection services are provided by the Department for Natural Resources and Environmental Protection. The Kentucky state park system is administered by the Department of Parks in the Development Cabinet, which also includes the Department of Energy, Kentucky Center for Energy Research, and the Department of Fish and Wildlife.

Labor services are administered by the Department of Labor; its areas of concern include labor-management relations, occupational safety and health, and occupational injury and disease compensation. The Manpower Services Bureau of the Department for Human Resources seeks to improve the employment capabilities of the unemployed and the underemployed.

Kentucky Presidential Vote by Political Parties, 1948–80

YEAR	ELECTORAL VOTE	KENTUCKY WINNER	DEMOCRAT	REPUBLICAN	STATES' RIGHTS DEMOCRAT	PROHIBITION	PROGRESSIVE	SOCIALIST
1948	11	*Truman (D)	466,756	341,210	10,411	1,245	1,567	1,284
1952	10	Stevenson (D)	495,729	495,029	—	1,161	—	—
1956	10	*Eisenhower (R)	476,453	572,192	—	2,145	—	—
1960	10	Nixon (R)	521,855	602,607	—	—	—	—
					STATES' RIGHTS			
1964	9	*Johnson (D)	669,659	372,977	3,469	—	—	—
					AMERICAN IND.			SOC. WORKERS
1968	9	*Nixon (R)	397,541	462,411	193,098	—	—	2,843
						AMERICAN	PEOPLE'S	
1972	9	*Nixon (R)	371,159	676,446	—	17,627	1,118	—
1976	9	*Carter (D)	615,717	531,852	2,328	8,308	—	—
							LIBERTARIAN	CITIZENS
1980	9	*Reagan (R)	617,417	635,274	—	—	5,531	1,304

*Won US presidential election.

¹⁶JUDICIAL SYSTEM

In accordance with a constitutional amendment approved in 1975 and effective January 1978, judicial power in Kentucky is vested in a unified court of justice. The highest court is the supreme court, consisting of a chief justice and six associate justices. It has appellate jurisdiction, and also bears responsibility for the budget and administration of the entire system. Justices are elected from seven supreme court districts for terms of eight years; they elect one of their number to serve for four years as chief justice.

The court of appeals consists of 14 judges, 2 elected from each supreme court district. The court divides itself into panels of at least 3 judges which may sit anywhere in the state. The judges also serve eight-year terms and elect one of their number to serve a four-year term as chief judge.

Circuit courts, with original and appellate jurisdiction, are held in each county. Circuit court judges are elected for terms of eight years. In circuits with more than one judge, the judges elect one of their number as chief judge for a two-year term. Under the revised judicial system, district courts, which have limited and original jurisdiction, replaced various local and county courts. There is no mandatory retirement age.

In 1977 there were 3,660 prisoners in state and federal prisons in state and federal prisons in Kentucky, of whom 96% were men. The Bureau of Corrections maintains 11 correctional institutions, including 2 career development centers, 2 forestry camps, and 2 farm centers. Commercial bail bonding has been abolished in Kentucky and replaced by a state-supported system; a pretrial release program was instituted in 1976.

In the past, Kentucky had a reputation for lawlessness. In 1890, more homicides were reported in Kentucky than in any other state except New York; blood feuds among Kentucky families were notorious throughout the country. By the late 1970s, however, Kentucky's crime rate was well below the national average.

¹⁷ARMED FORCES

The US Department of Defense had 61,241 personnel in Kentucky in 1978. US Army installations in the state include Fort Knox (site of the US gold depository) near Louisville, with 30,687 personnel, and Fort Campbell (partly in Tennessee), with 28,039 personnel. Kentucky received $177 million in federal defense contracts in 1978; the federal defense payroll for that year was $728 million.

As of 30 September 1979, there were 414,000 veterans of US military service living in Kentucky. Of these, World War I veterans numbered 9,000; World War II, 176,000; Korean conflict, 79,000; and Viet-Nam era, 122,000. Kentucky veterans received more than $319 million in benefits during 1977/78.

Kentucky Army and Air National Guard Units had 6,400 personnel as of 30 September 1978. State and local police forces totaled 6,847 in 1977, or 2 police employees per 1,000 population (only five states had a lower ratio). Total police expenditures were $117 million, of which 76% was spent on local police.

¹⁸MIGRATION

During the frontier period, Kentucky first attracted settlers from eastern states, especially Virginia and North Carolina. Prominent among early foreign immigrants were people of English and Scotch-Irish ancestry, who tended to settle in the Kentucky highlands, which resembled their families' recent Old World homelands.

Kentucky's black population increased rapidly during the first 40 years of statehood. By the 1830s, however, slavery had become less profitable in the state, and many Kentucky owners either moved to the Deep South or sold their slaves to new owners in that region. During the 1850s, nearly 16% of Kentucky's slave population—more than 43,000 blacks—were sold or moved from the state. A tiny percentage of Kentucky's blacks, probably fewer than 200, emigrated to Liberia under the auspices of the Kentucky Colonization Society.

The waves of European immigration that inundated many states during the late 19th century left Kentucky virtually untouched. In 1890, Kentucky's population was nearly 98% native-born. At that time, there were more than 284,000 blacks in the state—a number that was to fall precipitously until the 1950s because of migration to industrial cities in the Midwest. Until the 1970s there was also a considerable outmigration of whites, especially from eastern Kentucky.

¹⁹INTERGOVERNMENTAL COOPERATION

Among the many interstate regional commissions in which Kentucky participates are the Appalachian Regional Commission, the Interstate Mining Compact, the Interstate Oil and Gas Compact, the Southeastern Forest Fires Protection Compact, the Southern Regional Education Compact, the Southern Growth Policies Compact, and the Ohio River Valley Water Sanitation Compact. The Council of State Governments, founded in 1925 to foster interstate cooperation, has its headquarters in Lexington.

In 1978/79, Kentucky received more than $1.3 billion in federal aid. The US Department of Labor Mine Safety and Health Administration has Coal Mine Safety and Health District offices in Pikeville, Barbourville, and Madisonville, plus a Health and Safety Training Center in Lexington. Kentucky participates in the Tennessee Valley Authority.

²⁰ECONOMY

Between statehood and the Civil War, Kentucky was one of the preeminent agricultural states, partly because of good access to river transportation down the Ohio and the Mississippi to southern markets. Coal mining had become an important part of the economy by the late 19th century. Although agriculture is still important in Kentucky, manufacturing has grown rapidly since World War II and was, by the late 1970s, the most important sector of the economy as a source of both employment and personal income. Kentucky leads the nation in the production of coal and whiskey, and ranks 2d in tobacco output.

In contrast to the generally prosperous Bluegrass area and the growing industrial cities, eastern Kentucky, highly dependent on coal mining, has long been one of the poorest regions in the US. Beginning in the early 1960s, both the state and federal governments undertook programs to combat poverty in Appalachian Kentucky. Per capita personal income increased faster in this region than in the US as a whole between 1965 and 1976, and unemployment decreased between 1970 and 1978; however, personal income was still much lower, and unemployment higher, than in the rest of the state. The Appalachian Regional Commission, which includes representatives of the federal government and the 13 Appalachian states, funds various economic development projects in the region.

²¹INCOME

Kentucky has long been one of the poorest of the 50 states. In 1958, per capita income in Kentucky was $1,490, 73% of the national average and 44th in the US. In 1978, per capita income was $6,615, or 85% of the national average, for a rank of 40th.

Sources of personal income in 1977 were manufacturing, 27%; government, 16%; trade, 15%; services, 13%; transportation, communications, and public utilities, 7%; mining, 7%; contract construction, 6%; farms, 4%; and other sectors, 5%. Incomes were highest in the Louisville and Lexington-Fayette metropolitan areas; in Kentucky's share of the Cincinnati, Ohio, and Evansville, Ind., metropolitan regions; and in Franklin County (Frankfort). Among the poorest counties were Owsley, 75% of whose residents have incomes below the poverty level; Wolfe, 65%; and Wayne, 62%. In the state as a whole, 76,354 persons (about 22% of all Kentuckians) were below the federal poverty line in 1978. Per capita income in Appalachian Kentucky in 1965 was only 49% of the US average; by 1976, it had risen to 68%.

²²LABOR

According to federal statistics, Kentucky's civilian labor force was about 1,556,000 in 1978, of whom 928,000 were male and 628,000 were female. Among the 98,000 members of the labor force who were nonwhite, females were in the majority.

Among those actually employed in 1978, manufacturing accounted for 20%; wholesale and retail trade, 18%; government, 16%; services, 14%; agriculture, 5%; contract construction, 5%; transportation, communications, and public utilities, 4%; mining and quarrying, 4%; and other sectors, 14%.

A federal census of workers covered by unemployment insurance in March 1977 revealed the following nonfarm employment pattern for Kentucky:

	ESTABLISH-MENTS	EMPLOYEES	ANNUAL PAYROLL ('000)
Agricultural services, forestry, fishing	476	2,806	$ 19,660
Mining, of which:	1,530	47,140	833,865
Bituminous coal; lignite	(1,144)	(41,742)	(764,702)
Contract construction	6,697	44,072	580,079
Manufacturing	3,287	278,388	3,469,987
Transportation, public utilities	2,989	46,043	637,852
Wholesale trade	4,973	57,364	683,918
Retail trade	19,722	180,761	1,163,634
Finance, insurance, real estate	4,883	43,648	433,328
Services	15,710	159,483	1,186,740
Other	781	1,106	12,271
TOTALS	61,048	860,811	$9,021,334

Kentucky's overall unemployment rate was 5.3% in 1978; for nonwhites, slightly over 10%. Both rates were somewhat lower than the national averages. Unemployment was lowest in the Bluegrass region and in northern Kentucky, and highest in eastern Kentucky.

Although a small number of trade unions existed in Kentucky before the 1850s, it was not until after the Civil War that substantial unionization took place. During the 1930s, there were long, violent struggles between the United Mine Workers (UMW) and the mine owners of eastern Kentucky. The UMW won bargaining rights in 1938, but after World War II the displacement of workers because of mechanization, a drastic drop in the demand for coal, and evidence of mismanagement and corruption within the UMW served to undercut the union's position. Following the announcement by the UMW in 1962 that its five hospitals would be sold or closed, unemployed mine workers began protracted picketing of nonunion mines. Episodes of violence accompanied the movement, which succeeded in closing the mines but not in keeping them closed. The protests dissipated when public-works jobs were provided for unemployed fathers among the miners, beginning in late 1973. Increased demand for coal in the 1970s led to a substantial increase in jobs for miners, and the UMW, under different leaders, began a new drive to organize the Cumberland Plateau.

As of January 1980, 26% of all nonagricultural workers in Kentucky were union members. The largest unions in the state were the International Brotherhood of Teamsters, with 51,785 members; UMW, 23,070; United Auto Workers, 22,629; and United Steelworkers, 21,392.

²³AGRICULTURE

With cash receipts totaling $2 billion—51% from crops and 49% from livestock—Kentucky ranked 22d among the 50 states in farm marketing in 1978.

Kentucky tobacco, first marketed in New Orleans in 1787, quickly became the state's most important crop. Kentucky ranked 1st among tobacco-producing states until it gave place to North Carolina in 1929. Corn has long been one of the state's most important crops, not only for livestock feed but also as a major ingredient in the distilling of whiskey. Although hemp is no longer an important crop in Kentucky, its early significance to Kentucky farmers, as articulated in Congress by Henry Clay, was partly responsible for the establishment by the US of a protective tariff system. From 1849 to 1870, the state produced nearly all the hemp grown in the US.

Preliminary data for 1979 showed approximately 96,000 farms in Kentucky (down from 133,000 in 1964) with an average size of 150 acres (61 hectares). Kentucky's farm population was about 452,000 in 1970, less than half what it had been in 1950. Kentucky farms produced some 470,000,000 lb of tobacco worth $607,000,000 in 1978. Leading field crops in 1979 (in bushels) included corn for grain, 132,600,000; soybeans, 53,950,000; wheat, 11,020,000; sorghum, 2,312,000; and barley, 1,250,000.

²⁴ANIMAL HUSBANDRY

Since early settlement days, livestock raising has been an important part of Kentucky's economy. The Bluegrass region, which offers excellent pasturage and drinking water, has become renowned as a center for horse breeding and racing.

In 1977 there were 204,000 equine animals, including light horses, draft horses, mules and donkeys; there were 146,000 light horses, of which 45,800 were Thoroughbreds. As of 1980, the Kentucky Horse Council had identified approximately 50,000 horse owners in the state, and 1,075 horse farms. In 1979, $225,387,292 in horse sales was recorded at public auctions in the state. At Lexington, Thoroughbred auctions are usually held in January, July, and from September to November; Standardbreds are auctioned during September–November; and quarter horses, Appaloosas, and American saddle horses in April, June, and October–November.

Cattle production was Kentucky's leading source of agricultural income in 1978. In 1979, the production of 712,465,000 lb of cattle and calves yielded $472,196,000 in gross income, and the sale of 432,280,000 lb of hogs and pigs brought $170,188,000. In 1978, Kentucky ranked 13th among the 50 states in milk production, selling nearly 2.2 billion lb of whole milk.

The following table shows numbers of livestock on Kentucky farms for a three-year period.

	CATTLE AND CALVES	MILK COWS	HOGS AND PIGS
1979	2,600,000	265,000	1,400,000
1978	3,120,000	277,000	1,150,000
1977	3,300,000	280,000	1,140,000

²⁵FISHING

Fishing is of little commercial importance in Kentucky. In 1978, 2,966,000 lb of fish valued at $923,000 were landed in the state.

²⁶FORESTRY

In 1977 there were 12,161,000 acres (4,921,000 hectares) of forested land in Kentucky—48% of the state's land area, and 1.6% of the total forested area in the US.

The most heavily forested areas are in the river valleys of eastern Kentucky, in the Appalachians. Commercial timberland occupies 11,902,000 acres (4,817,000 hectares) of Kentucky forests, of which 11,007,000 acres (4,454,000 hectares) are privately owned.

There are two national forests—the Daniel Boone and the Jefferson—enclosing two national wilderness areas. National parks in the state include the Mammoth Cave National Park and the Cumberland Gap National Historical Park.

²⁷MINING

In 1978, Kentucky ranked 5th in the US in mineral production, with output valued at $3.5 billion. The state was 1st in the production of coal and 2d in fluorspar.

Most of Kentucky's coal came from the western fields until late in the 19th century, when the Cumberland Plateau coal reserves were discovered. In recent decades most extraction has been by strip-mining. In general, the Appalachian land companies, which own the coalfields and lease out mining rights, have been highly profitable, thanks to depletion allowances and tax exemptions. Much of the mining in Kentucky is done by out-of-state companies; a number of oil companies, such as Occidental Petroleum and Continental Oil, have acquired coal companies as a hedge against declining petroleum resources. Kentucky's bituminous coal reserves were estimated at 64.3 billion tons.

In 1978, Kentucky produced an estimated 131,215,000 tons of coal, with a value of $3 billion; 37,000,000 tons of crushed stone, valued at $93,800,000; 10,000,000 tons of sand and gravel, worth $20,000,000; and 709,000 tons of clay, worth $2,952,000.

28 ENERGY AND POWER

At the end of 1977, Kentucky had 36 electric generating plants: 21 steam, 7 hydroelectric, 6 gas turbine, and 2 internal combustion. Total installed capacity was 13.5 million kw in 1978, when 55.6 billion kwh of power were produced. Kentucky shares in the power produced by the Tennessee Valley Authority; only 46% of installed capacity and 40% of production were attributable to private sources.

In 1978, more than 14,097 wells in Kentucky produced 5,724,000 barrels of crude petroleum. At the end of 1978, Kentucky was estimated to have about 31,833,000 barrels of proved reserves, less than half the 1970 estimate. In 1978, Kentucky produced 57.3 billion cu feet of natural gas (1.6 billion cu meters). As of 31 December 1978, the state was estimated to have proved reserves totaling 718.9 billion cu feet (20.4 billion cu meters) of natural gas.

Oil shale is found in a band stretching from Lawrence County in the northeast through Madison and Washington counties in central Kentucky to Jefferson County in the north-central region of the state.

29 INDUSTRY

Although primarily an agricultural state during the 19th century, Kentucky was a leading supplier of manufactures to the South before the Civil War. Kentucky ranked 20th among the 50 states in value of shipments of manufactured goods in 1976, and 18th in value added by manufacture. Kentucky manufactures more than two-thirds of all American whiskey.

Value added in 1977 exceeded $9.4 billion, of which nonelectrical machinery accounted for 14%; electric and electronic equipment, 12%; chemical products, 11%; food and food products, 10%; transportation equipment, 10%; tobacco products, 9%; and other industries, 34%.

The following table shows value added by manufacture in 1972 and in 1977 for selected major industries.:

	1972	1977
Motor vehicles and equipment	NA	$916,800,000
Cigarettes	$464,400,000	728,700,000
Distilled liquor, except brandy	NA	320,600,000
Plastic materials, synthetics	191,800,000	299,900,000
Industrial organic chemicals	101,200,000	289,000,000
Blast furnace and steel mill products	167,000,000	236,200,000

As in the early days of the state, most industry is concentrated in the northern cities along the Ohio River. Most bourbon is distilled and tobacco processed in Louisville.

30 COMMERCE

In 1972, Kentucky ranked 28th among the states in wholesale trade, with total sales of $6.8 billion. Estimated retail sales in 1978 were $11.5 billion. Of that total, sales by grocery stores made up 24%; car dealers, 20%; general merchandise stores, 14%; gasoline service stations, 9%; building materials and hardware dealers, 8%; eating and drinking places, 7%; and other establishments, 18%. In 1977, Jefferson County alone had 24% of the state's total retail sales, and the city of Louisville more than 10%. The KFC Corp., which owns and franchises Kentucky Fried Chicken restaurants, has its headquarters in Louisville.

31 CONSUMER PROTECTION

The Consumer Protection Division of the Department of Law, created in 1972, is responsible for enforcement of the state's consumer protection laws and investigates and mediates consumer complaints. In 1978, the division received 5,400 written complaints from consumers, 2,096 of which it resolved. The most common complaints were against auto dealers (662), especially about defective new cars, and mail-order firms (440). Consumers may sue in small claims court for as much as $1,000; such judgments may be appealed. Consumers may also bring class-action suits. The Consumers' Advisory Council, a group of 16 citizens appointed by the governor, with the attorney general serving as chairman, advises the Department of Law on consumer affairs.

32 BANKING

Kentucky had 343 insured commercial banks in 1978, with total assets of nearly $16 billion. They held loans amounting to $5.4 billion and deposits totaling $13.6 billion, of which demand deposits were $5.5 billion and time deposits $8.1 billion.

As of 31 December 1978 there were 105 insured savings and loan associations in Kentucky, 94 of them federally chartered; 10 of the 11 state-chartered banks were mutual savings and loan associations. Together these had total assets of $5.2 billion and held $4.5 billion in savings accounts.

33 INSURANCE

In 1978, Kentuckians held nearly 6.5 million life insurance policies, with a total value of $37.8 billion. The average life insurance per family was $29,700. In 1977, Kentuckians paid $406 million in life insurance premiums. Life insurance benefits of $141.4 million were paid in 1978.

Premiums written by property and liability insurance companies in 1978 totaled $1.2 billion, including $439.6 million for automobile liability and physical damage insurance and $109.9 million in homeowners' coverage.

34 SECURITIES

There are no security exchanges in Kentucky. However, New York Stock Exchange member firms had 24 sales offices and 229 registered representatives in the state. Kentuckians reported $308.9 million in dividend income on their 1977 federal tax returns.

35 PUBLIC FINANCE

The Kentucky biennial state budget is prepared by the Executive Department for Finance and Administration in the fall of each odd-numbered year, and submitted by the governor to the general assembly for approval. The fiscal year runs from 1 July to 30 June. Following is a summary of budgeted revenues (available funds) and appropriations for 1977/78 and the governor's recommended budget for 1979/80:

AVAILABLE FUNDS	1977/78	1979/80
General fund	$1,487,111,994	$1,869,687,004
Federal funds	942,515,922	1,039,702,500
Road fund	525,305,100	422,985,900
Agency funds	410,540,810	489,368,627
Other funds	73,599,702	79,450,000
TOTALS	$3,439,073,528	$3,901,194,031
APPROPRIATIONS		
Department of Education	$ 758,016,284	$ 944,003,600
Human resources	809,129,374	907,978,700
Transportation	746,534,556	687,108,800
Public higher education	482,044,366	603,597,500
General government	152,768,808	197,952,800
Development	86,381,644	86,943,600
Other appropriations	306,804,256	449,653,004
TOTALS	$3,341,679,288	$3,877,238,004

For fiscal 1976/77, the total state debt was more than $4.2 billion. Per capita debt was $1,226, 17th in the US.

³⁶ TAXATION

Kentucky collected more than $1.8 billion in state taxes in 1978, ranking 20th among the 50 states.

As of 1979, the tax rate on personal income ranged from 2% on the first $3,000 to 6% on the amount over $8,000. Corporate income was taxed at a rate of 4% on the first $25,000, and 5.8% on earnings above $25,000. Kentucky imposes severance taxes on oil and coal, and also levies a 5% sales tax (excluding food and drugs), a gasoline tax, an inheritance tax, and excise taxes on alcoholic beverages, cigarettes, and motor vehicles.

In 1977, 1,222,755 Kentuckians filed federal income tax returns and paid a total tax of nearly $2 billion.

³⁷ ECONOMIC POLICY

The Department of Commerce seeks to encourage businesses to locate in Kentucky through its job creation program, which provides assistance in site selection as well as other services to US and Canadian firms. The department's International Division attempts to attract foreign industry and to increase exports of Kentucky manufactures. The Shows and Fairs program within the Department of Agriculture supports regional and national shows, such as the North American Livestock Exposition, as well as local agricultural fairs.

Since the early 1960s, Kentucky has attempted to alleviate the economic inequality between the Appalachian region and the rest of the state. One source of aid to Appalachia is a rebate to the coal-producing counties of a portion of the state severance tax on coal.

³⁸ HEALTH

In 1969–71, Kentucky ranked 39th among the 50 states in average live expectancy—70.1 years. The state's birthrate and death rate are both higher than the national average. The infant mortality rate in 1977 was 21 per 1,000 live births for nonwhites, and 13.7 for whites. In 1977, 10,392 legal abortions were performed in Kentucky, for a rate of 178 per 1,000 live births, well below the US average. Kentucky ranked 9th among the 50 states in deaths from heart diseases, 7th in deaths from cerebrovascular diseases, 7th in deaths from pneumonia, and above the national average in most other categories. Black lung (pneumoconiosis) has been recognized as a serious work-related illness among coal miners.

In 1978, Kentucky's 121 hospitals had 18,815 beds and recorded 637,963 admissions. At the end of 1977 there were 4,516 active physicians in Kentucky—a ratio of 132 per 100,000 population, 38th in the US. Three counties—Carlisle, Robertson, and Trigg—with a total population of 17,000, were without an active physician engaged in patient care. In 1979 there were 1,490 professionally active dentists in Kentucky.

Approximately $450 million in health insurance benefits was paid to community hospitals in the state in 1977. The average cost per patient per day was $145, the 5th lowest in the nation.

³⁹ SOCIAL WELFARE

In 1978, 164,400 Kentuckians, including 116,900 children, received aid to families with dependent children worth $122 million. About 322,000 Kentuckians participated in the federal food stamp program; the federal subsidy was $125.9 million. An estimated 603,000 Kentucky children (80% of eligible enrollment) participated in the school lunch program in 1978, at a federal cost of $35.3 million.

In 1977, 336,000 retired workers in Kentucky received $711 million in federal Social Security benefits; their average monthly payment of $216.30 was 7th lowest among the 50 states. Under the Black Lung Benefit Program, about 17,000 Kentucky miners totally disabled by black lung, 13,000 widows of miners, and 23,000 dependents were paid $107 million in benefits by the Social Security Administration. The average monthly payment to miners' families was $342; to widows' families, $249.

The state spent $20.4 million on vocational rehabilitation in 1978, and $92.1 million on workers' compensation in 1977. An average of 32,000 persons per week received unemployment insurance benefits totaling $101 million in 1978.

⁴⁰ HOUSING

According to the 1970 census, Kentucky had 984,000 occupied housing units. Only 81% of all units had full plumbing—the 2d-lowest percentage in the nation, outranking only Mississippi. From 1974 through 1978, 68,158 new housing units were authorized; their combined value was $834 million.

⁴¹ EDUCATION

Kentucky was relatively slow to establish and support its public education system, and the state has consistently ranked among the lowest in per capita spending on education and in the educational attainments of its citizens. Kentucky's illiteracy rate was 1.6% in 1970, well above the US average. In 1976, only 53% of Kentuckians 18 years of age or older had completed high school; this was the same percentage as West Virginia's, and only Mississippi's was lower.

In the fall of 1978, 684,000 students attended public schools in Kentucky, 470,000 in grades 1–8 and 214,000 in grades 9–12; private school enrollment was about 75,000. Public schools employed a total of 33,800 teachers in 1978/79, 21,000 elementary and 12,800 secondary.

During 1978/79 there were 42 institutions of higher education in Kentucky, of which 9 were public and 33 private; their total enrollment in fall 1978 exceeded 131,000. The University of Kentucky, established in 1865 at Lexington, is the state's largest public institution, with an enrollment on the Lexington campus of 22,362 in 1977/78. The University of Kentucky Community College System enrolled an additional 17,512 students. The University of Louisville (1798) had an enrollment of 17,398. Loans and grants to Kentucky students are provided by the Kentucky Higher Education Assistance Authority.

The Minimum Foundation Program was established by the general assembly in 1954 for the purpose of upgrading the level of basic education in the state. Funds were earmarked in the 1979/80 budget for diagnostic testing of students in grades 3, 5, 7, and 10 to ascertain which students required remedial education. In 1977/78, Kentucky received $243,234,083 in federal funds for a compensatory education program for approximately 150,000 educationally deprived youngsters.

⁴² ARTS

The Actors Theater of Louisville holds a yearly festival of new American plays. The city also has a resident ballet company. The Louisville Orchestra has recorded numerous works by contemporary American composers. The Kentucky Arts Commission supports a traveling exhibition program and professional artists' residencies in public schools.

Bluegrass, a modern form of country music punctuated by fiddle and banjo and usually played at a rapid tempo, takes its name from the style pioneered by Kentuckian Bill Monroe and his Blue Grass Boys.

⁴³ LIBRARIES AND MUSEUMS

In 1978/79 there were 113 public libraries in Kentucky, with a total of 6,820,222 volumes, including those in bookmobiles. The regional library system of 15 districts included university libraries and the state library at Frankfort, as well as city and county libraries.

The state has more than 60 museums. Art museums include the University of Kentucky Art Museum and the Headley-Whitney Museum in Lexington; the Allen R. Hite Art Institute at the University of Louisville; and the J. B. Speed Art Museum, also in Louisville. Among Kentucky's equine museums are the International Museum of the Horse in Lexington, and the Kentucky Derby and American Saddle Horse museums, both in Louisville. The John James Audubon Museum is located in Audubon State Park at Henderson.

Leading historical sites include Abraham Lincoln's birthplace at Hodgenville, and the Mary Todd Lincoln and Henry Clay homes in Lexington. The Kentucky Historical Society in Frankfort supports a mobile museum system that brings exhibits on Kentucky history to schools, parks, and local gatherings, and aids 109 local historical societies.

44 COMMUNICATIONS

There were 7,700 postal employees in Kentucky in 1977. In 1978, 2,215,495 telephones were in service in the state, 1,680,910 residential and 534,585 business. Only 89% of households in the state had telephones.

In 1922, Kentucky's first radio broadcasting station, WHAS, was established. By 1978 there were 205 radio stations, 119 AM and 86 FM. That year there were 11 commercial television broadcasting stations. The Kentucky Educational Television system had 13 transmitters, was on the air for 102 hours weekly, and attracted about 535,000 viewers in 1978. As of 1979 there were 127 cable television systems serving 201,464 subscribers in 304 communities.

45 PRESS

In 1978, Kentucky had 27 daily newspapers (5 morning, 22 evening), with a combined paid circulation of 775,835, and 12 Sunday papers, with a paid circulation of 617,577. The following table shows the leading Kentucky newspapers with their 1979 circulations:

AREA	NAME	DAILY	SUNDAY
Frankfort	State Journal (e, S)	10,147	11,105
Lexington	Herald (m)	63,926	101,664
	Leader (e)	33,191	
Louisville	Courier-Journal (m, S)	199,713	344,594
	Times (e)	157,638	

46 ORGANIZATIONS

The Thoroughbred Club of America has its headquarters in Lexington. Commercial organizations with headquarters in Kentucky include the Association of Dark Leaf Tobacco Dealers and Exporters, in Mayfield; the Burley Auction Warehouse Association, in Mt. Sterling; and the Burley Tobacco Growers Cooperative Association, in Lexington.

47 TOURISM, TRAVEL, AND RECREATION

Kentucky's income from tourism exceeded $1 billion in 1976. One of the state's top tourist attractions is Mammoth Cave, which contains an estimated 150 mi (241 km) of underground passages.

As of 1978, the state operated 15 resort parks (13 of them year-round), which were expected to attract 46.5 million visitors during the 1978–80 budget period. Another 22 state-operated recreational parks and 9 shrines were expected to attract 8.4 million visitors and 44,000 campers. Breaks Interstate Park, on the Kentucky-Virginia border, is noted for the Russell Fork River Canyon, which is 1,600 feet (488 meters) deep; the park is supported equally by the two states.

In 1979, the Kentucky State Horse Park opened in Lexington. The Kentucky State Fair is held annually in August at Louisville. In 1977/78, Kentucky issued licenses to 323,777 hunters and 602,153 fishermen.

48 SPORTS

The first horse race in Kentucky was held in 1783. The annual Kentucky Derby, first run on 17 May 1875, has become probably the single most famous event in US Thoroughbred racing. Held on the 1st Saturday in May at Churchill Downs in Louisville, the Derby is one of the three races comprising the Triple Crown for 3-year-olds. The Kentucky Futurity, an annual highlight of the harness racing season, is usually held on the 1st Friday in October at the Red Mile in Lexington.

In 1979, 2,418 Thoroughbred races were held in Kentucky, attracting a total attendance of 1,986,608. Total purses of $14,708,163 went to the horsemen; the betting handle amounted

to $233,835,109, of which the state's share was 5%. Harness races attracted 866,817 spectators. Total purses were $4,806,858, and the betting handle was $68,194,289.

Rivaling horse racing as a spectator sport is collegiate basketball. The University of Kentucky Wildcats won NCAA Division I basketball championships in 1948–49, 1951, 1958, and 1978, and the National Invitation Tournament in 1946 and 1976. The University of Louisville Cardinals captured the NCAA crown in 1980, having won an NIT title in 1956. Kentucky Wesleyan, at Owensboro, was the NCAA Division II titleholder in 1966, 1968–69, and 1973.

49 FAMOUS KENTUCKIANS

Kentucky has been the birthplace of one US president, four US vice presidents, the only president of the Confederacy, and several important jurists, statesmen, writers, artists, and sports figures.

Abraham Lincoln (1809–65), the 16th president of the US, was born in Hodgenville, Hardin (now Larue) County, and spent his developing years in Indiana and Illinois. Elected as the first Republican president in 1860 and reelected in 1864, Lincoln reflected his Kentucky roots in his opposition to secession and the expansion of slavery, and in his conciliatory attitude toward the defeated southern states. His wife, Mary Todd Lincoln (1818–82), was a native of Lexington.

Kentucky-born US vice presidents have all been Democrats. Richard M. Johnson (1780–1850) was elected by the Senate after a deadlock in the Electoral College; John C. Breckinridge (1821–75) became in 1857 the youngest man ever to hold the office; Adlai E. Stevenson (1835–1914) served in Grover Cleveland's second administration. The best known was Alben W. Barkley (1877–1956), who, before his election with President Harry S. Truman in 1948, was a US senator and longtime Senate majority leader.

Frederick M. Vinson (1890–1953) was the only Kentuckian to serve as chief justice of the US. Noteworthy associate justices were John Marshall Harlan (1833–1911), famous for his dissent from the segregationist *Plessy* v. *Ferguson* decision (1896), and Louis D. Brandeis (1856–1941), the first Jew to serve on the Supreme Court and a champion of social reform.

Henry Clay (b. Virginia, 1777–1852) came to Lexington in 1797 and went on to serve as speaker of the US House of Representatives, secretary of state, and US senator; he was also a three-time presidential candidate. Other important federal officeholders from Kentucky include Attorneys General John Breckinridge (b. Virginia, 1760–1806) and John J. Crittenden (1787–1863), who also served with distinction as US senator; Treasury Secretaries Benjamin H. Bristow (1830–96) and John G. Carlisle (1835–1910); and US Senator John Sherman Cooper (b. 1901).

Among noteworthy state officeholders, Isaac Shelby (b. Maryland, 1750–1826) was a leader in the movement for statehood, and the first governor of Kentucky. William Goebel (1856–1900) was the only US governor assassinated in office. Albert B. ("Happy") Chandler (b. 1898), twice governor, also served as US senator and as commissioner of baseball.

A figure prominently associated with frontier Kentucky is the explorer and surveyor Daniel Boone (b. Pennsylvania, 1734–1820). During the Civil War, Lincoln's principal adversary was another native Kentuckian, Jefferson Davis (1808–89); he moved south as a boy to a Mississippi plantation home, subsequently served as US senator from Mississippi, US secretary of war, and president of the Confederate States of America.

Other personalities of significance include James G. Birney (1792–1857) and Cassius Marcellus Clay (1810–1903), both major antislavery spokesmen. Clay's daughter Laura (1849–1941) and Madeline Breckinridge (1872–1920) were important contributors to the women's suffrage movement. Henry Watterson (1840–1921) founded and edited the *Louisville Courier-Journal* and was a major adviser to the Democratic Party. During the 1920s, Kentuckian John T. Scopes (1900–70) gained fame as the defendant in the "monkey trial" in Dayton, Tenn.; Scopes was charged with teaching Darwin's theory of evolution. Whitney M. Young (1921–71), a prominent black leader, served as head of the National Urban League.

Thomas Hunt Morgan (1866–1945), honored for his work in heredity and genetics, is Kentucky's lone Nobel Prize winner. Journalists born in Kentucky include Irvin S. Cobb (1876–1944), who was also a humorist and playwright, and Arthur Krock (1887–1974), a winner of four Pulitzer Prizes. Notable businessmen include Harland Sanders (b.Indiana, 1890–1980), founder of Kentucky Fried Chicken restaurants.

Kentucky has produced several distinguished creative artists. These include painters Matthew Jouett (1787–1827), Frank Duveneck (1848–1919), and Paul Sawyier (1865–1917); folk song collector John Jacob Niles (1891–1980); and novelists Harriette Arnow (b.1908) and Wendell Berry (b.1934). Robert Penn Warren (b.1905), a novelist, poet, and critic, won the Pulitzer Prize three times and was the first author to win the award in both fiction and poetry categories.

Among Kentuckians well recognized in the performing arts are film innovator D. W. Griffith (David Lewelyn Wark Griffith, 1875–1948), Academy Award–winning actress Patricia Neal (b.1926), and country music singer Loretta Lynn (b.1932). Kentucky's sports figures include basketball coach Adolph Rupp (b.Kansas, 1901–77), shortstop Harold ("Pee Wee") Reese (b.1919), football great Paul Hornung (b.1935), and world heavyweight boxing champions Jimmy Ellis (b.1940) and Muhammad Ali (Cassius Clay, b.1942).

[50]BIBLIOGRAPHY

Axton, W. F. *Tobacco and Kentucky.* Lexington: University Press of Kentucky, 1976.

Bakeless, John. *Daniel Boone, Master of the Wilderness.* Harrisburg, Pa.: Stackpole, 1965 (orig. 1939).

Caudill, Harry M. *Night Comes to the Cumberlands: A Biography of a Depressed Area.* New York: Little, Brown, 1962.

Channing, Steven A. *Kentucky: A Bicentennial History.* New York: Norton, 1977.

Clark, Thomas D. *Kentucky: Land of Contrast.* New York: Harper and Row, 1968.

Coleman, J. Winston. *Slavery Times in Kentucky.* Chapel Hill: University of North Carolina Press, 1940.

Cotterill, Robert S. *History of Pioneer Kentucky.* Cincinnati: Johnson and Hardin, 1917.

Coulter, E. M. *Civil War and Readjustment in Kentucky.* Gloucester, Mass.: Peter Smith, 1966 (orig. 1926).

Davis, William D. *Breckinridge: Statesman, Soldier, Symbol.* Baton Rouge: Louisiana State University Press, 1974.

Eaton, Clement. *Henry Clay and the Art of American Politics.* Boston: Little, Brown, 1957.

Federal Writers' Project. *Kentucky: A Guide to the Bluegrass State.* New York: Harcourt, Brace, 1973 (orig. 1939).

Fuller, Paul E. *Laura Clay and the Woman's Rights Movement.* Lexington: University Press of Kentucky, 1975.

Hollingsworth, Kent. *The Kentucky Thoroughbred.* Lexington: University Press of Kentucky, 1976.

Jones, Virgil C. *The Hatfields and the McCoys.* Chapel Hill: University of North Carolina Press, 1948.

Kentucky Department of Commerce. *Kentucky Deskbook of Economic Statistics, 1979–80.* Frankfort, 1979.

Moore, Arthur K. *The Frontier Mind: A Cultural Analysis of the Kentucky Frontiersman.* Lexington: University of Kentucky Press, 1957.

Walls, David S., and John B. Stephenson. *Appalachia in the Sixties: Decade of Reawakening.* Lexington: University Press of Kentucky, 1973.

Wilson, Mary Helen, comp. *A Citizens' Guide to the Kentucky Constitution.* Frankfort: Legislative Research Commission, 1977.

LOUISIANA

State of Louisiana

ORIGIN OF STATE NAME: Named in 1682 for France's King Louis XIV. **NICKNAME:** The Pelican State. **CAPITAL:** Baton Rouge. **ENTERED UNION:** 30 April 1812 (18th). **SONGS:** "Give Me Louisiana"; "You Are My Sunshine." **MOTTO:** Union, Justice, and Confidence. **COLORS:** Gold, white, and blue. **FLAG:** On a blue field, fringed on three sides, a white pelican feeds her three young, symbolizing the state providing for its citizens; the state motto is inscribed on a white ribbon. **OFFICIAL SEAL:** In the center, pelican and young are as depicted on the flag; the state motto encircles the scene, and the words "State of Louisiana" surround the whole. **BIRD:** Eastern brown pelican. **FLOWER:** Magnolia. **TREE:** Bald cypress. **GEM:** Agate. **FOSSIL:** Petrified palmwood. **INSECT:** Honeybee. **LEGAL HOLIDAYS:** New Year's Day, 1 January; Battle of New Orleans Day, 8 January; Martin Luther King's Birthday, 15 January, by proclamation of the governor; Robert E. Lee's Birthday, 19 January; Washington's Birthday, 3d Monday in February; Good Friday, March or April; National Memorial Day, last Monday in May; Confederate Memorial Day, 3 June; Independence Day, 4 July; Huey Long's Birthday, 30 August, by proclamation of the governor; Labor Day, 1st Monday in September; Columbus Day, 2d Monday in October; All Saints' Day, 1 November; Veterans Day, 11 November; Thanksgiving Day, 4th Thursday in November; Christmas Day, 25 December. Legal holidays in New Orleans, Jefferson, St. Bernard, St. Charles, and East Baton Rouge parishes also include Mardi Gras, February or March. **TIME:** 6 A.M. CST = noon GMT.

¹LOCATION, SIZE, AND EXTENT

Situated in the western south-central US, Louisiana ranks 31st in size among the 50 states.

The total area of Louisiana is 48,523 sq mi (125,675 sq km), including 44,930 sq mi (116,369 sq km) of land and 3,593 sq mi (9,306 sq km) of inland water. The state extends 237 mi (381 km) E-W; its maximum N-S extension is 236 mi (380 km). Louisiana is shaped roughly like a boot, with the heel in the SW corner and the toe at the extreme SE.

Louisiana is bordered on the N by Arkansas; on the E by Mississippi (with part of the line formed by the Mississippi River and part, in the extreme SE, by the Pearl River); on the S by the Gulf of Mexico; and on the W by Texas (with part of the line passing through the Sabine River and Toledo Bend Reservoir). The state's geographic center is in Avoyelles Parish, 3 mi (5 km) SE of Marksville.

The total boundary length of Louisiana is 1,486 mi (2,391 km). Louisiana's total tidal shoreline is 7,721 mi (12,426 km).

²TOPOGRAPHY

Louisiana lies wholly within the Gulf Coastal Plain. Alluvial lands, chiefly of the Red and Mississippi rivers, occupy the north-central third of the state. East and west of this alluvial plain are the upland districts, characterized by rolling hills sloping gently toward the coast. The coastal-delta section, in the southernmost portion of the state, consists of the Mississippi Delta and the coastal lowlands. The highest elevation in the state is Driskill Mountain at 535 feet (163 meters), in Bienville Parish; the lowest, 5 feet (2 meters) below sea level, in New Orleans.

Louisiana has the most wetlands of any state, about 11,000 sq mi (28,000 sq km) of floodplains and 7,800 sq mi (20,200 sq km) of coastal swamps, marshes, and estuarine waters. The largest lake, actually a coastal lagoon, is Lake Pontchartrain, with an area of more than 620 sq mi (1,600 sq km). Toledo Bend Reservoir, an artificial lake along the Louisiana-Texas border, has an area of 284 sq mi (736 sq km). The most important rivers are the Mississippi, Red, Pearl, Atchafalaya, and Sabine. Most drainage takes place through swamps between the bayous, which serve as outlets for overflowing rivers and streams.

Louisiana has nearly 2,500 coastal islands covering some 2,000 sq mi (5,000 sq km).

³CLIMATE

Louisiana has a relatively constant semitropical climate. Rainfall and humidity decrease, and daily temperature variations increase, with distance from the Gulf of Mexico. The normal daily temperature in New Orleans is 68°F (20°C), ranging from 53°F (12°C) in January to 82°F (28°C) in July. The all-time high temperature is 114°F (46°C), recorded at Plain Dealing on 10 August 1936; the all-time low, –16°F (–27°C), was set at Minden on 13 February 1899. The relative humidity at New Orleans ranges from 88% at 7 A.M. to 63% at 1 P.M., and the average annual rainfall is 57 in (145 cm). Snow falls occasionally in the north, but rarely in the south.

Prevailing winds are from the south or southeast. During the summer and fall, tropical storms and hurricanes frequently batter the state, especially along the coast. Among the most severe hurricanes in recent decades were Audrey, which entered Cameron Parish on 28 June 1957, causing 400–500 deaths and property damage of $150 million; and Betsy, which entered the coast near Grand Isle on 9 September 1965, causing 58 deaths and damages of $1.2 billion.

⁴FLORA AND FAUNA

Forests in Louisiana consist of four major types: shortleaf pine uplands, slash and longleaf pine flats and hills, hardwood forests in alluvial basins, and cypress and tupelo swamps. Important commercial trees also include beech, eastern red cedar, and black walnut. Among the state's wild flowers are the ground orchid and several hyacinths. Spanish moss (actually a member of the pineapple family) grows profusely in the southern regions, but is rare in the north. Two types of orchid are threatened, and the *Schwalbea americana* is endangered.

Louisiana's varied habitats—tidal marshes, swamps, woodlands, and prairies—offer a diversity of fauna. Deer, squirrels, rabbit, and bear are hunted as game, while muskrat, nutria, mink, opossum, bobcat, and skunk are commercially significant furbearers. Prized game birds include quail, turkey, woodcock, and various waterfowl, of which the mottled duck and wood

217

duck are native. Coastal beaches are inhabited by sea turtles, and whales may be seen offshore. Freshwater fish include bass, crappie, and bream; red and white crawfishes are the leading commercial crustaceans. Threatened animal species include both the green and loggerhead sea turtles. The American alligator, on the federal endangered species list, is listed by the state as threatened, but with exemptions for certain parishes. Other endangered animals include the sei and sperm whales, Florida panther, eastern brown pelican (the state bird), whooping crane, and red-cockaded woodpecker.

5 ENVIRONMENTAL PROTECTION

Louisiana's earliest and most pressing environmental problem was the chronic danger of flooding by the Mississippi River. In April and May 1927, the worst flood in the state's history inundated more than 1,300,000 acres (526,000 hectares) of agricultural land, left 300,000 people homeless, and would have swept away much of New Orleans had levees below the city not been dynamited. The following year, the US Congress funded construction of a system of floodways and spillways to divert water from the Mississippi when necessary.

Legislation enacted in 1979 consolidated much of the state's environmental protection effort in the Office of Environmental Affairs (OEA), within the Department of Natural Resources. Among its responsibilities are maintenance of air and water quality, solid-waste management, hazardous waste disposal, and control of radioactive materials. According to an OEA survey, hazardous waste disposal, past and future, and the protection of the wetlands head the list of state residents' environmental concerns. Louisiana's problem in protecting its wetlands differs from that of most other states in that its wetlands are more than wildlife refuges—they are central to the state's agriculture and fishing industries. Assessment of the environmental impact of various industries on the wetlands has been conducted under the Coastal Zone Management Plan of the Department of Transportation and Development.

The two largest wildlife refuges in the state are the Rockefeller Wildlife Refuge, comprising 82,000 acres (33,000 hectares) in Cameron and Vermilion parishes, and the Marsh Island Refuge, 78,000 acres (32,000 hectares) of marshland in Iberia Parish. Both are managed by the Department of Wildlife and Fisheries.

Among the most active citizens' groups on environmental issues are the League of Women Voters, the Sierra Club (Delta Chapter), and the Ecology Center of New Orleans.

6 POPULATION

At the time of the 1970 census, Louisiana ranked 20th among the 50 states, with a population of 3,641,306. The 1980 population, according to preliminary census data, was 4,194,299, representing an increase of over 15% since 1970.

As of 1970, 51.4% of Louisianians were female and 48.6% male. Louisianians are somewhat younger than the national average, but among the least mobile of Americans: in 1976, nearly 71% of all state residents over 14 years of age had never lived in any other state. The estimated population density in 1978 was 88 persons per sq mi (34 per sq km), 32% above the national average.

About 63% of Louisianians lived in metropolitan areas in 1977. New Orleans is the largest city, with a preliminary 1980 census population of 556,913, followed by Baton Rouge, 219,164; Shreveport, 194,506; Lafayette, 80,483; and Lake Charles, 77,043. Spurred by an expansion of state government employment, Baton Rouge, the capital, has grown with exceptional speed since 1940, when its population was 34,719. Among the state's largest metropolitan areas in 1977 were New Orleans, 1,133,000 (33d in the US); Baton Rouge, 435,000 (87th); and Shreveport, 357,000 (107th).

7 ETHNIC GROUPS

Louisiana, most notably the Delta region, is an enclave of ethnic heterogeneity in the South. At the end of World War II, the established population of the Delta, according to descent, included blacks, French, Spanish (among them Central and South Americans and Islenos, Spanish-speaking migrants from the Canary Islands), Filipinos, Italians, Chinese, American Indians, and numerous other groups.

Blacks made up about 28% of the population in 1976. They include descendants of "free people of color," some of whom were craftsmen and rural property owners before the Civil War (a few were slaveholding plantation owners); many of these, of mixed blood, are referred to locally as "colored Creoles," and have constituted a black elite in both urban and rural Louisiana. New Orleans had a black population of 267,000 (45%) in 1970 and elected its first black mayor, Ernest N. "Dutch" Morial, in 1977.

Two groups that have been highly identified with the culture of Louisiana are Creoles and Acadians (also called Cajuns). Both descend primarily from early French immigrants to the state, but the Cajuns trace their origins from the mainly rural people exiled from Acadia (Nova Scotia) in the 1740s, while the Creoles tend to be city people from France and, to a lesser extent, from Nova Scotia or Hispaniola (the term "Creole" also applies to the relatively few early Spanish settlers and their descendants). Although Acadians have intermingled with Spaniards and Germans, they still speak a French patois and retain a distinctive culture.

At the time of the 1970 census, 140,000 Louisianians (less than 4% of the population) were foreign-born or second-generation Americans. Italy, Germany, and the United Kingdom were the main countries of origin.

8 LANGUAGES

White settlers in Louisiana found several Indian tribes of the Caddoan confederacy, from at least five different language groups. In 1970, 747 of their descendants claimed an Indian language as their mother tongue. Place-names from this heritage include Coushatta, Natchitoches, and Ouachita.

Louisiana English is predominantly Southern. Notable features of the state's speech patterns are *pen* and *pin* as sound-alikes and, in New Orleans, the so-called Brooklyn pronunciation of *bird* as /boyd/. A *pave* is a paved highway, and a pecan patty is well known as *praline*.

In 1970, only 75% of all residents as well as native-born residents called English their native tongue. Major groups indicated their mother tongue as follows:

	NATIVE-BORN	FOREIGN-BORN
English	2,742,390	5,173
French	569,799	2,463
Italian	27,486	3,347
Spanish	26,026	16,613

Unique to Louisiana is a large enclave, west of New Orleans, where a variety of French called Acadian (Cajun) is the first language. From it, and from early colonial French, English has taken such words as *pirogue* (dugout canoe), *armoire* (wardrobe), *boudin* (blood sausage), and *lagniappe* (extra gift).

9 RELIGIONS

Spanish missionaries brought Roman Catholicism to Louisiana in the early 16th century, and many of them were killed in their attempts to convert the Indians. During the early days, the most active religious orders were the Jesuits, Capuchins, and Ursuline nuns. Until the Louisiana Purchase, the public practice of any but the Catholic religion was prohibited, and Jews were entirely banned.

LOCATION: 29° to 33°N; 89° to 94°W. **BOUNDARIES:** Arkansas line, 166 mi (267 km); Mississippi line, 596 mi (959 km); Gulf of Mexico coastline, 397 mi (639 km); Texas line, 327 mi (526 km).

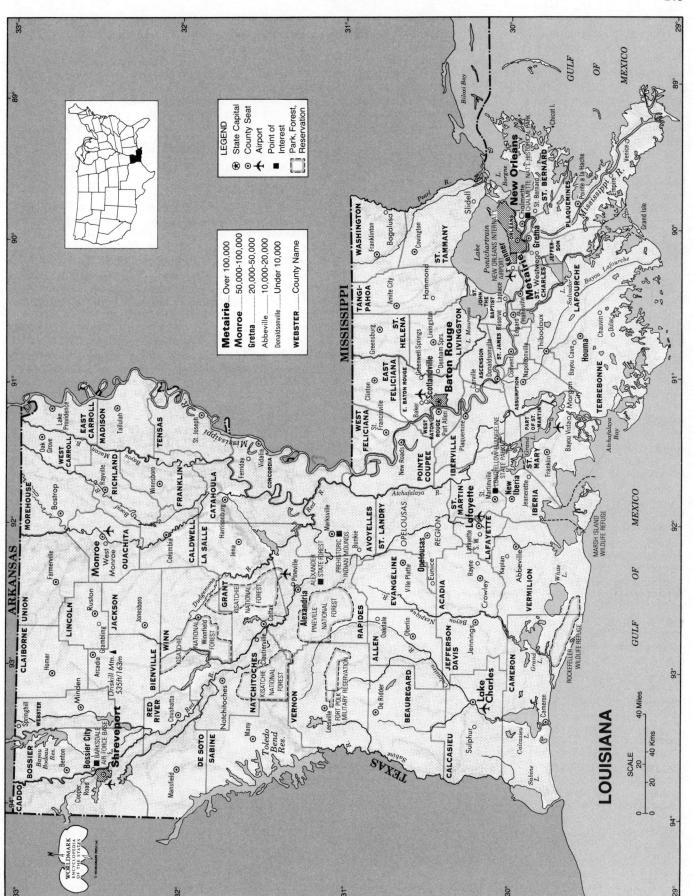

LOUISIANA

LEGEND
- ✪ State Capital
- ⊙ County Seat
- ✈ Airport
- ■ Point of Interest
- ⬚ Park, Forest, Reservation

Metairie	Over 100,000
Monroe	50,000-100,000
Gretna	20,000-50,000
Abbeville	10,000-20,000
Donaldsonville	Under 10,000
WEBSTER	County Name

SCALE
0   20   40 Miles
0   20   40 Kms

See US political: front cover H4; physical: back cover H4.

WORLDMARK
ENCYCLOPEDIA
OF THE STATES
© WORLDMARK PRESS Ltd.

Joseph Willis, a mulatto preacher who conducted prayer meetings at what is now Lafayette in 1804, organized the first Baptist church west of the Mississippi, at Bayou Chicot in 1812. In the Opelousas region, in 1806, the first Methodist church in the state was organized. The first Episcopal church was established in New Orleans in 1805, a Methodist church in 1813, a Presbyterian church in 1817, a synagogue in 1828, and a Baptist church in 1834. After the Civil War, blacks withdrew from white-dominated churches to form their own religious groups, mainly Baptist and Methodist.

As of 1979, the Roman Catholic Church was the largest Christian denomination, with 1,301,192 church members. In 1971, known adherents of Protestant groups totaled 898,053. The leading Protestant denominations were Southern Baptist, 602,687; United Methodist, 125,581; Episcopal, 41,348; and Presbyterian, 39,538. In 1979, 16,080 Jews resided in Louisiana, about two-thirds of them in New Orleans. Voodoo, in some cases blended with Christian ritual, is more widespread in Louisiana than anywhere else in the US, though the present number of practitioners is impossible to ascertain.

[10] TRANSPORTATION

New Orleans is a major center of domestic and international freight traffic. In volume of cargo handled, it is the busiest port on the Gulf of Mexico and 2d-leading port in the US. Although Louisiana's roads remained poor until the 1930s, the state was one of the nation's major rail centers by the end of the 19th century, and New Orleans was one of the first cities to develop a mass transit system.

Several short-run railroads were built in Louisiana during the 1830s. The first of these, and the first rail line west of the Alleghenies, was the Pontchartrain Railroad, which opened, using horse-drawn vehicles, on 23 April 1831. New Orleans was connected with New York before the Civil War, with Chicago by 1873, and with California in 1883 via a line that subsequently became part of the Southern Pacific. Railroads soon rivaled the Mississippi River in the movement of goods to and from New Orleans, and even today, the long-distance freight service provided by New Orleans' six trunk lines is a major reason for the preeminence of the port. As of 1980, Amtrak provided passenger links with Los Angeles, Chicago, and New York.

The New Orleans and Carrollton Railroads, a horse-drawn trolley system, began service in 1835; 59 years later, electric trolleys came into use. As of the 1980s, New Orleans Public Service was the only major privately owned trolley company in the US. New Orleans' 465 buses and 35 trolleys had some 76 million riders in 1979.

Louisiana's first road-building boom began after Huey Long entered the statehouse. When Long took office in 1928, the state had no more than 300 mi (480 km) of paved roads; by 1931 there were 1,583 (2,548). At the end of 1978, Louisiana had a total of 55,395 mi (89,150 km) of roads, 96% of them surfaced. That year, 1,834,306 automobiles and 712,167 trucks were registered in the state, and 2,258,857 driver's licenses were in force.

Early in the nation's history, the Mississippi River emerged as the principal route for north–south traffic, and New Orleans soon became the South's main port. The advent of the steamboat in 1812 solved the problem of upstream navigation, which previously had required three or four months for a distance that could be covered downstream in 15 days. (Barges moved by towboats eventually supplanted steamboats as cargo carriers.) An important breakthrough in international transportation was the deepening of the channel at the mouth of the Mississippi by means of jetties, the first of which were completed in 1879. As of 1980, the port of New Orleans had 15 mi (24 km) of public and private wharves, and its public docks had space for 101 vessels. The port is served by more than 100 steamship lines and by 20 common carrier and 110 contract carrier barge lines. During

1978, the port handled 7,664,000 tons of general cargo, a volume exceeded in the US only by the Port of New York and New Jersey. An offshore oil terminal, the Louisiana Superport, was under construction in 1980. Located south of New Orleans in the Gulf of Mexico, the supertanker facility has a designed capacity of 1,400,000 barrels of oil a day. Baton Rouge and Lake Charles are the state's other important deepwater ports.

As of 1978, Louisiana had 74 public and 213 private airfields. The busiest was New Orleans International Airport, which emplaned 3,018,722 passengers and handled 14,779 tons of freight. Louisiana also claims the world's largest heliport, in Morgan City, with 46 landing pads in 1979.

[11] HISTORY

The region now known as Louisiana is largely the creation of the Mississippi River; the process of land building still goes on in the Atchafalaya Basin and below New Orleans on the Mississippi Delta. Louisiana was never densely inhabited in prehistoric times, and at no time, probably, did as many as 15,000 Indians live inside the present boundaries of the state. The main relic of prehistoric inhabitants is the great earthwork at Poverty Point, near Marksville, but other Indian mounds are to be found in alluvial and coastal regions.

When white exploration and settlement of North America began, various tribes of Caddo Indians inhabited northwestern Louisiana, and small Tunican-speaking groups lived in the northeast. In the southwest were a number of rather primitive peoples of the Atakapa group; in south-central Louisiana the Chitimacha ranged through the marshes and lowlands. Various small Muskogean tribes, related to the Choctaw, lived east of the Mississippi in the "Florida parishes," so-called because they were once part of Spanish West Florida. The Natchez Indians, whose main villages were in present-day Mississippi near the city that still bears their name, played an important role in Louisiana's early history but were exterminated in the process.

Several Spanish explorers sailed along the coast of Louisiana, but Hernando de Soto was probably the first to penetrate the state's present boundaries, in 1541. Almost a century and a half passed before Robert Cavelier, Sieur de la Salle, departing from Canada, reached the mouth of the Mississippi on 9 April 1682, named the land there Louisiana in honor of King Louis XIV, and claimed it for France. La Salle's later attempt at a permanent settlement failed but in 1699, an expedition headed by Pierre le Moyne, Sieur d'Iberville, made a settlement on Biloxi Bay. In 1714, Louis Juchereau de St. Denis established Natchitoches, the first permanent European settlement in Louisiana; Iberville's brother, the Sieur de Bienville, established New Orleans four years later.

Louisiana did not thrive economically under French rule, whether as a royal colony or, from 1712 to 1731, under the proprietorship first of Antoine Crozat and then of John Law's Company of the Indies. On the other hand, French culture was firmly implanted there, and non-French settlers, especially Germans from Switzerland and the Rhineland, were quickly Gallicized. In 1762, on the verge of losing the rest of its North American empire to Great Britain in the French and Indian War, France ceded Louisiana to Spain. Governed by Spaniards, the colony was much more prosperous, though it never ceased to be a burden on the Spanish treasury. New settlers—Americans, Spaniards, Canary Islanders, and above all, Acadian refugees from Nova Scotia—added to the population. By 1800 there were about 50,000 inhabitants, a considerable number of them black slaves imported from Africa and the West Indies. The availability of slave labor, Eli Whitney's invention of the cotton gin, and Etienne de Boré's development of a granulation process for making cane sugar set the stage for future prosperity, though not under Spanish auspices. In 1800, by the secret Treaty of San Ildefonso, Napoleon forced the feeble Spanish government to return Louisiana to

France. Three years later, having failed to reestablish French rule and slavery in Haiti, Napoleon sold Louisiana to the US to keep it from falling into the hands of Great Britain.

President Thomas Jefferson concluded what was probably the best real estate deal in history, purchasing 800,000 sq mi (2,100,000 sq km) for $15,000,000 and thus more than doubling the size of the US at a cost of about 3 cents per acre. He made William C. C. Claiborne the governor of the huge new acquisition. The next year, that part of the purchase south of 33°N was separated from the remainder and designated the Territory of Orleans. The people of the territory then began the process of learning self-government, something with which they had had no experience under France and Spain. After the census of 1810 showed that the population had risen to 76,556, the people were authorized by Congress to draw up a state constitution. The constitutional convention met under the presidency of Julian Poydras in a coffeehouse in New Orleans and adopted, with a few changes, the constitution then in effect in Kentucky. In the meantime, in 1810, a revolt against Spain had taken place in West Florida. When the proposed Louisiana constitution reached Washington, Congress added that part of West Florida between the Mississippi and Pearl rivers to the new state, which entered the Union on 30 April 1812.

The key event in the Americanization of Louisiana was the campaign for New Orleans in December 1814 and January 1815, actually fought after the War of 1812 had ended. A force of British veterans under General Sir Edward Pakenham sailed into Lake Borgne and established itself below New Orleans at Chalmette. There they were met by detachments of Creoles, Acadians, blacks, and even Jean Lafitte's pirates, all from Louisiana, plus Tennesseans, Kentuckians, and Choctaw Indians, with the whole army under the command of Andrew Jackson. After several preliminary battles, the British were bloodily defeated when they launched an all-out assault on Jackson's line.

From 1815 to 1861, Louisiana was one of the most prosperous states in the South, producing sugar and cotton on its rich alluvial lands and grazing hogs and cattle in the wooded hills of the north and on the prairies of the southwest. Yeoman farmers and New Orleans workers far outnumbered the wealthy planters, but the planters, whose slaves made up almost half the population, dominated Louisiana politically and economically. When the secession crisis came in 1861, the planters led Louisiana into the Confederacy and, after four bloody years, to total defeat. The state suffered crippling economic losses during the Civil War, but the greatest loss was the lives of tens of thousands of young white men who died in defense of the South, and of thousands of blacks who died seeking and fighting for freedom. Louisiana did not fully recover from this disaster until the mid-20th century.

After the Civil War, Radical Republican governments elected by black voters ruled the state, but declining support from the North and fierce resistance from Louisiana whites brought the Reconstruction period to an end. Black people and their few white allies lost control of state government, and most of the former slaves became laborers on sugar plantations or sharecroppers in the cotton fields. There, as the years passed, they were joined by more and more landless whites. In 1898, blacks were disfranchised almost entirely by a new state constitution drawn up primarily for that purpose. This constitution also significantly reduced the number of poorer whites who voted in Louisiana elections.

The vast majority of Louisiana whites—whether hill farmers, Cajuns along the southern rivers and bayous, lumbermen in the yellow pine forests, or workers in New Orleans—were little better off than the black or white sharecroppers. Many economic changes had taken place: rice had become a staple crop on the southwestern prairies, and an oil boom had begun after the turn of the century. But just as before the Civil War, large

landowners, combined with New Orleans bankers, businessmen, and politicians, dominated state government, effectively blocking political and social reform. The Populist movement, which succeeded in effecting some change in other southern states, was crushed in Louisiana.

Not until 1928, with the election of Huey P. Long as governor, did the winds of change strike Louisiana; having been so long delayed, they blew with gale force. The years from 1928 through 1960 could well be called the Long Era: three Longs—Huey, who was assassinated in 1935; his brother Earl, who served as governor three times; and his son Russell, who became a powerful US senator—dominated state politics for most of the period. From a backward agricultural state, Louisiana evolved into one of the world's major petrochemical manufacturing centers. Offshore drilling sent clusters of oil wells 60 mi (97 km) out into the Gulf. The pine lands were reforested, and soybeans provided a new source of income. What had been one of the most parsimonious states became one of the most liberal in welfare spending, care for the aged, highway building, and education. The state could afford these expanding programs because of ever increasing revenues from oil and gas.

As Louisiana entered the 1980s, the major problems confronting the state were racial and labor tensions, inadequate disposal sites for industrial wastes, and (despite important new discoveries) the depletion of oil and gas resources. Even so, the state remained prosperous, a fact that little in the near future seemed likely to challenge.

12 STATE GOVERNMENT
Louisiana has had 11 constitutions, the most recent of which was enacted in 1974.

The state legislature consists of a 39-member senate and a 105-member house of representatives. All legislators are elected for concurrent four-year terms; they must be US citizens, at least 18 years old, and must have resided in the state for two years and in their districts for at least one year preceding election.

Major elected executive officials include the governor and lieutenant governor (independently elected), secretary of state, attorney general, treasurer, superintendent of education, commissioner of agriculture, commissioner of insurance, and commissioner of elections. All are elected for four-year terms. The governor must be a qualified elector, at least 25 years old, and must have been a US and Louisiana citizen for five years preceding election; after two consecutive terms, a governor may not succeed himself. The same eligibility requirements apply to the lieutenant governor, except that there is no limit on succession to the latter office. Other executive agencies are the State Board of Elementary and Secondary Education, whose eight elected members serve staggered six-year terms (another three members are appointed by the governor), and the Public Service Commission, whose five members also serve for six years.

To become law, a bill must receive majority votes in both the senate and the house and be signed by the governor, be left unsigned but not vetoed by the governor, or be passed again by two-thirds votes of both houses over the governor's veto. Appropriation bills must originate in the house but may be amended by the senate. The governor has an item veto on appropriation bills. Constitutional amendments require approval by two-thirds of the elected members of each house and ratification by a majority of the people voting on it at the next general election.

Voters in Louisiana must be US citizens, 18 years of age, and must have registered at least 30 days prior to the election.

13 POLITICAL PARTIES
The major political organizations are the Democratic Party and the Republican Party, each affiliated with the national party. However, differences in culture and economic interests have made Louisiana's politics extremely complex. Immediately fol-

lowing statehood, the primary political alignment was according to ethnic background, Anglo or Latin. By the 1830s, however, Louisiana politics reflected the national division of Jacksonian Democrats and National Republicans (by mid-decade replaced by the Whigs). By and large, the Whigs were favored by the Anglo-Americans, the Democrats by those of French and Spanish descent. When the Whig Party fell apart over slavery, many former Whigs supported the Native American (Know-Nothing) Party.

Louisiana was one of the three southern states whose disputed electoral votes put Republican Rutherford B. Hayes in the White House in 1877, in return for his agreement to withdraw federal troops from the South, thus putting an end to Reconstruction. The ensuing period of Bourbon Democratic dominance in Louisiana, a time of reaction and racism in politics (though a few blacks continued to hold office), lasted until the early 1890s, when worsening economic conditions inspired Populists and Republicans to challenge Democratic rule. The attempt failed largely because Democratic landowners were able to control the ballots of their black sharecroppers and "vote" them Democrat. The recognition that it was the black vote, however well controlled, that held the balance in Louisiana politics impelled the Democrats to seek its elimination as an electoral factor. The constitution of 1898 imposed a poll tax, a property requirement, a literacy test, and other measures that succeeded in reducing the number of registered black voters from 130,000 at the beginning of 1897 to 5,320 in March 1900 and to 1,342 by 1904. White registration also declined, from 164,000 in 1897 to 92,000 in 1904, since the new constitutional requirements tended to disfranchise poor whites as well as blacks.

Between 1900 and 1920, the New Orleans Ring, or Choctaw Club, was the dominant power in state politics. Growing political discontent led 5,261 Louisianians (6.6% of those voting) to cast their ballots for the Socialist presidential candidate in 1912. A few Socialists won local office that year in Winn Parish, a center of Populist activity in the 1890s and the birthplace of Huey Long in 1893.

During his relatively brief career as a member of the Railroad Commission, governor, and US senator, Long committed government resources to public service to an extent without precedent in the state. He also succeeded in substituting for the traditional Democratic Party organization a state machine geared primarily toward loyalty to himself and, after his assassination in 1935, to the Long family name, which kept its hold on the voters despite a series of scandals that publicized the corruption of his associates. When blacks began voting in increasing numbers during the 1940s, they tended to favor Democratic candidates from the Long camp. The Longs repaid their loyalty: when race became a bitterly divisive issue in the late 1940s and 1950s— Louisiana gave its presidential vote to the States' Rights "Dixiecrat" candidate in 1948—the Longs supported the national Democratic ticket.

The 1960s and 1970s saw a resurgence of the Republican Party and the election in 1979 of David C. Treen, the state's first Republican governor since Reconstruction. As of 31 March 1980 there were 1,741,160 registered Democrats and 1,119,547 registered Republicans. Both US senators and seven US representatives from the state were Democrats, and two US representatives were Republican. There were 96 Democrats and 9 Republicans in the house; all 39 state senators were Democrats.

Louisiana voters, who had been loyal to southerner Jimmy Carter in 1976, switched their allegiance to Ronald Reagan in November 1980, giving him a 51% majority of the popular vote. Russell Long, a Democrat, retained his US Senate seat without opposition on the ballot.

[14]LOCAL GOVERNMENT

The ecclesiastical districts, called parishes, into which Louisiana was divided in the late 17th century remain the primary political divisions in the state, serving functions similar to those of counties in other states.

By the late 1970s there were 64 parishes, nearly all of them governed by police jury. Juries for parishes of over 10,000 population have 5 to 15 members, or the number authorized as of 13 May 1974, whichever is greater; smaller parishes have at least 3 members on their juries. All police jury members are elected for four-year terms. Jefferson and Plaquemines are governed by commission-councils, East Baton Rouge by a city-parish council, and Orleans Parish (New Orleans) by a mayor and city council. Other parish officials include the sheriff, clerk of court, assessor, coroner, registrar of voters, and civil defense director. Each parish elects a school board whose members generally serve overlapping six-year terms.

Louisiana Presidential Vote by Political Parties, 1948–80

YEAR	ELECTORAL VOTE	LOUISIANA WINNER	DEMOCRAT	REPUBLICAN	STATES' RIGHTS DEMOCRAT	PROGRESSIVE	AMERICAN INDEPENDENT
1948	10	Thurmond (SRD)	136,344	72,657	204,290	3,035	—
1952	10	Stevenson (D)	345,027	306,925	—	—	—
					UNPLEDGED		
1956	10	*Eisenhower (R)	243,977	329,047	44,520	—	—
					NAT'L. STATES RIGHTS		
1960	10	*Kennedy (D)	407,339	230,980	169,572	—	—
1964	10	Goldwater (R)	387,068	509,225	—	—	—
1968	10	Wallace (AI)	309,615	257,535	—	—	530,300
					AMERICAN	SOC. WORKERS	
1972	10	*Nixon (R)	298,142	686,852	44,127	12,169	—
					LIBERTARIAN	COMMUNIST	
1976	10	*Carter (D)	661,365	587,446	3,325	7,417	10,058
						CITIZENS	
1980	10	*Reagan (R)	708,453	792,853	8,240	1,584	10,333

*Won US presidential election.

As of 1977, Louisiana also had more than 300 cities and towns. Prominent local officials include the mayor, chief of police, and a council or board of aldermen.

15 STATE SERVICES

Louisiana's ethics laws are administered by the Louisiana Commission on Government Ethics and the Louisiana State Board of Ethics for State Elected Officials, both within the Civil Service Department.

Educational services are provided through the Department of Education, which has jurisdiction over elementary, secondary, higher, and vocational-technical instruction, as well as the state schools for the visually impaired, hearing impaired, and other handicapped children. Highways, waterways, airports, and mass transit are the province of the Department of Transportation and Development. This department also oversees programs for soil and water conservation and provides assistance to coastal communities impacted by oil and gas exploration and production. The Motor Vehicle Office and State Police are within the Department of Public Safety.

Health and welfare services are administered mainly through the Department of Health and Human Resources, which provides welfare services under the Office of Family Security, services for the blind and vocational rehabilitation through the Office of Human Development, and special training for the mentally handicapped under the Office of Mental Retardation. Antipoverty programs, including Head Start, supplemental food, summer youth recreation, and Indian affairs programs, are administered by the Office of Community Services in the Department of Urban and Community Affairs, which also helps develop and administer housing and urban renewal programs.

16 JUDICIAL SYSTEM

Louisiana's legal system is the only one in the US to be based on civil or Roman law, specifically the Code Napoléon of France. Under Louisiana state law, cases may be decided by judicial interpretation of the statutes, without reference to prior court cases, whereas in other states and in the federal courts the common law prevails, and decisions are generally based on previous judicial interpretations and findings. In actual practice, Louisiana laws no longer differ radically from US common law, and most Louisiana lawyers and judges now cite previous cases in their arguments and rulings.

The highest court in Louisiana is the supreme court, with appellate jurisdiction. It consists of a chief justice and 6 associate justices, all of them elected from 6 supreme court districts (the first district has 2 judges) for staggered 10-year terms. There are 4 appellate circuits in the state, each divided into 3 districts; as of 1980, the 4 circuits were served by 32 judges, all of them elected for overlapping 10-year terms. Each of the state's district courts serves at least 1 parish and has at least 1 district judge, elected for a 6-year term; in 1980, there were 39 districts and 133 district judges. District courts have original jurisdiction in criminal and civil cases and appellate jurisdiction on cases from justices of the peace and some minor courts. City courts are the principal courts of limited jurisdiction.

Louisiana may have been the first state to institute a system of leasing convict labor; large numbers of convicts were leased, especially after the Civil War, until the practice was discontinued in the early 1900s. The abuses entailed in this system may be suggested by the fact that of 700 convicts leased in 1882, 149 died in service. At the end of 1978, 7,409 prisoners were in Louisiana's state and federal prisons, including 1,190 inmates of state prisons who were held in local jails because of overcrowding.

According to the FBI Crime Index, Louisiana's violent crime rate of 585 per 100,000 population ranked above the national average, while the rate of crimes against property—4,207—was below the US norm. New Orleans had the highest rate of homicide and nonnegligent manslaughter of any US metropolitan

area, 23.8 per 100,000 inhabitants, and the state as a whole ranked 1st in the nation with 15.8. Louisiana's rate of aggravated assault, 361, was 5th highest, and the rates for forcible rape (35) and larceny-theft (2,570) were also above the US norm.

In 1976/77, a total of $314,763,000 was spent on the state's criminal justice system, of which 50% went for police protection and 13% for the judicial system. That year there were 26,430 employees in Louisiana's criminal justice system, 16,088 of them in state and local police departments. Louisiana has a death penalty law, and judges may impose sentences of hard labor.

17 ARMED FORCES

As of mid-1978, Louisiana had five military installations with 34,006 personnel. There was one major army installation in the state, Ft. Polk at Leesville, with 15,729 personnel. In addition there were Air Force bases near Bossier City and Alexandria, and a naval air station and support station in the vicinity of New Orleans. During the year ending 30 September 1978, Louisiana firms received defense contracts totaling $505 million.

There were 453,000 veterans of US military service in Louisiana on 30 September 1979, of whom 9,000 had served in World War I, 188,000 in World War II, 94,000 during the Korean conflict, and 130,000 in the Viet-Nam era. Veterans' benefits during 1977/78 amounted to $332.6 million, of which $181.7 million was in compensation and pensions. In 1979, according to state figures, 106,755 veterans received direct cash payments averaging $2,499 per person.

Army and Air National Guard forces in Louisiana totaled 8,374 in 1979. The major National Guard installations are the Camp Beauregard Military Training Facility and the Jackson Barracks near New Orleans.

18 MIGRATION

Louisiana was settled by an unusually diverse assortment of immigrants. The Company of the Indies, which administered Louisiana from 1717 until 1731, at first began importing French convicts, vagrants, and prostitutes because of the difficulty of finding willing colonists. Next the company turned to struggling farmers in Germany and Switzerland, who proved to be more suitable and productive settlers. The importation of slaves from Africa and the West Indies began early in the 18th century.

Perhaps 10,000 Acadians, or Cajuns—people of French descent who had been exiled from Nova Scotia (Acadia) during the 1740s—migrated to Louisiana after the French and Indian War, attracted by generous land grants; they settled in the area of Lafayette and Breaux Bridge and along Bayou Lafourche and the Mississippi River. Probably the second largest group to migrate in the late 18th century came from the British colonies, and after the Revolution, the US. Between 1800 and 1870, Americans settled the area north of the Red River. Small groups of Canary Islanders and Spaniards from Málaga also settled in the south, and in 1791, a number of French people fled to Louisiana during the slave insurrection on Hispaniola.

During the 1840s and 1850s, masses of Irish and German immigrants came to New Orleans. In the late 1880s, a large number of midwestern farmers migrated to the prairies of southwest Louisiana to become rice farmers. Louisiana did not immediately begin losing much of its black population after the Civil War. In fact, the number of blacks who migrated to Louisiana from the poorer southeastern states during the postwar years may have equaled the number of blacks who migrated before the war or were brought into the state as slaves. In 1879, however, "Kansas fever" struck blacks from the cotton country of Louisiana and Mississippi, many of whom migrated to the wheat state; many later returned to their home states.

Beginning in World War II, large numbers of both black and white farm workers migrated north and west. During the 1960s, the state had a net outmigration of 15% of its black population, but the trend had slowed somewhat by 1975. Recent migration within the state has been from north to south, and from rural to urban areas, especially to Shreveport, Baton Rouge, and the suburbs of New Orleans. Overall, Louisiana suffered a net loss from migration of 326,000 from 1940 to 1970, but gained 26,000 from migration between 1970 and 1978.

[19]INTERGOVERNMENTAL COOPERATION

Among the interstate and regional efforts in which Louisiana participates are the Interstate Oil and Gas Compact, Louisiana-Ozarks Regional Commission, Gulf States Marine Fisheries Compact, Red River Compact, Sabine River Compact, the South Central Forest Fire Protection Compact, Southern Growth Policies Compact, Southern Interstate Energy Compact, and Southern Regional Education Compact.

Federal aid to Louisiana during 1978/79 exceeded $1.5 billion, of which $149.1 million was general revenue sharing.

[20]ECONOMY

Before the Civil War, when Louisiana was one of the most prosperous of southern states, its economy depended primarily on two then profitable crops—cotton and sugar—and on its position as the anchor of the nation's principal north–south trade route. But the upheaval and destruction wrought by the war, combined with severe flood damage to cotton crops, falling cotton prices, and the removal of the federal bounty on sugar, left the economy stagnant through the end of the 19th century, although New Orleans retained its commercial importance as an exporter of cotton and grain.

With the addition of two major crops, rice and soybeans, the rebirth of the timber industry as a result of reforestation and the demand for pine for paper pulp, and, most dramatically, the rise of the petrochemical industry, Louisiana's economy has regained much of its former vitality. Today, Louisiana ranks 2d only to Texas in the value of its mineral products, and in value per capita it exceeds that much larger and more populous state. As of 1978, the value of mineral production was $11.7 billion, 23% more than the value added by manufacture, about 8 times the value of all agricultural products, and more than 60 times the value of the commercial fishing catch.

By no means do all of Louisiana's citizens share in this new-found wealth. Wages have been rising—the average manufacturing wage is among the top third in the nation—but the state's unemployment rate has been higher than the national average, and the rates for women and blacks are especially high. Per capita income is still well below the national norm.

Louisiana is primarily an industrial state, but its industries are to a large degree based on its natural resources, principally oil, water, and timber. Timber is being replaced as fast as it is being removed. More attention is being paid to the care of Louisiana's inland and coastland waters than ever before, and the port of New Orleans is thriving. The central question for Louisiana's economic planners is, What happens when the oil runs out?

[21]INCOME

Louisiana's per capita personal income in 1970 was $3,023, for a rank of 46th in the US. By 1978, largely because of the oil boom, per capita income had risen to $6,640 (38th). Total personal income rose from $11 billion to $26.3 billion in current dollars, while the real growth (measured in constant 1972 dollars) was 47%, well above the national average of 32%. Median family income in 1975 was $12,576, 35th in the US.

Income, though increasing, is unequally distributed. In 1975, more than 19% of all Louisianians were below the federal poverty level, a proportion exceeded only in Mississippi. In 1972, on the other hand, 125,900 (about 1%) of the nation's top wealthholders lived in the state. In 1970, white families had more than double the median income of black families.

[22]LABOR

In 1978, Louisiana had a total civilian labor force of 1,619,000, or less than 59% of the population aged 16 or over. Only Missis-

sippi, Arkansas, Florida, and West Virginia had lower participation rates, and Louisiana's rate for females, 43%, ranked 49th among the 50 states. About 1,506,000 Louisianians were employed and 113,000 were unemployed, for a 1978 unemployment rate of not quite 7%. The total unemployment rate during 1977 was 7.6%, 5.7% for males and 9.1% for females. The rate for blacks was 13.4%, 11.8% for men and 15.4% for women; for white males, 4%; and for white females, 6.6%.

A federal census of workers covered by unemployment insurance in March 1977 revealed the following nonfarm employment pattern for Louisiana:

	ESTABLISH-MENTS	EMPLOYEES	ANNUAL PAYROLL ('000)
Agricultural services, forestry, fishing	793	4,340	$ 35,111
Mining, of which:	1,506	67,562	1,115,019
Oil, gas extraction	(1,340)	(57,315)	(926,212)
Contract construction	6,966	103,378	1,335,983
Manufacturing	3,796	196,092	2,719,654
Transportation, public utilities	3,798	92,486	1,177,605
Wholesale trade	6,720	82,020	994,192
Retail trade	21,588	225,384	1,486,924
Finance, insurance, real estate	6,871	63,762	653,543
Services	19,335	205,624	1,689,321
Other	1,106	1,571	19,017
TOTALS	72,479	1,042,219	$11,226,369

Government employees, not counted in this survey, totaled about 240,000 in 1978.

During the antebellum period, Louisiana had both the largest slave market in the US—New Orleans—and the largest slave revolt in the nation's history, in St. Charles and St. John the Baptist parishes in January 1811. New Orleans also had a relatively large free black population, and many of the slaves in the city were skilled workers, some of whom were able to earn their freedom by outside employment. Major efforts to organize Louisiana workers began after the Civil War. There were strikes in the cane fields in the early 1880s, and in the mid-1880s, the Knights of Labor began to organize the cane workers. The strike they called in 1886 was ended by hired strikebreakers, who killed at least 30 blacks. Back in New Orleans, the Knights of Labor led a general strike in 1892. The Brotherhood of Timber Workers began organizing in 1910, but had little to show for their efforts except the scars of violent conflict with the lumber-mill owners.

In 1976, 231,000 Louisianians belonged to labor unions and employee associations. Only 16% of all nonagricultural employees were union members, one of the lowest such percentages in the US. That year, a right-to-work law was passed, partly as a result of violent conflict between an AFL-CIO building trades union and an independent union over whose workers would build a petrochemical plant near Lake Charles. In 1979, a police strike began in New Orleans on the eve of Mardi Gras, causing the cancellation of most of the parades, but it collapsed the following month.

[23]AGRICULTURE

With a farm income of more than $1.4 billion in 1978, Louisiana ranked 30th among the 50 states. Nearly every crop grown in North America could be raised somewhere in Louisiana. In the south are strawberries, oranges, sweet potatoes, and truck crops; in the southeast, sugarcane; and in the southwest, rice and soybeans. Soybeans—which were introduced into Louisiana after World War I and are today the state's most valuable crop—are also raised in the cotton-growing area of the northeast and in a diagonal belt running east–northwest along the Red River. Oats, alfalfa, corn, potatoes, and peaches are among the other crops grown in the north.

As of 1979 there were an estimated 35,000 farms covering 10 million acres (4 million hectares). Louisiana long ranked 1st in the US in sugarcane production, but by the late 1970s, Florida and Hawaii had surpassed it. Cash receipts for the sugar crop in 1978 amounted to $109,647,000. That year, Louisiana ranked 4th in the value of its rice production, $168,188,000 for 22,425,000 hundredweight; 6th for cotton, $138,000,000 for 478,000 bales; and 9th for soybeans, $464,340,000 for 71,000,000 bushels. According to the Louisiana Department of Agriculture, three out of every five acres in production go for export to other states and countries rather than for domestic consumption, and Louisiana imports much more produce from other states and Mexico than it raises.

²⁴ANIMAL HUSBANDRY

In the mid-19th century, before rice production began there, southwestern Louisiana was a major cattle-raising area. Today, cattle are raised mainly in the southeast (between the Mississippi and Pearl rivers), in the north-central region, and in the west.

Livestock production in 1978 accounted for not quite one-third of agricultural income. At the end of 1979 there were 1,300,000 cattle and calves and 150,000 hogs and pigs. The cattle and calf output in 1979 totaled 335.6 million lb, valued at $236.3 million. Other farm products included 1 billion lb of milk valued at $135.8 million, 15 million lb of chickens worth $2 million, and 601 million eggs worth $35.2 million.

Fur trapping has some local importance. During the 1976/77 season, 3,246,988 pelts were taken in Louisiana, with a total value of $24,122,144. An experimental alligator harvest program was introduced in 1975; 16,045 alligators taken in 1979 had hides valued at $1,600,000.

²⁵FISHING

In 1978, Louisiana led all states in the size of its commercial landings, with 1.7 billion lb, ranked 3d by value of catch at $190.2 million. Cameron led all US ports in 1978 with a catch of 606 million lb. The ports of Dulac-Chauvin and Empire-Venice ranked 4th and 5th respectively, together accounting for another 593 million lb.

The most important species in 1977 were shrimp, 104 million lb, $87.2 million; menhaden, 756.7 million lb, $28.9 million; oysters, 10.1 million lb of meat, $10.3 million; and blue crabs, 16.3 million lb, $4.3 million. Louisiana led the nation in value of industrial fishery products in 1978 with $107.4 million. In 1979, 49,151 commercial fishing and dealers' licenses were issued.

Louisiana produces 99% of the US crayfish harvest. With demand far exceeding the natural supply, crayfish farming began about 1959. By 1977, crayfish farms covering some 40,000 acres (16,000 hectares) produced 2,450,331 lb of fish valued at $1,309,769. Catfish are also cultivated in Louisiana, on some 5,000 acres (2,000 hectares). Louisiana is the only state in which the craft of shrimp drying is still practiced.

²⁶FORESTRY

As of 1977 there were 14,558,000 acres (5,891,000 hectares) of forestland in Louisiana, representing about half the state's land area and 2% of all US forests. The principal forest types are loblolly and shortleaf pine in the northwest, longleaf and slash pine in the south, and hardwood in a wide area along the Mississippi River. More than 99% of Louisiana's forests—some 14,527,000 acres (5,879,000 hectares) in 1977—are commercial timberland, nearly all of it privately owned. In 1978, Louisiana ranked 1st in the nation in production of southern pine plywood, and 6th in production of pulpwood. The value of all products made from wood during that year was estimated at $4.5 billion.

As of 30 September 1979, Louisiana's two national forests, Kisatchie and Pineville, had a gross area of 1,022,703 acres (413,875 hectares) within their boundaries, including 597,639 acres (241,857 hectares) of National Forest System lands. Within the boundaries of Kisatchie's Evangeline Unit is the Alexander State Forest, established in 1923 for reforestation and the protection of seedlings.

The headquarters of the Southern Forest Survey of the US Forest Service and the offices of the largest of the nine US forest experimental stations are located in New Orleans.

²⁷MINING

In 1978, Louisiana ranked 2d among the 50 states in value of minerals produced, with $11.7 billion, most of that from fossil fuels. In order of value, the principal minerals were natural gas, crude petroleum, natural gas liquids, and sulfur. In 1978, Louisiana was 2d only to Texas in the production of petroleum, natural gas liquids, and sulfur, and was the leading producer of natural gas and of salt.

The principal mining regions are the south, especially the Gulf Coast, for salt, sulfur, and petroleum, much of which is found below salt domes; offshore for oil and gas; the northeast for gas. In 1978, Louisiana produced an estimated 13,547,000 tons of salt, 31% of the US output, and 2,389,000 tons of elemental sulfur, 22% of the US total.

²⁸ENERGY AND POWER

Oil and gas production have expanded greatly since World War II, but production reached its peak in the early 1970s, and proved reserves are declining.

At the end of 1978, power plants in Louisiana had a total installed capacity of 14.1 million kw. These generated a total of 61.8 billion kwh of power, about 30% from oil and 70% from gas. Energy sales in 1977 were 44.7 billion kwh, about three-fourths of that year's production, with the balance being exported to other states. As of 1980, two nuclear power plants were under construction: Waterford in St. Charles Parish (capacity, 1,165,000 kw), scheduled to begin operations by November 1981; and River Bend in West Feliciana Parish (1,036,000 kw), to begin partial operations by April 1984.

Louisiana produced 532,740,000 barrels of crude oil during 1978: 497,513,000 from the Gulf Coast, of which 309,177,000 was extracted offshore (nearly 75% of total US offshore production), and the balance from the rest of the state. Production that year was approximately 17% of the US total and was valued at $5 billion at the wellhead; some 24,500 wells produced an average of nearly 60 barrels per well per day. At the end of 1978, remaining proved reserves of oil in Louisiana amounted to 2.9 billion barrels (10% of the US total), down from 3.1 billion a year earlier, continuing a trend that began in 1971. About 40% of the crude oil imported through Louisiana's superport was expected to be refined in the state.

Louisiana supplies more than one-third of the US natural gas output. Production in 1978 was 7.1 trillion cu feet, leaving proved reserves of 49.7 trillion cu feet. There were 10,135 producing gas wells in 1978, down from 12,484 in 1977. Some 192.4 million barrels of natural gas liquids were also produced.

Energy conservation plans in Louisiana call for development of untapped energy sources, such as the state's lignite and geothermal reserves.

²⁹INDUSTRY

The Standard Oil Refinery (now owned by Exxon) that is today the largest in North America began operations in Louisiana in 1909, the same year construction started on the state's first long-distance oil pipeline. Since then, a huge and still-growing petrochemical industry has become a dominant force in the state's economy. Other expanding industries include wood products and, especially since World War II, shipbuilding.

In 1977, the total value added by manufacture was $9.5 billion, and the value of shipments of all manufactured goods amounted to $29.5 billion. The largest employers among industry groups were chemicals and chemical products, food and food products, transportation equipment, and paper and paper products, which together utilized 48% of the industrial work force. By value added, the leading groups were chemicals, 37%; petroleum refinery, 18%; food and food products, 8%; paper and paper products, 7%; transportation equipment, 6%; fabricated metal products, 4%; and lumber and wood products, 3%. The following table shows value added in 1972 and 1977 for selected industries:

	1972	1977
Petroleum refining	$408,700,000	$1,717,700,000
Agricultural chemicals	225,700,000	636,700,000
Ship, boat building and repairing	277,800,000	453,600,000
Plastics materials, synthetics	184,500,000	378,900,000
Paperboard mill products	157,500,000	274,200,000
Sugar, confectionery products	114,800,000	157,700,000

The principal industrial regions extend along the Mississippi River, from north of Baton Rouge to New Orleans, and also include the Monroe, Shreveport, Morgan City, and Lake Charles areas.

30 COMMERCE

Louisiana ranked 21st among the 50 states in wholesale trade in 1972, with sales amounting to $9.6 billion. Nearly half of that took place in metropolitan New Orleans, with metropolitan Baton Rouge and Shreveport together accounting for another 22%.

With sales of $12.4 billion, Louisiana ranked 21st in retail trade in 1977. The leading retail categories were grocery stores, with 24% of total sales; automotive dealers, 22%; department stores, 10%; eating and drinking places, 8%; and gasoline service stations, 7%. Metropolitan New Orleans accounted for 32% of all retail sales, followed by Baton Rouge, 13%, and Shreveport, 10%.

In 1976, Louisiana ranked 19th among the 50 states in value of its manufactures exported abroad, with $1.4 billion. The value of the state's foreign agricultural exports was $543 million in 1976/77 (15th in the US). Exports accounted for nearly 42% of Louisiana farm sales, a higher rate than that of any state except Illinois. Exports through the port of New Orleans during 1978 totaled $5.1 billion; imports, $4.9 billion. Among world regions, Africa supplied the greatest quantity of goods shipped to the port. Japan, Italy, West Germany, and the USSR, in that order, received the largest quantities of exported goods. The entire New Orleans customs district cleared $14.8 billion in exports and $14.2 billion in imports in 1978.

31 CONSUMER PROTECTION

The Office of Consumer Protection, in the Department of Urban and Community Affairs, is the principal investigative agency dealing with consumer interests, and the consumer protection section of the Justice Department is the enforcement agency. Leading complaints received by the Office of Consumer Protection during 1979 dealt with motor vehicle sales and service, mail order sales, home construction and repair, household goods and services, retail stores and services, mobile homes, and apartment and house rentals, in that order. The office operates a toll-free telephone line for consumer inquiries and complaints. A consumer advisory board, appointed by the governor, is designed to serve as a watchdog for consumer affairs.

32 BANKING

In 1978, Louisiana had 256 insured commercial banks with total assets of $19.1 billion, outstanding loans of $6.8 billion, and deposits of $16.2 billion, including $9.8 billion in time deposits and $6.4 billion in demand deposits. There were 120 insured savings and loan associations in the state as of 31 December 1978. Of these, 46 were federally chartered and 74 were state-chartered mutual savings associations. Total assets for both categories were $7 billion, of which the state banks accounted for 72%; outstanding mortgage loans totaled $5.9 billion, with the state institutions holding roughly the same percentage. In 1978, 100 chartered credit unions in Louisiana had assets exceeding $118 million.

Louisiana banks are regulated by the Office of Financial Institutions within the Department of Commerce.

33 INSURANCE

As of 1980, 1,373 insurance companies were licensed to do business in Louisiana, of which 154 were domestic firms.

There were 95 life insurance companies operating in the state in mid-1978. That year, Louisianians held 9,782,000 life insurance policies with a total value of $48.6 billion; the average family held $35,300 in coverage, slightly above the US average. Total benefits paid that year amounted to $399.5 million, of which $191.8 million comprised death benefits paid to 68,300 beneficiaries.

Premiums written by property and liability insurance firms in 1978 totaled $1.8 billion, of which automobile liability coverage accounted for $436 million; automobile physical damage insurance, $231 million; and homeowners insurance, $173 million. As of mid-1979, nearly $7.9 billion in flood insurance was in force, 2d only to Florida among the 50 states. Nonprofit funeral associations received assessments or premiums of $548,559 and paid claims of $498,102 in 1975; insurance in force amounted to $18,217,040.

The Louisiana Insurance Code requires that all insurance companies licensed in the state be examined at least once every three years.

34 SECURITIES

The New Orleans Commodity Exchange, specializing in cotton futures, was expected to begin operations in January 1981, at which time it would be the only commodity exchange in the South.

During 1979/80, some 800 securities offerings were authorized in the state by the commissioner of securities, and 290 broker-dealers and 2,850 agents were licensed. New York Stock Exchange member firms maintained 37 sales offices in Louisiana during 1978, with 342 registered representatives. Louisianians reported $215.4 million in dividend income on the 1977 federal income tax returns.

35 PUBLIC FINANCE

The budget is prepared by the state executive budget director and submitted annually by the governor to the legislature for amendment and approval. The fiscal year runs from 1 July through 30 June. The following table shows revised consolidated estimates for 1979/80 and recommendations for 1980/81:

REVENUES	1979/80	1980/81
State revenues:		
Taxes, licenses, fees, etc.	$2,811,619,000	$3,169,588,000
Revenues collected by agencies	204,650,852	198,184,055
Federal revenue sharing	49,136,000	20,518,000
Total federal grants	1,283,763,509	1,127,794,755
Total interagency transfers	196,368,135	217,104,373
Other sources:		
General fund surplus	387,533,150	253,728,125
Other funds	22,993,961	25,952,973
TOTALS	$4,956,064,607	$5,012,870,281
EXPENDITURES		
Public education	$1,582,423,353	$1,695,816,111
Health and human resources	1,269,624,470	1,389,393,967
Transportation and development	284,279,704	302,030,237
Department of Labor	145,353,568	138,215,197
Public safety	101,307,676	110,052,897
Corrections	86,239,618	98,854,870
Employee benefits	55,582,674	75,736,077
Other appropriations and requirements	692,995,837	914,792,725
Capital outlays	458,576,609	255,140,862
TOTALS	$4,676,383,509	$4,980,032,943

During 1976/77, New Orleans budgeted revenues of $270 million and expenditures of $259 million. Revenues in Baton Rouge were $119 million; expenditures, $116 million. In mid-1977, the state debt was $1.8 billion, and the total debt of all Louisiana governments was $5 billion, or $1,276 per capita (14th in the US).

36 TAXATION

For most of the state's history, Louisianians paid little in taxes. Despite increases in taxation and expenditures since the late 1920s, when Huey Long introduced the graduated income tax, Louisiana's state and local tax burden per capita, $636 in 1977, is still well below the national average.

Income taxes yielded $455 million in state revenues in 1978/79. As of 1980, the individual income tax ranged from 2% on the first $10,000 to 6% on income over $50,000. The corporate income tax ranged from 4% on the first $25,000 up to 8% on net income over $200,000.

The state sales and use tax of 3% yielded $585 million to the state in 1978/79; parishes and municipalities may impose additional sales taxes, so that the total tax rate in New Orleans, for example, was 6%. Natural resource severance taxes, whose rates vary according to the resource, brought in more than $466 million in 1978/79. The state also taxes gasoline sales, gifts and inheritances, soft drinks, alcoholic beverages, and tobacco products, among other items. Taxes on beer and chain stores contribute to local revenues, as does the property tax, although Louisiana relies less on this than most states do. The Louisiana Stadium and Exposition District and the Orleans Parish School Board impose a 4% tax on hotel and motel room occupancy.

During 1975/76, Louisiana paid total federal taxes of more than $4.4 billion and received federal expenditures amounting to $4.8 billion. Louisianians filed nearly 1.4 million federal income tax returns in 1977, paying almost $2.5 billion in tax.

37 ECONOMIC POLICY

The Office of Commerce and Industry in the Department of Commerce seeks to encourage investment and create jobs in the state and to expand the markets for Louisiana products. Louisiana's industrial development plan, known as "Right to Profit," offers tax incentives and aid for training and construction. During 1979, 11,016 permanent jobs were created, as well as 36,588 temporary construction jobs; capital investment exceeded $3.1 billion, up 26% from 1978. During 1978/79, 29 new firms located in Louisiana, and 50 did so in 1977/78. During this two-year period, state-aided training programs enrolled 4,575 workers, at an average cost of $182 per employee. The Music Commission, established in 1979, encourages the making of musical recordings in the state.

38 HEALTH

During 1969–71, Louisiana ranked 47th among the 50 states in average life expectancy at 68.76 years—72.88 for females, 64.85 for males. The infant mortality rate in 1977 was 12.4 per 1,000 live births for whites, 26.2 for nonwhites; the latter rate was among the highest in the US, as was the overall death rate from diseases of early infancy, 17.9 per 100,000 population. In 1977, some 14,600 legal abortions were performed in Louisiana.

The state had the 2d-highest death rate in the nation in 1977 from diabetes, 19.3 per 100,000 population. Death rates from heart disease (318), cancer (168), pneumonia and influenza (22), cirrhosis of the liver (10), and suicide (13) were below the national averages; from cerebrovascular diseases (88), accidents (62), and arteriosclerosis (15) above the US median. The overall death rate, 8.8 per 100,000 population, was average for 1977.

As of 1980, Louisiana had four state mental hospitals, one of which, Greenwell Springs State Hospital, formerly for tuberculosis patients, now cares primarily for alcoholics and acutely disturbed adolescents. There were nine state-run residential facilities for the mentally retarded serving some 3,500 residents and employing more than 4,800 personnel. The only leprosarium on the US mainland, established in 1894 by the state and taken over by the US Public Health Service in 1921, is at Carville. In

1978, the 159 hospitals in Louisiana had a total of 25,128 beds and recorded 765,584 admissions. Hospital personnel included 7,613 registered nurses and 5,084 licensed practical nurses. The average cost of hospital care in 1977 was $176 per day and $1,129 per stay, both well below the national average. There were 5,614 licensed physicians in the state in 1977 and 1,586 active dentists in 1979.

39 SOCIAL WELFARE

During the governorships of Huey and Earl Long, Louisiana developed a relatively progressive welfare system. Nevertheless, in 1976, Louisiana still ranked among the bottom fourth of all states in welfare spending, and most of the funds it did spend were from the federal government. In 1978, Louisiana ranked 44th among the 50 states in average monthly public assistance payments to families with dependent children (AFDC); a total of $98 million went to 202,400 recipients, three-fourths of them children. The previous year, 372,000 persons participated in the federal food stamp program, receiving coupons worth $130.9 million. An estimated 790,000 pupils benefited from the school lunch program in 1978, at a federal cost of $55.8 million; 85% of all students in participating schools were served.

During 1977, Social Security benefits exceeding $1.2 billion were paid to 571,200 Louisianians. Supplemental Security Income payments totaled $192.7 million in 1978. It is estimated that during 1979/80, 41,207 persons (45% of them severely disabled) received state-administered rehabilitation services and that 6,427 were successfully rehabilitated; of an estimated 1,740 blind persons, 236 were rehabilitated. During the same year, 50,000 children were registered in the Handicapped Children's Program for diagnosis and treatment of the indigent. During 1977, workers' compensation payments totaled $160.9 million. In 1978, a total of $138 million was paid in unemployment insurance to 29,000 average weekly beneficiaries.

40 HOUSING

The Indians of Louisiana built huts with walls made of clay kneaded with Spanish moss and covered with cypress bark or palmetto leaves. The earliest European settlers used split cypress boards filled with clay and moss; a few early 18th-century houses with clay and moss walls remain in the Natchitoches area. Examples of later architectural styles also survive, including buildings constructed of bricks between heavy cypress posts, covered with plaster; houses in the raised cottage style, supported by brick piers and usually including a wide gallery and colonettes; the Creole dwellings of the Vieux Carré in New Orleans, built of brick and characterized by balconies and French windows; and urban and plantation houses from the Greek Revival period of antebellum Louisiana.

According to the 1970 census there were 1,146,000 year-round housing units, of which 1,032,000 were occupied; of these 63% were owner-occupied and only 89% had full plumbing. Overcrowding is a problem: with New Mexico, Louisiana ranked 3d among the 50 states in density of occupants per room. In 1970, New Orleans had approximately 208,000 housing units, of which more than 29,000 had been built during the previous decade. Between 1976 and 1978, some 70,600 new units worth nearly $2 billion were authorized in the state. For the year ending 30 September 1978, Louisiana received $47.8 million in aid for low-rent public housing and more than $41.1 million in community development grants from the US Department of Housing and Urban Development.

41 EDUCATION

Most education in Louisiana was provided through private (often parochial) schools until Reconstruction. Not until Huey Long's administration, when spending for education increased greatly and free textbooks were supplied, did education become a high priority of the state. Throughout the 20th century, Louisiana has had the highest illiteracy rate in the nation, though the rate fell from 6.3% in 1960 to 2.8% in 1970. As of 1976, only 58% of adult Louisianians had completed high school, and nearly 9% had no more than four years of grade school.

During 1978/79, total enrollment in Louisiana schools was 845,813: 53,286 kindergarten, 537,585 elementary, and 254,942 secondary. Nonpublic school enrollment that year was 153,220: 11,313 kindergarten, 102,039 elementary, and 39,868 secondary. Black students made up 38% of the public school enrollment but less than 15% of the private school total.

Integration of New Orleans public schools began in 1960; two years later, the archbishop of New Orleans required that all Catholic schools under his jurisdiction be desegregated. However, it took a federal court order in 1966 to bring about integration in public schools throughout the state. By 1976, 38% of minority students in Louisiana were in schools with under 50% minority enrollment, and 25% were in schools with 99–100% minority enrollment. The civil rights revolution also affected other aspects of Louisiana education. During the 1977/78 school year, the mean salary for teachers was $12,692 ($12,877 for blacks, $12,372 for whites), and for principals, $18,321 ($18,291 for blacks, $18,333 for whites). In 1946/47, combined salaries of principals and teachers had averaged $1,765 for whites and $936 for blacks.

As of 1979, in addition to 53 vocational-technical schools, there were 32 institutions of higher education in Louisiana, of which 20 were public and 12 private. The center of the state university system is Louisiana State University (LSU), founded at Baton Rouge in 1855 and having a 1978/79 enrollment of 27,014; LSU also has campuses at Alexandria, Eunice, and Shreveport, and includes the University of New Orleans, with 13,909 students. Tulane, founded in New Orleans in 1834 and with a 1977/78 enrollment of 9,463, is one of the most distinguished private universities in the South. As of the late 1970s, Southern University at Baton Rouge (1879), with 8,097 students, was the largest predominantly black university in the US; other campuses were in New Orleans and Shreveport. Another mainly black institution is Grambling State University (1901), 9,249. The Governor's Commission on Education Services administers state loan, grant, and scholarship programs; in 1978/79, the Louisiana Student Loan Program guaranteed 7,068 loans averaging $1,320 apiece. The state Council for the Development of French in Louisiana organizes student exchanges with Quebec, Belgium, and France, and aids Louisianians studying French abroad.

Total state expenditures on public schools in 1977/78 exceeded $1.2 billion, or $1,481 for each student in average daily attendance (30th in the US).

[42] ARTS
New Orleans has long been one of the most important centers of artistic activity in the South. The earliest theaters were French, and the first of these was started by refugees from Hispaniola, who put on the city's first professional theatrical performance in 1791. The American Theater, which opened in 1824, attracted many of the finest actors in America, as did the nationally famous St. Charles. Showboats traveled the Mississippi and other waterways, bringing dramas, musicals, and minstrel shows to river towns and plantations as early as the 1840s, with their heyday being the 1870s and 1880s.

In the late 1970s, principal theaters included the New Orleans Theater of the Performing Arts, Le Petit Théâtre du Vieux Carré, and the Tulane Theater. The Free Southern Theater is a black touring company based in New Orleans. LSU at Baton Rouge has theaters for both opera and drama. Baton Rouge, Shreveport, Monroe, Lake Charles, and Hammond are among the cities with little theaters, and Baton Rouge, Lafayette, and Lake Charles have ballet companies. There are symphony orchestras in most of the larger cities, the one in New Orleans being the best known.

It is probably in music that Louisiana has made its most distinctive contributions to culture. Jazz was born in New Orleans around 1900; among its sources was the music played by brass bands at carnivals and at Negro funerals, and its immediate precursor was the highly syncopated music known as ragtime. Early jazz in the New Orleans style is called Dixieland; the transformation of jazz from the Dixieland ensemble style to a medium for solo improvisation was pioneered by Louis Armstrong. Traditional Dixieland may still be heard in New Orleans at Preservation Hall, Dixieland Hall, and the New Orleans Jazz Club. Equally distinctive is Cajun music, dominated by the sound of the fiddle and accordion. The French Acadian Music Festival, held in Abbeville, takes place in April.

[43] LIBRARIES AND MUSEUMS
Louisiana was served by 63 public libraries in 1980 and by 4 interregional library systems. In 1977/78, the public library system held 5,749,380 volumes and had a total circulation of 13,142,883. The New Orleans Public Library, with 11 branches and 749,073 books, features a special collection on jazz and folk music, and the Tulane University Library (1,308,725 volumes) has special collections on jazz and Louisiana history. Among the libraries with special black-studies collections are those of Grambling State University, Southern University at Baton Rouge, and Xavier University of Louisiana at New Orleans. The library of Northwestern State University at Natchitoches has special collections on Louisiana history, folklore, Indians, botany, and oral history.

As of 1979, Louisiana had more than 35 museums and historic sites. Leading art museums are the New Orleans Museum of Art, the Gallier House in the city's Vieux Carré district, and the R. W. Norton Art Gallery at Shreveport. The art museum of the Louisiana Arts and Science Center at Baton Rouge is located in the renovated Old Illinois Central Railroad Station. The oldest and largest museum in the state is the Louisiana State Museum, an eight-building historic complex in the Vieux Carré. There is a military museum in Beauregard House at Chalmette National Historical Park, on the site of the Battle of New Orleans, and a Confederate Museum in New Orleans. The Bayou Folk Museum at Cloutierville is in the restored home of author Kate Chopin; the Acadian House Museum at St. Martinsville is located in Longfellow-Evangeline State Park. Among the state's scientific museums are the Lafayette Natural History Museum and Planetarium, the Museum of Geoscience at Louisiana State University in Baton Rouge, and the Grindstone Bluff Museum and Environmental Education Center at Shreveport. Audubon Park and Zoological Gardens are in New Orleans.

[44] COMMUNICATIONS
The second rural free delivery route in the US, and the first in Louisiana, was established on 1 November 1896 at Thibodaux. By 1977, the US Postal Service had approximately 8,600 employees in the state.

As of 31 December 1978 there were 2,729,378 telephones, 2,072,435 residential and 656,943 business. On average, 95% of all households had telephone service. Bell companies owned 94% of the phones, the remainder being owned by 23 independent companies.

As of 1979, the stage had 171 commercial broadcasting stations: 95 AM, 61 FM, and 15 television. Three public television stations in 1979 broadcast an average of 16 hours a day, 7 days a week, reaching about 323,000 households in New Orleans, Baton Rouge, and Monroe. During 1978, 45 cable television systems in 87 communities had 202,063 subscribers.

[45] PRESS
At one time, New Orleans had as many as 9 daily newspapers (4 English, 3 French, 1 Italian, and 1 German), but by 1980 there were only 2, the *Times-Picayune* and *States-Item*, both owned by the Newhouse chain. In 1978, Louisiana had a total of 5 morning

dailies with 414,134 circulation, 21 evening dailies with 430,914, and 14 Sunday papers with 792,194. The following table shows the principal dailies with their 1978 circulations:

AREA	NAME	DAILY	SUNDAY
Baton Rouge	Advocate (m,S)	68,922	106,024
	State Times (e)	42,590	
New Orleans	States-Item (e)	113,973	
	Times-Picayune (m,S)	211,831	316,428
Shreveport	Journal (e)	36,436	
	Times (m,S)	89,587	126,611

Two influential literary magazines originated in the state. The *Southern Review* was founded at LSU in the 1930s by Robert Penn Warren and Cleanth Brooks. The *Tulane Drama Review*, founded in 1955, moved to New York University in 1967 but is still known by its original acronym, *TDR*.

⁴⁶ORGANIZATIONS

Among business or professional organizations with headquarters in Louisiana are the Federated Pecan Growers Associations of the US and the Louisiana Historical Association, in Baton Rouge; the National Rice Growers Association at Branch; the Federal Court Clerks Association, Louisiana Sugar Exchange, and the Southern Forest Products Association, all in New Orleans; and the American Board of Neurological Surgery and American Society of Parasitologists, at Tulane University. Blue Key, a national honor society, has its headquarters in Metairie.

Civil rights groups represented in the state include the National Association for the Advancement of Colored People (NAACP) and the Urban League. Especially active during the 1970s were the local branches of the American Civil Liberties Union, the Louisiana Coalition on Jails and Prisons, and its legal arm, the Southern Prisoners Defense Council, and the Fishermen's and Concerned Citizens Association of Plaquemines Parish, which organized a campaign against the continued domination of the parish by the descendants of Leander Perez, a racist judge who ruled there for 50 years until his death in 1969.

The Invisible Empire, Knights of the Ku Klux Klan, is headquartered in Denham Springs.

⁴⁷TOURISM, TRAVEL, AND RECREATION

As of 1980, approximately 73,500 persons were employed in the Louisiana tourist industry, which had an annual payroll of $460 million. Some 12 million visitors spent an estimated $2 billion in the state in 1977.

New Orleans is one of the major tourist attractions in the US. Known for its fine restaurants, serving such distinctive fare as gumbo, jambalaya, crayfish, and beignets, along with an elaborate French-inspired haute cuisine, New Orleans also offers jazz clubs, the graceful buildings of the French Quarter, and a lavish carnival called Mardi Gras (Fat Tuesday), which drew some 1 million participants in 1980. Beginning on the Wednesday before Shrove Tuesday, parades and balls, staged by private organizations called krewes, are held almost nightly. In other towns, country folk celebrate Mardi Gras in their own no less uproarious manner.

Among the many other annual events that attract visitors to the state are the blessing of the shrimp fleet at the Louisiana Shrimp and Petroleum Festival in Morgan City on Labor Day weekend, and the blessing of the cane fields during the Louisiana Sugar Cane Festival at New Iberia in September. October offers the International Rice Festival (including the Frog Derby) at Crowley, Louisiana Cotton Festival at Ville Platte (with a medieval jousting tournament), the Louisiana Yambilee Festival at Opelousas, and the Louisiana State Fair at Shreveport. Attractions of the Natchitoches Christmas Festival include 170,000 Christmas lights and spectacular fireworks displays. New Orleans has been selected as the site of the 1984 World's Fair.

During 1979/80, an estimated 4,516,000 people also visited 32 state parks and recreation sites totaling 13,903 acres (5,626 hectares). In 1977/78, licenses were issued to 358,811 hunters and 429,151 fishermen.

⁴⁸SPORTS

New Orleans' National Football League team, the Saints, plays in the Louisiana Superdome, a 74,726-seat stadium that hosted the Super Bowl in 1978. Super Bowl championships have also been held in Tulane Stadium. In baseball, Shreveport has a class AA minor league team.

During the 1850s, New Orleans was the horse-racing center of the US, and racing is still popular in the state. The principal tracks are the Louisiana Jockey Club at the Fair Grounds in New Orleans, and Evangeline Downs at Lafayette. Gambling has long been widespread in Louisiana, particularly in steamboat days, when races along the Mississippi drew huge wagers.

From the 1880s to World War I, New Orleans was the nation's boxing capital, and in 1893, the city was the site of perhaps the longest bout in boxing history, between Andy Bowen and Jack Burke, lasting 7 hours and 19 minutes, 110 rounds, and ending in a draw. The NBC New Orleans Open Golf Tournament, held in April, has been won by Billy Casper (twice), Gary Player, and Jack Nicklaus, among others.

In 1935, Tulane inaugurated the Sugar Bowl, an annual New Year's Day event. Since then the LSU Fighting Tigers have been frequent participants in the contest.

During 1978, some 20,000 mentally handicapped persons took part in the Louisiana Special Olympics program.

⁴⁹FAMOUS LOUISIANIANS

Zachary Taylor (b.Virginia, 1784–1850) is the only US president to whom Louisiana can lay claim. Taylor, a professional soldier who made his reputation as an Indian fighter and in the Mexican War, owned a large plantation north of Baton Rouge, which was his residence prior to his election to the presidency in 1848. Edward Douglass White (1845–1921) served first as associate justice of the US Supreme Court and then as chief justice.

Most other Louisianians who have held national office won more fame as state or Confederate officials. John Slidell (b.New York, 1793–1871), an antebellum political leader, also played an important role in Confederate diplomacy. Judah P. Benjamin (b.West Indies, 1811–84), of Jewish lineage, was a US senator before the Civil War; during the conflict he held three posts in the Confederate cabinet, after which he went to England and became a leading barrister. Henry Watkins Allen (b.Virginia, 1820–66) was elected governor of Confederate Louisiana in 1864, after he had been maimed in battle; perhaps the best administrator in the South, he installed a system of near-socialism in Louisiana as the fortunes of the Confederacy waned. During and after the Civil War, many Louisianians won prominence as military leaders. Leonidas Polk (b.North Carolina, 1806–64), the state's first Episcopal bishop, became a lieutenant general in the Confederate Army, dying in the Atlanta campaign. Zachary Taylor's son Richard (b.Kentucky, 1826–79), a sugar planter who also became a Confederate lieutenant general, is noted for his defeat of Nathaniel P. Banks's Union forces in the Red River campaign of 1864. Pierre Gustave Toutant Beauregard (1818–93) attained the rank of full general in the Confederate Army and later served as director of the Louisiana state lottery, one of the state's major sources of revenue at that time. In the modern era, General Claire Chennault (b.Texas, 1893–1958) commanded the famous "Flying Tigers" and then the US 14th Air Force in China during World War II.

Throughout the 20th century, the Longs have been the first family of Louisiana politics. Without question, the most important state officeholder in Louisiana history was Huey P. Long (1893–1935), a latter-day Populist who was elected to the governorship in 1928 and inaugurated a period of social and economic reform; in the process, he made himself very nearly an absolute dictator within Louisiana. After his election to the US Senate, the "King Fish" became a national figure, challenging Franklin D. Roosevelt's New Deal with his "Share the Wealth" plan and flamboyant oratory. Huey's brother Earl K. Long (1895–1960) served three times as governor and was one of the most colorful politicians in the nation. Huey's son, US Senator Russell B. Long (b.1918), was chairman of the Finance Committee—and, consequently, one of the most powerful men in Congress—from 1965 through 1980.

Also prominent in Louisiana history were Robert Cavelier, Sieur de la Salle (b.France, 1643–87), who was the first to claim the region for the French crown; Pierre le Moyne, Sieur d'Iberville (b.Canada, 1661–1706), who commanded the expedition that first established permanent settlements in the lands La Salle had claimed; his brother, Jean Baptiste le Moyne, Sieur de Bienville (b.Canada, 1680–1768), governor of the struggling colony and founder of New Orleans; and Bernardo de Galvez (b.Spain, 1746–86), who, as governor of Spanish Louisiana during the last years of the American Revolution, conquered British-held Florida in a series of brilliant campaigns. William Charles Coles Claiborne (b.Virginia, 1775–1817) was the last territorial and first state governor of Louisiana. The state's first Republican governor, Henry Clay Warmoth (b.Illinois, 1842–1932), came there as a Union officer before the end of the Civil War and was sworn in at age 26. Jean Etienne de Boré (b.France, 1741–1820) laid the foundation of the Louisiana sugar industry by developing a process for granulating sugar from Louisiana cane; Norbert Rillieux (birthplace unknown, 1806–94), a free black man, developed the much more efficient vacuum pan process of refining sugar.

Andrew Victor Schally (b.Poland, 1926), a biochemist on the faculty of the Tulane University School of Medicine, shared the Nobel Prize for medicine in 1977 for his research on hormones. Among other distinguished Louisiana professionals have been historian T. Harry Williams (1909–79), who won the Pulitzer Prize for his biography of Huey Long; architect Henry Hobson Richardson (1838–86); and four doctors of medicine, public health pioneer, Joseph Jones (b.Georgia, 1833–96), surgical innovator Rudolph Matas (1860–1957), surgeon and medical editor Alton V. Ocshner (b.South Dakota, 1896), and heart specialist Michael De Bakey (b.1908).

Louisiana's important writers include George Washington Cable (1844–1925), an early advocate of racial justice; Kate O'Flaherty Chopin (b.Missouri, 1851–1904); playwright and memoirist Lillian Hellman (b.1905); and novelists Truman Capote (b.1924) and Shirley Ann Grau (b.1929), winner of a Pulitzer Prize.

Louisiana has produced two important composers, Ernest Guiraud (1837–92) and Louis Gottschalk (1829–69). Jelly Roll Morton (Ferdinand Joseph La Menthe, 1885–1941) and Sidney Bechet (1897–1959) were important jazz musicians, and Louis "Satchmo" Armstrong (1900–1971) was one of the most prolific jazz innovators and popular performers in the nation. The distinctive rhythms of pianist and singer Professor Longhair (Henry Byrd, 1918–80) were an important influence on popular music.

Louisiana baseball heroes include Hall of Famer Melvin Thomas "Mel" Ott (1909–58) and pitcher Ron Guidry (b.1950). Terry Bradshaw (b.1948), a native of Shreveport, quarterbacked the Super Bowl champion Pittsburgh Steelers during the 1970s. Chess master Paul Morphy (1837–84) was born in New Orleans.

⁵⁰BIBLIOGRAPHY

Dufour, Charles L. *Ten Flags in the Wind: The Story of Louisiana.* New York: Harper and Row, 1967.

Federal Writers' Project. *Louisiana: A Guide to the State.* Rev. ed. New York: Hastings House, 1971 (orig. 1941).

Hair, William Ivy. *Bourbonism and Agrarian Protest in Louisiana, 1877–1900.* Baton Rouge: Louisiana State University Press, 1965.

Jackson, Joy. *New Orleans in the Gilded Age: Politics and Urban Progress, 1880–96.* Baton Rouge: Louisiana State University Press, 1969.

Louisiana, State of. *Executive Budget, 1980/81.* Baton Rouge, 1980.

Louisiana, State of. Secretary of State. *Roster of Officials, 1978.* Baton Rouge, 1978.

Louisiana Almanac, 1979–80. 10th ed. Gretna, La.: Pelican Publishing Co., 1979.

New Orleans, University of. College of Business Administration. Division of Business and Economic Research. *Statistical Abstract of Louisiana.* 6th ed. New Orleans, 1977.

Shugg, Roger W. *Origins of Class Struggle in Louisiana: A Social History of White Farmers and Laborers During Slavery and After, 1840–75.* Baton Rouge: Louisiana State University Press, 1939.

Sitterson, J. Carlyle. *Sugar Country: The Cane Sugar Industry in the South, 1753–1950.* Lexington: University of Kentucky Press, 1953.

Taylor, Joe Gray. *Louisiana: A Bicentennial History.* New York: Norton, 1976.

Taylor, Joe Gray. *Louisiana Reconstructed, 1863–77.* Baton Rouge: Louisiana State University Press, 1974.

Taylor, Joe Gray. *Negro Slavery in Louisiana.* Baton Rouge: Louisiana Historical Association, 1963.

Warmoth, Henry Clay. *War, Politics, and Reconstruction: Stormy Days in Louisiana.* New York: Macmillan, 1930.

Williams, T. Harry. *Huey Long.* New York: Knopf, 1971.

Winters, John D. *The Civil War in Louisiana.* Baton Rouge: Louisiana State University Press, 1963.

MAINE

State of Maine

ORIGIN OF STATE NAME: Either from the French for a historical district of France or from the early use of "main" to distinguish coast from islands. **NICKNAME:** The Pine Tree State. **CAPITAL:** Augusta. **ENTERED UNION:** 15 March 1820 (23d). **SONG:** "State of Maine Song." **MOTTO:** *Dirigo* (I direct). **COAT OF ARMS:** A farmer and sailor support a shield on which are depicted a pine tree, a moose, and water. Under the shield is the name of the state; above it, the state motto and the North Star. **FLAG:** The coat of arms on a blue field, with a yellow fringed border surrounding on three sides. **OFFICIAL SEAL:** Same as the coat of arms. **ANIMAL:** Moose. **BIRD:** Chickadee. **FISH:** Landlocked salmon. **FLOWER:** White pine cone and tassel. **TREE:** Eastern white pine. **INSECT:** Honeybee. **MINERAL:** Tourmaline. **LEGAL HOLIDAYS:** New Year's Day, 1 January; Washington's Birthday, 3d Monday in February; Patriots' Day, 3d Monday in April; Memorial Day, last Monday in May; Independence Day, 4 July; Labor Day, 1st Monday in September; Columbus Day, 2d Monday in October; Veterans Day, 11 November; Thanksgiving Day, 4th Thursday in November and day following; Christmas Day, 25 December. **TIME:** 7 A.M. EST = noon GMT.

¹LOCATION, SIZE, AND EXTENT

Situated in the extreme northeastern corner of the US, Maine is the nation's most easterly state, the largest in New England, and 39th in size among the 50 states.

The total area of Maine is 33,215 sq mi (86,027 sq km), including 30,920 sq mi (80,083 sq km) of land and 2,295 sq mi (5,944 sq km) of inland water. Maine extends 207 mi (333 km) E–W; the maximum N–S extension is 322 mi (518 km).

Maine is bordered on the N by the Canadian provinces of Quebec (with the line passing through the St. Francis River) and New Brunswick (with the boundary formed by the St. John River); on the E by New Brunswick (with the lower eastern boundary formed by the Chiputneticook Lakes and the St. Croix River); on the SE and S by the Atlantic Ocean; and on the W by New Hampshire (with the line passing through the Piscataqua River at the extreme SW) and Quebec.

Hundreds of islands dot Maine's coast. The largest is Mt. Desert Island; others include Deer Isle, Vinalhaven, and Isle au Haut. The total boundary length of Maine is 883 mi (1,421 km).

The state's geographic center is in Piscataquis County, 18 mi (29 km) N of Dover-Foxcroft. The easternmost point of the US is West Quoddy Head, at 66°57′W.

²TOPOGRAPHY

Maine is divided into four main regions: coastal lowlands, piedmont, mountains, and uplands.

The narrow coastal lowlands extend, on average, 10–20 mi (16–32 km) inland from the irregular coastline, but occasionally disappear altogether, as at Mt. Desert Island and on the western shore of Penobscot Bay. Mt. Cadillac on Mt. Desert Island rises abruptly to 1,532 feet (467 meters), the highest elevation on the Atlantic coast north of Rio de Janeiro, Brazil. The transitional hilly belt, or piedmont, broadens from about 30 mi (48 km) wide in the southwestern part of the state to about 80 mi (129 km) in the northeast.

Maine's mountain region, the Longfellow range, is at the northeastern end of the Appalachian Mountain system. This zone, extending into Maine from the western border for about 150 mi (240 km) and averaging about 50 mi (80 km) wide, contains nine peaks over 4,000 feet (1,200 meters), including Mt. Katahdin, which at 5,268 feet (1,606 meters) is the highest point in the state. The summit of Katahdin marks the northern terminus of the 2,000-mi (3,200-km) Appalachian Trail. Maine's up-

lands form a high, relatively flat plateau extending northward beyond the mountains and sloping downward toward the north and east. The eastern part of this zone is the Aroostook potato-farming region; the western part is heavily forested.

Of Maine's more than 2,200 lakes and ponds, the largest are Moosehead Lake, 117 sq mi (303 sq km), and Sebago Lake, 13 mi (21 km) by 10 mi (16 km). Of the more than 5,000 rivers and streams, the Penobscot, Androscoggin, Kennebec, and Saco rivers drain historically and commercially important valleys. The longest river in Maine is the St. John, but it runs for most of its length in the Canadian province of New Brunswick.

³CLIMATE

Maine has three climatic regions: the northern interior zone, comprising roughly the northern half of the state, between Quebec and New Brunswick; the southern interior zone; and the coastal zone. The northern zone is both drier and cooler in all four seasons than either of the other zones, while the coastal zone is more moderate in temperature year-round than the other two.

The annual mean temperature in the northern zone is 41°F (5°C); in the southern interior zone, 44°F (7°C); and in the coastal zone, 46°F (8°C). Record temperatures for the state are –48°F (–44°C), registered at Van Buren on 19 January 1925, and 105°F (41°C) at North Bridgton on 10 July 1911. The mean annual precipitation increases from 40.2 in (102 cm) in the north to 41.5 in (105 cm) in the southern interior and 45.7 in (116 cm) on the coast. Average annual snowfall for the state is 78 in (198 cm).

⁴FLORA AND FAUNA

Maine's forests are largely softwoods, chiefly red and white spruces, balsam fir (*Abies balsamea*), eastern hemlock, and white pine. Important hardwoods include beech, yellow and white birches, sugar and red maples, white oak, black willow, black and white ashes, and American elm, which has fallen victim in recent years to Dutch elm disease. Maine is home to most of the flowers and shrubs common to the north temperate zone, including an important commercial resource, the low-bush blueberry. Maine has 17 rare orchid species, of which 4 are considered threatened.

About 30,000 white-tailed deer are killed by hunters in Maine each year, but the herd does not appear to diminish. Moose hunting was banned in Maine in 1935; however, in 1980, 700 moose-hunting permits were issued for a six-day season. Other common forest animals include bobcat, beaver, muskrat, river otter, mink, fisher, raccoon, red fox, and snowshoe hare. The woodchuck is a conspicuous inhabitant of pastures, meadows, cornfields, and vegetable gardens. Seals, porpoises, and occasionally finback whales are found in coastal waters, along with virtually every variety of North Atlantic fish and shellfish, including the famous Maine lobster. Coastal waterfowl include the osprey, herring and great black-backed gulls, great and double-crested cormorants, and various duck species. Matinicus Rock, a small uninhabited island about 20 mi (32 km) off the coast near the entrance to Penobscot Bay, is the only known North American nesting site of the common puffin, or sea parrot.

The Canada lynx is a rare and threatened species. Endangered animals include the cougar and bald eagle.

5 ENVIRONMENTAL PROTECTION

The Department of Environmental Protection administers laws regulating the selection of commercial and industrial sites, air and water quality, the prevention and cleanup of oil spills, the licensing of oil terminals, the use of coastal wetlands, and mining. The Land Use Regulation Commission, established in 1969, extends the principles of town planning and zoning to Maine's 407 unorganized townships, 55 "plantations," and numerous coastal islands that have no local government and might otherwise be subject to ecologically unsound development.

6 POPULATION

Maine's 1970 census population was 993,663 (38th among the 50 states); the 1980 preliminary census total was 1,123,560.

The area that now comprises the State of Maine was sparsely settled throughout the colonial period. At statehood, Maine had 298,335 residents. The population doubled by 1860, but has remained relatively stagnant since that time. Recent estimates indicate the possibility of an upward shift in the growth rate, however, and Maine's population growth—over 13% between 1970 and 1980—was close to that of the US during the same period.

Maine's population features slightly higher than average concentrations of the very young and the very old. Indicative of shifting demographic patterns during the 1970s was the fact that, in 1976, 13% of Maine residents had lived in the state for five years or less but that 62% had lived in Maine all their lives, with both figures being above the national norms.

The population density for 1978 was 35 per sq mi (14 per sq km); more than half the population lives on less than one-seventh of the land, and almost half the state is virtually uninhabited. Although half of Maine's population is classified as urban, much of the urban population lives in towns and small cities. Among the state's few large cities are Portland, with about 63,000 people in 1978; Lewiston, 42,000; Bangor, 33,000; and Augusta, the capital, 22,500.

7 ETHNIC GROUPS

Maine's population is primarily Yankee, both in its English and Scotch-Irish origins and in its retention of many of the values and folkways of rural New England. The largest minority group consists of French Canadians; 1st- and 2d-generation Canadians accounted for 14% of the population in 1970, but those of French-Canadian origin represent at least 20% of the state's population.

The most notable ethnic issue in Maine during the 1970s was the legal battle of the Penobscot and Passamaquoddy Indians—living on two reservations covering 27,546 acres (11,148 hectares)—to recover 12,500,000 acres (5,059,000 hectares) of treaty lands. A compromise settlement calling for the establishment of a trust fund that would enable the Indians to purchase 300,000 acres (121,000 hectares) of unsettled lands was accepted by the two tribes in March 1980, pending US congressional approval.

As of 1970, Maine had 2,195 Indians, about 3,000 black Americans, and some 1,800 Asians.

8 LANGUAGES

Descendants of the Passamaquoddy and Penobscot Indians of the Algonkian family who inhabited Maine at the coming of the white man still lived there in 1970, and 352 of them claimed an Indian language as their first language. Algonkian place-names abound: Saco, Millinocket, Wiscasset, Kennebec, Skowhegan.

Maine English is celebrated as typical Yankee speech. Final /r/ is absent, a vowel sound between /ah/ and the /a/ in cat appears in car and garden, aunt and calf. Coat and home have a vowel that to outsiders sounds like the vowel in cut. Maple syrup comes from rock or sugar maple trees in a sap or sugar orchard, cottage cheese is curd cheese, and pancakes are fritters.

In 1970, 81% of the native-born residents reported English as their mother tongue, as did 79% of all residents. Speakers of the major first languages were as follows:

	NATIVE-BORN	FOREIGN-BORN
English	770,724	16,196
French	122,908	18,581
Italian	4,494	968
German	3,056	1,372
Polish	2,161	354

The decline of parochial schools and the great increase in numbers of young persons attending college have begun to erode the linguistic and cultural separateness that mark the history of the Franco-American experience in Maine.

9 RELIGIONS

In 1979, Maine had 269,460 Roman Catholics and an estimated 7,970 Jews. Protestant groups had 173,668 known adherents in 1971. The leading denominations were American Baptist Convention, with 41,294; United Church of Christ (Congregationalist), 38,626; United Methodist, 32,984; and Episcopal, 22,342.

10 TRANSPORTATION

Railroad development in Maine, which reached its peak in 1924, has declined rapidly since World War II, and passenger service has been dropped altogether. The Bangor and Aroostook, Maine Central, and Canadian Pacific railroads, along with five minor companies, carried freight on 1,756 mi (2,826 km) of main-line track in 1979.

About three-quarters of all communities and about half the population depend entirely on highway trucking for the overland transportation of freight. In 1978, Maine had 21,797 mi (35,079 km) of roads, 743,317 registered motor vehicles, and 683,290 licensed drivers. The Maine Turnpike and I-95, which coincide between Portland and Kittery, are the major highways.

River traffic has been central to the lumber industry; only since World War II has trucking replaced seasonal log drives downstream from timberlands to the mills, a practice that is now outlawed for environmental reasons. Maine has 10 established seaports, with Portland and Searsport the main depots for overseas shipping. There were 157 airfields (48 public, 109 private) in 1978; Bangor International Airport was the largest and most active, emplaning 142,717 passengers.

11 HISTORY

The first inhabitants of Maine—dating from 3000 to 1000 BC—are known to archaeologists as the Red Paint People because of the red ocher that has been found in their graves. This Paleolithic group had evidently disappeared long before the arrival of the Algonkian-speaking Abnaki (meaning "living at the sunrise"), or Wabanaki. Just at the time of European settlement, an intertribal war and a disastrous epidemic of smallpox swept away many of the Abnaki, some of whom had begun peaceful contacts with the English. After that, most Indian contacts with Europeans were with the French.

The first documented visit by a European to the Maine coast was that of Giovanni da Verrazano during his voyage of 1524, but one may infer from the record that the Abnaki he met there had encountered white men before. Sometime around 1600, English expeditions began fishing the Gulf of Maine regularly.

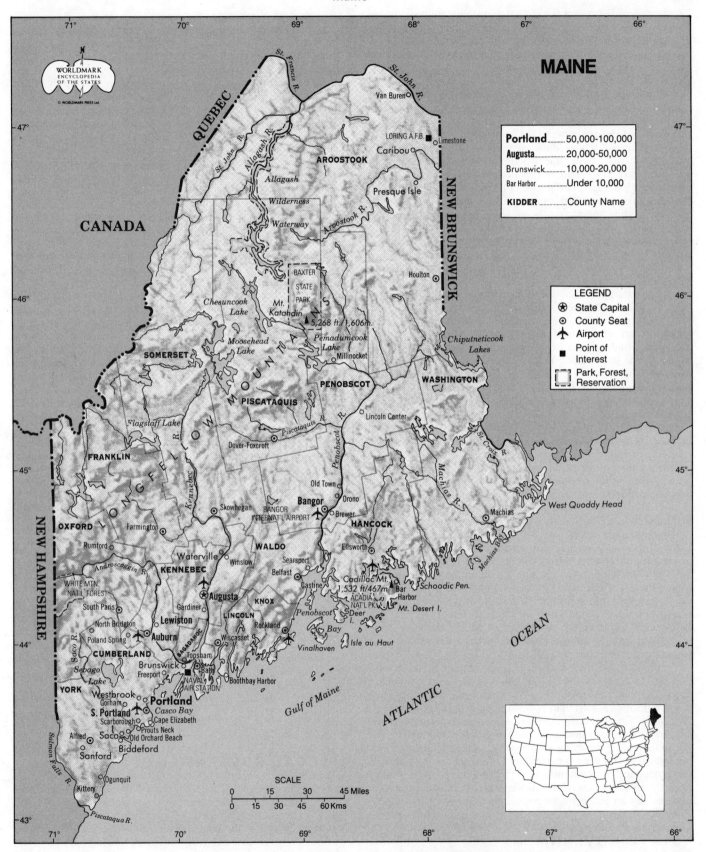

MAINE

Portland	50,000-100,000
Augusta	20,000-50,000
Brunswick	10,000-20,000
Bar Harbor	Under 10,000
KIDDER	County Name

LEGEND
⊛ State Capital
⊙ County Seat
✈ Airport
■ Point of Interest
⬚ Park, Forest, Reservation

SCALE
0   15   30   45 Miles
0   15   30   45   60 Kms

See US political: front cover N1; physical: back cover N1.

LOCATION: 43°04' to 47°28'N; 66°57' to 71°07'W. **BOUNDARIES**: Canadian line, 481 mi (774 km); Atlantic Ocean coastline, 228 mi (367 km); New Hampshire line, 174 mi (280 km).

The first recorded attempts to found permanent colonies, by the French on an island in the St. Croix River in 1604 and by the English at Sagadahoc in 1607, both failed. By 1630, however, there were permanent English settlements on several islands and at nearly a dozen spots along the coast.

The first grant of Maine lands was to Sir Ferdinando Gorges from the Council for New England, a joint-stock company that received and made royal grants of New England territory and which Gorges himself dominated. He and Captain John Mason received the territory between the Merrimack River (in present-day New Hampshire and Massachusetts) and Kennebec River in 1622. Seven years later, the two grantees divided their land at the Piscataqua River, and Gorges became sole proprietor of the "Province of Maine." The source of the name is not quite clear. It seems likely that some connection with the historical French province of the same name was intended, but the name was also used to distinguish the mainland from the islands.

Sir Ferdinando's various schemes for governing the territory and promoting a feudal-style settlement never worked. A few years after his death in 1647, the government of the Massachusetts Bay Colony began absorbing the small Maine settlements. Massachusetts purchased the title to Maine from the Gorges heirs in 1677, and Maine became a district of Massachusetts with the issuance of a new royal charter in 1691. During the first hundred years of settlement, Maine's economy was based entirely on fishing, trading, and exploitation of the forests. The origin of the Maine shipbuilding industry, the early settlement of the interior parts of southern Maine, and the beginning of subsistence farming all date from about the time that New England's supply center of white-pine masts for the Royal Navy moved from Portsmouth, N.H., to Falmouth (now the city of Portland).

The first naval encounter of the Revolutionary War occurred in Machias Bay, when, on 12 June 1775, angry colonials captured the British armed schooner *Margaretta*. On 8 October 1775, a British naval squadron shelled and set fire to Falmouth. Wartime Maine was the scene of two anti-British campaigns, both of which ended in failure: an expedition through the Maine woods in the fall of 1775 intended to drive the British out of Quebec, and a disastrous 1779 expedition in which a Massachusetts amphibious force, failing to dislodge British troops at Castine, scuttled many of its own ships near the mouth of the Penobscot River.

The idea of separation from Massachusetts began surfacing as early as 1785, but popular pressure for such a movement did not mount until the War of 1812. The overwhelming vote for statehood in an 1819 referendum was a victory for William King, who would become the first governor, and his fellow Jeffersonian Democratic-Republicans. Admission of Maine as a free state was joined with the admission of Missouri as a slave state in the Missouri Compromise of 1820.

Textile mills and shoe factories came to Maine between 1830 and 1860 as part of the industrialization of Massachusetts. After the Civil War, the revolution in papermaking that substituted wood pulp for rags brought a vigorous new industry to Maine. By 1900, Maine was one of the leading papermaking states in the US, and the industry continues to dominate the state today. The rise of tourism, the wartime contributions of the Maine shipbuilding industry, and the concurrent and often conflicting concerns for economic development and environmental protection have been the main themes of the 20th century. Politically, the state has pursued an independent course, though one of its leaders, Edmund Muskie, has played an influential role in the national Democratic Party since the 1960s.

12 STATE GOVERNMENT
The Maine constitution, based on that of Massachusetts but incorporating a number of more democratic features, remains much the same as when it was put into effect in 1820.

The bicameral legislature, consisting of a senate of from 31 to 35 members, depending on the number of districts (33 in 1980), and a 151-member house of representatives, convenes bienially in joint session to elect a seven-member Governor's Council, the secretary of state, attorney general, and state treasurer. All legislators serve two-year terms.

The governor, who serves a four-year term, is the only official elected statewide. All gubernatorial appointments, including judicial appointments, and the granting of reprieves, commutations, and pardons require the approval of the Governor's Council. A gubernatorial veto may be overridden by a two-thirds vote of members present and voting in each legislative chamber.

The state constitution may be amended by a two-thirds vote of the legislature and a majority vote at the next general election. To vote in Maine, one must be a US citizen and at least 18 years of age; there is no minimum residency requirement.

13 POLITICAL PARTIES
Maine's two major political parties are the Democratic and the Republican, each affiliated with the national party. Minor parties have not figured in Maine elections in this century, although an independent candidate, James B. Longley, beat the candidates of both major parties in the gubernatorial election of 1974.

During the early decades of statehood, Jeffersonian and Jacksonian Democrats remained in power quite consistently. In 1854, however, reformers rallied around the new Republican Party, which dominated Maine politics for the next hundred years. Maine's strong Republican tradition continued into the middle and late 1950s, when Margaret Chase Smith distinguished herself in the US Senate as a leader of national importance. The rise of Democrat Edmund S. Muskie, elected governor in 1954 and 1956 and to the first of four terms in the US Senate in 1960, signaled a change in Maine's political complexion. Muskie appealed personally to many traditionally Republican voters, but his party's resurgence was also the result of demographic changes, especially an increase in the proportion of French-Canadian voters. Of Maine's 691,697 registered voters in 1978, 34% were Democrats, 32% Republicans, and 34% unaffiliated.

Maine Presidential Vote by Major Political Parties, 1948–80

YEAR	ELECTORAL VOTE	MAINE WINNER	DEMOCRAT	REPUBLICAN
1948	5	Dewey (R)	111,916	150,234
1952	5	*Eisenhower (R)	118,806	232,353
1956	5	*Eisenhower (R)	102,468	249,238
1960	5	Nixon (R)	181,159	240,608
1964	4	*Johnson (D)	262,264	118,701
1968	4	Humphrey (D)	217,312	169,254
1972	4	*Nixon (R)	160,584	256,458
1976	4	Ford (R)	232,279	236,320
1980	4	*Reagan (R)	220,974	238,522

*Won US presidential election.

14 LOCAL GOVERNMENT
The principal units of local government in 1977 were the 24 cities and 475 towns. As is customary in New England, the basic instrument of town government is the annual town meeting, with an elective board of selectmen supervising town affairs between meetings; some of the larger towns employ full-time town managers. There is no local government in roughly half the state. Maine's 16 counties function primarily as judicial districts.

15 STATE SERVICES
The State Board of Education and its chief executive officer, the commissioner of education, administer the public education laws.

The Department of Transportation, established in 1972, includes bureaus responsible for highways, aviation, and railroads, the Maine Port Authority, the State Ferry Advisory Board, and the Bureau of Waterways, which operates three coastal-island ferry systems.

Various agencies responsible for health and social welfare were combined into the Department of Human Services in 1975. The Maine State Housing Authority, established in 1969, provides construction loans and technical assistance, and conducts surveys of the state's housing needs. The Commission on Governmental Ethics and Election Practices, an advisory and investigative body, was created in 1975 to serve as a watchdog over the legislature.

¹⁶JUDICIAL SYSTEM

The highest state court is the supreme judicial court, with a chief justice and six associate justices appointed by the governor and his council for seven-year terms, as are all other state judges. The supreme judicial court has statewide appellate jurisdiction in all civil and criminal matters. The superior court, which has original jurisdiction in cases involving trial by jury, is organized into regions by counties. District courts, whose jurisdictions cut across county lines and which sit in various designated towns and cities, hear petty criminal cases and a limited number of civil cases. A probate court judge is elected in each county. Maine's crime rate is far below the national average.

¹⁷ARMED FORCES

Major US military installations in Maine include Loring Air Force Base in Limestone, housing units of the Strategic Air Command; the Portsmouth Naval Shipyard in Kittery, site of an important Atlantic coast nuclear submarine repair facility; the Naval Air Station at Brunswick, home of a wing of antisubmarine patrol squadrons; and a large Coast Guard station in Portland that is home port for oceangoing cutters. Defense Department personnel in Maine totaled 8,603 in mid-1978. In that year, state firms received $341 million in defense contracts.

There were 153,000 veterans of US military service living in Maine as of 30 September 1979, including 4,000 veterans of World War I, 67,000 of World War II, 26,000 of the Korean conflict, and 44,000 from the Viet-Nam era. A total of $122 million in veterans' benefits were paid in 1977/78.

The Maine Army and Air National Guard consisted of 4,000 personnel in 1978. State and local police totaled 2,314 in 1977.

¹⁸MIGRATION

Throughout the colonial, Revolutionary, and early national periods, Maine's population grew primarily by immigration from elsewhere in New England. About 1830, after agriculture in the state had passed its peak, Maine farmers and woodsmen began moving west. Europeans and French Canadians came to the state, but not in sufficient numbers to offset this steady emigration.

Net losses from migration have continued through most of this century. Between 1940 and 1970, for example, the net loss was 163,000. However, preliminary census figures for 1970–77 disclosed a reversal of this tendency, with a net gain for the period estimated at 51,000.

¹⁹INTERGOVERNMENTAL COOPERATION

Regional agreements in which Maine participates include the Northern New England Medical Needs Compact, which promotes regional cooperation in planning medical care (especially for rural areas), and the Maine–New Hampshire School District Compact, which authorizes interstate public school districts. Maine also takes part in the Atlantic States Marine Fisheries Compact, New England Higher Education Compact, New England Interstate Water Pollution Control Compact, New England Police Compact, Northeastern Forest Fire Protection Compact, and New England Radiological Health Protection Compact.

In 1978/79, Maine received $508.1 million in federal aid, of which $45.5 was general revenue sharing.

²⁰ECONOMY

Maine's greatest economic strengths, as they have been since the beginning of European settlement, are its forests and waters, yielding wood products, waterpower, fisheries, and ocean commerce. Today, the largest industry by far is paper manufacturing, for which both forests and waterpower are essential.

Maine's greatest current economic weakness is its limited access to the national transportation network that links major production and manufacturing centers with large metropolitan markets. On the other hand, this relative isolation, combined with the state's traditional natural assets, has contributed to Maine's attractiveness as a place for tourism and recreation. Tourism accounted for 6% of the gross state product in 1976, trailing manufacturing (26%), other service industries (25%), and farming and fishing (8%), among other sectors.

²¹INCOME

Personal income in 1978 was $6,333 per capita, 46th in the US and the lowest in New England. Total personal income was $6.9 billion in 1978, when the state's ratio of $223,000 in income per sq mi of land area ($86,000 per sq km) was among the lowest in the US. Median family income in 1975 was $11,839 (43d in the US). During that same year, 12% of all state residents were below the federal poverty level.

²²LABOR

Maine's civilian labor force totaled 473,000 in 1978; about 59% of the work force was male and 41% female. The unemployment rate was 6.1%; of the 29,000 who were unemployed, only half received unemployment insurance.

A federal census of workers covered by unemployment insurance in March 1977 revealed the following nonfarm employment pattern in Maine:

	ESTABLISH-MENTS	EMPLOYEES	ANNUAL PAYROLL ('000)
Agricultural services, forestry, fishing	315	1,093	$ 13,495
Mining	24	224	3,331
Contract construction	3,104	14,712	187,390
Manufacturing	1,923	100,952	1,075,413
Transportation, public utilities	1,057	13,582	172,460
Wholesale trade	1,582	17,504	190,314
Retail trade	6,945	58,543	389,041
Finance, insurance, real estate	1,793	15,695	152,728
Services	6,480	59,672	453,074
Other	251	155	2,431
TOTALS	23,474	282,132	$2,639,677

Among the workers not covered by this survey are government employees, of whom Maine had 80,300 in 1978.

In 1978, the average Maine production worker earned $4.91 per hour for 40.2 hours of work, for a weekly total of $197, 26% below the US norm. Average weekly earnings for a Maine industrial worker ranked 43d in the US, lowest for any northern state except Rhode Island.

Labor union membership among Maine workers in nonagricultural jobs in 1976 amounted to 67,000, or 18% of those working in such jobs. Another 25,000 workers belonged to employee associations.

²³AGRICULTURE

Maine's total farm income in 1978 was $414 million (39th in the US). There were 7,600 farms and an estimated 1,710,000 acres (692,000 hectares) under cultivation in 1976. Maine's net income per farm is the highest in New England and in 1976 was more than double the national average.

Potatoes, grown primarily in Aroostook County, are by far the most important crop. Maine is one of the three largest potato-growing states in the US, producing 28,750,000 hundredweight in 1979. Other crops included commercial apples, 86,016,00 lb; oats, 2,400,000 bushels; and hay, 385,000 tons. Maine is also a leading producer of blueberries.

²⁴ANIMAL HUSBANDRY

Livestock products account for about three-fifths of Maine's agricultural income.

Maine's production of eggs, poultry, and dairy products grew steadily during the 1970s. By 1979, egg production exceeded 1.9 billion, yielding $110.3 million in gross income. During the same year, 87.8 million broilers yielded a gross income of $92.2 million; sales of 5.2 million chickens brought more than $4.3 million. South-central Maine is the leading poultry region.

There were 131,000 cattle and calves on Maine farms at the end of 1979, when production totaled 26.3 million lb worth $14.1 million. The milk output, 638 million lb, was valued at $83.6 million.

²⁵FISHING

Fishing has been important to the economy of Maine since its settlement. In 1978, 190.2 million lb of finfish and shellfish worth $68.8 million were landed at Maine ports. The most valuable Maine fishery product is the lobster, which accounts for about half the value of the total catch. Flounder, halibut, scallops, and shrimp are also caught. The state sought during the late 1970s to conserve and restore Atlantic salmon stocks in Maine's inland waterways.

Shipments of fishery products in 1977 included $50.8 million in canned and cured seafood and $32.2 million in fresh or frozen packaged fish.

²⁶FORESTRY

Maine's 17,749,000 acres (7,183,000 hectares) of forests in 1977 covered 90% of the state's land area, the largest percentage of any state in the US. About 16,894,000 acres (6,837,000 hectares) are classified as commercial timberland, 98% of it privately owned, and much of that by a few large paper companies. Timber operations in 1977 produced 851 million board feet of softwood lumber, 161 million board feet of hardwood lumber, and 2.8 million cords of pulpwood; about 30% of the annual timber cut is exported to other New England states and Canada. Forest growth exceeds 7 million cords a year.

²⁷MINING

The value of Maine's mineral output in 1978 was only $40 million (47th in the US). Quartz, feldspar, mica, graphite, asbestos, and gemstones such as tourmaline, beryl, amethyst, garnet, and topaz are mined, along with such metals as copper and zinc; granite and limestone are quarried. The 1979 mineral output included sand and gravel, 10,509,000 tons; stone, 1,300,000 tons; and clays, 101,000 tons.

²⁸ENERGY AND POWER

For more than three centuries, Maine has been exploiting its enormous waterpower potential. In recent decades, however, waterpower has been surpassed in importance by oil-fired steam plants and, most recently, by nuclear power. Since 1972, the Maine Yankee Atomic Power Co. station in Wiscasset has been generating nearly half of the state's electric power; in a referendum on 23 September 1980, voters decided that the station should remain open and that future nuclear power development should be allowed.

Installed generating capacity at the end of 1977 totaled 1,745,000 kw, consisting of 347,000 kw in hydroelectric plants, 460,000 kw in conventional steam plants, 830,000 kw in the Wiscasset nuclear plant, 45,000 kw in gas turbines, and 63,000 kw in internal-combustion plants. Power production in 1978 totaled 11.1 billion kwh.

All fuel oil and coal must be imported; natural gas, piped into the southwest corner of the state, is available in Portland and the Lewiston-Auburn area.

The Office of Energy Resources provides tax incentives and research and development grants to encourage use of solar pow-

er and energy conservation. The late 1970s saw some Maine homeowners switch to wood for heating as an alternative to oil.

²⁹INDUSTRY

Manufacturing in Maine has always been related to the forests. From the 17th century through much of the 19th, the staples of Maine industry were shipbuilding and lumber; today they are papermaking and wood products.

Maine has the largest paper-production capacity of any state in the nation. There are large papermills and pulpmills in more than a dozen towns and cities; major companies include International Paper, Boise-Cascade, Scott Paper, US Gypsum, and Great Northern Nekoosa. Wood-related industries—paper, lumber, wood products, and furniture—accounted for 43% of the value of Maine's manufactures in 1977, and paper alone, valued at $1.6 billion, represented one-third of the total.

Value added by manufacture in 1977 exceeded $2.3 billion, of which paper and paper products contributed 29%, leather and leather products 12%, and food and food products 9%. The following table shows value added by manufacture for selected industries in 1972 and 1977:

	1972	1977
Papermill products	$276,500,000	$520,900,000
Leather footwear	145,000,000	220,400,000
Textile mill products	89,800,000	168,000,000
Logs	48,800,000	138,700,000
Pulpmill products	NA	40,700,000

³⁰COMMERCE

In 1972, Maine's wholesale trade totaled $1.8 billion. Retail sales exceeded $3.6 billion in 1977, with grocery stores accounting for 23%, automotive dealers 20%, department stores 8%, eating and drinking places 7%, gasoline service stations 7%, and fuel oil dealers 6%.

Maine conducts substantial foreign commerce through Portland and Searsport. In 1977, Portland exported 27,300 tons of cargo (two-thirds of it wood pulp) and imported 18,795,996 tons (99.9% of it oil). In the same year, Searsport exported 57,501 tons of cargo (two-thirds potatoes) and imported a total of 1,075,835 tons of oil (81%), salt, gypsum, caustic soda, tapioca, and bauxite. The value of Maine's own exports amounted to $255 million of manufactured goods in 1976 and $28 million in agricultural products in 1976/77.

³¹CONSUMER PROTECTION

The Bureau of Consumer Protection was established in 1974 to protect state residents from unjust and misleading consumer credit practices, particularly in relation to the federal Truth-in-Lending Act. The bureau also administers state laws regulating home-repair finance, collection agencies, and insurance-premium finance companies.

³²BANKING

At the end of 1977, Maine had 70 state-chartered trust companies, savings and loan associations, and savings banks with 272 branches and combined assets of $4.2 billion, and 28 state-chartered credit unions with assets of $58 million. In addition, there were 17 national banks with 119 branches and assets exceeding $1.1 billion, 8 federal savings and loan associations with assets of $178 million, and 151 federal credit unions with assets of $239 million. Federal and state savings and loan associations held a combined total of $507.4 million in outstanding mortgage loans at the end of 1978.

³³INSURANCE

Four life insurance companies were licensed to do business in Maine in 1978, when 1,876,000 policies worth $11.4 billion were in force. The average coverage per family, $28,300, was the 5th lowest in the US, and the lowest of any northeastern state. Property and liability insurers wrote $356.3 million in premiums in 1978, of which 37% was for automotive coverage.

34 SECURITIES

There are no securities exchanges in Maine.

35 PUBLIC FINANCE

Maine's biennial budget is prepared by the Bureau of the Budget, within the Department of Finance and Administration, and submitted by the governor to the legislature for consideration. The fiscal year extends from 1 July to 30 June. The following table shows revenues and expenditures for 1978/79:

REVENUES	
Sales and use tax	$ 197,783,000
Individual income tax	112,512,000
Other taxes	269,935,000
Federal revenues	340,104,000
Other receipts	100,237,000
TOTAL	$1,020,571,000
EXPENDITURES	
Human services	$ 310,556,000
Education and culture	296,253,000
General government	141,469,000
Transportation	135,654,000
Manpower	68,740,000
Natural resources	38,054,000
Other outlays	30,937,000
TOTAL	$1,021,663,000

As of mid-1977, the outstanding state and local government debt exceeded $1 billion; the debt per capita was $948, 20% below the national average.

36 TAXATION

The leading source of tax revenue as of 1980 was a sales and use tax of 5%. The individual income tax ranged from 1% of the first $2,000 of taxable income to 10% of income over $25,000; the corporate income tax rates were 4.95% of the first $25,000 and 6.93% on net income in excess of $25,000. Other state levies include taxes on utilities, inheritance and estate taxes, liquor taxes, and taxes on specific agricultural and fishery products. Counties do not assess taxes, but they do make levies on municipalities and unorganized territories to meet county budgets. Real and personal property taxes and excise taxes on motor vehicles, aircraft, and mobile homes are the sources of local revenue.

Maine's total federal tax burden was $1.3 billion in 1975/76, when federal expenditures in the state reached nearly $1.7 billion. In 1977, state residents filed 445,959 federal income tax returns, paying $527 million in tax.

37 ECONOMIC POLICY

The Maine Guarantee Authority encourages industrial and recreational projects by insuring mortgage loans, authorizing municipalities to issue revenue bonds, and making direct loans for industrial facilities to local development corporations. State law exempts Maine food products from personal property taxes while they are awaiting shipment out of state, and exempts new or newly developed gold, silver, and base-metal mines from real property taxes for 10 years. In addition, the state exempts certified air or water pollution control facilities from sales and use taxes, and certified industrial waste disposal systems from real property taxes. A corporate franchise tax was repealed as of 31 December 1974, and the personal property tax on business inventories as of 1 April 1977.

38 HEALTH

The state of public health in Maine is generally favorable. As of 1969–71, life expectancy—70.93 years—ranked 21st in the US and was slightly above the national average for both males (67.24) and females (74.85). On the other hand, the death rate is somewhat higher than the US norm, reflecting a higher than average population in the upper age levels.

The birthrate in 1977 was 14.9 per 1,000 population; the death rate, 9.3. The infant mortality rate for whites in 1977 was 9.6 per 1,000 live births (the nonwhite population was too small for accurate statistical sampling). During 1977/78, 3,300 legal abortions were performed. Death rates for the leading causes of death were heart disease, 371 per 1,000 population; cancer, 201.

In 1978, Maine had 53 hospitals, with 7,324 beds. Hospital personnel included 3,280 registered nurses and 1,320 licensed practical nurses. The average cost of hospital care in 1977 was $186 per day and $1,397 per stay. Licensed medical personnel included 1,684 physicians in 1977 and 489 dentists in 1979.

39 SOCIAL WELFARE

Despite Maine's relatively low personal income and large proportion of residents below the poverty level, welfare payments per capita generally fall short of the national norms. In 1978, for example, payments of $52 million to Maine's 59,700 recipients of aid to families with dependent children resulted in an average monthly payment of $213 per family, compared with a national average of $254. During the same year, 94,000 Maine residents received food stamps at a federal cost of $33.1 million, and 146,000 students took part in the school lunch program, costing $10.6 million.

Social Security payments totaled $447.9 million in 1977. Supplemental Security Income benefits reached nearly $25 million in 1978, when payments for unemployment insurance were $49 million and expenditures on vocational rehabilitation totaled $5.5 million. Workers' compensation payments were $33.4 million in 1977.

40 HOUSING

Housing for Maine families has improved substantially since 1960, when the federal census categorized 57,000 of Maine's 364,650 housing units as deteriorated or dilapidated. Between 1960 and 1970, about 100,000 new units were built. Over 12% of all occupied units in 1970 lacked full plumbing, however.

Of an estimated 401,488 housing units in 1977, 261,976 were single-family units, 101,962 were in multifamily dwellings, and 37,550 were mobile homes. About one-sixth of all Maine homes are for seasonal rather than year-round use.

41 EDUCATION

Maine has a long and vigorous tradition of education at all levels, both public and private. Adult illiteracy in 1970 was 0.7%, well below the national average. Median educational attainment for the adult population in 1976 was 12.5 years.

In 1977/78, Maine had 761 public schools with a total enrollment of 242,203; the private school enrollment was 17,327.

Since 1968, the state's eight-campus system of state colleges and universities has been incorporated into a single University of Maine, which in 1976 had 18,010 full-time undergraduate students. The original and chief campus is at Orono; the other major element in the system is the University of Southern Maine at Portland and Gorham. The state also operates the Maine Maritime Academy at Castine and five vocational-technical institutes. Of the state's 19 private colleges and professional schools, Bowdoin College in Brunswick, Colby College in Waterville, and Bates College in Lewiston are the best known.

42 ARTS

Maine has long held an attraction for painters and artists, Winslow Homer and Andrew Wyeth among them. The state abounds in summer theaters, the oldest and most famous of which is at Ogunquit. The Portland Symphony is Maine's leading orchestra.

43 LIBRARIES AND MUSEUMS

In 1977, Maine public libraries had 3,716,951 volumes and a combined circulation of 5,015,872. Leading libraries and their holdings in 1977 included the Maine State Library at Augusta (494,867 volumes), the University of Maine at Orono (525,000), Bowdoin College at Brunswick (480,000), and the University of Southern Maine at Gorham (190,000).

Maine has at least 100 museums and historic sites. The Maine State Museum in Augusta houses collections in history, natural history, anthropology, marine studies, mineralogy, science, and technology. The privately supported Maine Historical Society in Portland maintains a research library and the Wadsworth-Longfellow House, the boyhood home of Henry Wadsworth Longfellow. The largest of several maritime museums is in Bath.

44 COMMUNICATIONS

In 1978 there were 769,565 telephones, 592,796 residential and 176,769 business. On average, virtually every household had telephone service.

Maine had 65 commercial radio stations (37 AM, 28 FM) during the same year, along with 7 commercial television stations. Educational television stations broadcast from Lewiston, Orono, Poland Spring, and Presque Isle. At the end of 1978, 34 cable televison systems served 92,959 subscribers in 75 communities.

45 PRESS

Maine had nine daily newspapers with a total circulation of 284,122 in 1978. The most widely read newspaper was the *Bangor Daily News* (mornings, 81,770), though its circulation was surpassed by the combined circulations of the *Portland Press Herald* (mornings, 55,307) and *Evening Express* (30,245), both published daily in Portland by the Guy Gannet Publishing Co. The same newspaper chain also published Maine's only Sunday newspaper, the *Maine Sunday Telegram* (115,000), and the *Central Maine Morning Sentinel* of Waterville.

There are some 35 general news weeklies, including the widely read, environmentally conscious *Maine Times* of Topsham. The most important monthly magazine is *Down East*, famous for its salty articles and stunning pictures of coastal Maine.

46 ORGANIZATIONS

Besides state chapters and branches of practically all the major national organizations, Maine has scores of clubs, societies, and associations of its own, including the Maine Historical Society, Maine Potato Council, Slavophile Society, Pro Life Education Association, and Maine Federation of Humane Societies. An organization with more than a statewide following is the International Backpackers Association, at Lincoln Center.

47 TOURISM, TRAVEL, AND RECREATION

Calling itself "Vacationland," the State of Maine is a year-round resort destination. Expenditures by tourists were estimated at $454.6 million in 1978, when most visitors came from New England (56%), the middle Atlantic states (20%), and Canada (8%).

Most out-of-state visitors continue to come in the summer, when the southern coast offers sandy beaches, icy surf, and several small harbors for sailing and saltwater fishing. Northeastward the scenery becomes more rugged and spectacular, and sailing and hiking are the primary activities. Hundreds of lakes, ponds, rivers, and streams offer opportunites for freshwater bathing, boating, and fishing. Whitewater canoeing lures the adventurous along the Allagash Wilderness Waterway in northern Maine. Maine has always attracted hunters, especially during the fall deer season. Wintertime recreation facilities include nearly 60 ski areas and countless opportunities for cross-country skiing and snowshoeing. In 1977/78, Maine issued licenses to 226,612 hunters and 251,689 fishermen.

48 SPORTS

The Maine Mariners of the American Hockey League play on their home ice at the Cumberland County Civic Center in Portland. Maine has one important racetrack for Thoroughbreds at Scarborough Downs, and harness racing is a popular attraction at racetracks and fairgrounds throughout the state.

49 FAMOUS "DOWN MAINERS"

The highest federal officeholder born in Maine was Hannibal Hamlin (1809–91), the nation's first Republican vice president, under Abraham Lincoln. James G. Blaine (b.Pennsylvania, 1830–93), a lawyer and politician, served 13 years as a US repre-

sentative from Maine and a term in the Senate; on his third try, he won the Republican presidential nomination in 1884 but lost to Grover Cleveland, later serving as secretary of state (1889–92) under Benjamin Harrison. Edmund S. Muskie (b.1914), leader of the Democratic revival in Maine in the 1950s, followed two successful terms as governor with 21 years in the Senate, until appointed secretary of state by President Jimmy Carter in 1980.

Other conspicuous state and national officeholders have included Rufus King (1755–1827), a member of the Continental Congress and Constitutional Convention and US minister to Great Britain; William King (1768–1852), leader of the movement for Maine statehood and the state's first governor; Thomas Bracket Reed (1839–1902), longtime speaker of the US House of Representatives; and Margaret Chase Smith (b.1897), who served longer in the US Senate—24 years—than any other woman.

Names prominent in Maine's colonial history include those of Sir Ferdinando Gorges (b.England, 1566?–1647), the founder and proprietor of the colony; Sir William Phips (1651–95), who became the first American knight for his recovery of a Spanish treasure, later serving as royal governor of Massachusetts; and Sir William Pepperrell (1696–1759), who led the successful New England expedition against Louisburg in 1745, for which he became the first native American baronet.

Maine claims an unusual number of well-known reformers and humanitarians: Dorothea Lynde Dix (1802–87), who led the movement for hospitals for the insane; Elijah Parish Lovejoy (1802–37), an abolitionist killed while defending his printing press from a proslavery mob in St. Louis, Mo.; Neal Dow (1804–97), who drafted and secured passage of the Maine prohibition laws of 1846 and 1851, later served as a Civil War general, and ran for president on the Prohibition Party ticket in 1880; and Harriet Beecher Stowe (b.Connecticut, 1811–96), whose *Uncle Tom's Cabin* (1852) was written in Maine.

Other important writers include poet Henry Wadsworth Longfellow (1807–82), born in Portland while Maine was still part of Massachusetts; humorist Artemus Ward (Charles Farrar Browne, 1834–67); Sarah Orne Jewett (1849–1909), novelist and short-story writer; Kate Douglas Wiggin (1856–1923), author of *Rebecca of Sunnybrook Farm*; Kenneth Roberts (1885–1957), historical novelist; and Robert Peter Tristram Coffin (1892–1955), poet, essayist, and novelist. Edwin Arlington Robinson (1869–1935) and Edna St. Vincent Millay (1892–1950) were both Pulitzer Prize–winning poets, and novelist Marguerite Yourcenar (b.Belgium, 1903), a resident of Mt. Desert Island, became in 1980 the first woman ever elected to the Académie Française. Winslow Homer (b.Massachusetts, 1836–1910) had a summer home at Prouts Neck, where he painted many of his seascapes.

50 BIBLIOGRAPHY

Bearse, Ray, ed. *Maine: A Guide to the Vacation State*. 2d ed., rev. Boston: Houghton Mifflin, 1969.

Clark, Charles E. *Maine: A Bicentennial History*. New York: Norton, 1977.

Isaacson, Dorris, ed. *Maine: A Guide "Down East."* 2d ed. Rockland: Courier-Gazette, Inc., for the Maine League of Historical Societies and Museums, 1970 (orig. 1937).

Maine, State of. State Development Office. *Facts about Industrial Maine*. Augusta, 1979.

Morris, Gerald E., ed. *The Maine Bicentennial Atlas*. Portland: Maine Historical Society, 1976.

Osborn, William C. *The Paper Plantation*. New York: Grossman, 1974.

Rich, Louise Dickinson. *State O'Maine*. New York: Harper and Row, 1964.

Rowe, William H. *The Maritime History of Maine*. New York: Norton, 1948.

Saltonstall, Richard. *Maine Pilgrimage: The Search for an American Way of Life*. Boston: Little, Brown, 1974.

MARYLAND

State of Maryland

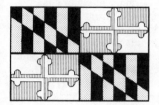

ORIGIN OF STATE NAME: Named for Henrietta Maria, queen consort of King Charles I of England. **NICKNAME**: The Old Line State; Free State. **CAPITAL**: Annapolis. **ENTERED UNION**: 28 April 1788 (7th). **SONG**: "Maryland, My Maryland." **MOTTO**: *Fatti maschii, parole femine* (Manly deeds, womanly words). **FLAG**: Bears the quartered arms of the Calvert and Crossland families (the paternal and maternal families of the founders of Maryland). **OFFICIAL SEAL**: Reverse: A shield bearing the arms of the Calverts and Crosslands is surmounted by an earl's coronet and a helmet and supported by a farmer and fisherman. The state motto (originally that of the Calverts) appears on a scroll below. The circle is surrounded by the Latin legend *Scuto bonæ voluntatis tuæ coronasti nos*, meaning "With the shield of thy favor hast thou compassed us," and "1632," the date of Maryland's first charter. Obverse: Lord Baltimore is seen as a knight in armor on a charger. The surrounding inscription, in Latin, means "Cecilius, Absolute Lord of Maryland and Avalon [New Foundland], Baron of Baltimore." **BIRD**: Baltimore oriole. **FISH**: Rockfish. **FLOWER**: Black-eyed Susan. **TREE**: White oak. **DOG**: Chesapeake Bay retriever. **INSECT**: Baltimore checkerspot butterfly. **SPORT**: Jousting. **LEGAL HOLIDAYS**: New Year's Day, 1 January; Birthday of Martin Luther King, Jr., 15 January; Lincoln's Birthday, 12 February; Washington's Birthday, 3d Monday in February; Maryland Day, 25 March; Good Friday, March or April; Memorial Day, 30 May; Independence Day, 4 July; Labor Day, 1st Monday in September; Defenders' Day, 12 September; Columbus Day, 12 October; Election Day, 1st Tuesday after 1st Monday in November, even-numbered years; Veterans Day, 11 November; Thanksgiving Day, 4th Thursday in November; Christmas Day, 25 December. **TIME**: 7 A.M. EST = noon GMT.

¹LOCATION, SIZE, AND EXTENT

Located on the eastern seaboard of the US in the South Atlantic region, Maryland ranks 42d in size among the 50 states.

Maryland's total area—10,577 sq mi (27,395 sq km)—comprises 9,891 sq mi (25,618 sq km) of land and 686 sq mi (1,777 sq km) of inland water. The state extends 199 mi (320 km) E–W and 126 mi (203 km) N–S.

Maryland is bordered on the N by Pennsylvania; on the E by Delaware and the Atlantic Ocean; on the S and SW by Virginia, the District of Columbia, and West Virginia (with the line passing through Chesapeake Bay and the Potomac River); and on the extreme W by West Virginia. Important islands in Chesapeake Bay, off Maryland's Eastern Shore (the Maryland sector of the Delmarva Peninsula), include Kent, Bloodsworth, South Marsh, and Smith.

The total boundary length of Maryland is 842 mi (1,355 km), including a general coastline of 31 mi (50 km); the total tidal shoreline extends 3,190 mi (5,134 km). The state's geographic center is in Prince Georges County, 4.5 mi (7.2 km) NW of Davidsonville.

²TOPOGRAPHY

Three distinct regions characterize Maryland's topography. The first and major area, falling within the Atlantic Coastal Plain, is nearly bisected by Chesapeake Bay, dividing Maryland into the Eastern Shore and the Western Shore. The Piedmont Plateau, west of the coastal lowlands, is a broad, rolling upland with several deep gorges cut by rivers. Farther west, from the Catoctin Mountains in Frederick County to the West Virginia border, is the Appalachian Mountain region, containing the state's highest hills. Backbone Mountain, in Garrett County in westernmost Maryland, is the state's highest point, at 3,360 feet (1,024 meters).

A few small islands lie in Chesapeake Bay, Maryland's dominant waterway. Extending 195 mi inland from the Atlantic and varying in width from 3 to 20 mi (5–32 km), the bay comprises 3,237 sq mi (8,384 sq km), of which 1,726 sq km (4,470 sq km)

are under Maryland's jurisdiction. Principal rivers include the Potomac, forming much of the southern and western border; the Patapsco, which runs through Baltimore; the Patuxent, draining the Western Shore; and the Susquehanna, crossing the Pennsylvania border and emptying into the Chesapeake Bay in northeastern Maryland. There are many lakes and creeks, none of any great size.

³CLIMATE

Despite its small size, Maryland exhibits considerable climatic diversity. Temperatures vary from an annual average of 48°F (9°C) in the extreme western uplands to 59°F (15°C) in the southeast, where the climate is moderated by Chesapeake Bay and the Atlantic Ocean. The average for Baltimore is 58°F (14°C), ranging from 37°F (3°C) in January to 79°F (26°C) in July. The record high temperature for the state is 109°F (43°C), set on 10 July 1936 in Allegany and Frederick counties; the record low, –40°F (–40°C), occurred on 13 January 1912 at Oakland in Garrett County.

Precipitation averages about 47 in (119 cm) annually in the southeast, but only 36 in (91 cm) in the Cumberland area west of the Appalachians; Baltimore averages 41 in (104 cm) each year. As much as 100 in (254 cm) of snow falls in western Garrett County, while 8–10 in (20–25 cm) is average for the Eastern Shore; Baltimore receives about 23 in (58 cm).

⁴FLORA AND FAUNA

Maryland's three life zones—coastal plain, piedmont, and Appalachian—mingle wildlife characteristic of both North and South. Most of the state lies within a hardwood belt in which red and white oaks, yellow poplar, beech, blackgum, hickory, and white ash are represented; shortleaf and loblolly pines are the leading softwoods. Honeysuckle, Virginia creeper, wild grape, and wild raspberry are also common. Wooded hillsides are rich with such wild flowers as Carolina crane's-bill, trailing arbutus, May apple, early blue violet, wild rose, and goldenrod; *Trillium virginiana* is an endangered plant.

The white-tailed (Virginia) deer, eastern cottontail, raccoon, and red and gray foxes are indigenous to Maryland, though urbanization has sharply reduced their habitat. Common small mammals are the woodchuck, eastern chipmunk, and gray squirrel. The brown-headed nuthatch has been observed in the extreme south, the cardinal and tufted titmouse are common in the piedmont, and the chestnut-sided warbler and the rose-breasted grosbeak are native to the Appalachians. Among saltwater species, shellfish—especially oysters, clams, and crabs—have the greatest economic importance. The Indiana bat, eastern cougar, Maryland darter, southern bald eagle, and Delmarva Peninsula fox squirrel are listed as endangered fauna in the state.

⁵ENVIRONMENTAL PROTECTION

Maryland's primary environmental protection agency is the Department of Natural Resources, whose divisions oversee fishery and wildlife management, state parks and forests, land reclamation, and scenic and wild rivers. The Environmental Health Administration, within the Department of Health and Mental Hygiene, is responsible for monitoring emissions and enforcing state air pollution regulations, providing for the safe collection and disposal of solid waste, controlling noise pollution, and overseeing the operations of sewage treatment plants. In addition, the Maryland Environmental Service, a public corporation established in 1970, has the power to design, construct, finance, and operate liquid and solid waste management systems in cooperation with local government and industry.

State programs are designed to ensure the safe utilization of Maryland's Atlantic and Chesapeake Bay shorelines and to reclaim areas in the western counties affected by open-pit mining. Authorities from Maryland, Virginia, and the federal government were working in 1980 to combat the effects of sewage pollution, chemical dumping, and pesticide runoffs on the marine life of Chesapeake Bay, and to assess the potential effects of development of the bay as an oil-refining center.

⁶POPULATION

The enormous expansion of the federal government and exodus of people from Washington, D.C., to the surrounding suburbs contributed to the rapid growth that made Maryland the 18th most populous state in 1970, with 3,923,897 residents. The state's population doubled between 1940 and 1970, and increased 5.6% between 1970 and 1978, when Maryland's estimated population was 4,143,000; the population density that year was 419 per sq mi (162 per sq km). Preliminary results of the 1980 census showed a further increase to 4,193,378.

Almost all the growth since World War II has occurred in the suburban areas around Washington, D.C., and Baltimore; as of 1978, about 83% of the state's population resided in these two regions. Metropolitan Baltimore, embracing Carroll, Howard, Harford, Anne Arundel, and Baltimore counties, expanded from 1,804,000 to 2,147,000 between 1960 and 1977 (14th in the US); the city of Baltimore, on the other hand, declined from 939,000 to 804,000 (8th in the US) during the same period, and the 1980 census indicated a further decrease to 783,320. Baltimore is the state's only major city; several west-central counties belong to the Washington metropolitan area, and Cecil County, in the northeast, is part of metropolitan Wilmington, Del.

⁷ETHNIC GROUPS

Black Americans, numbering 842,000 in 1976, constitute the largest racial minority in Maryland. About half the blacks live in the city of Baltimore, which was 46% black in 1970 and more so by the end of the decade.

Hispanic Americans, mostly from Puerto Rico and Central America, numbered 31,000 in 1976. The Asian population is relatively large: 6,520 Chinese, 5,170 Filipinos, 3,733 Japanese, and 8,370 other Asians in 1970. Maryland resettled 2,319 Vietnamese refugees in 1975.

Foreign-born residents and their native-born children represented 11.6% of the population in 1970. The leading countries of origin were Germany, Italy, and the Soviet Union; a significant proportion of the German and Russian immigrants were Jewish refugees arriving just before and after World War II. Maryland's American Indian population is small—only 4,239 in 1970.

⁸LANGUAGES

Several Algonkian tribes originally inhabited what is now Maryland; in 1970, 293 persons still claimed an Indian tongue as their first language. There are few Indian place-names.

The state's diverse topography has contributed to unusual diversity in its basic speech. Geographical isolation of the Delmarva Peninsula, proximity to the Virginia piedmont population, and access from southeastern and central Pennsylvania helped to yield a language mixture that now is dominantly Midland and yet reflects earlier ties to Southern English.

Regional features occur as well. In the northeast are found eastern Pennsylvania *pavement* (sidewalk) and *baby coach* (baby carriage). In the north and west are *poke* (bag), *quarter till*, *sick on the stomach*, *openseed peach* (freestone peach), and Pennsylvania German *ponhaws* (scrapple). In the southern portion are *light bread* (white bread), *curtain* (shade), *carry* (escort), *crop* as /krap/, and *bulge* with the vowel of *put*. East of Chesapeake Bay are *mosquito hawk* (dragonfly), *paled fence* (picket fence), *poor* rhyming with *mower*, and *Mary* with the vowel of *mate*. In central Maryland an earthworm is a *baitworm*.

English was reported as the mother tongue by 88% of the native-born and 85% of all residents in 1970. Speakers of the leading first languages were as follows:

	NATIVE-BORN	FOREIGN-BORN
English	3,327,032	22,637
German	61,993	18,872
Italian	40,366	9,779
Yiddish	37,925	8,307
Spanish	20,377	14,037

⁹RELIGIONS

Maryland was founded as a haven for Roman Catholics, and they remain the state's leading religious group, though their political supremacy ended in 1692, when Anglicanism became the established religion. Laws against "popery" were enacted by 1704, and Roman Catholic priests were harassed; the state constitution of 1776, however, placed all Christian faiths on an equal footing. The state's first Lutheran church was built in 1729, the first Baptist church in 1742, and the earliest Methodist church in 1760. Jews settled in Baltimore in the early 1800s, with a much larger wave of Jewish immigration in the late 19th century.

As of 1971 there were 785,571 Roman Catholics in Maryland. Adherents of the major Protestant denominations included United Methodist Church, 332,511; Southern Baptist Convention, 115,390; Lutheran Church in America, 101,754; and Episcopal Church, 73,577. In 1979 there were an estimated 185,760 Jews.

¹⁰TRANSPORTATION

Some of the nation's earliest efforts toward the development of a reliable transportation system began in Maryland. In 1695, a public postal road was opened from the Potomac River through Annapolis and the Eastern Shore to Philadelphia. Construction on the National Road (now US 40) began at Cumberland in 1811; within seven years, the road was a conduit for settlers in Ohio. The first commercial steamboat service from Baltimore started in 1813, and steamboats were active all along the Chesapeake during the 1800s. The Delaware and Chesapeake Canal, linking Chesapeake Bay and the Delaware River, opened in 1829.

Maryland's first railroad, the Baltimore and Ohio (B&O), was started in 1828; in 1835, it provided the first passenger train service to Washington, D.C., and Harpers Ferry, Va. (now W. Va.). By 1857, the line was extended to St. Louis, and its freight capacity helped build Baltimore into a major center of commerce. In the 1850s, the Pennsylvania Railroad began to buy up small Maryland lines and provide direct service to the northern

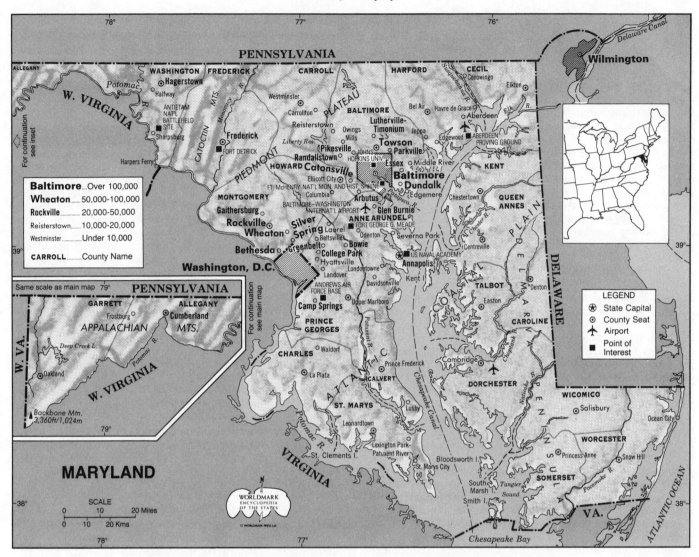

MARYLAND

SCALE
0   10   20 Miles
0 10   20 Kms

WORLDMARK
ENCYCLOPEDIA
OF THE STATES

© WORLDMARK PRESS Ltd.

Baltimore....Over 100,000
Wheaton.....50,000-100,000
Rockville......20,000-50,000
Reisterstown.....10,000-20,000
Westminster.......Under 10,000

CARROLL.....County Name

Same scale as main map

LEGEND
⊛ State Capital
⊙ County Seat
✈ Airport
■ Point of Interest

See US political: front cover L3; physical: back cover L3.

LOCATION: 37°53′ to 39°43′N; 75°04′ to 79°29′W. **BOUNDARIES**: Pennsylvania line, 196 mi (316 km); Delaware line, 122 mi (196 km); Atlantic Ocean coastline, 31 mi (50 km); Virginia line, 233 mi (375 km); District of Columbia line, 25 mi (40 km); West Virginia line, 235 mi (378 km).

cities. Today, some of the old Pennsylvania lines are operated by Amtrak, while the B&O provides commuter service between Baltimore and Washington. Trackage in Maryland totaled 1,099 mi (1,769 km) in 1974. The Maryland Transportation Department's Railroad Administration subsidizes four commuter lines, as well as freight lines in western Maryland and on the Eastern Shore. The Mass Transit Administration operates a fleet of more than 1,000 buses in metropolitan Baltimore and, as of 1980, was constructing the Baltimore Region Rapid Transit System, the first leg of which was scheduled for completion in 1982.

About half of Maryland's roads serve metropolitan Baltimore and Washington. As of 1978 there were 26,961 mi (43,390 km) of roadway; the major toll road is the John F. Kennedy Memorial Highway (I-95), linking Baltimore with Wilmington, Del., and with the New Jersey Turnpike. There were 2,550,003 licensed drivers and 2,766,917 motor vehicles registered in Maryland in 1978.

The Port of Baltimore, one of the nation's busiest, handled 33,523,875 tons of foreign goods in 1977/78. Of that total, exports accounted for 43%.

The Maryland Department of Transportation operates

Baltimore-Washington International Airport, the major air terminal in the state. In 1978/79, it handled 3,667,175 passengers and 116,252 commercial aircraft operations. Another 147 airfields (24 public, 123 private) also served the state in 1978.

¹¹HISTORY

The Indian tribes living in the region that was to become Maryland were Algonkian-speakers: the Accomac, Nanticoke, and Wicomico on the Eastern Shore, and the Susquehannock, Yacomico, and Piscataway on the Western Shore. The Susquehannock, the most powerful tribe at the time of English colonization, claimed all the land lying between the Susquehanna and Potomac rivers. Although the Algonkian Indians hunted for much of their food, many tribes (including the Susquehannock) also had permanent settlements where they cultivated corn (maize), vegetables, tobacco, and other crops. George Alsop in his *Character of the Province of Maryland* (1666) noted that Susquehannock women "are the Butchers, Cooks, and Tillers of the ground [but] the men think it below the honour of a Masculine to stoop to any thing but that which their Gun, or Bow and Arrows can Command." European penetration of the Chesapeake region began early in the 16th century, with the expeditions of Giovanni da Verrazano, a Florentine navigator, and the Spaniard Lucas Vázquez de Ayllón. Captain John Smith, leader of the English settlement at Jamestown, Va., was the first English explorer of Chesapeake Bay and produced a map of the area that was used for years.

The founding of Maryland is intimately tied to the career of another Englishman, George Calvert. A favorite of King James I, Calvert left the Church of England in 1624 to become a Roman Catholic. He announced his conversion in 1625 and—because Catholics were not allowed to hold public office in England at that time—then resigned his post as secretary of state and, against the king's wishes, retired from the royal court. As a reward for Calvert's service, the king bestowed upon him large Irish estates and a peerage with the title of Baron of Baltimore. Two years later, Calvert sailed for the New World, landing in Newfoundland, to which he had received title in 1621. After a severe winter, however, Calvert decided to seek his fortunes where the weather was warmer—in Virginia. Not well received there because of his religion, Calvert returned to England and asked King Charles I (James's successor) for land south of Virginia; instead he received a grant north of the Potomac. Virginia's agents in England contested Calvert's right to this land strenuously but unsuccessfully, and when he died in 1632 the title passed to his son Cecilius Calvert, 2d Baron Baltimore (usually called Lord Baltimore), who named the region Maryland after the queen consort of Charles I, Henrietta Maria. At this time, the land grant embraced not only present-day Maryland but also the present State of Delaware, a large part of Pennsylvania, and the valley between the north and south branches of the Potomac River. Not until the 1760s was the final boundary between Pennsylvania and Maryland (as surveyed by Charles Mason and Jeremiah Dixon) established by royal decree, and nearly a century passed before Maryland conceded to Virginia the land between the north and south branches of the Potomac.

The government of provincial Maryland was absolute, embodying the most extensive grant of royal powers to a colonial settlement. Lord Baltimore's main source of income as lord proprietary was the quitrents settlers paid for their land; in return for his authority, Calvert had to give the king only two Indian arrows yearly. Lord Baltimore assigned to his half-brother, Leonard Calvert, the task of organizing the settlement of the colony. On 22 November 1633, Calvert and approximately 250 settlers, including many Roman Catholics and two Jesuit priests, set sail for America on two ships, the *Ark* and the *Dove*. They landed at St. Clements Island on 25 March 1634. Two days later, Calvert purchased a site from the Indians, named it St. Marys (the first capital of Maryland), and assumed the governorship of the colony.

The early days of settlement were tumultuous. The refusal by a Virginia colonist, William Claiborne of Kent Island, to acknowledge Lord Baltimore's charter led to a small war that ended in 1638 with a temporary victory for Governor Calvert. The conflict in England during the 1640s found an echo in the struggle between Puritans and Roman Catholics in Maryland, a conflict that saw the two-year exile of Governor Calvert to Virginia, the assumption of power by English representatives (including Claiborne and one of the Puritan leaders) in 1652, a subsequent civil war, and finally the recognition of Lord Baltimore's charter by Oliver Cromwell in 1657.

Cecilius Calvert died in 1675. His successor was Charles Calvert, 3d Baron Baltimore, and the next lord proprietary. His tenure, which lasted until 1715, saw a decisive change in the character of the province. In 1689, with Protestants ascendant in both England and Maryland, the British crown assumed direct control over the province, and in 1692, the Church of England became Maryland's established religion. When Charles Calvert died, his successor, Benedict Leonard Calvert, 4th Baron Baltimore, was granted full proprietary rights—but only because he had em-

braced the Protestant faith. Proprietary rule continued through his legitimate heirs until the eve of the Revolution.

Throughout this period, the upper and lower houses of the colonial assembly—consisting, respectively, of the governor and his council and of delegates elected from the counties—quarreled over taxation and the extension of English statutes to free Marylanders. Having already secured most rights from the proprietor, the lower house was somewhat reluctant to vote for independence from the British crown, on whose authority the proprietary government now rested. After its initial hesitancy, however, Maryland cast its lot with the Revolution and sent approximately 20,000 soldiers to fight in the war. The Continental Congress met in Baltimore from December 1776 to March 1777 and in Annapolis from November 1783 to June 1784; these cities were thus among the eight that served as US capitals prior to the designation of a permanent seat of government in Washington, D.C.

Maryland was one of the last states to sign the Articles of Confederation, not ratifying them until other states dropped their claims to what later became the Northwest Territory. On 28 April 1788, Maryland became the 7th state to ratify the federal Constitution. The state constitution, drawn up in 1776, was weighted heavily in favor of propertyholders and the rural counties, at the expense of the propertyless and the city of Baltimore; the legislature removed the property qualifications in 1810.

Maryland's prosperity during the colonial and early federal period waxed and waned according to the world price of tobacco, the staple crop of tidewater and southern Maryland. Planters increasingly employed slave labor on farms and plantations, and the black population grew rapidly in the 18th century. German immigrants began moving into western Maryland, where wheat became the primary crop. The cultivation of wheat also helped make Baltimore's fortune. Founded in 1729 and incorporated in 1796, the city of Baltimore was blessed with a harbor well suited to the export and import trade. As commerce developed, shipbuilding emerged as a major economic activity. By the early 19th century, Baltimore was already the state's major center of commerce and industry.

The city and harbor were the site of extensive naval and military operations during the War of 1812. It was during the bombardment of Ft. McHenry in 1814 that Francis Scott Key, detained on a British frigate, composed "The Star-Spangled Banner," which became the US national anthem in March 1931.

After the War of 1812, Maryland history was marked by the continued growth of Baltimore and increasing division over immigration, slavery, and secession. The chartering in 1827 of the Baltimore and Ohio (B&O) Railroad, which eventually linked Maryland with the markets of the Ohio Valley and the West, added to the city's economic vitality. But distrust of the thousands of newcomers—especially of Irish immigrants and their Roman Catholicism—and fear of the economic threat they supposedly represented spurred the rise of nativist political groups, such as the Know-Nothings, who persecuted the immigrants and dominated Maryland politics in the 1850s.

Although not many Marylanders were in favor of secession, they were hostile to the idea of using force against the secessionist states. On 19 April 1861, as the 6th Massachusetts Regiment passed through Baltimore, it was attacked by a mob of southern sympathizers in a riot that left 4 soldiers and 12 civilians dead. Ten days later, the Maryland house of delegates, following the lead of Governor Thomas Hicks, rejected a bill of secession. Throughout the Civil War, Maryland was largely occupied by Union troops because of its strategic location and the importance for the northern cause of the B&O Railroad. Marylanders fought on both sides during the war, and one major battle took place on Maryland soil—the Battle of Antietam (1862), during which a Union army thwarted a Confederate thrust toward the north, but at an enormous cost to both sides. Confederate armies invaded the state on two other occasions, when General Robert E. Lee brought his troops through the state on the way to Gettysburg in 1863 and when Lieutenant General Jubal Early ravaged the Hagerstown area and threatened Baltimore in 1864. The Maryland legislature, almost totally pro-Union by 1864, passed a new constitution, which among other things abolished slavery.

The state's economic activity increased during Reconstruction, as Maryland, and especially Baltimore, played a major role in rebuilding the South. Maryland's economic base gradually shifted from agriculture to industry, with shipbuilding, steelmaking, and the manufacture of clothing and shoes leading the way. The decades between the Civil War and World War I were also notable for the philanthropic activities of such wealthy businessmen as Johns Hopkins, George Peabody, and Enoch Pratt, who endowed some of the state's most prestigious cultural and educational institutions. The years after World War I saw the emergence of a political figure without equal in Maryland's more recent history: Albert C. Ritchie, a Democrat who won election to the governorship in 1919 and served in that office until 1935, just one year before his death. Stressing local issues, states' rights, and opposition to prohibition, Ritchie remained in power until Harry W. Nice, a Republican but an advocate of New Deal reforms, defeated him in 1934.

The decades since World War II have been marked by intensive population growth, political scandal, and the passage of open housing and equal opportunity laws to protect Maryland's black citizens. Perhaps the most significant occurrence has been the redevelopment of Baltimore, which, though still the hub of the state's economy, had fallen into decay; by 1980, much of its downtown area and harbor facilities had been revitalized.

¹²STATE GOVERNMENT

Maryland's first state constitution was enacted in 1776. Subsequent constitutions were ratified in 1851, 1864, and 1867.

Under the 1867 constitution, as amended, the general assembly, Maryland's legislative body, consists of two branches: a 47-member senate and a 141-member house of delegates. All legislators serve four-year terms and must have been residents of the state for at least a year and of their district for at least six months prior to election. Senators must be at least 25 years of age, delegates 21.

Executives elected statewide are the governor and lieutenant governor (who run jointly), the comptroller of the Treasury, and the attorney general; all serve four-year terms. The state trea-

surer is elected by joint ballot of the general assembly, while the secretary of state is appointed by the governor. The governor, who may serve no more than two four-year terms in succession, also appoints other members of the executive council (cabinet) and the heads of major boards and commissions. The chief executive must be a US citizen at least 30 years of age, and must have been a resident of Maryland for five years prior to election.

Bills passed by majority vote of both houses of the assembly become law when signed by the governor or if left unsigned for 6 days while the legislature is in session or 30 days if the legislature has adjourned. The only exception is the budget bill, which becomes effective immediately upon legislative passage. Gubernatorial vetoes may be overridden by three-fifths votes in both houses. Proposed constitutional amendments also require approval by three-fifths of both houses of the legislature before submission to the voters at the next general election.

US citizens who are at least 18 years of age and have been residents of the state for 30 days prior to the election are eligible to vote.

¹³POLITICAL PARTIES

The Republican and Democratic parties, affiliates of the national organizations, are the dominant political groups in Maryland. Prior to the Civil War, the Democrats drew much of their strength from the slaveholding Eastern Shore, while their opponents, the Whigs, were popular in Baltimore and other centers of antislavery activity. The collapse of the Whigs on both the national and local levels corresponded with the rise in Maryland of the Native American ("Know-Nothing") Party, whose anti-immigrant and anti-Catholic attitudes appealed to Marylanders who saw their livelihood threatened by Roman Catholic immigrants from abroad. The Know-Nothings swept Baltimore in 1855 and won the governorship in 1857; Maryland was the only state to cast its electoral votes for the Know-Nothing presidential candidate, former President Millard Fillmore, in 1856. The Native American Party declined rapidly, however, and by 1860, Maryland was back in the Democratic column, voting for the secessionist John Breckinridge.

The Democrats dominate state politics today, although the Republicans remain strong in some suburbs and on the Eastern Shore. As of 1978 there were 1,888,313 registered voters, of whom 70% were Democrats, 23% Republicans, and 7% independents and members of minor parties. Maryland was one of the few states carried by Jimmy Carter in the November 1980

Maryland Presidential Vote by Political Parties, 1948–80

YEAR	ELECTORAL VOTE	MARYLAND WINNER	DEMOCRAT	REPUBLICAN	PROGRESSIVE	STATES' RIGHTS DEMOCRAT	SOCIALIST
1948	8	Dewey (R)	286,521	294,814	9,983	2,467	2,941
1952	9	*Eisenhower (R)	395,337	499,424	7,313	—	—
1956	9	*Eisenhower (R)	372,613	559,738	—	—	—
1960	9	*Kennedy (D)	565,808	489,538	—	—	—
1964	10	*Johnson (D)	730,912	385,495	—	—	—
					AMERICAN IND.		
1968	10	Humphrey (D)	538,310	517,995	178,734	—	—
					AMERICAN		
1972	10	*Nixon (R)	505,781	829,305	18,726	—	—
1976	10	*Carter (D)	759,612	672,661	—	—	—
						LIBERTARIAN	
1980	10	Carter (D)	726,161	680,606	—	14,192	—

*Won US presidential election.

presidential election. Carter drew 47% of the total vote, Ronald Reagan 44%, and John Anderson 8%.

Revelations of influence peddling and corruption afflicted both major parties during the 1970s. In 1973, Republican Spiro T. Agnew, then vice president of the US, was accused of taking payments from people who had done business with the state government while he was Baltimore Country executive and then governor prior to 1969. Agnew pleaded *nolo contendere* to a federal charge of income tax evasion and resigned from the vice-presidency on 10 October 1973. His gubernatorial successor, Democrat Marvin Mandel, was convicted of mail fraud and racketeering in 1977 for having used the powers of his office to assist the owners of a now-defunct racetrack in exchange for $350,000 in gifts and favors.

14 LOCAL GOVERNMENT

As of 1979 there were 23 counties, 152 incorporated cities and towns, and 102 unincorporated places of 1,000 or more in Maryland. Eight counties had charter governments, with (in most cases) elected executives and county councils; 12 had elected boards of county commissioners; and 3 home-rule counties also had commission governments, but with additional powers. County government is highly developed in Maryland, and there are numerous appointed county officials with responsibilities ranging from civil defense to liquor licensing.

The city of Baltimore is the only one in Maryland not contained within a county; it provides the same services as a county, and shares in state aid according to the same allocation formulas. The city (not to be confused with Baltimore County, which surrounds the city of Baltimore but has its county seat at Towson) is governed by a mayor and a nine-member city council. Other cities and towns are each governed by a mayor, with or without a council, depending on the local charter.

15 STATE SERVICES

The Maryland Board of Ethics, established in 1969, monitors compliance by state officeholders and employees with the state Code of Ethics, in order to avoid conflicts of interest; the Joint Committee on Legislative Ethics, created in 1972, has similar responsibilities with respect to general assembly members. The Fair Campaign Financing Commission provides for the public financing of elections and sets campaign spending limits.

The State Board of Education is an independent policymaking body, appointed by the governor, whose responsibilities include selection of a superintendent of schools to run the Education Department. The growth and development of postsecondary institutions is the responsibility of the State Board for Higher Education. The Department of Transportation oversees air, road, rail, bridge, and mass transit. The Department of Health and Mental Hygiene coordinates public health programs, regulates in-state medical care, and supervises the 24 local health departments. Social services and public assistance programs and employment security lie within the jurisdiction of the Department of Human Resources, which also includes the Maryland Office of Economic Opportunity, commissions on women and Hispanic affairs, and a Center for Displaced Homemakers.

Maryland's state prisons, police, and civil defense agencies are under the Department of Public Safety and Correctional Services, while the Department of Licensing and Regulation sets standards for businesses, professions, and trades.

16 JUDICIAL SYSTEM

The court of appeals, the state's highest court, comprises one chief judge and 6 associate judges. Each is appointed to the court by the governor but must be confirmed by the voters within two years of the appointment. Most criminal appeals are decided by the court of special appeals, consisting of a chief judge and 12 associate judges, selected in the same manner as judges of the high court; each case must be heard by a panel of at least 3 judges. All state judges serve 10-year terms.

In 1970, 12 district courts took the place of all justices of the peace, county trial judges, magistrates, people's courts, and the municipal court of Baltimore. District courts handle all criminal, civil, and traffic cases, with appeals being taken to one of eight circuit courts. Circuit court judges are elected, district court judges are appointed. The city of Baltimore and all counties except Montgomery and Harford have orphans' courts composed of two judges and one chief judge, all of them elected to four-year terms.

According to the FBI Crime Index for 1978, Maryland had a violent crime rate of 732 per 100,000 population (5th highest in the US) and a property crime rate of 5,082. Rates for specific crimes were murder and nonnegligent homicide, 8.2; forcible rape, 35.6; robbery, 310; aggravated assault, 379; burglary, 1,422; larceny/theft, 3,235; and motor vehicle theft, 425. Baltimore's violent crime rate of 1,875 was one of the highest in the US in 1978.

17 ARMED FORCES

As of 1978 there were 76,759 authorized US military personnel in Maryland. About 35,680 were stationed at Army facilities, including Ft. Meade in Baltimore, the Aberdeen Proving Ground in Harford Country, and Ft. Detrick in Frederick. Perhaps Maryland's best-known defense installation is Andrews Air Force Base in Camp Springs, a military airlift center which employed 12,087 in 1978. Annapolis is the home of the US Naval Academy, which in 1980 enrolled 4,363 midshipmen, 262 of them female. Total personnel at all naval facilities, including the National Naval Medical Center at Bethesda, was 26,168 in 1978. Federal defense contract awards to Maryland firms, mostly in Anne Arundel and Montgomery counties, exceeded $1.3 billion in 1977/78.

Some 629,000 veterans were living in the state as of 30 September 1979. Of these, veterans of wartime service were as follows: World War I, 9,000; World War II, 253,000; Korean conflict, 137,000; Viet-Nam era, 195,000. Veterans' benefits during 1977/78 totaled $290 million, of which $145 million was for compensation and pensions, $67 million for medical services, and $52 million for education and training.

Maryland's National Guard averaged about 7,400 members in 1978. In 1977 there were 9,584 local and 2,815 state police personnel.

18 MIGRATION

Maryland's earliest white settlers were English, many of whom farmed lands on the Eastern Shore. As tobacco crops wore out the soil, these early immigrants moved on to the fertile Western Shore and piedmont. During the 19th century, Baltimore ranked 2d only to New York as a port of entry for European immigrants. First to come were the Germans, followed by the Irish, Poles, East European Jews, and Italians; a significant number of Czechs settled in Cecil County during the 1860s. After the Civil War, many blacks migrated to Baltimore, both from rural Maryland and from other southern states.

Since World War II, intrastate migration has followed the familiar urban/suburban pattern: both the metropolitan area of Baltimore and the Maryland part of the metropolitan Washington, D.C., area have experienced rapid growth, while the inner cities have lost population. Overall, Maryland experienced a net gain from migration of 425,000 between 1960 and 1977, much of it from New York, Pennsylvania, and the District of Columbia.

19 INTERGOVERNMENTAL COOPERATION

Maryland is active in several regional organizations, including the Southern Regional Education Board, Atlantic States Marine Fisheries Commission, Coastal States Organizations, Ohio River Basin Commission (with 10 other states and the federal government), Susquehanna River Basin Commission (with Pennsylvania and New York), and the Potomac River Fisheries Commission (with Virginia). Representatives of Maryland, Virginia, and the District of Columbia form the Washington Metropolitan Area Transit

Authority, which coordinates regional mass transit. The Delmarva Advisory Council, representing Delaware, Maryland, and Virginia, works with local organizations on the Delmarva Peninsula to develop and implement economic improvement programs.

In 1978/79, federal aid to Maryland totaled $1.6 billion, including $137 million in general revenue sharing.

[20]ECONOMY

Throughout the colonial period, Maryland's economy was based on one crop—tobacco. Not only slaves but indentured servants worked the fields, and when they earned their freedom, they too secured plots of land and grew tobacco for the European market. By 1820, however, industry was rivaling agriculture for economic preeminence. Shipbuilding, metalworking, and commerce transformed Baltimore into a major city; within 60 years, it was a leading manufacturer of men's clothing and had the largest steel-making plant in the US.

Although manufacturing output continues to rise, the biggest growth areas in Maryland's economy are government, construction, trade, and services. With the expansion of federal employment during the late 1960s and early 1970s, many US government workers settled in suburban Maryland, primarily Prince Georges and Montgomery counties; construction and services in those areas expanded accordingly. The growth of state government boosted employment in Anne Arundel and Baltimore counties. Also of local importance are fishing and agriculture (primarily dairy and poultry farming) on the Eastern Shore and coal mining in Garrett and Allegany counties. As of 1978, Maryland's gross state product was $38 billion, more than double the 1970 total in current dollars, but no more than a 26% increase in real terms.

[21]INCOME

As of 1978, Maryland ranked 12th in per capita income with $8,306. Total personal income was $34.4 billion, to which services contributed 13%; manufacturing, 12%; state and local government, 9%; federal government, 9%; retail trade, 8%; transportation and public utilities, 5%; construction, 5%; wholesale trade, 4%; and other categories, 35%.

Montgomery County had the 2d-highest average household disposable income of any US county in 1978 ($28,658) and led the state in total per capita and personal income in 1977.

An estimated 313,000 Marylanders—less than 8% of the state's population—were below the federal poverty level in 1975.

[22]LABOR

Maryland's civilian labor force in 1978 numbered 2,032,000, of whom 1,918,000 were employed and 114,000 unemployed, for an unemployment rate of 5.6%. A federal census of workers covered by unemployment insurance in March 1977 revealed the following nonfarm employment pattern for Maryland:

	ESTABLISH-MENTS	EMPLOYEES	ANNUAL PAYROLL ('000)
Agricultural services, forestry, fishing	789	4,855	$ 46,347
Mining	116	2,085	30,012
Contract construction	8,649	89,016	1,267,436
Manufacturing, of which:	3,567	243,557	3,467,675
Primary metals	(59)	(24,893)	(489,087)
Electric, electronic equipment	(159)	(31,807)	(521,302)
Transportation, public utilities	2,863	67,399	928,127
Wholesale trade	5,014	70,556	969,115
Retail trade	20,575	278,564	2,037,067
Finance, insurance, real estate	7,113	86,170	940,124
Services, of which:	21,949	273,861	2,697,766
Health services	(5,468)	(75,858)	(825,965)
Other	671	920	11,767
TOTALS	71,306	1,116,983	$12,395,436

Not covered by this survey were the 45,200 Marylanders employed in 1978 in military and civilian capacities by the US Department of Defense, the more than 130,300 employees of other federal agencies, and 251,900 state and local government workers.

Baltimore was a leading trade union center by the early 1830s, although union activity subsided after the Panic of 1837. The Baltimore Federation of Labor was formed in 1889, and by 1900, the coal mines had been organized by the United Mine Workers. In 1902, Maryland passed the first workers' compensation law in the US; it was declared unconstitutional in 1904 but subsequently revived. As of 1976 there were 440,000 members of labor unions and 86,000 members of employee associations; both figures also include workers in the District of Columbia.

[23]AGRICULTURE

Maryland ranked 36th among the 50 states in agricultural income in 1978, with estimated receipts of $777.5 million, about one-third of that in crops.

Until the Revolutionary War, tobacco was the state's only cash crop; in 1979, an estimated 29,700,000 lb of tobacco were harvested (7th in the US). Corn and cereal grains are grown mainly in southern Maryland. Production in 1979 included 58,905,000 bushels of corn for grain, worth $164,934,000; 11,550,000 bushels of soybeans, $72,765,000; 4,312,000 bushels of barley, $7,115,000; and 4,218,000 bushels of wheat, $17,294,000. Fresh fruits and vegetables, cultivated primarily on the Eastern Shore, were valued at more than $25 million in 1979.

Maryland had some 16,000 farms covering 2,805,000 acres (1,135,000 hectares) in 1979. Of the 29,000 farm workers in 1978, 17,000 were family workers and 12,000 were hired hands.

[24]ANIMAL HUSBANDRY

Nearly two-thirds of Maryland's farm income derives from livestock and livestock products. The Eastern Shore is an important dairy and poultry region; cattle are raised in north-central and western Maryland, while the central region is notable for horse breeding.

Maryland ranked 6th among the 50 states in broiler production in 1979, with 244.8 million broilers worth $260.9 million. Also produced during 1979 were 6.5 million lb of chickens, worth $1.1 million; and 327 million eggs, $19.9 million.

An estimated 1.5 billion lb of milk were produced in 1979; in all, dairy products accounted for about 25% of total agricultural income. Maryland farms and ranches had 131,000 milk cows, 380,000 cattle and calves, and 235,000 hogs and pigs by the end of 1979; production of meat animals included 102.8 million lb of cattle ($64.5 million) and 61.2 million lb of hogs ($26.7 million).

[25]FISHING

A leading source of oysters, clams, and crabs, Maryland had a total commercial catch in 1978 of 56,437,000 lb, valued at $32,622,096. Shellfish accounted for 75% of the volume and 90% of the value of the catch. Leading items were oyster meats (44% of the total value), clam meats (29%), and crabs (16%). Striped bass was the most important finfish, accounting for 4% of the total value, followed by bluefin tuna, flounder, and menhaden. As of 1975, 16,233 commercial fishermen were active in Maryland, up from 11,817 in 1973. The state's 172 seafood-processing plants had an output worth $117,823,000 in 1978.

The Fisheries Administration of the Department of Natural Resources monitors fish populations, breeds and implants oysters, and stocks inland waterways with 900,000 finfish annually.

[26]FORESTRY

Maryland's 2,653,200 acres (1,073,700 hectares) of forestland in 1977 covered 42% of the state's land area. More than 95% of that was classified as commercial forest, nine-tenths of it privately owned. Hardwoods predominate, with red and white oaks and yellow poplar among the leading hardwood varieties.

The 1977 harvest included 146,361,000 board feet of timber,

58,300 cords of pulpwood, and 9,491 cords of fuel wood. Shipments of lumber and wood products were valued at $229.5 million; paper and allied products, $655.6 million.

Forest management and improvement lie within the jurisdiction of the Forest Service and Park Service, two state units administered by one director within the Department of Natural Resources. The Forest Service manages nine state forests and produces 7 million seedlings each year.

[27] MINING
Maryland ranked 35th among the states in mineral production in 1978, with a mineral output valued at $213 million. Coal is the leading mineral, accounting for about one-third of the total value. Excluding fossil fuels, Maryland mines and quarries in 1978 produced an estimated 17,630,000 tons of stone and 12 million tons of sand and gravel. Stone is quarried in Allegany, Baltimore, Cecil, Howard, and Montgomery counties, and sand and gravel statewide.

[28] ENERGY AND POWER
Maryland's installed electrical capacity was 9.2 million kw in 1978, when production of electricity exceeded 35.1 billion kwh. More than 99% of the generating capacity is privately owned, and about 35% of the state's electricity is produced by coal-fired plants. The Calvert Cliffs Nuclear Plant in Lusby, operated by Baltimore Gas and Electric, produced about 28% of the state's electricity in 1978.

Coal, Maryland's lone fossil fuel resource, is mined in Allegany and Garrett counties, along the Pennsylvania border. Reserves in 1976 were estimated at 1 billion tons of bituminous coal; the 1978 output totaled 3 million net tons. About 143 trillion Btu of natural gas from out of state were sold to Maryland consumers in 1978, down slightly from previous years, as gas companies put restrictions on new hookups. Revenues of approximately $446 million were up $16.8 million from 1977, however. More than 2 billion gallons of gasoline were sold to motorists in 1978, a 14% increase since the energy crisis year of 1974.

[29] INDUSTRY
During the early 1800s, Maryland's first industries centered around the Baltimore shipyards. Small ironworks cast parts for sailing vessels, and many laborers worked as shipbuilders. By the 1850s, Baltimore was also producing weather-measuring instruments and fertilizers, and by the 1930s, it was a major center of metal refining. The city remains an important manufacturer of automobiles and parts, machinery, and steel.

Value added by manufacturing in 1977 was $7.1 billion, up 51% from 1972. Of the 1977 figure, 14% was contributed by food and food products, 13% by electric and electronic equipment, 12% by primary metals, 10% by nonelectrical machinery, 10% by chemicals and allied products, 8% by transportation equipment, and 33% by other industries. The following table shows value added by selected industries in 1972 and 1977:

	1972	1977
Communications equipment	$432,900,000	$748,500,000
Blast furnace, basic steel products	489,600,000	645,400,000
Beverages	236,700,000	349,200,000
Soaps, cleaners, toiletries	195,600,000	250,400,000
Paperboard containers and boxes	93,700,000	186,500,000

In 1978, 36% of all manufacturing activity (by value) took place in the city of Baltimore, followed by Baltimore County (11%), Montgomery County (9%), and Prince Georges County (8%). Leading Maryland corporations include Martin Marietta of Bethesda (aerospace); Black & Decker Manufacturing of Towson (tools); Fairchild Industries of Germantown (aerospace); and Maryland Cup of Owings Mills (paper products).

[30] COMMERCE
Maryland's wholesale establishments registered $16.9 billion in trade during 1977, 66% more than in 1972. The city of Baltimore

accounted for 29% of all sales, followed by Prince Georges County, 16%; Baltimore County, 16%; and Montgomery County, 13%. Nearly 60% of the trade was in durable goods, with motor vehicles, parts, and supplies accounting for 20% of all sales. The largest nondurable items were groceries and related products (14%) and petroleum and petroleum products (9%).

Retail establishments in 1977 had $14.4 billion in sales, an increase of 53% since 1972. Baltimore, Prince Georges, and Montgomery counties, along with the city of Baltimore, together accounted for two-thirds of the total. Food stores yielded 22% of all sales; automobile dealers, 20%; department stores, 12%; eating and drinking places, 9%; and gasoline service stations, 8%.

The Port of Baltimore was the 5th-busiest foreign-trade port in 1978, as well as the fastest-growing foreign-trade port on the east coast. Imports were valued at $4.9 billion, nearly half of that from Europe and almost one-fourth from Japan; exports worth more than $6.4 billion were shipped primarily to Europe (48%) and Asia (32%), with Saudi Arabia, Federal Republic of Germany, France, Belgium-Luxembourg, United Kingdom, and Japan heading the list of principal destinations. Foreign exports of Maryland's own manufactures totaled $641 million in 1976 (29th in the US); exports of agricultural commodities in 1976/77 amounted to $136 million (34th in the US).

[31] CONSUMER PROTECTION
The state agency responsible for controlling unfair and deceptive trade practices is the Division of Consumer Protection within the Attorney General's Office. Under the division's jurisdiction is the Maryland Consumer Council, comprising representatives of consumer groups, business groups, and other interests. The consumer credit commissioner, within the Department of Licensing and Regulation, is responsible for enforcing the state's Consumer Loan Law, Retail Credit Accounts Law, Retail Installment Sales Act, and Equal Credit Opportunity Act (except for those provisions that apply to banks, over which the state bank commissioner has sole jurisdiction). The Consumer Services Division of the Motor Vehicle Administration, under the Department of Transportation, licenses motor vehicle dealers and manufacturers and professional driving schools; the division is also responsible for school bus safety inspections.

[32] BANKING
Maryland's 106 insured commercial banks in 1978 reported total assets of $13.8 billion; outstanding loans exceeded $5.3 billion, and deposits totaled nearly $11.4 billion. The Maryland National Bank (Baltimore), the largest in the state, ranked 50th in the US, with deposits of nearly $2.3 billion in mid-1979.

Of the 70 federally insured savings and loan associations in 1978, 55 were stated-chartered and 15 federally chartered. Total assets were $7.4 billion, and outstanding mortgage loans amounted to $6.4 billion. In 1977, Maryland had 32 credit unions with assets of $172 million; 317 consumer-loan and small-loan licensees had combined assets of $531.6 million. The volume of consumer loans declined from $404.3 million in 1977 to $293.3 million in 1978.

All state-chartered savings and loan associations are regulated by the Division of Building, Savings and Loan Associations of the Department of Licensing and Regulation.

[33] INSURANCE
Life insurance in force as of 31 December 1978 included 8,353,000 policies worth $56.4 billion. Payments of $539.7 million were made, including $235.3 million in death benefits. The average value of life insurance per family was $36,900.

Property and liability insurers wrote premiums in 1978 totaling $1.3 billion, including $193.4 million in automobile physical damage insurance, $427.2 million in automotive liability insurance, and $120.7 million in homeowners' coverage. Federal flood insurance totaling $508 million was in effect as of 30 June 1979. The Maryland Automobile Insurance Fund, a quasi-independent agency created in 1972, pays claims against uninsured motorists (i.e., hit-and-run drivers, out-of-state uninsured motorists, and state residents driving in violation of Maryland's compulsory automobile insurance law), and sells policies to Maryland drivers unable to obtain insurance from private companies.

The State Insurance Division of the Department of Licensing and Regulation licenses all state insurance companies, agents, and brokers, and must approve all policies for sale in the state.

³⁴SECURITIES

There are no securities or commodities exchanges in Maryland. New York Stock Exchange member firms had 44 sales offices and 507 registered representatives in the state in 1978. Marylanders reported $597 million in dividend income on their 1977 federal income tax returns. All securities dealers in Maryland are regulated by the Division of Securities within the Attorney General's Office.

³⁵PUBLIC FINANCE

The state budget, prepared by the Department of Budget and Fiscal Planning, is submitted annually by the governor to the general assembly for amendment and approval. The fiscal year runs from 1 July to 30 June.

The following table shows revenues and expenditures (excluding designated funds and certain transfers) for the fiscal years 1977/78 and 1978/79:

REVENUES	1977/78	1978/79
Income taxes	$ 996,920,000	$1,107,459,000
Retail sales and use taxes	628,059,000	699,188,000
Motor vehicle taxes and fees	415,057,000	431,010,000
Other taxes	354,245,000	395,457,000
Federal aid	834,945,000	881,964,000
Proceeds from bond issues	218,145,000	120,000,000
Charges for services	190,156,000	117,219,000
Interest and investment income	34,807,000	79,554,000
Other receipts	77,432,000	171,411,000
TOTALS	**$3,749,766,000**	**$4,003,262,000**

EXPENDITURES		
Education	$ 693,981,000	$ 740,997,000
Transportation	614,773,000	678,421,000
Health and mental hygiene	590,447,000	657,604,000
Human resources	350,067,000	375,058,000
Public safety and judicial system	207,704,000	339,723,000
Natural resources and recreation	43,577,000	44,809,000
Economic and community development	9,457,000	10,719,000
Agriculture	8,280,000	9,162,000
Personnel and retirement	260,790,000	458,869,000
Debt service	283,321,000	269,810,000
Capital outlays	282,384,000	207,801,000
General government	202,922,000	213,456,000
TOTALS	**$3,547,703,000**	**$4,006,429,000**

During the 1977/78 fiscal year, local governments spent nearly 40% of their total budgets for education, 11% for health and public welfare, 9% for public safety, 8% for highways, and 32% for other purposes. More than 54% of their revenues came from local sources, nearly 27% from the state, and the remaining 19% from the federal government. The following table shows general revenues and expenditures in 1976/77 for the city of Baltimore:

REVENUES	
Property taxes	$ 199,500,000
Sales and gross receipts taxes	26,600,000
Other taxes	63,100,000
Federal transfers	172,400,000
State and local transfers	531,000,000
Other receipts	89,400,000
TOTAL	**$1,082,000,000**

EXPENDITURES	
Education	$ 303,200,000
Public welfare	159,800,000
Highways	139,800,000
Police and fire	113,500,000
Health and hospitals	66,400,000
Housing and urban renewal	43,800,000
Other outlays	275,500,000
TOTAL	**$1,102,000,000**

The outstanding Maryland state and local government debt exceeded $6.4 billion as of 30 June 1977. The per capita debt of $1,557 was the 11th highest in the US. Baltimore's gross debt reached $498 million by the same date.

³⁶TAXATION

Among the taxes levied by the state are an individual income tax, ranging from 2% on the first $1,000 of taxable income to 5% on income over $3,000; a corporate income tax of 7%; a 5% sales and use tax; a state property tax of 20¢ per $100 assessed valuation; and motor vehicle use, franchise, pari-mutuel, cigarette, and alcoholic beverage taxes. All county and some local governments levy property taxes. All counties also tax personal income at rates ranging from 20% to 50% of those imposed by the state; the city of Baltimore taxes personal income at rates equal to 50% of the state levy.

Marylanders paid $7.2 billion in federal taxes in 1975/76 but received $8.3 billion in federal outlays. State residents filed 1.7 million federal income tax returns for 1977, paying $3.7 billion in tax.

³⁷ECONOMIC POLICY

The Department of Economic and Community Development, created in 1970, encourages new firms to locate in Maryland and established firms to expand their in-state facilities, promotes the tourist industry, and disseminates information about the state's history and attractions. The department helps secure industrial mortgage loans for businesses that create new jobs, and also provides small-business loans, low-interest construction loans, assistance in plant location and expansion, and an Office of Business Liaison to allow companies to maximize their use of state services. In addition, the department assists local governments in attracting federal funds for economic development and maintains programs to encourage minority businesses, the marketing of seafood, and the use of Ocean City Convention Hall. The Division of Economic Development maintains a representative in Brussels to promote European investment in Maryland. The Department of State Planning oversees state and regional development programs and helps local governments develop planning goals.

During the 1930s, Maryland pioneered in urban design with the new town of Greenbelt, in Prince Georges County. A wholly planned community, Columbia, was built in Howard County during the 1960s. More recently, redevelopment of Baltimore's decaying inner city has been aggressively promoted. Harborplace, a waterside pavilion featuring hundreds of shops and restaurants, formally opened in 1980, and an industrial park was being developed in a high-unemployment section of northwest Baltimore. Not far from Harborplace are the 33-story World Trade Center and other key elements of the Inner Harbor renewal project. Urban restoration has also been encouraged by urban homesteading: a Baltimorean can buy an old brick building for $1 with a commitment to live in it and fix it up. An analogous "shopsteading" program to attract merchants has also been encouraged.

³⁸HEALTH

One of the nation's most prestigious medical schools and a number of federal health facilities are located in Maryland. For the average Marylander, however, life expectancy in 1969–71 was no better than 70.22 years (36th in the US), 74.17 years for women and 66.47 for men. The infant mortality rate in 1977 was 11.5 per 1,000 live births for whites and 20.6 for nonwhites, in each case slightly below the US average. There were 23,700 legal abortions, for a rate of 24 per 1,000 women and about 3 abortions for each 7 live births.

Maryland's birthrate in 1977 (13.5 per 1,000 population) and death rate (7.8) were each below the respective national norms. The death rates for the leading causes of death were heart disease, 301 per 100,000 population; cancer, 177; and stroke, 57. As of 1970, the state had an estimated 98,600 alcoholics. The Alcoholism Control Administration monitors rehabilitation programs for alcoholics, while the Drug Abuse Administration oversees all drug treatment programs.

In 1978, Maryland had 85 hospitals, with 25,210 beds and an occupancy rate of 80.4%; hospital personnel included 11,426 registered nurses and 3,306 licensed practical nurses. Estimated hospital expenditures in 1978 exceeded $1.4 billion. The average cost of care in community hospitals in 1977 was $219 per day and $1,864 per stay, among the highest in the US.

Maryland's two medical schools are at Johns Hopkins University, which operates in connection with the Johns Hopkins Hospital and has superbly equipped research facilities, and at the University of Maryland in Baltimore. Federal health centers located in Bethesda include the National Institutes of Health and the National Naval Medical Center. In 1977, Maryland had 9,783 nonfederal physicians; there were 2,591 dentists in 1979.

[39] SOCIAL WELFARE

About 205,600 Marylanders, 70% of them children, received public assistance totaling $170 million under the aid to families with dependent children program in 1978; an additional $253 million was expended on Medicaid in 1977. Some 232,000 state residents took part in the food stamp program, paying $44.1 million for coupons worth $127.9 million. The school lunch program served 433,000 students at a federal cost of $27.7 million. The city of Baltimore accounts for a clear majority of public assistance recipients in the state.

Approximately 500,000 Marylanders received Social Security benefits in 1977, of whom 314,200 were retirees, 125,400 survivors, and 60,400 disabled workers. Benefits totaled $1.3 billion, with an average monthly payment of $245 for retired workers. Nearly $68 million in Supplemental Security Income benefits was paid in 1978, three-fourths of that to 30,800 disabled persons. During the same year, $15.3 million went for vocational rehabilitation. Workers' compensation programs paid $106.2 million in 1978, when unemployment insurance benefits exceeded $106 million, averaging $76.40 a week for each recipient.

[40] HOUSING

Maryland has sought to preserve many of its historic houses. Block upon block of two-story brick row houses, often with white stoops, fill the older parts of Baltimore, and stone cottages built to withstand rough winters are still found in the western counties. Greenbelt and Columbia exemplify changing modern concepts of community planning.

There were 1,235,000 year-round housing units in Maryland at the time of the 1970 census, of which 1,175,000 were occupied. Statewide, 28% of all units were built between 1960 and 1970, but that figure is misleading: in expanding Howard County (Columbia), over 50% of all existing units were built during that period, while in the city of Baltimore only 10% of the housing was new. According to the 1970 census, 59% of Maryland houses were owner-occupied and 4% lacked full plumbing facilities.

Between 1970 and 1978, more than 311,000 new units were authorized; residential contracts, valued at more than $7 billion during that period, represented slightly more than half the value of all construction contracts. The Community Development Administration of the Department of Economic and Community Development provides low-interest loans for the construction of rental housing and for the rehabilitation of housing in certain designated areas. The Maryland Housing Fund insures qualified lending institutions against losses on home mortgage loans.

[41] EDUCATION

Partly because of Maryland's large number of government and professional workers, educational attainments compare favorably with those of the other South Atlantic states. By 1970, the illiteracy rate had decreased to 0.9% of the adult population, slightly below the US average. In 1976, 69.3% of all Marylanders had completed high school, and a very high 18.6% had at least four years of college (the US average is 13.9%); the median number of school years completed was 12.6. Maryland students must pass state competency exams in order to graduate from high school.

During the 1978/79 school year there were 859 elementary, 329 secondary, and 147 combined schools serving the state. Enrollment for grades K–8 was 402,609 in public and 88,603 in private schools; for grades 9–12, 407,324 public and 37,569 private. Baltimore's total enrollment was 152,000. Statewide, there were 45,494 public school teachers, earning average salaries of $16,088, in 1977.

As of 1978 there were 29 four-year and 20 two-year accredited colleges and universities in the state. The total enrollment for all four-year institutions was 128,506. The Board of Trustees of the State Universities and Colleges, an 11-member panel (including one student) appointed by the governor, manages 4 state colleges, 2 state universities (Towson and Morgan), the University of Baltimore, and the University of Maryland. By far the largest is the University of Maryland, a land-grant school with a 1978 enrollment of 59,842 at 5 campuses, the largest being College Park, with 36,905 full-time students. The leading private institution in Maryland is Johns Hopkins University in Baltimore, with a full-time enrollment in 1978 of 9,551. The State Board for Community Colleges oversees 15 community and 2 regional two-year schools; their 1978 enrollment was 86,054. Private two-year colleges enrolled 1,009 students that year. The State Scholarship Board administers a general scholarship program as well as special grants for needy students, including war orphans and children of servicemen missing in action, orphans of firemen and policemen, teachers of persons with impaired hearing, and Viet-Nam veterans.

[42] ARTS

Though close to the arts centers of Washington, D.C., Maryland has its own cultural attractions. Baltimore, a major theatrical center in the 1800s, still contains many legitimate theaters. Center Stage in Baltimore is the designated state theater of Maryland, and the Olney Theatre in Montgomery County is the official state summer theater. Arts organizations are aided by the 11-member Maryland Arts Council.

The state's leading orchestra is the Baltimore Symphony, under the direction in 1980 of Sergiu Comissiona. Baltimore is also the home of the Baltimore Opera Company, and its jazz clubs were the launching pads for such musical notables as Eubie Blake, Ella Fitzgerald, and Cab Calloway. The Peabody Conservatory in Baltimore is one of the nation's most distinguished music schools.

[43] LIBRARIES AND MUSEUMS

Maryland's public libraries held 8,468,944 volumes in 1977/78 and had a combined circulation of 27,679,611. The center of the state library network is the Enoch Pratt Free Library in the city of Baltimore; founded in 1886, it had 33 branches, 2,226,309 volumes, and a circulation of 2,232,128 in 1978. Each county also has its own library system. The largest in 1978 were Montgomery, with 19 branches and 1,375,785 volumes; Baltimore, 21 branches and 1,214,767 volumes; and Prince Georges, 21 branches and 1,202,654 volumes. The largest academic libraries are those of Johns Hopkins (about 1,800,000 volumes in 1978) and the

University of Maryland at College Park (1,283,127). The Maryland Historical Society Library specializes in genealogy, heraldry, and state history. Maryland is also the site of several federal libraries, including the National Agricultural Library at Beltsville, with 1,632,945 volumes; the National Library of Medicine at Bethesda, 914,331; and the National Oceanic and Atmospheric Administration Library at Rockville, 500,000.

Of the approximately 70 museums and historic sites in the state, the major institutions are the US Naval Academy Museum in Annapolis and Baltimore's Museum of Art, Seaport and Maritime Museum, Maryland Academy of Sciences, the Maryland Historical Society, and Peale Museum, the oldest museum building in the US. Important historic sites include Ft. McHenry National Monument and Shrine in Baltimore (inspiration for "The Star-Spangled Banner," the national anthem) and Antietam National Battlefield Site near Sharpsburg.

[44] COMMUNICATIONS

Almost all telephone service in Maryland is provided by the Chesapeake and Potomac Telephone Co. In 1978 there were 3,386,804 telephones in the state, 2,536,110 residential and 850,694 business. Nearly 40% of the telephones were in Baltimore, and virtually every household in the state had service.

Of the state's 50 AM radio stations in 1979, 9 originated from Baltimore; the figure for FM stations was identical, except that 9 of the FM broadcasters (2 in Baltimore) were noncommercial. Four of the state's 10 television stations are in Baltimore. Maryland Public Broadcasting operates noncommercial television stations in Annapolis, Hagerstown, Owings Mills, and Salisbury; three additional outlets were planned as of 1980. There were 31 cable television systems with 106,878 subscribers in 91 Maryland communities by the end of 1978. Maryland also receives the signals of the Washington, D.C., broadcast stations.

[45] PRESS

The *Maryland Gazette*, established at Annapolis in 1727, was the state's first newspaper. Not until 1773 did Baltimore get its first paper, the *Maryland Journal and Baltimore Advertiser*, but by 1820 there were five highly partisan papers in the city. The *Baltimore Sun*, founded in 1837, reached its heyday after 1906, when H. L. Mencken became a staff writer. Mencken, who was also an important editor and critic, helped found the *American Mercury* magazine in 1924.

As of 1978, Maryland had 5 morning and 8 afternoon dailies with a total circulation of 692,382, and 4 Sunday papers with 665,449 in circulation, as well as 5 semiweekly newspapers and 75 weeklies. The most influential newspapers, both published in Baltimore, are the *Sun* (all-day 345,348, Sundays 359,929) and the *News-American* (evenings 160,838, Sundays 237,834). The *Washington Post* and *Washington Star* are also widely read in Maryland.

[46] ORGANIZATIONS

National medically oriented organizations with headquarters in Maryland include the National Federation of the Blind, National Retinitis Pigmentosa Foundation, and American Urological Association, all in Baltimore; the American Association of Colleges of Pharmacy, American Institute of Nutrition, and National Foundation for Cancer Research, Bethesda; the American Speech-Language-Hearing Association and Cystic Fibrosis Foundation, Rockville; and National Association of the Deaf, Silver Spring.

Leading commercial, professional, and trade groups include the Shellfish Institute of North America, in Baltimore; Aircraft Owners and Pilots Association and American Fisheries Society, Bethesda; International Association of Chiefs of Police, Gaithersburg; and Retail Bakers of America, Hyattsville. Lacrosse, a major sport in the state, is represented by the Lacrosse Foundation in Baltimore and the US Intercollegiate Lacrosse Association in Chestertown.

[47] TOURISM, TRAVEL, AND RECREATION

Maryland, not a tourist mecca, attracted 3,435,000 people in 1977; another 10,148,000 passed through the state, usually on their way to or from the nation's capital.

Among the state's attractions are Annapolis, the state capital and site of the US Naval Academy. On Baltimore's waterfront are monuments to Francis Scott Key and Edgar Allan Poe, historic Ft. McHenry, and the city's famed crab cakes and other seafood specialties. Ocean City is the state's major seaside resort, and there are many resort towns along Chesapeake Bay.

There are 30 state parks with camping facilities, as well as 79 private and 6 national campgrounds. In 1977/78, licenses were issued to 127,969 fishermen and 181,008 hunters.

[48] SPORTS

One of major league baseball's most successful teams, the American League's Orioles make their home in Baltimore. Under the leadership of manager Earl Weaver and such stars as Brooks Robinson, Frank Robinson, and Jim Palmer, the Orioles won the World Series in 1966 and 1970. Baltimore's other major professional team is the Colts of the National Football League; Hall of Famers Johnny Unitas, Raymond Berry, Gino Marchetti, and Lenny Moore were among those who starred for the Colts during their glory years of the 1950s and 1960s (with a substantially different team, the Colts won the Super Bowl in 1971). The Bullets of the National Basketball Association moved from Baltimore in the early 1970s to Landover in Prince Georges County and were renamed the Washington Bullets.

Ever since 1750, when the first Arabian Thoroughbred was imported by a Maryland breeder, horse racing has been a popular state pastime. The major tracks are Pimlico (Baltimore), Bowie, and Laurel; Pimlico is the site of the Preakness, the second leg of racing's Triple Crown. Six quarter-horse tracks are also located in the state, and several steeplechase events, including the prestigious Maryland Hunt Cup, are held annually.

In collegiate basketball, the University of Maryland won the National Invitation Tournament in 1972, and Morgan State took the NCAA Division II title in 1974. Another major sport is lacrosse: Johns Hopkins, Navy, the University of Maryland, and Washington College in Chestertown all have performed well in intercollegiate competition.

Every weekend from April to October, Marylanders compete in jousting tournaments held in four classes throughout the state. In modern jousting, designated as the official state sport, horseback riders attempt to pick up small rings with long, lancelike poles. The state championship is held in October.

[49] FAMOUS MARYLANDERS

Maryland's lone US vice president was Spiro Theodore Agnew (b.1918), who served as governor of Maryland before being elected as Richard Nixon's running mate in 1968. Reelected with Nixon in 1972, Agnew resigned the vice presidency in October 1973 after a federal indictment had been filed against him. Roger Brooke Taney (1777–1864) served as attorney general and secretary of the treasury in Andrew Jackson's cabinet before being confirmed as US chief justice in 1836; his most historically significant case was the Dred Scott decision in 1857, in which the Supreme Court ruled that Congress could not exclude slavery from any territory. Three associate justices of the US Supreme Court were also born in Maryland. Thomas Johnson (1732–1819), a signer of the Declaration of Independence, served as the first governor of the State of Maryland before his appointment to the Court in 1791. Samuel Chase (1741–1811) was a Revolutionary leader, another signer of the Declaration of Independence, and a local judicial and political leader before being appointed to the High Court in 1796; impeached in 1804 because of his alleged hostility to the Jeffersonians, he was acquitted by the Senate the following year. As counsel for the National Association for the Advancement of Colored People, Thurgood Marshall (b.1908) argued the landmark *Brown* v. *Board of Education* school desegregation case before the Supreme Court in 1954; President Lyndon Johnson appointed him to the Court 13 years later, thus making him the first black member of that body.

Other major federal officeholders born in Maryland include John Hanson (1721–83), a member of the Continental Congress and first president to serve under the Articles of Confederation (1781–82); Charles Carroll of Carrollton (1737–1832), a signer of the Declaration of Independence and US senator from 1789 to 1792; John Pendleton Kennedy (1795–1870), secretary of the Navy under Millard Fillmore and a popular novelist known by the pseudonym Mark Littleton; Reverdy Johnson (1796–1876), attorney general under Zachary Taylor; Charles Joseph Bonaparte (1851–1921), secretary of the Navy and attorney general in Theodore Roosevelt's cabinet; and Benjamin Civiletti (b.New York, 1935), attorney general under Jimmy Carter. Among the many important state officeholders are William Paca (1740–99), a signer of the Declaration of Independence and later governor; Luther Martin (b.New Jersey, 1748?–1826), Maryland's attorney general from 1778 to 1805 and from 1818 to 1822, as well as defense counsel in the impeachment trial of Chase and in the treason trial of Aaron Burr; John Eager Howard (1752–1827), distinguished Revolutionary soldier, governor, and US senator; and Albert C. Ritchie (1876–1936), governor from 1919 to 1935. William D. Schaefer (b.1921) has been mayor of Baltimore since 1972.

Lawyer and poet Francis Scott Key (1779–1843) wrote "The Star-Spangled Banner"—now the national anthem—in 1814. The prominent abolitionists Frederick Douglass (Frederick Augustus Washington Bailey, 1817?–95) and Harriet Tubman (1820?–1913) were born in Maryland, as was John Carroll (1735–1815), the first Roman Catholic bishop in the US and founder of Georgetown University. Elizabeth Ann Bayley Seton (b.New York, 1774–1821), canonized by the Roman Catholic Church in 1975, was the first native-born American saint. Stephen Decatur (1779–1820), a prominent naval officer, has been credited with the toast "Our country, right or wrong!"

Prominent Maryland business leaders include Alexander Brown (b.Ireland, 1764–1834), a Scotch-Irish immigrant who built the firm that is now the 2d-oldest private investment banking house in the US; George Peabody (b.Massachusetts, 1795–1869), founder of the world-famous Peabody Conservatory of Music; and Enoch Pratt (b.Massachusetts, 1808–96), who endowed the Enoch Pratt Free Library in Baltimore. Benjamin Banneker (1731–1806), a free black, assisted in surveying the new District of Columbia and published almanacs from 1792 to 1797. Ottmar Mergenthaler (b.Germany, 1854–99), who made his home in Baltimore, invented the linotype machine. Financier-philanthropist Johns Hopkins (1795–1873) was a Marylander, and educators Daniel Coit Gilman (b.Connecticut, 1831–1908) and William Osler (b.Canada, 1849–1919), also a famed physician, were prominent in the establishment of the university and medical school named in Hopkins's honor.

Maryland's best-known modern writer was H(enry) L(ouis) Mencken (1880–1956), a Baltimore newspaper reporter who was also a gifted social commentator, political wit, and student of the American language. Edgar Allan Poe (b.Massachusetts, 1809–49), known for his poems and eerie short stories, died in Baltimore, and novelist-reformer Upton Sinclair (1878–1968) was born there. Other writers associated with Maryland include James M. Cain (1892–1976), Leon Uris (b.1924), and John Barth (b.1930). Painters John Hesselius (b.Pennsylvania, 1728–78) and Charles Willson Peale (1741–1827) are also linked with the state.

Most notable among Maryland actors are Edwin Booth (1833–93) and his brother John Wilkes Booth (1838–65), notorious as the assassin of President Abraham Lincoln. Maryland was the birthplace of several jazz musicians, including James Hubert "Eubie" Blake (b.1883), William Henry "Chick" Webb (1907–39), and Billie Holiday (1915–59).

Probably the greatest baseball player of all time, George Herman "Babe" Ruth (1895–1948) was born in Baltimore. Other prominent ballplayers include Robert Moses "Lefty" Grove (1900–75), James Emory "Jimmy" Foxx (1907–67), and Al Kaline (b.1934). Former lightweight boxing champion Joe Gans (1874–1910) was a Maryland native.

⁵⁰BIBLIOGRAPHY
Bode, Carl. *Maryland: A Bicentennial History*. New York: Norton, 1978.

Cohen, Richard M., and Jules Witcover. *A Heartbeat Away: The Investigation and Resignation of Vice President Spiro T. Agnew*. New York: Viking, 1974.

Dozer, Donald. *Portrait of the Free State: A History of Maryland*. Cambridge, Md.: Tidewater, 1976.

Federal Writers' Project. *Maryland: A Guide to the Old Line State*. New York: Oxford University Press, 1940.

Harvey, Katherine. *The Best-Dressed Miners: Life and Labor in the Maryland Coal Region, 1835–1910*. Ithaca: Cornell University Press, 1969.

Maryland, State of. Department of Economic and Community Development. *Maryland Statistical Abstract 1979*. Annapolis, 1980.

Maryland, State of. Department of General Services. Hall of Records Commission. Archives Division. *Maryland Manual 1979–1980*. Edited by Edward C. Papenfuse. Annapolis, 1979.

Mencken, H. L. *A Choice of Days: Essays from "Happy Days," "Newspaper Days," and "Heathen Days."* Selected by Edward L. Galligan. New York: Knopf, 1980.

Walsh, Richard, and William Lloyd Fox (eds.). *Maryland: A History, 1632–1974*. Baltimore: Maryland Historical Society, 1974.

Warner, William. *Beautiful Swimmers: Watermen, Crabs, and the Chesapeake Bay*. Boston: Little, Brown, 1976.

MASSACHUSETTS

Commonwealth of Massachusetts

ORIGIN OF STATE NAME: Derived from the name of the Massachuset Indian tribe that lived on Massachusetts Bay; the name is thought to mean "at or about the Great Hill." **NICKNAME:** The Bay State. **CAPITAL:** Boston. **ENTERED UNION:** 6 February 1788 (6th). **SONG:** "All Hail to Massachusetts." **MOTTO:** *Ense petit placidam sub libertate quietem* (By the sword we seek peace, but peace only under liberty). **COAT OF ARMS:** On a blue shield an Indian depicted in gold holds in his right hand a bow, in his left an arrow pointing downward. Above the bow is a five-pointed silver star. The crest shows a bent right arm holding a broadsword. Around the shield beneath the crest is a banner with the state motto in green. **FLAG:** The coat of arms on a white field. **OFFICIAL SEAL:** Same as the coat of arms, with the inscription *Sigillum Reipublicæ Massachusettensis* (Seal of the Republic of Massachusetts). **BIRD:** Chickadee. **FISH:** Cod. **FLOWER:** Mayflower (ground laurel). **TREE:** American elm. **HORSE:** Morgan horse. **BEVERAGE:** Cranberry juice. **INSECT:** Ladybug. **LEGAL HOLIDAYS:** New Year's Day, 1 January; Martin Luther King, Jr., Day, 15 January; Washington's Birthday, 3d Monday in February; Patriots' Day, 3d Monday in April; Lafayette Day, 20 May; Memorial Day, last Monday in May; Independence Day, 4 July; Labor Day, 1st Monday in September; Columbus Day, 2d Monday in October; Veterans Day, 11 November; Thanksgiving Day, appointed by the governor, customarily the 4th Thursday in November; Christmas Day, 25 December. **TIME:** 7 A.M. EST = noon GMT.

¹LOCATION, SIZE, AND EXTENT

Located in the northeastern US, Massachusetts is the 4th largest of the 6 New England states, and ranks 45th in size among the 50 states.

The total area of Massachusetts is 8,257 sq mi (21,386 sq km), of which land comprises 7,826 sq mi (20,269 sq km) and inland water occupies 431 sq mi (1,116 sq km). Massachusetts extends about 190 mi (306 k) E–W; the maximum N–S extension is about 110 mi (177 km).

Massachusetts is bordered on the N by Vermont and New Hampshire; on the E by the Atlantic Ocean; on the S by the Atlantic Ocean and by Rhode Island and Connecticut; and on the W by New York.

Two important islands lie south of the state's fishhook-shaped Cape Cod peninsula: Martha's Vineyard (108 sq mi, or 280 sq km) and Nantucket (57 sq mi, or 148 sq km). The Elizabeth Islands, SW of Cape Cod and NW of Martha's Vineyard, consist of 16 small islands separating Buzzards Bay from Vineyard Sound.

The total boundary length of Massachusetts is 515 mi (829 km), including a general coastline of 192 mi (309 km); the tidal shoreline, encompassing numerous inlets and islands, is 1,519 mi (2,444 km). The state's geographic center is located in Worcester County, in the northern section of the city of Worcester.

²TOPOGRAPHY

Massachusetts is divided into four topographical regions: coastal lowlands, interior lowlands, dissected uplands, and residuals of ancient mountains. The coastal lowlands, located on the state's eastern edge, extend from the Atlantic Ocean 30–50 mi (48–80 km) inland and include Cape Cod and the offshore islands. The north shoreline of the state is characterized by rugged high slopes, but at the southern end, along Cape Cod, the ground is flatter and covered with grassy heaths.

The Connecticut River Valley—a lens-shaped trench characterized by red sandstone, curved ridges, open meadows, and good soil—is the main feature of west-central Massachusetts. The Berkshire Valley to the west is filled with streams in its northern end, including the two streams which join below Pittsfield to form the Housatonic River. Meadowlands lie at the valley's southern end.

East of the Connecticut River Valley are the eastern uplands, an extension of the White Mountains of New Hampshire. From elevations of 1,100 feet (355 meters) in midstate, this ridge of hills slopes down gradually toward the rocky northern coast.

In western Massachusetts, the Taconic Range and Berkshire Hills (which extend southward from the Green Mountains of Vermont) are characterized by numerous hills and valleys. Mt. Greylock, close to the New York border, is the highest point in the state, at 3,491 feet (1,064 meters). Northeast of the Berkshires is the Hoosac Range, an area of plateau land. Its high point is Spruce Hill at 1,974 feet (602 meters).

There are more than 4,230 mi (6,808 km) of rivers in the state. The Connecticut River, the longest, runs southward through west-central Massachusetts; the Deerfield, Westfield, Chicopee, and Millers rivers flow into it. Other rivers of note include the Charles and the Mystic, which flow into Boston harbor; the Taunton, which empties into Mount Hope Bay at Fall River; the Blackstone, passing through Worcester on its way to Rhode Island; the Housatonic, winding through the Berkshires; and the Merrimack, flowing from New Hampshire to the Atlantic Ocean via the state's northeast corner. Over 1,100 lakes dot the state; the largest, the man-made Quabbin Reservoir in central Massachusetts, covers 24,704 acres (9,997 hectares). The largest natural lake is Assawompset Pond in southern Massachusetts, occupying 2,656 acres (1,075 hectares).

Hilly Martha's Vineyard is roughly triangular in shape, as is Nantucket Island to the east. The Elizabeth Islands are characterized by broad, grassy plains.

Millions of years ago, three mountainous masses of granite rock extended northeastward across the state. The creation of the Appalachian Mountains transformed limestone into marble, mud and gravel into slate and schist, and sandstone into quartzite. The new surfaces were worn down several times. Then, during the last Ice Age, retreating glaciers left behind the shape of Cape Cod as well as a layer of soil, rock, and boulders.

³CLIMATE

Although Massachusetts is a relatively small state, there are significant climatic differences between its eastern and western sections. The entire state has cold winters and moderately warm summers, but the Berkshires in the west have both the coldest winters and the coolest summers. The normal January temperature in Pittsfield in the Berkshires is 22°F (−6°C), while the normal July temperature is 68°F (20°C). The interior lowlands are several degrees warmer in both winter and summer; the normal January temperature for Worcester is 26°F (−3°C), and the normal July temperature is 71°F (22°C). The coastal sections are the warmest areas of the state; the normal January temperature for Boston is 30°F (−1°C), and the normal July temperature is 74°F (23°C). The record high temperature in the state is 107°F (42°C), established at Chester and New Bedford on 2 August 1975; the record low is −34°F (−37°C), registered at Birch Hill Dam on 18 January 1957.

Precipitation ranges from 39 to 46 in (99–117 cm) annually, with an average for Boston of 42.5 in (108 cm); Worcester, 45.4 in (115 cm); and Pittsfield, 44.4 in (113 cm). The average snowfall for Boston is 42 in (107 cm), with the range in the Berkshires considerably higher. Boston's average wind speed is 13 mph (21 km/hr).

[4] FLORA AND FAUNA

Maple, birch, beech, oak, pine, hemlock, and larch cover the Massachusetts uplands. Common shrubs include rhodora, mountain laurel, and shadbush. Various ferns, maidenhair and osmund among them, grow throughout the state. Typical wild flowers include the Maryland meadow beauty and false loosestrife, plus several varieties of orchid, lily, goldenrod, and aster. Listed among rare and endangered plants are Eaton's quillwort, climbing fern, burhead, needlegrass, pipewort, mountain alder, whitewater crowfoot, Seneca snakeroot, prickly pear, and numerous rushes and sedges.

Massachusetts had 94 species of mammals in 1979, of which 59 were native land species, 28 were native marine mammals, and 7 had been introduced. Common native mammals include the white-tailed deer, bobcat, river otter, striped skunk, mink, ermine, fisher, raccoon, black bear, gray fox, muskrat, porcupine, beaver, red and gray squirrels, snowshoe hare, little brown bat, and masked shrew. Among the Bay State's 37 resident birds are the mallard, ruffed grouse, bobwhite quail, ring-necked pheasant, herring gull, great horned and screech owls, downy woodpecker, blue jay, mockingbird, cardinal, and song sparrow. Native inland fish include brook trout, chain pickerel, brown bullhead, and yellow perch; brown trout, carp, and smallmouth and largemouth bass have been introduced. Native amphibians include the Jefferson salamander, red-spotted newt, eastern American toad, gray tree frog, and bullfrog. Common reptiles are the snapping turtle, stinkpot, spotted turtle, northern water snake, and northern black racer. The venomous timber rattlesnake and northern copperhead are found mainly in Norfolk, Hampshire, and Hampden counties. The Cape Cod coasts are rich in a variety of shellfish, including clams, mussels, shrimps, and oysters. Among endangered mammals are the sperm, blue, sei, fin, right, and humpback whales.

[5] ENVIRONMENTAL PROTECTION

All environmental protection programs are administered by the Department of Environmental Quality Engineering of the Executive Office of Environmental Affairs.

The Division of Air Quality Control regulates atmospheric and noise pollution. Both sulfur dioxide and carbon monoxide levels decreased during the 1970s, although there was a slight rise in sulfur dioxide levels in 1979. The ozone quality exceeded state standards. Massachusetts maintains 75 air quality monitors statewide, with another 15–20 ozone monitors expected to go into operation during 1980.

All public water supplies are monitored by the Division of Water Supply. The Metropolitan District Commission operates the reservoirs and water supply lines for 35 cities in the Boston metropolitan area. It also operates the two major sewage treatment plants that serve 43 cities and towns in that region.

There are an estimated 340 solid waste disposal plants in the state; privately owned plants account for about 30% of the total refuse processed. As of 1980, the Northeast Massachusetts, Springfield, and Worcester districts were working with the state on resource recovery projects, including the use of solid wastes as an energy resource.

The Division of Forests and Parks maintains four bureaus concerned with public land management. Soil and water conservation districts covering 4,973,000 acres (2,013,000 hectares) are under the direction of the Division of Conservation Services. Approximately $2,209,000 was appropriated by the state and local governments for conservation programs in 1979.

[6] POPULATION

As New England's most populous state, Massachusetts has seen its population grow steadily since colonial times. However, since the early 1800s, its growth rate has lagged behind the rest of the nation's. Massachusetts' population according to the 1970 federal census was 5,689,170 (10th in the US), a 10.5% increase from 1960 but below the US growth rate of 13.3%. The state total for 1970 was 5,688,560 (610 fewer than the federal figure); the 1975 state census showed a population of 5,789,478. In 1970, about 54% of the state was suburban, 30% urban, and 16% rural. The median age was 29, slightly above the US average. A density of 727 people per sq mi (281 per sq km) made Massachusetts the 3d most densely populated of the 50 states, behind New Jersey and Rhode Island.

Preliminary census figures showed 5,728,288 people living in Massachusetts, an increase of no more than 0.7% since 1970. Reasons behind the population lag include a birthrate in 1977 of only 11.8 per 1,000, well below the US average, and a net outmigration of 54,000 people between 1970 and 1977, the largest drop of any New England state.

The state's biggest city is Boston, which according to preliminary census results had a population of 562,582 in 1980, a decline of 9% since the 1970 census was taken. Other large cities (with their 1980 populations) are Worcester, 161,384; Springfield, 152,212; New Bedford, 98,397; Cambridge, 95,362; Brockton, 94,990; Fall River, 92,240; Lowell, 92,160; Quincy, 84,068; and Newton, 83,586. More than one-half of all state residents live in the Greater Boston area, which in 1980 had a metropolitan population of 2,759,800, representing a decline of nearly 5% during the decade of the 1970s.

Massachusetts Counties, County Seats, and County Populations

COUNTY	COUNTY SEAT(S)[1]	LAND AREA (SQ MI)	POPULATION (1980)[3]
Barnstable	Barnstable	393	147,591
Berkshire	Pittsfield	941	144,928
Bristol	Taunton, New Bedford	554	474,345
Dukes	Edgartown	104	8,878
Essex	Salem, Lawrence, Newburyport	494	631,825
Franklin	Greenfield	708	64,333
Hampden	Springfield	619	442,884
Hampshire	Northampton	529	138,630
Middlesex	Cambridge (East), Lowell	825	1,366,980
Nantucket	Nantucket	46	5,072
Norfolk	Dedham	394	604,226
Plymouth	Plymouth	654	404,977
Suffolk	[2]	56	649,651
Worcester	Worcester, Fitchburg	1,509	643,968
	TOTALS	7,826	5,728,288

[1] Officially designated "shire town."
[2] No shire town. Suffolk County includes the city of Boston.
[3] Preliminary results.

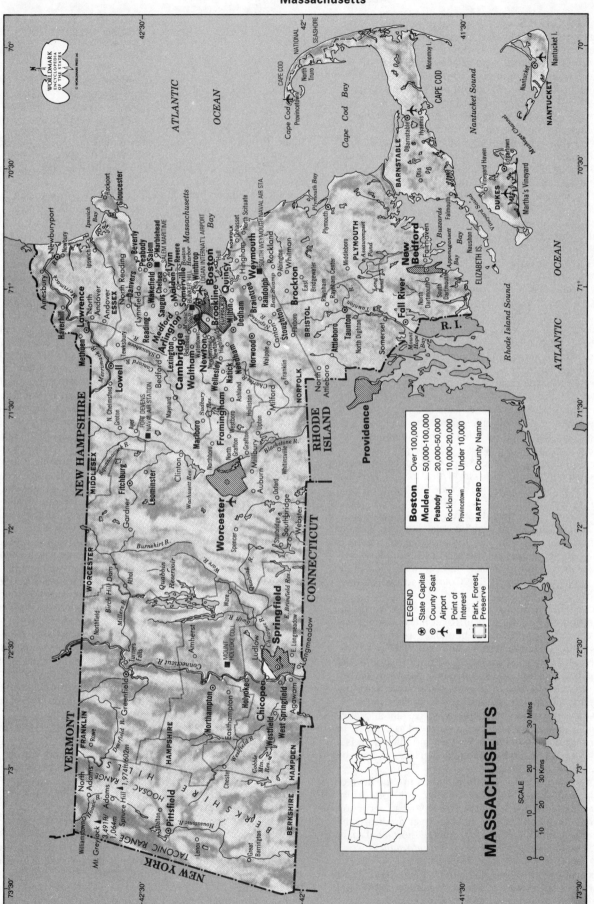

MASSACHUSETTS

LEGEND
⊗ State Capital
○ County Seat
✈ Airport
■ Point of Interest
⬚ Park, Forest, Preserve

Boston _____ Over 100,000
Malden _____ 50,000-100,000
Peabody _____ 20,000-50,000
Rockland _____ 10,000-20,000
Provincetown ___ Under 10,000
HARTFORD ___ County Name

SCALE
0   10   20   30 Miles
0   10 20 30 Kms

See US political: front cover M2; physical: back cover M2.

LOCATION: 41°14'17" to 42°53'13"N. 69°55'25' to 73°30'31"W. **BOUNDARIES:** Vermont line, 41 mi (66 km); New Hampshire line, 94 mi (151 km); Atlantic Ocean coastline, 192 mi (309 km); Rhode Island line, 46 mi (74 km); Connecticut line, 92 mi (148 km); New York line, 50 mi (81 km).

⁷ETHNIC GROUPS

Early industrialization helped make Massachusetts a mecca for many European migrants, particularly the Irish. As late as 1970, one-third of the Massachusetts population consisted of the foreign-born or the children of foreign-born Americans, with the largest groups being Canadian (8% of all state residents), Italian (5%), and Irish (4%). A Harvard University study of a small industrial town in 1935 showed the layering of ethnic stocks in the status and occupational systems. At the top, but also evident in all levels, were native-born Yankees of English descent. Just below the top were the "lace curtain" (2d- and 3d-generation economically successful) Irish and, in descending order, Armenians, Poles, Italians, and French Canadians. A 1962 study of one Boston district found that only 7% of the population was of native stock.

Massachusetts has always had some black population, and has contributed such distinguished figures as poet Phillis Wheatley and NAACP founder W. E. B. Du Bois (the first black Ph.D. from Harvard) to US cultural and public life. A sizable class of black professionals has developed, and the 20th century has seen an influx of working-class blacks from southern states. In 1976 there were 192,000 black Americans in Massachusetts, 3.3% of the population of the state; blacks comprised more than 16% of Boston's population. The state also has a sizable Spanish-speaking population, 88,000 as of 1976.

Greater Boston has a small, well-organized Chinatown; in the suburbs reside many business and professional Chinese, as well as those connected with the region's numerous educational institutions. Statewide, there were 14,012 Chinese in 1970. A smaller number of Japanese, 4,393, were in the state in 1970, along with 12,849 other peoples of Asian-Pacific origin. As of 1975, 1,169 Vietnamese refugees had been resettled in the Commonwealth of Massachusetts.

Small Indian settlements persist on Cape Cod, but all together Massachusetts had only 4,475 Indians in 1970. Cape Cod also has settlements of Portuguese fishermen, as has New Bedford.

⁸LANGUAGES

Some general Algonkian loanwords, a few place-names such as Massachusetts itself, Chicopee, Quebbin, and Naukeag, and the claim of 717 persons in 1970 that an Indian language was their mother tongue—these are the language echoes of the Massachuset, Pennacook, and Mahican Indians so historically important in the founding of Massachusetts Bay Colony and Old Colony, now Plymouth.

On the whole, Massachusetts English is classed as Northern, but early migration up the Connecticut River left that waterway a sometimes sharp, sometimes vague boundary, setting off special variations within the eastern half of the state. Two conspicuous but now receding features long held prestige because of the cultural eminence of Boston: the absence of /r/ after a vowel, as in *fear* and *port*, and the use of a vowel halfway between the short /a/ of *cat* and /ah/ in *half* and *past* as well as in *car* and *park*. Eastern Massachusetts speakers are likely to have /ah/ in *orange* and to pronounce *on* and *fog* with the same vowel as in *form*. In the east, a sycamore is a *buttonwood*, a tied and filled quilt is a *comforter*, a *creek* is a saltwater inlet, and pancakes may be called *fritters*.

Around Boston are heard the intrusive /r/ as in "the lawr of the land," the /oo̅/ vowel in *butcher*, *tonic* for soft drink, *submarine* for a large sandwich, and *milkshake* for a concoction lacking ice cream. West of the Connecticut River are heard the /aw/ sound in *orange*, /ah/ in *on* and *fog*, and the short /a/ of *cat* in *half* and *pass*; *buttonball* is a sycamore, and *comfortable* is a tied quilt.

English was reported in 1970 as the mother tongue by 75% of the native-born residents and by 71% of all residents. Principal first languages were reported as follows:

	NATIVE-BORN	FOREIGN-BORN
English	3,918,066	136,380
French	311,492	55,702
Italian	217,337	70,946
Polish	110,303	23,752
Yiddish	60,642	18,909
German	43,364	20,971
Spanish	33,792	14,395

⁹RELIGIONS

While Protestant sects have contributed greatly to the state's history and development, more than half the state's population is Roman Catholic, a fact that has had a profound effect on Massachusetts politics and policies.

Both the Pilgrims who landed on Plymouth Rock in 1620 and the Puritans who formed the Massachusetts Bay Company in 1629 came to the land to escape harassment by the Church of England. These early communities were based on strict religious principles and forbade the practice of differing religions. Religious tolerance was included in the Charter of 1692, to protect the Baptists, Anglicans, and Catholics who had by then arrived in the colony.

The major influx of Roman Catholics came in the 1840s with the arrival of the Irish in Boston. By the 1850s, they had migrated to other towns and cities and formed the backbone of the state's industrial work force. Later migration by Italian Catholics, German Catholics, and Eastern European Jews turned the state, by 1900, into a melting pot of religions and nationalities, although many of these minorities did not win substantial acceptance from the Protestant elite until the World War II era.

As of 1979 there were 3,031,244 Roman Catholics in Massachusetts, approximately 52% of the total population. The Boston archdiocese, one of the largest in the country, had 2,016,272 members. There were 654,030 known members of Protestant churches in 1971. The largest Protestant denominations were United Church of Christ, 186,477 adherents; Episcopal, 156,189; American Baptist Convention, 86,006; United Methodist, 80,524; Unitarian, 39,418; Lutheran Church in America, 26,909; and Congregationalist, 11,513. Of the state's estimated 250,060 Jewish population in 1979, about 165,000 lived in Boston.

Although small, the Church of Christ, Scientist is significant to Massachusetts history. Its first house of worship was founded in 1879 in Boston by Mary Baker Eddy, who four years earlier had published the Christian Science textbook, *Science and Health with Key to the Scriptures*. In Boston, the church continues to publish an influential newspaper, the *Christian Science Monitor*.

¹⁰TRANSPORTATION

The first rail line in the US, a 3-mi (5-km) stretch from the Neponset River to the granite quarries in Quincy, was built in 1826. The first steam railroad in New England, connecting Boston and Lowell, was completed seven years later. By the late 1830s, tracks were laid from Boston to Worcester and to Providence, R.I., and during the next two decades additional railroad lines opened up new cities for industrial expansion.

As of 1980, freight service was supplied by the Boston and Maine, Central Vermont (Canadian National), and Conrail, as well as by the smaller Fore River, Grafton and Upton, and Providence and Worcester lines. Boston is the northern terminus of Amtrak's Northeast Corridor, linking New England with Washington, D.C., via New York City and Philadelphia. In 1975, the state had 1,405 mi (2,261 km) of track.

Commuter service is coordinated by the Massachusetts Bay Transportation Authority (MBTA), formed in 1964 to consolidate bus, commuter rail, high-speed trolley, and subway services to the 79 municipalities in the Greater Boston area. The Boston subway, which began operation in 1897, is the oldest subway system in the US. In 1980, the system was 97 mi (156 km) long, with an additional 7 mi (11 km) under construction. Boston is also one of the few cities in the country with an operating trolley system. In 1980 there were 165 streetcars, 135 light rail trolleys, and 50 trackless trolleys (electric buses) in operation. In 1979, the entire MBTA district averaged about 553,000 commuters a day, a 3% increase over 1978, with an additional 8% increase forecast for 1980. According to 1970 census figures, about 39% of all Bostonians commuted to work by public transportation, the 2d-highest percentage in the nation, following New York City.

In 1978, 33,418 mi (53,781 km) of paved roadways crisscrossed the state. The major highways, which extend from and through Boston like the spokes of a wheel, include I-95, which runs north–south; the Massachusetts Turnpike (I-90), which runs west to the New York State border; I-93, which leads north to New Hampshire; State Highway 3 to Cape Cod; and State Highway 24 to Fall River. The other major road in the state is I-91, which runs north–south through the Connecticut River Valley. A total of $470 million in state highway funds was expended in 1977. In 1978, 3,719,718 motor vehicles were registered in the state. Of that number, 3,199,821 were automobiles, 424,500 were trucks, 11,543 were buses, and 83,854 were motorcycles. The state issued 3,726,326 driver's licenses in 1978.

Because it is the major American city closest to Europe, Boston is an important shipping center for both domestic and foreign cargo. In 1977, 25,975,275 tons of cargo, of which 7,547,246 tons were imports, passed through the Port of Boston. All port activity is under the jurisdiction of the Massachusetts Port Authority, which also operates Logan International Airport and Hanscom Field in Boston. Other important ports and their 1977 cargo totals were Fall River, 5,285,473 tons (1,947,067 imported); and Salem, 1,648,636 tons (923,402 imported).

There were 31 public and 109 private airports in the state in 1978. Logan International, near Boston, was the busiest, handling 98,271 departing aircraft, emplaning 6,286,825 passengers, and processing 84,867 tons of freight in 1977/78.

¹¹HISTORY

When the last of the glaciers receded from the land we call Massachusetts some 15,000 years ago, what remained was a rocky surface, scoured of most of its topsoil. In time, however, forests grew to support a rich variety of wildlife. When the first Indians arrived from the south, game abounded and fish were plentiful in streams and along the coast. These first Indians were hunter-gatherers; their successors not only foraged for food but also cleared fields for planting corn (maize) and squash. Periodically they burned away the woodland underbrush, a technique of forest management which stimulated the vegetation that supported game. When English settlers arrived, they encountered five main Algonkian tribes: the Nauset, a fishing people on Cape Cod; the Wampanoag in the southeast; the Massachuset in the northeast; the Nipmuc in the central hills; and the Pocumtuc in the west.

The earliest European explorers—including the Norsemen, who may have reached Cape Cod—made no apparent impact on these Algonkian groups, but in the wake of John and Sebastian Cabot's voyages (1497 and following), fishermen from England, France, Portugal, and Spain began fishing off the Massachusetts coast. By the mid-16th century, they were regularly going ashore to process and pack their catch. Within 50 years, fur trading with the Indians was established.

Permanent English settlement, which would ultimately destroy the Algonkian peoples, began in 1620 when a small band of Puritans left their haven at Leiden in the Netherlands to start a colony in the northern part of Virginia lands, near the Hudson River. Their ship, the *Mayflower,* was blown off course by an Atlantic storm, and they landed on Cape Cod before settling in an abandoned Wampanoag village they called Plymouth. Ten years later, a much larger Puritan group settled the Massachusetts Bay Colony, some miles to the north in Salem. Between 1630

and 1640, about 20,000 English people, chiefly Puritans, settled in Massachusetts, with offshoots moving to Connecticut and Rhode Island.

The leaders of the Massachusetts settlement, most notably John Winthrop, a country gentleman with some legal training, intended to make their colony an exemplary Christian society. Though church and state were legally separate, they were mutually reinforcing agencies; thus, when Roger Williams and Anne Hutchinson were separately found guilty of heresy in the 1630s, they were banished by the state. All male church members had a voice in both church and state leadership, though both institutions were led by college-educated men. In order to provide for future leaders, Harvard College (now Harvard University) was founded in 1636.

After the beginning of the English revolution in 1640, migration to Massachusetts declined abruptly. Farming soon overtook fishing and fur trading in economic importance; and after the trade in beaver skins was exhausted, the remaining Indian tribes were decimated in King Philip's War (1675–76). Shipbuilding and Atlantic commerce also brought prosperity to the Massachusetts Bay Colony, which was granted a new charter by King William and Queen Mary in 1692, merging Massachusetts and the colony of Plymouth. In that year, 19 people were executed for witchcraft on the gallows at Salem before Massachusetts authorities put a stop to the proceedings.

During the 18th century, settlement spread across the entire colony. Boston, the capital, had attained a population of 15,000 by 1730; it was an urbane community of brick as well as wooden buildings, with nearly a dozen church spires distinguishing its skyline by the 1750s. Religious revivals, also occurring elsewhere in America, swept Massachusetts in the 1730s and 1740s, rekindling piety and dividing the inhabitants into competing camps. Although the conflicts had ebbed by the 1750s, Massachusetts did not achieve unity again until the resistance to British imperial measures during the next two decades.

Up to this time, imperial government had rested lightly on Massachusetts, providing more advantages than drawbacks for commerce. The colony had actively supported British expeditions against French Canada, and supply contracts during the French and Indian War had enriched the economy. But the postwar recession after 1763 was accompanied by a new imperial policy that put pressure on Massachusetts as well as other colonies. None of the crown's three objectives—tight regulation of trade, the raising of revenue, and elimination of key areas of colonial political autonomy—were popular among the merchants, tradespeople, and farmers of Massachusetts. From 1765, when Bostonians violently protested the Stamp Act, Massachusetts was in the vanguard of the resistance.

At first, opposition was largely confined to Boston and surrounding towns, although the legislature, representing the entire colony, was active in opposing British measures. By December 1773, when East India Company tea was dumped into Boston harbor to prevent its taxation, most of the colony was committed to resistance. Newspaper polemics composed by Samuel Adams and his cousin John, among others, combined with the persuasive activities of the Boston Committee of Correspondence, helped convince a majority of Massachusetts residents that the slogan "no taxation without representation" stood for the preservation of their communities. When Parliament retaliated for the Tea Party by closing the port of Boston in 1774, rescinding the colony's 1692 charter and remaking the government to put it under London's control, Massachusetts was ready to rebel. Military preparations began immediately on both sides. After almost a year of confrontation, battle began at Lexington and Concord on 19 April 1775. By this time, Massachusetts had the backing of the Continental Congress.

For Massachusetts, the battlefield experience of the Revolution was largely confined to 1775, the climaxes being the Battle of Bunker Hill and the British evacuation of Boston the following year. Thereafter, Massachusetts soldiers were active throughout the colonies, but the theater of action shifted southward. A new republican constitution, adopted in 1780, was the first constitution of any state to be submitted to the electorate for ratification.

Social and economic conditions in post-Revolutionary Massachusetts were much like those of the colonial era. Although the Shays Rebellion, an uprising of central and western farmers led by Daniel Shays in 1786–87, challenged the political hegemony of commercially oriented eastern leaders, the latter succeeded in maintaining their hold on the state. Massachusetts was the center of Federalism from 1790 until the mid-1820s. Although Jeffersonian Republicans and Jacksonian Democrats achieved substantial followings, Federalist policies, embodied in the Whigs in the 1830s and the Republicans from the late 1850s, were dominant. This political continuity was based on the importance of national commercial and industrial development to the state.

Even before 1800, it was clear that Massachusetts could not sustain growth in agriculture. Its soil had never been excellent, and the best lands were tired, having been worked for generations with little regard for conservation. Much of Massachusetts' population departed for New York, Ohio, and beyond during the first decades of the 19th century. Those who stayed maintained a productive agriculture, more and more concentrating on fruits and dairying, but they also developed commerce and industry. At Waltham, Lowell, and Lawrence the first large-scale factories in the US were erected, and smaller textile mills throughout the state helped to make Massachusetts a leader in the cloth industry. At Springfield and Watertown, US armories led the way in metalworking, while shoes and leather goods brought prosperity to Lynn, and whale products and shipbuilding to New Bedford. By the 1850s, steam engines and clipper ships were both Bay State products.

The industrial development of Massachusetts was accompanied by a literary and intellectual flowering that was partly in reaction to the materialism and worldliness associated with urban and industrial growth. Concord, the home of Ralph Waldo Emerson, Henry David Thoreau, and a cluster of others, became the center of the transcendentalist movement in philosophy. Social reform also represented an assertion of moral values, whether in the fields of education, health care, temperance, or penology. Abolitionism, the greatest of the moral reform efforts, found some of its chief leaders in Massachusetts, among them William Lloyd Garrison and Wendell Phillips, as well as a host of supporters.

In the years following the Civil War, Massachusetts emerged as an urban industrial state. Its population, fed by immigrants from England, Scotland, Germany, and especially Ireland, grew rapidly in the middle decades of the century. Later, between 1880 and 1920, another wave of immigrants came from French Canada, Italy, Russia, Poland, Scandinavia, Portugal, Greece, and Syria. Still later, between 1950 and 1970, black southerners and Puerto Ricans settled in the cities.

From the election of Lincoln in 1860 through the 1920s, Massachusetts was led by Protestant Yankee Republicans; most Democrats were Catholics. Class, ethnic, and religious tensions were endemic, occasionally erupting into open conflict. Three such episodes gained national attention. In 1912, immigrant textile workers in Lawrence were pitted against Yankee capitalists in a highly publicized strike that dragged on for months. The Boston police strike of 1919 had the largely Irish-American force rebelling against Yankees in city and state government, and brought Governor Calvin Coolidge—who suppressed the strike and refused to reinstate the striking policemen—to national prominence. In 1921, Nicola Sacco and Bartolomeo Vanzetti, Italian immigrant anarchists, were convicted for a payroll robbery

and murder, though there was bitter controversy regarding the quality of the evidence against them. Before they were executed in 1927, their case and the issues it raised polarized political opinion throughout the US. Subsequently, electoral competition between Democrats and Republicans emerged as a less divisive outlet for class and ethnic tensions. Since 1959, the Democrats have enjoyed ascendancy statewide, and Republicans have won only when their candidates stood close to the Democrats on the issues. Party loyalties as such have waned, however.

The Massachusetts economy, relatively stagnant between 1920 and 1950, revived in the second half of the 20th century through a combination of university talent, capital resources, a skilled work force, and political clout. As the old industries and the mill cities declined, new high-technology manufacturing developed in Boston's suburban perimeter. Electronics, computers, and defense-oriented industries led the way, stimulating a general prosperity in which service activities such as banking, insurance, health care, and higher education were especially prominent. As a result, white-collar employment and middle-class suburbs flourished, though run-down mill towns and Yankee dairy farms and orchards still dotted the landscape.

In this respect, as in its politics, Massachusetts resembled much of the Northeast. It was a multiracial state in which the general welfare was defined by shifting coalitions of ethnic groups and special interests. From a national perspective, Massachusetts voters appeared liberal; the Bay State was the only one to choose Democrat George McGovern over President Richard M. Nixon in 1972, and was a secure base for Senator Edward M. Kennedy, a leading liberal Democrat, throughout the 1970s. Yet Boston was also the site of some of the most extreme anti-integration tension during the same era; Massachusetts was simultaneously a center of efforts in favor of the Equal Rights Amendment and against abortion. The old labels "conservative" and "liberal," though still in use, seemed scarcely more descriptive than party labels for understanding Massachusetts public life as the 1980s began.

¹²STATE GOVERNMENT

The first state constitution, drawn up soon after the signing of the Declaration of Independence, was rejected by the electorate. A revised draft was not approved by the state voters until 15 June 1780, following two constitutional conventions. This constitution, as amended, governs Massachusetts and is, according to the state, the oldest written constitution in the world still in effect.

The legislature of Massachusetts, known as the General Court, is composed of a 40-member senate and 160-member house of representatives, all of whom are elected every two years in even-numbered years. Members of the senate must have resided in their home district for at least five years; representatives, at least one year.

The governor and lieutenant governor are elected jointly every four years. The governor appoints all state and local judges, as well as the heads of the 10 executive offices. Both the governor and lieutenant governor must have resided in the state for at least seven years. Other elected officials include the attorney general, secretary of the commonwealth, treasurer and receiver-general, and auditor of the commonwealth. All serve four-year terms.

Massachusetts also has an eight-member executive council, elected every two years by district. The council has the power to review the governor's judicial appointments and pardons, and to authorize expenditures from the state treasury. The lieutenant governor also has a vote on the executive council except when the governor is absent, in which case the lieutenant governor presides over it as a nonvoting participant. Members of the council must have resided in the state for five years.

Any Massachusetts citizen may file a bill through a state legislator, or a bill may be filed directly by a legislator or by the governor. To win passage, a bill must gain a majority vote of both houses of the legislature. After a bill is passed, the governor has 10 days in which to sign it, return it for reconsideration (usually with amendments), veto it, or refuse to sign it ("pocket veto"). A veto may be overridden by a two-thirds majority in both houses.

Amendments to the constitution may be introduced by any house or senate member (legislative amendment) or by a petition signed by at least 25,000 qualified voters (initiative amendment) that is presented in a joint session of the General Court. If it is approved by two successive sessions of the legislature, the amendment is then submitted to the voters at the next general election.

To vote in a Massachusetts district, a person must be a US citizen, at least 18 years old, and a resident of that district; there is no time requirement for residency.

¹³POLITICAL PARTIES

The Federalist Party, represented nationally by John Adams, dominated Massachusetts in the late 18th and early 19th centuries. The state turned to the Whig Party in the second quarter of the 19th century. Predominantly Yankee in character, the Whigs supported business growth, promoted protective tariffs, and favored such enterprises as railroads and factories. The new Republican Party, to which most Massachusetts Whigs gravitated when their party split in the 1850s, was a prime mover of abolitionism and played an important role in the election of Abraham Lincoln as president in 1860. Republicans held most of the major state elective offices, as well as most US congressional seats, until the early 1900s.

The Democratic Party's rise starting in the 1870s was tied directly to massive Irish immigration. Other immigrant groups also gravitated toward the Democrats, and in 1876, the state's first Democratic congressman was elected. In 1928, the state voted for Democratic presidential candidate Alfred E. Smith, a Roman Catholic, the first time the Democrats won a majority in a Massachusetts presidential election. Since then Democrats have, for the most part, dominated state politics. In 1960, John F. Kennedy, who had been a popular US senator from Massachusetts, became the first Roman Catholic president in US history. In 1972, Massachusetts was the only state carried by Democratic presidential candidate George McGovern.

Approximately 3,031,000 voters registered for the 1980 presidential primary. Of these, 1,392,000 were Democrats, 431,000 were Republicans, and 1,208,000 were independents. As of 1979, the governorship and both US Senate seats were held by Democrats; the US House delegation consisted of 10 Democrats and 2 Republicans. The Massachusetts senate had 34 Democrats and 6 Republicans, while the house of representatives had 129 Democrats, 30 Republicans, and 1 independent.

In the November 1980 presidential election, Massachusetts voters left the Democratic fold for the first time in 24 years, choosing Ronald Reagan by a plurality of only a few thousand votes over President Jimmy Carter. At the same time, Bay Staters also approved a property tax limitation measure.

¹⁴LOCAL GOVERNMENT

As of 1979, Massachusetts had 14 counties, 39 cities, and 312 towns.

In 12 of the 14 counties, executive authority was vested in three county commissioners elected to four-year terms. The exceptions were Suffolk County, where executive powers are exercised by the mayor and city council of Boston, the board of aldermen in Chelsea, the city council of Revere, and the board of selectmen of Winthrop; and Nantucket County, where the five town selectmen have executive powers. Other county officials include the register of probate and family court, sheriff, clerk of courts, county treasurer, and register of deeds.

All Massachusetts cities are governed by mayors and city councils. Towns are governed by selectmen, who are usually elected to either one- or two-year terms. Town meetings—a carryover from the colonial period, when every taxpayer was given an equal voice in town government—still take place regularly. By state law, to be designated a city, a place must have at least 12,000 residents. Towns with more than 6,000 inhabitants may hold representative town meetings limited to elected officials.

¹⁵STATE SERVICES

State services are provided through the 10 offices of the governor's cabinet. Each of the offices is headed by a secretary appointed by the governor.

Educational services are administered by the Executive Office of Educational Affairs. Included under its jurisdiction are the State Board of Education and Board of Higher Education, the Massachusetts community college and state college systems, the University of Massachusetts, the State Art Commission, and the State Library.

The Executive Office of Transportation and Construction

Massachusetts Presidential Vote by Political Parties, 1948–80

YEAR	ELECTORAL VOTE	MASSACHUSETTS WINNER	DEMOCRAT	REPUBLICAN	SOCIALIST LABOR	PROGRESSIVE
1948	16	*Truman (D)	1,151,788	909,370	5,535	38,157
1952	16	*Eisenhower (R)	1,083,525	1,292,325	1,957	4,636
1956	16	*Eisenhower (R)	948,190	1,393,197	5,573	—
1960	16	*Kennedy (D)	1,487,174	976,750	3,892	—
1964	14	*Johnson (D)	1,786,422	549,727	4,755	—
						AMERICAN IND.
1968	14	Humphrey (D)	1,469,218	766,844	6,180	87,088
					SOC. WORKERS	AMERICAN
1972	14	McGovern (D)	1,332,540	1,112,078	10,600	2,877
1976	14	*Carter (D)	1,429,475	1,030,276	8,138	7,555
					LIBERTARIAN	
1980	14	*Reagan (R)	1,048,562	1,054,213	21,311	—

*Won US presidential election.

supervises the state Department of Public Works and has responsibility for the planning and development of transportation systems within the state, including the Massachusetts Port Authority, the Massachusetts Turnpike Authority, and the Massachusetts Bay Transportation Authority.

All public health, mental health, youth, and veterans' programs are administered by the Executive Office of Human Services. Also under its jurisdiction are the Department of Public Welfare and the Department of Corrections. The Executive Office of Public Safety includes the state Civil Defense Agency, Register of Motor Vehicles, and Highway Safety Bureau.

The Executive Office of Consumer Affairs regulates state standards and registers professional workers. The Public Utilities Commission and Alcoholic Beverage Control Commission are also part of this office, as are the divisions regulating banks and insurance. Housing services are provided through the Executive Office of Communities and Development. This office administers the Massachusetts Home Mortgage Finance Agency, the Housing Finance Agency, and the Mobile Homes Commission. The Executive Office of Environmental Affairs monitors the state's marine and wildlife, as well as its air, water, and food quality.

Labor and industrial relations are monitored through the Executive Office of Economic Development and Manpower Affairs. This office administers the minimum wage law, occupational safety laws, and child labor laws, among others, as well as unemployment and workers' compensation benefits. The Executive Office of Elder Affairs plans and implements programs for the elderly, including nutrition, home care, and education programs.

16 JUDICIAL SYSTEM
All statewide judicial offices are filled by the governor, with the advice and consent of the executive council.

The supreme judicial court, composed of a chief justice and 6 other justices, is the highest court in the state. It has appellate jurisdiction on matters of law and also advises the governor and legislature on legal questions. The superior courts, actually the highest level of trial courts, have a chief justice and 45 other justices; these courts hear law, equity, civil, and criminal cases, and make the final determination in matters of fact. The appeals court, consisting of a chief justice and 9 other justices, hears appeals of decisions by district and municipal courts. As of 1979 there were 62 district courts and 8 municipal courts, including the several departments of the Boston municipal court system. Other court systems in the state include the land court, probate and family court, housing court (with divisions in Boston and Hampden counties), and juvenile court (with divisions in Boston, Springfield, Worcester, and Bristol counties).

Except for the murder rate, which was nearly one-third the US average, crime rates for both the state and the Boston metropolitan area ranged at or slightly above the US averages. Specific figures for 1978 (with figures for the Boston area in parentheses) were murder and nonnegligent manslaughter, 3.7 per 100,000 inhabitants (4.6); forcible rape, 22.6 (26.3); robbery, 172.3 (241.7); aggravated assault, 263.3 (292.6); burglary, 1,515.1 (1,472.6); larceny-theft, 2,277.8 (2,220.7); and motor vehicle theft, 1,095.6 (1,357.0). A total of 308,933 crimes were committed in the state in 1978; of that number, 91% were property crimes. Capital punishment was restored to the state in 1979. Under Massachusetts gun control laws, all guns must be registered, and there is a mandatory one-year jail sentence for possession without a permit.

Of the 5,724 personnel in the state and local corrections systems, 2,388 worked for local correctional authorities in 1977.

17 ARMED FORCES
The six military installations located in Massachusetts in 1978 had 23,750 personnel. About half were stationed at Fort Devens in Ayer and at the two Army research and development centers at Natick and Watertown; the remainder were at the Navy's

South Weymouth Naval Air Station and at the Air Force bases at Bedford and North Truro. The state ranked 6th among the 50 states in the value of defense contracts awarded in 1978, with a total of about $2.8 billion.

Approximately 870,000 military veterans were living in the state in 1978. Veterans of World War I numbered 21,000; World War II, 375,000; Korean conflict, 170,000; and the Viet-Nam era, 250,000. About $599 million was paid in veterans' benefits in 1978, of which 52% went for compensation and pensions, 29% for medical and administrative costs, 13% for education and training, and 6% for other purposes.

The Massachusetts National Guard averaged nearly 11,000 members in 1980; the strength of the Air National Guard was nearly 2,500.

In 1977, state and local police forces had 17,162 employees. The rate of 3 police per 1,000 population was slightly above the US average. About $325 million was expended on state and local police, 87% of it for local forces.

18 MIGRATION
Massachusetts was founded by the migration of English religious groups to its shores, and for over a century their descendants dominated all activity in the state. The first great wave of non-English to enter Massachusetts were the Irish, who migrated in vast numbers during the 1840s and 1850s. By 1860, one-third of Boston's population was Irish, while nearly one-fourth of Middlesex and Norfolk counties and one-fifth of the inhabitants of Berkshire, Bristol, Essex, and Hampden counties were Irish-born. Other ethnic groups, such as the Scottish, Welsh, Germans, and Poles, were also entering the state at this time, but their numbers were small by comparison. During the late 1880s and 1890s, another wave of immigrants—from Portugal, Spain, Italy, Russia, and Greece—arrived. Irish and Italians continued to enter the state during the 20th century. As of the 1970 census, Massachusetts had more citizens of foreign stock (foreign-born or of foreign or mixed parentage) than any other state except Hawaii.

A slow but steady migration from Massachusetts farm communities began during the mid-1700s and continued well into the 1800s. The first wave of farmers resettled in northern Connecticut, Vermont, New Hampshire, and Maine. Later farmers moved to New York's Mohawk Valley, Ohio, and points farther west.

The only significant migration from other areas of the US to Massachusetts has been the influx of southern blacks since World War II. According to census estimates, Massachusetts gained 84,000 blacks between 1940 and 1975.

19 INTERGOVERNMENTAL COOPERATION
Massachusetts participates in numerous regional agreements, including the New England Corrections Compact, New England Police Compact, New England Higher Education Compact, New England Radiological Health Protection Compact, and New England Interstate Water Pollution Control Compact. The state is also involved in the Atlantic States Marine Fisheries Compact, the Northeastern Forest Fire Protection Compact, and the Connecticut River Valley Flood Control Compact.

Border agreements include the Connecticut-Massachusetts Boundary Compact (ratified by Massachusetts in 1908), the Massachusetts-New Hampshire compacts of 1889 and 1895, Massachusetts-New York Compact of 1853, and the Massachusetts-Rhode Island Compact of 1859.

During 1977/78, the state received $2.6 billion in federal aid. Estimated figures for 1978/79 were $2.7 billion, of which $218.6 million was general revenue sharing.

20 ECONOMY
From its beginnings as a farming and seafaring colony, Massachusetts became one of the most industrialized states in the country in the late 19th century and, more recently, a leader in the manufacture of high technology items.

During the colonial and early national periods, the towns of Salem, Gloucester, Marblehead, and Boston, among others, gave the state strong fishing and shipbuilding industries. Boston was also an important commercial port and a leading center of foreign commerce. Agriculture was important, but productivity of the rocky soil was limited, and by the mid-1800s, farming could not sustain the expanding population. The opening of the Erie Canal, and subsequent competition with cheaper produce grown in the West, hastened agriculture's decline in the Bay State.

Massachusetts' rise as a center of manufacturing began in the early 1800s, when cottage industries developed in small farming communities. Large factories were then built in towns with water power. The country's first "company town," Lowell, was built in the early 1820s to accommodate the state's growing textile industry. Throughout the rest of the 19th century, the state supplied the nation with most of its shoes and woven goods.

Manufacturing still accounts for a large share of the state's economy. The growth of such high technology industries as computers, word processors, and optical equipment has largely offset the loss to the state of the shoe and textile industries, which, though still active, have declined drastically as a result of foreign competition.

Contributions to the gross state product in 1977 were as follows: manufacturing, 26%; finance, insurance, and real estate, 18%; trade, 18%; services, 16%; government, 10%; and other sectors, 12%.

21 INCOME

In 1978, Massachusetts ranked 14th among the 50 states in per capita income, with $8,063 in current dollars. During the same year, the state ranked 10th in total personal income, with $46.6 billion. That latter figure represented nearly an 18% increase since 1970; however, the state's share of US income declined from 3.2% in 1960 to 2.7% in 1978. The median family income in 1975 was $15,531 (8th in the US).

The following table shows the average weekly wages for production workers in the major Massachusetts industries as of October 1979, according to the Massachusetts Division of Employment Security:

Chemicals and allied products	$340.13
Instruments	298.51
Stone, clay, glass	295.97
Transportation equipment	294.53
Nonelectrical machinery	280.31
Paper and allied products	277.76
Primary metals	271.23
Electronics and electrical equipment	255.58
Rubber, plastics	247.56
Printing and publishing	247.08
Textile mill products	213.42
Furniture and fixtures	196.10
Lumber and wood	190.35
Apparel	152.19

Weekly hours of production workers ranged from 33 hours for apparel workers to 43 hours for paper and allied products workers.

As of 1975, 7.1% of all Bay Staters had incomes below the federal poverty line, down from 8.6% in 1969 and below the US average of 11.4%. As of 1972, 2.7% of the nation's top wealth holders lived in the state.

22 LABOR

According to the US Department of Labor, 2,338,000 Massachusetts residents were employed full-time in 1978. The unemployment rate for all workers was 5.4%; the rate for white workers was 5.3%, and for nonwhites, 8.3%. The overall unemployment rate was 11.2% in 1975 and 9.5% in 1976.

Clerical workers made up about 19% of the labor force in 1978; professional and technical workers, 18%; service workers, 14%; operatives (except transport), 13%; crafts workers, 12%;

managers and administrators (nonfarm), 10%; sales workers, 6%; nonfarm laborers, 4%; transportation equipment operators, 3%; and farm workers, less than 1%. Women comprised 43% of the Massachusetts labor force.

A federal census of workers covered by unemployment insurance in March 1977 revealed the following nonfarm employment pattern for Massachusetts:

	ESTABLISH-MENTS	EMPLOYEES	ANNUAL PAYROLL ('000)
Agricultural services, forestry, fishing	1,412	6,205	$ 77,209
Mining	97	1,100	21,546
Contract construction	10,667	62,085	1,035,090
Manufacturing, of which:	10,294	619,567	8,007,105
Nonelectrical machinery	(1,520)	(80,509)	(1,163,407)
Electric, electronic equipment	(621)	(80,911)	(1,041,655)
Transportation, public utilities	4,289	111,676	1,650,425
Wholesale trade	8,993	118,749	1,654,371
Retail trade	33,179	388,304	2,567,206
Finance, insurance, real estate	9,322	138,095	1,591,601
Services, of which:	34,760	505,787	4,757,147
Health services	(8,556)	(176,520)	(1,726,932)
Educational services	(964)	(78,874)	(781,721)
Other	996	1,370	18,209
TOTALS	114,009	1,952,938	$21,379,909

Data reported to the Massachusetts Division of Employment Security for 1978 showed 2,077,171 insured employees earning $23.8 billion in 1978. As of 1970 there were 341,167 government workers, 127,498 self-employed workers, and 7,258 unpaid family workers in the state.

Some of the earliest unionization efforts took place in Massachusetts in the early 1800s, particularly in the shipbuilding and construction trades. However, the most important trade unions to evolve were those in the state's textiles and shoe industries. The workers had numerous grievances: shoebinders' salaries of $1.60–2.40 a week during the 1840s, workdays of 14 to 17 hours, wages paid in scrip that could be cashed only at company stores (which charged exorbitantly high prices), children working at dangerous machinery. In 1867, a seven-week-long shoemakers' strike at Lynn, the center of the shoe business, was at that time the longest strike in US history.

After the turn of the century, the state suffered a severe decline in manufacturing, and employers sought to cut back wages to make up for lost profits. This resulted in a number of strikes by both the United Textile Workers and the Boot and Shoe Workers Union. The largest strike of the era was at Lawrence in 1912, when textile workers (led by a radical labor group, the Industrial Workers of the World) closed the mills, and the mayor called in troops in an attempt to reopen them. Although the textile and shoe businesses are no longer major employers in the state, the United Shoe Workers of America, the Brotherhood of Shoe and Allied Craftsmen, United Textile Workers, and the Leather Workers International Union of America have their headquarters in Massachusetts. As of 1976 there were 651,000 members of labor unions and employee associations in the state, accounting for 28% of all employees (20th in the US); 81% of the union members belonged to AFL-CIO affiliates.

Massachusetts was one of the first states to enact child labor laws. In 1842, it established the 10-hour day for children under 12; in 1867, it forbade employment for children under 10. The nation's first Uniform Child Labor Law, establishing an 8-hour day for children aged 14 to 16, was enacted by Massachusetts in 1913. Massachusetts was also the first state to enact minimum wage guidelines (1912).

²³AGRICULTURE

As of 1979, only 650,000 acres (263,000 hectares), or 13% of the state's land area, was active farmland. Farming was mostly limited to the western Massachusetts counties of Hampshire, Franklin, and Berkshire, and southern Bristol County. Total agricultural income for 1979 was estimated at $242,779,000, 44th of the 50 states.

Although the state is not a major farming area, it is the largest producer of cranberries in the US. Production for 1978 was 111.8 million lb, 56% of the US total. Output totals for other crops in 1978 were as follows: corn for silage, 660,000 tons; hay, 262,000 tons; fresh vegetables, 45,200 tons; apples, 2,381 tons; tobacco, 729 tons; and maple syrup, 28,000 gallons. While of local economic importance, these figures are tiny fractions of US totals.

²⁴ANIMAL HUSBANDRY

Massachusetts is not a major producer of livestock. At the end of 1979, the state had 103,000 cattle and calves, 60,000 hogs and pigs, and 6,700 sheep and lambs. Production figures for 1979 were cattle and calves, 19,010,000 lb, worth $11,563,000; hogs and pigs, 18,640,000 lb, worth $8,201,000; sheep and lambs, 327,000 lb, worth $226,000; and turkeys, 2,993,000 lb, worth $2,035,000. The poultry industry also produced 1,580,000 chickens, worth $3,239,000, in 1978/79; and 340,000,000 eggs, worth $18,812,000, were sold during the same period.

In 1979, the state was the 5th-leading producer of ice cream, with 42,909,000 gallons. Other dairy products included milk, 572,000,000 lb; and cheese, 7,780,000 lb. Honey production was 420,000 lb.

²⁵FISHING

Massachusetts' fish catch is one of the largest in the US, but the fishing industry is not as important to the state economy as it once was.

The early settlers earned much of their income from the sea. The first shipyard in Massachusetts opened at Salem Neck in 1637, and during the years prior to independence the towns of Salem, Newburyport, Plymouth, and Boston were among the colonies' leading ports. By 1807, Massachusetts' fishing fleet made up 88% of the US total; for much of the 19th century, Nantucket and, later, New Bedford were the leading US whaling centers. But with the decline of the whaling industry came a sharp drop in the importance of fishing to the livelihood of the state. By 1978, the fishing industry ranked 13th in importance of the 15 industries monitored by the state. In that year there were 478 firms with 2,875 employees and a total annual payroll of $56,173,745.

Despite the decline, the value of the commercial catch in 1978—$152,251,000—was still the highest among the New England states and the 4th highest in the US. In the total catch of 376,878,000 lb, the major species were cod, haddock, mackerel, and lobster.

The state's long shoreline and many rivers make sport fishing a popular pastime for both deepsea and freshwater fishermen. The fishing season runs from mid-April through late October, with the season extended through February for bass, pickerel, panfish, and trout.

²⁶FORESTRY

Forestry is a minor industry in the state. A federal census in March 1977 found 19 firms with 112 employees and an annual payroll of $906,000 involved in forestry.

Forested lands cover about 2,952,000 acres (1,195,000 hectares), 0.4% of the US total. Of more importance is the manufacture of wood and paper products. In 1978 there were 396 lumber and wood products establishments with 5,400 employees and 322 paper and paper products manufacturers with 30,406 workers. The value added by all lumber and wood products manufactured in 1977 was $111.8 million; by paper and paper products manufacturers, $749.7 million.

There were 189 state parks and forests totaling 396,583 acres (160,492 hectares) in 1980. There are no national forests in Massachusetts.

²⁷MINING

Massachusetts accounts for only a small fraction of the nation's mineral output. In 1978, an estimated $82 million worth of minerals were mined in the state, 43d among the 50 states. Estimated production figures in tons for the year were sand and gravel, 17,000,000; stone, 8,964,000; lime, 186,000; and clays, 151,000.

²⁸ENERGY AND POWER

Massachusetts is highly dependent on oil for electric generation and home heating, and energy costs in the state are among the highest in the US. During the late 1970s, as much as 80% of the state's electric power output was generated from oil.

In 1978, about 37 billion kwh of electric power were produced; installed capacity was 10.1 million kw. Almost all generating capacity in the state is privately owned. Of the 31.5 billion kwh sold in 1977, 35% was for residential use, 37% commercial, 25% industrial, and 3% for other purposes. Boston Edison supplies electricity to the city of Boston; the rest of the state is served by 13 other companies, although a few municipalities do generate their own power. Power companies are regulated by the Department of Public Utilities, which establishes rates and monitors complaints from customers.

Massachusetts had no proved oil reserves as of 31 December 1978. After a lengthy court battle, oil exploration off the coast of Cape Cod began in 1979. Environmentalists and fishermen had sought to prevent development of an oil industry in the region, which is one of the richest fishing grounds in the country. No wells had been drilled as of early 1980, however.

The state consumes but does not produce natural gas. In 1978, about 165 trillion Btu of natural gas were sold at a cost of $605 million to 1,051,000 customers. Almost 54% of the gas sold was for residential use.

There are two nuclear power plants: one in Plymouth, with an operating capacity of 670 mw; and the other in Rowe, in western Massachusetts, with a capacity of 185 mw. Two pumped-storage hydroelectric plants, one at Bear Swamp and the other at Northfield Mountain, have a combined capacity of 1,600 mw. Forty run-of-the-river hydroelectric plants account for 200 mw; as of 1980 there were plans to construct additional plants, the largest being a 30-mw facility in Holyoke.

Because of the rising cost of home heating oil and the availability of wood, some Massachusetts residents were reportedly converting to wood stoves for home heating. Reliable data on the extent of this trend are not yet available.

The state encourages energy conservation and the development of alternative energy systems by granting tax credits to qualifying industries. Private researchers in the state are experimenting with solar energy systems and other alternatives to fossil fuels.

²⁹INDUSTRY

Massachusetts was the nation's first major industrial state, and during the latter part of the 19th century it was the US leader in shoemaking and textile production. By 1860, the state was a major producer of machinery and milled nearly one-fourth of the country's paper.

Massachusetts remains an important manufacturing center, placing 14th in the value of its shipments and 12th in value added by manufacture in 1976. Nearly all the major manufacturing sectors had plants in Massachusetts' eastern counties, with the largest concentration in Bristol, Essex, Middlesex, and Worcester counties, which collectively held 63% of the state's manufacturing jobs in 1977. Much of this industry is located along Route 128, a superhighway that circles Boston from Gloucester in the north to Quincy in the south and is unique in its concentration of high technology enterprises.

The following table shows value added by manufacture for selected industries in 1972 and 1977:

	1972	1977
Electronic computing equipment	$502,900,000	$1,702,300,000
Instruments and related products	876,200,000	1,570,200,000
Communications equipment	527,200,000	1,013,300,000
Textile mill products	417,500,000	556,800,000
Apparel and accessories	398,500,000	534,800,000
Metalworking machinery	265,600,000	366,700,000
Newspaper publishing	249,200,000	335,100,000
Book publishing	97,000,000	227,600,000

Massachusetts' future as a manufacturing center depends on its continued preeminence in the production of computers, optical equipment, and other sophisticated instruments. Among the major computer manufacturers in the state are Digital Equipment Corp. in Maynard, Honeywell in Cambridge, Wang Laboratories in Tewksbury, and Data General in Westboro; important instruments manufacturers include General Electric in Lynn, Itek in Lexington, and Foxboro in Foxboro. Other major manufacturers are Raytheon (Lexington), with assets of $2.3 billion in 1979; Gillette (Boston), with assets of $1.5 billion; and Polaroid (Cambridge), with assets of $1.2 billion.

³⁰COMMERCE

Massachusetts' machinery and electrical goods industries are important components of the state's wholesale trade, along with motor vehicle and automotive equipment, and paper and paper products. Overall, in 1972, 9,059 establishments with 114,800 employees produced about $19.2 billion in sales, 2.8% of the US total and 12th highest among the 50 states. The March 1977 employment census covered slightly fewer establishments—8,993—but more employees, 118,749. More than one-fourth of the wholesale establishments were located in Middlesex County.

The state ranked 10th in retail trade in 1977, with sales of $18,474,302,000, in 46,745 stores of all types. Food stores accounted for 23% of sales; automotive dealers, 16%; department stores, 10%; eating and drinking places, 10%; gasoline service stations, 7%; clothing stores, 6%; and other establishments, 28%. Middlesex County led the counties with 24% of all sales. Boston was the city with the highest retail sales, 10% of the total.

In 1978, the Boston customs district handled about $17.9 billion in imports (7% of the US total) and $10.3 billion in exports (10% of the US total). Foreign trade zones were established in both Boston and New Bedford in 1977. Foreign exports of the state's own manufactures totaled $2.5 billion in 1976.

³¹CONSUMER PROTECTION

The cabinet-level Executive Office of Consumer Affairs serves as an information and referral center for consumer complaints and oversees the activities of many regulatory agencies. The Office of the Attorney General also has a Consumer Protection Division that handles consumer complaints. The Massachusetts Consumer Council advises the governor and legislature; there are many local consumer councils.

³²BANKING

By the mid-1800s, Boston had developed into a major banking center whose capital financed the state's burgeoning industries. Today banking remains an important sector of the state's economy; in 1977, according to the federal employment census, 1,398 banks and their branches employed 39,725 workers, with an annual payroll of $389,735,000. Nearly 75% of these workers had jobs in commercial banks, 21% in mutual savings banks, and the rest in bank-related institutions.

As of 1978 there were 146 commercial banking companies in the state, with total assets of $23 billion. The largest banks, all located in Boston, were the First National Bank of Boston, with deposits of $7.8 billion and assets of $5.6 billion; the New England Merchants National Bank, with deposits of $1.5 billion and assets of $1.9 billion; the Shawmut Bank of Boston, with deposits of $1.5 billion and assets of $2.1 billion; and the State Street Bank and Trust Company, with deposits of $1.3 billion and assets of $1.8 billion.

A total of 166 savings and loan associations with assets of $7.2 billion were active in 1977. The 17 insured savings and loan associations in the Boston metropolitan area had assets of $1.4 billion in 1978.

State-chartered savings banks, trust companies, cooperative banks, credit unions, and consumer credit grantors are examined by the state Division of Banks and Loan Agencies, within the Executive Office of Consumer Affairs. The division also approves interest rates, administers the state's banking laws, and oversees bank practices and audits.

³³INSURANCE

Insurance is an important business in Massachusetts, and some of the largest life and property/casualty insurance companies in the nation have their headquarters in Boston. In 1978, the state's 771 insurance companies had 59,848 employees.

Bay Staters held 9,283,000 life insurance policies worth $71.8 billion in 1978. The average amount of life insurance per family was $33,500, and payments to 82,500 beneficiaries amounted to $274,500,000.

New England Mutual Life Insurance Co. of Boston was the first mutual company to be chartered in the US. It remains one of the larger firms in the business, with assets of $5.8 billion in 1978. John Hancock Mutual Life, also of Boston, was the 5th-largest life insurance company in the US in 1978, with assets of $16.2 billion. The Massachusetts Mutual Life Insurance Company had assets of $7.6 billion during the same year.

Of the 26 mutual property/casualty companies in Massachusetts, the largest is Liberty Mutual of Boston. In 1978, it had assets of $4.2 billion, 2d highest in the US. Automobile insurance premiums written in the state in 1978 totaled $948.7 million; in 1971, Massachusetts became the first state in the US to implement a no-fault automobile insurance law.

All aspects of the insurance business in Massachusetts, including the licensing of agents and brokers and the examination of all insurance companies doing business in the state, are controlled by the Division of Insurance, under the Executive Office of Consumer Affairs.

³⁴SECURITIES

The Boston Stock Exchange, founded in 1846, is the only stock exchange in Massachusetts. As of 31 December 1979, 931 issues were traded on the exchange, with a total volume for the year of 63,872,000 shares.

Mutual funds originated in Boston during the 1920s; by 1975, nearly $11.1 billion in assets were held in the funds managed in Boston (1st in the US).

The Securities Division of the Office of the Secretary of the Commonwealth is responsible for licensing and monitoring all brokerage firms in the state.

³⁵PUBLIC FINANCE

The Massachusetts budget is prepared by the Executive Office of Administration and Finance and is presented by the governor to the legislature for revision and approval. The fiscal year runs from 1 July to 30 June.

The following is a summary of estimated expenses and revenues for the 1978/79 and 1979/80 fiscal years:

REVENUES	1978/79	1979/80
Taxes	$3,520,200,000	$3,785,000,000
Department revenues (fees, licenses, permits, etc.)	419,400,000	476,700,000
Federal reimbursements	1,070,300,000	1,117,400,000
Federal revenue sharing	73,800,000	72,400,000
Transfer receipts	54,600,000	174,000,000
TOTALS	$5,138,300,000	$5,625,500,000

EXPENDITURES	1978/79	1979/80
Agency operations	$1,620,996,079	$1,745,012,618
Direct and medical service	1,448,054,804	1,558,187,697
Local aid	1,350,173,050	1,505,621,830
Other operations	720,416,248	774,382,877
TOTALS	$5,139,640,181	$5,583,205,022

The general obligation debt as of January 1980 was more than $2.8 billion, and the total state debt was nearly $3.5 billion.

36 TAXATION

Massachusetts' tax burden on a per capita basis is higher than the US average, but far from the highest. Total tax revenues received in 1977 were the 10th highest in the country.

As of 1979, the state levied a 5% tax plus a 7.5% surcharge on earned income and a 10% tax plus a 7.5% surcharge on unearned income. The corporate income tax rate was 9.5%. Commercial banks and other banking and trust companies pay a 12.54% tax on net income; public utilities, 6.5%.

A 5% gross receipts tax on sales was in effect in 1979, but such necessities as food, clothing, and home heating fuel were exempted. The estate tax ranges from 5% to 16%; estates worth less than $60,000 are not taxed. Other levies include room occupancy and meal taxes; taxes on alcoholic beverages, cigarettes, gasoline, and motor vehicles; and a pari-mutuel tax.

State residents and businesses paid nearly $9.7 billion in federal taxes in 1976, or $1,662 per capita. Massachusetts' share of federal spending that year was almost $9.5 billion.

Bay Staters filed nearly 2.4 million federal income tax returns for 1977, paying a total tax of $4.2 billion.

37 ECONOMIC POLICY

The Office of New Business Development of the Department of Commerce and Development (within the Executive Office of Economic Development and Manpower Affairs) provides business information and aids new businesses in securing venture capital and in exporting their products. Small businesses can also receive help in obtaining loans and mortgage insurance. The state provides training for new employees or provides a subsidy for companies that arrange for on-the-job training. In addition, cities and towns can issue revenue bonds for industrial expansion in their localities.

Among the many tax incentives offered to businesses are a 3% investment tax credit; an export sales tax exemption; property and sales tax exemptions for some machinery, parts, and inventory; credits against the state excise tax; and real estate tax reductions for building facilities in certain urban areas. Tax reductions are offered for the use of alternative energy sources (i.e., avoidance of fossil fuels), and five-year tax exemptions are granted for the development of products related to energy conservation. Also, losses for the first five years of business can be carried forward for tax purposes.

Massachusetts is divided into 13 regional planning districts. A regional planning commission in each district seeks to direct the economic and social growth of that district and to help the planning efforts of its localities.

38 HEALTH

The average life expectancy of a Massachusetts resident was 71.83 years in 1969–71, 15th highest in the US. The rate for males was 68.12, for females 75.45. In 1977 there were 11.8 live births per 1,000 population. The infant mortality rate was 11.6 per 1,000 live births among whites and 16.7 among nonwhites. Both mortality rates were better than the US average. That year there were 34,382 abortions, for a rate of 506 per 1,000 live births.

The death rates from heart disease and cancer in 1977 were above US averages. The major causes of death and their rates per 100,000 population were heart diseases, 353.2; malignant neoplasms, 198.5; cerebrovascular diseases, 78.9; accidents, 36.6; and pneumonia and influenza, 32.5.

In 1970, there were an estimated 211,000 alcoholics, 179,300 males and 31,700 females; the alcoholism rate of 5,850 per 100,000 adults was the 4th highest in the US. Programs for treatment and rehabilitation of alcoholics are administered by the Division of Alcoholism of the Department of Health, under the Executive Office of Human Services. The Division of Communicable and Venereal Diseases operates VD clinics throughout the state and provides educational material to schools and other groups. The Division of Drug Rehabilitation administers drug abuse treatment from a statewide network of hospital agencies and self-help groups. The state also runs a lead-poisoning prevention program.

As of 1978, Massachusetts had 28 psychiatric hospitals (3 federally operated) and 2 institutions for the mentally retarded. The patient population in 1976 was 4,122 in state and county facilities; in 1975, 659 mental patients were in private hospitals, and 63,572 were receiving outpatient psychiatric care. There were 4,810 full-time residents in institutions for the mentally retarded in 1978.

Massachusetts had 189 hospitals, with 45,456 beds and 936,260 admissions in 1978; there were 24,247 registered nurses, 7,767 licensed practical nurses, and 2,725 medical and dental residents. Among the best-known institutions are Massachusetts General Hospital, a leading research and treatment center, and the Massachusetts Eye and Ear Infirmary, a Boston clinic. The state has one of the highest physician-population ratios in the country: in 1977 there were 14,299 active physicians, or 248 per 100,000 residents, 38% above the US average. The state had 3,983 professionally active dentists in 1979. Four prominent medical schools are located in the state: Harvard Medical School, Tufts University School of Medicine, Boston University School of Medicine, and the University of Massachusetts School of Medicine. The average cost per stay in a Massachusetts community hospital in 1977, at $2,293, was the highest in the US, except for Washington, D.C. The average cost per day of $270 ranked 4th after Alaska, California, and Washington, D.C. Nearly $1.3 billion in health insurance benefits were paid in 1977, the 8th-highest total among the 50 states.

All health care facilities are registered by the Department of Public Health. The Bureau of Health Care Standards and Regulations inspects and licenses hospitals, clinics, school infirmaries, and blood banks every two years. Licensing of nursing homes is under the control of the Bureau of Long-Term Care Facilities; ambulances and their operators and attendants are certified by the Office of Emergency Services.

39 SOCIAL WELFARE

In 1978, 363,400 Massachusetts residents qualified for about $484 million in public assistance and $721 million in medical assistance under the Aid to Families with Dependent Children program. An estimated 522,000 state residents participated in the federal food stamp program, receiving coupons worth $233.7 million; the federal subsidy was $155.4 million. About 743,000 students, or about 65% of those enrolled, took part in the school lunch program, at a cost to the federal government of $42 million. Total federal public assistance grants were an estimated $805 million in 1978, 4.1% of the US total.

A total of $2.4 billion was paid to 897,800 recipients of Social Security benefits in 1977. Of that amount, 609,200 persons received retirement benefits totaling $1.6 billion, 188,400 persons received $517.9 million in survivors' benefits; and 100,200 disabled workers received benefits totaling $247.1 million. The average monthly retirement benefit (excluding persons with special benefits) of $251.30 was 3.4% above the US average.

Of more than 131,500 Massachusetts residents receiving $222.9 million in Supplemental Security Income in 1978, about 74,000 elderly persons received $101.3 million; 52,600 disabled persons got $109.8 million; and 4,900 blind persons were paid $11.8 million.

Massachusetts had 869 nursing homes with 50,900 beds and 48,100 patients in 1976. In 1978, nearly 242,000 state residents were enrolled in federally aided vocational training programs, at a cost to government of $211 million. Most of those enrolled were trained for office occupations and industrial trades. The state spent about $176.2 million in workers' compensation in 1977. In 1978, about $292 million in unemployment benefits were paid to 562,000 claimants.

40 HOUSING

Massachusetts' housing stock, much older than the US average, reflects the state's colonial heritage and its ties to English architectural traditions.

According to the 1970 census, 61% of the state's housing was built prior to 1939. Two major styles are common: colonial, typified by wood frame, two stories, center hall entry, and center chimney; and Cape Cod, 1½ story houses built by fishermen, typified by shallow basements, shingled roofs, clapboard fronts, and unpainted shingled sides weathered gray by the salt air. Many new houses are also built in these styles.

As of 1970 there were 1,890,319 housing units in the state. Of the 1,836,198 year-round structures, 55.1% were owner-occupied and 40.7% were rented; the remainder were vacant. Nearly 97% of all structures had plumbing. In 1978, 21,486 new housing units were authorized, of which 69% were in single-unit structures, a figure slightly above the US average.

The Department of Community Affairs, within the Executive Office of Communities and Development, administers federal housing programs for the state. The Massachusetts Housing Finance Agency finances the construction and rehabilitation of housing by private and community groups.

41 EDUCATION

Massachusetts has a long history of support for education. The Boston Latin School opened in 1635 as the first public school in the colonies. Harvard College—the first college in the US—was founded the following year. In 1647, for the first time, towns with more than 50 people were required by law to establish tax-supported school systems. More "firsts" followed: the country's first board of education, compulsory school attendance law, training school for teachers, state school for the retarded, and school for the blind. The drive for quality public education in the state was intensified through the efforts of educator Horace Mann, who during the 1830s and 1840s was also a leading force for the improvement of school systems throughout the US. Today the state boasts some of the most highly regarded private secondary schools and colleges in the country.

As of 1970, about 1.1% of the population was illiterate, slightly below the US average; 72.3% of state residents were high school graduates. During the 1978/79 school year there were 1,142,000 students enrolled in Massachusetts public schools, 777,000 in kindergarten through grade 8 and 365,000 in grades 9–12. There were 76,300 teachers, 65,600 in public schools and 10,700 in private schools. Among US city school systems, Boston's was 35th in size, with 76,889 students and 4,137 teachers in 160 schools in 1977/78. Violence broke out in South Boston schools when they were integrated in the mid-1970s.

The early years of statehood saw the development of private academies where the students could learn more than the basic reading and writing skills that were taught in the town schools at the time. Some of these private preparatory schools remain, including such prestigious institutions as Andover, Deerfield, and Groton. Enrollment in private schools totaled 124,000 in 1977/78, representing 3.3% of the US total.

There are 119 colleges and universities in the state. The major public university system is the University of Massachusetts, with campuses at Amherst and Boston and a medical school at Worcester. The Amherst campus, established in 1863, had an enrollment of 23,953 in the fall of 1977; the Boston campus,

established in 1965, had 8,363 students. The other public universities are Southeastern Massachusetts University in North Dartmouth and the University of Lowell. The 8 colleges and 2 specialized training schools in the Massachusetts State College system had 48,028 students in 1977, while the Massachusetts Board of Regional Community Colleges had 56,096 students at its 15 campuses.

Harvard University, which was established originally in Cambridge as a college for clergymen and magistrates, has grown to become one of the country's premier institutions; its 1977 student population was 21,095. Also located in Cambridge are Radcliffe College, founded in 1879, with 2,085 students in 1977, and the Massachusetts Institute of Technology, or MIT (1861), with 8,712 students. Mount Holyoke College, the first US college for women, was founded in 1837 and had a 1977 enrollment of 1,927. Other prominent private schools, their dates of origin, and their 1977 enrollment are Amherst College (1821), 1,502; Boston College (1863), 13,943; Boston Conservatory of Music (1867), 445; Boston University (1869), 24,414; Brandeis University (1947), 3,624; Clark University (1887), 3,060; Hampshire College (1965), 1,226; New England Conservatory of Music (1867), 761; Northeastern University (1898), 34,043; Smith College (1871), 2,635; Tufts University (1852), 6,937; Wellesley College (1875), 2,144; and Williams College (1793), 1,941.

Among the tuition assistance programs available to state residents are the Massachusetts General Scholarships, awarded to more than 250,000 college students annually; Massachusetts Honor Scholarships, for outstanding performance on the Scholastic Aptitude Test; special scholarships for war orphans and the children of deceased members of fire, police, and corrections departments; and the Higher Education Loan Plan, offered by the Massachusetts Higher Education Assistance Corp.

The State Board of Education, within the Executive Office of Educational Affairs, establishes standards and policies for the public schools throughout the state; its programs are administered by the Department of Education. Higher education planning and programs are under the control of the Board of Higher Education. Total expenditures for state public elementary and secondary schools in 1976/77 were nearly $2.5 billion.

42 ARTS

Boston is the center of artistic activity in Massachusetts, and Cape Cod and the Berkshires are areas of significant seasonal artistic activity.

Boston is the home of several small theaters, some of which offer previews of shows bound for Broadway. Of the regional theaters scattered throughout the state, the Williamstown Theater in the Berkshires and the Provincetown Theater on Cape Cod are especially noteworthy. Many art shows are held in Cape Cod towns during the summer months.

The Boston Symphony, one of the major orchestras in the US, was founded in 1881 and has had as its principal conductors Serge Koussevitzky, Charles Munch, Erich Leinsdorf, and Seiji Ozawa, among others. During the summer, the symphony is the main attraction of the Berkshire Music Festival at Tanglewood in Lenox. An offshoot of the Boston Symphony, the Boston "Pops" Orchestra, gained fame under the conductorship of Arthur Fiedler. Its mixture of popular, jazz, and light symphonic music continued in 1980 under the direction of Fiedler's successor, John Williams.

Boston is also the headquarters of the Opera Company of Boston, under the artistic direction of Sarah Caldwell. The Boston Ballet Company is the state's major dancing troupe.

43 LIBRARIES AND MUSEUMS

Massachusetts has one of the most important university libraries in the country, and numerous museums and historical sites commemorating its rich colonial history.

Three regional library systems serve the entire state. The Eastern Massachusetts system has 200 member libraries, as well as subregional libraries in Andover, Falmouth, Lowell, New Bedford, Quincy, Taunton, and Wellesley. The Central Massachusetts system has 70 member libraries, and the Western system 103. The major city libraries are the Boston Public Library, which in 1978 had 28 branches and a book stock of 4,472,684 volumes; the Worcester Public Library, with 6 branches and 855,817 books; and the Springfield Public Library, with 8 branches and 670,868 books. Statewide in 1978 there were 23,657,000 volumes in public libraries, with total circulation of 35,248,200. Public library income amounted to $55,401,575.

The Boston Athenaeum, with 600,000 volumes, is the most noteworthy private library in the state. Early in 1979, it agreed to sell its best-known works of art—the Gilbert Stuart portraits of George and Martha Washington—to the Smithsonian Institution and the Boston Museum of Fine Arts. The American Antiquarian Society in Worcester has a 650,000-volume research library of original source material dating from colonial times to 1876.

Harvard University's library system is one of the largest in the world, with 9,753,214 volumes in 1978. Other major academic libraries and their 1978 book holdings were Boston University, 1,265,366; University of Massachusetts (Amherst), 1,202,548; Smith College, 853,802; Boston College, 807,934; and Wellesley, 602,084.

Boston houses a number of important museums, among them the Museum of Fine Arts (its vast holdings of artwork include extensive Far East and French impressionists collections and American art and furniture), the Isabella Stewart Gardner Museum, the Museum of Science, the Massachusetts Historical Society, and the Children's Museum. Harvard University's museums include the Fogg Art Museum, the Peabody Museum of Archaeology and Ethnology, the Museum of Comparative Zoology, and the Botanical Museum. Other museums of note are the Whaling Museum in New Bedford, the Essex Institute in Salem, the Worcester Art Museum, the Clark Art Institute in Williamstown, the Bunker Hill Museum near Boston, and the National Basketball Hall of Fame in Springfield. In addition, many towns have their own historical societies and museums, including Historic Deerfield, Framingham Historical and Natural History Society, Ipswich Historical Society, Lexington Historical Society, and Marblehead Historical Society. Plimoth Plantation in Plymouth is a recreation of life in the 17th century, and Old Sturbridge Village, a working historical farm, displays 18th- and 19th-century artifacts. The state had over 270 museums in 1979.

44 COMMUNICATIONS
The first American post office was established in Boston in 1639. Today there are more than 650 post offices in Massachusetts and about 22,500 postal service employees, 3.3% of the US total.

Alexander Graham Bell first demonstrated the telephone in 1876 in Boston. As of 1978 there were 4,472,070 telephones in the state, 3,272,607 residential and 1,199,463 commercial; virtually every household had telephone service. During the same year, state residents made an estimated 7.1 billion local calls and 1.1 billion toll calls. The telephone system had 28,864,402 mi (46,452,838 km) of wire in cable, 18,338 mi (29,512 km) of aerial wire, 4,714 mi (7,586 km) of tube in coaxial cable, and 1,495 mi (2,406 km) of radio relay systems. Nearly all telephones in the state were owned by Bell System affiliates. Service is supplied by New England Telephone and Telegraph.

The state had 64 AM stations and 38 FM stations in 1978, when 12 television stations were also in operation. Educational programming was provided by Boston's WGBH, which is also a major producer of programming for the Public Broadcasting Service. As of the end of 1978 there were 30 cable television systems, with 219,001 subscribers in 79 communities.

45 PRESS
Milestones in US publishing history that occurred in the state include the first book printed in English colonies (Cambridge,

1640) and the first regularly issued American newspaper, the *Boston News-Letter* (1704). During the mid-1840s, two noted literary publications made their debut, the *North American Review* and the *Dial*, the latter under the editorial direction of Ralph Waldo Emerson and Margaret Fuller. The *Atlantic Monthly*, which remains an influential journal of literature, art, and politics, began publishing in 1857.

As of 30 September 1978 there were 47 daily newspapers in the state, 5 morning and 42 evening, with a combined circulation of 2,029,935. Nine Sunday papers had a combined circulation of 1,532,638. The *Boston Globe*, the most widely read newspaper in the state, has won numerous awards for journalistic excellence on the local and national levels. The *Christian Science Monitor* is highly respected for its coverage of national and international news. Major newspapers and their average daily circulations in 1979 were:

AREA	NAME	DAILY	SUNDAY
Boston	Christian Science Monitor (m)	165,677	—
	Globe (all day, S)	321,961 (m) 158,730 (e) }	670,267
	Herald American (m,S)	286,941	379,250

Massachusetts is also a center of book publishing, with more than 25 publishing houses. Among them are Little, Brown and Co., Houghton Mifflin, and Harvard University Press.

46 ORGANIZATIONS
Among the more important educational and research associations headquartered in Massachusetts are the National Association of Independent Schools, the National Commission for Cooperative Education, both in Boston, and the National Bureau of Economic Research in Cambridge. The Union of Concerned Scientists in Cambridge and the Center for Action on Endangered Species in Ayer are the major environmental and animal welfare associations in the state.

Academic and scientific organizations headquartered in Boston include the Academy of Applied Science, American Academy of Arts and Sciences, American Meteorological Society, American Society of Law and Medicine, the American Surgical Association, and the Optometric Research Institute. The World Academy of Art and Science is located in Cambridge, and the National Association of Emergency Medical Technicians is at Newton Highlands. The Protestant Guild for the Blind is in Watertown; the International Association for Religious Freedom is located at Lexington.

Among the many professional, business, and consumer organizations based in Boston are the American Institute of Management, National Consumer Law Center, Northern Textile Association, Wood Products Manufacturers Association, and the Wool Manufacturers Council. The American Orchid Society, the Nieman Foundation, and the World Science Fiction Society (presenter of the "Hugo" awards) are in Cambridge, and the Shoe Suppliers Association of America is in East Bridgewater.

The headquarters of the John Birch Society, an archconservative political association, is in Belmont. Oxfam-America, the US affiliate of the international humanitarian relief agency, is located in Boston. Major sports associations in the state are the Eastern College Athletic Conference in Centerville, the American Hockey League in Springfield, the Eastern Rugby Union of America in Cambridge, and the US Figure Skating Association in Boston. Action for Children's Television, a group concerned with the quality of broadcast programming, is located in Newtonville. The International Friendship League, which matches pen pals in 139 countries, has its headquarters in Boston.

47 TOURISM, TRAVEL, AND RECREATION
Massachusetts' beaches are a popular destination for summer travelers, but other areas have their own attractions.

In 1978, visitors to Massachusetts spent a total of 42,641,749 days in the state. About 39% of the visits were for recreation and entertainment, 37% to see friends or relatives, 11% for business, 9% for other personal reasons, and 4% for conventions. Nearly 43% of the visitor-days were spent during the summer. Tourist-related industries employed 51,064 workers, with a payroll of $263,627,000 in 1978. The largest employment—almost 41%—was on Nantucket Island, followed by Martha's Vineyard and Cape Cod.

Estimated travel expenditures for the year exceeded $1.2 billion. For those visitors who stayed in commercial lodging, spending was broken down as follows: lodging, 38%; eating and drinking establishments, 30%; gasoline stations, 7%; public transportation, 4%; amusements, 3%; and miscellaneous items, 18%.

The largest number of visitor-days were spent in Barnstable County (Cape Cod). Among its many attractions are beaches, fishing, good dining spots, several artists' colonies with arts and crafts fairs, antique shops, and summer theaters. Beaches, fishing, and quaint villages are also the charms of Nantucket and Martha's Vineyard.

Boston was the second most popular area for tourists. A trip to the city might include such old landmarks as Faneuil Hall, Old North Church, the USS *Constitution*, and Paul Revere's House, and such newer attractions as the John Hancock Observatory and the skywalk above the Prudential Tower. Boston Common, one of the earliest public parks in the country, is the most noteworthy municipal park.

The Berkshires are the summer home of the Berkshire Music Festival at Tanglewood and the Jacob's Pillow Dance Festival in Lee, and during the winter also provide recreation for cross-country and downhill skiers. Essex County on the North Shore of Massachusetts Bay offers many seaside towns and the art colony of Rockport. Its main city, Salem, contains the Witch House and Museum as well as Nathaniel Hawthorne's House of Seven Gables. Middlesex County, to the west of Boston, holds the university city of Cambridge as well as the battlegrounds of Lexington and Concord. In Concord are the homes of Henry David Thoreau, Ralph Waldo Emerson, and Louisa May Alcott. Norfolk County, south of Boston, has the homes of three US presidents: John Adams and John Quincy Adams in Quincy and John F. Kennedy in Brookline. The seaport town and former whaling center of New Bedford and the industrial town of Fall River are in Bristol County. Plymouth County offers Plymouth Rock, Plimoth Plantation, and a steam train ride through some cranberry bogs.

Massachusetts has 129 state-owned camping areas and more than 100 private campgrounds that accommodated a combined total of 1,483,000 campers in 1978. In 1977/78, the state issued licenses to 108,570 hunters and 185,896 fishermen.

48 SPORTS

All of the major league professional sports have franchises in Massachusetts. The Boston Red Sox of the American League make their home in Fenway Park, one of the oldest baseball stadiums in the country. The New England Patriots, who play in Foxboro, are members of the American Football Conference of the National Football League. The Boston Celtics, the most successful basketball team in National Basketball Association history, play in Boston Garden, as do the Boston Bruins of the National Hockey League. The New England Teamen of the North American Soccer League play their home games in Foxboro.

Suffolk Downs in East Boston features Thoroughbred horse racing; harness racing takes place at the New England Harness Raceway in Foxboro. Dog racing can be seen at Raynham Park in Raynham, Taunton Dog Track in North Dighton, and Wonderland Park in Revere.

Probably the most famous amateur athletic event in the state is the Boston Marathon, a race of more than 26 mi (42 km) held every Patriots' Day (3d Monday in April). It attracts many of the world's top long-distance runners. During the summer, a number of boat races are held, including the Colorado Cup Races off Martha's Vineyard.

49 FAMOUS BAY STATERS

Massachusetts has produced an extraordinary collection of public figures and leaders of thought. Its three US presidents were John Adams (1735–1826), a signer of the Declaration of Independence; his son John Quincy Adams (1767–1848); and John Fitzgerald Kennedy (1917–63). All three served in Congress. John Adams was also the first US vice president; John Quincy Adams served as secretary of state under James Monroe. Calvin Coolidge (b.Vermont, 1872–1933) was governor of Massachusetts before his election to the vice-presidency in 1920 and his elevation to the presidency in 1923. Two others who held the office of vice president were another signer of the Declaration of Independence, Elbridge Gerry (1744–1814), for whom the political practice of gerrymandering is named; and Henry Wilson (b.New Hampshire, 1812–75), a US senator from Massachusetts prior to his election with Ulysses S. Grant. George Bush (b.1924) was elected vice president on the Republican ticket in 1980.

Massachusetts' great jurists include US Supreme Court Justices Joseph Story (1779–1845), Oliver Wendell Holmes, Jr. (1841–1935), Louis D. Brandeis (b.Kentucky, 1856–1941), and Felix Frankfurter (b.Austria, 1882–1965). Important federal officeholders at the cabinet level were Henry Knox (1750–1806), the first secretary of war; Timothy Pickering (1745–1820), the first postmaster general and later secretary of war and secretary of state under George Washington and John Adams; Levi Lincoln (1749–1820), attorney general under Jefferson; William Eustis (1753–1825), secretary of war under Madison; Jacob Crowninshield (1770–1808), secretary of the Navy under Jefferson, and his brother Benjamin (1772–1851), who held the same office under Madison; Daniel Webster (b.New Hampshire, 1782–1852), US senator from Massachusetts who served as secretary of state under William Henry Harrison, John Tyler, and Millard Fillmore; Edward Everett (1794–1865), a governor and ambassador who served as secretary of state under Fillmore; George Bancroft (1800–1891), a historian who became secretary of the Navy under James K. Polk; Caleb Cushing (1800–1879), attorney general under Franklin Pierce; Charles Devens (1820–91), attorney general under Rutherford B. Hayes; Christian Herter (1895–1966), secretary of state under Dwight Eisenhower; Elliot L. Richardson (b.1920), secretary of health, education, and welfare, secretary of defense, and attorney general under Richard Nixon; Henry Kissinger (b.Germany, 1923), secretary of state under Nixon and Gerald Ford and a Nobel Peace Prize winner in 1973; and Robert F. Kennedy (1925–68), attorney general under his brother John, and later US senator from New York.

Other federal officeholders include some of the most important figures in American politics. Samuel Adams (1722–1803), the Boston Revolutionary leader, served extensively in the Continental Congress and was later governor of the Bay State. John Hancock (1737–93), a Boston merchant and Revolutionary, was the Continental Congress's first president, and later became the first elected governor of the state. In the 19th century, Massachusetts sent abolitionist Charles Sumner (1811–74) to the Senate. As ambassador to England during the Civil War, John Quincy Adams's son Charles Francis Adams (1807–86) played a key role in preserving US–British amity. At the end of the century, Henry Cabot Lodge (1850–1924) emerged as a leading Republican in the US Senate, where he supported regulatory legislation, protectionist tariffs, and restrictive immigration laws, and opposed women's suffrage and the League of Nations; his grandson, also Henry Cabot Lodge (b.1902), is an internationalist who has held numerous federal posts and was US senator.

Massachusetts has provided two US House speakers: John W. McCormack (1891–1980) and Thomas P. "Tip" O'Neill, Jr. (b.1912). Other well-known legislators include Edward W. Brooke (b.1919), the first black US senator since Reconstruction, and Edward M. Kennedy (b.1932), President Kennedy's youngest brother and a leading Senate liberal.

Among other historic colonial and state leaders were John Winthrop (b.England, 1588–1649), a founder of Massachusetts and longtime governor; William Bradford (b.England, 1590–1657), a founder of Plymouth, its governor, and author of its classic history; Thomas Hutchinson (1711–80), colonial lieutenant governor and governor during the 1760s and 1770s; and Paul Revere (1735–1818), the Patriots' silversmith-courier, who was later an industrial pioneer.

Literary genius has flourished in Massachusetts. In the 17th century, the colony was the home of poets Anne Bradstreet (1612–72) and Edward Taylor (1645–1729) and of the prolific historian, scientist, theologian, and essayist Cotton Mather (1663–1728). Eighteenth-century notables include the theologian Jonathan Edwards (b.Connecticut, 1703–58), poet Phillis Wheatley (b.Senegal, 1753–84), and numerous political essayists and historians. During the 1800s, Massachusetts was the home of novelists Nathaniel Hawthorne (1804–64), Louisa May Alcott (b.Pennsylvania, 1832–88), Horatio Alger (1832–99), and Henry James (b.New York, 1843–1916); essayists Ralph Waldo Emerson (1803–82) and Henry David Thoreau (1817–62); and such poets as Oliver Wendell Holmes, Sr. (1809–94), Henry Wadsworth Longfellow (b.Maine, 1807–82), John Greenleaf Whittier (1807–92), James Russell Lowell (1819–91), and Emily Dickinson (1830–86). Classic historical writings include the works of George Bancroft, William Hickling Prescott (1796–1859), John Lothrop Motley (1814–77), Francis Parkman (1823–93), and Henry B. Adams (1838–1918). Among 20th-century notables are novelists John P. Marquand (b.Delaware, 1893–1960) and John Cheever (b.1912); poets Elizabeth Bishop (1911–79), Robert Lowell (1917–77), Anne Sexton (1928–74), and Sylvia Plath (1932–63); and historian Samuel Eliot Morison (1887–1976). In philosophy, Charles Sanders Peirce (1839–1914) was one of the founders of pragmatism; Henry James's elder brother William (b.New York, 1842–1910) pioneered psychology; and George Santayana (b.Spain, 1863–1952), philosopher and author, grew up in Boston. Mary Baker Eddy (b.New Hampshire, 1821–1910) founded the Church of Christ, Scientist, during the 1870s.

Reformers have abounded in Massachusetts, especially in the 19th century. William Lloyd Garrison (1805–79), Wendell Phillips (1811–84), and Lydia Maria Child (1802–80) were outstanding abolitionists. Lucretia Coffin Mott (1793–1880), Lucy Stone (1818–93), Abigail Kelley Foster (1810–87), Margaret Fuller (1810–50), and Susan Brownell Anthony (1820–1906) were leading advocates of women's rights. Horace Mann (1796–1859), the state secretary of education, led the fight for public education; and Mary Lyon (1797–1849) founded Mount Holyoke, the first women's college. Efforts to improve the care and treatment of the sick, wounded, and handicapped were led by Samuel Gridley Howe (1801–76), Dorothea Lynde Dix (1802–87), and Clara Barton (1821–1912), founder of the American Red Cross. The 20th-century reformer and NAACP leader William Edward Burghardt Du Bois (1868–1963) was born in Great Barrington.

Leonard Bernstein (b.1918) is a composer and conductor of worldwide fame. Arthur Fiedler (1894–79) was the celebrated conductor of the Boston Pops Orchestra. Charles Bulfinch (1763–1844), Henry H. Richardson (b.Louisiana, 1838–86), and Louis Henri Sullivan (1856–1924) have been among the nation's important architects. Painters include John Singleton Copley (1738–1815), James Whistler (1834–1903), Winslow Homer (1836–1910), and Frank Stella (b.1936); Horatio Greenough (1805–52) was a prominent sculptor.

Among the notable scientists associated with Massachusetts are Nathaniel Bowditch (1773–1838), a mathematician and navigator; Samuel F. B. Morse (1791–1872), inventor of the telegraph; and Robert Hutchins Goddard (1882–1945), a physicist and rocketry pioneer.

Massachusetts' most famous journalist has been Isaiah Thomas (1750–1831). Its great industrialists include textile entrepreneurs Francis Lowell (1775–1817) and Abbott Lawrence (1792–1855). Elias Howe (1819–67) invented the sewing machine.

Massachusetts was the birthplace of television journalists Mike Wallace (b.1918) and Barbara Walters (b.1931). Massachusetts-born show business luminaries include director Cecil B. DeMille (1881–1959); actors Walter Brennan (1894–1974), Jack Haley (1901–79), Ray Bolger (b.1904), Bette Davis (b.1908), and Jack Lemmon (b.1925); and singers Donna Summer (b.1948) and James Taylor (b.1948). Outstanding among Massachusetts-born athletes was world heavyweight boxing champion Rocky Marciano (Rocco Francis Marchegiano, 1924–69), who retired undefeated in 1956.

⁵⁰BIBLIOGRAPHY

Andrews, Charles McLean. *The Colonial Period in American History*. New Haven: Yale University Press, 1934.

Bailyn, Bernard. *The Ordeal of Thomas Hutchinson*. Cambridge: Harvard University Press, 1974.

Boyer, Paul, and Stephen Nissenbaum. *Salem Possessed: The Social Origins of Witchcraft*. Cambridge: Harvard University Press, 1974.

Brown, Richard D. *Massachusetts: A Bicentennial History*. New York: Norton, 1978.

Butterfield, L. H., et al., eds. *Diary and Autobiography of John Adams*. Cambridge: Harvard University Press, 1962.

Federal Writers' Project. *Massachusetts: A Guide to Its Places and People*. Boston: Houghton Mifflin, 1973.

Gibney, Fred J. *Monograph of the Commonwealth of Massachusetts*. Boston: Massachusetts Office of Economic Affairs, 1980.

Gross, Robert. *The Minutemen and Their World*. New York: Hill and Wang, 1976.

Handlin, Oscar. *Boston's Immigrants*. Rev. ed. Cambridge: Harvard University Press, 1959.

Hart, Albert Bushnell, ed. *Commonwealth History of Massachusetts: Colony, Province, and State*. 5 vols. New York: States History Co., 1927–30.

Haskell, John D., Jr., ed. *Massachusetts: A Bibliography of Its History*. Boston: G. K. Hall, 1976.

Massachusetts, Commonwealth of. *A Manual for the Use of the General Court, 1979–80*. Boston: Causeway, 1979.

Massachusetts, Commonwealth of. Secretary of the Commonwealth. Citizen Information Service. *Citizen's Guide to State Services: A Selective Listing of Governmental Agencies*. Boston, 1976.

Morison, Samuel Eliot. *Builders of the Bay Colony*. Boston: Houghton Mifflin, 1958 (orig. 1930).

Morison, Samuel Eliot. *The Maritime History of Massachusetts, 1783–1860*. Boston: Houghton Mifflin, 1961.

Russell, Francis. *A City in Terror—1919—The Boston Police Strike*. New York: Viking, 1975.

Russell, Francis. *Tragedy in Dedham: The Story of the Sacco-Vanzetti Case*. New York: McGraw-Hill, 1971.

MICHIGAN

State of Michigan

ORIGIN OF STATE NAME: Possibly derived from the Fox Indian word *mesikami*, meaning "large lake." **NICKNAME:** The Wolverine State. **CAPITAL:** Lansing. **ENTERED UNION:** 26 January 1837 (26th). **SONG:** "Michigan, My Michigan" (unofficial). **MOTTO:** *Si quæris peninsulam amœnam circumspice* (If you seek a pleasant peninsula, look about you). **COAT OF ARMS:** In the center, a shield depicts a peninsula on which a man stands, at sunrise, holding a rifle. At the top of the shield is the word "Tuebor" (I will defend), beneath it the state motto. Supporting the shield are an elk on the left and a moose on the right. Over the whole, on a crest, is an American eagle beneath the US motto. **FLAG:** The coat of arms centered on a dark blue field, fringed on three sides. **OFFICIAL SEAL:** The coat of arms surrounded by the words "The Great Seal of the State of Michigan" and the date "A.D. MDCCCXXXV" (1835, the year the state constitution was adopted). **BIRD:** Robin. **FISH:** Trout. **FLOWER:** Apple blossom. **TREE:** White pine. **GEM:** Chlorastrolite. **STONE:** Petoskey stone. **LEGAL HOLIDAYS:** New Year's Day, 1 January; Martin Luther King Day, Monday nearest 15 January; Lincoln's Birthday, 12 February; Washington's Birthday, 3d Monday in February; Memorial Day, last Monday in May; Independence Day, 4 July; Labor Day, 1st Monday in September; Columbus Day, 2d Monday in October; Veterans Day, 11 November; Thanksgiving Day, 4th Thursday in November; Christmas Day, 25 December. **TIME:** 7 A.M. EST = noon GMT; 6 A.M. CST = noon GMT.

¹LOCATION, SIZE, AND EXTENT

Located in the eastern north-central US, Michigan is the 3d-largest state E of the Mississippi River and ranks 23d in size among the 50 states.

The total area of Michigan (excluding Great Lakes waters) is 58,216 sq mi (150,779 sq km), of which land takes up 56,817 sq mi (147,156 sq km) and inland water 1,399 sq mi (3,623 sq km). The state consists of the upper peninsula adjoining three of the Great Lakes—Superior, Huron, and Michigan—and the lower peninsula, projecting northward between Lakes Michigan, Erie, and Huron. The upper peninsula extends 334 mi (538 km) E–W and 215 mi (346 km) N–S; the lower peninsula's maximum E–W extension is 220 mi (354 km), and its greatest N–S length is 286 mi (460 km).

Michigan's upper peninsula is bordered on the N and E by the Canadian province of Ontario (with the line passing through Lake Superior, the St. Marys River, and Lake Huron); on the S by Lake Huron, the Straits of Mackinac separating the two peninsulas, and Lake Michigan; and on the SW and W by Wisconsin (with the line passing through the Menominee, Brule, and Montreal rivers). The lower peninsula is bordered on the N by Lake Michigan, the Straits of Mackinac, and Lake Huron; on the E by Ontario (with the line passing through Lake Huron, the St. Clair River, Lake St. Clair, and the Detroit River); on the SE by Ontario and Ohio (with the line passing through Lake Erie); on the S by Ohio and Indiana; and on the W by Illinois and Wisconsin (with the line passing through Lake Michigan and Green Bay). The state's geographic center is in Wexford County, 5 mi (8 km) NNW of Cadillac.

Among the most important islands are Isle Royale in Lake Superior; Sugar, Neebish, and Drummond islands in the St. Marys River; Bois Blanc, Mackinac, and Les Cheneaux islands in Lake Huron; Beaver Island in Lake Michigan; and Belle Isle and Grosse Ile in the Detroit River.

The state's total boundary length is 1,673 mi (2,692 km). The total freshwater shoreline is 3,121 mi (5,023 km).

²TOPOGRAPHY

Michigan's two peninsulas are generally level land masses. Flat lowlands predominate in the eastern portion of both peninsulas and in scattered areas elsewhere. The state's lowest point, 572 feet (174 meters), is found in southeastern Michigan along Lake Erie. Higher land is found in the western area of the lower peninsula, where elevations rise to as much as 1,600 feet (500 meters); the hilly uplands of the upper peninsula attain elevations of 1,800 feet (550 meters). The state's highest point, at 1,980 feet (604 meters), is Mt. Curwood, in Baraga County.

Michigan's political boundaries extend into four of the five Great Lakes, giving Michigan jurisdiction over 16,231 sq mi (42,038 sq km) of Lake Superior, 13,037 sq mi (33,766 sq km) of Lake Michigan, 8,975 sq mi (23,245 sq km) of Lake Huron, and 216 sq mi (559 sq km) of Lake Erie, for a total of 38,459 sq mi (99,608 sq km). In addition, Michigan has about 35,000 inland lakes and ponds, the largest of which is Houghton Lake, on the lower peninsula, with an area of 31 sq mi (80 sq km).

The state's leading river is the Grand, about 260 mi (420 km) long, flowing through the lower peninsula into Lake Michigan. Other major rivers that flow into Lake Michigan include the St. Joseph, Kalamazoo, Muskegon, Pere Marquette, and Manistee. On the eastern side of the peninsula, the Saginaw River and its tributaries drain an area of some 6,000 sq mi (15,500 sq km), forming the state's largest watershed. Other important rivers that flow into Lake Huron include the Au Sable, Thunder Bay, and Cheboygan. In the southeast, the Huron and Raisin rivers flow into Lake Erie. Most major rivers in the upper peninsula (including the longest, the Menominee) flow southward into Lake Michigan and its various bays. Tahquamenon Falls, in the eastern part of the upper peninsula, is the largest of the state's more than 150 waterfalls.

Most of the many islands belonging to Michigan are located in northern Lake Michigan and in Lake Huron, although the largest, Isle Royale, about 44 mi (71 km) long by 8 mi (13 km) wide, is found in northern Lake Superior. In northern Lake Michigan, Beaver Island is the largest, while Drummond Island, off the eastern tip of the upper peninsula, is the largest island in the northern Lake Huron area.

Michigan's geological development resulted from its location in what was once a basin south of the Laurentian Shield, a landmass covering most of eastern and central Canada and extending southward into the upper peninsula. Successive glaciers that swept down from the north dumped soil from the shield into the basin and eroded the basin's soft sandstone, limestone, and shale. With the retreat of the last glacier from the area about 6000 BC, the two peninsulas, the Great Lakes, and the islands in these lakes began to emerge, assuming their present shapes about 2,500 years ago.

³CLIMATE

Michigan has a temperate climate with well-defined seasons. The warmest temperatures and longest frost-free period are found most generally in the southern part of the lower peninsula; Detroit has a normal daily mean temperature of 50°F (10°C), ranging from 26°F (–3°C) in January to 73°F (23°C) in July. Colder temperatures and a shorter growing season prevail in the more northerly regions; Sault Ste. Marie has a normal daily mean of 40°F (4°C), ranging from 14°F (–10°C) in January to 64°F (18°C) in July. The coldest temperature ever recorded in the state is –51°F (–46°C), registered at Vanderbilt on 9 February 1934; the all-time high of 112°F (44°C) was recorded at Mio on 13 July 1936. Both sites are located in the interior of the lower peninsula, away from the moderating influence of the Great Lakes.

Detroit has an average annual precipitation of 31 in (79 cm); rainfall tends to decrease as one moves northward. The greatest snowfall is found in the extreme northern areas, where cloud cover created by cold air blowing over the warmer Lake Superior waters causes frequent heavy snow along the northern coast; Houghton and Calumet, on the Keweenaw Peninsula, average 183 in (465 cm) of snow a year, more than any other area in the state. Similarly, Lake Michigan's water temperatures create a snow belt along the west coast of the lower peninsula.

Cloudy days are more common in Michigan than in most states, due in part to the condensation of water vapor from the Great Lakes. Detroit has sunshine, on average, only 32% of the days in December and January, and only 54% year-round. The annual average relative humidity at Detroit is 77% at 7 A.M., dropping to 58% at 1 P.M.; at Sault Ste. Marie, the comparable percentages are 85% and 67%, respectively. The southern half of the lower peninsula is an area of heavy thunderstorm activity. Late spring and early summer are the height of the tornado season.

⁴FLORA AND FAUNA

Maple, birch, hemlock, aspen, spruce, and fir predominate in the upper peninsula, maple, birch, aspen, pine, and beech in the lower. Once common in the state, elms have largely disappeared because of the ravages of disease, while the white pine (the state tree) and red pine, which dominated northern Michigan forests and were prime objects of logging operations, have been replaced in cutover lands by aspen and birch. The area south of a line from about Muskegon to Saginaw Bay formerly held the only significant patches of open prairie land (found chiefly in southwestern Michigan) and areas of widely scattered trees, called "oak openings." Intensive agricultural development, followed by urban industrial growth, leveled much of this region's forests, although significant wooded acreage remains, especially in the less populated western regions.

Strawberries, raspberries, gooseberries, blueberries, and cranberries are among the fruit-bearing plants and shrubs that grow wild in many areas of the state, as do mushrooms and wild asparagus. The state flower, the apple blossom, calls to mind the importance of fruit-bearing trees and shrubs in Michigan, but wild flowers also abound, with as many as 400 varieties found in a single county. Protected plants include all members of the orchid, trillium, and gentian families, trailing arbutus, prince's-pine, bird's-foot violet, climbing bittersweet, flowering dogwood, mountain and Michigan hollies, and American lotus.

Michigan's fauna, like its flora, has been greatly affected by settlement and, in a few cases, by intensive hunting and fishing.

Moose are now confined to Isle Royale, as are nearly all the remaining wolves, which once roamed throughout the state. The caribou and passenger pigeon have been extirpated, but the elk and turkey have been successfully reintroduced in the 20th century. There is no evidence that the state's namesake, the wolverine, was ever found in Michigan, at least in historic times. Despite intensive hunting, resulting in a near-record kill of 158,360 deer during the 1977 hunting season (it is estimated that another 80,000 deer are bagged by poachers each year), the deer population remains high, with an estimated 300,000 in the upper peninsula and 700,000 in the lower peninsula. Other game animals include the common cottontail, snowshoe hare, raccoon, and various squirrels. In addition to the raccoon, important native furbearers are the river otter and the beaver, once virtually exterminated but now making a strong comeback.

More than 300 types of birds have been observed. Aside from the robin, the state bird, the most notable bird is Kirtland's warbler, which nests only in a 60-sq-mi (155-sq-km) section of jack-pine forest in north-central Michigan. Ruffed grouse, bobwhite quail, American woodcock, and various ducks and geese are hunted extensively. Populations of ring-necked pheasant, introduced in 1895, have dropped at an alarming rate in recent decades. Reptiles include the massasauga, the state's only poisonous snake.

Whitefish, perch, and lake trout (the state fish) are native to the Great Lakes, while perch, bass, and pike are indigenous to inland waters. In 1877, the carp was introduced, with such success that it has since become a nuisance. Rainbow and brown trout have also been planted, and in the late 1960s, the state enjoyed its most spectacular success with the introduction of several species of salmon.

The first Michigan list of threatened or endangered fauna in 1976 included 64 species, 15 endangered and 49 threatened. In 1977 and 1978, surveys indicated that Kirtland's warbler, the bald eagle, and the osprey were holding their own, while the greater prairie chicken, barn owl, and common tern were continuing to decline. Other endangered animals include the Indiana bat, gray wolf, Kirtland's water snake, blue pike, and five species of cisco.

⁵ENVIRONMENTAL PROTECTION

Michigan's initial conservation law, enacted in 1859, limited the hunting of deer and certain other wildlife to specific seasons. Later acts extended these provisions to other species, outlawed certain kinds of hunting and fishing equipment, and banned commercial hunting (1881).

The Michigan Forestry Commission was established in 1899, but only after the state's vast timber resources had been virtually wiped out by lumbermen. Four years later, a reforestation program was launched, the first state forest was set aside, and organized forest-fire fighting began. In 1921, the Michigan Department of Conservation was founded; it was renamed the Department of Natural Resources in 1968 and reorganized in 1973 to consolidate state environmental protection activities. The Michigan Environmental Review Board, established in 1974, advises the governor on environmental policy, holds public hearings, and reviews environmental impact statements. With the passage in 1970 of the Environmental Protection Act, Michigan became the first state to provide citizens with the statutory right to bring suit to protect the environment for the general good.

In the 1977/78 fiscal year, the Department of Natural Resources received an appropriation of $103,840,507. The largest amounts were budgeted for such traditional purposes as park-

LOCATION:41°41′ to 47°30′N; 82°26′ to 90°31′W. **BOUNDARIES**: Canadian line, 721 mi (1,160 km); Ohio line, 95 mi (153 km); Indiana line, 126 mi (203 km); Illinois line, 51 mi (82 km); Wisconsin line, 680 mi (1,094 km).

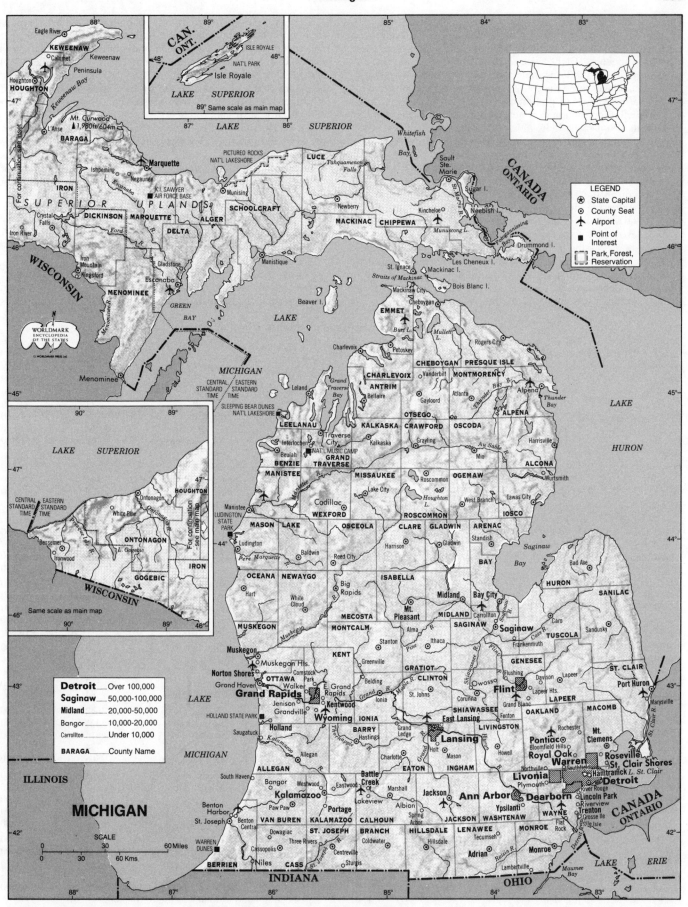

LEGEND
- State Capital
- County Seat
- Airport
- Point of Interest
- Park, Forest, Reservation

Detroit — Over 100,000
Saginaw — 50,000-100,000
Midland — 20,000-50,000
Bangor — 10,000-20,000
Carrollton — Under 10,000
BARAGA — County Name

MICHIGAN

SCALE
0   30   60 Miles
0   30   60 Kms

See US political: front cover J1; physical: back cover J1.

lands, wildlife, fisheries, and forests. A total of $1,941,370 was appropriated for air-pollution control; nearly 300 stations, supporting some 450 sensors, were part of a state and local air-sampling network. Eight water-quality monitoring programs, with a total of 215 stations, detected violations of water-quality standards and measured the waste-assimilative capacity of streams and the effectiveness of pollution-control programs. Increasing concern with the problem of water pollution led Michigan voters in 1968 to adopt overwhelmingly a $335-million bond issue for prevention and abatement facilities. Between 1 July 1976 and 30 June 1978, more than $818 million in federal and state grants were committed to a huge program to upgrade and expand existing sewage facilities and to build new ones. Serious problems remain in the Detroit industrial area, where, as of 1980, neither public nor industrial facilities were in compliance with federal and state water-quality standards.

The Resource Recovery Division licenses approximately 350 solid-waste processing facilities and 10,000 refuse transport units each year; promotion of recycling or resource-recovery facilities is also part of the division's responsibilities. A "bottle bill" requiring a deposit to be paid on all beverage cans and bottles sold in Michigan was approved by the voters in 1978.

The Land Resource Program Division is charged with responsibility for developing land-use objectives and guidelines that will permit planned growth while protecting and managing land resources for future use. State-owned lands, totaling 4,343,774 acres (1,757,869 hectares), about 12% of the state's total land area, are under the jurisdiction of the Lands Division. As of 30 June 1975, the state had 85 soil conservation and water conservation districts.

The accidental mixing of the fire-retardant chemical polybrominated biphenyl (PBB) with livestock feed in 1974 and the resultant controversy over the disposal of contaminated animals judged unfit for human consumption points up the problem of toxic or hazardous waste disposal. It was estimated in 1980 that of the 58 million tons of industrial waste produced in the state each year, about 12 million tons are toxic.

[6]POPULATION

Michigan ranked 7th among the 50 states in the 1970 census, with a population of 8,879,862. The preliminary 1980 census total was 9,236,891, for an increase of 4% during the decade.

During the long prehistoric period, Michigan was inhabited by only a few thousand Indians. As late as 1810, the non-Indian population of Michigan Territory was only 4,762. The late 1820s

Michigan Counties, County Seats, and County Populations[1]

COUNTY	COUNTY SEAT	AREA (SQ MI)	POPULATION (EST. 1978)	COUNTY	COUNTY SEAT	AREA (SQ MI)	POPULATION (EST. 1978)
Alcona	Harrisville	678	9,300	Lapeer	Lapeer	658	67,100
Alger	Munising	905	10,000	Leelanau	Leland	345	13,400
Allegan	Allegan	826	74,000	Lenawee	Adrian	753	87,300
Alpena	Alpena	565	33,400	Livingston	Howell	572	92,300
Antrim	Bellaire	476	16,300	Luce	Newberry	906	7,300
Arenac	Standish	367	13,500	Mackinac	St. Ignace	1,014	11,200
Baraga	L'Anse	901	8,600	Macomb	Mt. Clemens	480	693,400
Barry	Hastings	554	42,900	Manistee	Manistee	553	22,500
Bay	Bay City	447	121,600	Marquette	Marquette	1,828	73,800
Benzie	Beulah	316	10,600	Mason	Ludington	490	24,700
Berrien	St. Joseph	580	167,300	Mecosta	Big Rapids	560	34,800
Branch	Coldwater	506	38,900	Menominee	Menominee	1,038	26,500
Calhoun	Marshall	709	140,700	Midland	Midland	520	69,700
Cass	Cassopolis	491	45,400	Missaukee	Lake City	565	9,700
Charlevoix	Charlevoix	414	19,400	Monroe	Monroe	557	131,800
Cheboygan	Cheboygan	721	19,800	Montcalm	Stanton	712	45,400
Chippewa	Sault Ste. Marie	1,591	30,500	Montmorency	Atlanta	555	7,700
Clare	Harrison	571	23,800	Muskegon	Muskegon	501	158,800
Clinton	St. Johns	572	55,000	Newaygo	White Cloud	849	33,400
Crawford	Grayling	561	9,100	Oakland	Pontiac	867	1,009,400
Delta	Escanaba	1,177	40,300	Oceana	Hart	536	21,000
Dickinson	Iron Mt.	757	26,100	Ogemaw	West Branch	571	16,800
Eaton	Charlotte	571	82,100	Ontonagon	Ontonagon	1,316	10,700
Emmet	Petoskey	461	21,500	Osceola	Reed City	581	18,200
Genesee	Flint	642	451,000	Oscoda	Mio	563	6,700
Gladwin	Gladwin	503	18,300	Otsego	Gaylord	527	14,300
Gogebic	Bessemer	1,107	19,600	Ottawa	Grand Haven	563	149,400
Grand Traverse	Traverse City	462	48,400	Presque Isle	Rogers City	648	14,100
Gratiot	Ithaca	566	39,300	Roscommon	Roscommon	521	16,200
Hillsdale	Hillsdale	600	41,200	Saginaw	Saginaw	814	227,700
Houghton	Houghton	1,017	37,300	St. Clair	Port Huron	734	133,500
Huron	Bad Axe	819	35,800	St. Joseph	Centreville	506	51,800
Ingham	Mason	559	271,000	Sanilac	Sandusky	961	40,200
Ionia	Ionia	575	49,700	Schoolcraft	Manistique	1,181	9,300
Iosco	Tawas City	544	30,500	Shiawassee	Corunna	540	70,300
Iron	Crystal Falls	1,171	14,700	Tuscola	Caro	815	55,100
Isabella	Mt. Pleasant	572	52,100	Van Buren	Paw Paw	603	62,300
Jackson	Jackson	698	150,200	Washtenaw	Ann Arbor	711	254,500
Kalamazoo	Kalamazoo	562	208,000	Wayne	Detroit	605	2,390,600
Kalkaska	Kalkaska	566	11,400	Wexford	Cadillac	559	22,800
Kent	Grand Rapids	857	435,800				
Keweenaw	Eagle River	538	2,200	TOTALS		56,817	9,189,000
Lake	Baldwin	571	7,000				

[1]Entries do not add to total because of rounding.

marked the start of steady, often spectacular growth. The population increased from 31,639 people in 1830 to 212,267 in 1840 and 397,654 in 1850. Subsequently, the state's population grew by about 400,000 each decade until 1910, when its population of 2,810,173 ranked 8th among the 46 states. Industrial development sparked a sharp rise in population to 4,842,325 by 1930, which pushed Michigan ahead of Massachusetts into 7th place.

According to the 1970 census, Michigan's population was slightly younger than the national median age; the group in the upper age brackets showed the highest percentage of increase between 1960 and 1970, while a declining birthrate reduced the number of those under 5 years of age by 18%. Nevertheless, in 1976, Michigan had the lowest proportion of elderly citizens of any state in the northeast or north-central regions. State residents were among the least mobile in the US: as of 1976, only 1.3% of those 14 years of age or older had lived in Michigan for less than a year, and almost 65% had lived there all their lives.

With 74% of its population classified as urban in 1970, Michigan's population distribution virtually equaled the national average. Population density for the entire state in 1970 was 156 persons per sq mi (60 per sq km); half the population was concentrated in the Detroit metropolitan area. Population densities varied from 4,408 persons per sq mi (1,702 per sq km) in Wayne County to 4 per sq mi (1.5 per sq km) in Keweenaw County. The estimated density for the state in 1978 was 162 per sq mi (63 per sq km).

Detroit has always been Michigan's largest city since its founding in 1701, but its growth, like the state's, was slow until well into the 19th century. The city's population grew from 21,019 in 1850 to 285,704 in 1900, when it ranked as the 13th-largest city in the country. Within the next 30 years, the booming automobile industry pushed the city up into 4th place, with a population of 1,568,662 in 1930. Since 1950, when the total reached 1,849,568, Detroit has lost population, dropping to 1,514,063 in 1970 and to 1,314,206 in 1976, when it slipped to 6th place among US cities. As Detroit lost population, however, many of its suburban areas grew at an even greater rate, and the Detroit metropolitan area totaled 4,370,000 in 1977 (5th in the US), up from 3,950,000 in 1960.

In 1970, 90 cities aside from Detroit had populations of 10,000 or more, of which only 6 were located in the northern parts of the state. Preliminary 1980 census results showed Detroit with a population of 1,192,222; Grand Rapids, 181,602; Warren, 161,173; Flint, 159,576; Lansing, the state capital, 130,208; Livonia, 104,660; and Ann Arbor, 103,583.

[7] ETHNIC GROUPS

The 1970 census counted 16,854 Indians, nearly double the number in 1960. Most of them are scattered across the state; in 1972, only 2,069 Indians were living on the four federal reservations comprising a total of 16,635 acres (6,732 hectares). The Ottawa, Chippewa, and Potawatomi are the principal groups with active tribal organizations.

The black population of Michigan in 1970 was 991,066, 11% of the total population (3d highest among the northern states). Two-thirds of Michigan's black citizens live in Detroit, where they made up nearly 44% of the 1970 total—the highest percentage of any city of a million people or more. Detroit, which experienced severe race riots in 1943 and 1967, has had a black mayor since 1974.

There were 126,870 native-born Hispanic Americans living in the state in 1970; another 7,604 residents were immigrants from Mexico, and a few thousand more were born in other Spanish-speaking countries. Michigan's Asian population has also been increasing; its numbers included 6,407 Chinese, 5,221 Japanese, and 3,657 Filipinos in 1970.

The 1970 census determined that 1,684,265 Michgan residents (19%) were foreign-born or had at least one foreign-born parent. Those of Canadian descent were the most numerous, with 353,154

(4% of the total population); followed by Poles, with 214,085 (2.4%); and Germans, with 184,192 (2.1%). In addition, the United Kingdom and Italy were each represented by more than 100,000 Michiganians. Although state residents of first- or second-generation European descent are, almost without exception, decreasing in number and proportion, their influence remains great. Detroit continues to have numerous well-defined ethnic neighborhoods, and Hamtramck, a city surrounded by Detroit, is still dominated by its Polish element. Elsewhere in Michigan, Frankenmuth is the site of an annual German festival, and the city of Holland has an annual tulip festival that attracts about 400,000 people each spring. In the upper peninsula, the Finnish culture dominates in rural areas; in the iron and copper mining regions, descendants of immigrants from Cornwall in England, the original mining work force, and persons of Scandinavian background predominate.

[8] LANGUAGES

Before white settlement, Algonkian-language tribes occupied what is now Michigan, with the Menomini and Chippewa in the upper peninsula and Ottawa on both sides of the Straits of Mackinac. Numerous place-names recall their presence: Michigan itself, Mackinaw City, Petoskey, Kalamazoo, Muskegon, Cheboygan, and Dowagiac. Indian languages were claimed as a mother tongue by 3,058 Michigan residents in 1970.

Except for the huge industrial area in southeastern Michigan, English in the state is remarkably homogeneous in its retention of the major Northern dialect features of upper New York and western New England. Common are such Northern forms as *pail, wishbone, darning needle* (dragonfly), *mouth organ* (harmonica), *sick to the stomach, quarter to four* (3:45), and *dove* as past tense of *dive.* Common also are such pronunciations as the /ah/ vowel in *fog, frog,* and *on*; the /aw/ vowel in *horrid, forest,* and *orange; creek* as /krik/; *root* and *roof* with the vowel of *put*; and *greasy* with an /s/ sound. *Swale* (a marsh emptying into a stream) and *clock shelf* (mantel) are dying Northern words not carried west of Michigan. *Pank* (to pack down, as of snow) is confined to the upper peninsula, as is *pasty* (meat-filled pastry), borrowed from Cornish miners. A minister is a *dominie* in the Dutch area around Holland and Zeeland.

Southern blacks have introduced into the southeastern automotive manufacturing areas a regional variety of English that, because it has class connotations in the North, has become a controversial educational concern. Three of its features are perhaps more widely accepted than others: the coalescence of /e/ and /i/ before a nasal consonant, so that *pen* and *pin* sound alike; the loss of /r/ after a vowel, so that *cart* and *cot* also sound alike; and the lengthening of the first part of the diphthong /ai/, so that *time* and *Tom* sound alike, as do *ride* and *rod.* A federal court in 1979 ordered teachers in the Ann Arbor school system to learn "black English" so that they might be more sensitive to the needs of their black students. This decision was criticized by some Michiganians who feared it would serve to legitimate "incorrect" and ungrammatical usage.

In 1970, English was the first language of 84% of the native-born population and 81% of all state residents. Speakers of principal first languages were as follows:

	NATIVE-BORN	FOREIGN-BORN
English	7,090,769	120,096
Polish	239,321	41,222
German	209,704	51,462
Italian	79,680	33,436
Spanish	68,755	14,715
French	64,099	17,585
Yiddish	24,875	10,666

[9] RELIGIONS

The Roman Catholic Church was the only organized religion in Michigan until the 19th century. Detroit's Ste. Anne's parish, established in 1701, is the 2d-oldest Catholic parish in the country. In 1810, a Methodist society was organized near Detroit, and after the War of 1812, as settlers poured in from the East, Presbyterian, Congregational, Baptist, Episcopal, and Quaker churches were founded. The original French Catholics, reduced to a small minority by the influx of American Protestants, were soon reinforced by the arrival of Catholic immigrants from Germany, Ireland, and later from eastern and southern Europe. The Lutheran religion was introduced by German and Scandinavian immigrants; Dutch settlers were affiliated with the Reformed Church in America. The first Jewish congregations were organized in Detroit by German Jews, with a much greater number of eastern European Jews arriving toward the end of the 1800s. The Orthodox Christian Church and the Islamic religion have been introduced by immigrants from the Near East during the 20th century.

In 1979, Michigan had 1,987,528 Roman Catholics and an estimated 90,195 Jews. Among Protestant denominations, the most recent census of church members, taken in 1971, showed various Lutheran groups with a combined total of 516,338 adherents. Among other major Protestant groups, the United Methodist Church had 348,490 adherents; United Presbyterian Church, 188,675; Episcopal Church, 116,386; and United Church of Christ, 102,132. The Seventh-Day Adventists, who had their world headquarters in Battle Creek from 1855 to 1903, number 29,993, and the Church of Jesus Christ of Latter-day Saints (Mormon) had 13,434.

[10] TRANSPORTATION

Because of Michigan's location, its inhabitants have always depended heavily on the Great Lakes for transportation. Not until the 1820s did land transportation systems begin to be developed. Although extensive networks of railroads and highways now reach into all parts of the state, the Great Lakes remain major avenues of commerce.

The first railroad company in the Midwest was chartered in Michigan in 1830, and six years later the Erie and Kalamazoo, operating between Toledo, Ohio, and Adrian, became the first railroad in service west of the Appalachians. Between 1837 and 1845, the state government sought to build three lines across southern Michigan, before abandoning the project and selling the two lines it had partially completed to private companies. The pace of railroad construction lagged behind that in other midwestern states until after the Civil War, when the combination of federal and state aid and Michigan's booming economy led to an enormous expansion in trackage from fewer than 800 mi (1,300 km) in 1860 to a peak of 9,021 mi (14,518 km) in 1910. With the economic decline of northern Michigan and the resultant drop in railroad revenues, however, trackage declined to 6,032 mi (9,708 km) by 1974, 11th highest among the 50 states. Most railroad passenger service is provided by Amtrak between Detroit and Chicago, and much of the freight is carried by Conrail. The Michigan state government, through the Department of Transportation, has helped to revive the railroad system by operating some lines.

Railroads have been used only to a limited degree in the Detroit area as commuter carriers, although efforts have been made to improve this service. In the early 1900s, more than 1,000 mi (1,600 km) of interurban rail lines provided rapid transit service in southern Michigan, but automobiles and buses drove them out of business, and the last line shut down in 1934. Street railway service began in a number of cities in the 1860s, and Detroit took over its street railways in 1922. Use of these public transportation systems declined sharply after World War II. By the 1950s, streetcars had been replaced by buses, but by 1960, many small communities had abandoned city bus service altogether. During the 1970s, with massive government aid, bus service was restored to many cities and was improved in others,

and the number of riders has generally increased. The Southeastern Michigan Transportation Authority coordinates mass transit facilities in the metropolitan Detroit area. By 1980, a Detroit subway was part of the improved mass transit plan, to be financed by a federal grant of $600 million.

As the center of the automobile industry, Detroit and the state as a whole have a vested interest in increasing the use of motor vehicles. In 1978, Michigan had 119,359 mi (192,090 km) of rural and municipal roads, including 8,345 mi (13,430 km) of state roads, 88,364 mi (142,208 km) of local roads, 20,190 mi (32,493 km) of town and city streets, and 2,460 mi (3,959 km) of federal highways. There are no toll roads in Michigan, which was among the first states to complete most of its interstate highway system. Major toll-free expressways include I-94 (Detroit to Chicago), I-96 (Detroit to Grand Rapids), and I-75 (from the Ohio border to Sault Ste. Marie). In 1978 there were 5,123,926 registered passenger cars, 1,105,516 trucks, 15,738 buses, and 242,400 motorcycles. Licensed drivers were estimated to number 6,250,000 in 1978.

The completion in 1957 of the Mackinac Bridge, the 3d-longest suspension span in the world, eliminated the major barrier to easy vehicular movement between the state's two peninsulas. The International Bridge at Sault Ste. Marie, the Blue-Water Bridge at Port Huron, the Ambassador Bridge at Detroit, and the Detroit-Windsor Tunnel link Michigan with Canada.

The opening of the St. Lawrence Seaway in 1959 made it possible for a large number of oceangoing vessels to dock at Michigan ports. In 1976, the Detroit River handled 104,551,800 tons of freight; the St. Clair River, 96,360,200 tons; and the St. Marys River, 78,930,000. In that year, the port of Detroit handled 26,407,900 tons of cargo; the iron-ore port of Escanaba, 11,934,400 tons; the limestone-shipping port of Calcite, 11,313,500 tons; and the River Rouge port, which handles Ford Motor Co. shipments, 11,061,900 tons.

Michigan was a pioneer in developing air transportation service. The Ford Airport at Dearborn in the 1920s had one of the first air passenger facilities and was the base for some of the first regular airmail service. In 1976, Michigan had 378 airfields, 13 heliports, and 9 seaplane bases; of these, 126 were publicly owned and 274 privately owned. The major airport is Detroit Metropolitan, which in 1978 emplaned 4,805,448 passengers and handled nearly 78,000 scheduled aircraft departures.

[11] HISTORY

Indian hunters and fishermen inhabited the region now known as Michigan as early as 9000 BC. By 5000 BC these first peoples were making use of copper found in the upper peninsula—the first known use of a metal by peoples anywhere in the western hemisphere. Around 100 BC, their descendants introduced agriculture into southwestern Michigan. In the latter part of the prehistoric era, the various Indian groups appear to have suffered a decline in population, perhaps because of an epidemic or attacks by other peoples from the east.

In the early 17th century, when European penetration began, Michigan's lower peninsula was virtually uninhabited. In the upper peninsula there were small bands of Chippewa (Ojibwa) along the St. Marys River and the Lake Michigan shore; in the west, Menomini Indians lived along the present Michigan-Wisconsin border. Both tribes were of Algonkian linguistic stock, as were most Indians who later settled in the area, except for the Winnebago of the Siouan group in the Green Bay region of Lake Michigan, and the Huron of Iroquoian stock in the Georgian Bay area of Canada. In the 1640s, the Huron were nearly wiped out by other Iroquois tribes from New York, and the survivors fled westward with their neighbors to the north, the Ottawa Indians. Eventually, both tribes settled at the Straits of Mackinac before moving to the Detroit area early in the 18th century.

During the same period, the Potawatomi and Miami Indians moved from Wisconsin into southern Michigan.

For two centuries after the first Europeans came to Michigan, the Indians remained a vital force in the area's development. They were the source of the furs that the whites traded for, and they also were highly respected as potential allies when war threatened between the rival colonial powers in North America. However, after the War of 1812, when the fur trade declined and the possibility of war receded, the value of the Indians to the white settlers diminished. Between 1795 and 1842, Indian lands in Michigan were ceded to the federal government, and the Huron, Miami, and many Potawatomi were removed from the area. Some Potawatomi were allowed to remain on lands reserved for them, along with most of the Chippewa and Ottawa Indians in the north.

The first European explorer known to have reached Michigan was a Frenchman, Etienne Brulé, who explored the Sault Ste. Marie area arond 1620. Fourteen years later, Jean Nicolet explored the Straits of Mackinac and the southern shore of the upper peninsula en route to Green Bay. Missionary and fur trading posts, to which were later added military forts, were established at Sault Ste. Marie by Father Jacques Marquette in 1668, and then at St. Ignace in 1671. By the 1680s, several temporary posts had been established in the lower peninsula. In 1701, Antoine Laumet de la Mothe Cadillac founded at the site of present-day Detroit a permanent settlement where French craftsmen and farmers would make their home.

Detroit and Michigan grew little, however, because the rulers of the French colony of New France were obsessed with the fur trade, which did not attract large numbers of settlers. The colony's small population contrasted unfavorably with the large populations of the more diversified English colonies along the Atlantic, and this was a major factor in France's defeat in the French and Indian War. Fears that under British rule the area would be turned over to English farmers from the coastal colonies, with the consequent destruction of the Indian way of life, led the Indians at Detroit to rebel in May 1763, under the leadership of the Ottawa chief Pontiac. The uprising, which soon spread throughout the west, ended in failure for the Indians; Pontiac gave up his siege of Detroit after six months, and by 1764, the British were in firm control. Nevertheless, the British authorities did not attempt to settle the area. The need to protect the fur trade placed the people of Michigan solidly on the British side during the American Revolution, since a rebel triumph would likely mean the migration of American farmers into the west, converting the wilderness to cropland. The British occupied Michigan and other western areas for 13 years after the Treaty of Paris in 1783 had assigned these territories to the new United States. The US finally got possession of Michigan in the summer of 1796, but it merely continued the fur trade because Michigan's remoteness from the east coast made transportation to the area difficult and costly.

Michigan became a center of action in the War of 1812 when British-dominated commercial interests and their Indian allies sought to maintain the supremacy of the fur trade in the Great Lakes area. The capture of Detroit by the British on 16 August 1812 was a crushing defeat for the Americans. Although Detroit was recaptured by the Americans in September 1813, continued British occupation of the fort on Mackinac Island, which they had captured in 1812, enabled them to control most of Michigan. The territory was finally returned to American authority under the terms of the Treaty of Ghent at the end of 1814. With the opening in 1825 of the Erie Canal, which provided a cheap, all-water link between Michigan and New York City, American pioneers turned their attention to these northern areas, and during the 1820s, settlers for the first time pushed into the interior of southern Michigan.

Originally part of the Northwest Territory, Michigan had been set aside in 1805 as a separate territory, but with boundaries considerably different from those of the subsequent state. On the south, the territory's boundary was a line set due east from the southernmost point of Lake Michigan; on the north, only the eastern tip of the upper peninsula was included. In 1818 and 1834, areas as far west as Iowa and the Dakotas were added to the territory for administrative purposes. By 1833, Michigan had attained a population of 60,000, qualifying it for statehood. The territorial government's request in 1834 that Michigan be admitted to the Union was rejected by Congress, however, because of a dispute over Michigan's southern boundary. When Indiana became a state in 1816, it had been given a 10-mi (16-km) strip of land in southwestern Michigan, and Michigan now refused to accede to Ohio's claim that it should be awarded lands in southeastern Michigan, including the present site of Toledo. In 1835, Michigan militia defeated the efforts of Ohio authorities to take over the disputed area during the so-called Toledo War, in which no one was killed. Nevertheless, Ohio's superior political power in Congress ultimately forced Michigan to agree to relinquish the Toledo Strip. In return, Congress approved the state government that the people of Michigan had set up in 1835. As part of the compromise that finally brought Michigan into the Union on 26 January 1837, the new state was given land in the upper peninsula west of St. Ignace as compensation for the loss of Toledo.

Youthful Stevens T. Mason, who had led the drive for statehood, became Michigan's first elected governor, but he and the Democratic Party fell out of grace when the new state was plunged into financial difficulties during the depression of the late 1830s. The party soon returned to power and controlled the state until the mid-1850s. In Michigan, as elsewhere, it was the slavery issue that ended Democratic dominance. In July 1854, antislavery Democrats joined with members of the Whig and Free-Soil parties at a convention in Jackson to organize the Republican Party. In the elections of 1854, the Republicans swept into office in Michigan, with rare exceptions controlling the state until the 1930s.

Abraham Lincoln was not the first choice of Michigan Republicans for president in 1860, but when he was nominated they gave him a solid margin of victory that fall and again in 1864. Approximately 90,000 Michigan men served in the Union army, taking part in all major actions of the Civil War. Michigan's Zachariah Chandler was one of the leaders of the Radical Republicans in the US Senate who fought for a harsh policy toward the South during Reconstruction.

Michigan grew rapidly in economic importance. Agriculture sparked the initial growth of the new state and was responsible for its rapid increase in population. By 1850, the southern half of the lower peninsula was filling up, with probably 85% of the state's population dependent in some way on agriculture for a living. Less than two decades later, exploitation of vast pine forests in northern Michigan had made the state the top lumber producer in the US. Settlers were also attracted to the same area by the discovery of rich mineral deposits, which made Michigan for a time the nation's leading source of iron ore, copper, and salt.

Toward the end of the 19th century, as timber resources were being exhausted and as farming and mining reached their peak stages of development, new opportunities in manufacturing opened up. Such well-known Michigan companies as Kellogg, Dow Chemical, and Upjohn had their origins during this period. The furniture industry in Grand Rapids, the paper industry in Kalamazoo, and numerous other industries were in themselves sufficient to ensure the state's increasing industrial importance. But the sudden popularity of Ransom E. Olds's Oldsmobile runabout, manufactured first in Detroit and then in Lansing, inspired a host of Michiganians to produce similar practical, relatively inexpensive automobiles. By 1904, the most successful of the new models, Detroit's Cadillac (initially a cheap car) and the first Fords, together with the Oldsmobile, had made Michigan the leading automobile producer in the country—and, later, in the world. The key developments in Michigan's auto industry were the creation of General Motors by William C. Durant in 1908; Henry Ford's development of the Model T in 1908, followed by his institution of the moving assembly line in 1913–14; and Walter P. Chrysler's formation in 1925 of the automobile corporation named after him.

Industrialization brought with it urbanization. A state that had been overwhelmingly rural became steadily more urban; the census of 1920 for the first time showed a majority of Michiganians living in towns and cities. Nearly all industrial development was concentrated in the southern third of the state, particularly the southeastern Detroit area. The northern two-thirds of the state, where nothing took up the slack left by the decline in lumber and mining output, steadily lost population and became increasingly troubled economically. Meanwhile, the Republican Party, under such progressive governors as Fred Warner and Chase Osborn—and, in the 1920s, under a brilliant administrator, Alexander Groesbeck—showed itself far better able than the Democratic opposition to adjust to the complexities of a booming industrial economy.

The onset of the depression of the 1930s had devastating effects in Michigan. The market for automobiles collapsed; by 1932, half of Michigan's industrial workers were unemployed. The ineffectiveness of the Republican state and federal governments in reacting to the crisis led to a landslide victory for the Democrats. In traditionally Republican areas of rural Michigan, the defection to the Democratic Party in 1932 was only temporary, but in the urban industrial areas the faith of the factory workers in the Republican Party was, for the great majority, permanently shaken. These workers, now driven by the desire to gain greater job security, joined the recruiting campaign launched by the new Congress of Industrial Organizations (CIO). By 1941, with the capitulation of the Ford Motor Co., the United Automobile Workers (UAW) had organized the entire auto industry, and Michigan had been converted from an essentially open-shop state to a strongly pro-union one.

Eventually, the liberal leadership of the UAW and other CIO unions in the state allied itself with the Democratic Party to provide the funds and organization the party needed to mobilize worker support. The coalition elected G. Mennen Williams governor in 1948 and reelected him for five successive two-year terms. By the mid-1950s, the Democrats controlled virtually all statewide elective offices. Because legislative apportionment still reflected an earlier distribution of population, however, the Republicans maintained their control of the legislature and frustrated the efforts of the Williams administration to institute social reforms. In the 1960s, as a result of US Supreme Court rulings, the legislature was reapportioned on a strictly equal-population basis. This shifted a majority of legislative seats into the urban areas, enabling the Democrats generally to control the legislature since that time.

In the meantime, Republican moderates, led by George Romney, gained control of their party's organization. From Romney's election as governor in 1962 through 1980, the Republicans held the governorship without interruption, with William G. Milliken succeeding Romney in 1969. The 1970s saw a major effort to redevelop downtown Detroit into a business and convention center.

12 STATE GOVERNMENT
Michigan has had four constitutions. The first, adopted in 1835 when Michigan was applying for statehood, was followed by constitutions adopted in 1850, 1908, and 1963.

The legislature consists of a senate of 38 members, elected for terms of four years, and a house of representatives of 110 members, elected for two-year terms. The legislature meets annually for a session of indeterminate length. Special sessions may be called by the governor. Legislation may be adopted by a majority of each house, but to override a governor's veto, a two-thirds vote of the members of each house is required. A legislator must be at least 21 years of age, a US citizen, and a qualified voter of the district in which he or she resides.

Elected executive officials include the governor and lieutenant governor (who run jointly), secretary of state, and attorney general, all serving four-year terms pursuant to the 1963 constitution. Elections are held in even-numbered years between US presidential elections. The governor and lieutenant governor must be at least 30 years old, US citizens, and must have been registered voters in the state for at least four years prior to election. The governor appoints the members of the governing boards and/or directors of 19 executive departments, with the exception of the Department of Education, whose head is appointed by the elected State Board of Education.

Legislative action is completed when a bill has been passed by both houses of the legislature and signed by the governor. A bill also becomes law if not signed by the governor after a 14-day period when the legislature is in session. The governor may stop passage of a bill by vetoing it or, if the legislature adjourns before the 14-day period expires, by refusing to sign it.

The constitution may be amended by a two-thirds vote of both houses of the legislature and a majority vote at the next general election. An amendment also may be proposed by registered voters through petition and submission to the general electorate. Every 16 years the question of calling a convention to revise the constitution must be submitted to the voters; the question was last put on the ballot in 1978 and was rejected.

To be eligible to vote in Michigan, one must be a US citizen, 18 years of age, and must have been a resident of the state and precinct for 30 days.

13 POLITICAL PARTIES
From its birth in 1854 through 1932, the Republican Party dominated state politics, rarely losing statewide elections and developing strong support in all parts of the state, both rural and urban. The problems caused by the economic depression of the 1930s revitalized the Democratic Party and made Michigan a strong two-party state. Democratic strength was concentrated in metropolitan Detroit, while Republicans maintained their greatest strength in "outstate" areas, except for the mining regions of the upper peninsula, where the working class, hit hard by the depression, supported the Democrats.

Most labor organizations, led by the powerful United Automobile Workers union, have generally supported the Democratic Party since the 1930s. But in recent years, moderate Republicans have had considerable success in attracting support among previously Democratic voters.

As of early 1980, both of Michigan's US senators were Democrats, as were 13 of the state's 19-member US House delegation and solid majorities in both houses of the state legislature. However, between 1948 and 1976, the Republican candidate for president carried Michigan in five out of the eight elections. In July 1980, Detroit was the site of the Republican National Convention that selected Ronald Reagan as presidential nominee. In the November election, Reagan won 49% of Michigan's popular vote, compared with 42% for Jimmy Carter and 7% for John Anderson. Despite the Republican presidential victory, the Democrats held their majorities in the state legislature and among the state's US congressional delegation. Also in November, the voters rejected three proposals to cut state taxes; the most radical would have slashed property taxes by 60% and required the state to reimburse localities for their lost revenue.

Among minor parties, only Theodore Roosevelt's Progressive Party, which captured the state's electoral vote in 1912, has succeeded in winning a statewide contest. The strongest third-party showing since 1912 was that of George Wallace, who in 1968 captured 10% of the total vote cast for president.

¹⁴LOCAL GOVERNMENT

In 1979 there were 2,467 separate units of local government in Michigan, including 83 counties, 265 cities, and 1,245 townships, as well as hundreds of educational and special districts. Each county is administered by a county board of commissioners, whose members, ranging in number from 3 to 35 according to population, are elected for two-year terms. Executive authority is vested in 5 officers elected for four-year terms: the sheriff, prosecuting attorney, treasurer, clerk, and register of deeds. An increasing number of counties are placing overall administrative responsibility in the hands of a county manager or administrator.

Most cities are governed by home-rule legislation, adopted in 1909, enabling them to establish their own form of government under an adopted charter. Some charters provide for the election of a mayor, who usually functions as the chief executive officer of the city. Other cities have chosen the council-manager system, with a council appointing the manager to serve as chief executive and the office of mayor being largely ceremonial. Many villages are incorporated under home-rule legislation in order to provide services such as police and fire protection.

Each county is divided into two types of townships, geographical and political. Each geographical (or congressional) township has an area of 36 sq mi (93 sq km); in sparsely populated areas, parts of two or more geographical townships may be combined into one political township. Township government, its powers strictly limited by state law, consists of a supervisor, clerk, treasurer, and up to four trustees, all elected for four-year terms and together forming the township board.

¹⁵STATE SERVICES

Educational services are handled in part by the Department of Education, which distributes state school-aid funds, certifies teachers, operates the School for the Deaf at Flint, the School for the Blind at Lansing, and the state library system. The 13 state-supported colleges and universities are independent of the department's control, each being governed by an elected or appointed board. Although most of the funds administered by the Department of Transportation go for highway construction

and maintenance, some allocations support improvements of railroad, bus, ferry, air, and port services.

Health and welfare services are provided by the Department of Public Health, the Department of Mental Health, the Department of Social Services, and the Department of Civil Rights, as well as through programs administered by the Department of Labor, the Commission on Aging, the Michigan Women's Commission, the Indian Affairs Commission, the Spanish-Speaking Affairs Commission, and the Veterans Trust Fund. The state's Army and Air National Guard units are maintained by the Department of Military Affairs. Civil defense is part of the Department of State Police, and state prisons and other correctional facilities are maintained by the Department of Corrections. Resource protection services are largely under the Department of Natural Resources.

Housing services are provided by the State Housing Development Authority within the Department of Social Services. The Department of Labor establishes and enforces rules and standards relating to safety, wages, licenses, fees, and conditions of employment. The Michigan Employment Security Commission oversees unemployment benefits and assists job seekers.

¹⁶JUDICIAL SYSTEM

Michigan's highest court is the state supreme court, consisting of 7 justices elected for eight-year terms; the chief justice is elected by the members of the court. The high court hears cases on appeal from lower state courts and also administers the state's entire court system. The 1963 constitution provided for an 18-member court of appeals to handle most of the cases that previously had clogged the high court's calendar. Unless the supreme court agrees to review a court of appeals ruling, the latter's decision is final. Six appeals court justices are elected from each of three districts for six-year terms. The justices elect a chief justice of the appeals court.

The major trial courts in the state as of 1979 were the 52 circuit courts, encompassing 163 justices elected for six-year terms. The circuit courts have original jurisdiction in all felony criminal cases, civil cases involving sums of more than $10,000, and divorces. They also hear appeals from lower courts and state administrative agencies. Probate courts have original jurisdiction in cases involving juveniles and dependents, and also handle

Michigan Presidential Vote by Political Parties, 1948–80

YEAR	ELECTORAL VOTE	MICHIGAN WINNER	DEMOCRAT	REPUBLICAN	PROGRESSIVE	SOCIALIST	PROHIBITION
1948	19	Dewey (R)	1,003,448	1,038,595	46,515	6,063	13,052
						SOC. WORKERS	
1952	20	*Eisenhower (R)	1,230,657	1,551,529	3,922	655	10,331
1956	20	*Eisenhower (R)	1,359,898	1,713,647	—	—	6,923
					SOC. LABOR		
1960	20	*Kennedy (D)	1,687,269	1,620,428	1,718	4,347	2,029
1964	21	*Johnson (D)	2,136,615	1,060,152	1,704	3,817	
							AMERICAN IND.
1968	21	Humphrey (D)	1,593,082	1,370,665	1,762	4,099	331,968
							AMERICAN
1972	21	*Nixon (R)	1,459,435	1,961,721	2,437	1,603	63,321
					PEOPLE'S		LIBERTARIAN
1976	21	Ford (R)	1,696,714	1,893,742	3,504	1,804	5,406
					CITIZENS	COMMUNIST	
1980	21	*Reagan (R)	1,661,532	1,915,225	11,930	3,262	41,597

*Won US presidential election.

wills and estates, adoptions, and commitments of the mentally ill. In 1979 there were 105 probate judges elected for six-year terms and serving in 79 courts.

The 1963 constitution provided for the abolition of township justice-of-the-peace courts. To replace them, 97 district courts, served by 212 judges elected for six-year terms, have been established. These courts handle civil cases involving sums of less than $10,000, minor criminal violations, and preliminary examinations in all felony cases. Most municipalities have district courts, but Detroit is unique in having a recorder's court, consisting of 26 judges with jurisdiction over all criminal cases in the city; the court also has a separate 3-member traffic and ordinance division. The Detroit common pleas court, with 13 judges, handles civil cases involving sums up to $5,000.

The Department of Corrections in 1978 administered 13 prison and correctional institutions with a total inmate population of 14,337. The largest prison is the State Prison of Southern Michigan, at Jackson, with 5,516 inmates in 1978; it reportedly is the single largest walled prison in the world. A sharp rise in the number of individuals sentenced to prison terms created a need for additional prison facilities as the 1980s began.

Detroit became notorious during the 1970s as the "murder capital of the world," with more murders and other violent crimes between 1974 and 1977 than any other US city. Violent crimes (murder, nonnegligent manslaughter, forcible rape, and aggravated assault) reached a peak of 2,226 per 100,000 population in Detroit in 1976 but declined to 1,669 per 100,000 (3d behind Baltimore and New York City) in 1978. Michigan had an overall crime rate of 5,564 in 1978.

In 1846, Michigan became the first state to abolish capital punishment. Despite a sharp increase in the number of murders and other violent crimes, efforts to restore capital punishment failed during the 1970s.

17 ARMED FORCES

As of 30 September 1977, Department of Defense personnel in Michigan numbered 22,010, of whom more than half were civilians. Many of the military personnel are stationed at the K. I. Sawyer Air Force Base near Marquette; the Detroit Arsenal at Warren is the state's largest center for civilians. In 1978, Michigan firms received nearly $1.4 billion in defense contracts (13th in the US).

As of 30 September 1979 there were an estimated 1,188,000 veterans of the US military service living in Michigan. Of these, 21,000 saw service during World War I, 472,000 in World War II, 216,000 in the Korean conflict, and 367,000 during the Viet-Nam era. Veterans' benefits exceeded $564 million in 1978.

Approximately 10,900 personnel were allocated to Michigan's Army and Air National Guard units in 1978. In recent decades, the units have frequently been called out for riot duty and to aid in the aftermath of natural disasters such as tornadoes and heavy snowstorms. State and local police forces employed 24,155 persons in 1977, of whom 20,587 were local employees. In that year, police expenditures were estimated at $464 million, ranking Michigan 5th among the 50 states. Detroit's police force, with 5,703 officers and 610 civilian employees in 1977, also ranked 5th among US cities. Financial problems brought a substantial reduction of Detroit's police strength after that date.

18 MIGRATION

The earliest European immigrants were the French and English. The successive opening of interior lands for farming, lumbering, mining, and manufacturing proved an irresistible attraction for hundreds of thousands of immigrants after the War of 1812, principally Germans, Canadians, English, Irish, and Dutch. During the second half of the 19th century, lumbering and mining opportunities in northern Michigan attracted large numbers of Cornishmen, Norwegians, Swedes, and Finns. The growth of manufacturing in southern Michigan at the end of the century

brought many Poles, Italians, Russians, Belgians, and Greeks to the state. After World War II, many more Europeans immigrated to Michigan, plus smaller groups of Mexicans, other Spanish-speaking peoples from Latin America, and Arabic-speaking peoples, who by the late 1970s were more numerous in Detroit than in any other US city.

The first large domestic migration into Michigan came in the early 19th century from northeastern states, particularly New York and Pennsylvania, and from Ohio. Beginning in 1916, the demand for labor in Michigan's factories started the second major domestic migration to Michigan, this time by southern blacks, who settled mainly in Detroit, Flint, Pontiac, Grand Rapids, and Saginaw. During World War II, many southern whites migrated to the same industrial areas. Between 1940 and 1970, a net total of 518,000 migrants were drawn to Michigan. The economic problems of the auto industry in the 1970s caused a significant reversal of this trend, with the state suffering a net loss of 247,000 by outmigration between 1970 and 1978.

Intrastate migration has been characterized since the late 19th century by a steady movement from rural to urban areas. Most parts of northern Michigan have suffered a loss of population since the early years of this century, although a back-to-the-land movement, together with the growth of rural Michigan as a retirement area, appeared to reverse this trend during the 1970s. Since 1950, the central cities have experienced a steady loss of population to the suburbs in part caused by the migration of whites from areas that were becoming increasingly black.

19 INTERGOVERNMENTAL COOPERATION

The Commission on Intergovernmental Cooperation of the Michigan legislature represents the state in dealings with the Council of State Governments and its allied organizations. Since 1935, the state has joined 17 interstate compacts, dealing mainly with such subjects as gas and oil problems, law enforcement, pest control, civil defense, tax reciprocity, and water resources. The International Bridge Authority, consisting of members from Michigan and Canada, operates a toll bridge connecting Sault Ste. Marie, Mich., and Sault Ste. Marie, Ontario.

In 1978/79, federal aid to Michigan totaled almost $3.6 billion, of which $287 million was general revenue sharing.

20 ECONOMY

On the whole, Michigan benefited from its position as the center of the auto industry during the first half of the 20th century, when Detroit and other south Michigan cities were the fastest-growing industrial areas in the US. But the state's dependence on automobile production has caused grave and persistent economic problems since the 1950s. Michigan's unemployment rates in times of recession have far exceeded the national average, since auto sales are among the hardest hit in such periods. Even in times of general prosperity, the auto industry's emphasis on labor-saving techniques and its shifting of operations from the state have reduced the number of jobs available to Michigan workers. Although the state was relatively prosperous during the record automotive production years of the 1960s and 1970s, the high cost of gasoline and the encroachment of imports on domestic car sales had disastrous effects by 1980, when it became apparent that the state's future economic health required greater diversification of industry. On the other hand, some observers contend that the high wage rates and other benefits won by labor unions, whose power is strongly entrenched, make it difficult for Michigan to compete with other states in attracting new industries.

After manufacturing, agriculture, still dominant in the rural areas of southern Michigan, probably remains the most important element in the state's economy, although tourism, heavily promoted in recent years, is a rapidly growing source of income. In northern Michigan, forestry and mining activities continue but generally at levels far below earlier boom periods.

At the beginning of the 1980s, Michigan's immediate problems were the threat of bankruptcy to Chrysler, the 3d-leading auto-maker, and the very high rate of unemployment resulting from the deep decline in domestic car sales. As a result, the state and local governments faced severe financial difficulties because of reduced tax revenues and increased social welfare expenditures.

²¹INCOME

With a per capita personal income in 1978 of $8,442, Michigan ranked 10th among the 50 states. The state's grave recession in 1980 made it likely that both per capita income and its national ranking would tumble from the 1978 figure.

Total personal income in 1977 was $69.4 billion, of which labor and proprietors' income accounted for $55.5 billion. Leading sources of the latter were manufacturing, 44%; services, 14%; wholesale and retail trade, 14%; government, 13%; agriculture, 1%; and mining, less than 1%.

In 1975, 2,132,000 white families had a median income of $15,758, while 248,000 black families had a median income of $11,876. The number of persons below the federal poverty level in 1975 was 821,000, or 9% of the population. Some 7% of white families but 23% of all black families had incomes below the poverty level. Some 382,300 Michiganians (3% of the US total) were among the nation's top wealthholders in 1972.

²²LABOR

Michigan ranks 7th in the US in the size of its labor force and 6th in the extent to which that force is organized.

The civilian labor force totaled 4,118,000 persons in 1977 and 4,202,000 in 1978, of whom 289,000 (6.9%) were unemployed. Of the total work force in 1977, 1,686,300 persons were in the Detroit area; Grand Rapids, with 237,600, was a distant second.

Of those employed in 1978, males constituted 60.3% and females 39.7%. In 1977, 3,678,000 whites and about 440,000 nonwhites were in the work force. In age distribution, 2,937,000 of the workers were between the ages of 25 and 64, 1,100,000 were between the ages of 16 and 24, and 81,000 were 65 or older. Of all workers actually employed in 1976, 1,724,000 held white-collar jobs and 1,287,000 were in the blue-collar category; in addition, 533,000 persons held service jobs, and 79,000 were farm workers.

A federal census of workers covered by unemployment insurance in March 1977 revealed the following nonfarm employment pattern for Michigan:

	ESTABLISH-MENTS	EMPLOYEES	ANNUAL PAYROLL ('000)
Agricultural services, forestry, fishing	1,330	5,125	$ 57,850
Mining, of which:	457	12,283	208,648
Metals	(15)	(5,641)	(82,689)
Contract construction	15,491	98,946	1,913,023
Manufacturing, of which:	14,465	1,106,168	20,212,651
Fabricated metals	(2,259)	(132,828)	(2,206,465)
Nonelectrical machinery	(3,745)	(145,906)	(2,543,795)
Transportation equipment	(585)	(321,623)	(6,627,977)
Transportation, public utilities	4,752	131,606	2,158,162
Wholesale trade	12,443	153,359	2,434,913
Retail trade	46,665	527,160	3,909,828
Finance, insurance, real estate	13,105	140,445	1,635,681
Services	45,418	521,969	5,186,258
Other	1,738	1,914	28,498
TOTALS	155,864	2,698,975	$37,745,512

Government employees, not covered by this survey, numbered about 613,000 in 1978.

The unemployment rate in Michigan exceeded the national norm during the late 1970s and stood at 14.4% in May 1980, when the national rate was 7.8%. In 1977, when the total unemployment rate in Michigan was 8.2%, unemployment among young people aged 16–19 was more than 20%; unemployment among nonwhite males ranged from 33% to 53.3%, and for black females from 50% to 56%. Migrant workers, chiefly Mexicans and Mexican-Americans, were once widely used in harvesting farm products such as sugar beets and fruit, but their numbers have dropped, as has the number of other foreign workers.

Certain crafts and trades were organized in Michigan in the 19th century, with one national labor union, the Brotherhood of Locomotive Engineers, having been founded at meetings in Michigan in 1863, but efforts to organize workers in the lumber and mining industries were generally unsuccessful. Michigan acquired a reputation as an open-shop state, and factory workers showed little interest in unions at a time when wages were high. But the catastrophic impact of the depression of the 1930s completely changed these attitudes. With the support of sympathetic state and federal government officials, Michigan workers were in the forefront of the greatest labor organizing drive in American history. The successful sitdown strike by the United Automobile Workers against General Motors in 1936–37 marked the first major victory of the new Congress of Industrial Organizations. Since then, a strong labor movement has provided manufacturing workers in Michigan with some of the most favorable working conditions in the country. In 1977, the average hourly earnings of production workers reached $7.54, one-third above the national average. However, union membership declined from 1,255,000 in 1974 to 1,165,000 in 1976, and the share of union and employee association members in the eligible work force dropped from 38.3% to 32.7% during the same period.

Michigan's most powerful and influential industrial union since the 1930s has been the United Automobile Workers (UAW), with 1,358,000 members in 1976; its national headquarters is in Detroit. Under its long-time president Walter Reuther and his successors, Leonard Woodcock and Douglas Fraser, the union has also been a dominant force in the state Democratic Party. In recent years, as government employees and teachers have been organized, unions and associations representing these groups have become increasingly influential. Under the Michigan Public Employment Relations Act of 1965, public employees have the right to organize and to engage in collective bargaining, but are prohibited from striking. However, strikes of teachers, college faculty members, and government employees have been common since the 1960s, and little or no effort has been made to enforce the law.

²³AGRICULTURE

In 1978, Michigan's agricultural income was estimated at nearly $2.2 billion, placing Michigan 20th among the 50 states. The total was about evenly divided between crops and livestock and livestock products; dairy products, cattle, corn, and soybeans were the principal commodities in order of marketing receipts. The state in 1977 ranked 1st in output of tart cherries, cucumbers for processing, and navy beans; 2d in blueberries; and 3d in apples, asparagus, celery, and prunes and plums.

The growing of corn and other crops indigenous to North America was introduced in Michigan by the Indians around 100 BC, and a few Frenchmen tried to develop European-style agriculture during the colonial era. But little progress was made until well into the 19th century, when farmers from New York and New England poured into the interior of southern Michigan. By mid-century, 34,000 farms had been established, and the number increased to a peak of about 207,000 in 1910. The major cash crop at first was wheat, until soil exhaustion, insect infestations, bad winters, and competition from huge wheat farms to the west forced a deemphasis on wheat and a move toward agricultural diversity. Both the number of farms and the amount of farm acreage had declined by 1979 to 63,000 farms and slightly more than 11,000,000 acres (4,500,000 hectares).

The southern half of the lower peninsula is the principal agricultural region, and the area along Lake Michigan is a leader in fruit growing. Potatoes are profitable in northern Michigan, while eastern Michigan (the "Thumb" area near Lake Huron) is the country's leading bean producer. The Saginaw Valley leads the state in sugar beets. The south-central and southeastern counties are major centers of soybean production.

Leading field crops in 1979 included 237,500,000 bushels of corn for grain, valued at $374,063,000; 28,615,000 bushels of soybeans, worth $167,368,000; and 33,755,000 bushels of wheat, worth $125,279,000. Other crops and their 1979 outputs were commercial apples, 680,000,000 lb; cucumbers, 117,810 tons; and asparagus, 19,000 hundredweight for fresh market, 10,080 tons for processing.

24 ANIMAL HUSBANDRY

The same areas of southern Michigan that lead in crop production also lead in livestock and livestock products, except that the northern counties are more favorable for dairying than for crop production.

At the end of 1979 there were 1,310,000 cattle and calves in the state, 960,000 hogs and pigs, and 132,000 sheep and lambs. During that year, livestock production included 473,765,000 lb of cattle and calves, valued at $375,395,000, and 310,272,000 lb of hogs and pigs, worth $128,301,000.

In 1979, Michigan ranked 5th in output of creamed cottage cheese with production of 49,023,000 lb, ranked 6th in milk production with 4,830,000,000 lb, 6th in butter with 31,837,000 lb, and 8th in ice cream with 33,068,000 gallons. Poultry farmers produced nearly 1.5 billion eggs during the same year. In 1976, 5,670,000 lb of honey and 105,000 mink pelts were also marketed.

25 FISHING

Commercial fishing, once an important factor in the state's economy, is relatively minor today; the commercial catch in 1978 was 11,158,000 lb, valued at $3,529,000.

The common whitefish is the most commercially valuable fish, with a value of $2,058,388 in 1974. Alewife constitutes the largest catch in terms of weight, with 5,782,300 lb caught in 1974, but the catch, used in cat food, was worth only $117,516.

Sport fishing continues to flourish and is one of the state's major tourist attractions. A state salmon-planting program, begun in the mid-1960s, has made the salmon the most popular game fish for Great Lakes sport fishermen. The state has also sought, through breeding and stocking programs, to bring back the trout, which was devastated by an invasion of lamprey.

A bitter dispute raged during the 1970s between state officials and Ottawa and Chippewa commercial fishermen, who claimed that Indian treaties with the federal government exempted them from state fishing regulations. The state contends that without such regulations, Indian commercial fishing would have a devastating impact on the northern Great Lakes' fish population. A federal court in 1979 upheld the Indians' contention. As the 1980s began, the state was seeking both to secure a reversal of this decision and to negotiate a compromise settlement that would satisfy both Indian and non-Indian groups.

26 FORESTRY

In 1977, Michigan's forestland totaled 19,270,000 acres (7,798,000 hectares), or more than half the state's total land area. More than 97% of it is classed as commercial timberland, about two-thirds of it privately owned. The major wooded regions are in the northern two-thirds of the state, where great pine forests enabled Michigan to become the leading lumber-producing state in the last four decades of the 19th century. These cutover lands were reforested in the 20th century.

Michigan's lumber production totaled 350 million board feet in 1977, which put the state well down the list of lumber-producing states. In the sparsely populated western part of the upper peninsula, the lumber industry continues to be the major economic activity, however. In 1976, Michigan wood pulp production totaled 804,478 cords, which was less than 70% of the pulp consumed by Michigan mills. Shipments of lumber and wood products were valued at $659 million in 1977.

State and national forests cover 6,419,000 acres (2,598,000 hectares), or more than one-sixth of the state's land area; national forests encompass about 40% of this total. Reforestation programs have been devoted to preventing or curtailing forest fires, which devastated wide areas of forestland in earlier days.

27 MINING

In 1978, Michigan's estimated mineral output totaled $1.9 billion, 12th in the US. The state is a leading producer of iron ore, petroleum, cement, copper, salt, natural gas, gypsum, limestone, and sand and gravel.

The major mining area is the western part of the upper peninsula, where copper is mined in the Keweenaw peninsula. Iron ore deposits are found in three areas: west of Marquette, the Iron Mountain–Iron River area, and the extreme western area around Ironwood. A considerable amount of silver has been found associated with the copper deposits, and small amounts of gold have been mined in Marquette County. Limestone deposits are located chiefly in the eastern part of the upper peninsula and the northern part of the lower peninsula. Gypsum is found on the western side of Saginaw Bay and in the Grand Rapids area, while salt deposits appear both as brine and as rock throughout southern Michigan.

The leading minerals with estimated production in 1978 (excluding fossil fuels) were copper, 38,380 tons; silver, 354,000 troy oz; iron ore, 19,643,000 tons; sand and gravel, 47,000,000 tons; salt, 4,056,000 tons; gypsum, 2,176,000 tons; lime, 1,272,000 tons; and cement, 77,003,000 tons.

28 ENERGY AND POWER

Michigan's energy supply is provided primarily by private utility companies. Coal is the principal source of fuel used in generating electric power, while natural gas is the major fuel used for other energy needs.

The installed electric generating capacity of electric utilities and industrial plants at the end of 1978 was 22 million kw; electric energy production totaled 78 billion kwh. Hydroelectric plants, which had produced more than 10% of the state's electrical energy in 1947, produced barely 1% in 1977. Of electric energy generated by steam, coal was the fuel used to produce about 70% of the total; nuclear power produced 15%, oil 12%, and natural gas 3%.

The two major electric utilities are Detroit Edison, serving the Detroit area and portions of the eastern part of the lower peninsula, and Consumers Power, serving most of the remainder of the lower peninsula. The two companies had combined sales in 1976 of 58.1 billion kwh, out of total electric utility sales of 67.8 million kwh. Of these sales, 31% went to residential users, 66% to commercial and industrial users, and the remainder for street and highway lighting and other public uses. Rates of the utility companies are set by the Public Service Commission.

Michigan is dependent upon outside sources for most of its fuel needs. Petroleum production in 1978 totaled 34.6 million barrels, a tiny fraction of total US production; natural gas output was 159.2 billion cu feet, about six times the 1971 production but less than one-fourth the natural gas consumed in the state in 1977. Proved petroleum reserves were 190.2 million barrels at the end of 1978; natural gas reserves, 1.8 trillion cu feet. Bituminous coal reserves (estimated at 127 million tons in 1976) remain in southern Michigan, but production is negligible.

Efforts to make increased use of nuclear power were under attack by environmentalists at the end of the 1970s, causing delays in or the abandonment of several nuclear plant construction projects.

29 INDUSTRY

Manufacturing, a minor element in Michigan's economy in the

mid-19th century, grew rapidly in importance until, by 1900, an estimated 25% of the state's jobholders were factory workers. The rise of the automobile industry in the early 20th century completed the transformation of Michigan into one of the most important manufacturing areas in the world. In 1976, Michigan ranked 6th among the 50 states in the number of manufacturing employees, 3d in manufacturing payroll and capital expenditures, and 4th in the value added by manufacturing and value of shipments. Value added by manufacturing totaled $37.5 billion in 1977; value of shipments, $93.7 billion; and capital expenditures, $3.7 billion. The following table shows the value added by manufacturing for major sectors in 1972 and 1977:

	1972	1977
Transportation equipment	$8,544,300,000	$13,771,400,000
Nonelectrical machinery	2,968,500,000	5,135,800,000
Fabricated metal products	2,786,400,000	4,482,000,000
Primary metals	1,947,400,000	2,880,200,000
Food and food products	1,306,300,000	2,070,800,000
Chemicals and chemical products	1,221,100,000	1,989,000,000
Electric and electronic equipment	769,300,000	1,061,300,000
Printing and publishing	696,200,000	962,600,000
Rubber and plastic products	499,000,000	915,500,000
Apparel and textile products	411,200,000	820,400,000
Paper and paper products	480,100,000	783,400,000
Stone, clay, glass products	553,200,000	759,800,000
Furniture and fixtures	363,300,000	629,900,000

Motor vehicles and equipment completely dominate the state's economy, with a payroll of $5.4 billion in 1976, representing almost one-third of the state's manufacturing payroll; value added by automotive manufacture in 1977 was $13.1 billion, or 35% of the total. Production of nonelectrical machinery, primary and fabricated metal products, and metal forgings and stampings was directly related to automobile production.

The Detroit metropolitan area is the major industrial region, with a manufacturing payroll of $10.9 billion in 1977 and value added by manufacturing of $18.1 billion. This area includes not only the heavy concentration of auto-related plants in Wayne, Oakland, and Macomb counties, but also major steel, chemical, and pharmaceutical industries, among others. Flint, Grand Rapids, Saginaw, Ann Arbor, Lansing, and Kalamazoo are other major industrial centers. Among counties, manufacturing was of the greatest importance in the economy of Midland County (Dow Chemical), where 63% of all labor and proprietors' earnings in 1976 came from manufacturing. Genesee County, home of the General Motors plants in the Flint area, was second with 60% of its earnings coming from manufacturing.

Because the auto industry's Big Three—General Motors, Ford, and Chrysler—have their headquarters in the Detroit area, Michigan has had for many years three of the nation's largest industrial corporations. Until it was replaced in 1979 by Exxon, General Motors was the perennial leader among all manufacturers in the world: GM's assets in 1979 totaled $66.3 billion, and its net income was $2.9 billion. Ford (with $43.5 billion in assets) and Chrysler ($12 billion) ranked 4th and 17th, respectively. Dow Chemical, headquartered in Midland, was the 24th-largest corporation in 1979, and American Motors, with its offices at Southfield (although its factories are located outside Michigan), was 109th.

The auto industry's preponderance in Michigan manufacturing has come to be viewed in recent years as more of a liability than an asset. When times are good, as they were in the 1960s and early 1970s, automobile sales soar to record levels and Michigan's economy prospers. But when the national economy slumps, these sales plummet, pushing the state into a far deeper recession than is felt by the nation as a whole. In the 1970s, the escalating cost of gasoline and the slowness of Michigan automakers in providing small, fuel-efficient cars to meet foreign competition caused a severe decline in domestic motor vehicle

sales. Michigan's automakers produced 2,702,621 cars in the 1979 model year, or 29% of total US automobile output, compared with 34% in 1976.

The recession of 1979–80 forced Chrysler to obtain federally guaranteed loans of $1.5 billion and to borrow $150 million from the state in order to stave off bankruptcy. Chrysler reported losses totaling $1.1 billion in 1979—the largest operating loss that had ever been suffered by a US corporation. In 1980, however, the other two members of the Big Three were also hard hit; in the 3d quarter of 1980, Ford and General Motors reported record losses of $595 million and $567 million, respectively, with Chrysler losing another $490 million. The net deficit for the Big Three during the first nine months of 1980 exceeded $3.5 billion.

³⁰COMMERCE

In 1972, Michigan's wholesale trade establishments had sales exceeding $26.5 billion. Detroit had the largest number of establishments, 2,392, and the greatest sales, $6.1 billion. The leading categories of goods were motor vehicles and automobile parts and supplies (accounting for more than one-sixth of all sales), groceries, metals and minerals, and machinery.

In 1977, Michigan's retail establishments had total sales of $31.9 billion. Detroit led the cities with 9,768 establishments, 62,811 retail employees, and $2.7 billion in sales. The importance of retail trade to the local economy was greatest in northern Michigan, where in 16 counties the earnings from retail establishments accounted for 15–24% of total labor and proprietors' earnings. In the state as a whole in 1977, motor vehicle dealers, food outlets, and department stores had the largest sales.

Michigan, with its ports open to oceangoing vessels through the St. Lawrence Seaway, is a major exporting and importing state for the foreign market. In 1977, the Detroit Customs District, which includes all of Michigan, accounted for 10% of all US exports with an export value of $12.1 billion and 8% of all imports with $11.5 billion. Exports of Michigan's own manufactured products, $6.9 billion in 1976, accounted for well over half the state's total exports. Exports of transportation equipment accounted for $3.6 billion. Transportation equipment also accounts for much of the imports: a large number of the 888,146 cars built in Canada in 1977 for sale in the US were brought in through Detroit. Michigan's agricultural exports totaled $318 million in 1976/77.

³¹CONSUMER PROTECTION

The Michigan Consumer's Council, composed of the attorney general, secretary of state, director of the Department of Commerce, and three members appointed by the governor and three by the legislature was established in 1966 to protect consumers from harmful products, false advertising, and deceptive sales practices. Other state agencies, such as the Department of Licensing and Regulation, the State Insurance Bureau, and the Public Service Commission, also are responsible for protecting consumers.

A number of local governments have instituted consumer affairs offices, with Detroit's being especially active.

³²BANKING

Michigan's banks in the territorial and early statehood years were generally wildcat speculative ventures. More restrained banking activities date from the 1840s, when the state's oldest bank, the Detroit Bank and Trust, was founded. A crisis that developed in the early 1930s forced Governor William Comstock to close all banks in February 1933 in order to prevent collapse of the entire banking system. Federal and state authorities supervised a reorganization and reform of the state's banks that has succeeded in preventing any major problems from arising since that time.

In 1976, Michigan banks and credit agencies employed 66,121 persons and had total payrolls of $682.9 million. There were 364 insured commercial banks in 1978, with total assets of $46.7

billion. They held loans exceeding $17.5 billion and savings deposits of $39.2 billion. The National Bank of Detroit, with deposits exceeding $6.9 billion, was the largest bank in the state and the 18th-largest commercial bank in the US.

There are 64 insured savings and loan associations with total assets of $15.3 billion in 1978; their outstanding mortgage loans amounted to $13 billion. The First Federal Savings and Loan of Detroit and the Standard Federal Savings and Loan of Troy were the largest institutions. In 1977 there were 611 state-chartered credit unions, with assets of $2.3 billion, and 358 federally chartered credit unions, with assets of $1 billion.

[33] INSURANCE

In 1978, 23 insurance companies were based in Michigan. Life insurance benefit payments totaled $1.2 billion in 1978, including death benefits of $531.9 million. There were 5,557,000 life insurance policies in force, valued at $51.5 billion. The average Michigan family had life insurance coverage of $41,800, 19% above the national average. Property and liability companies wrote premiums of more than $3.8 billion in 1978, including $746 million in automobile liability coverage, $806.9 million in automobile physical damage insurance, and $362.3 million in homeowners insurance.

Most of Michigan's residents are covered by some form of health insurance. In 1975, 8,069,000 persons were covered by hospital insurance plans, 7,978,000 by surgical expense plans, 7,835,000 by regular medical expense plans, and 3,262,000 by major-medical expense programs. In 1977, health insurance company premiums hit $2.1 billion; benefit payments, $1.9 billion.

[34] SECURITIES

There are no securities or commodity exchanges in Michigan.

In 1978, New York Stock Exchange member firms had 124 sales offices and 1,076 registered representatives in the state. Michiganians reported more than $1 billion in dividend income on their 1977 federal tax returns.

[35] PUBLIC FINANCE

Michigan, the 7th most populous state in the US, had the 5th-largest state budget for the 1977/78 fiscal year.

The state constitution requires the governor to submit a budget proposal to the legislature each year. This executive budget, prepared by the Department of Management and Budget, is reviewed, revised, and passed by the legislature. During the fiscal year, which extends from 1 October to 30 September, if actual revenues drop below anticipated levels, the governor, in consultation with the legislative appropriations committees, must reduce expenditures to meet the constitutional requirement that the state budget be kept in balance. In 1977, the legislature created a budget stabilization fund; a portion of tax revenues collected in good times is held in reserve to be used during periods of recession, when the funding of essential state services is threatened. In 1978, a tax limitation amendment put a lid on government spending by establishing a fixed ratio of state revenues to personal income in the state. Further efforts to limit taxes were rejected by the voters in 1980.

State expenditures have expanded from $1 billion in 1957 to $2.9 billion in 1967, $5.2 billion in 1972, and $9.5 billion in 1978. The following is a summary of estimated revenues and expenditures for 1980/81 (in millions):

REVENUES	
Income tax	$2,099.6
Business tax	931.0
Sales and use tax	710.5
Other taxes	614.8
Lottery	177.0
Federal aid	123.6
Other receipts	250.7
TOTAL	$4,907.2

EXPENDITURES	
Department of Social Services	$1,489.9
Grant to School Aid Fund	884.8
Higher educational institutions	874.1
Department of Mental Health	547.7
Department of Corrections	199.2
Other current operations	781.1
Capital outlay	66.0
Debt service	64.3
TOTAL	$4,907.1

Detroit's revenues for the fiscal year ending 30 June 1977 exceeded $1 billion, including $213 million from the federal government and $329.4 million from city taxes. In 1977, Detroit had the 3d-highest property tax among US cities, $3.71 per $100 of assessed valuation. The following is a summary of estimated revenues and expenditures for 1979/80 (in millions):

REVENUES	
Local property tax	$ 162.8
Municipal income tax	157.9
Federal funds	364.0
State funds	255.2
Other receipts	550.5
TOTAL	$1,490.4

EXPENDITURES	
Public protection	$ 392.4
Physical environment	375.2
Development and management	211.4
Transportation	123.4
Housing supply and conditions	113.0
Health	89.4
Other outlays	185.6
TOTAL	$1,490.4

The total state debt in mid-1977 was nearly $2.2 billion, 13th largest among the 50 states, or $234 per capita (36th in the US).

[36] TAXATION

Until the 1930s, Michigan relied mainly on the property tax for revenues to support both local and state governments. A state sales tax, first imposed in 1933, and a state income tax, first levied in 1967, are now the main sources of state revenues. Property taxes are reserved entirely to local governments.

The state income tax in 1980 was 4.8% on all income, with exemptions of $1,500 for a single person, $3,000 for married couples, and $1,500 for each dependent. The state sales tax was 4% on most retail purchases, except food. An inheritance tax ranging from 2% to 17% was levied on inheritance of more than $100, with the first $65,000 to the spouse and the first $10,000 to other close relatives being exempt. Other state taxes and fees are levied on corporate and financial-institution income, cigarettes, alcoholic beverages, pari-mutuel wagering, and gasoline and other fuels.

Local government taxes in 1977 totaled $3.2 billion, of which $2.9 billion came from property taxes, $187.6 million from local income taxes, and $73.4 million from other taxes. Detroit levied a 2% city income tax, and several other communities had city income taxes with lower rates.

Michigan's share of the federal tax burden in 1977 was $15.2 billion; federal disbursements in the state totaled $12.3 billion. Michiganians filed nearly 3.6 million federal income tax returns in 1977, paying $7.9 billion in tax.

[37] ECONOMIC POLICY

Michigan has sought since territorial days to promote and assist economic development. Since the 1940s, improved coordination of such programs has been achieved through the agency now known as the Office of Economic Expansion, within the Department of Commerce. Local governmental units develop industrial parks and, together with the state, are authorized to provide a variety of tax incentives to encourage new companies to locate in the area or established companies to expand their operations.

Those in charge of industrial promotion must contend with Michigan's record as a state with one of the highest manufacturing pay scales in the country, entrenched and powerful labor organizations, and what some observers believe is a tax structure unfavorable to business. As a result, for each new business persuaded to locate in the state or old one convinced to remain, another of equal magnitude often has chosen to locate elsewhere.

[38] HEALTH

During 1969–71, life expectancy in Michigan averaged 70.63 years (29th in the US). Life expectancy for males was 67.09 years; for females, 74.48.

Live births in 1977 totaled 138,000, for a rate of 15.2 per 1,000 people, an increase from 14.4 per 1,000 in 1976 and the first upward movement shown for some years. The 1977 total included 114,000 whites and 24,000 nonwhites. Infant mortality in 1977 was 12.2 per 1,000 live births for whites and 23.1 per 1,000 for nonwhites. There were 53,600 legal abortions in 1977, up from 37,600 in 1974. The 1977 figure represented 25.1 abortions per 1,000 women and 392 abortions per 1,000 live births, both figures being below the national averages.

Major causes of death in 1977 (with their rates per 100,000 population) included heart disease, 317; cancer, 166; stroke, 75; accidents, 43; pneumonia and influenza, 18.2; diabetes, 17.7; cirrhosis of the liver, 14.9; arteriosclerosis, 12.7; suicide, 14.0; and early infancy diseases, 11.3. Michigan's overall death rate, 8.1 per 1,000 population, was not quite 9% below the US norm.

In 1978, Michigan had 244 hospitals, with 50,661 beds. They admitted 1,475,822 patients; had an average daily census of 39,457, and an occupancy rate of 78%; and employed 135,564 personnel, including 22,268 registered nurses and 11,673 licensed practical nurses. The average cost of hospital care in 1977 was $218 per day and $1,721 per stay. Michigan had 13,594 physicians in 1977 and 4,772 dentists in 1979.

[39] SOCIAL WELFARE

Until the 1930s, Michigan's few limited welfare programs were handled by the counties, but the relief load during the depression shifted the burden to the state and federal level. In recent decades, there have been enormous increases in social welfare programs. In 1976, Michigan ranked 5th among the states in expenditures for the five largest welfare programs, disbursing nearly $1.9 billion, of which the federal government supplied 52%.

In 1978, recipients of aid to families with dependent children numbered 619,900, and payments totaled $816,000,000, 3d highest among the 50 states. The average monthly payment was $337 per family. An average of 567,692 persons per month took part in the federal food stamp program, receiving bonus stamps valued at $124,925,000 for the 1977/78 fiscal year. Some 847,000 pupils participated in the school lunch program, with the federal government contributing $47,800,000 of the cost.

In 1977, 1,316,600 persons were receiving Social Security benefits, of whom 806,400 were retired workers, 312,600 were surviving dependents of deceased workers, and 197,600 were disabled workers. The total benefits paid were $3.5 billion; the average monthly benefit to retired workers was $262.10.

Under the Supplemental Security Income program, 117,600 aged, blind, and disabled persons received $201.1 million in 1978. About $30.9 million was spent on vocational rehabilitation programs in 1978, and $876 million on Medicaid payments. Workers' compensation payments totaled $434.7 million in 1977; unemployment insurance payments amounted to $479 million in 1978.

[40] HOUSING

The 1970 census counted 2,954,451 housing units in Michigan, of which 2,845,448 were year-round units. The percentage of owner-occupied housing units was 74.4%, the highest percent-

age in the US. The total number of year-round dwellings increased substantially by 1975 to 3,024,281.

As of 1970, the largest number of units, 1,608,360, had been built in 1949 or earlier; 623,100 dated from the 1950s; 613,988 from the 1960s. Some 97% of all occupied dwellings had full plumbing.

In 1978, the number of new housing units authorized was 61,100, valued at $2.1 billion. The value of property insured by the Federal Housing Authority in 1978 indicated that Michigan houses were priced below the national average. A limited amount of state aid for low-income housing is available through the State Housing Development Authority.

[41] EDUCATION

Historically, Michigan has strongly supported public education, which helps account for the fact that the percentage of students attending public schools is one of the highest in the US. But the cost of maintaining this extensive public educational system has become a major problem in recent years because of the declining school-age population.

Michigan's illiteracy rate in 1970, 0.9%, was below the US average. In 1976, almost 69% of persons 18 years and over had graduated from high school. Of the 6,159,000 residents in this age range, 111,000 had completed 0–4 years of school; 711,000, grades 5–8; 1,109,000, grades 1–3 in high school; 2,436,000, 4 years of high school; 1,016,000, 1–3 years of college; and 776,000, 4 or more years of college. The median number of school years completed was 12.5, equaling the national average.

In 1977 there were 4,030 public schools, including 2,865 elementary schools, 1,054 secondary schools, 24 combined elementary and secondary schools, and 87 special schools for the handicapped. Public school enrollments in 1978 included 1,357,000 elementary pupils and 640,000 secondary pupils. Detroit had the largest school enrollment with 238,000 pupils. In 1977 there were 762 private schools with a total enrollment of 171,000. Catholic, Lutheran, Seventh-Day Adventist, and Reformed and Christian Reformed churches have long had denominational schools. In the 1970s, a number of new Christian schools, particularly those of fundamentalist Baptist groups, were established.

In 1977, Michigan had 42 public institutions of higher education, with a combined enrollment of 420,300, and 48 private institutions, with a total of 61,500. The oldest and most prestigious state school is the University of Michigan, founded at its Ann Arbor campus in 1837. In 1979, it had a student enrollment of 46,017, including branches at Flint and Dearborn. Founded in 1855 as an agricultural school but later expanded into a university, Michigan State University, at East Lansing, had an enrollment of 43,459 in 1979. Wayne State University, in Detroit, had 34,818 students in 1979. There are 10 other state colleges and universities and 29 two-year community colleges. Among the state's private colleges and universities, the University of Detroit, a Jesuit school, is the only one that attempts to compete in undergraduate and graduate programs with the major state universities; it had an enrollment of 8,091 in 1979. Kalamazoo College (founded in 1833), Albion College (1835), Hope College (1866), and Alma College (1886) are among the better known of the private liberal arts colleges. Scholarships, merit awards, tuition grants, and guaranteed student loans are provided through the Student Financial Assistance Services office of the Department of Education.

In 1978, total expenditures for public schools amounted to $4.3 billion, or $466 per capita. Detroit's average teacher's salary of $19,390 placed the city behind only New York and Milwaukee among the country's largest cities. Expenditures for higher education in 1977 exceeded $1.6 billion.

[42] ARTS

Michigan's major center of arts and cultural activities is the Detroit area. The city's Ford Auditorium is the home of the

Detroit Symphony Orchestra; the Music Hall and the Masonic Auditorium present a variety of musical productions; the Fisher Theater is the major home for Broadway productions; and the Detroit Cultural Center supports a number of cultural programs. Nearby Meadow Brook, in Rochester, has a summer music program. At the University of Michigan, in Ann Arbor, the Power Center for the Performing Arts and Hill Auditorium host major music, theatrical, and dance presentations.

Programs relating to the visual arts tend to be academically centered; the University of Michigan, Michigan State, Wayne State, and Eastern Michigan University have notable art schools. The Cranbrook Academy of Arts, which was created by the architect Eliel Saarinen, is a significant art center, and the Ox-bow School at Saugatuck is also outstanding. The Ann Arbor Art Fair, begun in 1959, is the largest and most prestigious summer outdoor art show in the state.

The 1972 census listed 26 legitimate theater enterprises in Michigan, nearly all of which were civic theater operations. The Meadow Brook Theater at Rochester is perhaps the largest professional theater company; Detroit has a number of little theater groups. Successful summer theaters include the Cherry County Playhouse at Traverse City and the Star Theater in Flint. In film production, Michigan, and particularly Detroit, reportedly ranks 3d behind Hollywood and New York, with the emphasis on the production of industrial films and commercials for television.

The Detroit Symphony Orchestra, founded in 1914, and directed in 1980 by Antal Dorati, is nationally known. Grand Rapids and Kalamazoo have regional orchestras that perform on a part-time, seasonal basis. The National Music Camp at Interlochen is a mecca for young musicians in the summer. There are local ballet and opera groups in Detroit and in a few other communities. Michigan's best-known contribution to popular music was that of Berry Gordy, Jr., whose Motown recording company in the 1960s popularized the "Detroit sound" and featured such artists as Diana Ross and the Supremes, the Four Tops, the Temptations, and Stevie Wonder, among many others. In the 1970s, however, Gordy moved his operations to California.

43 LIBRARIES AND MUSEUMS

Michigan in 1978 had 360 public libraries, about 96 academic libraries, and numerous special libraries, with a combined total of nearly 17 million volumes and a circulation exceeding 32 million. The State Library in Lansing functions as the coordinator of library facilities in the state. The largest public library is the Detroit Public Library, which in 1978 had 2,460,509 bound volumes in its main library and 26 branches. Outstanding among its special collections are the Burton Historical Collection, a major center for genealogical research, and the National Automotive History Collection. Grand Rapids, Kalamazoo, Lansing, Flint, and Ann Arbor are among the larger public libraries.

Among academic libraries, the University of Michigan at Ann Arbor, with 5,049,501 books and 1,403,096 microfilm units in 1978, features the William L. Clements collection of books and manuscripts on the colonial period, and the Bentley Library's collection of books and manuscripts on Michigan, the largest such collection. In 1980, the Gerald R. Ford Presidential Library was opened on the university campus. The Michigan State University Library at East Lansing had 1,657,500 books and 1,050,000 microfilm units in 1978. At Wayne State University in Detroit, the Walter P. Reuther Library houses the largest collection of labor history records in the US.

The Detroit Institute of Arts is the largest art museum in the state and has an outstanding collection of African art. It is located in the Detroit Cultural Center, along with the Public Library and the Detroit Historical Museum, one of the largest local history museums in the country. The Kalamazoo Institute of Art, the Flint Institute of Art, the Grand Rapids Art Museum,

and the Hackley Art Gallery in Muskegon are important art museums. The University of Michigan and the Cranbrook Academy of Arts in Bloomfield Hills also maintain important collections.

The Detroit Historical Museum heads the more than 140 historical museums in the state, including the State Historical Museum in Lansing and museums in Grand Rapids, Flint, Kalamazoo, and Dearborn. In the latter city, the privately run Henry Ford Museum and Greenfield Village are leading tourist attractions.

The major historic sites open to the public include the late-18th-century fort on Mackinac Island and the reconstructed early-18th-century fort at Mackinaw City. The latter site has also been the scene of an archaeological program that has accumulated one of the largest collections of 18th-century artifacts in the country. Major investigations of prehistoric Indian sites have also been conducted in recent years.

44 COMMUNICATIONS

Michigan's remote position in the interior of the continent hampered the development of adequate communications services, and the first regular postal service was not instituted until the early 19th century. By 1977, the state had more than 1,000 post offices and 24,000 postal employees. Postal receipts at Detroit totaled $112,884,557 in 1978.

Telephone service began in Detroit in 1877. By 1978 there were 6,981,139 telephones in Michigan, 1,654,291 business and 5,326,848 residential, representing virtually every household. In 1977, the number of local calls totaled 11.8 billion, and there were 1.2 billion toll calls. Michigan Bell is the largest telephone company in the state, followed by General Telephone, serving mainly rural areas. Telegraph service, introduced in Michigan in the 1840s, is provided by Western Union.

Michigan had 127 AM radio stations and 109 FM stations in 1978. Radio station WWJ, owned by the *Detroit News*, began operating in 1920 as one of the country's first commercial broadcasting stations, and the *News* also started Michigan's first television station in 1947. By 1978 there were 24 commercial television stations and 7 educational stations in the state. There were 94 cable television systems serving 359,795 subscribers in 294 communities.

45 PRESS

Continuous newspaper coverage in Michigan dates from the appearance of the weekly *Detroit Gazette* in 1817. The state's oldest paper still being published is the *Detroit Free Press*, founded in 1831 and the state's first daily paper since 1835.

In 1978 there were 52 daily newspapers in Michigan with a total average daily circulation of 2,458,083. In addition, 17 Sunday editions had a total circulation of 2,366,033. There were also nearly 250 weekly or other nondaily newspapers. The number of daily papers has declined in recent decades; since 1959, Detroit has been the only Michigan city with more than one daily, and the *Detroit Free Press* was for some years the state's only major morning paper. The *Detroit News*, founded in 1873 by James E. Scripps, had the largest circulation of any evening paper in the US in 1978.

Outside Detroit, daily newspapers in eight of the larger cities were owned by the Booth Publishing chain, acquired by the Newhouse Newspapers in 1976. The Panax Corp. owned five small dailies and had interests in a number of weeklies in 1979.

The following table shows leading daily newspapers in Michigan with average daily and Sunday circulation in 1978:

AREA	NAME	DAILY	SUNDAY
Detroit	Free Press (m,S)	617,605	715,657
	News (e,S)	631,836	820,139
Flint	Journal (e,S)	105,428	105,494
Grand Rapids	Press (e,S)	126,286	142,777
Kalamazoo	Gazette (e,S)	58,607	65,053
Lansing	State Journal (e,S)	73,280	78,418
Pontiac	Oakland Press (e,S)	72,262	72,668
Saginaw	News (e,S)	52,436	55,168

⁴⁶ORGANIZATIONS

Few national organizations maintain their headquarters in Michigan, but the first chapters of the Kiwanis and Exchange service clubs were organized in the state.

The National Male Nurse Association at Saginaw and the National Hearing Aid Society in Livonia are two health organizations headquartered in Michigan. The most important trade association is the Motor Vehicle Manufacturers Association, with offices in Detroit. Its labor union counterpart, the United Automobile Workers, also has its international headquarters in that city.

Other organizations with headquarters in the state include the American Concrete Institute, Detroit; Society of Manufacturing Engineers, Dearborn; American Society of Agricultural Engineers, St. Joseph; American Association of Correctional Facility Officers, Marquette; and the National Association of Investment Clubs, Royal Oak.

⁴⁷TOURISM, TRAVEL, AND RECREATION

Tourism has been an important source of economic activity in Michigan since the 19th century and now rivals agriculture as the 2d most important segment of the state's economy.

In 1976, out-of-state visitors were estimated to have spent $3.8 billion in Michigan. An estimated 34,600 businesses, employing more than 346,000 people, are involved in providing recreation-related goods and services.

Michigan's tourist attractions are diverse and readily accessible to much of the country's population. The opportunities offered by Michigan's water resources are the number one attraction; no part of the state is more than 85 mi (137 km), from one of the Great Lakes, and most of the population lives only a few miles away from one of the thousands of inland lakes and streams. Southwestern Michigan's sand beaches along Lake Michigan offer sunbathing and swimming. Inland lakes in southern Michigan are favored by swimmers, while the Metropolitan Beach on Lake St. Clair, northeast of Detroit, claims to be the largest man-made lake beach in the world. Camping has enjoyed an enormous increase in popularity; many private campgrounds have been added recently to the extensive public camping facilities.

Although the tourist and resort business has been primarily a summer activity, the rising popularity of ice fishing, skiing, and other winter sports, autumn scenic tours, hunting, and spring festivals has made tourism a year-round business in many parts of the state. Historic attractions have been heavily promoted in recent years, following the success of Dearborn's Henry Ford Museum and Greenfield Village, which attract about 1.5 million paying visitors each year. Tours of Detroit automobile factories and other industrial sites, such as Battle Creek's breakfast-food plants, are also important tourist attractions.

Camping and recreational facilities are provided by the federal government at three national forests, comprising 2.7 million acres (1.1 million hectares); three facilities operated by the National Park Service (Isle Royale National Park and the Pictured Rocks National Lakeshore and Sleeping Bear Dunes National Lakeshore); and several wildlife sanctuaries.

State-operated facilities include 93 parks and recreational areas with 224,000 acres (90,600 hectares), and state forests and wildlife areas totaling 4,250,000 acres (1,720,000 hectares). Local parks encompass another 115,600 acres (46,800 hectares). Michigan also has 650 private campgrounds wih 35,000 fully equipped campsites, more than all the public campsites combined. In 1977, total attendance at state parks and recreation areas was 22,343,807. Holland (1,358,617 visitors) and Warren Dunes (1,256,654) state parks, located on Lake Michigan, had the largest overall park attendance; Ludington State Park, also on Lake Michigan, attracted the largest number of campers. State forest campgrounds were used by 311,539 campers in 1977. In 1977, 1,033,939 hunting licenses and 964,929 fishing licenses were sold.

⁴⁸SPORTS

Professional team sports in Michigan are centered in Detroit, home of the American League's Tigers (baseball), the Red Wings of the National Hockey League, the Lions of the National Football League, the Pistons of the National Basketball Association, and the Express of the North American Soccer League. In the late 1970s, the Detroit Lions and the Pistons moved their games to the new Silverdome Stadium in suburban Pontiac, while the Express has played there since the team's inception in 1978. To hold its remaining professional teams, the city of Detroit arranged to help refurbish Tiger Stadium, and the new city-owned Joe Louis Arena became the home of the Red Wings in 1979. This arena has also helped to revive professional boxing, which had enjoyed great popularity when Louis was the world heavyweight champion.

Horse racing, Michigan's oldest organized spectator sport, is controlled by the state racing commissioner, who regulates Thoroughbred and harness-racing seasons at tracks in the Detroit area and at Jackson. Attendance and betting at these races is substantial, although the modest purses rarely attract the nation's leading horses.

Interest in college sports centers on the football and basketball teams of the University of Michigan and Michigan State University, which usually are among the top-ranked teams in the country. Other colleges also have achieved national ranking in basketball, hockey, baseball, and track. Elaborate facilities have been built for these competitions; the University of Michigan's football stadium, seating 104,001, is the largest college-owned stadium in the country.

Among other sports, Michigan pioneered in the development of ski jumping. Ishpeming was the site of the first ski-jumping tournament in the country and is now the home of the National Ski Hall of Fame. The Detroit River has been a major center of speedboat racing since the 1920s. Bowling, tennis, and golf are also popular.

⁴⁹FAMOUS MICHIGANIANS

Only one Michiganian has held the offices of US president and vice president. Gerald R. Ford (Leslie King, Jr., b.Nebraska, 1913), the 38th US president, was elected to the US House as a Republican in 1948 and served continuously until 1973, becoming minority leader in 1965. Upon the resignation of Vice President Spiro T. Agnew in 1973, President Richard M. Nixon appointed Ford to the vice-presidency. When Nixon resigned on 9 August 1974, Ford became president, the first to hold the office without having been elected. Ford succeeded in restoring much of the public's confidence in the presidency, but his pardoning of Nixon for all crimes he may have committed as president helped cost Ford victory in the presidential election of 1976. Ford subsequently moved his legal residence to California.

Lewis Cass (b.New Hampshire, 1782–1866), who served as governor of Michigan Territory, senator from Michigan, secretary of war and secretary of state, is the only other Michigan resident nominated by a major party for president; he lost the 1848 race as the Democratic candidate. Thomas E. Dewey (1902–72), a native of Owosso, was the Republican presidential nominee in 1944 and 1948, but from his adopted state of New York.

Two Michiganians have served as associate justices of the Supreme Court: Henry B. Brown (b.Massachusetts, 1836–1913), author of the 1896 segregationist decision in *Plessy* v. *Ferguson*; and Frank Murphy (1890–1949), who also served as US attorney general and was a notable defender of minority rights during his years on the court. Another justice, Potter Stewart (b.1915), was born in Jackson but appointed to the court from Ohio.

Other Michiganians who have held high federal office include Robert McClelland (b.Pennsylvania, 1807–80), secretary of the interior; Russell A. Alger (b.Ohio, 1836–1907), secretary of war; Edwin Denby (b.Indiana, 1870–1929), secretary of the

Navy, who was forced to resign because of the Teapot Dome scandal; Roy D. Chapin (1880–1936), secretary of commerce; Charles E. Wilson (b.Ohio, 1890–1961) and Robert S. McNamara (b.California, 1916), secretaries of defense; George Romney (b.Mexico, 1907), secretary of housing and urban development; Donald M. Dickinson (b.New York, 1846–1917) and Arthur E. Summerfield (1899–1972), postmasters general; and W. Michael Blumenthal (b.Germany, 1926), secretary of the treasury.

Zachariah Chandler (b.New Hampshire, 1813–79) served as secretary of the interior but is best remembered as a leader of the Radical Republicans in the US Senate during the Civil War era. Other prominent US senators have included James M. Couzens (b.Canada, 1872–1936), a former Ford executive who became a maverick Republican liberal during the 1920s; Arthur W. Vandenberg (1884–1951), a leading supporter of a bipartisan internationalist foreign policy after World War II; and Philip A. Hart, Jr. (b.Pennsylvania, 1912–76), one of the most influential senators of the 1960s and 1970s. Recent well-known US representatives include Martha W. Griffiths (b.Missouri, 1912) and John Conyers, Jr. (b.1929).

In addition to Murphy and Romney, important governors have included Stevens T. Mason (b.Virginia, 1811–43), who guided Michigan to statehood; Austin Blair (b.New York, 1818–94), Civil War governor; Hazen S. Pingree (b.Maine, 1840–1901) and Chase S. Osborn (b.Indiana, 1860–1949), reform-minded governors; Alexander Groesbeck (1873–1953); G. Mennen Williams (b.1911); and William G. Milliken (b.1922), governor since 1969. Detroit's first black mayor, Coleman A. Young (b.Alabama, 1918), has effectively promoted programs to revive the city's tarnished image since taking office in 1974.

The most famous figure in the early development of Michigan is Jacques Marquette (b.France, 1637–75). Other famous historical figures include Charles de Langlade (1729–1801), a French-Indian soldier in the French and Indian War and the American Revolution; the Ottawa chieftain Pontiac (1720?–69), leader of an ambitious Indian uprising; and Gabriel Richard (b.France, 1767–1832), an important pioneer in education and the first Catholic priest to serve in Congress. Laura Haviland (b.Canada, 1808–98) was a noted leader in the fight against slavery and for black rights, while Lucinda Hinsdale Stone (b.Vermont, 1814–1900) and Anna Howard Shaw (b.England, 1847–1919) were important in the women's rights movement.

Nobel laureates from Michigan include diplomat Ralph J. Bunche (1904–71), winner of the Nobel Peace Prize in 1950, and Glenn T. Seaborg (b.1912), Nobel Prize winner in chemistry in 1951. Among leading educators, James B. Angell (b.Rhode Island, 1829–1916), president of the University of Michigan, led that school to the forefront among American universities, while John A. Hannah (b.1902), longtime president of Michigan State University, successfully strove to expand and diversify its programs. General Motors executive Charles S. Mott (b.New Jersey, 1875–1973) contributed to the growth of continuing education programs through huge grants of money.

In the business world, William C. Durant (b.Massachusetts, 1861–1947), Henry Ford (1863–1947), and Ransom E. Olds (b.Ohio, 1864–1950) are the three most important figures in making Michigan the center of the American automobile industry. Ford's grandson, Henry Ford II (b.1917), was the dominant personality in the auto industry from 1945 through 1979. Two brothers, John Harvey Kellogg (1852–1943) and Will K. Kellogg (1860–1951), helped make Battle Creek the center of the breakfast-food industry. William E. Upjohn (1850–1932) and Herbert H. Dow (b.Canada, 1866–1930) founded major pharmaceutical and chemical companies that bear their names. James E. Scripps (b.England, 1835–1906), founder of the *Detroit News*,

was a major innovator in the newspaper business. Pioneer aviator Charles A. Lindbergh (1902–74) was born in Detroit.

Among prominent labor leaders in Michigan were Walter Reuther (b.West Virginia, 1907–70), president of the United Automobile Workers, and his controversial contemporary, James Hoffa (b.Indiana, 1913–1975?), president of the Teamsters Union, whose disappearance and presumed murder remain a mystery.

The best-known literary figures who were either native or adopted Michiganians include Edgar Guest (b.England, 1881–1959), writer of enormously popular sentimental verses; Ring Lardner (1885–1933), master of the short story; Edna Ferber (1885–1968), best-selling novelist; Paul de Kruif (1890–1971), popular writer on scientific topics; Stewart Edward White (1873–1946), writer of adventure tales; Howard Mumford Jones (1892–1980), critic and scholar; and Bruce Catton (1899–1978), Civil War historian.

Other prominent Michiganians past and present include Frederick Stuart Church (1842–1924), painter; Liberty Hyde Bailey (1858–1954), horticulturist and botanist; Albert Kahn (b.Germany, 1869–1942), innovator in factory design; and (Gottlieb) Eliel Saarinen (b.Finland, 1873–1950), architect and creator of the Cranbrook School of Art, and his son Eero (1910–61), designer of the General Motors Technical Center in Warren and many distinctive structures throughout the US. Malcolm X (Malcolm Little, b.Nebraska, 1925–65) developed his black separatist beliefs while living in Lansing.

Popular entertainers born in Michigan include Danny Thomas (Amos Jacobs, b.1914), David Wayne (b.1914), Betty Hutton (b.1921), Ed McMahon (b.1923), Julie Harris (b.1925), Ellen Burstyn (Edna Rae Gillooly, b.1932), Della Reese (Dellareese Patricia Early, b.1932), Diana Ross (b.1944), Bob Seger (b.1945), and Stevie Wonder (Stevland Morris, b.1950), along with film director Francis Ford Coppola (b.1939).

Among sports figures who had notable careers in the state were Fielding H. Yost (b.West Virginia, 1871–1946), University of Michigan football coach; Joe Louis (Joseph Louis Barrow, b.Alabama, 1914), heavyweight boxing champion from 1937 to 1949; "Sugar Ray" Robinson (b.1920), who held at various times the welterweight and middleweight boxing titles; and baseball Hall of Famer Al Kaline (b.Maryland, 1934), a Detroit Tigers star.

⁵⁰BIBLIOGRAPHY

Bald, F. C. *Michigan in Four Centuries*. Rev. ed. New York: Harper and Row, 1961.

Catton, Bruce. *Michigan: A Bicentennial History*. New York: Norton, 1976.

Dunbar, Willis F., and George S. May. *Michigan: A History of the Wolverine State*. Rev. ed. Grand Rapids: Eerdmans, 1980.

Federal Writers' Project. *Michigan: A Guide to the Wolverine State*. New York: Oxford University Press, 1941.

Fuller, George N., ed. *Michigan: A Centennial History of the State*. 5 vols. Chicago: Lewis, 1939.

League of Women Voters of Michigan. *The State We're In: A Citizen's Guide to Michigan State Government*. Lansing, 1979.

May, George S. *Pictorial History of Michigan*. 2 vols. Grand Rapids: Eerdmans, 1967, 1969.

Michigan, State of. Department of Management and Budget. *Michigan Manual, 1979–80*. Lansing, 1979.

Michigan State University. Graduate School of Business Administration. Division of Research. *Michigan Statistical Abstract*. 14th ed. Edited by David I. Verway. East Lansing, 1979.

Sommers, Lawrence M., ed. *Atlas of Michigan*. East Lansing: Michigan State University Press, 1977.

Woodford, Frank B. and Arthur M. *All Our Yesterdays: A Brief History of Detroit*. Detroit: Wayne State University Press, 1969.

MINNESOTA

State of Minnesota

ORIGIN OF STATE NAME: Derived from the Sioux Indian word *minisota*, meaning "sky-tinted waters." **NICKNAME:** The North Star State. **CAPITAL:** St. Paul. **ENTERED UNION:** 11 May 1858 (32d). **SONG:** "Hail! Minnesota." **MOTTO:** *L'Etoile du Nord* (The North Star). **FLAG:** On a blue field bordered on three sides by a gold fringe, a version of the state seal is surrounded by a wreath with the statehood year (1858), the year of the establishment of Ft. Snelling (1819), and the year the flag was adopted (1893); five clusters of gold stars and the word "Minnesota" fill the outer circle. **OFFICIAL SEAL:** A farmer, with a powder horn and musket nearby, plows a field in the foreground, while in the background, before a rising sun, an Indian on horseback crosses the plains; pine trees and a waterfall represent the state's natural resources. The state motto is above, and the whole is surrounded by the words "The Great Seal of the State of Minnesota 1858." Another version of the seal in common use shows a cowboy riding across the plains. **BIRD:** Common loon. **FISH:** Walleye. **FLOWER:** Pink and white lady's-slipper. **TREE:** Red (Norway) pine. **GEM:** Lake Superior agate. **GRAIN:** Wild rice. **LEGAL HOLIDAYS:** New Year's Day, 1 January; Washington's and Lincoln's Birthdays, 3d Monday in February; Memorial Day, last Monday in May; Independence Day, 4 July; Labor Day, 1st Monday in September; Columbus Day, 2d Monday in October; Veterans Day, 11 November; Thanksgiving Day, 4th Thursday in November; Christmas Day, 25 December. By statute, schools hold special observances on Susan B. Anthony Day, 15 February; Arbor Day, last Friday in April; Minnesota Day, 11 May; Frances Willard Day, 28 September; Leif Erikson Day, 9 October. **TIME:** 6 A.M. CST = noon GMT.

¹LOCATION, SIZE, AND EXTENT

Situated in the western north-central US, Minnesota is the largest of the midwestern states and ranks 12th in size among the 50 states.

The total area of Minnesota is 84,068 sq mi (217,736 sq km), of which land accounts for 79,289 sq mi (205,358 sq km) and inland water 4,779 sq mi (12,378 sq km). Minnesota extends 406 mi (653 km) N–S; its extreme E–W extension is 358 mi (576 km).

Minnesota is bordered on the N by the Canadian provinces of Manitoba and Ontario (with the line passing through the Lake of the Woods, Rainy River, Rainy Lake, a succession of smaller lakes, the Pigeon River, and Lake Superior); on the E by Michigan and Wisconsin (with the line passing through Lake Superior and the St. Croix and Mississippi rivers); on the S by Iowa; and on the W by South Dakota and North Dakota (with the line passing through Big Stone Lake, Lake Traverse, the Bois de Sioux River, and the Red River of the North).

The length of Minnesota's boundaries totals 1,783 mi (2,870 km). The state's geographic center is in Crow Wing County, 10 mi (16 km) SW of Brainerd.

²TOPOGRAPHY

Minnesota, lying at the northern rim of the Central Plains region, consists mainly of flat prairie, nowhere flatter than in the Red River Valley of the west. There are rolling hills and deep river valleys in the southeast; the northeast, known as Arrowhead Country, is more rugged and includes the Vermilion Range and the Mesabi Range, with its rich iron deposits. Eagle Mountain, in the extreme northeast, rises to a height of 2,301 feet (701 meters), the highest point in the state; the surface of nearby Lake Superior, 602 feet (183 meters) above sea level, is the state's lowest elevation.

With more than 15,000 lakes and extensive wetlands, rivers, and streams, Minnesota has more inland water than any other states except Alaska and Texas. Some of the inland lakes are quite large: Lower and Upper Red Lake, 451 sq mi (1,168 sq km); Mille Lacs, 207 sq mi (536 sq km); and Leech Lake, 176 sq mi (456 sq km). The Lake of the Woods, at 1,485 sq mi (3,846 sq km), is shared with Canada, as is Rainy Lake, 345 sq mi (894 sq km). A total of 2,212 sq mi (5,729 sq km) of Lake Superior lies within Minnesota's jurisdiction.

Lake Itasca, in the northwest, is the source of the Mississippi River, which drains about three-fifths of the state and, after meeting with the St. Croix below Minneapolis–St. Paul, forms part of the eastern boundary with Wisconsin. The Minnesota River, which flows across the southern part of the state, joins the Mississippi at the Twin Cities. The Red River of the North, which forms much of the boundary with North Dakota, is part of another large drainage system; it flows north, crossing the Canadian border above St. Vincent and eventually emptying into Lake Winnipeg in Manitoba.

Most of Minnesota, except for small areas in the southeast, was covered by ice during the glacial ages. When the ice melted, it left behind a body of water known as Lake Agassiz, which extended into what we now call the Dakotas and Canada and was larger than the combined Great Lakes are today; additional melting to the north caused the lake to drain away, leaving flat prairie in its wake. The glaciers also left behind large stretches of pulverized limestone, enriching Minnesota's soil, and the numerous shallow depressions that have developed into its modern-day lakes and streams.

³CLIMATE

Minnesota has a continental climate, with cold, often frigid winters and warm summers. The growing season is 160 days or more in the south-central and southeastern regions, but 100 days or less in the northern counties. Normal daily mean temperatures range from 9°F (-13°C) in January to 66°F (19°C) in July for Duluth, and from 12°F (-11°C) in January to 72°F (22°C) in July for Minneapolis–St. Paul, often called the Twin Cities. The lowest temperature recorded in Minnesota was -59°F (-51°C), at Pokegama Dam on 16 February 1903; the highest, 114°F (46°C), at Moorhead on 6 July 1936. Precipitation is heaviest in the south and southeast, and lightest in the northwest, where it averages about 20 in (51 cm) per year. The mean annual precipitation in Duluth is 30 in (76 cm), with snowfall averaging 78 in (198 cm); mean annual precipitation in the Twin Cities is 26 in (66 cm), with snowfall averaging 46 in (117 cm).

⁴FLORA AND FAUNA

Minnesota is divided into three main life zones: the wooded lake regions of the north and east, the prairie lands of the west and southwest, and a transition zone in between. Oak, maple, elm, birch, pine, ash, and poplar still thrive, though much of the state's woodland has been cut down since the 1850s. Common shrubs include thimbleberry, sweetfern, and several varieties of honeysuckle. Familiar among some 1,500 native flowering plants are puccoon, prairie phlox, and blazing star; pink and white lady's-slipper is the state flower. White and yellow water lilies cover the pond areas, with bulrushes and cattails on the shore.

Among Minnesota's common mammals are the opossum, eastern and starnose moles, little brown bat, raccoon, mink, river otter, badger, striped and spotted skunks, red fox, bobcat, 13-lined ground squirrel (also known as the Minnesota gopher, symbol of the University of Minnesota), beaver, porcupine, eastern cottontail, moose, and white-tailed deer. The western meadowlark, Brewer's blackbird, Carolina wren, and Louisiana water thrush are among some 240 resident bird species; introduced birds include the English sparrow and ring-necked pheasant. Teeming in Minnesota's many lakes are such game fishes as steelhead, walleye, muskellunge, northern pike, and rainbow and brown trouts. The only poisonous snake is the rattler; other reptiles include various lizards and turtles.

Classification of rare, threatened, and endangered species is delegated to the Minnesota Department of Natural Resources. Among rare species noted by the department are the white pelican, short-eared owl, rock vole, pine marten, American elk, woodland caribou, lake sturgeon, and paddlefish; threatened species include the bobwhite quail, piping plover, and gray (timber) wolf. The trumpeter swan, American peregrine falcon, whooping crane, burrowing owl, and Higgins' eye pearly mussel are on the endangered list.

⁵ENVIRONMENTAL PROTECTION

The state's northern forests have been greatly depleted by fires, lumbering, and farming, but efforts to replenish them began as early as 1876, with the formation of the state's first forestry association. In 1911, the legislature authorized a state nursery, established forest reserves and parks, and created the post of chief fire warden to oversee forestry resources and promote reforestation projects. The Conservation Department, created in 1931, evolved into the present Department of Natural Resources, which is responsible for the management of forests, fish and game, public lands, minerals, and state parks and waters. The department's Soil and Water Conservation Board has jurisdiction over the state's 92 soil and water conservation districts. A separate Pollution Control Agency enforces air and water quality standards and oversees solid waste disposal and pollution-related land-use planning. The Environmental Quality Board coordinates conservation efforts among various state agencies. In 1978/79, an estimated $33.9 million was appropriated from the general fund for the Department of Natural Resources, and about $5.6 million for the Pollution Control Agency.

A long-standing controversy over toxic wastes was resolved in 1977, when the state supreme court in effect accepted the location proposed by the Reserve Mining Co. for on-land disposal of taconite wastes, a possible carcinogen, that the company had been discharging into Lake Superior; the lake dumping ended in March 1980, after nearly 25 years. Other pollution problems came to light during the 1970s with the discovery of asbestos in drinking water from Lake Superior, of contaminants from inadequately buried toxic wastes at St. Louis Park, and of the killing by agricultural pesticides of an estimated 100,000 fish in two southeastern Minnesota brooks. Another sensitive issue was settled in 1978, when the US Congress passed a measure banning logging and restricting mining in the huge federally owned Boundary Waters Canoe Area, in northeastern Minnesota.

⁶POPULATION

The 1970 census gave Minnesota a population of 3,804,971, ranking it 19th among the 50 states. The preliminary 1980 census total was 4,068,856, yielding an average density for the state of 51 per sq mi (20 per sq km).

Minnesota was still mostly wilderness until a land boom in 1848 attracted the first substantial wave of settlers, mainly lumbermen from New England, farmers from the Middle Atlantic states, and tradespeople from eastern cities. The 1850 census recorded a population of 6,077 in what was then Minnesota Territory. With the signing of major Indian treaties and widespread use of the steamboat, large areas were opened to settlement, and the population exceeded 150,000 by the end of 1857. Attracted by fertile farmland and enticed by ambitious recruitment programs overseas, large numbers of European immigrants came to settle in the new state from the 1860s onward. In 1880, the state population totaled 780,733; by 1920 (when overseas immigration virtually ceased), the state had 2,387,125 residents. Population growth leveled off during the 1920s and has fallen below the national average since the 1940s. As of 1976, Minnesotans were, on average, somewhat older than the nation as a whole and much less mobile: 64% of adult state residents had lived in Minnesota their whole lives, and only 2% had been living there less than a year.

Nearly 2 out of 3 Minnesotans live in metropolitan areas. The Minneapolis–St. Paul metropolitan area (including portions of Wisconsin) had an estimated 1977 population of 2,037,000 (15th in the US), a 3.6% decline since 1970. In Minneapolis itself, the population fell by nearly 19% from 1970 to 1978, at which time there were an estimated 353,992 residents. Preliminary 1980 census totals for the state's leading cities were as follows: Minneapolis, 370,091; St. Paul, 268,248; Duluth, 92,789; Bloomington, 81,640; and Rochester, 54,287.

⁷ETHNIC GROUPS

Minnesota was settled during the second half of the 19th century primarily by European immigrants, chiefly Germans, Swedes, Norwegians, Danes, English, and Poles, along with the Irish and some French Canadians. The Swedish newcomers were mainly farmers; Norwegians concentrated on lumbering, while the Swiss worked for the most part in the dairy industry. In 1890, Finns and Slavs were recruited to work in the iron mines; the state's meat-packing plants brought in Balkan nationals, Mexicans, and Poles after the turn of the century. By 1930, 50% of the population was foreign-born. Among first- and second-generation Americans of European origin, Germans and Scandinavians are still the largest groups. The other ethnic groups are concentrated in Minneapolis–St. Paul or in the iron country of the Mesabi Range, where ethnic enclaves still persist. As of 1970, the foreign-born and their American-born children in Minnesota numbered 707,000, nearly 19% of the state total.

As of 1970 there were still 23,128 Indians in Minnesota. Besides those living in seven small reservations and four villages, a cluster of Indian urban dwellers (chiefly Ojibwa) lived in St. Paul. Indian lands totaled 764,000 acres (309,000 hectares) in 1978, of which 93% were tribal lands.

There were only 39 black Americans in Minnesota in 1850; by 1976, blacks numbered 51,000, or 1.3% of the total population. In 1970 there were somewhat more than 10,000 Japanese, Chinese, Filipino, and other Asian and Pacific peoples; it is estimated that at least 9,000 refugees from Southeast Asia settled in Minneapolis–St. Paul in 1979–80. Hispanic Americans represent less than 1% of the population.

LOCATION: 43°34' to 49°23'N; 89°34' to 97°12'W. BOUNDARIES: Canadian line, 596 mi (959 km); Wisconsin line, 426 mi (686 km); Iowa line, 263 mi (423 km); South Dakota line, 182 mi (293 km); North Dakota line, 316 mi (509 km).

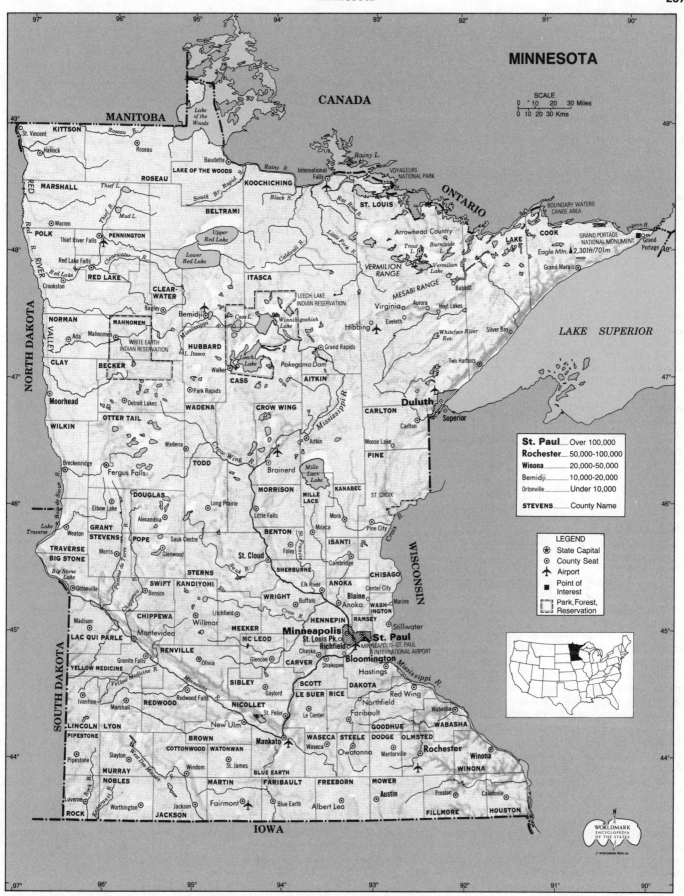

MINNESOTA

CANADA

MANITOBA

ONTARIO

NORTH DAKOTA

SOUTH DAKOTA

WISCONSIN

IOWA

LAKE SUPERIOR

SCALE
0 10 20 30 Miles
0 10 20 30 Kms

KITTSON
St. Vincent
Hallock
Roseau R.
Roseau
Lake of the Woods
Baudette
MARSHALL
Warren
ROSEAU
LAKE OF THE WOODS
KOOCHICHING
International Falls
Rainy R.
Rainy L.
VOYAGEURS NATIONAL PARK
ST. LOUIS
BOUNDARY WATERS CANOE AREA
COOK
GRAND PORTAGE NATIONAL MONUMENT
Pigeon R.
Grand Portage
Thief L.
Thief R.
Mud L.
BELTRAMI
Black R.
South Br. Rapid
Caldwell R.
Little Fork R.
Arrowhead Country
Burntside L.
Trout L.
Eagle Mtn. 2,301ft/701m
Grand Marais
POLK
RED RIVER
Thief River Falls
PENNINGTON
Upper Red Lake
VERMILION RANGE
Vermilion Lake
Babbitt
Red Lake Falls
Clearwater R.
Lower Red Lake
ITASCA
MESABI RANGE
Whiteface River Res.
Silver Bay
Red Lake
RED LAKE
Crookston
CLEAR- WATER
Bagley
LEECH LAKE INDIAN RESERVATION
Virginia
Aurora
Hoyt Lakes
Hibbing
Eveleth
Two Harbors
NORMAN
Ada
MAHNOMEN
Mahnomen
WHITE EARTH INDIAN RESERVATION
Bemidji
Cass L.
Winnibigoshish Lake
Grand Rapids
VALLEY
HUBBARD
L. Itasca
Leech Lake
Pokegama Dam
Duluth
CLAY
BECKER
Walker
CASS
AITKIN
Carlton
Superior
Moorhead
Detroit Lakes
Park Rapids
WADENA
CROW WING
CARLTON
WILKIN
OTTER TAIL
Wadena
Aitkin
Moose Lake
PINE
Breckenridge
Crow Wing R.
Brainerd
Mille Lacs Lake
ST. CROIX
Fergus Falls
TODD
MORRISON
KANABEC
Long Prairie
Little Falls
MILLE LACS
Mora
Pine City
Boise de Sioux R.
GRANT
DOUGLAS
Elbow Lake
Alexandria
BENTON
Milaca
ISANTI
WISCONSIN
Lake Traverse
STEVENS
POPE
Sauk Centre
Foley
Cambridge
TRAVERSE
Morris
Glenwood
St. Francis R.
Pomme de Terre R.
St. Cloud
SHERBURNE
CHISAGO
BIG STONE
STERNS
Sauk R.
Elk River
ANOKA
Center City
Big Stone Lake
SWIFT
KANDIYOHI
WRIGHT
Buffalo
Blaine
WASH- INGTON
Marine
Ortonville
Chippewa R.
Benson
Litchfield
Crow R.
Anoka
Stillwater
CHIPPEWA
MEEKER
HENNEPIN
RAMSEY
Madison
Willmar
St. Louis Pk.
Minneapolis
St. Paul
LAC QUI PARLE
Montevideo
MC LEOD
Richfield
MINNEAPOLIS—ST. PAUL INTERNATIONAL AIRPORT
RENVILLE
Glencoe
Chaska
Bloomington
Granite Falls
Olivia
CARVER
Shakopee
Hastings
YELLOW MEDICINE
Yellow Medicine R.
SIBLEY
SCOTT
Mississippi R.
Ivanhoe
Minnesota R.
Gaylord
LE SUER
RICE
DAKOTA
Red Wing
LINCOLN
LYON
REDWOOD
Redwood Falls
NICOLLET
St. Peter
Le Center
Northfield
Faribault
GOODHUE
Wabasha
Marshall
New Ulm
Faribault
WABASHA
PIPESTONE
BROWN
WASECA
STEELE
DODGE
OLMSTED
Pipestone
COTTONWOOD
WATONWAN
Mankato
Waseca
Owatonna
Mantorville
Rochester
Winona
MURRAY
Slayton
Windom
St. James
BLUE EARTH
WINONA
NOBLES
West Des Moines R.
MARTIN
FARIBAULT
FREEBORN
MOWER
Preston
Caledonia
Luverne
Worthington
Jackson
Fairmont
Blue Earth
Albert Lea
Austin
ROCK
JACKSON
FILLMORE
HOUSTON
Rock R.
Kanaranzi R.

St. Paul .... Over 100,000
Rochester 50,000-100,000
Winona 20,000-50,000
Bemidji 10,000-20,000
Ortonville .... Under 10,000
STEVENS .... County Name

LEGEND
⊗ State Capital
⊙ County Seat
✈ Airport
■ Point of Interest
⬚ Park, Forest, Reservation

WORLDMARK
ENCYCLOPEDIA OF THE STATES
© WORLDMARK PRESS Ltd.

See US political: front cover H1; physical: back cover H1.

[8] LANGUAGES

Many place-names echo the languages of the Yankton and Santee Sioux Indian tribes and of the incoming Algonkian-language Ojibwa, or Chippewa, from whom most of the Sioux fled to Dakota Territory. Such place-names as Minnesota itself, Minnetonka, and Mankato are Siouan in origin; Kabetogama and Winnibigoshish, both lakes, are Ojibwan. In 1970, 6,260 Minnesotans claimed Indian first languages.

English in the state is essentially Northern, with minor infiltration of Midland terms because of early movement up the Mississippi River into southern Minnesota and also up the Great Lakes into and beyond Duluth. Among older residents, traces of Scandinavian intonation persist, and on the Iron Range several pronunciation features reflect the mother tongues of mine workers from eastern Europe.

Although some minor variants now compete in frequency, on the whole Minnesota speech features such dominant Northern terms as *andirons, pail, mouth organ* (harmonica), *comforter* (tied and filled bedcover), *wishbone, clingstone peach, sweet corn, angleworm* (earthworm), and *sick to the stomach*, with *dove* as the past tense of *dive*. Minnesotans call the grass strip between street and sidewalk the *boulevard* and a rubber band a *rubber binder*, and many *cook coffee* when they brew it. Three-fourths of a sample population had *root* with the vowel of *put*; one-third, through school influence, pronounced /ah/ in *aunt* instead of the usual Northern short /a/, as in *pants*. Many younger speakers pronounce *caller* and *collar* alike.

Of the native-born, 76% claimed English as their mother tongue in 1970; of all residents, 75%. Speakers of leading first languages were as follows:

	NATIVE-BORN	FOREIGN-BORN
English	2,826,763	14,102
German	298,945	17,109
Polish	36,369	3,582
French	26,028	2,385
Spanish	10,953	2,988
Italian	10,538	2,250

[9] RELIGIONS

Minnesota's first Christian church was organized by Presbyterians in Ft. Snelling in 1835; the first Roman Catholic church, the Chapel of St. Paul, was dedicated in 1841 at a town then called Pig's Eye but now known by the same name as the chapel. Immigrants arriving in subsequent decades brought their religions with them, with Lutherans and Catholics predominating.

As of 1971 there were 1,527,190 known Protestant adherents, including 1,059,966 in four Lutheran denominations, 179,014 United Methodists, 88,149 United Presbyterians, 59,068 members of the United Church of Christ, and 42,139 Episcopalians. Roman Catholics numbered 1,019,495 in 1979, when the estimated Jewish population was 33,980. Minnesota is the headquarters for three national Lutheran religious groups: the American Lutheran Church, the Church of the Lutheran Brethren, and the Association of Free Lutheran Congregations.

[10] TRANSPORTATION

The development of an extensive railroad network after the Civil War was a key factor in the growth of lumbering, iron mining, wheat growing, and other industries. By 1976, Minnesota had 7,814 mi (12,575 km) of track, of which 3,007 mi (4,839 km) were in the Burlington Northern system. Amtrak serves Minneapolis–St. Paul en route from Chicago to Seattle.

As of 1980, 29 municipalities and metropolitan areas had state-aided mass transit systems. Planning and supervision of mass transportation in the Twin Cities metropolitan area is under the jurisdiction of the Metropolitan Transit Commission, a public corporation. The national Greyhound bus line was founded in Hibbing in 1914.

Minnesota had 127,918 mi (205,865 km) of roadway in 1978, of which 108,678 mi (174,901 km) were rural and 19,240 mi (30,964 km) municipal. The main interstate highways are I-35, linking Minneapolis–St. Paul with Duluth, and I-94, connecting the Twin Cities with Moorhead and Fargo, N.D. There were 1,962,130 registered automobiles, 704,688 trucks, 16,118 buses, and 420,470 motorcycles in 1978, when Minnesota had 2,234,646 licensed drivers.

The first settlements grew up around major river arteries, especially in the southeast; early traders and settlers arrived first by canoe or keelboat, later by steamer. The port of Duluth-Superior, at the western terminus of the Great Lakes–St. Lawrence Seaway (officially opened in 1959), is one of the 10 busiest US ports, averaging close to 40 million tons of domestic and international cargo annually, including bulk grain, coal, scrap iron, and refrigerated commodities. Since 1973, more than $100 million has been committed to port development on the Minnesota side, which is under the supervision of the Seaway Port Authority of Duluth, a public corporation. The ports of Minneapolis and St. Paul handle more than 15 million tons of cargo each year, with agricultural products and scrap iron moving downstream and petroleum products, chemicals, and cement moving upstream.

As of 1978, the state had 273 private and 147 public airports. Minneapolis–St. Paul International Airport handled 59,713 scheduled departing flights, emplaning 3,952,367 passengers.

[11] HISTORY

People have lived on the land that is now Minnesota for at least 10,000 years. The earliest inhabitants—belonging to what archaeologists classify as the Paleo-Indian (or Big Game) culture—hunted large animals, primarily bison, from which they obtained food, clothing, and materials for shelter. A second identifiable cultural tradition, from around 5000 BC, was the Eastern Archaic (or Old Copper) culture. These people hunted small as well as large game animals and fashioned copper implements through a cold hammering process. The more recent Woodland Tradition (1000 BC-AD 1700) was marked by the introduction of pottery and of mound burials. From the 1870s to the early 1900s, more than 11,000 burial mounds were discovered in Minnesota—the most visible remains of prehistoric life in the area. Finally, overlapping the Woodland culture in time was the Mississippian Tradition, beginning around AD 1000, in which large villages with permanent dwellings were erected near fertile river bottoms, and their residents, in addition to hunting and fishing, raised corn, beans, and squash. There are many sites from this culture throughout southern Minnesota.

At the time of European penetration in the 17th and early 18th centuries, the two principal Indian nations were the Dakota, or Minnesota Sioux, and, at least after 1700, the Ojibwa, or Chippewa, who were moving from the east into northern Minnesota and the Dakota homelands. Friendly relations between the two nations were shattered in 1736, when the Dakota slew a party of French missionaries and traders (allies of the Ojibwa) and their Cree Indian guides (distant relatives of the Ojibwa) at the Lake of the Woods, an act the Ojibwa viewed as a declaration of war. There followed more than 100 years of conflict between Dakota and Ojibwa, during which the Dakota were pressed toward the south and west, with the Ojibwa establishing themselves in the north.

Few scholars accept the authenticity of the Kensington Rune Stone, found in 1898, the basis of the claim that Minnesota was visited in 1362 by the Vikings. The first white men whose travels through the region have been documented were Pierre Esprit Radisson and his brother-in-law, Médart Chouart, Sieur de Groseilliers, who probably reached the interior of northern Minnesota in the 1650s. In 1679, Daniel Greysolon, Sieur Duluth, held council with the Dakota near Mille Lacs and formally claimed the region for King Louis XIV of France. The following year, Duluth negotiated the release of three captives of the Dakota Indians, among them a Belgian explorer and missionary, Father Louis Hennepin, who named the falls of the Mississippi (the site of present-day Minneapolis) after his patron saint, Anthony of Padua, and returned to Europe to write an exaggerated account of his travels in the region.

Duluth was in the vanguard of the French, English, and American explorers, fur traders, and missionaries who came to Minnesota during the two centuries prior to statehood. Among the best known was Nicolas Perrot, who built Ft. Antoine on the east side of Lake Pepin in 1686. In 1731, Pierre Gaultier de Varennes, Sieur de la Vérendrye, journeyed to the Lake of the Woods, along whose shores he erected Ft. St. Charles; subsequently, he or his men ventured farther west than any other known French explorer, reaching the Dakotas and the Saskatchewan Valley. His eldest son was among those slain by Dakota Indians at the Lake of the Woods in 1736.

Competition for control of the upper Mississippi Valley ended with the British victory in the French and Indian War, which placed the portion of Minnesota east of the Mississippi under British control; the land west of the Mississippi was ceded by France to Spain in 1762. Although the Spanish paid little attention to their northern territory, the British immediately sent in fur traders and explorers. One of the best known was Jonathan Carver, who spent the winter of 1766–67 with the Dakota on the Minnesota River. His account of his travels—a mixture of personal observations and borrowings from others—quickly became a popular success.

There was little activity in the region during the Revolutionary War, and for a few decades afterward, the British continued to pursue their interests there. The North West Company built a major fur trading post at Grand Portage, which quickly became the center of a prosperous inland trade, and other posts dotted the countryside. The company hired David Thompson away from the Hudson's Bay Company to map the area from Lake Superior west to the Red River; his detailed and accurate work, executed in the late 1790s, is still admired today. After the War of 1812, the US Congress passed an act curbing British participation in the fur trade, and the North West Company was eventually replaced by the American Fur Company, which John Jacob Astor had incorporated in 1808.

Under the Northwest Ordinance of 1787, Minnesota east of the Mississippi became part of the Northwest Territory; most of western Minnesota was acquired by the US as part of the Louisiana Purchase of 1803. The Red River Valley became a secure part of the US after an agreement with England on the northern boundary was reached in 1818.

In 1805, the US War Department sent Lieutenant Zebulon Pike and a detachment of troops to explore the Mississippi to its source. Pike failed to locate the source, but he concluded a treaty with a band of Dakota for two parcels of land along the river. Later, additional troops were sent in to establish US control, and in 1819, a military post was established in part of Pike's land, on a bluff overlooking the junction of the Mississippi and Minnesota rivers. First called Ft. St. Anthony, it was renamed in 1825 for Colonel Josiah Snelling, who supervised the construction of the permanent fort. For three decades, Ft. Snelling served as the principal center of civilization in Minnesota and the key frontier outpost in the northwest.

In 1834, Henry H. Sibley was appointed a manager of the American Fur Company on the upper Mississippi. He settled comfortably at Mendota, a trading post across the river from Ft. Snelling, and enjoyed immediate success. The company's fortunes took a downward turn in 1837, however—partly because of that year's financial panic, but even more important, because the same year also brought the first of a series of treaties with the

Dakota and Ojibwa transferring large areas of Indian land to the US government and thus curtailing the profitable relationship between fur traders and Indians.

The Indian treaties opened the land for lumbering, farming, and settlement. Lumbering spawned many of the early permanent settlements, such as Marine and Stillwater, on the St. Croix River, and St. Anthony (later Minneapolis) at the falls of the Mississippi. Another important town, St. Paul (originally Pig's Eye), developed as a trading center at the head of navigation on the Mississippi.

In 1849, Minnesota Territory was established. It included all of present-day Minnesota, along with portions of North and South Dakota east of the Missouri River. Alexander Ramsey, a Pennsylvania Whig, was appointed as the first territorial governor, and in 1851, the legislature named St. Paul the capital. Stillwater was chosen for the state prison, while St. Anthony was selected as the site for the university. As of 1850, the new territory had slightly more than 6,000 inhabitants, but as lumbering grew and subsequent Indian treaties opened up more land, the population boomed, reaching a total of more than 150,000 by 1857, with the majority concentrated in the southeast corner, close to the rivers.

On 11 May 1858, Minnesota officially became the 32d state, with its western boundaries pruned from the Missouri to the Red River. Henry Sibley, who was a Democrat, narrowly defeated Alexander Ramsey, running as a Republican, to become the state's first governor. But under Ramsey's leadership, the fast-growing Republican Party soon gained control of state politics and held it firmly through the early 20th century. In the first presidential election in which Minnesota participated, Abraham Lincoln, the Republican candidate, easily carried the state, and when the Civil War broke out, Minnesota was the first state to answer Lincoln's call for troops. In all, Minnesota supplied more than 20,000 men to defend the Union.

More challenging to the defense of Minnesota was the Dakota War of 1862. Grieved by the loss of their lands, dissatisfied with reservation life, and ultimately brought to a condition of near starvation, the Dakota appealed to US Indian agencies without success. The murder of five whites by four young Dakota Indians ignited a bloody uprising in which more than 300 whites and an unknown number of Indians were killed. In the aftermath, 38 Dakota captives were hanged for "voluntary participation in murders and massacres," and the Dakota remaining in Minnesota were removed to reservations in Nebraska. (Some later returned to Minnesota.) Meanwhile, the Ojibwa were relegated to reservations on remnants of their former lands.

Also during 1862, Minnesota's first railroad joined St. Anthony (Minneapolis) and St. Paul with 10 mi (16 km) of track. By 1867, the Twin Cities were connected with Chicago by rail; in the early 1870s, tracks crossed the prairie all the way to the Red River Valley. The railroads brought settlers from the eastern states (many of them Scandinavian and German in origin) to every corner of Minnesota; the settlers, in turn, grew produce for the trains to carry back to the cities of the east. The railroads soon ushered in an era of large-scale commercial farming. King Wheat provided the biggest cash crop, as wheat exports rose from 2 million bushels in 1860 to 95 million in 1890. Meanwhile, the falls of St. Anthony became the major US flour milling center; by 1880, 27 Minneapolis mills were producing more than 2 million barrels of flour annually.

Despite these signs of prosperity, discontent grew among Minnesota farmers, who were plagued by high railroad rates, damaging droughts, and a deflationary economy. The first national farmers' movement, the National Grange of the Patrons of Husbandry, was founded in 1867 by a Minnesotan, Oliver H. Kelley, and spread more rapidly in Minnesota than in any other state. The Farmers' Alliance movement, joining forces with the Knights of Labor, exerted a major influence on state politics in the 1880s, and in 1898, the Populist Party (in which a Minnesotan, Ignatius Donnelly, played a leading role nationwide) helped elect John Lind to the governorship on a fusion ticket.

Most immigrants during the 1860s and 1870s settled on the rich farmland of the north and west, but after 1880 the cities and industries grew more rapidly. When iron ore was discovered in the 1880s in the sparsely settled northeast, even that part of the state attracted settlers, many of them immigrants from eastern and southern Europe. Before the turn of the century, Duluth had become a major lake port, and by the eve of World War I, Minnesota had become a national iron mining center.

The economic picture changed after the war. As the forests became depleted, the big lumber companies turned to the Pacific Northwest. An agricultural depression hit the region, and flour mills moved to the Kansas City area and to Buffalo, N.Y. Minnesotans adapted to the new realities in various ways. Farmers planted corn, soybeans, and sugar beets along with wheat, and new food-processing industries developed. To these were added business machines, electronics, computers, and other high-technology industries. In 1948, for the first time, the dollar value of all manufactured products exceeded total cash farm receipts: Minnesota was becoming an urban, industrial commonwealth.

Economic dislocations and the growth of cities and industries encouraged challenges to the Republican leadership from Democrats and third parties. John Johnson, a progressive Democratic governor first elected in 1904, was especially active in securing legislation to regulate the insurance industry; his successor, Republican Adolph Eberhart, promoted numerous progressive measures, including one establishing direct primary elections. The Non-Partisan League, founded in 1915 by Minnesotan Arthur C. Townley, soon grew particularly strong in both North Dakota and Minnesota, where the elder Charles A. Lindbergh was its spokesman.

A political outgrowth of the Non-Partisan League known as the Farmer-Labor Party had many electoral successes in the 1920s and reached its peak with the election of Farmer-Labor candidate Floyd B. Olson to the governorship in 1930. Olson introduced a graduated income tax and other progressivist measures, but his death in office in 1936 was a crippling blow to the party. In 1938, the Republicans recaptured the governorship with the election of Harold E. Stassen. However, a successful merger of the Farmer-Labor and Democratic parties in Minnesota, engineered in 1943–44 by both local and national politicians, revived the progressivist tradition after World War II. Hubert Humphrey (later US vice president) and his colleagues Orville Freeman, Eugene McCarthy, and Eugenie Anderson emerged as leaders of this new coalition. The Democratic-Farmer-Labor Party controlled the state legislature for most of the 1970s, but it was unclear how much Humphrey's death in 1978 might weaken the DFL in the 1980s.

12 STATE GOVERNMENT

The constitutional convention that assembled at St. Paul on 13 July 1857 was marked by such bitter dissension that the Democrats and Republicans had to meet in separate chambers; the final draft was written by a committee of five Democrats and five Republicans and then adopted by a majority of each party, without amendment. Since Democrats and Republicans were also unwilling to sign the same piece of paper, two separate documents were prepared, one on blue-tinted paper, the other on white. The constitution was ratified by the electorate on 13 October and approved by the US Congress on 11 May 1858. An amendment restructuring the constitution for easy reference and simplifying its language was approved in 1974; for purposes of constitutional law, however, the original document (incorporating numerous other amendments) remains authoritative.

As reapportioned by court order after the 1970 census, the Minnesota legislature consists of a 67-member senate and a 134-member house of representatives. Senators serve four years and representatives two, at annual salaries of $18,500 as of 1980. Legislators must be US citizens, at least 21 years of age, and must have resided in the state for one year and in the legislative district for six months preceding election.

The governor and lieutenant governor are jointly elected for four-year terms; both must be at least 25 years old, US citizens, and must have been residents of Minnesota for a year prior to election. Other constitutional officers are the secretary of state, auditor, treasurer, and attorney general, all serving for four years. Numerous other officials are appointed by the governor, among them the commissioners of the 20 government departments and many heads and members of independent agencies.

Once a bill is passed by a majority of both houses, the governor may sign it, veto it in whole or in part, or pocket veto it by failing to act within 14 days of adjournment. (When the legislature is in session, however, a bill becomes law if the governor fails to act on it within 3 days.) A two-thirds vote of both houses is sufficient to override a veto. Constitutional amendments require the approval of a majority of both houses of the legislature and are subject to ratification by the electorate. Those voting in state elections must be at least 18 years old and must have been US citizens for three months and residents of the district for 30 days.

13 POLITICAL PARTIES

The two major political parties are the Democratic-Farmer-Labor Party (DFL) and the Independent-Republican Party (IR), as Minnesota's Republican Party is now officially called. The Republican Party dominated Minnesota politics from the 1860s through the 1920s, except for a period around the turn of the century. The DFL, formed in 1944 by merger between the Democratic Party and the populist Farmer-Labor Party, rose to prominence in the 1950s under the leadership of then US Senator Hubert Humphrey and others.

The DFL is the heir to a long populist tradition bred during the panic of 1857 and the early days of statehood, a tradition perpetuated by a succession of strong, though transient, third-party movements. The Grange, a farmers' movement committed to the cause of railroad regulation, took root in Minnesota in 1868; it withered in the panic of 1873, but its successors, the Anti-Monopoly Party and the Greenback Party, attracted large followings for some time afterward. They were followed by a new pro-silver group, the Farmers' Alliance, which spread to Minnesota from Nebraska in 1881 and soon became associated with the Minnesota Knights of Labor. The Populist Party also won a foothold in Minnesota, in alliance with the Democratic Party in the late 1890s.

The Farmer-Labor Party, the most successful of Minnesota's third-party movements, grew out of a socialist and isolationist movement known at first as the Non-Partisan League. Founded in North Dakota with the initial aim of gaining control of the Republican Party in that state, the league moved its headquarters to St. Paul and competed in the 1918 elections under the name Farmer-Labor Party, hastily adopted to attract what party leaders hoped would be its two main constituencies. The party scored a major success in 1922 when its candidate, Henrik Shipstead, a Glenwood dentist, defeated a nationally known incumbent, Republican Senator Frank B. Kellogg; Farmer-Labor candidate Floyd B. Olson won the governorship in 1930. The decline of the party in the late 1930s was hastened by the rise of Republican Harold Stassen, an ardent internationalist, who won the governorship in 1938 and twice won reelection.

The first DFL candidate to become governor was Orville Freeman in 1954. The DFL held the governorship from 1963 to 1967 and from 1971 to 1978, when US Representative Al Quie (IR) defeated his DFL opponent by 830,019 votes to 718,224.

Minnesota is famous as a breeding ground for presidential candidates. Governor Harold Stassen contended seriously for the

Republican nomination in 1948 and again in 1952. Vice President Hubert Humphrey was the Democratic presidential nominee in 1968, losing by a narrow margin to Richard Nixon. During the same year, US Senator Eugene McCarthy unsuccessfully sought the Democratic presidential nomination on an antiwar platform; his surprising showings in the early primaries against the incumbent, Lyndon B. Johnson, helped persuade Johnson to withdraw his candidacy. Eight years later, McCarthy ran for the presidency as an independent, drawing 35,490 votes in Minnesota (1.8% of the total votes cast) and 756,631 votes (0.9%) nationwide. Walter Mondale, successor to Hubert Humphrey's seat when Humphrey became Johnson's vice president in 1964, made an abortive bid for the 1976 Democratic presidential nomination before being chosen by Jimmy Carter as his running mate; he again ran with Carter in 1980. In that election, Minnesota was one of only six states to favor the Carter-Mondale ticket. Minnesotans gave the Republican Party a majority of the state's congressional delegation, but the Democrats retained control of the state legislature. Independent presidential candidate John Anderson won 174,997 votes in Minnesota, 8.5% of the total.

¹⁴LOCAL GOVERNMENT
Minnesota is divided into 87 counties and 13 regional administrations. As of 1979, the state had 1,795 townships (more than any other state) and 855 cities.

Each of Minnesota's counties is governed by a board of commissioners, ordinarily elected for four-year terms. Other elected officials include the auditor, treasurer, recorder, sheriff, attorney, and coroner; an assessor and engineer are customarily appointed. Besides administering welfare, highway maintenance, and other state programs, the county is responsible for planning and development and, except in large cities, for property assessment. During the 1970s, counties also assumed increased responsibility for solid waste disposal and shoreline management.

Each regional development commission, or RDC, consists of local officials (selected by counties, cities, townships, and boards of education in the region) and of representatives of public interest groups (selected by the elected officials). RDCs prepare and adopt regional development plans and review applications for loans and grants.

As of 1979, 103 cities had home-rule charters; the remaining 752 were statutory cities, restricted to the systems of government prescribed by state law. In either case, the mayor-council system was the most common. Besides providing such traditional functions as street maintenance and police and fire protection, some cities operate utilities, sell liquor, or run hospitals, among other services. Each township is governed by a board of three supervisors and by other officials elected for three-year terms at the town meeting, held annually on the 2d Tuesday in March.

¹⁵STATE SERVICES
Minnesota's ombudsman for corrections investigates complaints about corrections facilities or the conduct of prison officials. A six-member Ethical Practices Board supervises the registration of some 1,300 lobbyists, monitors the financing of political campaigns, and sees that some 1,000 elected and appointed state officials observe regulations governing conflict of interest and disclosure of personal finances. Minnesota law also provides that legislative meetings of any kind must be open to the public.

The state-aided public school system is under the jurisdiction of the Department of Education, which carries out the policies of a nine-member Board of Education appointed by the governor with the advice and consent of the senate. Responsible for higher education are the University of Minnesota Board of Regents, elected by the legislature; the State University Board and State Board for Community Colleges, both appointed by the governor; and other agencies. The Department of Transportation maintains roads and bridges, enforces public transportation rates, inspects airports, and has responsibility for railroad safety.

Minnesota's Department of Health investigates health problems, disseminates health information, regulates hospitals and nursing homes, and inspects restaurants and lodgings. Health regulations affecting farm produce are administered by the Department of Agriculture. State facilities for the mentally retarded are operated by the Department of Public Welfare, which administers state welfare programs and provides social services to the aged, the handicapped, and others in need.

Minnesota Presidential Vote by Political Parties, 1948–80

YEAR	ELECTORAL VOTE	MINNESOTA WINNER	DEMOCRAT¹	REPUBLICAN²	PROGRESSIVE	SOCIALIST	SOCIALIST LABOR³
1948	11	*Truman (D)	692,966	483,617	27,866	4,646	2,525
1952	11	*Eisenhower (R)	608,458	763,211	2,666	—	2,383
						SOC. WORKERS	
1956	11	*Eisenhower (R)	617,525	719,302	—	1,098	2,080
1960	11	*Kennedy (D)	779,933	757,915	—	3,077	962
1964	10	*Johnson (D)	991,117	559,624	—	1,177	2,544
							AMERICAN IND.
1968	10	Humphrey (D)	857,738	658,643	—	—	68,931
					PEOPLE'S		AMERICAN
1972	10	*Nixon (R)	802,346	898,269	2,805	4,261	31,407
					LIBERTARIAN		
1976	10	*Carter (D)	1,070,440	819,395	3,529	4,149	13,592
						CITIZENS	
1980	10	Carter (D)	954,173	873,268	31,593	8,406	6,136

*Won US presidential election.
¹Called Democratic-Farmer-Labor Party in Minnesota.
²Since 1976, called Independent-Republican in Minnesota.
³Appeared as Industrial Government Party on the ballot.

The Department of Public Safety registers motor vehicles, licenses drivers, enforces traffic laws, and regulates the sale of liquor. The Department of Military Affairs has jurisdiction over the Minnesota National Guard, and the Department of Corrections operates prisons, reformatories, and parole programs. The Housing Finance Agency aids the construction and rehabilitation of low- and middle-income housing. Laws governing occupational safety, wages and hours, and child labor are enforced by the Department of Labor and Industry, while the Department of Economic Security supervises public employment programs and administers unemployment insurance.

16 JUDICIAL SYSTEM

Minnesota's highest court is the supreme court, consisting of a chief justice and eight associate justices; all are elected without party designation for six-year terms, with vacancies being filled by gubernatorial appointment. The district court, divided into 10 judicial districts, is the principal court of original jurisdiction. Each judicial district has at least three district judges, elected to six-year terms. Judges in each district elect from their ranks a chief judge who serves in that capacity for a two-year term.

County courts, operating in all counties of the state except two—Hennepin (Minneapolis) and Ramsey (St. Paul), which have municipal courts—assume functions formerly exercised by probate, family, and local courts. They exercise civil jurisdiction in cases where the amount in contention is $5,000 or less, and criminal jurisdiction in preliminary hearings and misdemeanors. They also hear cases involving family disputes, and have concurrent jurisdiction with the district court in divorces, adoptions, and certain other proceedings. The probate division of the county court system presides over guardianship and incompetency proceedings and all cases relating to the disposition of estates. All county judges are elected for six-year terms.

The Department of Corrections operates a maximum-security state prison at Stillwater for adult males, a maximum-security state reformatory at St. Cloud for males under 21 years of age, and a correctional institution for women at Shakopee. Other facilities include two vocational institutions for adult offenders, a state training school for delinquent boys, and a forestry camp for juveniles. State correctional institutions had a total population of 1,986 as of 30 June 1978.

Crime rates are generally below the national average, and the rate of 2 reported cases of murder or nonnegligent manslaughter per 100,000 population was the 4th lowest in the US. Minnesota has no death penalty statute. The Crime Victims Reparations Board offers compensation to innocent victims of crime or to their dependent survivors.

17 ARMED FORCES

There were 4,341 authorized defense personnel stationed in Minnesota in 1977/78, near Minneapolis–St. Paul and Duluth international airports. Firms in the state received $730 million in defense contract awards during the same year.

As of 30 September 1979 there were 558,000 veterans living in Minnesota, including 13,000 who saw service in World War I, 215,000 in World War II, 88,000 during the Korean conflict, and 189,000 during the Viet-Nam era. Veterans in Minnesota received a total of $353.3 million in benefits in 1977/78.

The 113 units of the Minnesota National Guard had a total authorized strength of 11,940 as of 30 September 1978. Some 7,740 state and local police officers were on active duty in 1977.

18 MIGRATION

A succession of migratory waves began in the 17th and 18th centuries with the arrival of the Dakota and Ojibwa, among other Indian groups, followed during the 19th century by New England Yankees, Germans, Scandinavians, and finally southern and eastern Europeans. Especially since 1920, new arrivals from other states and countries have been relatively few, and the state experienced a net loss from migration of 302,000 between 1940 and 1977. As of 1976, 9% of all Minnesotans 14 years of age or older had moved to the state within the last five years, a proportion below the average for the US as a whole.

Within the state, there has been a long-term movement to metropolitan areas, and especially to the suburbs of major cities: from 1960 to 1970, the state's metropolitan population grew by nearly 20%, while the rest of the state's population declined by not quite 1%. However, this trend appeared to be reversing itself in the 1970s: from 1970 to 1977, the metropolitan area population grew by 5%, the rest of the state population by 7%.

19 INTERGOVERNMENTAL COOPERATION

Relations with the Council of State Governments are conducted through the Minnesota Commission on Interstate Cooperation, consisting of five members from each house of the state legislature and five administrative officers or other state employees; in addition, the governor, the president of the senate, and the speaker of the house are nonvoting members. Minnesota also participates in the Great Lakes Commission and the Minnesota-Wisconsin Boundary Area Commission.

In 1978/79, Minnesota received an estimated $1.5 billion in federal aid, including $137 million in general revenue sharing.

20 ECONOMY

Furs, wheat, pine lumber, and high-grade iron ore were once the basis of Minnesota's economy. As these resources diminished, however, the state turned to wood pulp, dairy products, corn and soybeans, taconite, and manufacturing, often in such food-related industries as meat packing, canning, and the processing of dairy products. During 1974–76, manufacturing accounted for 22% of the gross state product and trade for 20%, followed by finance, insurance, and real estate, 13%; government, 11%; services, 11%; transportation, communications, and public utilities, 9%; agriculture, 7%; construction, 5%; and mining, 2%. The share of GSP generated by government and trade rose significantly between the late 1960s and mid-1970s, while the relative contributions of manufacturing and construction declined.

Overall, the GSP rose from $13.4 billion to $31.2 billion between 1966 and 1976. Personal income has also been on the increase, with per capita income more than doubling during the same period. The state's growing skilled labor force and its position as a major marketing and distribution center were expected to promote continued economic growth in the decades ahead.

21 INCOME

In 1978, Minnesota ranked 18th among the 50 states in personal income per capita, amounting to $7,847; this was nearly four times the figure for 1960, when Minnesota placed 25th. Total personal income in 1978 was $31.5 billion, representing a real growth of 32% since 1970.

The following table (expressed in millions) shows total personal income and its components for 1975 and 1976:

	1975	1976
Farm earned income	$ 1,239	$ 797
Nonfarm earned income:		
Agricultural services, forestry, fisheries	47	51
Mining	254	293
Construction	1,058	1,194
Manufacturing	4,168	4,692
Wholesale trade	1,529	1,655
Retail trade	1,810	2,034
Finance, insurance, real estate	884	990
Transportation, communications, utilities	1,367	1,537
Services	2,539	2,816
Government	2,764	2,947
Other sources of income	4,938	5,509
TOTALS	$22,597	$24,515

Median family income in 1975 was $14,740, 18th in the US. There are wide regional variations: in 1976, median incomes for husband-wife families ranged from $7,871 in Clearwater County to $19,432 in Washington County, in the Twin Cities area, where Minnesota's high-income counties are clustered. As of 1975, 8% of all state residents and 6% of Minnesota's families were below the federal poverty level. Some 350,000 of the top US wealth-holders lived in the state in 1972.

22 LABOR

In 1978, the civilian labor force numbered 1,994,000, of whom nearly 42% were women. Adults under 35 represented 51% of the labor force in 1977, as against 43% in 1970. The most dramatic increase, however, was among women aged 25–34; 70% of this group had jobs or were seeking work in 1977, as against 30% in 1960.

A federal census of workers covered by unemployment insurance in March 1977 revealed the following nonfarm employment pattern for Minnesota:

	ESTABLISH-MENTS	EMPLOYEES	ANNUAL PAYROLL ('000)
Agricultural services, forestry, fishing	818	3,563	$ 35,703
Mining, of which:	161	14,798	201,241
Metals	(28)	(13,613)	(174,761)
Contract construction	9,192	61,345	1,155,164
Manufacturing, of which:	6,128	329,428	4,754,693
Food and food products	(655)	(40,380)	(537,179)
Nonelectrical machinery	(1,034)	(63,006)	(909,270)
Transportation, public utilities	3,835	71,986	1,101,571
Wholesale trade	8,435	101,910	1,445,822
Retail trade	23,239	275,367	1,765,036
Finance, insurance, real estate	7,433	86,010	985,944
Services	21,394	289,677	2,404,507
Other	1,084	1,301	16,678
TOTALS	81,719	1,235,385	$13,866,359

Minnesota had more than 274,000 government employees in 1976.

An average of 76,000 people in 1978 were unemployed, of whom 31,200 were covered by unemployment insurance. The unemployment rate was 3.8% for the general population—3.1% for men and 4.8% for women. As the economy dipped into recession, unemployment rose substantially, reaching 6% as of March 1980.

The history of unionization in the state includes several long and bitter labor disputes, notably, the Iron Range strike of 1916. The earliest known unions—two printers' locals, established in the late 1850s—died out during the Civil War, and several later unions faded in the panic of 1873. The Knights of Labor were the dominant force of the 1880s; the next decade saw the rise of the Minnesota State Federation of Labor, whose increasing political influence bore fruit in the landmark Workmen's Compensation Act of 1913 and the subsequent ascension of the Farmer-Labor Party. Some 385,000 workers, or 25% of nonfarm employees (15th in the US), belonged to a labor union as of 1976; another 51,000 Minnesotans were members of employee associations. The legislature enacted a fair employment practices law in 1955 and passed a measure in 1973 prescribing collective bargaining procedures for public employees and granting them a limited right to strike.

23 AGRICULTURE

Cash receipts from farm marketings totaled $5 billion in 1978, placing Minnesota 5th among the 50 states; crops made up about 47% of the total value. During the same year, Minnesota ranked 1st in the production of sugar beets and of sweet corn for processing, and 2d in oats, hay, and sunflowers.

The early farmers settled in the wooded hills and valleys in the southeastern quarter of the state, where they had to cut down trees and dig up stumps to make room for crops. With the coming of the railroads, farmers began planting the prairies with wheat, which by the late 1870s took up 70% of all farm acreage. In succeeding decades, wheat prices fell and railroad rates soared, fanning agrarian discontent. Farmers began to diversify, with dairy farming, oats, and corn becoming increasingly important. Improved corn yields since the 1940s have spurred the production of hogs and beef cattle and the growth of meat packing as a major industry.

As of 1979, the state had 104,000 farms with annual sales of $1,000 or more, covering 30,300,000 acres (12,262,000 hectares). There were 195,000 farm workers in 1978, of whom fewer than 20% were hired workers; wages averaged $3.29 an hour. Consumption of fertilizer, for the year ending 30 June 1978, totaled 1,950,000 tons. The main farming areas are in the south and southwest, where corn, soybeans, and oats are important, and in the Red River Valley along the western border, where oats, wheat, sugar beets, and potatoes are among the chief crops. The following table shows selected major crops in 1978:

	ACREAGE	PRODUCTION	VALUE ('000)
Corn for grain	6,190,000	643,760,000 bushels	$1,223,144
Soybeans	4,060,000	142,100,000 bushels	930,755
Hay	3,060,000	8,932,000 tons	366,212
Wheat	2,776,000	93,225,000 bushels	266,005
Sunflowers	683,000	521,335 tons	117,389
Oats	1,830,000	98,820,000 bushels	108,702
Barley	1,050,000	51,975,000 bushels	93,555
Potatoes	78,000	16,870,000 hundredweight	48,390
Sweet corn for processing	111,500	641,100 tons	29,106
Sugar beets	263,000	4,971,000 tons	NA

Agribusiness is Minnesota's largest basic industry, with about one-third of the state's labor force employed in agriculture or agriculture-related industries, most notably food processing. Although farm size has been increasing, Minnesota's farms are still considerably smaller than the national average, and Minnesota prides itself on the fact that more than 88% of its farm operators are full or part owners.

24 ANIMAL HUSBANDRY

Excluding the northeast, livestock raising is dispersed throughout the state, with cattle concentrated particularly in west-central Minnesota and in the extreme southeast, and hogs along the southern border. At the close of 1979, Minnesota had 3,750,000 cattle and calves; the state's total of 843,000 milk cows ranked 4th in the US. In addition, there were 4,900,000 hogs and pigs (3d in the US) and 264,000 sheep and lambs. Minnesota raised more turkeys in 1979 than any other state: 24,666,000, worth $165,756,000.

During 1979, Minnesota farms and ranches produced 1.3 billion lb of cattle and calves, valued at $967 million; 1.7 billion lb of hogs and pigs (3d in the US), $670 million; and 18.5 million lb of sheep and lambs, $11.8 million. Dairy products included 150.6 million lb of nonfat dry milk for human consumption, more than in any other state except California; 154.9 million lb of butter, 2d only to Wisconsin; and 480 million lb of cheese, also 2d behind Wisconsin. The state's total of 9.1 billion lb of milk outranked all but three states'. Production of chickens and broilers was 106.7 million lb, worth $24 million, and the egg output was 2.2 billion. During 1978, Minnesota produced 13.9 million lb of honey and 1.9 million lb of wool.

25 FISHING

Commercial fishermen in 1978 landed 9,043,000 lb of fish, valued at $1,822,000. The catch included herring and smelts from Lake Superior, whitefish and yellow pike from large inland lakes, and carp and catfish from the Mississippi and Minnesota rivers. Sport fishing attracts some 2 million anglers annually to the state's 2.6 million acres (1.1 million hectares) of fishing lakes and 7,000 mi (11,000 km) of fishing streams, many of them stocked by the Division of Fish and Wildlife of the Department of Natural Resources.

26 FORESTRY

Forests, which originally occupied two-thirds of Minnesota's land area, have been depleted by lumbering, farming, and forest fires. As of 1977, forestland covered 18,335,000 acres (7,420,000 hectares), or 36% of the state's total area. Most of the forestland is in the north, especially in Arrowhead Country in the northeast. Of the 16,100,000 acres (6,515,000 hectares) of commercial timberland in 1977, less than half was privately owned and more than one-third was under state, county, or municipal jurisdiction.

In 1975, Minnesota harvested 1,359,000 cords of pulpwood, at a value of $421,204,000; 185,500,000 board feet of lumber, logs, and bolts, valued at $22,260,000; and 136,500 cords of specialty wood products, valued at $11,555,500. Shipments of lumber and wood products totaled $847.3 million in 1977, and paper and allied products were worth more than $1.4 billion.

The Department of Natural Resources, Division of Forestry, promotes effective management of the forest environment and seeks to restrict forest fire occurrence to 1,100 fires annually, burning no more than 30,000 acres (12,000 hectares) in all. More than 20 million trees are planted each year by the wood fiber industry, other private interests, and federal, state, and county forest services—more than enough to replace those harvested or destroyed by fire, insects, or disease. There are at least 1,400 tree farms scattered throughout the state.

27 MINING

Minnesota ranked 14th among the 50 states in the value of its 1978 mineral output, amounting to more than $1.7 billion. The state ranked 1st in the production of iron ore, which traditionally accounts for well over 90% of the total mineral value; more than two-thirds of the iron ore produced in the US in 1978 was mined in Minnesota. Iron production is concentrated in the northeast, mainly in the Mesabi Range, which, since shipments began in 1892, has produced well over 2 billion tons of iron ore. A high-quality lode discovered earlier in the Vermilion Range continued to be exploited until the 1960s. Most iron production today is in the form of taconite (20–30% iron), from which a 60% concentrate is extracted in the form of hard pellets. In 1978, Minnesota produced an estimated 63,250,000 tons of recoverable iron ore, as well as 31,000,000 tons of sand and gravel and 8,600,000 tons of stone.

The largest known combined copper-nickel deposits in the US were discovered in the 1950s in northeastern Minnesota. Exploratory land use and environmental-impact studies were continuing as the 1980s began, with a view toward exploitation of this resource, valued in 1973 at more than $27 billion.

28 ENERGY AND POWER

Minnesota produced 35.3 billion kwh of electricity in 1978, when installed capacity reached 8.7 million kw. Steam generating plants accounted for 60% of installed capacity; most plants were coal-fired. There are three nuclear reactors, all owned by the Northern States Power Co.

Minnesota's 7 million acres (2.8 million hectares) of peat lands, the state's only known fossil fuel resource, constitute nearly half of the US total (excluding Alaska). If burned directly, the accessible fuel-quality peat deposit could supply all of Minnesota's energy needs for 50 years, at current rates of consumption. The feasibility of peat gasification was also under study as of 1980.

29 INDUSTRY

The exploitation of natural resources, especially the state's extensive timberlands and fertile prairie, was the basis of Minnesota's industrial development in the late 19th century, when Minneapolis became the largest sawmill and flour-milling center in the US. Canning and meat packing became important in the early 20th century, and food processing remains 2d only to nonelectrical machinery among Minnesota's leading industrial sectors. Computers are among the state's most important products.

The total value added by manufacture in 1977 exceeded $9.2 billion. Contributions of principal sectors were nonelectrical machinery, 22%; food and food products, 12%; fabricated metals, 10%; electrical and electronic equipment, 9%; paper and allied products, 8%; and printing and publishing, 7%. Value added by selected industries in 1972 and 1977 was as follows:

	1972	1977
Electronic computing equipment	NA	$775,900,000
Meat products	$247,100,000	333,300,000
Commercial printing	156,000,000	284,900,000
Refrigeration and service machinery	178,900,000	258,300,000
Dairy products	150,500,000	249,400,000
Preserved fruits and vegetables	135,500,000	241,300,000
Construction and related machinery	117,000,000	218,900,000

Industry is concentrated in the southeast, especially in the Twin Cities area, which in 1977 accounted for nearly two-thirds of the state's value added by manufacture. Among the well-known national firms with headquarters in the state are Minnesota Mining and Manufacturing (3M) in St. Paul; Honeywell, Control Data, General Mills, Pillsbury, and Land O'Lakes, all in Minneapolis; and Hormel in Austin.

30 COMMERCE

Access to the Great Lakes, the St. Lawrence Seaway, and the Atlantic Ocean, as well as to the Mississippi River and the Gulf of Mexico, helps make Minnesota a major marketing and distribution center for the upper Midwest. As of 1972, the state's wholesale trade establishments had sales totaling $14.7 billion (14th among the 50 states). Retail establishments had sales of $13.6 billion (19th in the US), with automotive dealers accounting for 20% of the total; food stores, 18%; department stores, 11%; gasoline service stations, 9%; and eating and drinking places, 9%. Much of this volume was concentrated in the Twin Cities area, where retail sales totaled $7.5 billion.

Agricultural exports to foreign countries amounted to $918 million in 1976/77 (10th among the 50 states), with dairy products, feed grains, flaxseed, and hides and skins among the notable export items. Export sales of manufactured goods totaled nearly $1.6 billion in 1976 (16th in the US); the chief manufactured exports included computers and computer software, food-processing and packaging machinery, and other industrial machinery and equipment. Nearly 800 Minnesota companies were involved in an export trade extending to more than 134 countries and providing jobs for approximately 125,000 state residents.

31 CONSUMER PROTECTION

The Office of Consumer Services, established within the Commerce Department in 1971, administers statutes governing fraudulent or deceptive business practices, attempts to resolve consumer complaints through voluntary arbitration, represents consumers before private organizations and governmental bodies, and provides consumer information and education. The Agriculture Department regulates the manufacture and distribution of food, feed, fertilizer, and other items. State antitrust and consumer laws are enforced by the Office of the Attorney General.

32 BANKING

As of 31 December 1978, Minnesota had 758 insured commercial banks with total assets of $24.4 billion, including $8.5 billion in commercial, industrial, and real estate loans. Deposits exceeded $19.9 billion, of which $6.8 billion were demand deposits. The leading commercial banking companies are Northwest Bancorporation and First Bank Systems, Inc., both of Minneapolis.

Minnesota had 56 insured savings and loan associations (46 federally chartered, 10 state-chartered) as of 31 December 1978, with assets totaling $9.2 billion, including $7.7 billion in outstanding mortgage loans. Also chartered by the state as of 1979 were 6 trust companies, 3 investment companies, 272 credit unions, 16 savings associations, 215 industrial loan companies, 129 small loan companies, 250 motor vehicle sales finance companies, 23 insurance premium finance companies, and 17 safe deposit bank companies, all of them licensed and regulated by the Banking Division of the Department of Commerce.

33 INSURANCE
Minnesotans held 6,286,000 life insurance policies valued at $55 billion as of 31 December 1978. Coverage per family averaged $37,600, 7% above the US average. Payments to beneficiaries in the same year totaled $465.3 million, including $165.9 million in death payments. The two most important Minnesota-based companies, Minnesota Mutual Life Insurance and Northwestern National, each had insurance in force with a value exceeding $1 billion in 1976.

Property and liability insurance companies wrote premiums totaling almost $1.8 billion in 1978; automotive liability insurance accounted for $395.4 million, automobile physical damage insurance for $229.1 million, and homeowners' coverage for $166.9 million. No-fault automobile insurance was enacted in 1974. Minnesotans held $305.4 million worth of flood insurance in mid-1979.

34 SECURITIES
The Minnesota Grain Exchange, founded in 1881, is the state's major commodity exchange. Enforcement of statutes governing securities, franchises, and corporate takeovers (as well as charitable organizations, public cemeteries, collection agencies, and bingo) is the responsibility of the Securities Division of the Department of Commerce.

New York Stock Exchange member firms had 46 sales offices and 622 registered representatives in Minnesota in 1978. Minnesotans reported $375.2 million in dividend income on their 1977 federal tax returns.

35 PUBLIC FINANCE
Minnesota spends a relatively large amount on state government and local assistance, especially on a per capita basis. In 1976/77, Minnesota tied North Dakota for 6th place in total general expenditures per capita ($961).

The state budget is prepared by the Department of Finance and submitted biennially by the governor to the legislature for amendment and approval. The fiscal year runs from 1 July to 30 June. The following table summarizes estimated revenues and expenditures for the 1977/79 biennium and of the proposed budget for 1979/81 (general fund only, in millions):

REVENUES	1977/79	1979/81
Individual income tax	$2,592.2	$3,047.4
Corporate income tax	577.1	618.9
General sales tax	1,134.1	1,351.4
Liquor and tobacco taxes	279.7	291.1
Departmental earnings	198.8	228.8
Miscellaneous receipts	1,097.6	1,149.6
TOTALS	$5,879.5	$6,687.2

EXPENDITURES		
Local assistance, of which:	$4,405.5	$5,158.2
School aid	(1,757.4)	(1,981.9)
Health, welfare, and corrections	(687.8)	(826.1)
Education	694.1	803.6
Health, welfare, and corrections (operations)	362.1	422.8
Other outlays	445.6	478.9
TOTALS	$5,907.3	$6,863.5

As of 30 June 1977, the total outstanding debt of state and local governments exceeded $5 billion; the per capita debt, $1,279, ranked 12th among the 50 states.

36 TAXATION
Minnesota ranked 13th among the 50 states in 1977 in total receipts from state and local taxes ($3.6 billion) and 9th in taxes collected per capita ($906). State taxes and fees collected in 1978 totaled $2.8 billion.

Corporate profits are taxed at 12%, according to a weighted formula based on the proportion of payroll, property, and sales within the state; there is a minimum tax of $100. Individual income is taxed at graduated rates in brackets that were indexed to the inflation rate beginning in the 1979 tax year. As of that year, rates ranged from 1.6% on the first $500 of taxable income to 17% on income over $44,043; in 1980, that top-bracket tax rate was the highest of any state's. There is also a 4% state sales tax on most items other than food, clothing, and medicine. Gift and inheritance taxes were repealed as of 1980. There is an estate tax, generally only on amounts above $200,000, with an additional $250,000 exemption for a surviving spouse. Rates range from 7% on the first $100,000 taxable to 12% on amounts over $1 million. The state also levies an employer's excise tax on compensation paid out by a company exceeding $250,000 in a given year, and certain other selective business taxes, as well as severance taxes on mineral production. Commercial, industrial, and residential property is subject to property tax, the principal source of revenue for local governing units.

In 1975/76, Minnesota paid out more than $5.6 billion in federal taxes and received $5 billion in federal expenditures. State residents filed 1,625,486 federal income tax returns in 1977, paying $2.7 billion in tax.

37 ECONOMIC POLICY
The Department of Economic Development counsels communities on their development potential and acts as a liaison between the business community and the state government. The department also seeks to encourage expansion of existing industries and to attract new industry to the state by providing data to help industrial planners and by disseminating information about the advantages of doing business in Minnesota. As of 1978, Minnesota was the only state that offered its own supplementary funding (through the Area Redevelopment Administration) for business development loans under the federal Economic Development Administration program. Minnesota's corporate income tax is structured to favor companies having relatively large payroll and property (as opposed to sales) within the state.

38 HEALTH
Shortly after the founding of Minnesota Territory, promoters attracted new settlers partly by proclaiming the tonic benefits of Minnesota's soothing landscape and cool, bracing climate; the area was trumpeted as a haven for retirees and for those afflicted with malaria or tuberculosis. Today, Minnesotans do in fact live longer than most Americans. As of 1969–71, women enjoyed an average lifespan of 76.80 years, longer than in any other state; men lived an average of 69.38 years, 3d highest in the US; and Minnesotans of both sexes lived an average of 72.96 years, 2d only to Hawaiians.

In 1977, approximately 60,000 infants were born in the state, or 15.2 per 1,000 population, slightly below the national average. Infant mortality was relatively low: an average of 10.8 per 1,000 whites and 17 per 1,000 nonwhites. There were 17,200 legal abortions in 1977; more than 80% of those having abortions were unmarried, and about 70% had no living children. In that year, 32,000 deaths, or 8.1 per 1,000 population (below the national average), were recorded. The death rates per 100,000 population for the two leading causes, heart disease and cancer, were 308 and 168, respectively. Rates for these and most other causes of death were below the national norms.

There were 3,646 resident mental patients in state and county hospitals as of 31 December 1976, and in 1975 there were 24,256 admissions and readmissions to all outpatient psychiatric facilities (excluding federally funded community health centers). In 1978, Minnesota had 188 hospitals, with 31,051 beds and average daily patient population of 22,274. Hospital personnel included 12,503 registered nurses and 5,147 licensed practical nurses. The average cost of hospital care in 1977 was $165 per day and $1,452 per stay, both figures below the national norm. As of 1976 there were also 517 nursing homes, with some 43,000 beds and an average of 41,000 resident patients. Minnesota had 7,356 licensed physicians in 1977, and 2,429 practicing dentists in 1979.

The Mayo Clinic, developed by Drs. Charles H. and William J. Mayo in the 1890s and early 1900s, was the first private clinic in the US and became a world-renowned center for surgery; today it is owned and operated by a self-perpetuating charitable foundation. The separate Mayo Foundation for Medical Education and Research, founded and endowed by the Mayo brothers in 1915, was subsequently affiliated with the University of Minnesota, which became the first US institution to offer graduate education in surgery and other branches of clinical medicine.

³⁹SOCIAL WELFARE

As of 1977, Minnesota ranked 9th among the 50 states in per capita state and local spending on public welfare, averaging $194, 21% above the US norm. The total budget for the Department of Public Welfare (including disbursement of federal funds) was an estimated $1.8 billion in the 1977/79 biennium, with $2.1 billion proposed for 1979/81. In January 1979, the department reported that, in an average month, the following numbers of clients were served under various federal and/or state welfare programs: under aid to families with dependent children (AFDC), 137,298; general assistance maintenance, 14,500; Medicaid, 123,997; general assistance medical care, 9,500; Minnesota supplemental aid, 11,000; catastrophic health expense protection, 170; and food stamps, 143,969. (Many recipients, of course, drew benefits from more than one program.)

Expenditures under the AFDC program totaled $169 million in 1978. The federal cost of the food stamp program was $56 million in 1977/78. During the same period, an estimated 589,000 schoolchildren—63% of those enrolled in participating schools—took part in the school lunch program, at a federal cost of $27.5 million. As of 1977, 419,000 Minnesotans were receiving Social Security retirement benefits totaling $989.5 million, and 125,600 drew survivors' benefits amounting to $334.6 million. The average monthly payment to retirees (excluding special benefits) was $235.90. In 1978, some 34,500 Minnesotans received Supplemental Security Income benefits of $37.6 million.

There were 54,700 disabled workers drawing $132.5 million in Social Security disability benefits in 1977. Some 29,300 Minnesotans were enrolled in vocational rehabilitation programs in 1977/78, at a cost of $18.4 million. Federally aided vocational training programs enrolled 439,000 persons in 1978, at a cost for 1977/78 of $102.5 million to state and local governments, with $13.4 million in federal subsidies. A total of $135.2 million was paid out in workers' compensation for 1977. During the following year, state and federal unemployment benefits totaled $125 million; the average weekly benefit was $96.66, 16% above the US norm.

⁴⁰HOUSING

According to the 1970 census, Minnesota had some 1,219,000 year-round housing units, of which 95% were occupied, 72% of those by their owners. Nearly 94% of the occupied housing had full plumbing. Building permits were issued for 37,800 housing units in 1978, 74% of them single-family homes, with a total valuation of more than $1.4 billion.

In the first five years of its existence, the state's Housing Finance Agency, founded in 1973, provided low-interest loans for some 5,600 new homes and more than 11,600 apartment units. In addition, state home improvement loans assisted some 16,600 households during the same period.

⁴¹EDUCATION

Minnesota's first public school system was authorized in 1849, but significant growth in enrollment did not occur until after the Civil War. Today, Minnesota has one of the best-supported systems of public education in the US. The illiteracy rate, as of 1970, was 0.6%, half the national average. By 1977, according to state data, 70% of all Minnesotans aged 25 or older were high school graduates, compared with 58% in 1970 and 44% in 1960. Among men 25–34 years old, 93% had completed 12 years of school, as against a national average of 85%; the figure for women in the same age group was also 93%, compared with 82% nationally. About 17% of adult Minnesotans held college degrees in 1977, compared with 8% in 1960.

In fall 1978, Minnesota had an estimated 522,000 public elementary school students, down 9% in only three years, and 299,000 secondary school students, a 3% drop from the 1975 level. There were 20,000 public elementary school teachers and 23,700 public high school teachers in 1979, earning an average salary of $15,400. Nonpublic schools had a total 1977 enrollment of 79,000, a decline of 25% in two years; there were 63,000 students at the elementary level and 16,000 attending nonpublic high schools. As of 1977/78 there were approximately 190,000 registered students in Minnesota's institutions of higher learning, at least three-fourths of them enrolled in public institutions.

The state has four major systems of public postsecondary education. The state university system—with campuses at Bemidji, Mankato, Marshall, Minneapolis–St. Paul, Moorhead, St. Cloud, and Winona—had an enrollment of about 34,000 in 1977/78. The community college system, consisting of 18 two-year colleges, had more than 30,000 students. A statewide network of 33 area vocational-technical institutes enrolled some 26,500 students as of 1976. Finally, the University of Minnesota (founded as an academy in 1851), with campuses in the Twin Cities, Duluth, Morris, Crookston, and Waseca, had 55,203 students in fall 1978. The state's oldest private college, Hamline University in St. Paul, was founded in 1854 and is affiliated with the United Methodist Church. There are more than a dozen other private institutions, many of them with ties to Lutheran or Roman Catholic religious authorities. Carleton College, at Northfield, is a notable independent institution.

Minnesota has an extensive program of student grants, work-study arrangements, and loan programs, in addition to reciprocal tuition arrangements with Wisconsin and North Dakota. In 1977/78, a total of $69.6 million was available to Minnesota students to help pay their expenses at institutions of higher learning inside and outside the state; the largest such program, the State Student Loan Program, instituted in 1973, made available a total of $37 million in student loans for 20,000 students in 1977/78. Grants-in-aid totaling $13.7 million benefited 18,220 students, and state scholarships worth $7.4 million were awarded to 9,726 students.

The 1977/79 biennial budget provided an estimated $3 billion for education, of which two-thirds represented state and federal aid to public schools. The proposed budget for the 1979/81 biennium included $3.4 billion (including federal aid) for education at all levels.

⁴²ARTS

The Walker Art Center in Minneapolis is an innovative museum with an outstanding contemporary collection, while the Minneapolis Institute of Arts exhibits more traditional works. The art gallery of the University of Minnesota is in Minneapolis, and the Minnesota Museum of Art is in St. Paul.

The Tyrone Guthrie Theater, founded in Minneapolis in 1963, is one of the nation's most prestigious repertory companies. The Minnesota Orchestra, founded in 1903 in Minneapolis, enlisted Neville Marriner as musical director in 1979; violinist Pinchas Zukerman became musical director of the St. Paul Chamber

Orchestra in 1980. The Minnesota Opera Company, in St. Paul, and the St. Olaf College Choir, at Northfield, also have national reputations.

State and regional arts groups as well as individual artists are supported by state and federal grants administered through the State Arts Board, an 11-member panel appointed by the governor. For the 1977/79 biennium the board had an estimated budget of $5.4 million.

⁴³LIBRARIES AND MUSEUMS
Minnesota has more than 320 public libraries, serving 95% of the state's population; about 90% of them are joined in a network of 13 regional library systems. The total number of books and audiovisual items was 11,339,371 in 1977, when public library circulation reached 23,687,162. The largest single public library system is the Minneapolis Public Library and Information Center (founded in 1885), which had 1,404,046 volumes in 1977. The leading academic library, with 3,224,076 volumes, is that maintained by the University of Minnesota at Minneapolis. Special libraries include the James Jerome Hill Reference Library (devoted to commerce and transportation) and the library of the Minnesota Historical Society, both located in St. Paul.

There are more than 100 museums and historic sites. In addition to several noted museums of the visual arts, Minnesota is home to the Mayo Medical Museum at the Mayo Clinic in Rochester. The Minnesota Historical Society Museum offers rotating exhibits on varied aspects of the state's history. Historic sites include the Ft. St. Charles recreation, on an island in the Lake of the Woods, and the Sauk Centre home of Sinclair Lewis.

⁴⁴COMMUNICATIONS
As of 31 December 1978 there were 3,056,266 telephones in Minnesota, 801,915 business and 2,254,351 residential. Virtually every household has telephone service. Commercial broadcasting began with the opening of the first radio station in 1922; as of 1979 there were 182 radio stations, of which 26 were noncommercial, and 18 television stations, 5 noncommercial. As of 1978, 95 cable television systems served 139 communities with 145,931 subscribers.

⁴⁵PRESS
The *Minnesota Pioneer*, whose first issue was printed on a small hand press and distributed by the publisher himself on 28 April 1849 in St. Paul, vies with the *Minnesota Register* (its first issue was dated earlier but may have appeared later) for the honor of being Minnesota's first newspaper. Over the next 10 years, in any case, nearly 100 newspapers appeared at locations throughout the territory, including direct ancestors of many present-day publications. As of 1978, the state had 5 morning dailies with a combined circulation of 404,987; 25 evening dailies, 683,831; and 11 Sunday papers, 1,042,390. The following table lists the leading dailies, with their paid circulations in 1978:

AREA	NAME	DAILY	SUNDAY
Minneapolis	Star (e)	226,828	
	Tribune (m,S)	226,899	607,872
St. Paul	Dispatch (e)	118,392	
	Pioneer Press (m,S)	100,502	244,261

As of 1979, 276 weekly newspapers and 177 periodicals were being published in Minnesota. Among the most widely read magazines published in Minnesota were *Family Handyman*, appearing 10 times a year, with a paid circulation of 920,219; *Catholic Digest*, a religious monthly serving 540,650 readers; and *Snow Goer*, published five times a year for snowmobile enthusiasts, with a paid circulation of 99,605.

⁴⁶ORGANIZATIONS
The Minnesota Historical Society, founded in 1849, is the oldest educational organization in the state and the official custodian of its history. The society is partly supported by state funds, as are such other semistate organizations as the Academy of Science (which promotes interest in science among high school students), the Minnesota State Horticultural Society, and the Humane Society.

The Sons of Norway and American Swedish Institute, both with headquarters in Minneapolis, seek to preserve the state's Scandinavian heritage. Among the various professional, commercial, educational, and hobbyist associations with headquarters in Minnesota are the American Association of Collectors and National Scholastic Press Association, Minneapolis; American Board of Radiology, American Ophthalmological Society, and American Board of Physical Medicine and Rehabilitation, Rochester; World Pen Pals, St. Paul; and Independent Bankers Association of America, Sauk Centre.

⁴⁷TOURISM, TRAVEL, AND RECREATION
With its lakes and parks, ski trails and campsites, and historical and cultural attractions, Minnesota provides ample recreational opportunities for residents and visitors alike. According to estimates by the Department of Economic Development, nearly 7.7 million tourists traveled in the state during 1976, spending more than $1.3 billion and generating the equivalent of 89,560 full-time jobs for Minnesotans. About half the tourists were from out of state.

Besides the museums, sports stadiums, and concert halls in the big cities, Minnesota's attractions include the 220,000-acre (89,000-hectare) Voyageurs National Park, near the Canadian border; Grand Portage National Monument, in Arrowhead Country, a former fur-trading center with a restored trading post; and Pipestone National Monument, in southwestern Minnesota, containing the red pipestone quarry used by Indians to make peace pipes. Lumbertown USA, a restored 1870s lumber community, is in Brainerd, and the US Hockey Hall of Fame is in Eveleth.

The state maintains and operates 65 parks, 9,240 mi (14,870 km) of trails, 12 scenic and natural areas, and 18 canoe and boating routes. Minnesota also has a total of 915 wildlife management areas, covering 988,000 acres (400,000 hectares). The parks have an estimated 7 million visitors annually. As of fiscal 1977/78 there were 1,339,098 licensed fishermen and 482,735 licensed hunters. An estimated 450,000 people enjoy boating each year on Minnesota's scenic waterways. Winter sports have gained in popularity, and many parks are now used heavily all year round. Snowmobiling, though it has declined slightly over the last few years, still attracts an estimated 340,000 enthusiasts annually, and cross-country skiing is rapidly accelerating in popularity.

⁴⁸SPORTS
The Twin Cities area has major league professional teams in baseball, football, hockey, and soccer. The Minnesota Twins, led by Harmon Killebrew and Tony Oliva, won the American League pennant in 1965; the Minnesota Vikings of the National Football League, featuring such stars as Fran Tarkenton and Chuck Foreman, were National Conference champions four times during the 1970s, although they failed in each of their Super Bowl bids. The North Stars of the National Hockey League and the Kicks of the North American Soccer League also represent the state.

In collegiate sports, the University of Minnesota Gophers are a Big Ten football team. The university is probably best known for its ice hockey team, which won the NCAA title three times during the 1970s and supplied the coach—Herb Brooks—and many of the players for the gold medal–winning US team in the 1980 Winter Olympics.

⁴⁹FAMOUS MINNESOTANS
No Minnesotan has been elected to the US presidency, but several have sought the office, including two who served as vice president. Hubert Horatio Humphrey (b.South Dakota, 1911–78) was vice president under Lyndon Johnson and a serious contender for the presidency in 1960, 1968, and 1972. A onetime mayor of Minneapolis, the "Happy Warrior" entered the US Senate in 1949, winning recognition as a vigorous proponent of liberal causes; after he left the vice-presidency, Humphrey won reelection to the Senate in 1970. Humphrey's protégé, Walter

Frederick "Fritz" Mondale (b.1928), a former state attorney general, was appointed to fill Humphrey's Senate seat in 1964, was elected to it twice, and after an unsuccessful try for the presidency, became Jimmy Carter's running mate in 1976; four years later, he and Carter ran unsuccessfully for reelection. Warren Earl Burger (b.1907) of St. Paul was named chief justice of the US Supreme Court in 1969. Three other Minnesotans have served on the court: Pierce Butler (1866–1939), William O. Douglas (1898–1980), and Harry A. Blackmun (b. Illinois, 1908).

Senator Frank B. Kellogg (b.New York, 1856–1937), who as secretary of state helped to negotiate the Kellogg-Briand Pact renouncing war as an instrument of national policy (for which he won the 1929 Nobel Peace Prize), also served on the Permanent Court of International Justice. Other political leaders who won national attention include Governors John A. Johnson (1861–1909), Floyd B. Olson (1891–1936), and Harold E. Stassen (b.1907), a perennial presidential candidate since 1948 but a serious contender in his early races. Eugene J. McCarthy (b.1916) served in the US Senate, was the central figure in a national protest movement against the Viet-Nam war and, in that role, unsuccessfully sought the 1968 Democratic presidential nomination won by Humphrey. McCarthy also ran for the presidency as an independent in 1976.

Several Minnesotans besides Kellogg have served in cabinet posts. Minnesota's first territorial governor, Alexander Ramsey (1815–1903), later served as a secretary of war, and Senator William Windom (1827–91) was also secretary of the treasury. Others serving in cabinet posts have included William DeWitt Mitchell (1874–1955), attorney general; Maurice H. Stans (b.1908), secretary of commerce; James D. Hodgson (b.1915), secretary of labor; and Orville Freeman (b.1918) and Bob Bergland (b.1928), both secretaries of agriculture. The first woman ambassador in US history was Eugenie M. Anderson (b.Iowa, 1909), like Humphrey an architect of the Democratic-Farmer-Labor Party.

Notable members of Congress include Knute Nelson (b.Norway, 1843–1923), who served in the Senate from 1895 to his death; Henrik Shipstead (1881–1960), who evolved into a leading Republican isolationist during 24 years in the Senate; Representative Andrew J. Volstead (1860–1947), who sponsored the 1919 prohibition act that bears his name; and Representative Walter Judd (b.1898), a prominent leader of the so-called China Lobby.

Daniel Greysolon, Sieur Duluth (b.France, 1636–1710), Father Louis Hennepin (b.Flanders, 1640?–1701), and Jonathan Carver (b.Massachusetts, 1710–80) were among the early explorers and chroniclers of what is now the State of Minnesota. Fur trader Henry H. Sibley (b.Michigan, 1811–91) was a key political leader in the territorial period and became the state's first governor; he also put down the Sioux uprising of 1862. Railroad magnate James J. Hill (b.Canada, 1838–1916) built one of the greatest corporate empires of his time, and Oliver H. Kelley (b. Massachusetts, 1826–1913), a Minnesota farmer, organized the first National Grange. John Ireland (b.Ireland, 1838–1918) was the first Roman Catholic archbishop of St. Paul, while Henry B. Whipple (b.New York, 1822–1901), longtime Episcopal bishop of Minnesota, achieved particular recognition for his work among Indians in the region.

The first US citizen ever to be awarded the Nobel Prize for literature was Sinclair Lewis (1885–1951), whose novel *Main Street* (1920) was modeled on life in his hometown of Sauk Centre. Philip S. Hench (b.Pennsylvania, 1896–1965) and Edward C. Kendall (b.Connecticut, 1886–1972), both of the Mayo Clinic, shared the 1950 Nobel Prize for medicine, and St. Paul native Melvin Calvin (b.1911) won the 1961 Nobel Prize for chemistry. The Mayo Clinic was founded in Minnesota by Dr. William W. Mayo (b.England, 1819–1911) and developed through the efforts of his sons, Drs. William H. (1861–1939) and Charles H. (1865–1939) Mayo. Oil magnate J. Paul Getty (1892–1976) was a Minnesota native.

Prominent literary figures, besides Sinclair Lewis, include Ignatius Donnelly (b.Pennsylvania, 1831–1901), a writer, editor, and Populist Party crusader; F. Scott Fitzgerald (1896–1940), well-known for classic novels including *The Great Gatsby*; and Ole Edvart Rølvaag (b.Norway, 1876–1931), who conveyed the reality of the immigrant experience in his *Giants in the Earth*. The poet and critic Allen Tate (b.Kentucky, 1899–1979) taught for many years at the University of Minnesota. Journalist Westbrook Pegler (1894–1969) and cartoonist Charles Schulz (b.1922) were both born in Minnesota, and economist Thorstein Veblen (b.Wisconsin, 1857–1929) lived there. Architects LeRoy S. Buffington (1847–1937) and Cass Gilbert (b.Ohio, 1859–1934) influenced their fields well beyond the state's borders, as did Minnesota artists like Wanda Gag (1893–1946) and Adolph Dehn (1895–1968).

Minnesota-born entertainers include Judy Garland (Frances Gumm, 1922–69) and Bob Dylan (Robert Zimmerman, b.1941). Football star William "Pudge" Heffelfinger (1867–1954) was a Minnesota native, and Bronislaw "Bronco" Nagurski (b.Canada, 1908) played for the University of Minnesota.

⁵⁰BIBLIOGRAPHY

Blegen, Theodore C. *Minnesota: A History of the State.* Rev. ed. Minneapolis: University of Minnesota Press, 1975 (orig. 1937).

Brook, Michael. *Reference Guide to Minnesota History: A Subject Bibliography of Books, Pamphlets, and Articles in English.* St. Paul: Minnesota Historical Society, 1974.

Chrislock, Carl H. *The Progressive Era in Minnesota, 1899–1918.* St. Paul: Minnesota Historical Society, 1971.

Coen, Rena N. *Painting and Sculpture in Minnesota, 1820–1914.* Minneapolis: University of Minnesota Press, 1976.

Federal Writers' Project. *Minnesota: A State Guide.* Rev. ed. New York: Hastings House, 1954 (orig. 1938).

Folwell, William W. *A History of Minnesota.* 4 vols. Rev. ed. St. Paul: Minnesota Historical Society, 1956–69 (orig. 1921–30).

Holmquist, June D., and Jean A. Brookins. *Minnesota's Major Historic Sites: A Guide.* 2d ed. St. Paul: Minnesota Historical Society, 1972.

Lass, William E. *Minnesota: A Bicentennial History.* New York: Norton, 1977.

Meyer, Roy. *History of the Santee Sioux: United States Indian Policy on Trial.* Lincoln: University of Nebraska Press, 1967.

Minnesota, State of. Department of Economic Development. *Minnesota Statistical Profile, 1978.* St. Paul, 1978.

Minnesota, State of. Secretary of State. *The Minnesota Legislative Manual, 1979–80.* St. Paul, 1979.

Mitau, G. Theodore. *Politics in Minnesota.* 2d rev. ed. Minneapolis: University of Minnesota Press, 1970.

Schwartz, George M., and G. A. Thiel. *Minnesota's Rocks and Waters: A Geological Story.* Minneapolis: University of Minnesota Press, 1954.

Upham, Warren. *Minnesota Geographic Names: Their Origin and Historic Significance.* St. Paul: Minnesota Historical Society, 1969 (orig. 1920).

MISSISSIPPI

State of Mississippi

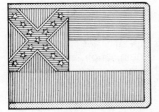

¹LOCATION, SIZE, AND EXTENT

Located in the eastern south-central US, Mississippi ranks 32d in size among the 50 states.

The total area of Mississippi is 47,716 sq mi (123,584 sq km), of which land takes up 47,296 sq mi (122,497 sq km) and inland water 420 sq mi (1,088 sq km). Mississippi's maximum E–W extension is 188 mi (303 km); its greatest N–S distance is 352 mi (566 km).

Mississippi is bordered on the N by Tennessee; on the E by Alabama; on the S by the Gulf of Mexico and Louisiana; and on the W by Louisiana (with the line partially formed by the Pearl and Mississippi rivers); and Arkansas (with the line formed by the Mississippi River). Several small islands lie off the coast.

The total boundary length of Mississippi is 1,015 mi (1,634 km). The state's geographic center is in Leake County, 9 mi (14 km) WNW of Carthage.

²TOPOGRAPHY

Mississippi lies entirely within two lowland plains. Extending eastward from the Mississippi River, the Mississippi Alluvial Plain, popularly known as the Delta, is very narrow south of Vicksburg, but stretches as much as a third of the way across the state farther north. The Gulf Coastal Plain covers the rest of the state. The latter plain includes several subregions, of which the Red Clay Hills of north-central Mississippi and the Piney Woods of the south and southeast are the most extensive. Mississippi's generally hilly landscape ascends from sea level at the Gulf of Mexico to reach its maximum elevation, 806 feet (246 meters), at Woodall Mountain, in the extreme northeastern corner of the state.

The state's largest lakes, Grenada, Sardis, Enid, and Arkabutla, are all man-made. Numerous smaller lakes—called oxbow lakes because of their curved shape—extend along the western edge of the state; once part of the Mississippi River, they were formed when the river changed its course. Mississippi's longest inland river, the Pearl, flows about 490 mi (790 km) from the eastern center of the state to the Gulf of Mexico, its lower reaches forming part of the border with Louisiana. The Big Black River, some 330 mi (530 km) long, begins in the northeast and cuts diagonally across the state, joining the Mississippi about 20 mi (32 km) below Vicksburg. Formed by the confluence of the Tallahatchie and Yalobusha rivers at Greenwood, the Yazoo flows 189 mi (304 km) southwest to the Mississippi just above Vicksburg.

³CLIMATE

Mississippi has short winters and long, humid summers. Summer temperatures vary little from one part of the state to another. Biloxi, on the Gulf coast, averages 81°F (27°C) in July, while Oxford, in the north-central part of the state, averages 80°F (27°C). During the winter, however, because of the temperate influence of the Gulf of Mexico, the southern coast is much warmer than the north; in January, Biloxi averages 53°F (12°C) to Oxford's 42°F (6°C). The lowest temperature ever recorded in Mississippi was –19°F (–28°C) on 30 January 1966 in Corinth; the highest, 115°F (46°C), was set on 29 July 1930 at Holly Springs.

Precipitation in Mississippi increases from north to south. The north-central region averages 53 in (135 cm) of precipitation a year; the coastal region, 62 in (157 cm). Some snow falls in northern and central sections. Mississippi lies in the path of hurricanes moving northward from the Gulf of Mexico during the late summer and fall. On 17–18 August 1969, Hurricane Camille ripped into Biloxi and Gulfport and caused more than 100 deaths throughout the state. Two tornado alleys cross Mississippi from the Southwest to northeast, from Vicksburg to Oxford and McComb to Tupelo.

⁴FLORA AND FAUNA

Post and white oaks, hickory, maple, and magnolia grow in the forests of the uplands; various willows and gums (including the the tupelo) in the Delta; and longleaf pine in the Piney Woods. Characteristic wild flowers include the green Virginia creeper, black-eyed Susan, and Cherokee rose.

Common among the state's mammals are the opposum, eastern mole, armadillo, coyote, mink, white-tailed deer, striped skunk, and diverse bats and mice. Birds include varieties of wren, thrush, warbler, vireo, and hawk, along with numerous waterfowl and seabirds, Franklin's gull, the common loon, and the wood stork among them. Black bass, perch, and mullet are common freshwater fish. Rare species in Mississippi include the hoary bat, American oystercatcher, mole salamander, pigmy killifish, Yazoo darter, and five species of crayfish. The state lists the black bear, cliff swallow, and scarlet snake among threatened species, and the panther, red wolf, Mississippi sandhill crane, and Bayou darter as endangered.

⁵ENVIRONMENTAL PROTECTION

Agencies with environmental responsibilities in Mississippi include the Department of Natural Resources and the Department of Wildlife Conservation, both established in 1978. The Gulf Coast Research Laboratory conducts research on marine resources, primarily in relation to the Mississippi Gulf coast. The Board of Health gives licenses for solid waste disposal.

The most controversial environmental issues as the 1980s began were the construction of the Grand Gulf and Yellow Creek nuclear reactors and the possible location of nuclear waste disposal sites in the southern part of the state.

⁶POPULATION

With a 1970 census population of 2,216,912, Mississippi ranked 29th among the 50 states. After remaining virtually level for 30 years, Mississippi's population during the 1970s grew at the rate of more than 1% per annum, reaching a preliminary census total of 2,503,250 in 1980.

According to the 1970 census, 48.4% of Mississippians were male, and 51.6% female. Mississippians were less mobile than residents of all but six other states: 69% of them had lived in the state all their lives. In 1978, the population density was 51 persons per sq mi (20 per sq km).

In 1970, nearly 45% of the population was urban, and 55% rural. Although this percentage was far below the national average—Mississippi remains one of the most rural states in the US—the urban population has tripled since 1930, when only 17% of state residents lived in cities. Mississippi's largest city, Jackson, had a preliminary 1980 census population of 200,338, more than double the 1950 total. Next came Biloxi, with 49,134 residents, followed by Meridian, 45,671; Greenville, 40,444; Hattiesburg, 40,278; and Gulfport, 39,450.

⁷ETHNIC GROUPS

Since 1860, blacks have constituted a larger proportion of the population of Mississippi than of any other state. By the end of the 1830s, blacks outnumbered whites 52% to 48%, and from the 1860s through the early 20th century, they made up about three-fifths of the population. Because of outmigration, the proportion of black Mississippians declined to less than 36% in 1976, when the state had an estimated 1,489,000 whites, 829,000 blacks, and no more than 25,000 members of other races. Except for a short period during Reconstruction when contract Chinese and some Italians were imported as a prospective substitute labor force, black labor was the backbone of the plantation economy of the Mississippi Delta.

The few Chinese who settled permanently in the state began as small traders serving black consumers. Until the 1940s, the Chinese—who numbered 1,441 in 1970—were an intermediate stratum between blacks and whites in the social hierarchy of the Delta counties. During 1975, 488 Indochinese refugees were settled in Mississippi, and more have come since that time. Conflicts arose during 1979 between refugee and native shrimp fishermen.

Mississippi has only a small Indian population remaining—4,113 in 1970. Most of them live on the Choctaw reservation in the east-central region.

⁸LANGUAGES

Of the original Chickasaw in northern Mississippi, the Natchez in the southwest, and the Choctaw in the southeast, 2,878 descendants claimed Choctaw or another Indian language as their mother tongue in 1970.

English in the state is largely Southern, with some South Midland speech in northern and eastern Mississippi because of population drift from Tennessee. Typical are the absence of final /r/ amd the lengthening and weakening of the diphthongs /ai/ and /oi/ as in *ride* and *oil*. South Midland terms in northern Mississippi include *tow sack* (burlap bag), *dog irons* (andirons), *plum peach* (clingstone peach), *snake doctor* (dragonfly), and *stone wall* (rock fence). In the eastern section are found *jew's harp* (harmonica) and *croker sack* (burlap bag). Southern speech in the southern half features *gallery* for porch, *mosquito hawk* for

dragonfly, and *press peach* for clingstone peach. Louisiana French has contributed *armoire* (wardrobe).

In 1970, 94% of both native-born residents and all residents held English to be their native language. Leading first languages and their speakers were as follows:

	NATIVE-BORN	FOREIGN-BORN
English	2,073,433	1,963
French	7,508	388
German	4,359	1,504
Spanish	3,750	836
Italian	3,064	651

⁹RELIGIONS

Protestants have dominated Mississippi since the late 18th century. The Baptists are the leading denomination, and many adherents are fundamentalists. Partly because of the strong church influence, Mississippi was among the first states to enact prohibition and among the last to repeal it.

During 1971, membership in the principal Protestant denominations was as follows: Southern Baptist Convention, 679,574 known adherents; United Methodist Church, 214,603; Presbyterians, 44,888. Most black Baptists belonged to the American Baptist Association or the National Baptist Convention of the USA. An organization called the Committtee of Concern (later the Mississippi Religious Leadership Conference) began in 1964 to raise funds for the rebuilding of at least 45 black churches that were damaged or destroyed during the civil rights conflict.

In 1979, Mississippi had 92,000 Roman Catholics and an estimated 3,395 Jews.

¹⁰TRANSPORTATION

At the end of 1976, the Illinois Central Gulf railroad line operated 2,824 mi (4,545 km) of track in Mississippi. Eleven other lines in the state serviced an additional 760 mi (1,223 km) of track.

At the end of 1978, Mississippi had 68,486 mi (110, 218 km) of roads, 60,689 mi (97,670 km) rural and 7,797 mi (12,548 km) municipal. Highways I-55, running north–south, and I-20 running east–west, intersect at Jackson. I-59 runs diagonally through the southeastern corner of Mississippi from Meridian to New Orleans. In 1978 there were 1,588,158 licensed drivers in Mississippi. A total of 1,602,867 motor vehicles was registered, including 1,124,059 automobiles and 441,107 trucks.

Mississippi has two deepwater seaports, Gulfport and Pascagoula, which together handle about 20 million tons of cargo a year. Smaller ports include Biloxi, on the Gulf of Mexico, along with Vicksburg and several smaller harbors along the Mississippi River.

There were 160 airfields in 1978, of which 77 were public and 83 private. The most important of these, Allen C. Thompson Field, near Jackson, emplaned 421,072 passengers that year.

¹¹HISTORY

The earliest record of human habitation in the region that is now the State of Mississippi goes back perhaps 2,000 years. The names of Mississippi's pre-Columbian inhabitants are not known. Upon the appearance of the first Spanish explorers in the early 16th century, Mississippi Indians numbered some 30,000 and were divided into 15 tribes. Soon after the French settled in 1699, however, only three large tribes remained: the Choctaw, the Chickasaw, and the Natchez. The French destroyed the Natchez in 1729–30 in retaliation for the massacre of a French settlement on the Natchez bluffs.

Spanish explorers, of whom Hernando de Soto was the most notable, explored the area that is now Mississippi in the first half

LOCATION: 30°06′32″ to 35°N; 88°5′53″ to 91°38′34″ W. **BOUNDARIES:** Tennessee line, 119 mi (192 km); Alabama line, 337 mi (542 km); Gulf of Mexico coastline, 44 mi (71 km); Louisiana line, 307 mi (494 km); Arkansas line, 208 mi (335 km).

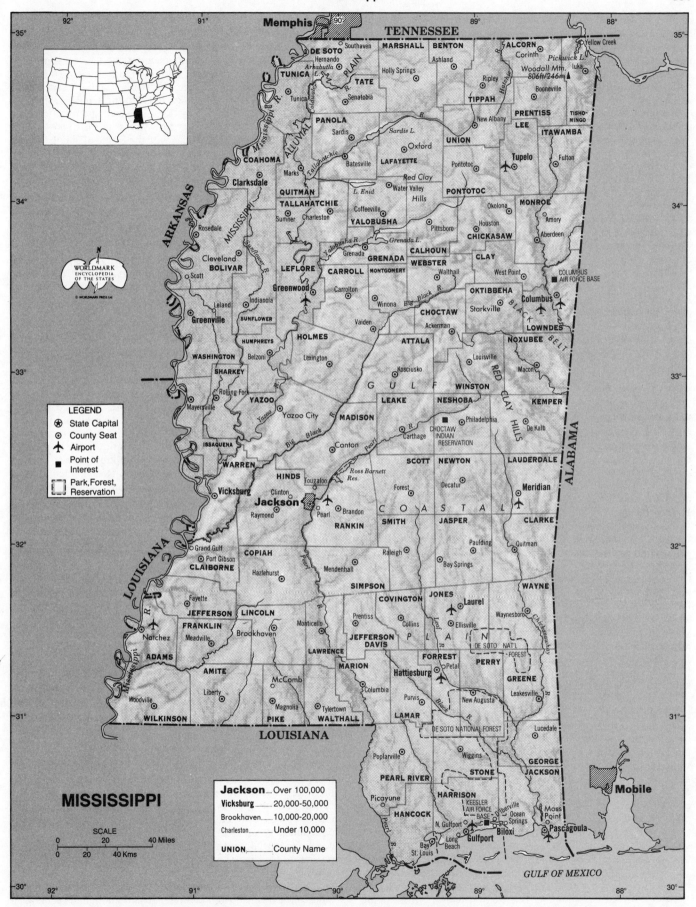

TENNESSEE

Memphis

MISSISSIPPI

ARKANSAS

LOUISIANA

ALABAMA

LOUISIANA

GULF OF MEXICO

LEGEND
- ⊛ State Capital
- ⊙ County Seat
- ✈ Airport
- ■ Point of Interest
- Park, Forest, Reservation

Jackson	Over 100,000
Vicksburg	20,000-50,000
Brookhaven	10,000-20,000
Charleston	Under 10,000
UNION	County Name

SCALE
0 20 40 Miles
0 20 40 Kms

WORLDMARK
ENCYCLOPEDIA
OF THE STATES
© WORLDMARK PRESS Ltd.

See US political: front cover J4; physical: back cover J4.

of the 16th century. De Soto found little of the mineral wealth he was looking for, and the Spanish quickly lost interest in the region. The French explorer Robert Cavelier, Sieur de la Salle, penetrated the lower Mississippi Valley from New France (Canada) in 1682. La Salle discovered the mouth of the Mississippi and named the entire area Louisiana in honor of the French king, Louis XIV.

An expedition under French-Canadian Pierre Lemoyne, Sieur d'Iberville, planted a settlement at Biloxi Bay in 1699. Soon the French opened settlements at Mobile (1702), Natchez (1716), and finally New Orleans (1718), which quickly eclipsed the others in size and importance. After losing the French and Indian War, France ceded Louisiana to its Spanish ally in 1762. The following year, Spain ceded the portion of the colony that lay east of the Mississippi to England, which governed the new lands as West Florida. During the American Revolution, the Spanish, who still held New Orleans and Louisiana, marched into Natchez, Mobile, and Pensacola (the capital) and took West Florida by conquest.

Although the US claimed the Natchez area after 1783, Spain continued to rule it. However, the Spanish were unable to change the Anglo-American character of the settlement. In fact, during the years of Spanish control, Americans continued to settle freely around Natchez. Spain agreed to relinquish its claim to the Natchez District by signing the Treaty of San Lorenzo on 27 October 1795, but did not evacuate its garrison there for another three years.

The US Congress organized the Mississippi Territory in 1798. Between 1798 and 1817, the territory grew enormously in population, attracting immigrants mainly from the older states of the South, but also from the Middle Atlantic states and even from New England. During this period, the territory included all the land area presently within the borders of Mississippi and Alabama. However, sectionalism and the territory's large size convinced Congress to organize the eastern half as the Alabama Territory in 1817. Congress then offered admission to the western half, which became the nation's 20th state—Mississippi—on 10 December.

Until the Civil War, Mississippi exemplified the American frontier, bustling, violent, and aggressive. By and large, Mississippians viewed themselves as westerners, not southerners. Nor was Mississippi, except for a few plantations around Natchez, a land of large planters. Rather, Mississippi's antebellum society and government were dominated by a coalition of prosperous farmers and small landowners. At the time of statehood, the northern two-thirds of Mississippi remained in the hands of the Choctaw and Chickasaw and was closed to settlement. Under intense pressure from the state government and from Andrew Jackson's presidential administration, these tribes signed three treaties between 1820 and 1832, ceding their Mississippi lands and agreeing to move to what is now Oklahoma.

The opening of fertile Indian lands for sale and settlement produced a boom of speculation and growth unparalleled in Mississippi history. Cotton agriculture and slavery—introduced by the French and carried on by the British and Spanish, but hitherto limited mostly to the Natchez area—swept over the state. As the profitability and number of slaves increased, so did attempts by white Mississippians to justify slavery morally, socially, and economically. The expansion of slavery also produced a defensive attitude which focused the minds of white Mississippians on two dangers: that the slaves outnumbered the whites and would threaten white society unless kept down by slavery; and that any attack on slavery, whether from the abolitionists or from Free-Soilers like Abraham Lincoln, was a threat to white society. The danger, they believed, was so great that no price was too high to maintain slavery, even secession and civil war.

After Lincoln's election to the US presidency, Mississippi became, on January 1861, the second southern state to secede. When the war began, Mississippi occupied a central place in Union strategy. The state sat squarely astride the major Confederate east–west routes of communication in the lower South, and the Mississippi River twisted along the state's western border. Control of the river was essential to Union division of the Confederacy. The military campaign fell into three phases: the fight for northeastern Mississippi in 1862, the struggle for Vicksburg in 1862–63, and the battle for east Mississippi in 1864–65. The Union advance on Corinth began with the Battle of Shiloh (Tenn.) in April 1862. The Union objective was the railroad that ran across the northeastern corner of Mississippi from Corinth to Iuka and linked Memphis, Tenn., to Atlanta, Ga. Losses in the ensuing battle, which eventually led to the occupation of Corinth by Union troops, exceeded 10,000 men on each side.

The campaign that dominated the war in Mississippi—and, indeed, along with Gettysburg provided the turning point of the Civil War—was Vicksburg. Perched atop high bluffs overlooking a bend in the Mississippi and surrounded by hills on all sides, Vicksburg provided a seemingly impregnable fortress. Union forces maneuvered before Vicksburg for more than a year before Grant besieged the city and forced its surrender on 4 July 1863. Along with Vicksburg went the western half of Mississippi. The rest of the military campaign in the state was devoted to the fight for the east, which Union forces still had not secured when the conflict ended in 1865. Of the 78,000 Mississippians who fought in the Civil War, nearly 30,000 died.

Ten years of political, social, and economic turmoil followed. Reconstruction was a tumultuous period during which the Republican Party encouraged blacks to vote and hold political office, while the native white Democrats resisted full freedom for their former slaves. The resulting confrontation lasted until 1875, when, using violence and intimidation, the Democrats recaptured control of the state from the Republicans and began a return to the racial status quo antebellum. Reconstruction left a scar on the minds of Mississippians. To the whites it seemed proof that blacks were incapable of exercising political power; to the blacks it proved that political and social rights could not long be maintained without economic rights.

The era from the end of Reconstruction to World War II was a period of economic, political, and social stagnation for Mississippi. White Mississippians pushed Negroes back into slavery in all but name. Segregation laws and customs placed strict social controls on blacks, and a new state constitution in 1890 removed the last vestiges of their political rights. Mississippi's agricultural economy, dominated by cotton and tenant farming, provided the economic equivalent of slavery for black sharecroppers. Ironically, as a continuing agricultural depression ground down the small white farmers, many of them also were driven into the sharecropper ranks. Whether former planter-aristocrats like John Sharp Williams or small-farmer advocates like James K. Vardaman and Theodore Bilbo held office, political life was dominated by the overriding desire to keep the blacks subservient. From Reconstruction to the 1960s, white political solidarity was of paramount importance. Otherwise, the whites reasoned, another reconstruction would follow.

The Great Depression of the 1930s pushed Mississippians, predominantly poor and rural, to the point of desperation, and the state's agricultural economy to the brink of disaster. In 1932, cotton sank to 5 cents a pound, and one-fourth of the state's farmland was forfeited for nonpayment of taxes. World War II unleashed the forces that would later revolutionize Mississippi's economic, social, and political order. The war brought the first prosperity to Mississippi in a century. By introducing outsiders to Mississippi and Mississippians to the world, the armed forces and the war began to erode the state's insularity. It also stimulated industrial growth and agricultural mechanization, and encouraged an exodus of blacks to better-paying jobs in other parts of the nation.

The seeds for the civil rights movement were sown in the war years. Within little more than a generation, from 1945 to 1975, legal segregation was destroyed, and black people exercised political rights for the first time since Reconstruction. The "Mississippi Summer" civil rights campaign—and the violent response to it, including the abduction and murder of three civil rights activists in June 1964—affected Mississippians as well as outsiders and helped turn public opinion toward racial accommodation.

By the late 1970s, according to any standard, Mississippi had become an industrial state. In the agricultural sector, cotton had been dethroned and crop diversification accomplished. In short, after a century, Mississippi had reentered the mainstream of American life.

¹²STATE GOVERNMENT

Mississippi has had four state constitutions. The first (1817) accompanied Mississippi's admission to the Union. A second constitution (1832) was superseded by that of 1868, redrafted under Republican rule to allow Mississippi's readmission to the Union after the Civil War. The state's present constitution, as amended, dates from 1890.

Mississippi's bicameral legislature includes a 52-member senate and a 122-member house of representatives. All state legislators are elected to 4-year terms. State representatives must be at least 21 years of age and senators 25 years old. All legislators must have been Mississippi residents for 4 years and residents of their district 2 years prior to election.

The governor, lieutenant governor, secretary of state, attorney general, state treasurer, auditor of public accounts, and superintendent of public education are independently elected to four-year terms. The governor and treasurer may not serve successive terms. The governor (and lieutenant governor) must be at least 30 years of age, a US citizen for 20 years, and a Mississippi resident for 5 years prior to election.

Constitutional amendments first must receive the approval of two-thirds of the members of each house of the legislature; a majority of voters must approve the amendment on a statewide ballot. The constitution also provides for the calling of a constitutional convention by majority vote of each house.

Every US citizen over the age of 18 may vote in Mississippi upon producing evidence of one year of residence in the state.

¹³POLITICAL PARTIES

Mississippi's major political parties are the Democratic Party and the Republican Party, each an affiliate of the national party organization. Mississippi Democrats have often been at odds with each other and with the national Democratic Party.

In the 1830s, party affiliation in the state began to divide along regional and economic lines: woodsmen and small farmers in eastern Mississippi became staunch Jacksonian Democrats, while the conservative planters in the western river counties tended to be Whigs. An early demonstration of the power of the Democrats was the movement of the state capital from Natchez in 1821 to a new city named after Andrew Jackson. During the pre–Civil War years, the secessionists were largely Democrats; the Unionists, western Whigs.

During Reconstruction, Mississippi had its first Republican governor. After the Democrats returned to power in 1875, they systematically deprived blacks of the right to vote, specifically by inserting in the constitution of 1890 a literacy clause that could be selectively interpreted to include illiterate whites but exclude blacks. Voter registration among blacks fell from 130,607 in 1880 to 16,234 by 1896.

In 1948, Mississippi Democrats seceded from the national party over the platform, which opposed racial discrimination. That November, Mississippi voters backed the State's Rights Democratic (Dixiecrat) presidential ticket. At the national Democratic convention in 1964, the black separatist Freedom Democratic Party asked to be allotted 40% of Mississippi's seats but was turned down. A further division in the party occurred during the 1960s between the (black) Loyalist Democrats and the (white) Regular Democrats, who were finally reunited in 1976. During the 1950s and early 1960s, the segregationist White Citizens' Councils were so widespread and influential in the state as to rival the major parties in political importance.

Since the passing of the federal Voting Rights Act of 1965, black Mississippians have registered and voted in substantial numbers. According to estimates by the Voter Education Project, only 22,000 (5%) of voting-age blacks were registered in 1960; by 1975, 286,000 (61%) were registered. In 1979 there were 327

Mississippi Presidential Vote by Political Parties, 1948–80

YEAR	ELECTORAL VOTE	MISSISSIPPI WINNER	DEMOCRAT	REPUBLICAN	STATES' RIGHTS DEMOCRAT	SOCIALIST WORKERS	LIBERTARIAN
1948	9	Thurmond (SRD)	19,384	4,995	167,538	—	—
1952	8	Stevenson (D)	172,553	112,966	—	—	—
					INDEPENDENT		
1956	8	Stevenson (D)	144,453	60,683	42,961	—	—
					UNPLEDGED		
1960	8	Byrd¹	108,362	73,561	116,248	—	—
1964	7	Goldwater (R)	52,616	356,512	—	—	—
					AMERICAN IND.		
1968	7	Wallace (AI)	150,644	88,516	415,349	—	—
					AMERICAN		
1972	7	*Nixon (R)	126,782	505,125	11,598	2,458	—
1976	7	*Carter (D)	381,309	366,846	6,678	2,805	2,788
					WORKERS' WORLD		
1980	7	*Reagan (R)	429,281	441,089	2,402	2,240	4,702

*Won US presidential election.

¹Unpledged electors won plurality of votes and cast Mississippi's electoral votes for Senator Harry F. Byrd of Virginia.

elected black officials in Mississippi (2d in the US), of whom 203 held city or county office, 56 (1st among the 50 states) were law enforcement officers, 62 were education officials, and 6 held federal or state legislative office.

As of early 1980, Democrats controlled all statewide elective offices, as well as the house and senate. The state had one Republican US senator (the first since Reconstruction) and one Democratic senator, and three of the five US representatives were Democrats. Mississippi was one of the most closely contested states in the South during the 1976 presidential election, and that again proved to be the case in 1980, when Ronald Reagan edged out Jimmy Carter by a plurality of fewer than 12,000 votes. Reagan won 49.4% of the total popular vote, Carter 48.1%, John Anderson 1.3%, and all other candidates 1.2%.

¹⁴LOCAL GOVERNMENT
Each of Mississippi's 82 counties is divided into 5 districts, each of which elects a member to the county board of supervisors. As of 1970, Mississippi had 24 municipalities with populations of 10,000 or more, 59 with populations of 2,500 to 10,000, and 62 with populations of 1,000 to 2,500. Most cities, including most of the larger ones, have a mayor and city council.

¹⁵STATE SERVICES
The Mississippi Ethics Commission, established by the state legislature in 1979, is composed of eight members who enforce a code of ethics requiring all state officials and elected local officials to file statements of sources of income.

The Mississippi Department of Education has special programs for illiterate adults, and the disabled. A separate Board of Trustees of Institutions of Higher Learning administers Mississippi's public college and university system. Health services fall under the jurisdiction of the Mississippi Board of Health, which operates state hospitals and hospital schools. The Department of Public Welfare provides assistance payments, child support, food stamp distribution, and such social services as foster home care and family planning.

Public protection is afforded by the Civil Defense Council, Military Department, Bureau of Narcotics, Department of Public Safety (including the Highway Safety Patrol), and Department of Corrections.

¹⁶JUDICIAL SYSTEM
The Mississippi supreme court consists of a chief justice, two presiding justices, and six associate justices, all elected to eight-year terms. The constitution stipulates that the supreme court must hold two sessions a year in the state capital; one session is to commence on the 2d Monday of September, the other on the 1st Monday of March. The principal trial courts are chancery courts, which try civil cases, and circuit courts, which try both civil and criminal cases; their judges are elected to four-year terms. Small claims courts are presided over by justices of the peace, who need not be lawyers.

There were 1,585 sentenced prisoners in state and federal prisons in Mississippi at the end of 1977. In the mid-1970s, federal courts mandated reform of Mississippi prisons; appropriations made for that purpose included $3.7 million in 1977 for the reform of Parchman state prison. During 1976/77, Mississippi spent $48 per capita on criminal justice, 3d lowest in the nation.

In 1978, Mississippi had a total FBI Crime Index rate of 2,555 per 100,000 population, about half the national average. The violent crime rate was also below the national norm, but the murder rate was high, 7th among the 50 states. The death penalty was reinstated in 1977.

¹⁷ARMED FORCES
Mississippi had five defense installations with 25,835 personnel in 1978. There were two US Air Force bases, Keesler (Biloxi) and Columbus. The three US naval installations were an oceanographic office at Bay St. Louis, an air station at Meridian, and a construction battalion center at Gulfport. In 1978, Mississippi received $1.4 billion in federal defense contracts, nearly the 1977 allocation.

There were 244,000 veterans of US military service living in Mississippi as of 30 September 1979. Of those who served in wartime, 6,000 were veterans of World War I, 110,000 of World War II, 48,000 of the Korean conflict, and 65,000 of the Viet-Nam era. Benefits totaling some $253 million were paid to Mississippi veterans during 1977/78.

As of 30 September 1978, the Mississippi Army and Air National Guard had 13,100 personnel. State and local police numbered 4,716 in 1977.

¹⁸MIGRATION
In the late 18th century, most Mississippians were immigrants from the South—primarily the Carolinas, Tennessee, Georgia, and Virginia—and predominantly of Scotch-Irish descent. The opening of lands ceded by the Indians beginning in the 1820s brought tens of thousands of settlers into northern and central Mississippi, and a resulting population increase between 1830 and 1840 of 175% (including an increase of 197% in the slave population).

After the Civil War, there was little migration into the state, but much outmigration, mainly of blacks. The exodus from Mississippi was especially heavy during the 1940s, when nearly 400,000 people, three-quarters of them black, left the state. During the 1960s, a net total of 279,000 blacks departed. Black outmigration slowed considerably during the 1970s, to a net of 42,000 between 1970 and 1975, while 44,000 whites settled in the state. Also during the 1970s there was considerable intrastate migration to Hinds County (Jackson) and the Gulf Coast.

¹⁹INTERGOVERNMENTAL COOPERATION
The Mississippi Commission on Interstate Cooperation oversees and encourages the state's participation in interstate bodies, especially the Council of State Governments and the National Conference of State Legislatures. Mississippi also participates in the Appalachian Regional Commission, Mississippi-Alabama Sea Grant Consortium, Southern Growth Policy Board, Southern Interstate Nuclear Board, Southern Regional Education Board, Tennessee River Valley Association, and Tennessee-Tombigbee Waterway Development Authority.

Mississippi received more than $1 billion in federal aid in 1978/79, including $100 million in general revenue sharing.

²⁰ECONOMY
Between the Civil War and World War II, Mississippi's economy remained poor, stagnant, and highly dependent on the market for cotton—a bitter legacy from which the state is only now beginning to recover. As in the pre–Civil War years, Mississippi exported its raw materials and imported manufactures. In the 1930s, however, state leaders began to realize the necessity of diversifying the economy; and by the mid-1960s, many more Mississippians recognized that political and economic inequality and racial conflict did not provide an environment attractive to the industries the state needed.

Once the turmoil of the 1950s and early 1960s had subsided, the impressive industrial growth of the immediate postwar years resumed. By the mid-1960s, manufacturing—attracted to the state, in part, because of low wage rates and a weak labor movement—surpassed farming as a source of jobs. During the following decade, the balance of industrial growth changed somewhat. The relatively low-paying garment, textile, and wood products industries, based on cotton and timber, grew less rapidly in both value added and employment than a number of heavy industries, including transportation equipment and electric and electronic goods.

²¹INCOME
As it has for much this century, Mississippi ranked last among the 50 states in per capita income in 1978, at $5,736. The state

ranked last in median family income ($9,999) in 1975, when it had a far higher proportion of its citizens (26%) below the federal poverty level than any other state. On the other hand, Mississippi has steadily been closing the gap between its low income level and the national norm. Per capita income has grown from 54% of the US average in 1960 to 65% in 1970, 69% in 1975, and 73% in 1978. Measured in constant 1972 dollars, per capita income grew 50% between 1970 and 1978.

²²LABOR

Preliminary data for December 1979 showed a labor force of approximately 973,000 in Mississippi. The projected labor force participation rate in 1978 was 78% for white males, but only 63% for nonwhite males, a decline from the 1960 rate of 72%. In 1960, nonwhite women had participated in the labor force at a higher rate (36%) than white women (33%); by 1978, however, white women participated at a rate of 46%, compared with 41% for black women. The overall participation, 54%, ranked 48th among the 50 states. The unemployment rate for nonwhites (14%) was four times as high as that for whites in 1978, and unemployment among nonwhites 16–19 years old was nearly ... by unemployment ... following nonfarm ...

	YEES	ANNUAL PAYROLL ('000)
	998	$ 23,052
	125	90,885
	796)	(77,030)
	468	330,192
	094	2,084,906
	767	391,568
	915	384,339
	091	643,895
	315	297,225
	831	611,819
	217	10,929
	821	$4,868,810

... issippi production ... mong the 50 states), ... Mississippi has a ... among the 50 states ... Mississippi nonfarm ... yee associations.

... the states in income ... lion.

... dominated by cotton, ... II was Mississippi's ... period, however, as ... per system, agriculture became more diversified, and soybeans had displaced cotton in 1979 as the most valuable crop. In 1978, Mississippi ranked 3d in cotton production, 5th in rice, 8th in soybeans, and 10th in peaches and pecans. Mississippi is also a leading producer of sweet potatoes, and ranked 6th in production in 1975. About 1,378,000 bales of cotton were harvested in 1978. Soybean output in 1979 totaled 118,900,000 bushels.

Federal estimates for 1978 showed some 78,000 farms with a total area of 16.2 million acres (6.6 million hectares). Mississippi's farm population in 1970 was approximately 277,000, down from 680,000 in 1960. The richest soil is in the Delta, where most of the cotton is raised. Livestock has largely taken over the Black Belt, a fertile area in the northwest.

²⁴ANIMAL HUSBANDRY

Cattle are raised throughout the state, though principally in the Black Belt and Delta. The main chicken-raising area is in the eastern hills.

There were 1,810,000 head of cattle on Mississippi farms at the beginning of 1980. In 1979, the state produced 453,030,000 lb of cattle, valued at $315,436,000. During the same year, 123,566,000 lb of hogs and pigs were produced, worth $52,391,000. Mississippi is a leading producer of broilers, ranking 5th in both 1978 and 1979. In 1979, 1.1 billion lb of chickens and broilers, worth $298.2 million, were raised in the state.

²⁵FISHING

In 1978, Mississippi ranked 5th among the 50 states in size of commercial fish landings, 377,534,000 lb, but 17th in value of its catch, $28,291,000. Menhaden and shrimp make up the bulk of the commercial landings. The saltwater catch also includes oysters and swordfish; the freshwater catch is dominated by buffalo fish, carp, and catfish. As of 1980, Mississippi ranked 1st among the states in catfish farming. During the year ending March 1980, catfish production in Mississippi had a total value of more than $57,000,000.

²⁶FORESTRY

Mississippi had approximately 16,912,000 acres (6,844,000 hectares) of forested land in 1977, 56% of the total area of the state, and 2.3% of all US forested lands. The state's most heavily forested region is the Piney Woods in the southeast. Some 16,892,000 acres (6,836,000 hectares) were commercial timberland, 90% of it privately owned; some of this land was also used for agricultural purposes. Shipments of forestry products in 1977 included paper and paper products, $596.3 million; softwood veneers and plywood, $174.6 million; and wooden household furniture, $108.4 million.

²⁷MINING

In 1978, Mississippi ranked 28th in the US in mineral production, with output valued at $519 million. Principal mineral products (excluding fossil fuels) were sand and gravel, 13,500,000 tons; stone, 2,240,000 tons; clays, 1,991,000 tons; and sulfur, 469,000 tons.

²⁸ENERGY AND POWER

There were 26 electric generating plants in Mississippi in 1978—16 steam, 9 gas turbine, and 1 internal combustion—with a total installed capacity of 5.5 million kw. During that year they generated a total of 19.6 billion kwh of electricity. Production increased nearly 7% annually between 1970 and 1978, and production capacity rose by almost 11% a year. Two large nuclear reactors were under construction in Mississippi in 1980: the Yellow Creek pressurized-water plant, built by the Tennessee Valley Authority at Iuka and scheduled for completion in 1984; and the Grand Gulf boiling-water plant, built by Mississippi Power and Light in Claiborne County and scheduled to open in 1982.

Mississippi is a major petroleum producer, ranking 12th in the US during 1978, when 2,956 oil wells were active. Production totaled 37,756,000 barrels; proved reserves, 187,587,000 barrels. Mississippi produced about 131.6 billion cu feet of natural gas during 1978, when proved reserves were estimated at 1.4 trillion cu feet. As of 1976, six leases covering 35,000 acres (14,000 hectares) had been granted for oil and gas production on the outer continental shelf of Mississippi.

²⁹INDUSTRY

In 1976, Mississippi ranked 29th among the states in both value of shipments of manufactured goods and in value added by manufacture. Value added doubled between 1972 and 1977, from $2.8 billion to $5.6 billion. Transportation equipment contributed the largest amount of the 1977 total, 10%; followed by lumber and wood products, 9%; electric and electronic equipment, 8%; food and food products, 8%; chemical and allied products, 8%; apparel and other textile products, 7%; nonelectrical machinery, 6%; and other sectors, 44%.

The following table shows value added in 1972 and 1977 for selected major industries:

	1972	1977
Men's and boys' furnishings	$171,700,000	$251,200,000
Household furniture	167,000,000	229,400,000
Meat products	88,900,000	150,000,000
Agricultural chemicals	92,100,000	145,200,000
Motor vehicle parts and accessories	NA	143,000,000

30 COMMERCE

With wholesale trade amounting to $3.7 billion in 1972, Mississippi ranked 33d among the 50 states. Mississippi also ranked 33d in 1977 retail sales, which amounted to $6.2 billion. Food stores accounted for 25% of the retail sales volume; automotive dealers, 25%; department stores, 7%; gasoline service stations, 7%; eating and drinking places, 6%; and other establishments, 30%.

Mississippi was the 13th-leading exporter of farm products in 1976/77, accounting for $648 million, or 2.7% of the US total. Exports of manufactures reached $698 million in 1976.

31 CONSUMER PROTECTION

The Office of Consumer Protection, established in 1975 within the Office of the Attorney General, may investigate complaints of unfair or deceptive trade practices and, in specific cases, may issue injunctions to halt them.

32 BANKING

Mississippi's 184 insured commercial banks had assets of $9.4 billion in 1978. They held loans amounting to nearly $3 billion and deposits of $8.3 billion, including $2.9 billion in demand deposits and $5.4 billion in time deposits.

At the end of 1978, Mississippi had 60 insured savings and loan associations, 30 federally chartered and 30 state chartered. Their assets totaled $2.5 billion, and their savings accounts exceeded $2.1 billion.

33 INSURANCE

In mid-1978, 20 companies sold life insurance in Mississippi. Some 4 million life insurance policies were in force, worth a total of $22.2 billion. Life insurance companies paid $80.1 million in death benefits to 20,700 beneficiaries in 1978. The average Mississippi family held $26,800 in life coverage, 24% below the national average and 49th among the 50 states. In 1978, premiums written for automobile liability and physical damage insurance totaled $275.9 million; $919.1 million in flood insurance was also in force.

34 SECURITIES

There are no securities exchanges in Mississippi. New York Stock Exchange member firms had 22 sales offices and 88 registered representatives in the state in 1978. Mississippians reported $115.4 million in dividend income on their 1977 federal tax returns.

35 PUBLIC FINANCE

The state budget is prepared annually by the Commission of Budget and Accounting, of which the governor is chariman ex officio, and submitted to the legislature for approval. The fiscal year runs from 1 July through 30 June.

The following table shows general revenues and expenditures for 1979/80 (estimated) and 1980/81 (recommended):

REVENUES	1979/80	1980/81
Sales tax	$421,300,000	$ 472,000,000
Individual income tax	164,000,000	174,000,000
Corporate income and franchise tax	91,185,000	102,000,000
Other receipts	243,073,778	264,940,200
TOTALS	$919,558,778	$1,012,940,200

EXPENDITURES	1979/80	1980/81
Education	$585,155,452	$607,862,136
Social welfare	76,277,712	78,326,777
Hospitals and hospital schools	49,726,392	54,820,779
Local assistance	46,418,000	51,745,000
Other expenditures	219,412,093	198,433,764
TOTALS	$976,989,649	$991,188,456

Consolidated expenditures (including federal and designated funds) recommended for 1980/81 totaled nearly $2.6 billion. As of 30 June 1977, the outstanding debt of state and local governments was $1.9 billion, or $793 per capita, 33% below the US average.

36 TAXATION

In 1978, Mississippi collected slightly more than $1 billion in state taxes, 31st in the US. As of 1980, the state income tax for both individuals and corporations was 3% on the first $5,000 and 4% on any additional income; the corporate income tax rate was one of the lowest in the nation. Mississippi also imposes severance taxes on oil, natural gas, and timber. A 5% retail sales tax is levied, along with taxes on inheritance, gasoline, tobacco, beer, wine, and numerous other items. In 1977, 681 local governments in Mississippi had property taxing authority.

In 1976, Mississippians paid $2.2 billion in federal taxes and received nearly $4 billion in federal expenditures; the state's ratio of federal spending to federal taxes paid was 3d highest among the 50 states. Mississippians filed 784,880 federal income tax returns in 1977, and paid $945 million in tax.

37 ECONOMIC POLICY

In 1936, the state began implementing a program called Balance Agriculture with Industry (BAWI), designed to attract manufacturing to Mississippi. The BAWI laws offered industry substantial tax concessions and permitted local governments to issue bonds to build plants that would be leased to companies for a 20-year period, after which the company would own them. Mississippi continues to offer low tax rates and numerous tax incentives to industry.

38 HEALTH

In 1969–71, average life expectancy in Mississippi was 68.09 years—72.40 for females, 64.06 for males—for a rank of 49th among the 50 states. In 1977 there were 45,485 live births in Mississippi; the birthrate was 19 per 1,000 population. That year the infant death rate for blacks and other minorities, 24.6 per 1,000 live births, was 2d only to Louisiana's among the 50 states; the rate for whites was 12.1. Mississippi's death rate from early childhood diseases was the highest in the US; from cardiovascular disease, 2d highest (tied with Florida). State estimates indicated that there were 270,000 hypertensives among Mississippians in 1980, only half of whom were aware of their condition. Though considerably less widespread than it once was, tuberculosis is still a serious health problem.

Mississippi had 114 hospitals, with 16,234 beds, in 1978; personnel included 4,377 registered nurses and 3,533 licensed practical nurses. The average cost of a hospital stay in 1977 was $135 per day, 2d lowest among the 50 states. In 1977 there were 2,471 licensed physicians, or 104 per 100,000 population, a ratio lower than in every state but South Dakota. During 1979, the state had 763 professionally active dentists.

39 SOCIAL WELFARE

During 1978, $38 million in aid to families with dependent children (AFDC) was paid to 168,500 Mississippians, 126,000 of whom were children. Average monthly AFDC payments of $61 per family were the lowest among the 50 states. About 298,000 Mississippians participated in the federal food stamp program during 1978, at a federal cost of $104.9 million. In 1978/79, 415,639 students participated in the state's school lunch program and 82,583 in the school breakfast program, at a total state and federal cost of

$68.8 million. That year, food was also provided for children under two nonschool programs: the Child Care Food Program, under which 29,500 children were served at 560 sites, through a federal subsidy of $7 million; and the Summer Special Food Service Program, serving 63,000 children at 384 sites, with a federal subsidy of $3.5 million.

In 1977, 233,800 retired workers in the state received federal Social Security benefits of $443.6 million; their average monthly payment was $195.80, the lowest in the US. Supplemental Security Income benefits totaling $71.8 million were paid in 1978. Unemployment insurance paid an average weekly benefit of $60.37 (50th in the US). Mississippi spent $42.2 million on workers' compensation and $16.8 million on vocational rehabilitation in 1977.

⁴⁰HOUSING

The 1970 census counted 697,000 year-round housing units, of which 637,000 were occupied. Only 77% of the occupied units had full plumbing—the lowest rate in the US.

In 1978, Mississippi received $18.5 million in federal aid for low-rent public housing and $26.1 million in community development grants. Nearly 26,000 units worth $629 million were authorized during 1976–78.

⁴¹EDUCATION

At the time of the 1970 census, Mississippi had the 2d-highest illiteracy rate in the US, 2.4%. Only 52% of Mississippians 18 and older had completed high school, the lowest rate in the nation. In 1970, adult whites of both sexes had completed an average of 12.1 years of schooling, whereas black men had averaged only 6.5 years, and black women 8.1.

Mississippi's reaction to the US Supreme Court decision in 1954 mandating public school desegregation was to repeal the constitutional requirement for public schools and to foster the development of segregated private schools. In 1964, the state's schools did begin to integrate, and compulsory school attendance was restored 13 years later. As of 1976, 29% of minority students were in schools in which minorities were less than 50% of the student body, and 15% were in 99–100% minority schools.

As of September 1979, there were 484,784 students enrolled in public schools in Mississippi, 270,752 elementary and 214,032 secondary. Between 1975 and 1977, nonpublic school enrollment fell from 37,000 to 12,000 at the elementary level and from 24,000 to 4,000 in the secondary grades, reflecting the return of Mississippi whites to public schools.

During 1978/79 there were 42 institutions of higher education with a total enrollment of 105,149; 8 were public universities, 16 were public junior colleges, and 18 (including 4 Bible colleges and theological seminaries) were private institutions. The University of Mississippi, established in 1844 and located in Lafayette County, had a total enrollment during 1978/79 of 9,655 (excluding its medical school at Jackson but including its law school). One of the most dramatic moments in the history of the civil rights movement came on 30 September 1962, when James Meredith became the university's first black student. Mississippi State University had 11,265 students in 1977; the University of Southern Mississippi, 9,689. Predominantly black institutions include Tougaloo College, Alcorn State University, Jackson State University, and Mississippi Valley State University. The Post-Secondary Financial Assistance Board provides loans for students who cannot obtain federally insured loans from banks, savings and loan associations, or credit unions.

⁴²ARTS

Jackson has a ballet company, a symphony orchestra, and two opera companies. Opera South, an integrated but predominantly black company, presents free operas during its summer tours and mounts two major productions yearly. The Mississippi Opera instituted a summer festival during its 1980/81 season. There are local symphony orchestras in Meridian, Tupelo, and Greenville.

The one established professional theater in the state, the Sheffield Ensemble in Biloxi, started as a children's theater but now also presents adult productions. The Greater Gulf Coast Arts Center has been very active in bringing arts programs into the coastal area.

A distinctive contribution to US culture is the music of black sharecroppers from the Delta, known as the blues. The Delta Blues Museum in Clarksdale has an extensive collection documenting blues history.

⁴³LIBRARIES AND MUSEUMS

There are 16 regional library systems in Mississippi (including municipal systems) and 28 county libraries. In 1977/78 there were 3.6 million volumes in Mississippi libraries, and total circulation of more than 7 million, including those from bookmobiles. The finest collection of Mississippiana is at the Mississippi State Department of Archives and History in Jackson. In the Vicksburg–Warren County Public Library are collections on the Civil War, state history, and oral history. Tougaloo College has special collections of African materials, civil rights papers, and oral history. The Gulf Coast Research Library of Ocean Springs has a marine biology collection.

There are more than 40 museums, including the distinguished Mississippi State Historical Museum at Jackson. Pascagoula, Laurel, and Jackson all have notable art museums. The Mississippi Museum of Natural Science in Jackson has been designated the state's official natural science museum by the legislature. In Meridian is a museum devoted to country singer Jimmie Rodgers, and in Jackson one to pitcher Dizzy Dean.

Beauvoir, Jefferson Davis's home at Biloxi, is a state shrine and includes a museum. The Mississippi governor's mansion, completed in 1845, restored in 1975, and purportedly the 2d-oldest executive residence in the US, is a registered National Historical Landmark.

⁴⁴COMMUNICATIONS

Mississippi had 466 post offices and about 4,700 postal employees in 1977. At the end of 1978 there were 1,464,192 telephones in Mississippi, 1,131,797 residential and 332,395 business. On average, only 84% of households in the state had telephone service, the lowest rate in the US. In 1978, the state had 173 commercial radio stations (105 AM, 68 FM) and 10 commercial television stations; 71 cable television systems had 191,724 subscribers in 115 communities.

⁴⁵PRESS

In 1978, Mississippi had 25 daily newspapers; 5 morning dailies, with 124,471 circulation, and 20 evening dailies, with 269,194 circulation. In addition there were 12 Sunday papers with a circulation of 308,520. The state's leading newspapers were all in Jackson, and all were owned by the same publisher: The *Clarion-Ledger* (m), 60,700; *Daily News* (e), 40,057; and the *Clarion-Ledger–News* (S), 111,982.

⁴⁶ORGANIZATIONS

Among the organizations that played key roles in the civil rights struggles in Mississippi during the 1950s and 1960s were the National Association for the Advancement of Colored People (NAACP), Congress of Racial Equality, Southern Christian Leadership Conference, and Student Nonviolent Coordinating Committee (SNCC; later the Student National Coordinating Committee); SNCC was the main organizer of the "Mississippi Summer" campaign. Of the national civil rights organizations still active in Mississippi, the NAACP is the largest, with members in every county. In contrast to the 1960s, most civil rights activities in the state are now organized around local social and economic programs, such as Head Start. The Freedom Information Service is a clearinghouse for information about civil rights activities in the state. The Citizens' Councils of America, headquartered in Jackson, is a state's rights group.

Other organizations with headquarters in Mississippi include the American Association of Public Health Physicians (Greenwood), Sons of Confederate Veterans (Hattiesburg), American Society of Photographers (Tupelo), National Association of Academies of Science (University of Mississippi), and the Amateur Field Trial Clubs of America.

⁴⁷TOURISM, TRAVEL, AND RECREATION

During 1977, some 6.4 million persons traveled to and through Mississippi, nearly 2.5 million to destinations within the state. Among Mississippi's major tourist attractions are its mansions and plantations, many of them in the Natchez area. McRaven, in Vicksburg, was built in 1797. The Delta and Pine Land Co. plantation near Scott is one of the largest cotton plantations in the US. At Greenwood is the Florewood River Plantation, a museum recreating 19th-century plantation life. The Mississippi State Fair is held annually in Jackson during the second week in October.

The Natchez Trace Parkway and Vicksburg National Military Park are popular attractions. There are 27 state parks. In 1977/78 licenses were issued to 311,953 hunters and 395,032 fishermen. The Gulf coast is popular for swimming and fishing.

⁴⁸SPORTS

There are no major league professional teams in Mississippi. Jackson has a minor league baseball team in the Texas League. The University of Mississippi has long been prominent in college football. From 1955 through 1970, "Ole Miss" teams won the Sugar Bowl five times and the Cotton Bowl once.

⁴⁹FAMOUS MISSISSIPPIANS

Mississippi's most famous political figure, Jefferson Davis (b. Kentucky, 1808–89), came to the state as a very young child, was educated at West Point, and served in the US Army from 1828 to 1835. He resigned a seat in Congress in 1846 to enter the Mexican War, from which he returned home a hero after leading his famous regiment, the 1st Mississippi Rifles, at the Battle of Buena Vista, Mexico. From 1853 to 1857, he served as secretary of war in the cabinet of President Franklin Pierce. Davis was representing Mississippi in the US Senate in 1861 when the state withdrew from the Union. In February 1861, he was chosen president of the Confederacy, an office he held until the defeat of the South in 1865. Imprisoned for two years after the Civil War (though never tried), Davis lived the last years of his life at Beauvoir, an estate on the Mississippi Gulf Coast given to him by an admirer. There he wrote *The Rise and Fall of the Confederate Government*, completed eight years before his death in New Orleans.

Lucius Quintus Cincinnatus Lamar (b.Georgia, 1825–93) settled in Oxford in 1855 and only two years later was elected to the US House of Representatives. A supporter of secession, he served as Confederate minister to Russia in 1862. After the war, Lamar was the first Mississippi Democrat returned to the House; in 1877, he entered the US Senate. President Grover Cleveland made Lamar his secretary of the interior in 1885, later appointing him to the US Supreme Court. Lamar served as associate justice from 1888 until his death.

Some of the foremost authors of 20th-century America owe their origins to Mississippi. Supreme among them is William Faulkner (Falkner, 1897–1962), whose literary career began in 1924 with the publication of *The Marble Faun*, a book of poems. His novels during the next 35 years included such classics as *The Sound and the Fury* (1929), *Light in August* (1932), and *Absalom, Absalom!* (1936). Faulkner received two Pulitzer Prizes (one posthumously), and in 1949 was awarded the Nobel Prize for literature.

Richard Wright (1908–60), born near Natchez, spent his childhood years in Jackson. He moved to Memphis as a young man, and from there migrated to Chicago; he lived his last years in Paris. A powerful writer and a leading spokesman for the black Americans of his generation, Wright is best remembered for his novel *Native Son* (1940) and for *Black Boy* (1945), an autobiographical account of his Mississippi childhood.

Two other native Mississippians of literary renown are Eudora Welty (b.1909) and Tennessee Williams (Thomas Lanier Williams, b.1911), each of whom is a Pulitzer Prize winner. Like Faulkner's, Welty's work is set in Mississippi; her best-known novels include *Delta Wedding* (1946), *The Ponder Heart* (1954), and *Losing Battles* (1970). Although Tennessee Williams has spent most of his life outside Mississippi, some of his most famous plays are set in the state. Other Mississippi authors are Hodding Carter (b.Louisiana, 1907–72), Shelby Foote (b.1916), Walker Percy (b.Alabama, 1916), and Willie Morris (b.1934).

Among the state's numerous musicians are William Grant Still (1895–1978), a composer and conductor, and Leontyne Price (Mary Leontine Price, b.1927), a distinguished opera soprano. Famous blues singers are Charlie Patton (1887–1934), William Lee Conley "Big Bill" Broonzy (1898–1958), Howlin' Wolf (Chester Arthur Burnett, b.1910), Muddy Waters (McKinley Morganfield, b.1915), John Lee Hooker (b.1917), and Riley "B. B." King (b.1925). Mississippi's contributions to country music include Jimmie Rodgers (1897–1933), Conway Twitty (b.1933), and Charley Pride (b.1939). Elvis Presley (1935–77), born in Tupelo, was one of the most popular singers in US history.

⁵⁰BIBLIOGRAPHY

Bettersworth, John K. *Your Mississippi*. Austin, Texas: Steck-Vaughn, 1975.

Brooks, Cleanth. *William Faulkner: The Yoknapatawpha Country*. New Haven: Yale University Press, 1963.

Federal Writers' Project. *Mississippi: A Guide to the Magnolia State*. Boston: Houghton Mifflin, 1973 (orig. 1938).

Ferris, William C. *Blues From the Delta*. Garden City, N.Y: Doubleday, 1978.

Kirwan, Albert D. *Revolt of the Rednecks, 1876–1925*. Lexington: University of Kentucky Press, 1951.

Loewen, James L., and Charles Sallis. *Mississippi: Conflict and Change*. New York: Pantheon, 1974.

McLemore, Richard A., ed. *A History of Mississippi*. 2 vols. Hattiesburg: University and College Press of Mississippi, 1973.

Miles, Edwin A. *Jacksonian Democracy in Mississippi*. Chapel Hill: University of North Carolina Press, 1960.

Mississippi State University, College of Business and Industry, Division of Research. *Mississippi Statistical Abstract, 1978*. 10th ed. Mississippi State, 1978.

Mitchell, George. *Blow My Blues Away*. Baton Rouge: Louisiana State University Press, 1971.

Moore, John H. *Agriculture in Antebellum Mississippi*. New York: Bookman, 1958.

Silver, James W. *Mississippi: The Closed Society*. 2d ed. New York: Harcourt, Brace, and World, 1966.

Skates, John Ray. *Mississippi: A Bicentennial History*. New York: Norton, 1979.

Sydnor, Charles S. *Slavery in Mississippi*. New York: Appleton-Century, 1933.

Welty, Eudora. *One Time, One Place: Mississippi in the Depression*. New York: Random House, 1971.

Wharton, Vernon L. *The Negro in Mississippi, 1865–90*. Chapel Hill: University of North Carolina Press, 1947.

MISSOURI

State of Missouri

ORIGIN OF STATE NAME: Probably from the Iliniwek Indian word *missouri*, meaning "owners of big canoes." **NICKNAME**: The Show Me State. **CAPITAL**: Jefferson City. **ENTERED UNION**: 10 August 1821 (24th). **SONG**: "Missouri Waltz." **MOTTO**: *Salus populi suprema lex esto* (The welfare of the people shall be the supreme law). **COAT OF ARMS**: Two grizzly bears standing on a scroll inscribed with the state motto support a shield portraying an American eagle and a constellation of stars, a grizzly bear on all fours, and a crescent moon, all encircled by the words "United We Stand Divided We Fall." Above are a six-barred helmet and 24 stars; below, the roman numeral MDCCCXX (1820), when Missouri's first constitution was adopted. **FLAG**: Three horizontal stripes of red, white, and blue, with the coat of arms, encircled by 24 white stars on a blue band, in the center. **OFFICIAL SEAL**: The coat of arms surrounded by the words "The Great Seal of the State of Missouri." **BIRD**: Bluebird. **FLOWER**: Hawthorn blossom. **TREE**: Dogwood. **ROCK**: Mozarkite (chert). **MINERAL**: Galena. **LEGAL HOLIDAYS**: New Year's Day, 1 January; Lincoln's Birthday, 12 February; Washington's Birthday, 3d Monday in February; Truman's Birthday, 8 May; Memorial Day, last Monday in May; Independence Day, 4 July; Primary Election Day, 1st Tuesday after 1st Monday in August (every four years); Labor Day, 1st Monday in September; Columbus Day, 2d Monday in October; Election Day, 1st Tuesday after 1st Monday in November (every four years); Veterans Day, 11 November; Thanksgiving Day, 4th Thursday in November; Christmas Day, 25 December. Though not a legal holiday, Missouri Day, the 3d Wednesday in October, is commemorated in schools each year. **TIME**: 6 A.M. CST = noon GMT.

¹LOCATION, SIZE, AND EXTENT

Located in the western north-central US, Missouri ranks 19th in size among the 50 states.

The total area of Missouri is 69,686 sq mi (180,487 sq km), of which land takes up 68,995 sq mi (178,697 sq km) and inland water 691 sq mi (1,790 sq km). Missouri extends 284 mi (457 km) E–W; its greatest N–S extension is 308 mi (496 km).

Missouri is bounded on the N by Iowa (with the line in the extreme NE defined by the Des Moines River); on the E by Illinois, Kentucky, and Tennessee (with the line passing through the Mississippi River); on the S by Arkansas (with a "boot heel" in the SE bounded by the Mississippi and St. Francis rivers); and on the W by Oklahoma, Kansas, and Nebraska (the line in the NW being formed by the Missouri River).

The total boundary length of Missouri is 1,438 mi (2,314 km). The state's geographic center is in Miller County, 20 mi (32 km) SW of Jefferson City.

²TOPOGRAPHY

Missouri is divided into four major land regions. The Dissected Till Plains, lying north of the Missouri River and forming part of the Central Plains region of the US, comprise rolling hills, open fertile flatlands, and well-watered prairie. The Osage Plains cover the western part of the state, their flat prairie monotony broken by low rounded hills. The Mississippi Alluvial Plain, in the southeastern corner, is made up of fertile black lowlands whose floodplain belts represent both the present and former courses of the Mississippi River. The Ozark Plateau, which comprises most of southern Missouri and extends into northern Arkansas and northeastern Oklahoma, constitutes the state's largest single region. The Ozarks contain Taum Sauk Mountain, at 1,772 feet (540 meters) the highest elevation in the state. Along the St. Francis River, near Cardwell, is the state's lowest point, 230 feet (70 meters).

Including a frontage of at least 500 mi (800 km) along the Mississippi River, Missouri has more than 1,000 mi (1,600 km) of navigable waterways. The Mississippi and Missouri rivers, the two largest in the US, respectively form the state's eastern bor-

der and part of its western border; Kansas City is located at the point where the Missouri bends eastward to cross the state, while St. Louis developed below the junction of the two great waterways. The White, Grand, Chariton, St. Francis, Current, and Osage are among the state's other major rivers. The largest lake is the man-made Lake of the Ozarks, covering a total of 93 sq mi (241 sq km).

Missouri's exceptional number of caves and caverns—23 were commercial tourist attractions in 1980—were formed during the last 50 million years through the erosion of limestone and dolomite by melting snows bearing vegetable acids. Coal, lead, and zinc deposits date from the Pennsylvanian era, beginning some 250 million years ago. The Mississippi Valley area is geologically active: massive earthquakes during 1811 and 1812 devastated the New Madrid area of the southeast.

³CLIMATE

Missouri has a continental climate, but with considerable local and regional variation. The average annual temperature is 50°F (10°C) in the northwest, but about 60°F (16°C) in the southeast. Kansas City has a normal daily mean temperature of 54.5°F (12.5°C), ranging from 28°F (−2°C) in January to 79°F (26°C) in July; St. Louis has an annual mean of 56°F (13°C), with 31°F (−1°C) in January and 79°F (26°C) in July. The coldest temperature ever recorded in Missouri was −40°F (−40°C), set at Warsaw on 13 February 1905; the hottest, 118°F (48°C), at Warsaw and Union on 14 July 1954.

The average annual precipitation for the state is about 40 in (100 cm), with some rain or snow falling about 110 days a year. The heaviest precipitation is in the southeast, averaging 48 in (122 cm); the northwest usually receives 32 in (81 cm) yearly. Snowfall averages 21 in (53 cm) in the north, 16 in (41 cm) in the southeast. During the winter, northwest winds prevail; the air movement is largely from the south and southeast during the rest of the year. Springtime is the peak tornado season.

⁴FLORA AND FAUNA

Representative trees of Missouri include the shortleaf pine, scarlet oak, smoke tree, pecan (*Carya illinoensis*), and peachleaf willow, along with species of tupelo, cottonwood, cypress, cedar, and dogwood (the state tree). American holly, which once flourished in the southeastern woodlands, is now considered rare; various types of wild grasses proliferate in the northern plains region. Missouri's state flower is the hawthorn blossom; other wild flowers include Queen Anne's lace, meadow rose, and white snakeroot. Showy and small white lady's-slipper, green adder's-mouth, purslane, corn salad, dotted monardo, and prairie white-fringed orchid are rare in Missouri. Among endangered plants are the water sedge, Loesel's twayblade, and marsh pink; the American elm, common throughout the state, is considered endangered because of Dutch elm disease.

Indigenous mammals are the common cottontail, muskrat, white-tailed deer, and gray and red foxes. The state bird is the bluebird; other common birds are the cardinal, solitary vireo, and the prothonotary warbler. A characteristic amphibian is the plains leopard frog; native snakes include garter, ribbon, and copperhead. Bass, carp, perch, jack salmon (walleye), and crayfish abound in Missouri's waters. The chigger, a minute insect, is a notorious pest.

The Missouri Department of Conservation and the Soil Conservation Service of the US Department of Agriculture jointly publish a list of rare and endangered species. Among rare animals are the black bear, black-tailed jackrabbit, Keen's bat, and snuffbox mussel. Listed as endangered are the river otter, cougar, gray and Indiana bats, caneback rattlesnake, Blanding's turtle, 2 subspecies of peregrine falcon, and 18 varieties of mussel.

[5] ENVIRONMENTAL PROTECTION

Missouri's first conservation law, enacted in 1874, provided for a closed hunting season on deer and certain game birds. In 1936, the state established a Conservation Commission to protect the state's wildlife and forest resources. Today, Missouri's principal environmental protection agencies are the Department of Conservation, which manages the state forests and maintains wildlife refuges; the Department of Natural Resources, responsible for state parks, energy conservation, and environmental quality programs, including air pollution control, water purification, land reclamation, soil and water conservation, and solid and hazardous waste management; and the State Environmental Improvement Authority, established in 1973 within the Department of Consumer Affairs, Regulation, and Licensing and empowered to offer financial aid to any individual, business, institution, or governmental unit seeking to meet pollution control responsibilities.

A constitutional amendment passed in 1976 mandates a sales tax of 0.125% exclusively for conservation purposes. The proposed 1980/81 budget allocated $32.6 million for the Department of Conservation, $71.9 million for the Department of Natural Resources, and $120 million in Environmental Improvement Authority loans.

[6] POPULATION

Missouri ranked 13th among the 50 states at the 1970 census, with a population of 4,677,983, an 8% increase over the 1960 census total of 4,319,813. The state's preliminary 1980 census population was 4,901,678, yielding a population density of 71 per sq mi (27 per sq km).

In 1830, the first year in which Missouri was enumerated as a state, the population was 140,455. Missouri's population just about doubled each decade until 1860, when the growth rate subsided; the population surpassed the 2 million mark at the 1880 census, 3 million in 1900 (when it ranked 5th in the US), and 4 million during the early 1960s. According to 1976 estimates, the population was 51.7% female, slightly older than the national average, and considerably less mobile: more than 62% of adult Missourians had resided in the state their whole lives.

In 1970, 70% of all Missourians lived in urban areas and 30% lived in rural areas; in 1830, the population distribution had been

4% urban and 96% rural. The largest cities and their preliminary 1980 census populations are St. Louis, 448,640; and Kansas City, 446,562. The St. Louis metropolitan area, embracing parts of Missouri and Illinois, comprised 2,385,900 people in 1978 (12th in the US), while metropolitan Kansas City, in Missouri and Kansas, had 1,324,600 (24th). St. Louis, Kansas City, and their surrounding metropolitan areas all experienced a net loss from migration between 1970 and 1978.

[7] ETHNIC GROUPS

After the flatboat and French traders and settlers had made possible the earliest development of Missouri and its Mississippi shore, the river steamer, the Civil War, the Homestead Act (1862), and the railroad changed the character of the state ethnically as well as economically. Germans came in large numbers, developing small diversified industries, and they were followed by Czechs and Italians. The foreign-born and their native-born American children numbered 312,000 in 1970, with Germany, Italy, and the United Kingdom being the leading countries of origin.

Black Americans have represented a rising proportion of Missouri's population in recent decades: 9% in 1960, 10.3% in 1970, 11.8% in 1976. Of the estimated 555,000 blacks in 1976, not quite half lived in St. Louis (which was more than 41% black); Kansas City's black community, 112,000 in 1970, supported a flourishing jazz and urban blues culture between the two world wars. In 1976, Missouri also had about 25,000 Hispanic Americans, mostly of Mexican origin. The Asian community is small: 2,382 Japanese, 2,815 Chinese, 2,010 Filipinos, and 6,222 other Asians as of 1970. In 1975, 2,669 Vietnamese refugees were resettled in the state.

Only a few American Indians remained in Missouri after 1836. The 1970 census showed an Indian population of 5,405; the state has no Indian reservations.

[8] LANGUAGES

White pioneers found Missouri Indians in the northern part of what is now Missouri, Osage in the central portion, and Quapaw in the south. Long after these tribes' removal to Indian Territory, only a few place-names echo their heritage: Missouri itself, Kahoka, Wappapello. In 1970, 908 state residents claimed an Indian mother tongue.

Four westward-flowing language streams met and partly merged in Missouri. Northern and North Midland speakers settled north of the Missouri River and in the western border counties, bringing their Northern *pail* and *sick to the stomach*, and their North Midland *fishworm* (earthworm), *gunnysack* (burlap bag), and *sick at the stomach*. But *sick in the stomach* occurs along the Missouri River from St. Louis to Kansas City and along the Mississippi south of St. Louis. South of the Missouri River, and notably in the Ozark Highlands, South Midland dominates, though with a few Southern forms, especially in the cotton-growing floodplain of the extreme southeast. *Wait on* (wait for), *light bread* (white bread), and *pullybone* (wishbone) are critical dialect markers for this area, as are *redworm* (earthworm), *towsack* (burlap bag), *snap beans* (string beans), *how* and *now* sounding like /haow/ and /naow/, and *Missouri* ending with the vowel of *me* rather than the final vowel of /uh/ heard north of the Missouri. In the extreme southeast are Southern *loaf bread*, *grass sack* (burlap bag), and *cold drink* as a term for a soft drink. In the eastern half of the state, a soft drink is generally *soda* or *sody*; in the western half, *pop*.

English was claimed as a mother tongue in 1970 by 89% of the

LOCATION: 36°30′ to 40°35′N; 89°06′ to 95°47′W. BOUNDARIES: Iowa line, 239 mi (385 km); Illinois line, 360 mi (579 km); Kentucky line, 59 mi (95 km); Tennessee line, 78 mi (125 km); Arkansas line, 331 mi (533 km); Oklahoma line, 35 mi (56 km); Kansas line, 267 mi (430 km); Nebraska line, 69 mi (111 km).

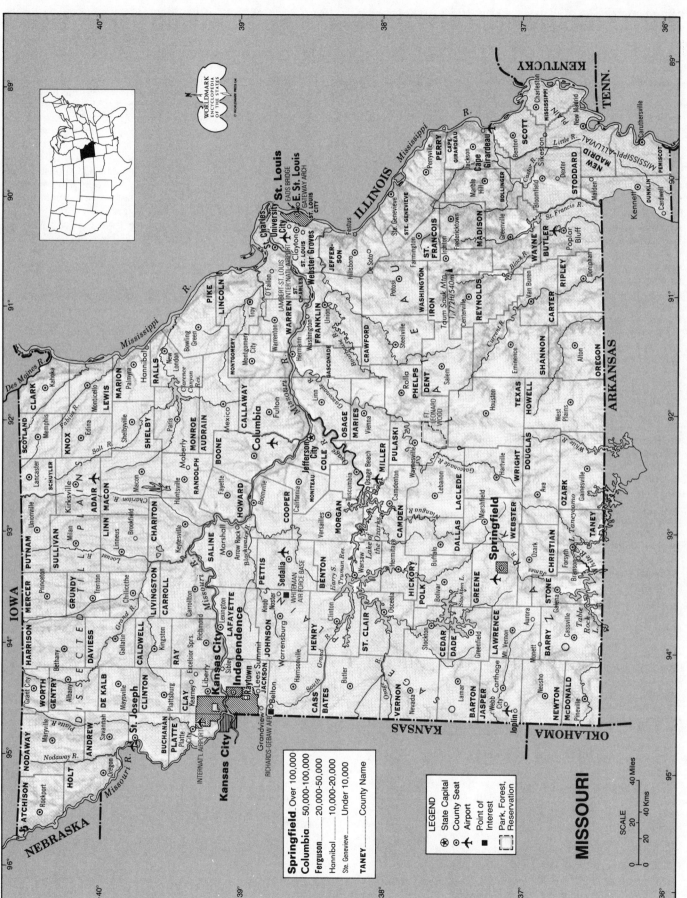

See US political: front cover H3; physical: back cover H3.

MISSOURI

LEGEND
- ⊛ State Capital
- ⊙ County Seat
- ✈ Airport
- ■ Point of Interest
- ⬚ Park, Forest, Reservation

Springfield Over 100,000
Columbia 50,000-100,000
Ferguson 20,000-50,000
Hannibal 10,000-20,000
Ste. Genevieve Under 10,000
TANEY County Name

SCALE
0   20   40 Miles
0   20   40 Kms

native-born and 88% of all state residents. Major resident groups claimed first languages as follows:

	NATIVE-BORN	FOREIGN-BORN
English	4,095,112	10,496
German	161,787	16,567
Italian	24,690	6,299
Spanish	18,374	5,107
French	12,110	1,870
Polish	11,870	2,298
Yiddish	11,869	4,362

[9] RELIGIONS

Beginning in the late 17th century, French missionaries brought Roman Catholicism to what is now Missouri; the first permanent Roman Catholic church was built about 1755 at Ste. Genevieve. Immigration from Germany, Ireland, Italy, and eastern Europe swelled the Catholic population during the 19th century, and Roman Catholicism remains the largest Christian denomination. Baptist preachers crossed the Mississippi River into Missouri in the late 1790s, and the state's first Methodist church was organized about 1806. Immigrants from Germany included not only Roman Catholics but also many Lutherans, the most conservative of whom organized the Lutheran Church–Missouri Synod in 1847. By 1979, the Missouri Synod, with its headquarters in St. Louis, had a total US baptized membership of 2,623,181.

In 1979, Missouri had 783,098 Roman Catholics, of whom 526,398 were in the archdiocese of St. Louis. There were 1,636,508 known Protestant adherents in 1971, the principal denominations being the Southern Baptist Convention, with 626,279; United Methodist Church, 286,967; Lutheran Church–Missouri Synod, 153,932; and the Christian Church (Disciples of Christ), 107,837. In 1979, Missouri's estimated Jewish population was 73,335, with about 75% in the St. Louis area and nearly 25% in the Kansas City vicinity.

[10] TRANSPORTATION

Centrally located, Missouri is a leading US transportation center. Both St. Louis and Kansas City are hubs of rail, truck, and airline transportation.

In 1836, delegates from 11 counties met in St. Louis to recommend construction of two railroad lines and to petition Congress for a grant of 800,000 acres (324,000 hectares) of public land on which to build them. More than a dozen companies were incorporated by the legislature, but they all collapsed with the financial panic of 1837. Interest in railroad construction revived during the following decade, and in 1849 a national railroad convention was held in St. Louis at which nearly 1,000 delegates from 13 states recommended the construction of a transcontinental railroad. By 1851, three railroad lines had been chartered, and construction by the Pacific Railroad at St. Louis was under way; the Pacific line reached Kansas City in 1865, and a bridge built over the Missouri River four years later enabled Kansas City to link up with the Hannibal and St. Joseph Railroad, providing a freight route to Chicago that did not pass through St. Louis. By 1974, the state had 6,082 mi (9,788 km) of rail lines. Amtrak provides passenger service directly from Chicago to St. Louis and to Kansas City, and between those two terminals via Jefferson City.

The first road developed in colonial Missouri was probably a trail between the lead mines and Ste. Genevieve in the early 1700s. A two-level cantilever bridge—the first in the world to have a steel superstructure—spanning the Mississippi at St. Louis was dedicated on 4 July 1874. By 1978 there were 117,550 mi (189,179 km) of roadway. The main interstate highways were I-70, linking St. Louis with Kansas City; I-44, connecting St. Louis with Springfield and Joplin; I-55, linking St. Louis with Chicago, Ill., to the north and paralleling the course of the Mississippi between St. Louis and Memphis, Tenn.; I-35, connecting Kansas City with Des Moines, Iowa; and I-29, paralleling the Missouri

River north of Kansas City. Motor vehicle registration for the state in 1978 was 3,245,088, including 2,360,828 passenger cars, 787,913 trucks, and 9,294 buses; 3,163,722 driver's licenses were in force during the same year.

The Mississippi and Missouri rivers have long been important transportation routes. Pirogues, keelboats, and flatboats plied these waterways for more than a century before the first steamboat, the *New Orleans*, traveled down the Mississippi in 1811. The Mississippi still serves considerable barge traffic, making metropolitan St. Louis one of the nation's most active inland port areas.

Pioneering aviators in Missouri organized the first international balloon races in 1907, and the first US-sponsored international aviation meet in 1910. Five St. Louis pilots made up the earliest US Army air corps, and a barnstorming pilot named Charles A. Lindbergh, having spent a few years in the St. Louis area, had the backing of businessmen from that city when he flew his *Spirit of St. Louis* across the Atlantic in 1927. Today, Kansas City International Airport and Lambert–St. Louis Municipal Airport are among the busiest airports in the country. These two emplaned 2,789,820 and 4,714,822 passengers, respectively, in 1978, when the state had 116 public and 255 private airfields.

[11] HISTORY

The region we now call Missouri has been inhabited for at least 4,000 years. The prehistoric Woodland peoples left low burial mounds, rudimentary pottery, arrowheads, and grooved axes; remains of the later Mississippian Culture include more sophisticated pottery and finely chipped arrowheads. When the first Europeans arrived in the late 17th century, most of the few thousand Indians living in Missouri were relatively recent immigrants, pushed westward across the Mississippi River because of pressures from eastern tribes and European settlers along the Atlantic coast. Indians then occupying Missouri belonged to two main linguistic groups: Algonkian-speakers, mainly the Sauk, Fox, and Iliniwek (Illinois) in the northeast; and a Siouan group, including the Osage, Missouri, Iowa, Kansa, and other tribes, to the south and west. Of greatest interest to the Europeans were the Osage, among whom were warriors and runners of extraordinary ability. The flood of white settlers into Missouri after 1803 forced the Indians to move into Kansas and into what became known as Indian Territory (present-day Oklahoma). During the 1820s, the US government negotiated treaties with the Osage, Sauk, Fox, and Iowa tribes whereby they surrendered, for the most part peaceably, all their lands in Missouri. By 1836, few Indians remained.

The first white men to pass through land eventually included within Missouri's boundaries apparently were Jacques Marquette and Louis Jolliet, who in 1673 passed the mouth of the Missouri River on their journey down the Mississippi; so did Robert Cavelier, Sieur de la Salle, who claimed the entire Mississippi Valley for France in 1682. Probably the first Frenchman to explore the Missouri River was Louis Armand de Lom d'Arce, Baron de Lahontan, who in 1688 claimed to have reached the junction of the Missouri and Osage rivers. The French did little to develop the Missouri region during the first half of the 18th century, although a few fur traders and priests established posts and missions among the Indians. A false report that silver had been discovered set off a brief mining boom in which no silver but some lead—available in abundance—was extracted. Missouri passed into Spanish hands with the rest of the Louisiana Territory in 1762, but development was still guided by French settlers; in 1764, the French fur trader Pierre Laclède established a trading post on the present site of St. Louis.

Although Spain fortified St. Louis and a few other outposts during the American Revolution and beat back a British-Indian attack on St. Louis in 1780, the Spanish did not attempt to settle

Missouri. However, they did allow Americans to migrate freely into the territory. Spanish authorities granted free land to the new settlers, relaxed their restrictions against Protestants, and welcomed slaveholding families from southern states, especially important after 1787, when slavery was banned in the Northwest Territory. Pioneers such as Daniel Boone arrived from Kentucky, and the Chouteau fur-trading family gained a lucrative monopoly among the Osage. Spanish rule ended abruptly in 1800 when Napoleon forced Spain to return Louisiana to France. Included in the Louisiana Purchase, Missouri then became part of the US in 1803. After the Lewis and Clark expedition (1804–6) had successfully explored the Missouri River, Missouri in general—and St. Louis in particular—became the gateway to the West.

Missouri was part of the Louisiana Territory (with headquarters at St. Louis) until 1 October 1812, when Missouri Territory (including present-day Arkansas, organized separately in 1819) was established. A flood of settlers between 1810 and 1820 more than tripled Missouri's population from 19,783 to 66,586, leading Missourians to petition the US Congress for statehood as early as 1818. But Congress, divided over the slavery issue, withheld permission for three years, finally approving statehood for Maine and Missouri under the terms of the Missouri Compromise (1820), which sanctioned slavery in the new state but banned it in the rest of the former Louisiana Territory north of Arkansas. Congress further required that Missouri make no effort to enforce a state constitutional ban on the immigration of free Negroes and mulattoes; once the legislature complied, Missouri became the 24th state on 10 August 1821. Alexander McNair became the state's first governor, and Thomas Hart Benton was one of the state's first two US senators; Benton remained an important political leader for more than three decades.

Aided by the advent of steamboat travel on the Mississippi and Missouri rivers, settlers continued to arrive in the new state, whose population surpassed 1 million by 1860. The site for a new capital, Jefferson City, was selected in 1821, and five years later the legislature met there for the first time. French fur traders settled the present site of Kansas City in 1821, and established a trading post at St. Joseph in 1827. Mormons came to Independence during the early 1830s but were expelled from the state and crossed the Mississippi back into Illinois. For much of the antebellum period, the state's economy flourished, with an emphasis on cotton, cattle, minerals (especially lead and zinc), and commerce—notably the outfitting of wagon trains for the Santa Fe and Oregon trails. On the eve of the Civil War, more than half the population consisted of Missouri natives; 15% of the white population was foreign-born, chiefly German and Irish. Black slaves represented only 9% of the total population—the lowest proportion of any slave state except Delaware—while only about 25,000 Missourians were slaveholders. Nevertheless, there was a great deal of proslavery sentiment in the state, and thousands of Missourians crossed into neighboring Kansas in the mid-1850s to help elect a proslavery government in that territory. State residents were also active in the guerrilla warfare between proslavery forces and Free Staters that erupted along the border with "bleeding Kansas." The slavery controversy was exacerbated by the US Supreme Court's 1857 decision in the case of Dred Scott, a slave formerly owned by a Missourian who had temporarily brought him to what is now Minnesota, where slavery was prohibited; Scott's suit to obtain his freedom was denied by the Court on the grounds that it was unconstitutional to restrict the property rights of slaveholders, in a decision that voided the Missouri Compromise reached 37 years earlier.

During the Civil War, Missouri remained loyal to the Union, though not without difficulty. When the conflict began, Governor Claiborne Fox Jackson called out the state militia "to repel the invasion" of federal forces, but pro-Union leaders such as

Francis P. Blair deposed Jackson on 30 July 1861. Missouri supplied some 110,000 soldiers to the Union and 40,000 to the Confederacy. As devastating as the battles fought on Missouri soil was the general lawlessness that prevailed throughout the state; pro-Confederate guerrilla bands led by William Quantrill and Cole Younger, as well as Unionist freebooters, murdered and looted without hindrance. In October 1864, a Confederate army under Major General Sterling Price was defeated at the Battle of Westport, on the outskirts of Kansas City, ending the main military action. At a constitutional convention held in January 1865, Missouri became the first slave state to free all blacks.

During Reconstruction, the Radical Republicans sought to disfranchise all citizens who failed to swear that they had never aided or sympathized with the Confederacy. But the harshness of this and other measures caused a backlash, and Liberal Republicans such as Benjamin Gratz Brown and Carl Schurz, allied with the Democrats, succeeded in ousting the Radicals by 1872. The subsequent decline of the Liberal Republicans inaugurated a period during which Democrats occupied the governorship uninterruptedly for more than three decades.

The 1870s saw a period of renewed lawlessness, typified by the exploits of Jesse and Frank James, that earned Missouri the epithet of the "robber state." Of more lasting importance were the closing of the frontier in Missouri, the decline of the fur trade and steamboat traffic, and the rise of the railroads, shifting the market economy from St. Louis to Kansas City, whose population tripled during the 1880s, while St. Louis was eclipsed by Chicago as a center of finance, commerce, transportation, and population. Missouri farmers generally supported the movement for free silver coinage, along with other Populist policies such as railroad regulation. Reform Governor Joseph W. Folk (1905–9) fostered the "Missouri idea" that all people really needed were honest leaders to enforce simple laws, and his immediate successors in the statehouse, Herbert S. Hadley (1909–13) and Elliott W. Major (1913–17), introduced progressive policies to Missouri. However, the ideal of honest government was soon subverted by Kansas City's corrupt political machine, under Thomas J. Pendergast, the most powerful Democrat in the state between the two world wars. Machine politics did not prevent capable politicians from rising to prominence—among them Harry S Truman, Missouri's first and thus far only native son to serve in the nation's highest office.

With the decline in Missouri's rural population from about three-fourths of the total in 1880 to less than one-third by 1970, the state's economy increasingly shifted from agriculture to industry. Although the overall importance of mining declined, Missouri remained the world's top lead producer, and the state has emerged as 2d only to Michigan in US automobile manufacturing. Postwar prosperity was threatened during the 1960s by the deterioration of several large cities, notably St. Louis, although Kansas City benefited from a building boom; both St. Louis and Kansas City subsequently undertook urban renewal programs to cope with the serious problems of air pollution, traffic congestion, crime, and substandard housing. During the 1970s, smaller metropolitan regions such as Springfield-Joplin and Jefferson City–Columbia experienced similar problems on a lesser scale.

¹²STATE GOVERNMENT

Missouri's first constitutional convention met in St. Louis on 12 May 1820, and on 19 July a constitution was adopted. The constitution was rewritten in 1865 and again in 1875, the latter document remaining in effect until 1945, when another new constitution was enacted and the state government reorganized. A subsequent reorganization, effective 1 July 1974, replaced some 90 independent agencies with 13 cabinet departments and the Office of Administration.

The legislative branch, or general assembly, consists of a 34-member senate and a 163-seat house of representatives. Senators are elected to staggered four-year terms, representatives for two; the age requirement for a senator is 30, for a representative 24. The state's elected executives are the governor and lieutenant governor (who run separately), secretary of state, auditor, treasurer, and attorney general; all serve four-year terms. The governor must be at least 30 years of age and must have been a US citizen for 15 years and a Missouri resident for 10 years prior to election.

A bill becomes law when signed by the governor within 15 days of legislative passage. A two-thirds vote by both houses is required to override a gubernatorial veto. Except for appropriations or emergency measures, laws may not take effect until 90 days after the end of the legislative session at which they were enacted. Constitutional amendments require a majority vote of both houses of the legislature and ratification by the voters at the next general election.

To vote in Missouri, one must be a US citizen and at least 18 years of age; the residency requirement is 30 days.

¹³POLITICAL PARTIES

The major political groups in Missouri are the Democratic Party and the Republican Party, each affiliated with the national party organization. Prior to 1825, the state had no organized political parties, and candidates ran as independents; however, each of Missouri's first four governors called himself a Jeffersonian Republican, allying himself with the national group from which the modern Democratic Party traces its origins. Except for the Civil War and Reconstruction periods, the Democratic Party held the governorship from the late 1820s to the early 1900s. Ten Democrats and six Republicans served in the statehouse from 1908 through 1980. The outstanding figures of 20th-century Missouri politics are both Democrats: Thomas Pendergast, the Kansas City machine boss whose commitment to construction projects bore no small relation to his involvement with a concrete manufacturing firm; and Harry S Truman, who began his political career as a Jackson County judge in the Kansas City area and in 1945 became 33d president of the US.

As of 1978, Missouri had 2,553,574 registered voters; there is no party registration. The state, which had voted for the Republican nominee only 3 times in the previous 14 presidential elections and had supported Democrat Jimmy Carter in 1976, gave 51% of its popular vote in the 1980 election to Republican Ronald Reagan. At the same time, Republican Christopher S. "Kit" Bond defeated the incumbent Democratic governor, Joseph P. Teasdale, who in 1976 had beaten Bond in a race for the same office. The voters also reelected Democratic Senator Thomas Eagleton and approved an amendment linking state tax increases to the rise in the consumer price index.

¹⁴LOCAL GOVERNMENT

As of 1977, Missouri had 114 counties, 916 municipalities, 326 townships, 574 school districts, and over 1,000 special districts.

Elected county officials generally include a public administrator, prosecuting attorney, sheriff, collector of revenue, assessor, treasurer, and coroner. The city of St. Louis, which is administratively independent of any county, has an elected mayor, comptroller, and a 29-member board of aldermen (including the president); the circuit attorney, city treasurer, sheriff, and collector of revenue, also elected, perform functions analogous to county officers. Most other cities are governed by an elected mayor and council, but as of 1980, Kansas City and 34 other communities additionally had appointed city managers.

¹⁵STATE SERVICES

Under the 1974 reorganization plan, educational services are provided through the Department of Elementary and Secondary Education and the Department of Higher Education. Within the former's jurisdiction are the state schools for the deaf, the blind, and the mentally retarded; adult education programs; teacher certification; and the general supervision of instruction in the state. The department is headed by a board of education whose eight members are appointed by the governor to eight-year terms; the board, in turn, appoints the commissioner of education, the department's chief executive officer. The Department of Higher Education—governed by a nine-member appointive board that selects the commissioner of higher education—sets financial guidelines for state colleges and universities, authorizes the establishment of new senior colleges and residency centers, and establishes academic, admissions, residency, and transfer policies. Transportation services are under the direction of the Department of Transportation, which is responsible for aviation, railroads, mass transit, and water transport, and the Department of Highways, which operates and maintains the state highway system. The Department of Revenue licenses all road vehicles and motor vehicle operators.

Missouri Presidential Vote by Political Parties, 1948–80

YEAR	ELECTORAL VOTE	MISSOURI WINNER	DEMOCRAT	REPUBLICAN	PROGRESSIVE	SOCIALIST
1948	15	*Truman (D)	917,315	655,039	3,998	2,222
1952	13	*Eisenhower (R)	929,830	959,429	—	—
1956	13	Stevenson (D)	918,273	914,289	—	—
1960	13	*Kennedy (D)	972,201	962,218	—	—
1964	12	*Johnson (D)	1,164,344	653,535	—	—
					AMERICAN IND.	
1968	12	*Nixon (R)	791,444	811,932	206,126	—
1972	12	*Nixon (R)	698,531	1,154,058	—	—
1976	12	*Carter (D)	998,387	927,443	—	—
					LIBERTARIAN	SOC. WORKERS
1980	12	*Reagan (R)	931,182	1,074,181	14,422	1,515

*Won US presidential election.

Health and welfare services are provided primarily through the Department of Social Services, which oversees all state programs concerning public health, public assistance, corrections, probation and parole, veterans' affairs, and the aging. The Department of Mental Health operates 5 state mental hospitals, 3 community mental health centers, and 14 other facilities throughout the state, providing care for the emotionally disturbed, the mentally retarded, alcoholics, and drug abusers. Among the many responsibilities of the Department of Consumer Affairs, Regulation, and Licensing are enforcement of antidiscrimination laws, development of low- and moderate-income housing, and provision of financial aid to private nonprofit hospitals and higher educational facilities.

Administered within the Department of Public Safety are the Missouri State Highway Patrol, National Guard, and civil defense, water safety, and alcoholic beverage control programs. The Department of Labor and Industrial Relations administers unemployment insurance benefits and workers' compensation. The lieutenant governor is designated as state ombudsman and volunteer coordinator.

[16]JUDICIAL SYSTEM

As of 1980, the supreme court, the state's highest court, consisted of seven judges and three commissioners. Judges are selected by the governor from three nominees proposed by a nonpartisan judicial commission; after an interval of at least 12 months, the appointment must be ratified by the voters on a separate nonpartisan ballot. The justices, who serve 12-year terms, select one of their number to act as chief justice. Commissioners, serving 4-year terms, were authorized in 1911 to alleviate the court's heavy workload; they may hear cases along with the justices, and their opinions, if approved by the court, may be issued as opinions of that body. When the present commissioners die or leave office for other reasons, they will be replaced by judges of the court of appeals. The mandatory retirement age is 70 for all judges in state courts.

The court of appeals, consisting of 29 judges in three districts, assumed its present structure by constitutional amendment in 1970. The eastern district, sitting in St. Louis, consists of 12 judges; the western district, in Kansas City, has 10; and the southern district, in either Springfield or Poplar Bluff, has 7. All appellate judges are selected for 12-year terms in the same manner as the supreme court justices.

The circuit court is the main trial court. Circuit court judges serve 6-year terms; in 1979 there were 132 judges in 43 circuits. Although many circuit court judges are still popularly elected, judges in St. Louis, Kansas City, and some other areas are selected on a nonpartisan basis.

The Division of Corrections of the Department of Social Services operates the Missouri State Penitentiary (Jefferson City), six other correctional facilities, and two urban "honor centers" (St. Louis and Kansas City) designed to help convicts become reintegrated into the community. As of 1977 there were 5,302 inmates in Missouri federal and state prisons. Crime rates for the state as a whole are generally at or below the national norm, but much higher in St. Louis, whose 1978 murder rate—46 per 100,000 residents—was the highest of any large US city. The rate for 1979 increased to 57 per 100,000; about 84% of the victims were black.

[17]ARMED FORCES

Missouri has played a key role in national defense since World War II, partly because of the influence of Stuart Symington, first as secretary of the Air Force (1947–50) and later as an influential member of the Senate Armed Services Committee. During 1977/78, authorized Department of Defense personnel at principal bases in Missouri totaled 26,030. Installations include Ft. Leonard Wood, near Rolla; Richards-Gebaur Air Force Base, Belton; and Whiteman AFB, Knob Noster. The Defense Map-

ping Agency Aerospace Center is in St. Louis. Defense contract awards for the same fiscal year totaled $3 billion (5th in the US).

There were 709,000 veterans living in the state as of 30 September 1979. Of these, 16,000 saw service in World War I, 300,000 in World War II, 135,000 in the Korean conflict, and 207,000 during the Viet-Nam era. Veterans' benefits amounted to $449.6 million in 1977/78, of which $206.8 million consisted of compensation and pensions.

Missouri had 10,400 National Guard personnel in 1978, and 13,425 state and local police employees in 1977. The 71st Fighter Wing, recognized by the federal government on 3 July 1946, was one of the first Air National Guard Units in the US.

[18]MIGRATION

Missouri's first European immigrants, French fur traders and missionaries, began settling in the state in the early 18th century. Under Spain, Missouri received few Spanish settlers, but many immigrants from the eastern US. During the 19th century, newcomers continued to arrive from the South and the East—slave-owning southerners (with their black slaves) as well as New Englanders opposed to slavery. They were joined by a wave of European immigrants, notably Germans and, later, Italians. By 1850, one out of three St. Louis residents was German-born; of all foreign-born Missourians in the late 1800s, more than half came from Germany.

More recently, the state has been losing population through migration—334,000 emigrated between 1940 and 1977. The dominant intrastate migration pattern has been the concentration of blacks in the major cities, especially St. Louis and Kansas City, and the exodus of whites from those same cities to the suburbs and, more recently, to small towns and rural areas.

[19]INTERGOVERNMENTAL COOPERATION

The Commission on Interstate Cooperation, established by the state legislature in 1941, represents Missouri before the Council of State Governments and its allied organizations. Regional agreements in which the state participates include boundary compacts with Arkansas, Iowa, and Kansas and various accords governing bridges across the Mississippi and Missouri rivers. Representatives from both Missouri and Kansas take part in the Kansas City Area Transportation Authority, which operates public transportation in the metropolitan region, embracing seven counties, four of them (Cass, Clay, Jackson, and Platte) in Missouri. Missouri also belongs to the Southern Interstate Energy Compact Commission and many other multistate bodies.

Federal aid to Missouri in 1978/79 was estimated at $1.5 billion, of which $128.7 million was general revenue sharing.

[20]ECONOMY

Missouri's central location and access to the Mississippi River contributed to its growth as a commercial center. By the mid-1700s, the state's first permanent settlement at Ste. Genevieve was shipping lead, furs, salt, pork, lard, bacon, bear grease, feathers, flour and grain, and other products to distant markets. The introduction of steamboat traffic on the Mississippi, western migration along the Santa Fe and Oregon trails, and the rise of the railroads spurred the growth of commerce during the 19th century. Flour and grist mills, breweries and whiskey distilleries, and meat-packing establishments were among the state's early industrial enterprises. Lead mining has been profitable since the early 19th century. Grain growing was well established by the mid-18th century, and tobacco was a leading crop 100 years later.

Missouri's economy remains diversified, with manufacturing, farming, trade, tourism, and mining as prime sources of income. Today, automobile manufacturing is by far the state's leading industry, while cattle, soybeans, hogs, and dairy items are the most important agricultural products. The state's historic past, varied topography, and modern urban attractions—notably the Gateway Arch in St. Louis—have made tourism a growth industry in recent decades. Mining, employing less than 1% of the state's nonagricultural workers, is no longer as important as it once was, although the state remains the leading US producer of lead and ranks 2d in the US in zinc production. The economic impact of state and local government and of defense-related federal expenditures has increased enormously since World War II.

21 INCOME

With an income per capita of $7,342 in 1978, Missouri ranked 31st among the 50 states. Total personal income was $35.7 billion, representing a real increase of 28% since 1970, when Missouri ranked 28th; the state had placed 23d in 1960. Median family income was $13,011 in 1975 (32d in the US), when 565,000 Missourians were below the federal poverty level.

22 LABOR

In 1978, Missouri's civilian labor force totaled 2,262,000, of whom 1,294,000 were male and 968,000 female; 2,148,000 were employed and 114,000 (5%) unemployed. By occupation, clerical workers made up about 17% of the labor force; professional and technical workers, 15%; service workers, 14%; crafts workers, 11%; machine operators (except transport), 11%; nonfarm managers and administrators, 10%; sales workers, 7%; nonfarm laborers, 6%; farm workers, 5%; and transport equipment operators, 4%. More than half of all unemployed workers in Missouri were in the St. Louis area in 1978, and about one-fourth in the Kansas City region. The economic impact of layoffs in 1980 at automobile plants around St. Louis was forecast at a loss of 26,700 jobs and $380 million in personal income.

A federal census of workers covered by unemployment insurance in March 1977 revealed the following nonfarm employment pattern for Missouri:

	ESTABLISH-MENTS	EMPLOYEES	ANNUAL PAYROLL ('000)
Agricultural services, forestry, fishing	890	4,456	$ 36,013
Mining	338	9,148	145,076
Contract construction	9,546	74,415	1,151,033
Manufacturing, of which:	6,773	436,695	5,807,119
Food and food products	(588)	(39,347)	(528,455)
Transportation equipment	(187)	(69,812)	(1,279,435)
Transportation, public utilities	4,115	110,396	1,738,928
Wholesale trade	9,884	120,410	1,614,811
Retail trade	29,354	304,197	2,093,843
Finance, insurance, real estate	9,240	101,598	1,076,329
Services	27,146	329,143	2,789,667
Other	1,338	1,694	20,643
TOTALS	98,624	1,492,152	$16,473,462

The survey did not include government employees, who numbered about 336,700 (20% federal) during 1978.

As early as the 1830s, journeyman laborers and mechanics in St. Louis, seeking higher wages and shorter hours, banded together to form trade unions and achieved some of their demands. Attempts to establish a workingman's party were unsuccessful, however, and immigration during subsequent decades ensured a plentiful supply of cheap labor. Union activity increased in the 1870s, partly because of the influence of German socialists. The Knights of Labor took a leading role in the labor movement from 1879 to 1887, the year that saw the birth of the St. Louis Trades and Labor Assembly; one year later, the American Federation of Labor came to St. Louis for its third annual convention, with Samuel Gompers presiding. The Missouri State Federation of Labor was formed in 1891, at a convention in Kansas City. By 1916, the state had 915 unions. Missouri remains a strong union state: 572,000 Missourians, representing 32% of the nonagricultural work force, belonged to labor organizations in 1976. Another 21,000 state residents were in employee associations.

23 AGRICULTURE

Missouri's agricultural income reached $4.2 billion in 1979, 9th among the 50 states. Of this total, about one-fourth came from soybeans, of which Missouri is the nation's 3d-leading producer. Soybean production is concentrated mainly in the northern counties and in the extreme southeast, with New Madrid County the leading producer in 1979. Saline County led the state in corn production, Barton County in wheat, and Stoddard County in grain sorghum.

All crops (including those used on farms as food or feed) had a value of $2.5 billion in 1978/79, including $1.1 billion from soybeans, $537.4 million from corn, $268 million from winter wheat, $128.7 million from grain sorghum, and $46.5 million from cotton. Farmers harvested 228.7 million bushels of corn, 186.8 million bushels of soybeans, 70.4 million bushels of winter wheat, 68 million bushels of grain sorghum, and 157,000 bales of cotton. Tobacco, hay, rice, apples, peaches, grapes, watermelons, and various seed crops are also grown in commercial quantities; Missouri leads the nation in the production of tall fescue seed and lespedeza seed.

24 ANIMAL HUSBANDRY

Cash receipts from sales of livestock and livestock products totaled $2.4 billion in 1979, accounting for 57% of Missouri's agricultural income. Hog raising is concentrated north of the Missouri River, cattle raising in the western counties, and dairy farming in the southwest. During 1979, Missouri ranked 6th in the US in number of beef cattle and calves, 5th in hogs and pigs, and 10th in milk cows.

In 1979, Missouri farms and ranches had 5.4 million cattle and calves, 4.6 million hogs, 7.7 million chickens (of which 6.2 million were hens and pullets of laying age), and 11 million turkeys. Some 1.9 billion lb of cattle valued at more than $1.3 billion were slaughtered in 1979, along with 1.6 billion lb of hogs worth $653.5 million. The state's 270,000 milk cows yielded 2.7 billion lb of milk. Other livestock products in 1979 included 211.3 million lb of turkeys, 120.7 million lb of chickens and broilers, 1.4 billion eggs, and 7.9 million lb of honey.

25 FISHING

Commercial fishing takes place mainly on the Mississippi, Missouri, and St. Francis rivers. In 1978, according to state data, 1,000,283 lb of fish valued at $242,849 were harvested from these three waterways: about 66% from the Mississippi, 33% from the Missouri, and 1% from the St. Francis. The harvest included 339,540 lb of buffalo species, 292,818 lb of carp, and 222,812 lb of catfish. Sport fishing is enjoyed throughout the state, but especially in the Ozarks, whose waters harbor walleye, rainbow trout, bluegill, and largemouth bass.

26 FORESTRY

As of 1977, Missouri had 12,876,000 acres (5,211,000 hectares) of forestland, of which more than 95% was commercial forest, about five-sixths of it privately owned. Most of Missouri's forestland is in the southeastern third of the state. Of the commercial forests, approximately two-thirds are of the oak/hickory type; shortleaf pine and oak/pine forests comprise about 7%, while the remainder consists of cedar and bottomland hardwoods.

According to the Forestry Division of the Department of Conservation, Missouri leads the US in the production of charcoal, cedar novelties, gunstocks, and walnut bowls and nutmeats; railroad ties, veneers, wine and beer casks, and other forest-related items are also produced. Timber production in 1979 totaled 650 million board feet, and shipments of all lumber and wood products in 1977 were valued at $357.1 million.

Some 250,000 acres (101,000 hectares) of state forests, managed by the Forestry Division, are used for timber production, wildlife and watershed protection, hunting, fishing, and other recreational purposes. A state-run nursery sells seedling trees and shrubs to Missouri landowners. Missouri's one national forest, Mark Twain in the southeast, encompassed 1,445,747 acres (585,075 hectares) of National Forest System lands as of 30 September 1979.

²⁷MINING

The estimated value of Missouri's mineral output in 1978 was $923 million, 22d among the 50 states. Lead is far and away the leading mineral product: the state's mines extracted 87% of the US total in 1978, and if Missouri were a separate country, only the Soviet Union would rival it as a world producer.

The estimated output of principal mineral products in 1978 included lead, 461,762 tons; zinc, 65,060 tons (2d only to Tennessee); copper, 11,925 tons; silver, 2,056 troy oz; cement, 4,756,000 tons; stone, 51,802,000 tons; sand and gravel, 15,000,000 tons; and lime, 1,782,000 tons. Iron ore, barite, clays, phosphate rock, asphalt, and small quantities of fossil fuels are also extracted.

²⁸ENERGY AND POWER

Missouri's electric power plants had an installed generating capacity of 13.9 million kw in 1978, when electrical output totaled 46.2 billion kwh, 57% more than in 1970. Sales of electric power, both private and public, totaled 36.6 billion kwh in 1977, of which 14.5 billion kwh went to residential users, 10.7 billion kwh to commercial users, 10.3 billion kwh to industrial users, and 1.1 billion kwh for other purposes. Coal-fired plants accounted for more than 90% of all power production in 1978; the state has no nuclear facilities.

Fossil fuel resources are limited. Reserves of bituminous coal totaled 5 billion tons as of 1 January 1976; 5.7 million tons were mined in 1978. Small quantities of crude petroleum and natural gas are also produced commercially. Gas utility industry revenues reached $699 million in 1978.

²⁹INDUSTRY

About one out of four nonfarm employees in Missouri is engaged in manufacturing. The leading industry groups, by employment, are transportation equipment (mainly automobiles and aerospace technology), food and food products, electric and electronic equipment, and fabricated metal products, together accounting for about 41% of all industrial jobs in 1977. Of the $12.8 billion in value added by manufacturing during the same year, transportation equipment accounted for 26%, food and food products 12%, chemicals 10%, electric and electronic equipment 7%, nonelectrical machinery 7%, fabricated metal products 7%, and all other sectors 31%.

The following table shows value added by selected industries in 1972 and 1977:

	1972	1977
Motor vehicles and car bodies	NA	$2,188,700,000
Soaps, cleaners, toiletries	$228,200,000	321,100,000
Grain mill products	143,200,000	308,200,000
Leather and leather products	NA	303,900,000
Drugs	165,700,000	288,600,000
Beverages	292,100,000	287,000,000
Dairy products	134,500,000	222,400,000
Blast furnace, basic steel products	138,300,000	215,100,000

St. Louis County, the city of St. Louis, and Jackson County (Kansas City) lead the state in manufacturing employment, together accounting for 60% of all industrial jobs. McDonnell-Douglas, with headquarters in St. Louis County, was the nation's 54th-ranked industrial corporation in 1979, with sales of $5.3 billion; its aerospace products have included all the Mercury capsules and Gemini space capsules. Other leading corporations headquartered in the St. Louis area are Monsanto, a chemical firm with 1979 sales of $6.2 billion (48th in the US); Ralston Purina, food and animal feed, $4.6 billion (67th); and General Dynamics, aerospace, $4.1 billion (83d). During the 1979 model year, Missouri automobile plants turned out 1,027,286 cars, 2d only to Michigan among the 50 states and 11% of the US total. Layoffs at the Chrysler, Ford, and General Motors facilities in

the St. Louis area in 1980 were a severe blow to the state's leading industry.

³⁰COMMERCE

Missouri has been one of the nation's leading trade centers ever since merchants in Independence (now part of the Kansas City metropolitan area) began provisioning wagon trains for the Santa Fe Trail. By 1972, wholesale trade was valued at $20.3 billion—9th in the US and 3d among the states west of the Mississippi River. Retail establishments had sales totaling $15.9 billion in 1977 (14th), of which automotive dealers accounted for 22%, food stores 21%, department stores 14%, gasoline service stations 9%, and eating and drinking places 8%. St. Louis County led all counties with 25% of total sales; the city of St. Louis accounted for another 9%. Kansas City led all cities with 11% of sales.

Foreign exports of Missouri agricultural commodities exceeded $1.1 billion in 1979, of which soybeans and soybean products accounted for 55%. Exports of manufactured goods were valued at more than $1.6 billion (15th in the US) in 1976.

³¹CONSUMER PROTECTION

The Department of Consumer Affairs, Regulation, and Licensing, created in 1974 through the consolidation of more than 30 state agencies, oversees community and economic development, regulates finance, insurance, and savings and loan institutions, and licenses such professions and occupations as accountancy, cosmetology, dentistry, medicine, nursing, pharmacy, and realty. The department's Office of Public Counsel represents consumer interests before the Public Service Commission, another branch of the department. In 1977, the department created the Consumer Information Center, which investigates all consumer complaints and publishes shopping guides.

³²BANKING

The first banks in Missouri, the Bank of St. Louis (established in 1816) and the Bank of Missouri (1817), had both failed by the time Missouri became a state, and the paper notes they had distributed proved worthless. Not until 1837 did the Missouri state government again permit a bank within its borders, and then only after filling its charter with elaborate restrictions. The Bank of Missouri, chartered for 20 years, kept its reputation for sound banking by issuing notes bearing the portrait of US Senator Thomas Hart Benton, nicknamed "Old Bullion" because of his extreme fiscal conservatism.

As of 1978, Missouri ranked 4th in the nation in the number of banks and 11th in total bank assets. The state had 714 insured commercial banks with assets totaling nearly $29 billion, outstanding loans of $9 billion, and deposits exceeding $23 billion. The state's largest commercial banks are the Mercantile Trust Co. and First National Bank (both in St. Louis), with assets in 1978 of $1.63 billion and $1.59 billion, respectively. During the same year, 29 multibank holding companies controlled 187 state-chartered banks with assets of $8 billion, and one-bank holding companies controlled 82 state-chartered banks with assets of nearly $2.2 billion. Assets of the state's 112 savings and loan associations in 1978 totaled $13.6 billion, and outstanding mortgage loans reached $11.2 billion. In addition, there were 370 state-chartered credit unions with $827 million in assets, as well as 421 small-loan offices, 41 financing institutions, and 77 motor vehicle time sales companies.

³³INSURANCE

In 1979, 1,195 insurance firms were doing business in Missouri, of which 128 were domiciled in the state. There were approximately 50,000 licensed agents and 7,500 licensed brokers.

Premiums written in Missouri in 1979 totaled more than $3.7 billion for all types of insurance, including $857.8 million in direct premiums for life insurance. About 8.9 million life insurance policies valued at $63.2 billion were in force at the close of 1978. The average coverage per family was $33,700, 4% below the US norm. Payouts totaled $654.1 million, of which death payments accounted for \$242.8 million, annuities \$152.5 million, and policy dividends \$138.7 million.

Companies licensed to write accident and health insurance in Missouri numbered 804 in 1979. Property and casualty companies wrote premiums totaling \$1.6 billion in 1978, including \$388.6 million in automotive liability insurance, \$304.1 million in automotive physical damage insurance, and \$169.2 million in homeowners' coverage. Flood insurance amounting to \$341.4 million was in force as of mid-1979.

³⁴SECURITIES
The Missouri Uniform Securities Act, also known as the "Blue Sky Law," and administered by the Securities Division of the Office of Secretary of State, requires the registration of stocks, bonds, debentures, notes, investment contracts, and oil, gas, and mining interests intended for sale in the state. In cases of fraud, misrepresentation, or other failure to comply with the act, the Missouri investor has the right to sue to recover the investment cost plus interest and legal fees. Government securities, stocks listed on the principal national exchanges, and securities sold under specific transactional agreements are exempt from registration.

Missouri has approximately 6,500 broker-dealers, agents, and investment advisers, all of whom, by law, must register with the state annually. Missourians reported \$531.7 million in dividend income on their 1977 federal tax returns. The state has no stock exchanges of its own.

³⁵PUBLIC FINANCE
The Missouri state budget is prepared by the Office of Administration's Division of Budget and Planning and submitted annually by the governor to the general assembly for amendment and approval. The fiscal year runs from 1 July to 30 June.

The following table summarizes estimated consolidated revenues and expenditures for 1979/80 and the proposed budget for 1980/81 (in millions):

	1979/80	1980/81
REVENUES		
Sales and use tax	\$ 769.4	\$ 817.8
Individual income tax	705.7	813.6
Corporate income tax	122.5	142.2
Insurance tax	56.4	62.9
Liquor and beer taxes	28.1	29.5
Inheritance tax	25.7	29.1
Corporation franchise tax	25.2	27.6
Interest on deposits and investments	34.9	39.4
Federal aid	1,298.6	1,275.6
Other funds	841.8	939.4
TOTALS	\$3,908.3	\$4,177.1
EXPENDITURES		
Human services	\$1,201.9	\$1,253.2
Elementary and secondary education	859.1	1,000.6
Higher education	309.8	347.9
Transportation and law enforcement	635.5	659.4
Natural and economic resources	293.5	278.2
Capital investments	102.9	121.1
Debt service	14.9	18.5
Other outlays	490.7	498.2
TOTALS	\$3,908.3	\$4,177.1

During 1976/77, St. Louis had general revenues of \$295 million and expenditures of \$269 million; the gross debt as of 30 June 1977 was \$163 million. Kansas City had general revenues of \$254 million, expenditures of \$235 million, and an outstanding debt of \$318 million for the 1977 fiscal year. The combined debt of the Missouri state and local governments in mid-1977 was \$3.1 billion, or \$644 per capita, well below the US average for the same period.

³⁶TAXATION
Missouri's total state tax revenues, traditionally low, ranked 21st in the nation in 1978. On a per capita basis, the state tax burden of \$548 ranked 49th in the US in 1977, exceeding only New Hampshire's.

The Missouri personal income tax in 1980 ranged from 1.5% on the first \$1,000 to 6% on amounts over \$9,000; the corporate tax rate was 5% of net income. The basic state sales tax is 3.125%; cities and towns may add an additional tax (St. Louis adds 1%, Kansas City 0.5%). Other taxes levied by the state include charges on motor fuel, cigarettes, and alcoholic beverages, along with motor vehicle and operator's license fees and taxes on credit institutions, insurance companies, and inheritances. Property and sales taxes are the leading sources of local revenue; St. Louis and Kansas City also levy income taxes of 1% within their respective jurisdictions.

During 1975/76, Missouri contributed \$6.6 billion in federal taxes and received \$8.8 billion in federal expenditures, for a spending/tax ratio of 1.33, one of the highest in the US. Missourians filed 1,851,806 federal tax returns for 1977, paying \$3.2 billion in tax.

³⁷ECONOMIC POLICY
Primary responsibility for economic development is vested in the Department of Consumer Affairs, Regulation, and Licensing, and especially in its Division of Commerce and Industrial Development, which seeks outside investment in the state, promotes the national and international marketing of Missouri products, provides technical assistance to existing businesses, and maintains an office in Düsseldorf in the Federal Republic of Germany. The division reported the creation in 1978 of 12,049 new jobs in 71 new plants and 78 expanding facilities. The Division of Community Development, within the same department, offers information, technical aid, and other public resources to foster local and regional planning. Special programs are provided for the Ozarks region and to rehabilitate urban neighborhoods.

General incentives for business include the state's reputation for fiscal conservatism, wage rates no better than the national average, and a tax structure toward which the corporate income tax contributes only about 3%.

³⁸HEALTH
The average life expectancy for both sexes in Missouri during 1969–71 was 70.69 years, 26th highest among the 50 states and close to the national average; 74.66 was the average life expectancy figure for women, 66.88 for men. The infant mortality rates in 1977 were 12.4 per 1,000 live births for whites and 23.6 for nonwhites; both rates were above the national norm. There were 14,900 legal abortions performed in 1977/78; the rate of 194 abortions per 1,000 live births was less than half the US average.

The overall death rate of 10.2 per 1,000 population in 1977 was among the highest in the US that year—a phenomenon attributable in part to the relatively high proportion of elderly Missourians in the population as a whole. Deaths from heart disease, cancer, stroke, accidents, pneumonia and influenza, and diabetes mellitus—the leading causes of death—were all above the national average.

In 1978, Missouri had 167 hospitals, with 35,437 beds; 972,727 admissions were recorded, for an average occupancy rate of 74%. Hospital personnel included 13,161 registered nurses and 5,957 licensed practical nurses. The average cost of hospital care in 1977 was \$171 per day and \$1,423 per stay, in each case below the US average. The state had 7,548 licensed physicians in 1977 and 2,303 professionally active dentists in 1979.

³⁹SOCIAL WELFARE
Outlays by federal, state, and local governments in Missouri for the five largest welfare programs totaled \$495 million in 1976. More than 193,000 Missourians (133,900 of them children) were recipients of aid to families with dependent children in 1978, at a

total cost of $152 million; Medicaid payments amounted to $195 million in 1977. During 1978, 189,000 state residents benefited from the food stamp program, at a federal cost of $64.2 million, while 668,000 Missouri schoolchildren took part in the school lunch program, with a federal subsidy of $36.1 million.

Social Security recipients numbered 845,100 in 1977, of whom 553,500 were retirees, 180,900 were survivors of deceased workers, and 110,700 were disabled. Payments exceeded $2 billion, with an average monthly payment to retired workers of $235.10. In 1978, federally administered Supplemental Security Income payments totaled $111 million. During the same year, vocational rehabilitation programs served 22,900 Missourians, of whom 7,900 were rehabilitated; the total cost was $21.5 million. The state expended $78.8 million on workers' compensation in 1977, and unemployment insurance benefits amounted to $136 million in 1978.

40 HOUSING

In 1970, Missouri had some 1,664,000 housing units, of which 1,521,000 were occupied; about 92% of the occupied units had full plumbing. From 1976 through 1978, nearly 80,000 new housing units were authorized, at a total value of more than $2.2 billion.

The Missouri Housing Development Commission is empowered to make and insure loans to encourage the construction of residential housing for persons of low or moderate income; funds for mortgage financing are provided through the sale of tax-exempt notes and bonds. Construction of multiunit public housing stagnated during the 1970s. In 1972, municipal authorities ordered the demolition of two apartment buildings in St. Louis's Pruitt-Igoe public housing complex, built 18 years earlier; the property remained vacant as the 1980s began.

41 EDUCATION

Although the constitution of 1820 provided for the establishment of public schools, it was not until 1839 that the state's public school system became a reality through legislation creating the office of state superintendent of common schools and establishing a permanent school fund. Missouri schools were officially segregated from 1875 to 1954, when the US Supreme Court issued its landmark ruling in *Brown* v. *Board of Education*; the state's school segregation law was not taken off the books until 1976. In that year, nearly 37% of all black students were in schools that were 99–100% black, a condition fostered by the high concentration of black Missourians in the state's two largest cities.

The adult illiteracy rate was 0.8% in 1970, well below the US average. In 1976, 64% of all Missourians 18 years of age or older were high school graduates; the median number of school years completed was 12.4. As of 1977, the state had a total of 2,249 public schools, of which 1,505 were elementary and 744 were secondary; public school enrollment during 1978/79 totaled 978,264: 657,196 in grades K–8 and 321,068 in grades 9–12. Private and parochial school enrollment was about 111,000 in fall 1977, an increase of 19% over the fall 1975 total.

Missouri had 23 public and 54 private institutions of higher education in 1977. The University of Missouri, established in 1839, was the first state-supported university west of the Mississippi River. By 1979, it had four campuses: Columbia (site of the world's oldest and one of the best-known journalism schools), Kansas City, Rolla, and St. Louis. The Rolla campus, originally founded in 1870 as a mining and engineering school, is still one of the nation's leading universities specializing in technology and science. The four campuses have a combined enrollment of more than 50,000, with nearly half of all students at the Columbia facility. Two leading independent universities, Washington and St. Louis, are located in St. Louis, as is the Concordia Seminary, an affiliate of the Lutheran Church–Missouri Synod and the center of much theological and political controversy during the

1970s. The Department of Higher Education maintains a student grant program for Missouri residents.

42 ARTS

Theatrical performances are offered throughout the state, mostly during the summer. In Kansas City, productions of Broadway musical comedies and light opera are staged at the Starlight Theater, seating 7,600 in an open-air setting. The Missouri Repertory Theater, on the University of Missouri campus in Kansas City, also has a summer season. In St. Louis, the 12,000-seat Municipal Opera puts on outdoor productions from June to early September, while the *Goldenrod*, built in 1909 and said to be the largest showboat ever constructed, is used today for vaudeville, melodrama, and ragtime shows. Other notable playhouses include the Ice House Theater in Hannibal and the Lyceum Theater in Arrow Rock.

Leading orchestras are the St. Louis Symphony and Kansas City Philharmonic; the Lyric Opera of Kansas City is another distinguished musical organization.

Between World Wars I and II, Kansas City was the home of a thriving jazz community that included Charlie Parker and Lester Young; leading bandleaders of that time were Benny Moten, Walter Page, and, later, Count Basie. Country music predominates in rural Missouri: the Ozark Opry at Osage Beach and the Baldknobbers Hillbilly Jamboree and Mountain Music Theater in Branson have seasons from May to October.

43 LIBRARIES AND MUSEUMS

Missouri had 79 county and 16 regional library systems in 1977/78, when the combined book stock of all public libraries in the state was 10,957,729, and their combined circulation 24,817,926. The Missouri State Library, in Jefferson City, is the center of the state's interlibrary loan network. The largest public library systems, those of Kansas City and St. Louis County, had 1,186,500 and 1,470,914 volumes, respectively, in 1977/78; the public library system of the city of St. Louis had 1,364,175. The University of Missouri–Columbia has the leading academic library, with 1,929,232 volumes in 1977/78. The State Historical Society of Missouri Library in Columbia contains more than 420,000 volumes. The federally administered Harry S Truman Library and Museum is at Independence.

Missouri has well over 100 museums and historic sites. The William Rockhill Nelson Gallery/Atkins Museum of Fine Arts in Kansas City and the St. Louis Art Museum each house distinguished general collections, while the Springfield Art Museum specializes in American sculpture, paintings, and relics of the westward movement. The Mark Twain Home and Museum in Hannibal has a collection of manuscripts and other memorabilia. Also notable are the Museum of Art and Archaeology, Columbia; the Kansas City Museum of History and Science; the Pony Express Stables Museum, St. Joseph; and the Jefferson National Expansion Memorial, McDonnell Planetarium, Missouri Botanical Garden, Museum of Science and Natural History, National Museum of Transport, and a zoo, all in St. Louis.

44 COMMUNICATIONS

In 1858, John Hockaday began weekly mail service by stagecoach between Independence and Salt Lake City, and John Butterfield, with a $600,000 annual appropriation from Congress, established semimonthly mail transportation by coach and rail from St. Louis to San Francisco. On 3 April 1860, the Pony Express was launched, picking up mail arriving by train at St. Joseph and racing it westward on horseback; the system ceased in October 1861, when the Pacific Telegraph Co. began operations. The first experiment in airmail service took place at St. Louis in 1911; Charles Lindbergh was an airmail pilot on the St. Louis–Chicago route in 1926. By 1978, Missouri had more than 900 post offices and 17,000 postal employees. Postal receipts in 1977/78 totaled $115.6 million in St. Louis and $85.4 million in Kansas City.

As of 31 December 1978, Missouri had 3,690,599 telephones, of which 2,772,969 were residential and 917,630 commercial. About 95% of all state residences had telephone service.

Radio broadcasting in Missouri dates from 1921, when a station at St. Louis University began experimental programming. On Christmas Eve 1922, the first midnight Mass ever to be put on the air was broadcast from the Old Cathedral in St. Louis. The voice of a US president was heard over the air for the first time on 21 June 1923, when Warren G. Harding gave a speech in St. Louis. FM broadcasting began in Missouri during 1948. As of 1978 there were 111 commercial AM stations and 77 FM stations. Missouri's first television station, KSD–TV in St. Louis, began in 1947, with WDAF–TV in Kansas City following in 1949. As of 1979, Missouri had 21 commercial and 3 noncommercial television stations; 7 commercial stations broadcast in the Kansas City area and 5 around St. Louis, with each region having a noncommercial station (the third one was at Springfield). By the end of 1978, the state had 87 cable systems serving 168,512 subscribers in 136 communities.

45 PRESS

The *Missouri Gazette*, published in St. Louis in 1808 by the politically independent and controversial Joseph Charless, was the state's first newspaper; issued to 174 subscribers, the paper was partly in French. In 1815, a group of Charless's enemies raised funds to establish a rival paper, the *Western Journal*, and brought in Joshua Norvell from Nashville to edit it. By 1820 there were five newspapers in Missouri. Since that time, many Missouri newspapermen have achieved national recognition. The best known is Sam Clemens (later Mark Twain), who started out as a "printer's devil" in Hannibal at the age of 13. Hungarianborn Joseph Pulitzer began his journalistic career in 1868 as a reporter for a German-language daily in St. Louis. Pulitzer created the *St. Louis Post-Dispatch* from the merger of two defunct newspapers in 1878, endowed the Columbia School of Journalism in New York City, and established by bequest the Pulitzer Prizes, which annually honor journalistic and artistic achievement.

As of 1978 there were 9 morning newspapers with a combined daily circulation of 726,694; 44 evening dailies with 936,787 circulation; and 19 Sunday papers with 1,159,385 circulation. The following table shows Missouri's leading dailies with their 1978 circulations:

AREA	NAME	DAILY	SUNDAY
Kansas City	Star (e,S)	286,032	400,215
	Times (m)	315,859	
St. Louis	Globe-Democrat (m)	271,248	
	Post-Dispatch (e,S)	252,198	433,317

46 ORGANIZATIONS

Kansas City is the home of the Veterans of Foreign Wars of the USA, with a national membership of about 1,850,000. Other leading organizations with headquarters in Kansas City include the Camp Fire Girls, People-to-People International, American Academy of Family Physicians, American Business Women's Association, American Nurses' Association, Fellowship of Christian Athletes, National Association of Intercollegiate Athletics, and National Secretaries Association.

Headquartered in St. Louis are the American Association of Orthodontists, American Optometric Association, American Pediatric Society, Catholic Hospital Association, Danforth Foundation, International Consumer Credit Association, and the National Hairdressers and Cosmetologists Association.

Other organizations include the National Council of State Garden Clubs, at Clayton; American Council on Education for Journalism, Columbia; National Innkeeping Association, Jefferson City; American Cat Fanciers Association, Branson; and the US Table Tennis Association, St. Charles.

47 TOURISM, TRAVEL, AND RECREATION

During 1977, travelers spent nearly $2.7 billion in Missouri on transportation, accommodations, meals, entertainment, recreation, and other items. This represented 2.2% of the US total, placing Missouri 15th among the 50 states in travel spending. About 100,000 jobs, with a payroll of $687 million, were attributable to the travel industry.

The principal attraction in St. Louis is the Gateway Arch, at 630 feet (192 meters) the tallest man-made national monument in the US. Designed by Eero Saarinen in 1948 but not constructed until 1964, three years after his death, the arch and the Museum of Westward Expansion form part of the Jefferson National Expansion Memorial on the western shore of the Mississippi River. In the Kansas City area are the modern Crown Center hotel and shopping plaza, the J. C. Nichols plaza, the Truman Sports Complex, Ft. Osage at Sibley, Jesse James's birthplace at Kearney, and Harry Truman's hometown of Independence. Memorabilia of Mark Twain are housed in and around Hannibal, in the northeast. The Lake of the Ozarks, with 1,375 mi (2,213 km) of shoreline, is one of the most popular vacation spots in mid-America. Other attractions include the Silver Dollar City handicrafts center near Branson; the Pony Express Stables and Museum at St. Joseph; and the "Big Springs Country" of the Ozarks, in the southeast.

As of 1979, Missouri had 43 state parks. Operated by the Department of Natural Resources, they offer camping, picnicking, swimming, boating, fishing, and hiking facilities. Lake of the Ozarks State Park is the largest, covering 16,872 acres (6,828 hectares).

Hunting and fishing are popular recreational activities throughout the state. In 1977, licenses were issued to 818,501 fishermen and 472,128 hunters.

48 SPORTS

Missouri has two major league baseball teams. The St. Louis Cardinals of the National League, now playing at Busch Memorial Stadium, have won the World Series eight times; their glory years came with Dizzy Dean and the "Gas House Gang" in the 1930s, the heyday of Stan Musial in the 1940s, and the era of Bob Gibson and Lou Brock in the 1960s. The Kansas City Royals, led by George Brett, won the American League pennant in 1980. The Kansas City Kings play in the National Basketball Association, while the St. Louis Blues compete in the National Hockey League. The St. Louis Cardinals of the National Football Conference and the Kansas City Chiefs of the American Football Conference (winners of the 1970 Super Bowl) are the state's two professional football teams.

Horse racing has a long history in Missouri. In 1812, St. Charles County sportsmen held two-day horse races; by the 1820s, racetracks were laid out in nearly every city and crossroads villages. Today, Thoroughbred racing can be seen during a summer and fall season at Cahokia Downs, outside St. Louis.

In collegiate sports, the University of Missouri competes in the Big Eight Conference.

49 FAMOUS MISSOURIANS

Harry S Truman (1884–1972) has been the only native-born Missourian to serve as US president or vice president. Elected US senator in 1932, Truman became Franklin D. Roosevelt's vice-presidential running mate in 1944 and succeeded to the presidency upon the latter's death on 12 April 1945. The "man from Independence"—whose tenure in office spanned the end of World War II, the inauguration of the Marshall Plan to aid European economic recovery, and the beginning of the Korean conflict—was elected to the presidency in his own right in 1948, scoring one of the most surprising upsets in US political history. Charles Evans Whittaker (b.Kansas, 1901–73) was a federal district and appeals court judge in Missouri before his appointment as Supreme Court associate justice in 1957. Among the state's outstanding US military leaders are Generals John J. Pershing (1860–1948) and Omar Bradley (b.1893).

Other notable federal officeholders from Missouri include Edward Bates (b.Virginia, 1793–1869), Abraham Lincoln's attorney general and the first cabinet official to be chosen from a state west of the Mississippi River; Montgomery Blair (b.Kentucky, 1813–83), postmaster general in Lincoln's cabinet; and Norman Jay Colman (b.New York, 1827–1911), the first secretary of agriculture. Missouri's best-known senator was Thomas Hart Benton (b.North Carolina, 1782–1858), who championed the interests of Missouri and the West for 30 years. Other well-known federal legislators include Francis P. Blair, Jr. (b.Kentucky, 1821–75), antislavery congressman, pro-Union leader during the Civil War, and Democratic vice-presidential nominee in 1868; Benjamin Gratz Brown (b.Kentucky, 1826–85), senator from 1863 to 1867, later governor of the state and Republican vice-presidential nominee (1872); Carl Schurz (b.Germany, 1829–1906), senator from 1869 to 1875 and subsequently US secretary of the interior, as well as a journalist and Union military leader; William H. Hatch (b.Kentucky, 1833–96), sponsor of much agricultural legislation as a US representative from 1879 to 1895; Richard P. Bland (b.Kentucky, 1835–99), leader of the free-silver bloc in the US House of Representatives; James Beauchamp "Champ" Clark (b.Kentucky, 1850–1921), speaker of the House from 1911 to 1919; W. Stuart Symington (b.Massachusetts, 1901), senator from 1952 to 1976 and earlier the nation's first secretary of the Air Force; and Thomas F. Eagleton (b.1929), senator since 1968 and, briefly, the Democratic vice-presidential nominee in 1972, until publicity about his having received electroshock treatment for depression forced him off the ticket.

Outstanding figures in Missouri history included two pioneering fur traders: William Henry Ashley (b.Virginia, 1778–1838), who later became a US representative; and Manuel Lisa (b.Louisiana, 1772–1820), who helped establish trade relations with the Indians. Meriwether Lewis (b.Virginia, 1774–1809) and William Clark (b.Virginia, 1770–1838) explored Missouri and the West during 1804–6; Lewis later served as governor of Louisiana Territory, with headquarters at St. Louis, and Clark was governor of Missouri Territory from 1813 to 1821. Dred Scott (b.Virginia, 1795?–1858), a slave owned by a Missourian, figured in a Supreme Court decision that set the stage for the Civil War. Missourians with unsavory reputations include such desperadoes as Jesse James (1847–82), his brother Frank (1843–1915), and Cole Younger (1844–1916), also a member of the James gang. Another well-known native was Kansas City's political boss, Thomas Joseph Pendergast (1872–1945), a power among Missouri Democrats until convicted of income tax evasion in 1939.

Among notable Missouri educators were William Torrey Harris (b.Connecticut, 1835–1909), superintendent of St. Louis public schools, US commissioner of education, and an authority on Hegelian philosophy; James Milton Turner (1840–1915), who helped establish Lincoln University for blacks at Jefferson City; and Susan Elizabeth Blow (1843–1916), cofounder with Harris of the first US public kindergarten at St. Louis in 1873. Distinguished scientists include agricultural chemist George Washington Carver (1864–1943), astronomers Harlow Shapley (1885–1972) and Edwin P. Hubble (1889–1953), Nobel Prize–winning nuclear physicist Arthur Holly Compton (b.Ohio, 1892–1962), and mathematician-cyberneticist Norbert Wiener (1894–1964). Engineer and inventor James Buchanan Eads (b.Indiana, 1820–87) supervised construction during 1867–74 of the St. Louis bridge that bears his name. Charles A. Lindbergh (b.Michigan, 1902–74) was a pilot and aviation instructor in the St. Louis area during the 1920s before winning worldwide acclaim for his solo New York–Paris flight.

Prominent Missouri businessmen include brewer Adolphus Busch (b.Germany, 1839–1913); William Rockhill Nelson (b.Indiana, 1847–1915), who founded the *Kansas City Star* (1880); and Joseph Pulitzer (b.Hungary, 1847–1911), who merged two failed newspapers to establish the *St. Louis Post-Dispatch* (1878) and later endowed the journalism and literary prizes that bear his name. Noteworthy journalists from Missouri include newspaper and magazine editor William M. Reedy (1862–1920), newspaper reporter Herbert Bayard Swope (1882–1958), and television newscaster Walter Cronkite (b.1916). Other distinguished Missourians include theologian Reinhold Niebuhr (1892–1971), civil rights leader Roy Wilkins (b.1901), and medical missionary Thomas Dooley (1927–61).

Missouri's most popular author is Mark Twain (Samuel Langhorne Clemens, 1835–1910), whose *Adventures of Tom Sawyer* (1876) and *Adventures of Huckleberry Finn* (1884) evoke his boyhood in Hannibal; novelist Harold Bell Wright (b.New York, 1872–1944) wrote about the people of the Ozarks; Robert Heinlein (b.1907) is a noted writer of science fiction and William S. Burroughs (b.1914) an experimental novelist. Poet-critic Thomas Stearns Eliot (1888–1965), awarded the Nobel Prize for literature in 1948, was born in St. Louis but became a British subject in 1927. Other Missouri-born poets include Sara Teasdale (1884–1933), Marianne Moore (1887–1972), and Langston Hughes (1902–67). Popular novelist and playwright Rupert Hughes (1872–1956) was a Missouri native, as was Zoë Akins (1886–1958), a Pulitzer Prize–winning playwright.

Distinguished painters who lived in Missouri include George Caleb Bingham (b.Virginia, 1811–79), who also served in several state offices; James Carroll Beckwith (1852–1917); and Thomas Hart Benton (1889–1975), the grandnephew and namesake of the state's famous political leader. Among the state's important musicians are ragtime pianist-composers Scott Joplin (b.Texas, 1868–1917) and John William "Blind" Boone (1864–1927); W(illiam) C(hristopher) Handy (b.Alabama, 1873–1958), composer of "St. Louis Blues," "Beale Street Blues," and other classics; composer-critic Virgil Thomson (b.1896), known for his operatic collaborations with Gertrude Stein; jazzman Coleman Hawkins (1907–69); and popular songwriter Burt Bacharach (b.1929). Photographer Walker Evans (1903–75) was a St. Louis native.

Missouri-born entertainers include actor Wallace Beery (1889–1949); actresses Jean Harlow (Harlean Carpenter, 1911–37), Jane Wyman (b.1914), and Betty Grable (1916–73); dancers Sally Rand (1904–79) and Josephine Baker (1906–75); film director John Huston (b.1906); and opera stars Helen Traubel (1903–72), Gladys Swarthout (1904–69), and Grace Bumbry (b.1937). In popular music, the state's most widely known singer-songwriter is Charles Edward Anderson "Chuck" Berry (b.California, 1926), whose works had a powerful influence on the development of rock 'n' roll.

St. Louis Cardinals' stars who became Hall of Famers include Jerome Herman "Dizzy" Dean (b.Arkansas, 1911–74), Stanley Frank "Stan the Man" Musial (b.Pennsylvania, 1920), and Robert "Bob" Gibson (b.Nebraska, 1935). Among the native Missourians who achieved stardom in the sports world are baseball manager Charles Dillon "Casey" Stengel (1890–1975), catcher Lawrence Peter "Yogi" Berra (b.1925), and sportscaster Joe Garagiola (b.1926).

[50] BIBLIOGRAPHY

Chappell, Philip Edward. *A History of the Missouri River*. Kansas City: Kansas State Historical Society, 1905.

DeVoto, Bernard Augustine. *Mark Twain's America*. Boston: Little, Brown, 1932.

Dorsett, Lyle W. *The Pendergast Machine*. New York: Oxford University Press, 1968.

Federal Writers' Project. *Missouri: A Guide to the "Show Me" State*. Rev. ed. New York: Hastings House, 1954 (orig. 1941).

Foley, William E. *A History of Missouri: 1673 to 1820*. Columbia: University of Missouri Press, 1971.

Glaab, Charles N. *Kansas City and the Railroads*. Madison: State Historical Society of Wisconsin, 1962.

Gerlach, Russel L. *Immigrants in the Ozarks*. Columbia: University of Missouri Press, 1976.

Greene, Lorenzo J. et al. *Missouri's Black Heritage*. St. Louis: Forum, 1980.

Hall, Leonard. *Stars Upstream: Life along an Ozark River*. Columbia: University of Missouri Press, 1969.

March, David D. *The History of Missouri*. 4 vols. New York and West Palm Beach: Lewis, 1967.

McCandless, Perry. *A History of Missouri: 1820 to 1860*. Columbia: University of Missouri Press, 1972.

Meyer, Duane. *The Heritage of Missouri: A History*. St. Louis: State Publishing Co., 1973.

Missouri, State of. Executive Office. *The Missouri State Budget, Fiscal Year 1981*. Jefferson City, 1980.

Missouri, State of. Secretary of State. *Official Manual, 1979–80*. Jefferson City, 1979.

Moore, Glover. *The Missouri Compromise, 1819–21*. Lexington: University of Kentucky Press, 1953.

Nagel, Paul C. *Missouri: A Bicentennial History*. New York: Norton, 1977.

Park, Eleanore G., and Kate S. Morrow. *Women of the Mansion: Missouri, 1821–1936*. Jefferson City: Midland, 1936.

Parrish, William E. *A History of Missouri: 1860 to 1875*. Columbia: University of Missouri Press, 1973.

Parrish, William E. et al. *Missouri: The Heart of the Nation*. St. Louis: Forum, 1980.

Primm, James Neal. *Economic Policy in the Development of a Western State: Missouri, 1820–60*. Cambridge: Harvard University Press, 1954.

Shoemaker, Floyd C. *Missouri and Missourians: Land of Contrasts and People of Achievement*. 5 vols. Chicago: Lewis, 1943.

Sprague, Marshall. *So Vast a Land: Louisiana and the Purchase*. Boston: Little, Brown, 1974.

State Historical Society of Missouri. *Historic Missouri: A Pictorial Narrative*. Columbia, 1977.

Truman, Harry S. *Memoirs*. 2 vols. Garden City, N.Y.: Doubleday, 1955–56.

Vestal, Stanley. *The Missouri*. New York: Farrar and Rinehart, 1945.

Wecter, Dixon. *Sam Clemens of Hannibal*. Boston: Houghton Mifflin, 1952.

MONTANA

State of Montana

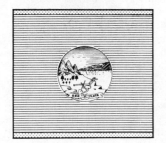

ORIGIN OF STATE NAME: Derived from the Latin word meaning "mountainous." **NICKNAME**: The Treasure State. (Also: Big Sky Country.) **CAPITAL**: Helena. **ENTERED UNION**: 8 November 1889 (41st). **SONG**: "Montana." **MOTTO**: *Oro y Plata* (Gold and Silver). **FLAG**: The state seal on a blue field, fringed in gold on the top and bottom borders. **OFFICIAL SEAL**: In the lower center are a plow and a miner's pick and shovel; mountains appear above them on the left, the Great Falls of the Missouri River on the right, and the state motto on a banner below. The words "The Great Seal of the State of Montana" surround the whole. **BIRD**: Western meadowlark. **FISH**: Black-spotted (cutthroat) trout. **FLOWER**: Bitterroot. **TREE**: Ponderosa pine. **GEMS**: Yogo sapphire; Montana agate. **GRASS**: Bluebunch wheatgrass. **LEGAL HOLIDAYS**: New Year's Day, 1 January; Lincoln's Birthday, 12 February; Washington's Birthday, 3d Monday in February; Memorial Day, last Monday in May; Independence Day, 4 July; Labor Day, 1st Monday in September; Columbus Day, 2d Monday in October; State Election Day, 1st Tuesday after the 1st Monday in November in even-numbered years; Veterans Day, 11 November; Thanksgiving Day, 4th Thursday in November; Christmas Day, 25 December. **TIME**: 5 A.M. MST = noon GMT.

¹LOCATION, SIZE, AND EXTENT
Located in the northwestern US, Montana is the largest of the 8 Rocky Mountain states and ranks 4th in size among the 50 states.

The total area of Montana is 147,138 sq mi (381,087 sq km), of which land takes up 145,587 sq mi (377,070 sq km) and inland water 1,551 sq mi (4,017 sq km). The state's maximum E–W extension is 570 mi (917 km); its extreme N–S distance is 315 mi (507 km).

Montana is bordered on the N by the Canadian provinces of British Columbia, Alberta, and Saskatchewan; on the E by North Dakota and South Dakota; on the S by Wyoming and Idaho; and on the W by Idaho. The total boundary length of Montana is *1,947 mi (3,133 km)*. The state's geographic center is in Fergus County, 12 mi (19 km) W of Lewistown.

²TOPOGRAPHY
Montana, as mountainous in parts as its name implies, has an approximate mean elevation of 3,400 feet (1,000 meters). The Rocky Mountains cover the western two-fifths of the state, with the Bitterroot Range along the Idaho border; the high, gently rolling Great Plains occupy most of central and eastern Montana. The highest point in the state is Granite Peak, at an elevation of 12,799 feet (3,901 meters), located in south-central Montana, near the Wyoming border. The lowest point, at 1,800 feet (550 meters), is in the northwest, where the Kootenai River leaves the state at the Idaho border. The Continental Divide passes in a jagged pattern through the western part of the state, from the Lewis to the Bitterroot ranges.

Ft. Peck Reservoir is Montana's largest body of inland water, covering 375 sq mi (971 sq km); Flathead Lake is the largest natural lake. The state's most important rivers are the Missouri, rising in southern Montana and flowing north and then east across the state, and the Yellowstone, which crosses southeastern Montana to join the Missouri at the North Dakota border. Located in Glacier National Park is the Triple Divide, from which Montana waters begin their journey to the Arctic and Pacific oceans and the Gulf of Mexico.

³CLIMATE
The Continental Divide separates the state into two distinct climatic regions: the west generally has a milder climate than the east, where winters can be especially harsh. Great Falls has a normal daily mean temperature of 45°F (7°C), ranging from 21°F

(−6°C) in January to 69°F (21°C) in July. The all-time low temperature, −70°F (−57°C), registered at Rogers Pass on 20 January 1954, is the lowest ever recorded in the conterminous US; the all-time high, 117°F (47°C), was set at Medicine Lake on 5 July 1937. Great Falls receives an average annual precipitation of 15 in (38 cm), but much of north-central Montana is arid. About 58 in (147 cm) of snow descends on Great Falls each year.

⁴FLORA AND FAUNA
Montana has three major life zones: subalpine, montane, and plains. The subalpine region, in the northern Rocky Mountains, is rich in wild flowers during a short midsummer growing season. The montane flora consists largely of coniferous forests, principally alpine fir, plus a variety of shrubs. The plains are characterized by an abundance of grasses, cacti, and sagebrush species.

Game animals of the state include elk, moose, white-tailed and mule deers, pronghorn antelope, bighorn sheep, and mountain goat. Notable among the amphibians is the axolotl; rattlesnakes and other reptiles occur in most of the state. Rare or threatened species include the grizzly bear, spotted bat, prairie falcon, and Arctic grayling. The black-footed ferret, Eskimo curlew, and Montana westslope cutthroat trout are on the endangered list.

⁵ENVIRONMENTAL PROTECTION
Montana's major environmental concerns are management of mineral and water resources and reclamation of strip-mined land. In 1973, the state legislature passed the Montana Resource Indemnity Trust Act, which, by 1975 amendment, imposes a coal severance tax of 30% on the contract sales price, with the proceeds placed in a permanent tax trust fund, in effect compensating Montanans for the loss of an irreplaceable resource. This tax, in conjunction with very tough strip-mining reclamation laws passed in the early 1970s, reflects the determination of Montanans to protect the beauty of the Big Sky Country while maintaining economic momentum.

⁶POPULATION
According to the 1970 census, Montana ranked 43d among the 50 states, with a population of 694,409. The 1980 preliminary census total was 783,674, for an average population density of 5 per sq mi (2 per sq km).

Only one-fourth of all Montanans live in metropolitan areas. Leading cities and their populations in 1980 were Billings, 68,317; and Great Falls, 56,568.

⁷ETHNIC GROUPS

According to state estimates, there are about 36,000 American Indians in Montana, of whom the Blackfeet and Crow are the most numerous.

The foreign-born and their native-born children made up nearly 18% of Montana's 1970 census population, with Canada, Germany, and Norway being the leading countries of origin. The black, Hispanic, and Asian populations are very small.

⁸LANGUAGES

Of the Indians of Siouan and Algonkian-Wakashan stock on Montana reservations in 1970, 37% claimed an Indian language as their first.

English in Montana fuses Northern and Midland features, the Northern proportion declining from east to west. Topography has given new meanings to *basin, hollow, meadow,* and *park* as kinds of clear spaces in the mountains.

In 1970, 84% of the native-born residents and 82% of all residents reported English as their mother tongue. Speakers of major first languages were as follows:

	NATIVE-BORN	FOREIGN-BORN
English	567,399	5,209
German	32,665	4,436
Indian languages	8,857	84
French	4,532	723
Spanish	3,430	530

⁹RELIGIONS

As of 1971, Protestant groups had 191,861 known adherents in Montana. Leading denominations included American Lutheran, 48,504; United Methodist, 28,790; and Latter-day Saints (Mormons), 22,847. Montana had 128,702 Roman Catholics in 1979 and an estimated 645 Jews.

¹⁰TRANSPORTATION

Montana's first railroad, the Utah and Northern, entered the state in 1880. Today, Montana is served by four major railroads, operating on about 4,900 mi (7,900 km) of track.

Because of its large size, small population, and difficult terrain, Montana was slow to develop a highway system. As of 1978, Montana had 77,852 mi (125,291 km) of roads, streets, and highways. There were 880,547 registered motor vehicles and about 580,000 licensed drivers in 1978.

Montana had 115 public and 57 private airfields in 1978. The leading airports are in Great Falls and Billings.

¹¹HISTORY

Much of Montana's prehistory has only recently been unearthed. The abundance of fossils of large and small dinosaurs, marine reptiles, miniature horses, and giant cave bears indicate that, from 100 million to 60 million years ago, the region had a tropical climate. Beginning some 2 million years ago, however, dramatic temperature changes profoundly altered what we now call Montana. At four different times, great sheets of glacial ice moved south through Canada to cover much of the north. The last glacial retreat, about 10,000 years ago, did much to carve the state's present topographic features. Montana's first humans probably came from across the Bering Strait; their fragmentary remains indicate a presence dating between 10,000 and 4000 BC.

The Indians encountered by Montana's first white explorers—probably French traders and trappers from Canada—arrived from the east during the 17th and 18th centuries, pushed westward into Montana by the pressure of European colonization. In January 1743, two traders, Louis-Joseph and François Verendrye, crossed the Dakota plains and saw before them what they called the "shining mountains," the eastern flank of the northern Rockies. However, it was not until 1803, when President Thomas Jefferson dispatched the Lewis and Clark Expedition to explore the upper reaches of the Missouri River, that the written history of Montana begins. On 25 April 1805, accompanied by a French trapper named Toussaint Charbonneau and his Shoshoni wife,

Sacagawea, Meriwether Lewis and William Clark reached the mouth of the Yellowstone River near the present-day boundary with North Dakota, and shortly thereafter, the first Americans entered Montana.

The fur trade dominated Montana's economy until 1858, when gold was discovered near the present community of Drummond. By mid-1862, a rush of miners from the gold fields of California, Nevada, Colorado, and Idaho had descended on the state. The temporary gold boom brought not only the state's first substantial white population but also an increased demand for government. In 1863, the eastern and western sectors of Montana were joined as part of Idaho Territory, which, in turn, was divided along the Bitterroot Mountains to form the present boundary between the two states. On 26 May 1864, President Abraham Lincoln signed the Organic Act, which created Montana Territory.

The territorial period was one of rapid and profound change. By the time Montana became a state on 8 November 1889, the remnants of Montana's Indian culture had been largely confined to federal reservations. A key event in this transformation was the Battle of the Little Big Horn River on 25 June 1876, when Lieutenant Colonel George Custer and his 7th US Cavalry regiment of fewer than 700 men were overwhelmed when they attacked an encampment of 15,000 Sioux and Northern Cheyenne led by Crazy Horse and Chief Gall. The following year, after a four-month running battle that traversed most of the state of Montana, Chief Joseph of the Nez Percé tribe surrendered to federal forces, signaling the end of organized Indian resistance.

As the Indian threat subsided, stockmen wasted little time in putting the seemingly limitless open range to use. In 1866, Nelson Story had driven the first longhorns up from Texas, and by the mid-1870s, sheep had also made a significant appearance on the open range. In 1886, at the peak of the open-range boom, approximately 664,000 head of cattle and nearly a million sheep grazed Montana's rangeland. Disaster struck during the "hard winter" of 1886/87, however, when perhaps as many as 362,000 head of cattle starved trying to find the scant forage covered by snow and ice. That winter marked the end of a cattle frontier based on the "free grass" of the open range and taught the stockmen the value of a secure winter feed supply.

Construction of Montana's railroad system between 1880 and 1909 breathed new life into mining as well as the livestock industry. Moreover, the railroads created a new network of market centers at Great Falls, Billings, Bozeman, Missoula, and Havre. By 1890, the Butte copper pits were producing more than 40% of the nation's copper requirements. The struggle to gain financial control of the enormous mineral wealth of Butte Hill led to the "War of the Copper Kings," in which the Amalgamated Copper Co., in conjunction with Standard Oil, bought out the competition and emerged as sole proprietor of "the richest hill on earth." In 1915, as a result of antitrust prosecution, Standard Oil gave up its copper holdings. The new company, Anaconda Copper Mining, virtually controlled the press, politics, and governmental processes of Montana until changes in the structure of the international copper market and the diversification of Montana's economy in the 1940s and 1950s reduced the company's power. Anaconda Copper was absorbed by the Atlantic Richfield Co. in 1976.

The railroads also brought an invasion of agricultural homesteaders. Montana's population surged from 243,329 in 1900 to 376,053 in 1910 and to 548,889 by 1920, while the number of farms and ranches increased from 13,000 to 57,000. Drought and a sharp drop in wheat prices after World War I brought an end to the homestead boom. From 1919 to 1925, nearly 11,000 farms were abandoned, and some 20,000 farm mortgages were foreclosed by banks. By 1926, half of Montana's commercial banks had failed. Conditions worsened with the drought and depression of the early 1930s, until the New Deal—enormously popular

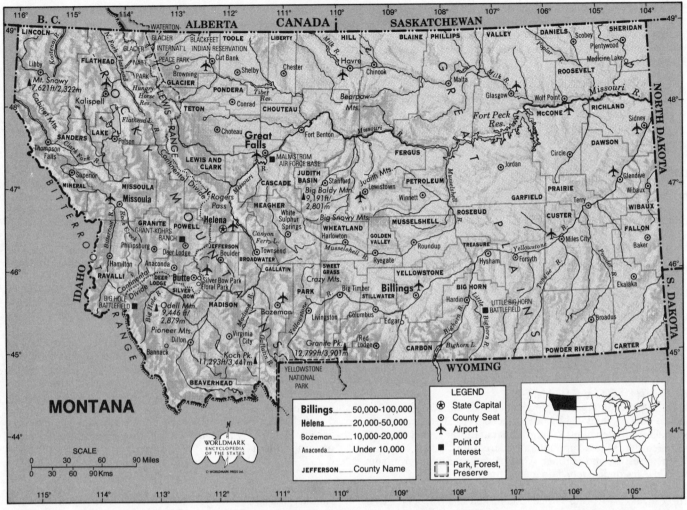

See US political: front cover D1; physical: back cover D1.

LOCATION: 44°21′26″ to 49°N; 104°02′26″ to 116°02′56″W. **BOUNDARIES:** Canadian line, 546 mi (879 km); North Dakota line, *212 mi (341 km)*; South Dakota line, *67 mi (108 km)*; Wyoming line, 384 mi (618 km); Idaho line, 738 mi (1,187 km).

in Montana—helped revive farming and silver mining and financed irrigation and other public works projects.

The decades since the end of World War II have seen moderate growth in Montana's population, economy, and social services. Manufacturing has developed slowly; the recent exploitation of fossil fuel reserves in eastern Montana has provided relatively few jobs. The expansion of coal strip-mining operations may prove to be the real key to Montana's future.

¹²STATE GOVERNMENT
Montana's original constitution, dating from 1889, was substantially revised by a 1972 constitutional convention, effective 1 July 1973. Under the present document, the state legislature consists of 50 senators, elected to staggered four-year terms, and 100 representatives serving for two years. The only elected officers of the executive branch are the governor and lieutenant governor (who run jointly), secretary of state, attorney general, superintendent of public instruction, and auditor. Each serves a four-year term.

To become law, a bill must pass both houses by a simple majority and be signed by the governor, remain unsigned for five days, or be passed over the governor's veto by a two-thirds vote of both houses. The state constitution may be amended by constitutional convention, by legislative referendum, or by voter initiative. To be adopted, each proposed amendment must be ratified at the next general election.

To vote in the State of Montana, one must be a US citizen and at least 18 years of age; there is a county residency requirement of 30 days for registration.

¹³POLITICAL PARTIES
Since statehood, Democrats have generally dominated in contests for the US House and Senate, and Republicans in elections for state and local offices and in national presidential campaigns (except during the New Deal years). It is remarkable that, as of mid-1980, only one Montana Republican had ever been elected to the US Senate, and then for only one term. Although the erosion of Montana's rural population since the 1920s has diluted the Republicans' agrarian base, the party has gained increasing financial and organizational backing from corporate interests, particularly from the mining and energy-related industries. The strength of the Democratic Party, on the other hand, lies in the strong union movement centered in Butte and its surrounding counties, augmented by smaller family farms throughout the state. Urbanization has also benefited the Democrats. Montana voted overwhelmingly for Republican presidential candidate Ronald Reagan in November 1980. They also gave the Republicans control of both houses of the state legislature, while electing a Democratic governor.

The most significant third party was the Populist Party, which drew much of its strength during the 1890s from Montana's depressed silver-mining communities, which saw new hope in the "free and unlimited coinage of silver" advocated by the Populists. In 1896, William Jennings Bryan captured 80% of the state's presidential vote, and Populist-Democrat Robert Smith won the governorship with 71%.

Montana Presidential Vote by Major Political Parties, 1948–80

YEAR	ELECTORAL VOTE	MONTANA WINNER	DEMOCRAT	REPUBLICAN
1948	4	*Truman (D)	119,071	96,770
1952	4	*Eisenhower (R)	106,213	157,394
1956	4	*Eisenhower (R)	116,238	154,933
1960	4	Nixon (R)	134,891	141,841
1964	4	*Johnson (D)	164,246	113,032
1968	4	*Nixon (R)	114,117	138,835
1972	4	*Nixon (R)	120,197	183,976
1976	4	Ford (R)	149,259	173,703
1980	4	*Reagan (R)	118,032	206,814

*Won US presidential election.

[14] LOCAL GOVERNMENT
As of 1977, Montana had 56 counties, 126 municipalities, 311 special districts, and 465 school districts. Typical elected county officials are three county commissioners, attorney, sheriff, clerk and recorder, school superintendent, treasurer, public administrator, assessor, and coroner. Unified city-county governments include Anaconda–Deer Lodge and Butte–Silver Bow.

[15] STATE SERVICES
The Citizens' Advocate Office, established in 1973, serves as a clearinghouse for problems, complaints, and questions concerning state government. The Department of Education oversees the state university system, while the superintendent of public instruction is responsible for the public schools. The Department of Highways is the main transportation agency. Health and welfare programs are the province of the Department of Health and Environmental Sciences and the Department of Social and Rehabilitation Services.

[16] JUDICIAL SYSTEM
Montana's highest court, the supreme court, consists of a chief justice and 6 associate justices. District courts are the courts of general jurisdiction; as of 1980 there were 19 judicial districts served by 32 district judges. Justice of the peace courts are essentially county courts whose jurisdiction is limited to minor civil cases, misdemeanors, and traffic violations. Supreme court justices are elected on nonpartisan ballots for eight-year terms, district court judges for six years, and justices of the peace for four years. Montana's crime rates were below the US averages in every category in 1978.

[17] ARMED FORCES
The principal military facility in Montana is Malmstrom Air Force Base (Great Falls), a Strategic Air Command facility employing 4,508 military personnel. An estimated 99,000 veterans of US military service were living in Montana in 1979. In 1977/78, expenditures on veterans totaled $72.4 million.

[18] MIGRATION
Montana's first great migratory wave brought Indians from the east during the 17th and 18th centuries. The gold rush of the 1860s and a land boom between 1900 and 1920 brought surges of white settlement, while the economically troubled 1920s and 1930s produced a severe wave of outmigration that continued through the 1960s. The trend reversed between 1970 and 1977, however, when Montana's net gain from migration was 32,000.

[19] INTERGOVERNMENTAL COOPERATION
Among the interstate agreements in which Montana participates are the Interstate Oil and Gas Compact, Western Corrections Compact, Western Interstate Energy Compact, Western Regional Education Compact, and Yellowstone River Compact (with North Dakota and Wyoming).

Federal aid to Montana in 1978/79 was estimated at $424.4 million, of which $25.2 million was general revenue sharing.

[20] ECONOMY
Resource industries—agriculture, mining, lumbering—dominate Montana's economy, although tourism is of increasing importance. In 1977, agriculture contributed $1 billion to the state economy; minerals, $687 million; travel, $264 million.

[21] INCOME
With an income per capita of $7,051 in 1978, Montana ranked 33d among the 50 states. Total income, $5.5 billion in 1978, represented a 44% increase since 1970 in constant dollars.

Median family income reached $13,608 (29th in the US) in 1975, when some 86,000 Montanans—11.5% of the state's population—were living below the federal poverty level.

[22] LABOR
Montana's labor force varies sharply with the season, swelling in the summer and shrinking in the winter. As of January 1979, the civilian labor force totaled 356,200 persons, of whom 329,600 were employed (21,300 in agriculture); by August, however, the labor force was 395,500, of whom 378,800 had jobs (46,000 in agriculture).

A federal census of workers covered by unemployment insurance in March 1977 revealed the following nonfarm employment pattern in Montana:

	ESTABLISH-MENTS	EMPLOYEES	ANNUAL PAYROLL ('000)
Agricultural services, forestry, fishing	205	710	$ 5,499
Mining	279	8,445	130,180
Contract construction	2,269	10,636	158,184
Manufacturing, of which:	1,003	23,806	320,294
Lumber, wood products	(392)	(9,089)	(129,352)
Transportation, public utilities	1,044	13,352	175,058
Wholesale trade	1,686	14,055	165,117
Retail trade	5,994	49,542	324,050
Finance, insurance, real estate	1,622	11,055	107,172
Services	5,350	43,763	313,943
Other	290	288	3,406
TOTALS	19,742	175,652	$1,702,903

Government employees, numbering about 58,000, were not included in this survey.

In 1976, the total union and employee association membership was 74,000, nearly 30% of the nonfarm work force (18th in the US). Unions have been strongest in the Butte area and in the mining and smelting industries.

[23] AGRICULTURE
Montana's farm income totaled nearly $1.4 billion in 1978, ranking 31st in the US. Montana was the nation's 6th-leading wheat producer in 1979, with an output of 116,475,000 bushels, valued at $404,028,000. Other major crops were barley, 40,560,000 bushels (5th), $64,530,000; and hay, 4,291,000 tons, $31,556,000. Oats, sugar beets, potatoes, flax, and dry beans are also grown.

[24] ANIMAL HUSBANDRY
Livestock production accounts for more than half of Montana's farm income. As of late 1979, the state had 2,645,000 cattle and

calves. Other livestock included 209,000 hogs and pigs and 494,000 sheep and lambs; the sheep industry suffered a decline during the 1960s and 1970s, largely because of increased use of synthetic fibers rather than wool in the US textile industry.

Livestock products in 1979 were 882,185,000 lb of cattle and calves, worth $646,595,000; hogs and pigs, 71,756,000 lb, $28,343,000; and sheep and lambs, 22,961,000 lb, $10,265,000. The wool clip was 4,173,000 lb in 1978.

25 FISHING
Montana's designated fishing streams offer some 10,000 mi (16,000 km) of good to excellent freshwater fishing.

26 FORESTRY
As of 1 January 1977, 22,559,000 acres (9,129,000 hectares) in Montana were classified as forestland; of that total, 14,359,000 acres (5,811,000 hectares) were commercial timberland, 32% in private hands, 4% state or locally owned, and 64% federally controlled. There are 10 national forests, comprising roughly 10% of the roadless area in the US. Most of the state's forestland is located in western Montana, which derives more than half its total personal income from forest-related industries.

27 MINING
The discovery of rich deposits of placer gold at Bannack, Virginia City, and Helena led to the settlement of southwestern Montana in the 1860s. Oil and natural gas, discovered in the 1920s, are scattered beneath the eastern two-thirds of the state, but especially near the North Dakota border; lignite is concentrated in the east, and bituminous coal in central and western Montana. Most metal mining—especially for copper, silver, and gold—takes place in the southwestern region, near Butte. Montana leads the US in the production of vermiculite and sapphires.

Montana's total mineral output was valued at $678 million (24th in the US) in 1978. Leading mineral products (excluding fossil fuels) included gold, 19,967 troy oz; silver, 2,918 troy oz; and copper, 74,214 tons.

28 ENERGY AND POWER
In 1978, Montana produced 16.9 billion kwh of electricity, mostly from hydropower; installed capacity was 3.1 million kw.

Fossil fuels account for the bulk of Montana's mineral income. In 1978, the state produced 30,087,000 barrels of crude oil, leaving proved reserves of 140,466,000 barrels; natural gas production totaled 57.4 billion cu feet, with proved reserves amounting to 991.7 billion. Coal reserves were estimated at 120.6 billion tons—1st in the US and more than 27% of the US total—in 1976, of which bituminous coal accounted for 1.4 billion tons; subbituminous, 103.4 billion; and lignite, 15.8 billion. Production of bituminous coal in 1978 was 26.6 million tons.

29 INDUSTRY
Montana's major manufacturing industries process raw materials from mines, forests, and farms. The total value added by manufacture for the state in 1977 amounted to $860,300,000. Major sectors and their value added in 1972 and 1977 included the following:

	1972	1977
Lumber and wood products	$149,500,000	$326,700,000
Food and food products	65,700,000	104,200,000
Petroleum and coal products	NA	87,200,000
Stone, clay, and glass products	24,900,000	48,600,000
Chemicals and allied products	9,700,000	29,600,000

30 COMMERCE
Wholesale establishments had sales of $1.5 billion in 1972, while retail sales exceeded $2.8 billion in 1977. Montana's foreign exports included $322 million in agricultural products (23d in the US) in 1976/77 and $44 million in manufactured goods (48th) in 1976. Wheat is the leading export item.

31 CONSUMER PROTECTION
Montana's consumer protection laws are administered by the Department of Business Regulation.

32 BANKING
In 1978, Montana had 160 insured commercial banks, with total assets of nearly $4.5 billion. Deposits were almost $4 billion, including $1.3 billion in demand deposits and $2.6 billion in time deposits. There were 12 insured savings and loan associations, all federally chartered, with total assets of $990.5 million.

33 INSURANCE
Montanans held 1,110,000 life insurance policies with a combined value of $8.2 billion in 1978. The average per family was $28,200, ranking 47th in the US and placing 20% below the national average. Property and liability insurers wrote premiums worth $271.6 million in 1978.

34 SECURITIES
There are no securities exchanges in Montana.

35 PUBLIC FINANCE
The Montana state budget is prepared biennially by the Office of Budget and Program Planning and submitted by the governor to the legislature for amendment and approval. The fiscal year runs from 1 July to 30 June. The following is a summary of consolidated revenues and expenditures for 1977/78 and 1978/79 (in millions):

	1977/78	1978/79
REVENUES		
Personal income taxes	$ 123.6	$ 141.4
Corporate income taxes	29.2	36.1
Coal, oil, and motor fuel taxes	89.0	99.3
Federal assistance	310.9	315.5
Other receipts and transfers	577.7	640.6
TOTALS	$1,130.4	$1,232.9
EXPENDITURES		
University system	$ 199.1	$ 207.1
Public schools	158.3	180.1
Highways	150.0	137.3
Labor and industry	116.8	111.7
Social and rehabilitation services	99.6	110.7
Other expenditures	327.3	356.1
TOTALS	$1,051.1	$1,103.0

As of mid-1977, the combined debt of Montana state and local governments was $531 million, or $697 per capita, among the lowest in the US.

36 TAXATION
As of 1980, Montana's personal income tax ranged from 2% on the first $1,000 to 11% on amounts over $35,000. The corporate income tax was 6.75% on net income, with a minimum tax of $50. The state levies a property tax but no sales or use tax.

Montana paid federal taxes totaling $979 million in 1975/76 and received $1.2 billion in federal expenditures. State residents filed 308,202 federal income tax returns in 1977, paying $459.2 million in tax.

37 ECONOMIC POLICY
To encourage economic development, Montana provides such incentives as a property tax reduction of 77%, during the first three years of operation, on new industrial property utilized by industries engaged in manufacturing; a property tax reduction of 50% for new or existing industries which locate in, or expand into, already established industrial areas within Montana; and a 79% property tax reduction for raw materials, work in progress, and other inventory items.

38 HEALTH
The average life expectancy in Montana during 1969–71 was 70.56 years (30th in the US), 66.73 for men and 75.08 for women. The infant mortality rates per 1,000 live births in 1977 were 13.6 for whites and 14.7 for nonwhites. The birthrate in 1977 was 17.5 per 1,000 population, the death rate 8.4. Leading causes of death (with their rates per 100,000 population) were heart disease, 281; cancer, 156; stroke, 76; and accidents, 75. The first three rates

were below the national norms, but Montana's accident rate was one of the highest in the US, and the suicide rate, 18.4, was 38% above the US average.

There were 65 hospitals in 1978, with 5,652 beds and an average daily occupancy rate of 63.9%. Hospital personnel included 2,049 registered nurses and 815 licensed practical nurses. The average cost of hospital care was $152 per day and $972 per stay; both figures were among the lowest in the US. Montana had 985 licensed physicians in 1977 and 442 active dentists in 1979.

39SOCIAL WELFARE

Montana played an important role in the development of social welfare. It was one of the first states to experiment with workers' compensation, enacting a compulsory compensation law in 1915; eight years later, Montana and Nevada became the first states to provide for old age pensions.

Public assistance payments to families with dependent children in 1978 totaled $15 million; the federal government expended $5.8 million for school lunches and $8.5 million on the food stamp program. In 1977, Social Security benefits were paid to 114,600 Montanans; their benefits totaled $280.2 million, with the average monthly payment to retired workers being $238.60. Other expenditures included Medicaid (1977), $44 million; Supplementary Security Income (1978), $9.6 million; unemployment insurance (1978), $30 million; vocational rehabilitation (1978), $3.7 million; and workers' compensation (1977), $23.8 million.

40HOUSING

In 1970, Montana had some 240,000 housing units, of which 217,000 were occupied; 66% of the units were owner-occupied, and 93% had full plumbing. The state authorized about 15,200 new housing units from 1976 through 1978.

41EDUCATION

Montana's illiteracy rate—0.6% in 1970—has ranked among the lowest in the US throughout the 20th century. As of 1976, more than 72% of all adult Montanans were high school graduates.

Estimated public school enrollments in fall 1978 were 109,000 in grades K–8 and 57,000 in grades 9–12; about 6,000 students were enrolled in private and parochial schools in 1977. The main components of the higher educational system are the University of Montana (Missoula) and Montana State University (Bozeman), both founded in 1893.

42ARTS

The C. M. Russell Museum in Great Falls honors the work of Charles Russell, whose mural *Lewis and Clark Meeting the Flathead Indians* adorns the capitol in Helena. Other fine art museums include the Museum of the Rockies in Bozeman, Yellowstone Art Center at Billings, and the Missoula Museum of the Arts.

43LIBRARIES AND MUSEUMS

Montana had 6 public library federations in 1977/78, serving 50 counties; the combined book stock of all Montana public libraries was 1,984,625, and their combined circulation was 3,981,513. Distinguished collections include those of the University of Montana (Missoula), with 613,008 volumes; Montana State University (Bozeman), 380,926; and the Montana State Library and Montana Historical Society Library, both in Helena.

Among the state's more than 80 museums and historic sites are the Montana Historical Society Museum, Helena; World Museum of Mining, Butte; Western Heritage Center, Billings; and Museum of the Plains Indian, Browning. National historic sites include Big Hole and Little Big Horn battlefields and the Grant-Kohrs Ranch at Deer Lodge, west of Helena.

44COMMUNICATIONS

In 1978, 93% of the state's households had telephone service, with the total number of telephones being 575,509—422,148 residential and 153,361 business. There were 66 commercial radio stations (45 AM, 21 FM) in 1978, and 12 television stations. During the same year, 35 cable television systems served 92,779 subscribers in 58 communities.

45PRESS

As of 1978, Montana had 4 morning dailies with a combined circulation of 149,353, 7 evening dailies with 46,862, and 7 Sunday newspapers with 192,994. The leading papers were the *Billings Gazette* (59,030 mornings, 61,280 Sundays) and *Great Falls Tribune* (39,235 mornings, 45,253 Sundays).

46ORGANIZATIONS

Among US organizations with headquarters in the state are the National Center For Appropriate Technology at Butte and the National High School Rodeo Association at Edgar.

47TOURISM, TRAVEL, AND RECREATION

Travel is Montana's 3d-largest industry. During 1975, approximately 4 million out-of-state visitors came to Montana.

Many tourists seek out the former gold rush camps, ghost towns, and dude ranches. Scenic wonders include all of Glacier National Park, covering 1,013,129 acres (410,000 hectares); the US portion of Waterton-Glacier International Peace Park; part of Yellowstone National Park, which also extends into Idaho and Wyoming; plus 10 national forests, 14 designated wilderness and primitive areas, and some 130 state parks. Rafting, backpacking, and rock hunting are popular outdoor activities. Montana also has some 30 ski centers and bills itself as the "Snowmobile Capital of America." Fishing and hunting are popular pastimes.

48SPORTS

There are no major league professional sports teams in Montana. The University of Montana and Montana State University both compete in the Big Sky Conference.

49FAMOUS MONTANANS

Prominent national officeholders from Montana include US Senator Thomas Walsh (b.Wisconsin, 1859–1933), who directed the investigation that uncovered the Teapot Dome scandal; Jeannette Rankin (1880–1973), the first woman member of Congress and the only US representative to vote against American participation in both world wars; Burton K. Wheeler (b.Mass., 1882–1975), US senator from 1923 to 1947 and one of the most powerful politicians in Montana history; and Michael Joseph "Mike" Mansfield (b.New York, 1903), who held the office of majority leader of the US Senate longer than anyone else.

Chief Joseph (b.Oregon, 1840?–1904), a Nez Percé Indian, repeatedly outwitted the US Army during the late 1870s; Crazy Horse (1849?–77) led a Sioux-Cheyenne army in battle at Little Big Horn. The town of Bozeman is named for explorer and prospector John M. Bozeman (b.Georgia, 1835–67).

Creative artists from Montana include Alfred Bertram Guthrie, Jr. (b.Indiana, 1901), author of *The Big Sky* and the Pulitzer Prize–winning *The Way West*; Dorothy Johnson (b.Iowa, 1905), whose stories have been made into such notable Western movies as *The Hanging Tree*, *The Man Who Shot Liberty Valance*, and *A Man Called Horse*; and Charles Russell (b.Missouri, 1864–1926), Montana's foremost painter and sculptor. Hollywood stars Gary Cooper (Frank James Cooper, 1901–61) and Myrna Loy (b.1905) were born in Helena. Newscaster Chet Huntley (1911–74) was born in Cardwell.

50BIBLIOGRAPHY

Federal Writers' Project. *Montana: A State Guide Book.* New York: Viking, 1939.

League of Women Voters of Montana. *Know Your State.* Missoula, 1973.

Malone, Michael P., and Richard B. Roeder. *Montana: A History of Two Centuries.* Seattle: University of Washington Press, 1976.

Spence, Clark C. *Montana: A Bicentennial History.* New York: Norton, 1978.

Toole, Kenneth R. *Twentieth-Century Montana: A State of Extremes.* Norman: University of Oklahoma Press, 1972.

Waldron, Ellis, and Paul Wilson. *Atlas of Montana Elections.* Missoula: University of Montana, 1978.

NEBRASKA

State of Nebraska

ORIGIN OF STATE NAME: From the Oto Indian word *Nebrathka*, meaning "flat water" (for the Platte River). **NICKNAME:** The Cornhusker State. **CAPITAL:** Lincoln. **ENTERED UNION:** 1 March 1867 (37th). **SONG:** "Beautiful Nebraska." **MOTTO:** Equality Before the Law. **FLAG:** The great seal appears in the center in gold and silver, on a field of blue. **OFFICIAL SEAL:** Agriculture is represented by a farmer's cabin, sheaves of wheat, and growing corn, the mechanic arts by a blacksmith. Above is the state motto; in the background, a steamboat plies the Missouri River and a train heads toward the Rockies. The scene is surrounded by the words "Great Seal of the State of Nebraska, March 1st 1867." **BIRD:** Western meadowlark. **FLOWER:** Goldenrod. **TREE:** Cottonwood. **GEM:** Blue agate. **ROCK:** Prairie agate. **GRASS:** Little bluestem. **INSECT:** Honeybee. **FOSSIL:** Mammoth. **LEGAL HOLIDAYS:** New Year's Day, 1 January; President's Day, 3d Monday in February; Arbor Day, 22 April; Memorial Day, last Monday in May; Independence Day, 4 July; Labor Day, 1st Monday in September; Columbus Day, 2d Monday in October; Veterans Day, 11 November; Thanksgiving, 4th Thursday in November and following Friday; Christmas Day, 25 December. **TIME:** 6 A.M. CST = noon GMT; 5 A.M. MST = noon GMT.

¹LOCATION, SIZE, AND EXTENT

Located in the western north-central US, Nebraska ranks 15th in size among the 50 states.

The total area of the state is 77,227 sq mi (200,018 sq km), of which land takes up 76,483 sq mi (198,091 sq km) and inland water 744 sq mi (1,927 sq km). Nebraska extends about 415 mi (668 km) E–W, and 205 mi (330 km) N–S.

Nebraska is bordered on the N by South Dakota (with the line formed in part by the Missouri River); on the E by Iowa and Missouri (the line being defined by the Missouri River); on the S by Kansas and Colorado; and on the W by Colorado and Wyoming. The boundary length of Nebraska totals 1,332 mi (2,143 km).

The state's geographic center is in Custer County, 10 mi (16 km) NW of Broken Bow.

²TOPOGRAPHY

Most of Nebraska is prairie; more than two-thirds of the state lies within the Great Plains proper. The elevation slopes upward gradually from east to west, from a low of 840 feet (256 meters) in the southeast to 5,426 feet (1,654 meters) in Kimball County.

Rolling alluvial lowlands in the eastern portion of the state give way to the flat, treeless plain of central Nebraska, which in turn rises to a tableland in the west. The Sand Hills of the north-central plain is an unusual region of sand dunes anchored by grasses that cover about 18,000 sq mi (47,000 sq km).

The Sand Hills region is dotted with small natural lakes; in the rest of the state the main lakes are artificial. The Missouri River—which, with its tributaries, drains the entire state—forms the eastern part of the northern boundary of Nebraska. Three rivers cross the state from west to east: the wide, shallow Platte River flows through the heart of the state for 310 mi (499 km); the Niobrara River traverses the state's northern region; and the Republican River flows through southern Nebraska.

³CLIMATE

Nebraska has a continental climate, with highly variable temperatures from season to season and year to year. The central region has an average normal temperature of 50°F (10°C), with a normal maximum of 76°F (24°C) and a normal minimum of 23°F (–5°C). The record low for the state is –47°F (–44°C), registered in Morrill County on 12 February 1899; the record high of 118°F (48°C) was recorded at Minden on 24 July 1936.

Normal yearly precipitation in the semiarid panhandle in the west is 17 in (43 cm); in the southeast, 31 in (79 cm). Snowfall in the state also varies by region; in 1977/78, the panhandle had 43 in (109 cm) and south-central Nebraska had 26 in (66 cm). Blizzards, droughts, and windstorms have plagued Nebraskans throughout their history.

⁴FLORA AND FAUNA

Nebraska's deciduous forests are generally oak and hickory; conifer forests are dominated by western yellow (ponderosa) pine. The tallgrass prairie may include various sloughgrasses and needlegrasses, along with big bluestem, and prairie dropseed. Mixed prairie regions abound with western wheatgrass and buffalo grass. The prairie region of the Sand Hills supports a variety of bluestems, gramas, and other grasses. Common Nebraska wild flowers are wild rose, phlox, petunia, columbine, goldenrod, and sunflower. Rare species of Nebraska's flora include the Hayden penstemon, yellow ladyslipper, paw-paw, and snow trillium.

Common mammals native to the state are the pronghorn sheep, white-tailed and mule deer, badger, kit fox, coyote, striped ground squirrel, prairie vole, and several skunk species. There are more than 400 kinds of birds, the mourning dove, barn swallow, and western meadowlark (the state bird) among them. Carp, catfish, trout, and perch are fished for sport. Rare animal species include the least shrew, least weasel, and bobcat. Among threatened species are the brook stickleback and mountain plover; the Arctic peregrine falcon, black-footed ferret, and swift fox (*Vulpes velox*) are listed as endangered species.

⁵ENVIRONMENTAL PROTECTION

The Department of Environmental Control was established in 1971 to protect and improve the quality of the state's water, air, and land resources. The director of the department also acts as secretary of the Environmental Control Council.

The major water pollution problems involve feedlot waste disposal and industrial discharges along the Platte River. Flood control falls under the jurisdiction of a separate agency, the Nebraska Natural Resources Commission.

⁶POPULATION

Nebraska ranked 35th in the US in 1970, with a census population of 1,485,333, a 5% increase over 1960.

In 1970 there were 725,431 men and 759,902 women in Ne-

329

braska. Some 62% of Nebraska's population lived in urban areas in 1970, compared with 54% in 1960. The census showed Douglas County, site of the city of Omaha, to be the most densely populated region, with 1,170 people per sq mi (452 people per sq km). Several western counties of the state averaged less than 2 people per sq mi (less than 1 per sq km).

According to preliminary census data, Nebraska had 1,564,727 residents in 1980. Omaha, the largest city, had a population of 312,929; Lincoln, 171,787.

⁷ETHNIC GROUPS

Large groups of Germans, Czechs, and Scandinavians were among Nebraska's early European settlers. In 1970, 86,160 Nebraskans (6% of the total) were first- and second-generation citizens of these nationality backgrounds. About 40,000 black Americans were in Nebraska (mainly in Omaha), and about 4,000 Asians, of whom Japanese-Americans (1,314) were the largest group.

There are about 8,000 Indians in three incorporated tribes—Omaha, Winnebago, and Santee Sioux—on three reservations.

⁸LANGUAGES

Many Plains Indians of the Macro-Siouan family roamed widely over what is now Nebraska. Omaha, Winnebago, and Santee tribes now reside there on reservations. Place-names derived from the Siouan language include Omaha, Ogallala, Niobrara, and Keya Paha. In all, 2,130 Nebraskans claimed Indian tongues as their first languages in 1970.

Nebraska English, except for slight South Midland influence in the southwest and some Northern influence from Wisconsin and New York settlers in the Platte River Valley, is almost pure North Midland. A few words, mostly food terms like *kolaches* (fruit-filled pastries), are derived from the language of the large Czech population. Usual pronunciation features are *on* and *hog* with the /o/ of *order*, *cow* and *now* as /kaow/ and /naow/, *because* with the /ah/ vowel, *cot* and *caught* as sound-alikes, and a strong final /r/. *Fire* sounds almost like *far*, and *our* like *are*; *greasy* is pronounced /greezy/.

In 1970, 83% of native-born Nebraskans claimed English as their mother tongue, as did 81% of all residents. Major resident groups reported their mother tongue as follows:

	NATIVE-BORN	FOREIGN-BORN
English	1,203,807	3,637
German	99,421	8,187
Czech	31,742	2,064
Polish	11,332	1,000
Spanish	11,245	2,044

⁹RELIGION

Nebraska's religious history derives from its patterns of immigration. German and Scandinavian settlers tended to be Lutheran; Irish, Polish, and Czech immigrants were mainly Roman Catholic. Methodism and other Protestant religions were spread by settlers from other midwestern states.

In 1979, the state's Catholic population was 331,824. Out of an estimated total of 896,127 Protestant adherents in 1971, 239,471 were members of Lutheran groups, 149,148 were United Methodists, and 68,858 were Presbyterians. The Jewish population was estimated at 7,905 in 1979, with most living in Omaha.

¹⁰TRANSPORTATION

Nebraska's development was profoundly influenced by two major railroads, the Union Pacific and the Burlington Northern, both of which were major landowners in the state in the late 1800s. These lines are still based in Nebraska, and three other railroads also operate there. All together, the six lines had 7,490 mi (12,054 km) of track in the state in 1977. Railroad freight traffic doubled from 1960 to 1976, when freight totaled 104,305,000 tons.

The state's road system, 96,657 mi (155,555 km) in 1978, is dominated by Interstate 80, the major east-west route and the largest public investment project in the state's history. Ninety-

five percent of the driving-age population of the state—about 1,194,000 people—held driver's licenses in 1979. A total of 1,387,382 motor vehicles were registered in 1976, of which 810,931 were automobiles and 132,136 farm vehicles.

There were 229 private and 93 public airports in the state in 1978. Omaha's airport is by far the busiest in the state, processing 829,483 passengers and 9,828 tons of freight in 1978.

¹¹HISTORY

Nebraska's first inhabitants, from about 10,000 BC. were nomadic Paleo-Indians. Successive groups were more sedentary, cultivating corn and beans. Archaeological excavations indicate that prolonged drought and dust storms prior to the 16th century caused these inhabitants to vacate the area. In the 16th and 17th centuries, other Indian tribes came from the east, some pushed by enemy tribes, others seeking new hunting grounds. By 1800, semisedentary Pawnee, Ponca, Omaha, and Oto, along with several nomadic groups, were in the region.

The Indians developed amiable relations with the first white explorers, French and Spanish fur trappers and traders who traveled through Nebraska in the 18th century, using the Missouri River as a route to the West. The area was claimed by both Spain and France, and was French territory at the time of the Louisiana Purchase, when it came under US jurisdiction. It was explored during the first half of the 19th century by Lewis and Clark, Zebulon Pike, Stephen H. Long, and John C. Frémont.

The Indian Intercourse Act of 1834 forbade white settlement west of the Mississippi River, reserving the Great Plains as Indian Territory. Nothing prevented whites from traversing Nebraska, however, and from 1840 to 1866, some 350,000 persons crossed the area on the Oregon, California, and Mormon trails, following the Platte River Valley, a natural highway to the West. Military forts were established in the 1840s to protect travelers from Indian attack.

The Kansas-Nebraska Act of 1854 established Nebraska Territory, which stretched from Kansas to Canada and from the Missouri River to the Rockies. The territory assumed its present shape in 1861. Still sparsely populated, Nebraska escaped the violence over the slavery issue that afflicted Kansas. The creation of Nebraska Territory heightened conflict between Indians and white settlers, however, as Indians were forced to cede more and more of their land. From mid-1860 to the late 1870s, western Nebraska was a battleground for Indians and US soldiers. By 1890, the Indians were defeated and moved onto reservations in Nebraska, South Dakota, and Oklahoma.

Settlement of Nebraska Territory was rapid, accelerated by the Homestead Act of 1862, under which the US government provided 160 acres (65 hectares) to a settler for a nominal fee, and the construction of the Union Pacific, the first transcontinental railroad. The Burlington Railroad, which came to Nebraska in the late 1860s, used its vast land grants from Congress to promote immigration, selling the land to potential settlers from the East and from Europe. The end of the Civil War brought an influx of Union veterans, bolstering the Republican administration, which began pushing for statehood. On 1 March 1867, Nebraska became the 37th state to join the Union. Farming and ranching developed as the state's two main enterprises. Facing for the first time the harsh elements of the Great Plains, homesteaders in central and western Nebraska evolved what came to be known as the sod-house culture, using grassy soil to construct sturdy insulated homes. They harnessed the wind with windmills to pump water, constructed fences of barbed wire, and developed dry-land farming techniques.

Ranching existed in Nebraska as early as 1859, and by the 1870s, it was well established in the western part of the state. Some foreign investors controlled hundreds of thousands of acres of the free range. The cruel winter of 1886/87 killed thousands of cattle and bankrupted many of these large ranches.

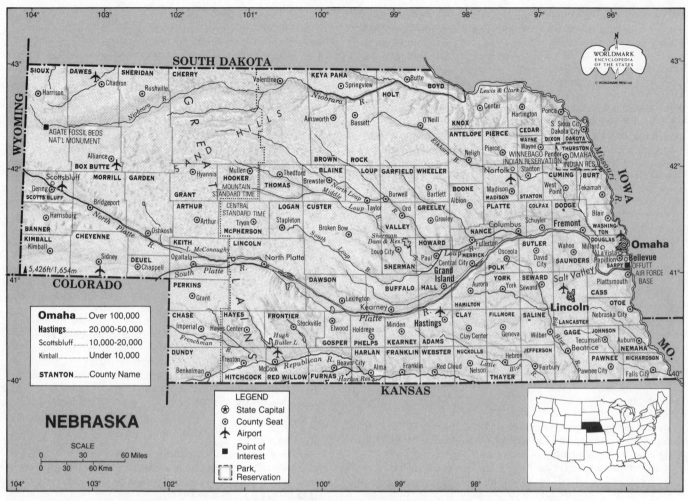

See US political: front cover F2; physical: back cover F2.

LOCATION: 40° to 43°00′02″N; 95°03′54″ to 104°03′09″w. **BOUNDARIES**: South Dakota line: land, 281 mi (452 km); Missouri River, 140 mi (225 km); Iowa line (Missouri River), 181 mi (291 km); Missouri line (Missouri River), 63 mi (101 km); Kansas line, 355 mi (571 km); Colorado line, 173 mi (279 km); Wyoming line, 139 mi (224 km).

By 1890, depressed farm prices, high railroad shipping charges, and rising interest rates were hurting the state's farmers, and a drought in the 1890s exacerbated their plight. These problems contributed to the rise of populism, a proagrarian, antimonopoly movement. Many of Nebraska's legislators embraced the new movement, helping to bring about the first initiative and referendum laws in any US state, providing for the regulation of stockyards and of telephone and telegraph companies, and instituting compulsory education.

World War I created a rift among Nebraskans, as excessive patriotic zeal was directed against residents of German descent. German-language newspapers were censored, ministers ordered to preach only in English (often to congregations that understood only German), and three university professors of German origin were fired. A Nebraska law (1919) prohibiting the teaching of any foreign language until high school was later declared unconstitutional by the US Supreme Court.

Tilling of marginal land to take advantage of farm prices inflated during World War I caused economic distress during the 1920s. Nebraska's farm economy was already in peril when the dust storms of the 1930s began, and conditions worsened as drought, heat, and grasshopper invasions plagued the state. Thousands of people, particularly from those southwest counties where dust bowl conditions were most severe, fled Nebraska for the west coast. Some farmers joined protest movements—dumping

milk, for example, rather than selling at depressed prices—while others marched on the state capital to demand a moratorium on farm debts—which they received. In the end, federal aid saved the farmers.

The onset of World War II brought prosperity to other sectors. Military airfields and war industries were placed in the state because of its safe inland location, bringing industrial growth that extended into the postwar years. Much of the new industry developed since that time is agricultural, including the manufacture of mechanized implements and irrigation equipment. Changes in farm procedures that revolutionized the state's agriculture include genetic improvement of seed through hybridization; use of pesticides, fungicides, and chemical fertilizers; and employment of close-row planting. Intensive use of irrigation, particularly center-pivot sprinkling systems, has relieved the fear of drought to some extent. On the other hand, irrigation has drastically lowered the water table, and runoff from agricultural chemicals poses a continuing threat to the purity of groundwater.

¹²STATE GOVERNMENT

The first state constitution was adopted in 1866; a second, adopted in 1875, is still in effect. A 1919–20 constitutional convention proposed and voters passed 41 amendments; by 1978, the document had been revised an additional 121 times.

Nebraska's legislature is unique among the states; since 1934, it has been a unicameral body of 49 members elected on a nonpartisan basis. Legislators are chosen in even-numbered years for four-year terms. Elected executives are the governor, lieutenant governor, secretary of state, auditor, treasurer, and attorney general, all of whom serve four-year terms. The governor and lieutenant governor are jointly elected; each must be a US citizen, at least 30 years old, and have been a resident of Nebraska for five years. After serving two consecutive terms, the governor is ineligible for the office for four years. The governor appoints the heads of 17 administrative departments.

A bill becomes law when passed by a majority of the legislature and signed by the governor. If the governor does not approve, he returns the bill with objections, and a three-fifths vote of the legislature is required to override the veto. A bill automatically becomes law if the governor does not take action within five days after receiving it.

A three-fifths majority of the legislature is required to propose an amendment to the state constitution. The people may propose an amendment by presenting a petition signed by 10% of the electorate. The amendments are then submitted for approval at the next regular election, or at a special election that can be called by a four-fifths vote of the legislature.

Voters in the state must be at least 18 years of age; there is a residency requirement of one day.

13 POLITICAL PARTIES

Historically, the Republican Party has dominated Nebraska politics: as of 1980, 23 Republican governors and 9 Democratic governors had been elected. Conservatism has typified Nebraska politics, although the voters have not been entirely predictable. For 40 years, for example, voters elected a liberal Republican, George Norris, first to the US House (1902–13) and then to the Senate (1913–43).

In the 1978 election, there were 402,097 registered Republicans, 382,693 Democrats, and 47,838 independents. As of 1979, two Democrats represented Nebraska in the US Senate, and two Republicans and one Democrat held seats in the House. The GOP picked up the third House seat in the 1980 elections, when Nebraskans also preferred the Republican presidential nominee, as they have in 10 of the last 11 presidential elections.

Nebraska Presidential Vote by Major Political Parties, 1948–80

YEAR	ELECTORAL VOTE	NEBRASKA WINNER	DEMOCRAT	REPUBLICAN
1948	6	Dewey (R)	224,165	264,774
1952	6	*Eisenhower (R)	188,057	421,603
1956	6	*Eisenhower (R)	199,029	378,108
1960	6	Nixon (R)	232,542	380,553
1964	5	*Johnson (D)	307,307	276,847
1968	5	*Nixon (R)	170,784	321,163
1972	5	*Nixon (R)	169,991	406,298
1976	5	Ford (R)	233,692	359,705
1980	5	*Reagan (R)	166,424	419,214

*Won US presidential election.

14 LOCAL GOVERNMENT

In 1978, Nebraska had 93 counties, 471 townships, 537 municipalities, and 1,282 school districts. An additional 1,192 special districts covered such services as fire protection, housing, irrigation, and sewage treatment.

Twenty-eight counties are run by elected boards of supervisors, and 65 by elected boards of commissioners. Municipalities are governed by mayors and are divided into five classifications by population: metropolitan cities, of which Omaha is the only one; primary cities, of which Lincoln is the only one; and, as of 1978, 28 first-class cities, 104 second-class cities, and 403 villages, some with populations of under 100.

15 STATE SERVICES

As of 1 June 1971, the Office of Public Counsel (Ombudsman) was empowered to investigate complaints from citizens in relation to the state government. The Accountability and Disclosure Commission, established in 1977, regulates the organization and financing of political campaigns, investigates reports of conflicts of interest involving state officials, and monitors lobbying groups.

The eight-member state Board of Education, elected on a nonpartisan basis, oversees elementary and secondary public schools and vocational education. The Board of Regents, which also consists of eight elected members, governs the University of Nebraska system. Special examining boards license architects, engineers, psychologists, and land surveyors.

The Department of Roads maintains and builds highways, and the Department of Aeronautics regulates aviation, licenses airports, and registers aviators. The Department of Motor Vehicles provides vehicle and driver services.

Public assistance, child welfare, medical care for the indigent, and a special program of services for crippled children are the responsibility of the Department of Public Welfare. The Department of Health operates community health services, provides nutritional services, and is responsible for disease control. The Department of Environmental Control monitors air and water quality, the Department of Water Resources manages the state's water supply, and the Game and Parks Commission manages park and wildlife.

The state's huge agricultural industry is aided and monitored by the Department of Agriculture, which is empowered to protect livestock, inspect food-processing areas, conduct research into crop development, and encourage product marketing.

16 JUDICIAL SYSTEM

The state's highest court is the supreme court, consisting of a chief justice and 6 other justices, all of whom are initially appointed by the governor. They must be elected after serving three years, and every six years thereafter, running unopposed on their own record. Below the supreme court are the district courts; 45 judges serve 21 districts in the state. These are trial courts of general jurisdiction. County courts handle criminal misdemeanors and those civil cases involving less than $5,000. In addition, there are a court of industrial relations, a worker's compensation court, two conciliation courts (family courts), two municipal courts (in Omaha and Lincoln), and juvenile courts in three counties. Nebraska's crime rate is well below the national average.

17 ARMED FORCES

The US military presence in Nebraska is concentrated near Omaha, where Offutt Air Force Base serves as the headquarters of the US Strategic Air Command. Total personnel at the base in 1978 was 13,922. In that year, Nebraska firms were awarded $72 million in defense contracts.

A total of 202,000 veterans of US military service resided in Nebraska as of 30 September 1979. Of these, about 5,000 served in World War I, 81,000 in World War II, 34,000 in the Korean conflict, and 63,000 in the Viet-Nam era. In 1978, a total of $147 million was spent on veterans' benefits.

Thirty communities have Army National Guard units. In 1979 there were 42 troop units with an allocated strength of 4,467 personnel. Nebraska also had ten Air National Guard units with 975 personnel, all of them stationed in Lincoln.

Of the 3,337 police officers in Nebraska in 1977, 2,579 were local police. Expenditures on police protection totaled $50 million, of which localities paid 72%.

[18] MIGRATION

The pioneers who settled Nebraska in the 1860s consisted mainly of Civil War veterans from the North and foreign-born immigrants. Some of the settlers migrated from the East and easterly parts of the Midwest, but many came directly from Europe to farm the land. The Union Pacific and Burlington Northern railroads, which sold land to the settlers, actively recruited immigrants in Europe. Germans were the largest group to settle in Nebraska (in 1900, 65,506 residents were German-born), then Czechs from Bohemia, and Scandinavians from Sweden, Denmark, and Norway. The Irish came to work on the railroads in the 1860s and stayed to help build the cities. Another wave of Irish immigrants in the 1880s went to work in the packinghouses of Omaha. The city's stockyards also attracted Polish workers. The 1900 census showed that over one-half of all Nebraskans were either foreign-born or the children of foreign-born parents.

For much of this century, Nebraska has been in a period of outmigration. From 1930 to 1960, the state suffered a net loss of nearly 500,000 people through migration, with more than one-third of the total leaving during the dust bowl decade, 1930–40. It appears that this trend was reversed during the 1970s. Within Nebraska, the largest migratory change has been a shift from farms to cities.

[19] INTERGOVERNMENTAL COOPERATION

Nebraska's Commission on Intergovernmental Cooperation represents the state in the Council of State Governments. As an oil-producing state, Nebraska is a member of the Interstate Compact to Conserve Oil and Gas. In addition, the state belongs to several regional commissions. Of particular importance are the Republican River Compact with Colorado and Kansas, and the Big Blue River Compact with Kansas. Nebraska also has boundary compacts with Iowa, South Dakota, and Missouri.

In 1978/79, the state received an estimated $474.6 million in federal aid, $42.5 million of it general revenue-sharing.

[20] ECONOMY

Agriculture has been and still is the basis of Nebraska's economy, with cattle, hogs, corn, and wheat leading the state's list of farm products. However, Nebraska is attempting to diversify its economy, and has been successful in attracting new business in large part because of its location near western coal and oil deposits.

Nearly one-half of the state's labor force is employed in agriculture, either directly or indirectly—as farm workers, as factory workers in the food-processing and farm equipment industries, or as providers of related services. Unemployment, generally well below the national average, was only 4.1% in 1977 and 2.9% in 1978.

[21] INCOME

Nebraska's per capita income was $7,391 in 1978 dollars, giving the state a rank of 29th in the nation. Measured in constant dollars, per capita income rose by 31% in Nebraska from 1970 to 1978, below the US average of 32%.

There were 147,000 people—9.6% of the state's population—living below the federal poverty level in 1975.

[22] LABOR

Nebraska's nonfarm labor force has increased rapidly in recent decades. According to state figures, the labor force totaled 716,000 in 1977, of whom 686,700 were employed. In 1978, women made up 44% of the state's labor force, well above the US average.

A federal census of workers covered by unemployment insurance in March 1977 revealed the following nonfarm employment pattern in Nebraska:

	ESTABLISHMENTS	EMPLOYEES	ANNUAL PAYROLL ('000)
Agricultural services, forestry, fishing	473	2,030	$ 20,445
Mining	189	1,829	25,965
Contract construction	4,548	29,993	434,472

	ESTABLISHMENTS	EMPLOYEES	ANNUAL PAYROLL ('000)
Manufacturing, of which:	1,832	89,643	1,115,320
Food and food products	(383)	(21,808)	(291,057)
Nonelectrical machinery	(243)	(13,419)	(181,022)
Transportation, public utilities	1,786	26,389	361,774
Wholesale trade	4,027	42,244	511,339
Retail trade	11,048	109,638	677,375
Finance, insurance, real estate	3,359	37,842	412,840
Services	9,474	99,259	716,660
Other	391	467	4,649
TOTALS	37,127	439,334	$4,280,839

The census excluded government employees, who numbered 126,600 in 1977.

Membership in unions or employees' associations in 1976 totaled 87,000, or 15% of the nonagricultural labor force, far below the US average. Most union members work in the food-processing industries. Nebraska has a right-to-work law.

[23] AGRICULTURE

With an agricultural income of over $5 billion in 1979, Nebraska ranked 6th among the 50 states. Of that total, about $3 billion came from livestock production and $1.6 billion from cash crops.

Territorial Nebraska was settled by homesteaders. Farmers easily adapted to the land in the relatively rainy eastern region, and corn soon became their major crop. In the drier central and western prairie regions, settlers were forced to learn new farming methods to conserve moisture in the ground. Droughts in the 1890s provided impetus for water conservation. Initially, oats and spring wheat were grown along with corn, but by the end of the 19th century, winter wheat became the main wheat crop. The drought and dust storms of the 1930s, which devastated the state's agricultural economy, once again drove home the need for water and soil conservation.

In 1979 there were 63,000 farms covering 48 million acres (19.4 million hectares), about 98% of Nebraska's total land area. The average of about 760 acres (306 hectares) per farm was one of the highest in the Farm Belt. In 1979, some 105,000 people worked on farms; of these, 21,000 were hired hands.

The most productive farms are located in the southern half of the state. Sorghum is grown mainly in eastern and central areas, corn in central Nebraska, and wheat all across the southern half of the state. Hamilton, York, and Buffalo counties lead in the production of corn for grain; Cheyenne and Kimball counties in wheat; and Gage, Lancaster, and Thayer counties in sorghum production. Crop production in 1979 (in bushels) included corn, 793.5 million; sorghum grain, 144.6 million; wheat, 86.7 million; soybeans, 54.7 million; and oats, 20.1 million.

Farms in Nebraska are major businesses, requiring large landholdings to justify investments. However, Nebraska farms still tend to be owned by single persons or families, rather than by large corporations.

[24] ANIMAL HUSBANDRY

In 1979, Nebraska was 2d in the US in commercial cattle slaughter (live weight) and 3d in number of cattle on farms. Beef cattle production accounts for more than one-half of the state's farm production cash receipts.

In 1974, 25,981 farms were devoted to livestock raising in Nebraska, with 21.5 million acres (8.7 million hectares) of grassland pasture. The Sand Hills region and the North Platte and central Platte valleys are the dominant cattle-raising areas. In 1979, Nebraska had a total of 6,450,000 cattle on farms, worth over $1.5 million. Hog raising is concentrated in the northeastern area; Nebraska's hog-raising business is the nation's 6th largest. The state had 4,150,000 hogs in 1979, and 175,000 sheep and lambs. In 1979, 2,835,410,000 lb of beef were produced in Nebraska and 1,509,879,000 lb of pork.

Dairy products included 1.3 billion lb of milk in 1979. About 802 million eggs were produced during the same year.

25 FISHING

Commercial fishing is negligible in Nebraska; in 1978, only 134,000 lb of fish, valued at $45,000, were caught. Sport fishing for bass, bluegill, perch, catfish, northern pike, and trout is popular.

26 FORESTRY

Arbor Day originated in Nebraska in 1872 as a way of encouraging tree planting in the state. The day is now observed throughout the US. Nebraska itself remains sparsely forested: only four states have less forestland. With 1,029,000 acres (416,000 hectares) as of 1977, the state had 0.13% of the US total.

The state's two national forests, one planted entirely by Nebraskans, occupied a total of 257,165 acres (104,071 hectares) as of 30 September 1979.

27 MINING

In 1978, the value of Nebraska's total mineral output was estimated at $147 million, 39th in the US.

Crude petroleum accounts for almost one-half of the value of mineral output, though Nebraska ranks no higher than 19th in US petroleum production. Aside from fossil fuels, the leading minerals are sand and gravel, about 17 million tons of which were mined in 1978.

28 ENERGY AND POWER

Nebraska is the only state with a power system totally owned by the public, through cooperatives and municipal plants. The state's installed capacity was 3.9 million kw in 1978, when electrical output totaled 15.2 billion kwh. Data for 1979 indicate that 46% of the electrical output came from the state's two nuclear power plants, 38% from coal, 9% from oil and natural gas, and 7% from hydroelectric plants.

As of 31 December 1978, crude petroleum reserves in the state were 29.3 million barrels; production in 1978 was estimated at 5.6 million barrels. Natural gas reserves as of 31 December 1978 were 72.8 billion cu feet, and production reached an estimated 2.9 billion cu feet in 1978. Most of the petroleum and gas reserves are in the panhandle region. Nebraska, which has no commercial coal industry, imported 36% more coal in 1976 than in 1970, most of it for electric utilities.

29 INDUSTRY

Nebraska has a small but growing industrial sector. During the 1960s, manufacturing employment increased by 28%, and the number of establishments grew by 22% between 1971 and 1977. Value added by manufacturing totaled $2.8 billion in 1977, a 63% increase over 1972. Of the 1977 total, food and food products led with 30% of the value added.

The following table shows value added by manufacturing in selected industries in 1972 and 1977:

	1972	1977
Grain-mill products	$149,900,000	$319,400,000
Meatpacking plants	219,200,000	240,200,000
Communications equipment	NA	170,400,000
Transportation equipment	68,500,000	116,600,000

The food-processing industry is based in Omaha. Iowa Beef Processors and Schuyler-Spencer Foods are the major beef-processing companies operating in the state. Grand Island, Hastings, Lexington, and Columbus have become important centers for the manufacture of farm equipment.

30 COMMERCE

In 1972, Nebraska had 4,262 wholesale trade establishments, with total sales of $6.4 billion and 33,000 employees. Trading in grain and livestock takes a major share of wholesale trade.

In 1977, Nebraska retail establishments had sales of $5.1 billion. Automotive sales accounted for 21% of the total; grocery stores, 18%; department stores and gas stations, 10% each.

Nebraska's exports of manufactured goods totaled $415.4 million in 1976, nearly three times the 1972 figure. Exports of farm commodities were about $1.1 billion in 1976/77 (6th in the US), with feed grains the leading export category.

31 CONSUMER PROTECTION

Nebraska has no separate state agency in charge of consumer protection. The Office of the Attorney General has a Consumer Protection Division, authorized under the state's Consumers Protection Act of 1974.

The Nebraska Public Service Commission regulates railroads, telephone and telegraph companies, and motor transport companies operating in the state.

32 BANKING

As of 31 December 1978 there were 452 insured commercial banks in Nebraska, with total assets of $9.6 billion. Total deposits equaled $8.2 billion, with $3.2 billion in demand deposits and $5 billion in time deposits.

There were 40 savings and loan associations in the state as of 31 December 1978. Total assets amounted to $4.5 billion; $3.7 billion in mortgage loans was outstanding. Also in 1978, 26 cooperative credit associations with assets of $93.6 million and 71 credit unions with $92 million in resources were operating in Nebraska.

During the late 1970s, Nebraska retail outlets and banks inaugurated the Nebraska Electronic Transfer System (NETS), enabling customers to purchase items by the use of card-activated banking machines that automatically transfer funds from a customer's bank account to the store's.

33 INSURANCE

The insurance industry is important in Nebraska's economy. The major company in the state is Mutual of Omaha.

Twenty-eight life insurance companies were based in the state in 1978. In that year, 2,698,000 policies were in force, with a total value of $22.2 billion. Benefit payments totaled $203.5 million, of which death benefits accounted for 35%. The average amount of life insurance per family was valued at $37,600, 7% above the US average.

In 1976, 34 Nebraska-based property and liability insurance companies earned $368 million in premiums, $91.1 million of it from within the state; 395 out-of-state companies earned $336.8 million in Nebraska premiums. Flood insurance coverage totaled $323.3 million as of 30 June 1979.

34 SECURITIES

The Bureau of Securities within the Department of Banking and Finance regulates the sale of securities in Nebraska. There are no stock exchanges in the state.

The Omaha Grain Exchange and the Omaha Livestock Market provide information on the daily movement, trade activity, and prices of grain and livestock on US commodity exchanges. No sales go through these offices, however.

New York Stock Exchange members firms had 43 sales offices and 265 registered representatives in Nebraska in 1978. State residents reported $143 million in dividend income on their 1977 federal tax returns.

35 PUBLIC FINANCE

The Nebraska state budget is prepared by the Budget Division of the Department of Administrative Services and is submitted annually by the governor to the legislature. The fiscal year runs from 1 July to 30 June.

Following is a summary of revenues and expenditures for 1976/77 and 1977/78 (in millions):

REVENUES	1976/77	1977/78
Taxes	$ 489	$ 613
Federal government	288	273
Local government	19	22
Other receipts	211	211
TOTALS	$1,007	$1,119

EXPENDITURES	1976/77	1977/78
Education	$ 312	$ 331
Highways	166	195
Public welfare	121	133
Health and hospitals	81	89
Natural resources	40	48
Other	263	246
TOTALS	$ 983	$1,042

As of 30 June 1977, the state debt outstanding was $59 million or $38 per capital (3d lowest in the US). The combined state and local debt, however, was $3.2 billion, or $2,020 per capita (6th highest in the US).

36 TAXATION
Until 1968, Nebraska had no income tax or sales tax but relied on its property tax for revenue. Rising government costs forced the adoption of these taxes, a move that had long been resisted by fiscal conservatives in the state.

State income tax in 1980 was computed as 15% of the federal tax liability. The corporate tax was 3.75% of the first $25,000 income and 4.125% of income over $25,000, based on federal tax liability for Nebraska operations. The state sales tax was 3%; Bellevue, Lincoln, and North Platte added an additional 1%, and Omaha 1.5%. In addition, there was a 13% excise tax on cigarettes, and a 9.5% tax on gasoline. Liquor and motor vehicle usage are also taxed.

Nebraska's federal tax burden in 1976 was $2.2 billion, or $1,433 per capital (26th in the US), and the state's share of federal spending was $1.8 billion, or $1,194 per capita (45th in the nation). State residents filed 630,627 federal income tax returns in 1977, paying slightly more than $1 billion in tax.

37 ECONOMIC POLICY
The Department of Economic Development was created in 1967 to promote industrial development and to diversify the state's economy. Business incentives include a tax exemption on inventory and a low workers' compensation contribution rate.

38 HEALTH
In 1969–71, Nebraska was 5th in the US in life expectancy. Average life expectancy was 72.6 years (76.61 for women, 68.85 for men), 1.85 years longer than the US average of 70.75. There were 25,000 live births in the state in 1977, or 16 per 1,000 population. Infant mortality was 12.6 per 1,000 live births for whites, 14.2 for nonwhites; the latter figure was 35% below the US average. About 5,400 legal abortions were performed, a rate of 216 per 1,000 live births. Nebraska's death rate was 9.2 per 1,000 population.

A total of 304,679 patients were admitted to 108 hospitals in 1978, 82,708 in Omaha. Hospital personnel included 4,570 registered nurses and 1,848 licensed practical nurses. Twenty-one counties in the state did not have hospitals in 1976; of those counties, five had populations of less than 1,000, and seven had populations of less than 2,000. The University of Nebraska's Hospitals (and its affiliated medical school) are in Omaha.

Nebraska had fewer physicians per capita than most other states in 1977. There were 2,167 physicians active in the state during that year, an average of 139 per 100,000 population, 20% below the US average. Dentists numbered 931 in 1979.

The average cost of a day in the hospital in 1977—$152—was much lower than the national average.

39 SOCIAL WELFARE
In 1978, 35,500 Nebraskans received $39 million worth of payments under the aid to families with dependent children (AFDC) program.

In 1978, an estimated 37,000 people participated in the federal food stamp program, receiving $10.5 million in coupons. Almost 66% (203,000) of children enrolled in Nebraska schools took part in the national school lunch program.

A total of 177,200 retired workers in the state received $425.2 million in Social Security retirement benefits in 1977. Survivors' benefits, paid to 52,600 people, amounted to $139.7 million. Under the Supplemental Security Income (SSI) program in 1978, the aged received about $5.3 million. An additional $5 million was paid through a state SSI program. Disability benefits under Social Security and SSI programs reached $59.4 million in 1977.

40 HOUSING
According to the 1970 census, there were 515,069 housing units in Nebraska, nearly 62% of which were owner occupied. In 1970, 40% of all housing units were in rural areas, 80% were single-unit structures, and 94% of homes had full plumbing facilities. In 1978, 10,600 new housing units authorized by the state had a total value of $275,000,000. About 92,000 new housing units were authorized between 1970 and 1978.

41 EDUCATION
Nebraska has more school districts (1,282 in 1978) than any other state, and education is the largest item of expenditure in the state budget. In 1970, the illiteracy rate was 0.6%, half the US average. In 1976, 74% of all Nebraskans 18 years or over were high school graduates.

In 1979 there were 1,698 public schools in Nebraska; 1,302 were elementary schools and 396 secondary schools. Enrollments for fall 1979 were elementary, 191,419; secondary, 96,151. Nebraska also had 226 nonpublic schools in 1978/79; 199 were elementary schools, 27 were secondary schools, and 19 offered both elementary and secondary education. There were 26,650 pupils enrolled in elementary grades; secondary, 10,394.

The University of Nebraska is the state's largest postsecondary institution, with campuses in Lincoln and Omaha. In 1979 there were also 4 state colleges, 14 private colleges, and 11 community-based technical colleges. In fall 1977, 67,002 students were enrolled in state colleges and universities, and 14,314 students were enrolled in private institutions of higher learning.

The Nebraska Department of Agriculture offers a loan program for postsecondary study to Nebraskans who live on farms or ranches, or at least 50% of whose family income is from farm or ranch labor.

42 ARTS
The Orpheum Theater in Omaha, renovated and reopened in 1975, provides performance space for opera, symphony concerts, ballet, plays, and popular music. The Art Guild and the Sheldon Art Gallery in Lincoln are leading centers for the visual arts. Modern sculptures line Route 80 as part of a state-sponsored artist-in-residence program.

Drama is presented at Lincoln and Omaha playhouses, and there are many resident community theaters. Omaha and Lincoln both have symphony orchestras, as do some smaller communities. Notable among the state's amateur groups is the Hastings Civic Symphony, founded in 1926. Even the sparsely populated Sand Hills region supports an orchestra. The Omaha Ballet Society sponsors dance performances in that city.

43 LIBRARIES AND MUSEUMS
The state's library system is divided into six regions covering all of Nebraska. In 1977, the state had 27 county libraries, 15 regional libraries, 26 academic and postsecondary libraries, 11 libraries in technical colleges, 19 institutional libraries, and 281 public libraries. In addition, libraries were maintained by the state, the Nebraska Library Commission, and the State Historical Society. A total of 3,689,004 volumes were in the public library system in 1977, and the total circulation was 7,338,751.

The Joslyn Art Museum in Omaha, with collections of ancient and modern paintings, graphics, decorative arts, sculpture, and archaeological artifacts, is the state's leading museum. Other important museums include the Nebraska State Historical Society and the University of Nebraska State Museum (natural history), both in Lincoln; the Western Heritage Museum in Omaha; the

Stuhr Museum of the Prairie Pioneer in Grand Island, and the Hastings Museum in Hastings. In all, the state had more than 90 museums in 1979.

The Agate Fossil Beds National Monument in northwestern Nebraska features fossils from the Miocene era.

⁴⁴COMMUNICATIONS

In 1978/79, Nebraska was served by 657 post offices and 5,400 employees of the US Postal Service. Forty-four telephone companies are regulated by the Public Service Commission; Northwestern Bell is the principal carrier. The state had 1,246,659 telephones in 1978, of which 928,091 were residential and 318,568 business. Virtually all households had telephones in 1978.

In 1978, 31 FM stations (about double the 1970 total) and 48 AM stations were operating commercially, and another 11 noncommercial FM stations were licensed. There were 14 commercial TV stations and a network of 9 PBS stations. As of December 1979, 51 cable television systems operated in the state, serving 88,328 subscribers in 56 communities.

⁴⁵PRESS

In 1978, Nebraska had 3 morning dailies with a combined circulation of 172,300, 16 evening dailies with a combined circulation of 320,580, and 5 Sunday newspapers with a total circulation of 388,916. The leading newspaper in 1979 was the *Omaha World-Herald*, with circulations as follows: morning, 124,765; evening, 111,092; and Sunday, 279,738. The *Lincoln Journal* had a daily circulation of 44,485 (evening) and a Sunday circulation (as the *Journal and Star*) of 69,167.

⁴⁶ORGANIZATIONS

A unique civic organization in Omaha, the Knights of Ak-Sar-Ben (Nebraska spelled backwards), sponsors an annual ball and festival, livestock shows, and horseracing. Proceeds are donated to conservation projects.

Among the national or regional organizations based in the state are the Great Plains Agricultural Council at the University of Nebraska in Lincoln, the American Shorthorn Society in Omaha, and the American Old Time Fiddlers Association in Lincoln.

⁴⁷TOURISM, TRAVEL, AND RECREATION

Tourism is not a major industry in Nebraska. The state depends on "pass through" traffic for travel revenues: of Nebraska's out-of-state visitors in 1976, fewer than 28% of the total number planned to visit only Nebraska, while 35% were bound for Colorado, California, or Wyoming. Expenditures by travelers in the state totaled about $600 million in 1976.

The 92 state parks and recreational areas are main tourist attractions; fishing, swimming, picnicking, and sightseeing are the principal activities. The Salt Valley recreational areas, with 1.8 million visitors, were the most popular attraction in 1977.

In 1977/78, licenses were issued to 202,210 fishermen and 151,132 hunters.

⁴⁸SPORTS

Nebraskans' favorite spectator sport is college football. Equestrian activities, including racing and rodeos, are also popular.

Pari-mutuel racing is licensed by the state, and tracks are operated by nonprofit organizations in Omaha, Lincoln, Grand Island, Columbus, and South Sioux City; quarter-horse tracks are in Broken Bow and Deshler. The racing season lasts from March to November. The state general fund receives 5% of all money in excess of $1 million wagered at each track and levies a tax on tickets to the meets.

The University of Nebraska Cornhuskers compete in the Big Eight football conference. The team often places high in national rankings and has been a frequent competitor in postseason play.

⁴⁹FAMOUS NEBRASKANS

Nebraska was the birthplace of only one US president, Gerald R. Ford (Leslie King, Jr., b.1913). When Spiro Agnew resigned the vice-presidency in October 1973, President Richard M. Nixon appointed Ford, then a US representative from Michigan, to the post. Upon Nixon's resignation on 9 August 1974, Ford thus became the first nonelected president in US history.

Four native and adoptive Nebraskans have served in the cabinet. J. Sterling Morton (b.New York, 1832–1902), who originated Arbor Day, was secretary of agriculture under Grover Cleveland. William Jennings Bryan (b.Illinois, 1860–1925), a US representative from Nebraska, served as secretary of state and was three times the unsuccessful Democratic candidate for president. Frederick A. Seaton (b.Washington, 1909–74) was Dwight Eisenhower's secretary of the interior, and Melvin Laird (b.1922) was Richard Nixon's secretary of defense.

George W. Norris (b.Ohio, 1861–1944), the "fighting liberal," served 10 years in the US House of Representatives and 30 years in the Senate. Norris's greatest contributions were in rural electrification (his efforts led to the creation of the Tennessee Valley Authority), farm relief, and labor reform; he also promoted the unicameral form of government in Nebraska. Theodore C. Sorensen (b.1928) was an adviser to and biographer of President John F. Kennedy.

Indian leaders important in Nebraska history include Oglala Sioux chiefs Red Cloud (1822–1909) and Crazy Horse (1849?–77). Moses Kinkaid (b.West Virginia, 1854–1920) served in the US House and was the author of the Kinkaid Act, which encouraged homesteading in Nebraska. Educator and legal scholar Roscoe Pound (1870–1964) was also a Nebraskan. In agricultural science, Samuel Aughey (b.Pennsylvania, 1831–1912) and Hardy W. Campbell (b.Vermont, 1850–1937) developed dry-land farming techniques. Botanist Charles E. Bessey (b.Ohio, 1845–1915) encouraged forestation. Father Edward Joseph Flanagan (b.Ireland, 1886–1948) was the founder of Boys Town, a home for underprivileged youth. Two native Nebraskans became Nobel laureates in 1980: Lawrence R. Klein (b.1920) in economics and Val L. Fitch (b.1923) in physics.

Writers associated with Nebraska include Willa Cather (b.Virginia, 1873–1947), who used the Nebraska frontier setting of her childhood in many of her writings and won a Pulitzer Prize in 1922; author and poet John G. Neihardt (b.Illinois, 1881–1973), who incorporated Indian mythology and history in his work; Mari Sandoz (1901–66), who wrote of her native Great Plains; writer-photographer Wright Morris (b.1910); and author Tillie Olsen (b.1913). Rollin Kirby (1875–1952) won three Pulitzer Prizes for political cartooning. Composer-conductor Howard Hanson (b.1896), born in Wahoo, won a Pulitzer Prize in 1944.

Nebraskans important in entertainment include actor-dancer Fred Astaire (Fred Austerlitz, b.1899); actors Harold Lloyd (1894–1971), Henry Fonda (b.1905), Robert Taylor (Spangler Arlington Brugh, 1911–69), Marlon Brando (b.1924), and Sandy Dennis (b.1937); television stars Johnny Carson (b.Iowa, 1925) and Dick Cavett (b.1936); and motion-picture producer Darryl F. Zanuck (b.1902).

⁵⁰BIBLIOGRAPHY

Creigh, Dorothy Weyer. *Nebraska: A Bicentennial History.* New York: Norton, 1977.

Federal Writers' Project. *Nebraska: A Guide to the Cornhusker State.* New York: Hastings House, 1947 (orig. 1939).

Nebraska, State of. Department of Economic Development. *Nebraska Statistical Handbook, 1978-1979.* Lincoln, 1977.

Nebraska, State of. *Executive Budget, 1980-1982.* Lincoln, 1980.

Nebraska, State of. Legislative Council. *Nebraska Blue Book, 1978-1979.* Lincoln, 1977.

Olson, James C. *History of Nebraska.* Lincoln: University of Nebraska Press, 1966 (orig. 1955).

Peirce, Neal B. *The Great Plains States of America.* New York: Norton, 1973.

Sandoz, Mari. *Love Song to the Plains.* Lincoln: University of Nebraska Press, 1966 (orig. 1961).

NEVADA

State of Nevada

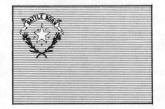

ORIGIN OF STATE NAME: Named for the Sierra Nevada, *nevada* meaning "snow-covered" in Spanish. **NICKNAME**: The Sagebrush State. (Also: The Silver State.) **CAPITAL**: Carson City. **ENTERED UNION**: 31 October 1864 (36th). **SONG**: "Home Means Nevada." **MOTTO**: All for Our Country. **FLAG**: On a blue field, two sprays of sagebrush and a golden scroll in the upper lefthand corner frame a silver star encircled by the word "Nevada"; the scroll, reading "Battle Born," recalls that Nevada was admitted to the Union during the Civil War. **OFFICIAL SEAL**: An ore-crushing mill, ore cart, and mine tunnel symbolize Nevada's mining industry; a plow, sickle, and sheaf of wheat represent its agricultural resources. In the background are a railroad, a telegraph line, and a sun rising over the mountains. Encircling this scene are 36 stars and the state motto. The words "The Great Seal of the State of Nevada" surround the whole. **ANIMAL**: Desert bighorn sheep. **BIRD**: Mountain bluebird. **FLOWER**: Sagebrush. **TREE**: Single-leaf piñon. **METAL**: Silver. **GRASS**: Indian ricegrass. **FOSSIL**: Ichthyosaur. **LEGAL HOLIDAYS**: New Year's Day, 1 January; Washington's Birthday, 3d Monday in February; Memorial Day, last Monday in May; Independence Day, 4 July; Labor Day, 1st Monday in September; Nevada Day, 31 October; Veterans Day, 11 November; Thanksgiving Day, 4th Thursday in November; Christmas Day, 25 December. **TIME**: 4 A.M. PST = noon GMT.

¹LOCATION, SIZE, AND EXTENT

Situated between the Rocky Mountains and the Sierra Nevada in the western US, Nevada ranks 7th in size among the 50 states.

The total area of Nevada is 110,540 sq mi (286,298 sq km), with land comprising 109,889 sq mi (284,612 sq km) and inland water covering 651 sq mi (1,686 sq km). Nevada extends 320 mi (515 km) E–W; the maximum N–S extension is 483 mi (777 km).

Nevada is bordered on the N by Oregon and Idaho; on the E by Utah and Arizona (with the line in the SE formed by the Colorado River); and on the S and W by California (with part of the line passing through Lake Tahoe). The total boundary length of Nevada is *1,480 mi (2,382 km)*. The state's geographic center is in Lander County, 26 mi (42 km) SE of Austin.

²TOPOGRAPHY

Almost all of Nevada belongs physiographically to the Great Basin, a plateau dominated by numerous mountain ranges. These ranges are short, up to 75 mi (121 km) long and 15 mi (24 km) wide, most with altitudes of 7,000–10,000 feet (2,100–3,000 meters). Chief among them are the Schell Creek, Ruby, Toiyabe, and Carson (within the Sierra Nevada). Nevada's highest point is Boundary Peak, 13,143 feet (4,006 meters), in the southwest.

Despite its arid climate, Nevada has a number of large lakes and saline marshes known as sinks. The largest lake is Pyramid, with an area of 188 sq mi (487 sq km), in the west. Nevada shares Lake Tahoe with California, and Lake Mead, created by Hoover Dam on the Colorado River, with Arizona. The streams of Nevada frequently disappear during dry spells; many of them flow into local lakes or sinks without reaching the sea. The state's longest river, the Humboldt, flows for 290 mi (467 km) through the northern half of the state into the Humboldt Sink. The Walker, Truckee, and Carson rivers drain the western part of Nevada. The canyon carved by the mighty Colorado, the river that forms the extreme southeastern boundary of the state, accounts for Nevada's lowest elevation, 470 feet (143 meters).

³CLIMATE

Nevada's climate is sunny and dry, with wide variation in daily temperatures. The normal daily temperature at Reno is 49°F (9°C), ranging from 32°F (0°C) in January to 69°F (21°C) in July. The all-time high, 122°F (50°C), was set at Overton on 23 June 1954; the record low, −50°F (−46°C), at San Jacinto on 8 January 1937.

Nevada is the driest state in the US, with an overall average annual precipitation of less than 4 in (10 cm). Snowfall is abundant in the mountains, however, reaching 60 in (152 cm) a year on the highest peaks.

⁴FLORA AND FAUNA

Various pine—among them the single-leaf piñon, the state tree—dominate Nevada's woodlands. Creosote bush is common in southern Nevada, as are many kinds of sagebrush throughout the state. Wild flowers include shooting star and white and yellow violets. Fifteen types of beech are listed as threatened.

Native mammals include the black bear, white-tailed and mule deer, pronghorn antelope, Rocky Mountain elk, cottontail rabbit, and river otter. Grouse, partridge, pheasant, and quail are the leading game birds, and a diversity of trout, charr, salmon, and whitefish thrive in Nevada waters. Rare and protected reptiles are the Gila monster and desert tortoise. Listed as endangered are the Utah cutthroat trout and Colorado squawfish.

⁵ENVIRONMENTAL PROTECTION

Preservation of the state's clean air, scarce water resources, and no longer abundant wildlife is the major environmental challenge facing Nevada. The Department of Fish and Game sets quotas on the hunting of deer, antelope, bighorn sheep, and other game animals. The Department of Conservation and Natural Resources has broad responsibility for environmental protection, state lands, forests, and water and mineral resources. Controversial environmental issues as the 1980s began were the proposed MX intercontinental ballistic missile system and to what extent resort development of Lake Tahoe should continue.

⁶POPULATION

Nevada ranked 47th in the US with a 1970 census population of 488,738. The preliminary census total for 1980 was 800,312, representing a 10-year growth of 63.8%, the highest in the US. The population boom dates from 1940, when the state had only 110,427 residents; the population tripled between 1950 and 1970. As might be expected, Nevadans are among the most mobile Americans: as of 1976, more than 35% of the adults had lived in the state for five years or less, and only 13% had lived there all their lives.

With a population density of 6 per sq mi (2 per sq km) in 1978, Nevada remains one of the nation's most sparsely populated states. More than 80% of Nevada's people live in cities, the largest of which, Las Vegas, had 162,960 residents according to preliminary 1980 census data. Reno had a population of 100,943; Carson City, the capital, 32,114.

⁷ETHNIC GROUPS

Some 38,000 black Americans made up about 6% of Nevada's population in 1976. The American Indian population was 7,933 in 1970; tribal landholdings totaled 1,067,000 acres (432,000 hectares) in 1978.

Nearly 14% of all state residents were foreign-born or children of the foreign-born in 1970. The leading countries of origin were Italy, Canada, and Germany.

⁸LANGUAGES

As of the 1970 census, 3,286 Nevadans reported Indian first languages. Midland and Northern English dialects are so intermixed in Nevada that no clear regional division appears; an example of this is the scattered use of both Midland *dived* (instead of dove) as the past tense of *dive* and the Northern /krik/ for *creek*.

In 1970, 80% of Nevada's native-born residents affirmed English as their mother tongue, as did 78% of all residents. Speakers of the principal first languages were as follows.

	NATIVE-BORN	FOREIGN-BORN
English	376,901	3,910
Spanish	12,952	3,884
German	8,117	2,425
Italian	7,004	1,507

⁹RELIGIONS

In 1979, Nevada had 110,000 Roman Catholics. Other Christian denominations had a total of 92,461 known adherents in 1971, of whom 47,269 belonged to the Church of Jesus Christ of Latter-day Saints (Mormons). In 1979 there were an estimated 14,700 Jews, 92% of them in metropolitan Las Vegas.

¹⁰TRANSPORTATION

As of 1974, Nevada had 1,573 mi (2,532 km) of railroads. Amtrak provides passenger service en route from Salt Lake City to Los Angeles.

In 1978 there were 49,899 mi (80,305 km) of roads and streets, 610,916 registered vehicles, and 527,118 licensed drivers. The major highways, I-80 and I-15, link Salt Lake City with Reno and Las Vegas, respectively. There were 58 public and 62 private airfields in 1978. The leading commercial air terminals are at Las Vegas and Reno.

¹¹HISTORY

The first inhabitants of what is now Nevada arrived about 12,000 years ago. They were fisherman, as well as hunters and food gatherers, for the glacial lakes of the ancient Great Basin were then only beginning to recede. Numerous sites of early human habitation have been found, the most famous being Pueblo Grande de Nevada (also known as Lost City). In modern times, four principal Indian groups have inhabited Nevada: Southern Paiute, Northern Paiute, Shoshoni, and Washo.

Probably the first white explorer to enter the state was the Spanish priest Francisco Garcés, who apparently penetrated extreme southern Nevada in 1776. The year 1826 saw Peter Skene Ogden of the British Hudson's Bay Company enter the northeast in a prelude to his later exploration of the Humboldt River; the rival American trapper Jedediah Smith traversed the state in 1826–27. During 1843–44, John C. Frémont led the first of his several expeditions into Nevada.

Nevada's first permanent white settlement, Mormon Station (later Genoa), was founded in 1850 in what is now western Nevada, a region that became part of Utah Territory the same year (the southeastern tip of Nevada was assigned to the Territory of New Mexico). Soon other Mormon settlements were started there and in Las Vegas Valley. The Las Vegas mission failed, but the farming communities to the northwest succeeded, even though friction between Mormons and placer miners in that area caused political unrest. Most of the Mormons in western Nevada departed in 1857 when Salt Lake City was threatened by an invasion of federal troops.

A separate Nevada Territory was established in 1861, and only three years later, on 31 October 1864, Nevada achieved statehood, although the present boundaries were not established until 18 January 1867. Two factors accelerated the creation of Nevada: the secession of the southern states whose congressmen had been blocking the creation of new free states; and the discovery, in 1859, of the Comstock Lode, an immense concentration of silver and gold which attracted thousands of fortune seekers and established the region as a thriving mining center.

Nevada's development during the remainder of the century was determined by the economic fortunes of the Comstock, whose affairs were dominated, first, by the Bank of California (in alliance with the Central Pacific Railroad) and then by the "Bonanza Firm" of John W. Mackay and his partners. The lode's rich ores were exhausted in the late 1870s, and Nevada slipped into a 20-year depression. A number of efforts were made to revive the economy, one being an attempt to encourage mining by increasing the value of silver. To this end, Nevadans wholeheartedly supported the movement for free silver coinage during the 1890s, and the Silver Party reigned supreme in state politics for most of the decade.

Nevada's economy revived following new discoveries of silver at Tonopah and gold at Goldfield early in the 20th century. A second great mining boom ensued, bolstered and extended by major copper discoveries in eastern Nevada. Progressive political ferment in this pre–World War I period added recall, referendum, and initiative amendments to the state constitution and brought about the adoption of women's suffrage (1914).

The 1920s was a time of subdued economic activity; mining fell off, and not even the celebrated divorce trade, centered in Reno, was able to compensate for its decline. Politically, the decade was conservative and Republican, with millionaire George Wingfield dominating state politics through a so-called bipartisan machine. Nevada went Democratic during the 1930s, when the hard times of the depression were alleviated by federal public-works projects, most notably the construction of the Hoover (Boulder) Dam, and by state laws aiding the divorce business and legalizing gambling (1931).

Gaming grew rapidly after World War II, becoming by the mid-1950s not only the mainstay of Nevada tourism but also the state's leading industry. Revelations during the 1950s and 1960s that organized crime had infiltrated the casino industry and that casino income was being used to finance narcotics and other rackets in major east coast cities led to a state and federal crackdown and the imposition of new state controls. Gaming operations were relatively scandal-free in the 1970s.

In the late 1970s, Nevada became the focus of the "sagebrush rebellion," a political attempt by some western states to gain possession of federal lands within their boundaries.

¹²STATE GOVERNMENT

Nevada's 1864 constitution, as amended, continues to govern the state. The state legislature consists of a senate with 20 members, each elected to a four-year term, and a house of representatives with 40 members, each serving two years. Executive officials elected statewide include the governor and lieutenant governor (who run separately), secretary of state, attorney general, treasurer, and controller, all of whom serve for four years. A two-thirds vote of the elected members of each house is required to override a gubernatorial veto.

Constitutional amendments may be submitted to the voters for ratification if they have received majority votes in each house in two successive sessions or under an initiative procedure calling for petitions signed by 10% of those who voted in the last general election. Legislative amendments need a majority vote, initiative

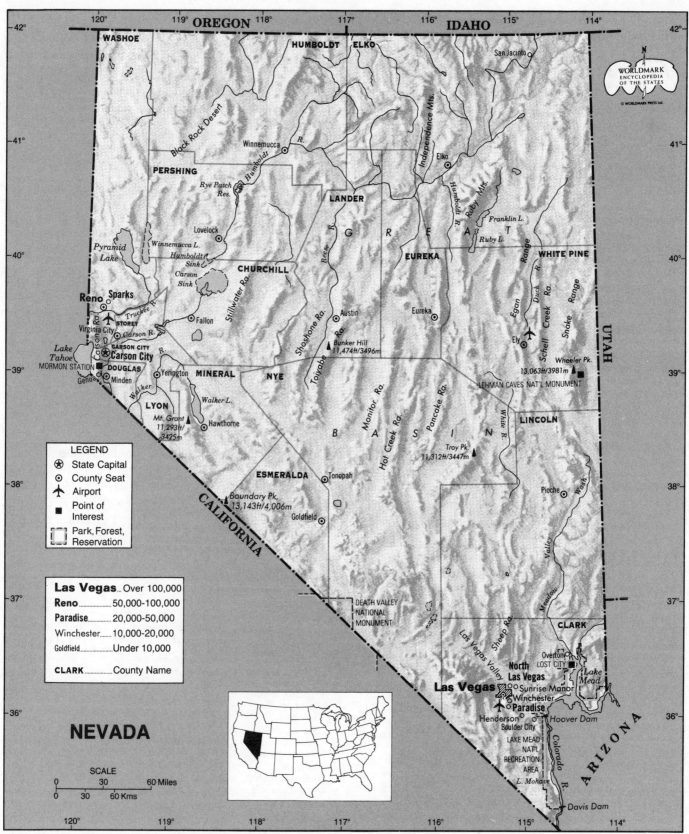

NEVADA

LEGEND

⊛ State Capital
⊙ County Seat
✈ Airport
■ Point of Interest
⬚ Park, Forest, Reservation

Las Vegas......Over 100,000
Reno..............50,000–100,000
Paradise...........20,000–50,000
Winchester......10,000–20,000
Goldfield............Under 10,000

CLARK..............County Name

SCALE
0   30   60 Miles
0   30   60 Kms

See US political: front cover C3; physical: back cover C3.

LOCATION: 35° to 42°N; 114° to 120°W. **BOUNDARIES**: Oregon line, *155 mi (249.5 km)*; Idaho line, *155 mi (249.5 km)*; Utah line, *345 mi (555 km)*; Arizona line, *205 mi (330 km)*; California line, *620 mi (998 km)*.

amendments require majorities in two consecutive elections. Voters must be US citizens, at least 18 years old, and must have lived in the state for 30 days and in the precinct for 10.

13 POLITICAL PARTIES

Registered Democrats outnumbered Republicans by 158,576 to 90,371 in 1978. The Democrats have failed to capitalize on this advantage, however, and since World War II neither party has dominated state politics, which are basically conservative. Ronald Reagan carried Nevada by nearly a two-to-one majority in 1980.

The free silver issue led the state's electors to cast their votes for the Populist candidate in 1892. Candidates of the Nevada Silver Party or a Democrat-Silver coalition held the governorship from 1895 to 1911, well after the silver controversy had subsided as a national issue.

Nevada Presidential Vote by Major Political Parties, 1948–80

YEAR	ELECTORAL VOTE	NEVADA WINNER	DEMOCRAT	REPUBLICAN
1948	3	*Truman (D)	31,290	29,357
1952	3	*Eisenhower (R)	31,688	50,502
1956	3	*Eisenhower (R)	40,640	56,049
1960	3	*Kennedy (D)	54,880	52,387
1964	3	*Johnson (D)	79,339	56,094
1968	3	*Nixon (R)	60,598	73,188
1972	3	*Nixon (R)	66,016	115,750
1976	3	Ford (R)	92,479	101,273
1980	3	*Reagan (R)	66,666	155,017

*Won US presidential election.

14 LOCAL GOVERNMENT

As of 1977, Nevada was subdivided into 16 counties, 1 independent municipality (Carson City), 16 other municipalities constituting the 16 county seats, and 132 special districts.

15 STATE SERVICES

The State Ethics Commission was created in 1977 to oversee financial disclosure by state officials. The Department of Education and the University of Nevada System are the main state educational agencies. The Department of Human Resources has divisions covering public health, rehabilitation, mental hygiene and mental retardation, welfare, youth services, and programs for the elderly. Regulatory functions are exercised by the Commerce Department (insurance, banking, real estate), the Public Service Commission, the Gaming Control Board, and other state agencies.

16 JUDICIAL SYSTEM

Nevada's supreme court consists of a chief justice and 4 other justices. As of 1980 there were 27 district court judges organized into 9 judicial districts. All judges are elected by nonpartisan ballot to six-year terms.

Nevada's overall crime rate—8,287 per 100,000 population in 1978—was the highest in the US. The rate for murder and nonnegligent manslaughter, 15.5 per 100,000 population, ranked 2d only to Louisiana's. Only Alaska had more forcible rapes, only New York State had more robberies, and no state had more burglary cases. Las Vegas, with its large transient population, had the highest crime rate of any US metropolitan area, 9,417, and Reno, with 8,613, was not far behind.

17 ARMED FORCES

Nevada had three installations in 1978, with 11,845 authorized personnel; the state has been the site of both ballistic missile and atomic weapons testing. In 1978, Nevada firms received $42 million in federal defense contracts. Most of the MX defense complex, a mobile missile system costing at least $33 billion and extending across 6,000 sq mi (16,000 sq km) of federal lands, was scheduled for construction in Nevada during the 1980s.

As of 30 September 1979, 95,000 military veterans were living in the state, including 1,000 from World War I, 41,000 of World War II, 19,000 of the Korean conflict, and 28,000 from the Viet-Nam era. Veterans' benefits in 1977/78 totaled $63 million.

National Guard personnel numbered 1,800 during 1978. State and local police personnel totaled 2,481 in 1977, when expenditures for police services came to $46 million.

18 MIGRATION

In 1870, about half of Nevada's population consisted of foreign immigrants, among them Chinese, Italians, Swiss, British, Irish, Germans, and French Canadians. Though their origins were diverse, their numbers were few—no more than 21,000 in all. Not until the 1940s did migrants come in large volume. Between 1940 and 1977, Nevada gained a total of 376,000 residents through migration, equal to 59% of the estimated 1977 population.

19 INTERGOVERNMENTAL COOPERATION

Nevada takes part in the Colorado River Compact, the Tahoe Regional Planning Compact, and the California-Nevada Interstate Compact, under which the two states administer water rights involving Lake Tahoe and the Carson, Truckee, and Walker rivers. The state also is a signatory to the Interstate Oil and Gas Compact and the Western Interstate Energy Compact.

Federal aid in 1978/79 totaled $206.9 million, of which $17 million was general revenue sharing.

20 ECONOMY

Nevada is disadvantaged by aridity and a shortage of arable land, but blessed with a wealth of mineral resources—gold, silver, copper, and other metals. Mining remains important, though overshadowed since World War II by tourism, which generates more than 50% of the state's income. Legalized gaming alone produces more than 40% of Nevada's tax revenues.

21 INCOME

Personal income in Nevada came to $6 billion in 1978; per capita income averaged $9,032, 3d in the US. The median family income of $14,961 ranked 15th in the US in 1975, when 53,000 Nevadans—less than 9% of the population—were below the federal poverty level.

22 LABOR

Nevada's total civilian labor force in 1978 was 334,000, of whom about 15,000 (4.5%) were unemployed. Of the total work force, some 200,000 were male and 134,000 female.

A federal census of workers covered by unemployment insurance in March 1977 revealed the following nonfarm employment pattern in Nevada:

	ESTABLISH-MENTS	EMPLOYEES	ANNUAL PAYROLL ('000)
Agricultural services, forestry, fishing	163	734	$ 8,604
Mining, of which:	136	3,591	56,706
Metals	(56)	(2,420)	(38,745)
Contract construction	1,750	18,024	317,658
Manufacturing	645	15,147	195,572
Transportation, public utilities	548	16,466	252,282
Wholesale trade	969	9,514	127,698
Retail trade	4,473	49,398	401,202
Finance, insurance, real estate	1,565	11,357	125,825
Services, of which:	5,119	111,557	1,162,895
Hotels, lodgings	(561)	(41,415)	(444,146)
Amusements, recreation	(365)	(36,566)	(349,711)
Other	289	453	5,273
TOTALS	15,657	236,241	$2,653,715

There were also about 50,000 government employees not covered by this survey.

In 1976, 69,000 workers belonged to labor unions, and 8,000 to employee associations. Nevada has a right-to-work law.

²³AGRICULTURE
Agricultural income in 1978 totaled $171.4 million (47th in the US), of which about one-fourth was from crops and three-fourths from livestock and animal products. Chief crops in 1979 included 1.6 million bushels of wheat, 1.3 million bushels of barley, 942,000 tons of hay, and 5.5 million hundredweight of potatoes. Virtually all the state's cropland requires irrigation.

²⁴ANIMAL HUSBANDRY
At the end of 1979, Nevada ranches and farms had 580,000 cattle and calves, 15,000 milk cows, and 122,000 sheep and lambs. Livestock products included 199 million lb of milk; 178.8 million lb of cattle and calves; 7.6 million lb of sheep and lambs; and 1.8 million eggs. The wool clip in 1978 was about 1.1 million lb.

²⁵FISHING
There is no commercial fishing industry in Nevada.

²⁶FORESTRY
Nevada in 1977 had 7,683,000 acres (3,109,000 hectares) of forestland, of which 5,143,000 acres (2,081,000 hectares) were in the National Forest System. Less than 2% of all forested land in Nevada was classified as commercial timberland.

²⁷MINING
Although mining plays an important part in the state's history and economy, Nevada ranked no better than 36th among the 50 states in 1978, with a mineral output of $205 million. Leading minerals were gold, 260,895 troy oz (2d in the US); silver, 804,000 troy oz; copper, 22,546 tons; zinc, 1,508 tons; lead, 720 tons; molybdenum, 99,000 lb; sand and gravel, 11,000,000 tons; and stone, 1,600,000 tons. Barite, lime, and salt are also produced.

²⁸ENERGY AND POWER
Nevada had an installed electrical capacity of 3.7 million kw in 1978, when 13.1 billion kwh of power were produced. That year, 8 billion kwh of electrical energy were sold in the state, the remainder being exported, principally to California. Hoover Dam, anchored in the bedrock of Black Canyon east of Las Vegas, was the largest hydroelectric installation. Eastern Nevada has some small oil deposits.

²⁹INDUSTRY
Industry in Nevada is limited but diversified, producing communications equipment, pet food, chemicals, and sprinkler systems, among other products. The total value added by manufacture in 1977 was $497.8 million, more than double the 1972 total. Major sectors and their value added in 1972 and 1977 were as follows:

	1972	1977
Stone, clay, glass products	$35,800,000	$82,200,000
Food and food products	30,000,000	66,000,000
Electric and electronic equipment	12,500,000	60,800,000
Chemicals and chemical products	35,500,000	59,600,000

³⁰COMMERCE
Wholesale trade in Nevada totaled about $900 million in 1972. Retail sales in 1977 exceeded $3 billion, with metropolitan Las Vegas accounting for 56% of the total, metropolitan Reno 29%. Foreign exports included $27 million in manufactured goods in 1976 and $10 million in agricultural products in 1976/77.

³¹CONSUMER PROTECTION
The Consumer Affairs Division of the Department of Commerce, with offices in Las Vegas and Carson City, protects consumers from deceptive or fraudulent sales practices, and represents consumers' interests in government. The Consumer Health Protection Services office, in the Department of Human Resources, is responsible for safe drinking water, radiological health, and inspection of motels, restaurants, and other institutions.

³²BANKING
During 1978 there were 9 insured commercial banks in Nevada, with total assets of $3.3 billion. Outstanding loans totaled $1.4 billion; deposits, $2.9 billion. In addition, there were 7 savings and loan associations with total assets exceeding $1.9 billion; mortgage loans outstanding reached $1.5 billion.

³³INSURANCE
Nevadans held 1,306,000 life insurance policies in 1978 with a total value of $10.1 billion. Life insurance per family averaged $38,100, 9% above the national average, and benefit payments totaled $80.2 million. Property and liability insurers wrote $262.5 million in premiums, of which 49% was automobile coverage.

³⁴SECURITIES
There are no securities exchanges in Nevada.

³⁵PUBLIC FINANCE
Nevada's budget is prepared biennially by the Budget Division of the Department of Administration and submitted by the governor to the legislature, which has unlimited power to change it. The fiscal year begins 1 July and ends 30 June.

The following table summarizes estimated general revenues and recommended appropriations for 1979/80 and 1980/81:

	1979/80	1980/81
REVENUES		
Gaming tax	$125,619,000	$143,505,000
Sales and use tax	119,782,000	137,750,000
Casino entertainment tax	17,942,000	19,377,000
Other receipts	37,302,923	41,254,802
TOTALS	$300,645,923	$341,886,802
EXPENDITURES		
Education	$172,791,419	$203,025,781
Human resources	62,612,655	69,754,705
Public safety	18,588,983	20,632,756
Other outlays	45,235,366	49,680,006
TOTALS	$299,228,423	$343,093,248

As of mid-1977, the total state and local government debt was $722 million, or $1,141 per capita.

³⁶TAXATION
Taken together, taxes on gaming and the casino entertainment tax totaled $130.9 million in 1978/79, or 44% of total state government revenues. As of 1980, Nevada also levied a 3% sales and use tax, along with taxes on liquor, real estate transfers, and numerous other items. There is no personal or corporate income tax. Nevadans filed 320,284 federal income tax returns in 1977, paying $699,044,000 in tax.

³⁷ECONOMIC POLICY
Federal projects have played an especially large role in the development of Nevada. During the depression of the 1930s, Hoover (Boulder) Dam was constructed to provide needed jobs, water, and hydroelectric power for the state. Other public works—Davis Dam (Lake Mohave) and the Southern Nevada Water Project—have served a similar purpose. The fact that some 87% of Nevada land is owned by the US government further increases the federal impact on the economy.

Nevada is not unique in its use of gambling as a source of state revenue: several other states derive more revenue from lotteries and pari-mutuel taxes than Nevada does from its casinos. What is unique is the large proportion of state revenues that gaming supplies. Nevada was the only state to allow casino gambling until the 1970s, when it was joined by New Jersey.

³⁸HEALTH
Nevada ranked lower in average life expectancy than any other nonsouthern state during 1969–71, with a figure of 69.03 years (46th in the US), 65.60 for males and 73.32 for females. Infant mortality during 1977 was 13.5 per 1,000 live births for whites, and 16.4 for nonwhites. The overall death rate was 7.7 per 1,000 population in 1977, when Nevada had the highest death rates of

any state for suicide and cirrhosis of the liver. In 1970, Nevada was estimated to have the highest alcoholism rate in the US, 6,770 per 100,000 population. Not surprisingly, in view of the state's liberal marriage and divorce laws, Nevada also had in 1977 by far the nation's highest rates for marriage, 164 per 1,000 population, 16 times the national average; and for divorce, at 16 per 1,000 population, more than 3 times the US norm.

In 1978 there were 25 hospitals, with 3,234 beds. Hospital personnel included 1,497 registered nurses and 711 licensed practical nurses. The average cost of hospital care in 1977 was $241 per day and $1,566 per stay. The state had 897 physicians in 1977 and 340 dentists in 1979.

39 SOCIAL WELFARE
Aid for families with dependent children totaled $8 million in 1978, when 16,000 Nevadans took part in the food stamp program at a federal cost of $6.2 million, and 63,000 children received school lunches subsidized with $3.6 million in federal funds. During 1977, 79,100 Nevadans received $206.8 million in Social Security benefits; workers' compensation payments added up to $37.7 million. Nevadans received $32 million in unemployment insurance payments the following year, when expenditures on vocational rehabilitation totaled $3.4 million.

40 HOUSING
The 1970 census counted 172,000 housing units in 1970, of which 160,000 were occupied; more than 97% had full plumbing. Between 1976 and 1978, 59,600 new units valued at $1.8 billion were authorized.

41 EDUCATION
With an illiteracy rate of 0.5% in 1970 and a high school completion rate of 76% in 1976, adult Nevadans have had more schooling than the US population as a whole. In 1979, 147,734 pupils were enrolled in Nevada's public schools: 8,958 kindergarten, 61,613 elementary, 68,942 secondary, and 8,221 ungraded special education. In 1977, 31,400 students were enrolled in institutions of higher learning, nearly all of them in the University of Nevada System, which, in 1980 included university campuses at Reno and Las Vegas and four community colleges.

42 ARTS
The Nevada State Council on the Arts receives and disburses funds from the National Endowment for the Arts and coordinates community arts programs. Major exhibits are mounted by the Las Vegas Arts League and the Sierra Arts Foundation in Reno. Reno also has a symphony orchestra.

43 LIBRARIES AND MUSEUMS
Nevada's public and special library systems in 1977/78 had a combined book stock of 1,008,131 volumes and a circulation of 3,117,151. The University of Nevada had 280,239 books in its Reno campus library system and 304,000 at Las Vegas; the Nevada State Library in Carson City had 63,565.

There are some 14 museums and historic sites. Notable are the Nevada State Museum in Carson City; the museum of the Nevada Historical Society, and the Fleischmann Atmospherium-Planetarium, University of Nevada, in Reno; and the Museum of Natural History, University of Nevada, at Las Vegas.

44 COMMUNICATIONS
In 1978 there were 697,837 telephones in Nevada, 477,532 residential and 220,305 business. Commercial broadcasting comprised 36 radio stations (22 AM, 14 FM) and 7 television stations in 1978. During the same year, 10 cable systems served 34,044 subscribers in 27 communities.

45 PRESS
In 1978, the state had 3 morning newspapers with a circulation of 81,367; 6 evening papers, 117,137; and 5 Sunday papers, 189,586. The leading newspaper was the *Las Vegas Review-Journal*, with an evening circulation of 75,246 and a Sunday circulation of 81,952. The *Nevada State Journal* (Reno) and *Reno Evening Gazette*, which have a combined Sunday edition, are also influential.

46 ORGANIZATIONS
Notable organizations with headquarters in Nevada include the National Council of Juvenile and Family Court Judges, Professional Chess Association, and Western History Association, all at Reno; and the American Science Fiction Association, National Association of Extension Home Economists, and National Friends of Public Broadcasting, all in Las Vegas.

47 TOURISM, TRAVEL, AND RECREATION
Tourism is Nevada's most important industry. Out-of-state visitors spent $1.3 billion in 1976, and gross casino revenues alone exceeded $1 billion in 1977. Tourists flock to "Vegas" not just for gambling but for the neon glitter of the city and for the top-flight entertainers who perform there. Other Nevada attractions include Pyramid Lake, Lake Tahoe, Lake Mead, and Lehman Caves National Monument.

There are 18 state parks and recreation areas. In 1977/78, licenses were issued to 160,331 fishermen and 44,653 hunters.

48 SPORTS
Although no major league sports teams represent Nevada, Las Vegas has hosted many professional boxing title bouts. Golfing and rodeo are also popular.

49 FAMOUS NEVADANS
Nevadans who have held important federal offices include Raymond T. Baker (1877–1935) and Eva B. Adams (b.1908), both directors of the US Mint, and Charles B. Henderson (b.California, 1873–1954), head of the Reconstruction Finance Corporation. Prominent US senators have been James W. Nye (b.New York, 1815–76), also the only governor of Nevada Territory; William M. Stewart (b.New York, 1827–1909), author of the final form of the 15th Amendment to the US Constitution, father of federal mining legislation, and a leader of the free-silver-coinage movement in the 1890s; and Francis G. Newlands (b.Mississippi, 1848–1917), author of the federal Reclamation Act of 1902.

Probably the most significant state historical figure is George Wingfield (b.Arkansas, 1876–1959), a mining millionaire who exerted great influence over Nevada's economic and political life in the early 20th century. Among the nationally recognized personalities associated with Nevada through birth or residence have been Sarah Winnemucca Hopkins (1844?–91), Paiute Indian spokeswoman; John W. Mackay (b.Ireland, 1831–1902), mining magnate and financier; sports promoter George L. "Tex" Rickard (b.Missouri, 1871–1929); Anne H. Martin (1875–1951), women's suffrage leader; and Howard R. Hughes (b.Texas, 1905–76), an aviation entrepreneur who became a casino and hotel owner and wealthy recluse in his later years.

Leading creative or performing artists have included operatic singer Emma Nevada (Emma Wixon, 1862–1940); painter Robert Caples (1908–79); and, among writers, Dan DeQuille (William Wright, b.Ohio, 1829–98); Lucius Beebe (b.Massachusetts, 1902–66); and Walter Van Tilburg Clark (b.Maine, 1909–71).

50 BIBLIOGRAPHY
Bushnell, Eleanore, and Don W. Driggs. *The Nevada Constitution: Origin and Growth*. 5th ed., rev. Reno: University of Nevada Press, 1980.

Elliott, Russell R. *History of Nevada*. Lincoln: University of Nebraska Press, 1973.

Laxalt, Robert. *Nevada: A Bicentennial History*. New York: Norton, 1977.

Nevada, State of. Secretary of State. *Political History of Nevada*. 7th ed. Carson City, 1979.

Paher, Stanley, W. *Nevada Ghost Towns and Mining Camps*. Berkeley, Calif.: Howell-North, 1970.

Ostrander, Gilman M. *Nevada: The Great Rotten Borough, 1859–1964*. New York: Knopf, 1966.

Smith, Grant H. *The History of the Comstock Lode, 1850–1920*. Reno: University of Nevada, 1943.

NEW HAMPSHIRE

State of New Hampshire

ORIGIN OF STATE NAME: Named for the English county of Hampshire. **NICKNAME:** The Granite State. **CAPITAL:** Concord. **ENTERED UNION:** 21 June 1788 (9th). **SONG:** "Old New Hampshire." **MOTTO:** Live Free or Die. **FLAG:** The state seal, surrounded by laurel leaves with nine stars interspersed, is centered on a blue field. **OFFICIAL SEAL:** In the center is a broadside view of the frigate *Raleigh*; in the left foreground is a granite boulder, in the background a rising sun. A laurel wreath and the words "Seal of the State of New Hampshire 1776" surround the whole. **STATE EMBLEM:** Within an elliptical panel appears a replica of the Old Man of the Mountains, with the state name above and motto below. **BIRD:** Purple finch. **FLOWER:** Purple lilac. **TREE:** White birch. **INSECT:** Ladybug. **LEGAL HOLIDAYS:** New Year's Day, 1 January; Washington's Birthday, 3d Monday in February; Fast Day, 4th Monday in April; Arbor Day, last Friday in April; Memorial Day, 30 May; Independence Day, 4 July; Labor Day, 1st Monday in September; Columbus Day, 2d Monday in October; Election Day, Tuesday following 1st Monday in November in even-numbered years; Veterans Day, 11 November; Thanksgiving Day, 4th Thursday in November; Christmas Day, 25 December. **TIME:** 7 A.M. EST = noon GMT.

¹LOCATION, SIZE, AND EXTENT

Situated in New England in the northeastern US, New Hampshire ranks 44th in size among the 50 states,

The total area of New Hampshire is 9,304 sq mi (24,097 sq km), comprising 9,027 sq mi (23,380 sq km) of land and 277 sq mi (717 sq km) of inland water. The state has a maximum extension of 93 mi (150 km) E–W and 180 mi (290 km) N–S. New Hampshire is shaped roughly like a right triangle, with the line from the far N to the extreme SW forming the hypotenuse.

New Hampshire is bordered on the N by the Canadian province of Quebec; on the E by Maine (with part of the line formed by the Piscataqua River) and the Atlantic Ocean; on the S by Massachusetts; and on the W by Vermont (following the west bank of the Connecticut River) and Quebec (with the line formed by Halls Stream).

The three southernmost Isles of Shoals lying in the Atlantic belong to New Hampshire. The state's total boundary line is 555 mi (893 km). Its geographic center lies in Belknap County, 3 mi (5 km) E of Ashland.

²TOPOGRAPHY

The major regions of New Hampshire are the coastal lowland in the southeast, the New England Uplands, covering most of the south and west; and the White Mountains (part of the Appalachian chain) in the north, including Mt. Washington, at 6,288 feet (1,917 meters) the highest peak in the northeastern US. With a mean elevation of about 1,000 feet (300 meters), New Hampshire's terrain is generally hilly, rocky, and in many areas, densely wooded.

There are some 1,300 lakes and ponds, of which the largest is Lake Winnipesaukee, covering 70 sq mi (181 sq km). The principal rivers are the Connecticut (forming the border with Vermont), Merrimack, Piscataqua, Saco, and Androscoggin. Near the coast are the nine rocky Isles of Shoals, three of which belong to New Hampshire.

³CLIMATE

New Hampshire has a changeable climate, with wide variations in daily and seasonal temperatures. Summers are short and cool, winters long and cold. Concord has a normal daily mean temperature of 46°F (8°C), ranging from 21°F (–6°C) in January to 70°F (21°C) in July. The record low temperature, –46°F (–43°C), was set at Pittsburg on 18 January 1925; the all-time high, 106°F (41°C) at Nashua, 4 July 1911. Annual precipitation at Concord

averages 36 in (91 cm); the average snowfall is 65 in (165 cm) a year, with more than 100 in (254 cm) yearly in the mountains.

⁴FLORA AND FAUNA

Well forested, New Hampshire supports an abundance of elm, maple, beech, oak, pine, hemlock, and fir trees. Among wild flowers, several orchids are considered rare; and three are classified as threatened. In 1980, Robbins' cinquefoil was proposed for the federal endangered species list.

Among native New Hampshire mammals are the white-tailed deer, muskrat, beaver, porcupine, and snowshoe hare. Threatened animals include the pine marten, arctic tern, purple martin, eastern bluebird, whip-poor-will, and osprey. The Indiana bat, lynx, bald eagle, shortnose sturgeon, sunapee trout, and Atlantic salmon are on the state's endangered species list.

⁵ENVIRONMENTAL PROTECTION

State agencies concerned with environmental protection include the Air Pollution Control Commission, the State Conservation Committeee, Fish and Game Commission, New Hampshire Water Resources Board, and New Hampshire Water Supply and Pollution Control Commission. The most controversial environmental issue during the late 1970s was nuclear power, as the Clamshell Alliance organized repeated demonstrations against the Seabrook nuclear power plant, whose first reactor was scheduled to begin operations in 1983.

⁶POPULATION

New Hampshire ranked 41st among the 50 states in the 1970 census, with a population of 737,681. The preliminary 1980 census figure was 919,114, representing a growth during the decade of nearly 25%, one of the highest in the US. The population density in 1980 was 102 per sq mi (39 per sq km).

In 1970, about 44% of the population lived in rural areas and only 56% in cities and towns, well below the US average. Leading cities with their 1980 census populations are Manchester, 90,757, and Nashua, 67,817; Concord, the capital, had about 32,000 in 1978. All three are located in the southeastern region, where more than two-thirds of all state residents live.

⁷ETHNIC GROUPS

The largest ethnic group in New Hampshire consists of 1st- and 2d-generation French Canadians, numbering 96,834 in 1970. The United Kingdom is the next-leading country of origin, followed by Ireland. About 3,000 black Americans live in New Hampshire, almost all of them in urban areas.

⁸LANGUAGES

Some place-names, such as Ossipee, Mascoma, and Chocorua, preserve the memory of the Pennacook and Abnaki Algonkian tribes living in the area before white settlement. Only 121 state residents claimed Indian first languages in 1970.

New Hampshire speech is essentially Northern, with the special features marking eastern New England: loss of final /r/, *park* and *path* with a vowel between those in *cat* and *father*, and /yu/ in *tube* and *new*. *Raspberries* sounds like /rawzberries/, a wishbone is a *luckybone*, gutters are *eavespouts*, and cows are summoned by "Loo!" Canadian French is heard in the northern region.

In 1970, 74% of all state residents reported English as their mother tongue. Speakers of the principal first languages were as follows:

	NATIVE-BORN	FOREIGN-BORN
English	535,163	9,027
French	96,251	16,308
Polish	6,604	1,345
Italian	5,168	885
German	4,011	2,200

⁹RELIGIONS

The first settlers of New Hampshire were Separatists, precursors of the modern Congregationalists (United Church of Christ), and their first church was probably built around 1633. The first Episcopal church was built in 1638, and the first Quaker meeting-house in 1701; Presbyterians, Baptists, and Methodists built churches later in the 18th century. The state remained almost entirely Protestant until the second half of the 19th century, when Roman Catholics (French Canadian, Irish, and Italian) began arriving in significant numbers, along with some Greek and Russian Orthodox Christians.

As of 1971, Protestant groups in New Hampshire had 105,518 known adherents. The leading denominations were United Church of Christ, 34,899; United Methodist, 17,437; and American Baptist, 16,482. There were 279,269 Roman Catholics in 1979, and an estimated 5,190 Jews.

¹⁰TRANSPORTATION

New Hampshire's first railroad, between Nashua and Lowell, Mass., was chartered in 1835 and opened in 1838. Two years later, Exeter and Boston were linked by rail. The state had more than 1,200 mi (1,900 km) of track in 1920, but by 1974, that total had declined to 751 mi (1,209 km). There is limited passenger service between Concord and Boston.

In 1978, the state had a total of 15,569 mi (25,056 km) of roads, of which 10,148 mi (16,332 km) were rural and 5,421 mi (8,724 km) municipal; the main north–south highway is I-93. As of 1978 there were 555,644 automobiles, 41,370 motorcycles, 1,328 buses, and 92,861 trucks registered in the state, as well as 613,402 licensed drivers.

New Hampshire had 55 airfields in 1978, 20 public and 35 private. The main airport is Grenier Field in Manchester.

¹¹HISTORY

The land called New Hampshire has supported a human population for at least 10,000 years. Prior to European settlement, Indian tribes of the Algonkian language group lived in the region. During the 17th century, most of New Hampshire's Indians, called Pennacook, were organized in a loose confederation centered along the Merrimack Valley.

The coast of New England was explored by Dutch, English, and French navigators throughout the 16th century. Samuel de Champlain prepared the first accurate map of the New England coast in 1604, and Captain John Smith explored the Isles of Shoals in 1614. By this time, numerous English fishermen were summering on New England's coastal banks, using the Isles of Shoals for temporary shelter and to dry their catch.

The first English settlement was established along the Piscataqua River in 1623. From 1643 to 1680, New Hampshire was a province of Massachusetts, and the boundary between them was not settled until 1740. During the 18th century, as settlers moved up the Merrimack and Connecticut river valleys, they came into conflict with the Indians. By 1760, however, the Pennacook had been expelled from the region.

Throughout the provincial period, people in New Hampshire made their living through fishing, farming, cutting and sawing timber, shipbuilding, and coastal and overseas trade. By the first quarter of the 18th century, Portsmouth, the provincial capital, had become a thriving commercial port. New Hampshire's terrain worked against Portsmouth's commercial interests, however, by dictating that roads (and later railroads) run in a north–south direction—making Boston, and not Portsmouth, New England's primary trading center. During the Revolutionary War, extensive preparations were made to protect the harbor from a British attack that never came. Although nearly 18,500 New Hampshire men enlisted in the war, no battle was fought within its boundaries. New Hampshire was the first of the original 13 colonies to establish an independent government—on 5 January 1776, six months before the Declaration of Independence.

During the 19th century, as overseas trade became less important to the New Hampshire economy, textile mills were built, principally along the Merrimack River. By midcentury, the Merrimack Valley had become the social, political, and economic center of the state. So great was the demand for workers in these mills that immigrant labor was imported during the 1850s; a decade later, French Canadian workers began pouring south from Quebec.

Although industry thrived, agriculture did not; New Hampshire hill farms could not compete against Midwestern farms. The population in farm towns dropped, leaving a maze of stone walls, cellar holes, and new forests on the hillsides. Those people who remained began to cluster in small village centers.

World War I, however, marked a turning point for New Hampshire industry. As wartime demand fell off, the state's old textile mills were unable to compete with newer cotton mills in the South, and New Hampshire's mill towns became as depressed as its farm towns; only in the north, the center for logging and paper manufacturing, did state residents continue to enjoy moderate prosperity. Industrial towns in the southern counties responded to the decline in textile manufacture by making other items, particularly shoes, but the collapse of the state's railroad network spelled further trouble for the slumping economy. The growth of tourism aided the rural areas primarily, as old farms became spacious vacation homes for "summer people," who in some cases paid the bulk of local property taxes.

During the 1960s, New Hampshire's economic decline began to reverse, except in agriculture. While growth in the state's northern counties remained modest, the combination of Boston's urban sprawl, interstate highway construction, and low state taxes encouraged people and industry to move into southern New Hampshire—a development accompanied by higher local taxes and concern over the state's vanishing open spaces.

¹²STATE GOVERNMENT

New Hampshire's constitution, adopted in 1784 and extensively revised in 1792, is the 2d-oldest state-governing document still in effect. Every 10 years, the people vote on the question of calling a convention to revise it; proposed revisions must then be approved by two-thirds of the voters at a referendum. Amendments may also be placed on the ballot by a three-fifths vote of both houses of the general court—the state legislature—which consists of a 24-member senate and a 400-seat house of representatives (largest of any state). Legislators serve two-year terms.

The only executive elected statewide is the governor, who serves a two-year term and is assisted by a five-member executive council, elected for two years by district. The council must approve all administrative and judicial appointments. The secretaries of state and treasury are elected by the legislature. The governor must be at least 30 years of age and must have been a state resident for 7 years prior to election.

A bill becomes law if signed by the governor, if passed by the legislature and left unsigned by the governor for five days while the legislature is in session, or if passed over a gubernatorial veto by two-thirds of the legislators present in each house. US citizens at least 18 years of age who have resided in the state for 30 days are eligible to vote in New Hampshire elections.

¹³POLITICAL PARTIES

New Hampshire is one of the few states where registered Republicans outnumber registered Democrats—177,370 to 146,854 in 1978. The state has almost always gone with the Republican presidential nominee in recent decades, but the two parties have been much more evenly balanced in local and state elections. New Hampshire's quadrennial presidential preference primary, traditionally the first state primary of the campaign season, accords to New Hampshirites a degree of national political influence and a claim on media attention far out of proportion to their numbers. In the 1980 presidential election, New Hampshire voters backed Ronald Reagan. Another Republican, Warren Rudman, ousted a Democratic incumbent, US Senator John Durkin, but Democrat Hugh Gallen was reelected as governor.

New Hampshire Presidential Vote by Major Political Parties, 1948–80

YEAR	ELECTORAL VOTE	NEW HAMPSHIRE WINNER	DEMOCRAT	REPUBLICAN
1948	4	Dewey (R)	107,995	121,299
1952	4	*Eisenhower (R)	106,663	166,287
1956	4	*Eisenhower (R)	90,364	176,519
1960	4	Nixon (R)	137,772	157,989
1964	4	*Johnson (D)	182,065	104,029
1968	4	*Nixon (R)	130,589	154,903
1972	4	*Nixon (R)	116,435	213,724
1976	4	Ford (R)	147,635	185,935
1980	4	*Reagan (R)	108,864	221,705

*Won US presidential election.

¹⁴LOCAL GOVERNMENT

New Hampshire has 10 counties, each governed by three commissioners. Other elected county officials include the sheriff, attorney, treasurer, register of deeds, and register of probate.

As of 1977, New Hampshire also had 13 municipalities and 221 townships. Municipalities have elected mayors and councils. The basic unit of town government is the traditional town meeting, held once a year, at which time selectmen and other local officials are chosen.

¹⁵STATE SERVICES

The Department of Education, governed by the State Board of Education (which appoints an education commissioner), has primary responsibility for public instruction. The New Hampshire Transportation Authority, Aeronautics Commission, Port Authority, and Department of Public Works and Highways share transport responsibilities, while the Department of Health and Welfare oversees public health, mental health, and medical licensing. The Department of Safety includes divisions of motor vehicles and state police. The Department of Labor and Department of Employment Security provide various labor services, including unemployment compensation and mediation.

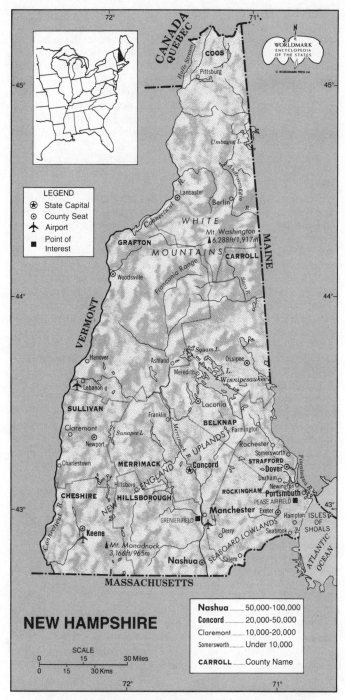

NEW HAMPSHIRE

See US political: front cover M2; physical: back cover M2.

LOCATION: 42°40' to 45°18'N; 70°37' to 72°34'W. **BOUNDARIES**: Canadian line, 60 mi (96 km); Maine line, 174 mi (280 km); Atlantic Ocean coastline, 13 mi (21 km); Massachusetts line, 95 mi (153 km); Vermont line, 213 mi (343 km).

¹⁶JUDICIAL SYSTEM

All judges in New Hampshire are appointed by the governor, subject to confirmation by the executive council; appointments are to age 70, with retirement compulsory at that time. The state's highest court, the supreme court, consists of a chief justice and 4 associate justices. The main trial court is the superior court, with one judgeship for each 60,000 state residents; there were 13 associate justices and a chief justice in 1979. Crime rates for all categories are among the lowest in the US.

[17] ARMED FORCES

The principal military installations in New Hampshire are the Portsmouth Naval Shipyard and Pease Air Force Base at Newington. Together they had 13,833 authorized personnel in 1977/78. Firms in the state received $227 million in defense contract awards in 1978.

As of 30 September 1979, veterans living in New Hampshire numbered 126,000, of whom 2,000 were veterans of World War I, 53,000 of World War II, 22,000 of the Korean conflict, and 38,000 of the Viet-Nam era. Veterans benefits totaled $84.9 million in 1977/78.

The Army and Air National Guard had 2,700 personnel in 1978. There were 336 state police and 1,582 local police in 1977.

[18] MIGRATION

From the time of the first European settlement until the middle of the 19th century, the population of New Hampshire was primarily of British origin. Subsequently, immigrants from Quebec, Ireland, Italy, and other countries began arriving in significant numbers. New Hampshire's population growth since 1960 has been fueled by migrants from other states, especially Massachusetts. The net gain from migration was 148,000 between 1960 and 1977.

[19] INTERGOVERNMENTAL COOPERATION

New Hampshire participates in the American and Canadian French Cultural Exchange Commission, Atlantic States Marine Fisheries Commission, Connecticut River Valley Flood Control Compact, and various New England regional compacts.

Federal aid to New Hampshire was estimated at $292.8 million in 1978/79; general revenue sharing contributed $23.2 million.

[20] ECONOMY

New Hampshire is one of the more industrialized states in the US, ranking well above the national median in proportion of labor force employed in manufacturing and in value added by manufacture. The electronics, chemical, and machinery industries are the major employers. Since World War II, tourism has been one of the state's fastest-growing sources of income.

[21] INCOME

New Hampshire's per capita income, which ranked 21st in the US in 1960 and 20th in 1970, had slipped to 32d by 1978, largely because of rapid population growth rather than any slowdown in real economic growth. At $7,277 in 1978 dollars, per capita income in the state was 7% below the US average.

In 1975, median family income was $14,258, ranking the state 24th in the US. During that same year, 7.9% of state residents and 5.9% of state families were below the federal poverty level.

[22] LABOR

New Hampshire's estimated civilian labor force totaled 428,000 in 1978. Of these, 412,000 were employed, yielding an unemployment rate of less than 4%, one of the lowest in the US.

A federal census of workers covered by unemployment insurance in March 1977 revealed the following nonfarm employment pattern for New Hampshire:

	ESTABLISHMENTS	EMPLOYEES	ANNUAL PAYROLL ('000)
Agricultural services, forestry, fishing	213	631	$ 5,839
Mining	26	169	3,172
Contract construction	2,721	11,990	170,595
Manufacturing	1,664	95,727	1,059,647
Transportation, public utilities	690	10,740	159,759
Wholesale trade	1,199	11,762	146,535
Retail trade	5,911	55,971	368,156
Finance, insurance, real estate	1,464	15,184	151,017
Services	5,500	54,129	431,044
Other	225	200[1]	2,802
TOTALS	19,613	256,503	$2,498,566

[1]Employed as of March 1977.

Government employees, who numbered about 52,000 in 1978, were not included in this survey.

Labor union membership in New Hampshire in 1976 totaled 43,000, of whom 36,000 were in AFL-CIO affiliates. Another 13,000 New Hampshirites belonged to employee associations.

[23] AGRICULTURE

Only in Rhode Island and Alaska do farmers earn less from farming than in New Hampshire. Farm income in 1978 was an estimated $87.6 million, less than 30% of which was in crops.

In 1976 there were about 2,600 farms occupying 560,000 acres (227,000 hectares); most of the land was used for pasture. Leading crops and their output in 1979 were hay, 188,000 tons, and commercial apples, 29,000 tons.

[24] ANIMAL HUSBANDRY

Dairy and poultry products are the mainstays of New Hampshire's agriculture. In 1979, the state had 30,000 milk cows, with a total milk yield of 342 million lb. Poultry items included 7,232,000 lb of chickens, worth $955,000, and 218,000,000 eggs, worth $12,767,000.

[25] FISHING

New Hampshire's commercial catch in 1978 consisted of 4,862,000 lb, much of it cod and lobster, worth $1,750,000.

[26] FORESTRY

New Hampshire had 5,014,000 acres (2,029,000 hectares) of forestland in 1977, of which 4,692,000 acres (1,899,000 hectares) were considered suitable for commercial use. Of that total, 88% was privately owned. Shipments of lumber and wood products were valued at $208.3 million in 1977, while paper and allied products were worth $467 million.

[27] MINING

Although New Hampshire has long been famous for its granite quarries—from which the state nickname derives—mineral resources are a very minor contributor to the state economy. In 1978, mineral production amounted to only $22 million, for a rank of 48th among the 50 states. The quarry output included 7,000,000 tons of sand and gravel and 896,000 tons of stone during the same year.

[28] ENERGY AND POWER

About 90% of all New Hampshire's electrical power was generated by water in the 1930s. By 1978, however, about 40% of the state's electricity came from oil-fired plants, another 40% from coal-fired plants, and only 20% from hydroelectric facilities. Power production totaled 5.1 billion kwh in 1978, when installed capacity was 1.6 million kw. Scheduled for completion by 1985 was the controversial $2.6-billion, two-reactor nuclear power plant at Seabrook, built by Public Service Co. of New Hampshire.

[29] INDUSTRY

During the provincial era, shipbuilding was New Hampshire's major industry. By 1870, cotton and woolen mills, concentrated in the southeast, employed about one-third of the labor force and accounted for roughly half the value of all manufactures. Today, the most important industry groups, ranked by employment, are electronic equipment, nonelectrical machinery, leather and leather products (mainly shoes), and rubber and miscellaneous plastic products.

The total value added by manufacture in 1977 was almost $2.2 billion, 69% higher than in 1972. The following table shows value added by major sectors in 1972 and 1977:

	1972	1977
Electric and electronic equipment	$169,300,000	$346,900,000
Nonelectric machinery	176,400,000	323,900,000
Instruments and related products	82,700,000	169,300,000
Paper and allied products	118,800,000	167,000,000
Leather and leather products	123,100,000	156,000,000
Rubber and miscellaneous plastic products	79,300,000	148,300,000
Textile mill products	93,000,000	125,600,000

[30] COMMERCE
New Hampshire wholesalers sold $1.1 billion worth of goods in 1972. Retailers had sales of almost $3.4 billion in 1977, the leading sectors being food stores, 24%; automotive dealers, 19%; department stores, 8%; eating and drinking places, 7%; and gasoline service stations, 7%.

Foreign exports of manufactured goods totaled $291 million in 1976 (36th in the US).

[31] CONSUMER PROTECTION
The Attorney General's Office is responsible for enforcing New Hampshire's consumer protection laws.

[32] BANKING
New Hampshire had 78 insured commercial banks in 1978, with total assets of $2.7 billion, outstanding loans of $1.3 billion, and deposits of $2.4 billion. The state's 17 insured savings and loan associations held total assets of $1 billion, savings capital of $858 million, and mortgage loans of $863 million.

[33] INSURANCE
In 1978 there were 1,454,000 life insurance policies in force in New Hampshire, with a total value of $11.1 billion. The average coverage per family was $34,700, slightly below the US average.

Property and liability insurers wrote premiums amounting to $342.2 million in 1978, of which automobile physical damage insurance accounted for $59.1 million; automotive liability insurance, $75 million; and homeowners' coverage, $45.2 million.

[34] SECURITIES
New Hampshire has no securities exchanges.

[35] PUBLIC FINANCE
The New Hampshire state budget is drawn up biennially by the Office of Administration and Control and then submitted by the governor to the legislature for amendment and approval. The fiscal year runs from 1 July to 30 June. The following is a summary of recommended expenditures for 1979/80 and 1980/81 (in millions):

	1979/80	1980/81
Health and welfare	$160.0	$180.9
Public works and highways	126.7	128.3
Higher Education Fund	95.3	97.2
Board of Education	59.1	61.7
Other outlays	186.1	215.6
TOTALS	$627.2	$683.7

Leading sources of revenue, in addition to federal aid, are the business profits tax, estimated to yield $54.6 million in 1980/81; corporation tax, $50.7 million; liquor licenses and fees, $39.4 million; and meals and rooms tax, $22.7 million.

As of mid-1977, the combined debt of state and local governments was $725 million, or $854 per capita, among the lowest such figures for any state.

[36] TAXATION
New Hampshire has no general income or sales tax but does levy 5% taxes on interest and dividends and on net corporate income. Levies on property, gasoline, alcoholic beverages, tobacco products, pari-mutuel betting, and many other items are also imposed. General revenues were only $544 per capita in 1976/77, ranking New Hampshire last among the 50 states.

During 1975/76, New Hampshire paid slightly more than $1.2 billion in federal taxes and received federal benefits amounting to about $10 million less. New Hampshirites filed 370,934 federal income tax returns in 1977, paying $610,973,000 in tax.

[37] ECONOMIC POLICY
Business incentives in New Hampshire include a generally favorable tax climate, specific tax incentives and exemptions, and relatively low wage rates. The Division of Economic Development, within the Department of Resources and Economic Development, is the agency primarily responsible for attracting new investment and industry.

[38] HEALTH
The average life expectancy in New Hampshire was 71.23 years in 1969–71 (20th in the US), 67.48 for males and 75.19 for females. Infant mortality rates are low—10.2 per 1,000 live births for whites, statistically not significant for nonwhites—and the death rates are below average for heart disease and stroke, two of the three leading causes of death.

In 1978 there were 33 hospitals, with 4,995 beds and an average occupancy rate of 71.8%. Hospital personnel included 2,637 registered nurses and 824 licensed practical nurses. The average cost of hospital care in 1977 was $168 per day and $1,194 per stay, both well below the national averages. New Hampshire had 1,512 licensed physicians in 1977 and 465 active dentists in 1979.

[39] SOCIAL WELFARE
Like its tax revenues, New Hampshire's expenditures on welfare are low for a northeastern state. Only eight states spent less for the five largest welfare programs than New Hampshire did during the 1976 fiscal year.

In 1978, 21,200 New Hampshirites received $22 million in aid to families with dependent children, 35,000 persons took part in the food stamp program at a federal cost of $11.9 million, and 95,000 students had school lunches with a federal outlay of $5.6 million. Medicaid absorbed $46 million in 1977, when Social Security benefits totaling $346 million were paid to 133,700 persons, the average monthly benefit for retired workers being $248.10. Federally administered Supplemental Security Income amounted to $5.5 million in 1978. Unemployment insurance benefits totaled $15 million in 1978; the average weekly payment was $74.35, 11% below the US norm.

[40] HOUSING
In 1970, housing units for year-round use numbered 247,000, a 28% increase over 1960. Of all occupied units, 68% were owner-occupied, the remainder rented; 95% had full plumbing. About 8% of New Hampshire homeowners owned two or more homes in 1970. More than 20,000 new housing units worth $622 million were authorized from 1976 through 1978.

[41] EDUCATION
New Hampshire residents have a longstanding commitment to education: the state's illiteracy rate was less than 2% in 1850, and an only slightly less impressive 0.7% in 1970. More than 70% of all adult state residents were high school graduates in 1976; 15% had four or more years of college.

In fall 1979, enrollment in public schools and approved public academies totaled 170,547: 87,044 in elementary schools, 29,540 in junior high schools, and 53,963 in high schools. The best-known institution of higher education is Dartmouth College (1977 enrollment, 4,195), which originated in Connecticut in 1754 as Moor's Indian Charity School and was established at Hanover in 1769. When the State of New Hampshire attempted to amend Dartmouth's charter to make the institution public in the early 19th century, the US Supreme Court handed down a precedent-setting ruling prohibiting state violation of contract rights. The leading public institution is the University of New Hampshire, which was founded at Hanover in 1866 and relocated at Durham in 1891, and had a 1977 enrollment of 12,175.

[42] ARTS
Hopkins Center at Dartmouth College features musical events throughout the year, while the Monadnock Music Concerts are held in several towns during the summer. The New Hampshire Music Festival takes place at Meredith. Theater by the Sea at Portsmouth presents classical and modern plays, and there is a year-round student theater at Dartmouth.

Principal galleries include the Currier Gallery of Art in Manchester, the Arts and Science Center in Nashua, the University Art Galleries at the University of New Hampshire in Durham, the Dartmouth College Museum and Galleries at Hanover, and the Lamont Gallery at Phillips Exeter Academy in Exeter.

⁴³LIBRARIES AND MUSEUMS

New Hampshire public libraries had a total book stock of 3,837,186 volumes and a combined circulation of 5,244,349 volumes in 1977/78. Leading academic and historical collections include Dartmouth College's Baker Memorial Library in Hanover (1,265,198 volumes); the New Hampshire State Library (636,948) and New Hampshire Historical Society Library (75,000), both in Concord; and the University of New Hampshire's Ezekiel W. Dimond Library (382,500) in Durham.

Among the more than 40 museums and historic sites are the New Hampshire Historical Society Museum and the Franklin Pierce Manse, both in Concord.

⁴⁴COMMUNICATIONS

New Hampshire had 673,049 telephones in 1978, 508,742 residential and 164,307 business. Virtually every household had telephone service. The state had 45 commercial radio stations (28 AM, 17 FM), but only 1 commercial television broadcaster. State residents also receive broadcasts from neighboring Massachusetts, Vermont, and Maine. Cable systems in 1978 served 75 communities with 89,944 subscribers.

⁴⁵PRESS

In 1978, New Hampshire had 9 daily newspapers with a combined circulation of 184,791 and 2 Sunday papers with 73,413. The best-known newspaper in the state is the *Manchester Union-Leader* (all day, 64,927), published by the ultraconservative William Loeb. The *New Hampshire Sunday News*, also published by Loeb, has a circulation of 66,909.

⁴⁶ORGANIZATIONS

National organizations with headquarters in New Hampshire include the Clamshell Alliance, Portsmouth; Student Conservation Association, Charlestown; National Association of State Foresters and American Association of Commodity Traders, both in Concord; American Society for Environmental Education, Durham; and the International Society of Developmental Biologists, Hanover.

⁴⁷TOURISM, TRAVEL, AND RECREATION

Tourism ranks 2d only to manufacturing in the economy of New Hampshire. An estimated 4.7 million persons traveled to or through the state in 1977.

Skiing, camping, hiking, and boating are the main outdoor attractions. There are more than 30 state parks, 200 youth camps, 60 golf courses, and 26 alpine ski areas, some of which also operate as summer resorts. Other attractions include Strawbery Banke, a restored village in Portsmouth; Daniel Webster's birthplace near Franklin; the Mt. Washington Cog Railway; and the natural "Old Man of the Mountains" granite head profile in the Franconia subrange of the White Mountains, on which the state's official emblem is modeled.

⁴⁸SPORTS

Major national and international skiing events are frequently held in the state, as are such other winter competitions as snowmobile races and the Sled Dog Derby. Thoroughbred, harness, and greyhound racing are the warm-weather spectator sports. The annual Whaleback Yacht Race is held in early August.

Dartmouth College competes in the Ivy League—the Big Green won or shared conference football championships six times during the 1970s—while the University of New Hampshire belongs to the Yankee Conference.

⁴⁹FAMOUS NEW HAMPSHIRITES

Born in Hillsboro, Franklin Pierce (1804–69), the nation's 14th president, serving from 1853 to 1857, was the only US chief executive to come from New Hampshire. Henry Wilson (Jeremiah Jones Colbath, 1812–75), US vice president from 1873 to 1875, was a native of Farmington.

US Supreme Court chief justices Salmon P. Chase (1808–73) and Harlan Fiske Stone (1872–1946) were New Hampshirites,

and Levi Woodbury (1789–1851) was a distinguished associate justice. John Langdon (1741–1819) was the first president pro tempore of the US Senate; two other US senators from New Hampshire, George Higgins Moses (b.Maine, 1869–1944) and Henry Styles Bridges (b.Maine, 1898–1961), also held this position. US cabinet members from New Hampshire included Henry Dearborn (1751–1829), secretary of war; Daniel Webster (1782–1852), secretary of state; and William E. Chandler (1835–1917), secretary of the Navy. Other political leaders of note were Benning Wentworth (1696–1770), royal governor; Meshech Weare (1713–86), the state's leader during the American Revolution; Josiah Bartlett (b.Massachusetts, 1729–95), a physician, governor, and signer of the Declaration of Independence; Isaac Hill (b.Massachusetts, 1789–1851), a publisher, governor, and US senator; and John Parker Hale (1806–73), senator, antislavery agitator, minister to Spain, and presidential candidate of the Free Soil Party.

Military leaders associated with New Hampshire during the colonial and Revolutionary periods include John Stark (1728–1822), Robert Rogers (b.Massachusetts, 1731–95), and John Sullivan (1740–95). Among other figures of note are educator Eleazar Wheelock (b.Connecticut, 1711–79), the founder of Dartmouth College; physicians Lyman Spaulding (1775–1821), Reuben D. Mussey (1780–1866), and Amos Twitchell (1781–1850), as well as Samuel Thomson (1769–1843), a leading advocate of herbal medicine; religious leaders Hosea Ballou (1771–1852), his grandnephew of the same name (1796–1861), and Mary Baker Eddy (1821–1910), founder of Christian Science; and labor oganizer and US Communist Party leader Elizabeth Gurley Flynn (1890–1964).

Sarah Josepha Hale (1788–1879), Horace Greeley (1811–72), Charles Dana (1819–97), Thomas Bailey Aldrich (1836–1907), Bradford Torrey (b.Massachusetts, 1843–1912), Alice Brown (1857–1948), and J(erome) D(avid) Salinger (b.New York, 1919) are among the writers and editors who have lived in New Hampshire, along with poets Edna Dean Proctor (1829–1923), Celia Laighton Thaxter (1835–94), Edward Arlington Robinson (b.Maine, 1869–1935), and Robert Frost (b.California, 1874–1963), one of whose poetry volumes is entitled *New Hampshire* (1923). Painter Benjamin Champney (1817–1907) and sculptor Daniel Chester French (1850–1931) were born in New Hampshire, while Augustus Saint-Gaudens (b.Ireland, 1848–1907) created much of his sculpture in the state.

Vaudevillian Will Cressey (1863–1930) was a New Hampshire man. More recent celebrities include newspaper publisher William Loeb (b.New York, 1905) and astronaut Alan B. Shepard, Jr. (b.1923).

⁵⁰BIBLIOGRAPHY

Brown, William R. *Our Forest Heritage.* Concord: New Hampshire Historical Society, 1958.

Clark, Charles E. *The Eastern Frontier: The Settlement of Northern New England, 1610–1763.* New York: Knopf, 1970.

Cole, Donald B. *Jacksonian Democracy in New Hampshire, 1800–51.* Cambridge: Harvard University Press, 1970.

Daniell, Jere R. *Experiment in Republicanism: New Hampshire Politics and the American Revolution, 1744–1794.* Cambridge, Mass.: Harvard University Press, 1970.

Federal Writers' Project. *New Hampshire: A Guide to the Granite State.* Boston: Houghton Mifflin, 1938.

Morison, Elizabeth Forbes and Elting E. *New Hampshire: A Bicentennial History.* New York: Norton, 1976.

New Hampshire, State of. Department of State. *Manual for the General Court, 1979.* Concord, 1979.

Squires, J. Duane. *The Granite State of the United States: A History of New Hampshire from 1623 to the Present.* 4 vols. New York: American Historical Co., 1956.

NEW JERSEY

State of New Jersey

ORIGIN OF STATE NAME: Named for the British Channel Island of Jersey. **NICKNAME:** The Garden State. **CAPITAL:** Trenton. **ENTERED UNION:** 18 December 1787 (3d). **MOTTO:** Liberty and Prosperity. **COLORS:** Buff and Jersey blue. **COAT OF ARMS:** In the center is a shield with three plows, symbolic of agriculture; a helmet above indicates sovereignty, and a horse's head atop the helmet signifies speed and strength. On the left stands Liberty; on the right, Ceres, goddess of vegetation and symbol of prosperity. The state motto and the date "1776" are displayed on a banner below. **FLAG:** The coat of arms on a buff field. **OFFICIAL SEAL:** The coat of arms surrounded by the words "The Great Seal of the State of New Jersey." **ANIMAL:** Horse. **BIRD:** Eastern goldfinch. **FLOWER:** Violet. **TREE:** Red oak. **MEMORIAL TREE:** Dogwood. **BUG:** Honeybee. **LEGAL HOLIDAYS:** New Year's Day, 1 January; Martin Luther King's Birthday, 15 January; Lincoln's Birthday, 12 February; Washington's Birthday, 3d Monday in February; Good Friday, March or April; Memorial Day, last Monday in May; Independence Day, 4 July; Labor Day, 1st Monday in September; Columbus Day, 2d Monday in October; Election Day, 1st Tuesday after 1st Monday in November; Veterans Day, 11 November; Thanksgiving Day, 4th Thursday in November; Christmas Day, 25 December. **TIME:** 7 A.M. EST = noon GMT.

¹LOCATION, SIZE, AND EXTENT

Situated in the northeastern US, New Jersey is the smallest of the Middle Atlantic states and ranks 46th among the 50 states.

The total area of New Jersey is 7,836 sq mi (20,295 sq km), of which 7,521 sq mi (19,479 sq km) constitute land and 315 sq mi (618 sq km) comprise inland water. New Jersey extends 166 mi (267 km) N–S; the extreme width E–W is 57 mi (92 km).

New Jersey is bordered on the N and NE by New York State (with the boundary formed partly by the Hudson River, New York Bay, and Arthur Kill, and passing through Raritan Bay); on the E by the Atlantic Ocean; on the S and SW by Delaware (with the line passing through Delaware Bay); and on the W by Pennsylvania (separated by the Delaware River). Numerous barrier islands lie off the Atlantic coast.

New Jersey's total boundary length is 480 mi (773 km), including a general coastline of 130 mi (209 km); the tidal shoreline is 1,792 mi (2,884 km). The state's geographic center is in Mercer County, 5 mi (8 km) SW of Trenton.

²TOPOGRAPHY

Though small, New Jersey has considerable topographic variety. In the extreme northwest corner of the state are the Appalachian Valley and the Kittatinny Ridge and Valley. This area contains High Point, the state's peak elevation, at 1,803 feet (550 meters) above sea level. To the east and south is the highlands region, an area of many natural lakes and of steep ridges, including the Ramapo Mountains, part of the Appalachian chain. East of the highlands is a flat area broken by the high ridges of the Watchungs and Sourlands and—most spectacularly—by the Palisades, a column of traprock rising some 500 feet (150 meters) above the Hudson River. The Atlantic Coast Plain, a flat area with swamps and sandy beaches, claims the remaining two-thirds of the state. Its most notable feature is the Pine Barrens, 760 sq mi (1,968 sq km) of pitch pines and white oaks. Sandy Hook, a peninsula more than 5 mi (8 km) long, extending northward into the Atlantic from Monmouth County, is part of the Gateway National Recreation Area.

Major rivers include the Delaware, forming the border with Pennsylvania, and the Passaic, Hackensack, and Raritan. The largest natural lake is Lake Hopatcong, about 8 mi (13 km) long.

Some 550 to 600 million years ago, New Jersey's topography was the opposite of what it is now, with mountains to the east and a shallow sea to the west. Volcanic eruptions about 225 million years ago caused these eastern mountains to sink and new peaks to rise in the northwest; the lava flow formed the Watchung Mountains and the Palisades. The shoreline settled into its present shape at least 10,000 years ago.

³CLIMATE

Bounded by the Atlantic Ocean and the Delaware River, most of New Jersey has a moderate climate with cold winters and warm, humid summers. Winter temperatures are slightly colder and summer temperatures slightly milder in the northwestern hills than in the rest of the state.

In Atlantic City, the average mean temperature is 54°F (12°C), ranging from 33°F (1°C) in January to 75°F (24°C) in July. Precipitation is plentiful, averaging 46 in (117 cm) annually; snowfall totals about 16 in (41 cm). The annual average humidity is 81% at 7 A.M., reaching a normal high of 87% in September.

Statewide, the record high temperature is 110°F (43°C), set in Runyon on 10 July 1936; the record low was –34°F (–37°C), set in River Vale on 5 January 1904. A 29.7-in (75.4-cm) accumulation on Long Beach Island in 1947 was the greatest 24-hour snowfall in the state's recorded history. Occasional hurricanes and violent spring storms have damaged beachfront property over the years, and floods along northern New Jersey rivers, especially in the Passaic River basin, are not uncommon.

⁴FLORA AND FAUNA

Although highly urbanized, New Jersey still provides a diversity of natural regions, including a sandy coastal zone, the hilly and wooded Allegheny zone, and the pine barrens in the south. Birch, beech, hickory, and elm all grow in the state, along with black locust, red maple, chestnut, and 20 varieties of oak; common shrubs include the spicebush, staggerbush, and mountain laurel. Vast stretches beneath pine trees are covered with pyxie, a small creeping evergreen shrub. Common wild flowers include meadow rue, butterflyweed, black-eyed Susan, and the ubiquitous eastern (common) dandelion. Among rare plants are Candy's lobelia, floating heart, and pennywort.

Among mammals indigenous to New Jersey are the white-tailed deer, black bear, gray and red foxes, raccoon, woodchuck, opossum, striped skunk, eastern gray squirrel, eastern chipmunk,

349

and common cottontail. The herring gull, sandpiper, and little green and night herons are common shore birds, while the red-eyed vireo, hermit thrush, English sparrow, robin, cardinal, and Baltimore oriole are frequently sighted inland. Fishermen prize the northern pike, chain pickerel, and various species of bass, trout, and perch. Declining or rare animals include the whip-poorwill, hooded warbler, eastern hognose snake, northern red salamander, and northern kingfish. The Atlantic green turtle, barred owl, bobolink, great blue heron, pied-billed grebe, corn snake, Atlantic tomcod, Atlantic sturgeon, and native brook trout are on the state's threatened species list. Fauna on the endangered list include six types of whale, four varieties of sea turtle, the Indiana bat, bald eagle, least tern, bog turtle, timber rattlesnake, Pine Barrens treefrog, Tremblay's salamander, and shortnose sturgeon.

⁵ENVIRONMENTAL PROTECTION

New Jersey claims one of the toughest air pollution laws in the US, and in 1971 became the first state to enact noise pollution control legislation. Laws and policies regulating the management of New Jersey's resources are administered by the Department of Environmental Protection (DEP). During 1978/79, the DEP spent $5,096,518 on environmental quality control programs. The DEP's overall budget was $35,067,325 in 1978/79, less than 1% of all state government expenditures.

New Jersey's high concentration of highways and heavy industry makes air pollution an especially serious concern, as anyone who has driven along the New Jersey Turnpike between North Bergen and Woodbridge can readily testify. The state maintains an air pollution monitoring network of 136 stations, including 104 particulate monitoring stations. About 60% of the state's air pollution as of 1978 was caused by vehicle emissions. Pollution control equipment is exempt from state taxes.

Major efforts to improve the state's water quality have not had dramatic results. As of 1978, all major rivers in northeastern New Jersey failed to meet state water quality standards, and a few, including the Passaic River, are among the most polluted waterways in the nation. Improvement of water quality is ham-

pered to some degree by inadequate sewage treatment facilities. More than 1 billion gallons of improperly or inadequately treated sewage (some of it carried by rivers from other states) entered New Jersey waters daily as of 1978, and about 5 million tons of sewage sludge and toxic wastes were dumped into the ocean each year. As many as half of the state's 800 wastewater treatment plants may have been functioning improperly in 1979.

For many years, massive landfills have been a familiar sight along the roads leading to the Lincoln Tunnel, which connects Weehawken with New York City. Most of the 15 million tons of solids generated in 1977 were disposed of by dumping. In 1978/79 there were 410 registered solid-waste disposal facilities, 80% of which met state engineering standards. By law, all disposal collectors must be registered with the DEP; 3,753 were registered in 1979. Of increasing concern to state officials and residents are unlawful disposal sites, especially those for toxic wastes produced by the chemical industry.

The state government was relatively late in acquiring land for preservation purposes. During the 1960s and 1970s, however, the state began buying land under a "Green Acres" program for conservation and recreation. Public pressure prevented the construction in the 1960s of a jetport on the Great Swamp in Morris County and halted a plan in the early 1970s by the US Army Corps of Engineers to build a dam on Tocks Island in the Delaware River.

Several large oil spills and the prospect of offshore petroleum drilling led to the enactment, in 1977, of a law establishing a special fund, financed by a tax on all oil entering the state, designated for the cleanup of offshore spills of oil or other hazardous materials. Federal and state laws seek to protect the coastal zone from pollution.

⁶POPULATION

The nation's most densely populated state, New Jersey ranked 9th among the 50 states in the 1970 census, with a total population of 7,171,112. The estimated 1978 population was 7,349,000, yielding an average density of 977 per sq mi (377 per sq km), nearly 16 times the national average. As of 1980, according to preliminary census data, there were 7,335,808 residents.

Sparsely populated at the time of the Revolutionary War, New Jersey did not pass the 1 million mark until the 1880 census. Most of New Jersey's subsequent growth has come through migration, especially from New York State. During the 1950s, when the population jumped from 4,835,329 to 6,066,782, the most significant growth came in commuter towns near New York City, Philadelphia, and the older northern New Jersey cities. The average annual population growth rate slowed from 2.3% in the 1950s to 1.7% in the 1960s and then to 0.2% between 1970 and 1978, as, for the first time since the 1930s, New Jersey showed a net loss from migration.

About 92% of all New Jerseyans lived in metropolitan areas in 1977, below the 1970 figure of 94%. Most of the state's major cities declined in population during the 1970s. Newark, the state's largest city, ranked 44th in the nation in 1977, with a population of 324,000, 26% below its 1950 total; only a year later, its population had fallen another 10,000, the result of both white and black middle-class flight. As of 1970, 54% of Newark residents were black, the highest percentage of any major city except Washington, D.C., and that percentage was rising throughout the decade. Preliminary 1980 census data showed Newark with 329,498 residents; Jersey City, 222,764; Paterson, 138,025; Elizabeth, 105,384; Trenton, 90,699; and Camden, 84,763.

Among metropolitan areas, Newark ranked 16th in the US in

New Jersey Counties, County Seats, and County Populations

COUNTY	COUNTY SEAT	LAND AREA (SQ MI)[1]	POPULATION (EST. 1978)[2]
Atlantic	Mays Landing	565	190,000
Bergen	Hackensack	237	865,200
Burlington	Mt. Holly	820	363,500
Camden	Camden	222	471,600
Cape May	Cape May	265	77,000
Cumberland	Bridgeton	499	130,200
Essex	Newark	127	829,900
Gloucester	Woodbury	329	200,000
Hudson	Jersey City	45	554,000
Hunterdon	Flemington	437	84,200
Mercer	Trenton	226	317,200
Middlesex	New Brunswick	311	591,100
Monmouth	Freehold	479	499,900
Morris	Morristown	473	404,000
Ocean	Toms River	637	331,500
Passaic	Paterson	190	466,800
Salem	Salem	347	62,400
Somerset	Somerville	304	207,800
Sussex	Newton	527	109,200
Union	Elizabeth	103	509,600
Warren	Belvidere	362	84,000
	TOTALS	7,505	7,349,000

[1]Areas, based on a 1960 state survey, differ from the federal total cited in the text.
[2]Total does not add because of rounding.

LOCATION: 38°55′40″ to 41°21′23″N; 73°59′50″ to 75°35′W. **BOUNDARIES:** New York line, 108 mi (174 km); Atlantic Ocean coastline, 130 mi (209 km); Delaware line, 78 mi (126 km); Pennsylvania line, 164 mi (264 km).

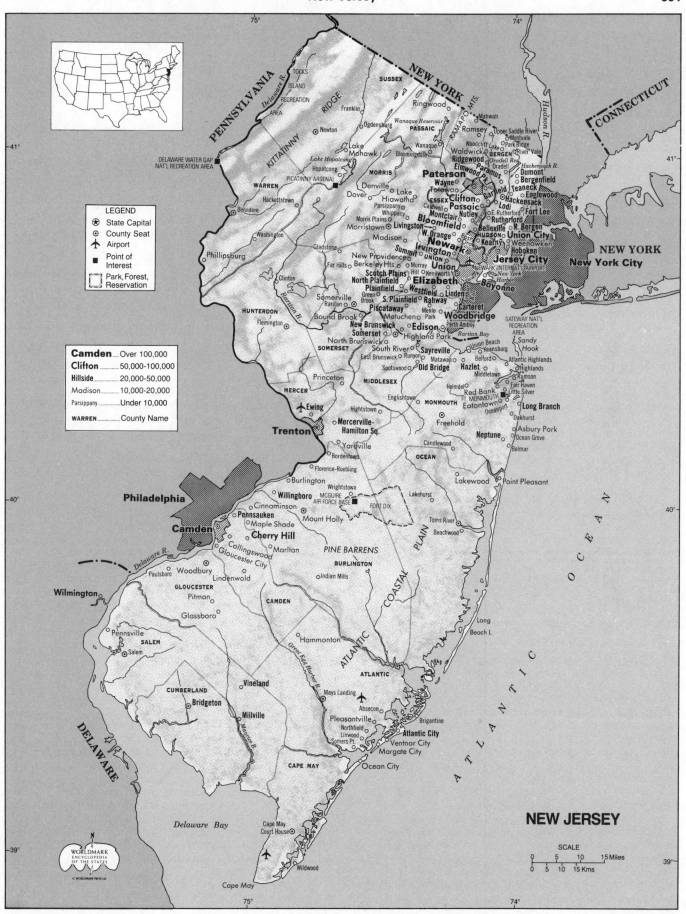

LEGEND
- ⊗ State Capital
- ⊙ County Seat
- ✈ Airport
- ■ Point of Interest
- ⬚ Park, Forest, Reservation

Camden——Over 100,000
Clifton——50,000-100,000
Hillside——20,000-50,000
Madison——10,000-20,000
Parsippany——Under 10,000
WARREN——County Name

NEW JERSEY

SCALE
0 5 10 15 Miles
0 5 10 15 Kms

WORLDMARK
ENCYCLOPEDIA
OF THE STATES

© WORLDMARK PRESS Ltd

See US political: front cover M2; physical: back cover M2.

1977, with a population of 1,969,000, down 4% since 1970. Metropolitan Jersey City had 564,000 residents (71st in the US), down 7% since 1970. Parts of New Jersey are included within the New York and Philadelphia metropolitan regions.

⁷ETHNIC GROUPS

New Jersey is one of the most ethnically heterogeneous states. About 2,156,000 people, or 30% of the population, were of foreign stock in 1970; 635,000 were foreign-born, and 1,521,000 were children of foreign or mixed parentage. The leading countries of origin were Italy, 7%; Germany, 3%; and Poland, 3%. The foreign-born continued to come during the 1970s, creating new subcommunities of Vietnamese, Soviet Jews, Caribbean blacks, and Hispanic Americans.

Blacks first came to New Jersey as slaves in the 1600s; the state abolished slavery in 1804, one of the last of the northern states to do so. Today black people comprise the state's largest ethnic minority, 782,000 as of 1976. Newark, Camden, Trenton, and Paterson all had black populations exceeding 25% in 1970. Newark, with a black majority, elected its first black mayor, Kenneth Gibson, in 1970, three years after the city was torn by racial disorders that killed 26 people and injured some 1,500 others. In 1980, Gibson was in his third term as mayor.

There were 384,000 Hispanic Americans in 1976, divided into distinct ethnic communities. The Puerto Rican population, which rose from 55,361 in 1960 to 135,676 in 1970, lived mostly in Newark, Jersey City, Elizabeth, Paterson, and Passaic. There were 71,233 Cubans in 1970, many of them in Union City and Elizabeth; their numbers were augmented by the migration of Cuban refugees in 1980. Smaller Spanish-speaking groups included Central Americans and Mexicans.

The largest group of Asians are the Chinese (9,233 in 1970), many of whom are in the restaurant business or grow Chinese vegetables for the Chinatown markets and other outlets in the New York metropolitan area. There were 5,681 Japanese, 5,623 Filipinos, and 22,721 other Asian/Pacific peoples in 1970.

American Indians numbered 4,706 in 1970. Not counted among the Indians in that census is a group claiming to be descended from Dutch settlers, black slaves, British and German soldiers, and Leni-Lenape and Tuscarora Indians; incorporated as the Ramapough Mountain Indians in 1978, they live in the Ramapo hills near Ringwood and Mahwah and numbered about 2,800 in 1980.

⁸LANGUAGES

European settlers found New Jersey inhabited largely by the Leni-Lenape, whose memory lingers in such place-names as Passaic, Totowa, Hopatcong, Kittatinny, and Piscataway. Only 592 state residents claimed Indian first languages in 1970.

English in New Jersey is rather evenly divided north and south between Northern and Midland dialects. Special characteristics of some New York metropolitan area speech occur in the northeast portion, such as the absence of /r/ after a vowel, a consonant like /d/ or /t/ instead of the /th/ sounds in *this* or *thin*, pronunciation of *bird* almost as if it were /boyd/, and of *won't* as /woont/. Limited chiefly to the northern half of the state are such pronunciations as *coop* rhyming with *stoop*, *food* with *good*, and *goal* and *fool*; *faucet* has the vowel of *father*. Dominant in the southern half are *run* (small stream), *baby coach* (baby carriage) in the Philadelphia trading area, *winnering owl* (screech owl), and *eel worm* (earthworm). Heard also are *out* as /aot/, *muskmelon* as /muskmillon/, and *keg* rhyming with *bag*, *scarce* with *fierce*, *spook* with *book*, and *haunted* with *panted*.

As in New York City, an influx of Spanish speakers from the Caribbean has created a teaching problem in schools, which now are offering special intensive programs in English as a second language.

In 1970, 75% of the native-born residents indicated English as their first language, as did 70% of all residents. Major resident groups reported these mother tongues:

	NATIVE-BORN	FOREIGN-BORN
English	4,907,855	91,844
Italian	385,420	118,303
German	178,652	90,826
Polish	173,106	41,578
Spanish	165,586	92,482
Yiddish	93,040	35,350

⁹RELIGIONS

With a history of religious tolerance, New Jersey has welcomed many denominations to its shores. Dutch immigrants founded a Reformed Church in 1662, the first in the state. After the English took control, Puritans came from New England and Long Island, Congregationalists from Connecticut, and Baptists from Rhode Island. Quaker settlements in Shrewsbury and western New Jersey during the early 1670s predated the better-known Quaker colony in Pennsylvania. Episcopalians, Presbyterians, German Lutherans, and Methodists arrived during the 18th century. The state's first synagogue was established in 1848, in Newark.

About the only religion not tolerated by New Jerseyans was Catholicism; the first Catholic parish was not organized until 1814, and laws excluding Catholics from holding office were on the books until 1844. The Catholics' numbers swelled as a result of Irish immigration after 1845, and even more with the arrival of Italians after 1880. Today, Roman Catholics constitute the state's single largest religious group, with a population of 2,885,940 in 1979. Passaic is the headquarters of the Byzantine-Ruthenian Rite in the Byzantine Catholic Church, whose membership in all the eastern seaboard states was 96,634.

The Jewish population was estimated at 440,915 in 1979. About 44% of all Jews lived in Bergen and Essex counties. As of 1971, the state had 933,056 known Protestant adherents. The largest denomination was the United Presbyterian Church, with 225,635 adherents, followed by United Methodist, 170,509; Episcopal, 168,357; Lutheran Church in America, 96,629; American Baptist Convention, 64,814; and Reformed Church in America, 62,735.

¹⁰TRANSPORTATION

Ever since the first traders sought the fastest way to get from New York to Philadelphia, transportation has been of central importance to New Jersey and has greatly shaped its growth.

Hoboken engineer John Stevens built, in the mid-1820s, the first steam locomotive operated in the US; over the protests of the dominant stagecoach operators, his son Robert obtained a charter in 1830 for the Camden and Amboy Railroad. The line opened in 1834, and six years later it held a monopoly on the lucrative New York–Philadelphia run. Other lines such as the Elizabeth and Somerville, the Morris and Essex, the Paterson and Hudson, and the Jersey Central were limited to shorter runs, largely because the Camden and Amboy's influence with the legislature gave it a huge competitive advantage. Camden and Amboy stock was leased to the Pennsylvania Railroad in 1871, and the ensuing controversey over whether New Jersey transit should be entrusted to an "alien" company led to the passage of a law opening up the state to rail competition. Industry grew around the rail lines, and the railroads became a vital link in the shipment of products from New York and northern New Jersey.

As of 1980, the major freight operations were run by Conrail, representing a consolidation of several bankrupt freight carriers, including the Penn Central, Central of New Jersey, Erie-Lackawanna, Reading, Lehigh Valley, and Lehigh and Hudson River railroads. Although some improvements have been made, the roadbeds are worn, the rolling stock old, and the tracks themselves in need of repair.

The same shortcomings prevail on the passenger lines operating in the state. Except for Amtrak trains serving Newark, Trenton, and a few other New Jersey cities along the main eastern rail corridor, the bulk of interstate passenger traffic consists of commuters to New York and Philadelphia on trains operated by Conrail, the Port Authority of New York and New Jersey (PA), and the Port Authority Transit Corp. (PATCO), a subsidiary of the Delaware River Port Authority. About 156,000 commuters traveled on Conrail trains daily in 1979; 158,000 daily on the 14-mi (23-km) Port Authority Trans Hudson (PATH) system from Newark, Jersey City, and Hoboken to Manhattan; and 40,000 weekly on the PATCO high-speed Lindenwold Line into Philadelphia. The state subsidized 3,025,000 passenger trips a month in 1978/79.

An average of 155,000 commuters traveled daily from New Jersey to New York by bus in 1979. Twenty-one state-subsidized bus companies operated 722 company-owned buses and 1,634 state-owned buses in 1978/79. In 1980, the Department of Transportation announced plans to take over Transport of New Jersey, the largest bus line in the state, intended as the first step of an eventual state takeover of all subsidized lines. Despite these state efforts, intrastate bus service remains fragmented; often it is easier to get from New York to any point in New Jersey than it is to make connections between cities within the state, and links between northern and southern cities are especially poor.

Although associated more with the West, the first stagecoach service began in New Jersey, as part of a New York–Philadelphia trek that took some five days in 1723. For a time, colonial law required towns along the way to provide taverns for the passengers, and it was not uncommon for coach operators who were also tavern owners to find some way to prolong the journey an extra night. They traveled on roads that were barely more passable than the Leni-Lenape trails from which they originated. Improvement was slow, but by 1828, the legislature had granted 54 turnpike charters.

Road building has continued ever since. As of 1 January 1979 there were 33,398 mi (53,749 km) of roads in the state, including 381 mi (613 km) of state toll roads, 321 mi (517 km) of interstate highways, 2,217 mi (3,568 km) of state highways, 6,803 mi (10,948 km) of county highways, 23,173 mi (37,293 km) of municipal roads and streets, 490 mi (789 km) of state park, forest, and institutional roads, and 13 mi (21 km) of national park roads. The major highways are the New Jersey Turnpike, opened in 1952 and extending 118 mi (190 km) between Bergen and Salem counties; and the Garden State Parkway, completed in 1955 and stretching 172 mi (277 km) from the New York State line to Cape May. The parkway was used by 201,900,000 vehicles in 1978, the turnpike by 120,600,000.

Many bridges and tunnels link New Jersey with New York State, Pennsylvania, and Delaware. The Holland Tunnel, built in 1927 and operated by the PA, carried 10,766,000 eastbound vehicles from Jersey City to Manhattan in 1979; the Lincoln Tunnel, built between 1937 and 1957 at Weehawken, was used by 16,966,000 eastbound vehicles. More than double that number, 40,024,000, entered New York City via the George Washington Bridge from Ft. Lee. The Port Authority also operates three bridges from Perth Amboy, Elizabeth, and Bayonne to Staten Island. Twenty-seven bridges cross the Delaware River, connecting New Jersey with Pennsylvania and Delaware. Among them are 4 operated by the Delaware River Port Authority, 19 by the Delaware River Joint Toll Bridge Commission, 2 by the Burlington County Bridge Commission, and 2 other spans.

At the gateway to New York Harbor, ports at Elizabeth and Newark have overtaken New York City ports in cargo volume, and contribute greatly to the local economy. Operated by the PA, Port Newark has almost 5 mi (8 km) of berthing space along Newark Bay, while nearby Port Elizabeth, with better than 3 mi (5 km) of berths, is a major handler of containerized cargo. These two terminals handled 2,307 ships and 11,704,967 tons of cargo (eight times the PA's total in New York City) in 1979,

while employing 5,948 workers. Privately owned ports are in use in Jersey City and Bayonne. The Ameriport System, centered in Philadelphia, operates facilities between Trenton and Wilmington, Del. Two terminals near Camden are operated by the South Jersey Port Corp.

The state's early aviation centers were Lakehurst and Newark. Lakehurst, whose dirigible operations attracted crowds of spectators during the 1920s and 1930s, was the scene of the crash on 6 May 1937 of the *Hindenburg*, a disaster that killed 36 people and spelled the end of commercial airship flights in the US. The state's first airmail service began in 1924 from New Brunswick's Hadley Field. Newark Airport in the late 1920s billed itself as the busiest air terminal in the world. The PA took over its operation from the city of Newark in 1948. Rebuilt during the 1960s and 1970s, Newark International Airport was by 1980 the state's busiest and the New York metropolitan area's fastest-growing airport, handling 9,297,000 passengers and 118,400 tons of cargo in 1979. Statewide in 1978 there were 30 public and 233 private airfields.

¹¹HISTORY

The first known inhabitants of what is now New Jersey were the Leni-Lenape (meaning "Original People"), who arrived in the land between the Hudson and Delaware rivers about 6,000 years ago. Members of the Algonkian language group, the Leni-Lenape were an agricultural people supplementing their diet with freshwater fish and shellfish. The peace-loving Leni-Lenape believed in monogamy, educated their children in the simple skills needed for wilderness survival, and clung rigidly to a tradition that a pot of food must always be warm on the fire to welcome all strangers.

The first European explorer to reach New Jersey was Giovanni da Verrazano, who sailed into what is now Newark Bay in 1524. Henry Hudson, an English captain sailing under a Dutch flag, piloted the *Half Moon* along the New Jersey shore and into Sandy Hook Bay in the late summer of 1609, a voyage that established a Dutch claim to the New World. Hollanders came to trade in what is now Hudson County as early as 1618, and in 1660, they founded New Jersey's first town, called Bergen (now part of Jersey City). Meanwhile, across the state, Swedish settlers began moving east of the Delaware River in 1639. Their colony of New Sweden had only one brief spurt of glory, from 1643 to 1653, under Governor Johan Printz.

The Leni-Lenape lost out to the newcomers, whether Dutch, Swedish, or English, despite a series of treaties that the Europeans thought fair. State and local records describe these agreements: huge tracts of land exchanged for trinkets, guns, and alcohol. The guns and alcohol, combined with smallpox (another European import), doomed the "Original People." In 1758, when a treaty established an Indian reservation at Brotherton (now the town of Indian Mills), only a few hundred Indians remained.

England assumed control in March 1664, when King Charles II granted a region from the Connecticut River to the Delaware River to his brother James, the duke of York. The duke, in turn, deeded the land between the Hudson and Delaware rivers, which he named New Jersey, to his court friends John Berkeley, 1st Baron Berkeley of Stratton, and Sir George Carteret, on 23 June 1664. Lord Berkeley and Sir George became proprietors, owning the land and having the right to govern its people. Subsequently, the land passed into the hands of two boards of proprietors in two provinces called East Jersey and West Jersey, with their capitals in Perth Amboy and Burlington, respectively. East Jersey was settled mainly by Puritans from Long Island and New England, West Jersey by Quakers from England. The split cost the colony dearly in 1702, when Queen Anne united East and West Jersey but placed them under New York rule. The colony did not get its own "home rule" until 1738, when native son Lewis Morris was named the first royal governor.

By this time, New Jersey's divided character was already established. Eastern New Jersey looked toward New York, western New Jersey toward Philadelphia. The level plain connecting those two major colonial towns made it certain that New Jersey would serve as a pathway. Along the makeshift roads that soon crossed the region—more roads than in any other colony—travelers brought conflicting news and ideas. During the American Revolution, the colony was about equally divided between Revolutionists and Loyalists. William Franklin (illegitimate son of Benjamin Franklin), royal governor from 1763 until 1776, strove valiantly to keep New Jersey sympathetic to England, but failed and was arrested. Throughout the Revolutionary period he remained a leading Loyalist and after the war he left for England.

Franklin's influence caused New Jersey to dally at first over independence, but in June 1776, the colony sent five new delegates to the Continental Congress—Abraham Clark, John Hart, Francis Hopkinson, Richard Stockton, and the Reverend John Witherspoon—all of whom voted for the Declaration of Independence. Two days before the Declaration was proclaimed, New Jersey adopted its first state constitution. William Livingston, a fiery anti-British propagandist, was the first elected governor of the state.

New Jersey played a pivotal role in the Revolutionary War, for the side that controlled both New York and Philadelphia would almost certainly win. George Washington and his battered troops made their winter headquarters in the state three times during the first four years of the war, twice in Morristown and once in Somerville. Five major battles were fought in New Jersey, the most important being the Battle of Trenton on 26 December 1776 and the Battle of Monmouth on 28 June 1778. At war's end, Princeton became the temporary capital of the US from 26 June 1783 to 4 November 1783.

The state languished after the Revolution, with many of its pathway towns ravaged by the passing of competing armies, its trade dependent on New York City, and its ironworks (first established in 1676) shut down because of decreased demand. The state's leaders vigorously supported a federation of the 13 states, in which all states, regardless of size, would be represented equally in one national legislative body. This so-called New Jersey Plan led to the establishment of the US Senate.

Railroads and canals brought life to the state in the 1830s and set it on a course of urbanization and industrialization. The 90-mi (145-km) Morris Canal linked northern New Jersey with the coalfields of Pennsylvania. Considered one of the engineering marvels of the 19th century, the canal rose to 914 feet (279 meters) from sea level at Newark Bay to Lake Hopatcong, then fell 760 feet (232 meters) to a point on the Delaware River opposite Easton, Pa. Old iron mines beside the canal found markets, the dyeing and weaving mills of Paterson prospered, and Newark, most affected by the emerging industries, became the state's first incorporated city in 1836. Another canal, the Delaware and Raritan, crossed the relatively flat land from Bordentown to New Brunswick. Along this waterway, Bordentown, Trenton, and New Brunswick boomed. Princeton, whose leaders fought to keep the canal away from the town, settled into a long existence as a college community built around the College of New Jersey, founded in Elizabeth in 1746 and transferred to Princeton in 1756.

The canals were doomed by railroad competition almost from the start. The Morris Canal was insolvent long before World War I, and the Delaware Canal, although operative until 1934, went into a long, slow decline after the Civil War. The first railroad, from Bordentown to South Amboy, closely paralleled the Delaware and Raritan Canal and in 1871 became an important part of the Pennsylvania Railroad. The coal brought in on railroad cars freed industry from water power; factories sprang up wherever the rails went. The Hudson County waterfront, eastern terminus for most of the nation's railway systems, became the most important railroad area in the US. Rail lines also carried vacationers to the Jersey shore, building an important source of income for the state.

The Civil War split New Jersey bitterly. Leaders in the Democratic Party opposed the war as a "Black Republican" affair. Prosperous industrialists in Newark and Trenton feared that their vigorous trade with the South would be impaired, Cape May hotelkeepers fretted about the loss of tourists from Virginia, and even Princeton students were divided. As late as the summer of 1863, after the Battle of Gettysburg, many state "peace Democrats" were urging the North to make peace with the Confederacy. Draft calls were vigorously opposed in 1863, yet the state sent its full quota of troops into service throughout the conflict. Most important, New Jersey factories poured forth streams of munitions and other equipment for the Union army. At war's end, political leaders stubbornly opposed the 13th, 14th, and 15th Amendments to the US Constitution, and blacks were not permitted to vote in the state until 1870.

During the last decades of the 19th century, New Jersey developed a reputation for factories capable of making the components necessary for thousands of other manufacturing enterprises. Few factories were large, although in 1873, Isaac M. Singer opened a huge sewing machine plant at Elizabeth that employed 3,000 persons. Oil refineries on the Hudson County waterfront had ever expanding payrolls, pottery firms in Trenton thrived, and Newark gained strength from many diversified manufactures and also saw its insurance companies become nationally powerful.

Twentieth-century wars stimulated New Jersey's industries. During World War I, giant shipyards at Newark, Kearny, and Camden made New Jersey the nation's leading shipbuilding state. The Middlesex County area refined 75% of the nation's copper, and nearly 75% of US shells were loaded in the state. World War II revived the shipbuilding and munitions industries, while chemical and pharmaceutical manufacturing, spawned by the World War I cutoff of German chemicals, showed further growth during the second world conflict. Paterson, preeminent in locomotive building during the 19th century, became the nation's foremost airplane-engine manufacturing center. Training and mobilization centers at Ft. Dix and Camp Kilmer moved millions of soldiers into the front lines.

The US Census Bureau termed New Jersey officially "urban" in 1880, when the state population rose above 1 million for the first time. Urbanization intensified throughout the 20th century and especially after World War II, as people left the old cities in New Jersey and other northeastern states to buy homes in developments on former farmlands. Places like Cherry Hill, Woodbridge, Clifton, and Middletown Township have boomed since 1945, increasing their population as much as sixfold. New Jersey has also experienced many of the problems of urbanization. Its cities have declined rapidly, and its once vaunted railway system is in a shambles. Traffic congestion is intense in the morning, when commuters stream into urban areas to work, and again in the evening, when they return home to what once was called "the country." That country now knows the problems of urban growth: increased needs for schools, sewers, police and fire protection, and road maintenance, along with rising taxes.

The state has not surrendered to its problems, however. In 1947, voters overwhelmingly approved a new state constitution, a terse, comprehensive document that streamlined state government, reformed the state's chaotic court system, and mandated equal rights for all. Governor Alfred E. Driscoll promptly integrated the New Jersey National Guard, despite strong federal objections; integration of all US armed forces soon followed. Voters since 1950 have passed a wide variety of multimillion-dollar bond issues to establish or rebuild nine state colleges. Rutgers, the state university, has been rapidly expanded. Funds have been allocated for the purchase and development of new park and forest lands. Large bond issues have financed the construction of highways, reservoirs, and rapid transit systems.

During the postwar period, New Jersey has had no predictable political pattern. It gave huge presidential majorities to Republican Dwight D. Eisenhower and Democrat Lyndon B. Johnson, narrowly supported Democrat John F. Kennedy, and favored Republican Gerald Ford over Democrat Jimmy Carter by a small margin. For more than 20 years, the state's two US senators, Clifford B. Case (R) and Harrison A. Williams (D), were recognized as like-minded liberals. Democrat Bill Bradley, former Princeton University and New York Knicks basketball star, was elected to Case's seat in 1978, after Case's own party repudiated him in the primary.

¹²STATE GOVERNMENT

New Jersey's first state constitution took effect in 1776. A second constitution was written in 1844, and a third in 1947. This last document, as amended, continues to govern the state today.

The state legislature consists of a 40-member senate and 80-member assembly. Senators, elected to four-year terms, must be at least 30 years of age and have been New Jersey residents for four years and district residents for a year. Assembly members, elected to two-year terms, must be at least 21 years of age and have been New Jersey residents for two years and district residents for a year. Both houses of the legislature meet in unlimited annual sessions.

New Jersey is one of only two states—the other is Maine—in which the governor is the only elective administrative official. Given broad powers by the state constitution, the governor appoints the heads, or commissioners, of the 19 major state departments with the advice and consent of the senate; not subject to senate approval are some 500 patronage positions. The governor is also commander-in-chief of the state's armed forces, submits the budget to the legislature each January, presents an annual message on the condition of the state, and may grant pardons and, with the aid of the Parole Board, grant executive clemency. Elected to a four-year term in the odd-numbered year following the presidential election, the governor may run for a second term but not for a third until four years have passed. A candidate for governor must be at least 30 years old and must have been a US citizen for 20 years and a New

Jersey citizen for 7 years in order to qualify for the ballot.

A bill may be introduced in either house of the legislature. Once passed, it goes to the governor, who may either sign it, return it to the legislature with recommendations for change, or veto it in its entirety. A two-thirds majority in each house is needed to override a veto.

Amendments to the state constitution may originate in either house. If, after public hearings, both houses pass the proposal by a three-fifths vote, the amendment is placed on the ballot at the next general election. If approved by a majority, but by less than a three-fifths vote in both houses, the amendment is referred to the next session of the legislature, at which time, if again approved by a majority, it is placed on the ballot. The amendment goes into effect 30 days after ratification by the electorate.

To vote in New Jersey, one must be at least 18 years old, a US citizen, and must have been a New Jersey resident for 30 days before the election.

¹³POLITICAL PARTIES

From the 1830s through the early 1850s, Democrats and Whigs dominated the political life of New Jersey. Exercising considerable, though subtle, influence in the decade prior to the Civil War was the Native American (Know-Nothing) Party, an anti-immigrant, anti-Catholic group that won several assembly and senate seats. Wary of breaking ties with the South and ambivalent about the slavery issue, New Jerseyans, especially those in Essex and Bergen counties, did not lend much support to the abolitionist cause. Early Republicans thus found it advantageous to call themselves simply "Opposition"; the state's first Opposition governor was elected in 1856. Republicans controlled the state for most of the 1860s; but with heavy support from business leaders, the Democrats regained control in 1869 and held the governorship through 1896. They were succeeded by a series of Progressive Republican governors whose efforts were largely thwarted by a conservative legislature. Sweeping reforms—including a corrupt practices act, a primary election law, and increased support for public education—were implemented during the two years that Woodrow Wilson, a Democrat, served as governor before being elected to the presidency. Between 1913 and 1980, 12 Democrats and 11 Republicans have captured the statehouse.

As of 1979 there were 3,556,481 registered voters, 48% of

New Jersey Presidential Vote by Political Parties, 1948–80

YEAR	ELECTORAL VOTE	NEW JERSEY WINNER	DEMOCRAT	REPUBLICAN	PROGRESSIVE	SOCIALIST	PROHIBITION	SOCIALIST LABOR	SOCIALIST WORKERS
1948	16	Dewey (R)	895,455	981,124	42,683	10,521	10,593	3,354	5,825
1952	16	*Eisenhower (R)	1,015,902	1,373,613	5,589	8,593	—	5,815	3,850
					CONSTITUTION				
1956	16	*Eisenhower (R)	850,337	1,606,942	5,317	—	9,147	6,736	4,004
					CONSERVATIVE				
1960	16	*Kennedy (D)	1,385,415	1,363,324	8,708	—	—	4,262	11,402
1964	17	*Johnson (D)	1,867,671	963,843	—	—	—	7,075	8,181
					AMERICAN IND.	PEACE & FREEDOM			
1968	17	*Nixon (R)	1,264,206	1,325,467	262,187	8,084	—	6,784	8,667
					PEOPLE'S	AMERICAN			
1972	17	*Nixon (R)	1,102,211	1,845,502	—	5,355	34,378	4,544	2,233
					US LABOR	LIBERTARIAN			COMMUNIST
1976	17	Ford (R)	1,444,653	1,509,688	7,716	1,650	9,449	3,686	1,662
					CITIZENS				
1980	17	*Reagan (R)	1,147,364	1,546,557	8,203	—	20,652	2,198	2,555

*Won US presidential election.

whom turned out to vote for members of the state assembly and state senate in 1979. The balloting left the assembly with 44 Democrats and 36 Republicans, and the senate with 27 Democrats and 13 Republicans. As of early 1980, the governor, Brendan Byrne, was a Democrat, as were both US senators and 10 of New Jersey's 15 US representatives. The Democratic margin in the House was cut to 8–7 by the election of November 1980, when New Jersey—where President Jimmy Carter had never won—gave a popular majority to Republican nominee Ronald Reagan. The final tally showed Reagan with 52% of the vote, Carter with 39%, and independent candidate John Anderson with 8%.

New Jersey's unenviable reputation for corruption in government dates back at least to 1838, when ballot tampering resulted in the disputed election of five Whigs to the US House of Representatives. (After a House investigation, the Whigs were barred and their Democratic opponents given the seats.) Throughout the remainder of the century, corruption was rampant in local elections: Philadelphians, for example, were regularly imported to vote in Atlantic City elections, and vote buying was a standard election-day procedure in Essex and Hudson counties. Wilson's 1911 reform bill eliminated some of these practices, but not the bossism that had come to dominate big-city politics. Frank Hague of Jersey City controlled patronage and political leaders on the local, state, and national level from 1919 to 1947; during the 1960s and 1970s, Hague's successor John V. Kenny, Jersey City mayor Thomas Whelan, and Newark mayor Hugh Addonizio, along with numerous other state and local officials, were convicted of corrupt political dealings. From 1969 to mid-1975, federal prosecutors indicted 148 public officials, securing 72 convictions. Brendan Byrne, who had never before held elective office, won the governorship in 1973, mainly on the strength of a campaign that portrayed him as the "judge who couldn't be bought." On the national level, New Jersey Representative Peter Rodino gained a reputation for honesty and fairness when he chaired the House Judiciary Committee's impeachment hearings against Richard Nixon. However, the state's image suffered a further blow in 1980, when, as a result of the FBI's "Abscam" investigation, charges of influence peddling were brought against several state officials, including members of the Casino Control Commission, whose function was to prevent corruption and crime in Atlantic City's gambling establishments. Later in the year, New Jersey Democrat Harrison Williams became the nation's first US senator to be indicted, on charges of bribery and conspiracy, as a result of the Abscam probe.

14 LOCAL GOVERNMENT

As of 1980, New Jersey had 21 counties, 53 cities, 257 boroughs, 233 townships, 21 towns, 3 villages, and 380 special districts.

Counties are classified by population and location. First-class counties (3 in 1980) have populations exceeding 600,000; second-class counties (7), populations of 200,000–600,000; third-class counties (7), populations of 50,000–200,000 but no Atlantic shore; fourth-class counties (0), under 50,000 population, no Atlantic shore; fifth-class counties (3), population more than 100,000, Atlantic shore; and sixth-class counties (1), less than 100,000 population, Atlantic shore. These classes determine the number of members on the main county governing body, the board of freeholders, which may range from three to nine. Elected to staggered three-year terms, the freeholders administer county and state programs. Under the Optional County Charter Law of 1972, four counties have an elected county executive, and one county has an appointed county manager. Other county officers include the clerk, sheriff, surrogate, prosecutor, boards of election and taxation, county counsel, administrator, medical examiner, chief probation officer, and jury commissioner.

Cities, boroughs, and towns may employ the mayor-council system, council-manager system, commission system, or other forms of their own devising. Most townships and villages are governed by committee or by a council and a mayor with limited powers. Cities, too, are classed by population and location: first-class cities are those over 150,000 in population; second-class, 12,000–150,000; third-class, all others except ocean resorts; and fourth-class, ocean resorts.

The budgets of all local units are supervised by the New Jersey Department of Community Affairs, which also offers municipal aid programs. By state law, all local budgets must be balanced, and budgetary increases ("budget caps") are limited to 5% a year for most items.

15 STATE SERVICES

The constitution of 1947 limited the number of state government departments to 20; as of 1980 there were 19. New Jersey in 1974 became the first state to establish a Public Advocate Department, empowered to provide legal assistance for indigent criminal defendants, mental patients, and any citizen with a grievance against a government agency or regulated industry. A temporary Code of Ethics was adopted by the legislature in 1976 and renewed for 1980–81; by executive order, more than 500 state executive officials must file financial disclosure statements.

The Education Department administers state and federal aid to all elementary and secondary schools, oversees pupil transportation, and has jurisdiction over the state library, museum, and historical commission. State-run colleges and universities and higher education policy are the province of the Department of Higher Education. All state-maintained highways and bus and rail transportation are the responsibility of the Department of Transportation, which also operates the New Jersey Transit Corp., whose function is to acquire and operate public transportation services.

The Human Services Department administers welfare, Medicaid, mental health, and mental retardation programs, as well as veterans' institutions and programs and other state-supported social services. Alcohol, drug abuse, and many other health-related programs are monitored by the Health Department, which also oversees hospitals and compiles statewide health statistics.

The Office of the Attorney General, officially titled the Department of Law and Public Safety, is the statewide law-enforcement agency. Its functions include criminal justice, consumer affairs, civil rights, alcoholic beverage control, and gaming enforcement; also within this department are the State Police, State Racing Commission, Violent Crimes Compensation Board, and a number of regulatory boards. The Defense Department controls the Army and Air National Guard. Correctional institutions, training schools, treatment centers, and parole offices are administered by the Corrections Department.

The newest agency, the Department of Energy, organized in 1977, monitors the supply and use of fuel and administers the state master plan for energy use and conservation; its Board of Public Utilities has broad regulatory jurisdiction, ranging from garbage collection to public broadcasting. Other agencies include the departments of agriculture, banking, civil service, community affairs, environmental protection, insurance, labor and industry, state, and treasury.

16 JUDICIAL SYSTEM

All judges in New Jersey, except municipal court judges, are appointed by the governor with the consent of the senate. Initial terms for supreme and superior court judges are seven years; after reappointment, judges may serve indefinitely.

The supreme court, the state's highest, consists of six associate justices and a chief justice, who is also the administrative head of the state court system. As the court of highest authority, the supreme court hears appeals on constitutional questions and of certain cases from the superior court, which comprises three divisions, chancery, law, and appellate. The chancery division has original jurisdiction over general equity cases, most probate cases, and divorce actions. All other original cases are tried within the law division. The appellate division hears appeals from the chancery and law divisions, from lower courts, and from most state administrative agencies. As of 1979 there were 22 appellate judges, 30 chancery judges, and 182 law judges. A state tax court, empowered to review local property tax assessments, equalization tables, and state tax determinations, has been in operation since July 1979; by statute it may have from 6 to 12 judges.

Each county has juvenile and domestic relations courts that handle cases involving delinquent minors, child abuse, child support, and children under foster care. Specially appointed judges preside over these courts in 12 counties; in the remaining 9 counties, superior court judges are assigned. County district courts hold jurisdiction over all civil matters involving sums of less than $3,000. Municipal court judges, appointed by local governing bodies for three-year terms, hear violations of municipal ordinances.

According to the FBI Crime Index, New Jersey's crime rate as of 1978—5,207 per 100,000 population—was slightly above the national average. Specific rates included murder and nonnegligent homicide, 5; forcible rape, 24; robbery, 192; aggravated assault, 202; burglary, 1,456; larceny-theft, 2,767; and motor vehicle theft, 561. The Newark metropolitan area had a crime rate of 5,557; 657 for violent crime and 4,900 for property crime.

¹⁷ARMED FORCES

Founded as a training base during World War I, Ft. Dix, near Trenton, remains the largest military base in New Jersey, with 12,972 authorized personnel in 1977/78. Other major army facilities are Ft. Monmouth in Eatontown and the Picatinny Arsenal in Dover. The largest naval facility is the Lakehurst Naval Air Center, with 4,178 authorized personnel in 1977/78; McGuire Air Force Base in Wrightstown had 12,694. Authorized personnel at all New Jersey military installations totaled 51,373 in 1977/78. In addition, the US Coast Guard operates a training center in Cape May. New Jersey firms received nearly $1.5 billion in defense contracts awards (10th in the US) in 1978.

Of the 1,107,000 estimated veterans living in New Jersey on 30 September 1979, World War I veterans numbered 23,000; World War II, 491,000; Korean conflict, 225,000; and Viet-Nam era, 297,000. Veterans' benefits in 1977/78 totaled $438 million, of which $237 million was for compensation and pensions, $103 million for medical services, $58 million for education and training, and $40 million for other purposes.

In the year ending 30 June 1979, 12,398 persons served in the New Jersey Army National Guard and 2,348 in the Air National Guard. In 1977 there were 25,154 state and local police personnel; the state's overall rate of 3.4 police per 1,000 population was the nation's 2d highest after New York.

¹⁸MIGRATION

New Jersey's first white settlers were intercolonial migrants: Dutch from New Amsterdam, Swedes from west of the Delaware River, and Puritans from New England and Long Island. By 1776, New Jersey's population was about 138,000, of whom perhaps 7% were black slaves.

Population growth lagged during the early 19th century, as discouraged farmers left their worn-out plots for more fertile western soil; farmers in Salem County, for example, went off to found new Salems in Ohio, Indiana, Iowa, and Oregon. Not until the rapid industrial growth of the mid-1800s did New Jersey attract great waves of immigrants. Germans and Irish were the first to arrive, the latter comprising 37% of Jersey City's population by 1870. The late 1800s and early 1900s brought newcomers from Eastern Europe, including many Jews, and a much larger number of Italians to the cities. By 1900, 43% of all Hudson County residents were foreign-born. More recently, migration from Puerto Rico and Cuba has been substantial.

From World War I on, there has been a steady migration of blacks from southern states; Newark's black population grew by 130,000 between 1950 and 1970. Black as well as Hispanic newcomers settled in major cities just as whites were departing for the suburbs. New Jersey's suburbs were also attractive to residents of New York City, Philadelphia, and other adjacent areas, who began a massive move to the state just after World War II; nearly all of these suburbanites were white. From 1940 to 1970, New Jersey gained a net total of 1,360,000 residents. Between 1970 and 1977, however, the state lost 67,000 residents through migration, and there was evidence that while the black population was still rising, whites were departing from New Jersey in increasing numbers.

¹⁹INTERGOVERNMENTAL COOPERATION

New Jersey participates in such regional bodies as the Interstate Sanitation Commission, Atlantic States Marine Fisheries Commission, and Mid-Atlantic Regional Fisheries Council. Of primary importance to the state are its relations with neighboring Pennsylvania and New York. With Pennsylvania, New Jersey takes part in the Delaware Valley Regional Planning Commission, Delaware River Joint Toll Bridge Commission, and Delaware River Port Authority; with New York, the Port Authority of New York and New Jersey, the Palisades Interstate Park Commission, and the Waterfront Commission, established to eliminate corruption and stabilize employment at the Hudson River ports. The Delaware River Basin Commission manages the water resources of the 12,750-sq-mi (33,000-sq-km) basin under the jurisdiction of New Jersey, New York, and Pennsylvania. The Tri-State Regional Planning Commission seeks to improve economic and environmental development of the New Jersey, New York, and Connecticut area; and the Delaware River and Bay Authority operates a bridge and ferry between New Jersey and Delaware.

In 1978/79, the state received $2.7 billion in federal assistance, including $223.8 million in general revenue sharing.

²⁰ECONOMY

New Jersey was predominantly agricultural until the mid-1800s, when the rise of the railroads stimulated manufacturing in northern New Jersey and opened the Jersey shore to resort development. The steady growth of population in the 1900s fostered the growth of service-related industries, construction, and trade, for which the state's proximity to New York and Philadelphia had long been advantageous.

Manufacturing accounted for about one-third of nongovernment employment as of September 1978. Although petroleum refining, chemicals and pharmaceuticals, food processing, and electric and electronic equipment are all important, the state is more noteworthy for the diversity of its manufactures than for any dominant company or product. Trade and tourism are the next leading sectors. The heaviest concentrations of jobs are in and near metropolitan New York and Philadelphia, but employment opportunities in the central and north-central counties have been increasing. Fresh market vegetables are the leading source of farm income.

During the 1970s, New Jersey's economy followed national trends, except that the mid-decade recession was especially severe. Conditions in most areas improved in the latter part of the decade, especially in Atlantic City, with the construction of gambling casinos and other entertainment facilities. Manufacturing in the central cities declined, however, as industries moved to suburban locations. The closing of the Ford Motor Co. assembly plant in Mahwah in 1980 did not augur well for the future of heavy industry in the state.

²¹INCOME

New Jersey's per capita income of $8,818 in 1978 ranked 6th among the 50 states. The total personal income of $64.6 billion ranked 8th, and New Jersey's average of $8.6 million per sq mi ($3.3 million per sq km) of land area was the highest of any state.

Median family income, $16,432, ranked 4th in 1975. On the other hand, real income rose only 18% between 1970 and 1978, well below the US average, and New Jersey's 1978 ranking in per capita income represented a decline from 2d place in 1970 to 3d in 1975.

During the 4th quarter of 1978, income by category of employment (excluding government workers) was as follows: manufacturing, 38%; personal services and amusements, 17%; retail trade, 12%; wholesale trade, 10%; finance, insurance, and real estate, 6%; contract construction, 6%; transportation, 5%; communications and utilities, 5%; and mining, agriculture, and other sectors, 1%.

About 586,000 New Jerseyans were below the federal poverty line in 1975 (2.4% of the US total). In 1972, 597,000 state residents made up 4.7% of the top US wealthholders.

²²LABOR

The civilian labor force was estimated at 3,431,000 in 1978, 58% male and 42% female. About 3,185,000 were employed and 246,000 unemployed, for an overall unemployment rate of 7.2% ranging from 6.2% for adult males to 17.6% for all teenagers. The overall rate dropped to below 6% in 1979.

The work force was distributed approximately as follows: clerical workers, 19%; professional and technical workers, 18%; service workers, 13%; nonfarm managers and administrators, 12%; craftsmen and kindred workers, 12%; equipment operators (except transport), 11%; salespeople, 7%; nonfarm laborers, 4%; transport equipment operators, 4%; and farm workers, less than 1%.

A federal census of workers covered by unemployment insurance in March 1977 revealed the following nonfarm employment pattern in New Jersey:

	ESTABLISH-MENTS	EMPLOYEES	ANNUAL PAYROLL ('000)
Agricultural services, forestry, fishing	1,810	5,658	$ 60,649
Mining	134	2,558	45,934
Contract construction	14,199	82,261	1,414,540
Manufacturing, of which:	14,496	780,513	11,197,815
Chemicals, chemical products	(956)	(95,988)	(1,624,338)
Nonelectrical machinery	(2,020)	(67,003)	(969,153)
Electric, electronic equipment	(818)	(76,058)	(1,073,772)
Transportation, utilities	6,517	165,223	2,542,773
Wholesale trade	12,774	192,546	2,896,728
Retail trade	41,120	433,180	3,305,609
Finance, insurance, real estate	13,791	141,624	1,623,857
Services	42,432	452,928	4,468,376
Other	2,297	3,046	50,459
TOTALS	149,570	2,259,537	$27,606,740

Government workers, not included in this survey, numbered 326,000 local, 92,000 state, and about 69,000 federal employees in 1978. Several migrant work camps are located near south Jersey tomato farms and fruit orchards, but the number of farm workers coming into the state is declining with the increased use of mechanical harvesters.

The state's first child labor law was passed in 1851, and in 1886, workers were given the right to organize. Labor's gains were slow and painful, however. In Paterson, no fewer than 137 strikes were called between 1881 and 1900, every one of them a failure. A 1913 strike of Paterson silkworkers drew nationwide headlines, but again few results. Other notable strikes were a walkout at a Carteret fertilizer factory in 1915 during which six picketers were killed by guards, a yearlong work stoppage by Passaic textile workers in 1926, and another Paterson silkworkers' strike in 1933, this one finally leading to union recognition

and significant wage increases. That same year, the state enacted a law setting minimum wages and maximum hours for women. This measure was repealed in 1971, in line with the trend toward nonpreferential labor standards. As of 1976, 824,000 New Jerseyans belonged to unions or employee associations.

²³AGRICULTURE

Although New Jersey is a leading producer of fresh market fruits and vegetables, its total farm income was only $374 million in 1978, 41st among the 50 states. As of 1978, New Jersey ranked 2d in the US in the production of cultivated blueberries, 3d in spinach, 4th in green peppers, tomatoes, and summer potatoes, and 5th in asparagus, sweet corn, and peaches.

Some 990,000 acres (401,000 hectares) were in farms in 1979. Of the 23,000 workers on 7,600 farms, about 11,000 were hired hands. The major farm counties are Hunterdon for grain, Gloucester and Cumberland for vegetables, fruits, and berries, Salem for vegetables, Atlantic for fruits and berries, and Monmouth for potatoes and nursery products.

In 1979, New Jersey produced 3,989,000 hundredweight of fresh market vegetables, worth $60,793,000. Leading crops (in hundredweight units) were sweet corn, 686,000; tomatoes, 528,000; lettuce, 479,000; green peppers, 440,000; snap beans, 176,000; eggplant, 145,000; and spinach, 82,000. New Jersey farmers also produced 90,000 tons of tomatoes for processing. Estimates for fruit crops in 1980 (in hundredweight units) included apples, 120,000,000, and peaches, 110,000,000. In 1979, 2,127,000 lb of blueberries, 253,000 hundredweight of cranberries, and 25,000 hundredweight of strawberries were also produced.

The expansion of housing and industry has increased the value of farm acreage throughout the state, and since World War II, many farmers have found it more profitable to sell their land than to keep it in crops. The state government sought to slow this trend through tax incentives during the 1970s.

²⁴ANIMAL HUSBANDRY

With cash receipts estimated at $104 million in 1978, New Jersey does not rank as a major livestock-producing state. At the close of 1979 there were 100,000 cattle and calves, 57,000 hogs and pigs, and 9,300 sheep and lambs on New Jersey farms.

Statewide meat production figures for 1979 included cattle, 26,825,000 lb; hogs and pigs, 15,525,000 lb; and sheep and lambs, 470,000 lb. Poultry farmers produced 1,298,000 lb of turkeys, 4,428,000 lb of chickens, and 342,000,000 eggs. Among the leading dairy products were milk, 494,000,000 lb; cheese, 25,569,000 lb; ice cream, 5,747,000 gallons; and ice milk, 3,040,000 gallons. In 1978, beekeepers produced 1,050,000 lb of honey and 18,000 lb of beeswax from 35,000 colonies of bees.

²⁵FISHING

New Jersey in 1978 had a commercial fish catch of 163.7 million lb, worth $44.4 million (11th in the US). Cape May–Wildwood was the 14th-largest fishing port in the US, bringing in 47.7 million lb of fish, worth $25.1 million. Clams and oysters were the leading species landed.

The Division of Fish, Game, and Shell Fisheries of the Department of Environmental Protection owns and operates 400,000 acres (162,000 hectares) of shellfish grounds, including 37,000 acres (15,000 hectares) of oyster and clam planting grounds, beneath tidal waters from the Raritan to the Delaware Bay. It also operates a fish hatchery at Hackettstown that produces some 500,000 trout annually, plus lesser amounts of largemouth bass, channel catfish, and sunfish.

Recreational fishermen catch finfish and shellfish along the Atlantic coast and in the rivers and lakes of northern New Jersey.

²⁶FORESTRY

About 40% of New Jersey's land area, or 1,928,000 acres (780,000 hectares), was forested in 1977. Of that, 96% was classified as commercial timberland, most of it privately owned. Not since the late 17th century, when lumber from forests in what is now Burlington, Camden, Cape May, and Salem counties was used to make ships in southern New Jersey ports, has the timber industry been of significant economic importance to the state. Shipments of lumber and wood products had a value of $268.5 million in 1977, less than 1% of all shipments of manufactured goods.

As of 1979, the Bureau of Parks maintained 260,124 acres (105,269 hectares) of state land, nearly 70% of that in 11 state forests. The bureau also operates 40 state parks, 12 natural areas, and 4 recreation areas.

27 MINING

Once a leading iron producer, New Jersey had a mineral output valued at $118 million in 1978, thereby ranking only 42d among the 50 states.

Throughout the 18th century, New Jersey iron deposits, primarily in the region that is now Morris County, provided most of the colonies' supply. The state's forges were later instrumental in providing weapons and munitions for the Revolutionary War. By the mid-1800s, zinc had replaced iron as the leading state mineral, and mines in Franklin and Ogdensburg led the nation in output. Although the mines in Franklin are now closed, New Jersey ranked 4th in the US in zinc production in 1978, with 31,873 tons, most of that from Sussex County. Other major minerals were stone, more than 13,300,000 tons; sand and gravel, 10,000,000 tons; sulfur, 131,000 tons; and clay, 96,000 tons.

28 ENERGY AND POWER

Though it contains some of the largest oil refineries in the US, New Jersey produces little of its own energy, importing much of its electric power and virtually all of its fossil fuels.

Installed capacity in the state's 30 electric generating plants totaled 12.4 million kw in 1978. Power production amounted to 30.4 billion kwh, of which 55% came from oil, 27% from nuclear fuels, and 18% from coal. The 1979 nuclear accident at Three Mile Island (TMI), though in Pennsylvania, had a major impact on New Jersey, since General Public Utilities, headquartered in Parsippany, is the holding company for the two firms that operate TMI Unit 2, damaged in the accident, and TMI Unit 1, undamaged but shut down since the incident occurred. New Jersey has three nuclear reactors of its own. Two of them, at Salem, are operated by Public Service Electric and Gas, the state's largest utility and the 10th largest in the US in 1979, with assets of $6.1 billion. A smaller unit is at Toms River.

Bayonne is a major terminal for oil and gas piped through the state; its depots are used by Exxon, Humble Oil, and Texaco, while Mobil employs facilities in Linden. Crude oil refineries produce gasoline, heating oil, and other petroleum products in Linden, Paulsboro, and Bayonne. In 1978, six companies began offshore drilling for oil and gas in the Baltimore Canyon area, about 100 mi (161 km) east of Atlantic City. Two years later, tests confirmed the presence of large gas deposits, but it was still uncertain whether recovery was commercially feasible.

29 INDUSTRY

New Jersey is one of the nation's major manufacturing states, ranking 1st in pharmaceuticals, 3d in plastics, and among the leaders in petrochemicals, instruments, food products, apparel, electrical machinery, and printing and publishing. The total value added by manufacturing was $23.2 billion in 1977.

New Jersey's earliest industries were glassmaking and ironworking. In 1791, Alexander Hamilton proposed the development of a planned industrial town at the Passaic Falls. The Society for Establishing Useful Manufactures, an agency charged with developing the town, tried but failed to set up a cotton mill at the site, called Paterson, in 1797. By the early 1800s, however, Paterson had become the country's largest silk manufacturing center; by 1850, it was producing locomotives as well. On the eve of the Civil War, industry already had a strong foothold in the state. Newark had breweries, hat factories, and

paper plants; Trenton, iron and paper; Jersey City, steel and soap; and Middlesex, clays and ceramics. The late 1800s saw the birth of the electrical industry, the growth of oil refineries on Bayonne's shores, and emerging chemical, drug, paint, and telephone manufacturing centers. All these products retain their places among the state's diverse manufactures.

As of 1977, the chemical industry led all sectors in manufacturing employment, with 13%, followed by electric and electronic equipment, 10%; nonelectrical machinery, 8%; apparel and other textile products, 8%; and fabricated metal products, 7%. By value added, the leading categories were chemical and allied products, 27%; food and food products, 9%; electric and electronic equipment, 8%; and nonelectrical machinery, 8%.

The following table shows value added by manufacture for selected industries in 1972 and 1977:

	1972	1977
Drugs	$1,497,500,000	$2,485,300,000
Soaps, cleansers, toiletries	1,006,200,000	1,535,600,000
Transport equipment	917,700,000	1,177,200,000
Industrial organic chemicals	683,000,000	996,500,000
Communications equipment	758,800,000	817,700,000
Plastics products, miscellaneous	460,700,000	760,500,000
Beverages	313,000,000	408,700,000
Pressed or blown glass	266,900,000	377,700,000
Ladies' outerwear	250,000,000	362,600,000
Commercial printing	228,600,000	339,100,000
Preserved fruits and vegetables	190,900,000	338,000,000

Nearly every major US corporation has facilities in the state. Major corporations headquartered in New Jersey include Allied Chemical in Morristown, American Cyanamid in Wayne, Campbell Soup in Camden, CPC International in Englewood Cliffs, Ingersoll-Rand in Woodcliff Lake, Johnson & Johnson in New Brunswick, Merck in Rahway, Nabisco in East Hanover, Schering-Plough in Kenilworth, Walter Kidde in Clifton, and Warner-Lambert in Morris Plains. Numerous corporations have moved their headquarters from New York to New Jersey since 1960.

30 COMMERCE

With one of the nation's busiest ports and many regional distribution centers, New Jersey is an important commercial state.

In 1972, New Jersey ranked 7th in the US in wholesale trade, with sales of $31.7 billion. Retail sales reached $24.3 billion in 1977 (9th among the 50 states). The major sales outlets were grocery stores, 22%; automotive dealers, 17%; department stores, 11%; eating and drinking places, 9%; and gasoline service stations, 7%. Bergen County led all counties with 14% of retail sales, and the borough of Paramus—with only 27,509 residents in 1978, but several huge shopping plazas—led all localities in sales with 3% and had the highest per capita retail sales in the US; many of the customers are New York City residents lured by New Jersey's lower and less inclusive sales tax. Other large shopping centers are in Eatontown, Livingston, Menlo Park, and Woodbridge. Three of the nation's largest supermarket chains have their headquarters in New Jersey: Great Atlantic and Pacific Tea Co. (A&P) in Montvale, the 6th-largest retailing company in the US; Grand Union in Elmwood Park; and Supermarkets General (Pathmark) in Woodbridge.

Port Newark and the Elizabeth Marine Terminal, foreign-trade zones operated by the Port Authority of New York and New Jersey, have been modernized and enlarged in recent years, and together account for 89% of the cargo unloaded in New York Harbor. In 1976, New Jersey exported nearly $2.7 billion of its own manufactures to foreign countries (10th in the US). Agricultural exports totaled $38 million in 1976/77.

31 CONSUMER PROTECTION

Consumer fraud cases are handled by the Division of Consumer Affairs of the Department of Law and Public Safety, which maintains regional offices in Camden and Newark, and in 1978/79 disposed of 5,166 cases at a savings to consumers of $587,452. The Division of Rate Counsel in the Public Advocate Department represents residents' interests before the various regulatory bodies, in some cases helping to postpone or reduce proposed utility rate increases.

³²BANKING

The colonies' first bank of issue opened in Gloucester in 1682. New Jersey's first chartered bank, the Newark Banking and Insurance Co., was the first of many banks to open in that city. By the mid-1800s, Newark was indisputably the financial center of the state, a position it still holds. Newark is the headquarters of the First National State Bank of New Jersey, the state's largest bank, with assets in mid-1979 of more than $1.4 billion (85th in the US). For the most part, however, commercial banking in New Jersey is overshadowed by the great financial centers of New York City and Philadelphia.

As of 1978 there were 184 commercial banks, with deposits of $27.3 billion and outstanding loans of $12.5 billion. The state's 175 savings and loan associations had assets of $20.3 billion and outstanding mortgage loans of $15.1 billion. There were 5,946 consumer credit associations in 1980.

Regulation of all banks within the state is the responsibility of the Department of Banking.

³³INSURANCE

In 1873, John Dryden (later a US senator) opened the first company to offer low-cost insurance for working people. Called the Widows' and Orphans' Friendly Society, the company was located in the basement of a Newark bank until 1878, one year after Dryden changed the name of the rapidly growing enterprise to the Prudential Insurance Co. Still based in Newark, Prudential is now the largest insurance company in the US, with 1979 assets of $54.7 billion. Another Newark company, Mutual Benefit Life, was the nation's 15th largest in 1979.

During 1978/79, New Jersey had 840 insurance companies and 93,836 licensed insurance agents and brokers. Some 11.8 million life insurance policies, worth $111.5 billion, were in force in 1978. The average family had $41,200 in life coverage, 17% above the national average. More than $1.3 billion in claims were paid to policyholders and their beneficiaries. Property and liability premiums totaling $3.2 billion were written in 1979, including $964.9 million in automobile liability coverage, $474.1 million in automobile physical damage insurance, and $280.7 million in homeowners insurance. Nearly $3.5 billion in flood insurance was in force in 1979.

No-fault automobile insurance has been compulsory in New Jersey since 1973. All insurance agents, brokers, and companies in the state are licensed and regulated by the Department of Insurance.

³⁴SECURITIES

There are no stock or commodity exchanges in New Jersey. Regulation of securities trading in the state is under the control of the Bureau of Securities of the Division of Consumer Affairs, within the Department of Law and Public Safety.

New York Stock Exchange member firms had 113 sales offices and 1,243 registered representatives in the state in 1978. In 1977, New Jerseyans reported nearly $1.3 billion in dividend income on their federal income tax returns.

³⁵PUBLIC FINANCE

From 1975 through 1980, current state expenditures rose at less than the rate of inflation, primarily because spending increases for most items were limited by state law to 5% a year. The annual budget, prepared by the Treasury Department's Division of Budget and Accounting, is submitted by the governor to the legislature for approval. The fiscal year runs from 1 July to 30 June.

The following is a summary of estimated revenues and expenditures for 1979/80 and 1980/81:

REVENUES	1979/80	1980/81
Major taxes	$2,933,500,000	$3,307,000,000
Property tax relief fund (income tax)	945,000,000	1,050,000,000
Miscellaneous taxes, fees, revenues	342,110,513	334,968,940
Other transfers and receipts	351,487,462	320,312,169
Balance from previous year	579,961,534	519,964,359
TOTALS	$5,152,059,509	$5,532,245,468

EXPENDITURES		
Direct state services	$1,969,024,127	$2,172,165,580
State aid	1,548,185,199	1,613,153,540
Property tax relief	943,021,000	1,043,000,000
Debt service	164,473,227	168,449,120
Casinos	74,000,000	81,500,000
Capital construction	37,742,675	35,889,958
TOTALS	$4,736,446,228	$5,114,158,198

Of the total state expenditures in 1980/81, 43% went for education, 8% for public assistance, 8% for Medicaid, 7% for mental health and mental retardation, 5% for transportation, 3% for debt service, and 26% for other purposes.

The public debt of state and local government as of 1977 was $8.9 billion, or $1,219 per capita (17th among the 50 states).

³⁶TAXATION

The repeated refusal of the state legislature to levy a personal income tax ended abruptly in 1976, when the state supreme court, having earlier ruled that local property taxes were an inadequate and unfair way to fund local school systems, ordered that the schools be closed down if the state did not come up with a suitable alternative. The legislature enacted a gross income tax of 2% on the first $20,000 of taxable income and 2.5% on amounts over $20,000, with the proceeds going for school aid, property tax relief to homeowners, and other designated purposes.

Estimated revenues from the income tax in 1980/81 exceeded $1 billion. A 5% sales and use tax was expected to yield nearly $1.3 billion in 1980/81. Also levied are several corporation taxes, along with taxes on motor fuels, cigarettes, inheritances, alcoholic beverages, insurance premiums, realty transfers, savings institutions, pari-mutuel income, public utilities, and railroads. Commuters from New York State pay a tax of 2–15% on income earned in New Jersey, in order to defray costs of subsidizing transportation between the two states.

The major local tax is the property tax, which in 1978/79 raised nearly $3.5 billion in revenues. Under the Homestead Tax Rebate Act of 1976, homeowners are eligible for property tax rebates, which in 1979 averaged about $185. Other exemptions and deductions from the property tax apply to senior citizens and to veterans and their widows.

In 1976, New Jersey paid $13.8 billion in federal taxes and received $9.3 billion in federal expenditures. The $1,886 in total federal taxes per capita was the 4th highest among the 50 states. New Jerseyans filed 3 million federal income tax returns in 1977, paying $6.6 billion in tax.

³⁷ECONOMIC POLICY

New Jersey's controlled budget and relatively low business tax burden have helped encourage new businesses to enter the state. In addition, the state government offers a number of development programs, administered under the Division of Economic Development of the Department of Labor and Industry.

The New Jersey Economic Development Authority provides long-term, low-interest financing in the form of industrial development bonds for new construction, expansion of existing facilities, and acquisition of new equipment. During 1978/79, the authority approved 313 new projects, loaned $343.2 million, and was responsible for the creation of more than 20,000 jobs. Also within the Division of Economic Development are offices that promote tourism; offer technical, marketing, and financial assistance to investors, entrepreneurs, and small businesses; and encourage motion-picture production within the state.

The main tax incentives offered are a 15-year local property tax abatement in the six largest cities and a 5-year abatement in 42 smaller municipalities. New Jersey's basic corporate tax rate of 7.5% compared favorably with rates of 10% in New York and 10.5% in Pennsylvania in 1980.

38 HEALTH

New Jerseyans' average life expectancy is not far from the national norm: 70.93 in 1969–71, ranking 22d in the US. Males lived an average of 67.52 years, females 74.38. During 1977, the infant mortality rate was 11.8 per 1,000 live births for whites, 24 for nonwhites. The birthrate that year was 12.8 per 1,000 population, 17% below the national average. There were 45,300 abortions in 1977/78; the abortion rate of 500 per 1,000 live births was 25% above the national norm. Another factor contributing to the low birthrate was a marriage rate 32% below the US average. Partly because the marriage rate was so low, New Jersey's divorce rate, 2.8 per 1,000 residents, was the lowest in the US in 1977.

The leading causes of death in the state are heart disease and cancer, for both of which New Jersey ranks well above the national average. Mortality rates per 100,000 residents in 1977 were as follows: diseases of the heart, 378; cancer, 203; cerebrovascular disease, 74; accidents, 34; pneumonia and influenza, 23; diabetes, 17; cirrhosis of the liver, 16; arteriosclerosis, 9; suicide, 8; and early infant diseases, 10. The level of protection from childhood diseases in 1978/79 ranged from 97% for diphtheria to 99% for rubella and measles.

The Department of Health monitors all drug abuse and public health programs in the state. During the 1979 fiscal year, 19,480 New Jerseyans sought alcoholism treatment, 18,500 were treated for drug abuse, and 750 cases of syphilis and 22,650 cases of gonorrhea were reported. Community health services offered family planning information to 87,309 women of childbearing age, more than 5% of the target population.

The state's four public psychiatric hospitals and its child and geriatric treatment centers had a total of 4,011 patients and 4,843 beds in 1978/79; the patient population in eight state-run mental retardation centers was 7,526. Private mental retardation centers and private supervised groups cared for 823 and 9,522 patients, respectively. As of 1978, 139 hospitals of all types had 44,157 beds and an 80% occupancy rate. Hospital personnel totaled 97,505, of whom 19,554 were registered nurses and 7,409 licensed practical nurses. Costs of hospital care in 1977, $182 per day and $1,579 per stay, were close to the US averages. The state's 467 nursing homes had, on average, 32,300 resident patients in 34,000 available beds in 1976. There were 13,349 licensed physicians in 1977 and 4,706 professionally active dentists in 1979. The state's only medical school is the College of Medicine and Dentistry of New Jersey, a public institution that combines facilities in Newark, Piscataway, Camden, and Green Brook.

Perhaps New Jersey's greatest contribution to health has come from its private industries. The brothers Johnson of New Brunswick (now the firm of Johnson & Johnson) inaugurated the manufacture and marketing of sterile dressings and bandages. Streptomycin is only one of the many pharmaceuticals developed by drug companies in the state.

39 SOCIAL WELFARE

Through the Department of Human Services, New Jersey administers the major federal welfare programs, as well as several programs specifically designed to meet the needs of New Jersey minority groups. Among the latter in 1978/79 were Cuban Refugee Assistance, involving expenditures of $4,126,699 to aid 2,524 persons, and Indochinese Refugee Assistance, $414,000 for

458 persons. The state also appropriated $29,425,780 for 212 community day-care centers serving 17,780 children.

In 1978, $502 million was spent on aid to families with dependent children, serving 457,400 New Jerseyans, 70% of them children. About 457,000 state residents purchased food stamps at a cost to the federal government of $154.9 million in subsidies. Under the school lunch program, $46.8 million was spent to feed 659,000 students; the rate, 42% of students in participating schools, was the lowest of any state.

Of the 1,118,200 Social Security beneficiaries who received more than $3.1 billion in 1977, 725,800 retired workers received $2.1 billion, and 243,500 survivors, $685.1 million; 148,900 disabled workers received $389.7 million. In 1978, 33,400 elderly persons received $40.5 million and 49,000 disabled persons received $82.4 million in Supplemental Security Income. About 297,000 participants in the Medicaid program received payments totaling $50.6 million.

In 1977, the state granted $245.3 million in workers' compensation benefits. About $22.8 million was spent on vocational rehabilitation programs in 1978; during that same year, unemployment insurance claims totaling $670 million for 752,000 workers were processed.

40 HOUSING

Before 1967, New Jersey took a laissez-faire attitude toward housing. With each locality free to fashion its own zoning ordinances, large tracts of rural land succumbed to "suburban sprawl"—single-family housing developments spread out in two huge arcs from New York City and Philadelphia. Meanwhile, the tenement housing of New Jersey's central cities was left to deteriorate.

Because poor housing was at least one of the causes of the Newark riot in 1967, the state established the Department of Community Affairs to coordinate existing housing aid programs and establish new ones; the department spent $9,326,582 for housing assistance in 1978/79. The state legislature also created the Mortgage Finance Agency and Housing Finance Agency to stimulate home buying and residential construction. In an effort to halt suburban sprawl, local and county planning boards were encouraged during the 1970s to adopt master plans for controlled growth. Court decisions in the late 1970s challenged the constitutionality of zoning laws that precluded the development of low-income housing in suburban areas.

As of 1970, the state had 2,303,000 year-round housing units, of which 2,218,000 were occupied. Of the latter, 61% were owner-occupied and nearly 98% had full plumbing. Some 103,600 new housing units worth $3 billion were authorized from 1976 through 1978.

41 EDUCATION

Public education in New Jersey dates from 1828, when the legislature first allocated funds to support education. Tuition charges were abolished in Newark, Jersey City, and Paterson by 1846, and by 1871, a public school system was established statewide.

A century later, the adult illiteracy rate was 1.1%. On this as on most other measures, the state is close to the US norm: median school years completed, 12.4; proportion of adult high school graduates, 66%; proportion of adults with four or more years of college, 15%.

As of 29 September 1978, New Jersey had 2,443 public schools, of which 1,746 were elementary, 196 middle, 390 secondary, 42 vocational, and 69 for the handicapped. The total enrollment, 1,337,327, represented a continuation of a 10-year decline that was expected to continue into the 1980s; Ocean County was the only area to show an increase. The student body was 74% white, 18% black (from a high of 48% in Essex County to a low of 0.4% in Sussex), 7% Hispanic (from 34% in Hudson to 0.4% in Hunterdon County), and 1% Asian. There were 44,369 elementary- and 30,621 secondary-school teachers. Nonpublic school enrollment in the fall of 1979 was 202,851.

Rutgers, the state university, began operations as Queen's College in 1766 and was placed under state control in 1956. Encompassing the separate colleges of Rutgers, Douglass, Livingston, and Cook, among others, the university's total enrollment as of the fall 1978 was 43,271. Nine state colleges run by the Department of Higher Education had a combined enrollment of 88,147. Also under the department's control are the New Jersey Institute of Technology, formerly the Newark College of Engineering, with 7,296 students; and the College of Medicine and Dentistry of New Jersey, with 1,678. The 17 community and county colleges had 88,680 students. The major private university in the state and one of the nation's leading institutions is Princeton University, founded in 1746, with an enrollment of 6,086 in 1977. Other major private universities are Seton Hall (1856) 9,132, Stevens Institute of Technology (1870) 2,300, and Fairleigh Dickinson (1942), 18,789 on three main campuses.

The New Jersey Department of Higher Education offers tuition aid grants and scholarships to state residents who attend colleges and universities in the state. Guaranteed loans for any qualified resident are available through the New Jersey Higher Education Assistance Authority.

Total expenditures for education in 1978 were $3.1 billion. The state ranked 3d nationwide in expenditures per pupil (based on average daily attendance); per capita school expenditures, $423, were the 14th highest of the 50 states.

[42] ARTS

During the late 1800s and early 1900s, New Jersey towns, especially Atlantic City and Newark, were tryout centers for shows bound for Broadway. As of 1980, the state had at least 25 theaters, most notably the McCarter Theater at Princeton.

Around the turn of the century, Ft. Lee was the motion-picture capital of the world. Most of the best-known "silents"—including the first, *The Great Train Robbery*, and episodes of *The Perils of Pauline*—were shot there, and in its heyday the state film industry supported 21 companies and 7 studios. New Jersey's early preeminence in cinema, an era that ended with the rise of Hollywood, stemmed partly from the fact that the first motion-picture system was developed by Thomas Edison at Menlo Park in the late 1880s.

The post–World War II era saw the development of community orchestras throughout the state. More than 50 such orchestras receive assistance from the New Jersey Orchestra Association, founded in 1966. The state has a long history of support for classical music: the libretto for *The Archers*, the first American opera to be commercially produced, was written in 1796 by William Dunlap of Perth Amboy. The state's leading orchestra is the New Jersey Symphony, which makes its home in Newark's Symphony Hall but performs throughout the state. The New Jersey State Opera also performs in Symphony Hall. Noteworthy dance companies include the Garden State Ballet, New Jersey Ballet, and Princeton Regional Ballet. A variety of performers, both classical and contemporary, appear during the summer at the Garden State Arts Center in Holmdel, an open amphitheater that seats more than 5,000. The jazz clubs of northern New Jersey and the seaside rock clubs in Asbury Park have helped launch the careers of many local performers. Financial assistance to the arts is provided through the New Jersey State Council of the Arts.

[43] LIBRARIES AND MUSEUMS

Statewide, some 330 public libraries in 1978 housed more than 21.4 million volumes and recorded a circulation of 34.3 million. The Newark Public Library was the largest municipal system, with 1,174,073 volumes and eight branches. Distinguished by special collections on Afro-American studies, art and archaeology, economics, and international affairs, among many others, Princeton University's library is the largest in the state, with 3,091,903 volumes in 1978; Rutgers University ranked 2d with 1,526,358. The New Jersey State Library in Trenton contained 396,302 vol-

umes, mostly on the state's history and government. One of the largest business libraries, emphasizing scientific and technical data, is the Bell Labs library system, based in Murray Hill.

New Jersey has more than 100 museums and historic sites. Among the most noteworthy are the New Jersey Historical Society in Newark and New Jersey State Museum in Trenton; the Newark Museum, containing both art and science exhibits; Princeton University's Art Museum and Museum of Natural History; and the Jersey City Museum. Also of interest are the early waterfront homes and vessels of Historic Gardner's Basin in Atlantic City, as well as Grover Cleveland's birthplace in Caldwell; the Campbell Museum in Camden (featuring the soup company's collection of bowls and utensils); Cape May County Historical Museum; Clinton Historical Museum Village; US Army Communications-Electronics Museum at Ft. Monmouth; Batsto Village at Hammonton; Morristown National Historic Park (where George Washington headquartered during the Revolutionary War); Sandy Hook Museum; and one of the most popular attractions, the Edison National Historic Site, formerly the home and workshop of Thomas Edison in West Orange.

[44] COMMUNICATIONS

Many communications breakthroughs—including Telstar, the first communications satellite—have been achieved by researchers at Bell Labs in Holmdel, Whippany, and Murray Hill. Three Bell Labs researchers shared the Nobel Prize in physics (1956) for developing the transistor, a device that has revolutionized communications and many other fields. In 1876, at Menlo Park, Thomas Edison invented the carbon telephone transmitter, a device that not only made the telephone commercially feasible but also embodied the principles of the radio microphone.

The first mail carriers to come to New Jersey were, typically enough, on their way between New York and Philadelphia. Express mail between the two cities began in 1737, and by 1764, carriers could speed through the state in 24 hours. In colonial times, tavern keepers generally served as the local mailmen. By 1978, the US Postal Service employed 27,600 workers in New Jersey, many of them at the nation's largest bulk-mail facility in Jersey City.

Nearly 98% of all telephones in the state are owned by New Jersey Bell, the remainder by Continental Telephone of New Jersey and the Delaware Valley Telephone Co. As of 31 December 1978 there were 6,335,199 telephones, 4,722,525 residential and 1,612,674 business. New Jerseyans made 8.1 billion local calls and 2.1 billion toll calls in 1978, when virtually every household in the state had telephone service.

Because the state lacks a major television broadcasting outlet, New Jerseyans receive more news about events in New York City and Philadelphia than in their own towns and cities. In 1979 there were 81 radio stations (48 AM, 33 FM) and 10 television stations, none of which commanded anything like the audiences and influence of the stations across the Hudson and Delaware rivers. The state government operates four television stations under the Public Broadcasting Authority. In 1978, in cooperation with public television's WNET (licensed in Newark but operated in New York), these stations began producing New Jersey's first nightly newscast. The Federal Communications Commission has urged New York and Philadelphia television stations to devote more air time to news from New Jersey, which accounts for about 30% of their combined audience. In mid-1979, cable television service was provided by 45 companies to 487,210 subscribers.

[45] PRESS

If New Jersey is a state without a clear identity, the lack of a powerful press must be at least partly responsible. Queen Anne in 1702 banned printers from the colony; the state's first periodical, founded in 1758, died two years later. New Jersey's first daily paper the *Newark Daily Advertiser*, did not arrive until 1832.

Although several present-day newspapers have amassed considerable circulation, most notably the *Newark Star-Ledger*, none has been able to muster statewide influence or match the quality or prestige of the nearby *New York Times* or *Philadelphia Inquirer*, both of which are read widely in the state, along with other New York City and Philadelphia papers. As of September 1978 there were 7 morning dailies with a total circulation of 668,336, 21 evening papers with 1,074,942 circulation, and 15 Sunday newspapers with 1,485,198 circulation. The following table shows leading New Jersey dailies with their 1978 circulation:

AREA	NAME	DAILY	SUNDAY
Asbury Park	Press (e,S)	102,564	135,368
Camden	Courier-Post (e)	122,442	
Hackensack	Record (e,S)	154,827	218,302
Jersey City	Jersey Journal (e)	67,603	
Newark	Star-Ledger (m,S)	413,914	567,264
Trenton	Times (e)	72,150	
	Times-Advertiser (S)		87,360

Numerous scholarly and historical works have been published by the university presses of Princeton and Rutgers. Prentice-Hall has its offices in Englewood Cliffs, and several New York City publishing houses maintain their production and warehousing facilities in the state. Notable among popular periodicals is the *New Jersey Monthly*, published in Princeton.

⁴⁶ORGANIZATIONS
Princeton is the headquarters of several education-related groups, including the Educational Testing Service, Graduate Record Examinations Board, Independent Educational Services, Law School Admission Council, and Woodrow Wilson National Fellowship Foundation. Seeing Eye of Morristown was one of the first organizations to provide seeing-eye dogs for the blind. Other medical and health-related organizations are National Industries for the Blind (Bloomfield) and the American Association of Veterinary State Boards (Teaneck). Birthright USA, an antiabortion counseling service, has its headquarters in Woodbury.

Among the many trade and professional organizations are the Hobby Industry Association of America in Elmwood Park, Science Fiction Writers of America in Hackettstown, American Littoral Society in Highlands, United Association of Railroad Veterans in Paterson, National Midwives Association in Princeton, and Consumers' Research in Washington. Hobby and sports groups include the National Association of Rocketry in New Providence, US Golf Association and World Amateur Golf Council in Far Hills, US Equestrian Team in Gladstone, National Intercollegiate Women's Fencing Association in Kearny, and Babe Ruth Baseball in Trenton.

⁴⁷TOURISM, TRAVEL, AND RECREATION
Tourism is a leading industry in New Jersey, accounting for at least $4 billion in annual income as of 1980. The Jersey shore has been a popular attraction since 1801, when Cape May began advertising itself as a summer resort. US President Ulysses S. Grant began a practice of summering in Long Branch that continued with his successors, Rutherford B. Hayes and James Garfield, who died near there in 1881.

Of all the shore resorts, the largest has long been Atlantic City, which by the 1890s was the nation's most popular resort city and by 1905 was the first major city with an economy almost totally dependent on tourism. That proved to be its downfall, as improvements in road and air transportation made more modern resorts in other states easily accessible to easterners. By the early 1970s, the city's only current claims to fame were the Miss America pageant and the game of Monopoly, whose standard version uses its street names. In an effort to restore Atlantic City to its former luster and revive its economy, New Jersey voters approved a constitutional amendment in 1976 to allow casinos in the resort. As of July 1980, 3 casinos employed some 11,000 persons; another 14 casinos were scheduled to open in the early

1980s. Casino taxes were earmarked to reduce property taxes of senior citizens.

Other state attractions include 10 ski areas in northwestern New Jersey, canoeing and camping at the Delaware Water Gap National Recreation Area, and amusement centers like Cowtown and Great Adventure in central Jersey.

State parks and forests attracted about 5,200,000 visitors in 1978/79, and more than 300,000 people visited state historic sites. New Jersey's inland lakes, 14,000 mi (22,500 km) of trout streams, and 26 towns with saltwater fishing facilities attracted the state's 155,086 fishing-license holders in 1977/78. Licenses were also issued to 178,115 hunters.

⁴⁸SPORTS
New Jersey did not have a major league professional team until 1976, when the New York Giants of the National Football League and the Cosmos of the North American Soccer League moved across the Hudson River into the newly completed Giants Stadium in the Meadowlands Sports Complex at East Rutherford. An indoor arena on that site, which was once marshland, has been planned as the permanent home of the New Jersey Nets of the National Basketball Association, along with a National Hockey League franchise. The Nets moved to the Garden State from Long Island in 1977.

The Meadowlands is also the home of a dual Thoroughbred–harness-racing track that was scheduled to host the prestigious Hambletonian for 3-year-old trotters in 1981. Other racetracks are Monmouth Park (Oceanport) and Atlantic City Race Course for Thoroughbreds, and Freehold Raceway for harness racing. The Trenton and Atlantic City speedways feature auto racing; midget cars race at Pinebrook Stadium, and motorcycles on courses in Madison Township and Englishtown. New Jersey has several world-class golf courses, including Baltusrol, the site of the 1980 US Open.

Princeton and Rutgers played what is claimed to be the first intercollegiate football game on 6 November 1869 at New Brunswick. Several important college games are held at Giants Stadium each fall, including one postseason game, the Garden State Bowl. Princeton also has a strong basketball tradition—Bill Bradley, later a forward for the New York Knickerbockers, starred for the Tigers during the early 1960s—and Rutgers was a collegiate basketball power during the 1970s.

⁴⁹FAMOUS NEW JERSEYANS
While only one native New Jerseyan, (Stephen) Grover Cleveland (1837–1908), has been elected president of the US, the state can also properly claim (Thomas) Woodrow Wilson (b. Virginia, 1856–1924), who spent most of his adult life there. Cleveland left his birthplace in Caldwell as a little boy, winning his fame and two terms in the White House (1885–89; 1893–97) as a resident of New York State. After serving as president, he retired to Princeton, where he died and is buried. Wilson, a member of Princeton's class of 1879, returned to the university in 1908 as a professor, and became its president in 1902. Elected governor of New Jersey in 1910, Wilson pushed through a series of sweeping reforms before entering the White House in 1913. Wilson's two presidential terms were marked by his controversial decision to declare war on Germany and his unsuccessful crusade for US membership in the League of Nations after World War I.

Two vice presidents hail from New Jersey: Aaron Burr (1756–1836) and Garret A. Hobart (1844–99). Burr, born in Newark and educated at what is now Princeton University, is best remembered for killing Alexander Hamilton in a duel at Weehawken in 1804. Hobart was born in Long Branch, graduated from Rutgers College, and served as a lawyer in Paterson until elected vice president in 1896; he died in office.

Four New Jerseyans have become associate justices of the US Supreme Court: William Paterson (b.Ireland, 1745–1806), Joseph P. Bradley (1813–92), Mahlon Pitney (1858–1924), and William

J. Brennan, Jr. (b.1906). Among the relatively few New Jerseyans to serve in the US cabinet was William E. Simon (b.1927), secretary of the treasury under Gerald Ford. Representative Peter W. Rodino (b.1909) was chairman of the House Judiciary Committee when it voted to impeach Richard Nixon in 1974.

Few New Jerseyans won important political status in colonial years because the colony was so long under New York's political and social domination. Lewis Morris (b.New York, 1671–1746) was named the first royal governor of New Jersey when severance from New York came in 1738. Governors who made important contributions to the state included William Livingston (b.New York, 1723–90), first governor after New Jersey became a state in 1776; Marcus L. Ward (1812–84), a strong Union supporter; and Alfred E. Driscoll (1902–75), who persevered in getting New Jersey a new state constitution in 1947 despite intense opposition from the Democratic Party leadership. Other important historical figures include Molly Pitcher (Mary Ludwig Hays McCauley, 1754?–1832), a heroine of the American Revolution, and Zebulon Pike (1779–1813), the noted explorer.

Several New Jersey persons have won Nobel prizes, including Woodrow Wilson, who won the Peace Prize in 1919. A three-man team at Bell Laboratories in Murray Hill won the 1956 physics award for their invention of the transistor: Walter Brattain (b.China, 1902), John Bardeen (b.Wisconsin, 1908), and William Shockley (b.England, 1910). Dr. Selman Waksman (b.Russia, 1888–1973), a Rutgers University professor, won the 1952 prize in medicine and physiology for the discovery of streptomycin. Theoretical physicist Albert Einstein (b.Germany, 1879–1955), winner of a Nobel Prize in 1921, spent his last decades in Princeton. One of the world's most prolific inventors, Thomas Alva Edison (b.Ohio, 1847–1931) patented over 1,000 devices from workshops at Menlo Park and West Orange.

The state's traditions in the arts began in colonial times. Patience Lovell Wright (1725–86) of Bordentown was America's first recognized sculptor. Jonathan Odell (1737–1818) was an anti-Revolutionary satirist, while Francis Hopkinson (b. Pennsylvania, 1737–91), lawyer, artist, and musician, lampooned the British. Authors of note after the Revolution included William Dunlap (1766–1839), who compiled the first history of the stage in America; James Fenimore Cooper (1789–1851), one of the nation's first novelists; Mary Mapes Dodge (b.New York, 1838–1905), noted author of children's books; Stephen Crane (1871–1900), famed for *The Red Badge of Courage* (1895); and Albert Payson Terhune (1872–1942), beloved for his collie stories.

Quite a number of prominent 20th-century writers were born in or associated with New Jersey. They include poets William Carlos Williams (1883–1963) and Allen Ginsberg (b.1926); satirist Dorothy Rothschild Parker (1893–1967); journalist-critic Alexander Woollcott (1888–1962); Edmund Wilson (1895–1972), a highly influential critic, editor, and literary historian; Norman Cousins (b.1915); Norman Mailer (b.1923); Thomas Fleming (b.1927); John McPhee (b.1931); Philip Roth (b.1933); Imamu Amiri Baraka (LeRoi Jones, b.1934); and Peter Benchley (b.New York, 1940).

Notable 19th-century artists were Asher B. Durand (1796–1886) and George Inness (b.New York, 1825–94). The best-known 20th-century artist associated with New Jersey was Ben Shahn (1898–1969); cartoonist Charles Addams (b.1912) was born in Westfield. Important New Jersey composers were Lowell Mason (b.Massachusetts, 1792–1872), called the "father of American church music," and Milton Babbitt (b.Pennsylvania, 1916), long active at Princeton. The state's many concert singers include Anna Case (b.1889), Paul Robeson (1898–1976), and Richard Crooks (1900–72). Ruth St. Denis (1878–1968), a noted dancer, grew up in the state.

Popular singers include Francis Albert "Frank" Sinatra (b.1915), Sarah Vaughan (b.1924), Dionne Warwick (b.1941), Paul Simon (b.1942), and Bruce Springsteen (b.1949). Jazz pianist, composer, and bandleader William "Count" Basie (b.1904) was born in Red Bank.

Other celebrities native to New Jersey include actors Jack Nicholson (b.1937), Meryl Streep (b.1948), and John Travolta (b.1954). Comedians Lou Costello (1906–59), Ernie Kovacs (1919–62), Jerry Lewis (b.1926), and Clerow "Flip" Wilson (b.1933) were also born in the state.

⁵⁰BIBLIOGRAPHY

Amick, George. *The American Way of Graft*. Princeton: Center for Analysis of Public Issues, 1976.

Burr, Nelson R. *A Narrative and Descriptive Bibliography of New Jersey*. Princeton: Van Nostrand, 1964.

Cross, Dorothy. *The Indians of New Jersey*. Trenton: Archaeological Society of New Jersey, 1958.

Cunningham, John T. *Made in New Jersey*. New Brunswick: Rutgers University Press, 1973.

Cunningham, John T. *New Jersey: America's Main Road*. Garden City, N.Y.: Doubleday, 1976.

Cunningham, John T. *Railroading in New Jersey*. New York: Associated Railroads, 1952.

Federal Writers' Project. *New Jersey: A Guide to the Present and Past*. Rev. ed. New York: Hastings House, 1977 (orig. 1939).

Fleming, Thomas. *The Forgotten Victory: The Battle for New Jersey*. New York: Reader's Digest, 1973.

Fleming, Thomas. *New Jersey: A Bicentennial History*. New York: Norton, 1977.

League of Women Voters of New Jersey. *New Jersey: Spotlight on Government*. 3d ed. New Brunswick: Rutgers University Press, 1978.

Link, Arthur F. *Wilson: The Road to the White House*. Princeton: Princeton University Press, 1947.

Lundin, Leonard. *Cockpit of the Revolution: The War for Independence in New Jersey*. Princeton: Princeton University Press, 1940.

Manual of the Legislature of New Jersey, 1980. Trenton: Edward J. Mullin, 1980.

McCormick, Richard P. *Experiment in Independence*. New Brunswick: Rutgers University Press, 1950.

New Jersey, State of. *Budget, Fiscal Year 1980/81*. Trenton, 1980.

Pomfret, John E. *Colonial New Jersey—A History*. New York: Scribner, 1973.

Rosenthal, Alan, and John Blydenburgh, eds. *Politics in New Jersey*. New Brunswick: Rutgers University Press, 1975.

NEW MEXICO

State of New Mexico

ORIGIN OF STATE NAME: Spanish explorers in 1540 called the area "the new Mexico." **NICKNAME:** Land of Enchantment. **CAPITAL:** Santa Fe. **ENTERED UNION:** 6 January 1912 (47th). **SONGS:** "O Fair New Mexico"; "*Así es Nuevo México.*" **MOTTO:** *Crescit eundo* (It grows as it goes). **FLAG:** The sun symbol of the Zia Indians appears in red on a yellow field. **OFFICIAL SEAL:** An American bald eagle with extended wings grasps three arrows in its talons and shields a smaller eagle grasping a snake in its beak and a cactus in its talons (the emblem of Mexico, and thus symbolic of the change in sovereignty over the state). Below the scene is the state motto; the words "Great Seal of the State of New Mexico 1912" surround the whole. **ANIMAL:** Black bear. **BIRD:** Roadrunner (chaparral bird). **FISH:** Cutthroat trout. **FLOWER:** Yucca. **TREE:** Piñon. **GEM:** Turquoise. **VEGETABLES:** Frijol; chili. **LEGAL HOLIDAYS:** New Year's Day, 1 January; Lincoln's Birthday, 12 February; Washington's Birthday, 3d Monday in February; Memorial Day, 30 May; Independence Day, 4 July; Labor Day, 1st Monday in September; Columbus Day, 2d Monday in October; Veterans Day, 11 November; Thanksgiving Day, 4th Thursday in November; Christmas Day, 25 December. **TIME:** 5 A.M. MST = noon GMT.

¹LOCATION, SIZE, AND EXTENT

New Mexico is located in the southwestern US. Smaller only than Montana of the 8 Rocky Mountain states, it ranks 5th in size among the 50 states.

The total area of New Mexico is 121,666 sq mi (315,115 sq km), of which land comprises 121,412 sq mi (314,457 sq km) and inland water 254 sq mi (658 sq km). Almost square in shape except for its jagged southern border, New Mexico extends about 352 mi (566 km) E–W and 391 mi (629 km) N–S.

New Mexico is bordered on the N by Colorado; on the E by Oklahoma and Texas; on the S by Texas and the Mexican state of Chihuahua (with a small portion of the south-central border formed by the Rio Grande); and on the W by Arizona. The total boundary length of New Mexico is 1,434 mi (2,308 km).

The geographic center of the state is in Torrance County, 12 mi (19 km) SSW of Willard.

²TOPOGRAPHY

The Continental Divide extends from north to south through central New Mexico. The north-central part of the state lies within the Southern Rocky Mountains, and the northwest forms part of the Colorado Plateau. The eastern two-fifths of the state fall on the western fringes of the Great Plains.

Major mountain ranges include the Southern Rockies, the Chuska Mountains in the northwest, and the Caballo, San Andres, San Mateo, and Guadalupe ranges in the south and southwest. The highest point in the state is Wheeler Peak, at 13,161 feet (4,011 meters); the lowest point, 2,817 feet (859 meters) is at Red Bluff Reservoir.

The Rio Grande traverses New Mexico from north to south and forms part of the state's southern border with Texas. Other major rivers include the Pecos, San Juan, Canadian, and Gila. The largest bodies of inland water are the Elephant Butte Reservoir and Conchas Reservoir, both created by dams.

The Carlsbad Caverns, the largest-known subterranean labyrinth in the world, penetrate the foothills of the Guadalupes in the southeast. The caverns embrace more than 37 mi (60 km) of connecting chambers and corridors and are famed for their stalactite and stalagmite formations.

³CLIMATE

New Mexico's climate ranges from arid to semiarid, with a wide range of temperatures. Average January temperatures vary from 25°F (–4°C) in the north to 44°F (7°C) in the southwest. July temperatures range from an average of 65°F (18°C) in the north to 80°F (27°C) in the south. The record high temperature for the state is 116°F (47°C), set most recently on 14 July 1934 at Orogrande; the record low, -50°F (–46°C), was set on 1 February 1951 at Gavilan.

Much of the state receives less than 20 in (51 cm) of precipitation, although some areas of the Southern Rockies receive as much as 30 in (76 cm). Nearly one-half the annual rainfall comes between June and August, and thunderstorms are common in the summer. Snow is much more frequent in the north than in the south; Albuquerque gets about 10 in (25 cm) of snow a year, and the northern mountains receive up to 100 in (254 cm).

⁴FLORA AND FAUNA

New Mexico is divided into six life zones: lower Sonoran, upper Sonoran, transition, Canadian, Hudsonian, and arctic-alpine. Characteristic vegetation in each zone includes, respectively, desert shrubs and grasses; piñon/juniper woodland, sagebrush, and chaparral; ponderosa pine and oak woodlands; mixed conifer and aspen forests; spruce/fir forests and meadows; tundra wild flowers and riparian shrubs. The yucca has three varieties in New Mexico and is the state flower. Six types of aster are considered threatened; several cacti are on the endangered list.

Indigenous animals include pronghorn antelope, javelina, and black-throated sparrow in the lower Sonoran zone; mule and white-tailed deer, ringtail, and brown towhee in the upper Sonoran zone; elk and wild turkey in the transition zone; black bear and hairy woodpecker in the Canadian zone; pine marten and blue grouse in the Hudsonian zone; and bighorn sheep, pika, ermine, and white-tailed ptarmigan in the Arctic-Alpine zone. Among notable desert insects are the tarantula, centipede, and vinegarroon. The coatimundi, Baird's sparrow, and brook stickleback are among rare animals. Threatened species include the Arizona shrew and Mexican tetra. The black-footed ferret, river otter, gray wolf, Gila monster, and Socorro isopod are on the endangered list.

⁵ENVIRONMENTAL PROTECTION

Agencies concerned with the environment include the Environmental Improvement Agency of the Department of Health and Social Services, the State Forest Conservation Commission, and the Natural Resources Conservation Commission.

Conservation of scarce water resources is the state's most widespread environmental concern. Only 0.2% of New Mexico consists of surface water—the lowest percentage in the US. Major water projects important for land-use planning, land reclamation, and flood control include the Middle and Lower Rio Grande Projects, Caballo Reservoir, Elephant Butte Reservoir, the Rio Grande Floodway, and Navajo Lake.

6 POPULATION

In 1970, New Mexico had a census population of 1,017,055, 37th in the US. The preliminary census total for 1980 was 1,290,551, for a density of 11 per sq mi (4 per sq km). About 70% of the population was urban and 30% rural in 1970.

Almost one-third of New Mexico's total population lives in the Albuquerque metropolitan area in Bernalillo County. Albuquerque itself had 328,829 residents, according to preliminary census data for 1980. The next-largest city is Santa Fe, the state capital, with 48,914 inhabitants.

7 ETHNIC GROUPS

New Mexico has two large minorities: Indians and Hispanics.

There were 72,788 Indians in the state in 1970, 7% of the total population. Part of Arizona's great Navaho reservation extends across the border into New Mexico. There are 2 Apache reservations, 19 Pueblo villages (including one for the Zia in Sandoval County), and lands allotted to other tribes. Indian lands cover 7,843,000 acres (3,174,000 hectares), 10% of New Mexico's area.

The Hispanic population is an old one, descending from Spanish-speaking peoples who lived there before the territory was annexed by the US. This group, with a much smaller one of immigrants from modern Mexico, makes up 31% of New Mexicans and 90% of the rural farm population.

About 5,000 Asians and 20,000 black Americans live in the state. The people of New Mexico are proud of their ethnoracial civic harmony, though there have been local conflicts between Anglos and Hispanos.

8 LANGUAGES

With large Indian and Spanish-speaking populations, New Mexico in 1970 reported English as the first language of only 55% of the native-born residents and 54% of all residents. But just a few place-names, like Tucumcari and Mescalero, echo in English the presence of the Apache, Zuñi, Navaho, and other tribes living there. Numerous Spanish borrowings include *vigas* (rafters) in the northern half, and *canales* (gutters) and *acequia* (irrigation ditch) in the Rio Grande Valley. New Mexico English is a mixture of dominant Midland, with some Northern features, such as *sick to the stomach*, in the northeast, and Southern and South Midland features such as *spoonbread* and *carry* (escort) in the eastern agricultural fringe.

In 1970, major resident groups claimed first languages as follows:

	NATIVE-BORN	FOREIGN-BORN
English	544,988	2,888
Spanish	317,377	12,306
Indian languages	50,389	6
German	10,395	2,207
Italian	3,419	681

9 RELIGIONS

The first religions in New Mexico were practiced by Pueblo and Navaho Indians. Franciscan missionaries arrived at the time of Coronado's conquest in 1540, and the first Roman Catholic church in the state was built in 1598. Roman Catholicism has long been the dominant religion, though from the mid-1800s there has also been a steady increase in the number of Protestants. The first Baptist missionaries arrived in 1849, the Methodists in 1850, and the Mormons in 1877.

The state's Roman Catholic churches had 370,777 members in 1979. There were 279,890 adherents of Protestant sects, including 116,869 Southern Baptists and 58,700 United Methodists.

The Jewish population was estimated at 5,685 in 1979. Cults in the state include the Penitentes and Pentecostals.

10 TRANSPORTATION

Important early roads included El Camino Real, extending from Veracruz on the east coast of Mexico up to Albuquerque, and the Santa Fe Trail, leading westward from Independence, Mo. By 1978, New Mexico had 72,617 mi (116,866 km) of roads and streets, including 930 mi (1,497 km) of interstate highway.

In 1978, 1,031,616 road vehicles were registered in the state, of which 641,219 were automobiles, 344,018 trucks, 42,691 motorcycles, and 3,688 buses.

Rail service did not begin in New Mexico until 1879. New Mexico had 2,120 mi (3,412 km) of railroad in 1975; the main rail lines serving the state are the Southern Pacific, Santa Fe, and Rock Island.

In 1978 there were 142 airports, 61 public and 81 private. Albuquerque has the state's main airport.

11 HISTORY

The earliest evidence of human occupation in what is now New Mexico, dating from at least 20,000 years ago, has been found in Sandia Cave near Albuquerque. This so-called Sandia man was later joined by other nomadic hunters—the Clovis and Folsom peoples from the northern and eastern portions of the state, and the Cochise culture, which flourished in southwestern New Mexico from about 10,000 to 500 BC. The Mogollón people tilled small farms in the southwest from 300 BC to about 100 years before Columbus came to the New World. Also among the state's early inhabitants were the Basket Makers, a seminomadic people who eventually evolved into the Anasazi, or Cliff Dwellers. The Anasazi, who made their home in the Four Corners region (where present-day New Mexico meets Colorado, Arizona, and Utah) were the predecessors of the modern Pueblo Indians.

The Pueblo people lived along the upper Rio Grande, except for a desert group east of Albuquerque, who lived in the same kind of apartmentlike villages as the river Pueblos. During the 13th century, the Navaho settled in the Four Corners area to become farmers, sheepherders, and occasional enemies of the Pueblos. The Apache, a more nomadic and warlike group who came at about the same time, would later pose a threat to all the non-Indians who arrived in New Mexico during the Spanish, Mexican, and American periods.

Francisco Vásquez de Coronado led the earliest major expedition to New Mexico, beginning in 1540, 80 years before the Pilgrims landed at Plymouth Rock. In 1598, Don Juan de Oñate led an expedition up the Rio Grande, where, one year later, he established the settlement of San Gabriel, near present-day Espanola; in 1610, the Spanish moved their center of activity to Santa Fe. For more than two centuries the Spaniards, who concentrated their settlements, farms, and ranches in the upper Rio Grande Valley, dominated New Mexico, except for a period from 1680 to about 1683, when the Pueblo Indians temporarily regained control of the region.

In 1821, Mexico gained its independence from Spain, and New Mexico came under the Mexican flag for 25 years. The unpopularity of government officials sent from Mexico City and the inability of the new republic to control the Apache led to the revolt of 1837, which was put down by a force from Albuquerque led by General Manuel Armijo. In 1841, as governor of the Mexican territory, Armijo defeated an invading force from the Republic of Texas, but he later made a highly controversial decision not to defend Apache Pass east of Santa Fe during the Mexican-American War, instead retreating and allowing US forces under the command of General Stephen Watts Kearny to enter the capital city unopposed on 18 August 1846.

Kearny, without authorization from Congress, immediately attempted to make New Mexico a US territory. He appointed the respected Indian trader Charles Bent, a founder of Bent's

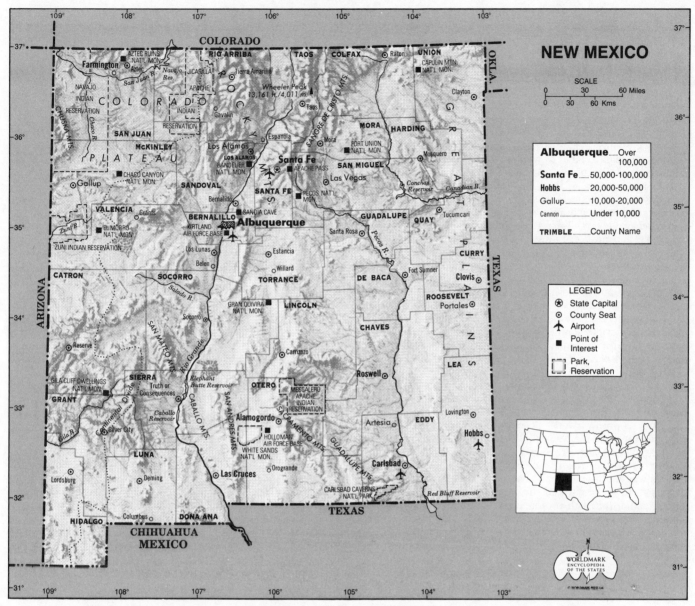

NEW MEXICO

SCALE
0   30   60 Miles
0   30   60 Kms

Albuquerque......Over 100,000
Santa Fe......50,000-100,000
Hobbs......20,000-50,000
Gallup......10,000-20,000
Cannon......Under 10,000

TRIMBLE......County Name

LEGEND
⊛ State Capital
⊙ County Seat
✈ Airport
■ Point of Interest
⬚ Park, Reservation

See US political: front cover E4; physical: back cover E4.

LOCATION: 31°20′ to 37°N; 103°02′ to 109°02′w. **BOUNDARIES**: Colorado line, 333 mi (536 km); Oklahoma line, 34 mi (55 km); Texas line, 498 mi (801 km); Mexico line, 180 mi (290 km); Arizona line, 389 mi (626 km).

Fort on the Santa Fe Trail, as civil governor, and then led his army on to California. After Kearny's departure, a Mexican and Indian revolt in Taos resulted in Bent's death; the suppression of the Taos uprising by another US Army contingent secured American control over New Mexico, although the area did not officially become a part of the US until the Treaty of Guadalupe-Hidalgo ended the Mexican-American War in 1848.

New Mexico became a US territory as part of the Compromise of 1850, which also brought California into the Union as a free state. Territorial status did not bring about rapid or dramatic changes in the life of those who were already in New Mexico. However, an increasing number of people traveling on the Santa Fe Trail—which had been used since the early 1820s to carry goods between Independence, Mo., and Santa Fe—were Americans seeking a new home in the Southwest. One issue that divided many of these new settlers from the original Spanish-speaking inhabitants was land. Native New Mexicans resisted, sometimes violently, the efforts of new Anglo residents and out-

side capital to take over lands that had been allocated during the earlier Spanish and Mexican periods. Anglo lawyers such as Thomas Benton Catron acquired unprecedented amounts of land from native grantees as payment of legal fees in the prolonged litigation that often accompanied these disputes. Eventually a court of private land claims, established by the federal government, legally processed 33 million acres (13 million hectares) of disputed land from 1891 to 1904.

Land disputes were not the only cause of violence during the territorial period. In 1862, Confederate General Henry Hopkins Sibley led an army of Texans up the Rio Grande and occupied Santa Fe; he was defeated at La Glorieta Pass in northern New Mexico by a hastily assembled army of volunteers from Colorado, in a battle that has been labeled the Gettysburg of the West. The so-called Lincoln County War of 1878–81, a range war pitting cattlemen against merchants and involving, among other partisans, William H. Bonney (Billy the Kid), helped give the territory the image of a lawless region unfit for statehood.

Despite the tumult, New Mexico began to make substantial economic progress. In 1879, the Atchison, Topeka, and Santa Fe Railroad entered the territory. General Lew Wallace, who was appointed by President Rutherford B. Hayes to settle the Lincoln County War, was the last territorial governor to enter New Mexico by stagecoach and the first to leave it by train.

By the end of the 19th century, the Indian threat that had plagued the Anglos, like the Spanish-speaking New Mexicans before them, had finally been resolved. New Mexicans won the respect of Theodore Roosevelt by enlisting in his Rough Riders during the Spanish-American War, and when he became president he returned the favor by working for statehood. New Mexico finally became a state on 6 January 1912, under President Taft.

In March 1916, irregulars of the Mexican revolutionary Pancho Villa crossed the international boundary into New Mexico, killing, robbing, and burning homes in Columbus. US troops under the command of General John J. Pershing were sent into Mexico on a long and unsuccessful expedition to capture Villa, while National Guardsmen remained on the alert in the Columbus area for almost a year.

The decade of the 1920s was characterized by the discovery and development of new resources. Potash salts were found near Carlsbad, and important petroleum reserves in the southeast and northwest were discovered and exploited. Oil development made possible another important industry, tourism, which began to flourish as gasoline became increasingly available. This period of prosperity ended, however, with the onset of the Great Depression.

World War II revived the economy, but at a price. In 1942, hundreds of New Mexicans stationed in the Philippines were among the US troops forced to make the cruel "Bataan march" to Japanese prison camps. Scientists working at Los Alamos ushered in the Atomic Age with the explosion of the first atomic bomb at White Sands Proving Ground in June 1945.

The remarkable growth that characterized the Sunbelt during the postwar era has been most noticeable in New Mexico. Newcomers from many parts of the country moved to the state, a demographic shift with profound social, cultural, and political consequences. Spanish-speaking New Mexicans, once an overwhelming majority, have become a diminishing minority. Nevertheless, the Hispanos have been able to maintain their political influence, and one Hispanic New Mexican, Dennis Chavez, who served for many years in the US Senate, was effective not only in advancing the cause of his people but also in bringing federal facilities to the state.

¹²STATE GOVERNMENT

The constitution of New Mexico was drafted in 1910, approved by the voters in 1911, and came into effect when statehood was achieved in 1912. A new constitution drawn up by a convention of elected delegates was rejected by the voters in 1969.

The legislature consists of a 42-member senate and a 70-member house of representatives. Senators serve four-year terms, and house members serve two-year terms. The legislature meets every year, for 60 calendar days in odd-numbered years and 30 calendar days in even-numbered years.

The executive branch consists of 10 elected officials, including the governor, lieutenant governor, secretary of state, auditor, treasurer, attorney general, and commissioner of public lands. These seven are elected for four-year terms; none may serve two successive terms. Three elected members of the Corporation Commission, which has various regulatory and revenue-raising responsibilities, serve six-year terms.

In general, constitutional amendments must be approved by majority vote in each house and by a majority of the electorate. Amendments dealing with voting rights, school lands, and linguistic requirements for education can be proposed only by three-fourths of each house, and then must be approved by three-fourths of the total electorate and two-thirds of the electorate in each county.

In order to vote in state elections, a person must be 18 years of age, a US citizen, and a state resident for at least 42 days.

¹³POLITICAL PARTIES

Although Democrats hold a very substantial edge in voter registration—there were 341,626 registered Democrats and only 149,801 registered Republicans in 1976—New Mexico has been a "swing state" in US presidential elections since it entered the Union. Between 1912 and 1980, New Mexicans voted for Democratic presidential candidates nine times and Republican presidential candidates nine times, in every election except 1976 choosing the candidate who was also the presidential choice of voters nationwide. In November 1980, Ronald Reagan carried the state with 55% of the popular vote to 37% for Jimmy Carter.

New Mexico Presidential Vote by Political Parties, 1948–80

YEAR	ELECTORAL VOTE	NEW MEXICO WINNER	DEMOCRAT	REPUBLICAN	PROGRESSIVE
1948	4	*Truman (D)	105,240	80,303	1,037
1952	4	*Eisenhower (R)	105,435	132,170	225
					CONSTITUTION
1956	4	*Eisenhower (R)	106,098	146,788	364
					SOC. LABOR
1960	4	*Kennedy (D)	156,027	153,733	570
1964	4	*Johnson (D)	194,015	132,838	1,217
					AMERICAN IND.
1968	4	*Nixon (R)	130,081	169,692	25,737
					AMERICAN
1972	4	*Nixon (R)	141,084	235,606	8,767
					SOC. WORKERS
1976	4	Ford (R)	201,148	211,419	2,462
					LIBERTARIAN
1980	4	*Reagan (R)	167,826	250,779	4,365

*Won US presidential election.

[14] LOCAL GOVERNMENT

There are 32 counties in New Mexico. Each is governed by three commissioners elected for two-year terms, except for Bernalillo, which is governed by five commissioners, and Los Alamos, which has a seven-member council. Municipalities are incorporated as cities, towns, or villages.

The Indian Reorganization Act of 1934 reaffirmed the right of Indians to govern themselves, adopt constitutions, and form corporations to do business under federal law. Indians also retain the right to vote in state and federal elections. Pueblo Indians elect governors from each of 19 pueblos, and they form a coalition called the All-Indian Pueblo Council. The Apache elect a tribal council headed by a president and vice-president. The Navaho—one-third of whom live in New Mexico—elect a chairman, vice-chairman, 7 judges, and 74 council members from the 96 chapters that make up their reservation in New Mexico and Arizona.

[15] STATE SERVICES

Agencies supervising the state transportation system include the Department of Aviation, the Civil Air Patrol, the State Highway Commission, the Department of Motor Transportation, the Department of Motor Vehicles, and the Traffic Safety Commission.

New Mexico was one of the first states to form a consolidated Department of Health and Social Services. Related service agencies include the Commission on Aging, Committee on Children and Youth, Department of Hospitals and Institutions, and the Mental Retardation Program Coordinating Council. The various public protection agencies include the Office of Civil and Defense Mobilization of the Attorney General's Office, the State Human Rights Commission, the Department of Corrections, and the New Mexico State Police.

The state's natural resources are protected by the Fish and Wildlife Service, the State Forest Conservation Commission, the Environmental Improvement Agency of the Department of Health and Social Services, the Water Quality Control Commission, and the State Park and Recreation Commission.

[16] JUDICIAL SYSTEM

The judicial branch consists of a supreme court, an appeals court, district courts, probate courts, magistrate courts, and other inferior courts as created by law.

The supreme court is composed of a chief justice and court associate justices; the appeals court, created to take over some of the supreme court's caseload, is composed of five judges. All are elected for eight-year terms.

The state's 32 countries are divided into 13 judicial districts, served by 37 district judges, each elected for a six-year term. District courts have unlimited general jurisdiction and are commonly referred to as trial courts. They also serve as courts of review for decisions of lower courts and administrative agencies. Each county has a probate court, served by a probate judge, who is elected from within the county for a two-year term.

In 1978, New Mexico's crime rates—especially the rates for forcible rape and aggravated assault—were far above the US average.

[17] ARMED FORCES

Air Force personnel totaled 16,270 in 1978; the major installations are Kirtland Air Force Base in the Albuquerque area, and Holloman at Alamogordo. Defense contract awards totaled $201 million in 1977/78.

In 1979 there were about 137,000 veterans living in New Mexico. Of these, 2,000 had served in World War I, 57,000 in World War II, 27,000 in the Korean conflict, and 42,000 during the Viet-Nam era. In 1977/78, total federal expenditures for veterans' programs amounted to $142.4 million.

In 1978, National Guard personnel numbered 4,000 and appropriations were $17.5 million. In 1977 there were 3,336 state and local police in the state, and 1,146 corrections officers.

[18] MIGRATION

Prior to statehood, the major influx of migrants came from Texas and Mexico; many of these immigrants spoke Spanish as their primary language. Wartime prosperity during the 1940s brought a wave of Anglos into the state. New Mexico experienced a net gain through migration of 78,000 people during 1940–60, a net loss of 130,000 during the economic slump of the 1960s, and another net gain of 80,000 between 1970 and 1977.

In 1970, New Mexico had 89,000 residents of foreign stock, of whom 23,000 were foreign-born. The overwhelming majority of foreign immigrants came from Mexico. The count of Mexican-born residents might be much higher if the number of illegal immigrants were known.

[19] INTERGOVERNMENTAL COOPERATION

New Mexico participates in the Western Interstate Commission for Higher Education, the Interstate Oil and Gas Compact, compacts governing use of the Rio Grande and the Canadian, Colorado, and Pecos rivers, and other interstate agreements.

In 1978/79, New Mexico received a total of $617,016,000 in federal assistance, of which $43,580,000 was in general revenue-sharing funds.

[20] ECONOMY

New Mexico was primarily an agricultural state until the 1940s, when military activities assumed major economic importance. Since then, the construction, mining, and tourism sectors have grown substantially. After a lag during the 1960s, New Mexico's economic growth outpaced the nation's during the late 1970s, though its per capita income remained the lowest in the Southwest. In particular, personal income for the state's Indian population was far behind that of New Mexico as a whole.

[21] INCOME

In 1978, per capita income in New Mexico was $6,505, 43d in the US. The state's rank remained low throughout the 1970s despite the fact that real income per capita grew 56% in 1970–78, compared with 32% for the US as a whole.

The 1970 census showed a median family income for the state of $7,849; 19% of all families were below the federal poverty line, and 15% had incomes over $15,000. Among families of Spanish-speaking or Spanish-surnamed persons, median family income was $6,576, with 25% below the poverty line. Median income for urban families was $8,493 in 1970; for all rural families, $6,355; and for farm families, $6,004.

[22] LABOR

In 1978, the total civilian labor force of New Mexico was estimated at 526,000. Of that total, 495,700 were employed and 30,300 (5.8%) unemployed. About 116,100 workers were government employees, with the federal government employing 34,900; state government, 31,700; and local governments, 49,500.

A federal census of workers covered by unemployment insurance in March 1977 revealed the following nonfarm employment pattern in New Mexico:

	ESTABLISH-MENTS	EMPLOYEES	ANNUAL PAYROLL ('000)
Agricultural services, forestry, fishing	230	1,286	$ 8,584
Mining, of which:	583	23,585	365,492
Oil, gas extraction	(461)	(10,324)	(151,054)
Contract construction	2,898	26,957	301,943
Manufacturing	1,113	31,350	305,158
Transportation, public utilities	987	18,526	241,542
Wholesale trade	1,837	16,899	186,694
Retail trade	7,596	73,166	454,656
Finance, insurance, real estate	2,178	17,281	164,750
Services	6,926	65,034	590,071
Other	742	671	9,390
TOTALS	25,090	274,755	$2,628,280

Because manufacturing is not a major industry in New Mexico, organized labor is neither large nor strong. In 1976 there were about 73,000 union members, of whom 65,000 were AFL-CIO members.

23 AGRICULTURE

The first farmers of New Mexico were the Pueblo Indians, who raised maize, beans, and squash. Wheat and barley were introduced from Europe, and indigo and chilies came from Mexico.

In 1978, New Mexico's estimated agricultural income was $993,463,000 (35th in the US). About 25% came from crops and 75% from livestock products. Leading crops include wheat, hay, and cotton. In 1979, wheat production was 8,756,000 bushels, valued at $35,024,000, and hay production was 1,158,000 tons, valued at $79,902,000. About 144,000 bales of cotton were grown in 1979. Other crops included sorghums, corn, and onions.

24 ANIMAL HUSBANDRY

Meat animals, especially cattle, represent the bulk of New Mexico's agricultural income. At the end of 1979 there were 1,600,000 head of beef cattle, 660,000 sheep and lambs, and 87,000 hogs and pigs on New Mexico farms. The main stock-raising regions are in the east, northeast, and northwest.

Beef production in 1979 was 639,090,000 lb, valued at $446,324,000; the lamb and mutton output totaled 19,878,000 lb, worth $12,851,000; and 25,782,000 lb of pork products were valued at $11,034,000.

25 FISHING

There is no commercial fishing in New Mexico. The native cutthroat trout is prized by sport fishermen, however, and numerous species have been introduced into state lakes and reservoirs.

26 FORESTRY

Although lumbering ranks low as a source of state income, the forests of New Mexico are of crucial importance because of the role they play in water conservation and recreation.

In 1977, 23% of New Mexico's land area—18,060,000 acres (7,309,000 hectares)—was forestland, 2.4% of the US total. Of the 5,537,000 acres (2,241,000 hectares) that were commercial timberland, 3,439,000 acres (1,392,000 hectares) were federally owned or managed; 171,000 acres (69,000 hectares) were owned by the state, counties, or municipalities; and 1,927,000 acres (780,000 hectares) were privately owned.

In 1979, 9,103,787 acres (3,684,184 hectares) of New Mexico's woodlands were in the Apache, Carson, Cíbola, Coronado, Gila, Lincoln, and Santa Fe national forests.

27 MINING

Mining is the major economic activity of New Mexico, and the source of much of the state's wealth. The state ranks 1st in potash, uranium, and perlite production, 3d in the production of copper, 4th in natural gas, and 7th in crude petroleum.

In 1976, mineral production amounted to $2.5 billion, of which $814.4 million came from crude petroleum, $695.5 million from natural gas, $239.9 million from copper, $231.9 million from natural gas liquids, $191.3 million from uranium, and $165.4 million from potash. The estimated value of the 1978 mineral output was $3 billion (7th in the US).

Major uranium deposits are located in the northwestern counties of McKinley and Valencia. In 1978, New Mexico mines yielded 15,628,000 lb of uranium ore, 47% of the US total. Other minerals (excluding fossil fuels) were copper, 140,906 tons; potash, 2,101,000 tons; and gold, 9,879 troy oz.

28 ENERGY AND POWER

New Mexico is a major producer of oil and natural gas, and has significant reserves of low-sulfur bituminous coal.

In 1978, the state produced 20 billion kwh of electric energy, based on an installed generating capacity of 4.7 million kw. In 1977, total electric energy sales were 7.6 billion kwh, of which 28% went for residential use, 34% for commercial use, 32% for industrial use, and 6% for other applications. Coal was the energy source for 66% of the power generated in 1976; natural gas, 31%; and other sources, 3%.

Most of New Mexico's natural gas and oil fields are located in the southeastern counties of Eddy, Lea, and Chaves, and in the northwestern counties of McKinley and San Juan. As of 31 December 1978, crude petroleum reserves were 485,640,000 barrels; production in 1978 was estimated at 78,130,000 barrels. Natural gas reserves were 13.3 trillion cu feet, and 1978 production was an estimated 1.1 trillion cu feet.

In 1978, 12,365,000 tons of coal were mined.

29 INDUSTRY

Value added by manufacturing totaled $790 million in 1977; only four states had lower totals. Manufacturing's share of total income and nonagricultural employment in New Mexico were both far below the national average.

The largest manufacturing sector was food and food products, accounting for 13% of value added, followed by electric and electronic equipment, 10%; printing and publishing, 8%; and chemicals, 5%. The following table shows value added by manufacturing for selected industries in 1972 and 1977:

	1972	1977
Lumber and wood products	$31,600,000	$63,600,000
Communications equipment	26,700,000	60,800,000
Stone, clay, glass products	31,700,000	57,000,000
Meat products	18,600,000	27,300,000

More than 50% of the manufacturing jobs in the state are located in and around Albuquerque, in Bernalillo County. Other counties with substantial manufacturing activity include Santa Fe, San Juan, Otero, McKinley, and Dona Ana.

30 COMMERCE

In 1972, wholesale establishments in the state registered sales of $1.5 billion, only 0.2% of the US total. Leading sectors of wholesale trade included petroleum and petroleum products, 17%; machinery, equipment, and supplies, 14%; farm products, 10%; lumber and construction materials, 7%; and groceries, 6%.

In 1977, retail establishments had sales of $3.9 billion. Leading sectors of retail trade included automotive dealers and service stations, 33%; food stores, 21%; general merchandise stores, 12%; and eating and drinking places, 9%.

New Mexico's foreign agricultural exports totaled $82 million in 1976/77; exports of manufactures were $69 million in 1976.

31 CONSUMER PROTECTION

Consumer protection in New Mexico is regulated by the Attorney General's Consumer Protection Division. This office may commence civil and criminal proceedings, represent the state before regulatory agencies, administer consumer protection programs, and handle consumer complaints.

32 BANKING

New Mexico's first bank, the First National Bank of Santa Fe, was organized in 1870. After the turn of the century, banking establishments expanded rapidly in the state, mainly because of growth in the livestock industry.

In 1978 there were 86 insured commercial banks in New Mexico, with total assets of $4.9 billion, time deposits of $2.6 billion, and demand deposits of $1.7 billion. In that same year, 33 savings and loan associations had total assets of $1.4 billion.

33 INSURANCE

There were an estimated 4,900 persons working in the insurance industry in New Mexico in 1978, when the industry as a whole was growing at an annual average rate of about 5%.

In 1978, 1,829,000 life insurance policies were in force in the state, and their total value was $13.6 billion; $109.2 million in benefits were paid. The average family had $33,200 in life insurance.

The $399.2 million of property and liability insurance premiums written in the state in 1978 included $169.2 million in automobile insurance and $42 million in homeowners insurance.

The insurance industry is regulated by the State Insurance Board.

³⁴SECURITIES

There are no securities exchanges in New Mexico. In 1978, however, New York Stock Exchange member firms had 19 sales offices and 124 full-time registered representatives in the state. New Mexicans reported $115 million in dividend income on their 1977 federal tax returns.

³⁵PUBLIC FINANCE

The governor of New Mexico submits a budget annually to the legislature for approval. The fiscal year runs 1 July–30 June.

The following is a summary of general revenues and expenditures for 1978/79 (actual) and 1979/80 (estimated), in millions:

	1978/79	1979/80
REVENUES		
Gross receipts tax	$261.4	$293.0
Income taxes	109.1	84.9
Mineral severance taxes	58.5	77.0
Other taxes	96.5	100.0
Other receipts	205.3	258.4
TOTALS	$730.8	$813.3
EXPENDITURES		
Public schools	$344.0	$374.3
Higher education	118.8	131.5
General government	210.4	234.6
Other expenses	—	18.7
TOTALS	$673.2	$759.1

Outstanding debt of the state and local governments totaled $886 million ($745 per capita) in 1977.

³⁶TAXATION

The state of New Mexico levies a gross receipts tax, various excise taxes, personal and corporate income taxes, property taxes, and mineral severance taxes. Of projected 1980/81 tax revenues, the gross receipts tax accounted for 50%; severance taxes, 16%; personal income tax, 9%; corporate income tax, 8%; and other taxes, 17%. As of 1979, personal income tax rates ranged from 0.8% on the first $2,000 of income to 9% on income over $100,000.

In 1977, 447,467 New Mexicans filed federal income tax returns; their federal tax bill amounted to $636,652,000.

³⁷ECONOMIC DEVELOPMENT

The Economic Development Division of the Department of Commerce and Industry promotes industrial and community development, seeks export markets for New Mexico's products, and encourages use of the state by the motion-picture industry. Funding for the department was $744,100 in 1979/80.

³⁸HEALTH

The average life span of New Mexicans in 1969–71 was 70.32 years (74.51 for females, 66.51 for males), 34th in the US. In 1977 there were 23,000 live births in New Mexico, or 19.4 per 1,000 population, and about 6,400 legal abortions, or 278 per 1,000 live births. In that same year there were about 8,000 deaths in the state (6.8 per 1,000 population), and the infant death rate in the state was 12.9 per 1,000 live births for whites and 18.7 for other groups. Deaths from heart disease and cancer were far below the national average.

There were 54 hospitals in 1978, with 6,503 beds and 193,010 admissions; personnel included 2,545 registered nurses and 1,218 licensed practical nurses. The state had 1,781 active physicians in 1977 and 511 active dentists in 1979.

³⁹SOCIAL WELFARE

In 1978, a total of 50,700 people received aid to families with dependent children; AFDC benefits totaled $31 million, and medical assistance to this same group amounted to $48 million. There were 99,000 participants in the federal food stamp pro-

gram, at a cost to the federal government of $37.5 million; 180,000 students participated in the school lunch program at a federal cost of $15.2 million.

Federally administered Supplemental Security Income in 1978 amounted to $34.3 million, of which $11.4 million went to the aged and $22.2 million to the disabled. In 1976, federal outlays for the five largest welfare programs in New Mexico amounted to $128 million, or 88% of the total welfare outlays in the state.

The state maintains the Carrie Tingley Crippled Children's Hospital in Truth or Consequences, the Meadows Home for the Aged in Las Vegas, the Miners Hospital of New Mexico in Raton, and the New Mexico School for the Visually Handicapped in Alamogordo.

⁴⁰HOUSING

In 1970, New Mexico had 325,715 housing units, with a per-person occupancy rate of 3.4; 10% of the units lacked full plumbing. The median value of all owner-occupied housing for that year was $13,100; the median value of owner-occupied rural housing was $7,900.

Residential construction is the major component of the state's construction industry, accounting for $597.4 million of total contracts worth $1.1 billion in 1978. More than 36,000 new housing units were authorized from 1976 through 1978.

⁴¹EDUCATION

New Mexico had an adult illiteracy rate of 2.2% (highest among the Mountain states and nearly double the US average) in 1970. In that year, 3% of those at least 25 years of age had no formal education; 24% had completed 1–8 years of elementary school; 17% had completed 1–3 years of high school; 30% had completed 4 years of high school; 13% had completed 1–3 years of college; and 13% had completed 4 years of college. The median number of school years completed was 12.2.

In 1977 there were 625 public schools and 78 private schools in New Mexico. The public school system had 270,105 students in 1978/79, when public school operating expenses totaled $427,473,512. In 1976, 42% of all children in public schools were Hispanic and 9% were Indian. New Mexico has sought to overcome these groups' traditional educational handicaps by devising programs that respect their cultural and linguistic distinctness.

New Mexico has 13 universities and colleges of all types, 9 public and 4 private; enrollment in fall 1977 totaled 55,264 students, of whom 93% were in public institutions. The leading public institutions are the University of New Mexico, with its main campus at Albuquerque, and New Mexico State University (Las Cruces).

⁴²ARTS

New Mexico is a state rich in Indian, Spanish, Mexican, and contemporary art. Major exhibits can be seen at the University of New Mexico Art Museum in Albuquerque, and the Art Museum of the Harwood Foundation in Taos. Taos itself is an artists' colony of renown.

The Santa Fe Opera, one of the nation's most distinguished regional opera companies, has its season during July and August.

⁴³LIBRARIES AND MUSEUMS

Public libraries in New Mexico had a combined total of 1,525,315 volumes and a circulation of 3,491,383 volumes in 1978. The largest municipal library is the Albuquerque Public Library, with more than 300,000 books. The largest university library is that of the University of New Mexico, with more than 925,000 volumes. There is a scientific library at Los Alamos and a state law library at Santa Fe.

New Mexico has more than 70 museums. Especially noteworthy are the Maxwell Museum of Anthropology at Albuquerque; the Museum of New Mexico, Museum of International Folk Art, and Institute of American Indian Arts Museum, all in Santa Fe; and several art galleries and museums in Taos. Historic sites include the Palace of the Governors (1610), the oldest US capitol and probably the nation's oldest public building, in Santa Fe; Aztec Ruins National Monument, near Aztec; and Gila Cliff Dwellings National Monument, 44 mi (71 km) north of Silver City.

44 COMMUNICATIONS

The first monthly mail service in New Mexico began in 1849. There were more than 350 post offices in 1977 and about 2,500 postal employees. In 1978, 813,090 telephones were in service in the state, 567,112 residential and 245,978 business; 90% of households had telephone service, well below the US average.

In 1977 there were 56 AM radio stations, 29 FM stations, 6 commercial TV stations, 2 public broadcasting stations, and 1 educational station affiliated with the University of New Mexico at Albuquerque. In 1978, 36 cable television systems served 110,119 subscribers in 76 communities.

45 PRESS

The first newspaper published in New Mexico was *El Crepúsculo de la Libertad* (Dawn of Liberty), a Spanish-language paper established at Santa Fe in 1834. The *Santa Fe Republican*, established in 1847, was the first English-language newspaper.

In 1978 there were 21 daily newspapers (1 morning, 20 evening) in the state. The leading dailies included the *Albuquerque Journal*, with a morning circulation in 1979 of 79,568 (118,879 on Sundays); and the *Santa Fe New Mexican*, with an evening circulation of 18,461 (22,415 on Sundays). The combined net paid circulation of all the dailies was 263,465 in 1979.

46 ORGANIZATIONS

National organizations with headquarters in New Mexico include the American Indian Law Students Association, Americans for Indian Opportunity, the National Indian Youth Council, Futures for Children, the Urban Libraries Council, and the National Association of Consumer Credit Administrators.

47 TOURISM, TRAVEL, AND RECREATION

The development of New Mexico's recreational resources has made tourism a leading economic activity. In 1978 there were 36,100 employees in travel-related industries, 11% more than in 1977. Hunting, fishing, camping, hiking, swimming, boating, and skiing are among the many outdoor attractions. In 1977/78 there were 115,701 hunting-license holders and 179,343 fishing-license holders.

The state has a national park—Carlsbad Caverns—and 10 national monuments: Aztec Ruins, Bandelier, Capulin Mountain, Chaco Canyon, El Morro (Inscription Rock), Fort Union, Gila Cliff Dwellings, Gran Quivira, Pecos, and White Sands. Visits to these national sites in 1978 totaled 1,940,550. Thirty-two state parks attracted 3,776,801 visitors during the same year.

Recreation and tourism are actively encouraged by the state. The industry grew by about 8% a year during the late 1970s but remained vulnerable to gasoline price increases and shortages.

48 SPORTS

New Mexico has no major professional sports teams, though Albuquerque does have a minor league baseball team in the Pacific Coast League. Thoroughbred and quarter-horse racing with pari-mutuel betting is an important spectator sport. Sunland Park, south of Las Cruces, has a winter-long schedule; from May to August there is racing and betting at Ruidoso Downs, La Mesa Park, and New Santa Fe Downs.

The Lobos of the University of New Mexico compete in the Western Athletic Conference, while the Aggies of New Mexico State belong to the Missouri Valley Conference. The Aggies won the conference football championship in 1978.

49 FAMOUS NEW MEXICANS

Among the earliest Europeans to explore New Mexico were Francisco Vásquez de Coronado (b.Spain, 1510–54) and Juan de Oñate (b.Mexico, 1549?–1624?), the founder of New Mexico. Diego de Vargas (b.Spain, 1643–1704) reconquered New Mexico for the Spanish after the Pueblo Revolt of 1680, which was led by Popé (d.1685?), a San Juan Pueblo medicine man. Later Indian leaders include Mangus Coloradas (1795?–1863) and Victorio (1809?–80), both of the Mimbreño Apache. Two prominent native New Mexicans during the brief period of Mexican rule were Manuel Armijo (1792?–1853), governor at the time of the American conquest, and the Taos priest José Antonio Martínez (1793–1867).

Army scout and trapper Christopher Houston "Kit" Carson (b.Kentucky, 1809–68) made his home in Taos, as did Charles Bent (b.Virginia, 1799–1847), one of the builders of Bent's Fort, a famous landmark on the Santa Fe Trail. A pioneer of a different kind was Jean Baptiste Lamy (b.France, 1814–88), the first Roman Catholic bishop in the Southwest, whose life is recalled in Willa Cather's *Death Comes for the Archbishop*. Among the more notorious of the frontier figures in New Mexico was Billy the Kid (William H. Bonney, b.New York, 1859–81); his killer was New Mexico lawman Patrick Floyd "Pat" Garrett (b.Alabama, 1850–1908).

Notable US senators from New Mexico were Thomas Benton Catron (b.Missouri, 1840–1921), a Republican who dominated New Mexico politics during the territorial period; Albert Bacon Fall (b.Kentucky, 1861–1944), who later, as secretary of the interior, gained notoriety for his role in the Teapot Dome scandal; Dennis Chavez (1888–1962), the most prominent and influential native New Mexican to serve in Washington; Carl A. Hatch (b.Kansas, 1889–1963), best known for the Hatch Act of 1939, which limited partisan political activities by federal employees; and Clinton P. Anderson (b.South Dakota, 1895–1975), who was also secretary of agriculture.

New Mexico has attracted many artists and writers. Painters Bert G. Phillips (b.New York, 1868–1956) and Ernest Leonard Blumenschein (b.Ohio, 1874–1960) started the famous Taos art colony in 1898. Mabel Dodge Luhan (b.New York, 1879–1962) did much to lure the creative community to Taos through her writings; the most famous person to take up residence there was English novelist D. H. Lawrence (1885–1930). New Mexico's best-known living artists are Georgia O'Keeffe (b.Wisconsin, 1887) and Peter Hurd (b.1904). Maria Povera Martinez (1887?–1980) was known for her black-on-black pottery.

Other prominent persons who have made New Mexico their home include rocketry pioneer Robert H. Goddard (b.Massachusetts, 1882–1945), Pulitzer Prize–winning editorial cartoonist Bill Mauldin (b.1921), novelist and popular historian Paul Horgan (b.New York, 1903), novelist N. Scott Momaday (b.Oklahoma, 1934), and golfer Nancy Lopez-Melton (b.California, 1957).

50 BIBLIOGRAPHY

Beck, W. A. *New Mexico: A History of Four Centuries*. Norman: University of Oklahoma Press, 1962.

Cather, Willa. *Death Comes for the Archbishop*. New York: Alfred Knopf, 1927.

Dozier, Edward P. *The Pueblo Indians of North America*. New York: Holt, 1970.

Federal Writers' Project. *New Mexico: A Guide to the Colorful State*. New York: Hastings House, 1962 (orig. 1940).

Larson, Robert W. *New Mexico's Quest for Statehood, 1846–1912*. Albuquerque: University of New Mexico Press, 1968.

New Mexico. Secretary of State. *New Mexico Blue Book 1977–78*. Santa Fe, n.d.

New Mexico, University of. Bureau of Business and Economic Research. *New Mexico Statistical Abstract, 1977*. Albuquerque, 1977.

Reeve, F. D. *New Mexico: A Short Illustrated History*. Denver: Sage Books, 1964.

Samora, Julian, and Patricia Vandel Simon. *A History of the Mexican-American People*. Notre Dame: University of Notre Dame Press, 1977.

Simmons, Marc. *New Mexico: A Bicentennial History*. New York: Norton, 1977.

NEW YORK

State of New York

ORIGIN OF STATE NAME: Named for the Duke of York (later King James II) in 1664. NICKNAME: The Empire State. CAPITAL: Albany. ENTERED UNION: 26 July 1788 (11th). SONG: "I Love New York." MOTTO: *Excelsior* (Ever upward). COAT OF ARMS: Liberty and Justice stand on either side of a shield showing a mountain sunrise; surmounted on the shield is an eagle on a globe. In the foreground are a three-masted ship and a Hudson River sloop, both representing commerce. Liberty's left foot has kicked aside a royal crown. Beneath the shield is the state motto. FLAG: Dark blue with the coat of arms in the center. OFFICIAL SEAL: The coat of arms surrounded by the words "The Great Seal of the State of New York." ANIMAL: Beaver. BIRD: Bluebird. FISH: Trout. FLOWER: Rose. TREE: Sugar maple. FRUIT: Apple. GEM: Garnet. LEGAL HOLIDAYS: New Year's Day, 1 January; Dr. Martin Luther King, Jr., Day, 3d Sunday in January; Lincoln's Birthday, 12 February; Washington's Birthday, 3d Monday in February; Memorial Day, last Monday in May; Flag Day, 2d Sunday in June; Independence Day, 4 July; Labor Day, 1st Monday in September; Columbus Day, 2d Monday in October; General Election Day, 1st Tuesday after the 1st Monday in November; Veterans Day, 11 November; Thanksgiving Day, 4th Thursday in November; Christmas Day, 25 December. TIME: 7 A.M. EST = noon GMT.

¹LOCATION, SIZE, AND EXTENT

Located in the northeastern US, New York State is the largest of the 3 Middle Atlantic states and ranks 30th in size among the 50 states.

The total area of New York is 49,576 sq mi (128,402 sq km), of which land takes up 47,831 sq mi (123,882 sq km) and the remaining 1,745 sq mi (4,520 sq km) consist of inland water. New York's width is about 320 mi (515 km) E–W, not including Long Island, which extends an additional 118 mi (190 km) SW–NE; the state's maximum N–S extension is about 310 mi (499 km). New York State is shaped roughly like a right triangle: the line from the extreme NE to the extreme SW forms the hypotenuse, with New York City as the right angle.

Mainland New York is bordered on the NW and N by the Canadian provinces of Ontario (with the boundary line passing through Lake Ontario and the St. Lawrence River) and Quebec; on the E by Vermont (with part of the line passing through Lake Champlain and the Poultney River), Massachusetts, and Connecticut; on the S by the Atlantic Ocean, New Jersey (part of the line passes through the Hudson River), and Pennsylvania (partly through the Delaware River); and on the W by Pennsylvania (with the line extending into Lake Erie) and Ontario (through Lake Erie and the Niagara River).

Two large islands lie off the state's SE corner. Long Island is bounded by Connecticut (through Long Island Sound) to the N, Rhode Island (through the Atlantic Ocean) to the NE, the Atlantic to the S, and the East River and the Narrows to the W. Staten Island (a borough of New York City) is separated from New Jersey by Newark Bay in the N, Raritan Bay in the S, and Arthur Kill channel in the W, and from Long Island by the Narrows to the E. Including these two islands, the total boundary length of New York State is 1,430 mi (2,301 km).

The state's geographic center is in Madison County, 6 mi (10 km) SSE of Oneida.

²TOPOGRAPHY

Two upland regions—the Adirondack Mountains and the Appalachian Highlands—dominate the topography of New York State.

The Adirondacks cover most of the northeast and occupy about one-fourth of the state's total area. The Appalachian Highlands, including the Catskill Mountains and Kittatinny Mountain Ridge (or Shawangunk Mountains), extend across the south-

ern half of the state, from the Hudson River Valley to the basin of Lake Erie. Between these two upland regions, and also along the state's northern and eastern borders, lies a network of lowlands, including the Great Lakes Plain; the Hudson, Mohawk, Lake Champlain, and St. Lawrence valleys; and the coastal areas of New York City and Long Island.

The state's highest peaks are found in the Adirondacks: Mt. Marcy, 5,344 feet (1,629 meters), and Algonquin Peak, 5,114 feet (1,559 meters). Nestled among the Adirondacks are many scenic lakes, including Lake Placid, Saranac Lake, and Lake George. The region is also the source of the Hudson and Ausable rivers. The Adirondack Forest Preserve covers much of this terrain, and both public and private lakes are mainly for recreational use.

The highest peak in the Catskills is Slide Mountain, at 4,204 feet (1,281 meters). Lesser upland regions of New York include the Hudson Highlands, projecting into the Hudson Valley; the Taconic Range, along the state's eastern border; and Tug Hill Plateau, set amid the lowlands just west of the Adirondacks.

Three lakes—Erie, Ontario, and Champlain—form part of the state's borders. The state has jurisdiction over 594 sq mi (1,538 sq km) of Lake Erie and 3,033 sq mi (7,855 sq km) of Lake Ontario. New York contains some 8,000 lakes: the largest lake wholly within the state is Oneida, about 22 mi (35 km) long, with a maximum width of 6 mi (10 km) and an area of 80 sq mi (207 sq km). Many smaller lakes are found in the Adirondacks and in the Finger Lakes region in west-central New York, renowned for its vineyards and great natural beauty. The 11 Finger Lakes themselves (including Owasco, Cayuga, Seneca, Keuka, Canandaigua, and Skaneateles) are long and narrow, fanning southward from a line that runs roughly from Syracuse westward to Geneseo.

New York's longest river is the Hudson, extending from the Adirondacks to New York Bay for a distance of 306 mi (492 km). The Mohawk River flows into the Hudson north of Albany. The major rivers of central and western New York State—the Black, Genesee, and Oswego—all flow into Lake Ontario. Rivers defining the state's borders are the St. Lawrence in the north, the Poultney in the east, the Delaware in the southeast, and the Niagara in the west. Along the Niagara River, Niagara Falls forms New York's most spectacular natural feature. The falls, with an estimated mean annual flow rate of more than 1,585,000 gallons (60,000 hectoliters) per second, are both a leading tourist attraction and a major source of hydroelectric power.

About 2 billion years ago, New York State was entirely covered by a body of water that periodically rose and fell. The Adirondacks and Hudson River Palisades were produced by undersea volcanic action during this Grenville period. At about the same time, the schist and other crystalline rock that lie beneath Manhattan were formed. The Catskills were worn down by erosion from what was once a high level plain. Glaciers from the last Ice Age carved out the inland lakes and valleys and determined the surface features of Staten Island and Long Island.

³CLIMATE

Although New York lies entirely within the humid continental zone, there is much variation from region to region. The three main climatic regions are the southeastern lowlands, which have the warmest temperatures and the longest season between frosts; the uplands of the Catskills and Adirondacks, where winters are cold and summers cool; and the snow belt along the Great Lakes Plain, one of the snowiest areas of the US.

Among the major population centers, New York City has an annual mean temperature of 55°F (13°C), with a normal maximum of 62°F (17°C) and a normal minimum of 47°F (8°C). Albany has an annual mean of 48°F (9°C), with a normal maximum of 62°F (17°C) and a normal minimum of 37°F (3°C). The mean in Buffalo is 47°F (8°C), the normal maximum 55°F (13°C), and the normal minimum 39°F (4°C). The record low temperature for the state is –52°F (–47°C), recorded at Stillwater Reservoir in the Adirondacks on 9 February 1934; the record high is 108°F (42°C), registered at Troy on 22 July 1926.

New York City has an annual mean snowfall of 29 in (74 cm), while Albany gets 66 in (168 cm); in the snow belt, Buffalo receives 89 in (226 cm) of snow, Rochester 86 in (218 cm), and Syracuse 110 in (279 cm). Although New York City has fewer days of precipitation than other major populated areas (121 days annually, compared with 168 for Buffalo), more of New York City's precipitation comes in the form of rain: 40 in (102 cm), compared with 33 in (84 cm) for Albany and 36 in (91 cm) for Buffalo. Buffalo is the windiest city in the state, with a mean hourly wind speed of about 12 mph (19 km/hr).

⁴FLORA AND FAUNA

Of the state's total area, roughly 37% is forested woodland, 8% is brushland, and 4% is wetland. Varieties of plant and animal life follow the state's broad topographic divisions.

New York has some 150 species of trees. Post and willow oak, laurel magnolia, sweet gum, and hop trees dominate the Atlantic shore areas, while oak, hickory, and chestnut thrive in the Hudson and Mohawk valleys and the Great Lakes Plain. Birch, beech, basswood, white oak, and commercially valuable maple are found on the Appalachian Plateau and in the foothills of the Adirondack Mountains. The bulk of the Adirondacks and Catskills is covered with red and black spruce, balsam fir, and mountain ash, as well as white pine and maple. Spruce, balsam fir, paper birch, and mountain ash rise to the timberline, while only the hardiest plant species grow above it. Larch, mulberry, locust, and several kinds of willow are among the many varieties that have been introduced throughout the state. Apple trees and other fruit-bearing species are important in western New York and the Hudson Valley.

Common meadow flowers include several types of rose (the state flower), along with dandelion, Queen Anne's lace, goldenrod, and black-eyed Susan. Wild sarsaparilla, Solomon's seal, Indian pipe, bunchberry, and goldthread flourish amid the forests. Cattails grow in profusion along the Hudson, and rushes cover the Finger Lakes shallows. Among protected plants in 1980 were all species of fern, bayberry, lotus, all native orchids, five species of rhododendron (including azalea), and trillium.

Some 600 species of mammals, birds, amphibians, and reptiles are found in New York, of which more than 450 species are common. Mammals in abundance include many mouse species, the snowshoe hare, common and New England cottontails, woodchuck, squirrel, muskrat, and raccoon. The deer population is controlled to an optimum herd size of 375,000; about 46,000 bucks and 25,000 does and fawns are killed each year. The wolverine, elk, and moose were all wiped out during the 19th century, and the otter, mink, marten, and fisher populations were drastically reduced; but the beaver, nearly eliminated by fur trappers, had come back strongly by 1940.

More than 260 bird species have been observed. The most common year-round residents are the crow, hawk, and several types of woodpecker. Summer visitors are many, and include the bluebird (the state bird). The wild turkey, which disappeared during the 19th century, was successfully reestablished in the 1970s. Introduced during the 1800s, the house (or English) sparrow has long outstayed its welcome.

The common toad, newt, and several species of frog and salamander inhabit New York waters. Garter snakes, water snakes, grass snakes, and milk snakes are common; rattlesnakes formerly thrived in the Adirondacks. There are 210 known species of fish; 130 species are found in the Hudson, 120 in the Lake Ontario watershed. Freshwater fish include species of perch, bass, pike, and trout (the state fish). Oysters, clams, and several saltwater fish species are found in Long Island Sound. Of insect varieties, the praying mantis is looked upon as a friend (since it eats insects that prey on crops and trees), while the gypsy moth has been singled out as an enemy in periodic state-run pest-control programs.

In 1980, the following species were classified as endangered by the state Department of Environmental Conservation: the Indiana bat, eastern cougar, eastern timber wolf, Eskimo curlew, northern and southern bald eagles, American and Arctic peregrine falcons, American osprey, bog turtle, longjaw cisco, blue pike, shortnose sturgeon, Karner blue butterfly, and Chittenango ovate amber snail.

There are three national wildlife refuges: Iroquois, in western New York; Montezuma, south of Lake Ontario; and Target Rock, on Long Island.

⁵ENVIRONMENTAL PROTECTION

New York was one of the first states to mount a major conservation effort. Since the early 1970s, well over $1 billion has been spent to reclaim the state from the ravages of pollution.

State conservation efforts date back at least to 1885, when a forest preserve was legally established in the Adirondacks and Catskills. Adirondack Park was created in 1892, Catskill Park in 1904. Then, as now, the issue was how much if any state forestland would be put to commercial use. Timber cutting in the forest preserve was legalized in 1893, but the constitution of 1895 forbade the practice. By the late 1930s, the state had spent more than $16 million on land purchases and controlled 2,159,795 acres (874,041 hectares) in the Adirondacks and some 230,000 acres (more than 93,000 hectares) in the Catskills. The constitutional revision of 1938 expressly outlawed the sale, removal, or destruction of timber on forestlands. That requirement was modified by constitutional amendment in 1957 and 1973, however, and the state is now permitted to sell forest products from the preserves in limited amounts.

All state environmental programs are run by the Department of Environmental Conservation, established in 1970. The department oversees pollution control programs, monitors environmental quality, manages the forest preserve, and administers fish and wildlife laws (including the issuance of hunting and fishing licenses). In 1978, 3,567,944 acres (1,443,901 hectares) of state-owned lands were under the department's jurisdiction.

Current funding for state environmental programs was esti-

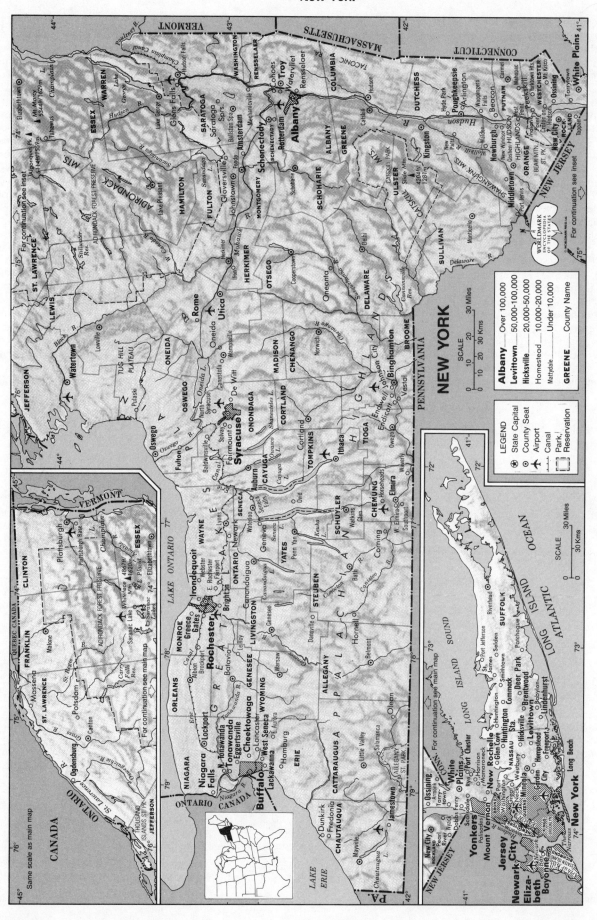

NEW YORK

SCALE

| 10 | 20 | 30 Miles |
| 10 | 20 | 30 Kms |

LEGEND

⊛ State Capital
⊙ County Seat
✈ Airport
Canal
Park/Reservation

Albany	Over 100,000
Levittown	50,000-100,000
Hicksville	20,000-50,000
Homestead	10,000-20,000
Mattydale	Under 10,000
GREENE	County Name

See US political: front cover L2; physical: back cover L2

LOCATION: 40°29'40" to 45°0'42"N; 71°47'25" to 79°45'54"W. **BOUNDARIES:** Canadian line, 445 mi (716 km); Vermont line, 171 mi (275 km); Massachusetts line, 50.5 mi (81 km); Connecticut line to Long Island Sound, 81 mi (130 km); Atlantic Ocean around Long Island to the New Jersey shore, 246 mi (396 km); New Jersey line, 92.5 mi (149 km); Pennsylvania line to beginning of Canadian line in Lake Erie, 344 mi (554 km).

WORLDMARK ENCYCLOPEDIA OF THE STATES
© WORLDMARK PRESS Ltd.

mated at $283 million in 1979/80, or 2% of the general budget. Sewage treatment, air pollution, and recycling programs have been funded through the $1.15-billion Environmental Quality Bond Act, approved by the voters on 7 November 1972. The act also provided for the purchase of forest preserves, park lands, and wetlands.

As of March 1980, the state had 43 air-pollution monitors in operation, 12 of these in New York City. An additional 16 sites were operated by the Long Island Lighting Co. Because of budget cuts by New York City, the state took over the operation of the city's air-monitoring network in 1978. Levels of atmospheric particles and sulfur dioxide in the state in 1977 bettered federal standards, and carbon monoxide levels have been reduced since 1972. The chief problem areas are Buffalo, where levels of particles (especially from the use of coke in steel-making) are high, and New York City, where little progress has been made in cutting carbon monoxide emissions from motor vehicles.

Before the 1960s, the condition of New York's waters was a national scandal. Raw sewage, arsenic, cyanide, and heavy metals were regularly dumped into the state's lakes and rivers, and fish were rapidly dying off. Two Pure Waters Bond Acts during the 1960s, the bond issue of 1972, and a state fishery program have helped reverse the damage. There were 526 municipally owned sewage-treatment plants in operation in 1980, when another 179 water-pollution control projects were under construction. The state has also taken action against corporate polluters, including a $7-million settlement with General Electric over that company's discharge of toxic polychlorinated biphenyls (PCBs) into the Hudson. In addition, the state had spent more than $30 million as of January 1980 on the cleanup of the Love Canal area, which was severely contaminated by the dumping of toxic wastes. Remaining problems include continued dumping of sewage and industrial wastes into New York Bay and Long Island Sound, sewage overflows into the Lower Hudson, industrial dumping in the Hudson Valley, nuclear wastes in West Valley in Cattaraugus County, and contamination of fish in Lake Erie.

New York has also reported progress in land-use management and solid-waste disposal. Under a consolidation program, solid-waste disposal sites were reduced from 854 in 1970 to 583 in 1978; the number of unsatisfactory sites dropped from 421 to 230 during that period. The Department of Environmental Conservation has become increasingly involved in land-use planning, and in 1976 became responsible for reclaiming mined lands.

[6]POPULATION

Although New York is no longer the most populous state, New York City remains the most populous US city, as it has been at least since 1790. Preliminary 1980 census figures showed a population in New York State of 17,476,978, a decline of more than 4% since the 1970 census.

New York State's population growth was slow during the colonial period. At the end of the 17th century, when the population of Virginia was nearing 60,000, New York still had fewer than 20,000 residents. The 1790 census showed a population of 340,120 for New York—less than for Virginia, Pennsylvania, North Carolina, and Massachusetts. The first great growth spurt came

New York Counties, County Seats, and County Populations

COUNTY	COUNTY SEAT	LAND AREA (SQ MI)	POPULATION (1977)[3]	COUNTY	COUNTY SEAT	LAND AREA (SQ MI)	POPULATION (1977)[3]
New York City		300	7,312,200	Monroe	Rochester	675	706,500
Bronx	Bronx	41	1,292,700	Montgomery	Fonda	408	54,500
Kings	Brooklyn	70	2,345,500	Nassau	Mineola	289	1,396,000
New York				Niagara	Lockport	532	236,600
(Manhattan)	New York City	23	1,387,500	Oneida	Utica	1,223	261,100
Queens	Jamaica	108	1,954,500				
Richmond				Onondaga	Syracuse	794	471,200
(Staten Island)	St. George	58	332,000	Ontario	Canandaigua	651	86,400
				Orange	Goshen	833	247,800
Rest of State		47,531	10,611,400	Orleans	Albion	396	38,700
Albany	Albany	526	286,700	Oswego	Oswego	964	110,700
Allegany	Belmont	1,047	50,500				
Broome	Binghamton	714	219,200	Otsego	Cooperstown	1,013	57,600
Cattaraugus	Little Valley	1,318	84,900	Putnam	Carmel	231	71,300
Cayuga	Auburn	698	77,700	Rensselaer	Troy	665	150,900
				Rockland	New City	176	257,100
Chautauqua	Mayville	1,081	146,600	St. Lawrence	Canton	2,768	117,000
Chemung	Elmira	415	99,000				
Chenango	Norwich	903	48,600	Saratoga	Ballston Spa	818	146,700
Clinton	Plattsburgh	1,059	83,400	Schenectady	Schenectady	207	155,500
Columbia	Hudson	645	57,000	Schoharie	Schoharie	624	28,700
				Schuyler	Watkins Glen	330	17,500
Cortland	Cortland	502	48,000	Seneca	Waterloo	330	33,600
Delaware	Delhi	1,443	47,500				
Dutchess	Poughkeepsie	813	231,800	Steuben	Bath	1,410	100,600
Erie	Buffalo	1,058	1,076,400	Suffolk	Riverhead	929	1,291,900
Essex	Elizabethtown	1,823	35,800	Sullivan	Monticello	980	62,700
				Tioga	Owego	524	49,300
Franklin	Malone	1,674	44,900	Tompkins	Ithaca	482	83,700
Fulton	Johnstown	498	55,100				
Genesee	Batavia	501	60,500	Ulster	Kingston	1,141	154,500
Greene	Catskill	653	38,000	Warren	Town of		
Hamilton	Lake Pleasant	1,735	5,000		Queensbury[1]	887	53,200
				Washington	Hudson Falls[2]	836	55,400
Herkimer	Herkimer	1,435	65,700	Wayne	Lyons	606	81,700
Jefferson	Watertown	1,294	90,800	Westchester	White Plains	443	871,900
Lewis	Lowville	1,291	25,500				
Livingston	Geneseo	638	57,000	Wyoming	Warsaw	598	38,600
Madison	Wampsville	661	65,600	Yates	Penn Yan	343	21,500
[1]Mail Lake George. [2]Mail Fort Edward. [3]Provisional.					TOTALS	47,831	17,923,600

between 1810 and 1820, when New York State's population grew by 43% to 1,372,812. The 1820 census was the first in which New York was top-ranked. The state held first place until the census of 1970, when California leapt to the top.

The 1970 census figure of 18,241,391 represented a 9% increase over the 1960 census total—a much lower growth rate than California's 27% or the overall US rate of 13% during the same period. In 1970, New York's population was 52% female and 48% male; nearly 9 out of every 10 New Yorkers (88%) lived in metropolitan areas. New Yorkers are also somewhat older than the national average, and considerably less mobile. According to the 1970 census, the densest region of the state was Manhattan, with 66,923 people per sq mi (25,839 per sq km); the least dense county was Hamilton, in the Adirondacks, with only 2.7 people per sq mi (1 per sq km).

Estimates for 1977 placed New York State's population at 17,923,600, a decline of 2% from 1970. The major reason for this decline was migration: a net total of 863,000 people left the state during this period, more than enough to make up for the 553,000 surplus of live births over deaths. The state's birthrate per 1,000 residents dropped from 21.3 in 1960 to 13.4 in 1977; both figures were below the national averages for those years. Meanwhile, the death rate showed much less of a decline, from 10.5 in 1960 to 9.3 in 1977; both figures were slightly above the national average.

In 1970, the state had 89 cities and villages of more than 10,000 people. First in the state as well as the nation was New York City, which, according to preliminary census estimates, had 7,015,608 residents in 1980. Of that total, Brooklyn had a population of 2,211,798; Queens, 1,883,682; Manhattan, 1,411,743; the Bronx, 1,158,788; and Staten Island, 349,597. Other leading cities according to the 1980 census were Buffalo, 357,002; Rochester, 241,509; Yonkers, 194,557; Syracuse, 170,292; and Albany, the state capital, 101,767.

The growth of New York City has been remarkable. In 1790, when the first national census was taken, the city had 49,401 residents. By 1850, its population had boomed to 696,115; by 1900, to 3,437,202, double that of Chicago, the city's closest rival. Manhattan alone housed more people in 1900 than any city outside New York. The data for 1977 are equally impressive. If Brooklyn, Queens, Manhattan, and the Bronx had each been a separate city, they would still have ranked 3d, 4th, 7th, and 8th in the nation. Even Staten Island, the smallest of the city's five boroughs, would have placed 43d in 1977. Despite recent population declines, rankings for 1980 are equally impressive.

[7] ETHNIC GROUPS

During the 19th and early 20th centuries, New York was the principal gateway for European immigrants. In the great northern migration that began after World War I, large numbers of blacks also settled there, and more recently there has been an influx of Hispanic Americans and, to a lesser extent, of Asians. Today, New York has the largest black and Puerto Rican populations of any state, the 3d-largest Asian community, and the 3d-largest percentage of foreign stock (the foreign-born and their native-born children).

According to the US Bureau of the Census, New York had 28,355 Indians in 1970, the 8th-highest Indian population in the nation. State data showed that 10,381 were registered as members of particular tribes, including 4,379 members of the Seneca Nation, 2,222 Mohawk, 1,107 Onondaga, and 803 Seneca of the Tonowanda Band—all descended from the original Iroquois Nation. As of 1970 there were seven reservations, inhabited by a total of 6,635 Indians.

Blacks have been in New York since before the Revolutionary War, and Rochester was a major center of the antislavery movement; Frederick Douglass, a former slave, settled and published his newspaper *North Star* there, while helping to run the Under-

ground Railroad. After World War I, blacks moving into New York City displaced the Italians then living in Harlem, which went on to become the cultural capital of black America. The black population of New York State was 2,234,000 as of 1976—8.4% of the state's population, below the national ratio and proportionately less than in some densely populated southern states. More than three of every four blacks lived in New York City, which has more black people than any other US city. There are black judges, legislators, and members of Congress, and many blacks are prominent in a variety of professions and arts. A large number, however, are at the bottom of the economic ladder; it is said that New York City could not survive without the black and Hispanic service workers who staff the city's hospitals, offices, hotels, and public institutions.

The Hispanic population as of 1976 was estimated at 1,439,000; there were 811,843 Puerto Ricans in New York City alone as of 1970, a net increase of 32.5% in 10 years. Cubans, Colombians, Central Americans, Filipinos, and Mexicans are also present in growing numbers, including a large but undetermined number of illegal immigrants.

The Asian population, excluding Filipinos, was 191,294 in 1970, among them 81,378 Chinese, 20,351 Japanese, and large numbers from India, Pakistan, and Korea. In 1975, 3,806 Vietnamese refugees were resettled in the state. A high proportion of the Asians live in New York City, which has the 2d-largest Chinatown in the US.

In 1970 there were some 5,995,000 New Yorkers of foreign stock, representing nearly one-third of the state's total population. Among 20th-century immigrants the leading nationalities were Italian (7.3% of the state population as of 1970), Russian (3.1%), Polish (3.1%), German (2.8%), and Irish (2.1%). These figures, however, do not reflect the large numbers of Irish and other nationalities who are not first- or second-generation but who would nevertheless identify themselves as members of an ethnic group. They also do not distinguish the large numbers of European Jewish immigrants who would identify themselves as Jews rather than by their country of origin.

The ethnic diversity of the state is reflected in the neighborhoods of Manhattan. In addition to Harlem, Chinatown, and "Spanish" or East Harlem, with its large Puerto Rican concentration, historically important communities include "Little Italy" in lower Manhattan; Yorkville on the Upper East Side, with its sizable German-Austrian and Eastern European population; and the Lower East Side, where Jews from Russia and Eastern Europe once predominated. Today, the old neighborhoods are not so distinct, and settlement patterns have shifted; many of the more successful ethnics have moved to the suburbs, and Manhattan's black and Puerto Rican populations have grown. In Brooklyn and the Bronx there are distinct clusters of Hasidic Jews, Haitians, and East Indians, among other groups. Outside of New York City there are also important ethnic enclaves in Buffalo, with its large Polish population, and northwestern New York, where most of the state's Canadians live.

[8] LANGUAGES

Just as New York for three centuries has channeled immigrant speakers of other languages into the English-speaking population, so it has helped to channel some of their words into English, with much more rapid dissemination recently because of the concentration of publishing and communications industries in New York City.

Little word-borrowing followed contacts by European settlers with the unfriendly Iroquois, who between the 14th and 17th centuries had dispersed the several Algonkian tribes of Montauk, Delaware, and Mahican Indians. In New York State the effect on English has been almost entirely the adoption of such place-names as Manhattan, Adirondack, Chautauqua, Skaneateles, and Schenectady. Of the Iroquois federation known as the

Five Nations there remained 5,948 persons in 1970 who claimed an Indian language as their mother tongue.

Although the speech of metropolitan New York has its own characteristics, in the state as a whole the Northern dialect predominates. New York State residents generally say /hahg/ and /fahg/ for *hog* and *fog*, /krik/ for *creek*, *greasy* with an /s/ sound, and *half* and *path* with the vowel of *cat*. They keep the /r/ after a vowel, as in *far* and *cord*; sharply differentiate *horse* and *hoarse* by pronouncing the former with the vowel of *haw* and the latter with the vowel of *hoe*; and call a clump of hard maples a *sugarbush*.

There are many regional variations. In the Hudson Valley, *horse* and *hoarse* tend to be pronounced alike, and a sugarbush is called a *sap bush*. In the eastern sector, New England *piazza* for porch and *buttonball* for sycamore are found, as is the Hudson Valley term *nightwalker* for a large earthworm. In the Niagara peninsula, Midland *eavespout* (gutter) and *bawl* (how a calf sounds) have successfully moved north from Pennsylvania to invade Northern speech. In the North Country, some Canadian influence survives in *stook* (shock), *boodan* (liver sausage), and *shivaree* (wedding celebration). In the New York City area, many speakers pronounce *bird* almost as if it were /boyd/, do not sound the /h/ in *whip* or the /r/ after a vowel—although the trend now is toward the /r/ pronunciation—may pronounce initial /th/ almost like /t/ or /d/, stand *on line* (instead of in a line) while waiting to buy a huge sandwich they call a *hero*, and may even pronounce *Long Island* with an inserted /g/ as /long-g-iland/. From the high proportion of New York Yiddish speakers (actually 44% of all those in the US in 1970), have come such terms as *schlock*, *schmaltz*, and *chutzpah*.

Serious communication problems have arisen in New York City, especially in the schools, because of the major influx since World War II of Spanish speakers from the Caribbean region and of speakers of so-called black English from the South, in addition to the ever-present large numbers of speakers of other languages. As a result, schools in some areas have emphasized teaching English as a second language and standard English as a second dialect.

In the 1970 census, 65% of all New Yorkers reported English as their first language, well below the national average of 79%. Only 71% of native-born New Yorkers had English as their mother tongue, again well below the national average of 82%. The following table shows the major languages named by New York State residents as their mother tongue in connection with the 1970 census:

	NATIVE-BORN	FOREIGN-BORN
English	11,508,409	377,824
Spanish	1,016,126	250,529
Italian	920,777	356,595
Yiddish	484,059	213,699
German	357,629	252,248
Polish	300,174	90,532
French	125,649	83,152
Greek	46,312	50,261
Russian	34,469	41,749
Chinese	21,426	49,512

Numerous other European and Asian languages are also spoken.

⁹RELIGIONS

With less than 9% of the total US population, New York is the home of nearly 13% of the nation's Roman Catholics and 37% of all US Jews. Both groups have had great impact on state politics during this century.

Prior to the 1800s, Protestant sects dominated the religious life of New York, although religion did not play as dominant a role in the public life of New Netherland as it did in New England, with its Puritan population. The first Jews were permitted by the Dutch to settle in New Amsterdam in 1654, but their numbers remained small for the next 200 years. Both the Dutch and later the English forbade the practice of Roman Catholicism. Full religious freedom was not permitted until the constitution of 1777, and there was no Roman Catholic church in upstate New York until 1797. During the early 19th century, Presbyterian, Methodist, Universalist, Baptist, and Quaker pioneers carried their faith westward across the state. Many Protestant churches took part enthusiastically in the abolitionist movement, and the Negroes who fled northward out of slavery formed their own Protestant churches and church organizations.

For Roman Catholics and Jews, the history of the 19th century is the story of successive waves of immigration: Roman Catholics first from Ireland and Germany, later from Italy and Poland; Jews first from Germany, Austria, and England, later (in vast numbers) from Russia and other Eastern European nations. The Jews who settled in New York City tended to remain there; the Roman Catholic immigrants were more dispersed throughout the state, with a large German and Eastern European group settling in Buffalo. Irish Catholics were the first group to win great political influence, but since World War II, Jews and Italian Catholics have played a leading role, especially in New York City.

As of 1 January 1979, New York had 6,571,635 Roman Catholic church members, of whom 4,322,546 were in the New York metropolitan region. By diocese the population was New York City (archdiocese), 1,825,090; Brooklyn, 1,458,951; Rockville Centre, 1,038,505; Buffalo, 914,152; Albany, 408,648; Syracuse, 385,919; Rochester, 369,711; and Ogdensburg, 170,659.

The Jewish population of New York State was estimated at 2,141,745 in 1979, about 12% of the state population. Approximately 93% of all Jews in the state lived in New York City or its suburbs. Leading centers of Jewish population were Brooklyn, 514,000; Queens, 379,000; Manhattan, 171,000; Bronx, 143,000; Nassau and Suffolk counties, 605,000; and Westchester County, 165,000.

Known adherents of Protestant sects totaled 2,092,948 in 1971, the latest year for which comprehensive data are available. Leading denominations included United Methodist, 529,369 members; Protestant Episcopal, 349,797; Presbyterian, 320,719; Lutheran Church in America, 191,090; American Baptist, 146,675; Lutheran Church–Missouri Synod, 129,401; United Church of Christ, 102,979; and Reformed Church in America, 92,379.

Because of diversified immigration, New York City has small percentages of Buddhists, Muslims, Hindus, and Orthodox Christians. There is also a wide variety of religious-nationalist sects and cults, including the Nation of Islam (Black Muslims), the Hare Krishna group, and the Unification Church of the Reverend Sun Myung Moon.

¹⁰TRANSPORTATION

New York City is a major transit point for both domestic and international passenger and freight traffic. The Port of New York and New Jersey is the nation's busiest harbor, and Kennedy International Airport in Queens handles the 4th largest volume of passenger traffic of any US airport. New York City is connected with the rest of the state by an extensive network of good roads, but road and rail transport within the metropolitan region are sagging with age.

The first railroad in New York State was the Mohawk and Hudson, which made its initial trip from Albany to Schenectady on 9 August 1831. A series of short intercity rail lines, built during the 1830s and 1840s, were united into the New York Central in 1853. Cornelius Vanderbilt gained control of the New York Central in 1867, and by 1873 had connected New York with Chicago. Under Vanderbilt and his son William, rail links were also forged between New York and Boston, Buffalo, Montreal, and western Pennsylvania.

The height of the railroads' power and commercial importance came during the last decades of the 19th century. After World War I, road vehicles gradually replaced the railroads as freight carriers. By 1972, only 28% of goods carried in New York were carried by rail, compared with 69% on the highways. In 1975, New York ranked 15th in railroad mileage, with 5,215 mi (8,393 km) of track, less than 3% of the total US mileage.

The decline in freight business, and the railroads' inability to make up the loss on passenger traffic, led to a series of reorganizations and failures: the best known is the merger of the New York Central with the Pennsylvania Railroad, and the subsequent bankruptcy of the Penn Central. Today, much of New York's rail network is operated by Conrail, a federally assisted private corporation that provides commuter service up the Hudson and to New Jersey and Connecticut. The National Railroad Passenger Corporation (Amtrak) owns and operates lines along the eastern corridor from Boston through New York City to Washington, D.C. The Long Island Railroad, an important commuter carrier, is run by the Metropolitan Transportation Authority (MTA), which also operates the New York City subways.

Construction of the New York City subway system began in 1900; service started on 27 October 1904. By 1978, the system was by far the largest in the US, and ranked 1st in the world in number of stations and cars, 2d in the length of its total route network, and 3d in number of passengers carried per day. The route network was about 230 mi (370 km) long, of which 137 mi (220 km) were underground; of 6,674 subway cars (about 20% of the world total), some 1,600 were air-conditioned. Operating round the clock, the system carried an average of 2.8 million paying passengers per day in 1978. Because most New York City residents depend on mass transit (subways and buses) to get to work each day, any disruption of service—as in the transit strikes of 1966 and 1980—affects the city's economy severely.

A clear indication of the importance of mass transit to New York City is the fact that although the five boroughs together account for over 40% of the state population, they also registered fewer than one-fourth of all passenger cars. In 1977, an estimated 8,255,000 vehicles were registered in New York State, including 6,701,000 passenger cars, 30,522 buses (1st in the US), and 142,100 motorcycles. A total of 837,704 trucks (9th in the US) were registered during the same year; state trucking companies had 408,500 employees in 1977, with a total payroll of more than $5.7 billion. As of 31 December 1977, the state had 108,693 mi (174,925 km) of roads, of which 15% were state highways, 19% were county roads, 50% were town highways, and 16% were city and village streets. Nearly 97% of all state roads were paved. The major toll road is the New York State Thruway, which extends 559 mi (900 km) from just outside New York City to the Pennsylvania border in southwestern New York. Toll-free expressways include the Adirondack Northway (I-87), from Albany to the Canadian border, and the North-South Expressway (I-81), from the Canadian to the Pennsylvania border. In 1976, the state spent an estimated $1.1 billion on highway maintenance, construction, and grants to local government, a figure slightly exceeded by receipts from highway tax revenue, tolls, bonds, and the federal government.

A number of famous bridges and tunnels connect the five boroughs of New York City with each other and with New Jersey. The Verrazano-Narrows Bridge, opened to traffic in 1964 and spanning New York Harbor between Brooklyn and Staten Island, remained in 1980 the world's longest suspension bridge. Equally famous, and especially renowned for its beauty, is the George Washington Bridge (1931). The Lincoln (1937–57) and Holland (1927) tunnels under the Hudson link Manhattan with New Jersey. Important links among the five boroughs include the Triborough Bridge, Bronx-Whitestone Bridge, Throgs Neck Bridge, Brooklyn Bridge, Brooklyn-Battery Tunnel, and Queens-Midtown Tunnel.

Until the early 1800s, almost all the state's trade moved on the Atlantic Ocean, Hudson River, and New York Bay. This waterway transportation system was expanded starting in the 1820s. Off the Hudson, one of the country's major arteries, branched the main elements of the New York Barge Canal System: the Erie Canal, linking the Atlantic with Lake Erie, and New York City with Buffalo; the Oswego Canal, connecting the Erie Canal with Lake Ontario; the Cayuga and Seneca Canal, connecting the Erie Canal with Cayuga and Seneca lakes; and the Champlain Canal, extending the state's navigable waterways from the Hudson to Lake Champlain, and so to Vermont and Quebec Province. By 1872, New York's canal system was carrying over 6 million tons of cargo a year; but an absolute decline in freight tonnage began after 1890 (the relative decline had begun 40 years earlier, with the rise of the railroads). In 1978, the canals carried only 1,553,310 tons of cargo, less than one-fourth the tonnage for 1880; the Champlain Canal actually carried more freight than the Erie, accounting for nearly 58% of the 1978 total.

Buffalo, on Lake Erie, is the most important inland port. In 1976, it handled 8,553,000 tons of domestic cargo and 3,714,000 tons of foreign cargo. Oswego, on Lake Ontario, handled 1,014,000 tons, nearly all of it to or from Canada. Albany, the major port on the Hudson, handled 10,146,000 tons of cargo, 75% of it domestic.

It would be hard to exaggerate the historic and economic importance of New York Harbor—haven for explorers, point of entry for millions of refugees, the nation's greatest seaport. Harbor facilities, including those of Bayonne, Jersey City, and Newark, N.J., add up to 755 mi (1,215 km) of frontage, with some 700 piers and wharves. The entire port is under the jurisdiction of the Port Authority of New York and New Jersey. In 1976, it handled 179,587,000 tons of cargo, 59,538,000 tons foreign and 120,049,000 tons domestic.

In 1977, New York State had 459 airfields, including 372 airports, 65 heliports, and 22 seaplane bases. Of the airports, 205 were municipal, 163 private, and 4 military. By far the busiest airports in the state are John F. Kennedy International and LaGuardia, both in New York City. In 1977, Kennedy handled 7,701,986 passengers, 100,842 aircraft departures, and 446,081 tons of cargo, while LaGuardia handled 7,586,096 passengers, 123,520 departures, and 49,421 tons of cargo. The Greater Buffalo International Airport, the largest outside New York City, handled 1,531,459 passengers and 17,446 tons of cargo in 1977.

¹¹ HISTORY

The region now known as New York State has been inhabited for at least 5,000 years. The first Indians probably came across the Bering Strait and most likely reached New York via the Niagara Peninsula. Remains have been found in southwestern New York of the Indians called Mound Builders (for their practice of burying their dead in large mounds), who cultivated food crops and tobacco. The Mound Builders were still living in the state well after AD 1000, although by this time most of New York was controlled by later migrants of the Algonkian linguistic group. These Algonkian tribes included the Mahican in the northeast, the Wappinger in the Hudson Valley and on Long Island, and the Leni-Lanape (or Delaware) of the Delaware Valley.

Indians of the Iroquoian language group invaded the state from the north and west during the early 14th century. In 1570, after European explorers had discovered New York but before the establishment of any permanent European settlements, the main Iroquois tribes—the Onondaga, Oneida, Seneca, Cayuga, and Mohawk—established the League of the Five Nations. For the next 200 years, members of the League generally kept peace among themselves but made war on other tribes, using not only traditional weapons but also the guns they were able to get from the French, Dutch, and English. In 1715, a sixth nation joined the League—the Tuscarora, which had fled the British in North

Carolina. For much of the 18th century, the Iroquois played a skillful role in balancing competing French and British interests.

The first European known to have entered New York Harbor was the Florentine navigator Giovanni da Verrazano, on 17 April 1524. The Frenchman Samuel de Champlain began exploring the St. Lawrence River in 1603. While Champlain was aiding the Huron Indians in their fight against the League in 1609, the English mariner Henry Hudson, in the service of the Dutch East India Company, entered New York Bay and sailed up the river that would later bear his name, reaching about as far as Albany. To the Dutch the area did not look especially promising, and there was no permanent Dutch settlement until 1624, three years after the Dutch West India Company had been founded. The area near Albany was first to be settled. The Dutch were mainly interested in fur trading, and agriculture in the colony—named New Netherland—was slow to develop. New Amsterdam was founded in 1626, when Director-General Peter Minuit bought Manhattan (from the Indian word *manahatin*, "hill island") from the Indians for goods worth—as tradition has it—about $24.

New Amsterdam grew slowly, and by 1650 had no more than 1,000 people. When the British took over New Netherland in 1664, only 8,000 residents lived in the colony. Already, however, the population was remarkably diverse: there were the Dutch and English, of course, but also French, Germans, Finns, Swedes, and Jews, as well as Negro slaves from Angola. The Swedes lived in what had been New Sweden, a territory along the Delaware River ceded to the Netherlands during the administration of Peter Stuyvesant. Equally famed for his wooden leg and his hot temper, Stuyvesant had become director general of the New Netherland colony in 1647. Three years later, after skirmishes with the English settlers of New England, the colony gave up all claims to the Connecticut Valley in the Treaty of Hartford.

Though small and weak, New Netherland was an annoyance to the English. The presence of Dutch traders in New York Bay made it difficult for England to enforce its monopolies under the Navigation Acts. Moreover, the Dutch colony was a political barrier between New England and two other English colonies, Maryland and Virginia. So, in 1664, King Charles II awarded "all the land from the west side of the Connecticutte River to the East Side of De La Ware Bay" to his brother, the Duke of York and Albany, the future King James II. The British fleet arrived in New York Bay on 18 August 1664. Stuyvesant wanted to fight, but his subjects refused, and the governor had no choice but to surrender. The English agreed to preserve the Dutch rights of property and inheritance, and to guarantee complete liberty of conscience. Thus New Netherland became New York. It remained an English colony for the next 112 years, except for a period in 1673 when Dutch rule was briefly restored.

The first decades under the English were stormy. After repeated demands from the colonists, a general assembly was called in 1683. The assembly adopted a Charter of Liberties and Privileges, but the document, approved by James before his coronation, was revoked after he became king in 1685. The assembly itself was dissolved in 1686, and James II acted to place New York under the Dominion of New England. The plan was aborted by the Glorious Revolution of 1688, when James was forced to abdicate. Power in New York fell to Jacob Leisler, a German merchant who had the backing of many artisans and small farmers. Leisler ruled until 1691, when a new royal governor arrived and had Leisler hanged for treason.

The succeeding decades were marked by conflict between the English and French and by the rising power of the provincial assembly in relations with the British crown. As early as 1690, a band of 150 Frenchmen and 100 Indians attacked and burned Schenectady. New York contributed men and money to campaigns against the French in Canada in 1709 and 1711 (during Queen Anne's War) and in 1746 (during King George's War). In 1756,

the English determined to drive the French out of the region once and for all. After some early reverses, the English defeated the French in 1760. The Treaty of Paris (1763), ending the French and Indian War, ceded all territory east of the Mississippi to England, except for New Orleans and two islands in the mouth of the St. Lawrence River. The Iroquois, their power weakened during the course of the war, signed treaties giving large areas of their land to the New York colony.

The signing of the Treaty of Paris was followed by English attempts to tighten their control over the colonies, in New York as elsewhere. New York merchants vehemently protested the Sugar Act and Stamp Act, and the radical Sons of Liberty made their first appearance in the colony in October 1765. Later, in 1774, after Paul Revere brought news of the Boston Tea Party to New York City, British tea was also dumped into that city's harbor. Nevertheless, New York hesitated before committing itself to independence. The colony's delegates to the Continental Congress in Philadelphia were not permitted by the Third Provincial Congress in New York to vote either for or against the Declaration of Independence on 4 July 1776. The Fourth Provincial Congress, meeting at White Plains, did ratify the Declaration five days later. On 6 February 1778, New York became the second state to ratify the Articles of Confederation.

Nearly one-third of all battles during the Revolutionary War took place on New York soil. The action there began when troops under Ethan Allen captured Fort Ticonderoga in May 1775, and Seth Warner and his New England forces took Crown Point. Reverses came in 1776, however, when George Washington's forces were driven from Long Island and Manhattan by the British; New York City was to remain in British hands for the rest of the war. Troops commanded by British General John Burgoyne recaptured Ticonderoga in July 1777, but were defeated in October at Saratoga, in a battle that is often considered the turning point of the war. In 1778, General Washington made his headquarters at West Point, which General Benedict Arnold tried unsuccessfully to betray to the British in 1780. Washington moved his forces to Newburgh in 1782, and marched into New York City on 25 November 1783, the day the British evacuated their forces. On 4 December, he said farewell to his officers at Fraunces Tavern in lower Manhattan, a landmark that still stands.

Even as war raged, New York State adopted its first constitution on 20 April 1777. The constitution provided for an elected governor and house of assembly, but the franchise was limited to property holders. The first state capital was Kingston, but the capital was moved to Albany in January 1797. After much debate, in which the Federalist Alexander Hamilton played a leading role, the state ratified the US Constitution (with amendments) on 26 July 1788. New York City served as the seat of the US government from 11 January 1785 to 12 August 1790, and the first US president, George Washington, was inaugurated in the city on 30 April 1789.

George Clinton was the state's first elected governor, serving from 1777 to 1795 and again from 1801 to 1804. The achievements under his governorship were considerable. In 1790, New York received $30,000 in exchange for giving up its land claims to Vermont. Commerce and agriculture expanded, partly because of Clinton's protectionist policies and partly because of the state's extremely favorable geographical situation.

The end of the War of 1812 signaled the opening of an era of unprecedented economic expansion for the state. By this time, the Iroquois were no longer a threat (most had sided with the British during the Revolutionary War, and many later fled to Canada). Migrants from New England were flocking to the state, which the census of 1820 showed was the most populous in the country. Small wonder that New York was the site of the early 19th century's most ambitious engineering project: construction of the Erie Canal. Ground was broken for the canal in 1817, during the first term of Governor De Witt Clinton, the nephew of George Clinton; the first vessels passed through the completed canal in 1825, during the younger Clinton's third term in office.

Actually, New York had emerged as the nation's leading commercial center before the canal was even started. The textile industry had established itself by the mid-1820s, and the dairy industry was thriving. The effects of the canal were felt most strongly in foreign trade—by 1831, 50% of US imports and 27% of US exports passed through the state—and in the canal towns of Utica, Syracuse, Rochester, and Buffalo, where business boomed.

Commercial progress during this period was matched by social and cultural advancement. New York City became a center of literary activity during the 1820s, and by the 1840s was already the nation's theatrical capital. A new state constitution drafted in 1821 established universal white male suffrage, but retained the property qualifications for Negroes. Slavery was abolished as of 4 July 1827 (few slaves actually remained in the state by this time), and New Yorkers soon took the lead in the growing antislavery movement. The first women's rights convention in the US was held in Seneca Falls in 1848—though women would have to wait until 1917 before winning the right to vote in state elections. Also during the 1840s, the state saw the first of several great waves of European immigration. The Irish and Germans were the earliest major arrivals during the 19th century, but before World War I they would be joined—not always amicably—by Italians and European Jews.

New Yorkers voted for Abraham Lincoln in the presidential election of 1860 and were among the readiest recruits to the Union side. Enthusiasm for the conflict diminished during the next two years, however. When the military draft reached New York City on 11 July 1863, the result was three days of rioting in which Negroes were lynched and the homes of prominent abolitionists were burned. But New York was not a wartime battleground, and overall the war and Reconstruction were very good for business.

The decades after the Civil War ushered in an era of extraordinary commercial growth and political corruption. This was the Gilded Age, during which entrepreneurs became multimillionaires and New York was transformed from an agricultural state to an industrial giant. In 1860, the leading manufactures in the state were flour and meal, men's clothing, refined sugar, leather goods, liquor, and lumber; 90 years later, apparel, printing and publishing, food, machinery, chemicals, fabricated metal products, electrical machinery, textiles, instruments, and transportation equipment had became the dominant industries.

The key to this transformation was the development of the railroads. The boom period for railroad construction started in the 1850s and reached its high point after 1867, when "Commodore" Cornelius Vanderbilt, who had been a steamboat captain in 1818, took over the New York Central. During the 1860s, native New Yorkers like Jay Gould and Russell Sage made their fortunes through investment and speculation. Especially during the century's last two decades, corporate names that today are household words began to emerge: Westinghouse Electric in 1886, General Electric (as Edison Electric) in 1889, Eastman Kodak in 1892. In 1882, another native New Yorker, John D. Rockefeller, formed the Standard Oil Trust; although the trust would eventually be broken up, the Rockefeller family would help shape New York politics for many decades to come.

The period immediately following the Civil War also marked a new high in political influence for the Tammany Society (or "Tammany Hall"), founded in 1789 as an anti-Federalist organization. From 1857 until his exposure by the press in 1871, Democrat William Marcy "Boss" Tweed ruled Tammany and effectively dominated New York City by dispensing patronage, buying votes, and bribing legislators and judges. Tammany went

into temporary eclipse after the Tweed Ring was broken up, and Republicans swept the state in 1872. The first result was a series of constitutional changes, including one abolishing the requirement that Negroes hold property in order to vote. A new constitution approved in 1894, and effective in 1895, remains the basic law of New York State today.

During the Union's first 100 years, New York's political life had projected into national prominence such men as Alexander Hamilton, John Jay, George and De Witt Clinton, Martin Van Buren, and Millard Fillmore. The state's vast population—New York held more electoral votes than any other state between 1810 and 1972—coupled with its growing industrial and financial power enhanced the prestige of state leaders during the nation's second century. Grover Cleveland, though born in New Jersey, became mayor of Buffalo, then governor of New York, and finally the 22d US president in 1885. Theodore Roosevelt was governor of New York, then became vice president and president of the US in 1901. In 1910, Charles Evans Hughes resigned the governorship to become an associate justice of the US Supreme Court; he also served as secretary of state, and in 1930 was appointed chief justice of the US. By the 1920s, Tammany had rebounded from the Tweed Ring breakup and from another scandal during the 1890s to reach its peak of prestige: Alfred E. Smith, a longtime member of Tammany, as well as an able and popular official, was four times elected governor and became in 1928 the first Roman Catholic candidate to be nominated by a major party for the presidency of the US. That same year saw the election of Franklin D. Roosevelt as governor of New York.

The 1930s, a period of depression, ushered in a new wave of progressive government. From 1933 until 1945, FDR was in the White House. Roosevelt's successor in the statehouse was Herbert H. Lehman, whose Little New Deal established the basic pattern of present state social welfare policies that had begun on a much more modest scale during Smith's administration. The Fusion mayor of New York City at this time—propelled into office by yet another wave of exposure of Tammany corruption—was the colorful and popular Fiorello H. La Guardia.

The decades since World War II have seen extraordinary expansion of New York social services, including construction of the state university system, but an erosion of the state's industrial base. Fiscal crises are not new to the state—reformers in the 1920s railed against New York City's "spendthrift" policies—but the greatly increased scale of government in the 1970s made the fiscal crisis of 1975 unprecedented in its scope and implications. The decreasing pace of population and industrial growth during the 1950s and 1960s, and the decline during the 1970s, also led to a dimming of New York's political fortunes. No native-born New Yorker has been elected president since FDR, and neither of the two presidents who were New York residents when elected—Dwight Eisenhower in 1952 and Richard Nixon in 1968, both Republicans—ever held elective office in the state. The single most dominant political figure in New York since World War II, Nelson A. Rockefeller, tried and failed three times to win the Republican presidential nomination before his appointment to the vice-presidency in 1974. Unable to overcome the hostility of his party's conservative wing, he was not renominated for the vice-presidency in 1976.

[12] STATE GOVERNMENT

New York has had four constitutions, adopted in 1777, 1822, 1846, and 1895. The 1895 constitution was extensively revised in 1938, and the basic structure of state government has not changed since then, although the document had been amended 195 times by the end of 1977.

The legislature consists of a 60-member senate and 150-member assembly. Senators and assembly members serve two-year terms and are elected in even-numbered years. Each house holds regular annual sessions; special sessions may be called by the governor or initiated by petition of two-thirds of the membership of each body. Either senators or assembly members may introduce or amend a bill. To pass, a bill requires a majority vote in both houses; a two-thirds majority (i.e., at least 40 votes in the senate and 100 votes in the assembly) is required to override the governor's veto. Members of both the senate and assembly must be US citizens and must have resided in the state for five years and in their district for 12 months. Legislative salaries are $23,500, but legislative leaders may receive up to $21,000 in addition.

The state's only elected executives are the governor, lieutenant governor, comptroller, and attorney general. Each serves a four-year term. The governor and lieutnant governor are jointly elected; there is no limit to the number of terms they may serve. The governor must be at least 30 years old, a US citizen, and a resident of the state for five years prior to the date of election. The lieutenant governor is next in line for the governorship (should the governor be unable to complete his term in office) and presides over the senate. Annual salary for the governor is $85,000; for the lieutenant governor, $60,000.

The governor appoints the heads of 17 of the 20 major executive departments. The exceptions are the comptroller and attorney general, who are elected by the voters, and the head of the Department of Education, who is named by the Regents of the University of the State of New York.

A bill becomes law when passed by both houses of the legislature and signed by the governor. While the legislature is in session, a bill may also become law if the governor fails to act on it within 10 days after he receives it. The governor may veto a bill or, if the legislature has adjourned, may kill a bill simply by taking no action on it for 30 days. The powers of the governor are enhanced by constitutional provisions that, in effect, permit the governor and the governor's legislative lieutenants to flood the legislature with bills during the last days of a session; this gives the opposition party little time to study each bill and gather votes against it. Bills that are not to the governor's liking, held up in the last-minute rush of new bills, can then be "pocket vetoed" when the legislature adjourns, with no possibility of a legislative override.

A proposed amendment to the state constitution must receive majority votes in both houses of the legislature during two suc-cessive sessions. Amendments so approved are then put on the ballot in November and are adopted or rejected by majority vote. The constitution also provides that, starting in 1957, the voters must be permitted every 20 years to decide whether a convention should be called to revise and amend the present constitution.

To vote in New York State, one must be a US citizen, at least 18 years of age, and a resident of the election district for 30 days. New York State has a permanent personal registration system; a registered voter who fails to vote in any general election during a two-year period must reregister.

[13] POLITICAL PARTIES

In addition to the Democratic and Republican parties, the major political groups, there has always been a profusion of minor parties in New York, some of which have significantly influenced the outcomes of national and state elections.

Party politics in the state crystallized into their present form around 1855. Up to that time, a welter of parties and factions—including such short-lived groups as the Anti-Masons (later Whigs), Bucktails, Clintonians, Hunkers, and Barnburners (split into Hard-shell and Softshell Democrats), Know-Nothings (Native American Party), Woolly Heads and Silver-Grays (factions of the Whigs), and the Liberty Party—jockeyed for power in the state. Roughly speaking, the Democratic Party evolved out of the Democratic Republican factions of the old Republican Party and were a unified party by the 1850s. The Democratic power base was—and has remained—the big cities, especially New York City. The most important big-city political machine from the 1860s through the 1950s, except for a few brief periods, was the Tammany Society ("Tammany Hall"). Tammany controlled the Democratic Party in New York City, and through that party the city itself.

The Republican Party in New York State emerged in 1855 as the heir of the Whigs, the Liberty Party, and the Softshell Democratic faction. The Republican Party's power base includes the state's rural counties, the smaller cities and towns, and (though not so much in the 1970s as in earlier decades) the New York City suburbs. Although New York Republicans stand to the right of the Democrats on social issues, they have usually been well to the left of the national Republican Party. The

New York Presidential Vote by Political Parties, 1948–80

YEAR	ELECTORAL VOTE	NEW YORK WINNER	DEMOCRAT	LIBERAL[1]	REPUBLICAN	PROGRESSIVE[2]	SOCIALIST	SOCIALIST WORKERS	PEACE AND FREEDOM
1948	47	Dewey (R)	2,557,642	222,562	2,841,163	509,559	40,879	2,675	—
1952	45	*Eisenhower (R)	2,687,890	416,711	3,952,815	64,211	2,664	2,212	—
1956	45	*Eisenhower (R)	2,458,212	292,557	4,340,340	—	—	—	—
1960	45	*Kennedy (D)	3,423,909	406,176	3,446,419	—	—	14,319	—
1964	43	*Johnson (D)	4,570,670	342,432	2,243,559		SOC. LABOR 6,118	3,228	—
1968	43	Humphrey (D)	3,066,848	311,622	3,007,932	AMERICAN IND.[3] 358,864	8,432	11,851	24,517
1972	41	*Nixon (R)	2,767,956	183,128	3,824,642	CONSERVATIVE[4] 368,136	4,530	7,797	COMMUNIST 5,641
1976	41	*Carter (D)	3,244,165	145,393	2,825,913	274,878	LIBERTARIAN 12,197	6,996	10,270
1980	41	*Reagan (R)	2,728,372	467,801	2,637,700	256,131	52,648	RIGHT TO LIFE 24,159	CITIZENS 23,186

*Won US presidential election. 1. Supported Democratic candidate except in 1980, when John Anderson ran on the Liberal line. 2. Ran in the state as the American Labor Party. 3. Appeared on the state ballot as the Courage Party. 4. Supported Republican candidate.

liberal "internationalist" strain of Republicanism was personified during the 1960s by Governor Nelson Rockefeller, US Senator Jacob Javits, and New York City Mayor John V. Lindsay (who later became a Democrat).

The disaffection of more conservative Republicans and Democrats within the state led to the formation of the Conservative Party in 1963. At first intended as a device to exert pressure on the state Republican establishment, the Conservative Party soon became a power in its own right, electing a US senator, James Buckley, in 1970. Its power decreased in the late 1970s as the Republican Party embraced some of its positions. The Conservative Party has its left-wing counterpart in the Liberal Party, which was formed in 1944 by dissidents in the American Labor Party who claimed the ALP was Communist-influenced. Tied strongly to labor interests, the Liberals have normally supported the national Democratic ticket, while opposing Tammany nominees in New York City and, occasionally, in statewide elections. Their power, however, has waned considerably in recent years.

In 1978–79, the state had 3,349,182 registered Democrats (53% in New York City), 2,406,337 registered Republicans (15% in New York City), 104,002 registered Conservatives (30% in New York City), and 75,938 registered Liberals (49% in New York City). In 1978, Hugh L. Carey was reelected as governor and his running mate, Mario M. Cuomo, was elected to his first term as lieutenant governor, winning 2,429,272 votes on the Democratic and Liberal lines; the Republican-Conservative ticket took 2,156,404 votes. The combined turnout represented 63% of registered voters for that year. As of March 1980, the Democrats and Republicans each held one seat in the US Senate; the Democrats held 26 seats in the House, the Republicans 13. In the legislature, as of March 1980, the Democrats controlled the assembly, with 86 seats to the Republicans' 64, while the Republicans controlled the senate, with 35 seats to the Democrats' 25.

In the November 1980 elections, Republican presidential nominee Ronald Reagan (with Conservative Party backing) won the state's 41 elctorl votes, apparently because John Anderson, running in New York State on the Liberal Party line, siphoned enough votes from the Democratic incumbent, Jimmy Carter, to give Reagan a plurality. In a close race for the US Senate, Republican-Conservative Alfonse D'Amato—who had defeated the incumbent, Jacob Javits, in the Republican Party primary—outpolled Elizabeth Holtzman, a liberal Democrat, and Javits, this time running on the Liberal Party ticket.

Minor parties have sometimes meant the difference between victory and defeat for major party candidates in state and national elections. In 1912, Theodore Roosevelt's Bull Moose Party cut into the state's normally Republican majority, taking 24.6% of the votes cast and allowing the Democrats under Woodrow Wilson to win the state. The Liberal Party line provided the victory margin in the state for Democratic presidential candidate John F. Kennedy in 1960. Other significant, though not victorious, minor-party presidential candidates have included the American Labor Party with Henry Wallace in 1948 (8% of the vote) and the Courage Party with George Wallace in 1968 (5%). Among radical parties, the Socialists qualified for the presidential ballot continuously between 1900 and 1952, reaching a peak of 203,201 votes (7% of the total) in 1920. The Socialist Workers Party has qualified for every presidential election but one since 1948, while the Communists were on the ballot in 1972 and 1976.

Until 1972, New York had more electoral votes than any other state. Its considerable bloc of 41 electoral votes (2d to California in 1980) still makes the state a powerful force on the national political scene.

[14] LOCAL GOVERNMENT

The state constitution, endorsing the principle of home rule, recognizes many different levels of local government.

At the end of 1979, New York had 62 counties, 62 cities, 931 towns, 556 villages, and 742 school districts. In addition, there were more than 6,400 special districts, covering such services as firefighting, fire prevention, lighting, drainage, waste removal, and parks.

Cities are contained within counties, with one outstanding exception: New York City is made up of five counties, one for each of its five boroughs. Traditionally, counties are run by an elected board of supervisors; however, a growing number of counties have vested increased powers in a single elected county executive. Two counties—Monroe and Schenectady—have appointed county managers. Most cities are governed by an elected mayor and by a city council, whose members are elected by district.

Those who do not live in cities live in towns, which may range in size from fewer than 100 people to more than 800,000. Towns are run by an elected town board; the most important board member is the town supervisor, who may also represent the town on the county board of supervisors. A group of people within a town may also incorporate themselves into a village, with their own elected mayor and board of trustees. Members of the village remain members of the town, and must pay taxes to both jurisdictions. The constitution grants the state legislature the power to decide which taxes the local governments may levy and how much debt they may incur.

New York City is governed by a mayor and city council, but much practical power resides in the Board of Estimate. On this board sit the city's three top elected officials—the mayor, comptroller, and City Council president. The board also includes the five borough presidents, elected officials who represent (and, to a limited extent, govern) each of the five boroughs. New York City government is further complicated by the fact that certain essential services are provided not by the city itself but by independent "authorities." The Port Authority of New York and New Jersey, for example, operates New York Harbor, sets interstate bridge and tunnel tolls, supervises the city's bus and air terminals, and operates the city's largest office complex, the World Trade Center; it is responsible not to the mayor but to the governors of New York and New Jersey. Similarly, the Metropolitan Transportation Authority, which controls the city's subways and some of its commuter rail lines, is an independent agency responsible to the state rather than the city.

[15] STATE SERVICES

Educational services are provided through the Education Department. Under this department's jurisdiction are the State Library, the State Museum, the New York State School for the Blind at Batavia, and the New York State School for the Deaf at Rome. The Education Department also issues licenses for the professions, including architecture, engineering and land surveying, massage, pharmacy, public accountancy, social work, and various medical specialties. The state university system is administered by a separate agency headed by a chancellor.

Transportation services are under the direction of the Department of Transportation, which has responsibility for highways, aviation, mass transit, railroads, water transport, transportation safety, and intrastate rate regulation. The Department of Motor Vehicles licenses all road vehicles, motor vehicle dealers, motor vehicle operators, and driving schools.

Human services are provided through several state departments. Among the programs and facilities operated by the Department of Health are the Birth Defects Institute, the New York State Veterans' Home, the New York State Kidney Disease Institute, and the New York State Burns Care Institute. The Department of Health licenses nursing home administrators, runs several special programs for veterans, and maintains 6 regional health offices throughout the state, as well as 10 district health offices. The state provides care for the mentally ill and the retarded through the Department of Mental Hygiene. The Department of Social Services supervises and sets standards for locally administered public and private welfare and health programs; it has special responsibilities for the visually handicapped and over Indian affairs. Other human services are provided through the Division of Veterans' Affairs, the Division of Human Rights, the Division for Youth, and the Office for the Aging.

Public protection services include state armed forces, corrections, and consumer protection. Included within the Division of Military and Naval Affairs are the Army National Guard, Air National Guard, and State Civil Defense Commission. The Division of State Police operates within the Executive Department, while prison facilities are administered by the separate Department of Correctional Services. The State Consumer Protection Board (Executive Department) coordinates the consumer protection activities of the various agencies and departments. The major legal role in consumer protection is played by the attorney general. Utilities are regulated by the Public Service Commission.

Housing services are provided through the Division of Housing and Community Renewal and through the quasi-independent New York State Housing Finance Agency, State of New York Mortgage Agency, and New York State Urban Development Corporation. The Division of Community Affairs (Department of State) aids in local and regional planning and coordination, and with economic development and antipoverty programs. The Department of Commerce has an Office of Minority Business Enterprise.

Natural resources protection services are centralized in the Department of Environmental Conservation. The administration of the state park and recreation system is carried out by the Office of Parks and Recreation. The Department of Agriculture and Markets serves the interests of farmers and also administers the state's Pure Food Law. Energy is the province of both the Public Service Commission and the state Energy Office created in 1976.

The Department of Labor provides most labor services for the state. Its responsibilities include occupational health and safety, manpower development and allocation, administration of unemployment insurance and other benefit programs, and maintenance of labor standards, including enforcement of minimum wage and other labor laws. The Labor Relations Board and State Mediation Board, both within the Department of Labor, try to settle labor disputes and prevent work stoppages.

[16] JUDICIAL SYSTEM

New York has a large and complex judicial and correctional system.

The state's highest court is the New York court of appeals, with appellate jurisdiction only. The court of appeals consists of a chief judge and five associate judges, elected by the voters for 14-year terms. In 1979, the chief judge received a salary of $72,292; the associate judges, $69,352. Below the court of appeals is the supreme court, which in 1979 consisted of 287 justices in 11 judicial districts. The supreme court of New York State does not sit as one body; instead, some supreme court justices are assigned original jurisdiction in civil and criminal matters, while other justices are assigned to the court's four appellate divisions. Supreme court justices are elected by district and serve 14-year terms at annual salaries of $56,098 for justices, $59,108 for appellate division justices, and $63,274 for the four presiding justices. No justice, either in the court of appeals or in the supreme court, may serve past the age of 70.

The New York court of claims, which sits in Albany, consists of 17 judges appointed by the governor to 9-year terms, with the advice and consent of the senate. This court hears civil cases involving claims by or against the state, and certain other cases. Legislation in 1973 permitted the one-time appointment of another 34 judges for 9-year terms.

Outside New York City, each county has its own county court and surrogate court. Larger counties also have their own family courts. The county district attorney has authority in criminal matters. Most cities (including New York City) have their own court systems. Village police justices and town justices of the peace handle minor violations and other routine matters.

The Department of Correctional Services maintains correctional facilities throughout the state, as well as regional parole offices. As of 31 December 1977, 19,380 inmates were in state facilities. Another 6,600 persons were in facilities operated by the New York City Department of Correction institutions; of these, 2,380 were serving sentences and 4,220 were awaiting court action. County jails admitted a total of 94,879 persons in 1977, the lowest number since 1969.

Although 11 states had higher overall crime rates, no state had a violent crime rate higher than New York's in 1978. About 55% of all crimes reported to the police in the state occurred in New York City, which had an FBI Crime Index total of 570,354 crimes, compared with totals of 233,344 for Los Angeles, 190,815 for Chicago, and 110,511 for Detroit. FBI data for the New York metropolitan area showed a violent crime rate of 1,370.6 crimes per 100,000 population, slightly less than three times the national average, and a property crime rate of 5,719.3, well above the national average of 4,622.4. In New York City alone there were 1,503 cases of murder or manslaughter, 3,882 forcible rapes, 74,029 robberies, 43,271 aggravated assaults, 164,447 cases of burglary, 200,110 cases of larceny-theft, and 83,112 motor vehicle thefts. Buffalo ranked 2d to New York City in the number of crimes reported in 1978, but its crime rate was about 33% lower.

[17] ARMED FORCES

New York State ranked 3d, behind California and Texas, in defense contracts received in 1978, and is home to the US Military Academy at West Point. About 11% of all US police employees work in the state, which leads the nation in combined state and local police manpower.

As of 1978 there were 33,963 Department of Defense personnel in the state; about one-third of them were civilians. The Army had 14,534 personnel; the Navy, 3,400; and the Air Force, 16,029. Almost half the Army personnel were at West Point. The academy, which was founded in 1802, enrolled 4,066 cadets (including 313 women) as of February 1980. The naval facilities in the state are concentrated in Brooklyn. Griffiss Air Force Base, near Rome, is the largest Air Force facility; the next largest is Plattsburgh Air Force Base, in the extreme northeastern corner of the state.

Firms in New York State were awarded an estimated $4.6 billion in defense contracts in 1978, more than 7% of the US total.

In 1978 there were 2,477,000 veterans of US military service in the state. Of these, 2,197,000 had seen service during wartime. Allowing for overlapping (some veterans served in more than one war), the estimates for living veterans of wartime service were as follows: World War I, 50,000; World War II, 1,144,000; Korea 505,000; Viet-Nam era, 610,000. Veterans' benefits totaling $1,408 million were paid to New Yorkers during 1977/78, of which about $663 million went for compensation and pensions, $139 million for education and training, and the balance for medical and insurance benefits.

The manpower strength of the Army National Guard in the state as of March 1980 was 14,802; the Air National Guard, 4,596.

State and local police forces employed 64,733 in 1977; of that total, 58,533 were local employees. Police expenditures in the state during 1977 were an estimated $1.3 billion, 2d behind California. New York City had 27,458 police as of 30 November 1979; expenditures for 1979/80 were estimated at $674 million. Despite force reductions because of budget cuts in the mid-1970s, New York City's police force in 1980 was about twice as large as Chicago's and three times that of Los Angeles.

¹⁸MIGRATION

Nowhere is it more evident than in New York that the US is a nation of immigrants. By 1664, New York already had English and Dutch, along with a sprinkling of French, Germans, Finns, Swedes, Jews, and Negroes.

The reason for New York's popularity among European immigrants is obvious. Since the early 1800s, New York has been—and still is—the primary port of entry for Europeans coming to the US. The Statue of Liberty, dedicated in 1886 and beckoning "your tired, your poor,/Your huddled masses yearning to breathe free" to the shores of America, was often the immigrants' first glimpse of America. The first stop for some 20 million immigrants in the late 19th and early 20th centuries was Ellis Island, where they were processed, often given Americanized names, and sent onward to an uncertain future.

The first great wave of European immigrants arrived in the 1840s, impelled by the potato famine in Ireland. By 1850, New York City had 133,730 Irish-born inhabitants; by 1890, 409,224. Although smaller in number, German immigration during this period was more widespread; during the 1850s, German-speaking people were the largest foreign-born group in Rochester and Buffalo, and by 1855 about 30,000 of Buffalo's 74,000 residents were German.

The next two great waves of European immigration—Eastern European Jews and Italians—overlapped. Vast numbers of Jews began arriving from Eastern Europe during the 1880s, by which time some 80,000 German-speaking Jews were already living in New York City. By 1910, the Jewish population of the city was about 1,250,000, growing to nearly 2,000,000 by the mid-1920s. The flood of Italians began during the 1890s, when the Italian population of New York City increased from 75,000 to more than 200,000; in 1950, nearly 500,000 Italian-born immigrants were living in the state. Migration from the 1840s onward followed a cyclical pattern; as one group dispersed from New York City throughout the state and the nation, it was replaced by a new wave of immigrants.

Yankees from New England made up the first great wave of domestic migration. Most of the migrants who came to New York between 1790 and 1840 were Yankees; it has been estimated that by 1850, 52,000 natives of Vermont (20% of that state's population) had become residents of New York. There was a slow, steady migration of Negroes from slave states to New York prior to the Civil War, but massive black migration to New York, and especially to New York City, began during World War I and continued well into the 1960s. The third great wave of domestic migration came after World War II, from Puerto Rico. Nearly 40,000 Puerto Ricans settled in New York City in 1946, and 58,500 in 1952/53. By 1960, the census showed well over 600,000 New Yorkers of Puerto Rican birth or parentage.

The fourth and most recent domestic migratory trend is unique in New York history—the net outward migration from New York to other states. During the 1960s, New York suffered a net loss of more than 100,000 residents through migration; between 1970 and 1977 the estimated net loss was 863,000. These general estimates hide a racial movement of historic proportions: during the 1960s, while a net total of 638,000 whites were moving out of the state, 396,000 blacks were moving in; during 1970–75, according to Census Bureau estimates, 701,000 whites left New York, while 60,000 blacks were arriving. It appears that most of the white emigrants went to suburban areas of New Jersey and Connecticut, but many also must have gone to two Sunbelt states, Florida and California. Overwhelmingly, the black arrivals came from the South. There was some evidence of a small net black migration from New York back to the South during the late 1970s.

Intrastate migration has followed the familiar pattern of rural to urban, urban to suburban. In 1790, the state was 88% rural; the rural population grew in absolute terms (though not as a percentage of the total state population) until the 1880s, when the long period of decline began. New York's farm population decreased by 21% during the 1940s, 33% during the 1950s, and another 38% during the 1960s. By 1977, an estimated 89% of all New Yorkers lived in metropolitan areas. Meanwhile, the suburban population has grown steadily. In 1950, 3,538,620 New Yorkers (24% of the state total) lived in suburbs; by 1976, this figure had grown to 7,215,582 (40% of all state residents). It should be remembered, of course, that this doubling of the suburban population reflects natural increase and direct migration from other states and regions, as well as the intrastate migratory movement from central cities to suburbs.

¹⁹INTERGOVERNMENTAL COOPERATION

New York State is a member of the Council of State Governments and its allied organizations. The Select Committee on Interstate Cooperation of the New York State legislature represents the state in dealings with the council.

The state participates in many interstate regional commissions. Among the more active are the Atlantic States Marine Fisheries Commission, Delaware River Basin Commission, Great Lakes Commission, Interstate Oil Compact Commission, Lake Champlain Bridge Commission, New England Interstate Water Pollution Control Commission, Northeastern Forest Fire Protection Commission, and Ohio River Valley Water Sanitation Commission.

The four most important interstate bodies for the New York metropolitan area are the Palisades Interstate Park Commission, Interstate Sanitation Commission, Tri-State Regional Planning Commission, and Port Authority of New York and New Jersey. The Palisades Interstate Park Commission was founded in 1900 (with New Jersey) in order to preserve the natural beauty of the Palisades region. The Interstate Sanitation Commission (with New Jersey and Connecticut; established in 1961) monitors and seeks to control pollution within the tri-state Interstate Sanitation District. The Tri-State Regional Planning Commission (with New Jersey and Connecticut) was originally founded in 1966 and took its present name in 1971; it studies and makes recommendations on a wide range of regional problems, and reviews applications for federal aid to the metropolitan region on matters ranging from airports to law enforcement. The Port Authority of New York and New Jersey, created in 1921 and the most powerful of the four, is a public corporation with the power to issue its own bonds. Its vast holdings include 4 bridges, 2 tunnels, 6 air terminals, 3 motor vehicle terminals, 7 marine terminals, the trans-Hudson rapid transit system, and the World Trade Center.

Federal aid to New York State totaled $8,372,465,000 in 1977/78. Federal revenue-sharing funds were estimated at $254,000,000 for 1979/80, or about 2% of the current state budget. Federal aid accounted for more than 18% of New York City revenues in the budget for 1979/80.

²⁰ECONOMY

From the Civil War through the 1950s, New York State led the nation in just about every category by which an industrial economy can be measured. With the rise of California and the growth of other Sunbelt states, New York can no longer be described in such superlatives.

The state is no stranger to economic transitions. In the colonial and early national periods, New York was a leading wheat-growing state. When the wheat crop declined, dairying and lumbering became the state's mainstays. Then New York emerged as the national leader in wholesaling, retailing, and manufacturing—and remained so, well into the 1960s. By 1973, however, the state was running neck and neck with California by most output measures, or had already been surpassed. The total labor force, the number of workers in manufacturing, and the number of factories all declined during the 1960s and 1970s.

In the late 1970s, the state remained a national power in printing and publishing, fashion and apparel, instruments, machinery, and electronic equipment. No state—and few countries—can match New York in the value of its banking, securities, and communications industries. Agriculture, forestry, fishing, and mining, though of local importance, are far less vital to the overall state economy. Roughly speaking, in 1977, manufacturing employed about 27% of the state's labor force; services, 26%; trade, 25%; public administration, 6%; and other sectors, 16%. New York's labor force is the most organized in the country. Wages and personal income are above the US average, though they lag behind those of several other industrial states.

New York City accounts for more than 40% of the state's income, nearly three-fourths of its wholesale trade, virtually the entire securities industry, and much of the banking and communications activity. It is also the nation's foremost manufacturing city and the country's busiest port. New York State cannot be economically healthy if the city does not remain so.

On that score, the indicators are not encouraging. The city's skilled laborers have been emigrating to the suburbs and to other states since World War II; replacing these skilled laborers, who are largely white and middle-class, have been mostly semiskilled or unskilled black and Puerto Rican migrants. About 1 of 6 New York City residents received some form of public assistance (including medical aid and supplemental security income benefits) in 1977. With the departure of the middle class has come a shrinking of the city's tax base, a factor that contributed to the fiscal crisis of 1975, when a package of short-term aid from Congress, the state government, and the labor union pension funds saved the city from default. According to the Bureau of Labor Statistics, the city did gain more than 100,000 new jobs in the late 1970s, but a long-term forecast issued in 1980 by Chase Econometrics predicted that the New York City area would lose about 130,000 jobs, mostly in manufacturing, by 1990.

21 INCOME

With an income per capita of $8,267 in 1978 dollars, New York ranked 13th among the 50 states. New York's total personal income for that year was $146.7 billion, 2d behind California, and 8.6% of the US total.

The following table shows contributions to earned income by major economic sectors in 1977:

Manufacturing	$ 23,613,700,000
Services	22,202,100,000
Government	16,854,000,000
Wholesale, retail trade	16,639,700,000
Finance, insurance, real estate	9,778,600,000
Transportation, communications, public utilities	8,987,800,000
Contract construction	3,515,100,000
Agriculture, forestry, fisheries	350,400,000
Mining	199,200,000
Other sources	268,500,000
TOTAL	$102,409,100,000

Surprisingly, despite New York State's—and especially New York City's—reputation for urban slums and poverty, the state actually has a lower percentage of persons with incomes below the poverty level (9% in 1975) than the national average (11%). New York's reputation for "Wall Street millionaires" is somewhat better deserved: in 1972, 12.3% of the nation's wealthiest people lived in the state, compared with 9.6% in California.

New York City, with 41% of the state's population, accounted for 42% of state income in 1977. On a per capita basis, Manhattan ranked 1st in the state, followed by the city's suburban counties, Westchester and Nassau. Monroe County (Rochester and suburbs) ranked 4th. Rural Lewis County in northeastern New York had the lowest per capita income, $4,565.

22 LABOR

The state ranks 2d to California in the size of its labor force, but 1st in the extent to which it is organized.

The civilian labor force totaled 7,762,000 in 1977, of whom 7,054,000 (91%) were employed and 708,000 (9%) were unemployed. Of the total labor force, 49% lived in the New York metropolitan area (including New Jersey suburbs), 15% in Nassau and Suffolk counties, and 7% in the Buffalo region.

US census data offer further insights into the structure of the work force. In 1970, 88% of the work force was white and 12% nonwhite. The participation of women increased by 22% between 1960 and 1970, when 2,878,973 workers were female and 4,579,774 were male. By occupation, clerical workers made up 23% of the labor force; professional and technical workers, 16%; service workers (except private household), 12%; craftsmen and foremen, 12%; machine operatives (except transport), 11%; managers and administrators (nonfarm), 9%; sales workers, 8%; and others, 9%.

A federal census of workers covered by unemployment insurance in March 1977 revealed the following nonfarm employment pattern in New York State:

	ESTABLISH-MENTS	EMPLOYEES	ANNUAL PAYROLL ('000)
Agricultural services, forestry, fisheries	2,904	10,463	$ 117,951
Mining	442	7,710	157,674
Contract construction	24,904	168,796	2,907,101
Manufacturing, of which:	33,190	1,506,583	21,763,672
Food, food products	(1,697)	(73,363)	(1,012,990)
Apparel, other textiles	(6,810)	(194,400)	(1,800,866)
Printing, publishing	(5,578)	(154,184)	(2,301,377)
Fabricated metal products	(2,317)	(81,942)	(1,105,393)
Nonelectrical machinery	(2,678)	(134,446)	(2,145,865)
Electric and electronic equipment	(1,414)	(149,582)	(2,183,501)
Transport equipment	(389)	(75,531)	(1,349,850)
Instruments and related products	(789)	(102,023)	(1,661,991)
Transportation, public utilities	13,888	399,674	6,758,339
Wholesale trade	37,052	428,454	6,736,206
Retail, trade, of which:	97,191	957,578	7,315,687
General merchandise stores	(2,529)	(147,245)	(1,006,348)
Food stores	(14,711)	(167,211)	(1,212,165)
Eating and drinking places	(25,084)	(247,423)	(1,329,158)
Finance, insurance, real estate, of which:	45,203	604,330	8,463,654
Banking	(4,446)	(193,966)	(2,478,631)
Insurance	(8,323)	(159,754)	(2,274,502)
Real estate	(26,314)	(117,761)	(1,185,558)
Services, of which:	106,684	1,430,055	15,736,647
Health services	(24,550)	(395,417)	(4,643,914)
Educational services	(3,083)	(140,168)	(1,388,910)
Membership organizations	(9,775)	(105,453)	(854,292)
Other	5,502	7,111	120,182
TOTALS	366,960	5,520,754	$70,077,113

There were about 1,259,900 government employees in New York State in 1977. Of these, 162,400 were employed by the federal government, 231,800 by the state, and 865,700 by local governments.

Unemployment in the state has exceeded the US average since 1971, reaching a high of 9.5% in 1975. In 1978, when the US average was 6%, New York's unemployment rate was 7.7%. Unemployment in New York City was 8.9% in 1978, above the state average but lower than in some other northern industrial cities. Among the minority races, the unemployment rate was 10.7%. This statistic reflects—and probably understates—the chronic unemployment among black teenagers and young adults in urban areas.

At the turn of the century, working conditions in New York were among the worst in the country. The flood of immigrants into the labor market and the absence of labor laws to protect them led to the development in New York City of cramped, ill-lit, poorly ventilated, and unhealthy factories—the sweatshops for which the garment industry became notorious. Since that time, working conditions in the garment factories have improved, primarily through the efforts of the International Ladies' Garment Workers Union and, later, its sister organization, the Amalgamated Clothing and Textiles Workers Union.

According to the US Department of Labor, 3,040,000 New Yorkers belonged to unions or employees' associations in 1976. That figure represented nearly 45% of the nonagricultural work force, the highest percentage in any state. Unions claimed 2,515,000 members, or nearly 83% of the state total; 2,168,000 union members belonged to AFL-CIO affiliates. Also in 1977, 31 national unions had their headquarters in the state; 30 of these were in New York City, a total exceeded only by Washington, D.C.

As of 1977, children under 16 were permitted to work no more than 8 hours a day, 40 hours a week, or 6 days a week; during a school week, the limit was 23 hours a week (3 hours per school day). At no time could they work between 7 P.M. and 7 A.M. These restrictions were relaxed for 16- and 17-year-olds.

Under the Taylor Law, public employees do not have the right to strike. Penalties for striking may be exacted against both the unions and their leaders. There were 13 work stoppages by state and local employees in 1977, involving a total of 5,700 workers.

²³ AGRICULTURE

New York ranked 25th in agricultural income in 1979, with an estimated total of $1,941,312,000. About 70% came from dairying. The state ranked 2d in the production of apples for that year, 4th in fresh vegetables, and 9th in potatoes and oats, but much lower for other crops.

Corn was the leading crop for the Indians and for the European settlers of the early colonial period. During the early 1800s, however, wheat was the major crop grown in eastern New York. With the opening of the Erie Canal, western New York (especially the Genesee Valley) became a major wheat-growing center as well. By the late 1850s, when the state's wheat crop began to decline, New York still led the nation in barley, flax, hops, and potato production and was a significant grower of corn and oats. The opening of the railroads took away the state's competitive advantage, however. As grain production shifted to the Midwest, the state emerged as a leading supplier of meat and dairy products.

New York remains an important dairy state, but urbanization has reduced its overall agricultural potential. By 1974, 21.9% of the state's land area was devoted to crop growing; however, only 1.3% of the population was living on farms, less than one-third the 1940 percentage.

Chautauqua County, in the extreme southwest, leads the state in grape production, while Wayne County, along Lake Ontario, excels in tree fruits, especially apples. The dairy industry is concentrated in the St. Lawrence Valley; grain growing dominates the plains between Syracuse and Buffalo. The major exception to this pattern is potatoes, which grow mostly in Suffolk County, on eastern Long Island.

The following table shows area and production of leading field crops in 1978:

CROP	AREA (ACRES)	PRODUCTION
Hay	2,475,000	5,297,000 tons
Corn, silage	682,000	8,866,000 tons
Corn, grain	600,000	47,400,000 bushels
Oats	300,000	17,700,000 bushels
Wheat	75,000	2,625,000 bushels
Potatoes	48,000	12,675,000 cwt

Farms in 1978 also produced 571,800 tons of fresh vegetables and 403,300 tons of vegetables for processing. Leading vegetable crops were cabbage, onions, sweet corn, and snap beans.

State vineyards produced 188,000 tons of grapes for wine and juice in 1978, while the apple crop totaled 1,030,000 lb. Maple syrup production was 330,000 gallons in 1978.

²⁴ ANIMAL HUSBANDRY

Only Wisconsin and California outrank New York in value of dairy items produced.

The St. Lawrence Valley is the state's leading cattle-raising region, followed by the Mohawk Valley and Wyoming County, in western New York. The poultry industry is more widely dispersed. In 1979, the state had 1,711,000 head of cattle, of which 904,000 were full-grown milk cows. Other livestock included 140,000 hogs and pigs, and 63,000 sheep and lambs.

The following table shows volume and value for selected livestock products in 1979:

PRODUCT	VOLUME (LB)	VALUE
Dairy:		
Milk	10,679,000,000	$1,278,276,000
Cheese (excluding cottage cheese)	304,480,000	NA
Creamed cottage cheese	124,444,000	NA
Ice cream (gallons)	61,903,000	NA
Butter	35,851,000	NA
Nonfat dry milk	42,152,000	NA
Meat animals		
Cattle and calves	333,580,000	202,883,000
Hogs and pigs	39,742,000	17,168,000
Sheep and lambs	3,397,000	1,678,000
Poultry:		
Chickens	29,385,000	2,703,000
Turkeys	4,427,000	1,859,000

The state was the nation's 14th largest egg producer during 1979, yielding 153,750,000 dozen. Duck raising is an industry of local importance on Long Island.

²⁵ FISHING

Fishing, though an attraction for tourists and sportsmen, plays only a marginal role in the economic life of the state.

In 1978, the catch by New York fishermen was estimated at 36,340,000 lb, or less than 1% of the US total. The catch was valued at $33,870,000, 2d behind New Jersey's in the Middle Atlantic states, and about equal to the value of crabs in Maryland. Even so, the catch represented only 0.02% of the total personal income for New Yorkers for that same year. Important species for commercial use are menhaden (for oils, animal feed, and fish meal) and, among shellfish, clams and oysters. Virtually all of New York's commercial fishing takes place in the Atlantic waters off Long Island.

Pollution and poor wildlife management seriously endangered the state's sport fishing in rivers and lakes. In recent decades, however, the Department of Environmental Conservation has taken an active role in restocking New York's inland waters. During 1976/77, state fisheries distributed 461,883,000 fry weighing 759,206 lb (344,370 kg). Walleyed pike and various species of trout make up most of the total.

²⁶ FORESTRY

About 57% of New York's surface area is forestland. The state, which occupies 1.3% of the total US land area, has 2.3% of the nation's forests.

The most densely forested counties are Hamilton, Essex, and

Warren in the Adirondacks, and Delaware, Greene, and Ulster in the Catskills. The total forested area was about 17,378,000 acres (703,000 hectares) in 1977, of which 83% was eligible for commercial exploitation. However, only 7% of the state's forestland was actually being exploited. The state produced only 1% of the national sawtimber output in 1977, mostly in hardwoods. Receipts from forestry products totaled $1,113,517,000 in 1978, when New York produced 10,780,000 board feet of sawtimber and 68,500 cords of pulpwood. The environmental and recreational value of New York's woodland is harder to measure, though no less significant.

The state Department of Environmental Conservation maintains 2,640,215 acres (1,068,461 hectares) in the Catskills and Adirondacks as forest preserves. State nurseries distributed 7,108,000 seedlings in 1978, 99% of them for use on lands that were not state owned.

27 MINING

New York is the nation's only supplier of wollastonite, a paper and paint filler, and produces a major share of the nation's emery, aluminum-titanium oxide, zinc, salt, aluminum oxide abrasives, calcium-magnesium chloride, talc, and ilmenite. The estimated value of the state's mineral output for 1978 (including fossil fuels) was $438,000,000, 29th in the US.

Recoverable metals are found almost entirely in St. Lawrence and Essex counties, in the northern Adirondacks. At Tahawus, in Essex County, the state claims to have the largest titanium mine in the country. Wollastonite is also found in Essex County. St. Lawrence County leads the state in zinc, iron ore, talc, lead, mercury, and silver output. Rock salt is mined in Livingston, Tompkins, and Yates counties. Emery is found in Westchester, while stone, sand, and gravel are quarried throughout the state. Overall, 422 mining and quarrying operations in New York in 1977 employed about 7,710 people, with an annual payroll of $157,674,000.

Estimated output of leading minerals in 1978 (in tons) included stone, 31,223,000; sand and gravel, 30,000,000; pig iron, 3,459,000; and salt, 5,928,000 (3d in US). In that same year, the state also produced 26,463 metric tons of zinc, 990 metric tons of lead, and 21,000 troy oz of silver.

28 ENERGY AND POWER

Although New York State's fossil fuel resources are limited, the state ranks 3d in the US in electric power production. About one-fourth of the state's annual electric power output comes from hydroelectric plants built and operated by the Power Authority of the State of New York.

Installed capacity in the state in 1978 was 31.8 million kw, of which 78% was privately owned. Electrical output totaled 115.5 billion kwh in 1978, of which 69% was supplied by the electric utility industry. Of the power supplied by these private sources, about 80% came from conventional steam turbines, 14% from nuclear-powered plants, 5% from hydroelectric plants, and 1% from gas turbines.

Two of the three largest nonfederal hydroelectric plants in the US are located in New York State. The largest, the Niagara Power Project, had a capacity of 2,400,000 kw at the start of 1979. The New York side of the St. Lawrence River Power Project ranks 3d in the US, with a capacity of 800,000 kw in 1979. Both plants were built and are operated by the Power Authority of the State of New York, which also built and operates a pumped-storage plant in Schoharie County (1,000,000 kw) and a nuclear power plant on Lake Ontario near Oswego (800,000 kw). Other nuclear plants in the state include two reactors at Indian Point (one operated by Consolidated Edison, and one by the State Power Authority), and units operated by the Long Island Lighting Co., the Niagara Mohawk Power Co., and the Rochester Gas & Electric Co.

Sales of public and private electric power totaled 101.3 billion kwh in 1977, of which 31% went to commercial users, 31% to industrial purchasers, 30% to residential users, and 8% for other purposes. Energy costs to industry are about 25% above the national average, and the energy bills for residents of large cities (especially New York City) are the highest in the nation. While the average usage per residential customer in the state rose from 2,598 kwh in 1960 to 5,315 kwh in 1977 (an increase of 105%), the average annual bill increased from $83.84 to $316.67, a 278% increase. New York City is supplied with electric power by Consolidated Edison, which had 2.7 million customers and operating revenues of $2.5 billion in 1977. The Public Service Commission, consisting of a chairman and five commissioners (all appointed by the governor), regulates rates and utility operations.

New York City has had two major power failures since the 1960s. The first, in November 1965, came as part of a much larger blackout on the east coast. The second, in July 1977, affected only the city and Westchester County, the area served by Consolidated Edison; power was not fully restored for 25 hours, and damage by looters was extensive.

Proved reserves of petroleum in New York State, as of 31 December 1978, were 8,996,000 barrels, or much less than 1% of the US total. Oil output in 1978 was 853,000 barrels—again, a tiny fraction of the national total. Exploration for oil off the coasts of Long Island and New Jersey began in 1978, after a long battle over the environmental impact of drilling, but by 1980 no wells had been brought in. Because New York has a large number of motor vehicles and because more than half of all occupied housing units in the state are heated by oil, the state is a very large net importer of petroleum products.

The state's estimated natural gas reserves as of December 1978 were 262.7 billion cu feet (7.4 billion cu meters); net production in 1978 totaled 13.3 billion cu feet (378 million cu meters). Although the state's natural gas output has risen steadily since 1966, both production and reserves represent only a tiny fraction of US totals. About 52% of natural gas sold in the state is used for residential heating and cooking.

The state has no commercially significant coal production. Most of its coal is consumed in electric power generation.

29 INDUSTRY

Until the 1970s, New York was the nation's foremost industrial state, ranking 1st in virtually every general category. However, US Commerce Department data show that by 1975 the state had slipped in manufacturing to 2d in number of employees, payroll, and value added, 4th in value of shipments of manufactured goods, and 6th in new capital spending.

According to the labor census of March 1977, New York had 33,190 manufacturing establishments with 1,506,583 employees and an annual payroll of $21,763,672,000. Industries employing the most workers were apparel and other textiles, printing and publishing, electric and electronic equipment, nonelectrical machinery, fabricated metal products, and transportation equipment, in that order. Value added by manufacturing totaled $44,676,900,000 in 1977. Of that 1977 figure, 14% was added by printing and publishing, 13% by instruments and related products, 11% by nonelectrical machinery, 10% by electric and electronic equipment, 9% by apparel and other textiles, 7% by food and food products, 7% by chemicals and chemical products, 6% by transportation equipment, 5% by fabricated metal products, and 18% by other industries.

Value added by manufacturing for selected New York industries in 1972 and 1977 was as follows:

	1972	1977
Periodicals publishing	$1,064,800,000	$1,903,500,000
Book publishing	952,000,000	1,382,300,000
Electronic components	910,100,000	1,256,200,000
Radio and television equipment	NA	1,234,600,000
Ladies' dresses	722,500,000	1,158,000,000

	1972	1977
Pharmaceuticals	879,200,000	1,019,200,000
Refrigeration machinery	693,600,000	982,600,000
Motor vehicle parts and accessories	NA	835,500,000
Electronic computing equipment	371,100,000	735,900,000
Toiletries	269,200,000	720,500,000

The Buffalo region, with its excellent transport facilities and abundant power supply, is the main center for heavy industry in the state. Plants in the region manufacture iron and steel, aircraft, automobile parts and accessories, and machinery, as well as flour, animal feed, and various chemicals. Steel products and automotive accessories are also produced in the Albany area. Light industry is dispersed throughout the state. Rochester is especially well known for its photographic and optical equipment and office machines; the city is the world headquarters of the Eastman Kodak Co., a world leader in photography with assets of $6.8 billion in 1978. Important clothing industry cities are Rochester, Utica, Syracuse, Troy, and especially New York City; Binghamton is a major producer of shoes. The state's leadership in electronic equipment is in large part attributable to the International Business Machines Corp. (IBM), which was founded by merger in 1911 at Endicott. In 1979, IBM ranked as the 8th leading US industrial corporation, with assets of $24.5 billion. Its world headquarters is at Armonk, in Westchester County. The presence of a large General Electric plant has long made Schenectady a leader in the manufacture of electric machinery. Schenectady is also a center of printing and publishing, as are Elmira and most especially New York City.

New York City excels not only in the apparel and publishing trades, but also in food processing, meat packing, chemicals, leather goods, metal products, and many other manufactures. In addition, the city serves as headquarters for many large industrial corporations whose manufacturing activities often take place entirely outside New York. Two of the top three largest US industrial corporations—Exxon and Mobil—had their headquarters in New York City in 1979, as did 19 of the top 100 firms.

Industries in New York were hit hard by the recession of the mid-1970s, but symptoms of a relative decline were evident more than a decade earlier. In fact, both the number of manufacturing establishments and the number of manufacturing employees peaked in 1954 and declined steadily thereafter, as industries moved to neighboring states and to the Sunbelt. Between 1972 and 1977, for example, the number of manufacturing establishments in New York dropped by more than 4%. For establishments with more than 20 employees, there was a decline of 12%. Employment in manufacturing decreased 8% during the same period. New capital spending in the state totaled $2,715,600,000 in 1977. The 1976 total for capital spending was less than 6% of the US total; Texas, California, Michigan, and Illinois all outspent New York in that year. In the late 1970s, the state Department of Commerce launched a new program of advertising and financial incentives to persuade business to remain in New York and to invest new capital in the state.

30 COMMERCE

New York's preeminence as the nation's leading commercial state is underscored by the fact that the wholesale trade of New York City alone exceeds that of any state except New York. The state ranks 2d in retail trade, behind California but well ahead of the other 48 states.

Wholesale trade employed 428,454 New Yorkers in 37,052 establishments in March 1977. There were 215,124 wholesale trade employees in New York City, 163,903 in Manhattan alone. In 1972, sales totaled $100.4 billion, or nearly 15% of the US total, far more than any other state. New York City's share was 72%. The most valuable categories of goods traded were apparel and textiles, groceries and related products, unprocessed farm products, machinery and equipment, minerals and metals (ex-

cluding petroleum), motor vehicles and parts, electrical goods, and petroleum and petroleum products. Except for apparel, this list appears to reflect the importance of New York City as a port and transportation center rather than the makeup of state or city industries.

According to the employment census of March 1977, 97,191 retail establishments in New York employed 957,578 workers, 363,751 of them in New York City. The census of retail trade for the same year showed a total of 142,202 retail establishments, of which 28% were "mom and pop" operations with no payroll. Retail sales in the state totaled $50.7 billion, of which food stores accounted for 25%; automotive dealers, 15%; general merchandise stores, 13%; eating and drinking places, 10%; gasoline service stations, 6%; and others 31%. New York State accounted for about 7% of all US retail sales, and New York City and its suburbs for about 60% of all retail sales in the state. In 1977, the state had more than 500 department stores, of which at least 56 were in New York City; of the 15 department stores employing 1,000 persons or more, New York City had 13.

The state's long border with Canada, its important ports on Lakes Erie and Ontario, and its vast harbor on New York Bay ensure it a major role in US foreign trade. About one-fourth of US imports and exports pass through the state's customs districts. The New York Customs District (including New York City, Albany, and Newark and Perth Amboy, N.J.) handled about $20 billion in exports and $26 billion in imports in 1977. Canadian border districts (including the Ogdensburg and Buffalo Customs Districts) handled $7.6 billion in exports and $8.5 billion in imports.

The following table shows foreign exports of New York State industrial and agricultural products for selected years:

	VALUE	US RANK	% OF US TOTAL
Manufactured goods:			
1966	$1,838,000,000	2	8.6
1969	2,296,000,000	5	7.9
1972	2,795,000,000	5	7.6
1976	5,320,000,000	5	6.4
Farm products:			
1963/64	78,000,000	24	1.3
1967/68	63,000,000	29	1.0
1971/72	44,000,000	33	0.5
1976/77	109,000,000	35	0.5

31 CONSUMER PROTECTION

Although the state government has a mixed record on consumer issues, one New York organization—the Consumers Union of the United States—has had great impact on the national consumer movement.

The State Consumer Protection Board was created in 1970, and consists of the chairman of the Public Service Commission, the superintendents of banking and insurance, the secretary of state, and the commissioners of health, agriculture and markets, environmental conservation, and commerce. Although the board represents consumer interests before federal, state, and local bodies (including the Public Service Commission), and encourages consumer education and research, it has no enforcement powers. These are vested in the Bureau of Consumer Frauds and Protection within the Department of Law, under the direction of the attorney general. The Public Service Commission, appointed by the governor, has regulatory authority over several areas of key interest to consumers, including gas, electric, and telephone rates. Especially during the 1960s and 1970s, consumer groups complained that the commission was more sensitive to the interests of the utility companies than to those of consumers.

State law outlaws unfair or deceptive trade practices and provides for small claims courts where consumers can take action at little cost to themselves. New York licenses and regulates automobile repair services, permits advertising of prescription drug prices, and requires unit pricing. A "cooling off" period for home purchase contracts is mandated, and standards have been established for mobile home construction. New York has no-fault automobile insurance. In 1974, the legislature outlawed sex discrimination in banking, credit, and insurance policy transactions; the state's fair trade law, which allowed price fixing on certain items, was repealed in 1975. The Fair Credit Reporting Act, passed in 1977, allows consumers access to their credit bureau files.

Consumer protection is also provided at the county and municipal level. In 1975 there were 11 county consumer offices and 11 city and town offices; one of the latter was operated by New York City.

Extremely influential both within the state and throughout the US is the Consumers Union (CU), established as a nonprofit corporation at Mt. Vernon in 1936. CU derives its income solely from sales of its magazine, *Consumer Reports*, and other publications. The magazine embraces many consumer interests, but the bulk of each issue consists of product reports on items as varied as stereos and canned chili. Product tests are conducted by CU's own research staff. Ratings of products may not be cited in advertising or used by product manufacturers or distributors for any commercial purpose.

[32] BANKING

New York City, the major US banking center, was the headquarters for six of the seven largest US banks in 1980. Banking is one of the state's leading industries, ranking 1st in the US in assets and employing 193,966 people in 4,446 establishments as of March 1977; of these, 891 establishments and 120,567 employees were in Manhattan alone.

In 1977, the New York State Banking Department listed 240 commercial banks, 113 chartered by the state and 127 chartered by the federal government. As of 31 December 1978, these banks held total assets of $261.2 billion; deposits totaled $179.3 billion, including $50.5 billion in demand deposits, $73 billion in time deposits, and $55.8 billion in other deposits.

There were 115 mutual savings banks in 1977. As of 31 December 1978, savings banks held total assets of $84.5 billion, time deposits of $76.5 billion, and demand deposits of $1.1 billion. Savings and loan associations in 1977 numbered 133, of which 60 were state chartered and 73 were federally chartered. Their assets totaled $24.9 billion at the close of 1978; time deposits were $20.7 billion. The state also had 1,211 credit unions (95 state, 1,116 federal) in 1977; their combined assets were $2.8 billion in 1978, and their time deposits during the same year reached a total of $2.4 billion.

About one-fifth of the assets of all insured commercial banks in the US are concentrated in the six largest New York banks. At the end of 1978, Citibank, the largest New York bank, ranked 4th in the world and 2d in the US; Chase Manhattan placed 6th in the world and 3d in the US: and the next four largest New York banks were also among the world leaders. Only one major state bank, Marine Midland in Buffalo, had its headquarters outside New York City.

The following is a list of leading New York commercial bank companies, with their assets and deposits at the end of 1978:

NAME	ASSETS ('000)	DEPOSITS ('000)
Citicorp[1]	$87,190,709	$61,115,062
Chase Manhattan Corp.	61,171,529	48,545,820
Manufacturers Hanover Corp.	38,392,178	32,056,693
J. P. Morgan & Co.[2]	37,666,216	28,615,659
Chemical New York Corp.	32,451,000	24,923,000
Bankers Trust New York Corp.	24,446,978	18,424,520
Marine Midland Banks, Inc.	14,225,462	11,426,846

[1] Holding company for Citibank NA.
[2] Holding company for Morgan Guaranty Trust Co.

[33] INSURANCE

Like banking, insurance is big business in New York. Three of the four top US life insurance companies have their headquarters in New York City, and the industry employed 159,754 workers according to the federal census of March 1977.

Premiums written in the state in 1977 totaled $14 billion for all types of insurance. The total included $3.6 billion for life insurance, $4.1 billion for accident and health insurance, $2.6 billion for automobile insurance, and $3.7 billion for other property insurance. Automobile insurance is compulsory for all owners of motor vehicles in the state. A no-fault system is in effect.

In 1978, New Yorkers held 27.2 million life insurance policies, with a value of $235.7 billion (2d in the US and more than 8% of the US total). There were 11.1 million ordinary policies, 8.3 million group policies, 5.9 million credit policies, and 1.9 million industrial policies. The average amount of life insurance per family increased from $8,600 in 1955 to $34,100 in 1978; the 1978 average was slightly below the US average.

In 1977, 66 New York companies and 52 out-of-state companies were licensed to sell life insurance in the state. Premiums paid to state companies totaled $14.8 billion; to out-of-state companies, $27.6 billion. The leading life insurance companies in the state in 1978 were Metropolitan (2d in US), Equitable Life Assurance (3d), New York Life (4th), Mutual of New York (11th), and Teachers Insurance & Annuity (12th).

A total of 528 fire and casualty companies were licensed in the state in 1977, including 208 New York companies, 287 out-of-state US companies, and 33 foreign companies. The leading companies, according to the state, were United States Fire, American Re-Insurance, Motors, Globe Indemnity, and American Home Assurance. About 7% of their total premiums was paid directly by New York State clients.

Five companies provided hospital insurance and eight offered medical and dental insurance in 1977. In 1976, 15,950,000 people were covered by hospital insurance in the state, 15,953,000 by surgical insurance, 15,869,000 by regular medical insurance, and 10,454,000 by major medical insurance.

The New York Insurance Exchange, designed primarily as a marketplace for high-risk commercial insurance and modeled after Lloyd's of London, began operations on 31 March 1980.

[34] SECURITIES

New York City is the capital of the US securities market.

The New York Stock Exchange (NYSE) is by far the largest organized securities market in the nation. It began as an agreement among 24 brokers in 1792; the exchange adopted its first constitution in 1817 and took on its present name in 1863. A clear sign of the growth of the NYSE is the development of its communications system. Stock tickers were first introduced in 1867; a faster ticker, installed in 1930, was capable of printing 500 characters a minute. By 1964, this was no longer fast enough, and a 900-character-a-minute ticker was introduced. Annual registered share volume increased from 1.8 billion in 1965 to 7.6 billion in 1978 following the introduction in 1976 of a new data line capable of handling 36,000 characters a minute.

The value of all shares traded on the NYSE totaled $210.4 billion in 1978, over 84% of the US total. Bond volume for the same year was $4.6 billion (par value). Listings included 2,194 stock issues of 1,581 companies, with a total market value of $822.7 billion; and 2,895 bond issues with a market value of $464.9 billion. The NYSE had 498 member organizations in 1978; the membership price ranged between $46,000 and $105,000, well below the all-time high of $625,000 in 1929.

The American Stock Exchange (AMEX) is the 2d leading US securities market, but the AMEX ranks far below the NYSE in both volume and value of securities. The AMEX traces its origins to the outdoor trading in unlisted securities that began on Wall and Hanover streets in the 1840s; the exchange was organized as the New York Curb Agency in 1908, and adopted its current name in 1953. Constitutional changes in 1976 for the first time permitted qualified issues to be traded on both the AMEX and NYSE as well as on other exchanges. This Intermarket Trading System (ITS) began in 1978. In 1978, 992.2 million shares valued at $15.2 billion were traded on the AMEX; the principal amount of all bonds traded in 1979 was $547.2 billion. The AMEX had 435 member firms in 1979. The price of a seat on the exchange ranged from $40,000 to $90,000; the all-time high, in 1929, was $254,000.

New York City is also a major center for trading in commodity futures. Leading commodity exchanges are the New York Coffee and Sugar Exchange; the New York Cocoa Exchange; the New York Cotton Exchange; the Commodity Exchange, Inc. (COMEX), specializing in gold, silver, and copper futures; and the New York Mercantile Exchange, which trades in futures for potatoes, platinum, palladium, silver coins, beef, and gold, among other items.

Bonds may be issued by cities, counties, towns, villages, school districts, and fire districts, as well as by quasi-independent authorities. Some 41 such agencies were established during the Rockefeller administration, primarily to undertake building programs during a period when state voters were regularly turning down bond issues. These authorities did not require voter approval to issue bonds; on the other hand, the bonds they did issue were backed by the "moral authority" of the state government, rather than by its "full faith and credit." That moral authority was put to the test in 1975, when the state government stepped in to save the New York State Urban Development Corporation from bankruptcy.

With the approval of the state legislature, New York City suspended the repayment of principal to its own noteholders in 1975, during the fiscal crisis. The noteholders were then encouraged to exchange their holdings for longer-term securities issued by the Municipal Assistance Corporation.

35 PUBLIC FINANCE

New York State and New York City have the 2d and 3d largest budgets (behind California) of any state or municipality in the US. The wide range of services offered, combined with a shrinking tax base, led to serious financial trouble for both the state and the city during the mid-1970s.

The New York State budget is prepared by the Division of the Budget and submitted annually by the governor to the legislature for amendment and approval. The fiscal year runs from 1 April to 31 March.

Under the Rockefeller administration, the state budget expanded rapidly from about $1.8 billion in 1958/59 to $8.5 billion in 1973/74. The following is a summary of revenues and expenditures by the State of New York for 1978/79 and 1979/80 (in thousands):

REVENUES	1978/79 (ACTUAL)	1979/80 (EST.)
Personal income taxes	$ 4,893,868	$ 5,860,000
User taxes and fees	3,905,259	4,078,000
Business taxes	1,904,790	2,050,000
Federal revenue sharing	256,531	254,000
Bond funds	124,720	124,100
Other receipts	851,212	741,300
TOTALS	$11,936,380	$13,107,400

EXPENDITURES		
Local assistance	$ 7,099,801	$ 7,628,346
State operations	3,204,479	3,532,131
Capital construction	381,763	516,633
Debt service	521,062	595,287
Other expenditures	724,268	834,894
TOTALS	$11,931,373	$13,107,291

Actual consolidated expenditures for 1978/79, including federal grants and other receipts that do not appear in the general budget, totaled $20.2 billion. Of that, 34% went to education, 30% to social development (including welfare), 11% to health, and 10% to transportation.

The annual budget for New York City is prepared by the comptroller and submitted to the Board of Estimate for revision and approval. The fiscal year is 1 July–30 June. In 1952/53, the city's budgeted appropriations totaled $1.5 billion; 20 years later that total had risen to $9.9 billion. The following is a summary of current budgeted revenues and expenditures for 1978/79 and 1979/80 (in millions):

REVENUES	1978/79	1979/80
Real estate tax	$ 3,142	$ 3,084
Other taxes	3,165	3,384
Federal aid	2,868	2,363
State aid	2,895	2,759
Capital funds	524	348
Other funds	872	901
TOTALS	$13,466	$12,839

EXPENDITURES		
Social services	$ 3,202	$ 2,640
Education	2,170	2,329
City University	440	480
Hospitals	400	427
Police	643	674
Fire	302	321
Pensions	1,197	1,220
Debt service	1,500	1,352
Municipal Assistance Corp.	493	368
Other expenditures	3,119	3,028
TOTALS	$13,466	$12,839

As of 1977, the total debt of state and local governments in New York was $46.1 billion, or 18% of the total for all 50 states; on a per capita basis, New York's debt ($2,573) ranked 2d among the 50 states, behind Alaska. New York City's inability to service its $12.3 billion debt in 1975 brought it to the brink of bankruptcy. For years the city had kept afloat through clever bookkeeping: postponing current expenses, using capital funds to finance current deficits, increasing fringe benefits instead of wages for its municipal employees, counting as current revenues millions of dollars in federal funds that had not been—and would not be—granted. In addition, New York City had been providing services—including a tuition-free university and an extensive network of municipal hospitals—matched by no other US city.

By 1975, with the city increasingly in the red, investors had decided that city notes were too risky; unable to raise cash, the city could not redeem the notes of earlier investors. A moratorium on repayments was declared, and a new bond-issuing body, the Municipal Assistance Corp. (MAC, or "Big Mac"), was created. Even so, extensive borrowing from union pension funds and the establishment by the US Congress of a short-term federal line of credit were necessary before bankruptcy was averted. New York City's debt as of 30 June 1979 was down to $7 billion; however, if MAC's debt of $5.9 billion is included, the city's gross debt was actually $12.9 billion.

36 TAXATION

On a per capita basis, New York's taxes are well above the national average, but far from the highest. State tax revenues rank 2d to California's.

Personal income tax rates in 1980 ranged from 2% on the first $1,000 to 14% on income over $23,000. The basic corporate tax was 10% on net income. The state imposes a 4% sales tax, but cities and towns may levy an additional tax. The estate tax ranges from 2% of the first $50,000 to a maximum of 21%. Other taxes include charges on motor fuel, cigarettes, alcoholic beverages, and motor vehicle usage, plus a bank tax, unincorporated business tax, insurance taxes, pari-mutuel taxes, and a real estate transfer tax. Receipts in 1978/79 totaled $11.6 billion, with $12.7 billion estimated for 1979/80.

More than half of New York City's tax revenues come from property taxes, which were estimated at $3 billion in 1979/80. The city also has a 4% sales tax.

New York ranked 2d to California in federal taxes paid and federal grants received in 1976. The state tax burden was $32 billion ($1,770 per capita), while its share of federal spending was $27.3 billion ($1,510 per capita). In 1977, New Yorkers filed nearly 6.9 million personal income tax returns and paid taxes totaling $13.3 billion.

³⁷ECONOMIC POLICY

To attract new businesses and to prevent established enterprises from leaving, the state launched an aggressive program of development incentives during the 1970s.

Among the incentives offered by New York are government-owned industrial park sites, state aid in the creation of county and city master plans, state recruitment and screening of industrial employees, programs for the promotion of research and development, and state help in bidding on federal procurement contracts. The state agency with primary responsibility for development planning is the Division of Industrial and Corporate Development within the Department of Commerce. Representatives of the division call on firms throughout the US, Canada, and Europe; the division also maintains representatives in Montreal and Toronto, Canada, and in Washington, D.C.

The state provides specific tax incentives for economic development. Among these are an investment tax credit of 4%, employment incentive credit of up to 6% on new buildings, machinery, and equipment; a job incentive credit applied both to corporate taxes and local property taxes; and a tax credit program designed to encourage the location of export-oriented industries in the state. Tax credits are also offered on the purchase and maintenance of pollution-control equipment.

³⁸HEALTH

Health presents a mixed picture in New York State. Life expectancy for state residents is shorter than the national average. But the state has some of the finest hospital and medical education facilities in the US—for those who can afford them.

New York tied with Arizona for 31st place in average life expectancy during 1969–71. The average life expectancy for both sexes was 70.55 years, compared with the national average of 70.75; 74.15 was the figure for women, 66.95 for men.

Infant deaths per 1,000 live births were 12.3 for whites and 21.7 for nonwhites in 1977; both rates equaled the national averages. New York State was one of the first states to liberalize its abortion laws, in 1970. A total of 147,655 legal abortions were performed in the state in 1977, of which 132,608 were on state residents. In New York City, there were 106,154 live births and 87,796 legal abortions—about 8 legal abortions for every 10 live births.

The state ranks above the national average in deaths due to heart disease, malignant neoplasms (cancer), influenza and pneumonia, and cirrhosis of the liver, but below the national average in deaths due to cerebrovascular diseases, arteriosclerosis, and accidents. Leading causes of death in 1977 (with their rates per 100,000 population) included heart disease, 389; cerebrovascular diseases, 72; cancer of the digestive organs and peritoneum, 62; cancer of the respiratory organs, 47; accidents, 32; diseases of the arteries, 22; and breast cancer, 21. Cardiovascular diseases of all types were responsible for 53% of all deaths recorded in 1977.

Marked progress has been made against many childhood diseases. Reported cases of diphtheria dropped from 22,630 in 1910 to 4 in 1977; measles, from 69,878 cases in 1910 to 4,763 in 1977 (up from a low of 673 in 1972); and whooping cough, from

24,848 cases in 1935 to 141 in 1977. In addition, reported cases of typhoid fever declined from 8,536 in 1910 to 37 in 1977, and of tuberculosis from 37,963 in 1910 to 2,434. Cases of rubella, however, increased from 805 in 1976 to 3,736 in 1977, reversing a steady decline from 15,164 in 1955.

Major public health problems in the 1970s included drug abuse, alcoholism, and venereal disease. There are no reliable estimates for the total number of addicts, although in 1978, 38,416 addicts were receiving treatment at state-run facilities, 74% of them in New York City. The majority of addicts under treatment were on methadone maintenance programs. Possession of small amounts of marijuana (up to ⅞ of an ounce, or about 25 grams) is a violation of a state law passed in 1977, and sale of small amounts is a misdemeanor. The law, however, is rarely enforced.

Rough estimates placed New York 5th in the nation in the number of alcoholics per 100,000 population in 1970—5,500, compared with the US average rate of 5,400, which rose to 5,750 in 1975. Of the estimated 647,300 alcoholics in the state in 1970, 516,200 were male and 131,100 female. Only 5,933 patients were admitted to facilities for alcoholism treatment (14 state run and one private) during 1977/78. The New York State Research Institute on Alcoholism opened in Buffalo in 1970, and the Advisory Committee on Alcoholism operates under the direction of the Department of Mental Hygiene.

In 1977, 58,282 cases of gonorrhea were reported (the lowest figure since 1971), but public health officials believe the problem is much more widespread than that. Reported cases of syphilis declined dramatically, however, from 64,146 in 1935 to 2,153 in 1977.

During 1977/78, 106,481 patients were admitted to state, private, and local psychiatric centers. There has been a gradual shift away from state treatment of psychiatric patients toward treatment in community mental health facilities. A total of 487,393 persons were treated either as inpatients or outpatients in all state and local programs during 1977/78; of these, 321,522 were treated in clinics, including 8 clinics operated by the New York City Bureau of Child Guidance. As of 31 March 1978, facilities for the mentally retarded had 20,008 residents.

In 1978, New York State had 368 hospitals, with 134,425 beds. Of that total, 289 were general hospitals and 46 were psychiatric hospitals. New York City had 85 community hospitals, with 39,036 beds, a drop from the mid-1970s totals as a result of city budgetary cutbacks. In the state as a whole, hospitals recorded 2,739,053 admissions, performed 1,390,281 surgical operations, had an occupancy rate of 85.1%, and employed 324,091 persons with a total payroll of $4.9 billion (65% of all hospital costs).

Medical personnel licensed to practice in the state as of April 1979 included 51,008 doctors, 14,560 dentists, 187,837 registered nurses, and 64,744 practical nurses. Colleges and universities in the state conferred 9,210 degrees in the health professions in 1977.

More than 88% of all New Yorkers are covered by hospital and surgical insurance. About $3.9 billion in health insurance benefits was paid in 1977. The average daily cost per patient in community hospitals in 1977 was $226, 10th highest in the US and 14% above the national average.

³⁹SOCIAL WELFARE

Social welfare is a major public enterprise in the state; the growth of poverty relief programs has been enormous. In 1977, 1,430,556 New Yorkers were receiving welfare benefits, a 21% drop from the high of 1,802,086 in 1972, but a 90% increase over the figure for 1965. The number of children qualifying under aid to families with dependent children rose from 548,011 in 1965 to 1,213,391 in 1977. In New York City, 942,480 city residents received public assistance in 1977, almost 68% of all state welfare recipients and about 13% of the city's population.

An estimated 1,458,000 New Yorkers (1st in the US) took part in the federal food stamp program in 1978. Coupons worth approximately $786,000,000 were issued, for which the federal subsidy was $389,000,000. During that year, 1,760,000 pupils participated in the national school lunch program, at a cost to the federal government of $143,100,000.

Federal Social Security benefits paid to 1,869,400 retired workers and their dependents in 1977 totaled $5.2 billion, for an average monthly payment of $264.40 (3d in the US). Survivors' benefits, paid to 597,100 state residents, were $1.7 billion in 1977. The aged received an additional $205,300,000 through the Supplemental Security Income program. Disability benefits in Social Security and supplemental programs totaled $1.5 billion.

The state had 1,027 nursing homes with 104,500 beds and 97,300 resident patients in 1976. The poor quality of many nursing homes was revealed in a statewide scandal in the mid-1970s, after which the legislature passed new laws regulating nursing home practices.

In 1978, 1,415,000 New Yorkers took part in federally aided vocational programs at a total cost of $551,900,000. In 1977, $475,700,000 was spent on workers' compensation. About 1,767,000 persons received unemployment insurance benefits in 1978. Benefits paid totaled $1.1 billion; the average weekly benefit was $83.74. Maximum weekly payments ranged from $25 to $125, depending on prior income.

40 HOUSING

Census data show that housing in New York State differs in many important ways from the national housing pattern.

In 1970, the state had 6,299,582 housing units, of which 2,924,281 were in New York City. The first striking feature of the state's housing stock is its age: nearly 56% of housing units in the state (62% in the city) were in structures built in 1939 or before, compared with the US average of 41%. Only 17% of New York State's dwelling units were built between 1960 and 1970, and only 14% of New York City's, while the US average was 25%. (The contrast between New York State and California is particularly great: as of 1970, 76% of all California dwelling units had been built since 1940, compared with 45% in New York State and 38% in New York City.) Although New York's housing stock is older than the nation's as a whole, housing costs are higher: both rental costs and the median value of single-family, owner-occupied dwellings in New York exceed the national average.

A second striking feature of housing in the state is the dominance of multiunit dwellings. New York State has the lowest percentage of owner-occupied housing of any state in the US except Hawaii. In 1970, 40% of the state's housing units were single-unit structures, compared with a national average of 69%; 31% of all units in the state (but only 15% of all units in the US) were in buildings with 10 housing units or more. Even within New York State, New York City is unique. In 1970, 58% of the city's housing units were in structures of 10 units or more; for Buffalo the comparable figure was 4%. There are great differences within New York City: in 1970, 77% of the housing units in the Bronx and 92% of those in Manhattan were in large multiunit structures, compared with 37% in Queens and 13% on Staten Island. Other housing differences in New York City offer far greater contrasts than units per structure: the posh penthouses on the East Side of Manhattan and the hovels of the South Bronx both count as "multiunit dwellings."

Because single-family homes tend to be more self-sufficient and better stocked with appliances, New York State ranks somewhat below the national standard for these conveniences. Thus a smaller percentage of New Yorkers had washing machines, clothes dryers, dishwashers, or freezers in 1970 than the US population at large. The only appliances for which New Yorkers ranked above the national average were television sets and room air conditioners (since private homes often have central systems rather than room air conditioners, and apartment dwellers rarely have a choice in the matter).

In 1970, New York had the lowest vacancy rate for rental units of any state in the country, and tied for the lowest vacancy rate in owner-occupied units. The tight housing market—which may have contributed to the exodus of New Yorkers from the state—was not helped by the slump in housing construction during the mid-1970s. In 1972, permits were issued for 111,282 units valued at $2.1 billion; by 1978, however, only 43,100 units worth $1.2 billion were authorized. The drop in construction of multiunit dwellings was even more noticeable: from 64,959 units in 1972 to about 19,000 units in 1978. The overall decline in construction was coupled with a drastic drop in new public housing: from 8,039 units in 1971 (4,392 of them in New York City) to only 1,009 in 1977 (718 in New York City).

Direct state aid to housing is limited. Consolidated expenditures for housing and community development were estimated at $236 million, about 1% of the consolidated state budget in 1979/80. Governmental and quasi-independent agencies dealing with housing include the Division of Housing and Community Renewal, which makes loans and grants to municipalities for slum clearance and construction of low-income housing; the New York State Housing Finance Agency, empowered to issue notes and bonds for various construction projects, not limited to housing; the State of New York Mortgage Agency, which may purchase existing mortgage loans from banks in order to make funds available for the banks to make new mortgage loans; the Urban Development Guarantee Fund of New York, which guarantees loans to small businesses and owners of housing unable to get credit through conventional financing sources; and the New York State Urban Development Corporation (UDC), a multibillion-dollar agency designed to raise capital for all types of construction, including low-income housing. In 1975, the UDC was unable to meet its debt-service obligations and defaulted on $130 million in short-term notes until the legislature created the Project Finance Agency to restore the corporation's credit. The UDC's difficulties were the first sign that the finances of both New York State and New York City were reaching a crisis.

41 EDUCATION

The educational establishment of New York State is larger and better funded than that of most countries. In 1978/79, the state ranked 2d behind California in both public school enrollment and educational funding. New York has one of the nation's largest public university systems, and an extensive system of private schools and universities. Whether this vast educational establishment could survive the declining enrollments expected during the 1980s was a source of concern as the decade opened.

In some ways, the average New Yorker is less educated than other Americans. The illiteracy rate in 1970 was 1.4%, above the US average of 1.2% and the highest for any northern state except Alaska. The percentage of high school graduates—66% in 1970—among all New Yorkers was slightly below the US average, but the percentage of black high school graduates was much better than the national average: 40% for New York, as compared with 31% for the US.

The quality of education is notoriously difficult to measure, but in New York City, at least, the signs were not encouraging during the 1970s. Standardized reading tests showed that only 45% of New York City public school students were reading at standard US grade level in 1974/75; the following year the figure dipped to 43%, with 21% reading two or more years below grade level. In the largely Hispanic areas of East Harlem and the South Bronx, no schools managed to meet the US standard. However, some school districts performed extremely well, and New York City's special high schools for gifted students are among the finest in the US.

In 1977/78, a total of 3,778,039 students were enrolled in all elementary and secondary schools in the state. Enrollment in public schools alone totaled 3,189,781 students; of these, nearly 6% were in kindergarten, 43% in grades 1–6, 49% in grades 7–12, and 2% in ungraded schools. Public schools in the state employed 196,546 professionals in 1977/78, of whom 170,706 were classroom teachers. About 30% of the teachers and 32% of the students were in New York City. The average dropout rate for public high schools in the state was 6% in 1976/77. Each of the boroughs of New York City had a dropout rate higher than the statewide average; the rate for Manhattan was 14%, up from 11% in 1975.

New York State had 1,940 nonpublic elementary and secondary schools in the fall of 1978. Of these, the 1,119 Roman Catholic schools had 77% of the total enrollment; there were 253,112 pupils in grades K–6 and 197,427 in grades 7–12. In addition, the state had 182 Jewish schools, with 47,404 pupils; 56 Lutheran schools, with 10,037 students; 36 Episcopalian schools, with 5,584 students; 46 Seventh Day Adventist schools, with 3,207 pupils; 39 schools (7,108 pupils) affiliated with other religious groups (including Society of Friends, Mennonites, Greek Orthodox, Russian Orthodox, Methodists, and Baptists); and 462 nondenominational schools, enrolling 64,379 students.

Enrollment in all institutions of higher learning totaled 936,861 in the fall of 1977. Of that total, 608,070 students were enrolled full-time at public colleges and universities, and 260,295 at private institutions. About 23% of all full-time students were in public two-year colleges. A total of 133,573 degrees were conferred in 1977, of which 18% were in education, 13% in business and management, 12% in social sciences, and 7% in the health professions. The remaining degrees were in a wide variety of other fields.

There are two massive public university systems: the State University of New York (SUNY) and the City University of New York (CUNY). Established in 1948, SUNY by 1978 was the largest university system in the country, with 4 university centers, 4 health sciences centers, 13 university colleges of arts and sciences, 4 specialized colleges, 6 agricultural and technical colleges, 5 statutory colleges (allied with private universities), and 30 locally sponsored community colleges. SUNY's total enrollment in 1978 was 348,361, of whom 222,081 students were full-time. Of the university centers, Buffalo enrolled 21,611 students; Albany, 15,216; Stony Brook, 14,314, and Binghamton, 10,231. The City University of New York was created in 1961, though many of its most important component institutions were founded much earlier. CUNY's total enrollment in the fall of 1979 was more than 176,900, of whom about 116,000 were full-time students. Under an open-enrollment policy adopted in 1970, every New York City resident with a high school diploma is guaranteed the chance to earn a college degree within the CUNY system (which CUNY campus the student attends is determined by grade point average).

The oldest private university in the state is Columbia University, founded in New York City as King's College in 1754. Columbia had 17,223 students in 1977; another 2,250 (all women) were enrolled in Barnard College, and there were 5,433 students (male and female) in Columbia University Teachers College. Other major private institutions include Cornell University (1865), with 18,651 students in 1977, of whom 10,895 were in endowed colleges, 7,012 in statutory colleges, and 744 in the medical center; Fordham University (1841), 15,163; New York University (1831), 31,197; St. John's University (1870), 17,023; Syracuse University (1870), 19,806; and the Univesity of Rochester (1850), 7,881. Among the state's many smaller but highly distinguished institutions are Hamilton College, the Juilliard School, the New School for Social Research, Rensselaer Polytechnic Institute, Rockefeller University, Sarah Lawrence College, Vassar College, and Yeshiva University.

The educational work of New York State is vested in the Department of Education, under the legislative direction of the Board of Regents of the University of the State of New York. The Board of Regents consists of 15 persons elected, one each year, to 15-year terms by the state legislature. The commissioner of education, who heads the state Department of Education, also serves as president of the University of the State of New York (which should not be confused with SUNY). Unique features of education in the state are the "Regents exams," uniform subject examinations administered to all high school students, and the Regents Scholarships Tuition Assistance Program (TAP), a higher education aid program which in 1977/78 distributed $242,636,000 in scholarships, fellowships, and grants to 371,995 students. Recipients of these awards must be in full-time attendance at an approved institution in New York State and must have resided in the state at least one year prior to enrollment. More than 235,000 student loans worth $446,108,978 were guaranteed by the state in 1978/79. The state passed a "truth in testing" law in 1979, giving students the right to see their graded college and graduate school entrance examinations, as well as information on how the test results were validated.

During 1978, the public school system consisted of 742 districts; New York City constituted a single district. Receipts of all public school systems in the state totaled nearly $8 billion in 1976/77, of which $3.1 billion came from state sources and $345 million from federal sources. New York City, which accounted for 33% of all educational revenues, received 59% of the federal aid. In 1977/78, the state ranked 2d to California in total expenditures (more than $8 billion), 2d behind Alaska in expenditures per pupil based on average daily attendance ($2,527), and 6th in per capita spending ($447). Teachers' salaries averaged $18,600 in 1979, 2d only to Alaska and 24% above the US average.

[42] ARTS

New York City is the cultural capital of the state, and leads the nation in both the creative and the performing arts.

The state's foremost arts center is Lincoln Center for the Performing Arts, in Manhattan. Facilities at Lincoln Center include Avery Fisher Hall (which opened as Philharmonic Hall in 1962), the home of the New York Philharmonic; the Metropolitan Opera House (1966), where the Metropolitan Opera Company performs; and the New York State Theater, which presents both the New York City Opera and the New York City Ballet. Also at Lincoln Center are the Juilliard School and the Library and Museum of the Performing Arts. The best-known arts center outside New York City is the Saratoga Performing Arts Center at Saratoga Springs. During the summer, the Saratoga Center presents performances by the New York City Ballet and the Philadelphia Orchestra. Artpark, a state park at Lewiston, has a 2,400-seat theater and offers art exhibits during the summer. Classical music, opera, and plays are performed at the Chautauqua Festival, which has been held every summer since 1874.

In addition to its many museums, New York City has more than 350 galleries devoted to the visual and plastic arts. The city's most famous "bohemian" district is Greenwich Village, which still holds an annual outdoor art show, but since the 1950s the havens for most artists have been SoHo (Manhattan south of Houston Street) and, more recently, NoHo (immediately north of Houston Street). During the late 1940s and early 1950s, abstract painters including Jackson Pollock, Mark Rothko, and Willem de Kooning helped make the city a center of the avant-garde. At the same time, poets such as Frank O'Hara and John Ashbery sought verbal analogues to developments in the visual arts, and an urbane, improvisatory literature was created. New York has enjoyed a vigorous poetic tradition throughout its history, most notably with the works of Walt Whitman (who served as editor of the *Brooklyn Eagle* from 1846 to 1848) and through Hart Crane's mythic vision of the city in his long poem, *The Bridge*. The emergence of New York as the center of the US publishing and communications industries fostered the growth of a literary marketplace, attracting writers from across the world. The simultaneous growth of the Broadway stage made New York City a vital forum for playwriting, songwriting, and theatrical production.

There are more than 35 Broadway theaters—large theaters in midtown Manhattan presenting full-scale, sometimes lavish productions with top-rank performers. "Off Broadway" productions are often of high professional quality, though typically in smaller theaters, outside the midtown district, often with smaller casts and less costly settings. "Off-Off Broadway" productions range from small experimental theaters on the fringes of the city to performances in nightclubs and cabarets. The New York metropolitan area has hundreds of motion picture theaters—more than 65 in Manhattan alone, not counting special series at the Museum of Modern Art and other cultural institutions. In the 1970s, New York City made a determined effort to attract motion picture production companies.

New York's leading symphony orchestra is the New York Philharmonic-Symphony Orchestra, whose history dates back to the founding of the Philharmonic Society of New York in 1842. Among the principal conductors of the orchestra have been Gustav Mahler, Josef Willem Mengelberg, Wilhelm Furtwängler, Arturo Toscanini, Leonard Bernstein, Pierre Boulez, and Zubin Mehta. Leading US and foreign orchestras and soloists appear at both Avery Fisher Hall and Carnegie Hall, built in 1892 and famed for its acoustics. Important orchestras outside New York City include the Buffalo Philharmonic, which performs at Kleinhans Music Hall, the Rochester Philharmonic, and the orchestra of the Eastman School of Music (University of Rochester).

New York City is one of the world centers of ballet. Of special renown are the New York City Ballet and its principal choreographer, George Balanchine. Many other ballet companies, including the American Ballet Theatre and the Alvin Ailey American Dance Theatre, make regular appearances in New York.

Jazz and popular artists perform at more than 60 night spots in New York City. The Westbury Music Fair (Long Island) presents a wide-ranging annual program of musical entertainment, and many leading US performers play the Catskill resorts regularly. New York City is a major link in the US songwriting, music publishing, and recording industries.

43 LIBRARIES AND MUSEUMS

New York State has three of the world's largest libraries, and New York City has several of the world's most famous museums.

The state had 715 public libraries, 245 academic libraries, and 1,278 special libraries in 1977. The New York State Library in Albany coordinates 22 public library systems covering every county in the state, with book holdings of 45,372,507 volumes and a combined circulation of 79,973,699 volumes. The libraries received $192,602,543 during that year, of which $4,845,547 came from the federal government, $31,148,479 from the state government, and the rest from local sources. The New York State Library alone had 1,637,000 volumes in 1977/78.

The leading public library systems and their operating statistics as of the late 1970s were the New York Public Library, 8,549,843 volumes and 9,164,156 circulation; the Nassau County system, 5,397,465 volumes and 10,867,631 circulation; the Brooklyn Public Library, 3,648,282 volumes and 6,398,092 circulation; Queens Borough Public Library, 3,225,655 volumes and 6,225,518 circulation; Suffolk Cooperative system, 3,204,580 volumes and 8,277,068 circulation; and Buffalo and Erie County system, 3,072,063 volumes and 5,297,965 circulation.

Chartered in 1895, the New York Public Library is the most complete municipal library system in the world. The library's main building, at 5th Avenue and 42d St., is one of the city's best-known landmarks; 82 operating branch libraries serve the

needs of Manhattan, the Bronx, and Staten Island. The New York Public Library (NYPL) is a repository for every book published in the US. Of its 8,549,943-volume book stock in 1979, 4,950,955 were in the research library and 3,598,888 were available for circulation. The library system also held 3,301,344 recordings, 1,468,398 microfilm and microfiche volumes, and 11,370,919 manuscripts. There are important collections in US history, economics, and black and Jewish studies. The NYPL also operates the Library and Museum of the Performing Arts at Lincoln Center.

Two private university libraries—at Columbia University (4,832,691 volumes) and Cornell University (4,095,234)—ranked among the world's major libraries. Other major university libraries in the state, with their 1978 book holdings, are State University of New York at Buffalo, 1,810,698; New York University, 1,800,000; the University of Rochester, 1,800,000; and Syracuse University, 1,752,453. Libraries at all branches of the State University of New York held a total of 9,470,491 catalogued volumes in 1979; the libraries of the City University of New York had over 3,600,000 volumes.

There are about 150 major museums in New York State, of which perhaps 80% are in New York City. In addition, some 300 sites of historic importance are maintained by local historical societies.

Major art museums in New York City include the Metropolitan Museum of Art, with more than 1 million art objects and paintings from virtually every period and culture; the Cloisters, a branch of the Metropolitan Museum devoted entirely to medieval art and architecture; the Frick collection; the Whitney Museum of American Art; the Brooklyn Museum; and two large modern collections, the Museum of Modern Art and the Solomon R. Guggenheim Museum (the latter designed by Frank Lloyd Wright in a distinctive spiral pattern). The Jewish Museum, the Museum of the American Indian, and the museum and reference library of the Hispanic Society of America specialize in cultural history. The sciences are represented by the American Museum of Natural History, famed for its dioramas of humans and animals in natural settings, and for its massive dinosaur skeletons; the Hayden Planetarium; and the New York Botanical Garden and New York Zoological Society Park (Bronx Zoo), both in the Bronx. Also of interest are the Museum of the City of New York, the Museum of the New-York Historical Society, and the South Street Seaport Museum.

The New York State Museum in Albany contains natural history collections and historical artifacts. Buffalo has several museums of note, including the Albright-Knox Art Gallery (for contemporary art), the Buffalo Museum of Science, and the Buffalo and Erie County Historical Society museum. Among the state's many other fine museums, the Everson Museum of Art (Syracuse), the Rochester Museum and Science Center, the National Baseball Hall of Fame and Museum (Cooperstown), and the Corning Museum of Glass deserve special mention.

44 COMMUNICATIONS

New York City is the hub of the entire US communications network.

Postal service was established in New York State in 1692; at the same time, the first General Letter Office was begun in New York City. By the middle of the 19th century, postal receipts in the state accounted for more than 20% of the US total. "Fast mail" service by train started in the 1870s, with the main routes leading from New York City to either Chicago or St. Louis via Indianapolis and Cincinnati. Mail was carried by air experimentally from Garden City to Mineola, Long Island, in 1911; the first regular airmail service in the US started in 1917, between New York City and Washington, D.C., via Philadelphia.

Since then, the volume both of mail and of postal business has grown enormously. Postal receipts in New York City alone totaled $559,199,925 in 1977/78. In the state as a whole, there were 81,400 postal employees (1st in the US, 12% of the national total) and more than 1,600 post offices in 1977.

As of 31 December 1978, New York State had 13,065,378 telephones, of which 3,647,527 were commercial and 9,417,851 residential. About 96% of all state residences had telephone service. During 1978, some 21.2 billion local calls and 1.6 billion toll calls originated in the state. The telephone system had 85,917,623 mi (138,271,268 km) of wire in cable, 99,864 mi (160,716 km) of aerial wire, 15,078 mi (24,266 km) of tube in coaxial cable, and 3,770 mi (6,067 km) of radio relay systems.

More than 91% of the telephones in the state are owned by Bell System affiliates. Telephone service is provided by the New York Telephone Co. and Continental Telephone Co. of Upstate New York. In 1978, the New York Telephone Co. had 76,725 employees and net operating revenues of $1.7 billion. Its parent company, American Telephone and Telegraph (AT&T), is the largest US utility and, by most standards of measurement, the largest private firm in the world. AT&T, which has its headquarters in New York City, had assets of $4.2 billion, net operating revenues of $1.1 billion, and a net income of $4.1 billion in 1978.

Domestic telegraph service is provided by the Western Union Telegraph Co. ITT World Communications, RCA Global Communications, and Western Union International offer telex service. All four companies have their headquarters in New York City.

New York State had 160 AM stations and 117 FM stations in 1978. Thirty-five of those stations broadcast an average of at least one hour per day in languages other than English; there were two all-Spanish stations, both in New York City. The city government operates its own radio stations, WNYC-AM and WNYC-FM, devoted largely to classical music and educational programming.

There were 29 commercial television stations in the state in 1978; of these, 7 were operating in New York City. The city is the headquarters for all the major US television networks, including the American Broadcasting Co., Columbia Broadcasting System, National Broadcasting Co., Westinghouse Broadcasting (Group W), Metromedia, and the Public Broadcasting Service (PBS). Educational television stations serve all the state's major populated areas, and the metropolitan area's PBS affiliate, WNET (licensed in Newark, N.J.), is a leading producer of programs for the network. As of December 1979, 185 cable television systems in the state had 1,080,807 subscribers, of whom 144,500 were in New York City. Virtually every household had at least one television set, and the percentage of households with two or more sets was above the US average during the 1970s.

45PRESS

A pioneer in the establishment of freedom of the press, New York is a leader in the US newspaper, magazine, and book publishing industries.

The first major test of press freedom in the colonies came in 1734, when a German-American printer, John Peter Zenger, was arrested on charges of sedition and libel. In his newspaper, the *New-York Weekly Journal*, Zenger had published articles criticizing the colonial governor of New York. Zenger's lawyer, Andrew Hamilton, argued that because the charges in the article were true, they could not be libelous. The jury's acceptance of this argument freed Zenger and established the right of the press to criticize those in power.

Two later decisions involving a New York newspaper also struck blows for press freedom. In *New York Times v. Sullivan* (1964), the US Supreme Court ruled that a public official could not win a libel suit against a newspaper unless he could show that its statements about him were not only false but also malicious or in reckless disregard of the truth. In 1971, the *New York Times* was again involved in a landmark case, when the federal government tried—and failed—to prevent the newspaper from pub-

lishing the Pentagon Papers, a collection of secret documents concerning the war in Viet-Nam.

All of New York City's major newspapers have claims to fame. The *Times* is the nation's "newspaper of record," excelling in the publication of full texts of lengthy excerpts of major speeches, press conferences, and government reports. It is widely circulated on microfilm to US libraries and is often cited in historical research. The *New York Post*, founded in 1801, is the oldest US newspaper published continuously without change of name. The *New York Daily News* has the largest daily and Sunday circulation of any newspaper in the state. The *Wall Street Journal*, published Monday through Friday, is the only truly national newspaper, presenting mostly business news in four regional editions. Many other historic New York papers first merged and then—bearing compound names like the *Herald-Tribune*, *Journal-American*, and *World-Telegram & Sun*—died in the 1950s and 1960s.

In 1979, New York had 21 morning newspapers, with a total average daily circulation of 4,256,355; 59 evening newspapers, with total circulation of 2,695,790; and 34 Sunday newspapers, with total circulation of 6,494,944. The following table shows leading newspapers in New York State, with their average daily and Sunday circulations in 1979:

AREA	NAME	DAILY	SUNDAY
Albany	Times-Union (m,S)	86,174	151,974
Buffalo	Courier-Express (m,S)	126,826	257,193
	News (e,S)	266,260	153,384
Long Island	Newsday (e,S)	494,998	519,207
New York City	Daily News (m,S)	1,824,836	2,656,981
	Post (e)	612,576	441,566[1]
	Times (m,S)	821,549	1,412,481
	Wall Street Journal (m)	593,154[2]	
Rochester	Democrat & Chronicle (m,S)	126,481 }	228,069
	Times-Union (e)	123,371 }	
Syracuse	Post-Standard (m,S)	88,634 }	239,520
	Herald-Journal (e,S)	120,342 }	

[1]Weekend edition published Saturdays.
[2]Eastern edition only.

The leading newspaper chain is the Gannett group, which had newspapers in 17 cities in 1979. All the major news agencies have offices in New York City, and the Associated Press has its headquarters there.

Many leading US magazines are published in New York City, including the newsmagazines *Time* and *Newsweek*, business journals like *Fortune*, *Forbes*, and *Business Week*, and hundreds of consumer and trade publications. *Reader's Digest*, with a paid circulation in 1979 of 18,094,192 (2d in the US), is published in Pleasantville. Two weeklies closely identified with New York are of more than local interest. While the *New Yorker* carries up-to-date listings of cultural events and exhibitions in New York City, the excellence of its journalism, criticism, fiction, and cartoons has long made it a literary standard-bearer for the entire nation. *New York* magazine influenced the writing style and graphic design of the 1960s and set the pattern for a new wave of state and local magazines that avoided boosterism in favor of independent reporting and commentary. Another weekly, the *Village Voice* (actually a tabloid newspaper) became the prototype for a host of alternative or "underground" journals during the 1960s.

New York City is also the center of the nation's book-publishing industry. Among those publishers listed by *Fortune* magazine as among the 500 largest US industrial corporations in 1979 were McGraw-Hill, Macmillan, and Harcourt Brace Jovanovich, all headquartered in Manhattan's midtown area. As of 1980, there were almost 400 publishing companies in Manhattan.

46ORGANIZATIONS

The United Nations is the best-known organization to have its headquarters in New York. The UN Secretariat, completed in 1951, remains one of the most familiar landmarks on the East Side of New York City.

Hundreds of US nonprofit organizations also have their national headquarters in New York City. General and service organizations operating out of New York City include the American Field Service, Boys Clubs of America, Girls Clubs of America, Girl Scouts of the USA, National Council of Young Men's Christian Associations of the USA (YMCA), Young Women's Christian Associations of the USA (YWCA), and Associated YM-YWHAs of Greater New York (the Jewish equivalent of the YMCA and YWCA). Among the cultural and educational groups are the American Academy of Arts and Letters, Authors League of America, Modern Language Association of America, PEN American Center, and New York Academy of Sciences.

Among the environmental and animal welfare organizations with headquarters in the city are the American Society for the Prevention of Cruelty to Animals (ASPCA), Friends of Animals, Fund for Animals, National Audubon Society, Bide-A-Wee Home Association, Environmental Defense Fund, and American Kennel Club.

Many medical, health, and charitable organizations have their national offices in New York City, including Alcoholics Anonymous, American Foundation for the Blind, National Society to Prevent Blindness, CARE, American Cancer Society, United Cerebral Palsy Associations, Child Welfare League of America, Children's Aid Society, American Diabetes Association, National Multiple Sclerosis Society, Muscular Dystrophy Association, and Planned Parenthood Federation of America.

Leading ethnic and religious organizations based in the city include the American Bible Society, National Conference of Christians and Jews, Hadassah, United Jewish Appeal, American Jewish Committee, American Jewish Congress, National Association for the Advancement of Colored People (NAACP), United Negro College Fund, Congress of Racial Equality, National Urban League, and Salvation Army.

There are many commercial, trade, and professional organizations headquartered in New York City. Among the better known are the American Arbitration Association, American Booksellers Association, American Institute of Chemical Engineers, American Society of Civil Engineers, American Society of Composers, Authors, and Publishers (ASCAP), Edison Electric Institute, American Insurance Association, Magazine Publishers Association, American Management Associations, American Society of Mechanical Engineers, American Institute of Physics, and American Society of Travel Agents.

Sports organizations centered in New York City include the National Football League, the American and National Leagues of Professional Baseball Clubs, National Basketball Association, Ladies Professional Golf Association, North American Soccer League, and the US Tennis Association. There are also several influential political and international-affairs groups: the American Civil Liberties Union, Council on Foreign Relations, Trilateral Commission, United Nations Association of the USA, and US Committee for UNICEF.

Major organizations with their headquarters outside New York City include the Consumers Union of the United States (Mt. Vernon), US Chess Federation (New Windsor), and the Thoroughbred Racing Association of North America (Lake Success). Virtually every other US organization has one or more chapters within the state.

47 TOURISM, TRAVEL, AND RECREATION

New York State is a popular destination for both domestic and foreign travelers. Although New York City draws over 45% of state tourist revenues, each of the major state regions has features of interest.

Cheaper transatlantic fares and the devaluation of the US dollar relative to foreign currencies during the 1970s made travel to the US more attractive to foreigners, and New York State reaped some of the benefits. Foreign tourist arrivals increased from 2,209,899 in 1977 to an estimated 3,196,543 in 1979, according to the New York State Department of Commerce. About 95% of these travelers visited New York City. Total spending by foreign tourists, not including transportation, exceeded $1.3 billion in 1979.

According to the National Travel Survey, New York State was the 4th most popular destination for domestic travelers in 1977, trailing California, Florida, and Texas. About 37% of domestic visits were to friends and relatives; 18% were for conventions or business; 14% for sightseeing and entertainment; 13% for outdoor recreation; and 18% for other reasons. The survey, however, left out trips of 100 mi (161 km) or less, and thus did not include the economically important trips from the New York metropolitan area to the Catskills and to Long Island.

Estimated travel expenditures in New York State in 1978 were $6.4 billion, of which 34% went for food, 14% for lodging, and 11% for entertainment and amusements. Tourist-related industries accounted for approximately 215,000 person-years of employment in 1978, or anywhere from 150,000 to 330,000 employees in mostly seasonal jobs.

According to the New York Convention and Visitors Bureau, New York City had about 17.5 million visitors in 1979. A typical visit to New York City might include a ferry ride to the Statue of Liberty; a three-hour boat ride around Manhattan; visits to the World Trade Center, the Empire State Building, the UN, Rockefeller Center, and the New York Stock Exchange; walking tours of the Bronx Zoo, Chinatown, and the theater district; and a sampling of the city's many museums, restaurants, shops, and shows.

Second to New York City as a magnet for tourists comes Long Island, with its beaches, racetracks, and other recreational facilities. Attractions of the Hudson Valley include the US Military Academy (West Point), the Franklin D. Roosevelt home at Hyde Park, Bear Mountain State Park, and several wineries. North of the Hudson Valley is Albany, with its massive government center, Governor Nelson A. Rockefeller Plaza, often called the Albany Mall; Saratoga Springs, home of an arts center, racetrack, and spa; and the Adirondack region, with its forest preserve, summer and winter resorts, and abundant hunting and fishing. Northwest of the Adirondacks, in the St. Lawrence River, are the Thousand Islands—actually some 1,700 small islands extending over about 50 mi (80 km), and popular among freshwater fishermen and summer vacationers.

Scenic sites in central New York include the resorts of the Catskills and the scenic marvels of the Finger Lakes region, including Taughannock Falls in Trumansburg, the highest waterfall east of the Rockies. Further west lie Buffalo and Niagara Falls; this region ranked as the state's 6th most important in tourist revenues in 1978. South of the Niagara Frontier is the Southwest Gateway, among whose dominant features are Chautauqua Lake and Allegany State Park, the state's largest.

In 1975, 209 state parks comprised 2,978,000 acres (1,205,000 hectares), 1st in the US. During 1977, a total of 2,091,897 individuals used state-operated recreational facilities (including public campsites and ski areas), while a total of 46,728,000 people visited the state parks. In that year, the state sold 1,743,747 licenses, of which 649,225 were for big-game hunting, 542,141 for fishing alone, 239,159 for hunting alone, 195,644 for both hunting and fishing, and 117,578 for other recreational purposes. The state registered 335,288 motorboats and 130,109 snowmobiles in 1977.

48 SPORTS

Teams represent the state and its largest cities in almost every major professional sport. Off-track betting is a legal, multimillion-dollar enterprise in New York City, and Lake Placid is a magnet for winter sports enthusiasts.

Both of the state's major-league baseball teams play in New York City. The Mets play at Shea Stadium in the Queens, while the Yankees are at Yankee Stadium in the Bronx. Few teams in any sport can match the Yankees' achievements: between 1901 and 1979, they won 32 league championships and 22 world championships, with teams starring such Hall of Famers as Babe Ruth, Lou Gehrig, Joe DiMaggio, and Lawrence Peter "Yogi" Berra. The "miracle" Mets won the World Series in 1969 and the National League championship in 1973.

The state has two major-league basketball teams: the Buffalo Braves (Memorial Auditorium) and the New York Knickerbockers (Madison Square Garden in Manhattan). The Knicks won playoff championships in 1970 and 1973; their stars during that era included Willis Reed, Walt Frazier, Dave DeBusschere, and Bill Bradley. The Buffalo Bills (War Memorial Stadium) and the New York Jets (Shea Stadium) compete in the National Football League. In ice hockey, the New York Islanders (Nassau Coliseum), winners of the Stanley Cup in 1980, New York Rangers (Madison Square Garden), and Buffalo Sabres are the state entries. The Lancers represent Rochester in the North American Soccer League. In addition to owning the Knickerbockers and Rangers, Madison Square Garden is a leading promoter of professional boxing, hosts professional and amateur track-and-field competitions, and presents many other sports and entertainment events.

Three metropolitan area teams moved across the Hudson to New Jersey during the 1970s: the Nets in basketball, the Giants in football, and the Cosmos in soccer.

Horse racing is important to New York State, both as a sport attraction and because of the tax revenues that betting generates. The main thoroughbred race tracks are Aqueduct in Queens and Belmont in Nassau County; Belmont is the home of the Belmont Stakes, one of the three jewels in the Triple Crown of US racing. Saratoga (Saratoga Springs) presents thoroughbred racing and also offers a longer harness-racing season. Thoroughbred racing is also offered at the Finger Lakes track in Canandaigua. The top tracks for harness racing are Roosevelt Raceway (Westbury, Long Island) and Yonkers Raceway; there are also harness tracks at Monticello (in the Catskills) and at Vernon and Syracuse, in western New York. Quarter-horse racing is run at Tioga Park, south of Oswego.

The New York City Off-Track Betting Corporation (OTB), which began operations in April 1971, takes bets on races at the state's major tracks, as well as on some out-of-state races. In 1979, OTB had 156 branch offices and a telephone betting account system. During 1978/79, OTB earned $150.1 million on a betting handle of $803.5 million. Off-track betting services operated on a smaller scale on Long Island and in upstate New York.

Among other professional sports facilities, the Watkins Glen automobile racetrack is the site of a Grand Prix race every October. Lake Placid, an important winter sports region, hosted the 1932 and 1980 Winter Olympics.

Educational institutions in the state offer a wide variety of athletic activities. Among the leading National Collegiate Athletic Association competitors during the 1970s were Hofstra, St. John's, and Syracuse in basketball, Cornell in ice hockey, and Cornell and Hobart in lacrosse.

⁴⁹FAMOUS NEW YORKERS

New York State has been the home of five US presidents, eight US vice presidents (three of whom also became president), many statesmen of national and international repute, and a large corps of writers and entertainers.

Martin Van Buren (1782–1862), the 8th US president, became governor of New York in 1829. He was elected to the vice-presidency as a Democrat under Andrew Jackson in 1832, and succeeded Jackson in the election of 1836. An unpopular presi-

dent, Van Buren ran for reelection in 1840 but was defeated, losing even his home state. The 13th US president, Millard Fillmore (1800–74), was elected vice president under Zachary Taylor in 1848. He became president in 1850, when Taylor died. Fillmore's party, the Whigs, did not renominate him in 1852; four years later he unsuccessfully ran for president as the candidate of the Native American (or Know-Nothing) Party.

New York's other US presidents had more distinguished careers. Although he was born in New Jersey, Grover Cleveland (1837–1908) served as mayor of Buffalo and as governor of New York prior to his election to his first presidential term in 1884; he was again elected president in 1892. Theodore Roosevelt (1858–1919), a Republican, was elected governor in 1898. He won election as vice president under William McKinley in 1900, and became the nation's 26th president after McKinley was murdered in 1901. Roosevelt pursued an aggressive foreign policy, but also won renown as a conservationist and trustbuster. Reelected in 1904, he was awarded the Nobel Peace Prize in 1906 for helping to settle a war between Russia and Japan. Roosevelt declined to run again in 1908. However, he sought the Republican nomination in 1912 and, when defeated, became the candidate of the Progressive (or Bull Moose) Party, losing the general election to Woodrow Wilson.

Franklin Delano Roosevelt (1882–1945), a fifth cousin of Theodore Roosevelt, first ran for national office in 1920, when he was the Democratic vice-presidential choice. A year after losing that election, FDR was crippled by poliomyelitis. He then made an amazing political comeback: he was elected governor of New York in 1928 and served until 1932, when US voters chose him as their 32d president. Reelected in 1936, 1940, and 1944, FDR is the only president ever to have served more than two full terms in office. Roosevelt guided the US through the Great Depression and World War II, and his New Deal programs greatly enlarged the federal role in promoting social welfare.

In addition to Van Buren, Fillmore, and Theodore Roosevelt, five US vice presidents were born in New York: George Clinton (1739–1812), who was also New York State's first elected governor; Daniel D. Tompkins (1774–1825); William A. Wheeler (1819–87); Schuyler Colfax (1823–85); and James S. Sherman (1855–1912).Two other US vice presidents, though not born in New York, were New Yorkers by the time they became vice president. The first was Aaron Burr (1756–1836), perhaps best known for killing Alexander Hamilton in a duel in 1804; Hamilton (b.Nevis, West Indies, 1757–1804) was a leading Federalist, George Washington's treasury secretary, and the only New York delegate to sign the US Constitution in 1787. The second transplanted New Yorker to become vice president was Nelson Aldrich Rockefeller (1908–79). Born in Maine, Rockefeller served as governor of New York State from 1959 to 1973, was for two decades a major force in national Republican politics, and was appointed vice president by Gerald Ford in 1974, serving in that office through January 1977.

Two native New Yorkers have become chief justices of the US: John Jay (1745–1829) and Charles Evans Hughes (1862–1948). A third chief justice, Harlan Fiske Stone (1872–1946), born in New Hampshire, spent most of his legal career in New York City and served as dean of Columbia University's School of Law. Among New Yorkers who became associate justices of the US Supreme Court, Benjamin Nathan Cardozo (1870–1938) is noteworthy.

Other federal officeholders born in New York include US secretaries of state William Henry Seward (1801–72), Hamilton Fish (1808–93), Elihu Root (1845–1937), Frank B. Kellogg (1856–1937), and Henry L. Stimson (1867–1950). Prominent US senators have included Robert F. Wagner (1877–1953), who sponsored many New Deal laws; Robert F. Kennedy (1925–68), who though born in Massachusetts was elected to represent New York in 1964; Jacob K. Javits (b.1904), who served continuously in the Senate from 1957 through 1980; and Daniel Patrick Moynihan (b.1927), a scholar, author, and former federal bureaucrat who has represented New York since 1977.

The most important—and most colorful—figure in colonial New York was Peter Stuyvesant (b.Netherlands, 1592–1672); as director general of New Netherland, he won the hearty dislike of the Dutch settlers. Signers of the Declaration of Independence in 1776 from New York were Francis Lewis (1713–1803); Philip Livingston (1716–78); Lewis Morris (1726–98), the half-brother of the colonial patriot Gouverneur Morris (1752–1816); and William Floyd (1734–1821).

Other governors who made important contributions to the history of the state include De Witt Clinton (1769–1828); Alfred E. Smith (1873–1944); Herbert H. Lehman (1878–1963); W. Averell Harriman (b.1891), who has also held many US diplomatic posts; and Thomas E. Dewey (1902–71). Hugh L. Carey (b.1919) was elected governor in 1975. Robert Moses (b.Connecticut, 1888) led in the development of New York's parks and highway transportation system. One of the best-known and best-loved mayors in New York City history was Fiorello H. La Guardia (1882–1947), reformer who held the office from 1934 to 1945. Edward I. Koch (b.1924) was elected to the mayoralty in 1977.

Native New Yorkers have won Nobel prizes in every category. Winners of the Nobel Peace Prize besides Theodore Roosevelt were Elihu Root in 1912 and Frank B. Kellogg in 1929. The lone winner of the Nobel Prize for literature was Eugene O'Neill (1888–1953) in 1936. The chemistry prize was awarded to Irving Langmuir (1881–1957) in 1932, John H. Northrop (b.1891) in 1946, and William Howard Stein (1911–80) in 1972. Winners in physics include Carl D. Anderson (b.1905) in 1936, Robert Hofstadter (b.1915) in 1961, Richard Phillips Feynman (b.1918) and Julian Seymore Schwinger (b.1918) in 1965, Murray Gell-Mann (b.1929) in 1969, Leon N. Cooper (b.1930) in 1972, Burton Richter (b.1931) in 1976, and Steven Weinberg (b.1933) and Sheldon L. Glashow (b.1923) in 1979.

Eleven New Yorkers have been awarded the Nobel Prize for physiology or medicine: Hermann Joseph Muller (1890–1967) in 1946, Arthur Kornberg (b.1918) in 1959, George Wald (b.1906) in 1967, Marshall Warren Nirenberg (b.1927) in 1968, Julius Axelrod (b.1912) in 1970, Gerald Maurice Edelman (b.1929) in 1972, David Baltimore (b.1938) in 1975, Baruch Samuel Blumberg (b.1925) and Daniel Carlton Gajdusek (b.1923) in 1976, Rosalyn Sussman Yalow (b.1921) in 1977, and Hamilton O. Smith (b.1931) in 1978.

The Nobel Prize for economic science was won by Kenneth J. Arrow (b.1921) in 1972 and Milton Friedman (b.1912) in 1976. New York is also the birthplace of national labor leader George Meany (1894–1980) and economist Walter Heller (b.1915). Other distinguished state residents were physicist Joseph Henry (1797–1878), Mormon leader Brigham Young (b.Vermont, 1801–77), botanist Asa Gray (1810–88), inventor-businessman George Westinghouse (1846–1914), and Jonas Edward Salk (b.1914), developer of a vaccine to prevent poliomyelitis.

Writers born in New York include the storyteller and satirist Washington Irving (1783–1859); poet Walt Whitman (1819–92); and playwrights Eugene O'Neill, Arthur Miller (b.1915), and Neil Simon (b.1927). Two of America's greatest novelists were New Yorkers: Herman Melville (1819–91), who was also an important poet; and Henry James (1843–1916), whose short stories are equally well known. Other novelists include James Fenimore Cooper (b.New Jersey, 1789–1851), Henry Miller (1891–1980), James Michener (b.1907), Joseph Heller (b.1923), James Baldwin (b.1924), and Gore Vidal (b.1925). Lionel Trilling (1905–75) was a well-known literary critic; Barbara Tuchman (b.1912), a historian, has won both scholarly praise and popular favor. New York City has produced two famous journalist-com-

mentators, Walter Lippmann (1889–1974) and William F. Buckley, Jr. (b.1925).

Broadway is the showcase of American drama and the birthplace of the American musical theater. New Yorkers linked with the growth of the musical include Jerome Kern (1885–1945), Lorenz Hart (1895–1943), Oscar Hammerstein 2d (1895–1960), Richard Rodgers (1902–79), Alan Jay Lerner (b.1918), and Stephen Sondheim (b.1930). George Gershwin (1898–1937), whose *Porgy and Bess* raised the musical to its highest artistic form, also composed piano and orchestral works. Other important US composers who are New Yorkers include Aaron Copland (b.1900), Elliott Carter (b.1908), and William Schuman (b.1910). New York is the adopted home of ballet director and choreographer George Balanchine (b.Russia,1904); his associate Jerome Robbins (b.1918) was born in New York City. Leaders in the visual arts include Frederic Remington (1861–1909), the popular illustrator Norman Rockwell (1894–1978) and Willem de Kooning (b.Netherlands, 1904).

Many of America's best-loved entertainers come from the state. A small sampling would include comedians Groucho Marx (Julius Marx, 1890–1977), Mae West (1892–1980), Eddie Cantor (Edward Israel Iskowitz, 1892–1964), James "Jimmy" Durante (1893–1980), Bert Lahr (Irving Lahrheim, 1895–1967), George Burns (b.1896), Milton Berle (Berlinger, b.1908), Lucille Ball (b.1911), and Danny Kaye (David Daniel Kominsky, b.1913); comedian-film directors Mel Brooks (b.1926) and Woody Allen (Allen Konigsberg, b.1935); stage and screen stars James Cagney (b.1904), Zero Mostel (Samuel Joel Mostel, 1915–77), and Lauren Bacall (Betty Joan Perske, b.1924); pop, jazz, and folk singers Cab Calloway (b.1907), Lena Horne (b.1917), Pete Seeger (b.1919), Sammy Davis, Jr. (b.1925), Harry Belafonte (b.1927), Joan Baez (b.1941), Barbra Streisand (b.1942), Carly Simon (b.1945), Arlo Guthrie (b.1947), and Billy Joel (b.1951); and opera stars Robert Merrill (b.1919), Maria Callas (Kalogeropoulos, 1923–77), and Beverly Sills (Belle Silverman, b.1929). Also noteworthy are producers Irving Thalberg (1899–1936), David Susskind (b.1920), Joseph Papp (b.1921), and Harold Prince (b.1928); and directors George Cukor (b.1899), Stanley Kubrick (b.1928), John Frankenheimer (b.1930), and Peter Bogdanovich (b.1939).

Among many prominent sports figures born in New York are first-baseman Lou Gehrig (1903–41), football coach Vince Lombardi (1913–70), pitcher Sanford "Sandy" Koufax (b.1935), and basketball stars Kareem Abdul-Jabbar (Lew Alcindor, b.1947) and Julius Erving (b.1950).

[50] BIBLIOGRAPHY

Auletta, Ken. *The Streets Were Paved With Gold*. New York: Random House, 1979.

Barlow, Elizabeth, *Frederick Law Olmsted's New York*. New York: Praeger, 1972.

Bellush, Jewel, and Stephen M. David. *Race and Politics in New York City*. New York: Praeger, 1971.

Berle, Beatrice Bishop. *80 Puerto Rican Families in New York City*. New York: Arno Press, 1975.

Bliven, Bruce. *New York: The Story of the World's Most Exciting City*. New York: Random House, 1969.

Brown, Claude. *Manchild in the Promised Land*. New York: Macmillan, 1965.

Caro, Robert A. *The Power Broker: Robert Moses and the Fall of New York*. New York: Vintage, 1975.

Edmiston, Susan, and Linda D. Cirino. *Literary New York: A History and Guide*. Boston: Houghton Mifflin, 1976.

Ellis, David M., *New York: State and History*. Ithaca: Cornell University Press, 1979.

Ellis, David M., James A. Frost, Harold C. Syrett, and Harry J. Carman. *A History of New York State*. Rev. ed. Ithaca: Cornell University Press, 1967.

Ellis, David M., James A. Frost, and William B. Fink. *New York: The Empire State*. 4th ed. Englewood Cliffs, N.J.: Prentice-Hall, 1975.

Federal Writers' Project. *New York: A Guide to the Empire State*. New York: Oxford University Press, 1962 (orig. 1940).

Federal Writers' Project. *New York City Guide*. New York: Octagon Books, 1970 (orig. 1939).

Flick, Alexander C., ed. *History of the State of New York*. 10 vols. in 5. Published under the auspices of the New York State Historical Association. Port Washington, N.Y.: Ira J. Friedman, 1962 (orig. 1933).

French, J. H. *Gazetteer of the State of New York*. Port Washington, N.Y.: Ira J. Friedman, 1969 (orig. 1860).

Furer, Howard B. *New York: A Chronological and Documentary History*. Dobbs Ferry, N.Y.: Oceana Publications, 1974.

Glazer, Nathan, and Daniel Patrick Moynihan. *Beyond the Melting Pot: The Negroes, Puerto Ricans, Jews, Italians, and Irish of New York City*. 2d ed. Cambridge, Mass.: MIT Press, 1970.

Hacker, Andrew. *The New Yorkers*. New York: Mason/Charter, 1975.

Heckscher, August, with Phyllis Robinson. *When La Guardia Was Mayor*. New York: Norton, 1978.

Henderson, Mary C. *The City and the Theatre: New York Playhouses from Bowling Green to Times Square*. Clifton, N.J.: J. T. White, 1973.

Hevesi, Alan G. *Legislative Politics in New York State*. New York: Praeger, 1975.

Howe, Irving. *World of Our Fathers*. New York: Harcourt Brace Jovanovich, 1976.

Irving, Washington. *A History of New York*. Edited by Edwin T. Bowden. New Haven, Conn.: College & University Press, 1964.

Kammen, Michael. *Colonial New York: A History*. New York: Scribner, 1975.

Kenney, Alice P. *Stubborn for Liberty: The Dutch in New York*. Syracuse: Syracuse University Press, 1975.

Kouwenhoven, John A. *The Columbia Historical Portrait of New York: An Essay in Graphic History*. New York: Harper & Row, 1973 (orig. 1952).

Myers, Gustavus. *The History of Tammany Hall*. New York: Burt Franklin, 1968 (orig. 1901).

Newfield, Jack, and Paul DuBrul. *Abuse of Power: The Permanent Government and the Fall of New York*. New York: Viking, 1977.

New York State. Department of Commerce. *Travel in New York State*. Research Bulletin no. 43. Albany, 1977.

New York, State of. Department of State. *Manual for the Use of the Legislature of the State of New York, 1977–1979*. Albany: Department of State, 1979.

New York, State of. Division of the Budget. *New York State Statistical Yearbook, 1979–1980*. Albany: Division of the Budget, 1979.

New York, State of. Governor. *Annual Budget Message, 1980–1981*. Albany: Office of the Governor, 1980.

Peirce, Neal R. *The Megastates of America: People, Politics and Power in the Ten Great States*. New York: Norton, 1972.

Ravitch, Diane. *The Great School Wars: New York City, 1805–1973*. New York: Basic Books, 1974.

Schneider, David Moses. *The History of Public Welfare in New York State*. Montclair, N.J.: Patterson, Smith, 1969.

Talese, Gay. *The Kingdom and the Power*. New York: World, 1969.

United States. Department of Commerce. Bureau of the Census. *County Business Patterns, 1977: New York*. Washington, D.C.: Government Printing Office, 1979.

NORTH CAROLINA

State of North Carolina

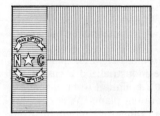

ORIGIN OF STATE NAME: Named in honor of King Charles I of England. **NICKNAME:** The Tarheel State. **CAPITAL:** Raleigh. **ENTERED UNION:** 21 November 1789 (12th). **SONG:** "The Old North State." **MOTTO:** *Esse quam videri* (To be rather than to seem). **FLAG:** Adjacent to the fly of two equally sized bars, red above and white below, is a blue union containing a white star in the center, flanked by the letters N and C in gold. Above and below the star are two gold scrolls, the upper one reading "May 20th 1775," the lower one "April 12th 1776." **OFFICIAL SEAL:** Liberty, clasping a constitution and holding aloft on a pole a liberty cap, stands on the left, while Plenty sits beside a cornucopia on the right; behind them, mountains run to the sea, on which a three-masted ship appears. "May 20, 1775" appears above the figures; the words "The Great Seal of the State of North Carolina" and the state motto surround the whole. **MAMMAL:** Gray squirrel. **BIRD:** Cardinal. **FISH:** Channel bass. **INSECT:** Honeybee. **FLOWER:** Dogwood. **TREE:** Pine. **GEM:** Emerald. **LEGAL HOLIDAYS:** New Year's Day, 1 January; Easter Monday, March or April; Memorial Day, last Monday in May; Independence Day, 4 July; Labor Day, 1st Monday in September; Veterans Day, 11 November; Thanksgiving Day, 4th Thursday in November, and the day following; Christmas Eve, 24 December; Christmas Day, 25 December. **TIME:** 7 A.M. EST = noon GMT.

¹LOCATION, SIZE, AND EXTENT

Located in the southeastern US, North Carolina ranks 28th in size among the 50 states.

The total area of North Carolina is 52,586 sq mi (136,198 sq km), of which land accounts for 48,798 sq mi (126,387 sq km) and inland water 3,788 sq mi (9,811 sq km). North Carolina extends 503 mi (810 km) E–W; the state's maximum N–S extension is 187 mi (301 km).

North Carolina is bordered on the N by Virginia; on the E by the Atlantic Ocean; on the S by South Carolina and Georgia; and on the W by Tennessee. A long chain of islands or sand banks, called the Outer Banks, lies off the state's Atlantic coast. The total boundary line of North Carolina is 1,270 mi (2,043 km), including a general coastline of 301 mi (484 km); the tidal shoreline extends 3,375 mi (5,432 km). The state's geographic center is in Chatham County, 10 mi (16 km) NW of Sanford.

²TOPOGRAPHY

North Carolina's three major topographic regions belong to the Atlantic Coastal Plain, the Piedmont Plateau, and the Appalachian Mountains.

The Outer Banks, narrow islands of shifting sandbars, screen most of the coastal plain from the ocean. Treacherous navigation conditions and numerous shipwrecks have earned the name of "Graveyard of the Atlantic" for the shoal waters off Cape Hatteras, which, like Cape Lookout and Cape Fear, juts out from the banks into the Atlantic. The shallow Pamlico and Albemarle sounds and broad salt marshes lying behind the Outer Banks serve as valuable habitats for marine life but as further hindrances to water transportation.

On the mainland, the coastal plain extends westward from the sounds for 100 to 150 mi (160–240 km) and upward from sea level to about 400 feet (120 meters). Near the ocean, the outer coastal plain is very flat and often swampy; this region contains all the natural lakes in North Carolina, the largest being Lake Mattamuskeet (67 sq mi, or 174 sq km), followed by Lakes Phelps and Waccamaw. The inner coastal plain is more elevated and better drained. Infertile sand hills mark its southwestern section, but the rest of the region constitutes the state's principal farming country.

The piedmont is a rolling plateau of red clay soil roughly 150 mi (240 km) wide, rising from 400 feet (120 meters) in the east to 1,500 feet (460 meters) in the west. The fall line, a sudden change in elevation, separates the piedmont from the coastal plain and produces numerous rapids in the rivers that flow between the regions.

The Blue Ridge, a steep escarpment that parallels the Tennessee border, divides the piedmont from North Carolina's westernmost region, containing the highest and most rugged portion of the Appalachian chain. The two major ranges are the Blue Ridge itself, which is 3,000–4,000 feet high (900–1,200 meters), and the Great Smoky Mountains, which have nearly 50 peaks higher than 6,000 feet (1,800 meters). Several smaller chains intersect these two ranges; one of them, the Black Mountains, contains Mt. Mitchell, at 6,684 feet (2,037 meters) the tallest peak east of the Mississippi River.

No single river basin dominates North Carolina. The Hiwassee, Little Tennessee, French Broad, Watauga, and New rivers flow from the mountains westward to the Mississippi River system. East of the Blue Ridge, the Chowan, Roanoke, Tar, Neuse, Cape Fear, Yadkin, and Catawba drain the piedmont and coastal plain. The largest artificial lakes are Lake Norman on the Catawba, Lake Gaston on the Roanoke, and High Rock Lake on the Yadkin.

³CLIMATE

North Carolina has a humid, subtropical climate. Winters are short and mild, while summers are usually very sultry; spring and fall are distinct and refreshing periods of transition. In most of North Carolina, temperatures rarely go above 100°F (38°C) or fall below 10°F (–12°C), but differences in altitude and proximity to the ocean create significant local variations. Average January temperatures range from lower than 36°F (2°C) in parts of the mountains to above 48°F (9°C) on the extreme southeastern coast, while average July temperatures in the same two regions are under 68°F (20°C) and over 80°F (27°C), respectively. The coldest temperature ever recorded in North Carolina is –29°F (–34°C), registered on 30 January 1966 on Mt. Mitchell; the hottest, 109°F (43°C), occurred on 7 September 1954 at Weldon.

In the southwestern section of the Blue Ridge, moist southerly winds rising over the mountains drop more than 80 in (203 cm) of precipitation per year, making this region the wettest in the eastern states; the other side of the mountains receives less than half that amount. The piedmont gets between 44 and 48 in (112–122 cm) of precipitation per year, while 44 to 56 in (112–142 cm) annually fall on the coastal plain. Average winter snowfalls vary from 50 in (127 cm) on Mt. Mitchell to only a trace amount at Cape Hatteras. In the summer, North Carolina weather responds to the Bermuda High, a pressure system centered in the mid-Atlantic. Winds from the southwest bring masses of hot, humid air over the state; anticyclones connected with this system frequently lead to upper-level thermal inversions, producing a stagnant air mass that cannot disperse pollutants until cooler, drier air from Canada moves in. During late summer and early autumn, the eastern region is vulnerable to high winds and flooding from hurricanes.

⁴FLORA AND FAUNA

North Carolina has approximately 300 species and subspecies of trees and almost 3,000 varieties of flowering plants. Coastal plant life begins with sea oats on the dunes and smooth cordgrass in the marshes, then gives way to myrtle, yaupon, and live oak further inland. Blackwater swamps support dense stands of cypress and gum trees. Pond pine favors the peat soils of the Carolina bays, while longleaf pine and turkey oak cover the sand hills and other well-drained areas. Weeds take root when a field is abandoned in the piedmont, followed soon by loblolly, shortleaf, and Virginia pine; sweet gum and tulip poplars spring up beneath the pines, later giving way to an oak-hickory climax forest. Dogwood decorates the understory, but kudzu—a rank, weedy vine introduced from Japan as an antierosion measure in the 1930s—is a less attractive feature of the landscape. The profusion of plants reaches extraordinary proportions in the mountains. The deciduous forests on the lower slopes contain Carolina hemlock, silver bell, yellow buckeye, white basswood, sugar maple, yellow birch, and beech, in addition to the common trees of the piedmont. There is no true treeline in the North Carolina mountains, but unexplained treeless areas called "balds" appear on certain summits.

The white-tailed deer is the principal big game animal of North Carolina, and the black bear is a tourist attraction in the Great Smoky Mountains National Park. The wild boar was introduced to the mountains during the 19th century; beavers have been reintroduced and are now the state's principal furbearers. The largest native carnivore is the bobcat.

North Carolina game birds include the bobwhite quail, mourning dove, wild turkey, and many varieties of duck and goose. Trout and smallmouth bass flourish in North Carolina's clear mountain streams, while catfish, pickerel, perch, crappie, and largemouth bass thrive in fresh water elsewhere. The sounds and surf of the coast yield channel bass, striped bass, flounder, and bluefish to sport fishermen. Among insect pests, the pine bark beetle is a threat to the state's forests and forest industries.

The gray wolf, elk, eastern cougar, and bison are extinct in North Carolina; the American alligator, protected by the state, has returned in large numbers to eastern swamps and lakeshores. Endangered species (all on the federal list) include the Florida manatee, Indiana and gray bats, bald eagle, American and Arctic peregrine falcons, eastern brown pelican, Atlantic ridley, and hawksbill turtles.

⁵ENVIRONMENTAL PROTECTION

State actions to safeguard the environment began in 1915 with the purchase of the summit of Mt. Mitchell as North Carolina's first state park. North Carolina's citizens and officials worked actively (along with those in Tennessee) to establish the Great Smoky Mountains National Park during the 1920s, the same decade that saw the establishment of the first state agency for wildlife conservation. In 1937, a state and local program of soil and water conservation districts began to halt erosion and waste of natural resources.

Interest in environmental protection intensified during the 1970s. In 1971, the state required its own agencies to submit environmental impact statements in connection with all major

project proposals; it also empowered local governments to require such statements from major private developers. Voters approved a $150-million bond issue in 1972 to assist in the construction of wastewater treatment facilities by local governments. The Coastal Management Act of 1974 mandated comprehensive land-use planning for estuaries, wetlands, beaches, and adjacent areas of environmental concern. The most controversial environmental action occurred mid-decade, when a coalition of state officials, local residents, and national environmental groups fought the proposed construction of a dam that would have flooded the New River Valley in northwestern North Carolina. Congress quashed the project when it designated the stream as a national scenic river in 1976.

Air quality in most of North Carolina's eight air quality control regions is good, although the industrialized areas of the piedmont and mountains experience pollution from engine exhausts and coal-fired electric generating plants. Water quality ranges from extraordinary purity in numerous mountain trout streams to serious pollution in major rivers and coastal waters. Soil erosion and municipal and industrial waste discharges have drastically increased the level of dissolved solids in some piedmont streams, while runoffs from livestock pastures and nitrates leached from fertilized farmland have overstimulated the growth of algae in slow-moving eastern rivers. Pollution also has made large areas of the coast unsafe for commercial shellfishing.

The Department of Natural Resources and Community Development, the state's main environmental agency, issues licenses to industries and municipalities and seeks to enforce clean air and water regulations.

⁶POPULATION

North Carolina had 5,084,411 inhabitants in 1970 (12th in the US). Preliminary census figures show a population of 5,846,159 in 1980, when the population density was 120 per sq mi (46 per sq km).

At the time of the first census in 1790, North Carolina ranked 3d among the 13 states, with a population of 393,751, but it slipped to 10th by 1850. In the decades that followed, North Carolina grew slowly by natural increase and suffered from net outmigration, while the rest of the nation expanded rapidly. Outmigration abated after 1890, however, and North Carolina's overall growth rate in the 20th century has been slightly greater than that of the nation as a whole. As of 1976, the state's population was slightly younger than the national average and very much less mobile: more than 70% of all state residents 14 years of age or older had lived in North Carolina their whole lives.

Although 45% of North Carolinians lived in urban areas in 1977, compared with 73% of all Americans, only 1 rural resident in 10 actually lived on a farm. Most North Carolinians live in and around a relatively large number of small and medium-sized cities and towns, many of which are concentrated in the Piedmont Crescent, between Charlotte, Greensboro, and Raleigh. Leading cities (and their 1980 preliminary census populations) are Charlotte, 310,799; Greensboro, 154,763; Raleigh, 148,299; and Winston-Salem, 131,211.

⁷ETHNIC GROUPS

North Carolina's white population is descended mostly from English settlers who arrived in the east in the 17th and early 18th centuries and from Scottish, Scotch-Irish, and German immigrants who poured into the piedmont in the middle of the 18th century. Originally very distinct, these groups assimilated with one another in the first half of the 19th century to form a relatively homogeneous body of native-born white Protestants. By 1860, North Carolina had the lowest proportion of foreign-born whites of any state; more than a century later, in 1970, only 1.9% of North Carolina residents were foreign-born or native-born children of foreign-born parents.

According to the 1970 federal census there were 44,406 Indians living in North Carolina, the 5th-largest number in any state.

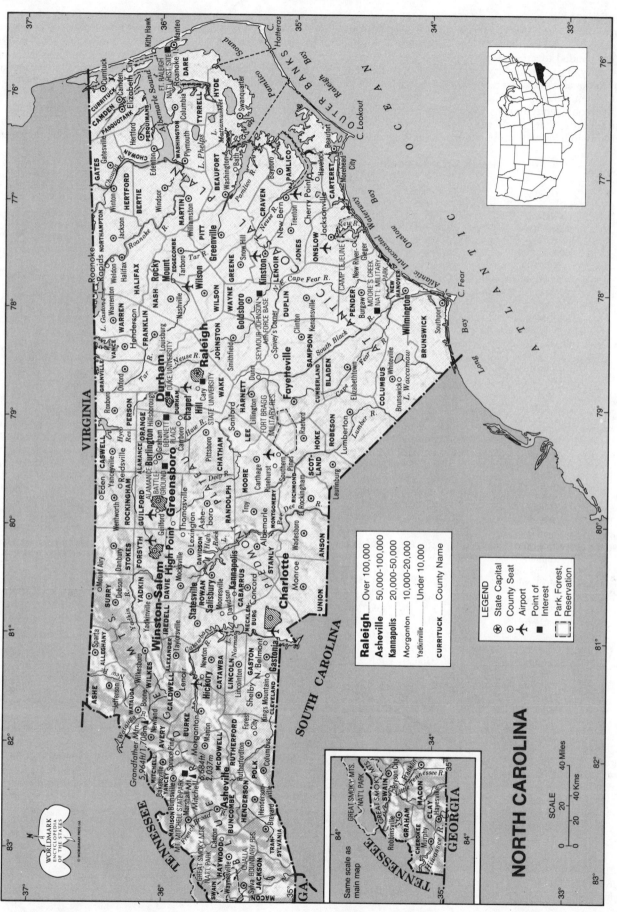

NORTH CAROLINA

LEGEND

Raleigh	Over 100,000
Asheville	50,000–100,000
Kannapolis	20,000–50,000
Morganton	10,000–20,000
Yadkinville	Under 10,000
CURRITUCK	County Name

⊛ State Capital
⊙ County Seat
✈ Airport
■ Point of Interest
▭ Park, Forest, Reservation

SCALE

0   20   40 Miles
0   20   40 Kms

Same scale as
main map

See US political: front cover L3; physical: back cover L3.

LOCATION: 33°27'37" to 36°34'25"N; 75°27' to 84°20'w. **BOUNDARIES:** Virginia line, 320 mi (515 km); Atlantic Ocean coastline, 301 mi (484 km); South Carolina line, 328 mi (528 km); Georgia line, 68 mi (109 km); Tennessee line, 253 mi (407 km).

WORLDMARK
ENCYCLOPEDIA
OF THE STATES
© WORLDMARK PRESS, Ltd.

The Lumbee of Robeson County and the surrounding area are the major Indian group. Their origins are mysterious, but they probably descend from many small tribes, decimated by war and disease, that banded together in the Lumber River swamps in the 18th century. The Lumbee have no language other than English, no traditional tribal culture, and are not recognized by the Bureau of Indian Affairs. The Haliwa, Waccamaw Siouan, Coharie, and Person County Indians are smaller groups in eastern North Carolina who share the Lumbee's predicament. The only North Carolina Indians with a reservation, a tribal language and culture, and federal recognition are the Cherokee, whose ancestors hid in the Smokies when the majority of their tribe was removed to Indian Territory (now Oklahoma) in 1838. The North Carolina Cherokee have remained in the mountains ever since, living in a community that now centers on the Qualla Boundary Reservation near Great Smoky Mountains National Park.

The 1,125,545 blacks in North Carolina comprised 95% of its nonwhite population in 1970 and 22% of its total population. Black slaves came to North Carolina from the 17th century through the early 19th; like most white immigrants, they usually

North Carolina Counties, County Seats, and County Populations

COUNTY	COUNTY SEAT	LAND AREA (SQ MI)[1]	POPULATION (1980 CENSUS)[2]	COUNTY	COUNTY SEAT	LAND AREA (SQ MI)[1]	POPULATION (1980 CENSUS)[2]
Alamance	Graham	428	98,964	Johnston	Smithfield	797	70,221
Alexander	Taylorsville	259	24,774	Jones	Trenton	467	9,673
Alleghany	Sparta	225	9,570	Lee	Sanford	256	36,754
Anson	Wadesboro	533	25,360	Lenoir	Kinston	400	59,391
Ashe	Jefferson	426	22,336	Lincoln	Lincolnton	297	42,484
Avery	Newland	245	14,422	Macon	Franklin	513	20,138
Beaufort	Washington	826	40,385	Madison	Marshall	450	16,791
Bertie	Windsor	698	20,918	Martin	Williamston	455	25,735
Bladen	Elizabethtown	883	30,069	McDowell	Marion	436	35,013
Brunswick	Southport	856	35,349	Mecklenburg	Charlotte	530	400,586
Buncombe	Asheville	657	160,265	Mitchell	Bakersville	215	14,391
Burke	Morganton	511	72,357	Montgomery	Troy	488	22,355
Cabarrus	Concord	363	85,513	Moore	Carthage	704	50,374
Caldwell	Lenoir	469	67,374	Nash	Nashville	544	66,338
Camden	Camden	239	5,820	New Hanover	Wilmington	185	97,926
Carteret	Beaufort	536	40,794	Northampton	Jackson	536	22,289
Caswell	Yanceyville	428	20,630	Onslow	Jacksonville	765	112,165
Catawba	Newton	394	104,788	Orange	Hillsborough	400	76,603
Chatham	Pittsboro	709	33,374	Pamlico	Bayboro	338	10,337
Cherokee	Murphy	452	18,940	Pasquotank	Elizabeth City	228	25,150
Chowan	Edenton	173	12,497	Pender	Burgaw	871	22,107
Clay	Hayesville	209	6,593	Perquimans	Hertford	246	9,466
Cleveland	Shelby	468	82,796	Person	Roxboro	401	29,110
Columbus	Whiteville	945	51,015	Pitt	Greenville	655	88,521
Craven	New Bern	699	70,631	Polk	Columbus	239	12,904
Cumberland	Fayetteville	654	246,522	Randolph	Asheboro	798	91,187
Currituck	Currituck	246	11,084	Richmond	Rockingham	475	45,383
Dare	Manteo	391	12,401	Robeson	Lumberton	949	101,401
Davidson	Lexington	549	112,618	Rockingham	Wentworth	569	83,164
Davie	Mocksville	265	24,451	Rowan	Salisbury	523	98,829
Duplin	Kenansville	815	40,658	Rutherford	Rutherfordton	563	53,299
Durham	Durham	295	150,035	Sampson	Clinton	945	49,243
Edgecombe	Tarboro	510	56,082	Scotland	Laurinburg	319	32,244
Forsyth	Winston-Salem	419	242,581	Stanly	Albemarle	398	48,192
Franklin	Louisburg	491	29,811	Stokes	Danbury	457	32,968
Gaston	Gastonia	356	161,288	Surry	Dobson	536	59,330
Gates	Gatesville	337	8,813	Swain	Bryson City	524	10,246
Graham	Robbinsville	292	7,194	Transylvania	Brevard	382	23,316
Granville	Oxford	537	33,855	Tyrrell	Columbia	390	3,988
Greene	Snow Hill	267	15,898	Union	Monroe	639	70,212
Guilford	Greensboro	655	314,839	Vance	Henderson	249	36,340
Halifax	Halifax	734	53,935	Wake	Raleigh	858	298,753
Harnett	Lillington	603	59,249	Warren	Warrenton	424	16,217
Haywood	Waynesville	551	46,449	Washington	Plymouth	343	14,786
Henderson	Hendersonville	378	58,088	Watauga	Boone	317	31,611
Hertford	Winton	353	23,109	Wayne	Goldsboro	557	96,513
Hoke	Raeford	389	20,293	Wilkes	Wilkesboro	757	58,323
Hyde	Swanquarter	613	5,725	Wilson	Wilson	375	62,723
Iredell	Statesville	572	82,461	Yadkin	Yadkinville	336	28,367
Jackson	Sylva	491	25,878	Yancey	Burnsville	312	14,955
				TOTALS		48,798	5,846,159

1. Column does not add to total because of rounding.
2. Preliminary results include a statistical discrepancy of less than 0.2%.

arrived in North Carolina after previous residence in other colonies. Although black slaves performed a wide variety of tasks and lived in every county of the state, they were most often field laborers on the large farms in the eastern region. The distribution of black population today still reflects the patterns of plantation agriculture: the coastal plain contains a much higher than average concentration of black inhabitants, with blacks outnumbering whites in four agricultural counties. The overall proportion of blacks in North Carolina rose throughout the 19th century but has fallen steadily in the 20th, as hundreds of thousands have migrated to northern and western states. Nevertheless, some of the earliest demonstrations of the civil rights movement, most notably a 1960 lunch counter sit-in at Greensboro, took place in the state.

[8] LANGUAGES

Although most of the original Cherokee Indians were removed to Indian Territory around 1838, descendants of those who resisted and remained have formed a strong Indian community in the Appalachian foothills; in 1970, 2,089 state residents claimed an Indian language as their native tongue. Among Indian place-names are Pamlico, Nantahala, and Cullasaja.

Many regional language features are widespread, but others sharply distinguish two subregions: the western half, including the piedmont and the Appalachian Highlands, and the eastern coastal plain. Terms common to South Midland and Southern speech occur throughout the state: both *dog irons* and *firedogs* (andirons), *bucket, spicket* (spigot), *seesaw, comfort* (tied and filled bedcover), *pullybone, ground squirrel* (chipmunk), *branch* (small stream), *light bread* (white bread), *polecat* (skunk), and *carry* (escort). Also common are *greasy* with the /z/ sound, *new* as /nyoo/ and *due* as /dyoo/, *swallow it* as /swaller it/, *can't* rhyming with *paint*, *poor* with the vowel sound /aw/, and *horse* and *hoarse* with different vowels.

Distinct to the western region are *snake feeder* (dragonfly), *blinds* (roller shades), *poke* (paper bag), *redworm* (earthworm), *a little piece* (a short distance), *plum peach* (clingstone peach), *sick on the stomach* (also found in the Pee Dee River Valley), *boiled* as /bawrld/, *fog* as /fawg/, *Mary* sounding like *merry*, and *bulge* with the vowel of *good*. Setting off eastern North Carolina are *lightwood* (kindling), *mosquito hawk* (dragonfly), *earthworm, press peach* (instead of plum peach), *you-all* as plural, and *sick in the stomach*. Distinctive eastern pronunciations include loss of /r/ after a vowel, *fog* as /fagh/, *scarce* and *Mary* with the vowel of *gate*, *bulge* with the vowel of *bun*, *shrimp* as /srimp/, and *foreign* and *forest* with the vowel sound /ah/. Along the coast, peanuts are *goobers* and a screech owl is a *shivering owl*.

English was reported as mother tongue in 1970 by 94% of both the native-born and all state residents. Speakers of leading first languages were as follows:

	NATIVE-BORN	FOREIGN-BORN
English	4,751,660	6,948
German	15,418	6,472
Spanish	11,506	2,273
French	9,928	1,355

[9] RELIGIONS

The majority of North Carolinians are Protestant. Of the predominantly white denominations in 1978, the churches of the North Carolina Baptist Convention reported 1,100,000 members, and the United Methodist Church claimed about 500,000. These two denominations embraced about 35% of the population in 1971; statistics for black churches are not available. In 1979, the state had 91,931 Roman Catholics and an estimated 13,620 Jews.

The Church of England was the established church of colonial North Carolina but was never a dominant force among the early immigrants. Scottish Presbyterians settled in the upper Cape Fear valley, and Scotch-Irish Presbyterians occupied the piedmont after 1757. Lutheran Evangelical Reformed Germans later moved into the Yadkin and Catawba valleys of the same region. The Moravians, a German sect, founded the town of Salem (later merging with Winston to become Winston-Salem) in 1766 as the center of their utopian community at Wachovia. Methodist circuit riders and Separate Baptists missionaries won thousands of converts among blacks and whites, strengthening their appeal in the Great Revival of 1801. In the subsequent generation, a powerful evangelical consensus dominated popular culture. After the Civil War, blacks left the white congregations to found their own churches, but the overall strength of Protestantism persisted. When many North Carolinians left their farms at the end of the 19th century, they moved to mill villages that were well supplied with churches, often at the mill owners' expense.

White church organizations have generally kept out of state politics except where matters of personal morality are concerned. In recent years, however, individual Protestant leaders have worked to reject the Equal Rights Amendment and to deny state-funded abortions to the poor. Resurgent political activism among fundamentalist Christians is a growing and prominent feature of contemporary North Carolina politics.

[10] TRANSPORTATION

Railroad construction was initially hampered in North Carolina by the reluctance of eastern legislators to approve heavy expenditures for the benefit of piedmont farmers. When political reform changed the balance of power in 1835, however, state subsidies for railroad construction followed. The state-owned North Carolina Railroad, completed in 1856, described an arc from Raleigh to Greensboro to Charlotte that became the backbone for the modern industrialized Piedmont Crescent. The builders of this and other early rail lines had hoped to channel trade into North Carolina ports, but development was slow. A generation after Appomattox, financial difficulties forced the ailing local railroads to merge into national lines whose rate structures forced regional commerce northward. The Southern Railway acquired a 99-year lease on the piedmont section of the North Carolina Railroad in 1895, while eastern routes fell to the Atlantic Coast Line and the Seaboard Air Line Railway. Northern interests thus owned all three major lines, and while they ended the dream of locally controlled development, the railroad barons did integrate North Carolina into the interregional trade patterns of the growing national economy. As of 1976, North Carolina had 4,168 mi (6,708 km) of track. Amtrak provides passenger service to most large North Carolina cities.

Shortly after consolidation, the railroads began to encourage "good roads" to facilitate wagon traffic between the railheads and the more remote farming districts. The new hard-surface roads soon proved ideal for automobiles and trucks, and in the 1920s, state roads came to rival the railroads as the principal means of transport. Ambitious bond issues paid for a statewide system of paved highways, giving the state more roads by the end of the decade than any other southern state except Texas. The state government took over the county roads in 1931. By 1978 there were 91,949 mi (147,978 km) of roads in the state, of which 82.5% were rural and 17.5% municipal; 3,253,000 automobiles were registered in 1978, and there were 3,599,341 licensed drivers. The major interstate highways are I–95, which stretches north–south across the coastal plain, and I–85, which parallels it across the piedmont. I–40 leads from Greensboro westward over the mountains, and I–26 and I–77 handle north–south traffic in the western section. A planned extension of I–40 will connect the piedmont and the coastal plain. Nearly all North Carolinians who commute to work travel by private automobile; intercity bus connections are poor, and commuter trains are nonexistent.

The Atlantic Intracoastal Waterway follows sounds, rivers, and canals down the entire length of eastern North Carolina, connecting the two state ports at Morehead City and Wilmington. Cargoes that flow through these cities to Europe, South America, and East Asia include tobacco, phosphates, lumber, logs, plywood, oil, and steel.

North Carolina had 76 public and 194 private airfields in 1978. Five regularly scheduled commercial airlines served 12 cities in 1978, emplaning some 4.5 million passengers; the airports at Charlotte, Raleigh-Durham, Greensboro–High Point, and Winston-Salem handled 80% of this traffic.

¹¹HISTORY

Peoples of the Archaic Culture came to North Carolina about 10,000 years ago. These early inhabitants hunted game with spears and gathered nuts, roots, berries, and freshwater mollusks. Around 500 BC, with the invention of pottery and the development of agriculture, the Woodland Culture began to emerge. The Woodland way of life—growing corn, beans, and squash, and hunting game with bows and arrows—prevailed on the North Carolina coast until the Europeans arrived.

Living in North Carolina by this time were Indians of the Algonkian-, Siouan-, and Iroquoian-language families. The Roanoke, Chowanoc, Hatteras, Meherrin, and other Algonkian-speaking tribes of the coast had probably lived in the area the longest; some of them belonged to the Powhatan Confederacy of Virginia. The Siouan groups were related to larger tribes of the Great Plains. Of the Iroquoian-speakers, the Cherokee probably had lived in the mountains since before the beginning of the Christian era, while the Tuscarora had entered the upper coastal plain somewhat later. After their defeat by the colonists in the Tuscarora War of 1711–13, the tribe fled to what is now upper New York State to become the sixth member of the Iroquois Confederacy.

Contact with whites brought war, disease, and enslavement to the Algonkian and Siouan tribes. Banding together, the survivors probably gave rise to the present-day Lumbee and to the other Indian groups of eastern North Carolina. The Cherokee tried to avoid the fate of the coastal tribes by selectively adopting aspects of white culture. In 1838, however, the federal government responded to the demands of land-hungry whites by expelling most of the Cherokee to Indian Territory along the Trail of Tears.

European penetration began when Giovanni da Verrazano, a Florentine navigator in French service, discovered the North Carolina coast in 1524. Don Lucas Vasquez de Ayllón led an unsuccessful Spanish attempt to settle near the mouth of the Cape Fear River two years later. Hernando de Soto tramped over the North Carolina mountains in 1540 in an unsuccessful search for gold, but the Spanish made no permanent contribution to the colonization of North Carolina.

Sixty years after Verrazano's voyage, North Carolina became the scene of England's first experiment in American empire. Sir Walter Raleigh, a courtier of Queen Elizabeth I, gained the queen's permission to send out explorers to the New World. They landed on the Outer Banks in 1584 and returned with reports so enthusiastic that Raleigh decided to sponsor a colony on Roanoke Island between Albemarle and Pamlico sounds. After a second expedition returned without founding a permanent settlement, Raleigh sent out a third group in 1587 under John White as governor. The passengers included White's daughter Eleanor and her husband, Ananias Dare. Shortly after landfall, Eleanor gave birth to Virginia Dare, the first child born of English parents in the New World. Several weeks later, White returned to England for supplies, but the threat of the Spanish Armada prevented his prompt return. By the time White got back to Roanoke in 1590, he found no trace of the settlers—only the word "Croatoan" carved on a tree. The fate of this "Lost Colony" has never been satisfactorily explained.

The next English venture focused on the more accessible Jamestown colony in the Chesapeake Bay area of Virginia. England tended to ignore the southern region until 1629, when Charles I laid out the territory between 30° and 36°N, named it Carolana for himself, and granted it to his attorney general, Sir Robert Heath. Heath made no attempt to people his domain, however, and Carolana remained empty of whites until stragglers drifted in from the mid–17th century onward. Events in England transformed Virginia's outpost into a separate colony. After the execution of Charles I in 1649, England had no ruling monarch until a party of noblemen invited Charles II back to England in 1660. Charles thanked eight of his benefactors three years later by making them lords proprietors of the province, now called Carolina. The vast new region eventually stretched from northern Florida to the modern boundary between North Carolina and Virginia, and from the Atlantic to the Pacific Ocean.

The proprietors divided Carolina into three counties and appointed a governor for each one. Albemarle County embraced the existing settlements in northeastern North Carolina near the waters of Albemarle Sound; it was the only one that developed a government within the present state boundaries. From the beginning, relations between the older pioneers and their newly imposed government were stormy. The English philosopher John Locke drew up the Fundamental Constitutions of Carolina, but his political blueprints proved unworkable. The proprietors' arbitrary efforts to collect royal customs touched off factional violence, culminating in Culpepper's Rebellion of 1677, one of the first American uprisings against a corrupt regime.

For a few years afterward, local residents had a more representative government, until the proprietors attempted to strengthen the establishment of the Anglican Church in the colony. In 1711, Cary's Rebellion was touched off by laws passed against the colony's Quakers. During the confusion, Tuscarora Indians launched a war against the white intruders on their lands. The whites won the Tuscarora War in 1713 with assistance from South Carolina, but political weakness in the north persisted. Proprietary officials openly consorted with pirates—including the notorious Edward Teach, alias Blackbeard—and royal inspectors questioned the fitness of proprietary government. South Carolina officially split off in 1719 and received a royal governor in 1721. Ten years later, all but one of the proprietors relinquished their rights for £2,500 each, and North Carolina became a royal colony. The remaining proprietor, Lord Granville, gave up his governing rights but retained ownership of one-eighth of the original grant; the Granville District thus included more than half of the unsettled territory in the North Carolina colony.

In the decades that followed, thousands of new settlers poured into North Carolina; by 1775, the population had swollen to 345,000, making North Carolina the 4th most populous colony. Germans and Scotch-Irish trekked down the Great Wagon Road from Pennsylvania to the piedmont. Scottish Highlanders spread over the upper Cape Fear Valley, as more Englishmen filled up the coastal plain. Backcountry settlers practiced self-sufficient farming, but eastern North Carolinians used slave labor to carve out rice and tobacco plantations. The westerners were often exploited by an eastern-dominated colonial assembly that sent corrupt and overbearing officials to govern them. Organizing in 1768 and calling themselves Regulators, unhappy westerners first petitioned for redress and then took up arms. Royal Governor William Tryon used eastern militia to crush the Regulators in a two-hour pitched battle at Alamance Creek in 1771.

The eastern leaders who dominated the assembly opposed all challenges to their authority, whether from the Regulators or from the British ministry. When England tightened its colonial administration, North Carolinians joined their fellow colonists in protests against the Stamp Act and similar impositions by Parliament. Meeting at Halifax in April 1776, the North Carolina provincial congress resolved in favor of American independence, the first colonial representative body to do so. Years later, citizens of Mecklenburg County recalled a gathering in 1775 during which their region declared independence, but subsequent historians have not verified their claim. The two dates on the North Carolina state flag nevertheless commemorate the Halifax Resolves and the "Mecklenburg Declaration of Independence."

Support for Britain appeared among recent Scottish immigrants, who answered the call to aid the royal governor but were ambushed by patriot militia at Moore's Creek Bridge on 27 February 1776. The incident effectively prevented a planned British invasion of the South. There was little further military action in North Carolina until late in the War for Independence, when General Charles Cornwallis invaded the state from South Carolina in the fall of 1780. Guerrilla bands harassed his troops, and North Carolina militia wiped out a Loyalist detachment at King's Mountain. Pursuing the elusive American army under General Nathanael Greene, Cornwallis won a costly victory at Guilford Courthouse in March 1781 but could neither eliminate his rival nor pacify the countryside. For the rest of 1781, Cornwallis wearied his men in marches and countermarches across North Carolina and Virginia before he finally succumbed to a trap set at Yorktown, Va., by an American army and a French fleet.

Numerous problems beset the new state. The government had a dire need of money, but when the victors sought to pay debts by selling land confiscated from the Loyalists, conservative lawyers objected strenuously, and a bitter political controversy ensued. Suspicious of outside control, North Carolina leaders hesitated before joining the Union. The state waited until November 1789 to ratify the US Constitution—a delay that helped stimulate the movement for adoption of a Bill of Rights. North Carolina relinquished its lands beyond the Great Smokies in 1789 (after an unsuccessful attempt by settlers to create a new state called Franklin), and thousands of North Carolinians migrated to the new western territories. The state did not share in the general prosperity of the early federal period. Poor transportation facilities hampered all efforts to expand commercial agriculture, and ignorance remained widespread. North Carolina society came to appear so backward that some observers nicknamed it the "Rip Van Winkle state."

In 1815, State Senator Archibald D. Murphey of Orange County began to press for public schools and for improved transportation to open up the piedmont. Most eastern planters resisted Murphey's suggestions, partly because they refused to be taxed for the benefit of the westerners and partly because they feared the destabilizing social effects of reform. As long as the east controlled the general assembly, the ideas of Murphey and his sympathizers had little practical impact, but in 1835, as a result of reforms in the state constitution, the west obtained reapportionment and the political climate changed. North Carolina initiated a program of state aid to railroads and other public-works, and established the first state-supported system of common schools in the South.

Like other southern whites, North Carolina's white majority feared for the security of slavery under a national Republican administration, but North Carolinians reacted to the election of Abraham Lincoln with caution. When South Carolina and six other states seceded and formed the Confederate States of America in 1861, North Carolina refused to join, instead making a futile attempt to work for a peaceful settlement of the issue. However, after the outbreak of hostilities at Ft. Sumter, S.C., and Lincoln's call for troops in April 1861, neutrality disappeared and pulic opinion swung to the Confederate side. North Carolina became the last state to withdraw from the Union, joining the Confederacy on 20 May 1861.

North Carolina provided more troops to the Confederacy than any other state, and its losses added up to more than one-fourth of the total for the entire South, but support for the war was mixed. State leaders resisted the centralizing tendencies of the Richmond government, and even Governor Zebulon B. Vance opposed the Confederacy's conscription policies. North Carolina became a haven for deserters from the front lines in Virginia. William W. Holden, a popular Raleigh editor, organized a peace movement when defeat appeared inevitable, and Unionist sentiment flourished in the mountain counties; nevertheless, most white North Carolinians stood by Vance and the dying Confederate cause. At the war's end, General Joseph E. Johnston surrendered the last major Confederate army to General William T. Sherman at Bennett House near Hillsborough on 26 April 1865.

Reconstruction marked a bitter political and social struggle in North Carolina. United in the Conservative Party, most of the prewar slaveholding elite fought to preserve as much as possible of the former system, but a Republican coalition of blacks and nonslaveholding white Unionists defended freedmen's rights and instituted democratic reforms for the benefit of both races. After writing a new constitution in 1868, Republicans elected Holden as governor, but the native whites fought back with violence and intimidation under the robes of the Ku Klux Klan. Holden's efforts to restore order were ineffectual, and when the Conservatives recaptured the general assembly in 1870, they impeached him and removed him from office. Election of a Conservative governor in 1876 signaled the end of the Reconstruction era.

Once in power, the Conservatives—or Democrats, as they renamed themselves—slashed public services and enacted legislation to guarantee the power of landlords over tenants and sharecroppers. They cooperated with the consolidation of railroads under northern ownership, and they supported a massive drive to build cotton mills on the swiftly flowing streams of the piedmont. By 1880, industry had surpassed its prewar level. But it was not until the turn of the century that blacks and their white allies were entirely eliminated as contenders for political power.

As the Industrial Revolution struck North Carolina, small farmers protested their steadily worsening condition. The Populist Party expressed their demands for reform, and for a brief period in the 1890s shared power with the Republican Party in the Fusion movement. Under the leadership of Charles Brantley Aycock, conservative Democrats fought back with virulent denunciations of "Negro rule" and a call for white supremacy. In 1900, voters elected Aycock governor and approved a constitutional amendment that barred all illiterates from voting, except for those whose ancestors had voted before 1867. This literacy test and "grandfather clause" effectively disenfranchised blacks, while providing a temporary loophole for uneducated whites. To safeguard white rights after 1908 (the constitutional limit for registration under the grandfather clause), Aycock promised substantial improvements in the school system to put an end to white illiteracy.

In the decades after Aycock's election, an alliance of business interests and moderate-to-conservative Democrats dominated North Carolina politics. The industrial triumvirate of textile, tobacco, and furniture manufacturers, joined by banks and insurance companies, controlled the state's economy. The Republican Party shriveled to a small remnant among mountain whites as blacks were forced out of the electorate. Political leaders emphasized fiscal responsibility, honest government, state assistance to aid economic growth, a tolerable level of social services, and a relative absence of racist extremism. Moderate business influence was so pervasive that political scientist V. O. Key labeled North Carolina a "progressive plutocracy" in the 1930s.

In the years since World War II, North Carolina has taken its place in the booming Sunbelt economy. The development of Research Triangle Park, equidistant from the educational facilities of Duke University, North Carolina State University, and the University of North Carolina at Chapel Hill, has provided a home for dozens of scientific laboratories for government and business. New industries, some of them financed by foreign capital, have apppeared in formerly rural areas, and a prolonged population drain has been reversed. The process of development has not been smooth, however. White backlash followed renewed activism among blacks in the 1960s, and the Republican Party (especially its conservative wing) rebounded as the national Democratic Party became closely identified with liberalism. In 1972, North Carolina elected its first Republican US senator and governor since Fusion days.

¹²STATE GOVERNMENT

North Carolina has operated under three constitutions, adopted in 1776, 1868, and 1971, respectively. The first was drafted hurriedly under wartime pressures and contained several inconsistencies and undemocratic features. The second, a product of Reconstruction, was written by native white Republicans and a sprinkling of blacks and northern-born Republicans. When conservative whites regained power, they left the basic framework of this constitution intact, though they added the literacy test, poll tax, and grandfather clause to it.

A century after the Civil War, the document had become unwieldy and partially obsolete. A constitutional study commission submitted to the general assembly in 1969 a rewritten constitution which the electorate ratified, as amended, in 1971. As of mid-1980, seven other amendments had been added, the most important of which permits the governor and lieutenant governor to serve two successive four-year terms.

Under the new constitution, the general assembly consists of a 50-member senate and a 120-member house of representatives. Senators must be at least 25 years old, must be qualified voters of the state, and must have been residents of the state for at least two years prior to election; representatives must be qualified voters of the state and must have lived in their district for at least a year.

The governor and lieutenant governor (who run separately) must be 30 years old; each must have been a US citizen for five years and a North Carolina resident for two years. The only state governor without a veto, North Carolina's chief executive has powers of appointment, supervision, and budgetary recommendation. The voters also elect a secretary of state, treasurer, auditor, superintendent of public instruction, attorney general, and commissioners of agriculture, insurance, and labor. These officials preside over their respective departments and sit with the governor and lieutenant governor as the council of state. The governor appoints the heads of the nine other major executive departments.

Bills become law when they have passed three readings in each house of the general assembly. Constitutional amendments may be proposed by a convention called by a two-thirds vote of both houses or may be submitted directly to the voters by a three-fifths consent of each house. In either case, the proposed amendments must be ratified by a popular majority before becoming part of the constitution.

Prospective voters in North Carolina must be US citizens who are at least 18 years old and have never been convicted of a felony. They must have lived in North Carolina for one year and in their home precinct for 30 days prior to the election.

¹³POLITICAL PARTIES

Prior to the Civil War, Whigs and Democrats were the two major political groups in North Carolina. The Republican Party emerged during Reconstruction as a coalition of newly enfranchised blacks, northern immigrants, and disaffected native whites, especially from nonslaveholding areas in the mountains. The opposing Conservative Party, representing a coalition of antebellum Democrats and former Whigs, became the Democratic Party after winning the governorship in 1876; from that time and for most of the 20th century, North Carolina was practically a one-party state. Beginning in the 1930s, however, as blacks reentered the electorate as supporters of the New Deal and the liberal measures associated with Democratic presidents, the Republican Party attracted new white members who objected to national Democratic policies. Republican presidential candidates picked up strength in the 1950s and 1960s, and Richard Nixon carried North Carolina in 1968 and 1972, when Republicans also succeeded in electing Governor James Holshouser and US Senator Jesse Helms. The Watergate scandal cut short this movement toward a revitalized two-party system. Although Helms—one of the most conservative members of the US Senate—won a decisive victory in 1978, voters chose only 5 Republican state senators out of 50 and only 15 Republican state representatives out of 120. Of the 2,357,649 registered voters in 1978, 73% were Democrats, 23% were Republicans, and 4% were unaffiliated.

In the 1980 presidential election, Republican Ronald Reagan narrowly won North Carolina, with a plurality of 49% of the popular vote, while another Republican, John P. East, won an

North Carolina Presidential Vote by Political Parties, 1948–80

YEAR	ELECTORAL VOTE	NORTH CAROLINA WINNER	DEMOCRAT	REPUBLICAN	STATES' RIGHTS DEMOCRAT	PROGRESSIVE
1948	14	*Truman (D)	459,070	258,572	69,652	3,915
1952	14	Stevenson (D)	652,803	558,107	—	—
1956	14	Stevenson (D)	590,530	575,069	—	—
1960	14	*Kennedy (D)	713,136	655,420	—	—
1964	13	*Johnson (D)	800,139	624,841	—	—
						AMERICAN IND.
1968	13	*Nixon (R)	464,113	627,192	—	496,188
						AMERICAN
1972	13	*Nixon (R)	438,705	1,054,889	—	25,018
					LIBERTARIAN	
1976	13	*Carter (D)	927,365	741,960	2,219	5,607
1980	13	*Reagan (R)	875,635	915,018	9,677	—

*Won US presidential election.

even closer race for the US Senate, defeating the Democratic incumbent, Robert Morgan, by less than 1% of the total votes cast. A conservative Democrat, Governor James B. Hunt, Jr., was easily reelected, however.

Minor parties have had a marked influence on the state. George Wallace's American Independent Party won 496,188 votes in 1968, placing 2d with more than 31% of the total vote. At least two Communist parties are presently active, the Revolutionary Communist Party and the Communist Workers Party (CWP). Both groups oppose the Ku Klux Klan and the American Nazi Party on the far right; five members of the CWP were killed in a confrontation with Klan sympathizers in Greensboro on 4 November 1979.

14 LOCAL GOVERNMENT

As of 1977, North Carolina had 100 counties, 472 municipalities, and 302 special districts.

Counties have been the basis of local government in North Carolina for more than 300 years, and are still the primary governmental units for most citizens. All counties are led by boards of commissioners; most boards have five members serving staggered four-year terms, but membership may vary from three to seven, and terms may be concurrent for two years as well as four. Most boards elect their own chairman from among their own members, but voters in some counties choose a chairman separately. More than half the counties employ a county manager to supervise day-to-day operations of county government. Counties are subdivided into townships, but these are for administrative convenience only; they do not exercise any independent government functions.

About 43% of all North Carolinians lived in incorporated cities and towns in 1970. County and municipal governments share many functions, but the precise allocation of authority varies in each case. Although the city of Charlotte and Mecklenburg County share a common school system, most often schools, streets, sewers, garbage collection, police and fire protection, and other services are handled separately. Most cities use the council-manager form of government, with council members elected from the city at large. Proliferation of suburban governments is prevented by a 1972 constitutional amendment that forbids the incorporation of a new town or city within 1 mi (1.6 km) of a city of 5,000 people, within 3 mi (4.8 km) of a city of 10,000, within 4 mi (6.4 km) of a city of 25,000, and within 5 mi (8 km) of any larger city.

15 STATE SERVICES

The Department of Public Instruction administers state aid to local public school systems and coordinates the community college system; a board of governors directs the 16 state-supported institutions of higher education. The Department of Cultural Resources offers a variety of educational and enrichment services to the public, maintaining historical sites, operating two major state museums, funding the North Carolina Symphony, and providing for the State Library. The Department of Transportation plans, builds, and maintains state highways, registers motor vehicles, and develops airport facilities.

Within the Department of Human Resources, the Division of Mental Health Services operates four regional psychiatric hospitals, four regional mental retardation centers, and three alcoholic rehabilitation centers; it also coordinates 41 area mental health programs that include community mental health centers, group homes for the mentally retarded and emotionally disturbed, sheltered workshops, and halfway houses. The Division of Social Services administers public assistance programs, and other divisions license medical facilities, promote public health, administer programs for juvenile delinquents and the vocationally handicapped, and operate a school for the blind and three schools for the deaf.

The Department of Crime Control and Public Safety encompasses the Highway Patrol and the National Guard, while the Department of Correction manages the prison system. Local law enforcement agencies receive assistance from the State Bureau of Investigation and the Police Information Network. The Community Assistance Division of the Department of Natural Resources and Community Development offers a variety of planning services to local government in the areas of housing, neighborhood renewal, and fiscal resources. The Department of Labor administers the state and federal Occupational Safety and Health Acts; inspects boilers, elevators, mines, and quarries; offers conciliation and arbitration services to settle labor disputes; and enforces state laws governing child labor, minimum wages, maximum working hours, overtime pay, and uniform wage payment.

16 JUDICIAL SYSTEM

North Carolina's general court of justice is a unified judicial system that includes appellate courts, superior courts, and district courts. The system splits the state geographically into four judicial divisions and 32 smaller judicial districts. District court judges are elected to four-year terms; judges above that level are elected for eight years.

The state's highest court, the supreme court, consists of a chief justice and 6 associate justices. It hears cases from the court of appeals as well as certain cases from lower courts. The court of appeals comprises 12 judges who hear cases in 3-judge panels. Superior courts have original jurisdiction in most major civil and criminal cases. There is a superior court justice in each district; 8 additional justices, appointed by the governor to four-year terms, rotate between the districts within their divisions. District courts try misdemeanors, civil cases involving less than $5,000, and all domestic cases. They have no juries, but cases may be appealed to superior court and be given a jury trial de novo.

As of 1980, the Department of Corrections operated 82 prisons and 7 youth centers. In addition, there were 100 county jails and 58 city jails. A total of 7,196 persons were employed in the corrections system in North Carolina in 1977. North Carolina's overall crime rate ranked 39th in the US in 1978, but the level of personal violence was alarmingly high: 10.8 murders and 318 aggravated assaults per 100,000 population.

North Carolina punishes crime severely. At the end of 1976, the state prison held 214 inmates per 100,000 population, an incarceration rate that ranked 3d in the US and was more than twice as high as the national average for state prisons. The US Supreme Court invalidated North Carolina's death penalty statute in 1976, and the sentences of all inmates then on death row reverted to life imprisonment. The state passed a new capital punishment statute in 1977 that apparently met the Court's objections.

17 ARMED FORCES

North Carolina holds the headquarters of the 3d Army at Ft. Bragg in Fayetteville and a major training facility for the Marine Corps at Camp Lejeune in Jacksonville. The Marine Corps air stations at Cherry Point and New River and Seymour Johnson Air Force Base in Goldsboro are the state's other important military installations. North Carolina firms received $437 million in defense contract awards in 1978.

There were 622,000 veterans living in North Carolina as of 30 September 1979; 11,000 saw service in World War I, 245,000 in World War II, 116,000 in the Korean conflict, and 200,000 during the Viet-Nam era. Veterans' benefits totaled $523.7 million in 1977/78.

The strength of the North Carolina National Guard was 11,700 in 1978. Police personnel numbered 12,158 in 1977; 78% were local forces.

18 MIGRATION

For most of the state's history, more people have moved away every decade than have moved into the state, and population growth has come only from net natural increase. In 1850, one-third of all free, native-born North Carolinians lived outside the state, chiefly in Tennessee, Georgia, Indiana, and Alabama. The state suffered a net loss of population from migration in every decade from 1870 to 1970.

Before 1890, the emigration rate was higher among whites than among blacks; since then, the reverse has been true, but the number of whites moving into North Carolina did not exceed the number of white emigrants until the 1960s. White immigrants exceeded white emigrants by 132,000 during the 1970–75 period. Between 1940 and 1970, 539,000 more blacks left North Carolina than moved into the state; most of these emigrants sought homes in the North and West. After 1970, however, black outmigration abruptly slackened as economic conditions in eastern North Carolina improved. The state's net loss from black emigration was only 4,000 during the first five years of the 1970s, and the 1980 census was expected to show a net gain from migration among North Carolina blacks.

[19] INTERGOVERNMENTAL COOPERATION

North Carolina adheres to 25 interstate compacts, including 4 that promote regional planning and development. The oldest of the 4, establishing the Board of Control for Southern Regional Education, pools the resources of southern states for the support of graduate and professional schools. The Southeastern Forest Fire Protection Compact promotes regional forest conservation, while the Southern Nuclear Board fosters cooperation in nuclear power development. The Southern Growth Policies Board, formed in 1971 at the suggestion of former North Carolina Governor Terry Sanford, collects and publishes data for planning purposes from its headquarters in Research Triangle Park.

The Tennessee Valley Authority operates three dams in western North Carolina to aid in flood control, to generate hydroelectric power, and to assist navigation downstream on the Tennessee River; most of the electricity generated is exported to Tennessee. Total federal aid in 1978/79 was $1.8 billion, including $170 million in general revenue sharing.

[20] ECONOMY

North Carolina's economy was dominated by agriculture until the closing decades of the 19th century, with tobacco the major cash crop; today, tobacco is still the central factor in the economy of the coastal plain. In the piedmont, industrialization accelerated after 1880, when falling crop prices made farming less attractive. During the "cotton mill crusade" of the late 19th and early 20th centuries, local capitalists put spinning or weaving mills on swift streams throughout the region, until nearly every hamlet had its own factory. Under the leadership of James B. Duke, the American Tobacco Co. (now American Brands, with headquarters in New York City) expanded from its Durham headquarters during this same period to control, for a time, virtually the entire US market for smoking products. After native businessmen had established a successful textile boom, New England firms moved south in an effort to cut costs, and the piedmont became a center of southern industrial development.

As more and more Tarheels left agriculture for the factory, their per capita income rose from 47% of the national average in 1930 to about 85% in 1978. The biggest employers are the textile and furniture industries. Wages in these labor-intensive fields remain comparatively low in all states, but especially low in North Carolina. As of 1978, North Carolina led the nation in the proportion of industrial workers in its nonagricultural work force, but had the lowest industrial wage rate and the 2d-lowest level of unionization.

Since the 1950s, state government has made a vigorous effort to recruit outside investment and to improve the state's industrial mix. Major new firms now produce electrical equipment, processed foods, technical instruments, fabricated metals, plastics, and chemicals. The greatest industrial growth, however, has come not from wholly new industries but from fields related to industries that were firmly established. Apparel manufacture spread across eastern North Carolina during the 1960s as an obvious extension of the textile industry, and other new firms produce chemicals and machinery for the textile and furniture business.

The major test for North Carolina's continued economic growth will be whether the state can break out of the low-skill, low-wage trap. Despite recent improvements, North Carolina is still poor; per capita income is not expected to match the national average until shortly before the year 2000. Labor-intensive traditional industries cannot be relied on to meet all the needs for sustained growth. The textile industry, moreover, faces the threat of foreign competition, and tobacco interests face a federal antismoking campaign.

[21] INCOME

In 1978, North Carolina's per capita personal income averaged $6,607, 41st among the 50 states. Measured in constant dollars, per capita income increased by 40% between 1970 and 1978, considerably faster than the national rate and nearly equal to the rate for the south Atlantic region. North Carolina's total personal income of $36.8 billion in 1978 represented 2.2% of the US total.

Per capita income levels in 1977 showed considerable geographical variation, ranging from $7,739 in urban Mecklenburg County (Charlotte) to $3,646 in mountainous Avery County. Only 19 counties out of 100 exceeded the statewide average of $5,916 in that year; all of the 19 contained sizable urban centers. Median family income was $11,384 (44th in the US) in 1975, when 14.7% of North Carolina residents and 12.1% of all families were below the poverty level.

[22] LABOR

North Carolina is unusual for combining a predominantly industrial and service-related work force with a dispersed pattern of rural residence. North Carolina's civilian labor force numbered 2,679,000 in 1978; 79.5% of these workers were white and 55.8% were male. The proportion of all women who participated in the work force that year was 55.5%, the 6th-highest level in the nation. The overall unemployment rate was 4.3% (the lowest in the US), although the rates for women and nonwhites were 5.8% and 9%, respectively.

A federal census of workers covered by unemployment insurance in March 1977 revealed the following nonfarm employment pattern in North Carolina:

	ESTABLISH-MENTS	EMPLOYEES	ANNUAL PAYROLL ('000)
Agricultural services, forestry, fishing	962	5,013	$ 34,745
Mining	163	4,682	55,808
Contract construction	13,058	104,034	1,008,073
Manufacturing, of which:	9,107	756,088	7,562,996
Tobacco manufactures	(33)	(22,097)	(312,295)
Textile mill products	(1,305)	(246,943)	(2,148,168)
Apparel, other textiles	(625)	(74,315)	(470,595)
Furniture and fixtures	(603)	(75,158)	(657,055)
Transportation, public utilities	3,701	94,042	1,255,689
Wholesale trade	9,633	109,889	1,309,015
Retail trade	33,065	298,246	1,995,885
Finance, insurance, real estate	8,817	90,410	923,074
Services	27,404	262,531	2,078,779
Other	1,353	1,881	21,610
TOTALS	107,263	1,726,816	$16,245,674

Another 318,000 North Carolinians, not included in this survey, were employed by the federal, state, and local governments in 1978.

North Carolina working conditions have brought the state considerable notoriety in recent years. As of April 1980, the average North Carolina factory worker received a wage of $4.82

per hour, the lowest industrial wage rate in the US and 68% of the national average. The overall labor climate is antiunion. In 1976, the state had 141,000 union members, accounting for only 6.8% of all nonagricultural employees—a percentage that ranked 49 among the 50 states, exceeding only that of South Carolina. Of the 100 union representation elections decided in 1978, the unions won 35 and lost 63. Work stoppages are rare.

North Carolina has a right-to-work law, and public officials are legally barred from negotiating with any collective bargaining unit. The major symbol of resistance to unionization in recent decades has been the J. P. Stevens Co., a textile firm found guilty of illegal labor practices 21 times between 1966 and 1979, the highest conviction rate in US history. The Amalgamated Clothing and Textile Workers Union (AFL–CIO) won the right to represent employees at seven J. P. Stevens mills in Roanoke Rapids but waged a 17-year battle to use it; not until 1980 was a contract finally approved. In the interim, Stevens was found guilty of refusing to bargain in good faith by the National Labor Relations Board and a US court of appeals, and union supporters had turned to a national boycott of Stevens products as an additional source of pressure on the company. Despite this settlement, Stevens maintained it would continue to block organizational efforts at its other plants.

23 AGRICULTURE

Agricultural income in North Carolina totaled $3.3 billion in 1978, 11th among the 50 states. North Carolina leads the nation in the production of tobacco and sweet potatoes, ranks 4th in peanuts, and is also a leading producer of corn, sorghum, and soybeans. Farm life plays an important role in the culture and traditions of the state.

The number of hired and family workers on North Carolina farms was 153,000 in 1979, down from 590,000 in 1950. According to state government statistics, the number of farms fell from 301,000 in 1950 to 98,000 in 1980, while the number of acres in farms declined from 17,800,000 to 12,300,000 (7,203,000 to 4,978,000 hectares); average farm size almost doubled during the same period. Nevertheless, at 126 acres (51 hectares), the average North Carolina farm is still less than one-third the size of the average US farm—a statistic that in part reflects the smaller acreage requirements of tobacco, the state's principal crop. The relatively large number of family farm owner-operators who depend on a modest tobacco allotment to make their small acreages profitable is the basis for North Carolina's opposition to the US government's antismoking campaign.

Although farm employment continues to decline, more than one-third of all North Carolina jobs are still linked to agriculture either directly or indirectly. North Carolina's most heavily agricultural counties are massed in the coastal plain, the center of tobacco production, along with a bank of northern piedmont counties on the Virginia border. Peanuts are the major crop of six counties in the northeast, while corn and soybean production is spread evenly over the coastal plain and spills over into the piedmont. Cotton is grown in scattered counties along the South Carolina border and in a band leading northward across the coastal plain. Beans, tomatoes, cucumbers, strawberries, and blueberries are commercial crops in selected mountain and coastal plain locations. Apples are important to the economy of the mountains, and the sand hills are a center of peach cultivation.

In 1980, tobacco production was estimated at 771,000,000 lb, worth $1 billion. Production and value data for North Carolina's other principal crops in 1979 was as follows: corn, 128,440,000 bushels, $359,632,000; soybeans, 45,825,000 bushels, $293,280,000; peanuts, 378,480,000 lb, $77,210,000; sweet potatoes, 4,920,000 hundredweight, $37,392,000; and hay, 589,000 tons, $34,751,000.

24 ANIMAL HUSBANDRY

Livestock and poultry production, increasingly important sectors of North Carolina's farm economy, accounted for about 40% of

agricultural income in 1978. Production figures in 1979 for cattle and calves were 277.7 million lb, worth $175 million; and hogs and pigs, 784.6 million lb, $331.9 million. As of December 1979 there were 1,080,000 cattle and 2,600,000 hogs on North Carolina farms and ranches. Dairy cows numbered 141,000 in 1979, when milk production reached nearly 1.6 billion lb.

The poultry business has also expanded. North Carolina is now the 3d-leading source of chickens in the US, with 72.1 million lb, worth $21.2 million, produced in 1979. The state ranks 4th in broilers, producing more than 1.5 billion lb, worth $386 million; 2d in turkeys, 397.3 million lb, $162.9 million; and 6th in eggs, 3.2 billion, $172.7 million.

25 FISHING

North Carolina's fishing industry ranks 2d only to Virginia's among the South Atlantic states, but its overall economic importance has declined. The total catch in 1978 was 299.5 million lb, valued at $40.6 million. Flounder, striped bass, and menhaden are the most valuable finfish; shrimp, oysters, and crabs are the most sought-after shellfish.

26 FORESTRY

As of 1977, forests covered 20,043,000 acres (8,111,000 hectares) in North Carolina, or about 64% of the state's total land area. North Carolina's forests constitute 2.7% of all US forestland, and fully 97.6% of the state's wooded areas have commercial value. The largest tracts are found along the coast and beyond the Blue Ridge, where most counties are more than 70% tree-covered. National forests embrace nearly 7% of North Carolina's timberlands, and state and local forests protect another 2%. The remainder is privately owned.

In the days of wooden sailing vessels, North Carolina pine trees supplied large quantities of "naval stores"—tar, pitch, and turpentine for waterproofing and other nautical purposes. Today the state produces mainly saw logs, pulpwood, and veneer logs. Shipments of lumber and wood products were valued at nearly $1.5 billion in 1977; wood household furniture, $1.2 billion; and paper and allied products, $1.6 billion.

27 MINING

At least 300 varieties of rock and minerals occur in North Carolina, and more than 70 have commercial importance. Iron production flourished briefly in the early 19th century but declined after 1830. Surprisingly, North Carolina was the nation's foremost source of gold before 1849. Most North Carolina minerals, however, are too scarce to be mined profitably today. The state's mineral industries ranked 33d in the nation in 1978, when the value of mineral products was $263 million.

Sand, gravel, and crushed stone account for the bulk of North Carolina's mining industry, but some other minerals have national importance. The state ranks 1st in the production of feldspar and mica, 3d in phosphate rock, and 4th in asbestos and clay; it also contains 80% of US lithium ore reserves. Other mineral products include kaolin, talc, pyrophylite, olivine, and cement. Sites near Grandfather Mountain and Spruce Pine have been identified as potential sources of uranium ore. Searching for gems and semiprecious stones is popular among amateur rockhounds in western North Carolina.

28 ENERGY AND POWER

Except for a modest volume of hydroelectric power, the energy consumed in North Carolina comes from outside sources. The state used 1.48 quadrillion Btu of energy in 1977, of which 51% came from petroleum, 36% from coal, 5% from natural gas, 4% from nuclear power, nearly 4% from hydropower, and minimal amounts from other sources. Residential users consumed about 19% of North Carolina's energy in that year, commercial users 12%, industrial users 26%, and transportation 43%.

Installed electrical capacity totaled 16.1 million kw in 1978, and production reached 65.1 billion kwh. Private utilities produced 98% of North Carolina's electricity in 1978. Duke Power

Co. was the largest supplier, with 1,080,551 customers. The Brunswick station operated by Carolina Power & Light (CP&L) was the only on-line nuclear generating facility in North Carolina; Duke Power had 10 new reactors either planned or under construction, and CP&L was building four reactors at its massive Shearon Harris plant south of Raleigh. An unusual generating facility is the 1.5-mw wind-powered plant (the world's largest as of 1980) that supplies electricity to a rural cooperative near Boone.

No petroleum or natural gas has been found in North Carolina, but major companies have expressed interest in offshore drilling, and plans for two coastal refineries are under way.

²⁹INDUSTRY

North Carolina has had a predominantly industrial economy for most of the 20th century. By 1976, North Carolina ranked 2d only to Texas among southern states in value added by manufacturing, and it placed 10th in the US overall. Today, the state is the nation's largest manufacturer of textiles, cigarettes, bricks, and furniture. The textile industry was the largest employer, followed by furniture, apparel, electric and electronic equipment, food processing, lumber and wood products, and nonelectrical machinery.

The total value added by manufacture exceeded $18.1 billion in 1977, with the textile industry contributing 24% of this total. Of the other major industries, tobacco added 11%, chemicals 9%, electrical equipment 8%, furniture 7%, food products 6%, and nonelectrical machinery 5%.

The following table shows value added by manufacture for selected industries in 1972 and 1977:

	1972	1977
Cigarettes	$1,198,500,000	$1,879,400,000
Weaving mill products	815,100,000	1,411,800,000
Knitting mill products	986,500,000	1,313,700,000
Household furniture	783,600,000	1,148,900,000
Yarn and thread	752,900,000	1,018,800,000
Plastics, synthetics	452,000,000	723,700,000
Drugs	NA	429,900,000
Communications equipment	NA	323,400,000

The industrial regions of North Carolina spread out from the piedmont cities; roughly speaking, each movement outward represents a step down in the predominant level of skills and wages and a step closer to the primary processing of raw materials. R. J. Reynolds Industries (tobacco and food products) has its headquarters at Winston-Salem, while Burlington Industries, Blue Bell Inc., and Cone Mills are major US textile corporations based in Greensboro. The furniture industry is centered in the High Point–Thomasville and Hickory-Statesville areas. Charlotte's factories produce electrical appliances, textiles, and chemicals and machinery for the textile industry. Broad rural areas of the piedmont also have many industrial installations: Gaston County near Charlotte contains the largest concentration of textile factories in the US.

³⁰COMMERCE

The wholesale trade of North Carolina was valued at $27.5 billion in 1977, 12th in the US. Wholesaling is concentrated in the Piedmont Crescent, with the Charlotte-Gastonia metropolitan area alone accounting for 40% of all 1977 sales. Charlotte is the regional distribution center for textile machinery, automobiles and parts, groceries, and chemicals. Retail sales, exceeding $16.8 billion in 1977, are much more widely distributed than wholesale. The leading retail sectors in 1977 were food stores, 23%; automotive dealers, 22%; gasoline service stations, 8%; department stores, 8%; and eating and drinking places, 7%.

The state ports at Wilmington and Morehead City handle a growing volume of international trade. Tobacco, wood pulp, and phosphates made up nearly three-fourths of all exports in 1977, while iron and steel, asphalt, and oil constituted two-fifths of all imports. North Carolina exported $964 million worth of agricultural commodities to foreign markets in 1976/77 (8th in the US); manufactured exports totaled $2.2 billion in 1976 (13th).

³¹CONSUMER PROTECTION

The Consumer Protection Section of the Department of Justice receives complaints concerning deceptive trade practices and unethical business competition. Although it assists in the resolution of disputes and prosecutes cases of consumer fraud and other criminal violations, it does not represent individual consumers in court. Another section of the department represents the public before the North Carolina Utilities Commission.

³²BANKING

North Carolina's 88 commercial banks held assets of $19.4 billion as of 31 December 1978; their outstanding loans totaled nearly $5.9 billion, and their deposits exceeded $15.8 billion. The state's branch banking law has permitted the growth of several large statewide banking firms: the North Carolina National Bank Corp. (NCNB) of Charlotte and the Wachovia Bank and Trust Co. of Winston-Salem are the two largest banks in the southeastern US and rank among the 50 largest banks in the US. The assets of NCNB were $6.4 billion by the end of 1979, while Wachovia's were $5.1 billion.

There were 155 insured savings and loan associations (44 federally chartered, 111 state-chartered) in North Carolina at the end of 1978; their assets measured $9.7 billion, and their outstanding mortgage loans amounted to $8.5 billion.

³³INSURANCE

North Carolina's insurance industry consisted of 84 domestic and 805 out-of-state companies in 1979; these carriers wrote combined premiums of $2.9 billion in 1977 and incurred losses of $1.6 billion. In 1978, 21 companies carried 11,979,000 life insurance policies worth $65.9 billion. This amounted to $32,800 of life insurance coverage per family, not quite 7% below the US average. Also in 1978, property and liability companies wrote premiums worth more than $1.3 billion, including $399.3 million in automobile liability coverage, $253.1 million in automobile physical damage insurance, and $152.6 million in homeowners' policies.

North Carolina has long required automobile liability insurance for all vehicles, and was the first state to establish a reinsurance facility to share the cost of insuring high-risk drivers among all insurers. In 1979, the general assembly stripped the insurance commissioner's office of most of its regulatory functions.

³⁴SECURITIES

There are no securities exchanges in North Carolina. The Securities Division of the Office of Secretary of State is authorized to protect the public against fraudulent issues and sellers of securities.

³⁵PUBLIC FINANCE

The North Carolina budget is prepared bienially and reviewed annually by the Office of Budget and Management, in consultation with the Advisory Budget Commission, an independent agency composed of four gubernatorial appointees and four members each from the senate and the house of representatives. It is then submitted to the general assembly for amendment and approval. The fiscal year runs from 1 July to 30 June. The following is a summary of consolidated revenues and expenditures for 1979/80 and 1980/81 (revised), in millions:

	1979/80	1980/81
REVENUES		
General fund, of which:	$2,845.4	$3,244.8
Individual income tax	(1,176.9)	(1,276.9)
Corporate income tax	(298.0)	(298.8)
Sales and use tax	(697.1)	(748.5)
Franchise tax	(201.4)	(224.1)
Federal funds	1,240.5	1,296.5
Highway fund	497.6	506.1
Other receipts	448.8	395.7
TOTALS	$5,032.3	$5,443.1

EXPENDITURES	1979/80	1980/81
Education, of which:	$2,235.2	$2,317.8
Public schools	(1,425.5)	(1,462.1)
University system	(581.4)	(662.6)
Human resources	1,199.3	1,276.0
Transportation	581.4	586.0
Other outlays	1,015.8	1,263.3
TOTALS	$5,031.7	$5,443.1

North Carolina's total outstanding state and local debt was $2.7 billion in 1977, or $488 per capita. Only one state, Idaho, had a lower per capita debt burden.

³⁶TAXATION

North Carolina anticipated more than $2.8 billion in tax revenues in 1980/81. The state's total revenues ranked 13th in the US in 1977, but the per capita share of North Carolina taxpayers ranked 27th at $729.

About 56% of state tax revenues in 1979/80 came from individual and corporate income tax. The personal income tax ranges in five steps from 3% on income over $2,000 to 7% on income exceeding $10,000. Most corporate incomes face a 6% levy. The sales and use tax of 3% accounted for 26% of 1979/80 state tax revenues; local governments may impose an additional 1% for their own use. Prescription drugs and certain other articles are exempt from sales tax, but food is not. As of 1980, the cigarette tax was 2¢ a pack, the lowest in the nation, and the gasoline tax was 9¢ a gallon. The state also levies inheritance, gift, insurance, beverage, and franchise taxes.

North Carolina state and local governments received general revenue totaling $5.7 billion in 1977. Of this sum, 27% was collected from the federal government, 49% came from state government, and 24% came from local governments. North Carolina taxpayers contributed $6.79 billion to the federal treasury in 1975/76 and received $6.82 billion in federal expenditures, or $1,249 per capita. North Carolinians filed 2,146,782 federal income tax returns in 1977, paying nearly $3 billion in tax.

³⁷ECONOMIC POLICY

North Carolina subsidized internal improvement companies at the beginning of the 19th century, and its government has actively stimulated economic growth ever since. During the administration of Governor Luther H. Hodges (1954–61), the state began to recruit outside investment directly, developing such forward-looking facilities as Research Triangle Park. After taking office in 1977, Governor James B. Hunt announced a policy of "balanced growth" to disperse future development into areas that have been neglected in the past, while taking steps to protect the environment and rural life-styles from the unwelcome effects of reckless industrial expansion.

A constitutional amendment approved in 1976 gives county governments the right to issue revenue bonds to finance pollution controls for industry and public utilities. The bonds must be repaid by the companies themselves, but the income from the interest paid on the bonds is tax-exempt, thus enabling the borrowers to obtain lower rates.

³⁸HEALTH

Health conditions and health care facilities in North Carolina vary widely from region to region. In the larger cities—and especially in proximity to the excellent medical schools at Duke University and the University of North Carolina at Chapel Hill—quality health care is as readily available as anywhere in the US. On the other hand, four isolated rural counties in the state had no more than a single doctor each in 1978.

The average life span was 69.21 years in 1969–71 (73.78 for women, 64.94 for men), placing North Carolina 44th among the 50 states. The birthrate has dropped from 24.1 live births per 1,000 population in 1960 to 15.3 per 1,000 in 1977, a rate slightly below the national average. In the same year, 15.8 infants per 1,000 live births died before their first birthday. The survival rate is slightly higher for North Carolina white babies than for all US white babies, but it is much lower for North Carolina nonwhite babies than for nonwhites elsewhere. There were 25,100 legal abortions in 1977, or 300 per 1,000 live births. Early childhood diseases are a more serious problem in North Carolina than in other states; these killers took more than 12 lives per 100,000 population in 1977, 14% above the national average. The leading causes of death in North Carolina are similar to those in the rest of the US, although North Carolinians die less frequently from heart disease and cancer than other Americans, and more frequently from stroke, accidents, and pneumonia and influenza.

A particularly serious public health problem in North Carolina is byssinosis, or brown lung disease. Caused by prolonged inhalation of cotton dust, byssinosis cripples the lungs of longtime textile workers, producing grave disability and even death. As of 1980, the Carolina Brown Lung Association estimated that some 25,000 present or former North Carolina textile workers showed symptoms of byssinosis, and that between 10,000 and 15,000 North Carolinians were disabled by it; textile industry estimates ran to less than one-tenth of those figures. Efforts of brown lung victims to claim workers' compensation for their disability have encountered stiff industry opposition, as have the efforts of public health officials to require reductions in the concentrations of airborne dust in the mills. By September 1980, 1,425 workers' compensation claims for brown lung had been filed with the state, of which 444 were found compensable, with total benefits of nearly $6.5 million.

The 158 hospitals in North Carolina contained 33,774 beds in 1978 and experienced a 76.4% occupancy rate. Hospital personnel included 13,278 registered nurses and 6,024 licensed practical nurses. Average hospital costs increased from $115 per day in 1975 to $149 per day in 1977, still below the US average of $198. The cost of an average hospital stay increased from $872 to $1,119 over the same period.

The supply of physicians has improved from a ratio of 113 per 100,000 population in 1970 to 148 in 1977, or 8,018 in all, but still below the national average. Professionally active dentists numbered 2,175 in 1979, or 1 for every 2,562 residents. The state has acted to increase the supply of doctors in eastern North Carolina by the establishment of a new medical school at East Carolina University in Greenville. Medical schools and superior medical research facilities are also located at Duke University Medical Center in Durham, North Carolina Memorial Hospital at the University of North Carolina in Chapel Hill, and the Bowman Gray School of Medicine at Wake Forest University in Winston-Salem.

³⁹SOCIAL WELFARE

North Carolina's social welfare programs are modest by national standards. Public assistance cases numbered 206,998 in May 1978, of whom not quite 40% were receiving monetary payments, while the remainder were receiving medical assistance. Aid to families with dependent children benefited 191,300 persons at a cost of $138 million in 1978. The average payment was $157 per family per month—a sum that, despite inflation, was actually $1 less than the average payment three years earlier; during the same period, average assistance per family increased from $219 to $254 in the nation as a whole. The school lunch program fed 965,000 pupils, or three-fourths of all students in participating schools in 1978, at a federal cost of $74.2 million. Food stamps costing the federal government $126.2 million helped pay the grocery bills for 345,000 persons in the same year.

Social Security benefits paid $1.8 billion to 842,800 retired North Carolina workers in 1977; at $217.50 per month, the average check ranked 43d in the nation. The Supplemental Security Income program paid an additional $174.5 million to 143,300 aged, disabled, and blind recipients in 1978. Medicare enrolled 599,000 North Carolinians for hospital insurance and 591,000 for medical insurance in 1977; trust fund outlays totaled $383 million in benefit payments.

State vocational rehabilitation centers served 49,800 clients in 1978 at a cost of $37.1 million. North Carolinians collected $72.6 million in workers' compensation awards in 1977. In an average week, 37,000 workers received unemployment insurance benefits of $71.65 each; 165,000 workers collected a total of $99 million in 1978.

⁴⁰HOUSING

The 1970 census counted some 1,618,000 units of year-round housing in North Carolina; of these, 82% were single units, 12% were in multiple-unit structures, and 6% were mobile homes. Owners occupied 65% of North Carolina homes, a slightly higher proportion than in the nation at large. The proportion of houses built within the previous 10 years (30.8%) almost equaled the proportion built before 1939 (31.6%). Many housing units had fewer amenities than the average American home: complete plumbing was a feature of only 86% of North Carolina units in 1970, compared with 94% of all US residences. Some 101,900 new housing units were authorized between 1976 and 1978; their combined value exceeded $2.8 billion.

⁴¹EDUCATION

North Carolina's commitment to public education is now exactly commensurate with its means, but its means are still quite slender. The state's rank in per pupil expenditure for public schools is the same as its national rank in per capita income—both stood at 41st in 1978. North Carolina established the first state university in the US and the first free system of common schools in the South—but the university preceded the common schools by 44 years. In other words, although North Carolina led the South in education for the masses, its first love has been education for the few.

The common school system began in 1839 after North Carolina received a windfall share of the federal government's surplus revenue. The system suffered neglect between 1865 and 1900, but revived when the imposition of a literacy test for voting made adequate schooling for whites a political necessity. Opportunities for whites improved thereafter (North Carolina led the nation in construction of rural schools in the 1920s), but the system labored under the burden of racial segregation for many decades longer. In 1957, Charlotte, Greensboro, and Winston-Salem were the first cities in the South to admit black students voluntarily to formerly all-white schools, but further progress came slowly. In 1971, the US Supreme Court, in the landmark decision *Swann v. Charlotte–Mecklenburg Board of Education*, upheld the use of busing to desegregate the Charlotte school system. Widespread desegregation followed throughout the state.

North Carolina reduced its illiteracy rate from 30.1% of the adult population in 1900 to 1.8% in 1970, but that was still higher than the national average of 1.2%. Median school years attended rose to 12.2 for adults over 18 in 1976, but that too was below the US norm. Moreover, in the same year, only 55% of North Carolina adults had completed high school, well below the US average of 67%. The state began a belated experiment in public kindergartens in 1969 and offered the program to all 5-year-olds in 1978. There were 1,459 public elementary schools with 824,388 pupils as of fall 1979; 554 public secondary schools enrolled 359,761 students; and 7,193 exceptional children attended 24 special education schools. Concern over declining academic standards led to the inauguration in 1978 of a statewide competency test which all high school students must pass in order to graduate. Nonpublic school enrollments expanded during most of the 1970s, reaching 57,000 in 354 schools in 1979/80. The popularity of nonpublic education is partly related to desegregation of the public schools, but during the 1970s, thousands of parents placed their children in private Christian academies to protect them from unwanted secular influences.

The University of North Carolina (UNC) was chartered in 1789 and opened at Chapel Hill in 1795. The system now embraces 16 campuses under a common board of governors; total enrollment stood at 107,327 in the fall of 1977. The three oldest and largest campuses, all of which offer research and graduate as well as undergraduate programs, are UNC–Chapel Hill, North Carolina State University at Raleigh (the first land-grant college for the study of agriculture and engineering), and UNC–Greensboro, formerly Women's College. North Carolina's 19 community colleges and 38 technical institutes are intermediate institutions between the public schools and the university system. There were 488,604 students enrolled in these schools in 1976/77.

Duke University at Durham is North Carolina's premier private institution and takes its place with the Chapel Hill and Raleigh public campuses as the third key facility for the Research Triangle. There are 29 other private colleges and universities, of which Wake Forest University in Winston-Salem and Davidson College in Davidson are most noteworthy. North Carolina also has 8 private junior colleges, 3 Bible colleges, and a theological seminary.

⁴²ARTS

North Carolina has been a pioneer in exploring new channels for state support of the arts. It was the first state to fund its own symphony, to endow its own art museum, to found a state school of the arts, to create a statewide arts council, and to establish a cabinet-level Department of Cultural Resources. The North Carolina Symphony, at Raleigh, received its first state appropriation in 1943. Eleven North Carolina cities support amateur or semiprofessional symphonies and opera groups, while music festivals in Greensboro and Brevard reach large summer audiences.

The North Carolina Dance Theater is a professional company attached to the North Carolina School of the Arts in Winston-Salem. At least six Tarheel cities support civic ballet companies, and the American Dance Theater, one of the nation's oldest and most respected summer dance festivals, has made its permanent home at Duke University since 1978. Summer stock theater is a long-standing tradition in the mountains: North Carolina's Pulitzer Prize–winning playwright Paul Green created the genre of outdoor historical drama with a 1937 production of *The Lost Colony* at Manteo, and nearly a dozen other historical dramas are now performed on summer evenings throughout the state.

Folk art has survived most completely in the remote coves and hollows of the Appalachians. Traditional mountain string music inspired bluegrass, a progenitor of modern country and western music. Festivals, fiddlers' conventions, gospel concerts, and other public occasions keep this heritage alive and spread it to a new generation and a wider audience. Traditional crafts—pottery, spinning, weaving, quilting, and woodcarving—are also taught, displayed, and disseminated at fairs and crafts centers, the most notable of which is Penland School of Handicrafts, near Spruce Pine, in the western part of the state.

⁴³LIBRARIES AND MUSEUMS

Public libraries, open in nearly every North Carolina community, are linked together through the State Library, ensuring that users in all parts of the state can have access to printed, filmed, and recorded materials. Total volumes in public libraries numbered 7,686,724 in 1977/78, when circulation reached 18,825,776. Major university research libraries are located at Chapel Hill, Raleigh, and Greensboro campuses of the University of North Carolina and at Duke University in Durham. The North Carolina Collection and Southern Historical Collection at the Chapel Hill campus are especially noteworthy.

North Carolina has at least 110 museums and historic sites. Established in 1956, the North Carolina Museum of Art, in Raleigh, is one of only two state-supported art museums in the US (the other is in Virginia). The North Carolina Museum of History (Raleigh) is housed in the Division of Archives and

History of the Department of Cultural Resources, which also administers 20 state historic sites and Tryon Place Restoration in New Bern. The Museum of Natural History in Raleigh is maintained by the state Department of Agriculture; smaller science museums exist in Charlotte, Greensboro, and Durham. The North Carolina Zoological Park opened in Asheboro in 1975.

44 COMMUNICATIONS
Government postal service in North Carolina began in 1755 but did not become regular until 1771, with the establishment of a central post office for the southern colonies. Mails were slow and erratic, and many North Carolinians continued to entrust their letters to private travelers until well into the 19th century. Rural free delivery in the state began on 23 October 1896 in Rowan County.

Telephone service began in Wilmington and Raleigh in October 1879, and long distance connections between Wilmington and Petersburg, Va., began later that same year. There were 26 telephone companies in North Carolina in 1976; the largest, Southern Bell, owned 53% of all telephone units. In 1978 there were 70 telephones in the state for every 100 inhabitants, and 92% of all households had telephone service, both below the national average. Overall, there were 3,906,567 telephones (2,950,454 residential, 956,113 business) in 1978.

There were 209 commercial AM radio stations in North Carolina in 1978, 85 commercial and 14 noncommercial FM stations; commercial television stations numbered 18, and there were 9 stations belonging to the noncommercial University of North Carolina Television Network. As of 1978, cable television served 155 communities and 242,144 subscribers.

45 PRESS
As of 1978, North Carolina had 10 morning newspapers with a combined circulation of 613,827, 42 evening dailies with 743,655, and 24 Sunday papers with 1,121,392. The following table shows the circulation of the largest dailies as of September 1978:

AREA	NAME	DAILY	SUNDAY
Charlotte	News (e)	55,240	
	Observer (m,S)	172,316	238,312
Durham	Herald (m,S)	42,097	57,770
Greensboro	Daily News (m,S)	83,217	115,963
Raleigh	News & Observer (m,S)	128,177	163,414
Winston-Salem	Journal (m,S)	71,856	94,540

North Carolina has been the home of several nationally recognized "little reviews" of literature, poetry, and criticism, including *The Rebel, Crucible, Southern Poetry Review, The Carolina Quarterly, St. Andrews Review, Pembroke Magazine,* and *Miscellany. The North Carolina Historical Review* is a scholarly publication of the Division of Archives and History. Published in Hendersonville is the bimonthly *Mother Earth News.*

46 ORGANIZATIONS
The North Carolina Citizens Association serves as the voice of the state's business community. A teachers' organization, the North Carolina Association of Educators, is widely acknowledged as one of the most effective political pressure groups in the state, as is the North Carolina State Employees Association. Every major branch of industry has its own trade association, most of which are highly effective lobbying bodies. Carolina Action, the North Carolina Public Interest Research Group, the Kudzu Alliance, and the Carolina Brown Lung Association represent related consumer, environmental, antinuclear power, and public health concerns.

Among the national organizations headquartered in the state are the Improved Benevolent Protective Order of Elks of the World in Winton, a black service group; the Association of Professors of Medicine, Winston-Salem; the Institute for Southern Studies, Chapel Hill; the Tobacco Association of the US, Raleigh; the American Football Coaches Association, Charlotte; and the US Power Squadrons, Raleigh.

47 TOURISM, TRAVEL, AND RECREATION
Travelers spent $2.1 billion in North Carolina in 1979. The travel industry supported 192,200 jobs that year, and in 1978 carried an annual payroll of $692 million. An estimated 47.8 million out-of-state travelers came to North Carolina or passed through it in 1979, of whom about half made the state their destination.

Tourists are attracted by North Carolina's coastal beaches, by golf and tennis opportunities in the piedmont (including the world-famous golf courses at Pinehurst), and parks and scenery in the North Carolina mountains. Sites of special interest are the Revolutionary War battlegrounds at Guilford Courthouse and Moore's Creek Bridge; Bennett Place, near Hillsborough, where the last major Confederate army surrendered; Ft. Raleigh, the site of the Lost Colony's misadventures; and the Wright Brothers National Memorial at Kitty Hawk. Cape Hatteras and Cape Lookout national seashores, which protect the beauty of the Outer Banks, received 1.8 million visitors in 1979. The Blue Ridge Parkway, a scenic motor route, operated by the National Park Service, that winds over the crest of the Blue Ridge in Virginia, North Carolina, and Georgia, attracted 14.8 million visitors. Another popular attraction, Great Smoky Mountains National Park, straddling the North Carolina–Tennessee border, received 11.2 million visitors, more than any other national park. Also in 1979, North Carolina's 26 state parks received more than 4.5 million visitors.

Licenses were sold to 456,063 fishermen and 374,573 hunters in 1977/78.

48 SPORTS
With no major league teams in North Carolina, the most important professional sports are golf and stock-car racing. The Greater Greensboro Open, the Kemper Open in Charlotte, and the Hall of Fame Classic at Pinehurst are major tournaments on the Professional Golfers' Association tour. The North Carolina Motor Speedway in Rockingham hosts the Carolina 500 and the American 500 annually, while the Charlotte Motor Speedway is the home of the World 600, the most lucrative race after the Daytona 500 on the National Association for Stock Car Auto Racing (NASCAR) circuit. In minor league baseball, Charlotte has an entry in the class-AA Southern Association, and four teams play in the North Carolina Division of the class-A Carolina League.

College basketball is the ruling passion of amateur sports fans in North Carolina. Organized in the Atlantic Coast Conference, the University of North Carolina at Chapel Hill, North Carolina State University, Wake Forest University, and Duke University consistently sponsor nationally competitive basketball teams and enlist spirited support from thousands of fans.

Unique North Carolina competitions include the annual Highland Games at Grandfather Mountain, where contestants engage in traditional Scottish sports, and the National Hollerin' Contest at Spivey's Corner, near Dunn.

49 FAMOUS NORTH CAROLINIANS
Three US presidents had North Carolina roots but all three reached the White House from Tennessee. Andrew Jackson (1767–1845), the 7th president, was born in an unsurveyed border region probably in South Carolina, but studied law and was admitted to the bar in North Carolina before moving to frontier Tennessee in 1788. James K. Polk (1795–1849), the 11th president, was born in Mecklenburg County but grew up in Tennessee. Another native North Carolinian, Andrew Johnson (1808–75), was a tailor's apprentice in Raleigh before moving to Tennessee at the age of 18. Johnson served as Abraham Lincoln's vice president for six weeks in 1865 before becoming the nation's 17th president when Lincoln was assassinated. William Rufus King (1786–1853), the other US vice president from North Carolina, also served in that office for only six weeks, dying before he could exercise his duties.

Three native North Carolinians have served as speaker of the

US House of Representatives. The first, Nathaniel Macon (1758–1837), occupied the speaker's chair from 1801 to 1807 and served as president pro tem of the US Senate in 1826–27. The other two were James K. Polk and Joseph G. "Uncle Joe" Cannon (1836–1926), who served as speaker of the House from 1903 to 1911, but as a representative from Illinois.

Sir Walter Raleigh (or Ralegh, b.England, 1552?–1618) never came to North Carolina, but his efforts to found a colony there led state lawmakers to give his name to the new state capital in 1792. Raleigh's "Lost Colony" on Roanoke Island was the home of Virginia Dare (1587–?), the first child of English parents to be born in America. More than a century later, the infamous Edward Teach (or Thatch, b.England, ?–1716) made his headquarters at Bath and terrorized coastal waters as the pirate known as Blackbeard.

Principal leaders of the early national period included Richard Caswell (b.Maryland, 1729–89), Revolutionary War governor; William Richardson Davie (b.England, 1756–1820), governor of the state and founder of the University of North Carolina; and Archibald De Bow Murphey (1777–1832), reform advocate, legislator, and judge. Prominent black Americans of the 19th century who were born or who lived in North Carolina were John Chavis (1763–1838), teacher and minister; David Walker (1785–1830), abolitionist; and Hiram Revels (1827–1901), first black member of the US Senate.

North Carolinians prominent in the era of Civil War and Reconstruction included antislavery author Hinton Rowan Helper (1829–1909), Civil War governor Zebulon B. Vance (1830–94), Reconstruction governor William W. Holden (1818–92), and carpetbagger judge Albion Winegar Tourgée (b.Ohio, 1838–1905). Among major politicians of the 20th century are Furnifold McLendell Simmons (1854–1940), US senator from 1901 to 1931; Charles Brantley Aycock (1859–1912), governor from 1901 to 1905; Frank Porter Graham (1886–1972), University of North Carolina president, New Deal adviser, and US senator, 1949–50; Luther H. Hodges (b.Virginia, 1898–1974), governor from 1954 to 1960, US secretary of commerce from 1961 to 1965, and founder of the Research Triangle Park; Samuel J. Ervin, Jr. (b.1896), US senator from 1954 to 1974 and chairman of the Senate Watergate investigation; and Terry Sanford (b.1917), governor from 1961 to 1965, US presidential aspirant, and president of Duke University. Civil rights leader Jesse Jackson (b.1941) began his career as a student activist in Greensboro. The most famous North Carolinian living today is probably evangelist Billy Graham (b.1918).

James Buchanan Duke (1856–1925) founded the American Tobacco Co. and provided the endowment that transformed Trinity College into Duke University. The most outstanding North Carolina–born inventor was Richard J. Gatling (1818–1903), creator of the "Gatling gun," the first machine gun. The Wright brothers, Wilbur (b.Indiana, 1867–1912) and Orville (b.Ohio, 1871–1948), achieved the first successful powered airplane flight at Kitty Hawk on the Outer Banks on 17 December 1903. Psy-chologist Joseph Banks Rhine (b.Pennsylvania, 1895–1980) was known for his research on extrasensory perception.

A number of North Carolinians have won fame as literary figures. They include Walter Hines Page (1855–1918), editor and diplomat; William Sydney Porter (1862–1910), a short-story writer who used the pseudonym O.Henry; playwright Paul Green (b.1894); and novelists Thomas Wolfe (1900–1938) and Reynolds Price (b.1933). Major scholars associated with the state have included sociologist Howard W. Odum (b.Georgia, 1884–1954) and historians W. J. Cash (1901–41), and John Hope Franklin (b.Oklahoma, 1915). Journalists Edward R. Murrow (1908–65), Tom Wicker (b.1926), and Charles Kuralt (b.1934) were all North Carolina natives.

Jazz artists Thelonious Monk (b.1918), John Coltrane (1926–67), and Nina Simone (b.1933) were born in the state, as were pop singer Roberta Flack (b.1939), folksinger Arthel "Doc" Watson (b.1923), bluegrass banjo artist Earl Scruggs (b.1924), and actor Andy Griffith (b.1926). North Carolina athletes include former heavyweight champion Floyd Patterson (b.1935), NASCAR driver Richard Petty (b.1937), football quarterbacks Sonny Jurgenson (b.1934) and Roman Gabriel (b.1940), baseball pitchers Gaylord Perry (b.1938) and Jim "Catfish" Hunter (b.1946), and basketball player Meadowlark Lemon (b.1932), long a star with the Harlem Globetrotters.

[50] BIBLIOGRAPHY

Barrett, John G. *The Civil War in North Carolina*. Chapel Hill: University of North Carolina Press, 1963.

Chafe, William H. *Civilities and Civil Rights: Greensboro, North Carolina and the Black Struggle for Freedom*. New York: Oxford University Press, 1980.

Clay, James W., Douglas M. Orr, Jr., and Alfred W. Stuart (eds.). *North Carolina Atlas: Portrait of a Changing Southern State*. Chapel Hill: University of North Carolina Press, 1975.

Lefler, Hugh T. *A Guide to the Study and Reading of North Carolina History*. Chapel Hill: University of North Carolina Press, 1969.

Lefler, Hugh T., and Albert Ray Newsome. *North Carolina: The History of a Southern State*. 3d ed., rev. Chapel Hill: University of North Carolina Press, 1973.

North Carolina, State of. Division of State Budget and Management. *North Carolina State Government Statistical Abstract, 1979*. 4th ed. Raleigh, 1979.

North Carolina, State of. Secretary of State. *North Carolina Manual, 1979–80*. Raleigh, 1980.

Powell, William S. *North Carolina: A Bicentennial History*. New York: Norton, 1977.

Powell, William S. *The North Carolina Gazetteer*. Chapel Hill: University of North Carolina Press, 1968.

Rights, Douglas L. *The American Indian in North Carolina*. Winston-Salem: John F. Blair, 1957.

Stick, David. *The Outer Banks of North Carolina, 1584–1958*. Chapel Hill: University of North Carolina Press, 1958.

NORTH DAKOTA

State of North Dakota

ORIGIN OF STATE NAME: The state was formerly the northern section of Dakota Territory; *dakota* is a Siouan word meaning "allies." **NICKNAME:** The Sioux State. (Also: Flickertail State.) **CAPITAL:** Bismarck. **ENTERED UNION:** 2 November 1889 (39th). **SONG:** "North Dakota Hymn." **MARCH:** "Spirit of the Land." **MOTTO:** Liberty and Union, Now and Forever, One and Inseparable. **FLAG:** The flag consists of a blue field with yellow fringes; on each side is depicted an eagle with outstretched wings, holding in one talon a sheaf of arrows, in the other an olive branch, and in his beak a banner inscribed with the words "*E Pluribus Unum*." Below the eagle are the words "North Dakota"; above it are 13 stars surmounted by a sunburst. **OFFICIAL SEAL:** In the center is an elm tree; beneath it are a sheaf of wheat, a plow, an anvil, and a bow and three arrows, and in the background an Indian chases a buffalo toward a setting sun. The depiction is surrounded by the state motto, and the words "Great Seal State of North Dakota October 1st 1889" encircle the whole. **BIRD:** Western meadowlark. **FISH:** Northern pike. **FLOWER:** Wild prairie rose. **TREE:** American elm. **GRASS:** Western wheatgrass. **STONE:** Teredo petrified wood. **LEGAL HOLIDAYS:** New Year's Day, 1 January; George Washington's Birthday, 3d Monday in February; Good Friday, March or April; Memorial Day, last Monday in May; Independence Day, 4 July; Labor Day, 1st Monday in September; Veterans Day, 11 November; Thanksgiving Day, 4th Thursday in November; Christmas Day, 25 December. **TIME:** 6 A.M. CST = noon GMT; 5 A.M. MST = noon GMT.

¹LOCATION, SIZE, AND EXTENT

Located in the western north-central US, North Dakota ranks 17th in size among the 50 states.

The total area of North Dakota is 70,665 sq mi (183,022 sq km), comprising 69,273 sq mi (179,417 sq km) of land and 1,392 sq mi (3,605 sq km) of inland water. Shaped roughly like a rectangle, North Dakota has three straight sides and one irregular border on the E. Its maximum length E–W is about 360 mi (580 km), its extreme width N–S about 210 mi (340 km).

North Dakota is bordered on the N by the Canadian provinces of Saskatchewan and Manitoba; on the E by Minnesota (with the line formed by the Red River of the North); on the S by South Dakota; and on the W by Montana. The total boundary length is 1,312 mi (2,111 km). The state's geographic center is in Sheridan County, 5 mi (8 km) SW of McClusky.

²TOPOGRAPHY

North Dakota straddles two major US physiographic regions: the Central Plains in the east and the Great Plains in the west. Along the eastern border is the generally flat Red River Valley, with the state's lowest point, 750 feet (229 meters); this valley was once covered by the waters of a glacial lake. Most of the eastern half of North Dakota consists of the Drift Prairie, at 1,300–1,600 feet (400–500 meters) above sea level. The Missouri Plateau occupies the western half of the state, and has the highest point in North Dakota—White Butte, 3,506 feet (1,069 meters)—in the Slope Country of the southwest. Separating the Missouri Plateau from the Drift Prairie is the Missouri Escarpment, which rises 400 feet (122 meters) above the prairie and extends diagonally from northwest to southeast.

North Dakota has two major rivers: the Red River of the North, flowing northward into Canada; and the Missouri River, which enters in the northwest and then flows east and, joined by the Yellowstone River, southeast into South Dakota.

³CLIMATE

North Dakota lies in the northwestern continental interior of the US. Characteristically, summers are hot, winters very cold, and rainfall sparse to moderate, with periods of drought. The average annual temperature is 40°F (4°C), ranging from 7°F (−14°C) in January to 69°F (21°C) in July. The record low temperature, −60°F (−51°C), was set at Parshall on 15 February 1936; the record high, 121°F (49°C), at Steele on 6 July 1936.

The average yearly precipitation is about 18 in (46 cm). The total annual snowfall averages 38 in (97 cm) at Bismarck and 32 in (81 cm) at Fargo.

⁴FLORA AND FAUNA

North Dakota is predominantly a region of prairie and plains, though the American elm, green ash, box elder, and cottonwood grow there. Cranberries, juneberries, and wild grapes are also common. Indian, blue, grama, and buffalo grasses grow on the plains; the wild prairie rose is the state flower.

Once on the verge of extinction, the white-tailed and mule deers and pronghorn antelope have been restored. The elk and grizzly bear, both common until about 1880, had disappeared by 1900; bighorn sheep, reintroduced in 1956, are beginning to flourish. North Dakota claims more wild ducks than any state except Alaska, and has the largest sharptailed grouse population in the US. The black-footed ferret and northern swift fox are listed by federal authorities as endangered in North Dakota.

⁵ENVIRONMENTAL PROTECTION

As of September 1978, the US Fish and Wildlife Service owned or leased 260,872 acres (105,572 hectares) of North Dakota land as national wildlife refuges. During that same year, 148,111 acres (59,939 hectares) consisted of North Dakota Game and Fish Department wildlife management areas.

The principal environmental issue confronting the state as the 1980s began was how to make use of the state's coal resources without irreparably damaging the land through strip-mining or polluting the clean air with coal-fired electrical plants.

⁶POPULATION

North Dakota ranked 45th in the US, with a 1970 census population of 617,761, representing a decline of 9% since 1930. The preliminary census population was 652,437 in 1980, when the population density, a little more than 9 per sq mi (4 per sq km), was less than one-sixth the US average. North Dakota was the most rural state in the US in 1977; more than three-fourths of the population lived outside metropolitan areas. Leading cities as of 1980 were Fargo, 61,281; Bismarck, the capital, 44,502; Grand Forks, 43,760; and Minot, 32,886.

⁷ETHNIC GROUPS

As of 1978, Indian lands covered 851,000 acres (344,000 hectares); the Indian population was 14,369 in 1970. Few Asians, black people, or Spanish-speaking Americans live in North Dakota.

First- and second-generation Americans of European origin made up 24% of the population in 1970. The leading groups were Norwegians 6%, Russians 5%, and Germans 3%.

8 LANGUAGES

Although a few Indian words are used in the English spoken near the reservations where Ojibwa and Sioux live in North Dakota, the only general impact of Indian speech on English is in such place-names as Pembina, Mandan, Wabek, and Anamoose. In 1970, 3,090 state residents claimed Indian first languages.

A few Norwegian food terms like *lefse* and *lutefisk* have entered the Northern dialect that is characteristic of North Dakota, and some Midland terms have intruded from the south.

In 1970, only 69% of the native-born and 68% of all state residents, called English their mother tongue. Major resident groups claimed these first languages:

	NATIVE-BORN	FOREIGN-BORN
English	415,032	2,684
German	86,807	7,229
French	5,416	337
Polish	3,164	169

9 RELIGIONS

The vast majority of North Dakota's inhabitants are Protestants. As of 1971, there were 300,905 known adherents of Protestant groups. Leading denominations were American Lutheran Church, with 169,208; United Methodist, 30,067; Lutheran Church–Missouri Synod, 27,647; United Presbyterian, 16,258; and Lutheran Church in America, 14,745.

As of 1979, the state had 172,979 Roman Catholic Church members and an estimated 1,085 Jews.

10 TRANSPORTATION

In 1978 there were 5,117 mi (8,235 km) of railway roadbed in North Dakota. In 1977, the chief railroads—the Burlington Northern, Soo Line, Milwaukee, and Chicago and Northwestern—transported 13,141,691 tons of revenue freight (mostly farm products and coal) originating in North Dakota and 4,032,076 tons terminating in the state.

North Dakota's highways and streets covered 106,641 mi (171,622 km) in 1978. There were 626,210 registered motor vehicles, and 403,050 driver's licenses were in force.

As of June 1979, five commercial airlines were operating in North Dakota: Air Wisconsin, Frontier, Republic, Northwest, and Real West. The state had 96 public and 121 private airfields in 1978, of which Hector Field at Fargo was the most active.

11 HISTORY

Human occupation of what is now North Dakota began about 13,000 BC in the southwestern corner of the state, which at that time was covered with lush vegetation. Drought drove away the aboriginal hunter-gatherers, and it was not until about 2,000 years ago that Indians from the more humid regions to the east moved into the easternmost third of the Dakotas. About AD 1300 the Mandan Indians brought an advanced agricultural economy up the Missouri River. They were joined by the Hidatsa and Arikara about three or four centuries later. Moving from the Minnesota forests during the 17th century, the Yanktonai Sioux occupied the southeastern quarter of the state. Their cousins west of the Missouri River, the Teton Sioux, led a nomadic life as hunters and mounted warriors. The Ojibwa, who had driven the Sioux out of Minnesota, settled in the northeast.

European penetration of the Dakotas began in 1738, when Pierre Gaultier de Varennes, Sieur de la Vérendrye, of Trois Rivières in New France, traded for furs in the Red River region. Later the fur trade spread farther into the Red and Missouri river valleys, especially around Pembina, where the North West Company and the Hudson's Bay Company had their posts. After the Lewis and Clark expedition (1804–16) explored the Missouri, the American Fur Company traded there, with buffalo hides the leading commodity.

In 1812, Scottish settlers from Canada moved up the Red River to Pembina. This first white farming settlement in North Dakota also attracted numerous métis, half-breeds of mixed Indian and European ancestry. An extensive trade in furs and buffalo hides, which were transported first by heavy carts and later by steamboats, sprang up between Pembina, Ft. Garry (Winnipeg, Canada), and St. Paul, Minn.

Army movements against the Sioux during and after the Civil War brought white men into central North Dakota, which in 1861 was organized as part of the Dakota Territory, including the present-day Dakotas, Montana, and Wyoming. The signing of treaties confining the agricultural Indians to reservations, the arrival of the Northern Pacific Railroad at Fargo in 1872, and its extension to the Missouri the following year led to the rise of homesteading on giant "bonanza farms." Settlers poured in, especially from Canada. This short-lived "Great Dakota boom" ended in the mid-1880s with drought and depressed farm prices. As many of the original American and Canadian settlers left in disgust, they were replaced by Norwegians, Germans, and other Europeans, so that by 1910, North Dakota was among the nation's leaders in percentage of foreign-born residents.

North Dakota entered the Union in 1889. From that time onward, Republicans dominated politics in the state. Their leader was Alexander McKenzie, a Canadian immigrant who built a reputation as an agent of the railroads, protecting them from regulation. Only in the depths of the 1893 depression did North Dakotans elect a Populist governor, but after two years they returned the Republicans to power. Between 1898 and 1915, the "Second Boom" brought an upsurge in population and railroad construction. In politics, Republican Progressives enacted reforms, but left unsolved the basic problem of how North Dakota farmers could stand up to the powerful grain traders of Minneapolis–St. Paul. Agrarian revolt flared in 1915, when Arthur C. Townley organized the Nonpartisan League. Operating through Republican Party machinery, Townley succeeded in having his gubernatorial candidate, Lynn J. Frazier, elected in 1916. State-owned enterprises were established, including the Bank of North Dakota, Home Builders Association, Hail Insurance Department, and state mill and grain elevator. However, the league was hurt by charges of "socialism" and, after 1917, by allegations of pro-German sympathies in World War I, as well as of mismanagement. In 1921, Frazier and Attorney General William Lemke were removed from office in the nation's first recall election.

The 1920s, a period of bank failures, low farm prices, drought, and political disunity, saw the beginnings of an exodus from the state. Matters grew even worse during the depression of the 1930s. Elected governor by hard-pressed farmers in 1932, William Langer took spectacular steps to save farms from foreclosure and to raise grain prices, until a conflict with the Roosevelt administration led to his removal from office on charges that he had illegally solicited political contributions.

World War II brought a quiet prosperity to North Dakota that lasted into the 1970s. Although the Republican Party continued to control the state legislature, Democrats held the governorship from 1960 on. The Arab oil embargo of 1973 and the rise of oil prices throughout the decade spurred drilling for oil (first discovered in 1951 in the trans–Missouri River country), encouraged the mining of lignite for electrical generation, and raised the prospect of a large-scale coal gasification industry for eastern markets.

12 STATE GOVERNMENT

North Dakota is governed by the constitution of 1889, as amended. Statewide elected officials include governor and lieutenant governor, secretary of state, auditor, treasurer, attorney general, commissioners of labor, insurance, and agriculture, and public service commissioner, all of whom serve four-year terms. The legislature is bicameral, with a 50-member senate and a

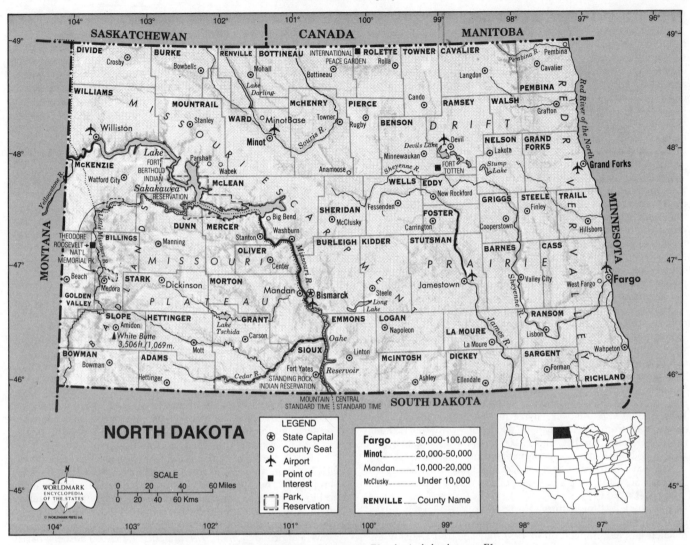

See US political: front cover F1; physical: back cover F1.

LOCATION: 45°56' to 49°N; 96°35' to 104°03'W. **BOUNDARIES**: Canadian line, 310 mi (499 km); Minnesota line, 420 mi (676 km); South Dakota line, 370 mi (595 km); Montana line, 212 mi (341 km).

100-member house of representatives. Senators are elected to staggered four-year terms, while representatives serve for two years. A two-thirds vote of the elected members of each house is required to override a gubernatorial veto.

Voters in North Dakota must be US citizens, at least 18 years of age, and must have been residents of the state at least 30 days prior to the election.

[13] POLITICAL PARTIES

Between 1889 and 1960, Republicans held the governorship for 58 of the 72 years. North Dakota politics were not monolithic, however, for aside from the Populist and Democratic opposition, the Republican Party was itself torn by factionalism, with Progressive and Nonpartisan League challenges to the conservative, probusiness party establishment. Between 1960 and 1980, the statehouse was in Democratic hands, though Republicans generally controlled the legislature.

In November 1980, North Dakotans cast 64% of the total popular vote for Ronald Reagan, sent Republican Mark Andrews to the US Senate, and favored Allen I. Olson for the governorship over Arthur Link, the Democratic incumbent. Republicans also captured a 41–9 majority in the state senate and a 74–26 lead in the house of representatives.

North Dakota Presidential Vote by Major Political Parties, 1948–80

YEAR	ELECTORAL VOTE	NORTH DAKOTA WINNER	DEMOCRAT	REPUBLICAN
1948	4	Dewey (R)	95,812	115,139
1952	4	*Eisenhower (R)	76,694	191,712
1956	4	*Eisenhower (R)	96,742	156,766
1960	4	Nixon (R)	123,963	154,310
1964	4	*Johnson (D)	149,784	108,207
1968	4	*Nixon (R)	94,769	138,669
1972	3	*Nixon (R)	100,384	174,109
1976	3	Ford (R)	136,078	153,470
1980	3	*Reagan (R)	79,189	193,695

*Won US presidential election.

[14] LOCAL GOVERNMENT

North Dakota in 1977 had 3,010 units of local government, including 53 counties, 368 municipalities, 1,360 townships, 527 school districts, and 702 special districts. Typical elected county officials are the sheriff, court clerk, county judge, county justice, and state's attorney. Municipalities range in size from the largest cities to 70 towns that had fewer than 100 people in 1970.

[15] STATE SERVICES

Educational services are under the jurisdiction of the Department of Public Instruction and the Board of Higher Education; there are state schools for the deaf and the blind. Health and welfare agencies include the State Health Department, Veterans Affairs Department, Social Service Board, and Indian Affairs Commission. Agricultural services include an extensive program of experiment and extension stations. The state bank, mill, and grain elevator established under Nonpartisan League influence remain to this day.

[16] JUDICIAL SYSTEM

North Dakota has a supreme court of five justices, seven district courts, and a system of local (county) courts. Supreme court justices are elected for 10-year terms, district court judges for 6-year terms.

According to the FBI Crime Index, North Dakota ranks 2d only to West Virginia as a low-crime state. For 1978, only 2,405 crimes per 100,000 population (67 violent, 2,338 nonviolent) were reported.

[17] ARMED FORCES

The main national defense installations are the Strategic Air Command bases at Minot and Grand Forks. North Dakota firms received $55 million in defense contract awards in 1978. As of 1979, 61,000 veterans were living in North Dakota, including about 2,000 from World War I, 27,000 from World War II, 8,000 from the Korean conflict, and 17,000 from the Viet-Nam era. A total of $52.4 million was spent on veterans' benefits in 1977/78.

National Guard personnel totaled 3,600 in 1978, when North Dakota had 1,141 state and local police.

[18] MIGRATION

During the late 19th century, North Dakota was largely settled by immigrants of German and Scandinavian stock. The state reached its peak population in 1930, but suffered a steady loss through migration until well into the 1970s. Between 1940 and 1977, the state's net loss from migration was estimated at 320,000.

[19] INTERGOVERNMENTAL COOPERATION

North Dakota participates in such interstate agreements as the Yellowstone River Compact, Western Interstate Energy Compact, and Interstate Oil and Gas Compact. A Minnesota–North Dakota Boundary Compact was ratified in 1961.

Federal assistance in 1978/79 totaled $295.2 million, of which $17.5 million was general revenue sharing.

[20] ECONOMY

North Dakota has been and still remains an important agricultural state, especially as a producer of wheat, much of which finds its way onto the world market. Like other midwestern farmers, North Dakotans suffered from high interest rates and a federal embargo on grain shipments to the Soviet Union as the 1980s began. Growth industries for the state are petroleum and coal mining, chiefly lignite. Manufacturing is limited mainly to food products and farm equipment.

The gross state product in 1977 totaled $4.7 billion, toward which trade contributed 22%; government, 16%; agriculture, 12%; finance, insurance, and real estate, 12%; services, 11%; construction, 7%; communications and public utilities, 7%; manufacturing, 6%; mining, 3%; and other sectors, 4%.

[21] INCOME

In 1978, North Dakota ranked 28th among the 50 states in per capita income, with $7,478. Total personal income reached $4.9 billion. The median family income was $13,626 in 1975, when 13,000 North Dakotans (8% of the state population) were below the federal poverty level.

[22] LABOR

North Dakota's labor force numbered 316,030 in 1978, of whom 14,150 (4.5%) were unemployed. A federal census of workers covered by unemployment insurance in March 1977 revealed the following nonfarm employment pattern in North Dakota:

	ESTABLISH-MENTS	EMPLOYEES	ANNUAL PAYROLL ('000)
Agricultural services, forestry, fishing	136	380	$ 4,080
Mining	146	2,187	37,469
Contract construction	1,977	10,662	171,355
Manufacturing	539	14,695	165,316
Transportation, public utilities	816	9,828	135,114
Wholesale trade	2,020	16,358	194,437
Retail trade	4,843	42,289	265,046
Finance, insurance, real estate	1,432	9,976	97,971
Services	3,574	38,138	284,272
Other	194	205	2,275
TOTALS	15,677	144,718	$1,357,335

Among the categories of workers excluded by this survey were government employees, who numbered 58,490 in 1978, and self-employed agricultural workers, 44,130.

During 1976, 38,000 North Dakotans belonged to labor unions and employee associations. A right-to-work law is in force.

[23] AGRICULTURE

North Dakota's agricultural income totaled $2.1 billion in 1978 (22d in the US). The state is the nation's 2d-leading wheat grower and the top producer of durum and other spring wheats, as well as of barley, flaxseed, and sunflowers.

In 1978 there were 41,500 farms in North Dakota occupying 41.7 million acres (16.9 million hectares), more than half of it cropland. The Red River Valley is important for wheat and other grains, flax, alfalfa, sugar beets, and potatoes. Various field crops thrive on the Drift Prairie. The dry western part of the state is suitable for livestock grazing and forage.

Wheat production in 1979 totaled 252,235,000 bushels; barley, 75,900,000 bushels; oats, 36,960,000 bushels; rye, 5,180,000 bushels; hay 5,780,000 tons; and potatoes, 18,240,000 hundredweight.

[24] ANIMAL HUSBANDRY

Livestock on North Dakota farms and ranches as of December 1979 included 2,000,000 cattle and calves, 370,000 hogs and pigs, and 236,000 sheep and lambs.

Sales of livestock products account for nearly one-third of North Dakota farm income. Leading products in 1979 were cattle, 740,460,000 lb; hogs, 109,351,000 lb; sheep, 11,694,000 lb; turkeys, 16,320,000 lb; chickens, 1,302,000 lb; milk, 874,000,000 lb; and eggs, 89,000,000.

[25] FISHING

There is little commercial fishing in North Dakota. In 1978, the catch totaled 635,000 lb, worth only $87,000.

[26] FORESTRY

North Dakota had 422,000 acres (171,000 hectares) of forestland in 1977, of which 27% was federally owned or managed. Although 405,000 acres (164,000 hectares) were classed as commercial timberland, forestry products are of very minor importance to the state's economy.

[27] MINING

North Dakota's mineral production was valued at $303 million in 1978 (30th in the US). Fossil fuels constitute the state's major mineral resource.

Coal production totaled 14 million tons, of which 86% was lignite; virtually all the coal was surface mined. Other mineral resources include petroleum, natural gas, and sand and gravel.

28 ENERGY AND POWER
Power stations in North Dakota generated 12.9 billion kwh of electricity in 1978, of which 55% was exported to other states.

North Dakota's proved petroleum reserves in 1978 totaled 161,213,000 barrels; production was 24,965,000 barrels. Natural gas reserves were 411.5 billion cu feet; production, 29.8 billion cu feet.

29 INDUSTRY
By number of employees, the leading manufacturing industries in North Dakota are food and related products, nonelectrical machinery, and printing and publishing. Value added by manufacturing in 1977 totaled $474.6 million. The following table shows value added by selected industries in 1977:

Farm and garden machinery	$62,700,000
Dairy products	29,300,000
Concrete, gypsum, plastic products	23,900,000
Preserved fruits and vegetables	19,500,000
Bakery products	16,800,000

30 COMMERCE
In 1977, wholesale trade establishments recorded $3.9 billion in sales. The leading wholesale lines by sales volume were farm-product raw materials, 34%; machinery, equipment, and supplies, 16%; groceries and related products, 13%; motor vehicles, auto parts, and supplies, 11%; and petroleum and petroleum products, 8%. Retail sales in 1977 were $2.2 billion.

North Dakota's agricultural exports totaled $554 million in 1976/77; sales of wheat and flour accounted for nearly three-fourths of the total. Exports of manufactured goods reached $85 million in 1976, six times the 1972 value.

31 CONSUMER PROTECTION
Allegations of consumer fraud and other illegal business practices are handled by the Consumer Fraud Division of the state Attorney General's Office. Other consumer services fall within the jurisdiction of the State Laboratories Consumer Affairs Office, which serves as a clearinghouse for consumer information and also mediates noncriminal disputes between consumers and businessmen, including landlords.

32 BANKING
North Dakota had 171 insured commercial banks with assets of $3.9 billion in 1978. The state's 11 savings and loan associations had $1.9 billion in assets and $1.6 billion in outstanding mortgage loans. There were 93 credit unions having 121,625 members, $201 million in assets, and $171.5 million in shares and deposits.

33 INSURANCE
In 1978, North Dakotans held 965,000 life insurance policies worth $8 billion. The average life insurance per family was $35,100. The nine life companies licensed to do business in the state paid benefits totaling $64.9 million. Premiums written by property and liability insurers in 1978 totaled $219 million.

34 SECURITIES
North Dakota has no securities exchanges.

35 PUBLIC FINANCE
North Dakota's biennial budget is prepared by the director of the Department of Accounts and Purchases by 15 July of each even-numbered year. The document is then submitted by the governor to the state legislature by 1 December, prior to its biennial session; the fiscal period begins 1 July of the following year.

General revenues and appropriated expenditures for 1975–77 and 1977–79 (estimated) were as follows:

REVENUES	1975–77	1977–79
Sales and use tax	$217,350,000	$182,778,000
Income tax	124,495,000	149,168,000
Business privilege tax	21,045,000	23,600,000
Other receipts	103,480,000	111,461,000
TOTALS	$466,370,000	$467,007,000

EXPENDITURES	1975–77	1977–79
Education	$259,618,711	$358,309,426
Health and welfare	74,025,339	100,014,603
General government	37,086,884	29,881,495
Other expenditures	71,798,627	85,611,887
TOTALS	$442,529,561	$573,817,411

Consolidated expenditures for 1977–79 (including federal aid and designated funds) totaled more than $1.1 billion, including $222.6 million for highways and an additional $131.3 million for health and welfare; the total for 1979–81 rose to $1.4 billion. The total debt of North Dakota state and local governments was $418 million in mid-1977; the per capita debt of $640 was among the lowest in the US.

36 TAXATION
As of 1980, the personal income tax ranged from 1% on the first $3,000 to 7.5% on taxable income over $30,000. The corporate tax rate ranged up to 8.5% of net profits exceeding $25,000. The state also taxed oil and gas production, insurance premiums, alcoholic beverages, tobacco products, mineral leases, and coal severance. There is a general sales and use tax of 3%.

In 1977, North Dakotans filed 268,908 federal income tax returns, paying $341.5 million in tax.

37 ECONOMIC POLICY
North Dakota has long sought to protect its agrarian interests, intervening in the marketplace to help farmers during periods of hardship, especially in the 1930s. Business incentives include a variety of job-training, financing, and tax-abatement programs.

38 HEALTH
North Dakotans ranked 4th among the 50 states in average life expectancy in 1969–71. The average for both sexes was 72.79 years, 69.23 for men and 77.01 for women. Death rates for all the leading causes except accidents are below the US averages.

As of January 1979, the state had 52 general hospitals, with 3,925 beds; 57 nursing homes, with 4,140 beds; and 31 intermediate-care facilities, with 1,888 beds. The cost of hospital care in 1977 averaged $141 per day and $1,171 per stay, both well below the national averages. Medical personnel licensed in North Dakota during 1978/79 included 777 physicians, 280 dentists, 76 optometrists, 76 chiropractors, 5,150 registered nurses, and 2,612 licensed practical nurses.

39 SOCIAL WELFARE
In 1977, North Dakota spent almost $70.4 million on state public welfare programs, with 62% of the funds coming from the federal government.

Benefits totaling $13.7 million under the aid to families with dependent children program were paid to nearly 4,700 families in 1978; a monthly average of 5,017 North Dakota households received $7.4 million in federal food stamps. In 1977, almost $20.3 million in Social Security benefits were paid to North Dakotans. Vocational rehabilitation cost $3.4 million in 1978, when about 5,000 workers claimed unemployment benefits totaling $22 million. Workers' compensation payments amounted to $11.6 million in 1976/77.

40 HOUSING
North Dakota had some 215,000 households in 1977. The 1970 census counted 200,334 year-round housing units, about 90% of them with full plumbing. Between 1976 and 1978, 18,600 new units were authorized at a value of $543 million.

41 EDUCATION
North Dakota's adult illiteracy rate was only 0.8% in 1970, well below the national average. By 1976, two-thirds of all adults were high school graduates, 12% had at least four years of college, and the median level of schooling was 12.5 years.

In 1979/80, 131,191 students were enrolled in public, private, and special schools, including 84,970 students in grades K–8, 45,891 in grades 9–12, and 330 in special institutions.

In fall 1978, 31,279 students were enrolled in North Dakota's 13 higher educational institutions. The chief universities are the University of North Dakota (Grand Forks), with 9,505 students, and North Dakota State University (Fargo), with 7,707. The Student Financial Assistance Agency offers scholarships for North Dakota college students, and the state Indian Scholarship Board provides aid to needy Indians attending colleges and junior colleges in the state.

42 ARTS
The Council on the Arts, a branch of the North Dakota state government, provides grants to local artists and groups, and encourages visits by out-of-state artists and exhibitions.

43 LIBRARIES AND MUSEUMS
During 1977–78, North Dakota public libraries had 1,183,192 volumes and a total circulation of 2,552,734. The leading academic library was that of the University of North Dakota (Grand Forks), with 292,689 volumes.

Among the most notable of the state's 30 museums and historical sites are the Art Galleries and Zoology Museum of the University of North Dakota. Theodore Roosevelt National Memorial Park, near Medora, features relics from the ranch where Roosevelt lived in the 1880s.

44 COMMUNICATIONS
During 1978, the state had 499,587 telephones (366,164 residential, 133,423 business), 72% of them owned by Bell companies. There were 38 commercial radio stations (27 AM, 11 FM), 12 commercial television stations, and 4 public television stations. Cable television systems served 53,217 subscribers in 38 North Dakota communities.

45 PRESS
As of 1978 there were two morning dailies, with a total average circulation of 27,556; nine evening dailies, with 135,963; and three Sunday papers, with 96,366 (the totals include an all-day paper). The leading dailies were the *Fargo Forum*, with an all-day circulation of 58,662 (Sunday, 63,070); the *Grand Forks Herald*, 35,655 evening, 36,832 Sunday; the *Minot Daily News*, 31,388 evening; and the *Bismarck Tribune*, 29,122 evening.

In addition, there were 91 weekly and semiweekly journals, with a total circulation of 181,566. The leading historical journal is the *North Dakota Quarterly*.

46 ORGANIZATIONS
The International Wild Waterfowl Association has its headquarters in Jamestown, and the Northwest Farm Managers' Association is located in Fargo. Most major national membership organizations have branches in the state.

47 TOURISM, TRAVEL, AND RECREATION
In 1977, nearly 1.9 million people traveled to North Dakota. Travel-related business receipts totaled $355.7 million in 1976, when tourism accounted for an estimated 16,200 jobs. State parks received 1,187,062 visitors in 1978.

Among the leading tourist attractions is the International Peace Garden, covering 2,200 acres (890 hectares) in North Dakota and Manitoba, and commemorating friendly relations between Canada and the US. Ft. Abraham Lincoln State Park, south of Mandan, has been restored to suggest the 1870s, when General Custer left the area for his "last stand" against the Sioux. The most spectacular scenery in North Dakota is part of the Theodore Roosevelt National Memorial Park, which had 833,306 visitors in 1978. So-called badlands, an integral part of the park, consist of strangely colored and intricately eroded buttes and other rock formations. Hunting and fishing are major recreational activities in North Dakota. In 1977/78 there were 102,178 licensed hunters and 159,907 licensed fishermen.

48 SPORTS
There are no major professional sports teams in North Dakota. In collegiate football, the University of North Dakota Sioux and the North Dakota State University Bison compete in the North Central Conference. The University of North Dakota also competes in collegiate ice hockey.

49 FAMOUS NORTH DAKOTANS
Preeminent among North Dakota politicians known to the nation was Gerald P. Nye (b. Wisconsin, 1892–1971), a US senator and a leading isolationist opponent of President Franklin D. Roosevelt's foreign policy, as was Senator William Langer (1886–1959). Another prominent senator, Porter J. McCumber (1858–1933), supported President Woodrow Wilson in the League of Nations battle. US Representative William Lemke (1878–1950) sponsored farm-relief legislation and in 1936 ran for US president on the Union Party ticket. Usher L. Burdick (1879–1960), a maverick isolationist and champion of the American Indian, served 18 years in the US House of Representatives.

Vilhjalmur Stefansson (b. Canada, 1879–1962) recorded in numerous books his explorations and experiments in the high Arctic. Orin G. Libby (1864–1952) made a significant contribution to the study of American history. Other North Dakota-nurtured writers and commentators include Maxwell Anderson (b. Pennsylvania, 1888–1959), a Pulitzer Prize–winning playwright; Edward K. Thompson (b. Minnesota, 1907), editor of *Life* magazine and founder-editor of *Smithsonian*; radio and television commentator Eric Sevareid (b. 1912); and novelist Larry Woiwode (b. 1941).

To the entertainment world North Dakota has contributed band leaders Harold Bachman (1892–1972), Lawrence Welk (b. 1903), and Tommy Tucker (Gerald Duppler, b. 1908); jazz vocalist Peggy Lee (Norma Delores Egstrom, b. 1920) and country singer Lynn Anderson (b. 1947); and actresses Dorothy Stickney (b. 1903) and Angie Dickinson (Angeline Brown, b. 1931).

Sports personalities associated with the state include outfielder Roger Maris (b. 1934), who in 1961 broke Babe Ruth's record for home runs in one season.

50 BIBLIOGRAPHY
Crawford, Lewis F. *History of North Dakota*. 3 vols. Chicago: American Historical Society, 1931.

Federal Writers' Project. *North Dakota: A Guide to the Northern Prairie State*. 2d ed. New York: Oxford University Press, 1950.

Goodman, L. R., and R. J. Eidem. *The Atlas of North Dakota*. Fargo: North Dakota Studies, Inc., 1976.

North Dakota, University of. Bureau of Business and Economic Research. *Statistical Abstract of North Dakota 1979*. Grand Forks: University of North Dakota Press, 1979.

Robinson, Elwyn B. *History of North Dakota*. Lincoln: University of Nebraska Press, 1966.

Tweton, D. Jerome, and Theodore Jelliff. *North Dakota—The Heritage of a People*. Fargo: North Dakota Institute for Regional Studies, 1976.

Tweton, D. Jerome, and Daniel F. Rylance. *The Years of Despair: North Dakota in the Depression*. Grand Forks: Oxcart Press, 1973.

Wilkins, Robert P. and Wynona H. *North Dakota: A Bicentennial History*. New York: Norton, 1977.

OHIO

State of Ohio

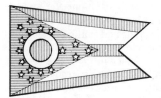

ORIGIN OF STATE NAME: From the Iroquois Indian word *oheo*, meaning "beautiful." **NICKNAME**: The Buckeye State. **CAPITAL**: Columbus. **ENTERED UNION**: 1 March 1803 (17th). **SONG**: "Beautiful Ohio." **MOTTO**: With God All Things Are Possible. **FLAG**: The flag is swallow-tailed, with three red and two white lateral stripes; at the staff is a blue triangular field covered with 17 stars (signifying Ohio's order of entry into the Union) grouped around a red disc superimposed on a white circular O. **OFFICIAL SEAL**: In the foreground are a sheaf of wheat and a sheaf of 17 arrows; behind, a sun rises over a mountain range, indicating that Ohio is the 1st state west of the Alleghenies. Surrounding the scene are the words "The Great Seal of the State of Ohio." **BIRD**: Cardinal. **FLOWER**: Scarlet carnation. **TREE**: Buckeye. **GEM**: Ohio flint. **BEVERAGE**: Tomato juice. **LEGAL HOLIDAYS**: New Year's Day, 1 January; Martin Luther King's Birthday, 3d Monday in January; President's Day, 3d Monday in February; Memorial Day, last Monday in May; Independence Day, 4 July; Labor Day, 1st Monday in September; Columbus Day, 2d Monday in October; Veterans Day, 11 November; Thanksgiving Day, 4th Thursday in November; Christmas Day, 25 December. **TIME**: 7 A.M. EST = noon GMT.

¹LOCATION, SIZE, AND EXTENT

Located in the eastern north-central US, Ohio is the 11th-largest of the 12 midwestern states and ranks 35th in size among the 50 states.

The state's total area is 41,222 sq mi (106,765 sq km), of which land comprises 40,975 sq mi (106,125 sq km) and inland water 247 sq mi (640 sq km). Ohio extends about 210 mi (338 km) E–W; its maximum N–S extension is 230 mi (370 km).

Ohio is bordered on the N by Michigan and the Canadian province of Ontario (with the line passing through Lake Erie); on the E by Pennsylvania and West Virginia (with the Ohio River forming part of the boundary); on the S by West Virginia and Kentucky (with the entire line defined by the Ohio River); and on the W by Indiana.

Five important islands lie off the state's northern shore, in Lake Erie: the three Bass Islands, Kelleys Island, and Catawba Island. Ohio's total boundary length is 997 mi (1,605 km).

The state's geographic center is in Delaware County, 25 mi (40 km) NNE of Columbus.

²TOPOGRAPHY

Ohio has three distinct topographical regions: the foothills of the Allegheny Mountains in the eastern half of the state; the Erie lakeshore, extending for nearly three-fourths of the northern boundary; and the central plains in the western half of the state.

The Allegheny Plateau in eastern Ohio consists of rugged hills and steep valleys that recede gradually as the terrain sweeps westward toward the central plains. The highest point in the state is Campbell Hill (1,550 feet, or 472 meters), located in Logan County about 50 mi (80 km) northwest of Columbus. The Erie lakeshore, a band of level lowland that runs across the state to the northwestern corner on the Michigan boundary, is distinguished by sandy beaches. The central plains extend to the western boundary with Indiana. In the south, undulating hills decline in altitude as they reach the serpentine Ohio River, which forms the state's southern boundary with Kentucky and West Virginia. The state's lowest point is on the banks of the Ohio River in the southwest, where the altitude drops to 433 feet (132 meters) above sea level.

Most of Ohio's 2,500 lakes are situated in the east, and nearly all are reservoirs backed up by river dams. The largest, Pymatuning Reservoir, on the Pennsylvania border, has an area of 14,650 acres (5,929 hectares). Grand Lake (St. Marys), located near the

western border, covering 12,500 acres (5,059 hectares), is the largest lake wholly within Ohio.

Ohio has two drainage basins separated by a low ridge extending from the northeast corner to about the middle of the western border with Indiana. North of the ridge, more than one-third of Ohio's area is drained by the Maumee, Portage, Sandusky, Cuyahoga, and Grand rivers into Lake Erie. South of the ridge, the remaining two-thirds of the state is drained mainly by the Muskingum, Hocking, Raccoon, Scioto, Little Miami, and Miami rivers into the Ohio River, which winds for about 450 mi (725 km) along the eastern and southern borders.

Ohio's bedrock of sandstone, shale, and limestone was formed during the Paleozoic era some 300–600 million years ago. The oldest limestone rocks are found in the Cincinnati anticline, a ridge of sedimentary rock layers about 3,000 feet (900 meters) thick that extends from north to south in west-central Ohio. Inland seas filled and receded periodically to form salt and gypsum, also creating peat bogs that later were pressurized into the coal beds of southeastern Ohio. At the end of the Paleozoic era, the land in the eastern region uplifted to form a plateau that was later eroded by wind and water into hills and gorges.

About 2 million years ago, glaciers covering two-thirds of the state leveled the western region into plains and deposited fertile limestone topsoil. As the glaciers retreated, the melting ice formed a vast lake, which overflowed southward into the channels that became the Ohio River. Perhaps 15,000 years ago, during the last Ice Age, the glacial waters ran off and reduced Lake Erie to its present size. Limestone rocks in Glacier Grooves State Park on Kelleys Island bear the marks of the glaciers' movements.

³CLIMATE

Lying in the humid continental zone, Ohio has a generally temperate climate. Winters are cold and summers mild in the eastern highlands. The southern region has the warmest temperatures and longest growing season—198 days on the average, compared with 150 to 178 days in the remainder of the state. More than half of the annual rainfall occurs during the growing season, from May to October.

Among the major cities, Columbus, in the central region, has an annual mean temperature of 52°F (11°C), with a normal maximum of 62°F (17°C) and a normal minimum of 41°F (5°C). Cleveland, in the north, has an annual mean of 50°F (10°C), with a normal maximum of 59°F (15°C) and minimum of 41°F (5°C). The mean temperature in Cincinnati, in the south, is 54°F (12°C), the normal maximum 64°F (18°C), and the normal minimum 44°F (7°C). Cleveland has an average of 127 days per year in which the temperature drops to 32°F (0°C) or lower, Columbus 124 days, and Cincinnati 99 days. The record low temperature for the state is –39°F (–39°C), set at Milligan on 10 February 1899. The record high is 113°F (45°C), registered near Gallipolis on 21 July 1934.

Cleveland has an average annual snowfall of 52 in (132 cm), while Columbus receives 28 in (71 cm), and Cincinnati 24 in (61 cm). Cincinnati has the most total precipitation, with 39 in (99 cm), compared with 37 in (94 cm) for Columbus and 35 in (89 cm) for Cleveland. Because of its proximity to Lake Erie, Cleveland is the windiest city, with winds that average 11 mph (18 km/hr) annually.

⁴FLORA AND FAUNA

More than 2,500 plant species have been found in Ohio. The southeastern hill and valley region supports pitch pine, bigleaf magnolia, and sourwood, with undergrowths of sassafras, witch-hazel, pawpaw, hornbeam and various dogwoods. At least 14 species of oak, 10 of maple, 9 of poplar, 9 of pine, 7 of ash, 7 of elm, 6 of hickory, 5 of birch, and 2 of beech grow in the state, along with butternut, eastern black walnut, wild black cherry, black locust, and sycamore. A relative of the horse chestnut (introduced to Ohio from Asia), the distinctive buckeye—first called the Ohio buckeye and now the official state tree—is characterized by its clusters of cream-colored flowers that bloom in spring and later form large, brown, thick-hulled nuts. The yellow-fringed orchid and wild kidney bean are threatened species, while painted trillium, white lady's-slipper, and rock elm are among more than 200 endangered plants.

The Buckeye State is rich in mammals. White-tailed deer, badger, mink, raccoon, red and gray foxes, coyote, beaver, eastern cottontail, woodchuck, least shrew, and opossum are found throughout the state's five wildlife districts; the bobcat, woodland jumping mouse, and red-backed mole are among many species with more restricted habitats. Common birds include the eastern great blue heron, green-winged teal, mourning dove, eastern belted kingfisher, eastern horned lark, blue-gray gnat-catcher, eastern cowbird, and a great variety of ducks, woodpeckers, and warblers; the cardinal is the state bird, and the ruffed grouse, mostly confined to the Allegheny Plateau, is a favorite game species. Bass, pickerel, perch, carp, pike, trout, catfish, sucker, and darter thrive in Ohio's lakes and streams. The snapping, midland painted, and spiny soft-shelled turtles, five-lined skink, northern water snake, midland brown snake, eastern hognose, and eastern milk snake appear throughout Ohio; the northern copperhead, eastern massasauga (swamp rattler), and timber rattlesnake are Ohio's only poisonous reptiles. Fowler's toad, bullfrog, green pickerel frog, and marbled and red-backed salamanders are common native amphibians.

Acting on the premise that the largest problem facing wildlife is the destruction of their habitat, the Division of Wildlife of the Department of Natural Resources has instituted an ambitious endangered species program. Among the numerous animals categorized by the state as endangered are the river otter, bobcat, Allegheny woodrat, sharp-shinned hawk, king rail, upland sandpiper, common tern, spotted turtle, five species of salamander, Ohio lamprey, shortnose gar, Great Lakes muskellunge, northern madtom, Tippecanoe darter, and Allegheny crayfish.

⁵ENVIRONMENTAL PROTECTION

Early conservation efforts in Ohio were aimed at controlling the ravages of spring floods and preventing soil erosion. After the Miami River floods of March 1913, which took 361 lives and resulted in property losses of more than $100 million in Dayton alone, the Miami Conservancy District was formed; five earth

dams and 60 mi (97 km) of river levees, all completed by 1922, had held back 857 cresting waters as of 1976. The cost of the Miami project was $40 million, but the estimated benefits from flood control have amounted to at least $90 million. In the Muskingum Conservancy District in eastern Ohio, construction of flood-control dams has prevented spring flooding and the washing away of valuable topsoil into the Ohio River. Again, the estimated benefits have been more than double the initial cost of $48 million. In the 1970s, the state's major environmental concerns were to clean up Lake Erie, to prevent industrial wastes from further polluting the water and lakeshore, and to control the air pollution attributable to coal burning and traffic congestion.

The state's regulatory agency for environmental matters is the Environmental Protection Agency established in 1972. The agency draws up both emergency plans and long-range programs to deal with pollution of air, water, and land resources. The EPA also coordinates state, local, and federal funding of environmental programs. The agency expended an estimated $20.9 million on environmental programs in the 1978/79 fiscal year.

The Ohio Department of Natural Resources is responsible for the development and use of the state's natural resources. The department manages state parks, forests, and nature preserves, assists in soil conservation, issues permits for dams, promotes conservation of oil and gas, and allocates strip-mining licenses. State-owned land under the department's jurisdiction totaled about 204,000 acres (83,000 hectares) in 1975. The department's funding for the preservation of the state's natural resources was estimated at $104.7 million in the 1978/79 fiscal year.

⁶POPULATION

Ohio ranked 6th in population among the 50 states at the 1970 census, with a population of 10,657,423. In 1977, Cleveland was the 19th-largest city in the US, Columbus ranked 22d, and Cincinnati placed 31st.

Ohio's population grew slowly during the colonial period and totaled 45,365 persons in 1800. Once the territory became a state in 1803, settlers flocked to Ohio and the population quintupled to 230,760 by 1810. The state's population doubled again by 1820, approached 2,000,000 in 1850, and totaled 3,198,062 by 1880. Ohio's annual rate of population increase slowed considerably after 1900, when its population was 4,157,545; nevertheless, in the period between 1900 and 1960, the total population more than doubled to 9,706,397.

The 1970 census figure of 10,657,423 represented an increase of nearly 10% over the 1960 census population, but this was lower than the overall US growth rate during the same period. In 1970, Ohio's population was 51.5% female and about 80% urban. The population density was 260 persons per sq mi (100 per sq km), more than four times the US average.

Ohio's rate of population increase slowed to less than 1% between 1970 and 1977. The main reason for the decline was the net migration (according to state estimates) of 435,051 residents to other states; this figure nearly equaled the 483,628 surplus of live births over deaths in the 1970–77 period. The state's annual birthrate per 1,000 population dropped from 18.7 in 1970 to 15.1 in 1977, or slightly below the national average; the death rate per 1,000 population declined slightly from 9.4 in 1970 to 9.1 in 1977, or slightly above the US rate. Preliminary census data for 1980 showed Ohio with a population of 10,758,421.

The 1970 census listed the populations of 225 cities and 711 villages in Ohio. Cleveland led the cities with a population of 750,903, but the exodus of 166,251 persons from the city between 1970 and 1977 was the major factor in reducing the city's

LOCATION: 38°23' to 41°59' N; 80°32' to 84°49' W. BOUNDARIES: Michigan line, 70 mi (113 km); Canadian line, 205 mi (330 km); Pennsylvania line, 92 mi (148 km); West Virginia line, 277 mi (446 km); Kentucky line, 174 mi (280 km); Indiana line, 179 mi (288 km).

OHIO

SCALE
0   10   20   30 Miles
0 10   20   30 Kms

Akron	Over 100,000
Euclid	50,000-100,000
Whitehall	20,000-50,000
Sylvania	10,000-20,000
Streetsboro	Under 10,000
ALLEN	County Name

LEGEND
✪ State Capital
⊙ County Seat
✈ Airport
■ Point of Interest

population to 609,197 by mid-1977. Cincinnati and other large cities also lost population during this period, largely because of the shift of the middle class from the inner cities to the suburbs or to other states. In 1980, according to preliminary census results, Cleveland's population was 572,532, followed by Columbus, 561,943; Cincinnati, 383,058; Toledo, 354,265; Akron, 236,820; Dayton, 193,319; and Youngstown, 115,429.

Ohio's 3 most populated cities and their suburbs ranked among the 35 largest metropolitan areas in the country in 1978. In that year, metropolitan Cleveland had an estimated population of 1,938,900; the Ohio portion of metropolitan Cincinnati, 1,098,300; and the metropolitan area of Columbus, 1,088,900.

⁷ETHNIC GROUPS

Ohio was first settled by migrants from the eastern states and from the British Isles and northern Europe, especially Germany. Cincinnati had such a large German population that its public schools were bilingual until World War I. With the coming of the railroads and the development of industry, Slavic and south Euro-

peans were recruited in large numbers. In 1970, more than 12% of Ohio's people were foreign-born or the children of foreign-born, the major groups being German (1.8%), Italian (1.6%), and Polish (1.1%). Ethnic clusters persist in the large cities, and some small communities retain a specific ethnic flavor, such as Fairport Harbor on Lake Erie, with its large Finnish population.

As of 1976 there were 1,003,000 blacks, representing 9% of the population. Most lived in the larger cities, especially Cleveland, which in 1970 was 38% black. Historically, Ohio was very active in the antislavery movement. Oberlin College, established in 1833 by dissident theological students, admitted blacks from its founding and maintained a "station" on the Underground Railway. Cleveland elected its first black mayor in 1967.

There were 85,000 Hispanic Americans in 1976. The largest number were of Mexican descent, but there were also many Puerto Ricans. American Indians numbered only 6,654 as of 1970. There are no reservations in Ohio, although there are some small Indian settlements in the northeast. In 1970 there

Ohio Counties, County Seats, and County Populations

COUNTY	COUNTY SEAT	AREA (SQ MI)	POPULATION (1978)[1,2]	COUNTY	COUNTY SEAT	AREA (SQ MI)	POPULATION (1978)[1,2]
Adams	West Union	588	23,700	Lorain	Elyria	495	271,200
Allen	Lima	410	108,300	Lucas	Toledo	351	464,200
Ashland	Ashland	426	45,200	Madison	London	464	32,200
Ashtabula	Jefferson	706	100,900	Mahoning	Youngstown	424	300,000
Athens	Athens	504	54,900	Marion	Marion	405	66,500
Auglaize	Wapakoneta	404	41,600	Medina	Medina	425	111,900
Belmont	St. Clairsville	539	81,700	Meigs	Pomeroy	436	22,200
Brown	Georgetown	491	31,100	Mercer	Celina	471	38,700
Butler	Hamilton	471	256,400	Miami	Troy	407	88,100
Carroll	Carrollton	396	26,100	Monroe	Woodsfield	456	16,400
Champaign	Urbana	433	32,600	Montgomery	Dayton	465	580,000
Clark	Springfield	402	150,600	Morgan	McConnelsville	421	13,500
Clermont	Batavia	459	120,100	Morrow	Mount Gilead	404	25,100
Clinton	Wilmington	412	33,000	Muskingum	Zanesville	670	81,900
Columbiana	Lisbon	535	114,200	Noble	Caldwell	404	11,100
Coshocton	Coshocton	563	34,700	Ottawa	Port Clinton	269	38,600
Crawford	Bucyrus	404	49,400	Paulding	Paulding	417	20,400
Cuyahoga	Cleveland	456	1,542,100	Perry	New Lexington	410	30,100
Darke	Greenville	605	53,600	Pickaway	Circleville	507	44,200
Defiance	Defiance	412	38,000	Pike	Waverly	444	21,900
Delaware	Delaware	459	53,100	Portage	Ravenna	506	133,300
Erie	Sandusky	265	76,400	Preble	Eaton	428	37,100
Fairfield	Lancaster	507	88,800	Putnam	Ottawa	486	31,200
Fayette	Wash. Court House	406	26,100	Richland	Mansfield	499	130,300
Franklin	Columbus	539	870,600	Ross	Chillicothe	687	63,000
Fulton	Wauseon	407	36,300	Sandusky	Fremont	416	62,400
Gallia	Gallipolis	471	29,900	Scioto	Portsmouth	611	82,800
Geauga	Chardon	408	72,900	Seneca	Tiffin	551	60,100
Greene	Xenia	416	129,000	Shelby	Sidney	410	41,300
Guernsey	Cambridge	529	39,100	Stark	Canton	581	377,700
Hamilton	Cincinnati	415	885,300	Summit	Akron	416	523,700
Hancock	Findlay	532	62,400	Trumbull	Warren	632	245,800
Hardin	Kenton	467	32,600	Tuscarawas	New Philadelphia	571	80,100
Harrison	Cadiz	411	17,600	Union	Marysville	434	30,000
Henry	Napoleon	420	29,400	Van Wert	Van Wert	409	30,500
Highland	Hillsboro	554	31,500	Vinton	McArthur	411	10,900
Hocking	Logan	421	22,200	Warren	Lebanon	408	92,900
Holmes	Millersburg	424	26,000	Washington	Marietta	641	61,400
Huron	Norwalk	497	53,400	Wayne	Wooster	561	96,300
Jackson	Jackson	420	29,900	Williams	Bryan	421	35,100
Jefferson	Steubenville	411	93,100	Wood	Bowling Green	621	105,000
Knox	Mt. Vernon	532	45,300	Wyandot	Upper Sandusky	406	21,800
Lake	Painesville	232	212,000				
Lawrence	Ironton	456	62,300		TOTALS	41,222	10,749,000
Licking	Newark	687	117,400				
Logan	Bellefontaine	469	37,500				

¹Provisional.
²Column does not add to total because of rounding.

were 5,555 Japanese, 5,305 Chinese, 3,490 Filipinos, and 13,569 other Asians. Ohio accepted 2,924 resettled Vietnamese in 1975.

8 LANGUAGES

Except for small Iroquoian groups like the Erie and Seneca, most of the Indian population before white settlement comprised four Algonkian tribes: Delaware, Miami, Wyandot, and Shawnee. In 1970, only 1,001 residents of Ohio had first learned an Indian language. Indian place-names include Ohio, Coshocton, Cuyahoga, and Wapakoneta.

Ohio English reflects three post-Revolutionary migration paths. Into the Western Reserve south of Lake Erie came Northern speech from New York and Connecticut. Still common there are the Northern pronunciation of the *ow* diphthong, as in *cow*, with a beginning like the /ah/ vowel in *father*, and the use of that /ah/ in *fog* and *college*; /krik/ is more common than /kreek/ for creek. *Tot* and *taught* do not sound alike. A dragonfly is a *devil's darning needle*; doughnuts may be *fried cakes*; a boy throws himself face down on a sled in a *bellyflop(per)*; and a tied and filled bedcover is a *comforter*.

Most of nonurban Ohio has North Midland speech from Pennsylvania. Generally, except in the northern strip, *cot* and *caught* are sound-alikes, and *now* is /naow/. South of Columbus, because of the influence of South Midland patterns from Kentucky and extreme southern Pennsylvania, corn bread may be *corn pone*, lima beans are *butter beans*, and a tied quilt is a *comfort*. *Spouting*, yielding to *gutters*, barely reaches across to Indiana; and *sick at the stomach, dived,* and *wait on me* are competing with expanding Northern *to the stomach, dove,* and *wait for me*. A new Midland term, *bellybuster*, originated around Wheeling and has spread north to compete with *bellyflop*. Northern and Midland merge in the mixed dialect west of Toledo.

From Kentucky, South Midland speakers took *you-all* into Ohio River towns, and in the southwestern tip of the state can be heard their *evening* for *afternoon, terrapin* for *tortoise,* and *frogstool* for *toadstool*. Recent northward migration for employment has introduced South Midland speech and black English, a southern dialect, into such industrial centers as Cleveland, Toledo, and Akron.

Localisms have developed. For the grass strip between sidewalk and street, Akron has *devil-strip* and Cleveland has *tree-lawn*. Foreign-language influence appears in such Pennsylvania Germanisms as *clook* (hatching hen), *snits* (dried apples), *smearcase* (cottage cheese) and *got awake*.

Of native-born Ohioans in 1970, 86% said English was their mother tongue; for all Ohioans the figure was 84%. Speakers of principal first languages were as follows:

	NATIVE-BORN	FOREIGN-BORN
English	8,932,055	48,141
German	299,275	60,534
Italian	125,792	36,621
Polish	113,194	18,829
Spanish	56,472	9,918
Yiddish	27,391	9,504
French	24,736	7,278

9 RELIGIONS

The first religious settlement in Ohio territory was founded among Huron Indians in 1751 by a Roman Catholic priest near what is now Sandusky. Shortly afterward, Moravian missionaries converted some Delaware Indians to Christianity; the first Protestant church was founded by Congregationalist ministers at Marietta in 1788. Dissident religious sects such as the Shakers, Amish, and Quakers moved into Ohio from the early 18th century onward, but the majority of settlers in the early 19th century were Presbyterians, Methodists, Baptists, Disciples of Christ, and Episcopalians.

The first Roman Catholic priest to be stationed permanently in Ohio was Father Edward Fenwick, who settled in Cincinnati in 1817. When the Protestant settlers there did not allow him to build a Catholic church in the town, he founded Christ Church (now St. Francis Church) just outside Cincinnati. In 1821, Father Fenwick became the first Catholic bishop in Ohio. The large influx of Irish and German immigrants after 1830 greatly increased the Catholic constituency in Cleveland, Cincinnati, Columbus, and Toledo. Among the German immigrants were many Lutherans and a large number of Jews, who made Cincinnati a center of Reform Judaism. In the mid-19th century, Cincinnati had the nation's 3d-largest Jewish community; the Union of American Hebrew Congregations, the most important Reform body, was founded there in 1873, and Hebrew Union College, a rabbinical training school and center of Jewish learning, was founded two years later.

In 1979, Ohio had a Roman Catholic population of 2,356,313, of which about 951,000 were in the Cleveland diocese and 500,000 in the archdiocese of Cincinnati. During the same year, the state's Jewish population was estimated at 151,870. Leading Jewish communities were in Cleveland, 75,000; Cincinnati, 28,500; and Columbus, 13,000.

There were more than 7,885 Protestant churches in 1971, when known adherents of all Protestant groups totaled 2,789,560. The largest Protestant denominations and their adherents in 1971 were United Methodist, 845,445; United Presbyterian, 313,787; United Church of Christ, 235,720; Lutheran Church of America, 189,321; Christian Church and Churches of Christ, 125,872; American Baptist Convention, 115,683; Southern Baptist Convention, 108,426; and Episcopal, 106,983.

10 TRANSPORTATION

Sandwiched between two of the country's largest inland water systems, Lake Erie and the Ohio River, Ohio has long been a leader in water transport. By means of its 130 terminals on the Ohio River and 8 deepwater ports on Lake Erie, Ohio ranks among the top 5 states in shipping. The state has more miles of railroad track in proportion to its area than any other state. In 1978, Ohio ranked 5th among the 50 states in miles of interstate highway, and also had more airport runways for its size than any other state.

The building of railroads in the mid-19th century greatly improved transportation within the state by connecting inland counties with Lake Erie and the Ohio River. The Mad River and Lake Erie Railroad, between Dayton and Sandusky, was completed in 1844, and two years later it was joined with the Little Miami Railroad, to provide through service to Cincinnati. Also in 1846, Cleveland was connected by rail with Columbus and Pittsburgh. Railroad building in the state reached a peak in the 1850s; at the outbreak of the Civil War, Ohio had more miles of track than any other state. By 1900, railroads were by far the most important system of transport.

In 1977, Ohio's railroads operated more than 7,500 mi (12,000 km) of track. A plan to connect Ohio's major cities by high-speed rail passenger service was in preparation in 1980. Freight service on 12 branch lines to 14 counties has been maintained, despite declining freight volume, through a state subsidy program.

Mass transit in Ohio's cities began in 1859 with horse-drawn carriages carrying paying passengers in Cleveland and Cincinnati, which added a cable car on rails about 1880. The electric trolley car, introduced to Cleveland in 1884, soon became the most popular mass transit system for the large cities. Interurban electric railways carried passengers to and from rural towns that had been bypassed by the railroads; there were 2,809 mi (4,521 km) of interurban track in the state by 1907. The use of electric railways declined with the development of the motor car in the 1920s, and by 1939, for example, the seven interurban lines serving Columbus had been abandoned. Today, suburbanites commute to their workplaces in Columbus and other cities by automobile, commuter railroads, and bus lines.

Rough roads were used by settlers in the early 19th century.

The National Road was built from Wheeling, W. Va., to Zanesville in 1826, and was extended to Columbus by 1833. The increasing use of the automobile in the 1930s led to massive state and federal road-building programs in Ohio as elsewhere. The major interstate highways across Ohio connect Cleveland and the Toledo area in the north (I-80, I-90), link Columbus with Zanesville and Wheeling (I-70) and with Cincinnati (I-73), and extend north–south from Cleveland and Akron to Marietta (I-77).

In 1978, Ohio had 1,515 mi (2,438 km) of interstate highways, 24,504 mi (39,435 km) of municipal roads, and 86,680 mi (139,498 km) of rural roads. In that year, 6,314,639 automobiles, 1,573,849 trucks, and 239,490 motorcycles were registered in the state; 8,178,585 driver's licenses were issued in 1978, 60% of them to males, the highest such percentage among the 50 states.

Inland waterways have long been important for transport and commerce in Ohio. The first settlers traveled into Ohio by flatboat down the Ohio River to establish such towns as Marietta and Cincinnati. Lake Erie schooners brought the founders of Cleveland and Sandusky. Steamboat service began on the Ohio River in 1811, and at Lake Erie ports in 1818. The public demand for water transportation in the interior of the state, where few rivers were navigable, led to construction of the Ohio and Erie Canal from Cleveland to Portsmouth, and of the Miami and Erie Canal from Cincinnati to Dayton; both were opened to traffic in 1827 but not completed for another 14 years. The canals gave Ohio's farmers better access to eastern and southern markets. Water transportation is still a principal means of shipping Ohio's manufactured products through the St. Lawrence Seaway to foreign countries, and the method by which many millions of tons of cargo, particularly coal, are moved via the Ohio River to domestic markets.

Ohio's ports ranked 4th in the nation in volume and 13th in value of foreign exports in 1976, with shipments totaling 20.9 million tons and valued at about $1.4 billion. The state's two largest port districts, Toledo and Ashtabula-Conneaut, accounted for about three-fourths of the state's foreign waterborne shipments, chiefly coal, soybeans, and corn.

Ohioans consider Dayton to be the birthplace of aviation because it was there that Wilbur and Orville Wright built the first motor-powered airplane in 1903. The state's major cities were served by 16 regularly scheduled commercial airlines in 1977. In 1978 there were 126 public airports and 458 private airfields in the state. The major air terminal is Cleveland's Hopkins International airport, which emplaned 3,485,207 passengers on 62,840 departing flights in 1978.

[11] HISTORY

The first people in Ohio, some 11,000 years ago, were primitive hunters. Their crude stone tools have been found with skeletal remains of long-extinct mammoths and mastodons. Centuries later, Ohio was inhabited by the Adena people, the earliest mound builders. Their descendants, the Hopewell Indians, built burial mounds, fortifications, and ceremonial earthworks, some of which are now preserved in state parks.

The first European travelers in Ohio, during the 17th century, found four Indian tribes: Wyandot and Delaware in northern Ohio, Miami and Shawnee in the south. All were hunters who followed game trails that threaded the dense Ohio forest. All together, these four tribes numbered about 15,000 people. European exploration was begun by a French nobleman, Robert Cavelier, Sieur de la Salle, who, with Indian guides and paddlers, voyaged from the St. Lawrence River to the Ohio, which he explored in 1669–70. In the early 1700s, French and English traders brought knives, hatchets, guns, blankets, tobacco, rum, and brandy to exchange for the Indians' deer and beaver skins. Profits from the fur trade were many times the value of the goods the Indians received.

Both the French and the English claimed possession of Ohio,

the French claim resting on La Salle's exploration, while the British claimed all territory extending westward from their coastal colonies. To reinforce the French claim, Celeron de Bienville led an expedition from Canada to Ohio in 1749 to warn off English traders, win over the Indians, and assert French possession of the land. Traveling by canoe, with marches overland, he found the Indians better disposed at that time to the English than to the French. The following year, a company of Virginia merchants sent Christopher Gist to map Ohio trade routes and to make friendship and trade agreements with the tribes. The clash of ambitions brought on the French and Indian War—during which the Indians fought on both sides—ending in 1763 with French defeat and the ceding of the vast western territory to the British. During the Revolutionary War, the American militiaman George Rogers Clark, with a small company of woodsmen-soldiers, seized British posts and trading stations in Ohio, and in the Battle of Piqua, defeated Indian warriors allied with the British. It was largely Clark's campaigns that won the Northwest Territory for the US.

The new nation had a huge public domain, extending from the Allegheny Mountains to the Mississippi River. To provide future government and development of the territory northwest of the Ohio River, the US Congress enacted the Land Ordinance of 1785 and the Northwest Ordinance of 1787. The Land Ordinance created a survey system of rectangular sections and townships, a system begun in Ohio and extended to all new areas in the expanding nation. The farsighted Northwest Ordinance provided a system of government under which territories could achieve statehood on a basis equal with that of the original colonies. When a specified area had a population of 60,000 free adult males, it could seek admission to the Union as an independent state.

The first permanent settlement in Ohio was made in 1788 by an organization of Revolutionary War veterans who had received land warrants as a reward for their military service. They trekked by ox-drawn wagons over the mountains and by flatboat down the Ohio River to the mouth of the Muskingum, where they built the historic town of Marietta. John Cleves Symmes, a New Jersey official, brought pioneer settlers to his Miami Purchase in southwestern Ohio; their first settlement, in 1789, eventually became the city of Cincinnati. Access to the fertile Ohio Valley was provided by the westward-flowing Ohio River, which carried pioneer settlers and frontier commerce. Flatboats made a one-way journey, as families floated toward what they hoped would be new settlements. Keelboats traveled both downstream and upstream—an easy journey followed by a hard one. The keelboat trade, carrying military supplies and frontier produce, created an enduring river lore. Its legendary hero is burly, blustering Mike Fink, "half horse and half alligator," always ready for a fight or a frolic, for riot or rampage.

Increasing settlement of the Ohio Valley aroused Indian resistance. War parties raided outlying villages, burned houses, and drove families away. Two military expeditions against the Indians were shattered by Chief Little Turtle and his Miami warriors. Then, in 1793, Major General "Mad Anthony" Wayne took command in the West. He built roads and forts in the Miami Valley, and trained a force of riflemen. On a summer morning in 1794, Wayne routed allied tribesmen, mostly Miami and Shawnee, in the decisive Battle of Fallen Timbers. In the ensuing Treaty of Greenville, Indian leaders surrendered claim to the southern half of Ohio, opening that large domain to uncontested American occupation.

When, in 1800, Connecticut ceded to the US a strip of land along Lake Erie claimed by its colonial charter and called the Western Reserve, that region became a part of the Northwest Territory. Now the future seemed unclouded, and from the older colonies came a great migration to the promised land. By 1802,

Ohio had enough population to seek statehood, and in November a constitutional convention assembled at Chillicothe. In 25 days and at a total cost of $5,000, the 35 delegates framed a constitution that vested most authority in the state legislature and gave the vote to all white male taxpayers. On 1 March 1803, Ohio joined the Union as the 17th state.

Beyond Ohio's western border, Indians still roamed free. In 1811, the powerful Shawnee chief Tecumseh led a tribal resistance movement (supported by the British) seeking to halt the white man's advance into the new territory and to regain lands already lost to the Americans. Ohio militia regiments led by General William Henry Harrison repulsed an Indian invasion near Toledo in the battle of Tippecanoe on 7 November 1811. Control of Lake Erie and of Great Lakes commerce was at stake when Commodore Oliver Hazard Perry won a decisive naval victory over a British fleet in western Lake Erie during the War of 1812. Tecumseh was slain in the Battle of Thames in Canada on 5 October 1813.

With peace restored in 1815, "Ohio fever" spread through New England. In a great migration, people streamed over the mountains and the lakes to a land of rich soil, mild climate, and beckoning opportunities. Across the Atlantic, especially in England, Ireland, and Germany, thousands of immigrants boarded ship for America. At newly opened land offices, public land was sold at $1.25 an acre. Forest became fields, fields became villages and towns, towns became cities. By 1850, Ohio was the 3d most populous state in the Union.

Having cleared millions of acres of forest, Ohioans turned to economic development. Producing more than its people consumed, the state needed transportation routes to eastern markets. The National Road extended across the central counties in the 1830s, carrying stagecoach passengers and wagon commerce from Pennsylvania and Maryland. The Ohio canal system, created between 1825 and 1841, linked the Ohio River and Lake Erie, providing a waterway to the Atlantic via New York's Erie Canal. In 1826, state lands were valued at $16 million; fifteen years later their value exceeded $100 million. The chief products were wheat, corn, pork, beef, salt, wool, and leather. By 1850, when farm and factory production outstripped the capacity of mule teams and canal barges, railroad building had begun. In the next decade, railroads crisscrossed the state.

In 1861, Ohio, like the rest of the nation, was divided. The northern counties, teeming with former New Englanders, were imbued with abolitionist zeal. But Ohio's southern counties had close ties with Virginia and Kentucky across the river. From southeastern Ohio came Clement L. Vallandigham, leader of the Peace Democrats—called Copperheads by their opponents—who defended states' rights, opposed all of President Lincoln's policies, and urged compromise with the Confederacy. While Ohio surpassed its quota by providing a total of 320,000 Union Army volunteers, the Copperhead movement grew strong enough to nominate Vallandigham for state governor in 1863. Responding to the news of Vallandigham's defeat by the rugged Unionist John Brough, Lincoln telegraphed: "Ohio has saved the nation." Ohio became directly involved in the war for two weeks in 1863, when Confederate General John Hunt Morgan led a Kentucky cavalry force on a daring but ineffectual raid through the southern counties.

Ohio gave the Union its greatest generals—Ulysses S. Grant, William Tecumseh Sherman, and Philip H. Sheridan—each of whom won decisive victories at crucial times. Also essential to the Union cause was the service of Ohio men in Lincoln's cabinet, including Treasury Secretary Salmon P. Chase and War Secretary Edwin M. Stanton.

Mid-19th-century Ohio was primarily an agricultural state, but war demands stimulated Ohio manufactures, and in the decade following the war the state's industrial products surpassed the value of its rich farm production. The greatest commercial development came in northern Ohio, where heavy industry grew dramatically. To Toledo, Cleveland, and Youngstown via Lake Superior came iron ore that was converted into iron and steel with coal from the Ohio Valley. In the 1870s, John D. Rockefeller of Cleveland organized the Standard Oil Co., which soon controlled oil refining and distribution throughout the nation. At the same time, B. F. Goodrich of Akron began making fire hose, the first rubber product in an industry whose prodigious growth would make Akron the "rubber capital of the world." In the middle of the state, the capital city, Columbus, became a center of the brewing, railroad equipment, and farm implement industries. Cincinnati factories made steamboat boilers, machine tools, meat products, railroad cars, and soap. Dayton became known for its paper products, refrigerators, and cash registers.

With industrial growth came political power. In the next half-century, Ohio virtually took possession of the White House. Presidents Grant, Rutherford B. Hayes, James A. Garfield, Benjamin Harrison, William McKinley, William Howard Taft, and Warren G. Harding were all Ohioans. The first four had been Civil War generals, but even these men were politicians more than commanders; moderation was their rule. Ohio, the heartland of the expanding nation, grew national in mind and character. The four great business pursuits—agriculture, commerce, mining, and manufacturing—were remarkably balanced in Ohio. With one in seven Ohioans being of foreign birth, the state had neither the greatest nor the least admixture of immigrants. Its ethnic strains were various. Following the earlier English, Irish, and German influx came Italian, Czech, Dutch, Finnish, Greek, Hungarian, Polish, Russian, Serbian, and Ukrainian immigrants, along with a growing number of blacks from the rural South. Thus Ohio was an advantageous background for a president; to any other part of the nation an Ohio candidate did not seem alien. In the 1920 campaign, both the Republican and Democratic nominees—Harding and James M. Cox—were Ohio men. Norman Thomas, a perennial Socialist candidate, was likewise an Ohioan.

During World War I, Ohio's heavy industry expanded and its cities grew. Progressivism developed in Toledo and Cleveland, where the respective mayors, Samuel M. "Golden Rule" Jones and Tom L. Johnson, both wealthy businessmen, strove for civic virtue and social justice. Their reforms resulted in the city-manager form of government that spread to other Ohio cities. In the postwar 1920s, Ohio's oil, rubber, and glass industries kept pace with accelerating automobile production. Yet none of these industries was immune to the prolonged depression of the 1930s. Widespread unemployment and a stagnant economy were not relieved until the outbreak of World War II. The war swept 641,000 Ohioans into military service and gave Ohio industry military contracts totaling $18 billion.

The state's economy prospered after World War II, with highway building, truck and tractor production, aircraft manufacture, and airport construction leading the field. The completion of the St. Lawrence Seaway made active ocean ports of Toledo and Cleveland, which exported grain, tractors, farm machinery, and electronic devices to foreign lands and received a wide variety of imports in return.

Major problems during this period involved pollution created by the dumping of industrial wastes (especially in Lake Erie) and urban decay resulting from the departure of middle-class families to the suburbs, an exodus that left the central cities to growing numbers of the poor and underprivileged. Related to these problems were troubles in the Ohio school system. Deteriorating neighborhoods produced inadequate revenues for schools and public services, and attempts at racial integration brought controversy and disturbance. When political office went to minority leaders—in 1967, Carl Stokes of Cleveland became the first black mayor of any major US city—friction and tension continued. Urban renewal barely kept pace with urban blight. A further shock to Ohioans was the shooting of 13 students, 4 of whom died, at Kent State University on 4 May 1970 by National Guardsmen who had been sent to the campus to preserve order during a series of demonstrations against US involvement in Indochina. The ensuing lawsuits helped keep the incident in the public eye well into the 1970s.

At the start of the 1980s, Ohio was still beset by serious social and economic problems. The state's population was static. Shrinking industrial employment had been only partly offset by new enterprises that offered services rather than material goods. Ohio's huge coal reserves were of limited usefulness because of their content of sulfur, an atmospheric pollutant.

On the positive side, Ohio had strengthened its state universities and developed a system of community colleges that brought vocational training within the reach of most of its citizens. Major conservancy programs embracing the watersheds of the Muskingum and the Miami rivers had become models for such undertakings in other states. These projects offered the benefits of flood control, soil conservation, and reforestation, as well as recreation areas capable of attracting numerous tourists.

[12] STATE GOVERNMENT

The Ohio constitution of 1803 was replaced by a second constitution in 1851. Amendments proposed by a constitutional convention in 1912 and subsequently approved by the voters so heavily revised the 1851 constitution as to make it virtually a new document. This modified constitution, with subsequent amendments, provides for county and municipal home rule, direct primary elections, recall of elected officials, and constitutional amendment by initiative and referendum.

Ohio's general assembly consists of a 99-member house of representatives, elected for two years, and a senate of 33 members serving four-year terms (half the members are chosen every two years). Regular sessions of the legislature convene the 1st Monday in January of odd-numbered years, and a second session is called on the same date of the following year. Each house may introduce legislation, and both houses must approve a bill before it can be signed into law by the governor. The governor's veto of a bill can be overridden by three-fifths majority votes of both houses. Legislators' salaries were $22,500 annually in 1980.

Officials elected statewide are the governor, lieutenant governor, secretary of state, attorney general, auditor, and treasurer, all of whom are elected to four-year terms. Effective in 1959, a constitutional amendment changed the governor's term from two to four years and forbade a governor from serving more than two successive terms. The governor appoints the heads of 21 executive departments. In 1980, the governor's annual salary was $50,000 and the lieutenant governor's, $30,000.

The constitution may be amended legislatively by a three-fifths vote of each house; the proposed amendment must then receive majority approval by the voters at the next general election. Amendments may also be proposed by petition of 10% of the electors who voted for governor in the last general election; a majority vote in a subsequent referendum is required for passage. The constitution provides that every 20 years (from 1932 onward) the voters must be given the chance to choose whether a constitutional convention should be held.

To vote in Ohio, one must be a US citizen, 18 years of age or older, and have been a resident of the county and voting precinct for at least 30 days.

[13] POLITICAL PARTIES

Ohio has sent seven native sons and one other state resident to the White House—equaling Virginia as the "mother of presidents." The state's two major political parties, Democratic and Republican, have dominated the political scene since 1856.

Ohioans scattered their votes among various political factions until 1836, when they rallied behind state resident William Henry Harrison and the Whig Party; they again supported Harrison in 1840, helping him win his second bid for the presidency. Whigs and Democrats divided the votes in 1844, 1848, and 1852; in 1856, however, Ohio supported the newly formed Republican Party, and after the Civil War, 7 of the country's next 12 presidents were Ohio-born Republicans, beginning with Grant and ending with Harding. From 1856 to 1976, Ohioans voted for the Republican candidate in all presidential elections except those in which the following five Democrats were elected: Woodrow Wilson (twice), Franklin D. Roosevelt (three times), Harry S. Truman, Lyndon B. Johnson, and Jimmy Carter. In 1920, when the presidential candidates of both major parties were Ohioans, the Republican, Warren G. Harding, carried Ohio as well as the nation.

Ohio Presidential Vote by Political Parties, 1948–80

YEAR	ELECTORAL VOTE	OHIO WINNER	DEMOCRAT	REPUBLICAN	PROGRESSIVE	SOC.LABOR	COMMUNIST	LIBERTARIAN
1948	25	*Truman (D)	1,452,791	1,445,684	37,487	—	—	—
1952	25	*Eisenhower (R)	1,600,367	2,100,391	—	—	—	—
1956	25	*Eisenhower (R)	1,439,655	2,262,610	—	—	—	—
1960	25	Nixon (R)	1,944,248	2,217,611	—	—	—	—
1964	26	*Johnson (D)	2,498,331	1,470,865	—	—	—	—
					AMERICAN IND.			
1968	26	*Nixon (R)	1,700,586	1,791,014	467,495	—	—	—
					AMERICAN			
1972	25	*Nixon (R)	1,558,889	2,441,827	80,067	7,107	6,437	—
					SOC. WORKERS			
1976	25	*Carter (D)	2,011,621	2,000,505	15,529	4,717	7,817	8,961
					CITIZENS			
1980[1]	25	*Reagan (R)	1,745,103	2,203,139	8,979	4,436	5,030	49,604

*Won US presidential election. [1]Candidates of nationwide minor parties were listed as independents on the Ohio ballot.

Political bossism flourished in Ohio during the last quarter of the 19th century, when the state government was controlled by Republicans Mark Hanna in Cleveland and George B. Cox in Cincinnati. Hanna played an influential role in Republican national politics; in 1896, his handpicked candidate, William McKinley, was elected to the presidency. But the despotism of the bosses and the widespread corruption in city goverments led to public demands for reform. In Toledo, a reform mayor, Samuel "Golden Rule" Jones, began to clean house in 1897. Four years later, another group of reformers, led by mayor Tom L. Johnson, ousted the Hanna machine and instituted honest government in Cleveland. At the time, journalist Lincoln Steffens called Cleveland "the best-governed city in the US" and Cincinnati "the worst." The era of bossism ended for Cincinnati in 1905, when the voters overthrew the Cox machine, elected a reform mayor on a fusion ticket, and instituted reforms that in 1925 made Cincinnati the first major US city with a nonpartisan city-manager form of government.

With the decline of big-city political machines, ticket splitting has become a regular practice among Ohio voters in state and local contests. Overall, between 1900 and 1980, 12 Republicans and 11 Democrats have held the governorship. Democrat Frank J. Lausche was elected to an unprecedented five two-year terms (1945–47, 1949–57); Republican James A. Rhodes has been elected governor four times (his fourth term is due to expire in 1983). In 1978, Ohioans elected a Republican governor (Rhodes) and lieutenant governor, but a Democratic secretary of state, attorney general, auditor, and treasurer. Democrats controlled both houses of the state legislature, but Republicans outnumbered Democrats in the state's congressional delegation.

In general, third parties have fared poorly in Ohio since 1856. An exception was the 1968 presidential election, in which American Independent Party candidate George Wallace garnered nearly 12% of Ohio's popular vote. Wallace's capture of many dissident Democrats probably provided the margin of victory for Richard M. Nixon, who carried the state by only 90,428 votes over the Democratic candidate, Hubert Humphrey. A more typical voting pattern was displayed in the 1976 presidential election, when the two major parties received 97.7% of the total votes cast, and only 2.3% of the votes were split among minor parties and independents. Of the state's 5,222,041 registered voters, nearly 80% voted, and Democrat Jimmy Carter won an extremely close election by only 11,116 votes. The result was not nearly so close in 1980, when Ronald Reagan, the Republican presidential nominee, won 51% of the popular vote to 41% for Jimmy Carter, 6% for John Anderson, and 2% for the minor-party candidates. John Glenn easily retained his seat in the US Senate, and the Republicans kept their hold on the state's US House delegation.

[14] LOCAL GOVERNMENT
Local government in Ohio is exercised by the 88 counties, more than 900 cities and villages, and about 1,300 townships.

Each county is administered by a board of three commissioners, elected to four-year terms, whose authority is limited by state law. The county government is run by eight officials elected to four-year terms: the auditor or financial officer, whose duties include levying taxes; the clerk of courts, who is elected as clerk of the court of common pleas and also serves as clerk of the county court of appeals; the coroner, who must be a licensed physician; an engineer; a prosecuting attorney; the recorder, who keeps records of deeds, mortgages, and other legal documents; a sheriff; and the treasurer, who collects and disburses public funds.

Within each county are incorporated areas with limited authority to govern their own affairs. Thirty voters in an area may request incorporation of the community as a village. A village reaching the population of 5,000 automatically becomes a city, which by law must establish executive and legislative bodies.

There are three types of city government: the mayor-council plan, which is the form adopted by a majority of the state's approximately 200 cities; the city-manager form, under which the city council appoints a professional manager to conduct nonpartisan government operations; and the commission type, in which a board of elected commissioners administers the city government. In practice, most large cities have adopted a home-rule charter, which permits them to select the form of government best suited to their requirements.

Cleveland experimented with the city-manager form of government from 1924 to 1932, at which time public disclosures of municipal corruption led the city's voters to return to the mayor-council plan. In 1967, Cleveland became the first major US city to elect a black mayor; Carl Stokes served two two-year terms but retired from politics in 1971. Cleveland again attracted national attention in 1978 when its 31-year-old mayor, Dennis J. Kucinich, publicly disputed the city's financial policies with members of the city council, and the city defaulted on $15 million in bank loans. Mayor Kucinich narrowly survived a recall election; in 1979, he was defeated for reelection by the state's lieutenant governor, George Voinovich.

Cincinnati has retained the city-manager form of government since 1925. The mayor, elected by the city council from among its nine members, has no administrative duties. Instead, the council appoints a city manager to an indefinite term as chief executive. In 1979, for the first time, the council appointed a black man, Sylvester Murray, as city manager. Columbus, the state capital since 1816, has a mayor-council form of government.

Townships are governed by three trustees and a clerk, all elected to staggered four-year terms. These elected officials oversee zoning ordinances, parks, road maintenance, fire protection, and other matters within their jurisdiction.

[15] STATE SERVICES
The State Department of Education administers every phase of public school operations, including counseling and testing services, the federal school lunch program, and teacher education and certification. The department also oversees special schools for the blind and deaf. The department's chief administrator is the superintendent of public instruction, appointed by a 23-member elective Board of Education.

Health and welfare services are provided by several departments. The Department of Health issues and enforces health and sanitary regulations. Violations of health rules are reviewed by a Public Health Council of seven members, including three physicians and a pharmacist. The Department of Mental Health and Mental Retardation administers 19 mental health institutions, develops diagnostic, prevention, and rehabilitation programs, and trains mental health professionals. The Department of Public Welfare helps the needy through aid to families with dependent children, public assistance payments, food stamps, and Medicaid. The Bureau of Employment Services and the Bureau of Workers' Compensation administer labor benefit programs.

Public protection services include those of the State Highway Patrol and the Bureau of Motor Vehicles, both within the Department of Highway Safety; the Department of Rehabilitation and Correction, which operates penal institutions; the Ohio Youth Commission, which administers juvenile correction centers; and the Environmental Protection Agency.

[16] JUDICIAL SYSTEM
The supreme court of Ohio, the highest court in the state, reviews proceedings of the lower courts and of state agencies. The high court has a chief justice and six associate justices elected to six-year terms. Below the supreme court are 11 courts of appeals, which exercise jurisdiction over their respective judicial districts. Each court has at least three judges elected to six-year terms; the district including Cleveland has nine appeals court judges, and the Cincinnati district has six.

Trial courts include 88 courts of common pleas, one in each county; judges are elected to six-year terms. Probate courts, domestic relations courts, and juvenile courts often function as divisions of the common pleas courts. In 1957, a system of county courts was established by the legislature to replace justices of the peace and mayors' courts at the local level. Large cities have their own municipal courts, as well as special juvenile courts and police courts.

Ohio has four state prisons for men, a boys' reformatory, and a reformatory for women. In 1977, state and federal prisons in Ohio had 12,846 inmates, of whom 577 were women. According to the FBI Crime Index, Ohio's crime rates rank below the national averages. In the FBI data for 1978, the state's crime rates per 100,000 population were murder and nonnegligent manslaughter, 7; forcible rape, 28; robbery, 183; assault, 196; burglary, 1,215; larceny, 2,630; and motor vehicle theft, 402. In that year, Cleveland ranked 5th among the largest US cities in violent crimes, with 1,578 reported crimes per 100,000 population.

17 ARMED FORCES

The US Department of Defense had 43,782 personnel in Ohio in 1977/78. The principal military installations are Wright-Patterson Air Force Base near Dayton, with 25,710 personnel, and Rickenbacker Air Force Base near Columbus, with 6,578. In 1977/78, the Defense Department awarded $1.2 billion in defense contracts to Ohio companies. An important Ohio defense contractor is the Chrysler plant at Lima, which in 1980 began producing the XM-1 turbine-powered tank; the Army expects to purchase more than 7,000 of these tanks by 1990.

In 1979, Ohio had 1,483,000 veterans, of whom an estimated 27,000 had served in World War I, 622,000 in World War II, 261,000 during the Korean conflict, and 447,000 during the Viet-Nam era. In fiscal year 1977/78, the Veterans Administration expended $747.6 million in pensions, medical assistance, and other veterans' benefits.

Army and Air National Guardsmen in Ohio numbered 16,400 in 1978. State and local police forces in 1977 employed 22,207 persons, of whom nearly 88% were in local police departments. Police expenditures for that year totaled $394 million.

18 MIGRATION

After the Ohio country became a US territory in 1785, Virginians, Connecticut Yankees, and New Jerseyites began arriving in significant numbers; tens of thousands of settlers from New England, Pennsylvania, and some southern states thronged into Ohio in subsequent decades. The great migration from the eastern states continued throughout most of the 19th century, and was bolstered by new arrivals from Europe. The Irish came in the 1830s, and many Germans began arriving in the 1840s. Another wave of European immigration brought about 500,000 people a year to Ohio during the 1880s, many of them from southern and eastern Europe. Former slaves left the South for Ohio following the Civil War, and a larger migratory wave brought blacks to Ohio after World War II to work in the industrial cities. In the 1910s, many emigrants from Greece, Albania, and Latvia settled in Akron to work in the rubber industry.

The industrialization of Ohio in the late 19th and the 20th centuries encouraged the migration of Ohioans from the farms to the cities. The large number of Ohioans who lived in rural areas and worked on farms declined steadily after 1900, with the farm population decreasing to under 1,000,000 during World War II and then to fewer than 400,000 by 1979. A more recent development has been the exodus of urbanites from Ohio's largest cities. From 1970 to 1977, Cleveland lost 166,251 residents; Cincinnati, 62,768; Dayton, 54,297; Columbus, 46,351; Toledo, 43,664; and Akron, 42,141. It is not clear how many of these former city dwellers moved to the suburbs and how many left the state. According to state estimates, Ohio lost more than 435,000 people through migration during this period.

19 INTERGOVERNMENTAL COOPERATION

The Ohio Commission on Interstate Cooperation represents the state in dealings with the Council of State Governments and its allied organizations. Ohio is a signatory to interstate compacts covering the Great Lakes Basin, the Ohio River Valley, and Pymatuning Reservoir. The state also participates in the Interstate Mining Compact, Interstate Oil and Gas Compact, and the Midwest Nuclear Compact.

Federal aid to Ohio for all purposes exceeded $3 billion in the 1978/79 fiscal year.

20 ECONOMY

Ohio's economy is remarkable for its balance. In the mid-19th century, Ohio became a leader in agriculture, ranking 1st among the states in wheat production in 1840, and 1st in corn and wool by 1850. With industrialization, Ohio ranked 4th in value added by manufacturing in 1900. Coal mining in the southeastern part of the state and easy access to Minnesota's iron ore via the Great Lakes contributed to the growth of the iron and steel industry in the Cleveland-Youngstown area; Ohio led the nation in the manufacture of machine tools and placed 2d among the states in steel production in the early 1900s. Automobile manufacturing and other new industries were developed after World War I. Hit hard by the depression of the 1930s, the state diversified its industry and enjoyed prosperity during and after World War II.

During the 1970s, the decline in the public demand for automobiles and other durable goods (which accounted for about 30% of state payrolls in 1978), coupled with the high inflation rate that has helped make Ohio's steel products less competitive in foreign markets, adversely affected the economy. Because the state is so highly industrialized, any decline in demand for durable goods threatens Ohio's economy.

In 1978, Ohio's gross state product totaled $103.2 billion. Contributing economic sectors were manufacturing, 35%; commerce, 17%; service industries, 11%; finance, insurance, and real estate, 11%; government, 9%; transportation, communications, and utilities, 9%; construction, 4%; mining, 2%; and farming, 2%.

In 1977, the metals and machinery industries accounted for nearly half of the state's total employment. Steel was produced primarily in Youngstown, automotive and aircraft parts in Cleveland, automobile tires and other rubber products in Akron, and office equipment in Dayton. The threat of recession in 1980 led to the closing of a US Steel plant in Youngstown and of two Firestone tire and rubber factories in the Akron area, and to widespread layoffs in the auto parts industry. This bad economic news was partially offset by the announcement in January 1980 that the Honda Motor Co. would build Japan's first US automobile assembly plant near Columbus, where Honda had already been manufacturing motorcycles.

21 INCOME

In 1978, Ohio ranked 6th among the 50 states in personal income with a total of $84.4 billion, but placed 20th in per capita income with an average of $7,855. The US Department of Commerce forecast a 29% increase in per capita income (in constant 1967 dollars) for Ohioans between 1980 and 1990—a rise equivalent to the projected US average.

In 1977, the sources of personal income were as follows: manufacturing, 39%; wholesale and retail trade, 15%; service industries, 14%; government, 12%; transportation and utilities, 7%; construction, 5%; finance, insurance, and real estate, 4%; and other sectors, 4%.

The median income of Ohio families in 1978 was $16,500. Of the state's 2,799,000 families in that year, 24% had annual incomes of $25,000 and more; 32% had incomes between $15,000 and $24,999; the incomes of 20% ranged from $10,000 to $14,999; and 24% had below $10,000. About 7.5% of Ohio families had incomes below the national poverty level in 1978.

²²LABOR

In 1978, Ohio ranked 6th among the 50 states in the size of its labor force, which totaled 4,943,000. In that year there were 4,675,000 wage and salary earners, of whom 59% were male and 41% were female. The total number of employed persons declined slightly during 1979 to an estimated 4,613,000 persons in February 1980. The US Commerce Department projected that total employment in Ohio would increase to about 5,485,000 by 1990.

A federal census of workers covered by unemployment insurance in March 1977 revealed the following employment pattern for Ohio:

	ESTABLISH-MENTS	EMPLOYEES	ANNUAL PAYROLL ('000)
Agricultural services, forestry, fishing	1,821	7,460	$73,697
Mining, of which:	1,109	27,295	457,968
Bituminous coal, lignite	(267)	(16,294)	(280,885)
Contract construction	19,414	142,499	2,558,676
Manufacturing, of which:	16,322	1,342,783	20,760,394
Primary metals	(650)	(148,851)	(2,674,571)
Fabricated metals	(2,248)	(157,917)	(2,460,068)
Nonelectrical machinery	(3,441)	(197,766)	(2,943,326)
Transportation equipment	(443)	(163,233)	(3,152,448)
Transportation, public utilities	6,674	184,312	3,015,900
Wholesale trade	16,484	226,237	3,231,380
Retail trade	58,569	673,037	4,672,180
Finance, insurance, real estate	17,945	186,225	2,002,312
Services, of which:	56,735	661,623	5,839,525
Health services	(13,697)	(231,660)	(2,463,231)
Other	1,945	2,538	30,484
TOTALS	197,018	3,454,009	$42,642,516

This survey excluded farm laborers, self-employed workers, government workers, and certain other employees. In 1978, Ohio had 663,069 government employees, of whom 89,444 were employed by the federal government and 111,740 by the state.

Of all Ohioans employed in 1977, nearly 78% worked in the state's metropolitan areas. There were 906,000 employees in the Cleveland metropolitan area, 510,700 in Columbus, and 497,400 in Cincinnati. In 1979, the unemployment rate in metropolitan areas ranged from 5% in Columbus and Cleveland to more than 7% in Toledo and Youngstown. Overall, the state's unemployment rate rose from 6.4% in February 1979 to 7% in February 1980.

The first workers' organization in Ohio was formed by Dayton mechanics in 1811. The Ohio Federation of Labor was founded in 1884; the American Federation of Labor was founded in Columbus in 1886, and Ohio native William Green became president of the AFL in 1924. But it was not until the 1930s that labor unions in Ohio were formed on a large scale. In 1934, the United Rubber Workers began to organize workers in Akron; through a successful series of sitdown strikes at the city's rubber plants, the union grew to about 70,000 members by 1937. In that year, the United Steelworkers struck seven steel plants in the Youngstown area and won the right to bargain collectively for 50,000 steelworkers. The number of union members increased from about 25% of the state's nonfarm employees in 1939 to more than 31% in 1976, when 1,289,000 workers belonged to labor unions. Another 177,000 Ohioans belonged to professional and state employee associations, bringing organized labor's total participation rate to nearly 36% (8th in the US). In 1978 there were 441 strikes or other labor stoppages involving 141,600 workers.

Strikes by public employees have troubled the major cities; in Youngstown, for example, police, fire, and sanitation workers all walked out during May 1980.

Progressive labor legislation in the state began in 1852 with laws regulating working hours for women and children and limiting men to a 10-hour workday. In 1890, Ohio became the first state to establish a public employment service. Subsequent labor legislation included a workers' compensation act in 1911, and child labor and minimum wage measures in the 1930s.

²³AGRICULTURE

Despite increasing urbanization and industrialization, agriculture retains its economic importance. In 1978, Ohio ranked 8th in farm value and 13th in agricultural income among the 50 states. In that year, the state's production of crops, dairy products, and livestock was valued at more than $3 billion.

Mechanization of agriculture contributed to the decline of Ohio's farm population from 1,089,000 in 1940 to 415,000 in 1979, and to a decrease in the number of farms from 234,000 to 97,000. The average size of farms has increased from 94 acres (38 hectares) in 1940 to 168 acres (68 hectares) in 1979. As of January 1980, Ohio had about 75,000 farmers and 25,000 farm laborers.

Grain is grown and cattle and hogs are raised on large farms in the north-central and western parts of the state, while smaller farms predominate in the hilly southeastern region. Truck farming has developed and expanded near the large cities; special crops for city markets include grapes along Lake Erie and vegetables in the northeast.

Ohio was the 2d-leading producer of tomatoes for processing in 1978, with 349,320 tons. Output of grapes, apples, peaches, and cherries totaled 169,000,000 lb. Field crops in 1979 (in bushels) included corn for grain, 417,450,000; soybeans, 145,080,000; wheat, 63,360,000; oats, 23,800,000. The most valuable crops were soybeans, with sales of $895,869,000, and corn, $654,562,000. Ohio farmers also produced 3,606,000 tons of hay and an estimated 261,000 tons of sugar beets in 1979.

²⁴ANIMAL HUSBANDRY

In 1978, production of meat and dairy products accounted for more than two-fifths of Ohio's farm income and was valued at nearly $1.3 billion. Ohio ranked 6th among the states in sales of dairy products, 7th in sales of hogs and pigs, and 7th in sales of eggs.

Cattle and hogs are raised in the central and western regions. At the end of 1979, Ohio had 2,070,000 hogs and pigs, 1,925,000 head of cattle, and 320,000 sheep and lambs. A total of 719,755,000 lb of hogs and pigs, 643,270,000 lb of cattle, and 23,322,000 lb of sheep and lambs were marketed in 1979.

Dairying is common in most regions of the state, but especially in the east and southeast. Cash receipts from sales of dairy products amounted to $449 million in 1978. In that year, 4.3 billion lb of milk were produced. The poultry industry is dispersed throughout the state. Cash receipts in 1978 from poultry and egg sales amounted to $135.8 million. In 1979, Ohio poultry farmers produced 6,750,000 chickens, 19,100,000 broilers, and 2,350,000 turkeys. Egg production totaled 2.2 billion.

²⁵FISHING

Commercial fishing, which once flourished in Lake Erie, has declined during the 20th century. Only 9,515,000 lb of fish worth $2,563,000 were landed in 1978.

²⁶FORESTRY

In 1977, Ohio had 6,504,000 acres (2,632,000 hectares) of forestland, representing nearly 25% of the state's total area but less than 1% of all US forests. Although scattered throughout the state, hardwood forests are concentrated in the hilly region of the southeast. Commercial timberlands in 1977 totaled 6,422,000 acres (2,599,000 hectares), of which 94% was privately owned.

The state's lumber and wood products industry supplies building materials, household furniture, and paper products. In 1977, shipments of major wood products included furniture, worth $327.3 million; prefabricated buildings and mobile homes, $161.7 million; lumber, $89.4 million; containers, $53.6 million, and partitions and fixtures, $45.4 million.

In 1977 there were about 227,000 acres (92,000 hectares) of state, county, and municipal timberland. State parks and recreation areas totaled 204,000 acres (83,000 hectares) in 1975. Reforestation programs involving the reseeding of more than 10,000 acres (4,000 hectares) per year ensure that timber growth exceeds the state's timber harvest, which totals more than 500 million board feet annually.

[27] MINING

In 1978, Ohio ranked 15th in mineral production, with a total value of $1.7 billion. The most valuable minerals are fossil fuels and stone. Mining of limestone, clay, and sand and gravel predominates in the southeast. In 1977, Ohio had 1,314 mines and quarries, of which 618 produced coal, 425 sand, 131 limestone, and 77 clay and shale; 63 produced other minerals.

Estimated output of major minerals in 1978 (in tons, excluding fossil fuels) were stone, 47,496,000; sand and gravel, 47,000,000; salt, 3,836,000; lime, 3,412,000; and cement, 2,044,000.

[28] ENERGY AND POWER

Ohio is blessed with energy resources. The state government estimated during the late 1970s that Ohio's coal reserves were sufficient to meet demand for 500 years, and that oil and natural gas reserves were also ample. On the other hand, nearly 98% of the state's electricity was produced by coal with an ash content ranging from 5% to 20%—a major atmospheric pollutant.

In 1978, Ohio ranked 5th among all states in electric power production. In that year, installed electric power capacity was 27 million kw, of which 97% was privately owned, and electrical output totaled 112 billion kwh (99% private). In 1977, the state's consumption of electric power amounted to 120.2 billion kwh, of which industries consumed 56%, residential users, 26%, commercial establishments, 15%, and other customers, 3%.

In the 1880s, petroleum was discovered near Lima and natural gas near Toledo, both in the northwest; these fossil fuels have since been found and exploited in the central and eastern regions. In 1978, the state produced 11,154,000 barrels of crude petroleum; proved reserves were estimated at 131,194,000 barrels. About 115.2 billion cu feet (3.3 billion cu meters) of natural gas were extracted, with reserves estimated at 1.6 trillion cu feet (45 billion cu meters). A total of 2,624 new oil and gas wells were drilled in 1977, of which 93% were productive. In the same year, Ohio's gas utilities served 2,722,000 customers, of whom 92% were residential users.

Coalfields lie beneath southeastern Ohio, particularly in Hocking, Athens, and Perry counties. In 1977, Ohio ranked 5th in the US in coal production, with total output of 46,940,131 tons, valued at $577,836,161. During that year, 314 surface mines produced 70% of the coal; 304 underground mines supplied the remaining 30%.

A potential energy source is a rich bed of shale rock, underlying more than half of Ohio, which was estimated to contain more than 200 trillion cu feet (5.7 trillion cu meters) of natural gas; but much research is needed before the gas can be extracted economically.

[29] INDUSTRY

Ohio has been a leading manufacturing state since the mid-1800s, and in 1977 it ranked 3d among the states in value added by manufacture.

During the last two decades of the 19th century, Ohio became the nation's leader in machine-tool manufacturing, the 2d-leading steel producer, and a pioneer in oil refining and in the production of automobiles and automotive parts, such as rubber tires. More recently, Ohio has become important as a manufacturer of glassware, soap, matches, paint, refrigerators, business machines—and even comic books and Chinese food products.

According to the 1977 federal census of manufacturers, value added by Ohio manufacturing establishments totaled $43.3 billion. The principal industries were nonelectrical machinery, primary metals, and fabricated metal products. Of the total value added in 1977, transportation equipment accounted for 15%; nonelectrical machinery, 14%; primary metals, 13%; fabricated metal products, 12%; chemicals, 8%; electrical and electronic equipment, 8%; rubber and plastics, 7%; food and food products, 7%; stone, clay, and glass products, 4%; and other sectors, 12%.

In 1977, four major metropolitan areas—Cleveland, Cincinnati, Dayton, and Columbus—employed 40% of all the state's industrial workers and accounted for 45% of the state total value added by manufacture.

The following table shows value added by manufacture for selected industries in 1972 and 1977:

	1972	1977
Motor vehicle parts and accessories	$1,897,400,000	$3,295,100,000
Blast furnace and steel mill products	1,882,900,000	3,099,000,000
Motor vehicles and car bodies	942,600,000	1,516,900,000
Soaps and toiletries	732,000,000	1,134,000,000
Iron and steel foundry products	542,000,000	1,070,600,000
Aircraft and parts	727,300,000	1,009,600,000
Household appliances	618,300,000	968,900,000
Tires and inner tubes	758,300,000	815,200,000
Petroleum refinery products	219,700,000	458,700,000
Glassware	268,400,000	394,600,000

Of the 100 leading US industrial corporations listed by *Fortune* magazine for 1979, 10 had their headquarters in Ohio. The sales leader was Procter and Gamble (Cincinnati), with sales totaling $9.3 billion, 23d in the US. Others were Goodyear Tire and Rubber (Akron), $8.2 billion; Standard Oil of Ohio (Cleveland), $7.9 billion; Marathon Oil (Findlay), $6.7 billion; Firestone Tire and Rubber (Akron), $5.3 billion; Armco (Middletown), $5 billion; TRW (Cleveland), $4.6 billion; Republic Steel (Cleveland), $4 billion; and Owens-Illinois (Toledo), $3.5 billion.

[30] COMMERCE

Ohio ranks 5th among the 50 states in overall commercial activity.

In 1977, wholesale trade amounted to $61.7 billion. In that year, the chief categories of wholesale goods traded (in order of largest sales) were machinery, equipment, and supplies, 15%; motor vehicles and automotive parts, 14%; groceries and related products, 12%; metals and minerals (except petroleum), 11%; chemicals, 8%; grains and other agricultural raw materials, 7%; electrical goods, 6%; petroleum and oil products, 6%; lumber and construction materials, 3%; and other items, 18%. Cuyahoga County, which includes Cleveland, accounted for 28% of the state's wholesale trade.

In 1978, Ohio's retail sales amounted to $40.9 billion, or about 5% of the US total. The principal retail store groups and their sales percentages were automotive, 23%; food, 21%; general merchandise, 16%; eating and drinking places, 9%; and furniture, furnishings, and appliances, 5%. Of total retail sales in 1978, metropolitan areas accounted for 79%, including Cleveland, 19%; Columbus, 11%; Cincinnati, 11%; Dayton, 7%; and Toledo, 7%.

In 1976, Ohio ranked 4th in the US as an exporter of manufactured goods, with foreign sales of $5.8 billion, or 7% of the US total. In that year, transportation equipment and nonelectrical machinery accounted for more than half of the state's export value, followed by electric and electronic equipment, fabricated metal products, chemicals, food products, and primary metals. In 1976/77, Ohio ranked 9th among the states in agricultural exports, with an estimated value of $957 million. Soybeans and feed grains accounted for nearly two-thirds of that total; other major agricultural exports were wheat and flour, protein meal, soybean oil, hides and skins, meat and meat products, lard and tallow, and dairy products.

[31] CONSUMER PROTECTION

The Division of Consumer Protection within the Ohio Department of Commerce is charged with informing the public of its rights under the Ohio Consumer Sales Practices Act. The division receives consumers' complaints and investigates violations of law. Although it does not have enforcement powers, the division may develop consumer fraud and other cases for prosecution by the Ohio attorney general.

[32] BANKING

Ohio's first banks, in Marietta and Chillicothe, were incorporated in 1808, and a state bank was authorized in 1845. As of 1978, Ohio's 481 insured commercial banks had total assets of $48.3 billion, including $16.1 billion in outstanding loans and $12.7 billion in securities. Commercial bank deposits totaled $39.2 billion, including demand deposits of $13.9 billion and time deposits of $25.3 billion.

In 1977 there were 405 savings and loan associations in the state, with total assets of nearly $31 billion. Their mortgage loans totaled $25.6 billion, and their savings capital was valued at $26.1 billion.

[33] INSURANCE

In 1978 there were 1,168 insurance companies licensed in Ohio, which wrote more than $30.8 billion in premiums and distributed benefits exceeding $4.7 billion. The number of insurance companies included 446 life, 399 stock fire and casualty, 104 mutual fire and casualty, 87 fraternal benefit societies, 67 mutual protective-property associations, and 65 others. Of that total, 232 were Ohio companies, 910 were from out of state, and 26 were foreign.

In 1978, life insurance companies in the state wrote premiums worth $26 billion and paid benefits of more than $1.9 billion. At the end of 1977, the total assets of Ohio life insurance companies were $7.1 billion; liabilities, $6.5 billion, and premium income, $976 million. The average Ohio family had $38,500 in life insurance (10% above the US norm) in 1978.

In 1978, fire, marine, and other insurance companies wrote direct premiums of nearly $4.8 billion and paid benefits of $2.8 billion.

[34] SECURITIES

The Cincinnati Stock Exchange (CSE) was organized on 11 March 1885 by 12 stockbrokers who agreed to meet regularly to buy and sell securities. The exchange was incorporated as a nonprofit organization two years later. As of 1980, four Cincinnati companies that had been listed on the CSE in 1885—including the Dayton and Michigan Railroad Co. and the Little Miami Railroad—still had their stock traded on the exchange.

The CSE is governed by an elected eight-member board of trustees, the majority of whom must approve new members of the exchange. The cost of a seat on the CSE, originally $50, has fluctuated widely, from a high of $38,500 in 1929 to a low of $2,050 in 1936; the cost of membership as of May 1980 was $2,500. New members must be individuals of sound financial standing with net capital of at least $25,000.

Corporations wishing to list their securities on the CSE must be approved by the board. For a security to be listed, the issuer must have net assets of at least $750,000, 75 or more shareholders, and at least 45,000 shares (or $1 million) of the issue outstanding. These requirements, which are less stringent than those of the larger exchanges, are designed to permit small but growing companies access to a regional investment market; the US Securities and Exchange Commission has permitted the CSE to trade in more than 300 stocks unlisted on larger exchanges. About 34.6 million shares were traded on the CSE during the whole of 1979.

As of 31 December 1978, firms belonging to the New York Stock Exchange had 145 sales offices and 1,292 full-time registered representatives in Ohio. Ohioans reported nearly $1.4 billion in dividend income on their 1977 federal tax returns.

[35] PUBLIC FINANCE

The state budget is prepared on a biennial basis by the Office of Budget and Management. It is submitted by the governor to the state legislature, which must act on it by the close of the current fiscal year (30 June). The general assembly has nearly total discretion in allocating general revenues, which are used primarily to support education, welfare, mental health facilities, law enforcement, property tax relief, and government operations. The assembly also allocates money from special revenue funds by means of specific legislative acts. More than one-half of all state expenditures come from the general fund.

The general fund for the 1979–81 biennium was estimated at $10.8 billion, compared with the 1977–79 total of $8.8 billion. Of the 1979–81 general fund, the major categories of expenditure were as follows: education, 45%; human services (including health and welfare), 34%; property tax relief, 6%; law enforcement and judiciary, 4%; general state government, 3%; local government, 2%; environment and natural resources, 1%; energy credits, 1%; and other sectors, 4%.

The following table summarizes general revenues and expenditures for the fiscal year 1978/79 (in millions):

REVENUES	
Sales and use tax	$1,427.0
Personal income tax	868.1
Corporation franchise tax	576.0
Public utility excise tax	358.3
Cigarette tax	189.5
Alcoholic beverages tax	152.8
Miscellaneous taxes	225.3
Federal aid	747.5
Other income	110.1
TOTAL	$4,654.6

EXPENDITURES	
Primary and secondary education	$1,436.4
Public welfare	1,217.5
Higher education	677.6
Mental health and retardation	320.6
General state government	254.3
Property tax relief	253.4
Law enforcement and judiciary	182.8
Local government	96.4
Debt service	53.3
Other expenses	41.2
TOTAL	$4,533.5

In 1976/77, the city of Cleveland collected general revenues totaling $340 million, of which the state and local governments provided 9% and the federal government 27%. Tax revenues totaled $96.2 million, of which property taxes supplied 41%. In the same year, Cleveland's expenditures totaled $374 million. Columbus had revenues of $187 million and expenditures of $204 million, while Cincinnati tallied $515 million in revenues and $483 million in expenditures.

The total debt owed by state and local governments in Ohio increased from $5.9 billion in 1970 to $8.9 billion in 1977. In the latter year, the per capita debt of Ohioans amounted to $833.

[36] TAXATION

Ohio ranked 6th among the 50 states in total tax revenues during the 1977/78 fiscal year, but was 36th in per capita state and local taxation, with an average tax burden of $700.52; the tax burden was the lowest of any northern industrial state, and was more than 20% below the national average.

In 1979, the state personal income tax ranged from 0.5% on the first $5,000 of taxable income to 3.5% on amounts over $40,000. The state sales and use tax was 4% on retail sales and rental of personal property, excepting groceries and prescription drugs. The corporate franchise tax rate was either 4% on the first

$25,000 of net income plus 8% on amounts above that figure, or $5 per each $1,000 of net worth, whichever is greater. The estate tax ranged from 2% on property valued up to $40,000 (excluding $5,000 for each estate and $30,000 for a surviving spouse) to 7% on estates valued over $500,000. Other taxes include charges on cigarettes, alcoholic beverages, gasoline, and motor vehicles. The state also imposes taxes on banks and insurance companies, public utilities, dealers in intangibles (stockbrokers), coal and other minerals, and pari-mutuels. In the fiscal year 1978/79, Ohio's tax receipts totaled nearly $3.8 billion.

Most local tax revenues come from property taxes, which exceeded $2.6 billion in 1977. In 1979, 424 cities levied personal income taxes ranging from 0.25% to 2%. Some counties levy sales taxes of 0.5%. Cleveland imposes a special sales tax, which in 1978/79 raised $50.7 million for the Greater Cleveland Regional Transit Authority. In 1977, 20 cents of a typical Ohioan's tax dollar went to the federal government, 39 cents to the state, and 41 cents to local governments.

Ohio residents filed 4,306,081 federal income tax returns in 1977 and paid more than $8.4 billion in tax.

³⁷ECONOMIC POLICY
Although Ohio seeks to attract new industries, about four-fifths of the state's annual economic growth stems from the expanding of existing businesses.

Ohio offers numerous business incentives to spur industrial development. The state's impacted-cities program encourages capital investment by offering private developers property tax abatements for commercial redevelopment. A 1976 state law permits municipal corporations to exempt certain property improvements from real property taxes for periods of up to 30 years. The state's guaranteed-loan program for industrial developers provides repayment guarantees on 90% of loans up to $1 million. The state also offers revenue bonds to finance a developer's land, buildings, and equipment at interest rates from 0.75% to 3% below the going mortgage interest rates.

The Ohio Department of Economic and Community Growth develops plans for economic growth in cooperation with city and county governments. It informs companies about opportunities and advantages in the state and promotes the sale of Ohio's exports abroad through offices in Tokyo and Brussels. By the late 1970s, the department had granted development funds totaling $10 million to communities in the economically depressed Allegheny region of the state.

³⁸HEALTH
Ohio ranked 25th in life expectancy among the states during 1969–71, with an average life expectancy of 70.82 years. The average life expectancy for women was 74.55 years; for men, 67.25 years.

The state's birthrate fell from 23.8 live births per 1,000 population in 1960 to 15.1 in 1977. In the latter year there were about 161,000 live births (139,000 for whites and 22,000 for other races). The decrease in the birthrate is due in large part to the increasing availability of legal abortions in Ohio. Between 1974/75 and 1977/78, the ratio of abortions to births more than doubled, from 188 to 384 legal abortions for every 1,000 live births; about 60,300 legal abortions were performed during the latter year. The infant death rate has decreased significantly since 1960, when there were 22.2 infant deaths per 1,000 live births among whites, 39.4 among nonwhites; by 1977, the rates had fallen to 12.7 for whites and 21 for other races.

Ohio ranks above the national average in deaths due to heart disease, cancer, stroke, and diabetes, but below the US average for deaths caused by accidents, pneumonia, cirrhosis of the liver, and suicide. The leading causes of death in 1977 (with rates per 100,000 population) included heart disease, 359; malignant neoplasms, 184; cerebrovascular diseases, 88; accidents, 40; pneumonia and influenza, 22; and diabetes, 18.

In 1977, Ohio had 241 hospitals, with 64,158 beds; they admitted 1,846,100 patients, for a daily average of 50,674 and a bed occupancy rate of about 79%. Hospital personnel included 30,216 registered nurses and 14,322 licensed practical nurses. General hospitals with psychiatric wards admitted 30,680 patients in 1975, and an additional 84,598 patients got help from outpatient psychiatric services. At the end of 1976 there were 8,125 resident patients in community mental health facilities; private facilities had 427 residents in 1975. Public institutions for the mentally retarded enrolled 6,577 persons in mid-1978.

In 1977, Ohio had 16,633 licensed physicians, of whom more than 25% practiced in Cuyahoga County. There were 5,064 professionally active dentists in 1979, of whom 24% were in the Cleveland area. Health insurance benefits paid to hospitals in 1977 exceeded $2.3 billion. The average cost per day to hospital patients was $187, and the average cost per hospital stay was $1,494; both figures were below the national average.

³⁹SOCIAL WELFARE
In 1976, Ohio ranked 7th among the states in expenditures for the five largest social welfare programs, which totaled $1.4 billion; the federal government provided about two-thirds of that amount.

The growth of welfare programs in the state was remarkably rapid during the 1970s. From 1970 to 1978, for example, aid to families with dependent children (AFDC) nearly tripled to $446,000,000. During 1977/78 there were 526,434 monthly AFDC recipients; the average monthly payment per family was $209.89.

In 1978, Supplemental Security Income payments were made to 123,900 needy persons and totaled about $170,700,000, of which 74% went to the disabled, 23% to the aged, and 3% to the blind. In December 1978, the average monthly payment amounted to $137 for disabled persons and $82 for aged recipients.

In 1979, federal expenditures for the food stamp program in Ohio totaled $303,579,770; food stamps were purchased by an average of 746,027 persons each month. In 1978, the school lunch program benefited 1,190,000 schoolchildren, at an estimated cost to the federal government of about $66,700,000.

Social Security old age, survivors, and disability insurance benefits were paid to 1,579,700 Ohioans in 1977; these payments totaled $4.1 billion, for an average monthly payment to retired workers of $251.60. Of the total benefits paid, 60% went to 970,800 retired workers and their dependents, 26% to 380,300 survivors of deceased workers, and 14% to 228,700 disabled workers. In 1979, the Medicaid program benefited an average of 308,408 persons per month at a cost for the year of $691,821,311.

Ohio spent about $45,600,000 on vocational rehabilitation in 1978 and $440,300,000 on workers' compensation in 1977. Some 266,000 persons claimed unemployment insurance benefits in 1978; total benefits amounted to $336,000,000, and the average weekly payment of $100.32 ranked 2d behind Iowa among the 50 states.

In 1978, payments totaling $58,000,000 under the Black Lung Benefit Program were paid to about 8,000 disabled miners, 9,000 miners' windows, and 8,000 dependents.

⁴⁰HOUSING
In 1978, Ohio had 3,634,500 occupied housing units; 69% were occupied by their owners and 31% were rented. An average of 2.8 persons lived in each house or apartment. Nearly 94% of the owner-occupied housing units belonged to whites, only 6% to blacks; about 82% of rented housing units were occupied by whites, and nearly 17% by blacks. The proportion of apartments rented to blacks was particularly high in the old, deteriorating centers of Cleveland and other large cities.

In 1978, the state authorized construction of 59,900 new housing units, of which 61% were single-unit structures. The total value of housing construction was estimated at more than $2.1 billion.

[41]EDUCATION

Ohio claims a number of "firsts" in US education: the first kindergarten, established by German settlers in Columbus in 1838; the first junior high school, also at Columbus, in 1909; the first municipal university, the University of Cincinnati, founded in 1870; and the first college to grant degrees to women, Oberlin, in 1837. The state's earliest school system was organized in Akron in 1847.

Only 0.8% of all Ohioans aged 14 years and over were found to be illiterate at the 1970 census. In 1976, state residents had completed a median of 12.4 years of school; of the total adult population, nearly 68% were high school graduates, and 11% had completed at least four years of postsecondary study. Analysis of aptitude and achievement test results for 1978 showed that Ohio's college-bound students had scored above the national average for the 10th successive year.

In fall 1978, the state's public schools enrolled an estimated 1,424,000 elementary pupils and 717,000 secondary pupils. In that year there were 104,355 full-time public school teachers, and 157,585 seniors graduated from public high schools. Catholic parochial schools had 166,254 elementary school pupils and 43,386 high school pupils in 1979.

In 1976, public schools enrolled 307,300 blacks and members of other minority groups, comprising about 14% of all public school pupils. De facto school segregation in Cleveland and other cities has been reduced in recent years, largely under court order. In March 1980, Cleveland began to desegregate its junior high schools by busing about 16,000 of 90,000 junior high school pupils, two-thirds of whom were blacks.

Vocational education has become increasingly important in Ohio. From 1963 to 1978, the number of public school students enrolled in job-training and career education programs increased nearly sevenfold to about 320,000. More than half of all high school juniors and seniors were enrolled in some vocational courses. Of the 1977 graduates of job-training programs, more· than 92% obtained employment.

In 1977, the state had 105 institutions of higher education, which enrolled 452,754 students. There are 12 state universities, including Ohio State University (Columbus), Ohio University (Athens), Miami University (Oxford), and other state universities at Akron, Bowling Green, Cincinnati, Cleveland, Dayton, Kent, Toledo, Wilberforce, and Youngstown. The largest, Ohio State, was chartered in 1870 and also has campuses at Dayton, Lima, Mansfield, Marion, Newark, and Wooster; the Columbus campus alone had 44,767 full-time undergraduates in 1977/78 (1st in the US) and a total enrollment of 51,084 (2d only to the University of Minnesota at Minneapolis–St. Paul). Ohio also has 5 two-year community colleges and 20 technical colleges. Well-known private colleges and universities include Antioch (Yellow Springs), Case Western Reserve (Cleveland), Kenyon (Gambier), Muskingum (New Concord), Oberlin, and Wooster. Twelve Roman Catholic colleges enrolled 26,680 students in 1979.

Ohio residents enrolled as full-time students at an eligible institution within the state may apply for instructional grants of $150–1,500 per year from the Student Assistance Office of the Ohio Board of Regents. Guaranteed loans are provided through the Ohio Student Loan Commission.

[42]ARTS

The earliest center of artistic activities in Ohio was Cincinnati, where a group of young painters did landscapes and portraits as early as 1840. The state's first art gallery was established there in 1854; the Cincinnati Art Academy was founded in 1869, and the Art Museum in 1886. Famous American artists who worked in Cincinnati during part of their careers include Thomas Cole, a founder of the Hudson River school of landscape painting, who was raised in Steubenville; Frank Duveneck, dean of the Cincinnati Academy; and Columbus-born George Bellows, whose real-istic "Stag at Sharkey's" is displayed at the Cleveland Museum of Art (founded in 1913). Other notable centers for the visual arts include the Akron Art Institute, Columbus Museum of Art, Dayton Art Institute, Toledo Museum of Art, and museums or galleries in Marion, Oberlin, Springfield, Youngstown, and Zanesville.

Cincinnati also was an early center for the theater; the Eagle Theater opened there in 1839, and shortly afterward the first showboat on the Ohio River began making regular stops at the city. The first US minstrel show appeared in Ohio in 1842; Al Field's famous minstrels, formed in Columbus in 1886, successfully toured the US for 41 years. As of 1980, Ohio had three professional theatrical companies: the Cincinnati Playhouse, the Cleveland Playhouse, and the Great Lakes Shakespeare Festival. The Ohio Community Theater Association had 99 members, including groups in Akron, Canton, Columbus, Mansfield, Toledo, and Youngstown. There were also 63 college theatrical groups and 674 high school drama programs.

Musical activities revolve around the Cincinnati Symphony, which was founded in 1895 and reorganized in 1909 with Leopold Stokowski as conductor, and the Cleveland Symphony, founded in 1918; especially since 1946, when George Szell began his 24-year tenure as conductor and music director, the Cleveland Orchestra has been considered one of the finest in the world. The nation's first college music department was organized at Oberlin College in 1865; the Cincinnati Conservatory of Music was established in 1867, and the Cleveland Institute of Music in 1920. There are civic symphony orchestras in Columbus, Dayton, Toledo, and Youngstown. Operas are performed regularly by resident companies in the three largest cities, Cleveland, Columbus, and Cincinnati.

[43]LIBRARIES AND MUSEUMS

Ever since early settlers traded coonskins for books and established, in 1804, the Coonskin Library (now on display at the Ohio Historical Center in Columbus), Ohioans have stressed the importance of the public library system. As of 1979, Ohio had 159 school district public libraries, 45 county district libraries, 21 municipal libraries, 18 association libraries, and 4 township libraries. Overall, the state public library system in 1978 had 29,035,335 volumes, a circulation of 62,066,322, and a total income of $102,804,190.

Major public library systems include those of Cincinnati, with 3,240,266 volumes in 1978; Cleveland, 2,713,079; Dayton, 1,338,985; Columbus, 1,186,077; and Toledo, 1,105,998. Columbus also has the library of the Ohio Historical Society, with 126,141 volumes. Leading academic libraries include those of Ohio State University, 3,126,131; Case Western Reserve University, 1,591,921; and the University of Cincinnati, 1,025,114.

Among the state's more than 200 museums are the Museum of Art, Natural History Museum, and Western Reserve Historical Society Museum in Cleveland; the Museum of Natural History, Art Museum, and Taft Museum in Cincinnati; and the Center of Science and Industry and Ohio Historical Center in Columbus. The Zanesville Art Center has collections of ceramics and glass made in the Zanesville area. Also noteworthy are the US Air Force Museum near Dayton, the Neil Armstrong Air and Space Museum at Wapakoneta, and the Ohio River Museum in Marietta. Cincinnati has a zoo and a conservatory of rare plants; Cleveland has botanical gardens.

Historic sites in Ohio include the Schoenbrunn Village State Memorial, a reconstruction of the state's first settlement by Moravian missionaries, near New Philadelphia; the early 19th-century Piqua Historical Area, with exhibits of Indian culture; and the Fort Meigs reconstruction at Perrysburg. Archaeological sites include the "great circle" mounds built by the Hopewell Indians at Newark; and Inscription Rock, marked by prehistoric Indians, on Kelleys Island.

⁴⁴COMMUNICATIONS

In 1978, about 96% of Ohio residences had telephones. In that year there were 7,784,619 telephones, of which 5,904,732 were residential and 1,879,887 business. Two Bell System affiliates owned and operated about three-fourths of these phones; 49 other companies serviced the remainder.

Many of the state's radio stations were established in the early 1920s, when the growth of radio broadcasting was fostered by the availability of low-priced sets manufactured by the Crosley Radio Corp. of Cincinnati. In 1978 there were 122 AM stations, 130 FM stations, and 24 television stations in commercial operation. The number of noncommercial television broadcasters increased from 8 in 1968 to 12 in 1978, when Akron, Columbus, Dayton, Cincinnati, Cleveland, Toledo, and several other cities all had educational stations. At the end of 1979 there were 180 cable television systems serving 692,155 Ohio subscribers in 526 communities.

⁴⁵PRESS

The first newspaper published in the region north and west of the Ohio River was the *Centinel of the North-Western Territory*, which was written, typeset, and printed in Cincinnati by William Maxwell in 1793. The oldest newspaper in the state still published under its original name is the *Scioto Gazette*, which appeared in 1800. The oldest extant weekly, the *Lebanon Western Star*, began publication in 1807, and the first daily, the *Cincinnati Commercial Register*, appeared in 1826. By 1840 there were 145 newspapers in Ohio.

Two of the state's most influential newspapers, the *Cleveland Plain Dealer* and the *Cincinnati Enquirer*, were founded in 1841. In 1878, Edward W. Scripps established the *Cleveland Penny Press* (now the *Press*), the first newspaper in what would become the extensive Scripps-Howard chain; he later added to his newspaper empire the *Cincinnati Post* (1881) and *Columbus Citizen* (1899; now the *Citizen-Journal*), as well as papers in Akron, Toledo, and Youngstown.

In 1978 there were 9 morning daily newspapers with net paid circulation of 862,997 copies; 87 daily evening papers with total circulation of 2,482,570; and 27 Sunday papers with 2,494,746 circulation. The following table lists leading Ohio newspapers with their daily circulation in 1979:

AREA	NAME	DAILY	SUNDAY
Akron	Beacon Journal (e, S)	165,532	215,662
Cincinnati	Enquirer (m, S)	184,138	287,113
	Post (e)	184,474	
Cleveland	Plain Dealer (m, S)	381,543	453,223
	Press (e)	308,543	
Columbus	Citizen-Journal (m)	111,777	
	Dispatch (e, S)	200,990	337,600
Dayton	Daily News (e, S)	144,687	219,217
	Journal-Herald (m)	100,018	
Toledo	Blade (e, S)	170,349	210,607
Youngstown	Vindicator (e, S)	101,614	149,696

⁴⁶ORGANIZATIONS

Service organizations with headquarters in Ohio include the Army and Navy Union, USA, at Lakemore, and the National Exchange Club, in Toledo. Among the state's cultural associations are the American Classical League, at Oxford; and the Guild of Carilloneurs in North America, American Music Scholarship Association, and the Music Teachers National Association, all in Cincinnati.

Commercial and professional organizations include the American Cemetery Association, American Ceramic Society, Order of United Commercial Travelers of America, and National Conference on Social Welfare, all in Columbus; American Society for Metals, in Metals Park; American Society for Personnel Administration, in Berea; Association for Systems Management, in Cleveland; and the Iron Castings Society, in Rocky River.

Sports associations operating out of Ohio are the American Amateur Baseball Congress and the Lighter-Than-Air Society, Akron; American Motorcyclist Association, Westerville; Amateur Trapshooting Association, Vandalia; and Indoor Sports Club, Napoleon. The International Brotherhood of Magicians has its headquarters in Kenton.

⁴⁷TOURISM, TRAVEL, AND RECREATION

Receipts of Ohio's tourist industry were estimated at $2.8 billion in 1975. In 1977, 18.3 million travelers spent 54.9 million nights in the state. About 43% of the visits were to relatives or friends, 22% for sightseeing, entertainment, and outdoor recreation, 13% for business purposes, and 22% for other reasons.

Leading tourist attractions include Ohio's presidential memorials and homes: the William Henry Harrison Memorial at North Bend, Ulysses S. Grant's birthplace at Point Pleasant, the James A. Garfield home at Mentor, the Rutherford B. Hayes home at Fremont, the William McKinley Memorial at Canton, the Taft National Historic Site in Cincinnati, and the Warren G. Harding home in Marion. Also of interest are the Thomas A. Edison birthplace at Milan, and Malabar Farm, in Richland County, home of author-conservationist Louis Bromfield.

Beaches and parks in the Lake Erie region are especially popular with tourists during the summer. Among the many attractions in the northern region are the Crosby Gardens in Toledo, reconstructions of Auglaize Village near Defiance and of Harbour Town in Vermilion, the Marblehead Lighthouse, and the Lake Erie Nature and Science Center in Cleveland.

The eastern Allegheny region has several ski resorts for winter sports enthusiasts. Popular tourist attractions include the Amish settlement around Millersburg, the National Road–Zane Grey Museum near Zanesville, and the restored Roscoe Village on the Ohio-Erie Canal. The southern region offers scenic hill country, the Kings Island entertainment complex at Kings Mills, and the showboat *Majestic*, the last of the original floating theaters, in Cincinnati.

In the western region, tourist sites include the Wright brothers' early flying machines in Dayton's Carillon Park, the Ohio Caverns at West Liberty, and the Zane Caverns near Bellefontaine. The central region is "Johnny Appleseed" country; the folk hero (a frontiersman whose real name was John Chapman) is commemorated in Mansfield by the blockhouse to which he directed settlers in order to save them from an Indian raid. At Columbus are reconstructed Ohio and German villages, plus the Exposition Center, site of the annual Ohio State Fair, held for 13 days in mid-August.

Ohio has 47 state parks, all of which offer camping facilities, and 77 other recreational areas; together these comprise about 204,000 acres (83,000 hectares). Among the most visited state parks are Alum Creek, East Harbor and Kelleys Island (both on Lake Erie), Grand Lake St. Marys, Hocking Hills, Hueston Woods, Mohican, Pymatuning (on the Pennsylvania border), Rocky Fork, Salt Fork, Scioto Trail, and West Branch.

The most popular sport fish are bass, catfish, bullhead, carp, perch, and rainbow trout. The deer shooting season is held in late November; hunters are limited to one deer per season. Professional trappers gathered 954,651 fur pelts in the state in the 1977/78 harvesting year, valued at $9,272,133. The most hunted species were muskrat, raccoon, and fox. Licenses were sold to 558,579 hunters and 870,688 fishermen in 1977/78.

⁴⁸SPORTS

Ohio is well represented in professional sports, with two major league teams in baseball and football, one in basketball, and major golf and bowling tournaments.

In baseball, as of 1980, the Cincinnati Reds had played 105 consecutive years in the National League, and the Cleveland Indians had competed for 80 years in the American League. During the 1970s, Cincinnati's Big Red Machine won four league titles and two World Series (1975–76). Cleveland last won a pennant in 1954 and a World Series in 1948. The Columbus Clippers and Toledo Mudhens are the state's minor-league entries.

The Cleveland Browns and Cincinnati Bengals belong to the National Football League (NFL). The Browns share Cleveland's Municipal Stadium with the baseball Indians; the Bengals and baseball Reds play in Cincinnati's Riverfront Stadium. The Browns—who entered the NFL in 1950 after winning four consecutive championships in the All-America Conference—have won three NFL titles, the last in 1964. The Bengals, who joined the NFL when the American Football League merged with it in 1970, have yet to win a championship. Paul Brown was the founder and original coach of both the Browns and the Bengals. The Pro Football Hall of Fame is located in Canton, where the pro sport originated in 1920.

The Cleveland Cavaliers have represented the state in the National Basketball Association since 1970; the Cincinnati Royals formerly played in the league from 1945 to 1972, when the club moved to Kansas City. Pro soccer made its debut in Ohio in 1979 with the Columbus Magic of the American Soccer League.

Akron has been headquarters for the Professional Bowlers Association (PBA) since its founding in 1958. The PBA's richest tournament is played there each year, and the PBA Hall of Fame is also located in Akron. The World Series of Golf is played annually in Akron, and the Memorial Golf Tournament in Columbus.

Major horse-racing tracks include Cleveland's Thistledown, Cincinnati's River Downs, Columbus's Scioto Downs, and other tracks at Toledo, Lebanon, Grove City, and Northfield. The Cleveland Gold Cup race is held annually at Thistledown, as is the Ohio Derby. The Little Brown Jug classic for three-year-old pacers takes place every year at the Delaware Fairgrounds, and the Ohio State race for two-year-old trotters is held during the state fair at Columbus.

In collegiate sports, Ohio State University has long been a football power, winning 22 Big Ten titles (through 1979). Under coach Woody Hayes from 1951 to 1978, the Buckeyes won 205 games (including 4 Rose Bowls), lost 61, and tied 10. Ohio State also has won NCAA championships in baseball, basketball, fencing, golf, swimming, track and field, and wrestling, while Cincinnati and Dayton universities have had highly successful basketball teams. Ohio's College Football Hall of Fame is located at King's Island Amusement Park, near Cincinnati.

The Amateur Trapshooting Association usually holds its grand tournament in August at Vandalia; the 1979 event drew an estimated 50,000 contestants. The All-American Soap Box Derby, attracting participants between the ages of 11 and 15 and crowds of about 75,000, was held at Dayton annually from 1934–72; since then, it has been held in Akron.

⁴⁹ FAMOUS OHIOANS

Ohio has been the native state of seven US presidents and the residence of another. Inventions by Ohioans include the incandescent light, the arc light, and the flying machine.

William Henry Harrison (b. Virginia, 1773–1841), the 9th US president, came to Ohio as an Army ensign in territorial times. After serving in the Indian wars under General Anthony Wayne, he became secretary of the Northwest Territory. As the territorial delegate to Congress, he fostered the Harrison Land Act, which stimulated settlement of the public domain. Named territorial governor in 1800, Harrison conducted both warfare and peace negotiations with the Indians. After the defeat of British and Indian forces in 1813, he became known as the "Washington of the West." After settling at North Bend on the Ohio River, he began a political career that carried him to the White House in 1841. Harrison caught a chill from a raw March wind and died of pneumonia, exactly one month after his inauguration.

From 1869 to 1881 the White House was occupied by three Ohio men. All were Republicans who had served with distinction as Union Army generals. The first, Ulysses Simpson Grant (1822–85), the 18th US president, was an Ohio farm boy educated at West Point. After service in the Mexican War, he left the Army, having been charged with intemperance. He emerged from obscurity in 1861 when he was assigned to an Illinois regiment. Grant rose quickly in command; after victories at Shiloh and Vicksburg, he was commissioned major general. In 1864, he directed the Virginia campaign that ended with Confederate surrender, and this rumpled, slouching, laconic man became the nation's hero. In 1868, he was elected president, and he was reelected in 1872. His second term was rocked with financial scandals, though none were directly connected to Grant. After leaving the presidency in 1877, he went bankrupt, and to discharge his debts he wrote his memoirs. That extraordinary book was completed four days before his death from throat cancer in 1885. Grant is buried in a monumental tomb in New York City.

Rutherford B. Hayes (1822–93), the 19th US president, was born in Delaware, Ohio, and educated at Kenyon College and Harvard Law School. Following Army service, he was elected to Congress, and in 1876 became the Republican presidential nominee. In a close and disputed election, he defeated New York's Governor Samuel J. Tilden. Hayes chose not to run for reelection, returning instead to Ohio to work on behalf of humanitarian causes. In 1893, Hayes died in Fremont, where the Hayes Memorial was created—the first presidential museum and library in the nation.

James A. Garfield (1831–81), 20th US president, was born in a log cabin in northern Ohio. Between school terms he worked as a farmhand and a mule driver on the Ohio Canal. After holding several Civil War commands, he served in Congress for 18 years. Elected president in 1880, he held office but a few months; he was shot by a disappointed office seeker in the Washington, D.C., railroad station on 2 July and died 11 weeks later.

Benjamin Harrison (1833–1901) 23d US president and grandson of William Henry Harrison, was born at North Bend. After graduation from Miami University, he studied law and began to practice in Indianapolis. Military command in the Civil War was followed by service in the US Senate and the Republic presidential nomination in 1888. As president, Harrison gave impetus to westward expansion, moved toward annexation of Hawaii, and enlarged the civil-service system.

US presidents in the 20th century include three more native Ohioans. William McKinley (1843–1901), was born in Niles. Elected in 1896 as the 25th president, he established the gold standard and maintained tariff protection for US manufactures. Early in his second term, while greeting a throng of people, he was shot to death by a young anarchist. William Howard Taft (1857–1930), of Cincinnati, was the 27th US president. He gained a national reputation in 1904 as President Theodore Roosevelt's secretary of war; five years later, he succeeded Roosevelt in the White House. Defeated in 1912, Taft then left Washington for a law professorship at Yale. In 1921, under President Warren G. Harding (1865–1923), he became US chief justice, serving in that office until a month before his death. Harding, the last Ohioan to win the White House, was born in Blooming Grove. He went into politics from journalism, after serving as editor of the *Marion Star*. After eight years in the US Senate, he was a dark-horse candidate for the Republican presidential nomination in 1920. He won the election from James M. Cox (1870–1957), another Ohio journalist-politician, and became the 29th US president. Harding, who died in office, was surrounded by graft and corruption in his own cabinet.

Three US vice presidents were natives of Ohio. Thomas A. Hendricks (1819–85) was elected on the Democratic ticket with Grover Cleveland in 1884. Charles W. Fairbanks (1852–1918) served from 1905 to 1909 under Theodore Roosevelt. Charles Gates Dawes (1865–1951) became vice president under Calvin Coolidge in 1925, the same year the Dawes Plan for reorganizing German finances brought him the Nobel Peace Prize; from 1929 to 1932, he served as US ambassador to Great Britain.

Of 11 Ohioans who had served on the Supreme Court by 1980, 3 were chief justices: Salmon P. Chase (b.New Hampshire, 1808–73), Morrison R. Waite (b.Connecticut, 1816–88), and Taft. Most notable among nearly 40 cabinet officers from Ohio were Secretary of State Lewis Cass (b.New Hampshire, 1782–1866), Treasury Secretaries Chase and John Sherman (1823–1900), and Secretary of War Edwin M. Stanton (1814–69). William Tecumseh Sherman (1820–91) was a Union general in the Civil War whose Georgia campaign in 1864 helped effect the surrender of the Confederacy. Although disappointed in his quest for the presidency, US Senator Robert A. Taft (1889–1953) was an enduring figure, best remembered for his authorship of the Taft-Hartley Labor Management Relations Act of 1947.

Nobel Prize winners from Ohio include Dawes and physicist Arthur Compton (1892–1962). Notable Pulitzer Prize winners include novelist Louis Bromfield (1896–1956), dramatist Russell Crouse (1893–1966), historian Paul Herman Buck (b.1899), and historian and biographer Arthur Schlesinger, Jr. (b.1917). Ohio writers of enduring fame are novelists William Dean Howells (1837–1920), Zane Grey (1875–1939), and Sherwood Anderson (1876–1941), poets Paul Laurence Dunbar (1872–1906) and Hart Crane (1899–1932), and humorist James Thurber (1894–1961). Among Ohio's eminent journalists are Whitelaw Reid (1837–1912), satirists David R. Locke (1833–88) and Ambrose Bierce (1842–1914), columnist O. O. McIntyre (1884–1938), newsletter publisher W. M. Kiplinger (1891–1967), and James Reston (b.Scotland, 1909), an editor and columnist for the *New York Times*, along with author-commentator Lowell Thomas (b.1892). Important in the art world were painters Thomas Cole (b.England, 1801–48), Frank Duveneck (b.Kentucky, 1848–1919), and George Bellows (1882–1925), as well as architects Cass Gilbert (1859–1934) and Philip Johnson (b.1906). Defense lawyer Clarence Darrow (1857–1938) was also an Ohioan.

Ohio educators whose books taught reading, writing, and arithmetic to the nation's schoolchildren were William Holmes McGuffey (b.Pennsylvania, 1800–73), Platt R. Spencer (1800–64), and Joseph Ray (1807–65). In higher education, Horace Mann (b.Massachusetts, 1796–1859) was the first president of innovative Antioch College, and William Rainey Harper (1856–1906) founded the University of Chicago.

Allied with industry are Ohio-born inventor-scientists. Thomas A. Edison (1847–1931) produced the incandescent lamp, the phonograph, and the movie camera. Charles Brush (1849–1929) invented the arc light. John H. Patterson (1844–1922) helped develop the cash register. The Wright brothers, Orville (1871–1948) and Wilbur (b.Indiana, 1867–1912), made the first flight in a powered aircraft. Charles F. Kettering (1876–1958) invented the automobile self-starter. Ohio's leading industrialist was John D. Rockefeller (b.New York, 1839–1937), founder of Standard Oil of Ohio. Harvey S. Firestone (1868–1938) started the tire company that bears his name. Edward "Eddie" Rickenbacker (1890–1973), an ace pilot in World War I, was president of Eastern Airlines.

The most notable Ohioans in the entertainment field are markswoman Annie Oakley (Phoebe Anne Oakley Mozee, 1860–1926); movie actors Clark Gable (1901–60) and Roy Rogers (Leonard Slye, b.1912); comedian Bob Hope (Leslie Townes Hope, b.England, 1903); actors Paul Newman (b.1925), Hal Holbrook (b.1925), and Joel Grey (b.1932); and jazz pianist Art Tatum (1910–56).

Leading sports figures from Ohio are boxing champion Jim Jeffries (1875–1953), racing driver Barney Oldfield (1878–1946), baseball pitcher Cy Young (1867–1955), baseball executive Branch

Rickey (1881–1965), track star Jesse Owens (b.Alabama, 1912–80), and golfer Jack Nicklaus (b.1940).

Astronauts from Ohio include John Glenn (b.1921), the first American to orbit the earth, who was elected US senator from Ohio in 1974; and Neil Armstrong (b.1930), the first man to walk on the moon.

[50] BIBLIOGRAPHY

Banta, R. E. *The Ohio*. New York: Rinehart, 1949.

Bromfield, Louis. *The Farm*. New York: Harper, 1933.

Clark, Edna. *Ohio Art and Artists*. Richmond, Va.: Garrett and Massie, 1932.

Condon, George E. *Cleveland: The Best Kept Secret*. Garden City, N.Y.: Doubleday, 1967.

Downes, Randolph C. *Frontier Ohio: 1788–1803*. Columbus: Ohio State Archaeological and Historical Society, 1935.

Ellis, William D. *The Cuyahoga*. New York: Holt, 1966.

Federal Writers' Project. *The Ohio Guide*. New York: Scholarly Press, 1979 (orig. 1940).

Galbreath, Charles B. *History of Ohio*. 5 vols. Chicago and New York: American Historical Society, 1925.

Hatcher, Harlan. *The Buckeye Country*. New York: Kinsey, 1940.

Havighurst, Walter. *Ohio: A Bicentennial History*. New York: Norton, 1976.

Hooper, Osman C. *History of Ohio Journalism*. Columbus: Spahr and Glenn, 1933.

Hopkins, Charles E. *Ohio the Beautiful and Historic*. Boston: Page, 1931.

Howe, Henry. *Historical Collections of Ohio*. 2 vols. Columbus: Henry Howe & Son, 1889.

Howells, William Dean. *A Boy's Town*. New York: Harper, 1890.

Hulbert, Archer B. *The Ohio River: A Course of Empire*. New York and London: Putnam, 1906.

Jordan, Philip D. *The National Road*. Indianapolis: Bobbs-Merrill, 1948.

Leech, Margaret. *In the Days of McKinley*. New York: Harper and Row, 1959.

Longworth de Chambrun, Clara. *Cincinnati: The Story of the Queen City*. New York: Scribner, 1939.

McCormick, Richard P. *The Second American Party System*. Chapel Hill: University of North Carolina Press, 1966.

Morgan, H. Wayne. *From Hayes to McKinley*. Syracuse, N.Y.: Syracuse University Press, 1969.

Notestein, Lucy. *Wooster of the Middle West*. New Haven, Conn.: Yale University Press, 1937.

Ohio Almanac 1980. 9th ed. Dayton: The Kids Come in Special Flavors, 1980.

Ohio State. Department of Budget and Management. *The State of Ohio Executive Budget for the Biennium July 1, 1979 to June 30, 1981*. Columbus, 1979.

Ohio State. Department of State. *Constitution of the State of Ohio*. Columbus: Anderson, 1979.

Ohio State. Department of State. *Official Roster, 1979–80*. Columbus, 1980.

Patterson, James T. *Mr. Republican: A Biography of Robert A. Taft*. Boston: Houghton Mifflin, 1972.

Reid, Whitelaw. *Ohio in the War*. 2 vols. Cincinnati: Moore, Wilstach and Baldwin, 1868.

Roseboom, Eugene Holloway, and Francis P. Weisenburger, *A History of Ohio*. New York: Prentice-Hall, 1934.

Thurber, James. *My Life and Hard Times*. New York: Harper, 1933.

Warner, Hoyt Landon. *Progressivism in Ohio*. Columbus: Ohio State University Press, 1964.

Wittke, Carl, ed. *History of the State of Ohio*. 6 vols. Columbus: Ohio State Archaeological and Historical Society, 1941–44.

OKLAHOMA

State of Oklahoma

ORIGIN OF STATE NAME: Derived from the Choctaw Indian words *okla humma*, meaning "land of the red people." **NICKNAME**: The Sooner State. **CAPITAL**: Oklahoma City. **ENTERED UNION**: 16 November 1907 (46th). **SONG**: "Oklahoma!" **POEM**: "Howdy Folks." **MOTTO**: *Labor omnia vincit* (Labor conquers all things). **FLAG**: On a blue field, a peace pipe and an olive branch cross an Osage warrior's shield, which is decorated with small crosses and from which seven eagle feathers descend; the word "Oklahoma" appears below. **OFFICIAL SEAL**: Each point of a five-pointed star incorporates the emblem of an Indian nation: (clockwise from top) Chickasaw, Choctaw, Seminole, Creek, and Cherokee. In the center, a frontiersman and Indian shake hands before the goddess of justice; behind them are symbols of progress, including a farm, train, and mill. Surrounding the large star are 45 small ones and the words "Great Seal of the State of Oklahoma 1907." **ANIMAL**: American buffalo (bison). **BIRD**: Scissor-tailed flycatcher. **FISH**: White bass (sand bass). **FLORAL EMBLEM**: Mistletoe. **TREE**: Redbud. **STONE**: Barite rose (rose rock). **REPTILE**: Collared lizard (mountain boomer). **GRASS**: Indian grass. **LEGAL HOLIDAYS**: New Year's Day, 1 January; Washington's Birthday, 3d Monday in February; Memorial Day, last Monday in May; Independence Day, 4 July; Labor Day, 1st Monday in September; Columbus Day, 2d Monday in October; Veterans Day, 11 November; Thanksgiving Day, 4th Thursday in November; Christmas Day, 25 December. **TIME**: 6 A.M. CST = noon GMT.

¹LOCATION, SIZE, AND EXTENT

Situated in the western south-central US, Oklahoma ranks 18th in size among the 50 states.

The total area of Oklahoma is 69,919 sq mi (181,090 sq km), of which land takes up 68,782 sq mi (178,145 sq km) and inland water 1,137 sq mi (2,945 sq km). Oklahoma extends 464 mi (747 km) E–W, including the panhandle in the NW, which is about 165 mi (266 km) long. The maximum N–S extension is 230 mi (370 km).

Oklahoma is bordered on the N by Colorado and Kansas; on the E by Missouri and Arkansas; on the S and SW by Texas (with part of the line formed by the Red River); and on the extreme W by New Mexico. The total estimated boundary length of Oklahoma is *1,581 mi (2,544 km)*. The state's geographic center is in Oklahoma County, 8 mi (13 km) N of Oklahoma City.

²TOPOGRAPHY

The land of Oklahoma rises gently to the west from an altitude of 287 feet (87 meters) at Little River in the southeastern corner to a height of 4,973 feet (1,516 meters) at Black Mesa, on the tip of the panhandle. Four mountain ranges cross this Great Plains state: the Boston Mountains (part of the Ozark Plateau) in the northeast, the Ouachitas in the southeast, the Arbuckles in the south-central region, and the Wichitas in the southwest. Much of the northwest belongs to the High Plains, while northeastern Oklahoma is mainly a region of buttes and valleys carved from shales and sandstones.

Not quite two-thirds of the state is drained by the Arkansas River, and the remainder by the Red River. Within Oklahoma, the Arkansas is joined by the Verdigris, Grand (Neosho), and Illinois rivers from the north and northeast, and by the Cimarron and Canadian rivers from the northwest and west. The Red River, which marks most of the state's southern boundary, is joined by the Washita, Salt Fork, Blue, Kiamichi, and many smaller rivers. There are few natural lakes but many artificial ones, of which the largest is Lake Eufaula, covering 102,500 acres (41,500 hectares).

³CLIMATE

Oklahoma has a continental climate with cold winters and hot summers. Normal daily mean temperatures in Oklahoma City range from 37°F (3°C) in January to 82°F (28°C) in July. The record low temperature of –27°F (–33°C) was set at Watts on 18 January 1930; the record high, 120°F (49°C), at Tishomingo on 26 July 1943.

Dry, sunny weather generally prevails throughout the state. Precipitation varies from an average of 15 in (38 cm) annually in the panhandle to 50 in (127 cm) in the southeast; the overall average is 31 in (79 cm). Snowfall averages 9 in (23 cm) a year in Oklahoma City, which is also one of the windiest cities in the US, with an average annual wind speed of 12.8 mph (20.6 km/hr).

Oklahoma is tornado prone. One of the most destructive windstorms was the tornado that tore through Ellis, Woods, and Woodward counties on 9 April 1947, killing 101 people and injuring 782 others.

⁴FLORA AND FAUNA

Grasses grow in abundance in Oklahoma. Bluestem, buffalo, sand lovegrass, and grama grasses are native, with the bluestem found mostly in the eastern and central regions, and buffalo grass most common in the western counties, known as the "short grass country." Deciduous hardwoods stand in eastern Oklahoma, and red and yellow cactus blossoms brighten the Black Mesa area in the northwest.

The white-tailed deer is found in all counties, and Rio Grande wild turkeys are hunted across much of the state. Pronghorn antelope inhabit the panhandle area, and elk survive in the Wichita Mountains Wildlife Refuge, where a few herds of American buffalo (bison) are also preserved. The bobwhite quail, ring-necked pheasant, and prairie chicken are common game birds. Native sport fish include largemouth, smallmouth, white, and spotted bass; channel, blue, and flathead catfish; crappie; and sunfish.

In 1980, the Department of Wildlife Conservation listed 11 species of wildlife as endangered: red wolf, black-footed ferret, Indiana bat, southern bald eagle, whooping crane, ivory-billed and red-cockaded woodpeckers, Bachman's warbler, American peregrine falcon, Eskimo curlew, and American alligator.

⁵ENVIRONMENTAL PROTECTION

Air quality control is a function of the Department of Health, which administers the Oklahoma Clean Air Act, with the assistance of the 59 local county health departments. The state agency also administers the federal Safe Drinking Water Act and Municipal Construction Grant Program. During the 1970s, approximately $245 million was distributed to cities and towns throughout the state for construction of water treatment facilities.

The Oklahoma Solid Waste Management Act of 1970 prohibits open burning and specifies sanitary landfills as a minimum requirement for solid waste treatment. Liquid waste disposal operates on a permit system; industries are required to stay within specified levels and must monitor themselves, reporting monthly to state authorities. Nuclear waste disposal is inspected and monitored from the Kerr-McGee radioactive materials processing facility at Gore. Allegations that Kerr-McGee's Cimarron plant was handling such materials in an unsafe manner sparked a prolonged controversy in the courts and in the press during the late 1970s.

Toxic industrial wastes remain an environmental concern, and old mines in the Tar Creek area of northeastern Oklahoma still exude groundwater contaminated by zinc, iron, and cadmium. Polychlorinated biphenyls (PCBs) produced by a World War I–era munitions factory near Ft. Gibson also present a long-term pollution problem. Measurements of PCBs in fish during 1979 exceeded federally mandated levels, and the State Board of Health has limited fishing in the region.

Lands devastated by erosion during the droughts of the 1930s were purchased by the federal government and turned over to the Soil Conservation Service for restoration. When grasses were firmly established in the mid-1950s, the land was turned over to the US Forest Service and is now leased for grazing.

⁶POPULATION

Oklahoma's estimated population reached 2,880,000 in July 1978, an increase of nearly 13% over the census total of 2,559,463 in 1970, when Oklahoma ranked 27th among the 50 states. The preliminary 1980 census population was 2,998,124, yielding an average density of 44 per sq mi (17 per sq km).

In 1977, nearly 56% of all Oklahomans lived in metropolitan areas, where the most rapid population increases have occurred. Metropolitan Oklahoma City experienced the largest numerical increase in population—more than 90,000—to a 1978 total of 789,400 residents, a 13% increase over 1970. Metropolitan Tulsa grew by more than 14% to 628,500, and Lawton by 11% to 119,900. According to preliminary census data, Oklahoma City proper had 401,002 residents in 1980; Tulsa, 355,500.

⁷ETHNIC GROUPS

Oklahoma has more Indians than any other state; the 1970 census counted 98,468, but the total number of Oklahomans of Indian descent may be as high as 600,000. Tulsa and Oklahoma City rank 2d and 3d behind Los Angeles among US cities in Indian population. On the whole, Indians have the lowest income level and highest unemployment rate of any ethnic group in the state.

Black slaves came with their Indian masters along the "Trail of Tears," experiencing the same hardships. There were about 7,000 free Negroes at the time of the Civil War. Langston University and the "all black town" of Langston were established in 1897. After the depression of the 1930s, blacks left the farms and small towns and concentrated in Oklahoma City and Tulsa. More than 50% of the state's black population, which totaled 179,000 in 1976, lives in Oklahoma City and Tulsa.

Mexicans came to Oklahoma during the 19th century as campesinos and were supplied to railroads, ranches, and coal mines. Later they worked in the cotton fields, until the depression of the 1930s and subsequent mechanization reduced the need for seasonal labor. Today, most 1st- and 2d-generation Mexicans live in Oklahoma City, Tulsa, and Lawton. Overall, there were about 38,000 residents of Hispanic origin in 1976.

Italians, Czechs, Germans, Poles, British, Irish, and others of European stock also came to Oklahoma during the 19th century. Foreign immigration has been small since that time, however, and in 1970, less than 4% of the population consisted of the foreign-born and their native-born children. Germany, the United Kingdom, and Canada were the leading countries of origin.

⁸LANGUAGES

Once the open hunting ground of the Osage, Comanche, and Apache Indians, what is now Oklahoma perforce welcomed the deported Cherokee and other transferred eastern tribes. The diversity of tribal and linguistic backgrounds is reflected in numerous place-names such as Oklahoma itself, Kiamichi, and Muskogee. Almost equally diverse is Oklahoma English, with its uneven blending of features of North Midland, South Midland, and Southern dialects.

English was the mother tongue in 1970 of 91% of both the native-born and the total population. Leading first languages were as follows:

	NATIVE-BORN	FOREIGN-BORN
English	2,317,389	3,911
German	32,361	5,067
Indian languages	29,329	28
Spanish	19,209	2,634

⁹RELIGIONS

Protestant groups predominate in Oklahoma, and Protestant fundamentalists constitute a third of the population. This group was influential in keeping the state "dry"—that is, banning the sale of alcoholic beverages—until 1959, and fundamentalists continue their successful opposition to the legalization of gambling and wagering.

According to 1980 state estimates, the leading Protestant groups include Southern Baptist, 632,462; United Methodist, 253,466; Church of Christ, 80,000; Assembly of God, 60,596; Christian Church (Disciples of Christ), 48,258; and Presbyterian groups, 41,677. In 1979, the state also had 113,847 Roman Catholics and an estimated 6,040 Jews.

Oral Roberts, a popular minister, has established a college and faith-healing hospital in Tulsa, and his "Tower of Faith" broadcasts by radio and television have made him a well-known preacher throughout the US.

¹⁰TRANSPORTATION

In 1930, the high point for railroad transportation in Oklahoma, there were 6,678 mi (10,747 km) of railroad track in the state. As of 1980 there were 5,005 mi (8,055 km) of track; the St. Louis-San Francisco Railway, running northeast–southwest, had the most track, followed by the Atchison, Topeka, and Santa Fe. In 1979, Amtrak terminated the state's last passenger train. Interurban transit needs, formerly served by streetcars (one of the most popular routes operated between Oklahoma City and Norman), are now supplied by buses.

The Department of Transportation is responsible for construction and maintenance of the state road system, which in 1978 included 12,990 mi (20,905 km) of state highways and 812 mi (1,307 km) of interstate highways. The main east–west highways are I-44, connecting Tulsa and Oklahoma City, and I-40; the major north–south route is I-35, which links Oklahoma City with Topeka, Kansas, and Ft. Worth, Texas. Overall, in 1978, Oklahoma had 109,723 mi (176,582 km) of roadway, 2,550,537 registered vehicles, and 1,874,344 licensed drivers.

The opening of the McClellan-Kerr Arkansas River Navigation System in 1971 linked Oklahoma with the Mississippi River and thus to Gulf coast ports. Tonnage carried on the system

LOCATION: 33°38′17″ to 37°N; 94°25′51″ to 103°W. **BOUNDARIES:** Colorado line, *58 mi (93 km);* Kansas line, *411 mi (661 km)*; Missouri line, *34 mi (55 km)*; Arkansas line, *198 mi (319 km)*; Texas line, *846 mi (1,361 km)*; New Mexico line, *34 mi (55 km).*

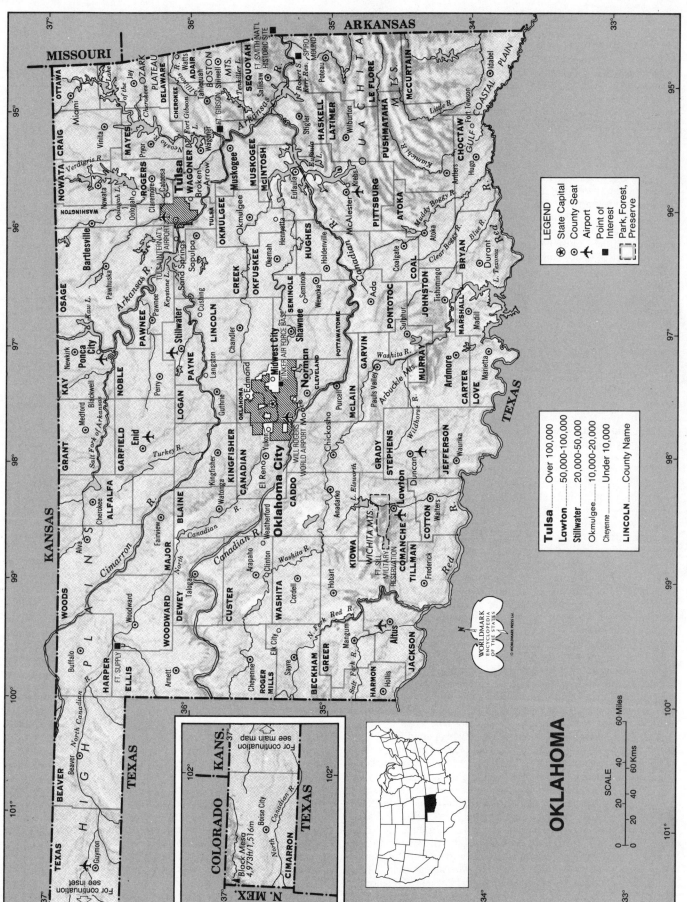

See US political: front cover G3; physical: back cover G3.

LEGEND

⊛ State Capital
⊙ County Seat
✈ Airport
■ Point of Interest
⬜ Park, Forest, Preserve

Tulsa Over 100,000
Lawton 50,000-100,000
Stillwater 20,000-50,000
Okmulgee 10,000-20,000
Cheyenne Under 10,000

LINCOLN County Name

OKLAHOMA

SCALE

0 20 40 60 Miles
0 20 40 60 Kms

WORLDMARK
ENCYCLOPEDIA
OF THE STATES
© WORLDMARK PRESS Ltd.

For continuation
see inset

For continuation
see main map

totaled 3.4 million tons in 1978, 23% more than in 1977. The leading public port in Oklahoma is Catoosa (Tulsa), which handled 1,113,804 tons of cargo in 1977.

Oklahoma had 129 public and 159 private airfields in 1978. Tulsa International Airport and Will Rogers World Airport in Oklahoma City are the largest airports in the state.

[11]HISTORY

There is evidence—chiefly from the Spiro Mound in eastern Oklahoma, excavated in 1930—that an advanced Indian civilization inhabited the region around AD 900–1100. By the time the Spanish conquistadores, led by Hernando de Soto and Francisco Vásquez de Coronado, arrived there in the 16th century, however, only a few scattered tribes remained. Two centuries later, French trappers moved up the rivers of Oklahoma and intermarried with the Indian population.

Except for the panhandle, which remained a no-man's-land until 1890, all of present-day Oklahoma became part of US territory with the Louisiana Purchase in 1803. Under the Indian Removal Act of 1830, Indian tribes from the southeastern US were resettled in what was then known as Indian Country. Although 4,000 Indians died along the "Trail of Tears" (from Georgia to Oklahoma) between the time of removal and the Civil War, the Five Civilized Tribes—Cherokee, Chickasaw, Choctaw, Creek, and Seminole—prospered in the new land. The eastern region they settled, comprising not quite half of modern Oklahoma and known as Indian Territory since the early 19th century though not formally organized under that name until 1890, offered rich soil and luxurious vegetation.

White settlers also came to farm the land, but their methods, learned in the northeast, depleted the soil, preparing the way for the dust bowl of the 1930s. Meanwhile, the increasing movement of people and goods between Santa Fe and New Orleans spurred further growth in the region. Military posts such as Ft. Gibson, Ft. Supply, and Ft. Towson were established between 1824 and the 1880s, with settlements growing up around them. A frontier spirit prevailed, and settlers ignored laws that interfered with their own personal interests.

During the early Civil War period, the Five Civilized Tribes—some of whose members were slaveholders—allied with the Confederacy. After Union troops captured Ft. Gibson in 1863, the Union Army controlled one-half of Indian Territory. From the end of the Civil War to the 1880s, the federal government removed the eastern tribes from certain lands that were especially attractive to the railroads and to interested white settlers. Skirmishes between the Indians and the federal troops occurred, culminating in a massacre of Cheyenne Indians on 27 November 1868 by then Colonel George Custer and his 7th Cavalry at the Battle of the Washita.

Amid a clamor for Indian lands, Congress opened western Oklahoma—formerly reserved for the Cherokee, Cheyenne, Fox, and other tribes—to homesteaders in 1889. Present-day Oklahoma City, Norman, Guthrie, Edmond, and Stillwater represent the eastern boundary for the 1889 "run" on Oklahoma lands; eight more runs were to follow. The greatest was in 1893, when about 100,000 people stormed onto the newly opened Cherokee outlet. The drive to get a land claim was fierce, and thousands of "Sooners" staked their claims before the land was officially opened. The western region became Oklahoma Territory, governed by a territorial legislature and a federally appointed governor in 1890; Guthrie was named the capital. Most of eastern Oklahoma continued to be governed by the Five Civilized Tribes.

Although an Oklahoma statehood bill was introduced in Congress as early as 1892, the Five Civilized Tribes resisted all efforts to unite Indian Territory with Oklahoma Territory until their attempt to form their own state was defeated in 1905. Congress passed an enabling act in June 1906, and Oklahoma became the 46th state on 16 November 1907 after a vote of the residents of both territories. Oklahoma City was named the state capital in 1910.

When President Theodore Roosevelt signed the statehood proclamation, Oklahoma's population was about 1,500,000—75% rural, 25% urban—most of them drawn by the state's agricultural and mineral resources. The McAlester coal mines had opened in 1871, and lead and zinc were being mined in Ottawa County. But it was oil that made the state prosperous. Prospecting began in 1882, and the first commercial well was drilled at Bartlesville in 1897. The famous Glenn Pool gusher, near Tulsa, was struck in 1905. Oil wells were producing more than 40 million barrels annually when Oklahoma entered the Union, and the state led all others in oil production until 1928.

Generally, the decade of the 1920s was a tumultuous period for Oklahoma. A race riot in Tulsa in 1921 was put down by the National Guard; the Ku Klux Klan claimed close to 100,000 Oklahomans that same year. The Klan was outlawed when Governor John C. Walton declared martial law in 1923, during a period of turmoil and violence that culminated in Walton's impeachment and conviction on charges of incompetence, corruption, and abuse of power. The 1930s brought a destructive drought, dust storms, and an exodus of "Okies," many of them to California. Colorful Governor William "Alfalfa Bill" Murray led the call for federal relief for the distressed dust bowl region—though he insisted on his right to administer the funds. When Oklahoma oil fields were glutting the market at 15 cents a barrel, Murray placed 3,106 producing wells under martial law from August 1931 to April 1933. Kansas, New Mexico, and Texas also agreed to control their oil production, and under the leadership of Governor E. W. Marland, the Interstate Oil Compact was created in 1936 to conserve petroleum and stabilize prices.

Oklahoma's first native-born governor, Robert Kerr, later to be senator for 14 years, held the statehouse during World War II and brought the state national recognition by promoting Oklahoma as a site for military, industrial, and conservation projects. Under postwar governors Roy Turner, Johnston Murray, and Raymond Gary, tax reductions attracted industry, major highways were built, a loyalty oath for state employees was declared unconstitutional, and Oklahoma's higher educational facilities were integrated. The term of Governor Howard Edmondson saw the repeal of prohibition in 1959, the establishment of merit and central purchasing systems, and the introduction of a state income tax withholding plan. Subsequent administrations have established free kindergartens for all children, encouraged the tourist industry, and developed new service industries, especially in the government sector.

[12]STATE GOVERNMENT

Oklahoma's first and only constitutional convention began its deliberations in Guthrie on 20 November 1906. The constitution was approved by the electorate on 11 September 1907.

The Oklahoma legislature consists of two chambers, a 48-member senate and a 101-member house of representatives. To serve in the legislature, senators must be 25 years of age, and representatives 21; senators hold office for four years, representatives for two. Elected executive officials include the governor, lieutenant governor, attorney general, state treasurer, superintendent of public instruction, and commissioner of insurance, all of whom serve four-year terms, and three corporation commissioners, who serve staggered six-year terms. The governor's appointment power extends to approximately 300 positions in 230 different agencies. The governor must be a US citizen, at least 31 years of age, and must have been a qualified voter in Oklahoma for at least 10 years preceding election.

Any member of either house may introduce legislation. A bill passed by the legislature becomes law if signed by the governor, if left unsigned by the governor for five days while the legislature is in session, or if passed over the governor's veto by two-thirds of the elected members of each house. Constitutional amendments may be placed on the ballot by majority vote in both houses, by initiative petition of 15% of the electorate, or by constitutional convention.

To vote in Oklahoma, one must be a US citizen, at least 18 years of age, and must have lived at least six months in the state, two months in the county, and 20 days in the election precinct.

13 POLITICAL PARTIES

The history of the two major political groups in Oklahoma, the Democratic and Republican parties, dates back to 1890, when Indian Territory and Oklahoma Territory were separately organized. Indian Territory was dominated by Democrats, reflecting the influence of southern immigrants, while Oklahoma Territory was primarily Republican because of immigration from the northern states. When the two territories joined for admission to the Union in 1907, Democrats outnumbered Republicans, as they have ever since. Democrats have continued to dominate the lesser state offices, but the Republicans won the governorship three times between 1962 and 1970, and the Republican presidential nominee outpolled his Democratic counterpart in seven of nine presidential elections between 1948 and 1980. The best showing by a minor party in a recent presidential race was the vote total of 191,731 garnered by American Independent Party candidate George Wallace in 1968.

As of 1979, the Democratic Party had 1,022,228 registered voters, while registered Republicans numbered 314,621; there were 24,345 registered independents.

Oklahomans gave the Republican Party a resounding victory in November 1980 by casting more than 60% of the popular vote for Ronald Reagan and by electing Don Nickles to the seat vacated by retiring Republican Senator Henry Bellmon. Democrats held the governorship and majorities in both legislative houses, however.

Oklahoma Presidential Vote by Major Political Parties, 1948–80

YEAR	ELECTORAL VOTE	OKLAHOMA WINNER	DEMOCRAT	REPUBLICAN
1948	10	*Truman (D)	452,782	268,817
1952	8	*Eisenhower (R)	430,939	518,045
1956	8	*Eisenhower (R)	385,581	473,769
1960	8	Nixon (R)	370,111	533,039
1964	8	*Johnson (D)	519,834	412,665
1968	8	*Nixon (R)	301,658	449,697
1972	8	*Nixon (R)	247,147	759,025
1976	8	Ford (R)	532,442	545,708
1980	8	*Reagan (R)	402,026	695,570

*Won US presidential election.

14 LOCAL GOVERNMENT

As of 1980, local governmental units in Oklahoma included 77 counties, 559 incorporated cities and towns, and several hundred unincorporated areas.

County government consists of three commissioners elected by districts, a county clerk, assessor, treasurer, sheriff, surveyor, and (in most counties) superintendent of schools. Towns of 1,000 population or more may incorporate as cities. Any city of 2,000 or more people may vote to become a home-rule city, determining its own form of government, by adopting a home-rule charter. As of 1979 there were 74 charter cities. Cities electing not to adopt a home-rule charter operate under aldermanic, mayor-council, or council-manager systems. A large majority of home-rule cities have council-manager forms.

15 STATE SERVICES

The Oklahoma Department of Education, functioning under a six-member appointed Board of Education and an elected superintendent of public instruction, has responsibility for all phases of education through the first 12 grades. Postsecondary study is under the general authority of the Oklahoma State Regents for Higher Education and 16 separate boards of regents associated with one or more institutions. Vocational and technical education, a federal-state cooperative program, is administered in Oklahoma under the Department of Vocational and Technical Education. The Department of Transportation has authority over the planning, construction, and maintenance of the state highway system. The Oklahoma Corporation Commission regulates transportation and transmission companies, public utilities, motor carriers, and the oil and gas industry, while the Oklahoma Aeronautics Commission participates in financing airports.

The Department of Health has as a major function the control and prevention of communicable diseases; it administers community health program funds and licenses most health-related facilities. The Department of Institutions, Social and Rehabilitative Services operates three homes for neglected children, three schools for delinquent youths, three schools for the mentally retarded, and various facilities and programs for the handicapped, the elderly, and the infirm.

Protective services are supplied through the Oklahoma Military Department, which administers the Army and Air National Guard; the Department of Corrections, overseeing nine adult prisons and nine community treatment centers; and the Department of Public Safety, with general safety and law enforcement responsibilities, among which are licensing drivers and patrolling the highways. Natural resource protection services are centered principally in the Oklahoma Conservation Commission; the Wildlife Commission administers the game and fish laws.

16 JUDICIAL SYSTEM

In 1967, following some of the worst judicial scandals in the history of the state, in which one supreme court justice was imprisoned for income tax evasion and another impeached on charges of bribery and corruption, Oklahoma approved a constitutional amendment to reform the state's judicial system. Under the new provisions, the supreme court, the state's highest court, consists of nine justices initially elected to six-year terms, but with additional terms pursuant to nonpartisan, noncompetitive elections; if a justice is rejected by the voters, the vacancy is filled by gubernatorial appointment, subject to confirmation by the electorate. The court's appellate jurisdiction includes all civil cases (except those which it assigns to the courts of appeals), while its original jurisdiction extends to general supervisory control over all inferior courts and agencies created by law.

The highest appellate court for criminal cases is the court of criminal appeals, a three-member body filled in the same manner as the supreme court. Courts of appeals, created by the legislature in 1968, are located in Tulsa and Oklahoma City; each has three elective judges with powers to hear civil cases assigned to them by the supreme court. When final, their decisions are not appealable to any other state court, a system unique to Oklahoma.

District courts have original jurisdiction over all justiciable matters and some review powers over administrative actions. There are 25 districts with 68 district judges and 77 associate judges, who are elected to four-year terms. Municipal courts hear cases arising from local ordinances.

As of 1979, about 4,300 prisoners and 12,000 persons on parole and probation were under state supervision. The FBI reported a crime index total of 4,130 crimes per 100,000 population, including rates of 353 for violent crime and 3,777 for property crime; all rates were below the respective US averages. Oklahoma law permits capital punishment by lethal injection for several felony crimes. As of 1980, it had never been utilized.

[17] ARMED FORCES

Oklahoma has two Army and four Air Force facilities. Of major importance are Ft. Sill, near Lawton, the training facility for the Artillery Branch, with 25,324 authorized personnel in 1977/78; and the Air Logistics Center at Tinker Air Force Base, with 22,903 personnel. The US Army Corps of Engineers is headquartered in Tulsa.

As of 30 September 1979, about 410,000 veterans were living in Oklahoma, of whom 9,000 saw service in World War I, 172,000 in World War II, 77,000 in the Korean conflict, and 127,000 during the Viet-Nam era. Expenditures on veterans totaled $324.5 million in 1977/78, of which $188.9 million went for compensation and pensions.

The Oklahoma National Guard consists of 104 units located in 77 communities throughout the state. Army units have about 9,200 authorized personnel, air units 2,000. State and local police forces employed some 6,300 sworn peace officers in 1980.

[18] MIGRATION

Early immigrants to what is now Oklahoma included explorers, adventurers, and traders who made the country conscious of the new territory, and Indian tribes forcibly removed from the East and Midwest. The interior plains of Oklahoma remained basically unchanged until white settlers came in the late 1880s.

Coal mining brought miners from Italy in the 1870s to the McAlester and Krebs area, and Poles migrated to Bartlesville to work in the lead and zinc smelters. British and Irish seasoned coal miners came to Indian Territory because they could earn higher wages there than in their native countries, and Czechs and Slovaks arrived from Nebraska, Kansas, Iowa, and Texas when railroad construction began. Mexicans also worked as railroad laborers, ranch hands, and coal miners before statehood. The oil boom of the early 20th century brought an influx of workers from the eastern and midwestern industrial regions.

In 1907, the population of Oklahoma was 75% rural and 25% urban; by the late 1970s, however, 72% of the state's labor force resided in urban areas. Oklahoma lost population during the 1930s because of dust bowl and drought conditions, and the trend toward outmigration continued after World War II; from 1940 through 1960, the net loss from migration was 653,000. During the 1960s, Oklahoma gained a net total of 13,000 immigrants. The gain for 1970–78 was 139,000.

[19] INTERGOVERNMENTAL COOPERATION

Oklahoma participates in a number of regional intergovernmental agreements, among them the Arkansas River Compact, Arkansas River Basin Compact, Interstate Oil and Gas Compact, Red River Compact, South Central Interstate Forest Fire Protection Compact, Southern Growth Policies Compact, and Southern Interstate Energy Compact. Oklahoma also takes part in the Ozarks Regional Commission along with Arkansas, Kansas, Louisiana, and Missouri.

Federal aid in 1978/79 totaled nearly $950 million, of which general revenue sharing accounted for $73 million.

[20] ECONOMY

Primarily an agricultural state through the first half of the 20th century, Oklahoma has assumed a broader economic structure since the 1950s. Manufacturing heads the list of growth sectors, followed by wholesale and retail trade, and finance, insurance, and real estate; oil and gas extraction continues to play a major role, but the federal share of Oklahoma's economy is declining. In 1977, 72 of the state's 77 counties produced oil or gas, and more than 29% of Oklahoma's total land area was productive or leased for that purpose. Mineral severance taxes are a major source of state and local revenue.

The gross state product increased at a compound annual rate of 4.4% between 1970 and 1977; the estimated GSP for 1980 was $17.4 billion (in 1972 dollars), of which manufacturing accounted for more than 24%, with the agricultural sector and the federal government contributing only 4% and 5% respectively.

[21] INCOME

Oklahoma led the nation in 1979 with the largest increase in annual per capita income of any state; even with a 15.4% increase, however, the average per capita income was only $8,226, below the US average of $8,706. Farm income in 1979 rose by 132%, and the income of self-employed farmers by 183%. Annual wages in durable goods manufacturing increased by nearly 23%, in oil and gas extraction by 21%, and in federal civilian employment by less than 5%.

As of 1978, Oklahoma ranked 34th among the 50 states in average income per capita. Median family income was $12,172 (40th in the US) in 1975, when 14% of all state residents were below the federal poverty level.

[22] LABOR

The civilian labor force in 1978 was estimated at 1,260,000 persons, of whom 735,000 were male and 525,000 were female. Oklahoma had an annual unemployment rate of 3.9% in 1978, while the US rate was 6%; in 1979, the respective percentages were 3.4% and 5.8%. The unemployment rate for Oklahoma women, 4.6%, was the lowest among southern states. Minority unemployment was 12.8%, above the national average.

A federal census of workers covered by unemployment insurance in March 1977 revealed the following nonfarm employment pattern in Oklahoma:

	ESTABLISH-MENTS	EMPLOYEES	ANNUAL PAYROLL ('000)
Agricultural services, forestry, fishing	527	2,765	$ 21,004
Mining, of which:	2,028	41,432	693,330
Oil, gas extraction	(1,825)	(31,981)	(506,119)
Contract construction	6,330	49,562	610,478
Manufacturing	3,399	171,889	2,157,882
Transportation, public utilities	2,300	56,137	808,362
Wholesale trade	5,236	55,075	687,825
Retail trade	18,462	171,708	1,106,244
Finance, insurance, real estate	5,147	46,936	471,757
Services	15,886	146,811	1,158,331
Other	916	1,161	12,988
TOTALS	60,231	743,476	$7,728,201

Government workers, not covered by this survey, numbered about 193,000 in 1978.

There were 161,000 union and employee association members in 1976. They represented 17% of all nonagricultural employment, ranking Oklahoma 42d among the 50 states.

[23] AGRICULTURE

Agriculture remains an important economic activity in Oklahoma, even though its relative share of personal income and employment has declined since 1950. Total farm income, estimated at $2.5 billion, ranked 17th in the US in 1978. Crops made up less than one-third of the total.

As of 1974, Oklahoma had 73,649 farms and ranches covering 33,349,000 acres (13,496,000 hectares). The state ranked 3d in the US for wheat production in 1979, with 216,600,000 bushels, worth $855,570,000. Peanut production ranked 5th, with 264,000,000 lb, valued at $52,800,000. Other crop figures for 1979 include hay, 4,030,000 tons, $223,665,000; sorghum for grain, 23,175,000 bushels, $53,766,000; soybeans, 7,590,000 bushels, $42,884,000; corn for grain, 8,250,000 bushels, $22,275,000; oats, 4,560,000 bushels, $8,208,000; and barley, 2,530,000 bushels, $5,819,000.

Virtually all of Oklahoma's wheat production is located in the western half of the state; cotton (450,000 bales in 1978) is grown in the southwest corner. Sorghum-producing regions include the panhandle, central to southwestern Oklahoma, and the northeast corner of the state.

24 ANIMAL HUSBANDRY

At the close of 1979 there were 5,500,000 cattle and calves (4th in the US), 110,000 milk cows, 370,000 hogs and pigs, and 93,000 sheep and lambs on Oklahoma farms and ranches. Livestock raising takes place throughout the state, but most cattle are found in the panhandle, Osage County, and in the central counties west of I–35. Dairying centers around the two metropolitan areas of Oklahoma City and Tulsa, with a third area on the western border with Texas.

Production figures for 1979 were as follows: cattle and calves, 2.1 billion lb, $1.5 billion (5th in the US); hogs and pigs, 113.8 million lb, $46.9 million; sheep and lambs, 5.3 million lb, $3.2 million; chickens and broilers, 155.3 million lb, $40 million; turkeys, 35.9 million lb, $15.1 million; eggs, 754 million, $39.9 million; and milk, 1 billion lb, $131.5 million.

25 FISHING

The estimated commercial catch in 1978 was 2,150,000 lb, valued at $570,000. Oklahoma ranks 3d in the nation in quantity of fresh water available for sport fishing—about 1,300,000 acres (526,000 hectares) of impounded water, as well as some 8,500 mi (13,700 km) of good river fishing. The prolific white bass (sand bass), Oklahoma's state fish, is abundant in most large reservoirs. Smallmouth and spotted bass, blue and flathead catfish, black and white crappie, and various sunfish have won favor with fishermen. Rainbow trout are stocked year round in the Illinois River, and walleye and sauger are stocked in most reservoirs. Catfish farming was an expanding industry during the 1970s.

26 FORESTRY

Forests covered 8,513,000 acres (3,445,000 hectares) in 1977, or nearly one-fifth of the state's land area. Just about half that was commercial forestland, mostly located in eastern Oklahoma and 87% privately owned. More than some 585,900 acres (237,100 hectares) of forestland have been cleared for farming since 1966, most of it becoming pasture.

Shipments of lumber and wood products, derived for the most part from hardwood timber, were valued at $260.1 million in 1977; shipments of paper and allied products amounted to $267 million. Ash and hickory wood are used for tool handles, while walnut and pecan are employed in furniture and gun stocks.

27 MINING

Production of crude minerals had an estimated value of nearly $3.8 billion in 1978, 4th highest in the US. More than 90% of the mineral output, by value, consists of fossil fuels. Oklahoma ranks 1st in production of iodine, 2d in high-purity helium and tripoli (used in polishing), 3d in crude helium, 4th in feldspar in feldspathic sand, and 5th in crude gypsum.

Large deposits of limestone are found in northeastern Oklahoma, while gypsum is extracted in the northwest, the west-central region, and the four southwesternmost counties. Oklahoma had been a leading producer of lead and zinc until market conditions in the 1970s brought this sector of the mining industry to a standstill. The state also has varying amounts of copper, asphalt, bentonite, clays, germanium, glass sand, granite, iron, manganese, sandstone, shale, silver, titanium, and uranium.

Output of selected minerals in 1978 (excluding fossil fuels) was as follows: stone, 26,310,000 tons; sand and gravel, 12,000,000 tons; and clays (including shale), 1,043,000 tons. In 1976, Oklahoma produced 1,134,000 tons of gypsum, 227,000 cu feet of high-purity helium, and 150,000,000 cu feet of crude helium.

28 ENERGY AND POWER

Electric power production in Oklahoma in 1978 was 41 billion kwh, based on an installed capacity of 9.8 million kw. That year,

electric energy sales in the state totaled 28.5 billion kwh, of which 55% went for commercial and industrial purposes.

Oklahoma is rich in fossil fuel resources, producing oil, natural gas, and coal. The search for oil showed a 96% increase in wells drilled during the decade 1968–78, from 2,996 to 5,859. Crude production, however, showed a continuing decline during the same period, from 223.6 million barrels in 1968 to 150.5 million barrels in 1978 (4.7% of the US total). Proved reserves of crude oil were estimated at 1.1 billion barrels at the close of 1978. During the same year, Oklahoma's natural gas output exceeded 1.6 trillion cu feet (3d in the US), leaving reserves of 11.5 trillion cu feet. Consumption of natural gas in the state in 1978 was 770.2 billion cu feet, representing 43% of marketed production in Oklahoma, and 3.9% of the total US consumption of natural gas.

Production of bituminous coal reached a record high of 6.1 million net tons in 1978, nearly all of it strip-mined. Reserves totaling 1.6 billion tons as of 1976 are concentrated in eastern Oklahoma.

29 INDUSTRY

Oklahoma's earliest manufactures were based on agricultural and petroleum production. As late as 1939, the food-processing and petroleum-refining industries together accounted for one-third of the total value added by manufacture. Although resource-related industries continue to predominate, manufacturing was much more diversified in 1977, with petroleum refining and food and kindred products accounting for only 9% and 8% of value added, respectively. The leading sectors were nonelectrical machinery (17%) and fabricated metal products (11%), followed by electric and electronic equipment (9%) and rubber and plastic products (8%). The total value added in 1977 was nearly $4.7 billion. The following table shows value added by manufacture in 1972 and 1977 for selected industries:

	1972	1977
Petroleum refining	NA	$406,200,000
Communication equipment	NA	305,900,000
Tires and inner tubes	$102,300,000	281,900,000
Oil-field machinery	66,900,000	198,500,000
Motor vehicle parts and accessories	NA	145,000,000
Construction machinery	76,600,000	136,200,000
Nitrogenous fertilizers	NA	86,000,000
Grain mill products	26,000,000	81,000,000
Men's and boys' work clothes	13,000,000	78,500,000

Industries with corporate headquarters in Oklahoma include Phillips Petroleum, located in Bartlesville; Kerr-McGee Petroleum, Oklahoma City; Continental Oil, Ponca City; and Halliburton Services, Duncan. Most manufacturing is concentrated around Tulsa and Oklahoma City, where a large General Motors plant opened in 1979.

30 COMMERCE

Wholesale establishments had sales totaling $13.4 billion in 1977, with sales of machinery, equipment, and supplies and farm-product raw materials accounting for slightly more than one-third of the total. Oklahoma and Tulsa counties accounted for 41% and 31%, respectively, of all sales by wholesalers in the state.

Retailers had sales totaling $9.2 billion in 1977, ranking 28th in the US. Automotive dealers accounted for 25% of the total, followed by grocery stores, 22%; department stores, 8%; eating and drinking places, 8%; and gasoline service stations, 7%. Oklahoma County accounted for 26% of total retail sales; Oklahoma City led all other cities with nearly 20%.

The value of foreign agricultural exports in 1976/77 was $410 million (19th in the US). In manufactured goods exported in 1976, Oklahoma ranked 33d with a value of $579 million.

31 CONSUMER PROTECTION

A Uniform Consumer Credit Code, passed in 1969, prohibits discrimination because of sex or marital status when credit is involved. It is administered by the Commission on Consumer Credit, which also maintains a program of consumer education and has the power to require lawful and businesslike procedures by lending agencies. The attorney general is responsible for enforcing the state's Consumer Protection Act.

32 BANKING

At the end of 1978, Oklahoma's 478 insured commercial banks held assets totaling $17 billion, outstanding loans of $5.1 billion, and deposits exceeding $14.5 billion. During the same year, 54 insured savings and loan associations (29 federally chartered, 25 state chartered) had combined assets of $4.8 billion, outstanding mortgage loans of nearly $4 billion, and savings capital of $3.9 billion. There were 54 credit unions, with assets of $479.9 million, at the end of 1979.

33 INSURANCE

Although approximately 1,400 insurance companies are licensed to sell insurance in Oklahoma, only about 100—including some 60 life insurance firms—have home offices in the state. There are about 24,000 licensed agents.

In 1979, Oklahomans purchased $4.7 billion of ordinary life insurance. Total benefit payments in 1978 were $311 million. Policies in force as of 31 December 1978 numbered 4.1 million, with a total value of $33.1 billion and an average value per family of $29,500, 16% below the US average. Property and liability companies wrote premiums totaling $972.9 million in 1978.

34 SECURITIES

There are no stock or commodity exchanges in Oklahoma.

35 PUBLIC FINANCE

The Oklahoma budget is prepared by the director of state finance and submitted by the governor to the legislature each January. The appropriated budget, however, represented only about 36% of all the revenue collections used for state functions in 1978/79, since major revenue sources are dedicated to specific uses by the constitution or by statute and are outside the annual legislative budgetary process. The fiscal year is 1 July–30 June.

The following table summarizes consolidated state revenues and expenditures for 1978/79 (in millions):

REVENUES	
State taxes	$1,347.7
Receipts from federal government	668.9
Licenses, permits, and fees	149.5
Sales and services	92.8
Income from money and property	120.4
Student fees in higher education	48.1
Other receipts	370.0
TOTAL	$2,797.4

EXPENDITURES	
Education	$1,189.8
Health and social services	786.3
Transportation	346.3
Public safety and defense	109.8
General government	78.4
Natural resources	216.4
Regulatory services	7.9
Other outlays	30.1
TOTAL	$2,765.0

State government's indebtedness as of 30 June 1979 was $230.9 million. Revenue bonds of quasi-governmental institutions, agencies, and authorities stood at $961.6 million as of the same date. The total indebtedness of state and local governments in Oklahoma surpassed $2.2 billion in mid-1977; the per capita figure of $799 was one-third below the US average.

36 TAXATION

In 1978/79, 48% of total state governmental revenue in Oklahoma came from state taxes and 28% from licenses, charges, and miscellaneous general revenue. Of the tax receipts, the state income tax accounted for $408.9 million; sales tax, $257.9 million; gross production tax on oil, gas, and other minerals, $242 million; and gasoline excise tax, $117.9 million. In 1977, Oklahoma ranked 35th in the US in state and local taxes per capita.

As of 1980, the state income tax ranged from 0.5% on the first $2,000 to 6% on amounts over $15,000. The corporate tax on net income was 4%, and the state sales and use tax 2%. Property taxes remain the principal source of revenue for local governments, representing nearly 70% of total local tax collections in 1977. Cities are authorized to impose a sales tax of up to 2%.

Oklahoma's federal tax burden in 1975/76 was $3.4 billion, while the state received a total of $4.3 billion in federal expenditures. In 1977, Oklahomans filed 1,051,218 federal income tax returns, paying more than $1.7 billion in tax.

37 ECONOMIC POLICY

Oklahoma entered the first years of statehood with a populist-inspired distrust of business, especially large corporations. In recent decades, however, government policies have generally favored business activity. Probusiness measures include a comparatively low property tax assessment level, a state oil depletion allowance of 30% to encourage oil exploration, a strong vocational education program to provide industrial manpower, and the creation of a state Department of Industrial Development, which encourages major US and foreign corporations to establish new manufacturing facilities in Oklahoma.

38 HEALTH

Average life expectancy in Oklahoma was 71.42 years in 1969–71 (19th in the US); men averaged 67.40 years, women 75.70. The overall estimated life expectancy rose to 73 years in 1977, when the infant mortality rate was 12.7 per 1,000 live births for whites and 17.7 for nonwhites; the latter figure was well below the US norm. Approximately 10,000 legal abortions were performed in Oklahoma in 1977, a ratio of 230 per 1,000 live births. The leading causes of death and their rates in 1977 were heart disease, 354 per 100,000 population; cancer, 182; cerebrovascular disease, 100; accidents, 60.2; and influenza and pneumonia, 28. On all these measures Oklahomans exceeded the national average; the state's overall death rate was 9.5 per 1,000 population.

Per capita consumption of alcoholic beverages doubled in Oklahoma between 1960 and the late 1970s. In 1976, the Department of Mental Health estimated that there were 168,900 problem drinkers in Oklahoma, 17,140 of them teenagers; men constituted two-thirds of Oklahoma alcoholics. There were 2,268 admissions to drug treatment programs in 1978. In 1979, 87 cases of syphilis and 12,755 cases of gonorrhea were reported.

Oklahoma had 3 state mental hospitals and 11 community health care centers in 1979. Overall, there were 141 hospitals in 1978, providing 17,482 beds and recording 512,410 admissions, for an average occupancy rate of 68%. Hospital personnel included 5,626 registered nurses and 3,448 licensed practical nurses. The average cost of hospital care in 1977 was $182 per day and $1,181 per stay, both below the US average. Oklahoma had 3,475 licensed physicians in 1977 and 1,192 active dentists in 1979. The Health Sciences Center of the University of Oklahoma is located in Oklahoma City.

39 SOCIAL WELFARE

Total expenditures in 1978/79 of the major state social welfare agency, the Department of Institutions, Social and Rehabilitative Services, exceeded $623 million, 58% from federal sources. Approximately 11,280 employees brought direct services to nearly 900,000 Oklahomans. Benefits in aid to families with dependent children totaled $74 million in 1978; Medicaid expenditures reached $199 million in 1977. During 1978, 135,000 Oklahomans received food stamps at a federal cost of $36.1 million, and some 402,000 children received school lunches requiring a federal expenditure of $23.4 million.

Social Security benefits of $1.1 billion were paid to 471,700 retired persons, survivors, and disabled workers in 1977; monthly payments to retired workers averaged $225.80. Federal Supplemental Security Income payments to 73,600 aged, disabled, and blind persons were $91.4 million. Vocational rehabilitation in 1978 required an expenditure of $18.6 million. During the same year, 38,000 Oklahomans received more than $31 million in unemployment insurance, for an average weekly benefit of $75.91. The state expended $72.1 million on workers' compensation in 1977.

40 HOUSING
Indian tepees and settlers' sod houses dotted the Oklahoma plains when the "eighty-niners" swarmed into the territory; old neighborhoods in cities and towns of Oklahoma still retain some of the modest frame houses they built. Nearly 70% of all housing units were owner-occupied in 1970, and most Oklahomans continue to prefer single-family dwellings, despite a recent trend toward condominiums. Modern underground homes and solar-heated dwellings can be seen in the university towns of Norman and Stillwater.

The 1970 census counted 939,681 housing units, of which 37% dated from 1939 or earlier and 26% from the 1960s; 94% of the occupied units had full plumbing. As of 1980 there were an estimated 1,150,000 housing units in the state.

41 EDUCATION
Oklahoma's educational enterprise is the largest expenditure item in the state budget, but the outlay barely kept pace with regional or national efforts during the 1970s—a fact reflected in teachers' salaries, which ranked 42d nationally in 1979. Per capita expenditures on education placed Oklahoma 34th among the 50 states in 1977/78.

The illiteracy rate—1.1% of the population as of 1970—is slightly below the national average. About 66% of all Oklahomans 18 years of age or older were high school graduates in 1976; during the same year, 29% of adult state residents had at least one year of college. The median figure for school years completed was 12.4, slightly below the US average. In 1978/79, Oklahoma's public school enrollment totaled 620,167, of which kindergartens accounted for 43,946; elementary schools, 259,668; junior high schools, 120,727; senior high schools, 165,086; and special and nondistrict schools, 30,740. A special education program for Indians covered 16,520 students in 179 schools. After the US Supreme Court outlawed public school segregation in 1954, integration proceeded rapidly in Oklahoma; by 1976, 80% of all minority students were in schools with a minority-group school enrollment of less than 50%.

Public higher educational institutions include 2 comprehensive, 6 regional, and 4 senior state universities, 13 state junior colleges, a community junior college, and a professional college. The comprehensive institutions, the University of Oklahoma (Norman) and Oklahoma State University (Stillwater), have more than 20,000 students each and offer the major graduate-level programs. The 15 private colleges and universities in Oklahoma increased their enrollment to 22,710 in 1978. Well-known institutions include Oral Roberts University and the University of Tulsa.

42 ARTS
Major arts centers are located in Tulsa and Oklahoma City, but there are many art and crafts museums throughout the state. The Oklahoma Arts and Humanities Council, now known as the State Arts Council of Oklahoma, was created by the Oklahoma legislature in 1965.

Oklahoma City's leading cultural institution is the Oklahoma Symphony. The Tulsa Philharmonic, Tulsa Ballet Theater, and Tulsa Opera all appear at the Tulsa Performing Arts Center, a municipally owned and operated facility; this six-level center consists of a 2,500-seat concert hall, 450-seat theater, and two multilevel experimental theaters.

The Myriad Center in Oklahoma City and the Lloyd Noble Center in Norman host rock, jazz, and country music concerts.

43 LIBRARIES AND MUSEUMS
Public libraries serve 29 counties in Oklahoma, while 14 bookmobiles aid in serving counties without libraries of their own. In 1978, a total of 3,693,668 volumes occupied public library shelves; total circulation was 8,090,257. The Five Civilized Tribes Museum Library in Muskogee has a large collection of Indian documents and art, while the Cherokee archives are held at the Cherokee National Historical Society in Tahlequah. The Morris Swett Library at Ft. Sill has a special collection on military history, particularly field artillery. The Oklahoma Department of Libraries in Oklahoma City has holdings covering law, library science, Oklahoma history, and other fields. Large academic libraries include those of the University of Oklahoma (Norman), with 1,686,957 volumes in 1978, and Oklahoma State University Library (Stillwater), with 1,210,406.

Oklahoma has more than 80 museums and historic sites. The Philbrook Art Center in Tulsa houses important collections of Indian, Renaissance, and Oriental art. Also in Tulsa are the Thomas Gilcrease Institute of American History and Art and the Rebecca and Tershorne Fenster Gallery of Jewish Art. The University of Tulsa's Alexander Hogue Gallery of Art features contemporary art, and the World Museum/Art Center has collections of European bronzes and marbles as well as antique cars. The National Cowboy Hall of Fame and Western Heritage Center, Oklahoma Heritage Center, Oklahoma Historical Society Museum, Oklahoma Museum of Art, and the Omniplex science museum are major attractions in Oklahoma City.

44 COMMUNICATIONS
The Butterfield Stage and Overland Mail delivered the mail to Millerton on 18 September 1858 as part of the first US transcontinental postal route. After the Civil War, the early railroads delivered mail and parcels to the Oklahoma and Indian territories. As of 1980 there were 8,131 postal employees and 632 post offices in the state.

The Southwestern Bell Co., employing 10,446 people, furnished 87% of the telephone service in the state as of 1980. Overall, Oklahoma had 2,226,430 telephones—588,462 business, 1,637,968 residential—at the end of 1978, when 95% of the state's households had telephone service.

There were 67 AM and 50 FM radio stations in the state as of 1978 and 12 commercial television channels in 1980. The Oklahoma Educational Television Authority maintains production facilities in Oklahoma City and operates stations in Oklahoma City, Tulsa, Cheyenne, and Eufaula. Cable television served 209,735 subscribers at the end of 1978.

45 PRESS
In 1978, Oklahoma had 9 morning dailies with a combined circulation of 425,259, 45 evening dailies with 452,381, and 46 Sunday newspapers with 894,932. Leading dailies and their circulation in 1978 were as follows:

AREA	NAME	DAILY	SUNDAY
Oklahoma City	Oklahoma Journal (m,S)	41,060	41,127
	Oklahoman (m,S)	179,960	283,364
	Oklahoma City Times (e)	93,107	
Tulsa	Daily World (m,S)	121,765	210,711
	Tribune (e)	77,833	

As of 1980 there were 191 established weeklies with a combined circulation of 383,100. Tulsa and Oklahoma City each have monthly city-interest publications, and the University of Oklahoma has a highly active university press.

46 ORGANIZATIONS
One of the nation's largest service groups, the US Jaycees, is headquartered in Tulsa. Trade organizations include the American Association of Petroleum Geologists, Association of Petro-

leum Writers, Gas Processors Association, all in Tulsa; and the American Poultry Association in Cushing. Among numerous sports-related groups are the Amateur Softball Association of America and International Softball Federation, both in Oklahoma City; the Football Writers Association of America in Edmond; and the International Rodeo Association, Pauls Valley.

⁴⁷TOURISM, TRAVEL, AND RECREATION

With the building of seven state resort lodges and the opening of state parks, tourism has become a growing sector of Oklahoma's economy. In 1977, $1.4 billion was taken in, and the estimate for the 1980 tourist season was $2.5 billion. During 1977/78, 32 state parks and 77 recreation areas operated by the Division of State Parks had nearly 20 million visitors.

The state also maintains and operates the National Hall of Fame for Famous American Indians, in Anadarko; Black Kettle Museum, in Cheyenne; the Ferguson Home in Watonga; the Murrell Home, south of Tahlequah; the Pawnee Bill Museum, in Pawnee; the Pioneer Woman Statue and Museum, in Ponca City; the Chisholm Trail Museum, in Kingfisher; the Western Trails Museum, in Clinton; and the Will Rogers Birthplace, near Oologah.

Licenses were issued to 279,141 hunters and 605,626 fishermen in 1977/78.

⁴⁸SPORTS

Oklahoma's lone major league professional team is the Tulsa Roughnecks of the North American Soccer League. Other professional franchises are, in Oklahoma City, the class-AAA baseball 89ers, the Stars of the Central Hockey League, and the football Dolls, a women's team. Tulsa has the class-AA baseball Drillers, the Twisters of the Professional Team Rodeo circuit, and the Central Hockey League Oilers.

Sports on the college level are still the primary source of pride for Oklahomans. As of mid-1980, the University of Oklahoma Sooners had won 5 national football titles in season-ending polls, 10 Big Eight Conference crowns (the last 7 in a row), a Big Eight basketball crown in 1979, and NCAA championships in wrestling, baseball, and gymnastics. The Oklahoma State University Cowboys have captured NCAA and Big Eight titles in basketball, baseball, and golf, and as of mid-1980 had won 27 national and 15 conference championships in wrestling.

Oklahoma City hosts the National Finals of Rodeo every December. In golf, Tulsa has been the site of several US Open tournaments. The Softball Hall of Fame is in Oklahoma City.

⁴⁹FAMOUS OKLAHOMANS

Carl Albert (b.1908), a McAlester native, has held the highest public position of any Oklahoman. Elected to the US House of Representatives in 1947, he became majority leader in 1962 and served as speaker of the House from 1971 until his retirement in 1976. Patrick Jay Hurley (1883–1963), the first Oklahoman appointed to a cabinet post, was secretary of war under Herbert Hoover and later ambassador to China.

William "Alfalfa Bill" Murray (b.Texas, 1869–1956) was president of the state constitutional convention and served as governor from 1931 to 1935. Robert S. Kerr (1896–1963), founder of Kerr-McGee Oil, was the state's first native-born governor, serving from 1943 to 1947; elected to the US Senate in 1948, he became an influential Democratic leader. A(lmer) S(tillwell) Mike Monroney (1902–80) served as US representative from 1939 to 1951 and senator from 1951 to 1969.

Oklahomans have been prominent in literature and the arts. Journalist and historian Marquis James (b.Missouri, 1891–1955) won a Pulitzer Prize in 1930 for his biography of Sam Houston and another in 1938 for *Andrew Jackson*, and Ralph Ellison (b.1914) won the 1953 National Book Award for his novel *Invisible Man*. The popular musical *Oklahoma!*, by Richard Rodgers and Oscar Hammerstein 2d, is based on *Green Grow the Lilacs* by Oklahoman Lynn Riggs (1899–1954). N(avarre) Scott Moma-

day (b.1934), born in Lawton, received a Pulitzer Prize in 1969 for *House Made of Dawn*. Woodrow Crumbo (b.1912) and Allen Houser (b.1914) are prominent Indian artists born in the state.

Just about the best-known Oklahoman was William Penn Adair "Will" Rogers (1879–1935), the beloved humorist and writer who spread cheer in the dreary days of the depression. Part Cherokee, Rogers was a horse rider, trick roper, and stage and movie star until he was killed in a plane crash in Alaska. Among his gifts to the American language are the oft-quoted expressions "I never met a man I didn't like" and "All I know is what I read in the newspapers." Other prominent performing artists include singer-songwriter Woody Guthrie (1912–67), composer of "This Land Is Your Land," among other classics; ballerina Maria Tallchief (b.1925); popular singer Patti Page (b.1927); and operatic soprano Roberta Knie (b.1938). Famous Oklahoma actors include (Francis) Van Heflin (1910–71), Ben Johnson (b.1918), Jennifer Jones (b.1919), Tony Randall (b.1920), James Garner (James Baumgardner, b.1928), and Cleavon Little (b.1939). Paul Harvey (b.1918) is a widely syndicated radio commentator, and Frank McGee (1921–74) was a noted television journalist.

James Francis "Jim" Thorpe (1888–1953) became known as the "world's greatest athlete" after his pentathlon and decathlon performances at the 1912 Olympic Games; of Indian ancestry, Thorpe also starred in baseball, football, and other sports. Bud Wilkinson (b.Minnesota, 1916) coached the University of Oklahoma football team to a record 47-game unbeaten streak in the 1950s. Baseball stars Paul Waner (1903–65) and his brother Lloyd (b.1906), Mickey Mantle (b.1931), Wilver Dornel "Willie" Stargell (b.1941), and Johnny Bench (b.1947) are native Oklahomans.

⁵⁰BIBLIOGRAPHY

Bicha, Karel D. *The Czechs in Oklahoma*. Norman: University of Oklahoma Press, 1980.

Blessing, Patrick. *The British and Irish in Oklahoma*. Norman: University of Oklahoma Press, 1980.

Brown, Kenny L. *Italians in Oklahoma*. Norman: University of Oklahoma Press, 1980.

Fischer, John. *From the High Plains*. New York: Harper and Row, 1978.

Franklin, Jimmie Lewis. *Blacks in Oklahoma*. Norman: University of Oklahoma Press, 1980.

Gibson, Arrell M. *The Oklahoma Story*. Norman: University of Oklahoma Press, 1978.

Gregory, Robert. *Oil in Oklahoma*. Muskogee, Okla.: Leake Industries, 1976.

Kirkpatrick, Samuel, et al. *The Oklahoma Voter*. Norman: University of Oklahoma Press, 1977.

Morgan, H. Wayne and Anne Hodges. *Oklahoma: A Bicentennial History*. New York: Norton, 1977.

Oklahoma, State of. State Election Board. *Directory of Oklahoma, 1979*. Oklahoma City, 1979.

Oklahoma, University of. College of Business Administration. Center for Economic and Management Research. *Statistical Abstract of Oklahoma, 1978*. Norman, 1978.

Oklahoma State University. College of Business Administration. *1980 Oklahoma Economic Outlook*. Stillwater, 1980.

Rohrs, Richard. *Germans in Oklahoma*. Norman: University of Oklahoma Press, 1980.

Smith, Michael. *Mexicans in Oklahoma*. Norman: University of Oklahoma Press, 1980.

Stewart, Ray. *Born Grown: Oklahoma City History*. Oklahoma City: Fidelity Bank, 1975.

Strain, Jack M. *An Outline of Oklahoma Government*. Edmond, Okla.: Central State University, 1978.

Strickland, Rennard. *Indians in Oklahoma*. Norman: University of Oklahoma Press, 1980.

Tobias, Henry J. *Jews in Oklahoma*. Norman: University of Oklahoma Press, 1980.

OREGON

State of Oregon

ORIGIN OF STATE NAME: Unknown; name first applied to the river now known as the Columbia. **NICKNAME:** The Beaver State. **CAPITAL:** Salem. **ENTERED UNION:** 14 February 1859 (33d). **SONG:** "Oregon, My Oregon." **DANCE:** Square dance. **MOTTO:** The Union. **COLORS:** Navy blue and gold. **FLAG:** The flag consists of a navy blue field with gold lettering and illustrations. Obverse: the shield from the state seal, supported by 33 stars, with the words "State of Oregon" above and the year of admission below. Reverse: a beaver. **OFFICIAL SEAL:** A shield, supported by 33 stars and crested by an American eagle, depicts mountains and forests, an elk, a covered wagon and ox team, wheat, a plow, a pickax, and the state motto; in the background, as the sun sets over the Pacific, an American merchant ship arrives as a British man-o'-war departs. The words "State of Oregon 1859" surround the whole. **ANIMAL:** Beaver. **BIRD:** Western meadowlark. **FISH:** Chinook salmon. **FLOWER:** Oregon grape. **TREE:** Douglas fir. **ROCK:** Thunderegg (geode). **INSECT:** Swallowtail butterfly. **LEGAL HOLIDAYS:** New Year's Day, 1 January; Lincoln's Birthday, 1st Monday in February; Washington's Birthday, 3d Monday in February; Memorial Day, last Monday in May; Independence Day, 4 July; Labor Day, 1st Monday in September; Veterans Day, 11 November; Thanksgiving Day, 4th Thursday in November; Christmas Day, 25 December. Designated as commemoration days are Oregon's Admission into the Union, 14 February; and Columbus Day, 12 October. **TIME:** 5 A.M. MST = noon GMT; 4 A.M. PST = noon GMT.

¹LOCATION, SIZE, AND EXTENT

Located on the Pacific coast of the northwestern US, Oregon ranks 10th in size among the 50 states.

The total area of Oregon is 96,981 sq mi (251,180 sq km), with land comprising 96,184 sq mi (249,116 sq km) and inland water 797 sq mi (2,064 sq km). Oregon extends 395 mi (636 km) E–W; the state's maximum N–S extension is 295 mi (475 km).

Oregon is bordered on the N by Washington (with most of the line formed by the Columbia River); on the E by Idaho (with part of the line defined by the Snake River); on the S by Nevada and California; and on the W by the Pacific Ocean. The total boundary length of Oregon is *1,444 mi (2,324 km)*, including a general coastline of 296 mi (476 km); the tidal shoreline extends 1,410 mi (2,269 km). The state's geographic center is in Crook County, 25 mi (40 km) SSE of Prineville.

²TOPOGRAPHY

The Cascade Range, extending north–south, divides Oregon into distinct eastern and western regions, each of which contains a great variety of landforms.

At the state's western edge, the Coast Range, a relatively low mountain system, rises from the beaches, bays, and rugged headlands of the Pacific coast. Between the Coast and Cascade ranges lie fertile valleys, the largest being the Willamette Valley, Oregon's heartland. The two-thirds of the state lying east of the Cascade Range consists generally of arid plateau cut by river canyons, with rolling hills in the north-central portion giving way to the Blue Mountains in the northeast. The Great Basin in the southeast is characterized by fault-block ridges, weathered buttes, and remnants of large prehistoric lakes.

The Cascades, Oregon's highest mountains, contain nine snow-capped volcanic peaks more than 9,000 feet (2,700 meters) high, of which the highest is Mt. Hood, at 11,235 feet (3,424 meters); a dormant volcano, Mt. Hood last erupted in 1865 (Mt. St. Helens, which erupted in 1980, is only 60 mi, or 97 km, to the northwest, in Washington). The Blue Mountains include several rugged subranges interspersed with plateaus, alluvial basins, and deep river canyons. The Klamath Mountains in the southwest form a jumble of ridges where the Coast and Cascade ranges blend together south of the Willamette Valley.

Oregon is drained by many rivers, but the Columbia, demarcating most of the northern border with Washington, is by far the biggest and most important. Originating in Canada, it flows more than 1,200 mi (1,900 km) to the Pacific Ocean. With a mean annual flow rate of 250,134 cu feet per second, the Columbia is the 3d-largest river in the US. It drains some 58% of Oregon's surface by way of a series of northward-flowing rivers, including the Deschutes, John Day, and Umatilla. The largest of the Columbia's tributaries in Oregon, and longest river entirely within the state, is the Willamette, which drains a fertile valley more than 100 mi (160 km) long. Better than half of Oregon's eastern boundary with Idaho is formed by the Snake River, which flows through Hells Canyon, one of the deepest canyons in North America.

Oregon has 19 natural lakes with a surface area of more than 3,000 acres (1,200 hectares), and many smaller ones. The largest is Upper Klamath Lake, which covers 58,922 acres (23,845 hectares) and is quite shallow. The most famous, however, is Crater Lake, which formed in the crater created by the violent eruption of Mt. Mazama several thousand years ago and is now a national park. Its depth of 1,932 feet (589 meters)—the greatest of any lake in the US—and its nearly circular expanse of bright blue water, edged by the crater's rim, make it a natural wonder.

³CLIMATE

Oregon has a generally temperate climate, but there are marked regional variations. The Cascade Range separates the state into two broad climatic zones: the western third, with relatively heavy precipitation and moderate temperatures, and the eastern two-thirds, with relatively little precipitation and more extreme temperatures. Within these general regions, climate depends largely on elevation and land configuration.

In January, average daily temperatures range from more than 46°F (8°C) along the southern coast to less than 21°F (-6°C) in some eastern regions. In July, portions of eastern Oregon have average temperatures above 71°F (22°C), while the Willamette Valley averages about 66°F (19°C). The record low temperature, -54°F (-48°C), was registered at Seneca on 10 February 1933; the all-time high, 119°F (48°C), at Pendleton on 10 August 1938.

The Cascades serve as a barrier to the warm, moist winds

451

blowing in from the Pacific, confining most precipitation to western Oregon. Some areas in the Coast Range receive more than 100 in (254 cm) of precipitation a year, and overall the west averages more than 40 in (102 cm). Most of eastern Oregon receives less than 20 in (51 cm) of precipitation, and some areas get less than 10 in (25 cm). Portland averages 38 in (97 cm) of precipitation a year, but only 7 in (18 cm) of snow; fog is common, and the sun shines, on average, during only 48% of the daylight hours, one of the lowest such percentages for any major US city. Up to 300 in (762 cm) of snow falls each year in the highest reaches of the Cascades.

⁴FLORA AND FAUNA

With its variety of climatic conditions and surface features, Oregon has a diverse assortment of vegetation and wildlife, including 78 native tree species. The coastal region is covered by a rain forest of spruce, hemlock, and cedar rising above dense underbrush. A short distance inland, the stands of Douglas fir—Oregon's state tree and dominant timber resource—begin, extending across the western slopes to the summit of the Cascade Range. Where the Douglas fir has been destroyed by fire or logging, alder and various types of berries grow. In the high elevations of the Cascades, Douglas fir gives way to pines and true firs. Ponderosa pine predominates on the eastern slopes, while in areas too dry for pine the forests give way to open range, which, in its natural state, is characterized by sagebrush, occasional juniper trees, and sparse grasses. The state's many species of smaller indigenous plants include Oregon grape—the state flower—as well as salmonberry, huckleberry, blackberry, and many other berries.

More than 130 species of mammal are native to Oregon, of which 28 are found throughout the state. Many species are protected, either entirely or through hunting restrictions. The bighorn sheep and sea otter, once extirpated in Oregon, have been reintroduced in limited numbers; the Columbian white-tailed deer, with an extremely limited habitat along the Columbia River, is still classified as endangered. Deer and elk are popular game mammals, with herds managed by the state: mule deer predominate in eastern Oregon, black-tailed deer in the west. Among introduced mammals, the nutria and opossum are now present in large numbers. At least 60 species of fish are found in Oregon, including five different salmon species, of which the Chinook is the largest and the coho most common. Salmon form the basis of Oregon's sport and commercial fishing, although dams and development have blocked many spawning areas, causing a decline in numbers and heavy reliance on hatcheries to continue the runs. Hundreds of species of birds inhabit Oregon, either year-round or during particular seasons. The state lies in the path of the Pacific Flyway, a major route for migratory waterfowl, and large numbers of geese and ducks may be found in western Oregon and marshy areas east of the Cascades. Extensive bird refuges have been established in various parts of the state. The northern bald eagle, northern spotted owl, and western snowy plover are considered threatened, while the California brown pelican, Aleutian Canada goose, and American and Arctic peregrine falcons are classified as endangered.

⁵ENVIRONMENTAL PROTECTION

Oregon has been among the most active states in environmental protection. In 1938, the polluted condition of the Willamette River led to the enactment, by initiative, of one of the nation's first comprehensive water pollution control laws, which helped restore the river's quality for swimming and fishing. An air pollution control law was enacted in 1951, and air and water quality programs were placed under the new Department of Environmental Quality in 1969. This department is Oregon's major environmental protection agency, enforcing standards for air and water quality, solid waste disposal, and noise abatement. A vehicle inspection program has been instituted to reduce

exhaust emissions in the Portland area. Two-thirds of Oregon's population is served by sewer systems, with state-backed bonds and grants assisting local jurisdictions.

Land-use planning has been a subject of controversy in Oregon, especially in rural areas. Voters in 1976 and 1978 defeated initiative measures that would have weakened a 1973 state law requiring each city and county to establish a comprehensive land-use plan. Local planning and zoning decisions are subject to review by an appointed Land Conservation and Development Commission, which also establishes land-use planning goals and guidelines.

In 1973, the legislature enacted what has become known as the Oregon Bottle Bill, the first state law prohibiting the sale of nonreturnable beer or soft-drink containers. Similar laws, aimed at reducing roadside litter, have since been enacted by several other states.

⁶POPULATION

Oregon ranked 31st among the 50 states at the 1970 census, with a population of 2,091,385. Like other western states, Oregon has experienced population growth more rapid than that of the US as a whole in recent decades. The 1970 census figure represented an 18% increase over the 1960 census population; the preliminary 1980 census total, 2,617,444, was 25% more than in 1970. Oregon's estimated population density in 1979 was 26 per sq mi (10 per sq km), less than half the national average.

As of 1970, about 40% of all Oregonians lived in the Portland region, while another 30% lived in the remainder of the Willamette Valley, particularly in and around Salem and Eugene. The city of Portland had an estimated 370,000 residents in 1979; the Portland Standard Metropolitan Statistical Area (which includes Vancouver, Wash.) had an estimated population of more than 1.1 million, ranking 34th in the US. Preliminary 1980 census figures were Portland, 364,246; Eugene, 104,672; and Salem, 89,161.

⁷ETHNIC GROUPS

Oregon's Indians numbered 13,510 in 1970, with the population evenly divided between rural and urban areas. The state has three reservations, and important salmon fishing rights in the north are reserved under treaty. About 30,000 black Americans lived in Oregon in 1976, most of them in the Portland area. People of Hispanic descent numbered about 40,000 in the same year. In 1970 there were 6,843 Japanese, 4,814 Chinese, and 1,633 Filipinos. Oregon added 2,063 resettled Vietnamese to its population in 1975.

French Canadians have lived in Oregon since the opening of the territory, and they have continued to come in a small but steady migration. In all, the 1970 census counted some 295,000 Oregonians of 1st- or 2d-generation immigrant stock, with Canada, Germany, and the United Kingdom ranking as the leading countries of origin.

⁸LANGUAGES

Place-names such as Umatilla, Coos Bay, Klamath Falls, and Tillamook reflect the variety of Indian tribes that white settlers found in Oregon territory. In 1970, 2,160 Indians—mostly of the Umatilla, Wasco, and Paiute tribes—claimed Indian languages as their mother tongue.

The Midland dialect dominates Oregon English, except for an apparent Northern dialect influence in the Willamette Valley. Throughout the state, *foreign* and *orange* have the /aw/ vowel, and *tomorrow* has the /ah/ of *father*.

In 1970, 87% of the native-born state residents and 85% of all residents claimed English as their mother tongue. Major resident groups reported their first languages as follows:

	NATIVE-BORN	FOREIGN-BORN
English	1,767,997	18,370
German	68,089	13,778
Spanish	17,815	3,652
French	8,881	1,907

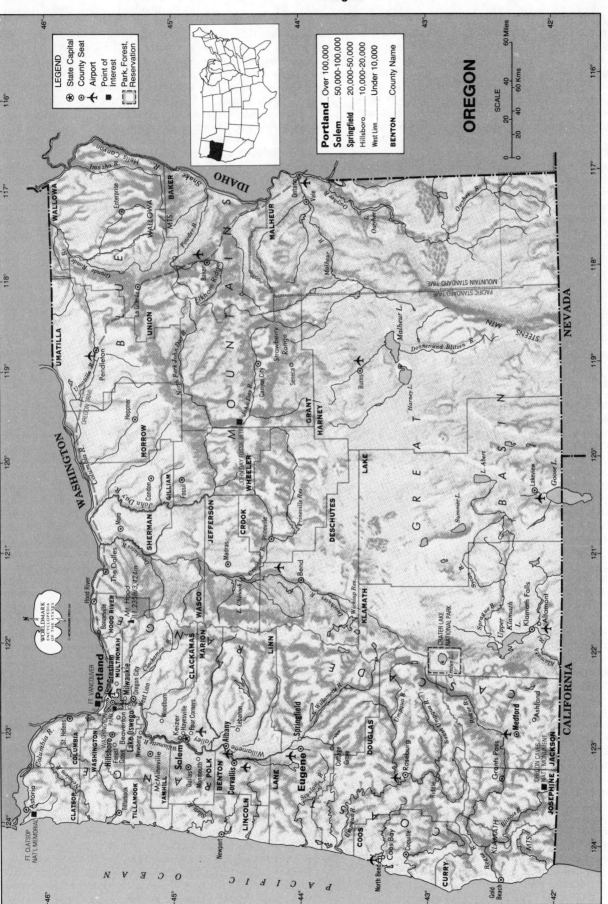

OREGON

LEGEND
⊗ State Capital
⊙ County Seat
✈ Airport
◾ Point of Interest
▢ Park, Forest, Reservation

Portland Over 100,000
Salem 50,000-100,000
Springfield 20,000-50,000
Hillsboro 10,000-20,000
West Linn Under 10,000
BENTON County Name

SCALE

0   20   40   60 Miles
0   20   40   60 Kms

See US political: front cover B2; physical: back cover B2.

LOCATION: 42° to 46°15'N; 116°33' to 124°32'W. **BOUNDARIES:** Washington line, 443 mi (713 km); Idaho line, 332 mi (534 km); Nevada line, 153 mi (246 km); California line, 220 mi (354 km); Pacific Ocean coastline, 296 mi (477 km).

⁹RELIGIONS

About one-third of Oregon's population is affiliated with an organized religion, well below the national average. The leading Christian denominations were the Roman Catholic Church, with 313,713 members in 1979, and the Church of Jesus Christ of Latter-day Saints (Mormon), with 59,178 adherents in 1971. Other major Protestant groups with their 1971 adherents were United Methodist, 58,731; United Presbyterian, 50,941; and Episcopal, 38,558. Jewish Oregonians were estimated to number 10,835 in 1979.

¹⁰TRANSPORTATION

With the state's major deepwater port and international airport, Portland is the transportation hub of Oregon. The state has about 3,700 mi (6,000 km) of track and is served by several major rail systems, including the Union Pacific, Southern Pacific, and Burlington Northern. Lumber and other wood products are the major commodities carried; about twice as much rail freight is shipped out of Oregon as is shipped in. Amtrak provides passenger service north–south through Portland, Salem, and Eugene, and east–west through Pendleton and Portland. Thirteen cities in Oregon operated local transit systems in 1979, with Portland's the largest.

Starting with pioneer trails and toll roads, Oregon's roads and highways had become a network extending 112,229 mi (180,615 km) by 1978. The main interstate highways are I-5, connecting the major Willamette Valley cities, and I-84 (formerly I-80N), running northwest from Ontario in eastern Oregon and then along the northern border. At the beginning of 1979 there were 2,304,625 motor vehicles, including 1,808,998 passenger cars, registered in Oregon, with 1,827,036 licensed drivers.

The Columbia River forms the major inland waterway for the Pacific Northwest, with barge navigation possible for about 425 mi (684 km) upstream to Lewiston, Idaho, via the Snake River. Wheat from eastern Oregon and Washington is shipped downstream to Portland for reloading onto oceangoing vessels. The Port of Portland operates four major cargo terminals. Oregon also has several important coastal harbors, including Astoria, Newport, and Coos Bay, the largest lumber export harbor in the US.

In 1978, Oregon had 302 airfields (92 public, 210 private), of which the largest and busiest, Portland International Airport, handled 40,568 scheduled departures and emplaned 2,058,535 passengers.

¹¹HISTORY

The land now known as Oregon has been inhabited for at least 10,000 years, the age assigned to woven brush sandals found in caves along what was once the shore of a large inland lake. Later, a variety of Indian cultures evolved. Along the coast and lower Columbia River lived peoples of the Northern Coast Culture, who ate salmon and other marine life, built large dugout canoes and cedar plank houses, and possessed a complex social structure, including slavery, that emphasized status and wealth. East of the Cascade Range were the dwellers of the arid plateau, hunter-gatherers who migrated from place to place as the food supply dictated.

The first European to see Oregon was probably Sir Francis Drake. In 1578, while on a raiding expedition against the Spanish, Drake reported sighting what is believed to be the Oregon coast before being forced to return southward by "vile, thicke and stinking fogges." For most of the next 200 years, European contact was limited to occasional sightings by mariners, who considered the coast too dangerous for landing. In 1778, however, British Captain James Cook, on his third voyage of discovery, visited the Northwest and named several Oregon capes. Soon afterward, American ships arrived in search of sea otter and other furs. A Yankee merchant captain, Robert Gray, discovered the Columbia River (which he named for his ship) in 1792, contributing to the US claim to the Northwest.

The first overland trek to Oregon was the Lewis and Clark Expedition, which traveled from St. Louis to the mouth of the Columbia, where it spent the winter of 1805/6. In 1811, a party of fur traders employed by New York merchant John Jacob Astor arrived by ship at the mouth of the Columbia and built a trading post named Astoria. The venture was not a success and was sold three years later to British interests, but some of the Astor party stayed, becoming Oregon's first permanent white residents. For the next 20 years, European and US interest in Oregon focused on the quest for beaver pelts. Agents of the British North West Company (which merged in 1821 with the Hudson's Bay Company) and some rival American parties explored the region, mapped trails, and established trading posts. Although Britain and the US had agreed to a treaty of joint occupation in 1818, the de facto governor from 1824 to the early 1840s was Dr. John McLoughlin, the Hudson's Bay Company chief factor at Ft. Vancouver in Washington, who ruled firmly but fairly over a network of posts.

Another major influence on the region was Protestant missionary activity, which began with the arrival of Jason Lee, a Methodist missionary, in 1834. Lee started his mission in the Willamette Valley, near present-day Salem. After a lecture tour of the East, he returned to Oregon in 1840 with 50 settlers and assistants. While Lee's mission was of little help to the local Indians, most of whom had been killed off by white men's diseases, it served as a base for subsequent American settlement and as a counterbalance to the Hudson's Bay Company.

The first major wagon trains arrived by way of the Oregon Trail in the early 1840s. On 2 May 1843, as a "great migration" of 875 men, women, and children was crossing the plains, about 100 settlers met at the Willamette Valley community of Champoeg and voted to form a provisional government. That government remained in power until 1849, when Oregon became a territory, three years after the Oregon Treaty between Great Britain and the US established the present US-Canadian boundary. As originally constituted, Oregon Territory included present-day Washington and much of Montana, Idaho, and Wyoming. A constitution prepared by an elected convention was approved in November 1857, and after a delay caused by North-South rivalries, on 14 February 1859, Congress voted to make Oregon, reduced to its present borders, the 33d state.

Oregon remained relatively isolated until the completion of the first transcontinental railroad link in 1883. State politics, which had followed a pattern of venality and influence buying, underwent a dramatic upheaval in the early 1900s. A group of reformers led by William S. U'Ren instituted what became known as the "Oregon System" of initiative, referendum, and recall, by which voters could legislate directly and remove corrupt elected officials.

Oregon's population grew steadily in the 20th century, as migration into the state continued. Improved transportation helped make the state the nation's leading lumber producer and a major exporter of agricultural products. Development was also aided by hydroelectric projects, many undertaken by the federal government. The principal economic changes since World War II have been the growth of the aluminum industry, a rapid expansion of the tourist trade, and creation of a growing electronics industry.

¹²STATE GOVERNMENT

The Oregon constitution drafted and approved in 1857 continues to govern the state today. The first decade of the 20th century saw the passage of numerous progressive amendments, including provisions for the direct election of senators, the rights of initiative, referendum, and recall, and a direct primary system.

The constitution establishes a 60-member house of representatives, elected for 2 years, and a senate of 30 members, serving 4-year terms. Major executive officials include the governor, secretary of state, attorney general, state treasurer, superintendent of public instruction, and commissioner of labor, all elected for 4 years. The governor, who may serve no more than 8 years in any 12-year period, must be a US citizen, at least 30 years of age, and must have been a resident of the state for 3 years before assuming office. Much policy in Oregon is set by boards and commissions whose members are appointed by the governor subject to confirmation by the senate.

Bills become law when approved by a majority of house and senate and either signed by the governor or left unsigned for 5 days when the legislature is in session or for 20 days after it has adjourned. Measures presented to the voters by the legislature or by petition become law when approved by a majority of the electorate. The governor may veto a legislative bill, but the legislature may override a veto by a two-thirds vote of those present in each house. Proposed constitutional amendments require voter approval to take effect, and they may be placed on the ballot either by the legislature or by initiative petition.

US citizens over age 18 are entitled to vote, subject to residency requirements of 6 months for a state or local election and 30 days for a presidential election.

13 POLITICAL PARTIES
Oregon has two major political parties, Democratic and Republican. Partly because of the role the direct primary system plays in choosing nominees, party organization is relatively weak. There is a strong tradition of political independence, evidenced in 1976 when Oregon gave independent presidential candidate Eugene McCarthy 3.9% of the vote—his highest percentage in any state—a total that probably cost Jimmy Carter Oregon's 6 electoral votes. Another independent, John Anderson, won 112,389 votes (9.5%) in the 1980 presidential election.

As of April 1980 there were 679,018 registered Democrats and 465,823 registered Republicans, along with 144,104 independents and minor party members. The Republicans held the governorship and both US Senate seats, while Democrats controlled both houses of the legislature. Oregon voters gave Republican presidential nominee Ronald Reagan a large plurality of the popular vote in November 1980, when US Senator Robert Packwood, also a Republican, won reelection to a third term.

14 LOCAL GOVERNMENT
As of 1980, Oregon had 36 counties and 240 incorporated cities. Towns and cities enjoy home rule, the right to choose their own form of government and enact legislation on matters of local concern. In 1958, home rule was extended to counties, but by 1978, only 6 counties had adopted home-rule charters. Most of Oregon's larger cities have council-manager forms of government. Typical elected county officials are three to five commissioners, assessor, district attorney, sheriff, and treasurer.

The state constitution gives voters strong control over local government revenue by requiring voter approval of property tax levies.

15 STATE SERVICES
Oregon has an ombudsman, appointed by the governor, who receives citizens' complaints but has no enforcement power. The Oregon Government Ethics Commission is a citizens' panel appointed by the governor and legislative leadership to investigate conflicts of interest involving public officials. Responsibility for educational matters is divided between the Board of Education, which oversees primary and secondary schools and community colleges; the Board of Higher Education, which controls the state college and university system; and the Educational Coordinating Commission, which monitors programs and advises the governor and legislature on policy.

State highways, airfields, and public transit systems are under the jurisdiction of the Department of Transportation, which is headed by an appointed commission. The largest state agency is the Department of Human Resources, whose separate divisions administer public assistance, children's services, corrections, and health, mental health, and unemployment insurance programs. State agencies involved in environmental matters include the Department of Environmental Quality, the Land Conservation and Development Commission, and the departments of Agriculture, Forestry, and Water Resources. State-owned lands are administered through the Land Board, consisting of the governor, secretary of state, and state treasurer.

16 JUDICIAL SYSTEM
Oregon's highest court is the supreme court, consisting of 7 justices who elect one of their number to serve as chief justice. It accepts cases on review from the 10-judge court of appeals, which has exclusive jurisdiction over all criminal and civil appeals from lower courts and over certain actions of state agencies. Circuit courts (with 75 circuit judges as of 1979) are the trial courts of original jurisdiction for civil and criminal matters. The more populous counties also have district courts, which hear

Oregon Presidential Vote by Political Parties, 1948–80

YEAR	ELECTORAL VOTE	OREGON WINNER	DEMOCRAT	REPUBLICAN	PROGRESSIVE	SOCIALIST
1948	6	Dewey (R)	243,147	260,904	14,978	5,051
1952	6	*Eisenhower (R)	270,579	420,815	3,665	—
1956	6	*Eisenhower (R)	329,204	406,393	—	—
1960	6	Nixon (R)	367,402	408,065	—	—
1964	6	*Johnson (D)	501,017	282,779	—	—
						AMERICAN IND.
1968	6	*Nixon (R)	358,866	408,433	—	49,683
						AMERICAN
1972	6	*Nixon (R)	392,760	486,686	—	46,211
1976	6	Ford (R)	490,407	492,120	—	—
					LIBERTARIAN	CITIZENS
1980	6	*Reagan (R)	456,890	571,044	25,838	13,642

*Won US presidential election.

minor civil, criminal, and traffic matters; some localities retain justices of the peace, also with jurisdiction over minor cases. All state judges in Oregon are elected by nonpartisan ballot for six-year terms.

Oregon's penal system is operated by the Corrections Division of the Department of Human Resources. As measured by the FBI Crime Index, Oregon's crime rate was above the national average in 1978, with especially high rates for forcible rape (41 per 100,000 population), aggravated assault (325), and larceny-theft (3,561).

17 ARMED FORCES

Oregon has no major military facilities, and had fewer than 3,000 authorized defense personnel in 1977/78. The US Coast Guard does maintain search-and-rescue facilities, and the Army Corps of Engineers operates a number of hydroelectric projects in the state. Military contract awards in 1977/78 totaled $92 million.

As of 30 September 1979, some 385,000 military veterans were living in Oregon, of whom 9,000 served in World War I, 167,000 in World War II, 66,000 during the Korean conflict, and 119,000 during the Viet-Nam era. Federal veterans' benefits totaled $229.6 million in 1977/78.

Oregon had 4,591 law enforcement officers in 1979, of whom 943 were state police. Air and Army National Guard forces totaled 6,900 in 1978.

18 MIGRATION

The Oregon Trail was the route along which thousands of settlers traveled to Oregon by covered wagon in the 1840s and 1850s. This early immigration was predominantly from midwestern states. After the completion of the transcontinental railroad, northeastern states supplied an increasing proportion of the newcomers.

Foreign immigration began in the 1860s with the importation of Chinese contract laborers, and reached its peak about the turn of the century. Germans and Scandinavians (particularly after 1900) were the most numerous foreign immigrants; Japanese, who began arriving in the 1890s, met a hostile reception in some areas. Canadians have also come to Oregon in significant numbers. Nevertheless, immigration from other states has predominated: by 1950, only four counties had a foreign-born population of more than 7%, and in no county did the proportion exceed 13%. Between 1940 and 1977, the state's net gain from migration was about 660,000.

19 INTERGOVERNMENTAL COOPERATION

Oregon, Idaho, and Washington are members of the Pacific Northwest Regional Commission, which allocates certain federal funds. Oregon also participates in such regional accords as the Columbia River Compact (also known as the Oregon-Washington Fisheries Compact), Klamath River Compact (with California), Pacific Marine Fisheries Compact, and several western groups concerned with corrections, education, and energy matters.

While Oregon received federal assistance for a variety of programs, federal involvement is particularly heavy in the areas of energy and natural resources, through federal development, operation, and marketing of hydroelectric power and federal ownership of forest and grazing lands. Approximately 52% of Oregon's land area is owned by the federal government—about half of that by the Forest Service and the remainder by the Bureau of Land Management. Federal aid to Oregon reached nearly $1.1 billion in 1978/79, of which $75.5 million was general revenue sharing.

20 ECONOMY

Since early settlement, Oregon's natural resources have formed the basis of its economy. Vast forests have made lumber and wood products the leading industry in the state, followed by agriculture and tourism. Since World War II, however, the state has striven to diversify its job base. The aluminum industry has been attracted to Oregon, along with computer and electronics firms, which now constitute the fastest-growing manufacturing sector. Meanwhile, the trend in employment has been toward white-collar and service jobs, with agriculture and manufacturing holding a declining share of the civilian labor force.

Despite diversification efforts, 70% of manufacturing jobs outside the Portland area were in the lumber and wood products field in 1978. As a result, the state's economy remains dependent on the health of the US construction industry: jobs are plentiful when US housing starts rise, but unemployment increases when nationwide construction drops off. The cyclical changes in demand for forest products is a chronic problem, with rural areas and small towns particularly hard-hit by the periodic closing of local lumber and plywood mills.

21 INCOME

Per capita income in Oregon in 1978 was $7,839, 19th among the 50 states. Total personal income was $19.2 billion, representing a real growth of 53% since 1970. Of a total labor and proprietary income of $15.4 billion, the major components were manufacturing, 25%; government, 16%; services, 15%; trade, 12%; construction, 7%; and other sectors, 25%.

Median family income in 1975 was $13,854, for a rank of 27th in the US. About 9% of all Oregonians were living below the federal poverty level during that year.

22 LABOR

Oregon's civilian labor force numbered 1,191,000 in 1978, of whom 1,119,000 were employed, giving the state an unemployment rate of 6%. Of the total labor force, 708,000 (59.4%) were male and 483,000 (40.6%) female.

A federal census of workers covered by unemployment insurance in March 1977 revealed the following nonfarm employment pattern for Oregon:

	ESTABLISH-MENTS	EMPLOYEES	ANNUAL PAYROLL ('000)
Agricultural services, forestry, fishing	800	5,726	$ 39,739
Mining	147	1,551	23,552
Contract construction	6,656	38,472	619,158
Manufacturing, of which:	5,081	191,472	2,797,480
Lumber, wood products	(1,894)	(71,434)	(1,068,532)
Transportation, public utilities	2,426	43,297	673,064
Wholesale trade	4,756	55,673	814,433
Retail trade	15,632	160,790	1,185,177
Finance, insurance, real estate	5,336	46,930	502,858
Services	15,858	148,774	1,232,091
Other	848	1,063	13,226
TOTALS	57,540	693,748	$ 7,900,778

Government employees, not included in this survey, numbered at least 158,000 in 1978.

In 1976, 275,000 Oregon workers—31.3% of all nonagricultural employees (15th in the US)—were members of a labor union or employee association. Average weekly earnings of production workers rose to $282 in 1978, 13% above the national average.

23 AGRICULTURE

Oregon ranked 32d in the US in agricultural output in 1978, with cash receipts of $1.3 billion. Crops accounted for more than three-fifths of the total. Wheat has been Oregon's leading crop since the state was first settled, but more than 170 farm and ranch commodities are now commercially produced. Oregon leads the nation in the production of winter pears, filberts, fresh plums, peppermint oil, blackberries, and several grass and seed crops. With 80–90% of Oregon's soft white wheat sold for export, mostly to Asian countries, agriculture has greatly boosted development of Portland's port facilities.

Farmland covers about 19.5 million acres (7.9 million hectares), or nearly one-third of Oregon's total area, with crops produced annually on about 4 million acres (1.6 million hectares). In 1978, the state had some 30,000 farms and an agricultural work force of 33,800. Quantity and value of selected crops in 1978 were as follows:

	VOLUME	VALUE
Wheat	51,925,000 bushels	$179,141,000
Hay	2,607,000 tons	127,700,000
Potatoes	28,488,000 hundredweight	94,000,000
Peppermint oil	3,306,000 lb	45,000,000
Ryegrass seed	240,980,000 lb	33,092,000
Pears	150,500 tons	32,974,000
Filberts	13,100 tons	10,480,000
Cultivated blackberries	20,100,000 lb	10,211,000

Irrigation is used throughout Oregon for many crops. About 1,900,000 acres (769,000 hectares) are irrigated, with a variety of different systems in use. While irrigation is expected to increase, the rate of growth will likely drop as water supplies become inadequate to meet new demand. Soil conservation programs are operated by local soil conservation districts, governed by elected boards under the general auspices of the State Soil and Water Conservation Commission.

²⁴ANIMAL HUSBANDRY

Most beef cattle are raised on the rangeland of eastern Oregon, while dairy operations are concentrated in the western portion of the state. Sheep and poultry are also raised largely in the west.

Cattle and calf production is Oregon's leading agricultural activity in terms of value, although income varies greatly with market conditions. Ranchers lease large tracts of federally owned grazing land under a permit system. In 1979, Oregon's cattle production was estimated at 1,510,000 head. Beef cattle and calf production was valued at $360.8 million. There were 94,000 dairy cows providing the basis for a dairy industry that includes a major cheese-processing industry on the northern Oregon coast; the 1979 milk output was 1.1 billion lb, and cheese production was nearly 31.9 million lb. Sheep and lambs were estimated at 460,000, with meat production totaling 24.4 million lb, worth $14 million, in 1979, and a wool clip of 3.5 million lb in 1978. Oregon's poultry farms produced 69.2 million lb of chickens and broilers in 1979, along with 24.5 million lb of turkeys, and 590 million eggs.

²⁵FISHING

Oregon's fish resources have long been of great importance to its inhabitants. For centuries, salmon provided much of the food for Indians, who gathered at traditional fishing grounds when the salmon were returning upstream from the ocean to spawn.

In 1978, Oregon ranked 10th among the states in the total value of its commercial catch. Commercial landings totaled 121.7 million lb in 1979, with an estimated value of $62.8 million. The catch included 10.3 million lb of salmon, valued at $21.5 million; groundfish, 60 million lb, $14.4 million; shrimp, 28.3 million lb, $11.9 million; crab, 14 million lb, $10.5 million; and albacore tuna, 3.1 million lb, $2 million.

Sport fishing, primarily for salmon and trout, is a major recreational attraction. The sport catch in 1977 was estimated at 15.8 million fish; trout made up 52% of the catch, salmon 22%, warm water game fish 10%, steelhead 10%, and other varieties 6%.

Hatchery production of salmon and trout has taken on increased importance, as development has destroyed natural fish-spawning areas. Some 69 million salmon, 12 million trout, and 4.8 million steelhead were released from hatcheries in 1977.

²⁶FORESTRY

Oregon is the nation's leading timber producer, and the forest products industry is the most important component of the state's economy. As of 1977, 30,023,000 acres (12,150,000 hectares) were in forestland, occupying not quite half the state's total area; 24,435,000 acres (9,889,000 hectares) were classified as commer-

cial timberland, or about 5% of the national total. The US government owns or manages 58% of the commercial timberland, with 4% under state or local control and 38% privately owned, mostly by large timber companies. The state had a net sawtimber volume of 430.9 billion board feet, about 17% of total US volume. Of this amount, 412.1 billion board feet were softwood timber, 21% of the nation's supply.

Logging of the Douglas fir forests of western Oregon is characterized by clear-cutting; selective logging of mature trees is practiced in much of the ponderosa pine forest of eastern Oregon. Sawmills and plywood mills are the main employers in many communities, and log trucks are a common sight on state highways. Since World War II, an increasing percentage of the timber harvest has gone to plywood production—35% in 1976, compared with 1% in 1940.

In 1977, the latest year for which comparative data are available, Oregon produced about 20% of the nation's lumber and 40% of its plywood. Forest products in 1978 included lumber from the Douglas fir region, 5.7 billion board feet, valued at $1.5 billion; lumber from the ponderosa pine region, 1.7 billion board feet, $522 million; plywood, 8.2 billion board feet, $1.5 billion; and pulp, paper, and paperboard, 4.7 million tons, $752.2 million. Exports of logs were worth $235.8 million in 1978.

Public timberlands are managed on a sustained yield basis, under which the amount cut each year is theoretically matched by new growth, so that the timber harvest may be indefinitely sustained. Major private timber owners operate tree farms, but not all of them practice sustained-yield management. Insect damage to forests is a major problem, particularly in the eastern part of the state. Forest research activities are conducted by the US Forest Service Experiment Station in Portland and by the Oregon State University School of Forestry at Corvallis.

²⁷MINING

The value of Oregon's mineral production was $123 million in 1978 (41st in the US), of which about 70% derived from sand, gravel, and crushed stone for construction materials. Oregon also contains the nation's only producing nickel mine, near Riddle, in Douglas County. While millions of dollars' worth of gold were mined in eastern and, to a lesser degree, southern Oregon in the late 19th century, production amounted to only 340 troy oz in 1978.

²⁸ENERGY AND POWER

Oregon ranks 3d in the US in hydroelectric power development. Multipurpose federal projects, including four dams on the Columbia River and eight in the Willamette Basin, account for about two-thirds of the state's hydroelectric capacity, with the rest coming from projects owned by private or public utilities. In recent decades, low-cost power from dams has proved inadequate to meet the state's energy needs, and nuclear and coal-fired steam plants have been built to supply additional electric power. Oregon's total electric power production in 1978 was 34.1 kwh; installed capacity was 8.1 million kw. The Bonneville Power Administration, the federal power marketing agency, operates a power distribution grid interconnecting Oregon, Washington, and parts of Idaho and Montana.

Despite intensive exploration, no oil has been found in Oregon, although commercially usable quantities of natural gas were discovered in the northwestern region in 1979. There is some coal in the southwest, but it has not been mined in recent years.

²⁹INDUSTRY

Manufacturing in Oregon is dominated by the lumber and wood products industry, which accounted for more than 38% of the state's value added by manufacture—$6.3 billion—in 1977. The other leading industries, with their share of the 1977 total value added, were food, 11%; paper and allied products, 9%; nonelectrical machinery, 8%; instruments, 6%; primary metals, 6%; and fabricated metals, 5%. In 1977, 44% of Oregon's industrial workers were employed in the Portland area. The Willamette Valley is the site of one of the nation's largest canning and freezing industries. In 1977, 502 food-processing establishments were licensed by the state; the canned pack of fruits, berries, and vegetables in that year exceeded 15 million cases, and 2.6 billion lb of fruit and vegetables were frozen.

The following table shows value added by manufacture for selected industry groups in 1972 and 1977:

	1972	· 1977
Lumber and wood products	$1,488,800,000	$2,410,900,000
Papermill products	128,500,000	270,000,000
Preserved fruits and vegetables	138,600,000	265,700,000
Office and computing machines	NA	119,800,000
Paperboard mill products	96,200,000	119,600,000

30 COMMERCE

Wholesale trade in Oregon exceeded $18.1 billion in 1977. Retail establishments had sales of $9.4 billion; the principal retail sectors were automotive dealers 22%, food stores 19%, department stores 11%, restaurants and taverns 9%, and gasoline service stations 7%.

Exports moving through Oregon customs districts were valued at about $2.3 billion in 1977, with imports valued at more than $2 billion. Wheat was the top export by value, followed by logs, wood chips for pulp, and lumber and plywood. The leading imports were passenger automobiles, followed by alumina for aluminum production. Oregon ranked 26th in the US in foreign exports of its own manufactures in 1976, shipping $824 million worth of goods abroad. Agricultural exports amounted to $182 million in 1976/77 (32d in the US).

31 CONSUMER PROTECTION

The Consumer Services Division of the Department of Commerce, with an associated Consumer Advisory Council, is responsible for coordinating state activities on consumer issues, but it has limited enforcement authority. The Consumer Protection Division of the Department of Justice is authorized to enforce Oregon's Unlawful Trade Practices Act. Also responsible for consumer protection are the Department of Agriculture (weights and measures); the Real Estate, Corporation, and Insurance divisions of the Department of Commerce; and the public utility commissioner.

32 BANKING

Consolidations and acquisitions have transformed Oregon's banking system from one characterized by a large number of local banks into one dominated by two large chains—the US National Bank of Oregon and the First National Bank of Oregon—each with branches throughout the state and each with assets of more than $3 billion in mid-1979. In all, the state had 60 insured commercial banks in 1978, with total assets of $11 billion and savings deposits of $9 billion. There were 28 insured savings and loan associations (15 of them federally chartered), with combined assets of nearly $6 billion, outstanding mortgage loans of almost $5 billion, and savings capital exceeding $4.7 billion.

33 INSURANCE

The number of licensed insurers in Oregon in the 1977/78 fiscal year totaled 1,033; direct premiums written for all types of insurance amounted to nearly $2.2 billion, and losses paid totaled $1.1 billion. At the end of 1978, Oregonians held 3,216,000 life insurance policies valued at $28.7 billion. The average life insurance per family was $29,700, 15% below the national average. Flood insurance in force in mid-1979 totaled $209 million.

34 SECURITIES

There are no securities or commodities exchanges in Oregon. Registration and regulation of securities issued within the state and of securities broker-dealers is the responsibility of the corporation commissioner in the Department of Commerce.

New York Stock Exchange member firms had 41 sales offices

and 371 registered representatives in Oregon in 1978. State residents reported $238.6 million in dividend income on their 1977 federal tax returns.

35 PUBLIC FINANCE

Oregon's biennial budget, covering a period from 1 July of each odd-numbered year to 30 June of the next odd-numbered year, is prepared by the Executive Department and submitted by the governor to the legislature for amendment and approval. Unlike some state budgets, Oregon's is not contained in a single omnibus appropriations bill; instead, each agency appropriation is considered as a separate measure. When the legislature is not in session, fiscal problems are considered by an emergency board of 17 legislators; this board may adjust budgets and allocate money from a special emergency fund but cannot enact new appropriations. The Oregon constitution prohibits a state budget deficit and requires that all general obligation bond issues be submitted to the voters.

The following table summarizes estimated revenues and expenditures for the 1977–79 budget period and the adopted budget for the 1979–81 period (in millions):

REVENUES	1977–79	1979–81
Individual taxes	$1,830	$ 2,498
Federal funds	1,475	1,906
Bond sales	1,553	1,686
Business taxes	1,410	1,690
Loan repayments	663	904
Interest	609	834
Charges for services	424	568
Liquor and other sales income	215	251
Licenses and fees	169	181
Other receipts	528	644
TOTALS	$8,876	$11,162

EXPENDITURES	1977–79	1979–81
Economic development and consumer services	$2,933	$ 3,393
Human resources	1,654	2,143
Education	1,740	2,135
Administration and support services	573	939
Transportation	513	948
Natural resources	225	258
Public safety	97	116
Legislative branch	20	22
Judicial branch	19	21
Other outlays	2	211
TOTALS	$7,776	$10,186

The city of Portland, Oregon's largest municipality, had total revenues of $155 million and expenditures of $154 million in 1977/78. Local governments are also prohibited from incurring deficits.

As of mid-1977, the total state and local government debt was $4.1 billion, or $1,715 per capita (7th among the 50 states).

36 TAXATION

Oregon's chief source of general revenue is the personal income tax, adopted in 1929; as of 1980, the tax ranged from 4% on the first $500 of taxable income to 10% on amounts over $5,000. A corporate income tax of 7.5% is also levied. Local governments rely on the property tax. Oregon does not have a general sales tax, although it does tax sales of gasoline and cigarettes.

The state constitution gives voters the right to vote on any substantial tax increase, either by the state or by local governments. State tax measures may be placed on the ballot by the legislature or by petition; local levies must be voted on yearly unless voter approval has been secured for a tax base that may increase by 6% a year without an additional vote.

Total state and local tax receipts in 1977/78 were $2.13 billion, of which 54% was received by the state. In 1975/76, Oregon remitted $3.4 billion in federal taxes and received $3.1 billion in federal expenditures. State residents filed 1,024,475 federal income tax returns in 1977, paying more than $1.8 billion in tax.

[37] ECONOMIC POLICY

During the 1970s, Oregon actively sought balanced economic growth in order to diversify its industrial base, reduce its dependence on the wood products industry, and provide jobs for a steadily growing labor force. Major agencies promoting Oregon as a potential industrial location—particularly for relatively non-polluting industries—are the Department of Economic Development and the local port districts. Business development in economically depressed areas is encouraged by a state-financed bond program to assist in the purchase of sites for new or expanding firms. Port districts and some cities have created industrial parks as sites for new plants.

[38] HEALTH

Life expectancy in Oregon averaged 72.13 years (76.2 for women, 68.43 for men) in 1969–71, 10th highest in the nation. In 1978 there were 38,882 live births, a rate of 15.8 per 1,000 population; this represented almost a 50% decline from the 1960 birthrate. The 1977 infant mortality rate was 12 infant deaths per 1,000 live births among whites and 14.7 among nonwhites. In the same year, some 15,000 legal abortions were performed, a rate of 388 abortions per 1,000 births. The leading causes of death, with rates per 100,000 population, were heart disease, 305; cancer, 177; cerebrovascular diseases, 88; and accidents, 58.

In 1978, Oregon had 85 hospitals, with 11,568 beds; hospital personnel included 6,454 registered nurses and 1,730 licensed practical nurses. The average cost of hospital care in 1977 was $218 per day and $1,349 per stay. There were 4,378 licensed physicians in 1977 and 1,685 active dentists in 1979. The only medical and dental schools in the state are at the University of Oregon Health Sciences Center in Portland.

[39] SOCIAL WELFARE

As in other states, social welfare problems in Oregon received an increasing share of government attention and funding during the 1970s. The Department of Human Resources, created in 1971 to coordinate social service activities, was operating more than 250 programs by 1980, when nearly one-fourth of the state budget was devoted to social welfare programs.

Public assistance payments to Oregonians in 1977 totaled $285 million, of which $142 million consisted of aid to families with dependent children and $143 million was medical assistance. A total of $999.5 million in Social Security benefits was paid to 387,400 Oregonians in the same year. Federal Supplemental Security Income payments totaled $29.4 million, of which the state paid $5 million. Some 139,000 Oregonians took part in the food stamp program in 1978, at a federal cost of $44.2 million, and 262,000 students were enrolled in the school lunch program, subsidized by $13.9 million in federal funds.

In 1978, Oregon spent $15.6 million on vocational rehabilitation; workers' compensation payments amounted to $195.4 million in 1977. The state's unemployment insurance program processed 283,000 initial claims in 1978 and paid $95 million.

[40] HOUSING

In general, owner-occupied homes predominate in Oregon, and there are few urban slums. During the 1970s, however, a growing percentage of new construction went for rental units. Between 1970 and 1978, the proportion of the housing stock in single-family units fell from 77% to 69%. In 1978 there were 950,844 housing units in Oregon, of which 909,816 were occupied—577,769 by owners and 332,047 by renters. A growing share of the state's housing stock was also in mobile homes (from 5.1% in 1970 to 9.4% in 1978).

As of 1978, about 30,130 housing units were receiving some type of subsidy, mostly from the Department of Housing and Urban Development. In the late 1970s, Oregon began to offer housing purchase assistance (through interest rates below the prevailing market) and construction subsidies to build units for low- and moderate-income renters.

[41] EDUCATION

On the whole, Oregonians are among the best educated of Americans. Their adult illiteracy rate was only 0.6%—half the national average—in 1970, and the median number of school years completed for those 18 years of age or older was 12.7 in 1976. In that year, more than 75% of adult state residents were high school graduates, and 15% had at least 4 years of college. There were 954 public elementary schools, 330 public secondary schools, and 189 private elementary and secondary schools in 1978. Average daily attendance in public schools in grades K–12 was 456,084; in private (mainly parochial) schools, 23,957.

Higher education in Oregon comprises 13 community colleges (with elected local boards), a state college and university system, and 21 independent institutions, of which 11 are small schools with a theological orientation. The state college and university system had a fall enrollment of 62,105 in 1978. The largest institution was Oregon State University in Corvallis (16,662), followed by the University of Oregon in Eugene (16,517) and Portland State University (16,073). Major private institutions include Lewis and Clark College, Reed College, and the University of Portland, all in Portland, along with Willamette University in Salem, Pacific University in Forest Grove, and Linfield College in McMinnville. A financial aid program for Oregon state college students is administered by the State Scholarship Commission, with more than $20 million earmarked for assistance in the 1979–81 budget period.

[42] ARTS

The Portland Art Museum, with an associated art school, is the city's center for the visual arts. The University of Oregon in Eugene has an art museum specializing in Oriental art.

The state's most noted theatrical enterprise is the annual Shakespeare Festival in Ashland, with a complex of theaters drawing actors and audiences from around the nation. The Oregon Symphony is situated in Portland, and Salem and Eugene have small symphonies of their own.

[43] LIBRARIES AND MUSEUMS

In 1978, Oregon had 381 academic, public, and special libraries, including branches, many linked by cooperative lending agreements; the total book stock of all public libraries was 4,439,609, and their combined circulation in 1977/78 was 13,116,443. Most cities and counties in Oregon have public library systems, the largest being the Multnomah County library system in Portland, with 17 branches and 1,101,524 volumes in 1977/78. The State Library in Salem, with 984,006 volumes in 1977, serves as a reference agency for state government.

Oregon has more than 50 museums and historic sites. Historical museums emphasizing Oregon's pioneer heritage appear throughout the state, with Ft. Clatsop National Memorial—featuring a replica of Lewis and Clark's winter headquarters—among the notable attractions. The Oregon Historical Society operates a major historical museum in Portland, publishes books of historical interest, and issues the *Oregon Historical Quarterly*. In Portland's Washington Park area are the Oregon Museum of Science and Industry, the Washington Park Zoo, an arboretum and other gardens, and a forestry museum.

[44] COMMUNICATIONS

As of 1978, about 95% of Oregon households had telephone service; there were 1,884,852 telephones, of which 1,362,558 were residential and 522,294 business. During the same year, Oregon had 80 AM and 33 FM commercial radio stations; 4 of the state's 12 commercial television stations were in Portland. A state-owned broadcasting system, which includes 4 television stations, provides educational radio and television programming. As of 1978, cable television served 209,318 subscribers.

45 PRESS

Oregon's first newspaper was the weekly *Oregon Spectator*, which began publication in 1846. Early newspapers engaged in what became known as the "Oregon style" of journalism, characterized by intemperate, vituperative, and fiercely partisan comments.

As of 1980, 24 daily and 95 weekly newspapers were published in Oregon. The state's largest newspaper, the *Oregonian*, published in Portland, is owned by the Newhouse group, which also owns the next-largest paper, the *Oregon Journal*, a Portland afternoon daily. The total circulation of Oregon's morning dailies in 1978 was 289,418; evening dailies, 387,380; and Sunday papers, 581,356. The following table lists leading Oregon newspapers with their 1978 circulations:

AREA	NAME	DAILY	SUNDAY
Eugene	Register-Guard (e,S)	60,398	65,785
Portland	Oregonian (m,S)	240,664	410,936
	Oregon Journal (e)	106,602	
Salem	Oregon Statesman (m,S)	44,860	55,762
	Capital Journal (e,S)	17,939	

46 ORGANIZATIONS

Among the many forestry-related organizations in Oregon are the International Woodworkers of America (AFL-CIO), Association of Western Pulp and Paper Workers, Pacific Lumber Exporters Association, Western Forest Industries Association, and Western Wood Products Association, all with their headquarters in Portland.

47 TOURISM, TRAVEL, AND RECREATION

Oregon's abundance and variety of natural features and recreational opportunities make the state a major tourist attraction, and tourism is generally considered the state's 3d-largest industry. In 1977, more than 12 million out-of-state visitors spent more than $700 million in Oregon, with the total economic impact estimated by the state at more than $1.7 billion. The Travel Information Section of the Department of Transportation maintains an active tourist advertising program, and Portland hotels busily seek major conventions.

Among the leading attractions are the rugged Oregon coast, with its offshore salmon fishing; Crater Lake National Park; the Rogue River, for river running and fishing; the Columbia Gorge, east of Portland; the Cascades wilderness; and Portland's annual Rose Festival. Oregon has one national park, Crater Lake, and three other areas—John Day Fossil Beds, Oregon Caves National Monument, and Ft. Clatsop National Memorial—managed by the National Park Service. The Forest Service administers the Oregon Dunes National Recreation Area, on the Oregon coast, and Lava Lands Visitor Complex near Bend. Oregon has one of the nation's most extensive state park systems: 234 parks and recreation areas cover 92,235 acres (37,326 hectares). Licenses were issued to 372,770 hunters and 732,111 fishermen in 1977/78.

48 SPORTS

Oregon's major professional teams, all based in Portland, are the Trail Blazers, winners of the National Basketball Asssociation championship in 1977, and the Timbers of the North American Soccer League. The Portland Beavers compete in baseball's class-AAA Pacific Coast League.

Horse racing takes place at Portland Meadows in Portland and, in late August and early September, at the Oregon State Fair in Salem; there is greyhound racing at the Multnomah Kennel Club near Portland. Pari-mutuel betting is permitted at the tracks, but off-track betting is prohibited.

The University of Oregon and Oregon State University belong to the Pacific 10 Conference.

49 FAMOUS OREGONIANS

Prominent federal officeholders from Oregon include Senator Charles McNary (1874–1944), a leading advocate of federal reclamation and development projects and the Republican vice-presidential nominee in 1940; Senator Wayne Morse (b.Wisconsin, 1900–1974), known as a maverick for much of his legislative career and an early opponent of US involvement in Viet-Nam; Representative Edith Green (b.1910), a leader in federal education assistance; and Representative Al Ullman (b.Montana, 1914), chairman of the House Ways and Means Committee until his defeat in 1980. Recent cabinet members from Oregon have been Douglas McKay (1893–1959), secretary of the interior; and Neil Goldschmidt (b.1940), secretary of transportation.

A major figure in early Oregon history was sea captain Robert Gray (b.Rhode Island, 1755–1806), discoverer of the Columbia River. Although never holding a government position, fur trader Dr. John McLoughlin (b.Canada, 1784–1857) in effect ruled Oregon from 1824 to 1845; he was officially designated the "father of Oregon" by the 1957 state legislature. Also of importance in the early settlement was Methodist missionary Jason Lee (b.Canada, 1803–45). Oregon's most famous Indian was Chief Joseph (1840?–1904), leader of the Nez Percé in northeastern Oregon; when tension between the Nez Percé and white settlers erupted into open hostilities in 1877, Chief Joseph led his band of about 650 men, women, and children from the Oregon-Idaho border across the Bitterroot Range, evading three army detachments before being captured in northern Montana.

Other important figures in the early days of statehood were Harvey W. Scott (b.Illinois, 1838–1910), longtime editor of the *Portland Oregonian*, and his sister, Abigail Scott Duniway (b.Illinois, 1834–1915), the Northwest's foremost advocate of women's suffrage, a cause her brother strongly opposed. William Simon U'Ren (b.Wisconsin, 1859–1949) was a lawyer and reformer whose influence on Oregon politics and government endures to this day. Journalist and Communist John Reed (1887–1920), author of *Ten Days That Shook the World*, an eyewitness account of the Bolshevik Revolution, was born in Portland, and award-winning science-fiction writer Ursula K. LeGuin (b.California, 1929) is a Portland resident.

Linus Pauling (b.1901), two-time winner of the Nobel Prize (for chemistry in 1954, for peace in 1962), is another Portland native. Other scientists prominent in the state's history include botanist David Douglas (b.Scotland, 1798–1834), who made two trips to Oregon and after whom the Douglas fir is named; and geologist and paleontologist Thomas Condon (b.Ireland, 1822–1907), discoverer of major fossil beds in eastern Oregon.

50 BIBLIOGRAPHY

Cogswell, Philip. *Capitol Names: Individuals Woven into Oregon's History*. Portland: Oregon Historical Society, 1977.

Corning, Howard. *Dictionary of Oregon History*. Portland: Binfords and Mort, 1956.

Dodds, Gordon B. *Oregon: A Bicentennial History*. New York: Norton, 1977.

Federal Writers' Project. *Oregon: End of the Trail*. New York: Hastings House, 1941.

Johansen, Dorothy, and Charles Gates. *Empire of the Columbia: A History of the Pacific Northwest*. 2d ed. New York: Harper and Row, 1967.

Loy, William. *Atlas of Oregon*. Eugene: University of Oregon Books, 1976.

Oregon, State of. Department of Economic Development. *Oregon: A Statistical Profile*. Portland, 1978.

Oregon, State of. Executive Department. *Adopted Budget, 60th Legislative Assembly, 1979–81*. Salem, 1979.

Oregon, State of. Executive Department. *Governor's Budget Recommendations, 1979–81*. Salem, 1979.

Oregon, State of. Secretary of State. *Oregon Blue Book, 1979–81*. Salem, 1979.

Vaughan, Thomas, and Terrence O'Donnell. *Portland: A Historical Sketch and Guide*. Portland: Oregon Historical Society, 1976.

PENNSYLVANIA

Commonwealth of Pennsylvania

ORIGIN OF STATE NAME: Named for Admiral William Penn, father of the founder of Pennsylvania. **NICKNAME**: The Keystone State. **CAPITAL**: Harrisburg. **ENTERED UNION**: 12 December 1787 (2d). **MOTTO**: Virtue, Liberty, and Independence. **COAT OF ARMS**: A shield supported by two horses displays a sailing ship, a plow, and three sheaves of wheat; an eagle forms the crest. Beneath the shield an olive branch and a cornstalk are crossed, and below them is the state motto. **FLAG**: The coat of arms appears in the center of a blue field. **OFFICIAL SEAL**: Obverse: A shield displays a sailing ship, a plow, and three sheaves of wheat, with a cornstalk to the left, an olive branch to the right, and an eagle above, surrounded by the inscription "Seal of the State of Pennsylvania." Reverse: A woman representing Liberty holds a wand topped by a liberty cap in her left hand and a drawn sword in her right, as she tramples a lion representing Tyranny; the legend "Both Can't Survive" encircles the design. **ANIMAL**: White-tailed deer. **BIRD**: Ruffed grouse. **DOG**: Great Dane. **FISH**: Brook trout. **FLOWER**: Mountain laurel. **INSECT**: Firefly. **TREE**: Hemlock. **LEGAL HOLIDAYS**: New Year's Day, 1 January; Lincoln's Birthday, 12 February; Washington's Birthday, 3d Monday in February; Memorial Day, last Monday in May; Flag Day, 2d Sunday in June; Independence Day, 4 July; Labor Day, 1st Monday in September; Columbus Day, 2d Monday in October; Veterans Day, 11 November; Thanksgiving Day, 4th Thursday in November; Christmas Day, 25 December. **TIME**: 7 A.M. EST = noon GMT.

¹LOCATION, SIZE, AND EXTENT

Located in the northeastern US, the Commonwealth of Pennsylvania is the 2d largest of the three Middle Atlantic states and ranks 33d in size among the 50 states.

The total area of Pennsylvania is 45,333 sq mi (117,412 sq km), of which land occupies 44,966 sq mi (116,462 sq km) and inland water 367 sq mi (950 sq km). The state extends 307 mi (494 km) E-W and 169 mi (272 km) N-S. Pennsylvania is rectangular in shape, except for an irregular side on the E and a break in the even boundary in the N-W, where the line extends N-E for about 50 mi (80 km) along the shore of Lake Erie.

Pennsylvania is bordered on the N by New York; on the E by New York and New Jersey (with the Delaware River forming the entire boundary); on the SE by Delaware; on the S by Maryland and West Virginia (demarcated by the Mason-Dixon line); on the W by West Virginia and Ohio; and on the NW by Lake Erie.

The total boundary length of Pennsylvania is 880 mi (1,416 km). The state's geographical center lies in Centre County, 2.5 mi (4 km) SW of Bellefonte.

²TOPOGRAPHY

Pennsylvania may be divided into more than a dozen distinct physiographic regions, most of which extend in curved bands from east to south. Beginning in the southeast, the first region (including Philadelphia) is a narrow belt of coastal plain along the lower Delaware River; this area, at sea level, is the state's lowest region. The next belt, dominating the southeastern corner, is the Piedmont Plateau, a wide area of rolling hills and lowlands. The Great Valley, approximately 10–15 mi (16–24 km) in width, runs from the middle of the state's eastern border to the middle of its southern border. The eastern, central, and western parts of the Great Valley are known as the Lehigh, Lebanon, and Cumberland valleys, respectively. West and north of the Great Valley, the Pocono Plateau rises to about 2,200 feet (700 meters). Next, in a band 50–60 mi (80–100 km) wide most of the way from the north-central part of the eastern border to the west-central part of the southern border are the Appalachian Mountains, a distinctive region of parallel ridges and valleys.

The Allegheny High Plateau, part of the Appalachian Pla-

teaus, makes up the western and northern parts of the state. The Allegheny Front, the escarpment along the eastern edge of the plateau, is the most striking topographical feature in Pennsylvania, being dissected by many winding streams to form narrow, steep-sided valleys; the southwestern extension of the Allegheny High Plateau contains the state's highest peak, Mt. Davis, at 3,213 feet (979 meters). A narrow lowland region, the Erie Plain, borders Lake Erie in the extreme northwestern part of the state.

According to federal sources, Pennsylvania has jurisdiction over 735 sq mi (1,904 sq km) of Lake Erie; the state government gives a figure of 891 sq mi (2,308 sq km). Pennsylvania contains about 250 natural lakes larger than 20 acres (8 hectares), most of them in the glaciated regions of the northeast and northwest. The largest natural lake within the state's borders is Conneaut Lake, about 30 mi (48 km) south of the city of Erie, with an area of less than 1.5 sq mi (3.9 sq km); the largest man-made lake is Lake Wallenpaupack, in the Poconos, occupying about 9 sq mi (23 sq km). Pennsylvania claims more than 21 sq mi (54 sq km) of the Pymatuning Reservoir, on the Ohio border.

The Susquehanna River and its tributaries drain more than 46% of the area of Pennsylvania, much in the Appalachian Mountains. The Delaware River forms Pennsylvania's eastern border and, like the Susquehanna, flows southeastward to the Atlantic Ocean. Most of the western part of the state is drained by the Allegheny and Monongahela rivers, which join at Pittsburgh to form the Ohio. The Beaver, Clarion, and Youghiogheny rivers are also important parts of this system.

During early geological history, the topography of Pennsylvania had the reverse of its present configurations, with mountains in the southeast and a large inland sea covering the rest of the state. This sea, which alternately expanded and contracted, interwove layers of vegetation (which later became coal) with layers of sandstone and shale. The northern parts of Pennsylvania were extensively affected by glaciation.

³CLIMATE

Although Pennsylvania lies entirely within the humid continental zone, its climate varies according to region and elevation. The region with the warmest temperatures and the longest growing

461

season is the low-lying southeast, in the Ohio and Monongahela valleys. The region bordering Lake Erie also has a long growing season, as the moderating effect of the lake prevents early spring and late autumn frosts. The first two areas have hot summers, while the Erie area is more moderate. The rest of the state, at higher elevations, has cold winters and cool summers.

Among the major population centers, Philadelphia has an annual mean temperature of 55°F (13°C), with a normal minimum of 45°F (7°C) and a normal maximum of 64°F (18°C). Pittsburgh has an annual mean of 50°F (10°C), with a minimum of 41°F (5°C) and a maximum of 60°F (16°C). In the cooler northern areas, Scranton has a normal annual mean ranging from 38°F (3°C) to 56°F (13°C); Erie, from 37°F (3°C) to 54°F (12°C). The record low temperature for the state is –42°F (–41°C), set at Smethport on 5 January 1904; the record high, 111°F (44°C), was reached at Phoenixville on 10 July 1936.

Philadelphia has about 40 in (102 cm) of precipitation annually, and Pittsburgh has 36 in (91 cm). Pittsburgh, however, has much more snow—45 in (114 cm), compared with 20 in (51 cm) for Philadelphia. Erie, in the snow belt, receives 91 in (231 cm) of snow a year. In Philadelphia, the sun shines an average of 58% of the time; in Pittsburgh, 50%.

The state has experienced several destructive floods. On 31 May 1889, the South Fork Dam near Johnstown broke after a heavy rainfall, and its rampaging waters killed 2,200 people and devastated the entire city in less than 10 minutes. Rains from Hurricane Agnes in June 1972 resulted in floods that caused 48 deaths and more than $1.2 billion worth of property damage in the Susquehanna Valley.

⁴FLORA AND FAUNA

Maple, walnut, poplar, oak, pine, ash, beech, and linden trees fill Pennsylvania's extensive forests, along with sassafras, sycamore, weeping willow, and balsam fir (*Abies fraseri*). Red pine and paper birch are found in the north, while the sweet gum is dominant in the extreme southwest. Mountain laurel (the state flower), Juneberry, dotted hawthorn, New Jersey tea, and various dogwoods are among the shrubs and small trees found in most parts of the state, and dewberry, wintergreen, wild columbine, and wild ginger are also common. The wild red rose is classified as threatened.

Numerous mammals persist in Pennsylvania, among them the white-tailed deer (the state animal), black bear, red and gray foxes, opossum, raccoon, muskrat, mink, snowshoe hare, common cottontail, and red, gray, fox, and flying squirrels. Native amphibians include the hellbender, Fowler's toad, and the tree, cricket, and true frogs; among reptilian species are the five-lined and black skinks and five varieties of lizard. The ruffed grouse, a common game species, is the official state bird; other game birds are the wood dove, ring-necked pheasant, bobwhite quail, and mallard and black ducks. The robin, cardinal, English sparrow, red-eyed vireo, cedar waxwing, tufted titmouse, yellow-shafted flicker, barn swallow, blue jay, and killdeer are common nongame birds. More than 170 types of fish have been identified, with brown and brook trout, grass pickerel, bigeye chub, pirate perch, and white bass among the common native varieties.

In 1978, the Pennsylvania Game Commission and the US Fish and Wildlife Service signed a cooperative agreement under which the federal government provides two dollars for each dollar spent by the state to determine the status of and improve conditions for threatened or endangered species. On the endangered list are the Indiana bat, Delmarva Peninsula fox squirrel, eastern cougar, bald eagle, American peregrine falcon, and Kirtland's warbler.

⁵ENVIRONMENTAL PROTECTION

Pennsylvania's environment was ravaged by uncontrolled timber cutting in the 19th century, and by extensive coal mining and industrial development until more recent times. Pittsburgh's most

famous landmarks were its smokestacks, and it was said that silverware on ships entering the port of Philadelphia would tarnish immediately from the fumes of the Delaware River. The anthracite-mining regions were filled with huge, hideous culm piles, and the bituminous and anthracite fields were torn up by strip-mining. In 1979, a different kind of threat to Pennsylvania's environment received worldwide attention when the nuclear power plant at Three Mile Island seriously malfunctioned.

In 1895, Pennsylvania appointed its first commissioner of forestry, in an attempt to repair some of the earlier damage. Gifford Pinchot, who twice served as governor of Pennsylvania, was the first professionally trained forester in the US (he studied at the Ecole Nationale Forestière in Paris), developed the US Forest Service, and served as Pennsylvania forest commissioner from 1920 to 1922.

In 1972, Pennsylvania voters ratified a state constitutional amendment adopted 18 May 1971, acknowledging the people's "right to clean air, pure water, and to the preservation of the natural, scenic, historic and esthetic values of the environment" and naming the state as trustee of these resources. Passage of the amendment came only two years after establishment of the Pennsylvania Department of Environmental Resources, which regulates mining operations, operates land and water management programs, and oversees all aspects of environmental control. Agencies in this department include bureaus responsible for land protection (solid waste management, mine subsidence regulation), surface mine regulation, water quality management, air quality control, community environmental control (municipal sewage facilities, water supply), radiation protection, forestry, state parks, soil and water conservation, dam safety, and storm water management. In 1979/80, the department had a budget of $133.4 million.

The Bureau of Air Quality and Noise Control, which enforces the Federal Clean Air Act as well as state laws and regulations, increased its expenditures from $307,805 in 1965/66 to $5,665,115 in 1977/78. During the same period, the sources of contamination covered by regulations increased from 3,000 to 140,000. Expenditures for water-pollution abatement increased from $1,480,401 in 1968/69 to $8,366,926 in 1977/78.

⁶POPULATION

As recently as 1940, Pennsylvania was the 2d most populous state in the US. By the 1970 census, however, Pennsylvania had slipped to 4th place, with a population of 11,793,909; the preliminary census population in 1980 was 11,824,561.

As of 1970, 47.9% of the population was male, 52.1% female; 71.5% of all Pennsylvanians lived in urban areas. The population density in 1978 was 261 per sq mi (101 per sq km), making Pennsylvania the 9th most densely populated state in the US. There are fewer young people and more persons aged 65 or over represented in the state's population than in the US as a whole. Pennsylvania's birthrate in 1977 was 13 per 1,000 population, 16% below the US average. At the same time, the death rate of 10.1 was nearly 15% above the national norm. A net outmigration of 272,000 between 1970 and 1977 was a further drag on population growth. Mobility statistics show how few new residents the state attracted during the last several decades: nearly three-fourths of all Pennsylvanians 14 years of age or older in 1976 were lifelong residents of the state, the highest such proportion in the US.

The largest city in the state, Philadelphia, was the 4th-largest US city as of 1970, with a population of 1,949,000. Like the

LOCATION: 39°43′16″ to 42°30′35″ N; 74°41′23″ to 80°31′08″ W. BOUNDARIES: New York line, 327 mi (526 km); New Jersey line, 166 mi (267 km); Delaware line, 25 mi (40 km); Maryland line, 101 mi (163 km); West Virginia line, 81 mi (130 km); Ohio line, 129 mi (208 km); Lake Erie shoreline, 51 mi (82 km).

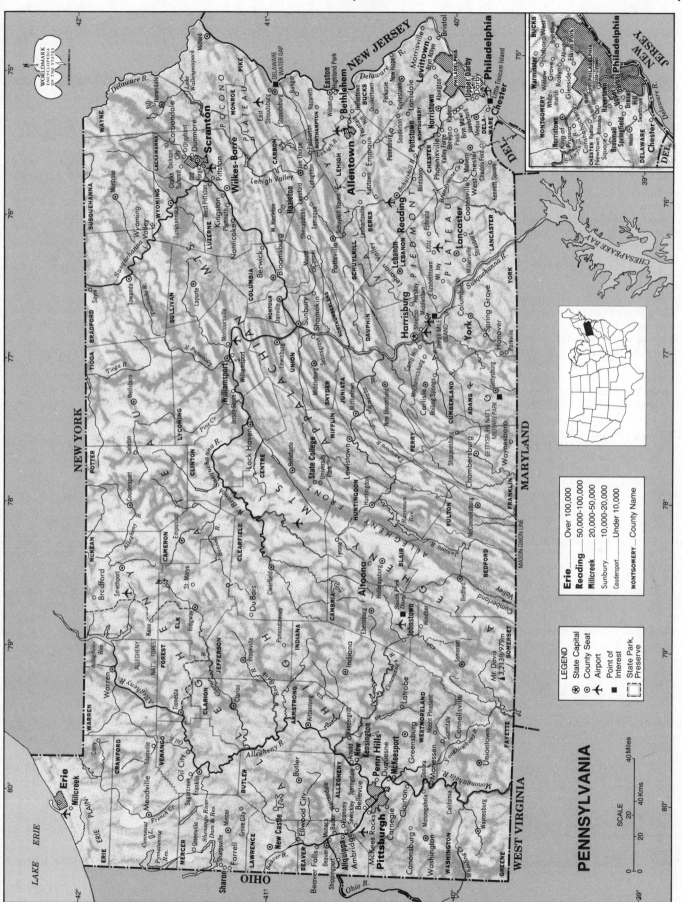

PENNSYLVANIA

LEGEND

Erie	Over 100,000
Reading	50,000-100,000
Millcreek	20,000-50,000
Sunbury	10,000-20,000
Coudersport	Under 10,000
MONTGOMERY	County Name

* State Capital
* County Seat
+ Airport
■ Point of Interest
State Park, Preserve

SCALE

40 Miles
20

40 Kms
20

WORLDMARK ENCYCLOPEDIA OF THE STATES

state's, Philadelphia's population declined during the decade, to an estimated 1,784,500 in 1977. The population of its metropolitan area also declined, from 4,824,000 in 1970 to 4,794,000 in 1977 (4th). Pittsburgh too lost population, from 677,000 in 1950 to 442,000 in 1977 (28th) in the city proper, and from 2,401,000 in 1970 to 2,294,000 in 1977 in its metropolitan area (13th).

Preliminary 1980 census counts for Pennsylvania's major cities were Philadelphia, 1,680,235; Pittsburgh, 423,962; Erie, 118,964; Allentown, 103,634; Scranton, 87,378; Reading, 78,582; Bethlehem, 70,389; Altoona, 57,000; Lancaster, 54,632; Harrisburg, 53,113; and Wilkes-Barre, 51,117.

[7] ETHNIC GROUPS

During the colonial period, under a religiously tolerant Quaker government, Pennsylvania was a haven for dissident sectarians from continental Europe and the British Isles. Some German sectarians, including the Amish, have kept up their traditions to this day. An initially friendly policy toward the Indians waned in the late 18th century under the pressures of population growth and the anxieties of the French and Indian War. The famous Carlisle Indian School (1879–1918) educated many leaders from various tribes throughout the US. In Pennsylvania itself, however, there were only 5,533 Indians as of 1970.

Modest numbers of black slaves were utilized as domestics, field workers, and iron miners in colonial Pennsylvania. Antislavery sentiment was stirred in the 18th century through the efforts of a Quaker, John Woolman, and other Pennsylvanians. An Act for the Gradual Abolition of Slavery was passed in 1780, and the important antislavery newspaper *The Liberator* appeared in Philadelphia in 1831. Today, black Americans are concentrated in the large cities. The black population in 1976 was about 1,021,000, amounting to nearly 9% of the population as a whole. Philadelphia was 34% black in 1970, Pittsburgh 20%.

The late 19th and early 20th centuries brought waves of immigrants from Ireland, Wales, various Slavic nations, and the eastern Mediterranean and the Balkans. Many of the new immigrants settled in the east-central anthracite coal-mining region. In 1970, 18% of all Pennsylvania residents were foreign-born or their native-born children, with Italy, Poland, and Germany the leading countries of origin. In the valleys surrounding Pittsburgh there are still self-contained ethnic enclaves, and there has been increased interest in preserving distinctive ethnic traditions.

Hispanic Americans in Pennsylvania numbered 125,000 in 1976. Most were Puerto Ricans, with smaller numbers of Cubans and Central Americans. Asians in 1970 included 7,053 Chinese, 5,461 Japanese, and 4,560 Filipinos. Pennsylvania resettled 7,159 Vietnamese refugees in 1975.

[8] LANGUAGES

Once home to several Algonkian tribes, Pennsylvania still has such Algonkian place-names as Punxsutawney, Aliquippa, Pocono, Towanda, Susquehanna, and Shamokin. An Iroquoian tribe gave its name to the region Conestoga. The word came to identify first the pioneers' covered wagons manufactured in the area, and then, in shortened form, a cheap cigar called a *stogie*. Only 907 Pennsylvanians in 1970 claimed an Indian language as their mother tongue.

Although not quite homogeneous, Pennsylvania's North Midland dialect is significant as the source of much midwestern and western speech. The only non-Midland sector is the northern tier of counties, settled from southern New York State, where features of the Northern dialect predominate.

Pennsylvania Counties, County Seats, and County Populations[1]

COUNTY	COUNTY SEAT	LAND AREA (SQ MI)	POPULATION (1977)	COUNTY	COUNTY SEAT	LAND AREA (SQ MI)	POPULATION (1977)
Adams	Gettysburg	526	62,800	Lancaster	Lancaster	946	347,900
Allegheny	Pittsburgh	728	1,493,600	Lawrence	New Castle	367	106,400
Armstrong	Kittanning	652	75,400	Lebanon	Lebanon	363	104,800
Beaver	Beaver	440	207,400	Lehigh	Allentown	348	263,600
Bedford	Bedford	1,018	43,000	Luzerne	Wilkes-Barre	886	338,600
Berks	Reading	862	302,100	Lycoming	Williamsport	1,216	113,200
Blair	Hollidaysburg	530	134,200	McKean	Smethport	992	52,000
Bradford	Towanda	1,148	60,700	Mercer	Mercer	670	126,500
Bucks	Doylestown	614	468,400	Mifflin	Lewistown	431	44,500
Butler	Butler	794	141,200	Monroe	Stroudsburg	611	57,700
Cambria	Ebensburg	692	187,800	Montgomery	Norristown	496	628,200
Cameron	Emporium	401	6,800	Montour	Danville	130	16,600
Carbon	Jim Thorpe	404	52,200	Northampton	Easton	376	225,700
Centre	Bellefonte	1,115	109,700	Northumberland	Sunbury	453	98,800
Chester	West Chester	761	298,200	Perry	New Bloomfield	551	33,500
Clarion	Clarion	597	41,600	Philadelphia	Philadelphia	129	1,784,500
Clearfield	Clearfield	1,139	78,900	Pike	Milford	542	14,300
Clinton	Lock Haven	899	37,600	Potter	Coudersport	1,092	16,800
Columbia	Bloomsburg	484	59,400	Schuylkill	Pottsville	784	157,600
Crawford	Meadville	1,012	85,200	Snyder	Middleburg	327	31,100
Cumberland	Carlisle	555	171,900	Somerset	Somerset	1,078	79,900
Dauphin	Harrisburg	518	223,500	Sullivan	Laporte	478	6,000
Delaware	Media	184	583,700	Susquehanna	Montrose	833	37,100
Elk	Ridgway	807	36,400	Tioga	Wellsboro	1,146	41,200
Erie	Erie	813	271,600	Union	Lewisburg	318	30,900
Fayette	Uniontown	802	156,400	Venango	Franklin	678	63,200
Forest	Tionesta	419	5,300	Warren	Warren	905	46,900
Franklin	Chambersburg	754	106,200	Washington	Washington	857	213,600
Fulton	McConnellsburg	435	11,600	Wayne	Honesdale	741	34,100
Greene	Waynesburg	578	39,100	Westmoreland	Greensburg	1,024	379,900
Huntingdon	Huntingdon	895	39,800	Wyoming	Tunkhannock	398	24,400
Indiana	Indiana	825	87,000	York	York	909	289,000
Jefferson	Brookville	652	47,200				
Juniata	Mifflintown	386	18,300		TOTALS	44,966	11,785,200
Lackawanna	Scranton	454	232,400				

[1] Totals do not add because of rounding.

On the whole, Pennsylvania North Midland is distinguished by the presence of *want off* a tram or bus, *snake feeder* (dragonfly), *run* (small stream), *waterspouts* and *spouts* (gutters), and *creek* as /krik/. With these features are found others that commonly occur in Southern, such as *corn pone, roasting ears,* and *spicket* (spigot). Western Pennsylvania, however, contrasts with the eastern half by the dominance of /nawthing/ for *nothing*, /greezy/ for *greasy*, /kao/ for *cow, sugar tree* (sugar maple), *hap* (quilt), and *clothes press* (closet), as well as by the influential merging of the /ah/ vowel and the /aw/ vowel so that *cot* and *caught* sound alike. Southeastern Pennsylvania has *flannel cakes* for pancakes and *ground hackie* for chipmunk; within this region, Philadelphia and its suburbs have distinctive *baby coach* for baby carriage, *pavement* for sidewalk, *hoagie* for a large sandwich, *put* in *broom* and *Cooper*, and the vowel of *father* in *on* and *fog*. In the east and northeast, a doughnut is a *cruller*, one is *sick in the stomach*, and *syrup* has the vowel of *sit*.

In much of central Pennsylvania, descendants of the colonial Palatinate German population retain their speech as Deitsch, often misnamed Pennsylvania Dutch, which has influenced English in the state through such loanwords as *toot* (bag), *rainworm* (earthworm), *snits* (dried apples), and *smearcase* (cottage cheese).

Of the native-born residents, 81% claimed English as a mother tongue in 1970, as did 79% of all residents. Other major resident groups claimed first languages as follows:

	NATIVE-BORN	FOREIGN-BORN
English	9,200,180	72,379
German	392,424	62,259
Italian	338,063	95,497
Polish	239,181	33,913
Slovak	143,311	20,830
Yiddish	93,729	27,233
Spanish	62,976	11,843

⁹RELIGIONS

With a long history of toleration, Pennsylvania has been a haven for numerous religious groups.

The first European settlers were Swedish Lutherans; German Lutherans began arriving in 1703. William Penn brought the Quakers to Pennsylvania during the 1680s, and the climate of religious liberty soon attracted other dissident groups, including German Mennonites, Dunkards, Moravians, and Schwenkfelders; French Huguenots; Scotch-Irish Presbyterians; and English Baptists. Descendants of the 16th-century Anabaptists, the Mennonites for the most part settled as farmers; they and the Quakers were the first religious groups openly to advocate abolition of slavery and to help runaway slaves to freedom via the Underground Railroad. The Amish—Mennonite followers of Jacob Amman—continue to dress in black clothing, shun the use of mechanized tools, automobiles, and electrical appliances, and observe Sundays by singing 16th-century hymns.

The Presbyterians, who built their first church in the state in 1704, played a major role both in the establishment of schools in the colony and in the later development of Pittsburgh and other cities in the western part of the state. Methodists held their first services in Philadelphia in 1768; for many years thereafter, Methodist circuit riders proselytized throughout the state.

Immigration during the 19th century brought a major change in patterns of worship. The Quakers gradually diminished in number and influence, while Roman Catholic and Greek Orthodox churches and Jewish synagogues opened in many of the mining and manufacturing centers. The bulk of the Jewish migration came after 1848 from Germany and after 1882, from East Europe and Russia. The Gilded Age saw the founding of a new group in Pittsburgh by clergyman Charles Taze Russell; first called the Russellites, members of this group are known today as Jehovah's Witnesses.

As of 1979, Roman Catholics comprised the largest religious group in the state, with a total population of 3,728,637; the Philadelphia archdiocese accounted for 1,377,258. Protestant groups had 3,350,920 known adherents in 1971. The largest denomination was the Lutheran Church in America, with 796,741 adherents. Other Protestant groups included United Methodists, 728,915; United Presbyterians, 573,905; Congregationalists (United Church of Christ), 310,389; Episcopalians, 193,399; and American Baptists, 113,850. The historically important Mennonites had 36,712 adherents in 1971; Friends USA (Quakers), 15,351; and Moravians, 12,697. About 7% of the nation's Jewish population lived in Pennsylvania as of 1979. Of the state's estimated 421,900 Jews, 295,000 lived in metropolitan Philadelphia.

¹⁰TRANSPORTATION

Like so many of its industrial assets, Pennsylvania's well-developed road and rail networks are showing signs of old age. Nevertheless, the state remains an important center of transportation, and its ports are among the busiest in the US.

The early years of railroad building left Pennsylvania with more miles of track than any other state. The first railroad charter, issued in 1819, provided for a horse-drawn railroad from the Delaware Valley to the headwaters of the Lehigh River. The state authorized construction of a line between Columbia and Philadelphia in 1828, and partial service began four years later as part of the State Works. The roadbed was state-owned, and private rail car companies paid a toll to use the rails. During this time, Pennsylvanians John Jervis and Joseph Harrison were developing steam-powered locomotives. Taking advantage of the new technology were separate rail lines connecting Philadelphia with Germantown (1834), Trenton, N.J. (1838), and Reading (1839), with the Lehigh Valley (1846), and with New York City (1855). In December 1852, the Pennsylvania Central completed lines connecting Philadelphia and Pittsburgh. Five years later, the Pennsylvania Railroad purchased the State Works, eliminating state competition and tolls. By 1880, the company (which had added many smaller coal-hauling lines to its holdings) was the world's largest corporation, with more than 30,000 employees and $400 million in capital. Although railroad revenues declined with the rise of the automobile, the Pennsylvania Railroad remained profitable until the 1960s, when the line merged with the New York Central to form the Penn Central. In 1970, the Penn Central separated its real estate holdings from its transportation operation, on which it declared bankruptcy.

As of 1978, the major lines using the state's 7,788 mi (12,534 km) of track were the Consolidated Rail Corp., or Conrail (which took over much of Penn Central's business), the Baltimore and Ohio, Delaware and Hudson, Bessemer and Lake Erie, Western Maryland, and Pittsburgh and Lake Erie. Amtrak operates passenger service to Philadelphia, Pittsburgh, and other cities along the east–west route, and from Philadelphia to New York and Washington, D.C., along the northeast corridor.

Mass transit systems in metropolitan Philadelphia and Pittsburgh and in Altoona, Allentown, Erie, Harrisburg, Johnstown, Lancaster, Reading, Scranton, Wilkes-Barre, and Williamsport served 467,678,610 passengers in 1976/77. The Philadelphia Rapid Transit System, the state's only subway, was established in 1902 and is operated by the Southeastern Pennsylvania Transportation Authority (SEPTA), which also runs buses, trolleys, trackless trolleys, and commuter trains in Philadelphia, Bucks, Chester, Delaware, and Montgomery counties. About a million passengers use the SEPTA system daily.

Throughout its history, Pennsylvania has been a pioneer in road transportation. One of the earliest roads in the colonies was a "king's highway," connecting Philadelphia to Delaware in 1677; a "queen's road" from Philadelphia to Chester opened in 1706. A flurry of road building connected Philadelphia with other eastern Pennsylvania communities between 1705 and 1735. The first interior artery, the Great Conestoga Road, was opened in 1741 and linked Philadelphia with Lancaster. Indian trails in western Pennsylvania were developed into roadways, and a thoroughfare to Pittsburgh was completed in 1758. During the mid-1700s, a Lancaster County artisan developed an improved wagon for transporting goods across the Alleghenies; called a Conestoga wagon after the region from which it came, this vehicle later became the prime means of transport for westward pioneers. Another major improvement in land transportation came with the opening in 1792 of the Philadelphia and Lancaster Turnpike, one of the first stone-surfaced roads in the US. The steel-cable suspension bridge built by John Roebling over the Monongahela River at Pittsburgh in 1846 revolutionized bridge building, leading to the construction of spans longer and wider than had previously been thought possible. During the 1920s, Pennsylvania farmers were aided by the building of inexpensive rural roads connecting them with their markets.

A major development in automotive transport, the limited-access highway, came to fruition with the Pennsylvania Turnpike, which opened in 1940. In 1978, this 479-mi (771-km) roadway served 57,218,000 passenger and 8,643,000 commercial vehicles. In all, Pennsylvania had 45,043 mi (72,490 km) of state-maintained highways, 68,328 mi (109,963 km) of local and county roads, 3,539 mi (5,695 km) of state park, reservation, and institutional roads, 810 mi (1,304 km) of national park roads, and 25 mi (40 km) of roads operated by the US Army Corps of Engineers. Besides the Turnpike, the major highways are I-80 (Keystone Shortway), crossing the state from East Stroudsburg to the Ohio Turnpike; I-81, from the New York to the Maryland border via Scranton, Wilkes-Barre, and Harrisburg; and I-79, from Erie to the West Virginia border via Pittsburgh. As of 1978, there were 6,894,869 motor vehicles registered, including 5,652,375 automobiles, 1,033,650 trucks, 183,045 motorcycles, and 25,799 buses. The total of 7,070,662 licensed drivers as of 1978 was the 5th highest in the US.

Blessed with access to the Atlantic Ocean and the Great Lakes and with such navigable waterways as the Delaware, Monongahela, Allegheny, and Ohio rivers, Pennsylvania was an early leader in water transportation, and Philadelphia, Pittsburgh, and Erie all developed as major ports. The peak period of canal building came during the 1820s and 1830s, which saw the completion of the Main Line of Public Works, used to transport goods between Philadelphia and Pittsburgh from 1834 to 1854; this system used waterways and a spectacular portage railroad that climbed over and cut through, via a tunnel, the Allegheny Mountains. Monumental as it was, the undertaking was largely a failure. Built too late to challenge the Erie Canal's domination of east–west trade, the Main Line was soon made obsolete by the railroads, as was the rest of the state's 800-mi (1,300-km) canal system.

Philadelphia, Pittsburgh, and Erie remain the state's major shipping ports. The Philadelphia Harbor (including ports in the Philadelphia metropolitan area) is the 2d largest on the east coast and 5th largest in the US, handling 49,710,565 tons of cargo in 1977. Pittsburgh, although no longer the dominant gateway to the Mississippi, is still a major inland port, handling 7,545,645 tons of cargo in 1977. Erie is the state's outlet to the Great Lakes.

As of 8 December 1978, Pennsylvania had 746 airfields, including 164 commercial airports, 368 private airfields, 197 heliports, 14 seaplane bases, and 3 gliderports. The busiest air terminal in the state, Greater Pittsburgh Airport, emplaned 4,635,645 passengers in 1978; Philadelphia International Airport was next with 4,138,542.

11 HISTORY

Soon after the glacier receded from what is now Pennsylvania, about 20,000 years ago, nomadic hunters from the west moved up the Ohio River, penetrated the passes through the Allegheny Mountains, and moved down the Susquehanna and Delaware rivers. By about AD 500, the earliest Indians, already accustomed to fishing and gathering nuts, seeds, fruit, and roots, were beginning to cultivate the soil, make pottery, and build burial mounds. Over the next thousand years, the Indians became semi-sedentary or only seasonal nomads.

Woodland Indians living in Pennsylvania, mostly of the Algonkian language family, were less inclined toward agriculture than other Indian tribes. The first Europeans to sail up the Delaware River found the Leni-Lenape ("original people"), who, as their name signified, had long occupied that valley, and whom the English later called the Delaware. Other Algonkian tribes related to the Leni-Lenape were the Nanticoke, who ranged along the Susquehanna River, and the Shawnee, who were scattered throughout central Pennsylvania. The other major Indian language group in Pennsylvania was Iroquoian. This group included the Susquehanna (Conestoga), living east of the Susquehanna and south to the shores of Chesapeake Bay, the Wyandot along the Allegheny River, and the Erie south of Lake Erie. Proving that tribes related by language could be deadly enemies, the Iroquoian Confederacy of the Five Nations, located in what is now New York, destroyed the Iroquoian-speaking Erie in the 1640s and the Susquehanna by 1680. The confederacy conquered the Leni-Lenape by 1720 but failed to destroy them, since they were less organized, less agrarian, and more scattered than were the Iroquoian tribes.

The first European to reach Pennsylvania was probably Cornelis Jacobssen, who in 1614 entered Delaware Bay for Dutch merchants interested in the fur trade. In 1638, the Swedes began planting farms along the Delaware River; they lived in peace with the Leni-Lenape and Susquehanna, with whom they traded for furs. Under Governor Johan Printz, the Swedes expanded into present-day Pennsylvania with a post at Tinicum Island (1643) and several forts along the Schuylkill River. The Dutch conquered New Sweden in 1655, but surrendered the land in 1664 to the English, led by James, the Duke of York, the brother of King Charles II and the future King James II.

The English conquest was financed partly by Admiral William Penn, whose son, also named William, subsequently joined the Society of Friends (Quakers), a radical Protestant sect persecuted for its ideas of equality and pacifism. Dreaming of an ideal commonwealth that would be a refuge for all persecuted peoples, Penn asked Charles II, who had never paid the debt owed to Penn's father, to grant him land west of the Delaware. The Duke of York willingly gave up his claim to that land, and Charles II granted it in 1681 as a proprietary colony to the younger Penn and named it Pennsylvania in honor of Penn's father.

As proprietor of Pennsylvania, Penn was given enormous power to make laws and wars (subject to approval by the king and the freemen of Pennsylvania), levy taxes, coin money, regulate commerce, sell land, appoint officials, administer justice, and construct a government. From the beginning, Penn virtually gave up his lawmaking power and granted suffrage to property holders of 50 acres or £50. Even before coming to Pennsylvania, he forged his first Frame of Government, a document that went into effect 25 April 1682 but lasted less than a year. Under it, a 72-member council, presided over by a governor, monopolized executive, legislative, and judicial power, though a 200-member assembly could veto or amend the council's legislation. Arriving in the colony in October 1682, Penn approved the location and layout of Philadelphia, met with the Leni-Lenape at Shackamaxon (Kensington) to acquire land and exchange vows of peace, called for elections to select an assembly, and proposed a Great Law (enacted in December) that ranged from prescribing weights and measures to guaranteeing fundamental liberties.

When the First Frame proved unwieldy, Penn on 2 April 1683 approved a Second Frame, which created an 18-member council and a 36-member assembly. A conspicuous friend of the deposed James II, Penn lost control of Pennsylvania from 1692 to 1694, and it was during this period that the legislature began to assert its rights. Penn returned to the colony in 1699, and on 28 October 1701 approved yet another constitution, called the Charter of Privileges. This document lodged legislative power in an annually elected unicameral assembly, executive power in a governor and council, which he now appointed, and judicial power in appointed provincial judges and an elected county judiciary. The Charter of Privileges remained in force until 1776.

As Pennsylvania's government evolved, its population grew steadily. Most of the first immigrants were from the British Isles and Germany. From 1681 to 1710, numerous English and Welsh Quaker migrants populated a 25-mi (40-km) zone surrounding Philadelphia. By 1750, most German immigrants were settled in a semicircular zone some 25–75 mi (40–120 km) from Philadelphia. A third and outermost ring, extending roughly 75 mi (120 km) west and north of the Germans, was populated beginning in 1717 by the Scotch-Irish; these lowland Scots, who had been resettled in Ulster in the 17th century, penetrated the interior of Pennsylvania west of the Susquehanna River, until turned in a southwesterly direction by the Alleghenies. Poor lands and distant markets made the Scotch-Irish indifferent farmers, but they were known as aggressive pioneers. By 1776, each major group—which remained quite distinct— constituted roughly a third of the 300,000 Pennsylvanians. Minorities included about 10,000 Scots, 10,000 Irish Catholics, 8,000 French Huguenots, 8,000 black slaves (despite Quaker hostility to slavery), and 1,000 Jews.

A key issue during the pre-Revolutionary period was the size and extent of the colony. Conflicting colonial charters, reflecting vague English ideas of American geography, made all of Pennsylvania's boundaries except the Delaware River disputed. After a protracted struggle, Pennsylvania and Maryland agreed upon a basis for Charles Mason and Jeremiah Dixon to run the famous line (1763–67) that divided North and South. Although Virginia and Pennsylvania both claimed the area around Pittsburgh, a joint commission agreed in 1779 to extend the Mason-Dixon line west the full five degrees prescribed in Penn's original charter. Five years earlier, the Penn family had abandoned to New York land north of the 42d parallel. This was confirmed as Pennsylvania's northern border in 1782, when the US Congress rejected Connecticut's claim to the Wyoming Valley area, where skirmishes (called the Yankee-Pennamite wars) had been going on since the 1760s.

Pennsylvania moved rapidly toward independence after the British victory in the French and Indian War. The Proclamation of 1763, preventing settlement west of the Alleghenies, outraged western Pennsylvania, while the Stamp Act (1765), Townshend Acts (1767), and Tea Act (1773) incensed Philadelphians. Although the Continental Congress began meeting in Philadelphia in September 1774, Pennsylvania revolted reluctantly. In July 1776, only three Pennsylvania delegates to the Second Continental Congress voted for independence, while two were opposed and two absented themselves from the vote. Nevertheless, the Declaration of Independence was proclaimed from Independence Hall on 4 July 1776. As the headquarters of the Congress, Philadelphia was an important British target. The American defeat at the Battle of Brandywine Creek on 11 September 1777 led to the British occupation of the city. The provisional capital was moved first to Lancaster and then to York, where the Articles of Confederation were drafted. Following battles at Germantown and Whitemarsh, General George Washington set up winter headquarters at Valley Forge, remaining there from December 1777 to June 1778. Faced with the threat of French naval power intervening on behalf of the Americans, the British

evacuated Philadelphia during the spring of 1778, and Congress reconvened there on 2 July. Philadelphia would serve as the US capital until 1783, and again from 1790 to 1800.

With independence, Pennsylvania adopted the state constitution of 1776, which established a powerful unicameral assembly elected annually by all freemen supporting the Revolution, a weak administrative supreme executive council (with a figurehead president), an appointed judiciary, and a council of censors meeting every seven years in order to take a census, reapportion the assembly, and review the constitutionality of state actions. In 1780, Pennsylvania passed the first state law abolishing slavery. Seven years later, Pennsylvania became the second state to ratify the US Constitution and join the Union. In 1790, Pennsylvania adopted a new constitution, modeled on the federal one, allowing all taxpaying males to vote. This document provided for a powerful governor, elected for a three-year term and eligible to succeed himself twice, a bicameral legislature (with senators elected every four years and a house elected annually), and an appointed judiciary.

Opposition to national taxes was evidenced by two disturbances in the 1790s. In 1794, western Pennsylvania settlers, opposed to a federal excise tax on distilled spirits, waged the Whiskey Rebellion. The insurrection was soon quashed by state troops under federal command. The levying of a federal property tax inspired the unsuccessful Fries Rebellion (1799) among Pennsylvania Germans.

By 1800, the first stages of industrialization were at hand. Pittsburgh's first iron furnace was built in 1792, and the increasing use of coal as fuel made its mining commercially feasible. The completion of the Main Line of Public Works, a canal and rail system connecting Philadelphia with Pittsburgh, was a major development of the early 19th century, which was otherwise a period of political turmoil and shifting party alliances.

By 1838, Pennsylvania adopted a new constitution curtailing the governor's power (he could serve only two three-year terms in a nine-year period), making many judgeships elective for specific terms, restricting the charter of banks, and disenfranchising black people. The 1840s saw not only an influx of Irish immigrants but also the rise of the Native American (Know-Nothing) Party, an anti-Catholic movement. The antislavery crusade, which gave birth to the Republican Party, influenced state politics during the following decade.

Although a Pennsylvania Democrat, James Buchanan, carried the state and won the presidency in 1856, the Republicans captured Pennsylvania for Abraham Lincoln in 1860, partly by their strong support for a protective tariff. Protectionism attracted Pennsylvania because, in addition to its enormously productive farms, it was heavily industrialized, leading the nation in the production of iron, lumber, textiles, and leather.

Pennsylvania rallied to the Union cause, supplying some 338,000 men, a figure exceeded only by New York. The state was the scene of the Battle of Gettysburg (1–3 July 1863), a turning point in the war for the Union cause. Under General George Gordon Meade, the Union troops (one-third of whom were Pennsylvanians) defeated Confederate forces under General Robert E. Lee, who was then forced to lead a retreat to Virginia.

The Civil War left the Republican Party dominant in Pennsylvania, but, in the post–Civil War years, the Republicans were themselves dominated by industry, particularly the Pennsylvania Railroad. Between 1890 and 1900, the state was the nation's chief producer of coal, iron, and steel, and for much of that period the main source of petroleum and lumber. Farmers' sons and daughters joined immigrants from abroad in flocking to the anthracite and bituminous coal regions and to Philadelphia, Pittsburgh, and other urban centers to work in mines, mills, and factories. As the state's industrial wealth increased, education, journalism, literature, art, and architecture flourished in Philadelphia and Pittsburgh. The 1876 Centennial Exhibition at Philadelphia illustrated America's advancement in the arts and industry.

Pennsylvania adopted a reform constitution in 1873, increasing the size of the senate and house to reduce the threat of bribery, prescribing rules to prevent treachery in legislation and fraud at the polls, equalizing taxation, limiting state indebtedness, restricting the governor to one four-year term in eight years, and creating the office of lieutenant governor. None of this, however, seriously hampered the Republican political machine, led by Simon Cameron, Matthew Quay, and Boies Penrose, which dominated the state from the 1860s to the 1920s. Though Progressive reforms were enacted in subsequent years, the Penrose machine grew ever more efficient, while industrial leaders—supported both by the Pennsylvania state government and by society at large—smashed labor's efforts to unite, particularly in the great steel strike of 1919.

During the nationwide boom years of the 1920s, Pennsylvania did little more than hold its own economically, and its industrial growth rate was low. The state's share of the nation's iron and steel output no longer exceeded that of the rest of the country combined. Coal, textiles, and agriculture—all basic to the state's economy—were depressed. When Penrose died in 1921, at least five factions sought to control the powerful Pennyslvania Republican Party. In this confusion, Gifford Pinchot, a Progressive disciple of Theodore Roosevelt, won the governorship for 1923–27 and reorganized the state's administration, but failed in his attempt to enforce prohibition and to regulate power utilities.

The disastrous depression of the 1930s brought major changes to Pennsylvania. Serving again as governor (1931–35), Pinchot fought for state and federal relief for the unemployed. The Republican organization's lack of enthusiasm for Pinchot and Progressivism helped revive the state Democratic Party long enough to secure the election in 1934—for the first time since 1890—of its gubernatorial nominee, George H. Earle. As governor, Earle successfully introduced a Little New Deal, supporting labor, regulating utilities, aiding farmers, and building public works. With government support, coal miners, steelworkers, and other organized labor groups emerged from the depression strong enough to challenge industry. Full employment and prosperity returned to Pennsylvania with the unprecedented demands on it for steel, ships, munitions, and uniforms during World War II. But the fact that Pennsylvania was not producing road vehicles and aircraft did not augur well for its industrial future.

Despite their professed opposition to government control, the Republican administrations (1939–55) that succeeded the Earle regime actually espoused and even enlarged Earle's program. They regulated industry, improved education, and augmented social services, at the same time increasing state bureaucracy, budgets, and taxes. The relative economic decline of Pennsylvania after World War II formed an ominous background for these Republican years. Although Pennsylvania remained the 2d-leading manufacturing state as late as 1947, it slipped to 3d place in 1954 and to 5th by 1958. Markets, transportation, banks, factories, machinery, and skilled labor remained abundant, however, and two Democratic governors were able to attract new industries to the state during the 1950s and early 1960s. Governor George Leader (1955–59) established the Pennsylvania Industrial Development Authority, and both he and his successor, David Lawrence, improved educational and mental health facilities, reformed government administration, and raised taxes. The economy was still not healthy in 1963, when Republican William W. Scranton entered the state house (1963–67). Warmly sympathetic to the poor, Scranton continued both to enlarge state responsibilities (through increased taxes) and to beg for federal aid for economic and social programs. He was rewarded with four years of steady economic growth. Pennsylvania's unemployment level, 2d highest in the nation from 1950 to 1962, had dropped below

the national average by 1966. Raymond P. Shafer (1967–71), Scranton's Republican successor, was as forward-looking as his predecessors in his efforts to rehabilitate the economy. The 1873 constitution was extensively revised at a constitutional convention held in 1968, during his administration.

Because the legislature refused to approve a state income tax to pay for Shafer's new social programs, Pennsylvania faced an unresolved financial crisis in 1971 when Democratic Milton J. Shapp became governor. During his first term (1971–75), Shapp weathered the storm by securing passage of the tax. He virtually eliminated state patronage by signing union contracts covering state employees. Not only did he continue to attract business to Pennsylvania, but he also championed the consumer with no-fault auto insurance, adopted in 1974. Shapp's second term, however, was wrecked by his pursuit of the 1976 presidential nomination and by rampant corruption among Pennsylvania Democrats. Shapp's successor, Republican Dick Thornburgh, had scarcely sat in the governor's chair before the nuclear accident at Three Mile Island confronted him with vexing questions concerning the safety and wisdom of atomic power.

[12] STATE GOVERNMENT

The 1873 constitution, substantially reshaped by a constitutional convention in 1968, is the foundation of state government in Pennsylvania.

The general assembly consists of a 50-member senate, elected to staggered four-year terms, and a 203-member house of representatives, elected every two years. Each house meets annually, and there are no limits to the length of each session. To qualify for the general assembly, a person must be a US citizen and have been a Pennsylvania resident for at least four years and a district resident for at least one; senators must be at least 25 years of age, representatives at least 21.

As head of the executive branch and chief executive officer of the state, the governor has the power to appoint heads of administrative departments, boards, and commissions, to approve or veto legislation, to grant pardons, and to command the state's military forces. The governor, who may serve no more than two four-year terms in succession, must be a US citizen, at least 30 years of age, and have been a Pennsylvania resident for at least 7 years prior to election. Elected with the governor is the lieutenant governor, who serves as president of the senate and chairman of the board of pardons, and assumes the powers of the governor if the governor is unable to continue in that office. Other officials also elected for four years are the auditor general, who oversees all state financial transactions; the state treasurer, who receives and keeps records of all state funds; and, beginning in 1980, the attorney general, who heads the Department of Justice. All other department heads, or secretaries, are appointed by the governor and confirmed by a majority of the senate.

A bill may be introduced in either house of the general assembly. After the measure is passed by majority vote in each house, the governor has 10 days in which to sign it, refuse to sign it (in which case it becomes law), or to veto it. Vetoes may be overridden by a two-thirds vote of the members of each house.

A proposed constitutional amendment must be approved by a majority of both house and senate members in two successive legislatures before it can be placed on the ballot. If approved by a majority of the voters in a general election, the amendment then becomes part of the constitution.

To vote in state elections, a person must be a US citizen, at least 18 years old, and have been a resident of Pennsylvania and of the district for at least 30 days preceding the election. Registration may take place at any time up to 30 days before an election.

[13] POLITICAL PARTIES

The Republican Party totally dominated Pennsylvania politics from 1860, when the first Republican governor was elected, to the early 1930s. During this period, there were 16 Republican and only 2 Democratic administrations. Most of the Republicans were staunchly probusiness, though one Republican Progressive, Gifford Pinchot, was elected governor in 1922 and again in 1930. A Democrat, George Earle, won the governorship in 1934, in the depths of the depression, but from 1939 through 1955, Republicans again held the office without interruption. Only since the mid-1950s has Pennsylvania emerged as a two-party state, with Democrats electing governors in 1954, 1958, 1970, and 1974, and Republicans winning the governorships in 1962, 1966, and 1978. Both US Senate seats have been held by Republicans since 1968.

As of 1978 there were 5,796,510 registered voters in the state, of whom 3,224,953 were Democrats, 2,321,807 were Republicans, and 249,750 were unaffiliated or members of other parties. Democratic voters were heavily concentrated in metropolitan Philadelphia and Pittsburgh. Pennsylvania, a pivotal state for Jimmy Carter in 1976, was swept by the Republican tide in the 1980 presidential election; Ronald Reagan, the Republican nominee, won nearly 50% of the popular vote, compared with 42% for Jimmy Carter, 6% for John Anderson, and 2% for the remaining candidates. By a margin of slightly more than 100,000 votes, Arlen Specter held for the Republicans the US Senate seat vacated after two terms by Richard Schweiker.

[14] LOCAL GOVERNMENT

As of 1978, Pennsylvania had 67 counties, 52 cities, 966 boroughs, 1 incorporated town, 1,551 townships, 505 school districts, and 2,513 authorities (special districts). Under home-rule laws, municipalities may choose to draft and amend their own charter. By January 1979, 5 counties, 8 cities, 15 boroughs, and 24 townships were operating under home rule.

Pennsylvania counties are responsible for enforcing state law and conducting state elections; other functions include property assessment, regional planning, and solid waste disposal. Counties also maintain hospitals, homes for the aged, community colleges, libraries, and other community facilities. The chief governing body in each county is a three-member board of commissioners, each elected to a four-year term. Other elected officials generally include the sheriff, district attorney, prothonotary (notary), clerk of courts, register of wills, recorder of deeds,

two jury commissioners, three auditors or a controller, and treasurer. Among the appointed officials is a public defender. Counties are divided by law into nine classes, depending on population. The only first-class county, Philadelphia, is also the only city-county in the state; its county offices were merged with the city government in 1952, pursuant to the home-rule charter of 1951.

There are four classes of cities. The only first-class city, Philadelphia, is governed by a mayor and 17-member city council. Other elected officials are the controller, district attorney, sheriff, register of wills, and three city commissioners. Major appointed officials include managing director, director of finance, city representative, and city solicitor. Both Pittsburgh, the only second-class city, and Scranton, the only second-class-A city, are governed under mayor-council systems that give the mayors strong discretionary powers. Of the remaining—third-class—cities in 1978, 26 were operating under commissions consisting of a mayor, four council members, a controller, and a treasurer; 18 had mayor-council forms of government; and 5 used council-manager systems.

Boroughs are governed under mayor-council systems giving the council strong powers. Other elected officials include tax assessor, tax collector, and auditor or controller. The state's first-class townships (92 in 1978), located mostly in metropolitan areas, are governed by elected commissioners who serve four-year overlapping terms. Second-class townships (1,459), mostly located in rural areas, have three supervisors who are elected at large to six-year terms. Other elected officials may include a tax assessor, tax collector, three auditors or a controller, and treasurer.

Authorities which may be set up by any other governmental unit (or group of units) to perform special functions, such as construction, financing, and maintenance of public works projects, have increased at a rapid pace since the 1960s.

[15] STATE SERVICES

Operating out of the governor's office is the Governor's Action Center, a state ombudsman program. Through a toll-free telephone network, the center guides individuals to appropriate state agencies and notifies state agencies of problems that demand their attention. Other executive agencies under the governor's jurisdiction include the Pennsylvania Council on Aging,

Pennsylvania Presidential Vote by Political Parties, 1948–80

YEAR	ELECTORAL VOTE	PENNSYLVANIA WINNER	DEMOCRAT	REPUBLICAN	PROGRESSIVE	SOCIALIST	PROHIBITION	SOC. LABOR
1948	35	Dewey (R}	1,752,426	1,902,197	55,161	11,325	10,538	1,461
						SOC. WORKERS		
1952	32	*Eisenhower (R)	2,146,269	2,415,789	4,222	1,508	8,951	1,377
1956	32	*Eisenhower (R)	1,981,769	2,585,252	—	2,035	—	7,447
1960	32	*Kennedy (D)	2,556,282	2,439,956	—	2,678	—	7,158
1964	29	*Johnson (D)	3,130,954	1,673,657	—	10,456	—	5,092
					PEACE & FREEDOM	AMERICAN IND.		
1968	29	Humphrey (D)	2,259,403	2,090,017	7,821	4,862	378,582	4,977
								AMERICAN
1972	27	*Nixon (R)	1,796,951	2,714,521	—	4,639	—	70,593
					COMMUNIST			US LABOR
1976	27	*Carter (D)	2,328,677	2,205,604	1,891	3,009	25,344	2,744
						LIBERTARIAN	SOC.WORKERS	
1980	27	*Reagan (R)	1,937,540	2,261,872	5,184	33,263	20,291	—

*Won US presidential election.

Human Relations Commission, Governor's Council on Opportunity for the Spanish-Speaking, Commission for Women, and Board of Ethics. The Liquor Control Board operates some 700 state liquor stores and claims to be the world's largest single purchaser of liquors and wines.

The Department of Education administers the state's public school laws, oversees community colleges, licenses private schools, and administers the state public library program. Educational policy is the province of the State Board of Education, a panel with 17 members appointed by the governor to six-year terms. Also within the department are various boards that make policies for and review developments within the state's higher educational system.

The Department of Transportation maintains state-operated highways, mass transit, rail service, and aviation facilities. The State Highway and Bridge Authority, Pennsylvania Transportation Assistance Authority, and Pennsylvania Turnpike Commission also have transport-related responsibilities. Agencies and departments providing health and welfare services include the Department of Aging, Department of Community Affairs, and Department of Health. All public assistance, social service, mental health, and mental retardation programs are administered by the Department of Public Welfare.

The Department of Justice is responsible for the state's correctional facilities. The National Guard, veterans' affairs, and the state veterans' homes are under the Department of Military Affairs; the Pennsylvania State Police is a separate state agency. The Pennsylvania Commission on Crime and Delinquency, created in 1978, allocated federal funds for crime control, juvenile justice, and delinquency prevention. The Pennsylvania Emergency Management Agency (formerly the State Council of Civil Defense) provides assistance in emergency situations involving natural or man-made disasters.

All environmental programs, mining operations, and state land and water management programs are under the supervision of the Department of Environmental Resources. The Governor's Energy Council seeks to augment the state's energy security through the planned development and conservation of energy resources. The Department of Labor and Industry administers safety, employment, and industrial standards; operates vocational rehabilitation and workers' compensation programs; and mediates labor disputes.

[16] JUDICIAL SYSTEM

Since 1968, all Pennsylvania courts have been organized under the Unified Judicial System. The highest court in the state is the supreme court, which, having been established in 1722, is the oldest appellate court in the US. The supreme court consists of seven justices, elected to 10-year terms on a nonpartisan ballot; the justice with the longest continuous service on the court automatically becomes chief justice. In general, the supreme court hears appeals from the commonwealth court. A separate appellate court, called the superior court, hears appeals from the courts of common pleas. There are seven superior court judges, also elected to 10-year terms, as are the commonwealth and common pleas court judges.

The commonwealth court, created in 1968 and composed of 9 judges, has original jurisdiction over civil actions brought by or against the state, and appellate jurisdiction over civil actions involving the state and its related agencies, nonprofit corporations, and eminent domain proceedings. The state's principal trial courts are the courts of common pleas, which have original jurisdiction over all civil and criminal cases not otherwise specified. As of 1979 there were 305 judges in 59 courts of common pleas, one for each judicial district.

Misdemeanors and other minor offenses are tried by district justices of the peace, who are elected to six-year terms. The Philadelphia municipal court consists of 22 judges, each serving a six-year term; 6 judges comprise the Philadelphia traffic court. Pittsburgh's magistrates court is composed of from 5 to 8 judges, appointed by the mayor to four-year terms.

As measured by the FBI Crime Index, Pennsylvania's overall crime rate in 1978 was 3,185 per 100,000 people; the violent crime rate was 301, the property crime rate 2,884. Rates for specific crimes were as follows: murder and nonnegligent manslaughter, 6.2; forcible rape, 18.7; robbery, 137; aggravated assault, 140; burglary, 900; larceny-theft, 1,643; and motor vehicle theft, 341. All these figures were well below the national norms. Although Philadelphia's crime rates were significantly above the state average—the violent crime rate was 453, the property crime rate 3,671—Philadelphia was actually one of the least crime-ridden of the nation's major metropolitan regions. Pittsburgh's violent crime rate was slightly above the state average, but its property crime rate was slightly below.

[17] ARMED FORCES

Several important US Army and Navy facilities are located in Pennsylvania. The US Army War College is in Carlisle, and there are Army depots in Chambersburg, Harrisburg, and Scranton. The largest naval facility in the state is the historically important Philadelphia Naval Shipyard. As of 1978 there were 58,155 Department of Defense personnel in the state, 36,842 of them in the Navy. Defense contracts worth more than $1.6 billion were awarded to Pennsylvania firms in 1977/78.

As of 30 September 1979 there were 1,747,000 veterans living in the state (3d in the US), of whom 34,000 served in World War I, 785,000 in World War II, 315,000 in the Korean conflict, and 488,000 during the Viet-Nam era. Veterans' benefits totaled $897 million in 1977/78, of which $477 million went for compensation and pensions, $268 million for medical services, $92 million for education and training, and $60 million for other purposes.

About 17,100 Pennsylvanians served in the National Guard during 1978. Of the 29,627 state and local police personnel in 1977, 24,057 were members of local forces. Total police expenditures were $493 million (4th in the US), of which $380 million went for local forces.

[18] MIGRATION

When William Penn's followers arrived in Pennsylvania, they joined small groups of Dutch, Swedish, and Finnish immigrants who were already settled along the Delaware River. By 1685, 50% of Pennsylvania's European population was British. In 1683, the Frankfort Land Co. founded the Mennonite community of Germantown on 6,000 acres (2,400 hectares) east of the Schuylkill River. One hundred years later there were 120,000 Germans, about one-fourth of the state's census population: the Moravians, from Saxony, settled primarily in Bethlehem and Nazareth, and the Amish in Lancaster and Reading.

During the 19th century, more immigrants settled in Pennsylvania than in any other state except New York. Between 1840 and 1890, the anthracite mines in east-central Pennsylvania attracted the Irish, Welsh, and Slavs; Scotch-Irish, Italian, Austrian, Hungarian, and Polish (and, after 1880, Russian) immigrants worked the western coalfields. The cities attracted Italian, French, and Slavic workers. East European and Russian Jews settled in Philadelphia and Pittsburgh between 1882 and 1900. By the turn of the century, the urban population surpassed the rural population for the first time.

During the 20th century, these patterns have been reversed. The trend among whites, particularly since World War II, has been to move out—from the cities to the suburbs, and from Pennsylvania to other states. Blacks, who began entering the state first as slaves and then as freemen, continued to migrate to the larger cities until the early 1970s, when a small outmigration began. Overall, between 1940 and 1977, Pennsylvania lost a net total of 1,480,000 residents through migration, the most for any state during that period.

[19]INTERGOVERNMENTAL COOPERATION

Pennsylvania participates in such regional bodies as the Atlantic States Marine Fisheries Commission, Appalachian Regional Commission, Great Lakes Basin Commission, Susquehanna River Basin Commission, Ohio River Valley Sanitation Commission, and Wheeling Creek Watershed Protection and Flood Prevention Commission.

Some of the most important interstate agreements concern commerce and development along the Delaware River. The Delaware River Basin Commission involves the governors of Delaware, New Jersey, New York, and Pennsylvania in the utilization and conservation of the Delaware and its surrounding areas. Through the Delaware River Port Authority, New Jersey and Pennsylvania control an interstate mass transit system. Representatives of the two states also sit on the Delaware River Valley Regional Planning Commission and on the Delaware River Joint Toll Bridge Commission.

During 1978/79, Pennsylvania received $4.1 billion in federal funds (3d among the 50 states), including $335 million in general revenue-sharing funds.

[20]ECONOMY

Dominated by coal and steel, Pennsylvania is an important contributor to the national economy, but its role has diminished considerably in this century. The state reached the height of its economic development by 1920, when its western oil wells and coalfields made it the nation's leading energy producer. By that time, however, Pennsylvania's oil production was already on the decline, and demand for coal had slackened. No longer did the state dominate US steel production: Pennsylvania produced 60% of the US total in 1900, but only 30% in 1940, and 24% in 1960. Philadelphia, a diversified manufacturing center, was beginning to lose many of its textile and apparel factories. The depression hastened the decline. Industrial production in 1932 was less than half the 1929 level, and mineral production, already in a slump throughout the 1920s, dropped more than 50% in value between 1929 and 1933. By 1933, 37% of the workforce was unemployed, and those who still had their jobs were settling for lower wages.

Massive federal aid programs and the production of munitions stimulated employment during the 1940s, but some sections of the state have never fully recovered from the damage of the depression years. Declines in coal and steel production and the loss of other industries to the Sunbelt have not been entirely counterbalanced by gains in other sectors, despite a steady expansion of machinery production, increased tourism, and the growth of service-related industries and trade. The outlook for the steel industry remained uncertain in the 1980s, as Pennsylvania's aging factories faced severe competition from more efficient foreign producers.

The gross state product in 1978 was estimated at $111.7 billion in current dollars, or 5.3% of the GNP. Measured in constant 1972 dollars, the gross state product increased only 9.4% between 1969 and 1977. Contributions to the 1978 total included manufacturing, 32%; trade, 16%; finance, insurance, and real estate, 13%; services, 12%; government, 9%; transportation, communications, and public utilities, 9%; construction, 4%; mining, 2%; and other sectors, 3%.

[21]INCOME

Although Pennsylvania is one of the nation's most industrialized states, its wage earners tend to receive less than their counterparts in other states, and its share of the nation's personal income is less than it was a decade ago.

Per capita income in 1978 was $7,733—21st among the 50 states and slightly below the US average. Total personal income for 1978, $90.9 billion, was only 22% higher than in 1970, well below the overall US growth rate of 32%. The state's share of the nation's income dropped from 6.4% in 1960 to 5.3% in 1978. Median family income in 1975 was $14,153, 26th in the US.

According to state figures, sources of personal income in 1978 were as follows: manufacturing, 34%; services, 17%; trade, 16%; government, 13%; transportation and public utilities, 8%; construction, 6%; finance, insurance, and real estate, 5%; mining, 2%; and farming, 1% (the total exceeds 100% because of rounding). More than 40% of all income was earned in the Philadelphia metropolitan area (including parts of New Jersey). Other major income areas were metropolitan Pittsburgh, 21%; Allentown-Bethlehem-Easton, 5%; northeastern Pennsylvania, including Scranton and Wilkes-Barre, 5%; and Harrisburg, 4%.

About 1,133,000 Pennsylvanians (9.7%) were below the federal poverty level in 1975; the percentage of blacks living in poverty was more than five times as high as that of whites. In 1972, 4.4% of the top wealthholders in the US lived in the state.

[22]LABOR

In 1978, Pennsylvania's civilian labor force totaled 5,252,000 (5th in the US), of whom 4,888,000 were employed. Employment was distributed among the following occupational categories: clerical workers, 18%; professional and technical workers, 15%; craftsmen, 14%; equipment operators (excluding transport), 14%; service workers, 13%; nonfarm managers and administrators, 9%; sales personnel, 6%; nonfarm laborers, 6%; transport equipment operators, 4%; and farm workers, 1%.

A federal census of workers covered by unemployment insurance in March 1977 revealed the following nonfarm employment pattern for Pennsylvania:

	ESTABLISH-MENTS	EMPLOYEES	ANNUAL PAYROLL ('000)
Agricultural services, forestry, fishing	1,752	8,371	$ 79,920
Mining, of which:	1,546	53,189	891,960
Bituminous coal, lignite	(644)	(34,844)	(609,880)
Contract construction	22,320	173,582	2,820,674
Manufacturing, of which:	17,472	1,343,748	18,249,627
Food products	(1,452)	(93,622)	(1,134,062)
Apparel, other textiles	(1,787)	(132,952)	(938,147)
Primary metals	(581)	(195,781)	(3,323,408)
Fabricated metal products	(1,836)	(100,748)	(1,418,788)
Nonelectrical machinery	(2,339)	(128,941)	(1,862,079)
Transportation, public utilities	8,657	210,990	3,134,785
Wholesale trade	17,515	219,988	3,011,270
Retail trade	64,108	692,965	4,594,907
Finance, insurance, real estate	18,368	226,163	2,494,465
Services	62,673	802,110	7,215,328
Other	1,780	2,698	50,131
TOTALS	216,191	3,733,804	$42,543,067

Among the categories of employees not included in this survey were government workers, of whom Pennsylvania had some 716,000 in November 1978.

The average adjusted unemployment for the state in 1978 was 6.9%, ranging from 4.5% for adult white males to nearly 20% for adult black males. In Philadelphia's central city the rates were even higher: 11.1% overall, ranging from 4.3% for adult white women to 23.9% for adult black men. Pittsburgh fared better, with an overall unemployment rate of 6.1% during the same year.

The history of unionism in Pennsylvania dates back to 1724, when Philadelphia workers organized the Carpenters' Company, the first crafts association in the colonies. Its Carpenters' Hall gained fame as the site of the First Continental Congress in 1774; the carpenters were also responsible for the first strike in the US, in 1791. The nation's first labor union was organized by Philadelphia shoemakers in 1794. By 1827, the Mechanics' Union of

Trade Associations, the country's first central labor body, was striking for a 10-hour workday and was the impetus behind the formation of the Organized Workingman's Party. Nine years later there were no fewer than 58 labor organizations in Philadelphia and 13 in Pittsburgh, but the Panic of 1837 resulted in a sharp decline of union strength and membership for many years. Union ranks were further depleted by the Civil War, despite the efforts of Pennsylvania labor leader William Sylvis, who later became an important figure in the national labor reform movement. After the Civil War ended, the Noble Order of the Knights of Labor was established in Philadelphia in 1869.

The coalfields were the sites of violent organizing struggles. Low wages and long hours sparked the first general mine strikes in 1835, which, like a subsequent walkout by anthracite miners in 1849, proved unsuccessful. During the 1850s and 1870s, a secret society known as the Molly Maguires led uprisings in the anthracite fields, but its influence ended after the conviction of its leaders for terrorist activities. The demise of the Molly Maguires did not stop the violence, however. Eleven persons were killed during a mine strike at Connellsville in 1891, and a strike by Luzerne County miners in 1897 resulted in 20 deaths. Finally, a five-month walkout by anthracite miners in 1902 led to increased pay, reduced hours, and an agreement to employ arbitration to settle future disputes.

Steelworkers, burdened for many years by 12-hour workdays and 7-day workweeks, called several major strikes during this period. An 1892 lockout at Andrew Carnegie's Homestead steel mill led to a clash between workers and Pinkerton guards hired by the company; after several months, the strikers went back to work, their resources exhausted. A major strike in 1919, involving half of the nation's steelworkers, shut down the industry for more than three months, but it too produced no immediate gains. The Steel Workers Organizing Committee, later the United Steelworkers, finally won a contract and improved benefits from US Steel in 1937, although other steel companies held out until the early 1940s, when the Supreme Court forced recognition of the union.

As of 1976, nearly 40% of all nonagricultural employees belonged to labor unions or employee associations, the 4th highest such percentage in the US. Of the 1,642,000 labor union members, 1,243,000 belonged to AFL-CIO affiliates. The most important union in the state is the United Steelworkers of America, headquartered in Pittsburgh. In 1977 there were 620 work stoppages involving 228,700 workers, resulting in 3,113,400 workdays lost.

23 AGRICULTURE

Pennsylvania ranked 21st among the 50 states in agricultural income in 1979, with receipts of nearly $2.2 billion.

During the colonial period, German immigrants farmed the fertile land in southeastern Pennsylvania, making the state a leader in agricultural production. Unlike farmers in other states who worked the soil until it was depleted and then moved on, these farmers carefully cultivated the same plots year after year, using crop rotation techniques that kept the land productive. As late as 1840, the state led the nation in wheat production, thanks in part to planting techniques developed and largely confined to southeastern Pennsylvania. However, westward expansion and the subsequent fall in agricultural prices hurt farming in the state, and many left the land for industrial jobs in the cities. Today, most farms in the state produce crops and dairy items for Philadelphia and other major eastern markets.

As of 1977 there were about 72,000 farms averaging 139 acres (56 hectares) in size. The leading farm areas were all in southeastern Pennsylvania. Lancaster County was by far the most productive, followed by the counties of Berks, Adams, Franklin, and York.

The following table shows leading field crops in 1979:

	OUTPUT (BU)	VALUE
Corn for grain	115,425,000	$323,190,000
Hay (tons)	4,293,000	236,115,000
Oats	8,122,000	34,519,000
Wheat	18,425,000	26,716,000
Soybeans	2,624,000	15,482,000
Barley	5,405,000	11,621,000

In 1977, Pennsylvania led the nation in the production of mushrooms with 198,606,000 lb, worth $137,017,000; it ranked 2d in the production of roses and 3d in production of carnations and chrysanthemums. Other crops included fresh vegetables, apples, pears, peaches, grapes, and cherries (sweet and tart). The value of fresh market vegetables exceeded $15 million in 1979; of vegetables for processing, $7.6 million.

24 ANIMAL HUSBANDRY

Most of Pennsylvania's farm income stems from livestock production, primarily in Lancaster County.

There were 1,900,000 cattle and calves, 840,000 hogs and pigs, and 85,000 sheep and lambs on Pennsylvania farms at the end of 1979. Sales of 489,940,000 lb of cattle and calves brought state farmers $321,641,000; 210,589,000 lb of hogs and pigs, $90,553,000; 3,906,000 lb of sheep and lambs, $2,588,000.

Pennsylvania was the 3d-leading producer of chickens in the US during 1979, selling 80,151,000 lb worth $14,858,000. Production of turkeys totaled 85,320,000 lb, worth $39,247,000. Egg production—3.8 billion eggs, worth $178 million—was 5th highest in the US.

Nearly 8 billion lb of milk (4th among the 50 states) worth $1 billion was produced by Pennsylvania dairy farms in 1979. The state ranked 4th in butter production, with 48,814,000 lb; 2d in ice cream, with 73,746,000 gallons; 4th in ice milk, with 15,570,000 gallons; and 9th in cheese, with 93,908,000 lb.

25 FISHING

Although there is little commercial fishing in Pennsylvania, its many lakes and streams make it a popular area for sport fishing. All recreational fishing in the state is supervised by the Fish Commission, established in 1866 and one of the oldest conservation agencies in the US. Almost 47 million fish were stocked from all sources in 1977/78. Walleye, trout, and salmon were the leading species.

26 FORESTRY

The hills of central Pennsylvania made up the bulk of the state's 18,540,856 acres (7,503,243 hectares) of forestland in 1979, when forests covered 64% of the total land area. As of 30 January 1978, 1,931,566 acres (781,680 hectares) of forestland managed by the state were spread across 42 counties. Nearly all of Pennsylvania's forests are usable as commercial timberland, about four-fifths of it privately owned. The National Forest Service administers the 508,695-acre (208,862-hectare) Allegheny National Forest in western Pennsylvania.

During the 1860s, Pennsylvania led the nation in lumber production, but overcutting and mismanagement nearly decimated the forests by 1900. Although more than 684 million seedlings from state nurseries were planted on public and private land between 1900 and 1978, the industry has never regained its former importance. In 1977, shipments of lumber and wood products exceeded $1 billion, but accounted for only 1.3% of the value of all shipments of manufactured goods. Paper and paper products played a much larger role, accounting for $3.3 billion in shipments in 1977.

27 MINING

Containing one of the nation's oldest and most extensive areas of coal production, Pennsylvania ranked 8th among the 50 states in total mining value in 1978, with $3 billion.

Coal is the state's most valuable mineral commodity, accounting for more than two-thirds of all mine income. Pennsylvania's 1978 production of 81,495,000 tons was the 3d highest in the US, representing 12% of US production. Pennsylvania is the only major US producer of anthracite coal, with an output of 6,445,000 tons in 1978; bituminous coal production totaled 75,050,000 tons, and 12,946,000 tons of coke were also produced. Next in value was portland cement, with a 1978 output of 7,014,000 tons, followed by stone, 67,075,000 tons. Other important minerals (excluding fossil fuels) were pig iron, 20,330,000 tons; sand and gravel, 19,000,000 tons; clay, 2,260,000 tons; lime, 2,056,000 tons; sulfur, 82,000 tons; and zinc, 21,053 tons.

Greene County led the state in value of mining output in 1975, followed by Clearfield, Armstrong, Somerset, and Northampton counties. Bituminous coal is mined in Washington, Clearfield, Greene, Cambria, Armstrong, Somerset, Clarion, Allegheny, and 19 other counties in the western part of the state; anthracite mining is concentrated in Schuylkill, Luzerne, Lackawanna, Northumberland, Carbon, Columbia, Sullivan, and Dauphin counties in the east. In 1977 there were 856 active coal mines, 140 underground and 716 surface. Demonstrated reserves as of 1976 were 23.7 billion tons of bituminous (3d in the US) and 7.1 billion tons of anthracite, 96% of the US total.

28 ENERGY AND POWER

Installed capacity of Pennsylvania's electric power plants in 1978 was 34.3 million kw, all of it privately owned. Power generation totaled 126.3 billion kwh, of which about 68% was from coal-fired plants, 18% from nuclear, 13% from oil, and 1% from hydroelectric installations and natural gas.

Pennsylvania's nuclear power production dropped abruptly on 28 March 1979, when a malfunction at the 906,000-kw Unit 2 plant operated by Metropolitan Edison (a subsidiary of General Public Utilities) at Three Mile Island near Harrisburg caused the reactor's containment building to fill up with radioactive water. Some radioactive steam was vented into the atmosphere, and thousands of residents of nearby areas were temporarily evacuated. A 12-member panel appointed by President Jimmy Carter to investigate the accident found serious flaws in the design of the plant's safety systems and in federal regulation of the nuclear power industry. More than a year after the malfunction, Unit 2 had still not been fully decontaminated. Metropolitan Edison's 819,000-kw Unit 1 plant was also shut down after the accident and was still closed as of mid-1980. Remaining nuclear plants in Pennsylvania are the Peach Bottom Units 2 and 3 (combined capacity 2,130,000 kw) owned by Philadelphia Electric in Lancaster County, and Beaver Valley Unit 1 (852,000 kw), at Shippingport, owned by Duquesne Light Co. and Ohio Edison.

Electric energy sales in the state in 1977 totaled 95.6 billion kwh, of which 47% was industrial, 32% residential, 19% commercial, and 2% for other purposes. The largest utility in the state is Philadelphia Electric, the 15th largest in the US with 1979 assets of more than $5.2 billion.

The nation's first oil well was struck in Titusville in 1859, and for the next five decades Pennsylvania led the nation in oil production. Reserves totaled 48,156,000 barrels in 1978, when output dropped to 2,820,000 barrels. The state's natural gas output was 91.8 billion cu feet. Natural gas reserves as of January 1979 were slightly more than 2 trillion cu feet. Virtually all the state's commercial oil and gas reserves lie beneath the Allegheny High Plateau, in western Pennsylvania.

29 INDUSTRY

At different times throughout its history, Pennsylvania has been the nation's principal producer of ships, iron, chemicals, lumber, oil, textiles, glass, coal, and steel. Although it is still a major manufacturing center, Pennsylvania's industrial leadership has diminished steadily during this century.

The first major industry in colonial Pennsylvania was shipbuilding, centered in Philadelphia. Iron works, brick kilns, candle factories, and other small crafts industries also grew up around the city. By 1850, Philadelphia alone accounted for nearly half of

Pennsylvania's manufacturing output, with an array of products including flour, preserved meats, sugar, textiles, shoes, furniture, iron, locomotives, pharmaceuticals, and books. The exploitation of the state's coal and oil resources and the discovery of new steel-making processes helped build Pittsburgh into a major industrial center.

Manufacturing accounted for 32% of Pennsylvania's estimated gross state product in 1978. According to the federal census of manufactures, manufacturing employment declined by 5% between 1972 and 1977, with jobs lost in nearly every category except machinery, metalworking, transportation equipment, and instruments, all of which showed slight increases. During the same period, shipments of manufactured goods grew from $48.3 billion to $80 billion, and value added by manufacture rose from $23.5 billion to $36 billion; inflation accounted for most of these increments. Leading industries by value added were primary metals, 16%; nonelectrical machinery, 10%; fabricated metal products, 8%; electric and electronic equipment, 8%; chemicals and chemical products, 8%; and transportation equipment, 6%.

The following table shows value added by manufacture for selected industries in 1972 and 1977:

	1972	1977
Basic steel and blast furnace products	$2,964,200,000	$4,452,800,000
Drugs	906,500,000	1,403,500,000
Electronic components	587,000,000	982,300,000
Petroleum refinery products	262,800,000	939,500,000
General industrial machinery	487,400,000	879,300,000
Textile mill products	695,200,000	808,400,000
Motor vehicles and equipment	NA	735,100,000
Construction and related machinery	453,500,000	723,900,000
Railroad equipment	NA	635,300,000
Ladies' outerwear	450,300,000	604,300,000
Metalworking machinery	341,500,000	574,300,000
Measuring and controlling machinery	337,300,000	558,700,000
Commercial printing	373,300,000	523,100,000
Glass products	298,700,000	436,000,000
Preserved fruits and vegetables	304,000,000	415,500,000

After New York City and Chicago, Pittsburgh is the 3d most popular site in the US for corporate headquarters, including many of the world's largest industrial corporations. Among the leading companies are Gulf Oil, with 1979 assets of $17.3 billion; US Steel, $11 billion; Westinghouse Electric, $6.8 billion; as well as Rockwell International, Aluminum Co. of America, National Steel, PPG Industries, and H. J. Heinz. Other major corporations headquartered in the state are Sun, a petroleum refiner in Radnor, $7.5 billion; and Bethlehem Steel in Bethlehem, $5.2 billion. Scott Paper, Crown Cork and Seal, and SmithKline (pharmaceuticals), have their headquarters in Philadelphia, Armstrong Cork in Lancaster, Hershey Foods in Hershey, and Hammermill Paper in Erie.

30 COMMERCE

A large ingredient in Philadelphia's early economy, trade remains important to the state, accounting for 16% of the estimated gross state product in 1978.

According to federal data, wholesale trade in 1972 totaled $31.9 billion, 6th highest in the US. The main items sold were groceries and related products; machinery, equipment, and supplies; motor vehicles and automotive parts and supplies; metals and minerals (excluding petroleum); electrical goods; and petroleum and petroleum products.

Pennsylvania ranked 5th in the US in retail trade in 1977, with $37.2 billion in sales. Philadelphia led all cities with nearly 12% of all sales, followed by Pittsburgh with 4%. The top sales categories were grocery stores, 20%; new car dealers, 17%;

department stores, 12%; gasoline service stations, 8%; and eating places, 7%. Philadelphian John Wanamaker opened the world's first department store in 1876; a century later, Pennsylvania had 511 department stores, 14 of them in Philadelphia and 10 in Pittsburgh.

During the colonial era, Philadelphia was one of the busiest Atlantic ports, and the leading port for the lucrative Caribbean trade. Philadelphia remains one of the country's leading foreign trade centers, although these days the main import suppliers are Nigeria, Saudi Arabia, and Algeria rather than the West Indies and Great Britain. During 1977, the Delaware River ports processed 72,567,468 tons of import cargo worth $8 billion, of which fully 80% consisted of mineral fuels, primarily crude oil. Also passing through the ports were 4,206,178 tons of exports worth $2 billion. Total exports of Pennsylvania manufactures had a value of $4.7 billion (7th in the US) in 1976; exports of the state's agricultural products totaled $137 million (33d) in 1976/77.

³¹CONSUMER PROTECTION

The Department of Justice's Bureau of Consumer Protection maintains regional offices in Erie, Harrisburg, Philadelphia, Pittsburgh, and Scranton. Also within the department is the Office of the Consumer Advocate, established in 1976, which represents citizens' interests before the Public Utilities Commission. The Bureau of Advocacy in the Department of Aging is designed to ensure that senior citizens' needs are being met by the programs of other state agencies. Pennsylvanians are encouraged to report instances of fraud, waste, or mismanagement of state funds through a toll-free telephone service maintained by the Taxpayer Information Program under the Department of the Auditor General. Other consumer services protect state residents against insurance fraud and illegal marketing of milk products.

³²BANKING

Philadelphia is the nation's oldest banking center, and Third St. between Chestnut and Walnut has been called the cradle of American finance. The first chartered commercial bank in the US was the Bank of North America, granted its charter in Philadelphia by the federal government in December 1781 and by Pennsylvania in April 1782. The first Bank of the US was headquartered in Philadelphia from its inception in 1791 to 1811, when its charter was allowed to expire. Its building was bought by Stephen Girard, a private banker whose new institution quickly became one of the nation's largest banks. As of 1979, the Girard Bank had assets of $4.4 billion, making it the 50th largest commercial bank in the US.

By the early 1800s, Philadelphia had reached its zenith as the nation's financial center. It was the home of the Bank of Pennsylvania, founded in 1793; the Bank of Philadelphia (1804); the Farmers and Mechanics Bank (1809); the Philadelphia Savings Fund Society (1816), the first mutual savings bank; and the most powerful of all, the Second Bank of the US (1816). After 1823, under the directorship of Nicholas Biddle, this bank became an international leader and the only rival to New York City's growing banking industry. When President Jackson vetoed the bank's recharter in 1831, Philadelphia lost its preeminence as a banking center.

Pittsburgh also rose to prominence during the Gilded Age, in great part because of the efforts of its most successful financier, Andrew Mellon. As of 1979, the Mellon Bank was the nation's 17th largest, with assets of $13.5 billion. Other major institutions include the First Pennsylvania Bank (26th), Philadelphia National Bank (32d), and Pittsburgh National Bank (33d). First Pennsylvania, in financial difficulty for several years, was saved from possible failure early in 1980 through a loan package engineered by the Federal Deposit Insurance Corporation.

As of 31 December 1978, Pennsylvania had 370 insured commercial banks with $18 billion in demand deposits, $37.3 billion in time deposits, and $72.2 billion in assets (5th in the US). The

417 savings and loan associations held $19.5 billion in assets and $16.3 billion in outstanding mortgage loans. There were 1,342 federally chartered credit unions with 1,212,002 members and $1.5 billion in assets, and 197 state-chartered credit unions with 202,030 members and $195,499,000 in assets.

³³INSURANCE

As in banking, Philadelphia has been a leading center for the insurance business. Most of the first insurance comanies underwrote only maritime insurance for goods in trade; fire and casualty insurance and life insurance did not become popular until the early 1800s. One of the oldest stock property and casualty firms, the Insurance Co. of North America, was formed in Philadelphia in 1792. It is now the largest in Pennsylvania and, as of 1979, was the 8th-largest diversified financial company in the US, with assets of nearly $9 billion.

Of the 1,121 insurance companies operating in Pennsylvania in 1977, 790 were out-of-state companies and 331 were based in the state. Premiums written in the state totaled $8.6 billion, of which Pennsylvania companies accounted for 37%.

The 385 life companies wrote $3 billion in premiums (9% by Pennsylvania companies) during 1977. As of 1978, Pennsylvanians held 24.8 million life insurance policies worth $156.2 billion, averaging $35,400 per family; policyholders received nearly $1.8 billion in benefits. The largest in-state company, Penn Mutual (18th largest in the US), had $3.7 billion in assets in 1979. Of the 600 fire and casualty insurers, 394 were out-of-state and 206 were Pennsylvania companies; nearly $3.8 billion in premiums were written, 32% by state firms.

All insurance companies operating in the state are regulated by the Insurance Department, as are all insurance brokers and agents. During 1978, the Bureau of Policyholders Service and Enforcement handled 35,371 consumer complaints and recovered $4.4 million for state policyholders. The department prepares shoppers' guides and was a leader in seeking to make the language of insurance policies more readable and comprehensible to the ordinary policyholder.

³⁴SECURITIES

Formally established in 1790, the Philadelphia Stock Exchange is the oldest stock exchange in the US. It was also the nation's most important exchange until the 1820s, when the New York Stock Exchange eclipsed it. Since World War II, the Philadelphia exchange has merged with stock exchanges in Baltimore (1949), Washington, D.C. (1953), and Pittsburgh (1969); in 1974, it established a trading floor in Miami. As the primary odd-lot market for Government National Mortgage Association securities, and as a leading market for odd-lot government securities and stock options, it ranks after only the New York and American exchanges in trading volume. In 1979, 173,191,319 shares of stock and 4,935,688 options contracts were traded by 410 member firms.

As of 1978, New York Stock Exchange member firms had 187 sales offices and 1,863 registered representatives in the state. Pennsylvanians reported $1.7 billion in dividend income on their 1977 federal tax returns.

Sales of securities are regulated by the Pennsylvania Securities Commission, which also licenses all securities dealers, agents, and investment advisers in the state.

³⁵PUBLIC FINANCE

Pennsylvania's budget is prepared annually by the Office of Budget and Administration and submitted by the governor (along with a plan for the next five fiscal years) to the general assembly for amendment and approval. By law, annual operating expenditures may not exceed available revenues and surpluses from prior years. The fiscal year runs from 1 July to 30 June.

The following table shows estimated general revenues and expenditures for the state government in 1979/80 and 1980/81 (in thousands):

REVENUES	1979/80	1980/81
Consumption taxes	$2,411,600	$2,573,400
Corporation taxes	1,847,400	1,894,700
Personal income taxes	1,675,900	1,763,600
Other taxes	267,500	306,500
Nontax revenues	191,200	228,600
TOTALS	$6,393,600	$6,766,800
EXPENDITURES		
Education	$3,064,769	$3,263,451
Health	1,198,799	1,319,342
Economic development, income maintenance	933,187	962,789
Social development	386,304	426,976
Public protection	271,299	293,771
Transportation and communications	168,080	146,938
Recreation and culture	79,105	79,015
Other expenses	272,887	293,162
TOTALS	$6,374,430	$6,785,444

The consolidated state budget, including revenues from the motor license fund, federal aid, and other fees and special fund revenues totaled $11.8 billion for 1980/81. The state debt as of 31 December 1979 was nearly $4.7 billion. As of mid-1977 the total state and local government debt was $16.7 billion, or $1,420 per capita.

During the 1970s, Philadelphia showed many of the fiscal ills typical of aging eastern cities: a stagnant economy, high tax base, deficit spending, deteriorating public works, and outmigration of upper-income whites to the suburbs. Early in 1980, the city's new mayor, William Green, announced a fiscal program involving cutbacks in some services, layoffs of city workers, and increased taxes. The following table summarizes Philadelphia's operating budget for 1978/79 (actual) and 1979/80 (estimated), in thousands:

REVENUES	1978/79	1979/80
Taxes	$727,800	$755,857
Nontax revenues	198,659	232,722
Revenues from other governments	392,741	426,587
Receipts from other city funds	22,603	27,920
Adjustments	20,433	2,156
TOTALS	$1,362,236	$1,445,242
EXPENDITURES		
Personal services	$587,785	$617,236
Purchase of services	338,606	388,936
Employee benefits	147,981	179,691
Debt service	148,195	150,614
Other expenditures	144,416	142,182
TOTALS	$1,366,983	$1,478,659

Pittsburgh's estimated operating revenues in 1979/80 were $179,020,267; expenditures, $179,467,951.

³⁶TAXATION

Pennsylvania's personal income tax, adopted in 1971, is levied at a rate of 2.2%. Business taxes include a corporation net income tax of 10.5%, capital stock and franchise tax, and taxes on public utilities, insurance premiums, and financial institutions. Pennsylvania's 6% sales and use tax exempts essential items like clothing, groceries, medicines, and residential utilities payments. An inheritance tax is levied at a rate of 6% for spouses and children and 15% for other heirs. Other taxable items include cigarettes, alcoholic beverages, and real estate transfers.

Municipalities may levy earned income, real estate, realty transfer, mercantile, amusement, and occupational taxes. As of 1977, all school districts levied real estate taxes. Among the major cities, Philadelphia, Pittsburgh, and Erie imposed income taxes.

In 1977, Pennsylvanians filed 4.6 million federal income tax returns, paying $8.5 billion in tax.

³⁷ECONOMIC POLICY

The Pennsylvania Industrial Development Authority and Pennsylvania Minority Business Development Authority help businesses build new facilities or renovate and expand older ones through low-interest long-term financing. New businesses may qualify for additional low-cost financing plans. Pennsylvania educational institutions are authorized to conduct research of benefit to in-state industries, and the Pennsylvania Science and Engineering Foundation Board promotes research-and-development activities and scientific and technical education throughout the state.

The Office of Business Ombudsman, within the Department of Commerce, helps the business community cut through government red tape by referring requests and complaints to appropriate state agencies. The Plant Location Division of the department's Bureau of Economic Development conducts in-state inspection tours and out-of-state promotional activities. Other departmental divisions assist Pennsylvania firms in developing export markets, aid foreign-owned firms who wish to establish facilities in the state, and compile and publish business statistics. Special programs are conducted by the Bureau of Minority Business Development and the Bureau of Appalachian Development.

The Department of Community Affairs coordinates local economic improvement programs. A portion of the state harness-racing fund is designated for construction and improvement of certain township and borough water-treatment and sewage-disposal facilities.

³⁸HEALTH

A checkered pattern dominates the state's medical history. During the mid-1700s, when Philadelphia's Dr. Benjamin Rush and the nation's first medical school were making the city a center for medical knowledge, rural Pennsylvanians were still treating themselves with herbs, charms, and incantations. As late as 1948, the American Public Health Association ranked the state among the worst in the quality of its public health services.

Pennsylvania's average life expectancy of 70.43 years—66.90 for males, 74.06 for females—ranked 33d in the US as of 1969–71. The infant mortality rate in 1977 was a high 12.6 per 1,000 live births for whites, 22.9 for nonwhites; both figures were above the US averages. An estimated 62,000 legal abortions were performed in 1977/78. Death rates for the leading causes of death—heart disease, cancer, and stroke—were well above the US average. Rates in 1978 per 100,000 population were as follows: heart disease, 412; cancer, 205; stroke, 87; accidents, 42; pneumonia and influenza, 24; diabetes, 18; cirrhosis of the liver, 14; arteriosclerosis, 15; suicide, 12; and early infant diseases, 10.

As of 30 June 1978, there were 9,103 residents in the 12 state mental retardation centers; another 5,800 persons were awaiting admission. State mental hospitals had 11,079 patients. Statewide in 1978 there were 313 hospitals of all types, with 86,474 beds; hospital personnel included 39,266 registered nurses and 14,092 licensed practical nurses. The average cost per stay in Pennsylvania hospitals in 1977, $1,584, was the 13th highest in the US, but the average cost per day, $189, ranked only 21st. There were 21,234 licensed physicians in the state in 1977, and 6,272 active dentists in 1979.

The University of Pennsylvania School of Medicine, which originated as the medical school of the College of Philadelphia in 1765, is the nation's oldest medical school. One of the nation's newest is the Hershey Medical Center of Pennsylvania State University. Other medical schools include the University of Pittsburgh School of Medicine, Temple University's School of Medicine, and Hahnemann Medical College, the last two in Philadelphia. The state also aids colleges of osteopathic medicine, podiatric medicine, and optometry in Philadelphia. Among the many medical certification boards in Philadelphia are the

American boards of allergy and immunology, internal medicine, ophthalmology, physicians, preventive medicine, and surgery.

³⁹ SOCIAL WELFARE

During 1978, 619,900 Pennsylvanians, of whom 419,200 were children, received $733 million in aid to families with dependent children. About 803,000 Pennsylvanians participated in the food stamp program at a cost to the federal government of $228.2 million. Close to $75.6 million in federal funds was spent on school lunches, providing food for 1,248,000 students, or 56% of the eligible enrollment.

In 1977, about 1,987,900 state residents received more than $5.3 billion in Social Security benefits; 1,277,400 retired workers received $3.4 billion, 458,400 survivors received $1.3 billion, and 251,900 disabled persons received $657 million. Supplemental Security Income totaling $269.3 million was paid to 169,500 Pennsylvanians in 1978.

About 30% of the beneficiaries of the federal Black Lung Benefit Program lived in Pennsylvania in 1978. Of the nearly 133,000 Pennsylvanians who received a total of $291 million in benefits, 41,000 were miners, 48,000 were miners' widows, and 44,000 were miners' dependents. As of 1977, 1,560,000 state residents received $913 million in Medicare hospital benefits and 1,529,000 received $344 million in Medicare medical payments.

About $52.5 million was spent on vocational rehabilitation in 1978, and $342 million on workers' compensation in 1977. The state spent $731 million on unemployment insurance benefits in 1978.

⁴⁰ HOUSING

Most of Pennsylvania's housing is owner-occupied. Of the 3,876,211 year-round housing units in the state in 1970, 2,549,277 were owned by their occupants, 1,156,133 were rented, and 170,801 were vacant. Only 5% of homeowners—but 14% of renters—were black. About 79% of all housing units were in metropolitan areas, 32% in metropolitan Philadelphia alone. Nearly 96% of all units had full plumbing, above the national average. Of the mobile homes in the state in 1970, 75,327 were owner-occupied and 12,268 were rented.

More than 146,000 new housing units worth $4.2 billion were authorized from 1976 to the end of 1978. Nearly three-fourths of them were single-family units. Faced with a decaying housing stock, Philadelphia during the 1970s encouraged renovation of existing units along with the construction of new ones.

⁴¹ EDUCATION

Pennsylvania lagged behind many of its neighbors in establishing a free public school system. From colonial times until the 1830s, almost all instruction in reading and writing took place in private schools. Called "dame schools" in the cities and "neighborhood schools" in rural areas, these primary courses were usually taught by women in their own homes. In addition, the Quakers, Moravians, and Scotch-Irish Presbyterians all formed their own private schools, emphasizing religious study. Many communities also set up secondary schools, called academies, on land granted by the state; by 1850, there were 524 academies, some of which later developed into colleges. A public school law passed in 1834 was not mandatory in the school districts but was still unpopular. Thaddeus Stevens, then a state legislator, is credited with saving the law from repeal in 1835. Two years later, more than 40% of the state's children were in public schools.

As of 1970, only 1% of the population was illiterate, slightly better than the US average. By 1976, adult Pennsylvanians had completed a median of 12.4 years of schooling. The proportion of adult high school graduates, 64.8%, was somewhat below the US average, and the figure for those 25 years of age or older, 60.5%, was considerably lower. About 12% of all state residents had completed four or more years of college, again below the national norm.

During the 1978/79 school year, 1,008,664 public school students were enrolled in grades K–6, and 1,038,082 in grades 7–12.

Enrollment in private elementary schools was 289,630; in private secondary schools, 116,855. More than half of the state's 1,667 private schools were Roman Catholic, and they accounted for at least four-fifths of all non-public school enrollment.

Enrollment in the 13 state-owned colleges in 1978/79 totaled 66,590. Indiana University of Pennsylvania, established in 1872, is the only state-controlled university; its enrollment reached 11,727 in 1978/79. Four universities have nonprofit corporate charters but are classified as state-related: Pennsylvania State University, Temple University, the University of Pittsburgh, and Lincoln University. Of these, Penn State was by far the largest, with a 1978/79 enrollment of 59,694. Founded in 1855 as the Farmers' High School of Pennsylvania, Penn State now has its main campus at University Park and 19 smaller campuses statewide. In 1977, there were 14 state-run community colleges.

The 14 state-aided private institutions (receiving designated grants from the legislature) had a combined enrollment of 44,031 in 1977. The largest of these schools is the University of Pennsylvania, founded in 1740 by Benjamin Franklin as the Philadelphia Academy and Charitable School; among its noteworthy professional schools is the Wharton School of Business. The state's many private colleges and universities, which may also receive state aid through a per-pupil funding formula, include Bryn Mawr College (founded in 1880), Bucknell University (1846) in Lewisburg, Carnegie-Mellon University (1900) in Pittsburgh, Dickinson College (1733) in Carlisle, Duquesne University (1878) in Pittsburgh, Haverford College (1833), Swarthmore College (1864), and Villanova University (1842). Enrollment at all private colleges and universities in the state totaled 138,614 in fall 1977. The Pennsylvania Higher Education Assistance Agency offers higher education grants, guarantees private loans, and administers work-study programs for Pennsylvania students.

During the 1978/79 school year, public school district revenues were nearly $4 billion. Per capita school expenditures of $412 in 1977/78 were only the 17th among the 50 states, but per pupil expenditures of $2,079 ranked 7th.

⁴² ARTS

Philadelphia was the cultural capital of the colonies, and rivaled New York as a theatrical center during the 1800s. By 1980, however, Philadelphia had only four legitimate theaters. A number of regional and summer-stock theaters are scattered throughout the state, the most noteworthy being in Bucks County, Lancaster, and Pittsburgh.

Pennsylvania's most significant contribution to the performing arts has come through music. One of America's first important songwriters, Stephen Foster, grew up in Pittsburgh. The Pittsburgh Symphony, which began performing in 1896, first achieved prominence under Victor Herbert. Temporarily disbanded in 1910, the symphony was revived under Fritz Reiner in 1927; subsequent music directors have included William Steinberg and André Previn. Even more illustrious has been the career of the Philadelphia Orchestra, founded in 1900. Among this orchestra's best-known permanent conductors have been Leopold Stokowski and Eugene Ormandy, both of whom recorded extensively. Ormandy was succeeded in 1980 by Riccardo Muti. An important dance company, the Pennsylvania Ballet, is based in Philadelphia, which also has the Curtis Institute of Music, founded in 1924.

⁴³ LIBRARIES AND MUSEUMS

Pennsylvania's public libraries stocked 18,792,319 volumes during 1977/78, with a total circulation of 34,899,356. The largest public library in the state, and one of the oldest in the US, is the Free Library of Philadelphia, with 3,054,442 volumes in 46 branches. The Carnegie Library in Pittsburgh has 2,012,945 volumes and 20 branches. Harrisburg offers the State Library of Pennsylvania, with 906,232 volumes. The Alverthorpe Gallery Library in Jenkintown contains the Rosenwald collection of illustrated books dating from the 15th century.

Philadelphia is the site of the state's largest academic collection, the University of Pennsylvania Libraries, with 2,821,000 volumes. Other major academic libraries are at the University of Pittsburgh, 2,283,082 volumes; Penn State, 1,515,600; Temple, 1,217,141; Carnegie-Mellon, 549,765; and Swarthmore, 513,101.

Pennsylvania has more than 240 museums and historic sites, many of them in Philadelphia. The Franklin Institute, established in 1824 as an exhibition hall and training center for inventors and mechanics, is a leading showcase for science and technology. Other important museums include the Philadelphia Museum of Art, Academy of Natural Sciences, Pennsylvania Academy of the Fine Arts, Afro-American Historical and Cultural Museum, American Catholic Historical Society, American Swedish Historical Foundation Museum, and Museum of American Jewish History.

The Carnegie Institute in Pittsburgh is home to several major museums, including the Carnegie Museum of Natural History and the Museum of Art. Also in Pittsburgh are the Buhl Planetarium and Institute of Popular Science and the Frick Art Museum. Other institutions scattered throughout the state include the Moravian Museum, Bethlehem; US Army Military History Institute, Carlisle; Erie Art Center, Museum, and Old Custom House; Pennsylvania Lumber Museum, Galeton; Pennsylvania Historical and Museum Commission and William Penn Memorial Museum, Harrisburg; Pennsylvania Dutch Folk Culture Society, Lenhartsville; Schwenkfelder Museum, Pennsburg; and Railroad Museum of Pennsylvania, Strasburg.

Several old forts commemorate the French and Indian War, and George Washington's Revolutionary headquarters at Valley Forge is now a national historical park. Brandywine Battlefield (Chadds Ford) is another Revolutionary War site. Gettysburg National Military Park commemorates the Civil War. Other historic sites include Independence National Historical Park, Philadelphia; the Daniel Boone Homestead, Birdsboro; John Brown's House, Chambersburg; James Buchanan's home, Lancaster; and Ft. Augusta, Sunbury, a frontier outpost.

44 COMMUNICATIONS

Philadelphia already had mail links to surrounding towns and to Maryland and Virginia by 1737, when Benjamin Franklin was named deputy postmaster of the city, but service was slow and not always reliable. During the remainder of the century, significant improvements in delivery were made, but some townspeople devised ingenious ways of transmitting information even faster than the mails. Philadelphia stock exchange brokers, for instance, communicated with agents in New York by flashing coded signals with mirrors and lights from a series of high points across New Jersey, thereby receiving stock prices on the same day they were transacted. By 1846, the first telegraph service in the state linked Harrisburg and Lancaster. There were some 39,000 postal service workers in the state in 1977. Receipts by Philadelphia post offices exceeded $180 million in 1977/78.

Telephone service is provided by Bell Telephone of Pennsylvania and the Delaware Valley Telephone Co. In 1978 there were 9,519,098 telephones in the state; of the 7,225,456 residential telephones, 1,237,446 were in Philadelphia, and of the 2,293,642 business phones, 445,895 were in that city. Statewide there were 40,693,502 mi (65,489,965 km) of wire in cable, 62,624 mi (100,784 km) of aerial wire, 15,518 mi (24,974 km) of tube in coaxial cable, and 4,723 mi (7,601 km) of radio relay system. Pennsylvanians made 11.5 billion local calls and 1.2 billion toll calls in 1978.

Pittsburgh's KDKA became the world's first commercial radio station in 1920. By 1979, it was one of 183 AM stations in the state; in addition, there were 146 FM radio stations and 37 television stations. Philadelphia alone had 10 AM, 15 FM, and 7 television stations; Pittsburgh, 14 AM, 12 FM, and 6 television stations. Public television stations are located in Allentown/Beth-

lehem, Erie, Hershey, Philadelphia, Pittsburgh, Scranton/Wilkes-Barre, and University Park.

A combination of high population density and hilly terrain (impeding television transmission) has made Pennsylvania a leader in cable television. In 1978 there were 329 systems serving 1,574 communities and 1,257,168 subscribers (1st in the US).

45 PRESS

Benjamin Franklin may have been colonial Pennsylvania's most renowned publisher, but its first was Andrew Bradford, whose *American Weekly Mercury*, established in 1719, was the third newspaper to appear in the colonies. Founded nine years later, the *Pennsylvania Gazette* was purchased by Franklin in 1730 and served as the springboard for *Poor Richard's Almanack*, which was read widely throughout the colonies between 1732 and 1758. By 1775, 6 of the colonies' 34 newspapers were in Pennsylvania, including German-language weeklies in Germantown and Bethlehem.

During the 1800s, newspapers sprang up in all the major cities and many small communities. By 1880, Pittsburgh had 10 daily newspapers, more than any other city its size. After a series of mergers and closings, however, it was left with only 2 by 1980. The *Philadelphia Bulletin*, begun in 1847, remains the city's most widely read newspaper, though it suffered losses in circulation and revenue during the 1970s. The *Inquirer* (1829), second in circulation among the Philadelphia dailies, has won numerous awards for its investigative reporting.

In 1978, Pennsylvania had 31 morning newspapers with a circulation of 1,377,861, 78 evening newspapers with 2,527,493 circulation, and 14 Sunday papers with 3,009,955 circulation (all-day papers are included in both morning and evening figures). The following table shows the circulation of leading dailies in 1978:

AREA	NAME	DAILY	SUNDAY
Allentown	Call (m,S)	102,556 }	156,130
	Chronicle (e,S)	22,466 }	
Harrisburg	News (e,S)	64,511 }	155,909
	Patriot (m,S)	47,017 }	
Philadelphia	Bulletin (e,S)	485,781	584,818
	Inquirer (m,S)	419,497	831,818
	News (e)	225,120	
Pittsburgh	Post-Gazette (m)	189,446	
	Press (e,S)	260,845	655,959
Wilkes-Barre	Times-Leader (all day)	69,898	

The most widely read magazine in the US, *TV Guide*, with a 1979 circulation of 19,547,763, is produced by Walter Annenberg's Triangle Publications in Radnor. *Farm Journal* and *Current History*, both monthlies, are published in Philadelphia, and there are monthlies named for both Philadelphia and Pittsburgh. Of more specialized interest are the gardening, nutrition, and health magazines and books from Rodale Press in Emmaus and automotive guides from the Chilton Co. in Radnor.

46 ORGANIZATIONS

Philadelphia is the home for two major service organizations: Big Brothers/Big Sisters of America and the Grand United Order of Odd Fellows. Cultural and educational organizations in that city include the American Academy of Political and Social Science, American Philosophical Society, and Middle States Association of Colleges and Schools. The Association for Children with Learning Disabilities is located in Pittsburgh, the College Placement Council in Bethlehem, and the American Philatelic Society in State College. Also in State College is the Environmental Coalition on Nuclear Power. The Society for Animal Rights, a humane organization, is located in Clarks Summit.

Commercial and trade groups in the state include the National Boating Federation, Bryn Athyn; American Society of Newspaper Editors, Easton; Anthracite Institute, Harrisburg; American

Mushroom Institute, Kennett Square; Insurance Institute of America, Malvern; Photographic Society of America, Philadelphia; National Freight Transportation Association, Swarthmore; and Society of Automotive Engineers, Warrendale. The Gray Panthers, a senior citizens' activist group, and Women's Strike for Peace are in Philadelphia. Valley Forge is the home of the Patriotic Order of the Sons of America.

Among the many sports organizations headquartered in Pennsylvania are the US Squash Racquets Association, in Bala-Cynwyd; US Women's Lacrosse Association, Boiling Springs; National Trotting and Pacing Association, Hanover; Pop Warner Junior League Football and US Rowing Society, Philadelphia; and Little League Baseball, Williamsport.

[47] TOURISM, TRAVEL, AND RECREATION

Travelers and tourists spent an estimated $5 billion in Pennsylvania in 1978; of that, $2.7 billion was spent by out-of-state visitors, and $2.3 billion by state residents. Some 181,000 Pennsylvanians were employed in travel-related services. Allegheny County, benefiting from heavy business travel to Pittsburgh, led the state with a 20% share of expenditures, followed by Philadelphia with 18%.

Philadelphia—whose Independence National Historical Park has been called the most historic square mile in America—offers the Liberty Bell, Independence Hall, and Carpenter's Hall, and many other sites. North of Philadelphia, in Bucks County, is the town of New Hope, with its numerous crafts and antique shops. The Lancaster area is "Pennsylvania Dutch" country, featuring tours and exhibits of Amish farm life. Gettysburg contains not only the famous Civil War battlefield but also the home of Dwight D. Eisenhower, opened to the public in 1980. Among the more popular sites are Chocolate World and Hersheypark in the town of Hershey. Annual parades and festivals include the Mummers Parade on 1 January in Philadelphia and the Kutztown Folk Festival, commemorating Pennsylvania Dutch life, held the first week of July.

No less an attraction are the state's outdoor recreation areas. By far the most popular for both skiing and camping are the Delaware Water Gap and the Poconos, also a favorite resort region. During 1978, more than 35 million people used the state park system, which included 95 parks, 41 forest picnic areas, and 2 environmental education centers. Pennsylvania has far more licensed hunters than any other state, 1,286,248 in 1978, when the state also had 1,005,163 fishermen.

[48] SPORTS

Pennsylvanians at both ends of the state have access to major professional sports.

Philadelphia's Veterans Stadium is the home of baseball's Phillies (winners of the 1980 World Series), football's Eagles, and soccer's Fury, while the 76ers of the National Basketball Association and the Flyers of the National Hockey League both play at the Spectrum. Wilt Chamberlain starred for the 76ers championship team in 1967; Bobby Clarke and Bernie Parent led the Flyers to the Stanley Cup in 1974 and 1975.

After several dismal decades, the Pittsburgh Steelers emerged as a National Football League powerhouse during the 1970s. Led by such stars as Franco Harris, Terry Bradshaw, and "Mean" Joe Greene, and coached by Chuck Noll, the Steelers won the Super Bowl in 1975, 1976, 1979, and 1980. The Pirates—who, like the Steelers, play at Three Rivers Stadium—had won five world series as of 1980, most recently in 1979, behind Dave Parker and Willie Stargell. The Pittsburgh Penguins compete in the National Hockey League.

Horse racing is conducted at Keystone Race Track in Bucks County, Penn National Race Course in Dauphin County, and at Commodore Downs in Erie County. Harness-racing tracks include Liberty Park in northeast Philadelphia, the Meadows in Washington County, and Pocono Downs in Luzerne County.

The state taxes admissions and pari-mutuel receipts. Each June, Pennsylvania hosts a major auto race, the Pocono 500.

In collegiate football, the University of Pittsburgh Panthers were voted national champions in the postseason wire-service polls for 1976/77. Penn State, under coach Joe Paterno, has been ranked at or near the top of the polls since the 1960s; its Nittany Lions are frequent winners of the Lambert Cup, as the best independent college team in the East. Villanova has long had an excellent track and field program. The Penn Relays, an important amateur track meet, are held in Philadelphia every April.

Each summer, Williamsport hosts baseball's Little League world series.

[49] FAMOUS PENNSYLVANIANS

Johan Printz (b.Sweden, 1592–1663), the 400-lb, hard-drinking, hard-swearing, and hard-ruling governor of New Sweden, was Pennsylvania's first European resident of note. The founder of Pennsylvania was William Penn (b.England, 1644–1718); a Quaker of sober habits and deep religious beliefs, he combined humanitarian ideals with the shrewd business sense of a promoter. Penn and his family were greatly aided by his Scotch-Irish chief lieutenant, James Logan (b.Ireland, 1674–1751), and hindered by colonial attorney general David Lloyd (b.Wales, 1656–1731). Most extraordinary of all Pennsylvanians, Benjamin Franklin (b.Massachusetts, 1706–90), a printer, author, inventor, scientist, legislator, diplomat, and statesman, served the Philadelphia, Pennsylvania, and US governments in a variety of posts.

Only one native Pennsylvanian, James Buchanan (1791–1868), has ever become US president. Buchanan was a state assemblyman, five-term US representative, two-term US senator, secretary of state, and minister to Russia and then to Great Britain before entering the White House as a 65-year-old bachelor in 1857. As president, he tried to maintain the Union by avoiding extremes and preaching compromise, but his toleration of slavery was abhorrent to abolitionists and his desire to preserve the Union was obnoxious to secessionists. Dwight D. Eisenhower (b.Texas, 1890–1969) retired to a farm in Gettysburg after his presidency was over. George M. Dallas (1792–1864), Pennsylvania's only US vice-president, was James K. Polk's running mate.

The six Pennsylvanians who have served on the US Supreme Court have all been associate justices: James Wilson (1742–98), Henry Baldwin (1780–1844), Robert C. Grier (1794–1870), William Strong (1808–95), George Shiras, Jr. (1832–1924), and Owen J. Roberts (1875–1955).

Many other Pennsylvanians have held prominent federal positions. Albert Gallatin (b.Switzerland, 1761–1849), brilliant secretary of the treasury under Thomas Jefferson and James Madison, later served as minister to France and then to Great Britain. Richard Rush (1780–1859) was Madison's attorney general and John Quincy Adams's secretary of the treasury. A distinguished jurist, Jeremiah Sullivan Black (1810–83) was Buchanan's attorney general and later his secretary of state. John Wanamaker (1838–1922), an innovative department store merchandiser, served as postmaster general under Benjamin Harrison. Philander C. Knox (1853–1921) was Theodore Roosevelt's attorney general and William Howard Taft's secretary of state. Financier Andrew C. Mellon (1855–1937) was secretary of the treasury under Warren G. Harding, Calvin Coolidge, and Herber Hoover. Recent Pennsylvanians in high office include Richard Helms (b.1913), director of the US Central Intelligence Agency from 1966 to 1973, and Alexander Haig (b.1924), former commander of NATO forces in Europe, chief of staff under Richard Nixon, and Ronald Reagan's choice for secretary of state.

Three US senators, Simon Cameron (1799–1889), Matthew Quay (1833–1904), and Boies Penrose (1860–1921), are best known as leaders of the powerful Pennsylvania Republican machine. Senator Joseph F. Guffey (1870–1959) sponsored legislation to stabilize the bituminous coal industry. After serving as reform mayor of Philadelphia, Joseph S. Clark (b.1901) also distinguished himself in the Senate, and Hugh Scott (b.1900) was Republican minority leader from 1969 to 1977. Outstanding representatives from Pennsylvania include Thaddeus Stevens (1792–1868), leader of radical Republicans during the Civil War era; David Wilmot (1814–68), author of the proviso attempting to prohibit slavery in territory acquired from Mexico; and Samuel J. Randall (1828–90), speaker of the House of Representatives from 1876 to 1881.

Other notable historical figures include Joseph Galloway (b.Maryland, 1729?–1803), a loyalist; Robert Morris (b.England, 1734–1806), a Revolutionary financier; and Betsy Ross (Elizabeth Griscom, 1752–1836), the seamstress who allegedly stitched the first American flag. Pamphleteer Thomas Paine (b.England, 1737–1809), pioneer Daniel Boone (1734–1820), and General Anthony Wayne (1745–96) also distinguished themselves during this period. In the Civil War, General George B. McClellan (1826–85) led the Union army on the Peninsula and at the Battle of Antietam, while at the Battle of Gettysburg, Generals George Gordon Meade (b.Spain, 1815–72) and Winfield Scott Hancock (1824–86) both showed their military prowess.

Important state governors include John W. Geary (1819–73), Samuel W. Pennypacker (1843–1916), Robert E. Pattison (b.Maryland, 1850–1904), Gifford Pinchot (b.Connecticut, 1865–1946), James H. Duff (1883–1969), George H. Earle (1890–1974), Milton J. Shapp (b.Ohio, 1912), William W. Scranton (b.Connecticut, 1917), George M. Leader (b.1918), and Dick Thornburgh (b.1932).

Pennsylvanians have won Nobel Prizes in every category except literature. General George C. Marshall (1880–1959), chief of staff of the US Army in World War II and secretary of state when the European Recovery Program (Marshall Plan) was adopted, won the 1953 Nobel Peace Prize. Simon Kuznets (b.Russia, 1901) received the 1971 Nobel Prize in economic science for work on economic growth, and Herbert A. Simon (b.Wisconsin, 1916) received the 1978 award for work on decision making in economic organizations; in 1980, Lawrence R. Klein (b.Nebraska, 1920) was honored for his design and application of econometric models. In physics, Otto Stern (b.Germany, 1888–1969) won the 1943 prize for work on the magnetic momentum of protons. In chemistry, Theodore W. Richards (1868–1928) won the 1914 Nobel Prize for determining the atomic weight of many elements, and Christian Boehmer Anfinsen (b.1916) won the 1972 award for pioneering studies in enzymes. In physiology or medicine, Philip S. Hench (1896–1965) won in 1950 for his discoveries about hormones of the adrenal cortex, Haldane K. Hartline (b.1903) won in 1967 for work on the human eye, and Howard M. Temin (b.1934) was honored in 1975 for the study of tumor viruses.

Many other Pennsylvanians were distinguished scientists. Ebenezer Kinnersly (1711–78) studied electricity, and Benjamin Franklin's grandson Alexander Dallas Bache (1806–67) was an expert on magnetism. Caspar Wistar (b.Germany, 1761–1818) and Thomas Woodhouse (1770–1809) pioneered the study of chemistry, while William Maclure (b.Scotland, 1763–1840) and James Mease (1771–1846) were early geologists. David Rittenhouse (1732–96) was a distinguished astronomer. John Bartram (1699–1777) and his son William (1739–1823) won international repute as botanists. Benjamin Rush (1745–1813) was Pennsylvania's most distinguished physician, as well as an influential political leader and social reformer. Philip Syng Physick (1768–1837) was a leading surgeon, and Nathaniel Chapman (b.Virginia, 1780–1853) was the first president of the American Medical Association. Rachel Carson (1907–64), a marine biologist and writer, became widely known for her crusade against the use of chemical pesticides. Pennsylvania inventors include steamboat builder Robert Fulton (1765–1815); David Thomas (1794–1882),

the father of the American anthracite iron industry; William Kelly (1811–88), who discovered the "air boiling" process for making steel; Charles M. Hall (1863–1914), creator of an inexpensive process to produce aluminum; and Christopher L. Sholes (1819–90), who helped invent the typewriter.

Pennsylvania played a large role in the economic development of the US. In addition to Mellon, outstanding bankers include Stephen Girard (b.France, 1750–1831), Nicholas Biddle (1786–1844), Anthony J. Drexel (1826–93), and John J. McCloy (b.1895). "Baron" Henry William Stiegel (b.Germany, 1729–85) made glass of remarkable quality. J. Edgar Thomson (1808–74), Thomas A. Scott (1823–81), and Alexander J. Cassatt (1839–1906) built the Pennsylvania Railroad into a vast transport network. Andrew Carnegie (b.Scotland, 1835–1919) and his lieutenants, including Henry Clay Frick (1849–1919) and Charles M. Schwab (1862–1939), created the most efficient steel-manufacturing company in the 19th century. Efficiency expert Frederick W. Taylor (1856–1915) was the initiator of scientific management. Wanamaker, Frank W. Woolworth (b.New York, 1852–1919), and Sebastian S. Kresge (1867–1966) were pioneer merchandisers. Pennsylvania labor leaders include Uriah S. Stephens (1821–82) and Terence V. Powderly (1849–1924), leaders of the Knights of Labor; Philip Murray (b.Scotland, 1886–1952), president of the CIO; and David J. MacDonald (1902–79), leader of the steelworkers. Among economic theorists, Henry George (1839–97) was the unorthodox advocate of the single tax. Florence Kelley (1859–1932) was an important social reformer, as is Bayard Rustin (b.1910).

Important early religious leaders, all born in Germany, include Henry Melchior Muhlenberg (1711–87), organizer of Pennsylvania's Lutherans; Count Nikolaus Ludwig von Zinzendorf (1700–1760), a Moravian leader; and Johann Conrad Beissel (1690–1768), founder of the Ephrata Cloister. David Brainerd (b.Connecticut, 1718–47) was a Presbyterian missionary to the Indians. Demetrius Augustine Gallitzin (b.Netherlands, 1770–1840), a Catholic missionary, founded the town of Loretto (1799); Charles Taze Russell (1852–1916), born a Congregationalist, founded the group that later became Jehovah's Witnesses. Among the state's outstanding scholars are historians Henry C. Lee (1825–1909), John Bach McMaster (1852–1932), Ellis Paxson Oberholtzer (1868–1936), and Henry Steele Commager (b. 1902); anthropologist Margaret Mead (1901–78), behavioral psychologist Burrhus Frederic Skinner (b.1904), urbanologist Jane Jacobs (b.1916), and language theorist Noam Chomsky (b.1928). Thomas Gallaudet (b.1787–1851) was a pioneer in education of the deaf.

Pennsylvania has produced a large number of distinguished journalists and writers. In addition to Franklin, newspapermen include John Dunlap (b.Ireland, 1747–1812), Benjamin Franklin Bache (1769–98), William L. McLean (1852–1931), and Moses L. Annenberg (1878–1942). Magazine editors were Sarah Josepha Buell Hale (b.New Hampshire, 1788–1879), Cyrus H. K. Curtis (b.Maine, 1850–1933), Edward W. Bok (b.Netherlands, 1863–1930), and Isidor Feinstein Stone (b.1907). Ida M. Tarbell (1857–1944) was perhaps Pennsylvania's most famous muckraker. Among the many noteworthy Pennsylvania-born writers are Charles Brockden Brown (1771–1810), Bayard Taylor (1825–78), novelist and physician Silas Weir Mitchell (1829–1914), Charles Godfrey Leland (1824–1903), Owen Wister (1860–1938), Richard Harding Davis (1864–1916), Gertrude Stein (1874–1946), Mary Roberts Rinehart (1876–1958), Hervey Allen (1889–1949), Christopher Morley (1890–1957), Conrad Richter (1890–1968), John O'Hara (1905–70), Donald Barthelme (b.1931), and John Updike (b.1932); James Michener (b.New York, 1907) was raised in the state. Pennsylvania playwrights include James Nelson Barker (1784–1858), Maxwell Anderson (1888–1959), George S. Kaufman (1889–1961), Marc Connelly (1890–1980), Clifford Odets (1906–63), and Ed Bullins (b.1935). Among Pennsylvania poets are

Francis Hopkinson (1737–91), Philip Freneau (b.New York, 1752–1832), Thomas Dunn English (1819–1902), Thomas Buchanan Read (1822–72), and Wallace Stevens (1879–1955).

Composers include Stephen Collins Foster (1826–64), Ethelbert Woodbridge Nevin (1862–1901), Charles Wakefield Cadman (1881–1946), and Samuel Barber (b.1910). Among Pennsylvania painters prominent in the history of American art are Benjamin West (1738–1820), renowned as the father of American painting, Charles Willson Peale (1741–1827), who was also a naturalist, Thomas Sully (b.England, 1783–1872), George Catlin (1796–1872), Thomas Eakins (1844–1916), Mary Cassatt (1845–1926), Man Ray (1890–1976), Andrew Wyeth (b.1917), and Andy Warhol (b.1927). Outstanding sculptors include William Rush (1756–1833), George Grey Barnard (1863–1938), and Alexander Calder (1898–1976). Distinguished Pennsylvania architects include Benjamin Henry Latrobe (b.England, 1764–1820), William Strickland (1787?–1854), Thomas U. Walter (1804–87), Charles Follen McKim (1847–1909), Paul Philippe Cret (b.France, 1876–1945), George Howe (1886–1955), William Lescaze (b.Switzerland, 1896–1969), Louis I. Kahn (b.Estonia, 1901–74), and Robert Venturi (b.1925).

Pennsylvania produced and patronized a host of actors, including Edwin Forrest (1806–72), Lionel (1878–1954), Ethel (1879–1959), and John (1882–1942) Barrymore; W. C. Fields (William Claude Dukenfield, 1880–1946); Ed Wynn (Isaiah Edwin Leopold, 1886–1966); William Powell (b.1892); Ethel Waters (1896–1977); Janet Gaynor (b.1906); James Stewart (b.1908): Broderick Crawford (b.1911); Gene Kelly (b.1912); Charles Bronson (Charles Buchinsky, b.1922); Mario Lanza (1925–59); Shirley Jones (b.1934); and comedians Bill Cosby (b.1937) and David Brenner (b.1945). Film directors Joseph L. Mankiewicz (b.1909), Arthur Penn (b.1922), and Sidney Lumet (b.1924), and film producer David O. Selznick (1902–65) also came from Pennsylvania.

Pennsylvania has produced outstanding musicians. Four important Pennsylvania-born vocalists are Marian Anderson (b.1902), Blanche Thebom (b.1919), Marilyn Horne (b.1934), and Anna Moffo (b.1934). Pianists include the versatile Oscar Levant (1906–72) and jazz interpreters Earl "Fatha" Hines (b.1905) and Erroll Garner (1921–77). Popular band leaders include Fred Waring (b.1900), Jimmy Dorsey (1904–57) and his brother Tommy (1905–56), and Les Brown (b.1912). Perry Como (b.1913) has achieved renown among popular singers. Dancers and choreographers from Pennsylvania include Martha Graham (b.1894), Paul Taylor (b.1930), and Gelsey Kirkland (b.1952).

Of the many outstanding athletes associated with Pennsylvania, Jim Thorpe (b.Oklahoma, 1888–1953) was most versatile, having starred in Olympic pentathlon and decathlon events and football. Baseball Hall of Famers include Honus Wagner (1874–1955), Stan Musial (b.1920), and Roy Campanella (b.1921). Outstanding Pennsylvania football players include Harold "Red" Grange (b.1903), George Blanda (b.1927), John Unitas (b.1933), Joe Namath (b.1943), and Tony Dorsett (b.1954). Other stars include basketball's Wilt Chamberlain (b.1936); golf's Arnold Palmer (b.1929); tennis' Bill Tilden (1893–1953); horse racing's Bill Hartack (b.1932); billiards' Willie Mosconi (b.1913); swimming's Johnny Weissmuller (b.1904); and track and field's Bill Toomey (b.1939).

Pennsylvania has also been the birthplace of a duchess—Bessie Wallis Warfield, the Duchess of Windsor (b.1896)—and of a princess—Grace Kelly, Princess Grace of Monaco (b.1929).

50 BIBLIOGRAPHY

Billinger, Robert D. *Pennsylvania's Coal Industry*. Gettysburg: Pennsylvania Historical Association, 1954.

Binder, Frederick Moor. *Coal Age Empire: Pennsylvania Coal and Its Utilization to 1860*. Harrisburg: Pennsylvania Historical and Museum Commission, 1974.

Bridenbaugh, Carl. *Cities in Revolt: Urban Life in America, 1743–76*. New York: Capricorn, 1964.

Clark, Victor S. *History of Manufactures in the United States*. 3 vols. New York: McGraw-Hill, 1929.

Cochran, Thomas C. *Pennsylvania: A Bicentennial History*. New York: Norton, 1978.

Federal Writers' Project. *Pennsylvania: A Guide to the Keystone State*. New York: Oxford University Press, 1940.

Hammond, Bray. *Banks and Politics in America: From the Revolution to the Civil War*. Princeton: Princeton University Press, 1957.

Klein, Philip S., and Ari Hoogenboom. *A History of Pennsylvania*. Rev. ed. University Park: Pennsylvania State University Press, 1980.

Murphy, Raymond E. and Marion. *Pennsylvania: A Regional Geography*. Harrisburg: Pennsylvania Book Service, 1937.

Pennsylvania, Commonwealth of. Bureau of Statistics, Research, and Planning. *1979 Pennsylvania Statistical Abstract*. 21st ed. Harrisburg, 1979.

Pennsylvania, Commonwealth of. Department of General Services. *The Pennsylvania Manual, 1978/79*. Vol. 104. Harrisburg, 1979.

Pennsylvania, Commonwealth of. *Governor's Executive Budget, 1980–81*. Harrisburg, 1980.

Pennsylvania Chamber of Commerce. *Pennsylvania Government Today*. State College, Pa.: Pennsylvania Valley Publishers, 1973.

Philadelphia, City of. *The Mayor's Fiscal 1981 Operating Budget*. Philadelphia, 1980.

Rizza, Paul F., et al. *Pennsylvania Atlas: A Thematic Atlas of the Keystone State*. Berlin, Conn.: Atlas Publishing, 1975.

Stevens, Sylvester K. *Pennsylvania: Birthplace of a Nation*. New York: Random House, 1964.

Stradley, Leighton P. *Early Financial and Economic History of Pennsylvania*. New York: Commerce Clearing House, 1942.

Wallace, Paul A. W. *Pennsylvania: Seed of a Nation*. New York: Harper and Row, 1962.

Warner, Sam Bass, Jr. *The Private City: Philadelphia in Three Periods of Its Growth*. Philadelphia: University of Pennsylvania Press, 1968.

RHODE ISLAND

State of Rhode Island and Providence Plantations

ORIGIN OF STATE NAME: Named for Rhode Island in Narragansett Bay, which was likened to the isle of Rhodes in the Mediterranean Sea. **NICKNAME:** The Ocean State. (Also: Little Rhody.) **CAPITAL:** Providence. **ENTERED UNION:** 29 May 1790 (13th). **SONG:** "Rhode Island." **MOTTO:** Hope. **COAT OF ARMS:** A golden anchor on a blue field. **FLAG:** In the center of a white field is a golden anchor and, beneath it, a blue ribbon with the state motto in gold letters, all surrounded by a circle of 13 gold stars. **OFFICIAL SEAL:** The anchor of the arms is surrounded by four scrolls, the topmost bearing the state motto; the words "Seal of the State of Rhode Island and Providence Plantations 1636" encircle the whole. **BIRD:** Rhode Island Red. **FLOWER:** Violet. **TREE:** Red maple. **MINERAL:** Bowenite. **ROCK:** Cumberlandite. **LEGAL HOLIDAYS:** New Year's Day, 1 January; Washington's Birthday, 3d Monday in February; Rhode Island Independence Day, 4 May; Memorial Day, last Monday in May; Independence Day, 4 July; Victory Day, 2d Monday in August; Labor Day, 1st Monday in September; Columbus Day, 2d Monday in October; Election Day, 1st Tuesday after 1st Monday in November, in even-numbered years; Veterans Day, 11 November; Thanksgiving Day, 4th Thursday in November; Christmas Day, 25 December. **TIME:** 7 A.M. EST = noon GMT.

¹LOCATION, SIZE, AND EXTENT

One of the six New England states in the northeastern US, Rhode Island is the smallest of all the 50 states. Rhode Island occupies only 0.03% of the total US area, and could fit inside Alaska, the largest state, nearly 486 times.

The total area of Rhode Island is 1,214 sq mi (3,144 sq km), of which land comprises 1,049 sq mi (2,717 sq km), and inland water 165 sq mi (427 sq km). The state extends 37 mi (60 km) E–W and 48 mi (77 km) N–S.

Rhode Island is bordered on the N and E by Massachusetts; on the S by the Atlantic Ocean (enclosing the ocean inlet, Narragansett Bay); and on the W by Connecticut (with part of the line formed by the Pawcatuck River). Three large islands—Prudence, Aquidneck (officially known as Rhode Island), and Conanicut—are situated within Narragansett Bay. Block Island, with an area of about 11 sq mi (28 sq km), lies some 9 mi (14 km) SW of Pt. Judith, on the mainland.

The total boundary length of Rhode Island is 160 mi (257 km). The state's geographic center is in Kent County, 1 mi (1.6 km) SSW of Crompton.

²TOPOGRAPHY

Rhode Island comprises two main regions. The New England Upland Region, which is rough and hilly and marked by forests and lakes, occupies the western two-thirds of the state, while the Seaboard Lowland, with its sandy beaches and salt marshes, occupies the eastern third. The highest point in the state is Jerimoth Hill, at 812 feet (247 meters), in the northwest.

Rhode Island's principal river, the Blackstone, flows from Woonsocket past Pawtucket and thence into the Providence River, which, like the Sakonnet, is an estuary of Narragansett Bay; the Pawcatuck River flows into Block Island Sound. The state has some 38 islands, the largest being Aquidneck (Rhode Island), with an area of about 45 sq mi (117 sq km).

³CLIMATE

Rhode Island has a humid climate, with cold winters and short summers. The average annual temperature is 50°F (10°C). At Providence the temperature ranges from an average of 28°F (−2°C) in January to 72°F (22°C) in July. The record high temperature, 104°F (40°C), was registered in Providence on 2 August 1975; the record low, −23°F (−31°C), at Kingston on 11 January

1942. In Providence, the average annual precipitation is 43 in (109 cm); snowfall averages 38 in (97 cm) a year. Rhode Island's weather is highly changeable, with storms and hurricanes an occasional threat.

⁴FLORA AND FAUNA

Though small, Rhode Island has three distinct life zones: sand-plain lowlands, rising hills, and highlands. Common trees are the tuliptree, pin and post oaks, and red cedar. Cattails are abundant in marsh areas, and 40 types of fern and 30 species of orchid are indigenous to the state. The smaller wall begonia, native to Rhode Island, is listed by the federal government as an endangered plant.

Urbanization and industrialization have taken their toll of native mammals. Swordfish, bluefish, lobsters, and clams populate coastal waters; brook trout and pickerel are among the common freshwater fish. As of 1980, Rhode Island had no official list of endangered and threatened species, although the bobcat, fisher, otter, and coyote, among other animals, were under consideration. The Indiana bat is on the federal endangered list.

⁵ENVIRONMENTAL PROTECTION

The Department of Environmental Management coordinates all of the state's environmental protection programs. The Division of Air Resources enforces controls on open-air dumps, open fires, and industrial pollution; the Division of Water Resources regulates waste-treatment facilities and the discharge of industrial waste into state waters and public sewer facilities; the Division of Land Resources oversees solid-waste disposal and individual home sewage disposal systems; and the Division of Coastal Resources reviews any development or operation affecting the tidelands. The department also supervises forests, parks, and recreational facilities, fish and game resources, and boating safety.

⁶POPULATION

Rhode Island ranked 39th in population among the 50 states, with a 1970 census total of 949,723. The preliminary total for 1980 was 945,761, a drop of 0.4%; outmigration of naval personnel and a shrinking birthrate contributed to the decrease. In 1978, Rhode Island was, at 891 persons per sq mi (344 per sq km), the nation's 2d most densely populated state, after New Jersey. According to the 1970 census, 92% of all Rhode Islanders lived in metropolitan areas, one of the highest such percentages in the

481

US. Providence, the capital, is the leading city, with a population in 1980 of 156,421, according to preliminary census data.

⁷ETHNIC GROUPS

Rhode Island's black population numbered 25,000 in 1976, or less than 3% of the state total. Among other minority groups, the 1970 census counted 1,761 Filipinos, 1,093 Chinese, and 629 Japanese. There were 1,390 American Indians.

Foreign-born Rhode Islanders or those of foreign or mixed parentage made up one-third of the population in 1970. Eight percent of all state residents were of Italian origin, and 7% French-Canadian.

⁸LANGUAGES

Many place-names in Rhode Island attest to the early presence of Mahican Indians: Sakonnet Point, Pawtucket, Matunuck, Narragansett. Only 117 state residents claimed Indian first languages in 1970, however.

In 1970, only 68% of the native-born and 64% of all residents said their mother tongue was English. English in Rhode Island is of the Northern dialect, with the distinctive features of eastern New England: absence of final /r/, and a vowel in *part* and *bath* intermediate between that in *father* and that in *bat*.

Major resident groups reported these first languages in 1970:

	NATIVE-BORN	FOREIGN-BORN
English	596,654	13,602
French	90,653	10,617
Italian	61,963	14,394
Portuguese	23,871	14,934
Polish	13,142	2,710

⁹RELIGIONS

The first European settlement in Rhode Island was founded by an English clergyman, Roger Williams, who left Massachusetts to find freedom of worship. The Rhode Island Charter of 1663 proclaimed "that a most flourishing civil state may stand and best be maintained with full liberty in religious concernments." Rhode Island has maintained this viewpoint throughout its history, and has long been a model of religious pluralism. The first Baptist congregation in the US was established in 1638 in Providence. In Newport stands the oldest synagogue (1763) and the oldest Quaker meetinghouse (1699) in the US.

There were 597,596 Roman Catholics in 1979, and an estimated 22,000 Jews. In 1971, known Protestant adherents totaled 110,454. Of these, 43,390 were Episcopalians, 26,386 belonged to the American Baptist Convention, and 11,080 to the United Church of Christ.

¹⁰TRANSPORTATION

Conrail, Amtrak, and five private railroads serve the state, operating on 139 mi (224 km) of track as of 1974. In 1977 there were 5,793 mi (9,323 km) of highways, streets, and roads; 679,256 motor vehicles were registered in 1978, and 580,544 driver's licenses were in force. The major route through New England, I-95, crosses Rhode Island. Some of the best deepwater ocean ports on the east coast are in Narragansett Bay, which in 1977/78 handled 6,642,510 tons of cargo. There were 8 public and 15 private airports in 1978. Theodore Francis Green Airport is the state's major air terminal, with 12 airlines providing some 100 scheduled flights daily.

¹¹HISTORY

Before the arrival of the first white settlers, the Narragansett Indians inhabited the area from what is now Providence south along Narragansett Bay. Their principal rivals, the Wampanoag, dominated the eastern shore region. Including such smaller tribes as the Nipmuc and Niantic, the Indians totaled about 10,000 by 1600.

In 1524, Florentine navigator Giovanni da Verrazano, sailing in the employ of France, became the first European to explore Rhode Island. The earliest permanent settlement was estab-

lished at Providence in 1636 by English clergyman Roger Williams and a small band of followers who left the repressive atmosphere of the Massachusetts Bay Colony to seek freedom of worship. Other nonconformists followed, settling Portsmouth (1638), Newport (1639), and Warwick (1642). In 1644, Williams journeyed to England, where he secured a parliamentary patent uniting the four original towns into a single colony, the Providence Plantations. This legislative grant remained in effect until the Stuart Restoration made it prudent to seek a royal charter. The charter, secured for Rhode Island and the Providence Plantations from Charles II in 1663, guaranteed religious liberty, permitted significant local autonomy, and strengthened the colony's territorial claims. Encroachments by white settlers on Indian lands led to the Indian uprising known as King Philip's War (1675–76), during which the Indians were soundly defeated.

The early 18th century was marked by significant growth in agriculture and commerce, including the rise of the slave trade. Having the greatest degree of self-rule, Rhode Island had the most to lose from British efforts after 1763 to increase the mother country's supervision and control over the colonies. On 4 May 1776, Rhode Island became the first colony formally to renounce all allegiance to King George III. Favoring the weak central government established by the Articles of Confederation, the state quickly ratified them in 1778, but subsequently resisted the centralizing tendencies of the federal constitution. Rhode Island withheld ratification until 29 May 1790, making it the last of the original 13 states to join the Union.

The principal trends in 19th-century Rhode Island were industrialization, immigration, and urbanization. The state's royal charter (then still in effect) gave disproportionate influence to the declining rural towns, conferred almost unlimited power on the legislature, and contained no procedure for its amendment. In addition, suffrage was restricted by the general assembly to owners of real estate and their eldest sons. Because earlier, moderate efforts at change had been virtually ignored by the assembly, political reformers decided to bypass the legislature and convene a People's Convention. Thomas Wilson Dorr, a patrician attorney who assumed the leadership of this movement, became the principal draftsman of a progressive "People's Constitution," ratified in a popular referendum in December 1841. A coalition of Whigs and rural Democrats used force to suppress the movement now known as Dorr's Rebellion, but they bowed to popular pressure and made limited changes via a new constitution, effective May 1843.

The latter half of the century was marked by continued industrialization and urbanization. Immigration became both more voluminous and more diverse. Politically the state was dominated by the Republican Party until the 1930s. The Democrats, having seized the opportunity during the New Deal, consolidated their power during the 1940s, and from that time onward have captured most state and congressional elections. Present-day Rhode Island, though predominantly urban, industrial, Catholic, and Democratic, retains an ethnic and cultural diversity surprising in view of its size but consistent with its pluralist traditions.

¹²STATE GOVERNMENT

Rhode Island is governed under the constitution of 1843. Through 1979 there had been 42 amendments to this document.

Legislative authority is vested in the general assembly, a bicameral body composed of 50 senators and 100 representatives. All legislators are elected for two-year terms from districts that are apportioned equally according to population after every federal decennial census. Legislators must be qualified voters in the state and must have been residents of the state and their district for 30 days prior to election. Among the more important checks enjoyed by the assembly is the power to override the governor's veto by a three-fifths vote of its members, the authority in joint session (Grand Committee) to name justices to the supreme court, and the power to establish all courts below the supreme court.

The chief officers of the executive branch are the governor, lieutenant governor, attorney general, secretary of state, and general treasurer. All are elected for two-year terms in even-numbered years. The governor and lieutenant governor must be qualified voters in Rhode Island and must have been residents of the US and the state for 30 days prior to election. In addition, they must never have been convicted of bribery. Nearly all department heads and commissioners are appointed by the governor with the approval of the senate. The governor may veto measures in their entirety but not specific items.

Constitutional amendments are enacted by majority vote of the whole membership of each house of the legislature, and by a simple majority at the next general election.

Voters must be US citizens, 18 years old or over, and have been residents of the state at least 30 days prior to an election.

[13] POLITICAL PARTIES

For nearly five decades, Rhode Island has been one of the nation's most solidly Democratic states. It has voted for the Republican presidential candidate only three times since 1928, elected only one Republican to the US Senate since 1934, and sent no Republicans to the US House from 1940 until 1980, when one Republican and one Democrat were elected. Also in 1980, Rhode Island was one of only six states to favor Jimmy Carter.

Rhode Island Presidential Vote by Major Political Parties, 1948–80

YEAR	ELECTORAL VOTE	RHODE ISLAND WINNER	DEMOCRAT	REPUBLICAN
1948	4	*Truman (D)	188,736	135,787
1952	4	*Eisenhower (R)	203,293	210,935
1956	4	*Eisenhower (R)	161,790	225,819
1960	4	*Kennedy (D)	258,032	147,502
1964	4	*Johnson (D)	315,463	74,615
1968	4	Humphrey (D)	246,518	122,359
1972	4	*Nixon (R)	194,645	220,383
1976	4	*Carter (D)	227,636	181,249
1980	4	Carter (D)	198,342	154,793

*Won US presidential election.

[14] LOCAL GOVERNMENT

As of 1980, Rhode Island was subdivided into 8 cities and 31 towns, the main units of local government. The state is one of the few without a significant county system: its five counties are merely units of judicial administration, and no unincorporated territory lies outside the limits of a city or town.

More than half the state's towns and cities have adopted home-rule charters, since that option was made available to them by constitutional amendment in 1951. Many smaller communities retain the New England town meeting form of government, under which the town's eligible voters assemble to enact the local budget, set the tax levy, and approve other local measures. Larger cities and towns are governed by a mayor and/or city manager and a council.

[15] STATE SERVICES

The Department of Education oversees all state educational services, including public higher education and the state school for the deaf. Roads, bridges, aeronautics, and public transit are under the jurisdiction of the Department of Transportation.

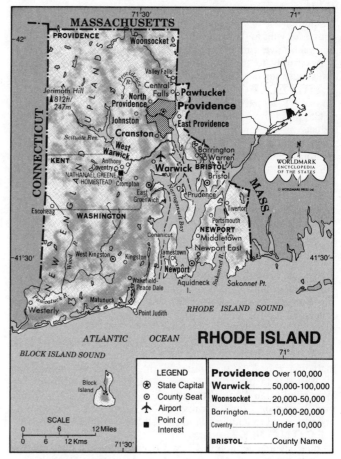

See US political: front cover M2; physical: back cover M2.

LOCATION: 41°18' to 42°01'N; 71°08' to 71°53'W. **BOUNDARIES:** Massachusetts line, 64 mi (103 km); Atlantic Ocean coastline, 40 mi (64 km); Connecticut line, 56 mi (90 km).

Health and welfare services are provided through the Department of Community Affairs, the Department of Elderly Affairs, the Department of Health, the Department of Mental Health, Retardation, and Hospitals, and the Department of Social and Rehabilitative Services. Public protection services are provided through the Department of Business Regulation, the Department of Corrections, and the state police (within the Executive Department). Resource protection services fall under the jurisdiction of the Department of Environmental Management; labor services, within the Department of Labor and the Department of Employment Security.

[16] JUDICIAL SYSTEM

The five-member supreme court is the state's highest appellate tribunal; it may also issue, upon request, advisory opinions on the constitutionality of a questioned act to the governor or either house of the legislature. Although other state judges hold office for life ("during good behavior"), supreme court justices can be removed by a mere resolution of the general assembly. In 1935, all five justices were ousted in this manner when a Democratic legislature replaced a court previously appointed by Republicans.

The second judicial level consists of the superior court and the family court. The former, the state's trial court, hears all jury trials in criminal cases and in civil matters involving more than $5,000. The family court deals with divorce, custody, juvenile crime, adoption, and related cases.

District courts do not hold jury trials. Civil matters that involve $5,000 or less, small claims procedures, and nonjury criminal cases, including felony arraignments and misdemeanors, are handled at the district level. All cities and towns operate probate courts for wills and estates. Providence and a few other communities each have a municipal or police court.

According to the FBI Crime Index for 1978, violent crime rates were far below the national average.

[17] ARMED FORCES

As of 1978, Department of Defense personnel in the state totaled 8,825, all of them at naval installations, including the US Naval Education Center in Newport and the Naval Construction Battalion Center in Davisville. Rhode Island firms received $156 million in defense contracts during 1977/78. A total of 237,000 US veterans were living in the state in 1979, of whom 5,000 saw military service during World War I, 104,000 during World War II, 45,000 in the Korean conflict, and 66,000 during the Viet-Nam era; veterans' benefits totaled $99 million in 1977/78.

In 1978, the state had 3,900 National Guard personnel and 2,574 state and local police.

[18] MIGRATION

During the 19th and early 20th centuries, the major immigrant groups who came to work in the state's growing industries were Irish, Italian, and French-Canadian. Significant numbers of British, Portuguese, Swedish, Polish, and German immigrants also moved to Rhode Island. Between 1940 and 1977, an estimated net total of 38,000 persons left the state.

[19] INTERGOVERNMENTAL COOPERATION

Rhode Island participates in many interstate regional bodies, including the Atlantic States Marine Fisheries Commission, New England Corrections Commission, New England Interstate Water Pollution Control Commission, and Northeastern Forest Fire Protection Commission.

Federal aid to Rhode Island totaled $412.4 million in 1978/79.

[20] ECONOMY

Rhode Island's economy is based overwhelmingly on industry; agriculture, mining, forestry, and fishing make only small contributions. The state's leading manufactured products are jewelry, silverware, machinery, primary metals, textiles, and rubber products. Unemployment rates in Rhode Island exceeded those of the US throughout the 1970s, and indications were that the state's economic growth was lagging behind that of the nation as a whole.

[21] INCOME

With an income per capita of $7,526 in 1978, Rhode Island ranked 26th among the 50 states. Total personal income reached $7 billion. Measured in constant 1972 dollars, the state's income increased by 17% during 1970–78, little more than half the US average.

[22] LABOR

In 1978, the civilian labor force for the state totaled 433,000, of whom 249,000 were men and 184,000 women. Since 1923, when the cotton textile industry began a sharp decline, Rhode Island has had one of the highest unemployment rates in the US.

Machine operators (except transport) made up about 20% of the labor force; clerical workers, 17%; professional and technical workers, 16%; service workers, 14%; crafts workers, 13%, managers and administrators (nonfarm), 9%; and others, 11%.

A federal census of workers covered by unemployment insurance in March 1977 revealed the following nonfarm employment pattern for Rhode Island:

	ESTABLISH-MENTS	EMPLOYEES	ANNUAL PAYROLL ('000)
Agricultural services, forestry, fishing	248	668	$ 7,757
Mining	21	182	2,599
Contract construction	2,282	12,741	205,165
Manufacturing	2,836	125,725	1,333,904
Transportation, public utilities	625	12,267	166,964
Wholesale trade	1,471	18,277	225,927
Retail trade	5,599	54,705	370,967
Finance, insurance, real estate	1,636	18,484	210,220
Services	5,757	65,971	555,096
Other	202	329	6,168
TOTALS	20,677	309,349	$3,084,767

About 125,000 Rhode Islanders belonged to labor unions and employee associations in 1976.

[23] AGRICULTURE

The state's total agricultural income in 1978 was $30.1 million, 49th in the US. Rhode Island has the fewest farms of any state, and the least area devoted to farming. Nursery and greenhouse products were the main agricultural commodity, valued at $8.6 million in 1979.

[24] ANIMAL HUSBANDRY

Cash income from livestock and livestock products totaled $11,210,000 in 1977, of which milk accounted for $6,100,000; eggs, $3,000,000; hogs and pigs, $900,000; cattle and calves, $500,000; turkeys, $100,000; chickens, $90,000; sheep and lambs, $20,000; and other livestock products, $500,000. In 1979, the state produced 50 million lb of milk and 59.2 million eggs. The Rhode Island Red, a strong, all-purpose fowl, was bred in the state during the 1850s, but is not commonly raised today.

[25] FISHING

The commercial catch in 1978 was 83.7 million lb, valued at $29.3 million. The principal edible fish caught were butterfish, scup, yellowtail and blackback flounders, cod, whiting, and herring. Shellfish landings, 9.2 million lb (mostly lobsters and clam meats), made up 44% of the total value of the catch.

[26] FORESTRY

In 1977, forest covered 404,000 acres (163,000 hectares), three-fifths of the state's land area. Some 395,000 acres (160,000 hectares) were usable as commercial timberland. However, Rhode Island's forests are more valuable for recreation and conservation than for commercial exploitation.

[27] MINING

Rhode Island's mineral production in 1978 totaled about $5.7 million, 49th in the US. The chief mineral resources are sand and gravel, granite, limestone, gemstones, and miscellaneous stone for crushing, with sand and gravel accounting for about 70% of the state's total mineral income. Undeveloped deposits of cumberlandite, an ore containing titanium and iron, are found at Iron Mine Hill, in the town of Cumberland.

[28] ENERGY AND POWER

Rhode Island is part of the New England regional power grid and imports most of its electric power. The state's installed capacity was 283,600 kw in 1978, and power production totaled 600 million kwh; both figures were the lowest in the US. Electric energy sales in Rhode Island in 1977 were 4.8 billion kwh, of which 1.8 billion kwh went for residential users, 1.6 billion kwh for commercial purchasers, and nearly all the rest for industry. The total number of gas utility customers for 1978 was 162,000.

[29] INDUSTRY

The Industrial Revolution began early in Rhode Island. The first spinning jenny in the US was built at Providence in 1787; three years later, in Pawtucket, Samuel Slater opened a cotton mill, one of the first modern factories in America. By the end of the 18th century, textile, jewelry, and metal products were being manufactured in the state.

Manufacturing remains Rhode Island's chief source of income. Shipments of manufactured goods totaled $5.4 billion in 1977, when value added by manufacturing surpassed $2.7 billion. Of the latter, fabricated metal products accounted for 12%; jewelry and silverware, 11%; primary metal industries, 9%; nonelectrical machinery, 8%; textile mill products, 8%; and other industries, 52%.

The following table shows value added by manufacturing for selected industries in 1972 and 1977:

	1972	1977
Costume jewelry	$117,200,000	$247,800,000
Metal-working machinery	55,900,000	110,500,000
Medical instruments, supplies	NA	67,900,000
Electric lighting and wiring equipment	36,500,000	63,700,000

³⁰COMMERCE

Wholesale trade totaled $2.1 billion in 1972. In 1977, retail establishments recorded sales of $2.8 billion. Of this total, 23% came from food store sales, 17% from automotive dealers, 12% from general merchandise stores, 9% from eating and drinking places, 8% from gasoline service stations, and 31% from other establishments. Foreign exports of manufactured goods were $268 million in 1976. Providence handles an increasing volume of imports, including lumber, oil, and automobiles.

³¹CONSUMER PROTECTION

The consumer protection division of the Department of the Attorney General, the Consumer's Council, and the consumer protection services within the Department of Health bear primary responsibility for enforcing consumer laws and regulations.

³²BANKING

In 1978, Rhode Island had 14 commercial banks with combined assets of $5.3 billion; deposits totaled $4.2 billion, and outstanding loans were nearly $2.7 billion. In 1977 there were six savings and loan associations, four of which were state chartered and two federally chartered; their combined assets reached $659 million, and outstanding mortgage loans added up to $564 million.

³³INSURANCE

In 1978, the state had eight life insurance companies; the 1,922,000 policies held by state residents had an aggregate value of $13.5 billion. The average amount of life insurance per family was $38,400, 9% above the US average. Automobile insurance premiums written in the state totaled $141.4 million.

³⁴SECURITIES

Rhode Island has no securities exchanges. However, New York Stock Exchange member firms had 11 sales offices and 137 registered representatives in the state in 1978.

³⁵PUBLIC FINANCE

The annual budget is prepared by the Division of the Budget within the Department of Administration, in conjunction with the governor, and submitted to the legislature for approval. The fiscal year runs from 1 July to 30 June.

The following is a summary of general revenues and expenditures in 1977/78 and 1978/79 (in millions):

	1977/78	1978/79
REVENUES		
Sales and use taxes	$140.6	$158.6
Personal income taxes	112.0	153.2
Other taxes	196.0	216.4
Departmental revenues	80.5	88.5
Federal assistance	13.8	10.3
TOTALS	$542.9	$627.0
EXPENDITURES		
Education	$193.6	$209.3
Corrections	115.5	125.6
Mental health, retardation, and hospitals	90.0	95.7
Transportation	46.2	44.5
Other expenditures	121.1	132.3
TOTALS	$566.4	$607.4

³⁶TAXATION

As of 1979, Rhode Island levied a state income tax equal to 19% of the taxpayer's federal income tax liability. The basic corporate tax rate was 8% of net income or 40 cents per $100 of net worth, whichever was greater. The sales and use tax was 6% on most items. The state also taxed motor fuel, cigarettes, alcoholic beverages, race-track admissions, and legacies and estates.

In 1977, Rhode Islanders filed 399,797 federal income tax returns, paying $608,715,000 in tax.

³⁷ECONOMIC POLICY

The Department of Economic Development seeks to promote the preservation and expansion of industry, commerce, and tourism. Business tax incentives offered by the state include elimination of local property taxes on manufacturers' machinery and equipment purchased after 1974, exemption from sales tax on all manufacturers' machinery and equipment, and a 2% investment tax credit for purchases of depreciable tangible property, including buildings.

³⁸HEALTH

The average life expectancy during 1969–71 for both sexes was 71.90 years (13th in the US), 68.31 years for men and 75.48 for women. As of 1977, the infant mortality rate was 11.2 per 1,000 live births for whites, 24 for nonwhites. Death rates from heart disease and cancer—the leading causes of death in 1977—were well above the national averages.

The state had 1,900 active physicians in 1977, and 509 active dentists in 1979. There were 21 hospitals, with 6,100 beds in 1978; hospital personnel included 2,866 registered nurses and 1,249 licensed practical nurses.

³⁹SOCIAL WELFARE

Aid to families with dependent children, paid to 49,100 Rhode Islanders in 1978, totaled $59 million. In 1977, $288 million in Social Security benefits were paid to 110,000 retired workers and their dependents. Outlays for other social programs in 1978 included $26.8 million for federal food stamps, $6.3 million for the school lunch program, and $65 million for unemployment insurance.

⁴⁰HOUSING

In 1970, the census counted 317,718 housing units, of which 9,976 were seasonal (principally summer cottages). More than 97% of year-round occupied units had full plumbing. The state authorized 15,300 new housing units worth $358 million from 1976 through 1978. Much of the new residential construction has taken place in the suburbs south and west of Providence.

⁴¹EDUCATION

In 1970, Rhode Island's illiteracy rate was 1.3%, the highest in New England. Only 61.7% of adult Rhode Islanders were high school graduates in 1976, the lowest such percentage for any northern state.

As of October 1977, 166,390 students were enrolled in 345 public schools. More than 60,000 students were enrolled in the state's 13 institutions of higher education in fall 1978. Leading institutions included Brown University (1764), with 5,225 undergraduates in fall 1978, the University of Rhode Island (1892), with 9,033, and Providence College (1917), with 5,930. The Rhode Island School of Design (1877) with 1,485 students in 1978, is located in Providence. The Higher Education Assistance Authority awards renewable state scholarships to about 5% of the annual graduating class of all secondary schools in the state.

⁴²ARTS

Newport and Providence have notable art galleries and museums. Theatrical groups include the Trinity Square Repertory Company, the Sock and Buskin Players of Brown University, and the Players, all in Providence. The Rhode Island Philharmonic performs throughout the state. Although the internationally famous Newport Jazz Festival is no longer held there, Newport continues to be the site of jazz and folk concerts.

[43] LIBRARIES AND MUSEUMS

In 1979, Rhode Island had 50 public libraries, 10 academic libraries, and 37 special libraries. In 1977/78, public libraries had a book stock of 2.3 million, and a combined circulation of 4 million. The Providence Public Library maintains several special historical collections. The Brown University Libraries, containing more than 2.3 million books, include the Annmary Brown Memorial Library, with its collection of rare manuscripts, and the John Carter Brown Library, with an excellent collection of early Americana.

Among the state's more than 30 museums and historic sites are the Haffenreffer Museum of Anthropology in Bristol, the Museum of Art of the Rhode Island School of Design in Providence, the Roger Williams Park Museum, also in Providence, the Nathanael Greene Homestead in Coventry, and the old Slater Mill in Pawtucket.

[44] COMMUNICATIONS

Rhode Island has some 100 post offices, stations, and branches; the first automated post office in the US postal system was opened in Providence in 1960. As of 1978 there were 698,115 telephones, of which 524,983 were residential and 173,132 commercial. In 1979, the state had 15 AM and 8 FM radio stations. Providence had four television stations, including an affiliate for each of the three major networks and one public broadcasting affiliate operated by the Department of Education. The state had one cable television system in 1978 serving 3,400 subscribers.

[45] PRESS

The *Rhode Island Gazette,* the state's first newspaper, appeared in 1732. In 1850, Paulina Wright Davis established *Una,* one of the first women's rights newspapers in the country.

In 1978, Rhode Island had seven daily newspapers, with a combined circulation of 949,723. The two largest newspapers, both published by the Providence Journal Co., were as follows:

AREA	NAME	DAILY	SUNDAY
Providence	Bulletin (e,S)	142,352	219,639
	Journal (m,S)	71,593	

[46] ORGANIZATIONS

Among the cultural and educational organizations with headquarters in Rhode Island are the Foundation for Gifted and Creative Children (Warwick) and the Rhode Island Historical Society (Providence). The American Mathematical Society is located in Providence. The Manufacturing Jewelers and Silversmiths of America (Providence) is a leading trade organization; the US International Sailing Association, the US Yacht Racing Union (both in Newport), and the Rooster Class Yacht Racing Association (Jamestown) are the main sports groups. National Gold Star Mothers has its headquarters in Warwick, as does the Foster Parents Plan.

[47] TOURISM, TRAVEL, AND RECREATION

An estimated 2,231,000 persons traveled to or through Rhode Island in 1977. Historic sites—especially the mansions of Newport and Providence—and water sports (particularly the America's Cup yacht races) are the main tourist attractions; Block Island is a popular resort. During 1978, licenses were issued to 14,931 hunters and 30,318 fishermen.

[48] SPORTS

Rhode Island's most famous sports competition is the America's Cup yacht races, held at Newport since 1851. Pawtucket has a minor league baseball team. Providence College has competed successfully in intercollegiate basketball, winning National Invitation Tournament titles in 1961 and 1963 and the NCAA Eastern Division crown in 1973. Swimming, boating, golf, tennis, softball, skiing, and hiking are popular participant sports. The International Tennis Hall of Fame is in Newport and a yachting hall of fame is under development there. Dog racing (Lincoln) and jai alai (Newport) are spectator sports with pari-mutuel betting.

[49] FAMOUS RHODE ISLANDERS

Important federal officeholders from Rhode Island have included US Senators Nelson W. Aldrich (1841–1915), Henry Bowen Anthony (1815–84), Theodore Francis Green (1867–1966), and John O. Pastore (b.1907), and US Representative John E. Fogarty (1913–67). J. Howard McGrath (1903–66) held the posts of US senator, solicitor general, and attorney general.

Foremost among Rhode Island's historical figures is Roger Williams (b.England, 1603?–83), apostle of religious liberty and founder of Providence. Other significant pioneers, also born in England, include Anne Hutchinson (1591–1643), religious leader and cofounder of Portsmouth, and William Coddington (1601–78), founder of Newport. Other 17th-century Rhode Islanders of note were Dr. John Clarke (b.England, 1609–76), who secured the colony's royal charter, and Indian leader King Philip, known also as Metacomet (1639?–76). Important participants in the War for Independence were Commodore Esek Hopkins (1718–1802) and General Nathanael Greene (1742–86). The 19th century brought to prominence Thomas Wilson Dorr (1805–54), courageous leader of Dorr's Rebellion; social reformer Elizabeth Buffum Chace (1806–99); and naval officers Oliver Hazard Perry (1785–1819), who secured important US victories in the War of 1812; and his brother, Matthew C. Perry (1794–1858), who led the expedition that opened Japan to foreign intercourse in 1854. Among the state's many prominent industrialists and inventors are Samuel Slater (b.England, 1768–1835), pioneer in textile manufacturing, and silversmith Jabez Gorham (1792–1869). Other significant public figures include Unitarian theologian William Ellery Channing (1780–1842); political boss Charles R. Brayton (1840–1910); Roman Catholic bishop and social reformer Matthew Harkins (b.Massachusetts, 1845–1921); Dr. Charles V. Chapin (1856–1941), pioneer in public health; and Leonard Woodcock (b.1911), a labor leader who also served as US ambassador to China.

Rhode Island's best-known creative writers are Gothic novelists H. P. Lovecraft (1890–1937) and Oliver LaFarge (1901–63), and its most famous artist is portrait painter Gilbert Stuart (1755–1828). Popular performing artists include George M. Cohan (1878–1942), Nelson Eddy (1901–67), Bobby Hackett (1915–76), and Van Johnson (b. 1916).

Important sports personalities include Baseball Hall of Famers Hugh Duffy (1866–1954), Napoleon Lajoie (1875–1959), and Charles "Gabby" Hartnett (1900–1972).

[50] BIBLIOGRAPHY

Carroll, Charles. *Rhode Island: Three Centuries of Democracy.* 4 vols. New York: Lewis, 1932.

Conley, Patrick T. *Democracy in Decline: Rhode Island's Constitutional Development, 1775–1841.* Providence: Rhode Island Historical Society, 1977.

Conley, Patrick T., and Matthew J. Smith. *Catholicism in Rhode Island.* Providence: Diocese of Providence, 1976.

Federal Writers' Project. *Rhode Island: A Guide to the Smallest State.* Boston: Houghton Mifflin, 1937.

James, Sydney V. *Colonial Rhode Island.* New York: Scribner, 1975.

Lovejoy, David S. *Rhode Island Politics and the American Revolution, 1760–1776.* Providence: Brown University Press, 1958.

McLoughlin, William G. *Rhode Island: A Bicentennial History.* New York: Norton, 1978.

Polishook, Irwin H. *Rhode Island and the Union, 1774–1795.* Evanston, Ill.: Northwestern University Press, 1969.

Providence Journal-Bulletin. *1979 Journal-Bulletin Rhode Island Almanac.* 93d ed. Providence, n.d.

Rhode Island. Secretary of State. *1979–80 Manual.* Edited by Edward F. Walsh. Providence, 1979.

Steinberg, Sheila, and Cathleen McGuigan. *Rhode Island: An Historical Guide.* Providence: Rhode Island Bicentennial Commission, 1976.

SOUTH CAROLINA

State of South Carolina

ORIGIN OF STATE NAME: Named in honor of King Charles I of England. **NICKNAME:** The Palmetto State. **CAPITAL:** Columbia. **ENTERED UNION:** 23 May 1788 (8th). **SONG:** "Carolina." **POET LAUREATE:** Helen von Kolnitz Hyer. **MOTTO:** *Animis opibusque parati* (Prepared in mind and resources); *Dum spiro spero* (While I breathe, I hope). **COAT OF ARMS:** A palmetto stands erect, with a ravaged oak (representing the British fleet) at its base; 12 spears, symbolizing the first 12 states, are bound crosswise to the palmetto's trunk by a band bearing the inscription "Quis separabit" (Who shall separate?). Two shields bearing the inscriptions "March 26" (the date in 1776 when South Carolina established its first independent government) and "July 4," respectively, hang from the tree; under the oak are the words "Meliorem lapsa locavit" (Having fallen, it has set up a better) and the year "1776." The words "South Carolina" and the motto *Animis opibusque parati* surround the whole. **FLAG:** Blue field with a white palmetto in the center and a white crescent at the union. **OFFICIAL SEAL:** The official seal consists of two ovals showing the original designs for the obverse and the reverse of South Carolina's great seal of 1777. Left (obverse): same as the coat of arms. Right (reverse): as the sun rises over the seashore, Hope, holding a laurel branch, walks over swords and daggers; the motto *Dum spiro spero* is above her, the word "Spes" (Hope) below. **ANIMAL:** White-tailed deer. **BIRD:** Carolina wren. **WILD GAME BIRD:** Wild turkey. **FISH:** Striped bass. **FLOWER:** Yellow jessamine. **TREE:** Palmetto. **GEM:** Amethyst. **STONE:** Blue granite. **LEGAL HOLIDAYS:** New Year's Day, 1 January; Martin Luther King's Birthday, 15 January; Lee's Birthday, 19 January; Washington's Birthday, 3d Monday in February; Confederate Memorial Day, 10 May; Jefferson Davis's Birthday, 3 June; Independence Day, 4 July; Labor Day, 1st Monday in September; Election Day, 1st Tuesday after 1st Monday in November (even-numbered years); Veterans Day, 11 November; Thanksgiving Day, 4th Thursday in November; Christmas Eve, 24 December, when declared by the governor; Christmas Day, 25 December; day after Christmas. **TIME:** 7 A.M. EST = noon GMT.

¹LOCATION, SIZE, AND EXTENT

Situated in the southeastern US, South Carolina ranks 40th in size among the 50 states.

The state's total area is 31,055 sq mi (80,433 sq km), of which land takes up 30,225 sq mi (78,283 sq km) and inland water 830 sq mi (2,150 sq km). South Carolina extends 273 mi (439 km) E–W; its maximum N–S extension is 210 mi (338 km).

South Carolina is bounded on the N and NE by North Carolina; on the SE by the Atlantic Ocean; and on the SW and W by Georgia (with the line passing through the Savannah and Chattooga rivers).

Among the 13 major Sea Islands in the Atlantic off South Carolina are Bull, Sullivans, Kiawah, Edisto, Hunting, and Hilton Head. The total boundary length of South Carolina is 824 mi (1,326 km), including a general coastline of 187 mi (301 km); the tidal shoreline extends 2,876 mi (4,628 km). The state's geographic center is located in Richland County, 13 mi (21 km) SE of Columbia.

²TOPOGRAPHY

South Carolina is divided into two major regions by the fall line that runs through the center of the state from Augusta, Ga., to Columbia and thence to Cheraw, near the North Carolina border. The area northwest of the line, known as the upcountry, lies within the Piedmont Plateau; the region to the southeast, called the low country, forms part of the Atlantic Coastal Plain. The rise of the land from ocean to the fall line is very gradual: Columbia, 120 mi (193 km) inland, is only 135 feet (41 meters) above sea level. In the extreme northwest, the Blue Ridge Mountains cover about 500 sq mi (1,300 sq km); the highest elevation, at 3,560 feet (1,085 meters), is Sassafras Mountain.

Among the many artificial lakes, mostly associated with electric power plants, is Lake Marion, the state's largest, covering 173 sq mi (448 sq km). Three river systems—the Pee Dee, Santee,

and Savannah—drain most of the state. No rivers are navigable above the fall line.

³CLIMATE

South Carolina has a humid, subtropical climate. Average temperatures range from 68°F (20°C) on the coast to 58°F (14°C) in the northwest, with colder temperatures in the mountains. Summers are hot: in the central part of the state, temperatures often exceed 90°F (32°C), with a record of 111°F (44°C) set at Camden on 28 June 1954. In the northwest, temperatures of 32°F (0°C) or less occur from 50 to 70 days a year; the record low for the state is −20°F (−29°C), set at Caesars Head Mountain on 18 January 1977. The normal daily temperature at Columbia is 34°F (1°C) in January and 70°F (21°C) in July.

Rainfall is ample throughout the state, ranging from 38 in (97 cm) in the central region to 52 in (132 cm) in the upper piedmont. Snow and sleet (totaling less than 2 in, or 5 cm, a year at Columbia) occur about three times annually, but more frequently and heavily in the mountains.

⁴FLORA AND FAUNA

Principal trees of South Carolina include palmetto (the state tree), balsam fir, beech, yellow birch, pitch pine, cypress, and several types of maple, ash, hickory, and oak; longleaf pine grows mainly south of the fall line. Rocky areas of the piedmont contain a wide mixture of moss and lichens. The coastal plain has a diversity of land formations—swamp, prairie, savannah, marsh, dunes—and, accordingly, a great number of different grasses, shrubs, and vines. Azaleas and camellias, not native to the state, have been planted profusely in private and public gardens. Bunched arrowhead and persistent trillium are endangered plants.

South Carolina mammals include white-tailed deer, black bear, opossum, gray and red foxes, cottontail and marsh rabbits, mink, and woodchuck. Three varieties of raccoon are indigenous, one of them unique to Hilton Head Island. The state is also home to

Bachman's shrew, originally identified in South Carolina by John Bachman, one of John J. Audubon's collaborators. Common birds include the mockingbird and Carolina wren (the state bird). Among endangered animals—all of which appear on the federal list—are the eastern brown pelican, southern bald eagle, Bachman's warbler, eastern cougar, Florida manatee, shortnose sturgeon, American alligator, Atlantic leatherback and ridley turtles, and seven whale species.

5 ENVIRONMENTAL PROTECTION

The Department of Health and Environmental Control, established in 1971, has primary responsibility for such environmental matters as water purity, solid waste disposal, air quality, nuclear energy, and food inspection. A plant in Barnwell County is one of three in the US used for storing low-grade nuclear waste.

During the 1970s, stringent measures were taken in the areas of sewage treatment, proper disposal of solid waste, and air pollution control. Water improvement programs brought 83% of South Carolina's major bodies of water within federal "fishable, swimmable" standards. The Water Resources Commission, created in 1967, formulates programs for the development and enlargement of the state's water supply.

6 POPULATION

South Carolina in 1970 ranked 26th in population among the 50 states, with 2,590,516 residents; the preliminary population from the 1980 census was 3,067,061, a gain of 18.4% since 1970. The population density in 1980 was 101 per sq mi (39 per sq km).

In 1978, South Carolina had about 1,429,000 men and 1,489,000 women. South Carolinians are much less mobile than the US population as a whole: as of 1976, about 69% of state residents had lived in South Carolina their whole lives. Although the state's population remains somewhat younger than the national average, the number of residents between 5 and 17 years of age decreased by nearly 6% during 1970–78, while those aged 65 or over increased by 34%.

The urban share of the population was about 48% in 1970. By 1977, 23 incorporated municipalities had more than 10,000 people, but only Columbia had a population in excess of 100,000. The largest cities as of the 1980 census were Columbia, 96,237; Charleston, 69,291; North Charleston, 54,281; and Greenville, 58,190. In 1978, the Charleston–North Charleston metropolitan area had an estimated 389,000 residents, ranking 97th in the US.

7 ETHNIC GROUPS

The white population of South Carolina is mainly of Northern European stock; the great migratory wave from Southern and Eastern Europe during the late 19th century left South Carolina virtually untouched. As of 1970, only 1.9% of South Carolinians were foreign-born or American-born children of foreign-born parents, with Germany, the United Kingdom, and Canada being the leading countries of origin.

Black Americans made up about 31% of the state's population in 1978. In the coastal regions and offshore islands there still can be found some vestiges of African heritage, notably the Gullah dialect. South Carolina has always had an urban black elite, much of it of mixed racial heritage. After 1954, racial integration proceeded relatively peacefully, with careful planning by both black and white leaders.

The 1970 census counted 2,241 American Indians, including about 1,200 living on the Catawba reservation in York County. There were also 1,222 Filipinos in 1970, and smaller numbers of other Asians; 759 Vietnamese refugees were resettled in South Carolina in 1975.

8 LANGUAGES

English settlers in the 17th century encountered first the Yamasee Indians and then the Catawba, both having languages of the Hokan-Siouan family. Few Indians remain today, and a bare handful of their place-names persist: Cherokee Falls, Santee, Saluda.

South Carolina English is marked by a division between the South Midland of the upcountry and the plantation Southern of the coastal plain, where dominant Charleston speech has extensive cultural influence even in rural areas. Many upcountry speakers of Scotch-Irish background retain /r/ after a vowel, as in hard, a feature now gaining acceptance among younger speakers in Charleston. On the other hand, a longtime distinctive Charleston feature, a centering glide after a long vowel, so that date and eight sound like /day-uht/ and /ay-uht/, is losing ground among younger speakers.

Along the coast and on the Sea Islands, some blacks still use the Gullah dialect, based on a Creole mixture of prerevolutionary English and African speech. The dialect is rapidly dying in South Carolina, though its influence on local pronunciations persists.

In 1970, 94% of the native-born and 96% of all state residents reported English as their mother tongue. Speakers of leading first languages were as follows:

	NATIVE-BORN	FOREIGN-BORN
English	2,409,598	3,955
German	7,745	3,125
Spanish	5,894	1,234
French	4,435	799
Italian	2,635	328

9 RELIGIONS

South Carolina is predominantly Protestant, and has been since colonial days. According to statistics furnished by the State Christian Action Council, Protestant denominations with more than 100,000 members in 1976 were the African Methodist Episcopal, Southern Baptist, Baptist Educational and Missionary Convention (black), and United Methodist churches; of these, the Southern Baptists are by far the most numerous, comprising about one-fourth of the population. The Episcopal Church had great influence during colonial times, but today it has fewer than 50,000 adherents. As of 1979, the state also had 58,399 Roman Catholics and an estimated 8,240 Jews.

10 TRANSPORTATION

Since the Revolutionary War, South Carolina has been concerned with expanding the transport of goods between the upcountry and the port of Charleston and the midwestern US. Several canals were constructed north of the fall line, and the 136-mi (219-km) railroad completed from Charleston to Hamburg (across the Savannah River from Augusta, Ga.) in 1833 was the longest in the world at that time. Three years earlier, the Best Friend of Charleston had become the first American steam locomotive built for public railway passenger service; by the time the Charleston-Hamburg railway was completed, however, the Best Friend had blown up, and a new engine, the Phoenix, had replaced it. Many other efforts were made to connect Charleston to the interior by railway, but tunnels through the mountains were never completed. Today, most freight service is furnished by the Southern Railway and the Seaboard Coast Line systems. Amtrak passenger trains pass north–south through the state, providing limited service to Charleston, Columbia, and other cities. In 1974, railway trackage totaled 3,016 mi (4,854 km).

The state road network in 1978 comprised 38,695 mi (62,274 km): interstate highways, 692 mi (1,114 km); primary roads, 9,331 mi (15,017 km); and secondary roads, 28,672 mi (46,143 km). I-26, running northwest–southeast from the upcountry to the Atlantic, intersects I-85 at Spartanburg, I-20 at Columbia, and I-95 on its way toward Charleston. There were 1,504,784 passenger vehicles and 397,053 trucks registered in 1978, when the number of licensed drivers totaled 1,814,389.

The state has three deepwater seaports. Charleston is one of the major ports on the Atlantic, and the harbors of Georgetown and Port Royal also handle significant waterborne trade. The Atlantic Intracoastal Waterway, crossing the state slightly inward from the Atlantic Ocean, is a major thoroughfare.

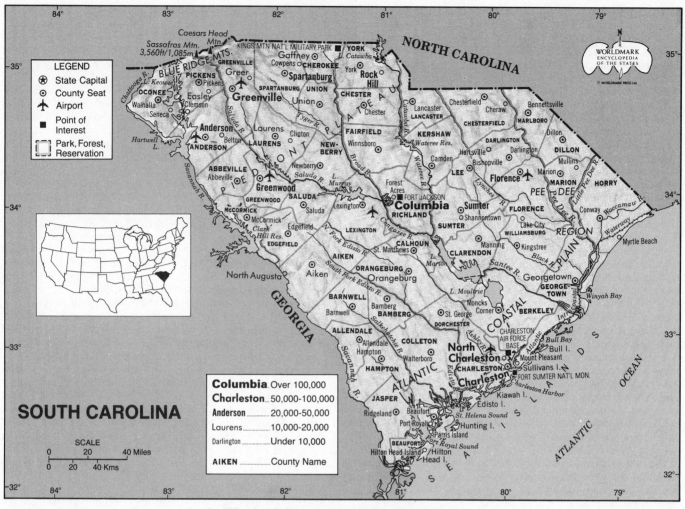

See US political: front cover K4; physical: back cover K4.

LOCATION: 32°02' to 35°12'56"N; 78°32'36" to 83°21'14"W. **BOUNDARIES**: North Carolina line, 327 mi (526 km); Atlantic Ocean coastline, 187 mi (301 km); Georgia line, 310 mi (499 km).

There were 64 public and 62 private airfields in 1978. Charleston, Columbia, and Greenville-Spartanburg are the major airports within the state; many travelers also enter South Carolina via the air terminals at Savannah, Augusta, and Atlanta, Ga., and at Charlotte, N.C.

[11]HISTORY

Prior to European settlement, the region now called South Carolina was populated by several Indian groups. Indians of Iroquoian stock, including the Cherokee, inhabited the northwestern section, while those of the Siouan stock—of whom the Catawba were the most numerous—occupied the northern and eastern regions. Indians of Muskogean stock lived in the south.

In the early 1500s, long before the English claimed the Carolinas, Spanish sea captains explored the coast. The Spaniards made an unsuccessful attempt to establish a settlement in 1526 at Winyah Bay, near the present city of Georgetown. Thirty-six years later, a group of French Huguenots under Jean Ribault landed at a site near Parris Island, but the colony failed after Ribault returned to France. The English established the first permanent settlement in 1670 under the supervision of the eight lords proprietors who had been granted "Carolana" by King Charles II. At first the colonists settled at Albemarle Point on the Ashley River; 10 years later, they moved across the river to the present site of Charleston.

Rice cultivation began in the coastal swamps, and black slaves were imported as field hands. The colony flourished, and by the mid-1700s, new areas were developing inland. Germans, Scotch-Irish, and Welsh, who differed markedly from the original aristocratic settlers of the Charleston area, migrated to the southern part of the new province. Although the upcountry was developing and was taxed, it was not until 1770 that the settlers there were represented in the government. For the most part, the colonists had friendly relations with the Indians. In 1715, however, the Yamasee were incited by Spanish colonists at St. Augustine, Fla., to attack the South Carolina settlements. The settlers successfully resisted, with no help whatsoever from the proprietors.

The original royal grant had made South Carolina a very large colony, but eventually the separate provinces of North Carolina and Georgia were established, two moves that destined South Carolina to be a small state. The colonists were successful in having the proprietors overthrown in 1719 and the government transferred to royal rule by 1721.

Skirmishes with the French, Spanish, Indians, and pirates, as well as a slave uprising in 1739, marked the pre-Revolutionary period. South Carolina opposed the Stamp Act of 1765 and took an active part in the American Revolution. The first British property seized by American Revolutionary forces was Ft. Charlotte in McCormick County in 1775. Among the many battles fought in South Carolina were major Patriot victories at Ft. Moultrie in Charleston (1776), Kings Mountain (1780), and Cowpens (1781), the last two among the war's most important engagements. Delegates from South Carolina, notably Charles Cotesworth Pinckney, were leaders at the federal constitutional convention of 1787. On 23 May 1788, South Carolina became the 8th state to ratify the Constitution.

Between the Revolutionary War and the Civil War, two issues dominated South Carolinians' political thinking: tariffs and slavery. Senator John C. Calhoun took an active part in developing the nullification theory by which a state claimed the right to abrogate unpopular federal laws. Open conflict over tariffs during the early 1830s was narrowly averted by a compromise on the rates, but in 1860, on the issue of slavery, no compromise was possible. At the time of secession, on 20 December 1860, more than half the state's population consisted of black slaves. The first battle of the Civil War took place at Ft. Sumter in Charleston Harbor on 12 April 1861. Federal forces soon captured the Sea Islands, but Charleston withstood a long siege until February 1865. In the closing months of the war, Union troops under General William Tecumseh Sherman burned Columbia and caused widespread destruction elsewhere. South Carolina contributed about 63,000 soldiers to the Confederacy out of a white population of some 291,000. Casualties were high: nearly 14,000 men were killed in battle or died after capture.

Federal troops occupied South Carolina after the war. During Reconstruction, as white South Carolinians saw it, illiterates, carpetbaggers, and scalawags raided the treasury, plunging the state into debt. The constitution was revised in 1868 by a convention in which blacks outnumbered whites by 76 to 48; given the franchise, blacks attained the offices of lieutenant governor and US representative. In 1876, bands of white militants called Red Shirts, supporting the gubernatorial candidacy of former Confederate general Wade Hampton, rode through the countryside urging whites to vote and intimidating potential black voters. Hampton, a Democrat, won the election, but was not permitted by the Republican incumbent to take office until President Rutherford B. Hayes declared an end to Reconstruction and withdrew federal troops from the state in April 1877.

For the next 100 years, South Carolina suffered through political turmoil, crop failures, and recessions. A major political change came in the 1880s with a large population increase upcountry and the migration of poor whites to cities. These trends gave farmers and industrial workers a majority of votes, and they found their leaders in Benjamin Ryan "Pitchfork Ben" Tillman, a populist who stirred up class and racial hatreds by attacking the "Charleston ring." Tillman was influential in wresting control of the state Democratic Party from the coastal aristocrats, and served as governor from 1890 to 1894 and then as US senator until his death in 1918. However, his success inaugurated a period of political and racial demagoguery that saw the gradual (though not total) disfranchisement of black voters.

The main economic transformation since 1890 has been the replacement of rice and cotton growing by tobacco and soybean cultivation and truck farming, along with the movement of tenant farmers, or sharecroppers, from the land to the cities. There they found jobs in textile mills, and textiles became the state's leading industry after 1900. With the devastation of the cotton crop by the boll weevil in the 1920s, farmers were compelled to diversify their crops, and some turned to cattle raising. Labor shortages in the North during and after World War II drew many thousands of blacks to Philadelphia, Washington, D.C., New York, and other cities. After 1954, public school desegregation proceeded very slowly but peaceably, and blacks were accepted alongside whites in the textile mills and other industries. Despite these changes, white South Carolinians remain staunchly conservative in political and social matters.

[12] STATE GOVERNMENT

South Carolina has had seven constitutions dating from 1776, 1778, 1790, 1861, 1865, 1868, and 1895, respectively. Beginning in 1970, most articles of the 1895 constitution were rewritten. The present document is more than 20,000 words long and has been amended well over 400 times since 1895.

The general assembly consists of a senate of 46 members, elected for four-year terms, and a house of representatives of 124 members, elected for two years. Senators must be 25 years of age, representatives 21; all legislators must be qualified voters in the districts they represent. Officials elected statewide include the governor and lieutenant governor (who run separately), attorney general, secretary of state, comptroller general, treasurer, adjutant general, secretary of agriculture, and superintendent of education, all elected to four-year terms. Eligibility requirements for the governor include a minimum age of 30, US citizenship for at least 5 years, and a 5-year state residency.

Most state agencies are governed by boards of at least five members appointed by the governor, but some of the largest agency boards are elected by the general assembly. Outside of his own office, the governor appoints very few department heads. South Carolina has nearly 130 agencies, boards, and commissions, of which at least 80 receive significant appropriations.

Legislative sessions are held annually. Bills may be introduced in either house, except for revenue measures, which are reserved to the house of representatives. The governor has a regular veto and an item veto on appropriation matters, either of which may be overridden by a two-thirds vote of those present in each house of the legislature; bills automatically become law after five days if the governor takes no action. The constitution may be amended by a two-thirds vote of each house of the general assembly and by a majority of those casting their ballots at the next general election. To take effect, however, the amendment must then be ratified by a majority vote of the next general assembly.

Citizens 18 years of age and older who have been state residents for 30 days are eligible to vote.

[13] POLITICAL PARTIES

South Carolina's major political organizations are the Democratic and Republican parties. From the end of Reconstruction, the Democratic Party dominated state politics. Dissatisfaction with the national party's position on civil rights in 1948 led to the formation of the States' Rights Democrat faction, whose candidate, South Carolina Governor J. Strom Thurmond, carried the state in 1948. Thurmond's subsequent switch to the Republicans while in the US Senate was a big boost for the state's Republican Party, which has captured South Carolina's eight electoral votes in four of the last five presidential elections, starting in 1964. However, all but 20 or so state legislators are Democrats, as are most municipal and county officials; although a Republican was elected governor in 1974, the Democrats swept all but one of the major statewide offices four years later. In 1980, Ronald Reagan carried South Carolina by a slim margin, but US Senator Ernest F. Hollings, a Democrat, won reelection.

Voters do not register according to political party in South Carolina. Instead, at primary elections, they simply take an oath that they have not participated in another primary. In 1979 there were 755,438 white registered voters and 267,291 blacks; black voter registration nearly doubled between 1964 and 1976, a period that saw black politicians play an increasingly influential role within the Democratic Party.

[14] LOCAL GOVERNMENT

As of 1977, South Carolina had 46 counties, 264 incorporated municipalities, 93 school districts, and 182 special districts of various types. Ten regional councils provide a broad range of technical and advisory services to county and municipal governments.

Under legislation enacted in 1975, all counties and municipalities have the same powers, regardless of size. Most municipalities operate under the mayor-council or city manager system; more than half the counties have a county administrator or manager. Customarily, each county has a council or commission, attorney, auditor, clerk of court, coroner, tax collector, treasurer, and sheriff. Many of these county officials are elected, but the only municipal officers elected are the mayor and the members of the council.

While the state shares revenues from many different sources with the counties and municipalities, these local units derive virtually all their direct revenue from the property tax. In recent years, the state's school districts have rapidly increased their own property tax levies, squeezing the counties' and municipalities' revenue base.

15 STATE SERVICES

The State Ethics Commission establishes rules covering possible conflicts of interest, oversees election campaign practices, and provides for officeholders' financial disclosure.

The Department of Education administers state and federal aid to the public schools, while the State Commission on Higher Education oversees the public colleges and universities, and the State Board for Technical and Comprehensive Education is responsible for postsecondary technical training schools. The state also runs special schools for the deaf and blind. Complementing both public and higher education is a state educational television network, under the jurisdiction of the South Carolina Educational Television Commission. Transportation services are provided by the Department of Highways and Public Transportation, which maintains most major roads, issues driver's licenses, and has jurisdiction over the Highway Patrol. The Aeronautics Commission licenses airplanes and pilots and oversees airport operations.

Through a variety of agencies, South Carolina offers a broad array of human services in the fields of mental health, mental retardation, vocational rehabilitation, veterans' affairs, care of the blind, and adoptions. An ombudsman for the aging handles complaints about nursing homes, which are licensed by the state. Public health programs pay special attention to diseases such as sickle-cell anemia and to the reduction of infant mortality. The South Carolina Law Enforcement Division provides technical aid to county sheriffs and municipal police departments. Emergency situations are handled by the Office of Disaster Assistance and the National Guard.

The State Housing Authority is authorized to subsidize interest rates on mortgages for middle- and low-income families. The Employment Security Commission oversees unemployment compensation and job placement, while the Department of Labor offers arbitration and mediation services and enforces health and safety standards. The Human Affairs Commission looks into unfair labor practices based on sex, race, or age.

16 JUDICIAL SYSTEM

South Carolina's unified judicial system is headed by the chief justice of the supreme court, who, along with four associate justices, is elected by the general assembly to a 10-year term. The supreme court is the final court of appeal; a five-member intermediate court of appeals for criminal cases was established in 1979, but legal questions (specifically, about the election of general assembly members to four of the five seats) prevented the court from convening.

Sixteen circuit courts hear major criminal and civil cases. As of 1980 there were 31 circuit court judges, all of them elected by the general assembly to six-year terms. The state also has a system of family courts for domestic and juvenile cases. In addition, there are magistrates courts (justices of the peace) in all counties, municipal courts, and county probate judges.

The state penal system is rapidly becoming centralized under the state Department of Corrections; there is a separate state system for juvenile offenders. In 1978 there were 7,526 inmates in correctional institutions, and youthful offenders numbered 2,309. Crime rates for that year exceeded the national averages for murder, forcible rape, and aggravated assault. South Carolina has a death penalty statute, but the death penalty has not been employed since the late 1950s.

17 ARMED FORCES

Ft. Jackson, in Columbia, is one of the Army's major training centers, with 19,207 authorized personnel in 1978. Air Force bases at Charleston, Sumter, and Myrtle Beach are all major installations, and the Charleston Harbor area has many naval facilities, including a nuclear submarine base. Parris Island has long been one of the country's chief Marine Corps training bases. Overall, the state has more than 100,000 defense personnel, of whom nearly two-thirds are with the Navy or Marines. South Carolina firms received $196 million in defense contract awards during 1977/78.

South Carolina Presidential Vote by Political Parties, 1948–80

YEAR	ELECTORAL VOTE	SOUTH CAROLINA WINNER	DEMOCRAT	REPUBLICAN	STATES' RIGHTS DEMOCRAT
1948	8	Thurmond (SRD)	34,423	5,386	102,607
1952	8	Stevenson (D)	172,957	168,043	—
					UNPLEDGED
1956	8	Stevenson (D)	136,278	75,634	88,509
1960	8	*Kennedy (D)	198,121	188,558	—
1964	8	Goldwater (R)	215,723	309,048	—
					AMERICAN IND.
1968	8	*Nixon (R)	197,486	254,062	215,430
					AMERICAN
1972	8	*Nixon (R)	186,824	477,044	10,075
1976	8	*Carter (D)	450,807	346,149	2,996
					LIBERTARIAN[1]
1980	8	*Reagan (R)	430,385	441,841	4,807

*Won US presidential election.   [1]Unofficial figure.

Veterans in South Carolina as of 30 September 1979 totaled 335,000, including some 5,000 from World War I, 124,000 from World War II, 66,000 from the Korean conflict, and 114,000 who served during the Viet-Nam era. Veterans' benefits during 1977/78 amounted to $291.5 million.

National Guard units had 10,800 personnel in 1978. State and local police departments had 6,424 employees in 1977, when expenditures on police protection totaled $88 million.

¹⁸MIGRATION

The original European migration into South Carolina consisted mostly of German, Welsh, and Scotch-Irish settlers. During the 19th century, many of the original settlers emigrated westward to Alabama, Mississippi, and Texas. In the 20th century, many blacks left the state for cities in the North. Between 1940 and 1970, South Carolina's net loss from outmigration was 601,000. During 1970–77, however, the state enjoyed a net gain of 100,000. During the 1970s, small numbers of Cubans, Vietnamese, and other foreign immigrants settled in the state.

¹⁹INTERGOVERNMENTAL COOPERATION

The South Carolina Interstate Cooperation Commission represents the state before the Council of State Governments. South Carolina also participates in the Atlantic States Marine Fisheries Compact, Southeastern Forest Fire Protection Compact, Southern Growth Policies Compact, Southern Interstate Energy Compact, Southern Regional Education Compact, Savannah River Compact, Appalachian Regional Commission, and the Coastal Plains Commission.

In 1978/79, the state received $987.2 million in federal funds, including $41.7 million in general revenue sharing.

²⁰ECONOMY

During its early days, South Carolina was one of the country's richest areas. Its economy depended on foreign commerce and agriculture, especially indigo, rice, and later cotton. After the Civil War, the state suffered severe economic depression. Not until the 1880s did the textile industry—today the state's major employer—begin to develop. Textiles and farming completely dominated the economy until after World War II, when efforts toward economic diversification attracted paper, chemical, and other industries to the state. During the postwar period, the state spent sizable amounts to improve its three ports, especially the harbor facilities of Charleston. South Carolina is blessed with an ample supply of electric power, an abundance of water and forests, adequate public highways, and good harbors. Largely because of its legacy of low-wage industries and an unorganized and poorly educated work force, the state continues to fall below national norms by most economic measures. Nevertheless, during the 1970s, real per capita income increased much faster than in the nation as a whole; rising foreign and domestic investment, coupled with an abundance of first-class tourist facilities along the coast, also boded well for South Carolina's economy in the 1980s.

²¹INCOME

South Carolina ranked 47th among the 50 states in 1978 with a per capita income of $6,242—8% below the average for the east and 20% below the national norm. In 1960, the state's per capita income was $1,396, or 37% below the US average.

Total income for 1978 exceeded $18.2 billion, representing a real increase of 46% since 1970. The two major sources of personal income were manufacturing, $4.9 billion , and government, $2.9 billion. State income tax data indicate that 33% of individual incomes were below $10,000 and 8% were below $5,000 in 1978. Median family income reached $12,188 (42d in the US) in 1975, when an estimated 17% of all South Carolinians and 13% of all families were below the federal poverty level. Counties with sizable military or other federal facilities generally rank highest in per capita income, while counties having majority black populations rank among the lowest.

²²LABOR

In 1978, South Carolina had a nonagricultural civilian labor force of 1,298,000, of whom 1,224,000 were employed and 74,000 were unemployed. The unemployment rate of 5.7% was below the 1978 national average; the rate for blacks and other minorities was 8.5%. A federal census of workers covered by unemployment insurance in March 1977 revealed the following nonfarm employment pattern for South Carolina:

	ESTABLISH-MENTS	EMPLOYEES	ANNUAL PAYROLL ('000)
Agricultural services, forestry, fishing	552	3,685	$ 30,524
Mining	67	1,531	15,636
Contract construction	6,096	76,939	920,409
Manufacturing, of which:	3,794	373,022	3,824,893
Textile mill products	(413)	(142,713)	(1,327,230)
Apparel, other textiles	(290)	(44,168)	(289,002)
Chemicals, allied products	(161)	(30,830)	(469,526)
Transportation, public utilities	1,775	33,254	419,673
Wholesale trade	4,108	42,931	480,028
Retail trade	16,870	147,378	931,944
Finance, insurance, real estate	4,460	39,302	397,598
Services	13,786	120,792	892,207
Other	751	948	9,350
TOTALS	52,259	839,782	$7,922,262

Another 217,000 South Carolinians, not covered by this survey, were federal, state, and local government employees in 1978.

In 1978, the average hourly payment for workers in durable goods was $4.71; in nondurable goods, $4.64. Average weekly earnings for production workers were $190, placing South Carolina 45th among the 50 states and 24% below the prevailing wage level for the US as a whole.

South Carolina has one of the lowest work stoppage rates in the nation, and only a small percentage of the total labor force is organized. Union membership in 1980 was only 67,475 (about 5% of the civilian labor force), including some 11,000 government employees. Textile, clothing, and ladies' garment workers' unions make up the bulk of the membership, followed by communications and electrical workers. Several large textile companies have made major efforts to prevent their workers from organizing unions; conflicts between management and workers have continued for years, but without serious violence. A right-to-work law was enacted in the 1950s.

²³AGRICULTURE

In 1978, South Carolina ranked 34th among the 50 states in farm income, with $1 billion; net income was $239.4 million, or about $6,650 per farm. For most of the 19th century, cotton was king, but today soybeans and tobacco outrank cotton in annual cash value. In 1978 there were 36,000 farms comprising 6,600,000 acres (2,670,000 hectares).

The principal farming area is a 50-mi (80-km) band across the upper coastal plain. The Pee Dee region in the east is the center for tobacco production. Cotton is grown mostly south of the fall line, and truck crops abound in the coastal and sand hill counties. South Carolina leads the nation in the sale of fresh peaches, which are produced mainly in the sand hills and piedmont.

The following table shows acreage, volume, and value of leading crops in 1978:

	ACRES HARVESTED	OUTPUT	VALUE
Soybeans	1,470,000	32,240,000 bushels	$219,912,000
Tobacco	71,000	150,520,000 lb	207,116,000
Corn for grain	623,000	30,250,000 bushels	68,063,000
Peaches	—	315,000,000 lb	46,500,000

[24]ANIMAL HUSBANDRY

Livestock and livestock products account for more than one-third of the state's farm income. Although production is well distributed throughout the state, Newberry and Orangeburg counties, in central South Carolina, lead in cash receipts from livestock products.

At the close of 1979 there were 625,000 cattle and calves, 50,000 milk cows, and 650,000 hogs and pigs. Production of cattle totaled 170.8 million lb, valued at $116.2 million, while hog production amounted to 168.8 million lb, worth $70.6 million. Dairy farms produced 524 million lb of milk, and poultry farmers marketed 1.6 billion eggs, worth $77.3 million, and 157.8 million lb of chickens and broilers, worth $37.8 million. Many farmers produce honey on a small scale.

[25]FISHING

The state's oceanfront saltwater inlets and freshwater rivers and lakes provide ample fishing opportunities. Major commercial fishing is restricted to saltwater species of fish and shellfish, mainly shrimp, crabs, and oysters. In 1978, the commercial catch totaled 20,609,116 lb, valued at $16,032,998. Among freshwater fish, some eels go to foreign markets, and catfish is also sold commercially.

[26]FORESTRY

South Carolina had 123,249,000 acres (4,957,000 hectares) of forestland in 1977—about 63% of the state's area and 1.7% of all US forests. Nearly all of South Carolina's forests are classified as commercial timberland, 91% of it privately owned. Several varieties of pine, both long- and shortleaf, are the major source of timber and of pulp for the paper industry. Shipments of lumber and wood products were valued at $795.4 million in 1977; shipments of paper and allied products, $1.1 billion.

[27]MINING

Mining is not a major industry. In 1978, South Carolina ranked 37th among the 50 states in mineral production, with a total value of $176 million. The only commercial minerals are kaolin and other types of clay, sand and gravel, stone, cement, phosphates, and granite. The 1978 mineral output included 17,912,000 tons of stone, 8,000,000 tons of sand and gravel, and 2,423 tons of clays.

[28]ENERGY AND POWER

Although it lacks fossil fuel resources, South Carolina produces more electricity than it consumes. Installed capacity totaled 12.1 million kw in 1978, when power production reached 44.3 billion kwh; about half the production came from nuclear reactors, and another third from coal-fired plants. Sales of electric energy in 1977 amounted to 34.5 billion kwh. Major power suppliers include three private companies and the state-owned Public Service Authority, known as Santee-Cooper. No municipality produces electrical power, but 23 own their own electrical and gas distribution systems. In addition, rural electrification authorities provide electrical and gas services. Gas utilities sold 114 trillion Btu of natural gas—all of it imported—to some 288,000 customers in 1978.

South Carolina is heavily involved in nuclear energy. As of 1980, four nuclear plants were producing electricity, and seven additional plants were under construction. The vast Savannah River plant in Aiken County produces plutonium; Chem-Nuclear Systems in Barnwell County stores low-level nuclear wastes; and a Westinghouse plant in Richland County makes fuel assemblies for nuclear reactors.

[29]INDUSTRY

South Carolina's principal industry since the 1880s has been textiles. Following World War II, the state began to attract a variety of new industries, major paper and chemical producers among them. Foreign investment has been especially significant: between 1970 and 1978, overseas investors pumped $2.3 billion into South Carolina's industrial economy. The Federal Republic of Germany led with 34% of the total, followed by the United Kingdom (20%) and France (18%). South Carolina's major manufacturing centers are concentrated north of the fall line and in the piedmont.

The total value added by manufacture was $8.1 billion in 1977, a 63% increase since 1972. The following table shows the value added by major sectors in 1972 and 1977:

	1972	1977
Textile mill products	$1,725,900,000	$2,523,500,000
Chemicals and chemical products	813,700,000	1,422,600,000
Nonelectrical machinery	406,400,000	660,800,000
Apparel, other textiles	359,600,000	450,100,000
Paper and allied products	292,600,000	411,000,000
Electric, electronic equipment	56,200,000	409,200,000
Fabricated metal products	114,700,000	315,000,000
Stone, clay, glass products	179,100,000	311,100,000
Food and food products	171,600,000	303,700,000
Lumber and wood products	170,800,000	303,300,000

[30]COMMERCE

Personal income from wholesale and retail trade exceeded $1.7 billion in 1978. Wholesalers reported a trade volume of $4.6 billion in 1972. Tobacco wholesale markets and warehouses are centered in the Pee Dee region, while soybean sales and storage facilities cluster around the port of Charleston; truck crops, fruits, and melons are sold in large quantities at the state farmers' market in Columbia. Retail trade in 1977 totaled $8.4 billion, of which food stores accounted for 24%, automotive dealers 21%, gasoline service stations 9%, department stores 8%, and other outlets 38%.

In 1978, the ports of Charleston, Georgetown, and Port Royal handled total tonnage of 4,047,835: 1,800,834 tons of imports and 2,247,001 tons of exports. Foreign imports were valued at $1.6 billion, overseas exports at $1.4 billion in 1977. Foreign exports of South Carolina's own manufactures were valued at $935 million in 1976 (24th in the US); agricultural exports totaled $312 million (25th) in 1976/77.

[31]CONSUMER PROTECTION

The Department of Consumer Affairs, established in 1974, has the authority to investigate consumer complaints and represent the public at regulatory proceedings.

[32]BANKING

In 1978, the states 727 banking offices had total assets of nearly $6 billion and deposits of more than $5 billion; outstanding loans amount to $3.4 billion. There were 75 saving and loan associations—47 federal and 28 state—with assets totaling $5.2 billion and mortgage loans of $4.5 billion. In addition, South Carolina had 202 credit unions with 460,677 members, representing almost 40% of all state households; assets amounted to $572.3 million, loans to $479.5 million.

[33]INSURANCE

The South Carolina Insurance Department licenses and supervises the 968 insurance companies doing business in the state; most of these represent national insurance organizations. In 1977, life insurance companies received $444.2 million in premiums from South Carolinians and paid $193.5 million in claims; property and casualty companies wrote premiums totaling $670.1 million and paid claims of $357.6 million; and accident and health insurance companies had $467.1 million in premiums and $347.8 million in claims.

As of 1978, state residents held 7,566,000 life insurance policies valued at $33.1 billion. The average family held $33,200 in life coverage, 5% below the national norm. A modified no-fault system of automobile insurance is in effect.

[34]SECURITIES

There are no securities exchanges in South Carolina. Enforcement of the state Securities Act is vested in the securities commissioner within the Office of the Secretary of State.

494   **South Carolina** [35—41]

³⁵ PUBLIC FINANCE

Contrary to general practice, South Carolina's governor is not the sole budget officer, but instead chairs the State Budget and Control Board, which also includes the state treasurer, comptroller general, and two legislators representing the senate and house, respectively. The budget board submits the budget to the general assembly in January as the basis for enactment of an appropriations bill, effective for the fiscal year beginning 1 July.

The state constitution requires that budget appropriations not exceed expected revenues (including reserve funds). If there should be a deficit, the next general assembly must provide for the deficit as a first order of business. Many tax revenues are earmarked for specific purposes: all gasoline taxes and related charges are designated for highways, and the sales tax finances public education, which accounts for more than half of all general fund expenditures. The state shares tax collections with its subdivisions—counties and municipalities—which determine how their share of the money will be spent.

The following table summarizes general fund revenues and expenditures for 1974/75 and 1978/79 (in millions):

REVENUES	1974/75	1978/79
Retail sales tax	$337.7	$ 525.9
Individual income tax	210.9	416.3
Corporate income tax	79.6	135.5
Other receipts	247.3	349.1
TOTALS	$875.5	$1,426.8
EXPENDITURES		
Education	$483.0	$ 787.5
Health	89.0	141.5
Social rehabilitation	53.5	101.7
Aid to subdivisions	70.1	86.6
Debt service	48.7	78.5
Other outlays	210.6	186.8
TOTALS	$954.9	$1,382.6

In mid-1977, South Carolina's public debt totaled $2.3 billion, or $806 per capita; though still below the US average, the latter figure represented a 142% increase since 1970, as compared with a 69% increase for the nation as a whole.

³⁶ TAXATION

South Carolinians bear a tax burden that is lighter than in most states. As of 1980, the chief levies were a personal income tax ranging from 2% on the first $1,000 to 7% on taxable income over $10,000; a corporate income tax of 6% (4.5% for banks, 8% for associations); a broad-based 4% sales tax; and taxes on gasoline, alcoholic beverages, business licenses, insurance, and gifts and estates. In addition to the property tax, municipalities and counties may impose business license fees—although no county charges these fees—plus charges for such services as garbage collection and water supply.

Taxes remitted to the federal government totaled $3.3 billion in 1975/76, when South Carolina received more than $3.9 billion in federal expenditures. South Carolinians filed 1,072,961 federal income tax returns for 1977, paying more than $1.4 billion in tax.

³⁷ ECONOMIC POLICY

Created in 1945, the State Development Board seeks to encourage economic growth and to attract new industries. During the 1970s, the state was successful in attracting foreign companies, especially to the piedmont.

The state exempts for five years all new industrial construction from local property taxes (except the school tax). Moreover, industrial properties are assessed very leniently for tax purposes. State and local governments have cooperated in building necessary roads to industrial sites, providing water and sewer services, and helping industries to meet environmental standards. Counties are authorized to issue industrial bonds at low interest rates. Gen-

erally conservative state fiscal policies, relatively low wage rates, and an antiunion climate also serve as magnets for industry.

³⁸ HEALTH

South Carolina's average life expectancy during 1969–71 was 67.96 years—63.85 for men, 72.29 for women—the lowest rates in the 50 states. The 1977 infant mortality rates of 13.1 per 1,000 live births for whites and 24.2 for nonwhites were among the nation's highest. Impeding efforts to improve health standards are a shortage of doctors (especially in rural areas and small towns), inadequate public education, poor housing, and improper sanitation.

As of 1977, death rates for the leading causes of death—heart disease and cancer—were below the US average, but the death rates for stroke, accidents, and early childhood diseases ranked high. The state has mounted major programs to detect heart disease and high blood pressure, reduce infant mortality, and expand medical education.

In 1978, South Carolina's health facilities included 93 general hospitals, 210 long-term care facilities, 5 mental hospitals, 3 rehabilitation facilities, 137 outpatient facilities, 180 public health centers (49 primary, 131 auxiliary), and 4 mental retardation centers, along with 2 major veterans' hospitals. The average cost of care in community hospitals in 1977 was $153 per day and $1,085 per stay, well below the national norms. Nonfederal medical personnel in 1979 were physicians, 3,514; dentists, 946; registered nurses, 10,803; licensed practical nurses, 5,476; and pharmacists, 1,784.

³⁹ SOCIAL WELFARE

Aid to families with dependent children amounted to $54 million in 1978. Federal Supplemental Security Income (SSI) payments came to $102.1 million, to which state-administered SSI added $1.5 million. Food stamps were issued to 240,000 persons and had a federal bonus value of $85.1 million. Virtually every school in the state participated in the school lunch program in 1977/78, at a federal cost of $42.2 million; some 400 schools took part in the school breakfast program, serving 11.8 million breakfasts.

In 1977, 420,800 people received Social Security benefits amounting to $909.6 million; the average monthly payment to retirees was $217.30. In the same year, 329,000 claims were filed for unemployment insurance; benefits totaled $66 million, with the average weekly payment being $73.31. Workers' compensation totaled $46.1 million in 1977, and vocational rehabilitation outlays reached $22.1 million in 1978.

⁴⁰ HOUSING

In 1970 there were 804,858 year-round housing units, of which 734,398 were owner-occupied. More than 17% of all occupied units lacked full plumbing, the highest such percentage in the US. Many residents live in mobile homes, which numbered 96,000 in 1977.

South Carolina made a determined effort to upgrade housing during the 1970s. The State Housing Authority, created in 1971, is empowered to issue bonds to provide mortgage subsidies for low- and middle-income families. Between 1974 and 1978, construction permits valued at $2.6 billion were issued for 91,637 new units, of which 81% were single-unit structures.

⁴¹ EDUCATION

For decades, South Carolina has ranked below the national averages in most phases of education, including expenditures per pupil, median years of school completed, teachers' salaries, and literacy levels. As of 1970, for example, the state's adult illiteracy rate was 2.3% (3d highest in the US); only 57% of South Carolinians were high school graduates (43d) in 1976, when the state's median school completion level was 12.2 years. During the 1970s, however, significant improvements were made through the adoption of five-year achievement goals, enactment of a statewide educational funding plan, provision of special programs for exceptional children and of kindergartens for all children, measurement of students' achievements at various stages, and expansion of adult education programs. As a result, South Carolina high school graduates now score only 4% lower than the national averages on standardized examinations. Although per pupil expenditures were only $1,340 in 1977/78 (42d in the US), South Carolina's educational funding is higher in relation to per capita income than that of most other states.

In 1977/78 there were 1,155 public schools, enrolling 618,281 pupils, and 219 private schools, with 45,620 pupils. During the same year there were 146,957 vocational pupils, 83,996 handicapped students, and 47,326 persons in adult programs. Enrollment of white students in private schools has expanded since the 1960s, partly in reaction to public school desegregation.

Higher educational institutions in 1978/79 enrolled 89,807 students, of whom 76% were attending public institutions. The state has three major universities: the University of South Carolina, with its main campus at Columbia; Clemson University, at Clemson; and the Medical University of South Carolina, in Charleston. In addition, there are 5 four-year state colleges, plus 9 four-year and two-year branches of the University of South Carolina. The state also has 20 four-year private colleges and universities, none of which enrolls more than 4,000 students; most are church affiliated. The Lutheran Theological Southern Seminary in Columbia is the only major private graduate institution. There were five private junior colleges, with a total enrollment of 2,660, in 1978/79. South Carolina has an extensive technical education system, supported by both state and local funds. There were 16 such institutions and 2 special schools, with a total enrollment of 147,748, in 1978/79. Tuition grants are offered for needy South Carolina students enrolled in private colleges in the state.

⁴²ARTS
South Carolina's three major centers for the visual arts are the Gibbes Art Gallery in Charleston, the Columbia Museum of Art and Science, and the Greenville County Museum of Art. Local theater groups in the larger municipalities produce five or six plays a year; Columbia's Town Theater claims to be the nation's oldest continuous community playhouse. Perhaps South Carolina's best-known musical event is the Spoleto Festival—held annually in Charleston during May and June and modeled on the Spoleto Festival in Italy—at which artists of international repute perform in original productions of operas and dramas. The South Carolina Arts Commission, created in 1967, seeks to encourage interest in the arts, especially at the public school level.

⁴³LIBRARIES AND MUSEUMS
Public libraries in South Carolina had a combined book stock of 3,791,964 volumes and a total circulation of 8,152,528 in 1977/78. The State Library in Columbia supervises the 39 county and regional libraries and also provides reference and research services for the state government. The University of South Carolina and Clemson University libraries, with 1,423,586 and 650,682 volumes respectively, have the most outstanding academic collections. Special libraries are maintained by the South Carolina Historical Society in Charleston, the Department of Archives and History in Columbia, and the South Carolina Society at the University of South Carolina.

There are at least 70 museums and historic sites, notably the Charleston Museum (specializing in history, natural history, and anthropology); the Citadel Archives-Museum, also in Charleston; and the University of South Carolina McKissick Museums (with silver, lapidary, and military collections) in Columbia. Charleston is also famous for its many old homes, streets, churches, and public facilities; at the entrance to Charleston Harbor stands Ft. Sumter, where the Civil War began. Throughout the state, numerous battle sites of the American Revolution have been preserved; many antebellum plantation homes have been restored, especially in the low country.

Among the state's best-known botanical gardens are the Cypress, Magnolia, and Middleton gardens in the Charleston area. Edisto Garden in Orangeburg is renowned for its azaleas and roses, and Huntington Gardens near Georgetown displays a wide variety of plants, animals, and sculpture.

⁴⁴COMMUNICATIONS
South Carolina is served by some 30 telephone companies, of which Southern Bell is by far the largest. In 1978 there were 1,981,232 telephones (1,487,452 residential, 493,780 business); roughly 90% of all households had telephone service. During the same year, the state had 163 commercial radio stations (108 AM, 55 FM), of which 88 belonged to the South Carolina Broadcasting Association. There were 11 television stations, most of them affiliated with the major US networks. South Carolina has one of the most highly regarded educational television systems in the nation, serving the public schools, higher educational institutions, state agencies, and the general public through a multichannel closed-circuit network and seven open channels. Cable systems broadcast television programming to 137,014 South Carolinians by the end of 1978.

⁴⁵PRESS
Of the leading morning newspapers still published in South Carolina, the *Charleston News and Courier* (with a paid circulation of 65,881 in 1979) was founded in 1803, the *Spartanburg Herald* (41,500) in 1872, the *Greenville News* (84,312) in 1874, and the *State* in Columbia (103,471) in 1891. Overall, as of 1978, South Carolina had 8 morning newspapers with a combined circulation of 394,519, 12 evening dailies with 198,035, and 8 Sunday newspapers with 474,381. North Carolina's *Charlotte Observer* also has many subscribers in nearby areas of South Carolina.

⁴⁶ORGANIZATIONS
Headquarters for most of the state's professional, trade, and industry groups are in Columbia, the capital. National organizations with headquarters in South Carolina include the International Studies Association, in Columbia; Association of Social and Behavioral Scientists, Orangeburg; National Philately Society, Sullivans Island; and Sports Car Collectors Society of America, Mt. Pleasant.

⁴⁷TOURISM, TRAVEL, AND RECREATION
In 1978, South Carolina had 40.5 million out-of-state visitors, of whom 17.2 million vacationed in the state. In that year, tourist spending exceeded $1.7 billion, double the 1974 total. More than three-fourths of the 1978 spending by vacationers was in Charleston and at the Myrtle Beach and Hilton Head Island vacation resorts.

South Carolina's 39 state parks attracted 11.5 million visitors in 1978. During the same year, the state registered 177,051 boats; licenses were issued to 218,743 hunters and 399,236 fishermen in 1977/78.

⁴⁸SPORTS
There are no major professional sports teams in South Carolina, and wagering on sports events is illegal. Several steeplechase horse races are held annually in Camden, and two important professional golf tournaments are held at Hilton Head Island every spring and summer.

In collegiate football, the Clemson Tigers won the Atlantic Coast Conference title in 1978; the University of South Carolina and South Carolina State also have football programs. Fishing, water skiing, and sailing are popular participant sports. Annually, on Labor Day, the Southern 500 stock-car race is held in Darlington.

⁴⁹FAMOUS SOUTH CAROLINIANS
Many distinguished South Carolinians made their reputations outside the state. Andrew Jackson (1767–1845), the 7th US president, was born in a border settlement probably inside present-day South Carolina, but studied law in North Carolina before establishing a legal practice in Tennessee. Identified more

closely with South Carolina is John C. Calhoun (1782–1850), vice president from 1825 to 1833; Calhoun also served as US senator and was a leader of the South prior to the Civil War.

John Rutledge (1739–1800), the first governor of the state and a leader during the American Revolution, served a term as US chief justice but was never confirmed by the Senate. Another Revolutionary leader, Charles Cotesworth Pinckney (1746–1825), was also a delegate to the US constitutional convention. A strong Unionist, Joel R. Poinsett (1779–1851) served as secretary of war and as the first US ambassador to Mexico; he developed the poinsettia, named after him, from a Mexican flower. Benjamin R. Tillman (1847–1918) was governor, US senator, and leader of the populist movement in South Carolina. Bernard M. Baruch (1870–1965), an outstanding financier, statesman, and adviser to presidents, was born in South Carolina. Another presidential adviser, James F. Byrnes (1879–1972), also served as US senator, associate justice of the Supreme Court, and secretary of state. The state's best-known recent political leader is J(ames) Strom Thurmond (b.1902), who ran for the presidency as a States' Rights Democrat ("Dixiecrat") in 1948, winning 1,169,134 popular votes and 39 electoral votes, and has served in the Senate since 1955.

Famous military leaders native to the state are the Revolutionary War general Francis Marion (1732?–95), known as the Swamp Fox, and James Longstreet (1821–1904), a Confederate lieutenant general during the Civil War. Mark W. Clark (b.New York, 1896), US Army general and former president of the Citadel, has lived in South Carolina since 1954. General William C. Westmoreland (b.1914) was commander of US forces in Viet-Nam.

Notable in the academic world are Francis Lieber (b.Germany, 1800–1872), a political scientist who taught at the University of South Carolina and, later, Columbia University in New York City, and wrote for the US the world's first comprehensive code of military laws and procedures; Mary McLeod Bethune (1875–1955), founder of Bethune-Cookman College in Florida and of the National Council of Negro Women; John B. Watson (1878–1958), a pioneer in behavioral psychology; and Charles H. Townes (b.1915), awarded the Nobel Prize in physics in 1964. South Carolinians prominent in business and the professions include architect Robert Mills (1781–1885), who designed the Washington Monument and many other buildings; William Gregg (b.Virginia, 1800–1867), a leader in establishing the textile industry in the South; David R. Coker (1870–1938), who developed many different varieties of pedigreed seed; and industrial builder Charles E. Daniel (1895–1964), who helped bring many new industries to the state.

South Carolinians who made significant contributions to literature include William Gilmore Simms (1806–70), author of nearly 100 books; Julia Peterkin (1880–1961), who won the Pulitzer Prize for *Scarlet Sister Mary*; DuBose Heyward (1885–1940), whose novel *Porgy* was the basis of the folk opera *Porgy and Bess*; and James M. Dabbs (1896–1970), a writer who was also a leader in the racial integration movement.

Entertainers born in the state include singer Eartha Kitt (b.1928) and jazz trumpeter John Birks "Dizzy" Gillespie (b.1917). Tennis champion Althea Gibson (b.1927) is another South Carolina native.

⁵⁰BIBLIOGRAPHY

Barry, John M. *Natural Vegetation of South Carolina.* Columbia: University of South Carolina Press, 1979.

Cauthen, Charles E. *South Carolina Goes to War, 1860–65.* Chapel Hill: University of North Carolina Press, 1950.

Jones, Lewis P. *South Carolina: A Synoptic History for Laymen.* Columbia: University of South Carolina Press, 1971.

Lander, Ernest M. *A History of South Carolina, 1856–1960.* Columbia: University of South Carolina Press, 1970.

Sirmans, M. Eugene. *Colonial South Carolina: A Political History, 1663–1763.* Chapel Hill: University of North Carolina Press, 1966.

South Carolina, State of. Division of Research and Statistical Services. *South Carolina Statistical Abstract, 1979.* Columbia, 1979.

South Carolina, State of. 103d General Assembly of South Carolina. *1980 South Carolina Legislative Manual.* 61st ed. Columbia, 1980.

Taylor, Rosser H. *Ante-Bellum South Carolina: A Social and Cultural History.* Chapel Hill: University of North Carolina Press, 1942.

Wallace, David Duncan. *History of South Carolina.* 4 vols. New York: American Historical Society, 1934.

Wood, Peter H. *Black Majority: Negroes in Colonial South Carolina from 1670 through the Stono Rebellion.* New York: Knopf, 1974.

Wright, Louis B. *South Carolina: A Bicentennial History.* New York: Norton, 1976.

SOUTH DAKOTA

State of South Dakota

ORIGIN OF STATE NAME: The state was formerly the southern part of Dakota Territory; *dakota* is a Sioux word meaning "friend." **NICKNAME**: The Coyote State. (Also: The Sunshine State.) **CAPITAL**: Pierre. **ENTERED UNION**: 2 November 1889 (40th). **SONG**: "Hail, South Dakota." **MOTTO**: Under God the People Rule. **COAT OF ARMS**: Beneath the state motto, the Missouri River winds between hills and plains; symbols representing mining (a smelting furnace and hills), commerce (a steamboat), and agriculture (a man plowing, cattle, and a field of corn) complete the scene. **FLAG**: The state seal, centered on a white or light blue field and encircled by a serrated sun, is surrounded by the words "South Dakota" above and "The Sunshine State" below. **OFFICIAL SEAL**: The words "State of South Dakota Great Seal 1889" encircle the arms. **ANIMAL**: Coyote. **BIRD**: Chinese ring-necked pheasant. **FLOWER**: Pasqueflower. **TREE**: Black Hills spruce. **GEM**: Fairburn agate. **MINERAL**: Rose quartz. **GRASS**: Western wheatgrass. **LEGAL HOLIDAYS**: New Year's Day, 1 January; Washington's Birthday, 3d Monday in February; Memorial Day, last Monday in May; Independence Day, 4 July; Labor Day, 1st Monday in September; Columbus Day, 2d Monday in October; Veterans Day, 11 November; Thanksgiving Day, 4th Thursday in November; Christmas Day, 25 December. **TIME**: 6 A.M. CST = noon GMT; 5 A.M. MST = noon GMT.

¹LOCATION, SIZE, AND EXTENT

Situated in the western north-central US, South Dakota ranks 16th in size among the 50 states.

The state has a total area of 77,047 sq mi (199,551 sq km), comprising 75,955 sq mi (196,723 sq km) of land and 1,092 sq mi (2,828 sq km) of inland water. Shaped roughly like a rectangle with irregular borders on the E and SE, South Dakota extends about 380 mi (610 km) E–W and has a maximum N–S extension of 245 mi (394 km).

South Dakota is bordered on the N by North Dakota; on the E by Minnesota and Iowa (with the line in the NE passing through the Bois de Sioux River, Lake Traverse, and Big Stone Lake, and in the SE through the Big Sioux River); on the S by Nebraska (with part of the line formed by the Missouri River and Lewis and Clark Lake); and on the W by Wyoming and Montana.

The total boundary length of South Dakota is 1,316 mi (2,118 km). The state's geographic center is in Hughes County, 8 mi (13 km) NE of Pierre. The geographic center of the US, including Alaska and Hawaii, is at 44°58′N, 103°46′W, in Butte County, 17 mi (27 km) W of Castle Rock.

²TOPOGRAPHY

The eastern two-fifths of South Dakota is prairie, belonging to the Central Lowlands. The western three-fifths fall within the Missouri Plateau, part of the Great Plains region; the High Plains extend into the southern fringes of the state. The Black Hills, an extension of the Rocky Mountains, occupy the southern half of the state's western border; the mountains, which tower about 4,000 feet (1,200 meters) over the neighboring plains, include Harney Peak, at 7,242 feet (2,207 meters) the highest point in the state. East of the southern Black Hills are the Badlands, a barren, eroded region with extensive fossil deposits. South Dakota's lowest elevation, 962 feet (293 meters), is at Big Stone Lake, in the northeastern corner.

Flowing south and southeast, the Missouri River cuts a huge swath through the heart of South Dakota before forming part of the southeastern boundary. Tributaries of the Missouri include the Grand, Cheyenne, Bad, and White rivers in the west and the James, Vermillion, and Big Sioux in the east. The Missouri River itself is controlled by four large dams—Gavins Point, Ft.

Randall, Big Bend, and Oahe—which provide water for irrigation, flood control, and hydroelectric power. Major lakes in the state include Traverse, Big Stone, Lewis and Clark, Francis Case, Sharpes, and Oahe.

³CLIMATE

South Dakota has an interior continental climate, with hot summers, extremely cold winters, high winds, and periodic droughts. The normal January temperature is 14°F (–10°C); the normal July temperature, 73°F (23°C). The record low temperature is –58°F (–50°C), set at McIntosh on 17 February 1936; the record high, 120°F (49°C), at Gannvalley on 5 July 1936.

Normal annual precipitation averages 25 in (64 cm) in Sioux Falls and is less farther west. Sioux Falls receives an average of 39 in (99 cm) of snow per year.

⁴FLORA AND FAUNA

Oak, maple, beech, birch, hickory, and willow all are represented in South Dakota's forests, while thickets of chokecherry, wild plum, gooseberry, and currant are found in the eastern part of the state. Pasqueflower (*Anemone ludoviciana*) is the state flower; other wild flowers include beardtongue, bluebell, and monkshood.

Familiar native mammals are the coyote (the state animal), porcupine, raccoon, bobcat, white-tailed and mule deer, white-tailed jackrabbit, and black-tailed prairie dog. Nearly 300 species of birds have been identified; the sage grouse, bobwhite quail, and ring-necked pheasant are leading game birds. Trout, catfish, pike, bass, and perch are fished for sport. South Dakota's list of threatened animals includes the river otter, mountain lion, northern swift fox, black bear, longnose sucker, brown snake, and Blandings turtle. The black-footed ferret, interior least tern, and pearl dace are endangered.

⁵ENVIRONMENTAL PROTECTION

Agencies concerned with natural resource preservation and environmental protection include the Department of Game, Fish, and Parks and the Department of Water and Natural Resources. The Health Department deals with solid waste disposal and air pollution. The South Dakota Natural Resources Coalition serves as an umbrella organization for various private conservation groups in the state.

[6]POPULATION

South Dakota ranked 44th in the US with a 1970 census population of 662,257. According to preliminary census data, the population in 1980 was 687,643, representing a 10-year increase of 3.8%; the average population density was 9 per sq mi (3 per sq km). Only 28% of all South Dakotans lived in metropolitan areas in 1977. The leading cities as of 1980 were Sioux Falls, with 80,747 residents, and Rapid City, 46,340.

[7]ETHNIC GROUPS

South Dakota's Indian population totaled 32,365 according to the 1970 census. That same year, tribal figures placed the population at around 42,000. Many lived on the 5,085,000 acres (2,058,000 hectares) of Indian lands in 1978, but Rapid City also had a large Indian population. As of 1976, the state had some 1,800 black Americans and 1,000 Asian-Pacific peoples. In 1970, about 16% of all South Dakotans were either foreign-born or children of the foreign-born; Germans, Norwegians, and Russians were the largest such groups.

[8]LANGUAGES

Despite hints given by such place-names as Dakota, Oahe, and Akaska, English has borrowed little from the language of the Sioux still living in South Dakota. *Tepee* is such a loanword, and *tado* (jerky) is heard near Pine Ridge. South Dakota English is transitional between the Northern and Midland dialects. Diffusion throughout the state is apparent, but many terms contrast along a curving line from the southeast to the northwest corner.

In 1970, 77% of the native-born residents, as well as 77% of all residents, reported English as their first language. Speakers of major first languages were as follows:

	NATIVE-BORN	FOREIGN-BORN
English	504,367	1,264
German	65,215	3,685
Indian languages	8,922	18

[9]RELIGIONS

Protestant groups had 325,673 adherents in 1971. Leading denominations were American Lutheran Church, with 114,831; United Methodist, 57,220; and Lutheran Church–Missouri Synod, 35,071. In 1979, the state had 139,705 Roman Catholics and an estimated 595 Jews.

[10]TRANSPORTATION

The Chicago, Milwaukee and Northwestern, Illinois Central Gulf, Burlington Northern, and Soo railroads operated 3,568 mi (5,742 km) of track in South Dakota as of 1979. Municipal and rural roads covered 82,518 mi (132,800 km) in 1978, when the state had 608,490 registered motor vehicles and 470,200 licensed drivers. There were 75 public and 67 private airfields, of which Joe Foss Field at Sioux Falls was the most active.

[11]HISTORY

People have lived in what is now South Dakota for at least 25,000 years. The original inhabitants, who hunted in the northern Great Plains until about 5000 BC, were the first of a succession of nomadic groups, followed by a society of semisedentary mound builders. After them came the prehistoric forebears of the modern riverine groups—Mandan, Hidatsa, and Arikara—who were found gathering, hunting, farming, and fishing along the upper Missouri River by the first European immigrants. These groups faced no challenge until the Sioux, driven from the Minnesota woodlands, began to move westward during the second quarter of the 18th century, expelling all other Native American groups from South Dakota by the mid-1830s.

Significant European penetration of South Dakota followed the Lewis and Clark expedition of 1804–6. White men came to assert US sovereignty, to negotiate Indian treaties, to "save Indian souls," and to traffic in hides and furs. Among the most important early merchants were Manuel Lisa, who pressed up the Missouri from St. Louis, and Pierre Chouteau, Jr., whose offices in St. Louis dominated trade on both the upper Mississippi and upper Missouri rivers from 1825 until his death in 1865, by which time all major sources of hides and furs were exhausted, negotiations for Indian land titles were in progress, and surveyors were preparing ceded territories for non-Indian settlers.

Territorial government, established in 1861, had its headquarters in Yankton and a jurisdiction that extended across the northern prairies and Great Plains. Through the subdivision of this organized territory, South Dakota emerged as a state in 1889, with the capital in Pierre. Included within the state were nine Indian reservations established, after protracted negotiations and three wars with the Sioux, by Indian Office personnel, with the backing of the US Army. Five reservations were established west of the Missouri for the Teton and Yanktonai Sioux, and four reserves east of the Missouri for the Yankton and several Isanti Sioux tribes. Sovereignty was thus divided between Indian agents, state officials, and tribal leaders, a division that did not always make for efficient government.

Through the late 19th and early 20th centuries, South Dakotans had limited economic opportunities, for they depended mainly on agriculture. Some 30,000 Sioux barely survived on farming and livestock production, supplemented by irregular government jobs and off-reservation employment. The 500,000 non-Indians lived mainly off cattle-breeding operations west of the Missouri, cattle-feeding enterprises and small grain sales east of the Missouri, mineral production (especially gold) in the Black Hills, and various service industries at urban centers throughout South Dakota.

The period after World War I saw extensive road building, the establishment of a tourist industry, and efforts to subdue and harness the waters of the Missouri. Like other Americans, South Dakotans were helped through the drought and depression of the 1930s by federal aid. Non-Indians were assisted by food relief, various work-relief programs, and crop-marketing plans, while Indians enjoyed an array of federal programs often called the "Indian New Deal."

The economic revival brought about by World War II persisted into the postwar era. Rural whites benefited from the mechanization of agriculture, dam construction along the Missouri, rural electrification, and arid-land reclamation. Federal programs were organized for reservation Indians, relocating them in urban centers where industrial jobs were available, establishing light industries in areas already heavily populated by Indians, and improving education and occupational opportunities on reservations.

Meanwhile, the Sioux continued to bring their historic grievances to public attention. For 70 days in 1973, some 200 armed Indians occupied Wounded Knee, on the Pine Ridge Reservation, where hundreds of Sioux had been killed by US cavalry 83 years earlier. In 1980, reviewing one of several land claims brought by the Sioux, the US Supreme Court upheld compensation of $105 million for land in the Black Hills taken from the Indians by the federal government in 1877.

[12]STATE GOVERNMENT

South Dakota is governed by the constitution of 1889, as amended. The legislature consists of a 35-seat senate and 70-seat house of representatives, all of whose members serve two-year terms. Chief executive officials are the governor, lieutenant governor, secretary of state, attorney general, treasurer, auditor, and commissioner of school and public lands, all of them elected for four-year terms.

Voters must be US citizens and at least 18 years of age; registration closes 15 days before an election.

[13]POLITICAL PARTIES

For the most part, South Dakota has voted Republican in presidential elections, even when native-son George McGovern was the Democratic candidate in 1972. Conservatism runs strong at the local level, although between the two world wars, populist groups gained a broad agrarian following.

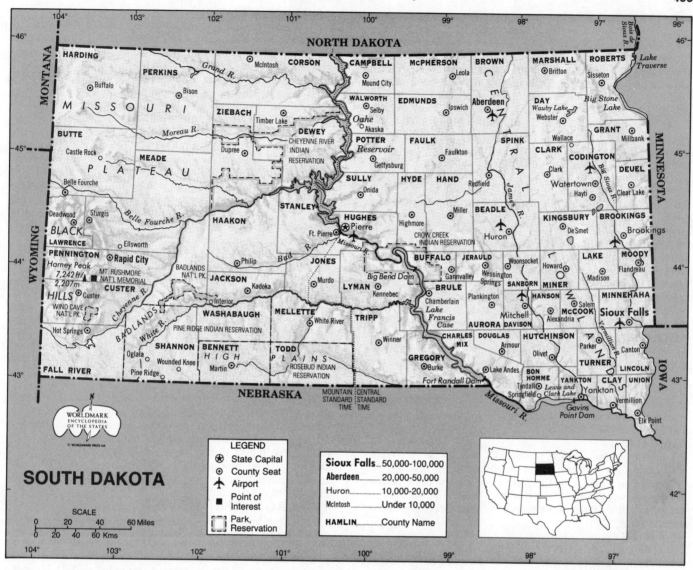

SOUTH DAKOTA

LEGEND
- ✪ State Capital
- ⊙ County Seat
- ✈ Airport
- ■ Point of Interest
- Park, Reservation

City	Population
Sioux Falls	50,000-100,000
Aberdeen	20,000-50,000
Huron	10,000-20,000
McIntosh	Under 10,000
HAMLIN	County Name

See US political: front cover F2; physical: back cover F2.

LOCATION: 42°28′47″ to 45°56′41″N; 96°26′11″ to 104°03′10″w. **BOUNDARIES**: North Dakota line, 361 mi (581 km); Minnesota line, 184 mi (296 km); Iowa line, 143 mi (230 km); Nebraska line, 423 mi (681 km); Wyoming line, 138 mi (222 km); Montana line, 67 mi (108 km).

South Dakota Presidential Vote by Major Political Parties, 1948–80

YEAR	ELECTORAL VOTE	SOUTH DAKOTA WINNER	DEMOCRAT	REPUBLICAN
1948	4	Dewey (R)	117,653	129,651
1952	4	*Eisenhower (R)	90,426	203,857
1956	4	*Eisenhower (R)	122,288	171,569
1960	4	Nixon (R)	128,070	178,417
1964	4	*Johnson (D)	163,010	130,108
1968	4	*Nixon (R)	118,023	149,841
1972	4	*Nixon (R)	139,945	166,476
1976	4	Ford (R)	147,068	151,505
1980	4	*Reagan (R)	103,855	198,343

*Won US presidential election.

South Dakotans chose Ronald Reagan in the 1980 presidential election. At the same time, Republican James Abdnor denied George McGovern's bid for a fourth term in the US Senate.

¹⁴LOCAL GOVERNMENT

As of 1977, South Dakota had 1,730 units of local government, including 67 counties, 311 municipalities, 1,010 townships, 194 school districts, and 148 special districts. Typical county officials include a treasurer, auditor, state's attorney, sheriff, register of deeds, and clerk of courts.

¹⁵STATE SERVICES

The secretary of public education oversees all elementary, secondary, higher, vocational, and cultural education programs. The Department of Social Services administers a variety of welfare programs, the Department of Labor aids the unemployed and underemployed, and the Department of Vocational Rehabilitation serves handicapped South Dakotans. Special agencies within the executive branch include the Office of Indian Affairs, State Economic Opportunity Office, and Office of Energy Policy.

¹⁶JUDICIAL SYSTEM

South Dakota has a supreme court with 5 justices, and eight circuit courts with 36 judges; all are elected on a nonpartisan ballot to staggered eight-year terms. In 1978, crime rates in every category were far below the national average.

[17] ARMED FORCES

Ellsworth Air Force Base, with 6,733 personnel in 1978, is the state's only defense installation. South Dakota firms received $20 million in federal defense contracts in 1978. As of 30 September 1979, about 75,000 veterans were living in the state, including 3,000 from World War I, 34,000 from World War II, 13,000 from the Korean conflict, and 18,000 from the Viet-Nam era. Veterans' benefits totaled $93 million during 1977/78.

South Dakota's National Guard numbered 3,900 as of 30 September 1978. In 1977, the state and local police numbered 1,318 personnel.

[18] MIGRATION

Since the 1930s, more people have left South Dakota than have settled in the state. Between 1940 and 1977, the net loss from migration totaled 281,000.

[19] INTERGOVERNMENTAL COOPERATION

South Dakota participates in the Belle Fourche River Compact (with Wyoming), the Interstate Oil and Gas Compact, and the Western Interstate Energy Compact, among other organizations; there are boundary compacts with Minnesota and Nebraska. In 1978/79, South Dakota received more than $316 million in federal aid, of which $22.4 million was general revenue sharing.

[20] ECONOMY

Agriculture dominates South Dakota's economy. Grains and livestock are the main farm products, and processed foods and farm equipment are leading manufactured items. Mining and tourism are also important. Projected contributions to total personal income for 1980 were agriculture, 17%; government, 17%; wholesale and retail trade, 13%; services, 11%; manufacturing, 6%; and other sectors, 36%.

[21] INCOME

Per capita income in 1978 was $6,841, ranking South Dakota 35th among the 50 states. Total personal income reached $4.7 billion, representing a real growth of 40% since 1970. Median family income was $12,051 (41st in the US) in 1975, when 88,000 South Dakotans, many of them Indians, were below the federal poverty level.

[22] LABOR

The state's civilian labor force numbered 328,000 in 1978, of whom 97% were employed and 3% unemployed. A federal census of workers covered by unemployment insurance in March 1977 revealed the following nonfarm employment pattern in South Dakota:

	ESTABLISH- MENTS	EMPLOYEES	ANNUAL PAYROLL ('000)
Agricultural services, forestry, fishing	195	622	$ 4,677
Mining	46	2,239	32,803
Contract construction	1,905	8,758	118,170
Manufacturing	671	22,447	251,208
Transportation, public utilities	930	10,924	140,742
Wholesale trade	1,800	15,078	159,416
Retail trade	5,154	41,171	244,284
Finance, insurance, real estate	1,481	9,538	91,980
Services	4,082	37,313	250,120
Other	177	223	1,595
TOTALS	16,441	148,313	$1,294,995

Among the workers not covered by this survey were government employees (57,000 in 1978) and agricultural workers (60,000 in 1979).

During 1976, 21,000 South Dakota workers belonged to labor unions, less than 10% of the nonfarm labor force. The state has a right-to-work law.

[23] AGRICULTURE

South Dakota ranked 18th among the 50 states in 1978 in agricultural income, with receipts of $2.2 billion. In 1979 there were an estimated 42,000 farms and ranches in the state, covering about 45 million acres (18 million hectares).

Leading crops and their values during 1979 were corn for grain, 210.9 million bushels, $400.7 million; hay, 7.9 million tons, $277 million; wheat, 60.1 million bushels, $219.5 million; soybeans, 21 million bushels, $123.6 million; oats, 98.5 million bushels, $123.1 million; and barley, 20 million bushels, $43 million.

[24] ANIMAL HUSBANDRY

The livestock industry is of great importance in South Dakota, particularly in the High Plains. In late 1979 there were 4,010,000 cattle and calves, 2,000,000 hogs and pigs, and 783,000 sheep and lambs. Livestock products in 1979 included 1.6 billion lb of cattle, 688.2 million lb of hogs, and 64.5 million lb of sheep. That same year, 1.6 billion lb of milk were produced, along with 512 million eggs, 5.3 million lb of chickens, and 24.6 million lb of turkeys.

[25] FISHING

Virtually all fishing is recreational. Commercial landings were worth only $314,000 in 1978.

[26] FORESTRY

In 1977, South Dakota's forestlands covered 1,702,000 acres (689,000 hectares), including 1,467,000 acres (594,000 hectares) of commercial timberland. Nearly two-thirds of the state's woodlands were publicly owned or managed. Shipments of lumber and wood products totaled $100.6 million in 1977.

[27] MINING

Although South Dakota is the nation's leading producer of gold, the overall value of the state's mineral output in 1978 was only $128 million, important to the local economy but no better than 40th among the 50 states. Production of gold, found in the Black Hills, totaled 285,812 troy oz in 1978. That same year, South Dakota quarries produced 6.2 million tons of sand and gravel and 3.7 million tons of stone. Some petroleum, silver, clays, and shale are also extracted.

[28] ENERGY AND POWER

In 1978, South Dakota had an installed electrical capacity of 2.2 million kw and produced 9.8 billion kwh of electricity, more than half of it sold to customers in other states. Nearly 70% of the power output came from hydroelectric sources and almost all the remainder from coal-fired plants. Utilities in South Dakota sold 27 trillion Btu of gas to 98,000 customers during 1978, with revenues of $51 million.

South Dakota has very modest fossil-fuel resources. Proved petroleum reserves totaled 2,738,000 barrels in 1978, when the oil output was 447,000 barrels. As of 1976, the state's lignite reserves were 426,000,000 tons; production was negligible in 1978, however.

[29] INDUSTRY

Food and related products, nonelectrical machinery, lumber and wood products, and printing and publishing together account for more than two-thirds of all South Dakota manufacturing employment. The total value added by manufacturing in 1977 was $608.5 million, with food and related items contributing nearly 40%. The following table shows value added by selected industries in 1972 and 1977:

	1972	1977
Meat products	$77,200,000	$155,000,000
Dairy products	23,700,000	31,000,000
Grain mill products	9,900,000	18,700,000
Farm machinery and equipment	7,000,000	18,700,000

[30] COMMERCE

Wholesale trade in South Dakota totaled $1.8 billion in 1972. Of the state's $2.2 billion in retail trade in 1977, grocery stores contributed 18%; automobile dealers, 18%; gasoline service stations, 11%; eating and drinking places, 9%; department stores, 6%; and other establishments, 38%. The state's foreign agricultural exports were valued at $210 million in 1976/77 (31st in the US); manufactured exports were $68 million in 1976.

31 CONSUMER PROTECTION

The Division of Consumer Affairs of the Office of the Attorney General enforces South Dakota's Deceptive Trade Practices Act, prosecutes cases of fraud and other illegal activities, and in cooperation with the Department of Commerce, mediates disputes between consumers and businesses.

32 BANKING

South Dakota in 1978 had 155 insured commercial banks with total assets of $4.2 billion, total deposits of $3.8 billion, and equity capital of $308 million. In 1978 there were 16 savings and loan associations with total assets of $948.7 million, outstanding mortgage loans of $763.4 million, and savings deposits of $804 million.

33 INSURANCE

During 1978, nine life insurance companies were licensed to do business in South Dakota. The 941,000 policies in force had a combined value of $7.9 billion. Benefit payments totaled $64.8 million in 1978, when the average family had $31,700 in coverage, 10% below the national norm. Automobile insurance accounted for 40% of the $216 million in premiums written by property and liability insurance companies in 1978.

Hospital and medical insurance benefits paid under the Medicare program totaled $59 million in 1977.

34 SECURITIES

Although South Dakota has no securities exchanges, New York Stock Exchange member firms had 10 sales offices and 44 registered representatives in the state during 1978. South Dakotans reported $60.6 million in dividend income on their 1977 federal tax returns.

35 PUBLIC FINANCE

The governor must submit the annual budget to the state legislature by 1 December; the fiscal year begins the following 1 July. The legislature may amend the budget at will, but the governor has an item veto.

The following table summarizes general revenues and expenditures for 1979/80 (estimated) and 1980/81 (governor's recommendation):

	1979/80	1980/81
REVENUES		
Sales and use tax	$146,415,000	$169,217,000
Insurance company tax	11,157,000	12,272,000
Cigarette tax	10,250,000	10,250,000
Inheritance tax	7,000,000	7,500,000
Other receipts	44,041,851	41,104,788
TOTALS	$218,863,851	$240,343,788
EXPENDITURES		
General budget bill	$146,879,470	$160,820,066
Other appropriations	77,232,746	80,090,700
TOTALS	$224,112,216	$240,910,766

Consolidated expenditures for 1979/80 (including federal aid) totaled $628.8 million, of which 33% went for public education, 30% for human assistance and development, 23% for transportation, and 14% for other purposes. The total state and local government debt was $358 million in 1977, or $519 per capita (47th among the 50 states).

36 TAXATION

South Dakota's per capita taxation is among the lowest in the US—$324.06 in 1978, or 38% below the national average. There is no personal or corporate income tax, and personal property taxes have been reduced since 1978. A state sales and use tax of 4% supplies more than two-thirds of South Dakota's general-fund receipts; as of 1979, 43 communities levied an additional 1% tax, and in five localities the rate ranged up to 2%. Taxes are also levied on gasoline sales, alcoholic beverages, tobacco products, mineral severance, inheritances, insurance premiums, and other items.

Federal taxes in South Dakota totaled $783 million in 1976, while federal expenditures in the state amounted to slightly more than $1 billion, for a net benefit of $218 million. In 1977, South Dakotans filed 256,880 federal income tax returns and paid $309,268,000 in tax.

37 ECONOMIC POLICY

Efforts to attract industry to South Dakota are under the jurisdiction of the Department of Economic and Tourism Development, which had a recommended budget of $2.2 million in 1980/81. Among the advantages noted by the department are low taxes, the availability of community development corporations to finance construction of new facilities, various property tax relief measures, inventory tax exemptions, and a favorable labor climate in which work stoppages are few and union activity is limited by a right-to-work law. South Dakota is one of the few states to have enacted a statute of limitations on product liability—in this case, six years—a measure cited as further proof of the state's attempt to create an atmosphere conducive to manufacturing.

38 HEALTH

South Dakotans had an average life expectancy of 72.08 years (11th in the US) in 1969–71; men averaged 68.49 years, women 76.19. The birthrate, death rate, and infant mortality rate all exceeded the national norms in 1977; death rates for heart disease, stroke, accidents, and early childhood disease were likewise above the national average.

In 1978, the state had 70 hospitals, with 5,676 beds; hospital personnel included 2,097 registered nurses and 916 licensed practical nurses. The average cost of hospital care in 1977 was $130 per day and $925 per stay, among the lowest of any state. In 1976 there were 154 nursing and related care facilities, with 8,400 beds and 7,900 residents. South Dakota had 683 active physicians in 1977 and 286 active dentists in 1979.

39 SOCIAL WELFARE

In 1975/76, outlays for the five largest welfare programs totaled $63 million, three-fourths of that from the federal government. Payments amounting to $18 million in aid for dependent children went to 20,600 South Dakotans in 1978. That same year, 117,300 state residents received Social Security benefits worth $267 million. Federally administered Supplemental Security Income paid $9.1 million to 8,200 South Dakotans. Other benefit programs included $7.2 million for food stamps, $6.4 million for school lunches, $3.6 million for vocational rehabilitation, and $10 million for unemployment insurance. Workers' compensation payments totaled $7.2 million in 1977.

40 HOUSING

The 1970 census counted 222,000 year-round housing units, of which 201,000 were occupied; 90% of the occupied units had full plumbing. Between 1976 and 1978, some 16,100 new housing units valued at $387 million were authorized.

41 EDUCATION

South Dakota tied with Nevada and Iowa for the lowest illiteracy rate in the US, 0.5% in 1970. As of 1976, 69% of adult South Dakotans were high school graduates, 11% had four or more years of college, and the median number of school years completed was 12.5.

Fall 1978 enrollment in public schools totaled 138,052; 90,261 in grades K–8, 47,791 in grades 9–12. Private school enrollment included 8,944 students in grades K–8 and 3,939 in grades 9–12. There were 11,088 teachers and supervisory staff in all these public and private schools.

More than 29,000 students were enrolled in higher educational institutions in fall 1978. There were six state-supported colleges and universities, of which the largest was the University of South Dakota (Vermillion and Springfield), with 6,559 students; South Dakota State University (Brookings) had 6,537. In addition, the state had eight private institutions of higher education. The Board of Regents offers financial aid programs.

⁴²ARTS
The South Dakota State Fine Arts Council, located at Sioux Falls, and the South Dakota Committee on the Humanities, at Brookings, aid and coordinate arts and humanities activities throughout the state. Artworks and handicrafts are displayed at the Dacotah Prairie Museum (Aberdeen), South Dakota Memorial Art Center (Brookings), Sioux Indian Museum and Crafts Center (Rapid City), Civic Fine Arts Association (Sioux Falls), and W. H. Over Museum (Vermillion). The South Dakota Symphony is based in Sioux Falls.

⁴³LIBRARIES AND MUSEUMS
In 1977/78, South Dakota had 60 public libraries with a combined total of 1,524,817 volumes and 2,930,603 circulation. Leading collections, each with more than 100,000 volumes, were those of South Dakota State University (Brookings), Northern State College (Aberdeen), Augustana College (Sioux Falls), the University of South Dakota (Vermillion), the South Dakota State Library (Pierre), and the Sioux Falls Public Library).

South Dakota has more than 50 museums and historic sites, including the Robinson Museum (Pierre), Siouxland Heritage Museums (Sioux Falls), and the Shrine to Music Museum (Vermillion). Badlands National Park, at Interior, exhibits many fossils found in the area. Wind Cave National Park, Hot Springs, has displays in geology and anthropology.

⁴⁴COMMUNICATIONS
South Dakota had some 430 post offices and 2,300 Postal Service employees in 1977. In 1978 there were 497,631 telephones, 369,578 residential and 128,053 business; on average, 95% of households had telephone service. Commercial broadcasters included 35 radio stations (29 AM, 6 FM) and 10 television stations. Cable television systems served 49,960 subscribers in 80 communities.

⁴⁵PRESS
In 1978, South Dakota had 1 morning newspaper, with an average daily circulation of 3,335; 12 evening papers, with a total of 173,981; and 4 Sunday papers, with 124,649. Leading newspapers included the *Rapid City Journal*, evenings 32,809, Sundays 33,294; and the *Sioux Falls Argus-Leader*, evenings 47,167, Sundays 54,120.

⁴⁶ORGANIZATIONS
The American Association of Conservation Information has its headquarters in Pierre. Most national membership organizations have branches in the state.

⁴⁷TOURISM, TRAVEL, AND RECREATION
Visitors spent an estimated $414 million in South Dakota in 1976. Most of the state's tourist attractions lie west of the Missouri River, especially in the Black Hills region. Mt. Rushmore National Memorial consists of the heads of four US presidents— George Washington, Thomas Jefferson, Abraham Lincoln, and Theodore Roosevelt—carved in granite in the mountainside. Wind Cave National Park and Jewel Cave National Monument are also in the Black Hills region. Just to the east is Badlands National Monument, consisting of fossil beds and eroded cliffs almost bare of vegetation. In 1977/78, South Dakota had 127,807 licensed hunters and 135,884 licensed fishermen.

⁴⁸SPORTS
There are no major league sports teams in South Dakota. The University of South Dakota Coyotes and the Jackrabbits of South Dakota State both compete in the North Central Division. Skiing and hiking are popular in the Black Hills.

⁴⁹FAMOUS SOUTH DAKOTANS
The only South Dakotan to win high elective office was Hubert H. Humphrey (1911–78), a native of Wallace who, after rising to power in Minnesota Democratic politics, served as US senator for 16 years before becoming vice president under Lyndon Johnson (1965–69).

Other outstanding federal officeholders from South Dakota include Newton Edmunds (1819–1908), second governor of the Dakota Territory; Charles Henry Burke (b.New York, 1861–1944), who as commissioner of Indian affairs improved education and health care for Native Americans; and Vermillion-born Peter Norbeck (1870–1936), a Progressive Republican leader, first while governor (1917–21), then as US senator until his death. The son of a German-American father and a Brulé Indian mother, Benjamin Reifel (b.1906) was the first American Indian elected to Congress from South Dakota; he later served as the last US commissioner of Indian affairs. George McGovern (b.1922) served in the US Senate from 1963 through 1980; an early opponent of the war in Viet-Nam, he ran unsuccessfully as the Democratic presidential nominee in 1972.

Associated with South Dakota are several distinguished Indian leaders. Among them were Red Cloud (b.Nebraska, 1822–1909), an Oglala warrior; Spotted Tail (b.Wyoming, 1833?–1881), the Brulé chief who was a commanding figure on the Rosebud Reservation; Sitting Bull (1834–90), a Hunkpapa Sioux most famous as the main leader of the Indian army that crushed George Custer's Seventh US Cavalry at the Battle of the Little Big Horn (1876) in Montana; and Crazy Horse (1849?–1877), an Oglala chief who also fought at Little Big Horn.

Ernest Orlando Lawrence (1901–58), the state's only Nobel Prize winner, received the physics award in 1939 for the invention of the cyclotron. The business leader with the greatest personal influence on South Dakota's history was Pierre Chouteau, Jr. (b.Missouri, 1789–1865), a fur trader after whom the state capital is named.

South Dakota artists include George Catlin (b.Pennsylvania, 1796–1872), Karl Bodmer (1809–93), Harvey Dunn (1884–1952), and Oscar Howe (b.1915). Gutzon Borglum (b.Idaho, 1871–1941) carved the faces on Mt. Rushmore. The state's two leading writers are Ole Edvart Rölvaag (b.Norway, 1876–1931), author of *Giants in the Earth* and other novels; and Frederick Manfred (b.Iowa, 1912), a Minnesota resident who served as writer-in-residence at the University of South Dakota, and has used the state as a setting for many of his novels.

⁵⁰BIBLIOGRAPHY
Cash, Joseph H., and Herbert T. Hoover, ed. *To Be an Indian: An Oral History*. New York: Holt, Rinehart, and Winston, 1971.

Clem, Adam L. *Prairie State Politics: Popular Democracy in South Dakota*. Washington, D.C.: Public Affairs Press, 1967.

Federal Writers' Project. *Guide to South Dakota*. New York: Oxford University Press, 1952.

Hoover, Herbert T. *The Sioux: A Critical Bibliography*. Bloomington: Indiana University Press, 1979.

Kingsbury, George W. *History of Dakota Territory*. 2 vols. Chicago: Clarke, 1915.

Milton, John R., ed. *The Literature of South Dakota*. Vermillion: Dakota Press, 1976.

Milton, John R. *South Dakota: A Bicentennial History*. New York: Norton, 1977.

Parker, Watson. *Gold in the Black Hills*. Norman: University of Oklahoma Press, 1966.

Schell, Herbert. *History of South Dakota*. 3d ed. Lincoln: University of Nebraska Press, 1975.

South Dakota. Office of the Governor. *State of South Dakota: Governor's Budget, Fiscal Year 1980–81*. Pierre, 1979.

TENNESSEE

State of Tennessee

ORIGIN OF STATE NAME: Probably from Indian name *Tenase*, which was the principal village of the Cherokee. **NICKNAME:** The Volunteer State. **CAPITAL:** Nashville. **ENTERED UNION:** 1 June 1796 (16th). **SONGS:** "When It's Iris Time in Tennessee"; "The Tennessee Waltz"; "My Homeland, Tennessee." **POET LAUREATE:** Pek Gunn. **MOTTO:** Agriculture and Commerce. **SLOGAN:** Tennessee—America at Its Best. **FLAG:** On a crimson field separated by a white border from a blue bar at the fly, three white stars on a blue circle edged in white represent the state's three main general divisions—East, Middle, and West Tennessee. **OFFICIAL SEAL:** The upper half consists of the word "Agriculture," a plow, a sheaf of wheat, a cotton plant, and the roman numeral XVI, signifying the order of entry into the Union; the lower half comprises the word "Commerce" and a boat. The words "The Great Seal of the State of Tennessee 1796" surround the whole. The date commemorates the passage of the state constitution. **WILD ANIMAL:** Raccoon. **BIRD:** Mockingbird. **FLOWER:** Iris. **WILDFLOWER:** Passion flower. **TREE:** Tulip poplar. **GEM:** Tennessee pearl. **ROCK:** Limestone. **INSECTS:** Ladybug, firefly. **LEGAL HOLIDAYS:** New Year's Day, 1 January; Washington's Birthday, 3d Monday in February; Good Friday, March or April; Decoration Day, last Monday in May; Independence Day, 4 July; primary and county elections, 1st Tuesday in August in even-numbered years; Labor Day, 1st Monday in September; Columbus Day, 2d Monday in October; General Election Day, 1st Tuesday after 1st Monday in November in even-numbered years; Veterans Day, 11 November; Thanksgiving Day, 4th Thursday in November; Christmas Day, 25 December. **TIME:** 7 A.M. EST = noon GMT; 6 A.M. CST = noon GMT.

¹LOCATION, SIZE, AND EXTENT

Situated in the eastern south-central US, Tennessee ranks 34th in size among the 50 states.

The total area of the state is 42,244 sq mi (109,412 sq km), of which land occupies 41,328 sq mi (107,040 sq km) and inland water 916 sq mi (2,372 sq km). Tennessee extends about 430 mi (690 km) E–W and 110 mi (180 km) N–S.

Tennessee is bordered on the N by Kentucky and Virginia; on the E by North Carolina; on the S by Georgia, Alabama, and Mississippi; and on the W by Arkansas and Missouri (with the line formed by the Mississippi River). The boundary length of Tennessee totals 1,306 mi (2,102 km). The state's geographic center lies in Rutherford County, 5 mi (8 km) NE of Murfreesboro.

²TOPOGRAPHY

Long, narrow, and rhomboidal in shape, Tennessee is divided topographically into six major physical regions: the Unaka Mountains, the Great Valley of East Tennessee, the Cumberland Plateau, the Highland Rim, the Central Basin, and the Gulf Coastal Plain. In addition, there are two minor physical regions: the Western Valley of the Tennessee River and the Mississippi Flood Plains.

The easternmost region is the Unaka Mountains, a part of the Appalachian chain. The Unakas actually include several ranges, the most notable of which is the Great Smoky Mountains. The region constitutes the highest and most rugged surface in the state and covers an area of about 2,600 sq mi (6,700 sq km). Several peaks reach a height of 6,000 feet (1,800 meters) or more; the tallest is Clingmans Dome in the Great Smokies, which rises to 6,643 feet (2,025 meters) and is the highest point in the state.

Lying due west of the Unakas is the Great Valley of East Tennessee. Extending from southwestern Virginia into northern Georgia, the Great Valley is a segment of the Ridge and Valley province of the Appalachian Highlands, which reach from New York into Alabama. This region, consisting of long, narrow ridges with broad valleys between them, covers more than 9,000 sq mi (23,000 sq km) of Tennessee. Since the coming of the Tennessee

Valley Authority (TVA) in 1933, the area has been dotted with artificial lakes and dams, which supply electric power and aid in flood control.

The Cumberland Plateau, which extends in its entirety from southern Kentucky into central Alabama, has an area of about 5,400 sq mi (14,000 sq km) in Middle Tennessee. The Plateau is a region of contrasts, including both the Cumberland Mountains, which rise to a height of 3,500 feet (1,100 meters) and the Sequatchie Valley, the floor of which lies about 1,000 feet (300 meters) below the surface of the adjoining plateau.

The Highland Rim, also in Middle Tennessee, is the state's largest natural region, consisting of more than 12,500 sq mi (32,400 sq km) and completely encircling the Central Basin. The eastern section is a gently rolling plain some 1,000 feet (300 meters) lower than the Cumberland Plateau. The western part has an even lower elevation and sinks gently toward the Tennessee River.

The Central Basin, an oval depression with a gently rolling surface, has been compared to the bottom of an oval dish, of which the Highland Rim forms the broad, flat brim. With its rich soil, the region has attracted people from the earliest days of European settlement and is more densely populated than any other area.

The westernmost of the major regions is the Gulf Coastal Plain. It embraces practically all of West Tennessee and covers an area of 9,000 sq mi (23,000 sq km). It is a broad plain, sloping gradually westward until it ends abruptly at the bluffs overlooking the Mississippi Flood Plains. In the northwest corner is Reelfoot Lake, the only natural lake of significance in the state, formed by a series of earthquakes in 1811 and 1812. The state's lowest point, 182 feet (55 meters) above sea level, is on the banks of the Mississippi in the southwest.

Most of the state is drained by the Mississippi River system. Waters from the two longest rivers—the Tennessee, with a total length of 652 mi (1,049 km), and the Cumberland, which is 687 mi (1,106 km) long—flow into the Ohio River in Kentucky and join

503

the Mississippi at Cairo, Ill. Formed a few miles north of Knoxville by the confluence of the Holston and French Broad rivers, the Tennessee flows southwestward through the Great Valley into northern Alabama, then curves back into the state and flows northward into Kentucky. Other tributaries of the Tennessee include the Clinch, Duck, Elk, Hiwassee, and Sequatchie rivers. The Cumberland River rises in southeastern Kentucky, flows across central Tennessee, and then turns northward back into Kentucky; its principal tributaries are the Harpeth, Red, Obey, Caney Fork, and Stones rivers and Yellow Creek. In the western part of the state, the Forked Deer and Wolf rivers are among those flowing into the Mississippi, which forms the western border with Missouri and Arkansas.

³CLIMATE
Generally, Tennessee has a temperate climate, with warm summers and mild winters. However, the state's varied topography leads to a wide range of climatic conditions.

The warmest parts of the state, with the longest growing season, are the Gulf Coastal Plain, the Central Basin, and the Sequatchie Valley. In the Memphis area in the southwest the average date of the last killing frost is 20 March, and the growing season is about 235 days. Memphis has an annual mean temperature of 62°F (17°C), 41°F (5°C) in January and 82°F (28°C) in July. In the Nashville area, the growing season lasts about 225 days. Nashville has an annual mean of 60°F (16°C), ranging from 38°F (3°C) in January to 80°F (27°C) in July. The Knoxville area has a growing season of 220 days. The city's annual mean temperature is 60°F (16°C), with averages of 43°F (6°C) in January and 78°F (6°C) in July. In some parts of the mountainous east, where the temperatures are considerably lower, the growing season is as short as 130 days. The record high temperature for the state is 113°F (45°C), set at Perryville on 9 August 1930; the record low, −32°F (−36°C), was registered at Mountain City on 30 December 1917.

Severe storms and high winds are relatively infrequent. The greatest rainfall occurs in the winter and early spring months, especially March; the early fall months, particularly September and October, are the driest. Average annual precipitation is 49 in (124 cm) in Memphis and 46 in (117 cm) in Nashville. Crop-damaging droughts are rare. Snowfall varies and is more prevalent in East Tennessee than in the western section; Nashville gets about 11 in (28 cm) a year, Memphis only 6 in (15 cm).

⁴FLORA AND FAUNA
With its varied terrain and soils, Tennessee has an abundance of flora, including at least 150 kinds of native trees. Tulip poplar (the state tree), shortleaf pine, and chestnut, black, and red oaks are commonly found in the eastern part of the state, while the Highland Rim abounds in several varieties of oak, hickory, ash, and pine. Gum maple, black walnut, sycamore, and cottonwood grow in the west, and cypress is plentiful in the Reelfoot Lake area. In East Tennessee, rhododendron, mountain laurel, and wild azalea blossoms create a blaze of color in the mountains. More than 300 native Tennessee plants, including digitalis and ginseng, have been utilized for medicinal purposes. Glade cress, Duck River bladderpod, and American yellowwood are listed as threatened plants; Cumberland rosemary is classified as endangered.

Mammals of Tennessee include the raccoon (the state animal), white-tailed deer, black bear, bobcat, muskrat, woodchuck, opossum, and red and gray foxes; the European wild boar was introduced by sportsmen in 1912. As of 1980, 259 bird species resided in Tennessee. Bobwhite quail, ruffed grouse, mourning dove, and mallard duck are the most common game birds. The state's 56 amphibian species include numerous frogs, salamanders, newts, and lizards; 58 reptile species include three types of rattlesnake. Of the 286 fishes that inhabit Tennessee's lakes and streams, catfish, bream, bass, crappie, pike, and trout are the leading game fish.

Tennessee's Wildlife Resources Agency conducts an endangered and threatened species protection program. Among threatened species are the river otter, Cooper's hawk, Bewick's wren, northern pine snake, Tennessee cave salamander, blue sucker, amber darter, and silverjaw minnow. The snail darter, cited by opponents of the Tellico Dam, is probably Tennessee's most famous endangered species. The eastern cougar, gray and Indiana bats, Bachman's sparrow, Mississippi kite, lake sturgeon, Ohio River muskellunge, and Cumber monkey face and Appalachian monkey face pearly mussels are also on the endangered list.

⁵ENVIRONMENTAL PROTECTION
The first conservationists were agricultural reformers who, even before the Civil War, recommended terracing to conserve the soil and curtail erosion. Such conservation techniques as crop rotation and contour plowing were discussed at county fairs and other places where farmers gathered. In 1854, the legislature established the State Agricultural Bureau, which sought primarily to protect farmlands from floods. Nevertheless, soil erosion, flooding, and other conservation problems remained severe until relatively recent times.

Counties were authorized to construct levees as early as 1871, but effective flood control was not achieved until establishment of the Tennessee Valley Authority in 1933. Eroded areas were reforested with seedling trees, and cover crops were planted to hold the soil.

Today, the state Department of Conservation is responsible for soil protection, development of state parks and forest preserves, and conservation and proper utilization of mineral and water resources. The state maintains forestry nurseries and provides seedlings at low cost to interested farmers. In 1971, the legislature enacted the Water Quality Control Act, which outlaws the dumping of raw sewage into streams, and gave the Department of Public Health the power to enforce it. Smoke control ordinances prevail in all the major cities.

Much attention has been given to mineral resources, and especially to the surface mining of coal. The Strip Mine Law of 1967, as modified in 1972, requires permits for strip-mining and makes compulsory the restoration of the soil with a vegetative cover. The law extends not only to coal mining but also to the mining of barite, clay, phosphate, and sand and gravel.

In the mid-1970s, a major controversy erupted over the then incomplete Tellico Dam, near Knoxville, and the proposed flooding of the Little Tennessee River. Opponents of the project filed suit under the Endangered Species Act of 1973 to protect the snail darter, a tiny perch that lived in the last free-flowing stretch of the river. Their suit, upheld in the US Supreme Court in 1978, stopped construction for a time, but in 1979, the dam's supporters in Congress succeeded in exempting it from the terms of all environmental legislation, and the project was completed.

⁶POPULATION
Tennessee, with a population of 3,923,687, ranked 17th among the 50 states at the 1970 census. Preliminary census totals for 1980 showed Tennessee with a population of 4,539,834, yielding an average density of 110 per sq mi (42 per sq km).

The first permanent white settlements in the state were made in the 1760s, when people from North Carolina and Virginia crossed the Unaka Mountains and settled in the fertile valleys. Between 1790 and 1800, the population increased threefold, from 35,690 to 105,600, and it doubled during each of the next two decades. After the Civil War, the population continued to increase, though at a slower rate, tripling between 1870 and 1970.

A pronounced urban trend became apparent after World War II. In 1960, for the first time in the state's history, census figures showed slightly more people living in urban than in rural places. By 1970, 59% of all Tennesseans lived in towns and cities of 2,500 or more. Memphis is the state's largest city; in 1980, according to preliminary census data, it had a population of 644,538. Nashville (Davidson County) had 439,599, followed by

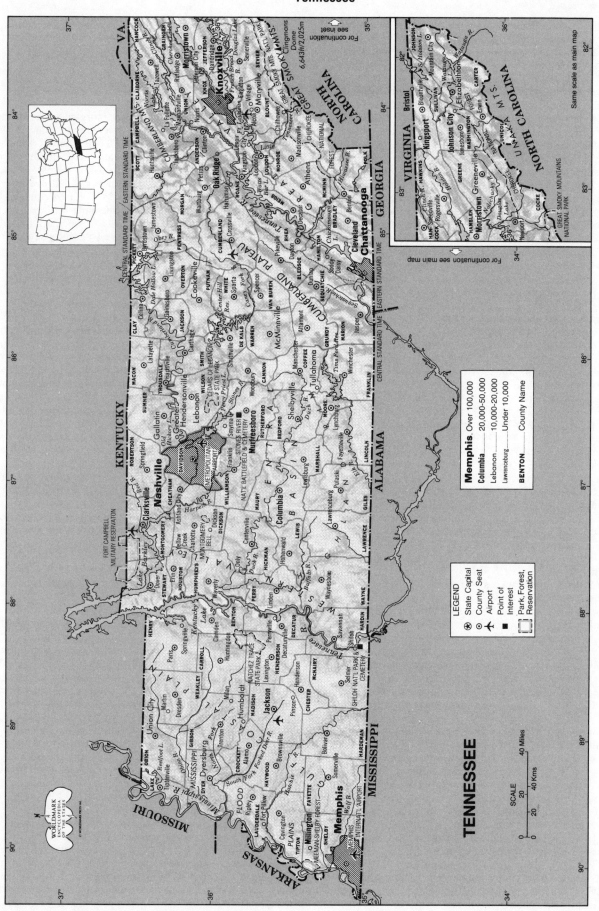

TENNESSEE

LEGEND
- ⊗ State Capital
- ⊙ County Seat
- ✈ Airport
- ■ Point of Interest
- ⬚ Park, Forest, Reservation

Memphis Over 100,000
Columbia 20,000-50,000
Lebanon 10,000-20,000
Lawrenceburg Under 10,000
BENTON County Name

SCALE
0   20   40 Miles
0   20   40 Kms

See US political: front cover J3; physical: back cover J3.

LOCATION: 34°58'59" to 36°40'41" N; 81°38'49", 90°18'35" w. **BOUNDARIES:** Kentucky line, 346 mi (557 km); Virginia line, 127 mi (204 km); North Carolina line, 255 mi (410 km); Georgia line, 75 mi (121 km); Alabama line, 150 mi (242 km); Mississippi line, 123 mi (198 km); Arkansas line, 163 mi (262 km); Missouri line, 67 mi (108 km).

Knoxville, 181,161; and Chattanooga, 165,238. The Memphis metropolitan area, including parts of Arkansas and Mississippi, had an estimated 888,800 residents in 1978, while metropolitan Nashville had 786,000.

[7]ETHNIC GROUPS

For nearly a century after the earliest white settlements, Tennessee was inhabited by three ethnoracial populations: whites of English and Scotch-Irish descent, Cherokee Indians, and black Americans. Settlers crossing the Appalachians met Indian resistance as early as the late 1700s. Eventually, however, nearly all the Cherokee were forced to leave; by 1970 there were only 2,276 Indians left in the state.

Blacks, originally brought into the state as slaves to work in the cotton fields of West Tennesssee, made up about 10% of the population in 1790. White Tennesseans were divided on the issue of slavery. The small farmers of the eastern region were antislavery, and in the late 1820s and 1830s there were more antislavery societies in Tennessee than in any southern state except North Carolina. The planters and merchants of southwest Tennessee, however, linked their sentiments and interests with those of the proslavery planters of the Mississippi Valley. The introduction of the cotton gin gave impetus to the acquisition of more slaves; by 1840, blacks accounted for 26% of the population, and Memphis had become a major market for the shipment of black slaves to large plantations farther south. Immediately after the Civil War, many blacks, now free, migrated from Virginia and North Carolina to East Tennessee to become farmers, craftsmen, and small businessmen. After 1880, though, the black proportion of the population declined steadily. In 1976 there were about 687,000 blacks in Tennessee, 16% of the total.

There are proportionately few 2d-generation descendants of European immigrants: 49,000 in 1970, the largest groups being of German and British descent.

[8]LANGUAGES

White settlers found Tennessee inhabited by Cherokee Indians in the eastern mountains, Shawnee in most of the eastern and central region, and Chickasaw in the west, all of them speakers of Hokan-Siouan languages. Subsequently removed to Indian Territory, they left behind such place names as Chickamauga, Chattanooga, and Chilhowee, as well as Tennessee itself. In 1970, only 278 state residents claimed Indian languages as their mother tongues.

Tennessee English represents a mixture of North Midland and South Midland features brought into the northeastern and north-central areas, of South Midland and Southern features introduced by settlers from Virginia and the Carolinas, and of a few additional Southern terms in the extreme western fringe, to which they were carried from Mississippi and Louisiana. Certain pronunciations exhibit a declining frequency from the Appalachians to the Mississippi River, such as /r/ after a vowel in the same syllable, as in *form* and *short*, and a rounded /aw/ before /r/ in *arm* and *barbed*. Others occur statewide, such as the /ah/ vowel in *forest* and *foreign*, *coop* and *Cooper* with the vowel of *book*, and simplification of the long /i/ vowel, so that *lice* sounds like *lass*. Common are such non-Northern terms as *wait on* (wait for), *pullybone* (along with Northern *wishbone*), *nicker* (neigh), *light bread* (white bread), and *snake feeder* (dragonfly), as well as *Jew's harp*, *juice harp*, and *French harp* (all for harmonica). In eastern Tennessee are found *goobers* (peanuts), *tote* (carry), *plum peach* (clingstone peach), *ash cake* (a kind of cornbread), *fireboard* (mantel), *redworm* (earthworm), *branch* (stream), and *peckerwood* (woodpecker). Appearing in western Tennessee are *loaf bread*, *cold drink* (soft drink), and *burlap bag*. In Memphis, a large long sandwich is a *poorboy*.

In 1970, 93% of both the native-born and of all state residents reported English as their mother tongue. Speakers of principal first languages were as follows:

	NATIVE-BORN	FOREIGN-BORN
English	3,642,022	4,599
German	13,281	3,659
Spanish	6,762	1,595
French	5,439	875
Italian	4,990	1,107

[9]RELIGIONS

Baptist and Presbyterian churches were organized on the frontier soon after permanent settlements were made. Many divisions have occurred in both groups. The Cumberland Presbyterian Church, which spread into other states, was organized near Nashville in 1810 because of differences within the parent church. Both the Baptists and the Presbyterians divided over slavery, and southern branches of each denomination persist to this day. Methodist circuit riders arrived with the early settlers, and they quickly succeeded in attracting many followers. Controversies over slavery and other sectional issues also developed within the Methodist Church, and, as with the Baptists and Presbyterians, divisions emerged during the 1840s. Unlike the other two denominations, however, Methodists were able to heal their differences and regroup.

Two other Protestant groups with large followings in the state had their origin on the Tennessee frontier in the first half of the 19th century: the Disciples of Christ and the Church of Christ. Both groups began with the followers of Thomas and Alexander Campbell and Barton W. Stone, among others, who deplored formal creeds and denominations and sought to return to the purity of early Christianity. As their numbers grew, these followers divided into Progressives, who supported missionary societies and instrumental music in church, and Conservatives, who did not. In 1906, a federal census of religions listed the Conservatives for the first time as the Church of Christ and the Progressives as the Disciples of Christ. The latter, now the Christian Church (Disciples of Christ) had 21,756 known adherents in 1971.

All Protestant groups had 1,872,473 known adherents in 1971. By far the largest group is the Southern Baptist Church; in 1971, it claimed 1,095,956 adherents. The United Methodists were second with 387,529 adherents, followed by the Presbyterian Church in the US, 77,140; and the Cumberland Presbyterian Church, 46,452. In 1979 there were 103,656 Roman Catholics and an estimated 17,230 Jews.

Tennessee has long been considered part of the Bible Belt because of the influence of fundamentalist Protestant groups that insist upon the literal accuracy of the Bible.

[10]TRANSPORTATION

Memphis, Nashville, Knoxville, and Chattanooga are the focal points for rail, highway, water, and air transportation. All are located on important rivers and interstate highways, and all have airports served by the major airlines.

Railroad building began in Tennessee as early as the 1820s. During the 1850s, the basis for 20th-century rail transportation was laid: the Louisville and Nashville Railroad linked Tennessee to the northern states, and the Memphis and Charleston line established ties with the East Coast. In 1975, Tennessee had 3,181 mi (5,119 km) of track; railroad employees numbered 10,300 and earned $157,700,000 in income. No east–west passenger trains operate in the state today (Amtrak serves Memphis on the Chicago–New Orleans route), but considerable freight is hauled.

The first roads, such as the Natchez Trace, which connected Nashville with the southwestern part of the state, often followed Indian trails. Many roads in the early 1800s were constructed by private individuals or chartered turnpike companies. The owners assessed all users—a practice encouraged by the state for many years. The introduction of the automobile shortly after the beginning of the 20th century brought the development of modern roads and highways. After 1916, the federal government began to share the high cost of highway construction, and the 1920s were a decade of extensive road building.

In 1978, Tennessee had 59,890 mi (96,384 km) of rural roads and 12,731 mi (20,489 km) of municipal roads. Only 1,564 mi (2,517 km) were unsurfaced, less than 8% of the 1950 figure. The major interstate highway is I-40, crossing east–west from Knoxville to Nashville and Memphis. In 1978, 2,994,110 motor vehicles were registered in the state, and 2,694,460 Tennesseans held driver's licenses.

The principal means of transportation during Tennessee's early history was water, and all of the early settlements were built on or near streams. The introduction of steamboats on the Cumberland River in the early 19th century helped make Nashville the state's largest city and its foremost trading center. By midcentury, however, Memphis, on the Mississippi River, had surpassed Nashville in population and trade, largely because of cotton. Tennessee has about 1,000 mi (1,600 km) of navigable waterways. In 1974, about 27.1 million tons of freight were carried by river traffic. Coal and coke were the major products transported, followed by sand and gravel, chemicals, petroleum products, and iron and steel.

As in other states, air transportation became significant in Tennessee during the 1920s. In 1978 there were 78 public and 72 private airfields. Memphis International Airport is the state's major air terminal, with 63,209 scheduled departures in 1978. Nashville's Metropolitan Airport serves about half as many aircraft and passengers.

¹¹HISTORY

The lower Tennessee Valley was heavily populated with hunter-gatherers some 10,000 years ago. Their descendants, called Paleo-Indians, were succeeded by other native cultures, including the Archaic Indians, Woodland Indians, and Early Mississippians. When the first Spanish arrived in the early 16th century, Creek Indians were living in what is now East Tennessee, along with the Yuchi. About 200 years later, the powerful Cherokee—the largest single tribe south of the Ohio River, occupying parts of North Carolina, South Carolina, Georgia, and East Tennessee—drove the Creek and Yuchi out of the area and established themselves as the dominant tribe. Their settlements, varying in size from a dozen families to more than 200, were known as the Upper or Overhill Towns. The Cherokee retained their tribal dominance until they were forced out by the federal government in the 1830s. In West Tennessee, the Chickasaw were the major group. They lived principally in northern Mississippi but used Tennessee lands as a hunting ground. Shawnee occupied the Cumberland Valley in Middle Tennessee until driven north of the Ohio River by the Cherokee and Chickasaw.

Explorers and traders from continental Europe and the British Isles were in Tennessee for well over 200 years before permanent settlements were established in the 1760s. Hernando de Soto, a Spaniard, came from Florida to explore the area as early as 1540. He was followed during the 17th century by the French explorers Jacques Marquette, Louis Jolliet, and Robert Cavelier, Sieur de la Salle. Englishmen were not far behind: by the mid-1700s, hundreds—perhaps thousands—had crossed the Appalachian barrier and explored the transmontane country beyond, which was claimed first by the colony of Virginia and later assigned to North Carolina. They came in search of pelts, furs, or whatever else of value they might find. A fiercely independent breed, they were accustomed to hardship and unwilling to stay for long in any civilized community. Perhaps the best known was Daniel Boone, who by 1760 had found his way into present-day Washington County.

With the conclusion of the French and Indian War in 1763, many people from North Carolina and Virginia began to cross the Alleghenies. Elisha Walden was among those who first led groups of "long hunters" into the wilderness. By 1770, small pockets of white settlement were developing in the valley between the Unaka and Cumberland mountains. In the two decades that followed, more than 35,000 people settled on soil soon to become the State of Tennessee.

Two major areas of settlement developed. The larger one, in the northeast along the Holston, Nolichucky, and Watauga rivers, was organized as the Watauga Association in 1791. The second major area was in the Cumberland Basin, where James Robertson, under the sponsorship of the Transylvania Company (formed by eastern land speculators), established a settlement he called Nashborough (now Nashville) in 1779. There more than 250 adult males signed the Cumberland Compact, which established a government. They pledged to abide by the will of the majority and expressed their allegiance to North Carolina.

The Revolutionary War did not reach as far west as Tennessee, but many of the frontiersmen fought in the Carolinas and Virginia. The most famous battle involving these early Tennesseans was that of Kings Mountain, in South Carolina, where Colonel John Sevier and others defeated a superior force of British soldiers and captured more than 1,000 prisoners. Hardly was the Revolution over when Tennesseans began to think about statehood for themselves. As early as 1784, leaders in three mountain counties—Greene, Sullivan, and Washington—established the Free State of Franklin. John Sevier was chosen as governor, and an assembly was formed. Only after border warfare developed and factionalism weakened their cause did Franklin's leaders abandon their plans and return their allegiance to North Carolina. But the spirit of independence—indeed, defiance—persisted.

In 1790, less than two years after Franklin collapsed, North Carolina ceded its western lands to the US. Tennessee became known as the Southwest Territory, with William Blount, a prominent North Carolina speculator and politician, as its governor. During his six-year tenure, a government was organized and a capital established at Knoxville. The population doubled to more than 70,000 in 1795, and steps were taken to convert the territory into a state. When the territorial legislature presented Congress with a petition for statehood, a lively debate ensued in the US Senate between Jeffersonian Democratic-Republicans, who urged immediate admission, and Federalists, who opposed it. The Jeffersonians triumphed, and on 1 June 1796, President George Washington signed a bill admitting Tennessee as the 16th state. Sevier became governor of the new state, Blount was elected to the US Senate, and Andrew Jackson became the state's first US representative.

Sevier dominated state politics for the first two decades of statehood, and he had little difficulty in thwarting the ambitions of Andrew Jackson and others who sought to challenge his leadership. Tennessee's population, about 85,000 when Sevier became governor, was more than 250,000 when he left the statehouse in 1809. Under Sevier's governorship, Nashville, Knoxville, and other early settlements became thriving frontier towns. Churches and schools were established, industry and agriculture developed, and Tennessee became a leading iron producer.

Andrew Jackson's rise to prominence came as a result of the Battle of New Orleans, fought at the conclusion of the War of 1812. Jackson, who had little difficulty raising troops in a state where volunteers for military service have always been abundant, lost only about a half dozen of his men, while British casualties exceeded 2,000. He returned to Nashville a hero, built a fine house which he named The Hermitage, received thousands of congratulatory messages, and conferred with friends about his political and military future. In 1823, Jackson was elected to the US Senate. Defeated the following year in a four-man race for the presidency, he ran again, this time successfully, in 1828, serving in that office for eight years.

Jackson became alienated from many people in the state after

1835, when he announced his support of Martin Van Buren for president instead of Knoxvillian Hugh Lawson White, an avowed candidate. A majority of Tennesseans joined the new Whig Party, which arose in opposition to Jackson's Democratic Party, and voted in the 1836 presidential election for White instead of for Van Buren. The Whigs won every presidential election in Tennessee from 1836 to 1852, including the election of 1844, which sent Tennessean James Knox Polk, a Democrat, to the White House. Polk's term (1845–49) brought another war, this one with Mexico. Although Tennessee's quota was only 2,800, more than 25,000 men volunteered for service. Among the heroes of that war were William Trousdale and William B. Campbell, both of whom later were elected governor.

Social reform and cultural growth characterized the first half of the 19th century. A penitentiary was built, and the penal code made somewhat more humane. Temperance newpapers were published, temperance societies formed, and laws passed to curtail the consumption of alcoholic beverages. In 1834, a few women, embracing the feminist cause, were influential in giving the courts, rather than the legislature, the right to grant divorces. Many important schools were established, including the Nashville Female Academy, the University of Nashville, and more than two dozen colleges.

More than most southern states, antebellum Tennessee was divided over the issue of slavery. Slaves had accompanied their owners into Tennessee in the 18th century, and by 1850, they constituted about one-fourth of the state's population. Although slaveholders lived in all sections of the state, they predominated in the west, where cotton was grown profitably, as well as in Middle Tennessee. In East Tennessee, where blacks made up less than 10% of the population, antislavery sentiment thrived. Most of those who supported emancipation urged that it be accomplished peacefully, gradually, and with compensation to the slave owners. Frances Wright, the Scottish reformer, founded the colony of Nashoba near Memphis in the 1820s as a place where freed blacks could learn self-reliance. After a few years the colony failed, however, and Wright took her colonists to Haiti. At the constitutional convention of 1834, hundreds of petitions were presented asking that the legislature be empowered to free the slaves. But while the convention endorsed several measures to democratize the constitution of 1796—abolishing property qualifications as a condition for office holding, for example—it decided against emancipation.

Considerable economic growth took place during this period. West Tennessee became a major cotton-growing area immediately after it was purchased from the Chickasaw in 1818, and Memphis, established in 1821, became the principal cotton-marketing center. The Volunteer State's annual cotton crop grew from less than 3,000 bales in 1810 to nearly 200,000 bales by midcentury. The counties of the Highland Rim produced tobacco in such abundance that, by 1840, Tennessee ranked just behind Kentucky and Virginia in total production. East Tennessee farmers practiced greater crop diversification, growing a variety of fruits and vegetables for market. Silk cultivation flourished briefly in the 1830s and 1840s.

Tennessee became a major battleground during the Civil War, as armies from both North and South crossed the state several times. Most Tennesseans favored secession. But the eastern counties remained staunchly Unionist, and many East Tennesseans crossed over into Kentucky to enlist in the Union Army. General Albert Sidney Johnston, the Confederate commander of the western theater, set up lines of defense across the northern border of the state and built forts on both the Cumberland and Tennessee rivers. In February 1862, Ft. Donelson and Ft. Henry were taken by General Ulysses S. Grant and naval Captain Andrew H. Foote, thereby opening the state to Union armies. Within two weeks Nashville was in the hands of the enemy. Northern troops pushed

farther south and west, taking key positions on the Mississippi River. Less than two months later, on 6 April, Union forces near the Mississippi state line engaged Johnston's army in the Battle of Shiloh. Both sides suffered tremendous losses, including Johnston himself, who bled to death after sustaining a thigh wound. In the meantime, President Abraham Lincoln had established a military government for the conquered state and appointed Andrew Johnson to head it. Johnson, who had served two terms as governor a decade earlier, had been elected to the US Senate in 1858, where he remained in 1861, the only southern senator to do so; he refused to follow his state into the Confederacy. In 1864, he was elected vice president under Lincoln.

Johnson's governorship did not mean the end of Confederate activities in Tennessee. Late in December 1862, Confederate forces made the first of two vigorous attempts to rid the state of the invader. General Braxton Bragg, who replaced Johnston as Confederate commander, established himself at Murfreesboro, 30 mi (48 km) southwest of Nashville, and threatened to retake the capital city. But at the Battle of Stones River, Union troops under General William S. Rosecrans forced Bragg to retreat to the southeast. Fighting did not resume until 19–20 September 1863, when the Confederates drove Union troops back to Chattanooga in the Battle of Chickamauga, one of the bloodiest engagements of the war. The second major Confederate drive occurred in November and December 1864, when General John B. Hood, commanding the Confederate Army of Tennessee, came out of Georgia and attacked the Union forces at Franklin and Nashville. Hood's army was destroyed, and these battles were the last major engagements in the state.

Returning to the Union in 1866, Tennessee was the only former Confederate state not to have a military government during Reconstruction. Economic readjustment was not as difficult as elsewhere in the South, and within a few years agricultural production exceeded antebellum levels. Extensive coal and iron deposits in East Tennessee attracted northern capital, and by the early 1880s, flour, woolen, and paper mills were established in all the urban areas. By the late 1890s, Memphis was a leading cotton market and the nation's foremost producer of cottonseed oil. Politically, the Democratic Party became firmly entrenched, and would remain so until the 1950s.

As the 20th century dawned, the major issue in Tennessee was the crusade against alcohol, a movement with deep roots in the 19th century. Though the major cities still were "wet," earlier legislation had dried up the rural areas and small towns, and the Tennessee Anti-Saloon League and Women's Christian Temperance Union (WCTU) kept the matter in the public eye. In 1908, with "wet" forces controlling the state government, Edward Ward Carmack, a rabid prohibitionist, powerful politician, newspaper editor, and former US senator, was shot and killed in the street in Nashville. His assailants were convicted but pardoned immediately by the governor. In the following year, with Carmack as a martyr to their cause, "dry" forces enacted legislation that, in effect, imposed prohibition on the entire state. The dominant Democratic Party was divided and demoralized to such an extent that the Republicans elected a governor—only the second since Reconstruction. The prohibition movement helped promote the cause of women's suffrage. A proposed state constitutional amendment giving women the right to vote failed in 1915, but in 1919, they were granted the franchise in municipal elections. One year later, Tennessee became the 36th state to ratify the 19th Amendment to the US Constitution, thereby granting women the right to vote nationwide.

The 1920s brought a resurgence of religious fundamentalism. When, in 1925, the legislature enacted a measure that prohibited the teaching of the theory of evolution in the public schools, a high school teacher named John T. Scopes decided to challenge the law. Three-time presidential candidate and fundamentalist spokesman William Jennings Bryan arrived in the tiny town of Dayton to aid in Scopes's prosecution, while the great civil liberties lawyer Clarence Darrow came from Chicago to lead the defense. The Scopes trial gave the Volunteer State unwanted notoriety throughout the civilized world. Scopes was convicted, and it was not until 1967 that the law was repealed.

The 1930s brought depression, but they also brought the Tennessee Valley Authority. Before TVA, residents of the Tennessee River Valley could boast of the beauty of the landscape, but of little else. The soil was so thin that little other than subsistence agriculture was possible, and many people lived on a cash income of less than $100 a year. There were some senators, such as George Norris of Nebraska and Tennessee's own Kenneth D. McKellar, who saw great possibilities in valley development. Harnessing the Tennessee River with dams could not only generate electricity inexpensively but also greatly improve navigation; aid flood control, soil conservation, and reforestation; and produce nitrate fertilizer. Efforts to establish such a program failed, however, until Franklin D. Roosevelt included it in his New Deal. The law establishing TVA was passed a few weeks after Roosevelt's inauguration in 1933, and dam construction began almost immediately. Before TVA, people in the valley consumed only 1.5 billion kwh of electricity; but consumption increased to 11.5 billion kwh by 1945 and to 57.5 billion kwh by 1960. Fewer than 2% of rural families in Tennessee had electricity in 1933, but by the late 1930s, power lines were being strung into remote areas, bringing to practically everyone the advantages that hitherto only urban residents had enjoyed. Inexpensive power became a magnet for industry, and industrial employment in the region nearly doubled in two decades. The building of a plant for the production of atomic weapons at Oak Ridge in 1942 was due in large measure to the availability of TVA power.

The TVA notwithstanding, the depression caused many manufacturers to close or curtail operations, and farm prices declined drastically. Cotton, which had earlier brought farmers more than 30 cents a pound, declined to 5.7 cents, and the prices of corn, tobacco, and other crops fell proportionately. The state still was in the grip of financial depression when World War II began. Thousands of men volunteered for service before conscription was introduced; when the US entered the war in 1941, several training posts were established in Tennessee. Tennessee firms manufacturing war matériel received contracts amounting to $1.25 billion and employed more than 200,000 people during the war. Industrial growth continued during the postwar period, while agriculture recovered and diversified. The chemical industry, spurred by high demand during and after World War II, became a leading sector, along with textiles, apparel, and food processing. Cotton and tobacco continued to be major crops, but by the early 1970s, soybeans had taken the lead, accounting for 22% of estimated farm income in 1980. Beef and dairy production also flourished.

Democratic boss Edward H. Crump, who ran an efficient political machine in Memphis, dominated state politics for most of the period between 1910 and the early 1950s, an era that saw the elevation of many Tennessee Democrats to national prominence. Considerable progress was made toward ending racial discrimination during the postwar years, though the desegregation of public schools was accomplished only after outbursts of violence at Clinton, Nashville, and Memphis. The killing of civil rights leader Martin Luther King, Jr., in Memphis in 1968 resulted in rioting by blacks in that city. The most notable political development during the 1970s was the resurgence of the Republican Party, making Tennessee one of the few true two-party states in the South.

¹²STATE GOVERNMENT

Tennessee's first constitution was adopted in 1796, just before the state was admitted to the Union. It vested executive authori-

ty in a governor elected for two years, who had to be at least 25 years of age and own at least 500 acres (202 hectares) of land. The governor could approve or veto bills adopted by the legislature, was commander-in-chief of the militia, and could grant pardons and reprieves, among other powers. Legislative power was placed in a general assembly, consisting of a house and senate, whose members served terms of two years. Candidates for the legislature were required to fulfill residence and age requirements and to own at least 200 acres (81 hectares). Property qualifications were not required for voting, and all freemen—including free Negroes—could vote.

The basic governmental structure established in 1796 remains the fundamental law today. The constitution has been revised several times, however. The spirit of Jacksonian democracy prompted delegates at the constitutional convention of 1834 to remove property qualifications as a requirement for public office, reapportion representation, transfer the right to select county officials from justices of the peace to the voters, and reorganize the court system. At the same time, though, free blacks were disfranchised. In 1870, another constitutional convention confirmed the abolition of slavery and the enfranchisement of black men but imposed a poll tax as a requirement for voting. Membership of the house was fixed at 99, and of the senate at 33, numbers retained today.

Yet another constitutional convention was held in 1953. Delegates increased the gubernatorial term from two to four years, gave the governor the power of item veto, eliminated the poll tax, authorized home rule for cities, and provided for the consolidation of county and city functions. Later conventions extended the term of state senators from two to four years, sought to improve and streamline county government, and placed a constitutional limit on state spending. A limited convention in 1965 required the apportionment of the legislature according to population. This change greatly increased the weight of urban, and particularly black, votes.

The governor appoints a cabinet of two dozen members. The speaker of the state senate automatically becomes lieutenant governor; the secretary of state, treasurer, and comptroller of the treasury are chosen by the legislature.

Legislation is enacted after bills are read and approved three times in each house and signed by the governor. If the governor vetoes a measure, the legislature may override the veto by majority vote of both houses. Not more often than once every six years, the legislature may submit to the voters the question of calling a convention to amend the constitution. If the vote is favorable, then delegates are chosen. Changes proposed by the convention must be approved by a majority vote in a subsequent election. Individual amendments also may be considered by the legislature from time to time, but the process is cumbersome.

People may vote in state and national elections if they are US citizens, at least 18 years of age, and have registered at least 30 days prior to the election.

¹³POLITICAL PARTIES

The major political groups are the Democratic and Republican parties, each affiliated with the national party organization. Minor parties have seldom affected the outcome of an election in Tennessee.

When Tennessee came into the Union in 1796, it was strongly loyal to the Democratic-Republican Party. The Jacksonian era brought a change in political affiliations, and for more than 20 years Tennessee had a vibrant two-party system. Jackson's followers formed the Democratic Party, which prevailed for a decade over the National Republican Party led by John Quincy Adams and Henry Clay. But by 1835, Tennesseans had become disillusioned with Jackson, and they joined the new Whig Party in large numbers. A Whig governor was elected in that year, and Whig presidential nominees consistently garnered Tennessee's electoral votes until the party foundered over the slavery issue in the 1850s.

After the Civil War and Reconstruction, Tennessee was part of the solid Democratic South for nearly a century. Only three Republican governors were elected during that period, and only then because bitter factionalism had divided the dominant party. East Tennessee remained a Republican stronghold, however; the 2d Congressional District, which includes Knoxville, was the only district in the country to elect a Republican continuously from 1860 on. Republicans Warren G. Harding and Herbert Hoover carried the state in the presidential elections of 1920 and 1928. But if the 1920s saw a tendency away from one-party domination, Franklin D. Roosevelt and the New Deal brought the Volunteer State decisively back into the Democratic fold. Tennesseans voted overwhelmingly Democratic in the four elections that Roosevelt won (1932–44).

After World War II, the one-party system in Tennessee was shaken anew. Dwight D. Eisenhower narrowly won the state in 1952 and 1956, although Tennessee Senator Estes Kefauver was the Democratic vice-presidential nominee in the latter year. Tennesseans chose Richard Nixon all three times he ran for president. In fact, between 1948 and 1976, the only Democratic nominees to carry the state came from the South (Lyndon Johnson and Jimmy Carter) or from a border state (Harry Truman).

In state elections, the Republicans made deep inroads into Democratic power during the 1960s and 1970s. In 1966, Howard Baker became the first popularly elected Republican US senator in state history. In 1970, voters elected Winfield Dunn as the first Republican governor in 50 years, and in the same year, they sent Republican Bill Brock to join Baker in the Senate. The Democrats regained the governorship in 1974 and Brock's seat in 1976, but Republicans again won the governorship in 1978 when Lamar Alexander defeated Jake Butcher. Except for 1969–71, the Democrats maintained their hold over the state legislature. Tennessee voters, who had provided Jimmy Carter with a large majority in 1976, delivered the state to Ronald Reagan in 1980 by a plurality of only 0.3% of the total votes cast.

¹⁴LOCAL GOVERNMENT

Local government in Tennessee is exercised by 95 counties and more than 300 municipalities. The county, a direct descendant of the Anglo-Saxon shire, has remained remarkably unaltered in Tennessee since it was brought from Virginia and North Carolina in frontier days. The constitution specifies that county officials must include at least a register, trustee (the custodian of county funds), sheriff, and coroner, all of whom hold office for four years and may succeed themselves. Other officials have been added by legislative enactment: county executives (known for many years as county judges or county chairmen), tax assessors, county court clerks, and superintendents of public schools.

City government is of more recent origin than county government and is, in fact, a creature of the state. There are three forms of municipal government: mayor-council (or mayor-alderman), council-manager, and commission. The mayor-council system is the oldest and by far the most widely employed. There were 326 municipalities in 1977, as well as 471 special districts.

¹⁵STATE SERVICES

The commissioner of education oversees the public schools as well as special, higher, and vocational-technical education. Highways, aeronautics, mass transit, and waterways are the responsibility of the Department of Transportation. The Department of Safety, including the State Highway Patrol, is charged with enforcing the safety laws on all state roads and interstate highways. Railroad regulation and the setting of railroad rates are the duties of the Public Service Commission. Public protection services are provided by the Military Department, which includes the Army and Air National Guard. The Department of Correction maintains prisons for adult offenders, a work-release program, and correctional and rehabilitation centers for juveniles.

The Department of Public Health licenses medical facilities, provides medical care for the indigent, operates tuberculosis treatment centers, and administers pollution control programs. The Department of Mental Health and Mental Retardation supervises mental hospitals, mental health clinics, and homes for retarded children. The Department of Human Services administers aid to the blind, aged, disabled, and families with dependent

Tennessee Presidential Vote by Political Parties, 1948–80

YEAR	ELECTORAL VOTE	TENNESSEE WINNER	DEMOCRAT	REPUBLICAN	STATES' RIGHTS DEMOCRAT	SOCIALIST	PROGRESSIVE
1948	11	*Truman (D)	270,402	202,914	73,815	1,288	1,864
					CONSTITUTION	PROHIBITION	
1952	11	*Eisenhower (R)	443,710	446,147	379	1,432	887
1956	11	*Eisenhower (R)	456,507	462,288	19,820	789	—
					NATL. STATES RIGHTS		
1960	11	Nixon (R)	481,453	556,577	11,298	2,450	—
1964	11	*Johnson (D)	635,047	508,965	—	—	—
					AMERICAN IND.		
1968	11	*Nixon (R)	351,233	472,592	424,792	—	—
							AMERICAN
1972	10	*Nixon (R)	357,293	813,147	—		30,373
						LIBERTARIAN	
1976	10	*Carter (D)	825,897	633,969	2,303	1,375	5,769
					NATL. STATESMAN		CITIZENS
1980	10	*Reagan (R)	783,051	787,761	5,021¹	7,116¹	1,112¹

*Won US presidential election. ¹National party candidate appeared on Tennessee ballot as independent.

children, and determines eligibility for families receiving food stamps. The Department of Employment Security administers unemployment insurance and provides job training and placement services. State laws governing workers' compensation, occupational and mine safety, child labor, and wage standards are enforced by the Department of Labor.

¹⁶JUDICIAL SYSTEM

The supreme court is the highest court in the state. It consists of five justices, not more than two of whom may reside in any one grand division of the state—East, Middle, or West Tennessee. The justices are elected by popular vote for terms of 8 years and must be at least 35 years of age. The court has appellate jurisdiction only, holding sessions in Nashville, Knoxville, and Jackson. The position of chief justice rotates every 19 months.

Immediately below the supreme court are two appellate courts (each sitting in three divisions), established by the legislature to relieve the crowded high court docket. The court of appeals, consisting of 12 judges in 1979, has appellate jurisdiction in most civil cases. The court of criminal appeals, consisting of 9 judges, hears cases from the lower courts involving criminal matters. Judges on both appellate courts are elected for eight-year terms.

Circuit courts have original jurisdiction in both civil and criminal cases. As of 1979, the state was divided into 31 circuits, with 58 judges. Tennessee is one of five states that still have chancery courts, vestiges of the English courts designed to hear cases where there was no adequate remedy at law. As of 1979 there were 19 chancery districts in the state, with a total of 27 chancellors. They administer cases involving receiverships of corporations, settle disputes regarding property ownership, hear divorce cases, and adjudicate on a variety of other matters. In some districts, judges of the circuit and chancery courts, all of whom are elected for eight-year terms, have concurrent jurisdiction.

At the bottom of the judicial structure are general sessions courts, which have replaced justice of the peace courts in nearly all counties. The latter, another vestige of medieval England, came under severe criticism beginning early in the 20th century because many of the justices were poorly trained, most failed to keep proper records, and some abused the fee system by which they were paid. A comprehensive juvenile court system was set up in 1911. Other courts created for specific services include domestic relations courts and probate courts.

Brushy Mountain Penitentiary at Petros is the state's maximum security prison. There are a prison farm at Ft. Pillow, a correctional rehabilitation center in Nashville, and a center for youthful offenders at Only. As of 31 December 1978, federal and state prisons in Tennessee had 5,480 inmates, 96% of them men.

According to the FBI Crime Index, Tennessee's crime rates rank below the national averages for all crimes except murder. FBI data for 1978 show that the state's crime rates per 100,000 population were murder and nonnegligent manslaughter, 9.4; forcible rape, 31; robbery, 152; aggravated assault, 190; burglary, 1,214; larceny, 1,766; and auto theft, 328.

¹⁷ARMED FORCES

Authorized personnel at US military installations in Tennessee totaled 30,376 in 1977/78, most of them at a naval air station near Memphis. Ft. Campbell, in Kentucky, extends into Tennessee north of Clarksville.

Tennessee supplied so many soldiers for the War of 1812 and the Mexican War that it became known as the Volunteer State. During the Civil War, more than 100,000 Tennesseans fought for the Confederacy and about half that number for the Union. In World War I, some 91,000 men served in the armed forces, and in World War II, 316,000 Tennesseans saw active duty. As of 30 September 1979, 541,000 veterans were living in Tennessee, of whom 10,000 served in World War I, 215,000 in World War II, 106,000 in the Korean conflict, and 166,000 during the Viet-Nam era. Veterans' benefits totaled $443.9 million in 1977/78.

The Army National Guard had more than 11,000 personnel in 1980, organized into more than 135 units and activities in 72 cities and towns. Tennessee's Air National Guard had more than 3,200 members, organized into 7 units in Nashville, Memphis, Chattanooga, and Knoxville. State and local police personnel numbered 9,810 in 1977.

¹⁸MIGRATION

The first white settlers in Tennessee, who came across the mountains from North Carolina and Virginia, were almost entirely of English extraction. They were followed by an influx of Scotch-Irish, mainly from Pennsylvania. About 3,800 German and Irish migrants arrived during the 1830s and 1840s. In the next century, Tennessee's population remained relatively stable, except for an influx of blacks immediately following the Civil War. There was a steady outmigration of blacks to industrial centers in the North during the 20th century. The state suffered a net loss through migration of 462,000 between 1940 and 1970, but gained 170,000 between 1970 and 1977.

The major in-state migration has been away from rural areas and into towns and cities. Blacks, especially, have tended to cluster in large urban centers. The population of Memphis, for example, is nearly 40% black.

¹⁹INTERGOVERNMENTAL COOPERATION

Tennessee participates in such interstate agreements as the Interstate Oil and Gas Compact, Southeastern Forest Fire Protection Compact, Southern Growth Policies Compact, Southern Interstate Energy Compact, and Southern Regional Education Compact. There are boundary accords with Arkansas, Kentucky, and Virginia, and an agreement with Alabama, Florida, Kentucky, and Mississippi governing development of the Tennessee-Tombigbee waterway.

Federal aid to Tennessee exceeded $1.5 billion in 1978/79, of which $126.4 million was general revenue sharing.

²⁰ECONOMY

Tennessee's economy is based primarily on industry. Since the 1930s, the number of people employed in industry has grown at a rapid rate, while the number of farmers has declined proportionately. The principal manufacturing areas are Memphis, Nashville, Chattanooga, Knoxville, and Kingsport-Bristol. Apparel production employs more workers than any other industry; chemical and allied products, electrical and electronic equipment, and food products follow in that order. The total industrial payroll in 1977 was more than $5 billion. Wage rates and average weekly earnings are well below the national average.

Farm operators have turned to raising dairy and beef cattle and soybeans rather than tobacco, cotton, and corn, which were the leading money crops for many years. Tourism is the third major contributor to the state's economy.

²¹INCOME

With a per capita income of $6,489 in 1978, Tennessee ranked 44th in the US. Among its neighbors, Tennessee had a higher per capita income than Alabama, Arkansas, and Mississippi but placed below Missouri, Kentucky, Virginia, North Carolina, and Georgia. Between 1960 and 1978, Tennessee's total income increased fivefold, from $5.6 billion to $28.3 billion.

In 1975, median family income was $11,341; only Kentucky, Arkansas, and Mississippi ranked lower. In that year, about 13% of Tennessee families and 16% of all Tennesseans were below the federal poverty level.

²²LABOR

In 1978, Tennessee had a total civilian labor force of 1,926,000, of whom 58% were male and 42% female. The overall unemployment rate for that year was 5.8%, but the rate for women was 7.3% and for minority groups 11.5%.

A federal census of workers covered by unemployment insurance in March 1977 revealed the following nonfarm employment pattern in Tennessee:

	ESTABLISH-MENTS	EMPLOYEES	ANNUAL PAYROLL ('000)
Agricultural services, forestry, fishing	652	3,406	$ 22,708
Mining	417	9,216	132,528
Contract construction	8,407	72,110	817,669
Manufacturing, of which:	5,909	486,878	5,241,418
Food products	(474)	(36,903)	(440,162)
Apparel, other textiles	(407)	(69,114)	(435,121)
Chemicals, allied products	(231)	(51,563)	(794,215)
Transportation, public utilities	2,906	63,768	893,553
Wholesale trade	7,320	94,317	1,178,951
Retail trade	25,522	243,396	1,608,673
Finance, insurance real estate	7,064	74,041	752,158
Services	21,969	233,794	1,927,372
Other	1,122	1,889	17,216
TOTALS	81,288	1,282,815	$12,592,246

This survey excluded farm laborers, self-employed workers, government workers, and certain other employees. In 1977, Tennessee had about 310,000 government employees, of whom 63,700 were employed by the federal government and 73,000 by the state.

In 1976, 288,000 Tennesseans were members of labor unions and another 55,000 belonged to professional and state employee associations. All together, 22% of the state's nonagricultural workers belonged to unions or employee associations. Tennessee has a right-to-work law. Weakness of the labor movement is one reason why average hourly earnings of production workers, $5.13 in 1978, were 17% below the US norm. In only nine states did factory workes have lower average weekly earnings.

23 AGRICULTURE
Tennessee ranked 27th among the 50 states in 1978 with farm receipts of more than $1.6 billion.

From the antebellum period to the 1950s, cotton was the leading crop, followed by corn and tobacco. But during the early 1960s, soybeans surpassed cotton as the principal source of income. In 1979, 70.7 million bushels of soybeans, valued at more than $449 million, were harvested. Tobacco production in 1978 was 142 million lb, at a value of $180 million. The main types of tobacco are burley, a fine leaf used primarily for cigarettes, and eastern and western dark-fired, which are used primarily for cigars, pipe tobacco, and snuff. Tennessee ranked 4th among the tobacco-producing states in total crop value in 1978. The corn harvest in 1979 was 51.5 million bushels, valued at $144 million. By the late 1970s, cotton had slipped to 4th place among Tennessee's leading cash crops; production in 1978 was 235,000 bales, at a value of $70 million.

In 1979, the Crop Reporting Service listed the average value of farm land and buildings at $669 per acre ($1,653 per hectare), more than twice the price of land six years earlier. In 1980, farmland in developing counties within close proximity of urban centers readily sold at $5,000 per acre ($12,400 per hectare). The number of farms declined from about 102,000 in 1975 to 94,000 in 1979.

24 ANIMAL HUSBANDRY
Livestock and livestock products account for more than half of Tennessee's agricultural income, and beef cattle are the state's most important commodity. Cattle are raised throughout the state, but principally in Middle and East Tennessee. In 1930, fewer than a million cattle and calves were raised on Tennessee farms; by late 1979, however, there were 2.3 million head. Production in 1979 totaled 600.6 million lb, valued at $364 million.

Hogs and pigs account for about 12% of farm income. The number of hogs and pigs produced has declined slightly during the past fifty years, but their value has increased considerably. In late 1979 there were 1.4 million hogs and pigs; production reached 511.2 million lb, worth $213.2 million. Sheep and lamb production has declined sharply in the past 50 years. In 1925, 368,000 head were raised, but by 1980, that number had declined to 12,000.

Poultry and eggs accounted for $158 million in income in 1979, shared almost equally among sales of chickens, broilers, and eggs. Poultry farmers produced 213.6 million lb of broilers, 229.6 million lb of chickens, and 998 million eggs that year, when Tennessee dairy farms yielded 2.1 billion lb of milk.

Horses are raised for market primarily in Middle and West Tennessee. The Tennessee Walking Horse is bred throughout the state but especially around Tullahoma.

25 FISHING
Fishing is a major attraction for sportsmen but plays a relatively small role in the economic life of Tennessee. The commercial catch in 1978 was estimated at only 8.8 million lb—mostly bluegill and white crappie—worth $2.4 million.

There are 17 TVA lakes and 7 other lakes, all maintained by the Army Corps of Engineers; 10 of these lakes span an area of 10,000 acres (4,000 hectares) or more, and there are thousands of miles of creeks and mountain streams, all of which attract fishermen. Tennessee has no closed season, except on trout.

In recent years, pollution has killed millions of fish and seriously endangered sport fishing. More than 300,000 fish were killed by industrial waste dumping in 1974 alone, particularly in the Memphis and Nashville areas.

26 FORESTRY
Forests covered 13,161,000 acres (5,326,000 hectares) in 1977, or about half the state's total land area. Commercial timberlands in 1977 totaled 12,820,000 acres (5,188,000 hectares), of which 90% was privately owned, half by farmers and the remainder by forest industries and other firms. The counties of the Cumberland Plateau and Highland Rim are the major sources of timber products, and in Lewis, Perry, Polk, Scott, Sequatchie, Unicoi, and Wayne counties, more than 75% of the total area is commercial forest.

About 80% of Tennessee's timber is in hardwoods, and more than one-half of that is in white and red oak. Of the softwoods, pine—shortleaf, loblolly, Virginia, pitch, and white—accounts for 75%. Red cedar, once in great abundance, now accounts for only 5% of the softwood supply.

Shipments of lumber and wood products totaled $616.7 million in 1977. There were more than 500 sawmills and planing mills in the state, employing 6,800 production workers. Most of the lumber produced by the mills is sold to the building trades, but some goes into furniture manufacture, cooperage (barrel making), poles, mine timbers, and fuel wood. Shipments of wood household furniture totaled $201.7 million in 1977. The leading forest-related industry is the manufacture of paper and paper products, shipments of which were nearly $1.4 billion in 1977.

27 MINING
Tennessee possesses a great variety of mineral resources. In 1978, the state ranked 26th among the 50 states in mineral production, with a total value of $584 million. Copper and zinc, the principal metals, are produced almost entirely in the Ducktown Basin near Chattanooga; iron, lead, manganese, and gold are mined in the same area. The sulfide copper ores are smelted and shipped to electrolytic refineries in New Jersey. Tennessee is the South's largest producer of sulfuric acid, a by-product of copper smelting. Coal, portland cement, sand and gravel, and stone are the principal nonmetals.

Bituminous coal is Tennessee's most valuable mineral commodity; $151 million worth of it was mined in 1976. For many years, coal was taken chiefly from underground mines, but by 1978, 59% of it was produced through surface mining. Most of the surface mines are small-scale operations using strip and auger methods. Thousands of acres have been marred because of the legislature's slowness in devising laws to restore and revegetate the stripped land.

Other minerals and their 1978 output include 96,900 tons of zinc and 12,444 tons of copper, along with 42,212,000 tons of stone, 13,000,000 tons of sand and gravel, and 1,814,000 tons of cement.

²⁸ENERGY AND POWER

The Tennessee Valley Authority (TVA) is the principal supplier of power in the state, providing electricity to more than 100 cities and 50 rural cooperatives. In 1978, Tennessee's installed electrical generating capacity was 14.6 million kw, virtually all of it publicly owned. Electrical output totaled 60.4 billion kwh (99% public). Electric energy sales amounted to 75.2 billion kwh, making Tennessee a net importer of electricity from neighboring states for that year. Two nuclear reactors, both owned by TVA, came on line in 1979, adding more than 2.3 million kw in generating capacity.

Most of the coal mined in the state is used for producing electricity, although some is utilized for home heating. Reserves in 1976 totaled 965 million tons; the 1978 output exceeded 10 million tons. Tennessee also had proved petroleum reserves totaling 2,489,000 barrels in 1978, when 593,000 barrels were produced; natural gas reserves were negligible.

²⁹INDUSTRY

On the eve of the Civil War, only 1% of Tennessee's population was employed in manufacturing, mostly in the iron, cotton, lumber, and flour-milling industries. Rapid industrial growth took place during the 20th century, however, and by 1976, Tennessee ranked 3d among the southeastern states and 15th in the US in value added by manufacture, with $10.7 billion. In 1977, Tennessee's four major metropolitan areas—Memphis, Nashville, Knoxville, and Chattanooga—employed 46% of all the state's industrial workers.

To the $12.6 billion added by manufacture in 1977, the principal contributors, with their percentages of the total, were chemicals, 18%; food and food products, 10%; nonelectrical machinery, 9%; electric and electronic equipment, 8%; and apparel, 7%. The following table shows value added by selected industries in 1972 and 1977:

	1972	1977
Industrial inorganic chemicals	$454,300,000	$1,008,400,000
Men's and boys' clothing	378,200,000	561,100,000
Motor vehicle parts and accessories	149,200,000	358,000,000
Refrigeration and heating equipment	137,400,000	326,900,000
Household furniture	237,800,000	293,800,000
Household appliances	189,900,000	278,400,000
Beverages	145,900,000	254,500,000

³⁰COMMERCE

Tennessee has been an important inland commercial center for more than 50 years. In 1972, the state's wholesale trade amounted to $14.6 billion (15th in the US). Sales in Memphis accounted for about half of this figure. In 1977, Tennessee had retail sales of $13.7 billion (20th in the US). The principal retail groups and their sales percentages were automotive dealers, 24%; grocery stores, 21%; department stores, 10%; gasoline service stations, 8%; and eating and drinking places, 7%. Metropolitan Memphis, Nashville, Knoxville, and Chattanooga together accounted for more than 64% of retail sales.

Of commodities shipped to other states in 1972, 80% of the volume went to southern destinations. Tennessee's foreign exports included nearly $1.3 billion in manufactured goods in 1976 and $390 million in agricultural commodities in 1976/77.

³¹CONSUMER PROTECTION

Although Tennessee has no consumer protection department, the state government has taken measures to protect consumer interests. "Blue-sky" laws, enacted in 1955 and modified several times since then, are designed to stop misrepresentation of stocks and bonds. The Tennessee Consumer Panel, established by the Public Service Commission, is a group of citizens in each county who deal directly with the commission.

³²BANKING

The first bank in Tennessee was the Bank of Nashville, chartered in 1807. Four years later, the Bank of the State of Tennessee was chartered at Knoxville; branches were established at Nashville, Jonesboro, Clarksville, and Columbia. In 1817, nearly a dozen more banks were chartered in various frontier towns. The Civil War curtailed banking operations, but the industry began again immediately after cessation of hostilities.

By 1978 there were 348 insured commercial banks with total assets of $19.9 billion, including $6.9 billion in outstanding loans and $4.6 billion in securities. Commercial bank deposits totaled $17.1 billion, including demand deposits of $6 billion and time deposits of $11.1 billion.

Also in 1978 there were 97 savings and loan associations in the state, with assets of $6.4 billion. Their outstanding mortgage loans reached $5.5 billion; savings accounts, $5.3 billion.

³³INSURANCE

In 1975, 982 insurance companies were licensed to operate in the state, including 48 Tennessee companies. The total included 456 life, 363 stock, fire, and casualty, 82 mutual fire and casualty, 23 county mutual fire, and 58 other companies.

Some 9,726,000 life insurance polices worth $54.8 billion were in force in 1978, when the average Tennessee family held $34,200 in coverage, slightly below the national average. More than $465 million in benefits was paid to Tennesseans during the same year. Property and liability insurers wrote premiums totaling nearly $1.4 billion, of which $338 million was automobile liability insurance, $236.2 million was automobile physical damage insurance, and $156.5 million was homeowners coverage. Tennesseans held $170.7 million in flood insurance as of 30 June 1979.

³⁴SECURITIES

There are no securities exchanges in Tennessee. An estimated 342,000 Tennesseans held shares on the New York Stock Exchange (NYSE) in mid-1975, and state residents reported $383.2 million in dividends on their 1977 federal income tax returns. NYSE member firms had 45 sales offices and 468 registered representatives in Tennessee at the close of 1978.

³⁵PUBLIC FINANCE

The state budget is prepared annually by the director of the budget and submitted by the governor to the legislature every January. The fiscal year lasts from 1 July to 30 June.

The consolidated state budget for the 1980/81 fiscal year was estimated at $3.7 billion. Within this consolidated total, the major categories of expenditure were education, 49%; health and social services, 15%; local government, 9%; transportation, 8%; law enforcement, 7%; and government operations, 6%.

The following table summarizes state revenues and state-funded appropriations for 1978/79 and estimates for 1979/80 (in millions):

REVENUES	1978/79	1979/80
Sales and use tax	$938.7	$1,000.0
Excise tax	186.1	203.6
Gasoline tax	178.9	167.5
Motor vehicle registration tax	89.9	92.0
Gross receipts tax	73.0	89.5
Other receipts	471.6	498.4
TOTALS	$1,938.2	$2,051.0

APPROPRIATIONS		
Primary and secondary education	$717.5	$756.1
Higher education	309.7	329.0
Public health	162.1	176.9
Corrections	81.8	98.4
Mental health and retardation	89.7	94.6
Other outlays	284.0	279.5
TOTALS	$1,644.8	$1,734.5

The total debt owed by the state and local governments in Tennessee increased from $2.6 billion in 1970 to $4.8 billion in 1977, when the per capita debt amounted to $1,115.

36 TAXATION

The Tennessee state government ranked 23d in the US in general revenues during the 1976/77 fiscal year with $2.6 billion, including intergovernmental receipts. It was 47th in per capita state and local taxation, however, with an average tax burden in 1977 of $564, 31% below the national average.

The major source of general state revenue is a sales and use tax, first levied in 1947; in 1980, the maximum rate was 6%, of which the state collected 4.5% and municipalities 1.5%. Other taxes include a 6% levy on dividend and interest income, a 6% corporate income tax, and levies on inheritances, alcoholic beverages, tobacco, gross receipts, motor vehicle registration, and other items. Tennessee is one of a few states that does not impose a tax on salaries and wages. Counties and municipalities depend on the real property taxes as their major source of income.

In 1975/76, Tennessee paid about $5.3 billion in federal taxes and received $6.5 billion in federal expenditures, for a net gain of $1.2 billion. Tennesseans filed 1.6 million federal income tax returns in 1977, paying almost $2.5 billion in tax.

37 ECONOMIC POLICY

Since World War II, Tennessee has aggressively sought new business and industry. The Department of Economic and Community Development helps prospective firms locate industrial sites in communities throughout the state, and its representatives work with firms in Canada, Europe, and the Far East, as well as domestic businesses. The department also administers special Appalachian regional programs in 50 counties and directs the state Office of Minority Business Enterprise.

Tennessee's right-to-work law and relatively weak labor movement constitute important industrial incentives. The counties and municipalities, moreover, offer tax exemptions on land, capital improvements, equipment, and machinery. During 1979, 90 manufacturing firms announced intentions of building new plants in Tennessee, and 151 existing companies revealed plans to expand facilities and employment. Foreign investment financed 16 new or expanded plants and nearly 1,000 new jobs in Tennessee during the same year.

38 HEALTH

Tennessee ranked 38th among the 50 states in average life expectancy during 1969–71, at 70.11 years. The average life expectancy for women was 74.26 years; for men, 66.15 years. The state's birthrate fell from 23 live births per 1,000 population in 1960 to 15.5 in 1977, when there were about 67,000 live births (52,000 white, 15,000 other races). Between 1975 and 1977, the ratio of legal abortions to live births increased from 178 to 246 for every 1,000 births; about 16,500 abortions were performed in 1977. The infant mortality rate in 1977 was 13.3 per 1,000 live births for whites and 22.6 for nonwhites.

The leading causes of death in Tennessee in 1977 (with rates per 100,000 population) were heart disease, 334; malignant neoplasms, 174; cerebrovascular diseases, 106; accidents, 57; pneumonia and influenza, 25; suicide, 14; arteriosclerosis, 13; diabetes, 13; early infancy diseases, 11; and cirrhosis of the liver, 10. The death rate overall, 9.1 per 1,000 population, was slightly above the US average. Tuberculosis, the major cause of death in 1927, was responsible for only 118 deaths in 1973. Among the leading public health problems is venereal disease, 34,109 cases of which were reported in 1975.

There were 160 hospitals, with 31,008 beds, in 1978. Hospitals admitted 933,101 patients, for an average occupancy rate of 78%; the average cost of hospital care in 1977 was $155 per day and $1,114 per stay, both far below the US average. General hospitals with psychiatric wards admitted 8,600 patients in 1975,

and an additional 24,300 patients got help from outpatient psychiatric services. In 1976 there were 3,900 resident patients in public mental hospitals and 2,500 in public institutions for the mentally retarded.

Tennessee has four medical schools: two in Nashville (Vanderbilt University and Meharry Medical School), one at Johnson City (East Tennessee State University), and one at Memphis (University of Tennessee). The state had 6,434 licensed physicians in 1977 and 2,034 professionally active dentists in 1979; hospital personnel included 10,068 registered nurses and 6,751 licensed practical nurses in 1978.

39 SOCIAL WELFARE

Social welfare outlays per poor resident in Tennessee (as determined by the federal poverty level) are only a little more than half the national average. A total of $552 million was spent by Tennessee on the five largest social welfare programs in 1976, and 84% of that came from federal funds.

Aid to families with dependent children amounted to $80 million in 1978; there were 159,600 AFDC recipients, 115,600 of them children. About 374,000 Tennesseans took part in the food stamp program, at a federal cost of $141.8 million. The school lunch program served 672,000 students (77% of all pupils in participating schools) and cost the federal government $42.3 million.

In 1977, more than $1.5 billion in Social Security benefits was paid to some 703,700 Tennesseans; 58% went to 415,600 retired workers, 24% to 163,900 survivors of deceased workers, and 18% to 124,200 disabled workers. Supplemental Security Income payments were made to 133,400 needy state residents in 1978, for a total of $166.1 million; 59% went to the disabled, 39% went to the aged, and 2% to the blind.

Tennessee spent $23.1 million on vocational rehabilitation in 1978 and $83.9 million on workers' compensation in 1977. An average of 35,000 Tennesseans received unemployment insurance benefits under state and federal programs in 1978, for a total of $114 million.

40 HOUSING

Surveys during the 1930s indicated that more than one-third of all homes in Memphis were substandard, while the situations in Knoxville, Nashville, and Chattanooga were not much better. The Public Works Administration provided federal aid for slum clearance and low-rent projects, and Tennessee created the Housing Development Agency, the Housing Rehabilitation Corporation, and other bodies to improve housing. In 1974 there were 75 urban renewal projects under way in 36 localities.

The 1970 census counted 1,213,187 occupied housing units in the state, 67% of which were owner-occupied, with a median of five rooms per unit. Some 14% of the occupied units lacked complete plumbing facilities, and 10% were without proper kitchen facilities. About 3% were mobile homes or trailers.

From 1976 through 1978, a total of 74,400 new units worth $1.9 billion were authorized.

41 EDUCATION

The state assumed very little responsibility for education until 1873, when the legislature established a permanent school fund and made schools free to all persons between the ages of 6 and 21. In 1917, an eight-year elementary and four-year secondary school system was set up. Thirty years later, enactment of the state sales and use tax enabled state authorities to increase teachers' salaries by about 100% and to provide capital funds for a variety of expanded educational programs. Today, nearly half the consolidated state budget is spent on education.

Despite these advances, the 1970 census found that 1.7% of all Tennesseans aged 14 years and over were illiterate. Of the total adult population in 1976, only 55% were high school graduates, compared with a national average of 67%. The state also lagged in median school years completed, with 12.2, below the averages of nine southern states. Public school expenditures per pupil in average daily attendance ranked 46th in the US in 1977/78.

In 1979/80, the Department of Education administered 1,704 public schools for grades K–12, 4 special schools, 29 vocational-technical schools, 4 regional technical institutes, a network of educational television stations, and a variety of public educational services. There were 616,060 students enrolled in the public elementary schools, 256,976 in public secondary schools, and 194,667 in state colleges and universities.

The University of Tennessee system, with principal campuses at Nashville, Knoxville, Memphis, Martin, and Chattanooga, enrolled some 35,250 students in fall 1980. Components of the State University and Community College System of Tennessee included Memphis State University (the largest, with 15,675 students), Tennessee Technological University at Cookeville, East Tennessee State University at Johnson City, Austin Peay State University at Clarksville, Tennessee State University at Nashville, and Middle Tennessee State University at Murfreesboro, along with 10 two-year community colleges enrolling 18,275 students on campuses throughout the state. Well-known private colleges are Vanderbilt University at Nashville (with 7,269 students in 1977), the University of the South at Sewanee (1,093), and Southwestern at Memphis (1,028). Vanderbilt has schools of medicine, law, divinity, nursing, business, and education, as well as an undergraduate program. Loan and grant programs are administered by the Tennessee Student Assistance Corporation.

[42] ARTS

Each of Tennessee's major cities has a symphony orchestra. The best known are the Memphis Symphony and the Nashville Symphony, the latter to make its home in the James K. Polk Cultural Center, which was scheduled to open in 1981. Included in this complex are three performing arts centers and the State Museum. The major operatic troupe is the Memphis Opera Theater.

Nashville is a center for country music. The Grand Ole Opry, Country Music Hall of Fame, and numerous recording studios are located there.

Among the leading art galleries are the Dixon Gallery and the Brooks Memorial Art Gallery in Memphis, the Tennessee Botanical Gardens and Fine Arts Center in Nashville, and the Dulin Gallery of Art in Knoxville.

[43] LIBRARIES AND MUSEUMS

Libraries and library associations were formed soon after Tennessee became a state. The Dickson Library at Charlotte was founded in 1811, and the Nashville Library Company in 1813. Not until 1854, however, was the first state-maintained library established. Andrew Johnson, the governor at that time, requested a library appropriation of $5,000, telling legislators that he wanted other Tennesseans to have the opportunities that had been denied him. Today, the institution he founded, the State Library at Nashville, with more than 250,000 volumes, has a renowned collection of state materials and is the repository for state records.

In all, there were more than 150 public libraries and nearly 50 academic libraries in Tennessee in 1977/78. Their combined book stock exceeded 5.6 million, and their total circulation surpassed 12.6 million volumes. The largest libraries are the Joint University Libraries at Nashville (1,405,293 volumes in 1977/78), Memphis–Shelby County Library (1,300,326), Memphis State University Library (728,068), University of Tennessee at Knoxville Library (628,859), Knoxville–Knox County Library (558,561), the East Tennessee State University Library at Johnson City (432,406), and Chattanooga–Hamilton County Library (302,192).

Tennessee has more than 75 museums and historic sites. The Tennessee State Museum in Nashville displays exhibits on pioneer life, military traditions, evangelical religion, and presidential lore. The Museum of Appalachia, near Norris, attempts an authentic replica of early Appalachian life, with more than 20,000 pioneer relics on display in several log cabins. Displays of solar,

nuclear, and other energy technologies are featured at the American Museum of Science and Energy, at Oak Ridge. There are floral collections at the Goldsmith Botanical Gardens in Memphis and the Tennessee Botanical Gardens and Fine Arts Center in Nashville.

[44] COMMUNICATIONS

The first postal service across the state, by stagecoach, began operations in the early 1790s. As of 1975 there were 737 post offices, branches, and stations. Postal revenues in that year were $44 million in Memphis and $31 million in Nashville.

As of 31 December 1978 there were 3,063,810 telephones, 742,271 business and 2,321,539 residential; on average, 93% of Tennessee households had telephone service. Bell System affiliates owned 84% of the phones, with General Telephone Co. of the Southeast and United Inter-Mountain Telephone also serving the state.

Tennessee had 155 commercial AM stations and 74 FM stations in 1978. Forty television stations were authorized for Tennessee as of 1979, with 26 in operation; there were 5 television stations each in Memphis, Nashville, and Chattanooga, and 3 in Knoxville. By the end of 1978, 81 cable systems served 168,168 subscribers in 126 communities.

[45] PRESS

In 1978 there were 7 morning newspapers with net paid circulation of 464,924; 25 evening dailies with a combined circulation of 655,523; and 13 Sunday papers with 1,002,156 circulation. The following table lists leading Tennessee newspapers with their daily circulation in 1978:

AREA	NAME	DAILY	SUNDAY
Chattanooga	News–Free Press (e,S)	65,017	78,135
Knoxville	Journal (m)	57,398	
	News-Sentinel (e,S)	101,628	157,625
Memphis	Commercial Appeal (m,S)	205,452	283,622
	Press-Scimitar (e)	104,125	
Nashville	Banner (e)	83,195	
	Tennessean (m,S)	129,408	229,022

More periodicals—184—were published in Tennessee in 1976 than in any other southeastern state. Several dozen trade publications, such as *Southern Lumberman*, appear in Nashville, the state's major publishing center.

[46] ORGANIZATIONS

Nashville is a center for Tennessee cultural and educational organizations. Among them are the American Association for State and Local History, Association of Colleges and Universities for International-Intercultural Studies, Association of Country Entertainers, Country Music Association, and Gospel Music Association.

Several national and regional trade associations are based in Tennessee, including the Walking Horse Breeders' and Exhibitors' Association (Lewisburg) and the Walking Horse Trainers' Association (Shelbyville). Knoxville is the headquarters of the Burley Tobacco Stabilization Association, and Springfield is the home of the Eastern Dark-Fired Tobacco Growers Association. The offices of the Southern Cotton Association, National Cotton Council of America, and Southern Hardwood Lumber Manufacturing Association are in Memphis, as are the headquarters of the American Contract Bridge League and the International Racquetball Association.

[47] TOURISM, TRAVEL, AND RECREATION

The natural beauty of Tennessee, combined with the activity of the Department of Tourist Development, has made tourism the state's 3d-largest industry. Tennessee was the first state to create a government department devoted solely to the promotion of tourism. In 1977, more than 16 million persons traveled to and through Tennessee, spending more than $1 billion in the state.

Leading tourist attractions include Fort Loudoun, built by the British in 1757; the American Museum of Science and Energy at

Oak Ridge; the William Blount Mansion at Knoxville; the Beale Street Historic District in Memphis, home of W. C. Handy, the "father of the blues"; Graceland, the Memphis estate of Elvis Presley; and Opryland USA and the Grand Ole Opry at Nashville. There are three presidential homes—Andrew Johnson's at Greeneville, Andrew Jackson's Hermitage near Nashville, and James K. Polk's at Columbia. Pinson Mounds, near Jackson, offers outstanding archaeological treasures and the remains of an Indian city. Reservoirs and lakes attract thousands of fishermen and water sports enthusiasts.

There are 29 state parks, almost all of which have camping facilities. All together, they cover 48,000 acres (19,000 hectares). Among the most visited state parks are the Meeman-Shelby Forest in Shelby County, Montgomery Bell in Dickson County, Cedars of Lebanon in Wilson County, and Natchez Trace in Henderson and Carroll counties. Extending into North Carolina, the Great Smoky Mountains National Park covers 235,438 acres (95,279 hectares) in Tennessee and drew more than 9 million visitors in 1979.

Licenses were issued to 483,978 hunters and 659,315 fishermen in 1977/78.

[48]SPORTS

Tennessee has been a baseball state for many years. Minor league teams in the class-AA Southern League are the Knoxville Vols, Chattanooga Lookouts, Nashville Sounds, and Memphis Chicks.

Tennessee's colleges and universities provide the major fall and winter sports. The University of Tennessee Volunteers and Vanderbilt University Commodores, in the Southeastern Conference, compete in football, basketball, and baseball; Vanderbilt won the conference title in baseball in 1980. Austin Peay and Middle Tennessee state universities belong to the Ohio Valley Conference.

[49]FAMOUS TENNESSEANS

Andrew Jackson (b.South Carolina, 1767–1845), the 7th president, moved to Tennessee as a young man. He won renown in the War of 1812 and became the first Democratic president in 1828. Jackson's close friend and associate, James Knox Polk (b.North Carolina, 1795–1849), came to Tennessee at the age of 10. He was elected the nation's 11th president in 1844 and served one term. Andrew Johnson (b.North Carolina, 1808–75), also a Democrat, remained loyal to the Union during the Civil War and was elected vice president with Abraham Lincoln in 1864. He became president upon Lincoln's assassination in 1865 and served out his predecessor's second term. Impeached because of a dispute over Reconstruction policies and presidential power, Johnson escaped conviction by one vote in 1868.

Supreme Court justices from Tennessee include John Catron (b.Pennsylvania, 1786–1865), Howell Jackson (1832–95), James C. McReynolds (b.Kentucky, 1862–1946), and Edward T. Sanford (1865–1930). Tennesseans who became cabinet officials include Secretary of State Cordell Hull (1871–1955), secretaries of war John Eaton (1790–1856) and John Bell (1797–1869), Secretary of the Treasury George Campbell (b.Scotland, 1769–1848), and attorneys general Felix Grundy (b.Virginia, 1777–1840) and James C. McReynolds.

Other nationally prominent political figures from Tennessee are Cary Estes Kefauver (1903–63), two-term US senator who ran unsuccessfully for vice president in 1956 on the Democratic ticket; Albert Gore (b.1907), three-term member of the US Senate; and Howard Baker (b.1925), who in 1966 became the first popularly elected Republican senator in Tennessee history. Three Tennesseans have been speaker of the US House of Representatives: James K. Polk, John Bell, and Joseph W. Byrns (1869–1936). Nancy Ward (1738–1822) was an outstanding Cherokee leader, and Sue Shelton White (1887–1943) played a major role in the campaign for women's suffrage.

Tennessee history features several military leaders and combat heroes. John Sevier (b.Virginia, 1745–1815), the first governor of the state, defeated British troops at Kings Mountain in the Revolution. David "Davy" Crockett (1786–1836) was a frontiersman who fought the British with Jackson in the War of 1812. Sam Houston (b.Virginia, 1793–1863) also fought in the War of 1812 and was governor of Tennessee before migrating to Texas. Nathan Bedford Forrest (1821–77) and Sam Davis (1842–63) were heroes of the Civil War. Sergeant Alvin C. York (1887–1964) won the Medal of Honor for his bravery in World War I.

Cordell Hull was awarded the Nobel Peace Prize in 1945 for his work on behalf of the United Nations. In 1971, Earl W. Sutherland, Jr. (b.Kansas, 1915–75), a biomedical scientist at Vanderbilt University, won a Nobel award for his discoveries concerning the mechanisms of hormones. Outstanding educators include Philip Lindsey (1786–1855), a Presbyterian minister and first president of the University of Nashville, and Alexander Heard (b.Georgia, 1917), nationally known political scientist and chancellor of Vanderbilt University.

Famous Tennessee writers are Mary Noailles Murfree (1850–1922), who used the pseudonym Charles Egbert Craddock; influential poet-critic John Crowe Ransom (1888–1974); author and poet James Agee (1909–55), posthumously awarded a Pulitzer Prize for his novel *A Death in the Family;* poet Randall Jarrell (1914–65), winner of two National Book Awards; and Wilma Dykeman (b.1920), novelist and historian. Sportswriter Grantland Rice (1880–1954) was born in Murfreesboro.

Tennessee has long been a center of popular music. Musician and songwriter William C. Handy (1873–1958) wrote "St. Louis Blues" and "Memphis Blues," among other classics. Bessie Smith (1898?–1937) was a leading blues singer. Elvis Presley (b.Mississippi, 1935–77) fused rhythm-and-blues with country-and-western styles to become one of the most popular entertainers who ever lived. Singer Dolly Parton (b.1946) was named Entertainer of the Year in 1978 by the Country Music Association.

[50]BIBLIOGRAPHY

Abernethy, Thomas P. *From Frontier to Plantation in Tennessee.* Chapel Hill: University of North Carolina Press, 1932.

Connelly, T. L. *Civil War Tennessee: Battles and Leaders.* Knoxville: University of Tennessee Press, 1979.

Corlew, Robert E. *Statehood for Tennessee.* Nashville: Tennessee Bicentennial Commission, 1976.

Dykeman, Wilma. *Tennessee: A Bicentennial History.* New York: Norton, 1975.

Federal Writers' Project: *Tennessee: A Guide to the State.* New York: Viking, 1939.

Folmsbee, Stanley J., Robert E. Corlew, and Enoch Mitchell. *History of Tennessee.* 4 vols. New York: Lewis, 1960.

Greene, Lee S., David H. Grubbs, and Victor C. Hobday. *Government in Tennessee.* Knoxville: University of Tennessee Press, 1975.

Hubbard, Preston. *Origins of TVA.* Nashville: Vanderbilt University Press, 1955.

Lewis, Thomas M. N., and Madeline Kneberg. *Tribes That Slumber: Indians of the Tennessee Region.* Knoxville: University of Tennessee Press, 1958.

Mooney, Chase. *Slavery in Tennessee.* Bloomington: Indiana University Press, 1957.

Smith, Samuel B., ed. *Tennessee History: A Bibliography.* Knoxville: University of Tennessee Press, 1974.

Taylor, A. Elizabeth. *Woman's Suffrage Movement in Tennessee.* New York: Bookman, 1957.

Tennessee, State of. Secretary of State. *Tennessee Blue Book, 1979–80.* Nashville, 1979.

Tennessee, University of. College of Business Administration. Center for Business and Economic Research. *Tennessee Statistical Abstract 1977.* Knoxville, 1977.

TEXAS

State of Texas

ORIGIN OF STATE NAME: Derived from the Caddo word *tayshas*, meaning "allies" or "friends." **NICKNAME**: The Lone Star State. **CAPITAL**: Austin. **ENTERED UNION**: 29 December 1845 (28th). **SONG**: "Texas, Our Texas." Also: "The Eyes of Texas." **MOTTO**: Friendship. **FLAG**: At the hoist is a vertical bar of blue with a single white five-pointed star; two horizontal bars of white and red cover the remainder of the flag. **OFFICIAL SEAL**: A five-pointed star encircled by olive and live oak branches, with the words "The State of Texas" surrounding. **BIRD**: Mockingbird. **FLOWER**: Bluebonnet. **TREE**: Pecan. **GEM**: Topaz. **STONE**: Palmwood. **GRASS**: Sideoats grama. **DISH**: Chili. **LEGAL HOLIDAYS**: New Year's Day, 1 January; Confederate Heroes Day, 19 January; Washington's Birthday, 3d Monday in February; Texas Independence Day, 2 March; San Jacinto Day, 21 April; Memorial Day, last Monday in May; Emancipation Day, 19 June; Independence Day, 4 July; Lyndon B. Johnson's Birthday, 27 August; Labor Day, 1st Monday in September; Columbus Day, 2d Monday in October; General Election Day, 1st Tuesday after 1st Monday in November; Veterans Day, 11 November; Thanksgiving Day, 4th Thursday in November; Christmas Day, 25 December. **TIME**: 6 A.M. CST = noon GMT.

¹LOCATION, SIZE, AND EXTENT

Located in the west south-central US, Texas is the largest of the 48 conterminous states. Texas's US rank slipped to 2d when Alaska entered the Union in 1959.

The total area of Texas is 267,338 sq mi (692,405 sq km), of which land comprises 262,134 sq mi (678,927 sq km) and inland water 5,204 sq mi (13,478 sq km). The state's land area represents 8.8% of the US mainland and 7.4% of the nation as a whole. The state's maximum E–W extension is 801 mi (1,289 km); its extreme N–S distance is 773 mi (1,244 km).

Texas is bordered on the N by Oklahoma and Arkansas (with part of the line formed by the Red River); on the E by Arkansas and Louisiana (with part of the Louisiana line defined by the Sabine River); on the SE by the Gulf of Mexico; on the SW by the Mexican states of Tamaulipas, Nuevo León, Coahuila, and Chihuahua (with the line formed by the Rio Grande); and on the W by New Mexico. The state's geographic center is in McCulloch County, 15 mi (24 km) NE of Brady.

Large islands in the Gulf of Mexico belonging to Texas are Galveston, Matagorda, and Padre. The boundary length of the state totals *3,029 mi (4,875 km)*, including a general Gulf of Mexico coastline of 367 mi (591 km); the tidal shoreline is 3,359 mi (5,406 km).

²TOPOGRAPHY

Texas's major physiographic divisions are the Gulf Coastal Plain in the east and southeast; the North Central Plains, covering most of central Texas; the Great Plains, extending from west-central Texas up into the panhandle; and the mountainous trans-Pecos area in the extreme west.

Within the Gulf Coastal Plain are the Piney Woods, an extension of western Louisiana that intrudes into East Texas for about 125 mi (200 km), and the Post Oak Belt, a flat region of mixed soil that gives way to the rolling prairie of the Blackland Belt, the state's most densely populated region. The Balcones Escarpment (so-called by the Spanish because its sharp profile suggests a balcony), a geological fault line running from the Rio Grande near Del Rio across central Texas, separates the Gulf Coastal Plain and Rio Grande Plain from the North Central Plains and south-central Hill Country, and in so doing divides East Texas from West Texas, watered Texas from dry Texas, and (culturally speaking) the Old South from the burgeoning West.

The North Central Plains extend from the Blackland Belt to the Cap Rock Escarpment, a natural boundary carved by erosion to heights of nearly 1,000 feet (300 meters) in some places. Much of this plains region is rolling prairie, but the dude ranches of the Hill Country and the mineral-rich Burnet-Llano Basin are also found here. West of the Cap Rock Escarpment are the Great Plains, stretching north–south from the Panhandle Plains to the Edwards Plateau, just north of the Balcones Escarpment. Along the western edge of the panhandle and extending into New Mexico is the Llano Estacado (Staked Plains), an extension of the High Plains lying east of the base of the Rocky Mountains.

The trans-Pecos region, between the Pecos River and the Rio Grande, contains the highest point in the state: Guadalupe Peak, with an altitude of 8,751 feet (2,667 meters), part of the Guadalupe Range extending southward from New Mexico into western Texas for about 20 mi (32 km). Also in the trans-Pecos region is the Diablo Plateau, which has no runoff to the sea and holds its scant water in lakes that often evaporate entirely. Farther south are the Davis Mountains, with a number of peaks rising above 7,000 feet (2,100 meters), and Big Bend country (surrounded on three sides by the Rio Grande), whose canyons sometimes reach depths of nearly 2,000 feet (600 meters). The Chisos Mountains, also exceeding 7,000 feet (2,100 meters) at some points, stand just north and west of the Rio Grande.

For all its vast expanse, Texas boasts few natural lakes. Caddo Lake, about one-third of which lies in Texas and two-thirds in Louisiana, is the state's largest natural lake, though its present length of 20 mi (32 km) includes waters added by dam construction in Louisiana. Each of two man-made reservoirs—Amistad, near Del Rio, and Toledo Bend, on the Sabine River—has storage capacities exceeding 3 million acre-feet, and the Sam Rayburn Reservoir (covering 179 sq mi, or 464 sq km) has a capacity of 2.9 million acre-feet. All together, the state contains more than 200 major reservoirs, 7 of which can store more than 1 million acre-feet of water. From the air, Texas looks as well-watered as Minnesota, but the lakes are artificial and much of the soil is dry.

One reason Texas has so many reservoirs is that it is blessed with a number of major river systems, although none is navigable for more than 50 mi (80 km) inland. Starting from the west, the Rio Grande, a majestic stream in some places but a trickling trough in others, imparts life to the Texas desert and serves as the international boundary with Mexico. Its total length of

1,896 mi (3,051 km), including segments in Colorado and New Mexico, makes the Rio Grande the nation's 2d-longest river, exceeded only by the Missouri-Mississippi river system. The Colorado River is the longest river wholly within the state, extending about 600 mi (970 km) on its journey across central and southeastern Texas to the Gulf of Mexico. Other important rivers include the Nueces, in whose brushy valley the range cattle industry began; the San Antonio, which stems from springs within the present city limits and flows, like most Texas rivers, to the Gulf of Mexico; the Brazos, which rises in New Mexico and stretches diagonally for about 840 mi (1,350 km) across Texas; the Trinity, which serves Ft. Worth and Dallas; the San Jacinto, a short river but one of the most heavily trafficked in North America, overlapping the Houston Ship Channel, which connects the Port of Houston with the Gulf; the Neches, which makes an ocean port out of Beaumont; the Sabine, which has the largest water discharge (6,800,000 acre-feet) at its mouth of any Texas river; the Red, forming part of the northern boundary; and the Canadian, which crosses the Texas panhandle from New Mexico to Oklahoma, bringing moisture to the cattle raisers and wheat growers of that region. In all, Texas has about 3,700 identifiable streams, many of which dry up in the summer and flood during periods of rainfall.

Because of its extensive outcroppings of limestone, extending westward from the Balcones Escarpment, Texas contains a maze of caverns. Among the better-known caves are Longhorn Cavern in Burnet County; Wonder Cave, near San Marcos; the Caverns of Sonora, at Sonora; and Jack Pit Cave, in Menard County, which, with 19,000 feet (5,800 meters) of passages, is the most extensive cave yet mapped in the state.

About 1 billion years ago, shallow seas covered much of Texas. After the seas receded, the land dropped gradually over millions of years, leaving a thick sediment that was then compressed into a long mountain range called the Ouachita Fold Belt. The sea was eventually restricted to a zone in West Texas called the Permian Basin, a giant evaporation pan holding gypsum and salt deposits hundreds of feet deep. As the mountain chain across central Texas eroded and the land continued to subside, the Rocky Mountains were uplifted, leaving deep cuts in Big Bend country and creating the Llano Estacado. The Gulf of Mexico area subsided rapidly, depositing sediment accumulations several thousand feet deep, while salt domes formed over vast petroleum and sulfur deposits. All this geologic activity also deposited quicksilver in the Terlingua section of the Big Bend, built up the Horseshoe Atoll (a buried reef in west-central Texas that is the largest limestone reservoir in the nation), created uranium deposits in southern Texas, and preserved the oil-bearing Jurassic rocks of the northeast.

³CLIMATE

Texas's great size and topographic variety make climatic description difficult. Brownsville, at the mouth of the Rio Grande, has had no measurable snowfall during all the years that records have been kept, but Vega, in the panhandle, averages 24 in (61 cm) of snowfall a year. In the eastern third of the state, rainfall averages 56 in (142 cm) annually, while in parts of extreme West Texas, rainfall averages less than 8 in (20 cm).

Generally, a maritime climate prevails along the Gulf coast, with continental conditions inland; the Balcones Escarpment is the main dividing line between the two zones, but they are not completely isolated from each other's influence. Texas has two basic seasons—a hot summer that may last from April through October, and a winter that starts in November and usually lasts until March. When summer ends, the state is too dry for autumn foliage, except in East Texas. Temperatures in El Paso, in the southwest, range from a mean January minimum of 32°F (0°C) to a mean July maximum of 94°F (34°C); at Amarillo, in the panhandle, from 24°F (–4°C) to 92°F (33°C); and at Galveston, on the Gulf, from 49°F (9°C) to 87°F (31°C). Perhaps the most startling contrast is in relative humidity, averaging 34% at noon in El Paso, 44% in Amarillo, and 72% in Galveston. In the Texas panhandle, the average date of the first freeze is 1 November; in the lower Rio Grande Valley, 16 December. The last freeze arrives in the panhandle on 15 April, and in the lower Rio Grande Valley on 30 January. The valley thus falls only six weeks short of having a 12-month growing season, while the panhandle approximates the growing season of the upper Midwest.

Record temperatures range from –23°F (–31°C) at Tulia, on 12 February 1899, and Seminole, on 8 February 1933, to 120°F (49°C) at Seymour in north-central Texas on 12 August 1936. The greatest annual rainfall was 109 in (277 cm), measured in 1873 at Clarksville, just below the Red River in northeast Texas; the least annual rainfall, 1.76 in (4.47 cm), was recorded at Wink, near the New Mexico line, in 1956. Thrall, in central Texas, received 38.2 in (97 cm) of rain in 24 hours on 9–10 September 1921. Romero, on the New Mexico border, received a record 65 in (165 cm) of snow in the winter of 1923–24, and Hale Center, near Lubbock, measured 33 in (84 cm) during one storm in February 1956. The highest sustained wind velocity in Texas history, 145 mph (233 km/hr), occurred when Hurricane Carla hit Matagorda and Port Lavaca along the Gulf coast on 11 September 1961.

Hurricanes strike the Gulf coast about once every decade, usually in September or October. A hurricane on 19–20 August 1886 leveled the port of Indianola; the town (near present-day Port Lavaca) was never rebuilt. Galveston was the site of one of the most destructive storms in US history: on 8–9 September 1900, a hurricane blew across the island of 38,000 residents, leaving at least 6,000 dead (the exact total has never been ascertained) and leveling most of the city. A storm of equal intensity hit Galveston in mid-August 1915, but this time the city was prepared; its new seawall held the toll to 275 deaths and $50 million worth of property damage. Because of well-planned damage-prevention and evacuation procedures, Hurricane Carla—at least as powerful as any previous hurricane—claimed no more than 34 lives. More recent hurricanes have frequently passed over the coastal area with no loss of life at all. Texas also lies in the path of "Tornado Alley," stretching across the Great Plains to Canada. The worst tornado in recent decades struck downtown Waco on 11 May 1953, killing 114 persons, injuring another 597, and destroying or damaging some 1,050 homes and 685 buildings.

Floods and droughts have also taken their toll in Texas. The worst flood occurred on 26–28 June 1954, when Hurricane Alice moved inland up the Rio Grande for several hundred miles, dropping 27 in (69 cm) of rain on Pandale above Del Rio. The Rio Grande rose 50 to 60 feet (15–18 meters) within 48 hours, as a wall of water 86 feet (26 meters) high in the Pecos River canyon fed it from the north. A Pecos River bridge built with a 50-foot (15-meter) clearance was washed out, as was the international bridge linking Laredo with Mexico. Periodic droughts afflicted Texas in the 1930s and 1950s; during the summer of 1980, Texans again wondered whether the extreme heat and lack of rain presaged another prolonged drought.

⁴FLORA AND FAUNA

More than 500 species of grasses covered Texas when the Spanish and Anglo-Americans arrived. Although plowing and lack of soil conservation destroyed a considerable portion of this rich heritage, grassy pastureland still covers about two-thirds of the

LOCATION: 25°50′ to 36°30′N; 93°31′ to 106°38′W. **BOUNDARIES**: Oklahoma line, *846 mi (1,362 km)*; Arkansas line, *102 mi (164 km)*; Louisiana line, *327 mi (526 km)*; Gulf of Mexico coastline, 367 mi (591 km); Mexico line, *889 mi (1,431 km)*; New Mexico line, *498 mi (801 km)*.

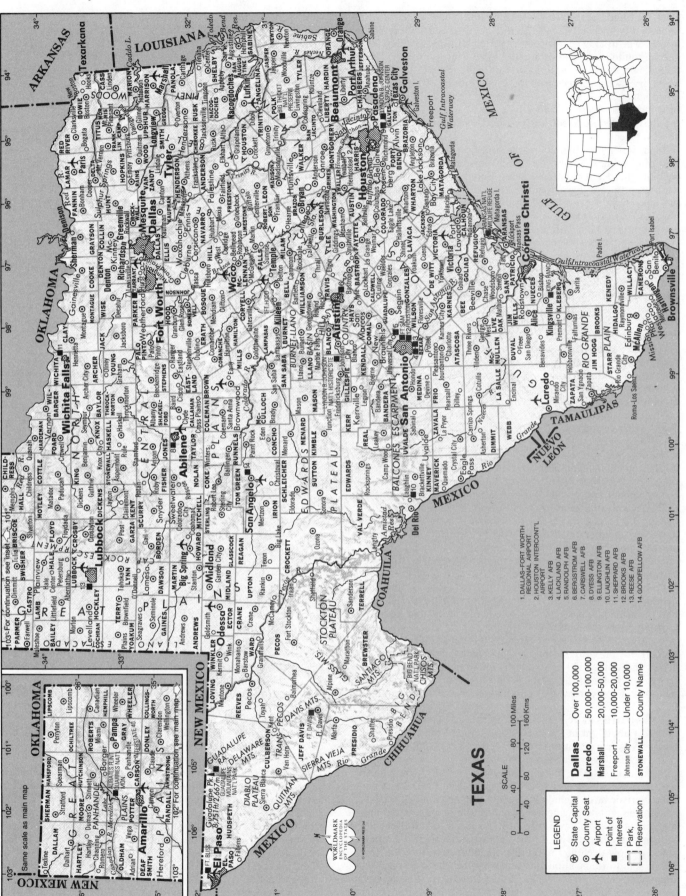

See US political: front cover G4; physical: back cover G4.

TEXAS

SCALE

0 40 80 120 160 Kms
0 40 80 100 Miles

LEGEND

⊗ State Capital
◉ County Seat
✈ Airport
■ Point of Interest
⬭ Park, Reservation

Dallas Over 100,000
Laredo 50,000-100,000
Marshall 20,000-50,000
Freeport 10,000-20,000
Johnson City Under 10,000
STONEWALL County Name

1. DALLAS-FORT WORTH REGIONAL AIRPORT
2. HOUSTON INTERCONT'L AIRPORT
3. KELLY AFB
4. LACKLAND AFB
5. BERGSTROM AFB
6. CARSWELL AFB
7. RANDOLPH AFB
8. DYESS AFB
9. ELLINGTON AFB
10. LAUGHLIN AFB
11. SHEPPARD AFB
12. BROOKS AFB
13. REESE AFB
14. GOODFELLOW AFB

WORLDMARK ENCYCLOPEDIA OF THE STATES

state. Bermuda grass is a favorite ground cover, especially an improved type called Coastal Bermuda, introduced after World War II. The prickly pear cactus is a mixed blessing: like the cedar and mesquite, it saps moisture and inhibits grass growth, but it does retain moisture in periods of drought and will survive the worst dry spells, so that (with the spines burned off) it can be of great value to ranchers as cattle feed in difficult times. The bean of the mesquite also provides food for horses and cattle when they have little else to eat, and its wood is a favorite in barbecues and fireplaces.

Texas has more than 200 native trees, of which the catclaw, flowering mimosa, huisache, black persimmon, huajillo, and weeping juniper (unique to the Big Bend) are common only in Texas. Cottonwood grows along streams in almost every part of the state, while cypress inhabits the swamps. The flowering dogwood in East Texas draws tourists to that region every spring, and the largest bois d'arc trees in the US are grown in the Red River Valley. Probably the most popular shade tree is the American (white) elm, which, like the gum tree, has considerable commercial importance. The magnolia is treasured for its grace and beauty; no home of substance in southeastern Texas would have a lawn without one. Of the principal hardwoods, the white oak is the most commercially valuable, the post oak the most common, and the live oak the most desirable for shade; the pecan is the state tree. Pines grow in two areas about 600 mi (970 km) apart—deep East Texas and the trans-Pecos region. In southeast Texas stands the Big Thicket, a unique area originally covering more than 3 million acres (1.2 million hectares) but now reduced to about one-tenth that by lumbering. Gonzales County, in south-central Texas, is the home of palmettos, orchids, and other semitropical plants not found anywhere else in the state. Texas wild rice and several cactus species are classified as endangered throughout the state.

Possibly the rarest mammal in Texas is the red wolf, which inhabits the marshland between Houston and Beaumont, one of the most thickly settled areas of the state; owing to human encroachment and possible hybridization with coyotes, the red wolf is steadily disappearing despite efforts by naturalists throughout the US to save it. On the other hand, Texans claim to have the largest number of white-tailed deer of any state in the Union, an estimated 3 million. Although the Hill Country is the white-tailed deer's natural habitat, the species has been transplanted successfully throughout the state.

Perhaps the most unusual mammal in Texas is the nine-banded armadillo. Originally confined to the Rio Grande border, the armadillo has gradually spread northward and eastward, crossing the Red River into Oklahoma and the Mississippi River into the Deep South. It accomplishes these feats of transport by sucking in air until it becomes buoyant and then swimming across the water. The armadillo is likewise notable for always having its young in litters of identical quadruplets. The chief mammalian predators are the coyote, bobcat, and mountain lion.

Texas attracts more than 825 different kinds of birds, with bird life most abundant in the lower Rio Grande Valley and coastal plains. Argument continues as to whether Texas is the last home of the ivory-billed woodpecker, which lives in inaccessible swamps, preferably in cutover timber. Somewhat less rare is the pileated woodpecker, which also inhabits the forested lowlands. Other characteristic birds include the yellow-trimmed hooded warbler, which frequents the canebrakes and produces one of the most melodious songs of any Texas bird; the scissor-tailed flycatcher, known popularly as the scissor-tail; Attwater's greater prairie chicken, now declining because of inadequate protection from hunters and urbanization; the mockingbird, the state bird; and the roadrunner, also known as paisano and chaparral. Rare birds include the Mexican jacana, with a fleshy comb and bright

yellow-green wings; the white-throated swift, one of the world's fastest flyers; the Texas canyon wren, with a musical range of more than an octave; and the Colima warbler, which breeds only in the Chisos Mountains. In the Aransas National Wildlife Refuge, along the central Gulf coast, lives the whooping crane, long on the endangered list and numbering 68 adults and 6 young in 1978. Controversy surrounds the golden eagle, protected by federal law but despised by ranchers for allegedly preying on lambs and other young livestock.

Texas has its fair share of reptiles, including more than 100 species of snake, 16 of them poisonous, including the deadly Texas coral snake. There are 10 kinds of rattlesnake, and some parts of West Texas hold annual rattlesnake roundups. Disappearing with the onset of urbanization are the horned toad, a small iguanalike lizard; the vinegarroon, a stinging scorpion; and the tarantula, a large black hairy spider that is scary to behold but basically harmless.

In addition to providing protection for the animals on federal lists of threatened and endangered species, the state has its own wildlife protection programs. Among the animals classified as nongame (not hunted) and therefore given special consideration are the lesser yellow bat, spotted dolphin, reddish egret, white-tailed hawk, wood stork, Big Bend gecko, rock rattlesnake, Louisiana pine snake, white-lipped frog, giant toad, toothless blindcat, and blue sucker. Along with the red wolf, Attwater's greater prairie chicken, and ivory-billed woodpecker, endangered species include the American alligator, jaguar, ocelot, Eskimo curlew, Houston toad, paddlefish, shovelnose sturgeon, and fountain darter.

⁵ENVIRONMENTAL PROTECTION

Conservation in Texas officially began with the creation of a State Department of Forestry in 1915; 11 years later, this body was reorganized as the Texas Forest Service, the name it retains today. The state's Soil Conservation Service was created in 1935; by 1979 there were 198 conservation districts overseen by the Texas State Soil and Water Conservation Board. The chief soil problem is wind erosion.

The scarcity of water is the one crisis every Texan must live with. Much of the state has absorbent soils, a high evaporation rate, vast areas without trees to hold moisture, and a rolling terrain susceptible to rapid runoff. The Texas Department of Water Resources directs the state's water supply and conservation programs. Various county and regional water authorities have been constituted, as have several water commissions for river systems. Probably the most complete system is that of the three Colorado River authorities—lower, central, and upper. The oldest of these is the Lower Colorado River Authority, created in 1934 by the Texas legislature to "control, store, preserve, and distribute" the waters of the Colorado River and its feeder streams. The authority exercises control over a 10-county area stretching from above Austin to the Gulf coast, overseeing flood control, municipal and industrial water supplies, irrigation, hydroelectric power generation, soil conservation, and recreation.

The most powerful conservation agency in Texas is the Railroad Commission, but whether its chief function is conservation or price fixing remains a source of continuing public controversy. Originally established to regulate railroads, the commission extended its power to regulate oil and natural gas by virtue of its jurisdiction over the transportation of those products by rail and pipeline. In 1917, the state legislature empowered the commission to prevent the waste of oil and gas. The key step in conservation arrived with the discovery of oil in East Texas in 1930. With a national depression in full swing and the price of oil dropping to $1 a barrel, the commission agreed to halt ruinous overproduction, issuing the first proration order in April 1931. In a field composed of hundreds of small ownerships, however, control was difficult to establish: oil was bootlegged, the commission's authority broke down, Governor Ross S. Sterling declared martial law, and the state's conservation edicts were not heeded until the federal government stepped in to enforce them. Today, the Railroad Commission acts to eliminate wasteful drilling procedures and decides which equipment and techniques are permissible. In addition, the commission requires careful accounting of all production and sales.

⁶POPULATION

According to preliminary 1980 census figures, Texas ranked 3d behind California and New York, with a population of 14,152,339. The state placed 4th at the 1970 census, with a population of 11,196,730, but surpassed Pennsylvania in 1974. The population density in 1980 was 54 per sq mi (21 per sq km), ranging from more than 100 per sq mi (39 per sq km) in the major cities to less than 1 in several counties.

At the first decennial census of 1850, less than five years after Texas had become a state, the population totaled 212,592. It reached 1,600,000 by the early 1880s (when the state ranked 11th), passed 4,000,000 during World War I, and jumped to 7,700,000 in 1950. The slowest period of growth occurred during the depression decade (1930–40), when the population rose only 10% and the state was surpassed by California. Growth rates have ranged between 17% and 27% during each of the last four decades.

The ratio between the sexes has changed during the 20th century. In 1920, the state had 155,000 more men than women; 40 years later, women outnumbered men by 90,000, and by 1976 the female lead was 359,000. At the same time, the Texas population has grown steadily older, a phenomenon linked to declining birthrates and increased life expectancies. In 1870, only one out of 68 Texans was 65 years of age or older; by 1978, one out of every 10.5 Texans was classified as a senior citizen. Surprisingly for a state whose population has grown so fast, fully 59% of all adult Texans have lived in the state their whole lives.

By 1970, 80% of all Texans lived in metropolitan areas, of which Texas has 25—more than any other state. The largest, Dallas–Ft. Worth, included an estimated 2,719,900 people (9th in the US) in an 11-county region in mid-1978. Close behind was the Houston area, covering 6 counties and having 2,595,400 residents (11th). San Antonio, with 3 counties, ranked 37th nationally at 1,037,800. Houston, the largest city, had a preliminary 1980 census population of 1,554,992. Next was Dallas, with 901,450, followed by San Antonio, 783,296; El Paso, 424,522; Ft. Worth, 382,349; Austin, 343,390; and Corpus Christi, 230,715. With the exception of El Paso, in the far western corner of the trans-Pecos region, most of the larger cities are situated along the Gulf coast or on or near an axis that extends north–south from Wichita Falls to Corpus Christi, in the heart of the Blackland Belt. (For the table of Texas counties, county seats, and county populations, see pp. 522–23.)

⁷ETHNIC GROUPS

Hispanic Americans constitute the largest ethnic minority in Texas, about 20.3% of the population in 1976. Black Americans accounted for 11.4%, and most of the rest were "Anglos"—a term denoting all whites except Spanish-surnamed or Spanish-speaking individuals. Although many Indian groups have lived in Texas, few Indians remain.

As white settlers pushed toward Texas during the 19th century, many Indian groups moved west and south into the region. The most notable tribes were the Comanche, Wichita, Kiowa, Apache, Choctaw, and Cherokee. Also entering in significant numbers were the Kickapoo and Potawatomi from Illinois, the Delaware and Shawnee from Missouri, the Quapaw from Arkansas, and the Creek from Alabama and Georgia. One of the few Texas tribes that has survived to the present time as an identifiable group is the Alabama-Coushatta, who inhabit a

4,351-acre (1,761-hectare) reservation in Polk County, 90 mi (145 km) northeast of Houston. The Tigua, living in Texas since the 1680s, were recognized by a federal law in 1968 that transferred all responsibility for them to the State of Texas. The two Indian reservations number about 500 persons each; overall, at the 1970 census, there were 17,957 Indians living in Texas.

Blacks have been integral to the history of Texas ever since a black Moor named Estevanico was shipwrecked near present-day Galveston in 1528. By 1860, Texas had 182,921 blacks, or 30% of the total population, of whom only 355 were free. Once emancipated, blacks made effective use of the franchise, electing two of their number to the state senate and nine to the house in 1868. After the return of the Democratic Party to political dominance, however, the power of blacks steadily diminished. Since then, their numbers have grown, but their proportion of the total population has dwindled, although both Houston and Dallas were about 25% black at the 1970 census. In 1976, an estimated 1,428,000 blacks lived in the state.

Hispanic Americans, the largest and fastest-growing minority in Texas, numbered 2,557,000 in 1976 (2d only to California). Mostly of Mexican ancestry, they are nevertheless a heterogeneous group, divided by history, geography, and economic circumstances. These differences have prevented them from becoming the political force their numbers would suggest, although Hispanos have been elected to the state legislature and to the US Congress. In 1980, the Houston independent school district, the state's largest, reported more Hispanic students than Anglos for the first time in its history.

All together, Texas has nearly 30 identifiable ethnic groups. Certain areas of central Texas are heavily Germanic and Czech. The first permanent Polish colony in the US was established at Panna Maria, near San Antonio, in 1854. Texas has one of the largest colonies of Wends in the world, principally at Serbin in central Texas. Significant numbers of Danes, Swedes, and Norwegians have also settled in Texas. As of 1970, foreign-born Texans and their native-born American children numbered 1,199,000, with Mexico, Germany, and the United Kingdom the leading countries of origin. The same census counted 7,635 Chinese, 6,537 Japanese, 3,442 Filipinos, and 45,026 other Asian-Pacific peoples. In 1975, 9,130 Vietnamese refugees were resettled in Texas.

⁸LANGUAGES

The 4,514 Indians who in 1970 claimed an Indian language as their mother tongue are mostly descendants of the Alabama-Coushatta that came to Texas in the 19th century. The few Indian place-names include Texas itself, Pecos, Waco, and Toyah.

Most of the regional features in Texas English derive from the influx of South Midland and Southern speakers, with a noticeable Spanish flavor from older as well as more recent loans. Settlers from the Gulf Coast states brought such terms as *snap beans* (green beans), the widespread *pail* (here probably of Southern rather than Northern origin), and *carry* (escort), with a 47% frequency in north Texas and 22% in the south. Louisiana *praline* (pecan patty) is now widespread, but *banquette* (sidewalk) appears only in the extreme southeast corner.

Southern and South Midland terms were largely introduced by settlers from Arkansas, Missouri, and Tennessee; their use ranges from northeast to west, but with declining frequency in the trans-Pecos area. Examples are *clabber cheese* (cottage cheese), *mosquito hawk* (dragonfly), *croker sack* (burlap bag), *mouth harp* (harmonica), *branch* (stream), and *dog irons* (andirons). A dialect survey showed *pallet* (bed on the floor) with a 90% overall frequency; *light bread* (white bread) and *pullybone* (wishbone), each 78%; and *you-all*, more than 80%. General Midland terms also widespread in the state are *sook!* (call to calves), *blinds* (roller shades), *piece* (a certain distance), and *quarter till five* (4:45).

Texas Counties, County Seats, and County Populations[1]

COUNTY	COUNTY SEAT	AREA (SQ MI)	POPULATION (EST. 1977)	COUNTY	COUNTY SEAT	AREA (SQ MI)	POPULATION (EST. 1977)
Anderson	Palestine	1,072	33,200	Duval	San Diego	1,814	12,100
Andrews	Andrews	1,504	11,400	Eastland	Eastland	952	18,700
Angelina	Lufkin	738	56,600	Ector	Odessa	907	103,300
Aransas	Rockport	275	11,100	Edwards	Rocksprings	2,076	2,200
Archer	Archer City	913	6,400	Ellis	Waxahachie	940	52,900
Armstrong	Claude	907	2,000	El Paso	El Paso	1,057	434,700
Atascosa	Jourdanton	1,206	20,200	Erath	Stephenville	1,085	18,900
Austin	Bellville	663	15,400	Falls	Marlin	764	16,300
Bailey	Muleshoe	835	7,800	Fannin	Bonham	905	23,100
Bandera	Bandera	763	6,500	Fayette	La Grange	934	17,600
Bastrop	Bastrop	890	20,000	Fisher	Roby	904	6,000
Baylor	Seymour	845	4,900	Floyd	Floydada	993	10,500
Bee	Beeville	842	22,800	Foard	Crowell	676	2,200
Bell	Belton	1,047	161,000	Ft. Bend	Richmond	869	86,600
Bexar	San Antonio	1,246	954,100	Franklin	Mt. Vernon	293	6,400
Blanco	Johnson City	719	4,000	Freestone	Fairfield	865	12,200
Borden	Gail	907	700	Frio	Pearsall	1,116	12,900
Bosque	Meridian	990	12,400	Gaines	Seminole	1,489	11,200
Bowie	Boston	891	73,100	Galveston	Galveston	399	195,400
Brazoria	Angleton	1,423	135,400	Garza	Post	914	5,300
Brazos	Bryan	586	77,400	Gillespie	Fredericksburg	1,055	11,300
Brewster	Alpine	6,204	7,300	Glasscock	Garden City	863	1,100
Briscoe	Silverton	874	2,600	Goliad	Goliad	871	4,800
Brooks	Falfurrias	904	7,700	Gonzales	Gonzales	1,056	16,100
Brown	Brownwood	938	29,600	Gray	Pampa	934	25,700
Burleson	Caldwell	670	10,600	Grayson	Sherman	940	84,100
Burnet	Burnet	996	15,800	Gregg	Longview	282	85,400
Caldwell	Lockhart	544	22,100	Grimes	Anderson	801	12,300
Calhoun	Port Lavaca	529	18,100	Guadalupe	Seguin	714	39,700
Callahan	Baird	856	9,600	Hale	Plainview	979	35,300
Cameron	Brownsville	896	176,500	Hall	Memphis	885	5,700
Camp	Pittsburg	192	8,400	Hamilton	Hamilton	844	7,500
Carson	Panhandle	900	6,500	Hansford	Spearman	907	6,200
Cass	Linden	941	26,400	Hardeman	Quanah	687	6,300
Castro	Dimmitt	880	10,600	Hardin	Kountze	897	37,200
Chambers	Anahuac	616	14,000	Harris	Houston	1,723	2,138,300
Cherokee	Rusk	1,049	32,400	Harrison	Marshall	894	45,800
Childress	Childress	699	6,500	Hartley	Channing	1,488	3,400
Clay	Henrietta	1,102	9,000	Haskell	Haskell	877	7,700
Cochran	Morton	783	4,900	Hays	San Marcos	650	34,700
Coke	Robert Lee	911	3,100	Hemphill	Canadian	904	4,000
Coleman	Coleman	1,280	10,300	Henderson	Athens	943	33,100
Collin	McKinney	836	101,300	Hidalgo	Edinburg	1,543	232,300
Collingsworth	Wellington	894	4,500	Hill	Hillsboro	1,010	22,400
Colorado	Columbus	949	17,200	Hockley	Levelland	908	21,000
Comal	New Braunfels	567	31,100	Hood	Granbury	426	11,000
Comanche	Comanche	944	12,100	Hopkins	Sulphur Springs	793	22,400
Concho	Paint Rock	1,004	2,800	Houston	Crockett	1,237	18,700
Cooke	Gainesville	905	24,500	Howard	Big Spring	911	37,400
Coryell	Gatesville	1,043	47,600	Hudspeth	Sierra Blanca	4,554	2,800
Cottle	Paducah	900	3,000	Hunt	Greenville	826	49,900
Crane	Crane	795	4,300	Hutchinson	Stinnett	875	25,900
Crockett	Ozona	2,794	4,200	Irion	Mertzon	1,073	1,100
Crosby	Crosbyton	911	8,600	Jack	Jacksboro	945	6,500
Culberson	Van Horn	3,851	3,600	Jackson	Edna	850	13,000
Dallam	Dalhart	1,494	6,700	Jasper	Jasper	907	28,000
Dallas	Dallas	859	1,469,600	Jeff Davis	Ft. Davis	2,259	1,400
Dawson	Lamesa	902	15,900	Jefferson	Beaumont	951	246,900
Deaf Smith	Hereford	1,510	20,300	Jim Hogg	Hebbronville	1,143	4,700
Delta	Cooper	276	4,600	Jim Wells	Alice	845	34,200
Denton	Denton	911	97,400	Johnson	Cleburne	740	58,600
DeWitt	Cuero	910	18,800	Jones	Anson	956	16,400
Dickens	Dickens	931	3,400	Karnes	Karnes City	758	12,600
Dimmet	Carrizo Springs	1,344	11,000	Kaufman	Kaufman	815	35,400
Donley	Clarendon	905	3,700	Kendall	Boerne	670	8,900

Texas Counties, County Seats, and County Populations[1]

COUNTY	COUNTY SEAT	AREA (SQ MI)	POPULATION (EST. 1977)	COUNTY	COUNTY SEAT	AREA (SQ MI)	POPULATION (EST. 1977)
Kenedy	Sarita	1,394	600	Red River	Clarksville	1,033	14,400
Kent	Jayton	880	1,200	Reeves	Pecos	2,608	15,800
Kerr	Kerrville	1,101	22,800	Refugio	Refugio	774	9,200
Kimble	Junction	1,274	4,000	Roberts	Miami	899	1,100
King	Guthrie	944	400	Robertson	Franklin	877	14,100
Kinney	Brackettville	1,393	2,300	Rockwall	Rockwall	147	9,700
Kleberg	Kingsville	851	32,800	Runnels	Ballinger	1,058	11,400
Knox	Benjamin	851	5,700	Rusk	Henderson	939	37,600
Lamar	Paris	894	38,100	Sabine	Hemphill	456	7,300
Lamb	Littlefield	1,022	17,500	San Augustine	San Augustine	473	8,500
Lampasas	Lampasas	726	11,600	San Jacinto	Coldspring	624	9,000
La Salle	Cotulla	1,500	5,700	San Patricio	Sinton	685	52,500
Lavaca	Hallettsville	975	17,600	San Saba	San Saba	1,120	5,300
Lee	Giddings	637	8,800	Schleicher	Eldorado	1,331	2,600
Leon	Centerville	1,102	8,900	Scurry	Snyder	904	18,000
Liberty	Liberty	1,180	40,300	Shackelford	Albany	887	3,300
Limestone	Groesbeck	931	18,200	Shelby	Center	778	20,300
Lipscomb	Lipscomb	934	3,700	Sherman	Stratford	916	3,900
Live Oak	George West	1,055	6,700	Smith	Tyler	934	111,500
Llano	Llano	941	9,100	Somervell	Glen Rose	197	3,700
Loving	Mentone	648	100	Starr	Rio Grande City	1,211	21,700
Lubbock	Lubbock	893	200,200	Stephens	Breckenridge	899	8,900
Lynn	Tahoka	915	8,900	Sterling	Sterling City	914	1,000
McCulloch	Brady	1,066	8,300	Stonewall	Aspermont	926	2,200
McLennan	Waco	1,000	161,500	Sutton	Sonora	1,493	4,900
McMullen	Tilden	1,159	800	Swisher	Tulia	896	10,100
Madison	Madisonville	480	8,900	Tarrant	Ft. Worth	861	779,800
Marion	Jefferson	380	8,500	Taylor	Abilene	912	105,000
Martin	Stanton	911	5,000	Terrell	Sanderson	2,391	1,800
Mason	Mason	935	3,300	Terry	Brownfield	899	13,800
Matagorda	Bay City	1,157	30,600	Throckmorton	Throckmorton	920	2,200
Maverick	Eagle Pass	1,289	24,000	Titus	Mt. Pleasant	418	18,900
Medina	Hondo	1,352	21,700	Tom Green	San Angelo	1,500	76,600
Menard	Menard	914	2,400	Travis	Austin	1,012	388,200
Midland	Midland	939	72,500	Trinity	Groveton	707	7,900
Milam	Cameron	1,028	19,700	Tyler	Woodville	919	14,500
Mills	Goldthwaite	734	4,300	Upshur	Gilmer	584	24,500
Mitchell	Colorado City	920	8,900	Upton	Rankin	1,312	4,600
Montague	Montague	932	16,500	Uvalde	Uvalde	1,588	19,800
Montgomery	Conroe	1,090	95,900	Val Verde	Del Rio	3,241	32,200
Moore	Dumas	909	14,900	Van Zandt	Canton	845	27,400
Morris	Daingerfield	260	13,700	Victoria	Victoria	892	60,600
Motley	Matador	980	1,900	Walker	Huntsville	790	34,000
Nacogdoches	Nacogdoches	902	42,600	Waller	Hempstead	509	15,800
Navarro	Corsicana	1,070	31,900	Ward	Monahans	827	12,500
Newton	Newton	949	12,500	Washington	Brenham	594	19,800
Nolan	Sweetwater	922	16,200	Webb	Laredo	3,306	85,000
Nueces	Corpus Christi	841	250,700	Wharton	Wharton	1,076	37,300
Ochiltree	Perryton	907	9,400	Wheeler	Wheeler	914	6,200
Oldham	Vega	1,478	2,600	Wichita	Wichita Falls	611	122,600
Orange	Orange	359	79,800	Wilbarger	Vernon	952	15,000
Palo Pinto	Palo Pinto	948	24,500	Willacy	Raymondville	591	16,800
Panola	Carthage	869	18,100	Williamson	Georgetown	1,104	51,400
Parker	Weatherford	903	35,600	Wilson	Floresville	802	14,000
Parmer	Farwell	859	10,300	Winkler	Kermit	887	9,600
Pecos	Ft. Stockton	4,740	14,300	Wise	Decatur	922	22,000
Polk	Livingston	1,100	18,700	Wood	Quitman	721	22,000
Potter	Amarillo	898	92,900	Yoakum	Plains	830	7,300
Presidio	Marfa	3,892	4,800	Young	Graham	888	17,300
Rains	Emory	210	4,600	Zapata	Zapata	957	5,300
Randall	Canyon	914	65,000	Zavala	Crystal City	1,291	11,500
Reagan	Big Lake	1,132	3,500	TOTALS		262,134	12,830,000
Real	Leakey	622	2,300				

[1]Columns may not add to totals because of rounding.

Some terms exhibit uneven distribution. Examples include *mott* (clump of trees) in the south and southwest, *sugan* (a wool-filled comforter for a cowboy's bedroll) in the west, Midland *draw* (dry steambed) in the west and southwest, South Midland *peckerwood* (woodpecker) in most of the state except west of the Pecos, *poke* (paper bag) in the central and northern areas, and *surly* (euphemism for *bull*) in the west. A curious result of dialect mixture is the appearance of a number of hybrids combining two different dialects, such as *freeseed peach* from *freestone* and *clearseed*, *fire mantel* and *mantel board* from *fireboard* and *mantel*, *flapcakes* from *flapjacks* and *pancakes*, and *horse doctor* from *horsefly* and *snake doctor*. The large sandwich is known as a *torpedo* in San Antonio and a *poorboy* in Houston.

Texas pronunciation is largely South Midland, with such characteristic forms as /caow/ and /naow/ for *cow* and *now* and /dyoo/ for *due*, although /doo/ is now more common in urban areas. In the German settlement around New Braunfels are heard a few loanwords such as *smearcase* (cottage cheese), *krebbel* (doughnut), *clook* (setting hen), and *oma* and *opa* for grandmother and grandfather.

Spanish has been the major foreign-language influence. In areas like Laredo and Brownsville, along the Rio Grande, as many as 90% of the people may be bilingual; in northeast Texas, however, Spanish is as foreign as French. In the days of the early Spanish ranchers, standard English adopted *hacienda*, *ranch*, *burro*, *canyon*, and *lariat*; in the southwestern cattle country are heard *la reata* (lasso), *remuda* (group of horses), and *resaca* (pond), along with *acequia* (irrigation ditch), *pilon* (something extra, as a tip), and *olla* (water jar). The presence of the large Spanish-speaking population was a major factor in the passage of the state's bilingual education law, as a result of which numerous school programs in both English and Spanish are now offered; in a ruling issued in January 1981, US District Judge William Wayne Justice ruled that by 1987 the state must expand such programs to cover all Spanish-speaking students. About one-sixth of all Texas counties—and a great many cities—are named for Mexicans or Spaniards or after place-names in Spain or Mexico.

About 78% of all native-born Texans claimed English as their mother tongue in 1970, and 74% of the total population. Major language groups reported their first language as follows:

	NATIVE-BORN	FOREIGN-BORN
English	8,291,388	24,633
Spanish	1,581,295	212,167
German	213,957	23,615
French	85,831	5,071
Polish	27,042	2,005
Italian	22,259	3,635

⁹RELIGIONS

Because of its Spanish heritage, Texas originally was entirely Roman Catholic except for unconverted Indians. Consequently the early history of Texas is almost identical with that of the Roman Catholic Church in the area. Under the Mexican Republic, the Catholic Church continued as the sole recognized religious body. In order to receive the generous land grants given by the Mexicans, Anglo-American immigrants had to sign a paper saying that they followed the Catholic religion. With an average grant of 4,605 acres (1,864 hectares) as bait, many early Protestants and atheists must have felt little hesitancy about becoming instant Catholics.

The Mexican government was careless about enforcing adherence to the Catholic faith in Texas, however, and many Baptists, Methodists, and Presbyterians drifted in from the east. The Methodist practice of having itinerant ministers range over frontier areas was particularly well suited to the Texas scene, and in 1837 the church hierarchy sent three preachers to the new republic. The first presbytery had been formed by that date, and Baptists had organized in Houston by 1840. Swedish and German immigrants brought their Lutheranism with them; the first German Lutheran synod was organized in Houston in 1851.

Geographically, Texas tends to be heavily Protestant in the north and east, and Catholic in the south and southwest. Leading Protestant denominations and their known adherents in 1971 were Southern Baptist Convention, 2,362,851; United Methodist Church, 855,733; Episcopal Church, 175,694; Presbyterian Church in the US, 147,194; Christian Church (Disciples of Christ), 117,597; Lutheran Church–Missouri Synod, 109,616; American Lutheran Church, 105,798; and Baptist Missionary Association of America, 104,751. Smaller evangelical denominations include the Church of the Nazarene, Assembly of God, and Church of the Brethren. Roman Catholics numbered 2,324,150 in 1979, when there were an estimated 71,515 Jews.

¹⁰TRANSPORTATION

Texas ranks 1st among the 50 states in total railroad mileage, highway mileage, and number of airports, and 2d only to California in motor vehicle registrations and in number of general aviation aircraft.

Transportation has been a severe problem for Texas because of the state's extraordinary size and sometimes difficult terrain; one of the more unusual experiments in US transport history was the use of camels in southwestern Texas during the mid-1800s. The Republic of Texas authorized railroad construction as early as 1836, but the financial panic of 1837 helped kill that attempt. Not until 1853 did the state's first railroad—from Harrisburg (now incorporated into Houston) to Stafford's Point, 20 mi (32 km) to the west—come into service. At the outbreak of the Civil War, 10 railroads were operating, all but 2 connected with seaports. Texas lacked sufficient capital to satisfy its railroad-building needs until the war was over, although the state legislature in 1852 had offered railroad companies eight sections (5,120 acres—2,072 hectares) of land per mile of road construction and doubled that offer two years later; the state generally held to the 10,240-acre (4,144 hectare) figure until all grants ceased in 1882. In all, Texas granted more than 50,000 sq mi (130,000 sq km) to railroad companies.

In 1870, Texas had fewer than 600 mi (960 km) of track; 10 years later it had 3,026 mi (4,870 km); in 1890, 6,045 mi (9,729 km); and by 1920, 16,049 mi (25,828 km). A peak was reached in 1932, when there were 17,078 mi (27,484 km) of track; by 1978, the trackage had dwindled to 13,035 mi (20,978 km). Three carriers—the Atchison, Topeka & Santa Fe, Missouri-Pacific, and Southern Pacific—control about three-fourths of the mileage. The only rail passenger service in Texas is provided by Amtrak, which runs three routes—roughly, from the Mexican border at Laredo, past Ft. Worth and Dallas, to Texarkana; from Beaumont through Houston and San Antonio to El Paso; and from Houston northwest to Temple. In 1977, Amtrak carried 274,046 passengers within Texas. Operating revenues of all railroads reached $1.4 billion (net revenues, $321.6 million) in 1977, when 242.3 million tons of freight were hauled. Texas has no commuter rail service. Ft. Worth has the state's only true subway—a 1-mi (1.6-km) line from a parking lot to a downtown shopping and office center—although Dallas–Ft. Worth Regional Airport has its own rail shuttle system.

In 1978, Texas had 262,059 mi (421,744 km) of roadway, 77% of it surfaced. The leading interstate highways are I-10 and I-20, respectively linking Houston and the Dallas–Ft. Worth areas with El Paso in the west, and I-35 and I-45, connecting Dallas–Ft. Worth with, respectively, San Antonio (via Austin) and Galveston (via Houston). There were 8,568,930 licensed drivers in 1978, as well as 10,370,510 registered vehicles, including 7,349,070 passenger cars, 218,966 motorcycles, and 2,770,884 trucks. Trucking is vital to the Texas economy because more than 1,800 communities are served by no other carrier freight.

River transport did not become commercially successful until the end of the 19th century, when the Houston Ship Channel was dredged along the San Jacinto River and Buffalo Bayou for more than 50 mi (80 km), and another channel was dredged down the Neches River to make a seaport out of Beaumont. With 13 major seaports and many shallow-water ports, Texas has been a major factor in waterborne commerce since the early 1950s. In 1977, Texas ports handled 315,315,824 tons of cargo, 33% of that by the Port of Houston, among the nation's three most active harbors. The Gulf Intracoastal Waterway begins in Brownsville, at the mouth of the Rio Grande, and extends across Texas for 423 mi (681 km) on its way to Florida and its connections with a similar waterway on the Atlantic. In 1977, the waterway transported 66,276,822 tons of cargo.

After American entry into World War I, Texas began to build airfields for training grounds; when the war ended, many US fliers returned to Texas and became civilian commercial pilots, carrying air mail (from 1926), dusting crops, and mapping potential oil fields. In 1979, the Texas Aeronautics Commission reported that the state had approximately 1,500 landing facilities—including 265 public and 261 private airports, 792 private farm and ranch airstrips, and 174 heliports—56,500 active pilots, and more than 13,000 aircraft. Air passenger service was available from 34 cities by 13 trunk and local service carriers, 8 foreign-flag air carriers, one intrastate air carrier, and 13 commuter air carriers. The Dallas–Ft. Worth Regional Airport, the nation's largest air terminal and its 12th-busiest in 1979, services about half of the aircraft departures in Texas, with another fourth handled by Houston Intercontinental Airport. Texas airports emplaned a combined total of 18,241,029 passengers on 315,992 departing aircraft in 1978.

[11] HISTORY

Although a site near Lewisville, in Denton County, contains artifacts that might be more than 37,000 years old, the generally accepted date for the earliest human presence in the region now known as Texas is the Llano civilization, dating from 12,000 years ago. Prehistoric Indians in Texas failed to develop as high a civilization as their neighbors to the west and east. When the first Europeans arrived in the 16th century, the Indians had developed little in the way of pottery or basketry, and had shown little aptitude for agriculture except in the extreme east and northeast, and possibly west of the Pecos. They were still largely hunter-gatherers on whom the more advanced culture of Mexico and the southeastern US had little effect.

Along the Gulf coast and overlapping into northeastern Mexico were the Coahuiltecan and Karankawa peoples, existing in a "cultural sink," so-called because anthropologists know little about their antecedents except that they were backward. They lived in a hostile environment, consuming berries in season, animal dung, spiders, and an occasional deer, bison, or javelina that had surrendered to time or been encircled by fire. In central Texas lived the Tonkawa, who hunted buffalo, slept in tepees, used dogs for hauling, and had a communal sensitivity akin to that of the Plains Indians. Unlike the Karankawa, who were tall, the Tonkawa were of average height, tattooed, and dressed in breechclouts—long for men, short for women. They proved extraordinarily susceptible to European diseases and evidently died out, whereas the Karankawa migrated to northern Mexico.

About two dozen tribes of Caddo in eastern and northeastern Texas were, at the time of European penetration, the most advanced Indians living within the state's present borders. Having developed agriculture, the Caddo were relatively sedentary and village oriented. Those belonging to the Hasinai Confederation called each other *tayshas*, a term that translates as "allies" or "friends." When the Hasinai told Spanish explorers that they were *tayshas*, the white men wrote the word as *Tejas*, which in time became *Texas*. The Caddo lived in the gentle portion of Texas, where woods, wild fruits, and berries abound, and where

game was plentiful until the advent of European civilization. Life was so good, in fact, that several members of an expedition under Robert Cavelier, Sieur de la Salle, reaching Matagorda Bay on 15 February 1685, chose to desert to the Caddo rather than remain with their fellow Frenchmen. Henri de Tonti, who entered the region somewhat later, reported that one Caddo tribe had a woman as chief. The Caddo were also unusual in their belief that three women, and not a single male deity, had created the world.

In trans-Pecos Texas, to the west, lived a fourth Indian group, the Jumano, probably descendants of the Pueblo culture. Some of the Jumano were nomadic hunters in the Davis and Chisos mountains. Others became farmers along the Rio Grande and the lower Rio Conchos, making and using some pottery and raising good crops of corn, beans, squash, and possibly cotton. Probably the successive droughts so common to the region began to thin out their ranks, and the coming of the Spanish removed them from the historical picture altogether.

The first white man to enter Texas was Spanish explorer Alonso Alvarez de Pineda, who sailed into the mouth of the Rio Grande in 1519. Basically, the Spanish left the Texas Indians alone for more than 150 years. Sometimes an accident placed Spaniards in Texas, or sometimes they entered by design, but generally the Spanish looked on Texas as too remote from Florida and the Mexico highlands—where most of their colonizing occurred—for successful settlement. A remarkable episode of this period involves the survivors of the Pánfilo de Narváez expedition, which had been commissioned to occupy the Gulf of Mexico coast from Mexico to Florida. Four shipwrecked men, led by Álvar Núñez Cabeza de Vaca, were washed ashore on a Texas sandbar on 6 November 1528; three were Spaniards, and one was the Moor Estevanico. For eight years they wandered virtually naked among the Texas Indians, sometimes as slaves and sometimes as free men, alternately blistered by the summer sun and freezing under winter ice storms. Using a deer bone as a needle, Cabeza removed an arrowhead from deep in an Indian's chest—a bit of surgical magic that earned him treatment as a demigod, for a time. Finally, the four Europeans reached the west coast of Mexico, from where Cabeza de Vaca returned home a hero. The other two Spaniards remained in Mexico, but Estevanico joined the Fray Marcos de Niza expedition as a guide, dying at the hands of Pueblo Indians in New Mexico in 1539. The trail he helped blaze through the High Plains of West Texas served as the route for the expedition a year later by Francisco Vásquez de Coronado. The first Texas towns and missions were begun by Spaniards in West Texas, outside present-day El Paso. Ysleta del Sur was founded in 1682, almost a decade before the earliest East Texas missions. But Ysleta was 500 mi (800 km) from anything else resembling a settlement in Texas, and the Spanish considered it a part of New Mexico.

What changed the Spaniards' attitude toward the colonization of Texas was the establishment of Ft. St. Louis by La Salle on the Gulf coast in 1685. Four years later, Captain Alonso de León, governor of Coahuila, sent out an expedition to expel the French. Father Damien Massanet, a Coahuilan priest, accompanied the León expedition and was charged with establishing a mission near wherever the captain built a fort. During the next several decades, these two men and their successors established a string of mission-forts across Texas. After fear of the French presence eased, Spain tended to neglect these establishments. But when the French entered Louisiana in force during the early 18th century, Spanish fears of French expansion were reignited. In 1718, the Spanish began to build a mission, San Antonio de Valero, and a fort, San Antonio de Bexar, at the site of the present city of San Antonio. As a halfway post between Mexico and the Louisiana border, San Antonio grew to be Texas's most important city during the Spanish period.

Until the 19th century, the US showed little interest in Texas. But the purchase of Louisiana Territory from the French by the US government in 1803 made Texas a next-door neighbor, and "filibusters" (military adventurers) began to filter across the border into Spanish territory. The best-known is Philip Nolan, an Irish-born intriguer who started spending time in Texas as early as 1790. Ostensibly, he was trading horses with the Indians, but the Spanish associated him with Aaron Burr's schemes to excise the Spanish southwest from its owners. In the summer of 1800, the Spanish governor of Texas, Juan Bautista Elguezábal, ordered that Nolan should be arrested if he returned. In December of that year, Nolan returned with a small force of 20 men and built a fort near Nacogdoches; he was killed fighting the Spanish on 4 March 1801. Nolan is remembered for having drafted the first Anglo-American map of Texas.

In 1810–11, the Mexicans launched their revolution against Spain, and though only an outpost, Texas as a Spanish-Mexican colony was naturally involved. In 1813, Texas formally declared its independence of Spain and its intention of becoming a Mexican state, with its capital at San Antonio. Various Anglo-Americans entered the new state to serve on behalf of Mexico. Pirates also aided the Mexican cause: on Galveston Island, Luis Aury preyed on Spanish shipping, and after 1816 his place was taken by Jean Laffite, who privateered against both Spanish and US shipping until the US Navy drove him out.

The Spanish finally gave up on Mexico in 1821, leaving Texas as a Mexican province with a non-Indian population of about 7,000. The only towns of significant size were Goliad, San Antonio (commonly called Bexar), and Nacogdoches. A year earlier, Moses Austin of Missouri had received permission from Spanish authorities to introduce Anglo-American colonists into Texas, presumably as a barrier against aggression by the US. When Spanish rule ended, his son, Stephen F. Austin, succeeded his late father as head of the colonization movement, securing permission from the new Mexican government to settle 300 families in the area between the lower Colorado and Brazos rivers. After Austin had settled his "Old Three Hundred" in 1821, he received permission to settle more, and within a decade his colonists numbered more than 5,000. The Mexicans invested Austin with the responsibilities and privileges of an *empresario*: authority to run commerce, maintain militia, administer justice, and hand out land titles. Other *empresarios* made similar arrangements. Green DeWitt, also of Missouri, settled several hundred families farther west and founded the town of Gonzales in 1825. Hayden Edwards received a grant to settle 800 families near Nacogdoches. Mexicans were also permitted to organize colonies. Texas thus began a pattern of growth from the outside that has continued to the present day.

Between 1821 and 1835, the population of non-Indian Texas expanded to between 35,000 and 50,000. Most new settlers were Anglo-Americans who brought their prejudices against Mexico with them, whether they were from the South or the North. They could not stomach Mexican culture, Mexican folkways, Mexican justice—and the Protestants among them disliked the omnipresence of the Roman Catholic Church. All of these Anglo-American settlers had ties to the US, and many undoubtedly longed for the time when they would live under the American flag again. The ineptitude of the Mexican government made the situation even worse. In 1826, Hayden Edwards organized the Republic of Fredonia and tried to drive the Mexicans from East Texas, but in the end he had to flee the province himself. Troubled by the rising spirit of rebellion, the Mexican Congress enacted the Law of 1830, which forbade most immigration and imposed duties on all imports. Anglo-Americans in Texas responded with the same anger that New Englanders had once shown when Britain imposed tax restrictions on the original American colonies.

At first, the Anglo-Texans insisted they were opposing Mexican political excesses, not the Mexican nation. Their hope lay with General Antonio López de Santa Anna, who was leading a liberal revolution against President Anastasio Bustamante. Skirmishes between the Anglo-Texans and Mexican officials remained sporadic and localized until 1833, when Santa Anna became president of Mexico and almost immediately dropped his liberal stance. Texans sent Austin to Mexico City to petition Santa Anna to rescind the Law of 1830, to allow the use of English in public business, and to make Texas (then an appendage of Coahuila) a separate state. After several months in Mexico City, Austin was arrested on his way back to Texas and was imprisoned for a year. When Santa Anna tried to enforce customs collections, colonists at Anahuac, led by William Barret Travis, drove the Mexican officials out of town. Santa Anna's answer was to place Texas under military jurisdiction. When the Mexican military commander, Colonel Domingo de Ugartechea, sent his soldiers to Gonzales to take a cannon there from the colonists, the Anglo-Texan civilians drove them off on 2 October 1835, in a battle that is generally considered to mark the start of the Texas Revolution.

On 3 November, a provisional government was formed. It called not for independence but for a return to the liberal Mexican constitution of 1824. Three commissioners, one of them Austin, were sent to Washington, D.C., to ask aid from the US. Sam Houston, who only six years earlier had resigned the governorship of Tennessee (when his wife left him) and had come to Texas after stays in Oklahoma and Arkansas, was named commander in chief of the upstart Texas army. Hostilities remained at a standstill until February 1836, when Santa Anna led an army across the Rio Grande. The Mexicans concentrated outside San Antonio at a mission-fort called the Alamo, where 187 or so Texans, commanded by Colonel William Barret Travis, had holed up in defense. The Mexicans besieged the Alamo until 6 March, when Santa Anna's forces, now numbering more than 4,000, stormed the fortress. When the battle ended, all the Alamo's defenders, including several native Mexicans, were dead. Among those killed were Travis and two Americans who became legends—James Bowie and Davy Crockett.

Four days before the battle of the Alamo, other Texans gathered at Washington-on-the-Brazos and issued a declaration of independence. As so often happens, a fight that had started on principle—in this case, a constitutional issue—grew into a fight for independence. The men who died at the Alamo believed they were fighting for restoration of the constitution of 1824. But three weeks after the Alamo fell, on 27 March 1836, the Mexicans killed 342 Texans who had surrendered at Goliad, thinking they would be treated as prisoners of war. Coming on the heels of the Alamo tragedy, the "Goliad massacre" persuaded Texans that only total victory or total defeat would solve their problems with Santa Anna. The Texas army under Sam Houston retreated before Santa Anna's oncoming forces, which held a numerical advantage over Houston's of about 1,600 to 800. On 21 April 1836, however, the Texans surprised the Mexicans during their siesta period at San Jacinto (east of present-day Houston). Mexican losses were 630 killed, 280 wounded, and 730 taken prisoner, while the Texans had only 9 killed and 30 wounded. This decisive battle—fought to the cry of "Remember the Alamo, remember Goliad!"—freed Texas from Mexico once and for all.

For 10 years, Texas existed as an independent republic, recognized by the US, Belgium, France, the United Kingdom, the Netherlands, and several German states. Sam Houston, the victorious commander at San Jacinto, became the republic's first nationally elected president. Although Texans are proud of their once-independent status, the fact is that the republic limped along like any new nation, strife-torn and short of cash. It was unable to reach agreement with Mexico on a treaty to clarify the border. Moreover, its original $1 million public debt increased eightfold in a decade, and its paper money depreciated alarmingly. Consequently, when Texas joined the Union on 29 December 1845, the date of the US congressional resolution recognizing the new state (the Lone Star flag, the republic's official banner, was not actually lowered and a governor inaugurated until 19 February 1846), its citizens looked on the action as a rescue. The annexation in great measure provoked the Mexican War, which in turn led to the conclusion of the Treaty of Guadalupe Hidalgo on 2 February 1848. Under the treaty, Mexico dropped its claim to the territory between the Rio Grande and the Nueces River. Later, by the Compromise of 1850, Texas relinquished for $10 million its claim on lands stretching into New Mexico, Colorado, Wyoming, Oklahoma, and Kansas.

With the coming of the Civil War, Texas followed its proslavery southern neighbors out of the Union into the Confederacy; Governor Houston, who opposed secession, was ousted from office. The state saw little fighting, and Texas thus suffered from the war far less than most of the South. The last battle of the war was fought on Texas soil at Palmito Ranch, near Brownsville, on 13 May 1865—more than a month after General Robert E. Lee's surrender at Appomattox Court House in Virginia.

During Reconstruction, Texas was governed briefly by a military occupation force and then by a Republican regime; the so-called carpetbag constitution of 1869, passed during this period, gave the franchise to blacks, a right that the Ku Klux Klan actively sought to deny them. Texas was allowed to rejoin the Union on 30 March 1870. Three years later, Republican Governor Edmund J. Davis was defeated at the polls by Richard Coke, and a Democratic legislature wrote a new constitution which was approved by the voters in 1876.

While most southern states were economically prostrate, the Texas economy flourished because of the rapid development of the cattle industry. Millions of Texas cattle walked the trails to northern markets, where they were sold for hard cash, providing a bonanza for the state. The widespread use of barbed wire to fence cattle ranches in the 1880s ended the open range and encouraged scientific cattle breeding. By 1900, Texas began to transform its predominantly agricultural economy to an industrial one. This process was accelerated by the discovery of the Spindletop oil field—the state's first gusher—near Beaumont in 1901, and by the subsequent development of the petroleum and petrochemical industries. World War I saw the emergence of Texas as a military training center. The rapid growth of the aircraft industry and other high-technology fields contributed to the continuing industrialization of Texas during and after World War II.

Texas politics remained solidly Democratic during most of the modern era, and the significant political conflict in the state was between the liberal and conservative wings of the Democratic Party. Populist-style reforms were enacted slowly during the governorships of James E. Ferguson—impeached and removed from office during his second term in 1917—and of his wife, Miriam A. "Ma" Ferguson (1925–27, 1933–35), and more rapidly during the two administrations of James V. Allred (1935–39). During the 1960s and 1970s, the Republican Party gathered strength in the state, electing John G. Tower as US senator in 1961 and William P. Clements, Jr., as governor in 1978—the first Republicans to hold those offices since Reconstruction. In general, the state's recent political leaders, Democrats as well as Republicans, have represented property interests and taken a conservative line.

On the national level, Texans have been influential since the 1930s, notably through such congressional leaders as US House Speaker Sam Rayburn and Senate Majority Leader Lyndon B. Johnson. Johnson, elected vice president under John F. Kennedy, was riding in the motorcade with the president when Kennedy was assassinated in Dallas on 22 November 1963. The city at-tained further national notoriety when Kennedy's alleged killer, Lee Harvey Oswald, was shot to death by Jack Ruby, a Dallas nightclub operator, two days later. Johnson served out the remainder of Kennedy's term, was elected to the presidency by a landslide in 1964, and presided over one of the stormiest periods in US history before retiring to his LBJ ranch in 1969. Memorials to him include the Lyndon B. Johnson Library at Austin and the renamed Lyndon B. Johnson Space Center, headquarters for the US manned spaceflight program, near Houston.

12 STATE GOVERNMENT
Texas has been governed directly under eight constitutions: the Mexican national constitution of 1824, the Coahuila-Texas state constitution of 1827, the independent Republic of Texas constitution of 1836, and the five US state constitutions of 1845, 1861, 1866, 1869, and 1876. This last document, with more than 200 amendments, is the foundation of state government today. An attempt to replace it with eight propositions that would, in effect, have given Texas a new constitution was defeated at the polls in November 1975.

The state legislature consists of a senate of 31 members elected to four-year terms, and a house of representatives of 150 members elected to two-year terms. The legislature meets on the 2d Tuesday in January of odd-numbered years for sessions of unlimited duration; the governor may also call special sessions. Senators and representatives receive the same pay, pursuant to a constitutional amendment of 1975: $600 per month and $30 per diem while the legislature is in session. The constitution requires that senators be 26 years of age and residents of the state for five years prior to election; for representatives, the requirements are 21 years of age and two years of residency.

The state's chief executives are the governor and lieutenant governor, separately elected to four-year terms. Other elected executives, also serving for four years, are the attorney general, comptroller, treasurer, commissioner of agriculture, and commissioner of the general land office. The remaining cabinet members are appointed by the governor, who also appoints members of the many executive boards and commissions. The governor, whose salary was $71,400 as of 1979, must be a US citizen, at least 30 years of age, and must have resided in the state for at least five years prior to election. A uniquely important executive agency is the Texas Railroad Commission, established in 1891 and consisting of three members, elected for six-year terms, who regulate the state's oil and gas production, coal and uranium mining, and trucking industry, in addition to the railroads. The commission thus wields extraordinary economic power, and the alleged influence by the regulated industries over the commission was a major source of political controversy as the 1980s began.

To become law, a bill must be approved by at least 16 senators and 76 representatives, and either signed by the governor or left unsigned for 10 days while the legislature is in session or 20 days after it has adjourned. A gubernatorial veto may be overridden by a two-thirds vote of each house, but such action is rare: the vote in April 1979 by state legislators to override the governor's veto of a minor wildlife regulation measure affecting only one county was the first successful attempt in 38 years. A constitutional amendment requires a two-thirds vote of each house and ratification by the voters at the next election.

In order to vote in Texas, one must be a US citizen and 18 years of age or over; there is a 30-day residency requirement.

13 POLITICAL PARTIES
The Democratic Party has dominated politics in Texas. William P. Clements, Jr., elected governor in 1978, is the first Republican since Reconstruction to hold that office. No Republican carried Texas in a presidential election until 1928, when Herbert Hoover defeated Democrat Al Smith, a Roman Catholic at a severe disadvantage in a Protestant fundamentalist state. Another Roman

Catholic, Democratic Presidential candidate John Kennedy, carried the state in 1960 largely because he had a Texan, Lyndon Johnson, on his ticket.

Prior to the Civil War, many candidates for statewide office ran as independents. After a period of Republican rule during Reconstruction, Democrats won control of the statehouse and state legislature in 1873. The major challenge to Democratic rule during the late 19th century came not from Republicans but from the People's Party, whose candidates placed second in the gubernatorial races of 1894, 1896, and 1898, aided by the collapse of the cotton market; imposition of a poll tax in 1902 helped disfranchise the poor white farmers and laborers who were the base of Populist support. The Populists and the Farmers' Alliance probably exercised their greatest influence through a Democratic reformer, Governor James S. Hogg (1891–95), who fought the railroad magnates, secured lower freight rates for farmers and shippers, and curbed the power of large landholding companies. Another Democratic governor, James E. "Farmer Jim" Ferguson, was elected on an agrarian reform platform in 1914 and reelected in 1916, but was impeached and convicted the following year for irregular financial dealings. Barred form holding state office, he promoted the candidacy of his wife, Miriam "Ma" Ferguson, whose first term as governor (1925–27) marked her as a formidable opponent of the Ku Klux Klan. During her second term (1933–35), the state's first New Deal reforms were enacted, and prohibition was repealed. The Fergusons came to represent the more liberal wing of the Democratic Party in a state where liberals have long been in the minority. After the progressive administration of Governor James V. Allred, during which the state's first old-age assistance program was enacted, conservative Democrats, sometimes called "Texas Tories," controlled the state until the late 1970s.

There is no voter registration by party in Texas; as of 1979, the state had 5,700,828 registered voters. In 1978, Clements was elected governor by a margin of less than 70,000 out of nearly 2,370,000 votes cast. Two years later, Texans gave the Republican presidential ticket of Ronald Reagan and George Bush (a longtime state resident and a US representative from Texas for two terms, beginning in 1967) a 55% majority of the popular vote. Democrats retained control of the state legislature, however, and won 19 of 24 US House seats—although the most liberal

member of the state's congressional delegation, Bob Eckhardt, a Harris County Democrat, lost to a young Republican conservative, Jack Fields.

Aside from the Populists, third parties have played a minor role in Texas politics. The Native American (Know-Nothing) Party helped elect Sam Houston governor in 1859. The best showing by a third-party candidate in a presidential election was in 1968, when George Wallace of the American Independent Party won 19% of the Texas popular vote.

Following passage of the federal Voting Rights Act of 1965, registration of black voters increased from about 375,000 in 1964 to 640,000 in 1976. Between 1895 and 1967, no black person served as a state legislator; by 1979, however, there were 14 black representatives. During the same year, 4 Mexican-Americans served in the senate and 17 in the house; 1 woman was in the senate, 11 in the house.

¹⁴LOCAL GOVERNMENT

The Texas constitution grants considerable autonomy to local governments. As of 1980, Texas had 254 counties, more than 1,000 cities and towns, about 1,100 school districts (down from 8,600 in 1910), and at least 1,400 special districts.

Each county is governed by a commissioners court of five members, consisting of four commissioners elected by precinct and a county judge or administrator elected at large. Other elected officials generally include a county clerk, attorney, treasurer, assessor-collector, and sheriff.

The 1970 census counted 219 cities having more than 5,000 population and thus entitled by law to adopt their own home-rule charters. As of June 1979, 138 cities had adopted the council-manager form of government, 47 had the commissioner-manager type, 25 had mayors and/or councils, and most of the remainder were governed by some form of commission.

In 1979, Texas had 24 regional councils consisting of representatives from two or more counties. The councils develop regional plans and seek to eliminate duplication and to promote economy and efficiency in local governments.

¹⁵STATE SERVICES

For a state of its size and population, Texas provides rather limited statewide services to its citizens. Texas has no ombudsman, ethics commission, consumer protection division, department of housing, or unified environmental protection agency.

Texas Presidential Vote by Political Parties, 1948–80

YEAR	ELECTORAL VOTE	TEXAS WINNER	DEMOCRAT	REPUBLICAN	STATES' RIGHTS DEMOCRAT	PROGRESSIVE	PROHIBITION
1948	23	*Truman (D)	750,700	282,240	106,909	3,764	2,758
					CONSTITUTION		
1952	24	*Eisenhower (R)	969,227	1,102,818	1,563	—	1,983
1956	24	*Eisenhower (R)	859,958	1,080,619	14,591	—	—
1960	24	*Kennedy (D)	1,167,935	1,121,693	18,170	—	3,868
1964	25	*Johnson (D)	1,663,185	958,566	5,060	—	—
					AMERICAN IND.		
1968	25	Humphrey (D)	1,266,804	1,227,844	584,269	—	—
					AMERICAN	SOC. WORKERS	
1972	26	*Nixon (R)	1,154,289	2,298,896	6,039	8,664	—
1976	26	*Carter (D)	2,082,319	1,953,300	11,442	1,723	—
					LIBERTARIAN		
1980	26	*Reagan (R)	1,881,147	2,510,705	37,643	—	—

*Won US presidential election.

Educational services in the public schools are administered by the Texas Education Agency, which is run by a commissioner of education appointed by a 24-member elected Board of Education; the State Textbook Committee, appointed by the board, oversees textbook purchases statewide. The Coordinating Board for the State College and University System, consisting of 18 appointed members, oversees public higher education. Transportation facilities are regulated by the State Highway and Public Transportation Commission, the Texas Railroad Commission, and the Texas Aeronautics Commission.

Health and welfare services are offered by the Department of Health and Department of Human Resources, while public protection is the responsibility of the National Guard, Department of Corrections, and Texas Youth Council, which maintains institutions for juvenile offenders. Labor services are provided by the Texas Employment Commission and Department of Labor and Standards.

[16] JUDICIAL SYSTEM

The Texas judiciary comprises the supreme court, the court of criminal appeals, 14 courts of civil appeals, and more than 300 district courts.

The highest court is the supreme court, consisting of a chief justice and eight associate justices, who are popularly elected to staggered six-year terms. As of 1979, each justice received a salary of $51,400 annually, and the chief justice earned $500 more. The court of criminal appeals, which has final jurisdiction in most criminal cases, consists of a presiding judge and eight associate judges, also elected to six-year terms. Appeals court judges' salaries were the same as those of supreme court justices in 1979.

Justices of the courts of civil appeals are elected to six-year terms and sit in 14 judicial districts; each court has a chief justice and at least two associate justices. Chief justices received annual salaries from the state of $45,900 in 1979, and each associate was paid $45,400; counties may supplement these salaries, but the total remuneration must be at least $1,000 less than justices of the higher courts receive.

In 1979 there were 330 district court judges, each elected to a four-year term. They received state salaries of $35,700, plus supplemental payments by local subdivisions. County, justice of the peace, and police courts handle local matters.

The state maintains 15 correctional institutions housing some 25,000 adult offenders. The maintenance cost to taxpayers in 1978 was $7.15 per inmate daily, $0.30 less than in 1976, one of the lowest rates in the nation; costs for inmate care are offset by income from the units' farm and livestock operations.

Texas has a high crime rate—substantially above the national average for murder, forcible rape, burglary, and larceny-theft, though below average for robbery, assault, and motor vehicle theft. Overall, according to the FBI Crime Index, Texas had a crime rate of 5,557 per 100,000 population, 435 for violent crimes and 5,122 for property crimes. Rates for specific crimes were murder, 14.2; forcible rape, 37.9; robbery, 164; aggravated assault, 219; burglary, 1,612; larceny-theft, 3,065; and motor vehicle theft, 444. Among major cities, Dallas's violent crime rate, 1,134 in 1978, was 55% higher than Houston's and nearly three times San Antonio's.

Texas criminal law provides for capital punishment by lethal intravenous injection for certain violent crimes.

[17] ARMED FORCES

In few states do US military forces and defense-related industries play such a large role as in Texas, which in 1978 had 134,256 military personnel and 58,317 civilians employed at major US military bases. During the same year, Texas ranked 2d only to California in the value of defense contract awards, worth more than $4.9 billion, or 8% of the US total.

Ft. Sam Houston, at San Antonio, is headquarters of the US 5th Army, while Ft. Bliss, at El Paso, is the home of the US Army Air Defense Center. Ft. Hood, near Killeen, is headquarters of the 3d Army Corps and other military units; with more than 46,000 military personnel in 1978, it is the state's largest single defense installation. Ft. Sam Houston is also the headquarters of the US Army Health Service Command and the site of the Academy of Health Sciences, the largest US military medical school, enrolling more than 25,000 officers and enlisted personnel and providing correspondence courses for another 30,000 students. Brooke Army Medical Center, the 2d-largest Army hospital in the US, is located at the same installation. William Beaumont Army Medical Center, at El Paso, is one of the nation's largest Army hospitals and most modern medical treatment centers.

Four principal Air Force bases are located near San Antonio: Brooks, Kelly, Lackland, and Randolph. Other major air bases are Bergstrom, near Austin; Carswell, Ft. Worth; Dyess, Abilene; Ellington, southwest of Houston; Goodfellow, San Angelo; Laughlin, Del Rio; Reese, Lubbock; and Sheppard, Wichita Falls. All US manned spaceflights are controlled from the Lyndon B. Johnson Space Center, operated by the National Aeronautics and Space Administration. Naval air training stations are located at Corpus Christi, Beeville, Dallas, and Kingsville. The Inactive Ships Maintenance Facility, at Orange, is home port for some of the US Navy's "mothball fleet."

Texas was a major military training center during World War II, when about 1 out of every 10 soldiers was trained there. Some 750,000 Texans served in the US armed forces during that war; the state's war dead numbered 23,022. Military veterans living in the state as of 30 September 1979 totaled 1,660,000, including 29,000 who served in World War I, 698,000 in World War II, 316,000 during the Korean conflict, and 514,000 during the Viet-Nam era. Expenditures on Texas veterans exceeded $1.3 billion in 1977/78, including $672.8 million for compensation and pensions and $258.6 million for education and training.

The Texas Army National Guard has dual status as a federal and state military force; its authorized strength was 17,800 as of April 1979. The Air Force National Guard had 3,300 personnel, and the Texas State Guard—an all-volunteer force available either to back up National Guard units or to respond to local emergencies—had some 2,500 members.

The famous Texas Rangers, a state police force first employed in 1823 (though not formally organized until 1835) to protect the early settlers, served as scouts for the US Army during the Mexican War. Many individual Rangers fought with the Confederacy in the Civil War; during Reconstruction, however, the Rangers were used to enforce unpopular carpetbagger laws. Later, the Rangers put down banditry on the Rio Grande. The force was reorganized in 1935 as a unit of the Department of Public Safety and is now called on in major criminal cases, helps control mob violence in emergencies, and sometimes assists local police officers. The Rangers have been romanticized in fiction and films, but one of their less glamorous tasks has been to intervene in labor disputes on the side of management. In 1977, Texas had a total of 30,354 state and local police employees; expenditures on police protection totaled $455 million, 78% of that for departments at the local level.

[18] MIGRATION

Estimates of the number of Indians living in Texas when the first Europeans arrived range from 30,000 to 130,000. Eventually they all were killed, fled southward or westward, or were removed to reservations. The first great wave of white settlers, beginning in 1821, came from nearby southern states, particularly Tennessee, Alabama, Arkansas, and Mississippi; some of these newcomers brought their black slaves to work in the cotton fields. During the 1840s, a second wave of immigrants arrived directly from Germany, France, and eastern Europe.

Interstate migration during the second half of the 19th century was accelerated by the Homestead Act of 1862 and the westward march of the railroads. Particularly notable since 1900 has been the intrastate movement from rural areas to the cities; this trend was especially pronounced from the end of World War II, when about half the state's population was rural, to the late 1970s, when nearly four out of every five Texans made their homes in metropolitan areas.

Texas's net gain from migration between 1940 and 1977 was 1,077,000, two-thirds of that during the 1970–77 period. This trend applied to whites much more than blacks, however; Texas lost 4,000 black residents through migration during the 1960s, before gaining 29,000 between 1970 and 1975. A significant proportion of postwar immigrants were seasonal laborers from Mexico, remaining in the US either legally or illegally.

[19]INTERGOVERNMENTAL COOPERATION

The Texas Advisory Commission on Intergovernmental Relations—including the lieutenant governor, the speaker of the state house of representatives, 3 state senators, and 3 representatives—works to improve coordination between state, local, and federal governments. The 19-member Texas Commission on Interstate Cooperation, similarly constituted but with greater legislative participation, represents Texas before the Council of State Governments. Texas is a member of the Interstate Mining Commission and Interstate Oil Compact Commission. The state is also a signatory to the Gulf States Marine Fisheries Compact, Southern Interstate Energy Compact, and Southern Regional Education Compact, and to accords apportioning the waters of the Canadian, Pecos, and Sabine rivers and the Rio Grande.

During 1978/79, Texas received an estimated $3.6 billion in federal aid, including a total of $336.7 million in general revenue sharing.

[20]ECONOMY

Traditionally, the Texas economy has been dependent on the production of cotton, cattle, timber, and petroleum. In recent years, cotton has declined in importance, cattle ranchers have suffered financial difficulties because of increased production costs, and lumber production has remained relatively stable. But in the 1970s, as a result of rising world petroleum prices, oil and natural gas emerged as by far the state's most important resource. The decades since World War II have also witnessed a boom in the electronics, computer, transport equipment, aerospace, and communications industries that have placed Texas 2d only to California in manufacturing among all the states of the Sunbelt region.

The Lone Star State's robust economy as the 1980s began was due chiefly to a plentiful labor market, high worker productivity, diversification of new industries, and less restrictive regulation of business activities than in most other states. The result has been a steady increase in industrial production, construction values, retail sales, and personal income, coupled with a relatively low rate of unemployment. Rapid industrial growth has exceeded the capital resources of the state banking system, however, making continued expansion dependent on investment capital from other states and abroad.

The booming economy enabled the state to surpass the $100-billion mark in annual personal income in 1978. That year, Texas ranked 3d among the 50 states in total personal income, but only 22d in income per capita. Sharp inequalities of income persist, and wages in manufacturing remain low, partly because of the relative weakness of the labor movement. One out of every five children was below the federal poverty level in 1975, and there are serious pockets of unemployment in cities bordering Mexico.

Among the most valuable manufactures are petroleum refinery products, chemicals, machinery, fabricated metals, electronic equipment, aircraft, and processed foods. Leading industrial

sites include the man-made Port of Houston and the aerospace plants in the Dallas–Ft. Worth area. The Lyndon B. Johnson Space Center, near Houston, is a center for the state's high-technology industries.

[21]INCOME

In 1978, Texas ranked 3d among the 50 states in personal income with $100.2 billion, or nearly 6% of the US total; per capita income during the same year reached $7,697, slightly below the national norm. The state's personal income enjoyed a real growth of 56% from 1970 to 1978, compared with the national growth average of 32%, while Texas's per capita income rank rose from 31st to 22d among the 50 states.

Major sources of personal income and their total contributions in the years 1976 and 1977 are represented in the following table (in millions):

	1976	1977
Total, of which:	$77,681	$87,279
Farm	1,198	1,183
Agricultural services, forestry, fisheries, and other	226	250
Mining	3,076	3,741
Construction	4,831	5,641
Manufacturing	11,863	13,599
Transportation and public utilities	4,732	5,450
Wholesale trade	4,997	5,595
Retail trade	6,618	7,492
Finance, insurance, and real estate	3,182	3,774
Services	9,114	10,312
Government	10,408	11,103
Dividends, interest, rent	11,565	13,021

Median family income in Texas averaged $12,672 in 1975, 34th among the 50 states and 10% below the US average. During the same year, 1,870,000 Texans in 381,000 families, many of them blacks and Mexican-Americans, were living below the federal poverty level; the totals represented 15% of all state residents and nearly 12% of all Texas families. Famed for its cattle barons and oil millionaires, Texas was the home of 563,200 of the nation's leading wealthholders in 1972 (the latest year for which statistics are available).

In 1977, about half the state's total personal income went to Texans living in the north-central region and on the Gulf Coast. Among metropolitan areas, the highest average per capita incomes went to residents of Midland, averaging $9,307 per person in 1977; Houston, $8,247; and Dallas–Ft. Worth, $7,704. The leading counties in 1977, distributed throughout the state, were Loving, $18,500; Kenedy, $12,166; and Glasscock, $11,977. The poorest counties, concentrated in south Texas along the Mexican border, were Starr, $2,515, and Maverick, $2,899.

[22]LABOR

With a civilian labor force of 5,994,000 in 1978, Texas ranked 3d among the 50 states; of that total, 59% were men and 41% women. More than 80% of males 16 years of age or older were in the labor force, and the female participation rate was over 51%; both rates exceeded the national average. In 1978, the number of unemployed workers averaged 288,000, or 4.8% of the labor force—the lowest unemployment rate of any highly industrialized state. The unemployment rate for males was only 3.7%; for females, 6.4%; and for all nonwhites, 9.5%. The largest number of unemployed persons lived in south Texas and the Rio Grande Valley; many of the unemployed and underemployed workers were Mexican aliens, some of them legal residents of the US, others not.

A federal census of workers covered by unemployment insurance in March 1977 revealed the following nonfarm employment pattern for Texas:

	ESTABLISH-MENTS	EMPLOYEES	ANNUAL PAYROLL ('000)
Agricultural services, forestry, fishing	2,766	16,181	$ 127,926
Mining, of which:	5,780	159,143	2,665,847
Oil, gas extraction	(5,193)	(121,042)	(1,933,248)
Contract construction	28,840	364,483	4,648,560
Manufacturing, of which:	16,302	908,883	11,939,947
Food and food products	(1,362)	(87,855)	(978,765)
Chemicals, allied products	(772)	(71,630)	(1,270,427)
Fabricated metals	(1,760)	(77,658)	(1,007,697)
Nonelectrical machinery	(2,523)	(112,960)	(1,595,049)
Electric, electronic equipment	(584)	(75,386)	(1,014,043)
Transport equipment	(571)	(63,360)	(963,997)
Transportation, public utilities	10,244	280,444	3,908,317
Wholesale trade	25,593	325,955	4,220,294
Retail trade	81,792	859,999	5,899,897
Finance, insurance, real estate	23,719	274,860	3,006,572
Services, of which:	74,599	791,747	6,722,073
Business services	(9,345)	(155,544)	(1,344,125)
Health services	(16,203)	(228,358)	(2,071,768)
Other	4,343	7,735	83,181
TOTALS	273,978	3,989,430	$43,222,614

Government workers, not covered by this survey, numbered 915,153 in 1978; 160,092 federal government employees earned wages exceeding $2.6 billion, while 755,061 state and local government employees earned wages of nearly $7.4 billion during the same year.

Organized labor has never been able to establish a strong base in Texas, and a state right-to-work law continues to make unionization difficult. The earliest national union, the Knights of Labor, declined in Texas after failing to win a strike against the railroads in 1886, when the Texas Rangers served as strikebreakers. That same year, the American Federation of Labor (AFL) began to organize workers along craft lines. One of the most protracted and violent disputes in Texas labor history occurred in 1935, when longshoremen struck Gulf Coast ports for 62 days. The Congress of Industrial Organizations (CIO) succeeded in organizing oil-field and maritime workers during the 1930s. As of 1976, labor union membership in the state totaled 563,000, of whom 84% belonged to unions affiliated with the AFL-CIO. The overall total represented 12% of the nonfarm work force—a very low percentage for a large industrial state. Another 131,000 Texans were members of employee associations. Manufacturing workers earned average weekly wages of $243 (average hourly wage, $5.88) in 1978, slightly below the US norm. Wage rates ranged from $9.95 an hour in brewing and $8.76 in petroleum refining to $3.52 in apparel and textiles and $3.40 in leather and leather products.

23 AGRICULTURE

Texas ranked 3d among the 50 states in agricultural production in 1978, with farm marketings totaling $7.9 billion; crops account for not quite two-fifths of the annual total. Texas leads the nation in output of cotton, grain sorghum, watermelons, cabbages, and spinach.

Since 1880, Texas has been the leading producer of cotton, which accounted for 35% of total US production and 37% of the state's crop sales in 1977. After 1900, Texas farmers developed bumper crops of wheat, corn, and other grains by irrigating dry land and transformed the "great Sahara" of West Texas into one of the nation's foremost grain-growing regions. Texans also raise practically every vegetable suited to a temperate or semitropical climate. Since World War II, farms have become fewer and larger, more specialized in raising certain crops and meat animals, more expensive to operate, and far more productive.

About 130 million acres (53 million hectares) are devoted to farms and ranches, representing more than three-fourths of the state's total area. The number of farms declined from 418,000 in 1940 to fewer than 160,000 in 1978, when the average farm was valued at $215,000. During the 1940–70 period, the farm population decreased from 2,160,000 persons to 471,000; as of 1978 there were 155,000 family workers and 82,000 hired laborers on Texas farms and ranches.

Productive farmland is located throughout the state. Grains are grown mainly in the temperate north and west, and vegetables and citrus fruits in the subtropical south. Cotton has been grown in all sections, but in recent years it has been extensively cultivated in the High Plains of the west and the upper Rio Grande Valley. Grain sorghum, wheat, corn, hay, and other forage crops are raised in the north-central and western plains regions. Rice is cultivated along the Gulf Coast, and soybeans are raised mainly in the High Plains and Red River Valley

Major crops in 1978 (except where indicated) are shown in the following table:

	HARVESTED ACREAGE ('000)	PRODUCTION	VALUE ('000)
Cotton, lint	6,200	3,800,000 bales	$1,046,976
Sorghum, grain	4,650	127,596,000 cwt	492,156
Corn	1,440	144,000,000 bushels	360,000
Hay	2,355	4,368,000 tons	233,688
Rice (1977)	501	23,400,000 cwt	223,470
Vegetables, fresh market	181	NA	213,907
Wheat	2,700	54,000,000 bushels	156,600
Soybeans	745	19,370,000 bushels	121,063

The leading vegetables, in terms of 1978 value, were onions, cabbages, potatoes, watermelons, cantaloupes, carrots, green peppers, lettuce, cucumbers, honeydew melons, and spinach. Cottonseed, barley, oats, peanuts, pecans, sugar beets, sugarcane, and sunflowers are also produced in commercial quantities.

Agribusiness contributed an estimated $30 billion to the economy in 1978. In that year, about 3% of all Texans whose livelihood was linked to agriculture worked on farms, while nearly 25% were engaged in marketing agricultural supplies and services. The total value of farmland, buildings, machinery, crop and livestock inventories, and other assets was estimated at $55 billion in 1979.

Irrigated land in 1978 totaled 8.9 million acres (3.6 million hectares), of which about 65% was in the High Plains; other areas dependent on irrigation included the lower Rio Grande Valley and the trans-Pecos region. Approximately 80% of the irrigated land is supplied with water pumped from wells. Because more than half of the state's irrigation pumps are fueled by natural gas, the cost of irrigation increased significantly as gas prices rose during the 1970s.

24 ANIMAL HUSBANDRY

Texas ranked 2d only to Iowa in livestock production, which contributed more than three-fifths of the state's total agricultural income. The state leads the US in output of cattle, goats, and sheep and lambs, and in the production of wool and mohair.

At the close of 1978, Texas had 13,900,000 head of cattle (12.5% of the US total), 310,000 milk cows, 2,415,000 sheep and lambs, 800,000 hogs, 1,360,000 goats, 16,800,000 chickens, and 475,000 turkeys. The combined value of all livestock was $5.1 billion, 75% more than in December 1977.

Cattle account for more than 90% of the farm value and about 70% of cash receipts from the sale of meat animals and livestock products. About 60% of cattle fattened for market are kept in feedlots located in the Texas panhandle and northwestern plains. The state's feedlots marketed 4,915,000 head of grain-fed cattle in 1978, about 18% of the US total. Meat animals slaughtered at 420 Texas plants in 1978 included 6,159,000 cattle, 428,000 calves, 1,062,000 hogs, 798,000 sheep and lambs, and 39,000 goats. Production of meat animals in 1979 included 5.1 billion lb of cattle and calves worth nearly $3.5 billion; 323.1 million lb of hogs and pigs, $128.3 million; and 114.5 million lb of sheep and lambs, $62.1 million.

About 90% of the dairy industry is located in eastern Texas. In 1979, milk production exceeded 3.4 million lb. Other dairy products included 22.9 million lb of cottage cheese and 38.8 million gallons of ice cream. Poultry sales, valued at more than $300 million, included 888 million lb of chickens and broilers and 7.3 million turkeys. Other livestock products in 1978 included wool, 18,500,000 lb; mohair, 8,100,000 lb; and honey, 8,695,000 lb.

Breeding of Palominos, Arabians, Appaloosas, Thoroughbreds, and quarter horses is a major industry in Texas. The animals are most abundant in the most heavily populated areas, and it is not unusual for residential subdivisions of metropolitan areas to include facilities for keeping and riding horses.

25 FISHING

Texas in 1978 recorded a commercial catch of 103.5 million lb (13th among the 50 states), valued at $148.9 million (5th). The leading commercial fishing ports are Brownsville–Port Isabel, Aransas Pass–Rockport, and Freeport.

Shrimp accounts for about 95% of the total value of the annual catch; other commercial shellfish include blue crabs, oysters, and squid. Species of saltwater fish with the greatest commercial value are sea trout, black drum, redfish, red snapper, and flounder. Early in 1980, the US government banned shrimp fishing for 45 days, effective in the summer of 1981, in order to conserve shrimp supplies. The future of the Texas fishing industry was placed further in doubt by the Mexican government's threat, revealed in December 1980, to renounce its fishing agreements with the US, including one governing the catch of red snapper and grouper in the Gulf of Mexico.

Sport fishing involves some 3 million Texans annually and pumps nearly $1 billion into local economies. Among the most sought-after native freshwater fish are large-mouth and white bass, crappie, sunfish, and catfish. In 1978, the Fisheries Division of the Texas Parks and Wildlife Department distributed 30 million walleye and more than 1 million striped bass to lakes and reservoirs.

26 FORESTRY

Texas forestland in 1977 covered 23,279,000 acres (9,421,000 hectares), representing more than 3% of the US total and about 14% of the state's land area. Commercial timberland comprised 12,513,000 acres (5,064,000 hectares), of which 94% was privately owned. Lands owned or managed by the federal government covered 740,000 acres (299,000 hectares), and state and local forestlands occupied 56,000 acres (23,000 hectares).

Most forested land, including practically all commercial timberland, is located in the Piney Woods region. In 1977, Texas timberlands yielded a harvest of 543,000,000 cu feet of softwoods and hardwoods; four of every five trees cut were pine. Primary forest products included 3,629,890 cords of pulpwood (87% softwood), more than 1 billion board feet of lumber (82% softwood), and nearly 1.4 billion sq feet of plywood. Although annual tree growth exceeds the yearly harvest by about one-third, acreage in commercial timberland continues to shrink as the result of real estate development, water impoundment, and the expansion of public parks and wilderness areas.

Production of timber alone was valued at $353.1 million in 1978, but that represents only a very small fraction of the state's forest-related industries. Shipments of lumber and wood products were valued at more than $1.7 billion in 1977; paper and allied products, $1.6 billion. Wood-preserving plants in Texas treated some 5.1 million crossties, 2.5 million fence posts, and

254,000 utility poles during the same year. Employment in the lumber and wood products industry totaled 36,368 in 1978, with a payroll of $349.3 million.

The Texas Forest Service manages state reforestation programs, coordinates pest control activities, and protects against forest fires. For reforestation purposes, there were 1,892 privately owned tree farm in 1978, aggregating 4,039,697 acres (1,634,813 hectares). The worst forest pest is the southern pine bark beetle, which kills more trees each year than are lost in forest fires. A pine beetle infestation in 1976 caused so much damage that the governor declared 34 counties in East Texas disaster areas; about half the infested timber was salvaged. In 1978, 3,531 forest fires burned a total of 48,794 acres (19,746 hectares). About half the fires resulted from the burning of debris.

27 MINING

Texas leads the US in mineral production, valued at nearly $20 billion in 1978. It is also the leading producer of mineral fuels, which accounted for 94% of the state's mineral value and 25% of the total US mineral output in 1978. All together, the state mines 24 different minerals, and ranks 1st among the 50 states in production of sulfur and magnesium chloride, 2d in clay bricks, and 5th in uranium. Production of petroleum, which exceeded 1 billion barrels in 1978, is concentrated in the panhandle and eastern part of the state. Construction materials are mined throughout the central and northern regions, sulfur and magnesium compounds on the Gulf Coast and in the west, and uranium in the Gulf Coastal Plain.

Mining accounted for about 4% of the state's personal income in 1978, when all mineral-related industries employed about 382,000 workers, or some 6% of the civilian labor force. Shipments of mineral-derived products, including fossil fuels, chemicals, primary metals, and clay, stone, and glass products, were valued at more than $50 billion in 1977. Apart from fuels, leading minerals in 1978 included cement, 8,809,000 tons, $376,333,000; stone, 62,525,000 tons, $148,950,000; sand and gravel, 56,000,000 tons, $135,000,000; salt, 10,465,000 tons, $56,057,000; and lime, 1,345,000 tons, $49,455,000. Data were withheld for some of the state's most important minerals—magnesium, uranium, iron ore, sulfur, and certain clays among them—in order to avoid disclosing individual company operations.

28 ENERGY AND POWER

Texas is an energy-rich state. Its vast deposits of petroleum and natural gas liquids account for nearly 30% of US proved liquid hydrocarbon reserves. Texas is also the largest producer and exporter of oil and natural gas to other states, and it leads the US in electric power production.

As of 31 December 1978, Texas power plants had a combined installed capacity of 54.3 million kw, nearly double the 1970 figure; their power output was 194.6 billion kwh, 8.5% of the US total. Gas-fired plants accounted for 80% of the production, coal 18%, and oil 2%. In 1977, domestic sales of electricity totaled 153 million kwh, of which industrial plants used 45%, homes 31%, businesses 22%, and other consumers 2%. The 12 largest investor-owned utilities accounted for about 70% of the state's generating capacity and together served more than 4 million customers in 1978. Major suppliers were Central Power & Light, Community Public Service, Dallas Power & Light, El Paso Power & Light, Gulf States Utilities, Houston Lighting & Power, Texas Electric Service, Texas Power & Light, West Texas Utilities, and three other southwestern utilities. In addition, 75 electric distribution cooperatives served some 750,000 rural customers in 245 counties by the end of 1978.

The state's first oil well was drilled in 1866 at Melrose in East Texas, and the first major oil discovery was made in 1894 at Corsicana, northwest of Melrose, in Navarro County. The famous Spindletop gusher, near Beaumont, was tapped on 10 January 1901. Another great oil deposit was discovered in the panhandle in 1921, and the largest of all, the East Texas field, in Rusk County, was opened in 1930. Subsequent major oil discoveries were made in West Texas, starting in Scurry County in 1948. Thirty years later, the state's crude oil production exceeded 1 billion barrels and was valued at $9.7 billion. Proved petroleum reserves at the end of 1978 were estimated at almost 7.7 billion barrels, representing nearly 28% of total US reserves. In addition, Texas had nearly 2.3 billion barrels of natural gas liquids, contributing to a combined liquid hydrocarbon reserve of not quite 10 billion barrels. As of 1979, Texas had 54 oil refineries with a capacity of 4,706,577 barrels of crude oil per day, or more than 27% of the US total. There were 6,086 oil wells and 3,292 gas wells in operation in 1978, when 3,884 exploratory wells were drilled. The petroleum industry—ranging from drilling technicians to fuel dealers and gasoline service station attendants—employed 313,237 workers in 1978 and paid wages totaling $5.2 billion.

In 1978, Texas produced more than 6.5 trillion cu feet of natural gas, valued at $6.6 billion; the output figure represented one-third of total US production. Production of natural gas liquids in 1978 amounted to 276 million barrels (45% of the national total), worth $2.1 billion. As of 31 December 1978, proved natural gas reserves were estimated at 54.6 trillion cu feet, 27% of the national total.

After the coal mines in the north-central region had been closed for many years, renewed interest in coal as an energy resource caused some mines to be reopened in the late 1970s. Coal production totaled 21 million tons in 1978, representing an increase of 24% over the previous year. More than 95% of the coal produced was lignite, nearly all of it used as fuel for electric generating plants close to the mines. Lignite reserves were estimated at 3.2 billion tons in 1976.

[29] INDUSTRY

Before 1900, Texas had an agricultural economy based, in the common phrase, on "cotton, cows, and corn." When the first US census of manufactures was taken in Texas in 1849, there were only 309 industrial establishments with 1,066 wage earners; payrolls totaled $322,368, and the value added by manufacture was a mere $773,896. The number of establishments increased tenfold by 1899, when the state had 38,604 wage earners and a total value added of $38,506,130. During World War II, the value added passed the $1-billion mark, and by 1976 the total was $27.6 billion, 7th among the 50 states and the highest in the South. By 1978, the leading industries, ranked by numbers of employees, were nonelectrical machinery, food processing, fabricated metal products, apparel and textiles, electric and electronic equipment, chemical products, and transportation equipment.

The total value added by manufacture in 1977 exceeded $32.9 billion. The following table shows value added by manufacture for the state's principal industrial sectors during the 1972 and 1977 production years:

	1972	1977
Chemicals and allied products	$3,189,800,000	$7,063,200,000
Petroleum and coal products	1,338,200,000	4,277,500,000
Nonelectrical machinery	1,449,900,000	3,686,100,000
Food and food products	1,716,600,000	3,051,500,000
Fabricated metal products	1,089,600,000	2,161,700,000
Electric and electronic equipment	988,900,000	2,121,700,000
Transportation equipment	1,260,600,000	2,028,200,000
Primary metals	1,001,700,000	1,469,400,000
Stone, clay, glass products	50,600,000	1,167,000,000
Printing and publishing	659,500,000	1,155,500,000
Clothing and textile products	551,900,000	985,800,000
Rubber and plastics	349,100,000	731,300,000
Lumber and wood products	369,400,000	702,800,000
Paper and paper products	342,000,000	676,100,000
Instruments, related products	177,000,000	455,100,000
Furniture and fixtures	199,000,000	304,400,000

Three of the state's leading industrial products—refined petroleum, industrial organic chemicals, and oil-field machinery—all stem directly from the petrochemical sector. Major oil refineries are located at Houston and other Gulf ports. Aircraft plants include those of North American Aviation and Chance-Vought at Grand Prairie, General Dynamics near Ft. Worth, and Bell Aircraft's helicopter division at Hurst. By the end of 1979, Texas was home to seven US industrial corporations wtih annual sales of $2 billion, all with headquarters in Houston or Dallas. Houston boasted Shell Oil, Tenneco, and Pennzoil, while Dallas was the headquarters of LTV, Dresser Industries, Texas Instruments, and Diamond Shamrock.

[30] COMMERCE

Texas ranked 4th among the 50 states in wholesale trade, with total sales of about $41.5 billion, in 1972. Wholesaling is an important source of personal income, accounting for 6.4% of the state total in 1977. The leading wholesaling centers are the Dallas–Ft. Worth, Houston, El Paso, Lubbock, and Odessa metropolitan areas.

Texas ranked 3d behind California and New York in retail sales, amounting to $45.8 billion, in 1977. About two-thirds of all retail stores are unincorporated businesses, and 90% of these are single-owner stores. Of the 1977 retail sales total, automotive dealers accounted for 25%, food stores 21%, department stores 10%, restaurants and taverns 8%, gasoline stations 8%, clothing stores 5%, hardware and other supply outlets 5%, and furniture and home furnishing stores 4%. Retail trade contributed 8.5% of the state's total personal income in 1977 and accounted for more than 10% of personal income in the Laredo, Lubbock, Brownsville–Harlingen–San Benito, Amarillo, and McAllen–Pharr–Edinburg metropolitan areas. Among the largest metropolitan areas, Houston provided 23% of the retail sales total, Dallas–Ft. Worth 22%, and San Antonio 7%. An amendment to the state constitution permits counties to vote on whether to allow sales of liquor by the drink. As of 31 August 1978, distilled spirits were legal in all or part of 164 counties; 14 counties permitted beverages with an alcohol content of 14% or less; and 76 counties were wholly dry.

Foreign exports through Texas customs districts in 1978 totaled $15.4 billion, imports $20.7 billion. The leading items shipped through Texas ports to foreign countries were grains, chemicals, fertilizers, and petroleum refinery products; principal imports included crude petroleum, minerals and metals (especially aluminum ores), liquefied gases, sugar, and molasses. Exports of the state's own agricultural products were valued at $2.1 billion in 1977/78, the main export items being cotton, worth $652.4 million, 38% of the US total; feed grains, $339.2 million, 6%; wheat and flour, $252.5 million, 6%; and rice, $196.5 million, 24%. Texas ranked 4th among the 50 states in 1976 as a producer of industrial goods for export, with nearly $1.8 billion.

[31] CONSUMER PROTECTION

Texas has no consumer protection agency. The consumer credit commissioner, appointed by the State Finance Commission, maintains a main office in Austin and branch offices in Houston and Dallas.

[32] BANKING

Texas has more banks than any other state and ranked 4th among the 50 states in commercial bank assets in 1978.

Banking was illegal in the Texas Republic and under the first state constitution, reflecting the widespread fear of financial speculation like that which had caused the panic of 1837. Because both the independent republic and the new state government found it difficult to raise funds or obtain credit without a banking system, they were forced to borrow money from merchants, thus permitting banking functions and privileges despite the constitutional ban. A formal banking system was legalized during the latter part of the 19th century.

In 1978, Texas had 1,390 commercial banks, with assets totaling $76.7 billion. As of 30 September 1978, 781 state banks held deposits totaling $22 billion, and 609 national banks had $41.7 billion in deposits. Bank loans outstanding amounted to $43.5 billion, of which business loans accounted for $16.5 billion; consumer loans, $10.9 billion; real estate loans, $8.9 billion; and loans to farmers, $2.2 billion. Of the total number of banks operating in the state during 1978, 101 banks with assets of $12.2 billion were located in Dallas County and 157 banks with $16.8 billion in Harris County (Houston). As of 31 December 1978, the state's leading commercial banks, each having more than $1 billion in domestic deposits, were First City National (the largest bank in Texas, with assets of $3.3 billion), Texas Commerce, and Bank of the Southwest, all in Houston; and Republic National, First National, and Mercantile National, in Dallas.

At the end of 1978, Texas had 318 insured savings-and-loan and building-and-loan associations (249 state-chartered, 69 federally chartered), with combined assets of $27.9 billion; these associations held $22.8 billion in outstanding mortgage loans and $22.9 billion in savings capital, and had a combined net worth (including surplus reserves and undivided profits) of more than $1.4 billion. In 1978 there were 1,432 credit unions with about 2.8 million members and assets totaling $4.7 billion.

The state's 10 largest bank holding companies in 1979 controlled about 43% of all bank deposits. Many out-of-state institutions have extended substantial loans to Texas businesses in recent years because the state's own banks have been unable to supply sufficient capital to meet the investment needs of the state's booming economy. In addition, at least 45 foreign banks have offices in the state, mostly in Houston, where they participate in the international financing of the petrochemical industry.

33 INSURANCE

As of 31 August 1978, 1,725 companies were licensed to handle insurance, including 654 Texas firms and 1,071 out-of-state companies. Texas ranked 1st among the 50 states in 1978 in number of life insurance companies and 3d in amount of life insurance in force; the state's 188 life companies had 23,961,000 policies in force, valued at $173.7 billion, and paid $1.4 billion in benefits. The average Texas family held $36,500 in life coverage, 4% above the US norm. Some 40 fraternal benefit societies issued 33,627 policies valued at $357.1 million during 1977; insurance in force totaled $1.9 billion at the end of the year.

The state's 429 stock fire and casualty insurance companies collected $3.1 billion in premiums and paid $1.4 billion in benefits in 1977, when 78 mutual fire and casualty companies wrote premiums amounting to $738.5 million and made payments of $350.9 million. During 1978, all property and liability insurers wrote premiums totaling $5.2 billion, including $1.1 billion in automotive liability insurance, $846 million in automobile physical damage insurance, and $530.3 million in homeowners' coverage.

The insurance industry, which employed 89,828 Texans and paid wages exceeding $1.1 billion in 1978, is regulated by the State Board of Insurance, consisting of three members appointed by the governor. The board appoints a state insurance commissioner who is responsible for directing the Texas Insurance Department.

34 SECURITIES

Although there are no securities exchanges in Texas, New York Stock Exchange member firms had 206 sales offices and 2,302 registered representatives in the state in 1978. Texans reported almost $1.3 billion in dividend income on their 1977 federal income tax returns.

The State Securities Board, established in 1957, oversees the issuance and sale of stocks and bonds in Texas. Registration fees under the Texas Securities Act of 1913 netted the state government $2.1 million in 1977/78; the stock share transfer tax has been repealed.

35 PUBLIC FINANCE

In general, public officials in Texas have sought to minimize state government spending, and budget surpluses have normally been recorded. At the end of the 1978/79 fiscal year, state revenues exceeded expenditures by $769.3 million, or nearly 9%. Because of high inflation and the rising cost of government during the 1970s, however, budget expenditures increased by 50% between 1975/76 and 1978/79. Under the "pay-as-you-go" amendment to the state constitution, in effect since 1945, the legislature may not appropriate more funds than the state comptroller certifies are available.

The governor's Office of Budget and Planning prepares a budget for the biennium that is reviewed by the Legislative Budget Board, consisting of the lieutenant governor, the speaker of the house, and eight other legislators. The proposed budget is then submitted to the legislature by the governor, approved or revised by the legislature subject to the governor's veto, and signed by the governor after final approval by majority vote of both houses. The Texas fiscal year extends from 1 September to 31 August.

The following table summarizes state revenues and expenditures for fiscal years 1977/78 and 1978/79 (in millions):

	1977/78	1978/79
REVENUES		
Taxes	$5,041.2	$5,400.7
Federal grants	2,037.7	2,284.9
Interest income	665.1	816.4
Licenses and fees	405.6	395.2
Land income	405.2	380.1
Other receipts	80.0	102.9
TOTALS	$8,634.8	$9,380.2
EXPENDITURES		
Education	$4,004.0	$4,327.5
State services, of which:	1,988.7	2,191.9
Welfare	(1,336.0)	(1,509.2)
Mental health, state homes, and corrections	(430.0)	(454.6)
Health and sanitation	(136.2)	(137.7)
Law enforcement	(86.5)	(90.4)
Highways and natural resources	1,049.6	1,154.7
Administration	227.5	241.5
Local government grants	263.6	293.3
Debt service	151.3	105.0
Other outlays	190.6	297.0
TOTALS	$7,875.3	$8,610.9

Budgeted expenditures for the 1979–81 biennium totaled $20.2 billion, of which slightly more than 50% was allocated to education.

The following table shows general revenues and expenditures for leading Texas cities in 1976/77 (in millions):

	DALLAS	HOUSTON	SAN ANTONIO
REVENUES			
Property tax	$113.0	$151.0	$ 38.1
Sales and gross receipts tax	54.4	86.4	20.8
Federal transfers	36.3	50.3	52.9
Other receipts	68.3	123.3	49.2
TOTALS	$272.0	$411.0	$161.0
EXPENDITURES			
Police protection	$ 41.0	$ 68.8	$ 26.5
Fire protection	24.1	46.9	16.6
Highways	23.1	30.6	15.2
Health and hospitals	4.5	16.1	8.2
Other outlays	155.3	227.6	120.5
TOTALS	$248.0	$390.0	$187.0

Houston's gross debt as of 30 June 1977 was $789 million; San Antonio's, $570 million; and Dallas's, $465 million. The combined state and local government debt in mid-1977 was $13.1 billion, 86% higher than in 1970 but still, at $1,018 per capita, below the national average.

³⁶TAXATION

Texas, whose total tax collections amounted to $5.4 billion in 1978/79, is one of the only six states that imposed neither a personal nor a corporate income tax in 1980. The principal source of state tax revenue is the 4% sales and use tax, which accounted for 40% of total 1978/79 tax collections. Other major sources of revenue in that year were oil and natural gas production taxes, providing 19% of the total; motor fuel taxes, 9%; motor vehicle sales tax, 8%; and cigarette and tobacco taxes, 5%. Other state levies include the corporation franchise tax, alcoholic beverage tax, public utility taxes, inheritance tax, and a tax on telephones.

Local property taxes provided more than one-third of county and city tax revenues in 1977. Property tax rates per $100 of assessed valuation varied widely throughout the state, from $.50 in Ward County to $1.92 in Duval County. The rate in Houston was $1.58; in Dallas, $1.35. In 1967, the state legislature authorized the cities to impose a sales tax of 1%; 913 cities had done so by 1979. The city sales tax is a major source of revenue for the municipalities, amounting in 1978/79 to $67 per capita in Houston and $61 in Dallas.

Although the state tax burden is well below the US average, tax collections per capita more than doubled between 1970 and 1977. In 1978, Texans approved a constitutional amendment limiting further tax increases. The legislature responded the following year by passing a tax-cut package totaling about $400 million, including a comprehensive property tax reform bill and a public education bill to provide greater equity between rich and poor school districts.

Federal tax collections in Texas during 1977/78 exceeded $25.1 billion: individual income and employment taxes, $17.9 billion; corporation income taxes, $5.1 billion; excise taxes, $1.8 billion; estate taxes, $337.9 million; and gift taxes, $19.2 million. During the same year, federal expenditures amounted to $24.6 billion, of which $9 billion consisted of Department of Defense outlays and $4.6 billion was general retirement and disability insurance, including Social Security.

³⁷ECONOMIC POLICY

The major factors responsible for the state's rapid economic expansion during the 1970s were the availability of reasonably priced real estate, plentiful fuel supplies, and a sizable, largely unorganized labor force. Texas state government has been notably probusiness: regulation is less restrictive than in many states, and there is no corporate income tax. The state government actively encourages outside capital investment in Texas industries, and the state's remarkable industrial productivity has produced a generally high return on investment.

The 12-member Texas Industrial Commission helps businesses locate or expand their operations in the state. A private organization, the Texas Industrial Development Council, in Bryan, also assists new and developing industries.

³⁸HEALTH

Medical care ranges from adequate to excellent in the state's largest cities, but many small communities are without doctors and hospitals. Texas suffers from a general shortage of health care personnel: although the number of students enrolled in medical education programs more than doubled during the 1970s, many hospitals were functioning without adequate numbers of registered nurses, laboratory technicians, and therapists as the 1980s began. These shortages were expected to continue, given the state's rapidly increasing population.

During 1969–71, Texas ranked 23d among the 50 states with an average life expectancy of 70.9 years (67.05 years for men, 74.99 for women). The infant mortality rate as of 1977 was 13.4 per 1,000 live births for whites and 21.7 for nonwhites. There were 70,900 legal abortions—24 per 1,000 women of childbearing age and 3 for each 10 live births—during 1977/78. Rates for live births (17.9 per 1,000 population), marriages (12.4), and divorces (6.4) all exceeded the national norms in 1977.

The overall death rate in 1977 was 7.8 per 1,000 population. Texas ranked below the national average in deaths due to heart disease, cancer, stroke, pneumonia and influenza, diabetes, cirrhosis of the liver, and arteriosclerosis, but above average in deaths from accidents, suicide, and early infancy diseases. The leading causes of death in 1977, with their rates per 100,000 popuulation, were heart disease, 262.2; cancer, 150.1; stroke, 80.2; accidents, 53.8; pneumonia and influenza, 21.5; suicide, 13.8; homicide, 13.8; early infancy diseases, 13; arteriosclerosis, 12.7; diabetes, 12.5; and cirrhosis of the liver, 10.9.

As of 1979, the Texas Department of Mental Health and Mental Retardation operated 7 state hospitals and 5 major mental health centers, plus 13 state training schools for the mentally retarded. There were 6,455 patients in mental care hospitals at the end of 1976, and 31,792 patients in psychiatric units of general hospitals at the close of 1975. Public institutions for the mentally retarded had 12,213 residents as of mid-1978. During that same year, Texas's 565 hospitals admitted 2,465,947 patients; on average, 71% of the state's hospital beds were occupied each day. Hospital personnel numbered 184,156, including 29,606 registered nurses and 18,824 licensed practical nurses. The average cost of hospital care in 1977 was $176 per day and $1,160 per stay, in both cases well below the US average. Texas had 19,429 licensed physicians in 1977, and 5,246 active dentists in 1979.

There are 7 medical schools, 2 dental colleges, and 54 schools of nursing in the state. The University of Texas has medical colleges at Dallas, Houston, Galveston, San Antonio, and Tyler. During the 1976/77 school year, 29,455 students were enrolled in health training programs and 11,525 graduated into professional careers.

³⁹SOCIAL WELFARE

Texas state expenditures on public welfare in 1978/79 totaled $1.5 billion, of which $1.3 billion was budgeted for the Department of Human Resources and the remaining $200 million represented disbursements to state schools, hospitals, and other social welfare and rehabilitation programs. The state has never enjoyed a reputation for lavishness in its public assistance efforts.

In 1978, payments to families with dependent children, made to 287,800 Texans (including 213,500 children), totaled $122 million; the monthly payment per family averaged $108, less than half the national norm and 9% below the state's 1970 support level. Medicaid payments, on the other hand, more than tripled during the 1970s, reaching $723 million in 1977. The following year, an estimated 731,000 Texans (354,000 fewer than in 1975) took part in the food stamp program, with a federal subsidy of $254.4 million. About 1,659,000 schoolchildren—470,000 more than in 1970—enjoyed school-provided lunches, at a federal cost that rose from $14.2 million in 1970 to $137.9 million in 1978.

Social Security benefits were paid in 1977 to 1,741,900 persons, of whom 61% were retired workers, 25% were survivors of deceased workers, and 14% were disabled. These pensions, amounting to nearly $4 billion, averaged $224.60 monthly for retired workers, almost 8% below the national average. Federally administered Supplemental Security Income (SSI) payments, made to 296,500 Texans, totaled $308.9 million in 1978. The average monthly benefit was $83 for a retiree and $121 for a disabled person—in each case, well below the US average, partly because Texas, alone among the 50 states, elected not to supplement federal SSI payments.

Texans enrolled in vocational rehabilitation programs in 1978 numbered about 73,000, of whom 17,700 were successfully rehabilitated; spending on the program totaled $60.3 million. Workers' compensation payments were $449.5 million in 1977. A weekly average of 46,000 beneficiaries received $159 million in unemployment benefits in 1978; the average weekly payment was $68.18, 47th among the 50 states, the lowest of any state west of the Mississippi, and 18.5% below the national norm.

⁴⁰ HOUSING

The variety of Texas architectural styles reflects the diversity of the state's topography and climate. In the early settlement period, Spanish-style adobe houses were built in southern Texas. During the 1840s, Anglo-American settlers in the east erected primitive log cabins. These were later replaced by "dog-run" houses, consisting of two rooms linked by an open passageway covered by a gabled roof, so-called because pet dogs slept in the open, roofed shelter, as did occasional overnight guests. During the late 19th century, southern-style mansions were built in East Texas, and the familiar ranch house, constructed of stone and usually stuccoed or whitewashed, with a shingle roof and a long porch, proliferated throughout the state; the modern ranch house in southwestern Texas shows a distinct Mexican-Spanish influence. Climate affects such modern amenities as air conditioning: a new house in the humid eastern region is likely to have a refrigeration-style cooler, while in the dry west and south an evaporating "swamp cooler" is the more common means of making hot weather bearable.

As of the 1970 census, Texas had some 3,808,000 year-round housing units, of which 3,432,000 units were occupied. Of the latter number, about 65% were lived in by the owner, and nearly 94% were equipped with modern plumbing. Between 1976 and 1978, the state authorized construction of 403,200 housing units, valued at $10.4 billion; at least 45% were multiunit dwellings. In 1978, for the fourth consecutive year, Houston led the nation's metropolitan areas in number of housing starts.

⁴¹ EDUCATION

Texas ranks 2d only to California in number of public schools and 3d behind California and New York State in public school enrollment. Only California has a more extensive public college and university system. School finance has been a chronic problem, however; per pupil expenditures for Texas public schools in 1977/78 were $1,352, 40th among the 50 states.

Although public instruction began in Texas as early as 1746, education was slow to develop during the period of Spanish and Mexican rule. The legislative foundation for a public school system was laid by the government of the Republic of Texas during the late 1830s, but funding was slow to develop. After annexation, in 1846, Galveston began to support free public schools, and San Antonio had at least four free schools by the time a statewide system of public education was established in 1854. Free segregated schooling was provided for black children beginning in the 1870s; their schools were ill-maintained and underfinanced. School integration was accomplished during the 1960s, nonviolently for the most part, and by 1976, only 14% of all minority-group children were attending schools where minorities made up 99–100% of the total enrollment.

In 1900, nearly 16% of all adult Texans were illiterate. By 1970, 2.2% of the population aged 14 and over was unable to read and write in any language—still one of the highest adult illiteracy rates in the U.S. In 1976, more than 64% of the population 18 years old and over had graduated from high school, and nearly 14% had four or more years of college; 6% of all adult Texans had fewer than five years of grade school, however, and the state's median of 12.4 school years lagged behind the US average.

Public school enrollment in 1977 was 2,083,508 in grades K–8 and 899,375 in grades 9–12. Professional personnel numbered 174,455, and the average salary was $13,266. Enrollment in nonpublic schools was estimated at 22,000 primary and 79,000 secondary during the same year.

Institutions of higher education in 1978 included 24 public senior colleges and universities, with 328,681 students; 59 public community college campuses, with 235,815 students; and more than three dozen private institutions with a combined enrollment exceeding 75,000. The leading public universities are Texas A & M (College Station), which opened in 1876 and enrolled 30,255 students in 1978/79, and the University of Texas (Austin), founded in 1883 and with 43,095 students enrolled in 1978/79; each institution is now the center of its own university system, including campuses in several other cities. Oil was discovered on lands owned by the University of Texas in 1923, and from 1924 through 1978 the university and Texas A & M shared more than $1 billion in oil-related rentals and royalties. Another state-supported institution, the University of Houston, enrolled 29,666 on its main campus in 1978/79, and Texas Tech (Lubbock) enrolled 22,696.

The first private college in Texas was Rutersville, established by a Methodist minister in Fayette County in 1840. The oldest private institution still active in the state is Baylor University (1845), at Waco, enrolling 9,524 students in 1978/79. Other major private universities and their enrollment in 1978/79 included Hardin-Simmons (Abilene), 1,749; Lamar (Beaumont), 12,846; Rice (Houston), 3,597; Southern Methodist, or SMU (Dallas), 8,623; and Texas Christian, or TCU (Ft. Worth), 5,874. Well-known black-oriented institutions of higher learning include Texas Southern University in Houston and Bishop College in Dallas.

Tuition charges to Texas colleges are among the lowest in the nation, averaging $2,829 at public colleges and $4,286 at private colleges in 1978/79. The Texas Student Assistance Corp. administers a guaranteed-loan program and tuition equalization grants for needy students.

⁴² ARTS

Although Texas has never been regarded as a leading cultural center, the arts have a long history in the state. The cities of Houston and Matagorda each had a theater before they had a church, and the state's first theater was active in Houston as early as 1838. Stark Young founded the Curtain Club acting group at the University of Texas in Austin in 1909, and the little theater movement began in that city in 1921. The performing arts now flourish at Houston's Theater Center, Jones Hall of Performing Arts, and Alley Theater, as well as at Dallas's Theater Center, National Children's Theater, and Theater Three. The Margo Jones repertory company in Dallas has a national reputation, and there are major repertory groups in Houston and San Antonio. During the late 1970s, Texas also emerged as a center for motion picture production.

Texas has 3 major symphony orchestras—the Dallas Symphony (with Eduardo Mata as music director), Houston Symphony, and San Antonio Symphony—and 25 orchestras in other cities. The Houston Grand Opera performs at Jones Hall; other opera companies perform regularly in Beaumont, Dallas, El Paso, Ft. Worth, and San Antonio. All these cities also have resident dance companies, as do Abilene, Amarillo, Austin, Corpus Christi, Denton, Galveston, Longview, Lubbock, Midland-Odessa, and Pampa.

Popular music in Texas stems from early Spanish and Mexican folk songs, Negro spirituals, cowboy ballads, and German-language songfests. Texans pioneered a kind of country and western music that is more outspoken and direct than Nashville's commercial product, and a colony of country-rock songwriters and musicians were active in the Austin area during the 1970s. Texans of Mexican ancestry have also fashioned a Latin-flavored music that is as distinctly "Tex-Mex" as the state's famous chili.

⁴³LIBRARIES AND MUSEUMS

Public libraries in Texas, serving 232 counties in 1977, had a combined book stock of 17,620,552 volumes and a circulation of 40,300,949 volumes. Funding for basic library service is provided by cities and counties, although state and federal library aid increased considerably during the 1970s. More libraries are supported by cities than by counties, partly because of fewer state restrictions on municipal library funding. The largest municipal library systems are those of Houston (2,106,247 volumes), Dallas (1,750,582), and San Antonio (1,006,420). The University of Texas at Austin, noted for outstanding collections in the humanities and in Latin American studies, ranked 10th among US university libraries in 1979, with 3,713,821 volumes. The Lyndon B. Johnson Presidential Library is also located in Austin, as are the state archives. Other notable academic libraries include those of Rice and Southern Methodist universities.

Among the state's more than 300 museums are Austin's Texas Memorial Museum; the Dallas Museum of Fine Arts; and the Amon Carter Museum of Western Art, the Ft. Worth Art Museums, and Kimbell Art Museum, all in Ft. Worth. Houston has the Museum of Fine Arts, Contemporary Arts Museum, and at least 30 galleries.

National historic sites in Texas are Ft. Davis (Jeff Davis County), President Johnson's boyhood home and Texas White House (Blanco and Gillespie counties), and the San Jose Mission (San Antonio). Other historic places include the Alamo, Dwight D. Eisenhower's birthplace at Denison, the Sam Rayburn home in Bonham, and the John F. Kennedy memorials in Dallas. A noteworthy prehistoric Indian site is the Alibates Flint Quarries National Monument, located in Potter County and accessible by guided tour.

⁴⁴COMMUNICATIONS

The US Postal Service had about 34,000 employees in Texas in 1977. Postal receipts in 1978/79 reached $199.1 million in Dallas and $165.7 million in Houston.

There were 10,245,165 telephones in service at the end of 1978, 7,393,901 residential and 2,851,264 commercial. Southwestern Bell, the state's largest telephone company, served 8,059,872 phones through 296 exchanges. Mountain Bell, also part of the Bell system, served the trans-Pecos region with 256,048 telephones. The major independent companies included the General Telephone Co. of the Southwest, with headquarters in San Angelo, serving 1,175,219 phones; Gulf States–United Telephone Co., Tyler, 106,570; and Continental Telephone, Dallas, 157,222. On average, 97% of Texas households had telephone service. Texans made more than 18.9 billion local calls in 1978 and nearly 1.4 billion toll calls. Installations included 70,215,116 mi (113,000,486 km) of wire in cable, 160,702 mi (258,625 km) of aerial wire, 11,696 mi (18,823 km) of tube in coaxial cable, and 7,653 mi (12,316 km) of radio relay systems. Dallas was one of Western Union's first US communications satellite stations, and it leads the state as a center for data communications.

The state has not always been in the communications vanguard, however. Texas passed up a chance to make a handsome profit from the invention of the telegraph when, in 1838, inventor Samuel F. B. Morse offered his newfangled device to the republic as a gift. When the Texas government neglected to respond, Morse withdrew the offer.

As of 1 January 1978, Texas had 286 commercial AM stations (1st in the US), 185 FM stations (2d), and 54 television stations (2d). The state's first radio station, WRR, was established by the city of Dallas in 1920—an interesting fact in view of Dallas's worldwide reputation as a bastion of free enterprise. The first television station, WBAP, began broadcasting in Ft. Worth in 1948. Cable television systems served 791,641 Texans in 261 communities in 1978.

⁴⁵PRESS

The first newspaper in Texas was a revolutionary Spanish-language sheet published in May 1813 at Nacogdoches. Six years later, the *Texas Republican* was published by Dr. James Long in the same city. In 1835, the *Telegraph and Texas Register* became the official newspaper of the Texas Republic, and it continued to publish until 1877. The first modern newspaper was the *Galveston News* (1842), a forerunner of the *Dallas Morning News* (1885). Other pioneering papers still in continuous publication include the *San Antonio Express* and the *Houston Post*.

By 1978, Texas had 25 morning dailies, with a combined circulation of 1,613,542; 89 evening dailies, with 1,821,011; and 89 Sunday papers, with 3,677,481. The newspapers with the largest daily circulations were as follows:

AREA	NAME	DAILY	SUNDAY
Austin	American-Statesman (m,e,S)	84,262 (m) 36,690 (e)	130,086
Dallas	Morning News (m,S)	273,880	336,806
	Times Herald (e,S)	241,208	332,462
Houston	Chronicle (e,S)	324,301	418,130
	Post (m,S)	299,546	359,423
San Antonio	Express (m,S)	81,251	177,552
	News (e,S)	75,973	
	Light (e,S)	125,206	184,238

In 1979 there were 509 weekly newspapers with total circulation of 1,520,000. The *Texas Almanac*, a comprehensive guide to the state, has been issued at regular intervals since 1857 by the A. H. Belo Corp., publishers of the *Dallas Morning News*. Leading magazines include the *Texas Monthly* and *Texas Observer*, both published in Austin.

⁴⁶ORGANIZATIONS

Dallas is the home of one of the nation's largest organizations, the Boy Scouts of America, with more than 4 million members in 1980. Important medical groups are the American Heart Association, also in Dallas, and the National Association for Retarded Citizens, Arlington. Professional societies include the American Association of Petroleum Landmen, Ft. Worth, and the Association of Engineering Geologists, Dallas. The Noncommissioned Officers Association has its home office in San Antonio, as does the Former Texas Rangers Association; the Airline Passengers Association is in Irving. Among the many organizations devoted to horse breeding are the American Quarter Horse Association, Amarillo; Palomino Horse Breeders of America, Mineral Wells; and the National Cutting Horse Association and American Paint Association, both in Ft. Worth. San Antonio is the home of the Texas Longhorn Breeders Association of America, among other cattlemen's groups.

⁴⁷TOURISM, TRAVEL, AND RECREATION

According to the Department of Highways and Public Transportation, 25,753,000 out-of-state visitors spent $4.3 billion in Texas in 1978. About 80% of the tourists entered the state by automobile, and 20% by air, rail, and bus. The largest number of US visitors came from Oklahoma, California, Louisiana, Missouri, and Michigan, together accounting for one-third of domestic automobile travelers; of the foreign tourists entering by car, 37% listed Mexico as their country of origin, and 34% gave Canada. The most-visited cities in 1978 were San Antonio, with 5,711,700 visitors; Houston, 5,653,900; Dallas, 4,394,100; El Paso, 3,681,100; Austin, 2,280,600; Galveston, 2,052,300; Ft. Worth, 1,910,900; Corpus Christi, 1,661,900; Amarillo, 1,449,500; Brownsville, 1,252,900; and Laredo, 1,195,700. (These figures do not include visitors from Mexico.)

Each of the state's seven major tourist regions offers outstanding attractions. East Texas has one of the state's oldest cities, Nacogdoches, with the nation's oldest public thoroughfare and a reconstruction of the Old Stone Fort, a Spanish trading post dating from 1779. Jefferson, an important 19th-century inland port, has many old homes, including Excelsior House. Tyler, which bills itself as the "rose capital of the world," features a 28-acre (11-hectare) municipal rose garden and puts on a Rose Festival each October. The Gulf Coast region of southeastern Texas offers the Lyndon B. Johnson Space Center, the Astrodome sports stadium and adjacent Astroworld amusement park, and a profusion of museums, galleries, and shops, all in metropolitan Houston; Spindletop Park, in Beaumont, commemorating the state's first great oil gusher; Galveston's sandy beaches, deep-sea fishing, and Sea-Arama Marineworld; and the Padre Island National Seashore.

To the north, the Dallas–Ft. Worth metropolitan area (including Arlington) has numerous cultural and entertainment attractions, including the Six Flags Over Texas amusement park and the state fair held in Dallas each October. Old Abilene Town amusement park, with its strong western flavor, is also popular with visitors. The Hill Country of south-central Texas encompasses many tourist sites, including the state capitol in Austin, Waco's Texas Ranger Museum (Ft. Fisher), the Lyndon B. Johnson National Historic Site, and frontier relics in Bastrop and Bandera.

South Texas has the state's most famous historic site—the Alamo, in San Antonio, which also contains HemisFair Plaza and Brackenridge Park. The Rio Grande Valley Museum, at Harlingen, is popular with visitors, as is the King Ranch headquarters in Kleberg County. The Great Plains region of the Texas panhandle offers Palo Duro Canyon—Texas's largest state park, covering 16,402 acres (6,638 hectares) in Armstrong and Randall counties—the Prairie Dog Town at Lubbock, Old West exhibits at Matador, and the cultural and entertainment resources of Amarillo. In the extreme northwestern corner of the panhandle is the XIT Museum, recalling the famous XIT Ranch, at one time the world's largest fenced ranch, which formerly covered more than 3 million acres (1.2 million hectares). Outstanding tourist sites in the far west are the Big Bend and Guadalupe Mountains national parks, the Jersey Lilly Saloon and Judge Roy Bean visitor center in Langtry, and metropolitan El Paso, just across the Rio Grande from Ciudad Juárez, Mexico's largest border city.

Texas's 32 state parks and 28 recreation areas attracted some 16 million visitors in 1978. In addition to Palo Duro Canyon, notable state parks include Big Creek (Ft. Bend County), Brazos Island (Cameron County), Caddo Lake (Harrison County), Dinosaur Valley (Somervell County), Eisenhower (Grayson County), Galveston Island, and Longhorn Cavern (Burnet County). In addition, there are 15 state historical parks—including San Jacinto Battleground (east Harris County), Texas State Railroad (Anderson and Cherokee counties), and Washington-on-the-Brazos (Washington County)—and 22 state historic sites and structures.

Hunting and fishing are extremely popular in Texas. Some 287,200 white-tailed deer were harvested in the 1977/78 season, when hunters also killed about 5,000,000 mourning doves, 1,000,000 ducks, 438,000 white-winged doves, 200,000 geese, and 28,500 Rio Grande turkeys. During that year, licenses were issued to 867,345 hunters and 1,482,821 fishermen.

⁴⁸SPORTS

Texas is a great state for sports enthusiasts. Perhaps the nation's most-publicized football team—known both for its prowess and its cheerleaders—is the Dallas Cowboys of the National Football League (NFL); coached by Tom Landry and led by such stars as Roger Staubach and Tony Dorsett, the Cowboys played in five Super Bowls between 1972 and 1979, winning two and losing three. The Houston Oilers captured American Football League championships in 1960 and 1961, subsequently joining the NFL's American Conference, where, led by rusher Earl Campbell, they have become a power in the Central Division.

The Astros, playing in the Astrodome, represent Houston in baseball's National League West; their best season was in 1980, when they won a divisional title but lost in the playoffs to the Philadelphia Phillies. The Texas Rangers of the American League play at Arlington, midway between Dallas and Ft. Worth. The class-AA Texas League, which has been in continuous existence since 1918 and had its heyday in the 1920s and 1930s, now includes teams in Amarillo, El Paso, Midland, and San Antonio, as well as four out-of-state clubs.

Texas is represented in the National Basketball Association by the Houston Rockets, San Antonio Spurs, and Dallas Mavericks. The Dallas Tornado and Houston Hurricane compete in the North American Soccer League.

College football is extremely popular in the state. Eight Texas college teams—the University of Texas, Texas A & M, Rice, Baylor, SMU, TCU, Texas Tech, and Houston—participate in the Southwest Conference, whose annual champion is the host team at the Cotton Bowl game held in Dallas on New Year's Day. Through January 1981, the University of Texas had won seven Cotton Bowl games; Houston, TCU, and Rice two apiece; and Texas A & M and SMU one each. Other college bowl games held in the state each year are the Astro-Bluebonnet Bowl in Houston and the Sun Bowl at El Paso.

Pari-mutuel betting on horse races is illegal in Texas, but quarter horse racing is popular, and rodeo is a leading spectator sport. Participant sports popular with Texans include hunting, fishing, horseback riding, boating, swimming, tennis, and golf. State professional and amateur golf tournaments are held annually. The Texas Sports Hall of Fame was organized in 1951; new members are selected each year by a special committee of the Texas Sports Writers Association.

⁴⁹FAMOUS TEXANS

Two native sons of Texas have served as president of the US. Dwight D. Eisenhower (1890–1969), the 34th president, was born in Denison, but his family moved to Kansas when he was two years old. Lyndon Baines Johnson (1908–73), the 36th president, was the only lifelong resident of the state to serve in that office. Born near Stonewall, he occupied center stage in state and national politics for a third of a century as US representative, Democratic majority leader of the US Senate, and vice president under John F. Kennedy, before succeeding to the presidency after Kennedy's assassination. Reelected by a landslide, Johnson accomplished much of his Great Society program of social reform, but saw his power and popularity wane because of the war in Viet-Nam. His wife, Claudia Alta Taylor "Lady Bird" Johnson (b.1912), was influential in environmental causes as First Lady.

Texas's other native vice president was John Nance Garner (1868–1967), former speaker of the US House of Representatives. George Bush (b.Massachusetts, 1924), who founded his own oil development company and has served in numerous federal posts, was elected vice president in 1980 on the Republican ticket. The only native Texan to serve on the US Supreme Court was Tom C. Clark (1899–1977), an associate justice from 1949 to 1967; he stepped down when his son Ramsey (b.1927) was appointed US attorney general, a post the elder Clark had also held.

Another prominent federal officeholder from Texas was Jesse H. Jones (1874–1956), who served as chairman of the Reconstruction Finance Corporation and secretary of commerce under Franklin D. Roosevelt. Oveta Culp Hobby (b.1905), publisher of the *Houston Post*, became the first director of the Women's Army Corps (WAC) during World War II and the first secretary of the Department of Health, Education, and Welfare under President Eisenhower. John Connally (b.1917), a protégé of Lyndon Johnson's, served as secretary of the Navy under Kennedy and, as governor of Texas, was wounded in the same attack that killed the president; subsequently he switched political allegiance, was secretary of the treasury under Richard Nixon, and has been active in Republican Party politics. Other federal officials from Texas include "Colonel" Edward M. House (1858–1938), principal adviser to President Wilson, and Leon Jaworski (b.1905), the Watergate special prosecutor whose investigations led to President Nixon's resignation.

The state's most famous legislative leader was Sam Rayburn (1882–1961), who served the longest tenure in the nation's history as speaker of the US House of Representatives—17 years in three periods between 1940 and 1961. James Wright (b.1922) was Democratic majority leader of the House in the 1970s, and Barbara C. Jordan (b.1936) won national attention as a forceful member of the House Judiciary Committee during its impeachment deliberations in 1974.

Famous figures in early Texas history include Moses Austin (b.Connecticut, 1761–1821) and his son, Stephen F. Austin (b.Virginia, 1793–1836), often called the "father of Texas." Samuel "Sam" Houston (b.Virginia, 1793–1863), adopted as a youth by the Cherokee, won enduring fame as commander in chief of the Texas revolutionary army, as president of the Texas Republic, and as the new state's first US senator; earlier in his career he had been governor of Tennessee. Mirabeau Bonaparte Lamar (b.Georgia, 1798–1859), the second president of the republic, founded the present state capital (now called Austin) in 1839. Anson Jones (b.Massachusetts, 1798–1858) was the last president of the republic, resigning the office when the annexation of Texas was completed in 1846.

Noteworthy state leaders include John H. Reagan (b.Tennessee, 1818–1905), postmaster general for the Confederacy; he dominated Texas politics from the Civil War to the 1890s, helping to write the state constitutions of 1866 and 1875, and eventually becoming chairman of the newly created Texas Railroad Commission. The most able Texas governor was probably James Stephen Hogg (1851–1906), the first native-born Texan to hold that office. Another administration with a progressive record was that of Governor James V. Allred (1899–1959), who served during the 1930s. Miriam A. "Ma" Ferguson (1875–1961) became in 1924 the first woman to be elected governor of a state, and she was elected again in 1932. With her husband, Governor James E. Ferguson (1871–1944), she was a factor in Texas politics for nearly 30 years. Texas military heroes include Audie Murphy (1924–71), the most decorated soldier of World War II (and later a film actor), and Admiral of the Fleet Chester W. Nimitz (1885–1966).

Figures of history and legend include James Bowie (b.Kentucky, 1796?–1836), who had a reputation as a brawling fighter and wheeler-dealer until he died at the Alamo; he is popularly credited with the invention of the bowie knife. David "Davy" Crockett (b.Tennessee, 1786–1836) served three terms as a US representative from Tennessee before departing for Texas; he, too, lost his life at the Alamo. Among the more notorious Texans was Roy Bean (b.Kentucky, 1825–1903), a judge who proclaimed himself "the law west of the Pecos." Gambler, gunman, and desperado John Wesley Hardin (1853–95) boasted that he "never killed a man who didn't deserve it." Bonnie Parker (1910–34) and Clyde Barrow (1909–34), second-rate bank robbers and murderers who were shot to death by Texas lawmen, achieved posthumous notoriety through the movie *Bonnie and Clyde* (1967).

Many Texas businessmen have profoundly influenced the state's politics and life-style. Clint Murchison (1895–1969) and Sid Richardson (1891–1959) made great fortunes as independent oil operators and spread their wealth into other enterprises: Murchison became owner-operator of the successful Dallas Cowboys professional football franchise, and Richardson, through the Sid Richardson Foundation, aided educational institutions through-

out the Southwest. Oilman H(aroldson) L(afayette) Hunt (b.Illinois, 1889–1974), reputedly the wealthiest man in the US, was an avid supporter of right-wing causes. Howard Hughes (1905–79), an industrialist, aviation pioneer, film producer, and casino owner, became a fabulously wealthy recluse in his later years. Stanley Marcus (b.1905), head of the famous specialty store Neiman-Marcus, became an arbiter of taste for the world's wealthy and fashionable men and women. Rancher Richard King (b.New York, 1825–85) put together the famed King Ranch, the largest in the US at his death. Charles Goodnight (b.Illinois, 1836–1929) was an outstanding rancher and cattle breeder.

Influential Texan historians include folklorist John A. Lomax (b.Mississippi, 1867–1948); Walter Prescott Webb (1888–1963), whose books *The Great Plains* and *The Great Frontier* helped shape American thought; and J. Frank Dobie (1888–1964), well-known University of Texas educator and compiler of Texas folklore. Dan Rather (b.1931) has earned an excellent reputation as a television reporter. Frank Buck (1884–1950), a successful film producer, narrated and appeared in documentaries showing his exploits among animals.

William Sydney Porter (b.North Carolina, 1862–1910) apparently embezzled funds from an Austin bank, escaped to Honduras, but returned to serve a three-year jail term—during which time he began writing short stories, later published under the pen name O. Henry. Katherine Anne Porter (1890–1980) also won fame as a short-story writer. Fred Gipson (b.1908) wrote *Hound Dog Man* and *Old Yeller*, praised by critics as a remarkable evocation of a frontier boy's viewpoint. Two novels by Larry McMurtry (b.1936), *Horseman, Pass By* (film title, *Hud*) and *The Last Picture Show*, became significant motion pictures. Robert Rauschenberg (b.1925) is a leading contemporary painter. Elisabet Ney (b.Germany, 1833–1907), a sculptor, came to Texas with a European reputation and became the state's first determined feminist; she wore pants in public, and seldom passed up an opportunity to outrage Texans' Victorian mores.

Prominent Texans in the entertainment field include Mary Martin (b.1913), who reigned over the New York musical comedy world for two decades; her son, Larry Hagman (b.1931), star of the "Dallas" television series; and Joshua Logan (b.1908), director of Broadway plays and Hollywood movies. Texans who achieved national reputations with local repertory companies were Margo Jones (1912–55) and Nina Vance (1914–80), who founded and directed theater groups in Dallas and Houston, respectively; and Preston Jones (1936–79), author of *A Texas Trilogy* and other plays.

Among Texas-born musicians, Scott Joplin (1868–1917) stands out as the father of ragtime music and composer of the opera *Treemonisha*. In a more modern vein, Janis Joplin (1943–70) was a leading rock singer. Willie Nelson (b.1933) wedded progressive rock with country music to start a new school of progressive "outlaw" music. Bob Wills (b.Oklahoma, 1905–75) was the acknowledged king of western swing. Musicians Trini Lopez (b.1937), Freddy Fender (Baldemar Huerta, b.1937), and Johnny Rodriguez (b.1951) have earned popular followings based on their Mexican-American backgrounds. Charlie Pride (b.Mississippi, 1938) became the first black country-western star. In the jazz field, pianist Teddy Wilson (b.1912) was a member of the famed Benny Goodman trio in the 1930s. Trombonist Jack Teagarden (1905–64) and trumpeter Harry James (b.1916) have also been influential.

The imposing list of Texas athletes is headed by Mildred "Babe" Didrikson Zaharias (1913–56), who gained fame as an All-American basketball player in 1930, won two gold medals in track and field in the 1932 Olympics, and was the leading woman golfer during the 1940s and early 1950s. Another Texan, John Arthur "Jack" Johnson (1878–1946), was boxing's first black heavyweight champion. Texans who won fame in football include quarterbacks Sammy Baugh (b.1914), Don Meredith (b.1938), and Roger Staubach (b.Ohio, 1942), running back Earl Campbell (b.1955), and coaches Dana X. Bible (1892–1980), Darrell Royal (b.Oklahoma, 1924), and Thomas Wade "Tom" Landry (b.1924). Among other Texas sports greats are baseball Hall of Famers Tris Speaker (1888–1958) and Rogers Hornsby (1896–1963); golfers Ben Hogan (b.1912), Byron Nelson (b.1912), and Lee Trevino (b.1939); auto racing driver A(nthony) J(oseph) Foyt (b.1935); and jockey William Lee "Willie" Shoemaker (b.1931).

⁵⁰BIBLIOGRAPHY

Arbingast, Stanley A., et al. *Atlas of Texas*. Austin: University of Texas, 1976.

Bainbridge, John. *The Super-Americans*. New York: Doubleday, 1961.

Binkley, William C. *The Texas Revolution*. Baton Rouge: Louisiana State University Press, 1952.

Conaway, James. *The Texans*. New York: Knopf, 1976.

Connor, Seymour V. (ed.). *The Saga of Texas*. 6 vols. Austin: Steck-Vaughn, 1965.

Connor, Seymour V. *Texas: A History*. New York: Crowell, 1971.

Dobie, J. Frank. *Coronado's Children*. New York: Grosset and Dunlap, 1963.

Dobie, J. Frank. *The Longhorns*. Boston: Little, Brown, 1941.

Dobie, J. Frank. *The Mustangs*. Boston: Little, Brown, 1952.

Duke, Cordia Sloan, and Joe B. Frantz. *6000 Miles of Fence: Life on the XIT Ranch of Texas*. Austin: University of Texas Press, 1961.

Federal Writers' Project. *Texas: A Guide to the Lone Star State*. Rev. ed. New York: Hastings House, 1969 (orig. 1940).

Fehrenbach, T. R. *Lone Star: A History of Texas and the Texans*. New York: Macmillan, 1968.

Frantz, Joe B. *Texas: A Bicentennial History*. New York: Norton, 1976.

Frantz, Joe B., and Julian E. Choate, Jr. *The American Cowboy*. Norman: University of Oklahoma Press, 1955.

Friend, Llerena. *Sam Houston: The Great Designer*. Austin: University of Texas Press, 1954.

Gambrell, Herbert. *Anson Jones: The Last President of Texas*. Austin: University of Texas Press, 1964.

Handbook of Texas. 3 vols. Edited by Walter Prescott Webb and H. Bailey Carroll, with supplement edited by Eldon Stephen Brandon. Austin: Texas State Historical Association, 1952–76.

Horgan, Paul. *Great River: The Rio Grande in North American History*. New York: Holt, Rinehart and Winston, 1954.

Miller, Merle. *Lyndon: An Oral Biography*. New York: Putnam, 1980.

Newcomb, W. W., Jr. *The Indians of Texas: From Prehistoric to Modern Times*. Austin: University of Texas Press, 1969.

Nunn, W. C. *Texas under the Carpetbaggers*. Austin: University of Texas Press, 1962.

Purcell, Mabel, et al. *This Is Texas*. Austin: L. P. Hawkins, 1977.

Richardson, Rupert N., et al. *Texas: The Lone Star State*. 3d ed. Englewood Cliffs, N.J.: Prentice-Hall, 1970.

Sibley, Marilyn McAdams. *The Port of Houston: A History*. Austin: University of Texas Press, 1968.

Spratt, John S. *The Road to Spindletop: Economic Change in Texas, 1875–1901*. Austin: University of Texas Press, 1970.

Texas, State of. Comptroller of Public Accounts. *1979 Annual Financial Report*. Austin, 1979.

Texas Almanac and State Industrial Guide, 1980–81. 50th ed. Dallas: A. H. Belo Corp., 1979.

Texas Fact Book, 1980. Edited by Rita J. Wright and Mildred C. Anderson. Austin: University of Texas, 1980.

Texas State Directory. 23d ed. Austin, 1980.

Tinkle, Lon. *Thirteen Days to Glory*. New York: McGraw-Hill, 1958.

Webb, Walter Prescott. *The Texas Rangers*. Boston: Houghton Mifflin, 1935.

Wright, Rita J. *Texas Sources: A Bibliography*. Austin: University of Texas, 1976.

UTAH

State of Utah

ORIGIN OF STATE NAME: Named for the Ute Indians. **NICKNAME:** The Beehive State. **CAPITAL:** Salt Lake City. **ENTERED UNION:** 4 January 1896 (45th). **SONG:** "Utah, We Love Thee." **MOTTO:** Industry. **COAT OF ARMS:** In the center, a shield, flanked by American flags, shows a beehive with the state motto and six arrows above, sego lilies on either side, and the numerals "1847" (the year the Mormons settled in Utah) below. Perched atop the shield is an American eagle. **FLAG:** Inside a thin gold circle, the coat of arms and the year of statehood centered on a blue field, fringed with gold. **STATE SEAL:** The coat of arms with the words "The Great Seal of the State of Utah 1896" surrounding. **ANIMAL:** Rocky mountain elk. **BIRD:** Sea gull. **FISH:** Rainbow trout. **FLOWER:** Sego lily. **TREE:** Blue spruce. **GEM:** Topaz. **EMBLEM:** Beehive. **LEGAL HOLIDAYS:** New Year's Day, 1 January; Lincoln's Birthday, 12 February; Washington's Birthday, 3d Monday in February; Arbor Day, last Friday of April; Memorial Day, last Monday in May; Independence Day, 4 July; Pioneer Day, 24 July; Labor Day, 1st Monday in September; Columbus Day, 2d Monday in October; Veterans Day, 11 November; Thanksgiving Day, 4th Thursday in November; Christmas Day, 25 December. **TIME:** 5 A.M. MST = noon GMT.

¹LOCATION, SIZE, AND EXTENT

Located in the Rocky Mountain region of the western US, Utah ranks 11th in size among the 50 states.

The area of Utah totals 84,916 sq mi (219,932 sq km), of which land comprises 82,096 sq mi (212,628 sq km) and inland water 2,820 sq mi (7,304 sq km). Utah extends 275 mi (443 km) E–W and 345 mi (555 km) N–S.

Utah is bordered on the N by Idaho; on the NE by Wyoming; on the E by Colorado and on the S by Arizona (with the two borders joined at Four Corners); and on the W by Nevada. The total boundary length of Utah is 1,226 mi (1,973 km). The state's geographic center is in Sanpete County, 3 mi (5 km) N of Manti.

²TOPOGRAPHY

The eastern and southern two-thirds of Utah belong to the Colorado Plateau, a region characterized by deep river canyons; erosion has carved much of the plateau into buttes and mesas. The Rocky Mountains are represented by the Bear River, Wasatch, and Uinta ranges in the north and northeast. These ranges, rising well above 10,000 feet (3,000 meters), hold the highest point in Utah, Kings Peak in the Uintas, at an altitude of 13,528 feet (4,123 meters).

The arid, sparsely populated Great Basin dominates the western third of the state. Drainage in this region does not reach the sea, and streams often disappear in the dry season. To the north are the Great Salt Lake, a body of hypersaline water, and the Great Salt Lake Desert (containing the Bonneville Salt Flats), both remnants of a vast prehistoric lake that covered the region during the last Ice Age. The lowest point in Utah—2,000 feet (610 meters) above sea level—occurs on Beaverdam Creek in Washington County, in the southwest corner of the state.

Separating the Great Basin from the Colorado Plateau and the Rockies to the east is the Wasatch Plateau, or Wasatch Front, which holds most of Utah's major cities and also has the greatest rainfall, particularly in the north. Two regions rich in fossil fuels are the Kaiparowits Plateau, in southern Utah, and the Overthrust Belt, a geologic formation underlying the northwestern part of the state.

The largest lake is the Great Salt Lake, estimated at 1,685 sq mi (4,364 sq km) in December 1976; other major bodies of water are Utah Lake, Bear Lake (shared with Idaho), and Lake Powell, formed by the Glen Canyon Dam on the Colorado River. Other important rivers include the Green, flowing into the Colo-

rado; the Sevier, which drains central and southern Utah; and the Bear, which flows into the Great Salt Lake.

³CLIMATE

The climate of Utah is generally semiarid to arid. Temperatures are favorable along the Wasatch Front, with relatively mild winters. At Salt Lake City, the normal daily mean temperature is 51°F (11°C), ranging from 28°F (–2°C) in January to 77°F (25°C) in July. The record high temperature, 116°F (47°C), was set at St. George on 28 June 1892; the record low, –50°F (–46°C), at Strawberry Tunnel West, near Thistle, on 5 January 1913. The average precipitation at Salt Lake City is 15 in (38 cm) per year. The annual snowfall is about 59 in (150 cm).

⁴FLORA AND FAUNA

Botanists have recognized more than 4,000 floral species in Utah's six major life zones. Common trees and shrubs include four species of pine and three of juniper; aspen, cottonwood, maple, hawthorn, and chokecherry also flourish, along with the Utah oak, Joshua tree, and blue spruce (the state tree). Among Utah's wild flowers are sweet William and Indian paintbrush; the sego lily is the state flower. Endangered plants include three varieties of cactus (purple-spined hedgehog, silver pincushion, and Wright fishhook) and the dwarf bear-poppy.

Mule deer are the most common of Utah's large mammals; other mammals include pronghorn antelope, Rocky Mountain bighorn sheep, lynx, grizzly and black bears, and white- and black-tailed jackrabbits. Among native bird species are the great horned owl, plain titmouse, and water ouzel; the golden eagle and great white pelican are rare species, and the sea gull (the state bird) is a spring and summer visitor from the California coast. The pygmy rattler occurs in southwest Utah, and the Mormon cricket is unique to the state. Among Utah's endangered fauna (as listed by the US government) are the Utah prairie dog, bonytail and humpback chubs, Colorado River squawfish, and woundfin.

⁵ENVIRONMENTAL PROTECTION

Divisions of the Department of Natural Resources oversee water and mineral resources, parks and recreation, forests, and wildlife; spending on natural resources totaled $32.4 million in 1978/79, of which $11.1 million came from state general revenues. The Department of Agriculture is concerned with soil conservation and pesticide control, while the Department of Social Services deals with air and water pollution.

The principal environmental controversies as the 1980s began involved exploitation of southeastern coal deposits; the planned construction of the MX missile system in western Utah and neighboring Nevada; and the threat by US Steel to close its Geneva plant, employing some 5,000 Utahns, if federally mandated air and water pollution controls proved too costly. Air pollution is a serious problem along the Wasatch Front, where automobiles abound.

⁶POPULATION

At the 1970 census, Utah had a population of 1,059,273, 36th in the US. Preliminary census returns showed 1,454,630 residents in 1980; natural increase, propelled by a birthrate that invariably exceeds the national average, was the prime component of growth. Utah's estimated population density was 16 per sq mi (6 per sq km) in 1978. Again because of the birthrate, Utahns tend to be much younger than the US as a whole: more than 12% of state residents were under 5 years of age in 1976, and fully 37%—the highest percentage among the 50 states—were younger than 18 years of age.

More than four-fifths of all Utahns live in cities and towns, mostly along the Wasatch Front. Salt Lake City is Utah's most populous urban center, with a 1977 population of 167,000 in the city proper and 822,000—65% of state residents—in its metropolitan region. Ogden, the next-largest city and part (for certain statistical purposes) of the Salt Lake City metropolitan area, had an estimated 68,360 residents in 1979; Provo, 56,040; and Orem, 48,610. The newly incorporated (1980) West Valley City in Salt Lake County has an estimated population of 70,000.

⁷ETHNIC GROUPS

Hispanic Americans constitute the largest ethnic minority in Utah, with a 1970 population estimated by the state at more than 40,000. In the late 1970s, Hispanics became increasingly active in urban politics.

American Indians are the 2d-largest minority group in Utah, numbering 11,273 in 1970. Indian lands covered 2,277,000 acres (921,000 hectares) in 1978, of which 2,242,000 acres (907,000 hectares) were tribal landholdings.

Nearly 10,000 Asian-Pacific peoples live in Utah, the largest group (4,713 in 1970) being Japanese-Americans. There are at least 1,000 Chinese and some Indochinese refugees. Utah also has about 7,000 black Americans.

Because of the rugged terrain, which makes for isolated rural settlements, there are still pockets of German, Greek, Dutch, and other European-descended peoples who retain their language and customs. Overall, Utah had 132,000 residents who were foreign-born or the children of foreign-born in 1970; the United Kingdom, Germany, and Canada were the leading countries of origin.

⁸LANGUAGES

Forebears of the Ute, Gosiute, and Paiute contributed to English only a few place-names, such as Utah itself, Uinta (and Uintah), Wasatch, and Tavaputs.

Utah English is primarily that merger of Northern and Midland carried west by the Mormons, whose original New York dialect later incorporated features from southern Ohio and central Illinois. Conspicuous in Mormon speech in the central valley, although less frequent now in Salt Lake City, is a reversal of vowels before r, so that *farm* and *barn* sound like *form* and *born* and, conversely, *form* and *born* sound like *farm* and *barn*.

In 1970, 89% of the native-born and 87% of all state residents had English as their native tongue. Speakers of principal first languages were as follows:

	NATIVE-BORN	FOREIGN-BORN
English	915,740	7,557
Spanish	27,497	2,132
German	12,408	6,393
Indian languages	7,473	12

⁹RELIGIONS

The dominant religious group in Utah is the Church of Jesus Christ of Latter-day Saints, popularly known as the Mormons. The church was founded by Joseph Smith, Jr., in 1830, the same year he published the *Book of Mormon*, the group's sacred text. The Mormons' arrival in Utah climaxed a long pilgrimage that began in New York State and led westward to Missouri, then back to Illinois (where Smith was lynched), and finally across Iowa, Nebraska, and Wyoming to Salt Lake City in 1847. The Latter-day Saints had 851,050 members in Utah in 1975 according to state figures—roughly 70% of the state population. They continue to play a central role in the state's political, economic, and cultural institutions.

Other leading Christian denominations and their 1975 memberships include various Baptist groups, 8,403; Greek Orthodox, 6,400; Presbyterian, 4,928; and Episcopal, 4,100. In 1979 there were 56,533 Roman Catholics and an estimated 2,300 Jews.

¹⁰TRANSPORTATION

Utah, where the golden spike was driven in 1869 to mark the completion of the first transcontinental railroad, had 1,734 mi (2,791 km) of track in 1974. Major railroads carried 27.2 million tons of freight in 1977, of which 48% terminated in the state. Amtrak provides passenger service to Salt Lake City, Ogden, Brigham City, and Milford.

Utah in 1978 had 48,982 mi (78,829 km) of roads and streets; there were 1,014,483 registered motor vehicles and 773,082 licensed drivers. The main east–west and north–south routes— I-80 and I-15, respectively—intersect at Salt Lake City.

Utah had 95 airfields (58 public, 37 private) in 1978. By far the busiest was Salt Lake City International Airport, handling 38,155 scheduled departures and emplaning 2,022,249 passengers.

¹¹HISTORY

Utah's historic Indian groups are primarily Shoshonean: the Ute in the eastern two-thirds of the state, the Gosiute of the western desert, and the Southern Paiute of southwestern Utah. The Athapaskan-speaking Navaho of southeastern Utah migrated from western Canada, arriving not long before the Spaniards. The differing life-styles of each group remained essentially unchanged until the introduction of the horse by the Spanish sometime after 1600. White settlement from 1847 led to two wars between whites and Indians, the Walker War of 1853–54 and the even more costly Black Hawk War of 1865–68, resulting finally in the removal of many Indians to reservations.

Mexicans and Spaniards are the first non-Indians known to have entered Utah, with Juan María Antonio Rivera reportedly near present-day Moab as early as 1765. In July 1776, a party led by two Franciscan priests, Francisco Atanasio Domínguez and Silvestre Vélez de Escalante, entered Utah from the east, traversed the Uinta basin, crossed the Wasatch Mountains, and visited the Ute encampment at Utah Lake. Trade between Santa Fe, the capital of the Spanish province of New Mexico, and the Indians of Utah was fairly well established by the early 1800s.

Until 1848, the 1,200-mi (1,900-km) Spanish Trail, the longest segment of which lies in Utah, was the main route through the Southwest. Following this trail, mountain men competing for fur explored vast areas of the American West, including most of Utah's rivers and valleys. In the 1840s, Utah was traversed by California-bound settlers and explorers, the most notable being John C. Frémont.

When Joseph Smith, Jr., founder of the Church of Jesus Christ of Latter-day Saints (Mormons), was lynched at Carthage, Ill., in June 1844, Brigham Young and other Mormon leaders decided to move west. By April 1847, the pioneer company of Mormons, including three blacks, was on its way to Utah, the reports of Frémont having influenced their choice of the Great Basin as a refuge. Advance scouts entered the Salt Lake Valley on 22 July, and the rest of the company two days later. Planting and

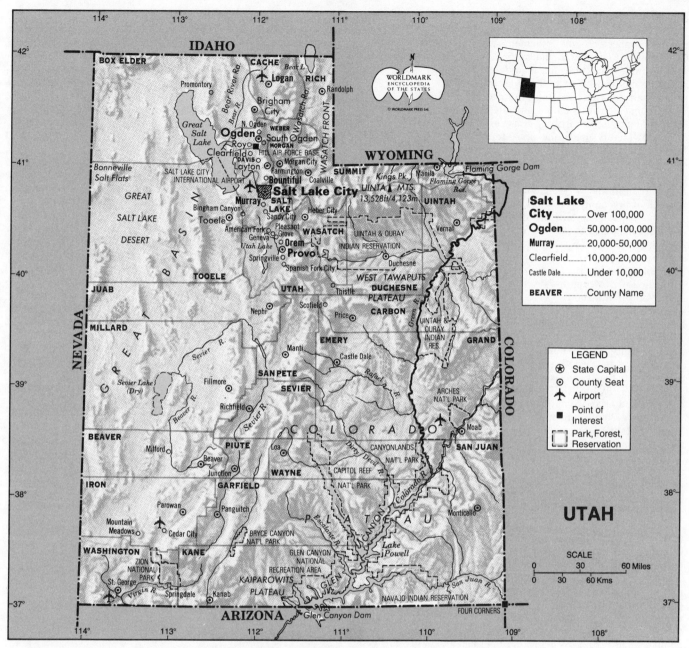

See US political: front cover D3; physical: back cover D3

LOCATION: 36°59′57″ to 41°59′39″N; 109°02′40″ to 114°02′26″W. **BOUNDARIES**: Idaho line, 154 mi (248 km); Wyoming line , 174 mi (280 km); Colorado line, 276 mi (444 km); Arizona line, 277 mi (446 km); Nevada line, 345 mi (555 km).

irrigating were begun immediately. Natural resources were regarded as community property, and the church organization served as the first government.

After the Treaty of Guadalupe-Hidalgo (1848) gave the US title to much of the Southwest, the Mormons established the provisional state of Deseret. Congress refused to admit Deseret to the Union, choosing instead to create Utah Territory "with or without slavery." The territory encompassed, in addition to present-day Utah, most of Nevada and parts of Wyoming and Colorado; land cessions during the 1860s left Utah with its present boundaries.

The territorial period lasted for 46 difficult years, marked by immigration, growth, and conflict. Reports that Utahns were in rebellion against federal authority led President James Buchanan to send an expeditionary force under Albert Sidney Johnston

to Utah in 1857. On 11 September, Mormon militiamen and their Indian allies, caught up in an atmosphere of war hysteria, massacred some 120 California-bound migrants at Mountain Meadows—the darkest event in Utah history and the only major disaster of the so-called Utah War. Peace was attained in June 1858, and Alfred Cumming assumed civil authority, replacing Brigham Young as territorial governor. Cumming's appointment signaled the beginning of prolonged hostility between Mormon leaders and federal authorities.

Almost 98% of Utah's total population was Mormon until after 1870, and the Mormon way of life dominated politics, economics, and social and cultural activities. As church president, Brigham Young remained the principal figure in the territory until his death in 1877. He contracted in 1868 with the Union Pacific to lay part of the track for the transcontinental railroad in Utah, and on 10 May 1869, the Central (now Southern) Pacific and Union Pacific were joined at Promontory. During the 1870s, new rail lines connected many settlements with the capital, Salt Lake City, spurring commerce and mining. Young had discouraged mining until agriculture and manufacturing were firmly established. Not until 1863, with the rediscovery of silver-bearing ore in Bingham Canyon, did the boom in precious metals begin. Those connected with mining, mostly non-Mormons, began to exert influence in the territory's business, politics, and social life.

Several factors made the non-Mormon minority fearful of Mormon domination: communitarian economic practices, lack of free public schools, encouragement of immigration by Mormon converts, church authoritarianism, and the mingling of church and state. But the most sensational reason was the Mormon practice of polygamy. Congress passed the Anti-Bigamy Act in 1862, but it was generally not enforced. After the Edmunds Act of 1882 was upheld by the US Supreme Court, arrests for polygamy greatly increased. Finally, in 1887, the Edmunds-Tucker Act dissolved the Mormon Church as a corporate entity, thereby threatening the survival of all Mormon institutions.

In fall 1890, Mormon President Wilford Woodruff issued a manifesto renouncing the practice of polygamy. The following year, the Republican and Democratic parties were organized in Utah, effectively ending political division along religious lines. A constitutional convention was held in 1895, and statehood became a reality on 4 January 1896. The new state constitution provided for an elected governor and a bicameral legislature, and restored the franchise to women, a privilege they had enjoyed from 1870 until 1887, when the Edmunds-Tucker Act had disfranchised Utah women and polygamous men.

The early 20th century saw further growth of the mineral industry. Many of those who came to mine copper and coal were foreign immigrants—Italians, Greeks, Slavs, Japanese, and Finns, among others—often recruited by labor agents. Militant union activity began slowly during the 1890s, until an explosion that killed 200 miners at Scofield on 1 May 1900 dramatized the plight of the miners and galvanized radical organizers in the state. It was in Utah in 1915 that a Swedish miner and songwriter named Joe Hill, associated with the Industrial Workers of the World ("Wobblies"), was executed for the murder of a Salt Lake City grocer and his son, a case that continues to generate controversy because of the circumstantial quality of the evidence against him.

Gradually, modern cities emerged, along with power plants, interurban railroads, and highways. By 1920, nearly half the population lived along the Wasatch Front. The influx of various ethnic groups diversified the state's social and cultural life, and the proportion of Mormons in the total population declined to about 68% in 1920. Less than a third of the people were engaged in agriculture and related occupations, although farm acreage had more than doubled, partly because of irrigation.

Utah businesses enjoyed the postwar prosperity of the 1920s. On the other hand, mining and agriculture were depressed throughout the 1920s and 1930s, decades marked by increased union activity, particularly in the coal and copper industries; in 1933, the United Mine Workers of America successfully unionized the Carbon County coalfields. The depression of the 1930s hit Utah especially hard. Severe droughts hurt farmers in 1931 and 1934, and high freight rates limited the expansion of manufacturing. With the coming of World War II, increased demand for food revived Utah's agriculture, and important military installations and war-related industries brought new jobs to the state. Utah was also the site of prisoner-of-war camps and of Topaz, a relocation camp for Americans of Japanese ancestry.

In the years since World War II, the state's population has doubled, while per capita income has declined relative to the national average—both trends indicative of a very high birthrate. Politics generally reflect prevailing Mormon attitudes.

[12] STATE GOVERNMENT

The state legislature, as established in the constitution of 1896, consists of a 29-member senate and a 75-seat house of representatives; senators serve for four years, representatives for two.

The chief executive officers, all elected for four-year terms, include the governor, lieutenant governor (who also serves as secretary of state), the attorney general, treasurer, and auditor. The governor must be at least 30 years of age and must have been a US citizen and state resident for at least 5 years. Gubernatorial vetoes may be overridden by two-thirds of the elected members of each house of the legislature.

Amending the constitution requires a two-thirds vote of the legislature and ratification by majority vote at the next general election. Voters must be US citizens, at least 18 years of age, and have been residents of the state 30 days prior to voting day.

[13] POLITICAL PARTIES

The Republican and Democratic parties, each affiliated with the national party organization, are the state's leading political groups. Democrats held the governorship throughout the 1970s, though Republicans have normally controlled the state legislature. As of 1979, the US House delegation was evenly split, but both US senators were Republicans. Generally, the state has voted Republican in presidential elections. Even more than party rivalry, the central facts of political life in Utah are conservatism and Mormon Church influence.

In November 1980, Utahns cast nearly 73% of their presidential votes for Ronald Reagan, less than 21% for Jimmy Carter, and 6% for other candidates. Governor Scott Matheson, a Democrat, and US Senator Jake Garn, a Republican, each won reelection.

Utah Presidential Vote by Major Political Parties, 1948–80

YEAR	ELECTORAL VOTE	UTAH WINNER	DEMOCRAT	REPUBLICAN
1948	4	*Truman (D)	149,151	124,402
1952	4	*Eisenhower (R)	135,364	194,190
1956	4	*Eisenhower (R)	118,364	215,631
1960	4	Nixon (R)	169,248	205,361
1964	4	*Johnson (D)	219,628	181,785
1968	4	*Nixon (R)	156,665	238,728
1972	4	*Nixon (R)	126,284	323,643
1976	4	Ford (R)	182,110	337,908
1980	4	*Reagan (R)	124,266	439,687

*Won US presidential election.

[14] LOCAL GOVERNMENT

Utah has 29 counties, each governed by three elected commissioners. Other elected county officials include clerk-auditor, sheriff, assessor, recorder, treasurer, county attorney, and surveyor. There were 112 municipalities with 800 or more residents in 1979. In addition, the state has about 100 smaller municipalities and at least 200 special districts.

[15] STATE SERVICES

The State Board of Education is responsible for public instruction, and the Utah State Board of Regents oversees the state college and university system. Highways, tramways, and airports are the responsibility of the Department of Transportation.

The Department of Community and Economic Development has an Office of Black Affairs, an Office of Hispanic Affairs, and a Division of Indian Affairs. Agencies dealing with the elderly, family services, public health, mental health, and corrections are under the Department of Social Services. The Department of Business Regulation licenses and regulates professions from accountancy to veterinary medicine.

16 JUDICIAL SYSTEM

Utah's highest court is the supreme court, consisting of a chief justice and 4 other justices, each serving a 10-year term. As of 1980 there were 24 district court judges, each one serving a 6-year term. Supreme court justices and district court judges are appointed by the governor from lists submitted by separate nominating commissions, one for the supreme court and one for each of seven judicial districts; each commission includes the chief justice and representatives of the governor, senate, house of representatives, and the Utah State Bar Association. Appointments must be ratified by the voters at the next general election.

Utah's crime rates are among the lowest in the US, and the incidence of violent crime is especially low. Utah has a death penalty statute and in 1977 executed a prisoner, Gary Gilmore, thus becoming the first state in a decade to carry out a sentence of capital punishment.

17 ARMED FORCES

Federal facilities in the state include Hill Air Force Base near Ogden and, in the Great Salt Lake Desert, Tooele Army Depot and Dugway Proving Ground, where nerve-gas tests have been conducted. Authorized military personnel in Utah totaled 30,857 in 1977/78. State firms were awarded $215 million in federal defense contracts in 1978.

As of 30 September 1979, 150,000 veterans were living in Utah, of whom 3,000 were veterans of World War I, 53,000 of World War II, 25,000 of the Korean conflict, and 57,000 of the Viet-Nam era. Veterans' benefits in 1977/78 totaled $110.5 million.

Utah's National Guard in 1978 had 4,800 personnel. There were 3,008 state and local police and 1,057 corrections personnel in 1977.

18 MIGRATION

After the initial exodus of Latter-day Saints from the eastern US to Utah, Mormon missionaries attracted other immigrants to the state, and some 90,000 foreign converts arrived between 1850 and 1905. Many non-Mormons were recruited from overseas to work in the mines, especially during the early 20th century. More recently, Utah had a net gain from migration of 52,000 between 1940 and 1977.

19 INTERGOVERNMENTAL COOPERATION

Utah participates in several regional agreements, including the Bear River Compact (with Idaho and Wyoming), Colorado River Compact, and the Upper Colorado River Basin Compact. The state is also a signatory to the Interstate Oil and Gas Compact, Western Corrections Compact, Western Interstate Energy Compact, and Western Regional Education Compact.

Federal aid in 1978/79 amounted to $455.6 million, of which $41 million was general revenue sharing.

20 ECONOMY

Government is the leading employer in Utah, and more than one-fourth of personal income is derived from that source. With more than 70% of Utah lands under US control and about 7% of the civilian work force on federal payrolls—another 5% is employed by defense industries or the military—the federal presence in Utah is both a major economic force and a controversial political issue. On the one hand, elected officials have sought federal funds for mammoth reclamation and power projects, such as the Flaming Gorge and Glen Canyon dams, both completed in the early 1960s. On the other hand, they resent (and sometimes publicly oppose) many federal programs concerned with social welfare, land use, or environmental protection.

Since 1965, employment has shifted away from agriculture, manufacturing, transportation, and communications, toward government, trade, and service occupations. Despite a decline in mining employment, the value of Utah's mineral industries tripled

in the three decades following World War II, and new oil, gas, and coal discoveries promise additional growth in that sector; tourism has also become a major factor in the economy.

21 INCOME

In 1978, Utahns' total personal income reached $8.7 billion, or $6,622 per capita. Although real income (as measured in constant 1972 dollars) more than doubled between 1960 and 1978, Utah's national rank in per capita income slipped from 31st to 39th during that period.

Median family income was $14,329 (23d in the US) in 1975, when 7% of Utah families and more than 8% of all Utahns were below the federal poverty level.

22 LABOR

In 1978, Utah's civilian labor force amounted to 540,000, of whom 519,000 were employed and 21,000 unemployed, with a resulting unemployment rate of 3.9%.

A federal census of workers covered by unemployment insurance in March 1977 revealed the following nonfarm employment pattern for Utah:

	ESTABLISH-MENTS	EMPLOYEES	ANNUAL PAYROLL ('000)
Agricultural services, forestry, fishing	180	673	$ 5,866
Mining	335	15,574	252,177
Contract construction	4,146	27,797	416,082
Manufacturing	1,594	70,571	888,238
Transportation, public utilities	842	21,815	324,735
Wholesale trade	2,229	27,819	357,546
Retail trade	7,137	84,121	523,748
Finance, insurance, real estate	2,653	22,562	210,781
Services	7,107	82,897	637,972
Other	525	905	8,751
TOTALS	26,748	354,734	$3,625,896

Government employees, not covered by this survey, totaled 125,765 in 1979, double the 1960 total; there were 36,815 federal, 32,220 state, and 56,730 local employees.

Average weekly earnings of production workers in 1978 totaled $224, 10% below the US average, and 2d lowest among the Rocky Mountain and Pacific states. Although Utah has a radical labor tradition, the union movement has weakened since World War II. In 1976, 62,000 of Utah's workers belonged to labor unions, 13,000 fewer than in 1970; employee associations had 31,000 members. Utah has a right-to-work law, enacted in 1955.

23 AGRICULTURE

Despite a dry climate and unpromising terrain, Utah ranked 38th in the US in agricultural income in 1978, with $477 million, mostly from livestock and livestock products. The first pioneers in Utah settled in fertile valleys near streams, which were diverted for irrigation. Since 1900, however, farmers have relied on inventive dry-land farming techniques and, more recently, on massive irrigation projects. As of 1978 there were an estimated 13,400 farms and ranches covering 12,900,000 acres (5,220,000 hectares).

The chief crops in 1979 were barley, 9 million bushels; wheat, 6.7 million bushels; hay, 1.2 million tons; and commercial apples, 51 million lb.

24 ANIMAL HUSBANDRY

Livestock and livestock products account for about three-fourths of Utah's agricultural income. At the close of 1979 there were 840,000 cattle and calves on Utah farms, 507,000 sheep and lambs, and 55,000 hogs and pigs. The 1979 cattle output was 220.8 million lb, valued at $150.8 million; sheep and lambs, 29.1 million lb, $17.2 million; and hogs and pigs, 13.3 million lb, $5.3 million. Dairy farms had 76,000 milk cows, producing 948 million lb of milk. The 1978 wool clip was 4.8 million lb.

25 FISHING

Fishing in Utah is for recreation only.

26 FORESTRY

In 1977, Utah held 15,557,000 acres (6,296,000 hectares) of forestland, consisting mostly of pine, juniper, spruce, scrub oak, and aspen. Of that, only 3,405,000 acres (1,378,000 hectares) were classed as commercial timberland, nearly three-fourths of it owned or managed by the federal government.

Shipments of lumber and wood products had a value of $121 million in 1977. Shipments of wood buildings and mobile homes were worth $59.9 million; of paper and paper products, $40.4 million.

27 MINING

Utah is an important mining state, producing significant quantities of copper, gold, silver, iron ore, lead, zinc, uranium, vanadium, tungsten, and salt, in addition to fossil fuels.

In 1978, the value of Utah's crude mineral output was nearly $1.1 billion (21st in the US). The following table shows volume and value for leading minerals in 1978 (excluding fossil fuels):

	VOLUME	VALUE
Copper	205,394 tons	$273,175,000
Gold	235,929 troy oz	45,664,000
Sand and gravel	12,000,000 tons	21,840,000
Iron ore	2,196,000 tons	21,224,000
Silver	2,900,000 troy oz	15,579,000
Salt	898,000 tons	13,532,000

The estimated value of the leading metals in 1979 was copper, $386.2 million; gold, $71.5 million; and silver, $26 million.

28 ENERGY AND POWER

During 1978, electric utilities in the state had an installed capacity of 2.4 million kw and produced 10 billion kwh of power. Over 90% of the production and capacity were in private hands.

Utah's proved oil reserves totaled 155.4 million barrels in 1978, when production was 31.5 million barrels. Reserves of natural gas amounted to 698.7 billion cu feet; production, 59.8 billion cu feet. Early in 1980 there were large new natural gas finds in northeastern Utah. The state's reserves of bituminous coal were estimated at nearly 6.6 billion tons in 1976; production reached 9.1 million tons in 1978. Coal resources of the Kaiparowits Plateau remained mostly undeveloped, largely because of environmental considerations.

29 INDUSTRY

Utah's manufacturing, diversified in products, is concentrated geographically in Salt Lake, Weber, Utah, and Cache counties, along the Wasatch Front. By number of employees, the leading sectors are nonelectrical machinery, primary metals, food and food products, and apparel and textiles.

The total value added by manufacturing in 1977 was almost $2 billion. The main industry groups were nonelectrical machinery, 16%; food, 10%; and transportation equipment, 9%. The following table shows value added by selected industries in 1972 and 1977:

	1972	1977
Petroleum refining	$42,000,000	$103,600,000
Communication equipment	24,200,000	99,300,000
Concrete, gypsum, plaster products	35,100,000	82,700,000
General industrial machinery	28,700,000	79,500,000
Construction, related machinery	NA	61,100,000

30 COMMERCE

Utah's wholesale business had sales exceeding $2.9 billion in 1972; nearly three-fourths of all sales were in Salt Lake County. Retail sales in 1977 surpassed $4.1 billion, half of that in Salt Lake County, and 70% of the total in the Salt Lake City–Ogden metropolitan area. The leading sales categories were automotive dealers, 23%; food stores, 20%; department stores, 11%; gasoline service stations, 9%; and eating and drinking places, 7%.

Foreign exports of Utah manufactured goods totaled $224 million in 1976; of agricultural products, $55 million in 1976/77.

31 CONSUMER PROTECTION

The Division of Consumer Affairs (Trade Commission) in the Department of Business Regulation is charged with enforcing Utah's Consumer Sales Practices Act.

32 BANKING

Utah in 1978 had 66 insured commercial banks, with total assets of $5.8 billion, outstanding loans of $1.1 billion, and deposits of nearly $5 billion. There were 13 insured savings and loan associations, with total assets of $3.4 billion, mortgage loans of $3 billion, and savings deposits of $2.4 billion.

33 INSURANCE

Utahns held some 2,108,000 life insurance policies in 1978; their total value was $14.9 billion, and the average coverage per family was $33,900, about 3% below the national average. Total benefit payments of $121 million included $46.1 million in death payments, $28 million in dividends, and $19 million in annuities. Premiums written by property and liability companies in 1978 totaled $338.2 million.

34 SECURITIES

The Intermountain Stock Exchange does a limited business in Salt Lake City. In addition, New York Stock Exchange member firms had 18 sales offices and 173 registered representatives in Utah in 1978. Utahns reported $93 million in dividend income on their 1977 income tax returns.

35 PUBLIC FINANCE

The annual budget is prepared by the State Budget Office and submitted by the governor to the legislature for amendment and approval. The fiscal year runs from 1 July through 30 June.

The following table summarizes state revenues and expenditures for calendar years 1978 and 1979 (in millions):

	1978	1979
REVENUES		
General sales tax	$ 258.5	$ 293.6
Individual income tax	188.1	226.7
Motor fuel tax	58.8	74.1
Corporate income tax	29.5	32.9
Other taxes	124.7	133.4
Federal aid	334.7	355.1
Other receipts	105.7	123.3
TOTALS	$1,100.0	$1,239.1
EXPENDITURES		
Education	$ 474.6	$ 524.5
Public welfare	148.6	173.2
Highways	128.6	160.4
Employment security	64.9	69.3
Health and hospitals	50.4	59.7
Natural resources	44.6	37.8
Other outlays	197.1	214.7
TOTALS	$1,108.8	$1,239.6

General revenues of all local government units in 1977/78 totaled $910.1 million; general expenditures, $880.5 million. As of mid-1978, the total local government debt was $623 million, of which school districts accounted for 46%, special districts 27%, municipalities 21%, and counties 6%.

36 TAXATION

The estimated total tax burden in 1979 was $3.3 billion, or $2,510 per capita. Of that total, federal taxes claimed more than $2.1 billion, state taxes $761 million, and local taxes $397 million.

The main source of state revenue is a 4% general sales and gross receipts tax. As of 1980, personal income tax rates ranged from 2.25% to 7.75%; the corporate income tax rate was 4%. Taxes are also levied on motor fuels, alcoholic beverages, tobacco products, and other items. Property taxes, the main source of local revenue, yielded $341.4 million in 1979.

Utahns filed 482,182 federal income tax returns in 1977, paying $717,628,000.

[37] ECONOMIC POLICY

The economic development of Utah has been dominated by two major forces: the relatively closed system of the original Mormon settlers and the more wide-open, speculative ventures of the state's later immigrants. The Mormons developed agriculture, industry, and a cooperative exchange system that excluded non-Mormons. The church actively opposed mining, and it was mostly by non-Mormon capital and non-Mormon foreign immigrants that the state's mineral industry was developed.

In recent years, these conflicts have been supplanted by a widespread fiscal conservatism that supports business activities and opposes expansion of government social programs at all levels. One Utah politician, Governor J. Bracken Lee, became nationally famous for his call to repeal the federal income tax. The Department of Community and Economic Development is the state agency responsible for the expansion of tourism and industry.

[38] HEALTH

Health conditions in Utah are exceptionally good. The average life span in 1969–71 was 72.90 (3d in the US), 69.49 for males and 76.55 for females. Infant mortality rates—9.9 per 1,000 live births for whites in 1977, and 14.9 for nonwhites—are among the lowest in the US, and the overall death rate (6 per 1,000 population in 1977) is one-third below the national average. The marriage rate exceeds the national norm, the divorce rate is far below it, and the birthrate—29.9 per 1,000 population in 1977—was 1st among the 50 states, and nearly double the rate for the nation as a whole. Only 3,100 legal abortions were performed in 1977/78, when the abortion rate was 79 per 1,000 live births.

In 1978 there were 41 hospitals in the state, with 5,084 beds and an average occupancy of 70%. Hospital personnel included 2,684 registered nurses and 960 licensed practical nurses. The average cost of hospital care was $209 per day and $1,088 per stay. There were 2,149 physicians licensed in Utah in 1977, and 853 active dentists in 1979.

[39] SOCIAL WELFARE

During 1979, public assistance payments totaled $128.4 million, of which $39.9 million was aid to families with dependent children, $85.1 million went for medical assistance, and $3.4 million came through other programs; 31,989 persons received AFDC payments, and 13,369 received Medicaid, the fastest growing of all social welfare programs in the state. The food stamp program benefited 36,127 Utahns in 1978/79, when the coupons had a subsidized value of $11.1 million. The national school lunch program enrolled 223,000 students in 1978 at a cost of $10.2 million.

As of December 1978, 141,721 persons in Utah were paid $33.1 million in monthly Social Security benefits. In 1978, federal Supplemental Security Income payments totaled $10.3 million.

During 1978, $7.7 million was spent on vocational rehabilitation, and $39 million on unemployment benefits. In 1976, benefits and withdrawals under the state-run public employees' retirement systems came to nearly $20.2 million. Other state social welfare outlays in 1978/79 included $3.8 million for children's day care, $2.1 million for foster care, and $3.2 million for the mentally retarded.

[40] HOUSING

The 1970 census counted 311,814 housing units in Utah, an increase of 19% over 1960. Of the total, 75% of the units were in single-unit structures, 22% in multiunit structures, and 3% in mobile homes. An additional 119,733 units were authorized between 1970 and 1977; their value, $2.6 billion, represented about 60% of all contract construction during that period. Nearly 98% of all occupied units in 1970 had full plumbing, ranking Utah 2d only to California among the 50 states.

[41] EDUCATION

Utahns are among the nation's leaders in educational attainments. Their illiteracy rate was only 0.6% (half the national average) in 1970, and their median number of school years completed (12.8) tied for 1st place with Colorado in 1976. That year, Utah had the highest proportion of adult high school graduates, 80.2%; nearly 18% had 4 years or more of college, and fewer than 1% had 4 years or less of grade school.

In fall 1979, Utah public schools had an enrollment of 332,575. There were 13,974 teachers in 1978/79, when per pupil expenditures reached $1,856.

Enrollment at Utah's higher educational institutions totaled 85,579 in 1979/80, 56,885 in public and 28,694 in private colleges and universities. Major public institutions include the University of Utah, with 21,603 students in 1979/80; Utah State University, 9,266; and Weber State College, 9,674. Brigham Young University (Provo), founded in 1875 and affiliated with the Latter-day Saints, is the main private institution, with 27,521 students.

[42] ARTS

Music has a central role in Utah's cultural life. Under the baton of the recently retired Maurice Abravanel, the Utah Symphony (Salt Lake City) earned a nationwide reputation, especially for its recording of the symphonies of Gustav Mahler. The Mormon Tabernacle Choir has won world renown, and Ballet West has developed into an important regional dance ensemble.

The Division of Fine Arts, in the Department of Community and Economic Development, sponsors exhibitions, artists in the schools, rural arts and folk arts programs, and statewide competitions in painting, sculpture, literature, drama, and music in cooperation with arts organizations throughout the state. In 1978, Utah had 16 art museums and galleries, several of them state-financed. The new Salt Lake City Art Center opened in 1979. Other major facilities are the Harris Fine Arts Center of Brigham Young University, Provo; Museum of Fine Arts of the University of Utah, Salt Lake City; and the Springville Art Museum.

[43] LIBRARIES AND MUSEUMS

In 1977/78, Utah had more than 50 public libraries with a combined book stock of 2,877,742 and circulation of 8,746,262. The Salt Lake County library system had 503,770 volumes; the Weber County system (including Ogden), 246,148. The leading academic libraries are the University of Utah (Salt Lake City), 1,811,271; and Brigham Young University (Provo), 1,550,000. Other collections are the Latter-day Saints' Library–Archives and the Utah State Historical Society Library, both in Salt Lake City.

During 1979, Utah had at least 49 museums, notably the Utah Museum of Natural History, Salt Lake City; Edge of the Cedars Indian Cultural Museum, Blanding; and Man and His Bread Museum, Logan. Utah had 320 historic sites as of 1980. Some are maintained as museums, including Beehive House and Wheeler Historical Farm, Salt Lake City; and the Brigham Young Winter Home, St. George.

[44] COMMUNICATIONS

There were 212 post offices in 1977, with 3,030 paid employees. As of 31 December 1978, Utah had 992,768 telephones, 732,790 residential, 259,978 business. Virtually every household had a telephone. Bell System affiliates provided 96% of the service.

A total of 66 radio stations broadcast in Utah in 1978; 34 were AM stations, 32 FM (15 of them noncommercial). There were 6 television stations in 1977; Salt Lake City had 5, including a noncommercial station, and Provo had the other, also noncommercial. Cable television served 23,908 subscribers in 18 communities in 1978.

[45] PRESS

Utah in 1978 had five daily newspapers with a combined circulation of 267,702, and four Sunday papers with 264,747 subscribers. The following table shows leading daily newspapers in 1978:

AREA	NAME	DAILY	SUNDAY
Ogden	Standard-Examiner(e,S)	47,439	48,565
Provo	Herald (e,S)	27,869	27,869
Salt Lake City	Deseret News (e)	74,087	
	Tribune (m,S)	106,459	176,386

⁴⁶ORGANIZATIONS

Salt Lake City is the world headquarters of the Church of Jesus Christ of the Latter-day Saints (Mormon). The city is also home to the Mental Retardation Association of America, the American Association for Vital Records and Public Health Statistics, and Executive Women International. The Western Literature Society is in Logan.

⁴⁷TOURISM, TRAVEL, AND RECREATION

Utah, with a billion-dollar tourist industry, offers exceptionally varied opportunities for travel and recreation. Temple Square, Pioneer Trail State Park, and Hogle Zoological Gardens are leading attractions of Salt Lake City, about 11 mi (18 km) east of the Great Salt Lake. At the Bonneville Salt Flats, west of the lake and near the border with Nevada, experimental automobiles have set world land-speed records.

Under federal jurisdiction are 5 parks—the Arches, Bryce Canyon, Canyonlands, Capitol Reef, and Zion—2 recreation areas, 6 monuments, and 1 historical site, Golden Spike. Of these the most visited are the Glen Canyon National Recreation Area and Zion National Park. There were 44 state parks in 1980.

Mountain climbing, skiing, fishing, hunting, and rock climbing are major outdoor recreations. Licenses were issued to 227,037 hunters and 369,144 fishermen in 1977/78.

⁴⁸SPORTS

Utah's only major league professional team is basketball's Utah Jazz, which moved from New Orleans at the close of the 1978/79 season. Basketball is also popular at the college level. The University of Utah's Running Utes won the NCAA championship in 1944 and the National Invitation Tournament in 1947, while the Cougars of Brigham Young were first in the Western Athletic Conference in 1979 and won NIT titles in 1951 and 1966.

In baseball, Salt Lake City and Ogden have teams in the class-AAA Pacific Coast League. Salt Lake City's Eagles are in the Central Hockey League.

⁴⁹FAMOUS UTAHNS

George Sutherland (b.England, 1862–1942) capped a long career in Utah Republican politics by serving as an associate justice of the US Supreme Court (1922–38). Other important federal officeholders from Utah include George Dern (b.Nebraska, 1872–1936), a mining man who was President Franklin D. Roosevelt's secretary of war from 1933 to 1936; Ivy Baker Priest (1905–75), US treasurer during 1953–61; and Ezra Taft Benson (b.Idaho, 1899), a high official of the Mormon Church and President Dwight Eisenhower's secretary of agriculture. Prominent in the US Senate for 30 years was Republican tariff expert Reed Smoot (1862–1941), also a Mormon Church official. The most colorful politician in state history, J(oseph) Bracken Lee (b.1899), was mayor of Price for 12 years before serving as governor during 1949–57 and mayor of Salt Lake City during 1960–72.

The dominant figure in Utah history is undoubtedly Brigham Young (b.Vermont, 1801–77), the great western colonizer. As leader of the Mormons for more than 30 years, he initiated white settlement of Utah in 1847 and until his death exerted almost complete control over life in the territory. Other major historical figures include Eliza R. Snow (b.Massachusetts, 1804–87), Mormon women's leader; Wakara, anglicized Walker (c.1808–55), the foremost Ute leader of the early settlement period; Colonel Patrick Edward Conner (b.Ireland, 1820–91), founder of Camp Douglas and father of Utah mining; George Q. Cannon (b.England, 1827–1901), editor, businessman, political leader, and a power in the Mormon Church for more than 40 years; and Lawrence Scanlan (b.Ireland, 1843–1915), first Roman Catholic bishop of Salt Lake City, founder of schools and a hospital.

Utah's most important scientist is John A. Widtsoe (b.Norway, 1872–1952), whose pioneering research in dry-land farming revolutionized agricultural practices. Noted inventors are gunsmith John M. Browning (1855–1926) and television innovator Philo T. Farnsworth (1906–71). Of note in business are mining entrepreneurs David Keith (b.Canada, 1847–1918), Samuel Newhouse (b.New York, 1853–1930), Susanna Emery-Holmes (b.Missouri, 1859–1942), Thomas Kearns (b.Canada, 1862–1918), and Daniel C. Jackling (b.Missouri, 1869–1956). Labor leaders include William Dudley "Big Bill" Haywood (1869–1928), radical Industrial Workers of the World organizer and Socialist, and Frank Bonacci (b.Italy, 1884–1954), United Mine Workers of America organizer and legislator.

Utah's artists and writers include sculptors Cyrus E. Dallin (1861–1944) and Mahonri M. Young (1877–1957), painter Henry L. A. Culmer (b.England, 1854–1914), author-critic Bernard A. DeVoto (1897–1955), poet-critic Brewster Ghiselin (b.Missouri, 1903), folklorist Austin E. Fife (b.Idaho, 1909), and novelists Maurine Whipple (b.1904), Virginia Sorensen (b.1912), and Edward Abbey (b.1927).

Actresses from Utah are Maude Adams (1872–1953), Loretta Young (b.1913), and Laraine Day (b.1920). Emma Lucy Gates Bowen (1880–1951), an opera singer, founded her own traveling opera company, and Willam F. Christensen (b.1902) founded Ballet West. Maurice Abravanel (b.Greece, 1903) conducted the Utah Symphony for many years.

Sports figures of note are former world middleweight boxing champion Gene Fullmer (b.1931) and former Los Angeles Rams tackle Merlin Olsen (b.1940).

⁵⁰BIBLIOGRAPHY

Alter, J. Cecil. *Utah, the Storied Domain: A Documentary History.* 3 vols. Chicago: American Historical Society, 1932.

Arrington, Leonard J., and Davis Bitton. *The Mormon Experience: A History of the Latter-day Saints.* New York: Knopf, 1979.

Morgan, Dale. *The Great Salt Lake.* New York: Bobbs-Merrill, 1947.

Papanikolas, Helen Z., ed. *The Peoples of Utah.* Salt Lake City: Utah State Historical Society, 1976.

Peterson, Charles S. *Utah: A Bicentennial History.* New York: Norton, 1977.

Poll, Richard D., et. al. *Utah's History.* Provo: Brigham Young University Press, 1978.

Stegner, Wallace. *The Gathering of Zion: The Story of the Mormon Trail.* New York: McGraw-Hill, 1964.

Utah, State of. Department of Finance. Utah State Archives and Records Service. *Utah Official Roster, 1979–80.* Salt Lake City, 1979.

Utah, University of. College of Business. Bureau of Economic and Business Research. *1979 Utah Statistical Abstract.* 8th ed. Salt Lake City, 1979.

VERMONT

State of Vermont

ORIGIN OF STATE NAME: Derived from the French words *vert* (green) and *mont* (mountain). **NICKNAME:** The Green Mountain State. **CAPITAL:** Montpelier. **ENTERED UNION:** 4 March 1791 (14th). **SONG:** "Hail, Vermont!" **MOTTO:** Freedom and Unity. **COAT OF ARMS:** Rural Vermont is represented by a pine tree in the center, three sheaves of grain on the left and a cow on the right, with a background of fields and mountains; a deer crests the shield. Below are crossed pine branches and the state name and motto. **FLAG:** The coat of arms on a field of dark blue. **OFFICIAL SEAL:** Bisecting Vermont's golden seal is a row of wooded hills above the state name; the upper half has a spearhead, pine tree, cow, and two sheaves of wheat, while two more sheaves and the state motto fill the lower half. **ANIMAL:** Morgan horse. **BIRD:** Hermit thrush. **FISH:** Brook trout (cold water); walleye pike (warm water). **FLOWER:** Red clover. **TREE:** Sugar maple. **INSECT:** Honeybee. **POET LAUREATE:** Robert Frost. **LEGAL HOLIDAYS:** New Year's Day, 1 January; Lincoln's Birthday, 12 February; Washington's Birthday, 3d Monday in February; Town Meeting Day, 1st Tuesday in March; Memorial Day, 30 May; Independence Day, 4 July; Bennington Battle Day, 16 August; Labor Day, 1st Monday in September; Columbus Day, 2d Monday in October; Veterans Day, 11 November; Thanksgiving Day, 4th Thursday in November; Christmas Day, 25 December. **TIME:** 7 A.M. EST = noon GMT.

¹LOCATION, SIZE, AND EXTENT

Situated in the northeastern US, Vermont is the 2d largest of the 6 New England states, and ranks 43d in size among the 50 states.

Vermont's total area of 9,609 sq mi (24,887 sq km) consists of 9,267 sq mi (24,002 sq km) of land and 342 sq mi (886 sq km) of inland water. Vermont extends 90 mi (145 km) E–W; its maximum N–S extension is 158 mi (254 km). The state resembles a wedge, wide and flat at the top and narrower at the bottom.

Vermont is bordered on the N by the Canadian province of Quebec; on the E by New Hampshire (separated by the Connecticut River); on the S by Massachusetts; and on the W by New York (with part of the line passing through Lake Champlain and the Poultney River).

The state's territory includes several islands and the lower part of a peninsula jutting south into Lake Champlain from the Canadian border, collectively called Grand Isle County. Vermont's total boundary length is 561 mi (903 km). Its geographic center is in Washington County, 3 mi (5 km) E of Roxbury.

²TOPOGRAPHY

The Green Mountains are the most prominent topographic region in Vermont. Extending north–south from the Canadian border to the Massachusetts state line, the Green Mountains contain the state's highest peaks, including Mansfield, 4,393 feet (1,339 meters), the highest point in Vermont; Killington, 4,241 feet (1,293 meters); and Ellen, 4,135 feet (1,260 meters). A much lower range, the Taconic Mountains, straddles the New York–Vermont border for about 80 mi (129 km). To their north is the narrow Valley of Vermont; farther north is the Champlain Valley, a lowland about 20 mi (32 km) wide between Lake Champlain—site of the state's lowest point, 95 feet (29 meters) above sea level—and the Green Mountains. The Vermont piedmont is a narrow corridor of hills and valleys stretching about 100 mi (161 km) to the east of the Green Mountains. The Northeast Highlands consist of an isolated series of peaks near the New Hampshire border.

Vermont's major inland rivers are the Missisquoi, Lamoille, and Winooski. The state includes about 75% of Lake Champlain on its western border and about 25% of Lake Memphremagog on the northern border.

³CLIMATE

Burlington's normal daily mean temperature is 44°F (7°C), ranging from 17°F (−8°C) in January to 67°F (19°C) in July. Winters are generally colder and summer nights cooler in the higher elevations of the Green Mountains. The record high temperature for the state is 105°F (41°C), registered at Vernon on 4 July 1911; the record low, −50°F (−46°C), at Bloomfield, 30 December 1933. Burlington's average annual precipitation of 32 in (81 cm) is less than the statewide average of 40 in (102 cm). Annual snowfall ranges from 55 to 65 in (140–165 cm) in the lower regions, and from 100 to 120 in (254–305 cm) in the mountain areas.

⁴FLORA AND FAUNA

Common trees of Vermont are the commercially important sugar maple (the state tree), the butternut, and various birches and ashes. Other recognized flora include 15 types of conifer, 130 grasses, and 192 sedges. As of 1980, Vermont classified 57 plants as endangered, including alpine woodsia and adder's-mouth.

Native mammalian species include white-tailed deer, coyote, red fox, and snowshoe hare. Several species of trout are prolific. Characteristic birds include the raven *(Corvus corax)*, gray or Canada jay, and saw-whet owl. Among endangered animals in Vermont are the Canada lynx, pine marten, and lake sturgeon.

⁵ENVIRONMENTAL PROTECTION

All natural resource regulation, planning, and operation are coordinated by the Agency of Environmental Conservation, established in 1970. The state is divided into 14 soil and water conservation districts covering about 5,935,000 acres (2,402,000 hectares); these are operated by local landowners, with the assistance of the state Natural Resources Conservation Council. Several dams on the Winooski and Connecticut river drainage basins help control flooding.

Legislation enacted in 1973 bans the use of throwaway beverage containers in Vermont, in an effort to reduce roadside litter.

⁶POPULATION

Vermont ranked 48th among the 50 states in population, with a 1970 census total of 444,732. Preliminary census data for 1980 put the total at 511,299, an increase of 15%.

In 1970, Vermont's population was 68% rural, the highest percentage of any state and the highest percentage in Vermont since 1920; the rural population increased 26% between 1960 and 1970, and the urban population declined by nearly 5%. The population density statewide was 48 per sq mi (19 per sq km) in 1970.

According to preliminary census data, Burlington had 37,727 residents in 1980; Rutland 18,427; and Montpelier, 8,249.

7 ETHNIC GROUPS

The largest ethnic minority, first- and second-generation French Canadians, makes up about 10% of the population. These Vermonters are congregated chiefly in the northern counties and in such urban centers as Burlington, St. Albans, and Montpelier. First- and second-generation Italians make up a little over 1% of the population.

The 1970 census counted few non-Caucasians. There were about 1,000 blacks and perhaps 1,000 others, including 229 American Indians.

8 LANGUAGES

A few place-names and very few Indian-language speakers remain as evidence of the early Vermont presence of the Algonkian Mohawk tribe and of some Iroquois in the north. Vermont English, although typically of the Northern dialect, differs from that of New Hampshire in several respects, including retention of the final /r/ and use of *eavestrough* in place of eavespout.

In 1970, 84% of the native-born and 81% of all state residents had English as their mother tongue. Speakers of major first languages were as follows:

	NATIVE-BORN	FOREIGN-BORN
English	357,473	4,893
French	34,560	7,633
Italian	4,185	1,037
German	2,962	1,486
Polish	2,722	484

9 RELIGIONS

From the early days of settlement to the present, Congregationalists (whose church is now called the United Church of Christ) have played a dominant role in the state. They are the leading Protestant denomination in the state, with 29,073 known adherents in 1971. Other major Protestant groups include the United Methodists, 23,202; Episcopalians, 12,966; and American Baptists, 10,576. The largest single religious organization in Vermont is the Roman Catholic Church, with 159,630 members in 1979. There is a small Jewish population (estimated at 2,465 in 1979), most of which lives in Burlington.

Vermont was the birthplace of both Joseph Smith and Brigham Young, founders of the Church of Jesus Christ of Latter-day Saints. The state had 1,744 Mormons in 1971.

10 TRANSPORTATION

Vermont's first railroad, completed in 1849, served more as a link to Boston than as an intrastate line; it soon went into receivership, as did many other early state lines. From a high of nearly 1,100 mi (1,770 km) of track in 1910, trackage shrank to 765 mi (1,231 km) in 1974.

Of the 15,218 mi (24,491 km) of highways in 1979, towns had jurisdiction over 12,921 mi (20,794 km), the state over 2.297 mi (3,697 km). A total of 379,249 motor vehicles were registered in 1978, when there were 328,069 licensed drivers.

Three of Vermont's 21 public and 3 private airports offered regularly scheduled commercial flights as of 1978. Burlington International Airport is the state's major air terminal.

11 HISTORY

Vermont has been inhabited continuously since about 10,000 BC. Archaeological finds suggest the presence of a pre-Algonkian group along the Otter River. Algonkian-speaking Abnaki settled along Lake Champlain and in the Connecticut Valley, and Mahican settled in the southern counties between 1200 and 1790. In 1609, Samuel de Champlain crossed the lake that now bears his name, becoming the first European explorer of Vermont. From the 1650s to the 1760s, French, Iroquois Indians from New York, Dutch, and English passed through the state over trails connecting Montreal with Massachusetts and New York. Few settled there. In 1666, the French built and briefly occupied Ft. Ste. Anne on Isle La Motte, and in 1690 there was a short-lived settlement at Chimney Point. Ft. Dummer, near Brattleboro, was the first permanent settlement, built in 1724 to protect the Massachusetts border.

Governor Benning Wentworth of New Hampshire, claiming that his colony extended as far west as did Massachusetts and Connecticut, had granted 131 town charters in the territory by 1764. In that year, the crown declared that New York's northeastern boundary was the Connecticut River. Owners of New Hampshire titles, fearful of losing their land, prevented New York from enforcing its jurisdiction. The Green Mountain Boys, organized by Ethan Allen in 1770–71, scared off the defenseless settlers under New York title and flouted New York courts.

Shortly after the outbreak of the Revolutionary War, Ethan Allen's men helped capture Ft. Ticonderoga, and for two years frontiersmen fought in the northern theater. On 16 August 1777, after a skirmish at Hubbardton, a Vermont contingent routed German detachments sent by British General Burgoyne toward Bennington, a battle that contributed to the general's surrender at Saratoga, N.Y. There were several British raids on Vermont towns during the war.

Vermont declared itself an independent republic with the name "New Connecticut" in 1777, promulgated a constitution abolishing slavery and providing universal manhood suffrage, adopted the laws of Connecticut, and confiscated Tory lands. Most Vermonters preferred to join the US, but the dominant Allen faction, with large holdings in the northwest, needed free trade with Canada, even at the price of returning to the British Empire. Political defeat of the Allen faction in 1789 led to negotiations that settled New York's claims and secured Vermont's admission to the Union on 4 March 1791.

With 30,000 people in 1781 and nearly 220,000 in 1810, Vermont was a state of newcomers spread evenly over the hills in self-sufficient homesteads. Second-generation Vermonters developed towns and villages with water-powered mills, charcoal-fired furnaces, general stores, newspapers, craft shops, churches, and schools. Those who ran these local institutions tended to be Congregationalist in religion, and successively Federalist, Whig, and Republican in party politics. Dissidents in the early 1800s included minority Protestants suffering legal and social discrimination, revivalist reformers attacking such targets as drink and Masonry, hardscrabble farmers, and Jacksonian Democrats.

Northwestern Vermonters smuggled to avoid the US foreign trade embargo of 1808, and widespread trade continued with Canada during the War of 1812. In September 1814, however, Vermont soldiers fought in the Battle of Plattsburgh, N.Y., won by Thomas Macdonough's fleet built at Vergennes the previous winter. The Mexican War was unpopular in the state, but Vermont, which had strongly opposed slavery, was an enthusiastic supporter of the Union during the Civil War.

The opening of the Champlain-Hudson Canal in 1823, and the building of the early railroad lines in 1846–53, made Vermont more vulnerable to western competition, killed many small farms and businesses, and stimulated emigration. The remaining farmers' purchasing power steadily increased, as they held temporary advantages in wool, then in butter and cheesemaking, and finally in milk production. The immigration of the Irish and French Canadians stabilized the population, and the expansion of light industry bolstered the economy.

During the 20th century and especially after World War II, autos, buses, trucks, and planes took over most passengers and much freight from the railroads. Manufacturing, especially light industry, prospered in valley villages. Vermont's picturesque landscape began to attract city buyers of second homes, first for summer, later for skiing and four-season recreation. Still rural in population distribution, Vermont became increasingly suburban in outlook, as new highways made the cities and hills mutually accessible.

¹²STATE GOVERNMENT

A constitution establishing Vermont as an independent republic was adopted in 1777. This document, as revised and amended, still governs the state.

The general assembly consists of a 150-member house of representatives and a 30-member senate. All legislators are elected to two-year terms. State elective officials include the governor, lieutenant governor (elected separately), treasurer, secretary of state, auditor of accounts, and attorney general, all of whom serve two-year terms.

The legislature meets biennially in odd-numbered years. All bills require a majority vote in each house for passage. Bills can be vetoed by the governor, and vetoes can be overridden by a two-thirds vote of each legislative house. A constitutional amendment must first be passed by a two-thirds vote in the senate, followed by a majority in the house during the same legislative session. It must then receive majority votes in both houses during the next legislative session before it can be submitted to the voters for approval.

Voters must be US citizens and 18 years of age; there is no minimum residency requirement.

¹³POLITICAL PARTIES

The Republican Party, which originally drew strength from powerful abolitionist sentiment, gained control of Vermont state offices in 1856 and for more than 100 years totally dominated state politics. No Democrat was elected governor from 1853 until 1962.

In 1978 there were 286,275 registered voters; no party affiliation is required. As of late 1979, Republicans controlled the governorship and both houses of the legislature. The lieutenant governor and one of the state's two US senators were Democrats.

Vermont has often shown its independence in national political elections. In 1832, it was the only state to cast a plurality vote for the Anti-Masonic presidential candidate, William Wirt; in 1912, the only state besides Utah to vote for William Howard Taft; and in 1936, the only state besides Maine to prefer Alf Landon to Franklin D. Roosevelt. Many Vermonters split their tickets in November 1980. Two incumbents—US Senator Patrick Leahy, a Democrat, and Governor Richard Snelling, a Republican—each won reelection, as Republican presidential nominee Ronald Reagan carried the state with a 44% plurality of the popular vote; Jimmy Carter took 38% and John Anderson 15%.

Vermont Presidential Vote by Major Political Parties, 1948–80

YEAR	ELECTORAL VOTE	VERMONT WINNER	DEMOCRAT	REPUBLICAN
1948	3	Dewey (R)	45,557	75,926
1952	3	*Eisenhower (R)	43,299	109,717
1956	3	*Eisenhower (R)	42,540	110,390
1960	3	Nixon (R)	69,186	98,131
1964	3	*Johnson (D)	108,127	54,942
1968	3	*Nixon (R)	70,255	85,142
1972	3	*Nixon (R)	68,174	117,149
1976	3	Ford (R)	77,798	100,387
1980	3	*Reagan (R)	81,952	94,628

*Won US presidential election.

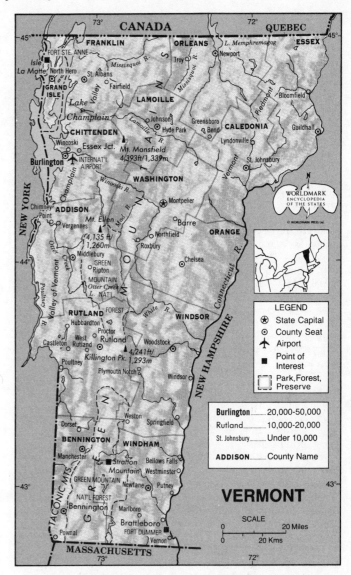

See US political: front cover M2; physical: back cover M2.
LOCATION: 42° 43′ 25″ to 45° 00′ 50″ N. 71° 27′ 57″ to 73° 26′ 03″ W.
BOUNDARIES: Canadian line, 89 mi (143 km); New Hampshire line, 242 mi (390 km); Massachusetts line, 41 mi (66 km); New York line, 189 mi (304 km).

¹⁴LOCAL GOVERNMENT

As of 1979 there were 14 counties, 9 cities, 237 organized towns, 5 unorganized towns, 50 incorporated villages, and 5 gores and grants (nongoverned areas) in Vermont. County officers, operating out of shire towns (county seats), include the probate court judge, assistant judges of the county court, county clerk, state's attorney, high bailiff, treasurer, and sheriff. All cities have mayor-council systems. Towns are governed by three selectmen, who serve staggered three-year terms; one is elected at each annual town meeting, held on the 1st Tuesday in March. Larger towns also have town managers.

¹⁵STATE SERVICES

Vermont's Department of Education oversees public elementary, secondary, higher education, and adult education programs. The Agency of Transportation includes the Department of Motor Vehicles, Transportation Board, and Hazardous Materials Committee. The Agency of Human Services coordinates programs for nursing homes, veterans' affairs, social welfare, employment and training, health, corrections, and parole. The Agency of Development and Community Affairs administers federal housing programs and offers aid to localities. The Department of Labor and Industry mediates labor disputes and operates the state Occupational Safety and Health Review Board.

16 JUDICIAL SYSTEM

Vermont's highest court is the supreme court, which consists of a chief justice and 4 associate justices. Other courts include the superior court (1 chief judge, 7 superior judges) and a district court divided into 6 territorial units embracing 16 circuits. All judges are appointed by the governor to six-year terms, subject to senate confirmation, from a list of qualified candidates prepared by the Judicial Nominating Board, which includes representatives of the governor, the legislature, and the Vermont bar association. There are also 28 assistant judges and 19 probate court judges, all of them elected to four-year terms.

Crime rates in virtually every category are far below the national average.

17 ARMED FORCES

An estimated $109 million in federal defense contracts was awarded to Vermont firms in 1978. Of the estimated 64,000 veterans living in Vermont in 1979, about 1,000 served in World War I, 25,000 in World War II, 9,000 in the Korean conflict, and 21,000 during the Viet-Nam era. Veterans' benefits in 1978 totaled $51 million.

18 MIGRATION

The earliest Vermont settlers were farmers from southern New England and New York; most were of English descent although some Dutch settlers moved to Vermont from New York. French Canadians came beginning in the 1830s, and by 1850, several thousand had moved into Vermont. As milling, quarrying, and mining grew during the 19th century, other Europeans arrived—small groups of Italians and Scots in Barre, and Poles, Swedes, Czechs, Russians, and Austrians in the Rutland quarry areas. Irish immigrants built the railroads in the mid-19th century. Steady outmigrations during the 19th and early 20th centuries kept population increases down, and in the decades of 1890–1900 and 1910–20, the population dropped. During the 1960s, the population of blacks more than doubled, though they still accounted for only 0.2% of the population in 1970.

19 INTERGOVERNMENTAL COOPERATION

Vermont belongs to such New England bodies as the Regional Commission, Interstate Water Pollution Control Commission, River Basin Commission, and Board of Higher Education. The state also takes part in the Connecticut River Valley Flood Control Commission, Lake Champlain Bridge Commission, and Interstate Commission on Lake Champlain Basin.

Federal aid to Vermont totaled $1.7 billion in 1978/79.

20 ECONOMY

During its early years of statehood, Vermont was overwhelmingly agricultural, with beef cattle, sheep, and dairying contributing greatly to the state's income. After World War II, agriculture was replaced by manufacturing and tourism as the backbone of the economy. Durable goods manufacturing (primarily electronics and machine parts), wholesale and retail trade, and other service industries have shown the largest growth in employment.

21 INCOME

Vermont ranked 42d in per capita income with $6,541 in 1978. Total personal income that year was $3.2 billion, 0.2% of the US total and the smallest amount of any state. The median family income was $12,415 (37th in the US) in 1975, when more than 13% of all Vermonters were below the federal poverty level.

22 LABOR

According to the US Department of Labor, 222,000 Vermonters were employed during 1978, about 42% of them women.

A federal census of workers covered by unemployment insur-

ance in March 1977 revealed the following nonfarm employment pattern for Vermont:

	ESTABLISH-MENTS	EMPLOYEES	ANNUAL PAYROLL ('000)
Agricultural services, forestry, fishing	129	572	$ 5,150
Mining	36	916	11,884
Contract construction	1,645	5,750	77,181
Manufacturing, of which:	941	40,729	495,318
Electric, electronic equipment	(31)	(7,252)	(122,026)
Transportation, public utilities	494	7,021	91,498
Wholesale trade	746	6,771	73,295
Retail trade	3,752	28,732	180,782
Finance, insurance, real estate	899	7,097	73,092
Services	3,518	38,940	277,391
Other	180	152[1]	1,738
TOTALS	12,340	136,680	$1,287,329

[1]As of 12 March 1977.

There were 39,000 members of unions or employee associations in Vermont in 1976.

23 AGRICULTURE

Although Vermont is one of the nation's most rural states, its agricultural income was only $313.5 million in 1978, 43d highest in the US. More than 90% of that came from livestock and livestock products. The leading crops were corn for silage, 1,470,000 tons; hay, 885,000 tons; and apples, 47,000,000 lb.

24 ANIMAL HUSBANDRY

The merino sheep and the Morgan horse (a breed developed in Vermont) were common sights on pastures more than a century ago, but today they have been for the most part replaced by dairy cattle. Vermont led the New England states in milk production in 1979 with 2.2 billion lb. Other dairy products included 71.2 million lb of cheese and 4.4 million lb of butter.

25 FISHING

Sport fishermen can find ample species of trout, perch, walleye pike, bass, and pickerel in Vermont's waters, many of which are stocked by the Department of Fish and Game. There is little commercial fishing.

26 FORESTRY

The Green Mountain State is covered by 4,512,000 acres (1,826,000 hectares) of forestland—76% of the state's total land area—much of it owned or leased by lumber companies. More than 25% of all manufacturing establishments in the state depend on the lumber industry. Shipments of forest products in 1977 included paper and paper products, $195.4 million; lumber and wood products, $137.5 million; and household furniture, $59.5 million. Vermont is the nation's leading producer of maple syrup; the 1978 output of 410,000 gallons represented more than 35% of the US total.

The largest forest reserve in Vermont is the Green Mountain National Forest, with 271,465 acres (109,858 hectares) in 1979.

27 MINING

Although Vermont is a leading producer of granite, marble, talc, and asbestos, the state's total estimated mining income for 1978 was only $48 million, 45th in the US.

The granite hills near Barre contain most of the state's actively worked granite deposits. Marble is mined in the West Rutland–Proctor area; slate is found in the southeast. Sand and gravel are quarried throughout the state. The estimated 1978 output included 3.5 million tons of sand and gravel and 2.4 million tons of stone.

28 ENERGY AND POWER

Because of the state's lack of fossil fuel resources, utility bills are higher in Vermont than in most states. During 1977, 60 plants with a capacity of 940,300 kw generated 4.5 billion kwh of power, nearly 79% of which was produced by the state's lone nuclear plant at Vernon, operated by Vermont Yankee Nuclear Power Corp.

[29] INDUSTRY

Value added by manufacturing exceeded $1 billion in 1977—a figure important to the state's economy though very small by national standards. Leading industry groups (and their percentage of value added) were electrical and electronic equipment, 21%; nonelectrical machinery, 18%; fabricated metal products, 10%; paper and paper products, 8%; printing and publishing, 7%; food and food products, 6%; and lumber and wood products, 5%;

Scales, machine tools, and electronics components are important manufactured items. The following table shows value added by manufacturing for selected industries in 1972 and 1977:

	1972	1977
Machine tools	NA	$89,400,000
Dairy products	$15,800,000	33,100,000
Household furniture	NA	29,900,000
Cut stone, stone products	27,700,000	29,000,000

[30] COMMERCE

Wholesale trade in 1972 exceeded $626.6 million. Retail trade totaled $1.7 billion in 1977, of which the leading sectors were food stores, 23%; automotive dealers, 18%; gasoline service stations, 8%; and eating and drinking places, 8%. Foreign exports of Vermont manufactures were estimated at $200 million for 1976.

[31] CONSUMER PROTECTION

The Consumer Protection Division of the Attorney General's Office handles most consumer complaints. The Vermont Public Service Board's Consumer Affairs Division monitors utility rates, and the Agency of Human Services' Office on Aging protects the rights of the state's senior citizens.

[32] BANKING

In 1978 there were 29 insured commercial banks with total assets of $2 billion and deposits exceeding $1.8 billion, and 7 savings and loan associations with assets of $230 million and deposits of $130.5 million.

[33] INSURANCE

More than 600 insurance companies are licensed to do business in Vermont. As of 1978, about 799,000 life insurance policies worth nearly $5.6 billion were held by Vermonters. The average Vermont family had $31,300 in life insurance coverage. Automobile insurance premiums written in the state in 1978 totaled $63.3 million; homeowners insurance premiums, $22.7 million.

[34] SECURITIES

There are no stock or commodity exchanges in Vermont. New York Stock Exchange member firms had 6 sales offices and 45 registered representatives in the state in 1978. Vermonters reported $79.2 million in dividend income on their federal tax returns in 1977.

[35] PUBLIC FINANCE

The budgets for two fiscal years are submitted by the governor to the general assembly for approval during its biennial session. The fiscal year runs from 1 July to 30 June.

The following table shows estimated general revenues and expenditures for the years 1978/79 and 1979/80:

REVENUES	1978/79	1979/80
Personal income taxes	$ 73,400,000	$ 76,700,000
Sales and use taxes	35,800,000	37,900,000
Corporate income taxes	22,000,000	23,100,000
Other taxes	56,108,000	58,760,000
Other receipts	15,650,000	15,000,000
TOTALS	$202,958,000	$211,460,000

EXPENDITURES	1978/79	1979/80
Education	$ 87,301,618	$ 91,251,503
Human services	61,695,914	61,943,066
Debt service	31,585,369	33,515,275
Other expenditures	24,084,073	28,807,303
TOTALS	$204,666,974	$215,517,147

These figures do not include activities supported by federal funds or by self-supporting revolving funds. Total expenditures for 1978/79 were $477,280,322; for 1979/80, $511,350,909.

The total outstanding debt of state and local governments in Vermont was $606 million, or $1,255 per capita, as of mid-1977.

[36] TAXATION

Vermont ranked 50th in the US in state and local tax receipts in 1977, with $391 million; the tax burden was $810 per capita. The state imposes personal and corporate income taxes, sales and use taxes, a franchise tax, and an inheritance tax. Taxes are also levied on beverages, electrical energy, insurance, meals and rooms, old age assistance, real estate transfers, and tobacco products, among other items.

In 1977, Vermonters filed 190,052 federal income tax returns and paid $239 million in tax.

[37] ECONOMIC POLICY

Incentives for industrial expansion include state and municipally financed industrial sites, state employment development and training funds, revenue bond financing, loans and loan guarantees for construction and equipment, and financial incentives for locating plants in areas of high unemployment. There are also exemptions from inventory taxes and sales tax on new equipment and raw materials.

[38] HEALTH

Vermont's average life expectancy during 1969–71 was 71.64 years, 18th among the 50 states. In 1977 there were about 7,000 live births (14.5 per 1,000 population); the infant mortality rate for whites was 10 per 1,000 live births, and there were 2,400 legal abortions.

Heart disease was the leading cause of death, though the rate of 321 per 100,000 population was below the US average. As of 1974 there were 8,440 alcoholics and 5,725 addicts and drug abusers in state rehabilitation programs. Of the 19 hospitals operating in 1978, 17 were general and 2 were psychiatric; hospital personnel included 1,438 registered nurses and 757 licensed practical nurses. The average costs per stay ($1,327) and per day ($158) were below the US average. The state had 1,049 licensed physicians in 1977, and 270 professionally active dentists in 1979.

[39] SOCIAL WELFARE

Participants in and benefits from leading social welfare programs in 1978 included aid to families with dependent children, 19,600 participants, $22 million in benefits; food stamps, 36,000, $10.3 million; school lunch program, 50,000, $3.8 million; Supplemental Security Income, 9,000, $13.1 million; and unemployment insurance, 6,000 (weekly average), $17 million. In 1977, 77,900 Vermonters received $191.1 million in Social Security payments.

[40] HOUSING

As rustic farmhouses gradually disappear, modern units (many of them vacation homes for Vermonters and out-of-staters) are being built to replace them. About 3,600 new units worth $101 million were authorized in 1978.

[41] EDUCATION

Vermont's illiteracy rate of 0.6% is about half the US average. Nearly 70% of all adult Vermonters are high school graduates, and 16% have completed at least four years of postsecondary study.

During the 1978/79 school year, 101,000 students were enrolled in Vermont's 468 public and private schools. The total 1977/78 enrollment in the state's 24 two- and four-year colleges was 29,506. The state operates the University of Vermont (Burlington), founded in 1791 and the oldest higher educational institution in the state, as well as the three state colleges, at Castleton, Johnson, and Lyndonville. Notable private institutions include Bennington College, Middlebury College, Goddard College (Plainfield), and Norwich University (Northfield), the oldest private military college in the US. The School for International Training at Brattleboro is the academic branch of the Experiment in International Living, a student exchange program. The Vermont Student Assistance Corp., a state agency, offers scholarships, incentive grants, and guaranteed loans for eligible Vermont students.

42 ARTS

The Vermont State Crafts Centers at Frog Hollow (Middlebury) and Windsor display the works of Vermont artisans. The Vermont Symphony Orchestra, in Burlington, makes extensive statewide tours. Marlboro College is the home of the summer Marlboro Music Festival, directed by pianist Rudolf Serkin. Among the summer theaters in the state are those at Dorset and Weston, and the University of Vermont Shakespeare Festival. The Middlebury College Bread Loaf Writers' Conference, founded in 1926, meets each August in Ripton.

43 LIBRARIES AND MUSEUMS

During 1977/78, the state's public libraries held 1,969,098 volumes and had a combined circulation of 2,423,710. The largest academic library was at the University of Vermont, with a book stock of 816,624.

Vermont has more than 60 museums and historic sites. Among them are the Bennington Museum, with its collection of Early American glass, pottery, furniture, and Grandma Moses paintings, and the Art Gallery–St. Johnsbury Athenaeum, featuring 19th-century American artists. The Shelburne Museum, housed in restored Early American buildings, contains collections of American primitives and Indian artifacts. Steamtown in Bellows Falls has a large collection of steam locomotives, and Old Constitution House in Windsor offers exhibits on Vermont history.

44 COMMUNICATIONS

As of 1977 there were about 1,800 postal service workers in Vermont. In 1978, 348,645 telephones were in use, of which 73% were residential; virtually every household had telephone service. There were 19 AM and 12 FM radio stations and 2 television stations in operation in 1978. In 1979, 40 cable television systems served 58,285 subscribers in 112 communities.

45 PRESS

In 1978 there were 8 daily papers with a combined circulation of 122,386, and 3 Sunday papers with 77,359 circulation. The leading daily in 1979 was the *Burlington Free Press* (48,051 mornings, 39,416 Sundays).

Vermont Life magazine is published quarterly under the aegis of the Agency of Development and Community Affairs.

46 ORGANIZATIONS

Associations headquartered in Vermont reflect the state's skiing and agricultural interests. They include the Eastern Ski Association in Brattleboro, Ski Touring Council in Troy, the Ayrshire Breeders' Association in Brandon, the Holstein-Friesian Association of America in Brattleboro, and the Natural Organic Farmers Association in Greensboro Bend.

47 TOURISM, TRAVEL, AND RECREATION

With the building of the first ski slopes in the 1930s (Woodstock claims the first ski area in the US) and the development of modern highways, tourism became a major industry in Vermont. As of 1978, it was the state's 2d largest, accounting for an estimated 15% of the gross state product. Travel-related industries earned about $800 million in 1977 and employed 23,000 full- and part-time workers. Perhaps 60–65% of all tourist expenditures come during the summer, when the state attracts campers to 37 state-owned campgrounds, 73 private campgrounds, and numerous private resorts. In the winter, the state's ski operators (38 in 1980) offer some of the finest skiing in the East. In 1977/78, the state issued licenses to 152,682 hunters and 135,038 fishermen.

48 SPORTS

Vermont ski areas have hosted national and international ski competitions in both Alpine and Nordic events. World Cup races have been run at Stratton Mountain, and the national cross-country championships have been held near Putney.

49 FAMOUS VERMONTERS

Two US presidents, both of whom assumed office on the death of their predecessor, were born in Vermont. Chester Alan Arthur (1829–86) became the 21st president after James A. Garfield's assassination in 1881 and finished his term. A machine politician, Arthur became a civil-service reformer in the White House. Calvin Coolidge (1872–1933), 28th president, was born in Plymouth Notch but pursued a political career in Massachusetts. Elected vice president in 1920, he became president on the death of Warren G. Harding in 1923, and was elected to a full term in 1924.

Other federal officeholders have included Matthew Lyon (1750–1822), a US representative imprisoned under the Sedition Act and reelected from a Vergennes jail; Jacob Collamer (1791–1865), who after serving three terms in the US House, was US postmaster general and then a US senator; Justin Smith Morrill (1810–98), US representative and senator who sponsored the Morrill tariff in 1861 and the Land Grant College Act in 1862; George Franklin Edmunds (1828–1919), a US senator who helped draft the Sherman Antitrust Act; Redfield Proctor (1831–1908), secretary of war, US senator, state governor, and the founder of a marble company; John Garibaldi Sargent (1860–1939), Coolidge's attorney general; Warren Robinson Austin (1877–1963), US senator and head of the US delegation to the UN; and George David Aiken (b.1892), US senator from 1941 to 1977.

Important state leaders were Thomas Chittenden (1730–97), leader of the Vermont republic and the state's first governor; Ethan Allen (1738–89), a frontier folk hero, leader of the Green Mountain Boys, and presenter of Vermont's claim to independence to the US Congress in 1778; Ira Allen (1751–1814), the brother of Ethan, who led the fight for statehood; Cornelius Peter Van Ness (b.New York, 1782–1852), who served first as Vermont chief justice and then as governor; and Erastus Fairbanks (1792–1864), a governor and railroad promoter.

Vermont's many businessmen and inventors include Thaddeus Fairbanks (1796–1886), inventor of the platform scale; Thomas Davenport (1802–51), inventor of the electric motor; plow and tractor manufacturer John Deere (1804–86); and Horace Wells (1815–48), inventor of laughing gas. Educator and philosopher John Dewey (1859–1952) was born in Burlington.

Robert Frost (b.California, 1874–1963) maintained a summer home near Ripton, where he helped found Middlebury College's Bread Loaf Writers' Conference. He was named poet laureate of Vermont in 1961. A famous Vermont performer is crooner and orchestra leader Rudy Vallee (Hubert Prior Rudy Vallee, b.1901).

50 BIBLIOGRAPHY

Bassett, T. D. S. *Outsiders Inside Vermont.* Canaan, N.H.: Phoenix Publishing, 1976 (orig. 1967).

Bearse, Ray, ed. *Vermont: A Guide to the Green Mountain State.* Boston: Houghton Mifflin, 1968.

Crockett, Walter H. *History of Vermont.* 5 vols. New York: Century, 1921.

Hill, Ralph Nading. *Contrary Country, a Chronicle of Vermont.* Brattleboro: Stephen Greene Press, 1961 (orig. 1950).

Hill, Ralph Nading. *Vermont: A Special World.* Montpelier: Vermont Life, 1969.

Newton, Earle. *The Vermont Story.* Montpelier: Vermont Historical Society, 1949.

Vermont, State of. Secretary of State. *Vermont Legislative Directory and State Manual, 1979–80.* Montpelier, 1979.

VIRGINIA

Commonwealth of Virginia

ORIGIN OF STATE NAME: Named for Queen Elizabeth I of England, the "Virgin Queen." **NICKNAME**: The Old Dominion. **CAPITAL**: Richmond. **ENTERED UNION**: 25 June 1788 (10th). **SONG**: "Carry Me Back to Old Virginia." **MOTTO**: *Sic semper tyrannis* (Thus ever to tyrants). **FLAG**: On a blue field with a white border at the fly, the state seal is centered on a white circle. **OFFICIAL SEAL**: Obverse: the Roman goddess Virtus, dressed as an Amazon and holding a sheathed sword in one hand and a spear in the other, stands over the body of Tyranny, who is pictured with a broken chain in his hand and a fallen crown nearby. The state motto appears below, the word "Virginia" above, and a border of Virginia creeper encircles the whole. Reverse: the Roman goddesses of Liberty, Eternity, and Fruitfulness, with the word "Perseverando" (By persevering) above. **BIRD**: Cardinal. **FLOWER**: Dogwood. **TREE**: Dogwood. **DOG**: Foxhound. **LEGAL HOLIDAYS**: New Year's Day, 1 January; Lee-Jackson Day, 3d Monday in January; Washington's Birthday, 3d Monday in February; Memorial Day, last Monday in May; Independence Day, 4 July; Labor Day, 1st Monday in September; Columbus Day, 2d Monday in October; Election Day, 1st Tuesday after 1st Monday in November; Veterans Day, 11 November; Thanksgiving Day, 4th Thursday in November; Christmas Day, 25 December. **TIME**: 7 A.M. EST = noon GMT.

¹LOCATION, SIZE, AND EXTENT

Situated on the eastern seaboard of the US, Virginia is the 4th largest of the South Atlantic states and ranks 36th in size among the 50 states.

The total area of Virginia is 40,817 sq mi (105,716 sq km), of which land occupies 39,780 sq mi (103,030 sq km) and inland water 1,037 sq mi (2,686 sq km). Virginia extends approximately 440 mi (710 km) E–W, but the maximum point-to-point distance from the state's noncontiguous Eastern Shore to the western extremity is 470 mi (756 km). The maximum N–S extension is about 200 mi (320 km).

Virginia is bordered on the NW by West Virginia; on the NE by Maryland and the District of Columbia (with the line passing through the Potomac River and Chesapeake Bay); on the E by the Atlantic Ocean; on the S by North Carolina and Tennessee; and on the W by Kentucky. The state's geographic center is in Buckingham County, 5 mi (8 km) SW of the town of Buckingham.

Virginia's offshore islands in the Atlantic include Chincoteague, Wallops, Cedar, Parramore, Hog, Cobb, and Smith. The boundaries of Virginia, including the Eastern Shore at the tip of the Delmarva Peninsula, total 1,356 mi (2,182 km), of which 112 mi (180 km) is general coastline; the tidal shoreline extends 3,315 mi (5,335 km).

²TOPOGRAPHY

Virginia consists of three principal physiographic areas: the Atlantic Coastal Plain, or Tidewater; the Piedmont Plateau, in the central section; and the Blue Ridge and Allegheny Mountains of the Appalachian chain, in the west and northwest.

The long, narrow Blue Ridge rises sharply from the piedmont, reaching a maximum elevation of 5,729 feet (1,746 meters) at Mt. Rogers, the state's highest point. Between the Blue Ridge and the Allegheny Mountains of the Appalachian chain in the northwest lies the Valley of Virginia, consisting of transverse ridges and six separate valleys. The floors of these valleys ascend in altitude from about 300 feet (90 meters) in the northern Shenandoah Valley to 2,400 feet (730 meters) in the Powell Valley. The Alleghenies average 3,000 feet (900 meters) in height.

The piedmont, shaped roughly like a triangle, varies in width from 40 mi (64 km) in the far north to 180 mi (290 km) in the extreme south. Altitudes in this region range from about 300 feet (90 meters) at the fall line in the east to a maximum of about 1,000 feet (300 meters) at the base of the Blue Ridge in the southwest. The Tidewater, which declines gently from the fall line to sea level, is divided by four long peninsulas cut by the state's four principal rivers—the Potomac, Rappahannock, York, and James—and Chesapeake Bay. On the opposite side of the bay is Virginia's low-lying Eastern Shore, the southern tip of the Delmarva Peninsula. The Tidewater has many excellent harbors, notably the deep Hampton Roads estuary. Also in the southeast lies the Dismal Swamp, a drainage basin that includes Lake Drummond, about 7 mi (11 km) long and 5 mi (8 km) wide near the North Carolina border. Other major lakes in Virginia are Smith Mountain—at 31 sq mi (80 sq km) the largest lake wholly within the state—Claytor, and South Holston. The John H. Kerr Reservoir, covering 76 sq mi (197 sq km), straddles the Virginia–North Carolina line.

³CLIMATE

A mild, humid coastal climate is characteristic of Virginia. Temperatures, most equable in the Tidewater, become increasingly cooler with the rising altitudes as one moves westward. The normal daily mean temperature at Richmond is about 58°F (14°C), ranging from 38°F (3°C) in January to 78°F (26°C) in July. The record high, 110°F (43°C), was registered at Balcony Falls (near Glasgow) on 15 July 1954; the record low, –29°F (–34°C), was set at Monterey on 10 February 1899. The frost-free growing season ranges from about 150 days in the west to 245 days in the east.

Precipitation at Richmond averages 43 in (109 cm) a year; the average snowfall amounts to nearly 14 in (36 cm) at Richmond but only 7 in (18 cm) at Norfolk.

⁴FLORA AND FAUNA

Native to Virginia are 12 varieties of oak, 5 of pine, and 2 each of walnut, locust, gum, and poplar. Pines predominate in the coastal areas, with numerous hardwoods on slopes and ridges inland; isolated stands of persimmon, ash, cedar, and basswood can also be found. Characteristic wild flowers include trailing arbutus, mountain laurel, and diverse azaleas and rhododendrons.

Among indigenous mammalian species are white-tailed (Virginia) deer, elk, black bear, bobcat, woodchuck, raccoon, opossum, nutria, red and gray foxes, and spotted and striped skunks, along with several species each of moles, shrews, bats, squirrels, deermice, rats, and rabbits; the beaver, mink, and river otter, once thought to be endangered, have returned in recent decades. Principal game birds include the ruffed grouse (commonly called pheasant in Virginia), wild turkey, bobwhite quail, mourning dove, woodcock, and Wilson's snipe. Tidal waters abound with croaker, hogfish, gray and spotted trout, and flounder; bass, bream, bluegill, sunfish, perch, carp, catfish, and crappie live in freshwater ponds and streams. Native reptiles include such poisonous snakes as the northern copperhead, eastern cottonmouth, and the timber rattler.

Endangered species in Virginia include the cougar, Delmarva fox squirrel, northern flying squirrel, Indiana bat, Virginia big-eared bat, southern bald eagle, red-cockaded woodpecker, spotfin chub, Roanoke logperch, canebrake rattlesnake, bog turtle, mudpuppy, and dwarf waterdog. Of more than 60 rare or endangered species in the state, at least one-fourth are found in the Dismal Swamp.

5 ENVIRONMENTAL PROTECTION

The Department of Conservation and Economic Development, established in the late 1920s and now under the jurisdiction of the secretary of commerce and resources, is charged with the protection and development of the state's forest and mineral resources, and with the management of state parks and other recreational areas. The Council on the Environment, within the same branch of the cabinet, is responsible for coordinating the state's environmental protection programs and for implementing the Virginia Environmental Quality Act of 1972. The Air Pollution Control Board, organized in 1966, monitors air quality throughout the state and enforces the emissions standards promulgated by the US Environmental Protection Agency. Under the Virginia Groundwater Act of 1973, the Water Control Board has developed programs and regulations to conserve water resources and has instituted water pollution controls, groundwater management plans, and flood protection programs. In the Tidewater and the Eastern Shore, state regulation of groundwater use is intended to prevent contamination of freshwater supplies by saltwater seepage.

Among Virginia's persistent environmental problems are air and water pollution in the Richmond-Petersburg-Hopewell industrial triangle, where chemical and other industrial plants are concentrated. The federal Office of Surface Mining Reclamation and Enforcement became embroiled during the late 1970s in a controversy with coal mine owners and state authorities as to whether the owners were attempting to evade federal strip-mining regulations by subleasing large holdings to small operators whose mines, less than 2 acres (0.8 hectare) in size, were then exempt from federal land-reclamation standards.

6 POPULATION

Virginia ranked 14th among the 50 states at the 1970 census, with a population of 4,648,494. The preliminary 1980 census total was 5,321,521, yielding a population density of 134 persons per sq mi (52 per sq km).

From the outset, Virginia was the most populous of the English colonies, with a population that doubled every 25 years and totaled more than 100,000 by 1727. By 1790, Virginia's population of 821,287 was about 21% of the US total and almost twice that of 2d-ranked Pennsylvania. Although surpassed by New York State at the 1820 census, Virginia continued to enjoy slow but steady growth until the Civil War, when the loss of its western counties (which became the new state of West Virginia) and the wartime devastation caused a decline of 23% for the decade of the 1860s. The population passed the 2-million mark in 1910, and the number of Virginians doubled between 1920 and 1970. The population growth rates for the four decades since 1940 were 23.9%, 19.5%, 17.2%, and 14.5%, in each case above the US average.

Not quite two-thirds of all Virginians live in metropolitan areas, the largest of which in 1978 were Virginia's share of metropolitan Washington, D.C., with more than 1,000,000 peo-

ple; the Norfolk–Virginia Beach–Portsmouth area, 800,100; metropolitan Richmond, 611,700; and Newport News–Hampton, 361,400. According to 1980 preliminary census figures, Virginia's most populous cities were Norfolk, 262,803; Virginia Beach, 260,680; Richmond, 219,429; Chesapeake, 165,328; Newport News, 144,795; Hampton, 122,383; Portsmouth, 104,068; and Alexandria, 102,494.

7 ETHNIC GROUPS

When the first federal census was taken in 1790, more than 306,000 blacks—of whom only 12,000 were free—made up more than one-third of Virginia's total population. After emancipation, blacks continued to be heavily represented, accounting in 1870 for 512,841 (42%) of 1,225,163 Virginians. Blacks numbered about 779,000 in 1976—but their proportion of the total estimated population was less than 16%. Richmond was 42% black in 1970, and Norfolk and Newport News each had a black population of 28%.

In 1976, Virginia had 56,000 Hispanic residents, chiefly Puerto Ricans, Cubans, and Filipinos. The 1970 census counted 7,496 Filipinos, 3,500 Japanese, 2,805 Chinese, and 6,958 other Asians; Virginia resettled 3,733 Vietnamese refugees in 1975. Fewer than 6% of all state residents were of foreign birth or had foreign-born parents in 1970, with Germany, the United Kingdom, and Canada being the principal foreign countries of origin. The American Indian population was only 4,853 during the same year.

8 LANGUAGES

English settlers encountered members of the Powhatan Indian confederacy, speakers of an Algonkian language, whose legacy consists of such place-names as Roanoke and Rappahannock. In 1970, 623 Virginians reported Indian first languages.

Although the expanding suburban area south of the District of Columbia has become dialectally heterogeneous, the remainder of the state has retained its essentially Southern speech features. Many dialect markers occur statewide, but subregional contrasts distinguish the South Midland of the Appalachians from the Southern of the piedmont and Tidewater. General are *batter bread* (a soft corn cake), *batter cake* (pancake), *comfort* (tied and filled bedcover), and *polecat* (skunk). Widespread pronunciation features include *greasy* with a /z/ sound; *yeast* and *east* as sound-alikes; *creek* rhyming with *peek*, and *can't* with *paint*; *coop* and *bulge* with the vowel of *book*; and *forest* with an /ah/ sound.

The Tidewater is set off by *creek* meaning a saltwater inlet, *fishing worm* for earthworm, and *fog* as /fahg/. Appalachian South Midland has *redworm* for earthworm, *fog* as /fawg/, *wash* as /wawsh/, *Mary* and *merry* as sound-alikes, and *poor* with the vowel of *book*. The Richmond area is noted also for having two variants of the long /i/ and /ow/ diphthongs as they occur before voiceless and voiced consonants, so that the vowel in the noun *house* is quite different from the vowel in the verb *house*, and the vowel in *advice* differs from that in *advise*. The Tidewater exhibits similar features.

Of the native-born residents in 1970, 92% claimed English as their mother tongue, as did 91% of all residents. Speakers of major first languages were as follows:

	NATIVE-BORN	FOREIGN-BORN
English	4,222,655	16,206
German	35,444	12,288
French	18,230	4,463
Italian	15,478	2,574
Polish	9,624	1,292

9 RELIGIONS

The Anglican Church (later, the Episcopal Church), whose members founded and populated Virginia Colony in the early days, was the established church during the colonial period. The first dissenters to arrive were Scotch-Irish Presbyterians in the late 17th century; they were followed by large numbers of German

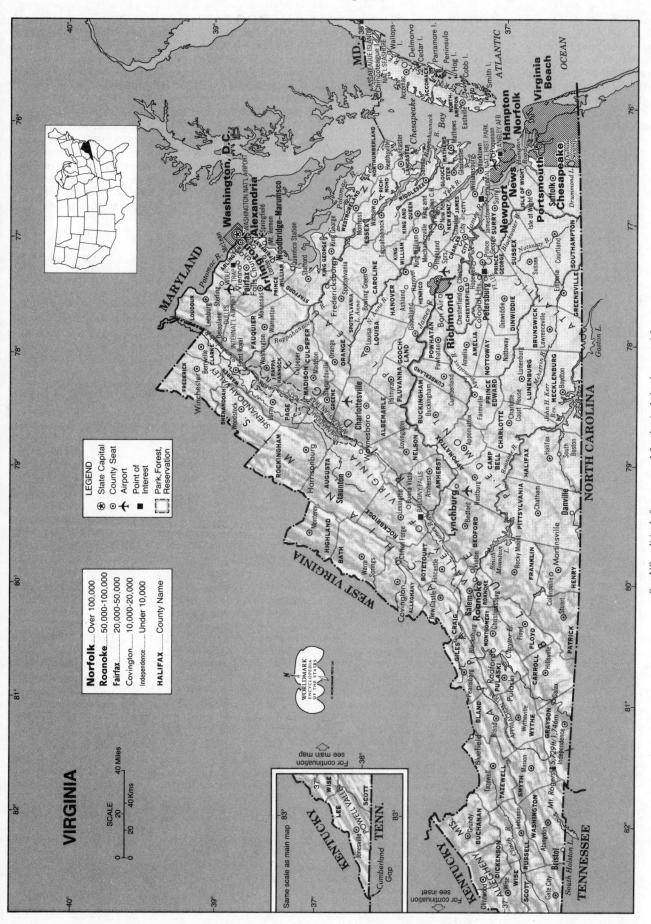

See US political: front cover L3; physical: back cover L3.

LOCATION: 36°31' to 39°27'N; 75°13' to 83°37'W. **BOUNDARIES:** West Virginia line, 438 mi (705 km); Maryland line, 233 mi (375 km); District of Columbia line, 12 mi (19 km); Atlantic Ocean coastline, 112 mi (180 km); North Carolina line, 320 mi (515 km); Tennessee line, 114 mi (184 km); Kentucky line, 127 mi (204 km).

Lutherans, Welsh Baptists, and English Quakers, who settled in the Valley of Virginia in the early 18th century. The general assembly's adoption in 1785 of the Virginia Statute for Religious Freedom, drafted by Thomas Jefferson, disestablished the Episcopal Church and made religious toleration the norm in Virginia. Although the Episcopal and Presbyterian churches retained the allegiance of the landed gentry during the 19th century, the Methodists and Baptists became the largest church groups in the state.

Protestant denominations had 1,767,209 known adherents in 1971, when the leading groups were the Southern Baptist Convention, with 642,930 adherents; United Methodist Church, 497,027; Presbyterian Church in the US, 144,057; and Episcopal Church, 136,755. As of 1979 there were 269,835 Roman Catholics in Virginia, and the Jewish population was estimated at 56,685.

[10]TRANSPORTATION

Virginia has one of the nation's most extensive highway systems, the leading port—Hampton Roads—by volume of exports in 1978, and two of the nation's busiest air terminals.

Virginia was a leader in early railroad development. Rail lines were completed between Richmond and Fredericksburg in 1836, from Portsmouth to Roanoke in 1837, between Petersburg and Lynchburg in 1854, and from Richmond to Washington, D.C., in 1872. Virginia's 1,290 mi (2,076 km) of track, two-thirds of it owned by the Baltimore and Ohio line, formed an important strategic supply link for Confederate and Union armies during the Civil War. Railroads remained the primary system of transportation until the rise of the automobile in the 1920s. As of 1980 there were 19 rail companies operating in the state, with total trackage of 4,021 mi (6,471 km). Principal north–south railroads

Virginia Counties, County Seats, and County Populations

COUNTY	COUNTY SEAT	LAND AREA (SQ MI)	POPULATION (EST. 1978)	COUNTY	COUNTY SEAT	LAND AREA (SQ MI)	POPULATION (EST. 1978)
Accomack	Accomac	602	31,900	King George	King George	183	9,800
Albemarle	Charlottesville	741	49,400	King William	King William	286	8,600
Alleghany	Covington	444	12,900	Lancaster	Lancaster	153	10,200
Amelia	Amelia	366	8,400	Lee	Jonesville	438	25,300
Amherst	Amherst	470	27,500	Loudoun	Leesburg	517	53,200
Appomattox	Appomattox	345	11,500	Louisa	Louisa	517	17,700
Arlington	Arlington	24	149,400	Lunenburg	Lunenburg	443	12,500
Augusta	Staunton	986	51,900	Madison	Madison	327	9,900
Bath	Warm Springs	540	5,500	Mathews	Mathews	105	8,200
Bedford	Bedford	778	31,100	Mecklenburg	Boydton	675	29,900
Bland	Bland	369	6,400	Middlesex	Saluda	138	7,400
Botetourt	Fincastle	549	21,500	Montgomery	Christiansburg	395	59,800
Brunswick	Lawrenceville	579	16,000	Nelson	Lovingston	471	11,700
Buchanan	Grundy	508	36,000	New Kent	New Kent	221	7,800
Buckingham	Buckingham	582	11,700	Northampton	Eastville	357	15,400
Campbell	Rustburg	529	44,300	Northumberland	Heathsville	223	9,500
Caroline	Bowling Green	549	17,000	Nottoway	Nottoway	308	14,000
Carroll	Hillsville	496	23,800	Orange	Orange	355	17,000
Charles City	Charles City	204	6,600	Page	Luray	316	18,900
Charlotte	Charlotte	471	12,700	Patrick	Stuart	469	16,200
Chesterfield	Chesterfield	469	127,900	Pittsylvania	Chatham	1,028	62,800
Clarke	Berryville	174	9,200	Powhatan	Powhatan	272	12,500
Craig	New Castle	336	4,100	Prince Edward	Farmville	357	15,700
Culpeper	Culpeper	389	21,900	Prince George	Prince George	298	21,900
Cumberland	Cumberland	292	7,300	Prince William	Manassas	354	134,700
Dickenson	Clintwood	335	20,000	Pulaski	Pulaski	340	33,000
Dinwiddie	Dinwiddie	506	21,400	Rappahannock	Washington	383	5,900
Essex	Tappahannock	264	8,100	Richmond	Warsaw	203	6,800
Fairfax	Fairfax	409	545,500	Roanoke	Salem	277	63,200
Fauquier	Warrenton	660	31,300	Rockbridge	Lexington	604	16,700
Floyd	Floyd	383	10,700	Rockingham	Harrisonburg	865	54,500
Fluvanna	Palmyra	288	10,100	Russell	Lebanon	483	28,600
Franklin	Rocky Mount	721	32,600	Scott	Gate City	539	24,700
Frederick	Winchester	432	28,300	Shenandoah	Woodstock	507	27,000
Giles	Pearisburg	363	16,700	Smyth	Marion	435	32,400
Gloucester	Gloucester	257	18,000	Southampton	Courtland	607	19,600
Goochland	Goochland	295	11,400	Spotsylvania	Spotsylvania	411	29,600
Grayson	Independence	454	15,600	Stafford	Stafford	277	37,100
Greene	Standardsville	153	7,300	Surry	Surry	306	5,700
Greensville	Emporia	302	10,000	Sussex	Sussex	496	10,800
Halifax	Halifax	806	30,100	Tazewell	Tazewell	522	49,500
Hanover	Hanover	471	52,100	Warren	Front Royal	219	19,800
Henrico	Richmond	234	173,900	Washington	Abingdon	578	41,500
Henry	Martinsville	394	56,100	Westmoreland	Montross	250	13,700
Highland	Monterey	416	2,800	Wise	Wise	412	44,300
Isle of Wight	Isle of Wight	360	20,400	Wythe	Wytheville	460	24,300
James City	Williamsburg	182	21,000	York	Yorktown	146	33,700
King and Queen	King and Queen	327	6,100	Independent cities	—	NA	2,019,600
				TOTALS		39,780	5,148,000

are the Richmond, Fredericksburg, and Potomac, the Seaboard Coast Line, and the Southern Railway System; major east–west lines include the Chesapeake and Ohio and the Norfolk and Western. Amtrak passenger trains serve the large cities, and the Auto-Train Corp. carries passengers and their automobiles from Lorton (south of Arlington) all the way to Florida.

Virginia's road network, at first built mainly for hauling tobacco to market, had expanded across the Blue Ridge by 1782, to the Cumberland Gap by 1795, and into the Shenandoah Valley by means of the Valley Turnpike in 1840. As of 1978, Virginia had 64,782 mi (104,257 km) of roadway, 3,511,197 registered vehicles, and 3,259,131 licensed drivers. Major interstate highways are I-95, extending north–south from Washington, D.C., via Richmond to the North Carolina border, and, eventually, to Florida; I-81, connecting northern Virginia with the southwest; and I-64, linking the Hampton Roads area with Staunton (and I-81) in the west. The 18-mi (29-km) Chesapeake Bay Bridge– Tunnel, completed in 1964, connects the Eastern Shore with the southeastern mainland. Popular scenic highways include the Blue Ridge Parkway, Colonial National Historical Parkway, and George Washington Memorial Parkway.

Coastal and ocean shipping are vital to Virginia's commerce. The Port of Hampton Roads, consisting of marine terminals in Chesapeake, Newport News, Norfolk, and Portsmouth, was linked as of 1980 by 81 steamship lines with 397 ports in 132 foreign countries. Virginia's 86 public airfields—including 14 commercial airports—were served by 22 major airlines and 10 commuter airlines in 1980. Dulles International Airport, with 10 US airlines and 3 foreign lines, handled more than 3,500,000 passengers and 62,500 tons of cargo in 1979; Washington National Airport, at Arlington, is a major center for domestic flights.

¹¹HISTORY

Distinctively fluted stone points found at Flint Run in Front Royal and at the Williamson Site in Dinwiddie County testify to the presence in what is now the Commonwealth of Virginia of nomadic Paleo-Indians after 8000 BC. Climatic changes and the arrival of other Indian groups about 3500 BC produced the Archaic Culture, which lasted until about AD 500. These Indians apparently were great eaters of oysters, and shell accumulations along riverbanks mark their settlement sites. The Woodland Period (AD 500–1600) marked the Indians' development of the bow and arrow and sophisticated pottery. At the time of English contact, early in the 17th century, Tidewater Virginia was occupied principally by Algonkian-speakers, planters as well as hunters and fishers, who lived in pole-framed dwellings forming small, palisaded towns. The piedmont area was the home of the Manahoac, Monacan, and Tutelo, all of Siouan stock. Cherokee lived in Virginia's far southwestern triangle.

The first permanent English settlement in America was established at Jamestown on 13 May 1607 in the new land named Virginia in honor of Elizabeth I, the "Virgin Queen." The successful settlement was sponsored by the London Company (also known as the Virginia Company), a joint-stock venture chartered by King James I in 1606. The charter defined Virginia as all of the North American coast between 30° and 45°N and extending inland for 50 mi (80 km). A new royal charter in 1609 placed Virginia's northern and southern boundaries at points 200 mi (320 km) north and south of Point Comfort, at the mouth of the James River, and extended its territory westward to the Pacific; a third charter, issued in 1612, pushed Virginia eastward to embrace the Bermuda Islands. Thus, Virginia at one time stretched from southern Maine to California and encompassed all or part of 42 of the present 50 states, as well as Bermuda and part of the Canadian province of Ontario.

Upon landing at Jamestown, the 100 or more male colonists— there were no women—elected from among 12 royally approved councillors a governor and captain general, Edward Maria Wing-

field. Much internal strife, conflict with the Indians, and a "starving time" that reduced the settlers to eating their horses caused them to vote to leave the colony in 1610, but just as they were leaving, three supply ships arrived; with them came Thomas West, Baron De La Warr (Lord Delaware), who stayed to govern the Virginia Colony until 1611. Finally, however, it was the energy, resourcefulness, and military skill of Captain John Smith that saved the colony from both starvation and destruction by the Indians. He also charted the coast and wrote the first American book, *A True Relation*, which effectively publicized English colonization of the New World.

Smith's chief Algonkian adversary was Powhatan, emperor of a confederacy in eastern Virginia that bore his name. Although Smith was taken prisoner by Powhatan, he was able to work out a tenuous peace later cemented by the marriage in 1614 of the emperor's favorite daughter, Pocahontas, to John Rolfe, a Jamestown settler who founded the colonial tobacco industry.

Three events marked 1619 as a red-letter year in Virginia history. First, women were sent to the colony in large numbers. Any man marrying one of a shipment of 90 "young maids" had to pay 120 lb of tobacco for the cost of her transportation. The women were carefully screened for respectability, and none had to marry if she did not find a man to her liking. The second key event was the arrival in Jamestown of the first blacks, probably as indentured servants, a condition from which slavery in the colony evolved; the first legally recognized slaveholder, in the 1630s, was Anthony Johnson, himself a black. The third and most celebrated event of 1619 was the convening in Jamestown of the first representative assembly in the New World, consisting of a council chosen by the London Company and a house of burgesses elected by the colonists. Thus, self-government through locally elected representatives became a reality in America and an important precedent for the English colonies.

King James I, for whom the colonial capital was named, was at first content with colonization under the London Company's direction. But in 1624, he charged the company with mismanagement and revoked its charter. Virginia remained a royal colony until 1776, although royal governors such as Sir Francis Wyatt and Sir George Yeardley continued to convoke the general assembly without the Crown's assent. A serious challenge to self-government came in 1629–35 with Governor John Harvey's "executive offenses"—including the knocking out of a councillor's teeth and the detaining of a petition of protest to the king—which sparked a rebellion led by Dr. John Pott. Harvey was bloodlessly deposed by the council—which, significantly, turned to the house of burgesses for confirmation of the action the council had taken.

Despite serious setbacks because of Indian massacres in 1622 and 1644, the colony's population expanded rapidly along the James, York, Rappahannock, and Potomac rivers, and along the Eastern Shore. In 1653, the general assembly attempted to collect taxes from the Eastern Shore, although that area had no legislative representation. At a mass meeting, Colonel Thomas Johnson urged resistance to taxation without representation. The resulting Northampton Declaration embodied this principle, which would provide the rallying cry for the American Revolution; the immediate result was the granting of representation to the Eastern Shore.

Virginia earned the designation Old Dominion through its loyalty to the Stuarts during England's Civil War, but the superior military and naval forces of Oliver Cromwell compelled submission to parliamentary commissioners in 1652. In the eight years that followed, the house of burgesses played an increasingly prominent role. Colonial governors, while at least nominally Puritan, usually conducted affairs with an easy tolerance that did not mar Virginia's general hospitality to refugee Cavaliers from the mother country.

With the restoration of the royal family in 1660, Sir William Berkeley, an ardent royalist who had served as governor before the colony's surrender to the Commonwealth, was returned to that office. In his first administration, his benign policies and appealing personality had earned him great popularity, but during his second term, his dictatorial and vindictive support of royal prerogatives made him the most hated man in the colony. When he seemed unable to defend the people against Indian incursions in 1676, they sought a general of their own. They found him in young Nathaniel Bacon, a charismatic planter of great daring and eloquence, whose leadership attracted many small planters impatient by this time with the privileged oligarchy directing the colony. Bacon's war against the Indians became a populist-style revolt against the governor, who fled to the Eastern Shore, and reform legislation was pushed by the burgesses. Berkeley regained control of the capital briefly, only to be defeated by Bacon's forces; but Jamestown was burned by the retreating Bacon, who died of fever shortly afterward. Berkeley's subsequent return to power was marked by so many hangings of offenders that the governor was summoned to the court of Charles II to answer for his actions. Bacon's Rebellion was cited as a precedent when the colonies waged war against George III a century later.

The 17th century closed on a note of material and cultural progress with the gubernatorial administration of Francis Nicholson. The College of William and Mary, the second institution of higher learning in America, was chartered in 1693, and Middle Plantation (renamed Williamsburg in 1722), the site of the college, became the seat of government when the capital was moved from Jamestown in 1699. The new capital remained small, although it was crowded when the legislature was in session. A new era of cultural and economic progress dawned with the administration of Alexander Spotswood (1710–22), sometimes considered the greatest of Virginia's colonial governors. He discouraged the colony's excessively heavy dependence on a single crop, tobacco; promoted industry, especially ironworks; took a humane interest in blacks and Indians; strengthened fortifications; ended the depredations of the notorious pirate Edward Teach, better known as Blackbeard; and, by leading his "Knights of the Golden Horseshoe" across the Blue Ridge, dramatized the opening of the transmontane region.

In the decades that followed, eastern Virginians moving into the Valley of Virginia were joined by Scotch-Irish and Germans moving southward from Maryland and Pennsylvania. Virginians caught up in western settlement lost much of their awe of the mother country during the French and Indian War (1756–63). A young Virginia militiaman, Colonel George Washington, gave wise but unheeded advice to Britain's Major General Edward Braddock before the Battle of Monongahela, and afterward emerged as the hero of that action.

Virginia, acting independently and with other colonies, repeatedly challenged agents of the Crown. In 1765, the house of burgesses, swept by the eloquence of Patrick Henry, adopted five resolutions opposing the Stamp Act, through which the English Parliament had sought to tax the colonists for their own defense. In 1768, Virginia joined Massachusetts in issuing an appeal to all the colonies for concerted action. The following year, Virginia initiated a boycott of British goods in answer to the taxation provisions of the hated Townshend Acts. In 1773, the Old Dominion became the first colony to establish an intercolonial committee of correspondence. And it joined the other colonies at the First Continental Congress, which met in Philadelphia in 1774, and elected Virginia's Peyton Randolph president.

Virginia was the first colony to instruct its delegates to move for independence at the Continental Congress of 1776. The congressional resolution was introduced by one native son, Richard Henry Lee, and the Declaration of Independence was written by another, Thomas Jefferson. In the same year, Virginians proclaimed their government a commonwealth and adopted a constitution and declaration of rights, prepared by George Mason. The declaration became the basis for the Bill of Rights in the US Constitution. Virginians were equally active in the Revolutionary War. George Washington was commander in chief of the Continental Army, and other outstanding Virginia officers were George Rogers Clark, Hugh Mercer, Henry "Light Horse Harry" Lee, William Campbell, Isaac Shelby, and an adopted son, Daniel Morgan. In addition, the greatest American naval hero was a Scottish-born Virginian, John Paul Jones. Virginia itself was a major battlefield, and it was on Virginia soil, at Yorktown on 19 October 1781, that British General Charles Cornwallis surrendered to Washington, effectively ending the war.

During the early federal period, Virginia's leadership was as notable as it had been during the American Revolution. James Madison is honored as the "father of the Constitution," and Washington, who was president of the constitutional convention, became the first US president in 1789. Indeed, Virginians occupied the presidency for all but 4 of the nation's first 28 years. Far more influential than most presidents was another Virginian, John Marshall, who served as US chief justice for 34 years, beginning in 1801.

During the first half of the 19th century, Virginians became increasingly concerned with the problem of slavery. From the early 1700s the general assembly had repeatedly prohibited the importation of slaves, only to be overruled by the crown, protecting the interests of British slave traders. In 1778, no longer subject to royal veto, the legislature provided that any slave brought into the state would automatically be freed upon arrival. (There was no immediate legal termination of the bondage of those already enslaved, or of their offspring.) The number of free blacks grew tenfold by 1810, and though some became self-supporting farmers and artisans, many could find no employment. Fearing that unhappy free blacks might incite those who were still slaves to rebellion, the general assembly in 1806 decreed that each slave emancipated in due course must then leave Virginia within a year or after reaching the age of 21. Nat Turner's slave revolt, which took the lives of at least 55 white men, women, and children in Southampton County in 1831, increased white fears of black emancipation. Nevertheless, legislation to end slavery in Virginia failed of adoption by only seven votes the following year.

The slavery controversy did not consume all Virginians' energies in the first half of the 19th century, an era that saw the state become a leading center of scientific, artistic, and educational advancement. But this era ended with the coming of the Civil War, a conflict about which many Virginians had grave misgivings. Governor John Letcher was a Union man, and most of the state's top political leaders hoped to retain the federal tie. Even after the formation at Montgomery, Ala., of the Confederate States of America, Virginia initiated a national peace convention in Washington, D.C., headed by a native son and former US president, John Tyler. A statewide convention, assembled in Richmond in April 1861, adopted an ordinance of secession only after President Abraham Lincoln sought to send troops across Virginia to punish the states that had already seceded and called upon the commonwealth to furnish soldiers for that task. Virginia adopted secession with some regret and apprehension but with no agonizing over constitutional principles, for in ratifying the Constitution the state had reserved the right to secede. Shortly afterward, Richmond, the capital of Virginia since 1780, became the capital of the Confederacy. It was also the home of the Tredegar Ironworks, the South's most important manufacturer of heavy weaponry.

Robert E. Lee, offered field command of the Union armies, instead resigned his US commission in order to serve his native state as commander of the Army of Northern Virginia and eventually as chief of the Confederate armies. Other outstanding Virginian generals included Thomas Jonathan "Stonewall" Jackson, J. E. B. "Jeb" Stuart, Joseph E. Johnston, and A. P. Hill. Besides furnishing a greater number of outstanding Confederate generals than any other state, the Old Dominion supplied some of the Union's military leaders, George H. Thomas, the "Rock of Chickamauga," among them. More than 30 Virginians held the rank of brigadier general or major general in the federal forces.

Virginia became the principal battlefield of the Civil War, the scene of brilliant victories won by General Lee's army at Bull Run (about 30 mi—48 km—southwest of Washington, D.C.), Fredericksburg, and Chancellorsville (Spotsylvania County). But the overwhelming numbers and industrial and naval might of the Union compelled Lee's surrender at Appomattox on 9 April 1865. Virginia waters were the scene of one of the most celebrated naval engagements in world history, the first battle of the ironclads, when the USS *Monitor* and CSS *Virginia* (*Merrimac*), rebuilt in the Portsmouth Shipyard, met at Hampton Roads. The war cost Virginia one-third of its territory when West Virginia was admitted to the Union as a separate state on 20 June 1863. Richmond was left in ruins, and agriculture and industry throughout the commonwealth were destroyed. Union General Philip H. Sheridan's systematic campaign of demolition in the Shenandoah Valley almost made good his boast that a crow flying over the valley would have to carry its own rations.

In 1867, Virginia was placed under US military rule. A constitutional convention held in Richmond under the leadership of carpetbaggers and scalawags drafted a constitution that disqualified the overwhelming majority of white Virginians from holding office and deprived about 95% of them of the right to vote. In this crisis, a compromise was negotiated under which white Virginians would accept Negro suffrage if they themselves were permitted to vote and hold office. The amended constitution, providing for universal manhood suffrage, was adopted in 1869, and Virginia was readmitted to the Union on 26 January 1870.

Although the bankrupt state was saddled with a debt of more than $45 million, the Conservative Democrats undertook repayment of the entire debt, including approximately one-third estimated to be West Virginia's share. Other Democrats, who came to be known as Readjusters, argued that the commonwealth could not provide education and other essential services to its citizens unless it disclaimed one-third of the debt and reached a compromise with creditors concerning the remainder. William Mahone, a railroad president and former Confederate major general, engineered victory for the Readjusters in 1880 with the aid of the Republicans. His election to the US Senate that year represented another success for the Readjuster-Republican coalition, which was attentive to the needs of both blacks and underprivileged whites.

Throughout the 1880s and 1890s, life in public places in Virginia continued in an unsegregated fashion that sometimes amazed visitors from northern cities. As the 19th century neared an end, however, Virginia moved toward legal separation of the races. In 1900, the general assembly by a one-vote majority enacted segregation on railroad cars. The rule became applicable the following year to streetcars and steamboats. In 1902, the Virginia constitutional convention enacted a literacy test and poll tax that effectively reduced the black vote to negligible size.

Two decades later, just when the Old Dominion seemed permanently set in the grooves of conservatism, two liberals, each with impeccable old-line backgrounds, found themselves battling for the governorship in a Democratic primary campaign that changed the course of Virginia's political history. Harry F. Byrd defeated G. Walter Mapp in the election of 1925 and immediately after taking office launched the state on an era of reform. In a

whirlwind 60 days, the general assembly revised the tax system, revised balloting procedures, and adopted measures to lure industry to Virginia. The Anti-Lynch Act of 1927 made anyone present at the scene of a lynching who did not intervene guilty of murder; there has never been a lynching in Virginia since its passage. Byrd also reorganized the state government, consolidating nearly 100 agencies into 14 departments. Later, as US senator, Byrd became so renowned as a conservative that many people forgot his earlier career as a fighting liberal.

Following the depression of the 1930s, Virginia became one of the most prosperous states of the Southeast. It profited partly from national defense contracts and military and naval expansion, but also from increased manufacturing and from what became one of the nation's leading tourist industries. Few states made so great a contribution as Virginia to the US effort in World War II. More than 300,000 Virginians served in the armed forces; 9,000 lost their lives and 10 were awarded the Medal of Honor. Virginians were proud of the fact that General George C. Marshall was a Virginia resident and a graduate of Virginia Military Institute, and even delighted in the knowledge that both General Dwight D. Eisenhower, commander in the European theater, and General Douglas MacArthur, commander in the Pacific, were sons of Virginia mothers.

The postwar period brought many changes in the commonwealth's public life. During the first administration of Governor Mills E. Godwin, Jr. (1966–70), the state abandoned its strict pay-as-you-go fiscal policy, secured an $81-million bond issue, and enacted a sales tax. Much of the increased revenue benefited the public school system; funding for the four-year colleges was greatly expanded, and a system of low-tuition community colleges was instituted.

In 1970, A. Linwood Holton, Jr., became the first Republican governor of Virginia since 1874. Pledging to "make today's Virginia a model in race relations," Holton increased black representation on state boards and in the higher echelons of government. (For many Americans, the new era in the South was symbolized by a nationally distributed news photo of Governor Holton escorting his 13-year-old daughter to a predominantly black public school.) He reversed the policies of his immediate predecessors, who had generally met the US Supreme Court's desegregation ruling in 1954 with a program of "massive resistance": eschewing violence but adopting every legal expedient to frustrate integration. By the mid-1970s, public school integration in Virginia had been achieved to a degree not yet accomplished in many northern states.

[12] STATE GOVERNMENT

Since 1776, Virginia has had five constitutions, all of which have expanded the power of the executive branch. The last constitution, framed in 1902 and heavily amended in 1970, still governs the state today.

The general assembly consists of a 40-member senate, elected to four-year terms, and a 100-member house of delegates, serving for two years. Senators and delegates must be at least 21 years of age and residents of their district. The assembly convenes annually on the 2d Wednesday in January for 60-day sessions in even-numbered years and 45-day sessions in odd-numbered years.

The governor, lieutenant governor, and attorney general, all serving four-year terms, are the only officials elected statewide; the governor, who must be at least 30 years of age, may not serve two successive terms. Most state officials, including the secretaries of administration and finance, commerce and resources, education, human resources, public safety, and transportation, are appointed by the governor but must be confirmed by both houses of the legislature. Bills become law when signed by the governor or left unsigned for 7 days while the legislature is in session; a bill dies if left unsigned for 30 days after the legislature has adjourned. A two-thirds majority in each house is needed to override a gubernatorial veto. The constitution may be amended by constitutional convention or by a two-thirds vote of two successive sessions of the general assembly; ratification by the electorate is required.

A qualified voter must be a US citizen, at least 18 years old, and have registered in the precinct of residence at least 30 days before the election. Elections for state offices are held in odd-numbered years.

13 POLITICAL PARTIES

Virginia has exercised a unique role in US politics as the birthplace not only of representative government but also of one of America's two major parties. The modern Democratic Party traces its origins to the original Republican Party (usually referred to as the Democratic-Republican Party, or the Jeffersonian Democrats), led by two native sons of Virginia, Thomas Jefferson and James Madison. Virginians have also been remarkably influential in the political life of other states: a survey published in 1949 showed that 319 Virginia natives had represented 31 other states in the US Senate and House of Representatives.

From the end of Reconstruction through the 1960s, conservative Democrats dominated state politics, with few exceptions. Harry F. Byrd was the state's Democratic political leader for 40 years, first as a reform governor (1926–30) and then as a conservative senator (1933–65). During the 1970s, Virginians, still staunchly conservative, turned increasingly to the Republican Party, whose presidential nominees had done well in the state since the early 1950s. Linwood Holton, the commonwealth's first Republican governor since Reconstruction, was elected in 1969 primarily because the Democrats were badly divided. His Republican successor, Mills E. Godwin, Jr., the first governor since the Civil War to serve more than one term, had earlier won election as a Democrat. The election in 1977 of another Republican, John N. Dalton, finally convinced many skeptics that Virginia had become a two-party state. This conviction was confirmed in 1978 when Virginians elected Republican John W. Warner as US senator and chose 6 Republicans and 4 Democrats for the state's US House delegation; the GOP's congressional

margin expanded to 9–1 in the 1980 elections, when Ronald Reagan easily carried the state. Harry F. Byrd, Jr., who succeeded his father in the US Senate in 1965 as a Democrat, was reelected as an independent in 1970 and 1976.

14 LOCAL GOVERNMENT

As of 1980, Virginia had 95 counties, 41 independent cities, and 189 incorporated towns.

During the colonial period, most Virginians lived on plantations and were reluctant to form towns. The general assembly in 1705 approved the formation of 16 "free boroughs"; although only Jamestown, Williamsburg, and Norfolk chose at that time to avail themselves of the option and become independent municipalities, their decision laid the foundation for the independence of Virginia's present-day cities from county government. In 1842, Richmond became the commonwealth's first charter city. Today, 41 cities elect their own officials, levy their own taxes, and are unencumbered by any county obligations. The 189 incorporated towns remain part of the counties.

In general, counties are governed by elected boards of supervisors; other typical county officials include the commissioner of accounts, commissioner of revenue, planning chairman, registrar, school superintendent, sheriff, treasurer, and real estate assessor. Most cities are governed by city managers and councils elected at large. Each incorporated town has an elected mayor and council.

15 STATE SERVICES

Under the jurisdiction of the secretary of education are the Department of Education, which administers the public school system, and the State Council of Higher Education, which coordinates the programs of the state-controlled colleges and universities. The secretary of transportation oversees the Department of Highways and Transportation, Department of Highway Transportation Safety, Department of Aviation, Virginia Port Authority, and Department of Military Affairs (National Guard).

Within the purview of the secretary of human resources are the Department of Health, Department of Mental Health and Mental Retardation, Department of Welfare, and Department of Rehabilitative Services, as well as special offices dealing with

Virginia Presidential Vote by Political Parties, 1948–80

YEAR	ELECTORAL VOTE	VIRGINIA WINNER	DEMOCRAT	REPUBLICAN	STATES' RIGHTS DEMOCRAT	PROGRESSIVE	SOCIALIST	SOCIALIST LABOR
1948	11	*Truman (D)	200,786	172,070	43,393	2,047	726	234
1952	12	*Eisenhower (R)	268,677	349,037	—	—	504	1,160
					CONSTITUTION			
1956	12	*Eisenhower (R)	267,760	386,459	42,964	—	444	351
					VA. CONSERVATIVE			
1960	12	Nixon (R)	362,327	404,521	4,204	—	—	397
1964	12	*Johnson (D)	558,038	481,334	—	—	—	2,895
					AMERICAN IND.	PEACE & FREEDOM		
1968	12	*Nixon (R)	442,387	590,319	320,272	—	1,680	4,671
					AMERICAN			
1972	12	*Nixon (R)	438,887	988,493	19,721	—	—	9,918
						LIBERTARIAN	US LABOR	SOC. WORKERS
1976	12	Ford (R)	813,896	836,554	16,686	4,648	7,508	17,802
							CITIZENS	
1980	12	*Reagan (R)	752,174	989,609	—	12,821	14,024[1]	1,986[1]

*Won US presidential election. [1]Candidates of the nationwide Citizens and Socialist Workers parties were listed as independents on the Virginia ballot; another independent, John Anderson, won 95,418 votes.

problems that affect children, women, the elderly, and the disabled. The State Police, Department of Corrections, and Department of Alcoholic Beverage Control are under the aegis of the secretary of public safety.

The secretary of commerce and resources oversees the Department of Housing and Community Development, Department of Labor and Industry, Department of Commerce, Department of Agriculture and Consumer Services, State Office of Minority Business Enterprise, and a profusion of boards and commissions. The secretary of administration and finance exercises jurisdiction over budgeting, accounting, and personnel services, as well as the Board of Elections.

Regulatory functions are concentrated in the quasi-independent State Corporation Commission, consisting of three commissioners elected by the legislature to staggered six-year terms. The commission regulates all public utilities; licenses banks, savings and loan associations, credit unions, and small loan companies; enforces motor carrier and certain aviation laws and sets railroad rates; supervises the activities of insurance companies; and enforces laws governing securities and retail franchising.

¹⁶JUDICIAL SYSTEM

The highest judicial body in the commonwealth is the supreme court, consisting of a chief justice and six other justices elected by the general assembly to 12-year terms. Judges in the state's 31 circuit courts, the main trial courts, are elected by the assembly to 8-year terms. Each circuit coincides with a judicial district in which sits at least one general district court judge, also serving an 8-year term, and at least four magistrates.

Virginia's state and federal prisons had 7,143 inmates in 1977. According to the FBI Crime Index, the state's crime rates per 100,000 population, below the national average in every category, were as follows in 1978: murder and nonnegligent manslaughter, 8.8; forcible rape, 22.7; robbery, 97; aggravated assault, 158; burglary, 991; larceny-theft, 2,567; and motor vehicle theft, 229. A capital punishment statute providing for death by electrocution is in effect.

¹⁷ARMED FORCES

The Hampton Roads area, one of the nation's major concentrations of military facilities, includes Langley Air Force Base, the Norfolk naval air station and shipyard, the naval air station at Virginia Beach, and Ft. Eustis at Newport News. Also among Virginia's major defense establishments are the army bases at Arlington and Petersburg. In 1978, Virginia ranked 8th among the 50 states in value of federal defense contracts, receiving awards worth $1.7 billion.

As of 30 September 1979, 661,000 veterans of US military service lived in Virginia. Of these, 10,000 saw service during World War I, 271,000 in World War II, 140,000 during the Korean conflict, and 213,000 during the Viet-Nam era. Veterans' benefits allocated to Virginia totaled $490.1 million in 1977/78.

Army and Air National Guard units comprised some 6,800 personnel in 1978. There were 11,149 state and local police employees in 1977.

¹⁸MIGRATION

Virginia's earliest European immigrants were English—only a few hundred at first, but 4,000 between 1619 and 1624, of whom fewer than 1,200 survived epidemics and Indian attacks. Despite such setbacks, Virginia's population increased, mostly by means of immigration, from about 5,000 in 1634 to more than 15,000 in 1642, including 300 blacks. Within 30 years, the population had risen to more than 40,000, including 2,000 blacks. In the late 17th and earth 18th centuries, immigrants came not only from England but also from Scotland, Wales, Ireland, Germany, France, the Netherlands, and Poland. In 1701, about 500 French Huguenots fled Catholic France to settle near the present site of Richmond, and beginning in 1714, many Germans and Scotch-Irish moved from Pennsylvania into the Valley of Virginia.

By the early 19th century, Virginians were moving westward into Kentucky, Ohio, and other states; the 1850 census showed that 388,000 former Virginians (not including the many thousands of slaves sold to other states) were living elsewhere. Some of those who left—Henry Clay, Sam Houston, Stephen Austin—were among the most able men of their time. The Civil War era saw the movement of thousands of blacks to northern states, a trend that accelerated after Reconstruction and again after World War I. Since 1900, the dominant migratory trend has been intrastate, from farm to city. Urbanization has been most noticeable since World War II in the Richmond and Hampton Roads areas. At the same time, the movement of middle-income Virginians to the suburbs and increasing concentrations of blacks in the central cities have been evident in Virginia as in other states.

Between 1940 and 1977, Virginia enjoyed a net gain from migration of 516,000, 191,000 during 1970–77 alone. Especially significant between 1970 and 1975 was a net gain through migration of 29,000 blacks, reversing the historic trend.

¹⁹INTERGOVERNMENTAL COOPERATION

Regional bodies in which Virginia participates include the Atlantic States Marine Fisheries Commission, Ohio River Valley Water Sanitation Commission, Potomac River Basin Commission, Southern Growth Policies Board, Southern Interstate Energy Board, and Washington Metropolitan Area Transit Authority. The Virginia Department of Intergovernmental Affairs, under the aegis of the secretary of administration and finance, coordinates the state's cooperative programs with other states.

In 1978/79, Virginia received federal aid totaling $1.7 billion, of which $141.6 million was general revenue sharing.

²⁰ECONOMY

Early settlements in Virginia depended on subsistence farming of native crops, such as corn and potatoes. Tobacco, the leading export crop during the colonial era, was joined by cotton during the early statehood period. Although cotton was never "king" in Virginia, as it was in many southern states, the sale of slaves to Deep South plantations was an important source of income for Virginians, especially during the 1830s, when some 118,000 slaves were exported for profit. Eventually, a diversified agriculture developed in the piedmont and the Shenandoah Valley. Manufacturing became significant during the 19th century, with a proliferation of cotton mills, tobacco-processing plants, ironworks, paper mills, and shipyards.

Agriculture and manufacturing remain important economic sectors, but today government outranks both in personal income and employment. Of the state's 1978 total personal income, federal sources, civilian as well as military, accounted for 12%; state and local government contributed another 8%, for a combined total of 20%. Manufacturing followed with 15%, services 12%, and commerce 11%. The federal government in 1979 employed 151,000 military personnel and 154,400 civilians in the state, while an estimated 60,000 federal employees in the District of Columbia were Virginia residents. Coal and timber are the leading resource industries, but only tourism has shown sufficient growth to counterbalance Virginia's increasing dependence on federal spending as a source of livelihood.

²¹INCOME

Virginia's per capita personal income in 1978 averaged $7,624, 24th among the 50 states and 4th in the South. Total personal income rose 149% in real terms between 1960—when Virginia placed 33d in income per capita—and 1978. Income relative to the US average rose from 86% to 98% during the same period. The improvement was due not only to the growth of the government and manufacturing sectors but also to a sharp rise in the number of persons employed, an increase in the number of higher-paying industrial jobs, and a decline of lower-paying agricultural positions. The following table shows selected major components of personal income in 1978 (in millions):

Total personal income,	$39,492
of which:	
Farm	401
Nonfarm:	
Government	7,875
Manufacturing	5,757
Services	4,691
Construction	1,957
Retail trade	2,839
Wholesale trade	1,533
Finance, insurance, real estate	1,426
Transportation	1,243
Communications, public utilities	840
Mining	458
Agricultural services, forestry,	
fishing, other industries	89
Dividends, interest, rent	4,517

Virginia ranked 19th in median family income with $14,579 in 1975. During that same year, 8.3% of Virginia families and 10.5% of all state residents were below the federal poverty level. Some 242,200 of the leading US wealthholders—less than 2% of the US total—lived in Virginia in 1972.

²²LABOR

In 1978, Virginia's civilian labor force totaled 2,429,000 persons, of whom 57% were male and 43% female. The labor force is somewhat younger than the national average and has a higher proportion of women, whose participation rate—54% in 1978—was 2d only to North Carolina's among southern states.

A federal census of workers covered by unemployment insurance in March 1977 revealed the following nonfarm employment pattern in Virginia:

	ESTABLISH-MENTS	EMPLOYEES	ANNUAL PAYROLL ('000)
Agricultural services,			
forestry, fishing	967	5,291	$ 39,291
Mining, of which:	792	23,281	351,816
Bituminous coal, lignite	(597)	(18,409)	(292,520)
Contract construction	12,018	99,303	1,167,465
Manufacturing, of which:	5,037	393,460	4,449,228
Tobacco products	(19)	(14,958)	(206,226)
Textile mill products	(98)	(45,770)	(421,024)
Chemicals, chemical			
products	(144)	(30,020)	(461,731)
Transportation			
equipment	(127)	(37,205)	(520,708)
Transportation, public			
utilities	3,659	83,448	1,102,648
Wholesale trade	6,271	82,882	1,054,156
Retail trade	26,787	301,860	2,073,245
Finance, insurance,			
real estate	8,841	88,709	931,390
Services	26,752	287,526	2,563,216
Other	1,090	1,455	18,457
TOTALS	92,214	1,367,215	$13,750,912

Government workers, not covered by this survey, included 154,400 federal civilian employees and 344,000 state and local government personnel in 1979.

Virginia had an unemployment rate of 5.4% in 1978, well below the national average. The rate for all men was 4.3%; for all women, 6.7%; and for nonwhites alone, 10.3%. A right-to-work law is in effect. Although the state has no equal employment statute, an equal pay law does prohibit employers from wage discrimination on the basis of sex, and the Virginia Employment Contracting Act establishes as state policy the elimination of racial, religious, ethnic, and sexual bias in the employment practices of government agencies and contractors. The labor movement has grown slowly, partly because of past practices of racial segregation that prevented workers from acting in concert.

Union membership totaled 252,000 in 1976, or only 14% of all industrial workers—about the same share as in 1912. In 1978, weekly earnings in manufacturing averaged $203, 18% below the national average.

²³AGRICULTURE

Virginia, ranking 33d among the 50 states in 1978 with farm marketings of more than $1.3 billion, is an important producer of tobacco, peanuts, sweet potatoes, apples, freestone peaches, and cucumbers. There were an estimated 59,000 farms aggregating some 9.7 million acres (3.9 million hectares) in 1979; the number of farms had declined by 44% since 1960, and the farm acreage by 28%; during the same period, the value of farm real estate increased sixfold. Farm employment in 1978 averaged 83,000, of whom 24,000 were hired laborers. Farm assets that year totaled $9.8 billion, of which real estate represented 74%, machinery and motor vehicles 15%, crop and livestock inventories 5%, household furnishings 3%, and financial assets 3%.

The Tidewater is still a major farming region, as it has been since the early 17th century. Corn, wheat, tobacco, peanuts, and truck crops are all grown there, and potatoes are cultivated on the Eastern Shore. The piedmont is known for its apples and other fruits, while the Shenandoah Valley is one of the nation's main apple-growing regions. The following table shows data for leading crops in 1978:

	ACRES ('000)	PRODUCTION	VALUE
Tobacco	73	135,157,000 lb	$173,972,000
Corn for grain	615	50,430,000 bushels	118,511,000
Hay	950	1,640,000 tons	106,600,000
Soybeans	445	12,460,000 bushels	84,728,000
Peanuts	103	319,300,000 lb	68,011,000
Apples	—	485,000,000 lb	37,830,000
Potatoes	27	2,970,000 hundredweight	17,523,000
Wheat	155	5,425,000 bushels	16,546,000
Barley	101	5,050,000 bushels	9,595,000
Tomatoes	6	1,150,000 hundredweight	7,631,000
Sweet potatoes	6	854,000 hundredweight	7,259,000
Cucumbers	9	731,000 hundredweight	6,295,000
Peaches	—	40,000,000 lb	5,720,000

²⁴ANIMAL HUSBANDRY

Cattle raising, poultry farming, and dairying, which together account for more than half of all cash receipts from farm marketings, play an increasingly important role in Virginia agriculture, especially in the Valley of Virginia and some central counties. At the close of 1979 there were 1,750,000 cattle and calves, 170,000 milk cows, 850,000 hogs and pigs, and 160,000 sheep and lambs. Production of meat animals that year included 506.4 million lb of cattle worth $318.4 million; 223.8 million lb of hogs, $95.1 million; and 12.2 million lb of sheep, $6.9 million. In 1978, 150,000 shorn sheep yielded 945,000 lb of wool valued at $765,000.

Milk production totaled 1.9 billion lb in 1979, when the output of cottage cheese totaled 7.3 million lb and of ice cream, 7.8 million gallons. Cash receipts from poultry and eggs in the 1978 marketing year amounted to $207.8 million, of which 48% came from chickens and broilers, 29% from turkeys, and 23% from eggs. The following year, poultry farmers produced 479.7 million lb of broilers, raised 9.2 million turkeys, and sold 939 million eggs. The honey output in 1978 exceeded 2.5 million lb valued at $1.8 million.

²⁵FISHING

The relative importance of Chesapeake Bay fisheries to Virginia's economy has lessened considerably in recent decades, although the state continues to place high in national rankings. In 1978, Virginia's commercial fish landings totaled 538.9 million lb (4th in the US), worth $60.6 million (9th). About 7,300 commercial fishermen ply Virginia coastal waters. The bulk of the catch consists of shellfish such as oysters, clams, and crabs, and finfish such as alewives and menhaden. Both saltwater and freshwater fish are avidly sought by hundreds of sport fishermen. A recent threat to Virginia fisheries is chemical and oil pollution of Chesapeake Bay and its tributaries.

26 FORESTRY

As of 1977, Virginia had 16,417,000 acres (6,644,000 hectares) of forestland, representing more than 64% of the state's land area and 2.2% of all US forests. Prevalent trees in the Tidewater include loblolly and other pines, gum, and oak. In the piedmont, hardwoods like oak, hickory, and yellow poplar predominate; softwoods include shortleaf and Virginia pines. The Blue Ridge and Appalachian region are covered with forests of pine, oak, hickory, yellow poplar, maple, and beech. Virtually every county has some commercial forestland and supports a wood products industry.

Commercial timberland in 1977 comprised 15,939,000 acres (6,450,000 hectares), of which 88% were privately owned, 10% were federally owned or managed, and about 2% belonged to the state, counties, and municipalities. More than 1 billion board feet of lumber are produced each year, and the output of small roundwood in 1978 totaled 1.8 million cords. Shipments of lumber and wood products were valued at more than $1 billion in 1977; wood household furniture, $525 million; and paper and allied products, nearly $1.2 billion.

A forest inventory completed during 1977 showed that annual forest growth of softwoods exceeds the commercial drain of timberland by 20%, a significant reversal of the results of the last previous survey in 1966; the 1979 inventory also revealed that annual hardwood growth was sufficient to sustain increased harvests of hardwood timber. Reforestation programs initiated by the Division of Forestry, within the Department of Conservation and Economic Development, have paid landowners to plant pine seedlings; state-funded tree nurseries produce 60–70 million seedlings annually. The division's tree seed orchards have developed improved strains of loblolly, shortleaf, white, and Virginia pine for planting in cutover timberland.

For recreational purposes there are approximately 2 million acres (800,000 hectares) of forested public lands, including Shenandoah National Park, Washington and Jefferson national forests, 20 state parks, and 8 state forests.

27 MINING

Virginia ranked 20th among the 50 states with a mineral output valued at $1.2 billion in 1978. Coal, of which Virginia is the nation's 6th-leading producer, accounts for more than 80% of the total annual mineral value. The state ranks 1st in production of kyanite, a heat-resistant aluminum silicate.

Bituminous coal is mined in the southwestern Appalachian region and the Richmond area. The piedmont and Blue Ridge are sources of kyanite, quartzite, slate, sandstone, and other construction materials. Minerals found in the Valley of Virginia, as well as in the Blue Ridge, include limestone, zinc ore, and dolomite; the coastal plain has large deposits of sand, gravel, and clay.

Coal reserves as of 1976 totaled 4.3 billion tons, 97% of it bituminous; production in 1978 was 31.9 million tons, with two-thirds coming from underground mines. Other leading minerals were zinc, 12,097 tons; lime, 769,000 tons; clays, 954,000 tons; stone, 44,410,000 tons; and sand and gravel, 10,600,000 tons.

28 ENERGY AND POWER

Virginia's installed electric generating capacity was 11.2 million kw in 1978, when production of electricity totaled 43.3 billion kwh, 97% of it provided by private utilities. Electric power is supplied to the eastern and central parts of the state by the Virginia Electric and Power Co. (Vepco), to the central and southwestern regions by Appalachian Power, in the southwest by Old Dominion Power, in the northwest by Potomac Edison, in the northeast by Potomac Electric Power, and on the Eastern Shore by Delmarva Power and Light. Also, 16 municipalities distribute power supplied by most of these companies, and 14 electric cooperatives serve rural areas. Sales of electric power in 1977 amounted to 44.5 billion kwh: 41% residential, 24% industrial, 24% commercial, and 11% other.

Although Virginia has no petroleum deposits, it does have a major oil refinery at Yorktown that uses imported petroleum. The state is supplied with natural gas by three major interstate pipeline companies. Liquefied natural gas plants operate in Chesapeake, Roanoke, and Lynchburg, and a synthetic gas plant has been built at Chesapeake.

Virginia's coal mines supplied fuel for 25% of electric power production in 1978; oil-fired plants produced 37%, nuclear 34%, hydroelectric 3%, and gas 1%. As a result of rising oil prices during the 1970s, the state's utilities have begun to convert some oil-fired electric plants to coal, a trend in which Vepco has been a national leader. Vepco is also committed to nuclear power: the state has four nuclear power reactors, all owned by Vepco, which in April 1980 was issued a limited operating license by the US Nuclear Regulatory Commission for its North Anna Unit 2 nuclear reactor at Mineral. The utility, whose operating revenues were nearly $2.1 billion in 1980, came under increasing scrutiny by environmentalists and federal officials during the late 1970s for a variety of problems, including the simultaneous shutdown of two nuclear reactors because of alleged safety problems late in 1979.

29 INDUSTRY

Beginning with the establishment of a glass factory at Jamestown in 1608, manufacturing grew slowly during the colonial era to include flour mills and, by 1715, an iron foundry. During the 19th century, the shipbuilding industry flourished, and many cotton mills, tanneries, and ironworks were built; light industries producing a wide variety of consumer goods developed mainly after 1900.

During the 1970s, manufacturing employment increased by 14% in Virginia, compared with the national average of about 10%. Textile, clothing, transportation equipment, and food-processing plants together employed more than one-third of all industrial workers in the state as of 1977, when value added by manufacture reached $10.8 billion. The following table shows value added by Virginia's leading industry groups in the years 1972 and 1977:

	1972	1977
Chemicals and chemical products	$844,400,000	$1,474,400,000
Food and food products	610,700,000	1,165,100,000
Tobacco products	580,500,000	1,100,000,000
Transportation equipment	NA	951,600,000
Electric, electronic equipment	370,800,000	856,000,000
Textile mill products	522,800,000	852,900,000
Paper and allied products	304,100,000	532,900,000
Apparel and textile products	281,000,000	475,500,000
Fabricated metal products	235,600,000	439,700,000
Nonelectrical machinery	191,700,000	437,400,000
Furniture and fixtures	341,700,000	419,600,000
Lumber and wood products	276,500,000	418,500,000
Printing and publishing	225,800,000	417,600,000
Rubber and plastics products	255,700,000	415,200,000
Primary metals	137,300,000	319,400,000

Richmond is a principal industrial area for tobacco processing, paper and printing, metals, clothing, and food products; nearby Hopewell is a locus of the chemical industry. Newport News, Hampton, and Norfolk are shipbuilding centers. In the western part of the state, Lynchburg is a center for electrical machinery, metals, clothing, and leather goods, and Roanoke for clothing and textiles, chemicals, and food. In the south, Martinsville has a concentration of furniture and textile manufacturing plants, and textiles are also dominant in Danville. The Newport News Shipbuilding and Dry Dock Co. is the state's single largest private employer, with some 23,000 workers in 1980.

³⁰COMMERCE

Virginia ranked 18th among the 50 states in wholesale trade in 1972, with sales totaling $10.1 billion. In 1977, the state placed 13th in retail sales, with $16.5 billion. The leading retail categories were food stores, 22%; automotive dealers, 21%; department stores, 10%; gasoline service stations, 9%; and restaurants and taverns, 7%. Fairfax County, in the Washington, D.C., metropolitan area, led all counties, with more than 11% of total sales; Richmond, the leading city, had 6%.

Virginia, a major container shipping center, handled 34 million tons of import and export cargo in 1978, mostly through the Hampton Roads estuary. Coal was the leading exported commodity, and residual fuel oils the principal import. Foreign exports of Virginia's own manufactured goods totaled $1.5 billion in 1976 (17th in the US); agricultural exports amounted to $225 million (30th in the US).

³¹CONSUMER PROTECTION

The Department of Law, headed by the attorney general, is responsible for enforcement of consumer protection legislation and for representing consumer interests at hearings of the State Corporation Commission. The Department of Agriculture and Consumer Services regulates food processors and handlers, product labeling, the use of potentially hazardous pesticides, and product safety.

³²BANKING

In 1978, Virginia's 262 commercial banks reported combined assets of $20.8 billion and total deposits of $17.8 billion. Their outstanding loans amounted to $7.9 billion, of which 38% went for commercial and industrial purposes and 62% for real estate mortgages. Leading commercial banks include the United Virginia Bank, First and Merchants National Bank, and Bank of Virginia, all headquartered in Richmond, and the Virginia National Bank, in Norfolk; each had deposits exceeding $1.6 billion in mid-1980. There were 84 savings and loan associations (54 state-charterd, 30 federally chartered), with total assets of $7.9 billion, in 1978; their mortgage loans amounted to $6.9 billion, their savings capital to $6.7 billion, and their total liabilities and net worth to $7.9 billion.

³³INSURANCE

Virginians held 5,117,000 life insurance policies worth $45.4 billion in 1978; the average coverage per family was $37,300, 6% above the national norm. Benefit payments totaled $560.2 million, of which death payments accounted for $257.9 million, annuities $79 million, policy dividends $113.2 million, and other disbursements $110.1 million.

In 1978, property and liability companies wrote premiums of $1.5 billion, including $467.2 million in automotive liability insurance, $245.6 million in automobile physical damage insurance, and $133.8 million in homeowners' coverage. Some 499,000 Virginians with Medicare hospital coverage received $254 million in payments during 1977, while 485,000 Medicare medical insurance enrollees received $97 million.

³⁴SECURITIES

There are no securities exchanges in Virginia. New York Stock Exchange member firms had 86 sales offices and 581 registered representatives in the state during 1978. Virginians reported $639.9 million in dividend income on their 1977 federal tax returns.

³⁵PUBLIC FINANCE

The biennial budget is prepared by the Virginia Department of Planning and Budget and submitted by the governor to the general assembly for amendment and approval. The constitution requires that the budget be balanced; in practice, there is generally a small surplus of revenues over expenditures. The fiscal year runs from 1 July through 30 June.

Consolidated revenues and expenditures budgeted for the 1980–82 biennium were as follows (in millions):

REVENUES	
General fund:	
Personal income tax	$ 2,599.7
Corporate income tax	408.4
Sales and use tax	1,281.6
Other revenues	1,127.5
Nongeneral fund:	
Grants and donations	2,732.9
Institutional revenue	1,121.0
Designated taxes	1,031.9
Sales of property and commodities	477.7
Other receipts	825.0
TOTAL	$11,605.7

EXPENDITURES	
Education	$ 3,741.4
Individual and family services	3,365.0
Transportation	2,125.9
General government	756.1
Administration of justice	579.0
State enterprises	456.3
Resource and economic development	287.5
Other outlays	184.0
TOTAL	$11,495.2

As of 30 June 1977, debts incurred by state and local governments totaled $4.3 billion, or $839 per capita, well below the US average.

³⁶TAXATION

Virginians bear a lighter tax burden than residents of most states. During 1976/77, for example, the state and local tax burden was $675 per capita, 28th among the 50 states and 17% below the national average. For the 1980–82 biennium, state taxes accounted for 51% of total state revenues. Of the tax total, the personal income tax provided 44%, sales and use tax 22%, and corporate income tax 7%.

As of 1981, state income tax rates ranged from 2% on adjusted gross income below $3,000 to 5.75% on the amount over $12,000. The basic corporate income tax rate was 6%. The state sales and use tax rate was 3%, plus a 1% levy by all counties and independent cities. Also taxed by the state are motor vehicles and insurance transactions. The real estate tax, tangible personal property tax, and utility taxes are levied by counties and cities.

Virginia remitted $7.3 billion in taxes to the federal government in 1975/76 and received $10.3 billion in federal expenditures, for a spending/tax ratio of 1.41, the highest of any state on the Atlantic coast; only California enjoyed a greater net surplus of federal transfers. State residents filed 2,069,415 personal income tax returns for 1977, paying $3.8 billion in tax.

³⁷ECONOMIC POLICY

The state government actively promotes a probusiness climate. Conservative traditions, low tax rates, low wage rates, a weak labor movement, and excellent access to eastern markets are the general incentives for companies to relocate into Virginia.

The Virginia Industrial Development Corp., a privately financed and privately capitalized lending facility operating under special charter from the general assembly, extends low-interest loans of up to $500,000 to creditworthy companies to purchase land, buildings, and machinery if conventional financing is not available. The state also may issue revenue bonds to finance industrial projects—a popular method of financing because the return to investors is tax-free. The bonds may also be used to finance the installation of pollution control equipment. At their discretion, localities may allow total or partial tax exemptions for such equipment and for certified solar energy devices.

Counties, cities, and towns may form local industrial development authorities to finance industrial projects, and may issue their own revenue bonds to cover the cost of land, buildings, machinery, and equipment. The authority's lease of the property normally includes an option to buy, thus permitting the lease-holding firm to claim depreciation allowances and investment tax credits. In addition, some 110 local development corporations have been organized.

38 HEALTH

Virginia ranked 40th among the 50 states in average life expectancy during 1969–71, at 70.08 years: 66.26 years for men, 74.17 for women. The infant mortality rate in 1977 was 13.3 deaths per 1,000 live births for whites and 23.4 for nonwhites—in each case, somewhat above the US average. Some 28,200 legal abortions were performed in 1977/78. Virginia's death rate of 7.8 per 1,000 population was below the US average for 1977, and Virginia's death rates for the leading causes of death—heart disease, cancer, and stroke—were likewise below the national norms.

In 1978, Virginia's 135 general hospitals had 32,138 beds and recorded 794,746 admissions, with an average daily occupancy rate of 76%. Hospital personnel included 12,232 registered nurses and 6,035 licensed practical nurses. The average cost of hospital care in 1977 was $167 per day and $1,306 per stay, well below the US norm. Virginia had 8,240 licensed physicians in 1977 and 2,599 active dentists in 1979.

A Virginia law allowing sterilization for eugenic purposes came under scrutiny in 1980 following disclosures that at least 7,000 Virginians had been sterilized—many without their knowledge or consent—between 1924 and 1972. A class action suit naming six state mental hospitals and several state officials as co-defendants was filed on behalf of the victims in December 1980.

39 SOCIAL WELFARE

Payments totaling $138 million in aid to families with dependent children were made in 1978, when the food stamp program enrolled 197,000 Virginians at a federal cost of $66.6 million. During the same year, the school lunch program benefited 743,000 pupils, with a federal outlay of $43.4 million.

In 1977, Social Security benefits were paid to 676,400 state residents; disbursements amounted to nearly $1.6 billion, with an average monthly benefit of $225.30 per retired worker, 7% below the US average. Federal Supplemental Security Income payments, made to 79,700 aged, blind, or disabled persons, totaled $94 million in 1978. Funds distributed under the Black Lung Benefit Program to coal miners afflicted with pneumoconiosis (and to their dependents or survivors) totaled $54 million during the same year. Some 27,300 Virginians took part in vocational rehabilitation programs costing $23.1 million in 1978; workers' compensation amounted to $100.3 million in 1977. Unemployment insurance payments, issued to an average of 24,000 beneficiaries weekly, totaled $97 million in 1978, when the average benefit was $83.51.

40 HOUSING

Virginia in 1970 had some 1,484,000 housing units, 1,391,000 of them occupied. Of the latter, 88% had full plumbing; a much higher percentage was anticipated in 1980. Between 1976 and 1978, the state authorized construction of 146,000 new units, about four-fifths of which were single-family homes. New residential construction in that period was valued at nearly $4.4 billion.

41 EDUCATION

Although Virginia was the first English colony to found a free school (1634), the state's public school system developed very slowly. Thomas Jefferson proposed a system of free public schools as early as 1779, but it was not until 1851 that such a system was established—for whites only. Free schools for blacks were founded after the Civil War, but they were poorly funded until recent years. Opposition by white Virginians to the US Supreme Court's desegregation order in 1954 was marked in certain communities by public school closings and the establishment of all-white private schools; in Prince Edward County, the most extreme case, the school board abandoned public education and left

black children without schools from 1959 to 1963. By the 1970s, however, school integration was an accomplished fact throughout the commonwealth.

As of 1970, Virginia's illiteracy rate was 1.4%. About 64% of all state residents 18 years of age or older were high school graduates in 1976, and more than 16% had at least four years of college; the median number of schools years completed was 12.4. Under a Standards of Quality Program adopted in 1972, students must pass minimum competency tests in reading and math in order to qualify for a high school diploma. During the 1978/79 school year, Virginia had 1,759 public schools, with 1,030,227 pupils; there were 252 private schools, with an estimated 32,000 pupils, in 1977/78.

Virginia has had a distinguished record in higher education since the College of William and Mary was founded at Williamsburg (then called Middle Plantation) in 1693, and especially after Thomas Jefferson established the University of Virginia at Charlottesville in 1819. In 1979/80, colleges and universities in the state enrolled more than 275,000 students, about three-fifths of them full-time; 23 community colleges on 33 campuses had 167,000 students in 1978/79. In addition to the University of Virginia and the College of William and Mary—with enrollments of 16,179 and 6,318, respectively, in 1978/79—public state-supported institutions include Virginia Polytechnic Institute and State University, at Blacksburg; Virginia Commonwealth University, Richmond; Old Dominion University, Norfolk; and George Mason University, Fairfax. Well-known private institutions include the Hampton Institute, at Hampton; Randolph-Macon College, Ashland; University of Richmond; Sweet Briar College, Sweet Briar; and Washington and Lee University, Lexington. Tuition assistance grants and scholarships are provided through the State Council of Higher Education, while the State Education Assistance Authority provides guaranteed student loans.

42 ARTS

Richmond and Norfolk are the principal centers for both the creative and performing arts in Virginia. In Richmond, the Mosque has been the scene of concerts by internationally famous orchestras and soloists for generations, and a modernistic coliseum now shelters many musical events. The intimate 500-seat Virginia Museum Theater presents new plays and classics with professional casts. Just outside the Richmond metropolitan area, the Barksdale Theater and its repertory company present serious plays and occasionally premiere a new script. In Norfolk, the performing arts are strikingly housed in Scope, a large auditorium designed by Pier Luigi Nervi; Chrysler Hall, an elegant structure with gleaming crystal; and the Wells Theater, an ornate building where John Philip Sousa, Will Rogers, and Fred Astaire once performed and which now houses the Virginia Stage Company, a repertory theater. The Virginia Opera Association, centered in Norfolk, is internationally recognized.

Wolf Trap Farm Park for the Performing Arts, in northern Virginia, provides theatrical, operatic, and symphonic performances featuring internationally celebrated performers. William and Mary's Phi Beta Kappa Hall in Williamsburg is the site of the Virginia Shakespeare Festival, an annual summer event inaugurated in 1979. Abingdon is the home of the Barter Theater, the first state-supported theater in the United States, whose alumni include Ernest Borgnine and Gregory Peck. This repertory company has performed widely in the United States and at the Elsinore Shakespeare Festival in Denmark. The John F. Kennedy Center for the Performing Arts in nearby Washington, D.C., is heavily patronized by Virginians.

43 LIBRARIES AND MUSEUMS

A total of 52 county or regional library systems served 77 Virginia counties in 1977/78; their combined book stock reached 8,307,089 volumes, and their combined circulation was 24,220,854. The Virginia State Library in Richmond and the libraries of the

University of Virginia (Charlottesville) and the College of William and Mary (Williamsburg) have the personal papers of such notables as Washington, Jefferson, Madison, Robert E. Lee, William H. McGuffey, and William Faulkner. The University of Virginia also has an impressive collection of medieval illuminated manuscripts, and the library of colonial Williamsburg has extensive microfilms of British records.

There are nearly 200 galleries, museums, and historic sites. In Richmond, the Virginia Museum of Fine Arts, the first state museum of art in the US, has a collection that ranges from ancient Egyptian artifacts to mobile jewelry by Salvador Dali. Other museums in Richmond are Wilton, the Randolphs' handsome 18th-century mansion, and the Maymont and Wickham-Valentine houses, elaborate 19th-century residences; Agecroft Hall and Virginia House, Tudor manor houses that were moved from England, are also open to the public. Norfolk has the Chrysler Museum, with its famous glassware collection; Myers House, an early Federal period home with handsome art and furnishings; and the Hermitage Foundation Museum, noted for its Oriental art. The Mariners Museum in Newport News has a superb maritime collection, and the much smaller but quite select exhibits of the Portsmouth Naval Shipyard Museum are also notable. Perhaps the most extensive "museum" in the US is Williamsburg's mile-long Duke of Gloucester Street, with such remarkable restorations as the Christopher Wren Building of the College of William and Mary, Bruton Parish Church, the Governor's Palace, and the colonial capitol.

More historic sites are maintained as museums in Virginia than in any other state. These include Washington's home at Mt. Vernon (Fairfax County), Jefferson's residence at Monticello (Charlottesville), and James River plantation houses such as Berkeley, Shirley, Westover, Sherwood Forest, and Carter's Grove. The National Park Service operates a visitor center at Jamestown.

44 COMMUNICATIONS

The state's communications network has expanded steadily since the first postal routes were established in 1738. Airmail service from Richmond to New York and to Atlanta began in 1928. As of 1977, the US Postal Service had 10,000 employees in Virginia, not including counties and cities falling within the Washington, D.C., metropolitan area.

Virginia in 1978 had 3,671,932 telephones, 938,615 residential and 2,733,317 business; 79% were owned by the Bell System. On average, 92% of all households had telephone service. During the same year, commercial broadcasters operated 137 AM radio stations, 73 FM stations, and 14 television stations. There were 81 cable systems serving 212,781 subscribers in 189 communities at the close of 1978.

45 PRESS

Although the crown forbade the establishment of a printing press in Virginia Colony, William Parks was publishing the *Virginia Gazette* at Williamsburg in 1736. Three newspapers were published regularly during the Revolutionary period, and in 1780 the general assembly declared that the press was "indispensable for the right information of the people and for the public service." The oldest continuously published Virginia daily, tracing its origins to 1784, is the *Alexandria Gazette*. The first Negro newspaper, *The True Southerner*, was started by a white man in 1865; several weeklies published and edited by blacks began soon after. By 1900 there were 180 newspapers in the state, but the number has declined drastically since then because of fierce competition, mergers, and rising costs.

In 1978, Virginia had 10 morning dailies with a combined circulation of 492,747, 23 evening dailies with 587,939 circulation, and 13 Sunday papers with 826,871 circulation. Leading Virginia newspapers with their 1978 circulations are shown in the following table:

AREA	NAME	DAILY	SUNDAY
Norfolk	Ledger-Star (e,S)	95,794 }	198,071
	Virginian-Pilot (m,S)	124,900 }	
Richmond	News Leader (e)	114,300	
	Times-Dispatch (m,S)	133,350	211,792
Roanoke	Times & World News	64,297(m) }	113,964
	(m,e,S)	48,413(e) }	

46 ORGANIZATIONS

Hundreds of national societies and organizations have their headquarters in Virginia. Service groups include the Independent Order of Odd Fellows, Arlington; United Way of America and the Association of Volunteer Bureaus, Alexandria; and American Youth Hostels, Delaplane. Veterans' organizations include the Veterans of World War I of the USA and the Retired Officers Association, Alexandria; and the Military Order of the Purple Heart, Arlington. The United Daughters of the Confederacy has national offices in Richmond.

Among the educational groups headquartered in the state are the American Astronautical Society and the American Society for Horticultural Science, both in Alexandria; the American Geological Institute, Falls Church; and Music Educators National Conference and National Art Education Association, both in Reston. Business and professional groups include the American Apparel Manufacturers Association, Alexandria; American Gas Association, Arlington; and National Automobile Dealers Association, McLean.

Sports societies with headquarters in Virginia include the American Canoe Association, Lorton; Boat Owners Association of the US, Alexandria; and National Rowing Association and Walking Association, both located in Arlington.

Other groups operating out of Virginia include the Future Farmers of America and National Sojourners, Alexandria; the Federation of Homemakers, Arlington; American Automobile Association, Falls Church; and the Association of Former Intelligence Officers, McLean. The US office of the World Federalists Association is at Arlington.

47 TOURISM, TRAVEL, AND RECREATION

By 1980, tourists spent an estimated $2.3 billion a year in Virginia. Attractions in the coastal region alone include the Jamestown and Yorktown historic sites, the Williamsburg restoration, and the homes of George Washington and Robert E. Lee. Also featured are the National Aeronautics and Space Administration's Langley Research Center, Assateague Island National Seashore, and the resort pleasures of Virginia Beach. The interior offers numerous Civil War Sites, including Appomattox; Thomas Jefferson's Monticello; Booker T. Washington's birthplace near Smith Mountain Lake; and the historic cities of Richmond, Petersburg, and Fredericksburg. In the west, the Blue Ridge Parkway and Shenandoah National Park, traversed by the breathtaking Skyline Drive, are favorite tourist destinations, as are Cumberland Gap and, in the Lexington area, the Natural Bridge, the home of Confederate General Thomas "Stonewall" Jackson, the George C. Marshall Library and Museum, and the Virginia Military Institute. Historic sites in Arlington and Alexandria attract many visitors to the Washington, D.C. area.

The state's many recreation areas include 20 state parks, 8 state forests, and 400 public and private campgrounds. Some of the most-visited sites are Mt. Rogers National Recreational Area, Prince William Forest Park, Chincoteague National Wildlife Refuge, and the Kerr Reservoir. Part of the famous Appalachian Trail winds through Virginia's Blue Ridge and Appalachian Mountains. The commonwealth, with more than 1,500 mi (2,400 km) of well-stocked trout streams, issued licenses to 431,138 fishermen and 449,176 hunters in 1977/78.

48 SPORTS

Although Virginia has no major league sports team, it does support two entries in baseball's class-AAA International League:

the Richmond Grays, affiliated with the Atlanta Braves, and Norfolk's Tidewater Tides, a farm team of the New York Mets.

In collegiate sports, the University of Virginia belongs to the Atlantic Coast Conference, while VMI competes in the Southern Conference. The 1979/80 season brought three national basketball crowns to the commonwealth: men's teams at the University of Virginia and Virginia Union University won the National Invitation Tournament and the NCAA Division II championships, respectively, and for the second consecutive year, Old Dominion University's Lady Monarchs won the national tournament sponsored by the Association for Intercollegiate Athletics for Women. The men's basketball team at Old Dominion won the NCAA Division II title in 1975.

Participant sports popular with Virginians include tennis, golf, swimming, skiing, boating, and water skiing. The state has at least 180 public and private golf courses.

[49] FAMOUS VIRGINIANS

Virginia is the birthplace of eight US presidents and many famous statesmen, noted scientists, influential educators, distinguished writers, and popular entertainers.

The 1st president of the US, George Washington (1732–99), also led his country's armies in the Revolutionary War and presided over the convention that framed its Constitution. Washington, who was unanimously elected president in 1789, served two four-year terms, and declined a third, was not, as has sometimes been assumed, a newcomer to politics: his political career began at the age of 27 with his election to the house of burgesses.

Thomas Jefferson (1743–1826), the nation's 3d president, offered this as his epitaph: "author of the Declaration of Independence and the Virginia Statute for Religious Freedom, and father of the University of Virginia." After serving as secretary of state under Washington and vice president under John Adams, he was elected president of the US in 1800 and reelected in 1804. Honored now as a statesman and political thinker, Jefferson was also a musician and one of the foremost architects of his time, and he has been called the first American archaeologist.

Jefferson's successor, James Madison (1751–1836), actually made his most important contributions before becoming chief executive. As a skillful and persistent negotiator throughout the Constitutional Convention of 1787, he earned the designation "father of the Constitution"; then, as coauthor of the *Federalist* papers, he helped produce a classic of American political philosophy. He was more responsible than any other statesman for Virginia's crucial ratification vote. Secretary of state during Jefferson's two terms, Madison occupied the presidency from 1809 to 1817.

Madison was succeeded as president in 1817 by James Monroe (1758–1831), who was reelected to a second term starting in 1821. Monroe, who had served as governor, US senator, minister to France, and secretary of state, is best known for the Monroe Doctrine, which has been US policy since his administration. William Henry Harrison (1773–1841) became the 9th president in 1841 but died of pneumonia one month after his inauguration; he had been a governor of Indiana Territory, a major general in the War of 1812, and a US representative and senator from Indiana. Harrison was succeeded by Vice President John Tyler (1790–1862), a native and resident of Virginia, who established the precedent that, upon the death of the president, the vice president inherits the title as well as the duties of the office.

Another native Virginian, Zachary Taylor (1784–1850), renowned chiefly as a military leader, became the 12th US president in 1849 but died midway through his term. The eighth Virginia-born president, (Thomas) Woodrow Wilson (1856–1924), became the 28th president of the US in 1913 after serving as governor of New Jersey.

John Marshall (1755–1835), was the third chief justice of the US and is generally regarded by historians as the first great American jurist, partly because of his establishment of the principle of judicial review. Four other Virginians—John Blair (1732–1800), Bushrod Washington (1762–1829), Philip P. Barbour (1783–1841), and Lewis F. Powell, Jr. (b.1907)—have served as associate justices.

George Washington's cabinet included two Virginians, Secretary of State Jefferson and Attorney General Edmund Randolph (1753–1813), who, as governor of Virginia, had introduced the Virginia Plan—drafted by Madison and calling for a House of Representatives elected by the people and a Senate elected by the House—at the Constitutional Convention of 1787. Among other distinguished Virginians who have served in the cabinet are James Barbour (1775–1842), secretary of war; John Y. Mason (1799–1859), secretary of the Navy and attorney general; Carter Glass (1858–1946), secretary of the treasury, author of the Federal Reserve System, and US senator for 26 years; and Claude Augustus Swanson (1862–1939), secretary of the Navy and, earlier, state governor and US senator.

Other prominent US senators from Virginia include Richard Henry Lee (1732–94), former president of the Continental Congress; James M. Mason (b.District of Columbia, 1798–1871), who later was commissioner of the Confederacy to the United Kingdom and France; John W. Daniel (1842–1910), a legal scholar and powerful Democratic Party leader; Thomas S. Martin (1847–1919), US Senate majority leader; and Harry F. Byrd (1887–1966), a governor of Virginia from 1926 to 1930 and US senator from 1933 to 1965. At one time, Byrd was regarded as the most influential member of the Senate. In 1980, Virginia was represented in the Senate by Harry F. Byrd, Jr. (b.1914), an independent; and Republican John W. Warner (b.District of Columbia, 1927), former secretary of the Navy and the husband of film star Elizabeth Taylor (b.England, 1932).

Some native-born Virginians have become famous as leaders in other nations. Joseph Jenkins Roberts (1809–76) was the first president of the Republic of Liberia, and Nancy Langhorne Astor (1879–1964) was the first woman to serve in the British House of Commons.

Virginia's important colonial governors included Captain John Smith (b.England, 1580?–1631), Sir George Yeardley (b.England, 1587?–1627), Sir William Berkeley (b.England, 1606–77), Alexander Spotswood (b.Tangier, 1676–1740), Sir William Gooch (b.England, 1681–1751), and Robert Dinwiddie (b.Scotland, 1693–1770).

Virginia signers of the Declaration of Independence, besides Jefferson and Richard Henry Lee, were Carter Braxton (1736–97); Benjamin Harrison (1726?–1791), father of President William Henry Harrison; Francis Lightfoot Lee (1734–97); Thomas Nelson, Jr. (1738–89); and George Wythe (1726–1806). Wythe is also famous as the first US law professor and the teacher, in their student days, of Presidents Jefferson, Monroe, and Tyler, and Chief Justice Marshall. Virginia furnished both the first president of the Continental Congress, Peyton Randolph (1721–75), and the last, Cyrus Griffin (1748–1810).

Other notable Virginia governors include Patrick Henry (1736–99), the first governor of the commonwealth, though best remembered as a Revolutionary orator; Westmoreland Davis (1859–1942); Andrew Jackson Montague (1862–1937); and Mills E. Godwin, Jr. (b.1914). A major historical figure who defies classification is Robert "King" Carter (1663–1732), greatest of the Virginia land barons, who also served as acting governor of Virginia and rector of the College of William and Mary.

Chief among Virginia's great military and naval leaders besides Washington and Taylor are John Paul Jones (b.Scotland, 1747–92); George Rogers Clark (1752–1818); Winfield Scott (1786–1866); Robert E. Lee (1807–70), the Confederate commander who earlier served in the Mexican War and as superintendent of West Point; Joseph E. Johnston (1807–91); George H. Thomas (1816–70); Thomas Jonathan "Stonewall" Jackson

(1824–63); James Ewell Brown "Jeb" Stuart (1833–64); and George C. Marshall (b.Pennsylvania, 1880–1959). Virginians' names are also written high in the history of exploration. Daniel Boone (b.Pennsylvania, 1734–1820), who pioneered in Kentucky and Missouri, was once a member of the Virginia general assembly. Meriwether Lewis (1774–1809) and William Clark (1770–1838), both native Virginians, led the most famous expedition in US history, from St. Louis to the Pacific coast (1804–6). Richard E. Byrd (1888–1957) was both an explorer of Antarctica and a pioneer aviator.

Woodrow Wilson and George C. Marshall both received the Nobel Peace Prize, in 1919 and 1953, respectively. Distinguished Virginia-born scientists and inventors include Cyrus H. McCormick (1809–84), who perfected the mechanical reaper; Matthew Fontaine Maury (1806–73), founder of the science of oceanography; and Dr. Walter Reed (1851–1902), who proved that yellow fever was transmitted by a mosquito. Among educators associated with the state are William H. McGuffey (b.Pennsylvania, 1800–1873), a University of Virginia professor who designed and edited the most famous series of school readers in American history; and Booker T. Washington (1856–1915), the nation's foremost black educator.

William Byrd II (1674–1744) is widely acknowledged to have been the most graceful writer in English America in his day, and Jefferson was a leading prose stylist of the Revolutionary period. Edgar Allan Poe (b.Massachusetts, 1809–49), who was taken to Richmond at the age of 3 and later educated at the University of Virginia, was the father of the detective story and one of America's great poets and short-story writers. Virginia is the setting of historical romances by three natives, John Esten Cooke (1830–86), Thomas Nelson Page (1853–1922), and Mary Johnston (1870–1936). Notable 20th-century novelists include Willa Cather (1873–1947), Ellen Glasgow (1874–1945), and James Branch Cabell (1879–1958). Willard Huntington Wright (1888–1939), better known as S. S. Van Dine, wrote many detective thrillers. Twice winner of the Pulitzer Prize for biography and often regarded as the greatest American master of that genre was Douglas Southall Freeman (1886–1953). Other important historians were Lyon Gardiner Tyler (1853–1935), son of President Tyler and also an eminent educator; Philip A. Bruce (1856–1933); William Cabell Bruce (1860–1946); Virginius Dabney (b.1901); and Alf J. Mapp, Jr. (b.1925). Some contemporary Virginia authors are poet Guy Carlton Drewry (b.1901); television writer-producer Earl Hamner (b.1923); novelist William Styron (b.1925); and journalists Virginia Moore (b.1903) and Tom Wolfe (Thomas Kennerly Wolfe, Jr., b.1931).

Celebrated Virginia artists include sculptors Edward V. Valentine (1838–1930) and Moses Ezekiel (1844–1917), and painters George Caleb Bingham (1811–79) and Jerome Myers (1867–1940). A distinguished protégé of Jefferson's, Robert Mills (b.South Carolina, 1781–1855), was a famous architect who designed the Washington Monument.

The roster of Virginians prominent in the entertainment world includes Bill "Bojangles" Robinson (1878–1949), Francis X. Bushman (1883–1966), Freeman Gosden (b.1899), Randolph Scott (b.1903), Joseph Cotten (b.1905), Margaret Sullavan (1911–60), John Payne (b.1912), George C. Scott (b.1927), Shirley MacLaine (b.1934), and Warren Beatty (b.1938).

Outstanding musical performers include John Powell (1882–1963), whose fame as a pianist once equaled his prominence as a composer; Virginia's most eminent contemporary composer is Thea Musgrave (b.Scotland, 1928). Popular musical stars include Kathryn Elizabeth "Kate" Smith (b.1909), Pearl Bailey (b.1918), Ella Fitzgerald (b.1918), June Carter (b.1929), Roy Clark (b.1933), and Wayne Newton (b.1942).

The Old Dominion's sports champions include golfers Bobby Cruickshank (b.1896), Sam Snead (b.1912), and Chandler Harper

(b.1914); tennis star Arthur Ashe (b.1943); football players Clarence "Ace" Parker (b.1912) and Bill Dudley (b.1921); and baseball pitcher Eppa Rixey (1891–1963). At age 15, Olympic swimming champion Melissa Belote (b.1957) won three gold medals. Helen Chenery "Penny" Tweedy (b.1922) is a famous breeder and racer of horses from whose stables have come Secretariat and other champions. Equestrienne Jean McLean Davis (b.1929) won 65 world championships.

[50]BIBLIOGRAPHY

Beverly, Robert. *History and Present State of Virginia*. Chapel Hill: University of North Carolina Press, 1947 (orig. 1705).

Bruce, Philip Alexander. *Economic History of Virginia in the Seventeenth Century*. 2 vols. New York: Macmillan, 1895–96.

Bruce, Philip Alexander. *Social Life of Virginia in the Seventeenth Century*. Lynchburg: J. P. Bell, 1927.

Buni, Andrew. *The Negro in Virginia Politics, 1902–65*. Charlottesville: University Press of Virginia, 1967.

Dabney, Virginius. *Richmond: The Story of a City*. Garden City, N.Y.: Doubleday, 1976.

Dabney, Virginius. *Virginia: The New Dominion*. Garden City, N.Y.: Doubleday, 1971.

Davis, Richard Beale. *Intellectual Life in Jefferson's Virginia, 1790–1830*. Chapel Hill: University of North Carolina Press, 1964.

Dowdey, Clifford. *Experiment in Rebellion*. Garden City, N.Y.: Doubleday, 1946.

Federal Writers' Project. *Virginia: A Guide to the Old Dominion*. New York: Oxford University Press, 1940.

Freeman, Douglas Southall. *George Washington*. 7 vols. New York: Scribner, 1948–57.

Friddell, Guy. *What Is It About Virginia?* Richmond: Dietz, 1966.

Gottmann, Jean. *Virginia in Our Century*. Charlottesville: University Press of Virginia, 1969.

Malone, Dumas. *Jefferson and His Time*. Vols. 1–2. Boston: Little, Brown, 1948, 1951.

Mapp, Alf J., Jr. *Frock Coats and Epaulets: Confederate Political and Military Leaders*. New York: A. S. Barnes, 1963.

Mapp, Alf J., Jr. *The Virginia Experiment: The Old Dominion's Role in the Making of America, 1607–1781*. 2d ed. LaSalle, Ill.: Open Court, 1975.

Moger, Allen W. *Virginia: Bourbonism to Byrd, 1870–1925*. Charlottesville: University Press of Virginia, 1968.

Morgan, Edmund S. *American Slavery, American Freedom: The Ordeal of Colonial Virginia*. New York: Norton, 1975.

Morton, Richard L. *Colonial Virginia*. 2 vols. Chapel Hill: University of North Carolina Press, 1960.

Peirce, Neal R. *The Border South States: People, Politics, and Power in the Five Border South States*. New York: Norton, 1975.

Rubin, Louis D., Jr. *Virginia: A Bicentennial History*. New York: Norton, 1977.

Stanard, Mary Newton. *The Story of Virginia's First Century*. Philadelphia: Lippincott, 1938.

Tyler, Lyon G. (ed.). *Narratives of Early Virginia: 1606–25*. New York: Scribner, 1959.

Virginia, Commonwealth of. *1980–82 Executive Budget*. Richmond, n.d.

Virginia, Commonwealth of. *Report of the Secretary of the Commonwealth to the Governor and General Assembly of Virginia*. Richmond, 1980.

Wertenbaker, Thomas J. *Norfolk, Historic Southern Port*. 2d ed. Durham, N.C.: Duke University Press, 1962.

Wertenbaker, Thomas J. *Torchbearer of the Revolution*. Princeton, N.J.: Princeton University Press, 1940.

Wright, Louis B. *The First Gentlemen of Virginia*. Charlottesville: University Press of Virginia, 1940.

WASHINGTON

State of Washington

ORIGIN OF STATE NAME: Named for George Washington. **NICKNAME**: The Evergreen State. **CAPITAL**: Olympia. **ENTERED UNION**: 11 November 1889 (42d). **SONG**: "Washington, My Home." **DANCE**: Square dance. **MOTTO**: *Alki* (By and by). **FLAG**: The state seal centered on a dark green field. **OFFICIAL SEAL**: Portrait of George Washington surrounded by the words "The Seal of the State of Washington 1889." **BIRD**: Willow goldfinch. **FISH**: Steelhead trout. **FLOWER**: Western rhododendron. **TREE**: Western hemlock. **GEM**: Petrified wood. **LEGAL HOLIDAYS**: New Year's Day, 1 January; Lincoln's Birthday, 12 February; Washington's Birthday, 3d Monday in February; Memorial Day, last Monday in May; Independence Day, 4 July; Labor Day, 1st Monday in September; Veterans Day and State Admission Day, 11 November; Thanksgiving Day, 4th Thursday in November; Christmas Day, 25 December. **TIME**: 4 A.M. PST = noon GMT.

¹LOCATION, SIZE, AND EXTENT

Located on the Pacific coast of the northwestern US, Washington ranks 20th in size among the 50 states.

The total area of Washington is 68,192 sq mi (176,617 sq km), of which land takes up 66,570 sq mi (172,416 sq km) and inland water 1,622 sq mi (4,201 sq km). The state extends about 360 mi (580 km) E–W and 240 mi (390 km) N–S.

Washington is bounded on the N by the Canadian province of British Columbia (with the northwestern line passing through the Juan de Fuca Strait and the Haro and Georgia straits); on the E by Idaho (with the line in the southwest passing through the Snake River); on the S by Oregon (with most of the line defined by the Columbia River); and on the W by the Pacific Ocean.

Islands of the San Juan group, lying between the Haro and Rosario straits, include Orcas, San Juan, and Lopez; Whidbey is a large island in the upper Puget Sound. The state's boundary length totals 1,099 mi (1,769 km), including 157 mi (253 km) of general coastline; the tidal shoreline extends 3,026 mi (4,870 km). Washington's geographic center is in Chelan County, 10 mi (16 km) WSW of Wenatchee.

²TOPOGRAPHY

Much of Washington is mountainous. Along the Pacific coast are the Coast Ranges extending northward from Oregon and California. This chain forms two groups: the Olympic Mountains in the northwest, mainly on the Olympic Peninsula between the Pacific Ocean and Puget Sound, and the Willapa Hills in the southwest. The highest of the Olympic group is Mt. Olympus, at 7,965 feet (2,428 meters). About 100 mi (160 km) inward from the Pacific coast is the Cascade Range, extending northward from the Sierra Nevada in California. This chain, 50–100 mi (80–160 km) wide, has peaks generally ranging up to 10,000 feet (3,000 meters), except for such volcanic cones as Mt. Adams, Mt. Baker, Glacier Peak, Mt. St. Helens, and Mt. Rainier, which at 14,410 feet (4,392 meters) is the highest peak in the state.

Between the Coast and Cascade ranges lies a long, trough-like depression—the Western Corridor—where most of Washington's major cities are concentrated. The northern section of this lowland is carved by Puget Sound, a complex, narrow arm of the Pacific wending southward for about 80 mi (130 km) and covering an area of 561 sq mi (1,453 sq km). Of all the state's other major regions, only south-central Washington, forming part of the Columbia Plateau, is generally flat.

The Cascade volcanoes were dormant, for the most part, during the second half of the 19th century and most of the 20th. Early in 1980, however, Mt. St. Helens began to show ominous signs of activity. On 18 May, the volcano exploded, blasting more than 1,300 feet (400 meters) off a mountain crest that had been 9,677 feet (2,950 meters) high. Tremendous plumes of steam and ash were thrust into the stratosphere, where prevailing winds carried volcanic dust thousands of miles eastward. The areas immediately surrounding Mt. St. Helens were deluged with ash and mudflows, choking local streams and lakes, particularly Spirit Lake. Millions of trees were destroyed; the ash fall also damaged crops in neighboring agricultural areas and made highway travel extremely hazardous. The known death toll was 34, with at least 28 other persons missing. Eruptions of lesser severity followed the main outburst; the mountain continued to pose a serious danger to life in the area as the estimated cost of the damage to property, crops, and livestock approached $3 billion.

East of the Cascade Range, much of Washington is a plateau underlain by ancient basalt lava flows. In the northeast are the Okanogan Highlands; in the southeast, the Blue Mountains and the Palouse Hills. All these uplands form extensions of the Rocky Mountain system.

Among Washington's numerous rivers, the longest and most powerful is the Columbia, entering Washington from Canada in the northeast corner and flowing for more than 1,200 mi (1,900 km) across the heart of the state and then along the Oregon border to the Pacific. In average discharge, the Columbia ranks 2d only to the Mississippi, with 262,000 cu feet (7,400 cu meters) per second. Washington's other major river, the Snake, enters the state from Idaho in the southeast and flows generally westward, meeting the Columbia River near Pasco.

Washington has numerous lakes, of which the largest is the artificial Franklin D. Roosevelt Lake, covering 123 sq mi (319 sq km). Washington has some 90 dams, providing water storage, flood control, and hydroelectric power. One of the largest and most famous dams in the US is Grand Coulee on the upper Columbia River, measuring 550 feet (168 meters) high and 4,173 feet (1,272 meters) long, with a storage capacity of more than 9.7 million acre-feet.

³CLIMATE

The Cascade Mountains divide Washington not only topographically but also climatically. Despite its northerly location, western Washington is as mild as the middle and southeastern Atlantic coast; it is also one of the rainiest regions in the world. Eastern Washington, on the other hand, has a much more continental climate, characterized by cold winters, hot summers, and sparse rainfall. Since the prevailing winds are from the west, the windward (western) slopes of the state's major mountains intercept most of the atmospheric moisture and precipitate it as rain or snow. Certain coastal areas, receiving more than 200 in (500 cm) of rain a year, support dense stands of timber in a temperate rain forest. But in the dry southeastern quadrant, there are sagebrush deserts.

Average January temperatures in western Washington range from a minimum of 20°F (–7°C) on the western slope of the Cascades to a maximum of 48°F (9°C) along the Pacific coast; July temperatures range from a minimum of 44°F (7°C) in the western slope of the Cascades to a maximum of 80°F (27°C) in the foothills. In the east, the temperature ranges are much more extreme: in January, from 8°F (–13°C) in the northeastern Cascades to 40°F (4°C) on the southeastern plateau; in July, from 48°F (9°C) on the eastern slope of the Cascades to 92°F (33°C) in the south-central portion of the state. The normal daily mean temperature in Seattle is 51°F (11°C), ranging from 38°F (3°C) in January to 65°F (18°C) in July; Spokane averages 47°F (8°C), ranging from 25°F (–4°C) in January to 68°F (20°C) in July. The lowest temperature ever recorded in the state is –48°F(–44°C), set at Mazama and Winthrop on 30 December 1968; the highest, at Ice Harbor Dam on 5 August 1961, was 118°F (48°C).

The average annual precipitation in Seattle is 43 in (109 cm), falling most heavily from October through March; Spokane receives only 17 in (43 cm), more than half of that from November through February. Snowfall in Seattle averages 15 in (38 cm) annually; in Spokane, 53 in (135 cm). High mountain peaks have permanent snowcaps or snowfields of up to 100 feet (30 meters) deep.

⁴FLORA AND FAUNA

More than 1,300 plant species have been identified in Washington. Sand strawberries and beach peas are found among the dunes, while fennel and spurry grow in salt marshes; greasewood and sagebrush predominate in the desert regions of the Columbia Plateau. Conifers include Sitka spruce, Douglas fir, western hemlock, and Alaska cedar; big-leaf maple, red alder, black cottonwood, and western yew are among the characteristic deciduous trees. Wild flowers include the deerhead orchid, Indian pipe, and wake-robin; the western rhododendron is the state flower.

Forest and mountain regions support Columbia black-tailed and mule deer, elk, and black bear; the Roosevelt elk, named after President Theodore Roosevelt, is indigenous to the Olympic Mountains. Other native mammals are the Canadian lynx, red fox, and red western bobcat. Smaller native mammals—western fisher, raccoon, muskrat, porcupine, marten, and mink—are plentiful. The whistler (hoary) marmot is the largest rodent. Game birds include the ruffed grouse, bobwhite quail, and ring-necked pheasant. Sixteen varieties of owl have been identified; other birds of prey include the prairie falcon, sparrow hawk, and golden eagle. The bald eagle is more numerous in Washington than in any other state except Alaska. Washington is also a haven for marsh, shore, and water birds. Various salmon species thrive in coastal waters and along the Columbia River, and the hair seal and sea lion inhabit Puget Sound. Listed as endangered are the northern Rocky Mountain wolf, Columbian white-tailed deer, American peregrine falcon, and Aleutian Canada goose.

⁵ENVIRONMENTAL PROTECTION

The Department of Ecology, established in 1970, is responsible for water, air, and noise pollution control, solid waste disposal, and shoreline management. Among other state agencies with environmental responsibilities are the State Parks and Recreation Commission, State Energy Office, and the Department of Fisheries, Game, and Natural Resources.

Principal air pollutants in 1976 were particulate emissions, 107,700 tons; sulfur oxides, 242,700 tons; carbon monoxide, 2,061,000 tons; hydrocarbons, 416,100 tons; and oxides of nitro-

gen, 320,600 tons. Fuel combustion and industrial processes were responsible for most of the first two pollutants, transportation (especially the automobile) for most of the last three. The Department of Ecology has estimated that 16,000 lb of solid waste per person per year are generated in Washington, including 7,986 lb of agricultural wastes, 1,694 lb of residential and commercial wastes, and 103 lb of industrial and hazardous wastes. The state had 79 open dumps, 63 sanitary landfills, and 645 resource recovery sites in 1978/79. During the same year, federal and state construction grants for municipal sewage-treatment facilities totaled $86,307,419, with 15% of that amount provided by the state.

Nuclear energy has been the source of considerable controversy in Washington, especially since the publication during the 1970s of reports of leakage from the Hanford Reservation, the nation's largest nuclear waste disposal site, managed by the US Department of Energy. A measure tightening controls on nuclear waste storage was approved by the voters in November 1980.

⁶POPULATION

Washington was the nation's 22d most populous state at the 1970 census, with 3,413,250 residents. Preliminary census data for 1980 showed a population of 4,109,634, representing a growth of 20% for the decade. Washington's estimated population density in 1980 was 62 per sq mi (24 per sq km), more than 11 times that of 1890, one year after statehood. From 1940 to 1977 alone, the state's population more than doubled; the increase during that period was about 1,945,000, of which the net gain from migration contributed 43%. As of 1976, only 37% of the population aged 14 years or over had resided in the state their whole lives.

In 1979, more than 2 out of 3 Washingtonians were concentrated in the Western Corridor, a broad strip in western Washington running north–south between the Coast and Cascade ranges. The leading city in the Western Corridor is Seattle, with a preliminary 1980 census population of 491,897. Other leading cities and their estimated 1979 populations are Spokane, 179,200; Tacoma, 157,800; Bellevue, 77,515; Everett, 54,600; Yakima, 52,700; Vancouver, 47,400; and Bellingham, 44,400. Olympia, the state capital, had 26,900 residents in 1979. The Seattle-Everett metropolitan area ranked 22d in the US in 1978, with an estimated population of 1,467,600; metropolitan Tacoma had 436,900 inhabitants (89th).

⁷ETHNIC GROUPS

Washington is ethnically and racially heterogeneous. As of 1970, foreign-born Washingtonians and their American-born children made up 19% of the state's population, with Canada, Germany, and the United Kingdom being the leading countries of origin.

The largest minority group consists of Hispanic Americans, numbering 74,000 according to federal estimates for 1976, 94,000 by state estimates for 1979. Most of the state's Spanish-speaking residents have come since World War II. Black Americans numbered 67,000, according to federal data, in 1976; the state estimate for 1979 was about 20,000 higher. Black immigration dates largely from World War II and postwar recruitment for defense-related industries.

Japanese-Americans have been farmers and small merchants in Washington throughout the 20th century. During World War II, the Nisei of Washington were interned. Chinese-Americans, imported as laborers in the mid-1800s, endured a wave of mob violence during the 1880s. According to state estimates, the Asian population was 70,000 in 1979; the 1970 census counted 20,335 Japanese, 11,462 Filipinos, 9,201 Chinese, and 12,422 other Asians. Immigration from Southeast Asia was an important factor during the late 1970s.

LOCATION: 45°32′40″ to 49°N; 116°54′45″ to 124°44′40″w. BOUNDARIES: Canadian line, 286 mi (460 km); Idaho line, 213 mi (343 km); Oregon line, 443 mi (713 km); Pacific Ocean coastline, 157 mi (253 km).

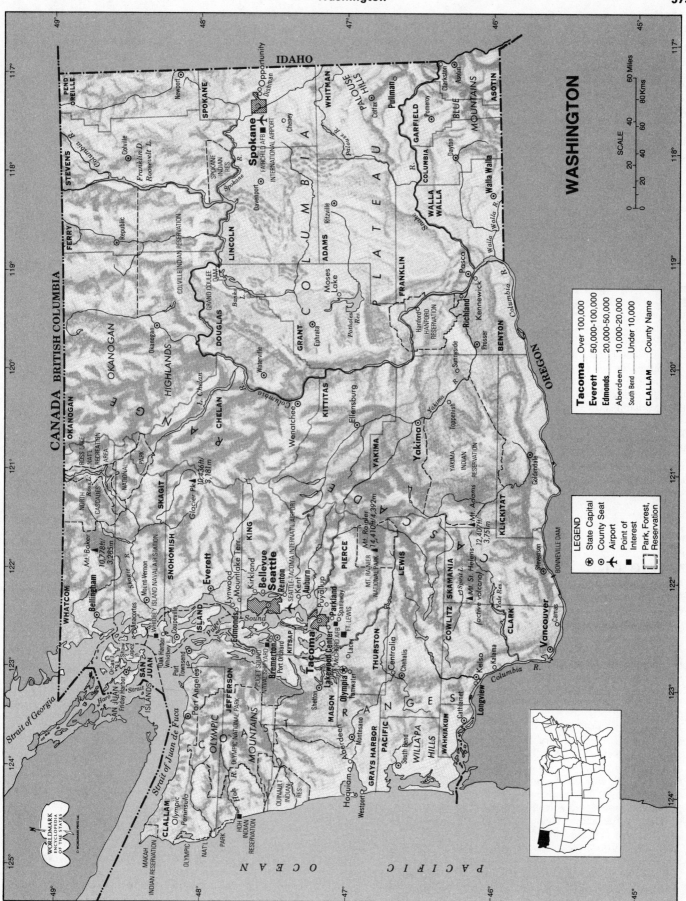

WASHINGTON

LEGEND
- ✪ State Capital
- ⊙ County Seat
- ✈ Airport
- ■ Point of Interest
- Park, Forest, Reservation

Tacoma	Over 100,000
Everett	50,000-100,000
Edmonds	20,000-50,000
Aberdeen	10,000-20,000
South Bend	Under 10,000
CLALLAM	County Name

SCALE

0   20   40   60 Miles

0   20   40   60   80Kms

See US political: front cover B1; US physical: back cover B1.

CANADA BRITISH COLUMBIA

IDAHO

OREGON

P A C I F I C   O C E A N

Strait of Georgia

Strait of Juan de Fuca

WORLDMARK ENCYCLOPEDIA OF THE STATES

There were an estimated 53,000 American Indians living in Washington in 1979; Indian lands in the state cover some 2.5 million acres (1 million hectares). A dispute developed in the 1970s over Indian fishing rights in the Puget Sound area; a decision in 1974 by US District Judge George Boldt that two 120-year-old treaties guaranteed the Indians 50% of the salmon catch in certain rivers was essentially upheld by the US Supreme Court in 1979.

[8] LANGUAGES

Early settlers took from Chinook some words like *potlatch* (gift-dispensing feast), *skookum* (strong), and *tillicum* (friend), but little other language influence came from the many Indian tribes inhabiting Washington except for such place-names as Chehalis, Walla Walla, Puyallup, and Spokane. In 1970, 4,032 state residents reported Indian languages as their mother tongue.

Northern and Midland dialects dominate, with Midland strongest in eastern Washington and the Bellingham area, Northern elsewhere. In the urban areas, minor eastern variants have been lost; in rural sections, however, older people have preserved such terms as *johnnycake* (corn bread) and *mouth organ* (harmonica). One survey showed Northern *quarter to* dominant in the state with 81%, with Midland *quarter till* having only a 5% response; Northern *angleworm* (earthworm) had 63%, but Midland *fishworm* and *fishing worm* only 17%. The north coast of the Olympic Peninsula, settled by New Englanders who sailed around Cape Horn, retains New England /ah/ in *glass* and *aunt*. In Seattle, *fog* and *frog* are Midland /fawg/ and /frawg/, but *on* is Northern /ahn/; *cot* and *caught* sound alike, as in Midland; but final /y/, as in *city* and *pretty*, has the Northern /ee/ sound rather than Midland short /i/ as in *pit*.

English in 1970 was the mother tongue of 86% of native-born Washingtonians, and of 83% of all residents. Major resident groups reported mother tongues as follows:

	NATIVE-BORN	FOREIGN-BORN
English	2,784,955	48,273
German	100,247	23,770
Spanish	39,396	7,666
Norwegian	38,846	11,504
Swedish	26,123	8,376
French	19,866	4,674
Italian	16,205	4,600

[9] RELIGIONS

First settled by Protestant missionaries, Washington remains a predominantly Protestant state. As of 1971 there were 742,829 known adherents of Protestant groups. The leading denominations were United Methodist, 116,723; American Lutheran, 98,815; and United Presbyterian, 75,818. In 1979 there were 486,462 Roman Catholics and an estimated 18,385 Jews.

[10] TRANSPORTATION

As of 1974, Washington had 4,807 mi (7,736 km) of railroad lines. Amtrak provides service from Seattle down the coast to Los Angeles, and eastward via Spokane to St. Paul, Minn., and Chicago.

There were 83,924 mi (135,063 km) of state highways, roads, and streets as of 1 January 1979, of which 49% were county roads, 13% National Forest System roads, 12% city streets, and 8% state highways; the remaining 18% traversed state forests, parks, Indian reservations, and other areas. Principal interstate highways include I-90, connecting Spokane and Seattle, and I-5, proceeding north–south from Vancouver in British Columbia through Seattle and Tacoma to Vancouver, Wash., and Portland, Ore. In 1978, the state had 2,485,248 licensed drivers and 3,066,948 registered motor vehicles.

Washington's principal ports include Seattle, Tacoma, and Bellingham, all part of the Puget Sound area and belonging to the Seattle Customs District; and Longview, Kalama, and Vancouver, along the Columbia River and considered part of the Portland (Ore.) Customs District. State-operated ferry systems transported almost 11 million passengers and about 9 million vehicles across Puget Sound in 1978/79.

In 1978, Washington had 117 public and 248 private airports, of which Seattle-Tacoma (SEATAC) International Airport was by far the most active, handling 8,364,446 arriving and departing passengers, 48,009 tons of mail, and 184,984 tons of air freight.

[11] HISTORY

The region now known as the State of Washington has been inhabited for at least 9,000 years, the first Americans having crossed the Bering Strait from Asia and entered North America via the Pacific Northwest. Their earliest known remains in Washington—some burned bison bones and a human skeleton—date from approximately 7000 BC.

The Cascades impeded communications between coastal Indians and those of the eastern plateau, and their material cultures evolved somewhat differently. Coastal Indians—belonging mainly to the Nootkin and Salishan language families—lived in a land of plenty, with ample fish, shellfish, roots, and berries. Timber was abundant for the construction of dugout canoes, villages with wooden dwellings, and some stationary wooden furniture. Warfare between villages was fairly common, with the acquisition of slaves the primary objective. The coastal Indians also emphasized rank based on wealth, through such institutions as the potlatch, a gigantic feast with extravagant exchanges of gifts. The plateau (or "horse") Indians, on the other hand, paid little attention to class distinctions. Social organization was simpler and intertribal warfare less frequent here than on the coast. After the horse reached Washington around 1730, the plateau tribes (mainly of the Shahaptian language group) became largely nomadic, traveling long distances in search of food. Housing was portable, often taking the form of skin or mat tepees. In winter, circular pit houses were dug for protection from the wind and snow.

The first Europeans known to have sailed along the Washington coast were 18th-century Spaniards; stories of earlier voyages to the area by Sir Francis Drake in 1579 and Juan de Fuca in 1592 are largely undocumented. In 1774, Juan Pérez explored the northwestern coastline to the southern tip of Alaska; an expedition led by Bruno Heceta and his assistant, Juan Francisco de la Bodega y Quadra, arrived a year later. Men from this expedition made the first known landing on Washington soil, at the mouth of the Hoh River, but the venture ended in tragedy when the Indians seized the landing boat and killed the Spaniards.

English captain James Cook, on his third voyage of exploration, arrived in the Pacific Northwest in 1778 while searching for a northwest passage across America. He was the first of numerous British explorers and traders to be attracted by the luxuriant fur of the sea otter. Cook was followed in 1792 by another Englishman, George Vancouver, who mapped the Pacific coast and the Puget Sound area. In the same year, an American fur trader and explorer, Captain Robert Gray, discovered the mouth of the Columbia River. As the maritime fur trade began to prosper, overland traders moved toward the Northwest, the most active organizations being the British Hudson's Bay Company and the Canadian North West Company.

American interest in the area also increased. Several US maritime explorers had already visited the Northwest when President Thomas Jefferson commissioned an overland expedition to inspect the territory acquired from France through the Louisiana Purchase (1803). That expedition, led by Meriwether Lewis and William Clark, first sighted the Pacific Ocean in early November 1805 from the north bank of the Columbia River in what is now Pacific County. In time, as reports of the trip became known, a host of British and American fur traders followed portions of their route to the Pacific coast, and the interest of missionaries was excited. In 1831, a delegation visited Clark in St. Louis,

Mo., where he was then superintendent of Indian affairs, to persuade him to send teachers who could instruct the Indians in the Christian religion. When news of the visit became known, there was an immediate response from the churches.

The first missionaries to settle in Washington were Marcus and Narcissa Whitman, representing the Protestant American Board of Missions; their settlement, at Waiilatpu in southeastern Washington (near present-day Walla Walla), was established in 1836. Although the early Protestant missions had scant success in converting the Indians, the publicity surrounding their activities encouraged other Americans to journey to the Pacific Northwest, and the first immigrant wagons arrived at Waiilatpu in 1840. The Indian population became increasingly hostile to the missionaries, however, and on 29 November 1847, Marcus and Narcissa Whitman and 12 other Americans were massacred.

As early as 1843, an American provisional government had been established, embracing the entire Oregon country and extending far into the area that is now British Columbia, Canada. Three years later, after considerable military and diplomatic maneuvering, a US-Canada boundary along the 49th parallel was establshed by agreement with the British. Oregon Territory, including the present state of Washington, was organized in 1848. In the early 1850s, residents north of the Columbia River petitioned Congress to create a separate "Columbia Territory." The new territorial status was granted in 1853, but at the last minute the name of the territory (which embraced part of present-day Idaho) was changed to Washington.

President Franklin Pierce appointed Isaac I. Stevens as the first territorial governor. Stevens, who served at the same time as a US superintendent of Indian affairs, negotiated a series of treaties with the Northwest Indian tribes, establishing a system of reservations. Although the Indian situation had long been tense, it worsened after the treaties were concluded, and bloody uprisings by the Yakima, Nisqualli, and Cayuse were not suppressed until the late 1850s. Court battles over fishing rights spelled out in those treaties were not substantially resolved until 1980.

On the economic front, discoveries of gold in the Walla Walla area, in British Columbia, and in Idaho brought prosperity to the entire region. The completion in 1883 of the Northern Pacific Railroad line from the eastern US to Puget Sound encouraged immigration, and Washington's population, only 23,955 in 1870, swelled to 357,232 by 1890. In the political sphere, Washington was an early champion of woman suffrage. The territorial legislature granted women the vote in 1883; however, the suffrage acts were pronounced unconstitutional in 1887.

Cattle and sheep raising, farming, and lumbering were all established by the time Washington became the 42d state in 1889. The Populist movement of the 1890s found fertile soil in the Evergreen State, and the financial panic of 1893 further stimulated radical labor and Granger activity. In 1896, the Fusionists—a coalition of Populists, Democrats, and Silver Republicans—swept the state. The discovery of gold in the Klondike, for which Seattle was the primary departure point, helped dim the Fusionists' prospects, and for the next three decades the Republican Party dominated state politics.

In 1909, Seattle staged the Alaska-Yukon-Pacific Exposition, celebrating the Alaska gold rush and Seattle's new position as a major seaport. World War I brought the state several major new military installations, and the Puget Sound area thrived as a shipbuilding center. The war years also saw the emergence of radical labor activities, especially in the shipbuilding and logging industries. Seattle was the national headquarters of the Industrial Workers of the World (IWW) and became, in 1919, the scene of the first general strike in the US, involving about 60,000 workers. The towns of Centralia and Everett were the sites of violent conflict between the IWW and conservative groups.

Washington's economy was in dire straits during the depression of the 1930s, when the market for forest products and field crops tumbled. The New Deal era brought numerous federally funded public works projects, notably the Bonneville and Grand Coulee dams on the Columbia River, providing hydroelectric power for industry and water for the irrigation of desert lands. Eventually, more than 1 million acres (400,000 hectares) were reclaimed for agricultural production. During World War II, Boeing led the way in establishing the aerospace industry as Washington's primary employer. Also during the war, the federal government built the Hanford Reservation nuclear research center; the Hanford plant was one of the major contractors in the construction of the first atomic bomb and later became a pioneer producer of atomic-powered electricity.

In 1962, "Century 21," the Seattle World's Fair, again promoted the area, as the Alaska-Yukon-Pacific Exhibition had a half-century earlier. The exhibition left Seattle a number of buildings—including the Space Needle and Coliseum—that have since been converted into a civic and performing arts center. The 1960s and 1970s, a period of rapid population growth (with Seattle and the Puget Sound area leading the way), also witnessed an effort by government and industry to reconcile the needs of an expanding economy with an increasing public concern for protection of the state's unique natural heritage. An unforeseen environmental hazard emerged in May 1980 with the eruption of Mt. St. Helens.

[12] STATE GOVERNMENT

Washington's constitution of 1889, as amended, continues to govern the state today. The legislative branch consists of a senate of 49 members elected to four-year terms, and a house of representatives with 98 members serving for two years. Executives elected statewide include the governor and lieutenant governor (who run separately), secretary of state, treasurer, attorney general, auditor, and officers for education, insurance, and land. The governor and lieutenant governor, who serve four-year terms, must be qualified voters in the state.

A bill becomes law if passed by a majority of the elected members of each house and then signed by the governor or left unsigned for 5 days while the legislature is in session or 20 days after it has adjourned; a two-thirds vote of members present in each house is sufficient to override a gubernatorial veto. Constitutional amendments require a two-thirds vote of the legislature and ratification by the voters at the next general election.

Voters in Washington must be US citizens, at least 18 years of age; the residency requirement is 30 days.

[13] POLITICAL PARTIES

Washington never went for a full-fledged Democrat in a presidential election until 1932, when Franklin D. Roosevelt won the first of four successive victories in the state. Until then, Washington had generally voted Republican, the lone exceptions being 1896, when the state's Populist voters carried Washington for William Jennings Bryan, and 1912, when a plurality of the voters chose Theodore Roosevelt on the Progressive ticket.

In recent decades, the state has tended to favor Republicans in presidential elections, but Democrats have more than held their own in other contests. In 1976, Washingtonians elected a Democratic governor, Dixy Lee Ray, and the Democrats held both US Senate seats, a majority of the state's congressional delegation, and large majorities in both houses of the state legislature. The rise of the Democratic Party has been linked to the careers of two US senators—Henry Jackson, who has held his seat since 1953, and Warren Magnuson, defeated in 1980 after serving since 1945. Republicans scored major victories in November 1980, electing Ronald Reagan for president, Slade Gorton as US senator, and John Spellman as governor, Dixy Lee Ray having been defeated in the Democratic primary. Reagan captured 50% of the vote, Jimmy Carter 37%, and John Anderson 11%.

[14]LOCAL GOVERNMENT

As of 1980, Washington had 39 counties, 154 cities, 111 towns, 300 school districts, and more than 1,000 special districts, including public utility, library, port, water, hospital, cemetery, and sewer districts.

Counties may establish their own institutions of government by charter; otherwise, the chief governing body is an elected board of three commissioners. Other elected officials generally include the sheriff, prosecuting attorney, coroner, auditor, treasurer, and clerk. Cities and towns are governed under the mayor-council or council-manager systems. Larger cities, Seattle among them, generally have their own charters and elected mayors.

[15]STATE SERVICES

The Public Disclosure Commission, consisting of five members appointed by the governor and confirmed by the senate, provides disclosure of financial data in connection with political campaigns, lobbyists' activities, and the holdings of elected officials and candidates for public office. Each house of the legislature has its own board of ethics.

Public education in Washington is governed by a Board of Education and superintendent of public instruction; the Council for Postsecondary Education coordinates the state's higher educational institutions. The Department of Transportation oversees the construction and maintenance of highways, bridges, and ferries and assists locally owned airports.

The Department of Social and Health Services, the main human resources agency, oversees programs for adult corrections, juvenile rehabilitation, public and mental health, Medicaid, nursing homes, income maintenance, and vocational rehabilitation. Also involved in human resources activities are the Human Rights Commission, Department of Labor and Industries, Employment Security Department, Department of Veterans Affairs, and Commission for the Blind. Public protection services are provided by the Washington State Patrol, the Department of Emergency Services (civil defense), and the Military Department (Army and Air National Guard).

[16]JUDICIAL SYSTEM

The state's highest court, the supreme court, consists of 9 justices serving six-year terms; 3 justices are elected by nonpartisan ballot in each even-numbered year. Every two years, the senior justice who has not previously been chief justice is named to that office. Appeals of lower court decisions are normally heard in the court of appeals, whose 16 judges are elected to six-year terms.

The superior courts, consisting in 1979 of 111 judges elected to four-year terms in 28 judicial districts, are the state trial courts.

During 1978, 135,630 cases were filed in superior court: 83,927 civil, 17,406 juvenile, 16,685 probate, 14,278 criminal, and 3,334 involving mental illness. Crime rates in 1978 were below the national averages for murder, robbery, aggravated assault, and motor vehicle theft, but above average for forcible rape, burglary, and larceny-theft.

[17]ARMED FORCES

The chief US military facilities in Washington in mid-1978 were a Trident nuclear submarine base at Bangor and the Puget Sound Naval Shipyard (Bremerton), Whidbey Island Naval Air Station, McChord Air Force Base (Tacoma), Fairchild Air Force Base (Airway Heights), and Ft. Lewis (Tacoma); authorized military personnel numbered 74,412. In 1977/78, federal defense contract awards exceeded $1.8 billion, 8th among the 50 states.

Veterans living in Washington as of 30 September 1979 numbered 612,000, of whom 11,000 saw service during World War I, 250,000 during World War II, 119,000 in the Korean conflict, and 201,000 during the Viet-Nam era. During 1977/78, veterans' benefits totaled $377.3 million, including $173 million for compensation and pensions and $81.6 million for education and training.

During 1979, Army and Air National Guard units had about 6,700 personnel. State and local police forces in Washington during 1977 had 7,981 members, 80% of them local.

[18]MIGRATION

The first overseas immigrants to reach Washington were Chinese laborers, imported during the 1860s; Chinese continued to arrive into the 1880s, when mob attacks on Chinese homes forced the territorial government to put Seattle under martial law and call in federal troops to restore order. The 1870s and 1880s brought an influx of immigrants from western Europe—especially Germany, Scandinavia, and the Netherlands—and from Russia and Japan.

In recent decades, Washington has benefited from a second migratory wave even more massive than the first. Between 1940 and 1977, the state enjoyed a net gain from migration of 835,000; many of those new residents were drawn from other states by Washington's thriving defense- and trade-related industries. Many immigrants from Southeast Asia arrived during the late 1970s.

[19]INTERGOVERNMENTAL COOPERATION

Washington participates in the Columbia River Compact (with Oregon), Pacific Marine Fisheries Compact, Western Corrections

Washington Presidential Vote by Political Parties, 1948–80

YEAR	ELECTORAL VOTE	WASHINGTON WINNER	DEMOCRAT	REPUBLICAN	PROGRESSIVE	SOCIALIST	PROHIBITION	SOCIALIST LABOR	CONSTITUTION
1948	8	*Truman (D)	476,165	386,315	31,692	3,534	6,117	1,133	—
1952	9	*Eisenhower (R)	492,845	599,107	2,460	—	—	633	7,290
1956	9	*Eisenhower (R)	523.002	620,430	—	—	—	7,457	
1960	9	Nixon (R)	599,298	629,273	—	—	—	10,895	1,401
1964	9	*Johnson (D)	779,699	470,366	—	—	—	7,772	—
					PEACE & FREEDOM		AMERICAN IND.		
1968	9	Humphrey (D)	616,037	588,510	1,669	—	96,990	491	—
					PEOPLE'S	LIBERTARIAN			AMERICAN
1972	9	*Nixon (R)	568,334	837,135	2,644	1,537	—	1,102	58,906
1976	9	Ford (R)	717,323	777,732	1,124	5,042	8,585	—	5,046
					CITIZENS			SOC. WORKERS	
1980	9	*Reagan (R)	650,193	865,244	9,403	29,213	—	1,137	—

*Won US presidential election.

Compact, Western Interstate Energy Compact, and Western Regional Education Compact, among other interstate bodies. Federal aid in 1978/79 exceeded $1.4 billion, of which $96 million was general revenue sharing.

[20] ECONOMY

The mainstays of Washington's economy are wholesale and retail trade, manufacturing (especially aerospace equipment, shipbuilding, food processing, and wood products), agriculture, lumbering, and tourism. Between 1968 and 1978, employment increased in such sectors as lumber and wood products, metals and machinery, food processing, trade, services, and government, while decreasing in aerospace—which remains, nevertheless, the state's single leading industry. Foreign trade, especially with Canada and Japan, was an important growth sector during the 1970s. The eruption of Mt. St. Helens in 1980 had an immediate negative impact on the forestry industry—already clouded by a slowdown in housing construction—crop growing, and the tourist trade.

[21] INCOME

With an income per capita of $8,450 in 1978, Washington ranked 9th among the 50 states. Total personal income was $31.9 billion, representing a real increase of 43% since 1970. The principal sources of personal income were manufacturing, 16%; government, 14%; wholesale and retail trade, 13%; dividends, interest, and rent, 13%; transfer payments, 13%; services, 12%; construction, 6%; transportation and utilities, 5%; finance, insurance, and real estate, 4%; and farming, mining, fishing, and all other sources, 4%.

Median family income in 1975 was $14,962, 14th in the US. During that same year, 8.5% of all state residents and 6.6% of all Washington families were below the federal poverty level, proportions that compared favorably with those for the West and for the US as a whole.

[22] LABOR

In 1978, Washington's civilian labor force numbered 1,754,000, of whom 1,032,000 were male and 722,000 female. Of those actually employed there were 969,000 males and 665,000 females, yielding an overall unemployment rate of 6.8%.

A federal census of workers covered by unemployment insurance in March 1977 revealed the following nonfarm employment pattern in Washington:

	ESTABLISH-MENTS	EMPLOYEES	ANNUAL PAYROLL ('000)
Agricultural services, forestry, fishing	1,241	7,957	$ 67,445
Mining	172	2,287	42,759
Contract construction	10,403	67,736	1,205,205
Manufacturing, of which:	5,960	255,859	4,069,395
Food and food products	(483)	(26,607)	(371,882)
Lumber, wood products	(1,784)	(48,113)	(723,010)
Transport equipment	(314)	(61,388)	(1,136,216)
Transportation, public utilities	3,174	61,125	986,645
Wholesale trade	6,891	80,161	1,164,470
Retail trade	22,182	231,011	1,779,914
Finance, insurance, real estate	8,189	76,038	897,801
Services	23,594	232,892	2,045,524
Other	1,204	1,468	16,942
TOTALS	83,010	1,016,534	$12,276,100

Government employees, not included in this survey, numbered 304,100 in 1978.

Although radical labor activities in the mines around the turn of the century, in the logging camps during World War I, and in Seattle in 1919 were suppressed by state and federal authorities, the impulse to unionize remained strong in Washington. The state's labor force is still one of the most organized in the US,

although (in line with national trends) the unions' share of the nonfarm work force declined from 44% in 1964 to 35.6% in 1976, when there were 453,000 union members; the latter percentage was exceeded only in New York State and Hawaii. In 1978, Washington production workers earned an average of $7.56 hourly and $297 a week, figures that ranked among the highest in the US at a time when, in Seattle at least, consumer prices were rising more slowly than in the US as a whole.

[23] AGRICULTURE

Orchard and field crops dominate Washington's agricultural economy, which yielded $2.2 billion in farm receipts in 1978, 19th among the 50 states. Fruits and vegetables are raised in the humid and in the irrigated areas of the state, while wheat and other grains grow in the drier central and eastern regions.

Washington is the nation's leading producer of apples. The 1979 crop, representing 32% of the US total, totaled 2.6 billion lb; among leading varieties, delicious apples ranked first (62%), followed by golden delicious (29%), and winesap (3%). Also produced in 1979 were wheat, 118 million bushels, valued at $466.1 million; hay, 2.5 million tons, $174.6 million; potatoes, 48.5 million hundredweight, $123.5 million; barley, 17 million bushels, $43.4 million; corn, 12.3 million bushels, $35.5 million; dry edible beans, 703,000 hundredweight, $18.1 million; and dry edible peas, 1.3 million hundredweight, $13.4 million. Sugar beets, pears, peaches, hops, and various seed crops are also grown.

[24] ANIMAL HUSBANDRY

Livestock products account for about 25% of Washington's agricultural income. By the end of 1979, farms and ranches had some 1.6 million cattle and calves, 126,000 hogs and pigs, and 65,000 sheep and lambs. Production of meat animals in 1979 included 458.7 million lb of cattle worth $309.5 million; 30.7 million lb of hogs, $13.5 million; and 4.4 million lb of sheep, $2.3 million.

During the same year, Washington dairy farmers had 192,000 milk cows that produced more than 2.8 billion lb of milk. Poultry farmers sold 103.5 million lb of chickens and broilers for more than $26.8 million. Egg production reached 1.2 billion, with cash receipts of $49.5 million.

[25] FISHING

In 1978, Washington's production of food fish reached 153.6 million lb, of which salmon accounted for 26%, shellfish 19%, miscellaneous saltwater species 53%, and freshwater food fish 2%. The processed value of the 1978 catch was nearly $222 million: salmon, $118 million; shellfish, $44.9 million; miscellaneous saltwater species, $56.9 million; and freshwater food fish, $2.2 million. The leading fishing ports, by value of landings, were Bellingham, Westport, and Seattle.

In 1978, about 60,000 Washingtonians were employed in the state's fishing industry, of whom 72% were in processing, handling, and distributing, 25% were classified as commercial fishermen, and 3% were Indians exercising their fishing rights. During the same year there were 7,678 licensed fishing boats, more than half of them weighing less than 5 tons.

Sport fishermen caught more than 1 million salmon and 125,000 steelhead trout during 1978/79. In 1978, nearly 30 million game fish were planted in Washington's streams and lakes; planted species included silver salmon and steelhead, cutthroat, brown, eastern brook, and Kokanee (silver) trout.

[26] FORESTRY

Washington's forests, covering 23,181,000 acres (9,381,000 hectares) in 1977, are an important commercial and recreational resource. Some 17,922,000 acres (7,253,000 hectares) were classified as commercial forestland, of which 49% was privately owned, 39% federally owned or managed, and 12% controlled by the state.

About 150,000 acres (61,000 hectares) encompassing 6.5 billion board feet of lumber are harvested annually. Shipments of lumber and wood products amounted to $4.1 billion in 1977, with lumber and plywood, logs for export, various chip products, pulp logs, and shakes and shingles the leading forest commodities; sales of paper and allied products exceeded $1.9 billion during the same year. The giant of Washington's forest industry is Weyerhaeuser, with headquarters in Tacoma; nationwide, the firm had sales in 1979 of $4.4 billion, assets worth nearly $5 billion, net income of $512.2 million, and 47,844 employees.

Federal, state, and private nurseries in Washington produced more than 120 million seedlings in 1978/79. Since 1975, more acres have been planted or seeded than have been cut down. Washington's forest-fire control program in 1978 covered some 12.5 million acres (5.1 million hectares) and cost the federal and state governments $6.7 million. Leading causes of forest fires in lands under the jurisdiction of the Department of Natural Resources in 1978 are shown in the following table:

	NUMBER	ACRES BURNED
Lightning	241	65
Burning debris	190	1,976
Recreation	131	97
Smokers	59	358
Railroad operations	56	18

[27] MINING

Washington's mineral output in 1978 had a value of $231 million, for a rank of 34th among the 50 states. Principal mineral products (excluding fossil fuels) were cement, 1,430,000 tons; sand and gravel, 19,000,000 tons; and stone, 12,404,000 tons. Clays, gold, silver, copper, uranium, peat, gypsum, lime, talc, and tungsten are also mined. Aluminum is refined electrolytically from imported ores.

[28] ENERGY AND POWER

With an installed capacity of 19.9 million kw in 1978, Washington power plants generated 99.8 billion kwh of electricity, about 90% of that from publicly owned hydroelectric facilities. Energy sales in the state totaled 58.8 billion kwh in 1977, of which 46% went to industrial users, and 35% to residential customers; most of the remainder was used for commercial purposes. The Hanford Reservation was the site of the first US nuclear energy plant.

The state's lone major fossil fuel resource is coal. Reserves were estimated at 1.6 billion tons in 1978, of which 83% was subbituminous, 16% bituminous, and 1% lignite. Production of coal totaled 4.7 million tons in 1978, all of it surface mined.

[29] INDUSTRY

Transportation equipment, lumber and wood products, food and food products, and paper and allied products are Washington's leading industries, together employing 61% of the state's manufacturing work force. The total value added by manufacture in 1977 was $8.6 billion, 83% higher than in 1972. The following table shows the leading industrial sectors and their value added in 1972 and 1977:

	1972	1977
Transportation equipment	$1,138,200,000	$2,069,100,000
Lumber and wood products	941,700,000	1,530,600,000
Food and food products	556,100,000	1,031,900,000
Primary metal industries	365,100,000	888,900,000
Paper and allied products	470,700,000	782,000,000
Nonelectrical machinery	169,700,000	377,200,000

The Seattle-Everett metropolitan area accounts for about half of all industrial employment and value added. By far the leading firm in Washington is Boeing, whose Everett manufacturing plant—construction site of the 747 wide-body superjet—occupied some 205 million cu feet by early 1980. The aerospace giant, which in 1979 had assets of $4.9 billion, sales of $8.1 billion, a net income of $505.4 million, and some 98,300 employees nationwide, was awarded the prime contract in March 1980 for construction of 3,400 cruise missiles for delivery to US bomber squadrons starting in 1982.

Aluminum refining is a major industry, producing more than 30% of the nation's supply and employing some 12,000 Washington workers. Refinery operations were threatened during the late 1970s by cutbacks in the availability of hydroelectric power.

[30] COMMERCE

Wholesalers in 1972 had a trade volume of $9.8 billion; by 1978, their gross income was nearly $24 billion. Total retail sales in 1977 reached $13.5 billion, of which food stores accounted for 21%, automotive dealers 20%, eating and drinking places 12%, and department stores 10%. The Seattle-Everett metropolitan area accounted for 43% of all retail sales, metropolitan Tacoma 11%, and metropolitan Spokane 9%.

In 1978, exports through the Seattle Customs District had a value of about $6.3 billion; imports, $6.7 billion. The leading exports were aircraft and aircraft parts (accounting for about one-third of the total), machinery, lumber and logs, fish and fish products, grains, motor vehicles and parts, fruits and vegetables, wood pulp, and paper products. Principal imports included crude petroleum (12%), lumber, natural gas, passenger cars, truck chassis and bodies, newsprint, aluminum oxide, motorcycles, radios, and television sets. Canada purchased about 28% of the exports and supplied 34% of the imports; Japan's approximate shares were 24% and 31%, respectively. In 1976, Washington exported $3.2 billion of its own manufactures to foreign countries (8th in the US); exports of agricultural commodities totaled $414 million in 1976/77 (18th).

[31] CONSUMER PROTECTION

The Office of the Attorney General, which enforces the state's Consumer Protection Act, investigates consumer complaints and, when necessary, seeks court action in connection with retail sales abuses, unfair automobile sales techniques, false advertising, and other fraudulent or deceptive practices. Consumer protection responsibilities of the Department of Agriculture include food labeling, sanitary food handling and storage, and weights and measures.

[32] BANKING

As of 31 December 1978, Washington had 93 insured commercial banks with $18 billion in assets; outstanding loans exceeded $6.8 billion, and deposits reached $7.4 billion. The largest commercial bank as of mid-1980 was the Rainier National Bank (Seattle), with assets of $3.6 billion. In 1978 there were 50 savings and loan associations (30 federally chartered, 20 state-chartered) with assets of $8.5 billion, including mortgage loans worth $7.3 billion.

[33] INSURANCE

Washingtonians held 5.1 million life insurance policies with a total face value of $45.4 billion as of 31 December 1978. The average life insurance coverage per family was $30,900, 12% below the national average. Benefits paid by life insurance companies in 1978 totaled $447.7 million, including $152.7 million in death payments, $105 million in annuities, and $99.1 million in policy dividends. During the same year, property and liability companies wrote premiums totaling more than $1.2 billion, of which $220.6 million was automobile physical damage insurance, $358 million was automotive liability insurance, and $144.4 million was homeowners' coverage. Flood insurance valued at $549.1 million was in force in mid-1979.

The Office of the Insurance Commissioner and State Fire Marshal regulates insurance company operations, reviews insurance policies and rates, examines and licenses agents and brokers, conducts fire safety inspections in hospitals, nursing homes, and other facilities, investigates fires of suspicious origin, and regulates the manufacture, sale, and public display of fireworks.

³⁴SECURITIES

The Spokane Stock Exchange, specializing in mining stocks, has an average monthly volume of more than 3 million shares. New York Stock Exchange member firms had 55 sales offices and 662 registered representatives throughout Washington in 1978; state residents reported $471.3 million in dividend income on their federal income tax returns for 1977.

³⁵PUBLIC FINANCE

Washington's biennial budget is prepared by the Office of Financial Management and submitted by the governor to the legislature for amendment and approval. The fiscal year runs from 1 July through 30 June.

The following table shows estimated revenues and expenditures for 1977/79 and 1979/81 (in millions):

	1977/79	1979/81
REVENUES		
Retail sales and use taxes	$2,162.1	$2,586.2
Business and occupational taxes	678.2	820.4
Property tax	506.9	693.0
Motor vehicle fuel tax	477.7	556.5
Other taxes	965.8	1,138.8
Federal grants	1,923.9	2,214.0
Other receipts	1,494.7	1,844.8
TOTALS	$8,209.3	$9,853.7
EXPENDITURES		
Education, of which:	$3,351.1	$4,295.0
Public schools	(1,871.3)	(2,692.3)
Higher education	(1,066.3)	(1,139.5)
Community colleges	(358.7)	(392.7)
Human resources	1,797.5	2,140.7
Transportation	819.8	1,069.1
General government	558.1	759.6
Revenue distribution to political subdivisions	436.9	490.5
Natural resources and recreation	346.3	428.8
Debt service	222.6	243.5
Other outlays	453.7	740.8
TOTALS	$7,986.0	$10,168.0

During 1976/77, the city of Seattle had general revenues of $256 million and expenditures of $232 million; the gross debt was $492 million. All state and local government units in Washington had a combined public debt in mid-1977 of $8.4 billion, or $2,302 per capita, 3d among the 50 states.

³⁶TAXATION

Taxes, licenses, permits, and fees account for more than three-fifths of Washington state government revenues. In 1977, the state and local tax burden per capita was $822, 18th among the 50 states.

Washington has no individual or corporate income tax. As of 1979, the state levied a general sales tax of 4.5%, with 0.5% allocated to localities; a cigarette tax of 16 cents a pack; a liquor excise tax of 10% on sales to restaurants and 15% on sales to individuals; an inheritance tax ranging from 1% to 25%, depending on inheritance size and beneficiary; a gift tax rated at 90% of the inheritance tax; an insurance premium tax of 1% for in-state insurers and 2% for out-of-state insurers; a gasoline sales tax of 12 cents per gallon; a business and occupation tax averaging 0.44%; a 1% tax on most service activities; a motor vehicle excise tax of 2.2%; a 6.5% excise tax on the value of the timber harvest from private land; and taxes on public utilities and pari-mutuel income. The state property tax, dedicated to the public schools, was levied in 1979/81 at a rate of $3.60 per $1,000 of assessed value. In 1978/79, state and local property tax collections totaled $1.06 billion.

During the 1975/76 fiscal year, Washington remitted more than $5.7 billion in taxes to the federal government and received nearly $7.3 billion in federal expenditures. Washingtonians filed 1.6 million federal tax returns for 1977, paying $3.1 billion in tax.

³⁷ECONOMIC POLICY

Divisions within the Department of Commerce and Economic Development seek to promote tourism and the motion picture industry, expand markets for Washington's products, aid existing businesses and attract new ones, provide special services for small and minority-owned enterprises, and stimulate investment and create jobs through grants and loans to municipalities and Indian reservations. The Office of Foreign Trade maintains representatives in Singapore and Tokyo.

³⁸HEALTH

As of 1969–71, Washington ranked 16th among the 50 states in average life expectancy: the figure for both sexes was 71.72 years (75.78 years for women, 68.07 for men). The birth rate in 1977 was 15.6 per 1,000 population; the infant mortality rate was 11.9 per 1,000 live births for whites and 14.4 for nonwhites, the latter figure being one-third below the US average. Some 31,400 legal abortions were performed in 1977/78. The death rate, 8.2 per 1,000 population, was below the national norm in 1977, and the rates for the leading causes of death—heart disease, cancer, and stroke—were all lower than average.

The following table shows cases of communicable diseases reported to the Department of Social and Health Services for 1964 and 1978:

	1964	1978
Influenza	137,209	170,511
Measles	22,799	442
Rubella	11,119	149
Gonorrhea	3,428	13,487
Tuberculosis	587	305
Syphilis	73	265

As of 30 June 1979 there were 410 health-care facilities in Washington, excluding state and federal institutions. Of these, 110 were general hospitals, with 13,256 beds; 6 were psychiatric institutions, with 346 beds; and 294 were nursing homes, with 26,849 beds. The average cost of care in community hospitals during 1977 was $231 per day and $1,271 per stay. In 1978 there were 11 federal hospitals in the state, with 2,441 beds and a monthly average of 1,836 patients. During 1978/79, 3,959 patients were admitted to mental hospitals, the average daily population of which was 1,169. Licensed health professionals as of 1 July 1979 included 35,951 registered nurses, 14,766 practical nurses, 11,142 physicians, 3,834 dentists, 860 chiropractors, 849 optometrists, 549 psychologists, and 453 osteopaths.

³⁹SOCIAL WELFARE

Washington's budgeted expenditures in 1979/81 for human resources constituted more than one-fifth of all state outlays. Public assistance programs received $968.3 million for the biennium; the state's share of the cost was $561 million, the federal share $407.3 million. Income maintenance was funded at $520.2 million, $303.6 million by the state and $216.6 million by the federal government. Nearly three-quarters of the total was set aside for aid to families with dependent children (AFDC), 8% for Supplemental Security Income, and the balance for other programs. During 1978/79, state grants totaling $164.4 million were paid in AFDC to an average of 137,594 monthly recipients; disability assistance, $58.7 million to 30,697 recipients; foster home care, $21.7 million to 6,207 recipients; and old-age assistance, $20 million to 17,038 Washingtonians. Washington's average monthly AFDC grant, $111.71 per recipient in February 1979, was the highest among all western states.

During 1978, 174,000 state residents took part in the food stamp program, at a federal cost of $57 million, and 362,000 children received school lunches subsidized by the federal government in the amount of $21.5 million. Social Security payments to 544,700 Washingtonians in 1977 exceeded $1.4 billion, with an average monthly benefit for retired workers of $251.90, 4% above the US average. A total of $45 million was allocated in the 1979/81 state budget for the vocational rehabilitation of nearly 30,000 persons. Workers' compensation in 1978/79 covered 1.3 million employees, with more than $201 million in benefits paid. Unemployment benefit payments in the same period reached $167.3 million; the average weekly benefit in 1978 was $86.80, slightly above the national average.

40 HOUSING

The 1970 census counted some 1,106,000 occupied housing units in Washington, of which two-thirds were owner-occupied and more than 97% had full plumbing. From 1976 through 1978, about 171,300 new units, worth $5.2 billion, were authorized.

41 EDUCATION

Washingtonians rank exceptionally high by most educational standards. As of 1970, the adult illiteracy rate was only 0.6%, half of the US average; more than 76% of all Washingtonians 18 years of age or older were high school graduates, 16% had four or more years of college, and only 1% had less than four years of grade school. Adult state residents had completed a median of 12.7 school years in 1976.

As of October 1979, public school enrollment for grades K–12 was 763,997; private schools enrolled 49,972. Of the $1.4 billion expended on the public schools in 1977/78, 68% went to basic education, 7% to services for the handicapped, 4% to vocational training, 5% each to food service and transportation, and 11% to all other programs. About 57% of public school funds came from the state, 34% from localities, and 9% from the federal government. The following table shows enrollments and expenditures per pupil over a 10-year period:

	ENROLLMENT (K–12)	EXPENDITURES PER PUPIL
1977/78	775,894	$1,804
1976/77	780,080	1,330
1975/76	784,771	1,210
1974/75	784,916	1,115
1973/74	787,815	1,006
1972/73	790,502	906
1971/72	805,049	837
1970/71	817,712	800
1969/70	820,591	741
1968/69	NA	662

As of 1979, Washington had 17 accredited colleges and universities (6 public, 11 private) and 27 community college campuses. The largest institution is the University of Washington (Seattle), founded in 1861 and enrolling 36,249 students in 1978. Other public institutions are Washington State University (Pullman), Eastern Washington University (Cheney), Central Washington University (Ellensburg), Western Washington University (Bellingham), and Evergreen State College (Olympia). Private institutions include Gonzaga University (Spokane), Pacific Lutheran University (Tacoma), Seattle University, Whitman College (Walla Walla), Whitworth College (Spokane), and the University of Puget Sound (Tacoma). The Council for Postsecondary Education provides 11,000 grants to Washington residents, with the amount of each grant dependent on need.

42 ARTS

The focus of professional performance activities in Washington is Seattle Center, home of the Seattle Symphony, Pacific Northwest Dance Ballet Company, and Seattle Repertory Theater; the Seattle Opera, which also performs there, is one of the nation's leading opera companies, offering five operas each season from September through May and presenting Richard Wagner's "Ring" cycle at the Pacific Northwest Festival in July. Tacoma and Spokane have notable local orchestras.

In 1978, Washington had 29 museums, universities, and other organizations exhibiting works of art on a permanent or periodic basis. Especially noteworthy are the Seattle Art Museum, with its Modern Art Pavilion; the Henry Art Gallery of the University of Washington at Seattle; the Washington State University Museum of Art at Pullman; the Whatcom Museum of History and Art, Bellingham; the Tacoma Art Museum; the State Capitol Museum (Olympia); and the Cheney Cowles Memorial Museum of the Eastern Washington State Historical Society (Spokane).

The Arts Commission, established in 1961, supports nonprofit arts groups as well as professional arts organizations and an artists-in-schools program. The commission's proposed operating budget for 1979/81 was $2,750,000, 78% more than in the preceding biennium.

43 LIBRARIES AND MUSEUMS

In 1978, Washington's system of public libraries held more than 8.1 million volumes and had a combined circulation of 24.2 million. Of Washington's 39 counties, 27 were served by the state's 15 county and multicounty libraries. Total library income in 1978 came to $35.6 million, most of that total derived from public funds.

The leading public library system was the Seattle Public Library, with 17 branches and 1,499,346 volumes in 1978. The principal academic libraries were at the University of Washington (Seattle) and Washington State University (Pullman), with 3,393,836 and 1,143,288 volumes, respectively. Olympia is the home of the Washington State Library, with a collection amounting to 430,738 volumes during the same year.

Washington has at least 100 museums and historic sites. The Washington State Historical Society Museum (Tacoma) features Indian and other pioneer artifacts; the State Capitol Museum (Olympia) and Cheney Cowles Memorial Museum (Spokane) also have important historical exhibits, as do the Thomas Burke Memorial Washington State Museum (Seattle) and the Pacific Northwest Indian Center (Spokane). Mt. Rainier National Park displays zoological, botanical, geological, and historical collections. The Pacific Science Center (Seattle) concentrates on aerospace technology; the Seattle Aquarium is a leading attraction of Waterfront Park.

44 COMMUNICATIONS

The US Postal Service had some 10,400 employees in Washington in 1977; postal receipts in Seattle totaled $94,814,291 during 1978/79. As of 31 December 1978 there were 2,998,511 telephones, 2,167,694 residential and 830,817 commercial; on average, 97% of all households had telephone service. During the same year, Washington had 157 commercial broadcasting stations—92 AM, 51 FM, and 14 television—while cable systems served 336,587 subscribers in 248 communities.

45 PRESS

In 1978, Washington had 5 morning newspapers (including all-day papers), with a combined circulation of 321,902; 19 evening dailies, with 795,562; and 13 Sunday papers, with 1,059,327. The following table shows the leading newspapers with their 1978 circulations:

AREA	NAME	DAILY	SUNDAY
Seattle	Post-Intelligencer (m,S)	191,286	233,841
	Times (e,S)	246,690	331,060
Spokane	Daily Chronicle (e)	61,269	
	Spokesman-Review (m,S)	71,603	121,474
Tacoma	News Tribune and Sunday Ledger (e,S)	101,572	105,418

46 ORGANIZATIONS

Among the national organizations with headquarters in Seattle are the American Association of Poison Control Centers, American Plywood Association, American Society of Plant Taxonomists, American Society of Primatologists, Federation of Western Outdoor Clubs, and the Northwest Fisheries Association. Groups with headquarters in other Washington cities include the Citizens Committee for the Right to Keep and Bear Arms, Bellevue; American Indian Development Association, Bellingham; American Institute of Fishery Research Biologists, Edmonds; Ecological Society of America and International Association of Industrial Accident Boards and Commissions, both at Olympia; and the American Academy on Mental Retardation, Tacoma.

⁴⁷TOURISM, TRAVEL, AND RECREATION

Seattle Center—featuring the 605-foot (184-meter) Space Needle tower, Opera House, and Pacific Science Center—helps make Washington's largest city one of the most exciting on the West Coast. Nevertheless, scenic beauty and opportunities for outdoor recreation are Washington's principal attractions for tourists from out-of-state.

Mt. Rainier National Park, covering 235,404 acres (95,265 hectares), encompasses not only the state's highest peak but also the most extensive glacial system in the conterminous US. Glaciers, lakes, and mountain peaks are also featured at North Cascades National Park (504,780 acres—204,278 hectares), while Olympic National Park (908,720 acres—367,747 hectares) is famous as the site of Mt. Olympus and for its dense rain forest and rare elk herds. Washington also offers two national historic parks (San Juan Island and part of Klondike Gold Rush), a national historic site (the Whitman Mission), and three national recreation areas (Coulee Dam, Lake Chelan, and Ross Lake). The most popular state parks are Deception Pass and Lake Sammamish, each of which received more than 1 million visitors in 1978/79.

Hunting is a highly popular pastime. In 1978, about 50,000 deer were killed out of an estimated population of more than 400,000; the elk harvest was approximately 12,500 out of a population of more than 50,000. Washington hunters also bagged at least 1,000,000 ducks, 500,000 pheasants, and more than 300,000 grouse and quail. Licenses were issued to 344,923 hunters and 567,242 fishermen in 1977/78. More than 180,000 motorboats were registered as pleasure craft with the US Coast Guard during the same year.

⁴⁸SPORTS

Seattle, home of the Kingdome, an enclosed stadium seating 59,438 for baseball and 64,572 for football, is well represented in professional sports. In baseball, the Mariners compete in the American League; the Seahawks play in the National Football League. Seattle's winningest franchise has been the SuperSonics of the National Basketball Association, who captured the league championship in 1979. In collegiate sports, the Huskies of the University of Washington, who play at Husky Stadium in Seattle (with a seating capacity of nearly 59,000), won the Rose Bowl games in 1960, 1961, and 1978.

⁴⁹FAMOUS WASHINGTONIANS

Washington's most distinguished public figure was US Supreme Court Justice William O. Douglas (b.Minnesota, 1898–1980), who grew up in Yakima and attended Whitman College in Walla Walla. In addition to his 37-year tenure on the Court, an all-time high, Douglas was the author of numerous legal casebooks as well as 27 other volumes on various subjects. Other federal officeholders from Washington include Lewis B. Schwellenbach (b.Wisconsin, 1894–1948), secretary of labor under Harry Truman, and Brockman Adams (b.Georgia, 1927), secretary of transportation under Jimmy Carter. Serving in the US Senate from 1945 to 1981, Warren G. Magnuson (b.Minnesota, 1905) held the chairmanship of the powerful Appropriations Committee. A fellow Democrat, Henry M. "Scoop" Jackson (b.1912) was first elected to the House in 1940 and to the Senate in 1952. Influential on the Armed Services Committee, Jackson ran unsuccessfully for his party's presidential nomination in 1976. Wil-

liam E. Boeing (b.Michigan, 1881–1956) pioneered Washington's largest single industry, aerospace technology.

Notable governors include Isaac I. Stevens (b.Massachusetts, 1818–62), Washington's first territorial governor; after serving as Washington's territorial representative to Congress, he died in the Civil War. Elisha P. Ferry (b.Michigan, 1825–95), territorial governor from 1872 to 1880, was elected as Washington's first state governor in 1889. John R. Rogers (b.Maine, 1838–1901), Washington's only Populist governor, was also the first to be elected for a second term. Clarence D. Martin (1886–1955) was governor during the critical New Deal period. Daniel J. Evans (b.1925) is the youngest man ever elected governor of Washington and also is the only one to have served three consecutive terms (1965–77).

Dixy Lee Ray (b.1914), governor from 1977 to 1981 and the only woman governor in the state's history, is a former head of the federal Atomic Energy Commission and a staunch advocate of nuclear power. Other notable women were Emma Smith De Voe (b.New Jersey, 1848–1927), a leading proponent of equal suffrage, and Bertha Knight Landes (b.Massachusetts, 1868–1943), elected mayor of Seattle in 1926; Landes, the first woman to be elected mayor of a large US city, was also an outspoken advocate of moral reform in municipal government.

Several Washington Indians attained national prominence. Seattle (1786?–1866) was the first signer of the Treaty of Point Elliott, which established two Indian reservations; the city of Seattle is named for him. Kamiakin (b.Idaho, c.1800–80) was the leader of the Yakima tribe during the Indian Wars of 1855, and Leschi (d.1858) was chief of the Nisqualli Indians and commanded the forces west of the Cascades during the 1855 uprising; Leschi was executed by the territorial government after the uprising was suppressed.

Washington authors have made substantial contributions to American literature. Mary McCarthy (b.1912) was born in Seattle, and one of her books, *Memories of a Catholic Girlhood* (1957), describes her early life there. University of Washington professor Vernon Louis Parrington (b.Illinois, 1871–1929) was the first Washingtonian to win a Pulitzer Prize (1928), for his monumental *Main Currents in American Thought*. Another University of Washington faculty member, Theodore Roethke (b.Michigan, 1908–63), won the Pulitzer Prize for poetry in 1953. Seattle-born Audrey May Wurdemann (1911–60) was awarded a Pulitzer Prize for poetry in 1934 for her volume *Bright Ambush*.

Singer-actor Bing Crosby (b.Harry Lillis Crosby, 1903–77), born in Tacoma, remained a loyal alumnus of Spokane's Gonzaga University. Modern dance choreographers Merce Cunningham (b.1919) and Robert Joffrey (b.1930) are both Washington natives. Photographer Edward S. Curtis (b.Wisconsin, 1868–1952) did most of the work on the *North American Indian* series while residing in Seattle. Modern artist Mark Tobey (b.Wisconsin, 1890–1976) spent much of his productive life in Seattle, and Robert Motherwell (b.1915) was born in Aberdeen. Washington's major contribution to popular music is rock guitarist Jimi Hendrix (1943–70).

⁵⁰BIBLIOGRAPHY

Bancroft, H. H. *History of Washington, Idaho, and Montana.* San Francisco: History Co., 1890.

Clark, Norman H. *Washington: A Bicentennial History.* New York: Norton, 1976.

Douglas, William O, *Of Men and Mountains.* New York: Harper, 1950.

Drury, Clifford M. *Marcus and Narcissa Whitman and the Opening of Old Oregon.* 2 vols. Glendale, Calif.: Clark, 1973.

Ficken, Robert E. *Lumber and Politics: The Career of Mark E. Reed.* Seattle: University of Washington Press, 1979.

Johansen, Dorothy O., and Charles M. Gates. *Empire of the Columbia.* 2d ed. New York: Harper and Row, 1967.

Kirk, Ruth. *Washington State: National Parks, Historic Sites, Recreation Areas, and Natural Landmarks*. Seattle: University of Washington Press, 1974.

Lee, W. Storrs (ed.). *Washington State: A Literary Chronicle*. New York: Funk and Wagnalls, 1969.

Meany, Edmond S. *History of the State of Washington*. New York: Macmillan, 1909.

Meinig, D.W. *The Great Columbia Plain: A Historical Geography, 1805–1910*. Seattle: University of Washington Press, 1968.

Snowden, Clinton A. *History of Washington*. 6 vols. New York: Century History, 1911.

Stewart, Edgar I. *Washington, Northwest Frontier*. 4 vols. New York: Lewis, 1957.

Tyler, Robert. *Rebels of the Woods: The I.W.W. and the Pacific Northwest*. Eugene, Ore.: University of Oregon Books, 1967.

Washington, State of. Office of Financial Management. *1979 Pocket Data Book*. Olympia, 1979.

Washington, State of. Office of the Governor. *Budget, 1979–81 Biennium*. Olympia, 1978.

Washington State Research Council. *The Book of Numbers: A Statistical Handbook on Washington State Government*. Olympia, 1979.

WEST VIRGINIA

State of West Virginia

ORIGIN OF STATE NAME: The state was originally the western part of Virginia. **NICKNAME:** The Mountain State. **CAPITAL:** Charleston. **ENTERED UNION:** 20 June 1863 (35th). **SONGS:** "The West Virginia Hills"; "West Virginia, My Home Sweet Home"; "This Is My West Virginia." **MOTTO:** *Montani semper liberi* (Mountaineers are always free). **COAT OF ARMS:** A farmer stands to the right and a miner to the left of a large ivy-draped rock bearing the date of the state's admission to the Union. In front of the rock are two hunters' rifles upon which rests a Cap of Liberty. The state motto is beneath and the words "State of West Virginia" above. **FLAG:** The flag has a white field bordered by a strip of blue, with the coat of arms in the center, wreathed by rhododendron leaves; across the top of the coat of arms are the words "State of West Virginia." **OFFICIAL SEAL:** The obverse is the same as the coat of arms; the reverse is no longer in common use. **ANIMAL:** Black bear. **BIRD:** Cardinal. **FISH:** Brook trout. **FLOWER:** *Rhododendron maximum* ("big laurel"). **TREE:** Sugar maple. **FRUIT:** Apple. **COLORS:** Old gold and blue. **LEGAL HOLIDAYS:** New Year's Day, 1 January; Lincoln's Birthday, 12 February; Washington's Birthday, 3d Monday in February; Memorial Day, 30 May; West Virginia Day, 20 June; Independence Day, 4 July; Labor Day, 1st Monday in September; Columbus Day, 2d Monday in October; Veterans Day, 11 November; Thanksgiving Day, 4th Thursday in November; Christmas Day, 25 December. **TIME:** 7 A.M. EST = noon GMT.

¹LOCATION, SIZE, AND EXTENT

Located in the eastern US in the South Atlantic region, West Virginia ranks 41st in size among the 50 states.

The area of West Virginia totals 24,181 sq mi (62,629 sq km), including 24,070 sq mi (62,341 sq km) of land and 111 sq mi (287 sq km) of inland water. The state extends 265 mi (426 km) E–W; its maximum N–S extension is 237 mi (381 km). West Virginia is one of the most irregularly shaped states in the US, with two panhandles of land, the northern, narrower one separating parts of Ohio and Pennsylvania, and the eastern panhandle separating parts of Maryland and Virginia.

West Virginia is bordered on the N by Ohio (with the line formed by the Ohio River), Pennsylvania, and Maryland (with most of the line defined by the Potomac River); on the E and S by Virginia; and on the W by Kentucky and Ohio (with the line following the Ohio, Big Sandy, and Tug Fork rivers).

The total boundary length of West Virginia is 1,180 mi (1,899 km). The geographical center of the state is in the Elk River public hunting area in Brayton County, 4 mi (6 km) E of Sutton.

²TOPOGRAPHY

West Virginia lies within two divisions of the Appalachian Highlands. Most of the eastern panhandle, which is crossed by the Allegheny Mountains, is in the Ridge and Valley region. The remainder, or more than two-thirds of the state, is part of the Allegheny Plateau, to the west of a bold escarpment known as the Allegheny Front, and tilts toward the Ohio River.

The mean elevation of West Virginia is 1,500 feet (457 meters), the highest of any state east of the Mississippi River. Its highest point, Spruce Knob, towers 4,863 feet (1,482 meters) above sea level. Major lowlands lie along the rivers, especially the Potomac, Ohio, and Kanawha. A point on the Potomac River near Harpers Ferry has the lowest elevation, only 240 feet (73 meters) above sea level. West Virginia has no natural lakes.

Most of the eastern panhandle drains into the Potomac River. The Ohio and its tributaries—the Monongahela, Little Kanawha, Kanawha, Guyandotte, and Big Sandy—drain most of the Allegheny Plateau section. Subterranean streams have carved out numerous caverns, including Seneca Caverns, Smoke Hole Caverns, and Organ Cave, from limestone beds in the Potomac and Greenbrier valleys.

During the Paleozoic era, when West Virginia was under water, a 30,000-foot (9,000-meter) layer of rock streaked with rich coal deposits was laid down over much of the state. Alternately worn down and uplifted during succeeding eras, most of West Virginia is thus a plateau where rivers have carved deep valleys and gorges and given the land an unusually rugged character.

³CLIMATE

West Virginia has a humid continental climate, with hot summers and cool to cold winters. The climate of the eastern panhandle is influenced by its proximity to the Atlantic slope and is similar to that of nearby coastal areas. Mean annual temperatures vary from 56°F (13°C) in the southwest to 48°F (9°C) in higher elevations. The yearly average is 53°F (12°C). The highest recorded temperature, 112°F (44°C), was at Martinsburg on 10 July 1936; the lowest, –37°F (–38°C), at Lewisburg on 30 December 1917.

Prevailing winds are from the south and west, and seldom reach hurricane or tornado force. Precipitation averages 45 in (114 cm) annually and is slightly heavier on the western slopes of the Alleghenies. Accumulations of snow may vary from about 20 in (51 cm) in the western sections to more than 50 in (127 cm) in the higher mountains.

⁴FLORA AND FAUNA

With its varied topography and climate, West Virginia provides a natural habitat for more than 3,400 species of plants in three life zones: Canadian, Alleghenian, and Carolinian. Oak, maple, poplar, walnut, hickory, birch, and such softwoods as hemlock, pine, fir, and spruce are the common forest trees. Rhododendron, laurel, dogwood, redbud, and pussy willow are among the more than 200 flowering trees and shrubs. Rare plant species include the box huckleberry, yellow coltsfoot, and thornless blackberry. The Cranberry Glades, an ancient lakebed similar to a glacial bog, contains the rare sundew, a carnivorous plant, and the bog rosemary.

West Virginia fauna includes at least 56 species and subspecies of mammals and more than 300 types of birds. The gray wolf, puma, elk, and bison of early times have disappeared, and beaver and river otter are nearly extinct. The white-tailed (Virginia) deer and the black bear (both protected by the state) as well as the wildcat are still found in the deep timber of the Allegheny ridges; raccoons, skunks, woodchucks, opossums, gray and red foxes, squirrels, and cottontail rabbits remain numerous. Common birds include the cardinal, tufted titmouse, brown thrasher, scarlet tanager, catbird, and a diversity of sparrows, woodpeckers, swallows, and warblers. Major game birds are the wild turkey, bobwhite quail, and ruffed grouse; hawks and owls are the most common birds of prey. Notable among more than 100 species of fish are smallmouth bass, rainbow trout, and brook trout (the state fish). The copperhead and rattlesnake are both numerous and poisonous. The southern bald eagle, American peregrine falcon, Kirtland's warbler, Indiana and Western Virginia big-eared bats, mountain lion, and tuberculed-blossom and pink mucket pearly mussels are on the endangered list.

⁵ENVIRONMENTAL PROTECTION
Major responsibility for environmental protection in West Virginia rests with the Air Pollution Control Commission and the Department of Natural Resources. In 1978/79, the former spent $1,031,280 and the latter $30,984,462.

The Department of Natural Resources grants awards to sewage treatment projects and issues permits for domestic and industrial waste treatment facilities, mine drainage projects, and coal preparation plants.

Most land reclamation springs from surface mining. The state levies a tax of $60 per bonded acre for reclaiming land from abandoned strip mines. In 1978/79, 1,008 acres (408 hectares) were reclaimed. Control of dam construction and coal refuse disposal was tightened after 118 persons died in the disastrous Buffalo Creek flood of 1972, which resulted from the collapse of a dam made of coal mine wastes near Logan.

⁶POPULATION
With a 1970 census total of 1,744,237, West Virginia ranked 34th among the 50 states in population.

The state's population grew rapidly in the 1880s and 1890s, as coal mining, lumbering, and railroads expanded to meet the needs of nearby industrial centers, but the pace of expansion slowed in the early 20th century. The population peaked at 2,005,552 in 1950; then mass unemployment, particularly in the coal industry, caused thousands of families to migrate to midwestern cities. An upswing began in the 1970s, and according to preliminary census data, the population was 1,928,524 in 1980.

In 1970, when nearly 75% of the American people lived in urban areas, only 39% of West Virginia's population was urban. West Virginia has no large cities. In 1980, Huntington, the largest city, had 63,626 residents; Charleston, 62,264; Wheeling, 43,141; and Parkersburg, 39,403. Huntington belongs to a metropolitan region that includes parts of eastern Kentucky and southern Ohio and had a population of 297,000 in 1977; the Charleston region had 261,000 residents.

⁷ETHNIC GROUPS
Nearly all Indian inhabitants had left the state before the arrival of European settlers. In the 1970 census, 751 Indians were counted.

The 64,400 blacks in the state in 1975 constituted about 4% of the population. The majority lived in industrial centers and coal-mining areas. Only 16,662, or about 1%, of West Virginians in 1970 were foreign-born. Another 57,358, or 3%, were second-generation Americans with at least one foreign-born parent. Most of the foreign-stock population came from Italy, the UK, Germany, and Poland. There were 6,261 Hispanic Americans, and fewer than 2,000 Asian and Pacific peoples.

⁸LANGUAGES
With little foreign immigration and with no effect from the original Iroquois and Cherokee Indians, West Virginia maintains Midland speech. There is a secondary contrast between the northern half and the southern half, with the former influenced by Pennsylvania and the latter by western Virginia.

The basic Midland speech sounds the /r/ after a vowel, as in *far*

and *short*, and has /kag/ for *keg*, /greezy/ for *greasy*, *sofy* instead of sofa, and *nicker* in place of neigh. The northern part has /yelk/ for *yolk*, /loom/ for *loam*, an /ai/ diphthong so stretched that *sat* and *sight* sound very much alike, *stone wall*, *run* for creek, and *teeter (totter)* for seesaw. The southern half pronounces *here* and *hear* as /hyeer/, *aunt* and *can't* as /aint/ and /kaint/, and uses *branch* for *creek*, and *tinter* for teeter.

In 1970, 93% of the native-born claimed English as their mother tongue, as did 92% of all the state's residents. Speakers of principal first languages were as follows:

	NATIVE-BORN	FOREIGN-BORN
English	1,608,321	2,852
Italian	12,292	3,661
German	6,865	1,800
Polish	6,301	1,049

⁹RELIGIONS
Throughout its history, West Virginia has been overwhelmingly Protestant. Most settlers before the American Revolution were Anglicans, Presbyterians, Quakers, or members of German sects, such as Lutherans, German Reformed, Dunkers, and Mennonites. The Great Awakening had a profound effect on these settlers, and they avidly embraced its evangelism, emotionalism, and emphasis on personal religious experience. Catholics were mostly immigrants from Ireland and southern and eastern Europe.

In 1971, the state had 706,179 known Protestants. The major denominations and the number of their adherents were United Methodist, 218,312; American Baptist Convention, 142,963; and Presbyterian, 36,489. The Catholic population was 101,502 in 1979; and the Jewish population was estimated at 4,090. Leading fundamentalist denominations were the Church of God (29,666) and the Church of the Nazarene (25,073).

¹⁰TRANSPORTATION
West Virginia has long been plagued by inadequate transportation. The first major pre–Civil War railroad line was the Baltimore and Ohio (B&O), completed to Wheeling in 1852. Later railroads, mostly built between 1880 and 1917 to tap rich coal and timber resources, also helped open up interior regions to settlement. Today, the railroads still play an important part in coal transportation; in 1977, 68% of coal was shipped by rail. Amtrak provides passenger service for parts of the state, which in 1974 had 3,508 mi (5,646 km) of railroads.

In 1977 there were 33,173 mi (53,387 km) of roads under the state system and 3,933 mi (6,330 km) of municipal and rural roads. The West Virginia Turnpike, completed from Charleston to Princeton in 1955 and regarded at that time as a marvel of engineering, was by 1977 far outclassed by the state's interstate highways, including the Appalachian Corridor highway system. There were 1,299,998 registered motor vehicles in the state as of 30 June 1978, and 1,367,000 licensed drivers in 1977.

Major navigable inland rivers are the Ohio, Kanawha, and Monongahela. In 1978, West Virginia had 28 public and 43 private airports; $7.2 million was spent on airport development. Kanawha County Airport is the state's main air terminal.

¹¹HISTORY
Paleo-Indian cultures in what is now West Virginia existed some 15,000 years ago, when hunters pursued buffalo and other large game. About 7000 BC they were supplanted by Archaic cultures, marked by pursuit of smaller game. Woodland (Adena) cultures, characterized by mound-building and agriculture, prevailed after about 1000 BC.

By the 1640s, the principal Indian claimants, the Iroquois and Cherokee, had driven out older inhabitants and made the region a vast buffer land. When European settlers arrived, only a few Shawnee, Tuscarora, and Delaware Indian villages remained.

The fur trade stimulated early exploration. In 1671, Thomas Batts and Robert Fallam explored New River and gave England a claim to the Ohio Valley, to which most of West Virginia be-

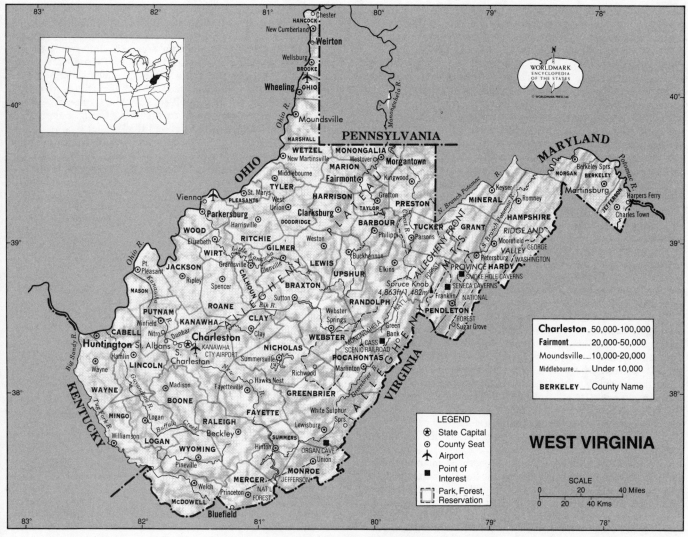

See US political: front cover K3; physical: back cover K3.
LOCATION: 37°12′8″ to 40°38′17″N; 77°43′11″ to 82°38′48″W. **BOUNDARIES**: Ohio line, 277 mi (446 km); Pennsylvania line, 119 mi (191 km); Maryland line, 235 mi (378 km); Virginia line, 438 mi (705 km); Kentucky line, 111 mi (179 km).

longs. France also claimed the Ohio Valley by virtue of an alleged visit by Robert Cavelier, Sieur de la Salle, in 1669. England eventually prevailed as a result of the French and Indian War.

Unsubstantiated tradition credits Morgan Morgan, who moved to Bunker Hill in 1731, with the first settlement in the state. By 1750, several thousand settlers were living in the eastern panhandle. In 1769, following treaties with the Iroquois and Cherokee, settlers began to occupy the Greenbrier, Monongahela, and upper Ohio valleys, and movement into other interior sections continued into the Revolutionary War, although wars with Indians occurred sporadically until the 1790s. The area that is now West Virginia was part of Virginia at the time of that state's entry into the Union, 25 June 1788.

Serious differences between eastern and western Virginia developed after the War of 1812. Eastern Virginia was dominated by a slaveholding aristocracy, while small diversified farms and infant industries predominated in western Virginia. Westerners rankled under property qualifications for voting, inadequate representation in the Virginia legislature, and undemocratic county governments, as well as poor transportation, inadequate schools, inequitable taxes, and economic retardation. A constitutional convention in 1829–30 failed to effect changes, leaving the west-

erners embittered. Another convention in 1850–51 met the west's political demands but exacerbated economic differences.

When Virginia seceded from the Union in 1861, western counties remaining loyal to the Union set up the Reorganized Government at Wheeling. Two years later, the Reorganized Government consented to the separation of present West Virginia from Virginia. After approval by Congress and President Lincoln, West Virginia entered the Union on 20 June 1863 as the 35th state. West Virginia won control over Jefferson and Berkeley counties in the eastern panhandle in 1871, giving it a greater share of the Baltimore and Ohio Railroad lines in the state.

Both Bourbon Democratic and Republican governors after the Civil War sought to improve transportation, foster immigration, and provide tax structures attractive to business. Industrialists such as Democrats Henry Gassaway Davis and Johnson N. Camden, who amassed fortunes in coal, oil, railroads, and timber, sat in the US Senate and dominated party affairs in West Virginia. Similarly, industrialists Nathan Goff, Jr., and Stephen B. Elkins wielded preponderant influence in the Republican Party from the 1870s until 1911. Native industrialists often collaborated with eastern interests to give the state a colonial economy dominated by absentee owners. Although Republican governors of the early 20th century were dominated by Elkins, they were attuned to Progressive ideas and were instrumental in the adoption of the direct primary, safety legislation for the coal mines, revision of corporate tax laws, and improvements in highways and education.

The Great Depression of the 1930s, from which West Virginia suffered acutely, ushered in a Democratic era. West Virginians embraced the New Deal and Fair Deal philosophies of Presidents Franklin D. Roosevelt and Harry S. Truman.

World Wars I and II produced significant changes in West Virginia, particularly through stimulation of chemical, steel, and textile industries in the Kanawha and Ohio valleys and the eastern panhandle. These industries lessened the state's dependence on extractive industries, historically the backbone of its economy, and gave cities and towns a more cosmopolitan character.

Overshadowing the economic diversification was the plight of the coal-mining areas, where, after World War II, mechanization and strip-mining displaced thousands of miners and resulted in a large exodus to other states. By 1960, West Virginia was considered one of the most economically depressed areas of the country, primarily because of conditions in the mining regions. Antipoverty programs of the Kennedy and Johnson administrations provided some relief, but much of it was temporary.

By the 1970s, the state's financial condition appeared more sound and economy more diversified. Moreover, the homogenizing effects of the automobile and of radio, television, and national marketing of goods and ideas changed West Virginia considerably. Its people, who in the 1920s and 1930s were as culturally isolated as their grandparents had been, were by the 1980s generally in the mainstream of American life.

12 STATE GOVERNMENT

Since becoming a state, West Virginia has had two constitutions. The first, adopted in 1863, served until 1872, when the present constitution was adopted.

The legislature consists of a senate with 34 members and a house of delegates with 100 members. Senators and delegates must be at least 25 and 18 years old, respectively. Both must have been residents of the state and of their districts for at least one year prior to taking their seats. Senators are elected to staggered four-year terms, and delegates serve for two years. The legislature meets annually in 60-day sessions, but special sessions may be called by the governor or by petition of three-fifths of the members of the legislature.

Elected officials of the executive branch of government are the governor, secretary of state, auditor, attorney general, commissioner of agriculture, and treasurer, all elected for four-year terms. The governor, who may serve no more than two terms in succession, must be at least 30 years old and have been a resident of the state for at least five years. He appoints the heads and members of 38 administrative divisions of state government.

Bills passed by the legislature become law when signed by the governor. Those that he vetoes may become law if repassed by majorities of both house memberships. Either house may propose an amendment to the state constitution. If both houses approve, it is submitted to the voters at the next regular election or at a special election.

The right to vote in an election is extended to all citizens over 18 years old who have registered and who have resided in the state for one year and in their respective counties for 30 days.

13 POLITICAL PARTIES

The Republican Party presided over the birth of West Virginia, but the Democrats have generally been in power for the last five decades. In 1940, a strong New Deal faction, headed by Matthew M. Neely and supported by organized labor, formed the "statehouse machine," which became a dominant factor in state politics. Only two Republicans, Cecil H. Underwood (1957–61) and Arch Moore, Jr. (1969–77), have been governor since 1933.

In 1978, West Virginia had 1,032,807 registered voters, of whom 694,313 were Democrats, 316,456 were Republicans, and 22,038 were affiliated with other parties. In 1976, Democrat John D. Rockefeller IV defeated Cecil H. Underwood for governor by a vote of 459,661 to 253,420. Two years later, Democrats won 74 of the 100 house of delegates seats and held 26 of the state senate seats. Robert Byrd was majority leader of the US Senate from 1977 through 1980, when the Democrats lost their majority. West Virginia held firm for Jimmy Carter in the November 1980 presidential balloting, and Rockefeller won reelection. But West Virginia's US House delegation, which had been entirely Democratic, was split evenly between Republicans and Democrats. Both US Senate seats were occupied by Democrats in 1981.

West Virginia Presidential Vote by Major Political Parties, 1948–80

YEAR	ELECTORAL VOTE	WEST VIRGINIA WINNER	DEMOCRAT	REPUBLICAN
1948	8	*Truman (D)	429,188	316,251
1952	8	Stevenson (D)	453,578	419,970
1956	8	*Eisenhower (R)	381,534	449,297
1960	8	*Kennedy (D)	441,786	395,995
1964	7	*Johnson (D)	538,087	253,953
1968	7	Humphrey (D)	374,091	307,555
1972	6	*Nixon (R)	277,435	484,964
1976	6	*Carter (D)	435,914	314,760
1980	6	Carter (D)	367,462	334,206

*Won US presidential election.

14 LOCAL GOVERNMENT

West Virginia has 55 counties. The chief county officials are the three commissioners, elected for six-year terms, who comprise the county court; the sheriff, assessor, county clerk, and prosecuting attorney, elected for four-year terms; the five-member board of education and the clerk of the circuit court, all elected for six-year terms. The sheriff is the principal peace officer but also collects taxes and disburses funds of the county court and board of education.

Cities and towns are divided into two classes. Those with more than 2,000 population may have their own charter and may adopt the mayor-council, commission, or city-manager type of government. Those with fewer than 2,000 people must have the mayor-council form of government.

15 STATE SERVICES

The Board of Education controls public education and teacher certification, and the Board of Regents governs higher education. The Department of Highways is responsible for construction and operation of state roads. Services of the State Health Department center around treatment of alcoholism and drug abuse, mental health, and environmental health services, maternal and child care, family planning, and control of communicable diseases. The Department of Welfare administers a variety of economic, medical, and social services.

In the area of public protection, the Department of Public Safety enforces criminal and traffic laws, and the Office of Emergency Services oversees civil defense and other emergency activities. The Public Service Commission regulates utilities. The Housing Development Fund concentrates on housing for low-and middle-income families and the elderly. The Department of Natural Resources has the major responsibility for protection of forests, wildlife, water, and other resources, for reclamation projects, and for operation of state parks and recreational facilities.

Responsibility in labor matters is shared by the Department of Labor, Department of Employment Security, Department of Mines, Workmen's Compensation Fund, and Labor-Management Relations Board.

16 JUDICIAL SYSTEM

The highest court in West Virginia, the supreme court of appeals, has five justices, including the chief justice, elected for 12-year terms. The court has broad appellate jurisdiction in both civil and criminal cases, and original jurisdiction in certain other cases.

West Virginia is divided into 31 judicial circuits, each with from 1 to 7 judges, for a total of 58, elected for eight-year terms. Each circuit serves from one to three counties and has jurisdiction over civil and criminal cases in amounts that exceed $100. Courts of limited jurisdiction in larger counties include intermediate, juvenile, domestic relations, and common pleas courts.

Local courts include the county magistrate courts and municipal courts. Magistrate courts have original jurisdiction in criminal matters but may not convict or sentence in felony cases. Municipal, police, or mayor's courts have authority to enforce municipal ordinances.

The Department of Corrections has charge of eight state institutions, ranging from the maximum security prison at Moundsville to youth correctional and rehabilitation centers. Counties and municipalities maintain their own jails.

In total crimes per 100,000 population in 1978, West Virginia ranked lowest among the states, with a rate of 2,270; the violent crime rate, 168, was about one-third the US average. The state abolished the death penalty in 1965.

17 ARMED FORCES

West Virginia has no military bases, academies, or training facilities. The Naval Telecommunications Station (Sugar Grove) is the main receiving facility for the Navy's global high-frequency radio communications and for point-to-point circuits destined for Washington, D.C. In 1978, defense contracts awarded West Virginia firms totaled $76 million.

In 1978, West Virginia had about 235,000 living war veterans, of whom 7,000 served in World War I, 110,000 in World War II, 41,000 in the Korean conflict, and 62,000 in the Viet-Nam era. In 1978, veterans received $209 million in benefits.

There were 4,400 National Guard personnel in 1978, and 969 state and 2,253 local police in 1977.

18 MIGRATION

West Virginia has considerable national and ethnic diversity. Settlers prior to the Civil War consisted principally of English, German, Scotch-Irish, and Welsh immigrants, many of whom came by way of Pennsylvania. A second wave of immigration from the 1880s to the 1920s brought thousands of Italians, Poles, Austrians, and Hungarians to the coal mines and industrial towns, which also attracted many blacks from the South. In 1970, 81% of the residents of the state were born in West Virginia.

Between 1950 and 1970, West Virginia suffered a 14% loss in population, chiefly from the coal-mining areas. Of the outmigrants, a majority went to contiguous states, the greatest loss being to Ohio. The migratory trend was reversed between 1970 and 1977; a net total of 43,000 people settled in the state.

19 INTERGOVERNMENTAL COOPERATION

The West Virginia Commission on Interstate Cooperation represents the state in the Council of State Governments. West Virginia participates in 22 regional compacts, including the Virginia–West Virginia Boundary Compact, Ohio River Valley Water Sanitation and Potomac Valley compacts, Southern Regional Education Board, Southern Interstate Energy Compact, and Interstate Mining Compact.

In 1977/78, federal funds accounted for 31% of the revenues in the state budget. General revenue-sharing funds amounted to $63.2 million in 1978/79. Allocations to West Virginia under the Appalachian development program in 1979 totaled $41 million.

20 ECONOMY

Agriculture was the backbone of West Virginia's economy until the 1890s, when extractive industries (including coal, oil, natural gas, and timber) began to play a major role. World War I stimulated important secondary industries, such as chemicals, steel, glass, and textiles. The strength of the state's economy lies in its diversity, as well as in the variety of natural resources. The beauty of the mountains and forests attracted an increasing number of tourists in the 1960s and 1970s.

21 INCOME

West Virginia's total personal income—$12 billion—ranked the state 32d in the US in 1978. The state's 1978 per capita income of $6,456 ranked 45th in the US. In 1975, 57,000—about 12%—of West Virginia families had incomes below the federal poverty level, as compared with 18% in 1969.

22 LABOR

West Virginia's labor force, which is mainly employed in mining and heavy industry, had the nation's lowest rate of participation by women (34%) in 1978. Unemployment in the state dropped between 1975 and 1978; unemployed persons in 1978 numbered 46,000 or 6.3% of the work force.

A federal census of workers covered by unemployment insurance in March 1977 revealed the following nonfarm employment pattern for West Virginia:

	ESTABLISH-MENTS	EMPLOYEES	ANNUAL PAYROLL ('000)
Agricultural services, forestry, fishing	189	874	7,258
Mining, of which:	1,395	68,277	1,056,988
Bituminous coal, lignite	(817)	(60,999)	(961,803)
Contract construction	3,477	24,234	365,977
Manufacturing, of which:	1,689	118,091	1,619,582
Primary metals	(47)	(23,261)	(464,091)
Chemicals	(64)	(18,703)	(319,397)
Transportation, public utilities	1,631	26,870	377,649
Wholesale trade	2,371	26,166	315,896
Retail trade	9,758	88,351	603,993
Finance, insurance, real estate	2,595	19,523	187,799
Services	8,665	76,960	608,104
Other	401	591	8,655
TOTALS	32,171	449,937	$5,151,901

Including government workers, the self-employed, and certain other employees, the state's total nonfarm labor force was 605,000.

Important milestones in the growth of unionism were the organization of the state as District 17 of the United Mine Workers of America (UMWA) in 1890 and the formation of the State Federation of Labor in 1903. The coal miners fought to gain union recognition by coal companies, and instances of violence were not uncommon between miners and operators throughout the early 1900s. Wages, working conditions, and benefits for miners improved rapidly after World War II. Membership in unions and employee associations in 1976 was 254,000, or 43% of the work force, with the UMWA the largest union.

Strikes, both legal and wildcat, contributed to decreases in coal production during the 1960s and 1970s. In 1977, 445 work stoppages idled 240,000 workers for a total of 2,549,000 days.

23 AGRICULTURE

With estimated farm marketings of $190.2 million, West Virginia ranked 46th among the 50 states in 1979. Until about 1890, small diversified farms dominated the economy, but, as in other states, farms have grown larger and the farm population has declined since that time. The farm population dropped from 533,000 in 1940 to only about 78,000 in 1970.

In 1974, the state had 3,496,606 acres (1,415,030 hectares), or nearly 23% of its land, devoted to farming. Its 16,909 farms averaged 207 acres (84 hectares) in size. Major farm sections are the eastern panhandle, a tier of counties along the Virginia border, the upper Monongahela Valley, and the Ohio Valley. Leading crops produced in 1979 were hay, 74,000 tons; corn, 4,543,000 bushels; commercial apples, 259,980,000 lb; and tobacco, 2,625,000 lb.

²⁴ANIMAL HUSBANDRY

Animal husbandry in 1978 accounted for 75% of West Virginia's agricultural cash receipts. The cattle industry, the largest component, produced 135,310,000 lb of beef in 1979, for a gross income of $78,863,000. Other major livestock products in 1979 were hogs and pigs, 25,903,000 lb; broilers, 63,726,000 lb; and turkeys, 47,394,000 lb. In 1978, the dairy industry yielded 344,000,000 lb of milk and 153,000,000 eggs.

²⁵FISHING

West Virginia fishing, valued at only $18,000 in 1978, has little commercial importance.

²⁶FORESTRY

In 1977, West Virginia had 11,669,000 acres (4,722,000 hectares) in forests, or 76% of its area and 1.6% of all US forestland. The state was once covered by a forest believed to have the greatest variety of hardwoods in the US, but because of excessive lumbering, the 10,000,000 acres (4,000,000 hectares) of virgin timber left in 1870 had all but disappeared by 1920. Reforestation is now a state priority, and more wood was grown than cut in 1977. Hardwoods, chiefly oaks, maples, poplars, and beeches, make up about 90% of the timber volume.

The three national forests wholly or partly in West Virginia are Monongahela, George Washington, and Jefferson. All nine state forests, totaling 79,308 acres (32,095 hectares), have recreational facilities.

²⁷MINING

In 1978, West Virginia ranked 6th among the states in production of minerals, which were valued at more than $3 billion. In order of value, the most important were coal, natural gas, petroleum, and natural gas liquids.

West Virginia ranked 1st in coal production until 1973, when it dropped to 2d behind Kentucky. In 1977, coal accounted for 93% of the state's total mineral output; underground mines produced 78% of the total. Major coal-mining regions lie within a north–south belt some 60 mi (97 km) wide through the central part of the state and include the Fairmont, New River–Kanawha, Pocahontas, and Logan-Mingo fields. The state, which had an estimated 57.3 billion tons of recoverable coal reserves in 1977, produced 84.7 million tons of coal in 1978. Liquefaction and gasification processes offer bright, if somewhat distant, prospects for the state's coal industry.

Other minerals produced in 1978 include more than 11.3 million tons of stone, 4 million tons of sand and gravel, and an estimated 1 million tons of salt.

²⁸ENERGY AND POWER

West Virginia has long been an important supplier of energy in the form of electric power and fossil fuels. In 1978, installed capacity was 13.1 million kw, and power output totaled 64 billion kwh. Out of 19.1 billion kwh of electricity sold in the state in 1977, 30% went to residential customers, 17% to commercial, and nearly 53% to industrial. The state's power facilities are all privately owned. The John Amos Plant, on the Kanawha River, is one of the world's largest investor-owned generating plants.

In 1978, West Virginia produced 2.4 million barrels of oil and 146.5 billion cu feet (4.1 billion cu meters) of natural gas. Proved petroleum reserves totaled 29.7 million barrels; natural gas, 2.7 trillion cu feet (76 billion cu meters).

²⁹INDUSTRY

An industrial state throughout much of its history, West Virginia enjoyed a 48% increase in value added by manufacture between 1972 and 1977. The total value added by manufacture in 1977 was $3.9 billion, the chief components being chemicals, 34%; primary metals, 19%; stone, clay, and glass products, 11%.

The following table shows value added by manufacturing for selected industries in 1972 and 1977:

	1972	1977
Industrial chemicals	$671,900,000	$918,800,000
Plastics, synthetics	252,900,000	362,300,000
Pressed or blown glass	183,400,000	249,400,000
Construction machinery	43,600,000	129,000,000

Major industrial areas are the Kanawha, Ohio, and Monongahela valleys and the eastern panhandle. Among large US companies operating in the state are Union Carbide, Wheeling-Pittsburgh Steel, E. I. du Pont de Nemours, Mobay Chemical, and Kaiser. In 1977, 82 manufacturers announced capital investments of $373 million in new plants or expansions, which would ultimately create 4,650 new jobs.

³⁰COMMERCE

In 1972, West Virginia's wholesale trade establishments had sales of $2.4 billion, ranking the state 36th in the US. Retail sales of nearly $5.7 billion in 1977 represented 0.7% of US sales and placed the state 34th among the 50 states. Sales in food stores made up 24% of the retail total; automotive dealers, 22%; general merchandise businesses, 14%; gasoline service stations, 9%; and other retailers, 31%.

In 1976, West Virginia's coal exports, over 27 million tons, constituted 47% of total US coal exports. Exports of manufactured goods, chiefly chemicals and primary metals, were valued at $580 million.

³¹CONSUMER PROTECTION

The state attorney general is empowered to investigate, arbitrate, and prosecute complaints involving unfair and deceptive trade practices, and to revoke charters and franchises. Assisting the attorney general is a nine-member Consumer Affairs Advisory Council, with five members representing the general public and four the consumer financing and retail businesses.

The Public Service Commission, consisting of three members, regulates rates, charges, and services of utilities and common carriers. Since 1977, it has included one member who is supposed to represent the "average" wage earner.

³²BANKING

West Virginia had 231 commercial banks in 1978, with assets of $8.6 billion, and 38 savings and loan associations, with assets of $1.2 billion. There were 7 building and loan associations and 159 supervised lenders licensed to make small loans in 1977.

³³INSURANCE

In 1978, 792 insurance companies were operating in West Virginia, collecting premiums of more than $1 billion. The 345 life, accident, and sickness companies collected $280.4 million and $190.9 million in life insurance and sickness and accident premiums, respectively, and paid out $153.6 million and $136.7 million in benefits. There were 3.4 million life insurance policies in force in 1978, with a total value of $19.5 billion; the average family had $28,100 in coverage (48th among the 50 states).

Fire and casualty firms, including automobile insurers, collected $442 million in premiums and disbursed $232 million in benefits. Blue Cross and Blue Shield, with premiums of $127 million and payments of $114.9 million, accounted for most of the hospital, medical, and dental insurance. The state insurance commissioner has responsibility for regulating the insurance business.

³⁴SECURITIES

There are no securities exchanges in West Virginia. New York Stock Exchange member firms had 19 sales offices and 101 registered representatives in the state in 1978. West Virginians reported $141.7 million in dividend income on their 1977 federal tax returns.

35 PUBLIC FINANCE

The state constitution requires the governor to submit to the legislature within 10 days after the opening of a regular legislative session a budget for the ensuing fiscal year (1 July–30 June). Budgets for fiscal 1977 and 1978 were as follows:

REVENUES	1976/77	1977/78
General revenue	$748,995,897	$811,089,791
Department of Highways	288,293,913	249,855,266
Federal funds	519,484,612	565,466,120
Special revenue funds	185,337,427	219,861,730
TOTALS	$1,742,111,849	$1,846,272,907
EXPENDITURES		
Education	$696,471,636	$571,705,316
Highways	480,484,521	517,789,900
Health and welfare	352,858,699	388,942,492
Other governmental costs	275,423,550	363,832,547
Bonded debt	10,918,327	13,835,431
Capital outlay	46,081,656	68,013,330
TOTALS	$1,862,238,389	$1,924,119,016

Total public debts of the state and municipalities in 1977 exceeded $1.9 billion, or $1,042 per capita (33d in the US).

36 TAXATION

West Virginia's diversified tax base yielded receipts of some $890 million in 1977/78. Personal income taxes, ranging from 2.1% to 9.6%, accounted for $182.9 million; a corporate income tax of 6%, $10.1 million; and consumers' sales taxes of 3% on goods and services, $146.6 million. The business and occupations tax, yielding $324.8 million, made up 40% of the general revenue fund. In 1979, the state decided to phase out taxes on food over a three-year period. Counties and localities mainly tax real and personal property.

West Virginians filed 645,340 federal income tax returns in 1977, paying a total of more than $1.1 billion.

37 ECONOMIC POLICY

The Industrial Development Division of the Department of Economic and Community Development has major responsibility for development planning. It assists companies with site locations, compliance with state and federal regulations, and employee training programs, as well as with construction of plants and access roads and provision of essential services.

The Economic Development Authority may make loans of up to 30% of the costs of land, buildings, and equipment at low interest rates for as long as 25 years. With the cooperation of the West Virginia Business Development Corp. and the federal Small Business Administration, it can offer 100% financing for some industries. Tax incentives include a credit of 10% on industrial expansion applicable to the business and occupations tax over a 10-year period.

38 HEALTH

Health conditions in West Virginia still lag behind those of the rest of the US. During 1969–71, the state's average life expectancy—69.48 years—was 41st among the 50 states. According to federal data, only one state had a higher death rate in 1977 and only two had higher infant mortality rates among the white population. The state also had the highest death rate from heart disease in that year. Increasing public health problems are alcoholism and drug abuse; in 1979/80, the West Virginia Department of Health treated 37,428 alcoholics and drug addicts. Pneumoconiosis (black lung) is an occupational hazard among coal miners.

In 1978, the state's 80 hospitals—including 8 state-run facilities—had 14,170 beds and 395,000 admissions. There were 2,531 physicians in 1977 and 703 dentists in 1979.

Medical education is provided by medical schools at West Virginia University and Marshall University and at the West Virginia School of Osteopathic Medicine. The emergency medical services program in the Department of Health has trained thousands of West Virginians in techniques for cardiopulmonary resuscitation.

39 SOCIAL WELFARE

Although rich in resources, West Virginia has more than its share of poverty. In 1978, 66,900 persons received $54 million in aid to families with dependent children. An estimated 283,000 persons received food stamps, with a federal subsidy amounting to $98.3 million. About 258,000 pupils participated in the school lunch program, at a federal cost of $18.3 million.

Social Security benefits in 1977 included $440.5 million for 191,500 retired workers and their dependents, $223 million for 88,300 survivors, and $172.9 million for 75,800 disabled persons. Federal Supplemental Security Income payments to the aged and disabled totaled $58.1 million. Under the Black Lung Benefit Program, 77,000 miners, widows, and dependents received $165 million in 1978. Workers' compensation payments were $109 million in 1977, and unemployment benefits reached $75 million in 1978.

40 HOUSING

In 1970, West Virginia had 547,214 occupied housing units, of which 376,767, or 69%, were owner-occupied, and 170,447, or 31%, were renter-occupied. Of these units, 84% had full plumbing, 92% had flush toilets, and 91% had tub or shower. In 1978, 4,400 new housing units valued at $125 million were authorized by the state.

41 EDUCATION

West Virginia has generally ranked below national standards in education. In 1970, the illiteracy rate was 1.4%; 53% of adult West Virginians were high school graduates in 1976, a criterion by which the state tied Kentucky and outranked only Mississippi.

In 1978/79, the state's public schools enrolled 387,688 students, with 230,647—including 27,439 in preschools and kindergarten—in elementary grades and 157,041 in secondary grades. Nonpublic schools enrolled 13,256 students, including 11,221 in church-related schools.

The state supports West Virginia University, Marshall University, and the West Virginia College of Graduate Studies (all offering graduate work), as well as 3 medical schools, 8 four-year colleges, and 4 two-year institutions. Public higher educational institutions enrolled 70,604 students in 1979. There are 10 private colleges. The West Virginia Higher Education Grant Program, administered by the Board of Regents, awards grants of $200–1,500 on the basis of need and merit to 5,000 undergraduates a year.

42 ARTS

Known for the quilts, pottery, and woodwork of its mountain artisans, West Virginia has shown considerable artistic enterprise. Huntington Galleries, the Sunrise Foundation at Charleston, and Oglebay Park, Wheeling, are major art centers. The Science and Culture Center at Charleston features West Virginia and Appalachian artists at work. The Mountain State Art and Craft Fair is held each summer at Ripley.

Popular outdoor musical dramas regularly presented at Grandview State Park include *Honey in the Rock*, based on the achievement of West Virginia statehood, and *Hatfields and McCoys*. Musical attractions range from symphony orchestras at Charleston and Wheeling to *Jamboree USA*, a weekly country music program at Wheeling.

43 LIBRARIES AND MUSEUMS

In 1978, West Virginia had 147 public libraries, with 2,336,816 volumes and a circulation of 5,543,713. Largest was the Kanawha County Public Library system at Charleston, with 442,117 volumes. The 26 college and university libraries housed 3,729,609 volumes, with 898,133 at West Virginia University, the largest academic library. The West Virginia University Medical Center at Morgantown and the state's Division of Archives and History Library and Library Commission Services to the Blind and Physically Handicapped maintain important specialized libraries.

There are more than 20 museums, including the State Museum and the Sunrise Foundation in Charleston, and the Charles Town Museum (with John Brown relics) and Oglebay Institute–Mansion Museum in Wheeling. Point Pleasant marks the site of a battle between colonists and Indians, and Harpers Ferry is the site of John Brown's raid.

44 COMMUNICATIONS

In 1978, West Virginia had 1,088 post offices, with about 4,800 employees. Of the 1,085,548 telephones in the state, 832,568 were residential and 252,980 were business; 89% of households had telephone service, well below the US average. In 1978, commercial broadcasting included 71 AM and 32 FM radio stations and 9 television stations; there were 3 public radio stations and 3 public television stations. Public stations operated under supervision of the West Virginia Educational Broadcasting Authority. In 1979, 184 cable television systems served 305,408 subscribers in 543 communities.

45 PRESS

In 1978, West Virginia had 28 daily newspapers and 72 weekly journals. Only two cities had dailies with more than 50,000 circulation.

The following table shows leading West Virginia newspapers with their 1979 circulations:

AREA	NAME	DAILY	SUNDAY
Charleston	Gazette (m,S)	56,002	105,789
	Daily Mail (e,S)	56,742	
Huntington	Herald-Dispatch (m,S)	43,007	50,287

The *West Virginia Hillbilly*, a folksy miscellany published weekly in Richwood, had a circulation of about 16,000. The only important newspaper chain in the state is Ogden Newspapers, which publishes four daily papers in Wheeling and Parkersburg.

There were 45 periodicals and trade journals published in the state in 1978. State publications include *Wild, Wonderful West Virginia* and *Goldenseal*, an illustrated journal of history and folklore.

46 ORGANIZATIONS

The Black Lung Association, based in Beckley, promotes safe working conditions in coal mines and benefits for disabled miners. The headquarters of the Appalachian Trail Conference is in Harpers Ferry. Nearly every national organization of importance has chapters or branches in the state.

47 TOURISM, TRAVEL, AND RECREATION

The tourist industry in West Virginia earned $647 million and employed 37,078 persons in 1976. Major attractions were Harpers Ferry Historical Park, the National Radio Observatory at Greenbank, the Naval Telecommunications Station at Sugar Grove, and White Sulphur Springs. Among 35 state parks are Cass Scenic Railroad, which includes a restoration of an old logging line; scenic Hawk's Nest; and Prickett's Fort, with recreations of pioneer life. State parks drew 6,761,226 visitors in 1978/79; state forests, 1,150,863. In 1977/78, licenses were issued to 316,665 hunters and 273,354 fishermen.

48 SPORTS

No major league professional teams are based in West Virginia. West Virginia University's basketball team won a National Invitation Tournament championship in 1942 and was NCAA Division I runner-up in 1959.

Horse-racing tracks operate in Chester and Charles Town. Dog races, legalized in 1975, are run in Wheeling. The state collects a daily license tax for each racing day and a percentage of gambling receipts.

49 FAMOUS WEST VIRGINIANS

Among West Virginians who have served in presidential cabinets are Nathan Goff, Jr. (1843–1920), Navy secretary; William L. Wilson (1843–1900), postmaster general; John Barton Payne (1855–1935), interior secretary; and Newton D. Baker (1871–1937), secretary of war during World War I. Lewis L. Strauss (1896–1974), was commerce secretary and chairman of the Atomic Energy Commission, and Cyrus R. Vance (b.1917) served as secretary of state. John W. Davis (1873–1955), an ambassador to Great Britain, ran as the Democratic presidential nominee in 1924. Dwight W. Morrow (1873–1931) was ambassador to Mexico. Prominent members of the US Senate have included Matthew M. Neely (1874–1958), who was also governor, Harley M. Kilgore (1893–1956), and Robert C. Byrd (b.1917).

Thomas J. "Stonewall" Jackson (1824–63) was a leading Confederate general during the Civil War. Brigadier General Charles E. "Chuck" Yeager (b.1923), a World War II ace, became the first person to fly faster than the speed of sound.

Major state political leaders, all governors (though some have held federal offices), have been E. Willis Wilson (1844–1905); Henry D. Hatfield (1875–1962); Arch A. Moore, Jr. (b.1923); and John D. "Jay" Rockefeller IV (b.New York, 1937).

The state's only Nobel Prize winner has been Pearl S. Buck (Pearl Sydenstricker, 1893–1973), who won the prize for literature for her novels concerning China. Alexander Campbell (b.Ireland, 1788–1866), with his father, founded the Disciples of Christ Church and was president of Bethany College in West Virginia. William H. Harvey (1851–1936), monetary reformer, was a proponent of the 19th-century free-silver movement. Geologist Israel C. White (1848–1927) became known for his anticlinal theory of oil and gas accumulation. Michael J. Owens (1859–1923) invented a bottle-making machine that stimulated the glass industry. Major labor leaders have included Walter Reuther (1907–70), president of the United Automobile Workers, and Arnold Miller (b.1923), president of the United Mine Workers.

Musicians include George Crumb (b.1929), a Pulitzer Prize–winning composer, and opera singers Eleanor Steber (b.1916) and Phyllis Curtin (b.1922). Melville Davisson Post (1871–1930) was a leading writer of mystery stories. Jerry West (b.1938) was a collegiate and professional basketball star, and a pro coach after his playing days ended; Rod Hundley (b.1934) and Hal Greer (b.1936) also starred in the National Basketball Association. Another West Virginian of note is Anna Jarvis (1864–1948), founder of Mother's Day.

50 BIBLIOGRAPHY

Ambler, Charles H., and Festus P. Summers. *West Virginia: The Mountain State*. 2d ed. Englewood Cliffs, N.J.: Prentice-Hall, 1958 (orig. 1940).

Cometti, Elizabeth, and Festus P. Summers, eds. *The Thirty-Fifth State: A Documentary History of West Virginia*. Parsons, W.Va.: McClain, 1966.

Conley, Phil, and William Thomas Doherty. *West Virginia History*. Charleston: Education Foundation, 1974.

Dillon, J. C., ed. *West Virginia Blue Book, 1978*. Charleston: Jarrett, 1978.

Federal Writers' Project. *West Virginia: A Guide to the Mountain State*. New York: Oxford University Press, 1941.

Moore, George E. *A Banner in the Hills: West Virginia's Statehood*. New York: Appleton-Century-Crofts, 1963.

Rice, Otis K. *The Allegheny Frontier: West Virginia Beginnings, 1730–1830*. Lexington: University Press of Kentucky, 1970.

Rice, Otis K. *West Virginia: The State and Its People*. Parsons, W.Va.: McClain, 1972.

West Virginia Research League, Inc. *1979 Statistical Handbook*. Charleston, 1979.

Williams, John Alexander. *West Virginia: A Bicentennial History*. New York: Norton, 1976.

WISCONSIN

State of Wisconsin

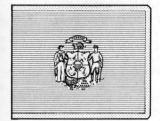

ORIGIN OF STATE NAME: Probably from the Ojibwa word *wishkonsing*, meaning "place of the beaver." **NICKNAME:** The Badger State. **CAPITAL:** Madison. **ENTERED UNION:** 29 May 1848 (30th). **SONG:** "On, Wisconsin!" **MOTTO:** Forward. **COAT OF ARMS:** Surrounding the US shield is the shield of Wisconsin, which is divided into four parts symbolizing agriculture, mining, navigation, and manufacturing. Flanking the shield are a sailor, representing labor on water, and a miner, labor on land. Above is a badger and the state motto; below, a horn of plenty and a pyramid of pig lead. **FLAG:** A dark blue field, fringed on three sides, surrounds the state coat of arms on each side. **OFFICIAL SEAL:** The seal consists of the coat of arms surrounded by the words "Great Seal of the State of Wisconsin," and 13 stars below. **ANIMAL:** Badger. **WILDLIFE ANIMAL:** White-tailed deer. **DOMESTIC ANIMAL:** Dairy cow. **BIRD:** Robin. **FISH:** Muskellunge. **FLOWER:** Wood violet. **TREE:** Sugar maple. **SYMBOL OF PEACE:** Mourning dove. **ROCK:** Red granite. **MINERAL:** Galena. **INSECT:** Honeybee. **LEGAL HOLIDAYS:** New Year's Day, 1 January; Lincoln and Washington Day, 3d Monday in February; Good Friday, March or April; Memorial Day, last Monday in May; Independence Day, 4 July; Labor Day, 1st Monday in September; Primary Day, 2d Tuesday in September in even-numbered years; Columbus Day, 2d Monday in October; Election Day, 1st Tuesday after 1st Monday in November in even-numbered years; Armistice Day, 11 November; Thanksgiving Day, 4th Thursday in November; Christmas Day, 25 December. **TIME:** 6 A.M. CST = noon GMT.

¹LOCATION, SIZE, AND EXTENT

Located in the eastern north-central US, Wisconsin ranks 26th in size among the 50 states.

The total area of Wisconsin is 56,154 sq mi (145,439 sq km), of which 54,464 sq mi (141,062 sq km) is land and 1,690 sq mi (4,377 sq km) inland water. The state extends 295 mi (475 km) E–W, and 320 mi (515 km) N–S.

Wisconsin is bordered on the N by Lake Superior and the State of Michigan (with the northeastern boundary formed by the Menominee River); on the E by Lake Michigan; on the S by Illinois; and on the W by Iowa and Minnesota (with the line defined mainly by the Mississippi and St. Croix rivers).

Important islands belonging to Wisconsin are the Apostle Islands in Lake Superior and Washington Island in Lake Michigan. The state's boundaries have a total length of 1,379 mi (2,219 km). Wisconsin's geographic center is in Wood County, 9 mi (14 km) SE of Marshfield.

²TOPOGRAPHY

Wisconsin can be divided into four main geographical regions, each covering roughly one-quarter of the state's land area. The most highly elevated of these is the Superior Upland, below Lake Superior and the border with Michigan. It has heavily forested rolling hills but no high mountains. Elevations range from about 700 feet (200 meters) to slightly under 2,000 feet (600 meters). A second upland region, called the Driftless Area, has a more rugged terrain, having been largely untouched by the glacial drifts that smoothed out topographical features in other parts of the state. Elevations here reach more than 1,200 feet (400 meters). The third region is a large, crescent-shaped plain in central Wisconsin; its unglaciated portion is a sandstone plain, broken by rock formations that from a distance appear similar to the buttes and mesas of Colorado. Finally, in the east and southeast along Lake Michigan, lies a large, glaciated lowland plain, fairly smooth in the Green Bay–Winnebago area but more irregular on the Door Peninsula and in the south.

Wisconsin's mean altitude is 1,050 feet (320 meters), with elevations generally higher in the north. The Gogebic Range, extending westward from Michigan's Upper Peninsula into northern Wisconsin, was an important center of iron mining in the early days of statehood. Timms Hill, in north-central Wisconsin, is the state's highest point, at 1,953 feet (595 meters). The lowest elevation is 581 feet (177 meters), along the Lake Michigan shoreline.

There are well over 8,000 lakes in Wisconsin. Lakes Michigan and Superior form part of the northern and eastern borders; the Wisconsin mainland has at least 575 mi (925 km) of lakeshore and holds jurisdiction over 10,062 sq mi (26,061 sq km) of their waters. By far the largest inland lake is Lake Winnebago, in eastern Wisconsin, covering an area of 215 sq mi (557 sq km).

The Mississippi River, which forms part of the border with Minnesota and the entire border with Iowa, is the main navigable river. The major river flowing through the state is the Wisconsin, which follows a south-southwest course for 430 mi (692 km) before meeting the Mississippi below Prairie du Chien, at the Iowa border. Other tributaries of the Mississippi include the St. Croix River, also part of the Minnesota border, and the Chippewa and Black rivers. Located on the Black River are Big Manitou Falls, at 165 feet (50 meters) the highest of the state's many scenic waterfalls. Waters from the Fox River and its major tributary, the Wolf, flow into Green Bay and thence into Lake Michigan, as does the Menominee, which is part of the Michigan state line.

Except in the Driftless Area, glaciation smoothed out many surface features, gouged out new ones, and left deposits of rock and soil creating distinctively shaped hills and ridges. Oval mounds, called drumlins, are still scattered over the southeast, and moraines, formed by deposits left at the edges of glaciers, are a prominent feature of eastern, central, and northwestern Wisconsin. In one section, called the Dells, the Wisconsin River has cut a gorge through 8 mi (13 km) of sandstone, creating caves and interesting rock formations.

³CLIMATE

Wisconsin has a continental climate, with low humidity. Summers are warm and winters very cold, especially in the north-central region, where the growing season is less than 100 days. Over the years 1973–77, north-central Wisconsin had a mean monthly temperature of 9°F (–13°C) in January and 68°F (20°C) in July. Southeastern Wisconsin had an average monthly temperature of 19°F (–7°C) in January and 73°F (23°C) in July. Over a 30-year period ending in 1970, the state's largest city, Milwaukee, had normal temperatures ranging from 11°F (–12°C) to 27°F (–3°C) in January and from 59°F (15°C) to 80°F (27°C) in July. The lowest temperature ever recorded in Wisconsin was –54°F (–48°C), at Danbury on 24 January 1922; the highest, 114°F (46°C), at Wisconsin Dells on 13 July 1936.

Precipitation in the state ranged in 1977 from a high of 40 in (102 cm) for the northwest to a low of 33 in (84 cm) in the south-central region. Normal annual precipitation in Milwaukee is 29 in (74 cm); June, July, and September are the rainiest months. Milwaukee's annual snowfall averages 46 in (117 cm); the average wind speed is 12 mph (19 km/hr).

⁴FLORA AND FAUNA

Common trees of Wisconsin include four oaks—bur, black, white, and red—along with black cherry and hickory. Jack pine, yellow birch, eastern hemlock, mountain maple, moosewood, and leatherwood grow in the north, with black spruce, black ash, balsam fir, and tamarack concentrated in the northern lowlands. Characteristic of southern Wisconsin's climax forests are sugar maple (the state tree), white elm, basswood, and ironwood, with silver maple, black willow, silver birch, and cottonwood on low, moist land. Prairies are thick with grasses; bogs and marshes are home to white and jack pines and jack oak. Forty-five varieties of orchid have been identified, as well as 20 types of violet, including the wood violet, the state flower. Threatened plants include lenticular sedge, ram's-head lady's-slipper, blue ash, prairie white-fringed orchid, prairie bush-clover, and snow trillium. Lake cress, harbinger-of-spring, pink milkwort, wild petunia, Lake Huron tansy, mountain cranberry, and dwarf bilberry are listed as endangered.

White-tailed deer, black bear, woodchuck, snowshoe hare, chipmunk, and porcupine are mammals typical of forestlands. The striped skunk, red and gray foxes, and various mice are characteristic of upland fields, while wetlands harbor such mammals as the muskrat, mink, river otter, and water shrew. The badger, dwelling in grasslands and semiopen areas, is rarely seen today. Game birds include the ring-necked pheasant, bobwhite quail, Hungarian partridge, and ruffed grouse; among 336 bird species native to Wisconsin are 42 kinds of waterfowl and 6 types of shorebird that are also hunted. Reptiles include 23 varieties of snake (2 of them poisonous), 13 types of turtle, and 4 kinds of lizard. Muskellunge (the state fish), northern pike, walleye, and brook trout are native to Wisconsin waterways.

Among threatened animals are the red-shouldered hawk, greater prairie chicken, glass lizard, Blanding's turtle, pickerel frog, and longear sunfish. The pine marten, Canada lynx, timber wolf, bald eagle, barn owl, osprey, queen snake, massasauga, slender madtom, and Higgin's eye pearly mussel are on the endangered list. The Office of Endangered and Nongame Species in the Department of Natural Resources develops programs designed to aid the recovery of listed flora and fauna.

⁵ENVIRONMENTAL PROTECTION

Conservation has been a concern in Wisconsin for more than a century. In 1867, a legislative commission reported that depletion of the northern forests by wasteful timber industry practices and frequent forest fires had become an urgent problem, partly because it increased the hazards of flooding. The legislature took no action for some time, but in 1897, a forestry warden was appointed and a system of fire detection and control was set up. A reforestation program was instituted in 1911; at about the same time, the state university began planting rows of trees in plains areas to protect soil from wind erosion, a method that was widely copied in other states. Fish and game wardens were appointed in 1885 and 1887, respectively. In 1927, the state began a program to clean its waters of industrial wastes, caused es-

pecially by pulp and paper mills and canneries. The legislature enacted a comprehensive antipollution program in 1966.

The present Department of Natural Resources, organized in 1967, brings together conservation and environmental protection responsibilities. The department supervises air, water, and solid waste pollution control programs and deals with the protection of forest, fish, and wildlife resources. A separate Solid Waste Recycling Authority was created in 1973 to develop solid waste disposal and recycling facilities.

Authorized funding for all state environmental programs amounted to $176.2 million for 1980/81, or nearly 3% of all appropriations. A substantial amount—$62 million in 1978/79—is allocated annually to municipalities for pollution abatement and solid waste management facilities. Funding for environmental programs came mainly from federal aid and from charges for boating, admission to state parks, and hunting and fishing licenses.

Although air pollution is heaviest in the industrial southeast, excessive levels have been monitored throughout the state. Since water pollution became a serious problem in the 1920s, pulp and paper mills have spent about $50 million to develop methods of recycling their industrial waste. A cleanup campaign during the 1970s led to significant declines in the level of suspended solids in industrial rivers. Nevertheless, more than 100 different chemicals were still being discharged into Wisconsin's rivers and streams as of 1979.

Wisconsin produces an estimated 13.5 million tons of solid waste annually. To assist local governments and landfill operators, the Bureau of Waste Management offers aid in locating acceptable landfill sites and planning for the collection, transportation, and disposal of solid wastes.

⁶POPULATION

Wisconsin ranked 16th in population among the 50 states in 1970, with a census population of 4,417,821.

During the 18th and early 19th centuries, the area that is now Wisconsin was very sparsely settled by perhaps 20,000 Indians and a few hundred white settlers, mostly involved in the fur trade. With the development of lead mining, the population began to expand, reaching a total of 30,945 (excluding Indians) by 1840. During the next two decades, the population increased rapidly to 775,881, as large numbers of settlers from the East and German, British, and Scandinavian immigrants arrived. Subsequent growth has been steady, if slower. Lumbering became important after the Civil War, and the north became more settled; in the late 19th century, industry expanded, and by 1930, the population became predominantly urban.

The 1970 census showed a population increase of nearly 12% since 1960, slightly below the national average. Average population density was 81 per sq mi (31 per sq km), above the US norm. Wisconsin is populated much less densely than the adjoining states of Illinois and Michigan, but more densely than Iowa and Minnesota. The state's estimated population in 1979 was 4,695,000, an increase of 6% over 1970. Of the 1979 population, an estimated 51.4% were females and 48.6% males. Nearly 12% of the population was 65 years of age or older, somewhat above the US average. According to preliminary 1980 census results, Wisconsin had a population of 4,689,055.

About two-thirds of all Wisconsinites live in urban areas, nearly all of them in the heavily urbanized southeastern region. Milwaukee, the largest city in Wisconsin and, as of 1978, the 17th largest in the US, had an estimated population of 620,162, 14% lower than in 1970. Other large cities in 1978 were Madi-

---

LOCATION: 42°29′34″ to 47°18′35″ N; 86°14′55″ to 92°53′31″ W.
BOUNDARIES: Michigan line, 680 mi (1,094 km); Illinois line, 182 mi (293 km); Iowa line, 91 mi (146 km); Minnesota line, 426 mi (686 km).

93° 92° 91° 90° 89° 88° 87°

LAKE   SUPERIOR

LAKE   SUPERIOR

47° 47°

APOSTLE ISLANDS

APOSTLE ISLANDS NAT'L LAKESHORE

Duluth

Superior

BAYFIELD

Washburn

DOUGLAS

Ashland

MICHIGAN

GOGEBIC RANGE

Hurley

46° 46°

ASHLAND

IRON

VILAS

MINNESOTA

WASHBURN

Hayward

L. Chippewa

CHEQUAMEGON

Eagle River

FOREST

Florence

FLORENCE

Menominee R.

Danbury

BURNETT

Grantsburg

SCENIC

POLK

Shell Lake

NATIONAL   FOREST

SUPERIOR   UPLAND

Rhinelander

Crandon

NICOLET

MARINETTE

BARRON

RUSK

LAC COURT OREILLES INDIAN RESERVATION

Phillips

ONEIDA

NAT'L

OCONTO

RIVERWAY

Balsam Lake

Rice Lake

PRICE

LANGLADE

FOREST

Peshtigo R.

BAY

Washington I.

45° 45°

ST. CROIX

LOWER ST. CROIX

Hudson

Ladysmith

Timms Hill ▲1,953 ft/ 609m

DUNN

CHEQUAMEGON NAT'L FOREST

TAYLOR

Medford

LINCOLN

Merrill

Antigo

Keshena

MENOMINEE

Oconto

Peshtigo

Fish Creek

Marinette

DOOR PENINSULA

ST. CROIX

Chippewa Falls

River Falls

Menomonie

CHIPPEWA

Eau Claire

CLARK

MARATHON

Wausau West **Wausau**

Rib Mtn. ▲ 1,941 ft/592m

MENOMINEE INDIAN RESERVATION

Shawano

SHAWANO

DOOR

KEWAUNEE

Sturgeon Bay

PIERCE

Ellsworth

Durand

PEPIN

EAU CLAIRE

Marshfield

WOOD

Neillsville

WAUPACA

OUTAGAMIE

Ashwaubenon

Green Bay

Allouez Little De Pere Chute

BROWN

Kewaunee

Carlton

BUFFALO

Alma

Whitehall

JACKSON

Black River Falls

Stevens Point

Wisconsin Rapids

Wisconsin R.

New London

Waupaca

Appleton

Menasha

Neenah

Kimberly

Kaukauna

CALUMET

Chilton

MANITOWOC

Two Creeks

Two Rivers

Manitowoc

TREMPEALEAU

MONROE

JUNEAU

Petenwell Flowage

ADAMS

PORTAGE

WAUSHARA

Wautoma

Berlin

WINNEBAGO

Oshkosh

Lake Winnebago

Greenbush

Plymouth

Sheboygan

44° 44°

LA CROSSE

Sparta

Tomah

Friendship

MARQUETTE

Green Lake

Montello

Ripon

Fond du Lac

SHEBOYGAN

La Crosse

Castle Rock Flowage

Mauston

GREEN LAKE

FOND DU LAC

Waupun

DODGE

Beaver Dam

Juneau

WASHING-TON

West Bend

Hartford

Germantown

OZAU-KEE

Port Washington

Cedarburg

Mequon

WORLDMARK ENCYCLOPEDIA OF THE STATES

© WORLDMARK PRESS Ltd.

VERNON

Genoa

Viroqua

Kickapoo R.

UPPER DELLS Wisconsin Dells

LOWER DELLS

Baraboo

Portage

COLUMBIA

Watertown

Oconomowoc

Menominee Falls

Whitefish Bay

Shorewood

Wauwatosa

Milwaukee

RICHLAND

Richland Center

Spring Green

SAUK

CAVE OF THE MOUNDS

BLUE MOUNDS

Sun Prairie

Madison

Middleton

Monona

Jefferson

JEFFERSON

Waukesha

West Allis

MILWAU-KEE

Cudahy

South Milwaukee

43° 43°

IOWA

CRAWFORD

Prairie du Chien

GRANT

Dodgeville

IOWA

Fort Atkinson

DANE

Whitewater

WAUKESHA

GENERAL MITCHELL FIELD

Racine

RACINE

Lancaster

Platteville

GREEN

ROCK

Janesville

WALWORTH

Delavan

Elkhorn

Burlington

Genoa City

Kenosha

LAKE

Darlington

Monroe

Beloit

Perrygo Place

KENOSHA

LAFAYETTE

ILLINOIS

42° 42°

WISCONSIN

SCALE

0   20   40   60 Miles

0   20   40   60 Kms

LEGEND

✹ State Capital

⊙ County Seat

✈ Airport

■ Point of Interest

Park, Forest, Reservation

Madison Over 100,000

Racine 50,000–100,000

Wausau 20,000–50,000

Kaukauna 10,000–20,000

Sturgeon Bay Under 10,000

WAUKESHA County Name

92° 91° 90° 89° 88° 87°

See US political: front cover J2; physical: back cover J2.

son, 171,113; Racine, 92,988; Green Bay, 89,289; and Kenosha, 80,718. Of these, Green Bay was the only city to gain population (about 2%) between 1970 and 1978. The state's largest metropolitan area, Milwaukee, had 1,427,000 residents as of 1 July 1977 (24th in the US).

[7] ETHNIC GROUPS

As early as 1839, Wisconsin attracted immigrants from Norway, Sweden, Denmark, and Finland, soon to be followed by large numbers of Germans and Irish. In 1850, the greatest number of foreign-born were English-speaking, but within a decade, the Germans had eclipsed them. Industrial development brought Belgians, Greeks, Hungarians, Lithuanians, Italians, and especially Poles, who continued to come steadily until the restriction of immigration in the early 1920s; in the 1930 census, Poles were the largest foreign-born group. By 1970, foreign-born residents and children of the foreign-born numbered 748,000 (17% of the total), the chief nationalities being German, Polish, and Norwegian.

Black Americans were in the region as early as 1822. Prior to World War I, however, there were no more than 3,000 blacks at any time. Migration during and after that war brought the number to 10,739 by 1930; by 1976, blacks were the largest racial minority in the state, numbering 147,000 (3% of Wisconsin's population). Most black Wisconsinites live in Milwaukee, which was nearly 15% black in 1970.

Asians are few in number: in 1970 there were 2,648 Japanese and 2,700 Chinese. A total of 1,821 Vietnamese were resettled in Wisconsin in 1975. As of 1976 there were 33,000 state residents of Hispanic origin.

Wisconsin had 18,924 American Indians of varying tribal groups and linguistic stocks according to the 1970 census. State estimates in 1978 placed the total living on reservations at 15,254, 40% of them Ojibwa; other tribes included the Menomini, Oneida, and Winnebago. There are 11 reservations, the largest being that of the Menomini. Wisconsin Indians have been involved in several protest demonstrations and succeeded in obtaining an abandoned Coast Guard station on Lake Michigan for use as an Indian center.

[8] LANGUAGES

Early French and English fur traders found in what is now Wisconsin several Indian tribes of the Algonkian family: Ojibwa along Lake Superior, Sauk in the northeast, Winnebago and Fox south of them, and Kickapoo in the southwest. Descendants of the Ojibwa and Winnebago still live in the state, 3,251 of them claiming an Indian language as their mother tongue in 1970. Numerous Indian place-names include: Antigo, Kaukauna, Kewaunee, Peshtigo, Menomonie, Oshkosh, Wausau, Waupun, and Winnebago.

Wisconsin English is almost entirely Northern, as are the areas that provided Wisconsin's first settlers—Michigan, northern Ohio, New York State, and western New England. Common are the Northern *pail, comforter* (tied and filled bedcover), *sick to the stomach, angleworm* (earthworm), *skip school* (play truant), and *dove* as the past of *dive*. Pronunciation features are *fog, frog,* and *on* with the vowel /ah/; *orange, forest,* and *foreign* with the /aw/ vowel; and *humor* as /hyumor/. Northern *fried cakes* is now yielding to *doughnuts,* and *johnnycake* is giving way to *corn bread.* Milwaukee has *sick in the stomach* and is known for the localism *bubbler* (drinking fountain). A small exception to Northern homogeneity is the cluster of South Midland terms brought by Kentucky miners to the southwestern lead-mining district, such as *dressing* (sweet sauce for a pudding), *eaves spout* as a blend of *eavestrough* with Midland *spouting, branch* for stream, *fishworm* for earthworm, and *blinds* for roller shades.

In 1970, 77% of the native-born claimed English as their mother tongue, as did 75% of the total population. First languages of major resident groups were as follows:

	NATIVE-BORN	FOREIGN-BORN
English	3,279,289	12,892
German	465,453	47,303
Polish	108,192	10,450
Italian	24,221	6,549
Spanish	24,035	4,566

[9] RELIGIONS

According to the Wisconsin Council of Churches, nearly 3.2 million state residents, about two-thirds of the population, were members of religious denominations in 1978, the largest groups being Roman Catholics and Lutherans.

The first Catholics to arrive were Jesuit missionaries seeking to convert the Huron Indians in the 17th century. Protestant settlers and missionaries of different sects, including large numbers of German Lutherans, came during the 19th century, along with Protestants from the Atlantic seaboard. Jews settled primarily in the cities: the state's first synagogue was built in Madison in 1858.

These groups often had conflicting aims. Evangelical sects favored strict blue laws (which they succeeded in retaining well into the 20th century) and temperance legislation, which was enacted in many communities. The use of Protestant prayers and the King James Bible in public schools was another source of public discord until these practices were declared unconstitutional by the state supreme court in 1890. A constitutional amendment allowing parochial school students to ride in public school buses was defeated in 1946 amid great controversy; 19 years later, however, it was enacted with little opposition. By that time, religious conflicts appeared to be on the decline.

As of 1978, the Wisconsin Council of Churches reported 1,536,360 Roman Catholics and 954,898 Lutherans, representing 49% and 30% of the state's religious membership, respectively; there were 1,582 Lutheran churches and 1,004 Catholic churches. Other Protestants included Methodists, 185,786; members of the United Church of Christ, 104,668; Baptists, 71,282; Presbyterians, 49,987; and Episcopalians, 30,830. There were an estimated 30,000 Jews, 80% of them in Milwaukee.

[10] TRANSPORTATION

Wisconsin's first rail line was built across the state, from Milwaukee to Prairie du Chien, in the 1850s. Communities soon began vying with one another to be included on proposed railroad routes. Several thousand farmers mortgaged property to buy railroad stock; the state had to rescue them from ruin when companies went bankrupt. By the late 1860s, two railroads—the Chicago and North Western and the Chicago, Milwaukee, and St. Paul—had become dominant in the state and were able to set high freight rates. However, Chicago emerged as the major rail center of the Midwest because of its proximity to eastern markets. In 1920 there were 35 railroads operating on 11,615 mi (18,693 km) of track; by 1977 there were only 15 railroads and 8,620 mi (13,873 km) of track. Passenger traffic declined from 20,188,000 to 125,000 during the same period. Freight revenues increased from $92,826,000 to $334,304,000 though tonnage declined by about 6% to 95,194,000 tons. Amtrak provides passenger service to Milwaukee, La Crosse, and several other cities.

As of 1 January 1978, Wisconsin had 106,547 mi (171,471 km) of roadway; about 57% of this mileage consisted of town roads, 30% state or county highways, 9% city streets, 3% village streets, and 1% park and forest roads. Almost 70% of the roads had all-weather surfaces. Registered vehicles included 2,239,107 automobiles and 578,004 trucks in 1978, when the state had 2,899,070 licensed drivers. A total of $254.4 million in federal and state funds was budgeted to highways and bridges in 1980/81.

The opening of the St. Lawrence Seaway in 1959 allowed oceangoing vessels access to Wisconsin via the Great Lakes, but failed to stimulate traffic to the extent anticipated. Overall, the state has 19 cargo-handling ports. The port of Superior (shared with Duluth, Minn.) on Lake Superior handled 33,419,210 tons of cargo in 1977, making it the 2d busiest of all Great Lakes ports.

At the end of 1978, Wisconsin had 349 airports, 100 of which were publicly owned. In 1979, General Mitchell Field, in Milwaukee, was served by eight major carriers and two commuter airlines; it handled 3,464,441 passenger arrivals and departures, and 57,212,710 lb of freight.

¹¹HISTORY

The region that is now Wisconsin has probably been inhabited since the end of the glacial period 10,000 years ago. Some of the earliest inhabitants were ancestors of the Menomini; these early immigrants from the north built burial mounds, conical ones at first, then large effigy mounds shaped like different animals. Other peoples arrived from the south and east, including ancestors of the Winnebago Indians (about AD 1400) and a tribe that built flat-top earthen pyramids. During the 17th century, the Ojibwa, Sauk, Fox, Potawatomi, Kickapoo, and other tribes came to Wisconsin. These tribes made their living from agriculture, hunting, and fishing, but with the arrival of Europeans the Indians became increasingly dependent on the fur trade—a dependence that had serious economic consequences when the fur trade declined in the early 19th century.

The first European believed to have reached Wisconsin was Jean Nicolet, who in 1634 landed on the shores of Green Bay while in the service of Samuel de Champlain. Two decades later, Médard Chouart des Groseilliers and Pierre Esprit Radisson, both fur traders, explored northern Wisconsin; in 1673, the Jesuit priest Jacques Marquette and the explorer Louis Jolliet crossed the whole area that is now Wisconsin, via the Fox and Wisconsin rivers, on their way to the Mississippi. Other Jesuits established missions, and French fur traders opened up posts; the French were succeeded by the British after the French and Indian War (the British ruled Wisconsin as part of Quebec Province from 1774 to 1783), and by Americans around 1816, when the US built forts at Prairie du Chien and Green Bay.

Under the Ordinance of 1787, Wisconsin became part of the Northwest Territory; it was subsequently included in the Indiana Territory, the Territory of Illinois, and then the Michigan Territory. In the early 1800s, lead mining brought an influx of white settlers. Indian resistance to white expansion collapsed after the 1832 Black Hawk War, in which Sauk and Fox Indians fleeing from Illinois were defeated and massacred by white militia near the site of present-day La Crosse, at the Battle of Bad Axe. Subsequently, the Winnebago and other tribes were removed to reservations outside the state, while the Ojibwa, Menomini, and some eastern tribes were among those resettled in reservations inside Wisconsin.

In 1836, the Wisconsin Territory was formed. Initially it included all of Iowa and Minnesota, along with a portion of the Dakotas, but in 1838, these areas became part of a newly organized Iowa Territory. The 1830s also saw the beginning of a land boom, fueled by migration of Yankees from New England and southerners who moved to the lead mining region of southwestern Wisconsin. The population and economy began to expand rapidly. Wisconsin voters endorsed statehood in 1846, and Congress passed enabling legislation that same year. After a first constitution was rejected by the voters, a revised document was adopted on 13 March 1848, and on 29 May, President James K. Polk signed the bill that made Wisconsin the 30th state.

Transportation facilities and industry did not develop as rapidly as proponents of statehood had expected. A canal was opened at the portage between the Fox and Wisconsin rivers in 1851, but the waterway was not heavily used. Railroads encountered difficulties in gaining financing, then suffered setbacks in the panic of 1857. Wisconsinites took a generally abolitionist stand, and it was in Wisconsin—at Ripon, on 28 February 1854—that the

Republican Party was formally established in the state. The new party developed an efficient political machine and later used much of its influence to benefit the railroads and lumber industry, both of which grew in importance in the decade following the Civil War. In that war more than 90,000 Wisconsin men fought on the Union side, and 12,000 died. During the late 19th century, Wisconsin was generally prosperous; dairying and food processing emerged as major industries, and Milwaukee grew into an important industrial center.

Wisconsin took a new political turn in the early 20th century, with the inauguration of Robert "Fighting Bob" La Follette as governor and the dawning of the Progressive Era. Both a Republican and an ardent reformer, La Follette fought against conservatives within his own party. In 1903, the legislature under his prodding passed a law providing for the nation's first direct statewide primary; other measures that he championed during his tenure as governor (1901–6) provided for increased taxation of railroads, regulation of lobbyists, creation of a civil service, and establishment of a railroad commission to regulate intrastate rates.

La Follette was also a conspicuous exponent of what came to be called the "Wisconsin idea": governmental reform guided by academic experts and supported by an enlightened electorate. Around the time he was governor, the philosophy of reform was energetically promoted at the University of Wisconsin (which had opened at Madison, the state capital, in 1849), and many professors were drafted to serve on government commissions and boards. In 1901, Wisconsin became the first state to establish a legislative reference bureau, intended to help lawmakers shape effective, forward-looking measures.

After La Follette left the governor's office to become a US senator, his progressivism was carried on by Republican governors James O. Davidson (1906–11) and especially Francis E. McGovern (1911–15). During one session in 1911, legislators enacted the first state income tax in the US, and one of the first workers' compensation programs. Other legislation passed during the same year sought to regulate the insurance business and the use of water power, create forest reserves, encourage farmer cooperatives, limit and require disclosure of political campaign expenditures, and establish a board of public affairs to recommend efficiency measures for state and local governments. This outburst of activity attracted national attention, and many states followed in Wisconsin's footsteps.

As US senator (1906–25), La Follette consistently opposed involvement in World War I and was one of only six senators to vote against US entry into the war; as a result, he was censured by the state legislature and the faculty of the University of Wisconsin, and there was a move to expel him from the Senate. His renomination and reelection in 1922 served to vindicate him, however, and he carried Wisconsin when he ran in 1924 for president on the national League for Progressive Political Action ticket.

After his death the following year, the reform tradition continued in Wisconsin. A pioneering old-age pension act was passed in 1925; seven years later, Wisconsin enacted the nation's first unemployment compensation act, with the encouragement of La Follette's son Philip, then serving his first term as governor. When Wisconsin went Democratic in November 1932, turning Philip out of office, he and his brother, Robert, Jr., an incumbent US senator, temporarily left the state Republican organization and in 1934 formed a separate Progressive Party; that statewide party, with the support of President Franklin Roosevelt and the Socialists, swept the 1934 elections and returned both brothers to office. During his second and third terms as governor, Philip La Follette successfully pressed for the creation of state agencies to develop electric power, arbitrate labor disputes, and set rules for fair business competition; his so-called Little New Deal corresponded to the New Deal policies of the Roosevelt administration.

After World War II, the state continued a trend toward increased urbanization, and its industries prospered. The major figure on the national scene in the postwar era was Senator Joseph R. McCarthy, who defeated Robert La Follette, Jr., in the 1946 Wisconsin Republican primary and went on to serve 10 years in the Senate. McCarthy launched an unsubstantiated attack in 1950 on alleged Communists and other subversives in the federal government. Especially after McCarthy's censure by the US Senate in 1954 and death in 1957, the Progressive tradition began to recover strength, and the liberal Democratic party grew increasingly influential in state politics. There was student unrest at the University of Wisconsin during the 1960s and early 1970s, and growing discontent among Milwaukee's black population. A major controversy in the 1970s concerned a court-ordered busing plan aimed at decreasing racial imbalances in Milwaukee's public schools.

12 STATE GOVERNMENT

Wisconsin's first constitutional convention, meeting in Madison in October 1846, was marked by controversy between conservative Whigs and allied Democrats, on the one hand, and progressive Democrats with a constituency made up of miners, farmers, and immigrants on the other. The latter, who favored the popular election of judges and exemption of homesteads from seizure for debt, among other provisions, carried the day, but this version of the constitution failed to win ratification. A second constitutional convention, convened in December 1847, agreed on a new draft, which made few major changes. This document, ratified by the electorate in 1848 and amended more than 100 times since then, remains in effect today.

The Wisconsin legislature consists of a senate with 33 members elected for four-year terms, and an assembly of 99 representatives elected for two-year terms. Legislators must be state residents for one year prior to election and residents of their districts at least 10 days before the election. Voters elect an assembly and half the senate membership in even-numbered years. Regular legislative sessions begin in January and usually last six to eight months. Each house elects its own president and other officers from among its members. Wisconsin's Legislative Reference Bureau provides extensive research assistance to legislators.

There are six elected state officers: governor and lieutenant governor (elected jointly), secretary of state, state treasurer, attorney general, and superintendent of public instruction. Since 1970, all have been elected for four-year terms. The governor and lieutenant governor must be qualified voters; there are no additional age or residency requirements. As the chief executive officer, the governor exercises his authority by his power of appointment, by presenting a budget bill and major addresses to the legislature, and by his power to veto bills and call special legislative sessions. Of 16 administrative departments in the executive branch, two—the Department of Justice and the Department of Public Instruction—are headed by the attorney general and the superintendent of public instruction, respectively. Ten departments are headed by secretaries appointed by the governor; part-time boards appoint the heads of the 4 remaining departments. There are also 19 independent agencies, of which 5 are headed by individual commissioners and 14 by commissions or boards; commissioners and board members are appointed by the governor in most cases.

A bill may be introduced in either house of the legislature, but must be passed by both houses to become law. The governor has six days (Sundays excluded) to sign or veto a measure. If the governor fails to act and the legislature is still in session, the bill automatically becomes law; if the legislature has adjourned sine die, however, the governor's failure to act has the effect of a veto. Vetoes can be overridden by a two-thirds majority of both houses. Constitutional amendments may be introduced in either house. They must be approved by a simple majority of both houses in two successive legislatures and then ratified by a majority of the electorate in a referendum.

Voters must be US citizens 18 years of age or older and must have resided in the state for at least 10 days prior to the election. The residency requirement is waived in voting for US president and vice president. Wisconsin has a statewide primary open to all without respect to party affiliation, a procedure which has been challenged legally by the national Democratic Party.

13 POLITICAL PARTIES

The Democratic Party dominated politics until the late 1850s; then, the newly founded Republicans held sway for almost 100 years. More recently, the Democrats have held a substantial edge, although a Republican governor was elected in 1978.

Wisconsin Presidential Vote by Political Parties, 1948–80

YEAR	ELECTORAL VOTE	WISCONSIN WINNER	DEMOCRAT	REPUBLICAN	PROGRESSIVE	SOCIALIST	SOCIALIST WORKERS	SOCIALIST LABOR
1948	12	*Truman (D)	647,310	590,959	25,282	12,547	—	399
1952	12	*Eisenhower (R)	622,175	979,744	2,174	1,157	1,350	770
					CONSTITUTION			
1956	12	*Eisenhower (R)	586,768	954,844	6,918	754	564	710
1960	12	Nixon (R)	830,805	895,175	—	—	1,792	1,310
1964	12	*Johnson (D)	1,050,424	638,495	—	—	1,692	1,204
1968	12	*Nixon (R)	748,804	809,997	—	—	1,222	1,338
					AMERICAN IND.	AMERICAN		
1972	11	*Nixon (R)	810,174	989,430	127,835	47,525	—	998
						SOCIALIST		LIBERTARIAN
1976	11	*Carter (D)	1,040,232	1,004,967	8,552	4,298	1,691	3,814
							CITIZENS	
1980	11	*Reagan (R)	981,584	1,088,845	1,519[1]	—	7,767	29,135

*Won US presidential election. [1]Listed as Constitution Party on Wisconsin ballot.

Jacksonian democracy was strong in Wisconsin in the early days, and until 1856, all territorial and state governors were Democrats, except for one Whig. In 1854, however, a coalition of Whigs, antislavery Democrats, and Free Soilers, meeting in Ripon, formed a Republican Party in the state—a key event in the establishment of the national Republican Party. Republicans quickly gained control of most elective offices; from 1856 to 1959 there were only three Democratic governors. The Republican Party was dominated in the late 19th century by conservatives, sympathetic to the railroads and the lumbering industry, but whose stands on pensions and jobs for Union veterans and ability to win federal funds for the state attracted support from farmers and small businessmen. Then, in the 1890s, Progressives within the party, led by Robert La Follette, began a successful battle for control that culminated in La Follette's election as governor in 1900.

The La Follette brand of progressivism remained strong in the state, although not always under the umbrella of Republicanism. In 1924, La Follette ran for president on the Progressive ticket; 10 years later, his sons Robert and Philip also broke away from the GOP, to head a Progressive Party slate. However, their newly organized national third party faded and folded when World War II made isolationism unpopular and Philip La Follette failed to be reelected governor. The Progressives rejoined the GOP in 1946.

Socialist parties have won some success in Wisconsin's political history. Socialists worked with progressive Republicans at the state level to pass important legislation in the early 20th century. In 1910, the Socialists scored two major political victories in Wisconsin: Emil Seidel was elected mayor of Milwaukee, becoming the first Socialist mayor of a major US city, and Victor Berger became the first Socialist ever elected to Congress.

There is no statewide system of registration by parties. As of 1979, Republicans controlled the governorship, but Democrats held the offices of secretary of state, state treasurer, and attorney general. Nearly 48% of Wisconsin voters cast their ballots for Ronald Reagan in the 1980 presidential election; Jimmy Carter won 43% of the vote, and John Anderson 7%. Gaylord Nelson, a liberal Democrat, lost his US Senate seat to a Republican, Robert W. Kasten, Jr., but the Democrats retained majorities in the legislature and in Wisconsin's congressional delegation.

¹⁴LOCAL GOVERNMENT

As of 31 December 1978, Wisconsin had 72 counties, 187 incorporated cities, 392 incorporated villages, 1,269 towns, 427 school districts, and 16 vocational, technical, and adult education districts. There were also 481 special districts, each providing a certain local service, such as sewerage or fire fighting, usually across municipal lines.

Each county is governed by a board of supervisors (which in the most populous counties has more than 40 members), elected for two years, except in Milwaukee County, where the term is four years. Six counties, including Milwaukee County, have elected county executives, serving four-year terms. Other county officials include district attorneys, sheriffs, clerks, treasurers, coroners, registers of deeds, and surveyors.

Towns are civil subdivisions of counties equivalent to townships in other states. Each town is a unit of 6 sq mi (16 sq km) marked off for governmental purposes. Cities and villages have home-rule powers limited by legislative review. Each incorporated village must have at least 150 residents; each incorporated city, 1,000. Most cities are governed by a mayor-council system; about 3% of all municipalities have a council-manager system, which was first authorized in Wisconsin in 1923. Executive power in a village is vested in an elected president, who presides over an elected board of trustees but has no veto power.

Wisconsin towns are generally small units; as of 1979, 82% had populations under 1,500, and 24% had fewer than 500 residents.

Each town is governed by a board of supervisors elected every two years; a town supervisor carries out policies set at an annual April town meeting.

¹⁵STATE SERVICES

In its first year of statehood, Wisconsin had only 14 paid officials and employees, including the 6 constitutional officers. By fiscal 1979, the state had nearly 54,000 full-time-equivalent employees. A 6-member Ethics Board, appointed by the governor, administers an ethics code for public officials and originates or investigates complaints against them. The board may refer cases for criminal prosecution and may hold civil hearings leading to such penalties as censure or removal from office.

The Department of Public Instruction administers public elementary and secondary education in the state, and the Board of Regents of the University of Wisconsin System has jurisdiction over all public higher education. A Board of Vocational, Technical, and Adult Education supervises programs in these areas, and an Education Communications Board oversees the state's educational radio and television networks.

The Transportation Department plans, constructs, and maintains highways and licenses motor vehicles and drivers. Physical and mental health, corrections, public assistance, children's services, and vocational rehabilitation fall within the purview of the Department of Health and Social Services. The Department of Industry, Labor, and Human Relations enforces antidiscrimination laws in employment, as well as minimum standards for wages and working conditions, provides training programs for the unemployed and disadvantaged, and sets safety standards for public buildings.

Public protection in general is provided by the Department of Justice, which is reponsible for investigating crimes of statewide magnitude and offering technical assistance to local law enforcement agencies. Regulations to protect consumers are administered and enforced by the Consumer Protection Division of the Department of Agriculture, Trade, and Consumer Protection, in cooperation with the Justice Department. The Army and Air National Guard are under the Department of Military Affairs.

The Housing Division of the Department of Local Affairs and Development offers technical and financial assistance to localities and maintains a housing data bank. The Department of Natural Resources monitors water and air quality and solid waste management; protects wildlife, fish, and forests; and maintains state parks. The Administration Department's Division of State Planning and Energy has an Energy Extension Service to furnish information and assistance to municipalities and businesses.

¹⁶JUDICIAL SYSTEM

The judicial branch is headed by a supreme court, consisting of seven justices, elected statewide on a nonpartisan basis for terms of 10 years. Only one justice may be elected on the judicial election day each April; vacancies are filled by gubernatorial appointment until an open election day becomes available. The justice with the greatest seniority serves as chief justice. The supreme court, which is the final authority on state constitutional questions, hears appeals at its own discretion and has original jurisdiction in limited areas.

The state's next highest court is the court of appeals, established by constitutional amendment in 1977. Its 12 judges (3 for each of four judicial districts) are elected by district and serve staggered six-year terms. These judges sit in panels of 3 for most cases, although some cases can be heard by a single judge. Decisions by the court of appeals may be reviewed by the supreme court.

The circuit court, the trial court of general jurisdiction, also hears appeals from municipal courts. Circuit court boundaries coincide with county boundaries, except that 3 judicial circuits comprise two counties each; thus, there are 69 judicial circuits. As of 1 January 1980 there were 190 trial judges, elected by district for six-year terms. All justices at the circuit court level or higher must have at least five years' experience as practicing attorneys in order to qualify for office.

Municipal courts have jurisdiction over local matters. Municipal judges are elected for terms of two or four years, generally serve on a part-time basis, and need not be attorneys.

A total of 181,556 criminal offenses was reported in Wisconsin during 1978, of which 175,372 were property crimes. The violent crime rate was 132 per 100,000 population in the state as a whole, 391 for the city of Milwaukee; both figures were far below the national average.

[17] ARMED FORCES

Wisconsin's principal military installation is an Air Force base at General Mitchell Field, Milwaukee, with 1,509 personnel.

A total of 3,932 Wisconsinites were killed in World War I, 7,980 in World War II, 800 in Korea, and 1,189 in Viet-Nam. An estimated 590,000 veterans were living in Wisconsin as of 30 September 1979. Of these, 15,000 saw service in World War I, 237,000 in World War II, 99,000 in the Korean conflict, and 186,000 in the Viet-Nam era. In the year ending 30 June 1978, 34,675 Wisconsin veterans received benefits exceeding $221 million.

Wisconsin's Army and Air National Guard units had 9,100 officers and enlisted men as of 30 September 1978. In 1977 there were 10,009 full-time police personnel; counties, cities, and other local governments employed 9,251 officers, or more than 92% of the total. In the year ending 30 June 1977, state and local expenditures for police amounted to $197 million.

[18] MIGRATION

Until the early 19th century, Wisconsin was inhabited mainly by Indians, some native to the area, and others arriving in waves of migration from the north, east, and south; the French and British brought few permament settlers. In the 1820s, southerners began to arrive from the lower Mississippi, and in the 1830s, easterners poured in from New York, Ohio, Pennsylvania, and New England.

Foreign immigrants began arriving in the 1820s, either directly from Europe or after temporary settlement in eastern states. Most of the early immigrants were from Ireland and England. Germans also came in large numbers, especially after the Revolution of 1848, and by 1860, they were predominant in the immigrant population, which was proportionately larger than in any other state except California. The state soon became a patchwork of ethnic communities—Germans in the counties near Lake Michigan, Norwegians in southern and western Wisconsin, Dutch in the lower Fox Valley and near Sheboygan, and other groups in other regions.

After the Civil War, and especially in the 1880s, immigration reached new heights, with Wisconsin receiving a large share of Germans and Scandinavians; the proportion of Germans declined, however, as new immigrants arrived from Finland and Russia and from southern and eastern Europe, especially Poland, prior to World War I. Despite this overseas immigration, Wisconsin suffered a net population loss from migration from 1900 to 1970, as Wisconsinites moved to other states. More recently, there has been a slight net gain, estimated at 34,000 persons for 1970–78.

Like other states, Wisconsin has become increasingly urbanized. In 1970, about three-fourths of the people lived southeast of an axis extending roughly from Green Bay through Madison to the Illinois state line. A significant trend since 1970 has been the decline in population in Milwaukee and other large cities; at the same time, suburbs have continued to grow.

[19] INTERGOVERNMENTAL COOPERATION

The legislature's Commission on Interstate Cooperation represents the state in its dealings with the Council of State Governments. Wisconsin also participates in the Education Commission of the States, Interstate Indian Commission, Great Lakes Commission, Upper Great Lakes Regional Commission, Minnesota-Wisconsin Boundary Area Commission, and the Mississippi River Parkway Commission.

In 1977/78, Wisconsin received nearly $1.2 billion in federal aid, including $53.4 million in general revenue sharing. Of the overall total, $374.7 million was channeled to local governments.

[20] ECONOMY

With the coming of the first Europeans, fur trading became a major economic activity; as more settlers arrived, agriculture prospered. Although farming—preeminently dairying—remains important, manufacturing is the mainstay of today's economy. Wisconsin's industries are diversified, with electrical and agricultural machinery and food products the leading items. Other important industries are paper and pulp products, lumber and wood products, leather goods, and fabricated metals. Economic growth has been concentrated in the southeast. There soils and climate are favorable for agriculture; a skilled labor force is available to industry; and capital, transportation, and markets are most readily accessible.

[21] INCOME

In 1978, Wisconsin ranked 25th among the 50 states in per capita income, which was $7,597, or more than double the 1970 figure. Earned income (labor and proprietors' income) in 1977 totaled $24.8 billion, of which manufacturing accounted for 35%; retail and wholesale trade, 16%; services, 14%; government, 13%; construction 6%; transportation and public utilities, 6%; farming, 6%; and other sectors, 4%. Median family income in 1975 was $15,064, 12th in the US.

On an adjusted basis (excluding transfer payments, retirement benefits, and other income not taxed by the state), per capita income in 1977 was $5,327. The highest per capita incomes were in Ozaukee and Waukesha counties (both suburbs of Milwaukee), with $7,206 and $7,003, respectively; the lowest was in Menominee County (an Indian reservation), with $712. An estimated 352,000 Wisconsinites, or less than 8% of the population, were below the federal poverty level in 1975; only three states had lower percentages that year.

[22] LABOR

As of February 1980, the civilian labor force (seasonally adjusted) amounted to 2,452,400 persons, of whom 2,329,500, or 95% were employed. Women represented 42% of the labor force as of 1978. Of all nonfarm workers, 580,100 were employed in manufacturing as of February 1980, nearly 40% of them in the Milwaukee area.

A federal census of workers covered by unemployment insurance in March 1977 revealed the following nonfarm employment pattern in Wisconsin:

	ESTABLISH-MENTS	EMPLOYEES	ANNUAL PAYROLL ('000)
Agricultural services, forestry, fishing	838	3,864	$ 44,542
Mining	202	1,942	37,955
Contract construction	10,424	60,948	1,097,543
Manufacturing, of which:	8,165	532,647	7,463,030
Food products	(1,134)	(55,500)	(785,267)
Fabricated metals	(791)	(52,495)	(750,500)
Nonelectrical machinery	(1,434)	(109,514)	(1,623,059)
Transportation, public utilities	3,755	70,841	998,729
Wholesale trade	7,821	86,052	1,140,413
Retail trade	29,034	296,550	1,846,311
Finance, insurance, real estate	8,113	83,153	900,699
Services	24,649	293,757	2,360,546
Other	888	994	11,914
TOTALS	93,889	1,430,748	$15,901,682

Among the categories of workers excluded from this survey were government employees, of whom Wisconsin had more than 312,000 in 1980. Farm employment was 199,000 in 1978.

Labor began to organize in the state after the Civil War. The Knights of St. Crispin, a shoemakers' union, grew into what was, at that time, the nation's largest union, before it collapsed during the Panic of 1873. In 1887, unions of printers, cigarmakers, and iron molders organized the Milwaukee Federated Trades Council, and in 1893, the Wisconsin State Federation of Labor was formed. A statewide union for public employees was established in 1932. As of 1976, labor union membership totaled 506,000, or 29% of all nonfarm employment. In addition, 51,000 Wisconsinites belonged to employee associations. In 1977, the state's legislature granted public employees (except public safety personnel) the right to strike, subject to certain limitations.

²³AGRICULTURE

Gross agricultural income in 1978 amounted to $3.6 billion, 8th among the 50 states; nearly $3 billion came from dairy products and livestock. The nation's leading dairy state, Wisconsin also leads the US in the production of hay, corn for silage, beets for canning, and peas and snap beans for processing. It also ranks 2d in the production of cranberries and tart cherries.

In the early years, Wisconsin developed an agricultural economy based on wheat, some of which was exported to eastern states and overseas via the port of Milwaukee. Farmers also grew barley and hops, finding a market for these products among early Milwaukee brewers. After the Civil War, soil exhaustion and the depredations of the chinch bug forced farmers to turn to other crops, including corn, oats, and hay, which could be used to feed hogs, sheep, cows, and other livestock.

Although agricultural income has continued to rise in recent years and the average size of farms has increased, farm acreage and the number of farms have declined. In 1978 there were 19 million acres (7.7 million hectares) of land, more than 54% of the total land area, distributed among 99,000 farms, a decline of 1,000 from 1977. Farmland is concentrated in the southern two-thirds of the state, especially in the southeast. Potatoes are grown mainly in central Wisconsin, cranberries in the Wisconsin Valley, and cherries in the Door Peninsula.

Leading field crops (in bushels) in 1979 were corn for grain, 306,940,000; oats, 55,860,000; soybeans, 10,030,000; wheat, 2,162,000; and barley, 1,176,000. About 12,555,000 tons of hay were harvested in 1979, and 11,760,000 tons of corn for silage in 1977. In 1978, Wisconsin farmers produced for processing 596,000 tons of sweet corn, 185,450 tons of snap beans, 146,200 tons of green peas, 95,000 tons of beets, and 58,500 tons of cucumber pickles; 870,000 barrels of cranberries and 6,100 tons of tart cherries were also harvested, along with 41,000,000 lb of commercial apples and 345,000 lb of mint for oil.

²⁴ANIMAL HUSBANDRY

Aided by the skills of immigrant cheesemakers and by the encouragement of dairymen who emigrated from New York—especially by the promotional efforts of the agriculturalist and publisher William D. Hoard—Wisconsin turned to dairying in the late 19th century. Today, Wisconsin has more milk cows than any other state and ranks 1st in the production of cheese, butter, and milk. More than one-third of the nation's cheese—and at least three-fourths of all Muenster cheese—is produced in the state. Dairy farms are prominent in nearly all regions, but especially in the Central Plains and Western Uplands. Wisconsin ranchers also raise livestock for meat production.

In 1978 there were 4,100,000 head of cattle, including 1,810,000 milk cows and heifers, along with 1,400,000 hogs and pigs; 5,714,000 chickens and 5,544,000 turkeys were on poultry farms during the same year. Cash receipts from marketings of meat animals amounted to $503.5 million in 1977, and meat products generated $366.6 million in value added by manufacture.

Dairy products account for about 60% of all cash receipts from agriculture; cash receipts from dairy products in 1977 amounted to $1.9 billion. In 1979, the state produced 1.4 billion lb of cheese, of which American cheese accounted for 926.3 million lb (1st in the US); Italian-style cheeses, 304.3 million lb (1st); brick and Muenster cheeses, 60.8 million lb; and Swiss cheese, 35.3 million lb. Wisconsin farms also yielded 22 billion lb of milk and 255.9 million lb of butter.

Cash receipts from marketings of poultry and eggs amounted to $116.8 million in 1977, when 981 million eggs were produced. During the same year, mink ranches produced 926,000 pelts of mink, more than any other state, and Wisconsin apiaries generated 9,625,000 lb of honey (5th in the US).

The Department of Agriculture, Trade, and Consumer Protection seeks to prevent and control diseases in domestic animals through field investigation, laboratory analysis, and quarantine.

²⁵FISHING

In 1978, Wisconsin ranked 22d among the 50 states in the value of its commercial fishing; 53,218,000 lb of fish were landed, at a total value of $4,186,000. During the 1977 season, sport fishermen caught an estimated 116 million fish, 90% of them bass, perch, and other panfish; trout, walleye, and northern pike made up most of the remaining 10%.

²⁶FORESTRY

Wisconsin was once about 85% forested. Although much of the forest was depleted by forest fires and wasteful lumber industry practices, vast areas reseeded naturally, and more than 820,000 acres (332,000 hectares) have been replanted. In 1977, Wisconsin had 14,908,000 acres (6,033,000 hectares) of forest (2% of the US total), covering 43% of the state's land area; two-thirds of all forestlands are privately owned. Hardwoods make up about two-thirds of the sawtimber. The most heavily forested region is in the north. The timber industry reached its peak in the late 19th century; in 1976, lumber production was estimated at 409,000,000 board feet.

Wisconsin's woods have recreational as well as commercial value. Two national forests—Chequamegon and Nicolet—located in northern Wisconsin, covered 1,466,734 acres (593,568 hectares) in 1979. The eight state forests were visited by about 3,500,000 people in 1977.

Forest management and fire control programs are directed by the Department of Natural Resources. The US Forest Service operates a Forest Products Laboratory at Madison, in cooperation with the University of Wisconsin.

²⁷MINING

When Wisconsin became a state, lead mining was an important activity in the southeast; later, for a time, there was substantial iron mining in the Gogebic Range. Today, however, mining plays only a small role in the state's economy. In 1978, Wisconsin ranked 38th among the states in the value of its mineral output, which amounted to $152 million. Chief minerals in 1978 were sand and gravel (about 30 million tons) and stone (22.3 million tons). Lead, lime, iron ore, sulfur, and zinc were also mined.

²⁸ENERGY AND POWER

The state's first hydroelectric plant was built at Appleton in 1882; many others were built later, especially along the Wisconsin River. Today, however, 95% of the state's electrical energy comes from other sources, mainly steam generating plants. Wisconsin itself has no significant coal, oil, or gas resources.

In 1978, electrical energy production totaled 38.7 billion kwh, and installed capacity was 10.2 million kw. As of 31 December 1977 there were 27 steam generating plants, accounting for 64% of the state's total installed generating capacity, and 15 gas turbine plants, accounting for 12%. The 78 hydroelectric plants accounted for less than 5%, and internal combustion plants for only 1%. The remaining 18% was attributable to four nuclear installations. In March 1980, the Dairyland Power Cooperative, citing federal regulatory pressures, announced plans to phase out its small Genoa nuclear power plant by 1990; the remaining plants are Point Beach Units 1 and 2, at Two Creeks, operated by the Wisconsin Michigan Power Co., and Kewaunee Unit 1, at Carlton, operated by the Wisconsin Public Service Corp.

²⁹INDUSTRY

As of 1976, Wisconsin ranked 11th in the nation in value added by manufacture, with $14.9 billion. Nonelectrical machinery, food products, fabricated metal products, and electrical equipment accounted for almost half of all industrial employment.

The total value added by manufacture increased to $16.8 billion in 1977. Of that total, nonelectrical machinery accounted for 22%; food products (especially beer, cheese, meat, and canned fruits and vegetables), 14%; paper and paper products, 10%; transportation equipment, 10%; fabricated metal products, 9%; electrical and electronic equipment, 9%; primary metal products, 5%; printing and publishing, 5%; chemicals and related products, 3%; and other items, 13%.

The following table shows value added by manufacture for selected industries in 1972 and 1977:

	1972	1977
Motor vehicles and equipment	$685,900,000	$1,341,000,000
Construction machinery	238,600,000	627,000,000
Farm and garden machinery	306,400,000	619,000,000
General industrial machinery	272,200,000	475,100,000
Iron and steel foundry products	214,500,000	473,100,000
Sanitary paper products	159,300,000	435,400,000
Malt beverages	NA	409,400,000
Cheese	207,100,000	369,700,000

Industrial activity is concentrated in the southeast, especially in the Milwaukee metropolitan area, which by itself accounts for about 40% of the total value added. Major corporations based in Milwaukee include Allis Chalmers and Bucyrus-Erie, manufacturers of industrial and agricultural machinery; and three of the nation's largest beer producers, Miller, Pabst, and Schlitz. Kimberley-Clark (paper and lumber products) has its headquarters in Neenah; the Parker Pen Co. is in Janesville; Oscar Mayer (meat packing and food products) is located in Madison; and Johnson (wax products) is in Racine.

³⁰COMMERCE

Wholesale trade in 1972 totaled $10.4 billion. Milwaukee County accounted for 23% of all wholesale establishments and 42% of the total trade volume.

Retail sales for 1979 amounted to $16.8 billion, compared with $14.9 billion in 1977 and $9.3 billion in 1972. Figures for 1977 show that nearly one-fourth of the retail sales volume was in Milwaukee County. Statewide, food stores accounted for 21% of the total retail sales volume; automotive dealers, 20%; department stores and other general merchandise stores, 13%; eating and drinking places, 10%; gasoline service stations, 8%; and other establishments, 28%.

The state engages in foreign as well as domestic trade through the Great Lakes ports of Superior-Duluth, Milwaukee, Green Bay, and Kenosha. Iron ore, wheat, and grain are shipped primarily from Superior-Duluth, while Milwaukee handles the heaviest volume of general merchandise. Wisconsin exported about $2.2 billion in manufactured goods (12th in the US) in 1976 and $263 million in agricultural products (27th) in 1976/77.

³¹CONSUMER PROTECTION

The Department of Agriculture, Trade, and Consumer Protection monitors food production, inspects meat, and administers grading programs; its Consumer Protection Division administers laws governing product safety and trade practices, in cooperation with the state Department of Justice. The Office of the Commissioner of Banking administers laws governing consumer credit, and the Department of Transportation investigates complaints from buyers of new and used automobiles.

³²BANKING

As of 31 December 1977 there were 1,058 commercial bank offices (including branches) in the state. Employment in banking was about 26,200 as of November 1979.

The 503 state-chartered banks and 128 federally chartered banks operating at the end of 1977 had assets totaling $21.8 billion, deposits exceeding $18.5 billion, and a combined net income of $158 million. The largest commercial bank, First Wisconsin National Bank (Milwaukee), had deposits of $2.1 billion in mid-1979. There were 118 savings and loan associations (85 state, 33 federal) as of 31 December 1977, with 2,168,838 investors and assets of nearly $9.9 billion. At the same time, Wisconsin's 663 state-chartered credit unions had assets of $1.1 billion.

The Office of the Commissioner of Banking licenses and charters banks, loan and collection companies, and currency exchanges.

³³INSURANCE

As of February 1980, an estimated 30,400 Wisconsinites were employed in the insurance industry, about 28,000 of them as insurance agents. There were 7,418,000 life insurance policies worth $58.1 billion in force in 1978; benefits paid totaled $215.7 million. The average family had $34,400 in life insurance, slightly below the US average. In 1978, automobile insurance premiums written in Wisconsin totaled $645.3 million; homeowners premiums that year reached $132.3 million.

The Office of the Commissioner of Insurance licenses insurance agents, enforces state and federal regulations, responds to consumer complaints, and develops consumer edcucation programs and literature. The office also operates the State Life Insurance Fund, which sells basic life insurance (maximum $10,000) to state residents, and the State Property Insurance Fund, which insures state-owned property, as well as county and municipal property on an optional basis.

³⁴SECURITIES

Wisconsin has no securities exchanges. However, as of 31 December 1977, member firms of the New York Stock Exchange had 81 sales offices and 503 full-time registered representatives in the state. The sale of securities is regulated by the Office of the Commissioner of Securities, which in 1976/77 registered 622 offerings having an aggregate value of $547 million. Wisconsinites reported $488 million in dividend income on their 1977 federal tax returns.

³⁵PUBLIC FINANCE

Budget estimates are prepared by departments and sent to the governor or governor-elect in the fall of each even-numbered year; the following January, the governor presents a biennial budget to the legislature, which passes a budget bill, often after many amendments.

In 1976/77, Wisconsin ranked 20th among the 50 states in state and local government revenues per capita, and 18th in expenditures per capita. The 1979–81 budget, approved by the legislature in 1979, amounted to almost $12.2 billion. Estimated revenues and expenditures were as follows (in millions):

REVENUES	1979/80	1980/81
General revenue	$3,374.4	$3,632.8
Federal revenue	1,363.6	1,429.7
Program revenue	522.1	553.1
Bond funds	166.1	—
Other receipts	559.1	566.2
TOTALS	$5,985.3	$6,181.8

EXPENDITURES		
State operations	$2,335.7	$2,312.7
Local assistance	1,764.8	1,884.7
Aid to individuals and organizations	896.0	939.6
Property tax relief and other expenses	988.8	1,044.8
TOTALS	$5,985.3	$6,181.8

Of the appropriations for 1980/81, 33% was allocated to education, 32% to human resources, 12% to environmental and natural resources, and 23% to other purposes. In 1976/77, the city of Milwaukee had general revenues of $253 million; general expenditures were $232 million.

Expenditures by state and local governments alike have risen dramatically since 1960 and now claim about one-fifth of all personal income. At one time, the state was constitutionally prohibited from borrowing money; this provision was at first circumvented by the use of private corporations, then eliminated in 1969 by constitutional amendment. As of November 1978, state indebtedness totaled $1.7 billion. The total indebtedness of state and local governments surpassed $4 billion in 1977.

[36] TAXATION

In 1976/77, state taxes amounted to $588 per capita, more than in all but five other states. The largest single source of state revenue is the income tax on individuals and corporations. Most local tax revenue comes from property taxes, and most of that goes for education.

Under legislation enacted in 1979, personal income tax rates on net taxable income ranged from 3.4% for the first $3,000 to 10% on amounts over $40,000. Beginning in 1980/81, tax brackets were to be altered annually to correspond with changes in the consumer price index, a tax-reform measure that was expected to save taxpayers $57 million in the first year alone. The general sales tax is 4%, and an inheritance tax is levied at rates ranging from 1.25% to 30%. Other state taxes include those on gasoline, cigarettes, liquor, beer, motor vehicles, insurance premiums, real estate transfers, and public utilities.

In 1976/77, total federal tax receipts from Wisconsin were $6.7 billion, or $1,454 per capita. During that same year, federal expenditures in Wisconsin were $4.8 billion or $1,044 per capita. Wisconsinites filed nearly 1.9 million federal income tax returns in 1977 and paid more than $3 billion in tax.

[37] ECONOMIC POLICY

The state seeks to promote relocation of new industries to Wisconsin, as well as expansion of existing ones, by providing advice and assistance through the Department of Business Development and some 200 local development corporations. Communities are authorized to issue tax-exempt bonds to enable industries to finance new equipment. In addition, all machinery and equipment used in production is tax-exempt under state law. Taxes on raw materials, work in progress, and finished goods inventories were to be eliminated entirely as of January 1981.

[38] HEALTH

Wisconsin has one of the best health records in the US. In 1969–71, Wisconsinites had the 8th-highest life expectancy in the nation, an average of 72.48 years—69.15 years for men, 76.04 for women. There were 14.8 live births per 1,000 population in 1977, a rate slightly below the national average. At the same time, infants had an excellent chance of survival. The infant mortality rate was 10.8 per 1,000 live births for the white population, 12% below the national average. The death rate for nonwhite infants was much higher—17.8 per 1,000—but still well under the comparable national norm.

About 16,200 legal abortions were performed in Wisconsin during 1977, a ratio of 236 abortions for every 1,000 live births. State law prohibits the use of public funds for abortions, except in cases of incest or rape or for grave health reasons. The state does provide funds for family planning counseling.

The death rate in 1977 was 8.5 per 1,000 population. Wisconsin ranked above the nation as a whole in death rates for heart disease, cerebrovascular disease, and arteriosclerosis, but below the national averages for cancer, pneumonia, diabetes, and cirrhosis of the liver, as well as for accidents and suicides. Leading causes of death in 1977 were heart disease (337.5 deaths per 100,000 population), cancer (174.9) and cerebrovascular disease (87.1).

As of 1978, Wisconsin had 171 hospitals, with 28,630 beds and an average daily patient population of 20,327. Hospital personnel totaled 66,284, including 12,397 registered nurses and 5,197 licensed practical nurses. The average cost of a hospital stay in 1977 came to $178 per day (10% below the national average). As of 31 December 1976 there were 932 resident patients in state and county mental hospitals; 273 patients were in private mental institutions at the end of 1975. Wisconsin had 530 nursing care facilities in 1976, with 47,900 resident patients.

In 1977 there were 6,984 practicing physicians; 2,654 dentists practiced professionally in 1979. Medical degrees are granted by the University of Wisconsin at Madison and by the Medical College of Wisconsin (formerly part of Marquette University), which receives state aid.

The Division of Health, a branch of the State Department of Health and Social Services, has responsibility for planning and supervising health services and facilities, enforcing state and federal regulations, administering medical assistance programs, and providing information to the public. State laws provide for generic drug substitution and require continuing physician education.

[39] SOCIAL WELFARE

Social welfare costs increased greatly during the 1970s. Federal, state, and county expenditures on the principal welfare programs in Wisconsin more than doubled between 1971/72 and 1976/77, reaching a total of $872.7 million, of which 57% came from the US government. From 1969 to 1978, aid to families with dependent children (at home or in foster homes or institutions) more than quadrupled, to a total of $267 million; over the same period, the number of recipients more than doubled, reaching 189,200 in 1978. As of 1976/77, Wisconsin ranked 10th among the 50 states in total state and local welfare expenditures (including support to welfare institutions), and ranked 8th in expenditures per capita.

Approximately 141,000 Wisconsin residents purchased food stamps in 1978, at a total federal cost of $35.3 million. Also in 1978, 524,000 pupils participated in the national school lunch program, at a federal cost of $25.3 million. A total of $1.9 billion was paid out in 1977 to some 740,800 Social Security beneficiaries, including 505,800 retirees, 154,100 survivors, and 80,900 disabled persons. The average monthly grant for retired persons was $250 (11th highest in the US). In addition, in 1978, Supplemental Security Income funds totaling $103 million were disbursed to 33,100 aged, 34,400 disabled, and 900 blind persons living in the state.

A total of $112.4 million in workers' compensation was paid during 1977. Some 23,100 persons participated in vocational rehabilitation programs in 1977/78, at an expenditure of $21.6 million. An average of 46,000 persons each week received state unemployment benefits in 1978; the average weekly amount was $94.36, 13% above the national norm.

[40] HOUSING

The 1970 census counted 1,414,000 housing units, of which 94% were occupied, in nearly two out of three cases by the owner. Better than 94% of the occupied units had full plumbing facilities. According to state estimates, roughly 10% were substandard in one or more ways, because of inadequate plumbing, improper wiring, poor heating, or deterioration through age. Rural areas had a higher proportion of deficient housing than urban areas, and substandard conditions were three times as common in units built before 1940. Overcrowding was not a serious problem; fewer than 7% of the occupied units averaged more than one resident per room. From 1976 through 1978, 114,300 new residential buildings were authorized. The total value of construction was nearly $3.5 billion.

The largest amount of public home financing is provided by the state Department of Veterans Affairs, which makes home loans to veterans. The Housing Finance Authority, created by the legislature in 1971, raises money through the sale of tax-exempt bonds and makes loans directly or indirectly to low- and moderate-income home buyers. Wisconsin's state building code, developed in 1913 to cover construction of all dwellings with three or more units, was revised in the late 1970s to cover new one- and two-family dwellings. Local housing codes prescribing standards for structural upkeep and maintenance in existing buildings were in force in all cities with populations of 50,000 or more as of 1977; about half the remaining cities and one-fourth of all villages also had housing codes during the same year.

⁴¹EDUCATION

Wisconsin has a tradition of leadership in education. The University of Wisconsin, one of the world's largest and most respected institutions of higher learning, was chartered by the state legislature in 1848. The constitution of that year also provided for free public education; however, there was no state tax for schools until 1885, and no effective compulsory attendance law until 1903. In 1911, the legislature enacted the first system of vocational, technical, and adult education in the nation.

Wisconsin's literacy rate in 1970 was 99.3%, one of the highest in the US. As of 1976, 70% of all Wisconsinites 18 years or older had completed high school, well above the US average.

In 1979/80, Wisconsin's elementary and secondary schools had a total enrollment of 1,021,106 students, of whom 857,855, or 84%, attended the state's 2,184 public schools. There were 57,383 faculty members and administrators in the public school system. Wisconsin's 923 nonpublic schools, with a total enrollment of 163,251, had a professional staff of 8,787 during the same year.

The University of Wisconsin System, which embraces all public institutions of higher learning in the state, had 147,645 students (excluding extension students) as of 1978/79, an increase of 9% since 1973/74. The University of Wisconsin at Madison, the system's largest campus, had 39,430 students as of 1978/79, of whom 26,192 were undergraduates; 47% of the undergraduates were women, but only 37% of the graduate students. The University of Wisconsin at Milwaukee, the system's 2d-largest center, had 24,818 graduate and undergraduate students as of 1978/79. Other campuses are Eau Claire, Green Bay, La Crosse, Oshkosh, Parkside (at Kenosha), Platteville, River Falls, Stevens Point, Stout (at Menomonie), Superior, and Whitewater. Also part of the University of Wisconsin System are 14 two-year centers offering courses in occupational and vocational fields (total 1978/79 enrollment, 8,337) and an Extension Division, offering agricultural and other courses (1977/78 enrollment, 199,924, mostly noncredit).

Marquette University in Milwaukee, with a graduate and undergraduate enrollment of 11,044 as of 1978/79, is the largest private institution. Other leading private colleges include Lawrence University in Appleton, Ripon College, and Beloit College. There are also three seminaries, a junior college, and five technical and professional schools, the largest of which is the Milwaukee School of Engineering, with a 1978/79 enrollment of 2,573 students.

Wisconsin also has a system of public vocational, technical, and adult education (VTAE), with a full-time-equivalent enrollment of about 52,000 in 1977/78. This system is operated by 16 separate VTAE districts, under the overall guidance of the state Board of Vocational, Technical, and Adult Education.

General public elementary and secondary education is administered by 427 local school districts, under the overall supervision of the Department of Public Instruction, which is headed by a state superintendent elected on a nonpartisan basis. The University of Wisconsin System was created under a 1971 law that merged the University of Wisconsin with the State University System, under a single Board of Regents. The Board of Regents appoints the president of the system and the chancellors of each of its 13 universities. The Wisconsin Higher Educational Aids

Board offers grants and guaranteed loans to qualified residents attending institutions within the state. The state Department of Veterans Affairs provides education grants and loans to Wisconsin veterans or to the surviving dependents of deceased veterans.

In 1977/78, total expenditures for public education in Wisconsin amounted to more than $2.7 billion. Of this amount, $1.8 billion, or 67%, was spent on public schools and their administration; another $794 million was allocated to the University of Wisconsin System; the remainder went for vocational education, communications, and other purposes. In 1976/77, Wisconsin spent $536.70 per capita on public education, placing it 16th among the 50 states. Per capita expenditures for public higher education amounted to $176.80, 9th among the 50 states.

⁴²ARTS

Wisconsin offers numerous facilities for drama, music, and other performing arts, including a three-theater Performing Arts Center in Milwaukee and the Dane County Coliseum in Madison. Milwaukee has a repertory theater, and there are many other theater groups around the state. Summer plays are performed at an unusual garden theater at Fish Creek in the Door Peninsula; there is also an annual music festival at that site.

The Pro Arte String Quartet in Madison and the Fine Arts Quartet in Milwaukee have been sponsored by the University of Wisconsin, which has also supported many other musical activities. Milwaukee is the home of the Milwaukee Symphony, of the Florentine Opera Company, and of a ballet company.

The Wisconsin Arts Board, consisting of 12 members appointed by the governor for three-year terms, aids individual artists and performing groups and assists communities in developing local arts programs. The board had a budget of $1.2 million during the 1980/81 fiscal year.

⁴³LIBRARIES AND MUSEUMS

In 1978, the state had about 350 public libraries, with a total of 11.7 million volumes. The Milwaukee Public Library, founded in 1878, maintains 12 branches and had more than 2 million bound volumes as of 1978; the Madison Public Library had 9 branches and more than 500,000 volumes. The largest academic library is that of the University of Wisconsin at Madison, with nearly 3.4 million bound volumes and 1.6 million microfilm units as of the same year. The best-known special library is that of the State Historical Society of Wisconsin at Madison, with about 200,000 books and 300,000 governmental publications and documents.

Wisconsin has some 145 museums and historical sites. The State Historical Society maintains a historical museum in Madison and other historical sites and museums around the state. The Milwaukee Public Museum contains collections on history, natural history, and art. The Milwaukee Art Center, founded in 1888, a major museum of the visual arts, emphasizes European works of the 17th to 19th centuries. The Madison Art Center, founded in 1901, has European, Japanese, Mexican, and American paintings and sculpture, as well as 17th-century Flemish tapestries. The Charles Allis Art Library in Milwaukee, founded in 1947, houses collections of Chinese porcelains, French antiques, and 19th-century American landscape paintings. Other leading art museums include the Elvehjem Museum of Art in Madison and the Theodore Lyman Wright Art Center at Beloit College.

The Circus World Museum at Baraboo occupies the site of the original Ringling Brothers Circus. Other museums of special interest include the Dard Hunter Paper Museum (Appleton), the National Railroad Museum (Green Bay), and the Green Bay Packer Hall of Fame. More than 500 species of animals are on exhibit at the Milwaukee County Zoological Park. Historical sites in Wisconsin include Villa Louis, a fur trader's mansion at Prairie du Chien; the Old Wade House in Greenbush; Old World Wisconsin, an outdoor ethnic museum near Eagle; Pendarvis, focusing on lead mining at Mineral Point; and the Taliesin estate of architect Frank Lloyd Wright, in Spring Green.

[44]COMMUNICATIONS

Nearly 800 post offices and more than 12,000 postal employees provide mail service to Wisconsin. As of 31 December 1978 there were 3,393,369 operating telephones, 2,524,884 residential and 868,485 business. Virtually all Wisconsin households had telephone service. In 1979 there were more than 200 commercial radio stations and 30 educational stations, including 9 operated by the Educational Communications Board (ECB) and 12 by the state Board of Regents. The state also had 18 commercial television stations, 5 of them based in Milwaukee, and 8 educational television stations, including 4 operated by the ECB and 1 by the University of Wisconsin (Madison). Seventy-nine cable television systems served 177,895 subscribers in 79 communities.

[45]PRESS

The state's first newspaper was the *Green Bay Intelligencer*, founded in 1833. Some early papers were put out by rival land speculators who used them to promote their interests; among these was the *Milwaukee Sentinel*, launched in 1837 and a major daily newspaper today. As immigrants poured in from Europe in succeeding decades, German, Norwegian, Polish, Yiddish, and Finnish papers sprang up. Wisconsin journalism has a tradition of political involvement. The *Milwaukee Leader*, founded as a Socialist daily by Victor Berger in 1911, was denied the use of the US mails because it printed antiwar articles; the *Madison Capital Times*, still important today, also started as an antiwar paper. Founded in 1882 by Lucius Nieman, the *Milwaukee Journal* won a Pulitzer Prize in 1919 for distinguished public service and remains the state's largest-selling and most influential newspaper.

In 1978, Wisconsin had 4 morning papers with a combined circulation of 258,300, 32 evening papers with 971,142, and 8 Sunday papers with 899,841. The following table shows leading dailies with their average 1978 circulations:

AREA	NAME	DAILY	SUNDAY
Green Bay	Press-Gazette (e,S)	56,461	69,120
Madison	Wisconsin State Journal (m,S)	73,413	122,851
Milwaukee	Capital Times (e)	34,581	
	Journal (e,S)	328,968	533,626
	Sentinel (m)	165,205	

As of 1979 there were also 23 semiweekly newspapers, 266 weeklies, and 1 biweekly, as well as 183 periodicals directed to a wide variety of special interests. Among the largest are *Hoard's Dairyman*, founded by William D. Hoard in 1870, with a paid semimonthly circulation of 223,100; *Model Railroader*, monthly, 178,819; *The Woman Bowler*, monthly, 150,000; *Bowling Magazine*, monthly, 140,000; *Coin Prices*, bimonthly, 106,980; *Coins*, monthly, 94,423; and *Old Cars*, biweekly, 92,000. *The Progressive*, a monthly published in Madison, helps carry on the Wisconsin liberal tradition. Other notable periodicals are the *Wisconsin Magazine of History*, published quarterly by the state historical society, and *Wisconsin Trails*, another quarterly, also published in Madison.

[46]ORGANIZATIONS

There are well over 500 statewide organizations, ranging from the State Bar Association and the Wisconsin Archaeological Society to the Wisconsin Orchid Society, the Wisconsin Association of Ex-Smokers, and the Wisconsin Association of Magicians. The State Historical Society of Wisconsin, founded in 1846, is one of the largest organizations of its kind; it has a museum, library, and research collections in Madison and is a prominent publisher of historical articles and books. The Forest Products Research Society, in Madison, has an international membership of about 5,000.

Other national organizations based in Wisconsin include the American Bowling Congress, American Society of Agronomy, Conservation Education Association, Crop Science Society of America, Experimental Aircraft Association, International Press Institute, Master Brewers Association of the Americas, Model Railroad Industry Association, National Funeral Directors Association, Outdoor Writers Association of America, Wilderness Watch, and World Council of Credit Unions.

[47]TOURISM, TRAVEL, AND RECREATION

An estimated 9.5 million tourists visited or passed through Wisconsin in 1977. Out-of-state tourists spent some $2.4 billion in the state in 1976; at the same time, Wisconsinites themselves made ample use of the state's scenic attractions and outdoor recreational opportunities. In addition to the famous Wisconsin Dells gorge, visitors are attracted to the Cave of the Mounds at Blue Mounds, the sandstone cliffs along the Mississippi River, and the rocky Lake Michigan shoreline of the Door Peninsula. Several areas in southern and northwestern Wisconsin, preserved by the state as the Ice Age National Scientific Reserve, still exhibit drumlins, moraines, and unusual geological formations.

There are three national parks in Wisconsin: Apostle Islands National Lakeshore, on Lake Superior, and the St. Croix and the Lower St. Croix scenic riverways. There are 55 state parks, covering 57,943 acres (23,449 hectares); 233 mi (375 km) of state park trails; 8 state forests; and some 5,200 campsites. The state also has 6 million acres (2.4 million hectares) of hunting land and 9,236 mi (14,865 km) of well-stocked trout streams. More than 8 million people visited the state parks in 1977, and some 116,000 hiked along the trails. During the same year, the state issued 337,114 deer hunting licenses, 214,709 licenses for small game, and 566,155 nonresident and annual resident fishing licenses; the state also registered 408,440 boats and 241,772 snowmobiles. The development of the snowmobile, in particular, has transformed the state into a major center for winter sports.

During 1979/80 there was an increase in jobs in some segments of the tourist industry. The $28-million Hyatt Regency Hotel, in Milwaukee, was the first downtown hotel to be built in that city in more than a decade.

[48]SPORTS

Wisconsin has professional teams in football, basketball, and baseball. The National Football League's Green Bay Packers, who play their home games in both Green Bay and Milwaukee, won five league championships and the first two Super Bowls during the 1960s under coach Vince Lombardi. Basketball fans follow the Milwaukee Bucks, who, led by Kareem Abdul-Jabbar (then known as Lew Alcindor), were National Basketball Association champions in 1970/71. In baseball, the Milwaukee Brewers play at Milwaukee County Stadium. Milwaukee is also the site of the annual Miller High Life Open in professional bowling, and of the Milwaukee Open in professional golf.

The University of Wisconsin Badgers compete in the Big Ten Conference. Basketball teams from Marquette University, in Milwaukee, won the NCAA Division I title in 1977 and the National Invitation Tournament championship in 1970.

[49]FAMOUS WISCONSINITES

Wisconsinites who have won prominence as federal judicial or executive officers include Jeremiah Rusk (b.Ohio, 1830–93), a Wisconsin governor selected as the first head of the Agriculture Department in 1889; William F. Vilas (b.Vermont, 1840–1908), who fathered rural free delivery as postmaster general under Grover Cleveland; Melvin Laird (b.Nebraska, 1922), a Wisconsin congressman who served as secretary of defense during the Viet-Nam era, 1969–73; and William Rehnquist (b.1924), named to the Supreme Court in 1971.

The state's best-known political figures achieved nationwide reputations as members of the US Senate. John C. Spooner (b.Indiana, 1843–1919) won distinction as one of the inner circle of Senate conservatives before he retired in 1907 amid an upsurge of Progressivism within his party. Robert La Follette (1855–1925) embodied the new wave of Republican Progressivism—and, later, isolationism—as governor and in the Senate.

His sons Robert, Jr. (1895–1953), and Philip (1897–1965) carried on the Progressive tradition as US senator and governor, respectively. Joseph R. McCarthy (1908–57) won attention in the Senate and throughout the nation for his anti-Communist crusade, using methods that gave a new term—McCarthyism—to the English language and led to his censure by the Senate in 1954. William Proxmire (b.Illinois, 1915), a Democrat, succeeded McCarthy in the Senate and eventually became chairman of the powerful Senate Banking Committee. Representative Henry S. Reuss (b.1912), also a Democrat, has served in the House since 1955 and is chairman of the Banking Committee. Democrat Clement Zablocki (b.1912), first elected to the House in 1948, is chairman of the Foreign Affairs Committee. Victor L. Berger (b.Transylvania, 1860–1929), a founder of the Social-Democratic Party, was first elected to the House in 1910; during World War I, he was denied his seat and prosecuted because of his antiwar views.

Besides the La Follettes, other governors who made notable contributions to the state include James D. Doty (b.New York, 1799–1865), who fought to make Wisconsin a separate territory and became the territory's second governor; William D. Hoard (b.New York, 1836–1918), a tireless promoter of dairy farming, both as private citizen and chief executive; James O. Davidson (b.Norway, 1854–1922), who attempted to improve relations between conservatives and progressives; Francis E. McGovern (1866–1946), who pushed through the legislature significant social and economic reform legislation; and Walter J. Kohler (1875–1940), an industrialist who, as governor, greatly expanded the power of the office.

Prominent figures in the state's early history include the Jesuit Jacques Marquette (b.France, 1637–75) and the explorer Louis Jolliet (b.Canada, 1645–1700) and the Sauk Indian leader Black Hawk (b.Illinois, 1767–1838), who was defeated in the Battle of Bad Axe. John Bascom (b.New York, 1827–1911) was an early president of the University of Wisconsin. Charles Van Hise (1857–1918), a later president, promoted the use of academic experts as government advisers; and John R. Commons (b.Ohio, 1862–1945), an economist at the university, drafted major state legislation. Philetus Sawyer (b.Vermont, 1816–1900), a prosperous lumberman and US senator, led the state Republican Party for 15 years, before Progressives won control. Carl Schurz (b.Germany, 1829–1906) was a prominent Republican Party figure in the years immediately before the Civil War. Lucius W. Nieman (1857–1935) founded the *Milwaukee Journal*, and Edward P. Allis (b.New York, 1824–89) was an important iron industrialist and state political figure.

Wisconsin was the birthplace of several Nobel Prize scientists, including Herbert S. Gasser (1888–1963), who shared a 1944 Nobel Prize for research into nerve impulses; William P. Murphy (b.1892), who shared a 1934 prize for research relating to anemia; and John Bardeen (b.1908), who shared the physics award in 1956 for his contribution to the development of the transistor. Stephen Babcock (b.New York, 1843–1931) was an agricultural chemist who did research important to the dairy industry. In addition, Wisconsin was the birthplace of the child psychologist Arnold Gesell (1880–1961) and of naturalist and explorer Chapman Andrews (1884–1960). John Muir (b.Scotland, 1838–1914), another noted naturalist and explorer, lived in Wisconsin in his youth. Conservationist Aldo Leopold (1887–1948) taught at the University of Wisconsin and wrote *A Sand County Almanac* while living there.

Frederick Jackson Turner (1861–1932), historian of the American frontier, was born in Wisconsin, as were the economist and social theorist Thorstein Veblen (1857–1929), and the diplomat and historian George F. Kennan (b.1904). Famous journalists include news commentator H. V. Kaltenborn (1878–1965), award-winning sports columnist Red Smith (Walter Wellesley Smith, b.1905), and television newsman Tom Snyder (b.1936).

Thornton Wilder (1897–1975), a novelist and playwright best known for *The Bridge of San Luis Rey* (1927), *Our Town* (1938), and *The Skin of Our Teeth* (1942), each of which won a Pulitzer Prize, heads the list of literary figures born in the state. Hamlin Garland (1860–1940), a novelist and essayist, was also a native, as were the sentimental poet Ella Wheeler Wilcox (1850–1919) and the novelist and playwright Zona Gale (1874–1938). The novelist Edna Ferber (b.Michigan, 1887–1968) spent much of her early life in the state.

Wisconsin is the birthplace of architect Frank Lloyd Wright (1869–1959) and the site of his famous Taliesin estate (Spring Green), Johnson Wax Co. headquarters (Racine), and First Unitarian Church (Madison). The artist Georgia O'Keeffe (b.1887) was born in Sun Prairie. Wisconsin natives who have distinguished themselves in the performing arts include Alfred Lunt (1893–1977), Frederic March (Frederic Bickel, b.1897–1975), Spencer Tracy (1900–1967), Agnes Moorehead (1906–74), and Orson Welles (b.1915). Magician and escape artist Harry Houdini (Ehrich Weiss, b.Hungary, 1874–1926) was raised in the state, and piano stylist Liberace (Wlad Ziu Valentino Liberace, b.1919) was born there. Speed skater Eric Heiden (b.1958), a five-time Olympic gold medalist in 1980, is another Wisconsin native.

50 BIBLIOGRAPHY

Current, Richard N. *The History of Wisconsin. Vol. 2: The Civil War Era, 1848–73*. Madison: State Historical Society of Wisconsin, 1976.

Current, Richard N. *Wisconsin: A Bicentennial History*. New York: Norton, 1976.

Curti, Merle, and Vernon Carstensen. *The University of Wisconsin: A History, 1848–1925*. 2 vols. Madison: University of Wisconsin Press, 1949.

Dictionary of Wisconsin Biography. Madison: State Historical Society of Wisconsin, 1960.

Epstein, Leon D. *Politics in Wisconsin*. Madison: University of Wisconsin Press, 1958.

Federal Writers' Project. *Wisconsin: A Guide to the Badger State*. Rev. ed. New York: Hastings House, 1954.

Gara, Larry. *A Short History of Wisconsin*. Madison: State Historical Society of Wisconsin, 1962.

Margulies, Herbert F. *The Decline of the Progressive Movement in Wisconsin, 1890–1920*. Madison: State Historical Society of Wisconsin, 1968.

Martin, Lawrence. *The Physical Geography of Wisconsin*. Madison: Wisconsin Geological and Natural History Survey, 1916.

Nesbit, Robert C. *Wisconsin: A History*. Madison: University of Wisconsin Press, 1973.

Ritzenthaler, Robert E. *Prehistoric Indians of Wisconsin*. Milwaukee: Milwaukee Public Museum, 1953.

Smith, Alice E. *The History of Wisconsin. Vol. 1: From Exploration to Statehood*. Madison: State Historical Society of Wisconsin, 1973.

Still, Bayrd. *Milwaukee: The History of a City*. Madison: State Historical Society of Wisconsin, 1948.

Thelen, David P. *Robert M. La Follette and the Insurgent Spirit*. Boston: Little, Brown, 1976.

Wisconsin, State of. Department of Administration. *1979-1981 Biennial Budget, Summary of Appropriations*. Madison, n.d.

Wisconsin, State of. Department of Administration. *Wisconsin Statistical Abstract,* 4th ed. Madison, 1979.

Wisconsin, State of. Legislative Reference Bureau. *1979–80 Blue Book*. Madison, 1979.

WYOMING

State of Wyoming

ORIGIN OF STATE NAME: Derived from the Delaware Indian words *maugh-wau-wa-ma*, meaning "large plains." **NICKNAME:** The Equality State. **CAPITAL:** Cheyenne. **ENTERED UNION:** 10 July 1890 (44th). **SONG:** "Wyoming." **MOTTO:** Equal Rights. **FLAG:** A blue field with a white inner border and a red outer border (symbolizing, respectively, the sky, purity, and the Indians) surrounds a bison with the state seal branded on its side. **OFFICIAL SEAL:** A female figure holding the banner "Equal Rights" stands on a pedestal between pillars topped by lamps symbolizing the light of knowledge; two male figures flank the pillars, on which are draped banners that proclaim "Livestock," "Grain," "Mines," and "Oil." At the bottom is a shield with an eagle, star, and Roman numerals XLIV, flanked by the dates 1869 and 1890. The whole is surrounded by the words "Great Seal of the State of Wyoming." **BIRD:** Meadowlark. **FLOWER:** Indian paintbrush. **TREE:** Cottonwood. **GEM:** Jade. **LEGAL HOLIDAYS:** New Year's Day, 1 January; Presidents' Day, 3d Monday in February; Memorial Day, last Monday in May; Independence Day, 4 July; Labor Day, 1st Monday in September; Columbus Day, 2d Monday in October; Election Day, 1st Tuesday after 1st Monday in November in even-numbered years; Veterans Day, 11 November; Thanksgiving Day, 4th Thursday in November; Christmas Day, 25 December. **TIME:** 5 A.M. MST = noon GMT.

¹LOCATION, SIZE, AND EXTENT

Located in the Rocky Mountain region of the northwestern US, Wyoming ranks 9th in size among the 50 states.

The total area of Wyoming is 97,914 sq mi (253,597 sq km), of which land comprises 97,203 sq mi (251,756 sq km) and inland water 711 sq mi (1,841 sq km). Shaped like a rectangle, Wyoming has a maximum E-W extension of 365 mi (587 km); its extreme distance N-S is 265 mi (426 km).

Wyoming is bordered on the N by Montana; on the E by South Dakota and Nebraska; on the S by Colorado and Utah; and on the W by Utah, Idaho, and Montana. The boundary length of Wyoming totals 1,269 mi (2,042 km). The state's geographic center lies in Fremont County, 58 mi (93 km) ENE of Lander.

²TOPOGRAPHY

The eastern third of Wyoming forms part of the Great Plains; the remainder belongs to the Rocky Mountains. Much of western Wyoming constitutes a special geomorphic province known as the Wyoming Basin. It represents a westward extension of the Great Plains into the Rocky Mountains, separating the Middle and Southern Rockies. Extending diagonally across the state from northwest to south is the Continental Divide, which separates the generally eastward-flowing drainage system of North America from the westward-flowing drainage of the Pacific states, Wyoming is thus an important watershed.

Wyoming's mean elevation is 6,700 feet (2,042 meters), 2d only to Colorado's among the 50 states. Gannett Peak, in western Wyoming, at 13,804 feet (4,207 meters), is the highest point in the state. With the notable exception of the Black Hills in the northeast, the eastern portion of Wyoming is generally much lower. The lowest point in the state—3,100 feet (945 meters)—occurs in the northeast, on the Belle Fourche River.

Wyoming's largest lake—Yellowstone—lies in the heart of Yellowstone National Park. In Grand Teton National Park to the south are two smaller lakes, Jackson and Jenny. All but one of Wyoming's major rivers originate within its boundaries and flow into neighboring states. The Green River flows into Utah; the Yellowstone, Big Horn, and Powder rivers into Montana; the Snake River into Idaho; the Belle Fourche and Cheyenne rivers into South Dakota; and the Niobrara River into Nebraska. The

lone exception, the North Platte River, enters Wyoming from Colorado and eventually exits into Nebraska.

³CLIMATE

Wyoming is generally semiarid, with local desert conditions. Normal daily temperatures in Cheyenne range from 15°F (–9°C) to 38°F (3°C) in January and 55°F (13°C) to 84°F (29°C) in July. The record low temperature, –63°F (–53°C) was set 9 February 1933 at Moran; the record high 114°F (46°C), 12 July 1900 at Basin. Normal precipitation is 15 in (38 cm) a year, most of that falling between March and September; the snowfall in Cheyenne averages 51 in (130 cm) annually.

⁴FLORA AND FAUNA

Wyoming has more than 2,000 species of ferns, conifers, and flowering plants. Prairie grasses dominate the eastern third of the state; desert shrubs, primarily sagebrush, cover the Great Basin in the west. Rocky Mountain forests consist largely of pine, spruce, and fir. Above the tree line, low-growing herbaceous species comprise the alpine flora.

The mule deer is the most abundant game mammal; others include the white-tailed deer, pronghorn antelope, elk, and moose. Wild turkey, bobwhite quail, and several grouse species are leading game birds; more than 50 species of nongame birds also inhabit Wyoming all year long. Some 80 species of fish are found, of which rainbow trout is the favorite game fish. Classified as protected are the black-footed ferret, fisher, lynx, otter, pika, and wolverine.

⁵ENVIRONMENTAL PROTECTION

The Environmental Quality Council, a 7-member board appointed by the governor, hears and decides all cases arising under the regulations of the Department of Environmental Quality. The department also embraces three 5-member advisory boards, for air, land, and water quality, respectively. The 10-member Conservation Commission administers 38 soil and water conservation districts. Conservation of scarce water resources and preservation of air quality are the state's main environmental concerns.

⁶POPULATION

Wyoming ranks 49th in the US in both population and population density; only Alaska is more sparsely populated. In 1870, when it was a territory, Wyoming had only 9,118 people. The

1970 census population was 332,416; by 1980, according to preliminary census results, Wyoming had 468,954 residents, an increase of 41%, largely from migration. The population density in 1980 was 5 per sq mi (2 per sq km). Leading cities that year were Casper, 50,704; Cheyenne, 47,207; and Laramie, 24,339.

[7] ETHNIC GROUPS

There are about 5,000 Indians in Wyoming. The largest tribe is the Arapaho, numbering more than 2,000. Wind River is the state's only reservation; tribal lands covered 1,791,000 acres (725,000 hectares) in 1978.

About 3,000 black Americans live in Wyoming, and some 1,000 Asian-Pacific peoples, about half of whom are Japanese-Americans. In 1970, 11% of the population was first- and second-generation of European descent, the largest groups being German and British.

[8] LANGUAGES

Some place-names—Oshoto, Shoshoni, Cheyenne, Uinta—reflect early contacts with regional Indians. In 1970, the first language of 34% of Wyoming's Shoshoni and Arapaho on reservations was an Indian tongue.

Some terms common in Wyoming, like *comforter* (tied quilt) and *angleworm* (earthworm), evidence the Northern dialect of early settlers from New York State and New England, but generally Wyoming English is North Midland with some South Midland mixture, especially along the Nebraska border. Geography has changed the meaning of *hole*, *basin*, *meadow*, and *park* to signify mountain openings.

English in 1970 was the first language of 86% of the native-born and 84% of all Wyoming residents. Major resident groups indicated these first languages:

	NATIVE-BORN	FOREIGN-BORN
English	278,610	1,548
Spanish	12,408	857
German	9,124	1,406
Italian	1,591	319
Indian languages	1,307	—

[9] RELIGIONS

Wyoming's churchgoing population is preponderantly Protestant. There were 112,281 known adherents of Christian denominations (excluding Roman Catholics) in 1971. The largest denominations were Mormon, with 28,954 members; United Methodist, 16,283; Episcopal, 12,569; and United Presbyterian, 11,263. The state's Roman Catholic population was about 50,000 in 1979, when Wyoming also had an estimated 310 Jews.

[10] TRANSPORTATION

Wyoming is served chiefly by the Burlington Northern, Chicago and Northwestern, Colorado and Southern, Colorado and Wyoming, and Union Pacific railroads. The total trackage in 1974 was 1,780 mi (2,865 km). Rural and urban roads, totaling 34,511 mi (55,540 km) in 1978, cross the state. An estimated 424,000 registered motor vehicles were operated by 319,049 licensed drivers in that year.

There were about 1,176 general aircraft based in Wyoming in 1977, 3,204 licensed pilots (1978), and 94 public and private airports (1978).

[11] HISTORY

The first human inhabitants of what is now Wyoming probably arrived about 11,500 BC. The forebears of these early Americans had most likely come by way of the Bering Strait and then worked their way south. Sites of mammoth kills south of Rawlins and near Powell suggest that the area was well populated. Artifacts from the period beginning in 500 BC include, high in the Big Horn Mountains of northern Wyoming, the Medicine Wheel monument, a circle of stones some 75 feet (23 meters) in diameter with 28 "spokes" that were apparently used to mark the seasons.

The first Europeans to visit Wyoming were French Canadian traders. The Vérendrye brothers, François and Louis-Joseph,

probably reached the Big Horn Mountains in 1743; nothing came of their travels, however. The first effective discovery of Wyoming was made by an American fur trader, John Colter, earlier a member of the Lewis and Clark expedition. In 1806–7, Colter traversed much of the northwestern part of the state, probably crossing what is now Yellowstone Park, and came back to report on the natural wonders of the area. After Colter, trappers and fur traders crisscrossed Wyoming. By 1840, the major rivers and mountains were named, and the general topography of the region was well documented.

Between 1840 and 1867, thousands of Americans crossed Wyoming on the Oregon Trail, bound for Oregon or California. Migration began as a trickle, but with the discovery of gold in California in 1848, the trickle became a flood. In 1849 alone it is estimated that more than 22,000 forty-niners passed through the state via the Oregon Trail. Fort Laramie in the east and Fort Bridger in the west were the best-known supply points; between the two forts, immigrants encountered Independence Rock, Devil's Gate, Split Rock, and South Pass, all landmarks on the Oregon Trail. Although thousands of Americans crossed Wyoming during this period, very few stayed in this harsh region.

The event that brought population as well as territorial status to Wyoming was the coming of the Union Pacific Railroad. Railroad towns such as Cheyenne, Laramie, Rawlins, Rock Springs, and Evanston sprang up as the transcontinental railroad leapfrogged across the region in 1867 and 1868; in the latter year, Wyoming was organized as a territory. The first territorial legislature distinguished itself in 1869 by passing a women's suffrage act, the first state or territory to do so. Wyoming quickly acquired the nickname "the Equality State."

In the 1870s, Wyoming became a center for cattlemen and foreign investors who hoped to make a fortune from free grass and the high price of cattle. Thousands of Texas longhorn cattle were driven to the southeastern quarter of the territory. In time, blooded cattle, particularly Hereford, were introduced. As cattle "barons" dominated both the rangeland and state politics, the small rancher and cowboy found it difficult to go into the ranching business. However, overgrazing, low cattle prices, and the dry summer of 1886 and harsh winter of 1886/87 all proved disastrous to the speculators. The struggle between the large landowners and small ranchers culminated in the so-called Johnson County War of 1891–92, in which the large landowners were arrested by federal troops after attempting to take the law into their own hands.

Wyoming became a state in 1890, but growth remained slow. Attempts at farming proved unsuccessful in this high, arid region, and Wyoming to this day remains a sparsely settled ranching state. What growth has occurred has been primarily through the minerals industry, especially the development of coal, oil, and natural-gas resources during the 1970s. Since World War II, uranium and trona (carbonate of soda) mining have also become important. Nevertheless, ranching continues to dominate the state's political and social outlook.

[12] STATE GOVERNMENT

Wyoming's state constitution was approved by the voters in November 1889 and accepted by Congress in 1890.

The legislature consists of a 30-member senate and a 62-member house of representatives. Senators are elected to staggered four-year terms. The entire house of representatives is elected every two years for a two-year term.

Heading the executive branch are five elected officials: the governor, secretary of state, auditor, treasurer, and superintendent of public instruction. Each serves a four-year term and, under Wyoming's cabinet form of government, each is also a member of seven state boards and commissions.

Voters must be US citizens, at least 18 years of age, and have been registered for at least 30 days before the election.

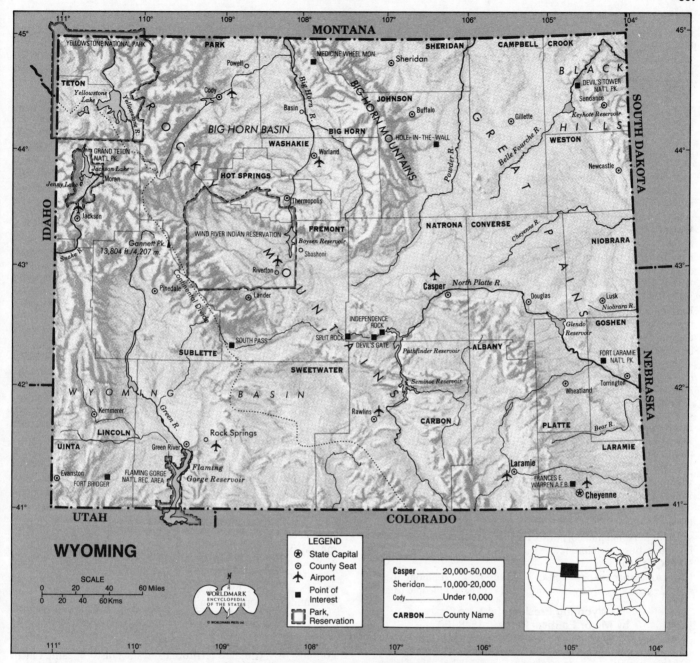

WYOMING

SCALE

| 0 | 20 | 40 | 60 Miles |
| 0 | 20 | 40 | 60 Kms |

WORLDMARK
ENCYCLOPEDIA
OF THE STATES
© WORLDMARK PRESS Ltd.

LEGEND
⊛ State Capital
⊙ County Seat
✈ Airport
■ Point of Interest
▢ Park, Reservation

Casper	20,000-50,000
Sheridan	10,000-20,000
Cody	Under 10,000
CARBON	County Name

See US political: front cover E2; physical: back cover E2.
LOCATION: 41° to 45° N; 104°03′ to 111°03′ W. **BOUNDARIES**: Montana line, 384 mi (618 km); South Dakota line, 137 mi (221 km); Nebraska line, 140 mi (225 km); Colorado line, 260 mi (418 km); Utah line 174 mi (280 km); Idaho line 174 mi (280 km).

[13] POLITICAL PARTIES

Except for the New Deal period during the 1930s and the national Democratic landslide of 1964, state government in Wyoming has been solidly in Republican hands. In the 90 years from 1890 to 1980, Republicans controlled the state senate for 84 years and the house of representatives 74 years. Wyoming is one of the very few states in which registered Republicans outnumber Democrats.

[14] LOCAL GOVERNMENT

Wyoming is subdivided into 23 counties, 90 municipalities, 55 school districts, and 217 special districts.

Each county has a clerk, treasurer, assessor, sheriff, attorney, coroner, a district court clerk, three commissioners, and from one to five county judges or justices of the peace.

[15] STATE SERVICES

The Board of Education has primary responsibility for educational services in Wyoming. Transportation services are provided by the Highway Commission; health and welfare matters fall under the jurisdiction of the Department of Health and Social Services. Among the many state agencies concerned with natural resources are the Department of Environmental Quality, Conservation Commission, Energy Conservation Committee, Land Use Commission, Oil and Gas Conservation Commission, and Water Development Commission. The Department of Labor and Statistics has primary responsibility for labor services in the state.

[16] JUDICIAL SYSTEM

Wyoming's judicial branch consists of a supreme court with a chief justice and 4 other justices, 9 district courts with 15 judges, and county judges and justices of the peace. Supreme court justices are appointed by the governor but must stand for retention at the next general election; once elected, they serve eight-year terms. District court judges are chosen in a similar manner, but serve six-year terms.

[17] ARMED FORCES

Wyoming has only one US military installation—the Francis E. Warren Air Force Base at Cheyenne, which had 4,171 personnel in 1978.

There were about 45,000 military veterans living in Wyoming in 1979. Of these, 1,000 were veterans of World War I, 20,000 of World War II, 7,000 of the Korean conflict, and 14,000 of the Viet-Nam era. Veterans' benefits were $48.9 million in 1977/78.

During 1978, some 2,200 persons were members of the National Guard; funding totaled $11.6 million. There were 1,175 state and local police in 1977.

[18] MIGRATION

Many people have passed through Wyoming, but relatively few have come to stay. Not until the 1970s, a time of rapid economic development, did the picture change. Between 1970 and 1977, Wyoming gained a net total of 48,000 residents through migration.

[19] INTERGOVERNMENTAL COOPERATION

Emblematic of Wyoming's concern for water resources is the fact that it belongs to seven compacts with neighboring states concerning the Bear, Belle Fourche, Colorado, Snake, Upper Niobrara, and Yellowstone rivers.

Wyoming has also joined the Interstate Oil and Gas Compact, the Western Interstate Energy Compact, and numerous other multistate bodies, including the Council of State Governments.

Federal aid in 1978/79 totaled $242,518,000, of which $12,589,000 was general revenue sharing.

[20] ECONOMY

The economic life of Wyoming is largely sustained by agriculture—chiefly feed grains and livestock—and mining, including petroleum and gas production. Unlike many western states, Wyoming did not enjoy any significant mining boom during the 19th century. But mining and petroleum production mushroomed during the 1970s, leading to a powerful upsurge in population. Unemployment is low, per capita income is high, and the absence of personal and corporate income taxes has helped foster a favorable business climate.

[21] INCOME

In personal income per capita, Wyoming ranks 2d among the 50 states, exceeded only by Alaska. In 1978, personal income totaled

Wyoming Presidential Vote by Major Political Parties, 1948–80

YEAR	ELECTORAL VOTE	WYOMING WINNER	DEMOCRAT	REPUBLICAN
1948	3	*Truman (D)	52,354	47,947
1952	3	*Eisenhower (R)	47,934	81,049
1956	3	*Eisenhower (R)	49,554	74,573
1960	3	Nixon (R)	63,331	77,451
1964	3	*Johnson (D)	80,718	61,998
1968	3	*Nixon (R)	45,173	70,927
1972	3	*Nixon (R)	44,358	100,464
1976	3	Ford (R)	62,239	92,717
1980	3	*Reagan (R)	49,427	110,700

*Won US presidential election.

$3.9 billion, or $9,096 per capita, more than double the 1970 figure and 16% above the US average. Wyoming's high per capita income is as much the result of its low population density as of its new mineral wealth; its income of $40,000 per sq mi ($15,500 per sq km) ranked 48th in the US in 1978. In 1975, 7% of Wyoming families had incomes below the federal poverty level.

[22] LABOR

In 1979, Wyoming's civilian labor force exceeded 230,000, compared with 208,000 in 1978. Of the 1978 total, about 88,000 held white-collar jobs, 69,000 were blue-collar workers, 27,000 were in service industries, 17,000 others worked on farms and ranches, and 7,000 were officially listed as unemployed.

A federal census of workers covered by unemployment insurance in March 1977 revealed the following nonfarm employment pattern in Wyoming:

	ESTABLISH-MENTS	EMPLOYEES	ANNUAL PAYROLL ('000)
Agricultural services, forestry, fishing	87	297	$2,313
Mining, of which:	646	21,221	385,042
Oil, gas extraction	(508)	(9,737)	(162,308)
Contract construction	1,583	10,673	150,474
Manufacturing	449	8,997	116,922
Transportation, public utilities	614	9,585	133,658
Wholesale trade	825	6,008	75,835
Retail trade	3,249	27,397	183,112
Finance, insurance, real estate	863	5,905	59,642
Services	3,182	20,601	153,087
Other	177	211	2,989
TOTALS	11,675	110,895	$1,263,074

In 1976, 25,000 employees belonged to labor unions, representing 16% of the working force in that year; 21,000 members were in unions affiliated with the AFL-CIO.

[23] AGRICULTURE

Agriculture—especially livestock and grain—is one of Wyoming's most important industries. In 1979, Wyoming had about 7,200 farms and ranches covering 35 million acres (14 million hectares). The state's average of 4,875 acres (1,973 hectares) per farm ranked 3d in the US. The value of the lands and buildings of Wyoming's farms and ranches in 1979 was nearly $4.2 billion. Total farm marketings in 1978 amounted to $527 million (37th in the US). Of this, livestock and animal products accounted for $447 million; crops, $80 million.

Field crops in 1979 (in bushels) included barley, 8,460,000; wheat, 6,354,000; corn for grain, 2,523,000; and oats, 2,024,000.

[24] ANIMAL HUSBANDRY

For most of Wyoming's territorial and state history, cattle ranchers have dominated the economy even though the livestock industry is not large by national standards (Wyoming's income from livestock marketings ranked 34th in 1978). At the end of 1979, Wyoming had 1,340,000 head of cattle, 1,050,000 sheep and lambs, and 32,000 hogs and pigs. During 1979, Wyoming produced 11,243,000 lb of red meat. Other livestock products in 1979 were milk, 117,000,000 lb, and eggs, 12,300,000. Estimated wool production in 1978 was 10,317,000 lb.

[25] FISHING

There is no important commercial fishing in Wyoming. Fishing is largely recreational, and fish hatcheries and fish planting programs keep the streams well stocked.

[26] FORESTRY

Wyoming had 10,028,000 acres (4,058,000 hectares) of forested land, equal to 16% of the state's land area, in 1977. Of this, 4,334,000 acres (1,754,000 hectares) were usable as commercial timberland. National forest system lands in the state covered 9,252,000 acres (3,744,000 hectares) in 1978.

27 MINING
The minerals industry expanded enormously during the 1970s. Total employment in mining has increased more than threefold since 1965, reaching 12,749 persons in 1977.

In order of value, petroleum, coal, natural gas, sodium compounds (especially trona), and uranium are the most important mineral products. In 1978, the total value of Wyoming's mineral output came to almost $2.6 billion (10th in the US).

Mineral production (excluding fossil fuels) in 1978 included uranium, 8,401,000 lb; sand and gravel, 5,200,000 tons; clays, 3,316,000 tons; stone, 2,822,000 tons; and sulfur, 58,000 tons. About 10,200,000 tons of trona and 3,000,000 tons of bentonite (a moisture-absorbing mineral) were mined in 1977.

28 ENERGY AND POWER
In 1977 there were 27 electrical generating plants in Wyoming, with a total installed capacity of about 3,297,000 kw. In 1978, 19.4 billion kwh of power were produced, 95% of that by private utilities.

Wyoming has extensive deposits of petroleum, natural gas, and coal. In 1978, Wyoming's proved petroleum reserves were estimated to be 804,567,000 barrels; crude oil production totaled 130,878,000 barrels. Natural gas reserves were 4.3 trillion cu feet; estimated production was 362.5 billion cu feet. Wyoming's coal mines yielded 58,328,000 tons of bituminous coal during the same year.

29 INDUSTRY
Although manufacturing increased markedly in Wyoming from 1972 to 1977—value added by manufacture jumped 165%, from $143.9 million to $380.7 million—it remains insignificant by national standards.

The following table shows value added by manufacturing for major sectors in 1972 and 1977:

	1972	1977
Petroleum, coal products	$53,000,000	$138,700,000
Chemicals, chemical products	NA	63,800,000
Stone, clay, glass products	21,700,000	51,200,000
Food, food products	19,400,000	32,400,000
Sawmills, planing mills	11,400,000	27,300,000

30 COMMERCE
Sales in wholesale trade were about $700 million in 1972. Retailers sold goods worth $1.7 billion in 1977. Of that total, automotive dealers and gasoline service stations accounted for 34%; food stores, 19%; general merchandise stores, 8%; and other retailers, 39%.

31 CONSUMER PROTECTION
The Consumer Protection Division of the Attorney General's Office handles consumer complaints.

32 BANKING
In 1978, Wyoming had 88 insured commercial banks with total assets of $2.7 billion. They had $1.5 billion in time deposits, $895 million in demand deposits, and $942 million in outstanding loans.

In 1977 there were 13 savings and loan associations with assets of $617 million. Their saving capital came to $515 million; outstanding mortgage loans, $522 million.

33 INSURANCE
There were about 615,000 life insurance policies in force in Wyoming during 1978; their total value was 5.4 billion. The average amount of life insurance per family was $34,400. Benefit payments in 1978 totaled $47.5 million.

In 1978, $149.6 million in liability insurance premiums were written in the state, $73 million in automobile insurance and $14.8 million in homeowners insurance.

34 SECURITIES
New York Stock Exchange member firms had 10 sales offices and 28 full-time registered representatives in the state in 1978. Wyomingites declared $52.5 million in dividend income on their 1977 federal tax returns. Wyoming has no securities exchanges.

35 PUBLIC FINANCE
Wyoming's biennial budget is prepared by the governor and submitted to the legislature at the beginning of each even-numbered calendar year. The fiscal year is 1 July–30 June.

Consolidated expenditures recommended by the governor for the 1980/82 biennium totaled nearly $1.4 billion, toward which federal funds were expected to contribute 24%. The following is a summary of general estimated revenues and recommended expenditures for 1980/82 (in millions):

REVENUES	
Sales and use taxes	$299.9
Mineral severance tax	91.5
Other current receipts	98.6
TOTAL	$490.0

EXPENDITURES	
University of Wyoming	$107.1
Other education	71.9
Hospitals, health, social services	117.6
General government	78.2
Other current expenses	132.4
TOTAL	$507.2

State and local government debt in 1977 totaled $466 million, or $1,148 per capita, slightly below the US average.

36 TAXATION
In 1978, the state government collected a total of $289 million in taxes. Sales and gross receipts tax revenues alone came to $164 million during the same period; excise taxes amounted to $3 million. There is no state personal or corporate income tax. The state retail sales tax is 3%.

Wyoming residents filed 174,853 federal income tax returns and paid $348,388,000 in taxes in 1977.

37 ECONOMIC POLICY
State policy in Wyoming has traditionally favored fiscal and social conservatism. A pro-business climate has generally prevailed: not until 1969, for example, was the minerals industry compelled to pay a severance tax on the wealth it was extracting from Wyoming soils. During the 1970s, the state government seemed increasingly aware of environmental problems (especially the lack of water) posed by economic growth.

38 HEALTH
Average life expectancy in Wyoming for 1969–71 was 70.29 years (35th among the 50 states), 66.19 for men and 75.19 for women. In 1977, however, the state's death rate—7.5 per 1,000 population—was below the national average. The death rates for heart disease, cancer, and cerebrovascular diseases were well below the national norm, but accidental deaths were 79% above it.

In 1978, Wyoming's 31 hospitals, with 2,529 beds, cared for an average of 1,592 patients daily. Hospital personnel included 951 registered nurses and 334 licensed practical nurses. In 1977, the state had a total of 466 licensed physicians; there were 216 dentists active in 1979.

39 SOCIAL WELFARE
In 1978, some 5,900 Wyoming residents received about $6 million in aid to families with dependent children. Medicaid exceeded $9 million, and federal Supplementary Security Income payments were $2.5 million. In 1977, 47,900 Social Security recipients were paid $119.9 million.

About $8 million in unemployment insurance benefits were awarded to Wyoming residents in 1978. Workers' compensation payments totaled $8.1 million in 1977.

40 HOUSING
The 1970 census counted 114,000 housing units in Wyoming, of which 66% were owner-occupied and 96% had full plumbing; both percentages exceeded the US average. Wyoming authorized 5,100 new housing units in 1978.

[41] EDUCATION

Wyoming's illiteracy rate in 1970 was 0.6%, one of the lowest in the US. More than 75% of all adults in the state were high school graduates in 1976.

In 1979/80, Wyoming had 390 public schools: 253 elementary, 133 secondary, and 4 especially for the handicapped. Student enrollment was 95,468, and teaching and nonteaching staff members totaled 14,129. School expenditures per capita in 1978 were $500 (3d in the US).

In the fall of 1978, 20,032 full- and part-time students were enrolled in Wyoming's higher educational institutions. The state controls and funds the University of Wyoming and seven community colleges. There are no private colleges or universities, although the National Outdoor Leadership School, based in Lander, offers courses in mountaineering and ecology.

[42] ARTS

The Wyoming Council on the Arts, consisting of 10 members appointed by the governor to three-year terms, funds local activities and organizations in the visual and performing arts, including painting, music, theater, and dance.

[43] LIBRARIES AND MUSEUMS

Wyoming was served by 23 county public library systems, with more than 1.4 million volumes, in 1977/78. Public library circulation exceeded 2.6 million during the same period. The University of Wyoming, in Laramie, had 626,282 volumes.

There are at least 39 museums and historical sites, including the Wyoming State Art Gallery and Wyoming State Museum in Cheyenne; the Buffalo Bill Historical Center (Cody), which exhibits paintings by Frederic Remington; and the anthropological, geological, and art museums of the University of Wyoming at Laramie.

[44] COMMUNICATIONS

In 1978 there were 346,548 telephones in Wyoming, of which 244,631 were residential and 101,917 business; 95% of homes in the state had telephone service.

In 1979, Wyoming had 42 radio stations, 30 AM and 12 FM, plus 4 commercial television stations. Twenty-eight cable television systems served 80,943 subscribers in 50 communities in 1978.

[45] PRESS

There are relatively few newspapers in Wyoming—only 10 dailies and 3 Sunday papers in 1978, with circulations of 93,752 and 62,307, respectively. The major dailies and their 1978 circulations were as follows:

AREA	NAME	DAILY	SUNDAY
Casper	Star-Tribune (m, S)	33,100	35,360
Cheyenne	Eagle (m, S)	8,148 }	19,762
	State Tribune (e, S)	11,824 }	

[46] ORGANIZATIONS

The Environmental Research Institute, with headquarters in Moose, is one of the very few national organizations located in Wyoming. Many national bodies have branches in the state.

[47] TOURISM, TRAVEL, AND RECREATION

There are two national parks in Wyoming—Yellowstone and Grand Teton—and nine state parks. Devils Tower and Fossil Butte are national monuments, and Fort Laramie is a national historic site. In 1976, they received more than 6.5 million visitors.

Yellowstone National Park, covering 2,219,823 acres (898,334 hectares), mostly in the northwestern corner of the state, is the oldest (1872) and largest national park in the US. The park features some 3,000 geysers and hot springs, including the celebrated Old Faithful. Just to the south of Yellowstone is Grand Teton National Park, 310,516 acres (125,662 hectares). Adjacent to Grand Teton is the National Elk Refuge, the feeding range of the continent's largest known herd of elk. Devils Tower, a rock formation in the northeast, looming 5,117 feet (1,560 meters) high, is the oldest national monument (1906).

Hunting and fishing are important recreational industries in Wyoming. In 1978, licenses were sold to 216,503 hunters and 294,902 fishermen.

[48] SPORTS

Sports in Wyoming are typically western. Skills developed by ranch hands in herding cattle are featured at rodeos held in Cheyenne.

Wyoming has no major professional sports teams. The University of Wyoming competes in the Western Athletic Conference; the Cowboys won conference titles in football during 1966–68 and shared the title in 1976.

[49] FAMOUS WYOMINGITES

The most important federal officeholder from Wyoming was Willis Van Devanter (b.Indiana, 1859–1941), who served on the US Supreme Court from 1910 to 1937. Known as a capable, conservative justice, he was often at odds with President Franklin Delano Roosevelt's New Deal legislation.

Many of Wyoming's better-known individuals are associated with the frontier. John Colter (b.Virginia, 1775?–1813), a fur trader, was the first white man to explore northwestern Wyoming. Jim Bridger (b.Virginia, 1804–81), perhaps the most famous fur trapper in the West, centered his activites in Wyoming. Late in life, William F. "Buffalo Bill" Cody (b.Iowa, 1846–1917) settled in the Big Horn Basin and established the town of Cody. A number of outlaws made their headquarters in Wyoming. The most famous were "Butch Cassidy" (Robert Leroy Parker, b.Utah, 1866–1908) and the "Sundance Kid" (Harry Longabaugh, birthplace in dispute, 1863?–1908), who, as members of the Wild Bunch, could often be found there.

Two Wyoming women, Esther Morris (b.New York, 1814–1902) and Nellie Tayloe Ross (b.Missouri, 1880–1979), are recognized as the first woman judge and the first woman governor, respectively, in the US; Ross also was the first woman to serve as director of the US Mint. Few Wyoming politicians have received national recognition, but Francis E. Warren (b.Massachusetts, 1844–1929), the state's first governor, served 37 years in the US Senate and came to wield considerable influence and power. Thurman Arnold (1891–1969) never was elected to a major office, but did gain a national reputation as a New Deal aide.

Without question, Wyoming's most famous businessman was James Cash Penney (b.Missouri, 1875–1971). Penney established his first "Golden Rule" store in Kemmerer and eventually built a chain of department stores nationwide. The water-reclamation accomplishments of Elwood Mead (b.Indiana, 1858–1936) and the botanical work of Aven Nelson (b.Iowa, 1859–1952) were highly significant. Jackson Pollock (1912–56), born in Cody, was a leading painter in the abstract expressionist movement.

[50] BIBLIOGRAPHY

Athearn, Robert G. *Union Pacific Country*. New York: Rand McNally, 1971.

Gressley, Gene M. *Bankers and Cattlemen*. New York: Knopf, 1966.

Larson, T. A. *History of Wyoming*. 2d ed., rev. Lincoln: University of Nebraska Press, 1978.

Larson, T. A. *Wyoming: A Bicentennial History*. New York: Norton, 1977.

Lavender, David. *Westward Vision: The Story of the Oregon Trail*. New York: McGraw-Hill, 1963.

Smith, Helen Huntington. *The War on Powder River*. New York: McGraw-Hill, 1966.

Woods, L. Milton, *The Wyoming Country Before Statehood*. Worland, Wyo.: Worland Press, 1971.

Wyoming. Department of Administration and Fiscal Control. Division of Research and Statistics. *Wyoming Data Handbook 1977*. 4th ed. Cheyenne, 1977.

Wyoming. Secretary of State. *1979 Wyoming Official Directory*. Cheyenne, 1979.

DISTRICT OF COLUMBIA

ORIGIN OF NAME: From "Columbia," a name commonly applied to the US in the late 18th century, ultimately deriving from Christopher Columbus. **BECAME US CAPITAL**: 1 December 1800. **MOTTO**: *Justitia omnibus* (Justice for all). **FLAG**: The flag, based on George Washington's coat of arms, consists of three red stars above two horizontal red stripes on a white field. **OFFICIAL SEAL**: In the background, the Potomac River separates the District of Columbia from the Virginia shore, over which the sun is rising. In the foreground, Justice, holding a wreath and a tablet with the word "Constitution," stands beside a statue of George Washington. To her left is the Capitol; to her right, an eagle and various agricultural products. Below is the District motto and the date 1871; above are the words "District of Columbia." **BIRD**: Wood thrush. **FLOWER**: American beauty rose. **TREE**: Scarlet oak. **LEGAL HOLIDAYS**: New Year's Day, 1 January; Martin Luther King's Birthday, 15 January; Washington's Birthday, 3d Monday in February; Memorial Day, last Monday in May; Independence Day, 4 July; Labor Day, 1st Monday in September; Columbus Day, 2d Monday in October; Veterans Day, 11 November; Thanksgiving Day, 4th Thursday in November; Christmas Day 25 December. **TIME**: 7 A.M. EST = noon GMT.

¹LOCATION, SIZE, AND EXTENT
Located in the South Atlantic region of the US, the District of Columbia has a total area of 67 sq mi (174 sq km), of which land takes up 61 sq mi (158 sq km) and inland water 6 sq mi (16 sq km). The District is bounded on the N, E, and S by Maryland, and on the W by the Virginia shore of the Potomac River. The total boundary length is 37 mi (59 km).

For statistical purposes, the District of Columbia (coextensive since 1890 with the city of Washington, D.C.) is considered part of the Washington, D.C., metropolitan area, which also embraces Charles, Montgomery, and Prince Georges counties in Maryland and Arlington, Fairfax, Loudoun, and Prince William counties in Virginia, along with several other Virginia jurisdictions, notably the city of Alexandria. The Greater Washington region comprises all these areas plus additional segments of Maryland, Virginia, and West Virginia.

²TOPOGRAPHY
The District of Columbia, an enclave of western Maryland, lies wholly within the Atlantic Coastal Plain. The major topographical features are the Potomac River and its adjacent marshlands; the Anacostia River, edged by reclaimed flatlands to the south and east; Rock Creek, wending its way from the northwestern plateau to the Potomac; and the gentle hills of the north. The District's highest point is in the northwest, at Tenleytown: 410 feet (125 meters). The average elevation is about 150 feet (46 meters); the low point is the Potomac, only 1 foot (30 cm) above sea level.

³CLIMATE
The climate of the nation's capital is characterized by chilly, damp winters and hot, humid summers. The normal daily mean temperature is 57°F (14°C), ranging from 36°F (2°C) in January to 79°F (26°C) in July. The record low, –15°F (–26°C), was set on 11 February 1899; the all-time high, 106°F (41°C), on 20 July 1930. Precipitation averages 39 in (99 cm) yearly; snowfall, 16 in (41 cm). The average annual relative humidity is 73% at 7 A.M. and 52% at 1 P.M.

⁴FLORA AND FAUNA
Although most of its original flora has been obliterated by urbanization, the District has long been known for its beautiful parks, and about 1,800 varieties of flowering plants and 250 shrubs and trees now grow there. Boulevards are shaded by stately sycamores, pin and red oaks, American lindens, and black walnut trees. Famous among the introduced species are the Japanese cherry trees around the Tidal Basin. Magnolia, dogwood, and gingko are also characteristic. The District's fauna is less exotic, with squirrels, cottontails, English sparrows, and starlings predominating.

⁵ENVIRONMENTAL PROTECTION
The Department of Environmental Services oversees air and noise pollution control, radiological health, food and milk sanitation, and beautification, among other programs.

⁶POPULATION
The District of Columbia outranked 10 states in population in 1970, with a census total of 756,510; preliminary results from the 1980 census showed a decline of 16% to 635,185, yielding a population density of 10,413 per sq mi (4,020 per sq km). Considered as a city, the District ranked 13th among the major US population centers in 1977. Even as the capital's population has declined, the number of Washington, D.C., metropolitan area residents has been increasing, from 2,109,000 in 1960 to 2,910,000 in 1970 and an estimated 3,017,000 in 1978 (8th in the US). The District's population is 100% urban and extremely mobile; only 32.4% of all residents have lived in Washington, D.C., for their entire lives.

⁷ETHNIC GROUPS
Black Americans have long been the largest ethnic group in the District of Columbia, accounting for 72% of the population in 1976, by far the highest such percentage in any major US city. Blacks comprise about 25% of the metropolitan area population, a proportion that has been relatively constant for more than 200 years. Ethnic minorities in 1970 included 2,582 Chinese, 1,662 Filipinos, 651 Japanese, and 956 American Indians. Contributing to Washington's ethnic diversity are the many foreign-born temporary or semipermanent residents attached to foreign embassies and missions.

Between 1970 and 1977, the population of groups other than white and black tripled within the Greater Washington area. Southeast Asians made up a significant proportion of the immigrants, as did Central and South Americans.

⁸LANGUAGES
In 1970, 81% of all District of Columbia residents and 86% of the native-born population claimed English as their mother tongue. Dialectically, the Washington, D.C., area is extremely heterogeneous. Speakers of principal first languages were as follows:

	NATIVE-BORN	FOREIGN-BORN
English	605,534	7,126
Spanish	6,053	5,937
German	5,471	2,631
French	4,733	2,644
Italian	2,934	1,715
Yiddish	3,820	994

[9] RELIGIONS

As of 1 January 1979, the Greater Washington area had 397,213 Roman Catholics; the District of Columbia alone had 95,508 Roman Catholics in 1971. There were 144,771 known adherents of Protestant groups in 1971, the leading denominations being Episcopal, 27,159; Southern Baptist Convention, 26,889; United Methodist, 24,835; and American Baptist Convention, 23,167. Data on some predominantly black Protestant groups were unavailable. The Jewish population in 1979 was estimated as 40,000 in the District and 160,000 in the Greater Washington area. Washington's resident foreign population includes followers of numerous other religions.

[10] TRANSPORTATION

Union Station, located north of the Capitol, is the District's one rail terminal, from which Amtrak provides passenger service to the northeast corridor and southern points. The Washington Metropolitan Area Transit Authority, or Metro, operates bus and subway transportation within the city and its Maryland and Virginia suburbs; 34 mi (55 km) of subway lines were in use by 1980, when US President Jimmy Carter signed a bill authorizing $1.7 billion as the federal contribution for completion of the 101-mi (163-km) system by the end of the decade.

Within the District as of 1978 were 1,101 mi (1,772 km) of streets and roads, including 89 mi (143 km) of streets in federal parks; 243,814 motor vehicles were registered, and 349,049 driver's licenses were in force. Three major airports handle the District's commercial air trafic: Washington National Airport, Dulles International Airport, and Baltimore-Washington International Airport. Of these, Washington National was the busiest airfield in 1978/79, handling 351,485 aircraft takeoffs and landings.

[11] HISTORY

Algonkian-speakers were living in what is now the District of Columbia when Englishmen founded the Jamestown, Va., settlement in 1607. The first white man known to have set foot in the Washington area was the English fur trader Henry Fleete, who in 1622 was captured by the Indians and held there for several years. Originally part of Maryland Colony, the region had been carved up into plantations by the latter half of the 17th century.

After the US Constitution (1787) provided that a tract of land be reserved for the seat of the federal government, both Maryland and Virginia offered parcels for that purpose; on 16 July 1790, Congress authorized George Washington to choose a site not more than 10 mi (16 km) square along the Potomac River. President Washington made his selection in January 1791 and then appointed Andrew Ellicott to survey the area and employed Pierre Charles L'Enfant, a French military engineer who had served in the Continental Army, to draw up plans for the federal city. L'Enfant's masterful design called for a wide roadway (now called Pennsylvania Avenue) connecting the Capitol with the President's House (Executive Mansion, now commonly called the White House) a mile away, and for other widely separated public buildings with spacious vistas. However, L'Enfant was late in completing the engraved plan of his design, and he also had difficulty in working with the three commissioners who had been appointed to direct a territorial survey; for these and other reasons, L'Enfant was dismissed and Ellicott carried out the plans. Construction was delayed by lack of adequate financing, and only one wing of the Capitol was completed and the President's House was still under construction when President John Adams and some 125 government officials moved into the Dis-

trict in 1800. Congress met there for the first time on 17 November, and the District officially became the nation's capital on 1 December. On 3 May 1802, the city of Washington was incorporated (the District also included other local entities), with an elected council and a mayor appointed by the president.

Construction proceeded slowly, while the city's population grew to about 24,000 by 1810. In August 1814, during the War of 1812, British forces invaded and burned the Capitol, the President's House, and other public buildings. These were rebuilt within five years, but for a long time Washington remained a rude, rough city. In 1842, English author Charles Dickens described it as a "monument raised to a deceased project," consisting of "spacious avenues that begin in nothing and lead nowhere." At the request of its residents, the Virginia portion was retroceded in 1846, thus confining the federal district to the eastern shore. The Civil War brought a large influx of Union soldiers, workers, and escaped slaves, and the District's population rose sharply from 75,080 in 1860 to 131,700 by the end of the decade, spurring the development of modern Washington.

In 1871, Congress created a territorial form of government; this territorial government was abolished three years later because of alleged local extravagances, and in 1878, a new form of government was established, headed by three commissioners appointed by the president. During the same decade, Congress barred District residents from voting in national elections or even for their own local officials. In the 1890s, Rock Creek Park and Potomac Park were established, and during the early 1900s, city planners began to rebuild the monumental core of Washington in harmony with L'Enfant's original design. The New Deal period brought a rise in the status of public employment, substantial growth of federal facilities, and the beginnings of large-scale public housing construction and slum clearance. After World War II, redevelopment efforts concentrated on demolishing slums in the city's southwest section. The White House was completely renovated in the late 1940s, and a huge building program coincided with the expansion of the federal bureaucracy during the 1960s.

Because it is the residence of the president, Washington, D.C., has always been noted for its public events, in particular the Presidential Inauguration and Inaugural Ball. The District has also been the site of many historic demonstrations, such as the appearance of Coxey's Army—some 300 unemployed workers—in 1894 and the massive March on Washington by civil rights demonstrators in 1963.

In recent years, the District's form of government has undergone significant changes. The 23d Amendment to the US Constitution, ratified on 3 April 1961, permits residents to vote in presidential elections, and beginning in 1971, the District was allowed to send a delegate to the US House of Representatives.

[12] DISTRICT GOVERNMENT

The District of Columbia is the seat of the federal government and houses the principal organs of the legislative, executive, and judicial branches. The District of Columbia committees of the US Senate and House of Representatives oversee affairs within Washington, D.C., though since the mid-1970s their jurisdiction has been limited. The District elects a delegate to the US House who participates in discussions and votes on bills within the District of Columbia Committee but may not vote on measures on the floor of the House. In 1978, Congress approved a constitutional amendment granting the district two US senators and at least one representative; to become law, the amendment requires the approval of 38 state legislatures by 1985.

[13] POLITICAL PARTIES

Washington, D.C., is the headquarters of the Democratic and Republican parties, the nation's major political organizations. The District itself is overwhelmingly Democratic: in 1978, out of 250,750 registered voters, 197,275 were Democrats, 21,169 were

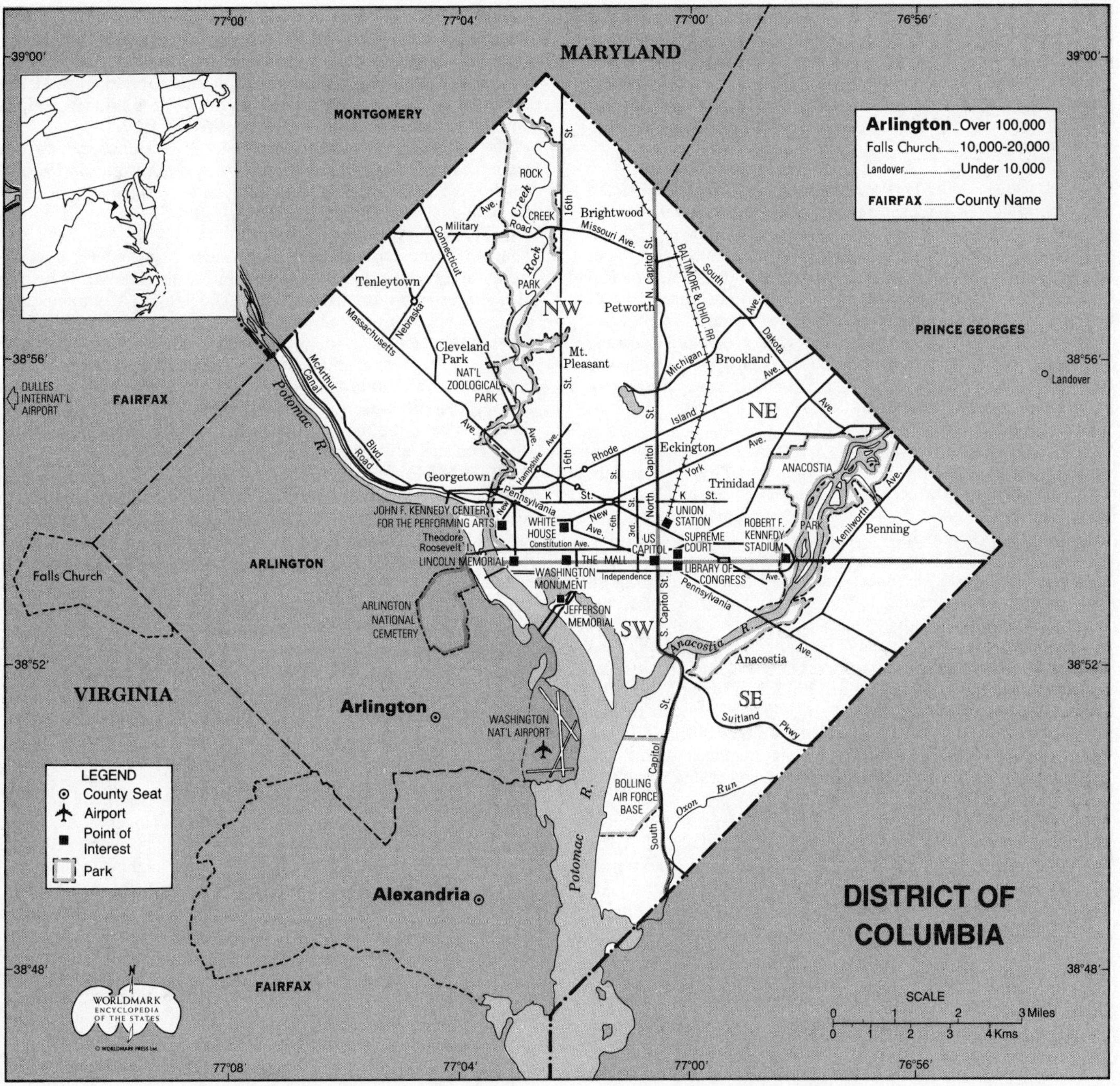
77°08′
77°04′
77°00′
76°56′
39°00′
38°56′
38°52′
38°48′
MARYLAND
MONTGOMERY
PRINCE GEORGES
FAIRFAX
ARLINGTON
VIRGINIA
Arlington
Alexandria
Falls Church
Landover
DULLES INTERNAT'L AIRPORT
Arlington Over 100,000
Falls Church 10,000-20,000
Landover Under 10,000
FAIRFAX County Name
NW
NE
SW
SE
ROCK CREEK PARK
Brightwood
Tenleytown
Petworth
Cleveland Park
NAT'L ZOOLOGICAL PARK
Mt. Pleasant
Brookland
Georgetown
Eckington
Trinidad
ANACOSTIA PARK
Benning
Anacostia
JOHN F. KENNEDY CENTER FOR THE PERFORMING ARTS
WHITE HOUSE
Theodore Roosevelt I.
LINCOLN MEMORIAL
THE MALL
WASHINGTON MONUMENT
JEFFERSON MEMORIAL
UNION STATION
SUPREME COURT
US CAPITOL
LIBRARY OF CONGRESS
ROBERT F. KENNEDY STADIUM
ARLINGTON NATIONAL CEMETERY
WASHINGTON NAT'L AIRPORT
BOLLING AIR FORCE BASE
Potomac R.
Anacostia R.
Oxon Run
BALTIMORE & OHIO RR
Military
Connecticut
Massachusetts
Nebraska
Missouri Ave.
Michigan
Rhode Island Ave.
New Hampshire Ave.
Pennsylvania
New York
Constitution Ave.
Independence Ave.
Suitland Pkwy
Kenilworth Ave.
McArthur Blvd.
Canal Road
16th St.
N. Capitol St.
S. Capitol St.
South Capitol St.
North Capitol St.
South Dakota Ave.
LEGEND
County Seat
Airport
Point of Interest
Park
WORLDMARK ENCYCLOPEDIA OF THE STATES
© WORLDMARK PRESS Ltd.
DISTRICT OF COLUMBIA
SCALE
0 1 2 3 Miles
0 1 2 3 4 Kms

See US political: front cover L3; US physical: back cover L3.

LOCATION: 38°47′ to 38°60′N; 76°55′ to 77°07′W. **BOUNDARIES**: Maryland line, 25 mi (40 km); Virginia line, 12 mi (19 km).

D.C. Presidential Vote by Major Parties, 1964–80

YEAR	ELECTORAL VOTE	D.C. WINNER	DEMOCRAT	REPUBLICAN
1964	3	*Johnson (D)	169,796	28,801
1968	3	Humphrey (D)	139,566	31,012
1972	3	McGovern (D)	127,627	35,226
1976	3	*Carter (D)	137,818	27,873
1980	3	Carter (D)	124,376	21,765

*Won US presidential election.

Republicans, 29,179 were independents, 1,876 were affiliated with the D.C. Statehood Party, and 1,251 were members of other groups. Residents of the District, permitted to vote for president since 1964, have unfailingly cast their ballots for the Democratic nominee. Democrats also dominate in local politics.

14 LOCAL GOVERNMENT

Local government in the District of Columbia operates under authority delegated by Congress. In 1973, for the first time in more than a century, Congress provided the District with a home-rule charter, allowing Washington, D.C., residents to elect their own mayor and a city council of 13 members, all serving four-year terms. Residents of the District approved the charter on 7 May 1974, and a new elected government took office the following year.

The mayor is the District's chief executive, and the council is the legislative branch; however, under constitutional authority, Congress can enact laws on any subject affecting the District, and all legislation enacted by the District is subject to congressional veto. The charter also provides for 36 neighborhood advisory commissions, whose seats (about 320 in all) are filled through nonpartisan elections.

¹⁵ DISTRICT SERVICES

Public education in the District is the responsibility of an elected Board of Education. Transportation services are provided through the Department of Transportation and the Washington Metropolitan Area Transit Authority, while health and welfare services fall within the jurisdiction of the Department of Human Resources. The Office of Consumer Protection, Department of Corrections, District of Columbia National Guard, and Metropolitan Police Department provide public protection services, and the Department of Housing and Community Development is the main housing agency. Employment security and job training are offered through the Department of Labor and the Apprenticeship Council.

¹⁶ JUDICIAL SYSTEM

All judges in Washington, D.C., are nominated by the president of the US from a list of persons recommended by the District of Columbia Nomination Commission, and appointed upon the advice and consent of the Senate. The US Court of Appeals for the District of Columbia functions in a manner similar to that of a state supreme court. The court consists of a chief judge and 8 associate judges, all serving 15-year terms. The Superior Court of the District of Columbia, the sole trial court, consists of 44 judges, also serving for 15 years. Washington, D.C., is also the site of the US Supreme Court and the US Department of Justice.

According to the FBI Crime Index, the violent crime rate in the District of Columbia was 1,412 per 100,000 population in 1978, a 37% decrease since 1970. Crimes in the District during 1978 included 189 cases of murder and nonnegligent manslaughter, 447 forcible rapes, 6,333 robberies, and 2,546 aggravated assaults.

¹⁷ ARMED FORCES

As of mid-1978, authorized Department of Defense personnel on military bases in the District of Columbia totaled 26,551. Of the District's 8 principal installations, 2 were Army facilities, 5 were Navy facilities, and 1—Bolling Air Force Base—was an Air Force installation. The Pentagon, headquarters of the US Department of Defense, covers 34 acres (14 hectares) of Arlington, Va., across the Potomac. Firms in the District received $537 million in federal defense contract awards in 1977/78.

As of 30 September 1979, 101,000 veterans of US military service were living in the District, of whom 2,000 served in World War I, 45,000 in World War II, 28,000 during the Korean conflict, and 22,000 during the Viet-Nam era. Veterans' benefits totaled $435.2 million during 1977/78.

Because Washington is often the scene of political demonstrations and because high federal officials and the District's foreign embassy personnel pose special police-protection problems, the ratio of police personnel to residents is higher than in any state: its 4,783 police employees represented a rate of 6.9 per 1,000 population, more than 2½ times the national average. There were 3,700 National Guard personnel in 1978.

¹⁸ MIGRATION

The principal migratory movements have been an influx of southern blacks after the Civil War and, more recently, the rapid growth of the Washington, D.C., metropolitan area, coupled with a shrinkage in the population of the District itself. Between 1950 and 1977, the District suffered a net loss from migration of 357,000, much of it to Maryland and Virginia.

¹⁹ INTERGOVERNMENTAL COOPERATION

The District of Columbia, a member of the Council of State Governments and its allied organizations, also participates in such interstate regional bodies as the Commission on Mental Health, Interstate Commission on Juveniles, Vehicle Equipment Safety Commission, and Washington Metropolitan Area Transit Authority Commission. Counties and incorporated cities in the Washington area are represented on the Metropolitan Washington Council of Governments, established in 1957.

The District relies heavily on federal assistance, which exceeded $1.1 billion in 1978/79. Federal aid per capita in 1977/78 reached $1,639, highest in the US and nearly five times the national average.

²⁰ ECONOMY

Tourism is the District's biggest business, the federal government the largest employer, and printing the leading industry. More than one-third of the total labor force is employed in professional, technical, administrative, and managerial positions. Government activity attracts an extraordinary number of professionals: in 1979, for example, the District had an estimated 28,200 lawyers, more than any state except New York and California. Among the principal socioeconomic trends in evidence during the 1970s were the increasing proportion of women in the work force and the upward mobility of blacks.

²¹ INCOME

With an income per capita of $10,022 in 1978, the District of Columbia outranked every state except Alaska. Total personal income was $6.8 billion, representing a real increase of 18% since 1970. Among black families in the Washington, D.C., metropolitan area, income levels have risen steadily: in 1959, 78% of all black families had incomes of less than $8,000, but by 1975, 59% of all black families had incomes above that mark. The proportion of District of Columbia residents below the federal poverty level declined from 17% to 12.5% between 1969 and 1975. Nevertheless, significant inequalities remain. The predominantly black District of Columbia had a median family income of $11,649 in 1977, far below the $21,954 median for families in Washington's predominantly white suburbs.

²² LABOR

The civilian labor force in the District of Columbia totaled 332,000 in 1978, of whom 303,000 were employed and 29,000 (8.7%) were unemployed. There were 164,000 women in the labor force, representing 49.4% of the total (highest in the US); 60% of all females 16 years of age or older were in the labor force, a higher percentage than in any state. The unemployment rate was 9.5% for men and 7.5% for women, a pattern atypical of the US as a whole.

A federal census of workers covered by unemployment insurance in March 1977 revealed the following nonfarm employment pattern for the District of Columbia:

	ESTABLISH-MENTS	EMPLOYEES	ANNUAL PAYROLL ('000)
Agricultural services, forestry, fishing	34	217	$ 1,975
Mining	17	65	1,870
Contract construction	488	9,147	149,910
Manufacturing, of which:	503	18,546	297,363
Printing, publishing	(307)	(13,660)	(210,492)
Transportation, public utilities	510	25,764	458,371
Wholesale trade	632	11,386	182,587
Retail trade	3,387	50,218	385,017
Finance, insurance, real estate	2,588	34,807	402,476
Services, of which:	7,521	147,813	1,784,205
Business services	(1,283)	(26,676)	(271,100)
Membership organizations	(1,429)	(25,770)	(392,928)
Other	257	311	7,109
TOTALS	15,937	298,274	$3,670,883

About 337,000 federal employees worked in the Washington, D.C., metropolitan area—including parts of Maryland and Virginia—in 1977. Local government employees in the District of Columbia numbered 49,000 in 1978.

The District of Columbia is the headquarters of the American Federation of Labor and Congress of Industrial Organizations (AFL–CIO), the dominant US labor organization, representing nearly 80% of the nation's total union membership. The AFL–CIO is a federation of 112 affiliated unions (1978), of which more than a third have their main office in the District. The National Federation of Independent Unions, the Assembly of Governmental Employees, and more than a dozen independent unions also have headquarters there.

23 AGRICULTURE
There is no commercial farming in the District of Columbia.

24 ANIMAL HUSBANDRY
The District of Columbia has no livestock industry.

25 FISHING
There is no commercial fishing in the District of Columbia.

26 FORESTRY
There is no forestland or forest products industry in the District of Columbia.

27 MINING
There is no mining in the District of Columbia, although a few mining firms have offices there.

28 ENERGY AND POWER
The District of Columbia had an installed electric energy capacity of 1.3 million kw in 1978, all of which was privately owned. Electrical output during the same year totaled 1.8 billion kwh. All power plants were oil-fired in 1978.

In 1978, the District had 150,000 gas utility customers, of whom 134,000 were residential and 16,000 were commercial. Revenues totaled $86 million in 1978. All fossil fuels must be imported from domestic and foreign suppliers outside the District.

29 INDUSTRY
Value added by manufacturing in 1977 reached $609.2 million, of which printing and publishing (most of it by or about the federal government) accounted for 83%. Within the District is the Government Printing Office (established by Congress in 1860), which operates one of the largest printing plants in the US. Food and fabricated metal products are the District's only other significant industries.

30 COMMERCE
Wholesaling in the District of Columbia totaled $1.7 billion in 1972. In 1977, the District's retail sales exceeded $2 billion, toward which eating and drinking places contributed 18%, food stores 17%, automotive dealers 10%, department stores 8%, and gasoline service stations 7%. Retailers in the Washington, D.C., metropolitan area had sales of $11.4 billion during the same year, with automotive dealers and food stores each accounting for 20%, department stores 13%, and eating and drinking places only 10%.

31 CONSUMER PROTECTION
The Office of Consumer Protection within the Executive Office of the Mayor has primary responsibility for consumer protection in the District. Business and professional licensing is accomplished through the Department of Licenses, Investigations, and Inspections.

32 BANKING
Banking in the District of Columbia began with the chartering of the Bank of Alexandria in 1792 and the Bank of Columbia in 1793; both banks terminated in the early 19th century. The oldest surviving bank in the District is the National Bank of Washington, founded as the Bank of Washington in 1809. As of mid-1980, the District's two largest commercial banks were the Riggs National Bank and the American Security Bank, with assets of $2.3 billion and $1.9 billion, respectively.

Overall, there were 17 insured commercial banks in 1978, with

assets totaling $6.3 billion and outstanding loans of $2.1 billion. As of 1978, 16 savings and loan institutions had combined assets of $4.7 billion and outstanding mortgage loans of $4.2 billion.

33 INSURANCE
In 1978, District of Columbia policyholders held life insurance polices worth $16.3 billion. The average coverage per family was $51,300, exceeded by only one state, Hawaii. Benefits totaled $116.2 million, of which death payments made up $57.9 million. Property and liability insurers wrote premiums worth $330.9 million in the District in 1978, of which $44.3 million was automotive liability insurance, $24.4 million was automobile physical damage insurance, and $21.9 million was homeowners' coverage.

34 SECURITIES
There are no securities exchanges in the District of Columbia. New York Stock Exchange member firms had 29 sales offices with 521 registered representatives in 1978. District of Columbia residents reported $146.8 million in dividend income on their 1977 federal tax returns.

35 PUBLIC FINANCE
The budget for the District of Columbia is prepared by the mayor and reviewed by the city council, but is subject to approval by Congress. The fiscal year runs from 1 October through 30 September.

The following table summarizes estimated revenues and expenditures for 1977/78 (in millions):

REVENUES	
Intergovernmental transfers	$ 726
Sales tax	314
Personal income tax	289
Property tax	197
Other receipts	157
TOTAL	$1,683
EXPENDITURES	
Social services	$ 423
Education	324
Public safety	194
Environment and housing	158
Government administration	122
Transportation	55
Utilities	42
Other expenditures	340
TOTAL	$1,658

The largest single source of revenue is federal aid. The local tax base is limited by a shortage of taxable real estate, much of the district being occupied by government buildings and federal reservations. The total public debt was $2.5 billion, or $3,673 per capita, as of mid-1977.

36 TAXATION
In 1980, the District of Columbia's personal income tax ranged from 2% on the first $1,000 to 11% on amounts over $25,000. The basic corporate tax was 9%, plus a 10% surtax. The District levies a 6% general sales and use tax, plus various excise taxes. As of 1975/76, federal receipts from the District totaled $1.4 billion, and federal expenditures exceeded $10.4 billion. District residents filed 324,534 income tax returns for 1977, paying $638.4 million in tax.

37 ECONOMIC POLICY
The economic policy of the District is set by Congress, which reviews the District's budget from year to year.

38 HEALTH
Health conditions in the nation's capital are no source of national pride. The District of Columbia has the lowest rate of life expectancy in the US: during 1969–71, the average life expectancy for both sexes was 65.71 years (70.52 for women, 60.92 for men). These figures reflect the high proportion of black people, whose

average life expectancy is, on the whole, five years less than that of whites in the US. Infant mortality rates—15 per 1,000 live births for whites and 29.7 for nonwhites in 1977—exceed those of every state. Legal abortions outnumber live births in the District, a distinction that no states and few cities share; there were 146 abortions for each 100 live births in 1977, more than three times the national average. The District also suffers the nation's highest death rate from early infancy diseases—26.7 deaths per 100,000 population in 1977, more than twice the US average—and an overall death rate of 10.4 per 1,000 population, tied with West Virginia as the national leader. In addition, the District has the nation's highest rate of death from cirrhosis of the liver, and its estimated alcoholism rate—5,430 alcoholics per 100,000 population in 1970—was also among the nation's leaders.

In 1978, there were 19 hospitals with 9,003 beds; they recorded 206,323 admissions, for an occupancy rate of 85%. Hospital personnel included 4,840 registered nurses and 1,450 licensed practical nurses. The average cost of hospital care in that year was $284 per day and $2,302 per stay—among the highest in the US. Medical personnel licensed to practice in the District included 3,356 nonfederal physicians in 1977 and 587 active dentists in 1979.

39 SOCIAL WELFARE

In 1976, outlays for the five largest welfare programs in the District of Columbia totaled $258 million, of which 57.4% was provided by the federal government, a lesser share than in 39 states. Aid to families with dependent children in 1978 totaled $91 million, with the average monthly payment being $238; Medicaid payments amounted to $120 million in 1977. During 1978, 91,000 District residents took part in the food stamp program, at a federal cost of $26.6 million; 71,000 children were served school lunches, with a federal subsidy of $7.4 million.

Social Security benefits in 1977 were paid to 89,800 residents; benefit payments totaled $205.2 million, with an average monthly stipend for retired workers of $215.70, 11% below the national average. Other social welfare expenditures included Supplemental Security Income (1978), $23.4 million; vocational rehabilitation (1978), $7.6 million; unemployment insurance (1978), $65 million; and workers' compensation (1977), $45.1 million.

40 HOUSING

The District of Columbia in 1970 had 278,000 housing units, of which 263,000 were occupied (70% rented); a majority of the units date from before 1939. Nearly 98% of all occupied units had full plumbing. The preponderance of rental units in a densely populated urban setting has led to overcrowding: about 12% of all units in 1970 averaged more than one person per room, a proportion exceeded only by Hawaii and Alaska. Some 41,500 new units were authorized between 1960 and 1969, but only 13,200 units during the following nine years. Construction also slowed down in the surrounding region, though not nearly so sharply.

41 EDUCATION

The District of Columbia's first public schools were opened in 1805. By 1978 there were 194 public schools with a total enrollment of 113,858 students, of whom 95% were black. Until 1954, public schools for whites and blacks were operated separately. The adult illiteracy rate in 1970 was 1.1%; nearly 66% of all residents 18 years of age or older were high school graduates, and the median for school completion was 12.6 years.

Of the District's institutions of higher education in 1977, 16 were private and 3 public; enrollment in private institutions predominated by 71,000 to 14,000. Some of the best-known private universities are American, Georgetown, George Washington, and Howard.

42 ARTS

The John F. Kennedy Center for the Performing Arts, officially opened on 8 September 1971, is the District's principal performing arts center. Its four main halls—the Opera House, Concert Hall, Eisenhower Theater, and American Film Institute Theater—display gifts from at least 30 foreign governments, ranging from stage curtains and tapestries to sculptures and crystal chandeliers. Major theatrical productions are also presented at the Arena Stage–Kreeger Theater, National Theater, Warner Theater, and Ford's Theater. In the summer, the Trapier Theater on the grounds of the Washington Cathedral presents a variety of dramas by classic playwrights from Shakespeare to Oscar Wilde, and the Sylvan Theater on the grounds of the Washington Monument presents a summer Shakespeare festival. Rep, Inc. is one of the few professional black theaters in the US; the New Playwrights' Theater of Washington, Inc., is a nonprofit group presenting new plays by American dramatists.

The District's leading symphony is the National Symphony Orchestra, which performs from October through April at the Concert Hall of the Kennedy Center; its principal conductor in 1980 was Mstislav Rostropovich. On a smaller scale, the Phillips Collection, National Gallery of Art, and Library of Congress offer concerts and recitals. The Washington Opera performs at the Kennedy Center's Opera House.

During the summer months, the Carter Barron Amphitheater presents popular music and jazz. Concerts featuring the Army, Navy, and Marine bands and the Air Force Symphony Orchestra are held throughout the District.

43 LIBRARIES AND MUSEUMS

Washington, D.C., is the site of the world's largest library, the Library of Congress, with a collection of more than 76 million items in at least 468 languages. The library, which is also the cataloging and bibliographic center for libraries throughout the US, has on permanent display a 1455 Gutenberg Bible, Thomas Jefferson's first draft of the Declaration of Independence, and Abraham Lincoln's first two drafts of the Gettysburg Address. Also in its permanent collection are the oldest known existing film (Thomas Edison's *The Sneeze*, lasting all of three seconds), maps believed to date from the Lewis and Clark expedition, original musical scores by Charles Ives, and huge libraries of Russian and Chinese texts. The Folger Shakespeare Library contains not only rare Renaissance manuscripts but also a full-size recreation of an Elizabethan theater. The District's own public library system had 24 branches, 1,899,409 volumes, and a circulation of 1,592,939 in 1977/78.

The Smithsonian Institution—endowed in 1826 by an Englishman, James Smithson, who had never visited the US—operates a vast museum and research complex that includes the National Air and Space Museum, National Museum of Natural History, National Museum of History and Technology, many of the District's art museums, and the National Zoological Park. Among the art museums operated by the Smithsonian are the National Gallery of Art, housing one of the world's outstanding collections of Western art from the 13th century to the present; the Freer Gallery of Art, housing a renowned collection of Near and Far Eastern treasures, along with one of the largest collections of the works of James McNeill Whistler, whose Peacock Room is one of the museum's highlights; the National Collection of Fine Arts; the National Portrait Gallery; and the Hirshhorn Museum and Sculpture Garden. Among the capital's other distinguished art collections are the Phillips Collection, the oldest museum of modern art in the US; the Museum of African Art, located in the Frederick Douglass Memorial Home; and the Corcoran Gallery of Art, devoted primarily to American paintings, sculpture and drawings of the last 300 years. Washington is also the site of such historic house-museums as Octagon House, Decatur House, and the Woodrow Wilson House. Many national associations maintain exhibitions relevant to their areas of interest.

44 COMMUNICATIONS

Postal receipts in Washington, D.C., the headquarters of the US Postal Service, totaled $175.5 million in 1978/79. As of 31 December 1978 there were 1,069,187 telephones, of which 512,042 were residential and 557,145 commercial. During that same year, the District had seven AM and seven FM radio stations and five commercial television stations.

⁴⁵PRESS

Because the District of Columbia is the center of US government activity, some 550 US and 280 foreign newspapers maintain permanent news bureaus there. The District has two major newspapers, the *Washington Post* and *Washington Star*. In 1978, the *Post*, a morning paper, had an average daily circulation of 559,371 and a Sunday circulation of 786,753; the *Star*, an evening paper, had a circulation of 328,612 weekdays and 308,910 Sundays. Press clubs active within the District include the National Press Club, Gridiron Club, American Newspaper Women's Club, Washington Press Club, and White House Correspondents Association.

There are more than 30 major Washington-based periodicals. Among the best known are the *National Geographic* (with a circulation of 10,560,885 as of 30 June 1980), *U.S. News & World Report*, *Smithsonian*, and *New Republic*. Important periodicals covering the workings of the federal government and Congress are the *Congressional Quarterly* and its companion, *CQ Weekly Report*.

⁴⁶ORGANIZATIONS

Nearly 2,000 national associations—and virtually all the major ones—maintain either their headquarters or a local office in the District of Columbia. Their presence and impact are constantly increasing.

General, patriotic, and service organizations with headquarters in the District include the Air Force Association, Daughters of the American Revolution, Order of the Eastern Star (Masons), and 4-H Clubs. Among the cultural, scientific, and educational groups are the American Film Institute, American Theatre Association, Federation of American Scientists, American Association for the Advancement of Science, National Academy of Sciences, National Geographic Society, Association of American Colleges, American Council on Education, National Education Association, American Association of University Professors, American Association of University Women, and US Student Association.

Among the environmental and animal protection organizations with headquarters in the District are the Animal Welfare Institute, Humane Society of the US, and National Wildlife Federation. There are numerous medical, health, and charitable organizations, including the American National Red Cross and National Federation of the Blind. Especially influential on matters affecting the elderly are the National Association of Retired Federal Employees, National Association of Retired Teachers, and American Association of Retired Persons. Notable ethnic and religious bodies (aside from religious denominations) are the National Association of Arab Americans, B'nai B'rith International, and US Catholic Conference.

There are many commercial, trade, and professional organizations in the District, including the National Society of Public Accountants, National Aeronautic Association, Air Line Pilots Association, American Bankers Association, Council of Better Business Bureaus, National Cable Television Association, Chamber of Commerce of the USA, American Chemical Society, International Association of Fire Fighters, Health Insurance Association of America, American Law Enforcement Officers Association, American Council of Life Insurance, National Association of Manufacturers, American Petroleum Institute, National Press Club, American Psychiatric Association, American Psychological Association, National Small Business Association, and American Trucking Association.

Virtually every major public interest group maintains an office in Washington, D.C. Notable examples (in addition to political parties and labor organizations) are the Consumer Federation of America, National Consumers League, National Abortion Rights Action League, National League of Cities, Common Cause, National Organization for the Reform of Marijuana Laws, US Conference of Mayors, National Organization for Women, National Rifle Association, and Zero Population Growth.

Among the important world organizations with headquarters in the District are the Organization of American States, International Monetary Fund, and International Bank for Reconstruction and Development (IBRD).

⁴⁷TOURISM, TRAVEL, AND RECREATION

The District of Columbia is one of the world's leading tourist centers, with 4,750,000 overnight visitors in 1979. The Washington Monument, Lincoln Memorial, Jefferson Memorial, White House, Capitol, US Supreme Court Building, Smithsonian Institution, Library of Congress, Ford's Theater, National Archives, National Gallery of Art, and Kennedy Center for the Performing Arts are only a few of the capital's extraordinary attractions. Across the Potomac, in Virginia, are Arlington National Cemetery, site of the Tomb of the Unknown Soldier and the grave of John F. Kennedy, and George Washington's home at Mt. Vernon, 15 mi (24 km) south of the capital.

⁴⁸SPORTS

Major professional sports teams representing the Washington, D.C., metropolitan area include the Redskins of the National Football League, the Bullets of the National Basketball Association (NBA), and the Capitals of the National Hockey League. The Redskins play at Robert F. Kennedy Stadium; the Bullets and Capitals have their home arena at the Capital Centre in Landover, Md. The Bullets have met with the most recent success, winning the NBA championship in 1978. Georgetown has a flourishing collegiate basketball program. The President's Cup Regatta, a speedboat race, is held annually off Hains Point.

⁴⁹FAMOUS WASHINGTONIANS

Although no US president has been born in the District of Columbia, all but George Washington (b.Virginia, 1732–99) lived there while serving as chief executive. Seven presidents died in Washington, D.C., including three during their term of office: William Henry Harrison (b.Virginia, 1773–1841), Zachary Taylor (b.Virginia, 1784–1850), and Abraham Lincoln (b.Kentucky, 1809–65). In addition, John Quincy Adams (b.Massachusetts, 1767–1848), who served as a congressman for 17 years after he left the White House, died at his desk in the House of Representatives, and William Howard Taft (b.Ohio, 1857–1930) passed away while serving as US chief justice. Retired Presidents Woodrow Wilson (b.Virginia, 1856–1924) and Dwight D. Eisenhower (b.Texas, 1890–1969) also died in the capital; Wilson is the only president buried there. Federal officials born in Washington, D.C., include John Foster Dulles (1888–1959), secretary of state; John Edgar Hoover (1895–1972), director of the FBI; and Robert C. Weaver (b.1907), who as secretary of housing and urban development was the first black American to hold cabinet rank. Walter E. Fauntroy (b.1933) has been the District's delegate to Congress since that office was established in 1971.

Among the outstanding scientists and other professionals associated with the District were Cleveland Abbe (b.New York, 1838–1916), a meteorologist who helped develop the US Weather Service; Henry Gannett (b.Maryland, 1846–1914), chief geographer with the US Geological Survey, president of the National Geographic Society (NGS), and a pioneer in American cartography; inventor Alexander Graham Bell (b.Scotland, 1842–1922), president of the NGS in his later years; Charles D. Walcott (b.New York, 1850–1927), director of the Geological Survey and secretary of the Smithsonian Institution; Emile Berliner (b.Germany, 1851–1929), a pioneer in the development of the phonograph; Gilbert H. Grosvenor (b.Turkey, 1875–1966), editor in chief of *National Geographic* magazine; and Charles R. Drew (1904–50), developer of the blood bank concept. Leading business executives who lived or worked in the District include William W. Corcoran (1798–1888), banker and philanthropist, and Katharine Graham (b.New York, 1917), publisher of the *Washington Post*; the two *Post* reporters who received much of the credit for uncovering the Watergate scandal are Carl Bernstein (b.1944), a native Washingtonian, and Robert "Bob" Woodward (b.Illinois, 1943). Washingtonians who achieved military fame include Benjamin O. Davis (1877–1970), the first black man to become an Army general, and his son, Benjamin O. Davis, Jr. (b.1912), who was the first black man to become a general in the Air Force.

The designer of the nation's capital was Pierre Charles L'Enfant (b.France, 1754–1825), whose grave is in Arlington National Cemetery; also involved in laying out the capital were surveyor Andrew Ellicott (b.Pennsylvania, 1754–1820) and mathematician-astronomer Benjamin Banneker (b.Maryland, 1731–1806), a black man who was an early champion of equal rights. Among Washingtonians to achieve distinction in the creative arts were John Philip Sousa (1854–1932), bandmaster and composer; Herblock (Herbert L. Block, b.Illinois, 1909), political cartoonist; and playwright Edward Albee (b.1928), winner of the Pulitzer Prize for drama in 1967 and 1975. Famous performers born in the District of Columbia include composer-pianist-bandleader Edward Kennedy "Duke" Ellington (1899–1974) and actress Helen Hayes (Helen Hayes Brown, b.1900). Alice Roosevelt Longworth (b.New York, 1884–1980) dominated the Washington social scene for much of this century.

[50]BIBLIOGRAPHY

Babb, Laura Longley (ed.). *The Washington Post Guide to Washington*. New York: McGraw-Hill, 1976.

Federal Writers' Project. *Washington, D.C.: A Guide to the Nation's Capital*. Rev. ed. New York: Hastings House, 1968 (orig. 1942).

Green, Constance M. *Washington: A History of the Capital*. Princeton, N.J.: Princeton University Press, 1976.

Gurney, Gene, and Harold Wise. *The Official Washington, D.C., Directory*. New York: Crown, 1977.

Gutheim, Frederick. *Worthy of the Nation: The Planning and Development of the National Capital City*. Washington, D.C.: Smithsonian, 1977.

Jacobsen, Hugh Newell (ed.). *A Guide to the Architecture of Washington, D.C.* New York: Praeger, 1965.

Kerwood, John R. (ed.). *The United States Capital: An Annotated Bibliography*. Norman: University of Oklahoma Press, 1972.

Lewis, David L. *District of Columbia: A Bicentennial History*. New York: Norton, 1976.

Shidler, Atlee E. *Trends and Issues in the Greater Washington Region: A Preliminary Report*. Washington, D.C.: Center for Municipal and Metropolitan Research, 1979.

PUERTO RICO*

Commonwealth of Puerto Rico
Estado Libre Asociado de Puerto Rico

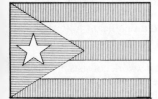

ORIGIN OF NAME: Spanish for "rich port." **NICKNAME:** Island of Enchantment. **CAPITAL:** San Juan. **BECAME A COMMONWEALTH:** 25 July 1952. **SONG:** *La Borinquena*. **MOTTO:** *Joannes est nomen ejus*. (John is his name.) **FLAG:** From the hoist extends a blue triangle, with one white star; five horizontal stripes—three red, two white—make up the balance. **OFFICIAL SEAL:** In the center of a green circular shield, a lamb holding a white banner reclines on the book of the Apocalypse. Above are a yoke, a cluster of arrows, and the letters "F" and "I," signifying King Ferdinand and Queen Isabella, rulers of Spain at the time of discovery; below is the Commonwealth motto. Surrounding the shield, on a white border, are the towers of Castile and lions, symbolizing Spain, crosses representing the conquest of Jerusalem, and Spanish banners. **ANIMAL:** Lamb. **REPTILE:** Coquí. **LEGAL HOLIDAYS:** New Year's Day, 1 January; Three Kings Day (Epiphany), 6 January; Birthday of Eugenio María de Hostos, 11 January; Washington's Birthday, 3d Monday in February; Abolition Day, 22 March; Good Friday, March or April; Birthday of José de Diego, 16 April; Memorial Day, last Monday in May; Independence Day, 4 July; Birthday of Luis Muñoz Rivera, 17 July; Constitution Day, 25 July; Birthday of José Celso Barbosa, 27 July; Labor Day, 1st Monday in September; Anniversary of the "Grito de Lares," 23 September; Veterans Day, 11 November; Discovery Day, 19 November; Thanksgiving Day, 4th Thursday in November; Christmas Day, 25 December. **TIME:** 8 A.M. Atlantic Standard Time = noon GMT.

¹LOCATION, SIZE, AND EXTENT

Situated on the NE periphery of the Caribbean Sea, about 1,000 mi (1,600 km) SE of Miami, Puerto Rico is the easternmost and smallest island of the Greater Antilles group. Its total area is 3,435 sq mi (8,897 sq km), including 3,421 sq mi (8,861 sq km) of land and 14 sq mi (36 sq km) of inland water.

Shaped roughly like a rectangle, the main island measures 111 mi (179 km) E–W and 36 mi (58 km) N–S. Offshore and to the E are two major islands, Vieques and Culebra.

Puerto Rico is bounded by the Atlantic Ocean to the N, the Virgin Passage and Vieques Sound to the E, the Caribbean Sea to the S, and the Mona Passage to the W. Puerto Rico's total boundary length is 378 mi (608 km).

²TOPOGRAPHY

About 75% of Puerto Rico's land area consists of hills or mountains too steep for intensive commercial cultivation. The Cordillera Central range, separating the northern coast from the semiarid south, has the island's highest peak, Cerro de Punta (4,389 feet—1,338 meters). Puerto Rico's best-known peak, El Yunque (3,496 feet—1,066 meters), stands to the east, in the Luquillo Mountains (Sierra de Luquillo). The north coast consists of a level strip about 100 mi (160 km) long and 5 mi (8 km) wide. Principal valleys are located along the east coast, from Fajardo to Cape Mala Pascua, and around Caguas, in the east-central region. Off the eastern shore are Vieques, with an area of 51 sq mi (132 sq km), and Culebra, covering 24 sq mi (62 sq km). Uninhabited Mona Island (19 sq mi—49 sq km), off the southwest coast, is a breeding ground for wildlife.

Puerto Rico has 50 waterways large enough to be classified as rivers, but none is navigable by large vessels. The longest river is the Río de la Plata, extending 46 mi (74 km) from Cayey to Dorado, where it empties into the Atlantic. There are few natural lakes but numerous artificial ones, of which Dos Bocas, south of Arecibo, is one of the most beautiful. Phosphorescent Bay, whose luminescent organisms glow in the night, is a tourist attraction on the south coast.

Like many Caribbean islands, Puerto Rico is the crest of an extinct submarine volcano. About 45 mi (72 km) north of the

island lies the Puerto Rico Trench, at over 28,000 feet (8,500 meters) one of the world's deepest chasms.

³CLIMATE

Tradewinds from the northeast keep Puerto Rico's climate more temperate than tropical. San Juan has a normal daily mean temperature of 79°F (26°C), ranging from 75°F (24°C) in January to 81°F (27°C) in July; the normal daily minimum is 72°F (22°C), the maximum 85°F (29°C). The lowest temperature ever recorded on the island is 39°F (4°C), the highest 103°F (39°C); the recorded temperature in San Juan has never been lower than 60°F (16°C) nor higher than 96°F (36°C).

Rainfall varies by region. The south coast receives only 29 in (74 cm) a year, while the highlands get 108 in (274 cm); the rain forest on El Yunque receives 180 in (457 cm). San Juan's average annual rainfall is 59 in (150 cm), the rainiest months being May through November.

The word "hurricane" derives from *hurakán*, a term the Spanish learned from Puerto Rico's Taíno Indians. Eight hurricanes have struck Puerto Rico in this century, most recently in 1979.

⁴FLORA AND FAUNA

During the 19th century, forests covered about three-fourths of Puerto Rico. Today, however, only one-fourth of the island is forested. Flowering trees still abound, and the butterfly tree, African tulip, and flamboyán (royal poinciana) add bright reds and pinks to Puerto Rico's lush green landscape. Among hardwoods, now rare, are nutmeg, satinwood, Spanish elm, and Spanish cedar. Pre-Columbian peoples cultivated yucca, yams, peanuts, hot peppers, tobacco, and cotton. Pineapple, guava, tamarind, and cashews are indigenous, and such fruits as mamey, jobo, guanábana, and quenepa are new to most visitors. Coconuts, coffee, sugarcane, plantains, mangoes, and most citrus fruits were introduced by the Spanish.

The only mammal found by the conquistadores on the island was a kind of barkless dog, now extinct. Virtually all present-day mammals have been introduced, including horses, cattle, cats, and dogs. The only troublesome mammal is the mongoose,

*All comparative data for the US exclude Puerto Rico unless otherwise noted.

brought in from India to control reptiles in the cane fields and now wild in remote rural areas. Mosquitoes and sand flies are common pests, but the only dangerous insect is the giant centipede, whose sting is painful but rarely fatal. Perhaps the island's best-known inhabitant is the coquí, a tiny tree frog whose call of "ko-kee, ko-kee" is heard all through the night. Marine life is extraordinarily abundant, including many tropical fish, crabs, and corals. Puerto Rico has some 200 bird species, many of which live in the rain forest. Thrushes, orioles, grosbeaks, and hummingbirds are common, and the reinita and pitirre are distinctive to the island. Several parrot species are rare, and the Puerto Rican parrot is endangered. Also on the endangered list are the yellow-shouldered blackbird and the Puerto Rican pigeon, whippoorwill, and boa.

5ENVIRONMENTAL PROTECTION

US environmental laws and regulations are applicable in Puerto Rico. Land-use planning, overseen by the Puerto Rico Planning Board, is an especially difficult problem, since residential, industrial, and recreational developers are all competing for about 30% of the total land area on an island that is already more densely populated than any state of the US except New Jersey. Pollution from highland latrines and septic systems and from agricultural and industrial wastes is a potential hazard; the rum industry, for example, has traditionally dumped its wastes into the ocean. Moreover, the US requirement that sewage receive secondary treatment before being discharged into deep seas may be unrealistic in view of the Commonwealth government's claim, in the late 1970s, that it cannot afford to build secondary sewage treatment facilities when 45% of its population lacks primary sewage treatment systems.

6POPULATION

Puerto Rico, with a 1970 census population of 2,717,033, had more people than 26 of the 50 states. The 1980 preliminary census total was 3,187,570, representing a 17% increase for the decade and a population density of 932 per sq mi (360 per sq km).

In 1975, Puerto Rico was 49% male and 51% female. Fully 36% of the population was under 15 years of age; nearly 56% was under 25, compared with 42% for the US. The birthrate declined steadily from 36 live births per 1,000 population in 1950 to 22.3 in 1975, but the latter figure was still 50% above the US average. The death rate, on the other hand, is nearly one-third lower than the US norm, and with the steady flow of migration from the US mainland to Puerto Rico during the 1970s, a continuation of rapid population growth appeared likely.

According to the 1970 census, the population was 58% urban and 42% rural. San Juan is Puerto Rico's capital and largest city, with a preliminary 1980 census population of 432,973, followed by Bayamón, 195,965; Ponce, 188,219; Carolina, 165,207; and Caguas, 118,020.

7ETHNIC GROUPS

Three main ethnic strands are the heritage of Puerto Rico: the Taíno Indians, most of whom fled or perished after the Spanish conquest; black Africans, imported as slaves under Spanish rule; and the Spanish themselves. With an admixture of Dutch, English, Corsicans, and other Europeans, Puerto Ricans today enjoy a distinct Hispanic-Afro-Antillean heritage. Of the total population of Puerto Rico, perhaps 50,000 are US mainlanders, or *continentales*.

Not quite two-thirds of all ethnic Puerto Ricans live on the island. Virtually all the remainder reside on the US mainland, where they made up less than 15% of the US Hispanic population in 1979.

8LANGUAGES

Spanish is the official language of Puerto Rico; English is required in schools as a second language. From 1898 through the 1920s, US authorities unsuccessfully sought to make English the island's primary language.

Taíno Indian terms that survive in Puerto Rican Spanish include such place-names as Arecibo, Guayama, and Mayagüez, as well as *hamaca* (hammock) and *canoa* (canoe). Among many African borrowings are food terms like *quimbombó* (okra), *guineo* (banana), and *mondongo* (a spicy stew).

9RELIGIONS

During the first three centuries of Spanish rule, Roman Catholicism was the only religion permitted in Puerto Rico. About 80% of the population is still Roman Catholic, and the Church maintains numerous hospitals and schools on the island. Most of the remaining Puerto Ricans belong to other Christian denominations, which have been allowed on the island since the 1850s. Pentecostal churches have attracted a significant following, particularly among the urban poor of the barrios.

10TRANSPORTATION

Puerto Rico's inland transportation network consists primarily of roads and road vehicles. Rivers are not navigable, and the only function of narrow-gauge rural railroads is to haul sugarcane to the mills during the harvesting season; other goods are transported by truck. A few public bus systems provide intercity passenger transport, the largest being the Metropolitan Bus Authority (MBA), a government-owned company serving San Juan and nearby cities. Each day, an average of 250 MBA buses transport more than 100,000 passengers. The predominant form of public transportation outside the San Juan metropolitan area is the *público*, or privately owned jitney, a small bus that carries passengers between fixed destinations; in many rural areas, it is the only form of public transit.

In 1978, Puerto Rico had 8,325 mi (13,398 km) of streets and roads, of which 92% were surfaced. Motor vehicle registrations in 1975/76 totaled 814,373, including 647,230 private cars—the island's ratio of better than one automobile for each five residents is one of the highest in the world, though far below the US average—21,484 trucks, 6,755 motorcycles, and 2,101 buses. Puerto Rico's motor vehicle fatality rate (deaths per 100 million vehicle-miles) was 6.41 in 1976, nearly double the US average.

Puerto Rico's ports and harbors annually handle about 45 million tons of cargo. San Juan, the island's principal port and one of the world's leading containerized cargo handling facilities, accommodates some 5,000 freighters from over two dozen nations each year. Ferries link the main island with Vieques and Culebra.

Puerto Rico receives direct flights from three dozen North American cities; in 1975/76, more than 2.3 million passengers arrived by air on the island, two-thirds of them from the continental US. Puerto Rico International Airport (San Juan) handles about five-sixths of all passenger traffic and air cargo, which amounted to 160,000 tons in 1975/76. Other leading air terminals are located at Ponce, Mayagüez, and Vieques. Puerto Rican International Airlines (Prinair) is the busiest commuter carrier under US jurisdiction, transporting 823,000 passengers in 1976. Antilles Air Boats provides service to neighboring island nations.

11HISTORY

Archaeological finds indicate that at least three Indian cultures settled on the island now known as Puerto Rico long before its discovery by Christopher Columbus on 19 November 1493. The first group, belonging to the Archaic Culture, are believed to have come from Florida. Having no knowledge of agriculture or pottery, they relied on the products of the sea; their remains have been found mostly in caves. The second group, the Igneri, came from northern South America. Descended from South American Arawak stock, the Igneri brought agriculture and pottery to the island; their remains are found mostly in the coastal areas. The third culture, the Taíno, also of Arawak origin, combined fishing with agriculture. A peaceful, sedentary tribe, the Taíno were adept at stonework and lived in many parts of the island; Taíno relics have been discovered not only along the coastal perimeter but also high in the mountains,

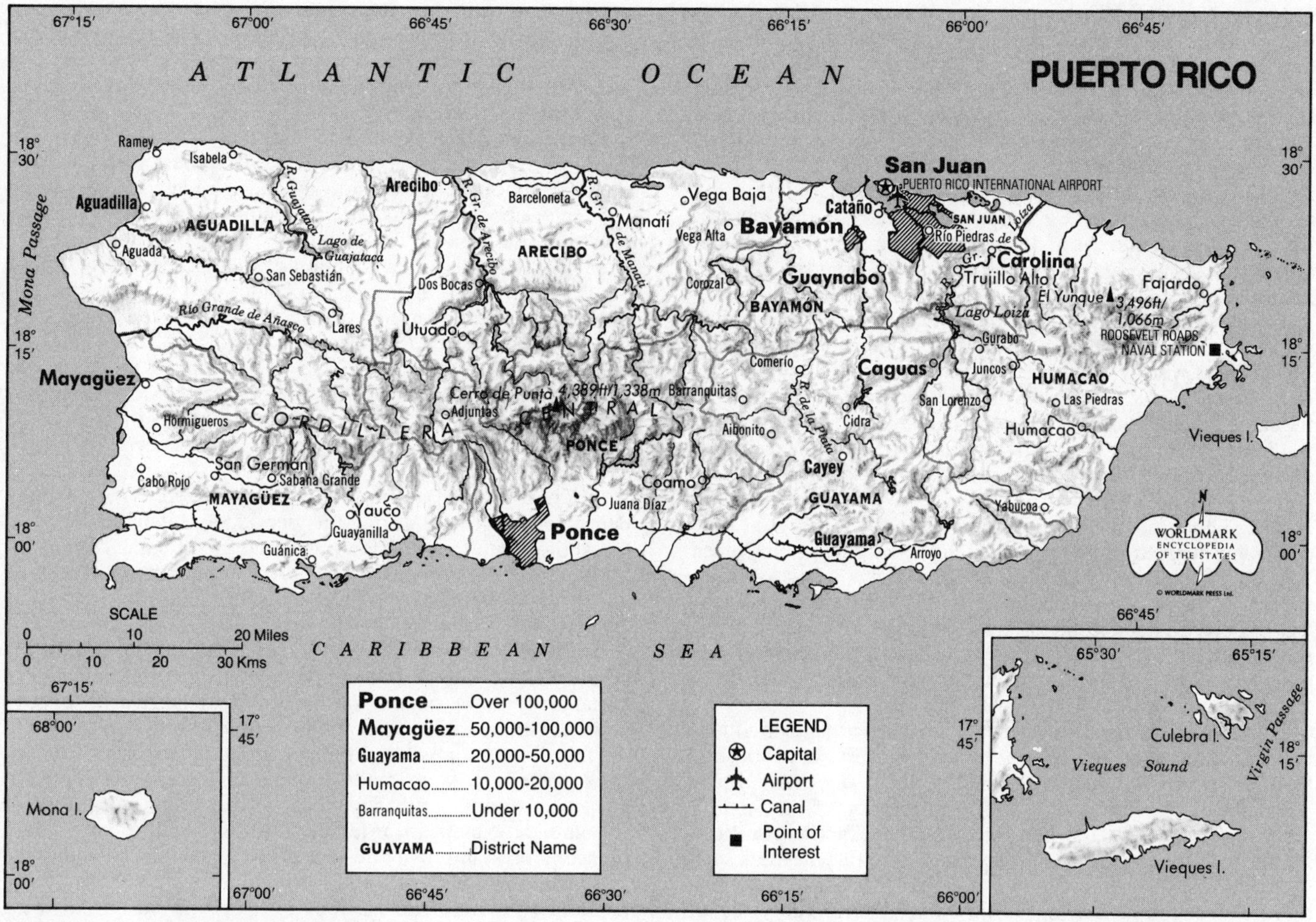
PUERTO RICO
ATLANTIC OCEAN
CARIBBEAN SEA
Mona Passage
San Juan
PUERTO RICO INTERNATIONAL AIRPORT
Aguadilla
AGUADILLA
Aguada
Ramey
Isabela
Lago de Guajataca
San Sebastián
Arecibo
ARECIBO
Barceloneta
Manatí
Vega Baja
Vega Alta
Bayamón
BAYAMÓN
Cataño
Guaynabo
Carolina
Trujillo Alto
Lago Loíza
El Yunque 3,496ft/ 1,066m
Fajardo
ROOSEVELT ROADS NAVAL STATION
Gurabo
Juncos
HUMACAO
Las Piedras
Humacao
Caguas
San Lorenzo
Cidra
Cayey
GUAYAMA
Guayama
Arroyo
Yabucoa
Vieques I.
Mayagüez
MAYAGÜEZ
Hormigueros
CORDILLERA CENTRAL
Cerro de Punta 4,389ft/1,338m
Adjuntas
Barranquitas
Aibonito
Comerío
Corozal
Dos Bocas
Utuado
Lares
Río Grande de Añasco
San Germán
Sabana Grande
Cabo Rojo
Yauco
Guayanilla
Guánica
Ponce
PONCE
Coamo
Juana Díaz
SCALE
0 10 20 Miles
0 10 20 30 Kms
Mona I.
Ponce .... Over 100,000
Mayagüez 50,000-100,000
Guayama 20,000-50,000
Humacao 10,000-20,000
Barranquitas .... Under 10,000
GUAYAMA .... District Name
LEGEND
Capital
Airport
Canal
Point of Interest
Culebra I.
Vieques Sound
Virgin Passage
Vieques I.
WORLDMARK ENCYCLOPEDIA OF THE STATES

LOCATION (main island only): 18°04′15″ to 18°31′N; 65°35′30″ to 67°15′W. **BOUNDARIES**: Total coastline, 378 mi (608 km).

where they performed ritual games in ball parks that have been restored in recent times. To the Indians, the island was known as Boriquén.

Columbus, accompanied by a young nobleman named Juan Ponce de León, landed at the western end of the island—which he called San Juan Bautista (St. John the Baptist)—and claimed it for Spain. Not until colonization was well under way would the island acquire the name Puerto Rico (literally, "rich port"), with the name San Juan Bautista applied to the capital city. The first settlers arrived on 12 August 1508, under the able leadership of Ponce de León, who sought to transplant and adapt Spanish civilization to Puerto Rico's tropical habitat. The small contingent of Spaniards compelled the Taíno, numbering perhaps 30,000, to mine for gold; the rigors of forced labor and the losses from rebellion reduced the Taíno population to about 4,000 by 1514, by which time the mines were nearly depleted. With the introduction of slaves from Africa, sugarcane growing became the leading economic activity. Since neither mining nor sugarcane was able to provide sufficient revenue to support the struggling colony, the treasury of New Spain began a subsidy, known as the *situado*, which until the early 19th century defrayed the cost of the island's government and defense.

From the early 16th century onward, an intense power struggle for the control of the Caribbean marked Puerto Rico as a strategic base of the first magnitude. After a French attack in 1528, construction of La Fortaleza (still in use today as the governor's palace) was begun in 1533, and work on El Morro fortress in San Juan commenced six years later. The new fortifications helped repel a British attack led by Sir Francis Drake in 1595; a second force, arriving in 1598 under George Clifford, earl of Cumberland, succeeded in capturing San Juan, but the British were forced to withdraw by tropical heat and disease. In 1625, a Dutch attack under the command of Boudewijn Hendrikszoon was repulsed, although much of San Juan was sacked and burned by the attackers. By the 18th century, Puerto Rico had become a haven for pirates, and smuggling was the major economic activity. A Spanish envoy who came to the island in 1765 was appalled, and his report to the crown inaugurated a period of economic, administrative, and military reform. The creation of a native militia helped Puerto Rico withstand a fierce British assault on San Juan in 1797, by which time the island had more than 100,000 inhabitants.

Long after most of the Spanish colonies in the New World had obtained independence, Puerto Rico and Cuba remained under Spanish tutelage. Despite several insurrection attempts, most of them inspired by the Liberator, Simón Bolívar, Spain's military might concentrated on these islands precluded any revolution. Puerto Rico became a shelter for refugees from Santo Domingo, Haiti, and Venezuela who were faithful to Spain, fearful of disturbances in their own countries, or both. As in Cuba, the sugar industry developed in Puerto Rico during this period under policies that favored foreign settlers. As a result, a new landowner class emerged—the *hacendados*—who were instrumental in strengthening the institution of slavery in the island. By 1830, the population was 300,000. Sugar, tobacco, and coffee were the leading export crops, though subsistence farming still covered much of the interior. Sugar found a ready market in the US, and trade steadily developed, particularly with the Northeast.

The 19th century also gave birth, however, to a new Puerto Rican civic and political consciousness. Puerto Rican participation in the short-lived constitutional experiments in Spain (1812–14 and 1820–23) fostered the rise of a spirit of liberalism, expressed most notably by Ramón Power y Giralt, at one time vice president of the Spanish Cortes (parliament). During these early decades, Spain's hold on the island was never seriously threatened. Although the Spanish constitution of 1812 declared that the people of Puerto Rico were no longer colonial subjects but were full-fledged citizens of Spain, the crown nevertheless maintained an alert, centralized, absolutistic government with all basic powers concentrated in the captain general.

Toward the middle of the 19th century, a *criollo* generation with strong liberal roots began a new era in Puerto Rican history. This group, which called for the abolition of slavery and the introduction of far-reaching economic and political reforms, at the same time developed and strengthened Puerto Rican literary tradition. The more radical reformers espoused the cause of separation from Spain and joined in a propaganda campaign in New York on behalf of Cuban independence. An aborted revolution, beginning in the town of Lares in September 1868 (and coinciding with an insurrection in Spain that deposed Queen Isabella II), though soon quelled, awakened among Puerto Ricans a dormant sense of national identity. "El Grito de Lares" (the Cry of Lares) helped inspire a strong anti-Spanish separatist current that never was able to challenge Spanish power effectively but which produced such influential leaders as Ramón Emeterio Betances and Eugenio María de Hostos.

The major reform efforts after 1868 revolved around abolitionism and *autonomía*, or self-government. Slavery was abolished in 1873 by the First Spanish Republic, which also granted new political rights to the islanders. The restoration of the Spanish monarchy two years later, however, was a check to Puerto Rican aspirations. During the last quarter of the century, leaders such as Luis Muñoz Rivera sought unsuccessfully to secure vast new powers of self-government. By this time, Puerto Rico was an island with a distinct Antillean profile, strong Hispanic roots, and a mixed population that, borrowing from its Indian-Spanish-African background and an influx of Dutch, English, Corsicans, and other Europeans, had developed its own folkways and mores.

The imminence of war with the US over Cuba, coupled with autonomist agitation within Puerto Rico, led Spain in November 1897 to grant to the island a charter with broad powers of self-rule. Led by Luis Muñoz Rivera, Puerto Ricans began to establish new organs of self-government, but no sooner had an elected government begun to function in July 1898 than US forces, overcoming Spanish resistance, took over the island. A cease-fire was proclaimed on 13 August, and sovereignty was formally transferred to the US with the signing in December of the Treaty of Paris, ending the Spanish-American War. The US government swept aside the self-governing charter granted by Spain and established military rule from 1898 to 1900. Civilian government was restored in 1900 under a colonial law, the Foraker Act, that gave the federal government full control of the executive and legislative branches, leaving some local representation in the lower chamber, or house of delegates. Under the Jones Act, signed into law by President Woodrow Wilson on 2 March 1917, Congress extended US citizenship to the islanders and granted an elective senate, but still reserved vast powers over Puerto Rico to the federal bureaucracy.

The early period of US rule saw an effort to Americanize all insular institutions, and even aimed at superseding the Spanish language as the vernacular. In the meantime, American corporate capital took over the sugar industry, developing a plantation economy so pervasive that, by 1920, 75% of the population relied on the cane crop for its livelihood. Glaring irregularities of wealth resulted, sharpening social and political divisions. This period also saw the development of three main trends in Puerto Rican political thinking. One group favored the incorporation of Puerto Rico into the US as a state; a second group, fearful of cultural assimilation, favored self-government; while a third group spoke for independence.

The depression hit Puerto Rico especially hard. With a population approaching 2 million by the late 1930s and with few occupational opportunities outside the sugar industry, the island's economy deteriorated, and mass unemployment and near-starvation were the results. Controlling the Puerto Rican legislature from 1932 to 1940 was a coalition of the Socialist Party, led by Santiago Iglesias, a Spanish labor leader who became a protégé of the American Federation of Labor, and the Republican Party, which had traditionally espoused statehood and had been founded in Puerto Rico by José Celso Barbosa, a black physician who had studied in the US. The coalition was unable to produce any significant improvement, although under the New Deal a US government effort was made to supply emergency relief for the "stricken island."

Agitation for full political and economic reform or independence gained ground during this period. A violent challenge to US authority in Puerto Rico was posed by the small Nationalist Party, led by Harvard-educated Pedro Albizu Campos. A broader attack on the island's political and economic ills was led by Luis Muñoz Marín and the Popular Democratic Party (PDP), founded in 1938; within two years, the PDP won control of the senate. Under Muñoz Marín, a new era began in Puerto Rico. Great pressure was put on Washington for a change in the island's political status, while social and economic reform was carried to the fullest extent possible within the limitations of the Jones Act. Intensive efforts were made to centralize economic planning, attract new industries through local tax exemptions (Puerto Rico was already exempt from federal taxation), reduce inequalities of income, and improve housing, schools, and health conditions. Meanwhile, a land distribution program helped the destitute peasants who were the backbone of the new party. All these measures—widely publicized as Operation Bootstrap—coupled with the general US economic expansion after World War II so transformed Puerto Rico's economy that income from manufacturing surpassed that from agriculture by 1955, and was five times as great by 1970. Annual income per capita rose steadily from $296 in 1950 to $1,384 in 1970.

The PDP, the dominant force in Puerto Rican politics from 1940 to 1968, favored a new self-governing relationship with the US, distinct from statehood or independence. The party succeeded not only in bringing about significant social and economic change but also in obtaining from Congress in 1950 a law allowing Puerto Ricans to draft their own constitution with full local self-government. This new constitution, approved in a general referendum on 3 March 1952, led to the establishment on 25 July of the Commonwealth of Puerto Rico (Estado Libre Asociado de Puerto Rico), which, according to a resolution approved in 1953 by the United Nations Committee on Information from Non-Self-Governing Territories, was constituted as an autonomous political entity in voluntary association with the United States.

An island-wide plebiscite in 1967 showed that 60% of those voting favored continuation and improvement of the commonwealth relationship, 39% preferred statehood, and less than 1% supported independence; the turnout among eligible voters was 65%. The result of the plebiscite, held to support a movement for additional home-rule powers, met with indifference from the US executive branch and outright opposition from the pro-statehood minority in Puerto Rico. Consequently, efforts to obtain passage by Congress of a "Compact of Permanent Union between Puerto Rico and the United States," although approved at the subcommittee level by the House of Representatives, failed to produce any change in the commonwealth arrangement.

The result was renewed agitation for either statehood or independence, with growing internal political polarization. The island's Republican Party rearranged itself after the plebiscite as the New Progressive Party (NPP) and came to power in 1968 as a result of a split in PDP ranks that led to the creation of the splinter People's Party. The two major blocs have been evenly balanced since that time, with the PDP returning to power in 1972 but losing to the NPP in 1976 and again, by a very narrow margin, in 1980. The independence movement, in turn, divided into two wings: the moderates favored social democracy, while the radicals pursued close ties with the Fidel Castro regime in Cuba. Capitalizing on the increased power of Third World countries in the United Nations and with Soviet support, the radicals challenged US policies and demanded a full transfer of sovereign rights to the people of Puerto Rico. Their position won the support of the UN Special Committee on the Situation with Regard to the Implementation of the Declaration on the Granting of Independence to Colonial Countries and Peoples (more generally known as the Committee of 24), which on 15 August 1979 reaffirmed "the inalienable right of the people of Puerto Rico to self-determination and independence...." The US government replied that the people of Puerto Rico had already exercised their right of self-determination in the 1967 plebiscite, and noted that Congress in 1979 had restated its "commitment to respect and support the right of the people of Puerto Rico to determine their own political future through peaceful, open and democratic processes." More advanced than most Caribbean countries in education, health, and social development, Puerto Rico was, nevertheless, a land of growing political tensions as the 1980s began.

[12] COMMONWEALTH GOVERNMENT

Since 1952, Puerto Rico has been a Commonwealth of the US, governed under the Puerto Rican Federal Relations Act and under a constitution based on the US model. The Puerto Rican constitution specifically prohibits discrimination "on account of race, color, sex, birth, social origin or condition, or political ideas."

The Commonwealth legislature comprises a senate (*Senado*) of 27 members, 2 from each of 8 senatorial districts and 11 elected at large; and a house of representatives (*Cámara de Representantes*) of 51 members, 1 from each of 40 districts and 11 at large. If a single party wins two-thirds or more of the seats in either house, the number of seats is expanded (up to a limit of 9 in the senate and 17 in the house), and additional minority party legislators are added at large. Senators must be at least 30 years of age, representatives 25; all legislators serve four-year terms.

The governor, who may serve an unlimited number of four-year terms, is the only elected executive. Candidates for the governorship must be US citizens, at least 35 years of age, and must have resided in Puerto Rico for at least five years.

A bill becomes law if approved by both houses and either signed by the governor or left unsigned for 10 days while the legislature is in session. A two-thirds vote of the elected members of each house is sufficient to override a gubernatorial veto. The constitution may be amended by a two-thirds vote of the legislature and ratification by popular majority vote.

Residents of Puerto Rico may not vote in US presidential elections. A Puerto Rican who settles in one of the 50 states automatically becomes eligible to vote for president, and, conversely, a state resident who migrates to Puerto Rico forfeits such eligibility. Puerto Rico has no vote in the US Senate or House of Representatives, but a nonvoting resident commissioner, elected every four years, may speak on the floor of the House, introduce legislation, and vote in House committees.

Qualified voters must be US citizens, at least 18 years of age, and must have resided in the Commonwealth for at least a year.

[13] POLITICAL PARTIES

Taking part in Puerto Rican elections during the late 1970s were two major and two smaller political parties. The Popular Democratic Party (PDP), founded in 1938, favors the strengthening and development of commonwealth status. The New Progressive Party (NPP), created in 1968 as the successor to the Puerto Rican Republican Party, is pro-statehood. Two smaller parties, each favoring independence for the island, are the Puerto Rican Independence Party, founded in the mid-1940s and committed to democratic socialism, and the more radical Puerto Rican Socialist Party, which has close ties with Cuba. In 1980, Governor Carlos Romero Barceló of the NPP, who had pledged to seek actively Puerto Rico's admission to the Union if elected by a large margin, retained the governorship by a plurality of less than 3,500 votes, in the closest election in the island's history,

Puerto Rico Gubernatorial Vote by Political Parties, 1948–80[1]

YEAR	WINNER	POPULAR DEMOCRAT (PDP)	NEW PROGRESSIVE (NPP)	REPUBLICAN	PUERTO RICAN INDEPENDENCE	SOCIALIST	LIBERAL REFORMIST
1948	Luis Muñoz Marín (PDP)	392,033	—	88,819	66,141	64,121	28,203
1952	Luis Muñoz Marín (PDP)	429,064	—	85,172	125,734	21,655	
1956	Luis Muñoz Marín (PDP)	433,010	—	172,838	86,386	—	—
1960	Luis Muñoz Marín (PDP)	457,880	—	252,364	24,103	—	—
1964	Roberto Sanchez Vitella (PDP)	487,280	—	284,627	22,201	26,867 (CHRISTIAN ACTION)	—
1968	Luis A. Ferré (NPP)	367,903	390,623	4,057	24,713	87,844 (PEOPLE'S)	—
1972	Rafael Hernández Colón (PDP)	609,670	524,039	—	52,070	2,910 (PR UNION)	1,608
1976	Carlos Romero Barceló (NPP)	634,941	682,607	—	58,556	9,761 (PR SOCIALIST)	—
1980	Carlos Romero Barceló (NPP)	756,434	759,868	—	87,275	5,225	—

[1]Residents of Puerto Rico are barred from voting in US presidential elections.

while the PDP won control of the senate and 52 out of 78 mayoralty contests.

Although Puerto Ricans have no vote in US presidential elections, the island does send voting delegates to the national conventions of the Democratic and Republican parties. In 1980, for the first time, those delegates were chosen by presidential preference primary.

Puerto Rico's political parties have generally committed themselves to peaceful change through democratic methods. One exception was the pro-independence Nationalist Party, whose followers were involved in an attempt to assassinate US President Harry S Truman in 1950 and in an outbreak of shooting in the House of Representatives that wounded five congressmen in 1954. A US-based terrorist group, the Armed Forces of Puerto Rican National Liberation (FALN), claimed credit during the late 1970s for bombings in New York and other major cities. FALN members briefly took over the Statue of Liberty in New York Harbor on 25 October 1977. Another group, the Macheteros, apparently based on the island, claimed responsibility for an attack on a US Navy bus in 1980 and for blowing up eight US Air Force planes at a Puerto Rico Air National Guard installation early in 1981.

14 LOCAL GOVERNMENT

The Commonwealth of Puerto Rico has 78 municipalities, each governed by a mayor and municipal assembly elected every four years. Many of the functions normally performed by municipal governments in the US—for instance, fire protection, education, water supply, and law enforcement—are performed by the Commonwealth government directly.

15 COMMONWEALTH SERVICES

The executive branch of Puerto Rico's highly centralized government is organized into 14 departments, 38 agencies, and 43 public corporations and other bodies. Most programs are administered through the departments of agriculture, commerce, consumer affairs, drug addiction services, education, health, housing, justice, labor, natural resources, social services, state, transportation and public works, and treasury. The Department of Health manages the public health system, providing hospitals, clinics, nursing homes, and preventive services for all island residents. A government corporation under the aegis of the Department of Social Services provides work for the blind, mentally retarded, and other disabled persons. Both the Commonwealth police force and the motor vehicles bureau are in the Department of Transportation and Public Works. Lodged within the Office of the Governor are the Bureau of the Budget, Planning Board, Women's Rights Improvement Commission, and Environmental Quality Board, as well as offices of economic opportunity, cultural affairs, and petroleum fuels affairs.

16 JUDICIAL SYSTEM

Puerto Rico's highest court, the Supreme Court, consists of a chief justice and eight associate justices, all appointed by the governor with the consent of the senate and serving until compulsory retirement at age 70. The court sits as three separate panels of three justices except in cases dealing with the constitutionality of Commonwealth law, for which the entire body convenes. Decisions of the Supreme Court of Puerto Rico regarding US constitutional questions may be appealed to the US Supreme Court.

The nine superior courts are the main trial courts; superior court judges are appointed to 12-year terms. In addition, there are 37 district courts, and 42 justices of the peace serve rural areas.

San Juan is the seat of the US District Court for Puerto Rico, which has the same jurisdiction as federal district courts on the US mainland.

Puerto Rico's crime rate, 2,826 per 100,000 population in 1975, was far below the US average, despite a murder rate that ranked with the highest among the states. Estimated crime rates that year included murder and nonnegligent manslaughter, 16 per 100,000 population; forcible rape, 22; aggravated assault, 322; robbery, 173; burglary, 1,126; larceny-theft, 807; and automobile theft, 360. The death penalty is constitutionally forbidden.

17 ARMED FORCES

Principal US military installations in Puerto Rico are the Roosevelt Roads Naval Reservation, near Ceiba, and the Naval Communications Station at Ponce. Ramey Field, a former Strategic Air Command base near Aguadilla, on the west coast, was phased out during the 1970s and the land transferred to the Commonwealth. Use of Vieques for training maneuvers, including shelling and bombing, forced many of that island's residents to move; aerial and naval target practice on Culebra by the US Navy was halted by protests and legal action.

As of 1978, an estimated 163,000 veterans of US military service were living on the island, including 3,000 who served in World War I, 45,000 in World War II, 51,000 during the Korean conflict, and 47,000 during the Viet-Nam era. Expenditures on veterans totaled $240.3 million in 1977/78. Puerto Ricans suffered 731 combat deaths in Korea and 270 in Viet-Nam.

National Guard personnel in Puerto Rico totaled 9,800 in 1978. The island's police force reached 9,463 in 1975.

18 MIGRATION

Although migration from Puerto Rico to the US mainland is not an entirely new phenomenon—several Puerto Rican merchants were living in New York City as early as 1830—there were no more than 70,000 islanders in the US in 1940. Mass migration, spurred by the booming postwar job market in the US, began in 1947. The outmigration was particularly large from 1951 through 1959, when the net outflow of migrants from the island averaged more than 47,000 a year. According to the 1970 census, 1,391,463 ethnic Puerto Ricans were living on the mainland, about 41% of them born there; at least 30 cities have Puerto Rican communities of 5,000 or more. Puerto Ricans are found in significant numbers not only in New York State but also in New Jersey, Illinois, Pennsylvania, California, Florida, and elsewhere.

During the 1970s, in part because of the economic decline of many US urban centers, the migration trend reversed dramatically. Official estimates show that the net flow of migrants returning to the island totaled 196,000 from 1970 to 1978.

One striking aspect of the US–Puerto Rico migration pattern is its fluidity. As US citizens, Puerto Ricans can move freely between the island and the mainland. Even in the year when the heaviest net outflow was recorded—74,603 in 1953—fully 230,307 persons emigrated from the US mainland to Puerto Rico, as 304,910 Puerto Ricans were migrating the other way. In 1974, the island's net gain from migration was 8,524—a relatively small figure that masked a huge volume of traffic, 1,630,525 persons to Puerto Rico and 1,622,001 from it. This extreme mobility, though sensitive to the job market, would not be possible were it not for the increased income available to Puerto Ricans on both the island and the US mainland, and the fact that Puerto Ricans who come to the continental US generally preserve their ties of family and friendship with those in the Commonwealth, thus finding it easy to return, whether for a short stay at Christmastime or for a new job on the island.

19 INTERGOVERNMENTAL COOPERATION

A member of the US Council of State Governments, Puerto Rico subscribes to the Compact for Education, the Interstate Compact for the Supervision of Parolees and Probationers, and the Southern Interstate Energy Compact. In its relations with the US government, the Commonwealth is in most respects like a state, except in the key areas of taxation and representation. US laws are in effect, federal agencies regulate aviation and broadcasting, and Puerto Ricans participate in such federally funded programs as Social Security and food stamps. US aid to Puerto Rico totaled $1.3 billion in 1978/79.

20 ECONOMY

Puerto Rico made enormous strides economically in only four decades, changing from a backward agricultural society into a highly industrialized one. In 1940, annual income per capita was $118, agricultural workers made as little as 6 cents an hour, and the illiteracy rate was 70%. By 1978, income per capita was $2,600, the average hourly farm wage at least $1.65, and the illiteracy rate about 11%—in each case, far below the US average, but also in each case a vast improvement over former times.

The following table shows changes in composition of domestic income between 1950 and 1977:

	1950	1977
Manufacturing	15.2%	33.9%
Government	12.1	17.2
Trade	17.4	13.2
Services	7.3	10.4
Finance	8.9	9.1
Transportation, public utilities	8.7	8.8
Agriculture	25.6	3.9
Construction, mining	4.8	3.5
	100.0%	100.0%

The island's most important industrial products are apparel, textiles, pharmaceuticals, rum, and refined sugar. Tourism is the backbone of a large service industry, and the government sector has also grown. Tourist revenues and remittances from workers on the US mainland largely counterbalance Puerto Rico's chronic trade deficit.

Puerto Rico's major problem is lack of jobs for an expanding population, a problem exacerbated when rising unemployment in the US persuades Puerto Ricans to return to the island.

21 INCOME

Per capita income in Puerto Rico, $2,934 in 1979, was far lower than in any of the 50 states during that same year, but far exceeded that of its Caribbean neighbors. Total income increased from $1.3 billion in 1960 to $5 billion in 1972 and $7.3 billion in 1978. Median family income on the island in 1977 was $7,150.

Inequalities of income continue to plague Puerto Rico despite the overall economic progress. Between 1959 and 1969, for example, the share of the total income received by the top 10% income group declined from 45% to 36%, but the share earned by the bottom 10% also declined, from 0.44% to 0.31%, a statistic which suggests that although economic expansion has stimulated the growth of the middle class, the poorest segment of Puerto Rican society has not benefited from industrialization. As of 1975, an estimated 62% of all Puerto Rico residents, 69% of all children, and 79% of all families with children and a woman as head of household were below the federal poverty level.

22 LABOR

Puerto Rico's civilian labor force in 1978 numbered 971,000, of whom 796,000 were employed. There were 651,000 males and 320,000 females in the labor force—about 61% of eligible men, but only 28% of the women. More than 80% were wage and salary workers, distributed as follows:

Private sector:	
Agriculture	19,500
Mining	900
Contract construction	36,000
Manufacturing	134,200
Transportation, public utilities	20,400
Wholesale trade	29,200
Retail trade	67,700
Finance, insurance, real estate	19,100
Service industries (except private household)	64,000
Private household service	11,000

Public sector:	
Federal government	10,200
Commonwealth and local governments	244,800
TOTAL	657,000

Although about 150,000 new jobs have been created since 1950, unemployment remains a chronic problem. In no year between 1950 and 1978 did the unemployment rate dip below 10%, and in 1977 it reached a high of 19.9%. The overall unemployment rate in 1978 was 18%—20.2% for men and 13.8% for women. Unemployment, highest among the young, was most severe in the construction industry during the late 1970s. Especially problematic was the case of returning migrants who left the mainland because of the tight US job market, only to discover that jobs were just as scarce, if not more so, back home in the Commonwealth.

Approximately one-fourth of the labor force belongs to trade unions, of which the largest is the Sugar Workers' Union. Wages tend to adhere closely to the US statutory minimum. Although hourly earnings rose significantly in all sectors during the 1970s, only in the hotel and motel trade—a traditionally low-paying industry in the US—did wages in Puerto Rico approximate those in the 50 states. The following table compares average hourly earnings for selected industries in Puerto Rico with those in the US in 1971 and 1978:

	PUERTO RICO, 1971	% OF US AVERAGE	PUERTO RICO, 1978	% OF US AVERAGE
Food processing	$1.94	57.4%	$3.46	58.7%
Tobacco	1.56	51.5	3.00	50.0
Textiles	1.71	66.0	2.80	63.3
Apparel	1.70	67.7	2.83	70.6
Chemicals	2.36	59.0	4.63	64.4
Leather	1.59	60.2	2.56	65.0
Metal products	2.17	57.6	4.04	62.2
Electrical goods	2.01	57.4	3.76	63.1
Stone, clay, glass products	2.27	60.5	3.66	56.5
Hotels and motels	2.09	99.1	3.46	97.2

23 AGRICULTURE

In 1940, agriculture employed 43% of the work force; by 1976, only 6% of Puerto Rico workers had agricultural jobs. Nowhere is this decline more evident than in the sugar industry. Production peaked at 1,300,000 tons in 1952, when 150,000 cane cutters were employed; by 1978, however, production was 300,000 tons, fewer than 20,000 cutters were in the fields, and the industry was heavily subsidized. The hilly terrain makes mechanization difficult, and manual cutting contributes to production costs that are much higher than those of Hawaii and Louisiana. Despite incentives and subsidies, tobacco is no longer profitable, and coffee production—well adapted to the highlands—falls far short of domestic consumption. Pineapple growing, managed by the Puerto Rican Land Authority, was also unprofitable during much of the 1970s. One of the few promising long-term agricultural developments has been the attempt to convert sugarcane lands to the cultivation of rice, a staple food in the diet of most Puerto Rico residents.

The following table shows acreage and production data for leading crops in 1976:

	ACRES	OUTPUT
Coffee	130,000	252,000 hundredweight
Sugar	127,000	300,000 tons
Starchy vegetables	30,000	4,376,000 hundredweight
Fruits, misc.	21,000	2,843,000 hundredweight
Pigeon peas	14,000	88,000 hundredweight
Vegetables	11,000	7,000,000 hundredweight
Pineapple	3,500	42,000 tons
Tobacco	3,000	46,500 hundredweight

²⁴ANIMAL HUSBANDRY

Puerto Rico was producing, by the mid-1970s, about 90% of the dairy products consumed on the island, and about 50% of the eggs. Dairy and beef production, concentrated in the coastal flatlands, increased markedly during the 1960s and 1970s, but the output of meat and poultry did not keep pace with demand; imports tripled in volume between 1961 and 1976, when more than two-thirds of the island's supply of beef, pork, and chicken was imported.

Livestock products in 1976 included 46.4 million lb of beef, 46.2 million lb of pork, 37.9 million lb of poultry, 348 million eggs, and 104.4 million gallons of dairy products.

²⁵FISHING

Although sport fishing, especially for blue marlin, is an important tourist attraction, the waters surrounding Puerto Rico are too deep to lend themselves to commercial fishery. Tuna brought in from African and South American waters is processed at five large plants on the western shore that together provide much of the canned tuna sold in eastern US markets. As of 1979, the canneries employed 6,700 persons. Fishery products worth $295.1 million were exported in 1976/77.

²⁶FORESTRY

Puerto Rico lost its self-sufficiency in timber production by the mid-19th century, as population expansion and increasing demand for food led to massive deforestation. Today, commercial timberland is scarce, and the island must import at least 90% of its wood and paper products.

²⁷MINING

The search for gold first brought the Spaniards to Puerto Rico, but they soon exhausted the known supply. The island was thought barren of mineral resources until recently, when deposits of copper, silver, and gold were discovered in the mountains of the northwest. Nickel deposits in the southwest are also being explored, and offshore drilling for oil and gas is under consideration. For the present, construction materials are Puerto Rico's most abundant resource. Marble is quarried for terrazzo tiles, and sand, gravel, and crushed stone are used for concrete. Limestone and clay deposits are also exploited.

²⁸ENERGY AND POWER

Puerto Rico is almost totally dependent on imported crude oil for its energy needs. The island has not yet developed any fossil fuel resources of its own, and its one experimental nuclear reactor, built on the south coast at Rincón in 1964, was shut down after a few years. Solar-powered hot water heaters have been installed in a few private homes and at La Fortaleza.

The Puerto Rico Electric Power Authority, a public agency with some 700,000 customers, is the sole producer of electricity on the island. Consumption increased from 412 million kwh in 1950 to 12.2 billion kwh in 1977. Inefficiency in the public transport system has encouraged Commonwealth residents to rely on private vehicles, thereby increasing the demands for imported petroleum. Domestic consumption of petroleum products in 1977 totaled 61.2 million barrels, of which 45% was residual fuel oil, 26% gasoline, 10% middle distillates, 8% refinery gas, 4% aviation fuel, and 7% other products.

²⁹INDUSTRY

Manufacturing contributed more than $3.2 billion to net income in Puerto Rico during 1977/78, more than three times the total for 1969/70. In 1949, about 55,200 Puerto Rican workers were employed in industrial jobs, 26% of them in sugar refining. By 1977, however, more than 134,000 persons had jobs in manufacturing. The major employment categories were apparel, 36,200; electrical machinery, 13,600; food processing, 13,250; instruments, 12,000; and pharmaceuticals, 9,360. In 1947, sugar alone accounted for more than 30% of industrial output, which amounted to only $218 million. Thirty years later, industrial output totaled more than $3.3 billion, of which pharmaceuticals contributed nearly

27%; electrical machinery, 13%; apparel, 8%; petrochemicals, 7%; food products, 7%; alcoholic beverages, 6%; and other manufactures, 32%, including 0.2% for sugar.

Among major US pharmaceutical companies, Warner-Lambert, Eli Lilly, and Johnson & Johnson each had 7 plants in Puerto Rico by 1979, Baxter Travenol Laboratories had 10, and Bristol-Myers had 4. Such major manufacturers of electrical and electronic equipment as General Electric, Motorola, and GTE Sylvania all have multiple subsidiaries on the island. Gulf + Western Industries, Hanes, Phillips–Van Heusen, and Warnaco have extensive apparel holdings.

³⁰COMMERCE

Wholesale trade in Puerto Rico in 1972 involved 2,074 establishments and total receipts of $2.5 billion. Of that total, 31% came from groceries and related products, 10% from machinery and equipment, 9% from drugs and chemicals, and 8% from petroleum. Retail trade during the same year involved 29,980 establishments and total receipts of nearly $3 billion, the major sectors being food stores, restaurants, and taverns, 31%; new and used car dealers, 15%; and department stores, 7%. Two large shopping centers, Plaza las Américas and Plaza Carolina, are in the San Juan area.

Foreign trade, unrestricted by the US government, is a significant factor in Puerto Rico's economy. Imports have always exceeded exports: in 1976/77, the island's imports were $6.1 billion and exports $4.5 billion. During that year, the continental US received 86% of Puerto Rico's exports (91% in 1965/66) and supplied about 60% of its imports (82% in 1966). The principal reason for the relative decline in imports from the continental US, which nearly tripled in value during the same period, is the rising volume and cost of oil imports, especially from Venezuela. Other leading import suppliers are Japan and the Bahamas; after the continental US, the main purchasers of Puerto Rican goods are the US Virgin Islands and the Netherlands. The pattern of exports has also changed. Sugarcane accounted for more than 50% of the export value during the early 1950s, but only 2% in 1976/77. Meanwhile, manufactured exports (excluding apparel), which represented only 12% of the total exports in 1950, accounted for at least half of all exports by the late 1970s. The following table shows how major commodity groups shared in Puerto Rico's imports and exports during the 1966 and 1977 fiscal years:

| | IMPORTS | | EXPORTS | |
	1966	1977	1966	1977
Food, live animals	17.9%	17.6%	17.0%	11.9%
Mineral fuels	7.3	27.1	7.8	11.2
Beverages, tobacco	NA	NA	12.7	4.8
Chemicals	6.2	9.0	6.5	34.2
Machinery and transport equipment	20.2	15.1	9.5	11.5
Other items	48.4	31.2	46.5	26.4
TOTALS	100.0%	100.0%	100.0%	100.0%

³¹CONSUMER PROTECTION

Consumer protection is the responsibility of Puerto Rico's cabinet-level Department of Consumer Affairs, with offices in Santurce.

³²BANKING

Puerto Rico's first bank began operations in 1850. The Commonwealth's largest commercial bank, the Banco Popular—with savings deposits of nearly $2 billion by mid-1980—was founded in 1893, near the end of the Spanish colonial era. As of 31 December 1978, Puerto Rico had 12 insured commercial banks (2 of them national banks with branches in New York City), whose total assets exceeded $7.6 billion; outstanding loans were $2.9 billion, and deposits totaled $6.2 billion. During the same year, 12 savings and loan associations, all federally chartered, had total assets of $1.6 billion, including $1.3 billion in outstanding mortgage loans.

The Government Development Bank, founded in 1948, serves as a fiscal agent for the Commonwealth government, municipalities, and public authorities and corporations, while also extending credit to private industry. In 1977, the bank had assets of $1.1 billion and provided loans of $653 million to public and private borrowers.

[33]INSURANCE
Puerto Ricans in 1975 paid $370 million in insurance premiums: disability, $120.1 million; life, $67.4 million; automobile physical damage, $46.8 million; automotive liability, $28.5 million; commercial multiple peril, $21.1 million; and other lines, $86.1 million. Losses paid by insurance companies during the same year totaled $223.9 million: disability, $91.3 million; life, $26 million; automobile physical damage, $25.7 million; automotive liability, $21.9 million; commercial multiple peril, $8.1 million; and other lines, $50.9 million. Flood insurance worth $133.1 million was in force in mid-1979. During 1977, 300,000 Puerto Rico residents were enrolled in hospital insurance programs and 158,000 had medical insurance coverage, both under Medicare; benefits paid through Medicare included $55 million for hospitalization and $23 million for medical treatment.

[34]SECURITIES
There are no securities exchanges in Puerto Rico. Bonds issued by the Government Development Bank, exempt from federal income taxes and from the income taxes of all US states and cities, are offered for sale on the world securities market. By 1977, $6 billion in bonds were outstanding.

[35]PUBLIC FINANCE
Puerto Rico's annual budget is prepared by the Bureau of the Budget and submitted by the governor to the legislature, which has unlimited power to amend it. The fiscal year extends from 1 July to 30 June. The following table shows revenues and expenditures by the Commonwealth government during 1976/77 and 1977/78 (in millions):

	1976/77	1977/78
REVENUES		
Taxes, of which:	$1,723	$1,791
Personal	(533)	(460)
Corporate	(180)	(236)
Indirect business	(1,010)	(1,095)
Social insurance contributions	372	402
US federal transfers	860	989
Other receipts	118	193
TOTALS	$3,073	$3,375
EXPENDITURES		
Compensation of employees	$1,450	$1,558
Transfer payments to persons	570	579
Interest	149	179
Subsidies	100	106
Other outlays	509	541
TOTALS	$2,778	$2,963

In 1959/60, transfers from the US government amounted to $44 million, or less than 13% of all revenues. By 1972/73, receipts from the US government represented 23% of all revenues; by 1977/78, more than 29%. The gross public debt of the Commonwealth government as of 30 June 1976 was $986 million; municipal governments had outstanding obligations totaling $171.8 million.

[36]TAXATION
The Puerto Rican Federal Relations Act stipulates that the Commonwealth is exempt from US internal revenue laws. The federal income tax is not levied on permanent residents of Puerto Rico, but federal Social Security and unemployment taxes are deducted from payrolls, and the Commonwealth government collects an income tax that ranged in 1978 from 12.6% on the first $2,000 of taxable income to 82.95% on income exceeding $200,000. That same year, the corporate income tax ranged from 22% to 45%, with numerous important exemptions; the estate tax ranged from 3% to 70%, and the gift tax from 2.25% to 52.5%. Property, franchise, and excise taxes are also levied, with the excise tax on new and used cars being an especially important source of revenue.

Transfers from the US federal government to the Commonwealth government totaled $989 million during 1977/78, when direct governmental remittances to the US were only $90 million. In 1976/77, the total inflow of US federal funds to Puerto Rico exceeded $1.8 billion; the outflow of funds from Puerto Rico to the US Treasury was $728 million, of which 54% represented contributions to Social Security.

[37]ECONOMIC POLICY
Inaugurated during the 1940s, Operation Bootstrap had succeeded by the late 1970s in attracting investments from nearly 400 of the 1,000 largest US corporations. More than 1,800 factories have been established throughout the island; industrial plants built since World War II produce nearly three-fourths of Puerto Rico's exports. The key Puerto Rican agency responsible for this transformation is the Administración de Fomento Económico, known as Fomento (Development), which helps select plant sites, build factories, hire and train workers, and arrange financing. Fomento also reorganized certain industries, taking a direct role, for example, in promoting export sales of Puerto Rican rum. At first, Fomento brought in apparel and textile manufacturers, who needed relatively unskilled workers. More recently, with the improvement in Puerto Rico's educational system, Fomento has emphasized such technologically advanced industries as chemicals and pharmaceuticals. Industrialization has also required heavy investment in roads, power, water facilities, and communications systems.

The key incentives to investment in Puerto Rico have been lower wage scales than in the continental US and the exemption of corporate profits from Commonwealth taxes for periods ranging from 10 to 30 years. More recently, the Commonwealth government has offered specific incentives to service industries, sought to reduce imports (especially of food), and promised that the phaseout of industrial tax exemptions will be gradual. Under the US Tax Reform Act of 1976, US companies may repatriate earnings from their Puerto Rican subsidiaries free of federal taxation without waiting for the Commonwealth exemption period to expire.

[38]HEALTH
Health conditions in Puerto Rico have improved remarkably since 1940, when the average life expectancy was only 46 years. A resident of Puerto Rico born in 1975 could expect to live 72.3 years, nearly equaling the US average. Similarly, the infant mortality rate declined from 113 per 1,000 live births in 1940 to 20 in 1976—a rate that was still about 25% above the US norm. The leading causes of death in 1940 were diseases brought on by malnutrition or infection: diarrhea, enteritis, tuberculosis, and pneumonia. By 1975—when Puerto Rico enjoyed one of the lowest mortality rates in the world, only 5.8 per 1,000 population—the leading causes of death were similar to those in most industrialized countries, though the death rates (per 100,000 population) were generally lower: heart disease, 167; cancer, 96; stroke, 50. Alcoholism and drug addiction are among the major public health problems.

In 1978, Puerto Rico had 60 hospitals, with 11,407 beds; of these, 16 were operated by the Commonwealth. Hospital personnel included 4,356 registered nurses and 3,186 licensed practical nurses. The island had an estimated 3,400 physicians in 1977, and 975 dentists in 1976. More than 15,000 Puerto Ricans are employed by the Department of Health.

[39] SOCIAL WELFARE

Residents of Puerto Rico are eligible for most of the programs that apply throughout the 50 states. Benefits have been limited, however, by a US public assistance payment ceiling of $24 million imposed annually between 1972 and 1978 (but raised to $72 million for 1979) and by the ineligibility of Commonwealth residents for Supplemental Security Income. The average monthly payment in aid to families with dependent children in 1978 was only $49, about one-fifth the US average. It has been estimated that some 70% of the population is eligible for food stamps; 1,446,000 Commonwealth residents, a total exceeded only in New York State, actually took part in the program during 1978, receiving a US federal bonus worth $637.4 million, more than was allocated to any state and about 12.5% of the total US government subsidy. During the same year, 549,000 children received school lunches at a cost to the US government of $57.4 million.

Because unemployment is high and wages are low, Social Security benefits are well below the US average. In 1977, $706.6 million was paid to 532,300 Social Security recipients; the average monthly payment for a retiree was $154, 37% below the US norm. Vocational rehabilitation programs served 12,000 islanders in 1978, at a cost of $21.2 million. Unemployment insurance, paid to an average of 36,000 claimants a week, totaled $96 million; the average weekly benefit was $45, slightly more than half the US average.

[40] HOUSING

Between 1950 and 1976, more than 340,000 new housing units were built on the island, of which about one-fourth were in public housing. One spur to housing construction was the widespread availability of federal financing through two US agencies, the Federal Housing Administration and the Veterans Administration, which together guaranteed housing loans amounting to more than $1.5 billion from 1970 through 1976. In 1977, at a time when the construction industry was lagging, the housing deficit was estimated by a US study group at 204,000 units.

Utilities and amenities in urban housing are superior to those in rural. In 1977, for example, 24% of rural families had sewer service, as compared with 71% of urban families; about 80% of rural families had an in-house water supply. Electric power in 1970 was provided to 93% of all homes, but of the 7% that did not have electrical service, three-fifths were rural.

[41] EDUCATION

Puerto Rico has made enormous strides in public education. In 1900, only 14% of the island's school-age children were actually in school; the proportion had increased to 50% by 1940 and 85% by the late 1970s. Of the total labor force in 1979, more than 27% had at least one year of college, 37% had 1–3 years of high school, and another 15% had completed intermediate school without further study. The government encouraged school attendance among the poor in the 1940s and 1950s by providing inexpensive shoes, free lunches, school uniforms, and small scholarships. Today, nearly one out of three Commonwealth budget dollars goes to education.

As of 1976 there were 710,000 students in public elementary and secondary schools, and another 103,000 in private schools, mostly Roman Catholic. Close to 22,000 children were in prekindergarten and kindergarten programs. During 1978, 123,000 students were in higher educational institutions, of whom 50,000 were in the University of Puerto Rico system, with its main campus at Río Piedras. The system also includes a university campus at Mayagüez and two-year colleges at Aguadilla, Arecibo, Bayamón, Carolina, Humacao, and Ponce. Leading private institutions are Inter-American University, with campuses at Hato Rey, San Germán, and seven other locations; and the Catholic University of Puerto Rico, at Ponce. Numerous student aid and loan programs are available.

[42] ARTS

The Tapia Theater in Old San Juan is the island's major showcase for local and visiting performers, including *zarzuela* (comic opera) troupes from Spain. The Institute of Puerto Rican Culture produces an annual theatrical festival, and 150 movie theaters provide year-round entertainment.

Puerto Rico has its own symphony orchestra and conservatory of music. Both were formerly directed by Pablo Casals, and the annual Festival Casals, which he founded, still attracts worldrenowned musicians to the island each May. Puerto Rico supports both a classical ballet company and the Areyto Dance Ensemble, which performs traditional folk dances. Salsa, a popular style pioneered by Puerto Rican musicians like Tito Puente, influenced the development of pop music on the US mainland during the 1970s.

[43] LIBRARIES AND MUSEUMS

In 1977/78, Puerto Rico's public libraries contained about 1,085,000 volumes and had a combined circulation of 725,000. The University of Puerto Rico Library at Río Piedras held 617,917 books in 1978; the library of the Puerto Rico Conservatory of Music, in San Juan, has a collection of music written by Puerto Rican and Latin American composers. La Casa del Libro, also in San Juan, is a library-museum of typographic and graphic arts. The Museo de Arte de Ponce (Luis A. Ferré Foundation) has paintings, sculptures, and archaeological artifacts, as well as a library. The Museo Histórico de Puerto Rico, in Santurce, specializing in Puerto Rican history and art, is housed in military buildings that date from 1535. The Marine Station Museum in Mayagüez exhibits Caribbean marine specimens and sponsors research and field trips.

[44] COMMUNICATIONS

The Puerto Rico Telephone Co. was founded in 1914 by two German sugar brokers, Sosthenes and Hernand Behn, best known today as the creators of International Telephone and Telegraph (ITT). In 1974, the Puerto Rican government bought the phone company from ITT and began a five-year, $500-million improvement program financed by bond issues. By mid-1978 there were more than 550,000 telephones on the island. Direct dialing to the continental US was inaugurated in 1968. The US Postal Service handles Puerto Rico's mail traffic.

WKAQ, the island's first radio station, came on the air in 1923. As of 1978, commercial broadcasters in Puerto Rico operated 53 AM, 32 FM, and 8 television stations. The first television station, WKAQ-TV, began broadcasting in 1954; by 1970, more than 82% of the island's homes had at least one television set. There are two public stations, affiliated with the US Public Broadcasting System. English-language cable transmissions served 16,000 subscribers in the San Juan area in 1978.

[45] PRESS

Puerto Rico has three major Spanish-language dailies: *El Nuevo Día*, with a 1978 circulation of 130,324 mornings, 109,490 Sundays; *El Mundo*, 116,773 mornings, 131,890 Sundays; and *El Vocero*, 186,500 mornings. The English-language *San Juan Star*, with a circulation of 40,595 mornings and 45,479 Sundays, won a Pulitzer Prize in 1961. Newspapers from New York, Miami, and Chicago are sold at major newsstands.

[46] ORGANIZATIONS

Important organizations on the island include the Puerto Rico Medical Association, Puerto Rico Manufacturers' Association, and the Puerto Rico Bar Association. Also maintaining headquarters in Puerto Rico are the Association of Island Marine Laboratories of the Caribbean, Puerto Rico Rum Producers Association, and Caribbean Hotel Association.

US-based agencies such as the National Puerto Rican Forum and the Puerto Rican Community Development Project assist Puerto Ricans living on the mainland. "Hometown clubs" consisting of "absent sons" (*hijos ausentes*) of various Puerto Rican towns are a typical feature of the barrios in New York and other cities in the continental US.

⁴⁷TOURISM, TRAVEL, AND RECREATION

Only government and manufacturing exceed tourism in importance to the Puerto Rican economy. The industry has grown rapidly, from 65,000 tourists in 1950 to 1,088,000 in 1970 and 1,376,000 in 1977, when each traveler stayed an average of four days and spent $308 per visit. More than 80,000 jobs—11% of total employment—were generated by tourism in 1977.

As of 30 June 1977, hotels and guest houses had a combined total of 8,582 rooms, about 70% of them in the San Juan area. Of all those who registered in hotels that year, 60% were from the 50 states (mostly from New York, New Jersey, and Florida, where many Puerto Ricans live), 27% were Puerto Rico residents, 5% were from the West Indies, and virtually all the remainder were from Canada, South America, and Europe, in that order.

Most tourists come for sunning, swimming, deep sea fishing, and the fashionable shops, night clubs, and casinos of San Juan's Condado Strip. Attractions of Old San Juan include two fortresses, El Morro and San Cristóbal, San José Church (one of the oldest in the New World), and La Fortaleza, the governor's palace. The government has been encouraging tourists to journey outside San Juan to such destinations as the Arecibo Observatory (with its radio telescope used for research astronomy, ionospheric studies, and radar mapping), the rain forest of El Yunque, Phosphorescent Bay, colonial-style San Germán, and the bird sanctuary and mangrove forest on the shores of Torrecilla Lagoon.

⁴⁸SPORTS

Baseball is very popular in Puerto Rico. There is a six-team professional winter league, in which many ball players from American and National league teams participate. Horseracing is also popular, especially at El Comandante, east of San Juan; offtrack betting is legal. Cockfighting is a favorite spectator sport in Puerto Rico, whose 139 *galleras* (arenas), mostly in rural areas, offer matches on weekends from November through August; the newest cockfighting arena, the air-conditioned Coliseo Gallístico, is located at Isla Verde. Boxing and basketball also attract wide followings. Puerto Rico, which has had its own Olympic Committee since 1948, sent a delegation to the 1980 Olympics in Moscow despite the US boycott.

Facilities for all water sports, golf, tennis, and horseback riding are available, but many Puerto Ricans prefer a more sedentary pastime—dominoes.

⁴⁹FAMOUS PUERTO RICANS

Elected to represent Puerto Rico before the Spanish Cortes in 1812, Ramón Power y Giralt (1775–1813), a liberal reformer, was the leading Puerto Rican political figure of the early 19th century. Power, appointed vice president of the Cortes, participated in the drafting of the new Spanish constitution of 1812, but died suddenly of yellow fever in Cádiz when he was only 38. Ramón Emeterio Betances (1827–98) became well known not only for his efforts to alleviate a cholera epidemic in 1855, but also for his crusade to abolish slavery in Puerto Rico and as a leader of a separatist movement that culminated in 1868 in the "Grito de Lares." Eugenio María de Hostos (1839–1903), a writer, abolitionist, and educator, spent much of his adult life in Latin America, seeking to establish a free federation of the West Indies to replace colonial rule in the Caribbean. He founded schools in Santo Domingo and in Chile, and wrote prolifically in the fields of law, literary criticism, and sociology. Luis Muñoz Rivera (1859–1916), a liberal journalist, led the movement that obtained for Puerto Rico the Autonomic Charter of 1897, and he headed the cabinet that took office in 1898. With the island under US rule, Muñoz Rivera served between 1911 and 1916 as Puerto Rico's resident commissioner to the US Congress. Other

important Puerto Rican historical figures include Juan Alejo Arizmendi (1760?–1814), the first Puerto Rican–born bishop, appointed to the See of San Juan; José Celso Barbosa (1857–1921), a US-trained physician who founded the Republican Party of Puerto Rico in 1899; and José de Diego (1866–1918), a noted poet and gifted orator, who, under the Foraker Act, became the first speaker of the island house of delegates and was a champion of independence for Puerto Rico.

The dominant political figure in 20th-century Puerto Rico was Luis Muñoz Marín (1898–1980), founder of the Popular Democratic Party in 1938 and president of the Puerto Rico senate from 1940 to 1948. Muñoz, the first native-born elected governor of the island (1948–64), devised the commonwealth relationship that has governed the island since 1952. Another prominent 20th-century figure, Antonio R. Barceló (1869–1939), led the Unionista Party after Muñoz Rivera's death, was the first president of the senate under the Jones Act, and was later the leader of the Liberal Party. In 1946, Jesús T. Piñero (1897–1952) became the first Puerto Rican appointed governor of the island by a US president; he had been elected as resident commissioner of Puerto Rico to the US Congress two years before. Pedro Albizu Campos (1891–1965), a Harvard Law School graduate, presided over the militant Nationalist Party and was until his death the leader of forces that advocated independence for Puerto Rico by revolution. In 1945, Gilberto Concepción de Gracia (1909–68), also a lawyer, helped found the more moderate Puerto Rican Independence Party. Herman Badillo (b.1929) was the first person of Puerto Rican birth to be a voting member of the US House of Representatives, as congressman from New York, and Maurice Ferré (b.1935), elected mayor of Miami in 1973, was the first native-born Puerto Rican to run a large US mainland city.

Women have participated actively in Puerto Rican politics. Ana Roqué de Duprey (1853–1933) led the Asociación Puertorriqueña de Mujeres Sufragistas, organized in late 1926, while Milagros Benet de Mewton (1868–1945) presided over the Liga Social Sufragista, founded in 1917. Both groups actively lobbied for the extension of the right to vote to Puerto Rican women, not only in Puerto Rico but in the US and other countries as well. Felisa Rincón de Gautier (b.1897), mayor of San Juan from 1946 to 1968, was named Woman of the Americas in 1954, the year she presided over the Inter-American Organization for Municipalities. Carmen Delgado Votaw (b.1935) was the first person of Puerto Rican birth to be elected president of the Inter-American Commission of Women, the oldest international organization in the field of women's rights.

Manuel A. Alonso (1822–89) blazed the trail for a distinctly Puerto Rican literature with the publication, in 1849, of *El Gíbaro*, the first major effort to depict the traditions and mores of the island's rural society. Following him in the development of a rich Puerto Rican literary tradition were, among many others, that most prolific of 19th-century Puerto Rican writers, Alejandro Tapia y Rivera (1826–82), adept in history, drama, poetry, and other forms of literary expression; essayist and critic Manuel Elzaburu (1852–92); novelist Manuel Zeno Gandía (1855–1930); and poets Lola Rodríguez de Tió (1843–1924) and José Gautier Benítez (1848–80). The former's patriotic lyrics, popularly acclaimed, were adapted to become Puerto Rico's national anthem. Among 20th-century Puerto Rican literary figures are poets Luis Lloréns Torres (1878–1944), Luis Palés Matos (1898–1959), and Julia de Burgos (1916–1953); and essayists and critics Antonio S. Pedreira (1898–1939), Tomás Blanco (b.1900), José A. Balseiro (b.1900), Margot Arce (b.1904), Concha Meléndez (b.1904), Nilita Vientós Gastón (b.1908), and María T. Babín (b.1910). In the field of fiction, René Marqués (1919–79), Abelardo Díaz Alfaro (b.1919), José Luis González (b.1926), and Pedro Juan Soto (b.1928) are among the best known outside Puerto Rico.

In the world of entertainment, Academy Award winners José Ferrer (b.1912) and Rita Moreno (b.1931) are among the most famous. Notable in classical music are cellist-conductor Pablo Casals (b.Spain, 1876–1973), a long-time resident of Puerto Rico; pianist Jesús María Sanromá (b.1902); and opera star Justino Díaz (b.1940). Well-known popular musicians include Tito Puente (b.New York, 1923) and José Feliciano (b.1945).

Roberto Clemente (1934–72), one of baseball's most admired performers and a member of the Hall of Fame, played on 12 National League All-Star teams and was named Most Valuable Player in 1966.

⁵⁰BIBLIOGRAPHY

Babín, María Teresa. *The Puerto Ricans' Spirit: Their History, Life and Culture*. New York: Collier, 1971.

Berbusse, Edward J. *The United States in Puerto Rico: 1898–1900*. Chapel Hill: University of North Carolina Press, 1966.

Brau, Salvador. *Historia de Puerto Rico*. San Juan: Editorial Coquí, 1966 (orig. 1904).

Hostos, Adolfo de. *Diccionario Histórico Bibliográfico Comentado de Puerto Rico*. San Juan: Academia Puertorriqueña de la Historia, 1976.

Keller, Allan. *The Spanish-American War: A Compact History*. New York: Hawthorn, 1969.

Lewis, Oscar. *La Vida: A Puerto Rican Family in the Culture of Poverty—San Juan and New York*. New York: Random House, 1966.

Morales Carrión, Arturo. *Historia del Pueblo de Puerto Rico: desde sus Origenes hasta el Siglo XVIII*. San Juan: Editorial Cordillera, 1971.

Morales, Carrión, Arturo. *Puerto Rico and the Non-Hispanic Caribbean*. Río Piedras: University of Puerto Rico, 1971.

Puerto Rico Federal Affairs Administration. *Puerto Rico, U.S.A.* Washington, D.C., 1979.

Rivera de Alvarez, Josefina. *Diccionario de Literatura Puertorriqueña*. 2 vols. San Juan: Instituto de Cultura Puertorriqueña, 1974.

US Commission on Civil Rights. *Puerto Ricans in the Continental United States: An Uncertain Future*. Washington, D.C., 1976.

US Department of Commerce. *Economic Study of Puerto Rico*. 2 vols. Washington, D.C., 1979.

Vivó, Paquita. *The Puerto Ricans: An Annotated Bibliography*. New York: Bowker, 1973.

Votaw, Carmen Delgado. *Puerto Rican Women: Some Biographical Profiles*. Washington, D.C.: National Conference of Puerto Rican Women, 1978.

Wagenheim, Kal. *Puerto Rico: A Profile*. New York: Praeger, 1970.

Wagenheim, Kal, and Olga Jiménez de Wagenheim (eds.). *The Puerto Ricans: A Documentary History*. New York: Praeger, 1973.

Wells, Henry. *The Modernization of Puerto Rico*. Cambridge: Harvard University Press, 1969.

UNITED STATES CARIBBEAN DEPENDENCIES

MINOR ISLANDS AND SHOALS

Navassa, a 2-sq-mi (5-sq-km) island between Jamaica and Haiti, was claimed by the US under the Guano Act of 1856. The island, located at 18°24′N and 75°1′W, is uninhabited except for a lighthouse station under the administration of the Coast Guard. A group of shoals and tiny islands in the western Caribbean—including Quita Sueño Bank (14°28′N, 81°7′W), Roncador Cay (13°14′N and 85°5′W), Serrana Bank (14°17′N and 80°24′W), and Serranilla Bank (15°55′N and 79°50′W)—were due to be turned over to Colombia in the early 1980s, pending ratification of a treaty by the US Senate.

VIRGIN ISLANDS OF THE UNITED STATES

The Virgin Islands of the United States lie about 40 mi (64 km) E of Puerto Rico and 1,000 mi (1,600 km) SSE of Miami, between 17°40′ and 18°25′N and 64°34′ and 65°3′W. The island group extends 51 mi (82 km) N–S and 50 mi (80 km) E–W, with a total area of at least 132 sq mi (342 sq km). Only 3 of the more than 50 islands and cays are of significant size: St. Croix, 84 sq mi (218 sq km) in area; St. Thomas, 28 sq mi (73 sq km); and St. John, 20 sq mi (52 sq km). The territorial capital, Charlotte Amalie, on St. Thomas, has one of the finest harbors in the Caribbean.

St. Croix is relatively flat, with a terrain suitable for sugarcane cultivation. St. Thomas is mountainous and little cultivated, but it has many snug harbors. St. John, also mountainous, has fine beaches and lush vegetation; about two-thirds of St. John's area has been declared a national park. The subtropical climate, with temperatures ranging from 70° to 90°F (21–32°C) and a mean temperature of 78°F (26°C), is moderated by northeast trade winds. Rainfall, the main source of fresh water, varies widely, and severe droughts are frequent. The average yearly rainfall is 45 inches (114 cm), with most occurring during the summer months. As of 1979, both the Anegada ground iguana and the St. Croix ground lizard were threatened with extinction.

The population of the US Virgin Islands was estimated at 118,960 in 1978, a 271% increase over the 1960 census total of 32,099 and nearly double the 1970 census population of 62,468; St. Croix had an estimated population of 60,830; St. Thomas, 55,560; and St. John, 2,570. St. Croix has two principal towns: Christiansted and Frederiksted. Economic development has brought an influx of new residents, mainly from Puerto Rico, other Caribbean islands, and the US mainland. In 1970, only 66% of the population was native-born. Most permanent inhabitants are descendants of slaves who were brought from Africa in the early days of Danish rule, and about 70% of the population is black. A small settlement of French fishermen on St. Thomas maintains its own language and traditions. English is the official and most widely spoken language.

Some of the oldest religious congregations in the western hemisphere are located in the Virgin Islands. A Jewish synagogue there is the 2d oldest in the New World, and the Lutheran Congregation of St. Thomas, founded in 1666, is one of the three oldest congregations in the US. The Catholic population in the Virgin Islands was over 23,000 in 1979; data on the Protestant and Jewish populations were unavailable.

In 1978, 36,347 motor vehicles were registered in the US Virgin Islands. Cargo shipping services operate from Baltimore, Jacksonville, and Miami via Puerto Rico. In addition, weekly shipping service is available from Miami. In 1978, 777 cruise ships bearing 547,568 passengers arrived at Virgin Islands ports.

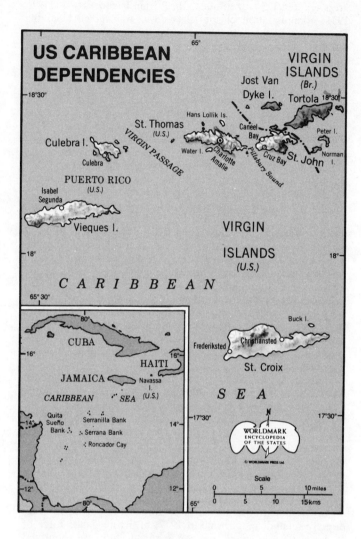

Both St. Croix and St. Thomas have airports, with St. Croix's facility handling the larger number of jet flights from the continental US and Europe. In 1978, 765,960 airline passengers landed in the US Virgin Islands; nearly 75% of these were tourists. In 1979, the islands had 3 cable offices, 7 radio stations (4 AM and 3 FM), and 3 television stations, including 1 public broadcasting channel. There were 36,973 telephones in 1978, and about 30,000 homes had television sets.

Excavations at St. Croix in the 1970s uncovered evidence of a civilization perhaps as ancient as AD 100. Christopher Columbus, who reached the islands in 1493, named them for the martyred virgin St. Ursula. At this time, St. Croix was inhabited by Carib Indians, who were eventually driven from the island by Spanish soldiers in 1555. In the 17th century, the archipelago was divided into two territorial units, one controlled by the British, the other (now the US Virgin Islands) controlled by Denmark. The separate history of the latter unit began with the settlement of St. Thomas by the Danish West India Co. in 1672. St. John was claimed by the company in 1683, and St. Croix was purchased from France in 1733. The holdings of the company were taken over as a Danish crown colony in 1754. Sugarcane, cultivated by slave labor, was the backbone of the islands' prosperity in the 18th and early 19th centuries. After brutally suppressing several slave revolts, Denmark abolished slavery in the colony in 1848. A long period of economic decline followed, until Denmark sold the islands to the US in 1917 for $25 million. Congress granted US citizenship to the Virgin Islanders in 1927. In 1931, administration of the islands was transferred from the Department of the Navy to the Department of the Interior, and the first civilian governor was appointed. In the late 1970s, the Virgin Islands government began to consider ways to expand self-rule. A UN delegation in 1977 found little interest in independence, however, and a locally drafted constitution was voted down by the electorate in 1979.

The chief executive of the Virgin Islands is the territorial governor. On 7 November 1970, Cyril E. King became the first governor of the islands elected by direct popular vote (governors had previously been appointed by the US president). Constitutionally, the US Congress has plenary authority to legislate for the territory. Enactment of the Revised Organic Act of the Virgin Islands on 22 July 1954 vested local legislative power—subject to veto by the governor—in a unicameral legislature, which in 1979 was composed of 15 members elected for two-year terms by popular vote. Seven legislators were from St. Croix, 7 from St. Thomas, and 1 from St. John. A two-thirds vote of the legislature is needed to override a veto by the governor. Since 1972, the islands have sent one nonvoting representative to the US House of Representatives.

Courts are under the US federal judiciary; the two federal district court judges are appointed by the US president. Territorial court judges, who preside over misdemeanor and traffic cases, are appointed by the governor and confirmed by the legislature. The district court has appellate jurisdiction over the territorial court.

Tourism has supplanted agriculture as the islands' principal economic activity. The number of tourists rose dramatically throughout the late 1960s and early 1970s, from 448,165 in 1964 to 1,116,127 in 1972/73. A series of murders on St. Croix in 1972/73 had a devastating effect on the tourist trade, particularly on overnight stays, and the occupancy rate for hotels dropped below 50% in 1973, 1974, and 1976. The tourist industry was rebuilt through a public relations campaign, however, and in 1978 the hotel occupancy rate was up to 74%. A total of 1,184,270 tourists visited the islands and spent over $240 million in 1978.

An estimated 30% of the labor force is employed in areas directly related to tourism. In 1977, of a total labor force of 40,778, 27% was employed in government, 15% in retail and wholesale trade, 12% in services, 9% in hotels, and 7% in manufacturing. The overall unemployment rate was 7.9%, but the rate among black youths may be much higher. Underemployment of black youths remains a major social problem and has been blamed for the islands' rising crime rate. Per capita income in 1978 was $5,376.

Much of the land formerly devoted to agriculture has been developed for tourism and industry. From 1917 to 1975, the total farm acreage on St. Croix was reduced by 56%, on St. Thomas by 78%, and on St. John by 92%. Overall, land devoted to agriculture declined from 69,892 acres (28,284 hectares) in 1917 to 24,703 acres (9,997 hectares) in 1975. Fruit and vegetables and livestock are raised on the farmland that remains.

Electrical energy production in 1978 was 426 million kwh, delivered to 33,911 customers. Power outages were frequent during the 1970s because of a lack of backup power to replace generators shut down for maintenance and repair. Work was suspended on a 35,000-kw steam unit in 1976 when funds for the project were depleted.

Rum is an important manufacture and export even though only 70 persons were actually employed in rum manufacturing in 1978. In 1977/78, the Virgin Islands received from the US government $24,480,815 in excise taxes on rum, based on shipments to the US of 2,981,731 gallons; rum excise taxes made up 17% of the islands' net government revenues in 1978/79. Virgin Islands rum claimed an 11% share of the US market during the late 1970s, 2d only to Puerto Rican rum. The Hess oil refinery on St. Croix employed 1,400 persons in 1979; production was threatened in 1980 by the shutoff of oil from Iran, which had formerly supplied about 50% of the crude oil. In the mid-1970s, the government began a campaign to attract the movie and advertising industries to the Virgin Islands.

Most basic goods must be imported to the islands, making for an unfavorable balance of trade. Petroleum is the major import category, for local use and for the Hess refinery. Imports in 1978 totaled $3.1 billion, of which 12% came from the US (including Puerto Rico); exports were $2.5 billion, of which 96% went to the US.

To encourage industrial development, the territorial government offers an extensive program of business incentives allowing a company to receive, for a period of 10 years, a nontaxable subsidy equal to 90% of income tax liability, exemptions from property and excise taxes, and a nontaxable subsidy equal to 90% of customs duties on raw materials.

The total operating budget for the US Virgin Islands in 1977/78 was $110,116,812. Major sources of consolidated revenues were US customs collections, 43%; taxes, 32%; federal contributions, 19%. Allocation of consolidated expenditures was as follows: subsidies for commercial and industrial development, 48%; education, 13%; government, 9%; health and medical programs, 8%; sanitation and waste removal, 4%; transportation and communications, 4%; other purposes, 14%.

The Department of Health provides hospital, medical, and public health services. A schedule of graduated fees has been established, based on ability to pay. There are two general hospitals, one on St. Thomas and the other on St. Croix. Both the neonatal and infant death rates in the Virgin Islands are much higher than the US averages.

As of 1980, monthly public assistance payments averaged $52 per recipient, an amount that had not been increased since 1970. Aid to families with dependent children, old-age assistance, and aid to the disabled amounted to $2.4 million in 1978, with onehalf coming from the federal government. About 21,000 children participated in the federal school lunch program at a cost to the US government of $2.2 million. The Community Action Agency operated 14 antipoverty programs with $679,118 in territorial budget appropriations and about $2.5 million in federal funds during 1977/78.

Education is compulsory in the US Virgin Islands, but the dropout rate is high. In 1977/78, a total of 25,014 children were enrolled in public schools and 6,909 in private schools. Overcrowding and lack of supplies are major problems in the schools, and many schools operate on double session. The Division of Vocational-Technical Education is responsible for retraining the unemployed, underemployed, and disadvantaged, as well as providing vocational training to secondary school students. In 1978, 2,019 secondary students in grades 9–12 participated in vocational programs, with 72 students engaged in on-the-job training. An additional 3,260 students were enrolled in prevocational programs at the junior high school level. A special adult education program had 2,747 students in 1977/78. The College of the Virgin Islands had 2,119 students, with 616 full-time undergraduates. In 1978, libraries in the Virgin Islands had a total circulaion of 67,700 volumes; the major library on the islands was located in Charlotte Amalie, St. Thomas.

UNITED STATES
PACIFIC DEPENDENCIES

AMERICAN SAMOA

American Samoa, an unincorporated insular US territory in the South Pacific Ocean, comprises that portion of the Samoan archipelago lying E of longitude 171°W. (The rest of the Samoan islands make up the independent state of Western Samoa.) While the Samoan group as a whole has an area of 1,205 sq mi (3,121 sq km), American Samoa consists of only seven small islands (between 14° and 15°S and 168° and 171°W) with a total area (land and water) of 76 sq mi (197 sq km). Five of the islands are volcanic, with rugged peaks rising sharply, and two are coral atolls. The climate is hot and rainy; normal temperatures range from 75°F (24°C) in August to 90°F (32°C) from December through February. The average annual rainfall is 130 inches (330 cm); the rainy season lasts from November through March. Hurricanes are common. The native flora includes tree ferns, coconut, hardwoods, and rubber trees. There are few wild animals.

As of the 1970 census, the population was 27,159, an increase of over 7,100 since 1960; the preliminary 1980 census total was 32,395, 19% more than in 1970. The inhabitants are almost pure Polynesian. Samoan and English are the principal languages. Most Samoans are Christians.

The capital and international port of the territory, Pago Pago, on the island of Tutuila, has one of the finest natural harbors in the South Pacific. American Samoa is a duty-free port. Passenger liners call there on South Pacific tours, and cargo ships arrive regularly from New Zealand, Australia, and the US west coast. There are regular air and sea services between American Samoa and Western Samoa, and regular flights connecting Pago Pago with Honolulu and the US mainland. During 1977/78, Pago Pago International Airport processed 10,418 flights and 171,664 passengers. As of 1979, telephone service was available to every village in American Samoa. Radiotelegraph circuits connect the territory with Hawaii, Fiji, and Western Samoa.

American Samoa was settled by Melanesian migrants in the 1st millennium BC. The Samoan islands were visited in 1768 by the French explorer Louis Antoine de Bougainville, who named them the Iles des Navigateurs as a tribute to the skill of their native boatmen. In 1889, the US, the United Kingdom, and Germany agreed to share control of the islands. The United Kingdom later withdrew its claim, and under the 1899 Treaty of Berlin, the US was internationally acknowledged to have rights extending over all the islands of the Samoan group lying east of 171°W, while Germany was acknowledged to have similar rights to the islands west of that meridian. The islands of American Samoa were officially ceded to the US by the various ruling chiefs in 1900 and in 1904, and on 20 February 1929 the US Congress formally accepted sovereignty over the entire group. From 1900 to 1951, the territory was administered by the US Department of the Navy, thereafter by the Department of the Interior.

The executive branch of the government is headed by the governor, who, along with the lieutenant governor, is elected by popular vote. (Before 1977 the two posts were appointed by the US president.) Village, county, and district councils have full authority to regulate local affairs. The legislature (Fono) is composed of the house of representatives and the senate. The 15 counties select, according to Samoan custom, 18 *matais* (chiefs) to four-year terms in the senate, while the 20 house members are elected for two-year terms by popular vote within the counties.

The secretary for Samoan affairs, who heads the Department of Local Government, is appointed by the governor. Under his administration are three district governors, the county chiefs, village mayors, and police officials. The judiciary, an independent branch of the government, functions through the high court and five district courts. Samoans living in the islands as of 17 April 1900 or born there since that date are nationals of the US; they may migrate freely to the US proper, and may become US citizens after fulfilling the requirements of the Immigration and Nationality Act.

The economy is primarily agricultural. The median family income in 1976 was $6,329—among the lowest for the US territories. Small plantations occupy about one-third of the land area; all but 5% of the land is communally owned. The principal crops are bananas, breadfruit, taro, papayas, pineapples, sweet potatoes, tapioca, coffee, cocoa, and yams. In 1977/78, 406,102 lb of vegetables, 330,825 lb of bananas, and 136,970 lb of taro were sold at local markets. Hogs and poultry are the principal livestock raised; dairy cattle are few.

American Samoa's labor force in 1978 was 9,663, of whom 3,725 were government employees. A California concern—Starkist Tuna—operates a modern tuna cannery, supplied with fish caught by Japanese fishing fleets; a second tuna cannery began operation in 1964. The two canneries provided employment for 1,457 men and women in 1978. The Pago Pago Intercontinental Hotel, opened in 1965 by the American Samoan Development Corp., and a new air terminal, which can accommodate Boeing 747 jets, have contributed to the further development of the tourist trade in the territory. The unemployment rate was 14% in 1978.

Owing largely to the cannery operations, American Samoa's balance of international trade has been highly favorable. In 1978, exports were valued at $104,155,656, nearly three times the 1970 total. American Samoa's trade is sensitive to fluctuations in the value of canned tuna shipments, since they comprise more than 90% of the territory's total exports. The islands are highly dependent on imports, which more than quadrupled between 1970 and 1978. In 1978, total imports were valued at $73,339,727. Fuel and oil make up 37% of the total; food, 16%; and jewelry, 11%.

Local revenues are supplemented by grants-in-aid and direct US appropriations. In 1977/78, grants-in-aid from the US Department of the Interior totaled $19,831,000, and other federal aid was $12,269,500. US currency is legal tender in the territory. Banking and credit are handled by the government-owned Development Bank of American Samoa, which had $3,578,638 in assets as of 30 June 1978.

American Samoans are entitled to free medical treatment, including hospital care. Besides district dispensaries, the government maintains a central hospital, a tuberculosis unit, and a leprosarium. In 1978, 11 staff physicians worked with 16 Samoan medical practitioners, 19 registered nurses, and 156 licensed practical nurses.

Education is a joint undertaking between the territorial government and the villages. School attendance is compulsory for all children from 6 through 18, and about 99% of the population 10 years of age and over is literate. The villages furnish the elementary school buildings and living quarters for the teachers; the territorial government pays all salaries, and provides buildings and supplies for all but primary schools. Since 1964, educational television has served as a basic teaching tool in the school system. In 1977/78 there were 6,464 pupils in elementary schools (grades 1–8) and 2,777 at the secondary level. American Samoa Community College had a fall 1978 enrollment of 777. The Department of Education budget was $9,384,832 in 1977/78; 11% of the funds were local, and 89% federal.

The Office of Tourism actively promotes development of the tourist industry. American Samoa attracted 11,157 tourists in 1978.

CANTON AND ENDERBURY ISLANDS
Canton Island (2°50′S and 171°40′W) is an atoll in the Central Pacific Ocean about 2,000 mi (3,220 km) W of Honolulu; it is about 4 mi (6 km) wide by 8 mi (13 km) long. To the SE is Enderbury Island (3°8′S and 171°5′W), an uninhabited atoll. The total area (land and water) of the islands is 27 sq mi (70 sq km). The islands were claimed by the US under the Guano Act of 1856 and were worked for guano until late in the 19th century. The United Kingdom, regarding them as in the Phoenix Islands group, claimed them in 1937 and built a radar station on Canton. The US formally claimed them in 1938 and placed them under Department of Interior jurisdiction. Both countries sent a few colonists to Canton in 1938, and it now serves as an emergency airfield. The two islands were made a US-UK condominium in 1939, an arrangement that ended in 1979. A new treaty ceding the islands to the independent Pacific nation of Kiribati had not yet been ratified by the US Senate as of 1980. Pending passage of the treaty, representatives of the US Department of the Interior and Kiribati were to monitor the islands.

GUAM
The largest and most populous of the Mariana Islands in the Western Pacific, Guam (13°30′N and 144°40′E) has a total area of 212 sq mi (549 km) and is about 30 mi (48 km) long and from 4 to 10 mi (6 to 16 km) wide. The island is of volcanic origin; in the south the terrain is mountainous, while the northern part is a plateau with shallow fertile soil. Cliffs on the northern end rise 500 feet (152 meters) above sea level. The central part of the island (where the capital, Agaña, is located) consists of undulating country.

Guam lies in the typhoon belt of the Western Pacific. In May 1976 a typhoon caused an estimated $300 million in damage and left 80% of the island's buildings in ruins. In general, Guam has a tropical climate with little seasonal variation. The average temperature is 79°F (26°C); annual rainfall is substantial, ranging from 85 inches (216 cm) at Apra Harbor to 110 inches (279 cm) in the mountains.

The 1970 census showed a population, including US military and civilian personnel and their families, of 84,996, a growth of 27% over the 1960 total. In July 1978, the population was estimated at 109,000, of whom 18,000 were uniformed military personnel and their dependents and 6,300 were aliens and other temporary residents; local residents numbered 84,700. The present-day Chamorro, who comprise about 62% of the permanent resident population, descend from the intermingling of the few surviving original Chamorro with Spanish, Filipino, and Mexican settlers, plus later arrivals from the US, United Kingdom, Korea, China, and Japan. Filipinos (21%) are the largest ethnic minority. Chamorro is the primary language of many Guamanians, but English is the official language. Roman Catholicism is the dominant religion.

There were about 270 mi (435 km) of roads in 1979. Apra, the only good harbor, ships goods to Japan, Taiwan, Hawaii, and the Trust Territory of the Pacific Islands. Four international airlines served Guam in 1979, with flights from California, Honolulu, Hong Kong, and Japan. Telephones numbered about 12,332 in 1978; overseas calls can be dialed directly.

The earliest known settlers on Guam were the original Cha-morro, who migrated from the Malay Peninsula to the Pacific around 1500 BC. When Ferdinand Magellan landed on Guam in 1521, it is believed that as many as 100,000 Chamorro lived on the island; by 1741, their numbers had been reduced to 5,000—most of the population either had fled the island or been killed through disease or war with the Spanish. A Spanish fort was established in 1565, and from 1696 until 1898, Guam was under Spanish rule. Under the Treaty of Paris that ended the Spanish-American War in 1898, the island was ceded to the US and placed under the jurisdiction of the Department of the Navy. During World War II, Guam was occupied by Japanese forces; the US recaptured the island in 1944 after 54 days of fighting. In 1950, the island's administration was transferred from the Navy to the US Department of the Interior. Under the 1950 Organic Act of Guam, passed by the US Congress, the island was established as an unincorporated territory of the US; Guamanians were granted US citizenship, and internal self-government was introduced.

The executive branch of government is headed by the governor, who with the lieutenant governor serves a four-year term. In 1970, the office was filled for the first time through direct election rather than presidential appointment.

A unicameral legislature of 21 senators from four districts is empowered to legislate on all local matters, including taxation and appropriations. The US Congress reserves the right to annul any law passed by the Guam legislature, but must do so within a year of the date it receives the text of any such law. A representative from Guam to the US House of Representatives has no vote on the floor, although he can vote in committee. A territorial constitution was drafted in 1977 and submitted to Guamanian voters in 1979. They rejected the document after critics contended that its provisions for self-government were inadequate.

Judicial authority is vested in the district court of Guam, and appeals may be taken to the regular US courts of appeal and ultimately to the US Supreme Court. An island court, a police court, and a juvenile court have jurisdiction over certain cases arising under Guamanian law. The judge of the district court is appointed by the US president; the judges of the other courts are appointed by the governor. Guam's laws were codified in 1953.

Guam is one of the most important US military bases in the Pacific, and the island's economy has been profoundly affected by the large sums of money spent by the US defense establishment. During the late 1960s and early 1970s, when the US was a major combatant in the Viet-Nam conflict, Guam served as a base for long-range US bombers on sorties over Indochina. In 1975, Guam was a way station for more than 100,000 Indochinese refugees. Military personnel on active duty in July 1978 totaled 8,779, of whom 5,703 were in the Navy, and 2,592 in the Air Force. Military expenditures on Guam reached $286,355,000 in 1977/78, including $84,364,000 in military pay, $78,734,000 in civilian pay, and $70,349,000 in military construction. Contending that military land ownership had impeded the island's economic development, Guam's civilian government sought the release of military landholdings during the late 1970s.

Prior to World War II, agriculture and animal husbandry were the primary economic activities. By 1947, however, most adults were wage earners employed by the US armed forces, although many continued to cultivate small plots to supplement their earnings. Median family income, $7,886 in 1970, had risen to $15,954 by 1977.

Melons, bananas, coconuts, rice, cocoa, pineapples, and indigo grow in the fertile valleys, but agriculture has not returned to prewar levels, partly because a considerable amount of arable land is taken up by military installations. In 1978, the agricultural sector produced 3,309 tons of fruits and vegetables worth $3,639,470; 1,149 tons of eggs valued at $2,527,800; and 524 tons of pork worth $889,950. The lack of available land in the port area is the major obstacle to development of a fisheries industry.

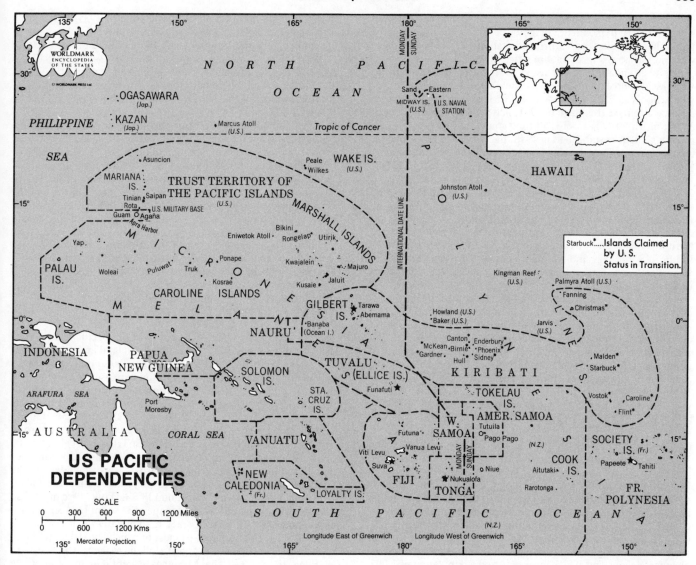

US PACIFIC DEPENDENCIES

Electric power is derived from fossil fuels; the Guam Power Authority, an autonomous agency, controls power generation and distribution. Power consumption was 461.4 million kwh in 1978. Revenues that year from power sales reached $25,166,000.

Guam has a vigorous and growing business community, as well as a rapidly growing tourist industry. Business revenues peaked at $786,423,000 in 1978. Manufacturing accounted for 24% of all business revenues; 90% of that share came from petroleum refinery operations. Retail trade made up 33% of business revenues in 1978 and employed 5,411 people in 1977. Guam's economy suffered a downturn in the mid-1970s, following the end of US military involvement in Southeast Asia. In 1976, unemployment reached a high of 12.6%; by 1978, however, the economic situation had improved, and unemployment was down to 7.5%.

Tourism expanded rapidly in the early 1970s, but the worldwide recession in mid-decade and the 1976 typhoon brought on a temporary decline. In 1978, 231,975 visitors, nearly 70% of them Japanese, spent about $116 million on the island.

The Guam Rehabilitation Act of 1963 was designed by the US Congress to fund the territory's capital improvement programs. Two further allocations in 1969 and 1977, totaling over $120 million, provided for further capital improvements and development of the island's power installations. More than $200 million in federal funds were authorized for typhoon relief in 1977–78.

Guam usually shows a large trade deficit. In 1978, exports were estimated at $34,192,000 (compared with $5,832,316 in 1970), while imports cost $272,000,000 ($96,402,314 in 1970). The bulk of Guam's trade is with the US, the Trust Territory of the Pacific Islands, and Japan. Refined petroleum and petroleum products are the major exports; and petroleum, food, and manufactured goods are the largest imports.

General revenues were $133,821,813 in 1977/78; current expenditures were $143,291,598, of which public education accounted for 34%. US income tax laws are applicable in Guam; all internal revenue taxes derived by the US from Guam are paid into the territorial treasury. US customs duties, however, are not levied; Guam is a duty-free port. In its trade with the US mainland, Guam is required to use US shipping.

By local custom, the aged, the indigent, and orphans are cared for by their families. However, the federal government has begun to play a larger role in public welfare. In 1978, $5,059,785 in public welfare benefits, more than twice the total for 1972, was paid to Guamanians. Of that amount, 61% went for aid to families with dependent children (AFDC), and 19,098 people received food stamps worth $13,254,356.

Typical tropical diseases are practically unknown today in Guam. Tuberculosis, long the principal killer, was brought under control by the mid-1950s. Hospital facilities include the Guam Memorial Hospital, which has a special tuberculosis wing, and a new medical center, opened in 1979. The US Naval Hospital serves military personnel. Village dispensaries function both as public health units and as first-aid stations. In addition, there were 66 physicians in private practice in 1977.

School attendance is compulsory from the age of 6 through 16. In 1978/79, enrollment in public schools totaled 28,529; in private schools, 5,223. The University of Guam in Agaña, which became a four-year college in 1961, had a 1978/79 enrollment of 3,104, of whom 1,657 were full-time students. The Guam Community College, established in 1978, had 2,486 students, including participants in high school and adult education programs.

HOWLAND, BAKER, AND JARVIS ISLANDS

Howland Island (0°48′N and 176°38′W), Baker Island (0°14′N and 176°28′W), and Jarvis Island (0°23′S and 160°1′W) are three small coral islands, each about 1 sq mi (2.6 sq km) in area, of the Line Islands group located in the Central Pacific Ocean. All three are administered directly from Washington as US unincorporated territories. Howland was discovered in 1842 by US sailors, claimed by the US in 1857, and formally proclaimed a US territory in 1935–36. It was worked for guano by US and British companies until about 1890.

Baker, 40 mi (64 km) S of Howland, and Jarvis, 1,100 mi (1,770 km) E of Howland, also were claimed by the US in 1857, and their guano deposits were similarly worked by US and British enterprises. Britain annexed Jarvis in 1889. In 1935, the US sent colonists from Hawaii to all three islands, which were placed under the US Department of the Interior in 1936. Baker was captured by the Japanese in 1942 and recaptured by the US in 1944. The three islands have no permanent residents but are visited annually by the US Coast Guard.

JOHNSTON ATOLL

Johnston Atoll, located in the North Pacific 715 mi (1,151 km) SW of Honolulu, consists of two islands, Johnston (16°44′N and 169°31′W) and Sand (16°45′N and 169°30′W), with a total land and water area of about 1 sq mi (2.6 sq km). It was discovered by English sailors in 1807 and claimed by the US in 1858. For many years, it was a bird reservation. Commissioned as a naval station in 1941, it remains an unincorporated US territory under the control of the US Department of the Air Force. In recent years, it has been used primarily for high-altitude testing of nuclear weapons and for storing nerve gas and other toxic and nontoxic chemical agents. The 1970 census reported a population of 1,007, but by 1978 only about 300 persons resided on the islands.

MALDEN AND STARBUCK ISLANDS

Malden Island (4°3′S and 154°59′W), formerly known as Independence Island, is about 35 sq mi (91 sq km) in area; the much smaller Starbuck Island (5°37′S and 155°33′W) was formerly known as Volunteer Island. Although regarded by the United Kingdom as part of the Phoenix Islands group, both islands are also claimed by the US. Once worked for their guano, they were uninhabited at the 1970 census. Starbuck was discovered in 1823 and claimed by the United Kingdom in 1866. Malden was discovered by the US in 1825 and claimed under the Guano Act of 1856; the United Kingdom claimed it in 1889. Malden contains Polynesian shrines of an undetermined period. A 1979 treaty ceding the islands to the independent Pacific nation of Kiribati had not yet been ratified by the US Senate as of 1980. Pending passage of the treaty, representatives of the US Department of the Interior and Kiribati were to monitor the islands.

MIDWAY

Midway (28°12′–17′N and 177°19′–26′W) consists of an atoll and two small islets, Eastern Island and Sand Island, about 1,300 mi (2,100 km) WNW of Honolulu. Their total land and water area is 2 sq mi (5 sq km). Their population was 2,220 as of the 1970 census.

Discovered and claimed by the US in 1859 and formally annexed in 1867, Midway became a submarine cable station early in the 20th century and an airlines station in 1935. Made a US naval base in 1941, Midway was attacked by the Japanese in December 1941 and January 1942. In one of the decisive battles of World War II, a Japanese naval attack on 3–6 June 1942 was repelled by US airplanes. There is a naval station at Midway, and the island is a US unincorporated territory under the administrative control of the US Department of the Navy.

PALMYRA ATOLL

Palmyra, an atoll in the Central Pacific Ocean, containing some 50 islets (with a total area of about 4 sq mi (10 sq km), is situated about 1,000 mi (1,600 km) SSW of Honolulu at 5°52′N and 162°5′W. It was discovered in 1802 by the USS *Palmyra*, formally annexed by the US in 1912, and was under the jurisdiction of the city of Honolulu until 1959, when Hawaii became the 50th state of the US. It is now the responsibility of the US Department of the Interior. The atoll is privately owned by the Fullard-Leo family of Hawaii. In 1979, the US government expressed interest in purchasing it as a nuclear waste storage area.

Kingman Reef, NW of Palmyra Atoll at 6°25′N and 162°23′W, was discovered in 1798, annexed by the US in 1922, and became a naval reservation in 1934. Now abandoned, it remains under the control of the US Department of the Navy.

TRUST TERRITORY OF THE PACIFIC ISLANDS

The US-administered Trust Territory of the Pacific Islands consists of 2,141 islands and atolls with a total land area of 716 sq mi (1,854 sq km) scattered over some 3,000,000 sq mi (7,800,000 sq km) of the Western Pacific Ocean, an expanse almost equal to the area of the continental US. The islands form part of Micronesia. Only about 100 of the islands support resident populations. The territory extends about 2,700 mi (4,350 km) from 130° to 172° E, and 1,500 mi (2,400 km) from 1° to 20°N; its approximate geographical center is the island of Truk, lying about 5,000 mi (8,000 km) SW of San Francisco and 2,000 mi (3,200 km) E of the Philippines. Three groups of islands are included in the territory: The Caroline Islands, to the S and W, include Palau, 191 sq mi (495 sq km), at 7°30′N and 138°8′E; Truk, 49 sq mi (127 sq km), at 7°25′N and 151°47′E; Ponape, 133 sq mi (344 sq km), at 6°58′N and 158°31′E; and Kosrae, 42 sq mi (109 sq km), at 5°19′N and 162°59′E. The Marshall Islands, of which Kwajalein (8°43′ to 9°15′N and 167°30′E) is the largest atoll, lie to the E. The Northern Mariana Islands (all the Marianas except Guam, a separate political entity) include Rota, 33 sq mi (85 sq km), at 14°7′–12′N and 145°8′–18′E; Saipan, 47 sq mi (122 sq km), at 15°5′–17′N and 145°41′–50′E; and Tinian, 39 sq mi (101 sq km), at 14°58′N and 145°38′E.

The Marianas are a volcanic archipelago. Other volcanic islands are found in the western Carolines, and there are volcanic outcroppings on Truk, Ponape, and Kosrae in the eastern Carolines. Other islands, mostly atolls, are of coral formation. The climate is tropical, with relatively little seasonal change; the temperature averages 70–85°F (21–29°C), and relative humidity is generally high, averaging about 78% throughout the islands. Average rainfall varies from 85 in (216 cm) per year in the Northern Marianas to 182 inches (462 cm) in the eastern Carolines. The Marshalls average 110 inches (279 cm) of rainfall per year, except in the north, where average rainfall is only about 20 inches (51 cm). In most of the territory, typhoons threaten from July through November, but the eastern islands are relatively free of these disturbances.

The islands generally are covered with moderately heavy tropical vegetation. Trees, including excellent hardwoods, grow on the slopes of the higher volcanic islands. Coconut palms flourish on the coral atolls. Insects are numerous (about 7,000 species) and ocean birds, including the tern, albatross, frigate, and heron, are common. The only native land mammals are four species of bats; water buffalo, deer, goats, and rats have been introduced by man. Ocean fauna is abundant, and includes tuna, barracuda, sharks, sea bass, eels, flying fish, octopus, many kinds of crustaceans, and porpoises.

As of 1979, endangered species on Palau Island in the Carolines included the dugong and Palau varieties of La Perouse's megapode, ground dove, owl, and fantail; and on Ponape Island, Ponape varieties of mountain starling and great white-eye. In the Marianas, endangered species included the La Perouse's megapode, mallard, reed warbler, and Tinian monarch flycatcher.

Total population in 1978 was estimated at 128,330; the 1973 census reported a total of 115,251, of which the Northern Marianas had 14,333. The principal islands, with their estimated 1978 populations, are Truk, 36,350; Ponape, 21,780; the Marshalls, 27,880; and the Northern Marianas, 14,850. Saipan is the administrative capital of the territory.

The local island people are classified broadly as Micronesians (literally, "peoples of the tiny islands"), and physically resemble the Malaysians. No native Micronesian culture encompasses the entire territory. Nine Micronesian languages, each with dialect variations, are spoken. Common cultural features are close kinship ties, a cult of ancestors, complex class distinctions, and local chieftainship. The Christian religion has been widely accepted, but earlier beliefs persist in certain forms. Japanese is widely spoken, but English is the official language.

Air Micronesia provides air service in the territory. International airports are on Saipan, Ponape, and Majuro. Construction began on a new airport facility on Truk in 1978. Services between the islands of each district are supplied by government-owned vessels operated by Micronesian companies. Most passenger movement among the territory's islands is by sea. Some of the larger centers have local telephone service; communication between most points is by radio. There were 6 AM and 1 FM radio stations and 4 television stations in 1978.

It is believed that Yap, Palau, and the Marianas were the islands first settled in Micronesia, probably by migrants from the Philippines and Indonesia. Excavations on Saipan have yielded evidence of settlement around 1500 BC. The Marshalls and the eastern and central Carolines were settled later by Melanesian migrants. The first European to reach the Marianas, in 1521, was Ferdinand Magellan, but as a whole the Micronesian islands were almost entirely unknown until the 19th century. By the late 19th century, Spain had extended its administrative control to include all three major island groups. Germany established a protectorate in the Marshall Islands in 1885 and, following Spain's defeat by the US in the Spanish-American War (1898), the Carolines and Marianas (with the exception of Guam, which was ceded to the US) were sold to Germany. With the outbreak of World War I, Japan took over the German-held islands, and on 17 December 1920 they were entrusted to Japan under a League of Nations mandate. Upon its withdrawal from the League in 1935, Japan began to fortify the islands, and in World War II they served as important military bases. Several of the islands were the scene of heavy fighting during the war. In the battle for control of Saipan in June 1944, some 23,000 Japanese and 3,500 US troops lost their lives in one day's fighting. As each island was occupied by US troops, it became subject to US authority in accordance with the international law of belligerent occupation. On 18 July 1947, the islands formally became a UN trust territory under US administration, in accordance with a special strategic areas trusteeship agreement. The territory was administered by the US Department of the Navy until 1 July 1951, when administration was transferred to the Department of the Interior. In 1953, the Northern Marianas, with the exception of Rota, were transferred to the Department of the Navy's administrative control; the Department of the Interior resumed jurisdiction over these islands in 1962.

The atolls of Bikini and Enewetak (formerly Eniwetok) have become world famous since 1946 as the sites of US nuclear and thermonuclear tests. The 167 inhabitants of Bikini and the 137 inhabitants of Enewetak were resettled on other islands, and the people of two other islands, Utirik and Rongelap, had to leave their homes temporarily in 1954 because of unforeseen radioactive fallout. The US government committed itself to clearing the nuclear debris on the islands, and in 1980 some former residents of Enewetak began to return home. However, a 1978 program to resettle Bikini was canceled when radiation tests showed that the island was still unsafe.

The trusteeship agreement under which the US has controlled the territory was expected to end in 1981. Accordingly, territorial government changed rapidly throughout the 1970s, as the island groups began to decide their political futures. In 1980, seven districts existed: the Palau, Yap, Truk, Ponape, and Kosrae (formerly Kusaie) districts in the Caroline Islands; the Marshall Islands District; and the Northern Mariana Islands District.

The 14 Mariana Islands were separated from the Caroline and Marshalls groups on 24 March 1976 by the Northern Marianas Covenant, which also provides for the Marianas' transition, by 1981, to US commonwealth status. The covenant followed a plebiscite, held in June 1975, in which 78.8% of Marianas' voters opted for US citizenship and constitutional integration with the US. Formation of the new entity, to be known as the Northern Marianas Islands, must await approval by the UN Security Council.

The political structure of the trust territory was further changed as the result of a referendum held on 12 July 1978, in which the Truk, Yap, Ponape, and Kosrae districts voted to approve a draft constitution for the Federated States of Micronesia, but the Marshalls and the Palau District rejected it. Under an agreement reached on 14 January 1980, the Marshalls were to proceed toward autonomy in domestic and foreign affairs, except in matters concerning security and defense. Negotiations for the future status of the Federated States of Micronesia hinged on the concept of free association, whereby the islands would exercise internal self-government with the financial and military backing of the US—a concept which the Palau District was also expected to embrace. By the end of 1980, US negotiators had apparently reached agreement with representatives of the Marshalls, the Federated States, and Palau on steps toward associated status. Any such agreements require ratification by plebiscite on the islands and approval by Congress and the US president, as well as acceptance by the UN.

As of 1980, authority over the trust territory (excluding the Northern Marianas) was vested in a high commissioner, appointed by the US president and under the immediate authority of the US secretary of the interior. Formerly, the high commissioner appointed a deputy commissioner for each district. However, by 1980 the districts of the Northern Marianas, Truk, Kosrae, Yap, and Ponape had elected their own governors, and the Federated States of Micronesia and the Marshall Islands District each had elected presidents. The Northern Marianas, the Federated States, the Marshall Islands, and the Palau District have their own legislatures. There are more than 100 municipalities headed by magistrates or mayors who are elected through universal adult suffrage. A municipality may consist of a group of villages on the larger islands; in the case of smaller islands, the municipality may consist of an entire island or group of islands.

The territorial judiciary in 1980 was independent of the office of the high commissioner. It was headed by a chief justice and an associate justice appointed by and responsible to the US secretary of the interior. A high court (consisting of an appellate division and a trial division), district courts, and community courts were under the administrative supervision of the chief justice. All judges of the district and community courts must be Micronesians, and two Micronesian judges sit on the trial division of the high court in murder cases. In all other cases involving local inhabitants, an assessor, often a district court judge, advises the court concerning local laws and customs.

All persons born in the trust territory are citizens of the territory; they are not US citizens and, if they desire US citizenship, must acquire it in the same way as other immigrants. (Residents of the Northern Marianas were granted US citizenship on 9 January 1978, when the district's new constitution took effect, but this special status was revoked in March 1980.) In general, only indigenous inhabitants may own land. Until 1962, persons not citizens or residents were required to obtain the specific authorization of the high commissioner to enter the territory. In that year, however, in response to recommendations by the UN Trusteeship Council to accelerate preparations for eventual self-government and independence, US President John Kennedy issued an executive order opening the territory to US citizens, shipping, and investment without prior security clearance. Law and order are maintained in the territory by an insular constabulary divided into district detachments.

The economy of the Trust Territory of the Pacific Islands is less well developed than that of other US territories. In 1978, the territory (excluding the Northern Marinas) received $135 million from the US government. Tax revenues that year brought $8.2 million; exports of fish, $4.5 million; exports of coconuts and coconut oil, $1.1 million; and tourism, $2.3 million. Wage income was $30.7 million. The Northern Marianas District is similarly dependent on federal assistance.

The traditional economic activities in the territory are subsistence agriculture, livestock raising, and fishing. Numerous tropical and semitropical food plants are cultivated, including taro, arrowroot, yams, tapioca, bananas, and coconuts. Hogs and chickens are widely raised; water buffalo, cattle, goats, and ducks are also commercially significant, particularly in the Northern Marianas. Lack of adequate soil conservation programs has impeded agricultural development, and erosion remains a major problem on most of the islands.

Seafood is an important part of the diet, and development of the islands' rich maritime resources began in the late 1970s. In 1977/78, about 1,100 tons of fish were caught by part-time fishermen and 9,151 tons by commercial fishermen, a 75% increase above the average for the previous 13 years.

Tourism also improved during the 1970s. In 1977, 22,260 visitors spent $2,337,000 on the islands, an increase in spending of 26% over the previous year. Most tourists come from the US, Japan, and the Philippines. Between 500 and 1,000 jobs are tied to the tourism industry.

The principal commercial products are coconut oil and tuna. In 1977, the value of exported coconut products was $1.1 million, and tuna exports reached $3.7 million. Two copra-crushing mills operate in the territory, one in Palau and one in the Marshall Islands; they have a combined capacity of 70,000 tons of coconut oil a year. Commerce in each district of the territory was conducted largely by 74 cooperatives operating as general importers, wholesalers, and retailers for their 12,466 members. Micronesian products centers on Guam and Kwajalein (Marshall Islands) serve as outlets for handicrafts and other cottage-industry products. Each district also has at least two outlets for the sale of local handicrafts. Imports, totaling about $41 million in 1977, vastly exceed exports, about $9 million in 1977. Trade is mainly with Japan and the US. The Northern Marianas had imports exceeding $19 million in 1977/78.

US currency is the official medium of exchange. Each district is served by a branch bank, and banking services are provided by institutions in Guam, Hawaii, and the continental US. The Trust Territory Economic Development Loan Fund makes loans to trading companies from a revolving fund appropriated by the US Congress. A moratorium on new loans was declared in 1975 pending final determination of the division of the fund between the Northern Marianas and the other districts.

The major communicable disease problem on the islands is digestive disorders. An epidemic of gastroenteritis in 1977 was the leading cause of death for the year. Cancer and heart disease are on the increase in the territory. Tuberculosis, once the most serious health problem in the territory, has now been controlled. As of 1978 there were seven district hospitals and two smaller field hospitals in the territory, and 173 dispensaries staffed by health assistants and nurses. The breakdown of health personnel in the Trust Territory of the Pacific Islands as of 30 September 1978 was as follows: doctors, 46; dentists, 21; registered nurses, 5; and other nurses, 163.

The territory seeks to provide universal free public education through primary and secondary levels, with advanced training in the trades and professions for those who can profit by further study. Adult and remedial education is also stressed; 4,500 adults were enrolled in education courses in 1978. Education is free and compulsory for children from 8 through 14 years of age, and more than 90% of the children in this age group attend school. Public and private school enrollment for the 1977/78 school year for the trust territory (including the Northern Marianas) was: elementary, 31,257; secondary, 7,982. The College of Micronesia, established in 1977, had 581 students in branches throughout the islands in 1977/78. During that year, the trust territory's 63 libraries had 142,780 books.

WAKE ISLAND

Wake Island, actually a coral atoll and three islets (Wake, Peale, and Wilkes) about 5 mi (8 km) long by 2 mi (3 km) wide, lies in the North Pacific 2,100 mi (3,380 km) w of Honolulu at 19°17′N and 166°35′E. The total land and water area is about 3 sq mi (8 sq km). Discovered by the British in 1796, it was long uninhabited. In 1898, a US expeditionary force en route to Manila landed on the island. The US formally claimed Wake in 1899. It was made a US naval reservation in 1934, and became a civil aviation station in 1935. Captured by the Japanese on 23 December 1941, it was subsequently the target of several US air raids. It was surrendered by the Japanese in September 1945 and has thereafter remained a US unincorporated territory under the jurisdiction, since 1972, of the Department of the Air Force.

As of the 1970 census, 1,647 persons lived on the island; by 1978, the population was estimated at 200, virtually all of them employees and dependents connected with military installations. Wake is a stopover and fueling station for civilian and military aircraft flying between Honolulu, Guam, and Japan.

UNITED STATES OF AMERICA

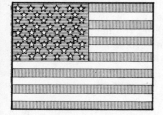

CAPITAL: Washington, D.C. **ANTHEM:** "The Star-Spangled Banner." **MOTTO:** In God We Trust. **FLAG:** The flag consists of 13 alternate stripes, 7 red and 6 white; these represent the 13 original colonies. Fifty five-pointed white stars, representing the present number of states in the Union, are placed in nine horizontal rows alternately of six and five against a blue field in the upper left corner of the flag. **OFFICIAL SEAL:** Obverse: An American eagle with outstretched wings bears a shield consisting of 13 alternating white and red stripes with a broad blue band across the top. The right talon clutches an olive branch, representing peace; in the left are 13 arrows, symbolizing military strength. The eagle's beak holds a banner with the motto "*E pluribus unum*" (From many, one); overhead is a constellation of 13 five-pointed stars in a glory. Reverse: Above a truncated pyramid is an all-seeing eye within a triangle; at the bottom of this triangle appear the roman numerals MDCCLXXVI (1776). The pyramid stands on a grassy ground, against a backdrop of mountains. The words *Annuit Cœptis* (He has favored our undertakings) and, on a banner, *Novus Ordo Seclorum* (A new order of the ages) surround the whole. **MONETARY UNIT:** The dollar ($) of 100 cents is a nonconvertible paper currency with a floating rate. There are coins of 1, 5, 10, 25, and 50 cents and 1 dollar, and notes of 1, 2, 5, 10, 20, 50, and 100 dollars (issuance of higher notes ceased in 1969). **FEDERAL HOLIDAYS:** New Year's Day, 1 January; Washington's Birthday, 3d Monday in February; Memorial Day, last Monday in May; Independence Day, 4 July; Labor Day, 1st Monday in September; Columbus Day, 2d Monday in October; Veterans Day, 11 November; Thanksgiving Day, 4th Thursday in November; Christmas Day, 25 December. **TIME:** Noon GMT = 7 A.M. EST, 6 A.M. CST, 5 A.M. MST, 4 A.M. PST, 3 A.M. Yukon Standard Time, 2 A.M. Alaska-Hawaii Standard Time, 1 A.M. Bering Standard Time.

¹LOCATION, SIZE, AND EXTENT

Located in the Western Hemisphere on the continent of North America, the US is the 4th-largest country in the world. Its total area, including Alaska and Hawaii and the outlying areas but excluding certain coastal and inland waters, is 3,631,407 sq mi (9,405,337 sq km). The conterminous US extends 2,897 mi (4,662 km) ENE–WSW and 2,848 mi (4,583 km) SSE–NNW. It is bordered on the N by Canada, on the E by the Atlantic Ocean, on the S by the Gulf of Mexico and Mexico, and on the W by the Pacific Ocean, with a total boundary length of 10,913 mi (17,563 km). Alaska, the 49th state, extends 2,261 mi (3,639 km) E–W and 1,358 mi (2,185 km) N–S. It is bounded on the N by the Arctic Ocean and Beaufort Sea, on the E by Canada, on the S by the Gulf of Alaska, Pacific Ocean and Bering Sea, and on the W by the Bering Sea, Bering Strait, Chukchi Sea, and Arctic Ocean, with a total boundary length of 8,178 mi (13,161 km). The 50th state, Hawaii, consists of islands in the Pacific Ocean, extending 1,576 mi (2,536 km) N–S and 1,425 mi (2,293 km) E–W, with a general coastline of 750 mi (1,207 km).

The geographic center of the US, including Alaska and Hawaii, is in Butte County, S.Dak., at 44°58′N, 103°46′W; the geographic center of the 48 conterminous states is in Smith County, Kans., at 39°50′N, 98°35′W.

Land boundaries between states have long since been determined; river boundaries, however, are subject to occasional variation. Offshore borders in the middle and south Atlantic region—including New Jersey, New York, Delaware, and Maryland—were in dispute in 1980 because of conflicting claims to areas leased by oil companies.

²TOPOGRAPHY

The great topographical divisions of the US are largely determined by the various mountain ranges that traverse the country from north to south.

Although the northern New England coast is rocky, along the rest of the eastern seaboard the Atlantic Coastal Plain rises gradually from the shoreline. Narrow in the north, the plain widens to about 200 mi (320 km) in the south and in Georgia merges with the Gulf Coastal Plain that borders the Gulf of Mexico and ultimately extends as far as Yucatán. West of the Atlantic Coastal Plain is the Piedmont Plateau, bounded by the Appalachian Mountains. The Appalachians, which extend from Maine southwest into central Alabama—with special names in some areas—are old mountains, largely eroded away, with rounded contours, and forested as a rule to the top. Few of their summits rise much above 3,500 feet (1,100 meters), although the highest, Mt. Mitchell in North Carolina, reaches 6,684 feet (2,037 meters).

Between the Appalachians and the Rocky Mountains, more than 1,000 mi (1,600 km) to the west, lies the vast interior plain of the US. Running south through the center of this plain and draining almost two-thirds of the area of the continental US is the Mississippi River. Waters starting from the source of the Missouri, the longest of its tributaries, travel almost 4,000 mi (6,400 km) to the Gulf of Mexico. The eastern reaches of the great interior plain are bounded on the north by the Great Lakes, which are thought to contain about half the world's total supply of fresh water. Under US jurisdiction are 22,178 sq mi (57,441 sq km) of Lake Michigan, 21,118 sq mi (54,696 sq km) of Lake Superior, 8,975 sq mi (23,245 sq km) of Lake Huron, 5,002 sq mi (12,955 sq km) of Lake Erie, and 3,033 sq mi (7,855 sq km) of Lake Ontario. The five lakes are now accessible to oceangoing

LOCATIONS: Conterminous US: 66°57′ to 124°44′W; 24°33′ to 49°23′N. Alaska: 130°W to 172°28′E; 51° to 71°23′N. Hawaii: 154°48′ to 178°22′W; 18°55′ to 28°25′N. **BOUNDARY LENGTHS:** Conterminous US: Canada, 3,987 mi (6,416 km); Atlantic Ocean, 2,069 mi (3,330 km); Gulf of Mexico coastline, 1,631 mi (2,625 km); Mexico, 1,933 mi (3,111 km); Pacific coastline, 1,293 mi (2,081 km). Alaska: Arctic Ocean coastline, 1,060 mi (1,706 km); Canada, 1,538 mi (2,475 km); Pacific coastline, including the Bering Sea and Strait and Chukchi coastlines, 5,580 mi (8,980 km). Hawaii: coastline, 750 mi (1,207 km).

vessels from the Atlantic via the St. Lawrence Seaway. The basins of the Great Lakes were formed by the glacial ice cap that moved down over large parts of North America some 25,000 years ago. The glaciers also determined the direction of flow of the Missouri River and, it is believed, were responsible for carrying soil from what is now Canada down into the central agricultural basin of the US. The great interior plain consists of two major subregions: the fertile Central Plains extending from the Appalachian Highlands to a line drawn approximately 300 mi (480 km) west of the Mississippi, broken by the Ozark Plateau; and the more arid Great Plains, extending from that line to the foothills of the Rocky Mountains. Although they appear flat, the Great Plains rise gradually from about 1,500 feet (460 meters) to more than 5,000 feet (1,500 meters) at their western extremity.

The Continental Divide, the Atlantic-Pacific watershed, runs along the crest of the Rocky Mountains. The Rockies and the ranges to the west are parts of the great system of young, rugged mountains shaped like a gigantic spinal column along western North, Central, and South America from Alaska to Tierra del Fuego. In the continental US, the series of western ranges, most of them paralleling the Pacific coast, are the Sierra Nevada, the Coast Ranges, the Cascade Range, and the Tehachapi and San Bernardino mountains. Between the Rockies and the Sierra Nevada–Cascade mountain barrier to the west lies the Great Basin, a group of vast arid plateaus containing most of the desert areas of the US, in the south eroded by deep canyons. The coastal plains along the Pacific are narrow, and in many places the mountains plunge directly into the sea. The most extensive lowland near the west coast is the Great Valley of California, lying between the Sierra Nevada and the Coast Ranges. There are 71 peaks in these western ranges of the continental US that rise to an altitude of 14,000 feet (4,300 meters) or more, Mt. Whitney in California at 14,494 feet (4,418 meters), being the highest. The greatest rivers of the Far West are the Colorado in the south, flowing into the Gulf of California, and the Columbia in the northwest, flowing to the Pacific. Each is more than 1,200 mi (1,900 km) long; both have been intensively developed to generate electric power, and both are important sources of irrigation.

Separated from the continental US by Canadian territory, the state of Alaska occupies the extreme northwest portion of the North American continent. A series of precipitous mountain ranges separates the heavily indented Pacific coast on the south from Alaska's broad central basin, through which the Yukon River flows from Canada in the east to the Bering Sea in the west. The central basin is bounded on the north by the Brooks Range, which slopes down gradually to the Arctic Ocean. The Alaskan Peninsula and the Aleutian Islands, sweeping west far out to sea, consist of a chain of volcanoes, many still active.

The state of Hawaii consists of a group of Pacific islands formed by volcanoes rising sharply from the ocean floor. The highest of these volcanoes, Mauna Loa, 13,675 feet (4,168 meters), is located on the largest of the islands, Hawaii, and is still active.

The lowest point in the US is Death Valley in California, 282 feet (86 meters) below sea level. At 20,320 feet (6,194 meters), Mt. McKinley in Alaska is the highest peak in North America. These topographic extremes suggest the geological instability of the Pacific Coast region. Major earthquakes destroyed San Francisco in 1906 and Anchorage, Alaska, in 1964, and the San Andreas Fault in California still causes frequent earth tremors. Washington State's Mt. St. Helens erupted in 1980, spewing volcanic ash over much of the Northwest.

[3]CLIMATE

There are great climatic variations between different regions of the US.

The eastern continental region is well watered, with annual rainfall generally in excess of 40 in (102 cm). It includes all the Atlantic seaboard and southeastern states and extends west to cover Indiana, southern Illinois, most of Missouri, Arkansas, Louisiana, and easternmost Texas. The eastern seaboard is affected primarily by the masses of air moving from west to east across the continent rather than by air moving in from the Atlantic. Hence its climate is basically continental rather than maritime. The midwestern and Atlantic seaboard states experience hot summers and cold winters; spring and autumn are clearly defined periods of climatic transition. Only Florida, with the Gulf of Mexico lying to its west, experiences moderate differences between summer and winter temperatures. Mean annual temperatures vary considerably between north and south: Boston, 51° F (11°C); New York City, 55°F (13°C); Charlotte, N.C., 61°F (16°C); Miami, 76°F (24°C). The Gulf and southern Atlantic states are often hit by severe tropical storms originating in the Caribbean Sea in late summer and early autumn.

The prairie lands lying to the west constitute a subhumid region. Precipitation usually exceeds evaporation by only a small amount; hence the region is more often familiar with drought than with excessive rainfall. Dryness generally increases from east to west. The average midwinter temperature in the extreme north—Minnesota and North Dakota—is about 9°F (–13°C) or less, while the average July temperature is 65°F (18°C). In the Texas prairie region to the south, January temperatures average 50–55°F (10–13°C) and July temperatures 80–85°F (27–29°C). Rainfall along the western border of the prairie region is as low as 18 in (46 cm) per year in the north and 25 in (64 cm) in the south. Precipitation is greatest in the early summer—a matter of great importance to agriculture, particularly in the growing of grain

Outlying Areas of the US[1]

NAME	AREA SQ MI	AREA SQ KM	CAPITAL	YEAR OF ACQUISITION	CENSUS POPULATION 1970	CENSUS POPULATION 1980[2]
Puerto Rico	3,435	8,897	San Juan	1898	2,712,033	3,187,570
Virgin Islands of the US	132	342	Charlotte Amalie	1916	62,468	93,000[4]
Trust Territory of the Pacific Islands, of which:	8,324[3]	21,559	Saipan	1947	90,940	129,000[4]
Northern Marianas	185	479	—	—	9,640	16,758
Other Pacific territories:						
American Samoa	76	197	Pago Pago	1899	27,159	32,395
Guam	212	549	Agaña	1898	84,996	105,816
Midway Islands	2	5	—	1867	2,220	NA
Wake Island	3	8	—	1899	1,647	200[4]

1. Excludes minor and uninhabited islands.
2. Preliminary results.
3. Dry lands and lagoons.
4. Estimate for 1977.

crops. In dry years, the prevailing winds may carry the topsoil eastward (particularly from the southern region) for hundreds of miles in clouds that obscure the sun.

The Great Plains constitute a semiarid climatic region. Rainfall in the southern plains averages about 20 in (51 cm) per year and in the northern plains about 10 in (25 cm), but extreme year-to-year variations are common. The tropical air masses that move northward across the plains originate on the fairly high plateaus of Mexico and contain little water vapor. Periods as long as 120 days without rain have been experienced in this region. The rains that do occur are often violent, and a third of the total annual rainfall may be recorded in a single day at certain weather stations. The contrast between summer and winter temperatures is extreme throughout the Great Plains. Maximum summer temperatures of over 110°F (43°C) have been recorded in the north as well as in the south. From the Texas panhandle north, blizzards are common in the winter, and tornadoes at other seasons. The average minimum temperature for January in Duluth, Minn., is –1°F (–18°C).

The higher reaches of the Rockies and the mountains paralleling the Pacific coast to the west are characterized by a typical alpine climate. Precipitation as a rule is heavier on the western slopes of the ranges. The great intermontane arid region of the West shows considerable climatic variation between its northern and southern portions. In New Mexico, Arizona, and southeastern California the greatest precipitation occurs in July, August, and September, mean annual rainfall ranging from 3 in (8 cm) in Yuma to 30 in (76 cm) in the mountains of northern Arizona and New Mexico. Phoenix, Ariz., has a mean annual temperature of 70°F (21°C), rising to 91°F (33°C) in July and falling to 51°F (11°C) in January. North of the Utah-Arizona line, the summer months usually are very dry; maximum precipitation occurs in the winter and early spring. In the desert valleys west of Great Salt Lake, mean annual precipitation adds up to only 4 in (10 cm). Although the northern plateaus are generally arid, some of the mountainous areas of central Washington and Idaho receive at least 60 in (152 cm) of rain per year. Throughout the intermontane region, the uneven availability of water is the principal factor shaping the habitat.

The Pacific coast, separated by tall mountain barriers from the severe continental climate to the east, is a region of mild winters and moderately warm, dry summers. Its climate is basically maritime, the westerly winds from the Pacific Ocean moderating the extremes of both winter and summer temperatures. Los Angeles in the south has an average temperature of 55°F (13°C) in January and 69°F (21°C) in July; Seattle in the north has an average temperature of 38°F (3°C) in January and 65°F (18°C) in July. Precipitation in general increases along the coast from south to north, extremes ranging from an annual average of 1.78 in (4.52 cm) at Death Valley, Calif. (the lowest in the US), to 144 in (366 cm) in Washington's Olympic Mountains.

Climatic conditions vary considerably in the vastness of Alaska. In the fogbound Aleutians and in the coastal panhandle strip that extends south along the Gulf of Alaska and includes the capital, Juneau, a relatively moderate maritime climate prevails. The interior is characterized by short, hot summers and long, bitterly cold winters, and in the region bordering the Arctic Ocean a polar climate prevails, the soil hundreds of feet below the surface remaining frozen the year round. Although snowy in winter, continental Alaska is relatively dry. Hawaii has a remarkably mild and stable climate with only slight seasonal variations in temperature, as a result of northeast ocean winds. The mean January temperature in Honolulu is 72°F (22°C), the mean July temperature 80°F (27°C). Rainfall is moderate—about 28 in (71 cm) per year—but much greater in the mountains; Mt. Waialeala on Kauai has a mean annual rainfall of 460 in (1,168 cm), highest in the world.

The lowest temperature recorded in the US was –79.8°F (–62°C) at Prospect Creek Camp, Alaska, on 23 January 1971; the highest, 134°F (57°C), at Greenland Ranch, in Death Valley, Calif., on 10 July 1913. The record annual rainfall is 578 in (1,468 cm) at Puu Kukui, Maui, in 1950; for a 24-hour period, 38.7 in (98.3 cm) at Yankeetown, Fla., on 5–6 September 1950; in 1 hour, 12 in (30 cm), at Holt, Mo., on 22 June 1947, and on Kauai, Hawaii, on 24–25 January 1956.

[4]FLORA AND FAUNA

As of 1974, excluding Alaska and Hawaii, about 32% of the US was forestland, 26% was grassland pasture, 16% was active cropland, 5% was idle or pastured cropland, and the remaining 21% encompassed "all other purposes"—a category (including military, urban, and designated wilderness areas) that has more than doubled since 1940.

At least 7,000 species and subspecies of indigenous US flora have been categorized. The eastern forests contain a mixture of softwoods and hardwoods that includes pine, oak, maple, spruce, beech, birch, hemlock, walnut, gum, and hickory. The central hardwood forest, which originally stretched unbroken from Cape Cod to Texas and northwest to Minnesota—still an important timber source— supports oak, hickory, ash, maple, and walnut. Pine, hickory, tupelo, pecan, gum, birch, and sycamore are found in the southern forest that stretches along the Gulf coast into the eastern half of Texas. The Pacific forest is the most spectacular of all because of the enormous size of its giant redwoods and Douglas firs. In the southwest are saguaro (giant cactus), yucca, candlewood, and the Joshua tree.

The central grasslands lie in the interior of the continent, where moisture is not sufficient to support the growth of large forests. The tall grassland or prairie (now almost entirely under cultivation) lies to the east of the 100th meridian. To the west of this line, where rainfall is frequently less than 20 in (51 cm) per year, is the short grassland. Mesquite grass covers parts of west Texas, southern New Mexico, and Arizona. Short grass may be found in the highlands of the latter two states, while tall grass covers large portions of the coastal regions of Texas and Louisiana and occurs in some parts of Mississippi, Alabama, and Florida. The Pacific grassland region includes northern Idaho, the higher plateaus of eastern Washington and Oregon, and the mountain valleys of California.

The intermontane region of the Western Cordillera is for the most part covered with desert shrubs. Sagebrush predominates in the northern part of this area, creosote in the southern, and the saltbrush near the Great Salt Lake and in Death Valley.

The lower slopes of the mountains running up to the coastline of Alaska are covered with coniferous forests as far north as the Seward Peninsula. The central part of the Yukon Basin is also a region of softwood forests. The rest of Alaska is heath or tundra. Hawaii has extensive forests of bamboo and ferns. Sugarcane and pineapple, although not native to the islands, now cover a large portion of the cultivated land.

Small trees and shrubs common to most of the US include hackberry, hawthorn, serviceberry, blackberry, wild cherry, dogwood, and snowberry. Wild flowers bloom in all areas, from the seldom seen blossoms of rare desert cacti to the hardiest alpine species. Wild flowers include forget-me-not, fringed and closed gentians, jack-in-the-pulpit, black-eyed Susan, columbine, and common dandelion, along with numerous varieties of aster, orchid, lady's-slipper, and wild rose.

An estimated 1,500 species and subspecies of mammals characterize the animal life of the continental US. Among the larger game animals are the white-tailed deer, moose, pronghorn antelope, bighorn sheep, mountain goat, black bear, and grizzly bear. The Alaskan brown bear often reaches a weight of 1,200–1,400 lb. Some 25 important furbearers are common, including the muskrat, red and gray foxes, mink, raccoon, beaver, opossum, striped skunk, woodchuck, common cottontail, snowshoe hare, and various squirrels. Human encroachment has transformed the mammalian habitat over the last two centuries. The American buffalo (bison), millions of which once roamed the plains, is now found only on select reserves. Other mammals, such as the elk and gray wolf, have been restricted to much smaller ranges.

Year-round and migratory birds abound. Loons, wild ducks, and wild geese are found in lake country; terns, gulls, sandpipers, herons, and other seabirds live along the coasts. Wrens, thrushes, owls, hummingbirds, sparrows, woodpeckers, swallows, chickadees, vireos, warblers, and finches appear in profusion, along with the robin, common crow, cardinal, Baltimore oriole, eastern and western meadowlarks, and various blackbirds. Wild turkey, ruffed grouse and ring-necked pheasant (introduced from Europe) are popular game birds.

Lakes, rivers, and streams teem with trout, bass, perch, muskellunge, carp, catfish, and pike; sea bass, cod, snapper, and flounder are abundant along the coasts, along with such shellfish as lobster, shrimp, clams, oysters, and mussels. Garter, pine, and milk snakes are found in most regions. Four poisonous snakes survive, of which the rattlesnake is the most common. Alligators appear in southern waterways, and the Gila monster makes its home in the Southwest.

During the 1960s and 1970s, numerous laws and lists designed to protect threatened and endangered flora and fauna were adopted throughout the US. Generally, each species listed as protected by the federal government is also protected by the states, but some states may list species not included on federal lists or on the lists of neighboring states. (Conversely, a species threatened throughout most of the US may be abundant in one or two states.) As of November 1980, the US Fish and Wildlife Service listed 234 endangered species, including 51 plants, and 49 threatened species, including 7 plants. The agency listed another 489 endangered and 28 threatened species by international agreement.

Threatened species, likely to become endangered if recent trends continue, include such plants as Rydberg milk-vetch, northern wild monkshood, Lee's pincushion cactus, and Lloyd's mariposa cactus. Among the endangered floral species (in imminent danger of extinction in the wild) are the Virginia round-leaf birch, San Clemente broom, Hawaiian wild broad-bean, Texas wild-rice, Furbish lousewort, Truckee barberry, Sneed pincushion cactus, spineless hedgehog cactus, Knowlton cactus, persistent trillium, and dwarf bear-poppy.

Threatened fauna include the grizzly bear, southern sea otter, gray wolf, Newell's Manx shearwater, American alligator, eastern indigo snake, bayou darter, several southwestern trout species, and Bahama and Schaus swallowtail butterflies. Among endangered fauna are the Indiana bat, key deer, black-footed ferret, northern swift fox, Florida panther, Sonoran pronghorn, gray wolf (except in Minnesota, where it is threatened), numerous whale species, bald eagle (endangered in most states, but only threatened in the Northwest and the Great Lakes region), Hawaiian creeper, Everglade kite, brown pelican, California clapper rail, blunt-nosed leopard lizard, red-cockaded woodpecker, American crocodile, green sea turtle, desert slender salamander, Houston toad, humpback chub, snail darter, blue pike, Tecopa pupfish, Stock Island tree snail, 18 species of pearly mussel, Socorro isopod, and mission blue butterfly.

5ENVIRONMENTAL PROTECTION

The Council on Environmental Quality, an advisory body contained within the Executive Office of the President, was established by the National Environmental Policy Act of 1969, which mandated an assessment of environmental impact for every federally funded project. The Environmental Protection Agency (EPA), created in 1970, is an independent body with primary regulatory responsibility in the fields of air and noise pollution, water and waste management, and control of toxic substances. Other federal agencies with environmental responsibilities include the Forest Service and Soil Conservation Service within the Department of Agriculture, the Fish and Wildlife Service and National Park Service within the Department of the Interior, the Department of Energy, and the Nuclear Regulatory Commission. In addition to the 1969 legislation, landmark federal laws protecting the environment include the Clean Air Act Amendments of 1970, controlling automobile emissions; the Water Pollution Act of 1972, setting clean water criteria for fishing and swimming; and the Endangered Species Act of 1973, protecting wildlife near extinction. A measure enacted in December 1980 established a $1.6-billion fund, financed largely by excise taxes on chemical companies, to clean up toxic waste dumps such as the one in the Love Canal district of Niagara Falls, N.Y.

Among the most influential environmental lobbies are the Sierra Club (founded in 1892; 183,000 members) and its legal arm, the Sierra Club Legal Defense Fund. Large conservation groups include the National Wildlife Federation (1936; 4,100,000) and the National Audubon Society (1905; 400,000). Smaller but highly active in the environmental protection movement are the Environmental Defense Fund (1967; 45,000), Friends of the Earth (1969; 22,000), and Environmental Action (1970; 20,000), all of which undertake research and litigation and monitor federal enforcement of environmental standards. The Greenpeace Foundation of America (1976; 30,000) has gained international attention by seeking to disrupt the hunts for whales and seals. Among the environmental movement's most notable successes have been the inauguration (and mandating in some states) of recycling programs, the banning in the US of the insecticide dichlorodiphenyltrichloroethane (DDT), the successful fight against construction of a supersonic transport (SST), and the protection of more than 100 million acres (40 million hectares) of Alaska lands, after a fruitless fight to halt construction of the trans-Alaska pipeline. The movement was much less successful in opposing certain large-scale water projects, and as the 1980s began, environmentalists faced pressure from business, labor, and civic interests seeking a relaxation of air quality standards where strict enforcement threatened local industries.

An assessment by the Council on Environmental Quality released in February 1980 noted that between 1974 and 1977, the number of "unhealthful" days on its air quality index declined by 15% in metropolitan areas, and the number of "very unhealthful" days decreased 32%; but two of every three days in 1977 remained "unhealthful" in Los Angeles and New York City. Since 1970, some 7,000 air-quality monitoring stations have been set up, and $13 billion was spent on cleaner air in 1978 alone. As of 1979, Congress had appropriated $28 billion for sewage treatment facilities, although projects valued at only $1.7 billion had been completed. Outstanding problems include "acid rain," precipitation contaminated by fossil fuel wastes; runoffs of agricultural pesticides, a pollutant deadly to fishing streams and very difficult to regulate; the continued dumping of raw or partially treated sewage from major cities into US waterways; the falling water tables in many western states; the decrease in arable land because of depletion, erosion, and urbanization; the need for reclamation of strip-mined lands and for regulation of present and future strip-mining; and the expansion of the US nuclear industry in the absence of any fully satisfactory technique for the handling and permanent disposal of radioactive wastes.

6POPULATION

The total population of the US rose from 179,323,175 as of 1960 to 203,211,926 in 1970, according to the census figures. In 1978, the population was estimated at 218,059,000, of whom 106,043,000 were male and 112,016,000 were female. By age, the population was distributed as follows: under 5 years, 15,361,000; 5–13,

31,378,000; 14–17, 16,637,000; 18–24, 28,687,000; 25–44, 58,097,000; 45–64, 43,845,000; 65 and over, 24,054,000. The US population is extremely mobile: 47% of the population moved in the years 1965–70, and as of 1970, only 56% of all Americans had lived in their native state their whole lives.

At the time of the first federal census, in 1790, the population of the country was 3,929,214. Between 1800 and 1850, the population almost quadrupled; between 1850 and 1900, it tripled; and between 1900 and 1950, it almost doubled. During the 1960s and 1970s, however, the growth rate slowed steadily, declining from 2.9% annually in 1960 to 2% in 1969, and to less than 1% in 1978. Provisional totals for 1980 placed the US population at 226,504,825.

By 1977, metropolitan areas had a total population of 157.9 million, representing a 22.6% increase over 1960. Suburbs have absorbed most of the shift in population distribution since 1950. Estimates for 1978 indicate that there are 37 urban areas with over 1 million population, of which the largest were New York, 9,221,800; Los Angeles–Long Beach, 7,080,900; Chicago, 7,029,600; Philadelphia, 4,770,400; and Detroit, 4,386,400.

State Areas, Entry Dates, and Populations

| | AREA | | | | ORDER OF | | POPULATION | | |
	SQ MI	SQ KM	RANK	CAPITAL	ENTRY	DATE OF ENTRY	AT ENTRY[1]	CENSUS 1970	CENSUS 1980[2]
Alabama	51,609	133,667	29	Montgomery	22	14 December 1819	127,901	3,444,165	3,863,698
Alaska	589,757	1,527,470	1	Juneau	49	3 January 1959	226,167	302,173	400,331
Arizona	113,909	295,024	6	Phoenix	48	14 February 1912	204,354	1,775,399	2,714,013
Arkansas	53,104	137,539	27	Little Rock	25	15 June 1836	57,574	1,923,322	2,280,687
California	158,693	411,015	3	Sacramento	31	9 September 1850	92,597	19,971,069	23,510,372
Colorado	104,247	270,000	8	Denver	38	1 August 1876	39,864	2,207,259	2,877,726
Connecticut*	5,009	12,973	48	Hartford	5	9 January 1788	237,946	3,032,217	3,096,951
Delaware*	2,057	5,328	49	Dover	1	7 December 1787	59,096	548,104	594,711
Florida	58,560	151,670	22	Tallahassee	27	3 March 1845	87,445	6,789,443	9,579,495
Georgia*	58,876	152,489	21	Atlanta	4	2 January 1788	82,548	4,589,575	5,396,425
Hawaii	6,450	16,706	47	Honolulu	50	21 August 1959	632,772	769,913	964,680
Idaho	83,557	216,413	13	Boise	43	3 July 1890	88,548	712,567	943,134
Illinois	56,400	146,076	24	Springfield	21	3 December 1818	55,211	11,112,772	11,321,350
Indiana	36,291	93,994	38	Indianapolis	19	11 December 1816	147,178	5,193,669	5,454,154
Iowa	56,290	145,791	25	Des Moines	29	28 December 1846	192,214	2,825,041	2,908,797
Kansas	82,264	213,064	14	Topeka	34	29 January 1861	107,206	2,249,071	2,355,536
Kentucky	40,395	104,623	37	Frankfort	15	1 June 1792	73,677	3,219,311	3,642,143
Louisiana	48,523	125,675	31	Baton Rouge	18	30 April 1812	76,556	3,641,306	4,194,299
Maine	33,215	86,027	39	Augusta	23	15 March 1820	298,335	993,663	1,123,560
Maryland*	10,577	27,394	42	Annapolis	7	28 April 1788	319,728	3,923,897	4,193,378
Massachusetts*	8,257	21,386	45	Boston	6	6 February 1788	378,787	5,689,170	5,728,288
Michigan	58,216	150,779	23	Lansing	26	26 January 1837	212,267	8,879,862	9,236,891
Minnesota	84,068	217,736	12	St. Paul	32	11 May 1858	172,023	3,804,971	4,068,856
Mississippi	47,716	123,584	32	Jackson	20	10 December 1817	75,448	2,216,912	2,503,250
Missouri	69,686	180,487	19	Jefferson City	24	10 August 1821	66,586	4,677,983	4,901,678
Montana	147,138	381,087	4	Helena	41	8 November 1889	142,924	694,409	783,674
Nebraska	77,227	200,018	15	Lincoln	37	1 March 1867	122,993	1,485,333	1,564,727
Nevada	110,540	286,299	7	Carson City	36	31 October 1864	42,491	488,738	800,312
New Hampshire*	9,304	24,097	44	Concord	9	21 June 1788	141,885	737,681	919,114
New Jersey*	7,836	20,295	46	Trenton	3	18 December 1787	184,139	7,171,112	7,335,808
New Mexico	121,666	315,115	5	Santa Fe	47	6 January 1912	327,301	1,017,555	1,290,551
New York*	49,576	128,402	30	Albany	11	26 July 1788	340,120	18,241,391	17,557,288
North Carolina*	52,586	136,198	28	Raleigh	12	21 November 1789	393,751	5,084,411	5,846,159
North Dakota	70,665	183,022	17	Bismarck	39	2 November 1889	190,983	617,761	652,437
Ohio	41,222	106,765	35	Columbus	17	1 March 1803[3]	43,365	10,657,423	10,758,421
Oklahoma	69,919	181,090	18	Oklahoma City	46	16 November 1907	657,155	2,559,463	2,998,124
Oregon	96,981	251,181	10	Salem	33	14 February 1859	52,465	2,091,385	2,617,444
Pennsylvania*	45,333	117,412	33	Harrisburg	2	12 December 1787	434,373	11,793,909	11,824,561
Rhode Island*	1,214	3,144	50	Providence	13	29 May 1790	68,825	949,723	945,761
South Carolina*	31,055	80,432	40	Columbia	8	23 May 1788	393,751	2,590,516	3,067,061
South Dakota	77,047	199,552	16	Pierre	40	2 November 1889	348,600	662,257	687,643
Tennessee	42,244	109,412	34	Nashville	16	1 June 1796	35,691	3,923,687	4,539,834
Texas	267,338	692,405	2	Austin	28	29 December 1845	212,592	11,198,655	14,152,339
Utah	84,916	219,932	11	Salt Lake City	45	4 January 1896	276,749	1,059,273	1,454,630
Vermont	9,609	24,887	43	Montpelier	14	4 March 1791	85,425	444,732	511,299
Virginia*	40,817	105,716	36	Richmond	10	25 June 1788	747,610	4,648,494	5,321,521
Washington	68,192	176,617	20	Olympia	42	11 November 1889	357,232	3,413,250	4,109,634
West Virginia	24,181	62,629	41	Charleston	35	20 June 1863	442,014	1,744,237	1,928,524
Wisconsin	56,154	145,439	26	Madison	30	29 May 1848	305,391	4,417,821	4,689,055
Wyoming	97,914	253,597	9	Cheyenne	44	10 July 1890	62,555	332,416	468,954

1. Census closest to entry date.
2. Preliminary results.

3. Date fixed in 1953 by congressional resolution.
*One of original 13 colonies.

⁷ETHNIC GROUPS

The majority of the population of the United States is of European origin, with the largest groups having ancestry traceable to the United Kingdom (12.6% of the total population in 1973), Germany (9.9%), Ireland (5.9%), and Italy (3.4%). Of those 33,575,000 Americans who were either foreign-born or the native-born children of foreign parents, 12.6% traced their ancestry to Italy, 10.8% to Germany, 9% to Canada, 7.3% to the United Kingdom, 7.1% to Poland, and 7% to Mexico. Major racial and national minority groups include blacks, Chinese, Japanese, Mexicans, Puerto Ricans, and other Spanish-speaking peoples of the Americas; together these groups comprised 16.5% of the population in 1974. Inequality in social and economic opportunities for ethnic minorities has become a key public issue in the post–World War II period.

Some American Indian societies survived warfare with land-hungry white settlers and retained their tribal cultures. Their survival, however, has been on the fringes of North American society, especially as a result of the implementation of a national policy of resettling Indian tribes on reservations. In 1890, according to the official census count, there were 248,253 Indians; in 1940, 333,909; and in 1970, at least 792,730. The ease with which Indians have moved into both white and black groups has made it difficult to measure their population growth, and state estimates often exceed the federal figures by a substantial margin. Groups of Indians are found most numerously in the southwestern states of Oklahoma, Arizona, New Mexico, and California. South Dakota has a large Sioux population, as does Oklahoma. North Carolina, ranking 5th behind New Mexico in total number of Indians, has a large population of Cherokee, and groups of the Onondaga, Seneca, and Tonawanda tribes live in New York. Since 1871, the Indians have been official wards of the federal government. The 1960s and 1970s saw successful court fights by Native Americans in Alaska, Maine, South Dakota, and other states to regain tribal lands or to receive cash settlements for lands taken from them in violation of treaties during the 1800s.

In 1976, 11.5% of the total US population was black. Some 53% of blacks still reside in the South, the region that absorbed the majority of slaves brought from Africa in the 18th and 19th centuries. Two important regional migrations of blacks have taken place: (1) the "Great Migration" to the North, commencing in 1915; and (2) the small but hitherto unprecedented westward movement beginning about 1940. Both migrations were fostered by the wartime demand for labor and by postwar job opportunities in northern and western urban centers. More than three out of four black Americans live in metropolitan areas, constituting, as of 1970, 71% of the population of Washington, D.C., 53% of Gary, Ind., 51% of Atlanta, and 46% of Baltimore; in New York City, which had the largest number of black residents (1,668,000), 21% of the population was black. Large-scale federal programs to ensure equality for blacks in voting rights, public education, employment, and housing were initiated after the historic 1954 Supreme Court ruling that barred racial segregation in public schools. By 1966, however, in the midst of growing and increasingly violent expressions of dissatisfaction by black residents of northern cities and southern rural areas, the federal Civil Rights Commission reported that integration programs were lagging. Throughout the 1960s and 1970s, the unemployment rate among nonwhites in the US was double that for whites, and school integration proceeded slowly, especially outside the South.

Included in the population of the US in 1970 were approximately 1.4 million persons whose lineage can be traced to Asian nationalities, chiefly Japanese (591,290), Chinese (435,062), and Filipinos (343,060). The Chinese population is highly urbanized and concentrated particularly in cities of over 100,000, mostly on the West Coast and in New York City. The Japanese population has risen steadily from a level of 72,157 in 1910. Hawaii is the most popular magnet of Japanese emigration; the Japanese population of Hawaii accounted in 1970 for 28% of the state's residents and 37% of the nation's total number of Japanese, with California contributing another 36%.

Mexican settlements are largely in the Southwest. Spanish-speaking Puerto Ricans, who often represent an amalgam of racial strains, have largely settled in the New York metropolitan area, where they partake in considerable measure of the hardships and problems experienced by other immigrant groups in the process of settling in the US. Since 1959, many Cubans have settled in Florida and other eastern states. In 1978 there were an estimated 12,046,000 Hispanic Americans, of whom 7,151,000 were of Mexican ancestry and 1,823,000 were Puerto Rican.

⁸LANGUAGES

The primary language of the US is English, enriched by words borrowed from the languages of Native Americans and immigrants, predominantly European.

When European settlement began, Indians living north of Mexico spoke about 300 different languages now held to belong to 58 different language families. Only 2 such families have contributed noticeably to the American vocabulary: Algonkian in the Northeast and Aztec-Tanoan in the Southwest. From Algonkian languages, directly or sometimes through Canadian French, English has taken such words as *moose*, *skunk*, *caribou*, *opossum*, *woodchuck*, *muskellunge*, and *raccoon* for New World animals; *hickory*, *kinnikinnick*, *squash*, and *tamarack* for New World flora; and *mugwump*, *succotash*, *hominy*, *mackinaw*, *moccasin*, *tomahawk*, *toboggan*, and *totem* for various cultural items. From Nahuatl, the language of the Aztecs, terms such as *tomato*, *mesquite*, *ocotillo*, *coyote*, *chili*, *tamale*, *chocolate*, and *ocelot* have entered English, largely by way of Spanish. A bare handful of words come from other language groups, such as *tepee* from Dakota Siouan, *catalpa* from Creek, *sequoia* from Cherokee, *hogan* from Navaho, and *sockeye* from Salish, as well as *cayuse* from Chinook.

Professional dialect research, initiated in Germany in 1878 and in France in 1902, did not begin in the US until 1931, in connection with the *Linguistic Atlas of New England* (1939–43). This kind of research, requiring trained field-workers to interview representative informants in their homes, subsequently was extended to the entire Atlantic Coast, the north-central states, the upper Midwest, the Pacific Coast, the Gulf states, and Oklahoma. As of 1980, only the New England atlas and the *Linguistic Atlas of the Upper Midwest* (1973–76) had been published, along with three volumes based on Atlantic Coast field materials; nearing publication were atlases of the north-central states, the Middle and South Atlantic states, the Gulf states, and Oklahoma. In other areas individual dialect researchers have produced more specialized studies. Scheduled for completion in 1982 is the definitive work on dialect speech, the American Dialect Society's monumental *Dictionary of American Regional English*, in preparation at the University of Wisconsin.

Dialect studies confirm that standard English is not uniform throughout the country. Major regional variations reflect patterns of colonial settlement, dialect features from England having dominated particular areas along the Atlantic Coast and then spread westward along the three main migration routes through the Appalachian system. Dialectologists recognize three main dialects—Northern, Midland, and Southern—each with subdivisions related to the effect of mountain ranges and rivers and railroads on population movement.

The Northern dialect is that of New England and its derivative settlements in New York; the northern parts of Ohio, Indiana, Illinois, and Iowa; and Michigan, Wisconsin, northeastern South Dakota, and North Dakota. A major subdivision is that of New England east of the Connecticut River, an area noted typically

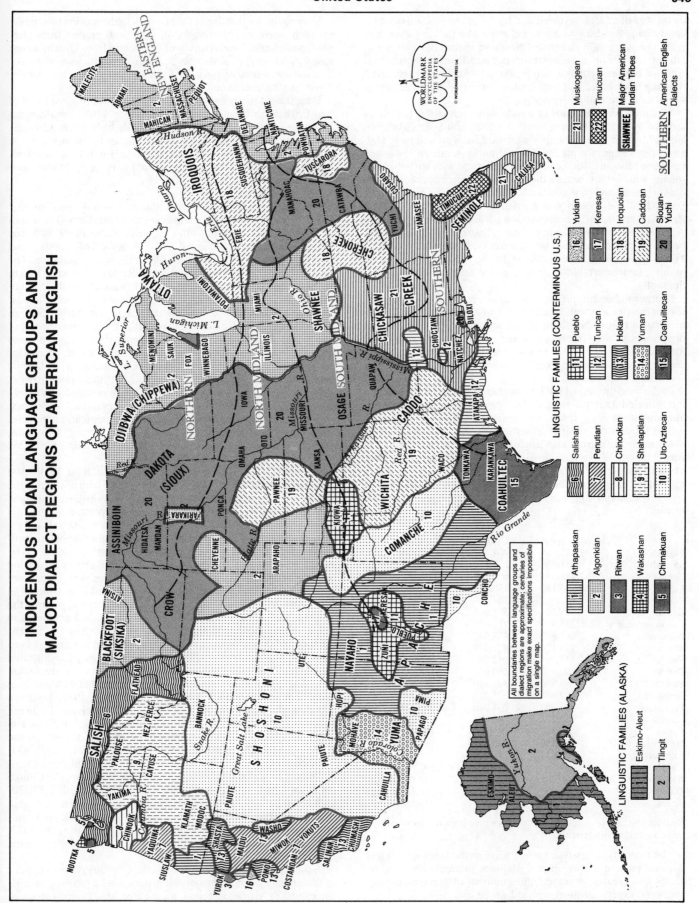

INDIGENOUS INDIAN LANGUAGE GROUPS AND MAJOR DIALECT REGIONS OF AMERICAN ENGLISH

WORLDMARK ENCYCLOPEDIA OF THE STATES
© WORLDMARK PRESS Ltd.

LINGUISTIC FAMILIES (CONTERMINOUS U.S.)

1 Athapaskan	6 Salishan
2 Algonkian	7 Penutian
3 Ritwan	8 Chinookan
4 Wakashan	9 Shahaptian
5 Chimakuan	10 Uto-Aztecan
11 Pueblo	16 Yukian
12 Tunican	17 Keresan
13 Hokan	18 Iroquoian
14 Yuman	19 Caddoan
15 Coahuiltecan	20 Siouan-Yuchi
21 Muskogean	22 Timucuan

SHAWNEE Major American Indian Tribes

SOUTHERN American English Dialects

All boundaries between language groups and dialect regions are approximate; centuries of migration make exact specifications impossible on a single map.

LINGUISTIC FAMILIES (ALASKA)

1 Eskimo-Aleut
2 Tlingit

by the loss of /r/ after a vowel, and by the pronunciation of *can't*, *dance*, *half*, and *bath* with a vowel more like that in *father* than that in *fat*. Generally, however, Northern speech has a strong /r/ after a vowel, the same vowel in *can't* and *cat*, a conspicuous contrast between *cot* and *caught*, the /s/ sound in *greasy*, *creek* rhyming with *pick*, and *with* ending with the same consonant sound as at the end of *breathe*.

Midland speech extends in a wide band across the US: there are two main subdivisions, North Midland and South Midland. North Midland speech extends westward from New Jersey, Delaware, and Pennsylvania into Ohio, Illinois, southern Iowa, and northern Missouri. Its speakers generally end *with* with the consonant sound that begins the word *thin*, pronounce *cot* and *caught* alike, and say *cow* and *down* as /caow/ and /daown/. South Midland speech was carried by the Scotch-Irish from Pennsylvania down the Shenandoah Valley into the southern Appalachians, where it acquired many Southern speech features before it spread westward into Kentucky, Tennessee, southern Missouri, Arkansas, and northeast Texas. Its speakers are likely to say *plum peach* for clingstone peach and *snake doctor* for dragonfly.

Southern speech typically, though not always, lacks the consonant /r/ after a vowel, lengthens the first part of the diphthong in *write* so that to Northern ears it sounds almost like *rat*, and diphthongizes the vowels in *bed* and *hit* so that they sound like /beuhd/ and /hiuht/. *Horse* and *hoarse* do not sound alike, and *creek* rhymes with *meek*. Corn bread is *corn pone*, and *you-all* is standard for the plural.

In the western part of the US, migration routes so crossed and intermingled that no neat dialect boundaries can be drawn, although there are a few rather clear population pockets.

The English of the original settlers has been accepted by so many immigrants from non-English-speaking countries that, according to the 1970 census, English was the native tongue of 79% of the population. Of the native-born, 82% claimed English as their native language. The following table shows the numbers of speakers of major languages named as mother tongue in the 1970 census:

	NATIVE STOCK	FOREIGN STOCK	
		TOTAL[1]	FOREIGN-BORN
English	149,312,435	11,404,678	1,697,825
Spanish	4,171,050	3,652,533	1,696,240
German	2,488,394	2,604,660	1,201,535
French	1,460,130	1,138,278	410,580
Polish	670,335	1,767,603	419,912
Italian	605,625	3,538,690	1,025,994
Indian languages	254,859	13,446	5,809
Norwegian	204,822	408,040	94,365
Yiddish	170,174	1,423,819	438,116
Swedish	113,119	512,983	131,408
Dutch	90,713	260,035	127,834
Slovak	86,950	423,416	82,561
Japanese	82,886	325,618	118,090
Portuguese	62,252	303,048	140,299
Finnish	58,124	156,044	38,290
Greek	56,839	401,860	193,745
Hungarian	52,156	395,341	161,253
Lithuanian	34,744	258,076	95,188
Chinese	30,764	314,667	190,260
Russian	30,665	303,950	149,277
Danish	29,089	165,373	58,218
Arabic	25,766	167,754	73,657

[1]Includes foreign-born residents as well as native-born residents with one or two foreign-born parents.

The majority of Spanish speakers live in the Southwest, Florida, and eastern urban centers. Refugee immigration since the 1950s has greatly increased the numbers of foreign-language speakers, especially from central Europe and Asia.

Very early, English borrowed from neighboring French speakers such words as *shivaree*, *butte*, *levee*, and *prairie*; from German, *sauerkraut*, *smearcase*, and *cranberry*; from Dutch, *stoop*, *spook*, and *cookie*; and from Spanish, *tornado*, *corral*, *ranch*, and *canyon*. From various West African languages, blacks have given English *jazz*, *voodoo*, and *okra*.

Educational problems raised by the presence of large blocs of non-English speakers led to the passage in 1976 of the Bilingual Education Act, enabling children to study basic courses in their first language while they learn English at the same time. A related school problem is that of black English, a Southern dialect variant that is the vernacular of many black students now in northern schools.

[9]RELIGIONS

US religious traditions are predominantly Judeo-Christian, and most Americans identify themselves as Protestants (of various denominations), Roman Catholics, or Jews. As of 1977–78, the US religious bodies counted 333,175 places of worship and 132,812,000 members, or about 61% of the total population. The largest Christian denomination is the Roman Catholic Church, with 49,836,000 members and 24,468 houses of worship. Immigration from Ireland, Italy, Eastern Europe, French Canada, and the Caribbean accounts for the predominance of Roman Catholicism in the Northeast, the Northwest, and some parts of the Great Lakes region, while Hispanic traditions and more recent immigration from Mexico and Latin America account for the historical importance of Roman Catholicism in California and throughout much of the Sunbelt. More than any other US religious body, the Roman Catholic Church maintains an extensive network of parochial schools. Jewish immigrants settled first in the Northeast, where the largest Jewish populations remain; in 1979, some 1,998,000 Jews lived in the greater New York area, out of an estimated total of 5,860,000. Eastern Orthodox churches have some 4,000,000 members.

As of 1978, US Protestant groups had at least 72,383,000 adherents, or nearly 55% of all those affiliated with any organized religion. Baptists predominate below the Mason-Dixon line and west to Texas. By far the nation's largest Protestant group, the Southern Baptist Convention had more than 13,000,000 adherents in 1979, representing at least 20% of the total populations of Alabama, Arkansas, Georgia, Kentucky, North Carolina, Oklahoma, Tennessee, and Texas; the American Baptist Convention claimed some 1,300,000 adherents in the same year. A concentration of Methodist groups extends westward in a band from Delaware to eastern Colorado; the largest of these groups, the United Methodist Church, had nearly 10,000,000 adherents in 1979, and the African Methodist Episcopal Church had 1,950,000. Lutheran denominations, reflecting in part the patterns of German and Scandinavian settlement, are most highly concentrated in the north-central states, especially Minnesota and the Dakotas. There are three major groups: the Lutheran Church in America, with 2,921,090 baptized members in 1979; Lutheran Church–Missouri Synod, 2,623,181; and American Lutheran Church, with 2,363,762. Other Protestant denominations and their estimated 1978 adherents were Episcopal Church in the USA, 2,818,130; United Presbyterian Chruch, 2,569,437; Churches of Christ, 2,500,000; and the United Church of Christ (Congregationalist), 1,778,000. One Christian group, the Church of Jesus Christ of Latter-day Saints (Mormon), with 2,591,700 adherents in 1979, was organized in New York State in 1830 and, since migrating westward, has played a leading role in Utah's political, economic, and religious life. Notable during the 1970s was a rise in the fundamentalist, evangelical, and Pentecostal movements.

Some 2,000,000 Muslims, followers of various Asian religions, a multiplicity of small Protestant groups, and a growing number of cults also participate in US religious life. Controversies as the 1980s began surrounded the proper role of organized religion in politics and the attitudes of religious bodies toward women, homosexuals, and abortion.

¹⁰TRANSPORTATION

The extent of the transportation industry in the US is indicated by the fact that railroads, motor vehicles, inland waterways, oil pipelines, and domestic airways carried a total of 2.3 trillion ton-miles of domestic intercity freight in 1977. Of this total, railroads accounted for 36.1% (compared with 68.4% in 1945); motor vehicles, 24.08% (6.2% in 1945); oil pipelines, 23.69%; inland waterways, 15.97%; and airlines 0.16%. The nation's major types of carriers had combined operating revenues of $76.8 billion for the year ending December 1977.

Railroads lost not only the largest share of intercity freight traffic, their chief source of revenue, but passenger traffic as well. Despite an attempt to revive passenger transport through the development of a national network (Amtrak) in the 1970s, the rail sector continued to experience heavy losses and declining revenues. In 1977 there were 320 rail companies in the US (compared with 471 in 1950) operating some 320,000 mi (515,000 km) of track (396,000 mi, or 637,000 km, in 1950). Railroads carried 276 million passengers in 1977, an increase of 6 million since 1975 but a decrease of 212 million since 1950.

Railroads have lost the bulk of their passenger trade to the private automobile, which, it is estimated, accounted for 85.1% of intercity passenger traffic in 1977. Airways accounted for 12.1% of the intercity traffic during the same year (4.4% in 1960). Intercity bus lines carried 335 million passengers in 1978. A survey of daily work-related travel in 1975 showed that 52,294,000 Americans drove alone to work in a car or a truck, 15,575,000 made use of car pools, and 4,825,000 used public transit, including 3,100,000 who took buses or streetcars and 1,179,000 who took subways or elevated trains.

The most conspicuous form of transportation is the automobile, and the extent and quality of the US road-transport system are without parallel in the world. In 1977, 84.1% of all US households owned automobiles, and 36.6% had more than one car. In 1978, factory sales totaled 12.87 million vehicles, of which 9.2 million were passenger cars. In the same year, 2 million imported cars, mainly from the Federal Republic of Germany (West Germany) and Japan, were sold (22% of passenger car sales). From the start of the automotive industry in 1896 through 1980, more than 350 million motor vehicles have been produced in the US. Some 153.9 million vehicles—a record number—were registered in 1978, including 116.6 million passenger cars and 32.2 million trucks and buses. In 1978, the US accounted for 37% of the world's registered motor vehicles. Motor vehicle travel in the US set a new record of 1.55 trillion vehicle-miles in 1978. Between 1973 and 1978, as average gasoline prices doubled and motor fuel shortages developed, fuel economy became an important consideration for car buyers and manufacturers; average annual fuel consumption per passenger car fell from 851 gallons in 1973 to 788 gallons in 1974 and was estimated at 715 gallons in 1978. Speed limits were reduced to 55 mph as a fuel economy measure, and the lower speeds had the beneficial side effect of temporarily reducing death rates from motor vehicle accidents. However, traffic fatalities climbed above 50,000 in 1978 and 1979, a trend attributed to the swing to more fuel-efficient but necessarily smaller and lighter vehicles.

The US has a vast network of roads, whose total length as of 31 December 1978 was 3,885,452 mi (6,253,041 km). Of these, 3,202,799 mi (5,154,415 km) were surfaced. During the 1970s, about $10 billion was spent annually on highway construction. By the late 1970s, new highway construction had slowed, and an increasing share of highway funds was allocated to the improvement of existing roads.

Major ocean ports or port areas are New York, the Delaware River area (Philadelphia), the Chesapeake Bay area (Baltimore, Norfolk, Newport News), New Orleans, Houston, and the San Francisco Bay area. The inland port of Duluth on Lake Superior handles more freight than all but the top-ranking ocean ports. The importance of this port, along with those of Chicago and Detroit, was enhanced with the opening in 1959 of the St. Lawrence Seaway. US overseas trade and domestic waterborne commerce in 1978 totaled 1.9 billion tons, 935 million tons (49%) of which involved foreign trade; the remainder was in domestic shipping—coastal, inland, and Great Lakes commerce. Waterborne freight consists primarily of bulk commodities such as petroleum and its products, coal and coke, iron ore and steel, sand, gravel and stone, grains, and lumber. The US merchant marine industry has been decreasing gradually since the 1950s. In 1977, the US had the 9th-largest registered merchant shipping fleet in the world, with 840 vessels of more than 1,000 gross registered tons.

In 1976 there were about 174,000 mi (280,000 km) of oil pipeline in operation, accounting for nearly one-fourth of total domestic freight traffic; the following year, the 789-mi (1,270-km) trans-Alaska pipeline came into service. This substantial system was to be further augmented by the 1,500-mi (2,400-km) Northern Tier pipeline, a project approved in 1980 that would carry oil from Alaska and California to the upper Midwest.

In 1978, the US had 35 scheduled passenger airlines, of which 33 flew primarily domestic routes. The gains in passenger service have been spectacular. In 1940, revenue passengers carried by the airlines totaled 2.7 million; by 1978, the figure was 275 million. In 1978, the US had 14,574 airports, of which 4,751 were public. US international carriers flew 319 million mi (513 million km) in scheduled international service, serving some 21 million passengers. In addition, eight charter airlines carried 3,102,000 domestic and 5,207,000 international passengers in 1978.

The federal government regulates and subsidizes almost all forms of transportation. It regulates railroads, pipelines, and motor carriers of passengers and freight through the Interstate Commerce Commission. The Federal Railroad Administration coordinates federal railroad support programs. Air transportation is regulated through the Federal Aviation Administration (FAA) and the Civil Aeronautics Board (which, under a policy of deregulation, was being phased out in 1980, with abolition scheduled for 1985). The FAA operates the National Airspace System, which develops and maintains guidance and control devices along designated air lanes. The government subsidizes shipping through the Maritime Subsidy Board of the Maritime Administration, sharing heavily in the costs of ship construction by private concerns.

¹¹HISTORY

The first Americans—distant ancestors of the American Indians—probably crossed the Bering Strait from Asia at least 12,000 years ago. By the time Christopher Columbus came to the New World in 1492, there were probably no more than 2 million Indians living in the land that was to become the US.

Following exploration of the American coasts by English, Portuguese, Spanish, Dutch, and French sea captains from the late 15th century onward, European settlements sprang up in the latter part of the 16th century. The Spanish established the first permanent settlement at St. Augustine in the future state of Florida in 1565, and another in New Mexico in 1599. During the early 17th century, the English founded Jamestown in Virginia Colony in 1607 and Plymouth Colony in present-day Massachusetts in 1620, and the Dutch established settlements at Ft. Orange (now Albany, N.Y.) in 1624, New Amsterdam (now New York City) in 1626, and at Bergen (now part of Jersey City, N.J.) in 1660. The Dutch conquered New Sweden—the Swedish colony in Delaware and New Jersey—in 1655. Nine years later, however, the English seized the New Netherland Colony, and they subsequently monopolized settlement of the East Coast except for Florida, where Spanish rule prevailed until 1821; in the Southwest, California, Arizona, New Mexico, and Texas also were part of the Spanish empire until the 19th century. Meanwhile, in the Great Lakes area south of present-day Canada, France set up a few trading posts and settlements but never established effective control; New Orleans was one of the few areas of the US where France pursued an active colonial policy.

From the founding of Jamestown to the outbreak of the American Revolution more than 150 years later, the British government administered its American colonies within the context of mercantilism: the colonies existed primarily for the economic benefit of the empire. Great Britain valued its American colonies especially for their tobacco, lumber, indigo, rice, furs, fish, grain, and naval stores, relying particularly in the southern colonies on black slave labor.

The colonies enjoyed a large measure of internal self-government until the end of the French and Indian War (1754–63), which resulted in the loss of French Canada to the British. To prevent further troubles with the Indians, the British government in 1763 prohibited the American colonists from settling beyond the Appalachian Mountains. Heavy debts forced London to decree that the colonists should assume the costs of their own defense, and to provide funds for that purpose a series of revenue acts followed. But soon the colonists began to insist that they could be taxed "only with their consent," and the struggle grew to become one of local versus imperial authority.

Growing cultural and intellectual differences also served to divide the colonies and the mother country. Life on the edge of the civilized world had brought about changes in the colonists' attitudes and outlook, emphasizing their remoteness from English life. In view of the long tradition of virtual self-government in the colonies, strict enforcement of imperial regulations and British efforts to curtail the power of colonial legislatures presaged inevitable conflict between the colonies and the mother country. When citizens of Massachusetts, protesting the tax on tea, dumped a shipload of tea belonging to the East India Company into Boston harbor in 1773, the British felt compelled to act in defense of their authority as well as in defense of private property. Punitive measures—referred to as the Intolerable Acts by the colonists—struck at the foundations of self-government.

In response, the First Continental Congress, composed of representatives from 12 of the 13 colonies—Georgia was not represented—met in Philadelphia in September 1774, and proposed a general boycott of English goods together with the organizing of a militia. British troops marched to Concord, Mass., on 19 April 1775 and destroyed the supplies that the colonists had assembled there. American "minutemen" assembled on the nearby Lexington green and fired "the shot heard round the world," although no one knows who actually fired the first shot that morning. The British soldiers withdrew and fought their way back to Boston.

Voices in favor of conciliation were raised in the Second Continental Congress that assembled in Philadelphia on 10 May 1775, this time including Georgia; but with news of the Restraining Act (30 March 1775), which denied the colonies the right to trade with countries outside the British Empire, all hopes for peace vanished. George Washington was appointed commander-in-chief of the new American army, and on 4 July 1776, the 13 American colonies adopted the Declaration of Independence, justifying the right of revolution by the theory of natural rights.

British and American forces met in their first organized encounter near Boston on 17 June 1775. Numerous battles up and down the coast followed. The British seized and held the principal cities but were unable to inflict a decisive defeat on Washington's troops. The entry of France into the war on the American side eventually tipped the balance. On 19 October 1781, the

British commander, Cornwallis, cut off from reinforcements by the French fleet on one side and besieged by French and American forces on the other, surrendered his army at Yorktown, Va. American independence was acknowledged by the British in a treaty of peace signed in Paris on 3 September 1783.

The first constitution uniting the 13 original states—the Articles of Confederation—reflected all the suspicions that Americans entertained about a strong central government. Congress was denied power to raise taxes or regulate commerce, and many of the powers it was authorized to exercise required the approval of a minimum of nine states. Dissatisfaction with the Articles of Confederation was aggravated by the hardships of a postwar depression, and in 1787—the same year that Congress passed the Northwest Ordinance, providing for the organization of new territories and states on the frontier—a convention assembled in Philadelphia to revise the articles. The convention adopted an altogether new constitution, the present Constitution of the United States, which greatly increased the powers of the central government at the expense of the states. This document was ratified by the states with the understanding that it would be amended to include a bill of rights guaranteeing certain fundamental freedoms. These freedoms—including the rights of free speech, press, and assembly, freedom from unreasonable search and seizure, and the right to a speedy and public trial by an impartial jury—are assured by the first 10 amendments to the constitution, adopted on 15 December 1791; the constitution did not, however, abolish slavery, nor did it grant women the right to vote. On 30 April 1789, George Washington was inaugurated as the first president of the US.

During Washington's administration the credit of the new nation was assured by acts providing for a revenue tariff and an excise tax; opposition to the excise on whiskey sparked the Whiskey Rebellion, suppressed on Washington's orders in 1794. Alexander Hamilton's proposals for funding the domestic and foreign debt and permitting the national government to assume the debts of the states were also implemented. Hamilton, the secretary of the treasury, also created the first national bank, and was the founder of the Federalist Party. Opposition to the bank as well as to the rest of the Hamiltonian program, which tended to favor northeastern commercial and business interests, led to the formation of an opposition party, the Democratic-Republicans, led by Jefferson. The Federalist Party, to which Washington belonged, regarded the French Revolution as a threat to security and property; the Republicans, while condemning the violence of the revolutionists, hailed the overthrow of the French monarchy as a blow to tyranny. The split of the nation's leadership into rival camps was the first manifestation of the two-party system, which has since been the dominant characteristic of the US political scene. (Jefferson's party should not be confused with the modern Republican Party, formed in 1854.)

The 1800 election saw the defeat of Federalist John Adams, Washington's successor as president, by Jefferson; a key factor in Adams's loss was the unpopularity of the Alien and Sedition Acts (1798), Federalist-sponsored measures that had abridged certain freedoms guaranteed in the Bill of Rights. Jefferson was responsible for the purchase from France of the Louisiana Territory, including all the present territory of the US west of the Mississippi drained by that river and its tributaries; exploration and mapping of the new territory, notably through the expeditions of Meriwether Lewis and William Clark, began almost immediately. Under Chief Justice John Marshall, the US Supreme Court, in the landmark case of *Marbury* v. *Madison*, established the principle of federal supremacy in conflicts with the states and enunciated the doctrine of judicial review.

During Jefferson's second term in office, the US became involved in a protracted struggle between Britain and Napoleonic France. Seizures of US ships and the impressment of US seamen

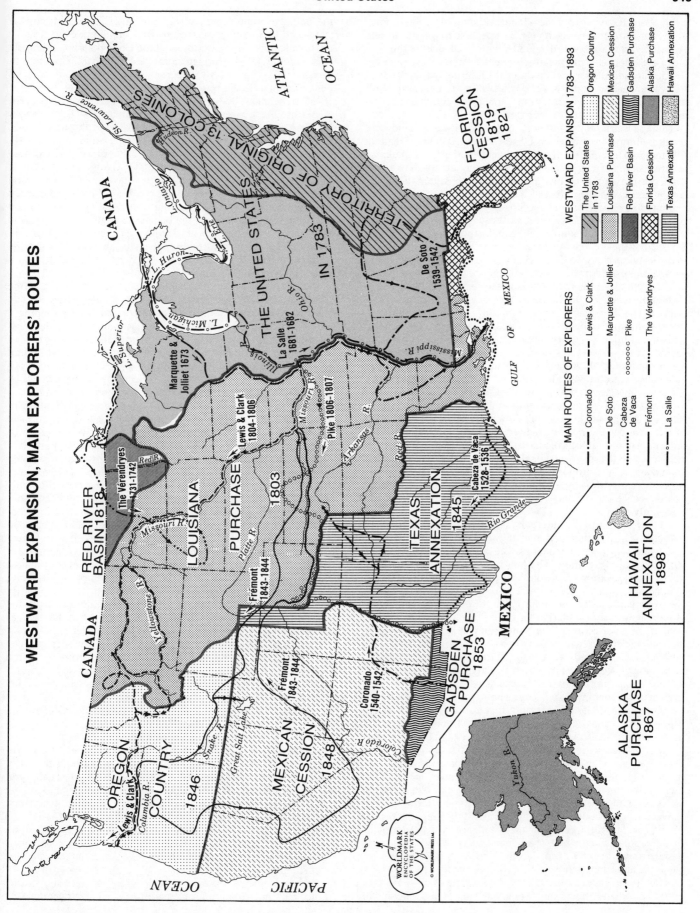

WESTWARD EXPANSION, MAIN EXPLORERS' ROUTES

ATLANTIC OCEAN

FLORIDA CESSION 1819-1821

CANADA

St. Lawrence R.

Hudson R.

L. Ontario

L. Erie

L. Huron

L. Michigan

L. Superior

Marquette & Jolliet 1673

TERRITORY OF ORIGINAL 13 COLONIES

THE UNITED STATES IN 1783

De Soto 1539-1542

La Salle 1681-1682

Ohio R.

Illinois R.

Mississippi R.

GULF OF MEXICO

WESTWARD EXPANSION 1783-1893

Oregon Country
Mexican Cession
Gadsden Purchase
Alaska Purchase
Hawaii Annexation

The United States in 1783
Louisiana Purchase
Red River Basin
Florida Cession
Texas Annexation

MAIN ROUTES OF EXPLORERS

Coronado
De Soto
Cabeza de Vaca
Frémont
La Salle

Lewis & Clark
Marquette & Jolliet
Pike
The Vérendryes

CANADA

RED RIVER BASIN 1818

The Vérendryes 1731-1742

Red R.

Missouri R.

LOUISIANA PURCHASE 1803

Lewis & Clark 1804-1806

Pike 1806-1807

Missouri R.

Arkansas R.

Red R.

Platte R.

Frémont 1843-1844

TEXAS ANNEXATION 1845

Cabeza de Vaca 1528-1536

Rio Grande

MEXICO

Yellowstone R.

OREGON COUNTRY 1846

Lewis & Clark

Columbia R.

Snake R.

Great Salt Lake

MEXICAN CESSION 1848

Frémont 1843-1844

Coronado 1540-1542

Colorado R.

GADSDEN PURCHASE 1853

PACIFIC OCEAN

WORLDMARK ENCYCLOPEDIA OF THE STATES
© WORLDMARK PRESS Ltd.

HAWAII ANNEXATION 1898

ALASKA PURCHASE 1867

Yukon R.

by the British navy forced the administration to pass the Embargo Act of 1807, under which no US ships were to put out to sea. After the act was repealed in 1809, continued British ship seizures and impressment of seamen were the ostensible reasons for the declaration of war on Britain in 1812 during the administration of James Madison. An underlying cause of the War of 1812, however, was the coveting by land-hungry westerners of southern Canada as potential US territory.

The war was largely a standoff. British successes on land were countered by a few surprising US naval victories. The Treaty of Ghent (24 December 1814), which ended the war, made no mention of impressment and provided for no territorial changes. The occasion for further maritime conflict with Britain, however, disappeared with the defeat of Napoleon in 1815.

Now the nation became occupied primarily with domestic problems and westward expansion. Because the US had been cut off from its normal sources of manufactured goods in Great Britain during the war, textiles and other industries developed and prospered in New England. To protect these infant industries, Congress adopted a high tariff policy in 1816.

Three events of the late 1810s and the 1820s were of considerable importance for the future of the country. The federal government in 1817 began a policy of forcibly resettling the Indians, already decimated by war and disease, in what later became known as Indian Territory (now Oklahoma); those Indians not forced to move were restricted to reservations. The Missouri Compromise (1820) was an attempt to find a nationally acceptable solution to the volatile dispute over the extension of black slavery to new territories. It provided for admission of Missouri into the Union as a slave state but banned slavery in territories to the west that lay north of 36°30′. As a result of the establishment of independent Latin American republics and threats by France and Spain to reestablish colonial rule, President James Monroe in 1823 asserted that the Western Hemisphere was closed to further colonization by European powers. The Monroe Doctrine declared that any effort by such powers to recover territories whose independence the US had recognized would be regarded as an unfriendly act.

From the 1820s to the outbreak of the Civil War, the growth of manufacturing continued, mainly in the North, and was accelerated by inventions and technological advances. Farming expanded with westward migration. The South discovered that its future lay in the cultivation of cotton. The cotton gin, invented by Eli Whitney in 1793, greatly simplified the problems of production; the growth of the textile industry in New England and Great Britain assured a firm market for cotton. Hence, during the first half of the 19th century, the South remained a fundamentally agrarian society based increasingly on a one-crop economy. Large numbers of field hands were required for cotton cultivation, and black slavery became solidly entrenched in the southern economy.

The construction of roads and canals paralleled the country's growth and economic expansion. The successful completion of the Erie Canal (1825), linking the Great Lakes with the Atlantic, ushered in a canal-building boom. Railroad building began in earnest in the 1830s, and by 1840, about 3,300 mi (5,300 km) of track had been laid. The development of the telegraph a few years later gave the nation the beginnings of a modern telecommunications network. As a result of the establishment of the factory system, a laboring class appeared in the North by the 1830s, bringing with it the earliest unionization efforts.

Western states admitted into the Union following the War of 1812 provided for free white male suffrage without property qualifications and helped spark a democratic revolution. As eastern states began to broaden the franchise, mass appeal became an important requisite for political candidates. The election to the presidency in 1828 of Andrew Jackson, a military hero and Indian fighter, was no doubt a result of this widening of the democratic process. By this time, the US consisted of 24 states and had a population of nearly 13 million.

The relentless westward thrust of the US population ultimately involved the US in foreign conflict. In 1836, US settlers in Texas revolted against Mexican rule and established an independent republic. Texas was admitted to the Union as a state in 1845, and relations between Mexico and the US steadily worsened. A dispute arose over the southern boundary of Texas, and a Mexican attack on a US patrol in May 1846 gave President James K. Polk a pretext to declare war. After a rapid advance, US forces captured Mexico City, and on 2 February 1848, Mexico formally gave up the unequal fight by signing the Treaty of Guadalupe Hidalgo, providing for the cession of California and the territory of New Mexico to the US. With the Gadsden Purchase of 1853, the US acquired from Mexico for $10 million large strips of land forming the balance of southern Arizona and New Mexico. A dispute with Britain over the Oregon Territory was settled in 1846 by a treaty that established the 49th parallel as the boundary. Thenceforth, the US was to be a Pacific as well as an Atlantic power.

Westward expansion exacerbated the issue of slavery in the territories. By 1840, abolition of slavery constituted a fundamental spect of a movement for moral reform, which also encompassed woman's rights, universal education, alleviation of working class hardships, and temperance. In 1849, a year after discovery of gold had precipitated a rush of new settlers to California, that territory (whose constitution prohibited slavery) demanded admission to the Union. A compromise engineered in Congress by Senator Henry Clay in 1850 provided for California's admission as a free state in return for various concessions to the South. But enmities dividing North and South could not be silenced. The issue of slavery in the territories came to a head with the Kansas-Nebraska Act of 1854, which repealed the Missouri Compromise and left the question of slavery in those territories to be decided by the settlers themselves. The ensuing conflicts in Kansas between northern and southern settlers earned the territory the name "bleeding Kansas." In 1860, the Democratic Party, split along northern and southern lines, offered two presidential candidates. The new Republican Party, organized in 1854 and opposed to the expansion of slavery, nominated Abraham Lincoln. Owing to the defection in Democratic ranks, Lincoln was able to carry the election in the electoral college, although he did not obtain a majority of the popular vote. To ardent supporters of slavery, Lincoln's election provided a reason for immediate secession. By February 1861, seven southern states had withdrawn from the Union and formed a separate government, known as the Confederate States of America, under the presidency of Jefferson Davis. Four other southern states later joined the Confederacy. The secessionists soon began to confiscate federal property in the South. On 12 April 1861, southerners opened fire on Ft. Sumter in the harbor of Charleston, S.C., and thus precipitated the US Civil War.

For the next four years, war raged between the Confederate and Union governments, largely in southern territories. An estimated 360,000 men in the Union forces died of various causes, including 110,000 killed in battle. Confederate dead were estimated at 250,000, including 94,000 killed in battle. The North, with great superiority in manpower and resources, finally prevailed. A Confederate invasion of the North was repulsed at the battle of Gettysburg, Pa., in July 1863; a Union army took Atlanta in September 1864; and Confederate forces evacuated Richmond, the Confederate capital, in early April 1865. With much of the South in Union hands, Confederate General Robert E. Lee surrendered to General Ulysses S. Grant at Appomattox Courthouse, Va. on 9 April.

The outcome of the war brought great changes in US life. Lincoln's Emancipation Proclamation of 1863 was the initial step in freeing some 4 million black slaves; their liberation was completed soon after the war's end by amendments to the Constitution. Lincoln's plan for the reconstruction of the rebellious states was compassionate but, only five days after Lee's surrender, Lincoln was assassinated by John Wilkes Booth as part of a conspiracy in which US Secretary of State William H. Seward was seriously wounded. During the reconstruction era of 1865–77, the defeated South was governed by Union Army commanders, and the resultant bitterness of southerners toward northern Republican rule, which enfranchised blacks, persisted for years afterward. Vice President Andrew Johnson, who succeeded Lincoln as president, tried to carry out Lincoln's conciliatory policies but was opposed by Radical Republican leaders in Congress, who demanded firm treatment of the South. On the pretext that he had failed to carry out an act of Congress, the House of Representatives voted to impeach Johnson in 1868, but the Senate failed by one vote to convict him and remove him from office. It was during Johnson's presidency that Secretary of State Seward negotiated the purchase of Alaska (which attained statehood in 1959) from Russia for $7.2 million.

The efforts of southern whites to regain political control of their states led to the formation of terrorist organizations like the Ku Klux Klan, which employed violence to prevent blacks from voting. By the end of the reconstruction era, whites had reestablished their political domination over blacks in the southern states and began to enforce patterns of segregation in education and social organization that were to last for nearly a century.

In many southern states, the decades following the Civil War were ones of economic devastation, in which rural whites as well as blacks were reduced to sharecropper status. Outside the South, however, a great period of economic expansion began. Transcontinental railroads were constructed, corporate enterprise spurted ahead, and the remaining western frontier lands were rapidly occupied and settled. The age of the big business tycoons dawned. As heavy manufacturing developed, Pittsburgh, Chicago, and New York emerged as the nation's great industrial centers. The Knights of Labor, founded in 1869, engaged in numerous strikes, and violent conflicts between strikers and strikebreakers were common. The American Federation of Labor, founded in 1886, established a nationwide system of craft unionism that remained dominant for many decades. During this period, too, the woman's rights movement organized actively to secure the vote (although woman's suffrage was not enacted nationally until 1920), and groups outraged by the depletion of forests and wildlife in the West pressed for the conservation of natural resources.

During the latter half of the 19th century, the acceleration of westward expansion made room for millions of immigrants from Europe. The country's population grew to more than 76 million persons by 1900. As homesteaders, prospectors, and other settlers tamed the frontier, the federal government forced Indians west of the Mississippi to cede vast tracts of land to the whites, precipitating a series of wars with various tribes. By 1890, only 250,000 Indians remained in the US, virtually all of them residing on reservations.

The 1890s marked the official closing of the US frontier for settlement and the beginning of US overseas expansion. By 1892, Hawaiian sugar planters of US origin had become strong enough to bring about the downfall of the native queen and to establish a republic, which in 1898, at its own request, was annexed as a territory by the US. The sympathies of the US with the Cuban nationalists who were battling for independence from Spain were aroused by a lurid press and by expansionist elements. A series of events climaxed by the sinking of the USS *Maine* in Havana harbor finally forced a reluctant President William McKinley to declare war on Spain on 25 April 1898. US forces overwhelmed those of Spain in Cuba, and as a result of the Spanish-American War the US added to its territories the Philippines, Guam, and Puerto Rico. A newly independent Cuba was drawn into the US orbit as a virtual protectorate through the 1950s. Many eminent citizens saw these new departures into imperialism as a betrayal of the time-honored US doctrine of government by the consent of the governed.

With the marked expansion of big business came increasing protests against the oppressive policies of large corporations and their dominant role in the public life of the nation. A demand emerged for strict control of monopolistic business practice through the enforcement of the antitrust laws. Two US presidents, Theodore Roosevelt (1901–9), a Republican, and Woodrow Wilson (1913–21), a Democrat, approved of the general movement for reform, which came to be called progressivism. Roosevelt developed a considerable reputation as a trustbuster, while Wilson's program, known as the New Freedom, called for reform of tariffs, business procedures, and banking. During Roosevelt's first term, the US leased the Panama Canal Zone and started construction of a 42-mi (68-km) canal, completed in 1914.

US involvement in World War I marked the country's active emergence as one of the great powers of the world. When war broke out in 1914 between Germany, Austria-Hungary, and Turkey on one side and Britain, France, and Russia on the other, sentiment in the US was strongly opposed to participation in the conflict, although a large segment of the American people sympathized with the British and the French. While both sides violated US maritime rights on the high seas, the Germans, enmeshed in a British blockade, resorted to unrestricted submarine warfare. On 6 April 1917, Congress declared war on Germany. Through a national draft of all able-bodied men between the ages of 18 and 45, some 4 million US soldiers were trained, of whom more than 2 million were sent overseas to France. By late 1917, when US troops began to take part in the fighting on the western front, the European armies were approaching exhaustion, and US intervention may well have been decisive in assuring the eventual victory of the Allies. In a series of great battles in which US soldiers took an increasingly major part, the German forces were rolled back in the west, and in the autumn of 1918 were compelled to sue for peace. Fighting ended with the armistice of 11 November 1918. President Wilson played an active role in drawing up the 1919 Versailles peace treaty, which embodied his dream of establishing a League of Nations to preserve the peace, but the isolationist bloc in the Senate was able to prevent US ratification of the treaty.

In the 1920s, the US had little enthusiasm left for crusades, either for democracy abroad or for reform at home; a rare instance of idealism in action was the Kellogg-Briand Pact (1928), an antiwar accord negotiated on behalf of the US by Secretary of State Frank B. Kellogg. In general, however, the philosophy of the Republican administrations from 1921 to 1933 was expressed in the aphorism "The business of America is business," and the 1920s saw a great business boom. The years 1923–24 also witnessed the unraveling of the Teapot Dome scandal: the revelation that President Warren G. Harding's secretary of the interior, Albert B. Fall, had secretly leased federal oil reserves in California and Wyoming to private oil companies in return for gifts and loans.

The great stock market crash of October 1929 ushered in the most serious and most prolonged economic depression that the country had ever known. By 1933, an estimated 12 million men and women were out of work; personal savings were wiped out on a vast scale through a disastrous series of corporate bankruptcies and bank failures. Relief for the unemployed was left to private charities and local governments, which were incapable of handling the enormous task.

The inauguration of the successful Democratic presidential candidate, Franklin D. Roosevelt, in March 1933 ushered in a new era of US history, in which the federal government was to assume a much more prominent role in the nation's economic affairs. Proposing to give the country a "New Deal," Roosevelt accepted national responsibility for alleviating the hardships of unemployment: relief measures were instituted, work projects were established, and deficit spending was accepted in preference to ignoring public distress. The federal Social Security program was inaugurated, as were various measures designed to stimulate and develop the economy through federal intervention. Unions were strengthened through the National Labor Relations Act, which established the right of employees' organizations to bargain collectively with employers. Union membership increased rapidly, and the dominance of the American Federation of Labor was challenged by the newly formed Congress of Industrial Organizations, which organized workers along industrial lines.

The depression of the 1930s was worldwide, and certain nations attempted to counter economic stagnation by building large military establishments and embarking on foreign adventures. Following German, Italian, and Japanese aggression, World War II broke out in Europe during September 1939. In 1940, Roosevelt, disregarding a long-standing tradition that no president should serve more than two terms, ran again for reelection. He easily defeated his Republican opponent, Wendell Willkie, who, along with Roosevelt, advocated increased rearmament and all possible aid to victims of aggression. The US was brought actively into the war by the Japanese attack on the Pearl Harbor naval base in Hawaii on 7 December 1941. The forces of Germany, Italy, and Japan were now arrayed over a vast theater of war against those of the US and the British Commonwealth; in Europe, Germany was locked in a bloody struggle with the USSR. US forces waged war across the vast expanses of the Pacific, in Africa, in Asia, and in Europe. Italy surrendered in 1943; Germany was successfully invaded in 1944 and conquered in June 1945; and after the US dropped the world's first atomic bombs on Hiroshima and Nagasaki, the Japanese capitulated in August. The Philippines became an independent republic soon after the war, but the US retained most of its other Pacific possessions, with Hawaii becoming the 50th state in 1959.

Roosevelt, who had been elected to a fourth term in 1944, died in April 1945 and was succeeded by Harry S Truman, his vice president. Under the Truman administration, the US became an active member of the new world organization, the United Nations. As the incompatibility of Soviet communism and Western democracy became evident, the Truman administration embarked on large-scale programs of military aid and economic support to check the expansion of communism. Aid to Greece and Turkey in 1948 and the Marshall Plan program, designed to accelerate the economic recovery of Western Europe, were outstanding features of US postwar foreign policy. The North Atlantic Treaty (1949) established a defensive alliance among a number of West European nations and the US. Truman's Point Four program gave technical and scientific aid to developing nations. When, following the North Korean attack on South Korea on 25 June 1950, the UN Security Council resolved that members of the UN should proceed to the aid of South Korea, US naval, air, and ground forces were immediately dispatched by President Truman. An undeclared war ensued, which eventually was brought to a halt by an armistice signed on 27 June 1953.

In 1952, Dwight D. Eisenhower, supreme commander of Allied forces in Europe during World War II, was elected president on the Republican ticket, thereby bringing to an end 20 years of Democratic presidential leadership. In foreign affairs, the Eisenhower administration continued the Truman policy of containing the USSR and threatened "massive retaliation" in the event of Soviet aggression, thus heightening the Cold War between the world's two great nuclear powers. Although Republican domestic policies were more conservative than those of the Democrats, the Eisenhower administration extended certain major social and economic programs of the Roosevelt and Truman adminis-

trations, notably Social Security and public housing. The early years of the Eisenhower administration were stirred with agitation (arising in 1950) over charges of Communist and other allegedly subversive activities in the US—a phenomenon known as McCarthyism, after Republican Senator Joseph R. McCarthy of Wisconsin, who aroused much controversy with unsubstantiated allegations that Communists had penetrated the US government, especially the Army and the Department of State. Even those who personally opposed McCarthy lent their support to the imposition of loyalty oaths and the blacklisting of persons with left-wing backgrounds.

A major event of the Eisenhower years was the US Supreme Court's decision of 1954 outlawing segregation of whites and blacks in public schools. In the aftermath of this ruling, desegregation proceeded slowly and painfully. In the early 1960s, sit-ins, "freedom rides," and similar expressions of passive resistance by blacks and their sympathizers led to a lessening of segregation practices in public facilities. Under Chief Justice Earl Warren, the high court also mandated the reapportionment of state and federal legislative districts according to a "one person, one vote" formula. It also broadly extended the rights of defendants in criminal trials to include the provision of a defense lawyer at public expense for an accused person unable to afford one, and the duty of police to advise an accused person of his or her legal rights immediately upon arrest.

In the early 1960s, during the administration of Eisenhower's Democratic successor, John F. Kennedy, the Cold War heated up as Cuba, under the regime of Fidel Castro, aligned itself with the Soviet Union. Attempts by anti-Communist Cuban exiles to invade their homeland in the spring of 1961 failed despite some US aid and encouragement. In October 1962, President Kennedy successfully forced a showdown with the Soviets over Cuba in demanding the withdrawal of Soviet-supplied "offensive weapons"—missiles—from the nearby island. On 22 November 1963, President Kennedy was assassinated while riding in a motorcade through Dallas, Tex.; hours later, Vice President Lyndon B. Johnson was inaugurated president. In the November 1964 elections, Johnson overwhelmingly defeated his Republican opponent, Barry M. Goldwater, and embarked on a vigorous program of social legislation unprecedented since Roosevelt's New Deal. His "Great Society" program sought to ensure black Americans' rights in voting and public housing, to give the underprivileged job training, and to provide persons 65 and over with hospitalization and other medical benefits (Medicare). Measures ensuring equal opportunity for minority groups may have contributed to the growth of the woman's rights movement in the late 1960s. This same period also saw the growth of a powerful environmental protection movement.

US military and economic aid to anti-Communist forces in Viet-Nam, which had its beginnings during the Truman administration (while Viet-Nam was still part of French Indochina) and was increased gradually by Presidents Eisenhower and Kennedy, escalated in 1965 when President Johnson sent US combat troops to South Viet-Nam and ordered US bombing raids on North Viet-Nam, after Congress (in the Gulf of Tonkin Resolution of 1964) had given him practically carte blanche authority to wage war in that region. By the end of 1968, American forces in Viet-Nam numbered 536,100 men, but US military might was unable to defeat the Vietnamese guerrillas, and the American people were badly split over continuing the undeclared (and, some thought, ill-advised or even immoral) war, with its high price in casualties and matériel. Reacting to widespread dissatisfaction with his Viet-Nam policies, Johnson withdrew in March 1968 from the upcoming presidential race, and in November, Republican Richard M. Nixon, who had been the vice president under Eisenhower, was elected president. Thus the Johnson years —which had begun with the new hopes of a Great Society but had soured with a rising tide of racial violence in US cities and the assassinations of civil rights leader Martin Luther King, Jr., and US Senator Robert F. Kennedy, among others—drew to a close.

President Nixon gradually withdrew US ground troops from Viet-Nam but expanded aerial bombardment throughout Indochina, and the increasingly unpopular and costly war continued for four more years before a cease-fire—negotiated by Nixon's national security adviser, Henry Kissinger—was finally signed on 27 January 1973 and the last US soldiers were withdrawn. The most protracted conflict in American history had resulted in 46,163 US combat deaths and 303,654 wounded soldiers, and had cost the US government $112 billion in military allocations. Two years later, the South Vietnamese army collapsed, and the North Vietnamese Communist regime united the country.

In 1972, during the last year of his first administration, Nixon initiated the normalization of relations—ruptured in 1949—with the People's Republic of China and signed a strategic arms limitation agreement with the Soviet Union as part of a Nixon-Kissinger policy of pursuing détente with both major Communist powers. Earlier, in July 1969, American technology had achieved a national triumph by landing the first astronaut on the moon. The Nixon administration sought to muster a "silent majority" in support of its Indochina policies and its conservative social outlook in domestic affairs. The most momentous domestic development, however, was the Watergate scandal, which began on 17 June 1972 with the arrest of five men associated with Nixon's reelection campaign during a break-in at Democratic party headquarters in the Watergate office building in Washington, D.C. Although Nixon was reelected in 1972, subsequent disclosures by the press and by a Senate investigating committee revealed a complex pattern of political "dirty tricks" and illegal domestic surveillance throughout his first term. The president's apparent attempts to obstruct justice by helping his aides cover up the scandal were confirmed by tape recordings of his private conversations (made by Nixon himself), which the Supreme Court ordered him to release for use as evidence in criminal proceedings. The House voted to begin impeachment proceedings, and in late July 1974, its Judiciary Committee approved three articles of impeachment. On 9 August, Nixon became the first president to résign the office. The following year, Nixon's top aides and former attorney general, John N. Mitchell, were convicted of obstruction of justice and were subsequently sentenced to prison.

Nixon's successor was Gerald R. Ford, who in October 1973 had been appointed to succeed Vice President Spiro T. Agnew when Agnew resigned following his plea of *nolo contendere* to charges that he had evaded paying income tax on moneys he had received from contractors while governor of Maryland. Less than a month after taking office, President Ford granted a full pardon to Nixon for any crimes he may have committed as president. In August 1974, Ford nominated Nelson A. Rockefeller as vice president (he was not confirmed until December), thus giving the country the first instance of a nonelected president and an appointed vice president serving simultaneously. Ford's pardon of Nixon, plus continued inflation and unemployment, probably contributed to his narrow defeat by a Georgia Democrat, Jimmy Carter, in 1976.

President Carter's forthright championing of human rights—though consistent with the Helsinki accords, the "final act" of the Conference on Security and Cooperation in Europe, signed by the US and 34 other nations in July 1974—contributed to strained relations with the Soviet Union and with some US allies. During 1978–79, the president concluded and secured Senate passage of treaties ending US sovereignty over the Panama Canal. His major accomplishment in foreign affairs, however, was his role in mediating a peace agreement between Israel and Egypt, signed at his Camp David, Md., retreat in September 1978. Domestically, the Carter administration initiated a national energy program to reduce US dependence on foreign oil by cutting gasoline and oil consumption and by encouraging the development of alternative energy resources. But the continuing decline of the economy because of double-digit inflation and high unemployment caused his popularity to wane, and confusing shifts in economic policy (coupled with a lack of clear goals in foreign affairs) characterized his administration during 1979 and 1980; a prolonged quarrel with Iran over more than 50 US hostages seized in Tehran on 4 November 1979 contributed to public doubts about Carter. Exactly a year after the hostages were taken, former California Governor Ronald Reagan defeated Carter in an election that saw the Republican party score major gains throughout the US.

¹²FEDERAL GOVERNMENT

The Constitution of the United States, signed in 1787, is the nation's governing document. In the first 10 amendments to the Constitution, ratified in 1791 and known as the Bill of Rights, the federal government is denied the power to infringe on rights generally regarded as fundamental to the civil liberties of the people. These amendments prohibit the establishment of a state religion and the abridgment of freedom of speech, press, and the right to assemble. They protect all persons against unreasonable searches and seizures, guarantee trial by jury, and prohibit excessive bail and cruel and unusual punishments. No person may be required to testify against himself, nor may he be deprived of life, liberty, or property without due process of law. The 13th Amendment (1865) banned slavery; the 15th (1870) protected the freed slaves' right to vote; and the 19th (1920) guaranteed the franchise to women. In all, there have been 26 amendments, the last of which, in 1971, reduced the voting age to 18. Still pending as of 1980 was the Equal Rights Amendment (ERA), approved by Congress in 1972, which would mandate legal equality between the sexes. As of 1980, 35 of the required 38 state legislatures had ratified ERA, although 3 of these subsequently sought to rescind passage; the amendment was further jeopardized by the presidential victory of Ronald Reagan, an opponent of ERA.

The US has a federal form of government, with the distribution of powers between the federal government and the states constitutionally defined. The legislative powers of the federal government are vested in Congress, which consists of the House of Representatives and the Senate. There are 435 members of the House of Representatives. Each state is allotted a number of representatives in proportion to its population as determined by the decennial census. Representatives are elected in every even-numbered year. A representative must be at least 25 years old, must be a resident of the state represented, and must have been a citizen of the US for at least seven years.

The Senate of the US consists of two senators from each state, elected for six-year terms. Senators must be at least 30 years old, must be residents of the states from which they are elected, and must have been citizens of the US for at least nine years. One-third of the Senate is elected in every even-numbered year.

Congress legislates concerning taxation, borrowing, regulation of international and interstate commerce, formulation of rules of naturalization, bankruptcy, coinage, weights and measures, post offices and post roads, courts inferior to the Supreme Court, provision for the armed forces, among many other matters. A broad interpretation of the "necessary and proper" clause of the Constitution has widened considerably the scope of congressional legislation based on the enumerated powers.

A bill that is passed by both houses of Congress in the same form is submitted to the president, who may sign it or veto it. If the president chooses to veto the bill, it is returned to the house in which it originated with the reasons for the veto. The bill may become law despite the president's veto if it is passed again by a two-thirds vote in both houses. A bill becomes law without the president's signature if retained for 10 days while Congress is in session. After Congress adjourns, if the president does not sign a bill within 10 days, an automatic veto ensues.

The president must be "a natural born citizen" at least 35 years old, and must have been a resident of the US for 14 years. Under the 22d Amendment to the Constitution, adopted in 1951, a president may not be elected more than twice. Each state is allotted a number of electors based on its combined total of US senators and representatives, and, technically, it is these electors who, constituted as the electoral college, cast their vote for president, with all of the state's electoral votes customarily going to the candidate who won the largest share of the popular vote of that state (the District of Columbia also has three electors, making a total of 538 votes). Thus, the candidate who wins the greatest share of the popular vote throughout the US may, in rare cases, fail to win a majority of the electoral vote. If no candidate gains a majority in the electoral college, the choice passes to the House of Representatives.

The vice president, elected at the same time and on the same party line as the president, serves as ex officio president of the Senate. The vice president assumes the power and duties of the president on the president's removal from office or as a result of the president's death, resignation, or inability to perform his duties. In the case of a vacancy in the vice-presidency, the president nominates a successor, who must be approved by a majority in both houses of Congress. The Congress has the power to determine the line of presidential succession in case of the death or disability of both the president and vice president.

Under the Constitution, the president is enjoined to "take care that the laws be faithfully executed." In reality, the president has a considerable amount of leeway in determining to what extent a law is or is not enforced. Congress's only recourse is impeachment, to which it has resorted only twice, in proceedings against presidents Andrew Johnson and Richard Nixon. Both the president and the vice president are removable from office after impeachment by the House and conviction at a Senate trial for "treason, bribery, or other high crimes and misdemeanors." The president has the power to grant reprieves and pardons for offenses against the US except in cases of impeachment.

The president nominates and "by and with the advice and consent of the Senate" appoints ambassadors, public ministers, consuls, and all federal judges, including the justices of the Supreme Court. As commander-in-chief, the president is ultimately responsible for the disposition of the land, naval, and air forces, but the power to declare war belongs to Congress. The president conducts foreign relations and makes treaties with the advice and consent of the Senate. No treaty is binding unless it wins the aproval of two-thirds of the Senate. The president's independence is also limited by the House of Representatives, where all money bills originate.

Subject to Senate confirmation, the president also appoints as his cabinet the secretaries who head the departments of the executive branch. As of 1980, the executive branch included the following cabinet departments: Agriculture (created in 1862), Commerce (1913), Defense (1947), Education (1980), Energy (1977), Health and Human Services (1980), Housing and Urban Development (1965), Interior (1849), Justice (1870), Labor (1913), State (1789), Transportation (1966), and the Treasury (1789). The Department of Defense—headquartered in the Pentagon, the world's largest office building—also administers the various branches of the military: Air Force, Army, Navy, defense agencies, and Joint Service Schools. The Department of Justice administers the Federal Bureau of Investigation, which originated in 1908; the Central Intelligence Agency (1947) is under the aegis of the Executive office. Among the several hundred quasi-independent agencies are the Federal Reserve System (1913),

serving as the nation's central bank, and the major regulatory bodies, notably the Environmental Protection Agency (1970), Federal Communications Commission (1934), Federal Power Commission (1920), Federal Trade Commission (1914), and Interstate Commerce Commission (1887).

Regulations for voting are determined by the individual states for federal as well as for local offices, and requirements vary from state to state. In the past, various southern states used literacy tests, poll taxes, "grandfather" clauses, and other methods to disfranchise black voters, but Supreme Court decisions and congressional measures, including a 1965 Voting Rights Act, nearly doubled black registration in Deep South states between 1964 and 1976.

[13]POLITICAL PARTIES

Two major parties, Democratic and Republican, have dominated national, state, and local politics since 1860. These parties are made up of clusters of small autonomous local groups primarily concerned with local politics and the election of local candidates to office. Within each party, such groups frequently differ drastically in policies and beliefs on many issues, but once every four years they successfully bury their differences and rally around a candidate for the presidency. Minority parties have been formed at various periods in US political history, but most have generally allied with one of the two major parties and none has achieved sustained national prominence; the most successful minority party in recent years—the American Independent Party in 1968—was little more than a vehicle for former Alabama Governor George C. Wallace, who won 13.5% of the total vote cast. Various extreme groups on the right and left, including a small US Communist Party, have had little political significance on a national scale; in 1980, the Libertarian Party became the first minor party since 1916 to appear on the ballot in all 50 states. Independent candidates have won state and local office, but no candidate has won the presidency without major party backing. Running as an independent in 1980, former US Representative John Anderson won 6.6% of the vote.

Traditionally, the Republican Party is more solicitous of business interests and gets greater support from business than does the Democratic Party. A majority of blue-collar workers, by contrast, have generally supported the Democratic Party, which favors more lenient labor laws, particularly as they affect labor unions; the Republican Party often (though not always) supports legislation that restricts the powers of labor unions. Republicans favor the enhancement of the private sector of the economy, while Democrats generally urge the cause of greater government participation and regulatory authority, especially at the federal level.

Within both parties there are sharp differences on a great many issues; for example, northeastern Democrats in the past almost uniformly favored strong federal civil rights legislation, which was anathema to the Deep South; eastern Republicans in foreign policy are internationalist-minded, while midwesterners of the same party constituted from 1910 through 1940 the hard core of isolationist sentiment in the country. More recently, "conservative" headings have been adopted by members of both parties who emphasize decentralized government power, strengthened private enterprise, and a strong US military posture overseas, while the designation "liberal" has been applied to those favoring an increased federal-government role in economic and social affairs, and disengagement from foreign military commitments.

President Nixon's resignation and the accompanying scandal surrounding the Republican Party hierarchy had a telling, if predictable, effect on party morale, as indicated by Republican losses in the 1974 and 1976 elections. The latent consequences of the Viet-Nam and Watergate years appeared to take their toll on both parties, however, in growing apathy toward politics and mistrust of politicians among the electorate. As of 1979, Democrats enjoyed a large advantage over Republicans in voter registration, held both houses of Congress, had a majority of state governorships, and controlled most state legislative bodies. The centers of Democratic strength were the South and the major cities; most of the solidly Republican states were west of the Mississippi. Ronald Reagan's successful 1980 presidential bid cut into traditional Democratic strongholds throughout the US. In the November elections, the Republicans also won control of the Senate and eroded state and local Democratic majorities.

¹⁴LOCAL GOVERNMENT

Governmental units within each state comprise counties, municipalities, and such special districts as those for water, sanitation, highways, parks, and recreation. There are more than 3,000 counties in the US; more than 18,000 municipalities, including cities, villages, towns, and boroughs; some 15,000 school districts; and at least 26,000 special districts. Additional townships, authorities, commissions, and boards make up the rest of the approximately 80,000 local governmental units.

The states are autonomous within their own spheres of government, and their autonomy is defined in broad terms by the 10th Amendment to the US Constitution, which reserves to the states such powers as are not granted to the federal government and not denied to the states. The states may not, among other restrictions, issue paper money, conduct foreign relations, impair the obligations of contracts, or establish a government that is not republican in form. Subsequent amendments to the Constitution and many Supreme Court decisions added to the restrictions placed on the states. The 13th Amendment prohibited the states from legalizing the ownership of one person by another (slavery); the 14th Amendment deprived the states of their power to determine qualifications for citizenship; the 15th Amendment prohibited the states from denying the right to vote because of race, color, or previous condition of servitude; and the 19th, from denying the vote to women.

During the last 100 years, the functions of the state have expanded. Local business—that is, business not involved in foreign or interstate commerce—is regulated by the state. The states create subordinate governmental bodies such as counties, cities, towns, villages, and boroughs, whose charters they either issue or, where home rule is permitted, approve. States regulate employment of children and women in industry, and enact safety laws to prevent industrial accidents. Education, public health, highway construction and safety, operation of a state highway patrol, and various kinds of personal relief are within each state's authority and functions. The state and local governments still are primarily responsible for providing public assistance, despite the large part the federal government plays in financing welfare.

The number, population, and geographic extent of the more than 3,000 counties in the US—including the analogous units called boroughs in Alaska and parishes in Louisiana—show no uniformity from state to state. The county is the most conspicuous unit of rural local government and has a variety of powers, including location and repair of highways, county poor relief, determination of voting precincts and of polling places, and organizing of school and road districts. City governments, usually headed by a mayor or city manager, have the power to levy taxes; to borrow; to pass, amend, and repeal local ordinances; and to grant franchises for public service corporations. Township government through an annual town meeting is an important New England tradition.

During the late 1960s and 1970s, several large city governments began to suffer severe fiscal crises brought on by a combination of factors. Loss of tax revenues stemmed from the migration of middle-class residents to the suburbs and the flight of many small and large firms seeking to avoid the usually higher costs of doing business in urban areas. Low-income groups, many of them unskilled black and Hispanic migrants from rural areas, have come to constitute large segments of city populations, placing added

US Popular Vote for President by National Political Parties, 1948–80

YEAR	WINNER	TOTAL VOTES CAST	% OF ELIGIBLE VOTERS	DEMOCRAT	REPUBLICAN	PROHI-BITION	SOCIALIST LABOR	SOCIALIST WORKERS	SOCIALIST	PROGRES-SIVE	STATES' RIGHTS DEMOCRAT	CONSTI-TUTION	OTHER¹
1948	Truman (D)	48,692,442	51	24,105,587	21,970,017	103,489	29,038	13,614	138,973	1,157,057	1,169,134	—	5,533
1952	Eisenhower (R)	61,551,118	62	27,314,649	33,936,137	73,413	30,250	10,312	20,065	140,416	—	17,200	8,676
1956	Eisenhower (R)	62,025,372	59	26,030,172	35,585,245	41,937	44,300	7,797	2,044	—	2,657	108,055	203,165
1960	Kennedy (D)	68,828,960	63	34,221,344	34,106,671	44,087	47,522	40,166	—	—	NATL. STATES RIGHTS 209,314	UNPLEDGED DEM. —	159,856
1964	Johnson (D)	70,641,104	62	43,126,584	27,177,838	23,266	45,187	32,701	—	—	6,953	UNPLEDGED DEM. 210,732	17,843
1968	Nixon (R)	73,203,370	61	31,274,503	31,785,148	14,915	52,591	41,390	COMMUNIST 1,076	PEACE & FREEDOM 83,720³	AMERICAN IND. 9,901,151	—	48,876
1972	Nixon (R)	77,727,590	55	29,171,791	47,170,179	12,818	53,811	94,415³	25,343	LIBERTARIAN 3,671	—	AMERICAN 1,090,673	104,889
1976	Carter (D)	81,552,331	54	40,829,046	39,146,006	15,958	US LABOR 40,041	91,310	58,992	173,019	170,531	160,773	866,655⁴
1980²	Reagan (R)	86,495,678	54	35,481,435	43,899,248	230,377	CITIZENS 32,319	RESPECT FOR LIFE 40,105	43,871	920,859	41,172	6,539	5,799,753⁵

1. Includes votes for state parties, independent candidates and unpledged electors.
2. Results as of 5 January 1981.
3. Total includes votes for several candidates in different states under the same party label.
4. Includes 756,631 votes for Eugene McCarthy, an independent.
5. Includes 5,719,437 votes for John Anderson, an independent.

burdens on locally funded welfare, medical, housing, and other services without providing the commensurate tax base for additional revenues. In late 1975, New York City hovered on the brink of insolvency and was compelled to make drastic budgetary cutbacks prior to receipt of an emergency loan from the federal government. A study by the congressional Joint Economic Committee of 300 cities with populations of more than 10,000 found that, as of 1980, cities in virtually every size category were increasing their expenditures faster than their revenues. Local government revenues (including transfers of funds from the federal and state governments) exceeded $176 billion in 1977.

¹⁵STATE SERVICES

All state governments provide services in the fields of education, transportation, health and social welfare, public protection (including state police and prison personnel), housing, and labor. The 1970s saw an expansion of state services in four key areas: energy, environment, consumer protection, and governmental ethics. As of 1979, all states had offices or departments of energy; 29 states had agencies or departments of environment,

while the others provided environmental protection through departments of health or natural resources. Each state provided some form of consumer advocacy, either through a separate department or agency or, more often, through the office of the attorney general. State government in the 1970s also showed the effects of the so-called post-Watergate morality. Laws mandating financial disclosure by public officials, once rare, had become common by 1979, when 31 states had offices designed specifically to oversee ethical compliance in government. Also on the increase were "sunshine laws," opening legislative committee meetings and administrative hearings to the public, and the use of an ombudsman either with general jurisdiction or with special powers relating, for example, to the problems of businesses, prisoners, the elderly, or racial minorities. Other trends in state administration, reflected on the federal level, include the separation of education from other services and the consolidation of social welfare programs in departments of human resources.

Federal aid to the states and territories totaled $77.9 billion in 1977/78. The largest outlays were distributed as follows: De-

Leading US Metropolitan Areas and Major Cities 1970–80

STANDARD METROPOLITAN STATISTICAL AREAS¹				MAJOR CITIES			
RANK			POPULATION ('000)		CENSUS POPULATION ('000)		AREA	% BLACK
1978	1970	NAME	1978 (EST.)	1970 (CENSUS)	NAME	1980²	1950	(SQ MI)³	(1970)
1	1	New York, N.Y.–N.J.	9,222	9,974	New York	7,016	7,892	300	21
2	2	Los Angeles–Long Beach, Calif.	7,081	7,042	Los Angeles	2,950	1,970	464	18
3	3	Chicago, Ill.	7,030	6,975	Chicago	2,969	3,621	223	33
4	4	Philadelphia, Pa.–N.J.	4,770	4,824	Philadelphia	1,680	2,072	129	34
5	5	Detroit, Mich.	4,386	4,435	Detroit	1,192	1,850	138	44
6	6	Boston–Lowell–Brockton–Lawrence–Haverhill, Mass.–N.H.	3,888	3,849	Boston	562	801	46	16
7	7	San Francisco–Oakland, Calif.	3,184	3,109	San Francisco	674	775	45	13
8	8	Washington, D.C.–Md.–Va.	3,017	2,910	Washington, D.C.	635	802	61	71
9	12	Dallas–Ft. Worth, Tex.	2,720	2,378	Dallas	901	434	266	25
10	9	Nassau–Suffolk, N.Y.	2,690	2,556	—	—	—	—	—
11	16	Houston, Tex.	2,595	1,999	Houston	1,555	596	434	26
12	10	St. Louis, Mo.–Ill.	2,386	2,411	St. Louis	449	857	61	41
13	11	Pittsburgh, Pa.	2,277	2,401	Pittsburgh	424	677	55	20
14	13	Baltimore, Md.	2,145	2,071	Baltimore	783	950	78	46
15	17	Minneapolis–St. Paul, Minn.–Wis.	2,063	1,965	Minneapolis	370	522	55	4
16	15	Newark, N.J.	1,951	2,057	Newark	329	439	24	54
17	14	Cleveland, Ohio	1,939	2,064	Cleveland	573	915	76	38
18	18	Atlanta, Ga.	1,852	1,596	Atlanta	405	331	132	51
19	20	Anaheim–Santa Ana–Garden Grove, Calif.	1,833	1,421	Anaheim	215	15	33	—
20	23	San Diego, Calif.	1,744	1,358	San Diego	870	334	317	8
21	27	Denver–Boulder, Colo.	1,505	1,240	Denver	489	416	95	9
22	19	Seattle–Everett, Wash.	1,468	1,425	Seattle	492	468	84	7
23	26	Miami, Fla.	1,451	1,268	Miami	335	249	34	23
24	21	Milwaukee, Wis.	1,417	1,404	Milwaukee	633	637	95	15
25	30	Tampa–St. Petersburg, Fla.	1,396	1,089	Tampa	269	125	85	20
26	22	Cincinnati, Ohio–Ky.–Ind.	1,389	1,387	Cincinnati	383	504	78	28
27	28	Riverside–San Bernardino–Ontario, Calif.	1,385	1,139	Riverside	170	47	72	5
28	25	Kansas City, Mo.–Kan.	1,325	1,274	Kansas City, Mo.	447	457	316	22
29	24	Buffalo, N.Y.	1,303	1,349	Buffalo	357	580	41	20
30	36	Phoenix, Ariz.	1,293	971	Phoenix	781	107	248	5
31	31	San Jose, Calif.	1,232	1,065	San Jose	626	95	136	3
32	29	Indianapolis, Ind.	1,156	1,111	Indianapolis	695	427	379	18
33	32	New Orleans, La.	1,141	1,046	New Orleans	557	570	197	45
34	35	Portland, Oreg.–Wash.	1,140	1,007	Portland	364	374	89	6
35	34	Columbus, Ohio	1,089	1,018	Columbus	561	376	135	19
36	33	Hartford–New Britain–Bristol, Conn.	1,045	1,035	Hartford	136	177	17	28
37	38	San Antonio, Tex.	1,038	888	San Antonio	783	408	184	8

1. Includes all 37 SMSA's estimated in 1978 to have a population of 1,000,000 or more.
2. Preliminary data.   3. As of 1970.

partment of Agriculture, $4.4 billion; Department of Commerce, $3.5 billion; Environmental Protection Agency, $3.4 billion; Department of Health, Education, and Welfare (divided as of May 1980 into the Department of Education and the Department of Health and Human Services), $29.7 billion, of which $5.7 billion came from the Office of Education, $10.7 billion from the Medicaid program, and $6.7 billion from the Social Security Administration; Department of Housing and Urban Development, $5.6 billion; Department of Labor, $10.6 billion; Department of Transportation, $8.6 billion ($5.7 billion of that from the Highway Trust Fund); and Department of the Treasury, $8.3 billion, of which $6.8 billion was general revenue sharing. New York State received more aid than any other state, $8.4 billion, followed by California, $8 billion. Illinois, Michigan, Pennsylvania, and Texas each received more than $3 billion in federal assistance.

¹⁶JUDICIAL SYSTEM

The Supreme Court, established by the US Constitution, is the nation's highest judicial body, consisting of the chief justice of the US and eight associate justices. All justices are appointed by the president with the advice and consent of the Senate. Appointments are for life "during good behavior," otherwise terminating only by resignation or impeachment and conviction.

The original jurisdiction of the Supreme Court is relatively narrow; as an appellate court, it is open to appeal from decisions of federal district courts, circuit courts of appeals, and the highest courts in the states, although it may dismiss an appeal if it sees fit to do so. The Supreme Court, by means of a writ of certiorari, may call up a case from a district court for review. Regardless of how cases reach it, the Court enforces a kind of unity on the decisions of the lower courts. It also exercises the power of judicial review, determining the constitutionality of state laws, state constitutions, congressional statutes, and federal regulations, but only when these are specifically challenged.

The Constitution empowers Congress to establish all federal courts inferior to the Supreme Court. On the lowest level and handling the greatest proportion of federal cases are the district courts—numbering 91 in 1980, including one each in Puerto Rico and the District of Columbia—where all offenses against the laws of the US are tried. Civil actions that involve cases arising under treaties and laws of the US and under the Constitution, where the amount in dispute is greater than $5,000, also fall within the jurisdiction of the district courts. District courts have no appellate jurisdiction; their decisions may be carried to the courts of appeals, organized into 11 circuits. These courts also hear appeals from decisions made by administrative commissions. For most cases, this is usually the last stage of appeal, except where the court rules that a statute of a state conflicts with the Constitution of the US, with federal law, or with a treaty. Special federal courts include the Court of Claims, Customs Court, and Tax Court.

State courts operate independently of the federal judiciary. Most states adhere to a court system that begins on the lowest level with a justice of the peace, and includes courts of general trial jurisdiction, appellate courts, and, at the apex of the system, a state supreme court. The court of trial jurisdiction, sometimes called the county or superior court, has both original and appellate jurisdiction; all criminal cases (except those of a petty kind) and some civil cases are tried in this court. The state's highest court, like the Supreme Court of the US, interprets the constitution and the laws of the state.

The grand jury is a body of from 13 to 23 persons that brings indictments against individuals suspected of having violated the law. Initially, evidence is presented to it by either a justice of the peace or a prosecuting county or district attorney. The trial or petit jury is used in trials of common law, both criminal and civil, except where the right to a jury trial is waived by consent of all parties at law. It judges the facts of the case, while the court is concerned exclusively with questions of law.

The judicial system is only one facet of a US legal establishment that comprised an estimated 531,500 lawyers in 1979 and 645,000 police and 255,000 corrections personnel in 1977; the criminal justice system alone cost an estimated $21.6 billion to administer during the 1976/77 fiscal year. A total of 278,141 prisoners (267,097 males, 11,044 females) were in state and federal institutions in 1977, and 173,300 convicts were on parole.

The Federal Bureau of Investigation Crime Index of offenses known to the police stood at 5,109 per 100,000 population in 1978. The rate for violent crimes was 487; for property crimes, 4,622. Rates for specific crimes in 1978 per 100,000 population were as follows: murder and nonnegligent manslaughter, 9; forcible rape, 31; robbery, 191; aggravated assault, 256; burglary, 1,424; larceny-theft, 2,744; and motor vehicle theft, 455. The US murder rate in 1976, 9.1 per 100,000 population, far exceeded that of every other industrialized nation except Northern Ireland in the United Kingdom, where, under conditions of civil war, the homicide rate was 13.7. Guns—widely available in the US—are the weapons used in nearly two-thirds of all murders. The crime rate in 1978 represented a 3% decrease since 1975 but a 71% rise over the 1967 rate. The most dramatic increases in the crime rate involved aggravated assault and forcible rape; it is not known, however, whether the doubling of these rates since 1967 was due to a real increase in the number of crimes or increased reporting of crimes that had previously gone unreported. Crime in the US is highly concentrated in metropolitan areas: the crime rate for all standard metropolitan statistical areas was 5,870 in 1978, 35% higher than the rate for small towns and cities, and nearly three times the rate for rural areas.

Prior to 1972, almost all of the states authorized capital punishment for the most serious crimes—notably first-degree murder—but the death penalty was often applied in an arbitrary and unequal manner. Between 1930 and 1978, 3,860 prisoners were executed under civil authority, of whom 2,066 were black. Of 3,335 prisoners executed for murder, 49% were black; of the 455 executed for rape, nearly 90% were black, an execution rate thought to reflect the historical prejudice of predominantly white juries against black people, especially in the South. It was this inequality of application, rather than a ruling that the death penalty was "cruel and unusual punishment," that led the Supreme Court to invalidate all death penalty statutes on the books in 1972, ordering that any subsequent capital punishment laws must provide safeguards against arbitrary and discriminatory treatment. Since then about two-thirds of the states have reinstituted capital punishment.

¹⁷ARMED FORCES

Compulsory induction into the armed services was terminated as of 1 July 1973; since that date, service in the military has been voluntary, although all men must register at age 18. As of 30 June 1978 there were 2,050,000 officers and personnel on active duty in the armed forces. The Army had 774,000 officers and other personnel; the Navy, 524,000; the Marine Corps, 190,000; and the Air Force, 562,000. In 1978 there were 353,000 black personnel in the armed forces, or 17.2% of the total, though blacks made up only 11.7% of the US population; blacks also represented just 4.3% of the total officer corps. Women numbered 151,000 in the armed forces as of February 1980; since 1970 their share of total enlisted and commissioned personnel has climbed from 1.1% to 7.4%. Personnel in the military reserve but not on active duty in mid-1978 numbered 2,118,000: Army, 1,178,000; Navy, 434,000; and Air Force, 506,000.

Since World War II, national defense has been the largest single item of expenditure in the federal budget. Although defense spending has increased enormously, its proportion of the total federal budget has decreased since the late 1950s (25% of the total estimated for 1980/81, as compared with nearly 51% in 1958/59). Estimated federal defense outlays in 1977 reached a record $100.9 billion, constituting about 24% of total world military expenditures. Federal defense contract awards in 1977/78 totaled $61.2 billion, of which firms in California, Texas, and New York accounted for nearly one-third. Defense-oriented industries employed 4,613,000 Americans in 1977 and shipped goods valued at $345.4 billion. The US is the world's leading arms exporter, registering military sales agreements worth $72.9 billion during 1970–78.

Strategic nuclear forces in 1980 included 1,054 intercontinental ballistic missiles (the maximum permissible under the 1972 treaty with the Soviet Union) and 430 combat aircraft of the Strategic Air Command; the Carter administration took the first steps toward deployment of the massive MX missile system in Utah and Nevada in 1979. Other hardware includes 10,900 Army tanks, with a new main battle tank force on order; 81 Navy attack submarines (74 of them nuclear-powered), 14 aircraft carriers (3 nuclear-powered), and 159 other major surface combat vessels; and 3,700 Air Force combat aircraft. Overseas deployment of US forces is concentrated in Western Europe (especially the Federal Republic of Germany), the Philippines, Japan, South Korea, and two US possessions, Guam and Midway.

As of 30 September 1979, an estimated 30,072,000 veterans of US military service were living in the 50 states, the outlying areas, and abroad. Of these, 26,310,000 served during wartime, many of them in more than one war: 209 in the Spanish-American War, 594,000 in World War I, 12,674,000 in World War II, 5,866,000 during the Korean conflict, and 8,910,000 in the Viet-Nam era. Benefits disbursed by the Veterans Administration totaled $20.9 billion in 1977/78, of which $9.6 billion went for compensation and pensions, $5.7 billion for medical assistance and administrative expenses, and $3.3 billion for education and readjustment assistance.

Army and Air National Guard units, distributed throughout the 50 states, may be summoned by a governor for military emergencies, riot control, disaster relief, and other purposes. As of 1978 there were 3,335 Army National Guard Units, with 347,000 personnel, and 1,020 Air National Guard Units, with 92,000 personnel.

The Federal Bureau of Investigation (FBI) investigates violations of federal law in more than 180 categories; state and local police matters and US intelligence activities overseas are among those categories excluded from its jurisdiction. Although lodged within the Department of Justice, the FBI enjoyed virtual autonomy until the death of longtime director J. Edgar Hoover in 1972. During the 1960s and 1970s, the FBI's political surveillance activities included illegal break-ins and attempts to harrass, entrap, or discredit members of civil rights and radical groups. State and local police forces had 573,582 personnel in 1977, 84% of them at the local level. Expenditures on police protection exceeded $10 billion during the same year.

18 MIGRATION

Between 1840 and 1930, some 37 million immigrants, the overwhelming majority of them Europeans, arrived in the US. Immigration reached its peak in the first decade of the 20th century, when nearly 9 million came. Following the end of World War I, the tradition of almost unlimited immigration was abandoned, and through the National Origins Act of 1924 a quota system was established as the basis of a carefully restricted policy of immigration. Under the McCarran Act of 1952, one-sixth of 1% of the number of inhabitants from each European nation residing in the continental US as of 1920 could be admitted annually. In practice, this system favored nations of Northern and Western Europe, with the United Kingdom, Germany, and Ireland being the chief beneficiaries. The quota system was radically reformed as of 1 July 1968, under a new law that established an annual

ceiling of 170,000 for Eastern Hemisphere immigrants and 120,000 for entrants from the Western Hemisphere. A uniform ceiling of 20,000 was placed on immigrants from any one country in the Eastern Hemisphere, while country quotas for Western Hemisphere immigrants were dropped. Preferential exemptions from numerical limitations have been granted to outstanding scientists and their families, parents of US citizens, children of resident

Net Migration by States and Other Selected Areas. 1940–77

	1940–1950	1950–1960	1960–1970	1970–1977[1]
Alabama	−342,000	−369,000	−233,000	50,000
Alaska	NA	41,000	16,000	68,000
Arizona	137,000	329,000	228,000	367,000
Arkansas	−415,000	−433,000	−71,000	135,000
California	2,658,000	3,142,000	2,113,000	809,000
Colorado	41,000	164,000	215,000	255,000
Connecticut	113,000	234,000	214,000	−23,000
Delaware	21,000	63,000	38,000	5,000
Florida	578,000	1,616,000	1,326,000	1,492,000
Georgia	−290,000	−212,000	51,000	136,000
Hawaii	NA	3,000	11,000	37,000
Idaho	−27,000	−40,000	−42,000	77,000
Illinois	75,000	124,000	−43,000	−397,000
Indiana	97,000	61,000	−16,000	−126,000
Iowa	−196,000	−234,000	−183,000	−36,000
Kansas	−91,000	−44,000	−130,000	−19,000
Kentucky	−366,000	−390,000	−153,000	81,000
Louisiana	−147,000	−49,000	−130,000	26,000
Maine	−27,000	−67,000	−69,000	51,000
Maryland	270,000	321,000	385,000	40,000
Massachusetts	23,000	−96,000	74,000	−54,000
Michigan	336,000	155,000	27,000	−229,000
Minnesota	−173,000	−98,000	−25,000	−6,000
Mississippi	−433,000	−433,000	−267,000	8,000
Missouri	−190,000	−134,000	2,000	−12,000
Montana	−40,000	−25,000	−58,000	32,000
Nebraska	−135,000	−117,000	−73,000	3,000
Nevada	34,000	86,000	144,000	112,000
New Hampshire	(2)	12,000	69,000	79,000
New Jersey	294,000	578,000	488,000	−67,000
New Mexico	16,000	52,000	−130,000	80,000
New York	270,000	210,000	−101,000	−863,000
North Carolina	−258,000	−328,000	−94,000	132,000
North Dakota	−121,000	−105,000	−94,000	−2,000
Ohio	245,000	407,000	−126,000	−468,000
Oklahoma	−434,000	−219,000	13,000	139,000
Oregon	286,000	16,000	159,000	199,000
Pennsylvania	−355,000	−475,000	−378,000	−272,000
Rhode Island	11,000	−26,000	13,000	−36,000
South Carolina	−230,000	−222,000	−149,000	100,000
South Dakota	−79,000	−95,000	−94,000	−13,000
Tennessee	−143,000	−274,000	−45,000	170,000
Texas	73,000	121,000	146,000	737,000
Utah	9,000	9,000	−11,000	45,000
Vermont	−19,000	−38,000	15,000	17,000
Virginia	169,000	15,000	141,000	191,000
Washington	392,000	87,000	249,000	107,000
West Virginia	−235,000	−446,000	−265,000	43,000
Wisconsin	−84,000	−53,000	4,000	34,000
Wyoming	−1,000	−20,000	−39,000	48,000
Other areas:				
D.C.	49,000	−160,000	−100,000	−97,000
Puerto Rico	NA	−493,000	−200,000	196,000
Virgin Islands	NA	−900	15,700	15,200
American Samoa	NA	−5,400	−1,700	−3,600
Guam	NA	−10,800	−4,200	6,700

[1]1970–78 for other areas.
[2]Less than 1,000.

aliens, and siblings and children of naturalized US citizens. The McCarran Act prohibits the immigration of Nazis, Communists, and Communist sympathizers to the US.

In the 12 months ending 30 September 1977, 462,300 immigrants entered the US, 290,000 of them under national quotas. Of the total number of immigrants, 223,200 were from countries in the Western Hemisphere, 74,000 from Europe, and 150,800 were from Asia. A direct result of the new quota system has been a sharp rise in the influx of Asians (primarily Chinese, Filipinos, Indians, Japanese, and Koreans), of whom 825,400 entered the country during 1971–77 (as compared with 153,334 during the entire decade of the 1950s).

Since 1961, the Federal government has supported and financed the Cuban Refugee Program. More than 500,000 Cubans were living in southern Florida by 1980, when at least 100,000 more Cuban refugees arrived. Following the defeat of the US-backed Saigon government, some 592,000 Vietnamese refugees came to the US between 1975 and 1978. Large numbers of aliens, mainly from the Caribbean, Latin America, and Asia, illegally establish residence in the US, having initially entered the country as tourists, students, or temporary visitors engaged in work or business. In 1977, 4,964,000 aliens were officially in residence. Recently, the Commonwealth of Puerto Rico, a possession of the US, has been an important source of migrants to the continental US. In the 1950–59 decade, almost all of Puerto Rico's net emigration of 430,522 persons went to the US. In the 1960s, annual net emigration was smaller, averaging about 11,000 a year through 1969. However, in 1970–77, the trend was reversed: a net flow of 196,000 Puerto Ricans returned to Puerto Rico in those years. Since Puerto Ricans are American citizens, no special authorization is required for their admission to the continental US.

The major migratory trends within the US have been the general westward movement during the 19th century; the long-term movement from farms and other rural settlements to metropolitan areas, a trend that showed signs of reversing in some states during the 1970s; the exodus of southern blacks to the cities of the North and Midwest, especially after World War I; a shift of whites from central cities to surrounding suburbs since World War II; and, also during the post–World War II period, a massive shift from the North and East to the Sunbelt.

¹⁹INTERGOVERNMENTAL COOPERATION

The US government interacts with the governments of other nations and with the governments of the several states, the outlying areas, and thousands of municipalities. Interstate cooperation is reflected through numerous compacts and organizations.

The US, whose failure to join the League of Nations was a major cause of the failure of that body, is a charter member of the United Nations (UN) and of its specialized agencies. It contributes almost one-third of the total funds required for the upkeep of the UN, far more than does any other nation. In the 1970s, the US participated in more than 70 intergovernmental organizations. Among these are international councils and commissions on rice, rubber, tea, wheat, wool, and other industries, along with the Indo-Pacific Fisheries Council and the International Whaling Commission. The US also participates actively in the Permanent Court of Arbitration, the World Health Organization, and the International Bank for Reconstruction and Development (commonly known as the World Bank). Hemispheric agreements include the Inter-American Committee on the Alliance for Progress, Inter-American Development Bank, Organization of the American States, and Pan-American Health Organization. The mutual defense pact between Australia, New Zealand, and the US (ANZUS) and the North Atlantic Treaty Organization (NATO) are the principal military alliances to which the US belongs.

The US spent $206 billion in foreign aid from the end of World War II through 1978, of which $154.6 billion was extended in outright grants and $51.4 billion in net credits. Of the total 1946–78 outlay, 62% was in economic assistance and 38% in military aid. Some 86.3% of military aid was in the form of grants. The Marshall Plan, or European Recovery Program, had as its chief purpose the reconstruction of Europe; during the period 1948–52, $14.5 billion in economic aid was disbursed. The Mutual Security Act (1953–61) provided for the distribution of $16.9 billion in military and economic aid, with 38.3% going to East and Southeast Asia, the largest regional recipient. Since 1961, foreign-aid funds have been administered by the Agency for International Development (AID). The Department of Defense now administers military aid. Through AID, the US, in addition to providing funds, goods, and equipment, makes available US experts in such fields as agriculture, industrial development, health, and housing. Also functioning chiefly in developing areas is the Peace Corps, created in 1961 and now grouped with other voluntary service programs in the ACTION Agency. As of 1980, this organization had more than 6,000 volunteers working in 64 countries, providing assistance in health, education, agriculture, and community development.

Most of the nations receiving US economic and military aid in the 1970s could be classified as developing. In recent decades, foreign-aid disbursement has been used increasingly as a vehicle for the pursuit of US foreign policy objectives. In the early 1960s, more than $10 billion was committed to Latin America in support of President Kennedy's Alliance for Progress program. In the latter half of that decade, the bulk of aid went to East Asia, with South Viet-Nam, South Korea, and Thailand as primary recipients. In the mid-1970s, the active role taken by the US in negotiating a Middle East peace settlement was reflected in sizable outlays to that region, chiefly to Israel, Egypt, and Syria, the principals in the dispute. Israel is now by far the largest aid beneficiary, receiving nearly $5 billion in grants and credits between 1975 and 1978, including $1.3 billion in 1978 alone (14.6% of total US foreign aid for that year). During the 1960s and 1970s, large amounts of assistance also went to India, Pakistan, Taiwan, Turkey, Yugoslavia, and West Berlin. In 1978, $8.9 billion in new funds was used for foreign grants and credits.

Interstate compacts and agencies generally reflect shared geographic concerns. Established in 1933 and headquartered in Lexington, Ky., the Council of State Governments is a coordinating body supported by contributions from all the states; its chief functions are research and publication. As of 1979, the council listed 45 interstate boundary compacts, as well as agreements governing bridge service, navigation of interstate waters, and the administration of shared port facilities. Three main compacts, comprising respectively the Atlantic, Pacific, and Gulf states, promote the conservation and utilization of the nation's fisheries. The Interstate Oil and Gas Compact, including 30 fossil fuel–producing states, oversees the management of these resources. Three regional compacts promote energy development, especially of nuclear power. Water apportionment in the Rocky Mountain, Midwest, Pacific Coast, and Sunbelt regions is governed by 23 accords. Seven flood-control compacts and 4 accords on water pollution deal with the water problems of the Northeast and the Great Lakes states. Eight regional planning compacts seek to coordinate economic growth policies.

Most states subscribe to some or all of the 9 agreements governing motor vehicle licensing, registration, and safety; the metropolitan areas of New York, Kansas City, and Washington, D.C. are each served by regional transportation compacts. There are 3 New England accords on health services; 44 states and the District of Columbia are joined in the Compact on Mental Health. The Compact for Education, including 46 states and 3 territories, establishes a commission to develop educational policy and to serve as an information center. Other major agreements govern interstate library services and qualifications for educational personnel. The Agreement on Detainers facilitates the organization and disposal of criminal cases; 46 states, the District of Columbia, and the federal government are members. Other compacts specify extradition procedures and correction services.

[20] ECONOMY

In variety and quantity, the natural resources of the US probably exceed those of any other nation, with the possible exception of the USSR. US industry not only consumes large amounts of bituminous coal and anthracite, sulfur, phosphate rock, and molybdenum, but there remains enough surplus of these raw materials for export. However, because of its vast economic growth, the US depends increasingly on foreign sources for a long list of raw materials. The extent of US dependence on oil imports was dramatically demonstrated during the 1973 Arab oil embargo, when serious fuel shortages developed in many sections of the country.

By mid-century, the US was a leading consumer of nearly every important industrial raw material. The industry of the US produced about 40% of the world's total output of goods, despite the fact that the country's population comprised about 6% of the world total and its land area about 7% of the earth's surface. Since then, US production has continued to expand, though at a slower rate than that of most other industrialized

Selected State Economic Indicators, 1978[1]

	INCOME PER CAPITA	% BELOW POVERTY LINE, 1975	LABOR FORCE ('000)	PRODUCTION			
				FARM COMMODITIES ('000,000)[2]	MINERALS, VALUE ('000,000)	ELECTRIC POWER (BILLION KWH)	MANUFACTURING, VALUE ADDED, 1977 ('000,000)
Alabama	$ 6,247	16.4	1,592	$ 1,927	$ 1,272	71.6	$ 8,348.7
Alaska	10,851	6.7	180	12	2,936	3.2	479.3
Arizona	7,374	13.8	993	1,480	1,963	30.5	3,387.6
Arkansas	6,183	18.5	926	2,703	574	19.7	4,865.0
California	8,850	10.4	10,632	10,425	4,432	139.9	55,452.3
Colorado	8,001	9.1	1,292	2,715	1,521	21.2	4,551.8
Connecticut	8,914	6.7	1,512	230	46	26.0	10,998.9
Delaware	8,604	8.2	273	323	2	7.3	1,618.0
Florida	7,505	14.4	3,689	3,249	1,770	94.6	9,332.1
Georgia	6,700	18.0	2,315	2,598	587	55.2	12,499.7
Hawaii	8,380	7.9	397	381	51	6.8	790.9
Idaho	6,813	10.3	405	1,497	280	10.0	1,418.5
Illinois	8,745	10.5	5,327	6,226	1,607	108.5	40,277.2
Indiana	7,696	8.1	2,570	3,532	702	68.0	22,593.7
Iowa	7,873	7.9	1,419	8,499	264	18.0	8,715.8
Kansas	8,001	8.0	1,158	4,747	1,504	24.7	5,385.3
Kentucky	6,615	17.7	1,555	2,053	3,517	55.6	9,440.1
Louisiana	6,640	19.3	1,619	1,435	11,737	61.8	9,503.1
Maine	6,333	12.0	473	414	40	11.1	2,346.6
Maryland	8,306	7.7	2,031	778	213	36.2	7,108.7
Massachusetts	8,063	7.1	2,836	243	82	37.0	16,895.4
Michigan	8,442	9.1	4,202	2,172	1,913	78.0	37,480.4
Minnesota	7,847	8.3	1,994	5,016	1,714	35.3	9,245.3
Mississippi	5,736	26.1	966	2,028	519	19.6	5,598.5
Missouri	7,342	12.0	2,262	3,648	923	46.2	12,813.5
Montana	7,051	11.5	370	1,369	678	16.9	860.3
Nebraska	7,391	9.6	771	5,000	147	15.2	2,821.8
Nevada	9,032	8.8	334	171	205	13.1	497.8
New Hampshire	7,277	7.9	428	88	22	5.1	2,162.6
New Jersey	8,818	8.1	3,431	374	118	31.2	23,165.2
New Mexico	6,505	19.3	525	993	3,033	20.0	790.0
New York	8,267	9.4	7,844	1,941	438	115.5	44,676.9
North Carolina	6,607	14.7	2,679	3,271	263	65.1	18,105.6
North Dakota	7,478	10.6	294	2,145	303	13.0	474.6
Ohio	7,812	9.4	4,943	3,027	1,697	112.1	43,294.0
Oklahoma	6,951	13.8	1,260	2,482	3,769	41.0	4,650.7
Oregon	7,839	8.9	1,191	1,299	123	34.1	6,255.7
Pennsylvania	7,733	9.7	5,252	2,165	3,028	126.3	35,984.7
Rhode Island	7,526	8.7	433	30	7	.6	2,764.8
South Carolina	6,242	17.2	1,298	1,000	176	44.3	8,095.4
South Dakota	6,841	13.1	328	2,213	128	9.8	608.5
Tennessee	6,489	15.8	1,926	1,641	584	60.4	12,635.0
Texas	7,697	15.2	5,994	7,867	20,173	194.6	32,922.9
Utah	6,622	8.5	540	477	1,082	10.0	1,971.5
Vermont	6,541	13.5	236	314	48	4.2	1,050.0
Virginia	7,624	10.5	2,429	1,258	1,194	43.3	10,765.4
Washington	8,450	8.5	1,754	2,193	231	99.8	8,628.9
West Virginia	6,456	15.1	720	190	3,060	64.0	3,908.1
Wisconsin	7,597	7.7	2,305	3,689	152	38.7	16,761.5
Wyoming	9,096	8.7	208	544	2,592	19.4	380.7

1. Except where indicated.
2. Receipts from farm marketings plus government cash payments.

nations. While the value of US exports of manufactured goods increased from $12.7 billion to $94.5 billion between 1960 and 1978, the US share of all world industrial exports decreased from 25.3% to 17%.

The US gross national product (GNP) nearly doubled between 1970 and 1977 to $1.9 trillion in current dollars; measured in constant 1976 dollars, the increase was 23.4%. The GNP per capita—$8,188 in 1977—ranks 3d in the world after the per capita GNP of Sweden and Canada, with the Federal Republic of Germany (FRG) not far behind. By and large, the US inflation rate is lower than that of most industrialized countries: for 1970–78, for example, consumer prices increased by an annual average of 6.7%, less than in every other Western country except Austria, FRG, Luxembourg, and Switzerland, and well below the price increase in Japan. The double-digit inflation of 1979–80 came as a rude shock to most Americans, however, and economists and politicians vied with each other in blaming international oil price rises, federal monetary policies, and US government spending for the problem. The US does exceed most industrialized nations in unemployment—the US rate was 6% in 1978, as compared with 2.2% in Sweden and 2.3% in Japan—and pockets of concentrated unemployment in the central cities, especially among young nonwhites, constitute one of the nation's most serious social and economic problems.

The following table shows major components of the GNP for 1950, 1970, and 1978 (in billions):

	1950	1970	1978
Agriculture, forestry, fisheries	$20.8	$28.7	$64.2
Mining	9.2	17.4	55.6
Construction	13.0	48.2	98.6
Manufacturing	83.8	250.3	510.2
Transportation	16.0	38.9	78.6
Communications	4.5	23.6	55.8
Electric, gas, and sanitary services	5.2	22.7	52.1
Wholesale and retail trade	51.3	167.3	362.6
Finance, insurance, real estate	31.2	140.2	290.2
Services	24.0	113.5	262.5
Government and government enterprises	23.8	129.1	255.9
Other	3.4	2.5	21.3
TOTALS	$286.2	$982.4	$2,107.6

Industrial activity within the country has been expanding southward and westward for much of the 20th century, most rapidly since World War II. Louisiana, Oklahoma, and especially Texas are centers of industrial expansion based on petroleum refining; aerospace and other high technology industries are the basis of the new wealth of Texas and California, the nation's leading manufacturing state. The industrial heartland of the US is the east–north-central region, comprising Ohio, Indiana, Illinois, Michigan, and Wisconsin, with steelmaking and automobile manufacturing among the leading industries. The Middle Atlantic states—New Jersey, New York, and Pennsylvania—and the Northeast are also highly industrialized, but of the major industrial states in these two regions, only Massachusetts has successfully reoriented itself toward the expanding industries of electronics and information processing.

Concentration and conglomeration continue to be salient aspects of US industry. Gradually the trend in judicial interpretation of the antitrust laws has been to recognize the inevitable domination of any industry by a small group of producers and to yield to the consideration that the forcible dissolution of large units of production would sacrifice the efficiency of large-scale enterprise. US industry has become increasingly oligopolistic, with a few large firms dominating specific areas of production.

[21] INCOME

Personal income in 1978 was estimated at $1.7 trillion; estimated disposable personal income (gross personal income less taxes) amounted to $1.5 trillion, as compared with $691.7 billion in 1970. Estimated personal savings, after deductions for personal consumption expenditures, were $77 billion.

Average per capita income in 1978 was $7,810 ($3,893 in 1970), but it varied considerably from state to state; the highest per capita incomes (more than $8,500) were recorded in Alaska, Wyoming, Nevada, Connecticut, California, New Jersey, Illinois, and Delaware, in that order. Among the lowest (under $6,300) were those in Mississippi, South Carolina, Arkansas, and Alabama. Median family income rose from $6,957 in 1965 to $14,094 in 1975. Median income in 1977 for white families (as defined by the head of the household) was $16,740; for Hispanic families, $11,421; and for black families, $9,563. Percentage distribution of personal income by family groups in 1974 and 1977 was as follows:

INCOME LEVEL	1974	1977
Under $3,000	5.0	3.6
$3,000–$4,999	7.7	5.7
$5,000–$5,999	4.4	3.5
$6,000–$6,999	4.4	3.7
$7,000–$9,999	13.8	10.9
$10,000–$14,999	24.2	18.5
$15,000–$19,999	18.1	17.8
$20,000–$24,999	10.5	13.9
$25,000 and over	11.9	22.4
TOTALS	100.0	100.0

In 1975, 9% (as compared with 13.9% in 1965) of families had incomes below the poverty level, as defined by the federal government. Of the nonwhite population, an estimated 29% in 1977 (32.2% in 1965), or about 8.3 million persons, were considered impoverished by government standards. About 90% of poverty-level families reside in metropolitan areas.

[22] LABOR

About 100,420,000 persons constituted the country's civilian labor force in 1978. Of this number, 6,047,000 (6%) were unemployed. A federal census of workers covered by unemployment insurance in March 1977 revealed the following employment pattern:

	ESTABLISH-MENTS	EMPLOYEES	ANNUAL PAYROLL ('000)
Agricultural services, forestry, fishing, of which:	44,997	242,997	$ 2,176,938
Agricultural services	(41,562)	(217,131)	(1,889,953)
Mining, of which:	27,755	830,178	13,703,983
Bituminous coal, lignite	(4,418)	(224,131)	(3,894,400)
Oil, gas extraction	(15,593)	(322,951)	(5,163,849)
Contract construction	439,381	3,571,973	53,943,405
Manufacturing, of which:	327,850	19,638,852	268,305,334
Food and food products	(24,294)	(1,498,119)	(18,790,491)
Printing and publishing	(44,651)	(1,127,876)	(14,093,848)
Chemicals and chemical products	(11,513)	(888,148)	(14,054,605)
Primary metal industries	(7,111)	(1,137,890)	(19,220,964)
Fabricated metal products	(31,118)	(1,516,661)	(21,114,349)
Nonelectrical machinery	(44,463)	(2,080,422)	(30,793,750)
Electric and electronic equipment	(13,565)	(1,710,806)	(22,614,455)
Transportation equipment	(9,147)	(1,793,451)	(30,914,572)
Transportation, public utilities, of which:	166,465	4,030,479	61,344,024
Trucking and warehousing	(80,865)	(1,146,153)	(16,602,620)
Communications	(23,723)	(1,146,019)	(18,281,551)

	ESTABLISH-MENTS	EMPLOYEES	ANNUAL PAYROLL ('000)
Wholesale trade	375,077	4,562,083	62,866,622
Retail trade	1,263,377	13,384,271	93,486,075
Finance, insurance, real estate, of which:	413,128	4,568,788	52,502,037
Banking	(42,418)	(1,288,258)	(13,426,404)
Insurance	(106,966)	(1,498,439)	(18,781,531)
Services, of which:	1,233,652	14,059,994	128,939,735
Business services	(145,005)	(2,307,384)	(21,585,362)
Health services	(283,274)	(4,339,178)	(44,769,345)
Other	60,613	85,965	1,102,136
TOTALS	4,352,295	64,975,580	$738,370,289

As of 1978, state, federal, and local governments employed 15,476,000 persons (18% of nonfarm employment). Agriculture employed 3,342,000 Americans during the same year.

Earnings of workers vary considerably with type of work and section of country. In 1977, the average weekly wage for industrial workers ranged from $162 in North Carolina to $395 in Alaska; the national average was $227. The average workweek varied, by state, from 38 to 41.8 hours, with the national rate at 40.3 hours (as compared with 41.2 hours in 1965).

In 1976, 24.8% of the nonagricultural work force were members of labor unions. The most important federation of organized workers in the US is the American Federation of Labor–Congress of Industrial Organizations (AFL–CIO). Of the 21,129,000 members of US unions in 1976, 16,657,000 belonged to the 112 unions affiliated with the AFL–CIO. The major independent unions and their 1976 memberships are the International Brotherhood of Teamsters (1,889,000) and the United Automobile Workers (1,358,000). Most of the other unaffiliated unions are confined to a single establishment or locality. US unions exercise economic and political influence not only through the power of strikes and slowdowns but also through the money and manpower they allocate to political campaigns (usually on behalf of Democratic candidates) and through the selective investment of multibillion-dollar pension funds.

The National Labor Relations Act of 1935 (the Wagner Act), the basic labor law of the US, was considerably modified by the Labor-Management Relations Act of 1947 (the Taft-Hartley Act) and the Labor-Management Reporting and Disclosure Act of 1959 (the Landrum-Griffin Act). Closed-shop agreements, which require employers to hire only union members, are banned. The union shop agreement, however, is permitted; it allows the hiring of nonunion members on the condition that they join the union within a given period of time.

As of 1976, 19 states had right-to-work laws, forbidding the imposition of union membership as a condition of employment. Under the Taft-Hartley Act, the president of the US may postpone a strike for 90 days in the national interest. The act of 1959 requires all labor organizations to file constitutions, bylaws, and detailed financial reports with the secretary of labor, and stipulates methods of union elections. The National Labor Relations Board seeks to remedy or prevent unfair labor practices and supervises union elections, while the Equal Employment Opportunity Commission seeks to prevent discrimination in hiring, firing, and apprenticeship programs.

Labor has found the acts of 1947 and 1959 harshly restrictive, although in practice many of their requirements are more a nuisance than an obstacle to the functioning of labor unions. However, the granting of the right to states to enact anti-labor legislation has undoubtedly retarded organization of nonunion workers, especially in the South. In the 1970s, the majority of labor disputes involved wages; union organization, plant administration, and job security were important secondary issues. A growing number of disputes involved civil servants and municipal employees such as teachers, transport workers, and police,

whose right to collective action is restricted in most states. The number of work stoppages and of workers involved reached a peak in the late 1960s and early 1970s, declining steadily thereafter. In 1977 there were 5,506 stoppages involving 2,040,000 workers, accounting for 35,822,000 worker-days idle. The National Mediation Board arbitrates disputes in the railroad and airline industries.

[23] AGRICULTURE

In 1977, the US produced a huge share of the world's agricultural commodities, including soybeans, 65%; tallow and greases, 57%; corn for grain (maize), 47%; edible vegetable oils, 28%; cotton, 22%; oats, 22%; tobacco, 16%; and wheat, 14%. Much US farm produce is exported; 60% or more of soybeans, tallow and greases, and corn, among other products, that cross international boundaries originates in the US. In 1978, US agricultural exports reached an all-time high of $29.4 billion and accounted for 21% of total US exports.

Gross farm income of $126 billion in 1978 included $111 billion in cash receipts (crops, $52 billion; livestock and livestock products, $59 billion); $3 billion in government payments; $1.4 billion in the value of products consumed on the farm; and $10.6 billion in other income. Average income per farm was $10,434; net income of farm operators from farming in 1978 was $27.9 billion.

About 16% of the total US land area was in crops in 1974; another 26% was grassland pasture. Between 1930 and 1979, the number of farms in the US declined from 6,546,000 to 2,330,000, although total farm acreage increased from 987 million acres (399 million hectares) to 1.05 billion acres (425 million hectares) during the same period (farm acreage decreased during the 1970s, however). Further, the size of the average farm tripled from 151 to 450 acres (61 to 182 hectares), a result of the consolidation effected by large-scale mechanized production. The fact that the same period also saw a sharp decline in the number of mortgaged farms suggests that the less efficient producer disappeared in the process of consolidation. The farm population, which comprised 35% of the total US population in 1910, declined to 25% during the Great Depression of the 1930s, and had dwindled to 3.7% in 1978.

A remarkable increase in the application of machinery to farms took place during and after World War II. Tractors, trucks, milking machines, grain combines, corn pickers, and pickup bailers became virtual necessities in farming. In 1920 there was less than one tractor in use for every 1,000 acres (405 hectares) of cropland harvested; by 1978 there were four. Two other elements essential to US farm productivity are chemical fertilizers and irrigation. Fertilizer use increased from 24.9 million tons in 1960 to 47.6 million tons in 1978, when the $6.3 billion allocated to fertilizers and lime represented more than 10% of farm operating expenses. Farmers also spend well over $1 billion each year on chemical pesticides and weed killers. Although only 4% of all cropland is irrigated, some of the irrigated lands—in particular, the Imperial and Central valleys in California—are among the most productive in the US.

Substantial quantities of corn, the most valuable crop produced in the US, are grown in almost every state; its yield and price are important factors in the economy of the regions where it is grown. The following table reports production and value of selected US crops in 1978:

	PRODUCTION ('000)	VALUE ('000)	ACREAGE HARVESTED ('000)
Corn for grain	7,086,666 bushels	$15,875,377	69,970
Soybeans for beans	1,870,181 bushels	12,458,598	63,003
Hay	142,209 tons	6,572,593	61,495
Wheat	1,797,528 bushels	5,349,483	56,839
Cotton	10,900 bales	3,064,000	12,370
Tobacco	2,026,000 lb	2,682,000	949
Sorghum for grain	747,790 bushels	1,501,737	13,581
Rice	133,170 bushels	1,087,000	3,059

MAJOR LAND-USE REGIONS AND MINERAL RESOURCES

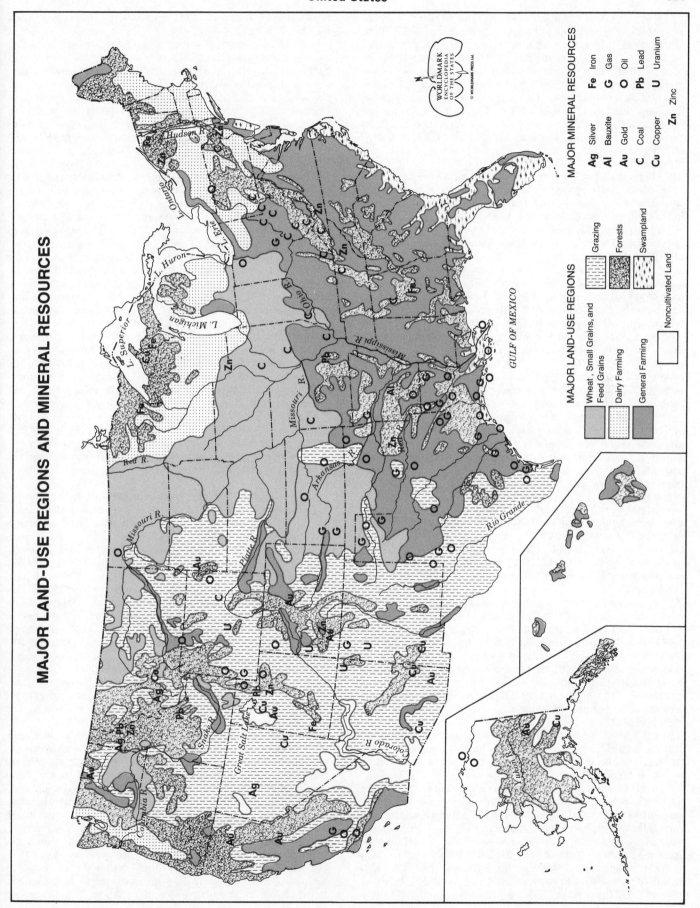

MAJOR LAND-USE REGIONS

Wheat, Small Grains, and Feed Grains

Dairy Farming

General Farming

Grazing

Forests

Swampland

Noncultivated Land

MAJOR MINERAL RESOURCES

Ag Silver   **Fe** Iron

Al Bauxite   **G** Gas

Au Gold   **O** Oil

C Coal   **Pb** Lead

Cu Copper   **U** Uranium

Zn Zinc

GULF OF MEXICO

Hudson R.

L. Ontario

L. Erie

L. Huron

L. Michigan

L. Superior

Red R.

Missouri R.

Ohio R.

Mississippi R.

Arkansas R.

Red R.

Rio Grande

Platte R.

Missouri R.

Snake R.

Great Salt Lake

Colorado R.

Columbia R.

Yukon R.

WORLDMARK ENCYCLOPEDIA OF THE STATES © WORLDMARK PRESS Ltd.

In 1979, the US also harvested 267 million hundredweight of vegetables for fresh market at a production value of $2.9 billion. Of this total, principal values were lettuce, $565,287,000; tomatoes, $522,190,000; strawberries, $243,971,000; and onions, $236,353,000. Arizona, Florida, California, and Texas are the major citrus-producing states. US citrus yields in 1979/80 included 12.1 million tons of oranges and tangerines, valued at $1.3 billion; 3 million tons of grapefruit, $300 million; and 789,000 tons of lemons, $161 million. Also produced in 1979 were 343 million hundredweight of potatoes, worth $1.2 billion, and 8.1 billion lb of commercial apples.

24 ANIMAL HUSBANDRY

The US produced an estimated 17% of the world's meat supply in 1978. Major cattle-producing states are, in order of rank, Texas, Iowa, Nebraska, Kansas, Missouri, Oklahoma, and California; leading producers of sheep and lambs are Texas, California, Wyoming, Colorado, South Dakota, and Utah; and ranking producers of hogs and pigs include Iowa, Illinois, Indiana, Missouri, and Minnesota.

The livestock population as of 1 January 1980 included an estimated 111 million head of cattle (approximately 10% were milk cows), 67 million hogs, and 12.5 million sheep and lambs. The number of cattle attained the 100-million mark for the first time in the nation's history in 1962, and reached a peak of 132 million in 1976; however it has been decreasing gradually since that year. In addition to about 399.7 million chickens on the nation's farms in 1979, 3.8 billion broilers were marketed by commercial producers, yielding $3.9 billion in gross income. Some 69.1 billion eggs were produced in 1979, representing an increase of 12% since 1960.

Improved techniques in breeding, feeding, and prevention of disease have accounted for great advances in animal husbandry in recent years, and especially for the greater yield of high-quality meat per animal and the larger production of milk per cow. Milk production totaled 123.6 billion lb in 1979, with Wisconsin, California, and New York together accounting for 37% of the total.

The peak year for creamery butter output was 1941. After that time, consumption declined, owing in part to the increasing use of butter substitutes. Wisconsin, Minnesota, and California account for more than half of all US butter production. Butter production totaled 984.6 million lb in 1979; in that year, the US was the world's largest producer of cheese, with more than 3.7 billion lb.

Total production of meat (commercial and farm) in 1979 was estimated at 37.6 billion lb, comprising 21.4 billion lb of beef, 434 million lb of veal, 293 million lb of lamb and mutton, and 15.4 billion lb of pork. The price of meat for consumers rose by about 30% during 1972–73 and by mid-1975 prices were nearly double the level of 1960; meat prices continued to rise, though more slowly, in the late 1970s. Domestic consumption levels continued to expand, with meat (and especially beef) remaining a prime source of protein in the US diet.

25 FISHING

The US, which ranked 5th in the world in commercial fish landings in 1977, nevertheless imports far more fish and fishery products than it exports. In 1978, US fishery exports were valued at $905.5 million; imports, $3.1 billion.

The 1978 commercial catch was 6 billion lb and had a value of $1.9 billion. Food and nonfood fish are caught in almost equal quantities, with nonfood fish being processed for fertilizer and oil. Of the total volume of fish caught in 1978, 1.1 billion lb were utilized by canneries, 2.2 billion lb were sold either fresh or frozen, 52 million lb were cured, and 2.6 billion lb were reduced to meal, scrap, and oil. Industrial products included 725.1 million lb of fresh meal and scrap and 294.9 million lb of fish oils. A total of 3,638 firms in the US were engaged in processing fishery

products in 1977, and 168,013 persons were employed as fishermen in 1975.

Menhaden, important for oil, meal, and fertilizer, was the leading species caught in 1978, accounting for 43% of all US commercial landings. Other leading varieties are crabs (2d in value and quantity), shrimp, salmon, tuna, flounder, herring, mackerel, cod, and clams. Alaska's fisheries provided 86% of all US commercial landings of salmon in 1978, and about 50% of the world's yield in 1977. Intense international competition for offshore fishing grounds prompted the enactment, in 1976, of a law extending the US fishing limit to 200 mi (322 km), effective 1 March 1977. Pollution is a problem of increasing concern to the US fishing industry; dumping of raw sewage, industrial wastes, spillage from oil tankers, and blowouts of offshore wells are the main threats to the fishing grounds. Overfishing is also a threat to the viability of the industry in some areas, especially Alaska.

Louisiana led the US in volume of commercial fish landings in 1978, followed by Alaska, California, and Virginia; by value, Alaska, California, Louisiana, Massachusetts, and Texas were the leaders, in that order. Leading fishing ports include Cameron, Dulac-Chauvin, and Empire-Venice in Louisiana, Pascagoula-Moss Point in Mississippi, San Pedro and San Diego in California, Gloucester and New Bedford in Massachusetts, and Kodiak and Dutch Harbor in Alaska.

Sport fishing is highly popular in the US, where an estimated 54 million persons fished in 1975. Along the Atlantic and Gulf coasts, recreational fishermen caught 709.6 million lb of fish and 192.7 million lb of shellfish that year. Bluefish, sea trout, flounder, striped bass, clams, and crabs were the most popular saltwater species.

26 FORESTRY

US forestlands cover about 740 million acres (299 million hectares). Major forest regions include the eastern, central hardwood, southern, Rocky Mountain, and Pacific coast areas. The National Forest System accounts for one-quarter of the nation's forestland.

Of the total acreage, about 66% is suitable for commercial exploitation, with 72% of these forests privately owned. Large lumber companies control extensive tracts of land in Maine, Oregon, and several other states.

Annual production of lumber in the US during 1975–77 ranged from 29.6 billion to about 37.8 billion board feet, of which softwoods accounted for roughly 83%. Consumption in 1977 required imports of a record 19.4 billion board feet. The US, the world's second-leading producer of newsprint, attained an output of 3.8 million tons in 1978. To satisfy its needs for about 7.1 million tons, it also imported heavily from Canada, the major world producer. Other forest products in 1978 included 50.5 million tons of wood pulp, 60.8 million tons of paper and paperboard (excluding newsprint), 155 million board feet of hardwood flooring, 3.6 billion sq feet of particleboard (¾-in basis), and 25.4 million gallons of turpentine. Rising petroleum prices in the late 1970s sparked a revival in the use of wood as home heating fuel, especially in the Northeast.

Throughout the 19th century, the federal government distributed forestlands lavishly as a means of subsidizing railroads and education. By the turn of the century, the realization that the forests were not inexhaustible led to the growth of a vigorous conservation movement, which was given increased impetus during the 1930s and again in the late 1960s. Federal timberlands are no longer open for private acquisition, and the government adds to the national forest domain by purchase. Recently, the states also have moved in the direction of retaining forestlands and continuing to add to their holdings when possible. As of 1979, the US Forest Service managed 154 national forests and 19 national grasslands; some 12.6 million acres (5.1 million hectares) have been designated as wilderness and 3.1 million acres

(1.3 million hectares) as primitive areas where timber cannot be harvested.

The federal government assists owners of private forestland to plant, grow, protect, and market trees. The Soil Bank Plan, operated through the federal government, encourages the planting of trees through federal payments to farmers. The Cooperative Forestry Act of 1950 (amended in 1978) provides federal subsidies for reforestation, with sums granted by the government matched by similar sums from the state.

[27]MINING

Rich in a variety of mineral resources, the US is a world leader in the production of many important mineral commodities, such as aluminum, cement, copper, pig iron, lead, phosphates, potash, salt, sulfur, uranium, and zinc. The value of mineral production

State Energy Resources, 1978

| | PETROLEUM | | NATURAL GAS | | COAL | | TOTAL | ELECTRICITY[1] | |
	RESERVES[2] (1,000 BARRELS)	PRODUCTION (1,000 BARRELS)	RESERVES[2] (1,000,000 CU FEET)	PRODUCTION (1,000,000 CU FEET)	RESERVES[3] (1,000,000 TONS)	PRODUCTION (1,000 TONS)[4]	INSTALLED CAPACITY (MW)	NUCLEAR CAPACITY (MW)	HYDRO CAPACITY (MW)
Alabama	33,107	11,188	751,219	55,926	3,092	20,553	18,108	4,344	2,588
Alaska	9,247,356	447,541	31,612,295	214,010	6,158	731	995	—	126
Arizona	—	—	—	—	326	9,054	8,948	—	2,111
Arkansas	94,038	19,419	1,627,064	105,747	392	519	5,425	902	1,081
California	3,471,301	347,102	5,095,082	304,990	—	—	36,674	1,478	9,340
Colorado	198,012	36,280	1,965,765	185,612	16,256	13,814	4,704	—	769
Connecticut	—	—	—	—	—	—	6,313	2,172	134
Delaware	—	—	—	—	—	—	1,644	—	—
Florida	169,361	47,262	160,296	50,987	—	—	27,973	3,260	30
Georgia	—	—	—	—	1	113	15,155	850	1,630
Hawaii	—	—	—	—	—	—	1,399	—	3
Idaho	—	—	—	—	4	—	1,762	—	1,700
Illinois	137,927	22,620	420,437	789	67,969	48,600	29,244	5,718	30
Indiana	26,515	4,785	56,710	173	10,714	24,182	15,732	—	93
Iowa	—	—	—	—	2,202	450	6,549	597	130
Kansas	350,367	55,163	12,287,341	843,927	998	1,226	6,802	—	2
Kentucky	31,833	5,685	718,929	57,336	26,001	135,689	13,451	—	747
Louisiana	2,893,401	458,755	49,674,148	7,061,561	—	—	12,864	—	—
Maine	—	—	—	—	—	—	2,024	810	345
Maryland	—	—	—	—	1,048	2,998	9,182	1,828	494
Massachusetts	—	—	—	—	—	—	9,690	863	1,639
Michigan	190,164	34,648	1,768,581	159,224	127	—	21,007	3,172	2,322
Minnesota	—	—	—	—	—	—	8,192	1,755	137
Mississippi	187,587	37,756	1,410,514	131,617	—	—	5,532	—	—
Missouri	—	—	—	—	5,014	5,665	13,827	—	844
Montana	140,466	30,087	991,668	57,387	120,569	26,600	3,144	—	2,066
Nebraska	29,291	5,587	72,839	2,904	—	—	3,871	1,303	235
Nevada	—	—	—	—	—	—	3,649	—	682
New Hampshire	—	—	—	—	—	—	1,567	—	379
New Jersey	—	—	—	—	—	—	12,382	1,720	389
New Mexico	485,640	78,130	13,261,489	1,068,933	4,598	12,632	4,512	—	24
New York	8,996	853	262,711	13,347	—	—	31,369	4,343	4,965
North Carolina	—	—	—	—	32	—	15,782	1,733	1,847
North Dakota	161,213	24,965	411,485	29,827	10,145	14,028	2,199	—	430
Ohio	131,194	11,154	1,560,478	115,239	19,230	41,237	26,964	962	2
Oklahoma	1,073,469	135,326	11,463,291	1,646,900	1,618	6,070	9,789	—	965
Oregon	—	—	—	—	18	—	7,947	1,216	5,687
Pennsylvania	48,156	2,820	2,093,516	97,763	30,837	81,477	33,280	5,195	1,651
Rhode Island	—	—	—	—	—	—	284	—	2
South Carolina	—	—	—	—	—	—	11,736	3,571	2,264
South Dakota	2,738	815	—	—	426	—	2,168	—	1,383
Tennessee	2,489	593	—	—	965	10,032	14,345	—	2,221
Texas	7,689,991	1,044,936	54,600,235	6,528,717	3,182	20,020	50,502	—	518
Utah	155,371	31,481	698,655	59,818	6,553	9,141	2,133	—	197
Vermont	—	—	—	—	—	—	940	563	193
Virginia	—	—	79,064	8,377	4,303	31,946	10,693	2,675	840
Washington	—	—	—	—	1,580	4,708	19,495	860	17,038
West Virginia	29,675	2,382	2,683,136	146,541	38,607	85,314	12,581	—	101
Wisconsin	—	—	—	—	—	—	9,772	1,673	399
Wyoming	804,567	130,878	4,315,775	362,479	55,372	58,328	3,625	—	220

1. Data on installed capacity, compiled from US Department of Energy publications, may differ slightly from figures cited in separate state articles.
2. As of 31 December 1978.
3. As of 1 January 1976.
4. Bituminous coal only.

in 1977 amounted to $77.1 billion; fuels accounted for more than 77% of the total mineral output, representing a value of $59.6 billion.

Other leading US minerals are copper and construction materials: cement, stone, and sand and gravel. Leading mineral-producing states are Texas, Louisiana, Oklahoma, and New Mexico, important for petroleum and natural gas, and Kentucky, West Virginia, and Pennsylvania, important for coal. Iron ore supports the nation's most basic nonagricultural industry, iron and steel manufacture. Although large, the domestic output of iron ore does not fulfill the nation's total requirements, and some 40 million tons are imported annually from abroad, largely from Canada and Venezuela. The major domestic sources are in the Lake Superior area: Minnesota and Michigan lead all other states in iron-ore yields.

The following table shows volume and value for selected mineral industries in 1977 (excluding fossil fuels):

	VOLUME	VALUE ('000)
Cement	79,300,000 tons	$2,896,700
Stone	955,000,000 tons	2,456,900
Sand and gravel	929,000,000 tons	2,028,000
Copper	1,504,000 tons	2,009,300
Iron ore	60,400,000 tons	1,417,400
Phosphate rock	52,100,000 tons	821,700
Lime	19,900,000 tons	666,500
Uranium	29,500,000 lb	582,200
Clays	53,200,000 tons	579,200
Salt (common)	43,400,000 tons	451,600
Molybdenum	125,000,000 lb	450,400
Silver	38,200,000 troy oz	176,300
Gold	1,100,000 troy oz	163,200

[28] ENERGY AND POWER

The US, with 5% of the world's population, consumed 29% of the world's energy in 1977. The US produced 31% of the world's electricity, 24% of its coal, and 39% of its natural gas, but only 13% of its crude oil, an energy imbalance that many observers believed would have serious economic and political implications for the 1980s.

Energy sources for US electric power are mainly coal, petroleum, natural gas, and waterpower. Bituminous coal and lignite were dominant until the 1950s, when the increasing use of crude oil and natural gas displaced the primacy of these fuels. Coal supplied about 44% of the energy produced for public use in 1978; crude petroleum, 16%; natural gas, 14%; waterpower, 13%; and nuclear sources, 13%. The increased use of natural gas was the most spectacular development in the commercial marketing of fuel after World War II; between 1950 and 1974, its share of total US energy production doubled from 20% to 40%, although by 1978 the proportion had declined to 35%. About 55% of all residences were heated by utility gas in 1977, and nearly 6% by bottled gas. Some 21%, chiefly in the Northeast and Northwest, used fuel oil, and 15% of housing units were electrically heated. The proportion of homes employing coal or coke declined from 35% to 0.6% between 1950 and 1977; a small but growing minority of homes were using wood or solar power devices as the 1980s began. For cooking purposes, electric stoves were the most popular, accounting for 49% of energy use; utility gas followed with 43%, and bottled and other gas fuels accounted for nearly all the remainder. In 1978, gas utility companies sold 14.7 quadrillion Btu of gas, of which 46% went to residential customers.

Proved recoverable reserves of crude oil totaled 27.8 billion barrels in 1978 and reserves of natural gas were about 200 trillion cu feet. Texas accounted for 7.7 billion barrels, or about 28% of the proved oil reserves, while the newly discovered deposits of Alaska accounted for 9.2 billion barrels. Natural gas reserves of Texas were 54.6 trillion cu feet in 1978; those of Louisiana, 49.7

trillion cu feet. Proved coal reserves totaled 438.3 billion tons in 1976, of which 52% was bituminous, 38% subbituminous, 8% lignite, and 2% anthracite. Montana led all states in coal reserves in 1976, with 120.6 billion tons; Illinois and Wyoming followed, with coal reserves amounting to 68 billion and 55.4 billion tons, respectively.

Mineral fuel production in 1978 included 665 million tons of bituminous coal, 19.3 trillion cu feet of natural gas, and approximately 3 billion barrels of crude petroleum; production of anthracite totaled 5.9 million tons in 1977. The 1973 Arab oil embargo and subsequent fuel shortages prompted a host of governmental measures aimed at increasing development of oil and gas resources; these included deployment of the trans-Alaska pipeline to facilitate exploitation of that state's considerable petroleum reserves and an easing of restrictions for oil drilling on the continental shelf. Further development of coal reserves has been hampered by a shortage of transportation facilities—either of railroad equipment or of the water needed to move coal as a slurry—and by concerns over mine safety and the environmental impact of surface mining. By the end of the 1970s, intensive exploration for oil and gas was under way along the Overthrust Belt, a region spanning 200,000 sq mi (518,000 sq km) of the Rocky Mountain states.

In 1978, public utilities and private industrial plants generated 2.2 trillion kwh of electricity, of which hydroelectric plants produced 280.5 billion, and steam and internal combustion plants 1.6 trillion; industrial plants produced 79 billion kwh for their own use. Installed generating capacity in all facilities totaled 580 million kw.

The 1970s saw increased development of plants and equipment designed to use atomic energy for commercial purposes. In 1978, nuclear-powered generators in operation had a total capacity of 53.6 million kw and generated 276 billion kwh of electricity (as compared with 4.3 million kw and 16.4 billion kwh in 1969). The expansion of the nuclear power industry was in doubt as of 1980, in the wake of a nuclear accident at Pennsylvania's Three Mile Island facility in March 1979. As the new decade began, growing attention was focused on the development of solar power, synthetic fuels, geothermal resources, and other energy technologies. Such energy conservation measures as mandatory automobile fuel-efficiency standards, enforcement of a 55-mph (89-km/hr) speed limit on the nation's highways, and tax incentives for home insulation have been promoted by the federal government, which also decontrolled oil and gas prices in the expectation that a rise in domestic costs to world-market levels would provide a powerful economic incentive for consumers to conserve fuel.

[29] INDUSTRY

The US is primarily an industrial nation. Manufacturing, the greatest single source of its wealth, accounts for a larger proportion of the income of the people, contributes more to the total gross national product, and is responsible for the employment of more people than any other category of economic activity. About 24% of the gross national product was derived from manufacturing in 1978, when the manufacturing sector employed 23% of the total labor force.

The Chicago metropolitan area in 1977 ranked as the nation's leading industrial center in terms of value added by manufacture. It was followed by Los Angeles–Long Beach, New York, Detroit, and Philadelphia. The east–north-central region leads all other sections by virtue of its huge concentration of heavy industry, including automaking. In 1978, US manufacturers had net sales of $1.5 trillion and a net profit (after state and federal taxes) of $81 billion. Value added by manufacture exceeded $511 billion in 1976, when new capital expenditures totaled $40.7 billion. The following table shows selected data for major industrial sectors in 1972 and 1976:

	NEW CAPITAL EXPENDITURES 1976 ('000,000)	VALUE ADDED BY MANUFACTURE ('000,000)	
	1976 ('000,000)	1972	1976
Nonelectrical machinery	$3,428	$37,543	$57,357
Transport equipment	3,131	39,799	55,657
Food and food products	3,817	35,615	52,760
Chemicals and chemical products	7,122	32,414	51,408
Electric and electronic equipment	2,240	30,558	41,746
Fabricated metal products	2,223	26,946	39,145
Primary metal industries	4,179	23,258	34,182
Printing and publishing	1,261	20,210	27,647
Paper and allied products	3,010	13,064	20,604
Apparel, other textile products	433	13,488	16,860
Stone, clay, glass products	1,504	12,587	16,773
Instruments and related products	783	10,580	16,386

Giant firms dominate industry in the US. During 1972, the 50 largest manufacturing firms accounted for 25% of the total value added and for more than 90% of the total value of shipments in sectors such as steel, automobiles, pharmaceuticals, aircraft, petroleum refining, computers, soap, tires, and communications equipment. In 1978, the 500 largest firms had $1.2 trillion in sales, four-fifths of the national total; employed 16.2 million persons, more than five-sixths of the industrial total; and registered $61.5 billion in net profits, about three-fourths of the total. Eighty-five companies earned more than $200 million each, with 14 showing net profits of over $1 billion. The 6 largest earners, with 1979 profits, were Exxon (formerly Standard Oil of New Jersey), $4.3 billion; International Business Machines, $3 billion; General Motors, $2.9 billion; Mobil Oil, $2 billion; Standard Oil, $1.8 billion; and Texaco, $1.76 billion. Large US oil companies showed significant profit gains following the world oil crisis of the early 1970s, replacing auto manufacturers as the leading moneymakers. The growth of multinational activities of US corporations has been rapid in recent years, with capital expenditures by US-owned foreign affiliates reaching $30.6 billion in 1978.

The history of US industry has been marked by the introduction of increasingly sophisticated technology in the manufacturing process. Advances in chemistry and electronics have revolutionized many industries through new products and methods: examples include the impact of plastics on petrochemicals, the use of lasers and electronic sensors as measuring and controlling devices, and the application of microprocessors to computing machines, home entertainment products, and a variety of other industries. Science has vastly expanded the number of metals available for industrial purposes, notably such light metals as aluminum, magnesium, and titanium. Integrated machines now perform a complex number of successive operations that formerly were done on the assembly line at separate stations. Those industries have prospered that have been best able to make use of the new technology, and the economies of some states—in particular, California and Massachusetts—are largely based on it. On the other hand, certain industries—especially clothing and steelmaking—have suffered from outmoded facilities that (coupled with high US labor costs) force the price of their products above the world market price. Automobile manufacturing was another ailing industry as the 1980s began.

³⁰COMMERCE

Domestic trade is a vast enterprise in the US, employing more than 18 million Americans, accounting for payrolls of over $150 billion, and sales of well over $2 trillion. Merchant wholesalers (who account for less than half of all wholesale trade) had sales of $754 billion in 1978, when retail sales were nearly $800 billion.

Major competitors of the small shopkeeper are the chain retailers; discount houses; manufacturers of millinery, clothing, shoes, ties, candy, and other products who operate their own outlets; and the great department stores. Corporate chains usually buy directly from producers and processors, thus avoiding the middleman. Multiunit chain stores account for only about one-third of the total retail trade, but in certain kinds of retail business the chain is the dominant mode of business organization. Chains handled about 81% of the variety store trade in 1978, about 94.5% of department store trade, 47.5% of the shoe business, and 57% of grocery store volume. With the great suburban expansion of the 1960s emerged the planned shopping center, usually designed by a single developer and intended to provide different kinds of stores in order to meet all the shopping needs of the particular area.

Installment credit is a major support for consumer purchases in the US. The total amount of installment credit outstanding by October 1979 was $305.2 billion, of which automobiles accounted for $114.9 billion. Commercial banks held 49% of debt outstanding; finance companies, 21.5%; credit unions, 16%; retailers, 8%. Noninstallment credit totaled $67.4 billion as of May 1979. Credit cards are used by a majority of US families; outstanding funds on bank credit-card accounts reached $24.4 billion in 1978, more than four times the 1970 total.

The US advertising industry is the world's most highly developed. With the expansion of television audiences particularly, spending for advertising has increased almost annually to successive record levels. Advertising expenditures in 1978 reached $43.7 billion, as compared with $18.1 billion in 1968 and $2 billion in 1940. Of the 1978 total, about $24 billion was spent in national media and $19.7 billion in local media. Newspaper advertising accounted for about $12.7 billion, television $8.9 billion, radio $3 billion, and magazines $2.6 billion. Direct mail advertising (chiefly letters, booklets, catalogs, and handbills) amounted to $6 billion. New York City is the center of the nation's advertising industry.

In the realm of foreign commerce, the US leads the world in value of both exports and imports. Exports of domestic merchandise, raw materials, agricultural and industrial products, and military goods amounted in 1978 to $143.7 billion, an all-time high. General imports for the same calendar year were valued at $172 billion, also a record. During the late 1970s, the US ran annual trade deficits of more than $20 billion, largely because of the rising cost of foreign oil. In 1973, the US imported $7.6 billion worth of petroleum products; the following year, that figure had more than tripled. In 1977, petroleum imports reached a peak of $41.8 billion; the decline of 6% in 1978 was partly the result of conservation and partly the result of a slackening in the world oil market. Another import category that proliferated throughout the mid-1970s was telecommunications apparatus—mainly TV sets from Japan—which showed a 196% increase between 1975 and 1978. Overall US imports increased 147% between 1973 and 1978, while US exports rose by 102%. One rapidly growing export category was computers, which rose from $1.2 billion in 1970 to $4.4 billion in 1978; grain exports rose from $2.6 billion to $11.6 billion during the same period.

The following table shows exports, including reexports, for 1978 (in millions):

Machinery, of which:	$38,110
Power-generating machinery	(4,797)
Electronic computers, parts, and accessories	(4,359)
Telecommunications apparatus	(2,689)
Air-conditioning and refrigeration equipment	(1,562)
Transport equipment, of which:	21,161
Automobiles, trucks, and parts	(12,148)
Aircraft, including parts and accessories	(8,204)
Food and live animals, of which:	18,333
Grains, coarse	(5,920)
Wheat and wheat flour	(4,532)
Fruits, vegetables, and nuts	(2,419)
Feed for animals	(1,921)
Meat and preparations	(958)

Chemicals, of which:	12,618
Plastic materials and resins	(2,088)
Medicinal and pharmaceutical preparations	(1,404)
Metals and metal products, of which:	6,101
Iron and steel mill products	(1,644)
Soybeans, except canned	5,210
Professional, scientific, and controlling instruments	3,904
Textiles and clothing	2,902
Tobacco and manufactures	2,125
Coal	2,046
Ores and metal scraps	1,839
Cotton, raw	1,740
Paper and related products	1,597
Petroleum and products	1,561
Other exports	24,413
TOTAL	$143,660

Imports for 1978 (in millions) were as follows:

Petroleum and petroleum products	$39,109
Machinery, of which:	24,752
Telecommunications apparatus	(6,136)
Engines and parts	(2,886)
Office machinery	(2,254)
Electronic tubes, transistors, semiconductors, and parts	(1,942)
Automobiles and parts	20,631
Metals and metal products, of which:	15,714
Iron and steel mill products	(6,687)
Chemicals	6,427
Clothing	5,657
Coffee	3,728
Paper and paper products, of which:	2,923
Newsprint	(2,101)
Ores and metal scraps	2,813
Softwood lumber	2,595
Footwear	2,585
Fish	2,212
Textiles other than clothing	2,200
Natural gas	2,000
Meat and meat products	1,856
Alcoholic beverages	1,744
Wood pulp	1,126
Other imports	33,954
TOTAL	$172,026

By value of combined exports and imports, the largest proportion of US foreign trade is with nations of the Western Hemisphere. These countries accounted for 35% of US exports and 33% of US imports in 1978, when imports from Asia exceeded those from the Western Hemisphere for the first time. Canada is the nation's single best customer and supplier, accounting for about 20% of both exports and imports in 1978. During the same year, trade with Western Europe yielded about 28% of US exports and 21% of US imports, and Asia accounted for 28% and 34%, respectively. Intensive negotiations were held between Washington, D.C., and Tokyo during 1979–80 in an attempt to lessen the growing US trade imbalance with Japan.

Principal trading partners in 1978 (in millions of dollars) were:

	EXPORTS	IMPORTS	BALANCE
Canada	28,372	33,529	−5,157
Japan	12,885	24,458	−11,573
Germany, Federal Republic of	6,957	9,961	−3,004
United Kingdom	7,119	6,513	606
Mexico	6,681	6,093	588
Saudi Arabia	4,370	5,307	−937
France	4,166	4,054	112
Taiwan	2,340	5,182	−2,842
Italy	3,360	4,103	−743
Netherlands	5,683	1,603	4,080
Venezuela	3,727	3,545	182
Korea, Republic of	3,160	3,747	−587
Iran	3,684	2,877	807
Brazil	2,978	2,831	147
Nigeria	985	4,714	−3,729
Belgium-Luxembourg	3,653	1,762	1,891
Hong Kong	1,625	3,474	−1,849
Indonesia	751	3,607	−2,856
Libya	425	3,779	−3,354
Algeria	374	3,482	−3,108
Switzerland	1,732	1,820	−88
Spain	1,884	1,255	629
Soviet Union	2,252	540	1,712
Israel	1,925	719	1,206
Other countries	32,572	33,071	−499
TOTALS	143,660	172,026	−28,366

Since 1950, the US has consistently had deficits in its overall payments with the rest of the world, despite the fact that it had an unbroken record of annual surpluses up to 1970 on current-account goods, services, and remittances transactions.

The nation's stock of gold declined from a value of $22.9 billion at the start of 1958 to $10.5 billion as of 31 July 1971, only two weeks before President Richard Nixon announced that the US would no longer exchange dollars for gold. On 12 February 1973, pressures on the US dollar compelled the government to announce a 10% devaluation against nearly all of the world's major currencies. International gold reserves thereupon rose from $14.4 billion in 1973 to $15.9 billion at the end of 1974; as of 30 June 1979, reserves stood at $21.2 billion.

³¹CONSUMER PROTECTION

Consumer protection has become a major government enterprise during the 20th century. The Federal Trade Commission (FTC), established in 1914, administers the Consumer Credit Protection Act, which governs the granting and use of credit, and the Fair Credit Reporting Act, which controls the activities of credit bureaus. The FTC also investigates unfair or deceptive trade practices, including price fixing and false advertising. The Securities and Exchange Commission, created in 1934, seeks to protect investors, while the Consumer Product Safety Commission, created in 1972, has the authority to establish product safety standards and to ban hazardous products. Overseeing the safety of air and highway transport is the National Transportation Safety Board, created in 1974. The Consumer Information Center of the General Services Administration (Pueblo, Colo.) and the Food Safety and Quality Service and Food and Nutrition Service of the Department of Agriculture also serve consumer interests. Legislation that would have established a Department of Consumer Affairs failed to win congressional approval several times during the 1970s, however.

Public interest groups have been exceptionally effective in promoting consumer issues. The Consumer Federation of America (CFA; founded in 1967), with 240 member organizations, is the largest US consumer advocacy body; its concerns include product pricing, credit, and the cost and quality of health care, education, and housing. The CFA also serves as a clearinghouse for consumer information. Consumers Union of the US, founded in 1936, publishes the widely read monthly *Consumer Reports*, which tests, grades, and comments on a variety of retail products. The National Consumers League, founded in 1899, was a pioneer in the consumer movement, focusing especially on labor laws and working conditions. Much of the growth of consumerism in the 1970s resulted from the public relations efforts of one man—Ralph Nader. Already a well-known consumer advocate concerned particularly with automobile safety, Nader founded Public Citizen in 1971 and an affiliated litigation group the following year. As of 1980, Public Citizen claimed 200,000 supporters; its activities include research committees on tax reform, health care, work safety, and energy, and its publications are often referred to as the work of "Nader's Raiders."

Other avenues open to consumers in most states include small claims courts, generally open to claims between $100 and $1,000 at modest legal cost. More than 1,000 federally funded legal aid offices assist with such cases as landlord-tenant disputes and complaints against utility companies. Complaints involving professional malpractice may be brought to state licensing or regulatory boards. Supported by the business community, the nearly 150 US Better Business Bureaus provide general consumer information and arbitrate some customer-company disputes.

³²BANKING

The Federal Reserve Act of 1913 provided the US with a central banking system. The Federal Reserve System dominates US banking, is a strong influence in the affairs of commercial banks, and exercises virtually unlimited control over the money supply.

Each of the 12 federal reserve districts contains a federal reserve bank. A board of nine directors presides over each reserve bank. Six are elected by the member banks in the district; of this group, three may be bankers; the other three represent business, industry, or agriculture. The Board of Governors of the Federal Reserve System (usually known as the Federal Reserve Board) appoints the remaining three, who may not be officers, directors, stockholders, or employees of any bank and who are presumed therefore to represent the public.

The Federal Reserve Board regulates the money supply and the amount of credit available to the public by asserting its power to alter the rediscount rate, by buying and selling securities in the open market, by setting margin requirements for securities purchases, by altering reserve requirements of member banks in the system, and by resorting to a specific number of selective controls at its disposal. The Federal Reserve Board's role in regulating the money supply is held by economists of the monetarist school to be the single most important factor in determining the nation's inflation rate.

Member banks increase their reserves or cash holdings by rediscounting commercial notes at the federal reserve bank at a rate of interest ultimately determined by the Board of Governors. A change in the rediscount rate, therefore, directly affects the capacity of the member banks to accommodate their customers with loans. Similarly, the purchase or sale of securities in the open market, as determined by the Federal Open Market Committee, is another device whereby the amount of credit available to the public is expanded or contracted. The same effect is achieved in some measure by the power of the Board of Governors to raise or lower the reserves that member banks must keep against demand deposits. Credit tightening by federal authorities in early 1980 pushed the prime rate—the rate that commercial banks charge their most creditworthy customers—above 20% for the first time since the financial panics of 1837 and 1839, when the rates reached 36%. As federal monetary policies eased, the prime rate had subsided to 11.25% by August 1980 before reaching 20% again in mid-December.

Combined assets of commercial and mutual savings banks as of 31 December 1978 amounted to nearly $1.5 trillion, of which $1.3 trillion represented the assets of commercial banks. Loans by these institutions as of that date totaled $840 billion, with commercial banks accounting for $737.6 billion of the total. Of commercial bank loans, $236.9 billion went into commercial and industrial lines and $214 billion into real estate loans. Aggregate deposits of all banks in 1978 amounted to nearly $1.2 trillion. Commercial banks again held the largest share, more than $1 trillion. Of the commercial total, demand deposits accounted for $400.3 billion and time deposits for $616.1 billion.

The nation's leading bank holding companies on the basis of total assets as of 31 December 1979 were BankAmerica (the largest commercial bank in the world, with $108.4 billion) in San Francisco, followed by Citicorp ($106.4 billion), Chase Manhattan ($64.7 billion), Manufacturers Hanover ($47.7 billion), J. P.

Morgan & Co. ($43.5 billion), and Chemical New York ($39.4 billion), all in New York City.

Under the provisions of the Banking Act of 1935, all members of the Federal Reserve System (and other banks that wish to do so) participate in a plan of deposit insurance (up to $100,000 for each individual account as of 1980) administered by the Federal Deposit Insurance Corporation (FDIC). At the end of March 1980, the deposits of 14,721 commercial banks out of a total of 15,259 were insured by the FDIC. All national banks, of which there were 4,437 in 1980, are regulated members of the Federal Reserve System; the "Fed" also counted 978 state banks as subject to its regulation, with the FDIC regulating the remaining 8,981 state banks.

As of 31 December 1978, 4,053 savings and loan associations were insured by the Federal Savings and Loan Insurance Corporation (FSLIC). Individual accounts are insured up to a limit of $40,000 for qualified investor's accounts and $100,000 for retirement accounts. Assets of all FSLIC-insured institutions totaled $510.7 million in 1978, of which $423.5 million consisted of mortgage. loans and contracts. The 12,757 federally chartered credit unions had 22.1 million members and combined assets of $34.7 billion in 1978; during the same year, there were 9,515 state chartered credit unions with 17.5 million members and $27.9 billion in assets.

As of December 1978, total currency in circulation was $113.4 billion.

³³INSURANCE

In 1978, 1,824 companies dispensed ordinary life, group, industrial, and other kinds of life insurance policies. The overwhelming majority of US families have some life insurance with a legal reserve company, the Veterans Administration, or fraternal, assessment, burial, or savings bank organizations. As of 31 December 1978, 400.5 million life insurance policies were in force, with a total value of $2.9 trillion. Payments to policyholders, annuitants, and beneficiaries totaled $28.6 billion. The average value of life insurance per family was $35,100, ranging from $23,900 in Arkansas to $51,500 in Hawaii.

Hundreds of varieties of insurance may be purchased. Besides life, the more important include accident, fire, hospital and medical expense, group accident and health, automobile liability, automobile damage, workers' compensation, ocean marine, and inland marine. During the 1970s, 26 states enacted a "no fault" form of automobile insurance, under which damages may be awarded automatically, without recourse to legal suit; Nevada, however, repealed its no-fault law, effective 1980.

Life insurance company assets totaled $390 billion on 31 December 1978. In the 1960s, these companies provided about half of the net new money borrowed annually by business and industry. The property and liability insurance industry, consisting of 2,940 companies, had about $135.5 billion in assets in 1977. Premiums written in 1978 totaled $81.5 billion: automotive liability coverage, $20.5 billion; automobile physical damage insurance, $12.9 billion; homeowners' insurance, $7.9 billion; commercial multiperil policies, $6.5 billion; workers' compensation coverage, $12.1 billion; and other lines, $21.6 billion. Flood insurance worth $57.6 billion was in force as of mid-1979.

³⁴SECURITIES

Stocks, stock options, commodities, commodity futures, and bonds of various types are traded on exchanges in major US cities. Of the dozen registered stock exchanges in the US, those of greatest importance as judged by the total value of securities bought and sold are the New York and American (both in New York), Midwest (in Chicago), Pacific (San Francisco and Los Angeles), Philadelphia, and Boston stock exchanges. In 1978, 7.6 billion shares with a market value of $210.4 billion were traded on the New York Stock Exchange; these record totals represented 80% by volume and 84% by value of all shares traded in the US that year. The American Stock Exchange ranked 2d in both volume and value, accounting for 11% and 6%, respectively. The total market value of all listed securities in 1978 was $1.3 trillion ($465 billion in bonds). Of the total stock value at the end of 1975, about 95% was in common stocks. Chicago and Minneapolis are centers for farm product trading.

Following World War II, there was a steady growth in the number of US stockholders, until the early 1970s, when a decline became evident; as of 1975 there were an estimated 25,270,000 shareowners, or 1 out of every 6 adult Americans. Increasingly such institutional investors as corporate pension funds and investment companies have entered the market for stock. As of early 1979, American Telephone & Telegraph had 2,939,000 common stockholders; General Motors, 1,249,000; Exxon, 695,000; International Business Machines, 605,000; and General Electric, 552,000. Americans reported $28.6 billion in domestic and foreign dividends on their 1977 federal income tax returns.

The Securities and Exchange Commission regulates securities trading and the disclosure of information to investors.

35 PUBLIC FINANCE

Under the Budget and Accounting Act of 1921, the president is responsible for preparing the federal government budget. In fact, the budget is prepared by the Office of Management and Budget (established in 1970), based on requests from the heads of all federal departments and agencies and advice from the Board of Governors of the Federal Reserve System, the Council of Economic Advisers, and the Treasury Department. The president submits a budget message to Congress in January. Under the Congressional Budget Act of 1974, the Congress establishes, by concurrent resolution, targets for overall expenditures and broad functional categories, as well as targets for revenues, the budget deficit, and the public debt. The Congressional Budget Office, established by the same act, monitors the actions of Congress on individual appropriations bills with reference to those targets. The president exercises fiscal control over executive agencies, which issue periodic reports subject to his perusal. Congress exercises control through the comptroller general, head of the General Accounting Office, who sees to it that all funds have been spent and accounted for according to legislative intent. The fiscal year runs from 1 October to 30 September.

During the 1970s, income security payments (including Social Security) became the largest expenditure item of the US government, overtaking outlays for national defense in 1974. Estimated federal receipts (by source) and expenditures (by general function) for the 1980 fiscal year (estimated, in billions) are indicated in the accompanying table, along with distribution percentages for the 1971, 1975, and 1979 fiscal years.

	1979/80	1978/79	1974/75	1970/71
RECEIPTS				
Individual income taxes	$238.7	46.8%	43.6%	45.8%
Social insurance taxes and contributions	162.2	30.4	30.7	25.8
Corporate income taxes	72.3	14.1	14.4	14.2
Excise taxes	26.3	4.0	5.9	8.8
Customs, estate, and gift taxes	13.4	2.7	3.0	3.3
Other receipts	10.9	2.0	2.4	2.1
TOTALS	$523.8	100.0%	100.0%	100.0%
EXPENDITURES				
Income security (including Social Security)	$190.9	32.4%	33.3%	26.2%
National defense	130.4	23.8	26.2	35.9
Health	56.6	10.0	8.5	7.0

	1979/80	1978/79	1974/75	1970/71
Education, manpower, and social services	30.7	6.0	4.9	4.6
Commerce and transportation	25.1	4.1	4.9	5.0
Veterans' benefits and services	20.8	4.0	5.1	4.6
Natural resources, environment, and energy	20.6	3.8	2.9	2.3
International affairs	10.4	1.2	2.1	1.9
Community and regional development	8.5	1.9	1.1	1.4
General science, space, and technology	5.9	1.0	1.2	2.0
General government	4.9	0.9	1.0	0.9
Agriculture	4.6	1.3	0.5	2.0
Interest	63.3	10.7	9.5	9.3
Other expenditures	13.2	2.6	3.1	0.9
Undistributed offsetting transactions	−22.3	−3.7	−4.3	−4.0
TOTALS	$563.6	100.0%	100.0%	100.0%

The public debt of the US subject to the statutory debt limit rose from $43 billion in 1940 to $259 billion in 1945, to $397.3 billion in 1971, and to $771.5 billion in 1978; the per capita federal debt increased from $325 in 1940 to $3,523 in 1978. Annual service on the federal debt reached $48.7 billion in 1978. Deficit financing was a fixture of US budgets throughout the 1970s.

At the end of World War II, combined expenditures, revenues, and debts of all state and local governments were almost in balance at $18 billion. Largely because of new borrowings for school and highway construction, however, the net outstanding debt of all state and local governments jumped from $69.9 billion in 1960 to $258 billion in mid-1977. The average debt per capita was $1,190 in mid-1977, ranging from $488 in North Carolina to $5,651 in Alaska. The following table shows general revenues and expenditures for state and city governments in 1977 (in billions):

REVENUES	STATES	CITIES
Taxes, of which:	$101.1	$26.1
Income	(34.7)	(NA)
Property	(2.3)	(15.7)
Sales	(52.4)	(3.5)
Transfers, of which:	48.6	24.2
Federal	(45.9)	(10.0)
State/local	(2.7)	(14.2)
Other receipts	20.2	10.6
TOTALS	$169.9	$60.9
EXPENDITURES		
Education	$ 64.0	$ 7.6
Highways	17.5	4.3
Public welfare	32.8	4.6
Health and hospitals	12.6	3.3
Police and fire	1.7	9.9
Natural resources	4.4	—
Sewer and sanitation	—	5.8
Other outlays	33.0	20.6
TOTALS	$166.0	$56.1

36 TAXATION

Measured as a proportion of the gross domestic product, the total US tax burden amounted to 29% in 1976, less than that in most industrialized countries. Federal, state, and local taxes are levied in a variety of forms, and together totaled $419.7 billion in 1977 (as compared with $51.1 billion in 1950 and $113.1 billion in

1960). The greatest source of revenue for the federal government is the personal income tax, which in 1980 was paid by citizens and noncitizens under the age of 65 with gross incomes of $3,300 or more, and by citizens over 65 years of age who earned $4,300 or more (both minimum levels as of 1980).

The personal income tax is a progressive tax that increases with increased income: in 1980, for example, the rate ranged, for a single person without dependents, from 14% on taxable income of less than $3,400 to as much as 70% on income of more than $56,000. Some 93 million personal income tax returns were filed in 1979.

Corporation taxes in 1980 consisted of a 17% levy on the first $25,000 of income, 20% on the next $25,000, and 46% on income in excess of $50,000; corporate incomes yielded $72.3 billion in revenues to the federal government in 1979/80.

Excise taxes include a 10% levy on certain motor vehicles, an 8% charge on personal air transportation, and a tax of 4 cents a gallon on some motor fuels (excluding gasohol); also taxed are alcoholic beverages, tobacco products, tires and tubes, telephone charges, capital gains, and gifts and estates. Effective 1 March 1980, a "windfall profits" tax was levied on producers of domestic crude oil; the tax, ranging up to 70%, is based on the difference between the selling price of the oil and its basic price according to Department of Energy regulations. This levy, which accompanied the decontrol of oil prices, is to last until January 1988 or until $227.3 billion is raised, whichever comes later; at that time, a 33-month phaseout period is to begin. Proceeds from the tax are allocated for income tax reductions, business tax incentives (mostly related to transportation and energy conservation), energy resource development, and energy aid for the poor.

Customs revenues were estimated at $8.4 billion for 1980/81. From the Civil War until the eve of World War I, when the lower Underwood tariff was enacted, a high tariff policy prevailed. Following the war, the Underwood tariff was abandoned and a high tariff policy was resumed; the Hawley-Smoot tariff of 1930 was the highest tariff in the history of the country. Beginning with the Trade Agreements Act of 1934, the policy of protection was modified but not reversed. Under this act, the principle of reciprocity became part of the tariff-making process. The US was authorized to make concessions in its own tariff rates for nations that countered with tariff concessions of their own. As a result, tariff rates have declined considerably since the 1930s. Imports are customarily valued at the American selling price, irrespective of the foreign value.

After World War II, Congress carefully restricted the presidential power to manipulate prevailing tariff rates. Under the Trade Agreements'Extension Act of 1951, the president is required to inform the US Tariff Commission of contemplated concessions in the tariff schedules. The commission then determines what the "peril point" is; that is, it informs the president how far the tariff may be lowered without injuring a domestic producer, or it indicates the amount of increase necessary to enable a domestic producer to avoid injury by foreign competition. Similarly, the same act provides an "escape clause," which, in effect, constitutes a method for rescinding a tariff concession granted on a specific commodity if the effect of the concession, once granted, has caused or threatens to cause "serious injury" to a domestic producer. Under the Trade Expansion Act of 1962, the president was granted much more flexibility, being empowered to negotiate tariff reductions of up to 50% under the terms of the General Agreement on Tariffs and Trade (GATT). In 1974, Congress authorized the president to reduce tariffs still further, especially on goods from developing countries. As the cost of imported oil rose in the mid-1970s, however, Congress became increasingly concerned with reducing the trade imbalance by discouraging the "dumping" of foreign goods on the US market. The Tariff Commission is required to impose a special duty on foreign goods offered for sale at what the commission determines is less than fair market value.

State tax collections in 1979 exceeded $125 billion, with California, New York, Pennsylvania, Illinois, Michigan, and Texas each collecting more than $5 billion. As of December 1979, only five states—Nevada, South Dakota, Texas, Washington, and Wyoming—had no income tax in any form. Atypically, Alaska (which in 1979 had the highest per capita tax burden, $2,012) abolished its corporate income tax in 1979 and its personal income tax in 1980, as increasing oil revenues more than made up the difference. At the same time, 45 states—all but Alaska, Delaware, Montana, New Hampshire, and Oregon—levied a sales tax. Property taxes are the main source of local revenue; a movement to limit property tax increases had its major success in California, with the passage of Proposition 13 in June 1978.

³⁷ECONOMIC POLICY

By the end of the 19th century, regulation rather than subsidy had become the characteristic form of government intervention in economic life. The abuses of the railroads in respect to rates and services gave rise to the Interstate Commerce Commission in 1887, which was subsequently strengthened by numerous acts that stringently regulate all aspects of US railroad operations.

The growth of large-scale corporate enterprises, capable of exercising monopolistic or near-monopolistic control of given segments of the economy, resulted in federal legislation designed to control trusts. The Sherman Antitrust Act of 1890, reinforced by the Clayton Act of 1914 and subsequent acts, established the federal government as regulator of large-scale business. This tradition of government intervention in the economy was reinforced during the depression of the 1930s, when the Securities and Exchange Commission and the National Labor Relations Board were established. The expansion of regulatory programs accelerated during the 1960s and early 1970s with the creation of the federal Environmental Protection Agency Equal Employment Opportunity Commission, Occupational Safety and Health Administration, and Consumer Product Safety Commission, among other bodies. Subsidy programs were not entirely abandoned, however. Federal price supports and production subsidies have made the government a major force in stabilizing US agriculture. Moreover, the federal government has stepped in to arrange for guaranteed loans for two large private firms—Lockheed in 1971 and Chrysler in 1980—where thousands of jobs would have been lost in the event of bankruptcy. As the 1980s began, there was a general consensus that, at least in some areas, government regulation was contributing to inefficiency and higher prices. Thus, the Carter administration moved to deregulate the airline, trucking, and communications industries, with other fields to follow.

Social legislation is a continually expanding area of federal and state government activity. Old age and survivors' insurance, unemployment insurance, and other aspects of the Social Security program, have, since the 1930s, been accepted areas of governmental responsibility. Federal responsibility has also been extended to insurance of bank deposits, to mortgage insurance, and to regulation of stock transactions. The government fulfills a supervisory and regulatory role in labor-management relations. Labor and management customarily disagree on what that role should be, but neither side advocates total removal of government from this field.

The Federal Reserve Board attempts to regulate the course of the business cycle by means of its control over the money supply. In the recessions of 1957, 1969–70, 1973–75, and 1979–80, for example, the board took "counterrecession" measures by adjusting its discount rates, altering reserve requirements, and conducting its open market operations so as to encourage bank credit and monetary expansion.

From the end of World War II until the end of 1952, US

government transfers of capital abroad represented an annual average of nearly $5.5 billion, or 88% of the overall national average, while private investments averaged roughly $730 million a year, or about 12%. During the 1960–73 period, the value of US-held assets abroad increased by nearly 12% annually, reaching $226.1 billion by 1973. This figure rose to $381.3 billion in 1977, reflecting a sixfold increase since 1945. Direct (corporate) investments, which represented the largest portion of the private capital, totaled $168 billion in 1978. Of this amount, $55.2 billion was invested in countries belonging to the European Economic Community, $37.2 billion in Canada, and $21.3 billion in Latin America.

Manufacturing accounted for 44.1% of direct US overseas investments in 1978. A sizable proportion of US capital (19.8% in 1978) is also invested in overseas petroleum endeavors. Of a total of $33.3 billion invested in petroleum, $14.7 billion was in Western Europe, $8.2 billion in Canada, and $2 billion in Latin America. US net liabilities in the Middle East totaled $2.1 billion, and liabilities in the petroleum sector alone exceeded $3.5 billion.

Earnings of US direct investments abroad in 1978 totaled $25.7 billion, as compared with $8.2 billion in 1970. Of the 1978 total, earnings from investments in petroleum enterprises exceeded $5.8 billion; in manufacturing, $10.8 billion; and in finance and insurance, $4.2 billion.

Direct foreign investments in the US have been rapidly increasing, with a record rate of $40.8 billion estimated for 1978. Of the investment volume, manufacturing represents 40%. The most important sources are the Netherlands, 24%; the United Kingdom, 18%; Canada, 15%; and Switzerland, 7%. As of 1977, foreign assets in the US totaled $311 billion, while US assets abroad exceeded $381 billion.

[38]HEALTH

The US health care system is among the most advanced in the world, and overall death rate and longevity figures compare favorably with those of most nations. However, the system serves different regions and ethnic groups unequally, and the rising cost of the system is also a continuing cause for concern. Between 1965 and 1978, total health care costs increased by 350%, and although numerous proposals for a national health insurance program were advanced during the 1970s, none was adopted.

Life expectancy in the US averaged 73.2 years in 1977. The life expectancy of women (77.1 years) was greater than that of men (69.3), and of whites (73.8) higher than nonwhites (68.8). The birthrate fell slowly from a postwar peak of 24.6 per 1,000 population in 1955, to a low of 14.8 in 1975, then rose slightly to 15.3 in 1978, with a total of 3,329,000 live births occurring during that year. Infant mortality declined from 38.3 per 1,000 live births in 1945 to 14.1 in 1977; however, the rate among nonwhites was 21.7, and the maternal death rate of 26.1 per 100,000 live births among nonwhites was more than three times the rate for whites. The rate of legal abortions increased from 19.6 per 1,000 women in 1974 to 26.9 in 1977, when the total of 1,320,300 legal abortions represented a rate of at least 2 abortions for each 5 live births. The marriage rate declined from 11.1 per 1,000 population in 1950 to 8.5 in 1960, before rising above 10 throughout the 1970s; the divorce rate, on the other hand, edged up steadily from 2.3 per 1,000 population in 1955 to 5.1 in 1978.

There has been a marked decline in the death rate from childhood diseases (including poliomyelitis, scarlet fever, diphtheria, measles, and whooping cough), from at least 100 per 1,000 children under 15 in 1900 to less than 0.05 by 1970. Tuberculosis has been brought under control with the use of new drugs, as have many other infectious diseases; less spectacular progress has been made against the diseases that strike later in life. By the late 1970s, about 70% of all deaths were attributable to cardiovascular diseases and cancer. The death rates from

cancer and cirrhosis of the liver increased between 1960 and 1978, as did the rates for homicide and suicide. The following table shows death rates per 100,000 population for the leading causes of death (excluding fetal deaths) in 1978:

	US AVERAGE	MEN WHITE	MEN NONWHITE	WOMEN WHITE	WOMEN NONWHITE
Heart disease	334.3	390.8	273.8	308.4	214.7
Cancer	181.9	206.4	184.9	167.7	122.1
Stroke	80.5	68.9	72.5	93.5	75.0
Accidents	48.4	68.3	78.2	28.5	26.8
Pneumonia and influenza	26.7	28.9	29.9	25.7	17.2
Diabetes mellitus	15.5	12.9	14.7	17.0	22.5
Cirrhosis of the liver	13.8	17.8	23.3	8.8	12.3
Arteriosclerosis	13.3	11.5	6.8	16.8	7.5
Suicide	12.5	20.2	11.1	6.9	3.1
Early childhood disorders	10.1	9.5	28.1	6.5	19.7
Bronchitis, emphysema, asthma	10.0	15.5	7.3	6.4	2.9
Homicide	9.4	9.2	52.6	2.9	11.8
Others	127.0	139.0	176.5	107.4	128.9
TOTALS	883.4	998.9	959.7	796.5	664.5

Although deaths from venereal diseases have been almost eradicated and syphilis has been curbed, the number of reported cases of gonorrhea has increased. In 1977, about 1,000,000 cases were reported, compared with 236,000 in 1955. The US had an estimated 5,750,000 alcoholics in 1975; 3,248 drug abuse treatment facilities cared for 213,400 clients in 1978 at a cost of $518.2 million. Cigarette smoking, linked to heart and lung disease, is one of the nation's most widespread public health problems; despite a federal antismoking campaign, 31% of adult women and 37% of adult men—46 million Americans in all—were regular smokers in 1976.

In 1975, 6,409,000 persons were treated in US mental health facilities; of this total, 28% were residents and 72% were outpatients (in 1955, 70% of all persons treated in mental health facilities were seen on an inpatient basis). Medical facilities in 1978 included 1,380,645 beds in 7,015 hospitals, of which 370 were under federal control, 1,780 were state or locally controlled, 3,339 were private nonprofit institutions, and 732 were investor-owned (for profit). A total of 37,243,182 admissions were recorded, and an occupancy rate of 75.5%; 263,606,079 outpatient visits included 82,871,521 visits to emergency rooms.

There were 149 physicians for each 100,000 persons in 1950. By 1977, when 438,000 physicians practiced in the US, the ratio was 198 per 100,000 population. The percentage of physicians serving as general practitioners dropped from 75% in 1930 to 13% in 1977, while the percentage of all physicians engaged in private practice decreased from 86% to 53%. Most of the 47% not in private practice were engaged in public health, industrial or military medicine, teaching, research, and hospital practice. During the period 1970–80, the number of US physicians increased at a rate equal to three times the population growth rate. However, some regions of the US did not benefit from this increase. Physicians tended to locate in urban or suburban settings, and rural areas actually showed a decline in physician/population ratio. In 1977, 12,324 newly licensed physicians were graduates of US and Canadian medical schools; 5,851 were from foreign schools. Other health care personnel included 1,112,000 registered nurses, 1,037,000 nursing aides (including orderlies and attendants), 402,000 practical nurses, 498,000 technologists and technicians, and 239,000 therapists and dietitians in 1978; and 117,223 dentists (54 per 100,000 population) in 1979.

Per capita expenditures for health and medical care rose from $78.20 in 1950 to $820.68 in 1978. Out of a total of $192.4 billion spent for health care in 1978, private expenditures reached $114.3 billion, of which $53 billion went toward payment of insurance premiums. The average cost of care in community hospitals in 1977 was $198 per day and $1,504 per stay. In 1948, 8% of all medical expenses were defrayed through health insurance arrangements; by 1976, 77% of the population had hospitalization insurance, and 76% had insurance covering surgery. The median annual premium for medical malpractice insurance increased from $1,300 in 1974 to $3,380 in 1977, prompting an increase from less than 2% to 8% in the proportion of physicians who chose not to be covered.

39 SOCIAL WELFARE

Social welfare programs in the US depend on both the federal government and the state governments for resources and administration. Old age, survivors, disability, and Medicare (health) programs are administered by the federal government; unem-

The US Health Care System 1977-79

	NUMBER	BEDS	POPULATION/ BED RATIO	AVERAGE COST PER DAY (1977)	REGISTERED NURSES	LICENSED PRACTICAL NURSES	PHYSICIANS (1977)	POPULATION/ PHYSICIAN RATIO	DENTISTS (1979)	POPULATION PER DENTIST
Alabama	148	25,242	148	$154	8,395	5,844	4,330	847	1,314	2,835
Alaska	26	1,697	237	359	867	306	442	864	232	1,815
Arizona	78	11,339	208	228	6,738	2,177	4,651	488	1,173	1,994
Arkansas	96	12,650	173	141	4,135	3,759	2,506	852	714	3,024
California	613	114,836	194	291	59,415	24,322	50,088	432	14,052	1,567
Colorado	101	14,666	182	199	7,752	2,790	5,299	486	1,701	1,562
Connecticut	64	18,791	165	242	8,986	2,817	7,354	421	2,194	1,431
Delaware	15	4,099	142	205	1,823	728	936	616	265	2,227
Florida	245	54,211	159	195	24,085	9,977	17,740	471	4,323	2,003
Georgia	189	31,146	163	174	11,652	6,680	6,928	720	2,167	2,320
Hawaii	27	3,813	235	213	2,003	1,228	1,709	490	599	1,509
Idaho	51	3,737	235	167	1,717	1,083	978	871	459	1,897
Illinois	285	75,484	149	212	35,309	10,346	19,592	572	5,999	1,880
Indiana	135	33,816	159	172	12,791	4,702	6,763	787	2,234	2,390
Iowa	141	21,613	134	154	8,614	3,398	3,490	825	1,396	2,096
Kansas	164	18,161	129	157	6,424	3,155	3,445	667	1,080	2,166
Kentucky	121	18,815	186	145	7,740	3,363	4,516	758	1,490	2,353
Louisiana	159	25,128	158	176	7,613	5,084	5,614	693	1,586	2,479
Maine	53	7,324	149	186	3,280	1,320	1,684	638	489	2,233
Maryland	85	25,210	164	219	11,426	3,306	9,783	419	2,591	1,612
Massachusetts	189	45,456	127	270	24,247	7,767	14,299	404	3,983	1,461
Michigan	244	50,661	181	218	22,268	11,673	13,594	671	4,772	1,919
Minnesota	188	31,051	129	165	12,503	5,147	7,358	540	2,429	1,653
Mississippi	114	16,234	148	135	4,377	3,533	2,471	958	763	3,129
Missouri	167	35,437	137	171	13,161	5,957	7,548	633	2,303	2,085
Montana	65	5,652	139	152	2,049	815	985	766	442	1,754
Nebraska	108	11,674	134	152	4,570	1,848	2,240	692	931	1,696
Nevada	25	3,234	204	241	1,497	711	897	695	340	1,887
New Hampshire	33	4,995	174	168	2,637	824	1,512	559	465	1,823
New Jersey	139	44,157	166	182	19,554	7,409	13,349	547	4,706	1,562
New Mexico	54	6,503	186	206	2,545	1,218	1,781	659	511	2,378
New York	368	134,425	132	226	61,935	17,226	45,147	396	12,611	1,434
North Carolina	158	33,774	165	149	13,278	6,024	8,018	677	2,175	2,562
North Dakota	60	5,830	112	141	2,200	1,095	786	816	312	2,098
Ohio	241	64,158	168	187	30,216	14,322	16,633	643	5,064	2,117
Oklahoma	141	17,482	165	182	5,626	3,448	3,475	800	1,192	2,375
Oregon	85	11,568	211	218	6,454	1,730	4,378	542	1,685	1,426
Pennsylvania	313	86,474	136	189	39,266	14,092	21,234	555	6,272	1,893
Rhode Island	21	6,700	140	235	2,866	1,249	1,900	489	509	1,839
South Carolina	88	16,919	172	153	5,462	3,187	3,670	765	1,130	2,564
South Dakota	70	5,676	122	130	2,097	916	683	1,000	286	2,453
Tennessee	160	31,008	141	155	10,068	6,751	6,434	565	2,034	2,112
Texas	565	79,071	165	176	29,606	18,824	19,070	665	5,757	2,235
Utah	41	5,084	257	209	2,684	960	2,149	588	853	1,499
Vermont	19	3,036	160	158	1,438	757	1,049	460	270	1,800
Virginia	135	32,138	160	167	12,232	6,035	8,240	605	2,599	1,981
Washington	127	16,138	234	231	9,064	4,077	6,702	538	2,611	1,415
West Virginia	80	14,170	131	149	4,618	2,680	2,531	734	703	2,650
Wisconsin	171	28,630	163	178	12,397	5,197	6,984	666	2,654	1,763
Wyoming	31	2,529	168	169	951	334	466	863	216	1,919
Other areas:										
D.C.	19	9,003	75	284	4,840	1,450	3,356	203	587	1,181
Puerto Rico	60	11,407	291[1]	NA	4,356	3,186	3,400	977	975[2]	3,406[1]

1. Based on 1977 population estimate.
2. As of 1976.

ployment insurance, dependent child care, and a variety of other public assistance programs are state-administered, although the federal government contributes to all of them through grants to the states. Total government and nonpublic agency expenditures for all social welfare programs, including income maintenance, health, education, and welfare services, reached $453 billion in 1976, of which 73% was supplied by public funds. Government outlays for social welfare in 1977 represented 20% of the gross national product.

In 1978, 10,325,000 Americans received $10.7 billion under the aid to families with dependent children (AFDC) program. Medical assistance (Medicaid) amounted to $17.7 billion in 1977, triple the figure for 1970. Attempts to get clients "off the welfare rolls and onto the payrolls" during the late 1960s and 1970s foundered on the reality that many welfare recipients were not easily employable, especially in a tight job market. Moreover, the job training and day care facilities necessary to allow some poor people to find and hold jobs proved no less expensive than direct public assistance. As of 1975, 284,000 children between 3 and 13 years of age were enrolled in day care centers; 86% of those children had working mothers.

The Food and Nutrition Service of the US Department of Agriculture oversees several food assistance programs. In 1978, 15,210,000 Americans took part in the food stamp program, at a cost to the federal government of $5.1 billion. Through 1978, participants were required to purchase the stamps at a discount; as of 1 January 1979, however, the purchase requirement was eliminated and income eligibility levels were reduced, reforms that added to the cost of the program. An estimated 27,048,000 pupils participated in the school lunch program in 1978, at a federal cost of $1.8 billion. During the same year, the federal government also expended $176 million for school breakfasts, $140 million for school milk programs, and $614 million for state-administered food aid for the needy.

The present Social Security program differs greatly from that created by the Social Security Act of 1935, which provided that retirement benefits be paid to retired workers aged 65 or older. Since 1939, Congress has attached a series of amendments to the program, including provisions for workers who retire at age 62, for widows, for dependent children under 18 years of age, for dependent children under 22 years of age who are enrolled in school, and for children who are disabled prior to age 18. Disabled workers between 50 and 65 years of age are also entitled to monthly benefits. Other measures increased the number of years a person may work; among these reforms was a 1977 law banning mandatory retirement in private industry before age 70. Retired workers were allowed to earn wages of up to $4,000 in 1978 without loss of Social Security benefits, with the amount due to be increased in $500 increments to $6,000 in 1982. In that year, the age of exemption from loss of benefits for earnings above $6,000 was to drop from 72 to 70. The actuarial basis for the Social Security system has also changed. In 1935 there were about nine US wage earners for each American aged 65 or more; by 1980, however, the ratio was closer to three to one.

In 1940, the first year benefits were payable, $35 million was paid out. By 1977, Social Security benefits totaled $84.6 billion, paid to more than 34 million beneficiaries. The average monthly benefit for a retired worker with no dependents in 1960 was $74; by 1978, the average benefit was $263 for a single retired worker and $239 for widow. Under legislation enacted in the early 1970s, increases in monthly benefits are pegged to the inflation rate, as expressed through the Consumer Price Index. Employers, employees, and the self-employed are legally required to make contributions to the Social Security fund. In 1977, some 83,100,000 workers were paying Social Security taxes under the Federal Insurance Contributions Act (FICA). As the amount of benefits and the number of beneficiaries have increased, so has the maximum FICA payment, which for 1981 was scheduled at $1,975, based on a rate of 6.65% on earnings up to $29,700; the 1960 maximum was $144. Among workers with many dependents, the Social Security tax deduction can now exceed the federal income tax deduction.

In January 1974, the Social Security Administration assumed responsibility for assisting the aged, blind, and disabled under the Supplemental Security Income program, In 1978, some 4,217,000 Americans—1,968,000 aged, 2,172,000 disabled, and 77,000 blind—received nearly $6.4 billion. Medicare, another program administered under the Social Security Act, provides hospital insurance and voluntary medical insurance for persons 65 and over, with reduced benefits available at age 62. Under the Medicare program, 26,094,000 persons had hospital insurance; 25,363,000 paid premiums for medical coverage in 1977.

The laws governing unemployment compensation originate in the states. Therefore, the benefits provided vary from state to state in duration (generally from 26 to 39 weeks) and amount (ranging from $60.37 to $106.66 weekly in 1978); the national average in 1978 was about $84 per week, with total benefits exceeding $8 billion. Workers' compensation payments in 1977 amounted to nearly $8.6 billion; outlays for vocational rehabilitation reached $986 million in 1978.

Private philanthropy plays a major role in the support of relief and health services. In 1978, individuals, foundations, and corporations gave $9.5 billion to US health and welfare agencies. The private sector plays an especially important role in pension management: private pension funds controlled $321 billion in 1978, while public funds amounted to $243.6 billion.

The federal agency ACTION, established in 1971, coordinates the Peace Corps program abroad and several US social service agencies. Chief among these is Volunteers in Service to America—VISTA—which was created in 1964 to marshal human resources against economic and environmental problems. ACTION also administers activities for the young and the aged, including the Retired Senior Volunteer Program and the Foster Grandparent Program, enlisting elderly persons to work with children who have special physical, mental, or emotional needs.

[40] HOUSING

The housing resources of the US far exceed those of any other country, with 82,420,000 housing units in 1977, 80,716,000 of which were occupied. There was an average of 2.4 persons per unit; some 65% of all US homes in 1977 were occupied by their owners, as against 55% in 1950. The majority of rental tenants are found in the large metropolitan areas. In 1977, 24,860,000 US homes were in cities, 30,037,000 in suburbs, and 27,523,000 outside metropolitan areas. In design and physical elements, houses in the US reflect variations in climate, materials, income, traditions, taste, and age. By 1978, 97% of US homes were equipped with running water, private toilet facilities, and private bathing facilities. During the same year, an estimated 77.8 million homes were wired for electricity; of these, 55% had room air conditioners, 42% had electric dishwashers, 75% had washing machines, 60% had electric or gas clothes dryers, 85% had color television sets, and virtually every electrified home had a refrigerator, electric coffeemaker, toaster, vacuum cleaner, radio, and black-and-white TV set. As of December 1977, about 34% of all housing units in the US had been built prior to 1940, 10% during 1940–49, 17% during 1950–59, 21% during 1960–70, and 18% since April 1970. The housing stock in central cities is much older than that of the US as a whole.

Construction of housing following World War II set a record-breaking pace, so that 1978 was the 30th successive year during which construction of more than 1 million housing units was begun. Between 1970 and 1973, 8 million housing units were constructed; by 1975, however, construction had dropped to 1,171,000 units, the lowest production in more than a decade. In

1978, new housing starts climbed back to 2,023,000, only to be squeezed again by a sluggish economy and high interest rates two years later. Housing construction contracts totaled $74.5 billion in 1978, a figure that represented 47% of the volume of all contract construction that year.

The great bulk of the housing stock as well as homes produced are one-family houses. Private firms or individuals are the main producers of houses, with about two-thirds of single-family, non-farm houses being built by professional builders and developers. The government participates in a variety of programs designed to stimulate housing construction and slum clearance, including issuance of housing loans through the Department of Housing and Urban Development (HUD), the guarantee of mortgages by the Veterans Administration, and the effort to expand the secondary market for HUD mortgages through the Government National Mortgage Association. The government also provides financial and technical assistance to local housing authorities through the Public Housing Administration in order to encourage construction of low-rent housing for lower-income groups. Between 1960 and 1975 the number of low-rent public housing units increased from 593,300 to 1,316,700; since then, however, construction has stagnated.

Perhaps the most significant change in the housing scene has been the shift to the suburbs made possible by the widespread ownership of automobiles. Much land, once rural, has been put to use for dwellings, shopping centers, and factories.

⁴¹EDUCATION
Between 1900 and 1970, illiteracy in the US (persons 14 years and older) declined from 11.3% to 1.2%. Illiteracy among blacks dropped from a rate of 80% in 1870 to 3.6% in 1969 (compared with 0.7% for whites). By 1979, more than two-thirds of all persons aged 25 years or older had completed high school, as compared with 41.1% in 1960 and 24.1% in 1940; 49.4% of all black adults had completed high school in 1979, as compared with only 13.2% in 1940. Some 16.4% of all adults had completed four or more years of college in 1979, as compared with 4.9% in 1940; the rate for blacks in 1979 was 7.9%. The rates of high school completion for men and women were roughly equal, but 20.4% of males had four or more years of college in 1979, compared with 12.9% of all adult females. As of 1979, Americans 18 years of age or older had completed a median of 12.4 years of school, as compared with 12.5 years in 1976; immigration from Asia and the Caribbean in the late 1970s may have contributed to the slight decrease.

Public schools are controlled and supported primarily by the states, each of which has its own system of public education and laws regulating private schools. Actual school administration, however, is usually in the hands of a state-authorized local school district, which is empowered to levy taxes. Supporting schools in this manner led to inequality of educational funding, because of variations in the extent to which residential suburbs could draw on commercial and industrial properties for their tax base. To an increasing extent, therefore, state governments have been called upon—sometimes by court order—to contribute to and equalize the costs of education. In 1977, intermediate and local districts raised 48% of the revenues needed for education; the states contributed 43% and the national government 9%. Expenditures per pupil in public elementary and secondary schools averaged $1,816 in 1976/77.

The individual states establish compulsory attendance requirements, generally for children between the ages of 7 and 16. Some 99% of the children in the 7–15-year-old group attended school in 1980. In the 1978 school year, some 58.6 million persons, or about 26.8% of the total population, were enrolled in schools or colleges. Of these, 28.4 million were enrolled in public school classes from kindergarten through the 8th grade, and 14.1 million were in secondary schools. Nonpublic schools enrolled 5.1 million students in 1977. In 1978, 9.8 million attended colleges and universities.

Public tax-supported schools predominate in elementary and secondary education. Schools affiliated with the Roman Catholic Church have traditionally enrolled the large majority of private school students, more than 3 million in 1979. As a result of reorganization and consolidation, the number of public schools declined from 248,279 in 1900 to 89,231 (62,600 elementary, 25,400 secondary, and 1,231 higher education) in 1977.

The number of public-school elementary teachers increased from 402,700 in 1900 to 541,500 in 1946 and 1,167,000 in 1977; secondary-school teachers, from 20,400 in 1900 to 289,500 in 1946 and 1,030,000 in 1977. The total number of teachers in all public and private educational institutions was about 2,446,000 in 1977. The public-school pupil/teacher ratio has improved gradually in recent decades, decreasing from 30.2 to 1 in elementary schools and 20.9 to 1 in secondary schools in 1955 to 21.3 to 1 and 18.4 to 1, respectively, in 1977.

Since 1957, the federal government has carried out a vigorous program of school desegregation; by 1965, 49% (1,476 of 3,031) of local school districts comprising white and black pupils were desegregated (compared with 18.5% in 1957). Of a total of 6.7 million black pupils attending school in 1974, 88.6% were enrolled in integrated schools; however, some 33.6% of all black pupils were enrolled in schools whose composition was at least 95% black. Of the 2.6 million Hispanic students in 1974, 33% were enrolled in schools with 95–100% Hispanic student populations. While desegregation has largely been accomplished in the public schools of the South, de facto segregation—resulting from residential patterns rather than the deliberate establishment of separate school systems—remains widespread, especially in urban areas. In order to compel conformity to federal desegregation guidelines, the courts in several localities have attempted to establish racial balance by ordering interdistrict busing of pupils.

Of 3,086 institutions of higher learning in the US in 1977/78, 1,618 were private and 1,468 public. College and university enrollment soared uninterruptedly from World War II through the 1960s; in the late 1970s, however, the rate began to slow considerably. By the fall of 1977, the nation's higher institutions enrolled 11,235,787 students (about 35% of them women) in degree-credit courses, representing a rise of 297% since 1960, but of only 24% since 1970. California, with 239 institutions, led all the states with 1,743,200 students in 1977.

Of the current income received by colleges and universities, 50.8% is derived from governmental sources and 20.7% from student fees, leaving the balance to be supplied from private sources and auxiliary enterprises. Rising costs for higher education, coupled with lack of growth among various sources of support, placed considerable pressure on US colleges and universities in the 1970s, many of which were forced to cut back drastically on staff and range of offerings. Most states provide guaranteed loans to state residents attending postsecondary schools, and the largest states generally offer multimillion-dollar tuition assistance programs for needy and deserving students. Grant and loan programs are offered on a national scale through the US Department of Education, the Veterans Administration, and other federal agencies, as well as through such private organizations as the National Merit Scholarship Corp.

The federal government allocates funds for vocational education to the states and some of the territories, which must match federal funds with state and local expenditures. Adult education agencies, both public and private, operate at all levels. In 1978, some 16.7 million persons were participating in federally aided adult vocational programs.

⁴²ARTS
The nation's arts centers are emblems of the importance of the performing arts in US life. New York City's Lincoln Center for

the Performing Arts, whose first concert hall opened in 1962, is now the site of the Metropolitan Opera House, three halls for concerts and other musical performances, two theaters, the New York Public Library's Library and Museum of the Performing Arts, and the Juilliard School; events at Lincoln Center attracted an audience of 4 million in 1979. The John F. Kennedy Center for the Performing Arts in Washington, D.C., opened in 1971; it comprises two main theaters, two smaller theaters, an opera house, and a concert hall.

In 1979 there were 1,540 symphony orchestras in the US, including 31 major orchestras with combined budgets totaling more than $2 billion. The largest budget, some $15 million, financed the Boston Symphony Orchestra, conducted by Seiji Ozawa; the New York Philharmonic, founded in 1842 and conducted by Zubin Mehta in 1979, is the nation's oldest professional musical ensemble. Other leading orchestras include those of Chicago (conducted by Sir Georg Solti), Cleveland (Lorin Maazel), Los Angeles (Carlo Maria Giulini), and Washington, D.C. (the National Symphony, led by Mstislav Rostropovich). In 1978/79, the US had 966 opera companies (73 in New York City alone), 95 of which had budgets above $100,000. More than 9.9 million people attended 8,554 operatic performances, both figures nearly double those of 1969/70. Expenses quadrupled during the same period, reaching $146.4 million in 1978/79. Particularly renowned for artistic excellence are the Lyric Opera of Chicago, San Francisco Opera, Opera Company of Boston, Santa Fe Opera, New York City Opera, and the Metropolitan Opera.

The recording industry is an integral part of the music world. In 1979, 502.2 million records (singles and albums) and 180.8 million prerecorded tapes were sold for gross receipts of, respectively, $2.4 billion and $1.3 billion. Popular music (mostly rock), performed in halls and arenas in every major city and on college campuses throughout the US, dominates record sales, the major categories in 1979 being rock 42%, pop 13%, country 10%, disco 9%, soul 9%, middle-of-the-road 5%, jazz 4%, classical 3%, children's 3%, comedy 1%, and other items 1%.

Though still financially insecure, dance is winning an increasingly wide following. From an audience of 1 million persons in 1964/65, dance now attracts an audience estimated at 17 million persons a year. The American Ballet Theater, founded in 1940, is the nation's oldest dance company still active today; the New York City Ballet, directed by George Balanchine, is equally acclaimed. Other important companies include those of Martha Graham, Merce Cunningham, and Paul Taylor.

Drama remains a principal performing art. In 1972 there were at least 1,029 theaters nationwide, of which 440 were nonprofit. Receipts of all theaters exceeded $227 million, with $146.3 million coming from New York's 281 theaters; Broadway shows had audiences of 9,780,000 in 1978/79.

Television and the motion picture industry have made film the dominant modern medium. The US had 12,218 movie theaters with 16,901 screens in 1979. Films registered record box-office receipts of $2.8 billion during the same year; 50 films grossed more than $8 million, and 37 topped $10 million. Though the industry's revenues are sizable, so are its expenses: the average cost of a new feature film was $8,482,200 in 1979, 51% above the 1978 average. At least 215 films, new and reissued, were released in 1979.

The National Endowment for the Arts, a federal agency established in 1965, provides funding for nonprofit arts organizations and individual artists. Recipients of its matching grants programs are determined by panels of artists on the basis of aesthetic merit. Musical organizations, including opera, received $8.7 million in 1980, the highest subsidy provided any of the performing arts; funding for dance companies increased from $177,000 in 1967 to $7.2 million in 1980. The privately endowed National Institute of Arts and Letters, founded in 1898, is a society of artists, writers, and composers limited to 250 American citizens at any one time.

⁴³LIBRARIES AND MUSEUMS

Of the 29,460 libraries in the US in 1978, 8,455 were public, with 5,963 branches; 4,129 were academic; 2,001 were medical; 1,259 were government; and 7,653 were religious, military, legal, and specialized independent collections.

The foremost library in the country is the Library of Congress, with holdings of more than 74 million items (including more than 18 million books and pamphlets) in 1978. Other great libraries are the public libraries in New York, Philadelphia, Boston, and Baltimore, and the John Crerar and Newberry libraries in Chicago. Noted special collections are those of the Pierpont Morgan Library in New York, the Huntington Library in San Marino, Calif., the Folger Shakespeare Library in Washington, D.C., the Hoover Library at Stanford University, and the rare book divisions of Harvard, Yale, Indiana, Texas, and Virginia universities. Among the leading university libraries, as judged by the extent of their holdings in 1978, are Harvard, Yale, Illinois (Urbana-Champaign), Michigan (Ann Arbor), California (Berkeley), Columbia, Stanford, Cornell, Texas (Austin), California (Los Angeles), and Chicago, each having more than 4 million bound volumes.

There are about 3,500 museums in the US. These include public, state, national, school, school-system, college and university, private company, children's, historic building, park, and other museums. The most numerous type is the historic building, followed in descending order by college and university museums, museums of science, public museums of history, and public museums of art.

Eminent US museums include the American Museum of Natural History, the Metropolitan Museum of Art, and the Museum of Modern Art, all in New York City; the National Gallery of Art and the Smithsonian Institution in Washington, D.C.; the Boston Museum of Fine Arts; the Art Institute of Chicago and the Chicago Museum of Natural History; the Franklin Institute and Philadelphia Museum of Art, both in Philadelphia; and the M. H. de Young Memorial Museum in San Francisco.

⁴⁴COMMUNICATIONS

All major electric communications systems are privately owned but regulated by the Federal Communications Commission (FCC). The US uses wire and radio services for communications more extensively than any other country in the world. It has about 38% of the world's telephones, in a system that connects with every continent. In 1978, 97% of US households had telephones; the total number of telephones reached 169 million (44.3 million business, 124.7 million residential) during the same year, accounting for a daily average of 737 million calls. The domestic telephone industry's total investment in plant and equipment reached $123.6 billion by 1978, and operating revenues were $31 billion in 1978. As of 1980, the FCC had begun to deregulate the telecommunications industry, allowing American Telephone and Telegraph (AT&T), the leading US communications firm, to enter the expanding field of computer-related data transmission. Western Union provides domestic telegraph service; there are six international carriers.

Radio serves a variety of purposes other than broadcasting. It is widely used by ships and aircraft for safety; it has become an important tool in the movement of buses, trucks, and taxicabs. Forest conservation, fire protection, and the police operate with radio as a necessary aid; it is used in logging operations, surveying, construction work, and dispatching of repair crews. Citizen's band radio became popular in the mid-1970s, especially among truck and automobile drivers seeking traffic information or emergency assistance from other drivers. In 1978, commercial broadcasting stations on the air comprised 4,399 AM radio stations, 2,855 FM radio stations, and 709 television stations. Some 272 educational television channels were in operation. In 1970, 97.7% of the nation's households had television sets. The expanding cable television industry, with 4,100 systems in the US as of December 1978, served 20% of all US households with television sets. Creation of new commercial radio stations and relaxation of certain broadcast restrictions were also part of the FCC's deregulation policy.

The Post Office Department of the US was replaced on 1 July 1971 by the US Postal Service, a financially autonomous federal agency. In 1978, 96.9 billion pieces of mail passed through 30,518 post offices with approximately 526,000 full-time employees. The Postal Service's operating revenues for 1978 were $14.1 billion, but its operation required an additional $1.7 billion in direct government subsidy. In addition to mail delivery, it provides registered, certified, insured, and COD mail service, issues money orders (5.6 billion in 1978), and operates a postal savings system.

⁴⁵PRESS

In 1978 there were 1,756 daily newspapers in the US, with a combined circulation of 61,990,000, and 696 Sunday newspapers, with a circulation of 53,990,000; 7,357 weekly newspapers had a paid circulation of over 35 million in 1979. The total circulation of US dailies fell to 60,655,000 in 1975 but has risen gradually since then. The following newspapers, all English-language, reported daily circulation of more than 500,000 in 1978:

	DAILY	SUNDAY
New York Daily News	1,824,836	2,656,981
Wall Street Journal	1,493,387*	—
Los Angeles Times	1,018,490	1,302,395
New York Times	821,549	1,412,481
Chicago Tribune	793,672	1,139,074
Chicago Sun-Times	683,573	719,577
Detroit News	631,836	820,139
Detroit Free Press	617,605	715,657
New York Post	612,576	—
Washington Post	559,371	786,753

*National circulation.

The Thomson, Hearst, Scripps-Howard, Gannett, Newhouse, and other chains are an important part of the newspaper business, but do not control it. Newspapers rely both on their own reporters and, to a marked degree, on the information furnished to them by the large press services. Outstanding among these is the Associated Press, a mutual nonprofit association including 1,365 US newspapers, which gathers news throughout the world and furnishes it at the rate of about 1 million words a day. United Press International functions in a similar manner. The United Features Syndicate and other syndicates supply by-lined columns, photographs, comic strips, and cartoons. Income of newspapers is derived mainly from advertising.

The 9,732 periodicals published during 1977 received $5.5 billion in advertising revenues. As of 30 June 1979, *TV Guide*, with a weekly circulation of 19,547,763, and *Reader's Digest*, with a monthly circulation of 18,094,192, were the best-selling consumer magazines by a wide margin. *Time* and *Newsweek* were the leading newsmagazines, with weekly circulations of 4,314,279 and 2,934,083 respectively.

The US book publishing industry consists of the major book companies (mainly in the New York metropolitan area), nonprofit university presses distributed throughout the US, and numerous small publishing firms. Of the 37,222 books published in the US in 1979, 29,657 were new books and 7,565 were new editions; another 4,086 titles were imported. The average price per hardcover edition was $22.80 in 1979. Receipts from sales of all books in 1977 totaled $4.8 billion, with general adult and juvenile books accounting for 40%; textbooks, 30%; and technical, scientific, and professional books, 15%. Thousands of paperbacks (many of them reprints of hardcover titles) are also published, and millions of copies sold.

⁴⁶ORGANIZATIONS

There are thousands of independent associations and societies in the US, many of which have numerous local branches and chapters. A number of industrial and commercial organizations exercise considerable influence on management policies. The National Association of Manufacturers and the US Chamber of Commerce, with numerous local branches, are the two central bodies of business and commerce. Various industries have their own associations, concerned with cooperative research and questions of policy alike.

Practically every profession in the US is represented by one or more professional organizations. Among the most powerful of these are the American Medical Association, comprising regional, state, and local medical societies; the American Bar Association, also comprising state and local associations; the American Hospital Association; and the National Education Association.

Many private organizations are dedicated to programs of political and social action. Prominent in this realm are the National Association for the Advancement of Colored People (NAACP), the Urban League, the American Civil Liberties Union (ACLU), Common Cause, and the Anti-Defamation League. The League of Women Voters, which provides the public with nonpartisan information about candidates and election issues, sponsored televised debates between the major presidential candidates in 1976 and 1980. The National Organization for Women and the National Rifle Association have each mounted nationwide lobbying campaigns on issues affecting their members.

The great privately endowed philanthropic foundations and trusts play an important part in encouraging the development of education, art, science, and social progress in the US. In 1978, foundations, corporations, and charitable bequests donated a total of $6.8 billion in philanthropic gifts. Prominent foundations include the Carnegie Corporation and the Carnegie Endowment for International Peace, the Ford Foundation, the Guggenheim Foundation, the Mayo Association for the Advancement of Medical Research and Education, and the Rockefeller Foundation. Private philanthropy was responsible for the establishment of many of the nation's most eminent libraries, concert halls, museums, and university and medical facilities; private bequests were also responsible for the establishment of the Pulitzer Prizes. Merit awards offered by industry and professional groups include the "Oscars" from the Academy of Motion Picture Arts and Sciences, the "Emmys" of the National Academy of Television Arts and Sciences, and the "Grammys" of the National Academy of Recording Arts and Sciences.

Funds for a variety of community health and welfare services are funneled through United Way campaigns, which raised $1.3 billion in 1978. The American Red Cross had 34.3 million contributors in 1978, who helped support the $358.6 million cost of its services and activities, ranging from disaster relief to blood donor programs. Private organizations supported by contributions from the general public lead the fight against specific diseases.

The Boy Scouts of America, the Girl Scouts of America, rural 4-H Clubs, the Young Men's and the Young Women's Christian Associations, and the Young Men's and Young Women's Hebrew Associations are among the organizations devoted to recreation, sports, camping, and education.

The largest religious organization in the US is the National Council of the Churches of Christ in the USA, which embraces 32 Protestant and Orthodox denominations whose adherents total about 40 million. Many organizations, such as the American Philosophical Society, the American Association for the Advancement of Science, and the National Geographic Society, are dedicated to the enlargement of various branches of human knowledge. National, state, and local historical societies abound, and there are numerous educational, sports, and hobbyist groups.

The larger veterans' organizations are the American Legion,

the Veterans of Foreign Wars of the US, the Catholic War Veterans, and the Jewish War Veterans. Fraternal organizations, in addition to such international organizations as the Masons, include indigenous groups, such as the Benevolent and Protective Order of Elks, the Loyal Order of Moose, and the Woodmen of the World. Many, such as the Ancient Order of Hibernians in America, commemorate the national origin of their members. One of the largest fraternal organizations is the Roman Catholic Knights of Columbus.

⁴⁷TOURISM, TRAVEL, AND RECREATION

Foreign visitors to the US (excluding Canadian and Mexican citizens) numbered at least 5,732,000 in 1978, nearly triple the total for 1968. Of the 1978 visitors, 2,450,000 came from Europe, 1,479,000 from Central and South America and the Caribbean, and 880,000 from Japan (20,000 in 1960). Travelers to the US from all foreign countries spent $8.5 billion in 1978, including $1.2 billion for fares on US carriers to and from their home countries. Canadians accounted for more than 26% of foreign tourist spending, Mexicans more than 17%. With a few exceptions, such as Canadians entering from the Western Hemisphere, all visitors to the US are required to have passports and visas.

A total of $13.2 billion was spent by 7.8 million US tourists abroad in 1978, of which $4.6 billion went for transportation costs (predominantly air). Of the balance, Canada collected $1.4 billion and Mexico $2.1 billion. Europe and the Mediterranean attracted $2.9 billion in US tourist spending; the average per tourist was $35 a day or $717 per trip (transatlantic fares excluded). The Caribbean and Central America absorbed $888 million; South America, $306 million.

Some 136 million US domestic travelers took trips to destinations at least 100 mi (161 km) away from home during 1977. Fully four-fifths of all trips were by car, truck, or camper; another 12% were by air. Visiting friends or relatives was the purpose of 37% of the trips, while another 20% traveled for business or convention reasons.

For the 26% of domestic journeys that had entertainment, sightseeing, and outdoor recreation as the primary goal, state and national parks were leading destinations. In 1975, the nation's 3,804 state parks, covering a total of 9.8 million acres (4 million hectares), registered 465 million day visits and 51 million overnight stays. Expenditures for state park maintenance and services totaled $649 million. By 1979, the 320 areas of the National Park System—including 92 national monuments, 59 national historic sites, 39 national parks, the White House and numerous memorials, battlefields, scenic rivers, and other sites—claimed more than 6.7 million acres (2.7 million hectares) of federal land. The system registered 282 million visits (including 16 million overnight stays) during the same year. The following table shows some of the most popular sites and the number of visitors they attracted in 1978:

	ACREAGE ('000)	RECREATIONAL VISITS ('000)
Acadia National Park, Me.	39	2,600
Blue Ridge Parkway, Ga., N.C., Va.	82	12,700
Cape Cod National Seashore, Mass.	45	5,000
Cape Hatteras National Seashore, N.C.	30	1,800
C&O (Chesapeake and Ohio) Canal National Historical Park, Md., Va.	21	3,100
Colonial National Historical Park, Va.	10	7,600
Gateway National Recreation Area, N.Y., N.J.	26	8,600
George Washington Memorial Parkway Va., Md.	7	5,900
Glacier National Park, Mont.	1,014	1,600
Glen Canyon National Recreation Area, Ariz., Utah	1,237	2,100
Golden Gate National Recreation Area, Calif.	39	9,000

	ACREAGE ('000)	RECREATIONAL VISITS ('000)
Grand Canyon National Park, Ariz.	1,218	2,700
Grand Teton National Park, Wyo.	311	3,200
Great Smoky Mountains National Park, N.C., Tenn.	517	8,700
Gulf Islands National Seashore, Fla., Miss.	140	3,900
Hot Springs National Park, Ark.	6	1,200
Lake Mead National Recreation Area, Ariz., Nev.	1,497	6,600
Natchez Trace Parkway, Miss., Tenn., Ala.	48	9,700
Olympic National Park, Wash.	909	2,500
Rocky Mountain National Park, Colo.	264	3,000
Sequoia National Park, Calif.	403	1,000
Shenandoah National Park, Va.	194	2,000
Valley Forge National Historic Park, Pa.	2	3,100
Yellowstone National Park, Idaho, Mont., Wyo.	2,220	2,600
Yosemite National Park, Calif.	761	2,600

Americans spent at least $81.2 billion on recreational activities in 1977, ranging from spectator sports to home gardening. Toys, sports supplies and equipment, and pleasure craft alone absorbed $21.8 billion. Participant sports are a favorite form of recreation: as of 1980, an estimated 100 million persons jogged or walked regularly, 32 million played tennis, and 16 million enjoyed golf. Skiing is a popular recreation in New England and the western mountain ranges, while sailing, power boating, rafting, and canoeing are popular water sports. Wilderness areas provide year-round hiking, climbing, hunting, and fishing. In 1977/78, state authorities issued 32.8 million fishing licenses and 25.8 million hunting licenses.

⁴⁸SPORTS

Baseball, long honored as the national pastime, is the nation's leading professional team sport, with two major leagues having 26 teams (2 in Canada); in summer 1979, 43.6 million attended major league games. In addition, there is an extensive network of minor league baseball teams, each of them related to a major league franchise. The National Basketball Association, created in 1946, included 22 teams which drew 9.9 million fans during the 1978/79 season. The average salaries of basketball players rose from $32,000 in 1969 to $185,000 in 1979, by far the highest of any professional sport. In autumn 1979, 13.1 million Americans attended regular season games of the National Football League's 28 teams. Attendance at National Hockey League (NHL) games exceeded 7.7 million in 1978/79; of 21 NHL teams, 6 were Canadian, as were 80% of the players. Some 5.6 million persons attended the games of 3 Canadian and 21 US teams during the 1978/79 North American Soccer League season. Radio and television contracts are integral to the popular and financial success of all professional team sports.

Several other professional sports are popular nationwide. Horse racing, which lured some 76 million Americans to the track in 1978, is the nation's most popular spectator sport. Annual highlights of Thoroughbred racing are the three jewels of the Triple Crown—Kentucky Derby, Preakness, and Belmont Stakes—last won by Seattle Slew in 1977 and Affirmed in 1978. In 1974, $8.9 billion was legally wagered on horse racing, including licensed off-track betting in New York; illegal bets on horseraces totaled an estimated $1.4 billion during the same year. Attendance at greyhound racetracks totaled 20.2 million in 1978. The prize money that Henry Ford won in a 1901 auto race helped him start his now famous car company two years later; since then, automobile manufacturers have backed sports car, stock car, and motorcycle racing at tracks throughout the US. From John L. Sullivan to Muhammad Ali, the personality and power of the great boxing champions have drawn millions of spectators to

LANDS UNDER FEDERAL JURISDICTION

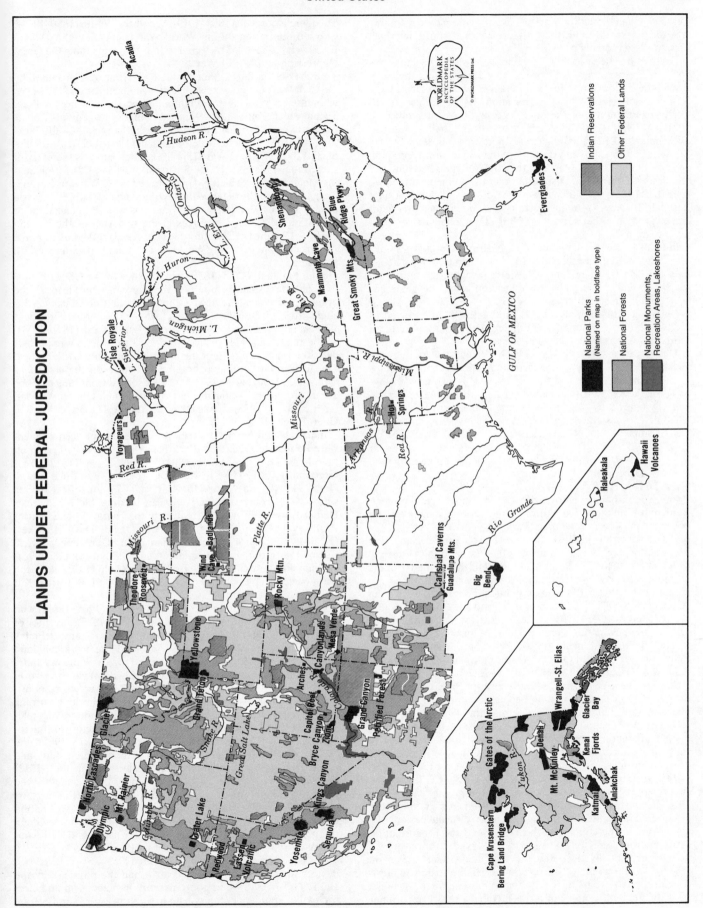

Acadia

Hudson R.

L. Ontario

L. Erie

L. Huron

L. Michigan

L. Superior

Isle Royale

Voyageurs

Red R.

Missouri R.

Missouri R.

Theodore
Roosevelt

Wind
Cave
Badlands

Platte R.

Ohio R.

Mammoth
Cave

Shenandoah

Blue
Ridge Pkwy.

Great Smoky Mts.

Mississippi R.

Hot
Springs

Arkansas R.

Red R.

Everglades

GULF OF MEXICO

Rocky Mtn.

Yellowstone

Grand Teton

Glacier

North Cascades

Mt. Rainier

Olympic

Columbia R.

Snake R.

Great Salt Lake

Crater Lake

Redwood

Lassen
Volcanic

Yosemite

Kings Canyon

Sequoia

Bryce Canyon

Capitol Reef
Zion

Arches

Canyonlands
Mesa Verde

Grand Canyon

Petrified Forest

Colorado R.

Carlsbad Caverns
Guadalupe Mts.

Big
Bend

Rio Grande

WORLDMARK
ENCYCLOPEDIA
OF THE STATES
© WORLDMARK PRESS Ltd.

Indian Reservations

Other Federal Lands

National Parks
(Named on map in boldface type)

National Forests

National Monuments,
Recreation Areas, Lakeshores

Haleakala

Hawaii
Volcanoes

Cape Krusenstern
Bering Land Bridge

Gates of the Arctic

Yukon R.

Denali

Mt. McKinley

Wrangell-St. Elias

Glacier
Bay

Kenai
Fjords

Katmai

Aniakchak

ringside. Glamour and top prizes also provide national followings for tennis and golf, the only professional sports in which women are nationally prominent.

Football has been part of US college life since the game was born on 6 November 1869 with a New Jersey match between Rutgers and Princeton. In 1978, the 478 varsity teams of the National Collegiate Athletic Association (NCAA) drew crowds totaling 32 million; the National Association of Intercollegiate Athletics (NAIA) included 225 teams from smaller colleges. Collegiate basketball is almost as important; in 1978/79, the NCAA's 715 varsity teams drew more than 30 million spectators, and another 490 teams played in the NAIA. Colleges recruit top athletes with sports scholarships in order to win media attention, keep the loyalty of alumni, and thereby boost fund raising. Baseball, hockey, swimming, gymnastics, crew, track and field, and a variety of other sports also fill the intercollegiate competitive program.

In 1978, 415,661 students played baseball at 13,466 high schools; several hundred thousand played football at some 14,000 schools. Ever since 1891, when James Naismith invented basketball for his Springfield, Mass., physical education class, the game has been popular in secondary schools: in 1978, 619,601 boys played the game at 16,978 high schools, and 449,695 girls played in 15,290 schools. Community youth leagues also support these sports, as well as ice hockey and soccer.

The Amateur Athletic Union (AAU), founded in 1888, directs competition in 21 sports, including national championships in swimming and track and field. The AAU is also the advisory body for the US Olympic team. St. Louis hosted the 1904 summer Olympics; Los Angeles was home to them in 1932 and was scheduled to host them again in 1984. The winter games were held in Squaw Valley, Calif., in 1960, and at Lake Placid, N.Y., in 1932 and 1980. The US boycotted the summer games at Moscow in 1980 to protest the Soviet invasion of Afghanistan the previous December.

⁴⁹FAMOUS AMERICANS

Printer, publisher, inventor, scientist, statesman, and diplomat, Benjamin Franklin (1706–90) was America's outstanding figure of the colonial period. George Washington (1732–99), leader of the colonial army in the American Revolution, became first president of the US and is known as the "father of his country." Chief author of the Declaration of Independence, founder of the US political party system, and third president was Thomas Jefferson (1743–1826). His leading political opponents were John Adams (1735–1826), second president, and Alexander Hamilton (b.West Indies, 1755–1804), first secretary of the treasury, who ensured the new nation's credit. James Madison (1751–1836), a leading figure in drawing up the US Constitution, served as fourth president. John Quincy Adams (1767–1848), sixth president, was an outstanding diplomat and secretary of state.

Andrew Jackson (1767–1845), seventh president, was an ardent champion of the common people and opponent of vested interests. Outstanding senators during the Jackson era were John Caldwell Calhoun (1782–1850), spokesman of the southern planter aristocracy and leading exponent of the supremacy of states' rights over federal powers; Henry Clay (1777–1852), the great compromiser, who sought to reconcile the conflicting views of the North and the South; and Daniel Webster (1782–1852), statesman and orator, who championed the preservation of the Union against sectional interests and division. Abraham Lincoln (1809–1865) led the US through its most difficult period, the Civil War, in the course of which he issued the Emancipation Proclamation. Jefferson Davis (1808–89) served as the only president of the short-lived Confederacy. Stephen Grover Cleveland (1837–1908), a conservative reformer, was the strongest president in the latter part of the 19th century. The foremost presidents of the 20th century have been Nobel Peace Prize winner

Theodore Roosevelt (1858–1919); Woodrow Wilson (1856–1924), who led the nation during World War I; and Franklin Delano Roosevelt (1882–1945), elected to four terms spanning the Great Depression and World War II.

Of the outstanding US military leaders, four were produced by the Civil War: Union generals Ulysses Simpson Grant (1822–85), who later served as the eighteenth president, and William Tecumseh Sherman (1820–91); and Confederate generals Robert Edward Lee (1807–70) and Thomas Jonathan "Stonewall" Jackson (1824–63). George Catlett Marshall (1880–1959), army chief of staff during World War II, in his later capacity as secretary of state under President Harry S Truman (1884–1972) formulated the Marshall Plan, which did much to revitalize Western Europe. Douglas MacArthur (1880–1964) commanded US forces in Asia during World War II, oversaw the postwar reorganization of Japan, and directed UN forces in the first year of the Korean conflict. Dwight D. Eisenhower (1890–1969) served as supreme Allied commander during World War II, later becoming the 34th president.

John Marshall (1755–1835), chief justice of the US from 1801 to 1835, established the power of the Supreme Court through the principle of judicial review. Other important chief justices include Edward Douglass White (1845–1921), former president William Howard Taft (1857–1930), and Earl Warren (1891–1974), whose tenure as chief justice from 1953 to 1969 saw important decisions on desegregation, reapportionment, and civil liberties. The justice who enjoyed the longest tenure on the court was William O. Douglas (1898–1980), who served from 1939 to 1975; other prominent associate justices included Oliver Wendell Holmes (1841–1935), Louis Dembitz Brandeis (1856–1941), and Hugo Black (1886–1971).

Indian chiefs renowned for their resistance to white encroachment were Pontiac (c.1720–69), Black Hawk (1767–1838), Tecumseh (1768–1813), Osceola (c. 1804–38), Cochise (1812?–74), Geronimo (c. 1829–1909), Sitting Bull (c. 1831–90), Chief Joseph (1840?–1904), and Crazy Horse (1849?–77). Historical figures who have become part of American folklore include pioneer Daniel Boone (1734–1820); silversmith, engraver, and patriot Paul Revere (1735–1818); frontiersman David "Davy" Crockett (1786–1836); the scout and Indian agent Christopher "Kit" Carson (1809–68); James Butler "Wild Bill" Hickok (1837–76); William Frederick "Buffalo Bill" Cody (1846–1917), and the outlaws Jesse Woodson James (1847–82) and Billy the Kid (William H. Bonney, 1859–81).

Outstanding inventors were Robert Fulton (1765–1815), who developed the steamboat; Eli Whitney (1765–1825), inventor of the cotton gin and mass production techniques; Samuel Finley Breese Morse (1791–1872), who invented the telegraph; and Elias Howe (1819–67), who produced the sewing machine. Alexander Graham Bell (b.Scotland, 1847–1922) gave the world the telephone. Thomas Alva Edison (1847–1931) was responsible for hundreds of inventions, among them the long-burning incandescent electric lamp, the phonograph, automatic telegraph devices, a motion picture camera and projector, the microphone, and the mimeograph. Lee De Forest (1873–1961), the "father of the radio," developed the audion vacuum tube and many other inventions. Two brothers, Wilbur Wright (1867–1912) and Orville Wright (1871–1948), designed, built, and flew the first successful motor-powered airplane. Amelia Earhart (1898–1937) and Charles Lindbergh (1902–74) were aviation pioneers. Pioneers in the space program include John Glenn (b.1921), the first US astronaut to orbit the earth, and Neil Armstrong (b.1930), the first man to set foot on the moon.

Benjamin Thompson, Count Rumford (1753–1814), developed devices for measuring light and heat, and the physicist Joseph Henry (1797–1878) did important work in magnetism and electricity. Outstanding botanists and naturalists were John Bartram

(1699–1777); his son William Bartram (1739–1832); Louis Agassiz (b.Switzerland, 1807–73); Asa Gray (1810–88); Luther Burbank (1849–1926), developer of a vast number of new and improved varieties of fruits, vegetables, and flowers; and George Washington Carver (1864–1943), known especially for his work on industrial applications for peanuts. John James Audubon (1785–1851) won fame as an ornithologist and artist.

Distinguished physical scientists include Samuel Pierpont Langley (1834–1906), astronomer and aviation pioneer; Josiah Willard Gibbs (1839–1903), mathematical physicist whose work laid the basis for physical chemistry; Henry Augustus Rowland (1848–1901), who did important research in magnetism and optics; and Albert Abraham Michelson (b.Germany, 1852–1931), who measured the speed of light and became the first of a long line of US Nobel Prize winners. The chemists Gilbert Newton Lewis (1875–1946) and Irving Langmuir (1881–1957) developed a theory of atomic structure.

The theory of relativity was conceived by Albert Einstein (b.Germany, 1879–1955), generally considered the greatest mind in the physical sciences since Newton. Percy Williams Bridgman (1882–1961) was the father of operationalism and studied the effect of high pressures on materials. Arthur Holly Compton (1892–1962) made discoveries in the field of X rays and cosmic rays. The physical chemist Harold Clayton Urey (b.1893) discovered heavy hydrogen. Isidor Isaac Rabi (b.Austria, 1898), nuclear physicist, has done important work in magnetism, quantum mechanics, and radiation. Enrico Fermi (b.Italy, 1901–54) created the first nuclear chain reaction, in Chicago in 1942, and contributed to the development of the atomic and hydrogen bombs. Also prominent in the splitting of the atom were Leo Szilard (b.Hungary, 1898–1964), J. Robert Oppenheimer (1904–67), and Edward Teller (b.Hungary, 1908). Ernest Orlando Lawrence (1901–58) developed the cyclotron. Carl David Anderson (b.1905) discovered the positron. Mathematician Norbert Wiener (1894–1964) developed the science of cybernetics.

Outstanding figures in the biological sciences include Theobald Smith (1859–1934), who developed immunization theory and practical immunization techniques for animals; the geneticist Thomas Hunt Morgan (1866–1945), who discovered the heredity functions of chromosomes; and neurosurgeon Harvey William Cushing (1869–1939). Selman Abraham Waksman (b.Russia, 1888–1973), a microbiologist specializing in antibiotics, was co-discoverer of streptomycin. Edwin Joseph Cohn (1892–1953) is noted for his work in the protein fractionalization of blood, particularly the isolation of serum albumin. Philip Showalter Hench (1896–1965) isolated and synthesized cortisone. Wendell Meredith Stanley (1904–71) was the first to isolate and crystallize a virus. Jonas Salk (b.1914) developed an effective killed-virus poliomyelitis vaccine, and Albert Bruce Sabin (b.1906) contributed oral, attenuated live-virus polio vaccines.

Adolf Meyer (b.Switzerland, 1866–1950) developed the concepts of mental hygiene and dementia praecox and the theory of psychobiology; Harry Stack Sullivan (1892–1949) created the interpersonal theory of psychiatry. Social psychologist George Herbert Mead (1863–1931), behaviorist B(urrhus) F(rederic) Skinner (b.1904) and learning theorist Jerome S. Bruner (b.1915) have been influential in the 20th century.

A pioneer in psychology who was also an influential philosopher was William James (1842–1910). Other leading US philosophers include Charles Sanders Peirce (1839–1914); Josiah Royce (1855–1916); John Dewey (1859–1952), also famous for his theories of education; George Santayana (b.Spain, 1863–1952); Rudolf Carnap (b.Germany, 1891–1970); Willard Van Orman Quine (b.1908); and John Rawls (b.1921). Educators of note include Horace Mann (1796–1859), Henry Barnard (1811–1900), and Charles William Eliot (1834–1926). Noah Webster (1758–1843) was the outstanding US lexicographer, and Melvil

Dewey (1851–1931) was a leader in the development of library science. Thorstein Veblen (1857–1929) wrote books that have strongly influenced economic and social thinking. Also important in the social sciences have been sociologist Talcott Parsons (b.1902) and anthropologist Margaret Mead (1901–78).

Social reformers of note include Dorothea Lynde Dix (1802–87), who led movements for the reform of prisons and insane asylums; Elizabeth Cady Stanton (1815–1902) and Susan Brownell Anthony (1820–1906), leaders in the woman suffrage movement; Clara Barton (1821–1912), founder of the American Red Cross; economist Henry George (1839–97), advocate of the single-tax theory; Eugene Victor Debs (1855–1926), labor leader and an outstanding organizer of the Socialist movement in the US; Jane Addams (1860–1935), who pioneered in settlement house work; Robert Marion La Follette (1855–1925), a leader of progressive political reform in Wisconsin and in the US Senate; Margaret Higgins Sanger (1883–1966), pioneer in birth control; Norman Thomas (1884–1968), Socialist Party leader; and Martin Luther King, Jr. (1929–68), a central figure in the black civil rights movement and winner of the Nobel Peace Prize in 1964.

Religious leaders include Roger Williams (c.1603–83), an early advocate of religious tolerance in the US; Jonathan Edwards (1703–58), New England preacher and theologian; Elizabeth Ann Seton (1774–1821), the first American canonized in the Roman Catholic Church; William Ellery Channing (1780–1842), a founder of American Unitarianism; Joseph Smith (1805–44), founder of the Church of Jesus Christ of Latter-day Saints (Mormon) and his chief associate, Brigham Young (1801–77); and Mary Baker Eddy (1821–1910), founder of the Christian Science Church. Paul Tillich (b.Germany, 1886–1965) and Reinhold Niebuhr (1892–1971) were outstanding Protestant theologians of international influence.

Famous US businessmen include Pierre Samuel du Pont (1739–1817), John Jacob Astor (Johann Jakob Ashdour, b.Germany, 1763–1848), Cornelius Vanderbilt (1794–1877), Andrew Carnegie (b.Scotland, 1835–1919), John Pierpont Morgan (1837–1913), John Davison Rockefeller (1839–1937), Andrew William Mellon (1855–1937), and Henry Ford (1863–1947).

The first US author to be widely read outside the US was Washington Irving (1783–1859). James Fenimore Cooper (1789–1851) was the first popular US novelist. Three noted historians were William Hickling Prescott (1796–1859), John Lothrop Motley (1814–77), and Francis Parkman (1823–93). The writings of two men of Concord, Mass.—Ralph Waldo Emerson (1803–82) and Henry David Thoreau (1817–62)—influenced philosophers, political leaders, and ordinary men and women in many parts of the world. The novels and short stories of Nathaniel Hawthorne (1804–64) explore New England's Puritan heritage. Herman Melville (1819–91) wrote the powerful novel *Moby Dick*, a symbolic work about a whale hunt that has become an American classic. Mark Twain (Samuel Langhorne Clemens, 1835–1910) is the best-known US humorist. Other leading novelists of the later 19th and early 20th centuries include William Dean Howells (1837–1920), Henry James (1843–1916), Edith Wharton (1862–1937), Stephen Crane (1871–1900), Theodore Dreiser (1871–1945), and Sinclair Lewis (1885–1951), first US winner of the Nobel Prize for literature (1930). Later Nobel Prize–winning US novelists include Pearl S. Buck (1892–1973), in 1938; William Faulkner (1897–1962), in 1949; Ernest Hemingway (1899–1961), in 1954; John Steinbeck (1902–68), in 1962; Saul Bellow (b.Canada, 1915), in 1976; and Isaac Bashevis Singer (b.Poland, 1904), in 1978.

Noted US poets include Henry Wadsworth Longfellow (1807–82), Edgar Allan Poe (1809–49), Walt Whitman (1819–92), Emily Dickinson (1830–86), Edwin Arlington Robinson (1869–1935), Robert Frost (1874–1963), Wallace Stevens (1879–1955), William Carlos Williams (1883–1963), Marianne

Presidents of the US, 1789–1881

NAME	BORN	DIED	OTHER MAJOR OFFICES HELD	RESIDENCE AT ELECTION
1 George Washington	Westmoreland County, Va., 22 February 1732	Mt. Vernon, Va., 14 December 1799	Commander in Chief, Continental Army (1775–83)	Mt. Vernon, Va.
2 John Adams	Braintree (later Quincy), Mass., 30 October 1735	Quincy, Mass. 4 July 1826	Representative, Continental Congress (1774–77); US vice president (1789–97)	Quincy, Mass.
3 Thomas Jefferson	Goochland (now Albemarle) County, Va., 13 April 1743	Monticello, Va., 4 July 1826	Representative, Continental Congress (1775–76); governor of Virginia (1779–81); secretary of state (1790–93); US vice president (1797–1801)	Monticello, Va.
4 James Madison	Port Conway, Va., 16 March 1751	Montpelier, Va., 28 June 1836	Representative, Continental Congress (1780–83; 1786–88); US representative (1789–97); secretary of state (1801–9)	Montpelier, Va.
5 James Monroe	Westmoreland County, Va., 28 April 1758	New York, N.Y., 4 July 1831	US senator (1790–94); governor of Virginia (1799–1802); secretary of state (1811–17); secretary of war (1814–15)	Leesburg, Va.
6 John Quincy Adams	Braintree (later Quincy), Mass., 11 July 1767	Washington, D.C., 23 February 1848	US senator (1803–8); secretary of state (1817–25); US representative (1831–48)	Quincy, Mass.
7 Andrew Jackson	Waxhaw, Carolina frontier, 15 March 1767	The Hermitage, Tenn., 8 June 1845	US representative (1796–97); US senator (1797–98)	The Hermitage, Tenn.
8 Martin Van Buren	Kinderhook, N.Y., 5 December 1782	Kinderhook, N.Y., 24 July 1862	US senator (1821–28); governor of New York (1829); secretary of state (1829–31); US vice president (1833–37)	New York
9 William Henry Harrison	Charles City County, Va., 9 February 1773	Washington, D.C., 4 April 1841	Governor of Indiana Territory (1801-13); US representative (1816–19); US senator (1825–28)	North Bend, Ohio
10 John Tyler	Charles City County, Va., 29 March 1790	Richmond, Va., 18 January 1862	US representative (1816–21); governor of Virginia (1825–27); US senator (1827–36); US vice president (1841)	Richmond, Va.
11 James K. Polk	Mecklenburg County, N.C., 2 November 1795	Nashville, Tenn., 15 June 1849	US representative (1825–39); governor of Tennessee (1839–41)	Nashville, Tenn.
12 Zachary Taylor	Orange County, Va., 24 November 1784	Washington, D.C., 9 July 1850	—	Louisiana
13 Millard Fillmore	Cayuga County, N.Y., 7 January 1800	Buffalo, N.Y., 8 March 1874	US representative (1833–35; 1837–43); US vice president (1849–50)	Buffalo, N.Y.
14 Franklin Pierce	Hillsboro, N.H., 23 November 1804	Concord, N.H., 8 October 1869	US representative, (1833–37); US senator (1837–42)	Concord, N.H.
15 James Buchanan	Mercersburg, Pa., 23 April 1791	Lancaster, Pa., 1 June 1868	US representative (1821–31); US senator (1834–45); secretary of state (1845–49)	Lancaster, Pa.
16 Abraham Lincoln	Hodgenville, Ky., 12 February 1809	Washington, D.C., 15 April 1865	US representative (1847–49)	Springfield, Ill.
17 Andrew Johnson	Raleigh, N.C., 29 December 1808	Carter Station, Tenn., 31 July 1875	US representative (1843–53); governor of Tennessee (1853–57; 1862–65); US senator (1857–62); US vice president (1865)	Greeneville, Tenn.
18 Ulysses S. Grant	Point Pleasant, Ohio, 27 April 1822	Mount McGregor, N.Y., 23 July 1885	Commander, Union Army (1864–65); secretary of war (1867–68)	Galena, Ill.
19 Rutherford B. Hayes	Delaware, Ohio, 4 October 1822	Fremont, Ohio, 17 January 1893	US representative (1865–67); governor of Ohio (1868–72; 1876–77)	Fremont, Ohio
20 James A. Garfield	Orange, Ohio, 19 November 1831	Elberon, N.J., 19 September 1881	US representative (1863–80)	Mentor, Ohio

PARTY	% OF POPULAR VOTE	% OF ELECTORAL VOTE[2]	TERMS IN OFFICE[5]	VICE PRESIDENTS	NOTABLE EVENTS	
Federalist	—	50.0 50.0	30 April 1789–4 March 1793 4 March 1793–4 March 1797	John Adams John Adams	Federal government organized; Bill of Rights enacted (1791); Whiskey Rebellion suppressed (1794); North Carolina, Rhode Island, Vermont, Kentucky, Tennessee enter Union.	1
Federalist	—	25.7	4 March 1797–4 March 1801	Thomas Jefferson	Alien and Sedition Acts passed (1798); Washington, D.C., becomes US capital (1800).	2
Dem.-Rep.	—	26.4[3] 92.0	4 March 1801–4 March 1805 4 March 1805–4 March 1809	Aaron Burr George Clinton	Louisiana Purchase (1803); Lewis and Clark Expedition (1803–6); Ohio enters Union.	3
Dem.-Rep.	—	69.7 58.9	4 March 1809–4 March 1813 4 March 1813–4 March 1817	George Clinton Elbridge Gerry	War of 1812 (1812–14); protective tariffs passed (1816); Louisiana, Indiana enter Union.	4
Dem.-Rep.	—	84.3 99.5	4 March 1817–4 March 1821 4 March 1821–4 March 1825	Daniel D. Tompkins Daniel D. Tompkins	Florida purchased from Spain (1819–21); Missouri Compromise (1820); Monroe Doctrine (1823); Mississippi, Illinois, Alabama, Maine, Missouri enter Union.	5
National Republican	30.9	38[4]	4 March 1825–4 March 1829	John C. Calhoun	Period of political antagonisms, producing little legislation; road and canal construction supported; Erie Canal opens (1825).	6
Democrat	56.0 54.2	68.2 76.6	4 March 1829–4 March 1833 4 March 1833–4 March 1837	John C. Calhoun Martin Van Buren	Introduction of spoils system; Texas Republic established (1836); Arkansas, Michigan enter Union.	7
Democrat	50.8	57.8	4 March 1837–4 March 1841	Richard M. Johnson	Financial panic (1837) and subsequent depression.	8
Whig	52.9	79.6	4 March 1841–4 April 1841	John Tyler	Died of pneumonia one month after taking office.	9
Whig	—	—	4 April 1841–4 March 1845	—	Monroe Doctrine extended to Hawaiian Islands (1842); Second Seminole War in Florida ends (1842).	10
Democrat	49.5	61.8	4 March 1845–4 March 1849	George M. Dallas	Boundary between US and Canada set at 49th parallel (1846); Mexican War (1846–48), ending with Treaty of Guadalupe Hidalgo (1848); California gold rush begins (1848); Florida, Texas, Iowa, Wisconsin enter Union.	11
Whig	47.3	56.2	4 March 1849–9 July 1850	Millard Fillmore	Died after 16 months in office.	12
Whig	—	—	9 July 1850–4 March 1853	—	Fugitive Slave Law (1850); California enters Union.	13
Democrat	50.8	85.8	4 March 1853–4 March 1857	William R. King	Gadsden Purchase (1853); Kansas-Nebraska Act (1854); trade opened with Japan (1854).	14
Democrat	45.3	58.8	4 March 1857–4 March 1861	John C. Breckinridge	John Brown's raid at Harpers Ferry, Va. (now W. Va.; 1859); South Carolina secedes (1860); Minnesota, Oregon, Kansas enter Union.	15
Republican	39.8 55.0	59.4 91.0	4 March 1861–4 March 1865 4 March 1865–15 April 1865	Hannibal Hamlin Andrew Johnson	Confederacy established, Civil War begins (1861); Emancipation Proclamation (1863); Confederacy defeated (1865); Lincoln assassinated (1865); West Virginia, Nevada attain statehood.	16
Republican	—	—	15 April 1865–4 March 1869	—	Reconstruction Acts (1867); Alaska purchased from Russia (1867); Johnson impeached but acquitted (1868); Nebraska enters Union.	17
Republican	52.7 55.6	72.8 78.1	4 March 1869–4 March 1873 4 March 1873–4 March 1877	Schuyler Colfax Henry Wilson	Numerous government scandals; financial panic (1873); Colorado enters Union.	18
Republican	48.0	50.1	4 March 1877–4 March 1881	William A. Wheeler	Federal troops withdrawn from South (1877); civil service reform begun.	19
Republican	48.3	58.0	4 March 1881–19 Sept. 1881	Chester A. Arthur	Shot after 4 months in office, dead 2½ months later.	20

Presidents of the US, 1881–1981

	NAME	BORN	DIED	OTHER MAJOR OFFICES HELD	RESIDENCE AT ELECTION
21	Chester A. Arthur	Fairfield, Vt., 5 October 1829	New York, N.Y., 18 November 1886	US vice president (1881)	New York, N.Y.
22	Grover Cleveland	Caldwell, N.J., 18 March 1837	Princeton, N.J., 24 June 1908	Governor of New York (1882–84)	Albany, N.Y.
23	Benjamin Harrison	North Bend, Ohio, 20 August 1833	Indianapolis, Ind., 13 March 1901	US senator (1881–87)	Indianapolis, Ind.
24	Grover Cleveland	(see above)	(see above)	(see above)	New York, N.Y.
25	William McKinley	Niles, Ohio, 29 January 1843	Buffalo, N.Y., 14 September 1901	US representative (1877–83; 1885–91); governor of Ohio (1892–96)	Canton, Ohio
26	Theodore Roosevelt	New York, N.Y., 27 October 1858	Oyster Bay, N.Y., 6 January 1919	Governor of New York (1899–1900); US vice president (1901)	Oyster Bay, N.Y.
27	William H. Taft	Cincinnati, Ohio, 15 September 1857	Washington, D.C., 8 March 1930	Governor of Philippines (1901–4); secretary of war (1904–8); chief justice of the US (1921–30)	Washington, D.C.
28	Woodrow Wilson	Staunton, Va., 28 December 1856	Washington, D.C., 3 February 1924	Governor of New Jersey (1911–13)	Trenton, N.J.
29	Warren G. Harding	Blooming Grove, Ohio, 2 November 1865	San Francisco, Calif., 2 August 1923	US senator (1915–21)	Marion, Ohio
30	Calvin Coolidge	Plymouth Notch, Vt., 4 July 1872	Northampton, Mass., 5 January 1933	Governor of Massachusetts (1919–20); US vice president (1921–23)	Boston, Mass.
31	Herbert Hoover	West Branch, Iowa, 10 August 1874	New York, N.Y., 20 October 1964	Secretary of commerce (1921–29)	Stanford, Calif.
32	Franklin D. Roosevelt	Hyde Park, N.Y., 30 January 1882	Warm Springs, Ga., 12 April 1945	Governor of New York (1929–1933)	Hyde Park, N.Y.
33	Harry S Truman	Lamar, Mo., 8 May 1884	Kansas City, Mo., 26 December 1972	US senator (1935–45); US vice president (1945)	Independence, Mo.
34	Dwight D. Eisenhower	Denison, Tex., 14 October 1890	Washington, D.C., 28 March 1969	Supreme allied commander in Europe (1943–44); Army chief of staff (1945–48)	New York
35	John F. Kennedy	Brookline, Mass., 29 May 1917	Dallas, Tex., 22 November 1963	US representative (1947–52); US senator (1953–60)	Massachusetts
36	Lyndon B. Johnson	Stonewall, Tex., 27 August 1908	Johnson City, Tex., 22 January 1973	US representative (1937–48); US senator (1949–60); US vice president (1961–63)	Johnson City, Tex.
37	Richard M. Nixon	Yorba Linda, Calif., 9 January 1913	—	US representative (1947–51); US senator (1951–53); US vice president (1953–61)	New York, N.Y.
38	Gerald R. Ford	Omaha, Nebr., 14 July 1913	—	US representative (1949–73); US vice president (1973–74)	Grand Rapids, Mich.
39	Jimmy Carter	Plains, Ga., 1 October 1924	—	Governor of Georgia (1971–75)	Plains, Ga.
40	Ronald Reagan	Tampico, Ill., 6 February 1911	—	Governor of California (1967–75)	Los Angeles, Calif.

[1]Percentage of electors actually voting.

[2]In elections of 1789, 1792, 1796, and 1800, each elector voted for two candidates for president. The candidate receiving the highest number of votes was elected president; the next highest, vice president. Percentages in table are of total vote cast. From 1804 onward, electors were required to designate which vote was for president and which for vice president, and an electoral majority was required.

PARTY	% OF POPULAR VOTE	% OF ELECTORAL VOTE[2]	TERMS IN OFFICES[5]	VICE PRESIDENTS	NOTABLE EVENTS	
Republican	—	—	19 Sept. 1881–4 March 1885	—	Chinese immigration banned despite presidential veto (1882); Civil Service Commission established by Pendleton Act (1883).	21
Democrat	48.5	54.6	4 March 1885–4 March 1889	Thomas A. Hendricks	Interstate Commerce Act (1887).	22
Republican	47.8	58.1	4 March 1889–4 March 1893	Levi P. Morton	Sherman Silver Purchase Act (1890); North Dakota, South Dakota, Montana, Washington, Idaho, Wyoming enter Union.	23
Democrat	46.1	62.4	4 March 1893–4 March 1897	Adlai E. Stevenson	Financial panic (1893); Sherman Silver Purchase Act repealed (1893); Utah enters Union.	24
Republican	51.0 51.7	60.6 65.3	4 March 1897–4 March 1901 4 March 1901–14 Sept. 1901	Garret A. Hobart Theodore Roosevelt	Spanish-American War (1898): Puerto Rico, Guam, Philippines ceded by Spain; independent Republic of Hawaii annexed; US troops sent to China to suppress Boxer Rebellion (1900); McKinley assassinated.	25
Republican	— 56.4	— 70.6	14 Sept. 1901–4 March 1905 4 March 1905–4 March 1909	— Charles W. Fairbanks	Antitrust and conservation policies emphasized; Roosevelt awarded Nobel Peace Prize (1906) for mediating settlement of Russo-Japanese War; Panama Canal construction begun (1907); Oklahoma enters Union.	26
Republican	51.6	66.5	4 March 1909–4 March 1913	James S. Sherman	Federal income tax ratified (1913); New Mexico, Arizona enter Union.	27
Democrat	41.8 49.2	81.9 52.2	4 March 1913–4 March 1917 4 March 1917–4 March 1921	Thomas R. Marshall Thomas R. Marshall	Clayton Antitrust Act (1914); US Virgin Islands purchased from Denmark (1916); US enters World War I (1917); Treaty of Versailles signed (1919) but not ratified by US; constitutional amendments enforce prohibition (1919), enfranchise women (1920).	28
Republican	60.3	76.1	4 March 1921–2 Aug. 1923	Calvin Coolidge	Teapot Dome scandal (1923–24).	29
Republican	— 54.1	— 71.9	3 Aug. 1923–4 March 1925 4 March 1925–4 March 1929	— Charles G. Dawes	Kellogg-Briand Pact (1928).	30
Republican	58.2	83.6	4 March 1929–4 March 1933	Charles Curtis	Stock market crash (1929) inaugurates Great Depression.	31
Democrat	57.4 60.8 54.7 53.4	88.9 98.5 84.6 81.4	4 March 1933–20 Jan. 1937 20 Jan. 1937–20 Jan. 1941 20 Jan. 1941–20 Jan. 1945 20 Jan. 1945–12 April 1945	John N. Garner John N. Garner Henry A. Wallace Harry S Truman	New Deal social reforms; prohibition repealed (1933); US enters World War II (1941)	32
Democrat	— 49.5	— 57.1	12 April 1945–20 Jan. 1949 20 Jan. 1949–20 Jan. 1953	Alben W. Barkley	United Nations founded (1945); US nuclear bombs dropped on Japan (1945); World War II ends (1945); Philippines granted independence (1946); Marshall Plan (1947); Korean conflict begins (1950); era of McCarthyism.	33
Republican	55.1 57.4	83.2 86.1	20 Jan. 1953–20 Jan. 1957 20 Jan. 1957–20 Jan. 1961	Richard M. Nixon Richard M. Nixon	Korean conflict ended (1953); Supreme Court orders school desegregation (1954); Alaska, Hawaii enter Union.	34
Democrat	49.7	56.4	20 Jan. 1961–22 Nov. 1963	Lyndon B. Johnson	Conflicts with Cuba (1961–62); aboveground nuclear test ban treaty (1963); Kennedy assassinated.	35
Democrat	— 61.1	— 90.3	22 Nov. 1963–20 Jan. 1965 20 Jan. 1965–20 Jan. 1969	— Hubert H. Humphrey	Great Society programs; Voting Rights Act (1965); escalation of US military role in Indochina; race riots, political assassinations.	36
Republican	43.4 60.7	55.9 96.7	20 Jan. 1969–20 Jan. 1973 20 Jan. 1973–9 Aug. 1974	Spiro T. Agnew Spiro T. Agnew Gerald R. Ford	First lunar landing (1969); arms limitation treaty with Soviet Union (1972); US withdraws from Viet-Nam (1973); Agnew resigns in tax scandal (1973); Nixon resigns at height of Watergate scandal (1974).	37
Republican	—	—	9 Aug. 1974–20 Jan. 1977	Nelson A. Rockefeller	First combination of unelected president and vice president; Nixon pardoned (1974).	38
Democrat	50.1	55.2	20 Jan. 1977–20 Jan. 1981	Walter F. Mondale	Carter mediates Israel-Egypt peace accord (1978); Panama Canal treaties ratified (1979); tensions with Iran (1979–81).	39
Republican	50.8	90.9	20 Jan. 1981–	George H. Bush	—	40

[3]Electoral vote tied between Jefferson and Aaron Burr; election decided in House of Representatives.

[4]No candidate received a majority; election decided in House.

[5]In the event of a president's death or removal from office, his duties are assumed to devolve immediately upon his successor, even if he does not immediately take the oath of office.

Chief Justices of the US, 1789–1981

	NAME	BORN	DIED	APPOINTED BY	SUPREME COURT TERM	MAJOR COURT DEVELOPMENTS
1	John Jay	New York City, 12 December 1745	Bedford, N.Y., 17 May 1829	Washington	October 1789– June 1795	Organized court, established procedures.
2	John Rutledge	Charleston, S.C. September 1739	Charleston, S.C. 18 July 1800	Washington	—	Rutledge presided for one term in 1795, but Senate refused to confirm his appointment.
3	Oliver Ellsworth	Windsor, Conn., 29 April 1745	Windsor, Conn. 26 November 1807	Washington	March 1796– December 1800	—
4	John Marshall	Fauquier County, Va., 24 September 1755	Philadelphia, 6 July 1835	Adams	February 1801– July 1835	Established principle of judicial review (*Marbury* v. *Madison,* 1803); formulated concept of implied powers (*McCulloch* v. *Maryland,* 1819).
5	Roger Brooke Taney	Calvert County, Md., 17 March 1777	Washington, D.C., 12 October 1864	Jackson	March 1836– October 1864	Held that slaves could not become citizens, ruled Missouri Compromise illegal (*Dred Scott* v. *Sandford,* 1857).
6	Salmon Portland Chase	Cornish, N.H., 13 January 1808	New York City, 7 May 1873	Lincoln	December 1864– May 1873	Ruled military trials of civilians illegal (*Ex parte Milligan* 1866); Chase presided at A. Johnson's impeachment trial.
7	Morrison Remick Waite	Old Lynne, Conn., 29 November 1816	Washington, D.C., 23 March 1888	Grant	March 1874– March 1888	Held that businesses affecting the "public interest" are subject to state regulation (*Munn* v. *Illinois,* 1877).
8	Melville Weston Fuller	Augusta, Me., 11 February 1833	Sorvento, Me., 4 July 1910	Cleveland	October 1888– July 1910	Issued first opinions on cases under the Sherman Antitrust Act, (*US* v. *E.C. Knight Co.,* 1895; *Northern Securities Co.* v. *US,* 1904); held the income tax unconstitutional (*Pollock* v. *Farmers' Loan,* 1895).
9	Edward Douglass White	Lafourche Parish, La., 3 November 1845	Washington, D.C., 19 May 1921	Taft	December 1910– May 1921	Further qualified the Sherman Antitrust Act (*Standard Oil Co.* v. *US,* 1911) by applying the "rule of reason."
10	William Howard Taft	Cincinnati, Ohio, 15 September 1857	Washington, D.C., 8 March 1930	Harding	July 1921– February 1930	Held against congressional use of taxes for social reform (*Bailey* v. *Drexel Furniture,* 1922).
11	Charles Evans Hughes	Glens Falls, N.Y., 11 April 1862	Osterville, Mass., 27 August 1948	Hoover	February 1930– June 1941	Upheld constitutionality of National Labor Relations Act and Social Security Act; invalidated the National Industrial Recovery Act (*Sehechter* v. *US,* 1935); F. Roosevelt's attempt to pack Court opposed.
12	Harlan Fiske Stone	Chesterfield, N.H., 11 October 1872	Washington, D.C., 22 April 1946	F. Roosevelt	July 1941– April 1946	Upheld Court's power to invalidate state laws (*Southern Pacific Co.* v. *Arizona,* 1945).
13	Frederick Moore Vinson	Louisa, Ky., 22 January 1890	Washington, D.C., 8 September 1953	Truman	June 1916– September 1953	Overturned federal seizure of steel mills (*Youngstown Sheet and Tube Co.* v. *Sawyer,* 1952), Vinson dissenting.
14	Earl Warren	Los Angeles, Calif., 19 March 1891	Washington, D.C., 9 July 1974	Eisenhower	October 1953– June 1969	Mandated public school desegregation (*Brown* v. *Board of Education,* 1954); required reapportionment of state legislatures (*Baker* v. *Carr,* 1962); upheld rights of suspects in police custody (*Miranda* v. *Arizona,* 1966).
15	Warren Earl Burger	St. Paul, Minn., 17 September 1907	—	Nixon	June 1969–	Legalized abortion (*Roe* v. *Wade,* 1973); rejected the claim of executive privilege as justification for the withholding of evidence in a criminal case (*US* v. *Nixon,* 1974).

Moore (1887–1972), and Hart Crane (1899–1932). Ezra Pound (1885–1972) and Nobel laureate Thomas Stearns Eliot (1888–1965) lived and worked abroad for most of their careers. Wystan Hugh Auden (b.England, 1907–73), who became an American citizen in 1946, published poetry and criticism. Elizabeth Bishop (1911–79), Robert Lowell (1917–77), Allen Ginsberg (b.1926), and Sylvia Plath (1932–63) are among the best-known poets of the postwar period. Robert Penn Warren (b.1904) has won the Pulitzer Prize for both fiction and poetry. Carl Sandburg (1878–1967) was a noted poet, historian, novelist, and folklorist. The foremost US dramatists are Eugene (Gladstone) O'Neill (1888–1953), who won the Nobel Prize for literature in 1936; Tennessee Williams (Thomas Lanier Williams, b.1911); Arthur Miller (b.1915); and Edward Albee (b.1928).

Two renowned painters of the early period were John Singleton Copley (1738–1815) and Gilbert Stuart (1755–1828). Outstanding 19th-century painters were James Abbott McNeill Whistler (1834–1903), Winslow Homer (1836–1910), Thomas Eakins (1844–1916), Mary Cassatt (1845–1926), Albert Pinkham Ryder (1847–1917), and John Singer Sargent (1856–1925). More recently, Edward Hopper (1882–1967), Georgia O'Keeffe (b.1887), Thomas Hart Benton (1889–1975), Charles Burchfield (1893–1967), Ben Shahn (1898–1969), Mark Rothko (b.Russia, 1903–70), Jackson Pollock (1912–56), Robert Rauschenberg (b.1925), and Jasper Johns (b.1930) have achieved international recognition.

Sculptors of note include Augustus Saint-Gaudens (1848–1907), Gaston Lachaise (1882–1935), Jo Davidson (1883–1952), Alexander Calder (1898–1976), and Louise Nevelson (b.Russia, 1900). Henry Hobson Richardson (1838–86), Louis Henry Sullivan (1856–1924), Frank Lloyd Wright (1869–1959), Louis I. Kahn (b.Estonia, 1901–74), and Eero Saarinen (1910–61) were outstanding architects. Contemporary architects of note include R. Buckminster Fuller (b.1895), Edward Durell Stone (b.1902), Philip Johnson (b.1906), and I(eoh) M(ing) Pei (b.China, 1917). The US has produced many fine photographers, notably Mathew B. Brady (c.1823–96), Alfred Stieglitz (1864–1946), Edward Steichen (1879–1973), Edward Weston (1886–1958), Ansel Adams (b.1902), and Margaret Bourke-White (1904–71).

Outstanding figures in the motion picture industry are D. W. (David Lewelyn Wark) Griffith (1875–1948), Charles Spencer "Charlie" Chaplin (b.England, 1889–1978), Walter E. "Walt" Disney (1906–66), and Orson Welles (b.1915). John Ford (1895–1973), Howard Hawks (b.1896), and Alfred Hitchcock (b.England, 1899–1980) were influential motion picture directors. Director-choreographer Bob Fosse (b.1927) has won Oscar, Tony, and Emmy awards; Woody Allen (Allen Konigsberg, b.1935) has written, directed, and starred in comedies on stage and screen. Classic American actors and actresses include the Barrymores, Ethel (1879–1959), and her brothers Lionel (1878–1954) and John (1882–1942); Humphrey Bogart (1899–1957); Spencer Tracy (1900–1967); Clark Gable (1901–60); Greta Garbo (b.Sweden, Greta Gustafsson, 1905); Henry Fonda (b.1905) and his daughter, Jane (b.1937); Bette Davis (b.1908); Katharine Hepburn (b.1909); Judy Garland (Frances Gumm, 1922–69); and Marlon Brando (b.1924). Among great entertainers are W. C. Fields (William Claude Dukenfield, 1880–1946), Jack Benny (b.Benjamin Kubelsky, 1894–1974), Fred Astaire (b.Fred Austerlitz, 1899), Bob Hope (Leslie Townes Hope, b.England, 1903), Bing Crosby (Harry Lillis Crosby, 1904–78), and Frank Sinatra (Francis Albert Sinatra, b.1915). The first great US "showman" was Phineas Taylor Barnum (1810–91).

Foremost composers are Edward MacDowell (1861–1908), Charles Ives (1874–1954), Ernest Bloch (b.Switzerland, 1880–1959), Roger Sessions (b.1896), Roy Harris (b.1898), Aaron Copland (b.1900), Elliott Carter (b.1908), Samuel Barber (b.1910), John Cage (b.1912), and Leonard Bernstein (b.1918). George Crumb (b.1929) and Philip Glass (b.1937) have won more recent followings. The songs of Stephen Collins Foster (1826–64) have achieved folksong status. Leading composers of popular music are John Philip Sousa (1854–1932), Jerome Kern (1885–1945), Irving Berlin (b.Israel Baline, Russia, 1888), Cole Porter (1893–1964), George Gershwin (1898–1937), Richard Rodgers (1902–1979), Woody Guthrie (1912–67), and Bob Dylan (Robert Zimmerman, b.1941). Leading jazz figures include the composers Scott Joplin (1868–1917) and Edward Kennedy "Duke" Ellington (1899–1974); and performers Louis Armstrong (1900–1971), Billie Holiday (Eleanora Fagan, 1915–59), John Birks "Dizzy" Gillespie (b.1917), Charlie "Bird" Parker (1920–55), John Coltrane (1926–67), and Miles Davis (b.1926). Many foreign-born musicians have enjoyed personal and professional freedom in the US; principal among them were pianists Artur Schnabel (b.Austria, 1882–1951), Arthur Rubinstein (b.Poland, 1887), Rudolf Serkin (b.Bohemia, 1903), Vladimir Horowitz (b.Russia, 1904), and violinists Jascha Heifetz (b.Russia, 1901) and Isaac Stern (b.Soviet Union, 1920). Among distinguished instrumentalists born in the US are Benny Goodman (b.1909), a classical as well as jazz clarinetist, and concert pianist Van Cliburn (Harvey Lavan, Jr., b.1934). Singers Paul Robeson (1898–1976), Marian Anderson (b.1902), Maria Callas (Maria Kalogeropoulos, 1923–77), Leontyne Price (b.1927), and Beverly Sills (Belle Silverman, b.1929) achieved international acclaim. Isadora Duncan (1878–1927) was one of the first US dancers to win fame abroad. George Balanchine (b.Russia, 1904), Agnes De Mille (b.1908), and Jerome Robbins (b.1918) are leading choreographers. Martha Graham (b.1893) pioneered in modern dance.

Among the many noteworthy sports stars are baseball's Tyrus Raymond "Ty" Cobb (1886–1961) and George Herman "Babe" Ruth (1895–1948); football's Samuel Adrian "Sammy" Baugh (b.1914), Jim Brown (b.1936), Francis A. "Fran" Tarkenton (b.1940), and O(renthal) J(ames) Simpson (b.1947); golf's Robert Tyre "Bobby" Jones and Mildred "Babe" Didrikson Zaharias (1914–56); William "Bill" Tilden (1893–1953) and Billie Jean (Moffitt) King (b.1943) in tennis; Joe Louis (Joseph Louis Barrow, b.1914) and Muhammad Ali (Cassius Marcellus Clay, b.1942) in boxing; William Felton "Bill" Russell (b.1934) and Wilton Norman "Wilt" Chamberlain (b.1936) in basketball; Mark Spitz (b.1950) in swimming; Eric Heiden (b.1958) in speed skating; and Jesse Owens (1913–80) in track and field.

Of the 156 Nobel Prizes awarded to US citizens as of 1980, 43 were in physics, 24 in chemistry, 55 in physiology or medicine, 9 in literature, 9 in economics, and 16 for peace.

⁵⁰BIBLIOGRAPHY

Adams Family Correspondence. 4 vols. Edited by L. H. Butterfield et al. Cambridge, Mass.: Belknap Press, 1963–73.

Adams Family Diaries. 6 vols. Edited by L. H. Butterfield et al. Cambridge, Mass.: Belknap Press, 1964–74.

Ahlstrom, Sydney E. *A Religious History of the American People*. New Haven: Yale University Press, 1972.

Allen, Harold B. (ed.). *Readings in American Dialectology*. New York: Appleton-Century-Crofts, 1971.

Bailey, Thomas Andrew. *A Diplomatic History of the American People*. New York: Appleton-Century-Crofts, 1955.

Barnouw, Erik. *A History of Broadcasting in the US*. 3 vols. New York: Oxford University Press, 1966–70.

Barone, Michael, et al. *The Almanac of American Politics, 1980*. New York: Dutton, 1979.

Becker, Carl Lotus. *The Declaration of Independence: A Study in the History of Political Ideas*. New York: Knopf, 1942.

Berlin, Ira. *Slaves without Masters: The Free Negro in the Antebellum South*. New York: Pantheon, 1976.

The Book of the States. Chicago: Council of State Governments, 1935–date.

Boorstin, Daniel J. *The Americans: The Colonial Experience*. New York: Random House, 1958.

Boorstin, Daniel J. *The Americans: The National Experience.* New York: Random House, 1965.

Boorstin, Daniel J. *The Americans: The Democratic Experience.* New York: Random House, 1973.

Brown, Dee. *Bury My Heart at Wounded Knee: An Indian History of the American West.* New York: Holt, Rinehart and Winston, 1971.

Catton, Bruce. *The Centennial History of the Civil War.* 3 vols. Garden City, N.Y.: Doubleday, 1961–65.

Chase, Gilbert. *Our American Music from the Pilgrims to the Present.* New York: McGraw-Hill, 1966.

Coles, Robert. *Children of Crisis.* 5 vols. Boston: Little, Brown, 1967–77.

Commager, Henry Steele (ed.). *Documents of American History.* New York: Appleton-Century-Crofts, 1949.

Congressional Directory . . . Washington, D.C.: Government Printing Office, 1809–date.

Congressional Quarterly's Guide to US Elections. Washington, D.C., 1975. Supplement, 1977.

Dickstein, Morris. *Gates of Eden: American Culture in the 1960s.* New York: Basic Books, 1977.

Dictionary of American Biography. 16 vols. New York: Scribner, 1927–72. Supplements, 1973–80.

Encyclopedia of Associations: Vol. I. *National Organizations of the U.S.* 14th ed. Detroit: Gale Research, 1980.

Freidel, Frank, with Richard K. Showman (ed.). *Harvard Guide to American History.* Rev. ed. Cambridge, Mass.: Belknap Press, 1974.

Goodwyn, Lawrence. *Democratic Promise: The Populist Movement in America.* New York: Oxford University Press, 1977.

Greeley, Andrew M. *The American Catholic: A Social Portrait.* New York: Basic Books, 1978.

Haley, Alex. *Roots: The Saga of an American Family.* New York: Doubleday, 1976.

Hart, James David (ed.). *Oxford Companion to American Literature.* 4th ed. New York: Oxford University Press, 1965.

Howe, Irving. *The World of Our Fathers.* New York: Harcourt Brace Jovanovich, 1976.

Jordan, Winthrop P. *White over Black: American Attitudes toward the Negro, 1550–1812.* Chapel Hill: University of North Carolina Press, 1968.

The Justices of the United States Supreme Court, 1789–1969: Their Lives and Major Opinions. 4 vols. Edited by Leon Friedman and Fred L. Israel. New York: Chelsea House and Bowker, 1970.

Kammen, Michael. *People of Paradox: An Inquiry Concerning the Origins of American Civilization.* New York: Knopf, 1972.

Kelly, Alfred Hinsey, and Winfred Audif Harbison. *The American Constitution: Its Origins and Development.* New York: Norton, 1955.

Key, V. O. *Southern Politics in State and Nation.* New York: Vintage, 1949.

Kissinger, Henry. *The White House Years.* Boston: Little, Brown, 1979.

Lerner, Max. *America as a Civilization: Life and Thought in the United States Today.* New York: Simon and Schuster, 1957.

Mardan, Charles F. and Gladys Meyer. *Minorities in American Society.* 5th ed. New York: Van Nostrand, 1978.

Mencken, Henry Louis. *The American Language.* New York: Knopf, 1936. Supplements, 1945, 1948.

Morison, Samuel Eliot. *The European Discovery of America: The Northern and Southern Voyages.* 2 vols. New York: Oxford University Press, 1971–74.

Morison, Samuel Eliot. *The Oxford History of the American People.* New York: Oxford University Press, 1965.

Morris, Richard Brandon (ed.). *Encyclopedia of American History.* New York: Harper & Row, 1970.

Nevins, Allan. *Ordeal of the Union.* 8 vols. New York: Scribners, 1947–71.

Notable American Women, 1607–1950: A Biographical Dictionary. 3 vols. Edited by Edward T. James et al. Cambridge, Mass.: Belknap Press, 1973.

Peirce, Neal R. *The Megastates of America: People, Politics, and Power in the Ten Great States.* New York: Norton, 1972.

Reed, Carroll E. *Dialects of American English.* Amherst: University of Massachusetts Press, 1973.

Richardson, E. P. *Painting in America.* New York: Crowell, 1965.

Rose, Barbara. *American Art since 1900.* New York: Praeger, 1975.

Sherwin, Martin J. *A World Destroyed: The Atomic Bomb and the Grand Alliance.* New York: Knopf, 1977.

Silberman, Charles E. *Criminal Violence, Criminal Justice.* New York: Norton, 1979.

Slotkin, Richard. *Regeneration through Violence: The Mythology of the American Frontier, 1600–1860.* Middletown, Conn.: Wesleyan University Press, 1975.

Smith, Page. *A New Age Now Begins: A People's History of the American Revolution.* 2 vols. New York: McGraw-Hill, 1976.

Smith, Page. *The Shaping of America: A People's History of the Young Republic.* Vol. 3. New York: McGraw-Hill, 1980.

Spiller, Robert, et al. (eds.). *Literary History of the United States.* 4th ed. rev. New York: Macmillan, 1974.

Stampp, Kenneth Milton. *The Peculiar Institution: Slavery in the Ante-Bellum South.* New York: Knopf, 1956.

Terkel, Studs. *Hard Times: An Oral History of the Great Depression.* New York: Pantheon, 1970.

Tocqueville, Alexis Charles Henri Maurice Cherel de. *Democracy in America.* New York: Knopf, 1945.

US Bureau of the Census. *Historical Statistics of the United States, Colonial Times to 1970.* Washington, D.C.: Government Printing Office, 1975.

US Bureau of the Census. *Statistical Abstract of the United States.* Washington, D.C.: Government Printing Office, 1879–date.

US Geological Survey. *National Atlas of the United States.* Washington, D.C., 1970.

United States Government Manual. Washington, D.C.: Federal Register Division, National Archives and Records Service, General Service Administration, 1935–date.

White, Theodore. *Breach of Faith: The Fall of Richard Nixon.* New York: Atheneum, 1975.

Who's Who in America: A Biographical Dictionary of Notable Living Men and Women. Chicago: Marquis, 1899–date.

Wills, Garry. *Inventing America: Jefferson's Declaration of Independence.* New York: Doubleday, 1978.

Wood, Michael. *America in the Movies.* New York: Basic Books, 1976.

Zaretsky, Irving I., and Mark P. Leone (eds.). *Religious Movements in Contemporary America.* Princeton: Princeton University Press, 1976.

Glossary

ANTEBELLUM: before the US Civil War.

BLUE LAWS: laws forbidding certain practices (e.g., conducting business, gaming, drinking liquor), especially on Sundays.

CAPITAL BUDGET: a financial plan for acquiring and improving buildings or land, paid for by the sale of bonds.

CAPITAL PUNISHMENT: punishment by death.

CIVILIAN LABOR FORCE: all persons 16 years of age or older who are not in the armed forces and who are now holding a job, have been temporarily laid off, are waiting to be reassigned to a new position, or are unemployed but actively looking for work.

COMMERCIAL BANK: a bank that offers to businesses and individuals a variety of banking services, including the right of withdrawal by check.

CONTINENTAL CLIMATE: the climate typical of the US interior, having distinct seasons, a wide range of daily and annual temperatures, and dry, sunny summers.

CONSOLIDATED BUDGET: a financial plan that includes the general budget, federal funds, and all special funds.

CONSTANT DOLLARS: money values calculated so as to eliminate the effect of inflation on prices and income.

COUNCIL-MANAGER SYSTEM: a system of local government under which a professional administrator is hired by an elected council to carry out its laws and policies.

CREDIT UNION: a cooperative body that raises funds from its members by the sale of shares and makes loans to its members at relatively low interest rates.

CURRENT DOLLARS: money values that reflect prevailing prices, without excluding the effects of inflation.

DEMAND DEPOSIT: a bank deposit that can be withdrawn by the depositor with no advance notice to the bank.

ELECTORAL VOTES: the votes that a state may cast for president, equal to the combined total of its US senators and representatives and nearly always cast entirely on behalf of the candidate who won the most votes in that state on Election Day.

ENDANGERED SPECIES: a type of plant or animal threatened with extinction in all or part of its natural range.

FEDERAL POVERTY LEVEL: a level of money income below which a person or family qualifies for US government aid.

FISCAL YEAR: a 12-month period for accounting purposes.

FOOD STAMPS: coupons issued by the government to low-income persons for food purchases at local stores.

GENERAL BUDGET: a financial plan based on a government's normal revenues and operating expenses, excluding special funds.

GENERAL COASTLINE: a measurement of the general outline of the US seacoast. See also **TIDAL SHORELINE.**

GREAT AWAKENING: during the mid-18th century, a Protestant religious revival in North America, especially New England.

GROSS STATE PRODUCT: the total value of goods and services produced in the state.

GROWING SEASON: the period between the last 32°F (0°C) temperature in spring and the first 32°F (0°C) temperature in autumn.

HOME-RULE CHARTER: a document stating how and in what respects a city, town, or county may govern itself.

INSTALLED CAPACITY: the maximum possible output of electric power at any given time.

MAYOR-COUNCIL SYSTEM: a system of local government under which an elected council serves as a legislature and an elected mayor is the chief administrator.

MEDICAID: a federal-state program that helps defray the hospital and medical costs of needy persons.

MEDICARE: a program of hospital and medical insurance for the elderly, administered by the federal government.

METROPOLITAN AREA: in most cases, a city and its surrounding suburbs.

NO-FAULT INSURANCE: an automobile insurance plan that allows an accident victim to receive payment from an insurance company without having to prove who was responsible for the accident.

NORTHERN, NORTH MIDLAND: major US dialect regions; see pp. 644–46.

OMBUDSMAN: a public official empowered to hear and investigate complaints by private citizens about government agencies.

POCKET VETO: a method by which a state governor (or the US president) may kill a bill by taking no action on it before the legislature adjourns.

PER CAPITA: per person.

PROVED RESERVES: the quantity of a recoverable mineral resource (such as oil or natural gas) that is still in the ground.

PUBLIC DEBT: the amount owed by a government.

RELIGIOUS ADHERENTS: the followers of a religious group, including (but not confined to) the full, confirmed, or communicant members of that group.

RETAIL TRADE: the sale of goods directly to the consumer.

REVENUE SHARING: the distribution of federal tax receipts to state and local governments.

RIGHT-TO-WORK LAW: a measure outlawing any attempt to require union membership as a condition of employment.

SAVINGS AND LOAN ASSOCIATION: a bank that invests the savings of depositors primarily in home mortgage loans.

SOCIAL SECURITY: as commonly understood, the federal system of old age, survivors, and disability insurance.

SOUTHERN, SOUTH MIDLAND: major US dialect regions; see pp. 644–46.

SUNBELT: the southernmost states of the US, extending from Florida to California.

SUPPLEMENTAL SECURITY INCOME: a federally administered program of aid to the aged, blind, and disabled.

TIDAL SHORELINE: a detailed measurement of the US seacoast that includes sounds, bays, other outlets, and offshore islands.

TIME DEPOSIT: a bank deposit that may be withdrawn only at the end of a specified time period or upon advance notice to the bank.

VALUE ADDED BY MANUFACTURE: the difference, measured in dollars, between the value of finished goods and the cost of the materials needed to produce them.

WHOLESALE TRADE: the sale of goods, usually in large quantities, for ultimate resale to consumers.

Abbreviations and Acronyms

AD—Anno Domini
AFDC—aid to families with dependent children
AFL–CIO—American Federation of Labor–Congress of Industrial Organizations
A.M.—before noon
AM—amplitude modulation
American Ind.—American Independent Party
Amtrak—National Railroad Passenger Corp.
b.—born
BC—Before Christ
Btu—British thermal unit(s)
bu—bushel(s)
c.—circa, about
C—Centigrade
CIA—Central Intelligence Agency
cm—centimeter
Co.—company
Conrail—Consolidated Rail Corp.
Corp.—corporation
CST—Central Standard Time
cu—cubic
cwt—hundredweight(s)
d.—died
D—Democrat
e—evening
E—east
ed.—edition, editor
e.g.—exempli gratia (for example)
EPA—Environmental Protection Agency
est.—estimated
EST—Eastern Standard Time
et al.—et alii (and others)
etc.—et cetera (and so on)
F—Fahrenheit
FBI—Federal Bureau of Investigation
FCC—Federal Communications Commission
FM—frequency modulation
Ft.—fort
GMT—Greenwich Mean Time
GNP—gross national product
GOP—Grand Old Party, i.e., the Republican Party
GSP—gross state product

I—interstate (highway)
in—inch(es)
Inc.—incorporated
K—kindergarten
km—kilometer(s)
km/hr—kilometers per hour
kw—kilowatt(s)
kwh—kilowatt-hour(s)
lb—pound(s)
m—morning
mi—mile(s)
mph—miles per hour
mw—megawatt(s)
MST—Mountain Standard Time
Mt.—mount
Mtn.—mountain
N—north
NA—not available
NAACP—National Association for the Advancement of Colored People
Natl.—National
NATO—North Atlantic Treaty Organization
NCAA—National Collegiate Athletic Association
n.d.—no date
OASDI—old age, survivors, and disability insurance
oz—ounce(s)
P.M.—after noon
PST—Pacific Standard Time
R—Republican
Ra.—range
rev. ed.—revised edition
s—south
S—Sunday
Soc.—Socialist
sq—square
St.—saint
TV—television
UN—United Nations
Unicef—United Nations Children's Fund
US—United States
USIA—United States Information Agency
w—west

NAMES OF STATES AND OTHER SELECTED AREAS

	STANDARD ABBREVIATION(S)	POSTAL ABBREVIATION		STANDARD ABBREVIATION(S)	POSTAL ABBREVIATION
Alabama	Ala.	AL	Nebraska	Nebr. (Neb.)	NE
Alaska	*	AK	Nevada	Nev.	NV
Arizona	Ariz.	AZ	New Hampshire	N.H.	NH
Arkansas	Ark.	AR	New Jersey	N.J.	NJ
California	Calif.	CA	New Mexico	N.Mex. (N.M.)	NM
Colorado	Colo.	CO	New York	N.Y.	NY
Connecticut	Conn.	CT	North Carolina	N.C.	NC
Delaware	Del.	DE	North Dakota	N.Dak. (N.D.)	ND
District of Columbia	D.C.	DC	Ohio	*	OH
Florida	Fla.	FL	Oklahoma	Okla.	OK
Georgia	Ga.	GA	Oregon	Oreg. (Ore.)	OR
Hawaii	*	HI	Pennsylvania	Pa.	PA
Idaho	*	ID	Puerto Rico	P.R.	PR
Illinois	Ill.	IL	Rhode Island	R.I.	RI
Indiana	Ind.	IN	South Carolina	S.C.	SC
Iowa	*	IA	South Dakota	S.Dak. (S.D.)	SD
Kansas	Kans. (Kan.)	KS	Tennessee	Tenn.	TN
Kentucky	Ky.	KY	Texas	Tex.	TX
Louisiana	La.	LA	Utah	*	UT
Maine	Me.	ME	Vermont	Vt.	VT
Maryland	Md.	MD	Virginia	Va.	VA
Massachusetts	Mass.	MA	Virgin Islands	V.I.	VI
Michigan	Mich.	MI	Washington	Wash.	WA
Minnesota	Minn.	MN	West Virginia	W.Va.	WV
Mississippi	Miss.	MS	Wisconsin	Wis.	WI
Missouri	Mo.	MO	Wyoming	Wyo.	WY
Montana	Mont.	MT	*No standard abbreviation